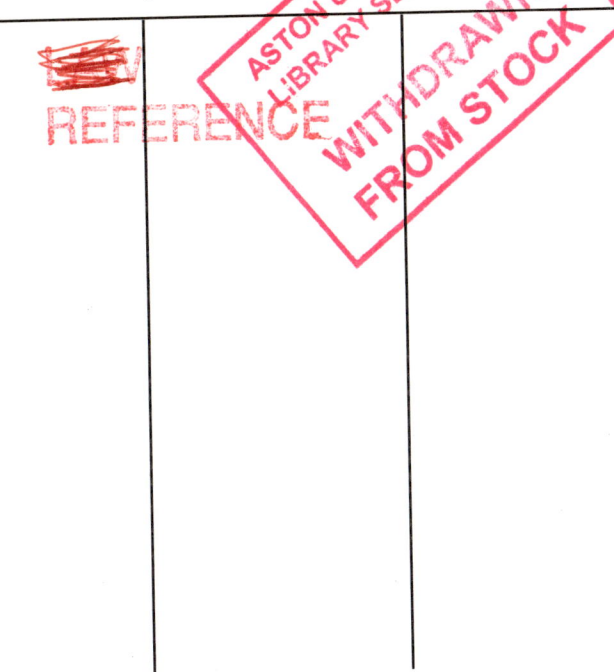

YEARBOOK OF THE UNITED NATIONS 1999

Volume 53

Yearbook of the United Nations, 1999

Volume 53 Sales No. E.01.I.4

Prepared by the Yearbook Section of the Department of Public Information, United Nations, New York. Although the *Yearbook* is based on official sources, it is not an official record.

Chief Editor: Kathryn Gordon

Senior Editors: Elizabeth Baldwin-Penn, Melody C. Pfeiffer

Editors/Writers: Federigo Magherini, Isolda Oca

Contributing Editors/Writers: Peter Jackson, Nancy Seufert-Barr, Juanita B. Phelan, Luisa Balacco, Alexandre Slavashevich, Sharon McPherson, Anvita Sharma

Senior Copy Editor: Alison M. Koppelman

Copy Editor: Peter Homans

Production Coordinator: Leonard M. Simon

Editorial Assistants: Lawri M. Moore, Margaret O'Donnell, Rodney Pascual

Senior Typesetter: Sunita Chabra

Indexer: David Golante

Jacket design adapted by Patricia Doelger

YEARBOOK OF THE UNITED NATIONS 1999

Volume 53

Department of Public Information
United Nations, New York

Yearbook of the United Nations, 1999
Vol. 53
ISBN: 92-1-100856-5
ISSN: 0082-8521

UNITED NATIONS PUBLICATIONS
SALES NO. E.01.I.4

Printed in the United States of America

Foreword

THE YEAR 1999 was a tumultuous time for the United Nations. New conflicts erupted in several parts of the world, and several long-running ones continued to defy peacemaking efforts. In the wake of horrific violence and gross human rights violations in East Timor and Kosovo, the Organization was charged with the responsibility of helping to rebuild shattered societies almost from scratch.

Although peacekeeping and post-conflict peace-building commanded a large share of the attention and resources of the United Nations during the year, the Organization also faced growing humanitarian, economic and social challenges, such as natural disasters, refugee flows, AIDS and the changes wrought by globalization. As the new millennium approached, the United Nations took further steps to ensure that its work and objectives could respond to the needs of the twenty-first century. This included expanded partnerships with civil society and the private sector. Meanwhile, with the admission of Kiribati, Nauru and Tonga, United Nations membership rose to 188 States and our global constituency grew to 6 billion people.

I trust that this volume of the *Yearbook of the United Nations* will contribute to a better understanding of the Organization's work to build peace and a better future for the world's peoples, in a rapidly changing and globalizing world.

KOFI A. ANNAN

Secretary-General of the United Nations
New York, November 2001

Contents

Part Two: *Human Rights*

Part Three: *Economic and social questions*

Part Four: *Legal questions*

Part Six: *Intergovernmental organizations related to the United Nations*

Appendices

Indexes

About the 1999 edition of the *Yearbook*

This volume of the *YEARBOOK OF THE UNITED NATIONS* continues the tradition of providing the most comprehensive coverage of the activities of the United Nations. It is an indispensable reference tool for the research community, diplomats, government officials and the general public seeking readily available information on the UN system and its related organizations.

Efforts by the Department of Public Information to achieve a more timely publication have resulted in having to rely on provisional documentation and other materials to prepare the relevant articles. Largely, Security Council resolutions and presidential statements, Economic and Social Council resolutions and some other texts in the present volume are provisional.

Structure and scope of articles

The *Yearbook* is subject-oriented and divided into six parts covering political and security questions; human rights issues; economic and social questions; legal questions; institutional, administrative and budgetary questions; and intergovernmental organizations related to the United Nations. Chapters and topical headings present summaries of pertinent UN activities, including those of intergovernmental and expert bodies, major reports, Secretariat activities and, in selected cases, the views of States in written communications.

Activities of United Nations bodies. All resolutions, decisions and other major activities of the principal organs and, on a selective basis, those of subsidiary bodies are either reproduced or summarized in the appropriate chapter. The texts of all resolutions and decisions of substantive nature adopted in 1999 by the General Assembly, the Security Council and the Economic and Social Council are reproduced or summarized under the relevant topic. These texts are preceded by procedural details giving date of adoption, meeting number and vote totals (in favour–against–abstaining) if any; and information on their approval by a sessional or subsidiary body prior to final adoption. The texts are followed by details of any recorded or roll-call vote on the resolution/decision as a whole.

Major reports. Most reports of the Secretary-General, in 1999, along with selected reports from other UN sources, such as seminars and working groups, are summarized briefly.

Secretariat activities. The operational activities of the United Nations for development and humanitarian assistance are described under the relevant topics. For major activities financed outside the UN regular budget, selected information is given on contributions and expenditures.

Views of States. Written communications sent to the United Nations by Member States and circulated as documents of the principal organs have been summarized in selected cases, under the relevant topics. Substantive actions by the Security Council have been analysed and brief reviews of the Council's deliberations given, particularly in cases where an issue was taken up but no resolution was adopted.

Related organizations. The *Yearbook* also briefly describes the 1999 activities of the specialized agencies and other related organizations of the UN system.

Multilateral treaties. Information on signatories and parties to multilateral treaties and conventions is taken from *Multilateral Treaties Deposited with the Secretary-General: Status as at 31 December 1999* (ST/LEG/SER.E/18 (vols. I & II)), Sales No. E.00.V.2.

Terminology

Formal titles of bodies, organizational units, conventions, declarations and officials are given in full on first mention in an article or sequence of articles. They are also used in resolution/decision texts, and in the SUBJECT INDEX under the key word of the title. Short titles may be used in subsequent references.

How to find information in the *Yearbook*

The user may locate information on the United Nations activities contained in this volume by the use of the Table of Contents, the Subject Index, the Index of Resolutions and Decisions and the Index of Security Council Presidential Statements. The volume also has five appendices: Appendix I comprises a roster of Member States; Appendix II reproduces the Charter of the United Nations, including the Statute of the International Court of Justice; Appendix III gives the structure of the principal organs of the United Nations; Appendix IV provides the agenda for each session of the principal organs in 1999; and Appendix V gives the addresses of the United Nations information centres and services worldwide.

For more information on the United Nations and its activities, visit our Internet site at:

http://www.un.org

ABBREVIATIONS COMMONLY USED IN THE *YEARBOOK*

ACABQ	Advisory Committee on Administrative and Budgetary Questions
ACC	Administrative Committee on Coordination
CEDAW	Committee on the Elimination of Discrimination against Women
CIS	Commonwealth of Independent States
DPRK	Democratic People's Republic of Korea
DRC	Democratic Republic of the Congo
ECA	Economic Commission for Africa
ECE	Economic Commission for Europe
ECLAC	Economic Commission for Latin America and the Caribbean
ECOWAS	Economic Community of West African States
ESC	Economic and Social Council
ESCAP	Economic and Social Commission for Asia and the Pacific
ESCWA	Economic and Social Commission for Western Asia
EU	European Union
FAO	Food and Agriculture Organization of the United Nations
FRY	Federal Republic of Yugoslavia (Serbia and Montenegro)
FYROM	The former Yugoslav Republic of Macedonia
GA	General Assembly
GDP	gross domestic product
GNP	gross national product
IAEA	International Atomic Energy Agency
ICAO	International Civil Aviation Organization
ICJ	International Court of Justice
ICRC	International Committee of the Red Cross
ICTR	International Tribunal for Rwanda
ICTY	International Tribunal for the Former Yugoslavia
IDA	International Development Association
IFAD	International Fund for Agricultural Development
ILO	International Labour Organization
IMF	International Monetary Fund
IMO	International Maritime Organization
INCB	International Narcotics Control Board
INSTRAW	International Research and Training Institute for the Advancement of Women
ITC	International Trade Centre (UNCTAD/WTO)
ITU	International Telecommunication Union
JIU	Joint Inspection Unit
LDC	least developed country
MINURCA	United Nations Mission in the Central African Republic
MINURSO	United Nations Mission for the Referendum in Western Sahara
MIPONUH	United Nations Civilian Police Mission in Haiti
MONUA	United Nations Observer Mission in Angola
MONUC	United Nations Mission in the Democratic Republic of the Congo
NATO	North Atlantic Treaty Organization
NGO	non-governmental organization
NSGT	Non-Self-Governing Territory
OAS	Organization of American States
OAU	Organization of African Unity
ODA	official development assistance
OECD	Organisation for Economic Cooperation and Development
OHCHR	Office of the United Nations High Commissioner for Human Rights
OIOS	Office of Internal Oversight Services
OPEC	Organization of Petroleum Exporting Countries
OSCE	Organization for Security and Cooperation in Europe
PLO	Palestine Liberation Organization
SC	Security Council
SDR	special drawing right
UN	United Nations
UNAMSIL	United Nations Mission in Sierra Leone
UNCTAD	United Nations Conference on Trade and Development
UNDCP	United Nations International Drug Control Programme
UNDOF	United Nations Disengagement Observer Force (Golan Heights)
UNDP	United Nations Development Programme
UNEP	United Nations Environment Programme
UNESCO	United Nations Educational, Scientific and Cultural Organization
UNFICYP	United Nations Peacekeeping Force in Cyprus
UNFPA	United Nations Population Fund
UNHCR	Office of the United Nations High Commissioner for Refugees
UNIC	United Nations Information Centre
UNICEF	United Nations Children's Fund
UNIDO	United Nations Industrial Development Organization
UNIFIL	United Nations Interim Force in Lebanon
UNIKOM	United Nations Iraq-Kuwait Observation Mission
UNMIBH	United Nations Mission in Bosnia and Herzegovina
UNMIK	United Nations Interim Administration Mission in Kosovo
UNMOGIP	United Nations Military Observer Group in India and Pakistan
UNMOP	United Nations Mission of Observers in Prevlaka
UNMOT	United Nations Mission of Observers in Tajikistan
UNOMIG	United Nations Observer Mission in Georgia
UNOMSIL	United Nations Observer Mission in Sierra Leone
UNOPS	United Nations Office for Project Services
UNPSG	United Nations Police Support Group
UNRWA	United Nations Relief and Works Agency for Palestine Refugees in the Near East
UNTAET	United Nations Transitional Administration in East Timor
UNTSO	United Nations Truce Supervision Organization
UPU	Universal Postal Union
WFP	World Food Programme
WHO	World Health Organization
WIPO	World Intellectual Property Organization
WMO	World Meteorological Organization
WTO	World Trade Organization
YUN	*Yearbook of the United Nations*

EXPLANATORY NOTE ON DOCUMENTS

References in square brackets in each chapter of Parts One to Five of this volume give the symbols of the main documents issued in 1999 on the topic. The following is a guide to the principal document symbols:

A/- refers to documents of the General Assembly, numbered in separate series by session. Thus, A/54/- refers to documents issued for consideration at the fifty-fourth session, beginning with A/54/1. Documents of special and emergency special sessions are identified as A/S- and A/ES-, followed by the session number.

A/C.- refers to documents of the Assembly's Main Committees, e.g. A/C.1/- is a document of the First Committee, A/C.6/-, a document of the Sixth Committee. A/BUR/- refers to documents of the General Committee. A/AC.- documents are those of the Assembly's ad hoc bodies and A/CN.-, of its commissions; e.g. A/AC.105/- identifies documents of the Assembly's Committee on the Peaceful Uses of Outer Space, A/CN.4/-, of its International Law Commission. Assembly resolutions and decisions since the thirty-first (1976) session have been identified by two arabic numerals; the first indicates the session of adoption; the second, the sequential number in the series. Resolutions are numbered consecutively from 1 at each session. Decisions of regular sessions are numbered consecutively, from 301 for those concerned with elections and appointments, and from 401 for all other decisions. Decisions of special and emergency special sessions are numbered consecutively, from 11 for those concerned with elections and appointments, and from 21 for all other decisions.

E/- refers to documents of the Economic and Social Council, numbered in separate series by year. Thus, E/1999/- refers to documents issued for consideration by the Council at its 1999 sessions, beginning with E/1999/1. E/AC.-, E/C.- and E/CN.-, followed by identifying numbers, refer to documents of the Council's subsidiary ad hoc bodies, committees and commissions. For example, E/CN.5/- refers to documents of the Council's Commission for Social Development, E/C.2/-, to documents of its Committee on Non-Governmental Organizations. E/ICEF/- documents are those of the United Nations Children's Fund (UNICEF). Symbols for the Council's resolutions and decisions, since 1978, consist of two arabic numerals: the first indicates the year of adoption and the second, the sequential number in the series. There are two series: one for resolutions, beginning with 1 (resolution 1999/1); and one for decisions, beginning with 201 (decision 1999/201).

S/- refers to documents of the Security Council. Its resolutions are identified by consecutive numbers followed by the year of adoption in parentheses, beginning with resolution 1(1946).

ST/-, followed by symbols representing the issuing department or office, refers to documents of the United Nations Secretariat.

Documents of certain bodies bear special symbols, including the following:

ACC/-	Administrative Committee on Coordination
CD/-	Conference on Disarmament
CERD/-	Committee on the Elimination of Racial Discrimination
DC/-	Disarmament Commission
DP/-	United Nations Development Programme
HS/-	Commission on Human Settlements
ITC/-	International Trade Centre
TD/-	United Nations Conference on Trade and Development
UNEP/-	United Nations Environment Programme

Many documents of the regional commissions bear special symbols. These are sometimes preceded by the following:

E/ECA/-	Economic Commission for Africa
E/ECE/-	Economic Commission for Europe
E/ECLAC/-	Economic Commission for Latin America and the Caribbean
E/ESCAP/-	Economic and Social Commission for Asia and the Pacific
E/ESCWA/-	Economic and Social Commission for Western Asia

"L" in a symbol refers to documents of limited distribution, such as draft resolutions; "CONF." to documents of a conference; "INF." to those of general information. Summary records are designated by "SR.", verbatim records by "PV.", each followed by the meeting number.

United Nations sales publications each carry a sales number with the following components separated by periods: a capital letter indicating the language(s) of the publication; two arabic numerals indicating the year; a Roman numeral indicating the subject category; a capital letter indicating a subdivision of the category, if any; and an arabic numeral indicating the number of the publication within the category. Examples: E.99.II.A.2; E/F/R.99.II.E.7; E.99.X.1.

Report of the Secretary-General

Report of the Secretary-General on the work of the Organization

Following is the Secretary-General's report on the work of the Organization, submitted to the General Assembly and dated 31 August 1999. The Assembly took note of it on 11 October (**decision 54/408**).

Introduction

Facing the humanitarian challenge

1. Confronting the horrors of war and natural disasters, the United Nations has long argued that prevention is better than cure; that we must address the root causes, not merely their symptoms. Our aspiration has yet to be matched by effective action, however. As a consequence the international community today confronts unprecedented humanitarian challenges.

2. The year 1998 was the worst on record for weather-related natural disasters. Floods and storms killed tens of thousands of people worldwide and displaced millions more. When the victims of earthquakes are included, some 50,000 lives were lost last year to natural disasters. Meanwhile what had seemed a gradual but hopeful trend towards a world with fewer and less deadly wars may have halted. Armed conflicts broke out or erupted anew in Angola, Guinea-Bissau, Kashmir and Kosovo, and between Eritrea and Ethiopia. Other long-established wars, notably that in the Democratic Republic of the Congo, ground on largely unreported by the global media. Moreover, the impact of wars on civilians has worsened because internal wars, now the most frequent type of armed conflict, typically take a heavier toll on civilians than inter-State wars, and because combatants increasingly have made targeting civilians a strategic objective. This brutal disregard for humanitarian norms—and for the Geneva Conventions on the rules of war, whose fiftieth anniversary we recently commemorated—also extends to treatment of humanitarian workers, who are all too frequently denied access to victims in conflict zones or are themselves attacked.

3. Confronted with renewed armed conflict and the rapidly escalating human and financial costs of natural disasters, our task is twofold. On the one hand, we must strengthen our capacity to bring relief to victims; chapter III of the present report, together with my report to the Security Council on the protection of civilians in armed conflict, addresses in detail how our humanitarian response strategies can be improved. On the other hand, we must devise more effective strategies to prevent emergencies from arising in the first place. The case for better and more cost-effective prevention strategies is my central theme in this introduction.

The scope of the challenge

4. The world has experienced three times as many great natural disasters in the 1990s as in the 1960s, while emergency aid funds have declined by 40 per cent in the past five years alone, according to the International Federation of Red Cross and Red Crescent Societies.

5. In the Caribbean, hurricanes Georges and Mitch killed more than 13,000 people in 1998, Mitch being the deadliest Atlantic storm in 200 years. A much less publicized June cyclone in India caused damage comparable to Mitch and an estimated 10,000 deaths.

6. Major floods hit Bangladesh, India, Nepal and much of East Asia, with thousands killed. Two thirds of Bangladesh was inundated for months, making millions homeless. More than 3,000 died in China's catastrophic Yangtze flood, millions were displaced, and the financial cost is estimated to have been an astonishing $30 billion. Fires ravaged tens of thousands of square kilometres of forest in Brazil, Indonesia and Siberia, with devastating consequences for human health and local economies. In Afghanistan, earthquakes killed more than 9,000 people. In August 1999, Turkey suffered one of the most devastating earthquakes in recent history.

7. In terms of violent conflicts, the most worrying development in 1998 was a significant increase in the number of wars. This is particularly troubling because the incidence and severity of global warfare had been declining since 1992—by a third or more according to some researchers.

8. The humanitarian challenge is heightened by the fact that the international community does not respond in a consistent way to humanitarian emergencies. Media attention is part of the problem. The crisis in Kosovo, for example, received saturation coverage. The more protracted and deadly war between Eritrea and Ethiopia, and the resumption of Angola's savage civil war, received very little. Other wars went almost entirely unreported. Partly for that reason, responses to appeals for humanitarian and security assistance have been similarly skewed. Such assistance should not be allocated on the basis of media coverage, politics or geography. Its sole criterion should be human need.

9. I am particularly alarmed by the international community's poor response to the needs of victims of war and natural disasters in Africa. Where needs are pressing, if we are not true to our most basic principles of multilateralism and humanitarian ethics, we will be accused of inconsistency at best, hypocrisy at worst.

Understanding causes: the first step to successful prevention

10. Devising preventive strategies that work requires that we first have a clear understanding of underlying causes. With respect to disasters the answers are relatively straightforward; war is a more complicated story.

11. Human communities will always face natural hazards—floods, droughts, storms or earthquakes; but today's disasters are sometimes man-made, and human action—or inaction—exacerbates virtually all of them. The term "natural disaster" has become an increasingly anachronistic misnomer. In reality, human behaviour transforms natural hazards into what should really be called unnatural disasters.

12. Poverty and population pressures increase the costs of natural hazards because more and more people have been forced to live in harm's way—on flood plains, earthquake-prone zones and unstable hillsides. It is no accident that more than 90 per cent of all disaster victims worldwide live in developing countries.

13. Unsustainable development practices also contribute to the ever greater impact of natural hazards. Massive logging operations reduce the soil's capacity to absorb heavy rainfall, making erosion and flooding more likely. The destruction of wetlands reduces the ability of the land to soak up run-off, which in turn increases the risk of flooding. In 1998, an estimated 25 million people were driven off their lands into overcrowded and often disaster-prone cities by these and related forms of environmental malpractice.

14. While the earth has always experienced natural cycles of warming and cooling, the 14 hottest years since measurements first began in the 1860s have occurred in the past two decades, and 1998 was the hottest year on record. Although still contested in some quarters, the evidence is steadily accumulating that the current wave of warming and the extreme climatic events associated with it are the product of increased carbon emissions, a large fraction of which is generated by human activity.

15. The causes of war are inherently more difficult to explain than those of natural events. Social behaviour is not subject to physical laws in the same way as cyclones or earthquakes; people make their own history, often violently and sometimes inexplicably. Causality is therefore complex and multidimensional, and it differs, often fundamentally, from war to war.

16. We can, however, identify some conditions that increase the probability of war. In recent years poor countries have been far more likely to become embroiled in armed conflicts than rich ones. Yet poverty per se appears not to be the decisive factor; most poor countries live in peace most of the time.

17. A study recently completed by the United Nations University shows that countries that are afflicted by war typically also suffer from inequality among domestic social groups. It is this, rather than poverty, that seems to be the critical factor. The inequality may be based on ethnicity, religion, national identity or economic class, but it tends to be reflected in unequal access to political power that too often forecloses paths to peaceful change.

18. Economic decline is also strongly associated with violent conflict, not least because the politics of a shrinking economy are inherently more conflictual than those of economic growth. In some instances the impact of radical market-oriented economic reforms and structural adjustment programmes imposed without compensating social policies can undermine political stability. More generally, weak Governments—and, of course, so-called failed States—have little capacity to stop the eruption and spread of violence that better organized and more legitimate Governments could have prevented or contained.

19. The shift from war-proneness to war itself can be triggered by the deliberate mobilization of grievances, and by ethnic, religious or nationalist myth mongering and the promotion of dehu-

manizing ideologies, all of them too often propagated by hate media. The widespread rise of what is sometimes called identity politics, coupled with the fact that fewer than 20 per cent of all States are ethnically homogeneous, means that political demagogues have little difficulty finding targets of opportunity and mobilizing support for chauvinist causes. The upsurge of "ethnic cleansing" in the 1990s provides stark evidence of the appalling human costs that this vicious exploitation of identity politics can generate.

20. In other cases armed conflict has less to do with ethnic, national or other enmities than the struggle to control economic resources. The pursuit of diamonds, drugs, timber concessions and other valuable commodities drives a number of today's internal wars. In some countries, the capacity of the State to extract resources from society and to allocate patronage to cronies or political allies is the prize to be fought over. In others, rebel groups and their backers command most of the resources—and the patronage that goes with them.

Strategies for prevention

21. Taking prevention more seriously will help to ensure that there are fewer wars and less consequential disasters to cope with in the first place. There is a clear financial incentive for doing so. In the 1960s natural disasters caused some $52 billion in damage; in the 1990s the cost has already reached $479 billion. The costs of armed conflict are equally sobering. The Carnegie Commission on Preventing Deadly Conflict estimates that the cost to the international community of the seven major wars in the 1990s, not including Kosovo, was $199 billion. This was in addition to the costs to the countries actually at war. The Carnegie researchers argued that most of these costs could have been saved if greater attention had been paid to prevention.

22. More effective prevention strategies would not only save tens of billions of dollars, but hundreds of thousands of lives as well. Funds currently spent on intervention and relief could be devoted to enhancing equitable and sustainable development instead, which would further reduce the risks of war and disaster.

23. Building a culture of prevention is not easy, however. While the costs of prevention have to be paid in the present, its benefits lie in the distant future. Moreover, the benefits are not tangible; they are the wars and disasters that do not happen. So we should not be surprised that preventive policies receive support that is more often rhetorical than substantive.

24. This is not all. History tells us that single-cause explanations of either war or natural disaster are invariably too simplistic. This means that no simple, all-embracing, solutions are possible either. To address complex causes we need complex, interdisciplinary solutions. The fundamental point is that implementing prevention strategies—for wars or disasters—requires cooperation across a broad range of different agencies and departments.

25. Unfortunately, international and national bureaucracies have yet to remove the institutional barriers to building the cross-sector cooperation that is a prerequisite of successful prevention. For example, in national Governments as well as international agencies, departments that are responsible for security policy tend to have little knowledge of development and governance policies, while those responsible for the latter rarely think of them in security terms. Overcoming the barriers posed by organizational division requires dedicated leadership and a strong commitment to creating "horizontal" interdisciplinary policy networks that include our partners in international civil society.

Disaster prevention

26. Disaster prevention seeks to reduce the vulnerability of societies to the effects of disasters and also to address their man-made causes. Early warning is especially important for short-term prevention. Advance warning of famine facilitates relief operations; advance warning of storms and floods allows people to move out of harm's way in time. Improvements in wide-area satellite surveillance technologies are revolutionizing the collection of early warning data relevant to disaster prevention.

27. United Nations agencies are playing an increasingly important early warning role. For example, the Food and Agriculture Organization of the United Nations (FAO) provides vital warning on impending famines, while the World Meteorological Organization provides support for tropical cyclone forecasting and drought monitoring. The Internet is facilitating the real-time dissemination of satellite-derived and other warning data.

28. Greater efforts are also being put into contingency planning and other preparedness measures for disaster-prone countries, while major improvements in risk-assessment and loss-estimation methodologies have been identified through the International Decade for Natural Disaster Reduction. As a result of these and other innovations, national Governments are increasingly aware of the dangers and costs imposed by

inappropriate land use and environmental practices.

29. There is also growing consensus on what must be done. Stricter limits should be placed on residential and commercial development in hazardous areas—vulnerable flood plains, hillsides prone to slippage, or fault zones. Construction codes should ensure more resilient buildings as well as infrastructure that can maintain essential services when disaster does strike. Sounder environmental practices are also necessary, particularly with respect to deforestation of hillsides and the protection of wetlands. Moreover, because poverty rather than choice drives people to live in disaster-prone areas, disaster prevention strategies, to be truly effective, should be integrated into overall development policies.

30. The experience of the International Decade for Natural Disaster Reduction shows that a key to successful longer-term prevention strategies is broad-based cross-sectoral and interdisciplinary cooperation. The campaign to reduce carbon emissions and slow global warming illustrates what can be achieved with such cooperation. Working closely together and guided by the expert consensus that evolved in the Intergovernmental Panel on Climate Change, the scientific community and national and local Governments, together with non-governmental organizations, have been highly successful in alerting the international community to the threats posed by global warming.

31. Here too, we have ample evidence for the benefits of prevention. As severe as last year's floods in China were, the death toll would have been far higher without the extensive disaster prevention efforts China has undertaken over the years. Floods on a similar scale in 1931 and 1954 claimed more than 140,000 and 33,000 lives respectively—in contrast to 3,000 in 1998. Likewise, hurricane Mitch claimed between 150 and 200 lives in one Honduran village, but none in an equally exposed village nearby, where a disaster reduction pilot programme had been in operation for some time.

32. We should not underestimate the challenges, however. In some areas, we still lack a broad scientific consensus on core issues and many questions remain unanswered. The problem often lies not so much in achieving consensus among scientists as in persuading Governments to resist pressures from vested interests opposed to change.

33. Resources are a pervasive concern. Some Governments, particularly in the poorest developing countries, simply lack the funds for major risk-reduction and disaster-prevention programmes. International assistance is critical here; and, because preparedness and prevention programmes can radically reduce the future need for humanitarian aid and reconstruction costs, such assistance is highly cost-effective.

34. Education is essential, and not just in schools. Many national Governments and local communities have long pursued appropriate and successful indigenous risk-reduction and mitigation strategies. Finding ways to share that knowledge, and to couple it with the expertise of the scientific community and the practical experience of non-governmental organizations, should be encouraged.

35. For all of these reasons it is essential that the pioneering work carried out during the International Decade for Natural Disaster Reduction be continued. In July 1999, the programme forum on the Decade set out a strategy for the new millennium, "A safer world in the twenty-first century: risk and disaster reduction". It has my full support.

Preventing war

36. For the United Nations, there is no higher goal, no deeper commitment and no greater ambition than preventing armed conflict. The main short- and medium-term strategies for preventing non-violent conflicts from escalating into war, and preventing earlier wars from erupting again, are preventive diplomacy, preventive deployment and preventive disarmament. "Post-conflict peace-building" is a broad policy approach that embraces all of these as well as other initiatives. Longer-term prevention strategies address the root causes of armed conflict.

37. Whether it takes the form of mediation, conciliation or negotiation, preventive diplomacy is normally non-coercive, low-key and confidential in its approach. Its quiet achievements are mostly unheralded; indeed it suffers from the irony that when it does succeed, nothing happens. Sometimes, the need for confidentiality means that success stories can never be told. As former Secretary-General U Thant once remarked, "the perfect good offices operation is one which is not heard of until it is successfully concluded or even never heard of at all". It is not surprising, therefore, that preventive diplomacy is so often unappreciated by the public at large.

38. In some trouble spots, the mere presence of a skilled and trusted Special Representative of the Secretary-General can prevent the escalation of tensions; in others more proactive engagement may be needed. In September and October 1998, interventions by my Special Envoy for Afghanistan prevented escalating tensions between Iran and Afghanistan from erupting into war. That vital mission received little publicity, yet its cost

was minimal and it succeeded in averting what could have been a massive loss of life.

39. Preventive diplomacy is not restricted to officials. Private individuals as well as national and international civil society organizations have played an increasingly active role in conflict prevention, management and resolution. So-called "citizen diplomacy" sometimes paves the way for subsequent official agreements. For example, former United States President Jimmy Carter's visit to Pyongyang in June 1994 helped to resolve a crisis over the nuclear weapons programme of the Democratic People's Republic of Korea and set in motion a process that led directly to an agreement in October that year between that country and the United States of America. In the Middle East peace process, it was a small Norwegian research institute that played the critical initial role in paving the way for the 1993 Oslo Agreement.

40. In addressing volatile situations that could lead to violent confrontation, Governments are increasingly working in partnership with civil society organizations to defuse tensions and seek creative resolutions to what are often deep-seated problems. In Fiji, for example, collaboration between non-governmental organizations and government officials, aided by quiet diplomacy on the part of regional States, resulted in the promulgation of a new constitution and forestalled what many observers believed was a real possibility of violent conflict.

41. Early warning is also an essential component of preventive strategy and we have steadily improved our capacity to provide it, often in partnership with regional organizations, such as the Organization of African Unity. The failures of the international community to intervene effectively in Rwanda and elsewhere were not due to a lack of warning, however. In the case of Rwanda, what was missing was the political willingness to use force in response to genocide. The key factors here were the reluctance of Member States to place their forces in harm's way in a conflict where no perceived vital interests were at stake, a concern over cost, and doubts—in the wake of Somalia—that intervention could succeed.

42. Complementing preventive diplomacy are preventive deployment and preventive disarmament. Like peacekeeping, preventive deployment is intended to provide a "thin blue line" to help contain conflicts by building confidence in areas of tension or between highly polarized communities. To date, the only specific instance of the former has been the United Nations mission to the former Yugoslav Republic of Macedonia. Such deployments have been considered in other conflicts and remain an underutilized but potentially valuable preventive option.

43. Preventive disarmament seeks to reduce the number of small arms and light weapons in conflict-prone regions. In El Salvador, Mozambique and elsewhere this has entailed demobilizing combat forces as well as collecting and destroying their weapons as part of the implementation of an overall peace agreement. Destroying yesterday's weapons prevents their being used in tomorrow's wars.

44. Preventive disarmament efforts are also increasingly directed towards slowing small arms and light weapons trafficking, the only weapons used in most of today's armed conflicts. These weapons do not cause wars, but they can dramatically increase both their lethality and their duration. I firmly support the various initiatives to curtail this lethal trade that are currently being pursued within the United Nations, at the regional level and by non-governmental organization coalitions.

45. What has come to be known as post-conflict peace-building is a major and relatively recent innovation in preventive strategy. During the 1990s, the United Nations developed a more holistic approach to implementing the comprehensive peace agreements it negotiated. From Namibia to Guatemala, post-conflict peace-building has involved inter-agency teams working alongside non-governmental organizations and local citizens' groups to help provide emergency relief, demobilize combatants, clear mines, run elections, build impartial police forces and set in motion longer-term development efforts. The premise of this broad strategy is that human security, good governance, equitable development and respect for human rights are interdependent and mutually reinforcing.

46. Post-conflict peace-building is important not least because there are far more peace agreements to be implemented today than there were in the past. In fact, three times as many agreements have been signed in the 1990s as in the previous three decades. Some agreements have failed, often amid great publicity, but most have held.

47. Long-term prevention strategies, in addressing the root causes of conflict, seek to prevent destructive conflicts from arising in the first place. They embrace the same holistic approach to prevention that characterizes post-conflict peace-building. Their approach is reflected in the recent United Nations University study that found that inclusive government is the best guarantor against internal violent conflicts. Inclusiveness requires that all the major groups in a society participate in its major institutions—government, administration, police and the military.

48. These conclusions are consistent with the so-called "democratic peace thesis", which states that democracies rarely go to war against each other, and that they have low levels of internal violence compared with non-democracies. The former proposition is still the subject of lively debate among academic experts—in part because of the changing meanings of "democracy" across time and geography. The latter proposition is less controversial: in essence, democracy is a non-violent form of internal conflict management.

49. Long-term prevention embraces far too many strategies to be considered in detail in this essay. Here, I will simply highlight three that are worthy of consideration but have thus far received relatively little attention in the international community.

50. First, the international community should do more to encourage policies that enhance people-centred security in conflict-prone States. Equitable and sustainable development is a necessary condition for security, but minimum standards of security are also a precondition for development. Pursuing one in isolation from the other makes little sense. Security from organized violence is a priority concern of people everywhere, and ensuring democratic accountability and transparency in the security sector should receive greater support and encouragement from donor States and the international financial institutions. Moreover, since the overwhelming majority of today's armed conflicts take place within, not between, States, it makes good security sense in many cases to shift some of the resources allocated to expensive external defence programmes to relatively low-cost initiatives that enhance human—and hence national—security.

51. Second, greater effort should be put into ensuring that development policies do not exacerbate the risks of conflict—by increasing inequality between social groups, for example. In this context, the idea of "conflict impact assessments" should be explored further. Such assessments seek, via consultation with a broad range of stakeholders, to ensure that particular development or governance policies at the very least do not undermine security and at best enhance it. The model here is the well-established environmental impact assessment process, which accompanies major development and extractive industry projects in many countries.

52. Third, the changing realities of the global economy mean new challenges—and new opportunities. During the past decade, development assistance has continued to decline, while private capital flows to the developing world have risen significantly. This has reduced the relative influence of donor States and international institutions in developing countries, while increasing the presence of international corporations. The private sector and security are linked in many ways, most obviously because thriving markets and human security go hand in hand. Global corporations can do more than simply endorse the virtues of the market, however. Their active support for better governance policies can help create environments in which both markets and human security flourish.

53. The common thread running through almost all conflict prevention policies is the need to pursue what we in the United Nations refer to as good governance. In practice, good governance involves promoting the rule of law, tolerance of minority and opposition groups, transparent political processes, an independent judiciary, an impartial police force, a military that is strictly subject to civilian control, a free press and vibrant civil society institutions as well as meaningful elections. Above all, good governance means respect for human rights.

54. We should not delude ourselves, however, into thinking that prevention is a panacea, or that even the best-resourced prevention policies will guarantee peace. Prevention philosophy is predicated on the assumption of good faith, the belief that Governments will seek to place the welfare of the people as a whole over narrow sectional interests. Sadly, we know that this is often not the case. Indeed, many of the requirements of good governance that are central to prevention stand in stark contradiction to the survival strategies of some of the most conflict-prone Governments.

55. While providing incentives for progressive change can sometimes help, it is not something that the international community does often or particularly well. The prospect of closer association with the European Union has served as a powerful tool for promoting tolerance and institutional reforms in several East and Central European countries, but few if any counterparts exist at the global level.

56. The fact that even the best prevention strategies can fail means that we can never completely escape the scourge of war. It follows that, for the foreseeable future, the international community must remain prepared to engage politically—and if necessary militarily—to contain, manage and ultimately resolve conflicts that have got out of hand. This will require a better functioning collective security system than exists at the moment. It will require, above all, a greater willingness to intervene to prevent gross violations of human rights.

57. Demonstrable willingness to act in such circumstances will in turn serve the goal of prevention by enhancing deterrence. Even the most

repressive leaders watch to see what they can get away with, how far they can tear the fabric of human conscience before triggering an outraged external response. The more the international community succeeds in altering their destructive calculus, the more lives can be saved.

58. Collective security in the international system is, of course, the responsibility of the Security Council and responding to crises and emergencies will always be a major focus of its activity. Article 1 of the Charter reminds us that one of the purposes of the United Nations is to take "effective collective measures for the prevention and removal of threats to the peace". Yet reaction, not prevention, has been the dominant Security Council approach to dealing with conflict over the years. Recently, however, the Council has shown increased interest in tackling prevention issues. This has been evident in the Council's extensive debate on post-conflict peace-building and in its response to my report on the causes of conflict and the promotion of durable peace and sustainable development in Africa, which endorsed a range of conflict prevention measures.

59. I greatly welcome these developments. During the coming year, I intend to continue the dialogue on prevention with the members of the Council, which started with the first Security Council retreat I convened in June 1999.

* * *

60. Today, no one disputes that prevention is better, and cheaper, than reacting to crises after the fact. Yet our political and organizational cultures and practices remain oriented far more towards reaction than prevention. In the words of the ancient proverb, it is difficult to find money for medicine, but easy to find it for a coffin.

61. The transition from a culture of reaction to a culture of prevention will not be easy for the reasons I have outlined, but the difficulty of our task does not make it any less imperative. War and natural disasters remain the major threats to the security of individuals and human communities worldwide. Our solemn duty to future generations is to reduce these threats. We know what needs to be done. What is now needed is the foresight and political will to do it.

Chapter I

Achieving peace and security

Introduction

62. During the 1990s, we have witnessed major changes in the patterns of global conflict and in the international community's responses to them. Today, more than 90 per cent of armed conflicts take place within, rather than between, States. With relatively few inter-State wars, traditional rationales for intervention have become decreasingly relevant, while humanitarian and human rights principles have increasingly been invoked to justify the use of force in internal wars, not always with the authorization of the Security Council. Sanctions have been used far more frequently in the 1990s than ever before, but with results that are ambiguous at best.

63. One of the more encouraging developments of the last decade has been an increase in the number of conflicts settled by negotiation. Three times as many peace agreements were signed in the 1990s as in the previous three decades, reflecting a more than 30 per cent decline in the overall number and intensity of armed conflicts around the world from 1992 to 1997. With the sharp upturn in the number of wars in 1998, however, it seems doubtful that the positive trend of the previous five years will be sustained.

64. Comprehensive peace agreements have led to complex implementation processes involving many different agencies. While some traditional peacekeeping operations remain, peacekeepers throughout this decade have been involved in the broader post-conflict peace-building processes associated with the implementation of peace agreements. Post-conflict peace-building involves the return and reintegration of refugees and internally displaced persons, reconciliation, rebuilding judicial systems, strengthening the promotion and protection of human rights, electoral assistance and assistance in rebuilding war-torn political, economic and social infrastructures, as well as more traditional peacekeeping tasks.

65. In response to the changing international normative climate, the number of legal instruments, particularly relating to humanitarian and human rights law, has increased considerably. Growing public concern about gross human rights violations provided much of the political impetus for the creation of the International Criminal Court; concern about the humanitarian costs of landmines fuelled the successful campaign to ban them.

66. The past decade has also been a period of tension and difficulty for the United Nations as it has sought to fulfil its collective security mandate. Earlier this year, the Security Council was precluded from intervening in the Kosovo crisis by profound disagreements between Council members over whether such an intervention was legitimate. Differences within the Council reflected the lack of consensus in the wider international community. Defenders of traditional in-

terpretations of international law stressed the inviolability of State sovereignty; others stressed the moral imperative to act forcefully in the face of gross violations of human rights. The moral rights and wrongs of this complex and contentious issue will be the subject of debate for years to come, but what is clear is that enforcement actions without Security Council authorization threaten the very core of the international security system founded on the Charter of the United Nations. Only the Charter provides a universally accepted legal basis for the use of force.

67. Disagreements about sovereignty are not the only impediments to Security Council action in the face of complex humanitarian emergencies. Confronted by gross violations of human rights in Rwanda and elsewhere, the failure to intervene was driven more by the reluctance of Member States to pay the human and other costs of intervention, and by doubts that the use of force would be successful, than by concerns about sovereignty.

Preventive diplomacy and peacemaking

68. Early warning is now universally agreed to be a necessary condition for effective preventive diplomacy. It is not, unfortunately, a sufficient condition, as the tragedy in Kosovo has demonstrated. As the crisis unfolded, I twice addressed the Security Council in the hope that consensus could be achieved for effective preventive action. Regrettably, diplomatic efforts failed, and the destructive logic of developments on the ground prevailed.

69. What lessons should be drawn from this and other recent failures in conflict prevention? First, that if the primacy of the Security Council with respect to the maintenance of international peace and security is rejected, the very foundations of international law as represented by the Charter will be brought into question. No other universally accepted legal basis for constraining wanton acts of violence exists. Second, that conflict prevention, peacekeeping and peacemaking must not become an area of competition between the United Nations and regional organizations. We work together best when we respect each other's prerogatives and sensitivities. Third, that prevention can only succeed with strong political commitment from Member States and if the provision of resources is adequate.

70. Healing the wounds of a war-torn society is never an easy task. It presents a particularly difficult challenge in Kosovo, which remains embedded in the complicated and contentious political fabric of the Balkans. We recognize the real potential for further disruption of the fragile ethnic equilibrium in a number of the surrounding countries.

71. While the crisis in Kosovo has dominated global media headlines during the past year, equally or more serious crises in other parts of the world have been largely ignored. If this neglect were restricted to the media it would not be of great consequence, but media inattention reflects the attitude of much of the international community, as has become evident in the decline in support for humanitarian appeals for Africa.

72. Security developments in Africa continue to cause the gravest concern. In West and Central Africa in particular, the threat that internal conflicts will spread and lead to armed confrontations between sovereign African States is an especially worrying development.

73. This risk is perhaps best illustrated by the ongoing hostilities in the Democratic Republic of the Congo, in which a large number of African countries have become involved. My Special Envoy, Moustapha Niasse, whom I dispatched to the region in the spring, has been working in support of the diplomatic solution put forward by President Frederick Chiluba, on behalf of the Southern African Development Community. President Chiluba's efforts have the support of the Organization of African Unity (OAU) and the United Nations.

74. The prospects for peace in the Democratic Republic of the Congo have improved. On 10 July, all the belligerents except the Rassemblement congolais pour la démocratie signed a ceasefire agreement in Lusaka. The Security Council welcomed the agreement and authorized the deployment of United Nations military and civilian personnel in the region to facilitate the implementation of the ceasefire. After concerted efforts by South Africa, the United Republic of Tanzania, Zambia and others, the disagreement between the Kisangani and Goma factions of the Rassemblement congolais pour la démocratie over who should sign the ceasefire agreement appears to have been resolved. Once the agreement is signed, the United Nations will dispatch a multidisciplinary technical survey team to the region to assess the security and infrastructure of the areas provisionally identified for future deployments.

75. The peace process in Burundi has also shown some progress, with the Arusha negotiations, under the leadership of former President Julius Nyerere, having reached a crucial stage.

76. In Sierra Leone, whose people have been the victims of one of the most brutal conflicts of recent times, the United Nations Observer Mission in Sierra Leone (UNOMSIL) has worked assiduously to help facilitate a negotiated solution.

In close cooperation with the Economic Community of West African States (ECOWAS), its Monitoring Group (ECOMOG) and other interested Member States, UNOMSIL actively supported the process of negotiations between the Government and the Revolutionary United Front, which led to the signing on 7 July 1999 of the Lomé Peace Agreement. Following the signing of the Peace Agreement, the Security Council authorized an expansion of UNOMSIL. Recognizing the close relationship between the promotion of human rights and sustainable peace, UNOMSIL, in collaboration with the Office of the United Nations High Commissioner for Human Rights, continues to monitor and report on human rights abuses in Sierra Leone with a view to ending further violations.

77. The outbreak of war between Eritrea and Ethiopia in May 1998 was also a cause of profound disquiet. I immediately contacted the leaders of both parties, urging restraint and offering assistance in resolving the conflict peacefully. I have maintained contacts with both sides. I also requested Ambassador Mohammed Sahnoun to assist the mediation efforts of OAU as my Special Envoy. Ambassador Sahnoun participated in various meetings organized by OAU and visited the Eritrean and Ethiopian capitals to press for the acceptance of the peace plan, the OAU Framework Agreement.

78. The conflict between Eritrea and Ethiopia has also had a tragic regional impact, particularly with regard to the conflict in Somalia. The United Nations Political Office for Somalia continues to assist regional efforts at peacemaking in Somalia that are led by the Intergovernmental Authority on Development (IGAD). However, a lack of consensus on the mode of power-sharing among the various factions has precluded settlement of the conflict. The main challenge in the year ahead will be to strengthen international peacemaking efforts and to identify initiatives that can be supported by all the relevant actors.

79. I have also been closely following the continuing complex humanitarian emergency in the Sudan, where developments again highlight the need to address the root causes of the conflict in order to speed the search for a political solution. In 1998, I visited the area and reiterated my offer of good offices to the parties and the mediators. Following a number of internal and external consultations, we have taken further steps to support and invigorate the IGAD peace initiative on the Sudan. Assisting this process, which sadly has not been sustained, remains our primary objective in the quest to help the parties achieve a just and lasting settlement.

80. The United Nations has been involved for many years in Western Sahara, where recent consultations with the Government of Morocco and the Frente POLISARIO have finally resolved a longstanding impasse over a referendum for self-determination. A new date, 31 July 2000, has been set for the referendum.

81. Africa is not, of course, the only area of security concern for the United Nations. Relations with Iraq took a turn for the worse during the year, despite a brief period of compliance with the Memorandum of Understanding signed by Deputy Prime Minister Tariq Aziz and myself in February 1998. In the face of continuing Iraqi non-compliance, the use of force by two Member States and the division in the Security Council that followed it was predictable. Our principal demands remain unchanged, however: Iraq must fully comply with all relevant Security Council resolutions; the international community must be assured that Iraq no longer has the capacity to develop or use weapons of mass destruction; missing Kuwaiti and third country nationals must be accounted for; and Kuwait's irreplaceable archives must be returned. Meanwhile, the people of Iraq continue to suffer the effects of sanctions, although since December 1996 the oil-for-food programme has helped to alleviate some of the suffering by allowing the delivery of humanitarian goods to the country.

82. The overall situation in the Middle East remains troubling. The international community has expressed its strong support for a comprehensive, just and lasting peace in the Middle East based on relevant Security Council resolutions and the principle of land for peace. The recent resumption of the peace process and indications of a real commitment to achieving a settlement by the key protagonists are grounds for cautious optimism.

83. In some conflicts, however, hostility is so intense, and distrust so pervasive, that progress becomes extraordinarily difficult to achieve. This is still the case in Afghanistan. My Special Envoy for Afghanistan, Lakhdar Brahimi, visited the region in October 1998 and late in February this year for talks with the authorities of neighbouring countries, as well as with the Taliban and the United Front. In July of this year, the "six plus two" group held a meeting in Tashkent following which my Special Envoy again visited the region. The United Nations Special Mission to Afghanistan succeeded in convening two rounds of intra-Afghan talks in Ashgabat in February and March 1999. The parties managed to reach an agreement in principle on the sharing of government institutions. Unfortunately, in mid-spring, the Taliban leadership announced that it would not

resume the negotiations started under United Nations auspices. In July, the Taliban launched an offensive against the United Front but failed to gain a decisive advantage. In August, severe fighting continued with grave humanitarian consequences. Notwithstanding these setbacks, I intend continuing my efforts to persuade both sides to resume consultations and to draw in interested Member States and the Organization of the Islamic Conference, where this may be helpful, in order to explore the prospects for an eventual peace agreement.

84. The recent upsurge of fighting along and across the line of control in Kashmir, especially in the Kargil area, is a reminder of the fragility of the situation in this region. The process initiated in Lahore needs to be put back on track as there are serious grounds for concern, not least because of the dangers of an unintended escalation in a subcontinent in which nuclear devices have been tested.

85. On 5 May 1999, after intensive diplomatic efforts, Indonesia, Portugal and the United Nations concluded a set of agreements calling for the United Nations to conduct a popular consultation of the East Timorese people on whether they would accept the special autonomy status offered by Indonesia. Rejection of autonomy would lead to East Timor's separation from Indonesia and transition, under United Nations authority, to independent statehood. The United Nations Mission in East Timor (UNAMET) was established by the Security Council on 11 June 1999. A region-wide structure established by the Mission's Electoral Unit completed a successful registration process despite adverse security conditions. UNAMET also organized and conducted a comprehensive voter education campaign, worked with local authorities and East Timorese groups to foster reconciliation, and deployed civilian police and military liaison officers to advise local police and liaise with the Indonesian military on security issues. Following the successful consultation on 30 August, the United Nations will remain in East Timor to assist in implementing the result.

86. The situation in Myanmar is of continuing concern. My Special Envoy, Alvaro de Soto, visited Myanmar in October 1998 to hold consultations with the Myanmar authorities, as well as with other political actors, including Daw Aung San Suu Kyi, General Secretary of the National League for Democracy. Despite our concerted efforts, I am unfortunately unable to report on any genuine, substantive response by the Government of Myanmar to the appeals made to it, in successive resolutions, by the General Assembly.

87. The United Nations Political Office in Bougainville, which was established in August 1998, has played a critical role in facilitating the search for a peaceful resolution of the crisis in Bougainville, Papua New Guinea. The National Government of Papua New Guinea and the Bougainville parties have asked the Office to supervise the process of disarmament, which will allow implementation of the programme of rehabilitation and reconstruction of the island to begin as soon as possible. The new Government of Papua New Guinea has stressed that the continuation of the peace process is one of its most important objectives.

88. There have been a number of encouraging signs of improved security relations in Latin America over the past year. The Governments of Ecuador and Peru finally took the steps needed to bring their long-standing border dispute to an end, while Argentina and Chile have also agreed to settle the dispute over their frontier.

Peacekeeping

89. The past year has been a tumultuous one for United Nations peacekeeping. We are facing major new challenges with the creation of the large-scale, and in many ways unprecedented, operation in Kosovo, with preparations for a complex new mission in the Democratic Republic of the Congo, the expansion of the mission in Sierra Leone, the strong likelihood of a new operation in Eritrea and Ethiopia, the continuing evolution of the situation in Timor, and the recent agreement by the Government of Angola for a continued United Nations presence in that country.

90. The closure of two major missions, the United Nations Observer Mission in Angola and the United Nations Preventive Deployment Force, and the completion of a follow-on operation, the United Nations Police Support Group in Croatia, have brought the current number of peacekeeping operations to 16.

91. A sudden deterioration in the security situation led to the evacuation of the United Nations Observation Mission in Sierra Leone in January 1999. The restoration of security in Freetown allowed UNOMSIL to return in March to help in supporting the peace process, which culminated in the signing of the Lomé Peace Agreement on 7 July. The implementation of that Agreement will involve an expanded peacekeeping presence, which we are currently examining with ECOWAS.

92. The volatility and danger of the environments in which the United Nations operates are underlined by the number of casualties suffered by United Nations peacekeepers. From 1 January

1998 to 19 August 1999, 34 United Nations personnel gave their lives in peacekeeping operations. We owe them a debt of gratitude that can never be repaid.

93. Perhaps the most disturbing trend has been the growing contempt for international norms. In addition to the savage attacks on civilians, peacekeepers have also been targeted, or used as pawns to manipulate international public opinion. In this context, I warmly welcome the entry into force of the Convention on the Safety of United Nations and Associated Personnel and I would strongly encourage further ratifications by Member States. In response to these developments, the Department of Peacekeeping Operations is undertaking a systematic review of the problem of violence against peacekeepers. I look forward to informing Member States of its findings as this work progresses.

94. Just as the year was tumultuous for peacekeeping, it was similarly testing for the Department of Peacekeeping Operations. In accordance with the wishes of the General Assembly, gratis personnel were phased out by the end of February. As a consequence, the Department as a whole has been reduced by almost 20 per cent during the past year. In order to adjust to the new realities, while continuing to perform its mandated functions, the Department underwent a significant restructuring. The creation or expansion of several missions, the closure and liquidation of others, and mandated planning for possible future operations have occurred in this context. Ironically, the logistics and communications area—vital for the deployment of new missions as well as the liquidation of old ones—was hardest hit by the reduction of staff.

95. This experience shows once again that preparedness requires capacities beyond those needed for current activities. The demand for peacekeeping and other field operations is, by its very nature, difficult to predict and such operations must often be established at short notice. The credibility and effectiveness of any new operation is affected by the promptness with which it is deployed. Delays provide an opportunity for those who oppose the peace process, or the terms of a settlement, to seize the initiative before United Nations personnel arrive. In determining resource requirements for the Organization, including its Headquarters staff, I trust that Member States will bear this in mind.

96. In spite of the unpredictability of events over the past year, some things remained constant. One was the continued emphasis on multidimensional peacekeeping, which is now the norm for the Organization. Multidimensional peacekeeping operations tackle a number of challenges concurrently: helping to maintain ceasefires and to disarm and demobilize combatants; assisting the parties to build or strengthen vital institutions and processes and respect for human rights, so that all concerned can pursue their interests through legitimate channels rather than on the battlefield; providing humanitarian assistance to relieve immediate suffering; and laying the groundwork for longer-term economic growth and development on the understanding that no post-conflict system can long endure if it fails to improve the lot of impoverished people. The Organization is continuing to develop the methods to coordinate these diverse activities more effectively.

97. I have previously reported on ways in which the United Nations programmes, funds and agencies are brought together by my appointed Special Representatives in support of integrated security and development strategies. Additional innovations this year have included our work with the World Bank in the Central African Republic, where the United Nations responsibilities in security, elections and institutional reform have been matched by the Bank's efforts to assist with economic stabilization and to promote longer-term growth. The United Nations Mission in the Central African Republic (MINURCA) played an important supportive role that enabled the peaceful and successful conduct of legislative elections in November/December 1998. MINURCA is to provide support for the presidential elections scheduled for September 1999. Unfortunately, funding for MINURCA is suffering from a worrying lack of enthusiasm among donors, and lack of funding will undoubtedly hamper the efforts of MINURCA to support and observe the elections.

98. Similarly, in Tajikistan, there was initially a very low donor response to appeals for funds to support demobilization projects, an important aspect of the mandate of the United Nations Mission of Observers in Tajikistan. The resulting delays again point to the drawbacks of funding essential elements of a mandate through voluntary contributions, rather than through assessed contributions as is normally the case in peacekeeping operations. There has nevertheless been significant progress in advancing the peace process, and we are cautiously optimistic that the Mission's mandate will be fulfilled.

99. The case of Kosovo is the latest in a series of innovations in peacekeeping and post-conflict peace-building that have been pursued in the 1990s in cooperation with regional and subregional organizations. In Kosovo, we are cooperating with the European Union in reconstruction and rehabilitation programmes, and with the

Organization for Security and Cooperation in Europe in institution-building. Both of those organizations operate under the authority of my Special Representative. We are also working closely with the international military forces responsible for security in Kosovo to ensure unity of civilian and military efforts.

100. In 1999 the Secretariat, in collaboration with the International Committee of the Red Cross, finalized principles and rules on the observance of international humanitarian law by peacekeepers; these rules have been issued as a Secretary-General's bulletin. I hope that the promulgation of that bulletin will help to clarify the scope of the application of international humanitarian law to United Nations forces and operations and ensure that the required standards are observed.

Post-conflict peace-building

101. Post-conflict peace-building seeks to prevent the resurgence of conflict and to create the conditions necessary for a sustainable peace in war-torn societies. It is a holistic process involving broad-based inter-agency cooperation across a wide range of issues. It encompasses activities as diverse as traditional peacekeeping and electoral assistance.

102. Achieving the necessary coordination and complementarity between agencies in conflict and fragile post-conflict situations continues to present a major challenge to the United Nations and its partners. Recognizing the scope of this challenge, in 1997 I designated the Department of Political Affairs, in its capacity as convener of the Executive Committee on Peace and Security, as the focal point for post-conflict peace-building.

103. The past year has seen a number of developments in United Nations post-conflict peace-building operations. Activities in the field include forward planning for a future United Nations presence in the Central African Republic when the mandate of MINURCA expires; establishing a new office dedicated to peace-building in Guinea-Bissau; sustaining the major United Nations presence in Guatemala and consolidating long-standing peace processes in Cambodia and El Salvador and elsewhere.

104. After a year of divisive and destructive conflict in Guinea-Bissau, prospects for a return to normality have improved, albeit gradually. The United Nations Peace-building Support Office is working with the Government and people to coordinate an integrated response to the challenges of peace-building. In Liberia, the United Nations Peace-building Support Office is about to complete its second year of operation. Despite limited financial resources, the Office has supported a number of projects dealing with national reconciliation and rebuilding respect for the rule of law and human rights.

105. The United Nations Verification Mission in Guatemala is mandated by the General Assembly to carry out a range of post-conflict peace-building activities in addition to verifying the peace agreements, providing good offices and undertaking advisory and public information activities. Since 1997, considerable emphasis has been placed on human rights, particularly indigenous rights; social investment; decentralization of State activities; rural development; fiscal and judicial reforms; and the reform of public security and national defence. In 1998, these initiatives provided the basis for a constitutional reform package, which was approved by Congress but which the people failed to ratify in a national referendum in May 1999. As presidential and legislative elections approach in November 1999, continuing commitment to the peace agenda will be crucial to its sustainability.

106. In neighbouring El Salvador, the United Nations Development Programme (UNDP) is responsible for assisting the Government with peace accord issues that remain unresolved. UNDP works in close coordination with the Department of Political Affairs, which retains responsibility for good offices. One of the greatest challenges facing the newly inaugurated Government is consolidation of the institutions that were created, or reformed, as part of the peace process, particularly those responsible for dealing with the country's public security crisis and the protection and promotion of human rights.

107. Institution-building, particularly of the judicial sector, and the protection and promotion of human rights are the key tasks of the International Civilian Mission in Haiti (MICIVIH). As in previous years, there remains much to be done to strengthen State institutions and civil society organizations. The reduced participation of the Organization of American States in MICIVIH, as from 1 July 1999, will necessarily affect our continued role, although core functions will continue to be performed. Meanwhile, the United Nations and the international community have pledged to support the holding of legislative and local government elections by the end of 1999—a crucial requirement for Haiti's future progress.

108. During the past year, there have been welcome developments in Cambodia. With the establishment of a new Government and the collapse of the Khmer Rouge movement, the country is finally at peace and able to devote its attention to reconstruction. My Personal Representative in Cambodia and the United Nations

agencies in the country remain committed to assisting the Government in its nation-building efforts, including the strengthening of democratic institutions and assistance in the promotion and protection of human rights.

Electoral assistance

109. In the late 1980s and early 1990s, the implementation of comprehensive peace agreements in Angola, Cambodia, El Salvador, Mozambique and Nicaragua required the presence of major United Nations electoral missions to help organize the mandated elections. Often viewed as the final step in a long-term peacemaking process, elections symbolize the re-establishment of national authority in a new multi-party system of government. Experience has demonstrated, however, that the relationship of elections to the long-term process of peace-building is highly complex. As the "age of democratization" has entered into a new phase, the Organization has shifted its electoral assistance strategy to encompass a broader understanding of post-conflict peace-building. Elections that have in the past served predominantly as an exit strategy out of conflict situations are now seen as providing an opportunity for institution-building and the introduction of programmes for good governance.

110. Elections are a necessary, but not sufficient, condition for creating viable democracies. That requires the establishment or strengthening of democratic infrastructures such as electoral commissions, electoral laws and election administration structures and the promotion of a sense of citizenship and its attendant rights and responsibilities. The recent experience of the United Nations in Nigeria shows how a partnership in electoral assistance can build a base for long-term post-electoral assistance activities.

111. The United Nations wealth of experience in electoral assistance allows the Organization to tailor its programmes to meet the particular demands of its Member States with great efficacy.

The United Nations, regional organizations and security

112. During the 1990s, regional organizations have played an increasingly active role in regional security affairs, not only in the realms of preventive diplomacy, peacekeeping and confidence-building, but also with respect to peace enforcement. The relationship between the United Nations and regional organizations is complex, usually fruitful, but sometimes difficult. Several lessons have emerged from recent experience.

113. First, it is imperative that regional security operations be mandated by the Security Council if the legal basis of the international security system is to be maintained. Frequently, such operations will also need the wider political support that only the United Nations can provide, and peace settlements will often require United Nations involvement under Security Council authority.

114. Second, security policies that work in one region may not in others. Most regions do not have organizations with the capacity to carry out major peacekeeping or peace enforcement operations. Some regional organizations—most notably OAU—would like to develop a peacekeeping capacity and it is important for the international community to assist them. This is a long-term undertaking, however, and one in which the parties can count on the United Nations to play an active supporting role.

115. Third, today's complex humanitarian emergencies require equally complex multidisciplinary responses, which only the United Nations has the qualifications and experience to provide. Whether responding to crises or implementing comprehensive peace agreements, the United Nations has an unparalleled ability to coordinate action across a wide range of sectors and disciplines.

116. I support moves towards greater cooperation with regional organizations. However, as multilateral activity expands, both the Secretariat and Member States are finding that the human and financial resources allotted for new operations have not kept pace with increased demands, and are at times barely adequate. It is crucial that this situation be addressed with energy and resolve if the United Nations is to avoid a cycle in which expectations exceed capacity, bringing inevitable disappointment and a decline in confidence in the potential of the Organization.

Disarmament

117. During the past year, existing disarmament agreements were threatened by a number of developments which are likely not only to undermine global security but also to cause an increase in global military expenditures. The disarmament machinery in the United Nations was not fully utilized during the year, and no consensus was reached on the convening of a fourth special session of the General Assembly devoted to disarmament, which could set universal goals for the immediate future. However, the United Nations has remained committed to upholding existing norms and to facilitating the necessary political will among Member States to establish new agreements to achieve global security at the low-

est level of armaments commensurate with legitimate self-defence and security requirements.

118. The development of longer-range missiles and their testing by several countries, together with the development of missile defences and the fact that large numbers of missiles are ready to be launched on warning, seriously threaten peace and security. Multilaterally negotiated norms against the spread of ballistic missile technology for military purposes and restraint in missile development would considerably reduce the threat posed by ballistic missiles, whether armed with conventional weapons or capable of delivering weapons of mass destruction. Furthermore, they would substantially improve prospects for progress on bilateral and multilateral disarmament and arms control negotiations, including the prevention of an arms race in outer space.

119. The systematic and progressive reduction of nuclear weapons, with the ultimate goal of their complete elimination, will remain one of the priority tasks of the international community. Little was achieved in this area in the past year, however. Long-standing differences over how to tackle questions of nuclear disarmament continued to prevent the start of negotiations on a treaty banning the production of fissile material, which, in the autumn of 1998, had seemed possible. Meanwhile, we have continued to support ongoing negotiations on the establishment of a nuclear-weapon-free zone in Central Asia, and a text of the treaty is evolving.

120. Efforts to promote entry into force of the Comprehensive Nuclear-Test-Ban Treaty continue, and a conference to consider the issue is scheduled for the autumn. It is crucial that the three nuclear-weapon States that have not yet ratified the Treaty, as well as those States whose ratification is required for its entry into force, deposit their instruments promptly. The path to the 2000 Review Conference of the Parties to the Treaty on the Non-Proliferation of Nuclear Weapons will be smoother if there has been tangible progress in this and other areas of nuclear disarmament.

121. Disarmament activity—in the form of treaties, components of peacekeeping mandates or confidence-building measures—both supports, and is supported by, progress in social and economic development. Promotion of mine awareness, progress in mine clearance, and the provision of medical, psychological and technical assistance to mine victims, who are mainly women and children, sustain the process of socio-economic reconstruction and development in countries emerging from conflict. In May, the worldwide efforts to abolish landmines took a major step forward with the convening of the First Meeting of the States Parties to the Ottawa Convention, which bans anti-personnel mines and mandates their destruction. A further step towards reducing the devastation wrought by landmines will be taken in December, when the parties to Amended Protocol II of the Convention on Certain Conventional Weapons, which constitutes a partial prohibition on landmines, will hold their first annual conference.

122. Other practical disarmament measures, such as the collection and destruction of small arms and light weapons, can reduce the potential for violence and enhance stability, thus facilitating the development process. The reduction of military budgets, especially in post-conflict countries, will increase the resources available for development. The latter issue will, we hope, be considered in depth by the re-established high-level Steering Group on Disarmament and Development.

123. The failure of the Conference on Disarmament, for the third year in succession, to agree on a programme of work and the lack of consensus on holding a special session of the General Assembly on disarmament are a source of grave and ongoing concern.

Sanctions

124. It is increasingly accepted that the design and implementation of sanctions mandated by the Security Council need to be improved, and their humanitarian costs to civilian populations reduced as far as possible. This can be achieved by more selective targeting of sanctions, as proponents of so-called "smart sanctions" have urged, or by incorporating appropriate and carefully thought through humanitarian exceptions directly in Security Council resolutions. I support both approaches.

125. Intense debate continues, both within and outside the United Nations, on how effective the existing sanctions regimes have been, whether comprehensive, like those against Iraq, or more targeted, as in the case of the Libyan Arab Jamahiriya. Questions remain on how best to address the problems arising from their application.

126. Since 1997, the Government of Switzerland has facilitated a dialogue between sanctions practitioners and experts, known as "the Interlaken process". Its goal has been to explore the potential effectiveness of targeted financial sanctions, which may include freezing the financial assets and blocking the financial transactions of targeted entities or individuals. Although their efficacy remains to be tested, and several issues require resolution, the technical feasibility of such sanctions has now been established, as reflected in a report submitted to the Security Council in June 1999.

Chapter II

Cooperating for development

Overview

127. In an increasingly interdependent world, the challenges of development can be met only through well-planned, coordinated and adequately funded international action. The United Nations and its partners have extraordinary capacities in the development field. The challenge is to use them more effectively and synergistically. In the reform programme I initiated in 1997, the United Nations Development Group was created to help meet this challenge. During the past year, the Group has been developing and implementing the new modes of collaboration necessary to meet our development goals.

Reform tools: common country assessment and United Nations Development Assistance Framework

128. Through the common country assessment and the United Nations Development Assistance Framework (UNDAF), the United Nations has for the first time the tools needed to provide strategic and coordinated support for the development goals of national Governments. The common country assessment provides a common analysis for use by the United Nations, donors and other institutions, so that all have a shared understanding of the challenges and potential risks they face. The United Nations Development Assistance Framework is the planning and programming mechanism that coordinates the United Nations response to meeting these challenges.

129. We are also taking steps to ensure that those United Nations programmes, funds and agencies, including the regional commissions, that do not have a presence in the field are fully involved in the preparation and implementation of United Nations Development Assistance Frameworks and common country assessments. Since 1997, some 60 countries have initiated common country assessments; 18 countries participated in the UNDAF pilot project started in 1997, and 19 more are expected to commence an UNDAF before the end of 1999.

Strengthening leadership: the resident coordinator system

130. Throughout the last year, the United Nations Development Group has intensified efforts to improve the resident coordinator system. These have included new selection procedures for resident coordinators to broaden the basis for recruitment and improve the gender balance; performance appraisals of resident coordinators and country teams; improved annual reporting procedures for resident coordinators and a review of lessons learned; and greater support from Headquarters, including better training for resident coordinators and country teams.

Maximizing resources: harmonization and United Nations Houses

131. In response to a call by the General Assembly for greater harmonization and simplification of the policies and procedures used by United Nations bodies, 100 country teams have now planned to have their individual programming cycles begin at the same time, and all country programmes will have harmonized cycles by 2004.

132. The housing of United Nations entities in common premises (United Nations Houses) will foster a greater sense of community and common purpose. To date, some 36 United Nations Houses have been designated around the world; the establishment of 20 more is being considered in 1999. In a number of countries, we are promoting "virtual" United Nations Houses that will connect separate offices via an in-country intranet and thus improve the sharing of information, practices and expertise.

Improving impact: inter-agency support

133. The United Nations Development Group has set up a number of inter-agency groups to provide support to country teams. The Working Group on the Right to Development reviewed the provisional UNDAF guidelines and made specific proposals on how better to incorporate respect for human rights. The Working Group prepared a guidance note for all resident coordinators and will develop a human rights training module. The Group will also disseminate examples of good practice to help country teams learn from each other.

134. The Sub-Group on Gender, formed in June 1998, reviewed the pilot United Nations Development Assistance Frameworks and made recommendations for more effective incorporation of gender perspectives into the core indicators of the common country assessments and the final UNDAF guidelines.

135. Ad hoc task forces and working groups have pooled knowledge gained by the United Nations Development Group on specific topics for the benefit of country teams. In 1998/99, these included the Working Groups on poverty and girls' education, and the Task Forces on globalization, sector programmes and collaboration with the Bretton Woods institutions.

Working together: building partnerships for development

136. During the past year, the United Nations placed greater emphasis on communicating its research, publications and debates to its various partners—nationally, regionally and internationally. This has contributed to greater understanding and awareness of key development issues and to more innovative development thinking. In addition, a database set up jointly by the United Nations Children's Fund (UNICEF), the United Nations Population Fund (UNFPA) and UNDP has deepened mutual understanding and provided valuable input for civil society organizations. A survey carried out by the World Food Programme (WFP) in 1998 found that WFP is collaborating with more than 1,100 non-governmental organizations worldwide, of which three quarters are national and local groups.

137. In response to my statement to business leaders at the World Economic Forum at Davos in 1999, the United Nations Development Group has explored private sector partnerships on a range of development issues. UNDP, for example, has joined with Internet giant Cisco Systems in creating NetAid, a multi-city concert to be broadcast over the Internet to raise public awareness and generate financial support for reducing poverty in developing countries. UNICEF's partnerships with the private sector include a global campaign that has succeeded in eliminating polio in many parts of the world.

138. The United Nations has also made concerted efforts to increase collaboration with the international financial institutions. In February 1999, the Economic and Social Council held a high-level meeting with the Executive Board members of the World Bank and the International Monetary Fund (IMF). Top World Bank officials, including President Wolfensohn and 11 Vice-Presidents, have participated in other exchanges, in the General Assembly, the Economic and Social Council and various open meetings. Discussions have also been held with World Bank officials on the Comprehensive Development Framework and other areas for cooperation, such as the common country assessment and UNDAF. Within the United Nations, including the specialized agencies, there have been a number of discussions on how to make United Nations engagement with the World Bank more effective. The United Nations has also collaborated actively with the regional development banks, particularly in regard to the financial crises in East Asia and elsewhere. Similarly, there has been practical collaboration at the country level and in following up UNDAF/Country Assistance Strategy pilots in Mali and Viet Nam.

139. The United Nations has continued to stress that governance grounded in democracy, the rule of law and respect for human rights is the best foundation for sustainable development. Cooperation has increased markedly between the Office of the United Nations High Commissioner for Human Rights, UNDP, the international financial institutions and the specialized agencies on integrating human rights norms into the development process. The next stage will be to draw upon the practical experiences of Governments throughout the world to identify where, and what sort of, assistance is most needed.

The link between relief and development

140. Inter-agency task forces engaged in post-conflict peace-building have become increasingly common in the 1990s as the number of comprehensive peace agreements has grown. This development has highlighted the need to ensure that emergency relief and recovery assistance programmes are linked effectively to longer-term development initiatives. Recognizing the importance of this linkage, we have initiated a dialogue between the principal actors in the humanitarian, human rights, security and development fields; its goal is to facilitate more effective interdepartmental and inter-agency cooperation. The first meeting of the Executive Committees on Peace and Security, Political Affairs and the United Nations Development Group in November 1998 was an important step in this process.

Capacity-building in statistics

141. In May 1998, the Economic and Social Council, recognizing the importance of statistics and indicators, requested the United Nations Secretariat, bilateral funding agencies and the Bretton Woods institutions to work together to provide support for national statistical capacity-building in Member States. The Department of Economic and Social Affairs, in collaboration with UNFPA, has undertaken various initiatives to implement the 2000 world population and housing census. The Department has also supported regional approaches for census-taking in Central Asia, the Southern African Development Community and the Pacific. Intraregional cooperation among organizations responsible for collecting national and regional statistics is also being supported.

Eradication of poverty

142. Despite improvements over the past 50 years in nutrition, health, education and life expectancy and in reducing material poverty, we

still have far to travel: over 1.5 billion people live on less than $1 a day; almost 1 billion adults—a majority of them women—are unable to read or write; 830 million people are malnourished; and 750 million people have no access to adequate shelter or health care. Gender inequalities continue to hamper economic growth and well-being.

143. Increased natural disasters, the hangover from the East Asian economic crisis, the continuing economic decline of the former Soviet Union, the growing toll of AIDS, especially in Africa, and new outbreaks of war have exacerbated poverty in many parts of the world in 1998.

144. The eradication of poverty is one of the central goals of the United Nations and its agencies, but its achievement remains elusive. While declining aid flows are part of the problem, increasing aid is not a panacea. In some cases, aid has made a real difference in reducing poverty; in others, it has made little or no impact. What makes the difference is how the aid is used. Where foreign assistance is misused, it is of little benefit to those in need.

145. The United Nations has long recognized that development policy is about more than economics narrowly defined. Development cannot occur in a vacuum. It requires that minimal levels of human security are met and that there is inclusive political participation and respect for human rights. As the only international organization with a mandate that embraces security, development and human rights, the United Nations is uniquely well placed to tackle the eradication of poverty in a holistic manner. This requires broad inter-agency cooperation, which is increasingly common practice in today's United Nations. For example, work carried out jointly by the International Labour Organization (ILO), the Department of Economic and Social Affairs, UNDP, the World Bank and IMF formed the basis for my report to the Economic and Social Council in July 1999 on the role of employment and work in poverty eradication: the empowerment and advancement of women.

146. Better poverty eradication policy requires improved risk assessment and early warning strategies—as have been developed jointly by the International Fund for Agricultural Development, FAO and WFP. More generally over the past year, the United Nations has been working with its partners to produce more holistic development policies. The Administrative Committee on Coordination sent an action plan, entitled "Freedom from poverty", and based on its statement on poverty of March 1998, to all United Nations resident coordinators and country teams in October 1998. The plan forms the basis for a new initiative, led by the United Nations Development Group, to help programme countries to meet the goal of halving absolute poverty by 2015.

147. In December 1998, the United Nations Development Group developed an action plan for country-level responses to the challenges of globalization and the financial crisis in East Asia. Seventy-eight countries have either developed a separate strategy for poverty reduction (43 countries) or dedicated part of their overall development plan to poverty reduction (35 countries). United Nations country teams have established inter-agency thematic working groups on gender (in 58 countries), food security (in 48 countries) and a range of other issues related to poverty eradication. In 1998, the Economic and Social Commission for Western Asia (ESCWA), drawing on studies carried out in 1996/97, began to develop poverty alleviation policies.

148. By the end of 1998, the Poverty Strategies Initiative of UNDP had provided support to over 100 countries in the area of poverty analysis, mapping and monitoring and developing national poverty reduction strategies. This initiative involved extensive collaboration at the country level with the World Bank, the regional commissions, ILO, UNICEF, the Department of Economic and Social Affairs and UNFPA.

149. The United Nations Development Fund for Women (UNIFEM) and UNDP initiated a global knowledge network designed to help produce effective pro-poor budgets that were also sensitive to gender and environmental concerns. WFP assisted almost 75 million people, more than half of them women and children, helping to build sustainable food security assets for the poor and responding to their needs in emergency situations. A UNFPA study in South-East Asia on the effects of the financial crisis revealed increasing poverty in the region, and recommended specific policy responses.

150. In May 1999, the United Nations Centre for Human Settlements (Habitat) and the World Bank launched the Cities Alliance to coordinate their support for cities in the developing world. The Alliance focuses in particular on urban squatters, upgrading slums and improving urban governance and management systems. UNDP, with support from Habitat, the United Nations Industrial Development Organization (UNIDO), the United Nations Educational, Scientific and Cultural Organization (UNESCO) and the United Nations Conference on Trade and Development (UNCTAD), launched the World Alliance of Cities against Poverty as follow-up to the Habitat II process.

151. The United Nations International Drug Control Programme has helped Governments in

Latin America and Asia develop "business plans" to reduce incentives for the cultivation of illicit drugs and promote alternative development activities. Meanwhile, United Nations agencies have continued their collaboration with civil society organizations with a view to achieving one of the goals of the Microcredit Summit, namely, to provide 100 million of the poorest families with access to credit and other financial services.

Social development

152. One of the most significant achievements of the international conferences on social development issues convened by the United Nations during the 1990s has been the consensus on the need for people-centred approaches to both social and economic problems. In 1999, the five-year review of the International Conference on Population and Development, held at Cairo in 1994, was conducted in New York. Preparatory work also began for the five-year reviews, to be held in 2000, of the Fourth World Conference on Women and the World Summit for Social Development, and of Habitat II, which will occur in 2001.

153. The review process of the Cairo Conference culminated in a special session of the General Assembly, held from 30 June to 2 July 1999, at which the Assembly adopted key actions for the further implementation of the Programme of Action of the International Conference on Population and Development. This drew on reports prepared by the Department of Economic and Social Affairs on the basis of several technical workshops and symposia, and an on-the-ground assessment of progress made in 114 developing countries and 18 developed countries since the Cairo Conference. The document adopted by the General Assembly focused on population and development concerns; gender equity and the empowerment of women; reproductive health and rights; partnerships and collaborations. It also called for a greater effort by all countries to address the shortfall in resources needed to implement the commitments made at Cairo.

154. At the country level, inter-agency working groups have been established to assist with the integrated follow-up to the conferences. The 1998 annual reports of resident coordinators indicated that 573 thematic groups were functioning around the world. Many of these groups deal with social development concerns, such as basic social services (16 groups), health and nutrition (29), education (24), population and development (7), reproductive health (5), drugs (6) and human rights (15).

155. The use of new information technologies has assisted public information outreach on social development issues. For example, in March 1999 the UNIFEM inter-agency global videoconference, *A World Free of Violence against Women*, linked Member States, United Nations bodies and activists around the world.

156. In addition, ESCWA is implementing a project to provide an integrated regional follow-up by the Arab States to the United Nations conferences, which was launched in October 1998. The project addresses issues related to the themes of the major conferences, including women, population, human settlements and social development. The project also builds on the experiences of UNICEF, UNFPA and UNIFEM.

157. Four particular areas of activity are highlighted below.

A new initiative for girls' education

158. Led by UNICEF, the United Nations Development Group is planning to launch a new 10-year initiative for girls' education. The initiative will bring together a broad coalition of actors, including those outside the United Nations system, to support enhanced provision of girls' education at country level. The Conferences on Population and Development and on Women, and the Social Summit, have demonstrated widespread recognition of the benefits that enhancing the education of girls confers, including increased family incomes, later marriages and reduced fertility rates, reduced infant and maternal mortality rates, better nourished and healthier children, greater opportunities and choices for more women, and greater participation of women in development and in political and economic decision-making.

Focus on youth

159. Contributing to young people's development has important implications for human development and human rights, including strengthening democratic processes and decreasing gender and ethnic discrimination and disparities. The United Nations has continued to build partnerships and strengthen its commitment to supporting young people around the world. In 10 United Nations country teams, inter-agency working groups have been established on children, youth and adolescents.

160. The United Nations International Drug Control Programme sponsored a Youth Vision Drug Abuse Forum bringing together young people from around the world to exchange ideas on tackling drug-related problems. The General Assembly at its special session on the world drug problem agreed on the importance of reducing the demand for drugs as well as cutting off the

supply. The World AIDS Campaign focused on young people in both 1998 and 1999.

161. UNIFEM, UNFPA, UNDP and UNESCO, in partnership with civil society organizations, sponsored the Global Meeting of Generations initiative that fosters dialogue between generations to further human development in the twenty-first century. UNICEF, with the support of the Rockefeller Foundation and the United Nations Foundation, collaborated with a number of United Nations and non-governmental organization partners to develop and support interregional dialogues aimed at formulating policies and programmes which take account of the needs of young people. UNFPA continued to foster regional and national cooperation in adolescent reproductive health by sponsoring a number of events in the Caribbean, sub-Saharan Africa, Asia and the Arab States.

Advocating higher and more focused social spending

162. The 20/20 initiative, by which recipient countries agree to dedicate 20 per cent of their national budgets—and donors give 20 per cent of their development assistance—to social development spending, has drawn attention to the need to increase spending on social development priorities and has stimulated debate on donor and in-country policies. UNICEF, UNDP, UNFPA and the World Bank collaborated both at the international level and in specific countries on this issue over the past year, building on work begun after the Social Summit.

163. Thirty-five social sector expenditure reviews have been completed to date. In October 1998, at the second international meeting on the 20/20 initiative, representatives from 48 countries adopted the Hanoi consensus, which emphasizes the need for increased investment in social services.

United Nations collaboration in the fight against HIV/AIDS

164. The challenge posed by the global AIDS epidemic is growing increasingly serious. By the end of 1998, over 30 million people were infected by HIV/AIDS and almost 14 million had succumbed to the disease. Half of the 6 million new cases of HIV infection in 1998 were young people aged 15 to 24. According to the *World Health Report 1999*, AIDS is now the most deadly infectious disease in the world, killing even more people than tuberculosis.

165. In a number of poor countries, HIV/AIDS is having a major negative impact on progress towards achieving social development goals. For example, according to a report produced by the Department of Economic and Social Affairs in 1998, the nine countries most affected by AIDS will have experienced a 10-year reduction in life expectancy by the year 2000, and a 16-year reduction by 2010-2015. By 2005-2010, infant mortality in the most affected countries could be 28 per cent higher than it would have been in the absence of AIDS, and mortality under age 5 could be 51 per cent higher. Social and economic losses create a downward spiral, reversing hard-won development gains and depriving those infected of any chance of a decent livelihood.

166. In 1998, the United Nations International Drug Control Programme became the seventh sponsor of the Joint and Co-sponsored United Nations Programme on HIV/AIDS (UNAIDS), joining UNICEF, UNDP, UNFPA, UNESCO, the World Health Organization (WHO) and the World Bank. UNAIDS achievements include the production of a series of guides to the strategic planning process for national responses to HIV/AIDS (with UNAIDS support, 13 countries in Asia and Africa have now completed their strategic plans); the publication of over 100 guides to best practices, which include advocacy material, technical updates and case studies; preparations for a new International Partnership against HIV/AIDS in Africa; the establishment of an inter-agency working group on HIV/AIDS with the participation of 115 United Nations country teams; and the launch of a joint initiative by UNAIDS, UNIFEM and UNFPA to build the capacity of women's organizations and Governments to address the challenges of HIV/AIDS.

Sustainable development

167. The seventh session of the Commission on Sustainable Development in 1999 attracted a record number of ministerial participants, confirming the role of the Commission as the main high-level intergovernmental forum on sustainable development. Participants agreed to address the most pressing problems of sustainable development and management of the world's oceans and seas; to promote sustainable development in tourism; and to encourage further action to achieve more sustainable production and consumption. In addition, the five-year review of progress on the Barbados Programme of Action for the Sustainable Development of Small Island Developing States, which represent more than one fifth of the membership of the United Nations, will be held in September 1999.

168. The United Nations Development Group and other bodies in the United Nations system have continued to work together on sustainable development and environmental issues. In January 1999, the United Nations Environ-

ment Programme (UNEP) and Habitat, in collaboration with UNDP and the World Bank, launched a joint regional initiative to improve water management in African cities. The Office to Combat Desertification and Drought continues to provide assistance to a number of countries. To date, 49 countries have benefited.

169. The United Nations Revolving Fund for Natural Resources Exploration promoted environment-friendly mining activities in Mozambique and Suriname and distributed guidebooks on CD-ROM to over 50 countries. In 1998, UNDP completed 75 conversion projects in 19 countries under the Montreal Protocol, which supports the conversion of contaminated industrial sites into usable, safe land. The Office of the United Nations High Commissioner for Refugees (UNHCR) and WFP together identified sustainable environmental management practices in areas hosting large numbers of refugees. ESCWA continued to work towards developing environmental indicators for the Arab region.

170. In 1998, the Department of Economic and Social Affairs, the World Energy Council and UNDP jointly launched the world energy assessment to provide background scientific and technical data for bodies involved in furthering the work of Agenda 21. Through their partnership in the Global Environment Facility (GEF), UNDP, UNEP and the World Bank have helped 138 countries to prepare national strategies to implement their commitments under the United Nations Framework Convention on Climate Change and the Convention on Biological Diversity.

171. Reform of the United Nations Secretariat has improved user access to the analytical and technical work of the Department of Economic and Social Affairs. This in turn will help ensure that the results of policy deliberations in intergovernmental forums, particularly the Commission on Sustainable Development, contribute more effectively to United Nations support for national sustainable development policies.

Africa

172. Working with national and regional partners to improve the lives of people in Africa remains a priority for the United Nations Development Group. The challenges are clear. An estimated 44 per cent of Africans, and 51 per cent of those in sub-Saharan Africa, are living in absolute poverty. Of the 30 million people infected by HIV/AIDS in the world, 23 million live in sub-Saharan Africa; 91 per cent of all AIDS deaths in the world have occurred in 34 countries—29 of which are in Africa. If Africa is to reach the Social Summit's target of halving absolute poverty by 2015, annual GDP must rise by at least 7 per cent until 2015. Growth is currently around 3 per cent and is expected to reach 3.5 per cent in 2000. Africa's debt burden increased from $344 billion in 1997 to $350 billion in 1998, a sum equivalent to 300 per cent of exports of goods and services. Africa received less than $5 billion in foreign direct investment, a mere 3 per cent of global flows.

Enhancing United Nations collaboration for the development of Africa

173. I presented my report on the causes of conflict and the promotion of durable peace and sustainable development in Africa to the Economic and Social Council at its substantive session of 1999. It highlighted the need for substantial and sustained economic growth and social development to meet the challenges faced by African countries. Against this background, the United Nations Development Group, with some of the Executive Committees, has developed an action plan to identify common activities and the most appropriate contributions from individual agencies.

174. The Administrative Committee on Coordination continues to stress the need to tie United Nations initiatives in Africa—the United Nations New Agenda for the Development of Africa in the 1990s and its implementing arm, the United Nations System-wide Special Initiative—into other development undertakings, such as the Tokyo International Conference on African Development, the Heavily Indebted Poor Countries Debt Initiative, the Alliance for African Industrialization and the coordinated follow-up to the United Nations conferences. The first annual regional coordination meeting of the United Nations system in Africa was held at Nairobi, in March 1999, chaired by the Deputy Secretary-General. It adopted the System-wide Special Initiative and the New Agenda as the framework for coordinating the United Nations approach to the development of Africa.

175. Under the auspices of the United Nations Development Group, 10 African countries have participated in the UNDAF pilot phase. Ten more UNDAFs are expected in Africa by the end of 1999 in preparation for the programme cycles beginning in 2001.

Tackling the challenges of poverty in Africa

176. The Jobs for Africa programme is an integral part of the System-wide Special Initiative and meets commitments made at the Social Summit. It aims to develop and strengthen the capacity of national and regional institutions and networks in 10 participating countries to combat

poverty by generating productive employment. Following up on the Summit and taking on the fight against poverty was also the topic for a subregional meeting organized by the Economic Commission for Africa (ECA) in March 1999.

177. The United Nations Development Programme has sponsored a number of long-term national studies to enable Governments to define objectives for poverty eradication, taking into account the effects of globalization and investment flows. A regional decision-making information system was set up in Zimbabwe in 1999 with outreach to other African countries. The programme has benefited 14 countries to date, and another 30 have made formal requests for support.

178. The Africa 2000 initiative of UNDP, providing support to rural women in Africa for sustainable development activities, had sponsored over 700 projects by the end of 1998. At a cost of $1.5 billion, WFP is providing assistance to approximately 21 million people in Africa through 100 projects. In southern Africa, WFP has been working with national partners through its vulnerability analysis and mapping units to promote the use of vulnerability monitoring and analysis to develop contingency plans for tackling regional natural disasters.

179. The United Nations Centre for Human Settlements established the African Forum on Urban Poverty in September 1998. Its Urban Management Programme, supported by UNDP and the World Bank, already covers 26 African countries. The Sustainable Cities Programme, implemented jointly with UNEP, operates in eight African countries.

Focusing on health and education for Africa

180. Led by UNESCO, UNICEF and the World Bank, education activities under the Special Initiative focused during the year on improving primary education in 16 countries where primary school enrolment is low. United Nations agencies were also involved in improving the quality of education in Cameroon, Côte d'Ivoire, Ethiopia, Madagascar, Malawi, Uganda and the United Republic of Tanzania.

181. UNAIDS, together with its sponsors (UNICEF, UNDP, UNFPA, UNESCO, WHO, the World Bank and the United Nations International Drug Control Programme), intensified its campaign against HIV and AIDS in Africa. Seeking as broad a base as possible for its campaign, UNAIDS has brought together Governments, regional bodies, bilateral development agencies, multilateral organizations and the corporate sector, with commitments from large pharmaceutical corporations, the entertainment industry and the Global Business Council on AIDS, as well as civil society organizations.

182. Africa, whose peoples are major victims of malaria, is a principal beneficiary of the WHO-led Roll Back Malaria campaign, which aims to cut deaths from malaria by 50 per cent by 2010 and 75 per cent by 2015. Other United Nations initiatives, such as National Immunization Days, have also helped women and children in many African countries.

183. The work of UNFPA in assisting countries in Africa to implement the Programme of Action of the International Conference on Population and Development has led to concrete improvement in reproductive health care in 19 countries. Four countries have introduced legislation outlawing the practice of female genital mutilation.

184. A major focus of the development activities of WFP is on enhancing women's capacity to increase household food security.

Building national capacity for good governance and trade

185. Collaboration with national, regional and international partners in Africa is central to the United Nations efforts to strengthen national capacity for good governance and trade. The Special Initiative governance group established the Africa Governance Forum and is creating comprehensive databases to analyse government practices. The Forum met in June 1999 in Mali to examine the link between governance and conflict management. In addition, UNIFEM's programme on governance and leadership is promoting greater gender balance in decision-making by voters, candidates and elected representatives in Africa.

186. UNDP, together with UNCTAD, UNIDO, UNESCO, the World Trade Organization (WTO), the African Development Bank, OAU and ECA, organized a forum in March 1999 to consider how to create a positive environment for investment and to enhance competitiveness.

187. The Special Initiative trade group, led by UNCTAD in collaboration with WTO and the International Trade Centre, has developed an integrated framework for trade-related technical assistance. The UNCTAD Asia-Africa Business Networking Forum (March 1999) is itself an example of the United Nations continuing support for South-South cooperation.

United Nations Fund for International Partnerships

188. Since the establishment of the United Nations Fund for International Partnerships in March 1998, four funding rounds have been

completed and almost $140 million awarded to 79 projects covering population and women (33 projects), children's health (15 projects), environment (20 projects) and selected United Nations causes (11 projects) which include the provision of support to the Secretary-General's reform programme. Funds have also been earmarked for emergency assistance relief efforts to the Kosovo region.

189. At the beginning of 1999, a more streamlined and efficient funding process was launched. Separate "programme framework groups" were established to provide guidance for the preparation of specific projects. The groups include population and women, focusing particularly on adolescent girls and the quality of reproductive health services; children's health, focusing particularly on decreasing childhood mortality and reducing smoking; and the environment, focusing particularly on biodiversity and energy and climate change.

Chapter III

Meeting humanitarian commitments

190. The past year was fraught with humanitarian disasters. The extraordinary rise in the number and scale of natural disasters was particularly striking. New armed conflicts broke out with enormous loss of life, massive forced displacement and human suffering in Eritrea, Ethiopia and the southern Balkans, while protracted emergencies continued in Afghanistan, Angola, Sierra Leone, the Sudan and elsewhere.

191. Timely humanitarian action in many countries continued to be compromised by the deliberate targeting of civilians and humanitarian workers and denial of access to humanitarian assistance. Responding to this unacceptable flouting of humanitarian norms, the Security Council initiated a series of open debates on the protection of civilians in armed conflict.

Coordinating humanitarian action

192. The Office for the Coordination of Humanitarian Affairs has continued to strengthen its three core functions: coordination of humanitarian action, policy development and humanitarian advocacy.

193. Coordination efforts focused on improving the environment for humanitarian action in a number of ways, including negotiation with parties to conflicts over access and security; reinforcement of the principles of humanitarian action; and advocacy with the Security Council and other bodies. The need for greater respect for, adherence to, and application of, international laws and norms relating to the rights of civilians has been a central focus in this year of the fiftieth anniversary of the Geneva Conventions. In January and February 1999, the Security Council held two open sessions on this issue. The resulting presidential statement requested that I submit a report on the protection of civilians to the Security Council in September 1999, identifying innovative ways in which the Council, acting within its mandate, could strengthen its capacity to ensure the protection of civilians in conflict.

194. For the first time, the consolidated inter-agency appeals were launched simultaneously (in December 1998 for 1999). As at 31 July, the response to the appeals was about 49 per cent of the amount sought. Excluding south-eastern Europe, however, the response was 31.6 per cent, only marginally better than in 1998. The geographical and sectoral commitment of funds has been extremely uneven, meaning that not even minimum levels of assistance could be guaranteed in certain sectors and that some countries were left critically underfunded. The poor response to crises in Africa, at a time when many donor countries are enjoying a period of prolonged prosperity, was particularly distressing.

195. Effective coordination is particularly important in designing the inter-agency response to the needs of internally displaced persons, since there is no single international lead agency. Work carried out jointly by my Special Representative for internally displaced persons, the Office of the United Nations High Commissioner for Human Rights and the Office for the Coordination of Humanitarian Affairs has formed the basis for a policy paper of the Inter-Agency Standing Committee, which will soon be finalized, on protection of internally displaced persons. It identifies ways of ensuring that protection responsibilities are discharged effectively and sets out a system that can rapidly assign responsibilities to different agencies in emergency situations. Other initiatives during the past year included the undertaking of a review of country situations affected by internal displacement, the preparation of a compendium of good field practice and the development of a global database of internally displaced persons.

196. As the number of major natural and environmental disasters has increased, efforts to enhance the coordination of United Nations responses to them have included the launch of three major inter-agency appeals—for hurricane Mitch and for the floods in Bangladesh and China. In addition, 17 United Nations disaster assessment and coordination teams were dispatched during the year. Situation reports on over 60 natural dis-

asters were disseminated. Twenty-eight international appeals were launched, and over $1 billion was raised. The Office for the Coordination of Humanitarian Affairs and UNDP jointly organized an international disaster management workshop in Beijing in June 1999 to examine ways of enhancing response-preparedness and capacity-building and bridging the gap between emergency relief and early recovery. Regional workshops and seminars were also held. These focused on the development of contingency plans and the strengthening of disaster assessment and coordination teams in disaster-prone regions.

197. A series of thematic events and regional conferences was organized to mark the end of the International Decade for Natural Disaster Reduction. This culminated in a programme forum, held at Geneva in July 1999 and involving all partners in the Framework of Action for the Decade. A comprehensive disaster reduction strategy for the twenty-first century was adopted by the forum, and reviewed by the Economic and Social Council. The latter evaluated the achievements of the Decade and adopted a resolution to ensure continuation of United Nations multisectoral and concerted disaster reduction activities in the future.

198. The Executive Committee on Humanitarian Affairs, under the chairmanship of the Emergency Relief Coordinator, has achieved greater synergy in dealing with issues that have strong security, peacekeeping and political implications for humanitarian assistance. FAO and WHO have recently been invited to participate in the meetings of the Executive Committee. The Inter-Agency Standing Committee remained the principal forum for inter-agency coordination, consultation and decision-making on humanitarian issues.

199. The Inter-Agency Standing Committee has set up working groups on a number of issues. These include natural disasters, improving the consolidated appeal process, human rights and humanitarian action, internally displaced persons, gender and humanitarian response, training, small arms, assistance to countries in the Commonwealth of Independent States, post-conflict reintegration and millennium initiatives. The admission of the World Bank as a member in March 1999 has further strengthened the effectiveness of the Committee. Major priority has also been given to strengthening the systems for coordination in the field, particularly the capacity of humanitarian coordinators, through, for example, the joint consultation of resident and humanitarian coordinators that was held in December 1998. Generic guidelines for strategic frameworks have also been developed from work piloted in Afghanistan.

Delivering humanitarian services

200. In the past year, the United Nations assisted countries and regions affected by over 60 natural disasters, as well as by man-made emergencies. These included Afghanistan, Angola, Armenia, Azerbaijan, Burundi, the Republic of the Congo, the Democratic Republic of the Congo, the Democratic People's Republic of Korea, Eritrea, Ethiopia, Georgia, Guinea-Bissau, Liberia, the Russian Federation, Rwanda, Sierra Leone, Somalia, the Sudan, Tajikistan, Uganda, the former Yugoslavia and the Great Lakes region of Africa. This assistance has often involved innovative joint initiatives. Some examples are the collaboration on health issues between the Pan American Health Organization and UNICEF against cholera in Central America; initiatives undertaken by UNHCR and UNICEF in West Africa on child soldiers and unaccompanied children; and initiatives on gender by UNICEF and WFP.

201. Attacks on humanitarian personnel continued to pose major problems. In 1998, 22 United Nations staff members and many more local and international personnel from non-governmental organizations involved in complex emergencies lost their lives. The loss of humanitarian personnel in several direct attacks in Angola and Somalia illustrated the growing extent of this problem. The World Food Programme lost 12 staff members in 1998. As a result, it has sought to improve staff security by providing at least three days of basic security awareness training for all agency personnel and making key improvements in the security of field facilities.

202. Disbursements of food aid increased in 1998. WFP assisted nearly 75 million people, with contributions amounting to $1.7 billion in 1998, a 33 per cent increase over 1997. In recognition of the challenges posed by its increased involvement in relief assistance, WFP established the Protracted Relief and Recovery Operation, a programme aimed at ensuring a seamless transition from emergency relief and life-saving activities to post-crisis recovery.

203. The health assistance programmes of WHO focused on assessing the health needs of those affected by emergencies and disasters, providing health information, assisting in health sector coordination and planning and implementing priority programmes in areas such as mental health, control of epidemics, immunization, pharmaceuticals and nutrition. Priority was given to strengthening the coordination between national health authorities and the international community, as well as to bridging the gap between recovery, rehabilitation and health development activities. Special efforts were made to

eradicate polio and to control malaria in countries affected by emergencies, to improve health systems in the Palestinian self-rule areas, and to observe the equitable distribution of commodities imported under Security Council resolution 986 (1995) and the rehabilitation of health services in Iraq.

204. Humanitarian conventions are increasingly flouted in modern warfare, and children are major victims. In addressing the needs of children in conflict, UNICEF has continued to press for commitments from Governments and military bodies to act more effectively to protect children. It has urged an end to the use of child soldiers and the universal adoption of the global ban on anti-personnel landmines. Its in-country programmes to protect children in conflict zones have included mine-awareness programmes, and the negotiation of ceasefire agreements to allow the provision of food or immunization to those in need.

205. My Special Representative for Children and Armed Conflict has been working to increase global awareness of the impact of conflict on children and to mobilize the political support of both Governments and civil society to strengthen the protection, rights and welfare of children in armed conflict and its aftermath. At the country level, he undertook a series of visits to countries in, or affected by, armed conflict and sought to obtain commitments from the parties to conflicts and other key actors to providing better protection and welfare for children. Efforts are also under way to promote the inclusion of the protection and needs of children in peace processes, targeting several countries that are undergoing peace-building efforts. In August 1999, the Security Council adopted a resolution stressing the need for greater and more effective efforts to protect children in armed conflicts.

206. In recognizing children and women as bearers of rights who may play a central role in peace-building efforts, UNICEF has contributed to developing and conducting children's rights and gender awareness training for peacekeeping forces. As disasters and crises can affect women and men differently, the Inter-Agency Standing Committee has also developed a common policy on the integration of a gender perspective into humanitarian assistance programmes.

207. The majority of those affected by disasters live in the countryside. Here, FAO has played an important role in assessing damage to local production capacities, providing early warning of impending food emergencies, producing information on crop and food supplies and rendering technical advice to the numerous actors involved in agricultural emergency assistance. FAO has also provided considerable support to disaster-stricken farmers, helping to bridge the gap between relief and rehabilitation.

208. Many of today's gravest humanitarian crises are exacerbated by the use of mines, which in many areas continue to pose deadly threats to civilians long after hostilities have ceased. Responding to the threats posed by landmines, the Mine Action Service of the Department of Peacekeeping Operations has coordinated a number of inter-agency assessment missions, which have defined the problems and challenges facing individual countries and communities and proposed common and comprehensive responses. In addition, it has worked with its partners to develop and implement programmes in mine awareness, victim assistance, mine clearance and advocacy. These and other activities have been strongly supported by Member States, both through contributions to the Voluntary Trust Fund for Mine Action and through the many ratifications of the Ottawa Convention, which allowed it to enter into force on 1 March 1999.

209. The humanitarian community increasingly recognizes that it is part of its responsibility to ensure that relief programmes pave the way for sustainable development. UNDP and humanitarian agencies are working together to ensure that a concern for long-term sustainable human development informs relief operations. Programmes for the demobilization of former combatants, comprehensive mine action, the return and reintegration of refugees and internally displaced persons and the restoration of the institutions of good governance reflect this concern.

210. The United Nations Relief and Works Agency for Palestine Refugees in the Near East (UNRWA) combines humanitarian and development objectives in providing relief and social services to approximately 3.6 million Palestine refugees. A special feature of the Agency's operations has been its ability to maintain essential services, often on an emergency basis, in war and conflict situations. However, the Agency's continuing financial deficit, which reached $70 million against its 1999 budget of $322 million, has inevitably had a negative effect on the level and standard of services.

Assisting refugees

211. By the end of 1998, there were 21.4 million refugees and persons of concern to UNHCR compared with 22.3 million in 1997. Just over half (11.4 million) were refugees; the remainder comprised internally displaced persons, returnees, asylum-seekers and stateless people. The vast majority of

refugees and persons of concern were in Africa, Asia and Europe.

212. In contrast to previous years, there were no large refugee movements in 1998 or in the beginning of 1999. Though numerous, the emergencies the humanitarian community dealt with were relatively small in size and of low visibility. This pattern changed dramatically in the last week of March 1999. From then, over the next three months, 850,000 Kosovar Albanians were forced from their homes—one of the largest and most rapid refugee exoduses of modern times. UNHCR and its partners, with the logistical support of the North Atlantic Treaty Organization, mounted a huge relief operation to assist those who streamed into Albania, the former Yugoslav Republic of Macedonia and Montenegro. More than 90,000 refugees were moved to countries in Europe and beyond under the auspices of the humanitarian evacuation programme. When peace was restored to Kosovo, the refugees returned almost as suddenly and in as large numbers as they had left. In just two weeks, more than 400,000 refugees crossed back into Kosovo.

213. The Kosovo crisis provides a graphic example of the close relationship between human rights abuses, war and refugee flows. The humanitarian and human rights communities both increasingly accept that responses to humanitarian crises must also tackle human rights failings. In Kosovo, the United Nations High Commissioner for Human Rights broke new ground by dispatching envoys to gather information about human rights violations and establishing field offices expressly for this purpose.

214. Africa provides many more tragic examples. The crises in Guinea-Bissau and Sierra Leone forced hundreds of thousands to flee their homes. Renewed fighting in the Democratic Republic of the Congo not only provoked new movements of refugees and displaced persons, but also made it extremely hazardous for humanitarian agencies to continue to provide relief. Late in 1998, the armed conflict between Eritrea and Ethiopia led to a new spate of displacement and mass expulsions in the Horn of Africa, while the internal war in the Republic of the Congo impelled 25,000 Congolese refugees from the Pool region to cross into Bas-Congo in the Democratic Republic of the Congo.

215. There was only limited voluntary repatriation in 1998. Ethiopian refugees were able to return from the Sudan; refugees returned from Ethiopia to north-west Somalia, indicating the restoration of some degree of peace and stability to at least parts of the Horn of Africa. In West Africa, the repatriation of Tuareg refugees to Mali and the Niger was completed, while sizeable numbers of Liberians returned home, either spontaneously (160,000 refugees) or with UNHCR assistance (110,000 since 1997). In Central America, long-standing Guatemalan refugee problems moved towards a successful conclusion thanks to a combination of voluntary repatriation and local integration in Mexico.

216. In other situations, however, continuing violence or a breakdown in political negotiations disrupted plans for refugees to return, leading in extreme cases to further exoduses. This was notably the case in Angola, where renewed hostilities caused a new wave of refugees and generated even greater numbers of internally displaced persons, forcing UNHCR to suspend its repatriation programme. Armed conflict in southern Sudan ruled out plans for the voluntary repatriation of some 240,000 refugees from Ethiopia and Uganda; some 124,000 Somali refugees in Kenya were likewise unable to return to their country of origin; around 120,000 Sahrawi refugees continued to live in exile, waiting for a successful conclusion to negotiations on Western Sahara; refugees from Burundi, numbering some 270,000, had to remain in the United Republic of Tanzania, where their presence was a major source of tension between the two States.

217. Solutions proved equally elusive in other parts of the world. In May 1998, internal conflict again broke out in Georgia, prompting 40,000 people to flee from the Gali area. Many were being displaced for the second time. The repatriation of Afghan refugees from Pakistan and the Islamic Republic of Iran was impeded by continuing instability in Afghanistan, where the reintegration and rehabilitation activities of UNHCR came to a virtual halt. The repatriation of hundreds of thousands of Tamil refugees to Sri Lanka from India proved impossible as a result of the intensity of the Sri Lankan civil war. UNHCR urged the Governments of Bangladesh and Myanmar to accelerate the voluntary repatriation of the estimated 20,000 Muslim refugees who remain in Cox's Bazar, Bangladesh. The repatriation programme resumed in November 1998.

218. The challenges facing UNHCR in these volatile and often stalemated situations are compounded by the fact that safe refuge in neighbouring States, or in countries further afield, is becoming increasingly difficult to secure for victims of war or human rights abuses. Countries in both the developing and the industrialized world are increasingly reluctant to accept the basic obligations of refugee protection. Poor countries argue that they have had to bear a disproportionate burden of the global refugee problem for too long.

219. Responding to these and other concerns, UNHCR has intensified its efforts under its protection mandate, giving prominence to advocacy activities such as the global campaign to promote States' accession to international instruments for the protection of refugees and to the conventions on statelessness. At the same time, it has taken steps to ensure that protection needs are better integrated into assistance programmes.

Chapter IV

Engaging with globalization

220. Globalization is a summary term for the increasingly complex interactions between individuals, enterprises, institutions and markets across national borders. The manifold challenges it poses, challenges that cannot successfully be addressed by nation States acting on their own, provide the most immediate and obvious reason for strengthening multilateral cooperation. Globalization is manifest in the growth in trade, technology and financial flows; in the continuing growth and increasing influence of international civil society actors; in the global operations of transnational corporations; in the vast increase in transboundary communication and information exchanges, most notably via the Internet; in transboundary transmission of disease and ecological impact; and in the increased internationalization of certain types of criminal activity. Its benefits and risks are distributed unequally, and the growth and prosperity it provides for many is offset by the increasing vulnerability and marginalization of others—and by the growth of "uncivil society". During the past year, the United Nations has been examining the various dimensions of globalization—economic, social, environmental and gender—in some detail.

Economic and social dimensions

221. Only a year ago, a worldwide global recession was seen as a distinct possibility. Fortunately, such an outcome has thus far been avoided. Two years of crisis-induced international financial turbulence have nonetheless reduced global economic growth substantially. Other than Japan, the developed economies—conventionally viewed as the engines of growth in the world economy—have barely been affected, but the vast majority of developing and transition economies have experienced at the very least a slowdown—and in some cases a reversal—in economic growth, with its concomitant setbacks in social progress. The more favourable trends of the pre-crisis era may well be restored, but this will take time, and the losses of 1998 and 1999 can never be made up. Meanwhile, the world remains vulnerable to similar disruptions in the future, underlining the need for action to prevent such a possibility.

222. In the majority of countries, growth for the foreseeable future will fall short of what is necessary to reduce the number of people living in poverty. In developing countries as a whole, 1.5 billion people continue to live on less than $1 per day. Unfortunately the commitment of the international community to the eradication of poverty has yet to produce results.

223. During the year, the United Nations provided a valuable platform for dialogue on the financial crisis, the persistence of poverty, the marginalization of Africa and the least developed countries and other dimensions of globalization.

224. At the intergovernmental level, the General Assembly is increasingly engaged with globalization issues. In September 1998, the Assembly held a two-day high-level dialogue on the theme of the social and economic impact of globalization. This innovative process, which involved ministerial round tables and panels, drew together perspectives from Governments, civil society, the private sector and the United Nations system and demonstrated the United Nations unique ability to engage a broad range of stakeholders on issues of critical importance to the international community.

225. Recognizing both the challenges and opportunities that today's globalized financial markets present, particularly for developing and transition economies, the General Assembly decided in 1997 to consider convening a high-level international intergovernmental forum on financing for development, not later than 2001. In the first half of 1999, the Working Group of the General Assembly on Financing for Development agreed that the forum would address national, international and systemic issues relating to financing for development in a holistic manner in the context of globalization and interdependence. The Working Group proposed that the forum involve all relevant stakeholders, including IMF and the World Bank. In this regard, the Economic and Social Council has recommended setting up a joint task force of United Nations and Bretton Woods institutions to facilitate the further involvement of those institutions in the finance for development process launched by the General Assembly.

226. The Economic and Social Council conducted a number of internal debates on the socio-economic dimensions of globalization during the year, and is working more and more with its counterparts in the Bretton Woods institutions in tackling these broad issues. The second special high-level meeting of the Economic and

Social Council with the Bretton Woods institutions was held in 1999 and was complemented by a number of exchanges between the Council and the Executive Directors of the World Bank and IMF. A further visit to the Council in the autumn of 1999 by the Executive Directors of the Bank and IMF, following their annual meetings, is being arranged. The Development Committee recommended that the United Nations further refine the principles and good practice in social policy prepared by the World Bank as follow-up to the World Summit for Social Development.

227. The functional commissions of the Economic and Social Council—those addressing social development, the advancement of women and population and development—continued their work on the follow-up to United Nations conferences. Each of these broad issues is profoundly affected by globalization. Major achievements were the finalization of the optional protocol to the Convention on the Elimination of All Forms of Discrimination against Women and the five-year review of the International Conference on Population and Development, conducted at a special session of the General Assembly in June/July 1999. At its substantive session of 1999 the Economic and Social Council focused on the related issues of poverty, employment and gender equality, and the development of Africa.

228. The impact of globalization on gender in the world of work is both important and complex. It is the focus of a major study, the *1999 World Survey on the Role of Women in Development*, which has involved ILO, UNCTAD, the Department of Economic and Social Affairs and the World Bank, and which I will submit to the General Assembly.

229. The Commission for Social Development considered the impact of globalization on access to social services and recommended greater international coordination in the planning and financing of such services. The Commission on Population and Development considered the relationship between population growth, structure and distribution and sustained economic growth and sustainable development. The deliberations of that Commission highlighted how demographic challenges are affected by globalization, particularly with respect to the international movement of people and the spread of infectious diseases such as HIV.

230. The Commission on Sustainable Development dealt with a number of important challenges posed by globalization, including the management of the oceans, tourism, which is one of the fastest growing industries in the world economy, and the development challenges confronting small island developing States. It has proposed, among other ideas, steps for strengthening the work of the General Assembly on ocean affairs and policy guidelines for sustainable tourism. It also looked at the Barbados Programme of Action for the Sustainable Development of Small Island Developing States for the review which is to take place in the General Assembly in September 1999.

231. The Commission on Human Rights, recognizing that the driving forces of globalization can have major implications for human rights, particularly in developing countries, requested all treaty bodies, special rapporteurs, independent experts and working groups to address the impact of globalization on human rights within their respective mandates. The Subcommission on the Promotion and Protection of Human Rights was asked to submit a comprehensive study on this issue to the Commission at its next session.

232. At Headquarters, the new management arrangements and other reforms have enabled the Secretariat and other bodies to contribute more effectively to the ongoing dialogue on globalization. The Deputy Secretary-General leads a task force of senior officials which is coordinating the United Nations response to a range of globalization issues. The Executive Committee on Economic and Social Affairs has issued reports on the need for the reform of the global financial architecture and on the debt problems of developing countries. New reports are being prepared on development finance and the social dimensions of macroeconomic policy as a contribution to the debate on socio-economic questions related to globalization.

233. One of the consequences of globalization has been the reaffirmation of regional identity. Addressing regional issues and enhancing cooperation with regional institutions via the regional commissions remains central to the work of the Organization. During the past year, the regional commissions have provided the vehicle for in-depth consultations involving Governments and civil society on the agenda of the Millennium Assembly. Globalization has also become a major research focus for the regionally dispersed campuses of the United Nations University and many of the other United Nations research institutes around the world.

234. The challenges of globalization are too great for Governments and international organizations to deal with on their own. Meeting in October 1998, the Administrative Committee on Coordination placed the challenges arising from globalization and the adverse effects of the financial crisis centrally on its agenda. Following that meeting, the United Nations Development

Group was requested to develop an action plan for United Nations country teams to work together with national partners in response to the challenges of globalization and the financial crisis in East Asia. Drawing on existing strategies, the plan presented a range of specific options under four broad areas of activity: (1) monitoring the impact of the crisis, particularly on vulnerable groups; (2) assisting individual countries to carry out the necessary structural and institutional reforms; (3) helping to strengthen and build basic social services and safety nets for the least fortunate; and (4) forging closer links with the World Bank.

235. At the first regular session of 1999 of the Administrative Committee on Coordination, in April, the members concluded that, to meet the challenges of globalization, the United Nations system needed to cooperate more effectively with the private sector and civil society, as well as with Governments. Cooperation can be deepened through partnerships, and it was for this reason that I proposed at Davos that the power and reach of the corporate sector be engaged to further the goals of the Organization. At the second regular session, in October 1999, the members of the Committee will endeavour to reach some overall conclusions on the capacity of the United Nations system to respond flexibly and effectively to the challenges of globalization in the next century.

236. Despite the need to involve all stakeholders in devising responses to globalization, much of the responsibility for addressing its negative consequences rests with the world's most advanced economies. That is why I wrote to the leaders of the G-8 prior to their summit in Cologne in June 1999, urging them to act to prevent the majority of the world's population being left on the margins of the global economy. I urged them to boost their own economic growth, to provide additional official development assistance and debt relief and to bring the representatives of the developing countries and economies in transition into the deliberations on a new international financial system. Although some progress has been made in these areas, far more needs to be done.

237. Progress was made at the Cologne summit on the issue of relieving the debt burden of the heavily indebted poor countries. However, financial and operational details still need to be discussed by the Ministers of Finance at the next session of the Interim Committee, and in the Economic and Social Council this year emphasis was placed on ensuring adequate financing for the full implementation of the G-7 decisions at Cologne. With regard to official development assistance the picture is bleak, however. Between 1990 and 1998, the share of GDP devoted to official development assistance in the developed economies fell from 0.33 per cent to 0.23 per cent.

238. Countries enter the global trading system from very different starting points, and globalization and liberalization affect them unevenly. There have been notable developing country successes where domestic reforms have provided increased dynamism to international trade and investment. Yet problems of access to markets, capital and technology remain pervasive, and many developing countries find it extremely difficult to make the institutional transformations necessary for a beneficial integration into the world economy. In November 1999, the third session of the Ministerial Conference of the World Trade Organization will be held at Seattle, and it now seems likely that the Conference will launch a new round of multilateral trade negotiations. In the Economic and Social Council this year, the idea of making this round into a "development round" enjoyed considerable support. A new trade and development round could provide major opportunities for developing countries to negotiate their integration into the world economic system on the basis of a positive agenda. UNDP and UNCTAD are joining forces to help developing countries to formulate negotiating positions for the Conference.

Globalization and the environment

239. Changes in the global environment do not respect national boundaries and represent one of the most critical challenges of globalization. Nowhere is this more evident than in the threats posed to the world's population by global warming. These threats can only be addressed by far-reaching multilateral agreement, but the political consensus necessary to achieve this has not been easy to obtain. The fourth session of the Conference of the Parties to the United Nations Framework Convention on Climate Change was held in Buenos Aires in November 1998 to begin the process of deciding the rules for implementation of the mechanisms agreed in Kyoto in 1997 and to adopt a two-year plan of action.

240. The Tenth Meeting of the Parties to the Montreal Protocol on Substances that Deplete the Ozone Layer was held at Cairo in November 1998. Its agenda focused on strengthening international efforts to reverse the destruction of the Earth's protective ozone layer. For the first time, it took up the challenge of making policies to protect the ozone layer consistent with the ongoing efforts to reduce emissions of the greenhouse gases that cause climate change.

241. In February 1999, at Cartagena, the Conference of the Parties to the Convention on Biological Diversity examined the risks that biotechnology may pose for biological diversity and human health, its socio-economic implications for developing countries and the relevance of biosafety concerns in developing a precautionary approach to risk prevention. The international community is pursuing a protocol on biosafety that, among other aims, seeks to ensure that living modified organisms are transported into countries only with their prior informed consent.

242. Headway continues to be made in the global chemical safety agenda. International consensus was finally reached on the need for a legally binding treaty to promote chemical safety by preventing unwanted trade in hazardous chemicals and pesticides. In this regard, the Rotterdam Convention on the Prior Informed Consent Procedure for Certain Hazardous Chemicals and Pesticides in International Trade was opened for signature in September 1998. In January 1999, at the second negotiating session, solid progress was made in the drafting of a global treaty to reduce and eliminate environmental emissions and discharges of persistent organic pollutants. The Criteria Expert Group has now met. The third negotiating session will be held at Geneva in September 1999, and a series of regional workshops are planned.

243. The Global International Water Assessment, a major initiative led by UNEP and financed by the Global Environment Fund, was launched to assess key issues and problems facing the aquatic environment over the next four years. The Assessment focuses on the problems of shared, transboundary waters. It is designed not only to analyse current problems but also to develop scenarios for the future condition of the world's water resources. Policy options will be analysed with a view to providing sound scientific advice for decision makers and managers concerned with water resources.

244. At the European regional level, the third Ministerial Conference on Environment and Health was held in London in June 1999. The Protocol on Water and Health, attached to the United Nations/Economic Commission for Europe Convention on the Protection and Use of Transboundary Watercourses and International Lakes, was signed by 35 countries, including 16 countries in transition. The Conference built on foundations laid at previous environment and health conferences (Frankfurt, 1989, and Helsinki, 1994). It marked a new commitment to improving the environment and health in the twenty-first century in view of the need for international cooperation to deal with transboundary problems, such as air pollution, the continuing lack of access to safe water and sanitation, and transport, where solutions have yet to be found to the adverse effects of increasing traffic levels on health and the environment.

245. Achieving effective, legally binding agreements to safeguard the environment remains a major challenge, particularly with respect to creating environmentally sensitive international trade regimes. UNEP, together with UNCTAD, is analysing the social and environmental impact of the economic trends associated with globalization. It is focusing in particular on clarifying potential areas of conflict and convergence between the global trade and environmental agendas. It is also assessing the value of using economic instruments to help to implement environmental agreements.

246. UNEP has pursued my call at the World Economic Forum at Davos for engagement with the private sector, for example through the adoption of the International Declaration on Cleaner Production. There has also been substantial progress in the work of UNEP with the financial services industry and the telecommunication and tourism sectors, including through a new initiative with tour operators.

"Uncivil society"

247. Globalization has brought many benefits but it has also been associated with the unrelenting growth of cross-border illegal activities, which have created a netherworld economy, running into the hundreds of billions of dollars, which threatens the institutions of the State and civil society in many countries. Production, trafficking and abuse of illicit drugs and the spread of transnational organized crime are the main challenges faced by the Office for Drug Control and Crime Prevention, which consists of the United Nations International Drug Control Programme and the Centre for International Crime Prevention, in confronting "uncivil society".

248. At the twentieth special session of the General Assembly, Member States made a historic commitment to eliminate, or significantly reduce, the illicit cultivation of the opium poppy, coca bush and cannabis by 2008. The critical importance of demand reduction in the campaign to curtail drug consumption within 10 years was also highlighted.

249. On the supply side, the United Nations International Drug Control Programme is playing a catalytic role in developing an overall strategy for eliminating illicit crops and drug trafficking. This strategy is predicated on the assumption that the drug problem needs to be addressed holistically, which in turn requires close

cooperation between the Programme and its national and international partners, as well as the international financial institutions. Reducing incentives to cultivate illegal crops requires improving the overall quality of life in rural communities; this in turn means that greater attention must be paid to providing farmers with legal economic alternatives, including basic health, education and social services. On the demand side, the Programme has launched a new initiative to assist Governments in establishing an epidemiological database that will inform officials about the extent and type of drug abuse occurring within their borders. This will help them to develop more effective prevention, treatment and rehabilitation policies.

250. The Centre for International Crime Prevention has continued to promote efforts to address the growing challenges of transnational crime. In March 1999, it launched three global programmes against transnational organized crime, trafficking in human beings and corruption. The Ad Hoc Committee on the Elaboration of a Convention against Transnational Organized Crime has made considerable headway in drafting the convention and its three protocols on trafficking in human beings, migrants and firearms.

251. The rapid expansion of the global financial system and the Internet has increased the challenges posed by money-laundering. In response, the global programme against money-laundering of the Office for Drug Control and Crime Prevention is currently designing a global initiative, the United Nations Offshore Forum, to be launched early in 2000, to prevent the misuse of the offshore financial sector for the laundering of criminal proceeds. The wider objectives of this initiative are to improve transparency in international transactions and to stimulate greater international cooperation in dealing with transnational criminal activity involving offshore financial centres. The global programme against money-laundering will also continue to help Governments to meet the commitment they made at the twentieth special session of the General Assembly to adopt national money-laundering legislation and programmes by 2003.

Implications of globalization for security

252. Globalization has a number of implications for global and national security, some positive, some negative. Global market forces can generate wealth and spread prosperity, but where development is uneven the result can be increased political tensions and risks of instability—as we have recently witnessed following the East Asian financial crisis. Ironically, the same crisis reduced defence spending in the region, checking what some had characterized as a regional arms race. In Western Europe, the logic of market forces has deepened European integration, giving all parties a clear vested interest in the peaceful resolution of inter-State disputes.

253. Many commentators see an important association between the spread of economic liberalism, which is one of the hallmarks of globalization, and the expansion of political liberalism. More than 60 per cent of the world's States now have some form of democratic government. Proponents of what has been called the "democratic peace thesis" point out that democracies almost never fight each other and have far lower levels of internal armed conflict than non-democracies. They argue that insofar as the expansion of market forces facilitates the emergence of democracy, globalization has a positive impact on global security.

254. Globalization also has a dark side. Global demand for particular commodities, such as timber, diamonds and drugs, has provided the funds that have allowed warring factions to sustain fighting over many years. The same Internet that has facilitated the spread of human rights and good governance norms has also been a conduit for propagating intolerance and has diffused information necessary for building weapons of terror.

255. Rising levels of industrial development also mean that more and more States have access to the basic technologies needed to make weapons of mass destruction, while the increasingly open global market makes controlling traffic in the precursors of weapons of mass destruction increasingly difficult.

Chapter V

The international legal order and human rights

Introduction

256. As the nineteenth century gave way to the twentieth, Peace Conferences held at The Hague in 1899 and 1907 sought to humanize our world and to introduce rules to mitigate human suffering during armed conflict. The quest for the peaceful settlement of disputes had as its *raison d'être* the reduction of human suffering wrought by war. The efforts of the League of Nations and the United Nations to codify and progressively develop international law have seen their greatest vindication in the twentieth century in the international legal regime for the protection of human rights.

257. Today, declarations, conventions, treaties, bodies of principles and codes of conduct cover almost every conceivable aspect of the relationship between the individual and the State. Legal instruments exist to protect the rights of the child, to protect the rights of women to equality of treatment, to spell out the duties of Governments in respect of the observance of civil and political rights and economic, social and cultural rights, to proscribe racial discrimination, to prevent torture, to protect minorities and to promote and protect cultural diversity. We enter the new millennium with an international code of human rights that is one of the great accomplishments of the twentieth century.

258. Alas, human rights are flouted wantonly across the globe. Genocide, mass killings, arbitrary and summary executions, torture, disappearances, enslavement, discrimination, widespread debilitating poverty and the persecution of minorities still have to be stamped out. Institutions and mechanisms have been established at the United Nations to eradicate these blights on our civilization. They include the working groups and special rapporteurs of the Commission on Human Rights, the institutions and mechanisms established to promote the realization of economic, social and cultural rights and the right to development, and the Office of the United Nations High Commissioner for Human Rights.

259. When we face egregious violations of human rights, documenting and exposing them has been, and will remain, of the utmost importance. In the future, it is our hope that the International Criminal Court, building on the examples set by the International Tribunals already established, will not only bring criminal despots and tyrants to justice but also act as a deterrent against gross violations of human rights everywhere.

260. The agreement reached to establish the International Criminal Court is a watershed in the history of international cooperation for the promotion of human welfare and for the universal realization of human rights. Developments in this area are of such great potential import for the international legal order that they warrant detailed attention.

The International Criminal Court

261. Eighty-four States have now signed the Rome Statute of the International Criminal Court. Four have ratified the statute, which will enter into force after ratification by 60 States. At the request of the General Assembly in December 1998, I convened the Preparatory Commission for the International Criminal Court established by the Rome Conference. The Commission held its first session in February 1999 and its second in July-August. A third session will be held in November-December.

262. The Preparatory Commission has made some progress in drafting the Rules of Procedure and Evidence and the Elements of Crimes for the future Court, but much remains to be done if the deadline of 30 June 2000 set by the Rome Conference is to be met. In the meantime, I urge Member States to ratify the statute and take the necessary steps for its implementation.

The International Tribunals

263. At the request of the General Assembly in December 1998, I appointed five independent experts to review all aspects of the functioning of the two International Tribunals. The review is general in scope but will focus on judicial management, especially case management in the pretrial phase. Its aim will be to ascertain whether resources can be deployed more efficiently. The review team is to report to the General Assembly towards the end of 1999.

264. The judgements of the two Tribunals have continued to clarify key aspects of international humanitarian law. These include the scope of grave breaches of the Geneva Conventions of 1949; the application of, and the distinction between, the concepts of international and non-international armed conflict; the rules of international humanitarian law which are applicable in armed conflict of a non-international character; the meaning and scope of crimes against humanity, including their relation to armed conflict; the definition of torture in international humanitarian law; the definition of rape in international criminal law; the criminality of the planning and preparation of violations of international humanitarian law; the meaning and scope of command responsibility; the legitimacy of duress as a defence against charges of war crimes and crimes against humanity; and elements of the offence of aiding and abetting in the planning, preparation or execution of a crime under international law.

265. Two main challenges confront the Tribunals. First, further steps must be taken to reduce the time the accused are held in custody awaiting trial and the time taken to conduct the trials themselves. Second, the Tribunal for the Former Yugoslavia faces the additional, and immense, task of investigating crimes committed in Kosovo.

International Tribunal for the Former Yugoslavia

266. In the past year, the International Tribunal for the Former Yugoslavia issued four indictments against nine individuals including, most notably, Slobodan Milosevic, President of the Federal Republic of Yugoslavia. Since its incep-

tion, the Tribunal has issued 27 public indictments against 90 individuals.

267. At the time this report was being prepared, the Tribunal was holding 30 people in custody. Five of those were awaiting appeals; 10 were being tried; 15 were awaiting trial. During the past year, the trials of eight accused were commenced, while judgements were handed down in respect of six accused, bringing the total of those subjected to judgement to seven. Five of the accused were found guilty of at least some of the charges against them; the other was found not guilty on all counts. In addition, the appeal of one accused against conviction and sentence was rejected by the Appeals Chamber, which at the same time allowed appeals by the Prosecutor against his acquittal on certain counts.

268. During the year, the President of the Tribunal wrote four times to the President of the Security Council protesting at the failure of the Federal Republic of Yugoslavia to cooperate with the Tribunal, its continuing failure to arrest and transfer three persons indicted by the Tribunal and its persistent refusal to permit the Prosecutor and her investigators to enter Kosovo.

269. As a consequence of events in Kosovo, the Office of the Prosecutor established temporary operational bases in Albania and the former Yugoslav Republic of Macedonia. The Prosecutor also received my authorization to recruit up to 300 type-II gratis personnel from Member States to undertake specialized forensic work in Kosovo as soon as international forces were deployed. To date, 11 States have finalized agreements with the Organization to provide experts for this purpose.

270. Austria and Sweden concluded agreements on enforcing the sentences of the Tribunal, bringing to five the number of those agreements concluded to date. Negotiations are under way with other States to secure similar agreements.

271. On 16 October 1998, the General Assembly elected three judges to staff a new, third Trial Chamber. They took up their duties on 16 November 1998. Judge Gabrielle Kirk McDonald announced her resignation from the Tribunal, with effect from 17 November 1999. Following consultations with the Presidents of the Security Council and the General Assembly, I appointed Patricia McGowan Wald, a national of the United States of America, to serve out the remainder of Judge McDonald's term of office, which ends in November 2001. The Prosecutor of the two Tribunals, Louise Arbour, announced her resignation with effect from 15 September 1999. On 11 August 1999, the Security Council appointed my nominee, Carla Del Ponte, a national of Switzerland, as Prosecutor of both Tribunals, effective 15 September 1999.

International Tribunal for Rwanda

272. During the past year, the International Tribunal for Rwanda issued two indictments against five individuals. Since its inception, it has served 28 indictments on 48 people. Thirty-eight people are currently in custody under the authority of the Tribunal; 5 accused are waiting for appeals to be heard; 3 are being tried; and 30 are awaiting trial. Five accused have already been found, or pleaded, guilty on counts involving genocide. All five have been sentenced. Appeals are pending from all of these judgements or sentences.

273. Mali became the first State to conclude an agreement on enforcing the sentences of the Tribunal. Negotiations are under way with other States for the conclusion of further such agreements.

274. On 3 November 1998, the General Assembly elected nine judges to the Tribunal's Trial Chambers. At the Tribunal's plenary session in June 1999, Judge Navanethem Pillay was elected President of the Tribunal, replacing Judge Laïty Kama, who was ineligible for re-election to that post.

The way forward

275. Throughout this report, I have sought to emphasize that peace, development and human rights are interrelated. I have also noted that the combination of underdevelopment, globalization and rapid change poses particular challenges to the international human rights regime. This makes it doubly important that we insist on the responsibility of Governments to uphold human rights regardless of their political, economic, social or cultural systems and notwithstanding their economic and social situation. Stated simply: the pursuit of development, the engagement with globalization, and the management of change must all yield to human rights imperatives rather than the reverse.

276. Respect for human rights, as proclaimed in the international instruments, is central to our mandate. If we lose sight of this fundamental truth, all else will fail.

Chapter VI

Managing change

Creating a culture of communication

277. The creation of a new culture of communication within the United Nations is central to our preparations for meeting the challenges of the twenty-first century. In pursuing this goal, the Department of Public Information is imple-

menting a new outreach strategy, in partnership with organizations in civil society throughout the world. The aim is to find new ways to publicize United Nations activities and to highlight our successes. In support of this aim, the Department has worked during the year to promote greater openness and transparency by making more information more widely available, and by improving contact between United Nations officials and the world's media. At the same time, the United Nations programme for broadcasters and journalists from developing countries, which the Department sponsors and runs each year, is engaging younger generations of practitioners and helping to build networks of media professionals who can raise awareness of the work of the United Nations around the world.

278. The Department plans to improve the speed of delivery of United Nations news by initiating a Web-based United Nations News Service which will use e-mail to alert journalists to important news stories emanating from the Organization. Wherever possible, such news alerts will be tailored to the journalists' interests and will be linked to a United Nations News Centre on the home page which will provide greater details about each story outlined in the news alert. Tele- and videoconferencing press briefings by senior United Nations officials from Headquarters and other news-making sites will also help to bring United Nations news to the desks of reporters around the world. United Nations information centres will play a key role by gathering supplementary information from regional centres and monitoring domestic media coverage.

279. The Department has overall responsibility for the United Nations Internet web site, which is undergoing constant refinement. In 1999, a new audio-visual home page was created on the site. United Nations radio and television programmes are now available almost immediately to Internet users around the globe. The United Nations home page (www.un.org) is accessed 3 million times a week, from 133 countries. Use has increased dramatically over the past three years: from 11.5 million hits in 1996 to 98.5 million in 1998, and a projected 150 million in 1999. Intergovernmental support will be vital to sustain the web site in all United Nations languages and keep it up to date, both in content and in the light of technological advances.

280. More than 800,000 schools from over 100 countries have accessed the Department's Cyberschoolbus (www.un.org/cyberschoolbus), an on-line interactive education project which brings together diverse communities of students and educators to learn about the work of the United Nations. The Schools Demining Schools project, for example, raised funds from schoolchildren in donor countries to help to clear mines around schools in war-torn countries. It also helped raise awareness about mines among students who corresponded by e-mail with mine-clearance teams in Afghanistan and Mozambique.

281. During the year, the Department presented a wide range of exhibitions and special events at Headquarters in New York and elsewhere in collaboration with United Nations agencies and outside partners, such as the Walt Disney Company, the American Foundation for AIDS Research (AmFAR) and the Freedom Forum. The Department has received a record number of requests for assistance for projects to mark the year 2000.

282. Among its services to the general public, the Department continues to target young people both through direct, face-to-face contact—such as guided tours, briefings and special events—and workshops for students and teachers. In December 1998, almost 400 young people from 125 schools in 7 countries attended a student conference on human rights at Headquarters. Videoconferencing is also an increasingly important means of connecting young audiences everywhere with the United Nations. In addition, a special effort is being made to involve young people from around the world in the global communications strategy for the Millennium Assembly.

283. To communicate effectively, the United Nations has to be able to get its message across to citizens of Member States as well as Governments. The United Nations information centres play a vital role here by organizing events and disseminating information in local languages that demonstrate how the work of the United Nations is relevant to the daily lives of people everywhere. Their presence on the ground and familiarity with local conditions allow the centres to deliver the Organization's message more effectively to domestic audiences. The United Nations global vision finds a local voice through the relationships that the centres develop with the local community.

284. During the past year, the information centres, in cooperation with Governments and non-governmental organizations, have focused on educational and youth activities, such as model United Nations conferences, after-school educational programmes and community service projects.

285. The Dag Hammarskjöld Library has further increased its "virtual library" capacity by using the Internet to link to United Nations depository libraries and other major libraries around the world. An increasing number of

documents are now posted in Arabic, Chinese, French, Russian and Spanish, as well as English, while a new search engine guides users to major reference sources and the most frequently requested United Nations reports. A newsletter is distributed electronically to more than 330 depository libraries around the world, drawing their attention to newly released United Nations documents. The Library is offering on-line training courses and, as part of its outreach to civil society, particularly in developing countries, is conducting regional training programmes to draw attention to the availability of on-line information at the United Nations.

Administration and management

286. A new vision for management is central to my programme for the reform of the Organization. The strategy which is implementing that vision seeks to create simplified structures and a leaner and more efficient Secretariat run by empowered managers who are committed to managerial excellence and accountability. With the support of staff and management, we are making steady progress towards meeting our goals of streamlining procedures across a range of areas.

287. The Management Policy Office has established an ongoing dialogue with programme managers regarding the implementation of productivity measures that will improve the delivery of mandated programmes while containing, or reducing, costs. It is my intent that efficiency savings will be deposited in a new Development Account and made available for additional projects.

288. Advanced information technologies have improved communication with staff and encouraged discussion on reform throughout the Organization. The Change Management Forum is the leading vehicle for debate, while the UN21 Awards have continued to recognize staff for innovative ideas. The establishment of a Human Resources Cyber Forum has allowed an on-line exchange of views on reform issues. The Ideas Data Bank, set up to encourage staff to offer ideas for management improvements, now contains almost 100 proposals.

289. We are committed to continue improving management practices, notably in reporting and monitoring systems and in enhancing management capacity and accountability.

Human resources management

290. The strategy for human resources management adopted by the General Assembly in 1994 was reconfirmed and expanded in 1996 and 1998. Implementation of the strategy is progressing steadily, with managerial delegation, empowerment and accountability being pursued on an incremental basis making use of a variety of monitoring mechanisms and the strengthening of specific methods of accountability.

291. An electronically accessible performance assessment system is now in place. It aligns performance appraisal more closely with results, identifies staff development needs and holds managers accountable for both managing and staff development. The streamlining of recruitment, placement and promotion procedures is under way and in its initial phase will halve the time needed for each. A recently installed tracking capability will monitor progress.

292. We are building the managerial resources of the Secretariat through an integrated series of staff development and career support programmes. The introduction of a human resources review programme, which will culminate in action plans agreed with individual programme managers, has added a new dimension to human resources planning.

Financial management

293. The Department has continued to develop its results-based approach to financial budgeting. In line with this, current budget proposals include a parallel set of performance indicators, which will highlight the expected outcome for the resources committed. These will form the basis for a prototype budget to be submitted for review to the General Assembly by the autumn of 1999.

294. As in the past, we have provided Member States with regular updates on the financial situation of the Organization. This remains critical. Despite the fact that 117 Member States—a record high—met in full their regular budget assessments for 1998 and all prior years, as at mid-1999 the United Nations was still owed $2.5 billion. As a result, there has been no reduction in the debt to Member States for troops and equipment used in peacekeeping operations. This debt remains at almost $900 million—the same level as for the past three years. Unless there is a significant payment of arrears by Member States, we do not envisage paying off any of this debt in 1999. The United Nations therefore has little, if any, financial flexibility, and those Member States waiting for payment face few prospects for relief.

295. Concerns have recently grown over the added burden of some humanitarian and peacekeeping activities where the additional financing has not been forthcoming as promptly as required, or where the Organization has been asked to meet costs from funds already allocated for its regular programme of work.

Information technology

296. Upgrades to the Secretariat's information technology infrastructure have improved our ability to disseminate information internally and to Member States. Major achievements have included the replacement of more than 4,000 personal computers, the upgrading of the local area network, a rolling programme to install the latest industry-standard office automation software packages, and improvements to the satellite communication system, which can now support increased traffic from the main duty stations and peacekeeping missions. At the same time, the provision of electronic mail, greater technical support and the decision to host web pages of permanent missions in New York have revolutionized communications with Member States.

297. We have continued our programme to develop and install an up-to-date integrated management information system (IMIS) at all duty stations. We are now testing the last elements of this system. At present, eight major duty stations use the system for personnel matters. All Headquarters financial management needs are also now met through the system; away from Headquarters, capability will be in place by the end of 2000. The new payroll capacity of the system will also be deployed by the end of 2000. Further technological advances will allow those working in the field to have remote access to the integrated management system. The system has become ever more versatile, and other United Nations agencies are installing it or those component features which are responsive to their needs.

298. We have made concerted efforts in the past year to ensure Y2K compliance. The Year 2000 Management Group identified core operations for the Organization as a whole and oversaw the drawing up of contingency plans in the event of breakdown of mission-critical operations. In addition, the Administrative Committee on Coordination reviewed the preparedness of members of the United Nations system and identified lead agencies to coordinate work in each location.

Facilities management

299. During the past year, we have given particular attention to the maintenance and renovation of the Headquarters complex of buildings, which has now been in constant use for almost 50 years. In response to growing overhaul and maintenance needs, we are drawing up a programme of long-term capital investment for the refurbishment of Headquarters. Coupled with our commitment to energy conservation programmes, this should help to improve the working environment for our staff and others who use our facilities.

Legal affairs

Legislative assistance

300. A number of bodies involved in the legislative process, in particular the International Law Commission and the United Nations Commission on International Trade Law (UNCITRAL), benefited from the legal research services of the Office of Legal Affairs during the year. The Office also provided legal advice to law-making bodies to assist their deliberations and promote the successful conduct of their negotiations, including the International Law Commission; UNCITRAL; the Sixth Committee of the General Assembly and its working groups; the Ad Hoc Committee established by General Assembly resolution 51/210 of 17 December 1996; the Special Committee on the Charter of the United Nations and on the Strengthening of the Role of the Organization; the Preparatory Commission for the International Criminal Court; and the First Meeting of the States Parties to the Ottawa Convention.

301. The Office of Legal Affairs also provided assistance in running conferences convened for the negotiation and adoption of a number of important multilateral agreements and provided support to the institutions created by the United Nations Convention on the Law of the Sea (the Meeting of States Parties, the Commission on the Limits of the Continental Shelf, the International Seabed Authority and the International Tribunal for the Law of the Sea). Other international organizations sought advice from the Office in developing regulations, rules and standards in their respective areas of competence, for example, in the field of maritime law.

302. The Office participated in the drafting of several legal instruments, including my bulletin on fundamental principles and rules of international humanitarian law applicable to United Nations forces in situations of armed conflict.

303. The Office also provided guidance to States in taking measures for the implementation of the United Nations Convention on the Law of the Sea and offered technical assistance to States engaged in commercial law reform, targeting in particular those States considering the adoption of texts prepared by UNCITRAL.

Legal advice

304. The Office assisted in the preparation and drafting of agreements between the United Nations and a number of other international organizations. This assistance included helping to prepare a draft relationship agreement with the Preparatory Commission for the Comprehensive Nuclear-Test-Ban Treaty Organization. It also as-

sisted in preparing and drafting agreements between the United Nations and individual States—most notably, status-of-mission agreements and agreements with States for the enforcement of the sentences of the two International Tribunals. The Office also provided legal assistance for the negotiation of contracts, leases and other legal transactions in which the Organization was involved.

305. Legal advice on a range of peacekeeping operations was provided, including the preparation of agreements between Indonesia and Portugal on the status of East Timor; between the United Nations and the International Organization for Migration and between the United Nations and Australia on the conduct of the popular consultation for East Timorese living outside East Timor; and on the status of the United Nations Mission in East Timor. It drafted appeals procedures and operational directives for the Identification Commission of the United Nations Mission for the Referendum in Western Sahara and prepared the legislative instruments necessary for the United Nations Interim Administration Mission in Kosovo (UNMIK) to commence operations and gave advice on a range of complex legal issues arising from that Mission's administration of Kosovo.

306. It followed up on the report of the Group of Experts for Cambodia and developed a proposal for a tribunal for the prosecution of Khmer Rouge leaders.

307. The Office of Legal Affairs also provided legal advice, assistance and representation in relation to the resolution of a number of disputes around the world. The Office represented the United Nations in suits brought by the Organization or against it, including a large number of commercial claims arising from peacekeeping missions. It acted to secure respect for the United Nations privileges and immunities by representing me before the International Court of Justice in the advisory proceedings concerning a *Difference Relating to Immunity from Legal Process of a Special Rapporteur of the Commission on Human Rights.* It also acted for the Organization before the two International Tribunals and drew up general guidance for the Secretariat on how to respond to requests from the Tribunals for access to United Nations documentation and for testimony from force commanders and other United Nations personnel.

308. The Office assisted the Member States concerned in the resolution of legal issues related to the implementation of Security Council resolution 1192(1998), and other Council resolutions concerning the bombing of Pan Am flight 103. In addition, it was charged with the task of preparing for, and effecting, the transfer of the two persons suspected of the bombing from the Libyan Arab Jamahiriya to the Netherlands.

309. General guidance was provided to the Secretariat on the conduct of its business, and advice was given to political organs on questions of procedure, participation, representation and membership arising from their work. Legal advice was offered on questions relating to the enforcement of sanctions imposed by the Security Council and on implementing the oil-for-food programme.

310. The Office served as a focal point for contacts between the legal advisers of the United Nations system of organizations and promoted coordination between them on matters of legal policy.

International treaty system

311. The Office discharged my functions as depositary of 508 multilateral treaties. In the past year, the Office handled over 1,800 separate actions in connection with those treaties, considering and addressing the many legal questions arising. The Office discharged the Secretariat's function under the Charter of registering treaties and international agreements entered into by Member States, processing over 2,500 registration submissions during the past year.

Information outreach

312. A range of activities were undertaken during the year to improve the dissemination of information on international law and the work of United Nations legal bodies. In particular, the Office continued to implement a new programme aimed at promoting understanding of the United Nations Convention on the Law of the Sea and ensuring its consistent and effective application.

313. The Office made significant improvements to its publications programme. It reduced the backlog in the production of the *Treaty Series* and introduced measures that should eliminate it completely by 2001. It also increased efforts to address the backlog in the preparation of the *Repertory of Practice of United Nations Organs.* It set up an electronic database for production of the monthly *Statement of Treaties and International Agreements Registered or Filed and Recorded with the Secretariat* and *Multilateral Treaties Deposited with the Secretary-General* and initiated measures to post all printed volumes of the *Treaty Series* on the Internet by 2001. It improved and updated its web sites on the Organization's treaty collection, the International Law Commission, the International Criminal Court and the codification, development and promotion of international law.

314. The international law audio-visual library was expanded to facilitate loans of audio-visual material to Governments and educational institutions; and training seminars and briefing sessions on uniform commercial law were organized to promote awareness of texts prepared by UNCITRAL and encourage States to adopt them.

Challenges

315. In the year ahead, the Office anticipates major challenges in addressing the complex legal issues arising from the implementation of the mandate of UNMIK in Kosovo, and in assisting Member States in their preparations for the establishment of the International Criminal Court. Additional challenges are emerging from the upsurge of activity around the world aimed at reforming and modernizing commercial law and the concomitant need to harmonize and unify the laws of international trade.

Project services

316. The United Nations Office for Project Services, the only entirely self-financing entity in the United Nations system, executes projects on behalf of United Nations agencies and other organizations around the world. Among the many services it provides are project management, loan administration, procurement of goods and services and recruitment of project personnel. The Office combines corporate and public values, putting private sector practices at the service of the ideals of the Charter of the United Nations.

317. In 1998, the total project portfolio of the Office for Project Services reached $3.5 billion, and new business acquisitions exceeded $1 billion for the first time. Actual delivery amounted to $713 million. This represents the value of all inputs—goods, services and consultants—contracted by the Office to execute projects entrusted to it by its clientele. It also includes the authorization of $175 million in loan disbursements for projects that the Office is supervising for the International Fund for Agricultural Development.

318. The Office for Project Services continued to work on behalf of UNDP in such traditional areas as environmental management, governance and the eradication of poverty. It also worked with new partners, including the Department of Political Affairs, the Department of Peacekeeping Operations, the Office of the United Nations High Commissioner for Human Rights and the Office of the United Nations High Commissioner for Refugees, in areas outside the strict purview of development.

319. Several milestones in 1999 highlighted the benefits of new partnerships with other entities of the United Nations system. On behalf of the Department of Political Affairs for example, support was provided to the Commission for Historical Clarification in investigating and documenting human rights abuses in Guatemala. The Office established the Commission's infrastructure, comprising 14 local offices in nine regions of the country, hired the interviewers who documented the country's long history of political violence, contracted services locally and internationally, procured equipment and provided training. The Commission presented its final report to me in February 1999.

320. The Office for Project Services also assisted the Electoral Assistance Division of the Department of Political Affairs, UNDP and the Government of Mexico in the production of a state-of-the-art CD-ROM, which provided guidelines on electoral assistance and was released in Mexico City in March 1999.

321. In June 1999, the Office's Mine Action Unit responded to the request of the Department of Peacekeeping Operations for assistance in laying the groundwork for United Nations mine-clearance operations in Kosovo—a prerequisite for the large-scale return of refugees. The Unit is setting up a Mine Action Coordination Centre in Pristina, hiring a manager and key personnel, and procuring equipment as needed. The Geneva Office, home of the Rehabilitation and Social Sustainability Unit, is well placed to provide management services to United Nations organizations engaged in the reconstruction of Kosovo.

322. The Office for Project Services has made client diversification a top priority so as to broaden its financial base and better serve the needs of the international community. In 1999, as part of its move towards decentralization, the Office signed an agreement with FAO and opened a regional office in FAO headquarters in Rome. The Office hopes that its presence there will encourage new alliances with other United Nations partners as well as bilateral and multilateral development organizations.

323. In keeping with its innovative approach, the Office for Project Services seeks where possible to turn challenges into opportunities. Its own work on Y2K compliance, for example, has translated into new projects in several countries to help Governments deal with the challenges posed by the "millennium bug". Relocation to new offices in autumn 1999 has led to the development of a new expertise in architectural and construction management that can be tapped by other members of the United Nations system. The Office now has teams for business and proj-

ect development that can design services to match the changing needs of its many partners.

324. As the United Nations embarks on a new relationship with the private sector, it can benefit from the experience of the Office for Project Services in outsourcing from, and working with, business to adopt best corporate practice while remaining faithful to the principles of the Charter.

Accountability and oversight

325. In its fifth year of existence, the Office of Internal Oversight Services has continued to strive for increased management accountability within the Organization. During this period, a culture of internal oversight has become accepted and strengthened, and the working methods of the Office have become well established.

326. The Office of Internal Oversight Services has developed a number of mechanisms for enhancing internal oversight of separately administered organs. It has concluded memoranda of understanding for the provision of internal audit services with the Office of the United Nations High Commissioner for Refugees, the International Trade Centre UNCTAD/WTO and the United Nations Compensation Commission. Audit services are also provided to the United Nations International Drug Control Programme and the United Nations Joint Staff Pension Fund. These arrangements have operated for several years and reflect the commitment of the Office to promoting sound management and accountability throughout the United Nations system.

327. The Fifth Committee of the General Assembly and the Committee for Programme and Coordination have taken an increasing interest in the work of the Office for Internal Oversight Services. The number of reports published by the Office has increased each year, more than 50 per cent being in response to mandates from the General Assembly.

328. In 1999, the Office for Internal Oversight Services has looked in particular at peacekeeping operations, humanitarian and other field-related activities, as well as the progress achieved in the Secretariat and its overseas offices in preparing information technology systems for the year 2000. Special emphasis was given to monitoring the progress of implementing United Nations reform, particularly in human resources management and other support services.

Audit and management consulting

329. During the past year, the Audit and Management Consulting Division of the Office for Internal Oversight Services conducted audits of various Secretariat activities, including administrative support, peacekeeping missions and technical cooperation projects; the United Nations Offices at Geneva, Nairobi and Vienna; the Office of the Humanitarian Coordinator in Iraq; the field operation in Rwanda of the Office of the United Nations High Commissioner for Human Rights; the United Nations International Drug Control Programme projects in China, Thailand and the Netherlands Antilles; the Centre for International Crime Prevention and its International Scientific and Professional Advisory Council; UNEP and its Regional Office for West Asia and Regional Coordination Unit for East Asian Seas; the Fukuoka and Rio de Janeiro offices of the United Nations Centre for Human Settlements (Habitat); the United Nations Compensation Commission; and the International Tribunals for the Former Yugoslavia and Rwanda. Audits were also conducted at the Economic and Social Commission for Western Asia, the secretariat of the Economic Commission for Latin America and the Caribbean and its subregional headquarters for the Caribbean, the Economic Commission for Africa and the Economic Commission for Europe.

330. Peacekeeping operations and other field activities continued to receive priority. The Audit and Management Consulting Division conducted audits of peacekeeping missions in Angola, Bosnia and Herzegovina, Eastern Slavonia, Haiti, Israel, Lebanon, and the Syrian Arab Republic and the United Nations Logistics Base at Brindisi, Italy. In addition, the Division has assigned resident auditors to the United Nations Mission in Bosnia and Herzegovina, the United Nations Observer Mission in Angola and the Office of the Humanitarian Coordinator in Iraq.

331. The UNHCR Section of the Division audited UNHCR field operations in 20 countries. These audits, which also covered implementing partners, including government agencies and local and international non-governmental organizations, have contributed to improved internal controls and financial reporting. The Section paid particular attention to procurement to ensure that this was fair and transparent, even under emergency conditions.

332. Recognizing the need to make the United Nations computer system Y2K compliant, the Audit and Management Consulting Division participated as an ex officio member of the Headquarters year 2000 implementation team. It also conducted a major campaign to raise awareness at offices outside Headquarters by sending year 2000 questionnaires and follow-up reports to 22 offices, programmes and regional commis-

sions around the world. The Division also conducted information technology audits of the United Nations Office at Nairobi and the International Tribunals for Rwanda and the former Yugoslavia, and undertook a special consultancy to assist the International Computing Centre at Geneva in assessing the adequacy, timeliness and completeness of its planning and preparations for meeting the year 2000 problem.

333. The Office of Internal Oversight Services submitted the results of several audits and reviews to the General Assembly at its fifty-third session, including those of the United Nations health insurance programme, the employment of retirees, the increase in costs of the development contract for the Integrated Management Information System, and the review of procurement-related arbitration cases.

Evaluation

334. The Office of Internal Oversight Services reviewed the support given by the Department for Disarmament Affairs to international disarmament bodies, namely, the First Committee of the General Assembly, the Disarmament Commission and the Conference on Disarmament. The Office found that delegations were generally satisfied with the level of support provided by the Department to multilateral bodies. The evaluation did however identify a number of shortcomings related to the activities of the regional centres; the United Nations Disarmament Information Programme; technical information provided to Member States; cooperation with regional organizations; and development of contacts with specialized agencies, research bodies and non-governmental institutions.

335. The Office of Internal Oversight Services assessed the achievements of the United Nations electoral assistance programme from 1992 to 1998. The final report focused on *(a)* the role of the Electoral Assistance Division of the Department of Political Affairs in the context of the changing nature of the electoral assistance network, and international norms and codes of practice; *(b)* overlapping roles and responsibilities in the area of electoral assistance among units and organizations of the United Nations system; *(c)* internal and external assessments of the Electoral Assistance Division's major activities; and *(d)* the adequacy of existing standard operating procedures and lessons learned processes.

336. The Office of Internal Oversight Services also conducted triennial reviews of the implementation of the recommendations made by the Committee for Programme and Coordination at its thirty-sixth session on the evaluation of the Department of Public Information and of the termination phase of peacekeeping operations. The review of the Department of Public Information found that the Department was acting on a number of the Committee's recommendations: it was using traditional media, such as radio, and new electronic media more actively, and it was developing a more effective news-gathering and delivery system. However, progress was uneven and the effect of measures adopted in 1997 and 1998—following the reorientation of United Nations public information activities—will have to be reviewed again later.

337. The review of peacekeeping operations found that the Department of Peacekeeping Operations has made significant advances in learning lessons from past experience, in collaborating with the Department of Public Information on the information aspects of peacekeeping missions, and in closing down missions. However, there was little progress on establishing an indexed archive of standard operating procedures developed by completed missions. The Office will keep this issue under review.

Inspection and monitoring

338. In response to concerns raised by the Committee for Programme and Coordination at its thirty-eighth session on the need to place more emphasis on qualitative analysis in future programme assessments, the Office prepared a report on ways in which the full implementation and the quality of mandated programmes and activities could be ensured and could be better assessed by and reported to Member States. Three options were proposed, which were considered by the Committee at its thirty-ninth session. The Committee requested me further to explore ways in which the full implementation of mandates could be ensured and better assessed, in accordance with General Assembly resolution 53/207, and to report on this matter to the Committee at its fortieth session.

339. Progress in building up the provision of common services, and improving the efficiency of support services in New York, Geneva and Vienna in the areas identified in the programme for reform was also reviewed during the past year. The review revealed that the reform process had provided new impetus to improve cost-effectiveness through the expansion of common services. In its inspection report, the Office of Internal Oversight Services recommended measures to enhance central support services, and to remove barriers to the expansion of common services, such as distrust, "turf" protection and the lack of communication among heads of organizations. It also stressed the need for Member

States to support fully the strengthening of common services.

Investigations

340. The Investigations Section of the Office of Internal Oversight Services, based in New York and Nairobi, continued to promote the principle of accountability by recommending that staff and contractors be held responsible for violations of United Nations rules and criminal acts perpetrated against the Organization. As provided by its mandate, the Section was involved in a range of inquiries. In 1999, the Section investigated allegations of corruption, examined partnerships with the private sector and completed its first investigation at a regional commission. The Section also worked with national law enforcement agencies to help bring before the courts those who had committed criminal acts against the Organization. One case involved the theft of $400,000 worth of United Nations property by a contractor to a peacekeeping mission. Another involved fraudulent travel expenses in a peacekeeping mission amounting to an estimated $1.2 million.

341. The Section investigated allegations of corruption in a major programme's field office. The investigation concluded that the evidence did not support the allegations. However, the Section recommended that the programme's management establish policies and procedures for investigating allegations impartially, expeditiously and transparently. This case represented a major step in the Organization's determination to enforce high ethical and legal standards in its commercial dealings with outside entities.

342. Following reports of the illegal export and improper retention of intellectual property by those associated with another programme's project, the Section examined United Nations/private sector partnerships involving electronic commerce. The investigation uncovered extensive solicitations of funds and unauthorized commercial agreements between United Nations staff and private individuals and companies. It also uncovered private sector interests in a United Nations–sponsored programme providing technical assistance to economically disadvantaged countries. The Office of Internal Oversight Services made recommendations to remedy these abuses and for tighter controls on private sector partnerships. The Senior Management Group has now formally taken up this question.

343. A review, conducted jointly with the Audit and Management Consulting Division, of the International Tribunal for the Former Yugoslavia disclosed that the three organs of the Tribunal—the Chambers, the Office of the Prosecutor, and the Registry—were generally managed in an efficient and effective manner. The review recommended improvements in some key administrative and financial areas, however. A report has been submitted to the General Assembly.

344. The Investigations Section also conducted proactive investigations throughout the Organization examining the potential for fraud and made recommendations to combat this. The investigations focused on staff entitlements, such as education and security grants, which are susceptible to abuse.

PART ONE

Political and security questions

Chapter I

International peace and security

The year 1999 was a tumultuous one for United Nations peacekeeping as it faced new challenges with the creation of large-scale, and in many ways unprecedented, operations, while it worked to maintain ongoing operations worldwide in pursuit of its Charter objective of maintaining and promoting international peace and security. The Security Council, in November, reaffirmed its responsibility under the Charter to take action in that regard and expressed its readiness to consider appropriate preventive action in response to matters likely to threaten international peace and security. The Council expressed concern that the destabilizing accumulation of small arms had contributed to the duration and intensity of armed conflict and called for measures to discourage arms flows to countries engaged in or emerging from armed conflict. It welcomed the convening in 2001 of an international conference on the illicit arms trade. The Council also suggested practical measures to promote the success of the process of peace-building.

During the year, the United Nations deployed 21 peacekeeping operations worldwide, with some 18,410 military personnel and civilian police serving under UN command as at 31 December 1999. The year began with 16 operations in place. Four missions ended during the year, one in Europe, two in Africa and one in Asia; and five new ones were established, one in Europe, two in Africa and two in Asia. The total number of missions in place at the end of the year stood at 17.

Besides its peacekeeping operations, the United Nations addressed conflict situations in other areas through a number of political and human rights missions and the deployment of the Secretary-General's Special Representatives in Afghanistan, Angola, Burundi, the Democratic People's Republic of Korea, Guatemala, Guinea-Bissau, Liberia, Papua New Guinea and Somalia.

The Special Committee on Peacekeeping Operations, the body responsible for reviewing UN peacekeeping operations in all their aspects, and its open-ended Working Group made proposals and recommendations to guide the principles, definitions and implementation of mandates, on enhancing the capacity of UN peacekeeping and on cooperation with regional arrangements. It also reviewed its own relationship with the General Assembly and recommended procedures for enhancing that relationship.

The cost of UN peacekeeping operations amounted to $837.8 million for the 12-month period ending 30 June 1999, compared with $879.3 million for the previous 12-month period, while unpaid assessed contributions from Member States to peacekeeping budgets amounted to $1,687.6 million as at June 1999, compared to $1,739.9 million in 1998.

The Assembly considered various aspects of peacekeeping financing, including the apportionment of costs, financial performance and proposed budgets, peacekeeping support accounts and the Peacekeeping Reserve Fund. It also reviewed implementation of the new procedures for the reimbursement of contingent-owned equipment and the management of peacekeeping assets, including the operation of the United Nations Logistics Base in Brindisi, Italy.

Prevention of armed conflicts and peace-building

Preventive diplomacy and peacemaking

In his report on the work of the Organization [A/54/1], the Secretary-General stated that it was universally agreed that early warning was to be a necessary condition for effective preventive diplomacy. However, it was not a sufficient condition, as the tragedy in Kosovo in the Federal Republic of Yugoslavia (Serbia and Montenegro) demonstrated (see PART ONE, Chapter V). The lessons to be drawn from that and other recent failures in conflict prevention were: if the primacy of the Security Council with respect to the maintenance of international peace and security was rejected, the foundations of international law as represented by the Charter would be brought into question since no other universally accepted legal basis for constraining wanton acts of violence existed; conflict prevention, peacekeeping and peacemaking should not become an area of competition between the United Nations and regional organizations; and prevention could succeed only with strong political commitment from Member States, together with the provision of adequate resources.

The Secretary-General drew attention to three long-term prevention strategies that deserved further consideration. First, the international community should do more to encourage policies that enhanced people-centred security in conflict-prone States. Second, greater effort should be put into ensuring that development policies did not exacerbate the risks of conflict, such as increasing inequality between social groups. In that context, the idea of "conflict impact assessments"—consultation with a broad range of stakeholders to ensure that particular development or governance policies did not undermine security—should be explored further. Third, the changing realities of the global economy had meant new challenges and opportunities. In addition, development assistance had declined while private capital flows to the developing world had risen significantly. In that regard, the active support of global corporations for better governance policies could help create environments in which both markets and human security flourished.

The common thread running through almost all conflict prevention policies, said the Secretary-General, was the need to pursue good governance, which, above all, meant respect for human rights. Prevention philosophy was predicated on the assumption of good faith, the belief that Governments would seek to place the welfare of the people as a whole over narrow sectional interests. However, many of the requirements of good governance that were central to prevention stood in stark contradiction to the survival strategies of some of the most conflict-prone Governments. The fact that even the best prevention strategies could fail meant that the scourge of war could never be escaped completely. Therefore, for the foreseeable future, the international community had to remain prepared to engage politically, and if necessary militarily, to contain, manage and ultimately resolve conflicts that had got out of hand.

The Secretary-General observed that collective security in the international system was the responsibility of the Security Council and responding to crises and emergencies would always be a major focus of its activity. On the other hand, the Charter stated that one of the purposes of the United Nations was to take effective collective measures for the prevention and removal of threats to the peace. Yet reaction, not prevention, had been the dominant Council approach to dealing with conflict over the years. Recently, however, the Council had shown increased interest in tackling prevention issues. That was evident in the extensive debates on post-conflict peace-building and the promotion of durable peace and sustainable development in Africa. Nevertheless, UN political and organizational cultures and practices remained oriented far more towards reaction than prevention. The transition from a culture of reaction to a culture of prevention would not be easy, but the difficulty of the task did not make it any less imperative, said the Secretary-General.

SECURITY COUNCIL ACTION

On 29 and 30 November [meetings 4072 & 4073], the Security Council discussed its role in the prevention of armed conflicts. On 30 November [meeting 4073], following consultations among Council members, the President made statement **S/PRST/1999/34** on behalf of the Council:

The Security Council has considered, within its primary responsibility for the maintenance of international peace and security, its role in the prevention of armed conflicts. The Council emphasizes the need fully to respect and implement the principles and provisions of the Charter of the United Nations and norms of international law, in particular, in this context, those related to prevention of armed conflicts and settlement of disputes by peaceful means. It affirms its commitment to the principles of the political independence, sovereign equality and territorial integrity of all States. The Council also affirms the need for respect for human rights and the rule of law. It will give special attention to the humanitarian consequences of armed conflicts. The Council recognizes the importance of building a culture of prevention of armed conflicts and the need for a contribution from all principal organs of the United Nations in that regard.

The Council stresses the importance of a coordinated international response to economic, social, cultural or humanitarian problems, which are often the root causes of armed conflicts. Recognizing the need for the development of effective long-term strategies, it emphasizes the need for all United Nations organs and agencies to pursue preventive strategies and to take action within their respective areas of competence to assist Member States to eradicate poverty, strengthen development cooperation and assistance and promote respect for human rights and fundamental freedoms.

The Council recognizes that early warning, preventive diplomacy, preventive deployment, preventive disarmament and post-conflict peace-building are interdependent and complementary components of a comprehensive conflict-prevention strategy. The Council emphasizes its continuing commitment to addressing the prevention of armed conflicts in all regions of the world.

The Council is aware of the importance of its early consideration of situations which might deteriorate into armed conflicts. In this context, it underlines the importance of the settlement of disputes by peaceful means, in accordance with Chapter VI of the Charter of the United Nations. The Council re calls that parties to any dispute, the continuance of which is likely to endanger the maintenance of international peace and security, have an obligation to seek peaceful means of settlement.

The Council reaffirms its responsibility under the Charter to take action on its own initiative in order to maintain international peace and security. The results of the Council's mission to Jakarta and Dili from 6 to 12 September 1999 demonstrate that such missions undertaken with the consent of the host country and with clear goals can be useful if dispatched in a timely and appropriate manner. The Council expresses its intention to support, with appropriate follow-up action, efforts by the Secretary-General to prevent conflict through such areas as fact-finding missions, good offices and other activities requiring action by his envoys and Special Representatives.

The Council emphasizes the important role of the Secretary-General in the prevention of armed conflicts. The Council expresses its readiness to consider appropriate preventive action in response to the matters brought to its attention by States or the Secretary-General and which it deems likely to threaten international peace and security. It invites the Secretary-General to present to the members of the Council periodic reports on such disputes, including, as appropriate, early warnings and proposals for preventive measures. In this regard the Council encourages the Secretary-General to improve further his capacity to identify potential threats to international peace and security and invites him to indicate any requirements to fulfil that capacity, including the development of the expertise and resources of the Secretariat.

The Council recalls that the United Nations Preventive Deployment Force, as the first United Nations preventive deployment mission, has prevented the spillover of conflict and tensions from the region to the host country. The Council will continue to consider the establishment of such preventive missions in appropriate circumstances.

The Council will also consider other preventive measures such as the establishment of demilitarized zones and preventive disarmament. While fully conscious of the responsibilities of other United Nations organs, it emphasizes the crucial importance of disarmament and the non-proliferation of weapons of mass destruction and the means of their delivery for the maintenance of international peace and security. In particular, progress in preventing and combating the excessive and destabilizing accumulation of and illicit trafficking in small arms and light weapons is of vital importance to the prevention of armed conflicts. The Council will also take appropriate measures in situations of post-conflict peace-building aimed at preventing the recurrence of armed conflicts, including through adequate programmes for the disarmament, demobilization and reintegration of ex-combatants. The Council acknowledges the increasingly important role of the civilian components of multifunctional peacekeeping operations and will look towards their playing a greater role in wider preventive efforts.

The Council recalls the provisions of Article 39 of the Charter concerning measures to prevent armed conflicts. Such measures may include targeted sanctions, in particular arms embargoes and other enforcement measures. In imposing such measures the Council will pay special attention to their likely effectiveness in achieving clearly defined objectives, while avoiding negative humanitarian consequences as much as possible.

The Council recognizes the link between the prevention of armed conflicts, the facilitation of the peaceful settlement of disputes and the promotion of security for the civilian population, in particular the protection of human life. Furthermore, the Council underlines the fact that the existing international criminal tribunals represent useful instruments to combat impunity and can, by helping to deter crimes against humanity, contribute to the prevention of armed conflicts. In this context, the Council acknowledges the historic significance of the adoption of the Rome Statute of the International Criminal Court.

The Council recognizes the important role that regional organizations and arrangements are playing in the prevention of armed conflicts, including through the development of confidence- and security-building measures. The Council also emphasizes the importance of supporting and improving regional capacities for early warning. It emphasizes the importance of cooperation between the United Nations and regional organizations in preventive activities in accordance with Chapter VIII of the Charter. The Council welcomes meetings between the United Nations, including the Security Council, and regional organizations, and encourages participants to continue to keep those meetings focused on issues related to prevention of armed conflicts.

The Council will continue to review its activities and strategies for the prevention of armed conflicts. It will consider the possibility of holding further orientation debates and strengthening its cooperation with the Economic and Social Council. The Council will also consider the possibility of a meeting at the level of Ministers for Foreign Affairs on the issue of prevention of armed conflicts during the Millennium Assembly.

The Council will remain seized of the matter.

Small arms and conflict prevention

On 24 September [meeting 4048], the Security Council held a ministerial meeting on the question of small arms in the context of the challenges facing the international community in that regard.

Addressing the Council, the Secretary-General said that he was pleased to join its effort to tackle one of the key challenges in preventing conflict in the next century. Small arms and light weapons were primary tools of violence in many conflicts and their proliferation had also aggravated the violence associated with terrorism and organized crime. Even in societies not beset by civil war, the easy availability of small arms had in many cases contributed to violence and political instability, he said. There was probably no single tool of conflict so widespread, so easily available and so difficult to restrict as small arms, which survived from conflict to conflict, perpetuating the cycle of violence.

The Secretary-General stated that the United Nations had played a leading role in putting the issue of small arms firmly on the international agenda (see also PART ONE, Chapter VII). The General Assembly, in resolution 53/77 E [YUN 1998, p. 525], had decided to convene a conference on all aspects of illicit arms trafficking no later than 2001.

The Secretary-General drew attention to his report to the Council on the protection of civilians in armed conflict [S/1999/957], in which he stated that controlling the easy availability of small arms was a prerequisite for a successful peace-building process, as it was for conflict prevention. In that report, he appealed to the Council to devote greater attention to conflict prevention and to provide effective leadership in that area. He stressed the importance of including in peace agreements and mandates of all UN peacekeeping operations specific measures for disarmament and demobilization.

The Secretary-General mentioned some positive developments in the struggle against small arms proliferation, and particularly illicit arms trafficking, including: the declaration by the Economic Community of West African States of a moratorium on the production and transfer of small arms, covering 16 countries, and the United Nations Development Programme (UNDP) assistance in implementing that moratorium; the holding by the Organization of African Unity of a regional conference on small arms in preparation for the international conference on illicit arms trafficking; and joint action by the European Union in preventing and combating illicit trafficking in conventional arms. More specifically, in Albania, UNDP, in close collaboration with the Department for Disarmament Affairs, had been engaged in a "Weapons for Development" project. In the Americas, the Organization of American States had adopted in November 1997 the Inter-American Convention against the Illicit Manufacturing of and Trafficking in Firearms, Ammunition, Explosives and Other Related Materials [YUN 1997, p. 519].

The momentum for combating small arms proliferation had also come from civil society. The establishment early in 1999 of the International Action Network on Small Arms had helped to gain the public support necessary for success in curbing the spread of small arms.

UN efforts to promote peace and security, whether through conflict prevention, development, diplomacy or intervention, depended to a great extent on how it tackled the smaller, more specific challenges of limiting the tools of war and violence.

The Secretary-General also addressed the issue of small arms in his progress report on the causes of conflict and the promotion of durable peace and sustainable development in Africa [S/1999/1008] (see next chapter).

SECURITY COUNCIL ACTION

The Security Council President, following consultations among Council members, made statement **S/PRST/1999/28** on behalf of the Council:

The Security Council recalls its primary responsibility under the Charter of the United Nations for the maintenance of international peace and security, in view of which its attention is drawn inevitably to small arms and light weapons as the most frequently used weapons in the majority of recent armed conflicts.

The Council notes with grave concern that the destabilizing accumulation of small arms has contributed to the intensity and duration of armed conflicts. The Council also notes that the easy availability of small arms can be a contributing factor to undermining peace agreements, complicating peace-building efforts and impeding political, economic and social development. In this regard, the Council acknowledges that the challenge posed by small arms is multifaceted and involves security, humanitarian and development dimensions.

The Council is deeply concerned that countries involved in, emerging from, or close to protracted armed conflicts are particularly vulnerable to violence resulting from the indiscriminate use of small arms in armed conflict. In this regard, the Council recalls the report of the Secretary-General of 8 September 1999 on the protection of civilians in armed conflict and its resolution 1265(1999) of 17 September 1999.

The Council emphasizes that the right of individual and collective self-defence recognized in Article 51 of the Charter and the legitimate security demands of all countries should be fully taken into account. The Council recognizes that small arms are traded globally for legitimate security and commercial considerations. Bearing in mind the considerable volume of this trade, the Council underlines the vital importance of effective national regulations and controls on small arms transfers. The Council also encourages the Governments of arms-exporting countries to exercise the highest degree of responsibility in these transactions.

The Council emphasizes that the prevention of illicit trafficking is of immediate concern in the global search for ways and means to curb the wrongful use of small arms, including their use by terrorists.

The Council welcomes the various initiatives that are currently under way, globally and regionally, to address the issue. These initiatives at the regional level include the moratorium of the Economic Community of West African States on the production and trade in small arms, the Inter-American Convention Against the Illicit Manufacturing of and Trafficking in Firearms, Ammunition, Explosives, and Other Related Materials, the European Union Joint Action on Small Arms, and the European Union Code of Conduct on Arms Exports. At the global level, the Council welcomes the negotiation process on the elaboration of an international convention against transnational organized crime, including a draft protocol against the illicit manufacturing of and trafficking in firearms, ammunition and other related materials.

The Council emphasizes the importance of regional cooperation in tackling the issue of illicit trafficking in small arms. Initiatives, such as the work done by the Southern African Development Community and the Southern African Regional Police Commissioners Coordinating Organization, illustrate how regional cooperation can be harnessed to tackle small arms proliferation. The Council recognizes that while regions may sometimes benefit from the experiences of others, one region's experience cannot be extended to others without taking into account their different characteristics.

The Council also welcomes and encourages efforts to prevent and combat the excessive and destabilizing accumulation of and illicit trafficking in small arms, and invites Member States to involve civil society in these efforts.

The Council notes with satisfaction the growing attention paid within the United Nations system to the problems associated with the destabilizing accumulation of small arms. The Council welcomes the initiative by the Secretary-General for Coordinated Action on Small Arms, designed to ensure a coherent and coordinated approach to the small arms issue within the United Nations system.

The Council notes that although the humanitarian impact of small arms in a conflict situation is verifiably serious, a detailed analysis is not available. The Council therefore requests the Secretary-General to include specifically the humanitarian and socio-economic implications of the excessive and destabilizing accumulation and transfer of small arms and light weapons, including their illicit production and trade, in relevant studies he is currently undertaking.

The Council calls for effective implementation of arms embargoes, imposed by the Council in its relevant resolutions. The Council encourages Member States to provide the sanctions committees with available information on alleged violations of arms embargoes and recommends that the chairmen of the sanctions committees invite relevant persons from organs, organizations and committees of the United Nations system, as well as other intergovernmental and regional organizations and other parties concerned, to provide information on issues relating to the implementation and enforcement of arms embargoes.

The Council also calls for measures to discourage arms flows to countries or regions engaged in or emerging from armed conflicts. The Council encourages Member States to establish and abide by voluntary national or regional moratoria on arms transfers with a view to facilitating the process of reconciliation in these countries or regions. The Council recalls the precedents for such moratoria and the international support extended for their implementation.

The Council recognizes the importance of incorporating, as appropriate, within specific peace agreements, with the consent of the parties, and on a case-by-case basis within United Nations peacekeeping mandates, clear terms for the disarmament, demobilization and reintegration of ex-combatants, including the safe and timely disposal of arms and ammunition. The Council requests the Secretary-General to provide the negotiators of peace accords with a record of best practice based upon experience in the field.

The Council requests the Secretary-General to develop a reference manual for use in the field on ecologically safe methods of weapons destruction in order better to enable Member States to ensure the disposal of weapons voluntarily surrendered by civilians or retrieved from former combatants. The Council invites Member States to facilitate the preparation of such a manual.

The Council welcomes the recommendations of the Group of Governmental Experts on Small Arms (A/54/258), including the convening of an international conference on the illicit arms trade in all its aspects no later than 2001, noting the offer by Switzerland to host the conference. The Council encourages Member States to participate actively and constructively in the conference and any preparatory meetings, taking into account the recommendations contained in this statement, with a view to ensuring that the conference makes a meaningful and lasting contribution to reducing the incidence of illicit arms trafficking.

Post-conflict peace-building

Post-conflict peace-building was a major and relatively recent innovation in the preventive strategy, said the Secretary-General in his report on the work of the Organization [A/54/1]. The issue was important, not least because there were far more peace agreements to be implemented than in the past. In fact, three times as many agreements were signed in the 1990s as in the previous three decades, and the United Nations had developed a more holistic approach to implementing the comprehensive peace agreements it had negotiated.

From Namibia to Guatemala, post-conflict peace-building had involved inter-agency teams working with non-governmental organizations (NGOs) and local citizens' groups to help provide emergency relief, demobilize combatants, clear mines, run elections, build impartial police forces and set in motion longer-term development efforts. Achieving the necessary coordination and complementarity between agencies in conflict and fragile post-conflict situations continued to present a major challenge to the

United Nations and its partners. The preceding year had seen a number of developments in UN post-conflict peace-building operations, including forward planning for a future presence in the Central African Republic when the mandate of the United Nations Mission in the Central African Republic (MINURCA) expired; establishing a new office dedicated to peace-building in Guinea-Bissau; sustaining the major UN presence in Guatemala; and consolidating long-standing peace processes in Cambodia and El Salvador and elsewhere. In Guinea-Bissau, the United Nations Peace-building Support Office was working with the Government and people to coordinate an integrated response to the challenges of peace-building. In Liberia, the United Nations Peace-building Support Office was about to complete its second year of operation, supporting projects dealing with national reconciliation and rebuilding respect for the rule of law and human rights.

In his progress report on the causes of conflict and the promotion of durable peace and sustainable development in Africa [S/1999/1008] (see next chapter), the Secretary-General said that he had written to the International Monetary Fund (IMF) and the World Bank to encourage them to give greater financial and organizational support to post-conflict peace-building efforts. He suggested the establishment of a group comprising IMF, the World Bank and the United Nations to study how best they could support countries emerging from conflict or assist countries that became flooded with refugees as a result of instability in the region.

ACC consideration. The Administrative Committee on Coordination (ACC), at its first regular session of 1999 (Geneva, 9-10 April) [ACC/1999/4], was informed that guidelines were being finalized for the strategic framework process in peace-building, launched in 1997 [YUN 1997, p. 38], and that it was proposed that the strategic framework be applied next to Sierra Leone. The design of such a framework would be undertaken in consultation with ACC members, drawing on and learning from the experience gained in connection with the strategic framework for Afghanistan [YUN 1998, p. 35].

SECURITY COUNCIL ACTION

On 8 July [meeting 4021], the Security Council met to consider the maintenance of peace and security and post-conflict peace-building, focusing on the disarmament, demobilization and reintegration of ex-combatants in a peacekeeping environment. The President, following consultations among Council members, made statement **S/PRST/1999/21** on behalf on the Council:

The Security Council recalls its primary responsibility under the Charter of the United Nations for the maintenance of international peace and security. The Council also recalls the statements made by its President in relation to activities of the United Nations in preventive diplomacy, peacemaking, peacekeeping and post-conflict peace-building.

The Council has considered the matter of disarmament, demobilization and reintegration of ex-combatants in a peacekeeping environment as part of its overall and continuing effort to contribute to enhancing the effectiveness of United Nations peacekeeping and peace-building activities in conflict situations around the world.

The Council is seriously concerned that in a number of conflicts, armed fighting among various parties or factions continues despite the conclusion of peace agreements by the warring parties and the presence of United Nations peacekeeping missions on the ground. It recognizes that a major contributory factor to such a situation has been the continued availability of large amounts of armaments, in particular small arms and light weapons, to conflicting parties. The Council emphasizes that in order to achieve settlement, parties to a conflict must work towards the successful disarmament, demobilization and reintegration of ex-combatants, including child soldiers whose special needs should be seriously addressed.

The Council recognizes that disarmament, demobilization and reintegration cannot be seen in isolation, but rather as a continuous process which is rooted in and feeds into a broader search for peace, stability and development. Effective disarmament of ex-combatants represents an important indicator of progress towards post-conflict peace-building and normalization of the situation. The demobilization effort is only possible when there is some level of disarmament and its success can only be achieved when there is effective rehabilitation and reintegration into society of ex-combatants. Disarmament and demobilization must take place in a secure and safe environment, which will give ex-combatants the confidence to lay down their arms. Taking into account the fact that the process is closely linked to economic and social issues, the question must be addressed comprehensively so as to facilitate a smooth transition from peacekeeping to peace-building.

The Council emphasizes that for disarmament, demobilization and reintegration to be successful, there must be political will and a clear commitment by the parties concerned to achieve peace and stability. At the same time, it is vital that such commitment by the parties be reinforced by political will and consistent, effective and determined support from the international community to guarantee the achievement of sustainable peace, including through its contributions of long-term assistance for development and trade.

The Council affirms its commitment to the principles of the political independence, sovereignty and territorial integrity of all States in conducting peace-building activities, and the need for States to comply with their obligations under international law. Bearing this in mind, the Council stresses the need for the implementation, with the consent of the parties, of practical measures to promote the success of the process which, *inter alia*, may include the following:

(a) The inclusion, as appropriate, within specific peace agreements and, on a case-by-case basis, within United Nations peacekeeping mandates, of clear terms for disarmament, demobilization and reintegration of ex-combatants, including the safe and timely disposal of arms and ammunition;

(b) The establishment by Governments contributing to peacekeeping operations of databases of experts on disarmament, demobilization and reintegration of ex-combatants. In this context, training in disarmament and demobilization could be a useful component of national programmes for the preparation of peacekeeping troops;

(c) The prevention and reduction of the excessive and destabilizing flow, accumulation and illegitimate use of small arms and light weapons. In this context, the relevant Security Council resolutions and existing United Nations arms embargoes should be strictly implemented.

The Council is of the view that techniques for executing and coordinating programmes related to the process of disarmament, demobilization and reintegration of ex-combatants and the problems associated with it should be given in-depth consideration. It takes note with appreciation of the efforts by the Secretary-General, United Nations bodies, Member States and international and regional organizations aimed at developing general principles and practical guidelines for disarmament, demobilization and reintegration of ex-combatants in a peacekeeping environment.

The Council underlines the need to address this issue on a regular basis and, in this regard, requests the Secretary-General to submit to the Council, within a period of six months, a report containing his analysis, observations and recommendations, in particular those relating to principles and guidelines as well as practices, experiences and lessons learned to facilitate its further consideration of the matter. The report should pay special attention to the problems of disarmament and demobilization of child soldiers and their reintegration into society.

The Council will remain seized of the matter.

Peacekeeping operations

General aspects

In his August 1999 report on the work of the Organization [A/54/1], the Secretary-General stated that the preceding year had been a tumultuous one for United Nations peacekeeping. New challenges included the creation of the large-scale, and in many ways unprecedented, operation in Kosovo, preparations for a complex new mission in the Democratic Republic of the Congo, the expansion of the mission in Sierra Leone, the strong likelihood of a new operation in Eritrea and Ethiopia, the continuing evolution of the situation in East Timor and the agreement for a continued UN presence in Angola. The volatility and danger of the environments in which the United Nations operated were underlined by the number of casualties suffered by its peacekeepers. Between January 1998 and August 1999, 34 UN personnel had lost their lives in peacekeeping operations. However, the most disturbing trend was the growing contempt for international norms, as civilians and peacekeepers were targeted or used as pawns to manipulate international public opinion. In response, the Department of Peacekeeping Operations (DPKO) was undertaking a systematic review of the problem of violence against peacekeepers. The year was also testing for DPKO as it underwent significant restructuring due to its reduction by almost 20 per cent as a result of the phasing out of gratis personnel, while continuing to perform its mandated functions. The logistics and communications area, which was vital for both the deployment of new missions and the liquidation of old ones, was hardest hit by the staff reductions. That experience showed again that preparedness required capacities beyond those needed for current activities. The Secretary-General hoped that, in determining resource requirements for the Organization, Member States would bear that in mind.

The Special Committee on Peacekeeping Operations [A/54/87], whose mandate was to review the whole question of peacekeeping operations in all their aspects, held an organizational meeting on 24 March. It held a general debate from 24 to 26 March and its open-ended Working Group met between 30 March and 23 April.

Standby arrangements and rapid deployment

In 1999 [A/54/87], the Special Committee on Peacekeeping Operations welcomed the increased commitment by Member States in providing specialized units to the UN standby arrangements system. It noted that the system should be further developed to enhance rapid deployment capabilities, including broadening the base of Member States making resources available, especially specialized capabilities and working with the Secretariat to improve deployment response times. Where critical mission start-up *matériel* and services were subject to extended procurement lead times, the Special Committee encouraged the Secretariat to maintain a minimum stock of such items on hand and recommended that the appropriate General Assembly bodies explore additional contracting authority mechanisms to permit accelerated procurement for such items.

The Special Committee stressed the importance of the Organization being able to respond and deploy rapidly to a peacekeeping operation upon the adoption of a Security Council mandate. To enhance that capability, it called for the full establishment of the Rapidly Deployable Mission Headquarters by adding the requisite military expertise. DPKO was encouraged to identify key staff for temporary field assignment, especially in the case of new operations.

The Special Committee emphasized that the contingent-owned equipment concept was vital to mission and mission support planning and mission budgeting, on the part of the United Nations and the Member State concerned. It was also an indispensable element in an effective UN rapid deployment capability. The Special Committee supported linking the concept to the standby arrangements system to realize its full rapid deployment capability potential. Member States that had subscribed to the standby arrangements system were called on to initiate, in collaboration with the Secretariat, development of applicable contingent-owned equipment memoranda of understanding.

Reports of Secretary-General. In a 30 March report [S/1999/361], the Secretary-General presented information on the number of Member States that had indicated their willingness to provide resources to the standby arrangements system in 1998 [YUN 1998, p. 40]. He noted that much still remained to be done, both to widen the involvement of Member States in the standby arrangements system and to improve the availability and utilization of the resources pledged by them.

In a later report [S/2000/194], the Secretary-General stated that six Member States had joined the system during the year, bringing the number of participants to 87 as at 31 December 1999 and a total of 147,500 personnel. Information on specific capabilities they were prepared to offer had been provided by 65 States, 43 of which were able to complete the standby arrangements planning data sheet with detailed technical information on their contributions. Formalization of standby contributions by the signing of a memorandum of understanding had been completed by 10 more States (Chad, Chile, France, Mongolia, Pakistan, Paraguay, Spain, Tunisia, United Kingdom, Zimbabwe), bringing the total number to 31. Some 60 per cent of the confirmed standby resources had a response time for deployment of up to 30 days; 20 per cent had a response time of 30 to 60 days; 15 per cent had a response time of between 60 and 90 days; and the remaining 5 per cent had a response time of more than 90 days or had not stated a response time.

The DPKO Standby Arrangements Unit continued to promote the system among African Member States. Common briefings and bilateral consultations involving Benin, Burkina Faso, Côte d'Ivoire, Mali, the Niger and Togo assisted those States to draw up lists of capabilities. It was expected that those countries would be in a better position to prepare planning data and ultimately sign the relevant memorandum of understanding. Special emphasis would be put on increasing civilian police and support capacity as contributions from those States. Efforts were also made to increase the participation of civilian police in the standby arrangements system, including the holding of a civilian police workshop (New York, 30 July) on the theme "Enhancing representation of police in the standby arrangements system".

In relation to improving response time, the Secretary-General reported that the goal was to get a better balance of resources with a response time of not more than 30 days. The planning element of the Multinational Standby Forces High Readiness Brigade had been established and operated out of Denmark. The Brigade, while not a UN formation, was established by small and medium-sized Member States already participating in the standby arrangements system in order to meet the criteria for rapid deployment and training and compatibility of command and control procedures and equipment. The Brigade would be available at high readiness for peacekeeping operations where rapid response was important, including humanitarian tasks. The response time should be 15 to 30 days. At the ninth meeting of the Brigade Steering Committee (Stockholm, Sweden, 7-8 October), participating Member States decided that the mechanism had reached the level of readiness required to declare it available to the United Nations as from the end of January 2000.

The Secretary-General observed that the system of standby arrangements had proved its ability to expedite planning and had begun to demonstrate its usefulness as a tool to shorten the time required for the finalization of the memorandum of understanding in support of peacekeeping operations. While the United Nations still did not have a true rapid reaction capability, the standby arrangements were a positive step.

In a report on implementation of the recommendations of the Special Committee on Peacekeeping Operations [A/AC.121/43], the Secretary-General stated that Member States had increased their commitment to the standby arrangements system of specialized units, including engineering and medical units. In view of the ongoing need for such capacity, the Secretariat would continue to emphasize development of those elements. A concerted effort was also made to enlist more African Member States in the standby arrangements system; the number of African States in the database had almost doubled and stood at 22 as at February 1999.

Consultations with troop contributors

At its 1999 session [A/54/87], the Special Committee on Peacekeeping Operations encouraged the Security Council to continue to take more formal steps to ensure the rigorous, timely and systematic implementation of the arrangements for consultations with troop contributors, set out in the Council President's statement S/PRST/1996/13 [YUN 1996, p. 18] and amplified in a 1998 note by the Council President [YUN 1998, p. 1333]. The Special Committee stressed the need, in the case of upcoming operations or the expansion of existing operations, to invite prospective troop contributors to consultations at the earliest possible stage to provide them with access to information required and to enable them to make an informed decision on participation. It stated that the consultations on mandates and those on operational questions were chaired by the Council President and by the Secretariat, respectively, and encouraged the Secretary-General to ensure that his reports were made available to the troop contributors in a timely fashion prior to any consultations.

The Special Committee requested that the weekly situation reports distributed to Council members be made available to all troop contributors, including those that had expressed an interest in contributing to peacekeeping operations. The Secretariat should consider ways to inform troop contributors more frequently of the situation on the ground and ensure the availability of the monthly peacekeeping strength reports. The Special Committee drew the Secretariat's attention to the fact that its policies directly affecting the participation of Member States in peacekeeping operations had not always benefited from full transparency and consultation. It called on the Secretariat to ensure that the Special Committee was consulted when developing policy on issues affecting peacekeeping personnel.

The Special Committee emphasized that consultation with the Member State concerned was necessary when mission authorities took any action, including repatriation or investigation in the event of misconduct by peacekeeping personnel. It stressed that national contingent commanders had the sole authority for any disciplinary actions in respect of misconduct by a member of their contingent. However, national legislation might preclude a Member State from taking any disciplinary action following repatriation of its involved personnel if mission authorities had already taken in-theatre action. Noting that the Secretariat had undertaken several measures to strengthen the United Nations ability to address misconduct by peacekeeping personnel, the Committee requested the Secretariat to develop, in consultation with Member States, guidelines governing action to be taken in such instances.

The Special Committee noted that the arrangements regarding consultations with troop-contributing countries were not exhaustive and did not preclude a variety of forms of consultation, including between the Council President (or its members) and contributors, countries especially affected by the conflict situation under discussion and other countries from the region concerned. The Special Committee encouraged the Council to be mindful of that point.

Civilian police

The Special Committee on Peacekeeping Operations encouraged efforts by the Secretariat to hold a follow-up meeting to the 1998 civilian police seminar [YUN 1998, p. 41] and to coordinate further initiatives in that area. It reiterated the need to strengthen the DPKO Civilian Police Unit, as well as to enhance the role of the Civilian Police Advisor, and noted the Secretariat's failure to fill all posts in the Unit, despite General Assembly authorization, contained in resolution 52/248 [YUN 1998, p. 51], thereby jeopardizing the Unit's ability to maintain its progress on civilian police issues. It requested the Secretariat to explain and clarify the staffing procedures for recruiting and selecting seconded personnel to the Unit.

The Special Committee reiterated that the Secretariat should develop draft guidelines on general principles regarding the role of civilian police as soon as possible and provide an update in the next progress report. It welcomed the completion of a draft set of standard operating procedures for civilian police operations, including a detailed code of conduct, the publication of selection and training standards and the extraction of lessons learned from previous civilian police operations.

The Special Committee said that care should be taken to ensure that police and military tasks were clearly differentiated. It emphasized that the Training Unit's activities should take into account the increased requirements of civilian police in peacekeeping operations and called for enhanced cooperation between Member States in training civilian police personnel for UN peacekeeping operations. The Secretary-General was asked to provide an update on the training workshops being conducted by DPKO in his next progress report.

Safety and security

The Special Committee on Peacekeeping Operations expressed grave concern at the growing number of attacks and acts of violence against UN and associated personnel. Recalling statement S/PRST/1997/13 by the Security Council President on the subject [YUN 1997, p. 1473], the Special Committee took note of progress achieved in the legal protection of the security of UN and associated personnel, including the entry into force of the Convention on the Safety of United Nations and Associated Personnel [YUN 1994, p. 1289]. It urged those States that had not done so to consider becoming parties to the Convention as soon as possible, and took note of the need to explore the scope of further ensuring the safety and security of UN and associated personnel.

Reaffirming that safety and security constituted integral elements of the planning and conduct of peacekeeping operations, the Special Committee stressed the need for peacekeeping forces to be properly configured and discrepancies between mandates and resources avoided. It recognized that elaboration of a comprehensive security plan at the commencement of a peacekeeping operation was essential and noted DPKO's initiative to conduct a comprehensive review of security requirements. In response to the Secretary-General's requests for assistance, the Committee encouraged the Secretariat to seek the views of Member States in an open-ended working group or seminar on safety and security of UN personnel in peacekeeping operations. It stressed the need for adequate budgetary provisions to ensure the security of peacekeeping personnel and noted the Secretariat's development of the conceptual approach over the Composite Observation and Monitoring Force.

The Special Committee encouraged the Secretariat to ensure an efficient and continuous flow of information to Member States in all phases of peacekeeping operations, especially prior to evacuation, in the immediate wake of tragic developments or in periods of crisis. When a crisis affected the safety of peacekeeping personnel, the Secretariat should make full information immediately available to the permanent missions concerned. It should also review continuously the safety of flight operations and, in the event of a tragic occurrence, share without delay the results of any subsequent investigation with all contributors to the mission. The Special Committee recommended that the DPKO Situation Centre coordinate fully with other relevant UN departments and agencies with a view to becoming the main point of contact for permanent missions in such circumstances.

Status-of-forces agreements

The Special Committee on Peacekeeping Operations expressed disappointment that the compendium of instances in which the Organization was due restitution, as a result of non-compliance with status-of-forces agreements or other agreements, was still not completed. It reiterated the need for the Secretary-General to fulfil the 1996 request [YUN 1996, p. 36] of the Advisory Committee on Administrative and Budgetary Questions (ACABQ) to provide the compendium and to withhold claims submitted by Member States concerned until the matter of expenditures was resolved.

Noting that a draft version of the model status-of-forces agreement had been prepared, the Special Committee urged its early finalization and promulgation and recommended that the Secretariat ensure that it contained specific and practical measures to reinforce and guarantee the responsibility of host Governments to ensure the physical security of UN and associated personnel employed in peacekeeping operations.

Training

The Special Committee on Peacekeeping Operations, acknowledging the work accomplished by the DPKO Training Unit, remained concerned that training materials were not available in all the UN official languages. It encouraged the Secretariat to continue its efforts in that regard and to include information on the matter in the next progress report.

The Special Committee welcomed the publication of selection and training standards for military observers and civilian police, as well as the use of current technology in providing a directory of current UN publications on CD-ROM. It requested the Secretary-General to seek appropriate staffing levels to ensure that the Training Unit was able to maintain its current programmes, including the United Nations Training Assistance Teams programme and other essential capacities, such as the planning and conduct of regional peacekeeping training programmes and the maintenance of the peacekeeping databases. The Secretariat should continue to find innovative means to supplement the current departmental training capacity, in collaboration with Member States.

The Special Committee, noting the increasingly close and direct contact between UN peacekeeping personnel and local populations during peacekeeping operations, stressed the importance of participants in such operations being given specific training that addressed local cultural sensitivities, including gender-sensitivity training; it encouraged the Secretariat, as well as Member States, to include and develop that aspect in their efforts to promote training norms for UN peacekeeping personnel.

Comprehensive review of peacekeeping

Special Committee on Peacekeeping Operations

As requested by the General Assembly in resolution 53/58 [YUN 1998, p. 44], the Special Committee on Peacekeeping Operations continued its comprehensive review of the whole question of peacekeeping operations in all their aspects [A/54/87]. The Committee, which met between 24 March and 23 April, had before it the Secretary-General's report on the implementation of its recommendations [A/AC.121/43].

The Special Committee stressed that peacekeeping operations should strictly observe the principles and purposes enshrined in the United Nations Charter and emphasized that respect for the principles of sovereignty, territorial integrity and political independence of States, as well as non-intervention in matters within domestic jurisdiction were crucial to efforts, including peacekeeping operations, to promote international peace and security. Respect for the basic principles of peacekeeping, such as the consent of the parties, impartiality and the non-use of force in self-defence, was essential to its success. The Special Committee was of the view that peacekeeping operations should not be used as a substitute for addressing the root causes of conflict, which should be addressed in a coherent, well-planned, coordinated and comprehensive manner with political, social and developmental instruments. Consideration should be given to ways in which those efforts could continue without interruption after the departure of a peacekeeping operation to ensure a smooth transition to lasting peace and security.

The Special Committee noted statement S/PRST/1998/38 by the Security Council President [YUN 1998, p. 37] with regard to the inclusion of peace-building elements in the mandates of peacekeeping operations, with a view to ensuring a smooth transition to a successful post-conflict phase, and stressed the importance of those elements being explicitly defined and clearly identified before being incorporated into the mandates of peacekeeping operations. The Committee emphasized the role of the General Assembly in the formulation of post-conflict peace-building activities.

The Special Committee stressed the importance of providing peacekeeping operations with clearly defined mandates, objectives and command structures, as well as secure financing, and the need to ensure, in the formulation and implementation of mandates, congruity between mandates, resources and objectives. Changes in mandates should be accompanied by commensurate adjustments in the resources available to the peacekeeping operation to carry out its new mandate and should be based on a thorough and timely reassessment by the Security Council, including military advice, of the implications on the ground. The need to ensure the unity of command of UN peacekeeping operations was stressed.

The Special Committee also stressed the need for greater coordination to avoid overlap and duplication of efforts within the UN system and encouraged the Secretariat to continue developing effective administrative and logistics mechanisms and procedures. The Secretariat should pursue more actively structural changes that enhanced the Organization's capacity for the effective planning, conduct and support of peacekeeping operations. The Secretary-General was urged to review the structures in DPKO in consultation with UN oversight bodies and report on the outcome of the review to the Special Committee. Consideration should be given to all offers by Member States to participate in peacekeeping operations and the Member States concerned should be advised of the reasons underlying DPKO's decision not to accept their offered contribution.

The Special Committee called on the Secretariat to work closely with the international criminal tribunals (see PART FOUR, Chapter II) on matters relating to testimony by UN peacekeepers and keep Member States continuously apprised of all developments in that regard.

The Secretariat's intention to consult with the Special Committee prior to finalizing the sample rules of engagement was welcomed, and the Special Committee called on the Secretary-General to consult with Member States, through the Special Committee, prior to making any significant changes to those rules, and with both current and prospective personnel contributors prior to any similar changes to mission rules of engagement.

Concerning organization, planning and coordination of peacekeeping operations, the Special

Committee noted the proposed structural changes to DPKO and requested the Secretary-General to include an assessment of that new structure in his next progress report. It emphasized the need to strengthen working-level consultations among UN departments and agencies to avoid duplication and overlap and to improve effectiveness. The Secretariat should promulgate a policy on the use of the standby arrangements system, including procedures for the selection of troop contributors for new missions and for replacements in established missions. It should consult first with contributors to the system and other Member States regarding necessary capabilities to overcome deficiencies referred to by the Secretary-General in his 30 March report (see p. 52). The Special Committee welcomed the progress made to improve the coordination of military and civilian components of peacekeeping operations and encouraged the Secretariat to continue its integrated approach at Headquarters and field levels.

Also welcoming the progress in developing a flexible and comprehensive logistic strategy to accommodate a wide range in variety and complexity of peacekeeping operations, the Special Committee noted the list of outputs that the Secretariat intended to pursue over the next year and supported the intended structure of the Operational Support Manual, especially plans to harmonize it with other related manuals.

The Special Committee recommended the speedy implementation of the field assets control system to more missions so that an assessment could be completed. It requested that an update on the review of the contents of the start-up kits and the status of implementing the field assets control system be included in the next progress report.

Stressing that the norms of international humanitarian law should be strictly observed by all personnel associated with UN-mandated peacekeeping operations, the Special Committee urged that the guidelines for peacekeepers be finalized as soon as possible in consultation with the Special Committee. It emphasized the need to differentiate between peacekeeping operations and humanitarian assistance. However, if the protection of humanitarian assistance was a mandated task of a UN peacekeeping operation, both should be coordinated to ensure that they were not working at cross purposes and that humanitarian assistance was impartial. The Special Committee emphasized that the conduct of peacekeeping operations and humanitarian activities did not absolve host Governments and parties to the conflicts from their responsibility towards the victims of a conflict among populations.

The Special Committee endorsed the role that effective public information could play in enhancing personnel safety and security, and encouraged the Secretariat to incorporate that feature into its public information policy for peacekeeping operations. It encouraged Member States to contribute to the Trust Fund to support public information and related efforts in UN peacekeeping operations and the incorporation of public information planning and the identification of resources into the earliest possible phases of mission planning. The Special Committee endorsed the inclusion of a public information authority from host Governments in the status-of-forces agreements/status-of-mission agreements and urged the enhancement of a public information capability at the mission level by widening public access to reliable and objective information.

The activities of the Lessons Learned Unit during the preceding year and its objectives for the coming year were noted. The Special Committee invited the Secretariat to consider the validation of conclusions drawn by the Unit and requested the Unit to consider how it might enhance the relevance of its work at the tactical and field levels.

GENERAL ASSEMBLY ACTION

On 6 December [meeting 71], the General Assembly, on the recommendation of the Fourth (Special Political and Decolonization) Committee [A/54/577], adopted **resolution 54/81 A** without vote [agenda item 90].

Comprehensive review of the whole question of peacekeeping operations in all their aspects

The General Assembly,

Recalling its resolution 2006(XIX) of 18 February 1965 and all other relevant resolutions,

Recalling in particular its resolution 53/58 of 3 December 1998,

Taking note of the report of the Secretary-General on the work of the Organization,

Affirming that the efforts of the United Nations in the peaceful settlement of disputes, including through its peacekeeping operations, are indispensable,

Convinced of the need for the United Nations to continue to improve its capabilities in the field of peacekeeping and to enhance the effective and efficient deployment of its peacekeeping operations,

Considering the contribution that all States Members of the Organization make to peacekeeping,

Noting the widespread interest in contributing to the work of the Special Committee on Peacekeeping Operations expressed by many Member States, in particular troop-contributing countries,

Bearing in mind the continuous necessity of preserving the efficiency and strengthening the effectiveness of the work of the Special Committee,

1. *Welcomes* the report of the Special Committee on Peacekeeping Operations;

2. *Endorses* the proposals, recommendations and conclusions of the Special Committee, contained in paragraphs 43 to 130 of its report;

3. *Urges* Member States, the Secretariat and relevant organs of the United Nations to take all necessary steps to implement the proposals, recommendations and conclusions of the Special Committee;

4. *Reiterates* that those Member States that become personnel contributors to United Nations peacekeeping operations in years to come or participate in the future in the Special Committee for three consecutive years as observers shall, upon request in writing to the Chairman of the Special Committee, become members at the following session of the Special Committee;

5. *Decides* that the Special Committee, in accordance with its mandate, shall continue its efforts for a comprehensive review of the whole question of peacekeeping operations in all their aspects and shall review the implementation of its previous proposals and consider any new proposals so as to enhance the capacity of the United Nations to fulfil its responsibilities in this field;

6. *Requests* the Special Committee to submit a report on its work to the General Assembly at its fifty-fourth session;

7. *Decides* to keep open during its fifty-fourth session the item entitled "Comprehensive review of the whole question of peacekeeping operations in all their aspects".

In other action, the Assembly, on 23 December, decided that the agenda item "Comprehensive review of the whole question of peacekeeping operations in all their aspects" would remain for consideration during the fifty-fourth session (**decision 54/465**).

Review of evaluation of peacekeeping operations: termination phase

OIOS report. At its thirty-ninth session (New York, 7 June-2 July) [A/54/16], the Committee for Programme and Coordination (CPC) had before it an April note by the Secretary-General [E/AC.51/1999/5] transmitting the Office of Internal Oversight Services (OIOS) triennial review of the implementation of the 1996 CPC recommendations on the evaluation of peacekeeping operations' termination phase [YUN 1996, p. 40].

The report stated that DPKO had made a concerted effort to follow through on the CPC recommendations. Significant progress was reported in connection with learning lessons of experience, the collaboration between DPKO and the Department of Public Information on the information aspects of peacekeeping missions and the liquidation of missions. However, little progress was made in establishing an indexed archive of standard operating procedures developed in completed missions.

On 8 June, CPC noted that DPKO had substantially improved its management of the termination phase of peacekeeping operations and endorsed the conclusions of the triennial review.

Operations in 1999

On 1 January 1999, 16 UN peacekeeping operations were in place—3 in Africa, 1 in the Americas, 3 in Asia, 6 in Europe and 3 in the Middle East. During the year, 4 operations ended and 5 were launched. The total number of operations deployed in 1999 was 21; the number in place at the end of the year was 17.

Africa

In Africa, two new peacekeeping operations became active in 1999. The Security Council established the United Nations Mission in Sierra Leone (UNAMSIL) on 22 October for an initial period of six months to assist in the implementation of the Peace Agreement signed in Lomé, Togo, on 7 July, thereby ending the mandate of the United Nations Observer Mission in Sierra Leone (UNOMSIL). In November, the Council established the United Nations Organization Mission in the Democratic Republic of the Congo (MONUC) to help implement the Lusaka Ceasefire Agreement (see next chapter). On 26 February, the mandate of the United Nations Observer Mission in Angola (MONUA) expired.

The United Nations Mission for the Referendum in Western Sahara (MINURSO) continued to monitor the ceasefire and otherwise conduct peacekeeping tasks. In December, the Council extended its mandate until 29 February 2000.

Americas

In the Americas, the United Nations Civilian Police Mission in Haiti (MIPONUH) continued its task of helping to professionalize the Haitian police force. In November, the Security Council decided to continue MIPONUH to ensure a phased transition to an International Civilian Support Mission in Haiti by 15 March 2000 (see PART ONE, Chapter III).

Asia

In Asia, the United Nations Iraq-Kuwait Observation Mission (UNIKOM) continued to monitor the demilitarized zone along the border between the two countries. In November, the Security Council extended the mandate of the United Nations Mission of Observers in Tajikistan (UNMOT) until 15 May 2000. Elsewhere in Asia, the United Nations Military Observer Group in India and Pakistan (UNMOGIP), established in 1949, remained in place to monitor the ceasefire in Jammu and Kashmir (see PART ONE, Chapter IV). In June, the Council established the United Nations Mission in East Timor (UNAMET), initially to organize and conduct a popular consultation on East Timor's constitutional future and to implement its results. UNAMET's mandate ended on 25 October with the establishment of the United Nations Transitional Administration in East Timor (UNTAET), responsible for the Territory's overall administration (see PART ONE, Chapters IV and VIII).

Europe

In Europe, the mandate of the United Nations Preventive Deployment Force (UNPREDEP), established by Security Council resolution 983(1995) [YUN 1995, p. 597] to monitor the border areas of the former Yugoslav Republic of Macedonia, ended on 28 February 1999. The Council extended the mandate of the United Nations Mission in Bosnia and Herzegovina (UNMIBH), which included the International Police Task Force (IPTF), until 21 June 2000; the mandate of the United Nations Observer Mission in Georgia (UNOMIG) until 31 January 2000; and the mandate of the United Nations Mission of Observers in Prevlaka (UNMOP) until 15 January 2000. The United Nations Interim Administration Mission in Kosovo, Federal Republic of Yugoslavia (FRY) (Serbia and Montenegro), was established on 10 June to provide an interim administration for Kosovo, while establishing and overseeing the development of provisional democratic self-governing institutions to ensure conditions for a peaceful and normal life for the inhabitants. In the Mediterranean, the mandate of the 35-year-old United Nations Peacekeeping Force in Cyprus (UNFICYP) was extended to 15 June 2000.

Middle East

Three long-standing operations continued in the Middle East: the United Nations Truce Supervision Organization (UNTSO), the United Nations Interim Force in Lebanon (UNIFIL) and the United Nations Disengagement Observer Force (UNDOF) (see PART ONE, Chapter VI).

Other missions

In addition to peacekeeping, the United Nations continued to support a number of political and human rights missions worldwide. With regard to the African region, the Security Council supported the Secretary-General's decision to establish a post-conflict Peace-building Support Office in Guinea-Bissau to harmonize and integrate the activities of the UN system in Guinea-Bissau leading up to elections and to facilitate implementation of the 1998 Abuja Agreement [YUN 1998, p. 153]. The Council in October authorized the establishment until 15 April 2000 of the United Nations Office in Angola to explore effective measures for restoring peace and to assist the Angolan people in capacity-building, humanitarian assistance and the promotion of human rights. The Council also welcomed the continuing efforts of the Secretary-General and the United Nations Political Office for Somalia (UNPOS), located in Nairobi, Kenya. It encouraged the Secretary-General to review the UN role in Somalia, as a prelude for an enhanced role there, including the possible relocation of UNPOS and other programmes to Somalia. The Council also concurred with the Secretary-General's decision to upgrade the United Nations Office in Burundi, in the light of the critical stage the current peace process had reached. It noted the Secretary-General's intention to extend the mandate of the United Nations Peace-building Support Office in Liberia until the end of December 2000. (See next chapter for further details on those missions.) In August, the Council, prior to the establishment in November of its mission in the Democratic Republic of the Congo, authorized the deployment of up to 90 UN military liaison personnel, together with civilian, political and humanitarian staff, to the capitals of the States signatories to the Ceasefire Agreement of 1 August 1999 and the provisional headquarters of the Joint Military Commission (see next chapter).

In Europe, the Council authorized Member States and relevant international organizations to establish an international security presence in Kosovo, FRY, to, among other things, deter renewed hostilities, demilitarize armed groups and establish a secure environment for the return of refugees and displaced persons.

As to Asia and the Pacific, the Security Council established a new monitoring mission in Iraq—the United Nations Monitoring, Verification and Inspection Commission (UNMOVIC)—to replace the United Nations Special Commission (UNSCOM). UNMOVIC would continue to monitor Iraq's compliance with Security Council resolutions on its disarmament (see PART ONE, Chapter IV).

With regard to the Americas, the General Assembly renewed the mandate of the United Nations Verification Mission in Guatemala (MINUGUA) until 31 December 2000. Also, the Assembly, consequent upon its decision to establish an International Civilian Support Mission in Haiti (MICAH), decided that the mandate of the International Civilian Mission in Haiti (MICIVIH), conducted jointly with the Organization of American States, would continue until the commencement of MICAH. The Security Council requested the Secretary-General to coordinate and expedite the transition from MICIVIH to MICAH.

The Assembly welcomed the establishment of the Civil Affairs Unit within the United Nations Special Mission to Afghanistan. It supported the Secretary-General's intention to strengthen the Mission with a view to assuring its primary role in conducting UN peacemaking activities in Afghanistan, including the progressive moving of its head office to Kabul.

In November, the Council noted the Secretary-General's intention to extend the mandate of the United Nations Political Office in Bougainville, Papua New Guinea, for a further 12 months to continue to assist in the promotion of political dialogue among parties to the Lincoln Agreement [YUN 1998, p. 319] (see PART ONE, Chapter IV). The United Nations Command continued to implement the maintenance of the 1953 Korean Armistice Agreement [YUN 1953, p. 136].

During the year, the Security Council authorized two missions by multinational forces, one in East Timor and one in the Kosovo province of FRY.

Roster of 1999 operations

UNTSO

United Nations Truce Supervision Organization

Established: June 1948.

Mandate: To assist in supervising the observance of the truce in Palestine.

Strength as at December 1999: 152 military observers.

UNMOGIP

United Nations Military Observer Group in India and Pakistan

Established: January 1949.

Mandate: To supervise the ceasefire between India and Pakistan in Jammu and Kashmir.

Strength as at December 1999: 45 military observers.

UNFICYP

United Nations Peacekeeping Force in Cyprus

Established: March 1964.

Mandate: To prevent the recurrence of fighting between the two Cypriot communities.

Strength as at November 1999: 1,219 troops, 35 civilian police.

UNDOF

United Nations Disengagement Observer Force

Established: June 1974.

Mandate: To supervise the ceasefire between Israel and the Syrian Arab Republic and the disengagement of Israeli and Syrian forces in the Golan Heights.

Strength as at November 1999: 1,053 troops.

UNIFIL

United Nations Interim Force in Lebanon

Established: March 1978.

Mandate: To confirm the withdrawal of Israeli forces from southern Lebanon, restore peace and security, and assist the Lebanese Government in ensuring the return of its effective authority in the area.

Strength as at June 1999: 4,495 troops.

UNIKOM

United Nations Iraq-Kuwait Observation Mission

Established: April 1991.

Mandate: To monitor the demilitarized zone along the border between Iraq and Kuwait.

Strength as at September 1999: 900 troops, 193 military observers.

MINURSO

United Nations Mission for the Referendum in Western Sahara

Established: April 1991.

Mandate: To monitor and verify the implementation of a settlement plan for Western Sahara and assist in the holding of a referendum in the Territory.

Strength as at December 1999: 27 troops, 203 military observers, 81 civilian police observers.

UNOMIG

United Nations Observer Mission in Georgia

Established: August 1993.

Mandate: To verify compliance with a ceasefire agreement between the parties to the conflict in Georgia and investigate ceasefire violations; expanded in 1994 to include monitoring the implementation of an agreement on a ceasefire and separation of forces and observing the operation of a multinational peacekeeping force.

Strength as at October 1999: 101 military observers.

UNMOT

United Nations Mission of Observers in Tajikistan

Established: December 1994.

Mandate: To assist in monitoring a temporary ceasefire agreement between the parties to the conflict in Tajikistan.

Strength as at October 1999: 37 military observers, 2 civilian police.

UNPREDEP

United Nations Preventive Deployment Force

Established: March 1995.

Terminated: February 1999.

Mandate: To monitor border areas in the former Yugoslav Republic of Macedonia.

Strength as at February 1999: 1,049 troops, 35 military observers, 26 civilian police.

UNMIBH

United Nations Mission in Bosnia and Herzegovina (including the International Police Task Force (IPTF))

Established: December 1995.

Mandate: To monitor and facilitate law enforcement activities in Bosnia and Herzegovina, train and assist law enforcement personnel in carrying out their responsibilities, advise government authorities on the organization of civilian law enforcement agencies, and assess threats to public order and the agencies' capability to deal with such threats.

Strength as at December 1999: 1,795 civilian police.

UNMOP

United Nations Mission of Observers in Prevlaka

Established: January 1996.

Mandate: To monitor the demilitarization of the Prevlaka peninsula.

Strength as at December 1999: 27 military observers.

MONUA

United Nations Observer Mission in Angola

Established: July 1997.

Terminated: February 1999.

Mandate: To assist the Angolan parties in consolidating peace and national reconciliation, enhancing confidence-building and creating an environment conducive to long-term stability, democratic development and rehabilitation of the country.

Strength as at February 1999: 562 troops, 38 military observers, 54 civilian police.

MIPONUH

United Nations Civilian Police Mission in Haiti

Established: November 1997.

Mandate: To continue to assist the Government of Haiti by supporting and contributing to the professionalization of the Haitian National Police, including monitoring Haitian National Police field performance.

Strength as at November 1999: 281 civilian police.

MINURCA

United Nations Mission in the Central African Republic

Established: March 1998.

Mandate: To assist in maintaining and enhancing security and stability in Bangui and the immediate vicinity of the city; to supervise, control storage and monitor the final disposition of all weapons retrieved in the course of the disarmament exercise; and to assist in a short-term police trainers programme and in other capacity-building efforts of the national police and provide advice on the restructuring of the national police and special police forces.

Strength as at October 1999: 930 troops, 24 civilian police.

UNOMSIL

United Nations Observer Mission in Sierra Leone

Established: July 1998.

Terminated: October 1999.

Mandate: To monitor the military and security situation in the country and the disarmament and demobilization of former combatants; to assist in monitoring respect for international humanitarian law, including at disarmament and demobilization sites; and to monitor the voluntary disarmament and demobilization of members of the Civil Defence Forces.

Strength as at September 1999: 105 military observers.

UNAMET

United Nations Mission in East Timor

Established: June 1999.

Terminated: October 1999.

Mandate: To organize a popular consultation on the proposed constitutional framework providing for a special autonomy for East Timor within Indonesia or leading to separation from it; expanded to include preparation for a United Nations Transitional Administration in East Timor.

Authorized strength: 280 civilian police, 50 military liaison officers.

UNTAET

United Nations Transitional Administration in East Timor

Established: October 1999.

Mandate: To provide security and maintain law and order, establish an effective administration, assist in the development of civil and social services, ensure the coordination and delivery of humanitarian assistance, rehabilitation and development assistance, support capacity-building for self-government and assist in the establishment of conditions for sustainable development.

Authorized strength: 1,640 civilian police, 8,950 troops, 200 military observers.

UNAMSIL

United Nations Mission in Sierra Leone

Established: October 1999.

Mandate: To cooperate with the Government of Sierra Leone and other parties in the implementation of the Peace Agreement signed in Lomé, Togo, on 7 July 1999, including, among other things, to assist in the implementation of the disarmament, demobilization and reintegration plan, monitor adherence to the ceasefire agreement of 18 May 1999, facilitate the delivery of humanitarian assistance and provide support to the elections.

Authorized strength: 6,000 military personnel, including 260 military observers.

UNMIK

United Nations Interim Administration Mission in Kosovo

Established: June 1999.

Mandate: To promote, among other things, the establishment of substantial autonomy and self-government in Kosovo, perform basic civilian administrative functions, organize and oversee the development of provisional institutions, facilitate a political process to determine Kosovo's future status, support reconstruction of key infrastructure, maintain civil law and order, protect human rights and assure the return of refugees and displaced persons.

MONUC

United Nations Organization Mission in the Democratic Republic of the Congo

Established: November 1999.

Mandate: To establish contacts with the signatories to the Ceasefire Agreement, provide technical assistance in implementation of the Agreement, provide information on security conditions, plan for the observation of the ceasefire, facilitate the delivery of humanitarian assistance and assist in the protection of human rights.

Authorized strength: 500 military observers.

Financial and administrative aspects of peacekeeping operations

General aspects

Expenditures for peacekeeping activities amounted to $837.8 million for the period from 1 July 1998 to 30 June 1999, compared to $879.3 million during the previous 12-month period.

The financial situation of UN peacekeeping operations continued to be affected by serious cash shortages, necessitating borrowing from and among peacekeeping funds, while substantial amounts of obligations for reimbursement to Member States for troop costs and contingent-owned equipment remained unpaid.

As at 30 June 1999, the total unpaid assessed contributions for peacekeeping operations amounted to $1,687.6 million, compared with $1,739.9 million in 1998. Available cash for all operations totalled $668.9 million, while total liabilities were about twice as high, at $1,363.6 million.

Notes of Secretary-General. In accordance with General Assembly resolution 49/233 A [YUN 1994, p. 1338], the Secretary-General submitted to the Assembly's Fifth (Administrative and Budgetary) Committee a February note [A/C.5/53/50] updating the budgetary information on requirements for all peacekeeping operations from 1 July 1998 to 30 June 1999 and reflecting the appropriations provided to date by the Assembly for those operations for that period, inclusive of support account requirements. The updated level of requirements of $843,819,800 represented an increase of $17,862,300 over the initial estimated budgetary requirements of $825,957,500.

In May [A/C.5/53/60], the Secretary-General submitted proposed budgetary requirements for the period from 1 July 1999 to 30 June 2000 of $644,199,100, including $182,937,000 for military personnel costs and $264,945,400 for civilian personnel costs.

By **decision 54/462 A** of 23 December, the Assembly decided that the Fifth Committee should continue its consideration of the sub-item on the financing of United Nations peacekeeping operations at its resumed fifty-fourth (2000) session. On the same date, the Assembly decided that the agenda item "Administrative and budgetary aspects of the financing of the United Nations peacekeeping operations" should remain for consideration during its fifty-fourth session (**decision 54/465**).

Review exercise

In its June report [A/54/87], the Special Committee on Peacekeeping Operations stressed that all Member States should pay their assessed contributions in full, on time and without conditions. The delay in reimbursements to troop contributors, which caused hardship to all troop- and equipment-contributing countries, especially developing countries, remained a concern for the Special Committee. It encouraged the Secretary-General to sensitize all departments involved in the peacekeeping reimbursement process to the need to resolve current delays as soon as funds were available. The Secretariat should continue to expedite the processing of all claims, especially the backlog claims. It should also address the medical aspects of peacekeeping operations, such as the identification of medically high-risk areas, pre-deployment immunization costs and costs incurred for necessary post-repatriation treatment of peacekeeping personnel, and refine the mission start-up budgeting mechanism, which should include provisions for the enhancement of the security of UN and associated personnel, as well as the resources to allow the United Nations to discharge its obligation to contributing Member States in accordance with negotiated contingent-owned equipment memorandum agreements or understandings.

The Special Committee requested the Secretary-General, as a matter of priority, to address the operational and financial liquidation of completed operations, to take steps for the timely and efficient disbursement from trust funds on urgent UN-authorized peacekeeping operational activities, to identify clearly those trust funds and their impact on peacekeeping operations and to advise the Committee of the steps taken to ensure their timely disbursement. He was also asked to keep the Committee informed of the terms of reference of any trust fund that might be established in the future for peacekeeping operations.

Apportionment of costs

In 1999, the General Assembly again considered the question of the placement of Member States into groups for the apportionment of peacekeeping expenses. First specified in resolution 3101(XXVIII) [YUN 1973, p. 222], the groups were subsequently adjusted several times, most recently by resolution 52/230 [YUN 1998, p. 49]. The original four groups were: (A) permanent members of the Security Council; (B) specifically named economically developed Member States not permanent members of the Council; (C) economically less developed Member States; and (D) economically less developed Member States that were specifically named.

In a 23 June note verbale [A/53/1009], South Africa requested relocation from group B to group C. It stated that it had been placed in group B since 1973 because of the policy of the then Government to project South Africa as an economically developed Member State. However, South Africa was a developing country with an average per capita gross national product of $3,400 per annum, which was lower than that of some countries placed in group C, and it was the only less developed Member State to be placed in group B. Facing the dilemma of redressing the poverty and suffering brought about by years of apartheid rule, the country could ill afford the added burden of its allocation in group B.

On 29 September [A/54/233], South Africa requested the inclusion of a sub-item entitled "Relocation of South Africa to the group of Member States set out in paragraph 3 *(c)* of General Assembly resolution 43/232" [YUN 1989, p. 793] under agenda item 151 of the Assembly's fifty-fourth session. In an explanatory memorandum, South Africa reiterated the reasons set out in its June note verbale.

The Assembly, by **decision 54/462 A** of 23 December, decided that the Fifth Committee should continue consideration of the sub-item at its resumed (2000) fifty-fourth session. By the same decision, the Assembly decided that the Fifth Committee should also continue consideration of the sub-item "Relocation of Ukraine to the group of Member States set out in paragraph 3 *(c)* of General Assembly resolution 43/232".

Also on 23 December, the Assembly decided that, as an ad hoc arrangement, Kiribati (**decision 54/456**), Nauru (**decision 54/457**) and Tonga (**decision 54/458**) should be included in the group of Member States set out in paragraph 3 *(d)* of resolution 43/232 for the apportionment of peacekeeping appropriations.

Arrears of Belarus and Ukraine

On 23 December [meeting 88], the General Assembly, on the recommendation of the Fifth Committee [A/54/684], adopted **resolution 54/242** without vote [agenda item 151].

Administrative and budgetary aspects of the financing of the United Nations peacekeeping operations

The General Assembly,

Recalling its decision 49/470 of 23 December 1994,

1. *Decides* that, from the date of adoption of the present resolution and without prejudice to the relevant financial regulations and rules of the United Nations, all financial contributions of Belarus and Ukraine to the Organization, including those for which assessments were issued prior to 1996, shall be taken into account when determining whether the amount of their arrears, as calculated in accordance with decision 49/470, equals or exceeds the amount of the contributions due from Belarus and Ukraine for the preceding two full years in accordance with Article 19 of the Charter of the United Nations;

2. *Emphasizes* that this decision shall not exempt Belarus and Ukraine from their obligation to pay all outstanding contributions, and calls upon Belarus and Ukraine to make proposals for the treatment of their arrears concerning the financing of peacekeeping operations;

3. *Decides* to keep this matter under review.

Financial performance and proposed budgets

In April [A/53/895 & Add.1-8], ACABQ considered the financial performance reports for the period from 1 July 1997 to 30 June 1998 and the proposed budgets for 1 July 1999 to 30 June 2000 of UNDOF, UNIFIL, UNIKOM, UNFICYP, UNOMIG, UNMOT, UNMIBH, including the liaison offices in Belgrade and Zagreb and UNMOP, the United Nations Support Mission in Haiti (UNSMIH), the United Nations Transition Mission in Haiti (UNTMIH), MIPONUH and the United Nations Logistics Base in Brindisi, Italy. It also considered the financial performance reports for the United Nations Observer Mission in Liberia (UNOMIL) for the periods 1 July 1996 to 30 June 1997 [YUN 1998, p. 156] and 1 July 1997 to 30 June 1998 [A/53/802]; the United Nations Transitional Administration for Eastern Slavonia, Baranja and Western Sirmium (UNTAES) and the Civilian Police Support Group for the period 1 July 1997 to 30 June 1998 [A/53/742] and the final disposition of the assets of those operations [A/53/838 & Corr.1]; the Military Observer Group of MINUGUA for the period 15 February to 31 May 1997 [A/53/775]; and the revised estimates for MIPONUH for the period 1 July 1998 to 30 June 1999 [A/53/789 & Add.1].

ACABQ, noting that $1.8 billion of assessed contributions from Member States remained unpaid as at 30 June 1998, recommended that the Secretariat draw the attention of the General Assembly to the latest information on the status of contributions for each peacekeeping operation at the time it took up the budgets of the missions. It believed that further attempts should be made to standardize the presentation and full disclosure of contributions from host Governments, made under status-of-forces agreements and on a voluntary basis, as well as from other sources. All peacekeeping budgets should disclose the estimated income from staff assessment and other sources, and budget reports should include for each mission a clear explanation of the method of reimbursement for contingent-owned equipment and details of the relevant mission factors employed. Salary and common staff cost adjustments should also be implemented in all budgets where mission appointees were a significant percentage of the international staff.

ACABQ noted that additional requirements were incurred in a number of missions as a result of cancellation by a contractor unable to provide services stipulated in the initial contract. It recommended that contracts entered into with vendors should include penalty clauses or an escrow arrangement to protect the mission in case of breach of contract. There was a need also to improve planning so that estimates for procurement could be more accurate. Concerning savings in respect of air operations, ACABQ recommended that missions include aircrew subsistence allowance in contracts for air operations and requested the Secretariat to report on the question in future budgets. The Secretary-General should look into the possibility of negotiating the inclusion of spare parts, as the next step to the global system contract for the purchase of vehicles. The recording and accounting for support services provided to other entities of the UN system in the mission area, including those provided to non-UN bodies, needed to be improved. The return of contingent-owned equipment to troop-contributing countries, even if it was obsolete and in a condition to be written off, should be reviewed with a view to devising a more practical and economical procedure, and measures should be taken to control the sharp increases in mission vehicle insurance costs, by stricter safety and security measures in the missions and through negotiation of rates with insurance providers.

In addition to carrying out a review of the return of contingent-owned equipment (see p. 66), ACABQ recommended that the Secretary-General provide information on the guidelines that had been developed for the liquidation of peacekeeping missions. Also, in view of the new procedures for settling claims relating to contingent-owned equipment and death and disability, the Secretariat should review the need to continue the suspension of financial regulations 4.3 and 4.4 and report to the Assembly at its fifty-fourth session.

GENERAL ASSEMBLY ACTION

On 8 June [meeting 101], the General Assembly, on the recommendation of the Fifth Committee

[A/53/522/Add.3], adopted **resolution 53/237** without vote [agenda item 143 *(a)*].

Report of the Advisory Committee on Administrative and Budgetary Questions on the financing of the United Nations peacekeeping operations

The General Assembly,

Having considered the report of the Advisory Committee on Administrative and Budgetary Questions,

Endorses the observations and recommendations of the Advisory Committee on Administrative and Budgetary Questions and, in this connection:

(a) Requests the Secretary-General to conduct the review recommended in paragraph 41 of the report of the Advisory Committee, in consultation with Member States, through established mechanisms;

(b) Also requests the Secretary-General to include in his next report on the support account information on the implications of the implementation of the review recommended in paragraph 48 of the report of the Advisory Committee.

Accounts and auditing

At its resumed fifty-third session, the General Assembly considered the financial report and audited financial statements for UN peacekeeping operations for the 12-month period from 1 July 1997 to 30 June 1998 [A/53/5, vol. II]. The question of peacekeeping financing had been deferred in 1998 by decision 53/458 [YUN 1998, p. 48].

GENERAL ASSEMBLY ACTION

The General Assembly, by **decision 53/473** of 8 June, deferred consideration, until the main part of its fifty-fourth session in 1999, of the financial report and the audited financial statements for UN peacekeeping operations and the report of the Board of Auditors, the April report of the Secretary-General on implementation of the recommendations of the Board of Auditors concerning peacekeeping operations for the period ended 30 June 1998 [A/53/932], and the related report of ACABQ [A/53/940].

On 29 October [meeting 43], the Assembly, on the recommendation of the Fifth Committee [A/54/506], adopted **resolution 54/13 A** without vote [agenda item 117 *(a)*].

Financial reports and audited financial statements, and reports of the Board of Auditors

The General Assembly,

Reaffirming its resolutions 50/222 of 11 April 1996, 51/218 E of 17 June 1997 and 52/212 B of 31 March 1998,

Having considered the report of the Board of Auditors on United Nations peacekeeping operations for the period from 1 July 1997 to 30 June 1998, the related report of the Advisory Committee on Administrative and Budgetary Questions and the report of the Secretary-General on the implementation of the recommendations of the Board of Auditors concerning United Nations peacekeeping operations for that period,

1. *Endorses* the recommendations of the Board of Auditors contained in its report, subject to the provisions of the present resolution;

2. *Decides* to consider the recommendations of the Board of Auditors on contingent-owned equipment and the recommendation contained in paragraph 70 of its report under sub-item *(a)*, entitled "Financing of the United Nations peacekeeping operations", of agenda item 151, entitled "Administrative and budgetary aspects of the financing of the United Nations peacekeeping operations".

The Secretary-General submitted to the Assembly in December a report [A/54/140/Add.2] on implementation of recommendations of the Board of Auditors concerning peacekeeping operations [A/53/5, vol. II], which, according to his April report [A/53/932], had not been fully implemented.

Peacekeeping support account

The Secretary-General, in response to General Assembly resolution 52/248 [YUN 1998, p. 51], submitted a March report on the support account for peacekeeping operations for the period 1 July 1997 to 30 June 1998 [A/53/854]. The financial performance report showed that of the authorized amount of $32,426,500 for post and non-post requirements, expenditures totalled $28,560,700, resulting in an unutilized balance of $3,865,800.

In an addendum of the same date [A/53/854/Add.1], the Secretary-General submitted support account proposals for the period 1 July 1999 to 30 June 2000 estimated at $36,065,600, which provided for a staffing establishment of 406 posts, including six new ones.

ACABQ report. ACABQ, in April [A/53/901], recommended that the Assembly approve the overall staffing of 400 temporary posts and total staffing and non-staffing requirements of $34,887,100 for the period from 1 July 1999 to 30 June 2000. The unencumbered balance of $3,865,800 from 1 July 1997 to 30 June 1998 should be applied to the resources required for the period 1 July 1999 to 30 June 2000.

GENERAL ASSEMBLY ACTION (June)

On 8 June [meeting 101], the General Assembly, on the recommendation of the Fifth Committee [A/53/522/Add.3], adopted **resolution 53/12 B** without vote [agenda item 143 *(a)*].

Support account for peacekeeping operations

The General Assembly,

Recalling its resolutions 45/258 of 3 May 1991, 47/218 A of 23 December 1992, 48/226 A of 23 December 1993, 48/226 B of 5 April 1994, 48/226 C of 29 July 1994, 49/250 of 20 July 1995, 50/11 of 2 November 1995, 50/221 A of 11 April 1996, 50/221 B of 7 June 1996, 51/226 of 3 April 1997, 51/239 A of 17 June 1997,

51/239 B and 51/243 of 15 September 1997, 52/220 of 22 December 1997, 52/234 and 52/248 of 26 June 1998, 53/12 A of 26 October 1998 and 53/208 B of 18 December 1998, and its decisions 48/489 of 8 July 1994, 49/469 of 23 December 1994 and 50/473 of 23 December 1995,

Having considered the reports of the Secretary-General on the support account for peacekeeping operations and the related report of the Advisory Committee on Administrative and Budgetary Questions,

Reaffirming the need to continue to improve the administrative and financial management of peacekeeping operations,

Recognizing the need for adequate support during all phases of peacekeeping operations, including the liquidation and termination phases,

1. *Takes note* of the reports of the Secretary-General on the support account for peacekeeping operations, in particular the performance report on the use of support account resources for the period from 1 July 1997 to 30 June 1998;

2. *Also takes note* of the observations and recommendations contained in the report of the Advisory Committee on Administrative and Budgetary Questions;

3. *Notes* the initial efforts made in the implementation of the request contained in paragraph 7 of its resolution 51/239 A and paragraph 14 of its resolution 52/248, and requests the Secretary-General to ensure full compliance with the provisions of the present resolution;

4. *Also notes* that the backstopping activities for peacekeeping operations require ongoing reviews which should take into account the overall evolution of peacekeeping trends;

5. *Requests* the Secretary-General to reflect the issues related to this analysis in his annual report on the support account;

6. *Also requests* the Secretary-General to continue his efforts to avoid duplication, overlap and fragmentation in all departments involved in the backstopping of peacekeeping operations;

7. *Concurs* with the recommendations of the Advisory Committee contained in paragraphs 3 and 4 of its report;

8. *Notes* the improvement in the format and content of the reports of the Secretary-General on the support account, and requests him to make further improvements in accordance with resolution 51/239 A and the related reports of the Advisory Committee;

9. *Requests* the Secretary-General to adopt a standard format for support account reports in accordance with resolution 53/208 B;

10. *Invites* the Advisory Committee to submit its reports in accordance with paragraph 12 of resolution 53/208 B;

11. *Affirms* the need for adequate funding for the backstopping of peacekeeping operations;

12. *Reaffirms* that the expenses of the Organization, including the backstopping of peacekeeping operations, shall be borne by Member States and, to that effect, that the Secretary-General should request adequate funding to maintain the capacity of the Department of Peacekeeping Operations of the Secretariat;

13. *Stresses* that the Secretary-General should continue to submit annually comprehensive proposals on the total requirement for human and financial resources from all sources of funding for all departments involved in the backstopping of peacekeeping operations;

14. *Notes* the observations of the Advisory Committee contained in paragraph 28 of its report, and requests the Secretary-General to ensure that the delegation of authority to field missions is in accordance with the Charter of the United Nations, the regulations and rules of the Organization and the relevant resolutions of the General Assembly;

15. *Notes with concern* the reduction in the level of resources for the Training Unit, which may affect the capacity of the Unit to perform its important functions in the backstopping of peacekeeping operations;

16. *Requests* the Secretary-General to examine further the requirements of the Training Unit and to include the results of that review in the next support account budget proposal with a view to enhancing the training function of the Department of Peacekeeping Operations;

17. *Emphasizes* the need for the coordination of the internal and external audits of the Department of Peacekeeping Operations and the peacekeeping missions, with a view to avoiding duplication and overlap;

18. *Decides* to maintain for the period from 1 July 1999 to 30 June 2000 the funding mechanism for the support account used in the current period, from 1 July 1998 to 30 June 1999, as provisionally approved in paragraph 3 of its resolution 50/221 B;

19. *Approves* four hundred support account–funded temporary posts for the period from 1 July 1999 to 30 June 2000;

20. *Regrets* that a comprehensive review of a rapidly deployable mission headquarters, as requested in paragraph 7 of its resolution 53/12 A, has not been carried out, and requests the Secretary-General to make the comprehensive review available before the report on the support account for the period from 1 July 2000 to 30 June 2001 is submitted;

21. *Requests* the Secretary-General to ensure that the necessary military and civilian police expertise in the Department of Peacekeeping Operations is maintained;

22. *Endorses* the recommendation contained in paragraph 24 of the report of the Advisory Committee that the six additional posts for the rapidly deployable mission headquarters be accommodated through redeployment within the existing support account establishment throughout the Secretariat;

23. *Decides* to monitor closely the functions and activities to be performed by the rapidly deployable mission headquarters, in particular its functions related to other structures in the Secretariat, and to revert to the issue in the context of future reports of the Secretary-General on the support account;

24. *Approves* the support account post and non-post requirements for the period from 1 July 1999 to 30 June 2000 in the amount of 34,887,100 United States dollars;

25. *Decides* to apply the unencumbered balance of 3,865,800 dollars for the period from 1 July 1997 to 30 June 1998 to the resources required for the period from 1 July 1999 to 30 June 2000 and to appropriate the balance of 31,021,300 dollars, to be prorated among the individual active peacekeeping operation budgets, to

meet the financing requirements of the support account for the period from 1 July 1999 to 30 June 2000;

26. *Decides also* to delete paragraph 24 of the report of the Secretary-General on the support account for peacekeeping operations, and requests the issuance of a corrigendum to that effect.

In December [A/54/648], the Secretary-General submitted revised requirements to be funded from the support account for peacekeeping of 67 additional posts for the period 1 July 1999 to 30 June 2000, as a result of increased backstopping requirements at Headquarters due to the establishment of two new peacekeeping missions (UNMIK and UNTAET) and the expansion of UNOMSIL as UNAMSIL, MINURCA and MINURSO. The revised budgetary requirement amounted to $38,388,700, an increase of $3,501,600.

ACABQ recommended that the Assembly approve those requirements [A/54/661].

GENERAL ASSEMBLY ACTION (December)

On 23 December [meeting 88], the General Assembly, on the recommendation of the Fifth Committee [A/54/684], adopted **resolution 54/243 A** without vote [agenda item 151].

Support account for peacekeeping operations

The General Assembly,

Recalling its resolutions 45/258 of 3 May 1991, 47/218 A of 23 December 1992, 48/226 A of 23 December 1993, 48/226 B of 5 April 1994, 48/226 C of 29 July 1994, 49/250 of 20 July 1995, 50/11 of 2 November 1995, 50/221 A of 11 April 1996, 50/221 B of 7 June 1996, 51/226 of 3 April 1997, 51/239 A of 17 June 1997, 51/239 B and 51/243 of 15 September 1997, 52/220 of 22 December 1997, 52/234 and 52/248 of 26 June 1998, 53/12 A of 26 October 1998, 53/208 B of 18 December 1998 and 53/12 B of 8 June 1999 and its decisions 48/489 of 8 July 1994, 49/469 of 23 December 1994 and 50/473 of 23 December 1995,

Having considered the report of the Secretary-General on the support account for peacekeeping operations and the related report of the Advisory Committee on Administrative and Budgetary Questions,

Reaffirming the need to continue to improve the administrative and financial management of peacekeeping operations,

Recognizing the need for adequate support during all phases of peacekeeping operations, including the liquidation and termination phases,

1. *Takes note* of the report of the Secretary-General concerning the revised post requirements for the support account for peacekeeping operations for the period from 1 July 1999 to 30 June 2000;

2. *Endorses* the observations and recommendations contained in the report of the Advisory Committee on Administrative and Budgetary Questions;

3. *Requests* the Secretary-General, when submitting his support account proposal for the period from 1 July 2000 to 30 June 2001, to implement fully the observations set out in paragraph 11 of the report of the Advisory Committee;

4. *Notes* that the backstopping activities for peacekeeping operations require ongoing reviews which should take into account the overall evolution of peacekeeping trends;

5. *Affirms* the need for adequate funding for the backstopping of peacekeeping operations;

6. *Reaffirms* that the expenses of the Organization, including the backstopping of peacekeeping operations, shall be borne by Member States and, to that effect, that the Secretary-General should request adequate funding to maintain the capacity of the Department of Peacekeeping Operations of the Secretariat;

7. *Approves* sixty-seven additional support account-funded temporary posts for the period from 1 July 1999 to 30 June 2000;

8. *Authorizes* the Secretary-General to enter into commitments not exceeding 3,501,600 United States dollars for the additional staff costs, and requests the Secretary-General to report thereon to the General Assembly in the context of the performance report for the period from 1 July 1999 to 30 June 2000.

Peacekeeping Reserve Fund

In April [A/53/912], the Secretary-General provided information on the status of the Peacekeeping Reserve Fund, established by General Assembly resolution 47/217 [YUN 1992, p. 1022] as a cash flow mechanism to ensure the Organization's rapid response to the needs of peacekeeping operations; its level was set at $150 million. As at 31 December 1998, the Fund had an available balance of $103.7 million. Total receipts to the Fund amounted to $112.4 million. An annex to the report provided information on the utilization of the Fund by month from April 1996 to December 1998.

In May [A/53/961], ACABQ, in its comments on the Secretary-General's report, recalled that in its report on UN peacekeeping operations [A/53/940] it had stated that, in view of the substantial decrease in the level of peacekeeping operations, the current level of the Fund, at $150 million, should be reconsidered by the Assembly.

The Assembly, by **decision 53/479** of 8 June, took note of the Secretary-General's report and the related report of ACABQ and concurred with ACABQ's recommendations and observations.

Reimbursement issues

Equipment

Audit of contingent-owned equipment

ACABQ, in its May report on UN peacekeeping operations [A/53/940], stated that the Board of Auditors, at ACABQ's request [YUN 1998, p. 55], had conducted a special audit of contingent-owned equipment [A/53/5, vol. II], which confirmed many of the observations made in

ACABQ's previous reports, in particular that the capacity of the Secretariat to manage the new contingent-owned equipment arrangements was lacking.

ACABQ was particularly concerned by the implication of applying the new contingent-owned equipment procedures retroactively to missions whose mandates had terminated before July 1996. It reiterated its view that the potential existed for double payment with respect to services provided by the United Nations to contingents, which might overlap with services of self-sustenance. With respect to the Board of Auditors' recommendation that the Administration review the retroactive application of the new arrangements for reimbursement of contingent-owned equipment, ACABQ pointed out that issues related to the retroactive application of the new arrangements were temporary as they related to the transition from the old to the new system of reimbursement. It was doubtful whether the results of the review would affect retroactive payments already agreed to between troop-contributing countries and the United Nations. ACABQ did not therefore see any merit in conducting a review.

Concerning the Board's recommendation that DPKO review the generic fair market value of major equipment as set out in the policies and procedures manual and submit proposals to the General Assembly for revision, ACABQ recommended that the United Nations supplement its in-house expertise with the assistance of independent outside expertise in the review and assessment of the generic fair market value of equipment, and that the review be undertaken in 2000 for the results to be included in the peacekeeping budgets for the period 1 July 2001 to 30 June 2002.

Implementation of reformed reimbursement procedures

ACABQ, in May [A/53/944 & Corr.1], considered the 1998 report of the Secretary-General [YUN 1998, p. 55] on the first full year of implementation of the reformed procedures for determining reimbursement to Member States for contingent-owned equipment, as recommended by the Phase IV Working Group on the subject [ibid., p. 54]. ACABQ paid particular attention to those elements on which the Secretary-General and the Working Group differed. They related to the legally binding aspects of the memorandum of understanding; levels of reimbursement for loss or damage in cases of hostile action or forced abandonment; UN responsibility for loss or damage during transportation; universality of missions factors; establishing dates for applying procedures in current missions; retroactive implementation; review of major equipment standards; office supplies; laundry and cleaning; tentage and accommodation; liability of the United Nations under the lease system; a revised manual of policies and procedures; and expertise in the review and assessment of the generic fair market value of equipment.

ACABQ reiterated the importance of including in memoranda of understanding clear information on the obligations of Member States, including the five-year period for submission of claims. It requested that future peacekeeping budgets should include complete information on reimbursement arrangements for troop-contributing countries and that performance reports should provide data on actual amounts paid or to be paid as compared with initial estimates.

Special Committee consideration. The Special Committee on Peacekeeping Operations [A/54/87] called for the timely implementation of the recommendations of the Phase IV Working Group on Reimbursement of Contingent-owned Equipment. It regretted the delay of the Secretary-General's report on the first year of implementation of those recommendations and called on him to convene the Phase V Working Group as soon as possible.

GENERAL ASSEMBLY ACTION

The General Assembly, by **decision 53/480** of 8 June, requested the Secretary-General to convene the Phase V Working Group and decided to continue consideration of the question of reformed procedures for determining reimbursement to Member States for contingent-owned equipment at its fifty-fourth session.

In October, the Assembly considered the Secretary-General's 1998 report on the first full year of implementation of the reformed procedures [YUN 1998, p. 55]. It also had before it the related report of ACABQ (see above). On 29 October [meeting 43], the Assembly, on the recommendation of the Fifth Committee [A/54/509], adopted **resolution 54/19 A** without vote [agenda item 151 *(a)*].

Reformed procedures for determining reimbursement to Member States for contingent-owned equipment

The General Assembly,

Recalling its resolution 45/248 B, section VI, of 21 December 1990 and rule 153 of the rules of procedure of the General Assembly,

Recalling also its resolution 49/233 A of 23 December 1994,

Reaffirming its resolutions 50/222 of 11 April 1996 and 51/218 E of 17 June 1997,

Having considered the report of the Phase IV Working Group on Reimbursement of Contingent-owned Equipment as transmitted by the Chairman of the Working Group to the Chairman of the Fifth Committee, the report of the Secretary-General on the first full year of implementation of the reformed procedures for determining reimbursement to Member States for contingent-owned equipment and the related report of the Advisory Committee on Administrative and Budgetary Questions,

1. *Reaffirms* that the Fifth Committee is the appropriate Main Committee of the General Assembly entrusted with responsibilities for administrative and budgetary matters;

2. *Requests* the Secretary-General, while implementing the approved reformed procedures for determining reimbursement to Member States for contingent-owned equipment, to avoid any double payment;

3. *Approves* a general policy whereby the United Nations should only assume financial responsibilities in accordance with the decisions of the General Assembly;

4. *Emphasizes* that the intent of the new procedures on reimbursement of contingent-owned equipment is to ensure equitable reimbursement to the troop-contributing countries while ensuring the interests of Member States and the United Nations;

5. *Endorses* the recommendations of the Phase IV Working Group on Reimbursement of Contingent-owned Equipment, subject to the provisions of the present resolution;

6. *Also endorses* the recommendations of the Advisory Committee on Administrative and Budgetary Questions in its report, with the exception of the following proposals, relating to:

(*a*) The levels of reimbursement for loss or damage to contingent-owned equipment in cases of hostile action or forced abandonment, as contained in paragraph 15;

(*b*) The review regarding United Nations responsibility for loss or damage during transportation, as contained in paragraph 16;

(*c*) Tentage and accommodation, as contained in paragraph 27;

(*d*) The use of independent outside expertise in the review and assessment of the generic fair market value of equipment, as contained in paragraph 31;

7. *Reaffirms* that, with regard to all new missions activated since 1 July 1996, only the reformed procedures for reimbursement to Member States for contingent-owned equipment are applicable;

8. *Requests* the Secretary-General to take all necessary measures to ensure the full participation of delegations in the work of the Phase V Working Group;

9. *Emphasizes* that the revision of the contingent-owned equipment manual should be a continuous process, and requests the Secretary-General to revise the manual only after the completion of the work of the Phase V Working Group, in order to incorporate recommendations made by the Phase II, III, IV and V Working Groups, as approved by the General Assembly;

10. *Requests* the Board of Auditors to continue to audit the implementation of the reformed procedures for determining reimbursement to Member States for contingent-owned equipment and to report thereon in the context of its annual report to the General Assembly.

Management of peacekeeping assets

Liquidation of missions

ACABQ, in its April report on financing of UN peacekeeping missions [A/53/895], considered notes by the Secretary-General on the financing of the United Nations Operation in Somalia [A/C.5/53/52]; the United Nations Mission in Haiti [A/C.5/53/55]; the United Nations Protection Force, the United Nations Confidence Restoration Operation in Croatia, UNPREDEP and the United Nations Peace Forces headquarters [A/C.5/53/56]; and the United Nations Assistance Mission for Rwanda [A/C.5/53/57].

The purpose of the notes was to inform the General Assembly about the status of the liquidation of those missions and the reasons for delays, and to indicate what remained to be done before final reports were submitted.

ACABQ recommended that, in conjunction with the submission of the final reports on those missions, the Secretary-General should provide information on the guidelines developed for the liquidation of UN peacekeeping missions and on what further steps would be taken by the Secretariat and the Assembly to increase the efficiency and timely liquidation of missions. In view of the new procedures for the settlement of claims relating to contingent-owned equipment and death and disability, the Secretariat should review the need to continue the suspension of regulations 4.3 and 4.4 of the Financial Regulations and report to the Assembly at its fifty-fourth session.

GENERAL ASSEMBLY ACTION

On 8 June, the General Assembly, on the recommendation of the Fifth Committee [A/53/990], adopted **decision 53/477** without vote [agenda items 127, 128, 132 & 134].

Financing of the United Nations Protection Force, the United Nations Confidence Restoration Operation in Croatia, the United Nations Preventive Deployment Force and the United Nations Peace Forces headquarters; financing of the United Nations Operation in Somalia II; financing of the United Nations Mission in Haiti; and financing of the United Nations Assistance Mission for Rwanda

At its 101st plenary meeting, on 8 June 1999, the General Assembly, on the recommendation of the Fifth Committee:

(*a*) Took note of the notes by the Secretary-General and the relevant section of the report of the Advisory Committee on Administrative and Budgetary Questions;

(*b*) Requested the Secretary-General to take all necessary action to address the outstanding issues in connection with the preparation of the related final performance information;

(*c*) Approved, on an exceptional basis, the special arrangements for the United Nations Operation in Somalia II with regard to the application of article IV of the Financial Regulations of the United Nations, whereby appropriations required in respect of obligations owed to Governments providing contingents and/or logistic support for the Operation shall be retained beyond the period stipulated under financial regulations 4.3 and 4.4, as set out in the annex to the present decision;

(*d*) Decided to include in the provisional agenda of its fifty-fourth session the items entitled "Financing of the United Nations Protection Force, the United Nations Confidence Restoration Operation in Croatia, the United Nations Preventive Deployment Force and the United Nations Peace Forces headquarters", "Financing of the United Nations Operation in Somalia II", "Financing of the United Nations Mission in Haiti" and "Financing of the United Nations Assistance Mission for Rwanda".

ANNEX
Special arrangements with regard to the application of article IV of the Financial Regulations of the United Nations

1. At the end of the twelve-month period provided for in financial regulation 4.3, any unliquidated obligations of the financial period in question relating to goods supplied and services rendered by Governments for which claims have been received or which are covered by established reimbursement rates shall be transferred to accounts payable; such accounts payable shall remain recorded in the Special Account for the United Nations Operation in Somalia II until payment is effected.

2. (*a*) Any other unliquidated obligations of the financial period in question owed to Governments for goods supplied and services rendered, as well as other obligations owed to Governments, for which required claims have not yet been received, shall remain valid for an additional period of four years following the end of the twelve-month period provided for in financial regulation 4.3;

(*b*) Claims received during this four-year period shall be treated as provided for under paragraph 1 of the present annex, if appropriate;

(*c*) At the end of the additional four-year period, any unliquidated obligations shall be cancelled and the then remaining balance of any appropriations retained therefor shall be surrendered.

OIOS report. In September, the Secretary-General submitted to the Assembly the OIOS report on the audit of the liquidation of peacekeeping missions [A/54/394 & Corr.1].

The report analysed the main findings and recommendations of audits carried out by OIOS between 1996 and 1999 of the liquidation of eight peacekeeping missions with combined asset acquisition costs of over $900 million. The audits showed that the liquidation process could be streamlined further by developing standard operating procedures in key areas, planning and organizing the liquidation process more efficiently and ensuring adequate staff resources. Good management during the operational period of a mission was also crucial to successfully completing the liquidation in a timely manner.

The audits' major findings included: provisional guidelines for the liquidation of field missions, issued in 1996 [YUN 1996, p. 39], needed to be updated and further developed; DPKO had not established a formal mechanism to consolidate lessons learned into the operations of new and ongoing missions; DPKO needed to resolve several issues relating to the disposal of UN-owned equipment, including the installation of the field asset control system in all missions and development of standard systems and procedures to control receipt, movement and disposal of UN-owned equipment, the transfer by liquidating missions of expendable items to other missions where they often could not be used, the uneconomical transfer of low-value assets to the UN Logistics Base for upgrading, and the use of depreciated values rather than fair market values in determining the cost-effectiveness of transferring UN-owned equipment; no delegation of authority had been granted to missions to assess mission personnel for the loss or damage of UN-owned equipment; financial management problems often delayed completion of the liquidation; property sales documents for the transfer of UN-owned equipment to third parties often did not provide adequate legal protection to the Organization; the frequent rotation of chief procurement officers sometimes led to delays in providing essential services; failure to ensure full staffing levels often hindered the efficiency of critical areas; and DPKO's draft field administration manual did not provide sufficient guidance to missions to establish board of inquiry procedures, leading to unnecessary processing of cases and delayed processing of other cases.

OIOS made a number of recommendations to DPKO, including that it should: finalize and regularly update the provisional liquidation guidelines to include areas not currently covered, expand on those areas inadequately covered and delete outdated information and instructions; designate a focal point to be responsible for ensuring that administrative aspects of lessons learned were incorporated into standard operating procedures for missions; ensure adequate resources to implement the field asset control system in all missions, to develop standard operating procedures for the receipt, movement within the mission and disposal of assets and for Headquarters to monitor the implementation of the system, and provide field asset control system procedures for the proper segregation of duties between the property control and inventory unit and the account holders; develop standard operating procedures for disposing of assets by direct commercial sale and auction; request that the Controller delegate limited authority to peacekeeping missions for assessing mission personnel for the loss or damage of UN-owned equipment resulting from negligence; ensure that mission vacancies were promptly filled, in particular in key areas; and revise the provisions of the draft field administration manual dealing with boards of inquiry procedures.

Procurement

The Special Committee on Peacekeeping Operations [A/54/87] stressed the importance of timely, efficient, transparent and cost-effective procurement of goods and services in support of peacekeeping operations and was disappointed at the delays in fully implementing the United Nations Common Supplier Database. It welcomed the Secretariat's efforts to make procurement information available to prospective vendors and encouraged further innovative, accessible and user-friendly approaches for accelerated dissemination of accurate procurement information in a timely manner. The Special Committee requested the Secretary-General to implement fully and expeditiously General Assembly resolution 52/226 A [YUN 1998, p. 1254].

The Special Committee recognized that shortened procurement times were required for the United Nations to react swiftly to conflicts and to deploy rapidly. It requested the Secretary-General to undertake a comprehensive review of the procurement process and to include in his annual report on procurement reform a section addressing field procurement, with particular emphasis on a more flexible and timely contracting mechanism for new missions, including local procurement, where applicable.

On the issue of transparency, the Special Committee noted with dissatisfaction that little further work was anticipated in promoting the level of detail in which the United Nations Common Supplier Database could report on procurement activity. It noted the Secretariat's assurances that, if requested, details of each and every item would be made accessible to any Member State. It encouraged interested Member States to contribute in cash or in kind to the programme for providing procurement information via video and CD-ROM.

Contract management

In July, the Secretary-General transmitted to the General Assembly an OIOS report on the investigation into the award of a fresh rations contract in a UN peacekeeping operation [A/54/169]. The investigation, which concerned the actions of the operation's Chief Administrative and Chief Financial Officers, indicated mismanagement and abuse of authority, including violations of UN procurement policy and financial rules. The financial damage to the Organization was in the range of $17,000. OIOS recommended the filing of disciplinary charges against the two officers, that the contractor be given no further contracts without demonstrating that he could meet all the specifications and that company "A" should be monitored.

The Secretary-General concurred with the OIOS recommendations.

In September, the Secretary-General transmitted a further OIOS report on the audit of the management of service and ration contracts in peacekeeping missions [A/54/335]. In 1998, OIOS performed an audit of service and ration contract management at five peacekeeping missions—MONUA, the United Nations Mission in Haiti, UNIFIL, UNDOF and UNFICYP—comprising contracts with an annual contract value of $37 million. The objectives were to: ascertain the role of the missions, DPKO and the Procurement Division in the management of contracts; assess the effectiveness of service and ration contract management in missions; and determine steps to improve the contract management process.

OIOS found that there was a general trend in peacekeeping operations to move towards large-scale contracts for the provision of support services and rations; that was an economical and efficient way of providing support to missions. However, most of the missions reviewed did not have a contract management unit, which resulted in an uncoordinated approach to managing complex contracts; standard systems had not been developed for missions to track ration deliveries against contractual provisions; no comprehensive programmes had been established by DPKO to train personnel in contract management techniques; and inadequate monitoring of invoice payments could result in loss of early payment discounts and disputes with vendors leading to arbitration.

OIOS made the following recommendations. DPKO, in consultation with the Procurement Division, should: review the time frames required for the procurement of service and ration contracts and take steps to shorten the time involved; complete the project for development of clear contract specifications for all categories of rations; develop standard operating procedures for managing service and ration contracts that should include guidelines for evaluating performance of contractors; establish a contract management function within new missions; formulate a plan, with implementation time frames, for developing a ration management receiving and inspection system and test the system before implementation; assess training requirements of mission contract management personnel and develop a programme to enable them to manage complex service and ration contracts successfully; establish procedures to review cost proposals that were significantly lower than others to determine their reasonableness and validity; and negotiate prompt payment discount terms in future service and ration contracts that missions could realistically meet.

In its response, DPKO stated that the recent surge in peacekeeping activities was overstretching the resources of the Field Administration and Logistics Division to such an extent that it was barely able to address the immediate operational problems of missions. It would, therefore, create the systems and procedures recommended by the auditors when resources were available. OIOS agreed that it was essential that adequate resources be available to implement the long-overdue procedures recommended in its report. DPKO should, therefore, request additional funds to enable it to develop the procedures on a timely basis.

Property losses

ACABQ, in its May report on UN peacekeeping operations [A/53/940], expressed concern at what appeared to be a very cumbersome and involved process of reporting property losses and observed that there was a need to improve considerably the coordination between the various units involved in handling those losses. The functioning of Property Survey Boards appeared inefficient, involved and lengthy. ACABQ recommended that urgent steps be taken by the Secretariat to correct weaknesses identified by the Board of Auditors [A/53/5, vol. II], including staff training and temporary deployment of qualified staff to clear any existing backlog.

In June, the General Assembly considered the issue of property losses in connection with the Secretary-General's reports on the financing and liquidation of the United Nations Transitional Authority in Cambodia [YUN 1998, p. 317] and the financing of the Military Observer Group of MINUGUA [A/53/775]. The Assembly, in **resolutions 53/230** (see PART ONE, Chapter IV) and **53/235** (see PART ONE, Chapter III) of 8 June, requested the Secretary-General to provide an updated report on losses of UN property in peacekeeping operations at its fifty-fourth session.

Report of Secretary-General. In response to that request, the Secretary-General, in December [A/54/669 & Corr.1], submitted a report on the subject, which provided data on property losses for all peacekeeping missions operational or under liquidation during 1996-1997, except the United Nations Assistance Mission in Rwanda. Data on losses at the UN Logistics Base in Brindisi were also included.

Information showed that 7,728 items belonging to UN missions, excluding the United Nations Peace Forces (UNPF), were lost during that period due to accidents, negligence, acts of hostility, theft and other reasons, with an inventory value of $11,458,097 and a residual value of $3,312,948. Data for UNPF, presented in a separate annex because of the vast size of its property holdings, showed losses of 11,117 items, with an inventory value of $37,961,668 and a residual value of $21,590,143.

The Secretary-General said that the Secretariat had made progress in its efforts to safeguard UN property. To provide an auditable chain of accountability, the field asset control system was developed to ensure that UN property was properly recorded, accounted for and controlled, and that appropriate decisions were made on the procurement, delivery, redistribution, replenishment, storage, write-off and disposal of mission equipment. The system, which was expected to be fully operational in all missions by the end of 1999, could account for all non-expendable assets valued at $1,500 or more per unit at the time of purchase and with a serviceable life of five years or more, as well as items of lesser value, but not those valued below $500.

However, the system was not sufficient to ensure adequate protection of UN property; it was crucial that missions be provided with sufficient experienced personnel, particularly during their early and final phases. Nevertheless, losses due to heightened insecurity in mission areas and acts of war or hostilities were unavoidable. Experience showed that the commitment of host Governments to ensuring the protection of mission personnel and assets was also a crucial factor in terms of facilitating security.

With regard to the accountability procedures to deter loss of or damage to UN assets, all personnel were subject to UN financial and personnel regulations and rules, were regularly reminded to take care of the property assigned to them, and were made aware of the consequences if found responsible for the loss or damage.

However, the Secretariat considered that an efficient recovery mechanism was one of the best means to ensure accountability of those responsible for losses. In that connection, prompt action by the Property Survey Boards in the missions and at Headquarters was essential. The

Secretariat was reviewing a proposal to amend the delegation of authority to the field that would permit local property survey boards to assess UN personnel up to $500. With regard to the accountability of UN military and civilian police observers, in a number of cases the amounts retained under the current practice of withholding two weeks of mission subsistence allowance entitlements prior to the departure of those concerned, in respect of cases in which they were involved, pending the taking of a decision by the Headquarters Property Survey Board, had proved to be insufficient to compensate the Organization. Since contingent personnel and members of formed police units did not serve in an individual capacity, cases of loss or damage to UN property by those categories of personnel were handled directly with the Governments involved.

The Secretariat was preparing a follow-up to the report of the Secretary-General on management irregularities causing financial losses to the Organization [A/53/849]. In preparing the report, the Secretary-General had been asked to take into account, among other related financial issues, measures to improve internal control and accountability. (See PART FIVE, Chapter II, for further details.)

UN Logistics Base

Reports of Secretary-General. In a January report [A/53/815], the Secretary-General presented the proposed budget for the period 1 July 1999 to 30 June 2000 for the maintenance of the United Nations Logistics Base in Brindisi, which amounted to $7,783,800. That represented a 9 per cent increase in total resources in relation to the period 1 July 1998 to 30 June 1999, which reflected a 14.6 per cent increase in civilian personnel costs and a 2.3 per cent increase in operational costs. The increase was partially offset by a 20 per cent decrease under other programmes. The budget provided for a staffing establishment of 20 international and 28 locally recruited staff. In addition, 55 posts were funded under general temporary assistance, which the Secretary-General proposed should be regularized, bringing the number of locally recruited staff to 83.

In May [A/C.5/53/62 & Corr.1], the Secretary-General submitted to the Fifth Committee the amounts to be apportioned in respect of each peacekeeping mission, including the prorated share of the support account and of the Logistics Base.

ACABQ report. In an April report [A/53/895/Add.8], ACABQ provided its comments on the financial performance report of the Logistics Base for the period 1 July 1997 to 30 June 1998 [YUN 1998, p. 59] and on the proposed budget.

ACABQ recommended: inclusion of information on miscellaneous income in future performance reports and proposed budgets; acceptance of the Secretary-General's proposal to apply the unencumbered balance of $1,373,600 to the resources required for the period 1 July 1999 to 30 June 2000; and approval of his proposed cost estimates for that period after a reduction of $327,300 relating to general temporary assistance. In that regard, ACABQ did not find justification for the 12 additional general temporary assistance staff requested and recommended that, should any surges in activity arise, related costs should be charged to the missions concerned. Also, commencing with the budget for the 2000-2001 biennium, the standard procedures for dealing with staff assessment should be applied to the Base.

In relation to the cost-benefit analysis contained in the budget report for the Base for the period 1 July 1998 to 30 June 1999 [YUN 1998, p. 58], ACABQ concurred with the Secretary-General's conclusion that the Base would continue to provide an effective level of cost-utility for the support of new peacekeeping operations for the foreseeable future.

GENERAL ASSEMBLY ACTION

On 8 June [meeting 101], the General Assembly, on the recommendation of the Fifth Committee [A/53/522/Add.3], adopted **resolution 53/236** without vote [agenda item 143 *(a)*].

Financing of the United Nations Logistics Base at Brindisi, Italy

The General Assembly,

Recalling section XIV of its resolution 49/233 A of 23 December 1994,

Recalling also its decision 50/500 of 17 September 1996 on the financing of the United Nations Logistics Base at Brindisi, Italy, and its subsequent resolutions thereon, the latest of which was resolution 52/1 B of 26 June 1998,

Having considered the reports of the Secretary-General on the financing of the Logistics Base and the related reports of the Advisory Committee on Administrative and Budgetary Questions,

Stressing the importance of establishing an accurate inventory of assets,

1. *Takes note* of the reports of the Secretary-General on the financing of the United Nations Logistics Base at Brindisi, Italy;

2. *Notes with satisfaction* the effective and timely completion of the clearing of the backlog in the inventory, and requests the Secretary-General to give priority to the full implementation of a single database for the field assets control system;

3. *Endorses* the observations and recommendations contained in the report of the Advisory Committee on Administrative and Budgetary Questions;

4. *Concurs* with the observations of the Advisory Committee on the cost-benefit analysis;

5. *Urges* the International Civil Service Commission to finalize its work on the review of the rate of post adjustment for the Logistics Base and report thereon before the end of the main part of the fifty-fourth session of the General Assembly;

6. *Requests* the Secretary-General, in the context of the next budget submission, to indicate clearly, as recommended by the Advisory Committee, the resources required for the Logistics Base to perform its basic functions;

7. *Encourages* the Secretary-General to take additional steps with a view to wider use of the Logistics Base by the specialized agencies and programmes of the United Nations system, taking into account the observations of the Advisory Committee contained in paragraphs 12 and 34 of its report;

8. *Approves* the cost estimates for the Logistics Base amounting to 7,456,500 United States dollars for the period from 1 July 1999 to 30 June 2000;

9. *Decides* to apply the unencumbered balance of 1,373,600 dollars in respect of the period from 1 July 1997 to 30 June 1998 to the resources required for the period from 1 July 1999 to 30 June 2000, and also decides to prorate the balance of 6,082,900 dollars among the individual active peacekeeping operation budgets to meet the financing requirements of the Logistics Base for the period from 1 July 1999 to 30 June 2000;

10. *Authorizes* the Secretary-General to provide for a civilian establishment consisting of ten Professional, ten Field Service and eighty-three locally recruited staff;

11. *Decides* to consider during its fifty-fourth session the question of the financing of the United Nations Logistics Base at Brindisi.

Personnel matters

Special Committee consideration. The Special Committee on Peacekeeping Operations [A/54/87] recommended that active-duty military and civilian police personnel should be adequately represented in DPKO and actively involved in its work. Member States should be given sufficient time to select and nominate their officers, preferably no less than 90 days, upon issuance of vacancy announcements. The Special Committee noted that the phasing out of Type II gratis personnel in DPKO had been completed, but expressed concern at the lack of an effective transition plan with respect to staff recruitment to minimize disruption, loss of continuity and expertise. It welcomed the Secretariat's assurances that vacancies would be announced to Member States in a more timely fashion, as well as the plan to implement a three-year cyclical recruitment/rotation programme. It encouraged the development and implementation of innovative strategies to further the participation of female personnel in all aspects of peacekeeping operations and recommended that an analysis of the effectiveness of such strategies be included in the Secretary-General's reports on peacekeeping operations.

The Special Committee stressed the importance of having senior military commanders, police commissioners and key staff personnel well selected and prepared prior to their deployment to a peacekeeping operation, and recommended a more thorough review of candidates. It reiterated its request to the Secretary-General for improvement of the current method by which senior military commanders and police commissioners were selected, and that he consider the feasibility of mandatory interviews. The criteria for selection should include professional experience and other personal qualities, such as good judgement, common sense and an ability to work in a multinational peacekeeping environment.

The Special Committee was encouraged by the establishment of the three-month training programme for potential chief administrative officer/senior management candidates. Recruitment of highly qualified chief administrative officers remained a concern as peacekeeping operations and their administration became increasingly complex. It noted the Secretariat's assurance that there were no plans to engage outside commercial firms in recruiting chief administrative officers and encouraged the Secretariat to include in the training programme the role of the chief administrative officer in the preparation of mission budgets.

Death and disability benefits

Reports of Secretary-General. Pursuant to General Assembly resolution 51/239 A [YUN 1997, p. 50], the Secretary-General submitted his sixth quarterly report on death and disability benefits [A/C.5/53/51]. As at 31 December 1998, 208 claims were awaiting processing, of which 63 were part of the backlog. A total of 104 claims were received by the Secretariat during the period 1 September to 31 December 1998.

The Assembly, by **decision 53/461 B** of 7 April, took note of the report.

The Secretary-General submitted his seventh quarterly report [A/C.5/53/58], which showed that, as at 31 March 1999, the number of claims awaiting processing had increased to 222, of which 47 were part of the backlog. During the period 1 January to 31 March 1999, 195 claims were received by the Secretariat, of which 181 were processed.

The Assembly, by **decision 53/461 C** of 8 June, took note of the seventh quarterly report.

In August and October, the Secretary-General submitted his eighth [A/C.5/53/66] and ninth [A/C.5/54/13] quarterly reports. As at 30 June, the number of claims awaiting processing had further increased to 285, as a result of the receipt of 113 new claims. A total of 47 claims represented part of the backlog. Only 50 claims were processed from 1 April to 30 June. As at 30 September, the number of claims awaiting processing had reached 317. Ninety-nine new claims were received and 67 were processed. The number of backlog claims had been reduced to nine.

The Assembly, by **decision 54/459 A** of 23 December, took note of the Secretary-General's eighth and ninth reports and of the progress made in clearing the backlog.

Special Committee consideration. The Special Committee on Peacekeeping Operations [A/54/87] requested the Secretariat, in order to alleviate the hardship of affected families, promptly to settle compensation claims on account of death and disability suffered while in service with UN peacekeeping operations. Claims filed prior to 1 July 1997 should be settled expeditiously. Recognizing that, in certain cases, the long treatment period of a disability might prevent a State from filing a claim in a timely manner, the Special Committee requested the Secretariat to accept preliminary notification from the concerned Member State to that effect and the disability claim at a later stage on the basis of such notification. The Secretariat should also monitor, in cooperation with the Member State concerned, disability cases, preferably on a semi-annual basis, from the date of occurrence through medical certification, until the Government presented the claim, or for a maximum of five years to maintain contact with the situation and to support the affected persons morally.

Other peacekeeping matters

Demining

The Secretary-General, in his February report on the implementation of the recommendations of the Special Committee on Peacekeeping Operations [A/AC.121/43], said that during 1998 the United Nations Mine Action Service (UNMAS) had coordinated and fielded six assessment missions and was mounting a Level I Survey programme to measure the impact of mine contamination on specific communities in affected countries. It continued to serve as the point of contact with all mine action programmes in the field. An Inter-Agency Coordination Group was established at Headquarters and UNMAS had established a Steering Committee to serve as a vehicle for identifying priority issues and areas, the coordination of missions and programmes and the development of a unified policy.

The Special Committee on Peacekeeping Operations [A/54/87], recognizing the role of UNMAS as the focal point for coordinating mine action, welcomed the progress reported by the Secretary-General and encouraged continued coordination between UN departments, funds and programmes in that respect. It also encouraged Member States to contribute and make pledges to the Voluntary Trust Fund for Assistance in Mine Action. The Special Committee reiterated its request that the Secretary-General provide an update on the experiences of the United Nations in demining in peacekeeping operations, taking into account inputs from those involved in such activities.

Cooperation with regional arrangements

Enhancing African peacekeeping capacity

The Secretary-General, responding to a request from the Special Committee on Peacekeeping Operations [YUN 1997, p. 63; YUN 1998, p. 62], submitted a February report on the enhancement of African peacekeeping capacity [A/54/63-S/1999/171]. He said that the Organization of African Unity (OAU) and subregional African organizations were playing an increasing role in the management of conflicts on the continent and in contributing to the maintenance of international peace and security. The reinforcement of the capacity of African countries to participate in peacekeeping missions remained a key priority, whether through a UN peacekeeping mission or one authorized by the Security Council, but conducted by a regional organization or group of States. The United Nations continued to work closely with regional and subregional organizations in specific peacekeeping and peacemaking efforts in Africa. It had established a political liaison office with OAU in Addis Ababa, Ethiopia, and was collaborating with OAU in enhancing its capacity to address conflict. The United Nations was prepared to facilitate development of expertise for the creation of the OAU Situation Room; OAU could also send some of its staff members to UN Headquarters for familiarization with its methods of operation. The Secretariat was also ready to deploy liaison officers to peacekeeping operations of OAU and of subregional organizations in Africa that the Security Council had authorized and at the headquarters of those organizations.

The Secretariat had also focused on enhancing awareness among African States of the functions of the standby arrangements system, and of the potential benefits of participation. It was reviewing the possibility of dispatching a standby arrangements team to Africa for further briefings and discussion. On 21 January 1999, the Secretariat, in cooperation with OAU, convened in New York a third meeting of African and non-African countries on the enhancement of African peacekeeping capacity. The meeting approved a training strategy and arrangements for information exchange proposed by the United Nations and endorsed, in principle, the establishment of a working group of those States directly involved in training assistance. The Secretariat intended to develop further its cooperation with OAU and the donor community in strengthening African peacekeeping capacity. DPKO, in coordination with OAU, had undertaken to serve as the focal point for the collection and dissemination of information on African capacity for peacekeeping. Over the preceding two years, the United Nations had conducted a number of training activities through its training assistance team and train-the-trainers programmes.

The Secretary-General said that resources to support the Secretariat's efforts to enhance African peacekeeping capacity were provided on a small scale and on a case-by-case basis. The United Nations Trust Fund for Improving Preparedness for Conflict Prevention and Peacekeeping in Africa, established to assist those efforts, had to date received only one contribution, from the United Kingdom. He strongly encouraged Member States to contribute to the Fund and drew the attention of donors to the OAU Peace Fund.

The Secretary-General proposed additional steps to enhance African peacekeeping capacity, including the provision of funding to allow African military officers to participate in short-term exchanges with UN peacekeeping staff; deployment of UN liaison officers to regional organizations; promotion of further cooperation by African States within the UN standby arrangements system and further use of the system to match needs with resources; and establishment of a special peacekeeping programme for African police officers.

Special Committee consideration. The Special Committee on Peacekeeping Operations [A/54/87], reaffirming the important contribution that regional arrangements and agencies could make to peacekeeping, emphasized that no enforcement action should be taken under regional arrangements or regional agencies without the Security Council's authorization. It urged the strengthening of cooperation between the United Nations and relevant regional arrangements and agencies to enhance the capabilities of the international community in the maintenance of international peace and security and encouraged the Secretary-General to take steps towards that end. The Committee noted the successful experience of cooperation between the United Nations and a number of regional and subregional arrangements and agencies.

The Special Committee noted the Secretary-General's report on enhancement of African peacekeeping capacity and the recommendations contained therein, and asked Member States to establish the proposed working group on training assistance to African countries in the field of peacekeeping.

The Special Committee was of the view that efforts to enhance the capacity of African countries in the various aspects of peacekeeping were complementary to the obligations of all Member States under the Charter and were not intended to replace or reduce engagement of non-African countries in peacekeeping operations in the continent. International efforts to enhance the collective capacity of African countries to participate in peacekeeping operations should focus on enhancing OAU's institutional capacity, in particular its Mechanism for the Prevention, Management and Resolution of Conflicts, through the provision of financial and technical assistance. In that connection, the Special Committee underlined the relevance and importance of the OAU Peace Fund and urged Member States to contribute to it. It encouraged Member States to contribute to current efforts to enhance the participation of African countries in peacekeeping operations and reiterated its view that the United Nations, in consultation with OAU and with the cooperation of Member States, should play an active role, especially in coordinating all those efforts. It urged Member States to contribute to the Trust Fund established by the Secretary-General for that purpose. It also encouraged Member States to provide financial and other support to current peacekeeping operations conducted by African subregional organizations.

The Special Committee noted that the DPKO Lessons Learned Unit was finalizing its study on cooperation between the United Nations and regional arrangements and agencies, and urged that the study be made available to Member States and regional arrangements and agencies as soon as possible.

Chapter II

Africa

Countries in Africa that had experienced serious political problems in 1998 continued to do so in 1999, although in some cases the situation improved slightly during the year. The political problems of the continent, mostly brought about by ethnic conflict, were mitigated by some successful efforts by the United Nations, as well as by regional organizations and others, to negotiate settlements between warring factions. Advances were made in the search for negotiated solutions in Sierra Leone and the Democratic Republic of the Congo (DRC) and between Ethiopia and Eritrea, opening a possible path towards sustainable peace in those troubled areas. Despite the progress that generated cautious optimism about the future, tensions remained high and warfare continued in a number of countries.

During 1999, the Secretary-General reported on action taken with regard to his 1998 recommendations on the causes of conflict and the promotion of durable peace and sustainable development in Africa. He stated that progress had been made in the areas of democratic elections, good governance, accountability, transparency and the rule of law. Problems that continued to need attention included conflict, corruption, debt burdens, trade barriers and the AIDS epidemic. Massive investment was required to accomplish such goals as improving education, providing health care, improving infrastructure, reducing poverty, establishing good governance and reintegrating refugees and displaced persons, and he appealed to States for assistance.

In the Great Lakes region, the situation in the DRC was complicated by the presence of foreign troops supporting the opposing parties—the Government, assisted by Angola, Chad, Namibia, the Sudan and Zimbabwe, and the armed militias reportedly supported by Burundi, Rwanda and Uganda. The conflict in the eastern part of the country continued and was accompanied by serious violations of international humanitarian law, including murders and attacks on the civilian population. Following efforts to find a negotiated settlement, the DRC, one of the two main rebel movements and five regional States signed the Lusaka Ceasefire Agreement in July. The Agreement provided for a ceasefire to be monitored by the United Nations, the Organization of African Unity (OAU) and Zambia; withdrawal of foreign forces; and re-establishment of the State administration throughout the country. In the light of the Agreement, the Security Council, acting on the recommendation of the Secretary-General, established the United Nations Organization Mission in the Democratic Republic of the Congo (MONUC), at a strength of 90 military personnel, to help implement the terms. However, fighting and troop mobilization resumed after the Agreement was reached, and the commitments were not implemented by the end of the year.

Rwanda, in general, experienced diminished tension and improved security in 1999. Steps were taken towards building democracy and reconciliation between ethnic groups, including successful local elections and the establishment of commissions on human rights and on national unity and reconciliation. Despite the positive moves, the National Assembly of Rwanda extended the period of transition to democracy by another four years on the grounds that more time was needed to promote reconciliation and to draft a new constitution.

The peace process for Burundi continued in early 1999, with the all-party peace negotiations taking place in Arusha, United Republic of Tanzania. The Seventh Regional Summit on Burundi in January expressed satisfaction over the progress achieved by the negotiations and decided to suspend the remaining sanctions imposed by the countries of the Great Lakes on Burundi. In July, the peace process resumed at a meeting among the numerous Burundi parties, under the chairmanship of the Facilitator of the peace process, Julius K. Nyerere. After extended talks, Mr. Nyerere criticized the Burundi parties for the lack of progress. The killing of civilians, murder of UN officials and the Government's policy of forced removal of civilians brought the peace process to a near standstill by the end of the year.

In Angola, hostilities resumed at the beginning of the year between the government forces and those of the National Union for the Total Independence of Angola (UNITA). The Government led a successful military campaign that resulted in a significant change in the political situation in September. State authority was re-established in much of the territory previously occupied by UNITA, bringing a measure of stability to those areas. The Security Council reiterated its view that the primary cause of the crisis was the refusal of UNITA to comply with its obligations under the 1994 Lusaka Protocol and relevant Council resolutions. The United Nations Observer Mission in Angola (MONUA) was withdrawn and, in its place, a UN office was established to explore ways for restoring peace and assisting in development.

The situation in Sierra Leone improved considerably towards the end of the year, which began with an inauspicious event—an attack by rebel forces on the capital, Freetown, which left many killed and mutilated and much destruction. The rebels were repelled after two weeks by forces of the Monitoring Group (ECOMOG) of the Economic Community of West African States (ECOWAS). Following diplomatic efforts led by ECOWAS and the United Nations, the Lomé Peace Agreement was signed in July, by which the parties agreed to form a Government of National Unity. In August, the Security Council authorized the expansion of its mission in Sierra Leone, with a new mandate to work together with ECOMOG troops in implementing the Agreement. In late 1999, the leaders of the two main rebel factions returned to Freetown, a new Government of National Unity was formed that included members of the main opposition parties, and a disarmament programme was launched. Nevertheless, the situation remained precarious as ceasefire violations and human rights abuses continued. When ECOWAS indicated its intention to withdraw its troops from Sierra Leone, the Secretary-General recommended another expansion of the UN mission there.

The 1998 border dispute between Eritrea and Ethiopia escalated into a full-scale war in 1999. The Security Council condemned the use of force by both parties and demanded an immediate halt in the hostilities and protection for the civilian population. OAU took the lead in the search for a negotiated settlement, with the support of the United Nations, among others. Although both sides accepted the terms of the OAU Framework Agreement, they disagreed on how it should be applied. Experts from OAU, the United Nations, Algeria and the United States met in Algeria to work out technical arrangements for its implementation.

In the Central African Republic, progress was made towards implementing the Bangui Agreements with the holding of the presidential elections in September. The Security Council twice extended the mandate of the United Nations Mission in the Central African Republic (MINURCA) at the request of the Government. However, the transition to a new government was impeded by the tense political climate and the opposition's challenge to the outcome of the elections. The Secretary-General recommended a gradual transition from UN peacekeeping involvement to post-conflict peace-building, with MINURCA gradually handing over its security functions to local security and law enforcement forces.

Progress was made in implementing the Abuja Agreement on Guinea-Bissau, signed in 1998 by President João Bernardo Vieira and his former Chief of Staff, General Ansoumane Mane, to end fighting between forces supporting the two parties. In early January 1999, an interim Government of National Unity was appointed, following which an ECOWAS interposition force was deployed. The Secretary-General established the United Nations Peace-building Support Office in Guinea-Bissau to promote national reconciliation and assist with the organization of elections. When President Vieira was forcibly removed from office by the military junta led by General Mane in May, ECOWAS withdrew its force. Nevertheless, presidential and legislative elections were held, as scheduled, in November.

The United Nations continued its efforts to hold a referendum in Western Sahara for the self-determination of its people, as agreed in 1990 by Morocco and the Frente Popular para la Liberación de Saguia el-Hamra y de Río de Oro (POLISARIO). The identification of voters and the initiation of the appeals process were implemented as planned, but the identification of members of certain tribes caused delays. At the end of the year, the Secretary-General observed that it appeared unlikely that a referendum could be held earlier than 2002.

The Security Council suspended the 1992 sanctions imposed on the Libyan Arab Jamahiriya after the Secretary-General reported on the arrival in the Netherlands of the two suspects charged with the 1988 Pan Am flight 103 bombing. They were to be tried by a Scottish court sitting in the Netherlands. However, by the end of the year, the sanctions had not been lifted.

The political, military and humanitarian situation in Somalia deteriorated in 1999, despite peace initiatives by regional and international organizations. Somalia remained a country with no functioning central government.

Promotion of peace in Africa

During the year, the United Nations carried out activities to implement the recommendations made by the Secretary-General in his 1998 report on the causes of conflict and the promotion of durable peace and sustainable development in Africa [YUN 1998, p. 66]. In that report, the Secretary-General stated that the Organization's cardinal mission was the lasting prevention of conflict as the means to achieve human security and development, stressing the importance of early warning capabilities, early action through peacekeeping deployment and/or humanitarian intervention, post-conflict peace-building efforts, promoting economic growth and strengthening good governance. The development-related aspects of the Secretary-General's report were considered by the Economic and Social Council and the General Assembly (see PART THREE, Chapter III). The Secretary-General submitted a September report to the Security Council, in which he concentrated on his recommendations regarding peace and security in Africa (see below).

Communications. On 28 April [A/53/931-S/1999/491], Germany requested circulation to the General Assembly and the Security Council of the conclusions of the Council of the European Union (EU) on the Secretary-General's 1998 report. Welcoming the report and its follow-up as contributing to raising the international community's awareness of the need to promote durable peace and sustainable development in Africa, the EU expressed its commitment to participating in the follow-up process and commended the Secretary-General's efforts to mobilize the international community in support of Africa through the UN system, within a coordinated framework. As the most important donor to African countries, the EU said, it would continue to contribute to the creation of durable peace and sustainable development, in particular through efforts to assist in creating a stable and democratic environment, eradicating poverty and integrating African countries into the world economy. It would continue to support conflict prevention and resolution under UN auspices, also considering that increased attention should be given to illicit arms flows to and in Africa, as well as to safeguarding the civilian and humanitarian character of refugee camps and settlements.

By a 2 August letter [A/54/209-S/1999/859], Cameroon transmitted the report of the Subregional High-level Seminar on the Examination and Implementation of the Recommendations Contained in the Report of the Secretary-General of the United Nations on the Causes of Conflict and the Promotion of Durable Peace and Sustainable Development in Africa (Yaoundé, 19-21 July), which was part of the programme of activities of the UN Standing Advisory Committee on Security Questions in Central Africa. The seminar covered subjects related to resolution of conflicts and crises, including peacemaking, peacekeeping and peace-building measures and promotion of humanitarian law, good governance and sustainable development. It recommended a number of measures for African countries to take in the areas of inclusive democracy, peaceful settlement of disputes, illicit trafficking in light weapons and cooperation in defence and security, among others.

Report of Secretary-General. In a September report [S/1999/1008], the Secretary-General described progress in implementing recommendations contained in his 1998 report, including the activities of the Security Council's ad hoc Working Group to review the recommendations pertaining to peace and security. The Working Group had developed concrete proposals for action: support for regional and subregional initiatives in the areas of conflict prevention and maintenance of peace; establishment of an international mechanism to assist host Governments in maintaining the security and neutrality of refugee camps; strengthening of Africa's peacekeeping capacity; strengthening the effectiveness of arms sanctions regimes imposed by the Council; addressing urgently the question of arms flows; and enhancing the Council's ability to monitor activities authorized by it but carried out by Member States or a coalition of States. The Secretary-General also described action being taken by the Economic and Social Council and the General Assembly (see PART THREE, Chapter III).

In the area of peacemaking, the Secretary-General had appointed special envoys and representatives who had been actively involved in negotiations initiated by regional organizations to help resolve conflicts in Burundi, the Democratic Republic of the Congo (DRC), Ethiopia-Eritrea and Sierra Leone. Noting that the proliferation of initiatives had complicated and at times frustrated UN peacemaking efforts, the Secretary-General said he had consulted closely with the Organization of African Unity (OAU) and subregional organizations to avoid rival mediation efforts and to concentrate the resources and comparative advantage of all involved in conflict prevention and resolution. In that context, he had, in the case of Somalia, established a forum that grouped together all Security Council members and the countries and regional organizations that had undertaken peacemaking initiatives. Another useful mechanism was the establishment of "Friends of the Secretary-General" or "Friends of (country)" (for example, the

Group of Friends of Guinea-Bissau) to bring together countries and organizations with particular interest and influence or a contribution to make in peacemaking efforts in a given country. He had also made use of contact groups and special conferences, such as the Special Consultation on Guinea and the Special Conference on Sierra Leone.

Other efforts being considered to respond to situations of conflict included targeting sanctions (rendering Council sanctions a more effective and less blunt instrument); criminalizing violations of Council arms embargoes; reducing the purchase of arms and munitions to below 1.5 per cent of gross domestic product; addressing the problem of illicit arms flows and small arms; and identifying international arms merchants.

With regard to supporting African peacekeeping, the Secretariat convened a special meeting in coordination with OAU on 21 January to discuss ways of implementing the recommendations on enhancing African peacekeeping capacity. The 51 participants broadly supported the UN proposals for training and information exchange and considered the establishment of a regular forum for strengthening coordination, better utilization of resources and follow-up action. The United Nations and OAU were also working on a staff exchange programme. The Secretariat undertook to serve as a clearing house for the collection and dissemination of information on enhancing African capacity for peacekeeping, and its database was posted on the Internet. The Secretariat also provided expert advice, through the United Nations Training Assistance Team, to various bilateral and multilateral training activities in Africa and train-the-trainer courses. In 1998 and 1999, the Secretariat participated in the conduct and organization of some 15 multinational peacekeeping training programmes, most of which were held in Africa. Increased focus was also given to the training and organization of civilian police for peacekeeping. In coordination with the Economic Community of West African States (ECOWAS), the Secretariat participated in June in the organizational seminar of a newly established regional peacekeeping centre in Côte d'Ivoire. It also participated in the preparatory seminar for the Central African regional peacekeeping exercise planned for 2000. The United Nations Standby Arrangement (SBA) System teams visited six southern African States and provided briefings in New York to 18 other African countries; as a result, 11 additional African States joined SBA, bringing the number of African members to 23. The United Nations Trust Fund for Improving Preparedness for Conflict Prevention and Peacekeeping in Africa had been used over the preceding two years for training in such areas as mission management and logistics. In February, the Secretary-General submitted a related report to the General Assembly and the Security Council on enhancement of African peacekeeping capacity [A/54/63-S/1999/171] (see preceding chapter).

As to humanitarian assistance, the Secretary-General described the coordination of those efforts in Africa (see PART THREE, Chapter III), including aid to refugees and displaced persons (see PART THREE, Chapter XII).

Post-conflict peace-building was the focus of a number of UN activities. For example, the United Nations Peace-building Support Office in Guinea-Bissau, established in 1999, was mandated to help restore and consolidate peace and democracy by supporting national reconciliation efforts, organizing elections and seeking the commitment of the Government and other parties to adopting a programme of voluntary arms collection. The United Nations Peace-building Support Office in Liberia contributed to the consolidation of peace by facilitating negotiations between ECOWAS and the Government, conducting training courses for members of the police, encouraging the Government to ratify human rights conventions and assisting in the destruction of weapons. The United Nations Mission in the Central African Republic (MINURCA) assisted in the conduct of presidential elections. The work of the United Nations Observer Mission in Sierra Leone (UNOMSIL) included disarmament, demobilization, human rights promotion and humanitarian assistance.

As part of its efforts to build a durable peace and promote economic growth, the United Nations focused on securing respect for human rights and the rule of law, promoting transparency and accountability in public administration, enhancing Governments' administrative capacity and strengthening democratic governance.

Sustainable development was promoted through UN activities aimed at creating a positive environment for investment, investing in human resources, establishing public health priorities, focusing on social justice, eliminating all forms of discrimination against women, restructuring international aid, reducing debt burdens, opening international markets and supporting regional cooperation and integration.

The Secretary-General observed that Africa, on the eve of the new millennium, revealed a remarkable combination of accomplishments and unresolved problems, of opportunities seized and chances missed. There were places in Africa, he noted, where problems persisted, such as arms trading, conflicts, poor governance, silence and inaction regarding AIDS, corruption, crushing debt burdens, trade barriers and declining aid, which made it extremely hard for nations to attract investment and stave off further marginalization from the global economy. However, there were also places—many more than was commonly recognized—where dramatic changes for the better were taking place. Citing the examples of Nigeria and South Africa in particular, the Secretary-General noted that democratic elections were gradually becoming the norm in Africa, and good governance, accountability, transparency and the rule of law were gaining ground. Many African nations were liberalizing trade and exchange controls, privatizing moribund State industries, building up communications infrastructures and reforming their legal and regulatory frameworks.

Through the sustained diplomatic efforts of African countries themselves, important breakthroughs had been made in the search for negotiated solutions in some of the protracted conflicts—for example, the Lomé Agreement for Sierra Leone and the Lusaka accords for the DRC. Significant progress had also been made in efforts to negotiate peace in the conflict between Ethiopia and Eritrea (see p. 130).

Although a beginning had been made in strengthening cooperation between the United Nations and African regional organizations and for the enhancement of African peacekeeping capacity, the necessary resources had not been made available. The Secretary-General appealed to Member States to be generous, bilaterally, multilaterally and to the UN and OAU trust funds. Increased official development assistance (ODA) remained necessary and action on debt was urgent. With the will and wherewithal on the part of both Africa and the international community, peace and development in Africa could be given decisive new momentum, he stated.

Security Council consideration. The Security Council, on 29 and 30 September [meeting 4049], discussed the situation in Africa, specifically the Secretary-General's September report. Opening the debate, the Secretary-General said that political and military engagement, both African and international, was needed to bring stability and to address the root causes of the upheavals on the continent. He called on States to do what was reasonable and doable—to provide more resources for humanitarian assistance and post-conflict peace-building, to act more decisively on debt, to increase ODA, to contribute training and technology and to become politically engaged.

In his statement to the Council, the OAU Secretary-General welcomed recent developments in the DRC and Sierra Leone leading towards a peaceful resolution of the conflicts there. He noted, however, that a number of countries remained a source of concern—conflicts in Angola and between Ethiopia and Eritrea, and the situations in Burundi, the Comoros, the Republic of the Congo and Liberia. In almost all those conflicts, Africans had been at the forefront in seeking solutions and the United Nations had been OAU's main peace partner. The Secretary-General cautioned that the signing of a peace agreement, even though significant, was but the beginning of a long and arduous path to peace, with the potential for renewed conflict if the components for peacemaking and peacekeeping were not adequate, timely and appropriate. OAU lacked the necessary and adequate resources to ensure the full and successful implementation of the agreements that had so far been signed, much less those yet to be agreed by the parties to the conflicts. Africa was undertaking a process of political, economic and social reform and renewal, but for the process to remain sustainable, it needed the active support of the international community, he concluded.

At the end of the discussion on the Secretary-General's progress report, the President announced that the Council had concluded the current stage of its consideration of the agenda item. The Council took no further action on the item during the remainder of the year.

GENERAL ASSEMBLY ACTION

On 22 December, the General Assembly adopted **resolution 54/234** on the causes of conflict and the promotion of durable peace and sustainable development in Africa (see PART THREE, Chapter III).

On 23 December, the Assembly decided that the agenda item on that topic would remain for consideration during its resumed fifty-fourth (2000) session (**decision 54/465**).

In related action, the Assembly adopted **resolution 54/55 A** concerning the activities of the United Nations Standing Advisory Committee on Security Questions in Central Africa (see PART ONE, Chapter VII).

Great Lakes region

The United Nations, in cooperation with regional organizations, continued its peacemaking efforts in the Great Lakes region of Africa, which continued to suffer from political and military turmoil in 1999. While progress was made in negotiations on the situations in the Democratic Republic of the Congo (DRC) and Burundi, fighting continued sporadically in both countries between government troops and armed militias. Rwanda, on the other hand, enjoyed a period of diminished combat and positive steps were made towards democracy and reconciliation between armed groups. The situation in the region was complicated by the movement of militias, armies and refugees across borders.

The DRC, in particular, remained volatile despite a mid-year respite from the fighting between political and ethnic factions. The year opened with a continuation of the war in the eastern part of the country, begun in 1998 by the Congolese Rally for Democracy party, which was supported by the armies of Burundi, Rwanda and Uganda. As the fighting escalated and foreign forces became involved, the Government sought military assistance from five other countries—Angola, Chad, Namibia, the Sudan and Zimbabwe. Following regional negotiations, a ceasefire agreement was signed in July in Lusaka, Zambia, by the DRC and the five regional States, which called for a UN peacekeeping force to ensure implementation of the agreement. However, the agreed ceasefire provisions were not observed by the armed groups and fighting resumed. As a result of the agreement, the Security Council in August authorized the deployment of up to 90 military liaison personnel to assist in developing modalities for implementing the provisions, and later established the United Nations Organization Mission in the Democratic Republic of the Congo to carry out that function. The Secretary-General appointed Moustapha Niasse as his Special Envoy to pursue the peace process with a possible UN role in negotiating a settlement.

In Burundi, signs of progress towards a peaceful settlement between the many armed factions were seen in early 1999, as the series of all-party peace negotiations, begun in 1998, continued in Arusha, United Republic of Tanzania. The Seventh Regional Summit on Burundi in January welcomed the progress achieved by those negotiations and decided to suspend the remaining sanctions imposed by the regional countries on Burundi. However, fighting broke out again and, despite renewed attempts at negotiations, the prospects for success were clouded by the killing of civilians and UN officials, the forced removal of civilians by the Government, and the influx of Burundian and Rwandan rebels from neighbouring countries.

Rwanda experienced a period of reduced fighting and tensions eased in 1999, particularly when compared with the previous five years. Furthermore, it made initial moves towards democracy through such steps as holding local elections, establishing commissions on human rights and on national reconciliation, and better supervision by parliament over aspects of government.

The Secretary-General in December appointed Berhanu Dinka as his Special Representative for the Great Lakes Region.

Peacemaking efforts

On 29 December [S/1999/1296], the Secretary-General informed the Security Council of his decision to appoint Berhanu Dinka as his Special Representative for the Great Lakes Region. In that capacity, he would sound out the views of countries in the region regarding the proposed organization of an international conference on the Great Lakes; represent the Secretary-General at meetings and deliberations under the Arusha peace process on Burundi; and address the regional dimensions of the conflict in the DRC through, among other things, close interaction with the Special Representative in the DRC. The Council took note of the decision on 30 December [S/1999/1297].

In an April resolution on the DRC (**resolution 1234(1999)**), the Security Council reaffirmed the importance of holding, at the appropriate time, an international conference on peace, security and stability in the Great Lakes region under the auspices of the United Nations and OAU, with the participation of the Governments of the region and all others concerned. The Council, in a June statement by its President (**S/PRST/1999/17**), encouraged the international community to help facilitate such a conference.

Communication. The EU, in a statement transmitted to the Security Council by Germany on 21 June [S/1999/700], expressed concern about the flow of arms and military equipment and personnel to and within the Great Lakes region, which, it said, was fuelling conflicts in the Great Lakes and Central Africa, as well as in other parts of the continent, and was mostly financed through the trafficking of diamonds, gold and other precious materials, and other illicit activities. The EU believed that a search for a long-term solution should give high priority to measures to curb arms supplies, their illicit circulation and the illicit trafficking that financed them.

Democratic Republic of the Congo

Throughout 1999, the Democratic Republic of the Congo (DRC) was afflicted by the war in the eastern part of the country, which flared up in August 1998 [YUN 1998, p. 79]. The war escalated as several Congolese rebel movements received support from the armies of Burundi, Rwanda and Uganda. In the light of that situation, the DRC Government requested help from the armies of five other countries: Angola, Chad, Namibia, the Sudan and Zimbabwe. The presence of those armies, in addition to the involvement of various militias such as the Interahamwe, the Mai-Mai, the former Rwandan Armed Forces, the Front pour la défense de la démocratie and the Lord's Resistance Army, created a climate of great insecurity, which was complicated by serious violations of international humanitarian law, such as murders and attacks on the civilian population (see PART TWO, Chapter III).

Following many attempts to end the conflict in the DRC, the Lusaka Ceasefire Agreement was signed on 10 July by the DRC and the five other regional States. Later, the Agreement was signed by one rebel group, the Movement for the Liberation of the Congo, but not by the Congolese Rally for Democracy. Under the Agreement, which contained both military and political provisions and called for observer participation by one country (Zambia) and two organizations (the United Nations and OAU), the parties agreed to seek a UN peacekeeping force in the DRC to ensure implementation. However, the ceasefire provisions were not observed by the armed groups, fighting and troop mobilization continued, the militias were not disarmed and massacres were carried out by armed elements. Many of the commitments outlined in the Agreement (including withdrawal of foreign forces, facilitation of humanitarian assistance, equal rights for all ethnic groups and re-establishment of the State administration throughout the country) were not implemented by year's end. In particular, the Government of President Laurent Désiré Kabila refused to hold an all-inclusive national dialogue (inter-Congolese political negotiations) on the future of the country with the participation of political parties and civil society, preferring instead a "national debate" limited to the issues it was prepared to discuss.

Following the signing of the Agreement, the Secretary-General made recommendations on a peacekeeping force to the Security Council, which in August authorized the deployment of up to 90 UN military liaison personnel, together with the necessary civilian, political, humanitarian and administrative staff, to assist in developing modalities for implementing the Agreement, among other things. In November, the Council, recognizing the Lusaka Agreement as the most viable basis for a resolution of the conflict, established the United Nations Organization Mission in the Democratic Republic of the Congo (MONUC), composed of those staff already authorized. The Council encouraged all Congolese to participate in the national dialogue to be organized on the future government.

While some progress was made in the implementation of the Ceasefire Agreement, a number of setbacks also occurred and the military and security situation deteriorated in November and December. In addition to lack of security and freedom of movement for peacekeeping personnel, fighting continued in some parts of the country.

The Secretary-General appointed Moustapha Niasse (Senegal) as his Special Envoy for the DRC peace process. Mr. Niasse's mandate was to pursue the peace process, including through a possible UN role in promoting a negotiated settlement.

Political and military developments

The DRC, in the early months of 1999, addressed several letters to the Security Council to inform the members of the situation in the country and the reported involvement of foreign troops and militias. It initially named Rwanda and Uganda as the countries sending troops into the DRC and later added Burundi.

By a 6 January letter [S/1999/13], the DRC informed the Council of a massacre of some 500 civilians, including many women, children and elderly people, allegedly committed by troops of a Rwandan-Ugandan coalition, in the south-east of the DRC. The killings were a sequel to reprisals against Mai-Mai warriors who were reported to have attacked enemy positions in South Kivu province the day before. According to reports, the massacres, which lasted from 30 December 1998 to 1 January 1999, were perpetrated by soldiers of the Rwandan-Ugandan coalition, and more specifically by soldiers of the Rwandan Patriotic Army, and the victims were Christian members of the indigenous population. The DRC urged the Council to condemn the invasion of Congolese territory by Rwandan and Ugandan troops, to call on the two countries to withdraw their troops and halt all atrocities against the Congolese population and to initiate an inquiry into the massacres. In April [S/1999/493], the DRC revised the figure of murdered Congolese civilians to 814.

Despite the difficulties raised by the war, said the DRC in a letter of 15 January [S/1999/46], the Government had made progress towards the restoration and democratization of the political system. In the political arena, efforts were made to establish structures to prepare for free, democratic elections at all political levels of Congolese society. With regard to the economy, measures were taken to control inflation and halt the currency depreciation. In the legal and human rights field, a Ministry of Human Rights was established to promote respect for human rights and efforts were made to improve the legal system. In the same letter, the DRC expressed concern about the border security situation, noting that the country was located in a conflict zone that had for decades undergone crises, including the Rwandan genocide of 1994. The DRC claimed that the Great Lakes region had been destabilized because armed bands used the territories of host countries to attack their enemies and States violated the national sovereignty of other countries on the pretext of their own national security.

By a 24 February letter [S/1999/205], the DRC transmitted to the Council a document entitled "White paper on massive violations of human rights and of the basic rules of international humanitarian law by the aggressor countries (Uganda, Rwanda and Burundi) in the eastern part of the DRC", which covered the period from 2 August to 5 November 1998. It transmitted a second document on 28 June [S/1999/733], covering the period from 6 November 1998 to 15 April 1999. The DRC acknowledged the support of Angola, Chad, Namibia and Zimbabwe in its efforts to repulse foreign aggression and regain its territorial integrity but noted that it had spared no effort at the diplomatic level to find an acceptable solution. The DRC stated that the Security Council was doing nothing to promote international peace and security by indiscriminately calling for the withdrawal of all foreign forces without distinction between aggressors and those aiding the legitimate Government.

The DRC, in a 15 March letter [S/1999/276], claimed that on 5 March Rwandan elements of the Rwandan-Ugandan coalition troops had massacred 100 civilians in the town of Kamituga, South Kivu province. The Government urged the Council to expedite an international inquiry into the recent massacres in South Kivu.

Concerning a related development in the border region, Uganda and the DRC commented on who was responsible for the murder on 1 March of 12 people, including 8 tourists, in a national park in Uganda. Uganda, on 8 March [S/1999/252], transmitted the comments of its President, who said the criminals were the Interahamwes (Hutus living in the DRC). On 3 March [S/1999/229], the DRC condemned the act and denied all responsibility for those events. It expressed concern at the attempt to destabilize the Great Lakes region and called for an international investigation.

Security Council consideration. By a 4 March letter [S/1999/278], the DRC requested the Security Council to hold an open debate on the question of a peaceful settlement of the conflict in the DRC. The Council considered the situation on 19 March [meeting 3987].

Addressing the Council, the DRC said that the sole obstacle to a peaceful solution to the Congolese crisis was Rwanda's determination to remain on Congolese territory. Negotiations were continuing at the regional level within OAU, but, as a result of the impasse in the negotiating process, the DRC felt it timely to appeal to the international community to induce the aggressors to engage in negotiations to ensure regional peace and stability. The DRC believed that resolution of the crisis required a regional conference of the Great Lakes countries that would bring together leaders and their respective opposition forces under the auspices of OAU and the United Nations. The DRC's concern was to end the martyrdom of the population in the eastern and Kivu provinces, which remained under the occupation of the regular armed forces of Rwanda and Uganda. The DRC agreed to sign a ceasefire agreement, to be followed by the deployment of a buffer force along its borders with Burundi, Rwanda and Uganda, and a timetable for the withdrawal of the aggressor troops. Until the international community took additional steps to bring peace to the entire Great Lakes region, the DRC expected the Council to recognize that the DRC was the victim of armed aggression; to condemn that aggression; to demand respect by the aggressors for international humanitarian law; to demand withdrawal of the troops of aggression; to deploy an interposing force along common borders; and to convene an international conference on restoring peace in the Great Lakes region.

Rwanda believed that the peace process, particularly the Lusaka process, was well under way and that the Council should continue to support it. Rwanda's security had been affected by the presence in the DRC of large numbers of armed elements of Rwandan nationality, including former government forces and militia responsible for the 1994 genocide. Their ability to reorganize and rearm on Congolese territory, with the support of the Congolese Government, was a destabilizing factor for Rwanda. In Rwanda's view, a comprehensive resolution of the DRC crisis should be reached through dealing with the governance and leadership crisis there, through the neutralization and dismantling of the non-State armies operating in the DRC, and through the isolation of those embracing genocide in the region. Rwanda called on the DRC to dismantle the dozen non-State armies that were being used in aggression against the territorial integrity of neighbouring States.

Uganda said it was committed to a diplomatic solution to the conflict in the DRC and stated that it had neither territorial ambitions nor economic interests beyond normal trade relations. According to Uganda, the crisis in the DRC had a regional dimension that originated with the 1994 genocide in Rwanda. Former Rwandan forces and militias had crossed into the DRC and had launched attacks against Uganda from Congolese territory. Uganda had responded in self-defence by recapturing its territory and following its attackers into Zairian (currently DRC) territory in hot pursuit. Furthermore, in 1998 DRC President Kabila had invited Uganda to deploy its forces inside the DRC to flush out the Allied Democratic Forces, a rebel group that had been infiltrated into his country by the Sudan. Zimbabwe, Angola and Namibia, later joined by Chad and the Sudan, had provided foreign military assistance at Mr. Kabila's request, on the pretext that the DRC had been invaded by Uganda and Rwanda. The DRC Government had committed itself to the principle of a national conference to determine the political future of the country involving all political stakeholders, although the question of whether the rebels should participate directly or through proximity talks had not been settled.

Namibia said that on 18 January it had hosted a summit of the countries that were involved in the fighting in the DRC. That meeting resolved that a ceasefire should be signed without delay; however, what followed were continued attacks on government and allied forces. In its view, the Security Council needed to become actively involved.

Most speakers warned of the implications for the region of the ongoing conflict in the DRC and supported the regional mediation efforts currently under way, particularly those led by the Southern African Development Community (SADC) known as the Lusaka process, and those of OAU and the United Nations. Several countries supported the call for an international conference on peace and security in the Great Lakes region, while others called for an African approach. The United States, expressing concern about the ethnicization of the conflict, said it would consider supporting a peacekeeping operation in the DRC if there were a comprehensive agreement among the belligerents to end the conflict and to observe a ceasefire, and the mandate would be to observe and monitor, not to enforce the peace or maintain the security of the borders. Burkina Faso and the United Kingdom also supported a peacekeeping force.

Appointment of Special Envoy. The Secretary-General informed the Security Council on 1 April [S/1999/379] of his appointment of Moustapha Niasse (Senegal) as his Special Envoy for the DRC peace process. Mr. Niasse's mandate would be to: demonstrate to the leaders concerned the Secretary-General's commitment to regional efforts to restore peace; assess progress made in the Lusaka process; identify obstacles to signing the ceasefire agreement; have contacts with Congolese political and civil leaders with the aim of assessing the prospects for broader political participation and national reconciliation; sound out African leaders on a possible UN role in promoting a negotiated settlement; ascertain possible material and financial support for a settlement from non-African countries; and report to the Secretary-General on his mission, with recommendations on practical measures that the United Nations could take to assist the peace process. Mr. Niasse, who was expected to visit the area in April, would be assisted by the Secretary-General's Special Representative for the Great Lakes Region, Berhanu Dinka. On 5 April [S/1999/380], the Council agreed with the Secretary-General's decision to appoint a Special Envoy.

Communications. The EU, by a 17 February declaration on peace efforts in the DRC [S/1999/176], noted some positive signals with regard to a possible ceasefire agreement. It welcomed President Kabila's preparedness to enter into negotiations with all parties to the conflict, including the rebel movement. It stated its readiness to consider a rehabilitation programme for the DRC in the event of cessation of hostilities and internal progress on peace, democracy and respect for human rights.

On 25 March [S/1999/329], the DRC stated that Rwandan, Burundian and Ugandan aggressors had massacred more than 250 Congolese civilians in the occupied territory in eastern DRC during March. It called for an investigation into violations of international humanitarian law with a view to prosecuting the guilty parties. On 7 April [S/1999/396], the DRC forwarded a joint statement issued on the occasion of the visit by President Kabila to Kenya. Kenyan President Daniel arap Moi and President Kabila agreed that the subject of national debate in the DRC should include the process of acceding to power through popular elections, the question of a new constitutional dispensation and the formulation of laws to govern the formation and operation of political parties. President arap Moi offered Nairobi as the venue for the all-inclusive talks and agreed to consult with all parties with a view to inviting the DRC Government and all Congolese groups that were stakeholders to attend.

SECURITY COUNCIL ACTION

On 9 April [meeting 3993], the Security Council unanimously adopted **resolution 1234(1999).** The draft text [S/1999/400] was prepared during consultations among Council members.

The Security Council,

Recalling the statements by its President of 31 August 1998 and of 11 December 1998,

Expressing its concern at the further deterioration of the situation in the Democratic Republic of the Congo and the continuation of hostilities,

Expressing its firm commitment to preserving the national sovereignty, territorial integrity and political independence of the Democratic Republic of the Congo and all other States in the region,

Recalling that the Assembly of Heads of State and Government of the Organization of African Unity, during its first ordinary session held in Cairo from 17 to 21 July 1964, adopted in its resolution AHG 16(1) the principle of the inviolability of national frontiers of African States, as stated in paragraph 2 of the communiqué issued on 17 August 1998 by the Central Organ of the Organization of African Unity Mechanism for Conflict Prevention, Management and Resolution,

Concerned at reports of measures taken by forces opposing the Government in the eastern part of the Democratic Republic of the Congo in violation of the national sovereignty and territorial integrity of the country,

Expressing its concern at all violations of human rights and international humanitarian law in the territory of the Democratic Republic of the Congo, including acts of and incitement to ethnic hatred and violence by all parties to the conflict,

Deeply concerned at the illicit flow of arms and military materiel in the Great Lakes region,

Recalling the inherent right of individual or collective self-defence in accordance with Article 51 of the Charter of the United Nations,

Welcoming the appointment by the Secretary-General of his Special Envoy for the peace process in the Democratic Republic of the Congo,

Stressing that the present conflict in the Democratic Republic of the Congo constitutes a threat to peace, security and stability in the region,

1. *Reaffirms* the obligation of all States to respect the territorial integrity, political independence and national sovereignty of the Democratic Republic of the Congo and other States in the region, including the obligation to refrain from the threat or use of force against the territorial integrity or political independence of any State or in any other manner inconsistent with the purposes of the United Nations, and further reaffirms the need for all States to refrain from any interference in each other's internal affairs, in accordance with the Charter of the United Nations;

2. *Deplores* the continuing fighting and the presence of forces of foreign States in the Democratic Republic of the Congo in a manner inconsistent with the principles of the Charter, and calls upon those States to bring to an end the presence of those uninvited forces and to take immediate steps to that end;

3. *Demands* an immediate halt to the hostilities;

4. *Calls* for the immediate signing of a ceasefire agreement allowing the orderly withdrawal of all foreign forces, the re-establishment of the authority of the Government of the Democratic Republic of the Congo throughout its territory, and the disarmament of non-governmental armed groups in the Democratic Republic of the Congo, and stresses, in the context of a lasting peaceful settlement, the need for the engagement of all Congolese in an all-inclusive process of political dialogue with a view to achieving national reconciliation and to the holding on an early date of democratic, free and fair elections, and for the provision of arrangements for security along the relevant international borders of the Democratic Republic of the Congo;

5. *Welcomes* the intention of the Government of the Democratic Republic of the Congo to hold an all-inclusive national debate as a precursor to elections, and encourages further progress in this respect;

6. *Calls upon* all parties to the conflict in the Democratic Republic of the Congo to protect human rights and to respect international humanitarian law, in particular, as applicable to them, the Geneva Conventions of 1949 and the Additional Protocols thereto, of 1977, and the Convention on the Prevention and Punishment of the Crime of Genocide of 1948;

7. *Condemns* all massacres carried out on the territory of the Democratic Republic of the Congo, and calls for an international investigation into all such events, including those in the province of South Kivu and other atrocities as referred to in the report submitted by the Special Rapporteur on the situation of human rights in the Democratic Republic of the Congo in accordance with Commission on Human Rights resolution 1998/61 of 21 April 1998, with a view to bringing to justice those responsible;

8. *Condemns* the continuing activity of, and support to, all armed groups, including the ex-Rwandese armed forces, Interahamwe, and others in the Democratic Republic of the Congo;

9. *Calls* for safe and unhindered access for humanitarian assistance to those in need in the Democratic Republic of the Congo, and urges all parties to the conflict to guarantee the safety and security of United Nations and humanitarian personnel;

10. *Welcomes* the commitment by the parties to the conflict in the Democratic Republic of the Congo to stop fighting in order to allow an immunization campaign, and urges all parties to the conflict to take concrete action in order to provide greater protection to children exposed to armed conflict in the Democratic Republic of the Congo;

11. *Expresses its support* for the regional mediation process by the Organization of African Unity and the Southern African Development Community to find a peaceful settlement to the conflict in the Democratic Republic of the Congo, and calls upon the international community to continue to support those efforts;

12. *Urges* all parties to the conflict to continue to work constructively through the regional mediation process towards the signing of a ceasefire agreement and settlement of the conflict in the Democratic Republic of the Congo, and calls upon all States in the re-

gion to create the conditions necessary for the speedy and peaceful resolution of the crisis and to desist from any act that may further exacerbate the situation;

13. *Expresses its support* for the Special Envoy of the Secretary-General for the peace process in the Democratic Republic of the Congo, calls upon all parties to the conflict to cooperate fully with him in his mission in support of regional mediation efforts and national reconciliation, as set out in his mandate, and urges Member States and organizations to respond readily to requests from the Special Envoy for assistance;

14. *Reaffirms* the importance of holding, at the appropriate time, an international conference on peace, security and stability in the Great Lakes region under the auspices of the United Nations and the Organization of African Unity, with the participation of all the Governments of the region and all others concerned;

15. *Reaffirms its readiness* to consider the active involvement of the United Nations, in coordination with the Organization of African Unity, including through concrete sustainable and effective measures, to assist in the implementation of an effective ceasefire agreement and in an agreed process for political settlement of the conflict;

16. *Requests* the Secretary-General of the United Nations to work closely with the Secretary-General of the Organization of African Unity in promoting a peaceful resolution of the conflict, to make recommendations on the possible role of the United Nations to this end, and to keep the Council informed of developments;

17. *Decides* to remain actively seized of the matter.

Sirte peace agreement

On 20 April [S/1999/450], the Libyan Arab Jamahiriya transmitted to the Security Council the text of the Peace Agreement for the Great Lakes Region, signed in Sirte, Libya, on 18 April by the Presidents of Chad, the DRC, Eritrea and Uganda, and the head of State of Libya, Colonel Muammar Al-Qadhafi, who was coordinator of the peace process in the Great Lakes region.

By that agreement, the signatories affirmed the security and integrity of the borders of all States; decided to cease hostilities in order to pave the way for dialogue and a peaceful solution; agreed to deploy a neutral African peacekeeping force in the area inside the DRC where Burundian, Rwandan and Ugandan troops were situated and that all foreign forces in the DRC would be withdrawn as soon as a peace agreement was reached; and agreed that the withdrawal of Rwandan and Ugandan troops would be timed with the arrival of the African peace forces. The signatories condemned all acts of violence and mass murder and affirmed the need to punish and disarm those responsible. They encouraged the DRC to initiate a national dialogue for all parties. In addition, they pledged to refrain from taking actions to overthrow the DRC Government and stressed the continuity of the role of the peace coordinator in creating the climate and mechanism for accelerating the peace process. Libya affirmed that it had been decided to deploy ceasefire monitors from Liberia, Libya and Zambia.

Uganda also forwarded the text of the Sirte agreement to the Council on 21 May [S/1999/623]. It added that the agreement was linked to the Lusaka peace process and described it as a declaration of commitment to the ongoing regional peace process under the facilitation of President Frederick Chiluba of Zambia. A ceasefire agreement would have to be negotiated and finalized by all the belligerents in the DRC to enable the cessation of hostilities, the putting in place of an interposition force, the enhancement of internal dialogue and the withdrawal of all foreign troops. Uganda called on Colonel Qadhafi to liaise with President Chiluba.

In a 29 April letter [S/1999/493], the DRC recalled the agreement signed in Sirte, reiterated its request that the Council demand that Rwanda and Uganda adhere strictly to resolution 1234(1999) (see above), particularly to those paragraphs demanding an immediate halt to the hostilities and calling on those two States to end their military presence in the DRC. The DRC urged the Council to demand that Rwanda and Uganda conclude a ceasefire agreement with the DRC, to create the conditions for a peaceful settlement, including the withdrawal of their troops, and to refrain from action that might aggravate the situation.

Communiqués and statements

The Presidents of Rwanda, Uganda and the United Republic of Tanzania issued a communiqué on the DRC on 5 May [A/54/95-S/1999/551]. At a meeting in Dodoma, United Republic of Tanzania, on 4 and 5 May, the leaders focused on finding a solution to the conflict in the framework of the SADC Lusaka peace initiative and process. They took note of the Sirte peace agreement as a contribution to the Lusaka peace process and urged the parties to the conflict to arrange a ceasefire agreement. The leaders reaffirmed the need for an all-inclusive national dialogue to discuss the new political dispensation in the DRC and welcomed President Kabila's expressed readiness to hold direct talks with the rebels.

Following the visit of a delegation from the DRC to Uganda (28 May–1 June), the two countries issued a joint communiqué [S/1999/635] expressing their commitment to implementing the broad principles stipulated in the Sirte peace agreement. They concurred that sustainable peace, security and stability could be achieved only through real democracy in all the countries of the region, and welcomed the DRC efforts to open a national dialogue.

On 4 June [S/1999/654], Uganda transmitted the joint communiqué issued at the conclusion of a meeting in Dar-es-Salaam between the Presidents of Rwanda, Uganda and the United Republic of Tanzania. They welcomed the commitment made by the DRC and Uganda towards achieving a peaceful solution to the conflict in the DRC. They also welcomed the unilateral cessation of hostilities declared by Rwanda, which they said would enhance the chances for a negotiated and comprehensive ceasefire agreement in accordance with the Lusaka peace process.

In a 2 June statement [S/1999/683], the EU Presidency called on the warring parties in the DRC to abide by the terms of resolution 1234(1999) and urged them to reach a ceasefire, to operate an orderly withdrawal of forces and to prepare for the deployment of a multinational peacekeeping force, which would be followed by an international conference on the Great Lakes region. The EU would be prepared to consider financial assistance to the DRC if its plan for a "national debate", as proposed by President Kabila, was organized by an independent authority, if all parties were allowed to take part and if its agenda was approved by all participants and enabled a dialogue on the institutions and conditions for establishing civil peace, the rule of law and democracy.

SECURITY COUNCIL ACTION

On 24 June [meeting 4015], the President of the Security Council, following consultations among Council members, made statement **S/PRST/1999/17** on behalf of the Council:

> The Security Council recalls the statements by its President of 31 August 1998 and 11 December 1998. It reaffirms its resolution 1234(1999) of 9 April 1999 on the situation in the Democratic Republic of the Congo and calls on all parties to comply with this resolution. It expresses its continued concern at the continuing conflict in the Democratic Republic of the Congo.
>
> The Council reaffirms its commitment to preserving the national unity, sovereignty, territorial integrity and political independence of the Democratic Republic of the Congo and all other States in the region. It further reaffirms its support for the regional mediation process facilitated by the President of the Republic of Zambia on behalf of the Southern African Development Community in cooperation with the Organization of African Unity and with support from the United Nations to find a peaceful settlement to the conflict in the Democratic Republic of the Congo.
>
> The Council takes note of the constructive efforts being made to promote a peaceful settlement of the conflict in the context of the above-mentioned regional mediation process, including the meeting and agreement signed at Sirte, Libyan Arab Jamahiriya, on 18 April 1999. It calls on all parties to demonstrate commitment to the peace process and to participate with a constructive and flexible spirit in the forthcoming summit in Lusaka scheduled for 26 June 1999. In this context, the Council calls upon the parties immediately to sign a ceasefire agreement which includes the appropriate modalities and mechanisms for its implementation.
>
> The Council reaffirms its readiness to consider the active involvement of the United Nations, in coordination with the Organization of African Unity, including through concrete sustainable and effective measures, to assist in the implementation of an effective ceasefire agreement and in an agreed process for political settlement of the conflict.
>
> The Council emphasizes the need for a peaceful settlement of the conflict in the Democratic Republic of the Congo in order to permit the economic reconstruction of the country, so as to enhance development and foster national reconciliation.
>
> The Council stresses the need for a continuing process of genuine national reconciliation and democratization in all States of the Great Lakes region. It reaffirms the importance of holding, at the appropriate time, an international conference on peace, security and stability in the Great Lakes region and encourages the international community to help facilitate such a conference.
>
> The Council expresses its appreciation and full support for the continuing efforts of the Secretary-General and his Special Envoy for the peace process in the Democratic Republic of the Congo.
>
> The Council will remain actively seized of the matter.

Lusaka Ceasefire Agreement

On 10 July, Angola, the DRC, Namibia, Rwanda, Uganda and Zimbabwe signed in Lusaka, Zambia, the Ceasefire Agreement on the DRC [S/1999/815]. Under the Agreement, which was witnessed by Zambia, OAU, SADC and the United Nations, the six regional leaders agreed to the cessation of hostilities between the belligerent forces in the DRC. The Agreement stipulated that all air, land and sea attacks would cease within 24 hours of the signing, as well as the movement of military forces and all acts of violence against the civilian population. Other provisions concerned the release of prisoners of war, the immediate disengagement of forces where they were in direct contact, the facilitation of humanitarian assistance by opening up humanitarian corridors, equal rights for all ethnic groups and nationalities in the DRC, and control of illicit trafficking of arms and the infiltration of armed groups.

Under the terms of the Agreement and upon conclusion of the inter-Congolese political negotiations, State administration would be re-established throughout the DRC. The DRC Government and the opposition would enter into an open national dialogue under a neutral facilitator to be agreed upon by the Congolese parties. There would be a mechanism for the formation of a national, restructured and integrated army, including the forces of the Congolese parties who were signatories to the Agreement. A mechanism would also be established for disarming militias and armed groups. In that connection, the parties committed themselves to locating, identifying, disarming and assembling all members of armed groups in the DRC. The final withdrawal of all foreign forces from DRC territory would be carried out in accordance with a schedule in an annex to the Agreement, and a withdrawal schedule to be prepared by the United Nations, OAU and the Joint Military Commission (JMC) to be set up by the parties as a peacekeeping force until the deployment of UN forces. The parties agreed to request the Security Council to deploy a peacekeeping force in the DRC to ensure implementation of the Agreement and mandate the force to track down all armed groups in the DRC.

Another annex described modalities for the implementation of the Ceasefire Agreement and covered the cessation of hostilities, disengagement of forces, release of hostages, withdrawal of foreign forces, national dialogue and reconciliation, re-establishment of the State administration, the JMC mandate, the proposed UN peacekeeping mandate, disarmament of armed groups, formation of a national army, redeployment of forces of the parties to defensive positions in conflict zones, and normalization of the security situation along the DRC borders.

In a 9 July statement [S/1999/787], the EU Presidency said that the EU supported the Agreement; it appealed to the parties to implement it as soon as possible.

Deployment of UN personnel

Report of Secretary-General. Following the signing of the Lusaka Ceasefire Agreement, the Secretary-General submitted a 15 July report [S/1999/790] to the Security Council on its implications for the United Nations and made recommendations concerning possible preliminary UN action. Noting that the Congolese Rally for Democracy and the Movement for the Liberation of the Congo had declined to sign the Agreement, he expressed the hope that the rebels would sign it without further delay and that it could be implemented promptly and in full.

The Secretary-General reviewed the tasks proposed for a UN force: working with JMC and OAU in implementation of the Agreement; observing and monitoring the cessation of hostilities; investigating violations of the ceasefire and ensuring compliance; supervising the disengagement of forces; supervising the redeployment of forces to defensive positions; providing humanitarian assistance to and protecting displaced persons, refugees and others; informing the parties of its peacekeeping operations; collecting weapons from civilians; supervising the withdrawal of foreign forces; and verifying all information relating to military forces of the parties. The Agreement also envisaged a number of peace enforcement operations, including the "tracking down" and disarming of armed groups; screening mass killers, perpetrators of crimes against humanity and others; handing over suspected *genocidaires* to the International Criminal Tribunal for Rwanda; and repatriation. The armed groups were identified as the former Rwandan government forces and Interahamwe militia, the Allied Democratic Front, the Lord's Resistance Army, the Forces for the Defence of Democracy of Burundi, the Former Uganda National Army, the Uganda National Rescue Front II, the West Nile Bank Front and the National Union for the Total Independence of Angola.

The Secretary-General stated that the conflict in the DRC had inflicted further terrible suffering on a country already burdened with poverty and neglect. An estimated 700,000 persons were displaced within the country, in addition to some 300,000 refugees located on its territory, and the United Nations had received harrowing accounts of famine and epidemics. The conflict had also been characterized by appalling, widespread and systematic human rights violations, including mass killings, ethnic cleansing, rape and destruction of property. The Secretary-General stated that the peace agreement could be viewed as a first step towards an eventual recovery.

In order to be effective, any UN peacekeeping mission would have to be large and expensive, requiring the deployment of thousands of troops and civilian personnel. In the light of the numerous difficulties envisaged, the Secretary-General recommended that the Security Council immediately authorize the deployment of up to 90 military personnel, together with the necessary civilian, political, humanitarian and administrative staff, to the capitals of the States signatories to the Lusaka Agreement and the provisional headquarters of JMC. As a second stage, he would then recommend a further deployment of up to 500 military observers whose functions would be to establish contacts with the parties; liaise with JMC; assist JMC in investigating ceasefire violations; make a security assessment of the country; obtain from the parties guarantees of cooperation; determine the locations of the forces of all parties; observe the ceasefire and disengagement of the forces; facilitate the provision of humanitarian assistance; and assist the Department of Peacekeeping Operations in refining its concept of operations for subsequent deployments.

The Secretary-General noted that in due course he would appoint a Special Representative to lead the observer mission, which he proposed calling the United Nations Observer Mission in the Democratic Republic of the Congo. He had also ordered the dispatch of a small advance team to the region to clarify the role to be played by the United Nations, to be followed by a technical survey team to the DRC to pave the way for deployments and assess the logistical capacity in the mission area. In the meantime, the Congolese parties needed to proceed with their national debate in order to work towards national reconciliation. The Secretary-General could foresee the need for a well-funded, well-planned and long-term programme for the disarmament, demobilization and reintegration into society of former combatants, as well as measures to address the human rights violations that had characterized the conflict. The necessary first step would be the signing of the Agreement by the two rebel groups that had not done so.

(The Movement for the Liberation of the Congo signed the Agreement on 1 August.)

SECURITY COUNCIL ACTION (August)

On 6 August [meeting 4032], the Security Council unanimously adopted **resolution 1258(1999)**. The draft text [S/1999/852] was prepared in consultations among Council members.

The Security Council,

Reaffirming its resolution 1234(1999) of 9 April 1999, and recalling the statements by its President of 31 August 1998, 11 December 1998, and 24 June 1999,

Bearing in mind the purposes and principles of the Charter of the United Nations, and the primary responsibility of the Security Council for the maintenance of international peace and security,

Reaffirming the sovereignty, territorial integrity and political independence of the Democratic Republic of the Congo and all States in the region,

Determined to resolve with all parties concerned the grave humanitarian situation in the Democratic Republic of the Congo in particular, and in the region as a whole, and to provide for the safe and free return of all refugees and displaced persons to their homes,

Recognizing that the current situation in the Democratic Republic of the Congo demands an urgent response by the parties to the conflict with support from the international community,

Recalling the relevant principles contained in the Convention on the Safety of United Nations and Associated Personnel adopted on 9 December 1994,

Welcoming the report of the Secretary-General of 15 July 1999 on the United Nations preliminary deployment in the Democratic Republic of the Congo,

1. *Welcomes* the signing of the Ceasefire Agreement on the conflict in the Democratic Republic of the Congo by the States concerned, in Lusaka on 10 July 1999, which represents a viable basis for a resolution of the conflict in the Democratic Republic of the Congo;

2. *Also welcomes* the signing of the Ceasefire Agreement on 1 August 1999 by the Movement for the Liberation of the Congo, expresses deep concern that the Congolese Rally for Democracy has not signed the Agreement, and calls upon the latter to sign the Agreement without delay in order to bring about national reconciliation and lasting peace in the Democratic Republic of the Congo;

3. *Commends* the Organization of African Unity and the Southern African Development Community for their efforts to find a peaceful settlement of the conflict in the Democratic Republic of the Congo, and commends in particular the President of the Republic of Zambia, and also the Secretary-General, the Special Envoy of the Secretary-General for the peace process in the Democratic Republic of the Congo, the Representative of the Secretary-General to the Great Lakes Region and all those who contributed to the peace process;

4. *Calls upon* all parties to the conflict, in particular the rebel movements, to cease hostilities, to implement fully and without delay the provisions of the Ceasefire Agreement, to cooperate fully with the Organization of African Unity and the United Nations in the implementation of the Agreement and to desist from any act that may further exacerbate the situation;

5. *Stresses* the need for a continuing process of genuine national reconciliation, and encourages all Congolese to participate in the national debate to be organized in accordance with the provisions of the Ceasefire Agreement;

6. *Stresses also* the need to create an environment conducive to the return in safety and dignity of all refugees and displaced persons;

7. *Notes with satisfaction* the prompt establishment of the Political Committee and the Joint Military Commission by the States signatories to the Ceasefire Agreement as part of their collective effort to implement the Agreement;

8. *Authorizes* the deployment of up to ninety United Nations military liaison personnel, together with the necessary civilian, political, humanitarian and administrative staff, to the capitals of the States signatories to the Ceasefire Agreement and the provisional headquarters of the Joint Military Commission, and, as security conditions permit, to the rear military headquarters of the main belligerents in the Democratic Republic of the Congo and, as appropriate, to other areas the Secretary-General may deem necessary, for a period of three months, with the following mandate:

- To establish contacts and maintain liaison with the Joint Military Commission and all parties to the Agreement;
- To assist the Joint Military Commission and the parties in developing modalities for the implementation of the Agreement;
- To provide technical assistance, as requested, to the Joint Military Commission;
- To provide information to the Secretary-General regarding the situation on the ground, and to assist in refining a concept of operations for a possible fur-

ther role of the United Nations in the implementation of the Agreement once it is signed by all parties;

–To secure from the parties guarantees of cooperation and assurances of security for the possible deployment in-country of military observers;

9. *Welcomes* the intention of the Secretary-General to appoint a Special Representative to serve as the head of the United Nations presence in the subregion relating to the peace process in the Democratic Republic of the Congo and to provide assistance in the implementation of the Ceasefire Agreement, and invites him to do so as soon as possible;

10. *Calls upon* all States and parties concerned to ensure the freedom of movement, security and safety of United Nations personnel in their territory;

11. *Calls* for safe and unhindered access for humanitarian assistance to those in need in the Democratic Republic of the Congo, and urges all parties to the conflict to guarantee the safety and security of all humanitarian personnel and to respect strictly the relevant provisions of international humanitarian law;

12. *Requests* the Secretary-General to keep it regularly informed of developments in the Democratic Republic of the Congo and to report at the appropriate time on the future presence of the United Nations in the Democratic Republic of the Congo in support of the peace process;

13. *Decides* to remain actively seized of the matter.

On 24 August [S/1999/920], the Secretary-General proposed that 26 countries be included in the list of countries contributing military personnel to the preliminary deployment of UN liaison officers to the DRC and other countries of the subregion. In a response of 27 August [S/1999/921], the Council President informed the Secretary-General that the members agreed with his proposal.

Communications (August-October). In several letters to the Security Council, the DRC stated that, despite the signing of the Lusaka Agreement, foreign troops on its territory were responsible for renewed fighting. In a 14 August communication [S/1999/898], the DRC said that 41 Congolese had been burned alive in Kasala and called on the Council to take measures to enforce its call for the withdrawal of foreign forces. On 16 August [S/1999/881], the DRC said that armed forces of the Rwandan-Ugandan coalition had attacked the city of Kisangani in eastern DRC. It requested the Council to adopt sanctions against those two countries. On 23 August [S/1999/913], the DRC requested the Council to authorize the Secretary-General to designate special envoys in Rwanda and Uganda with a mandate to secure their commitment to the ceasefire agreement. On 1 October [S/1999/1029], the DRC transmitted a document in which it described alleged violations of the Lusaka Ceasefire Agreement and Council resolution 1234(1999) (see p. 85) during August. The DRC claimed that armed confrontations between Rwanda and Uganda on its territory attested to the gravity of the war of aggression being waged against the DRC by the Rwandan-Ugandan-Burundian coalition. The document described massacres at several locations and an armed clash between Rwandans and Ugandans that had impeded the national vaccination campaign and listed violations of human rights.

On 30 August [S/1999/930], Rwanda transmitted a press release issued by its Vice-President stating that its Government looked forward to the speedy implementation of the Lusaka Agreement, aspects of which addressed both Rwanda's security concerns and the wider problems of the DRC. The Vice President said that, despite the recent clashes in Kisangani between the Rwandese Patriotic Army and the Uganda People's Defence Force in August, relations between Rwanda and Uganda had been and were still good. The Vice President noted that talks on 16 and 17 August had achieved a speedy resolution and demonstrated the good relations. He also observed that divisions within the Congolese Rally for Democracy were contrary to Rwanda's advice to the DRC opposition to form a united front.

Finland forwarded several statements by the EU Presidency regarding the situation in the DRC. On 3 September [A/54/331-S/1999/959], the EU affirmed its support for the Lusaka Agreement, provided that all the parties implemented it in accordance with its terms. The EU was ready to support national reconciliation, rehabilitation and democratization in the DRC and the process of reintegration of displaced people in the Great Lakes region into their countries of origin. On 22 September [S/1999/1005], the Presidency expressed concern about the delays in implementation and the continued military activities and hostile propaganda. The EU called on the United Nations and OAU to support implementation and expressed its willingness to support various components of the Agreement, such as UN and OAU peacekeeping operations, JMC and the national dialogue. Reiterating that willingness on 11 October [A/54/482-S/1999/1076], the EU stated that it remained concerned at the slow pace at which the main provisions of the Agreement were being applied and at which the main bodies for implementing it were being established. It welcomed the fact that the first JMC meeting was scheduled for 11 October. The EU was considering supporting JMC financially.

Report of Secretary-General (November). In November [S/1999/1116 & Corr.1], the Secretary-General, pursuant to Security Council resolution 1258(1999) (see p. 89), reported on the preliminary UN deployment in the DRC. He noted that the two opposition parties that had not signed the Ceasefire Agreement at the time it was concluded—the Movement for the Liberation of the Congo and the Congolese Rally for Democracy—had done so by the end of August. The Political Committee established by the Agreement met on 3 September and agreed that the United Nations and OAU should be full participants in its work and in that of JMC. On 11 and 12 October, JMC met in Kampala, Uganda, with the participation of all the signatories to the Agreement, as well as the United Nations and OAU. It decided to deploy observers at four sites within the DRC to verify the parties' positions and to investigate ceasefire violations. At the invitation of the UN representatives, all the parties, with the exception of Angola and the DRC, provided guarantees in writing that they would safeguard the personal security of UN military and civilian personnel deployed in the mission. The JMC meeting was followed by another meeting of the Political Committee (15 October, Lusaka), which expressed concern about the slow pace at which the United Nations was handling the request for the deployment of peacekeepers in the DRC. It called on the Congolese parties to expedite consultations on the appointment of a neutral facilitator for the inter-Congolese negotiations so that the national dialogue could start.

The Secretary-General noted that there had been accusations and counter-accusations of ceasefire violations by the parties and troop movements were said to be continuing. Some reports also indicated a build-up of foreign troops around Mbuji-Mayi and Kisangani and a serious confrontation took place between Rwandan and Ugandan troops in Kisangani in August/September. The presence of former Rwandan government forces (ex-FAR) and Interahamwe militia elements in the region underscored the intricate and interconnected nature of the peace process in the Great Lakes region, he stated.

The UN advance team had been sent to the subregion to make contact with Governments participating in the ceasefire process so that it could make recommendations for the initial deployment of UN personnel. Having established a military headquarters and liaison presence in Kinshasa with a total of 39 staff members, it was prepared to deploy officers to other parts of the DRC, as well as to dispatch a technical survey team to assess the security conditions and infrastructure in 13 proposed deployment locations. The deployment of UN liaison officers in the country could proceed once the Government had provided the United Nations with acceptable security guarantees. Military liaison officers had also been sent to Harare, Kampala, Kigali and Windhoek, the capitals of the State signatories to the Lusaka Agreement. Officers were also sent to Bujumbura and to Lusaka, the provisional seat of JMC.

Despite the agreed ceasefire, insecurity remained a major obstacle to humanitarian operations and hampered access to the internally displaced—over 800,000 people. More than 180,000 DRC citizens had fled to neighbouring countries and over 250,000 were refugees in the DRC. Inter-ethnic fighting in the north-east had forced over 100,000 people to flee their homes. The major constraint for the humanitarian community was that priority life-saving operations were severely underfunded.

Proper implementation of the Lusaka Agreement required close coordination between the United Nations, the parties, JMC and OAU. Two UN liaison officers had been dispatched to OAU headquarters for consultations in that regard. To support the peace process and help mobilize the necessary resources for JMC, the United Nations had established a trust fund.

As outlined in his earlier report, the Secretary-General planned to deploy up to 500 military observers. In addition to military personnel and their logistical support, the humanitarian and human rights aspects of the conflict required deployment of civilian personnel, including political, humanitarian, human rights and child protection officers, as well as administrative personnel, led by a Special Representative.

The Secretary-General recommended that the Council extend the mandate of the UN personnel already in the DRC until 15 January 2000. By then, on the basis of the conclusions of the technical survey team, he expected to be able to provide details on the possible establishment of a UN peacekeeping operation. He requested that the Council authorize him to set up a UN observer mission in the DRC and the deployment of up to 500 military observers with the necessary logistical and personnel support. He called on the parties to cooperate with the UN mission and stressed that the provision of an acceptable security guarantee and the acceptance by the DRC Government of the need for UN deployment throughout the country were preconditions to the mission's ability to function effectively. JMC had a central role to play in the peace process under the terms of the Lusaka Ceasefire Agreement, and the deployment of four UN military liaison officers, initially in Lusaka, was intended to provide support for that body. He proposed that the United Nations provide JMC with the necessary logistical and other operational support and called on Governments and other donors to do likewise.

SECURITY COUNCIL ACTION (5 November)

On 5 November [meeting 4060], the Security Council unanimously adopted **resolution 1273 (1999)**. The draft text [S/1999/1130] was prepared during prior consultations among Council members.

The Security Council,

Recalling its resolutions 1234(1999) of 9 April 1999 and 1258(1999) of 6 August 1999 and the statements by its President of 31 August 1998, 11 December 1998 and 24 June 1999,

Reaffirming the sovereignty, territorial integrity, and political independence of the Democratic Republic of the Congo and all States in the region,

Reaffirming also that the Ceasefire Agreement signed at Lusaka on 10 July 1999 represents a viable basis for a resolution of the conflict in the Democratic Republic of the Congo,

Welcoming the report of the Secretary-General of 1 November 1999,

Noting with satisfaction the deployment of United Nations military liaison personnel to the capitals of the States signatories to the Ceasefire Agreement and to the Joint Military Commission established by them, and underlining the importance of their full deployment as provided for in its resolution 1258(1999),

Noting that the Joint Military Commission and the Political Committee have held meetings as mandated under the Ceasefire Agreement,

Urging all parties to the Ceasefire Agreement to cooperate fully with the technical assessment team dispatched to the Democratic Republic of the Congo by the Secretary-General as indicated in his report of 15 July 1999, in order to allow it to assess conditions and to prepare for subsequent United Nations deployments in the country,

1. *Decides* to extend the mandate of the United Nations military liaison personnel deployed under paragraph 8 of resolution 1258(1999) until 15 January 2000;
2. *Requests* the Secretary-General to continue to report to it regularly on developments in the Democratic Republic of the Congo, including on the future presence of the United Nations in the country in support of the peace process;
3. *Calls upon* all parties to the Ceasefire Agreement signed at Lusaka to continue to abide by its provisions;
4. *Decides* to remain actively seized of the matter.

Appointment of Special Representative. By a 13 November letter [S/1999/1171], the Secretary-General informed the Security Council of his intention to appoint Kamel Morjane (Tunisia) as his Special Representative for the DRC, with immediate effect. On 16 November [S/1999/1172], the Council took note of the appointment.

SECURITY COUNCIL ACTION (30 November)

On 30 November [meeting 4076], the Security Council unanimously adopted **resolution 1279 (1999)**. The draft text [S/1999/1207] was prepared in consultations among Council members.

The Security Council,

Recalling its resolutions 1234(1999) of 9 April 1999, 1258(1999) of 6 August 1999 and 1273(1999) of 5 November 1999 and the statements by its President of 31 August 1998, 11 December 1998 and 24 June 1999,

Bearing in mind the purposes and principles of the Charter of the United Nations, and the primary responsibility of the Security Council for the maintenance of international peace and security,

Reaffirming the sovereignty, territorial integrity and political independence of the Democratic Republic of the Congo and all States in the region,

Reaffirming also that the Ceasefire Agreement signed at Lusaka on 10 July 1999 represents the most viable basis for a resolution of the conflict in the Democratic Republic of the Congo, and noting the role it requests the United Nations to play in the implementation of the ceasefire,

Expressing its concern at the alleged violations of the Ceasefire Agreement, and urging all parties to refrain from any declarations or action that could jeopardize the peace process,

Stressing the responsibilities of the signatories for the implementation of the Ceasefire Agreement, and calling on them to permit and facilitate the full deployment of United Nations military liaison officers and other personnel necessary for the fulfilment of their mandate throughout the territory of the Democratic Republic of the Congo,

Welcoming the pledges of support made to the Joint Military Commission by States and organizations, and calling upon others to contribute, together with the signatories to the Ceasefire Agreement, to the funding of the body,

Noting with concern the humanitarian situation in the Democratic Republic of the Congo, and calling upon all Member States to contribute to current and future consolidated humanitarian appeals,

Expressing its concern at the severe consequences of the conflict for the security and well-being of the civilian population throughout the territory of the Democratic Republic of the Congo,

Expressing its concern also at the adverse impact of the conflict on the human rights situation in the Democratic Republic of the Congo, particularly in the eastern parts of the country, and the continuing violations of human rights and international humanitarian law committed throughout the territory of the Democratic Republic of the Congo,

Having considered the recommendations of the Secretary-General contained in his report of 1 November 1999,

Reiterating the importance of the successful completion of the mission of the technical assessment team dispatched to the Democratic Republic of the Congo to assess conditions and to prepare for possible subsequent United Nations deployment in the country as well as to obtain firm guarantees from the parties to the conflict over the safety, security and freedom of movement of United Nations and associated personnel,

Recalling the relevant principles contained in the Convention on the Safety of United Nations and Associated Personnel adopted on 9 December 1994,

Underlining the importance of the full deployment of the United Nations military liaison personnel as provided for by resolution 1258(1999),

1. *Calls upon* all parties to the conflict to cease hostilities, to implement fully the provisions of the Ceasefire Agreement signed at Lusaka, and to use the Joint Military Commission to resolve disputes over military issues;

2. *Stresses* the need for a continuing process of genuine national reconciliation, encourages all Congolese to participate in the national dialogue to be organized in coordination with the Organization of African Unity, and calls upon all Congolese parties and the Organization of African Unity to finalize agreement on the facilitator for the national dialogue;

3. *Welcomes* the appointment by the Secretary-General of his Special Representative for the Democratic Republic of the Congo to serve as the head of the United Nations presence in the subregion relating to the peace process in the Democratic Republic of the Congo and to provide assistance in the implementation of the Ceasefire Agreement;

4. *Decides* that the personnel authorized under its resolutions 1258(1999) and 1273(1999), including a multidisciplinary staff of personnel in the fields of human rights, humanitarian affairs, public information, medical support, child protection, political affairs and administrative support, which will assist the Special Representative, shall constitute the United Nations Organization Mission in the Democratic Republic of the Congo until 1 March 2000;

5. *Decides* also that the Mission, led by the Special Representative of the Secretary-General, consistent with resolutions 1258(1999) and 1273(1999), shall carry out the following ongoing tasks:

(a) Establish contacts with the signatories to the Ceasefire Agreement at their headquarters levels, as well as in the capitals of the States signatories;

(b) Liaise with the Joint Military Commission and provide technical assistance in the implementation of its functions under the Ceasefire Agreement, including in the investigation of ceasefire violations;

(c) Provide information on security conditions in all areas of its operation, with emphasis on local conditions affecting future decisions on the introduction of United Nations personnel;

(d) Plan for the observation of the ceasefire and disengagement of forces;

(e) Maintain liaison with all parties to the Ceasefire Agreement to facilitate the delivery of humanitarian assistance to displaced persons, refugees, children, and other affected persons, and assist in the protection of human rights, including the rights of children;

6. *Underlines* the fact that the phased deployment of United Nations military observers with the necessary support and protection elements in the Democratic Republic of the Congo will be subject to its further decision, and expresses its intention to take such a decision promptly on the basis of further recommendations of the Secretary-General, taking into account the findings of the technical assessment team;

7. *Requests* the Secretary-General to accelerate the development of a concept of operations based on assessed conditions of security, access and freedom of movement and cooperation on the part of the signatories to the Ceasefire Agreement;

8. *Also requests* the Secretary-General to keep it regularly informed and to report to it as soon as possible on the situation in the Democratic Republic of the Congo and submit his recommendations on further deployment of United Nations personnel in the country and on their protection;

9. *Requests* the Secretary-General, with immediate effect, to take the administrative steps necessary for the equipping of up to 500 United Nations military observers with a view to facilitating future rapid United Nations deployments as authorized by the Council;

10. *Decides* to remain actively seized of the matter.

Communications (December). On 3 December [S/1999/1217], Finland transmitted a 26 November statement by the Presidency of the EU expressing support for the ceasefire measures in the DRC, in particular those decided by JMC. EU members declared their readiness to augment their financial and practical assistance to the Commission. The EU stressed the need to ensure a peaceful disarmament, demobilization and reintegration of the militia groups in the region and respect for human rights. In particular, it underlined that members of the ex-FAR/Interahamwe accused of genocide should be brought to justice. It affirmed its support for an eventual international conference on security and cooperation in the Great Lakes region.

On 14 December [S/1999/1251], Namibia forwarded a press release on the SADC regional summit on the DRC held in Windhoek on 12 December, which was attended by the heads of State of the DRC, Namibia and Zimbabwe and the Defence Minister of Angola. The summit welcomed the inauguration of JMC and the deployment of regional joint military commissions in some locations in the DRC to verify ceasefire implementation. The summit noted with concern that there had been violations of the ceasefire, particularly in the area of Ikela and Basankusu by Rwandan- and Ugandan-sponsored rebel groups. The participants called on the Security Council to authorize an early deployment of the UN peacekeeping forces to expedite the implementation of the Ceasefire Agreement. The summit welcomed the deployment of OAU military observers in the DRC and commended the efforts by the OAU Secretary-General to assist the Congolese people to identify a neutral facilitator for the national dialogue.

Later developments. In early December [S/2000/30], JMC adopted for approval by the Political Committee papers submitted by its four working groups on the following questions: determination of humanitarian corridors, release of hostages, exchange of prisoners of war and working relations with the United Nations Office for the Coordination of Humanitarian Affairs and the International Committee of the Red Cross; working out mechanisms and budget estimates for disarming, tracking down and quartering of armed groups, as well as procedures for handing over mass killers and other war criminals; drafting mechanisms and procedures for the disengagement of forces; and working out mechanisms, procedures and a calendar for the withdrawal of foreign forces.

JMC adopted a proposal for the peaceful resolution of the situation at Ikela, where a force of about 700 Congolese, Namibian and Zimbabwean troops had been encircled by rebel forces.

On 15 December, the OAU Secretary-General, following consultations with the parties, announced that agreement was reached on the selection of former President Ketumile Masire of Botswana as facilitator for the inter-Congolese political negotiations.

Despite such political advances, the military and security situation in the DRC deteriorated towards the end of the year. In November, the Government launched an offensive from Mbandaka into rebel-held territory. Heightened military activity by some of the "armed groups" identified in the Lusaka Ceasefire Agreement was also reported in eastern DRC. They included ex-FAR and Interahamwe militia, Burundian rebels and various Mai-Mai groups. Rebel sources also reported that the armed groups had acquired new equipment. Reports from South Kivu suggested the danger of large-scale violence among different ethnic groups there. The Government, at a press conference on 29 December and in a letter to the Security Council dated 22 December [S/1999/1275], charged that rebels had buried alive 15 women in Kivu province. An alleged massacre of 23 women and three children was reported near the town of Kalima, allegedly by rebels, on 14 December.

The United Nations continued its efforts to support implementation of the Agreement. On 11 December, the Special Representative assumed his duties in Kinshasa. The preliminary UN deployment in the DRC continued to encounter difficulties in positioning military liaison officers in key locations relating primarily to security needs and freedom of movement to inspect locations and to assess the military, political, logistics and infrastructure situations. By the end of the year, teams of UN military liaison officers were positioned at eight locations, but were not granted approval to go to other locations. On the basis of information sent back from deployment locations and data available in neighbouring capitals and in Kinshasa, MONUC had built up a picture of the military, logistical and humanitarian situation of many locations considered important to UN deployment.

GENERAL ASSEMBLY ACTION

By a 7 September note verbale [A/53/1048], the DRC requested that the Secretary-General keep the item "Armed aggression against the Democratic Republic of the Congo" of the General Assembly's fifty-third session on the agenda of the fifty-fourth (1999) session, and that the question be debated in plenary session without being referred to a Main Committee. On 13 September [A/54/349], Uganda called on the Secretary-General to reject that request in view of the Ceasefire Agreement and the fact that the peace process had already been launched and UN military liaison officers had been deployed. Rwanda, on 14 September [A/54/369], requested that the item be removed from the agenda of the fifty-fourth session.

By **decision 53/488** of 13 September, the Assembly decided to include in the draft agenda of its fifty-fourth session the item on armed aggression against the DRC. The Assembly did not consider the item at the fifty-fourth session in 1999; on 23 December, it decided that the item would remain for consideration during the resumed part of the session in 2000 (**decision 54/465**).

On 8 December, the Assembly adopted **resolution 54/96 B** on special assistance for the economic recovery and reconstruction of the DRC (see PART THREE, Chapter III).

Rwanda

In 1999, Rwanda showed signs of improved security and positive developments which indicated a movement towards democracy and reconciliation among ethnic groups [E/CN/4/2000/41]. The security situation improved noticeably in the north-west of the country, the site of armed conflict in 1998 [YUN 1998, p. 88], resulting in a corresponding decline in alleged abuses by the Rwandan armed forces. Fighting diminished in eastern DRC in 1999, resulting in fewer incursions of armed infiltrators into north-west Rwanda. Steps towards democracy included successful local elections; the establishment of two new commissions (on human rights and on national unity and reconciliation); steps towards drafting a new constitution; a new law to professionalize the civilian police force; a revision of the 1991 press law; and more effective supervision by parliament over all aspects of government. Despite the positive moves, however, the National Assembly of Rwanda extended the period of transition from genocide to democracy by another four years on the grounds that more time was needed to promote reconciliation and complete drafting of a new constitution.

An exception to the generally diminished tension occurred on 23 December, when armed Interahamwe crossed from the DRC and attacked the resettlement site of Tamira, killing 29 persons and wounding 40. The attack was apparently planned and the victims carefully selected.

The humanitarian situation remained precarious in Rwanda despite several good harvests. Some 150,000 people remained vulnerable owing to lack of services, and approximately 32,000 refugees returned from the DRC during the year.

Inquiry into UN response to 1994 genocide

The Secretary-General, in an 18 March letter [S/1999/339], informed the Security Council of his intention to set up an independent inquiry into the actions taken by the United Nations at the time of the 1994 genocide in Rwanda [YUN 1994, p. 282]. In view of the enormity of the genocide, he stated, questions continued to surround the actions of the United Nations immediately before and during the period of the crisis. The primary purpose of the inquiry would be to establish the facts and to draw conclusions as to the UN response to the tragedy. The President of the Council stated on 26 March [S/1999/340] that the members supported the Secretary-General's proposed course of action.

The Independent Inquiry, which was chaired by Ingvar Carlsson, former Prime Minister of Sweden, and included Han Sung-Joo, former Foreign Minister of the Republic of Korea, and Lieutenant-General Rufus M. Kupolati of Nigeria, submitted its report to the Secretary-General on 15 December [S/1999/1257]. On the same date, the Secretary-General forwarded the report to the Council. The Inquiry's terms of reference were to establish a chronology of key events pertaining to UN involvement in Rwanda from October 1993 to July 1994; to evaluate the mandate and resources of the United Nations Assistance Mission for Rwanda (UNAMIR) and how they affected the UN response to the events relating to the massacres; and to draw conclusions and identify the lessons to be learned from the tragedy. The Inquiry had unrestricted access to all UN documentation and persons involved.

The report stated that approximately 800,000 people were killed during the 1994 genocide in Rwanda. The systematic slaughter of men, women and children took place over the course of about 100 days between April and July 1994, during which atrocities were committed by militia and the armed forces, but also by civilians against other civilians. The international community did not prevent the genocide, nor did it stop the killing once the genocide had begun. The failure by the United Nations to prevent and subsequently to stop the genocide was a failure by the UN system as a whole. The fundamental failure was the lack of resources and political commitment devoted to the situation in Rwanda and to the UN presence there. There was a persistent lack of political will by Member States to act, or to act with enough assertiveness, thus affecting the response by the Secretariat and decision-making by the Security Council; it was also evident in the difficulties in obtaining sufficient troops for UNAMIR. Despite the Mission's chronic lack of resources and political priority, serious mistakes were made with the resources that were at the disposal of the United Nations.

The Inquiry noted that the 1948 Convention on the Prevention and Punishment of the Crime of Genocide [YUN 1948-49, p. 959] established the criteria for determining genocide and the Security Council had used the same criteria in outlining the mandate of the International Criminal Tribunal for Rwanda (see PART FOUR, Chapter II), which had determined that the mass killings of Tutsi in Rwanda in 1994 constituted genocide. The Inquiry concluded that the genocide was planned and incited by Hutu extremists against the Tutsi.

The Inquiry found that the UN response before and during the genocide failed in a number of respects. The responsibility for the failure to prevent and stop the genocide lay with a number of different actors, in particular the Secretary-General, the Secretariat, the Security Council, UNAMIR and the broader membership of the United Nations. The Organization and Member States concerned owed a clear apology to the Rwandan people. In addition, efforts should be made to bring to justice those Rwandans who planned, incited and carried out the genocide against their countrymen. The overriding failure in the UN response before and during the genocide was summarized by the Inquiry as a lack of resources and a lack of will. UNAMIR, the main component of the UN presence in Rwanda, was not planned, dimensioned, deployed or instructed in a way that provided for a proactive and assertive role in dealing with a peace process in serious trouble. The Mission's mandate was based on an analysis of the peace process that proved erroneous and that was never corrected, despite significant warning signs that the original mandate had become inadequate. In the time of deepest crisis, the Mission experienced a lack of political leadership, lack of military capacity, severe problems of command and control and lack of coordination and discipline. Despite facing a deteriorating security situation that should have motivated a more assertive and preventive UN role, no steps were taken to adjust the mandate to the reality of the needs in Rwanda.

The Inquiry addressed the matter of the 11 January 1994 cable sent by UNAMIR Force Commander Brigadier-General Romeo A. Dallaire to the Secretary-General's Military Adviser, Major-General Maurice Baril, stating that Dallaire had received information regarding a strategy to provoke the killing of Belgian soldiers and the Belgian battalion's withdrawal from Rwanda. He had also been informed that trained men were scattered throughout Kigali, that all Tutsi in Kigali were to be registered, probably for their extermination, and that there was a major arms cache for that purpose. In response to Dallaire's request to take military action, senior Secretariat officials responded that such an operation went beyond UNAMIR's mandate. The Inquiry believed that serious mistakes were made in dealing with the cable, both in UNAMIR and in the Secretariat. The leadership of the Department of Peacekeeping Operations did not brief the Secretary-General and the Security Council was not informed. The Inquiry also found it incomprehensible that more was not done to follow up on the information received. However, it saw no reason to criticize the Secretariat's decision on the mandate issue but felt that the matter should have been raised with the Council. Further, the threat against the Belgian contingent should have been followed up more clearly.

Regarding failure to respond to the genocide, the Inquiry noted that UNAMIR was in disarray. It was also under rules of engagement not to use force except in self-defence. The operation was prevented from performing its political mandate, incapable of protecting the civilian population or civilian UN staff and at risk itself. Further, UNAMIR was sidelined in relation to the national evacuation operations conducted by Belgium, France, Italy and the United States. The responsibility for that situation, said the Inquiry, had to be shared between the leadership of UNAMIR, the Secretariat and troop-contributing countries.

As to the withdrawal of the Belgian contingent following the killing of 10 of its members, the Inquiry believed it was essential to preserve the unity of UN command and control and that troop-contributing countries, despite domestic political pressures, should refrain from unilateral withdrawal to the detriment and even risk of ongoing peacekeeping operations. The subsequent Council decision to reduce UNAMIR to a minimal force rather than make every effort to muster the political will to stop the killing led to widespread bitterness in Rwanda; it was a decision that the Inquiry found difficult to justify and it felt that the Council bore a responsibility for its lack of political will to do more.

Rwanda was to prove a turning point in UN peacekeeping, and came to symbolize a lack of will to commit to peacekeeping and, above all, to take risks in the field, said the Inquiry. From its inception, UNAMIR suffered from a lack of resources and logistics. During the massacres, the Mission and the Secretariat continued to focus on achieving a ceasefire and too little attention was given to the massacres. Furthermore, there was a weakness in the capacity for political analysis, in particular within UNAMIR but also at Headquarters. The Mission also failed to protect civilians, political leaders and Rwandan UN staff members who expected or sought protection.

The Inquiry believed that there were institutional lessons to be learned from the Rwandan crisis with regard to the capacity and willingness of the United Nations to conduct peacekeeping operations, and there were lessons to be learned relating to the relationship between the United Nations and Rwanda. The aftermath of the genocide was still a reality—in the suffering, in the efforts to build reconciliation, in bringing those responsible to justice, and in the continued problems of those displaced and the needs of the survivors. It was also a reality in the continued existence of the Interahamwe as an armed force in the Great Lakes region, and in the continued instability in that region.

The Inquiry made a number of recommendations for future peacekeeping efforts: (1) the Secretary-General should initiate an action plan to prevent genocide involving the whole UN system; (2) efforts should be made to improve UN peacekeeping capacity, including the availability of resources and clarity as to which rules of engagement should apply; (3) the United Nations—and in particular the Security Council and troop-contributing countries—should be prepared to prevent acts of genocide or gross violations of human rights; (4) the UN early warning capacity should be improved, both with outside actors and within the Secretariat; (5) protection of civilians in conflict situations should be improved; (6) the security of UN and associated personnel, including local staff, needed to be improved; (7) cooperation between officials responsible for the security of different categories of staff in the field needed to be ensured; (8) an effective flow of information needed to be ensured; (9) improvements should be made in the flow of information to the Council; (10) the flow of information on human rights issues should be improved; (11) national evacuation operations should be coordinated with UN missions on the ground; (12) further study should be given to suspending participation of a Member State on the Security Council in exceptional circumstances, such as the Rwandan crisis; (13) the international community should support efforts in Rwanda to rebuild the society; and (14) the United Nations should acknowledge its part of the responsibility for not having done enough to prevent or stop the genocide in Rwanda.

Arms embargo

International Commission of Inquiry

The Sudan, in a 14 January letter to the Security Council [S/1999/66], referred to the November 1998 report of the International Commission of Inquiry [YUN 1998, p. 91] mandated to collect information on the supply of arms to former Rwandan government forces in the Great Lakes region in violation of Security Council resolutions 918(1994) [YUN 1994, p. 285], 997(1995) [YUN 1995, p. 386] and 1011(1995) [ibid., p. 380]. The Sudan denied the allegations that between 5,000 and 8,000 ex-FAR and Interahamwe were located in southern Sudan and training at three locations. It said that the allegations were derived from suspect sources and that they were attempts to drag the Sudan into the conflict in the DRC. The allegations, in the Sudan's view, demonstrated that the Commission had exceeded its mandate.

Sanctions Committee

On 29 December [S/1999/1292], the Chairman of the Security Council Committee established pursuant to resolution 918(1994) concerning the arms embargo against Rwanda [YUN 1994, p. 285] submitted to the Council a report on its 1999 activities. The Committee was mandated to seek information regarding the implementation of the embargo, consider information concerning violations and make recommendations for strengthening it. The Committee recalled that it had no specific monitoring mechanism to ensure implementation and that it relied solely on the cooperation of States and organizations to provide pertinent information. During the year, no violations were brought to the attention of the Committee.

UNAMIR financing

In February [A/C.5/53/57], the Secretary-General submitted to the General Assembly a note providing information on the status of unfinished work related to the financial liquidation of UNAMIR. With the withdrawal of the military component of UNAMIR from Rwanda completed in April 1996 [YUN 1996, p. 62], most of the Mission's administrative staff were also compelled to leave at that time. From 20 April to 31 December 1996, the liquidation continued from administrative offices in Nairobi; thereafter, a small liquidation team was assembled at UN Headquarters until 31 December 1997.

As at 30 June 1998, combined expenditures for the period since the inception of the United Nations Observer Mission Uganda-Rwanda, established in 1993 and integrated within UNAMIR later that year, amounted to $445,735,700 gross, inclusive of unliquidated obligations of $29,303,000, after taking into account savings arising from unutilized obligations pertaining to prior periods and other adjustments. The resulting unencumbered balance amounted to $16,694,700. A number of outstanding issues remained to be finalized, in particular the reconciliation of outgoing shipments with inventory data of missions to which, according to UNAMIR records, equipment had been transferred. In addition, action had yet to be taken on government claims for the contingent-owned equipment reported as lost, stolen or abandoned in Rwanda in April 1994, for which no provision had been made in UNAMIR budgets. Resolution of the outstanding issues was essential to establish the actual resource requirements of the Mission. Accordingly, it was anticipated that final performance information, together with the final report on the disposition of assets, could be prepared and submitted to the Advisory Committee on Administrative and Budgetary Questions (ACABQ) and the Fifth (Administrative and Budgetary) Committee during the fifty-fourth (1999) session of the Assembly.

On 8 June, the Assembly, by **decision 53/477**, included in the provisional agenda of its fifty-fourth session the item on UNAMIR financing. On 23 December, it decided that the Fifth Committee should continue its consideration of the item at its resumed fifty-fourth session in 2000 (**decision 54/462 A**). On the same date, the Assembly decided that the agenda item would remain for consideration during its fifty-fourth session (**decision 54/465**).

Burundi

Although 1999 started on a positive note with progress continuing during the January peace negotiations among the numerous disputing Burundi factions, renewed outbreaks of armed violence during the crucial phase of the peace process indicated the potential difficulties of the political situation of Burundi.

The joint communiqué of the Seventh Regional Summit on the Conflict in Burundi, in

January, expressed its satisfaction over the progress achieved by the peace negotiations and decided to suspend all the remaining sanctions imposed by the countries of the Great Lakes region on Burundi. The lifting of the embargo was subject to review and depended on progress in the peace process. However, at the fifth session of the Arusha peace process in July, the Facilitator, Mwalimu Julius K. Nyerere, expressed deep dissatisfaction at the lack of progress. In August, there was renewed fighting between the Burundian army and the rebels, resulting also in the deaths of many civilians. In October, two UN officials and other civilians on a humanitarian mission were killed near the border with the United Republic of Tanzania.

Mr. Nyerere died on 14 October. The participants in the peace talks expressed their determination to continue outside negotiations, and consultations began immediately with a view to appointing a new mediator. In December, former President of South Africa Nelson Mandela was appointed to replace Mr. Nyerere.

Political situation

Although the Arusha peace process continued throughout 1999, no concrete progress was made on the crucial questions of security and democracy [E/CN.4/2000/34]. Following rebel attacks on Bujumbura, a few political parties within Burundi demanded the suspension of the Arusha process and threatened to pull out of the negotiations. Following the July Lusaka Agreement on the DRC (see p. 87), local media reported cross-border movements of rebels from the DRC into Burundi in an apparent attempt to avoid disarmament. At a September meeting in Vienna, donors confirmed the resumption of bilateral aid conditional on the results of the Arusha talks. They did, however, maintain expanded humanitarian assistance.

In a statement to the General Assembly in October, the Burundian Minister for Foreign Affairs and Cooperation said that the ending of hostilities was a condition for the signing of a peace agreement in the framework of the peace negotiations. He also called on the rebel movements to take part in the talks and said that the Government was prepared to hold discussions with all the groups, even outside the framework of the Arusha process. Despite their exclusion from the Arusha talks, the Forces pour la défense de la démocratie, the armed wing of the Conseil national pour la défense de la démocratie (CNDD), and the Forces nationales pour la libération, the armed wing of the Parti pour la libération du peuple hutu, reaffirmed their willingness to negotiate, but also their determination to continue the armed struggle. Although the international community and the Secretary-General expressed concern about the forced displacement and regroupment of the population, Burundi justified its policy by the need to protect the civilian population from the fighting. The suspension of the embargo in January was not followed up by sufficient development assistance and had no positive effects on the country's economy.

Communications (January). Burundi's National Assembly President, Léonce Ngendakumana, in a 12 January statement [S/1999/53], informed the Security Council that a comprehensive peace process had been designed on two fronts: one internal, the other external. The internal process had resulted in a domestic political partnership for peace involving the National Transition Assembly and the Government in the process of national reconstruction. The partnership took concrete shape with the agreement on the political platform of the transition regime, signed on 6 June 1998, and the Constitutional Act of Transition, issued on that day [YUN 1998, p. 98]. On the external front, the comprehensive peace negotiations, which began in June 1998 in Arusha [ibid., p. 99], were proceeding smoothly. Burundi appealed to the international community to support the comprehensive peace process to ensure that war and violence ceased, economic sanctions were lifted, and bilateral and multilateral cooperation, as well as external financing, were resumed.

In a statement delivered at the donor conference for Burundi in New York on 11 and 12 January [S/1999/54], sponsored by the Department of Political Affairs, the United Nations Development Programme (UNDP) and the Canadian Government, Burundi noted that it had made significant progress along the path to peace with the third session of the Arusha negotiations held in October 1998 [YUN 1998, p. 99]. There were, however, three constraints on the negotiating environment: the economic sanctions imposed by the subregion, continued violence and the freeze on bilateral and multilateral cooperation. Because of those constraints, Burundi's current situation was extremely precarious and there were major threats both to the survival of its population and to the Government's efforts to achieve lasting peace. An added constraint was the external debt burden, which in 1997 was equivalent to over 130 per cent of Burundi's gross domestic product. The weight of that burden had been exacerbated by the freeze in financial assistance by a large number of Burundi's partners. Therefore, Burundi called on its partners to convince the countries of the subregion immediately to lift the embargo against it; convince the Facilitator of the peace process that the effective participation of the armed groups of the rebellion was absolutely necessary; support Burundi's efforts to seek a resolution of the crisis through political negotiations; and resume bilateral and multilateral cooperation without delay.

Seventh Regional Summit

The Seventh Regional Summit on the Conflict in Burundi, which was held in Arusha on 23 January, was attended by the Presidents of Kenya, Rwanda, Uganda and the United Republic of Tanzania, the Prime Minister of Ethiopia and representatives of the DRC and Zambia, with the participation of the OAU Secretary-General and the Facilitator of the peace process, Mr. Nyerere. The Summit was also briefed by the Burundi President, Major Pierre Buyoya. In a joint communiqué [A/53/804-S/1999/74, S/1999/83], the Summit expressed its satisfaction over the progress achieved so far in the peace negotiations and decided to suspend all the remaining sanctions imposed by the countries of the Great Lakes region on Burundi. The Summit called on all parties to sustain the momentum of the peace negotiations until the conclusion of a final peace accord that would guarantee the restoration of lasting peace, genuine democracy and security for all. The countries of the region would monitor closely the progress of the negotiations. The Summit decided that the suspension of the sanctions would be subject to review, based on the progress made.

In a 1 February letter [S/1999/106], Burundi informed the Security Council President of the lifting of the economic sanctions imposed on Burundi since 31 July 1996 [YUN 1996, p. 84].

Communications (February/March). By a 25 February letter [S/1999/207], Burundi informed the Council President of the visits of its Minister for External Relations and Cooperation to Kenya, Rwanda, Uganda and the United Republic of Tanzania. The Minister expressed Burundi's gratitude to those countries for supporting the lifting of sanctions and officially requested their support for Burundi's membership in the future East African Community.

In a 19 March statement [S/1999/299], the Presidency of the EU welcomed the continuing talks within the Arusha peace process to find a peaceful solution to the conflict in Burundi. The EU took note of Burundi's resolve to conclude negotiations successfully in 1999 and encouraged all parties to contribute constructively to that goal. It also noted that the suspension of the embargo by regional States signalled their support for the talks. However, the EU was deeply concerned about reports of continuing violence by rebel groups and security forces and appealed to both sides to cease their acts of violence immediately. It urged the parties to organize the talks in a way that would help to achieve the desired result as soon as possible; it was willing to consider further financial support and appealed to other donors to act likewise. The EU was also willing to provide long-term assistance to Burundi's socio-economic rehabilitation and reconstruction, but emphasized that such support was linked to a successful pursuance and accomplishment of the peace process.

Peace negotiations

The fifth session of the peace negotiations took place in Arusha from 5 to 17 July under the mediation of the Facilitator, Mwalimu Julius K. Nyerere. In a 21 July statement [S/1999/816], Burundi noted that Mr. Nyerere had made serious charges against the Burundian Government, which it categorically rejected, including that the Government was responsible for the deadlock in Arusha. It stated that the continuation of hostilities made the peace process totally meaningless and the exclusion of certain armed bands from the negotiations was an impediment. The Government reported that rebel groups were using extreme violence against the Burundian population and that its role was not to organize armed bands but to protect the population against such violence. It appealed to all the partners in the peace process to work for peace seriously and realistically.

On 16 August [S/1999/883], the United Republic of Tanzania transmitted to the Council President the concluding remarks by Mr. Nyerere made at the plenary closing meeting of the fifth session, noting that, although the Facilitator was distressed at the lack of progress made at the negotiations, he did not single out any party. The Facilitator stated that some delegations had attempted to block any kind of progress, using the excuse of the continued violence in Burundi, which continued despite the Facilitator's insistence that the Government and armed groups suspend hostilities during the period of negotiations. Another problem concerned armed groups that were not party to the agreement to suspend hostilities but were requested to participate in the negotiations. In that regard, the issue of Jean-Bosco, representing a breakaway group from CNDD, was discussed. Mr. Nyerere had made suggestions to facilitate his attendance and all of them were rejected by the Government. In an effort to involve everybody in the negotiations, he had asked for other suggestions. Before the next session, scheduled for 6 September,

Mr. Nyerere would carry out consultations to speed up the work.

Burundi, on 23 July [S/1999/817], forwarded to the Council President the text of a note verbale it had sent to the United Republic of Tanzania concerning serious threats to security on the common border. Burundi drew attention to the intensification of attacks inside its territory and preparations by Burundian rebels to infiltrate from Tanzania. Burundi requested Tanzania to take all necessary measures to stop the upsurge in infiltrations by Burundian rebels and the arrival in Tanzania of a new influx of rebel combatants, troops and former members of the Rwandan armed forces, who were dreading the approaching ceasefire in the DRC and would like to disrupt security in Burundi at a time when the Arusha negotiations were reaching a crucial phase. Burundi called for an urgent security meeting between the Ministers of Defence of the two countries.

Renewed violence

In a 27 August statement [A/54/302], the EU Presidency deplored recent clashes between the army and the rebels in Burundi, which had resulted in many civilian victims. It called on the Government to work in close collaboration with observers from the UN Human Rights Office, and to set up an internal inquiry to establish any responsibility of the members of the army involved and to bring the latter to justice. The EU drew the attention of the Government to the fragility of the final phases of the Arusha peace process and to the dangers that such incidents represented.

On 3 September [A/54/330-S/1999/958], the EU condemned the 28 August killings of civilians by rebels in Bujumbura and urged all parties to refrain from any violence and fully respect human rights. It called on all Burundians to preserve the ongoing process of national reconciliation, in particular the Arusha negotiations, which were entering a critical phase. The EU stressed to all Burundians that peace and stability could be achieved only through a negotiated political settlement and encouraged all Burundians to support the negotiations.

In an 8 October statement [S/1999/1060], the EU strongly deplored the renewed outbreak of violence and internal conflict in Burundi, mainly in the southern part of the country and around Bujumbura. It was particularly concerned about the forced removals by the Burundi army of some 260,000 civilians in the countryside around Bujumbura. The EU called on the Government to stop the policy of forced removals and to allow the people to return to their property as quickly as possible. In the meantime, the Government was urged to provide the people with improved sanitary conditions and temporary accommodations. The EU noted that the Government had assured UN representatives and international non-governmental organizations (NGOs) free access to all of the camps concerned to enable them to provide humanitarian assistance. It asked the authorities to afford the Office of the High Commissioner for Human Rights in Burundi and its observers the same access. It hoped that all Burundi rebel movements would join the Arusha peace process and that all the parties to the Burundi conflict would choose the path of negotiation rather than that of violence and conflict.

Murder of UN staff. Burundi, on 13 October [A/54/460], informed the Secretary-General of the murder on 12 October of several members of a humanitarian assistance mission in Rutana province. Among them were Luis Manuel Zuñiga of the United Nations Children's Fund and Saskia Louis Von Meijenfeldt of the World Food Programme. The Government condemned the acts perpetrated by terrorists and urged humanitarian and international cooperation agencies operating in Burundi not to give way to intimidation, adding that it would make every effort to protect all personnel working for humanitarian organizations. It reiterated its urgent request for regional cooperation, in particular with the United Republic of Tanzania, in tracking down and eliminating such terrorism. The Government would conduct all the necessary investigations and would bring the full force of the law and justice to bear against all perpetrators of the crimes.

On 18 October [A/54/493-S/1999/1085], the EU Presidency strongly condemned the attack and called for the perpetrators of the massacre to be brought to justice. It appealed to all the Burundian parties to put an end without delay to all acts of violence and to reach an early agreement on the terms of a ceasefire and a return to civil peace, reconciliation and democracy.

Burundi, on 2 November [S/1999/1118], transmitted to the Council President a preliminary report on the investigation of the attack in Rutana province. The witnesses reported that the attack was carried out by genocidal professional terrorists and lasted only 10 minutes, after which the attackers withdrew towards Tanzania, the direction from which they had come. The report concluded that the preparation for the investigation mission was inadequate and both the delegation and the local authorities underestimated the danger. A judicial brief would be prepared indicting persons unknown.

On 9 November [S/1999/1151], the United Republic of Tanzania condemned the cold-blooded murder of the UN personnel and innocent Burundian civilians. It rejected allegations by Burundi that the perpetrators came from Tanzania. However, it reiterated its commitment to support Burundi in the search for a peaceful settlement to its political problems.

UN Office in Burundi

On 12 April [S/1999/425], the Secretary-General informed the Security Council that he had decided to upgrade the level of the United Nations Office in Burundi (UNOB) by appointing Cheikh Tidiane Sy (Senegal), the current head of the Office, as the Representative of the Secretary-General in Burundi.

On 15 April [S/1999/426], the Council President informed the Secretary-General that the Council members took note of his decision.

The Secretary-General, on 2 November [S/1999/1136], informed the Council of his intention to extend the mandate of UNOB until the end of 2000. It seemed unlikely that the peace process would culminate in the conclusion of a general peace agreement in Arusha by the end of 1999 and peace efforts would probably continue in the year 2000. Once the peace agreement was reached, there would be a need for UNOB to undertake responsibilities in the post-conflict peace-building phase to help in the consolidation of peace and security. That would entail assisting in the implementation of the peace agreement and the establishment of new institutions, as well as providing support for the various reforms envisaged in the agreement.

On 5 November [S/1999/1137], the Council took note of the Secretary-General's intention.

SECURITY COUNCIL ACTION (12 November)

On 12 November [meeting 4068], the Security Council President made statement **S/PRST/1999/32** on behalf of the Council:

> The Security Council notes with concern the recent outbreaks of violence in Burundi and the delays in the peace process. It calls upon all the parties to put an end to this violence and pursue negotiations towards the peaceful resolution of Burundi's ongoing crisis.
>
> The Council reiterates its support for the Arusha peace process and for the efforts to build an internal political partnership in Burundi. It notes with great sadness the death of Mwalimu Julius Nyerere, while at the same time rededicating its efforts to the cause of peace he served. The Council firmly believes that the process chaired by the late Mwalimu Nyerere offers the best hope for peace in Burundi and should be the foundation for all-party talks leading to the conclusion of a peace agreement. The States of the region, in close consultation with the United Nations, need to act quickly to appoint a new mediation team that is acceptable to the Burundian parties to the negotiations.
>
> The Council commends those Burundian parties, including the Government, that demonstrated their commitment to continue negotiations, calls on those parties that remain outside the process to cease hostilities and calls for their full participation in Burundi's inclusive peace process.
>
> The Council condemns the murder of United Nations personnel in Burundi in October. It calls on the Government to undertake and cooperate with investigations, and for the perpetrators to be brought to justice. The Council urges all parties to ensure the safe and unhindered access of humanitarian assistance to those in need in Burundi and to guarantee fully the security and freedom of movement of United Nations and humanitarian personnel. The Council recognizes the important role of the States of the region, in particular the United Republic of Tanzania, which is host to hundreds of thousands of Burundian refugees and home to the Julius Nyerere Foundation, which has provided outstanding support to the talks.
>
> The Council calls upon States of the region to ensure the neutrality and civilian character of refugee camps and to prevent the use of their territory by armed insurgents. It also calls on the Government of Burundi to halt the policy of forced regroupment and to allow the affected people to return to their homes, with full and unhindered humanitarian access throughout the process. It condemns the attacks by armed groups against civilians and calls for an end to these unacceptable incidents.
>
> The Council recognizes Burundi's dire economic and social conditions and affirms the need for the donor community to expand assistance for Burundi.

Peace process Facilitator

The Facilitator of the Burundi peace process, Mwalimu Julius K. Nyerere, died on 14 October.

In a 17 October note verbale to the Secretary-General [S/1999/1068], Burundi paid tribute to Mr. Nyerere for the enormous amount of work he accomplished in pursuit of peace and national reconciliation in Burundi. Burundi stated that it was essential to capitalize on the work already achieved in the Arusha process but it was important to correct the weaknesses in methodology and management. It was necessary for a new Facilitator to be appointed without delay, said Burundi. Presenting some criteria to guide the search for the new Facilitator, Burundi added that it was up to the international community to propose a new Facilitator and that it had no objection to that person utilizing the means of the former facilitation team if they had proved their effectiveness.

The former President of South Africa, Nelson Mandela, was appointed Facilitator of the Burundi peace process in December.

UN Adviser to peace process

The Secretary-General, on 2 November [S/1999/1138], informed the Security Council President of his decision to extend until June 2000 the appointment of Ayité Jean-Claude Kpakpo (Benin) as Senior UN Adviser to the Facilitator of the Burundi peace process.

On 5 November [S/1999/1139], the President informed the Secretary-General that his decision had been brought to the attention of the Council members.

Angola

At the beginning of the year, the situation in Angola continued to deteriorate as hostilities resumed between government forces and the National Union for the Total Independence of Angola (UNITA). As a result of the successful military campaign launched by the Government in September, a major change in the political situation took place with the re-establishment of State authority in the vast territory previously occupied by UNITA. By the end of the year, government forces had gained control of a number of key UNITA areas, including its strongholds in the central highlands, bringing a measure of stability to some regions. The protracted conflict and the risks of spillover into neighbouring countries remained a concern for the international community. The hostilities caused immense suffering for the Angolan people and at the end of the year there were an estimated 2 million internally displaced persons. In January, the Security Council condemned the downing, under suspicious circumstances, of aircraft chartered by the United Nations.

Implementation of the 1994 Lusaka Protocol [YUN 1994, p. 348], the agreement signed by the two sides by which the State administration would be extended throughout the country, came to a virtual standstill. The Government maintained that it did not consider Jonas Savimbi, the UNITA leader, a credible partner for dialogue, given his record of not implementing his previous undertakings in good faith. Nevertheless, President José Eduardo dos Santos affirmed in November that the Protocol was still a valid basis for the peace process, and he outlined a programme of action, without any timetable, that would culminate in the holding of legislative and presidential elections. The Security Council reiterated that the primary cause of the crisis in Angola was UNITA's refusal to comply with its obligations under the Lusaka Protocol and relevant Council resolutions, and stressed that lasting peace could be achieved only through a political settlement.

The United Nations Observer Mission in Angola (MONUA) was gradually withdrawn during the year after its mandate expired at the end of February; the United Nations and the Government of Angola established a joint commission to oversee the liquidation of the Mission. The United Nations Office in Angola was established in its place to liaise with the political, military, police and other civilian authorities, with a view to exploring measures for restoring peace and assisting in capacity-building, humanitarian assistance and the promotion of human rights.

The Committee established pursuant to Council resolution 864(1993) [YUN 1993, p. 256] assessed the implementation of sanctions against UNITA and made recommendations on ways to strengthen their effectiveness. In line with the Committee's recommendations, the Council established expert panels to make recommendations on strengthening sanctions, particularly with respect to restricting the flow of arms, petroleum and petroleum products, diamonds and funds to and from UNITA.

Political and military developments

The situation in Angola in 1999 continued the downward spiral that began the previous year. The conflict between government and UNITA forces widened and all progress towards implementation of the 1994 Lusaka Protocol [YUN 1994, p. 348], signed by President dos Santos and Jonas Savimbi, halted. That agreement covered, among other things, the withdrawal, quartering and demilitarization of all UNITA forces; the disarming of civilians; integration of forces into a national military; police functions; the electoral process; and national reconciliation. A major change in the overall situation occurred late in the year following the successful military campaign by the Government. As a result, the Government was able to re-establish its authority in much of the area previously occupied by UNITA. The hostilities continued to cause suffering for the Angolan people and the destruction of much of the country's infrastructure.

With the resumption of hostilities and the determination by the Angolan Government that the MONUA mandate should be ended, the Security Council did not renew the Mission's mandate when it expired on 26 February.

Report of Secretary-General (January). The Secretary-General, in response to Security Council resolution 1213(1998) [YUN 1998, p. 118], reported on 17 January on the United Nations Observer Mission in Angola (MONUA) [S/1999/49].

Since his previous report in October 1998 [YUN 1998, p. 115], said the Secretary-General, the overall situation in Angola had taken a turn towards a military confrontation with serious humanitarian consequences. The peace process had collapsed and Angola was in a state of war. The dialogue between the Government and Jonas Savimbi, which was interrupted in June 1998 after UNITA refused the extension of State administration in its strongholds, was non-existent. Several statements made by the parties, together with the intensifying hostilities, effectively ended any hope for the resumption of the implementation of the provisions of the Protocol in the foreseeable future. Although Mr. Savimbi had reaffirmed, in a letter of 3 December 1998, his commitment to the Protocol, his subsequent messages to the Secretary-General and his Special Representative, Issa B. Y. Diallo, gave no indication that UNITA intended to resume its obligations under the Protocol. However, Mr. Savimbi indicated his wish to meet with Mr. Diallo, as well as the need for the presence of international observers in Angola to serve as "useful witnesses". For his part, President dos Santos, speaking to the Fourth Congress of the Movimento Popular da Libertação de Angola (MPLA) in December 1998, said that the only path to lasting peace was the total isolation of Mr. Savimbi and his group. The President called for the early conclusion of the implementation of the Protocol and the termination of the MONUA mandate. At the same time, he indicated the need to begin preparations for the next legislative and presidential elections, to be held within two to three years. In his end-of-year address, the President again rejected any dialogue with Mr. Savimbi. Public statements by both parties indicated their apparent intention to continue and escalate the fighting. The Special Representative, in collaboration with representatives of the three observer States (Portugal, the Russian Federation and the United States), continued to maintain contacts with the parties, including the newly established UNITA Restoration Committee (UNITA-Renovada) and UNITA deputies to the National Assembly. Because of the Angolan Government's position, the Special Representative had not been able to meet directly with Mr. Savimbi or any of his senior representatives.

Government and military officials, as well as representatives from MPLA and UNITA-Renovada, had made claims that the United Nations was responsible for the deterioration of the security situation and for the failure to demilitarize UNITA forces. The negative public atmosphere created by the Angola media campaign against the United Nations was compounded by incidents of harassment and non-cooperation with MONUA. The exposure of UN personnel in Angola to grave security risks was demonstrated by the presumed shooting down near Huambo, an area of active military operations, of two UN aircraft, with a total of 15 passengers and eight crew members, on 26 December 1998 [YUN 1998, p. 120] and 2 January 1999. The two parties denied any responsibility for those incidents and initially denied the United Nations access to search the areas where the aircraft had gone down. The Secretary-General described the incidents as crimes apparently intended to intimidate the United Nations and force it to curtail its operations. In response to those developments, it was decided to limit air operations in Angola and to expedite the withdrawal of all UN personnel to Luanda, as also requested by the Government, ending all humanitarian air operations. By some accounts, Angola was on the verge of a humanitarian catastrophe.

The military situation in Angola had deteriorated since early December 1998 with the commencement of a large-scale military operation in the central highlands, the Secretary-General reported. The widening hostilities had had a negative impact on the general law and order situation in the country, and the attitude of local officials had prevented civilian police observers and human rights monitors from carrying out patrols and visits to prisons or detention centres. MONUA reported grave human rights violations against the civilian population as a result of the escalation of hostilities. At the beginning of 1999, the total number of new internally displaced persons had risen to 500,000 from 4,000 in April 1998.

In response to Security Council resolutions 1202(1998) [YUN 1998, p. 116] and 1213(1998) [ibid., p. 118], the Secretary-General included in his report recommendations regarding ways for Member States to improve the implementation of sanctions against UNITA (see p. 111), as called for by Council resolution 864(1993) [YUN 1993, p. 256]. For example, he suggested that Member States, particularly those neighbouring Angola, provide regular information necessary to enable the Sanctions Committee to investigate violations of the mandatory measures; Angola and neighbouring States could monitor major border crossings and airports to prevent illegal movement across the border; and an expert study could be commissioned on ways to trace violations of the measures regarding arms trafficking, oil supply and the diamond trade, as well as the movement of UNITA funds.

In the light of the deteriorating security situation and the inability of MONUA to carry out its mandate, it had become clear that the conditions for a meaningful UN peacekeeping role in Angola had ceased to exist. The Government had informed the United Nations, and announced in the media, that it did not intend to support the extension of MONUA beyond its current mandate. As for UNITA, although it had made statements in favour of a continued UN presence, it had not taken any initiative to restore meaningful contacts with the United Nations or to resume implementation of the Lusaka Protocol. The United Nations had brought four years of relative peace to Angola, the longest such period Angola had enjoyed since its independence, but it could not play an effective role without the parties' cooperation. In the circumstances, the Secretary-General found that MONUA had no other option but to continue to reduce its presence within Angola and proceed with repatriation of UN personnel and property. Upon the expiration of MONUA's mandate on 26 February, the United Nations would proceed with its technical liquidation, which would last four to six months. However, the United Nations should remain actively involved in finding a possible resolution of the fratricidal conflict which had lasted longer than any other in Africa, the Secretary-General stated. He therefore intended to designate a senior official to serve as his Special Envoy for Angola, who would be based in New York. The human rights work of the United Nations in Angola should continue, as should humanitarian assistance to the Angolan people. However, the United Nations could not carry out those tasks without guarantees of access and assurances for the safety and security of humanitarian personnel and operations. The Secretary-General called on the two parties to provide such guarantees and cooperate fully with the humanitarian organizations working in Angola.

SECURITY COUNCIL ACTION (January)

The Security Council, in January, adopted a resolution and issued a presidential statement on the situation in Angola.

On 12 January [meeting 3965], the Council unanimously adopted **resolution 1221(1999)**. The draft [S/1999/27] was submitted by Brazil, Canada, France, Gabon, Malaysia, Namibia, Portugal and the Russian Federation.

The Security Council,

Reaffirming its resolution 696(1991) of 30 May 1991 and all subsequent relevant resolutions, in particular resolutions 1196(1998) of 16 September 1998 and 1219(1998) of 31 December 1998,

Recalling the statement by its President of 23 December 1998,

Expressing its outrage at the downing on 2 January 1999 of a second United Nations-chartered aircraft over territory controlled by the União Nacional para a Independência Total de Angola, which brings to six the number of aircraft lost in this area in recent months,

Expressing its deep concern regarding the fate of the passengers and crews of the above-mentioned aircraft, and its deep regret at the loss of life in these incidents,

Stressing that attacks against personnel who act on behalf of the United Nations are unacceptable and unjustifiable by whomsoever committed,

Deploring the lack of cooperation by the União Nacional para a Independência Total de Angola in clarifying the circumstances of these tragic incidents, which occurred over territory under its control, and in permitting the prompt dispatch of the United Nations search and rescue mission,

Acting under Chapter VII of the Charter of the United Nations,

1. *Condemns* the downing of the two aircraft chartered by the United Nations, deplores the loss under suspicious circumstances of other commercial aircraft, and demands that all such attacks cease immediately;

2. *Reaffirms its resolve* to establish the truth about the circumstances of and to determine the responsibility for the downing of the two aircraft chartered by the United Nations and the loss under suspicious circumstances of other commercial aircraft over territory controlled by the União Nacional para a Independência Total de Angola through an immediate and objective international investigation of these tragic incidents, and reiterates its call upon all concerned, especially the União Nacional para a Independência Total de Angola, to cooperate fully with and to facilitate such an investigation;

3. *Concludes* that the leader of the União Nacional para a Independência Total de Angola, Mr. Jonas Savimbi, has not complied with the demands contained in its resolution 1219(1998);

4. *Reiterates its demand* that the leader of the União Nacional para a Independência Total de Angola, Mr. Jonas Savimbi, cooperate immediately and in good faith in the search for and rescue of possible survivors of the above-mentioned incidents;

5. *Welcomes* the concrete actions undertaken by the Government of Angola to follow up the commitment made by the President of Angola to the Special Envoy of the Secretary-General on 5 January 1999 regarding the cooperation to be extended to the United Nations search and rescue efforts, and encourages it to continue to extend such cooperation;

6. *Requests* the International Civil Aviation Organization to provide all possible support to the investigation of those incidents as soon as conditions on the ground permit, and urges Member States with investigative capability and expertise to assist the United Nations, upon request, in the investigation of those incidents;

7. *Stresses* the obligation of Member States to comply with the measures imposed against the União Nacional para a Independência Total de Angola contained in resolutions 864(1993) of 15 September 1993, 1127(1997) of 28 August 1997 and 1173(1998) of 12 June 1998;

8. *Expresses its readiness* to pursue reports of violations of the measures referred to in paragraph 7 above, to take steps to reinforce the implementation of these measures and to consider the imposition of additional measures, including in the area of telecommunica-

tions, on the basis of a report to be prepared by the Security Council Committee established pursuant to resolution 864(1993), by 15 February 1999, drawing on the expertise of relevant bodies and organizations, including the International Telecommunication Union;

9. *Encourages* the Chairman of the Committee referred to in paragraph 8 above to consult with the Organization of African Unity and the Southern African Development Community on ways to strengthen the implementation of the measures referred to in paragraph 7 above;

10. *Decides* to remain actively seized of the matter.

On 21 January [meeting 3969], following consideration of the Secretary-General's 17 January report (see p. 102), the Council President made statement **S/PRST/1999/3** on behalf of the Council:

The Security Council expresses its alarm at the serious deterioration in the political and military situation in Angola. It reaffirms its belief that lasting peace and national reconciliation cannot be achieved through military means, and urges the Government of Angola and especially the União Nacional para a Independência Total de Angola to resume a constructive dialogue on the basis of the "Acordos de Paz", the Lusaka Protocol and relevant Council resolutions in order to seek a peaceful resolution of the conflict and spare the Angolan people further war and suffering. In this context, it reaffirms that the primary cause of the crisis in Angola is the refusal by the União Nacional para a Independência Total de Angola to comply with the basic provisions of the Lusaka Protocol and reiterates its demand that the União Nacional para a Independência Total de Angola comply with its obligations to demilitarize and to permit the extension of State administration to territories it controls.

The Council shares the assessment and judgements of the Secretary-General on the political and military situation in Angola contained in his report of 17 January 1999. It underscores the contribution of the United Nations to the past four years of relative peace in Angola. It expresses its deep regret that the present political and security situation in the country and the lack of cooperation with the United Nations Observer Mission in Angola, especially by the União Nacional para a Independência Total de Angola, have prevented the Mission from carrying out its mandated role fully.

The Council underlines the great importance it attaches to a continued multidisciplinary presence of the United Nations under the direction of a representative of the Secretary-General in Angola. It recognizes that such a continued presence depends on the safety of United Nations personnel and requires the agreement of the Government of Angola and the cooperation of all concerned. In this context, it appeals to the Government of Angola to provide such agreement and to the União Nacional para a Independência Total de Angola to cooperate fully. It welcomes the intention of the Secretary-General to consult urgently with the Government of Angola on such a United Nations presence and to report to the Council in this regard.

The Council again calls upon Member States to support the peace process in Angola through full and immediate implementation of the measures against the União Nacional para a Independência Total de Angola contained in resolutions 864(1993) of 15 September 1993, 1127(1997) of 28 August 1997 and 1173(1998) of 12 June 1998, and reiterates its readiness to take steps to reinforce the implementation of those measures on the basis of the recommendations contained in section IV of the report of the Secretary-General of 17 January 1999.

The Council expresses its profound concern at the humanitarian impact of the conflict on the Angolan people. It urges the international community to support the Government of Angola in fulfilling its primary responsibility for the humanitarian needs of the Angolan people and, in this regard, urges Member States to fund generously the 1999 United Nations Consolidated Inter-Agency Appeal for Angola. It calls upon all concerned to concur and cooperate with United Nations humanitarian assistance activities on the basis of the principles of neutrality and non-discrimination, to guarantee the security and freedom of movement of humanitarian personnel, and to ensure necessary, adequate and safe access and logistics by land and air. It urges all concerned to cooperate with the human rights activities of the United Nations, which help to lay a basis for lasting peace and national reconciliation.

The Council will remain actively seized of the matter.

Communications (January/February). Angola, on 21 January [S/1999/65], forwarded to the Security Council a note verbale of 20 January from Higino Carneiro, Angola's Vice-Minister of Territorial Administration, to the Special Representative of the Secretary-General in Angola, concerning the 2 January crash of the UN-chartered aircraft in Bailundo. Mr. Carneiro was responding to a request that a UN team be allowed to visit Bailundo, with guarantees for its security. He informed Mr. Diallo that contacts had been established with the Command of the Northern Centre (Huambo) so as to coordinate all actions for security guarantees. The visit would have to take place between 20 and 23 January.

On 28 January [S/1999/86], Zambia transmitted to the Council a press release issued the day before by its Foreign Ministry. Zambia was responding to allegations by Angola that Zambian authorities were involved in sending logistic and military support to Mr. Savimbi. Zambia stated that it had no evidence or reason to believe the existence or credibility of such information. Zambia, on 20 February [S/1999/182], transmitted a press statement of 17 February by its Foreign Minister on the Angolan claims of Zambian support for Mr. Savimbi. In 1998, the Minister said, several international verification teams had investigated the claims and had cleared Zambia of the allegations. Zambia stated that it had complied with the Council resolutions against UNITA and had communicated that information to the United Nations.

Expiration of MONUA mandate

Communication. President dos Santos of Angola, in an 11 February letter to the Secretary-General [S/1999/166], said his Government considered that conditions for maintaining MONUA's presence in Angola had ceased to exist. Mr. Savimbi had withdrawn from the Lusaka Protocol process to restart and spread the war on a large scale throughout the country beginning in December 1998. Angola claimed that Mr. Savimbi had been removed from the UNITA leadership and therefore it would continue discussions with the new leaders elected at a recent party congress. Angola also indicated that it was not opposed to the idea of the appointment of a special representative who, from New York, could maintain contact with the Government in monitoring the situation in Angola.

Report of Secretary-General (February). On 24 February, the Secretary-General submitted a report on MONUA [S/1999/202] to the Security Council, as the Council had requested in its statement of 21 January (see p. 105). The situation in Angola remained grave, he said, with a marked escalation in fighting between government and UNITA forces.

On 27 January, the National Assembly of Angola adopted a resolution accusing the international community of acquiescence, complacency and bias and of making it easy for Mr. Savimbi to rearm and prepare for war. The Assembly reiterated its view that MONUA's mandate should end. In another resolution, the Assembly declared Mr. Savimbi a war criminal and called for his arrest. The new Angolan Minister of Defence warned seven neighbouring countries that had allegedly provided Mr. Savimbi with material and logistical support that Angola reserved the right of retaliation and hot pursuit. One of those countries, Zambia, had publicly denied those allegations.

The Government and UNITA-Renovada held a joint meeting in Luanda on 18 February [S/1999/268 & Corr.1] to review the implementation of the Lusaka Protocol and agreed that the presidential elections, required under the terms of that document, would be cancelled. The Government informed the Special Representative that, in its view, a continued UN presence in Angola was not necessary (see above), but that the United Nations should continue its activities through the specialized agencies, under the coordination of UNDP.

The United Nations, through the Special Representative, continued to make efforts to maintain contacts with all parties concerned. In a letter to the Secretary-General, Mr. Savimbi claimed that the war was the exclusive responsibility of the Government and the UNITA leadership maintained its position that MONUA should continue in its original format as a facilitator of rapprochement between the parties.

The fighting increased on 26 January when UNITA launched an unexpected offensive, threatening oil fields on the western coast. In the central highlands, the Angolan Armed Forces (FAA) were reported to have made substantial gains. UNITA forces continued to shell Malange and captured the Capenda hydroelectric project south-west of the town. There were large numbers of civilian casualties in Malange, which was overwhelmed by the influx of almost 100,000 internally displaced persons (IDPs). UNITA announced that its forces had captured two diamond mines in the north-east of the country. The presence of troops from the DRC, who were reportedly being trained by FAA, had been confirmed in the Lubango and Matala areas.

After extensive negotiations, on 25 January a UN investigation team, with a UNITA escort, reached the site of the crash of the UN flight that went down on 2 January. The team, which had only an hour at the location, found bullet holes in the tail section and determined that it was unlikely that any of those on board could have survived the crash.

The escalation of hostilities contributed to the dramatic deterioration in the human rights situation, with the civilian population bearing the full brunt of the warfare. Indiscriminate UNITA shelling of Malange killed at least several dozen persons in early January and injured many more. The number of abuses committed against members of the Roman Catholic Church increased, with mission property and personnel being targeted for harassment, torture and killings. The humanitarian situation had shown no sign of improvement, and indications pointed to a further deterioration of the condition of vulnerable populations. The effects of the conflict had led to further displacements of the civilian population during February, with the total number of confirmed IDPs having reached over 550,000 persons. Moreover, the Office of the United Nations High Commissioner for Refugees (UNHCR) reported that 19,000 Angolan refugees had recently arrived in the DRC, fleeing the fighting. In spite of the deteriorating security situation, UN agencies and programmes resumed their air operations to most provincial capitals in mid-January, but the ability of the humanitarian community to operate in Angola had been seriously affected by the constraints on access.

The Secretary-General reported that all UN team sites and regional headquarters were relocated to Luanda by 23 February. Since the beginning of 1999, 325 MONUA military and civilian police observers had been repatriated. As at 20 February, MONUA military and police personnel numbered 654. It was estimated that 260 troops would be needed to provide the necessary protection for UN property during the liquidation phase following the expiration of MONUA's mandate. The Secretary-General trusted that the Angolan Government, in accordance with the status-of-forces agreement, would continue to ensure the security of UN personnel. The technical liquidation of MONUA and its predecessors, whose combined presence in Angola spanned 10 years, was estimated to take six months to complete and would require administrative, logistical and other personnel. The Secretary-General would continue consultations with the Government concerning the modalities of the future UN presence.

SECURITY COUNCIL ACTION (February)

On 26 February [meeting 3983], the Security Council unanimously adopted **resolution 1229 (1999)**. The draft text [S/1999/203] was prepared in consultations among Council members.

The Security Council,

Reaffirming its resolution 696(1991) of 30 May 1991 and all subsequent relevant resolutions, in particular resolutions 864(1993) of 15 September 1993, 1127(1997) of 28 August 1997 and 1173(1998) of 12 June 1998, as well as resolutions 1219(1998) of 31 December 1998 and 1221(1999) of 12 January 1999,

Recalling the statements by its President of 23 December 1998 and of 21 January 1999,

Reaffirming its commitment to preserve the sovereignty and territorial integrity of Angola,

Reiterating that the primary cause of the present situation in Angola is the failure of the União Nacional para a Independência Total de Angola, under the leadership of Mr. Jonas Savimbi, to comply with its obligations under the "Acordos de Paz", the Lusaka Protocol and relevant Security Council resolutions,

Expressing its concern at the humanitarian effects of the present situation on the civilian population of Angola,

Reiterating that lasting peace and national reconciliation can be achieved only through peaceful means, and in this regard reaffirming the importance of the "Acordos de Paz", the Lusaka Protocol and relevant Security Council resolutions,

Underscoring the contribution of the United Nations to the past four years of relative peace in Angola, and expressing its deep regret that the present political and security situation in the country has prevented the United Nations Observer Mission in Angola from carrying out its mandated role fully,

Taking note of the letter dated 11 February 1999 from the President of the Republic of Angola to the Secretary-General,

Reaffirming its view that a continued presence of the United Nations in Angola can contribute greatly to national reconciliation, and noting the ongoing consultations with the Government of Angola to obtain its agreement regarding the practical arrangements for this presence,

Having considered the report of the Secretary-General of 24 February 1999,

1. *Takes note* that the mandate of the United Nations Observer Mission in Angola expires on 26 February 1999;

2. *Endorses* the recommendations contained in paragraphs 32 and 33 of the report of the Secretary-General of 24 February 1999 regarding the technical liquidation of the Mission;

3. *Affirms* that notwithstanding the expiration of the mandate of the Mission, the status-of-forces agreement applicable to the Mission remains in force, pursuant to relevant provisions thereof, until the departure of the final elements of the Mission from Angola;

4. *Decides* that the human rights component of the Mission shall continue its current activities during the liquidation period;

5. *Requests* the Secretary-General to designate a channel to liaise with the Government of Angola pending the conclusion of the consultations with the Government of Angola regarding the follow-up configuration of the United Nations presence in Angola;

6. *Calls upon* all concerned to cooperate with the United Nations humanitarian assistance activities throughout the national territory of Angola on the basis of the principles of neutrality and non-discrimination and to guarantee the security and freedom of movement of humanitarian personnel;

7. *Expresses its deep concern* at the lack of progress in investigating the downing of the two aircraft chartered by the United Nations and the loss under suspicious circumstances of other commercial aircraft over areas controlled by the União Nacional para a Independência Total de Angola, and reiterates its call upon all concerned, especially the União Nacional para a Independência Total de Angola, to cooperate fully with and to facilitate an immediate and objective international investigation of those incidents;

8. *Endorses* the recommendations contained in the report of 12 February 1999 of the Security Council Committee established pursuant to resolution 864 (1993), reiterates its readiness to take steps to reinforce the measures against the União Nacional para a Independência Total de Angola contained in resolutions 864(1993), 1127(1997) and 1173(1998), and calls upon all Member States to implement those measures fully;

9. *Decides* to remain actively seized of the matter.

Downing of commercial aircraft

The Foreign Ministry of the Russian Federation, in a 20 May statement [S/1999/593], transmitted to the Secretary-General, said a Russian civilian aircraft, chartered by an Angolan company to transport food and other civilian cargo on domestic Angolan routes, was shot down on 12 May in Lunda Norte province. According to Russia, UNITA captured the Russian flight crew and took responsibility for shooting the aircraft down. The Ministry demanded the immediate and unconditional release of all Russian citizens captured by UNITA and held illegally.

SECURITY COUNCIL ACTION (May)

On 19 May [meeting 4007], following consultations among Security Council members, the President made statement **S/PRST/1999/14** on behalf of the Council:

The Security Council strongly condemns the criminal act by the União Nacional para a Independência Total de Angola against commercial aircraft, namely the shooting down of an Antonov-26 aircraft on 12 May 1999 near Luzamba and the taking of its Russian crew hostage, while the fate of its Angolan passengers remains unknown.

The Council expresses its grave concern at the fate of those who were on board the downed aircraft, demands the immediate and unconditional release of the Russian crew members and all other foreign nationals that may be held hostage in Angola by the União Nacional para a Independência Total de Angola and also demands information on the fate of the Angolan passengers. It stresses that the União Nacional para a Independência Total de Angola and its leader, Mr. Jonas Savimbi, carry full responsibility for their security.

The Council calls upon the Government of Angola and all other concerned parties to cooperate in obtaining the release of the Russian crew members as well as in ascertaining the fate of passengers and crew members of other commercial aircraft lost under suspicious circumstances over territory controlled by the União Nacional para a Independência Total de Angola.

The Council will remain actively seized of the matter.

In **resolution 1237(1999)** (see p. 112), the Council condemned the continued attacks by UNITA and called on Member States to enforce measures imposed against UNITA since 1993.

Communications (June-August). On 9 June [S/1999/684], Germany forwarded to the Council an 8 June statement by the EU Presidency supporting the Council's condemnation of the shooting down of the Russian commercial aircraft. It noted that the fate of neither the Russian crew nor the Angolan passengers had been cleared up, nor could the investigation into the shooting down of other aircraft over UNITA-controlled territory, including the downings of two UN aircraft, be concluded. The EU appealed to UNITA to release the hostages and called on the Government and, in particular, UNITA to cooperate with the United Nations.

Finland forwarded a 22 July statement on Angola by the EU Presidency [S/1999/821]. The EU deplored the resumption of civil war in Angola, for which the responsibility lay primarily with UNITA, and reiterated its commitment to maintaining pressure on UNITA through the implementation of UN sanctions. UNITA was urged to resume dialogue with the Government of Angola, with a view to the demilitarization of UNITA and the extension of State administration throughout the country.

The Central Organ of the OAU Mechanism for Conflict Prevention, Management and Resolution issued a communiqué, forwarded to the Council on 10 May [S/1999/533], on the recent visit of the OAU Secretary-General to Angola. The Central Organ requested him to continue his efforts to address the political and humanitarian aspects of the conflict in Angola and appealed to States to implement UN sanctions against UNITA.

Angola, in its capacity as Coordinator of the Council of Ministers of the Community of Portuguese-speaking Countries, transmitted a 22 July statement by the Council on the subject of Angola on 3 August [S/1999/847]. The Ministers reiterated their solidarity with the Government of Angola, condemned the attacks against civilians by UNITA military forces, and noted with pleasure UN humanitarian assistance efforts in Angola.

SECURITY COUNCIL ACTION (August)

On 24 August [meeting 4036], following consultations among Security Council members, the Council President made statement **S/PRST/1999/26** on behalf of the Council:

The Security Council expresses its deep concern at the deteriorating political, military and humanitarian situation in Angola, at the suffering of the people and at the dramatic increase in the number of internally displaced persons, which has now reached well over two million people, not including the unknown number of internally displaced persons in areas which are currently inaccessible to humanitarian agencies.

The Council reiterates that the primary cause of the current crisis in Angola is the failure by the leadership of the União Nacional para a Independência Total de Angola to comply with its obligations under the Lusaka Protocol, and it again demands that the União Nacional para a Independência Total de Angola comply immediately and without conditions with its obligations to demilitarize and permit the extension of state administration to areas under its control. It reaffirms its belief that lasting peace and national reconciliation can only be achieved through political dialogue.

The Council expresses its concern at the critical condition of the internally displaced persons who suffer from lack of food, medicines, shelter, arable land and other necessities. The Council further expresses its grave concern at the number of malnourished children and at the outbreak of diseases such as polio and meningitis due to the lack of access to clean water and hygiene. In this regard the Council commends the excellent work by the Government of Angola and the United Nations system in their efforts towards the eradication of diseases in Angola. The Council also expresses its concern at the plight of those vulnerable groups, such as children, women, the elderly and the handicapped, who are particularly at risk and in need of special assistance.

The Council expresses its concern that the continuing conflict in Angola has increased the cost of humanitarian assistance. It notes the insufficient level of contributions to the 1999 United Nations Consolidated Inter-Agency Appeal for Angola and reiterates its appeal to the donor community to contribute generously, financially and in kind, to the humanitarian appeal to enable the agencies to address effectively the plight of the internally displaced persons. The Council welcomes the announcement by the Government of Angola of an emergency plan for humanitarian assistance.

The Council also expresses its concern that the continuing conflict and lack of access jeopardize the ability of the agencies to continue to deliver assistance to those in need. The Council urges the Government of Angola and particularly the União Nacional para a Independência Total de Angola to provide access to all internally displaced persons in Angola and to facilitate the mechanisms necessary for the delivery of humanitarian assistance to all populations in need throughout the country. The Council urges both parties, particularly the União Nacional para a Independência Total de Angola, to guarantee the safety and security and freedom of movement of humanitarian personnel, including United Nations and associated personnel, providing assistance to internally displaced persons. The Council strongly urges respect for the principle of neutrality and impartiality in the delivery of assistance. The Council commends the determination and courage of those working to relieve human suffering in Angola, including the Office for the Coordination of Humanitarian Affairs, the World Food Programme and the United Nations Children's Fund and other agencies.

The Council urges both parties to ensure full respect for human rights and international humanitarian law. In this connection, the Council urges the União Nacional para a Independência Total de Angola to cease committing atrocities, including killing civilians and attacking humanitarian aid workers, and demands the release of all foreign citizens, including the Russian aircrews, held by the União Nacional para a Independência Total de Angola. It expresses its concern at reports of re-mining activities as well as the laying of mines in new areas in the country.

The Council will remain actively seized of the matter.

Establishment of UN Office in Angola

In response to statement S/PRST/1999/3, the Secretary-General, in an 11 August letter [S/1999/871], reported on the status of his consultations with Angola on a continued UN multidisciplinary presence in that country. Following a positive response from Angola, the Secretary-General expressed his intention to proceed with the establishment of the United Nations Office in Angola (UNOA). Practical arrangements would be made for the earliest establishment of the office and the conclusion with Angola of a status-of-mission agreement. The staff of the office would liaise with the political, military, police and other civilian authorities, with a view to exploring ways to restore peace and assist the Angolan people in the area of human rights. The United Nations Humanitarian Assistance Coordination Unit would continue to operate in its existing configuration.

SECURITY COUNCIL ACTION (October)

On 15 October [meeting 4052], the Security Council unanimously adopted **resolution 1268(1999)**. The draft text [S/1999/1061] was prepared during the Council's prior consultations.

The Security Council,

Reaffirming its resolution 696(1991) of 30 May 1991 and all subsequent relevant resolutions, in particular resolutions 1229(1999) of 26 February 1999 and 1237(1999) of 7 May 1999,

Recalling the statements by its President of 21 January 1999 and 24 August 1999,

Reaffirming its commitment to preserve the sovereignty and territorial integrity of Angola,

Reiterating that the primary cause of the present situation in Angola is the failure of the União Nacional para a Independência Total de Angola, under the leadership of Mr. Jonas Savimbi, to comply with its obligations under the "Acordos de Paz", the Lusaka Protocol and relevant Security Council resolutions,

Reiterating also that lasting peace and national reconciliation can only be achieved through peaceful means, and in this regard reaffirming the importance of the "Acordos de Paz", the Lusaka Protocol and relevant Security Council resolutions,

Expressing its concern at the humanitarian effects of the present situation on the civilian population in Angola,

Welcoming the letter from the Secretary-General to the President of the Security Council dated 11 August 1999, and the letters referred to therein from the Minister for Foreign Affairs of the Republic of Angola to the Secretary-General dated 26 July 1999 and from the Secretary-General to the Minister for Foreign Affairs of the Republic of Angola dated 2 August 1999,

Reaffirming its view that a continued United Nations presence in Angola can contribute greatly to the promotion of peace, national reconciliation, human rights and regional security,

1. *Authorizes* the establishment, for an initial period of six months until 15 April 2000, of the United Nations Office in Angola staffed with the personnel nec-

essary to liaise with the political, military, police and other civilian authorities, with a view to exploring effective measures for restoring peace, assisting the Angolan people in the area of capacity-building, humanitarian assistance and the promotion of human rights, and coordinating other activities;

2. *Decides* that, pending further consultations between the United Nations and the Government of Angola, the United Nations Office in Angola shall consist of up to thirty substantive professional staff, as well as the necessary administrative and other support personnel;

3. *Stresses* that the United Nations Humanitarian Assistance Coordination Unit will continue to operate and to be funded in its present configuration;

4. *Calls upon* all parties concerned and in particular the União Nacional para a Independência Total de Angola to ensure the safety, security and freedom of movement of the United Nations and associated personnel and to respect fully their status;

5. *Calls upon* the Government of Angola and the Secretary-General to conclude as soon as possible a status-of-mission agreement;

6. *Expresses its readiness* to review the configuration and mandate of the United Nations presence in Angola upon the recommendation of the Secretary-General in consultation with the Government of Angola;

7. *Requests* the Secretary-General to provide every three months a report on developments in Angola, including his recommendations about additional measures the Council might consider to promote the peace process in Angola;

8. *Decides* to remain actively seized of the matter.

The Government of Angola informed the Secretary-General on 18 October [S/1999/1099] that it consented to the installation of a UN office in the country. Angola reiterated that, under current circumstances, a UN presence could be of great use only if its activity was restricted to the area of humanitarian assistance and capacity-building and strengthening of government institutions in the field of human rights. Angola reaffirmed its position that the UNOA mandate should be to serve as a liaison between the Government and the Secretary-General, with a view to ensuring follow-up to the situation in Angola by the Security Council on those matters. As to the Humanitarian Assistance Coordination Unit, Angola supported its role and had no objection to its current configuration, i.e., independent from UNOA. Concerning public information questions, the Government believed that, given the nature and scope of the mission, the installation of a broadcasting station and the allocation of a special space in the media would not be required. Angola concluded that the necessary conditions for the conclusion and signing of the headquarters agreement were in place.

In an 11 November reply, the Secretary-General took note of the Government's position and stressed that the substantive staff of the new office would perform the functions outlined in Council resolution 1268(1999).

Later developments. In late 1999 [S/2000/23], the situation in Angola underwent a major change following the successful military campaign launched by the Government in September, resulting in the re-establishment of State authority in the territory previously occupied by UNITA in the central, northern and eastern regions. The Government maintained that it did not consider Mr. Savimbi a credible partner for dialogue, given his record of not implementing his previous undertakings in good faith. At the same time, President dos Santos stated on 11 November that all Mr. Savimbi's supporters who surrendered to government forces would be allowed to carry out political activities. He also stressed that the Lusaka Protocol was still a valid basis for the peace process in Angola and outlined a programme of action that would culminate in the holding of legislative and presidential elections. However, no dates for elections were announced. In the meantime, the Government reinforced its military action on the ground and continued a campaign aimed at the political isolation of UNITA. To that effect, consultations were conducted by the Government with various countries, particularly those in the subregion, in an attempt to deny Mr. Savimbi lines of communication and logistic support. In that context, meetings were held with representatives of the Congo, the DRC, Namibia and Zambia on issues related to security along Angola's border, and some bilateral understandings were reportedly reached in that regard. UNITA-Renovada remained active, calling for the termination of the conflict by Mr. Savimbi's group and urging the Government to resume the demobilization of UNITA fighters to be incorporated in the proposed "fourth branch" of FAA.

The Human Rights Division of MONUA pursued its activities in cooperation with the Government, State institutions and civil society. By the end of the year, several capacity-building projects had been developed, focusing on the training of prosecutors and judges, improving infrastructure, public access to law and court proceedings, and the need for law reform. A UN police training project awaited approval by the authorities. Since the relocation of all MONUA personnel to Luanda in early 1999, the Division had had to discontinue its activities outside the Angolan capital, except in Benguela province where it had set up human rights centres.

The humanitarian situation in the country remained precarious as a result of continued military activities, with disruptions in the rehabilitation of social and economic structures and services. The war-affected civilian population was estimated at 3.7 million people, of whom nearly 2 million were IDPs. The security situation had seriously constrained international humanitarian work.

The United Nations and the Angolan Government cooperated on administrative aspects of the liquidation of MONUA through a joint commission. After lengthy negotiations, the Government on 11 November offered the United Nations $8.3 million to purchase the Mission's assets and the sale was expected to be completed by the end of January 2000. With regard to the two UN aircraft that were shot down in central Angola in December 1998 and January 1999, MONUA representatives and Angolan military authorities met in December 1999 to coordinate the return of UN teams to the crash sites.

In the Secretary-General's view, the protracted conflict in Angola and the risks of spillover into neighbouring countries remained a source of major concern for the international community. UNITA bore the primary responsibility for the current state of affairs. Its refusal to comply with obligations under the Lusaka Protocol, in particular its failure to demilitarize its forces and to allow State administration to be extended throughout the country, had precipitated the resumption of widespread hostilities.

Other matters

Sanctions Committee

During 1999, the Security Council Committee established pursuant to resolution 864(1993) [YUN 1993, p. 256] to monitor sanctions against UNITA explored ways to ensure the implementation of the mandatory measures. In **resolutions 1221(1999)** and **1229(1999)**, the Council stressed the obligation of Member States to comply with the measures imposed against UNITA in 1993 and strengthened in resolutions 1127(1997) [YUN 1997, p. 106] and 1173(1998) [YUN 1998, p. 108] and expressed its readiness to consider additional measures.

In response to the Council's request in resolution 1221(1999), the Chairman of the Committee, in a 12 February report [S/1999/147], reviewed and supported recommendations made by the Secretary-General in his January report [S/1999/49] to improve the implementation of the sanctions. They included: Member States should provide information on the implementation of those measures; the Council and the Committee should review the implementation process with a view to identifying and eliminating gaps; Member States should provide the Committee with information necessary for it to investigate possible violations; Angola and neighbouring States should monitor all major border crossings and airports to prevent illegal movement across the border; and an expert study should focus on ways to trace violations of the measures. In addition, the Committee proposed that States consider enacting legislation making violations of the sanctions a criminal offence; prohibit logistical assistance and military services to UNITA; obtain information on transfer of military equipment to UNITA and activities involving illicit diamond trade with UNITA; and track the financial flows of UNITA and its officials. The Committee also suggested that Member States, particularly those neighbouring Angola, provide information on illegal arms flows to Angola, the illicit trade in diamonds, the supply of petroleum products to UNITA, and proposals for tightening the embargo. By a note of 18 February [S/1999/168], the President stated that the Council had approved the report of the Committee and endorsed its recommendations.

Angola, in a 9 March letter to the Chairman of the Committee [S/1999/267], said that some African countries had compromised efforts to stem the flow of political and material support to the militarist wing of Mr. Savimbi. It pointed to Zambia and gave examples of evidence of such support. It alleged that Zambian enterprises and some individuals were involved in the sale and purchase of lethal materials and food for UNITA and that the Zambian Government had provided direct support for UNITA. Zambia responded to the charges on 19 March [S/1999/306]. It rebutted the allegations after having conducted investigations of the reported evidence.

Establishment of expert panels

On 4 May [S/1999/509], the Sanctions Committee Chairman transmitted to the Council a conceptual framework for the expert studies to be undertaken to trace violations in arms trafficking, oil supplies and the diamond trade, as well as the movement of UNITA funds, as proposed by the Committee [S/1999/147] and endorsed by the Council in resolution 1229(1999). It was proposed that the expert studies be conducted in two parts—one panel, on the sources of revenue, funding and petroleum supplies of UNITA, would focus on the resources that enabled UNITA to operate, and the other panel, on the sources of military support to UNITA, would study violations of Council-imposed sanctions on the sale and supply to UNITA of arms, materiel and military assistance, including mercenaries. The expert panels would have a mandate to collect information on the sources and methods of violations of sanctions and to recommend measures to end those violations and improve the implementation of sanctions. Each panel would have a mandate of six months and the Committee Chairman would provide oversight of the studies. The panels would be supported as an expense of the Organization and through a UN trust fund established for that purpose.

SECURITY COUNCIL ACTION

On 7 May [meeting 3999], the Security Council unanimously adopted **resolution 1237(1999)**. The draft text [S/1999/521] was sponsored by Canada, Portugal, the Russian Federation and the United States.

The Security Council,

Reaffirming its resolution 696(1991) of 30 May 1991 and all subsequent relevant resolutions, in particular resolutions 864(1993) of 15 September 1993, 1127(1997) of 28 August 1997 and 1173(1998) of 12 June 1998, as well as resolution 1229(1999) of 26 February 1999,

Reaffirming its commitment to preserve the sovereignty and territorial integrity of Angola,

Reiterating that the primary cause of the present crisis in Angola is the refusal of the União Nacional para a Independência Total de Angola, under the leadership of Mr. Jonas Savimbi, to comply with its obligations under the "Acordos de Paz", the Lusaka Protocol and relevant Security Council resolutions,

Expressing its alarm at the humanitarian effects of the present crisis on the civilian population of Angola,

Emphasizing its strong concern at reports of the provision of military assistance, including mercenaries, to the União Nacional para a Independência Total de Angola,

Having considered the recommendations contained in section IV of the report of the Secretary-General of 17 January 1999 concerning improvement of the implementation of the measures imposed against the União Nacional para a Independência Total de Angola, and having endorsed the recommendations contained in the report of 12 February 1999 of the Security Council Committee established pursuant to resolution 864 (1993),

Welcoming the recommendations contained in the annex to the letter dated 4 May 1999 from the Chairman of the Committee established pursuant to resolution 864(1993),

A

1. *Stresses* that lasting peace and national reconciliation in Angola can be achieved only through a political settlement of the conflict, and in this regard reaffirms the importance of the "Acordos de Paz" and the Lusaka Protocol;

2. *Welcomes and endorses* the planned visits by the Chairman of the Security Council Committee established pursuant to resolution 864(1993) to Angola and other concerned countries to discuss ways to improve the implementation of the measures against the União Nacional para a Independência Total de Angola specified in paragraph 5 below;

B

Determining that, as a result of the refusal of the União Nacional para a Independência Total de Angola to comply with its obligations under the "Acordos de Paz", the Lusaka Protocol and relevant Security Council resolutions, the current situation in Angola continues to constitute a threat to international peace and security in the region,

Emphasizing its concern at reports of violations of the measures with respect to arms and related materiel, petroleum, diamonds and financial assets, imposed against the União Nacional para a Independência Total de Angola by resolutions 864(1993), 1127(1997) and 1173(1998), and in this context acting under Chapter VII of the Charter of the United Nations,

3. *Deplores* the deteriorating situation in Angola, which is primarily due to the refusal of the União Nacional para a Independência Total de Angola, under the leadership of Mr. Jonas Savimbi, to comply with its obligations under the "Acordos de Paz", the Lusaka Protocol and relevant Security Council resolutions;

4. *Condemns* the continued, indiscriminate attacks by the União Nacional para a Independência Total de Angola against the civilian population of Angola, particularly in the cities of Huambo, Kuito and Malange;

5. *Stresses* the obligation of all Member States to comply fully with the measures imposed against the União Nacional para a Independência Total de Angola by resolutions 864(1993), 1127(1997) and 1173(1998);

6. *Endorses* the letter dated 4 May 1999, and the annex thereto, from the Chairman of the Committee established pursuant to resolution 864(1993), and decides to establish the expert panels referred to therein for a period of six months with the following mandate:

(a) To collect information and investigate reports, including through visits to the countries concerned, relating to the violation of the measures imposed against the União Nacional para a Independência Total de Angola with respect to arms and related materiel, petroleum and petroleum products, diamonds and the movement of funds of the União Nacional para a Independência Total de Angola as specified in the relevant resolutions, as well as information on military assistance, including mercenaries;

(b) To identify parties aiding and abetting the violations of the above-mentioned measures;

(c) To recommend measures to end such violations and to improve the implementation of the above-mentioned measures;

7. *Requests* the Chairman of the Committee established pursuant to resolution 864(1993) to submit to the Council no later than 31 July 1999 an interim report of the expert panels regarding their progress and preliminary findings and recommendations and to submit to the Council within six months of the formation of the expert panels their final report with recommendations;

8. *Calls upon* all States, relevant United Nations bodies and concerned parties, as appropriate, including non-governmental organizations and enterprises, to cooperate in a full and timely manner with the expert panels to facilitate the implementation of their

mandate, including by making available to the expert panels information relating to their mandate;

9. *Calls upon* the Governments of the States concerned in which the expert panels will carry out their mandate to cooperate fully with the expert panels in the fulfilment of their mandate, including responding positively to requests from the expert panels for security, assistance and access in pursuing investigations, including:

(*a*) Adoption by them of any measures needed for the expert panels and their personnel to carry out their functions throughout the respective territories with full freedom, independence, and security;

(*b*) Provision by them to the expert panels or to the Chairman of the Committee established pursuant to resolution 864(1993) of information in their possession which the expert panels request or is otherwise needed to fulfil their mandate;

(*c*) Freedom of access for the expert panels and their personnel to any establishment or place they deem necessary for their work, including border points and airfields;

(*d*) Appropriate measures to guarantee the safety and security of the personnel of the expert panels and guarantees by them of full respect for the integrity, security and freedom of witnesses, experts and any other persons working with the expert panels in the fulfilment of their mandate;

(*e*) Freedom of movement for the personnel of the expert panels, including freedom to interview any person in private, at any time, as appropriate;

(*f*) The grant of relevant privileges and immunities in accordance with the General Convention on the Privileges and Immunities of the United Nations;

10. *Expresses its concern* at the delays in the investigation into the downing on 26 December 1998 and 2 January 1999 of two aircraft chartered by the United Nations and the loss under suspicious circumstances of other commercial aircraft over areas in Angola controlled by the União Nacional para a Independência Total de Angola as well as the crash on 26 June 1998 in Côte d'Ivoire of the aircraft carrying the Special Representative of the Secretary-General to Angola and other United Nations personnel, and reiterates its call upon all concerned to cooperate fully with and to facilitate an immediate and objective international investigation of these incidents;

C

11. *Endorses* the recommendation contained in the annex to the letter dated 4 May 1999 from the Chairman of the Committee established pursuant to resolution 864(1993) that the expert panels should be supported as an expense of the Organization and through a United Nations trust fund established for this purpose, requests the Secretary-General to take the necessary steps towards this end, and urges States to make voluntary contributions to this trust fund;

12. *Reiterates its call* upon all concerned to cooperate with the United Nations humanitarian assistance activities on the basis of the principles of neutrality and non-discrimination, to facilitate the delivery of humanitarian assistance to all those in need throughout the territory of Angola and to guarantee unconditionally the security and freedom of movement of humanitarian personnel;

13. *Expresses its strong support* for further consultations between the Secretary-General and the Government of Angola regarding the follow-up configuration of the United Nations presence in Angola;

14. *Decides* to remain actively seized of the matter.

Reports of Sanctions Committee Chairman. The Chairman of the Sanctions Committee, Robert R. Fowler (Canada), visited Southern and Central Africa, Europe and Algeria in mid-1999 to assess the implementation of the sanctions imposed against UNITA.

In May, the Chairman travelled to Angola, Botswana, the DRC, Namibia, South Africa, Zambia and Zimbabwe to discuss ways to improve the sanctions [S/1999/644]. He described Angola as a country of extraordinary potential wealth, including an anticipated level of petroleum production unequalled in Africa, but a country troubled by an impending humanitarian catastrophe. The number of IDPs in Angola had reached 1.6 million out of a population of some 11 million. Of those, more than 800,000 had been displaced since fighting resumed in December 1998. More than 1 million Angolans had lost their lives in more than 20 years of civil war. In his meetings with heads of State and other high officials in Angola and neighbouring States, the Chairman said widespread concern was expressed at the likelihood of continuing warfare. Those with whom he met expressed willingness to consider practical measures to decrease the revenue available to UNITA, principally from diamond sales, and to increase its costs in acquiring petroleum, armaments and other supplies.

A number of Southern African States were alleged to be involved in the violation of sanctions, but, in most cases, that was believed to be the consequence of private interests acting without the knowledge of their Governments. Countries outside the region, including in particular several in Central and West Africa and Eastern Europe, were also widely rumoured to be implicated in systematic violation of the sanctions. The Chairman made a number of recommendations on ways to determine whether and, if so, how sanctions were being violated, including deploying UN sanctions monitors in the region, requesting Member States with intelligence-gathering capacities to provide information on violations; air surveillance and interdiction of UNITA supply flights; collaboration between the Committee and the Southern African Development Community (SADC) members on sanctions; and collaboration between the Committee and the International Criminal Police Organization (Interpol) on application of sanctions.

Diamond revenues constituted the essential component of UNITA's capacity to wage war, bringing in approximately $200 million in revenue in 1998, according to some reports. Having met with government officials responsible for the diamond industries in Botswana, Namibia and South Africa and representatives of De Beers Consolidated Mines Limited and other companies, the Chairman recommended that the licensed foreign diamond buyers in Angola, the major diamond mining companies active there and the industry councils in the major diamond-cutting centres liaise with the Committee in devising practical measures to limit UNITA's access to legitimate diamond markets. The expert panels should make recommendations on the feasibility of the appointment of expert monitors at the major diamond exchanges, to identify and confiscate UNITA diamonds illegally brought to market. Their objective was not to inflict any collateral damage on the legitimate diamond trade.

With regard to the application of sanctions, the Chairman noted that several Member States in the region had not enacted legislation giving force to the Council's sanctions and he recommended that they do so, making violations a criminal offence with specific legal penalties. He suggested further that the Secretary-General and the President of the Council brief all Member States on the application of the sanctions, to outline the obligation of Member States and advise them on how that obligation might best be acquitted. The Chairman also proposed that the expert panels be empowered to commission background studies by bodies with expertise useful to their work. They should identify "best practices", such as procedural or legal measures, for applying sanctions. Furthermore, the Special Rapporteur of the Commission on Human Rights on the question of the use of mercenaries should be invited to contribute to their work.

Following his visit to Europe and participation in the OAU Council of Ministers meeting (Algiers, Algeria, 9 July), the Chairman, in a July report to the Council [S/1999/829], made further recommendations regarding the sanctions against UNITA. He travelled to Algeria, Belgium, France, Ukraine and the United Kingdom to identify measures to improve the sanctions' effectiveness and to request Member States, companies and individuals to provide the Committee with information on violations. The Chairman recommended that donor States be encouraged to provide financial and material assistance to SADC in support of its efforts to enhance regional capacity for the implementation and monitoring of sanctions. The North Atlantic Treaty Organization (NATO) and the EU were urged to reaffirm their inclusion of compliance with Security Council decisions, including sanctions against UNITA, among criteria for accession by new members. Further recommendations included collaboration between the World Customs Organization and the Committee and its expert panels in the implementation of the sanctions, and the establishment of a working group consisting of Interpol representatives and members of the expert panels. After meeting with representatives of the diamond industry in several countries, the Chairman recommended that interested Member States, including in particular those that exported or imported diamonds, work together to harmonize procedures and documentation for the import and export of rough diamonds, possibly through the World Customs Organization, in consultation with the diamond industry and drawing on any advice of the expert panels.

At the conclusion of both reports, the Chairman affirmed that the Committee and the Council would continue to review UNITA's willingness to engage in political dialogue and calibrate Council-imposed sanctions accordingly.

The Security Council was briefed on 29 July [meeting 4027] by the Chairman of the Committee. The aim of the Sanctions Committee, he said, was to limit UNITA's capacity to wage war by diminishing its revenues derived from the sale of diamonds and to increase the cost of its arms procurement. The Committee's work was premised on the belief that the war could be ended only through political dialogue and it intended to limit the ability of UNITA to pursue the war option. The sanctions invoked against UNITA were focused, as opposed to broad, pervasive, comprehensive sanctions that could cause collateral damage. In applying sanctions, it was necessary to apply triage or prioritization so that the Council's efforts were expended mainly in areas with the fastest return. The responsibility for enforcing sanctions was that of individual Member States, whether through legislation, regulation or decree.

Expert panel meetings. By a 30 July letter and later addendum [S/1999/837 & Add.1], the Chairman transmitted to the Council a list of 10 experts appointed to the expert panels established by resolution 1237(1999). In order to facilitate the sharing of information and expertise, it was decided that the two original panels (one dealing with arms and the other with UNITA resources) would as a practical matter function as one panel. The panel met on 26 and 27 August in New York and on 24 and 25 September in Geneva and issued an interim report on 30 September [S/1999/1016]. The members agreed on a plan of work and considered how best to prioritize their work within the five categories established by the Council, namely, diamonds, finances, petroleum products, representation and travel, and weapons. The panel decided to establish a base in southern Africa and arrangements for the office were expected to be completed by October. The panel agreed to establish an information database and a web site and to undertake visits to a number of countries.

1999 activities

Summarizing the Sanctions Committee's activities during the year [S/2000/83], the Chairman remarked that public awareness of the sanctions increased substantially in 1999 and the effectiveness of the measures appeared to have been enhanced. The work of the expert panel in identifying the sources and methods of violations of the sanctions and in offering practical recommendations for further action could render them still more effective and thus further impair the ability of UNITA to pursue its objectives through military means.

Communications. Ukraine, in a 17 August press statement [S/1999/900], stated that it had repeatedly denied as groundless the allegations implicating Ukraine in violations of Council sanctions, including those against UNITA. Ukraine remained concerned that such allegations still occasionally appeared in the media. In that regard, the Chairman of the Sanctions Committee, during his visit to Europe in July (see p. 114), had discussed the allegations [S/1999/829], and senior officials said they were without foundation. The authorities of Ukraine offered to submit to the Committee information on the results of their investigations into specific alleged violations of the sanctions against UNITA [S/2000/83]. That information was subsequently provided to the Chairman.

The Chairman forwarded to the Council communications dealing with action taken by the diamond industry in regard to sanctions—a letter from the Managing Director of De Beers Consolidated Mines Limited [S/1999/1048] and a press release issued by the International Diamond Manufacturers Association in Antwerp, Belgium [S/1999/1163].

The Managing Director, Gary Ralfe, said that De Beers had never bought diamonds from UNITA and, since the promulgation of resolution 1173(1998), it had not bought Angolan diamonds without the requisite certificate of origin. The company had decided to take additional action: to suspend buying anywhere in the world any parcels of Angolan diamonds, with one exception where it had a contractual arrangement; to withdraw from the Codiam joint venture in Angola and thereby have no further interest in diamond buying offices in Angola; and to review its other buying operations in Central and West Africa, namely the DRC and Guinea, with a view to withdrawal. De Beers issued a press release on 5 October on its decision, which was motivated by its concern for the situation in Angola.

The International Diamond Manufacturers Association affirmed its readiness to work with the United Nations to achieve greater compliance with sanctions. It was also working within the diamond community to ensure zero tolerance in respect of any violation of the sanctions.

Financing of UN missions in Angola

In April [A/53/908], the Secretary-General presented the financial performance report of MONUA for the period from 1 July 1997 to 30 June 1998. Expenditures for the period totalled $170,428,100 gross ($166,466,100 net), as compared with an appropriation of $175,000,000 gross ($170,741,200 net), resulting in an unencumbered balance of $4,571,900 gross ($4,275,100 net), attributable primarily to reduced requirements under civilian personnel, premises/accommodation, transport and air operations, other equipment and air and surface freight, which were offset in part by additional requirements under communications, supplies and services and the absorption of the cost of the financing of the United Nations Logistics Base in Brindisi, Italy.

The financing of MONUA was also the subject of a May report [A/53/937] containing the proposed budget for 1 July 1999 to 30 June 2000, amounting to $7,000,000 gross ($6,642,300 net). The proposed budget would cover the liquidation of the mission for the 12-month period. The estimated requirements were $122,875,600 less than the approved budget of $130,431,600 gross for the period 1 July 1998 to 30 June 1999.

Commenting on the MONUA financial reports in May [A/53/957], ACABQ considered that the overall monitoring of expenditures for the Mission had been weak. It noted the similar findings of the Board of Auditors in its 1998 report on UN peacekeeping operations and of the Office of Internal Oversight Services (OIOS) on the audits of the procurement process at the United Nations Angola Verification Mission (UNAVEM) [YUN 1998, p. 123], which became MONUA in 1997 [YUN 1997, p. 104]. In regard to the unencumbered balance, ACABQ recommended that it be applied to the next budget period, from 1 July 1999 to 30 June 2000. ACABQ recommended that the General Assembly appropriate $7,000,000 gross

($6,642,300 net) for 1 July 1999 to 30 June 2000 and that it take into account the unencumbered balance of $4,571,900 gross ($4,275,100 net) from the MONUA budget and the unencumbered balance of $149,720 gross ($49,625 net) in respect of UNAVEM and UNAVEM II mentioned in the Secretary-General's May report.

GENERAL ASSEMBLY ACTION

On 8 June [meeting 101], the General Assembly, on the recommendation of the Fifth Committee [A/53/745/Add.1], adopted **resolution 53/228** without vote [agenda item 123].

Financing of the United Nations Angola Verification Mission and the United Nations Observer Mission in Angola

The General Assembly,

Having considered the reports of the Secretary-General on the financing of the United Nations Observer Mission in Angola and the related report of the Advisory Committee on Administrative and Budgetary Questions,

Bearing in mind Security Council resolutions 626(1988) of 20 December 1988, by which the Council established the United Nations Angola Verification Mission, 696(1991) of 30 May 1991, by which the Council decided to entrust a new mandate to the United Nations Angola Verification Mission (thenceforth called the United Nations Angola Verification Mission II), 976(1995) of 8 February 1995, by which the Council authorized the establishment of a peacekeeping operation (thenceforth called the United Nations Angola Verification Mission III), 1118(1997) of 30 June 1997, by which the Council decided to establish, as from 1 July 1997, the United Nations Observer Mission in Angola, and its subsequent resolutions, the latest of which was resolution 1229(1999) of 26 February 1999,

Recalling its resolution 43/231 of 16 February 1989 on the financing of the Verification Mission and its subsequent resolutions and decisions thereon, and resolution 53/211 of 18 December 1998 on the financing of the Observer Mission,

Reaffirming that the costs of the Observer Mission are expenses of the Organization to be borne by Member States in accordance with Article 17, paragraph 2, of the Charter of the United Nations,

Recalling its previous decisions regarding the fact that, in order to meet the expenditures caused by the Observer Mission, a different procedure is required from that applied to meet expenditures of the regular budget of the United Nations,

Taking into account the fact that the economically more developed countries are in a position to make relatively larger contributions and that the economically less developed countries have a relatively limited capacity to contribute towards such an operation,

Bearing in mind the special responsibilities of the States permanent members of the Security Council, as indicated in General Assembly resolution 1874(S-IV) of 27 June 1963, in the financing of such operations,

Noting with appreciation that voluntary contributions have been made to the Observer Mission,

Mindful of the fact that it is essential to provide the Observer Mission with the necessary financial resources to enable it to fulfil its responsibilities under the relevant resolutions of the Security Council,

1. *Takes note* of the status of contributions to the United Nations Angola Verification Mission and the United Nations Observer Mission in Angola as at 30 April 1999, including the contributions outstanding in the amount of 144.9 million United States dollars, representing 12 per cent of the total assessed contributions from the inception of the Verification Mission to the period ending 30 June 1997 and from the inception of the Observer Mission to the period ending 30 June 1999, notes that some 6 per cent of the Member States have paid their assessed contributions in full, and urges all other Member States concerned, in particular those in arrears, to ensure payment of their outstanding assessed contributions;

2. *Expresses concern* about the financial situation with regard to peacekeeping activities, in particular as regards the reimbursement of troop contributors, which bear additional burdens owing to overdue payments by Member States of their assessments;

3. *Expresses its appreciation* to those Member States which have paid their assessed contributions in full;

4. *Urges* all other Member States to make every possible effort to ensure payment of their assessed contributions to the Verification Mission and the Observer Mission in full and on time;

5. *Endorses* the observations and recommendations contained in the report of the Advisory Committee on Administrative and Budgetary Questions;

6. *Requests* the Secretary-General to take all necessary action to ensure that the liquidation of the Observer Mission is administered with a maximum of efficiency and economy;

7. *Expresses concern* that the Secretary-General did not submit a report before the second part of the resumed fifty-third session of the General Assembly on the status of implementation of measures taken or initiated to address appropriately the issues, observations and recommendations contained in the report of the Office of Internal Oversight Services and other related actions taken by the Observer Mission and the Secretariat, as requested in paragraph 9 of Assembly resolution 52/8 C of 26 June 1998 and in paragraph 8 of its resolution 53/211, and requests the Secretary-General to submit that report no later than 30 June 1999;

8. *Decides* to appropriate to the Special Account for the United Nations Observer Mission in Angola the amount of 7,441,540 dollars gross (7,083,840 dollars net) for the liquidation of the Observer Mission for the period from 1 July 1999 to 30 June 2000, inclusive of the amount of 369,153 dollars for the support account for peacekeeping operations and the amount of 72,387 dollars for the United Nations Logistics Base at Brindisi, Italy, to be apportioned, as an ad hoc arrangement, among Member States in accordance with the composition of groups set out in paragraphs 3 and 4 of its resolution 43/232 of 1 March 1989, as adjusted by the General Assembly in its resolutions 44/192 B of 21 December 1989, 45/269 of 27 August 1991, 46/198 A of 20 December 1991, 47/218 A of 23 December 1992, 49/249 A of 20 July 1995, 49/249 B of 14 September 1995, 50/224 of 11 April 1996, 51/218 A to C of 18 December 1996 and 52/230 of 31 March 1998 and its deci-

sions 48/472 A of 23 December 1993 and 50/451 B of 23 December 1995, and taking into account the scale of assessments for the years 1999 and 2000, as set out in its resolution 52/215 A of 22 December 1997;

9. *Decides also* that, in accordance with the provisions of its resolution 973(X) of 15 December 1955, there shall be set off against the apportionment among Member States, as provided for in paragraph 8 above, their respective share in the Tax Equalization Fund of the estimated staff assessment income of 357,700 dollars approved for the period from 1 July 1999 to 30 June 2000;

10. *Decides further* that, for Member States that have fulfilled their financial obligations to the Verification Mission and the Observer Mission, there shall be set off against their apportionment, as provided for in paragraph 8 above, their respective share of the unencumbered balance of 149,720 dollars gross (49,625 dollars net) in respect of the period from 3 January 1989 to 30 September 1994;

11. *Decides* that, for Member States that have not fulfilled their financial obligations to the Verification Mission and the Observer Mission, their share of the unencumbered balance of 149,720 dollars gross (49,625 dollars net) in respect of the period from 3 January 1989 to 30 September 1994 shall be set off against their outstanding obligations;

12. *Decides also* that, for Member States that have fulfilled their financial obligations to the Verification Mission and the Observer Mission, there shall be set off against their apportionment, as provided for in paragraph 8 above, their respective share of the unencumbered balance of 4,571,900 dollars gross (4,275,100 dollars net) in respect of the period from 1 July 1997 to 30 June 1998;

13. *Decides further* that, for Member States that have not fulfilled their financial obligations to the Verification Mission and the Observer Mission, their share of the unencumbered balance of 4,571,900 dollars gross (4,275,100 dollars net) in respect of the period from 1 July 1997 to 30 June 1998 shall be set off against their outstanding obligations;

14. *Invites* voluntary contributions to the Observer Mission in cash and in the form of services and supplies acceptable to the Secretary-General, to be administered, as appropriate, in accordance with the procedure and practices established by the General Assembly;

15. *Decides* to include in the provisional agenda of its fifty-fourth session the item entitled "Financing of the United Nations Angola Verification Mission and the United Nations Observer Mission in Angola".

Procurement procedures

The Secretary-General, in a June report [A/53/1018] submitted in response to General Assembly resolutions 52/8 C [YUN 1998, p. 123] and 53/211 [ibid., p. 125], commented on measures taken by the United Nations to address the issues, observations and recommendations contained in a 1998 OIOS report on audits of the procurement process in UNAVEM [ibid., p. 123].

The Secretary-General concurred with the OIOS findings that there were serious management deficiencies and apparent breaches of financial regulations and rules, as well as improprieties and irregularities in the procurement process, which in some cases resulted in significant losses to the Organization and might have fostered fraud and financial abuse. Nevertheless, no evidence of fraud or financial abuse had been established in the ensuing investigations. As a result of the investigations, the procurement section of the Mission was reorganized and personnel replaced and all peacekeeping missions were given guidance on reviewing requisitions. The Procurement Manual was updated and made available to the field missions on the Internet. More training of procurement officers was offered, with emphasis on the need to strengthen internal controls over the procurement and finance processes in the field.

GENERAL ASSEMBLY ACTION

On 29 October [meeting 43], the General Assembly, on the recommendation of the Fifth Committee [A/54/504], adopted **resolution 54/17 A** without vote [agenda item 129].

Financing of the United Nations Angola Verification Mission and the United Nations Observer Mission in Angola

The General Assembly,

Recalling its resolutions 52/8 A of 31 October 1997, 52/8 C of 26 June 1998, 53/211 of 18 December 1998 and 53/228 of 8 June 1999,

Regretting the delay in the submission of the report of the Secretary-General requested in the aforementioned resolutions,

1. *Takes note* of the report of the Secretary-General on the findings, observations and recommendations contained in the report of the Office of Internal Oversight Services on the audits of the procurement process in the United Nations Angola Verification Mission;

2. *Notes with concern* that one of the recommendations of the Office of Internal Oversight Services was based on incomplete information provided to the Office;

3. *Requests* the Secretary-General to continue to examine carefully the internal audit recommendations before taking remedial action;

4. *Expresses concern* over the lack of a consistent policy for the implementation of audit recommendations in respect of cases of fraud and financial abuse;

5. *Requests* the Secretary-General to ensure that audit recommendations in respect of cases of fraud and financial abuse are implemented in a consistent manner throughout the Secretariat;

6. *Calls* for further efforts to provide proper training and guidance to procurement officers in the field, especially in view of the expansion of United Nations peacekeeping activities;

7. *Looks forward* to the report of the Secretary-General on the procurement of goods for quartering areas of the United Nations Angola Verification Mission;

8. *Calls upon* the Secretary-General to provide additional information on the measures being taken by the

Secretariat further to improve procurement activities in the field and to enhance control and accountability, within the context of the report on management irregularities causing financial losses to the Organization, as requested by the General Assembly in its resolution 53/225 of 8 June 1999, and requests the Secretary-General to submit a report to the General Assembly, prior to the second part of its resumed fifty-fourth session, providing a concrete plan to correct procurement-related problems in peacekeeping operations, which should include the following:

(a) All remedial measures taken to address problems identified with regard to the United Nations Observer Mission in Angola and other peacekeeping operations;

(b) Standardization of the corrective measures that have already been taken for all existing and future peacekeeping operations;

(c) A description of how accountability was pursued in the cases of individuals who were found to have engaged in fraud, mismanagement or abuse, and how accountability measures will be applied in the future.

The Assembly, on 23 December, decided that the Fifth Committee should continue its consideration of the agenda item on the financing of UNAVEM and MONUA at the Assembly's resumed fifty-fourth session in 2000 (**decision 54/462 A**).

By **decision 54/465** of the same date, the Assembly decided that the agenda item would remain for consideration during its fifty-fourth session.

OIOS report. In November [A/54/548], OIOS issued a report on the investigation into the procurement of quartering area goods in UNAVEM. A $6.9 million contract was awarded to a local trading company, based on a four-week delivery schedule. The award was part of a tender exercise conducted in May 1995, in which six other vendors were also awarded smaller contracts. The investigation determined that planning for the tender exercise was inadequate, and that the procurement processes of the Mission were flawed. In addition, the local trading company failed repeatedly to meet crucial deadlines, objected to provisions that would hold it accountable, and provided goods, most notably tents, that failed to meet specifications and required additional material and work to make them usable. The quartering area project was a critical component of the peace process under the Lusaka Protocol, which called for the establishment of quartering areas in Angola for the purpose of demobilization of combatants. Problems encountered were a lack of a budget for eight months after the signing of the Protocol, limited planning, non-implementation of recommendations of the Headquarters Committee on Contracts, deficiencies in the invitation to bid and the selection process, and the delayed decision over whether the procurement would be at UN Headquarters or at the Mission site. Despite delays, the demobilization did occur through the efforts of Mission staff. The evidence did not support a finding that Mission staff personally benefited or sought to wilfully mislead UN Headquarters, or that there was actual financial loss.

In the light of its findings, OIOS made the following recommendations, with which the Secretary-General concurred: (1) when exigent procurement was required, such procurement action could and should be initiated, even in the absence of budgetary provision, to an extent just short of that which financially obligated the Organization; (2) institutionally sanctioned mechanisms should be developed to avoid procurement problems, including special procedures for procurement under emergency situations; (3) the Office of Legal Affairs should review the UNAVEM case to determine if the local trading company or others managed by its directors should be precluded from conducting business with the United Nations; and (4) legal advisers in missions should be consulted for complicated and expensive procurement action.

Central African Republic

During 1999, the United Nations Mission in the Central African Republic (MINURCA) made a significant contribution towards restoring and consolidating peace in the country. Progress towards implementing the 1997 Bangui Agreements [YUN 1997, p. 91] was achieved with the holding of the presidential elections in September. In January, President Ange-Félix Patassé requested the extension of MINURCA until after the presidential elections. On the recommendation of the Secretary-General, the Security Council extended MINURCA's mandate in February and again in October until 15 February 2000.

Various aspects of the situation in the Central African Republic complicated the transition to post-conflict peace-building, including the tense political climate, challenges regarding the results of the presidential elections, accusations of acquisition of weapons and recruitment of militias by political leaders, the condition of the military, which was still capable of destabilizing the political and security environment, the need for economic and social reform, and the security situation in the region. The Secretary-General, in October, recommended a short but gradual transition from UN peacekeeping involvement to post-conflict peace-building. During the transition period, MINURCA would continue to discharge its security functions in Bangui, which it would gradually hand over to local security and law enforcement forces. At the end of the year, the Secretary-General proposed the establishment of the United Nations Peace-Building Support Office in the Central African Republic. That small political office would be established after the end of the political presence of MINURCA on 15 February 2000 with an initial duration of one year.

Political situation and MINURCA

Throughout 1999, the Secretary-General reported regularly to the Security Council on the activities of MINURCA and on the political situation in the country. Established by Council resolution 1159(1998) [YUN 1998, p. 134], MINURCA took over the functions of the Inter-African Mission to Monitor the Implementation of the Bangui Agreements (MISAB). The 1997 Bangui Agreements [YUN 1997, p. 91] aimed to bring about a comprehensive settlement of a crisis in the Central African Republic, which stemmed from an army rebellion that broke out in 1996, resulting in a large supply of weapons remaining in the hands of the ex-rebels and the militia.

Report of Secretary-General (January). In his fourth (29 January) report on MINURCA [S/1999/98], the Secretary-General described developments in the Central African Republic since his third report [YUN 1998, p. 140]. With regard to the legislative elections held on 22 November and 13 December 1998, he stated that the Mouvance présidentielle had won 54 seats, while the coalition of opposition parties won 55. However, following the formal proclamation of the results by the Constitutional Court, one opposition legislator announced his support for the Mouvance présidentielle, which then claimed a majority in the Assembly and the right to the presidency and other key positions. In response to that development, the opposition parties walked out of the Assembly shortly after it convened on 4 January 1999. Roadblocks and barricades were set up in parts of Bangui, and MINURCA was placed on alert and increased its patrols until calm was restored. Despite intensive consultations with the parties conducted by the Secretary-General's Special Representative, Oluyemi Adeniji, the impasse persisted. In the meantime, President Patassé had nominated a Prime Minister and the Assembly had elected its President. Although the President initially announced the creation of a Government comprising 23 members, including four from the opposition, three of the opposition members had left the Government and were replaced by persons chosen by the President.

With regard to economic and financial reforms, the Secretary-General noted that the Government has not been able to meet a number of important obligations, including the regular payment of salaries, pensions and student bourses; the privatization of public enterprises, including the oil company PETROCA; and the maintenance of government revenues at an acceptable level. As a result, the International Monetary Fund (IMF) was not in a position to recommend the release of the second allocation of 6 billion CFA francs under the enhanced structural adjustment facility agreement.

In his third report to the Council, the Secretary-General had invited the Council to consider extending MINURCA's mandate until the presidential elections scheduled for the latter half of 1999. In order to address certain concerns raised by Council members and to assess more closely the situation on the ground, the Secretary-General sent Hédi Annabi, Assistant Secretary-General for Peacekeeping Operations, as his Personal Envoy to the Central African Republic from 19 to 23 January 1999. Mr. Annabi was asked to make the following points to the Government: the impasse regarding the composition of the Bureau of the National Assembly should be resolved in a manner consistent with the Bangui Agreements; every effort should be made to implement the remaining provisions of those Agreements by moving forward with the restructuring of the armed forces; the Government should comply with the provision of its agreements with the international financial institutions, ensuring the regular payment of salaries and other commitments; and the country should on no account allow itself to be drawn into the conflict in the neighbouring DRC. Mr. Annabi made it clear to his interlocutors in the Central African Republic that the Council's response to the Secretary-General's proposal to extend MINURCA's mandate until the presidential elections would depend on concrete action to address those concerns. The President and other senior officials, stressing that they strongly supported MINURCA's continued presence, stated that the Government had tried to reach agreement with the opposition parties on the formation of a government; the restructuring of the armed forces was highly desirable but lack of funds had made it difficult to achieve; the Prime Minister would ensure that the Government met the obligations incumbent upon it with regard to the international financial institutions; and the Government had no intention of becoming involved in the Congolese conflict.

Annexed to the Secretary-General's report was a 23 January letter from President Patassé, in which he made a number of commitments in line with the concerns expressed by the Personal Envoy and the international financial institutions.

The Secretary-General observed that MINURCA remained a source of much-needed stability, both in the Central African Republic and in the subregion as a whole. He therefore remained convinced that MINURCA should stay in the Central African Republic until the presidential elections and indeed assist the Government in preparing and establishing a secure environment for those elections and monitor and verify their conduct. To that end, MINURCA's military component should be retained at its current strength of 1,350 military personnel and 25 civilian police advisers, supported by 179 international and local staff. The Secretary-General suggested that the Council decide on an initial extension for six months, until 31 August, subject to a further determination that the Government had made acceptable progress in carrying out the reforms outlined in President Patassé's letter.

Communications. The Secretary-General transmitted to the Security Council a letter of 8 December 1998 from the President of the Central African Republic requesting the extension of the MINURCA mandate until the presidential elections [S/1999/116].

On 4 February [S/1999/121], he transmitted a letter from James D. Wolfensohn, President of the World Bank, in which he provided an assessment of the prospects of the Central African Republic's financial consolidation and economic reform programme being implemented with the Bretton Woods institutions and the link between the programme and the peacekeeping arrangements. He noted that security had improved, the first round of legislative elections had passed peacefully and the economic situation had stabilized. Should MINURCA forces withdraw, however, the prospects for continued economic improvement and security would weaken, especially when the task of restructuring the armed forces remained incomplete. He stated that the premature withdrawal of international support in any of the key areas could easily undermine and even reverse the fragile progress made so far. He asked the Secretary-General to consider those factors when preparing his recommendations to the Security Council.

In a 9 February letter [S/1999/132], the President of the Central African Republic requested the Council to extend MINURCA's mandate until the presidential elections. He described the state of the Government at the executive, jurisdictional and judicial and legislative levels. Enclosed with the letter were a press release on the National Assembly special session, held from 4 to 18 January, a list of parliamentary committees and their membership and a note on the progress of the structural adjustment programme.

SECURITY COUNCIL ACTION (18 February)

On 18 February [meeting 3979], the Security Council, following consultations among its members, authorized the President to make statement **S/PRST/1999/7** on its behalf:

The Security Council, noting the letter dated 9 February 1999 from the President of the Central African Republic to the President of the Council, notes with satisfaction the commitment expressed by the President of the Central African Republic to maintain peace in the Central African Republic through dialogue and consultation. In this context, it strongly reaffirms that the complete implementation of the Bangui Agreements and of the National Reconciliation Pact is essential to peace and national reconciliation in the Central African Republic.

The Council calls upon the Government of the Central African Republic to continue to take concrete steps to implement political, economic, social and security reforms as referred to in the report of the Secretary-General of 23 February 1998 and to fulfil the commitments expressed in the letters dated 8 January 1998 and of 23 January 1999 from the President of the Central African Republic to the Secretary-General. It recalls that the success, the future mandate and the ongoing presence of the United Nations Mission in the Central African Republic are closely linked to the fulfilment of these commitments, in particular the immediate resumption of a constructive political dialogue.

The Council expresses its concern about the consequences that the current political tensions have for the stability and the functioning of the institutions of the Central African Republic. It reaffirms that the Government, the political leaders and the people of the Central African Republic bear the primary responsibility for national reconciliation, the maintenance of a stable and secure environment and the reconstruction of their country. It emphasizes the importance of continuing efforts in the Central African Republic to settle outstanding contentious issues peacefully and democratically in accordance with the Bangui Agreements. It stresses the need for both the "mouvance présidentielle" and the opposition parties to cooperate closely and work actively with the aim of achieving the political consensus indispensable to stability in the Central African Republic.

The Council considers that a smooth preparation of free and fair presidential elections, for which proper steps should be taken as soon as possible, requires a certain level of political consensus and the opening of a genuine dialogue between all the constituent parties of the National Assembly. It also considers that consensual preparation for the presidential elections can only reinforce the legitimacy of the next President of the Republic and also secure a sustainable civil peace. It fully supports the Special Representative of the Secretary-General in his call to the Central African political leaders and authorities to resolve the political impasse so the country can move forward, and welcomes the current efforts undertaken to this end.

The Council will remain seized of the matter.

Communication. By a 24 February letter [S/1999/200], the Central African Republic transmitted to the Security Council a press release issued the day before by the National Political Council of the Mouvement de libération du peuple centrafricain, in which it stated its willingness to work with the opposition to ease the political tensions. It appealed to the opposition deputies to return to the hall of the National Assembly and to the Security Council to renew the mandate of MINURCA so that it could supervise the presidential elections.

Extension of Mission (February)

On 26 February [meeting 3984], the Security Council unanimously adopted **resolution 1230 (1999)**. The draft text [S/1999/122] was submitted by Canada, Côte d'Ivoire, Egypt, France, Gabon, Japan, Kenya, Senegal, Togo and the United States.

The Security Council,

Reaffirming its resolutions 1125(1997) of 6 August 1997, 1136(1997) of 6 November 1997, 1152(1998) of 5 February 1998, 1155(1998) of 16 March 1998, 1159(1998) of 27 March 1998, 1182(1998) of 14 July 1998 and 1201(1998) of 15 October 1998,

Welcoming the holding of free and fair legislative elections on 22 November and 13 December 1998,

Welcoming also the report of the Secretary-General of 18 December 1998 and the addendum thereto, of 14 January 1999, and the report of the Secretary-General of 29 January 1999, and taking note of the recommendations contained therein,

Taking note of the request of 8 December 1998 from the President of the Central African Republic to the Secretary-General, and the letter dated 23 January 1999 from the President of the Central African Republic to the Secretary-General,

Reiterating the importance of the work done by the joint committee of the Government of the Central African Republic and the United Nations Mission in the Central African Republic to address the restructuring of the Central African Armed Forces, and stressing the necessity quickly to adopt the draft law and decrees on national defence and the structure of the defence forces,

Reaffirming the link between socio-economic progress and the consolidation of peace in the Central African Republic, and in that context taking note of the letter dated 23 December 1998 from the President of the World Bank to the Secretary-General,

Recalling the importance of regional stability and the need to consolidate the progress achieved so far, and in particular to assist the people of the Central African Republic to consolidate the process of national reconciliation taking into account the need to maintain a secure and stable environment conducive to economic recovery and to the holding of free and fair presidential elections,

Stressing the importance of cooperation and understanding by the Government of the Central African Republic, the newly elected legislators and the political groupings, so as to ensure the effective functioning of the National Assembly,

Emphasizing the need for the Government of the Central African Republic to set the presidential election dates as soon as possible, in accordance with article 23 of the Constitution of the Central African Republic,

1. *Decides* to extend the mandate of the United Nations Mission in the Central African Republic until 15 November 1999;

2. *Expresses its intention* to commence the reduction of Mission personnel fifteen days after the conclusion of the presidential elections in the Central African Republic, with a view to full termination of the Mission no later than 15 November 1999;

3. *Decides* to review every forty-five days, on the basis of reports of the Secretary-General, the mandate of the Mission in the light of the progress achieved towards implementation of the commitments made by the President of the Central African Republic to the Secretary-General in his letter dated 23 January 1999;

4. *Welcomes* the intention of the Secretary-General to discuss with the President of the Central African Republic plans for a possible progressive reduction of the military component and in anticipation of the 15 November 1999 termination date of the Mission, commensurate with the advances in the restructuring of the Central African Armed Forces of the Mission taking into account the need to ensure the stability and security of Bangui;

5. *Urges* the international community to lend its support to the restructuring of the security forces of the Central African Republic, including the gendarmerie, through bilateral and multilateral assistance programmes, and reaffirms the role of the Mission in providing advice in the restructuring of the security forces and, in this connection, in coordinating and channelling international support to this end;

6. *Strongly reaffirms* that the complete implementation of the Bangui Agreements and of the National Reconciliation Pact is essential to peace and national reconciliation in the Central African Republic, and urges the Government of the Central African Republic to continue to take concrete steps to implement political, economic, social and security reforms as referred to in the report of the Secretary-General of 23 February 1998 and to fulfil the commitments expressed in the letter dated 8 January 1998 from the President of the Central African Republic to the Secretary-General and in the letter dated 23 January 1999 from the President of the Central African Republic to the Secretary-General;

7. *Calls upon* all parties in the Central African Republic, with the assistance of the Special Representative of the Secretary-General, to take the necessary measures to resolve the current political impasse, with a view to enhancing the national reconciliation process;

8. *Calls upon* the Government of the Central African Republic to establish the new electoral commission as soon as possible in order to organize the presidential

elections, and to establish and adhere to a timetable for the holding of those elections;

9. *Authorizes* the Mission to play a supportive role in the conduct of the presidential elections, in conformity with the tasks previously performed during the legislative elections of 22 November and 13 December 1998, recognizing the major responsibility that the United Nations Development Programme will have in the co-ordination of electoral assistance;

10. *Also authorizes* the Mission to supervise the destruction of confiscated weapons and ammunition under its control, as recommended in paragraph 29 of the report of the Secretary-General of 18 December 1998;

11. *Encourages* an increased role for an increased number of troops of the Central African Armed Forces to support the presidential elections process, to include the deployment of the Central African Armed Forces troops to electoral sites to assist the Mission personnel in the provision of security and logistical support, and notes in this exceptional case that those troops of the Central African Armed Forces assisting the Mission in this context would operate during that time under United Nations rules of engagement;

12. *Welcomes* the commitments made by the President of the Central African Republic in his letter to the Secretary-General dated 23 January 1999, and urges the Government of the Central African Republic to fulfil these commitments, in particular:

(*a*) To expedite the legislative process regarding national defence and the structure of defence forces with a view to adopting draft laws and decrees as prepared by the joint committee of the Government of the Central African Republic and the Mission, by 15 April 1999;

(*b*) To take steps to limit the mission of the Special Force for the Defence of the Republican Institutions to the protection of the republican institutions and of high-level authorities, excluding all police and maintenance of law and order tasks;

(*c*) To continue to implement with the support of the Mission the demobilization and reintegration programme funded by the United Nations Development Programme;

(*d*) To establish no later than 1 April 1999 an implementation programme in accordance with the timetable established by the joint committee of the Government of the Central African Republic and the Mission which should specify the key elements of the restructuring programme of the Central African Armed Forces to be implemented, among them the need to create well-balanced geographical and multi-ethnic recruitment, the improvement of working conditions, including payment of salary and salary arrears, the provision of adequate infrastructure, equipment and support materials, and the redeployment of some of the restructured units outside Bangui;

13. *Urges* the Government of the Central African Republic to meet the requirements of the financial consolidation and economic reform programmes agreed upon with the international financial institutions;

14. *Requests* the Government of the Central African Republic to refrain from any involvement in external conflicts, in conformity with the commitment expressed in the letter dated 23 January 1999 from the President of the Central African Republic to the Secretary-General;

15. *Urges* Member States to support financially and materially the restructuring programme of the Central African Armed Forces so as to facilitate its prompt implementation, and expresses its appreciation to those that have already done so;

16. *Emphasizes* that economic rehabilitation and reconstruction constitute important tasks facing the Government and people of the Central African Republic and that significant international assistance is indispensable for sustainable development in the Central African Republic, stresses the commitment of the international community to a long-term programme of support for the Central African Republic, and further urges the Economic and Social Council, the United Nations Development Programme, the International Monetary Fund, the World Bank and the appropriate regional financial institutions to contribute to the designing of such a programme;

17. *Requests* the Secretary-General to consider, in keeping with the statement of its President of 29 December 1998, what role the United Nations might play in the transition from peacekeeping to post-conflict peace-building in the Central African Republic, and further requests him, in consultation with the Government of the Central African Republic, to submit recommendations in this regard, by 31 May 1999 on a possible United Nations presence in the Central African Republic after the 15 November 1999 termination of the Mission;

18. *Also requests* the Secretary-General to submit by 15 April 1999 and every forty-five days thereafter a report on the implementation of the mandate of the Mission, on developments in the Central African Republic, in particular on the election process, on progress towards the implementation of the commitments expressed in the letters dated 8 January 1998 and of 23 January 1999 from the President of the Central African Republic to the Secretary-General and on the implementation of the Bangui Agreements and the National Reconciliation Pact, including on commitments related to ensuring the country's economic recovery, the restructuring of the security forces and the functioning of the Special Force for the Defence of the Republican Institutions;

19. *Commends* the efforts of the Special Representative of the Secretary-General and the personnel of the Mission to promote peace and national reconciliation in the Central African Republic;

20. *Recalls* the urgent need for Member States to contribute voluntarily to the trust fund established by the Secretary-General to support the activities of the Mission;

21. *Decides* to remain actively seized of the matter.

Report of Secretary-General (April). In response to Security Council resolution 1230 (1999), the Secretary-General, on 14 April, submitted his fifth report on MINURCA and on developments in the Central African Republic [S/1999/416]. He stated that the opposition legislators had returned to the National Assembly on 2 March and their participation in the Assembly's seven standing commissions had helped to reduce tensions somewhat. Since then, the opposition had actively participated in elaborating several draft laws fundamental to the reform process. However, although some of the reforms the Government had pledged to make were being carried out, progress was slow.

Some of the reforms outlined in his report of 29 January that had been partially achieved were: the participation of the opposition in the National Assembly; the submission for adoption by the Assembly of draft laws on the restructuring of the armed forces; and some progress towards privatization. He urged further action to bring those issues to a satisfactory conclusion, especially the early adoption and speedy implementation of the draft laws on restructuring and the conclusion of the nationalization process in respect of the State oil company.

In response to the request made by the Council in its resolution 1230(1999), the Secretary-General noted the withdrawal of units of the presidential guard (Special Defence Force of the Republican Institutions (FORSDIR)) from road-block duties. However, complaints of their transgressions were still being received. He called on the Government to ensure the exclusion of FORSDIR from all police and law-and-order functions, which should be performed by the police. The latter were receiving human rights and other training from the civilian police component of MINURCA. MINURCA would also accelerate the selection of suitable personnel from the Central African armed forces and their training for election-related duties.

Some progress was made with respect to the presidential elections scheduled for August/September. The streamlined membership of the Mixed and Independent Electoral Commission (CEMI) was a positive development. However, the late start in inaugurating the new CEMI delayed decisions on funding, revision of the electoral register and practical and logistical preparations. The Secretary-General stated that there was urgent need for the Government and CEMI to advance their electoral plans as soon as possible, while ensuring full transparency. Objections had been expressed by the opposition concerning local control of CEMI by sous-préfets, who were considered loyal to the President.

In the economic sphere, the Secretary-General noted the steps taken towards the privatization of some State-run enterprises, the reorganization of the Finance Ministry, the restructuring of the banking sector and the efforts being made to improve the Government's revenue position in order to ensure the timely payment of wages and debt servicing. The World Bank and IMF would continue to monitor progress made and, pending the fulfilment of several conditions, would continue to offer support for economic programmes.

Report of Secretary-General (May). On 28 May, the Secretary-General submitted his sixth report [S/1999/621], pursuant to the Security Council's request in resolution 1230(1999) to review every 45 days MINURCA's mandate in the light of progress achieved towards implementation of commitments made by the President of the Central African Republic in his 23 January letter [S/1999/98].

Despite the impasse over the distribution of posts in its Bureau, the National Assembly had been functioning normally since the Secretary-General's April report and had taken action on the modification of the electoral code and the reform of the armed forces and the economy.

The political activity focused on the establishment, functioning and membership of CEMI, the inauguration of which had been seriously delayed as a result of a series of disagreements between the Mouvance présidentielle and the opposition. CEMI comprised 27 members, including 9 members each from the Mouvance présidentielle and the opposition, with other members representing government ministries and independents. Following objections by the opposition concerning the President's decision to entrust CEMI's administration in the provinces to the sous-préfets and interventions by MINURCA and the donor community in that regard, the President issued a decree establishing a control mechanism designed to ensure the impartial functioning of CEMI.

With regard to a UN presence in the Central African Republic following the withdrawal of MINURCA, the Secretary-General recommended, in general terms and subject to the results of the presidential election, the establishment of a small political office in Bangui to continue the work of post-conflict peace-building. The Secretary-General felt that it was premature to submit detailed recommendations but suggested that the possible functions of such an office could include: facilitating continued dialogue and reconciliation; supporting the strengthening of the democratization process; and mobilizing support for economic, social and security reforms.

With regard to the UN role in the presidential elections, the Secretary-General described plans made by MINURCA, including the re-establishment of its electoral unit with a staff of three. The Mission expected to establish eight permanent observation sites and two temporary sites throughout the country as bases for monitoring activities. The minimum number of long-term electoral observers required was 30. The deployment of 200 short-term observers was planned for an intensive observation of the polling period. The civilian observers would be deployed once the observation sites had been prepared and their security ensured. Additional specialists in logistics and communications were to be provided by Canada and Egypt. The Secretary-General envisaged that the existing authorized force structure of MINURCA of 1,350 military personnel would accommodate the additional specialists. However, he stated that he would not hesitate to request additional troops to restore the security of the Mission if he considered it to be at risk.

The Secretary-General observed that the security situation in the Central African Republic remained calm. However, following the agreement reached in Sirte, Libyan Arab Jamahiriya, on 18 April, Chad had begun to withdraw its 2,000 troops from the northern part of the DRC. The withdrawal was closely monitored by MINURCA. As the Chadians withdrew, the Congolese rebels could advance directly across the river from Bangui and MINURCA was keeping a close eye on that situation.

The Secretary-General noted that, since his April report, the economic reform programme of the country had made major progress in several areas. The National Assembly had adopted a series of laws designed to promote economic and social reforms, particularly the law for the privatization of PETROCA. In the light of the overall improved performance in programme implementation, external support from the Bretton Woods institutions, the African Development Bank, the EU and other bilateral donors could follow. Nevertheless, efforts were needed to improve revenue collection.

Report of Secretary-General (July). On 15 July, the Secretary-General presented his seventh report [S/1999/788] on MINURCA's mandate in the light of progress achieved towards implementing the commitments made by the President of the Central African Republic in January. The report also provided an update on the presidential electoral preparations. The President had set the first round for 29 August; the second round, if necessary, would be held on 19 September.

The Secretary-General stated that there had been armed clashes and unrest in Bangui in June involving Chadian nationals. Following the intervention by elements of FORSDIR in an altercation in a cattle market between Chadian cattle herdsmen and Central African citizens, at least five Chadians and one FORSDIR member were killed. Later, Central African students at the University of Bangui attacked Chadian students. There was also a riot when a Central African tried to rob a Chadian merchant. MINURCA troops were deployed to assist in those incidents. The Secretary-General's Special Representative raised with the Prime Minister and the President the issue of the President's commitment to restrict FORSDIR to its mandate, which did not include the maintenance of law and order. He called on the President to withdraw FORSDIR from Bangui airport and from border posts, and to prevent FORSDIR from performing law and order duties. President Patassé stated that he could not take any of those measures except at risk to his own safety.

As to electoral preparations, the Secretary-General said that CEMI had adopted a budget of 1.9 billion CFA francs (CFAF) (approximately $3 million). The Government had budgeted a sum of CFAF 1 billion, of which CFAF 500 million had been deposited into an escrow account from which CEMI could draw. UNDP had coordinated several meetings of donors at which the following pledges were made: Japan, CFAF 187 million (paid in full); United States, $120,000 (paid in full); EU, CFAF 450 million; UNDP, $200,000; and France, CFAF 300 million. Egypt donated two computers. The Secretary-General observed that there had been delays in CEMI's operations and that the election dates set could be met only if further delays were avoided.

The Secretary-General expressed concern at the sudden upsurge in tension in Bangui arising from the incidents involving the Chadian community and at the fact that parties preparing for the elections had begun to exchange mutual accusations and amass arms. Bearing in mind security considerations, including the flight of thousands of Congolese government troops into the country, the Secretary-General recommended increasing the strength of MINURCA through the deployment of an additional 148 troops, bringing the authorized total of the military component to 1,498 all ranks. That figure included the additional communications and logistical personnel essential to support the elections.

Regarding the restructuring of the armed forces, the Secretary-General noted that there were delays, as the legal aspects of the programme had still not been promulgated. There had been a lack of progress in confining FORSDIR to its statutory duties and the Secretary-General proposed that the Security Council consider additional steps to encourage President Patassé to fulfil the commitments he had made in that regard.

The Secretary-General welcomed the IMF decision to make available to the Central African Republic an additional 8.24 million special drawing rights (SDR) in the context of the mid-term review of the first annual enhanced structural adjustment facility (ESAF) arrangement. However, IMF's favourable review of the economic situation in the country had to be set against the additional arrears accumulated by the Government and the delays in implementing reforms.

Presidential elections

The first round of presidential elections was held on 19 September and the results were announced on 3 October. President Patassé received an absolute majority of 51.63 per cent of the vote, making it unnecessary to hold a second round of voting.

Report of the Secretary-General (October). On 7 October, the Secretary-General submitted his eighth report on MINURCA and the situation in the Central African Republic [S/1999/1038]. He noted that the report's submission had been delayed due to the postponement of the first round of the presidential election to 19 September and the announcement of the results on 3 October, as well as the overall political and security situation in the country.

The Secretary-General stated that, since his previous report, events were dominated by the preparations for the presidential elections by CEMI, assisted by MINURCA, the electoral campaign and the elections themselves on 19 September. The postponements in the elections were due to defective lists of voters, lack of printed ballots and disruptions from opposition candidates. As the election date drew near, the political situation grew increasingly charged. Unsubstantiated accusations that MINURCA and the international community were less than impartial grew louder and MINURCA staff came under threat. Several clashes took place among militants of some political parties. Several opposition candidates campaigned for a further postponement of the elections and some stated that they would not accept a victory by President Patassé and would call for mass protests were he to be declared the winner. On 29 August, 10 candidates were duly registered and the election campaign took place over a two-week period, throughout which MINURCA provided technical advice, guarded sensitive electoral materials and maintained security at electoral sites. MINURCA was assisted by 360 Central African armed forces soldiers, made available by the Government with financial support from France. The concept of operations with regard to the deployment of long-term and short-term electoral observers described by the Secretary-General in his sixth report was followed. MINURCA also deployed the essential additional military personnel and equipment to support the elections. Canada provided 31 communications personnel and Egypt sent 91 logistic and medical personnel and 15 armoured personnel carriers.

MINURCA stepped up its information activities ahead of the election in order to sensitize the population to the electoral process and to explain the UN role in supporting CEMI. Radio MINURCA broadcast programmes on civil education and the role of the population in the election. Statements by the Secretary-General and the Security Council President were widely circulated before the elections.

Voter turnout on 19 September was estimated at close to 60 per cent. There were some technical problems owing to the shortage of ballot papers in Bangui and some provincial towns. MINURCA assisted CEMI in resupplying the ballot papers in the provincial towns concerned, where voting was extended to 22 and 23 September. There were a few isolated attempts to intimidate voters and disrupt the electoral process, which were quickly dealt with by local authorities. On 22 September, MINURCA observers and those of the Francophonie and the EU issued separate statements in which, while acknowledging some irregularities, they declared that the election had been conducted in a peaceful, transparent and credible atmosphere. On the same day, a group of local NGOs, which had also monitored the election, released a statement concurring with the positive conclusions of the international observers.

On 3 October, the President of the Constitutional Court announced the official results of the election, according to which President Patassé received an absolute majority of 51.63 per cent of the vote. He pronounced that President Patassé had been re-elected as President with a mandate of six years and that no second round of voting would be held. The Court did not accept the results from the extension of voting to 22 and 23 September that had occurred in a few areas. Overall turnout was 56.4 per cent.

With regard to human rights, MINURCA continued to receive reports of arbitrary detentions and ill-treatment of prisoners, and religious and ethnic tensions continued to surface. Some incidents of intimidation and harassment against the Muslim community were also reported. MINURCA implemented a broad programme of human rights training for 180 new police recruits. It also completed a specialized programme of training for 383 police officials.

The situation of refugees remained a matter of serious concern. More than 52,000 refugees of various nationalities were in the country, of whom more than 13,000 were from the DRC. Following the fall of Gbadolite to Congolese rebels, thousands of civilian and military refugees from the DRC started crossing to the Central African Republic and another influx occurred when Zongo, across the river from Bangui, fell to rebels on 30 July. The total influx into the Central African Republic reached about 20,000, including some 7,000 Congolese government troops. The presence of the refugees, particularly the soldiers, created burdens for the limited infrastructure and social amenities and also created fears that the election campaigns would be hampered. However, logistic support provided by the Libyan Arab Jamahiriya enabled the repatriation of all Congolese military personnel to Kinshasa.

Regarding the economic situation, IMF approved the release of the second allocation of CFAF 7 billion under the ESAF agreement. In addition, China and Nigeria provided bilateral budget support to enable the Government to meet some of its obligations, such as its contractual payments to the Bretton Woods institutions, the payment of some salary arrears and payments to retiring soldiers. Although the Government did not lack the political will to institute the much-needed economic reforms, there was a need for further rigorous measures for greater transparency in the conduct of government operations. Prospective investors were waiting to make a proper evaluation of the political terrain before entering into economic cooperation. Progress was made in the area of privatization of government-owned enterprises: PETROCA had been liquidated and the privatization of the Union bancaire en Afrique centrale was proceeding well.

Regarding the restructuring and demobilization of the armed forces, the four bills that were adopted by the National Assembly were not promulgated into law by the President. He referred them to the Constitutional Court, which advised that several provisions in each of the laws violated the Constitution. A committee was established to incorporate the observations of the Court into amended draft bills for the consideration of the National Assembly. The Government, however, had begun to take first steps in the restructuring of the armed forces. It had earmarked funds to pay the salary arrears and other benefits of some 630 soldiers to be retired. To date, donors had made no commitments to provide the much-needed $3.1 million for the demobilization and reintegration of members of the armed forces. With regard to FORSDIR, there had been no change in its functions, despite several interventions by the Special Representative.

In response to resolution 1230(1999), the Secretary-General described various aspects of the situation in the Central African Republic that needed to be borne in mind in the context of a transition to post-conflict peace-building, including the tense political climate; the continuing challenge to the results of the presidential elections; accusations of acquisition of weapons and recruitment of militias by political leaders; the condition of the military, which was still capable of destabilizing the political and security environment; the need for economic and social reform; and the security situation in the region. He therefore recommended a short but gradual transition from UN peacekeeping involvement to post-conflict peace-building. During the transition period, MINURCA would continue to assist in the implementation of major reforms and promote national reconciliation. It would also facilitate, in coordination with relevant UN agencies and programmes and the Bretton Woods institutions, a smooth transformation from the current international involvement to post-conflict peace-building. The MINURCA military component would continue to discharge its security functions in Bangui, which it would gradually hand over to local security and law enforcement forces. The proposed transition would also allow MINURCA to complete a six-month training course for 180 local police.

During the transition, MINURCA would gradually reduce its military strength. A first batch of three infantry companies would depart in mid-December, with a second batch of two infantry companies and a logistic support element departing in January 2000. A third group, consisting of an infantry company, a light tank company and a medical unit, would then depart by 15 February 2000, leaving an element of 185 military personnel, which would be needed to provide security for UN personnel and protect its assets during the liquidation of MINURCA. During the transition period, the Mission's substantive and administrative personnel would also be reduced gradually, taking into account any requirements by a post-conflict peace-building presence. The Secretary-General intended to dispatch a small multidisciplinary mission to Bangui to finalize the possible mandate and requirements of a post-conflict peace-building presence of the United Nations in the country. The presence would take the form of a small political office, to be established after the end of the political presence of MINURCA on 15 February 2000.

The Secretary-General noted that the General Assembly, in **resolution 53/238** (see p. 129), had appropriated $33.4 million for the operation of MINURCA for the period from 1 July to 15 November 1999 and its subsequent liquidation and administrative closing until 30 June 2000. He had obtained authorization from ACABQ to enter into commitments to incur additional expenditure in the amount of $6.7 million for the estimated costs associated with the supportive role that MINURCA played in the conduct of the presidential elections. As at 15 September, unpaid assessed contributions to the MINURCA special account amounted to $67.6 million. With regard to the trust fund for the support of activities of MINURCA, contributions as at 30 September totalled $0.87 million, with expenditures authorized in the full amount of contributions received.

Extension of Mission (October)

On 22 October [meeting 4056], the Security Council unanimously adopted **resolution 1271(1999)**. The draft [S/1999/1078] was prepared in consultations among Council members.

The Security Council,

Reaffirming all its relevant resolutions, in particular resolutions 1159(1998) of 27 March 1998, 1201(1998) of 15 October 1998 and 1230(1999) of 26 February 1999,

Noting with satisfaction the successful conclusion of the presidential elections held on 19 September 1999,

Commending the United Nations Mission in the Central African Republic and the Special Representative of the Secretary-General on the support provided to the electoral process,

Affirming the commitment of all States to respect the sovereignty, political independence and territorial integrity of the Central African Republic,

Welcoming the report of the Secretary-General of 7 October 1999, and noting with approval the recommendations contained therein,

Recalling the importance of the process of national reconciliation, and urging all the political forces of the Central African Republic to continue their efforts towards cooperation and understanding,

Emphasizing the necessity of proceeding speedily to the restructuring of the Central African Armed Forces,

Reaffirming the importance of regional stability and of the consolidation of the climate of peace in the Central African Republic, which constitute essential elements for the restoration of peace in the region,

Reaffirming also the link between socio-economic progress and the consolidation of the stability of the Central African Republic,

Recalling the relevant principles set out in the Convention on the Safety of United Nations and Associated Personnel, adopted on 9 December 1994,

Noting the desire expressed by the Government of the Central African Republic for an extension of the presence of the Mission beyond 15 November 1999,

1. *Decides* to extend the mandate of the United Nations Mission in the Central African Republic until 15 February 2000 with a view to ensuring a short and gradual transition from United Nations peacekeeping involvement in the Central African Republic to a post-conflict peace-building presence with the aid of the relevant United Nations agencies and programmes and of the International Monetary Fund and the International Bank for Reconstruction and Development;

2. *Welcomes* the recommendation of the Secretary-General in paragraph 58 of his report of 7 October 1999 that the reduction of the military and civilian strength of the Mission be conducted in three stages;

3. *Calls firmly once again* upon the Government of the Central African Republic to continue to take tangible measures to implement the political, economic, social and security reforms mentioned in the report of the Secretary-General of 23 February 1998 and to honour the commitments set forth, inter alia, in the letter dated 23 January 1999 from the President of the Central African Republic addressed to the Secretary-General, and reaffirms the role of the Special Representative of the Secretary-General for the Central African Republic in assisting the promotion of reforms and national reconciliation;

4. *Strongly encourages* the Government of the Central African Republic to coordinate closely with the Mission in the progressive transfer of the functions of the Mission in the security field to the local security and police forces;

5. *Urges* the Government of the Central African Republic to complete, with the advice and technical support of the Mission, the initial steps of the restructuring programme of the Central African Armed Forces and of the demobilization and reintegration programme of the Central African Armed Forces retired military personnel, appeals to the international community to give its support to those programmes, and welcomes the proposal of the Secretary-General to convene a meeting in New York in the coming months to solicit funds in order to finance those programmes;

6. *Welcomes* the proposal of the Secretary-General to despatch a small multidisciplinary mission to Bangui in order to examine, in accordance with the wishes expressed by the Government of the Central African Republic, the conditions for the maintenance of the United Nations presence beyond 15 February 2000 in accordance with the recommendations made by the Secretary-General and contained in his reports of 28 May 1999 and 7 October 1999, and requests the Secretary-General to inform the Council as soon as possible concerning his detailed proposals in this regard;

7. *Reaffirms* the importance of the role of the Mission in supervising the destruction of confiscated weapons and ammunition under its control;

8. *Requests* the Secretary-General to submit by 15 January 2000 a report on the implementation of the mandate of the Mission and, in particular, on the progressive transfer of the functions of the Mission in the security field to the local security and police forces, on the evolution of the situation in the Central African Republic, on the progress achieved in the implementation of the commitments set forth in the letters dated 8 December 1998 and 23 January 1999 from the President of the Central African Republic addressed to the Secretary-General, and on the implementation of the Bangui Agreements and the National Reconciliation Pact, including the commitments relating to economic recovery, the restructuring of the security forces and the functioning of the Special Force for the Defence of the Republican Institutions;

9. *Decides* to remain actively seized of the matter.

Later developments. Despite the confirmation by national and international observers that the 19 September presidential election in the Central African Republic was transparent and credible, the opposition lodged a petition with the Constitutional Court challenging the results. However, since the Court did not hand down a decision within 60 days of the filing of the petition, it seemed that the issues raised regarding the election could be regarded as closed [S/2000/24]. On 25 November, the National Assembly voted for the Government's programme of action, which included the restructuring of the security forces; creation of a multi-ethnic national security institution; expansion in the economic sector, particularly in agriculture, mining and tourism; and fiscal reforms, particularly in the area of revenue generation. In the spirit of national unity, the Prime Minister appointed several cabinet members from civil society and opposition parties. A number of provisions of the National Reconciliation Pact had been implemented, including the Family Code, the establishment of a National Population Commission, the independence of the judiciary and the privatization of public enterprises.

By mid-December, the first four UN infantry companies were repatriated from Bangui and, on 29 December, elements of the Central African gendarmerie, police and armed forces began to take over the duties previously carried out by MINURCA military contingents. The government authorities created a Mixed General Command comprising the police, gendarmerie and army elements to facilitate the transfer of security functions and to coordinate with MINURCA on relevant matters.

In the economic area, the World Bank approved a fiscal consolidation of SDR 14.4 million based on the progress in privatization and on the strong commitment to revenue generation.

Proposed mandate for BONUCA

In a 3 December letter [S/1999/1235], the Secretary-General submitted to the Security Council, in response to resolution 1271(1999), his proposals regarding the maintenance of a UN presence in the Central African Republic following the withdrawal of MINURCA on 15 February 2000. His recommendations were based on the observations of the small multidisciplinary mission that visited Bangui from 15 to 19 November.

The primary mission of the post-MINURCA presence would be to support the Government's efforts to consolidate peace and national reconciliation, strengthen democratic institutions, and facilitate the mobilization of international political support and resources for national reconstruction and economic recovery.

The Secretary-General proposed the establishment of the United Nations Peace-Building Support Office in the Central African Republic (BONUCA). That Office, whose duration would initially be for one year, would be headed by a Representative of the Secretary-General at the D-2 level. In drawing up the budget for BONUCA, the Secretary-General intended to include provisions that would enable the Office to make modest contributions towards the development and implementation of some of the post-conflict peace-building functions under its purview, including those related to disarmament and the consolidation of the rule of law. Every effort would be made to ensure that BONUCA was operational on 15 February 2000.

On 10 December [S/1999/1236], the Security Council informed the Secretary-General that his proposal to establish BONUCA had been brought to the attention of its members.

Financing of MINURCA

The Secretary-General, in January [A/53/791], submitted to the General Assembly the financial performance report of MINURCA from 27 March to 30 June 1998. By resolution 52/249 [YUN 1998, p. 143], the Assembly had appropriated an amount of $18,560,600 gross ($18,335,500 net) for that period. Expenditures totalled $16,667,600 gross ($16,543,700 net), exclusive of budgeted voluntary contributions in kind in the amount of $916,900, which resulted in an unencumbered balance of $1,893,000 gross ($1,791,800 net). The unencumbered balance was attributable to delays in deploying military contingents and civilian police, international civilian vacancies and reduced requirements under operational costs.

In a May report [A/53/939], the Secretary-General presented the revised budget for MINURCA for the period 1 July 1998 to 30 June 1999, amounting to $65,863,850 gross ($64,678,250 net), inclusive of budgeted voluntary contributions in kind of $2,448,200, an increase of some 36 per cent in gross terms over resources provided for the period from 1 July 1998 to 28 February 1999. The proposed budget for the period 1 July 1999 to 30 June 2000 amounted to $32,167,200 gross ($31,372,000 net), inclusive of budgeted voluntary contributions in kind of $784,400.

Having considered those reports, ACABQ, in May [A/53/971], recommended that the Assembly appropriate and assess an additional amount of $31,382,800 gross ($30,587,600 net) for the period from 1 July 1999 to 30 June 2000.

GENERAL ASSEMBLY ACTION

On 8 June [meeting 101], the General Assembly, on the recommendation of the Fifth Committee [A/53/989], adopted **resolution 53/238** without vote [agenda item 161].

Financing of the United Nations Mission in the Central African Republic

The General Assembly,

Having considered the reports of the Secretary-General on the financing of the United Nations Mission in the Central African Republic and the related report of the Advisory Committee on Administrative and Budgetary Questions,

Bearing in mind Security Council resolution 1159(1998) of 27 March 1998, by which the Council decided to establish the United Nations Mission in the Central African Republic, and the subsequent resolutions by which the Council extended the mandate of the Mission, the latest of which was resolution 1230(1999) of 26 February 1999,

Recalling its resolution 52/249 of 26 June 1998 on the financing of the Mission,

Reaffirming that the costs of the Mission are expenses of the Organization to be borne by Member States in accordance with Article 17, paragraph 2, of the Charter of the United Nations,

Recalling its previous decisions regarding the fact that, in order to meet the expenditures caused by the Mission, a different procedure is required from that applied to meet expenditures of the regular budget of the United Nations,

Taking into account the fact that the economically more developed countries are in a position to make relatively larger contributions and that the economically less developed countries have a relatively limited capacity to contribute towards such an operation,

Bearing in mind the special responsibilities of the States permanent members of the Security Council, as indicated in General Assembly resolution 1874(S-IV) of 27 June 1963, in the financing of such operations,

Noting with appreciation that voluntary contributions have been made to the Mission,

Mindful of the fact that it is essential to provide the Mission with the necessary financial resources to enable it to fulfil its responsibilities under the relevant resolutions of the Security Council,

1. *Takes note* of the status of contributions to the United Nations Mission in the Central African Republic as at 30 April 1999, including the contributions outstanding in the amount of 15.9 million United States dollars, representing 34 per cent of the total assessed contributions from the inception of the Mission to the period ending 30 November 1998, notes that some 26 per cent of the Member States have paid their assessed contributions in full, and urges all other Member States concerned, in particular those in arrears, to ensure payment of their outstanding assessed contributions;

2. *Expresses concern* about the financial situation with regard to peacekeeping activities, in particular as regards the reimbursement of troop contributors, which bear additional burdens owing to overdue payments by Member States of their assessments;

3. *Expresses its appreciation* to those Member States which have paid their assessed contributions in full;

4. *Urges* all other Member States to make every possible effort to ensure payment of their assessed contributions to the Mission in full and on time;

5. *Endorses* the observations and recommendations contained in the report of the Advisory Committee on Administrative and Budgetary Questions;

6. *Requests* the Secretary-General to take all necessary action to ensure that the Mission is administered with a maximum of efficiency and economy;

7. *Also requests* the Secretary-General, in order to reduce the cost of employing General Service staff, to continue efforts to recruit local staff for the Mission against General Service posts, commensurate with the requirements of the Mission;

8. *Approves,* on an exceptional basis, the special arrangements for the Mission with regard to the application of article IV of the financial regulations of the United Nations, whereby appropriations required in respect of obligations owed to Governments providing contingents and/or logistic support for the Mission shall be retained beyond the period stipulated under financial regulations 4.3 and 4.4, as set out in the annex to the present resolution;

9. *Decides* to appropriate to the Special Account for the United Nations Mission in the Central African Republic the amount of 34,309,800 dollars gross (33,860,700 dollars net) for the operation of the Mission in respect of the period from 1 July 1998 to 30 June 1999, in addition to the amount of 29,105,850 dollars gross (28,369,350 dollars net) already appropriated under the terms of General Assembly resolution 52/249 and inclusive of the amount of 18,111,200 dollars gross (17,728,700 dollars net) authorized by the Advisory Committee under the terms of section IV of Assembly resolution 49/233 A of 23 December 1994;

10. *Decides also,* as an ad hoc arrangement, taking into account the amount of 29,105,850 gross (28,369,350 dollars net) already apportioned under the terms of General Assembly resolution 52/249, to apportion among Member States the additional amount of 34,309,800 dollars gross (33,860,700 dollars net) for the period from 1 July 1998 to 30 June 1999, in accordance with the composition of groups set out in paragraphs 3 and 4 of its resolution 43/232 of 1 March 1989, as adjusted by the Assembly in its resolutions 44/192 B of 21 December 1989, 45/269 of 27 August 1991, 46/198 A of 20 December 1991, 47/218 A of 23 December 1992, 49/249 A of 20 July 1995, 49/249 B of 14 September 1995, 50/224 of 11 April 1996, 51/218 A to C of 18 December 1996 and 52/230 of 31 March 1998 and its decisions 48/472 A of 23 December 1993 and 50/451 B of 23 December 1995, and taking into account the scale of assessments for the years 1998 and 1999, as set out in its resolution 52/215 A of 22 December 1997;

11. *Decides further* that, in accordance with the provisions of its resolution 973(X) of 15 December 1955, there shall be set off against the apportionment among Member States, as provided for in paragraph 10 above, their respective share in the Tax Equalization Fund of the estimated additional staff assessment income of 449,100 dollars approved for the Mission for the period from 1 July 1998 to 30 June 1999;

12. *Decides* to appropriate the amount of 33,367,875 dollars gross (32,572,675 dollars net) for the operation and liquidation of the Mission for the period from

1 July 1999 to 30 June 2000, inclusive of the amount of 1,659,640 dollars for the support account for peacekeeping operations and the amount of 325,435 dollars for the United Nations Logistics Base at Brindisi, Italy, to be apportioned as an ad hoc arrangement among Member States in accordance with the scheme set out in the present resolution and the scale of assessments for the years 1999 and 2000, as set out in its resolution 52/215 A;

13. *Decides also* that, in accordance with the provisions of its resolution 973(X), there shall be set off against the apportionment among Member States, as provided for in paragraph 12 above, their respective share in the Tax Equalization Fund of the estimated staff assessment income of 795,200 dollars approved for the period from 1 July 1999 to 30 June 2000;

14. *Decides further* that, for Member States that have fulfilled their financial obligations to the Mission, there shall be set off against their apportionment, as provided for in paragraph 10 above, their respective share of the unencumbered balance of 1,893,000 dollars gross (1,791,800 dollars net) in respect of the period from 1 July 1997 to 30 June 1998;

15. *Decides* that, for Member States that have not fulfilled their financial obligations to the Mission, their share of the unencumbered balance of 1,893,000 dollars gross (1,791,800 dollars net) in respect of the period from 1 July 1997 to 30 June 1998 shall be set off against their outstanding obligations;

16. *Invites* voluntary contributions to the Mission in cash and in the form of services and supplies acceptable to the Secretary-General, to be administered, as appropriate, in accordance with the procedure and practices established by the General Assembly;

17. *Decides* to include in the provisional agenda of its fifty-fourth session the agenda item entitled "Financing of the United Nations Mission in the Central African Republic".

ANNEX

Special arrangements with regard to the application of article IV of the financial regulations of the United Nations

1. At the end of the twelve-month period provided for in financial regulation 4.3, any unliquidated obligations of the financial period in question relating to goods supplied and services rendered by Governments for which claims have been received or which are covered by established reimbursement rates shall be transferred to accounts payable; such accounts payable shall remain recorded in the Special Account for the United Nations Mission in the Central African Republic until payment is effected.

2. *(a)* Any other unliquidated obligations of the financial period in question owed to Governments for goods supplied and services rendered, as well as other obligations owed to Governments, for which required claims have not yet been received shall remain valid for an additional period of four years following the end of the twelve-month period provided for in financial regulation 4.3;

(b) Claims received during this four-year period shall be treated as provided for under paragraph 1 of the present annex, if appropriate;

(c) At the end of the additional four-year period, any unliquidated obligations shall be cancelled and the then remaining balance of any appropriations retained therefor shall be surrendered.

On 23 December, the Assembly decided that the agenda item on the financing of MINURCA would remain for consideration at its resumed fifty-fourth session in 2000 (**decision 54/465**).

Eritrea-Ethiopia

In 1999, the border dispute between Eritrea and Ethiopia, which broke out in May 1998, escalated into a full-scale war. Both countries accused each other of aggression and of violating an air strike moratorium.

The Security Council, in February, condemned the use of force by both parties and demanded an immediate halt in the hostilities, particularly air strikes. It urged all States to end immediately all arms sales to Eritrea and Ethiopia. OAU continued to take the lead in finding a solution to the conflict, with the support of the United Nations, the EU and the international community. In February, Eritrea accepted as the viable solution to the conflict the OAU Framework Agreement, which provided for the withdrawal of Eritrea from Badme and the restoration of Ethiopian civilian administration to the area. Ethiopia had already accepted the Agreement in 1998. Nevertheless, hostilities between the two countries continued throughout the year. The Security Council received frequent briefings on the situation in Eritrea and Ethiopia and OAU continued its peacemaking efforts.

Border dispute

Communications (January). In a 1 January press release transmitted to the Security Council President [S/1999/5], Ethiopia stated that since the Eritrean troops invaded Ethiopia in May 1998 [YUN 1998, p. 145], 338,318 persons had been forced from their homes. Ethiopia recalled that it had shown its commitment to find a peaceful resolution to the conflict and had accepted the proposals for a Framework Agreement put forward by OAU in November 1998 [ibid., p. 149] and endorsed by the United Nations and the EU, calling for the withdrawal of Eritrean forces from Badme, to the positions held before 6 May 1998. Eritrea had not accepted the Agreement but had proposed amendments that were not even discussed by OAU. On 6 January [S/1999/11], Ethiopia transmitted to the Council a statement by its Foreign Minister to members of the diplomatic community in Addis Ababa on Eritrea's aggression and rejection of the OAU peace proposal. He stated that the OAU Ambassadorial Committee formed to investigate the origins of the crisis had found Eritrea to be the aggressor. He accused Eritrea of two types of crime: invasion and occupation of Ethiopian territory on 12 May 1998; and disdain towards peacemaking efforts. He called on Eritrea to withdraw from occupied Ethiopian territories and for the restoration of the status quo ante and on the international community to put pressure on Eritrea so that the peace process might succeed.

Eritrea, in an 8 January press release [S/1999/21], addressed the Ethiopian Foreign Minister's allegations, stating that it had sought clarifications on a number of issues in the Framework Agreement but had not rejected it. Ethiopia had not accepted the Agreement in toto but an amended version or its own interpretation of key clauses. Eritrea denied that the OAU Ambassadorial Committee had proved Eritrean aggression or that Eritrea wanted to stop OAU from investigating who had administered Badme before 12 May 1998. Eritrea's reservations concerned the singular focus on Badme and the incidents of 6-12 May to the exclusion of preceding incidents of Ethiopian aggression and occupation. Eritrea accused Ethiopia of repeated acts of aggression against it; violation of basic principles of international law through illegal expulsion of Eritreans and confiscation of property; the detention in special concentration camps of thousands of Eritrean youths on the basis of their ethnicity; the use of force as a means of settling the border dispute; and the rejection of immediate cessation of hostilities.

Eritrea, in 12 and 15 January statements [S/1999/32, S/1999/43], reported on Ethiopia's alleged preparations for war and the death of Eritreans in Ethiopian detention camps. Eritrea stated that a binding agreement was needed on a cessation of all hostilities, including a total ban on air strikes. However, Ethiopia was opposed to such an agreement and had repeatedly declared its intent to launch war. Although Eritrea did not consider war as an option, it reserved its right to self-defence.

In a 13 January press release [S/1999/36], Ethiopia refuted Eritrea's allegation that Ethiopia was planning an attack. It noted that Eritrea was resorting to gimmicks to avoid responding to the OAU peace proposal and to the OAU request to withdraw from Ethiopian territory. Ethiopia accused Eritrea of embarking on a wave of shelling, specifically as the OAU Central Organ meeting in December 1998 approached, to provoke Ethiopia to a reaction.

Germany forwarded a 15 January statement by the EU Presidency [S/1999/63] reiterating its full support for OAU's Framework Agreement and for OAU's ongoing commitment to mediate in the conflict between Eritrea and Ethiopia. The EU urged both countries to cooperate fully with the OAU mediation and renew their efforts to achieve a peaceful negotiated settlement. Both parties were called on to refrain from any military action and to work for a de-escalation of the conflict, including measures to improve the humanitarian situation.

In a 25 January press release [S/1999/70], Ethiopia stated that it found encouraging the latest efforts by the international community to put pressure on Eritrea to implement the OAU peace proposal. However, the issue was Eritrea's withdrawal from Ethiopian territory. It stated that Eritrea was not awaiting clarification on the OAU proposal but was preparing, under the pretext of an allegedly Ethiopian-initiated resumption of the war, to continue as aggressor in the conflict. Ethiopia called for the international community to apply pressure on Eritrea in the political, diplomatic and economic areas.

SECURITY COUNCIL ACTION

On 29 January [meeting 3973], the Security Council unanimously adopted **resolution 1226(1999)**. The draft text [S/1999/90] was prepared during consultations among Council members.

The Security Council,

Reaffirming its resolution 1177(1998) of 26 June 1998,

Expressing grave concern over the risk of armed conflict between Ethiopia and Eritrea and the escalating arms build-up along the common border between the two countries,

Noting that armed conflict between Ethiopia and Eritrea would have a devastating effect on the peoples of the two countries and the region as a whole,

Recognizing that the rehabilitation and reconstruction efforts of both the Ethiopian and Eritrean Governments during the last eight years have given hope to the rest of the continent, all of which would be put at risk by armed conflict,

Commending the efforts of concerned countries and regional bodies aimed at facilitating a peaceful solution to the border dispute between Ethiopia and Eritrea,

1. *Expresses its strong support* for the mediation efforts of the Organization of African Unity and for the Framework Agreement as approved on 17 December 1998 by the Summit of the Central Organ of the Mechanism for Conflict Prevention, Management and Resolution of the Organization of African Unity, and affirms that the Framework Agreement provides the best hope for peace between the two parties;

2. *Endorses* the decision by the Secretary-General to send his Special Envoy for Africa to the region in support of the efforts of the Organization of African Unity;

3. *Stresses* that it is of primary importance that the Framework Agreement be accepted, and calls for cooperation with the Organization of African Unity and full implementation of the Framework Agreement without delay;

4. *Welcomes* the acceptance by Ethiopia of the Framework Agreement;

5. *Welcomes* Eritrea's engagement in the process undertaken by the Organization of African Unity, notes the fact that the Organization of African Unity has responded to Eritrea's request for clarifications of the Framework Agreement, and in this regard strongly urges Eritrea to accept the Framework Agreement as the basis for a peaceful resolution of the border dispute between Ethiopia and Eritrea without delay;

6. *Calls upon* both parties to work for a reduction in tensions by adopting policies leading to the restoration of confidence between the Governments and peoples of Ethiopia and Eritrea, including urgent measures to improve the humanitarian situation and respect for human rights;

7. *Strongly urges* Ethiopia and Eritrea to maintain their commitment to a peaceful resolution of the border dispute, and calls upon them in the strongest terms to exercise maximum restraint and to refrain from taking any military action;

8. *Welcomes* the Secretary-General's continued engagement in support of the peace process undertaken by the Organization of African Unity;

9. *Decides* to remain actively seized of the matter.

Also on 29 January [S/1999/97], Eritrea transmitted a statement to the Council President regarding resolution 1226(1999). It accused Ethiopia not only of declaring war but of continuing to operate through a policy of threats of launching the war, diplomatic intimidation and engaging in a concerted campaign to solicit international blessing for the war that it intended to unleash. Eritrea reiterated that it did not believe in the logic of force or in the diplomacy of intimidation and renewed its call for the cessation of hostilities. It expressed dismay at the Council's disregard of the crimes of mass deportation, incarceration and expropriation of Eritreans and Ethiopians of Eritrean origin by Ethiopia, which had been corroborated by independent witnesses such as Amnesty International.

In a 29 January letter to the Security Council [S/1999/102] and a 2 February press statement [S/1999/104], Ethiopia commented on resolution 1226(1999). It was encouraged by the Council's adoption of the resolution, which left no room for misinterpretation and did not reward aggression. Ethiopia was waiting for Eritrea's acceptance of the OAU peace proposal to ensure its implementation. It viewed the resolution as a step in the right direction for strengthening OAU's hand so that it could implement the peace proposal.

Outbreak of hostilities

In a 4 February press statement [S/1999/115], Ethiopia reported shelling by Eritrea at the Badme/Sheraro front within days of Eritrean President Isaias Afwerki's statement in which he insisted that Eritrea would not fire the first bullet. It accused Eritrea of renewing hostilities just as the international community was starting to apply increased pressure on the Government to accept the OAU Framework Agreement. It also stated that Eritrea was engaging in a propaganda campaign alleging that Ethiopia was launching an attack. Ethiopia urged the international community to see Eritrea's actions for what they were and apply more tangible pressure so that there might be a peaceful resolution to the conflict.

On 5 February [S/1999/119], Ethiopia issued a press release alleging that Eritrea had carried out an aerial bombing of a fuel depot and its surroundings in Adigrat, which, it stated, was a violation of the 1998 moratorium on air strikes brokered by the United States and agreed to by Eritrea and Ethiopia [YUN 1998, p. 146]. Eritrea's bombing of Adigrat, especially during the time the UN Special Envoy was in the region to support OAU's peace proposal, showed that it did not have any intention of pursing a peaceful resolution to the conflict.

In a press statement of the same date [S/1999/117], Eritrea denied Ethiopia's charges that Eritrea had launched an air attack and stated that Ethiopia was concocting stories as it was planning to launch a full-scale war against Eritrea. It countered that Ethiopia had opened a new front in central Eritrea by deploying 55,000 troops, while claiming that Eritrea had deployed troops on the Tsorona front. Eritrea stated that Ethiopia, rather than informing the United States as broker of the air strikes moratorium of its real intention, preferred to fabricate a story. Eritrea remained on record as calling for an immediate cessation of all hostilities.

Burkina Faso transmitted to the Security Council a 6 February statement by OAU's current Chairman [S/1999/126] expressing deep concern about the deterioration in the situation along the borders of Ethiopia and Eritrea. The Chairman observed that it would be extremely unfortunate if the situation were to get out of control while OAU, with the assistance of the United Nations and the international community, was pursuing efforts to find a peaceful settlement. The Chairman reiterated to both parties the appeal that the fourth summit meeting of the Central Organ made to them in Ouagadougou in December 1998 [YUN 1998, p. 149] to continue to cooperate with the OAU High-level Delegation and create the necessary conditions for the rapid implementation of the Framework Agreement and to continue to exercise restraint. Both countries were urged to put an immediate and unconditional end to the hostilities that had resumed along their borders.

Eritrea, on 8 February [S/1999/128], expressed disappointment about what it called the international impunity that was encouraging Ethiopia to indulge in dangerous military adventures. It claimed that Ethiopia continued to use force to violate Eritrean sovereignty and grab Eritrean territory. It reported that Ethiopia, after a long lull, had launched a renewed offensive on 5 February; had issued a new map of a "greater Tigray", illegally redrawing the international boundary between Eritrea and Ethiopia that was based on established colonial treaties; resorted to the repeated use of force; escalated the conflict by launching the first air strike on 5 June 1998; continued to perpetrate unparalleled violations of the human rights of innocent Eritreans; announced its intention of solving the dispute militarily; unleashed the war that it had been threatening all along; and violated the air moratorium by employing its air force in its ongoing offensive. Eritrea accused the international community of maintaining an unbalanced stance. To expedite an early resolution to the conflict, it called on the international community to abandon its double standard by condemning Ethiopia for its continued use of force.

Ethiopia transmitted to the Council an 8 February statement by the OAU Secretary-General [S/1999/131], in which he reiterated his deep concern at the escalation of the conflict and urged both Eritrea and Ethiopia immediately to put an end to the fighting and recommit themselves to a peaceful solution to the dispute. He emphasized that the Framework Agreement, endorsed by the OAU Central Organ and supported by the United Nations and the international community, remained a viable and sound framework for a peaceful solution. He repeated that OAU and its High-level Delegation remained available to engage the parties to the dispute and awaited Eritrea's response to the clarifications OAU had provided on elements of the Agreement.

In a 10 February statement [S/1999/134], Ethiopia stated that it had always cooperated with the third parties that had made their good offices available in order to avert escalation of the crisis between it and Eritrea. Ethiopia had accepted the peace plan put forward by the United States and Rwanda in June 1998 [YUN 1998, p. 147] and the OAU Framework Agreement, while Eritrea had always rejected them. It alleged that the final Eritrean response to the OAU peace plan came on 6 February 1999 after it had violated the air strike moratorium, when it mounted a large-scale military offensive on the Badme-Shiraro front, imposing war on Ethiopia. Thus, Ethiopia had only one option, which was to exercise its right of self-defence under Article 51 of the Charter of the United Nations. Ethiopia called on the international community to prevail upon Eritrea to accept and implement the OAU Framework Agreement.

SECURITY COUNCIL ACTION

On 10 February [meeting 3975], the Security Council unanimously adopted **resolution 1227 (1999)**. The draft [S/1999/133] was prepared during consultations among Council members.

The Security Council,

Reaffirming its resolutions 1177(1998) of 26 June 1998 and 1226(1999) of 29 January 1999,

Expressing its grave concern regarding the border conflict between Ethiopia and Eritrea and the resumption of hostilities between the parties,

Recalling the commitment of Ethiopia and Eritrea to a moratorium on the threat of and use of air strikes,

Stressing that the situation between Ethiopia and Eritrea constitutes a threat to peace and security,

1. *Condemns* the recourse to the use of force by Ethiopia and Eritrea;
2. *Demands* an immediate halt to the hostilities, in particular the use of air strikes;
3. *Also demands* that Ethiopia and Eritrea resume diplomatic efforts to find a peaceful resolution to the conflict;
4. *Stresses* that the Framework Agreement as approved on 17 December 1998 by the Summit of the Central Organ of the Mechanism for Conflict Prevention, Management and Resolution of the Organization of African Unity remains a viable and sound basis for a peaceful resolution of the conflict;
5. *Expresses its full support* for the efforts of the Organization of African Unity, the Secretary-General and his Special Envoy for Africa, and concerned Member States to find a peaceful resolution to the present hostilities;
6. *Calls upon* Ethiopia and Eritrea to ensure the safety of the civilian population and respect for human rights and international humanitarian law;
7. *Strongly urges* all States to end immediately all sales of arms and munitions to Ethiopia and Eritrea;
8. *Decides* to remain actively seized of the matter.

Both Eritrea and Ethiopia made statements to the Council, which they transmitted by letter to the Council President.

In its statement [S/1999/140], Eritrea alleged that Ethiopia broke the de facto truce that had existed since June 1998 and restarted an all-out offensive against Eritrea. Eritrea summarized independent eyewitness reports stating that Ethiopia had expended an estimated $300 million on arms in order to retake the disputed border area of Badme. Eritrea expressed regret that the Council had not condemned Ethiopia for its irresponsible resort to force to solve a border conflict and allowed Ethiopia to wage war with impunity. It stated that Ethiopia alone bore full responsibility for the start and escalation of the conflict to a full-scale war and urged the Council to take note of that fact and to act appropriately.

Ethiopia, in its statement [S/1999/162], said that Eritrea had never engaged constructively in resolving the crisis peacefully but had carried out provocative military actions to create an atmosphere of general crisis and to divert the attention of the international community from addressing the core issue, namely, Eritrean withdrawal from Ethiopian territory. The Ethiopian Government had no option but to exercise its legitimate right of self-defence in the light of those developments. Ethiopia placed on record its strong reservation in respect of paragraph 7 of resolution 1227(1999).

Communications. On 11 February [S/1999/143], Eritrea reaffirmed its commitment not to start war but it would exercise its legitimate right of self-defence in the face of aggression. It further stated that it had not conducted any air strikes violating the moratorium, nor had it committed any human rights violations. It was disappointed that the Security Council had not addressed the human rights issue. Eritrea also expressed astonishment that the Council had taken the unprecedented step of embargoing the sales of arms in this case, as it had never embargoed the sale of arms to States that were a cause of regional instability and insecurity.

In a 15 February press release [S/1999/154], Ethiopia expressed disappointment at the Council's double standard as reflected in paragraph 7 of resolution 1227(1999). It emphasized that the aggressor in the conflict was Eritrea and that the Council's adoption of the resolution was a sudden turnaround that signalled denial to the victim of the aggression of its rights of self-defence.

The EU, in an 11 February statement [S/1999/159], noted with dismay the recent outbreak of open war between Ethiopia and Eritrea, condemned the use of force by the two countries and urged them to respect the air strike moratorium. It expressed its support for resolution 1227(1999), particularly paragraph 7, and called on the two sides to agree unilaterally to a cessation of hostilities. The EU stood ready to provide assistance and dispatch a special troika mission to promote a rapid solution to the conflict based on the OAU Framework Agreement.

On 16 February [S/1999/157], Eritrea asserted that the Ethiopian regime opposed an arms embargo because of its desire to occupy Eritrean territory by force and purchase weapons. Over the preceding eight months, Ethiopia had spent an estimated $400 million on weapons, even as it was soliciting food aid from the World Food Programme (WFP) in the amount of $100 million. Eritrea accused Ethiopia of further attacks on 14 and 15 February on the Burie front, on which Ethiopia had no territorial claims.

In other communications to the Council in February, Eritrea [S/1999/188] and Ethiopia [S/1999/192] again exchanged charges, each accusing the other of aggression and pursuing the escalation of the conflict.

Eritrean acceptance of Framework Agreement

In identical letters of 27 February to the Secretary-General and the Security Council [S/1999/215], Eritrea indicated its acceptance of the OAU Framework Agreement. It called on the Council to condemn Ethiopia's territorial ambitions and aggression, ensure the implementation of its relevant resolutions and ensure that observers were sent to verify facts on the ground and facilitate demarcation of the border.

SECURITY COUNCIL ACTION

The Security Council, on 27 February [meeting 3985], following consultations among its members, authorized its President to make statement **S/PRST/1999/9** on its behalf:

> The Security Council reaffirms its resolutions 1177(1998) of 26 June 1998, 1226(1999) of 29 January 1999 and 1227(1999) of 10 February 1999, which called upon Ethiopia and Eritrea to refrain from armed conflict and to accept and implement the Framework Agreement as approved on 17 December 1998 by the Summit of the Central Organ of the Mechanism for Conflict Prevention, Management and Resolution of the Organization of African Unity.
>
> The Council demands an immediate halt to all hostilities and calls upon the parties to refrain from the further use of force.
>
> The Council welcomes the acceptance by Eritrea, at the level of head of State, of the Framework Agreement and recalls the prior acceptance of the Agreement by Ethiopia. The Framework Agreement remains a viable and sound basis for a peaceful resolution of the conflict.
>
> The Council reaffirms the sovereignty and territorial integrity of Ethiopia and Eritrea.
>
> The Council expresses its willingness to consider all appropriate support to implement a peace agreement between the two parties.
>
> The Council expresses its continuing support for the efforts of the Organization of African Unity, the Secretary-General and his Special Envoy, Mr. Mohammed Sahnoun, and concerned Member States to find a peaceful resolution to the border dispute.
>
> The Council remains actively seized of the matter.

In a 28 February letter [S/1999/221], the OAU Chairman and its Secretary-General welcomed Eritrea's acceptance of the Framework Agreement, which, they felt, presented a fair, balanced and sound basis to end the dispute. They urged an immediate end to the fighting so that the modalities for a peaceful resolution in accordance with the Framework Agreement could be pursued.

In a 2 March statement [S/1999/239], the EU also welcomed Eritrea's acceptance of the Framework Agreement and considered the OAU proposal to be the only basis for a peaceful solution, as the EU ministerial troika that visited Addis Ababa and Asmara on 19 and 20 February had concluded. The EU urged both parties immediately to cease hostilities on all fronts, to refrain from any further use of violence and to implement the Framework Agreement without any further delay.

On 5 March [S/1999/241], during discussions with an OAU delegation, Eritrea reaffirmed its acceptance of the Framework Agreement; committed itself to an immediate ceasefire and cessation of hostilities; and stated that it had established a high-level body fully mandated to initiate and finalize the implementation of the Agreement's provisions.

Communications (March-May). On 1 March [S/1999/226], Ethiopia transmitted to the Security Council a resolution adopted by the House of People's Representatives on the war of aggression by Eritrea against Ethiopia and on Council resolution 1227(1999). Expressing its deep anguish at that resolution, particularly paragraph 7, the House appealed to the Council to redress the injustice done to Ethiopia and take appropriate measures against Eritrea.

In a 6 March statement marking 300 days of Eritrean occupation [S/1999/249], Ethiopia said that, although it had pushed the Eritrean military out of Badme, Eritrean troops continued to occupy Ethiopian territory in the Zalambessa-Aiga, Bada-Bure and Egala regions.

Also on 6 March [S/1999/246], Ethiopia's Prime Minister, Meles Zenawi, expressed his frustration regarding the treatment Ethiopia had received from the Council, which had, it said, placed the victim of aggression and the aggressor on the same footing. After continuous pleadings to the Council to ensure the withdrawal of Eritrean troops from its territory, Ethiopia had itself liberated the Badme area from Eritrean occupation. The Eritrean acceptance of the Framework Agreement was a tactical ploy to buy time, he charged. Large chunks of Ethiopian territory still remained under Eritrean occupation. The Prime Minister asked the Council to condemn the Eritrean aggression, call on Eritrean occupying forces to withdraw from all remaining occupied Ethiopian territory, and affirm that Eritrea bore full responsibility for the loss of lives, the humanitarian crisis and the destruction of property.

On 12 March [S/1999/274], Eritrea transmitted to the Security Council OAU's written clarification to the issues it had raised on 12 December 1998 regarding the Framework Agreement, prior to the meeting of the OAU Central Organ. While it was studying the clarifications, received on 26 January, the process was cut short by Ethiopia's launch of an all-out offensive on 6 February. Eritrea drew the Council's attention to the clarity of OAU's answers to the issues of the "environs" of Badme and redeployment, and concluded that, since Ethiopia had not raised any questions about the clarifications, it was in agreement with them.

In further communications during March [S/1999/247, 250, 258, 259, 260, 269, 273], Eritrea and Ethiopia continued to exchange charges, each accusing the other of prevaricating on the acceptance and implementation of the OAU Framework Agreement and the violation of Security Council resolutions.

On 15 April [S/1999/427], Eritrea forwarded a press release to the Council on the Ethiopian bombing of the town of Adi-Kaieh, the environs of Mendefera and the village of Forto, during which a school had been hit and children wounded.

In a 26 April press release [S/1999/482], Eritrea reaffirmed its strict adherence to the Framework Agreement and its readiness to implement it. Eritrea had informed the Secretary-General's Special Envoy, Mohamed Sahnoun, that the Government stood ready to play its role within the Follow-up Committee to be established by OAU, with the active participation and assistance of the United Nations.

In a 12 May press release [S/1999/550], Eritrea stated that it had reiterated to the OAU High-level Delegation that visited Asmara on 11 May its adherence to the Framework Agreement. Eritrea called for both parties to sign formal and binding agreements, confirming acceptance of the Agreement, concerning the "mechanisms" and "technicalities" of implementation, and on a ceasefire so as to create a climate conducive for implementation. Eritrea also urged the OAU delegation to ensure that Ethiopia's illegal expulsion of Eritrea's Ambassador to OAU would be rectified.

In a 14 May statement [S/1999/561], Ethiopia said that it had reiterated to the OAU High-level Delegation that visited Addis Ababa on 13 May its commitment to the Framework Agreement, which called on Eritrea to withdraw from all occupied Ethiopian territories.

Security Council press statement (19 May). Following informal consultations on 19 May, the members of the Security Council issued a press statement in which they welcomed Mr. Sahnoun's recent visit to the region and reaffirmed their support for the Secretary-General's efforts, in coordination with OAU, to promote a peaceful solution to the conflict. They urged both parties to comply immediately and in full with resolution 1227(1999) and appealed to them for an end to inflammatory rhetoric. They also expressed concern about the humanitarian situation.

Communications (June). In a 14 June letter [S/1999/678], the Ethiopian Minister for Foreign Affairs expressed his fear that the Security Council and the international community had missed an important opportunity to contribute towards the fair settlement of the conflict. The reasons were lack of political support for the OAU High-level Delegation; the differing interpretations of the Framework Agreement, particularly what was meant by "Badme and its environs"; the absence of resolve to call on Eritrea to withdraw from all the territories it occupied by force, not only Badme; the lack of readiness of the Eritrean regime to reverse its aggression; and the Council's complete abdication of responsibility and attempts to appease Eritrea. Ethiopia particularly deplored the fact that the 19 May press statement was devoid of any reference to the need for Eritrea to heed the voice of OAU and concluded that the Framework Agreement was a peace document to which only lip service was given.

Responding on 17 June [S/1999/696], the Eritrean Minister for Foreign Affairs stated that Ethiopia had reneged on its earlier commitment to the Framework Agreement by putting forth new preconditions. Not only was that Agreement unambiguous in terms of redeployment of troops, it also provided for the determination of the origin of the crisis "through an investigation that will be carried out on the incidents of 6 May 1998 and on any other incident prior to that date . . . including the incidents of July-August 1997". Eritrea charged Ethiopia with wanting to be exonerated from the acts of aggression that it had perpetrated in the preceding years and to legitimize the Eritrean territories that it had occupied in the process. It stated that, with regard to international law, the status quo in Africa was anchored in the respect of the boundaries inherited from colonial rule, the sacrosanct OAU principle governing the behaviour of neighbouring countries, and Ethiopia violated that principle. Eritrea also accused Ethiopia not only of violating the moratorium on air strikes but also of deporting about 60,000 Eritreans and Ethiopians of Eritrean origin in the most inhuman manner and of confiscating their lifelong earnings.

Security Council press statement (23 June). Following consultations on 23 June, the Security Council members issued a press statement on the conflict between Ethiopia and Eritrea, in which they deplored the continuing hostilities and demanded that both parties immediately and unconditionally agree to a ceasefire. The parties were called on to cooperate with the OAU High-level Delegation in implementing the Framework Agreement. The Council expressed concern that both parties continued to purchase weapons when a large number of their populations faced famine and urged all States to halt immediately the sale of arms and munitions to Ethiopia and Eritrea. To permit the provision of assistance to the local population, the Council requested both countries to grant humanitarian access to areas of military conflict.

On 24 June [S/1999/712], Eritrea, in response to the Council's press statement, emphasized that it had not initiated the hostilities with Ethiopia and again announced its readiness to implement the Framework Agreement. Ethiopia, on 29 June [S/1999/731], stated that it had been disappointed for some time by the Council's reaction to Eritrean aggression, which had failed to reflect any sympathy for the victim. The Council now chose to remind Ethiopia of its responsibility for feeding its people.

Communication (July). In a 3 July press release [A/53/1012-S/1999/755], Eritrea accused Ethiopia of violating the 1961 Vienna Convention on Diplomatic Relations [YUN 1961, p. 512] and the various agreements between OAU and Ethiopia as host country. It said Ethiopia had expelled all Eritrean diplomatic and technical staff in June 1998; deported all local staff; denied the Eritrean Ambassador and his deputy freedom of movement; declared Eritrea's Permanent Representative to OAU persona non grata, ordered him to leave the country within 24 hours and confiscated documents of the mission; and sent to the Ambassador's residence armed agents who ransacked it and took Embassy employees away.

Modalities for implementation of Framework Agreement

In a 15 July statement [S/1999/789], Ethiopia stated that the thirty-fifth session of the Assembly of Heads of State and Government of OAU (Algiers, Algeria, 12-14 July) had unanimously endorsed the Modalities for the Implementation of the OAU Framework Agreement. The substance of the Modalities was the call for the return to the status quo ante that had prevailed until 6 May 1998. Ethiopia accused Eritrea of removing the substance of the proposal by trying to amend it and then saying that it accepted it. Eritrea had told the Algiers summit that it had a different cut-off date for return to the status quo ante—not 6 May 1998 but July 1997—and claimed that facts to corroborate its position had been submitted to the High-level Delegation. Another amendment was a demand for compensation for an alleged 56 villages that had been uprooted and for Eritrean urban deportees. Those amendments were presented after the Modalities had been endorsed by the summit by acclamation. Ethiopia concluded that Eritrea had not accepted the Modalities and called on the international community not to tolerate Eritrea's prevarications.

On 16 July [S/1999/794], Eritrea transmitted to the Security Council its President's speech to the Algiers summit on 14 July, its President's letter to the OAU Chairman formally accepting the Modalities, and the Modalities.

On 23 July [S/1999/820], Finland transmitted to the Secretary-General a 21 July statement in which the EU welcomed the decision of the Algiers summit to approve the Modalities and reiterated its support to the Framework Agreement and the Modalities. The EU also urged Ethiopia and Eritrea to subscribe immediately to the Modalities, end all hostilities, proceed to the signature of a ceasefire agreement and fully implement the Framework Agreement.

Eritrea, in an 8 August press release [S/1999/857], officially accepted the OAU proposal on Technical Arrangements, which were worked out by technical experts from OAU, the United Nations, Algeria and the United States. On 6 September [S/1999/948], Eritrea reported that Ethiopia had formally rejected the Technical Arrangements.

Ethiopia transmitted to the Security Council a 4 September statement by its Ministry of Foreign Affairs [S/1999/949], which claimed that the Technical Arrangements were inconsistent with the Framework Agreement and its Modalities. Ethiopia stated that new provisions related to a peacekeeping mission were contained in the Technical Arrangements, and matters involving sovereignty and governance in the areas of redeployment indicated that the return to the status quo ante was not fully assured. It sought clarifications from OAU.

In statements of 14 September and 11 and 30 October [S/1999/973, S/1999/1045, S/1999/1108], Ethiopia stated that it was the victim of aggression and, if the return of all its territories and a full and unequivocal return to the status quo ante were guaranteed, it would be ready to fulfil its obligations on the basis of the OAU peace proposals. However, it also stated that the Technical Arrangements failed to guarantee its fundamental principle, which was the unequivocal return to the status quo ante.

In a 5 November press release [S/1999/1140], Eritrea maintained that the restoration of the status quo ante was nothing more than respect of, and a reversion to, the colonial boundaries that the Ethiopian regime had violated. The primary aim of the OAU peace package was to ensure respect of colonial boundaries and hence restoration of the stable status quo ante through demarcation. Ethiopia was obstructing that by refusing to contemplate demarcation of the boundary in accordance with inherited and sacrosanct colonial boundaries. Interim redeployment of troops of both countries was not going to restore the status quo ante, but was necessary to create a climate conducive for demarcation. The peace package had detailed provisions for restoring the status quo ante by securing the cessation of hostilities and the placement of a peacekeeping mission to monitor interim redeployment of troops to guarantee the demarcation of the boundary.

In response, Ethiopia, on 9 November [S/1999/1147], asserted that the return to the status quo ante meant the redeployment of troops to the positions they occupied prior to 6 May 1998. The final status of the territories would later be determined through delimitation and demarcation (based on colonial treaties and applicable international law), processes that were completely separate from the restoration of the status quo ante.

In an 8 December press release [S/1999/1228], Eritrea reported that Ethiopia had formally rejected the peace package in its entirety, demanding that Eritrea declare its recognition of Ethiopian sovereignty over the "contested territories". Eritrea charged that the demand contravened the fundamental tenets of the Framework Agreement and the Modalities, which stated that the status of those territories should be determined through demarcation. In a 16 December statement [S/1999/1256], Eritrea said that Ethiopia would never contemplate peace unless it was arbitrarily awarded, prior to demarcation, all the sovereign Eritrean territories that it claimed.

Special Envoy

On 2 November [S/1999/1132], the Secretary-General informed the Security Council that he had decided to extend the appointment of his Special Envoy in Africa, Mohamed Sahnoun (Algeria), who had been actively engaged in efforts to help resolve the conflict between Eritrea and Ethiopia. He had also decided to ask Mr.

Sahnoun to follow developments in other countries in the Horn of Africa, especially Somalia and the Sudan, and to represent him in meetings on the two countries of the Intergovernmental Authority on Development and its Partners Forum. On 5 November [S/1999/1133], the Council informed the Secretary-General that it took note of his decision.

Security in Horn of Africa

In a 14 May letter [S/1999/563], Ethiopia drew the Security Council's attention to eyewitness accounts of a large-scale military activity of destabilization by Eritrea in Somalia in support of one of the warring factions through shipments by air and sea of arms in violation of resolution 733(1992) [YUN 1992, p. 199]. It stated that Eritrea was organizing anti-Ethiopian terrorist groups from around the world for deployment in Somalia and along the common border between Ethiopia and Somalia. The Council was asked to condemn Eritrea's activities in Somalia and its violation of the embargo on all deliveries of weapons and military equipment to Somalia.

In response, Eritrea, on 26 May [S/1999/611], said that it had no vested interest in destabilizing Somalia where it was working to promote national reconciliation without partiality towards selected factions. Eritrea charged Ethiopia with acts of aggression, human rights violations and incursions against neighbouring countries and with accusing its victims for the very transgressions that it was guilty of. It accused Ethiopia of several incursions into Somalia and of training and arming different warring factions under the pretext of containing "the threat from terrorist groups". Eritrea cited Ethiopian shipments of arms to Somalia in 1997, 1998 and 1999, with a policy of creating clan-based mini-States so that it could manipulate a weak and divided Somalia.

Djibouti, in a 24 May letter [S/1999/600], referred to reported and corroborated accounts of Eritrean weapons and personnel involvement in Somalia. It accused Eritrea of destabilizing neighbouring countries in general and Ethiopia in particular and of violating Council resolutions concerning the complete embargo on all deliveries of weapons and military equipment to Somalia. It called on the Council to take urgent measures to thwart Eritrea's provocative and destabilizing activities in the region. In a 28 May letter [S/1999/622], Eritrea stated that its 26 May statement was an appropriate response to Djibouti's unfounded accusations, which echoed those of Ethiopia.

Germany transmitted to the Secretary-General an 18 June statement by the EU Presidency [S/1999/701] regarding the Ethiopian/Eritrean intervention in Somalia. It expressed concern at the illicit delivery of weapons, military equipment and military assistance to factions and other groups in Somalia in violation of the arms embargo imposed by the Security Council. Aware of the security implications of the situation in Somalia for the countries in the region, the EU called on Ethiopia and Eritrea to stop military intervention in Somalia.

In response to the EU statement, Ethiopia, on 24 June [S/1999/713], asserted that the EU, rather than calling on Eritrea to withdraw its troops, preferred to put pressure on the victim of aggression, slowing down development cooperation and taking unprecedented positions at international financial forums to punish Ethiopia, which for many years had been striving to draw attention to the growing crisis in Somalia. It stated that it was public knowledge that Eritrea was supplying arms to a faction directly linked to terrorist groups based in Somalia. Ethiopia called on the EU to re-examine its position so as to make a constructive contribution to promoting peace in the Horn of Africa.

Human rights situation

Communications. Eritrea transmitted to the Secretary-General a 9 January press release concerning the deaths of Eritreans in Ethiopian detention camps [A/53/793-S/1999/34]. The press release also drew attention to the deportation of over 48,000 Eritreans from Ethiopia on the basis of their ethnicity and the confiscation of their property.

In a 14 February press release [A/53/839-S/1999/184], Eritrea claimed that Ethiopia had released 38 Eritrean exchange students who had been in prison camps for eight months. Some 1,500 Eritrean civilians remained in the camps and their death toll continued to rise.

In communications submitted to the Security Council and General Assembly in May, June, July and October [A/53/966-S/1999/578, A/53/997-S/1999/660, A/53/1013-S/1999/756, A/54/489-S/1999/1084], Eritrea accused Ethiopia of human rights violations of Eritreans and Ethiopians of Eritrean origin.

Independent investigations. On 29 January [A/53/814-S/1999/95], Eritrea transmitted to the Secretary-General an Amnesty International report concerning gross violations of the human rights of Eritreans and Ethiopians of Eritrean origin by the Ethiopian Government. Amnesty International representatives had visited Ethiopia in October 1998 and Eritrea in January 1999 to examine allegations from both sides of human rights abuses arising from the May 1998 conflict.

They had met government officials and interviewed returnees from both countries. The report stated that Ethiopia's policy of deporting people of Eritrean origin, which began after war broke out in May 1998, had developed into a systematic, country-wide operation to arrest and deport anyone of full or part Eritrean descent. A total of 52,000 Eritreans had been deported from Ethiopia since May 1998, 6,300 in January 1999. Ethiopia's Prime Minister had stated that the deportees posed a threat to national security and that they had forfeited their Ethiopian citizenship by voting in Eritrea's independence referendum in 1993.

At least 22,000 Ethiopians had returned to Ethiopia from Eritrea since May 1998. No evidence was found to support Ethiopia's allegations that 40,000 of its citizens had been seriously ill-treated and forcibly deported. Amnesty International reiterated its appeal to the Ethiopian Government to put an end to the deportations, ill-treatment of deportees and arbitrary detentions of thousands of Eritreans.

An International Committee of the Red Cross (ICRC) press release, transmitted to the Council by Ethiopia on 13 May [S/1999/558], reported that ICRC delegates had visited some 300 Eritrean prisoners of war between 17 and 19 April, registered them and interviewed them in private. ICRC continued regular visits to Bilate camp in Ethiopia to verify that living conditions were in keeping with international humanitarian law. It was still pursuing efforts to gain access to Ethiopian prisoners in Eritrea.

Guinea-Bissau

In 1999, further progress was made in the implementation of the 1998 Abuja Agreement on Guinea-Bissau, which ended an armed conflict between forces supporting President João Bernardo Vieira and his former Army Chief of Staff, General Ansoumane Mane.

On 8 January 1999, an interim Government of National Unity led by Prime Minister Francisco Fadul was appointed but, largely due to logistical and financial difficulties, the date of the elections was postponed to 28 November. Following a resumption of fighting on 31 January, President Vieira and General Mane, on 3 February in Bissau, signed a new ceasefire agreement. Subsequently, foreign troops were withdrawn and the interposition force of the ECOWAS Monitoring Group (ECOMOG) was deployed. To assist Guinea-Bissau in its peace-building efforts, the Secretary-General, at the request of the interim Government, established in March the United Nations Peace-building Support Office in Guinea-Bissau, the main tasks of which were to promote national reconciliation and assist with the organization of the elections.

The peace process suffered a setback on 7 May when President Vieira was forcibly removed from office by the military junta led by General Mane and ECOWAS withdrew the interposition force. Nevertheless, legislative and presidential elections were held, as scheduled, on 28 November. The United Nations provided electoral assistance and coordinated international observation of the elections. As the first round of the presidential elections was inconclusive, the second round was scheduled for 16 January 2000.

Implementation of Abuja Agreement

Throughout the year, the Secretary-General reported on the situation in Guinea-Bissau, as requested by the Security Council, in particular on the implementation of the Abuja Agreement signed on 1 November 1998 [YUN 1998, p. 153] by President Vieira and General Mane.

The fighting had begun as a result of the President's dismissal of General Mane over allegations relating to arms smuggling to separatist rebels in Senegal. During the 1998 uprising, at President Vieira's request, Guinea and Senegal had sent troops to Guinea-Bissau to support the President's forces. Under the terms of the Abuja Agreement, the two sides agreed to uphold a ceasefire; withdraw all foreign troops from Guinea-Bissau; deploy an interpositional force of ECOWAS to guarantee security along the Guinea-Bissau/Senegal border and to keep the warring parties apart; form a Government of national unity; and hold general and presidential elections by March 1999.

Report of Secretary-General (March). In response to Security Council resolution 1216(1998) [YUN 1998, p. 154], the Secretary-General submitted a 17 March report [S/1999/294] on developments in Guinea-Bissau since the signing of the Abuja Agreement and the Additional Protocol of 15 December 1998 [YUN 1998, p. 154], which dealt with the composition of the new Government. On 8 January 1999, in conformity with the formula outlined in the Additional Protocol, members of the transitional Government of National Unity were appointed, some nominated by President Vieira and the remainder by the self-proclaimed junta led by General Mane. Despite the announcement that the new Government would be sworn in on 22 January, Prime Minister Fadul was reported to have stated that the Government would begin functioning only after foreign troops invited by President Vieira had left Guinea-Bissau. The resumption of fighting on 31 January further delayed the installation of the Government.

Immediately following the renewed fighting, President Gnassingbe Eyadema of Togo, the current Chairman of ECOWAS, launched efforts to secure a new ceasefire, an agreement for which President Vieira and General Mane signed on 3 February. At a meeting with President Eyadema on 17 February, both leaders, in their final communiqué later forwarded to the Security Council [S/1999/173], undertook never again to resort to arms and agreed that the Government of National Unity should be inaugurated as soon as possible. Three days later, that Government was formally inaugurated in Bissau. However, the functioning of the Government was hampered by a lack of adequate facilities, staff and other resources, and the disruption of the economic and monetary system.

Deployment of ECOMOG troops took place between 26 December 1998 and 2 January 1999. By mid-March, the ECOMOG interposition force stood at 600 troops, composed of contingents from Benin, the Gambia, the Niger and Togo, and the withdrawal of foreign troops was nearly complete. ECOMOG established its headquarters in Bissau, from where its troops were dispatched for patrol and reconnaissance operations. ECOMOG forces provided security at the seaport, which had reopened, and at the airport, reopened for humanitarian flights but not for commercial traffic. With some 100,000 people displaced throughout the country, ECOMOG helped ensure access for humanitarian supplies to reach the affected populations. ECOMOG also began disarming the forces of the two ex-belligerents and launched a demining programme. As for deployment along the Guinea-Bissau/Senegal border, ECOMOG indicated that the task, as called for under the Abuja Agreement, would require more troops.

Owing to delays in implementing the peace accords, it had become clear that it was not possible to hold elections by March, as called for in the Abuja Agreement. Both parties had expressed their interest in holding elections as soon as possible and requested UN assistance in that regard, specifically the coordination of international assistance, the provision of technical assistance to electoral authorities and the coordination of international observation of the polls.

The Secretary-General observed that the post-conflict situation in Guinea-Bissau remained very fragile. The economy, basic social services and State institutions needed to be rebuilt virtually from scratch. The significant action taken so far towards implementing the Abuja Agreement were steps in the right direction. The Secretary-General was heartened by the undertaking made by President Vieira and General Mane, in the presence of President Eyadema, never to resort to arms again.

Establishment of UNOGBIS

The Secretary-General, in a letter to the Security Council of 26 February [S/1999/232], proposed that a United Nations Peace-building Support Office (UNOGBIS) be established in Guinea-Bissau to help create an environment for restoring peace, democracy and the rule of law and for the organization of elections; to facilitate the implementation of the Abuja Agreement; to seek the parties' commitment to disarmament; and to integrate UN activities in the country. The Office would be headed by a representative of the Secretary-General, assisted by several political affairs and human rights officers, an electoral officer, a military adviser and support staff. The Council, on 3 March [S/1999/233], welcomed the proposal. On 26 April [S/1999/494], the Secretary-General informed the Council of his decision to appoint Samuel Nana-Sinkam (Cameroon) as his representative in Guinea-Bissau. The Council took note of the decision on 30 April [S/1999/495].

SECURITY COUNCIL ACTION

On 6 April [meeting 3991], the Security Council unanimously adopted **resolution 1233(1999)**. The draft [S/1999/369] was prepared during consultations among Council members.

The Security Council,

Reaffirming its resolution 1216(1998) of 21 December 1998 and the statements by its President of 6 November, 30 November and 29 December 1998,

Gravely concerned at the security and humanitarian situation in Guinea-Bissau,

Expressing its firm commitment to preserving the unity, sovereignty, political independence and territorial integrity of Guinea-Bissau,

Welcoming the report of the Secretary-General of 17 March 1999 and the observations contained therein,

Noting with appreciation the formal undertaking by the President of Guinea-Bissau and the leader of the Self-Proclaimed Military Junta on 17 February 1999 never again to resort to arms,

Welcoming the establishment and swearing-in on 20 February 1999 of the new Government of National Unity in Guinea-Bissau, which constitutes a significant step forward in the peace process,

Noting with concern that serious obstacles continue to hamper the effective functioning of the new Government, including, in particular, the failure of civil servants and other professional cadres seeking refuge in other countries to return,

Welcoming the deployment of troops constituting the Interposition Force of the Monitoring Group of the Economic Community of West African States by States in the region to implement their peacekeeping mandate and the withdrawal of all foreign forces from Guinea-Bissau pursuant to the Abuja Agreement of 1 November 1998,

Reiterating the need to conduct general and presidential elections pursuant to the Abuja Agreement and in accordance with national constitutional requirements as soon as possible, and noting the expression by the parties of their firm interest in having elections held as soon as possible,

1. *Reiterates* that the primary responsibility for achieving lasting peace in Guinea-Bissau rests with the parties, and strongly calls upon them to implement fully all the provisions of the Abuja Agreement and subsequent undertakings;

2. *Commends* the parties for the steps taken so far in the implementation of the Abuja Agreement, in particular the establishment of the new Government of National Unity, and strongly urges them to adopt and implement all measures necessary to ensure the smooth functioning of the new Government and all other institutions, including, in particular, confidence-building measures and measures to encourage the early return of refugees and internally displaced persons;

3. *Commends also* the Community of Portuguese Speaking Countries, States members of the Economic Community of West African States and leaders in and outside the region, in particular the President of the Republic of Togo in his capacity as Chairman of the Economic Community of West African States, for the key role they are playing to bring about national reconciliation and to consolidate peace and security throughout Guinea-Bissau;

4. *Expresses its appreciation* to those States which have already provided assistance for the deployment in Guinea-Bissau of the Monitoring Group of the Economic Community of West African States;

5. *Reiterates its urgent appeal* to all States and regional organizations to make financial contributions to the Monitoring Group, including through the United Nations trust fund established to support peacekeeping in Guinea-Bissau, to provide technical and logistical support to assist the Monitoring Group to carry out its peacekeeping mandate and to help facilitate the full implementation of all the provisions of the Abuja Agreement, and to that end invites the Secretary-General to consider convening a meeting in New York with the participation of the Economic Community of West African States in order to assess the needs of the Monitoring Group and to examine ways in which contributions could be mobilized and channelled;

6. *Calls upon* the parties concerned promptly to agree on a date for the holding of elections as soon as possible, which are all-inclusive, free and fair, and invites the United Nations and others to consider, as appropriate, providing any needed electoral assistance;

7. *Supports* the decision of the Secretary-General to establish a post-conflict Peace-building Support Office in Guinea-Bissau under the leadership of a representative of the Secretary-General, which will provide the political framework and leadership for harmonizing and integrating the activities of the United Nations system in Guinea-Bissau during the transitional period leading up to general and presidential elections and will facilitate, in close cooperation with the parties concerned, the Economic Community of West African States, the Monitoring Group, as well as other national and international partners, the implementation of the Abuja Agreement;

8. *Encourages* all agencies, programmes, offices and funds of the United Nations system, including the Bretton Woods institutions, as well as other international partners, to lend their support to the Support Office and to the Representative of the Secretary-General in order to establish, together with the Government of Guinea-Bissau, a comprehensive, concerted and coordinated approach to peace-building in Guinea-Bissau;

9. *Reiterates* the need for the simultaneous disarmament and encampment of ex-belligerent troops, welcomes the progress made by the Monitoring Group in that regard, and strongly urges the parties to continue to cooperate through the Special Commission established for that purpose, to conclude expeditiously those tasks and to create conditions for the reunification of the national armed and security forces;

10. *Emphasizes* the need for urgent demining of affected areas to pave the way for the return of refugees and displaced persons and for the resumption of agricultural activities, encourages the Monitoring Group to continue its demining activities, and calls upon States to provide the necessary assistance for demining;

11. *Calls upon* all concerned to respect strictly the relevant provisions of international law, including international humanitarian law and human rights law, to ensure safe and unimpeded access by humanitarian organizations to those in need and to ensure the protection and freedom of movement of United Nations and international humanitarian personnel;

12. *Reiterates its appeal* to States and organizations concerned to provide urgent humanitarian assistance to internally displaced persons and refugees;

13. *Welcomes* the planned round-table conference of donors on Guinea-Bissau to be held at Geneva on 4 and 5 May 1999, under the sponsorship of the United Nations Development Programme, to mobilize assistance for, inter alia, humanitarian needs, consolidation of peace and the socio-economic rehabilitation of Guinea-Bissau;

14. *Requests* the Secretary-General to keep the Security Council regularly informed and to submit a report to it by 30 June 1999 and every ninety days thereafter on developments in Guinea-Bissau, the activities of the Support Office and the implementation of the Abuja Agreement, including the implementation by the Monitoring Group of its mandate;

15. *Decides* to remain seized of the matter.

ECOWAS reports. On 16 April [S/1999/432], the Secretary-General transmitted to the Security Council the report on Guinea-Bissau prepared by the ECOWAS Executive Secretary pursuant to Council resolution 1216(1998) [YUN 1998, p. 154]. The report covered the period from the date of the deployment of ECOMOG in Guinea-Bissau and described the status of implementation of the Abuja Agreement, as well as the political, military, social and humanitarian situation. The report noted that, despite the significant progress in the disarmament process through the cooperation of the parties and the professionalism of ECOMOG troops, the situation on the ground remained precarious. Priority needed to be given to strengthening the ECOMOG force by deploying an additional battalion of 850 soldiers, and any assistance that could be provided to ECOWAS to effect that deployment would be appreciated.

On 19 April [S/1999/445], Togo forwarded to the Council the text of the agreement defining the operations, composition and status of ECOMOG in Guinea-Bissau, signed on 22 March by representatives of ECOWAS and the two parties to the conflict.

Resumed fighting and coup d'état

On 7 May, following resumed fighting in Guinea-Bissau, President Vieira was removed from office by the forces of the self-proclaimed junta. Towards the end of May, ECOMOG withdrew from the country and it was generally recognized that the Abuja Agreement was no longer applicable.

Communications. In May, several countries and international organizations addressed letters to the Security Council expressing concern over the seizure of power in Guinea-Bissau by the self-proclaimed military junta.

Burkina Faso, on 10 May [S/1999/533], forwarded a communiqué issued by the Central Organ of the OAU Mechanism for Conflict Prevention, Management and Resolution, in which it condemned the coup d'état at a time when ECOWAS and the international community were trying to find a durable solution to the conflict, and it demanded the immediate restoration of constitutional legality and respect for the interim agreement negotiated between the parties under ECOWAS auspices. On 12 May [S/1999/552], Togo forwarded a communiqué of 7 May issued by President Eyadema, current ECOWAS Chairman, condemning the violation of the Abuja Agreement and the Additional Protocol. He further deplored the fact that the parties to the conflict had not exercised restraint, which would have made it possible to continue the process of reconciliation for which the Government of National Unity had been formed. Similarly, Mali, on 9 May [S/1999/569], condemned the hostilities and demanded that the provisions of the Abuja Agreement and the Additional Protocol be respected so that elections could be held. Germany, on 18 May [S/1999/581], forwarded a statement by the EU Presidency, in which it appealed to the military junta, the Government and the other authorities of Guinea-Bissau to renew efforts to promote national reconciliation and development. On 25 May [S/1999/606], Cape Verde transmitted an 18 May communiqué issued by the members of the Community of Portuguese Speaking Countries (CPLP). Noting the commitments undertaken by the interim President of Guinea-Bissau, the military junta and the Government of National Unity to respect democracy, human rights and the rule of law, CPLP underlined the importance of holding free and fair elections.

The final communiqué of the meeting of Ministers for Foreign Affairs of ECOWAS (Lomé, 24-25 May) was forwarded to the Council by Togo on 26 May [S/1999/613]. Stressing that the coup d'état was contrary to the Abuja Agreement, the meeting agreed that ECOMOG be withdrawn from Guinea-Bissau. It also agreed on the need to monitor the situation closely.

Report of Secretary-General (July). In response to resolution 1233(1999), the Secretary-General reported to the Security Council on the situation in Guinea-Bissau on 1 July [S/1999/741]. Prior to the overthrow of the President, a round-table conference, sponsored by UNDP, was convened on 4 May in Geneva to assist the Government of Guinea-Bissau in its reconciliation and reconstruction efforts. Pledges amounting to some $200 million were made to cover activities in the areas of consolidation of peace and democracy, elections, demobilization and reinsertion of ex-combatants into civilian life, mine clearance and reunification of the armed forces.

Following President Vieira's ouster on 7 May, Prime Minister Fadul confirmed that legislative and presidential elections would proceed on 28 November, as announced by President Vieira before his removal from office. An interim President, the Speaker of the National Assembly, Malam Bacai Sanha, was inaugurated pending elections. To address the changed circumstances in Guinea-Bissau, ECOWAS, at a meeting in Lomé on 24 and 25 May (see above), condemned the coup d'état and agreed that ECOMOG troops would be withdrawn, despite the request of the Government of National Unity to the contrary.

Although it was generally recognized that the Abuja Agreement was no longer applicable, all parties concerned reaffirmed their commitment to holding elections as scheduled and preparations continued. In view of the situation, the Secretary-General stated that the mandate of UNOGBIS should be revised. In addition to its original mandate, UNOGBIS would support national efforts towards national reconciliation, particularly during the transitional period, and encourage initiatives to build confidence and maintain friendly relations between Guinea-Bissau, its neighbours and its international partners. In a letter to the Council of 28 June [S/1999/737], the Secretary-General described the revised mandate, which, he said, took into account the new realities on the ground and would enable UNOGBIS to contribute to restoring peace and sustainable development. The Council took note of that information on 30 June [S/1999/738].

The post-conflict situation in Guinea-Bissau remained complex as the events of 7 May had altered the pace and nature of the peace process, and the killings and destruction that accompanied that turn of events had created bitterness, the Secretary-General said. However, he was encouraged by the stated commitment of the transitional authorities to restore peace based on national reconciliation, respect for the rule of law and the return to constitutional order. He intended to set up a trust fund in support of UNOGBIS activities.

UNOGBIS activities and other developments

The Security Council, having discussed the Secretary-General's July report (above), issued a press statement on 6 July expressing support for his decision to establish UNOGBIS with its revised mandate and to create a trust fund for the Office. Meanwhile, in Guinea-Bissau, the situation stabilized by the end of September, despite some sporadic acts of violence.

Report of Secretary-General (September). In response to Security Council resolution 1233(1999), the Secretary-General submitted a 29 September report on developments in Guinea-Bissau and on UNOGBIS activities [S/1999/1015]. The internal political climate had stabilized by that time and the country continued to move in an orderly fashion towards the legislative and presidential elections scheduled for 28 November. The interim President had increasingly assumed the role defined by the Constitution and the day-to-day administration of the country was in the hands of the interim Prime Minister, while the National Assembly was carrying out its legislative functions. The military hierarchy had reaffirmed its commitment to stay out of politics and reorient the armed forces into a more professional service subordinate to civilian authorities. Notwithstanding those positive developments, the internal political situation remained fragile and the hold of the interim administration on political power was somewhat tenuous.

In keeping with the UNOGBIS mandate, the Secretary-General's Representative was cooperating with the transitional authorities to help ensure that the elections were held as scheduled, in an orderly, fair and transparent manner. At the request of the Government, the United Nations was providing, through UNDP, technical assistance for the electoral process and would be coordinating the observation of the elections. Experts were provided in the fields of electoral informatics, logistics, registration and civic education. By late September, 14 political parties were registered by the interim Government for participation in the elections, and some of them had nominated their candidates. The general census and voter registration began on 22 August and was completed on 2 September. The National Electoral Commission was active and Presidents of provincial electoral commissions had been appointed. Donor countries had already provided \$3.5 million of the estimated \$4.5 million electoral expenses.

Members of the interim Government expressed commitment to the national reconciliation process and, in that regard, UNOGBIS helped to launch a number of initiatives, including a National Conference on Reconciliation on 13 and 14 August, which brought together representatives of the interim administration, the military establishment, women and youth organizations, trade unions and the diaspora. The internal security situation was calm but somewhat tense due to the circulation of small arms among the civilian population and the omnipresence of the military, manning checkpoints and roadblocks. The disarmament and mobilization programme had not been revived. UNOGBIS, in cooperation with other UN bodies, was developing a programme of incentives to encourage civilians to surrender arms. Externally, the tenuous stability along the border with Senegal, in the wake of the recent upsurge of fighting in the Casamance region, was a major concern for the transitional Government. Another concern was the reported large presence, across the border in Guinea, of armed elements believed to be supporters of former President Vieira. Faced with those concerns, the Government asked the United Nations to consider deploying international military observers to monitor the situation along the borders with Guinea and Senegal and provide a measure of confidence among the population during the electoral process. In response, the Secretary-General sent a small mission to Guinea-Bissau to assess the situation and make recommendations.

The human rights situation in Guinea-Bissau continued to improve during the reporting period. To promote human rights and the rule of law, UNOGBIS worked with civil society groups and the offices of the Attorney General and other judicial officials. The Judiciary had been speeding up hearings of the 600 political and military prisoners in detention. The humanitarian situation was also improving. Refugees were returning from neighbouring States and an estimated 50,000 internally displaced persons had decided to settle with host families. Some $4.4 million of humanitarian assistance was required to resettle the returnees. Poverty was a concern, owing to the difficulties prevailing in health, education, water supply, energy and housing.

The Secretary-General said that progress had been made since his last report but that the transition process was still encountering difficulties. Although the internal security situation remained relatively stable, concerns about subregional instability persisted. UNOGBIS had been able to pursue its mandate. Its further success would depend not only on the political will of the Government and the political forces in the country, but also on the availability of resources. The Secretary-General had established a trust fund for that purpose. He hoped that elections would encourage the international community to resume cooperation with Guinea-Bissau and contribute to reconstruction. In view of the situation and in order to assist Guinea-Bissau in the post-electoral period, the transitional Government had requested that the UNOGBIS mandate be extended for one year after its expiry on 31 December 1999. The Secretary-General would revert to the Council on that issue after the elections and consultations with the new Government.

Mission report. On 13 October [S/1999/1091], the Secretary-General informed the Security Council that he had received the report of the small mission he had sent to Guinea-Bissau and neighbouring countries, namely the Gambia, Guinea and Senegal, to look into the transitional Government's request for international military observers along the borders with Guinea and Senegal. The mission found that the situation along those borders was tenuous and recommended the deployment of approximately 200 military observers to monitor developments. The Secretary-General concluded that it would be preferable to take the following measures, while keeping the option of deploying military observers under review: to send his Representative to visit those countries and ECOWAS headquarters to brief them on the report and to encourage Guinea, Guinea-Bissau and Senegal to set up joint monitoring mechanisms along their borders; to develop a programme of visits by his Representative, the UN country team and the diplomatic community to towns and villages in Guinea-Bissau during the weeks prior to the elections; and to encourage Member States to send electoral observers. Such measures would provide some confidence among the population during the electoral process and indicate that the international community would be watching that process. On 26 October [S/1999/1092], the Security Council took note of the interim proposals.

Presidential and legislative elections

Following the elections in Guinea-Bissau on 28 November, the Secretary-General, on 9 December [S/1999/1252], informed the Council that, since none of the contending presidential candidates received the required majority of the vote, a second round was expected to be held in January 2000. Following consultations with the transitional Government, he proposed that the UNOGBIS mandate be extended for three months, until 31 March 2000. He would revert to the Council again following the second round of voting. The Council on 14 December [S/1999/1253] took note of the proposal.

Report of Secretary-General (December). In response to Security Council resolution 1233(1999), the Secretary-General, on 23 December [S/1999/1276], issued a further report on the situation in Guinea-Bissau, covering developments since his report of 29 September, a period dominated by preparations for and the holding of elections. During the preparations, the principal leaders in the country, including the interim President, the Prime Minister, the leaders of political parties and the military establishment, reaffirmed their commitment to holding elections as scheduled. In addition to supporting the ongoing peace process, the military authorities also committed themselves to transforming the armed forces into a republican army subordinate to civilian authorities following the elections. The political and military leaders reaffirmed the supremacy of the Constitution, which provided for the rule of law. Meanwhile, relations between Guinea-Bissau and its neighbours continued to improve, strengthened by the efforts of the Secretary-General's Representative who visited Guinea and Senegal in November. Internally, there was a relaxation in the political climate. Newspapers resumed publication, new journals emerged and private radio stations began broadcasting again.

Twelve presidential candidates contested the office of the presidency. In the legislative elections, candidates from 13 political parties contested 102 seats in the National Assembly. The National Electoral Commission was responsible for the organization and conduct of the elections. The United Nations, through UNDP, provided technical assistance in many areas, including developing an operational plan, which entailed the procurement, delivery and collection of polling station materials, computerization of the voters' lists, identification of polling stations and the training and deployment of poll workers. To support the process, the international community provided financial resources and in-kind contributions. The Commission registered 502,678 voters, representing 91.2 per cent of the eligible voting population, and initiated a civic education campaign on the electoral process. A televised round-table discussion was held on 26 November during which the presidential candidates addressed the electorate and answered questions. UNOGBIS, in collaboration with UNDP and the United Nations Population Fund (UNFPA), organized a seminar to promote the participation of women in political life on 19 and 20 November. On the eve of the elections, the Secretary-General issued a statement calling on all concerned parties, including the military, to ensure that the elections were conducted in a free, fair and transparent manner and without interference. He also affirmed the readiness of the United Nations to support the new Government in building a climate for peace and reconciliation. UNOGBIS coordinated the international observation of the elections, with the participation of 88 observers.

Over 80 per cent of eligible voters participated in the elections, which, in general, proceeded in an orderly manner despite some minor delays. On 30 November, international observers declared that the voting had taken place in a climate of "civility, serenity, transparency and sincerity" and in accordance with the electoral laws.

On 9 December, the Commission published the official results, which showed that the Party for Social Renewal, headed by Kumba Yala, had won the largest share (38) of the 102 seats in the Assembly. Guinea-Bissau Resistance came next with 28 seats. The remainder were shared by six parties. In the presidential elections, Kumba Yala obtained 38.81 per cent of the vote, followed by interim President Sanha with 23.37 per cent. Consequently, a second round of voting was scheduled for 16 January 2000.

By the end of the year, the military still maintained a high visible presence and continued to perform routine police functions. A World Bank mission visited Guinea-Bissau and carried out a comprehensive feasibility study, and a United Nations Secretariat team worked on a plan for disarmament and demobilization.

As part of its efforts to promote human rights, UNOGBIS carried out joint visits with the Government to detention facilities and encouraged the acceleration of trial proceedings. It also provided assistance for the training of 20 magistrates to help speed up the judicial process. On 13 December, the authorities announced the release of 59 of the estimated 600 prisoners detained since the events of 7 May.

By the end of the year, the country was in a transitional phase from humanitarian relief to reconstruction and rehabilitation. UN organizations, in particular the Food and Agriculture Organization of the United Nations (FAO) and WFP, provided assistance to vulnerable groups, with FAO concentrating on the agricultural sector and WFP on the needs of hospitals, nutritional centres and school canteens. Other UN assistance was provided for rebuilding infrastructure damaged by the fighting. The voluntary repatriation of Bissau Guinean refugees from neighbouring countries continued under UNHCR auspices and assistance was provided for some 6,000 refugees from neighbouring countries, mainly Senegalese from the Casamance region.

The Secretary-General observed that the holding of the legislative and presidential elections in an open, fair and transparent manner was an important step forward in the transition to democracy and the restoration of peace and normalcy in Guinea-Bissau. Since no candidate had won the presidential elections, the formation of a new Government was not expected before February 2000 following the second round of elections. Therefore, as an interim measure and following consultations with the current interim Government and with the Council, it was agreed to extend the UNOGBIS mandate for three months, until 31 March 2000.

Liberia

During 1999, the United Nations Peace-building Support Office in Liberia (UNOL) continued to work towards the consolidation of peace and democracy in close cooperation with the Liberian Government and ECOWAS. Efforts to destroy all weapons began on 26 July and ended on 18 October, during which time a total of 19,296 arms and 3,164,849 rounds of ammunition of all sizes were destroyed.

ECOWAS met twice to consider issues relating to regional peace and security, particularly the situation prevailing at the border zone between Guinea and Liberia.

In July, following a one-day visit to Liberia, the Secretary-General requested the Economic Commission for Africa (ECA) to assist in coordinating activities for the resuscitation of the Mano River Union linking Guinea, Liberia and Sierra Leone.

UNOL

In a 12 October letter to the Security Council President [S/1999/1064], the Secretary-General stated that, during 1999, UNOL had continued to assist the Liberian Government in facilitating communication with the United Nations on matters relating to peace-building and in providing political support to efforts to mobilize international assistance for reconstruction. It had provided political and technical assistance in the destruction of the large quantities of weapons and ammunition that had been collected during Liberia's civil war and had been active in reducing tension between Liberia and its neighbours, particularly Guinea and Sierra Leone. UNOL, in cooperation with the United Nations Observer Mission in Sierra Leone and ECA, had joined efforts with ECOWAS to support initiatives to resuscitate the Mano River Union, a mechanism for subregional cooperation among Guinea, Liberia and Sierra Leone. It had also worked in support of subregional efforts to achieve a political settlement of the Sierra Leone crisis and facilitated the implementation of the Lomé Peace Agreement (see below, under "Sierra Leone").

In view of UNOL's catalytic contributions to Liberia's post-conflict peace-building efforts, the Liberian Government had asked that its mandate be extended to the end of December 2000. The Secretary-General stated his intention to agree to the extension. On 15 October [S/1999/1065], the Council took note of that intention.

Sanctions Committee

The Security Council Committee established pursuant to resolution 985(1995) [YUN 1995, p. 355] to monitor sanctions against Liberia, issued a report on 31 December [S/1999/1301], covering its activities in 1999. The arms embargo was imposed by the Council by resolution 788(1992) [YUN 1992, p. 192].

The Committee observed that it did not have any specific monitoring mechanism to ensure the effective implementation of the arms embargo and thus relied solely on the cooperation of States and organizations in a position to provide pertinent information. In 1999, communications from Ukraine and the United Kingdom on alleged violations of the arms embargo were discussed by the Committee. The Chairman, on behalf of the Committee, addressed letters to Burkina Faso, Liberia and Ukraine concerning the alleged shipment of arms from Ukraine to Sierra Leone via Burkina Faso and Liberia and informed them of their possible violation of Council resolutions 1132(1997) [YUN 1997, p. 135] and 985(1995). The Committee received a reply from Ukraine but not from Burkina Faso and Liberia.

UNOMIL financing

In January [A/53/802], the Secretary-General submitted to the General Assembly the financial performance report of the United Nations Observer Mission in Liberia (UNOMIL) for the period 1 July 1997 to 30 June 1998. UNOMIL's mandate came to an end in 1997 [YUN 1997, p. 123]. Resources of $12,226,700 gross ($11,667,900 net) were made available to UNOMIL for the period. Expenditures amounted to $10,027,600 gross ($9,514,600 net), resulting in an unencumbered balance of $2,199,100 gross ($2,153,300 net). Regarding the amount of $8,952,900 gross ($8,434,900 net) appropriated by General Assembly decision 52/407 [ibid., p. 127] for the administrative closing and liquidation of UNOMIL, expenditures totalled $8,798,700 gross ($8,303,100 net), resulting in an unencumbered balance of $154,200 gross ($131,800 net).

The Assembly also had before it related reports of ACABQ [A/53/895, A/53/896].

GENERAL ASSEMBLY ACTION

On 8 June [meeting 101], the General Assembly, on the recommendation of the Fifth Committee [A/53/984], which had before it reports of the Secretary-General on UNOMIL financing submitted in 1998 [YUN 1998, p. 156], adopted **decision 53/478** without vote [agenda item 133].

Financing of the United Nations Observer Mission in Liberia

At its 101st plenary meeting, on 8 June 1999, the General Assembly, on the recommendation of the Fifth Committee, having considered the reports of the Secretary-General on the financing of the United Nations Observer Mission in Liberia and the related reports of the Advisory Committee on Administrative and Budgetary Questions, and recalling its resolution 51/3 C of 13 June 1997 and its decision 52/407 of 31 October 1997 on the financing of the Observer Mission:

(a) Endorsed the observations and recommendations contained in the report of the Advisory Committee;

(b) Decided, as an ad hoc arrangement, and taking into account the amount of 5,111,775 United States dollars gross (4,729,575 dollars net) already apportioned under the terms of General Assembly resolution 51/3 C, to apportion among Member States the additional amount of 3,841,125 dollars gross (3,705,325 dol-

lars net) in respect of the period from 1 July 1997 to 30 June 1998, in accordance with the scheme set out in paragraph 7 of resolution 51/3 C, and taking into account the scale of assessments for the year 1997, as set out in its resolution 49/19 B of 23 December 1994 and decision 50/471 A of 23 December 1995, and the scale of assessments for the year 1998, as set out in its resolution 52/215 A of 22 December 1997;

(c) Decided also that, in accordance with the provisions of its resolution 973(X) of 15 December 1955, there shall be set off against the apportionment among Member States, as provided for in subparagraph *(b)* above, their respective share in the Tax Equalization Fund of the estimated additional staff assessment income of 135,800 dollars approved for the Observer Mission in respect of the period from 1 July 1997 to 30 June 1998;

(d) Decided further that, for Member States that have fulfilled their financial obligations to the Observer Mission, there shall be set off against the apportionment, as provided for in subparagraph *(b)* above, their respective share of an equivalent amount of 3,841,125 dollars gross (3,705,325 dollars net) from the unencumbered balance of 4,601,200 dollars gross (4,238,000 dollars net) in respect of the period from 1 July 1996 to 30 June 1997;

(e) Decided that, for Member States that have not fulfilled their financial obligations to the Observer Mission, their share of an amount of 3,841,125 dollars gross (3,705,325 dollars net) from the unencumbered balance of 4,601,200 dollars gross (4,238,000 dollars net) in respect of the period from 1 July 1996 to 30 June 1997 shall first be set off against their outstanding obligations;

(f) Decided also that Member States that have fulfilled their financial obligations to the Observer Mission shall be credited their respective share in the remaining portion of the unencumbered balance of 4,601,200 dollars gross (4,238,000 dollars net) in respect of the period from 1 July 1996 to 30 June 1997 after the application of 3,841,125 dollars gross (3,705,325 dollars net) as provided for in subparagraph *(d)* above, that is, 760,075 dollars gross (532,675 dollars net);

(g) Decided further that, for Member States that have not fulfilled their financial obligations to the Observer Mission, their share in the remaining portion of the unencumbered balance of 4,601,200 dollars gross (4,238,000 dollars net) in respect of the period from 1 July 1996 to 30 June 1997 after the application of 3,841,125 dollars gross (3,705,325 dollars net), that is, 760,075 dollars gross (532,675 dollars net), shall first be set off against their outstanding obligations;

(h) Decided that Member States that have fulfilled their financial obligations to the Observer Mission shall be credited their respective share of the unencumbered balance of 154,200 dollars gross (131,800 dollars net) in respect of the period from 1 July 1997 to 30 June 1998;

(i) Decided also that, for Member States that have not fulfilled their financial obligations to the Observer Mission, their share in the unencumbered balance of 154,200 dollars gross (131,800 dollars net) in respect of the period from 1 July 1997 to 30 June 1998 shall first be set off against their outstanding obligations;

(j) Took note of the report of the Secretary-General on the final disposition of the assets of the Observer Mission;

(k) Reaffirmed its decision 52/485 of 26 June 1998, and reiterated that all reports on the final disposition of assets should contain detailed information on and justification of written-off and lost items;

(l) Requested the Board of Auditors to conduct an audit of the final disposition of assets of the Observer Mission, in particular of sold and written-off assets, and to include its recommendations in the audit report for the period from July 1998 to June 1999;

(m) Decided to include in the provisional agenda of its fifty-fourth session the item entitled "Financing of the United Nations Observer Mission in Liberia".

On 23 December, the Assembly decided that the Fifth Committee should continue to consider the question of UNOMIL financing at its resumed fifty-fourth (2000) session (**decision 54/462 A**).

Liberia-Guinea

On 11 August [S/1999/876], Liberia reported to the Secretary-General that an armed incursion into Liberian territory from Guinea, in the Foya District of Lofa County, had taken place on 10 August. Liberia had submitted a note of protest to Guinea and demanded that it take the necessary measures to bring the situation under control. Liberia stated that the incident was the second incursion from Guinea, the first having occurred on 21 April.

ECOWAS action

By a 30 August letter to the President of the Security Council [S/1999/929], Togo informed the Security Council President that a meeting of the ECOWAS ad hoc Committee of Ministers for Foreign Affairs was held in Lomé on 26 August. The Ministers condemned the attack by Liberian dissidents from Guinea, which threatened the peace and security of Liberia and could destabilize the subregion and mar relations between Guinea and Liberia. They agreed to establish a commission comprising ECOWAS, Guinea and Liberia, in order to find a solution to common security problems threatening the peace and stability of the two countries. The Ministers called on Guinea and Liberia to observe the relevant provisions of the ECOWAS Treaty and the Protocol on Non-Aggression, signed in Lagos, Nigeria, on 22 April 1978.

On 20 September [S/1999/992], Togo transmitted to the Council President the Declaration of the Ad Hoc Committee of Heads of State and Government of ECOWAS, signed in Abuja, Nigeria, on 16 September. The Ad Hoc Committee strongly condemned the attacks on Guinea and Liberia, which threatened the peace and security of both countries and could also destabilize the region and mar the relations between the two ECOWAS member States. The Committee, in accordance with the Mano River Union Treaty, agreed that: the three countries of the Union, namely Guinea, Liberia and Sierra Leone, should exchange among themselves the list of persons suspected of involvement in subversive activities against their respective countries, with a view to their expulsion; a Joint Security Committee would be established by the three countries to monitor and ensure the security of their common borders; the three countries would reactivate the Mano River Union with the participation of the ECOWAS secretariat as an observer and hold their summit in Freetown, Sierra Leone, during the first week of November; and the heads of State of Guinea and Liberia should establish early a direct line of communication to facilitate regular consultation.

Liberia–Sierra Leone

A joint communiqué was issued on the occasion of a visit to Togo by Charles Ghankay Taylor, President of Liberia (Kara, 4-5 June) [S/1999/656]. President Taylor assured Gnassingbe Eyadema, President of Togo and current Chairman of ECOWAS, of his support for negotiations to achieve lasting peace and reconciliation in Sierra Leone. Both Presidents welcomed the signing, on 18 May in Lomé, of the ceasefire agreement between the Government of Sierra Leone and the Revolutionary United Front of Sierra Leone and appealed to States to refrain from supplying the parties with arms, ammunition, mercenaries or other forms of logistical support (see below, under "Sierra Leone").

Libyan Arab Jamahiriya

On 5 April, the Security Council suspended, but did not lift, the sanctions imposed on the Libyan Arab Jamahiriya under resolution 748(1992) [YUN 1992, p. 55] and strengthened under resolution 883(1993) [YUN 1993, p. 101]. That action was taken on receipt of the Secretary-General's report on the arrival in the Netherlands of the two Libyan suspects charged with the 1988 bombing of Pan Am flight 103. As agreed among the parties concerned—Libya, the United Kingdom and the United States—the two suspects were to face trial under a Scottish court sitting in the Netherlands. The sanctions covered air links with, provisions of military supplies to, restrictions on diplomatic and consular personnel of, and restrictions on suspected terrorist nationals of Libya. On 30 July, the Secretary-General reported to the Council that Libya had complied with the requirements of resolutions 731(1992) [YUN 1992, p. 53] and 748(1992). Despite that confirmation and notwithstanding the efforts of the League of Arab States (LAS), the Organization of the Islamic Conference, the Organization of African Unity (OAU) and the Movement of Non-Aligned Countries, the sanctions had not been lifted by the end of the year.

Arrangements for trial of Pan Am 103 bombing suspects

On 19 March [S/1999/311], the Secretary-General submitted to the Security Council a letter of the same date from Libya stating its agreement that the two Libyan nationals suspected of bombing Pan Am flight 103 over Lockerbie, Scotland, in 1988 would be available for the Secretary-General to take custody of them on or before 6 April. The points of agreement were: a Scottish court would be convened in the Netherlands to try the two suspects in accordance with Scottish law, in the presence of international observers appointed by the Secretary-General and in consultation with Saudi Arabia and South Africa; if the suspects were found guilty, they would serve their sentence in Scotland, under the supervision of the United Nations and the auspices of the Libyan Consulate in Scotland; and the sanctions imposed on Libya would be suspended on the arrival of the two suspects in the Netherlands and would be lifted definitively after the Secretary-General had submitted to the Security Council within 90 days a report stating that Libya had complied with the Council's resolutions.

On 23 March [S/1999/312], the Council President made a statement to the press welcoming Libya's letter. The Council members reaffirmed existing Council resolutions as the basis for bringing about a full and final resolution of the situation. They looked forward to the implementation of that handover, taking into account the information provided by the French authorities regarding the 1989 bombing of Union de transports aériens (UTA) flight 772 [YUN 1997, p. 160], and to the immediate suspension of sanctions with a view to lifting them as soon as circumstances permitted, in accordance with relevant Council resolutions.

Suspension of sanctions

Report of Secretary-General (April). On 5 April [S/1999/378], the Secretary-General reported to the Security Council that, as requested in Council resolution 1192(1998) [YUN 1998, p. 161], the two Libyan nationals charged with the bombing of Pan Am flight 103 had arrived safely in the Netherlands on board a UN aircraft. The accused were detained by the Dutch authorities pending their transfer for the purpose of trial before the Scottish court sitting in the Netherlands. He also reported that he had been informed by the French authorities that, regarding the bombing of UTA flight 772, the conditions set forth in resolution 1192(1998) had been met, without prejudice to the other requests concerning the bombing of Pan Am flight 103. Concerning the reaffirmation in that resolution of paragraph 16 of resolution 883(1993) [YUN 1993, p. 101], which requested the Secretary-General to report within 90 days of the date of the suspension of the sanctions on Libya's compliance with the remaining provisions of Council resolution 748(1992), the Secretary-General stated that, following the suspension of the measures, he would proceed with the preparation of that report. Libya had already provided information and assurances on the matter.

Also on 5 April, the Security Council issued a press release welcoming the Secretary-General's report on the arrival of the two suspects and the cooperation of the Libyan Government with the French authorities regarding flight UTA 772. The Council noted that the conditions for the immediate suspension of sanctions had been fulfilled and the sanctions were therefore effectively suspended.

SECURITY COUNCIL ACTION (April)

On 8 April [meeting 3992], following consultations among Security Council members, the President made statement **S/PRST/1999/10** on behalf of the Council:

The Security Council recalls its resolutions 731(1992) of 21 January 1992, 748(1992) of 31 March 1992, 883(1993) of 11 November 1993 and 1192(1998) of 27 August 1998.

The Council welcomes the letter dated 5 April 1999 from the Secretary-General to the President of the Security Council, reporting that the two persons accused of the bombing of Pan Am flight 103 have arrived in the Netherlands for the purpose of trial before the court described in paragraph 2 of resolution 1192(1998) and that, with regard to the bombing of UTA 772, the French authorities had informed the Secretary-General that he might indicate, in reporting to the Council under paragraph 8 of resolution 1192(1998), that the conditions set forth in resolution 1192(1998) had been met, without prejudice to the other requests concerning the bombing of Pan Am flight 103.

The Council expresses its deep appreciation to the Secretary-General, the Governments of the Republic of South Africa and the Kingdom of Saudi Arabia and other countries for their commitment towards reaching a satisfactory conclusion relating to Pan Am flight 103.

The Council further notes the role played by the League of Arab States, the Organization of the Islamic Conference, the Organization of African Unity and the Movement of Non-Aligned Countries in this regard.

The Council notes that, with the letter from the Secretary-General dated 5 April 1999, the conditions set forth in paragraph 8 of resolution 1192(1998) for the immediate suspension of the measures set forth in resolutions 748(1992) and 883(1993) have been fulfilled. In this regard, the Council recalls that, in accordance with resolution 1192(1998), the measures set forth in resolutions 748(1992) and 883(1993) were immediately suspended upon receipt of the letter of the Secretary-General on 5 April 1999 at 1400 hours eastern standard time. This development was immediately acknowledged through a statement of the President of the Security Council to the press on 5 April 1999 following consultations of the whole.

The Council remains seized of the matter.

Communications (April). In an 8 April letter to the President of the Security Council [S/1999/397], LAS welcomed the suspension of the measures imposed on Libya and emphasized the importance of the Council adopting a resolution confirming the suspension and the need to lift the measures as soon as possible, within not more than 90 days, as provided for in Council resolution 883(1993) and confirmed in resolution 1192(1998). LAS invited the Council to call on all States that had taken measures and decisions to implement resolutions 748(1992) and 883(1993) to announce their suspension.

Also on 8 April [S/1999/407], Germany drew the Secretary-General's attention to a statement by the EU Presidency, which welcomed Libya's transfer to the Netherlands of the two bombing suspects, as well as its cooperation with the French authorities in the case of UTA flight 772, thus bringing about the suspension of UN and EU Lockerbie-related sanctions against Libya. The EU stressed that full compliance with the provisions of the relevant Council resolutions would enable Libya to regain its position as a full member of the international community.

On 22 April [S/1999/466], the Islamic Group at the United Nations expressed the view that the suspension of sanctions should have been embodied in a Council resolution so as to place the question in its correct legal framework and requested the Council to adopt a resolution definitively lifting the sanctions imposed on Libya. The Islamic Group also stated that, as the legal process had gone before the Scottish court as agreed to by all parties concerned, all parties should comply with whatever verdict was reached by that court.

Report of Secretary-General (June). On 30 June [S/1999/726], the Secretary-General presented his report to the Security Council regarding the suspension and lifting of sanctions against Libya. He summarized the international response from the EU, LAS, the Group of African States at the United Nations, the Coordinating Bureau of the Movement of Non-Aligned Countries and the Islamic Group at the United Nations to the events of 5 April, when the conditions set forth in resolutions 1192(1998), 883(1993) and 748(1992) had been fulfilled.

With respect to the investigation of the bombing of UTA flight 772, the French authorities informed him that their requests had, on the whole, been satisfied and that they expected Libya to abide by the obligations that followed from the judgement handed down by French courts: on 10 March, six Libyan nationals had been convicted of that crime in absentia; and on 31 March, 17 decisions were issued regarding payment of indemnities to the plaintiffs. It was thus concluded that Libya had complied with the relevant requirements of Council resolutions 731(1992) and 748(1992).

Regarding the bombing of Pan Am flight 103, the first issue was Libya's cooperation with the Scottish court sitting in the Netherlands to try the two bombing suspects. On 7 June, the Scottish court granted a request by the defence lawyers to delay the trial for six months. The trial was scheduled to start on or before 4 February 2000. Since Libya was only expected to comply with requirements regarding access to witnesses, relevant documents and other material evidence during the trial, the Secretary-General pointed out that he was not in a position to provide any factual information on compliance. However, Libyan authorities had provided assurances that they would cooperate with the Scottish court. Regarding the requirement concerning the payment of compensation, Libya was not expected to pay compensation to the families of the Pan Am 103 victims before the trial was completed. However, Libya had publicly stated on several occasions that it would comply with the conclusions of the Scottish court and, if required, would pay the necessary compensation. As to the issue of Libya's renunciation of terrorism, Libya had stated on numerous occasions that it was opposed to terrorism in all its forms and had condemned all terrorist acts. The Secretary-General recalled that Libya, in a number of letters to the Security Council, had pledged to sever relations with all groups involved in international terrorism of any kind and affirmed that there were no terrorist training camps in its territory.

The Secretary-General observed that his report did not provide a comprehensive view of all the events and developments related to the bombings of the two civilian aircraft but rather a limited picture in line with the Council's mandate.

The Secretary-General reported that on 11 June he had hosted a tripartite meeting between Libya, the United Kingdom and the United States to assist them in clarifying their positions regarding the requirements of the relevant resolutions for the lifting of measures imposed against Libya. The Secretary-General hoped that further contacts between the parties would help to develop a constructive dialogue and eventually lead to the normalization of relations among them.

SECURITY COUNCIL ACTION (July)

On 9 July [meeting 4022], following consultations among Security Council members, the President made statement **S/PRST/1999/22** on behalf of the Council:

> The Security Council recalls its resolutions 731(1992) of 21 January 1992, 748(1992) of 31 March 1992, 883(1993) of 11 November 1993 and 1192(1998) of 27 August 1998 and the statement by its President of 8 April 1999.
>
> The Council welcomes the report of the Secretary-General of 30 June 1999 submitted in fulfilment of the request contained in paragraph 16 of resolution 883(1993).
>
> The Council welcomes the positive developments identified in the report and the fact that the Libyan Arab Jamahiriya has made significant progress in compliance with the relevant resolutions. It welcomes also the commitment given by the Libyan Arab Jamahiriya to implement further the relevant resolutions by continuing cooperation in order to meet all the requirements contained therein. It encourages all parties concerned to maintain their spirit of cooperation. The Council recalls that the measures set forth in resolutions 748(1992) and 883(1993) have been suspended, and reaffirms its intention to lift those measures as soon as possible, in conformity with the relevant resolutions.
>
> The Council expresses its gratitude to the Secretary-General for his continued efforts in his role as set out in paragraph 4 of resolution 731(1992) and paragraph 6 of resolution 1192(1998), and requests him to follow developments regarding this matter closely and to report to the Council accordingly.
>
> The Council remains actively seized of the matter.

Communications (July and November). By a 6 July letter to the Security Council President [S/1999/752], Libya stated that, following the Secretary-General's June report and according to its resolutions 883(1993) and 1192(1998), the Council was obliged to lift the sanctions imposed on Libya. It asserted that matters of a bilateral nature could be dealt with at the bilateral level and should not be linked to Council resolutions or the sanctions imposed by the Council. Libya again expressed it willingness to engage in a dialogue with any State on any bilateral matters and urged the Council not to allow itself to be used by anyone for the purpose of achieving certain political goals.

By a 9 July letter [S/1999/770], South Africa, on behalf of the Movement of Non-Aligned Countries, requested the Council to consider adopting a resolution reflecting the decision of the Twelfth Summit of Heads of State or Government of the Movement (Durban, 2-3 September 1998) that sanctions against Libya should be totally terminated once the suspects had appeared for trial.

On 27 July [S/1999/827], Libya transmitted to the Council President a decision adopted by the OAU Assembly of Heads of State and Government at its thirty-fifth ordinary session (Algiers, 12-14 July) on the crisis between Libya and the United States and the United Kingdom. The Assembly called on the Council immediately and permanently to lift the sanctions against Libya and requested the OAU Chairman to request the Secretary-General and the Council President to take appropriate measures to ensure the speedy and permanent lifting of sanctions.

In an 18 November letter to the Council [S/1999/1183], Libya expressed its readiness to cooperate with the other parties involved in establishing the truth and identifying those responsible for blowing up Pan Am flight 103 over Lockerbie in 1988. It stated that the Council should have rescinded the measures imposed on Libya 90 days after the arrival of the suspects in the Netherlands and on receipt of a report from the Secretary-General. Although that period of time had elapsed and the Council had received the Secretary-General's report, the Council had been unable to rescind the measures because of a threat by the United States to use its veto against any such resolution. Libya urged the other parties to abide by the undertakings they had given and to discharge the obligations imposed on them by the relevant Council resolutions with respect to cooperation with the Scottish court in the Netherlands. It again called on the Council to rescind, fully and immediately, the measures imposed on Libya under resolutions 748(1992) and 883(1993).

Sanctions Committee

The Committee established pursuant to Security Council resolution 748(1992) concerning the Libyan Arab Jamahiriya (Sanctions Committee) issued a report on 31 December covering its activities in 1999 [S/1999/1299]. During the year, the Committee held two meetings and handled over 50 incoming communications relating to various aspects of the implementation of the mandatory sanctions, as well as a comparable number of replies.

The Committee approved 25 medical emergency evacuation flights in 1999, compared to 91 in 1998. It also approved procedures for the travel of Libyan pilgrims to the Hajj and for humanitarian flights.

On 26 January, the Committee considered communications from the United States and UN sources concerning numerous alleged flight violations of the sanctions regime on Libya. The Committee requested its Chairman to address letters to Chad, the Democratic Republic of the Congo, Eritrea, Libya, the Niger, the Sudan and Uganda in order to seek additional information regarding that issue. The Committee also sent letters to Chad and the Gambia, which had confirmed violations, noting that the flights in question were unacceptable breaches of the sanctions regime.

1986 attack against Libya

In a 15 April letter to the Security Council President [S/1999/457], Libya stated that the families of the victims continued to seek justice and the punishment of those responsible for the American aggression against Libya on 15 April 1986 [YUN 1986, p. 247]. It enclosed an indictment issued by a Libyan court against a number of American officials who planned and executed the aggression, a list of names of the dead and wounded and an account of the damage done to private and public property. Libya expected the Council to take measures, as provided for in the Charter, to impel the United States authorities to respond to the notice served on the officials responsible through the Belgian Embassy in Libya and to the verbal notification sent to the Office of the United States Secretary of State through the Foreign Ministry of the United Arab Emirates, and to do everything to bring about the appearance of the United States citizens concerned before the Libyan courts in the two cases brought against them.

The General Assembly, on 9 December (**decision 54/424**), deferred consideration of the agenda item "Declaration of the Assembly of Heads of State and Government of the Organization of African Unity on the aerial and naval military attack against the Socialist People's Libyan Arab Jamahiriya by the present United States Administration in April 1986" and included it in the provisional agenda of its fifty-fifth (2000) session.

Sierra Leone

In 1999, the civil war in Sierra Leone that had resumed at the end of 1998 intensified as rebel forces of the former junta, the Armed Forces Revolutionary Council (AFRC) and the Revolutionary United Front (RUF), attacked Freetown on 6 January, overrunning much of the capital. Fierce fighting resulted in thousands killed, and many civilians were severely mutilated by the rebel forces. Those forces were repelled after two weeks by a counter-attack of the forces of the ECOWAS Monitoring Group (ECOMOG). At the time of the attack, most of the international staff of the United Nations Observer Mission in Sierra Leone (UNOMSIL) and UN agencies had already been evacuated due to the deteriorating security situation. Following the incursion, diplomatic efforts by the Government, the United Nations and ECOWAS to find a peaceful resolution of the eight-year civil conflict intensified. Negotiations between the Government and RUF, which began in May in Lomé, Togo, resulted in the signing of a ceasefire agreement on 18 May, followed by the signing of the Lomé Peace Agreement on 7 July.

In August, the Security Council authorized an expansion of UNOMSIL, and, in October, gave the mission a new mandate, renaming it the United Nations Mission in Sierra Leone (UNAMSIL). The authorized size of the force was set at 6,000 military personnel, including 260 military observers. The UN force was mandated to work together with ECOMOG troops to help in the implementation of the Lomé Peace Agreement and to cooperate with the Government and other parties in that regard. It was also to assist the Government in implementing the disarmament plan, ensure freedom of movement of UN personnel, monitor the ceasefire and facilitate the delivery of humanitarian aid.

The return of RUF leader Foday Sankoh and AFRC leader Johnny Paul Koroma to Freetown in October gave impetus to the implementation of the Agreement. That was followed by President Ahmad Tejan Kabbah's announcement of the composition of the new Government of National Unity, which included members of AFRC/RUF.

By the end of the year, progress had been achieved in implementing the Agreement, but the overall situation in the country remained precarious as ceasefire violations, human rights abuses and movement of rebel forces continued. When ECOMOG announced its intention to withdraw its forces from Sierra Leone, the Secretary-General sought the Council's approval to expand UNAMSIL to approximately 10,000 military personnel.

Renewed conflict

A serious situation prevailed in Sierra Leone in the early days of 1999. Rebel attacks, which began in late December 1998 [YUN 1998, p. 180], resulted in heavy casualties among civilians, as well as looting and destruction of property, sending thousands of people fleeing towards Freetown. ECOMOG, which was obliged to fall back from its positions in the east, brought in reinforcements over the new year, and UNOMSIL withdrew most of its personnel from Freetown to Conakry, Guinea, leaving a small core team led by the Secretary-General's Special Representative, Francis G. Okelo.

The border with Liberia was also a source of tension. President Charles Taylor of Liberia, having announced the closure of the border between Liberia and Sierra Leone [YUN 1998, p. 181], claimed that an attack was being planned against Liberian territory by Liberian factions based inside Sierra Leone. Both the Force Commander of ECOMOG and the Foreign Minister of Sierra Leone accused Liberia of providing military support to the rebels, which Liberia denied in a 6 January letter to the Security Council [S/1999/17]. Liberia also renewed its request to the United Nations to deploy observers on its border with Sierra Leone.

Report of Secretary-General (January). In view of the serious developments in Sierra Leone, the Secretary-General submitted a special report on the situation on 7 January [S/1999/20]. He stated that the situation had deteriorated markedly on 6 January when rebels penetrated to the centre of Freetown and UNOMSIL completed its evacuation of the city. On 7 January [S/1999/18], the President of Togo and current Chairman of ECOWAS, Gnassingbe Eyadema, appealed to the President of Sierra Leone and the leader of the rebel forces to order a halt to the fighting.

Rebel attacks in the east and west involved the killing of civilians, the destruction of homes and abductions. Overland access to the interior was cut, and the capacity to provide humanitarian assistance was sharply reduced as all expatriate staff of most humanitarian organizations were relocated outside the country. Rebel advances were preceded by the displacement of large numbers of civilians fleeing the violence.

The Secretary-General endorsed the conclusions of the 28 December 1998 meeting of the ECOWAS Committee of Six on Sierra Leone (Côte d'Ivoire, Ghana, Guinea, Liberia, Nigeria, Togo) [YUN 1998, p. 181], which included an appeal to the rebels to cease fighting and to recognize the Government of President Kabbah. The Secretary-General urged ECOWAS to meet at summit level to consider how it could best support the legitimate Government of Sierra Leone. As for UNOMSIL, its future was less clear than at the time of his December 1998 report [YUN 1998, p. 177]. It could still facilitate discussions; help reactivate the programme to disarm and demobilize former Sierra Leone fighters; continue to support initiatives for the reconstitution of a national army and reform of the national police; and continue to monitor the human rights situation. Therefore, the Secretary-General recommended that UNOMSIL's mandate be extended for two months, until 13 March. He intended to reduce the number of military observers, retaining in Conakry a small number to return to Sierra Leone when conditions permitted, along with the necessary civilian substantive and logistical support staff under the leadership of his Special Representative.

SECURITY COUNCIL ACTION (January)

On 7 January [meeting 3963], following consultations among Council members, the President made statement **S/PRST/1999/1** on behalf of the Council:

> The Security Council expresses its grave concern at the attacks by armed rebels of the former junta and Revolutionary United Front in the capital of Sierra Leone and at the resulting suffering and loss of life. It condemns the unacceptable attempt by the rebels to overthrow by violence the democratically elected Government of Sierra Leone. The Council also condemns the continued campaign by the rebels to terrorize the population of Sierra Leone and, especially, the atrocities committed against women and children. The Council demands that the rebels lay down their arms immediately and cease all violence. The Council reiterates once more its firm support for the legitimate and democratically elected Government of President Ahmad Tejan Kabbah.
>
> The Council strongly condemns all those who have afforded support, including through the supply of arms and mercenaries, to the rebels in Sierra Leone. In this context, it expresses its grave concern at reports that such support to the rebels is being afforded in particular from the territory of Liberia. It reaffirms the obligation of all Member States to comply strictly with existing arms embargoes. In that context, the Council urges the Committee established pursuant to resolution 985(1995) and the Committee established pursuant to resolution 1132 (1997) to pursue active measures to investigate violations of the embargoes and to report to the Council, with recommendations as appropriate.
>
> The Council stresses the importance of dialogue and national reconciliation for the restoration of lasting peace and stability to Sierra Leone. The Council welcomes the efforts to resolve the conflict being undertaken by the Government of President Kabbah, and further endorses the approach set out in the final communiqué of the meeting of the Committee of Six on Sierra Leone of the Economic Community of West African States, held in Abidjan on 28 December 1998. It welcomes the offers made by leaders in the region aimed at resolving the conflict and, in that context, urges them, including the Economic Community of West African States Committee of Six, to facilitate the peace process. It also calls upon the Secretary-General to do all he can to assist in these efforts, including through his Special Representative.
>
> The Council also expresses its concern at the serious humanitarian consequences of the escalating fighting in Sierra Leone. It calls upon all States and international organizations to provide appropriate humanitarian assistance and upon all parties in Sierra Leone to afford humanitarian access. The Council notes that United Nations agencies are working with the increasing numbers of refugees in neighbouring countries and calls upon all States to ensure that the humanitarian agencies are adequately resourced to meet the additional demand.
>
> The Council commends the forces of the Monitoring Group of the Economic Community of West African States in Sierra Leone for the courage and determination they have demonstrated over the last year in their efforts to maintain security in Sierra Leone. It also commends the key contribution of the United Nations Observer Mission in Sierra Leone and the Special Representative of the Secretary-General in efforts to restore stability in the country. The Council urges all States urgently to provide resources, including logistical and other support, to help maintain an effective peacekeeping presence in Sierra Leone.
>
> The Council expresses its intention to continue to monitor the situation closely and to consider urgently any further action which may be necessary.

The Council again took up the question of Sierra Leone on 12 January [meeting 3964]. It had before it the Secretary-General's December 1998 [YUN 1998, p. 177] and January 1999 (see p. 152) reports. The Council adopted **resolution 1220 (1999)** unanimously. The draft text [S/1999/26] was prepared during consultations among Council members.

> *The Security Council,*
>
> *Recalling* its resolution 1181(1998) of 13 July 1998 and the statement by its President of 7 January 1999,
>
> *Expressing its deep concern* over the recent deterioration of the situation in Sierra Leone, and encouraging all efforts aimed at resolving the conflict and restoring lasting peace and stability,
>
> *Having considered* the third progress report of the Secretary-General of 16 December 1998 on the United

Nations Observer Mission in Sierra Leone and his special report on the Mission of 7 January 1999, and noting the recommendations contained therein,

1. *Decides* to extend the mandate of the United Nations Observer Mission in Sierra Leone until 13 March 1999;

2. *Takes note* of the intention of the Secretary-General, as expressed in paragraph 37 of his special report, to reduce the number of military observers in the Mission and to retain in Conakry a small number who would return to Sierra Leone when conditions permit, together with the necessary civilian substantive and logistical support staff under the leadership of his Special Representative;

3. *Requests* the Secretary-General to keep the Council closely informed on the situation in Sierra Leone and to submit a further report to the Council with recommendations on the future deployment of the Mission and the implementation of its mandate by 5 March 1999;

4. *Decides* to remain actively seized of the matter.

Communications (January/February). Germany forwarded to the Secretary-General a 12 January statement by the EU Presidency [S/1999/47], in which it condemned the latest attempt to overthrow the democratically elected Government of Sierra Leone and reiterated its support for President Kabbah and his Government. It expressed its concern at reports that arms and personnel were being supplied, in particular from the territory of Liberia, and called on all States to comply with existing arms embargoes (see p. 170). It endorsed the approach of the ECOWAS Committee of Six.

Ukraine, on 15 January [S/1999/44], also expressed concern over the situation and condemned those who had given assistance, including the supply of arms and mercenaries, to the rebels. Ukraine expressed alarm that some mercenaries in Sierra Leone had been identified as nationals of Ukraine. Ukraine had no evidence to that effect and refuted the allegations.

Sierra Leone forwarded to the Council on 21 January [S/1999/68] a 16 January statement by the Government describing the situation in the country and the background to the conflict. The Government said that ECOMOG had regained control of Freetown and life there was returning to normal. It restated its willingness to enter into a dialogue with RUF. Sierra Leone again accused Liberia of being involved in the Sierra Leone conflict. Those charges had also been made in a letter to the Secretary-General of 5 January [S/1999/73], in which President Kabbah said that there was evidence that the rebel offensive in Sierra Leone had been initiated and sustained by the Government of Liberia, despite denials by President Taylor. Sierra Leone reported that it had proof that arms, personnel and logistics for the rebels were supplied by Liberia with the intent to destabilize Sierra Leone, and that mercenaries had entered Sierra Leone from Liberia. The rebels had provided diamonds from Sierra Leone to President Taylor to finance their activities. Citing the risk that an escalated conflict would lead to destabilization of the subregion, Sierra Leone called on the Security Council to take action to arrest the deteriorating situation.

Liberia, in a statement of 19 February [S/1999/193], addressed the concerns expressed regarding its alleged complicity in the Sierra Leonean crisis. Affirming its support of the democratically elected Government of President Kabbah, Liberia said that its citizens had been used as mercenaries in the conflict by successive Governments of Sierra Leone, RUF/AFRC, the Kamajors and ECOMOG. It appealed to all parties to abolish the use of Liberians as mercenaries and called for their repatriation. It requested the United Nations to assist Sierra Leone and Liberia in identifying, documenting and processing Liberians fighting in Sierra Leone for repatriation. Liberia called for the appointment of members of the Joint Security Liaison Committee provided for in the Mano River Union Non-Aggression and Security Cooperation Treaty between Liberia, Sierra Leone and Guinea. It also renewed its requests that Sierra Leone accept the joint patrol and monitoring of the Liberian/Sierra Leonean border and that the Security Council send UN monitors to join ECOMOG forces at that border. President Taylor repeated that request in a letter to the Secretary-General dated 23 February [S/1999/213].

On 10 and 23 February [S/1999/138, S/1999/186], Sierra Leone transmitted statements of 7 and 21 February by President Kabbah to the nation, in which he reiterated his willingness to meet with RUF leaders to facilitate the peace process and called on the Council to consider further action, not excluding the threat of force, against the rebels and their supporters, in order to give effect to its previous demands that the rebels cease all violence and seek dialogue for peace.

Report of Secretary-General (March). The Secretary-General, in response to resolution 1220(1999), reported on 4 March [S/1999/237] on the aftermath of the rebel attack on Freetown on 6 January. After four days, the rebels were forced to withdraw by a counter-attack. The fighting resulted in the deaths of between 3,000 and 5,000 persons, including rebel fighters, ECOMOG soldiers, members of the Civil Defence Force defending the capital and civilians. Many civilians were severely mutilated by the rebels. Up to 150,000 people were displaced in and around Freetown and many buildings were destroyed.

President Kabbah had indicated his readiness to engage in a dialogue with the rebel leaders and to allow Foday Sankoh, the leader of RUF who was being tried by the courts, to meet other RUF leaders, provided that RUF accepted the legitimacy of the Government. In a national broadcast on 28 February, the President agreed that Mr. Sankoh and RUF members could hold their internal consultations in Lomé or Bamako (Mali). He stressed that, following those consultations, the RUF leader should be returned to Freetown to resume his appeal against his conviction for treason and related offences. In his broadcast statement, circulated to the Security Council on 1 March [S/1999/224], the President called for the immediate release of all civilians being held by the rebels, including children and women whom the rebels had abducted during the attack on Freetown.

The United Nations participated in diplomatic efforts aimed at strengthening ECOMOG, while opening up dialogue with the rebels. Those efforts culminated in a 29 January meeting in Conakry of the heads of State of the three troop-contributing countries of ECOMOG—Ghana, Guinea and Nigeria. At that meeting, Presidents Rawlings, Conte and Abubakar agreed on the need to convene an ECOWAS summit on Sierra Leone, to be followed by a visit by representatives of the ECOWAS Committee of Six on Sierra Leone to New York to brief the Security Council. That Committee comprised those three countries, as well as Côte d'Ivoire, Liberia and Togo. The Secretary-General's Special Representative met with RUF representatives on 21 February in Abidjan, Côte d'Ivoire, to ascertain the RUF commitment to the peace process.

UNOMSIL human rights officers visited Freetown in January and February to assess the situation. They found that the ultimate responsibility for the fighting, for most of the civilian casualties and for the related humanitarian emergency in Freetown rested with the rebel forces. According to medical sources, many hundreds of civilians were treated for the amputation of limbs or other mutilations, and there were reports of widespread rape and other forms of sexual abuse by rebel elements. The humanitarian situation had deteriorated drastically following the fighting and the number of refugees in neighbouring countries was estimated at 450,000 and internally displaced persons at 700,000. The suffering of vulnerable civilian populations was exacerbated by increasing levels of malnutrition, appalling sanitation conditions and inadequate health care. Humanitarian aid was reaching some parts of the country, but delivery was impaired by the ongoing hostilities outside Freetown. Though ECOMOG had driven the rebels from Freetown and restored order in its immediate vicinity, the capital was still threatened by rebel forces in the peninsula.

The Secretary-General condemned the merciless murders, inhuman mutilations and other human rights violations and widespread property damage inflicted by the rebels. He urged the international community to continue to support ECOMOG, which was to be congratulated on its success in repelling the rebels, and to consider bilateral assistance to Sierra Leone. He intended to pursue further with President Taylor some of Liberia's suggestions. As he had indicated earlier, UNOMSIL had been scaled back since its relocation to Conakry and comprised only a small core of essential personnel, but in the light of the discussions on the start of a dialogue, UNOMSIL should remain in a position to render further assistance to the peace process. He therefore recommended the extension of UNOMSIL's mandate for three months, until 13 June. The Secretary-General's intention was to re-establish UNOMSIL in Freetown as soon as possible. He would begin by increasing the current number of military observers from 8 to 14 and redeploy the necessary staff to support the relocation.

SECURITY COUNCIL ACTION (March)

On 11 March [meeting 3986], the Security Council unanimously adopted **resolution 1231(1999)**. The draft text [S/1999/262] was prepared during consultations among Council members.

The Security Council,

Recalling its resolutions 1181(1998) of 13 July 1998 and 1220(1999) of 12 January 1999 and the statement by its President of 7 January 1999,

Expressing its continued concern over the fragile situation in Sierra Leone,

Affirming the commitment of all States to respect the sovereignty, political independence and territorial integrity of Sierra Leone,

Having considered the fifth report of the Secretary-General of 4 March 1999 on the United Nations Observer Mission in Sierra Leone, and noting the recommendations contained therein,

1. *Decides* to extend the mandate of the United Nations Observer Mission in Sierra Leone until 13 June 1999;

2. *Welcomes* the intention of the Secretary-General to re-establish the Mission in Freetown as soon as possible and, to that end, to increase the current number of military observers and human rights personnel as referred to in paragraphs 46 and 54 of his report and to redeploy the necessary staff to support the relocation to Freetown, subject to strict attention to the security situation there;

3. *Condemns* the atrocities perpetrated by the rebels on the civilian population of Sierra Leone, including, in particular, those committed against women and children, deplores all violations of human rights and inter-

national humanitarian law which have occurred in Sierra Leone during the recent escalation of violence as referred to in paragraphs 21 to 28 of the report of the Secretary-General, including the recruitment of children as soldiers, and urges the appropriate authorities to investigate all allegations of such violations with a view to bringing the perpetrators to justice;

4. *Calls upon* all parties to the conflict in Sierra Leone fully to respect human rights and international humanitarian law and the neutrality and impartiality of humanitarian workers, and to ensure full and unhindered access for humanitarian assistance to affected populations;

5. *Expresses its grave concern* at continued reports that support is being afforded to the rebels in Sierra Leone, including through the supply of arms and mercenaries, in particular from the territory of Liberia;

6. *Acknowledges* the letter dated 23 February 1999 from the President of Liberia to the Secretary-General and the statement of the Government of Liberia of 19 February 1999 on the action it is taking to curtail the involvement of Liberian nationals in the fighting in Sierra Leone, including measures to encourage the return of Liberian fighters and directives to the Liberian national security agencies to ensure that no cross-border movement of arms takes place and that there is no transshipment of arms and ammunition through Liberian territory, and requests the Secretary-General to continue to consider, in coordination with the countries of the Mano River Union and other States members of the Economic Community of West African States, the practicability and effectiveness of the deployment of United Nations monitors along with forces of the Monitoring Group of the Economic Community of West African States at the Liberia/Sierra Leone border;

7. *Reaffirms* the obligation of all States to comply strictly with the provisions of the embargo on the sale or supply of arms and related materiel imposed by its resolution 1171(1998) of 5 June 1998;

8. *Expresses its intention* to keep the issue of external support to the rebels in Sierra Leone under close review and to consider further steps to address this in the light of developments on the ground;

9. *Expresses its support* for all efforts, in particular by States members of the Economic Community of West African States, aimed at peacefully resolving the conflict and restoring lasting peace and stability to Sierra Leone, encourages the Secretary-General, through his Special Representative for Sierra Leone, to facilitate dialogue to these ends, welcomes the statement of the President of Sierra Leone of 7 February 1999 expressing the readiness of his Government to continue its efforts for dialogue with the rebels, and calls upon all parties involved, especially the rebels, to participate seriously in those efforts;

10. *Commends* the efforts of the Monitoring Group towards the restoration of peace, security and stability in Sierra Leone, and calls upon all Member States to provide the Monitoring Group with financial and logistical support and to consider the provision of prompt bilateral assistance to the Government of Sierra Leone in the creation of a new Sierra Leonean army to defend the country;

11. *Requests* the Secretary-General to keep the Council closely informed on the situation in Sierra Leone and, in this regard, to submit an additional report to the Council with recommendations on the future deployment of the Mission and on the implementation of its mandate by 5 June 1999;

12. *Decides* to remain actively seized of the matter.

Peacemaking efforts

The Sierra Leone Government's initiatives to meet with leaders of the rebel forces, supported by diplomatic activity in the subregion, particularly within ECOWAS, led to the signing of a ceasefire agreement on 18 May and the start of a dialogue between the Government and RUF on 25 May.

Internal RUF talks

On the occasion of the thirty-eighth anniversary of the independence of Sierra Leone on 27 April, President Kabbah, in a public address later circulated to the Security Council [S/1999/508], said that the internal RUF talks taking place in Lomé (26 April–10 May) provided an opportunity to open a new chapter in Sierra Leone's history by launching a peaceful transition to national reconstruction.

SECURITY COUNCIL ACTION

On 15 May [meeting 4005], following consultations among Council members, the President made statement **S/PRST/1999/13** on behalf of the Council:

The Security Council stresses that an overall political settlement and national reconciliation are essential to achieving the peaceful resolution of the conflict in Sierra Leone. In this context, it welcomes the recent holding of internal talks by a rebel delegation in Lomé, and urges the Government of Sierra Leone and rebel representatives to ensure that there are no further obstacles to a start of direct talks without delay.

The Council calls upon all concerned to remain committed to the process of negotiation and to demonstrate flexibility in their approach to the process. In this context, the Council underlines its strong support for the mediation efforts of the United Nations within the Lomé process, in particular the work of the Special Representative of the Secretary-General to facilitate dialogue, and for the key role being played by the President of Togo.

The Council commends, once again, the continued efforts of the Government of Sierra Leone and the Monitoring Group of the Economic Community of West African States towards the restoration of peace, security and stability in Sierra Leone, and calls for sustained support for the Monitoring Group from the international community.

The Council condemns the recent killings, atrocities, destruction of property and other violations of human rights and international humanitarian law perpetrated on civilians by the rebels in recent attacks, in particular at Masiaka and Port Loko. It calls upon the rebels to cease such actions immediately and urges the rebel leadership to release all hostages and abductees without delay.

The Council urges both parties to commit themselves to a cessation of hostilities for the duration of the Lomé talks, to ensure that this is fully respected on the ground and to work constructively and in good faith for a ceasefire agreement. It calls upon both sides to refrain from any hostile or aggressive act which could undermine the talks process.

The Council welcomes the intention of the Secretary-General to increase, as security conditions permit, the presence on the ground of the United Nations Observer Mission in Sierra Leone within currently authorized levels, in anticipation of a cessation of hostilities. The Council also welcomes the intention of the Secretary-General to send an assessment team to Sierra Leone to examine how an expanded Mission with a revised mandate and concept of operations might contribute to the implementation of a ceasefire and peace agreement in the event of a successful outcome to the negotiations between the Government of Sierra Leone and the rebels, and expresses its readiness to consider recommendations from the Secretary-General to that end.

The Council stresses, however, that it will be prepared to consider deploying monitors throughout Sierra Leone only when a credible ceasefire is in place and is being respected by all sides and there is a commitment by all parties to a framework peace agreement.

The Council underlines the importance, in the context of a lasting solution to the conflict in Sierra Leone, of a plan for the internationally supervised disarmament, demobilization and reintegration of ex-combatants, including child soldiers. It also draws attention to the need for the secure and timely disposal of collected arms, in accordance with any peace agreement reached.

The Council reaffirms the obligation of all States to comply strictly with the provisions of the embargo on the sale or supply of arms and related materiel imposed by its resolution 1171(1998) of 5 June 1998.

The Council reiterates its grave concern at the humanitarian situation in Sierra Leone and urges all parties, in particular the rebel leadership, to guarantee safe and unhindered humanitarian access to all those in need.

The Council reiterates that a peaceful and lasting solution to the conflict in Sierra Leone remains the responsibility of the Government and people of Sierra Leone, but again emphasizes the strong commitment of the international community to support a sustainable peace settlement.

The Council will remain seized of the matter.

Ceasefire agreement

On 18 May, President Kabbah and Mr. Sankoh signed a ceasefire agreement, the text of which was forwarded to the Security Council by Togo [S/1999/585]. The two sides agreed to a ceasefire as from 24 May, and decided that the dialogue between the Government of Sierra Leone and RUF would commence on 25 May. The ceasefire agreement provided for guarantees of safe and unhindered humanitarian access to populations in need and the immediate release of all prisoners of war and non-combatants. The parties also agreed to request the United Nations to deploy military observers as soon as possible to observe compliance with the agreement by the Government forces (ECOMOG and Civil Defence Forces) and RUF, including former AFRC forces.

The ECOWAS meeting of Foreign Ministers (Lomé, 24-25 May) [S/1999/613] observed that the developments in Sierra Leone were generally positive and expressed satisfaction that a ceasefire agreement had been signed. The Ministers called on the parties to find a peaceful solution to the crisis and to create an environment conducive to the observance of the ceasefire so as to facilitate the deployment of additional UN observers. To that end, they expressed their appreciation to the Secretary-General for having dispatched a team to assess the logistical support needed for the deployment of the additional observers. The meeting noted the recent incursion of Sierra Leonean rebels into Guinean territory, where numerous atrocities were perpetrated and property destroyed. The Ministers appealed to the international community to provide ECOWAS with the necessary material and financial assistance to facilitate rapid resolution of the crisis in Sierra Leone.

In a 24 May communiqué [S/1999/599], the OAU Acting Chairman welcomed the ceasefire agreement and invited the parties to bring their negotiations to a satisfactory conclusion. Presidents Taylor of Liberia and Eyadema of Togo, on the occasion of a visit on 4 and 5 June of the former to Togo, issued a joint communiqué [S/1999/656] in which they praised ECOWAS efforts to find a solution to the crisis in Sierra Leone, welcomed the signing of the ceasefire agreement and expressed satisfaction at the launching on 25 May of a dialogue among Sierra Leoneans. The two Presidents appealed to States to refrain from supplying the parties to the conflict with arms or other logistical support and commended the neighbouring States for taking in hundreds of thousands of refugees from Sierra Leone.

Report of Secretary-General (June). The Secretary-General described the peace process in a 4 June report to the Security Council [S/1999/645], noting significant progress in the signing of the ceasefire agreement and the start of dialogue between the Government and RUF in Lomé on 25 May. To a large extent, those steps reflected the outcome of initiatives undertaken by the Government, which were accompanied by diplomatic activity by the current ECOWAS Chairman, President Eyadema; the ECOMOG troop-contributing countries, namely, Ghana, Guinea, Mali and Nigeria; the Governments of the United Kingdom and the United States and the United States Presidential Special Envoy, Jesse Jackson; and the Secretary-General's Special Representative for Sierra Leone, Francis G. Okelo. Although Mr. Sankoh was still pursuing his appeal against his conviction and sentence to death for treason, the Government had granted him judicial leave to pursue the dialogue process. On 29 May, the Government and RUF reached an understanding on his status. The Government undertook to take legal steps to grant him an absolute and free pardon and Mr. Sankoh said that his delegation would proceed with the dialogue.

The internal RUF talks (see p. 156) resulted in a position paper reflecting the RUF/AFRC demands: an amnesty for all members of RUF and AFRC, the rebel groups that had organized the coup d'état in Sierra Leone in 1997 [YUN 1997, p. 132]; and the establishment of a four-year transitional Government. The main functions of that Government would include: the drafting of a new constitution; the reform of the national security forces and civil service; the encampment, disarmament, demobilization and reintegration of all combatants; and the establishment of a national electoral commission. RUF demanded the departure from Sierra Leone of all foreign troops and mercenaries and the termination of the status-of-forces agreement between Sierra Leone and Nigeria. It stipulated that a neutral peace-monitoring group should be deployed. In response, the Government said that the proposal for an amnesty would be examined with a view to achieving peace, while taking into account gross human rights violations. It endorsed the importance of the transformation of RUF into a political party. On 2 June, the two sides asked UNOMSIL to establish a committee to effect the release of prisoners of war and non-combatants.

In response to Council resolution 1231(1999), the Secretary-General had begun to explore with ECOWAS the possibility of deploying UN monitors, along with ECOMOG forces, on the Sierra Leone/Liberia border.

The military and security situation in Sierra Leone remained fluid and complex. ECOMOG had opened the roads between Freetown and various western and north-western towns, but RUF/AFRC continued to dominate many areas, particularly in the northern and eastern provinces and the Kono diamond mining region. They had also carried out raids both before and after 24 May when the ceasefire took effect. Meanwhile, the two sides accused each other of ceasefire violations. The Government made efforts to restructure the Civil Defence Forces and reform the police force. The disarmament, demobilization and reintegration programme had been at a near standstill, but a pilot phase of a readjusted programme was resumed. The United Nations Children's Fund (UNICEF) was providing services, in cooperation with ECOMOG and UNOMSIL, to children who had been released by RUF/AFRC.

The reporting period (5 March–4 June) was marked by a resurgence of rebel atrocities against civilians, mostly in the towns of Masiaka and Port Loko. They included summary executions, mutilations, limb amputations, abductions and sexual abuse, as well as large-scale destruction of property. The Special Representative expressed to RUF/AFRC the deep concerns of the United Nations over the reported abuses of human rights and violations of international humanitarian law. There were a few reports of ill-treatment of the civilian population by ECOMOG and government troops, as well as reports of widespread recruitment of children by the Civil Defence Forces in some provinces. President Kabbah announced the establishment of a new Human Rights Commission for Sierra Leone.

Since the Secretary-General's previous report, the already desperate humanitarian situation had worsened. Rebel gains had increased the number of needy people while limiting aid workers' access to affected areas. It was estimated that well over 1 million civilians countrywide required some form of humanitarian assistance. Humanitarian aid was provided in government-controlled areas to about 370,000 individuals.

At the beginning of June, UNOMSIL consisted of 24 military observers, as well as 29 international and 24 national staff members. The planned deployment in June of a further 16 observers would restore the Mission's military capacity to its December 1998 level. The security situation permitting, the Secretary-General expressed his intention of deploying up to the authorized limit of 70 military personnel, with an additional 15 medical personnel. In view of the likelihood of UN involvement with the peace talks, he intended to increase the civilian staff by two political officers and to restore the human rights section to its previous level of five persons. With its restored strength, the military component would monitor the ceasefire within the limits of its resources. It would continue to establish, maintain and improve contacts with local RUF commanders with a view to establishing joint military commissions. The functions of those commissions would be to identify and locate forces on the ground; obtain written assurances from rebel commanders of their commitment to the ceasefire and guarantees of security for UN personnel; and build confidence, facilitate contacts and resolve disputes.

To determine the activities that might be carried out by an enlarged UNOMSIL, the Secretary-General had dispatched a military assessment and planning team to Sierra Leone at the end of May to develop a revised concept of operations. His recommendations on the size, mandate and configuration of an eventual expanded mission would depend on the provisions of any peace agreement and on considerations on the ground, notably security. One important consideration in redefining UNOMSIL's mandate would be the future strength, activities and state of deployment of ECOMOG. The Secretary-General envisaged the need for UNOMSIL to ensure the security of UN personnel if it were to assist in the implementation of an eventual peace agreement, which would require a sizeable number of infantry and additional observers, along with the necessary equipment and logistical support. The new mandate would likely include: monitoring and supervising the ceasefire; supervising, monitoring and assisting in the encampment, disarmament and demobilization of former combatants; providing security to UN personnel; providing assistance to humanitarian efforts; and providing planning and logistical support for an eventual election. The Secretary-General would revert to the Council with detailed proposals for a revised mandate and concept of operations as soon as a peace agreement was signed.

The Secretary-General said that it appeared that a political settlement might be within reach to break the cycle of violence that had held the country in its grip since 1991, and he called on all parties to adhere strictly to the terms of the ceasefire agreement. He also pointed to the need for the international community to support ECOMOG, for the process of disarmament to be resumed and for an end to recruitment of children as soldiers. He called on all States to comply with the arms embargo to non-governmental forces in Sierra Leone imposed by the Security Council in resolution 1171(1998) [YUN 1998, p. 169]. Given the current situation, including the signing of the ceasefire agreement and the start of the dialogue, the Secretary-General recommended the extension of UNOMSIL for another six months, until 13 December 1999.

SECURITY COUNCIL ACTION (June)

On 11 June [meeting 4012], the Security Council unanimously adopted **resolution 1245(1999)**. The draft text [S/1999/664] was prepared during consultations among Council members.

The Security Council,

Recalling its resolutions 1181(1998) of 13 July 1998, 1220(1999) of 12 January 1999 and 1231(1999) of 11 March 1999 and the statements by its President of 7 January and 15 May 1999,

Acknowledging the cooperation provided by the Economic Community of West African States and its Monitoring Group,

Expressing its continued concern over the fragile situation in Sierra Leone,

Affirming the commitment of all States to respect the sovereignty, political independence and territorial integrity of Sierra Leone,

Having considered the sixth report of the Secretary-General of 4 June 1999 on the United Nations Observer Mission in Sierra Leone, and noting the recommendations contained therein,

1. *Decides* to extend the mandate of the United Nations Observer Mission in Sierra Leone until 13 December 1999;

2. *Stresses* that an overall political settlement and national reconciliation are essential to achieving a peaceful resolution of the conflict in Sierra Leone, and welcomes the holding of talks in Lomé between the Government of Sierra Leone and rebel representatives;

3. *Calls upon* all concerned to remain committed to the process of negotiation and to demonstrate flexibility in their approach to the process, underlines its strong support for all those involved in the mediation efforts of the United Nations within the Lomé process, in particular the Special Representative of the Secretary-General in his work to facilitate dialogue, and for the key role being played by the President of Togo as current Chairman of the Economic Community of West African States, and emphasizes the strong commitment of the international community to support a sustainable peace settlement;

4. *Takes note* of the intention of the Secretary-General, as expressed in paragraphs 52 to 57 of his report, to revert to the Council with recommendations on an expanded Mission presence in Sierra Leone with a revised mandate and concept of operations in the event of a successful outcome to the negotiations between the Government of Sierra Leone and rebel representatives in Lomé, and underlines the fact that further eventual deployment of the Mission should be considered, taking into account security conditions;

5. *Requests* the Secretary-General to keep the Council closely informed on the situation in Sierra Leone;

6. *Decides* to remain actively seized of the matter.

Lomé Peace Agreement

Following two weeks of intense negotiations in Lomé under the auspices of the current ECOWAS Chairman, President Eyadema of Togo, the Government of Sierra Leone and RUF signed a peace agreement on 7 July. The text of the Peace Agreement [S/1999/777] and of the final communiqué on the peace talks [S/1999/769] were forwarded to the Security Council by Togo.

The Agreement provided for, among other things: an immediate ceasefire to be monitored by Ceasefire Monitoring Committees at the district level and, at the national level, through a Joint Monitoring Committee chaired by UNOMSIL; the immediate release of Mr. Sankoh; liberation of prisoners of war and non-combatants; transformation of RUF into a political party and its access to public office; amnesty to be granted to Mr. Sankoh and to conflict-related combatants, exiles and other RUF members; establishment of commissions for reconciliation, implementation of the Agreement, review of the 1991 Constitution, preparation of general elections and management of resources; adaptation of the ECOMOG and UNOMSIL mandates to the new exigencies of peace and national reconciliation; security guarantees; encampment, disarmament, demobilization and reintegration of combatants; restructuring and training of the armed forces of Sierra Leone; withdrawal of mercenaries; and protection of civil and political human rights.

Communications (July). On 16 July [S/1999/792], Sierra Leone forwarded to the Council an address made by President Kabbah when the Lomé Peace Agreement was submitted for ratification. Noting that the Agreement was the second such agreement that the Government had signed with RUF, the first being the 1996 Abidjan Peace Accord [YUN 1996, p. 123], President Kabbah stated that the Lomé Agreement was more likely to succeed because other nations were involved in the negotiation process, the international community would be involved in monitoring its implementation and security guarantees were included.

Also on 16 July [S/1999/795], Finland forwarded a statement by the EU Presidency welcoming the signature of the Peace Agreement and commending the role of those involved. The EU emphasized that the accountability of individual perpetrators of grave human rights violations was important in ensuring a fair justice system and, ultimately, reconciliation and stability in Sierra Leone.

Report of Secretary-General (July). In a 30 July report [S/1999/836], the Secretary-General described the main provisions of the Lomé Peace Agreement and made recommendations for immediate measures to strengthen UNOMSIL. Following consultations with all interested parties, he would submit additional recommendations to the Council. The Secretary-General visited Freetown on 8 July, immediately following the signing of the Agreement, and expressed hope for its implementation.

The Parliament of Sierra Leone unanimously ratified the Peace Agreement on 15 July and later adopted the legislation necessary for its implementation. Mr. Sankoh indicated that he was ready to come to Freetown, pending arrangements for accommodation and security. The military and security situation had improved significantly since the ceasefire agreement took effect, despite some minor violations. RUF and AFRC continued to dominate much of the northern and eastern provinces and ECOMOG remained in control of the Freetown peninsula. For the first time in years, the delivery of humanitarian assistance seemed within grasp.

The signing of the Agreement required UNOMSIL to perform new and significantly expanded tasks in coordination with ECOMOG, whose presence, at that juncture, remained indispensable. Revised mandates needed to be worked out and to include the division of labour between the United Nations and ECOWAS, the need to provide a credible level of security throughout the country, the appropriate size and composition of the peacekeeping force, the deployment of units to various regions of the country and arrangements for logistical support. In the interim, the Secretary-General proposed to deploy additional UN military observers, increasing their number from 50 to 210, along with the necessary equipment and administrative support. The expanded UNOMSIL military observer component would be mandated to: strengthen contacts between UNOMSIL and RUF troops in the countryside; extend its ceasefire activities to a wider geographical area; assist ceasefire-monitoring mechanisms; monitor the military and security situation in the country; assist and monitor the disarmament and demobilization of combatants; work closely with humanitarian organizations with a view to ensuring the widest possible access for humanitarian assistance; work closely with human rights officers; coordinate with ECOMOG; and assist in preparing plans for deployment of neutral peacekeeping troops.

The Lomé Peace Agreement called for an expanded role for UNOMSIL, which would require additional human and administrative resources, including political affairs, civil affairs, human rights, legal affairs and information officers. They would be involved in monitoring and supporting implementation of the Agreement through such activities as liaising with government bodies at the district level; and liaising on and monitoring matters relating to political reform, economic reconstruction and investment, human rights, refugees and displaced persons, elections, education and health.

The signing of the Agreement was a great step forward for Sierra Leone, the Secretary- General stated, and provided an opportunity for the people to bring an end to the conflict. He noted that some of the terms of the Agreement, in particular the provisions on amnesty, were difficult to reconcile with the goal of ending the culture of impunity, which had inspired the creation of UN Tribunals for Rwanda and the former Yugoslavia, and the future International Criminal Court. Hence he had instructed the Special Representative to enter a reservation when he signed the Peace Agreement stating that, for the United Nations, the amnesty could not cover international crimes of genocide, crimes against humanity, war crimes and other serious violations of international humanitarian law. The international community and the United Nations had an important responsibility to assist Sierra Leone and to ensure that momentum was maintained in the peace process. He therefore recommended that the Council approve, as an immediate step, the provisional expansion of UNOMSIL.

In an 11 August addendum to his report [S/1999/836/Add.1], the Secretary-General informed the Council that the full cost of the provisional expansion of UNOMSIL was estimated at $24.3 million for a 10-month period ending 30 June 2000. That provided for the gradual phasing in of an additional 140 military observers, the establishment of a second-line medical capability with 35 medical personnel, the expansion of the Mission by 59 international civilian and 21 local staff, and logistical support. The projected cost of UNOMSIL for the 1999-2000 financial period would amount to $40.7 million, excluding additional requirements to be determined when the Secretary-General's recommendations for the mandate and structure of the enhanced UN peacekeeping presence in Sierra Leone were finalized.

SECURITY COUNCIL ACTION (August)

On 20 August [meeting 4035], the Security Council unanimously adopted **resolution 1260(1999)**. The draft text [S/1999/874] was prepared during consultations among Council members.

The Security Council,

Recalling its resolutions 1171(1998) of 5 June 1998, 1181(1998) of 13 July 1998, 1231(1999) of 11 March 1999 and other relevant resolutions as well as the statement by its President of 15 May 1999,

Recalling also that in accordance with its resolution 1245(1999) of 11 June 1999 the mandate of the United Nations Observer Mission in Sierra Leone extends until 13 December 1999,

Affirming the commitment of all States to respect the sovereignty, political independence and territorial integrity of Sierra Leone,

Having considered the report of the Secretary-General of 30 July 1999,

1. *Welcomes* the signing of the Peace Agreement between the Government of Sierra Leone and the Revolutionary United Front of Sierra Leone in Lomé on 7 July 1999, and commends the President of Togo, the Special Representative of the Secretary-General, the Economic Community of West African States and all those involved in facilitating the negotiations in Lomé on their contribution to this achievement;

2. *Commends* the Government of Sierra Leone for its courageous efforts to achieve peace, including through legislative and other measures already taken towards implementation of the Peace Agreement, commends also the leadership of the Revolutionary United Front for taking this decisive step towards peace, and calls upon them both to ensure that the provisions of the Agreement are fully implemented;

3. *Commends also* the Monitoring Group of the Economic Community of West African States on the outstanding contribution it has made to the restoration of security and stability in Sierra Leone, the protection of civilians and the promotion of a peaceful settlement of the conflict, and urges all States to continue to provide technical, logistical and financial support to the Monitoring Group to help it to maintain its critical presence and continue to perform its role in Sierra Leone, including through the United Nations trust fund established to support peacekeeping and related activities in Sierra Leone;

4. *Authorizes* the provisional expansion of the United Nations Observer Mission in Sierra Leone to up to 210 military observers along with the necessary equipment and administrative and medical support to perform the tasks set out in paragraph 38 of the report of the Secretary-General, and decides that these additional military observers shall be deployed as security conditions permit and shall operate for the time being under security provided by the Monitoring Group as indicated in paragraph 39 of the report;

5. *Underscores* the importance of the safety, security and freedom of movement of United Nations and associated personnel, notes that the Government of Sierra Leone and the Revolutionary United Front have agreed in the Peace Agreement to provide guarantees in this regard, and urges all parties in Sierra Leone to respect fully the status of United Nations and associated personnel;

6. *Authorizes* the strengthening of the political, civil affairs, information, human rights and child protection elements of the Mission as set out in paragraphs 40 to 51 of the report of the Secretary-General, including through the appointment of a deputy Special Representative of the Secretary-General and the expansion of the Office of the Special Representative of the Secretary-General;

7. Encourages the ongoing consultations among the parties concerned on future peacekeeping arrangements in Sierra Leone, including the respective tasks, strength and mandates of the Monitoring Group and the United Nations, and welcomes the intention of the Secretary-General to revert to the Council with comprehensive proposals concerning a new mandate and concept of operations for the Mission;

8. *Calls upon* the Revolutionary United Front of Sierra Leone and all other armed groups in Sierra Leone to begin immediately to disband and give up their arms in accordance with the provisions of the Peace Agreement, and to participate fully in the disarmament, demobilization and reintegration programme in Sierra Leone;

9. *Urges* all States and international organizations to provide resources to help ensure the successful conduct of the disarmament, demobilization and reintegration programme, in particular through the trust fund established by the International Bank for Reconstruction and Development for this purpose;

10. *Stresses* the urgent need to promote peace and national reconciliation and to foster accountability and respect for human rights in Sierra Leone, and in this context takes note of the views expressed in paragraph 54 of the report of the Secretary-General, welcomes the provisions in the Peace Agreement on the establishment of the Truth and Reconciliation Commission and the Human Rights Commission in Sierra Leone, and calls upon the Government of Sierra Leone and the Revolutionary United Front to ensure that those Commissions are established promptly within the time frame provided for in the Peace Agreement;

11. *Welcomes* the adoption of the Human Rights Manifesto by the parties concerned in Sierra Leone and stresses the need for international assistance to address the human rights issues in Sierra Leone as a step towards accountability in the country, as referred to in paragraph 20 of the report of the Secretary-General;

12. *Stresses* the need for the international community and the Government of Sierra Leone to design and implement programmes to address the special needs of war victims, in particular those who have suffered maiming mutilation, and, in this regard, welcomes the commitment of the Government of Sierra Leone as set out in article XXIX of the Peace Agreement to establish a special fund for this purpose;

13. *Stresses* the urgent and substantial need for humanitarian assistance to the people of Sierra Leone, in particular in the large proportion of the country hitherto inaccessible to relief agencies, and urges all States and international organizations to provide such assistance as a priority, in response to the revised consolidated inter-agency appeal issued in July 1999;

14. *Calls upon* all parties to ensure the safe and unhindered access of humanitarian assistance to those in need in Sierra Leone, to guarantee the safety and security of humanitarian personnel and to respect strictly the relevant provisions of international humanitarian law;

15. *Stresses* the need for sustained and generous assistance for the longer term tasks of reconstruction, economic and social recovery and development in Sierra Leone, and urges all States and international organizations to participate in and contribute actively to these efforts;

16. *Welcomes* the commitment of the Government of Sierra Leone to work with the United Nations Children's Fund and the Office of the Special Representative of the Secretary-General for Children and Armed Conflict and other international agencies to give particular attention to the long-term rehabilitation of child combatants in Sierra Leone, and encourages those involved also to address the special needs of all children affected by the conflict in Sierra Leone, including through the disarmament, demobilization and reintegration programme and the Truth and Reconciliation Commission and through support to child victims of mutilation, sexual exploitation and abduction, to the rehabilitation of health and education services, and to the recovery of traumatized children and the protection of unaccompanied children;

17. *Welcomes* the decision of the Secretary-General, as indicated in paragraph 44 of his report, that the United Nations should develop a strategic framework approach for Sierra Leone in consultation with national and international partners;

18. *Requests* the Secretary-General to keep the Council closely informed on the situation in Sierra Leone and to submit an additional report to the Council as soon as possible, including recommendations for the mandate and structure of the enhanced United Nations peacekeeping presence that may be required in the country;

19. *Decides* to remain actively seized of the matter.

The Secretary-General, in a 24 August letter [S/1999/918] to the Council concerning resolution 1260(1999), proposed that 11 countries be added to the 13 already contributing military observers to UNOMSIL. On 27 August [S/1999/919], the Council agreed with the proposal.

ECOMOG revised mandate

At a meeting in Lomé on 25 August, ECOWAS adopted a new mandate for ECOMOG in Sierra Leone, which was transmitted to the Security Council on 19 October by Togo [S/1999/1073]. Under the new mandate, ECOMOG would: maintain the peace and security of Sierra Leone; provide protection for UNOMSIL and the personnel working in the disarmament, demobilization and reintegration programme; provide security for UNOMSIL military observers, human rights monitors, humanitarian aid workers and the staff of the disarmament, demobilization and reintegration programme; disarm all fighters of RUF, the Civil Defence Force, former Sierra Leone armed forces and paramilitary groups, in conjunction with UNOMSIL; conduct cordon and search operations to recover hidden arms; establish checkpoints to monitor movement of arms and prevent illegal movement of arms into or out of the country; provide protection and escort duties to government officials, UN officials and NGO personnel involved in humanitarian relief activities; deploy troops in all disarmament centres and arms collection sites and provide security to encamped ex-combatants; establish safe corridors and locations for the settlement of refugees and the distribution of humanitarian relief materials; provide security for the weapons and ammunition retrieved during disarmament and demobilization; assist in the destruction of recovered arms and ammunition; conduct security patrols, including the guarding of key points; monitor and investigate ceasefire violations; and clear landmines.

Report of Secretary-General (September). In a 28 September report on UNOMSIL and the situation in Sierra Leone, the Secretary-General described the state of implementation of the Lomé Peace Agreement and made recommendations for the mandate and structure of the enhanced UN peacekeeping presence that would be needed. Since his previous report, both the Government and RUF had reaffirmed their commitment to the peace process. President Kabbah had maintained close contact with Mr. Sankoh and had established contact with Johnny Paul Koroma, the AFRC leader. On 7 August, the first meeting of the Joint Implementation Committee established under the Agreement took place in Freetown under the chairmanship of the Foreign Minister of Togo, representing the ECOWAS Chairman. The Committee welcomed the steps taken towards implementation, including the removal of legal impediments to enabling RUF to participate in the governance of Sierra Leone; the submission of all nominations for cabinet and other positions; and the consultations between UNOMSIL and ECOMOG on their cooperation under the Agreement.

A number of incidents had occurred that threatened the security of UNOMSIL and ECOMOG personnel and revealed a serious rift between RUF and AFRC, including the detention of such personnel by AFRC supporters at Occra Hills; the detention of RUF leaders by the same group; a brief detention of a UNOMSIL helicopter by RUF; and the detention of an NGO member. The subsequent issuance by Mr. Koroma of a list of grievances about the Peace Agreement had further revealed the existing problems between RUF and AFRC. The delay in the start of the disarmament, demobilization and reintegration programme was another cause for concern, as was the continuing absence of Mr. Sankoh and Mr. Koroma from Sierra Leone and their failure to take up their duties in implementing the Peace Agreement. In order to move the process forward, the Secretary-General said, those two personalities should take up their positions in the Government of National Unity and encourage their supporters to participate in the disarmament programme.

The security situation remained rather tense during the reporting period, though the ceasefire was generally holding, apart from minor incidents. The Committee on the Release of Prisoners of War and Non-Combatants, chaired by UNOMSIL, met regularly. The Government of Sierra Leone, ECOMOG and the Civil Defence Force had assured UNOMSIL that they had released all persons detained by them; however, compliance by RUF and AFRC was still awaited. It was believed that the rebel groups were holding several thousand civilians, including 3,000 children reported missing since the rebel incursion into Freetown in January. Some progress was made with regard to the human rights provisions of the Peace Agreement. UNOMSIL had assisted the Sierra Leone Human Rights Committee in monitoring implementation. However, the human rights institutions and mechanisms provided for in the Agreement had not been established. The Office of the United Nations High Commissioner for Human Rights was advising national institutions on preliminary steps. The Secretary-General's Special Representative for Children and Armed Conflict, Olara Otunnu, visited Sierra Leone from 30 August to 3 September to assess the conditions of children; he outlined an agenda for action, aimed at ensuring the rehabilitation and welfare of children in the aftermath of the war.

The humanitarian needs of more than 2.6 million Sierra Leoneans in the RUF/AFRC-controlled northern and eastern regions of the country remained largely unmet. In the immediate wake of the 3 June statement on allowing access throughout the country for humanitarian delivery, the humanitarian community was able to assess and in some cases launch limited humanitarian operations and food distribution in several key towns in rebel-controlled areas, revealing high levels of malnutrition in both children and adults. Malaria, respiratory infections and nutrition-related illnesses were rampant. Severe malnutrition also persisted in the southern and eastern provinces. In response, aid agencies had increased food, medical, agriculture, child protection, water and sanitation activities. Friction between armed groups had jeopardized humanitarian operations in some areas. Humanitarian assistance needs were expected to triple concurrently with the increase of access to previously closed areas. The inter-agency consolidated appeal, which was requesting donors to provide $22 million, had received only 27 per cent of that amount (see also PART THREE, Chapter III).

In August, the Government of Sierra Leone, in cooperation with the World Bank, the United Kingdom and UNOMSIL, developed an operational plan for the disarmament, demobilization and reintegration into society of an estimated 45,000 fighters. The plan was to be executed by the Government in cooperation with ECOMOG, UNOMSIL and UN agencies. Under the plan, each ex-combatant would surrender his weapons and receive a cash payment. ECOMOG, under UN supervision, would collect, register, disable and destroy the weapons at the designated reception centres. Figures varied, but the strength of RUF was estimated at 15,000, approximately the same size as the Civil Defence Force. AFRC comprised some 6,000 men, slightly fewer than the armed forces of Sierra Leone, which had a nominal roll of 7,000. Some 2,000 fighters were thought to belong to various paramilitary groups. UNICEF estimated that about 12 per cent of all groups were children.

In view of the expressed intent of the Peace Agreement that a neutral peacekeeping force should comprise both ECOMOG and UNOMSIL, the Secretary-General, in a letter to President Olusegun Obasanjo of Nigeria, proposed a division of labour. Mr. Obasanjo informed the Secretary-General of his intention to withdraw, between August and December, 10,000 troops from ECOMOG. At that time, the great majority of the 12,000 ECOMOG troops were Nigerian. The President agreed, however, to the Secretary-General's proposal to deploy a UN peacekeeping force to include some Nigerian and other ECOWAS troops. The withdrawal of Nigerian troops began on 31 August, but was then suspended following a meeting between President Obasanjo and President Kabbah. Nigeria indicated that the withdrawal would resume in October. Nevertheless, it appeared that, even as it drew down its forces in Sierra Leone, ECOMOG would be ready to continue to provide security for the areas where it was located, particularly around Freetown and Lungi, and to proceed with disarmament and demobilization. As a result of further meetings with Nigerian officials, during which they clarified their plans in Sierra Leone, the Secretary-General said that it seemed appropriate to proceed on the basis that a robust UN peacekeeping force should be deployed to ensure implementation of the Peace Agreement. It would be an advantage if a substantial element of the UN force was contributed by Governments already participating in ECOMOG, thereby providing troops familiar with the conditions on the ground.

Revised mandate of UNOMSIL (UNAMSIL)

In view of the need for an enhanced UN peacekeeping role in Sierra Leone, the Secretary-General, in his September report [S/1999/1003], said that the main purpose of the force would be to assist the Government in carrying out its programme to disarm and demobilize all former combatants and thereafter to help create the conditions of confidence and stability required for the smooth implementation of the peace process. The tasks of ensuring the security of Freetown and the international airport at Lungi, protection for the Government and operations against rogue elements unwilling to participate in the peace process would remain ECOMOG's responsibility. As the situation remained volatile, the UN force should be large and capable and should operate on the basis of robust rules of engagement. The Secretary-General envisaged the following mandate for such a force: assisting the Government in implementing the disarmament, demobilization and reintegration plan; establishing a presence at key locations, including at disarmament/reception centres and demobilization centres; ensuring the security and freedom of movement of UN personnel; monitoring the ceasefire; encouraging the parties to create confidence-building mechanisms; facilitating delivery of humanitarian assistance; supporting the operations of UN civilian officials; and providing support to the elections.

The UN military force would require some 6,000 personnel and the number of civilian administrative personnel would have to be increased accordingly. The concept of operations for the force was predicated on ECOMOG remaining in Sierra Leone. In the eventuality of the withdrawal of Nigerian troops, a reassessment would be required of the security conditions, and, in the eventuality of a full ECOMOG withdrawal, a much stronger UN force of about 10 infantry battalions would be required. In addition to the military personnel, the Secretary-General intended to redeploy to Sierra Leone up to six civilian police to advise the Government and local police officials on police practice, training, re-equipment and recruitment.

The Secretary-General, having received the concurrence of ACABQ for financing the mission from July to October in the amount of $5.5 million, sought an additional $6.3 million to provide for the Mission's deployment of additional personnel and equipment. More contributions were needed to finance the long processes of demobilization and reintegration.

The Secretary-General observed that Sierra Leone was in urgent need of security in order for it to carry out the programme of disarming and demobilizing approximately 45,000 ex-combatants, many of them children. In order to restore confidence, some steps had to be taken immediately, among them the return of Mr. Sankoh and Mr. Koroma to assume their functions within the Government. The United Nations could play its part in bolstering security in Sierra Leone by the swift deployment of a robust force as proposed. The Secretary-General therefore recommended to the Security Council that it authorize the deployment of the UN force, which, together with the UNOMSIL military observers and civilian components, would be known as the United Nations Mission in Sierra Leone (UNAMSIL).

Communication. On 6 October [S/1999/1030], Liberia informed the Council that a delegation headed by Mr. Sankoh and Mr. Koroma, the leaders of RUF and AFRC, respectively, arrived in Freetown from Monrovia on 3 October. They had held consultations, facilitated by President Taylor, on implementation of the Lomé Peace Agreement.

SECURITY COUNCIL ACTION

On 22 October [meeting 4054], the Security Council unanimously adopted **resolution 1270(1999)**. The draft [S/1999/1069] was prepared during consultations among Council members.

The Security Council,

Recalling its resolutions 1171(1998) of 5 June 1998, 1181(1998) of 13 July 1998, 1231(1999) of 11 March 1999 and 1260(1999) of 20 August 1999 and other relevant resolutions, and the statement by its President of 15 May 1999,

Recalling also the report of the Secretary-General of 8 September 1999 and its resolution 1265(1999) of 17 September 1999 on the protection of civilians in armed conflict,

Affirming the commitment of all States to respect the sovereignty, political independence and territorial integrity of Sierra Leone,

Having considered the report of the Secretary-General of 23 September 1999,

Determining that the situation in Sierra Leone continues to constitute a threat to international peace and security in the region,

1. *Welcomes* the important steps taken by the Government of Sierra Leone, the leadership of the Revolutionary United Front of Sierra Leone, the Monitoring Group of the Economic Community of West African States and the United Nations Observer Mission in Sierra Leone towards implementation of the Peace Agreement since its signing in Lomé on 7 July 1999, and recognizes the important role of the Joint Implementation Committee established by the Peace Agreement under the chairmanship of the President of Togo;

2. *Calls upon* the parties to fulfil all their commitments under the Peace Agreement to facilitate the restoration of peace, stability, national reconciliation and development in Sierra Leone;

3. *Takes note* of the preparations made for the disarmament, demobilization and reintegration of excombatants, including child soldiers, by the Government of Sierra Leone through the National Committee for Disarmament, Demobilization and Reintegration, and urges all concerned to make every effort to ensure that all designated centres begin to function as soon as possible;

4. *Calls upon* the Revolutionary United Front, the Civil Defence Force, former Sierra Leone Armed Forces/Armed Forces Revolutionary Council and all other armed groups in Sierra Leone to begin immediately to disband and give up their arms in accordance with the provisions of the Peace Agreement, and to participate fully in the disarmament, demobilization and reintegration programme;

5. *Welcomes* the return to Freetown of the leaders of the Revolutionary United Front and the Armed Forces Revolutionary Council, and calls upon them to engage fully and responsibly in the implementation of the Peace Agreement and to direct the participation of all rebel groups in the disarmament and demobilization process without delay;

6. *Deplores* the recent taking of hostages, including personnel of the Observer Mission and Monitoring Group, by rebel groups, and calls upon those responsible to put an end to such practices immediately and to address their concerns about the terms of the Peace Agreement peacefully, through dialogue with the parties concerned;

7. *Reiterates its appreciation* for the indispensable role Monitoring Group forces continue to play in the maintenance of security and stability in and the protection of the people of Sierra Leone, and approves the new mandate for the Monitoring Group, adopted by the Economic Community of West African States on 25 August 1999;

8. *Decides* to establish the United Nations Mission in Sierra Leone with immediate effect for an initial period of six months and with the following mandate:

(a) To cooperate with the Government of Sierra Leone and the other parties to the Peace Agreement in the implementation of the Agreement;

(b) To assist the Government of Sierra Leone in the implementation of the disarmament, demobilization and reintegration plan;

(c) To that end, to establish a presence at key locations throughout the territory of Sierra Leone, including at disarmament/reception centres and demobilization centres;

(d) To ensure the security and freedom of movement of United Nations personnel;

(e) To monitor adherence to the ceasefire in accordance with the ceasefire agreement of 18 May 1999 through the structures provided for therein;

(f) To encourage the parties to create confidence-building mechanisms and support their functioning;

(g) To facilitate the delivery of humanitarian assistance;

(h) To support the operations of United Nations civilian officials, including the Special Representative of the Secretary-General and his staff, human rights officers and civil affairs officers;

(i) To provide support, as requested, to the elections, which are to be held in accordance with the present constitution of Sierra Leone;

9. *Also decides* that the military component of the United Nations Mission in Sierra Leone shall comprise a maximum of 6,000 military personnel, including 260 military observers, subject to periodic review in the light of conditions on the ground and the progress made in the peace process, in particular in the disarmament, demobilization and reintegration programme, and takes note of paragraph 43 of the report of the Secretary-General of 23 September 1999;

10. *Further decides* that the United Nations Mission in Sierra Leone shall take over the substantive civilian and military components and functions of the Observer Mission as well as its assets, and to that end decides that the mandate of the Observer Mission shall

terminate immediately on the establishment of the United Nations Mission in Sierra Leone;

11. *Commends* the readiness of the Monitoring Group to continue to provide security for the areas where it is currently located, in particular around Freetown and Lungi, to provide protection for the Government of Sierra Leone, to conduct other operations in accordance with their mandate to ensure the implementation of the Peace Agreement, and to initiate and proceed with disarmament and demobilization in conjunction and full coordination with the United Nations Mission in Sierra Leone;

12. *Stresses* the need for close cooperation and coordination between the Monitoring Group and the United Nations Mission in Sierra Leone in the performance of their respective tasks, and welcomes the intended establishment of joint operations centres at headquarters and, if necessary, also at subordinate levels in the field;

13. *Reiterates* the importance of the safety, security and freedom of movement of United Nations and associated personnel, notes that the Government of Sierra Leone and the Revolutionary United Front have agreed in the Peace Agreement to provide guarantees in this regard, and calls upon all parties in Sierra Leone to respect fully the status of United Nations and associated personnel;

14. *Decides*, acting under Chapter VII of the Charter of the United Nations, that in the discharge of its mandate the United Nations Mission in Sierra Leone may take the necessary action to ensure the security and freedom of movement of its personnel and, within its capabilities and areas of deployment, to afford protection to civilians under imminent threat of physical violence, taking into account the responsibilities of the Government of Sierra Leone and the Monitoring Group;

15. *Underlines* the importance of including in the United Nations Mission in Sierra Leone personnel with appropriate training in international humanitarian, human rights and refugee law, including child and gender-related provisions, negotiation and communication skills, cultural awareness and civilian-military coordination;

16. *Requests* the Government of Sierra Leone to conclude a status-of-forces agreement with the Secretary-General within thirty days of the adoption of the present resolution, and recalls that, pending the conclusion of such an agreement the model status-of-forces agreement, dated 9 October 1990 should apply provisionally;

17. *Stresses* the urgent need to promote peace and national reconciliation and to foster accountability and respect for human rights in Sierra Leone, underlines in this context the key role of the Truth and Reconciliation Commission, the Human Rights Commission and the Commission for the Consolidation of Peace established under the Peace Agreement, and urges the Government of Sierra Leone to ensure the prompt establishment and effective functioning of these bodies with the full participation of all parties and drawing on the relevant experience and support of Member States, specialized bodies, other multilateral organizations and civil society;

18. *Emphasizes* that the plight of children is among the most pressing challenges facing Sierra Leone, welcomes the continued commitment of the Government of Sierra Leone to work with the United Nations Children's Fund, the Office of the Special Representative of the Secretary-General for Children and Armed Conflict and other international agencies to give particular attention to the long-term rehabilitation of child combatants in Sierra Leone, and reiterates its encouragement of those involved to address the special needs of all children affected by the conflict;

19. *Urges* all parties concerned to ensure that refugees and internally displaced persons are protected and are enabled to return voluntarily and in safety to their homes, and encourages States and international organizations to provide urgent assistance to that end;

20. *Stresses* the urgent need for substantial additional resources to finance the disarmament, demobilization and reintegration process, and calls upon all States, international and other organizations to contribute generously to the multidonor trust fund established by the International Bank for Reconstruction and Development for that purpose;

21. *Stresses also* the continued need for urgent and substantial humanitarian assistance to the people of Sierra Leone, as well as for sustained and generous assistance for the longer-term tasks of peace-building, reconstruction, economic and social recovery and development in Sierra Leone, and urges all States and international and other organizations to provide such assistance as a priority;

22. *Calls upon* all parties to ensure safe and unhindered access of humanitarian assistance to those in need in Sierra Leone, to guarantee the safety and security of humanitarian personnel and to respect strictly the relevant provisions of international humanitarian and human rights law;

23. *Urges* the Government of Sierra Leone to expedite the formation of professional and accountable national police and armed forces, including through their restructuring and training, without which it will not be possible to achieve long-term stability, national reconciliation and the reconstruction of the country, and underlines the importance of support and assistance from the international community in this regard;

24. *Welcomes* the continued work by the United Nations on the development of the strategic framework for Sierra Leone aimed at enhancing effective collaboration and coordination within the United Nations system and between the United Nations and its national and international partners in Sierra Leone;

25. *Notes* the intention of the Secretary-General to keep the situation in Sierra Leone under close review and to revert to the Council with additional proposals if required;

26. *Requests* the Secretary-General to report to the Council every forty-five days to provide updates on the status of the peace process, on security conditions on the ground and on the continued level of deployment of Monitoring Group personnel, so that troop levels and the tasks to be performed can be evaluated as outlined in paragraphs 49 and 50 of the report of the Secretary-General of 23 September 1999;

27. *Decides* to remain actively seized of the matter.

Appointment of Special Representative and UNAMSIL Commander

On 16 November [S/1999/1186], the Secretary-General informed the Security Council of his intention to appoint Oluyemi Adeniji (Nigeria) as his Special Representative for Sierra Leone and Head of UNAMSIL. The Council took note of the appointment on 19 November [S/1999/1187]. Similarly, the Secretary-General on 22 November [S/1999/1199] informed the Council of his intention to appoint Major-General Vijay Kumar Jetley (India) as Force Commander of UNAMSIL, and the Council took note of his intention on 26 November [S/1999/1200].

Further developments

Report of Secretary-General (December). On 6 December [S/1999/1223], the Secretary-General reported that some progress had been made in the implementation of the Lomê Agreement, but the overall situation in the country remained precarious. He noted that the military and security situation had deteriorated in October and November as a result of an increase in ceasefire violations and human rights abuses by rebel elements.

Following their return to Freetown on 3 October, the leaders of RUF and AFRC held a series of meetings with combatants to inform them of the Lomê Agreement and the disarmament, demobilization and reintegration programme. On 20 October, President Kabbah announced the composition of the Government of National Unity, comprising 20 ministers (including four members of RUF/AFRC), five ministers of State and 13 deputy ministers (including four members of RUF/AFRC). Also on 20 October, President Kabbah appointed Mr. Sankoh as the Chairman of the Commission for the Management of Strategic Resources, National Reconstruction and Development, and Mr. Koroma as the Chairman of the Commission for the Consolidation of Peace. RUF was registered provisionally as a political party on 22 November as the Revolutionary United Front Party (RUFP); the registration would become official when RUFP had met the remaining criteria—having a constitution and party premises.

Despite those political steps forward, ceasefire violations continued, including fighting between RUF and AFRC, extensive movement of troops and weapons by the former and the targeting of humanitarian personnel. ECOMOG troops were fired on by some rebels and on two occasions UNAMSIL troops were detained briefly. UNAMSIL and ECOMOG worked together in monitoring the situation and in the implementation of the disarmament, demobilization and reintegration programme. That programme began when four new demobilization centres were opened on 4 November (one already existed in Lungi). Several reception sites were set up to disarm combatants before their transfer to the demobilization centres. As at 2 December, of an estimated total of 45,000 combatants, the number of registered ex-combatants at the official sites was 4,217. The process continued to suffer because of several security and organizational problems.

The human rights situation in Sierra Leone also deteriorated markedly towards the end of the year, with an escalation of attacks on civilians by former rebel elements in some areas, frequently involving rape, abduction and harassment, in addition to looting and destruction of property. Both RUF and AFRC had shown a reluctance to release adult and child abductees. Deteriorating security conditions throughout the country reversed gains in access for humanitarian assistance.

Meanwhile, the United Nations proceeded with plans to deploy the mandated 6,000 troops. A UN technical team was dispatched to Sierra Leone in late October to assist in deployment plans.

The Secretary-General stated that the continued violence against the people of Sierra Leone and international personnel was unacceptable and perpetrators should expect to be held accountable for their actions. While the United Nations was expediting the deployment of its troops, ECOMOG was expected to continue to provide national security functions and assist in the disarmament process, requiring a force of several thousand troops.

The Security Council discussed the Secretary-General's report on 10 December [meeting 4078].

Communication and further report. By a 23 December letter [S/1999/1285], the Secretary-General provided the Council with an update on UNAMSIL, which was expected to be fully deployed in January 2000. The Secretariat had expedited the deployment, and a substantial number of UNAMSIL troops, in particular from Ghana, Kenya and India, were already in Sierra Leone. The full deployment of 6,000 troops was predicated on the continuing presence of ECOMOG and the Secretary-General contacted leaders from the region to impress on them the need to maintain a sizeable ECOMOG presence in Sierra Leone. On 7 December, President Obasanjo of Nigeria notified the Secretary-General of his intention to withdraw all Nigerian forces from ECOMOG. Later, he confirmed that Nigeria would gradually withdraw its troops from ECOMOG, first by deploying the two battalions it had pledged to contribute to UNAMSIL and then repatriating two of its battalions serving with ECOMOG in early January 2000. By the end of January, two other Nigerian battalions would be withdrawn. The remaining contributors to

ECOMOG, Ghana and Guinea, were also preparing to withdraw their troops, which would make ECOMOG unable to continue performing its vital functions of providing security at Freetown and the international airport at Lungi, and protecting the Government. UNAMSIL had neither the mandate nor the means to perform those tasks.

The Secretary-General was concerned that the repatriation of ECOMOG troops would create a dangerous security gap. He therefore recommended the expansion of UNAMSIL with the addition of up to four infantry battalions and necessary military support elements, to approximately 10,000 military personnel. The mandate should be broadened to enable it to assume those functions currently performed by ECOMOG, in particular the provision of security at Lungi airport and at key installations, buildings and institutions in and around Freetown. In order to be able to deter any attempt to derail the peace process, the additional troops would have to be robustly equipped, including the necessary force multipliers.

At informal consultations on 29 December [S/2000/13], the Council discussed the Secretary-General's recommendations and requested the Secretariat to provide it with more information. During the last week of December, ECOMOG continued to withdraw from several key locations in the provinces and RUFP challenged the implementation of some of the aspects of the peace process.

On 29 December in Freetown, Mr. Sankoh issued a position paper on alleged violations of the Lomé Peace Agreement. RUFP criticized the Government and the international community for not providing the financial resources necessary to allow its participation in various ceasefire monitoring mechanisms or the transformation of RUF into a political party. RUFP stated that it would not allow the deployment of UNAMSIL in areas under its control until the district-level ceasefire monitoring committees were in place. On 31 December, the National Committee on Disarmament, Demobilization and Reintegration decided that UNAMSIL deployment should proceed immediately and that the Government would find a way to establish ceasefire monitoring committees in various parts of the country and to allow the participation of RUFP representatives in them.

UNOMSIL/UNAMSIL financing

The Secretary-General, in February [A/53/454/Add.1], presented to the General Assembly the proposed budget for 1 July 1999 to 30 June 2000 for the maintenance of UNOMSIL, which amounted to $16,412,400 gross ($15,560,400 net). In October [A/54/455], he submitted a revised budget for the same period amounting to $34,382,400 gross ($32,870,100 net). It incorporated additional requirements for the provisional expansion of UNOMSIL, which was authorized by the Security Council in resolution 1260(1999) of 20 August. Also in October [A/54/490], ACABQ considered the proposed budget and recommended approval of the appropriation and assessment proposed by the Secretary-General.

Following the Security Council's establishment of UNAMSIL, the Secretary-General submitted a November report [A/54/633] on its financing. It set out additional requirements for the establishment and maintenance of UNAMSIL, which took over the substantive civilian and military components of UNOMSIL, for the 1999/2000 financial period, estimated at $174,138,000 gross ($173,257,800 net). The full proposed budget for UN operations in Sierra Leone amounted to $208,520,400 gross ($206,127,900 net) and incorporated the proposed budget of $34,382,400 gross for the provisional expansion of UNOMSIL (see above). It included total commitment authorities amounting to $52,971,600 gross ($52,687,600 net) already granted by ACABQ.

In December [A/54/647], ACABQ recommended that the Assembly appropriate and assess the amount of $200 million gross for the maintenance and provisional expansion of UNOMSIL and the establishment and maintenance of UNAMSIL for 1 July 1999 to 30 June 2000.

GENERAL ASSEMBLY ACTION

On 23 December [meeting 88], the General Assembly, on the recommendation of the Fifth Committee [A/54/686], adopted **resolution 54/241 A** without vote [agenda items 150 & 172].

Financing of the United Nations Observer Mission in Sierra Leone and financing of the United Nations Mission in Sierra Leone

The General Assembly,

Having considered the reports of the Secretary-General on the financing of the United Nations Observer Mission in Sierra Leone and the United Nations Mission in Sierra Leone and the related reports of the Advisory Committee on Administrative and Budgetary Questions,

Bearing in mind Security Council resolutions 1181(1998) of 13 July 1998, by which the Council established the United Nations Observer Mission in Sierra Leone, 1260(1999) of 20 August 1999, by which the Council authorized the provisional expansion of the Observer Mission, and 1270(1999) of 22 October 1999, by which the Council established the United Nations Mission in Sierra Leone for an initial period of six months,

Recalling its resolution 53/29 of 20 November 1998 on the financing of the Observer Mission,

Reaffirming that the costs of the Observer Mission are expenses of the Organization to be borne by Member States in accordance with Article 17, paragraph 2, of the Charter of the United Nations, and recognizing that the costs of the United Nations Mission in Sierra Leone are also to be borne by Member States in accordance with Article 17, paragraph 2, of the Charter,

Recalling its previous decision concerning the Observer Mission, and recognizing that, with regard to the United Nations Mission in Sierra Leone, in order to meet the expenditures caused by the Mission, a different procedure is required from that applied to meet expenditures of the regular budget of the United Nations,

Taking into account the fact that the economically more developed countries are in a position to make relatively larger contributions and that the economically less developed countries have a relatively limited capacity to contribute towards such an operation,

Bearing in mind the special responsibilities of the States permanent members of the Security Council, as indicated in General Assembly resolution 1874(S-IV) of 27 June 1963, in the financing of such operations,

Noting with appreciation that voluntary contributions have been made to the Observer Mission and the United Nations Mission in Sierra Leone,

Mindful of the fact that it is essential to provide the United Nations Mission in Sierra Leone with the necessary financial resources to enable it to fulfil its responsibilities under the relevant resolutions of the Security Council,

1. *Takes note* of the status of contributions to the United Nations Observer Mission in Sierra Leone as at 30 November 1999, including the contributions outstanding in the amount of 1.2 million United States dollars, representing 8 per cent of the total assessed contributions, notes that some 37 per cent of the Member States have paid their assessed contributions in full, and urges all other Member States concerned, in particular those in arrears, to ensure the payment of their outstanding assessed contributions;

2. *Expresses its appreciation* to those Member States which have paid their assessed contributions in full;

3. *Urges* all other Member States to make every possible effort to ensure payment of their assessed contributions to the Observer Mission and to the United Nations Mission in Sierra Leone in full and on time;

4. *Expresses concern* at the delay experienced by the Secretary-General in deploying and providing adequate resources to some recent peacekeeping missions, in particular those in Africa;

5. *Emphasizes* that all future and existing peacekeeping missions shall be given equal and non-discriminatory treatment in respect of financial and administrative arrangements;

6. *Also emphasizes* that all peacekeeping missions shall be provided with adequate resources for the effective and efficient discharge of their respective mandates;

7. *Requests* the Secretary-General to make the fullest possible use of facilities and equipment at the United Nations Logistics Base at Brindisi, Italy, in order to minimize the costs of procurement for the United Nations Mission in Sierra Leone, and for this purpose requests the Secretary-General to speed up the implementation of the asset management system at all peacekeeping missions in accordance with General Assembly resolution 52/1 of 15 October 1997;

8. *Endorses* the observations and recommendations contained in the reports of the Advisory Committee on Administrative and Budgetary Questions;

9. *Requests* the Secretary-General to report to the General Assembly on the experience gained in the use of resident auditors in peacekeeping missions and the implications of the implementation of the recommendation of the Office of Internal Oversight Services referred to in paragraph 12 of the report of the Advisory Committee;

10. *Notes* that a technical assessment mission will be undertaken to assess the needs relating to mine clearance, and requests that the necessary funding for operational demining needs be made available for these activities;

11. *Requests* the Secretary-General to take all necessary action to ensure that the United Nations Mission in Sierra Leone is administered with a maximum of efficiency and economy;

12. *Also requests* the Secretary-General, in order to reduce the cost of employing General Service staff, to continue efforts to employ locally recruited staff for the United Nations Mission in Sierra Leone against General Service posts, commensurate with the requirements of the Mission;

13. *Decides* to continue to use the Special Account established in accordance with General Assembly resolution 53/29 for the Observer Mission, for the United Nations Mission in Sierra Leone beginning 22 October 1999;

14. *Decides also* to appropriate the amount of 200 million dollars gross (197,765,100 dollars net) for the maintenance and provisional expansion of the Observer Mission and the establishment and maintenance of the United Nations Mission in Sierra Leone for the period from 1 July 1999 to 30 June 2000, inclusive of the amount of 52,971,600 dollars gross (52,687,600 dollars net) previously authorized by the Advisory Committee under the terms of section IV of General Assembly resolution 49/233 A of 23 December 1994 on the administrative and budgetary aspects of the financing of peacekeeping operations;

15. *Decides further*, as an ad hoc arrangement, to apportion the amount of 161,666,667 dollars gross (159,860,123 dollars net) for the Observer Mission and the United Nations Mission in Sierra Leone for the period from 1 July 1999 to 21 April 2000 in accordance with the composition of groups set out in paragraphs 3 and 4 of General Assembly resolution 43/232 of 1 March 1989, as adjusted by the Assembly in its resolutions 44/192 B of 21 December 1989, 45/269 of 27 August 1991, 46/198 A of 20 December 1991, 47/218 A of 23 December 1992, 49/249 A of 20 July 1995, 49/249 B of 14 September 1995, 50/224 of 11 April 1996, 51/218 A to C of 18 December 1996 and 52/230 of 31 March 1998 and its decisions 48/472 A of 23 December 1993, 50/451 B of 23 December 1995 and 54/456 to 54/458 of 23 December 1999, and taking into account the scale of assessments for the years 1999 and 2000, as set out in its resolutions 52/215 A of 22 December 1997 and 54/237 A of 23 December 1999;

16. *Decides* that, in accordance with the provisions of its resolution 973(X) of 15 December 1955, there shall be set off against the apportionment among Member States, as provided for in paragraph 15 above, their respective share in the Tax Equalization Fund of the estimated staff assessment income of 1,806,544 dollars approved for the Observer Mission and the United Nations Mission in Sierra Leone for the period from 1 July 1999 to 21 April 2000;

17. *Decides also,* as an ad hoc arrangement, to apportion the amount of 38,333,333 dollars gross (37,904,977 dollars net) among Member States for the period from 22 April to 30 June 2000 for the maintenance of the United Nations Mission in Sierra Leone at a monthly rate of 16,666,667 dollars gross (16,480,425 dollars net), in accordance with the scheme set out in the present resolution and taking into account the scale of assessments for the year 2000, as set out in its resolutions 52/215 A and 54/237 A, subject to the decision of the Security Council to extend the mandate of the Mission beyond 21 April 2000;

18. *Decides further* that, in accordance with the provisions of its resolution 973(X), there shall be set off against the apportionment among Member States, as provided for in paragraph 17 above, their respective share in the Tax Equalization Fund of the estimated staff assessment income of 428,356 dollars approved for the United Nations Mission in Sierra Leone for the period from 22 April to 30 June 2000;

19. *Emphasizes* that no peacekeeping mission shall be financed by borrowing funds from other active peacekeeping missions;

20. *Encourages* the Secretary-General to continue to take additional measures to ensure the safety and security of all personnel under the auspices of the United Nations participating in the United Nations Mission in Sierra Leone;

21. *Invites* voluntary contributions to the United Nations Mission in Sierra Leone in cash and in the form of services and supplies acceptable to the Secretary-General, to be administered, as appropriate, in accordance with the procedure and practices established by the General Assembly;

22. *Decides* to keep under review during its fifty-fourth session the items entitled "Financing of the United Nations Observer Mission in Sierra Leone" and "Financing of the United Nations Mission in Sierra Leone".

In other action, the Assembly, by **decision 54/462 A** of 23 December, decided that the Fifth Committee should continue its consideration of the financing of UNOMSIL and UNAMSIL at the Assembly's resumed fifty-fourth session in 2000. On the same date, the Assembly decided that the agenda items on UNOMSIL and UNAMSIL financing would remain for consideration during its fifty-fourth session (**decision 54/465**).

Security Council Committee

By a series of letters issued during the year [S/1999/111, S/1999/350, S/1999/381, S/1999/1013, S/1999/1026], the Chairman of the Security Council Committee established pursuant to resolution 1132(1997) [YUN 1997, p. 135], which imposed sanctions against Sierra Leone, reported on notifications received from States on the export of arms and related materiel to Sierra Leone. The Committee had received notifications from Ukraine and the United Kingdom on the export of certain logistical equipment for peacekeeping purposes and use in Sierra Leone by ECOMOG and/or the Government, including vehicles, satellite telephones, personnel carrier trucks, arms, radio handsets and radio communications equipment. The Committee also received a notification from Sierra Leone [S/1999/174] that it had decided to import two helicopter gunships and arms to be used for peacekeeping purposes.

The Committee, on 31 December [S/1999/1300 & Corr.1], transmitted to the Council an account of its 1999 activities. During the year, the Committee held six meetings and one informal consultation at the expert level. The Committee reaffirmed the need for cooperation with ECOWAS and UNOMSIL in reporting on compliance with the arms embargo and other aspects of the sanctions regime. In an effort to improve compliance with the travel ban in effect under that regime, the Committee agreed to request additional information from the Permanent Mission of Sierra Leone to the United Nations to update the list of members of the former military junta and RUF who were banned from entering other States. On 16 April, the Committee approved a request from the Government for an exemption from the travel ban in order to permit the travel to Togo of Mr. Sankoh and a delegation of AFRC/RUF in order to facilitate the peace process. Other exemptions were made for delegations to attend international conferences. In May, the Committee considered reports of alleged violations of the sanctions regime, involving shipment of arms from Ukraine, via Burkina Faso, to Liberia, then to rebel forces in Sierra Leone. It sought additional information from those countries (see above, under "Liberia").

The Committee agreed that it should consider ways to improve the monitoring and implementation of the sanctions against Sierra Leone. Reports from ECOMOG and/or UNAMSIL could strengthen the effectiveness of the arms embargo by assisting the Committee in its efforts.

Somalia

Despite peacemaking efforts by regional and international organizations, the political, military and humanitarian situation in Somalia deteriorated in 1999. Reports of illicit delivery of weapons and military equipment exacerbated the divisions among the warlords, while the United Nations Political Office for Somalia (UNPOS) did not have the mandate or the capacity to verify the reports. Because of the absence of law and order, criminals and terrorists were attracted to Somalia, a country with no functioning central government, and used it as a transit point for the trafficking of narcotic drugs.

In August, the Secretary-General reported that, although a negotiated settlement of the crisis continued to be elusive, he believed that the United Nations should play an enhanced role in Somalia. He proposed that the Organization work with the Intergovernmental Authority on Development (IGAD) for national reconciliation, that a general review be made of the UN role in Somalia and that a trust fund be established to support the emerging process. In September, Djibouti introduced an initiative for the international community to assume a more active role in Somalia and proposed bold, decisive measures against the warlords.

In December, the General Assembly, in **resolution 54/96 D**, called on the international community to provide assistance in response to the United Nations Consolidated Inter-Agency Appeal for relief, rehabilitation and reconstruction assistance for Somalia (see PART THREE, Chapter III).

Alleged external involvement

Communications (May). In a 14 May letter to the Security Council [S/1999/563], Ethiopia drew the Council's attention to dangerous developments in Somalia, allegedly caused by Eritrea involving itself in the internal conflict by embarking on a large-scale military activity of destabilization. On 24 May [S/1999/600], Djibouti also expressed to the Council its apprehension regarding accounts of Eritrean weapons and personnel being involved in the situation in Somalia. Eritrea responded to the accusations in a 26 May statement [S/1999/611] (see above, under "Eritrea-Ethiopia").

Deteriorating situation

At informal consultations on 27 May, the Security Council received a briefing by the Secretariat on the latest developments in Somalia, in particular the political, security and humanitarian situation. On the same date [meeting 4010], the President made statement **S/PRST/1999/16** on behalf of the Council:

The Security Council expresses its alarm at the serious deterioration in the political, military and humanitarian situation in Somalia and concern at the reports of increasing external interference in Somalia.

The Council reaffirms its commitment to a comprehensive and lasting settlement of the situation in Somalia, bearing in mind respect for the sovereignty, territorial integrity and political independence and unity of Somalia, in accordance with the principles of the Charter of the United Nations. It reiterates that full responsibility for achieving national reconciliation and for restoring peace rests with the Somali people.

The Council expresses its support for the activities of the Standing Committee on Somalia and calls upon all Somali factions to cease all hostilities immediately and to cooperate with the regional and other efforts to achieve peace and reconciliation.

The Council is deeply concerned at recent reports of the illicit delivery of weapons and military equipment to Somalia, in violation of the arms embargo imposed by resolution 733(1992) of 23 January 1992, which could exacerbate the crisis in Somalia and endanger the peace and security of the region as a whole.

The Council reiterates its call upon States to observe the arms embargo and to refrain from any actions which might exacerbate the situation in Somalia. It further requests Member States having information about violations of the provisions of resolution 733(1992) to provide this information to the Security Council Committee established pursuant to resolution 751(1992) of 24 April 1992.

The Council expresses its deep concern at the humanitarian impact of the long-lasting crisis and, in particular, condemns attacks or acts of violence against civilians, especially women, children and other vulnerable groups, including internally displaced persons. It also condemns attacks on humanitarian workers, in violation of the rules of international law.

The Council calls upon the Somali factions to cooperate on the basis of the principles of neutrality and non-discrimination with the United Nations agencies and other organizations carrying out humanitarian activities. The Council urges all parties to guarantee the security and the freedom of movement of humanitarian personnel and to ensure unhindered access to those in need of assistance. In this regard, it also commends the existing coordination of all efforts of the international community to meet the humanitarian needs of the Somali people, undertaken by the Somali Aid Coordination Body, comprising donors, United Nations agencies and non-governmental organizations.

The Council urges all States to contribute generously to the appeal of the United Nations to ensure continued relief and rehabilitation efforts in all regions of Somalia, including those aimed at the strengthening of civil society.

The Council welcomes the continuing efforts of the Secretary-General and the United Nations Political Office for Somalia in Nairobi.

The Council requests the Secretary-General to submit periodic reports on the situation in Somalia.

The Council will remain seized of the matter.

Peace initiatives

Report of Secretary-General (August). In a 16 August report [S/1999/882], the Secretary-General, in response to the request in Security Council statement S/PRST/1999/16, reported on developments in Somalia since his last report in September 1997 [YUN 1997, p. 143]. He stated that peacemaking efforts by some Somali political leaders, the IGAD Partners Forum, OAU and the League of Arab States (LAS) continued throughout the reporting period.

In June 1999, the Secretary-General reported, ministers of the EU and some African, Caribbean and Pacific countries met in Brussels. They expressed the view that only a process leading to a Somali-driven national reconciliation conference inclusive of all geographic areas and all segments of Somali society could lead to national and international acceptance of a transitional government. They reaffirmed that European Development Fund resources would be made available to Somalia once it adhered to the Lomé IV Convention, an update of the 1975 trade pact between the European Economic Community and the African, Caribbean and Pacific countries [YUN 1975, p. 330].

Describing the internal situation in Somalia, the Secretary-General stated that north-west Somalia/Somaliland continued to enjoy relative peace. In March, Mohamed Ibrahim Egal, leader of Somaliland, proposed that it should assist the clans in the south in reaching peace and subsequently enter into negotiations on an appropriate formula for reuniting the country. In other regions, including Mogadishu, efforts to establish regional administrations led to inconclusive results.

Regarding reports of arms and/or fighters being shipped into Somalia by Eritrea and Ethiopia, both countries had denied any involvement. UNPOS, located in Nairobi, Kenya, had neither the mandate nor the capacity to verify those reports.

A common strand in discussions by UN officials with Somali interlocutors was a strong feeling that the days of the "warlords" were over, said the Secretary-General, and most of them called for a renewed UN effort to disarm militia members in the country. Through his representative, the Secretary-General had emphasized his continued interest in finding a solution to the Somali problem. However, he had stressed that the onus for peace rested with Somalis themselves and that members of the international community could only assist them in those efforts.

As outlined in the Consolidated Inter-Agency Appeal for Somalia 1999 (see PART THREE, Chapter III), the main UN objective was to prevent the current situation in the south from developing into famine and to continue the groundwork for establishing stability, self-reliance and security in the north. To meet those goals, the United Nations had adopted a number of sectoral interventions in the areas of food security, health and nutrition, water and sanitation, education and public administration, as well as cross-cutting interventions to ensure programme coherence and protection of civilian populations, promotion and protection of human rights and inter-agency planning and coordination.

The effects of the continuing internal armed conflict on the population had been compounded by extensive flooding in the southern regions followed by drought in most areas of Somalia. The security of those providing humanitarian aid to Somalia continued to be a grave cause for concern due to murders, robbery and kidnapping of international staff.

The Secretary-General observed that little or no development had taken place in Somalia for 10 years and it ranked among the poorest and most deprived countries in the world. It continued to have no functioning central government to provide basic services, such as the police, judiciary, civil service, postal service, communications and electricity. The economy was in dire straits. Somalia had been attracting criminals and subversives and was being used as a transit point for the trafficking of narcotic drugs and as a haven for terrorists. The country was divided on clans lines, with each clan fearful of the incursions of others. The violence, where it was not simple banditry, was mainly defensive in nature. The missing ingredient was trust and without it there could be no peace or security in Somalia and no central government could be re-established.

While a negotiated settlement of Somalia's crisis had continued to be elusive, some important steps forward had been made. Djibouti, in its capacity as Chairman of IGAD, had proposed a number of ideas to speed up the IGAD process that were worthy of serious consideration. The Somalis themselves, tired of violence, were increasingly taking political initiatives through regional conferences organized by traditional leaders and attended by civil society, women's groups in particular. There was also increased criticism of the role of the Somali faction leaders. Approximately half of Somali territory was peaceful. While struggles continued over control of some key southern towns, the violence was criminal rather than political in origin. Many Somali leaders had informed UNPOS that they were willing to join a national meeting. However, several leaders believed that no progress was possible while Eritrea and Ethiopia continued to be at war and involved faction leaders in that war. The task of re-establishing a functioning state in Somalia would require not only an enormous effort of political will on the part of the Somali people and their leaders, but a massive rebuilding operation would also be a necessary accompaniment of any peace process. The two processes would have to be carefully coordinated, with international support being carefully calibrated to reinforce those tendencies in Somali society that were working constructively together.

The Secretary-General believed that the stage had been reached for the United Nations to play an enhanced role in Somalia. He proposed that consideration be given to action on two fronts. First, the United Nations, working impartially and objectively with interested Member States, especially with the IGAD process, should do more to help bring about national unity and the restoration of a national government. He proposed a general review of the UN role in Somalia, including possible relocation of some programmes and agencies, and the establishment of a trust fund for Somalia to provide financial support for the emerging process. In addition, consideration might be given to whether, in advance of political agreements on the formation of a national government, action could be taken by the international community to assist Somalia to recover its sovereignty in certain limited fields, for example the protection of offshore natural resources. Efforts could also be made to limit the introduction of illegal arms and weapons into the country. The Secretary-General urged international financial institutions such as the World Bank and the European Development Fund, in administering the Lomé IV Convention, to allow financial assistance to flow into Somalia even before a formal central government and other institutions were re-established.

Communications. By a 23 September letter [S/1999/1007], the President of Djibouti transmitted to the Security Council the portion of his statement in the General Assembly the day before, in which he discussed Somalia. He said the challenge in Somalia was to establish an authority to fill the vacuum that was continuously exploited by the warlords and announced a set of proposals to achieve that goal: a reconciliation conference with representatives from civil society, jointly with the warlords, should agree on steps towards national harmony, including acceptance of the principle that the Somali people were free to exercise their democratic right to choose their own regional and national leaders, in accordance with an agreed time frame; the warlords had to agree to convert their factions into political parties that would compete in elections, commit to disarmament, submit to the primacy of law, and respect the creation of a Somali police force; and the United Nations, as in Guinea-Bissau, should establish a post-conflict peace-building office in Somalia to initiate projects in support of the process, including coordinating and monitoring legislative and presidential elections. If those proposals were spurned by the warlords, they would be charged with crimes against humanity and made accountable for their actions. Sanctions would be imposed on warlords not agreeing to the demands of the international community, including confinement to their area, bans on travel abroad and on foreign support or any type of assistance, and a freeze on their assets. If those measures failed to accomplish the objectives, the alternative would be for regional organizations to which Somalia belonged—principally OAU and LAS, with support of the United Nations—to redress the situation under "all necessary means".

On 2 November [S/1999/1134], the Secretary-General informed the Security Council that he intended to extend UNPOS into the biennium 2000-2001, given that its role was very important and useful and that the Council had expressed support for continued UN involvement in the search for peace in Somalia. He also advised that the activities of UNPOS would be expanded and its staff strengthened.

On 5 November [S/1999/1135], the Council took note of the Secretary-General's decision.

SECURITY COUNCIL ACTION

On 12 November [meeting 4066], following consultations among Council members, the President made statement **S/PRST/1999/31** on behalf of the Council:

> The Security Council recalls the report of the Secretary-General of 16 August 1999 on the situation in Somalia.
>
> The Council reaffirms its commitment to a comprehensive and lasting settlement of the situation in Somalia, bearing in mind respect for the sovereignty, territorial integrity and political independence and unity of Somalia, in accordance with the principles of the Charter of the United Nations.
>
> The Council expresses its grave concern at the increasingly evident effects of the lack of a functioning central government in Somalia. It regrets the fact that most children receive no health care and that two generations have had no access to formal education. It is concerned that some Somali natural resources are being exploited, mainly by foreigners, without regulation and monitoring. It expresses its deep distress over reports that the absence of law and order in the country risks creating a haven for criminals of all kinds.

The Council welcomes the progress that has been made in the development of a greater uniformity of approach on the part of the international community in addressing the crisis in Somalia. It recognizes that the Standing Committee on Somalia, created a year ago, has been instrumental in monitoring the evolution of the Somali situation and working for a greater coordination of efforts by the various external actors, in order to avoid contrasting influences and to give weight to common actions. It calls for the strengthening of the coordination of these efforts aimed at securing peace and stability in Somalia.

The Council expresses its full support for the efforts exerted by the Intergovernmental Authority on Development to find a political solution to the crisis in Somalia. In this context, it welcomes the initiative of the President of Djibouti aimed at restoring peace and stability in Somalia, which was outlined in his letter of 23 September 1999 to the President of the Security Council. It endorses the call made by the President of Djibouti to the warlords to recognize fully and accept the principle that the Somali people are free to exercise their democratic right to choose their own regional and national leaders. The Council looks forward to the finalization of the proposals of the President of Djibouti at the forthcoming summit of the Intergovernmental Authority on Development and stands ready to work with the Intergovernmental Authority and the Standing Committee to help bring about national unity and the restoration of a national government in Somalia. It calls upon the leaders of the Somali factions and all others concerned to cooperate constructively and in good faith in the efforts to resolve the crisis.

The Council strongly calls upon all States to observe and improve the effectiveness of the arms embargo imposed by resolution 733(1992) of 23 January 1992 and to refrain from any actions which might exacerbate the situation in Somalia. It urges Member States having information about violations of the provisions of resolution 733(1992) to provide this information to the Security Council Committee established pursuant to resolution 751(1992) of 24 April 1992, with a view to supporting the work of the Committee.

The Council expresses its grave concern at the continuing deterioration of the humanitarian situation in Somalia. It urges all States to contribute generously to the appeals of the United Nations to ensure continued relief and rehabilitation efforts in all regions of Somalia, including those aimed at the strengthening of civil society. In this context, it encourages enhancement of the operational capacity of humanitarian agencies in Somalia through donor support.

The Council expresses its appreciation for all United Nations agencies, other organizations and individuals carrying out humanitarian activities in all regions of Somalia. It calls upon the Somali factions to ensure the safety and freedom of movement of all humanitarian personnel and to facilitate the delivery of humanitarian relief. In this context, it strongly condemns attacks and acts of violence against, and the murder of, humanitarian workers in Somalia, and reiterates its position that those responsible for these acts should be brought to justice.

The Council expresses its satisfaction that despite all the difficulties, approximately half of Somali territory continues to enjoy relative peace. In this context, it notes that local administrations in some parts of the country are beginning to provide some basic services to the people of Somalia.

The Council welcomes the efforts of civil society in Somalia. It is encouraged by the political initiatives of Somalis, through regional conferences, often organized by traditional leaders and informal cross-clan contacts, to find a peaceful solution to the crisis. In this context, it underlines the active role of Somali women's groups.

The Council welcomes the continuing efforts of the Secretary-General and the United Nations Political Office for Somalia in Nairobi.

The Council encourages the Secretary-General to review the role of the United Nations in Somalia, as a prelude to the United Nations playing an enhanced role, aimed at achieving a comprehensive and lasting settlement of the situation in Somalia. This review would include the possible relocation of some United Nations programmes and agencies, as well as the United Nations Political Office, to Somalia. The review should also consider the security situation carefully, as well as the resources that would be necessary to provide a secure environment for United Nations operations in Somalia.

The Council takes note of the recommendation in the report of the Secretary-General of 16 August 1999 that the international community should consider establishing mechanisms which would allow financial assistance to flow into secure and stable areas of Somalia even before a formal central government and other institutions are re-established, with a view to promoting the sovereignty, territorial integrity and political independence and unity of Somalia.

The Council will remain seized of the matter.

Communications. By a 29 November letter to the Security Council [S/1999/1206], Djibouti transmitted the declaration of the seventh Summit of Heads of State and Government of IGAD (Djibouti, 26 November) and the resolution on the Somali peace initiative and proposals of the President of Djibouti adopted at the Summit. The heads of State and Government stated that those in Somalia who had so far sought to promote peace in their respective regions should be encouraged, and called for the early realization of the UN trust fund for Somalia. They agreed on the speedy working out of the detailed implementation mechanism of the new initiative in cooperation with other members of IGAD. They condemned the third parties who had chosen to exacerbate the crisis in Somalia. They recommended further elaboration of the proposals made by the President of Djibouti to the General Assembly in September and urged the international community to support them.

In a 3 December statement transmitted to the Secretary-General [S/1999/1259], the EU Presidency welcomed the IGAD decision to endorse the Djibouti President's proposals. The EU looked forward to examining the detailed proposals and the mechanism for their implementation that IGAD would produce in collaboration with the Standing Committee on Somalia. The EU support would be considered in the light of the conclusions of the meeting of the Committee on Somalia of the IGAD Partners Forum held in Rome on 19 and 20 October.

Arms embargo

On 28 December [S/1999/1283], the Chairman of the Security Council Committee established pursuant to resolution 751(1992) [YUN 1992, p. 202] concerning Somalia transmitted to the Council President the Committee's report covering its activities in 1999. The Committee had been established to monitor the military and weapons embargo against Somalia imposed by resolution 733(1992) [ibid., p. 199].

On 12 May, the Committee approved, on a no-objection basis, a request from Denmark regarding importation of explosives for a humanitarian demining project in north-west Somalia.

In the light of reports of the illicit delivery of weapons and military equipment to Somalia and the call by the Council for States to observe the arms embargo and its request to Member States to provide the Committee with information on violations, the Committee held a meeting on 20 December to exchange ideas on effective implementation of the arms embargo and on strengthening its work, especially in the light of the Djibouti initiative (see above).

The Committee observed that it had no specific monitoring mechanism to ensure the effective implementation of the arms embargo and recalled that it relied solely on the cooperation of States and organizations to provide information on violations.

UNOSOM II financing

The Secretary-General, in February [A/C.5/53/52], reported to the General Assembly on the financing of the United Nations Operation in Somalia (UNOSOM and UNOSOM II). UNOSOM was established by the Security Council by resolution 751(1992) [YUN 1992, p. 202], and its mandate was last extended by resolution 954(1994) [YUN 1994, p. 325]. The force was withdrawn from Somalia in March 1995. The February financial report provided information on the status of unfinished work related to the financial liquidation of UNOSOM and UNOSOM II. As at 31 December 1998, unliquidated obligations retained in the special account amounted to $134.2 million, compared with $213.3 million in 1997. As at the same date, from the total amount of $1,645.9 million assessed on Member States since the Operation's inception, $284.5 million remained uncollected. Owing to an acute cash deficit in the Operation's special account, reimbursement to troop contributors for certified claims totalling $69.2 million for equipment, supplies and services provided by them to the Operation had been put on hold pending receipt of assessed contributions.

Owing to the difficulties experienced by the UNOSOM administration during the life of the Operation, the originally envisaged time frame for the completion of its liquidation process proved unrealistic. The following outstanding issues remained: completion of the analysis and reconciliation of accounts recoverable locally; processing of inter-office transactions and write-off actions; review and finalization of contingent-owned equipment reimbursement cases and of government claims for supplies, goods, and services provided to UNOSOM; and preparation and processing of the pending Property Survey Board cases for the contingent-owned equipment. Resolution of the outstanding issues by the Department of Peacekeeping Operations and the Office of Programme Planning, Budgeting and Accounts was essential to establish authoritatively the actual resource requirements of the Operation and to facilitate the determination by the General Assembly of the appropriate course of action.

On 8 June, by **decision 53/477**, the General Assembly approved the Fifth Committee's recommendation on the financing of UNOSOM II (see preceding chapter). By **decision 54/462 A** of 23 December, the Assembly decided that the Fifth Committee should continue consideration of the financing of UNOSOM II at the resumed fifty-fourth session in 2000.

Sudan

The Sudan's relations with neighbouring States improved somewhat in 1999. In May, the Sudan and Eritrea committed themselves to restoring diplomatic relations and, in December, the Sudan and Uganda agreed to re-establish relations and promote peace in the region.

With regard to the civil conflict, the Sudan and the Sudan People's Liberation Movement (SPLM) agreed to the extension of the ceasefire that was due to expire on 15 July. A UN humanitarian assessment mission to the SPLM-controlled areas in the Nuba Mountains took place in late June with the full cooperation of both parties (see PART THREE, Chapter III).

In **resolution 54/96 J** of 17 December, the General Assembly called on the international community to continue to contribute generously to the emergency needs, recovery and development of the Sudan and urged all parties involved to offer all feasible assistance to guarantee the success of Operation Lifeline Sudan.

Internal conflict

Communications. In a 14 January statement [S/1999/62], the EU Presidency strongly requested the Sudanese Government and all other parties concerned in the internal armed conflict to extend indefinitely the ceasefire in the Bahr al-Ghazal area in southern Sudan, agreed to in October 1998 [YUN 1998, p. 185], which would expire on 15 January, to facilitate humanitarian assistance to the suffering people in that region. The EU stated that it supported the IGAD Partners Forum's mission to the Sudan, which was scheduled for the end of January.

In a statement of 21 October [A/54/527-S/1999/1125], the EU welcomed the decision of the Sudanese Government and SPLM to extend the ceasefire in southern Sudan for three more months, thereby securing humanitarian aid to war-torn areas. It reiterated its appeal to both parties to proceed to a permanent and comprehensive humanitarian ceasefire and to resume peace negotiations in Nairobi, as called for by the IGAD peace process initiated in 1994 [YUN 1994, p. 837].

Sudan-Uganda

On 18 February [S/1999/169], the Sudan informed the Security Council that Uganda continued to interfere in its internal affairs by hosting a conference of the so-called Sudanese armed opposition (Kampala, 8-12 February) to overthrow the Sudanese Government. The conference, in which terrorist groups allegedly participated, published a final declaration reaffirming the need to continue the policy of violence to destabilize the country. The Sudan called on the Council to put an end to Uganda's interference in its internal affairs, not only to preserve the stability of the Sudan but also peace throughout the region.

In a 20 December letter [S/1999/1270], Uganda informed the Council of the agreement signed by President Yoweri Museveni of Uganda and President Omar al-Bashir of the Sudan to re-establish relations between their two countries and promote peace in the region. The talks leading to the agreement were organized by the Carter Center, an NGO that promoted peace and health worldwide. According to the agreement, both countries committed themselves to renounce the use of force; prevent acts of terrorism; not support rebel groups, opposition groups or hostile elements from each other's territory; and refrain from hostile propaganda campaigns against each other. They condemned the abuse of innocent civilians and offered amnesty and reintegration assistance to all former combatants who renounced the use of force. They agreed to open offices in Kampala and Khartoum and restore full diplomatic relations by the end of February 2000.

Sudan-Eritrea

By a 3 May letter [S/1999/504], Eritrea transmitted to the Security Council an agreement reached between Eritrea and the Sudan. In response to the mediation of Qatar, a summit meeting was held in Doha on 2 May attended by President Issaias Afewerki of Eritrea and President Omar al-Bashir of the Sudan. The two countries agreed to: restore diplomatic relations; respect international laws regulating peaceful coexistence; respect political choices; refrain from hosting conferences threatening the security of neighbouring countries; work to resolve differences; and establish joint committees to examine remaining issues.

Sudan–United States

In letters of 15 April [S/1999/424] and 23 September [S/1999/997], the League of Arab States (LAS) transmitted to the Security Council resolutions adopted by the LAS Council condemning the August 1998 United States bombing of the Shifa pharmaceutical plant in Khartoum [YUN 1998, p. 185] and the alleged threat of renewed aggression against the Sudan by the United States. The LAS Council asked the Secretary-General to take the necessary action with regard to the follow-up mechanism and cooperate with the relevant organizations, primarily the Security Council and the United Nations, for the implementation of resolutions adopted by the LAS Council.

Western Sahara

The United Nations continued its efforts in 1999 to conduct a referendum to enable the people of Western Sahara to choose, freely and democratically, between independence and integration with Morocco, as outlined in the 1990 settlement plan approved by the Security Council in resolution 658(1990) [YUN 1990, p. 920]. The plan, agreed to by both Morocco and the Frente Popular para la Liberación de Saguia el-Hamra y de Río de Oro (POLISARIO), set out the conditions for the referendum. To implement the plan, the Security Council, by resolution 690(1991) [YUN 1991, p. 794], had established the United Nations Mission for the Referendum in Western Sahara (MINURSO), composed of civilian, military and police units. In October 1998 [YUN 1998, p. 195], the Secretary-General had proposed a package of measures to move forward the identification, appeals and repatriation of refugees process.

At the beginning of the year, informal consultations between the United Nations and Morocco and POLISARIO continued to address the concerns of the parties, clarify points of the Secretary-General's 1998 package of measures to move the various processes forward and facilitate the signing of protocols. Following intensive discussions among the parties, amended protocols and operational directives were provided to them by the United Nations. In June, with the cooperation of both parties, the identification process and the initiation of the appeals process resumed as planned. However, in August, two issues caused delays in the identification operation for certain tribes in group H61, namely the appointment of sheikhs and that of their advisers. Other delays were caused by the staggered opening of the appeals centres and difficulties in meeting staff requirements, which affected parts of the timetable for the referendum process.

The appeals process, launched by the Identification Commission in July, included 84,251 names in the first provisional voting list out of the 147,249 identified during the first two phases of the process. In November, the overall total of those identified to vote by the Commission since 1994 reached 190,023.

During the early part of the year, the Moroccan authorities agreed to formalize the presence in the Territory of the Office of the United Nations High Commissioner for Refugees (UNHCR). UNHCR, in close coordination with MINURSO, continued its preparatory work for the repatriation of Saharan refugees as provided for under the settlement plan. Morocco and POLISARIO agreed, in principle, to the draft plan of action for the cross-border confidence-building measures submitted by UNHCR in May, pursuant to Security Council resolution 1238(1999).

At the end of the year, the Secretary-General observed that the prospect of holding a referendum in Western Sahara was becoming very distant. The problem posed by the number of appeals and the opposing positions taken by both parties on the issue of admissibility did not allow for the referendum to be held earlier than 2002.

SECURITY COUNCIL ACTION (January)

During informal consultations on 21 January, the Security Council received a briefing from the Under-Secretary-General for Peacekeeping Operations on MINURSO's activities and on modalities for the implementation of the Secretary-General's proposals of October 1998 [YUN 1998, p. 195].

On 28 January [meeting 3971], the Council unanimously adopted **resolution 1224(1999)**. The draft text [S/1999/78] was prepared in consultations among Council members.

The Security Council,

Recalling all its previous resolutions on the question of Western Sahara,

1. *Decides* to extend the mandate of the United Nations Mission for the Referendum in Western Sahara until 11 February 1999;

2. *Requests* the Secretary-General to keep the Council informed of all significant developments in the implementation of the settlement plan and the agreements reached between the parties, and, as appropriate, on the continuing viability of the mandate of the Mission;

3. *Decides* to remain seized of the matter.

Report of Secretary-General (January). In response to Security Council resolution 1215(1998) [YUN 1998, p. 198], the Secretary-General submitted a 28 January progress report [S/1999/88] on the implementation of the 1990 settlement plan. He recalled that in December 1998 [YUN 1998, p. 197] POLISARIO had formally accepted the package of measures in the settlement plan, while the Government of Morocco had expressed concerns and sought clarifications about voter identification and the appeals procedure. The consultations between the United Nations and the Moroccan authorities that began in late December 1998 intensified in January 1999 and continued in Rabat and New York. In reply to Morocco's memorandum containing the Government's formal response to the draft protocols and concerns on several key elements of the proposed package, the Secretary-General, on 13 January, addressed those concerns and provided clarifications on all points raised in the memorandum. The Secretary-General's Special Representative, Charles F. Dunbar, the Chairman of the Identification Commission, Robin Kinloch, and UNHCR remained in close contact with the two parties in order to finalize the various draft protocols as soon as possible. Following a meeting with the Moroccan Minister of the Interior in Rabat on 18 January, Mr. Dunbar and Mr. Kinloch began a series of daily consultations on 21 January with a Moroccan delegation to discuss the draft protocols on voter identification and the appeals procedures contained in the proposed package. Meanwhile, MINURSO provided extensive clarifications on the package of measures.

As at 26 January, the strength of the military component of MINURSO was 316, including 60 members of the engineering support unit from Pakistan. That unit commenced repatriation on 22 January and was scheduled to complete the process by the first week of February. The Secretary-General intended to retain two Pakistani officers with the Mission as military observers, to continue to provide the necessary technical guidance and expertise on matters related to mines and unexploded ordnance. MINURSO's civilian police component stood at 26, of an authorized establishment of 81 officers.

The Moroccan authorities indicated that they were finalizing their response to the draft status-of-forces agreement, which was an indispensable condition for the full and timely deployment of MINURSO's formed military units. In order to provide further clarification of certain provisions of the agreement and to assist in bringing about its prompt signature, a UN legal officer, accompanied by MINURSO representatives, held discussions in Rabat and New York. As a result, all issues except one were settled.

During the reporting period, UNHCR continued its preparatory activities in the camps in Tindouf, Algeria, including construction of its operational base and enlargement of its field office. The resumption of the pre-registration exercise in the two remaining camps in Tindouf continued to be subject to the implementation of the other measures in the package of proposals. UNHCR maintained an active presence in the Tindouf refugee camps in order to understand better the needs of the refugees and to promote confidence-building, for which it continued to receive the required cooperation from POLISARIO. On 7 and 8 January, in Geneva, Morocco confirmed its decision to formalize the UNHCR presence in the Territory. Preliminary discussions were held between the Moroccan delegation and UNHCR on the draft protocol for the repatriation of refugees, which was submitted to Morocco, POLISARIO, Algeria and Mauritania early in November 1998. UNHCR informed the Moroccan authorities that it was ready to discuss the protocol once a working group was established. POLISARIO and Algeria submitted their respective proposals for amendments to the draft protocol on 12 January.

The Secretary-General recommended that MINURSO's mandate be extended until 28 February 1999, in the hope that ongoing discussions would lead to a full and detailed agreement in order to reactivate the referendum process and move towards the transition period. However, should the prospects remain elusive, the Secretary-General would ask his Personal Envoy to reassess the situation and the viability of the MINURSO mandate.

SECURITY COUNCIL ACTION (February)

At informal consultations on 2, 9 and 10 February, the Security Council considered the Secretary-General's January report on Western Sahara and received briefings from the Under-Secretary-General and the Assistant Secretary- General for Peacekeeping Operations on the negotiations on the package of measures proposed by the Secretary-General in December 1998 [YUN 1998, p. 197] and on the status-of-forces agreement.

On 11 February [meeting 3976], the Council unanimously adopted **resolution 1228(1999)**. The draft text [S/1999/130] was prepared in consultations among Council members.

The Security Council,

Recalling all its previous resolutions on the question of Western Sahara, and reaffirming in particular resolutions 1204(1998) of 30 October 1998 and 1215(1998) of 17 December 1998,

Welcoming the report of the Secretary-General of 28 January 1999 and the observations and recommendations contained therein,

1. *Decides* to extend the mandate of the United Nations Mission for the Referendum in Western Sahara until 31 March 1999 to allow for consultations in the hope and expectation of agreement on the protocols on identification, appeals and repatriation planning activities, as well as on the essential issue of the implementation calendar, without undermining the integrity of the Secretary-General's proposed package of measures or calling into question its main elements, for the prompt resumption of voter identification and initiation of the appeals process;
2. *Requests* both parties to take concrete action to enable the Office of the United Nations High Commissioner for Refugees to carry out the necessary preparatory work for the repatriation of Saharan refugees eligible to vote, and their immediate families, according to the settlement plan;
3. *Requests* the Secretary-General to report to the Council by 22 March 1999 on the implementation of the present resolution;
4. *Supports* the intention of the Secretary-General to ask his Personal Envoy to reassess the viability of the mandate of the Mission should the prospects for putting the package of measures into effect remain elusive at the time of submission of the next report of the Secretary-General;
5. *Decides* to remain seized of the matter.

Report of Secretary-General (March). In a 22 March report [S/1999/307], submitted in response to resolution 1228(1999), the Secretary-General stated that during the reporting period his Special Representative, the Chairman of the Identification Commission and other Commission officers continued discussions with the Moroccan authorities on the package outlined in December 1998. During those discussions, the Moroccan authorities asked that the modalities for organizing the identification and appeals be consistent with the objective of holding the referendum by March 2000; that the appeals procedure be launched no later than one month after the date of resumption of identification; and that the provisional list of potential voters, from among the applicants identified so far, be published on that date. On 22 March, Morocco accepted, in principle, the proposed package on the understanding that certain amendments would be incorporated in the identification and appeals protocols and that operational directives, together with a revised timetable, would be provided to the parties. The United Nations also held informal consultations on the developments with POLISARIO. MINURSO expected to provide, at the end of March, the revised texts of the identification and appeals protocols, which would incorporate necessary amendments, including revised dates. It would also provide to the parties detailed operational directives and a revised timetable for the implementation of the protocols.

As at 15 March, the strength of the MINURSO military component was 230. The status-of-forces agreement between the United Nations and Morocco was signed on 11 February. An arrangement regarding the implementation of the provisions on the carriage of weapons was expected to be elaborated in the near future. A military agreement between MINURSO and the Royal Moroccan Army was signed in March regarding exchange of information on mines and unexploded ordnance. MINURSO was engaged in efforts to reach a similar agreement with POLISARIO. In February, communications equipment was stolen from a MINURSO station east of the defensive sand-wall (berm). The Mission conducted an inquiry but did not succeed in recovering it.

UNHCR made progress in establishing itself in the Territory and in preparing the ground in order to complete its preparatory work for the repatriation of Saharan refugees. However, UNHCR was unable to resume the pre-registration exercise in the remaining two refugee camps in Tindouf since POLISARIO maintained its earlier position that the exercise remained subject to the implementation of the other measures in the package of proposals.

The Secretary-General designated Robin Kinloch, Chairman of the Identification Commission, as Acting Special Representative, effective 1 April, in the light of the resignation of Charles F. Dunbar.

The Secretary-General recommended that MINURSO's mandate be extended until 30 April 1999.

SECURITY COUNCIL ACTION (March)

On 30 March [meeting 3990], the Security Council unanimously adopted **resolution 1232(1999)**. The draft text [S/1999/354] was prepared in consultations among Council members.

The Security Council,

Recalling all its previous resolutions on the question of Western Sahara,

Welcoming the report of the Secretary-General of 22 March 1999 and the observations and recommendations contained therein,

Welcoming also the agreement in principle to the Secretary-General's package of measures by the Government of Morocco, and recalling its acceptance by the Frente Popular para la Liberación de Saguia el-Hamra y de Río de Oro,

1. *Decides* to extend the mandate of the United Nations Mission for the Referendum in Western Sahara until 30 April 1999 to allow for an understanding to be reached among all concerned on detailed modalities for the implementation of the identification and appeals protocols, including a revised implementation schedule, in a manner that would preserve the integrity of the Secretary-General's package of measures;

2. *Requests* both parties to move ahead with the necessary discussions to reach an agreement on the refugee repatriation protocol, so that all aspects of the work needed to prepare the way for the repatriation of refugees may begin, including confidence-building measures, and in that regard welcomes the decision of the Frente Popular para la Liberación de Saguia el-Hamra y de Río de Oro to allow the resumption of pre-registration activities of the Office of the United Nations High Commissioner for Refugees in Tindouf;

3. *Welcomes* the signature, by the Government of Morocco and the Force Commander of the Mission, of the agreement on mines and unexploded ordnance mentioned in paragraph 13 of the report of the Secretary-General, and urges the Frente Popular para la Liberación de Saguia el-Hamra y de Río de Oro to engage in a similar effort;

4. *Requests* the Secretary-General to report to the Council by 23 April 1999 on the implementation of the present resolution;

5. *Decides* to remain seized of the matter.

Report of Secretary-General (April). In a 27 April report on the latest developments in Western Sahara [S/1999/483], submitted in response to resolution 1232(1999), the Secretary-General stated that during the reporting period his Acting Special Representative held consultations on the package to accelerate the referendum process with the Coordinator for POLISARIO and with the Moroccan Minister of the Interior and other officials. The amended protocols on identification and appeals, together with detailed operational directives for their implementation, were communicated to the parties on 9 April. Following intensive discussions between the United Nations and the two parties in New York, those documents and the outline calendar were finalized and transmitted to the parties on 26 April. The amended protocols and the operational directives provided for the resumption of identification work on 1 June and its completion (subject to later confirmation by Morocco that it would provide two sheikhs for the identification of H61 Ait Ousa tribe applicants) in November, and for the start of the appeals process on 1 July and its completion by February 2000. In the revised outline calendar for the referendum process, the transition period would begin in February 2000, with a view to holding the referendum in July 2000.

As at 23 April, MINURSO's military component stood at 203 and the civilian police component was 22. Following the 12 March military agreement between MINURSO and the Royal Moroccan Army for the marking and destruction of mines and unexploded ordnance in the Mission area, the first clearance operation was successfully completed. A similar military agreement was concluded by MINURSO with POLISARIO on 5 April. With regard to the communications equipment stolen from MINURSO in February, POLISARIO and the Algerian authorities offered to assist in the investigation.

Pending the establishment of a UNHCR/Morocco formal working group, a UNHCR mission was dispatched to Rabat to discuss with the Ministry of the Interior the amendments provided verbally by the latter to the refugee repatriation protocol. A UNHCR mission also visited Tindouf in April to discuss with POLISARIO the resumption of the pre-registration exercise in the two remaining camps.

The Secretary-General observed that the timely implementation of the revised calendar was predicated upon many critical assumptions, including authorization by the Security Council to begin preparations in July for the full deployment of MINURSO troops; the total cooperation of the parties in the identification of individual applicants from groups H41, H61 and J51/52 so as to maintain a rigorous programme without the delays and interruptions experienced in the past; the expectation that the appeals process would not be turned into a second round of identification for all applicants found ineligible; the completion by the end of 1999 of planning arrangements for repatriation; the deployment of formed military units, additional military observers and civilian police by January 2000; the reduction and confinement of troops on both sides; the demining of repatriation routes; the proclamation of a general amnesty; and a repatriation process that would be completed within 16 weeks. The Secretary-General recommended that, should the parties agree to the proposed protocols and operational directives, the Council consider extending MINURSO's mandate for a period of six months, until 30 October 1999.

SECURITY COUNCIL ACTION (April)

On 30 April [meeting 3994], the Security Council unanimously adopted **resolution 1235(1999)**. The draft text [S/1999/489] was prepared in consultations among Council members.

The Security Council,

Recalling all its previous resolutions on the question of Western Sahara,

Taking note of the report of the Secretary-General of 27 April 1999 and the observations and recommendations contained therein,

1. *Decides* to extend the mandate of the United Nations Mission for the Referendum in Western Sahara until 14 May 1999;
2. *Requests* the Secretary-General to keep the Council informed of all significant developments in the implementation of the settlement plan and the agreements reached between the parties, and, as appropriate, on the continuing viability of the mandate of the Mission;
3. *Decides* to remain seized of the matter.

Communications (April/May). In May, the Secretary-General transmitted to the Security Council letters from POLISARIO and Morocco commenting on the five documents (see below) that he had transmitted to them following discussions between their representatives and the United Nations in New York from 12 to 26 April.

In a 28 April letter [S/1999/555], the POLISARIO Secretary-General reminded the UN Secretary-General that POLISARIO had made a major concession regarding the identification of the disputed tribal groupings. It did so on the understanding that the agreement meant that the identification of tribal groupings H41, H61 and J51/52 and the appeal procedures would take place simultaneously and under conditions of complete strictness, impartiality and transparency. He stated that major changes to the original texts, particularly the protocol on appeal procedures, as well as new procedures were included in the version transmitted to both parties on 8 April. During later discussions, POLISARIO put forward amendments concerning the methods of proof recognized by the Identification Commission and, in particular, by the appeals sections. It indicated strong reservations concerning the oral testimony accorded to every individual, whereas the settlement plan authorized only the sheikhs to make use of it. It expressed fears that the change would lead to the sections being inundated with an endless number of appeals, resulting ultimately in repeat identifications and a forced reappraisal of the work already done. Nevertheless, POLISARIO formally accepted the 26 April version of the proposed package on the understanding that: the appeal and identification operations for the disputed tribal groupings would be carried out under conditions of exemplary strictness, transparency and fairness; and the Identification Commission would continue to carry out its mission demonstrating its authority, independence and impartiality as in the past. The success of the entire process depended on that demand, which remained the keystone of the entire structure.

In a 7 May letter [S/1999/554], Morocco's Minister for Foreign Affairs and Cooperation stated that Morocco agreed to the timetable and the measures proposed by the Secretary-General, which were linked to the resumption of the identification operation on 1 June and the start of the appeal procedures on 1 July. However, he also expressed reservations to the relevant protocols and operational guidelines: the admissibility procedure had not reflected the possibility of each applicant making use of all the possible guarantees for ensuring a fair re-examination of his case, which might eliminate thousands of applicants who considered that they had been unjustifiably or unfairly eliminated from the electorate and desired to have their right restored; the provision related to the periodic communication of partial results of identification, which did not indicate that the next identification stage, which essentially concerned Morocco, would be carried out within a strictly limited period of time. In that regard, there was a need to prevent a recurrence of practices such as the "revision" of the identification results and the use of corroborating testimony as a condition for the eligibility of applicants not included in the Spanish census of 1974. The Foreign Minister therefore proposed that future identification operations be accompanied by every possible guarantee for fairness and that the communication of the results be on a weekly basis to ensure better monitoring and greater transparency.

Report of Secretary-General (May). In a 13 May addendum to his April report [S/1999/483/Add.1], the Secretary-General transmitted to the Security Council the text of the five documents he had sent to Morocco and POLISARIO following the discussions between their representatives and the United Nations (New York, 12-26 April), namely: the protocol on the identification of the remaining individual applications from candidates belonging to tribal groupings H41, H61 and J51/52; operational directives for the identification of the remaining individual applications from candidates belonging to those tribal groupings; the appeals process for the referendum in Western Sahara; operational directives for the implementation of the appeals process; and the time frame for the implementation of the settlement plan. The Secretary-General drew the Council's attention to the positions of Morocco and POLISARIO contained in their letters to him (see above). He intended to carry out preparations to resume the identification operation on 15 June and to begin the appeals process on 15 July.

SECURITY COUNCIL ACTION (May)

On 14 May [meeting 4002], the Security Council unanimously adopted **resolution 1238(1999)**. The draft text [S/1999/556] was prepared during consultations among Council members.

The Security Council,

Recalling all its previous resolutions on the question of Western Sahara,

Welcoming the report of the Secretary-General of 27 April 1999 and the observations and recommendations contained therein,

Welcoming also the acceptance by the Government of Morocco and the Frente Popular para la Liberación de Saguia el-Hamra y de Río de Oro of the detailed modalities for the implementation of the Secretary-General's package of measures relating to the identification of voters, the appeals process and the revised implementation timetable as a good foundation for the completion of this phase of the settlement plan and taking note of their respective letters,

1. *Decides* to extend the mandate of the United Nations Mission for the Referendum in Western Sahara until 14 September 1999 in order to resume the identification process, start the appeals process and conclude all outstanding agreements needed to implement the settlement plan, and reaffirms the rights of the applicants, with an expectation that the appeals process will not be turned into a second round of identification;

2. *Supports* the proposed increase in staff of the Identification Commission from twenty-five to thirty members, and the proposed increase also in the necessary support activities, in order to strengthen the Commission and enable it to continue working with full authority and independence, in accordance with its mandate as authorized by the Security Council, and to accomplish its tasks expeditiously;

3. *Requests* the Secretary-General to report every forty-five days on significant developments in the implementation of the settlement plan, in particular on the following issues which will form, inter alia, the basis of its consideration of a further extension of the mandate of the Mission: full and unequivocal cooperation of the parties during the resumption of voter identification and during the start of the appeals pro-

cess; agreement by the Government of Morocco on the modalities for implementing paragraph 42 of the status-of-forces agreement; agreement of the parties on the protocol relating to refugees; and confirmation that the Office of the United Nations High Commissioner for Refugees is fully operational in the region;

4. *Also requests* the Office of the High Commissioner to provide the Security Council with recommendations for confidence-building measures and time lines for their implementation;

5. *Requests* the Secretary-General to submit to the Council a revised timetable and financial implications for the holding of the referendum for the self-determination of the people of Western Sahara in accordance with the settlement plan and the agreements with the parties for its implementation;

6. *Decides* to remain seized of the matter.

Appointment. On 18 May [S/1999/590], the Secretary-General informed the Security Council that he had appointed William Eagleton (United States) as his Special Representative for Western Sahara. The Council took note of the appointment on 21 May [S/1999/591].

Special Committee consideration. The Special Committee on the Situation with regard to the Implementation of the Declaration on the Granting of Independence to Colonial Countries and Peoples considered the question of Western Sahara on 22 June [A/54/23]. The Committee granted a request for a hearing to Moulud Said of POLISARIO and reviewed a June working paper on developments concerning the Territory over the previous year [A/AC.109/1999/11]. The paper summarized the activities of the good offices of the Secretary-General and action taken by the Security Council and the General Assembly. It stated that, on 23 April, the Commission on Human Rights adopted a resolution, in which it took note with satisfaction of the agreements reached between the parties and urged them to implement the agreements fully and in good faith (see PART TWO, Chapter II).

Communication. In a 21 June statement [A/54/151-S/1999/718], the EU reiterated its full support for the settlement plan proposed by the Secretary-General and welcomed the agreements reached concerning further steps to implement it. It hoped that the proposals could be implemented without further delay in line with the deadlines set out in the Secretary-General's 28 April report. The EU called on both parties to cooperate fully throughout the voter identification and the appeals process.

Reports of Secretary-General (June, August and September). In a 25 June report on the Western Sahara situation [S/1999/721], the Secretary-General stated that his Special Representative, Mr. Eagleton, and his Deputy Special Representative, Mr. Kinloch, had met with the senior officials of Morocco, POLISARIO, Mauritania and Algeria to discuss their commitment to the implementation of the settlement plan. The newly appointed Chairman of the Identification Commission, Eduardo Vetere, participated in the visits to Nouakchott and Algiers and took up his functions in Laayoune.

The final programme of identification for the remaining individual applicants from tribal groupings H41, H61 and J51/52 was issued on 1 June and the identification operation resumed on schedule on 15 June at one centre in the Territory and another in the Tindouf area. Two more centres were opened on 21 June in southern Morocco. As at 24 June, 2,328 persons had been interviewed by the Identification Commission since 15 June, bringing the total number identified since 28 August 1994 to 149,577. Special efforts would be made to increase the staffing of the Commission to required levels by mid-July. A training centre for former and new Identification Commission staff opened in Agadir on 15 June, with a basic one-week staff training course. Trainees would also spend a week in the Tindouf area for additional training.

As at 25 June, the military component of MINURSO was 230 military observers and the strength of the civilian police component had increased to 52. Consultations with Moroccan authorities were initiated to formalize an agreement regarding the carriage of weapons. Both parties continued to extend their full support to military agreements on the marking and destruction of unexploded ordnance and exchange of related information, with 60 per cent of tasks west of the berm and 20 per cent east of the berm completed.

An agreement was reached with the Moroccan Government on 21 May to undertake a joint reconnaissance visit to the Territory to gather relevant information for planning the return of refugees, including on existing infrastructure, such as schools, hospitals, housing facilities and transit centres. The pre-registration exercise resumed in the Tindouf refugee camps on 24 May. A total of 12,798 refugees (constituting 1,672 families) had been pre-registered by UNHCR in Camp El-Aiun. Pending conditions conducive to safe return, the majority of the refugees expressed reservations about repatriation to the Territory west of the berm, owing to fear of their security and safety. UNHCR provided refugees with information on its mandate and on repatriation operations and conducted a refugee-needs assessment. The pre-registration exercise was scheduled to resume in Nouadhibou and Zouerate in northern Mauritania in mid-July, at the same time as MINURSO was scheduled to start the identification process at those locations. UNHCR prepared a draft plan of action for its cross-border confidence-building measures aimed at creating confidence and trust within the refugee camps and in the Territory.

The Secretary-General observed that the agreements with the two parties on the resumption of the identification process and the initiation of the appeals process were being implemented as planned, with the cooperation of both parties. It was important that both parties stay the course, particularly with regard to the launching of the appeals process on 15 July, in conjunction with the publication of the first part of the provisional voters list. All efforts would be made to meet the staffing requirements for the process.

In a 12 August report [S/1999/875], the Secretary-General stated that the reporting period was marked by the death of His Majesty King Hassan II of Morocco on 23 July. At the King's funeral, the Secretary-General met His Majesty King Mohammed VI and senior Moroccan government officials, as well as President Abdelaziz Bouteflika of Algeria. King Mohammed renewed his commitment to Morocco's territorial integrity through the holding of a "confirmative" referendum under the auspices of the United Nations. President Bouteflika reiterated that the Western Sahara issue should be dealt with by the United Nations within the framework of the 1997 Houston agreements [YUN 1997, p. 149], while the issue of Algeria's bilateral relations with Morocco would be addressed between the two countries. On 31 July, Morocco's Minister of the Interior expressed concern regarding the results of the second phase of the identification operation and what he considered to be its restrictive terms for eligibility.

During the reporting period, identification operations continued in Laayoune and in Tan Tan and Goulimine in southern Morocco. Two new identification centres were opened in Assa in southern Morocco and in Nouadhibou in Mauritania. As at 23 July, 9,674 individual applicants from tribal groupings H41, H61 and J51/52 had been interviewed since the resumption of identification on 15 June, which brought the total to 155,923.

On 9 July, Morocco's Interior Minister reiterated his concern about several thousand applicants eliminated during the identification process. The Secretary-General replied that those applicants would have a full opportunity to seek and obtain redress through the appeals process if it was concluded that they were withdrawn without valid reason.

The appeals process was launched by the Identification Commission on 15 July, when the first part of the provisional list of persons authorized to vote was communicated to the two parties by the Special Representative and made public. The first part included 84,251 names of applicants found eligible to vote, out of 147,249 identified during the first two phases of the process from 28 August 1994 to 22 December 1995 and from 3 December 1997 to 3 September 1998. For the sake of transparency, the Commission provided the parties with the list of reviewed cases. On 4 August, Morocco again expressed concern about the review issue. Additional appeals centres were opened in Morocco, Mauritania and the Territory and a second mobile centre was also opened in the Tindouf area to cover the El-Aiun, Dakhla and Awsard camps. As at 11 August, 18,914 persons had presented themselves to the centres and submitted 22,159 requests for file transcripts; 520 asked to consult their own original files and 1,999 appeals were filed.

On 20 and 21 July, the Interior Minister visited Laayoune and met with sheikhs, Moroccan observers and other officials. He addressed the public and noted that the provisional list contained 46,255 voters from Morocco (and the Territory), 33,786 from the Tindouf camps and 4,210 from Mauritania. He alleged bias by certain members of the Identification Commission.

Two issues caused delays in the identification operation for certain tribes in group H61, namely, the appointment of sheikhs and that of their advisers. Under the identification protocol, the parties were to appoint two sheikhs each for the identification of applicants from the Ait Ousa tribe, the first pair before 1 June and the second pair before 1 August. Morocco's appointment of the latter was awaited. With regard to the advisers to the sheikhs, the issue pertained only to the group of 13 tribes listed in the protocol. Morocco objected that the advisers designated by POLISARIO were not members of the tribes concerned. The Commission and the UN Secretariat were of the opinion that, under the protocol, the adviser who could be designated for each of the 13 tribes did not necessarily have to be a member of the tribe concerned. The identification of applicants from the group of tribes had to be postponed pending a resolution of the issue.

The Commission decided, with the consent of both parties, to deploy all available staff to the appeals process and to suspend identification operations for three weeks, starting on 2 August, because of the shortage of staff and the persisting problems in connection with the identification operations.

As at 9 August, the MINURSO military component stood at 230, while the civilian police component stood at 78. A draft proposal on the carriage of weapons prepared by MINURSO was under review by the UN Secretariat. Satisfactory progress was made in implementing the military agreements between MINURSO and each party on the marking and disposal of unexploded ordnance and related exchange of information.

A UNHCR mission visited Laayoune to discuss with MINURSO outstanding political issues, logistics planning, confidence-building measures and administrative matters. They both agreed on the need for a common approach and decided to hold a joint follow-up workshop in Laayoune in September. Morocco's Interior Minister expressed the Government's full support to enable UNHCR to complete its work for the return of refugees, as provided for in the settlement plan. The Special Representative, together with UNHCR, visited Tindouf and met with POLISARIO senior officials to review planning for the repatriation of refugees and other issues. The draft plan of action on confidence-building measures presented to the Security Council in June was submitted to the parties to secure their cooperation on implementation procedures and a time frame. The draft plan would be discussed with both parties in late August. Joint MINURSO-UNHCR road reconnaissance trips were carried out east and west of the berm. By early-August, 22,656 individuals (3,075 families) had been pre-registered in Camp El-Aiun. The pre-registration also resumed in Nouadhibou and Zouerate in northern Mauritania, where 548 individuals (121 families) were pre-registered.

The Secretary-General observed that it should be recognized that delays in solving certain issues in the identification operation, and the staggered opening of the appeals centres, compounded by difficulties in meeting staffing requirements, had affected parts of the timetable for the referendum process.

In an 8 September report [S/1999/954], the Secretary-General stated that his Special Representative had held consultations with both parties to secure the continuation of the appeals process and the simultaneous identification of the remaining applicants from tribal groupings H41, H61 and J51/52, as well as preparatory work for the repatriation of refugees and other Saharans residing outside the Territory who were eligible to vote. The consultations settled two outstanding issues in the identification process—the appointment by each side of a second Ait Ousa sheikh and the designation of advisers to the H61 sheikhs—which led to the resumption of identification operations. Identification Commission staff deployed to appeals centres in July and August were reassigned to identification operations after the closing of five appeals centres. As at 3 September, 47,796 appeals had been received by MINURSO and 14,750 applicants had accessed their identification files. The Commission provided 34,243 file transcripts to applicants. The majority of appeals received were against non-inclusion in the first part of the provisional list of persons eligible to vote. In accordance with the six-week period allotted, the Commission closed the receipt of appeals at the centres. At the same time, it continued the preparations for hearings on admissibility and substance of appeals. Shortage of qualified staff remained a major constraint and staffing requirements would be evaluated once the total number of appeals was known. In the meantime, OAU increased the strength of its observer delegation to MINURSO.

The strength of MINURSO's military component remained at 230, while the civilian police component stood at 80. An additional 25 police officers had been requested to assist the Commission. At the request of POLISARIO, due to its annual congress, the UNHCR pre-registration exercise in the Tindouf camps was suspended but was expected to resume on 10 September. The UNHCR plan of action for confidence-building measures was under discussion with the parties, as was the draft repatriation planning protocol. Discussions between MINURSO and the Moroccan authorities were in progress on modalities for implementing the status-of-forces agreement concerning the carriage of weapons by MINURSO troops.

As Emmanuel Roucounas (Greece), the Independent Jurist for Western Sahara since 1995, would no longer be able to serve in that capacity, the Secretary-General would appoint a new Independent Jurist in due course.

Given the delays that had occurred in the identification operations, the Secretary-General stated that he was not yet in a position to submit a revised timetable and financial implications, including recommendations that the Security Council authorize preparations for MINURSO's full deployment. In the meantime, he recommended that the Council consider extending MINURSO's mandate until 14 December 1999.

SECURITY COUNCIL ACTION (September)

The Security Council acted on the Secretary-General's recommendation to extend MINURSO's mandate by unanimously adopting, on 13 September [meeting 4044], **resolution 1263(1999)**. The draft [S/1999/964] was prepared during consultations among Council members.

The Security Council,

Recalling all its previous resolutions on Western Sahara,

Welcoming the report of the Secretary-General of 8 September 1999 and the observations and recommendations contained therein,

Welcoming also the resumption of the identification of voters and the commencement of the appeals process,

1. *Decides* to extend the mandate of the United Nations Mission for the Referendum in Western Sahara until 14 December 1999 in order to complete the identification of voters as envisaged in paragraph 21 of the report of the Secretary-General, to implement confidence-building measures and conclude all outstanding agreements needed to implement the settlement plan, and to continue with the appeals process, and reaffirms the rights of the applicants, with the expectation that the appeals process will not be turned into a second round of identification;

2. *Requests* the Secretary-General to report every forty-five days on significant developments in the implementation of the settlement plan;

3. *Also requests* the Secretary-General to submit to the Security Council before the end of the current mandate a comprehensive assessment of steps taken towards the completion of the appeals process, and of staffing requirements as outlined in the report, as well as preparations for the repatriation of refugees and the start of the transitional period;

4. *Decides* to remain seized of the matter.

Reports of Secretary-General (October and December). The Secretary-General, on 28 October [S/1999/1098], reported that his Special Representative continued to consult with both parties regarding the appeals process and the simultaneous identification of remaining applicants from "contested" tribal groupings and the preparatory work for the repatriation of refugees. The Secretary-General met with Morocco's Foreign Minister and POLISARIO's Coordinator with MINURSO at Headquarters on 29 September and 28 October, respectively. The number of applicants interviewed by the Identification Commission as at 22 October totalled 177,067. By the closing date for the submission of appeals on 18 September, MINURSO had received 79,125 appeals (a preliminary figure). Preliminary statistical analysis of the appeals showed that the overwhelming majority (65,072) were against exclusion from the first part of the provisional list of persons eligible to vote. An estimated 36 additional members of the Commission would be required, above the 30 authorized, to handle 80,000 appeals over a period of 10 to 12 months, which did not include eventual appeals from the individual applicants of the "contested" tribal groupings.

The number of refugees pre-registered in the Tindouf camps totalled 68,556 since the exercise began in 1998. The refugees continued to express their doubts of the UN ability to guarantee their safety and security during the transitional period under the settlement plan.

The Secretary-General observed that, with the large number of appeals submitted, there would be a lengthy appeals process involving almost all applicants rejected in the first instance, as well as a large number of applicants whose inclusion in the provisional voter list had been challenged. Depending on the results of MINURSO's analysis of the admissibility of those appeals, a thorough consideration would be needed of all relevant consequences relating to the application of the appeals procedures, to the staff, financial and other resources required, and to the timetable for holding the referendum.

In a 6 December report [S/1999/1219], the Secretary-General stated that his Special Representative met with Mauritania's President Maaouya Ould Sid'Ahmed Taya, POLISARIO Secretary-General Mohamed Abdelaziz, Algeria's Prime Minister and Foreign Minister and Morocco's King Mohammed VI, Prime Minister and Minister for Foreign Affairs and the new Minister of the Interior. All of them declared support for the settlement plan and Algeria, Mauritania and POLISARIO expressed concern about the prospect of delays caused by the large number of appeals. POLISARIO maintained that a large number of appeals could be eliminated by adhering strictly to the provisions concerning their admissibility. The Moroccan authorities invoked Security Council resolution 1263(1999), which reaffirmed the rights of the applicants to appeal. The Special Representative was continuing discussions with the Moroccan authorities on the appeals issue as well as on a new round of appeals after the issuance of the second provisional voter list.

Identification operations since 15 June 1999 from the tribal groupings H41, H61 and J51/52 had identified 42,774 applicants. A relatively small percentage of applicants from those groupings had been found eligible. On 30 November, the overall total of those identified since 1994 reached 190,023. MINURSO's preliminary analysis of the 79,000 appeals filed by applicants following the publication of the first part of the provisional voter list on 15 July indicated that: appeals were filed by almost all the applicants who did not meet the criteria; the great majority of the appeals filed indicated the names of witnesses who purportedly would provide, at the appeals hearings, new facts to support the applicants' claim for inclusion; the Commission was constrained in handling the appeals by the parties' radically opposed interpretations of the procedures regarding grounds for appeals and admissibility of applications; and the Special Representative had not received any indication that either party would change its view on the issue. The second part of the provisional list of the tribal groupings was expected in mid-January 2000 and could evoke a high number of appeals. Hearings on such numerous appeals posed serious logistical and organizational strains on the Commission.

On 23 November, POLISARIO's Secretary-General presented the Special Representative with a list of 191 Moroccan prisoners of war who had been freed that day on humanitarian grounds, from among those taken prisoner during the 1975-1989 Western Sahara armed conflict. The list was forwarded to the Government of Morocco and to the ICRC, which was available to organize their repatriation.

As at 2 December, MINURSO's military strength remained at 230 and the civilian police component stood at 81.

UNHCR held meetings with senior officials of Algeria, POLISARIO and Morocco concerning the repatriation of Saharan refugees. During the meetings, the parties reiterated their agreement, in principle, to the draft plan of action for the cross-border confidence-building measures pursuant to Security Council resolution 1238(1999). The number of refugees pre-registered in the camps since the beginning of the exercise in 1998 totalled 87,860. Regarding the draft refugee repatriation protocol, submitted to the parties pursuant to Security Council resolution 1204(1998) [YUN 1998, p. 196], UNHCR was not in a position to finalize such a document because of the absence of a solution to the outstanding issues.

The Secretary-General observed that the prospect of holding the referendum within a reasonable period of time was becoming more distant. The problems posed by the number of appeals and the opposing positions taken by the parties on the issue of admissibility seemed to allow little possibility of holding the referendum before 2002. He recommended that MINURSO's mandate be extended to 29 February 2000.

SECURITY COUNCIL ACTION (December)

On 14 December [meeting 4080], the Security Council adopted by vote (14-0-1) **resolution 1282(1999)**. The draft text [S/1999/1239] was submitted by France, the Russian Federation, the United Kingdom and the United States.

The Security Council,

Recalling all its previous resolutions on Western Sahara, in particular resolutions 1238(1999) of 14 May 1999 and 1263(1999) of 13 September 1999,

Welcoming the report of the Secretary-General of 6 December 1999 and the observations and recommendations contained therein,

1. *Decides* to extend the mandate of the United Nations Mission for the Referendum in Western Sahara until 29 February 2000 in order to complete the identification of voters, issue a second provisional voters list, and initiate appeals for tribal groupings H41, H61 and J51/52;

2. *Welcomes* the reiteration by the parties of their agreement in principle to the draft plan of action for cross-border confidence-building measures, including person-to-person contacts, submitted pursuant to resolution 1238(1999), and calls on them to cooperate with the United Nations High Commissioner for Refugees and the Mission for the initiation of these measures without further delay;

3. *Takes note* of the concern that the problems posed by the current number of candidates who have exercised their right of appeal and the opposing positions taken by the parties on the issue of admissibility seem to allow little possibility for holding the referendum before 2002 or even beyond, and supports the intention of the Secretary-General to instruct his Special Representative to continue his consultations with the parties on these issues, seeking a reconciliation of their opposing views regarding the appeals process, the repatriation of refugees and other crucial aspects of the United Nations settlement plan;

4. *Takes note also* of the assessment by the Secretary-General, however, that difficulties may be encountered in reconciling the opposing views of the parties, and therefore requests the Secretary-General to report before the end of the present mandate on prospects for progress in implementing the settlement plan within a reasonable period of time;

5. *Decides* to remain seized of the matter.

VOTE ON RESOLUTION 1282(1999):

In favour: Argentina, Bahrain, Brazil, Canada, China, France, Gabon, Gambia, Malaysia, Netherlands, Russian Federation, Slovenia, United Kingdom, United States.

Against: None.

Abstaining: Namibia.

Speaking before the vote, Namibia stated that it did not consider the text to represent faithfully the Secretary-General's December report. The text ignored crucial concerns expressed previously by the Council, the most obvious of which was that the appeals process should not be turned into a new round of identification. In addition, the text painted a negative picture that would send a wrong message to the international community.

GENERAL ASSEMBLY ACTION

On 6 December [meeting 71], the General Assembly, having considered the Secretary-General's report [A/54/337] summarizing developments in Western Sahara from 30 September 1998 to 31 August 1999, on the recommendation of the Fourth (Special Political and Decolonization) Committee [A/54/584], adopted **resolution 54/87** without vote [agenda item 18].

Question of Western Sahara

The General Assembly,

Having considered in depth the question of Western Sahara,

Reaffirming the inalienable right of all peoples to self-determination and independence, in accordance with the principles set forth in the Charter of the United Nations and in General Assembly resolution 1514(XV) of 14 December 1960, containing the Declaration on the Granting of Independence to Colonial Countries and Peoples,

Recalling its resolution 53/64 of 3 December 1998,

Recalling also the agreement in principle given on 30 August 1988 by the Kingdom of Morocco and the Frente Popular para la Liberación de Saguia el-Hamra y de Río de Oro to the proposals of the Secretary-General of the United Nations and the Chairman of the Assembly of Heads of State and Government of the Organization of African Unity in the context of their joint mission of good offices,

Recalling further Security Council resolutions 658(1990) of 27 June 1990 and 690(1991) of 29 April 1991, by which the Council approved the settlement plan for Western Sahara,

Recalling all the Security Council and General Assembly resolutions relating to the question of Western Sahara,

Reaffirming the responsibility of the United Nations towards the people of Western Sahara, as provided for in the settlement plan,

Noting with satisfaction the entry into force of the ceasefire in accordance with the proposal of the Secretary-General, and stressing the importance it attaches to the maintenance of the ceasefire as an integral part of the settlement plan,

Also noting with satisfaction the agreements reached by the two parties during their private direct talks aimed at the implementation of the settlement plan, and stressing the importance it attaches to a full, fair and faithful implementation of the settlement plan and the agreements aimed at its implementation,

Further noting with satisfaction the progress made in the implementation of the settlement plan since December 1997,

Taking note of Security Council resolutions 1131 (1997) of 29 September 1997, 1198(1998) of 18 September 1998, 1204(1998) of 30 October 1998, 1215(1998) of 17 December 1998, 1224(1999) of 28 January 1999, 1228(1999) of 11 February 1999, 1232(1999) of 30 March 1999, 1235(1999) of 30 April 1999, 1238(1999) of 14 May 1999 and 1263(1999) of 13 September 1999,

Welcoming the acceptance by the two parties of the detailed modalities for the implementation of the Secretary-General's package of measures relating to the identification of voters, the appeals process and the revised implementation timetable,

Having examined the relevant chapter of the report of the Special Committee on the Situation with regard to the Implementation of the Declaration on the Granting of Independence to Colonial Countries and Peoples,

Having also examined the report of the Secretary-General,

1. *Takes note* of the report of the Secretary-General;

2. *Again notes with satisfaction* the agreements reached between the Kingdom of Morocco and the Frente Popular para la Liberación de Saguia el-Hamra y de Río de Oro for the implementation of the settlement plan during their private direct talks under the auspices of James Baker III, the Personal Envoy of the Secretary-General, and urges the parties to implement those agreements fully and in good faith;

3. *Commends* the Secretary-General and his Personal Envoy for their efforts in reaching those agreements as well as the two parties for the cooperation they have shown, and urges them to continue this cooperation in order to facilitate the speedy implementation of the settlement plan;

4. *Urges* the two parties to continue their cooperation with the Secretary-General and his Personal Envoy, as well as with his Special Representative, and to refrain from undertaking anything that would undermine the implementation of the settlement plan and the agreements reached for its implementation;

5. *Notes with satisfaction* the progress achieved in connection with the implementation of the settlement plan, and in this respect calls upon the two parties to cooperate fully with the Secretary-General, his Personal Envoy and his Special Representative in implementing the various phases of the settlement plan;

6. *Urges* the two parties to implement faithfully and loyally the Secretary-General's package of measures relating to the identification of voters, the appeals process and the revised implementation timetable;

7. *Reaffirms* the responsibility of the United Nations towards the people of Western Sahara, as provided for in the settlement plan;

8. *Reiterates its support* for further efforts of the Secretary-General for the organization and the supervision by the United Nations, in cooperation with the Organization of African Unity, of a referendum for self-determination of the people of Western Sahara that is impartial and free of all constraints, in conformity with Security Council resolutions 658(1990) and 690(1991), by which the Council approved the settlement plan for Western Sahara;

9. *Takes note* of Security Council resolutions 1131 (1997), 1238(1999) and 1263(1999);

10. *Requests* the Special Committee on the Situation with regard to the Implementation of the Declaration on the Granting of Independence to Colonial Countries and Peoples to continue to consider the situation in Western Sahara, bearing in mind the positive ongoing implementation of the settlement plan, and to report thereon to the General Assembly at its fifty-fifth session;

11. *Invites* the Secretary-General to submit to the General Assembly at its fifty-fifth session a report on the implementation of the present resolution.

Further developments. The identification of applicants from the H41, H61 and J51/52 tribal groupings, which began on 15 June, was completed by MINURSO on 30 December as scheduled [S/2000/131].

UN Mission for the Referendum in Western Sahara

The United Nations Mission for the Referendum in Western Sahara (MINURSO) reported that the situation remained calm during 1999 and that there had been no indications that either side intended to resume hostilities. Its military component's strength remained at 230 for most of the year. Under the command of Brigadier-General Claude Buze (Belgium), who was appointed Force Commander on 1 November [S/1999/1109, S/1999/1110], the military component continued to monitor the ceasefire between the Royal Moroccan Army and the POLISARIO forces, which came into effect on 6 September 1991 [YUN 1991, p. 796]. The strength of the civilian police component stood at 81 at the end of the year, under the command of Inspector General Om Prakash Rathor (India), who assumed his functions as the new Police Commissioner for MINURSO on 5 November. The civilian police continued to assist the Identification Commission at the identification centres.

Financing of MINURSO

In January [A/53/810], the Secretary-General reported on MINURSO's financial performance for the period from 1 July 1997 to 30 June 1998. Expenditures totalled $40,878,900 gross ($39,062,500 net), resulting in an unencumbered balance of $6,523,200 gross ($5,357,200 net), attributable to the delayed deployment of contingent personnel and initial delays in the deployment of civilian personnel.

In a February report [A/53/820], the Secretary-General presented the proposed budget to maintain MINURSO for the 12-month period from 1 July 1999 to 30 June 2000, which amounted to $49,023,000 gross ($45,071,400 net). In a May report [A/53/943], ACABQ recommended that the General Assembly appropriate the requested amount subject to the Security Council's extension of MINURSO's mandate beyond 14 May 1999.

GENERAL ASSEMBLY ACTION

On 8 June [meeting 101], the General Assembly, on the recommendation of the Fifth Committee [A/53/544/Add.1], adopted **resolution 53/18 B** without vote [agenda item 125].

Financing of the United Nations Mission for the Referendum in Western Sahara

The General Assembly,

Having considered the reports of the Secretary-General on the financing of the United Nations Mission for the Referendum in Western Sahara and the related report of the Advisory Committee on Administrative and Budgetary Questions,

Bearing in mind Security Council resolution 690(1991) of 29 April 1991, by which the Council decided to establish the United Nations Mission for the Referendum in Western Sahara, and the subsequent resolutions by which the Council extended the mandate of the Mission, the latest of which was resolution 1238(1999) of 14 May 1999,

Recalling its resolution 45/266 of 17 May 1991 on the financing of the Mission and its subsequent resolutions and decisions thereon, the latest of which was resolution 53/18 A of 2 November 1998,

Reaffirming that the costs of the Mission are expenses of the Organization to be borne by Member States in accordance with Article 17, paragraph 2, of the Charter of the United Nations,

Recalling its previous decisions regarding the fact that, in order to meet the expenditures caused by the Mission, a different procedure is required from that applied to meet expenditures of the regular budget of the United Nations,

Taking into account the fact that the economically more developed countries are in a position to make relatively larger contributions and that the economically less developed countries have a relatively limited capacity to contribute towards such an operation,

Bearing in mind the special responsibilities of the States permanent members of the Security Council, as indicated in General Assembly resolution 1874(S-IV) of 27 June 1963, in the financing of such operations,

Noting with appreciation that voluntary contributions have been made to the Mission,

Mindful of the fact that it is essential to provide the Mission with the necessary financial resources to enable it to fulfil its responsibilities under the relevant resolutions of the Security Council,

1. *Takes note* of the status of contributions to the United Nations Mission for the Referendum in Western Sahara as at 30 April 1999, including the contributions outstanding in the amount of 59.3 million United States dollars, representing 17 per cent of the total assessed contributions from the inception of the Mission to the period ending 31 March 1999, notes that some 6 per cent of the membership has paid its assessed contributions in full, and urges all other Member States concerned, in particular those in arrears, to ensure payment of their outstanding assessed contributions;

2. *Expresses concern* about the financial situation with regard to peacekeeping activities, in particular as regards the reimbursement of troop contributors, which bear additional burdens owing to overdue payments by Member States of their assessments;

3. *Expresses its appreciation* to those Member States which have paid their assessed contributions in full;

4. *Urges* all other Member States to make every possible effort to ensure payment of their assessed contributions to the Mission in full and on time;

5. *Takes note* of the observations, and endorses the recommendations contained in the report of the Advisory Committee on Administrative and Budgetary Questions;

6. *Requests* the Secretary-General to take all necessary action to ensure that the Mission is administered with a maximum of efficiency and economy;

7. *Also requests* the Secretary-General, in order to reduce the cost of employing General Service staff, to continue efforts to recruit local staff for the Mission

against General Service posts, commensurate with the requirements of the Mission;

8. *Decides* to appropriate to the Special Account for the United Nations Mission for the Referendum in Western Sahara the amount of 52,124,911 dollars gross (48,173,311 dollars net) for the operation of the Mission for the period from 1 July 1999 to 30 June 2000, inclusive of the amount of 2,593,381 dollars for the support account for peacekeeping operations and the amount of 508,530 dollars for the United Nations Logistics Base at Brindisi, Italy;

9. *Decides also,* as an ad hoc arrangement, to apportion among Member States the amount of 10,714,566 dollars gross (9,902,291 dollars net) for the period from 1 July to 14 September 1999, in accordance with the composition of groups set out in paragraphs 3 and 4 of General Assembly resolution 43/232 of 1 March 1989, as adjusted by the Assembly in its resolutions 44/192 B of 21 December 1989, 45/269 of 27 August 1991, 46/198 A of 20 December 1991, 47/218 A of 23 December 1992, 49/249 A of 20 July 1995, 49/249 B of 14 September 1995, 50/224 of 11 April 1996, 51/218 A to C of 18 December 1996 and 52/230 of 31 March 1998 and its decisions 48/472 A of 23 December 1993 and 50/451 B of 23 December 1995, and taking into account the scale of assessments for the year 1999, as set out in its resolution 52/215 A of 22 December 1997;

10. *Decides further* that, in accordance with the provisions of its resolution 973(X) of 15 December 1955, there shall be set off against the apportionment among Member States, as provided for in paragraph 9 above, their respective share in the Tax Equalization Fund of the estimated staff assessment income of 812,275 dollars approved for the period from 1 July to 14 September 1999;

11. *Decides,* as an ad hoc arrangement, to apportion among Member States the amount of 41,410,345 dollars gross (38,271,020 dollars net) for the period from 15 September 1999 to 30 June 2000, at a monthly rate of 4,343,743 dollars gross (4,014,443 dollars net), in accordance with the scheme set out in the present resolution and the scale of assessments for the years 1999 and 2000, as set out in its resolution 52/215 A, and subject to the decision of the Security Council to extend the mandate of the Mission beyond 14 September 1999;

12. *Decides also* that, in accordance with the provisions of its resolution 973(X), there shall be set off against the apportionment among Member States, as provided for in paragraph 11 above, their respective share in the Tax Equalization Fund of the estimated staff assessment income of 3,139,325 dollars approved for the period from 15 September 1999 to 30 June 2000;

13. *Decides further* that, for Member States that have fulfilled their financial obligations to the Mission, there shall be set off against their apportionment, as provided for in paragraph 9 above, their respective share of the unencumbered balance of 6,523,200 dollars gross (5,357,200 dollars net) in respect of the period from 1 July 1997 to 30 June 1998;

14. *Decides* that, for Member States that have not fulfilled their financial obligations to the Mission, their share of the unencumbered balance of 6,523,200 dollars gross (5,357,200 dollars net) in respect of the period from 1 July 1997 to 30 June 1998 shall be set off against their outstanding obligations;

15. *Invites* voluntary contributions to the Mission in cash and in the form of services and supplies acceptable to the Secretary-General, to be administered, as appropriate, in accordance with the procedure and practices established by the General Assembly;

16. *Decides* to include in the provisional agenda of its fifty-fourth session the agenda item entitled "Financing of the United Nations Mission for the Referendum in Western Sahara".

On 23 December, the Assembly decided that the item on MINURSO financing remained for consideration at its resumed fifty-fourth (2000) session (**decision 54/465**) and that the Fifth Committee should continue consideration of the item at that time (**decision 54/462 A**).

Other questions

Comoros

The Inter-Comorian Conference, convened by OAU in Antananarivo, Madagascar (19-23 April), resulted in the signing of the Antananarivo Agreement by all the Comorian parties with the exception of the Anjouanese side. The Agreement provided a framework for a lasting solution to the crisis in the Comoros, which began in 1997 with the announcement by the islands of Anjouan (Nzwani) and Mohéli (Mwali) of their secession, by establishing unity and territorial integrity. However, while efforts were being made to implement the Agreement, a coup d'état took place in the Comoros on 30 April.

Communications. In a statement of 30 April [S/1999/568], Mali condemned the coup and appealed for the restoration of legitimacy, constitutional order, democratic institutions and the rule of law. It reiterated its support for OAU efforts to establish peace in the Comoros and implement the Addis Ababa Agreement [YUN 1998, p. 206] and the Antananarivo process. Mali called on all the Comorian parties to work together for the return of peace and national reconciliation.

On 10 May [S/1999/533], OAU transmitted to the Security Council a communiqué on the situation in the Comoros. OAU reiterated its unequivocal condemnation of the coup d'état; reaffirmed its support for the Antananarivo Agreement; renewed its request to the Anjouanese Party to sign the Agreement; decided to withdraw the military component of the OAU Observer Mission in the Comoros; and called on all OAU member States and the international community to withhold any cooperation with the Comorian military authorities.

In a 2 July letter [S/1999/763], the Comoros updated the Security Council on the social and political developments since the intervention of the Comorian armed forces in April. It stated that its armed forces had gained the support of all sectors of the Comorian population, as well as the majority of the local political parties, and that dialogues and consultations that the new authorities undertook with the various sectors, including political parties, trade unions, village communities and civil society, had resulted in progress towards national reconciliation. The new national authorities reaffirmed their intention to respect the spirit of the Antananarivo Agreement as the guarantor of the peaceful coexistence of all Comorians. In a resolution, signed by a majority of political parties in the Comoros, OAU was requested to convene as early as possible the committee for the follow-up of the Agreement.

By **decision 53/490** of 13 September, the General Assembly included in the draft agenda of its fifty-fourth (1999) session the item on the question of the Comorian island of Mayotte. On 17 December, the Assembly decided to defer consideration of the item and include it in the agenda of its fifty-fifth (2000) session (**decision 54/439**).

Côte d'Ivoire

On 25 December [S/1999/1288], Mali condemned the military coup d'état that took place in Côte d'Ivoire on 24 December. It called on those responsible to return to constitutional legality, reiterated its strong solidarity with the people of Côte d'Ivoire and expressed its determination to support efforts to establish democratic legality in the country.

In identical 30 December letters to the Secretary-General and the Security Council [S/1999/1303], Mali transmitted the final communiqué of the first meeting of the Ministers for Foreign Affairs members of the Mediation and Security Council of ECOWAS (Bamako, 29 December), which was devoted to the situation in Côte d'Ivoire and its implications for the subregion. The Ministers strongly condemned the military coup d'état and urged the Ivorian Committee of National Salvation: to set up an independent structure to revise the Constitution and electoral code; to put in place a transition Government; to release all political detainees; and to respect and guarantee human rights throughout the country. The Ministers invited the military junta to ensure the safety of all ECOWAS citizens and foreigners resident in Côte d'Ivoire.

Mozambique

In accordance with decision 53/458 [YUN 1998, p. 206], the General Assembly retained on its agenda in 1999 the item on financing of the United Nations Operation in Mozambique (ONUMOZ). ONUMOZ began operations in 1992 [YUN 1992, p. 196] and was liquidated in 1995 [YUN 1995, p. 368].

On 13 September, the Assembly decided to include the item in the draft agenda of its fifty-fourth session (**decision 53/495**).

On 23 December, the Assembly decided that the item would remain for consideration at its resumed fifty-fourth (2000) session (**decision 54/465**) and that the Fifth Committee should continue its consideration of the item at that session (**decision 54/462 A**).

Niger

On 9 April, a coup d'état took place in the Niger during which the President, Ibrahim Mainassara Baré, was assassinated.

Communications. In a 12 April declaration [S/1999/418], Mali expressed its indignation regarding President Baré's assassination, which it condemned. Mali hoped that an inquiry would be opened on the circumstances of the assassination and appealed to Niger's political circles to uphold the Republic's legality and foster respect for democratic principles.

In a 14 April statement [S/1999/434], the EU condemned the coup d'état and deplored the suspension of the 1996 Constitution and the dissolution of the elected Parliament and of the Government. It called on the military leadership to set a timetable for a return to democracy as quickly as possible. The EU was forced, in view of the major setback in the Niger's democratic development, to re-examine its cooperation with that country, in compliance with the mechanisms laid down by the Lomé IV Convention (an updated trade pact between the European Economic Community and the African, Caribbean and Pacific Group [YUN 1975, p. 330]).

Cooperation between OAU and the UN system

In response to General Assembly resolution 53/91 [YUN 1998, p. 207], the Secretary-General submitted an October report [A/54/484] on cooperation between the United Nations and the Organization of African Unity (OAU). Since 1997, the Secretaries-General of the two organizations had carried out regular exchanges of information and mutual briefings on key African questions and had held meetings twice a year, along with their senior advisers. In 1999, such meetings were held during the OAU summit in Algiers in July and in New York in September to discuss priority areas of cooperation and coordination.

The Secretary-General summarized the cooperation of the two organizations in the areas of peace and security, involving the Department of Political Affairs, the Department of Peacekeeping Operations, the Office for the Coordination of Humanitarian Affairs and the Office of the United Nations High Commissioner for Human Rights. He also reviewed cooperation in economic and social development, involving the Department of Economic and Social Affairs, the Economic Commission for Africa, the United Nations Development Programme, the United Nations Population Fund, the Office of the United Nations High Commissioner for Refugees, the United Nations Conference on Trade and Development, the International Labour Organization, the United Nations Educational, Scientific and Cultural Organization, the World Health Organization, the World Bank, the International Monetary Fund, the World Intellectual Property Organization, the International Fund for Agricultural Development and the United Nations Industrial Development Organization. The Universal Postal Union and the United Nations International Drug Control Programme were also cooperating with OAU.

On 29 September [A/54/424], Algeria transmitted to the Secretary-General the declarations and decisions adopted by the Assembly of Heads of State and Government of OAU during it summit in July.

On 17 November [A/54/621], the Chairman of the Group of African States at the United Nations transmitted to the Secretary-General the Sirte Declaration, adopted by OAU in September, which aimed to strengthen the unity of the African continent and its peoples.

GENERAL ASSEMBLY ACTION

On 8 December [meeting 73], the General Assembly adopted **resolution 54/94** [draft: A/54/L.38 & Add.1] without vote [agenda item 31].

Cooperation between the United Nations and the Organization of African Unity

The General Assembly,

Having considered the report of the Secretary-General on cooperation between the United Nations and the Organization of African Unity,

Recalling the provisions of Chapter VIII of the Charter of the United Nations on regional arrangements or agencies, which set forth the basic principles governing their activities and establishing the legal framework for cooperation with the United Nations in the area of the maintenance of international peace and security, as well as resolution 49/57 of 9 December 1994, the annex to which contains the Declaration on the Enhancement of Cooperation between the United Nations and Regional Arrangements or Agencies in the Maintenance of International Peace and Security,

Recalling also the agreement of 15 November 1965 on cooperation between the United Nations and the Organization of African Unity as updated and signed on 9 October 1990 by the Secretary-General of the United Nations and the Secretary-General of the Organization of African Unity,

Recalling further all its resolutions on the enhancement of cooperation between the United Nations and the Organization of African Unity, including resolution 53/91 of 7 December 1998,

Recalling that, in its resolutions 46/20 of 26 November 1991, 47/148 of 18 December 1992 and 48/25 of 29 November 1993, it, inter alia, urged the Secretary-General and the relevant agencies of the United Nations system to continue to extend their support for the establishment of the African Economic Community,

Recalling also its resolution 48/214 of 23 December 1993 on the implementation of the United Nations New Agenda for the Development of Africa in the 1990s,

Taking note of the Algiers Declaration and the declarations and decisions adopted by the Assembly of Heads of State and Government of the Organization of African Unity at its thirty-fifth ordinary session, held at Algiers from 12 to 14 July 1999,

Taking note also of the decisions contained in the Sirte Declaration adopted by the Assembly of Heads of State and Government of the Organization of African Unity at its fourth extraordinary session, held at Sirte, Libyan Arab Jamahiriya, on 8 and 9 September 1999,

Mindful of the need for continued and closer cooperation between the United Nations and its specialized agencies and the Organization of African Unity in the field of peace and security and in the political, economic, social, technical, cultural and administrative fields,

Taking note of the report of the Secretary-General on the causes of conflict and the promotion of durable peace and sustainable development in Africa,

Noting that the Mechanism for Conflict Prevention, Management and Resolution in Africa of the Organization of African Unity is steadily developing its capacity in conflict prevention and resolution,

Noting also the efforts of the Organization of African Unity, and the assistance of the United Nations, to promote the peaceful settlement of disputes and conflicts and the continuation of the process of democratization in Africa,

Welcoming decision CM/Dec.482(LXX) of 1999, adopted by the Council of Ministers of the Organization of African Unity, concerning the establishment of a special committee on children and armed conflict, in the light of the gravity of the situation of children affected by armed conflict,

Deeply concerned that, despite the policies of reform being implemented by African countries, their economic situation remains critical and African recovery and development continue to be severely hindered by, inter alia, the persistence of lower commodity prices and the heavy debt burden, and they are substantially affected by the levels of official development assistance and foreign direct investment, as well as the ongoing conflicts in some regions of the continent,

Aware of the efforts being made by the Organization of African Unity and its member States in the area of economic integration and of the need to accelerate the process of implementation of the Treaty establishing the African Economic Community,

Recalling the convening of the Organization of African Unity Ministerial Conference on Refugees, Returnees and Displaced Persons in Africa at Khartoum, on 13 and 14 December 1998,

Acknowledging the assistance already rendered by the international community to refugees, internally displaced persons and host countries in Africa,

Stressing that the gravity of the situation of refugees and internally displaced persons and of host countries in Africa requires urgent and increased international assistance,

Recalling the convening by the Organization of African Unity of the first Ministerial Conference on Human Rights in Africa at Grand-Baie, Mauritius, from 12 to 16 April 1999,

Recognizing the importance of developing and maintaining a culture of peace, tolerance and harmonious relationships based on economic development, democratic principles, good governance, social justice and international cooperation,

1. *Takes note* of the report of the Secretary-General on cooperation between the United Nations and the Organization of African Unity and of his efforts to strengthen that cooperation and to implement the relevant resolutions;

2. *Notes* the contribution made by the United Nations Liaison Office with the Organization of African Unity since its establishment in April 1998;

3. *Notes with appreciation* the continued and increasing participation of the Organization of African Unity in the work of the United Nations, its organs and specialized agencies, and its constructive contribution to that work;

4. *Calls upon* the United Nations organs, in particular the Security Council and the Economic and Social Council, to enhance the involvement of the Organization of African Unity in all their activities concerning Africa;

5. *Expresses its appreciation* for the report of the Secretary-General on the causes of conflict and the promotion of durable peace and sustainable development in Africa, and encourages the early implementation of the recommendations contained therein by the United Nations, its organs and specialized agencies, in their respective areas of competence, as well as by Member States;

6. *Calls upon* the United Nations to enhance its cooperation, coordination and exchange of information with the Organization of African Unity, in the following areas:

(*a*) Prevention of conflict through the promotion of a culture of peace, tolerance and harmonious relations in Africa;

(*b*) Peaceful settlement of disputes and maintenance of international peace and security in Africa, as provided for under Chapter VIII of the Charter of the United Nations;

7. *Invites* the United Nations to intensify its assistance to the Organization of African Unity in strengthening the institutional and operational capacity of its Mechanism for Conflict Prevention, Management and Resolution in Africa, in particular in the following areas:

(*a*) Development of its early-warning system;

(*b*) Technical assistance and training of civilian and military personnel, including a staff exchange programme;

(*c*) Exchange and coordination of information, including between the early-warning systems of the two organizations;

(*d*) Logistical support, including in the area of demining;

(*e*) Mobilization of financial support, including through the trust funds of the United Nations and the Organization of African Unity;

8. *Urges* the United Nations to encourage donor countries, in consultation with the Organization of African Unity, to provide adequate funding and training for African countries in their efforts to enhance their peacekeeping capabilities, with a view to enabling those countries to participate actively in peacekeeping operations within the framework of the United Nations;

9. *Calls upon* all Member States and regional and international organizations, in particular those of the United Nations system, as well as non-governmental organizations, to provide appropriate assistance to refugees and internally displaced persons, as well as to the African host countries, and to ensure the security and neutrality of refugee camps and settlements;

10. *Encourages* the United Nations, through the Special Representative of the Secretary-General on the impact of armed conflict on children, to assist the Organization of African Unity and its special committee on children and armed conflict in their efforts to ensure the protection and the welfare of children affected by conflicts in Africa;

11. *Notes with appreciation* the assistance provided by the United Nations and its agencies to African countries in the context of strengthening the democratization process, and calls for the continuation of this support in the areas of education for democracy, election observation, human rights, freedom and the rule of law, including technical support to the African Commission on Human and People's Rights;

12. *Welcomes* the priority accorded by the United Nations system to African development and, in this regard, stresses the need to continue and increase economic and technical assistance to African countries;

13. *Urges* the Secretary-General, Member States and regional and international organizations, in particular those of the United Nations system, to support the strengthening of the African Economic Community;

14. *Requests* the agencies of the United Nations system working in Africa to include in their programmes at the national, subregional and regional levels activities that will enhance African regional economic cooperation and integration;

15. *Calls upon* the United Nations agencies to intensify the coordination of their regional programmes in Africa in order to enhance linkages among them, ensure the effective harmonization of their programmes with those of the African regional and subregional economic organizations and create a positive environment for investment;

16. *Emphasizes* the urgent need to implement effectively the recommendations arising from the mid-term review of the implementation of the United Nations New Agenda for the Development of Africa in the 1990s;

17. *Invites* the Secretary-General to encourage the closer involvement of the Organization of African Unity in the implementation, follow-up and evaluation of the United Nations New Agenda for the Development of Africa in the 1990s and beyond, including the conduct of the final review of the implementation of the New Agenda in 2002;

18. *Calls upon* the international community to support and enhance the capacity of African countries to take advantage of the opportunities offered by globalization and to overcome the challenges it poses, as a means of ensuring sustained economic growth and sustainable development;

19. *Invites* the Secretary-General to develop new effective strategies for the implementation of the recommendations of the annual meeting of the secretariats of the Organization of African Unity and the United Nations, held from 6 to 8 May 1998, as agreed upon by the two organizations in their follow-up meeting held on 21 September 1999;

20. *Calls upon* the relevant organizations of the United Nations system to ensure the effective and equitable representation of African men and women at senior and policy levels at their respective headquarters and in their regional field of operations;

21. *Requests* the Secretary-General to report to the General Assembly at its fifty-fifth session on the implementation of the present resolution.

Regional cooperation

By a 28 January letter to the Security Council [S/1999/89], Uganda transmitted the text of the joint communiqué of the East African heads of State summit (Arusha, United Republic of Tanzania, 22 January) on African regional cooperation.

On 24 November [A/54/636-S/1999/1201], Gabon transmitted to the Secretary-General the final communiqué of the summit of heads of State, Government and delegation of the Gulf of Guinea (Libreville, 19 November). The participants agreed to establish a consultation framework for cooperation among and the development of the countries of the Gulf of Guinea for the prevention, management and settlement of conflicts among them, to be known as the Commission of the Gulf of Guinea.

On 29 November [S/1999/1206], the Intergovernmental Authority on Development transmitted to the Security Council a declaration on subregional cooperation, trust-building among members States and the resolution of conflicts in the subregion (Djibouti, 26 November).

Chapter III

Americas

During 1999, the United Nations continued to advance the cause of lasting peace, human rights, sustainable development and the rule of law in the Americas. The Organization monitored the political and security situation in Central America; with the exception of Haiti, progress had been made in the consolidation of stability and greater democratization throughout the subregion.

The United Nations Verification Mission in Guatemala (MINUGUA), established in 1994, continued to fulfil its mandate by verifying compliance with the implementation of the peace accords signed in 1996 between the Government of Guatemala and the Unidad Revolucionaria Nacional Guatemalteca. In December, the General Assembly extended the mandate of MINUGUA until 31 December 2000. The Commission for Historical Clarification submitted its report on the human rights violations that had been committed during the 34-year internal armed conflict. General elections, held in November and December, culminated with the election of Alfonso Portillo as President.

Haiti continued to experience a serious political and institutional crisis, which stalled the implementation of structural reforms and contributed to a worsening of the human rights situation. General elections, scheduled for November, were postponed to March 2000. In view of the situation, the United Nations continued its cooperation in 1999 with the Organization of American States through the jointly fielded International Civilian Mission to Haiti (MICIVIH), established in 1993 to monitor the human rights situation. The United Nations Civilian Police Mission in Haiti (MIPONUH), established in 1997, supervised, supported and trained the Haitian National Police. In December, the General Assembly established the International Civilian Support Mission in Haiti (MICAH) to consolidate the responsibilities of MIPONUH and MICIVIH into one mission. In view of the fact that MIPONUH's mandate was to expire on 30 November 1999, the Security Council decided to continue the Mission to ensure a phased transition to MICAH by 15 March 2000. The Assembly also decided that MICIVIH's mandate would terminate with the commencement of MICAH.

Throughout the year, the UN system actively participated in the reconstruction process following the devastation brought about by hurricane Mitch, which struck the region in late 1998 (see PART THREE, Chapter III).

In November 1999, the General Assembly again called on States to refrain from promulgating laws and measures such as the ongoing United States economic embargo against Cuba.

Central America

As requested by the General Assembly in resolution 53/94 [YUN 1998, p. 212], the Secretary-General submitted a September 1999 report on the situation in Central America [A/54/311], covering progress achieved by Central American countries in the areas of peace, freedom, democracy and development since August 1998. The report focused on the five signatories to the Esquipulas II process [YUN 1987, p. 188] (Costa Rica, El Salvador, Guatemala, Honduras, Nicaragua). In accordance with the new Central American agenda and the composition of Central American summit meetings, reference was also made to the situation in Belize and Panama.

The Secretary-General said that, in spite of challenges to stability, including the devastation caused by hurricane Mitch in 1998 [YUN 1998, p. 876], increasingly plural and democratic political processes continued to develop in the region. New Governments were democratically elected in Belize (26 August 1998), El Salvador (7 March 1999) and Panama (2 May 1999). In Guatemala, a national referendum on constitutional reform was peacefully and transparently conducted on 16 May. High participation in the Panamanian elections (76 per cent) continued to be an exception, however, and it was hoped that national and regional attention would focus increasingly on mechanisms to broaden citizen participation in the electoral process, particularly with regard to women and indigenous people. The vitality and inclusiveness of democratic governance in Central America was a fundamental counterpart to ongoing efforts to achieve economic growth, stability and equity, added the Secretary-General.

Public security in the region was threatened by the continued escalation in the rate of common crime and social violence, compounded by regional and international criminal networks. Irregularities and long delays in the processing of accused persons undermined public confidence in the judicial process. Attacks by vigilante groups on persons suspected of common crimes were reported. Violence against women continued to be an acute problem, although institutions had been created or strengthened to protect women's security and rights. Civilian police forces with limited resources had struggled to respond adequately to the public security crisis and had suffered increasing losses of officers in the line of duty, particularly in El Salvador. In spite of those trends, advances had been made in bringing public security forces under civilian control. To that end, in El Salvador, the Government had sought to strengthen prevention policy and to affirm the role of the National Council for Public Security. In Honduras, the National Assembly had ratified reforms that consolidated the transition to civilian command of the armed forces. With regard to Guatemala, the process of strengthening the capacity and expanding the deployment of the new National Civil Police continued, while constitutional reforms aimed at redefining the role of the military were still pending.

Regional and extraregional cooperation on a range of shared security and human rights issues, including illegal drug trafficking, migration, anti-personnel landmines and arms trafficking, had been recurring themes addressed through the presidential and ministerial summit process, including a meeting with the Presidents of the United States (March), the European Union (EU) (May/June) and the Organization of American States (OAS) (June). In January, the Secretary-General of the Central American Integration System (SICA) signed an agreement of co-operation with the International Organization for Migration, which called for joint action in several areas, including regional norms development and the human rights of the migrant population, with a focus on women and children.

Across the region there were indications of a growing gap in human development between zones of relative affluence in the capitals and principal cities and the extreme poverty of marginalized rural and urban areas. Related patterns of social inequality and exclusion between social groups were reflected in regional data on distribution of income and access to employment, health and education. Indigenous peoples, representing 20 per cent of the Central American population (80 per cent of whom lived in Guatemala), and women in particular suffered high rates of socio-economic and political exclusion. The Central American Governments also had to contend with regional disparities among their countries in terms of human development, economic performance and their respective political and legal frameworks, all of which were obstacles to achieving integrated and sustainable arrangements for economic growth and stable political processes.

The reconstruction and transformation process following hurricane Mitch, the worst natural disaster to strike the region in over a century, dominated the regional agenda during the year. A report by the Economic Commission for Latin America and the Caribbean (ECLAC) revealed that the hurricane had left more than 9,000 dead and affected 24 per cent of the regional population, or almost 7 million people, including 77 per cent of the population of Honduras and 19 per cent of the Nicaraguan people, resulting in the displacement and migration of victims, principally to Costa Rica and the United States.

At the first meeting of the Consultative Group on Reconstruction and Transformation (Washington, D.C., 10-11 December 1998), convened by the Inter-American Development Bank (IDB), the international community pledged $6 billion in disaster relief, reconstruction assistance and debt forgiveness. At the follow-up meeting of the Consultative Group (Stockholm, Sweden, 25-28 May), pledges for $9 billion were made, including $5.3 billion from the World Bank and IDB, and the remainder in the form of bilateral assistance. In addition to national proposals, the Central American countries presented a joint reconstruction plan within the framework of SICA that focused on reducing environmental, economic and social vulnerabilities and on deepening the Central American integration process. Participants at the meeting expressed, through the Stockholm Declaration, the shared commitments to reduce the social and ecological vulnerability of the peoples of the region; reconstruct and transform Central America on the basis of an integrated focus on transparency and governability; consolidate democracy and good governance; promote human rights; coordinate donor activities; and renew efforts to reduce the external debt of countries in the region. Special meetings of the Central American Presidents were held in February and March. The latter summit, which took place in Antigua, Guatemala, resulted in the Antigua Declaration, which, among other things, recognized the impact of hurricane Mitch. (See also PART THREE, Chapter III.)

Regarding regional and extraregional trade and economic cooperation, ECLAC reported that the gross national product (GNP) of the region grew by 4.4 per cent compared with 4.3 per cent in 1997. The slight improvement was due to the growth of external demand, capital inflows and a sustained effort to increase capital investment. The capacity of Governments to transform underlying structural problems in order to permit sustainable economic growth depended in particular on reducing external debt. In June, the Group of Eight countries (Canada, France, Germany, Italy, Japan, Russian Federation, United Kingdom, United States) made commitments of substantial relief, particularly for Honduras and Nicaragua, which were also being considered for inclusion in the International Monetary Fund/World Bank Heavily Indebted Poor Countries Initiative.

On 28 and 29 May, Mexico hosted the thirteenth summit of the Rio Group, with heads of State from Latin America and the Caribbean. Global financial turbulence, the acute socio-economic situation of the Central American countries and rapid multilateral disaster response for Central America dominated the agenda. The Rio Group met with EU representatives (Rio de Janeiro, Brazil, 28-29 June) and adopted the Rio Declaration, which confirmed shared principles and goals regarding trade integration, as well as mutual commitment to the preservation of democratic institutions and to free, just and open electoral processes. The Central American Governments maintained their commitments to the agenda set forth in the Santiago Declaration of April 1998 [YUN 1998, p. 211], in order to establish a free trade area of the Americas by 2005.

Regional institution-building efforts continued with further consolidation in the role of SICA, the Central American Economic Integration Secretariat and the Central American Economic Integration Bank. The system of regional institutions was further expanded to include the Central American Court of Justice. The Presidents agreed to meet at least once a year to make strategic and political decisions on integration, while a Council of Ministers had operated as the main decision-making body on the integration of foreign affairs, economy, social affairs and the environment.

At the twenty-ninth regular session of OAS (Guatemala City, 6-8 June), participants adopted, among other things, a resolution regarding the ongoing mine-clearing programme in Central America, noting the setback to operations as a result of hurricane Mitch. That objective had also been given renewed support with OAS participation in the Joint Declaration on the Elimination of Anti-personnel Landmines, signed at a meeting of the Central American Ministers of External Relations (Managua, Nicaragua, 12-13 April).

As for UN efforts in Central America, the Secretary-General stated that the United Nations remained committed to the process of peace-building. In El Salvador, he continued to entrust the United Nations Development Programme (UNDP) with following up on the implementation of outstanding commitments of the 1992 Peace Agreement [YUN 1992, p. 222] and to assist the Government to that end.

In Guatemala, the United Nations continued to verify compliance with the 1996 Agreement on a Firm and Lasting Peace [YUN 1996, p. 168]. UNDP worked with distinct sectors of society to promote democratic governance, sustainable human development and capacity-building at the regional level, while at the national level it continued to support the consolidation of peace- and consensus-building in El Salvador, Guatemala and Nicaragua. It also played an important role in preventing or minimizing future social conflict by facilitating the demobilization and integration of ex-combatants and by strengthening the civilian police force. In Guatemala and Nicaragua, UNDP promoted pilot projects for the creation of "judicial centres" where citizens could find the police, the local judge and magistrates and legal assistance (including informal means of conflict resolution) in a single, highly visible location. Regarding hurricane Mitch, in January and February the Office for the Coordination of Humanitarian Assistance, UNDP, the United Nations Children's Fund (UNICEF), the World Health Organization and the Pan American Health Organization undertook an inter-agency evaluation mission to analyse, along with Governments, donors, disaster managers and UN system partners, action taken during the emergency and to formulate guidelines to enhance preparedness for future natural disasters. Consultations between SICA and the United Nations focused on launching a new phase of more intense collaboration, building on previous experiences and including the development of new national and regional initiatives. UN agencies continued to assist Governments in achieving diverse objectives that contributed to lasting peace and sustainable development. The World Bank hosted the fourth annual Conference on Development in Latin America and the Caribbean (El Salvador, June). The Bank confirmed that structural adjustment policies had not been sufficient to diminish poverty and improve the quality of life in the region; those policies needed to be complemented by further institutional reform, including the areas of justice and education.

The Secretary-General observed that, although Governments and their peoples continued to advance the cause of lasting peace, human rights, sustainable development and the rule of law, Governments still faced difficulties, particularly in reconciling the imperatives of economic growth, stability and equity. Successfully balancing those needs was at the root of lasting peace. The Secretary-General hoped that the alarming levels of social and criminal violence would continue to be addressed by Governments through strengthened civilian police, more efficient judicial systems, independent ombudsmen and permanent respect for human rights and the rule of law. He supported the efforts of the international community to reduce external debt significantly and to provide emergency and long-term aid.

Communication. On 17 November [A/54/630], Belize, Costa Rica, the Dominican Republic, El Salvador, Guatemala, Honduras, Nicaragua and Panama transmitted the Declaration of Guatemala II, signed by them in Guatemala City on 19 October. They agreed to adopt the Strategic Framework for the Reduction of Vulnerability and Disasters in Central America and to establish the Central American Five-Year Plan for the Reduction of Vulnerability to and the Impact of Disasters (2000-2004). They also agreed to support foreign debt relief for Honduras and Nicaragua. The Declaration, among other things, expressed support for the full transfer of control of the Panama Canal to the Government of Panama, scheduled to take place on 31 December 1999, and for an effective mechanism to settle trade and investment disputes in an institutional framework.

GENERAL ASSEMBLY ACTION

On 15 December [meeting 80], the General Assembly adopted **resolution 54/118** [draft: A/54/L.24/Rev.1 & Add.1] without vote [agenda item 47].

The situation in Central America: procedures for the establishment of a firm and lasting peace and progress in fashioning a region of peace, freedom, democracy and development

The General Assembly,

Considering the relevant resolutions of the Security Council, particularly resolution 637(1989) of 27 July 1989, and its own resolutions, particularly resolution 43/24 of 15 November 1988, in which it requests the Secretary-General to continue his good offices and to afford the fullest possible support to the Central American Governments in their efforts to achieve the objectives of peace, reconciliation, democracy, development and justice established in the agreement on "Procedures for the establishment of a firm and lasting peace in Central America" of 7 August 1987,

Reaffirming its resolutions in which it recognizes and stresses the importance of international economic, financial and technical cooperation and assistance, both bilateral and multilateral, aimed at promoting economic and social development in the region with a view to furthering and supplementing the efforts of the Central American peoples and Governments to achieve peace and democratization, particularly resolution 52/169 G of 16 December 1997, concerning international assistance to and cooperation with the Alliance for the Sustainable Development of Central America, as well as its resolution 53/1 C of 2 November 1998, concerning emergency assistance to Central America, owing to the destruction caused by hurricane Mitch,

Emphasizing the importance of the development of the Central American Integration System, which has as its main objective the promotion of the integration process; the Alliance for the Sustainable Development of Central America as the integrated programme for national and regional development, which contains the commitments and priorities of the countries of the area for the promotion of sustainable development; the establishment of the subsystem and of the regional social policy; the model of democratic Central American security; and the implementation of other agreements adopted at the presidential summit meetings, which taken together constitute the global frame of reference for consolidating peace, freedom, democracy and development and the basis for the promotion of mutually advantageous relations between Central America and the international community,

Recognizing the progress made in the fulfilment of the commitments contained in the Guatemala Peace Agreements, implementation of which is being verified by the United Nations Verification Mission in Guatemala, including the submission of the report of the Commission for Historical Clarification, the finalization of the programme for the repatriation of the Guatemalan refugees in Mexico, the compliance with the expenditure ceilings contained in the Agreements, the expansion of the deployment of the new National Civil Police, the approval by the Congress of the new Land Act and the establishment of the Office for the Defence of Indigenous Women,

Taking note with satisfaction of the successful implementation of the Peace Agreements and of the consolidation of the process of democratization in El Salvador, as a result of the efforts of the country's people and Government,

Recognizing with satisfaction the role played by the peacekeeping operations and observer and monitoring missions of the United Nations, which carried out successfully their mandate in Central America pursuant to the relevant resolutions of the Security Council and the General Assembly, respectively,

Welcoming the changes and progress made by the Central American peoples, whose efforts have brought about, inter alia, the strengthening of civil society and authority, the creation of new political forms, the holding of free and pluralistic elections, the creation of mechanisms for the protection and promotion of human rights, freedom of expression, the strengthening of democratic institutions and of the rule of law, judicial reform processes and the adoption of a fairer development model providing greater opportunities for the Central American peoples,

Emphasizing the importance of the end of a critical period in Central American history and the start of a new phase free from armed conflict, with freely elected Governments in each country and with political, economic, social and other changes which can create a climate conducive to the promotion of economic growth and further progress towards the consolidation and further development of democratic, just and equitable societies,

Reaffirming that firm and lasting peace and democracy in Central America are a dynamic and ongoing process that faces serious structural challenges, whose continuation and consolidation are closely related to progress in human development, especially the alleviation of extreme poverty, the promotion of economic and social justice, judicial reform, the safeguarding of human rights and fundamental freedoms, respect for minorities and the satisfaction of the basic needs of the most vulnerable groups among the peoples of the region, issues which have been a primary source of tension and conflict and which deserve to be discussed with the same urgency and dedication as was the case in the settlement of armed conflicts,

Deeply concerned by the devastating effects of hurricane Mitch and other natural disasters on the population and economies of the region's countries and by the possible consequences of a significant setback as regards the efforts of the Central American peoples and the international community to overcome the aftermath of the armed conflicts and as regards the progress made with respect to political stability, democratization and sustainable development,

Emphasizing the solidarity of the international community with the victims of hurricane Mitch, as demonstrated by friendly States' generous response to the emergency situation and in particular by the meetings of the Consultative Group for the Reconstruction and Transformation of Central America, held in Washington, D.C., in December 1998 and in Stockholm in May 1998, resulting in the Stockholm Declaration, in which the objectives and principles of reconstruction and transformation were established, and of which five countries agreed to initiate the follow-up process,

1. *Takes note with appreciation* of the report of the Secretary-General;

2. *Commends* the efforts of the peoples and the Governments of the Central American countries to reestablish peace and democracy throughout the region and promote sustainable development by implementing the commitments adopted at the summit meetings, and supports the decision of the presidents that Central America should become a region of peace, freedom, democracy and development;

3. *Recognizes* the need to continue to follow closely the situation in Central America according to the objectives and principles established in the Stockholm Declaration in order to support national and regional efforts to overcome the underlying causes that have led to armed conflicts, avoid setbacks and consolidate peace and democratization in the area and promote the objectives of the Alliance for the Sustainable Development of Central America, especially in the transitional period for overcoming the devastating effects of hurricane Mitch and other natural disasters, which entail extraordinary efforts for the reconstruction and transformation of the worst affected countries in the region, in particular Honduras and Nicaragua;

4. *Emphasizes* the importance of the global frame of reference and the establishment of national and regional development priorities as the basis for promoting the effective, consistent and sustainable progress of the Central American peoples, and for providing international cooperation in accordance with the new circumstances in and outside the region;

5. *Welcomes* the progress achieved in implementing the Guatemala Peace Agreements, calls upon all parties to take further measures to implement the commitments in the Peace Agreements, and urges all sectors of society to combine efforts and work with courage and determination to consolidate peace;

6. *Also welcomes* the efforts made by the people and the Government of El Salvador to fulfil the commitments set forth in the Peace Agreements, thus contributing substantially to the strengthening of the democratization process in the country;

7. *Requests* the Secretary-General, the bodies and programmes of the United Nations system and the international community to continue to support and verify in Guatemala the implementation of all the peace agreements signed under United Nations auspices, compliance with which is an essential condition for a firm and lasting peace in that country;

8. *Recognizes* the importance of the Central American Integration System as the body set up to coordinate and harmonize efforts to achieve integration, a process aimed at establishing, gradually and progressively, the Central American Union, and calls upon the international community, the United Nations system and other international organizations, both governmental and non-governmental, to extend generous and effective cooperation with a view to improving the competence and efficiency of the Central American Integration System in the fulfilment of its mandate;

9. *Encourages* the Central American Governments to continue to carry out their historic responsibilities by fully implementing the commitments they have assumed under national, regional or international agreements, especially the commitments to implement the social programme to overcome poverty and unemployment, establish a more just and equitable society, improve public safety, strengthen the judiciary, consolidate a modern and transparent public administration and eliminate corruption, impunity, acts of terrorism and drug and arms trafficking, all of which are necessary and urgent measures for establishing a firm and lasting peace in the region;

10. *Reiterates its deep appreciation* to the Secretary-General, his special representatives, the groups of countries for the peace processes in El Salvador (Colombia, Mexico, Spain, United States of America and Venezuela), and Guatemala (Colombia, Mexico, Norway, Spain, United States of America and Venezuela), to the Support Group for Nicaragua (Canada, Mexico, Netherlands, Spain and Sweden), to the European Union and to other countries that have contributed significantly and to the international community in general for its support and solidarity in the building of peace, democracy and development in Central America;

11. *Reaffirms* the importance of international cooperation, in particular cooperation with the bodies, funds and programmes of the United Nations system,

and the donor community in the new stage of consolidating peace and democracy in Central America, and urges them to continue to support Central American efforts to achieve those goals, bearing in mind the global framework of the new regional development strategy, which is in keeping with the collective aspirations and needs of the Central American peoples;

12. *Notes with appreciation* the demonstrations of international solidarity and support for the region's reconstruction and transformation efforts following the severe damage caused by hurricane Mitch, which will enable the region to attain normality and continue its efforts to consolidate democracy and attain sustainable development;

13. *Reaffirms* the need to maintain sustained assistance to the region in order to create the conditions needed for balance between the challenges of reconstruction, economic growth and equitable social development that will ensure firm and lasting peace in the region, and stresses the need to improve preparedness and the integration of natural disaster reduction components into development planning;

14. *Requests* the Secretary-General to continue to lend his full support to the initiatives and activities of the Central American Governments, particularly their efforts to consolidate peace and democracy through the implementation of a new, comprehensive sustainable development programme and the initiative to establish the Central American Union, emphasizing, inter alia, the potential repercussions of natural disasters, in particular of hurricane Mitch, for the peace processes and the vulnerable economies of the region, and to report to the General Assembly at its fifty-fifth session on the implementation of the present resolution;

15. *Decides* to include in the provisional agenda of its fifty-fifth session the item entitled "The situation in Central America: procedures for the establishment of a firm and lasting peace and progress in fashioning a region of peace, freedom, democracy and development".

On 23 December, the Assembly, by **decision 54/465**, decided that the agenda item on the situation in Central America remained for consideration during its resumed fifty-fourth (2000) session.

Guatemala

In 1999, the peace process in Guatemala continued to be implemented and gained greater support and acceptance throughout all sectors of society, despite delays and setbacks in fiscal, judicial and military reforms and a worsening human rights situation. The year also witnessed two major events as far as reconciliation and parliamentary representation were concerned: the presentation of the report of the Commission for Historical Clarification, established in 1994 to clarify the human rights violations and acts of violence connected with the armed conflict [YUN 1994, p. 407], and the holding of general elections.

The United Nations Verification Mission in Guatemala (MINUGUA) continued to verify the implementation of the 1996 Agreement on a Firm and Lasting Peace [YUN 1996, p. 168] and the 1996 Agreement on the Implementation, Compliance and Verification Timetable for the Peace Agreements (the Timetable Agreement) [YUN 1997, p. 176], signed by the Government of Guatemala and the Unidad Revolucionaria Nacional Guatemalteca (URNG). The Secretary-General transmitted to the General Assembly reports by the MINUGUA Director covering the Mission's activities throughout 1999. The Assembly renewed the mandate of the Mission until 31 December 2000.

Commission for Historical Clarification

On 23 April, the Secretary-General transmitted the executive summary, conclusions and recommendations of the report of the Commission for Historical Clarification (CEH), "Guatemala: Memory of Silence" [A/53/928]. The report contained the results of the investigation carried out by CEH on human rights violations and acts of violence that had been committed during the 34-year civil war. The Commission registered a total of 42,275 victims, of whom 23,671 were victims of arbitrary execution and 6,159 of forced disappearance. Eighty-three per cent of the victims were identified as Mayan and 17 per cent were Ladino. Together with the results of other studies of political violence in Guatemala, CEH estimated that the number of persons killed or disappeared reached over 200,000. Human rights violations and acts of violence attributable to State actions represented 93 per cent of those registered by CEH, and were especially severe from 1978 to 1984, a period during which 91 per cent of the CEH documented violations were committed. Eighty-five per cent of the violations and acts registered by CEH were attributable to the Army alone and 18 per cent to the Civil Patrols, which were organized by the armed forces. Acts of violence attributable to the guerrillas represented 3 per cent of the registered violations. Human rights violations committed by the State included massacres of the Mayan people, forced disappearances, arbitrary executions, rape of women, the use of death squads, the denial of justice and forced and discriminatory military recruitment. CEH concluded that State agents, within the framework of counter-insurgency operations carried out between 1981 and 1983, committed acts of genocide against groups of Mayan people. Guerrilla groups had carried out arbitrary executions, massacres, forced disappearances and kidnapping and forced recruitment. Private individuals also committed acts of violence in defence of their own interests and were generally economically powerful people at either the national or local level.

CEH presented a series of recommendations relating to reparatory measures, including the creation of a national reparation programme for the victims and their relatives, a search for the disappeared and an active exhumation policy; measures to foster a culture of mutual respect and observance of human rights; measures to strengthen the democratic process; and the promotion of peace and national harmony. In order to fulfil its recommendations, CEH recommended that the Guatemalan Congress establish a body responsible for implementing and monitoring its recommendations under the name of "Foundation for Peace and Harmony". It presented the Foundation's mandate, composition, appointment procedure, constitution, installation, period of operation, human and material resources and financing. CEH asked the Secretary-General to lend his support, through MINUGUA, so that its recommendations might be implemented. It also asked him to appoint the Foundation's independent member and to establish an international mechanism to provide the Foundation with technical support and to channel donations from the international community.

The Secretary-General stated in November that human rights organizations, a large part of organized civil society and URNG had endorsed the report [A/54/526]. The Government, although it appreciated the Commission's work, disagreed with the recommendation to establish a commission to purify the armed forces and a foundation to follow up the implementation of CEH recommendations, on the grounds that their mandates would duplicate the mandates of other entities involved in the peace process. With regard to the Foundation, the Government later stated that it was open to other options involving the participation of representatives of organized social sectors. On 9 April, under the auspices of the Council for Human Rights, a large group of organizations of civil society agreed to form the Multi-institutional Forum for Peace and Harmony, to advance the implementation of the Commission's recommendations and, especially, the establishment of a Foundation for Peace and Harmony.

Regarding the Commission's request to the Secretary-General, MINUGUA had helped disseminate the report and had used its good offices to secure an agreement between the Government and organizations of civil society on setting up the Foundation. The Secretary-General expressed his intention to appoint the independent member and establish the international technical support mechanism once the Foundation's rules of procedure had been determined. He was of the opinion that it was essential to establish a forum made up of State bodies and organizations of civil society to assume jointly the task of reconciliation. The forum could give priority to actions recommended by CEH, including promotion of and support for historical research; the search for the disappeared; measures to honour and preserve the memory of the victims; compensation for the victims; the initiation of a policy of exhumation; the promotion of a culture of mutual respect; and the formulation and promotion of a legislative agenda based on the CEH report.

MINUGUA

The mandate of MINUGUA, which was extended to 31 December 1999 by General Assembly resolution 53/93 [YUN 1998, p. 221], included verification of all agreements signed by the Government of Guatemala and URNG covering human rights, the parties' compliance with the ceasefire, separation and concentration of the respective forces, and disarmament and demobilization of former URNG combatants. The Mission's functions also comprised good offices, advisory and support services and public information. The parties to the agreements had requested that the duration of the mandate of MINUGUA be the same as that of the implementation timetable, namely four years, up to 31 December 2000.

Report of Secretary-General. In response to General Assembly resolution 53/93, the Secretary-General submitted a September report [A/54/355] covering the state of implementation of the peace agreements (see p. 201) and the structure and staffing of MINUGUA. He said that the Mission's configuration was well suited to the multiple and varied tasks with which it was charged, and, therefore, he proposed that only a modest change in its regional structure be made in 2000. The change, which would contemplate a geographical redeployment of the Mission's regional structure and not a change in geographical coverage, would result in a more flexible distribution of resources. Accordingly, the Mission would close three sub-offices and increase its capacity for flexibility by introducing an additional (third) mobile office. The number of coordinators and political affairs officers (8 and 25, respectively) would remain unchanged. The Secretary-General recommended that the Assembly authorize the renewal of MINUGUA's mandate for a further period of one year, until 31 December 2000. He noted that the financial requirements, inclusive of support staff and operational costs for the period from 1 January to 31 December 2000, were estimated at $31.4 million.

Verification of compliance

In response to General Assembly resolution 53/93, the Secretary-General, in November, submitted his fourth report [A/54/526] on the verification of compliance with the agreements signed by the Government of Guatemala and URNG [YUN 1996, p. 168].

The implementation of the commitments entered into by the two parties was governed by the Timetable Agreement [YUN 1997, p. 176], which divided the period from 1997 to 2000 into three phases. The report covered part of the third phase (1998-2000), from 1 August 1998 to 31 August 1999, which coincided with the last year in office of the Government of President Álvaro Arzú, the signatory of most of the peace agreements, and with the period leading up to the general elections of 7 November 1999. In the light of those circumstances, the Secretary-General not only reviewed the verification results for the reporting period, but also included general conclusions on compliance with each agreement and recommendations on the outstanding peace agenda. At the beginning of the year, the Commission to Follow up the Implementation of the Peace Agreements had established seven priorities for 1999 that included the commitments to give sustainability to the reconstruction effort undertaken in the wake of hurricane Mitch (see PART THREE, Chapter III), the preparation of various legislative bills related to the constitutional reform adopted by the Congress in October 1998 [YUN 1998, p. 218], fiscal matters, rural development, compensation, civic participation and coordination and consultation, including monitoring the work of the commissions set up under the peace agreements.

Compliance with the 1994 Comprehensive Agreement on Human Rights [YUN 1994, p. 407] included the institution on 12 April 1999 of a National Programme of Compensation for and/or Assistance to the Victims of Human Rights Violations during the Armed Conflict to provide compensation and/or assistance through civic, socio-economic and moral reparation programmes and projects. Pilot projects initiated prior to the formulation of the Programme confirmed that compensation was a complex matter for a country emerging from almost four decades of armed conflict, with a toll of some 200,000 dead and disappeared persons. Nonetheless, the Secretary-General said the State had a legal and moral duty towards the victims and, therefore, it was important to extend the Compensation Programme through the year 2000 and subsequent years as a continuing, long-term effort.

Regarding compliance with the 1994 Agreement on Resettlement of the Population Groups Uprooted by the Armed Conflict [YUN 1994, p. 407], during the period under review 5,853 Guatemalan refugees were repatriated. The process of organized return of the Guatemalan refugees in Mexico ended on 30 June 1999. Some 43,000 refugees had been repatriated during the past 15 years, while 22,000 who were still living in Mexico had chosen to remain there. Access to land and legal security of tenure were priority issues for the uprooted population and key areas in the implementation of the Agreement. As to the internally displaced population, 1,500 families had applied for assistance in the purchase of 23 estates; as at 31 October, two estates had been purchased. A number of factors continued to imperil the resettlement process, including the absence of land management and micro-regional development plans. There were worrisome delays in implementing commitments on productive integration in the context of regional policies of sustainable development and strengthening the system of development councils.

As to the 1994 Agreement on the Establishment of the Commission to Clarify Past Human Rights Violations and Acts of Violence That Have Caused the Guatemalan Population to Suffer [YUN 1994, p. 407], the Secretary-General, on 25 February, received and made public the CEH report entitled "Guatemala: Memory of Silence" (see p. 199).

Under the 1995 Agreement on Identity and Rights of Indigenous Peoples [YUN 1995, p. 432], priority was given to the continuation of consultations between the Government and indigenous organizations on the Agreement's implementation. The Joint Commission on Land Rights reached agreement on a preliminary bill establishing the Land Trust Fund, which was approved by the Congress on 13 May. The Act established the principal mechanism for facilitating access to land ownership for peasants who possessed no land or insufficient land. The Office for the Defence of Indigenous Women's Rights was established within the Presidential Commission for Coordinating Executive Policy in the Field of Human Rights. The Office would have administrative, technical and financial management capacities and the power to promote and develop, together with governmental entities, proposals for public policy and plans and programmes for the prevention of, protection against and eradication of all forms of violence and discrimination against indigenous women.

Commitments to ensure the sustainability of the reconstruction activities undertaken in the wake of hurricane Mitch were emphasized under the 1996 Agreement on Social and Economic Aspects and the Agrarian Situation [YUN 1996, p. 165]. A Fiscal Pact Preparatory Commission was established in March 1999 as part of the fiscal pact process, which was responsible, among other things, for preventing a decline in tax collection. The Secretary-General said that a decision on ending the prolonged fiscal stalemate could not be delayed any longer without serious consequences for social and institutional development and, therefore, for governability.

Among positive aspects of government action in the area of rural development were the definition by the Ministry of Agriculture, Livestock and Food of areas for long-term strategic action and of priorities for 1999 based on the key elements of the peace agreements; the submission of a document on national agrarian policy which contained components for the definition of a rural development strategy; the modernization of the Ministry; the adoption by the Congress of the Land Trust Fund Act; the increase in public investment in rural areas; the beginning of the process of regulating public land; the execution of pilot land registry plans; the expansion of forestry incentives; and the continuation of consultations between the Government and indigenous organizations within the Joint Commission on Rights relating to Indigenous Peoples' Land. Scant progress was made in launching comprehensive land management plans in both urban and rural areas which took into account multiculturalism and indigenous communities' forms of land ownership. That situation was a matter of concern since a substantial part of the damage caused by hurricane Mitch occurred because of the absence of such plans. The land registry process had made limited progress and was extremely weak, owing to its excessive dependence on external resources and the very limited allocation of national funds.

In the health sector, progress had been made in the commitment to allocate a higher percentage of spending to preventive health, which had improved the health infrastructure and had expanded the coverage of health services, especially in rural areas, despite the fact that there was still a need to reduce the rate of infant mortality. The results achieved were due in large measure to the creation of the Integrated Health Care System (SIAS), which, in less than two years, had provided services throughout the country to low-income people. At times, though, the quality of the SIAS services was somewhat deficient, due to a shortage of medicines, equipment and basic supplies and a lack of training on the part of its rank-and-file workers. Accordingly, the Secretary-General called on SIAS to consolidate its institutions, learn to do without the voluntary work of community staff, overcome its dependence on cooperation workers from Cuba, and improve its agreements with non-governmental organizations (NGOs) in terms of time frame, payments, monitoring and supervision.

In the education sector, the goal of increasing the amount of public spending actually disbursed was achieved in 1998 and progress had been made in reducing illiteracy, in educational support programmes and in increasing educational coverage, especially in rural areas. Nevertheless, progress had been hindered because the target of access for all those between the ages of 7 and 12 to at least three years of schooling by the year 2000 had not been achieved; although there was an overall reduction in illiteracy, the rates for the indigenous population remained higher than for the rest of the population; and little progress had been made in fulfilling other commitments, such as the execution of a national programme of civic education and providing out-of-school education and training. The National Programme for Educational Self-Management provided support for over 175,000 children in 1998, mainly in rural areas, thereby narrowing the traditional gap between urban and rural educational coverage. The Secretary-General stressed that the urgency of instituting educational reform required greater efforts by all sectors involved.

With regard to housing, coverage had increased and the commitment to allocate 1.5 per cent of annual tax revenues to that sector had been fulfilled, although the quality of the service provided was very poor. The Secretary-General noted that there was a need to reformulate completely the policy for access to low-income housing, since the current regulatory framework did not include the components established in the peace agreements. The Government had implemented an emergency agenda for the post-hurricane Mitch reconstruction period that had helped repair the damage to the economic infrastructure and to solve some of the most pressing social problems in the areas affected, including health, loss of jobs and temporary housing. However, important components of the reconstruction effort had been carried out without respect for the provisions of the peace agreements. As regards participation, once the immediate emergency was over, the implementation of reconstruction activities became over-centralized and the failure to involve regional and municipal forums precluded the participation of organized sectors of the population in designing and planning those activities. In the case of housing, the relocation and reconstruction programme was carried out without considering such factors as coordination between central and local government agencies, land management, urban planning and environmental protection. In addition, as at July, the food-for-work programme put in place by the Ministry of Labour had not covered women workers. As wage conditions enjoyed by workers prior to hurricane Mitch had deteriorated noticeably and had not improved a year after the emergency, the Secretary-General called for improved labour conditions in the country.

Under the 1996 Agreement on the Strengthening of Civilian Power and on the Role of the Armed Forces in a Democratic Society [YUN 1996, p. 167], the commitment to increase the judiciary's budget by 50 per cent in relation to 1995 was implemented. Other positive developments included the establishment of the ad hoc commission to follow up the recommendations of the Commission on the Strengthening of the Justice System, and the leading role assumed by that Commission, particularly during the process of selecting members of the new Supreme Court of Justice and the Courts of Appeal. The judiciary had continued to implement its modernization plan; however, it was proceeding slowly and had not had the impact necessary to meet the population's demands for justice. The deployment of the National Civil Police (PNC), a central element of the peace agreements, was extended throughout the country, despite constraints on the infrastructure and equipment of the units that had been deployed. The slow deployment and weak structure of the Criminal Investigation Service were not consistent with the importance that the Agreement attached to criminal investigation in developing the new PNC structure.

The restructuring of the armed forces in accordance with the provisions of the peace agreements had been carried out from a quantitative standpoint, in the reduction in the size and budget of the military. The qualitative restructuring remained to be carried out due, in part, to the delays in the discussion of the constitutional reform. In addition, MINUGUA reported that the military, which had 104 units before the signing of the peace agreements, still had 95 units deployed in the same geographical locations as during the armed conflict, even in areas where extremely serious human rights violations had occurred. In view of the situation, the Mission had conducted verification of the deployment to identify the functions carried out by each unit. The Secretary-General said that the qualitative implementation of the commitments and the ambiguities of the current deployment demonstrated the urgency of adopting a new military doctrine to define the military's functions in a democratic, peaceful society. He called on the Government to comply in 1999 with the commitment to disband the Presidential General Staff and replace it with a civilian unit responsible for the security of the President and Vice-President.

As far as the 1996 Agreement on Constitutional Reforms and the Electoral Regime [YUN 1997, p. 178] was concerned, a reform package—comprising 50 amendments to the Constitution—was submitted for ratification in a referendum held on 16 May 1999. Although the vast majority of political forces came out in favour of the reform, the outcome of the referendum was negative, raising serious legal difficulties as to the alteration of the mandate of the armed forces, the reform of the career judicial service and official recognition of indigenous languages. Despite that setback, the Secretary-General said that there was a conviction among the main political parties and many elements of civil society that the outcome of the referendum had not diminished the legitimacy and validity of the peace agreements.

Some aspects of the 1996 Agreement on the Basis for the Legal Integration of the URNG [YUN 1996, p. 169] were implemented with the launching of most of the subprogrammes for the initial integration of demobilized combatants. However, serious difficulties remained, due to, among other things, limited progress made in other peace agreements linked to the integration process and delays in the implementation of production projects for some two thirds of all demobilized combatants.

The Secretary-General observed that 1999 was the last year in office of the Government that had signed the majority of the peace agreements. The general elections would bring changes in the executive branch, the Legislative Assembly and the local governments. The current Government and the new authorities would have to implement electoral, fiscal, judicial and military reforms. According to the Secretary-General's Chef de Cabinet, there was a broad consensus among diverse sectors of Guatemalan society as to the need to continue and expand implementation of the peace agenda.

In a later report [A/55/175], the Secretary-General stated that the first general elections since the signing of the 1996 Agreement on a Firm and Lasting Peace took place on 7 November. Alfonso Portillo, the candidate of the Frente Republicano Guatemalteco (FRG), was elected President after winning the second round of presidential elections on 26 December. URNG participated for the first time as a political party in the elections, winning nine congressional seats and 13 mayoral posts as a member of the Alianza Nueva Nación. FRG won 63 of the 113 congressional seats.

On 15 November, with regard to the 1994 Comprehensive Agreement on Human Rights, the Follow-up Commission submitted to the President of the Congress the preliminary draft of a bill setting up a commission for peace and harmony, the text of which had been agreed on with civil society organizations, based on a preliminary draft prepared by the Multi-institutional Forum for Peace and Harmony and in keeping with the Mission's recommendations. The bill was presented to the full Congress on the last day of its regular session and was referred to the Congressional Committee for Peace and Mine Clearance, which issued a favourable ruling. However, it could not be voted on by the full Congress because the special December session did not have a quorum.

The Judicial Civil Service Act, an important landmark in the modernization of the judiciary, was adopted on 30 November, and, in December, the Ad Hoc Commission, which had taken over from the Commission on the Strengthening of the Justice System, completed its work.

The proposed "doctrinal manual of the Guatemalan armed forces", submitted in late 1999 by the previous Government, focused almost exclusively on military aspects, and therefore did not meet expectations of fulfilling the commitment of a new military doctrine. The newly elected Government had taken over the manual, which it viewed as a working draft, and expressed its willingness to include more sectors in its discussion.

Human rights

In December [A/54/688], the Secretary-General transmitted to the General Assembly the MINUGUA head's tenth report on human rights, which described the Mission's activities between 1 January and 30 November 1999.

One of the most significant events that took place was the verification of political rights in the context of the first round of general elections on 7 November. The Mission monitored a registration plan launched in June by the Supreme Electoral Tribunal and provided logistical support specifically aimed at the most inaccessible areas. Overall, MINUGUA investigated over 200 complaints and incidents during the electoral period, though, in many cases, the complainants failed to provide the minimum information needed to determine plausibility. Threats or intimidation against members of political parties, candidates and officials of the Supreme Electoral Tribunal were reported. On election day, the Mission was present throughout Guatemala, serving as a deterrent to potential conflicts. It also toured 286 of the country's 330 municipalities and visited 750 polling stations. The Mission's observations suggested that in nearly 80 per cent of the municipalities visited, political rights were exercised under normal conditions, while minor problems occurred in just under 20 per cent of the municipalities.

During the first nine months of 1999, the Mission admitted 316 complaints, compared with 219 during the previous reporting period [YUN 1998, p. 218]. The increase was partly due to the fact that 66.12 per cent of all violations of the State's legal obligation to prevent, investigate and punish stemmed from cases admitted during previous periods, regarding massacres and disappearances. Verifications of the violations indicated an increase in the practice of torture and cruel, inhuman or degrading treatment, as well as an increase in violations of the right to individual liberty, due process of law, political rights and the right to freedom of association and assembly. The Mission stressed that greater efforts were needed to promote a culture of independence within the judiciary branch, as well as greater professionalism among judges and prosecutors. A fact-finding mission to Guatemala was carried out by the Special Rapporteur of the Commission on Human Rights on the independence of judges and lawyers (see PART TWO, Chapter II).

The weaknesses of the judiciary and the Public Prosecutor's Office were compounded by the fact that some institutions of the executive branch had interfered and, at times, refused to cooperate with the justice system. In the case of the assassination of Monsignor Juan José Gerardi Conedera [YUN 1998, p. 219], the lack of cooperation or interference had been blatant. In fact, evidence pointed to a parallel investigation in the Gerardi case that was carried out with the participation of intelligence services without the knowledge of the judicial authorities. Parallel investigations were carried out in other cases, disrupting and confusing the work of the Public Prosecutor's Office, thereby perpetuating impunity for the crime. The Mission recommended that the Government should enforce the prohibition contained in the peace agreements against the involvement of military intelligence organizations in civilian matters, particularly in judicial investigations.

During the reporting period, the deterioration in the human rights situation was also due to the actions of PNC. However, MINUGUA noted improvements in its performance, particularly a more active policy to combat the phenomenon of lynching. It also noted a reduction in violations stemming from the excessive use of force in eviction or similar operations resulting in large numbers of victims. At the same time, cases of torture associated with the investigation of crimes and offences had been reported.

The worsening human rights situation, three years after the signing of the peace agreements, was cause for concern. Despite MINUGUA's recommendations, no progress had been made towards fulfilling the commitment to perfect the norms and mechanisms to protect human rights through the ratification or signing of new instruments. The Mission therefore urged the Government to deposit with the UN Secretary-General its instrument of ratification of the Optional Protocol to the International Covenant on Civil and Political Rights [YUN 1966, p. 431] and to recognize the competence of the Committee against Torture and the Committee on the Elimination of Racial Discrimination, so that the respective Committees could receive communications from individuals. The Mission once more stressed the need for the Government to complete the process of ratification of the 1994 Inter-American Convention on Forced Disappearance of Persons, by depositing the relevant instruments with OAS, as an effective means of fostering in the international community recognition of enforced disappearance as a crime against humanity. As to the ownership, use and bearing of firearms by individuals, the Mission called on the State to develop effective and reliable mechanisms of control, given the indiscriminate proliferation of that type of weapon and its widespread marketing.

GENERAL ASSEMBLY ACTION

On 8 December [meeting 73], the General Assembly adopted **resolution 54/99** [draft: A/54/L.27 & Add.1] without vote [agenda item 47].

United Nations Verification Mission in Guatemala

The General Assembly,

Recalling its resolution 53/93 of 7 December 1998, in which it decided to authorize the renewal of the mandate of the United Nations Verification Mission in Guatemala from 1 January to 31 December 1999,

Taking into account the ninth report on human rights of the Mission,

Taking into account also the report of the Commission for Historical Clarification,

Stressing the role played by the Mission in support of the Guatemala peace process, and emphasizing the need for the Mission to continue to enjoy the support of all parties,

Taking into account the fact that the parties have expressed their interest in the continued presence of the Mission in Guatemala,

Having considered the report of the Secretary-General on the work of the Mission and the recommendations therein, which are aimed at ensuring that the Mission can respond adequately to the demands of the peace process until 31 December 2000,

1. *Welcomes* the ninth report on human rights of the United Nations Verification Mission in Guatemala;

2. *Also welcomes* the report of the Commission for Historical Clarification and its recommendations;

3. *Takes note with satisfaction* of progress made in the implementation of the peace agreements, in particular the finalization of the programme for the repatriation of Guatemalan refugees in Mexico, compliance with the spending targets included in the agreements, increased deployment of the new National Civil Police, the approval by Congress of the new Land Trust Fund and the establishment of the Office for the Defence of Indigenous Women;

4. *Also takes note with satisfaction* of the ongoing efforts at consensus-building carried out within the commissions created under the peace agreements, as well as of the contribution of the Women's Forum;

5. *Underscores* the fact that, as pointed out by the Commission to Follow up the Implementation of the Peace Agreements, key reforms remain outstanding, including the fiscal, judicial, military and electoral reforms, and therefore stresses the critical importance of continued compliance with the peace agreements in 2000;

6. *Encourages* the Government to implement its decision to adopt a new military doctrine and disband the current Presidential Military Staff, in keeping with the peace agreements;

7. *Underscores* the fact that meeting the tax revenue targets set in the Agreement on Social and Economic Aspects and the Agrarian Situation is essential to the sustainability of the implementation of the peace agreements;

8. *Notes* that, while significant achievements have been registered in the implementation of the Comprehensive Agreement on Human Rights, important shortcomings persist, and calls upon the Government to redouble its efforts in the promotion of human rights, taking into account the recommendations contained in the reports on human rights of the Mission, and to do its utmost to assist in the investigation of the murder of Monsignor Juan José Gerardi Conedera;

9. *Calls upon* the Government to follow up on the recommendations of the Commission for Historical Clarification, with a view to promoting national reconciliation, upholding the right to truth and providing redress, in accordance with Guatemalan law, for the victims of human rights abuses and violence committed during the thirty-six-year armed conflict;

10. *Welcomes* the commitment to the implementation of the peace agreements made by the presidential candidates of the major political parties and their support for the extension of the mandate of the Mission;

11. *Encourages* the parties and all sectors of Guatemalan society to continue efforts to achieve the goals of the peace agreements, in particular the observance of

human rights, including the rights of indigenous peoples, equitable development, participation and national reconciliation;

12. *Invites* the international community and, in particular, the agencies, programmes and funds of the United Nations, to continue to take the implementation of the peace agreements as the framework for their technical and financial assistance programmes and projects, and stresses the continued importance of close cooperation among them;

13. *Stresses* the role of the Mission as a key instrument in the consolidation of peace, promotion of the observance of human rights and building of confidence in the implementation of the peace agreements;

14. *Decides* to authorize the renewal of the mandate of the Mission from 1 January to 31 December 2000;

15. *Requests* the Secretary-General to submit, as early as possible, an updated report to the General Assembly at its fifty-fifth session, with his assessment and recommendations with regard to the peace process after 31 December 2000;

16. *Also requests* the Secretary-General to keep the General Assembly fully informed of the implementation of the present resolution.

Financing of Military Observer Group

In April [A/53/898], the Advisory Committee on Administrative and Budgetary Questions (ACABQ) presented its comments on a 1998 report [YUN 1998, p. 221] on the financing of the Military Observer Group of MINUGUA for the period from 15 February to 31 May 1997. The Military Observer Group had been deployed for three months—from 3 March to 27 May 1997 [YUN 1997, p. 172]—to verify the Agreement on the Definitive Ceasefire of 4 December 1996 [YUN 1996, p. 168] between the Government of Guatemala and URNG.

The Committee recommended that Member States be credited their share of the unencumbered balance of $184,200 gross ($140,500 net) for the financing period. Regarding the treatment of interest ($38,653) and miscellaneous income ($68,983), totalling $107,636, it advised the General Assembly either to credit that amount, along with any surplus from the eventual liquidation of the remaining obligations in the Special Account for the Military Observer Group, to the Peacekeeping Reserve Fund, or to credit Member States their respective share. As to obligations owed to Governments that provided contingents and/or logistic support that had been retained beyond the period stipulated under the financial regulations of the United Nations, ACABQ recommended approval of the special arrangements under article IV of the regulations, similar to those annexed to General Assembly resolution 52/240 [YUN 1998, p. 205].

GENERAL ASSEMBLY ACTION

On 8 June [meeting 101], the General Assembly, on the recommendation of the Fifth (Administrative and Budgetary) Committee [A/53/981], adopted **resolution 53/235** without vote [agenda item 142].

Financing of the Military Observer Group of the United Nations Verification Mission in Guatemala

The General Assembly,

Having considered the report of the Secretary-General on the financing of the Military Observer Group of the United Nations Verification Mission in Guatemala and the related reports of the Advisory Committee on Administrative and Budgetary Questions,

Recalling Security Council resolution 1094(1997) of 20 January 1997, in which the Council authorized the attachment to the United Nations Mission for the Verification of Human Rights and of Compliance with the Commitments of the Comprehensive Agreement on Human Rights in Guatemala of a group of one hundred and fifty-five military observers and requisite medical personnel for a period of three months,

Recalling also its resolution 51/228 of 3 April 1997 on the financing of the Observer Group,

Reaffirming that the costs of the Observer Group are expenses of the Organization to be borne by Member States in accordance with Article 17, paragraph 2, of the Charter of the United Nations,

Recalling its previous decisions regarding the fact that, in order to meet the expenditures caused by the Observer Group, a different procedure is required from that applied to meet expenditures of the regular budget of the United Nations,

Taking into account the fact that the economically more developed countries are in a position to make relatively larger contributions and that the economically less developed countries have a relatively limited capacity to contribute towards such an operation,

Bearing in mind the special responsibilities of the States permanent members of the Security Council, as indicated in General Assembly resolution 1874(S-IV) of 27 June 1963, in the financing of such operations,

Mindful of the fact that it is essential to continue to provide the account for the Observer Group with the necessary financial resources to enable it to meet its outstanding liabilities,

1. *Takes note* of the status of contributions to the Military Observer Group of the United Nations Verification Mission in Guatemala as at 30 April 1999, including the contributions outstanding in the amount of 298,613 United States dollars, representing 7 per cent of the total assessed contributions from the inception of the Observer Group to the period ending 31 May 1997, notes that some 55 per cent of the Member States have paid their assessed contributions in full, and urges all other Member States concerned, in particular those in arrears, to ensure payment of their outstanding assessed contributions;

2. *Expresses concern* about the financial situation with regard to peacekeeping activities, in particular as regards the reimbursement of troop contributors, which bear additional burdens owing to overdue payments by Member States of their assessments;

3. *Expresses its appreciation* to those Member States which have paid their assessed contributions in full;

4. *Urges* all other Member States to make every possible effort to ensure payment of their assessed contributions to the Observer Group in full and on time;

5. *Endorses* the observations and recommendations contained in the report of the Advisory Committee on Administrative and Budgetary Questions, subject to the provisions of the present resolution;

6. *Approves*, on an exceptional basis, the special arrangements for the Observer Group with regard to the application of article IV of the financial regulations of the United Nations, whereby appropriations required in respect of obligations owed to Governments which provided contingents and/or logistic support for the Observer Group shall be retained beyond the period stipulated under financial regulations 4.3 and 4.4, as set out in the annex to the present resolution;

7. *Decides* that Member States that have fulfilled their financial obligations to the Observer Group shall be credited their respective share of the unencumbered balance of 184,200 dollars gross (140,500 dollars net) in respect of the period ending 31 May 1997 and their respective share of the miscellaneous income of 68,983 dollars and interest income of 38,653 dollars;

8. *Decides also* that, for Member States that have not fulfilled their financial obligations to the Observer Group, their share in the unencumbered balance of 184,200 dollars gross (140,500 dollars net) in respect of the period ending 31 May 1997 and their respective share of the miscellaneous income of 68,983 dollars and interest income of 38,653 dollars shall be set off against their outstanding obligations;

9. *Decides further* to transfer to the Peacekeeping Reserve Fund any surplus arising from the eventual liquidation of the remaining obligations in the Special Account for the Military Observer Group of the United Nations Verification Mission in Guatemala;

10. *Takes note* of the report of the Secretary-General on the disposition of assets of the Observer Group;

11. *Requests* the Secretary-General to ensure the safety of United Nations assets and that there are accountability procedures in place to deter and penalize those responsible for the losses of the United Nations property and to report thereon to the General Assembly at its fifty-fourth session;

12. *Notes with concern* that the provisions of its decision 52/485 of 26 June 1998 have not been complied with, and reiterates that all reports on the final disposition of assets should contain detailed information on and justification for items written off and lost;

13. *Requests* the Board of Auditors to conduct an audit of the final disposition of assets of the Observer Group, in particular of assets sold and written off, and include its recommendations in the audit report for the period July 1998 to June 1999.

ANNEX

Special arrangements with regard to the application of article IV of the financial regulations of the United Nations

1. At the end of the twelve-month period provided for in financial regulation 4.3, any unliquidated obligations of the financial period in question relating to goods supplied and services rendered by Governments for which claims have been received or which are covered by established reimbursement rates shall be transferred to accounts payable; such accounts payable shall remain recorded in the Special Account for the Military Observer Group of the United Nations Verification Mission in Guatemala until payment is effected.

2. *(a)* Any other unliquidated obligations of the financial period in question owed to Governments for goods supplied and services rendered, as well as other obligations owed to Governments, for which required claims have not yet been received shall remain valid for an additional period of four years following the end of the twelve-month period provided for in financial regulation 4.3;

(b) Claims received during this four-year period shall be treated as provided for under paragraph 1 of the present annex, if appropriate;

(c) At the end of the additional four-year period, any unliquidated obligations shall be cancelled and the then remaining balance of any appropriations retained therefor shall be surrendered.

Pursuant to resolution 53/235, the Secretary-General submitted a December report [A/54/669 & Corr.1] that provided statistics on losses of UN property in peacekeeping operations from 1 January 1996 to 31 December 1997, including those pertaining to MINUGUA.

On 23 December, the Assembly, by **decision 54/465**, decided that the item on the financing of the Military Observer Group of MINUGUA remained for consideration during its resumed fifty-fourth (2000) session.

On the same date, the Assembly decided that the Fifth Committee should continue to consider the item at the resumed session (**decision 54/462 A**).

Nicaragua

In a report on international assistance for the rehabilitation and reconstruction of Nicaragua [A/55/125-E/2000/91] (see PART THREE, Chapter III), the Secretary-General noted that in June the National Assembly elected the Attorney for the Defence of Human Rights and his deputy. The election led to the installation of the Attorney's Office for the Defence of Human Rights, created by law in 1996 as an independent State institution. At the Government's request, UNDP initiated a project, with the support of the Nordic countries, to create the necessary conditions for it to function, providing office space and equipment, communication facilities, technical assistance and managerial and organizational support. In November, the Special Attorney for Children and Adolescents took up his post. The most significant change in government policy towards children's rights had been the approval by the National Assembly (May 1998) and entry into force (November 1998) of the Code for Children and Adolescents. While the Code had yet to demonstrate its impact on the situation of Nicaraguan children, the preparatory work for its approval, strongly supported by UNICEF, visibly increased the presence of the subject of children and adolescent rights on the Government's agenda, in the media and as an issue for debate among the public in general. The promotion of public sensitivity about the problem of child labour advanced. The Ministry of Labour supported the implementation of national legislation prohibiting labour for children under 14 years of age.

A comprehensive programme that had assisted governmental efforts to return properties confiscated by the Sandinist Government between 1979 and 1990 to their former owners or at least to compensate them had entered a second phase in 1998 with support from Sweden, UNDP and Nicaragua. While much remained to be done, the programme had decreased significantly the problem of property conflicts.

Governance, democratization and consolidation of the rule of law had been set as priorities by the Nicaraguan Government. The need to reform the judicial system led to the formulation of a national programme to modernize justice, implemented by the Government with financial support from a wide range of Governments and organizations. Under the umbrella of the programme, various initiatives were carried out, such as the modernization of laws and codes, the restructuring of the Supreme Court of Justice and the Attorney-General's Office, the installation of the Institute of Forensic Medicine and the integrated reform of the penitentiary system. In December 1999, the Justice Commission of the National Assembly presented a project for a new penal code.

In recent years, a range of projects for ex-combatants, comprising productive reintegration, capacity-building, construction of family habitats and legal support for the set-up of multiple service cooperatives, had benefited more than 15,000 persons. Since November 1998, the Institute for Rural Development, with contributions from UNDP and France, had been implementing the second phase of a programme which provided assistance in the process of the consolidation of peace and the creation of a basis for productive and social development. The first stage of the project responded to the needs of more than 6,000 families of former combatants in over 40 municipalities. In the early 1990s, the Nicaraguan Government sought the support of the International Organization for Migration to create a programme to allow Nicaraguan professionals to return and reintegrate fully into Nicaraguan society. The qualified Nicaraguan professionals return programme, which was supported by the EU, ended in August 1999, having transferred 466 professionals and their dependants to Nicaragua, thereby reintegrating a total of more than 1,500 persons.

Communications. In response to a 1998 letter submitted by Nicaragua [YUN 1998, p. 223], Costa Rica, on 13 January [A/53/795], demanded respect for the Jérez-Cañas Treaty, the Cleveland Award and the Judgement of 30 September 1916 of the Central American Court of Justice, which, it said, stipulated that Costa Rica had a real, perpetual and immutable right of use in relation to navigation on the San Juan River. On 23 March [A/53/882], Nicaragua said that there was no dispute between it and Costa Rica concerning matters of territorial sovereignty over the San Juan River [YUN 1998, p. 224] or any other matter. By a reply of 9 April [A/53/905], Costa Rica also declared that no dispute existed between it and Nicaragua regarding territorial sovereignty.

On 3 December [A/54/652], Nicaragua informed the Secretary-General that Honduras had ratified on 30 November the Maritime Delimitation Treaty (the Ramírez-López Treaty), an agreement which Honduras had negotiated with Colombia in 1986. According to Nicaragua, the Treaty's ratification by Honduras breached the provisions of a ruling issued by the Central American Court of Justice on 30 November 1999. Nicaragua was not a party to the Treaty, which, it maintained, would deprive it of 30,000 square kilometres of continental shelf off its Atlantic coast.

In order to reduce tensions between the two countries, OAS had appointed a special envoy who had been instrumental in arranging confidence-building measures, such as a pull-back of forces, joint naval patrols and the demilitarization of the border. On 30 December [A/54/696], by a joint communiqué issued in Miami (United States), Nicaragua and Honduras undertook to adopt measures designed to avoid the occurrence of violent actions that endangered peace, security and stability in the Central American region and reaffirmed their desire to resolve their differences through peaceful means.

Haiti

During 1999, Haiti continued to experience a serious political and institutional crisis, which stalled the implementation of essential structural reforms and contributed to a worsening of the human rights situation. General elections, which were scheduled to take place in November 1999, were postponed to March 2000. Improvements were reported in the restructuring and functioning of the Haitian National Police (HNP), though major structural weaknesses in the justice system undermined the rule of law and civil liberties.

The United Nations continued to support Haiti in its difficult transition process towards greater democracy and development. The United Nations Civilian Police Mission in Haiti (MIPONUH) monitored and assisted HNP, while the joint UN/OAS International Civilian Mission to Haiti (MICIVIH) provided institutional assistance, helped in the promotion and protection of human rights and verified observance of individual rights and fundamental freedoms.

In December, following a request for continued UN assistance by Haiti's President René Préval and within the UN framework of developing a long-term strategy of support for the Haitian people, the General Assembly established the International Civilian Support Mission in Haiti (MICAH) to consolidate the results, as well as some of the activities, of MIPONUH and MICIVIH. Since MIPONUH's mandate was to expire on 30 November 1999, the Security Council decided to continue the Mission to ensure a phased transition to MICAH by 15 March 2000. MICIVIH's mandate was also extended until the commencement of MICAH.

Civilian Police Mission

Reports of Secretary-General (February and May). On 19 February [S/1999/181], the Secretary-General updated the activities of MIPONUH and developments in the mission area since his November 1998 report [YUN 1998, p. 228]. The Mission had been established by Security Council resolution 1141(1997) of 28 November 1997 [YUN 1997, p. 193] to assist the Government of Haiti by supporting and contributing to the professionalization of HNP in close cooperation with MICIVIH.

The Secretary-General said that there had been disturbing developments in the political situation in Haiti, raising renewed concerns about the country's stability and its transition to democracy. On 11 January, President Préval, following failure to complete the ratification process of his nominee for the position of Prime Minister [YUN 1998, p. 229], declared that the terms of all deputies, one third of the senators and all the local authorities had expired. Noting that he lacked the legal authority to either dissolve Parliament or extend its mandate, he appealed to all sectors of society to find a constitutional solution to the crisis. On 20 January, the Council of Ministers adopted a resolution calling for the relevant authorities to freeze the bank accounts of the National Assembly and withhold the salaries of parliamentarians, cancel their diplomatic passports and confiscate their firearms. Certain parties characterized the declaration as a coup d'état and as a step towards totalitarianism.

Following a briefing to the Security Council on 19 January by the Under-Secretary-General for Peacekeeping Operations, Bernard Miyet, the President of the Council made a statement to the press, in which he urged a negotiated solution to the crisis and broad agreement on the formation of a credible Provisional Electoral Council (CEP). On 26 January [A/53/830-S/1999/156], the Government responded by pointing out that President Préval had not dissolved Parliament; it was still sitting with nine senators whose terms would expire in 2001, and there had been no untimely interruption of the democratic process, as the President had not vested himself with dictatorial powers.

Concerned about the deepening political crisis, the Secretary-General requested his Representative, Julian Harston, and MICIVIH's Executive Director, Colin Granderson, to meet for consultations in New York from 20 to 22 January with the "Friends of the Secretary-General for Haiti". At the meeting, the participants agreed to engage jointly in parallel discussions with the President, the Prime Minister and political parties to assist in resolving the situation, while using the statement of the Security Council President as a basis for joint and individual initiatives. President Préval initiated a dialogue with opposition leaders in order to achieve consensus on the establishment of CEP and the holding of elections. On 3 February, after having had a further briefing on the situation in Haiti, the President of the Security Council, in a press statement, urged Haiti's political leaders to overcome their differences and to create the basis for free and fair elections.

As at 15 February, MIPONUH was composed of 282 civilian police officers (CIVPOL) from 10 countries, including a 140-strong special police unit deployed along with the necessary support personnel. The substantive police element remained deployed in Port-au-Prince and in all nine départements, while the special police unit was based in the capital. Among other activities, MIPONUH conducted weekly training on administration, arrest procedures, community relations, crowd control, data processing, judiciary-police relations, record keeping and report writing to enhance the competence and effectiveness of HNP. The Mission continued to coordinate its activities closely with those of UNDP and bilateral programmes, such as those of Canada, France and the United States. Following a deterioration in the security situation after 11 January, the MIPONUH special police unit provided assistance to MIPONUH personnel and increased its activities in the protection of Mission property.

The Secretary-General noted that HNP, which numbered 6,100, had performed in an efficient and exemplary manner since 11 January and had remained politically neutral. The overall human rights record of HNP had improved and reports of ill-treatment during arrests and interrogations had decreased. However, individual acts of abuse and misconduct by some officers remained a problem.

Developments in the justice system were uneven. The Ministry of Justice had failed to take steps to implement the short- and long-range plan of reform submitted by the Preparatory Commission on Legal and Judicial Reform in July 1998 [YUN 1998, p. 227]. With a view to strengthening the Office of the Ombudsman, UNDP had financed training of its personnel, human rights seminars for HNP and publications to inform the public on the role of the Ombudsman. However, financial difficulties impeded the capacity of the Office to fulfil its mandate.

The performance of the Haitian economy was encouraging throughout 1998, with a 3.1 per cent growth in GNP in real terms, and the national currency, the gourde, was stabilized. For the first time in years, agricultural production increased significantly, inflation was reduced to 8 per cent and the budget deficit was kept to 1.3 per cent of GNP. Improvements in tax collection and the launching of a voluntary early retirement programme for civil servants also inspired optimism. On the downside, hurricane Georges, which struck the island in September 1998 [YUN 1998, p. 875], and—as a result of the institutional crisis—unratified loan agreements with major donors had a negative impact on the economy. The report of the resident coordinator of January 1999 emphasized that the United Nations was able to provide assistance according to national priorities, through the Joint United Nations Programme on HIV/AIDS (UNAIDS) (see PART THREE, Chapter XIII), hurricane-related disaster relief, the police project, and measures to enhance the participation of the public in local government, environmental protection and the promotion of equality, health and advocacy. Development activities of the UN system included, among other programmes, an advocacy campaign on violence against women by all UN agencies; a United Nations Educational, Scientific and Cultural Organization workshop on the culture of peace; a rights of the child and justice for minors programme by UNICEF; the finalization of the UNDP-assisted national environment plan; and sensitization of the public on reproductive health sponsored by the United Nations Population Fund.

The Secretary-General observed that there had been an increasing polarization in Haiti and new risks to the consolidation of democracy. The absence of a functioning Parliament had created a serious institutional vacuum. The political crisis was affecting adversely social and economic development. Without a functioning government and legislature, it was becoming increasingly difficult to utilize international assistance or to implement developmental projects. The Secretary-General expressed concern over the lack of real progress in implementing the reform of the judicial system and called on the international community to provide assistance to the Office of the Ombudsman.

On 19 May [S/1999/579], the Secretary-General described the activities of MIPONUH and developments in the mission area since February. He also proposed initial recommendations on a viable transition to other forms of international assistance for Security Council consideration.

The Secretary-General said that encouraging steps had been taken towards resolving the protracted political crisis in Haiti. President Préval had held talks with leaders of a coalition of opposition parties—the so-called Espace de concertation—as well as with popular, business and labour organizations. UN officials, "Friends of Haiti" representatives and former President of Costa Rica Oscar Arias also endeavoured to establish common ground between all parties concerned. In February, the Cour de cassation (Supreme Court) dismissed an action by members of Parliament challenging President Préval's declaration on the expiration of their mandate by deciding that the Court did not have the legal authority to rule on the dispute between the legislative and executive branches of government. On 6 March, President Préval and the representatives of the Espace de concertation reached agreement on the principles for the establishment of a new CEP and a new government. On 16 March, the President appointed the nine members of CEP; on 25 March, the Prime Minister, Jacques-Edouard Alexis, announced his new Cabinet. The Prime Minister, who also held the portfolio of Minister of Interior, called his Administration transitional and said that its top priority would be to organize legislative and local elections. The newly appointed CEP held talks with a number of political parties on the promulgation of a new electoral decree, in the hope of holding the first round of elections before the end of the year. Following a request from CEP for UN technical assistance, a member of the Department of Political Affairs visited Haiti on an electoral assessment mission from 27 to 30 April. As a result of his recommendations, UNDP decided to provide electoral advisers and assistance to CEP. A monitoring committee and a technical task force had been established by the Secretary-General's Representative.

Increased insecurity was reflected in a number of high-profile murders and attempted murders, while other disquieting developments included demonstrations, blockades, strikes and other violent incidents. The unrest was due to tensions among the different political forces, as well as economic desperation and political frustration on the part of the population.

MIPONUH continued to provide HNP with training in its day-to-day work, while technical advice was given to the leadership of the police force at the supervisory level. Close links had developed between HNP's crowd-control unit and the UN special police unit. CIVPOL provided border-monitoring training to those police officers stationed near the frontier with the Dominican Republic. On 14 March, a helicopter carrying six members of the Argentine National Gendarmerie and seven members of the International Charter Incorporated helicopter company was involved in an accident in which all 13 people on board were killed. A UN inquiry was to follow.

The Secretary-General said that the HNP continued to perform in a professional and neutral manner, despite the increased number of demonstrations and violent protests that had occurred throughout the country since February. HNP had been the target of attacks from some political forces in what appeared to be a campaign to destabilize and undermine the police service. Although HNP had made considerable progress, a top priority remained combating police involvement in drug trafficking and other criminal activities.

Structural weaknesses in the judicial system continued to undermine the rule of law and civil liberties and remained the most significant obstacle to the effective protection of human rights. The newly appointed Minister of Justice noted that real judicial reform could not take place without the election of a new Parliament.

It was expected that a common country assessment, a key step under the Secretary-General's reform programme for the creation of a United Nations Development Assistance Framework, would be completed at year's end, thus providing UN agencies with the elements to define a long-term assistance programme and to harmonize their interventions. The UN Disaster Management Team held meetings to prepare for the hurricane season. UNDP finalized four preparatory projects in the areas of governance, protection of the environment, productive employment and the prevention and management of disasters. Other UN-sponsored activities included the launching by UNICEF of a national programme for salt iodization; the signing of an agreement between the Food and Agriculture Organization of the United Nations and the Government to promote sustainable agriculture and soil and water conservation; and the development of a programme funded by UNAIDS that focused on the transmission of AIDS from mother to child.

The Secretary-General said CEP would face a number of challenges in organizing the parliamentary and local elections before the end of 1999. A secure and stable environment was a precondition for a free and fair electoral campaign. In view of Security Council resolution 1212(1998) [YUN 1998, p. 229], which had expressed the Council's intention not to extend MIPONUH's mandate beyond 30 November 1999 and had called on the Secretary-General to present recommendations on a viable transition to other forms of international assistance, the Government would have to assume full responsibility for the further strengthening and effective functioning of HNP. In consultation with the Secretary-General's Representative, HNP was developing a two-year technical assistance programme designed to provide the police service with the expertise to carry out training and institution-building and to ensure the necessary continuity to the efforts of MIPONUH following its termination.

ECONOMIC AND SOCIAL COUNCIL ACTION

On 16 February [E/1999/7-S/1999/170], the President of the Economic and Social Council (ESC) sought advice from the President of the Security Council on the interpretation of paragraph 8 of resolution 1212(1998), by which the Council invited UN bodies and agencies, especially ESC, to contribute to designing a long-term programme of support for Haiti. On 7 April [E/1999/12-S/1999/403], the Council confirmed that, through resolution 1212(1998), it had invited ESC to contribute to designing a programme of support.

On 7 May, ESC, by **resolution 1999/4**, created an Ad Hoc Advisory Group on Haiti and asked it to submit its recommendations on how to ensure that adequate, coherent, well-coordinated and effective assistance could be provided by the international community to Haiti in order to achieve sustainable development (see PART THREE, Chapter III).

On 31 July [E/1999/115-S/1999/865], the ESC President informed the Security Council that, on 27 July, ESC, on the basis of a report presented by the Ad Hoc Advisory Group, adopted **resolution 1999/11**, by which it called on the Secretary-General to take steps to develop on a priority basis a long-term strategy and programme of support for Haiti. It also called on the General Assembly to review all aspects of the mandate and operations of MICIVIH, and to consider devising a UN special training and technical assistance programme for HNP. Also on 31 July [A/54/274-E/1999/116], a similar letter was submitted by the ESC President to the General Assembly.

On 20 August [E/1999/117-S/1999/905], the President of the Security Council informed the ESC President that, in order to ensure sustainable development in Haiti, the effort of the international community had to be geared towards supporting the Government in addressing the capacity-building of its governmental institutions.

Report of Secretary-General (August). On 24 August [S/1999/908], the Secretary-General described the activities of MIPONUH and developments in the mission area since May and presented recommendations on a possible transition to other forms of international assistance to HNP following the expiration of MIPONUH's mandate, as requested by the Security Council in resolution 1212(1998).

The period under review was marked by continuing negotiations, interrupted by repeated discord, and slow progress between the political parties and the Government on how to continue to provide essential services, such as police and customs services, and how to further the cause of democracy through the organization of legislative and municipal elections. No agreement had been reached on how to alleviate the legislators' loss of power, the result of President Préval's 11 January declaration on the expiration of their mandate (see p. 209). On 24 May, Prime Minister Alexis presented his Government Action Plan, outlining in detail the priorities and resource allocations for each of the 15 government ministries. The plan was well received by some political parties.

Since May, a few highly visible developments and incidents had heightened the perception of an increase in public insecurity. On 28 May, police officers allegedly killed 11 detainees in Port-au-Prince. The Secretary-General's Representative called for the immediate suspension of any officer suspected of involvement. The authorities arrested four police officers and a special commission was established to investigate the crime further. A number of violent street demonstrations had also taken place.

The newly established CEP conducted in-depth consultations to organize local and legislative elections. On 11 June, CEP announced that it had drafted an electoral text to replace the Electoral Law of 1995. Although that action had elicited favourable comments from a large number of political parties, President Préval expressed reservations about it. On 16 July, the President and the Prime Minister, on behalf of the Government, signed an electoral law, which CEP had modified to reflect the President's concerns. The tentative date for the first round of elections was set for mid-December 1999, although it was later changed to March 2000 (see p. 213). Donor countries had pledged to assist with the election costs.

Police training procedures were designed to facilitate the transition to the post-MIPONUH era. As part of that process, and in order to enable HNP to pursue its professionalization without interruption, efforts were made to install technical advisers as counterparts to key police officers before the expiration of the Mission's mandate. A draft schedule by the MIPONUH civilian police Commissioner proposing the deployment of advisers (32 from the United Nations, 17 from the Canadian International Development Agency, 12 from the United States International Criminal Investigative Training Assistance Programme, and 1 from the French bilateral programme) was reviewed by donor representatives during a coordination meeting on 13 July and was being considered by the Director-General of HNP and other participants in police training in Haiti.

HNP continued to be the target of criticism from a number of political actors, who had called for the resignation of high-ranking security officials. Numerous demonstrations had dramatized calls for changes in the police hierarchy. In addition to accusations of involvement in extrajudicial killings and reports of ill-treatment during arrests and interrogations, HNP addressed allegations of involvement in drug trafficking.

Developments in the justice system were uneven. On 21 May, a Court for Minors was inaugurated, which constituted an important element in judicial institution-building. Conditions had improved at the National Penitentiary but overcrowding and poor infrastructure were reported in the majority of prisons. A considerable number of detainees continued to be held in prolonged pre-trial detention in violation of international treaties ratified by Haiti. The prison administration continued to receive technical assistance from UNDP. The Office of the Ombudsman had indicated that, to the extent permitted by its budgetary and human resources, it would strive to carry out some of the services previously provided by MICIVIH. In June, the Special Rapporteur of the Commission on Human Rights on violence against women visited Haiti (see PART TWO, Chapter II).

UNDP launched, in June 1999, a technical assistance project to assist CEP in organizing the local and legislative elections. An inter-agency meeting (Barahona, Dominican Republic, 20-21 May), attended by UN country teams from Haiti and the Dominican Republic, discussed operational arrangements for a more coordinated intervention on both sides of the border, with a focus on migration and human rights.

Within the context of devising a post-MIPONUH support programme, HNP continued to develop a two-year technical assistance programme that foresaw the recruitment of international police advisers to work throughout Haiti with HNP. Subject to the availability of resources, police advisers would continue to assist the Government with the training and professionalization of HNP. The Secretary-General said that it would appear appropriate to review the extent to which some of the functions exercised by MIPONUH and MICIVIH could be combined in one integrated mission. He added that the new mission could discharge responsibilities in the areas of human rights monitoring and institution-building to provide support to both the justice sector and HNP. The Economic and Social Council recommended the continued presence in Haiti of an office of a representative of the Secretary-General to continue his good offices and to manage any new civilian mission mandated by the United Nations. Following the expiration of MIPONUH's mandate, such an office could help the Government with the transition from the Security Council–mandated assistance to a new model of police development in the context of the continuing consolidation of democracy. In addition, the office would manage any new UN civilian mission, facilitate continuing dialogue among key actors in Haiti and the international community, support the democratization process, help to mobilize international political and financial support for Haiti and provide the political framework and focal point for integrating and coordinating the activities of the international community.

The Secretary-General observed that the international community should support CEP's aspiration to have a new legislature in place by 10 January 2000, even though it was unlikely that both rounds of elections could be held before the end of 1999. At the same time, the security situation in Haiti remained a matter of concern. In order to avoid further deterioration in the months leading to the elections, a coordinated effort by the Government, the police service and Haiti's political and civil leaders was required.

Communications (September). On 10 September [S/1999/969], the Secretary-General informed the President of the Security Council that following consultations he intended to appoint Alfredo Lopes Cabral (Guinea-Bissau) to succeed Julian Harston (United Kingdom) as his Representative in Haiti and head of MIPONUH. On 14 September [S/1999/970], the Council took note of the Secretary-General's intention.

Further reports of Secretary-General. On 18 November [S/1999/1184], the Secretary-General described the activities of MIPONUH and developments in the mission area since his August report. He stated that preparations for the next legislative and local elections had continued to lag, violent crime had not diminished and HNP had been the target of renewed attacks. On 29 September, despite an initial proposal by CEP to hold the elections in November and December 1999, the Government, following discussions between President Préval and CEP, announced 19 March 2000 as the date for the first round of legislative elections. In the official electoral timetable published on 6 October, CEP set 30 April 2000 as the date for the second round of elections, which would make it impossible for a new Parliament to be in place by the second week of January, as stipulated in the Constitution. A new electoral alliance of right-wing parties, the Front civico-politique haïtien, was formed on 15 September, while the Espace de concertation formally presented itself as an electoral alliance on 20 September. The security situation was characterized by continuing demonstrations, blockades and incidents of violence, some of which were related to discontent over the country's dire economic situation and difficult living conditions.

In the area of police training, MIPONUH had attained the objectives established for it by the Director-General of HNP. In view of the planned departure of the Mission at the end of November, the emphasis had shifted to the training of the trainers to prepare HNP for the post-MIPONUH period. CIVPOL had similarly continued to discharge its mentoring responsibilities, which focused on the fight against capital crimes and drug trafficking, as well as on the maintenance of law and order and logistics and administration.

Seven working groups were established in September by the Ministry of Justice and Public Security to work on judicial reform and draft legislation. Despite financial limitations, the Office of the Ombudsman opened its first regional office on 5 November and announced that its second one would open at the beginning of January 2000. The Office reported that, from its inception in November 1997 to the end of 1998, it had received almost 300 complaints, including 35 concerning HNP and 35 related to the judicial system. The Ombudsman observed that the institution was not well known among the population and recommended a more active presence in the field to reinforce its activities.

As to the formulation of a long-term programme of development and assistance for Haiti, the first step in implementing Economic and Social Council resolution 1999/11 was the launching of a common country assessment to conduct an in-depth analysis of the country's strategic development sectors and to identify priorities for social and economic development. New activities by resident agencies intensified and UNDP continued to support developing cooperation efforts. Regarding support to Haiti after 30 November, the Government had taken the lead in exploring possible modalities for the strengthening and effective functioning of HNP. Senior police officials had presided over a series of meetings with representatives of the international donor community to develop a strategy for Government-donor cooperation built on the concept of a core of police advisers to be provided by the United Nations and bilateral donors. Parallel to those efforts, a needs assessment mission visited Haiti (11-15 October) to prepare the ground for the future UN presence (see below). Consultations between the Government, the Friends of Haiti, the Secretary-General's Representative, the UN resident coordinator and the MICIVIH Executive Director, as well as an Economic and Social Council delegation that visited Haiti, had facilitated planning for the new and integrated mission. An 8 November letter from President Préval to the Secretary-General, requesting an institutional support mission, whose members would be neither uniformed nor armed, to support democracy, strengthen the judiciary and professionalize HNP, was annexed to the report.

The Secretary-General observed that challenges in planning the next elections, including registering some 4 million eligible voters, conducting effective civic education programmes and distributing electoral materials, required the active support of CEP by the Government and the international community. Responsibility for ensuring a peaceful and secure environment prior to and during the elections rested with the Haitian authorities, in particular the political leaders and HNP.

The Secretary-General said that, in pursuance of Security Council resolution 1212(1998), he was preparing to withdraw MIPONUH following the expiration of its mandate on 30 November, unless the Council decided otherwise. An appropriate repatriation schedule for the civilian police contingent was being prepared. He stressed that the assistance of the international community in the process of democratization, professionalization of the police and reinforcement of the justice system would continue to be necessary.

In a later report [S/2000/150], the Secretary-General stated that the Security Council, by **resolution 1277(1999)** (see p. 215), had decided to continue MIPONUH in order to ensure a phased transition to an International Civilian Support Mission in Haiti (MICAH) by 15 March 2000. The Secretary-General had been requested to coordinate and expedite the transition from MIPONUH and MICIVIH to MICAH.

The period from mid-November to early December was marked by the expulsion of more than 20,000 migrant workers of Haitian nationality or descent from the Dominican Republic. The situation stirred up public sentiment and led to some calls for the restoration of the Haitian armed forces. Negotiations between the two countries led to the signature on 2 December of an accord providing, among other things, for the humane treatment of repatriates and requiring the Government of the Dominican Republic to give advance notification of any future expulsion plans to their Haitian counterparts. The pre-electoral registration process started on 15 November and was completed on 12 December.

In December 1999, jury trials were held in several jurisdictions in the country after a long period of interruption, thereby suggesting an increased commitment by the authorities to restoring the credibility and confidence of the people in the judicial system.

Needs assessment mission. A needs assessment mission, led by the UN Department of Political Affairs in cooperation with the Department of Peacekeeping Operations, visited Haiti (11-15 October) [A/54/629]. The mission envisaged the establishment of a new integrated UN mission that would combine some of the functions of MIPONUH and MICIVIH to assist the Government of Haiti in the areas of human rights monitoring and institution-building.

The assessment mission proposed main objectives and plans of action, as well as activities, for improving the climate of respect for human rights and reinforcing the institutional effectiveness of the police and the judiciary. The implementation of the mission's recommendations would require resources estimated at approximately $24 million, of which $10 million would need to be funded from the regular budget and $14 million from voluntary contributions, the latter in respect of the technical assistance component of the programme.

SECURITY COUNCIL ACTION

On 30 November [meeting 4074], the Security Council adopted **resolution 1277(1999)** by vote (14-0-1). The draft [S/1999/1202] was sponsored by Argentina, Brazil, Canada, France, the United States and Venezuela.

The Security Council,

Recalling all its relevant resolutions, in particular resolution 1212(1998) of 25 November 1998, and those adopted by the General Assembly and the Economic and Social Council,

Taking note of the letter dated 8 November 1999 from the President of the Republic of Haiti to the Secretary-General, requesting the establishment of an international civilian support mission in Haiti,

Taking note also of the reports of the Secretary-General of 24 August and 18 November 1999,

Commending the valuable contributions of the Representative of the Secretary-General, the United Nations Civilian Police Mission in Haiti, the International Civilian Mission in Haiti and the technical assistance programmes of the United Nations Development Programme and bilateral donors, in assisting the Government of Haiti by supporting and contributing to the professionalization of the Haitian National Police Force as an integral element of the consolidation of Haiti's system of justice, as well as by their efforts in developing national institutions,

Recognizing that the people and Government of Haiti bear the ultimate responsibility for national reconciliation, the maintenance of a secure and stable environment, the administration of justice and the reconstruction of their country, and that the Government of Haiti bears particular responsibility for the further strengthening and effective functioning of the Haitian National Police Force and the justice system,

1. *Decides* to continue the United Nations Civilian Police Mission in Haiti in order to ensure a phased transition to an International Civilian Support Mission in Haiti by 15 March 2000;

2. *Requests* the Secretary-General to coordinate and expedite the transition from the United Nations Civilian Police Mission in Haiti and the International Civilian Mission in Haiti to the International Civilian Support Mission in Haiti and to report to the Security Council on the implementation of the present resolution by 1 March 2000;

3. *Decides* to remain seized of the matter.

VOTE ON RESOLUTION 1277(1999):

In favour: Argentina, Bahrain, Brazil, Canada, China, France, Gabon, Gambia, Malaysia, Namibia, Netherlands, Slovenia, United Kingdom, United States.

Against: None.

Abstaining: Russian Federation.

The Russian Federation stated that it would abstain from voting on the draft because the Council was in breach of its own decision by extending the Mission's mandate. The fact that in the text the words "to continue" were used instead of "to extend the mandate" did not change the essence of the matter. In addition, President Préval, on 8 November [S/1999/1184], had thanked the United Nations for the work of MIPONUH and had expressed the desire that the new mission be established whose members would be neither uniformed nor armed. That approach was at variance with the draft.

International Civilian Mission to Haiti

On 10 May [A/53/950], the Secretary-General reviewed the situation of human rights and democracy in Haiti and updated the activities of MICIVIH since his November 1998 report [YUN 1998, p. 231]. The Mission continued to cooperate with MIPONUH, which in turn provided MICIVIH with logistical and administrative support. MICIVIH, a joint UN/OAS Mission, was established in 1993 [YUN 1993, p. 338] to verify full observance of human rights and fundamental freedoms, provide institution-building and support the development of a programme to promote and protect human rights.

Monitoring the human rights dimension of police conduct continued to be one of the most important activities of the Mission. The police had met the challenges of the political crisis—a concerted campaign of denigration against HNP leadership, numerous demonstrations and spates of armed crimes—in a professional manner. Police authorities had yet to take broad, effective action to reduce beatings and other forms of ill-treatment. Statistics regarding such allegations fluctuated, though figures for 1998 (423) showed a marked increase, compared to 1997 (284). Inquiries by the General Inspectorate and by HNP's General Directorate led to the dismissal of 288 police officers by the end of 1998. Forty-one police officers were being detained on drug-trafficking charges as of the beginning of April 1999. By and large, the judiciary was slow to prosecute complaints of human rights violations allegedly committed by police officers, though there had been a few exceptions. Self-appointed vigilante brigades and other informal police aides had been operating in the capital and in some rural areas. At the same time, MICIVIH, in coordination with MIPONUH, continued to train police officers on human rights and conflict resolution.

As of March, MICIVIH had recorded a total prison population of some 3,665 detainees, which resulted in overcrowding and poor infrastructure in some detention facilities. A code of conduct for prison guards and a set of internal regulations that had been pending since 1997 had still not been approved or implemented, though some steps had been taken to hold prison guards accountable for abuses. The Mission strengthened its working ties with the unit which supervised those legal assistants assigned to identify cases of illegal detention, prolonged pre-trial detention, miscalculation of prison sentences and other serious irregularities in prison dossiers, with a view to seeking solutions.

Though the period under review revealed no signs of overall progress in the judicial system, MICIVIH continued its monitoring and technical support activities. The Justice Minister had requested MICIVIH's assistance on matters related to impunity and compensation and the defining of short-term priorities. In response to the latter request, MICIVIH transmitted a document calling for, among other things, the development of the Ecole de la magistrature into a proper training school for judges; the development of a police and judicial criminal investigation capacity; the implementation of the 1998 strategic plan for judicial reform [YUN 1998, p. 227]; and the establishment of a functioning judicial inspectorate to closely supervise judicial work as one of the fundamental steps towards improving judicial performances.

The Mission's human rights promotion programmes were greatly reduced, pending the start of a new budget year and a review of its activities. MICIVIH, nevertheless, continued to distribute information through documentaries and a monthly bulletin. A major focus had been the development of a pilot programme of seminars on human rights, women's rights and civic education with the State Secretariat for Literacy. The Mission continued to work with local human rights organizations, mainly in terms of training, to assist in strengthening their capacity for human rights monitoring. The consolidation of a network of committees set up, with MICIVIH assistance, to monitor prisons and police custody cells remained a priority, particularly in the light of the Mission's eventual departure.

The Secretary-General concluded that, given the adverse consequences of the protracted crisis in Haiti, it was apparent that much still remained to be accomplished prior to the Mission's withdrawal with regard to the strengthening of State institutions and civil society organizations.

On 6 August [A/54/211], the Secretary-General updated the General Assembly on developments concerning MICIVIH. He said that the OAS Secretary-General on 4 June had informed him that, owing to financial constraints, a reduction of the OAS component of MICIVIH was necessary. As at 1 July, OAS had withdrawn 34 members of its personnel and only one OAS contracted staff, the Executive Director, remained. As a result, five of MICIVIH's nine regional offices had been closed since that date. Discussions between the United Nations and OAS focused on the payment by OAS of its share of the joint expenses incurred up to the time of the reduction of OAS personnel, and the new modalities of cooperation, including financial arrangements, for the remaining period of the MICIVIH mandate, on the basis of a significantly reduced OAS component. The United Nations and OAS nevertheless agreed to continue their cooperation in MICIVIH as a joint mission. The UN Secretary-General believed that the joint mission would be able to carry out its core activities at a meaningful, though reduced, level. It was therefore envisaged that the UN component of MICIVIH would remain at the same authorized level for the duration of its mandate. Since much remained to be accomplished in Haiti with regard to the strengthening of State institutions and civil society organizations, the Secretary-General called on the Assembly to renew the mandate of the UN component of the Mission.

On 22 November [A/54/625], the Secretary-General reviewed the activities of MICIVIH since May.

The milieu in which HNP operated during the period was marked by violent street demonstrations, armed crime and public pressure to act against criminals, as well as political pressures, threats and attacks against police officers. Against that background, the human rights situation deteriorated sharply. HNP remained a fragile institution, weakened by internal shortcomings (administrative, disciplinary and operational) and external pressures (ebbing public support and an aggressive campaign by the political movement Fanmi Lavalas against its leadership). The sudden resignation of the Secretary of State for Public Security in early October and the assassination of the person rumoured to replace him brought to the forefront questions about the capacity of HNP to provide effective security during the election period. The credibility and reputation of HNP were damaged by accusations that it was allegedly responsible for the summary execution of 11 individuals arrested in the Carrefour-Feuilles area in the outskirts of Port-au-Prince on 28 May. Following initial investigations, seven policemen were detained in connection with that crime. The executions were among 50 killings allegedly caused by the police between April and early June 1999, more than the total for the whole of 1998.

The shortcomings and systemic weaknesses that plagued the functioning of the judicial system were most apparent in the areas of respect for judicial procedures and in the preparation of cases for trial. In order to address those problems, in August MICIVIH presented updated lists of detainees held in pre-trial detention since 1995 and 1996. The Mission's suggestion to establish a commission to study the long-outstanding cases was adopted by the Minister of Justice. In other action, MICIVIH helped prepare a draft agreement under which an institution for juveniles run by a priest and the Ministries of Justice and of Social Affairs would work together on literacy and trade training programmes for women and juveniles.

On 28 September, MICIVIH published its report on impunity and compensation, which analysed legal proceedings related to the prosecution of human rights abuses that had occurred during the coup d'état period (September 1991 to October 1994), looked at initiatives by the Government, civil society organizations and the international community in response to the issue of impunity and compensation and concluded with a wide range of recommendations. The Government announced that it would create a commission of judges to investigate serious human rights violations, in particular three massacres with strong symbolic value attributed to security forces.

MICIVIH's programme of human rights promotion and advocacy was severely disrupted by the downsizing of the Mission, as a consequence of which many of its training and seminar programmes were suspended. As the reduced Mission moved closer to the end of its mandate, its work focused increasingly on developing and carrying out projects in partnership with government ministries, organizing training-of-trainer courses, reinforcing the capacity of local NGOs and working with a network of committees set up to monitor prisons and police custody. Some 40 members of human rights organizations from throughout the country took part in a seminar from 8 to 13 November, organized by MICIVIH on behalf of the Office of the United Nations High Commissioner for Human Rights, the aim of which was to deepen the participants' theoretical and practical knowledge of national and international human rights mechanisms, recourses and themes. One of the Mission's major projects was the completion of a video documentary, entitled *A Work in Progress: Human Rights in Haiti,* the Creole version of which was launched on 30 September.

The Secretary-General observed that Haiti had reached a critical juncture, with a political and security climate that was far from conducive to launching the electoral process. The persistent professional and ethical shortcomings of a yet to be reformed judicial system continued to be a source of endemic due process violations, as well as an obstacle to the police's performance in the area of law and order. Despite improvements in the penal system and the conditions of detention, formidable obstacles remained. New State institutions, such as the Office of the Ombudsman, remained embryonic and required the support of the State and of the international community with regard to their unmet resource needs and institutional development. MICIVIH had helped put in place some of the essential building blocks of the rule of law through its activities. However, Haiti was still in the early stages of transition towards a full-fledged democracy. There remained a number of areas in which the United Nations could continue to provide support in response to the request of Haitian authorities for assistance in strengthening institutions and civil society. The Secretary-General called on the General Assembly to consider the establishment of a new mission to consolidate the gains achieved by the Haitians with the support of MIPONUH and MICIVIH. By **resolution 54/193** (see p. 218), the Assembly approved the establishment of the new mission, the International Civilian Support Mission in Haiti, to consolidate the results achieved by MIPONUH, MICIVIH and previous UN missions.

International Civilian Support Mission in Haiti

In November [A/C.5/54/38], the Secretary-General submitted the programme budget implications for the extension of the MICIVIH mandate for the first part of 2000 and the subsequent establishment of the International Civilian Support Mission in Haiti (MICAH) until 6 February 2001. He recalled General Assembly resolution 53/206 [YUN 1998, p. 1284], which had decided that a provision of $86,200,000 should be reflected in the proposed programme budget for the biennium 2000-2001 for special political missions. Accordingly, should the Assembly decide to extend MICIVIH's mandate and establish MICAH, the estimated requirements from the UN regular budget of $10,353,200 ($9,173,100 for MICAH and $1,180,100 for MICIVIH) would be charged against the $86,200,000 provision. It was also estimated that $14,734,200 from extrabudgetary resources would be required to support the technical assistance component.

In December [A/54/659], ACABQ said that the total estimated resource requirements to be funded from the regular budget and from extrabudgetary resources might not be sufficient to cover all the potential requirements identified in the report of the needs assessment mission (see p. 215).

GENERAL ASSEMBLY ACTION

On 17 December [meeting 84], the General Assembly adopted **resolution 54/193** [draft: A/54/L.36] without vote [agenda item 48].

International Civilian Support Mission in Haiti

The General Assembly,

Recalling all its relevant resolutions, in particular its resolution 53/95 of 8 December 1998 on the situation of democracy and human rights in Haiti,

Taking note of Security Council resolution 1212(1998) of 25 November 1998, in which the Council decided to extend the mandate of the United Nations Civilian Police Mission in Haiti until 30 November 1999 and, in particular, paragraph 11, in which the Secretary-General was requested to make recommendations on a viable transition to other forms of international assistance,

Having considered the report presented by the Ad Hoc Advisory Group on Haiti to the Economic and Social Council and the recommendations contained therein, and noting with satisfaction the contribution made by the Economic and Social Council,

Welcoming Economic and Social Council resolution 1999/11 of 27 July 1999, in which the Economic and Social Council, inter alia, emphasized the need to establish the necessary mechanisms to develop on a priority basis a long-term strategy and programme of support for Haiti,

Taking note of the relevant resolutions adopted on the question by the Organization of American States, commending the contribution of the organization to the International Civilian Mission in Haiti, and inviting the organization to pursue its cooperation with the United Nations in Haiti,

Taking into account the recommendations of the Secretary-General contained in his reports on the United Nations Civilian Police Mission in Haiti to the Security Council and in his reports to the General Assembly on the International Civilian Mission in Haiti and on the needs assessment mission,

Recognizing the efforts made by the Secretary-General, his representatives, the Organization of American States and its Secretary-General and the group of Friends of the Secretary-General on Haiti and their constant support and contribution to the continuing consolidation of the political, economic and social institutions in Haiti, and supporting fully the efforts already undertaken by the Civilian Mission and the Civilian Police Mission, as well as those by individual Member States,

Encouraged by the efforts made by the people and the Government of Haiti to consolidate democracy and to improve respect for human rights and the rule of law,

Recognizing that the people and the Government of Haiti bear the ultimate responsibility for the reconstruction of their country, in particular for national reconciliation and the maintenance of a secure and stable environment, and taking note of the plan of action developed by the Haitian Government, in particular for the administration of justice,

Taking note of the request of 8 November 1999 from the President of Haiti to the Secretary-General,

1. *Affirms* the will of the United Nations to continue to accompany Haiti in its democratic, economic and social development, in particular during the next crucial period;

2. *Decides*, at the request of the President of Haiti, to establish the International Civilian Support Mission in Haiti to consolidate the results achieved by the International Civilian Mission in Haiti, the United Nations Civilian Police Mission in Haiti and previous United Nations missions;

3. *Also decides* that the initial mandate of the International Civilian Support Mission in Haiti will begin at the closing of the United Nations Civilian Police Mission in Haiti and continue until 6 February 2001 and that the mandate of the International Civilian Mission in Haiti will continue until the commencement of the International Civilian Support Mission in Haiti;

4. *Further decides* that the personnel and goods of the International Civilian Mission in Haiti and the United Nations Civilian Police Mission in Haiti will be transferred to the International Civilian Support Mission in Haiti, as needed;

5. *Decides*, pursuant to the request of the Government of Haiti, that the International Civilian Support Mission in Haiti shall have, in accordance with the recommendations of the Secretary-General, the following mandate:

(a) To support the democratization process and assist the Haitian authorities with the development of democratic institutions;

(b) To assist the Haitian authorities in the reform and the strengthening of the Haitian system of justice, including its penal institutions, and to promote the Office of the Ombudsman;

(c) To support the efforts of the Government of Haiti to professionalize the Haitian National Police through a special training and technical assistance programme and help the Government to coordinate bilateral and multilateral aid in this area;

(d) To support the efforts of the Government of Haiti aimed at the full observance of human rights and fundamental freedoms;

(e) To provide technical assistance for the organization of democratic elections and to collaborate with the Government of Haiti in the coordination of bilateral and multilateral assistance;

6. *Underlines* the importance of full coordination and transparency, including among multilateral and bilateral contributors, and, in this regard, decides that the Representative of the Secretary-General and head of the Mission will have overall authority over all United Nations activities in Haiti and, as appropriate, act as the focal point for coordinating the activities of the international community and facilitating its continuing dialogue with key political and social actors in Haiti, assisted by a committee of representatives of police contributors and international donors and in close liaison with the Government of Haiti;

7. *Endorses* the recommendations of the Economic and Social Council contained in resolution 1999/11,

inter alia, its request that the Secretary-General take the necessary steps, in agreement with the Government of Haiti, and making use of the appropriate United Nations presence there, to develop on a priority basis a long-term strategy and programme of support for Haiti;

8. *Recommends* that the United Nations Resident Coordinator continue to be the Deputy to the Representative of the Secretary-General, that continued use be made of the resident coordinator system, including completion of a Common Country Assessment, and that preparations be made for the United Nations Development Assistance Framework in order to contribute to the establishment of an effective development programme involving all relevant organizations in the United Nations system;

9. *Requests* the Secretary-General to coordinate with the Government of Haiti and interested Member States on modalities to ensure support from the international community for the electoral processes under way in Haiti, and, in this regard, requests the United Nations Development Programme to continue its work relating to support of the Haitian electoral processes;

10. *Authorizes* the Secretary-General to utilize the amounts allocated in the regular budget for the International Civilian Mission in Haiti, under its current mandate, for activities undertaken by the International Civilian Support Mission in Haiti;

11. *Requests* the Secretary-General to establish a trust fund for the Mission, and invites Member States to make voluntary contributions, which will cover additional costs for the implementation of its mandate;

12. *Also requests* the Secretary-General to submit a report on the Mission to the General Assembly every four months;

13. *Decides* to include in the provisional agenda of its fifty-fifth session the item entitled "The situation of democracy and human rights in Haiti".

In **resolution 54/187** (see PART TWO, Chapter I), the Assembly called on the Government of Haiti to ensure the necessary political and security environment to hold free and fair elections and to continue structural reforms in the police and the judicial system, as well as the prison sector.

Financing of missions

In January [A/53/789], the Secretary-General submitted the revised budget for the maintenance of MIPONUH for the period from 1 July 1998 to 30 June 1999, amounting to $29,994,700 gross ($28,562,700 net), excluding budgetary voluntary contributions in kind totalling $3,428,400. Of that amount, $12,290,015 gross ($11,603,615 net) represented the additional requirements resulting from the continuation of the Mission's mandate and for some transportation, data-processing and other equipment that was not included previously.

In February [A/53/846], ACABQ recommended that the General Assembly approve the appropriation and assessment of $12,264,015 gross ($11,577,615 net) for the period from 1 July 1998 to 30 June 1999, in addition to $17,704,685 gross ($16,959,085 net) that had been appropriated and assessed under Assembly resolution 52/246 [YUN 1998, p. 234]. In a letter of 9 February, annexed to the report, ACABQ's Chairman authorized the Secretary-General to enter into additional commitments in the amount of $3,000,000 for MIPONUH's maintenance for the same period.

GENERAL ASSEMBLY ACTION (April)

On 7 April [meeting 97], the General Assembly, on the recommendation of the Fifth Committee [A/53/873], adopted **resolution 53/222 A** without vote [agenda item 141].

Financing of the United Nations Support Mission in Haiti, the United Nations Transition Mission in Haiti and the United Nations Civilian Police Mission in Haiti

The General Assembly,

Having considered the report of the Secretary-General on the financing of the United Nations Support Mission in Haiti, the United Nations Transition Mission in Haiti and the United Nations Civilian Police Mission in Haiti and the related report of the Advisory Committee on Administrative and Budgetary Questions,

Bearing in mind Security Council resolutions 1063(1996) of 28 June 1996, by which the Council established the United Nations Support Mission in Haiti, and 1086(1996) of 5 December 1996, by which the Council extended the mandate of the Mission until 31 July 1997,

Bearing in mind also Security Council resolution 1123(1997) of 30 July 1997, by which the Council established the United Nations Transition Mission in Haiti for a single four-month period,

Bearing in mind further Security Council resolutions 1141(1997) of 28 November 1997, by which the Council established the United Nations Civilian Police Mission in Haiti, and 1212(1998) of 25 November 1998, by which the Council extended the mandate of the Mission until 30 November 1999,

Recalling its resolution 51/15 A of 4 November 1996 on the financing of the Support Mission and its subsequent decisions and resolutions thereon, the latest of which was resolution 52/246 of 26 June 1998,

Reaffirming that the costs of the Missions are expenses of the Organization to be borne by Member States in accordance with Article 17, paragraph 2, of the Charter of the United Nations,

Recalling its previous decisions regarding the fact that, in order to meet the expenditures caused by the Missions, a different procedure is required from that applied to meet expenditures of the regular budget of the United Nations,

Taking into account the fact that the economically more developed countries are in a position to make relatively larger contributions and that the economically less developed countries have a relatively limited capacity to contribute towards such an operation,

Bearing in mind the special responsibilities of the States permanent members of the Security Council, as indicated in General Assembly resolution 1874(S-IV) of 27 June 1963, in the financing of such operations,

Noting with appreciation that voluntary contributions have been made to the Missions by certain Governments,

Mindful of the fact that it is essential to provide the Missions with the necessary financial resources to enable them to fulfil their responsibilities under the relevant resolutions of the Security Council,

1. *Takes note* of the status of contributions to the United Nations Support Mission in Haiti, the United Nations Transition Mission in Haiti and the United Nations Civilian Police Mission in Haiti as at 28 February 1999, including the contributions outstanding in the amount of 17.9 million United States dollars, representing 20 per cent of the total assessed contributions from the inception of the Support Mission to the period ending 30 June 1999, notes that some 37 per cent of the Member States have paid their assessed contributions in full, and urges all other Member States concerned, in particular those in arrears, to ensure the payment of their outstanding assessed contributions;

2. *Expresses concern* about the financial situation of the Organization, in particular with regard to reimbursements to troop contributors, which bear additional burdens owing to overdue payments by Member States of their assessments;

3. *Expresses its appreciation* to those Member States which have paid their assessed contributions in full;

4. *Urges* all other Member States to make every possible effort to ensure payment of their assessed contributions to the Missions in full and on time;

5. *Endorses* the observations and recommendations contained in the report of the Advisory Committee on Administrative and Budgetary Questions;

6. *Requests* the Secretary-General to take all necessary action to ensure that the Civilian Police Mission is administered with a maximum of efficiency and economy;

7. *Also requests* the Secretary-General, in order to reduce the cost of employing General Service staff, to continue efforts to recruit local staff for the Civilian Police Mission against General Service posts, commensurate with the requirements of the Mission;

8. *Decides* to appropriate the amount of 12,264,015 dollars gross (11,577,615 dollars net) for the maintenance of the Civilian Police Mission for the period from 1 July 1998 to 30 June 1999, in addition to the amount of 17,704,685 dollars gross (16,959,085 dollars net) already appropriated under the terms of General Assembly resolution 52/246 and inclusive of the amount of 3 million dollars gross and net authorized by the Advisory Committee under the terms of section IV of Assembly resolution 49/233 A of 23 December 1994;

9. *Decides also,* as an ad hoc arrangement, and taking into account the amount of 17,704,685 dollars gross (16,959,085 dollars net) already apportioned in accordance with its resolution 52/246, to apportion among Member States the additional amount of 12,264,015 dollars gross (11,577,615 dollars net) for the period from 1 July 1998 to 30 June 1999, in accordance with the composition of groups set out in paragraphs 3 and 4 of General Assembly resolution 43/232 of 1 March 1989, as adjusted by the Assembly in its resolutions 44/192 B of 21 December 1989, 45/269 of 27 August 1991, 46/198 A of 20 December 1991, 47/218 A of 23 December 1992, 49/249 A of 20 July 1995, 49/249 B of 14 September 1995, 50/224 of 11 April 1996, 51/218 A to C of 18 December 1996 and 52/230 of 31 March 1998 and its decisions 48/472 A of 23 December 1993 and 50/451 B of 23 December 1995, and taking into account the scale of assessments for the years 1998 and 1999, as set out in its resolution 52/215 A of 22 December 1997;

10. *Decides further* that, in accordance with the provisions of its resolution 973(X) of 15 December 1955, there shall be set off against the apportionment among Member States, as provided for in paragraph 9 above, their respective share in the Tax Equalization Fund of the estimated additional staff assessment income of 686,400 dollars approved for the Civilian Police Mission for the period from 1 July 1998 to 30 June 1999;

11. *Invites* voluntary contributions to the Civilian Police Mission in cash and in the form of services and supplies acceptable to the Secretary-General, to be administered, as appropriate, in accordance with the procedure and practices established by the General Assembly;

12. *Decides* to keep under review during its fifty-third session the agenda item entitled "Financing of the United Nations Support Mission in Haiti, the United Nations Transition Mission in Haiti and the United Nations Civilian Police Mission in Haiti".

In January [A/53/789/Add.1], the Secretary-General presented the proposed budget for the period from 1 July 1999 to 30 June 2000 for the maintenance of MIPONUH from 1 July to 30 November 1999 and for the liquidation of the Mission from 1 December 1999 to 30 June 2000, which amounted to $19,246,400 gross ($18,223,200 net), including budgeted voluntary contributions in kind amounting to $1,714,200.

In April [A/53/895/Add.7], ACABQ recommended, with regard to the Secretary-General's 1998 report on the financing of the United Nations Support Mission in Haiti (UNSMIH), the United Nations Transition Mission in Haiti (UNTMIH) and MIPONUH [YUN 1998, p. 235], that the unencumbered balance of $906,800 gross ($865,200 net) for the period from 1 July 1997 to 30 June 1998 be credited to Member States in a manner to be determined by the Assembly. In addition, it recommended that the special arrangements for the application of article IV of the financial regulations of the United Nations, approved for UNSMIH in Assembly resolution 51/15 B [YUN 1997, p. 188], be applied to UNTMIH and MIPONUH. With regard to the Secretary-General's report on the financing of MIPONUH from 1 July 1999 to 30 June 2000, the Committee recommended that the Assembly approve the proposed appropriation and assessment of $17,532,200 gross ($16,509,000 net) for the maintenance and liquidation of the Mission.

GENERAL ASSEMBLY ACTION (June and December)

On 8 June [meeting 101], the General Assembly, on the recommendation of the Fifth Committee [A/53/873/Add.1], adopted **resolution 53/222 B** without vote [agenda item 141].

Financing of the United Nations Support Mission in Haiti, the United Nations Transition Mission in Haiti and the United Nations Civilian Police Mission in Haiti

The General Assembly,

Having considered the reports of the Secretary-General on the financing of the United Nations Support Mission in Haiti, the United Nations Transition Mission in Haiti and the United Nations Civilian Police Mission in Haiti and the related reports of the Advisory Committee on Administrative and Budgetary Questions,

Bearing in mind Security Council resolutions 1063(1996) of 28 June 1996, by which the Council established the United Nations Support Mission in Haiti, and 1086(1996) of 5 December 1996, by which the Council extended the mandate of the Mission until 31 July 1997,

Bearing in mind also Security Council resolution 1123(1997) of 30 July 1997, by which the Council established the United Nations Transition Mission in Haiti for a single four-month period,

Bearing in mind further Security Council resolutions 1141(1997) of 28 November 1997, by which the Council established the United Nations Civilian Police Mission in Haiti, and 1212(1998) of 25 November 1998, by which the Council extended the mandate of the Mission until 30 November 1999,

Recalling its resolution 51/15 A of 4 November 1996 on the financing of the Support Mission and its subsequent decisions and resolutions thereon, the latest of which was resolution 53/222 A of 7 April 1999,

Reaffirming that the costs of the Missions are expenses of the Organization to be borne by Member States in accordance with Article 17, paragraph 2, of the Charter of the United Nations,

Recalling its previous decisions regarding the fact that, in order to meet the expenditures caused by the Missions, a different procedure is required from that applied to meet expenditures of the regular budget of the United Nations,

Taking into account the fact that the economically more developed countries are in a position to make relatively larger contributions and that the economically less developed countries have a relatively limited capacity to contribute towards such an operation,

Bearing in mind the special responsibilities of the States permanent members of the Security Council, as indicated in General Assembly resolution 1874(S-IV) of 27 June 1963, in the financing of such operations,

Noting with appreciation that voluntary contributions have been made to the Missions by certain Governments,

Mindful of the fact that it is essential to provide the Missions with the necessary financial resources to enable them to fulfil their responsibilities under the relevant resolutions of the Security Council,

1. *Takes note* of the status of contributions to the United Nations Support Mission in Haiti, the United Nations Transition Mission in Haiti and the United Nations Civilian Police Mission in Haiti as at 30 April 1999, including the contributions outstanding in the amount of 23.8 million United States dollars, representing 21 per cent of the total assessed contributions from the inception of the Support Mission to the period ending 30 June 1999, notes that some 27 per cent of the Member States have paid their assessed contributions in full, and urges all other Member States concerned, in particular those in arrears, to ensure payment of their outstanding assessed contributions;

2. *Expresses concern* about the financial situation with regard to peacekeeping activities, in particular as regards the reimbursement of troop contributors, which bear additional burdens owing to overdue payments by Member States of their assessments;

3. *Expresses its appreciation* to those Member States which have paid their assessed contributions in full;

4. *Urges* all other Member States to make every possible effort to ensure payment of their assessed contributions to the Missions in full and on time;

5. *Endorses* the observations and recommendations contained in the report of the Advisory Committee on Administrative and Budgetary Questions;

6. *Requests* the Secretary-General to take all necessary action to ensure that the Civilian Police Mission is administered with a maximum of efficiency and economy;

7. *Also requests* the Secretary-General, in order to reduce the cost of employing General Service staff, to continue efforts to recruit local staff for the Civilian Police Mission against General Service posts, commensurate with the requirements of the Mission;

8. *Decides,* on an exceptional basis, that the special arrangements approved in its resolution 51/15 B of 13 June 1997 for the Support Mission, with regard to the application of article IV of the financial regulations of the United Nations, whereby appropriations required in respect of obligations owed to Governments providing contingents and/or logistic support to the Support Mission shall be retained beyond the period stipulated under financial regulations 4.3 and 4.4, as set out in the annex to the present resolution, shall be applied to the Transition Mission and the Civilian Police Mission;

9. *Decides also* to appropriate the amount of 18,641,616 dollars gross (17,618,416 dollars net) for the maintenance and liquidation of the Civilian Police Mission for the period from 1 July 1999 to 30 June 2000, inclusive of the amount of 927,537 dollars for the support account for peacekeeping operations and the amount of 181,879 dollars for the United Nations Logistics Base at Brindisi, Italy, to be apportioned as an ad hoc arrangement among Member States, in accordance with the composition of groups set out in paragraphs 3 and 4 of General Assembly resolution 43/232 of 1 March 1989, as adjusted by the Assembly in its resolutions 44/192 B of 21 December 1989, 45/269 of 27 August 1991, 46/198 A of 20 December 1991, 47/218 A of 23 December 1992, 49/249 A of 20 July 1995, 49/249 B of 14 September 1995, 50/224 of 11 April 1996, 51/218 A to C of 18 December 1996 and 52/230 of 31 March 1998 and its decisions 48/472 A of 23 December 1993 and 50/451 B of 23 December 1995, and taking into account the scale of assessments for the years 1999 and 2000, as set out in its resolution 52/215 A of 22 December 1997;

10. *Decides further* that, in accordance with the provisions of its resolution 973(X) of 15 December 1955, there shall be set off against the apportionment among Member States, as provided for in paragraph 9 above, their respective share in the Tax Equalization Fund of the estimated staff assessment income of 1,023,200 dollars approved for the Civilian Police Mission for the period from 1 July 1999 to 30 June 2000;

11. *Decides* that, for Member States that have fulfilled their financial obligations to the Missions, there shall be set off against the apportionment, as provided for in paragraph 9 above, their respective share of the unencumbered balance of 906,800 dollars gross (865,200 dollars net) in respect of the period ending 30 June 1998;

12. *Decides also* that, for Member States that have not fulfilled their financial obligations to the Missions, their share of the unencumbered balance of 906,800 dollars gross (865,200 dollars net) in respect of the period ending 30 June 1998 shall be set off against their outstanding obligations;

13. *Invites* voluntary contributions to the Civilian Police Mission in cash and in the form of services and supplies acceptable to the Secretary-General, to be administered, as appropriate, in accordance with the procedure and practices established by the General Assembly;

14. *Requests* the Secretary-General to include in all future reports, both on budget performance and budget estimates, information on inventory in a standard and simplified format;

15. *Decides* to include in the provisional agenda of its fifty-fourth session the item entitled "Financing of the United Nations Support Mission in Haiti, the United Nations Transition Mission in Haiti and the United Nations Civilian Police Mission in Haiti".

ANNEX

Special arrangements with regard to the application of article IV of the financial regulations of the United Nations

1. At the end of the twelve-month period provided for in financial regulation 4.3, any unliquidated obligations of the financial period in question relating to goods supplied and services rendered by Governments for which claims have been received or which are covered by established reimbursement rates shall be transferred to accounts payable; such accounts shall remain recorded in the Special Account for the United Nations Transition Mission in Haiti and the Civilian Police Mission in Haiti until payment is effected.

2. *(a)* Any other unliquidated obligations of the financial period in question owed to Governments for goods supplied and services rendered, as well as other obligations owed to Governments, for which required claims have not yet been received, shall remain valid for an additional period of four years following the end of the twelve-month period provided for in financial regulation 4.3;

(b) Claims received during this four-year period shall be treated as provided for under paragraph 1 of the present annex, if appropriate;

(c) At the end of the additional four-year period, any unliquidated obligations shall be cancelled and the then remaining balance of any appropriations retained therefor shall be surrendered.

On 23 December, the Assembly decided that the Fifth Committee should continue its consideration of the financing of the United Nations Mission in Haiti (UNMIH), UNSMIH, UNTMIH and MIPONUH at its resumed fifty-fourth (2000) session (**decision 54/462 A**).

On the same date, the Assembly decided that the items on the situation of democracy and human rights in Haiti and the financing of UNMIH, UNSMIH, UNTMIH and MIPONUH remained for consideration at that session (**decision 54/465**).

Other questions

Cuba–United States

Report of Secretary-General. In August [A/54/259], the Secretary-General, in response to General Assembly resolution 53/4 [YUN 1998, p. 236], submitted information received from 58 States, the EU and eight UN organs and specialized agencies on the implementation of the resolution, by which the Assembly had called on States to refrain from unilateral application of economic and trade measures against States, and urged them to repeal or invalidate such measures. The preamble to resolution 53/4 had made particular reference to the Helms-Burton Act, promulgated by the United States in 1996, which had strengthened sanctions against Cuba.

GENERAL ASSEMBLY ACTION

The General Assembly, on 9 November [meeting 50], adopted **resolution 54/21** [draft: A/54/L.11] by recorded vote (155-2-8) [agenda item 33].

Necessity of ending the economic, commercial and financial embargo imposed by the United States of America against Cuba

The General Assembly,

Determined to encourage strict compliance with the purposes and principles enshrined in the Charter of the United Nations,

Reaffirming, among other principles, the sovereign equality of States, non-intervention and non-interference in their internal affairs and freedom of international trade and navigation, which are also enshrined in many international legal instruments,

Recalling the statements of the heads of State or Government at the Ibero-American Summits concerning the need to eliminate the unilateral application of economic and trade measures by one State against another that affect the free flow of international trade,

Concerned about the continued promulgation and application by Member States of laws and regulations, such as that promulgated on 12 March 1996 known as the "Helms-Burton Act", the extraterritorial effects of which affect the sovereignty of other States, the legitimate interests of entities or persons under their jurisdiction and the freedom of trade and navigation,

Taking note of declarations and resolutions of different intergovernmental forums, bodies and Governments that express the rejection by the international community and public opinion of the promulgation and application of regulations of the kind referred to above,

Recalling its resolutions 47/19 of 24 November 1992, 48/16 of 3 November 1993, 49/9 of 26 October 1994, 50/10 of 2 November 1995, 51/17 of 12 November 1996, 52/10 of 5 November 1997 and 53/4 of 4 October 1998,

Concerned that, since the adoption of its resolutions 47/19, 48/16, 49/9, 50/10, 51/17, 52/10 and 53/4, further measures of that nature aimed at strengthening and extending the economic, commercial and financial embargo against Cuba continue to be promulgated and applied, and concerned also about the adverse effects of such measures on the Cuban people and on Cuban nationals living in other countries,

1. *Takes note* of the report of the Secretary-General on the implementation of resolution 53/4;
2. *Reiterates its call* on all States to refrain from promulgating and applying laws and measures of the kind referred to in the preamble to the present resolution in conformity with their obligations under the Charter of the United Nations and international law, which, inter alia, reaffirm the freedom of trade and navigation;
3. *Once again urges* States that have and continue to apply such laws and measures to take the necessary steps to repeal or invalidate them as soon as possible in accordance with their legal regime;
4. *Requests* the Secretary-General, in consultation with the appropriate organs and agencies of the United Nations system, to prepare a report on the implementation of the present resolution in the light of the purposes and principles of the Charter and international law and to submit it to the General Assembly at its fifty-fifth session;
5. *Decides* to include in the provisional agenda of its fifty-fifth session the item entitled "Necessity of ending the economic, commercial and financial embargo imposed by the United States of America against Cuba".

RECORDED VOTE ON RESOLUTION 54/21:

In favour: Afghanistan, Algeria, Andorra, Angola, Antigua and Barbuda, Argentina, Armenia, Australia, Austria, Azerbaijan, Bahamas, Bahrain, Bangladesh, Barbados, Belarus, Belgium, Belize, Benin, Bhutan, Bolivia, Botswana, Brazil, Brunei Darussalam, Bulgaria, Burkina Faso, Cambodia, Canada, Cape Verde, Chad, Chile, China, Colombia, Comoros, Congo, Costa Rica, Côte d'Ivoire, Croatia, Cuba, Cyprus, Czech Republic, Democratic People's Republic of Korea, Democratic Republic of the Congo, Denmark, Djibouti, Dominica, Dominican Republic, Ecuador, Egypt, Equatorial Guinea, Eritrea, Ethiopia, Fiji, Finland, France, Gabon, Gambia, Germany, Ghana, Greece, Grenada, Guatemala, Guinea, Guinea-Bissau, Guyana, Haiti, Honduras, Hungary, Iceland, India, Indonesia, Iran, Ireland, Italy, Jamaica, Japan, Jordan, Kazakhstan, Kenya, Kuwait, Lao People's Democratic Republic, Lebanon, Lesotho, Libyan Arab Jamahiriya, Liechtenstein, Lithuania, Luxembourg, Madagascar, Malawi, Malaysia, Maldives, Mali, Malta, Mauritius, Mexico, Monaco, Mongolia, Mozambique, Myanmar, Namibia, Nepal, Netherlands, New Zealand, Nigeria, Norway, Pakistan, Panama, Papua New Guinea, Paraguay, Peru, Philippines, Poland, Portugal, Qatar, Republic of Korea, Republic of Moldova, Romania, Russian Federation, Rwanda, Saint Kitts and Nevis, Saint Lucia, Samoa, San Marino, Seychelles, Sierra Leone, Singapore, Slovakia, Slovenia, Solomon Islands, South Africa, Spain, Sri Lanka, Sudan, Suriname, Swaziland, Sweden, Syrian Arab Republic, Tajikistan, Thailand, The former Yugoslav Republic of Macedonia, Togo, Trinidad and Tobago, Tunisia, Turkey, Turkmenistan, Uganda, Ukraine, United Arab Emirates, United Kingdom, United Republic of Tanzania, Uruguay, Venezuela, Viet Nam, Yemen, Zambia, Zimbabwe.

Against: Israel, United States.

Abstaining: Estonia, Georgia, Latvia, Micronesia, Morocco, Nicaragua, Senegal, Uzbekistan.

Communications. By a 1 June letter to the Secretary-General [A/54/122], Cuba transmitted the text of a legal complaint submitted by the people of Cuba against the Government of the United States for human damages, which had been filed with the Civil and Administrative Division of the People's Provincial Court of the City of Havana on 31 May.

On 16 September [A/54/375], Cuba transmitted to the Secretary-General a Proclamation issued by its National Assembly of People's Power, which denounced the United States economic blockade on Cuba as an act of genocide.

Peru-Ecuador

By a 14 June letter [A/54/158] to the Secretary-General, Ecuador and Peru transmitted a declaration signed by their respective Presidents on 13 May, formalizing the conclusion of the process of demarcating their common land boundary, carried out in accordance with the 1998 Brasilia Presidential Act [YUN 1998, p. 239], and of the entry into force of the agreements constituting a comprehensive settlement of their differences.

Chapter IV

Asia and the Pacific

An overriding concern of the United Nations in the Asia and Pacific region in 1999 was securing Iraq's compliance with its unmet obligations under Security Council resolution 687(1991). Since the cessation of UN disarmament inspections and long-term monitoring operations in Iraq, following the withdrawal from that country in December 1998 of the United Nations Special Commission and the International Atomic Energy Agency (IAEA), and the ensuing military strikes against it by the United States and the United Kingdom, Iraq had not allowed the UN inspectors to return. In December 1999, the Council, following consideration of the recommendations of three panels on Iraq that it created in January, adopted, albeit not unanimously, a resolution that preserved disarmament standards for Iraq, with a series of steps to terminate sanctions; established a new reinforced monitoring and verification arrangement in the form of the United Nations Monitoring, Verification and Inspection Commission to address the remaining disarmament tasks; reiterated Iraq's obligation to cooperate in accounting for missing persons and to return properties it had seized from Kuwait; and provided for Iraq's humanitarian concerns resulting from the sanctions, including lifting the ceiling on its oil production and export capacities under the oil-for-food formula on which the 1995 humanitarian programme for the Iraqi people was based. In the meantime, the Council extended the humanitarian programme thrice during the year, the last time until 8 June 2000.

In Afghanistan, where a long-standing war continued to rage, the United Nations Special Mission to Afghanistan succeeded early in the year in bringing the two warring parties together in two rounds of talks. In April, however, the Taliban, the party with significant territorial and military advantage, declined to continue the talks and thereafter mounted a major offensive intended finally to defeat the United Front, the other party to the conflict. In the waves of fighting that followed, without decisive result, tens of thousands of civilians were forcibly displaced. Concluding that the shuttle missions of his Special Envoy for Afghanistan between the warring parties and the countries bordering Afghanistan had limited impact, the Secretary-General and the Special Envoy agreed to shift the latter's activities to the Special Mission. In October, the Council demanded, under penalty of sanctions, that the Taliban turn over Usama bin Laden, a Saudi Arabian national indicted by the United States for terrorist activities, to appropriate authorities to face trial. As the Taliban failed to comply, the sanctions took effect on 14 November.

In Tajikistan, the Commission on National Reconciliation, the joint implementing body of the Government, and the United Tajik Opposition (UTO), the two parties to the 1997 General Agreement on the Establishment of Peace and National Accord in Tajikistan, reached several milestones towards its goal of national reconciliation and democratization. They included UTO's official declaration in August of the disbandment of its armed forces, paving the way for the Supreme Court's lifting in that month of the 1993 ban on political parties; and the September referendum that approved the amendments to the Constitution, leading to presidential elections in November. Preparations were under way for the parliamentary elections—the last major step to be achieved under the General Agreement—scheduled to take place before February 2000. The Secretary-General observed that those achievements were due in no small measure to the extraordinary efforts of the United Nations Mission of Observers in Tajikistan, with the active support of the Contact Group of Guarantor States and International Organizations, and of the Mission in Tajikistan of the Organization for Security and Cooperation in Europe. To prepare for and monitor the parliamentary elections, the Council extended the Mission's mandate until 15 May 2000.

On the Korean peninsula, the United Nations Command continued to discharge its responsibilities relating to the 1953 Armistice Agreement. In view of the continued report by IAEA that the cooperation of the Democratic People's Republic of Korea (DPRK) with it remained limited, the General Assembly, in November, reiterated its call on the DPRK to cooperate fully in the fulfilment of its nuclear safeguards agreement with IAEA.

The Secretary-General dispatched a Group of Experts to Cambodia to assist it in addressing the issue of bringing to justice those responsible for past serious violations of Cambodian and international law. Following a review of the Group's report, the Prime Minister decided that the perpetrators should be tried by a Cambodian court, rather than by an international tribunal, as recommended by the Group. The Assembly, in December, appealed to the Government to ensure that those most responsible be brought to account in accordance with international standards of justice, fairness and due process of law.

In a popular consultation held on 30 August, the people of the Non-Self-Governing Territory of East Timor voted overwhelmingly against the offer of special autonomy within Indonesia in favour of transition to independence. The offer, embodied in one of the 5 May Agreements concluded under the Secretary-General's good offices between Indonesia and Portugal (the administering Power) and with the UN Secretariat, called for the consultation under UN auspices, for which the Council created the United Nations Mission in East Timor. Following the announcement of the consultation result, the already serious security situation prevailing before the consultation erupted into violence unleashed by rampaging anti-independence militias, with the alleged acquiescence of the Indonesian military and police, resulting in numerous deaths, the displacement of hundreds of thousands of East Timorese and a grave humanitarian situation. As conditions deteriorated into chaos, the Council, in September, authorized an international force led by Australia to restore law and order and pave the way for an orderly transition of authority in East Timor under UN administration. For that purpose, the Council, in October, established the United Nations Transitional Administration in East Timor for an initial three-month period until 31 January 2000.

The United Nations Political Office in Bougainville (UNPOB), Papua New Guinea, continued to monitor and report on the implementation of the 1998 Lincoln Agreement on Peace, Security and Development on Bougainville by the parties to that Agreement, as well as by the Peace Monitoring Group composed of Australia, Fiji, New Zealand and Vanuatu. At the request of the Government, the Secretary-General, with the concurrence of the Council, extended UNPOB's mandate for a further 12-month period to 31 December 2000.

Among other matters brought to the attention of the United Nations were the long-standing dispute between India and Pakistan over Jammu and Kashmir, violations reported by Iran and Iraq of their 1987 ceasefire agreement and of the area of separation between them, as well as the continued occupation by Iran of Greater Tunb, Lesser Tunb and Abu Musa, three islands claimed by the United Arab Emirates.

Iraq

Throughout 1999, relations between the Security Council and Iraq were marked by a stalemate precipitated by the withdrawal on 16 December 1998 of the United Nations Special Commission (UNSCOM) and the International Atomic Energy Agency (IAEA)—both mandated by the Council's ceasefire resolution 687(1991) [YUN 1991, p. 172] to disarm Iraq of its weapons of mass destruction and to ensure that it did not reconstitute or reacquire them—and the military strike that ensued against Iraq by the United States and the United Kingdom. Although UNSCOM and IAEA ceased operations in Iraq, they each submitted to the Council, in addition to the required biannual reports, a comprehensive report on the status of the disarmament of Iraq and of the monitoring and verification activities in that country for which each was responsible.

To assist in its consideration of options for the full implementation of resolution 687(1991) and all other related resolutions regarding Iraq, the Council, in January, set up three panels to deal with the unresolved issues concerning disarmament in the context of the established ongoing monitoring and verification (OMV) systems, Iraq's humanitarian situation, and prisoners of war (POWs) and Kuwaiti property.

In December, drawing on the recommendations of the three panels, the Council, by resolution 1284(1999), created the United Nations Monitoring, Verification and Inspection Commission (UNMOVIC) to replace UNSCOM, assume the latter's responsibilities connected with verifying Iraq's compliance with its weapons-related obligations under resolution 687(1991) and other relevant resolutions, and establish and operate a reinforced OMV system and address unresolved disarmament issues within that framework. The resolution retained the linkage between compliance by Iraq and lifting of the sanctions against it, but introduced the principle of their suspension commensurate with compliance achieved. It also removed the ceiling for Iraqi oil exports, exempted from travel restrictions those Hajj pilgrimage flights that were not also transporting cargo into or out of Iraq, and asked an expert group to recommend alternatives for increasing Iraq's production and export capacity.

Before the resolution was adopted, Iraq categorically rejected the draft text, insisting that, since it had honoured its fundamental obligations under the relevant resolutions, it was incumbent on the Council to adopt forthwith a resolution providing for the complete and unconditional lifting of the sanctions. It could not accept the new and arbitrary conditions to be imposed on Iraq, as they constituted a threat to its sovereignty and national interests.

In view of the continuing sanctions, the Council extended the humanitarian programme for three 180-day periods (26 November 1998–24 May 1999; 25 May–20 November 1999, later extended to 4 and then to 11 December; and 11 December 1999–8 June 2000).

On 23 December, the General Assembly decided that the agenda item on the financing of the activities arising from Security Council resolution 687(1991) would remain for consideration during its resumed fifty-fourth (2000) session (**decision 54/465**) and that the Fifth (Administrative and Budgetary) Committee should continue consideration of the item at the resumed session (**decision 54/462 A**).

By **decisions 54/425** and **54/426** of 9 December, the Assembly deferred consideration of, respectively, Israel's armed aggression against Iraqi nuclear installations and its grave consequences for the established international system on the peaceful uses of nuclear energy, the non-proliferation of nuclear weapons and international peace and security; and the consequences of Iraq's occupation of and aggression against Kuwait. It included both items in the provisional agenda of its fifty-fifth (2000) session.

UN Special Commission and IAEA post-withdrawal activities

UN Special Commission

UNSCOM remained in being until 17 December 1999, when the Security Council replaced it with a new body (see p. 229). Richard Butler (Australia) remained as Executive Chairman until the end of his two-year tenure on 30 June. Thereafter, the Deputy Executive Chairman, Charles Duelfer (United States), acted as officer-in-charge until the successor body was created.

Report of UNSCOM (January). The Executive Chairman forwarded to the Security Council on 25 January two UNSCOM reports [S/1999/94]: one on the current status of the disarmament of Iraq's proscribed missile, chemical and biological weapons and the other on the status of the OMV operations in Iraq to ensure that it did not reconstitute or retain prohibited chemical and biological weapons and missiles with a range greater than 150 kilometres.

The first report contained a comprehensive record of those disarmament issues for which UNSCOM was responsible: a description of UNSCOM's mandate, the methodology for its execution, and the impact of its working environment on its accounting for proscribed weapons; the outstanding priority issues in each weapons area, as summarized in the Executive Chairman's 1998 consolidated biannual reports [YUN 1998, p. 247]; three appendices on the current status of the material balances of proscribed operational weapons and capabilities in each weapons area, with tabulated records of, among others, items in question, declared quantities and disposal status, UNSCOM's comments and accounting status; and an appendix describing Iraqi actions to obstruct disarmament. In the biological weapons area, each element of Iraq's full, final and complete disclosure (FFCD), submitted in three versions but without significant new information—the first rejected by UNSCOM as incomplete and the third declared by international experts as deficient in all areas—was dealt with in detail, with the tabulated record of UNSCOM's assessment and comments. A summary of biological disarmament efforts from 1991 to 1998 was also provided.

The second report, on the status of OMV operations in Iraq, gave an overview of the system, underscoring the key elements for its effectivity and credibility, namely, Iraq's adherence to its obligations and cooperation with monitoring activities, UNSCOM's unhindered access to sites and information, and resources available to it for implementing its mandate.

Attention was drawn to the shortcomings of the OMV operations in terms of funding and availability of experts. Suggestions for the system's improvement were put forward, among them a specialized training programme for inspection teams and the creation of two monitoring sub-centres or operational bases, in Mosul in the north and Basrah in the south, to enable access to practically all of the sites designated for monitoring within two hours.

The report pointed out that the UNSCOM OMV system was based on the assumption that the mandated objective of the full verification and disposal of Iraq's proscribed weapons would be achieved. It stated that the current review took account of the possibility that that would prove not to be the case, but that UNSCOM might nevertheless be required to operate its OMV system under the shadow of Iraq possibly retaining prohibited materials; and that, once sanctions were reduced or lifted, UNSCOM would face a considerable increase in its OMV work.

Further reports (April and October). As called for by Security Council resolution 1051(1996) [YUN 1996, p. 218], UNSCOM submitted to the Council, through the Secretary-General, two biannual reports, on 9 April [S/1999/401] and 8 October [S/1999/1037]. The April report, covering the period 6 October 1998–11 April 1999, outlined developments in 1998 that had led to the suspension of UNSCOM's activities, its withdrawal from Iraq and subsequent resumption of activities, its final withdrawal in December and the ensuing military action against that country. It briefly described UNSCOM's disarmament and OMV activities until then. The report recorded that neither the declarations on Iraq's activities, facilities, materials and other items that might be used for prohibited purposes, due on 15 January 1999, nor any notifications on national implementation measures, had been received. Moreover, after 15 December 1998, Iraq ceased to provide the notification forms on its import of notifiable items. The report concluded that, not having received the cooperation required of Iraq, UNSCOM remained unable to give the Council the assurances it required regarding the final disposition of Iraq's proscribed weapons programmes and their possible reconstitution.

The October report covered the period 12 April–11 October 1999, during which UNSCOM focused on facilitating an eventual resumption of UN disarmament and monitoring operations in Iraq. To that end, it continued to organize, analyse and computerize the large store of data accumulated during its operations to make them more readily usable. It prepared recommendations for a reconstituted OMV system, including steps for its implementation. Notifications received from Governments on the supply to Iraq of dual-use materials were analysed and registered. At the Council's request, UNSCOM provided written information and oral briefings on various matters at informal Council consultations. It settled some of its liabilities, including reimbursing Chile for expenditures for helicopter support, France for a camera system and Germany for aerial support between April 1995 and September 1996. In the light of discussions with Bahrain, the Secretary-General and the IAEA Director General proposed, on 29 September, an interim arrangement to hold the field office in that country (relocated to Manama in July) in caretaker status to enable the quick resumption of work when conditions allowed.

Communications from Iraq. On 28 July [S/1999/831], Iraq protested the destruction of seven specimens of VX nerve gas at UNSCOM's premises (Canal Hotel) in Baghdad by a team directed to do so by the Executive Chairman. It claimed that the existence of those specimens, revealed only after the team's arrival in Baghdad, supported its suspicion that the specimens had been deliberately used to contaminate the warhead remnants sent to the United States for analysis in 1998 [YUN 1998, p. 249] so as to result in findings of VX traces. Iraq demanded an inventory by an impartial body of all items at UNSCOM's premises in Baghdad to bring out facts that would vindicate Iraq. It repeated that demand on 16 August [S/1999/897], in the light of a 5 August report of the Organization for the Prohibition of Chemical Weapons (OPCW) on the work of its special team for Iraq, which included an inventory of materials in the two UNSCOM laboratories at the Baghdad Monitoring and Verification Centre (BMVC). The inventory referred to five bottles identified as "Iraq GD-hexane", a toxic agent Iraq claimed it never submitted to UNSCOM, and to seven comparison samples of VX nerve agent, marked to be kept in a container designed to ensure the secure transportation of dangerous materials, such as explosives. Iraq took the reference to imply the presence of explosives in the UNSCOM wing of the BMVC, a claim denied by the former Executive Chairman. Iraq said the references, as well as opposition by the United States and the United Kingdom to submitting those VX samples to analysis, made clear that the Canal Hotel VX samples were destroyed, not for the danger they posed, but to get rid of proof of UNSCOM's illegitimate activities.

On 1 August [A/54/202], Iraq took exception to the Secretary-General's statement in his report to the General Assembly on the role of the United Nations in the field of verification [A/54/166], namely, that UNSCOM activities to verify Iraq's compliance with relevant Security Council resolutions ceased on 16 December 1998, without stating why or how those activities were conducted. Iraq claimed that UNSCOM had exceeded its mandate and significantly deviated from its original course, that the former Executive Chairman, on orders from United States officials and without the Council's or the Secretary-General's authorization, withdrew UNSCOM personnel from Iraq in November and December, and that, in consultation with such officials, he prepared a report that provided grounds for the 16 December military strike on Iraq.

Earlier, on 27 February [S/1999/219], Iraq claimed that efforts to contain the spread of foot-and-mouth disease in a number of governorates were severely hampered by the shortage of vaccine owing to UNSCOM's destruction of equipment in the laboratory devoted to producing it.

That statement, the Executive Chairman asserted on 11 March [S/1999/285], did not accord with the pertinent facts. The Daura facility for the production of vaccines was, by Iraq's admission in 1995, not a purely civilian facility, but had been used for biological-warfare-agent production, research and development. The installations, facilities and 28 pieces of equipment used for those purposes were destroyed in 1996 and special air-handling equipment was disabled. Some 40 major pieces originally imported for the production of foot-and-mouth disease vaccine remained, as UNSCOM could not establish their use in Iraq's biological warfare programme. Iraq unilaterally halted vaccine production in September 1992.

IAEA

IAEA report (February). In connection with the establishment of the disarmament and OMV panel on Iraq [S/1999/100], the IAEA Director General transmitted to the Security Council a report on 8 February 1999 [S/1999/127], summarizing the status of the implementation of the Agency's mandate in Iraq up to its withdrawal on 16 December 1998 [YUN 1998, p. 267], which could facilitate that panel's work. The summary incorporated information provided in the 1997 [YUN 1997, p. 225] and 1998 [YUN 1998, p. 264] six-monthly reports.

The report identified and examined the three areas where questions and concerns remained: the lack of certain technical documentation relating to engineering drawings of centrifuge and nuclear-weapon mechanical designs, and Iraq's inability to provide further information regarding the identification and location of a foreign national alleged to have offered assistance to its clandestine nuclear weapons programme, as well as documentary evidence of the timing and modalities of the abandonment of the programme. However, the uncertainties those created presented no technical impediment to the full implementation of the IAEA OMV plan, which took them into account. Provided IAEA was allowed full and free access in Iraq, it would be able to proceed with that implementation, and to investigate further the remaining questions and concerns and any other aspect of Iraq's clandestine nuclear programme arising out of new information acquired by IAEA. The scope of the activities to be carried out was based on the technically coherent picture of Iraq's clandestine nuclear programme derived from IAEA's intensive verification activities since 1991; the remaining uncertainties were compensated for by prudent assumptions regarding Iraq's nuclear capabilities.

Direct annual implementation costs were estimated at about $10 million, not including substantial logistical costs and other assistance provided through UNSCOM.

Further report (April) and communications. Pursuant to Security Council resolution 1051(1996), IAEA submitted its consolidated six-monthly report for the period 1 October 1998 to 1 April 1999 [S/1999/393 & Corr.1].

According to the report, the BMVC-based Nuclear Monitoring Group, since its establishment in August 1994 until IAEA's withdrawal from Iraq in 1998, carried out some 1,625 OMV inspections, the majority without prior notice and some in cooperation with UNSCOM. The results of the analyses of the environmental samples taken in connection with the 1998 visits to Iraq's presidential sites [YUN 1998, p. 266], received and evaluated during the reporting period, did not indicate the presence of proscribed materials or of proscribed activities at any of those sites. Seven of eight requests for the release or relocation of equipment and materials, or for the change of use of monitored facilities, were approved, as were the intended export to Iraq of items under some 30 transactions, for which notifications were received under the export/import mechanism jointly administered with UNSCOM. In addition, the report included excerpts from IAEA's February report on the status of its verification activities.

In lieu of its second six-monthly report, IAEA recorded in a 6 October letter [S/1999/1035] that it had not received the semi-annual declarations required of Iraq regarding changes in its use of facilities, installations and sites, as well as the inventory and location of materials, equipment and isotopes that were under IAEA monitoring. The declarations were due on 15 January and 15 July. IAEA indicated that it maintained an operational plan for resuming OMV operations in Iraq on short notice. For the full implementation of its mandate, however, retention of its right to unrestricted access was essential, as provided for in relevant Council resolutions and in the IAEA OMV plan.

On 10 December [S/2000/120], IAEA notified the Council that, in keeping with the safeguards agreement between Iraq and IAEA pursuant to the Treaty on the Non-Proliferation of Nuclear Weapons, adopted by the General Assembly in resolution 2373(XXII) [YUN 1968, p. 17], it needed to carry out a physical inventory verification by 14 December of the nuclear material subject to safeguards in Iraq to ensure that it remained accounted for, unaltered and under IAEA seal. Required under the safeguards system once a year, or not less than every 14 months, that task was subsumed under the more comprehensive and intrusive disarmament and OMV activities mandated by Council resolution 687(1991) and related resolutions. The last inventory verification took place on 14 October 1998. IAEA stressed that the dispatch of the safeguards mission did not in any way obviate the need to resume OMV operations and clarification of outstanding disarmament questions as soon as possible.

By **resolution 54/26** of 15 November (see p. 962), the General Assembly stressed the need for the resumption without delay of IAEA's OMV activities in Iraq.

Transitional arrangements

UN Monitoring, Verification and Inspection Commission

The Security Council President, on 30 January [S/1999/100], announced that the Council, while continuing discussions on options for the full implementation of all of its resolutions regarding Iraq, would establish three panels on that country. The first panel, on disarmament and current and future OMV issues, would involve the participation and expertise of UNSCOM, IAEA, the UN Secretariat and others. It would assess all information, including OMV data, relating to the state of disarmament in Iraq and make recommendations on how to re-establish an effective disarmament/OMV regime in that country. The second panel, on humanitarian issues, would involve the participation and expertise of the United Nations Office of the Iraq Programme, the secretariat of the Sanctions Committee for Iraq and the UN Secretariat. It would assess Iraq's current humanitarian situation and recommend measures for its improvement. The third panel, on POWs and Kuwaiti property, including archives, and involving the participation and expertise of the Secretariat and any other relevant expertise, would assess Iraq's compliance relating to POWs and Kuwaiti property, as stipulated by relevant Council resolutions. The panels would submit their recommendations to the Council no later than 15 April. The current Council President, Celso L. N. Amorim (Brazil), would chair each panel.

Report of disarmament/OMV panel. On 27 and 30 March [S/1999/356], the Chairman of the panels transmitted the report of the panel on disarmament and OMV issues, as well as those of the panels on humanitarian issues (see p. 251) and on POWs and Kuwaiti property (see p. 235). Composed of 20 experts, the first panel met in New York from 23 to 27 February and from 22 to 27 March to consider information on the OMV regime; the export/import monitoring mechanism; the nuclear, missile, chemical and biological weapons areas; and overhead imagery. The panel's mandate reflected the Council's assessment that the presence of inspectors on the ground remained the most effective way to provide assurance that Iraq did not retain, reacquire or rebuild its proscribed weapons programmes. Bearing in mind the need to ensure full implementation of all relevant Council resolutions regarding Iraq, particularly resolutions 687(1991) [YUN 1991, p. 172], 707(1991) [ibid., p. 188], 715(1991) [ibid., p. 194] and 1051(1996) [YUN 1996, p. 218], the panel needed to answer the fundamental question of whether it was feasible to address the remaining disarmament issues and areas of uncertainty through their integration into a reinforced OMV regime developed to its full potential.

The panel heard briefings by UNSCOM and IAEA on the current status of disarmament and OMV in the four proscribed weapons areas, which concentrated on specific, outstanding priority issues. It also considered Iraqi documentation containing its views on the subject. The briefings indicated that, despite the well-known difficult circumstances, both bodies had effectively uncovered and eliminated the bulk of Iraq's proscribed weapons programmes: IAEA was able to evolve a technically coherent picture of Iraq's nuclear weapons programme and UNSCOM achieved considerable progress in establishing material balances of Iraq's proscribed weapons. As to the disarmament issues still to be resolved, reference was made to a possible "point of impasse" in further investigating those issues under current procedures.

The briefings demonstrated that it was technically possible to pursue resolution of the remaining issues within the OMV framework, provided adequate arrangements were established to ensure the full exercise of the rights contemplated in the UNSCOM and IAEA OMV plans. An adequate legal framework for implementing a rigorous and effective OMV system, integrating into it the investigation of unresolved issues relating to proscribed weapons programmes, was provided for in those plans. From a legal perspective, specific operations aimed at clarifying certain questions and detecting the retention of proscribed items that escaped being destroyed, removed or rendered harmless were fully guaranteed. The reinforced OMV system should make maximum use of synergies, cross-checks and cross-fertilizations between the activities of the four disciplines (nuclear, missile, chemical, biological) and the export/import monitoring mechanism. Such an integrated approach could enable rapid and effective work towards confirming

Iraq's disarmament status. The BMVC, which might be strengthened further, would continue to play a pivotal role.

The panel advanced some parameters under which unresolved or not sufficiently resolved disarmament issues could be integrated into OMV. It insisted that Iraq should confirm the rights and privileges of UNSCOM and IAEA inspectors and support staff and, consistent with past experience, confirm that their health and safety would be protected at all times within its territory.

To achieve its objectives, the reinforced OMV system would require Iraq to provide immediate and unobstructed access to all sites, as well as documentation to determine the legitimacy of activities under monitoring. It should ensure access to information and materials related to past proscribed activities and to the Iraqi personnel involved for interviews without interference. It should not conceal, remove or destroy relevant evidence, or interfere with monitoring equipment. It should adopt national legislation for the implementation of its obligations under Council resolutions.

The panel suggested the possibility of restructuring UNSCOM as a collegiate body, comprising a core of technical experts, including from IAEA and OPCW, Security Council members, the Under-Secretary-General for Disarmament Affairs and other Secretariat representatives, which could provide independent advice, guidance and general oversight, at the expert and diplomatic levels, on OMV activities and problems. Its functions could include consideration of matters relating to the execution of the OMV plan; reports from the Executive Chairman on the conduct of operations; issues submitted for resolution or recommendation to the Council; Iraqi complaints regarding the conduct of inspections; developing rosters of monitoring experts; and advising on personnel policy. The collegiate body should meet at least every three months, possibly with a non-permanent Council member presiding. The restructured UNSCOM should ensure a clear UN identity and be guided by the principles of full independence, rigour and transparency to ensure the effectiveness of its work and credibility of its results. Weight should be given to training aimed at developing and reinforcing core inspection skills, with emphasis on understanding national sensitivities during inspections. OMV information, whether provided by Iraq or other Member States or generated by inspections, should be held confidential and assessed strictly in terms of its credibility and relevance to the mandate. Difficulties encountered in the past, including instances of obstruction and/or deception, should be taken into account; at the same time, unnecessary confrontation or disproportionate reactions should be avoided. Confidentiality should also be maintained during all stages of the planning and execution phases. There should be a single point of contact with the press and public comment by the verification entity should be restricted to the factual, leaving to the Council evaluations or comments with obvious political implications.

The panel concluded that a reinforced OMV system, integrating intrusive inspections and investigation of relevant elements of past proscribed activities, was viable. It was in fact the same system as conceived in the plans approved by resolution 715(1991), developed to its full potential.

The panel observed that, the longer inspection and monitoring activities remained suspended, the more difficult the comprehensive implementation of Council resolutions would become. The current absence of inspectors had exponentially increased the risk of compromising the already achieved level of assurance regarding Iraq's compliance with its weapons-related obligations, given the difficulty of re-establishing the necessary OMV baseline. The panel considered the status quo as not a practical alternative and recommended that an effective, rigorous and credible international inspection regime be restored in Iraq. The reinforced OMV would be more intrusive than the one so far practised, and the Council had to devise ways to ensure Iraq's acceptance of it.

On 13 April [S/1999/415], the Council President circulated the personal remarks of the panels' Chairman at the 7 April Council consultations of the whole, strongly urging the Council to give due consideration to the disarmament/OMV panel's suggestions, in spite of the cautious diplomatic but by no means opaque language in which they were couched.

SECURITY COUNCIL ACTION

On 17 December [meeting 4084], the Security Council adopted **resolution 1284(1999)** by vote (11-0-4), based on a draft by the United Kingdom [S/1999/1232].

The Security Council,

Recalling its previous relevant resolutions, including its resolutions 661(1990) of 6 August 1990, 687(1991) of 3 April 1991, 699(1991) of 17 June 1991, 707(1991) of 15 August 1991, 715(1991) of 11 October 1991, 986(1995) of 14 April 1995, 1051(1996) of 27 March 1996, 1153(1998) of 20 February 1998, 1175(1998) of 19 June 1998, 1242(1999) of 21 May 1999 and 1266(1999) of 4 October 1999,

Recalling the approval by the Council in its resolution 715(1991) of the plans for future ongoing monitoring and verification submitted by the Secretary-General and the Director General of the International Atomic Energy Agency in pursuance of paragraphs 10 and 13 of resolution 687(1991),

Welcoming the reports of the three panels on Iraq, and having undertaken a comprehensive consideration of those reports and the recommendations contained in them,

Stressing the importance of a comprehensive approach to the full implementation of all relevant Security Council resolutions regarding Iraq and the need for Iraqi compliance with those resolutions,

Recalling the goal of establishing in the Middle East a zone free from weapons of mass destruction and all missiles for their delivery and the objective of a global ban on chemical weapons as referred to in paragraph 14 of resolution 687(1991),

Concerned at the humanitarian situation in Iraq, and determined to improve that situation,

Recalling with concern that the repatriation and return of all Kuwaiti and third-country nationals or their remains, present in Iraq on or after 2 August 1990, pursuant to paragraph 2 *(c)* of resolution 686(1991) of 2 March 1991 and paragraph 30 of resolution 687(1991), have not yet been fully carried out by Iraq,

Recalling that in its resolutions 686(1991) and 687(1991) the Council demanded that Iraq return in the shortest possible time all Kuwaiti property it had seized, and noting with regret that Iraq has still not complied fully with that demand,

Acknowledging the progress made by Iraq towards compliance with the provisions of resolution 687(1991), but noting that, as a result of its failure to implement the relevant Council resolutions fully, the conditions do not exist which would enable the Council to take a decision pursuant to resolution 687(1991) to lift the prohibitions referred to in that resolution,

Reiterating the commitment of all Member States to the sovereignty, territorial integrity and political independence of Kuwait, Iraq and the neighbouring States,

Acting under Chapter VII of the Charter of the United Nations, and taking into account the fact that operative provisions of the present resolution relate to previous resolutions adopted under Chapter VII of the Charter,

A

1. *Decides* to establish, as a subsidiary body of the Council, the United Nations Monitoring, Verification and Inspection Commission, which replaces the Special Commission established pursuant to paragraph 9 *(b)* of resolution 687(1991);

2. *Decides also* that the Monitoring, Verification and Inspection Commission will undertake the responsibilities mandated to the Special Commission by the Council with regard to the verification of compliance by Iraq with its obligations under paragraphs 8, 9 and 10 of resolution 687(1991) and other related resolutions, that the Commission will establish and operate, as was recommended by the panel on disarmament and current and future ongoing monitoring and verification issues, a reinforced system of ongoing monitoring and verification, which will implement the plan approved by the Council in resolution 715(1991) and address unresolved disarmament issues, and that the Commission will identify, as necessary in accordance with its mandate, additional sites in Iraq to be covered by the reinforced system of ongoing monitoring and verification;

3. *Reaffirms* the provisions of the relevant resolutions with regard to the role of the International Atomic Energy Agency in addressing compliance by Iraq with paragraphs 12 and 13 of resolution 687(1991) and with other related resolutions, and requests the Director General of the International Atomic Energy Agency to maintain this role with the assistance and cooperation of the Monitoring, Verification and Inspection Commission;

4. *Reaffirms* its resolutions 687(1991), 699(1991), 707(1991), 715(1991), 1051(1996), 1154(1998) of 2 March 1998, and all other relevant resolutions and statements by its President, which establish the criteria for Iraqi compliance, affirms that the obligations of Iraq referred to in those resolutions and statements with regard to cooperation with the Special Commission, unrestricted access and provision of information will apply in respect of the Monitoring, Verification and Inspection Commission, and decides in particular that Iraq shall allow Commission teams immediate, unconditional and unrestricted access to any and all areas, facilities, equipment, records and means of transport which they wish to inspect in accordance with the mandate of the Commission, as well as to all officials and other persons under the authority of the Iraqi Government whom the Commission wishes to interview so that it may fully discharge its mandate;

5. *Requests* the Secretary-General, within 30 days of the adoption of the present resolution, to appoint, after consultation with and subject to the approval of the Council, an Executive Chairman of the Monitoring, Verification and Inspection Commission who will take up his mandated tasks as soon as possible and, in consultation with the Executive Chairman and the Council members, to appoint suitably qualified experts as a College of Commissioners for the Commission, which will meet regularly to review the implementation of the present and other relevant resolutions and provide professional advice and guidance to the Executive Chairman, including on significant policy decisions and on written reports to be submitted to the Council through the Secretary-General;

6. *Requests* the Executive Chairman of the Monitoring, Verification and Inspection Commission, within 45 days of his appointment, in consultation with and through the Secretary-General, to submit to the Council for its approval an organizational plan for the Commission, including its structure, staffing requirements, management guidelines, recruitment and training procedures, incorporating as appropriate the recommendations of the panel on disarmament and current and future ongoing monitoring and verification issues, and recognizing in particular the need for an effective, cooperative management structure for the new organization, for staffing with suitably qualified and experienced personnel, who would be regarded as international civil servants subject to Article 100 of the Charter of the United Nations, drawn from the broadest possible geographical base, including as he deems necessary from international arms control organizations, and for the provision of high quality technical and cultural training;

7. *Decides* that the Monitoring, Verification and Inspection Commission and the International Atomic Energy Agency, not later than 60 days after they have both started work in Iraq, will each draw up, for approval by the Council, a work programme for the discharge of their mandates, which will include both the implementation of the reinforced system of ongoing monitoring and verification, and the key remaining disarmament tasks to be completed by Iraq pursuant to its obligations to comply with the disarmament requirements of resolution 687(1991) and other related resolutions, which constitute the governing standard of Iraqi compliance, and further decides that what is required of Iraq for the implementation of each task shall be clearly defined and precise;

8. *Requests* the Executive Chairman of the Monitoring, Verification and Inspection Commission and the Director General of the International Atomic Energy Agency, drawing on the expertise of other international organizations as appropriate, to establish a unit which will have the responsibilities of the joint unit constituted by the Special Commission and the Director General under paragraph 16 of the export/import mechanism approved by resolution 1051(1996), and also requests the Executive Chairman, in consultation with the Director General, to resume the revision and updating of the lists of items and technology to which the mechanism applies;

9. *Decides* that the Government of Iraq shall be liable for the full costs of the Monitoring, Verification and Inspection Commission and the International Atomic Energy Agency related to their work under the present and other related resolutions on Iraq;

10. *Requests* Member States to give full cooperation to the Monitoring, Verification and Inspection Commission and the International Atomic Energy Agency in the discharge of their mandates;

11. *Decides* that the Monitoring, Verification and Inspection Commission shall take over all assets, liabilities and archives of the Special Commission, and that it shall assume the part of the Special Commission in agreements existing between the Special Commission and Iraq and between the United Nations and Iraq, and affirms that the Executive Chairman, the Commissioners and the personnel serving with the Monitoring, Verification and Inspection Commission shall have the rights, privileges, facilities and immunities of the Special Commission;

12. *Requests* the Executive Chairman of the Monitoring, Verification and Inspection Commission to report every three months, through the Secretary-General, to the Council, following consultation with the Commissioners, on the work of the Commission, pending submission of the first reports referred to in paragraph 33 below, and to report immediately when the reinforced system of ongoing monitoring and verification is fully operational in Iraq;

B

13. *Reiterates* the obligation of Iraq, in furtherance of its commitment to facilitate the repatriation of all Kuwaiti and third-country nationals referred to in paragraph 30 of resolution 687(1991), to extend all necessary cooperation to the International Committee of the Red Cross, and calls upon the Government of Iraq to resume cooperation with the Tripartite Commission and the Technical Subcommittee established to facilitate work on this issue;

14. *Requests* the Secretary-General to report to the Council every four months on compliance by Iraq with its obligations regarding the repatriation or return of all Kuwaiti and third-country nationals or their remains, to report every six months on the return of all Kuwaiti property, including archives, seized by Iraq, and to appoint a high-level coordinator for these issues;

C

15. *Authorizes* States, notwithstanding the provisions of paragraphs 3 *(a)*, 3 *(b)* and 4 of resolution 661(1990) and subsequent relevant resolutions, to permit the import of any volume of petroleum and petroleum products originating in Iraq, including financial and other essential transactions directly relating thereto, as required for the purposes and on the conditions set out in paragraphs 1 *(a)* and 1 *(b)* and subsequent provisions of resolution 986(1995) and related resolutions;

16. *Underlines*, in this context, its intention to take further action, including permitting the use of additional export routes for petroleum and petroleum products, under appropriate conditions otherwise consistent with the purpose and provisions of resolution 986(1995) and related resolutions;

17. *Directs* the Security Council Committee established by resolution 661(1990) to approve, on the basis of proposals from the Secretary-General, lists of humanitarian items, including foodstuffs, pharmaceutical and medical supplies, as well as basic or standard medical and agricultural equipment and basic or standard educational items, decides, notwithstanding paragraph 3 of resolution 661(1990) and paragraph 20 of resolution 687(1991), that supplies of these items will not be submitted for the approval of that Committee, except for items subject to the provisions of resolution 1051(1996), and that they will be notified to the Secretary-General and financed in accordance with the provisions of paragraphs 8 *(a)* and 8 *(b)* of resolution 986(1995), and requests the Secretary-General to inform the Committee in a timely manner of all such notifications received and actions taken;

18. *Requests* the Committee established by resolution 661(1990) to appoint, in accordance with resolutions 1175(1998) and 1210(1998) of 24 November 1998, a group of experts, including independent inspection agents appointed by the Secretary-General in accordance with paragraph 6 of resolution 986(1995), decides that this group will be mandated to approve speedily contracts for the parts and equipment necessary to enable Iraq to increase its exports of petroleum and petroleum products, according to lists of parts and equipment approved by that Committee for each individual project, and requests the Secretary-General to continue to provide for the monitoring of these parts and equipment inside Iraq;

19. *Encourages* Member States and international organizations to provide supplementary humanitarian assistance to Iraq and published material of an educational character to Iraq;

20. *Decides* to suspend, for an initial period of six months from the date of the adoption of the present resolution and subject to review, the implementation of paragraph 8 *(g)* of resolution 986(1995);

21. *Requests* the Secretary-General to take steps to maximize, drawing as necessary on the advice of specialists, including representatives of international humanitarian organizations, the effectiveness of the arrangements set out in resolution 986(1995) and related resolutions, including the humanitarian benefit to the Iraqi population in all areas of the country, and further requests the Secretary-General to continue to enhance as necessary the United Nations observation process in Iraq, ensuring that all supplies under the humanitarian programme are utilized as authorized, to bring to the attention of the Council any circumstances preventing or impeding effective and equitable distribution and to keep the Council informed of the steps taken towards the implementation of this paragraph;

22. *Also requests* the Secretary-General to minimize the cost of the United Nations activities associated with the implementation of resolution 986(1995) as well as the cost of the independent inspection agents and the certified public accountants appointed by him, in accordance with paragraphs 6 and 7 of resolution 986(1995);

23. *Further requests* the Secretary-General to provide Iraq and the Committee established by resolution 661(1990) with a daily statement of the status of the escrow account established by paragraph 7 of resolution 986(1995);

24. *Requests* the Secretary-General to make the necessary arrangements, subject to Security Council approval, to allow funds deposited in the escrow account established by resolution 986(1995) to be used for the purchase of locally produced goods and to meet the local cost for essential civilian needs which have been funded in accordance with the provisions of resolution 986(1995) and related resolutions, including, where appropriate, the cost of installation and training services;

25. *Directs* the Committee established by resolution 661(1990) to take a decision on all applications in respect of humanitarian and essential civilian needs within two working days of receipt of these applications from the Secretary-General, and to ensure that all approval and notification letters issued by the Committee stipulate delivery within a specified time, according to the nature of the items to be supplied, and requests the Secretary-General to notify the Committee of all applications for humanitarian items which are included in the list to which the export/import mechanism approved by resolution 1051(1996) applies;

26. *Decides* that Hajj flights which do not transport cargo into or out of Iraq are exempt from the provisions of paragraph 3 of resolution 661(1990) and resolution 670(1990), provided timely notification of each flight is made to the Committee established by resolution 661(1990), and requests the Secretary-General to make the necessary arrangements, for approval by the Security Council, to provide for reasonable expenses related to the Hajj to be met by funds in the escrow account established by resolution 986(1995);

27. *Calls upon* the Government of Iraq:

(a) To take all steps to ensure the timely and equitable distribution of all humanitarian goods, in particular medical supplies, and to remove and avoid delays at its warehouses;

(b) To address effectively the needs of vulnerable groups, including children, pregnant women, the disabled, the elderly and the mentally ill among others, and to allow freer access, without any discrimination, including on the basis of religion or nationality, by United Nations agencies and humanitarian organizations to all areas and sections of the population for evaluation of their nutritional and humanitarian condition;

(c) To prioritize applications for humanitarian goods under the arrangements set out in resolution 986 (1995) and related resolutions;

(d) To ensure that those involuntarily displaced receive humanitarian assistance without the need to demonstrate that they have resided for six months in their places of temporary residence;

(e) To extend full cooperation to the mine-clearance programme of the United Nations Office for Project Services in the three northern governorates of Iraq and to consider the initiation of the demining efforts in other governorates;

28. *Requests* the Secretary-General to report on the progress made in meeting the humanitarian needs of the Iraqi people and on the revenues necessary to meet those needs, including recommendations on necessary additions to the current allocation for oil spare parts and equipment, on the basis of a comprehensive survey of the condition of the Iraqi oil-production sector, not later than 60 days from the date of the adoption of the present resolution, and updated thereafter as necessary;

29. *Expresses its readiness* to authorize additions to the current allocation for oil spare parts and equipment, on the basis of the report and recommendations requested in paragraph 28 above, in order to meet the humanitarian purposes set out in resolution 986(1995) and related resolutions;

30. *Requests* the Secretary-General to establish a group of experts, including oil industry experts, to report within 100 days of the date of adoption of the present resolution on Iraq's existing petroleum production and export capacity and to make recommendations, to be updated as necessary, on alternatives for increasing Iraq's petroleum production and export capacity in a manner consistent with the purposes of relevant resolutions, and on the options for involving foreign oil companies in Iraq's oil sector, including investments, subject to appropriate monitoring and controls;

31. *Notes* that in the event of the Council acting as provided for in paragraph 33 below to suspend the prohibitions referred to in that paragraph, appropriate arrangements and procedures will need, subject to paragraph 35 below, to be agreed by the Council in good time beforehand, including suspension of provisions of resolution 986(1995) and related resolutions;

32. *Requests* the Secretary-General to report to the Council on the implementation of paragraphs 15 to 30 of the present resolution within 30 days of the adoption of this resolution;

D

33. *Expresses its intention,* upon receipt of reports from the Executive Chairman of the Monitoring, Verification and Inspection Commission and from the Director General of the International Atomic Energy Agency that Iraq has cooperated in all respects with the

Commission and the Agency in particular in fulfilling the work programmes in all the aspects referred to in paragraph 7 above, for a period of 120 days after the date on which the Council is in receipt of reports from both the Commission and the Agency that the reinforced system of ongoing monitoring and verification is fully operational, to suspend with the fundamental objective of improving the humanitarian situation in Iraq and securing the implementation of the Council's resolutions, for a period of 120 days renewable by the Council, and subject to the elaboration of effective financial and other operational measures to ensure that Iraq does not acquire prohibited items, prohibitions against the import of commodities and products originating in Iraq, and prohibitions against the sale, supply and delivery to Iraq of civilian commodities and products other than those referred to in paragraph 24 of resolution 687(1991) or those to which the mechanism established by resolution 1051(1996) applies;

34. *Decides* that in reporting to the Council for the purposes of paragraph 33 above, the Executive Chairman of the Monitoring, Verification and Inspection Commission will include as a basis for his assessment the progress made in completing the tasks referred to in paragraph 7 above;

35. *Decides* that if at any time the Executive Chairman of the Monitoring, Verification and Inspection Commission or the Director General of the International Atomic Energy Agency reports that Iraq is not cooperating in all respects with the Commission or the Agency or if Iraq is in the process of acquiring any prohibited items, the suspension of the prohibitions referred to in paragraph 33 above shall terminate on the fifth working day following the report, unless the Council decides to the contrary;

36. *Expresses its intention* to approve arrangements for effective financial and other operational measures, including on the delivery of and payment for authorized civilian commodities and products to be sold or supplied to Iraq, in order to ensure that Iraq does not acquire prohibited items in the event of suspension of the prohibitions referred to in paragraph 33 above, to begin the elaboration of such measures not later than the date of receipt of the initial reports referred to in paragraph 33 above, and to approve such arrangements before the Council decision in accordance with that paragraph;

37. *Also expresses its intention* to take steps, based on the report and recommendations requested in paragraph 30 above, and consistent with the purpose of resolution 986(1995) and related resolutions, to enable Iraq to increase its petroleum production and export capacity, upon receipt of the reports relating to the cooperation in all respects with the Monitoring, Verification and Inspection Commission and the Agency referred to in paragraph 33 above;

38. *Reaffirms its intention* to act in accordance with the relevant provisions of resolution 687(1991) on the termination of prohibitions referred to in that resolution;

39. *Decides* to remain actively seized of the matter, and expresses its intention to consider action in accordance with paragraph 33 above no later than 12 months from the date of the adoption of the present resolution provided the conditions set out in paragraph 33 above have been satisfied by Iraq.

VOTE ON RESOLUTION 1284(1999):

In favour: Argentina, Bahrain, Brazil, Canada, Gabon, Gambia, Namibia, Netherlands, Slovenia, United Kingdom, United States.

Against: None.

Abstaining: China, France, Malaysia, Russian Federation.

China pointed out that implementation of the resolution was highly questionable without Iraqi cooperation. China had always believed that Iraq was obligated to implement the relevant Council resolutions; however, the Council also had to assess objectively Iraq's implementation and gradually lift or at least suspend the sanctions accordingly. It said a draft put to the vote on which there was no consensus, even if adopted, would not help resolve the long-standing issue of Iraq.

France said two matters were regrettable: the refusal to break the isolation of the Iraqi population and, in that connection, to permit the resumption of civil aviation; and the lack of a real exception to the sanctions for religious activities, such as the Hajj and the Omra pilgrimage, since everything remained in the hands of the Sanctions Committee. The resolution did not include the specifics for the financial mechanism to be applicable during the period of sanctions suspension. The criteria for the suspension and lifting of sanctions were ambiguous and thus subject to interpretation difficulties. Its abstention notwithstanding, France would plead for wisdom to prevail in the interpretation of paragraphs 33 and 34 so that a reasonable financial mechanism could be adopted.

The Russian Federation stated that, while it could not support the resolution, it would not hinder its adoption since, at its insistence, serious changes offering an opportunity to break the Iraqi stalemate had been introduced into the text. That should not be taken to mean that Russia was obliged to play along with attempts to enforce implementation. It agreed that Iraq had to fulfil its obligations, but that the Council had to act in an unbiased manner and not allow its work to be politicized. Russia was not trying to shield Iraq, but a repetition of the previous situation under UNSCOM was unacceptable.

Malaysia said the resolution was driven by political rather than humanitarian considerations and left out the important issue of financial modalities. It established no definite benchmark or time frame for the final lifting of sanctions and persisted in effecting stringent controls that impacted negatively on innocent civilians. Its formulation on the Hajj issue was such as not to resolve the problems occurring every Hajj season. Malaysia regretted that its proposal to hear Iraq's views before acting on the draft was not accommodated. While there was broad agreement on continued monitoring and on the urgency to resolve the key remaining disarmament issues, any reinforced OMV system should take account of Iraq's dignity as a sovereign State, as well as of the religious and cultural sensitivities of its people.

Communication from Iraq. Prior to the resolution's adoption, Iraq, on 5 December [S/1999/1218], categorically rejected the draft text as a "malicious and biased rewriting" of existing Council resolutions, saying that, since it had honoured its fundamental obligations under those resolutions, it was incumbent on the Council to follow suit and adopt forthwith a resolution providing for the complete and unconditional lifting of the sanctions against Iraq. It could not accept the "new and arbitrary conditions" that the draft sought to impose on Iraq as they constituted "a threat to its sovereignty and national interests".

Iraq-Kuwait

Kuwait, on 14 January [S/1999/40], drew attention to an article in the 10 January Iraqi paper *Al-Thawrah* by Iraq's Deputy Prime Minister, maintaining that Kuwait was created by the United Kingdom to contain Iraq and deny it access to its coasts, which historically had always been part of Iraqi territory. The article went on to say that Iraq's overtures to settle the demarcation of the boundaries between it and Kuwait had been met with delays and obstacles, while Kuwait continued to construct oil-production facilities and military installations and to create farm settlements on what was Iraqi territory.

Kuwait called the article a distortion of internationally recognized historical facts, namely, that Kuwait was a State with recognized boundaries before Iraq was established as a political entity in 1921. More seriously, the article constituted a complete repudiation of Security Council resolution 687(1991) [YUN 1991, p. 172], setting forth Iraq's obligations in the aftermath of its aggression against Kuwait, and resolution 833(1993) [YUN 1993, p. 400] on the completion of demarcating for the first time the precise coordinates of the international boundary between Iraq and Kuwait.

POWs and Kuwaiti property

Report of POW/Kuwaiti property panel. The Chairman of the three panels on Iraq, established pursuant to the Security Council President's note of 30 January (see p. 229), transmitted the report of the panel on POWs and Kuwaiti property to the Council on 30 March [S/1999/356]. The panel, composed of UN Secretariat officials, agreed to base its assessment on briefings and written submissions of those with first-hand information, including those directly concerned, and not to engage in any investigative work of its own. The panel met on 18 February and on 3, 4 and 9 March to consider information from a variety of sources.

POWs

For its work on POWs, the panel considered written submissions from the International Committee of the Red Cross (ICRC) and from Max van der Stoel, Special Rapporteur on the situation of human rights in Iraq; a non-paper by Iraq; and oral briefings from the Special Envoy of the Secretary-General in Baghdad, the Permanent Representative of Kuwait to the United Nations, the Vice-Chairman of the Kuwaiti National Committee on Missing Persons and Prisoner of War Affairs, the Chairman of the Committee for Saudi Prisoners of War in Iraq, and the French, United Kingdom and United States representatives in the Tripartite Commission, formally created by the 1991 Riyadh Agreement (see p. 236) to ascertain the fate of missing military personnel and civilians.

In assessing Iraqi compliance relating to POWs as stipulated by Council resolutions, the panel took as the legal framework for its own work the relevant Council resolutions and international humanitarian law provisions, as well as other pertinent international agreements.

The panel noted that, at the end of the Gulf War, ICRC arranged for the global repatriation of more than 70,000 Iraqi and 4,000 Kuwaiti and allied POWs, and over 1,300 civilian internees and detained civilians of Kuwaiti or third-State nationality. Others reportedly returned to Kuwait after the 1991 insurrection in southern Iraq. Although the efforts of the Tripartite Commission, which, under the chairmanship of ICRC had held 23 meetings by September 1998, had yielded limited results, it was deemed the most appropriate mechanism to deal with the issue of missing persons. Its Technical Subcommittee (TSC), set up in 1994 to expedite the search for all persons for whom inquiry files had been opened, met monthly in the demilitarized zone on the Iraq-Kuwait border, holding its thirty-sixth meeting on 2 December 1998. Iraq notified ICRC, however, that it would not participate in the next scheduled 1999 meeting of either the Commission or TSC. ICRC was unable to obtain Iraq's agreement to grant it access to those detained in Iraq.

According to ICRC, individual files for persons not accounted for submitted by the July 1996 deadline set by the Commission numbered 608 from Kuwait (including 7 files for Saudi nationals), 17 from Saudi Arabia and 789 from Iraq. Three Kuwaiti files had since been closed, leaving 605 open, relating to 570 Kuwaiti nationals and 35 third-State nationals legally in Kuwait at the time of its occupation by Iraq. According to Saudi Arabia, 24 of its nationals (21 of them civilians) remained unaccounted for; approximately 5,300 Iraqis, in that country as refugees under the auspices of the Office of the United Nations High Commissioner for Refugees (UNHCR), refused repatriation to Iraq after the Gulf War.

Iraq held that there were no POWs or detainees in its territory and that the issue was one of missing persons. Of the 126 cases to which it had responded, 121 were arrested and sent to detention centres in southern Iraq, but their fate could not be established after their escape from detention during the unrest in the area; five cases were identified as those of persons killed in Kuwait or in combat, one of whose remains was returned, thus closing that file. Eight other cases were solved or withdrawn by Kuwait. As for the rest of the files, Iraq claimed that all documents that could provide a basis for a search had been destroyed, burned or lost in the riots in the south. While reaffirming that it held no POWs, Iraq said it was not possible to reach agreement with ICRC on the question of visits to detention sites, for it was under no obligation to accept proposals that would extend the scope and duration of the search for the missing.

The panel observed that, were Iraq's compliance with its obligations to be assessed in the light of current circumstances, the status of the remaining 605 persons unaccounted for, whether POWs, civilian detainees or missing persons, would be crucial, as each of those categories of individuals entailed for the detaining Power different obligations under the relevant legal instruments. Given the limitation of not being able to investigate the facts, the panel found itself unable to make a definitive determination. The absence of a direct legal link between the Council resolutions and 1991 agreements concluded by Iraq and the coalition forces in Riyadh, Saudi Arabia (the Riyadh Agreements), did not exonerate Iraq from its obligation to cooperate with the Tripartite Commission under those agreements. The panel thus urged Iraq to reconsider its decision not to participate in the Commission and TSC. In reaffirming the humanitarian character of the issues, it stressed the need to avoid politicizing them and the imperative to provide information to the families of the missing. Although progress had been below the level expected and desired by the international community, the Tripartite Commission and TSC offered the best chance of progress for the issue; it was therefore the responsibility of all involved to cooperate fully with them. The panel recommended that, since the Council had addressed the POW issue in its resolutions, the Secretary-General should keep it informed of progress on the situation through a semi-annual or annual report, based on information collected by the Secretariat from Iraq, Kuwait and the Commission. The panel believed that, for progress to be achieved, it was fundamental to show good will in ascertaining the fate of the missing by transparency and openness.

Kuwaiti property

For its assessment of Iraqi compliance relating to Kuwaiti property, including archives, the panel took as its legal framework those provisions of Security Council resolutions 686(1991) and 687(1991) requiring Iraq immediately to begin to return all Kuwaiti property it had seized, the return to be completed in the shortest possible period. Considered as part of that framework were relevant provisions of the Hague Regulations Concerning the Laws and Custom of War on Land, annexed to the 1907 IV Hague Convention, generally recognized as part of customary international law, in so far as they related to respect for property and the 1949 Geneva Convention relative to the Protection of Civilian Persons in Time of War.

The panel outlined the actions taken relating to the return of Kuwaiti property in 1991 [YUN 1991, p. 195], 1994 [YUN 1994, p. 476] and 1996 [YUN 1996, p. 234]. It noted that in June 1997 and December 1998, Iraq's Permanent Representative to the United Nations informed the Coordinator for the return of Kuwaiti property that several small items identified by markings as belonging to Kuwait had been found in local markets but not returned due to the absence in Iraq of a field representative of the Coordinator. The matter of the missing archives and military equipment previously reported to the United Nations was again brought to the attention of Iraq in October 1997 and March 1998.

In his oral presentation, the Secretary-General's Special Envoy in Baghdad said he had raised the missing-property issue in December 1998 as an important one to be resolved; Iraq's Deputy Prime Minister replied that it could be easily settled in the context of the comprehensive review of Iraq's disarmament compliance that was shortly to have been undertaken by the Council [YUN 1998, p. 259]. The panel also heard from Kuwait's Permanent Representative that no private property had been returned but for which compensation claims had been presented to the United Nations Compensation Commission; that, while much of the outstanding property could be subject to claims, the return of the archives was essential—no compensation could be paid for them, nor for museum objects, being unique items; and that Kuwaiti anti-aircraft weapons were intact and emplaced around Baghdad and at other Iraqi sites. Documentation provided by the Compensation Commission indicated that, since the Commission had no enforcement mechanism, it could do nothing for claimants seeking compensation for loss of irreplaceable objects and other tangible properties stolen by Iraq. It had also rejected some other Kuwaiti claims for lack of supporting evidence. The panel recognized the difficulty in providing such evidence, given the destruction or loss of documentation during Iraq's occupation of and departure from Kuwait.

Given Kuwait's emphasis on the return of irreplaceable items, especially the archives and military equipment, besides the still unaccounted-for items of the Islamic and National Museums of Kuwait, the panel encouraged Iraq to exert additional efforts to find Kuwaiti property in its territory and to continue to return those found through the Secretariat. Since no mechanism existed to foster the return of property, progress could be achieved through periodic reports by the parties to a Secretariat focal point, who would maintain an updated list of items yet to be returned, together with supporting evidence. On the basis of such data, the Secretary-General would submit an annual progress report to the Council. A field representative of the Coordinator should be appointed as soon as possible to facilitate the handover of any property found by Iraq. The panel suggested that the Compensation Commission could consider making settlements, even for claims submitted beyond the deadline, for replaceable items claimed to have been lost in Iraqi possession. Kuwait should submit an updated list of items whose return need not be pursued, provided compensation was arranged.

The panel asserted that Iraq was under obligation to return the missing archives of the Emir, the Prime Minister, the Cabinet and the Foreign Ministry and had also to respond to Kuwait's repeated claims that there was still military equipment to be returned. The absence of a credible explanation from Iraq on the missing archives and military material, the panel observed, did not allow it to conclude that Iraq was in full compliance with its obligation to implement paragraph 2 of resolution 686(1991).

By section B of **resolution 1284(1999)**, the Council reiterated Iraq's obligation and commitment to repatriate all Kuwaiti and third-country nationals or return their remains, as well as to return all Kuwaiti property, including archives, it had seized; it asked the Secretary-General to report on Iraq's compliance and to appoint a high-level coordinator for those issues.

UN Iraq-Kuwait Observation Mission

The United Nations Iraq-Kuwait Observation Mission (UNIKOM), established by Security Council resolution 687(1991) [YUN 1991, p. 172], continued in 1999 to discharge its functions in accordance with its terms of reference, as expanded by resolution 806(1993) [YUN 1993, p. 406].

UNIKOM operations involved surveillance, control, investigation and liaison. Surveillance of the demilitarized zone (DMZ), an area about 200 to 240 kilometres long and extending 10 kilometres into Iraq and 5 kilometres into Kuwait, was based on ground and air patrols and observation points. Control operations included static checkpoints, random checks and maintenance of a mobile reserve force. For operational purposes, the DMZ was divided into the northern and southern sectors, with 10 and 7 patrol/observation bases, respectively. Investigation teams were stationed in those sectors and at UNIKOM headquarters. Continuous liaison was maintained with Iraqi and Kuwaiti authorities at all levels.

The military observers were responsible for patrol, observation, investigation and liaison activities. The infantry battalion, deployed at Camp Khor, Kuwait, at a company camp in Al-Abdali, at platoon camps in the two DMZ sectors, and in the easternmost patrol/observation base on the DMZ's Iraqi side, conducted armed patrols within those areas and manned checkpoints at border-crossing sites, making random checks in cooperation with Iraqi and Kuwaiti liaison officers. It also provided security for UNIKOM personnel and installations.

UNIKOM maintained headquarters at Umm Qasr in Iraq, liaison offices in Baghdad and Kuwait City and a support centre at Camp Khor.

Reports of Secretary-General (March and September). UNIKOM's activities were described in two reports by the Secretary-General, covering the periods 24 September 1998 to 23 March 1999 [S/1999/330] and 24 March to 23 September 1999 [S/1999/1006 & Corr.1].

The reports noted that the situation in the DMZ remained generally calm. However, the military strike against Iraq in December 1998 [YUN 1998, p. 262] and the subsequent skirmishes over the no-fly zones in the north and south of the country affected some operational aspects of the Mission. UNIKOM flights by fixed-wing aircraft in Iraq and by helicopter on the DMZ's Iraqi side remained suspended since December 1998, when Iraqi authorities informed UNIKOM that they could not guarantee the safety of such flights due to Iraq's conflict with the United States and the United Kingdom regarding the no-fly zones. For security reasons, therefore, deployment of military observers from those countries had since been restricted to patrol and observation bases on the Kuwaiti side of the DMZ and to UNIKOM headquarters.

DMZ violations increased to 122 during the first period but dropped to 49 during the second period. The ground and maritime violations were mostly by Iraqi police or military personnel and civilians, while the air violations were by aircraft generally flying too high to be identified. UNIKOM received six official complaints, five from Kuwait and one from Iraq; none could be verified as the complaints were received long after the alleged incidents occurred. Twenty-one other incidents in the DMZ were recorded during the second period. UNIKOM also provided security and logistic support for ICRC humanitarian activities.

The Secretary-General observed that UNIKOM received the cooperation of the Iraqi and Kuwaiti authorities in the performance of its tasks and recommended that it be maintained in view of its continued contribution to the maintenance of calm and stability in the DMZ.

SECURITY COUNCIL ACTION

The Security Council informed the Secretary-General on 6 April [S/1999/384] and on 6 October [S/1999/1033] that, in the light of his reports, it had reviewed the question of the termination or continuation of UNIKOM and its modalities of operation and concurred with his recommendation that UNIKOM be maintained. The Council would review the question again by 6 April 2000.

Composition

As at 1 September, UNIKOM, under the command of Major-General Esa Kalervo Tarvainen (Finland), had an overall strength of 1,299, comprising 193 military observers from 32 Member States; an infantry battalion of 767 from Bangladesh; 133 support personnel, including a 50-member engineering unit and a 34-member logistic unit from Argentina, a helicopter unit of 35 from Bangladesh and a medical unit of 14 from Germany; plus a civilian staff of 205, of whom 57 were recruited internationally.

On 5 November [S/1999/1154], the Secretary-General informed the Security Council of his intention to appoint General John Augustine Vize (Ireland) to succeed Major-General Tarvainen, who was to relinquish his post on 30 November; the Council agreed to the appointment on 10 November [S/1999/1155]. General Vize assumed the post of Force Commander on 1 December.

Financing

On 8 June [meeting 101], the General Assembly considered the Secretary-General's reports on the financial performance of UNIKOM for the period 1 July 1997–30 June 1998 [A/53/782] and its proposed budget for 1 July 1999–30 June 2000 [A/53/817], together with related reports of the Advisory Committee on Administrative and Budgetary Questions (ACABQ) [A/53/895 & Add.2]. On the recommendation of the Fifth Committee [A/53/987], the Assembly adopted **resolution 53/229** without vote [agenda item 124 *(a)*].

Financing of the United Nations Iraq-Kuwait Observation Mission

The General Assembly,

Having considered the reports of the Secretary-General on the financing of the United Nations Iraq-Kuwait Observation Mission and the related reports of the Advisory Committee on Administrative and Budgetary Questions,

Recalling Security Council resolutions 687(1991) of 3 April 1991 and 689(1991) of 9 April 1991, by which the Council decided to establish the United Nations Iraq-Kuwait Observation Mission and to review the question of its termination or continuation every six months,

Recalling also its resolution 45/260 of 3 May 1991 on the financing of the Observation Mission and its subsequent resolutions and decisions thereon, the latest of which was resolution 52/238 of 26 June 1998,

Reaffirming that the costs of the Observation Mission that are not covered by voluntary contributions are expenses of the Organization to be borne by Member States in accordance with Article 17, paragraph 2, of the Charter of the United Nations,

Recalling its previous decisions regarding the fact that, in order to meet the expenditures caused by the Observation Mission, a different procedure is required from that applied to meet expenditures of the regular budget of the United Nations,

Taking into account the fact that the economically more developed countries are in a position to make relatively larger contributions and that the economically less developed countries have a relatively limited capacity to contribute towards such an operation,

Bearing in mind the special responsibilities of the States permanent members of the Security Council, as indicated in General Assembly resolution 1874(S-IV) of 27 June 1963, in the financing of such operations,

Expressing its appreciation for the substantial voluntary contributions made to the Observation Mission by the Government of Kuwait and the contributions of other Governments,

Mindful of the fact that it is essential to provide the Observation Mission with the necessary financial resources to enable it to fulfil its responsibilities under the relevant resolutions of the Security Council,

1. *Takes note* of the status of contributions to the United Nations Iraq-Kuwait Observation Mission as at 30 April 1999, including the contributions outstanding in the amount of 9.8 million United States dollars, representing some 4 per cent of the total assessed contributions from the inception of the Mission to the period ending 30 April 1999, notes that some 21 per cent of the

Member States have paid their assessed contributions in full, and urges all other Member States concerned, in particular those in arrears, to ensure payment of their outstanding assessed contributions;

2. *Expresses its continued appreciation* of the decision of the Government of Kuwait to defray two thirds of the cost of the Observation Mission, effective 1 November 1993;

3. *Expresses concern* about the financial situation with regard to peacekeeping activities, in particular as regards the reimbursement of troop contributors, which bear additional burdens owing to overdue payments by Member States of their assessments;

4. *Expresses its appreciation* to those Member States which have paid their assessed contributions in full;

5. *Urges* all other Member States to make every possible effort to ensure payment of their assessed contributions to the Observation Mission in full and on time;

6. *Endorses* the observations and recommendations contained in the report of the Advisory Committee on Administrative and Budgetary Questions;

7. *Requests* the Secretary-General to take all necessary action to ensure that the Observation Mission is administered with a maximum of efficiency and economy;

8. *Also requests* the Secretary-General, in order to reduce the cost of employing General Service staff, to continue efforts to recruit local staff for the Observation Mission against General Service posts, commensurate with the requirements of the Mission;

9. *Decides* to appropriate to the Special Account for the United Nations Iraq-Kuwait Observation Mission the amount of 53,991,024 dollars gross (51,996,124 dollars net) for the maintenance of the Observation Mission for the period from 1 July 1999 to 30 June 2000, inclusive of the amount of 2,686,445 dollars for the support account for peacekeeping operations and the amount of 526,779 dollars for the United Nations Logistics Base at Brindisi, Italy, a two-thirds share of this amount, equivalent to 34,664,080 dollars, to be funded through voluntary contributions from the Government of Kuwait, subject to the review by the Security Council with regard to the question of termination or continuation of the Mission;

10. *Decides also,* as an ad hoc arrangement, taking into consideration the funding through voluntary contributions from the Government of Kuwait of the two-thirds share of the cost of the Observation Mission, equivalent to 34,664,080 dollars, to apportion among Member States the amount of 19,326,944 dollars gross (17,332,044 dollars net), representing one third of the cost of the maintenance of the Mission for the period from 1 July 1999 to 30 June 2000, the said amount to be apportioned at a monthly rate of 1,610,579 dollars gross (1,444,337 dollars net), in accordance with the composition of groups set out in paragraphs 3 and 4 of General Assembly resolution 43/232 of 1 March 1989, as adjusted by the Assembly in its resolutions 44/192 B of 21 December 1989, 45/269 of 27 August 1991, 46/198 A of 20 December 1991, 47/218 A of 23 December 1992, 49/249 A of 20 July 1995, 49/249 B of 14 September 1995, 50/224 of 11 April 1996, 51/218 A to C of 18 December 1996 and 52/230 of 31 March 1998 and its decisions 48/472 A of 23 December 1993 and 50/451 B of 23 December 1995, and taking into account the scale of assessments for the years 1999 and 2000, as set out in its resolution 52/215 A of 22 December 1997, subject to the review by the Security Council with regard to the question of termination or continuation of the Mission;

11. *Decides further* that, in accordance with the provisions of its resolution 973(X) of 15 December 1955, there shall be set off against the apportionment among Member States, as provided for in paragraph 10 above, their respective share in the Tax Equalization Fund of the estimated staff assessment income of 1,994,900 dollars approved for the Observation Mission for the period from 1 July 1999 to 30 June 2000;

12. *Decides* that, taking into consideration the funding through voluntary contributions from the Government of Kuwait of the two-thirds share of the cost of the Observation Mission, for Member States that have fulfilled their financial obligations to the Mission, there shall be set off against the apportionment, as provided for in paragraph 10 above, their respective share of the unencumbered balance of 1,339,300 dollars gross (1,028,100 dollars net), representing one third of the unencumbered balance of 3,395,500 dollars gross (3,084,300 dollars net) in respect of the period from 1 July 1997 to 30 June 1998;

13. *Decides also* that, for Member States that have not fulfilled their financial obligations to the Observation Mission, their share of the unencumbered balance of 1,339,300 dollars gross (1,028,100 dollars net) in respect of the period from 1 July 1997 to 30 June 1998 shall be set off against their outstanding obligations;

14. *Decides further* that two thirds of the net unencumbered balance of 3,084,300 dollars, equivalent to 2,056,200 dollars, shall be returned to the Government of Kuwait;

15. *Expresses concern* that the Secretary-General did not submit to the General Assembly during the main part of its fifty-third session the separate report on developments relating to the issue of overpayment of mission subsistence allowance and compensatory time off, including measures taken with respect to those responsible for the overpayment on the basis of the conclusion of the inquiry, as requested in paragraph 18 of Assembly resolution 52/238, and requests the Secretary-General to submit that report to the Assembly no later than 30 June 1999;

16. *Invites* voluntary contributions to the Observation Mission in cash and in the form of services and supplies acceptable to the Secretary-General, to be administered, as appropriate, in accordance with the procedure and practices established by the General Assembly;

17. *Decides* to include in the provisional agenda of its fifty-fourth session, under the item entitled "Financing of the activities arising from Security Council resolution 687(1991)", the sub-item entitled "United Nations Iraq-Kuwait Observation Mission".

On 29 October [meeting 43], the Assembly considered the Secretary-General's report on the results of efforts to recover overpayment of mission subsistence allowance in UNIKOM [A/53/1023], together with the related ACABQ report [A/54/418]. On the Fifth Committee's recommendation [A/54/510], the Assembly adopted **resolution 54/18 A** without vote [agenda item 130 *(a)*].

Financing of the United Nations Iraq-Kuwait Observation Mission

The General Assembly,

Recalling its resolutions 52/238 of 26 June 1998 and 53/229 of 8 June 1999,

Having considered the report of the Secretary-General on the financing of the United Nations Iraq-Kuwait Observation Mission and the related report of the Advisory Committee on Administrative and Budgetary Questions,

1. *Notes with deep concern* the mishandling of this matter by the Administration, as observed by the Advisory Committee on Administrative and Budgetary Questions in paragraph 4 of its report;

2. *Requests* the Board of Auditors to undertake a comprehensive audit of the United Nations Iraq-Kuwait Observation Mission, in particular the question of the payment of mission subsistence allowance, as a matter of priority;

3. *Requests* the Secretary-General to submit a comprehensive report on this question within a period not exceeding three months following the adoption of the present resolution, for consideration during the first part of its resumed fifty-fourth session;

4. *Decides* to continue its consideration of this question during the first part of its resumed fifty-fourth session in the light of the reports of the Board of Auditors and the Secretary-General, and decides that, pending its decision, all actions on this question should remain in abeyance.

By **decision 54/462 A** of 23 December, the Assembly decided that the Fifth Committee should continue its consideration of the item on the financing of UNIKOM at the resumed fifty-fourth (2000) session.

Arms and related sanctions

The Security Council's yearly reviews of the sanctions provisions against Iraq, pursuant to its resolution 687(1991) [YUN 1991, p. 172], remained suspended in 1999, in accordance with resolution 1194(1998) [YUN 1998, p. 257]. As it later reaffirmed in resolution 1205(1998) [ibid., p. 258], the Council would act in accordance with the relevant provisions of resolution 687(1991) on the duration of the prohibitions referred to in that resolution.

Communications from Iraq. By a 14 January statement [S/1999/41], Iraq called for the immediate lifting of the embargo against it, based on what had been achieved to disarm it of weapons of mass destruction, which should be considered as meeting in full Iraq's weapons-related obligations under resolution 687(1991).

On 8 November [S/1999/1170], the Speaker of Iraq's National Assembly drew attention to the grave consequences of the unjust embargo imposed on Iraq, which was entering its ninth year, and to continued United States and United Kingdom military assaults on Iraq under the so-called aerial exclusion (also no-fly) zones, which were destroying vital infrastructure and basic utilities. The Speaker urged an immediate halt to the "daily" attacks by the United States and the United Kingdom and pleaded for the lifting of the embargo that was inflicting untold suffering on the Iraqi people.

Sanctions Committee activities

The Security Council Committee established by resolution 661(1990) [YUN 1990, p. 192] (Sanctions Committee for Iraq), in its annual report [S/2000/133], described its activities from 1 August 1998 to 20 November 1999. In addition to its implementation activities under Council resolutions 986(1995) [YUN 1995, p. 475], and 1175(1998) [YUN 1998, p. 274] relating to the humanitarian programme for the Iraqi people (see p. 251), the Committee processed 6,070 notifications and applications from States and international organizations to send humanitarian goods to Iraq under resolutions 661(1990) and 687(1991). Of that total, 98 for foodstuffs and 46 for medical supplies were acknowledged. The remaining 5,926 applications, for the supply of other categories of goods, were processed under the no-objection procedure, of which 2,654, estimated at $4,413,446,701, were approved; 427, valued at $7,623,378,005, were placed on hold for further information or clarification; 2,823, valued at $24,892,308,758, were blocked; and 22, valued at $6,715,325, were withdrawn or nullified.

Pursuant to resolution 1153(1998) [YUN 1998, p. 271], the Committee Chairman discussed with the Permanent Representatives of Iraq and of Saudi Arabia suggested arrangements to facilitate the participation of Iraqi pilgrims in the Hajj, possibly involving third parties to assist in those arrangements. The Chairman was informed, however, of Iraq's insistence that funds for the Hajj be made directly to Iraq, regarding which the Committee reached no consensus. Iraq's representative confirmed in March that, as Iraq did not agree with the Committee's suggestions, it would not communicate further on the matter.

The Committee received seven requests for humanitarian flights to Iraq: one for medical evacuation (United Kingdom), four for sending humanitarian supplies (Cyprus, Russian Federation, United Arab Emirates) and two for transporting other personnel to Iraq (Austria, Venezuela). The first five requests were approved and letter exchanges were in progress on the remaining two. On the United Arab Emirates request for weekly flights to Baghdad, the Committee reiterated its inability to grant blanket approvals for regular flights to Iraq.

The Committee considered several financial matters. It did not approve a request by Lebanon that the funds held by Lebanese nationals and companies at the Rafidain Bank in Beirut be released to their depositors. Concerning a request from the Danish Agency for Trade and Industry inquiring whether Iraq's frozen account in a Danish bank could be reactivated to cover the administrative expenses of Iraq's Embassy in Stockholm, Sweden, the Committee responded that it was not in a position to authorize the unfreezing of Iraqi accounts as such. Following its own request for clarification as to why the funds had to be moved from Denmark to Sweden, the inquiry was withdrawn. The Committee granted permission to a Danish company to invest in a project in which Iraq had a 5 per cent minority share, provided the profits generated were placed in a frozen account. It did not object to a request from Bahrain for the release of funds of Yemeni citizens with Al-Rafadeen Bank, provided the funds released were not made available directly or indirectly to any Iraqi citizens or entities.

The Committee continued discussions on air travel to and from Baghdad for diplomats and their families with the Dean of the Diplomatic Corps in that city, who submitted a new proposal on the question. It approved the United Arab Emirates request to include private vehicles as "personal effects" in its passenger shipping service to and from Iraq, denied Iraq's request to have its deteriorating vessel *Al-Bahr al-Arabi* towed out of the territorial waters of the United Arab Emirates to the port of Umm Qasr, and approved the operation of a ferry service to transport pilgrims from Bahrain to Iraq.

Other matters considered, but on which no decisions were reached, included a request from Turkey, first introduced in 1996, to resume importing petroleum and petroleum products from Iraq for domestic purposes, and another from Iraq for access to the Committee's summary records and for participation in its formal meetings on matters on which Iraq's opinion might be needed. In May, the Committee approved IAEA's request to implement seven new technical projects in Iraq, provided they were implemented together with appropriate monitoring mechanisms. It also advised IAEA, in August, that its query as to whether it could send a fact-finding mission to Iraq, at the latter's request, was not within the Committee's purview. The Committee agreed in principle to the 1999 aerial pesticide campaign of the Food and Agriculture Organization of the United Nations (FAO), provided the campaign complied with procedures established for that purpose and the related dual-use items to be shipped to Iraq were submitted for the Committee's consideration on a case-by-case basis.

In addition, the Committee raised with Iran the smuggling of Iraqi oil through Iranian waters, as reported by the Multinational Interception Force operating in the Gulf region, and was awaiting a reply. It informed Saudi Arabia that it reached no consensus on that country's request for advice on an Iraqi aircraft transporting Iraqi Hajj pilgrims to Jeddah on 17 March, which Saudi Arabia detained at the Jeddah airport but would allow it to return to Iraq without its passengers, unless an immediate response was received from the Committee.

During the year, the Committee issued four reports on the implementation of arms and related sanctions against Iraq, in accordance with the guidelines [YUN 1991, p. 198] approved by Council resolution 700(1991) [ibid.] for facilitating full international implementation of resolution 687(1991). The reports were transmitted to the Council on 3 February [S/1999/110], 4 May [S/1999/519], 2 August [S/1999/848] and 29 October [S/1999/1113].

Each report indicated that, during the period under review, no State had brought to the Committee's attention any information relating to possible violations of the arms and related sanctions against Iraq committed by other States or foreign nationals; no State or international organization had consulted the Committee on whether certain items fell within the provisions of paragraph 24 of resolution 687(1991), or on cases relating to dual-use or multiple-use items; and no international organization had reported any relevant information requested under the guidelines.

Communication. On 21 October [S/1999/1088], Iraq accused the United States of circulating to the Committee, at its 12 October meeting, a document entitled "Saddam Hussein's Iraq", containing information on Iraq's policy of expulsion, destruction of homes, threats to its neighbours and failure to comply with Security Council resolutions, intended to influence the Committee's work and deflect it from the exercise of its proper mandate.

Oil-for-food programme

In accordance with Security Council resolutions 1210(1998) [YUN 1998, p. 279] and 1242(1999) (see p. 246), each extending for a 180-day period the provisions of resolution 986(1995) [YUN 1995, p. 475], which authorized States to import Iraqi petroleum and petroleum products as a temporary measure to finance a humanitarian programme to alleviate the adverse consequence of the sanctions regime on the Iraqi people (also known as the oil-for-food programme) [YUN 1996, p. 225], the Secretary-General and the Sanctions Committee for Iraq separately submitted a report 90 days after entry into force of each resolution and again before the end of the next 90 days. The 180-day periods under the first and second resolutions were extended, respectively, from 26 November 1998 to 24 May 1999 (phase V) and from 25 May to 20 November (phase VI). The latter period was subsequently extended until 4 December by resolution 1275(1999) and until 11 December by resolution 1280(1999) (see pp. 249 and 250).

The reports described progress in implementing the arrangements specified by the resolutions, taking account of the provisions of the 1996 Memorandum of Understanding between the UN Secretariat and the Government of Iraq [YUN 1996, p. 226] and the procedures established by the Sanctions Committee for the resolutions' implementation [ibid., p. 228]. They also described the distribution of humanitarian relief, on behalf of the Government, in the three northern governorates of Arbil, Dihouk and Suleimaniyeh under the United Nations Inter-Agency Humanitarian Programme, to complement government distribution in central and southern Iraq, thereby ensuring equitable distribution to all segments of the Iraqi population.

The provisions of resolution 986(1995) were extended for a further 180-day period beginning on 12 December by resolution 1281(1999) (see p. 250), inaugurating phase VII of the programme. Shortly thereafter, by section C of resolution 1284(1999) (see p. 230), the Council authorized a series of measures, including removal of the ceiling for the export of Iraqi oil, to secure additional funds for the programme and speed up its implementation, on the basis of the report of a panel created to review the humanitarian situation in Iraq and make recommendations for its improvement.

Programme review

On 28 April 1999 [S/1999/481], the Secretary-General reported to the Security Council on the results of a comprehensive review and assessment of the humanitarian programme's implementation and of Iraq's overall humanitarian situation. Undertaken by the Office of the Iraq Programme (OIP), with the participation of the UN agencies and programmes involved and the United Nations Office of the Humanitarian Coordinator in Iraq acting as focal point, the review covered the period from the programme's inception, which began with phase I on 10 December 1996, through phase IV, which ended on 25 November 1998.

Highlighted were the programme's development and incremental enhancement by encompassing, in addition to Iraq's priority humanitarian requirements, a range of additional sectors and support activities; the consequent raising, by Council resolution 1153(1998) [YUN 1998, p. 271], of the oil sales ceiling to $5.256 billion during a given 180-day period and authorization of the export of oil-production spare parts and equipment to enable Iraq to produce oil up to that ceiling; and the Secretary-General's recommendations to improve procedures for contracting, processing and approving applications, the procurement and shipment of humanitarian supplies and their timely distribution, as well financial and banking arrangements.

The report pointed out, however, that, regardless of improvements to the programme's scope and implementation, the humanitarian needs were of a magnitude that could not be met within the parameters set by resolution 986(1995) and succeeding resolutions, particularly 1153(1998). The enhanced programme's objectives could not be fully achieved due primarily to revenue shortfalls. Of the $3.436 billion funding level envisaged by the Secretary-General's 1998 supplementary report [YUN 1998, p. 270] and authorized by resolution 1153(1998), only $1.9 billion (including $300 million for oil spare parts and equipment) could be made available for the enhanced distribution plan under phase IV—an amount not much greater than that provided for each of the previous three phases. Thus, with the exception of the agriculture and electricity sectors, none of the additional projects set out in the supplementary report could be implemented.

The Secretary-General again asked the Sanctions Committee to endeavour to reduce the number of applications placed on hold; review the distribution plan's annexes at the outset so as to identify those items likely to be put on hold, or to require further information and end-use verification, and to so inform the applicants concerned in writing within 48 hours; endorse the 11 February OIP proposal to improve the current reimbursement system from the 13 per cent account (the account for the three northern governorates) to the 53 per cent account (the account for the 15 central and southern governorates); expedite applications for oil spare parts and equipment to enable sustained oil production; recognize the technical complexity of rehabilitation projects in such sectors as electricity, and promptly approve complementary spare parts and equipment when their linkage to those projects was appropriately explained by Iraq; authorize OIP, in case of a fund shortfall during a given phase, to transfer approved but unfunded applications from that phase to the next without resubmitting them to the Committee; and exercise flexibility in response to unforeseen events, such as epidemics and natural disasters.

The Secretary-General also recommended that Iraq, in developing its distribution plan, which was central to the entire system of procurement, approval and distribution of humanitarian supplies, should adopt a genuinely multisectoral approach towards improving the population's nutrition and health. It should urgently address the growing imbalance between the procurement of pharmaceuticals and equipment with a view to establishing a pragmatic basis for procurement decisions in the health sector, utilize excess supplies currently in storage, and set up a comprehensive infrastructure and equipment inventory to serve as a basis for procurement decisions. It should also review difficulties relating to the late submission of health-sector applications, including contracts for the targeted nutrition programme.

Phase V

Referring to the exception he had made to Iraq's telecommunications requirements set out in annex VII to the phase V distribution plan [YUN 1998, p. 280], the Secretary-General informed the Security Council on 13 May [S/1999/559] that he had that day approved the revised part seven of the plan's executive summary and revised annex VII, submitted by Iraq following a joint technical review of those requirements by experts from the International Telecommunication Union and relevant Iraqi ministries. Approval was given on the understanding that the implementation of the revised plan for telecommunications would be governed by resolutions 986(1995) and 1210(1998) and the 1996 Memorandum of Understanding between the UN Secretariat and Iraq, and without prejudice to the Sanctions Committee procedures.

Reports of Secretary-General (February and May). Pursuant to resolution 1210(1998), the Secretary-General issued two progress reports covering the two 90-day periods under phase V, which began on 26 November 1998. The first, issued on 22 February 1999 [S/1999/187], and the second, on 18 May [S/1999/573 & Corr.2], provided information on all implementation aspects up to 31 January and 31 March, respectively.

The February report drew attention, as had previous others, to certain constraints preventing full implementation of the approved distribution plan for the current phase, the most serious being the growing revenue shortfall, projected to reach some $950 million. Consequently, Iraq was asked to revise the plan's fund allocations in line with resolutions 1153(1998) and 1210(1998) and promptly to submit costed annexes and projects. By 31 January, a reimbursable sum of $111 million for food under phases II to IV remained to be transferred from the 13 per cent account to the 53 per cent account.

Drawn to Iraq's urgent attention were the slow distribution of medicine and medical supplies from central to governorate warehouses and thence to health facilities, resulting in the accumulation in warehouses of some $275 million worth of such items; the bulk of applications for targeted nutrition inputs under phases IV and V, which had yet to be submitted to the Secretariat; and the need for intersectoral linkages and coordinated planning, as well as timely submission of applications and delivery of supplies to make for effective programme management in the central and southern governorates.

The report noted the severe disruption of UN observation activities due to events in Iraq in November and December 1998, as well as the Secretary-General's 4 February 1999 decision to withdraw from Iraq UN personnel of British and United States nationality in the absence of government assurances for their security and safety.

In his May report, the Secretary-General reiterated his observations and recommendations resulting from the review and assessment of the overall humanitarian programme (see p. 242). Annex I to the report, detailing the status of the UN Iraq Account established under resolution 867(1995), recorded that, by 15 April, of the $5.256 billion authorized under resolution 1210(1998), $1,606.4 million had been deposited into that account, bringing total oil sales since inception to $10,993.2 million. The cumulative amounts allocated from that sum to the seven different accounts specified in paragraph 8 of resolution 986(1995) included $5,508 million for the purchase of humanitarian supplies by Iraq for the 15 central and southern governorates and $1,350.2 million for similar purchases for distribution to the three northern governorates by the United Nations Inter-Agency Humanitarian Programme.

Sanctions Committee reports (March and May). The Sanctions Committee reports for the first and second 90-day periods of phase V were transmitted to the Council on 15 March [S/1999/279] and 19 May [S/1999/582], respectively. They noted that the export of petroleum from Iraq had proceeded smoothly, with excellent cooperation among the oil overseers, the independent inspection agents (contracted through Saybolt Nederland BV), Iraq's State Oil Marketing Organization and the national oil purchasers. The overseers continued to advise the Committee on oil pricing mechanisms, oil contract approval and modifications, management of the revenue objective and other pertinent questions related to export and monitoring. They continued to work closely with the Saybolt inspection agents monitoring oil loadings and transfers to ensure the effective monitoring of the relevant oil installations and liftings. For the third consecutive year, both had received Iraq's full cooperation. The reports stressed that the Committee continued to attach high priority to the processing of contracts to supply humanitarian goods to Iraq under the expanded programme.

The March report noted that, in view of projections that phase IV revenues would not be sufficient to fund all applications received, at Iraq's request 132 phase IV applications worth some $358,938,878 had been transferred to phase V by 24 February. Of those, 34 food-sector applications valued at $179,607,075 had received Committee approval. Due to projected phase V revenue shortfalls, circulation to the Committee of 98 phase IV applications for other sectors, valued at $179,331,803 and rolled over to phase V, was being held in abeyance pending Iraq's submission of the requested adjustment to phase V sectoral allocations. In addition, 112 applications, valued at $213,730,123 and already evaluated by the Secretariat, remained in phase IV due to insufficient revenues.

Confirmation of the arrival of goods at the four entry points to Iraq (Al-Walid, Trebil, Umm Qasr and Zakho) by the UN independent inspection agents—performed by Lloyd's Register Inspection Ltd. and, from 1 February, by Cotecna Inspection S.A.—went according to plan, except for an interruption during the military strike against Iraq in December 1998 [YUN 1998, p. 262]. As in previous phases, the inspection agents enjoyed Iraq's full cooperation.

According to the reports, the level of oil exports increased during the second 90-day period, with more crude oil being exported from the southern terminal at Mina al-Bakr—an imbalance the Committee wanted corrected without delay through the maximum use of the northern Kirkuk-Yumurtalik pipeline. The reports recorded, as at 10 May, a total of 178 oil contracts approved under phase V, corresponding to about 671 million barrels of oil; and 374 liftings completed, amounting to 485.4 million barrels valued at $2,808 million. At current prices, total phase V revenues were estimated to approximate $3.9 billion (including $180 million in pipeline fees).

Applications received, as at 14 May, for the export of humanitarian supplies to Iraq totalled 1,071. Of the 786 of them circulated to the Committee, 674 were found eligible for payment from the UN Iraq Account, in the amount of $1,654 million. Consignments of humanitarian supplies from previous phases confirmed as having arrived in Iraq in total or in partial shipments totalled 2,514 in the first half of phase V and 3,161 in the second half.

Since Council resolution 1175(1998) [YUN 1998, p. 274] authorized the export to Iraq of oil-production parts and equipment, up to 14 May 1999, the number of applications to ship such items had reached 792, with a value of $434,633,918. Of those, 80 were returned for clarification, 14 were declared null and void, 7 were under review by Committee experts, and 638 were circulated to the Committee. Of the latter, 481, valued at $264,526,444, were approved; 134, valued at $53,915,885, were placed on hold; and 23 were pending under the no-objection procedure. As at 14 May, a total of 54 full or partial shipments of parts and equipment had arrived in Iraq.

Issues considered by the Committee included: a February proposal by OIP regarding the reimbursement from the 13 per cent account to the 53 per cent account for government bulk purchases of food and medicines; the transfer of 1 per cent of oil sales proceeds from the UN Iraq Account for the payment envisaged in paragraph 6 of resolution 778(1992) [YUN 1992, p. 320], concerning which the Under-Secretary-General for Management was advised that the amount agreed upon by the Committee for that purpose should be $10 million every 90 days, as specified by paragraph 8 *(g)* of resolution 986(1995); options to resolve the financial issue relating to the Hajj pursuant to paragraph 3 of resolution 1210(1998); and the stock of pharmaceuticals and medical supplies and equipment accumulating in Iraq's warehouses, currently valued at $291 million.

Communications. A number of communications on various subjects were received from Iraq during phase V. On 4 January [S/1999/9], it questioned the amount of $29,140,708 withheld from the proceeds of oil sales under phase IV, as not consistent with paragraph 8 *(g)* of resolution 986(1995). Iraq asked that the excess amounts withheld be returned to the UN Iraq Account and that the Iraqi Central Bank be provided with the financial statements relating to the Account's operations.

On 23 February [S/1999/199], Iraq sought the Secretary-General's intervention with the Sanctions Committee for the release of 102 spare-parts contracts currently on hold at the instigation of the United States and the United Kingdom, under the usual pretext of requiring more information or time for their technical evaluation. Iraq repeated that request on 18 April [S/1999/442] for similar contracts on hold for as long as six months. It spoke of a deliberate obstruction focused on contracts pertaining to the southern oil companies, including for Mina al-Amiq, a terminal being readied to supplement Mina al-Bakr, on the grounds that that terminal was not covered by the export plan.

On 29 April [S/1999/500], Iraq urged a reconsideration of the amount of oil revenue to be transferred from the UN Iraq Account to the United Nations Compensation Fund, namely, not more than 30 per cent of the annual value of Iraq's export of petroleum and petroleum products. Since oil revenues continued to fall short of meeting Iraq's most basic humanitarian needs, Iraq called for a stop to such fund transfers. It reiterated that demand on 11 June [S/1999/674], especially since resolution 687(1991) on the Gulf War ceasefire [YUN 1991, p. 172] had asked that in determining the appropriate level of the amount to be withheld, account should be taken of the Iraqi people's requirements, Iraq's payment capacity, its external debt service and the needs of the Iraqi economy. Iraq referred to the allocation of $125.4 million to cover the Compensation Commission's operating expenses, and queried the whereabouts of $427.4 million unaccounted for by the status report on the UN Iraq Account as at 15 April 1999 [S/1999/573 & Corr.2]. Besides inquiring into the disposition of that amount, Iraq called for a halt to the withholding of amounts for compensation payments and for a review of that Commission's budget.

On 11 May [S/1999/549], Iraq set out in detail the setbacks suffered during the implementation of phases I to V, confirming the humanitarian programme's failure just when the humanitarian situation in Iraq was worsening. It called on the Secretary-General to announce that the programme had not and could not mitigate the suffering of the Iraqi people; and that the only way to do that was for the Council to lift the sanctions on Iraq without further conditions. Iraq's National Assembly on 26 June [S/1999/742] further called for an immediate lifting of the sanctions in view of their cumulative catastrophic effects since 1990, as well as of the inability of the humanitarian programme significantly to alleviate the Iraqi people's suffering.

In reply to the OIP Executive Director's press statement that in just over two years some $570 million worth of medicines and medical supplies had arrived in Iraq, but that only 48 per cent had been distributed, Iraq, on 16 May [S/1999/572], said the sum allocated to the health sector under phases I-V was $1,029 million; delivery of more than 42 per cent of items ordered were still being awaited.

To a United States allegation that Iraq was re-exporting infant dried milk powder imported under the humanitarian programme, Iraq replied on 22 August [S/1999/910] that the shipment in question consisted, not of infant powdered milk, which Iraq had never imported under the programme, but of 75 cartons of baby's talcum powder and 25 cartons of teats and infant feeding bottles, which were being returned to the supplier as not in conformity with standard specifications. On 1 October [S/1999/1017] and again on 29 December [S/1999/1298], Iraq protested interceptions and time-consuming inspections by United States naval forces of civilian vessels in the Persian Gulf carrying humanitarian goods for Iraq under duly documented bills of lading, thus delaying delivery of those urgently needed goods.

Other related communications. Iraq, on 28 February [S/1999/220], drew attention to the United States bombing of a radio relay station that was a key component of the operational control system for the Kirkuk-Yumurtalik pipeline, 40 kilometres south-west of Mosul, within the so-called air-exclusion (no-fly) zone in northern Iraq illegally imposed by the United Kingdom and the United States. The attack killed one and injured three others. Iraq stressed that no air defence or other installations were in the area for kilometres around. By identical letters of 2 March to the Security Council [S/1999/225] and the Secretary-General [S/1999/228], Iraq reported that two later raids, on a residential complex for the North Oil Company's Ayn Zalah oilfield, 55 kilometres north-west of Mosul, that killed one and injured nine others, had completely halted the flow of crude oil through the northern pipeline. That meant a daily loss of 1 million barrels of oil, or $9 million in revenues, over and above the human and material losses. Iraq said the action was at odds with the Sanction Committee's insistence that more than half of oil produced had to be exported through the Kirkuk-Yumurtalik pipeline.

By identical letters, dated 2 April, to the Secretary-General [S/1999/373] and the Council [S/1999/374], Iraq called on them to take a clear and unambiguous position on the repeated acts of aggression against Iraq in the face of another bombing by United States and United Kingdom warplanes, this time on the main oil pumping station serving the Mina al-Bakr terminal in Hamdan, in the southern governorate of Basrah. On the same date [S/1999/370], Iraq said it awaited measures which the Council might deem fit to take in response to that aggression.

On 15 March [S/1999/281], Iraq reported that on 23 February customs authorities found a staff member of FAO smuggling rugs out of the country in violation of Iraqi laws. On 5 July [S/1999/757], Iraq protested against an alleged sabotage by an employee of an Australian company contracted for by the United Nations to clear mines in the northern governorates. The employee allegedly buried a number of boxes in areas contiguous to Khanaqin district villages, which, it was later revealed, contained locusts' eggs intended to be unleashed on Khanaqin and other central and southern governorates. Iraq demanded an investigation and the termination of the Australian company's contract.

Iraq, on 11 April [S/1999/411], had also appealed for an urgent supply of vaccine in sufficient quantities to halt an epidemic of foot-and-mouth disease that threatened the large-scale destruction of livestock, which would exacerbate the suffering of the Iraqis.

SECURITY COUNCIL ACTION

On 21 May [meeting 4008], the Security Council unanimously adopted **resolution 1242(1999)**. The draft [S/1999/588] was sponsored by Argentina, the United Kingdom and the United States.

The Security Council,

Recalling its previous relevant resolutions, in particular its resolutions 986(1995) of 14 April 1995, 1111(1997) of 4 June 1997, 1129(1997) of 12 September 1997, 1143(1997) of 4 December 1997, 1153(1998) of 20 February 1998, 1175(1998) of 19 June 1998 and 1210(1998) of 24 November 1998,

Convinced of the need as a temporary measure to continue to provide for the humanitarian needs of the Iraqi people until the fulfilment by the Government of Iraq of the relevant resolutions, including notably resolution 687(1991) of 3 April 1991, allows the Council to take further action with regard to the prohibitions referred to in resolution 661(1990) of 6 August 1990, in accordance with the provisions of those resolutions,

Convinced also of the need for equitable distribution of humanitarian supplies to all segments of the Iraqi population throughout the country,

Determined to improve the humanitarian situation in Iraq,

Reaffirming the commitment of all Member States to the sovereignty and territorial integrity of Iraq,

Acting under Chapter VII of the Charter of the United Nations,

1. *Decides* that the provisions of resolution 986(1995), except those contained in paragraphs 4, 11 and 12, shall remain in force for a new period of 180 days beginning at 0001 hours eastern standard time on 25 May 1999;

2. *Also decides* that paragraph 2 of resolution 1153(1998) shall remain in force and shall apply to the 180-day period referred to in paragraph 1 above;

3. *Requests* the Secretary-General to continue to take the actions necessary to ensure the effective and efficient implementation of the present resolution, and to continue to enhance as necessary the United Nations observation process in Iraq in such a way as to provide the required assurance to the Council that the goods produced in accordance with the present resolution are distributed equitably and that all supplies authorized for procurement, including dual-usage items and spare parts, are utilized for the purpose for which they have been authorized;

4. *Notes* that the Security Council Committee established by resolution 661(1990) is reviewing various options, in particular the proposal made by the Secretary-General, as requested by paragraph 4 of resolution 1210(1998), to resolve the difficulties encountered in the financial process, referred to in his report of 19 November 1998;

5. *Decides* to conduct a thorough review of all aspects of the implementation of the present resolution 90 days after the entry into force of paragraph 1 above and again prior to the end of the 180-day period, upon receipt of the reports referred to in paragraphs 6 and 10 below, and expresses its intention, prior to the end of the 180-day period, to consider favourably renewal of the provisions of the present resolution as appropriate, provided that the said reports indicate that those provisions are being satisfactorily implemented;

6. *Requests* the Secretary-General to report to the Council 90 days after the date of entry into force of paragraph 1 above and again prior to the end of the 180-day period, on the basis of observations of United Nations personnel in Iraq, and of consultations with the Government of Iraq, on whether Iraq has ensured the equitable distribution of medicine, health supplies, foodstuffs, and materials and supplies for essential civilian needs, financed in accordance with paragraph 8 *(a)* of resolution 986(1995), including in his reports any observations he may have on the adequacy of the revenues to meet Iraq's humanitarian needs, and on Iraq's capacity to export sufficient quantities of petroleum and petroleum products to produce the sum referred to in paragraph 2 of resolution 1153(1998);

7. *Also requests* the Secretary-General to report to the Council if Iraq is unable to export petroleum and petroleum products sufficient to produce the total sum provided for by paragraph 2 above and, following consultations with relevant United Nations agencies and the Iraqi authorities, make recommendations for the expenditure of the sum expected to be available, consistent with the priorities established in paragraph 2 of resolution 1153(1998) and with the distribution plan referred to in paragraph 5 of resolution 1175(1998);

8. *Decides* that paragraphs 1, 2, 3 and 4 of resolution 1175(1998) shall remain in force and shall apply to the new 180-day period referred to in paragraph 1 above;

9. *Requests* the Secretary-General, in consultation with the Government of Iraq, to submit to the Council, by 30 June 1999, a detailed list of parts and equipment necessary for the purpose described in paragraph 1 of resolution 1175(1998);

10. *Requests* the Committee established by resolution 661(1990), in close coordination with the Secretary-General, to report to the Council 90 days after the entry into force of paragraph 1 above, and again prior to the end of the 180-day period, on the implementation of the arrangements in paragraphs 1, 2, 6, 8, 9 and 10 of resolution 986(1995);

11. *Urges* all States, and in particular the Government of Iraq, to provide their full cooperation in the effective implementation of the present resolution;

12. *Appeals* to all States to continue to cooperate in the timely submission of applications and the expeditious issue of export licences, facilitating the transit of humanitarian supplies authorized by the Committee established by resolution 661(1990), and to take all other appropriate measures within their competence in order to ensure that urgently required humanitarian supplies reach the Iraqi people as rapidly as possible;

13. *Stresses* the need to continue to ensure respect for the security and safety of all persons directly involved in the implementation of the present resolution in Iraq;

14. *Decides* to keep these arrangements under review, including, in particular, those in paragraph 2 above, to ensure the uninterrupted flow of humanitarian supplies into Iraq, and expresses its willingness to review the relevant recommendations of the report of the panel established to review humanitarian issues as appropriate with regard to the 180-day period referred to in paragraph 1 above;

15. *Decides* to remain seized of the matter.

Communications from Secretary-General. In the light of the foregoing resolution, the Secretary-General transmitted to the Council a 24 May exchange of letters [S/1999/601] between the UN Secretariat and Iraq constituting their agreement to extend for the new 180-day period the provisions of the 1996 Memorandum of Understanding between them on the implementation of Council resolution 986(1995).

Responding to paragraph 9 of the resolution, the Secretary-General, on 2 July [S/1999/746 & Add.1], transmitted Iraq's detailed list of spare parts and equipment necessary for Iraq to produce oil exports up to the sum of $5.256 billion set by resolution 1153(1998). Examined by a Saybolt expert group during its visit to Iraq (6-12 June) to review the situation on the ground, the list was valued at twice the amount approved by the resolution, but deemed commensurate with the production levels achieved and stated targets, in barrels per day: 3 million by December 1999, 3.2 million by March 2000 and 3.5 million by December 2000. The expert group observed that the spare-parts-and-equipment distribution plan under phase VI aimed to stabilize and, where possible, to increase crude oil production while undertaking prudent repair and maintenance; to enhance operational efficiency; and to undertake projects to improve product quality and address environmental and safety issues.

Phase VI

Pursuant to paragraph 1 of Security Council resolution 1242(1999) (see p. 246), the new 180-day extension (phase VI) of the humanitarian programme established by resolution 986(1995) began on 25 May. The corresponding distribution plan was approved by the Secretary-General on 11 June [S/1999/671], on the understanding that, should total revenues generated exceed the $5.256 billion target authorized in resolution 1242(1999), he would invite Iraq to submit proposals for utilizing the excess revenue and make recommendations to the Council. The accompanying list of supplies and goods was made available to the Sanctions Committee, which concluded that, based on the limited information in the annexes, no prohibited items could be identified.

Report of Secretary-General (August). In a report of 19 August [S/1999/896 & Corr.1] on the first 90-day period of phase VI, the Secretary-General described developments in the programme's implementation up to 31 July. He reported a steady increase in the price of crude oil since the phase began, rising by about $5 in June and $2.50 in July, to $17 a barrel. Were prices to remain at that level, estimated revenues from contracts approved and under review would reach $6.3 billion (including pipeline fees). While exceeding the authorized target of $5.256 billion for phase VI, it was still insufficient to cover the shortfall of about $3.1 billion under phases IV and V. In anticipation of the Security Council's review pursuant to paragraph 14 of resolution 1242(1999), Iraq was invited to submit proposals for utilizing the additional revenue for the Secretary-General's consideration and recommendation to the Council.

The findings detailed in the report led the Secretary-General to appeal to the Council and the Sanctions Committee to expedite approval of the applications for oil spare parts and equipment submitted under phases IV to VI and the appointment of additional oil overseers; to review further all applications placed on hold, including those related to the current drought; and to resolve the difficulties in the current system of reimbursement for Iraq's bulk purchases of humanitarian supplies from the 13 per cent account to the 53 per cent account. Based on a report by a UN team sent to the Mina al-Bakr oil-loading site in April, in response to a complaint about the deteriorating working conditions there, the Secretary-General asked Iraq urgently to ensure a safe working environment for Saybolt's oil inspection agents and local staff at the site.

In welcoming the World Food Programme (WFP) and Iraqi initiatives to ensure a mechanism for more timely and equitable food distribution to the three northern governorates, the Secretary-General asked Iraq to procure better quality commodities through more reputable contractors. Based on a July survey of child and maternal mortality conducted by the United Nations Children's Fund (UNICEF) and the Government, Iraq should expedite the implementation of and increase funding for the targeted nutrition programmes in the 15 central and southern governorates, as provided for in the distribution plans for phases IV to VI.

Communication. On 11 September [S/1999/968], Iraq criticized the Secretary-General's report for a number of reasons, among them that it was wanting in objectivity in a number of respects and was not prepared in consultation with the Government of Iraq, as required by resolution 986(1995); its report on the UN Iraq Account did not include information on how, when and on what basis expenditures were made from the programme's various accounts; it made no assessment of OIP's activities and said nothing of the hundreds of applications languishing in its filing cabinets; it made no reference to the fundamental reasons why the humanitarian programme had not been satisfactorily implemented; and it was silent on the impact of the use of depleted uranium by the United States and the United Kingdom on the health of Iraqis. Iraq took exception to being asked to deal with more reputable contractors. The programme should support Iraq's suggestion that contracts should contain a clause safeguarding Iraq's rights and ensure that the goods supplied met specifications.

SECURITY COUNCIL ACTION

On 4 October [meeting 4050], the Security Council unanimously adopted **resolution 1266(1999)**. The draft [S/1999/1020] was sponsored by the Netherlands.

The Security Council,

Recalling its previous relevant resolutions, in particular resolutions 986(1995) of 14 April 1995, 1111(1997) of 4 June 1997, 1129(1997) of 12 September 1997, 1143(1997) of 4 December 1997, 1153(1998) of 20 February 1998, 1175(1998) of 19 June 1998, 1210(1998) of 24 November 1998 and 1242(1999) of 21 May 1999,

Recalling also the report of the Secretary-General of 19 August 1999, in particular paragraphs 4 and 94 thereof,

Determined to improve the humanitarian situation in Iraq,

Reaffirming the commitment of all Member States to the sovereignty and territorial integrity of Iraq,

Acting under Chapter VII of the Charter of the United Nations,

1. *Decides* that paragraph 2 of resolution 1153(1998), as extended by resolution 1242(1999), shall be modified to the extent necessary to authorize States to permit the import of petroleum and petroleum products originating in Iraq, including financial and other essential transactions directly related thereto, sufficient to produce an additional sum, beyond that provided for by resolution 1242(1999), equivalent to the total shortfall of revenues authorized but not generated under resolutions 1153(1998) and 1210(1998), 3.04 billion United States dollars, within the period of 180 days from 0001 hours eastern standard time on 25 May 1999;
2. *Decides* to remain seized of the matter.

Communication from Secretary-General. On 12 October [S/1999/1053], the Secretary-General informed the Council that he had approved the proposed adjustments to the allocations in the phase VI distribution plan submitted by Iraq, as it appeared likely that increased oil revenues would exceed the $3.04 billion required for that plan's implementation. Recalling his report that Iraq's oil industry continued to be in a lamentable state, the Secretary-General recommended approval of the additional $300 million for oil spare parts and equipment, bringing that sector's adjusted allocation to $600 million. The adjustments were approved with the understanding that the food-and-nutrition and health sectors received priority, the food basket was increased to the approved 2,300 kilocalories per person per day, and the allocation for the targeted nutrition programme was increased to provide adequate warehousing, transportation and related infrastructure. Acceptance of the revised sectoral allocations did not imply endorsement of those for either the housing construction programme or banking equipment and supplies. The availability of phase VI revenues to fund the full extent of new contracts arising from Iraq's plan to use the revenue increases, as authorized by resolution 1266(1999), would need to be considered vis-à-vis the transfer of some $510 million phase IV-approved applications and the yet to be determined transfers from phase V.

Report of Secretary-General (November). In a 12 November report on the second 90-day period of phase VI [S/1999/1162 & Corr.1], the Secretary-General gave an account of implementation activities up to 31 October. As at that date, of the $8.3 billion authorized by Council resolutions 1242(1999) and 1266(1999), $4,807.6 million had been deposited to the UN Iraq Account for phase VI, bringing total oil sales since the programme's inception to $18,141.5 million. The cumulative amounts allocated from that total to the seven different accounts specified in paragraph 8 of resolution 986(1995) included Iraq's purchases of humanitarian supplies totalling $9,242.3 million for its 15 central and southern governorates and $2,247.5 million for its three northern governorates. The sum of $239.6 million was due for reimbursement for Iraq's bulk purchases for the northern governorates.

The programme had delivered 12 million tonnes of food and related items, which continued to be distributed efficiently through the rationing system, and health-sector supplies worth over $729 million. Owing to increased contractual volume and higher oil prices, phase VI revenues were projected to reach $7.2 billion, including pipeline fees, but which were still $1.3 billion short of the revenue target authorized by resolution 1266(1999). In the current favourable revenue situation, the Secretary-General reiterated that Iraq provide a food basket of 2,300 kilocalories minimum per person per day countrywide, in line with its undertaking in the enhanced distribution plan, and that funding for targeted nutrition programmes be increased.

In view of the programme's sizeable expansion, the Secretary-General urged the further streamlining of the applications approval process by every means possible, an increase in OIP staff commensurate with its growing workload, and the expeditious appointment of additional oil overseers. He reiterated his recommendation for Council approval of Iraq's request for an additional $300 million for oil spare parts and equipment, and called for an early decision on each application currently on hold, to facilitate which he also urged Iraq and its suppliers to provide timely technical specifications and end-user information. He asked the Council to consider widening the programme's scope to include end-user training so as to maximize the use of programme resources. In noting the disruption of UN observation activities due to lack of Iraqi escorts, the Secretary-General called on Iraq to ensure freedom of movement and to rescind its new regulations requiring travel permits for UN staff.

Communication. On 29 November [S/1999/1209], Iraq commented that the Secretary-General's report did not refer to the adverse impact that the holds on contracts by the United States and the United Kingdom had on the implementation of the humanitarian programme; that the programme's exorbitant administrative expenses and other extravagant deductions from the oil revenues were depriving Iraq of funds for its humanitarian needs; and that the report neglected to mention the Sanctions Committee's inability to improve its procedures so that long processing delays had led to the accumulation of more than $5 billion in the UN Iraq Account, instead of being used immediately for the purchase of humanitarian items. Iraq set out its detailed observations on all sectors encompassed by the programme.

Sanctions Committee reports (August and November). The Sanctions Committee reports for the first and second 90-day periods of phase VI, respectively dated 24 August [S/1999/907] and 17 November [S/1999/1177], noted a continuing trend of increased oil export levels, largely from Mina al-Bakr. They recorded, as at 10 November, a total of 158 contracts approved under phase VI for the export of some 762 million barrels of oil and 389 liftings completed, equivalent to 506.9 million barrels worth $9,157 million.

Data on the export of humanitarian supplies indicated that phase VI applications received totalled 942. Of that number, 623 were circulated to the Committee, which found 452 eligible for payment, in the amount of $1,124 million, from the UN Iraq Account. Meanwhile, 2,395 phase V applications were also received: 2,071 were circulated to the Committee, of which 1,165 were eligible for payment in the amount of $2.9 billion. Consignments of humanitarian supplies from previous phases confirmed as having arrived in Iraq in full or in part numbered 4,012 during the first half of phase VI and 4,850 during the second half from the current and previous phases. Circulation of an increasing number of applications was being delayed because they contained payment mechanisms inconsistent with Committee guidelines and procedures.

As for the export of oil-production spare parts and equipment to Iraq, 1,108 applications had been circulated to the Committee, of which 783, worth $396.5 million, were approved; 385 such shipments had arrived in Iraq in full or in part.

The Committee affirmed its commitment to reach a solution to filling the overseer vacancies. It discussed the absence of audit reports on the operations of UN agencies in northern Iraq, contracts containing payment-mechanism clauses, the reimbursement from the 13 per cent account to the 53 per cent account, the need to increase oil revenues (authorized for phase IV) and the impact of holds on contracts for, as well as monitoring in Iraq of, oil-production spare parts and equipment.

Communication from Secretary-General. On 22 October [S/1999/1086], the Secretary-General transmitted a note from the OIP Executive Director drawing attention to the growing number of applications placed on hold, which, by 12 October, made up 23.7 per cent of applications circulated under phase V, and saying the Sanctions Committee was also taking longer (34 days on average) to review such applications. Moreover, specific activities or projects could not be completed because of holds on interrelated or complementary applications. The Secretary-General therefore asked the Committee to undertake an early review of all applications currently on hold and expedite a decision, as appropriate, in each case.

The foregoing was preceded by Iraq's 23 August communication [S/1999/902] complaining about the large number of contracts blocked or on hold. Iraq subsequently wrote that, as at 30 December, contracts on hold numbered 778, with a total value of $1.27 billion [S/2000/2].

SECURITY COUNCIL ACTION

On 19 November [meeting 4070], the Security Council unanimously adopted **resolution 1275**

(1999). The draft [S/1999/1180] was prepared during prior Council consultations.

The Security Council,

Recalling its resolutions 1242(1999) of 21 May 1999 and 1266(1999) of 4 October 1999,

Acting under Chapter VII of the Charter of the United Nations,

1. *Decides* to extend the period referred to in paragraphs 1, 2 and 8 of resolution 1242(1999) and in paragraph 1 of 1266(1999) until 4 December 1999;

2. *Decides* to remain seized of the matter.

On 3 December [meeting 4077], the Council adopted **resolution 1280(1999)** by vote (11-0-3), based on a draft [S/1999/1215] sponsored by the United States.

The Security Council,

Recalling its resolutions 1242(1999) of 21 May 1999, 1266(1999) of 4 October 1999 and 1275(1999) of 19 November 1999,

Acting under Chapter VII of the Charter of the United Nations,

1. *Decides* to extend the period referred to in paragraphs 1, 2 and 8 of resolution 1242(1999) and in paragraph 1 of resolution 1266(1999) until 11 December 1999;

2. *Decides* to remain seized of the matter.

VOTE ON RESOLUTION 1280(1999):

In favour: Argentina, Bahrain, Brazil, Canada, Gabon, Gambia, Namibia, Netherlands, Slovenia, United Kingdom, United States.
Against: None.
Abstaining: China, Malaysia, Russian Federation.
Not Participating: France.

China explained that extending phase VI for one week would neither help to improve Iraq's humanitarian situation nor advance consultations among the permanent Council members on an omnibus text on Iraq currently being drafted. China's appeals, which had not received due attention, were for the parties to seek common ground, while reserving differences and avoiding confrontation, in devising a roll-over programme that best met the needs of Iraqi civilians. The Russian Federation, which felt that the one-week extension was not in keeping with the realities of the grave humanitarian situation in Iraq, was unable to support the resolution as it took no account of the logical amendment proposed by France for a longer "technical" rollover, which would have allowed the programme to remain in operation.

France said it did not participate in the voting because the measure proposed could not be realized within so short an extension.

Communication. Iraq, on 5 December [S/1999/1218], refused to comply with resolutions 1275(1999) and 1280(1999). Given the implementation experience during the humanitarian programme's six phases, the successive extensions of phase VI for two weeks and one week authorized by those resolutions were impractical and farcical. Iraq was willing to cooperate in a six-month extension, however, and hoped to see improvements in the programme, as proposed by the Secretary-General and some Council members.

Phase VII

On 10 December [meeting 4079], the Security Council unanimously adopted **resolution 1281 (1999)**. The draft [S/1999/1230] was sponsored by the United States.

The Security Council,

Recalling its previous relevant resolutions, in particular resolutions 986(1995) of 14 April 1995, 1111(1997) of 4 June 1997, 1129(1997) of 12 September 1997, 1143(1997) of 4 December 1997, 1153(1998) of 20 February 1998, 1175(1998) of 19 June 1998, 1210(1998) of 24 November 1998, 1242(1999) of 21 May 1999, 1266(1999) of 4 October 1999, 1275(1999) of 19 November 1999 and 1280(1999) of 3 December 1999,

Convinced of the need as a temporary measure to continue to provide for the humanitarian needs of the Iraqi people until the fulfilment by the Government of Iraq of the relevant resolutions, including notably resolution 687(1991) of 3 April 1991, allows the Council to take further action with regard to the prohibitions referred to in resolution 661(1990) of 6 August 1990, in accordance with the provisions of those resolutions,

Convinced also of the need for equitable distribution of humanitarian supplies to all segments of the Iraqi population throughout the country,

Determined to improve the humanitarian situation in Iraq,

Reaffirming the commitment of all Member States to the sovereignty and territorial integrity of Iraq,

Acting under Chapter VII of the Charter of the United Nations,

1. *Decides* that the provisions of resolution 986 (1995), except those contained in paragraphs 4, 11 and 12, shall remain in force for a new period of 180 days beginning at 0001 hours eastern standard time on 12 December 1999;

2. *Also decides* that paragraph 2 of resolution 1153(1998) shall remain in force and shall apply to the 180-day period referred to in paragraph 1 above;

3. *Requests* the Secretary-General to continue to take the actions necessary to ensure the effective and efficient implementation of the present resolution and to continue to enhance as necessary the United Nations observation process in Iraq in such a way as to provide the required assurance to the Council that the goods produced in accordance with the present resolution are distributed equitably and that all supplies authorized for procurement, including dual-usage items and spare parts, are utilized for the purpose for which they have been authorized;

4. *Decides* to conduct a thorough review of all aspects of the implementation of the present resolution 90 days after the entry into force of paragraph 1 above, and again prior to the end of the 180-day period, upon receipt of the reports referred to in paragraphs 5 and 10 below, and expresses its intention, prior to the end of the 180-day period, to consider favourably renewal of the provisions of the present resolution, as appropri-

ate, provided that the said reports indicate that those provisions are being satisfactorily implemented;

5. *Requests* the Secretary-General to report to the Council 90 days after the date of entry into force of paragraph 1 above and again prior to the end of the 180-day period, on the basis of observations of United Nations personnel in Iraq, and of consultations with the Government of Iraq, on whether Iraq has ensured the equitable distribution of medicine, health supplies, foodstuffs, and materials and supplies for essential civilian needs, financed in accordance with paragraph 8 *(a)* of resolution 986(1995), including in his reports any observations he may have on the adequacy of the revenues to meet Iraq's humanitarian needs and on Iraq's capacity to export sufficient quantities of petroleum and petroleum products to produce the sum referred to in paragraph 2 of resolution 1153(1998);

6. *Requests* the Secretary-General to report to the Council if Iraq is unable to export petroleum and petroleum products sufficient to produce the total sum provided for by paragraph 2 above and, following consultations with the relevant United Nations agencies and the Iraqi authorities, make recommendations for the expenditure of sums expected to be available, consistent with the priorities established in paragraph 2 of resolution 1153(1998) and with the distribution plan referred to in paragraph 5 of resolution 1175(1998);

7. *Decides* that paragraph 3 of resolution 1210(1998) shall apply to the new 180-day period referred to in paragraph 1 above;

8. *Also decides* that paragraphs 1, 2, 3 and 4 of resolution 1175(1998) shall remain in force and shall apply to the new 180-day period referred to in paragraph 1 above;

9. *Requests* the Secretary-General, in consultation with the Government of Iraq, to submit to the Council no later than 15 January 2000 a detailed list of parts and equipment necessary for the purpose described in paragraph 1 of resolution 1175(1998);

10. *Requests* the Security Council Committee established by resolution 661(1990), in close coordination with the Secretary-General, to report to the Council 90 days after the entry into force of paragraph 1 above, and again prior to the end of the 180-day period, on the implementation of the arrangements in paragraphs 1, 2, 6, 8, 9 and 10 of resolution 986(1995);

11. *Urges* all States, and in particular the Government of Iraq, to provide their full cooperation in the effective implementation of the present resolution;

12. *Appeals* to all States to continue to cooperate in the timely submission of applications and the expeditious issue of export licences, facilitating the transit of humanitarian supplies authorized by the Committee established by resolution 661(1990), and to take all other appropriate measures within their competence in order to ensure that urgently needed humanitarian supplies reach the Iraqi people as rapidly as possible;

13. *Stresses* the need to continue to ensure respect for the security and safety of all persons directly involved in the implementation of the present resolution in Iraq;

14. *Decides* to keep these arrangements under review, including in particular those in paragraph 2 above, to ensure the uninterrupted flow of humanitarian supplies into Iraq, and expresses its determination to act without delay to address the recommendations of the report of the panel established to review humanitarian and other issues in Iraq in a further, comprehensive resolution;

15. *Decides* to remain seized of the matter.

In the light of the new 180-day extension of the humanitarian programme (phase VII) from 12 December, the UN Secretariat and Iraq, by an 11 December exchange of letters [S/1999/1241], agreed to extend for the same period the provisions of the 1996 Memorandum of Understanding between them on the implementation of resolution 986(1995).

Panel on humanitarian issues

Panel report. In accordance with the Security Council President's note of 30 January, which established three panels on Iraq (see p. 229), the Chairman of those panels on 30 March [S/1999/356] transmitted the report of the panel mandated to assess the current humanitarian situation in Iraq and recommend measures for its improvement. The panel, which was composed of four senior UN Secretariat officials, met between 19 February and 29 March.

In addition to reports and data from OIP, the panel considered written submissions from the United Nations Development Programme (UNDP), UNICEF, the United Nations Population Fund, UNHCR, the United Nations Office for Project Services (UNOPS), WFP, the Special Rapporteur of the Commission on Human Rights on the situation of human rights in Iraq, FAO, the United Nations Educational, Scientific and Cultural Organization, the World Health Organization, ICRC, the International Federation of Red Cross and Red Crescent Societies, the European Community Humanitarian Office and the Middle East Council of Churches. The panel heard briefings by the Special Envoy of the Secretary-General for Iraq, representatives of several UN offices, bodies and agencies, the UN independent oil monitors (Saybolt Nederland BV) and the Permanent Observer of the League of Arab States.

The report provided a comparative analysis between the current situation and that which prevailed before the events leading to the Gulf War (1990-1991). It noted that the Iran-Iraq war (1980-1988) had already taken a heavy toll on Iraqi society. Nonetheless, towards the end of the 1980s, Iraq's social and economic indicators were generally above the regional and developing country averages.

Data provided to the panel on conditions in Iraq under the effects of war and sanctions pointed to a continuing degradation of the economy, with an acute deterioration in the living conditions of the population and severe strains on its social fabric. As summed up by UNDP, the country had experienced a shift from relative affluence to massive poverty. Iraqi infant mortality rates were currently among the highest in the world. Low birth weight affected at least 23 per cent of all births, and chronic malnutrition affected every fourth child under five years old. Only 41 per cent of the population had regular access to clean water. Eighty-three per cent of all schools were in need of substantial repairs. Communicable diseases, which had been under control, returned on an epidemic scale in 1993 and had become part of the endemic pattern of the precarious health situation.

Regardless of improvements that might be brought about in the implementation of the current humanitarian programme, including speedier approval procedures, better government performance and higher funding levels, the magnitude of Iraq's humanitarian needs could not be met within the parameters of resolution 986(1995) and succeeding resolutions, in particular 1153(1998). Nor was the programme intended to meet all of the Iraqi people's needs. In the light of Iraq's near absolute dependence on oil exports to generate foreign exchange, the precarious state of the oil industry infrastructure, if allowed to deteriorate further, would have disastrous effects on the country's ability to cover the costs of basic humanitarian needs. That those were being met through handouts did not contribute to stimulating the economy and had a negative impact on agriculture, while increasing State control over a population whose private initiative was already under severe internal and external constraints.

The gravity of the humanitarian situation of the Iraqi people was indisputable and could not be overstated. Data and qualitative assessments of bona fide observers and sheer common-sense analysis of economic variables converged to corroborate that evaluation.

The panel made a series of recommendations that it believed might lead to incremental improvements. Those on the paramount question of securing additional funds for the purchase of urgently needed humanitarian supplies included: lifting the ceiling of allowable oil exports from Iraq and facilitating the speedy provision of oil-production parts and equipment; authorizing bilateral production-sharing agreements between Iraq and foreign oil companies that would supply maintenance and related equipment, thereby freeing the $300 million earmarked for parts and equipment; authorizing private investment flows into the oil industry and other secondary export industries, as well as into agriculture; encouraging the international community to provide supplementary funding within and outside the oil-for-food programme, either bilaterally or through multilateral organizations and non-governmental organizations (NGOs); temporarily reducing, by an agreed percentage, the revenue allocated to the United Nations Compensation Commission, or borrowing from it; temporarily suspending the implementation of paragraph 8 *(g)* of resolution 986(1995), which provided for the transfer of up to $10 million every 90 days from the UN Iraq Account to the escrow account for the purpose envisaged in paragraph 6 of resolution 778(1992) [YUN 1992, p. 320]; authorizing, at the request of States holding frozen Iraqi assets, the release of such assets to the UN Iraq Account or to another mechanism; minimizing the costs of the UN activities associated with implementing resolution 986(1995); and, as a confidence-building measure, furnishing Iraq with a daily statement of the status of the UN Iraq Account.

Foodstuffs, pharmaceuticals and medical supplies, as well as basic or standard medical and agricultural equipment and educational items, included in the pre-approved list of humanitarian supplies, could be contracted for and procured directly by the Government without notification to or approval by the Sanctions Committee. Dual-use items should be processed under the export/import mechanism in accordance with resolution 1051(1996) [YUN 1996, p. 218] and submitted to the Sanctions Committee for approval under the no-objection procedure. The export of other goods to Iraq should be authorized by the Committee within two business days upon receipt of the application indicating the goods, the agreed price and the estimated time of arrival.

Other recommendations called on Iraq to ensure the timely distribution of humanitarian goods, particularly medical supplies, and to clear the unjustifiable bottlenecks at its warehouses; to address the needs of vulnerable groups (street children, the disabled, elderly and mentally ill) in central and southern Iraq and allow UN agencies and bona fide NGOs freer access to restricted areas and sections of the population to evaluate their nutritional and general humanitarian condition; to refine its list of priorities in terms of packaging contracts through the humanitarian programme; to ensure adequate humanitarian assistance for the involuntarily displaced without their having to demonstrate the required six-month residence in their current domicile; and to extend full cooperation to the mine-clearance programme in northern Iraq, facilitate the work of UNOPS, and consider initiating demining efforts in other areas of the country.

The panel reiterated its understanding that the humanitarian situation in Iraq would continue to be a dire one in the absence of a sustained revival of the Iraqi economy, which in turn could not be achieved solely through remedial humanitarian efforts.

On 17 December, the Security Council incorporated the panel's main recommendations into section C of **resolution 1284(1999)**.

UN Compensation Commission and Fund

The United Nations Compensation Commission, established in 1991 [YUN 1991, p. 195] for the resolution and payment through the United Nations Compensation Fund, established at the same time, of claims against Iraq for losses and damage resulting from its 1990 invasion and occupation of Kuwait [YUN 1990, p. 189], continued in 1999 to expedite the prompt settlement of claims. The Commission was headquartered in Geneva, where its Governing Council held all of its sessions.

Governing Council. The Commission's Governing Council held four regular sessions during the year (thirty-first (15-18 March) [S/1999/470], thirty-second (22-24 June) [S/1999/856], thirty-third (28-30 September) [S/2000/68] and thirty-fourth (7-9 December) [S/2000/69]) at which it considered the reports and recommendations of the Panels of Commissioners appointed to review specific instalments of various categories of claims. Each report described in detail the measures taken by the Panel to determine whether a given claim fell within the Commission's jurisdiction, to verify its validity, to evaluate compensable losses and to arrive at the compensation amounts to be recommended. The Governing Council also acted on the Executive Secretary's report submitted at each session, which, in addition to providing a summary of the previous period's activities, covered corrections to approved claim awards, claim withdrawals, the processing and payment of approved claims, the appointment of Commissioners and the 1999 progress report on the Commission's 1997-2003 work programme.

In March, the Council considered Panel reports on specific instalments of corporate claims under category E, grouped as follows: one on tourism and non-tourism claims (E2), four on construction and engineering claims (E3) and one on Kuwaiti private-sector claims (E4). Also considered was a Panel report on the third instalment of F1 claims filed by 14 Governments on behalf of national entities or nationals for losses related to departure and evacuation costs or damage to physical property. The session report tabulated those groups of claims, together with the total amounts of compensation claimed and amounts recommended for award, as approved by the Council. Discussions continued on priority of payment and payment mechanisms for the second payment phase due to begin on completion of the first phase, in July 1999. In keeping with Council decision 17 [YUN 1994, p. 478], each individual claimant in categories A (for departure from Iraq or Kuwait during 2 August 1990–2 March 1991), B (for serious personal injury or death) and C (for damages up to $100,000) had been accorded priority in the first phase and paid an initial amount of up to $2,500 each.

Considered at the June session were: a special Panel report concerning 636 unresolved category A claims from Pakistan; four Panel reports and recommendations on the seventh instalment of C, the third instalment of D (individual claims for damages above $100,000) and the second and third instalments of E1 (oil-sector claims by corporations, other private legal entities and public-sector enterprises) categories of claims; as well as the Executive Secretary's report on corrections to approved awards to Governments and international organizations on behalf of 10,757 category A claimants. The session noted that the Panel report on the category C claims marked the completion of the processing of such claims. The Council approved the Panel's recommendations on the groups of claims mentioned. Each of those decisions, as well as those taken at the following two sessions, included: a table indicating the countries or organizations concerned, the numbers of claims recommended and not recommended for payment, the compensation amounts claimed and recommended, and a request that a copy of the Panel report be provided to the Secretary-General, Iraq, and the respective Governments and international organizations. The Council also adopted a decision concerning the priority of payment and mechanisms for the second payment phase.

The September session examined five reports and recommendations by the Panels for the fourth, eighth and ninth instalments of E3 non-Kuwaiti construction and engineering claims; and for the second and fourth instalments of E4 private-sector Kuwaiti claims. The Council approved the recommendations for those groups and categories of claims. It also corrected additional approved category A awards, based on the Executive Secretary's report, and approved awards in the first three instalments of category D claims, in accordance with the relevant Panel's recommended adjustments. The Council further decided that, where previously undistributed funds were returned to Governments for payment to claimants who had since been located, each Government should distribute those funds to claimants within four months and report thereon to the Commission within two additional months. In the light of increased income received by the Compensation Fund, the Council decided that its working group should begin discussing the mechanism for the third payment phase. In addition, the Council appointed a new Commissioner, on the Secretary-General's nomination, and changed the chairmen of two Panels.

The December session considered four reports with recommendations by Panels for the fourth instalment of category D claims; the third instalment of E2 non-Kuwaiti corporate transport-sector claims; and the first instalments of F2 and F3 claims filed by Jordan and Kuwait, respectively, on behalf of their government ministries and other entities. Also considered was the Executive Secretary's report recommending corrections to the approved awards in the fifth and sixth instalments of category A claims and to those in the first to the seventh instalments of C claims. The Council approved the Panels' and Executive Secretary's recommendations. It noted that the Committee on Administrative Matters, at its 18 November meeting, approved the proposed budget for the 2000-2001 biennium in the amount of $99,629,600.

Communications from Iraq. Between February and December, Iraq drew to the Secretary-General's attention examples of illegal and arbitrary measures applied by the Compensation Commission in processing what it said were unjustified claims and asked his intervention to ensure the Commission's compliance with international law and principles of justice. In that regard, Iraq complained of neither having been given detailed information nor the opportunity to present its views on the following: a large and complex Kuwaiti E claim referred to in the Commission's procedural order No. 8 [S/1999/112]; 15 category E1 oil-sector claims [S/1999/180]; 20 category F claims filed by Jordan on behalf of government ministries and entities [S/1999/113] and 25 similar claims filed by Saudi Arabia [S/1999/1243], although Iraq had received the corresponding procedural orders for both groups of F claims. Iraq insisted that it be provided with details of the Jordanian claims [S/1999/570].

Other matters

Iraqi complaints

Iraq asserted on 15 January [S/1999/45] that the continued forceful imposition of the northern and southern air-exclusion (no-fly) zones over Iraqi territory by the United States and the United Kingdom—and also by France initially—were illegal and violated UN resolutions and international law regarding sovereignty. Iraq claimed that, with its official acceptance of the provisions of Security Council resolution 687(1991) [YUN 1991, p. 172], a formal ceasefire to the Gulf War became effective and brought to an end the authorizations of military intervention implicit in resolution 678(1990) [YUN 1990, p. 204]. Furthermore, the pretext of humanitarian protection for the Kurds in the north and the Shia in the south, which had demarked the no-fly zones, was based on claims about human rights violations. The refusal of China and the Russian Federation to condone the zones and France's withdrawal from their unilateral enforcement underscored the lack of Council support for the illegal imposition of the zones and incursions by the United States and the United Kingdom.

Affirming its absolute rejection of the no-fly zones, Iraq regarded as violations of its airspace the zone-enforcement sorties by United States and United Kingdom aircraft based in Kuwait, Saudi Arabia and Turkey, all of which Iraq tracked throughout 1999 and reported regularly through identical letters to the Secretary-General and the Council. Alleged wanton military attacks in the process, causing civilian deaths and injuries, as well as destruction to private and public property, were recorded in a number of additional communications [S/1999/101, S/1999/447, S/1999/819, S/1999/880, S/1999/893, S/1999/901, S/1999/978, S/1999/1009, S/1999/1149, S/1999/1208]. Iraq warned of the dangerous repercussions for international peace and security stemming from UN silence in the face of such brutal acts of aggression [S/1999/153], adding that, as the aggressors were permanent Council members, their actions were conducive to the collapse of the collective security regime enshrined in the UN Charter [S/1999/842].

Iraq also alleged violations of its territorial waters by Kuwait [S/1999/364, S/1999/467, S/1999/540, S/1999/553, S/1999/931, S/1999/1077], whose patrols increasingly subjected Iraqi fishing boats and other marine craft to searches, confiscations of fishing permits, even detention and torture of Iraqi fishermen. Kuwait denied certain of those allegations as fabrications [S/1999/616] and, in turn, claimed the incursion into its territorial waters by two Iraqi naval units, necessitating the crews' detention and interrogation [S/1999/784], and by an Iraqi boat allegedly exporting oil-for-food humanitarian goods out of Iraq [S/1999/885].

In the light of the admission by the United States Department of Defense that the United States and the United Kingdom had fired more than 1 million depleted uranium rounds weighing 315 tons during the Gulf War, Iraq reaffirmed its previously announced position that it held those States responsible for the environmental and health-related consequences of such use [A/54/75-S/1999/345]. In that connection, Iraq submitted several reports [S/1999/195, S/1999/410, S/1999/668, S/1999/891, S/1999/1039, S/1999/1254] concerning its disposal of unexploded ordnance—left behind by what it called the 1991 30-Power aggression against it—which continued to be found in large quantities in the country.

Also during 1999, Iraq protested against the increasing land and air incursions into its northern territory by Turkey, which maintained that the object was to pursue and root out terrorist groups posing a threat to its national security. Iraq rejected that as a legitimate reason for Turkey's open violation of its sovereignty and territorial integrity and drew attention to several large-scale incursions between April and November [S/1999/560, S/1999/580, S/1999/778, S/1999/1028, S/1999/1222, S/1999/1225], which, it claimed, left in their wake serious losses of Iraqi lives and property.

In other communications, Iraq protested against the illegal entry, through Turkey, into northern Iraq of a United States official at the head of a British and Turkish delegation [S/1999/103]; the so-called Iraq Liberation Act passed by the United States Congress to finance and arm terrorist groups seeking to undermine Iraq's stability and challenge its unity [S/1999/651]; and United States use of UN agencies working in northern Iraq as covers for its agents to carry out acts of espionage and sabotage [S/1999/690], as well as its sponsorship of military training for opponents of President Saddam Hussein [S/1999/1129].

Afghanistan

The war in Afghanistan between the Taliban and the United Front (UF), which was fuelled by ever-increasing numbers of foreign-supplied arms and combatants, as well as by revenue from opium production that reached record levels during the year, continued throughout 1999. The Taliban, holding significant military and territorial advantage, attempted to prosecute the war to victory, while UF defended its hold on the remaining territories outside Taliban control. Although the United Nations Special Mission to Afghanistan (UNSMA) and certain neighbouring countries succeeded in bringing the parties together in two rounds of talks in February and March, the Taliban, in April, declined to continue the talks unless UF accepted to join the "Islamic Emirate of Afghanistan". Only nine days after the "six plus two" group—the six countries bordering Afghanistan: China, Iran, Pakistan, Tajikistan, Turkmenistan and Uzbekistan; plus the Russian Federation and the United States—issued a 19 July declaration calling for a resumption of the talks and agreeing not to give military support to any Afghan party, the Taliban mounted a major offensive intended decisively to defeat UF. The waves of fighting, which see-sawed without significant gains on either side, left in their wake more death and destruction and tens of thousands of civilians forcibly displaced.

In view of the limited impact of the activities of the Special Envoy for Afghanistan, Lakhdar Brahimi (Algeria), on the military and political situation, he and the Secretary-General decided to freeze his activities until conditions warranted his renewed intervention. To improve the Organization's political effectiveness, the Secretary-General proposed to strengthen UNSMA to enable it to assume the primary role of UN peacemaking and to deploy its offices to facilitate regular liaison with belligerents and non-belligerents alike, proposals which the General Assembly supported in December.

Acting on evidence that the Taliban provided training and sanctuary for international terrorists, notably Usama bin Laden, a Saudi national indicted by the United States for terrorist activities and intentions against the United States and its nationals, the Security Council, in October, demanded that the Taliban turn Mr. bin Laden over to appropriate authorities for trial. Council sanctions on the Taliban for failure to comply with that demand went into effect on 14 November.

Meanwhile, UN agencies, in cooperation with international humanitarian organizations and NGOs, attempted to provide emergency relief to the neediest of war victims, especially the forcibly displaced, as well as to victims of an earthquake in February. The Mine Action Programme of the United Nations Office for the Coordination of Humanitarian Affairs (OCHA) recorded the successful clearance of some 400 square kilometres of mined areas since its inception. UNHCR helped in the orderly repatriation of large numbers of Afghan refugees from Pakistan and Iran. As to the year's record levels of opium cultivation and production, the Secretary-General instructed the United Nations International Drug Control Programme to coordinate response to it, in cooperation with the Secretariat's Department of Political Affairs and UNSMA.

(For Afghanistan's credentials to the fifty-fourth session of the General Assembly, see PART FIVE, Chapter IV.)

Situation in Afghanistan

Reports of Secretary-General (March, June and September). The situation in Afghanistan during 1999 was described by the Secretary-General in four progress reports, submitted in response to General Assembly resolution 53/203 A [YUN 1998, p. 289]. The first three were quarterly, issued on 31 March [A/53/889-S/1999/362], 21 June [A/53/1002-S/1999/698] and 21 September [A/54/378-S/1999/994]; the fourth was an annual report, issued in the last quarter of the year (see p. 258). The reports gave accounts of the political and military developments in the country; the peacemaking activities of the Special Envoy, of UNSMA and at UN Headquarters in New York; UN assistance and programmes to alleviate the progressively deteriorating humanitarian and human rights situations of the war victims; and UN efforts to curb terrorism within and from Afghanistan, as well as to reduce the illicit cultivation, production and trafficking of drugs.

The September report underscored the adoption, by the high-level meeting of the "six plus two" group (Tashkent, Uzbekistan, 19-20 July)—attended also by the Taliban and UF—of the Tashkent Declaration on Fundamental Principles for a Peaceful Settlement of the Conflict in Afghanistan [A/54/174-S/1999/812]. By the Declaration, the group urged the resumption of political negotiations under UN auspices aimed at establishing a broad-based, multi-ethnic and fully representative Government; agreed not to provide military support to any Afghan party and to prevent the use of its members' territories for that purpose so as to help bring about a cessation of hostilities; and outlined two stages for the negotiations: the first stage to agree on an immediate ceasefire without preconditions and to engage in confidence-building measures, including prisoner-of-war (POW) exchanges and lifting blockades to enable reciprocal trade and delivery of humanitarian assistance; the second to draw up basic principles for Afghanistan's future State structure. The Declaration further urged the Afghan parties, particularly the Taliban, to cease providing refuge and training to international terrorists and called on the international community to respond to the 1999 Inter-Agency Consolidated Appeal for Emergency Humanitarian and Rehabilitation Assistance for Afghanistan (see p. 837).

However, immediately following that hopeful event, the Taliban launched a major offensive on 28 July in northern Afghanistan, aimed at capturing the remaining part of the country outside their control. Besides noting the involvement of thousands of non-Afghan nationals and boy soldiers, mainly on the side of the Taliban forces, and the external supply of materiel to both warring parties, the report spoke of brutalities inflicted on civilians, as had occurred during past Taliban offensives, and the deteriorating humanitarian situation.

Communications. Among a series of identical letters addressed to the Secretary-General and the Security Council, Afghanistan, on 10 March [A/53/860-S/1999/261], forwarded a declaration reiterating its conviction that geniune intra-Afghan dialogue was the only solution to the Afghan turmoil, its resolve to defend Afghanistan's national unity, political independence and territorial integrity should the Taliban and its sponsors continue to reject a peaceful solution, its calls on Pakistan to stop supporting the Taliban, and its condemnation of the Taliban's massacre of civilians in the north-western provinces and support of terrorism and narcotics trafficking.

On 12 April [A/53/906-S/1999/409], Afghanistan reported that, during arrangements for the second (March) round of talks, the Taliban was preparing for a massive assault on government positions, towards which Pakistan had been contributing arms and ammunition shipments throughout March, in addition to dispatching a regiment of paramilitary force to the western suburbs of Kabul.

On 24 July [A/53/1027-S/1999/824], Afghanistan quoted a 22 July Pakistani news report that 5,000 armed Pakistani "students" had been dispatched to help in the "decisive offensive" against anti-Taliban fighters, that from 3,000 to 5,000 Pakistani militants from a number of Islamic fundamentalist parties had arrived in Kabul and that a brigade of some 400 Arab Islamic militants from the Middle East, under the control of the Saudi terrorist Usama bin Laden, had taken up positions along Kabul's front line. Afghanistan also set out the main points of its statement to the "six plus two" Tashkent meeting, including the imperative to unite the nation through a broad-based Government representing all of the country's ethnic groups and extending equal rights to all, its rejection of continued foreign military intervention, its opposition to terrorism and its commitment to fight the illicit drug production.

President Burhanuddin Rabbani of Afghanistan, on 1 August [S/1999/838], expanded on Pakistan's support of the Taliban, adding that he expected the Security Council to address the issue and adopt measures against Pakistan. On 17 August [A/53/1038-S/1999/884], he called for immediate and adequate UN assistance for the victims of the Pakistan/Taliban campaign of ethnic cleansing and forcible deportation in the Shomali Plains and in Parwan and Kapisa provinces. On 5 November [A/54/532-S/1999/1142 & Corr.1], Afghanistan forwarded a 3 November Afghan Online Press editorial urging the United Nations to be wary about offering diplomatic recognition to the Taliban and to remain tough in its dealings with it, along with a report in *The Guardian* (London) of 20 October stating that the Taliban, in the course of its July offensive, drove some 130,000 people from their homes and caused immense human and physical wreckage.

In August, Uzbekistan appealed to the "six plus two" group to observe its commitment not to render military assistance to any Afghan party [A/54/203-S/1999/849]; the European Union (EU) called on Afghanistan's neighbouring States to prevent the flow of arms and personnel from and through their territories, and to use their influence with Afghan factions to support UN peace efforts [S/1999/886]; and Iran, on the anniversary of the still unresolved 1998 murder of its consular staff and journalist in Mazar-e-Sharif [YUN 1998, p. 294], pursued its demand that the Taliban apprehend and bring the perpetrators to justice, calling on the Council to implement its decisions in that regard so as to underscore the inviolability of diplomatic premises and dispel the Taliban's notion that it could disregard international law and UN resolutions with impunity [A/54/204-S/1999/851, S/1999/855].

SECURITY COUNCIL ACTION

On 22 October [meeting 4055], the Security Council President made statement **S/PRST/1999/29** on the Council's behalf:

The Security Council has considered the report of the Secretary-General of 21 September 1999 concerning the situation in Afghanistan and its implications for international peace and security.

The Council reiterates its grave concern at the continued Afghan conflict, which is a serious and growing threat to regional and international peace and security. It strongly condemns the Taliban for the launching in July 1999, only one week after the meeting of the "six plus two" group in Tashkent, of a new offensive, despite the repeated demands by the Council to cease fighting. This has undermined international efforts to facilitate the restoration of peace in Afghanistan. The fighting following the offensive has resulted in enormous suffering to the civilian population of Afghanistan. The Taliban has a primary responsibility for this.

The Council reiterates that there is no military solution to the conflict in Afghanistan and that only a negotiated political settlement aimed at the establishment of a broad-based, multi-ethnic and fully representative government acceptable to all Afghans can lead to peace and reconciliation. It recalls its demand that the parties to the conflict, especially the Taliban, resume negotiations under United Nations auspices without delay and preconditions in full compliance with the relevant resolutions of the General Assembly and the Council. The Council notes that the United Front of Afghanistan has repeatedly made clear that it is willing to talk with the Taliban in order to reach a solution to the country's problems.

The Council reiterates that outside interference in the internal affairs of Afghanistan, including the involvement of foreign combatants and military personnel and the supply of weapons and other materials used in the conflict, should cease immediately. It calls upon all States to take resolute measures to prohibit their military personnel from planning and participating in combat operations in Afghanistan, and immediately to withdraw their personnel and to assure that the supply of ammunition and other war-making materials is halted. The Council expresses its deep distress over reports indicating the involvement in the fighting in Afghanistan, on the side of the Taliban forces, of thousands of non-Afghan nationals, mostly from religious schools and some of whom are below the age of fourteen.

The Council reaffirms its full support for the efforts of the United Nations, in particular the activities of the United Nations Special Mission to Afghanistan and those of the Special Envoy of the Secretary-General for Afghanistan, in facilitating the political process towards the goals of national reconciliation and a lasting political settlement with the participation of all parties to the conflict and all segments of Afghan society, and reiterates its position that the United Nations must continue to play its central and impartial role in international efforts towards a peaceful resolution of the Afghan conflict.

The Council expresses its grave concern at the seriously deteriorating humanitarian situation in Afghanistan. It calls upon all Afghan parties, and in particular the Taliban, to take the necessary steps to secure the uninterrupted supply of humanitarian aid to all in need of it and in this connection not to create impediments to the activities of the United Nations humanitarian agencies and international humanitarian organizations.

The Council once again urges all Afghan factions to cooperate fully with the Special Mission and international humanitarian organizations, and calls upon them, in particular the Taliban, to take the necessary steps to ensure the safety and freedom of movement of such personnel.

The Council welcomes the Tashkent Declaration on Fundamental Principles for a Peaceful Settlement of the Conflict in Afghanistan, adopted by the "six plus two" group on 19 July 1999, particularly the agreement of members of the group not to provide military support to any Afghan party and to prevent the use of their territories for such purposes. It urges the members of the group and the Afghan factions to implement these principles in support of the efforts of the United Nations towards a peaceful resolution of the Afghan conflict.

The Council strongly condemns the continuing use of Afghan territory, especially areas controlled by the Taliban, for the sheltering and training of terrorists and planning of terrorist acts, and reaffirms its conviction that the suppression of international terrorism is essential for the maintenance of international peace and security. It insists that the Taliban cease the provision of sanctuary and training for international terrorists and their organizations, take effective measures to ensure that the territory under its control is not used for terrorist installations and camps or for the preparation or organization of terrorist acts against other States or their citizens, and cooperate with efforts to bring indicted terrorists to justice. The Council demands once again that the Taliban turn over indicted terrorist Usama bin Laden to appropriate authorities as set out in its resolution 1267(1999) of 15 October 1999. It reaffirms its decision to implement on 14 November 1999 the measures contained in that resolution, unless the Secretary-General reports that the Taliban has fully complied with the obligation set out in paragraph 2 of that resolution.

The Council is deeply disturbed also by a significant increase in the cultivation, production and trafficking of drugs in Afghanistan, especially in areas controlled by the Taliban, which will contribute to the war-making capabilities of the Afghans and will have even more serious international consequences. It demands that the Taliban, as well as others, halt all illegal drug activities. The Council calls upon Member States, in particular those neighbouring Afghanistan, and all others concerned to undertake concerted measures to stop the trafficking of illegal drugs from Afghanistan.

The Council deplores the worsening human rights situation in Afghanistan. It expresses particular alarm at the continuing disregard by the Taliban of the concerns expressed by the international community. The Council underlines the unacceptability of the forced displacement of the civilian population, in particular that conducted by the Taliban during their recent offensive, summary executions, the deliberate abuse and arbitrary detentions of civilians, violence and continuing discrimination against women and girls, the separation of men from their families, the use of child soldiers, the widespread burning of crops and destruction of homes, the indiscriminate bombing and other violations of human rights and international humanitarian law in Afghanistan. It calls upon all Afghan parties, especially the Taliban, to put an end to such practices, to adhere to the international norms and standards in this sphere, to take urgent measures to improve the human rights situation and, as an immediate first step, to ensure the protection of civilians.

The Council reiterates that the capture by the Taliban of the Consulate-General of the Islamic Republic of Iran and the murder of the Iranian diplomats and a journalist in Mazar-e-Sharif constitute flagrant violations of international law. It demands that the Taliban cooperate fully with the United Nations in investigating these crimes with a view to prosecuting those responsible.

The Council looks forward to the next report of the Secretary-General on the situation in Afghanistan, and encourages him to review options for the Council and the General Assembly.

The Council deplores the failure of the leadership of the Taliban to take measures to comply with the demands made in its previous resolutions, especially to conclude a ceasefire and to resume negotiations, and in this context reaffirms its readiness to consider the imposition of measures, in accordance with its responsibility under the Charter of the United Nations, with the aim of achieving the full implementation of its relevant resolutions.

Further report of Secretary-General (November). The Secretary-General's fourth progress report, dated 16 November [A/54/536-S/1999/1145] (see p. 261), summarized developments since the issuance of his 23 November 1998 annual report [YUN 1998, p. 289].

GENERAL ASSEMBLY ACTION

On 17 December [meeting 84], the General Assembly adopted **resolution 54/189 A** [draft: A/54/L.58] without vote [agenda items 20 (*f*) & 50].

The situation in Afghanistan and its implications for international peace and security

The General Assembly,

Recalling its resolutions 50/88 B of 19 December 1995, 51/195 B of 17 December 1996, 52/211 B of 19 December 1997 and 53/203 A of 18 December 1998,

Recalling also Security Council resolutions 1193(1998) of 28 August 1998, 1214(1998) of 8 December 1998 and 1267(1999) of 15 October 1999 and all statements of the President of the Security Council on the situation in Afghanistan,

Noting all recent declarations by participants of regional international meetings and by international organizations on the situation in Afghanistan,

Reaffirming its strong commitment to the sovereignty, independence, territorial integrity and national unity of Afghanistan, and respecting its multicultural, multi-ethnic and historical heritage,

Convinced that there is no military solution to the Afghan conflict and that only a political settlement aimed at the establishment of a broad-based, multi-ethnic and fully representative government acceptable to the Afghan people can lead to peace and reconciliation,

Stressing the importance of non-intervention and non-interference in the internal affairs of Afghanistan, and deeply concerned at all forms of continued external support, which is causing the prolongation and intensification of the conflict,

Expressing its grave concern at the failure of all Afghan parties, in particular the Taliban, to put an end to the conflict, which seriously threatens stability and peace in the region, and welcoming the willingness of the United Front to talk to the Taliban in order to find a solution to the country's problems,

Deeply concerned by the increasingly ethnic nature of the conflict, by reports of persecution on the grounds of ethnic origin and religious persuasion and by the threat this poses to the unity of the Afghan State,

Strongly condemning the sharp escalation of the conflict, in particular after the launching of a new offensive by the Taliban in July 1999, only one week after the meeting of the "six plus two" group in Tashkent, despite the repeated demands by the Security Council and continuing attempts by the Special Envoy of the Secretary-General for Afghanistan to avert the Taliban offensive,

Noting with concern the resulting exacerbation of the enormous suffering of the Afghan people, including the massive loss of human life, summary executions, deliberate abuse and arbitrary detention of civilians, refugee flows, use of child soldiers, harassment, forcible displacement of innocent civilians and extensive destruction,

Expressing its grave concern at persistent violations of human rights and at breaches of international humanitarian law in Afghanistan, as exemplified by reports of mass killings and atrocities committed by combatants against civilians and prisoners of war, including the finding in the report of the United Nations investigation team for Afghanistan, submitted by the Office of the United Nations High Commissioner for Human Rights, that serious violations of human rights and international humanitarian law took place in Afghanistan in 1997 and 1998,

Noting with alarm the massive displacement by the Taliban of the civilian population and, in particular, of women and children, in the Shomali Plains, as well as the indiscriminate destruction of their homes and agricultural land, thereby eliminating their source of income,

Expressing its grave concern at the continuing and substantiated reports of systematic human rights violations against women and girls, including all forms of discrimination against them, notably in areas under the control of the Taliban,

Strongly condemning the capture by Taliban militia of the Consulate-General of the Islamic Republic of Iran and the murder of Iranian diplomats and a journalist in Mazar-e Sharif, and stressing that these unacceptable acts, which constitute flagrant violations of established international law, must not go unpunished,

Deeply disturbed by the continuing use of Afghan territory, especially areas controlled by the Taliban, for the recruitment, sheltering and training of terrorists, including international terrorists, and the planning of terrorist acts within and outside Afghanistan,

Deeply disturbed also by the continuing use of Afghan territory, especially areas controlled by the Taliban, for the increasing cultivation and trafficking of drugs, as well as by the significant rise in the illicit production of opium, which contribute to the war-making capabilities of the Afghans and have dangerous repercussions reaching Afghanistan's neighbours and far beyond,

Reiterating that the United Nations, as a universally recognized and impartial intermediary, must continue to play the central role in international efforts towards a peaceful resolution of the Afghan conflict,

Expressing its appreciation for the efforts made in this regard by the United Nations Special Mission to Afghanistan and by the Special Envoy of the Secretary-General for Afghanistan, and noting with concern that, following years of continuing negotiation, insufficient cooperation with the Special Envoy of the Secretary-General by the parties to the conflict has led to the freezing of his activities,

Noting and welcoming the meeting of the "six plus two" group under the auspices of the United Nations, with the participation of representatives of the warring Afghan parties, held in Tashkent on 19 and 20 July 1999, and the Tashkent Declaration on Fundamental Principles for a Peaceful Settlement of the Conflict in Afghanistan adopted on 19 July 1999, as well as the working meeting of the "six plus two" group at the level of foreign ministers, held in New York in September 1999,

Regretting recent reports by the Secretary-General indicating that the "six plus two" group has not yet had the desired impact on the warring parties in Afghanistan,

Welcoming the contacts between the United Nations Special Mission to Afghanistan and various non-warring Afghan parties and personalities, and supporting calls by these independent Afghans for an end to the fighting and any proposals that might advance the cause of peace, including the meeting, held in Rome from 22 to 25 November 1999, of a group of Afghan personalities aimed at the convening of a genuine *loya jirgah* to promote a political settlement,

1. *Takes note* of the report of the Secretary-General, and endorses the observations and recommendations set out therein;

2. *Stresses* that the main responsibility for finding a political solution to the conflict lies with the Afghan parties, and urges all of them to respond to the repeated calls for peace by the United Nations;

3. *Calls upon* all Afghan parties, in particular the Taliban, to cease immediately all armed hostilities, to renounce the use of force and to engage, without delay or preconditions, in a political dialogue under United Nations auspices aimed at achieving a lasting political settlement of the conflict by creating a broad-based, multi-ethnic and fully representative government, which would protect the rights of all Afghans and observe the international obligations of Afghanistan;

4. *Welcomes* the intra-Afghan meetings in Ashgabat at the beginning of 1999 and in Tashkent in July 1999, and urges all Afghan parties to take further confidence-building measures with a view to resuming direct intra-Afghan talks;

5. *Urges* the Taliban and other Afghan parties to refrain from all acts of violence against civilians, including women and children;

6. *Strongly condemns* the sharp escalation of the conflict, in particular after the launching of a new offensive by the Taliban in July 1999;

7. *Notes with distress* reports indicating the involvement in the fighting in Afghanistan, mainly on the side of the Taliban forces, of two thousand to five thousand non-Afghan nationals, mostly from religious schools, some of whom are still children;

8. *Strongly condemns* the fact that foreign military support to the Afghan parties continued unabated through 1999, and calls upon all States to refrain strictly from any outside interference and to end immediately the supply of arms, ammunition, military equipment, training or any other military support to all parties to the conflict in Afghanistan;

9. *Calls upon* all States to take resolute measures to prohibit their military personnel from planning and participating in combat operations in Afghanistan and immediately to withdraw their personnel and to assure that the supply of ammunition and other war-making materials is halted;

10. *Reiterates its position* that the United Nations must continue to play its central and impartial role in

international efforts towards a peaceful resolution of the Afghan conflict;

11. *Reaffirms its full support* for the efforts of the United Nations in facilitating the political process towards the goal of national reconciliation and a lasting political settlement with the participation of all parties to the conflict and all segments of Afghan society, and fully supports, in particular, the comprehensive efforts of the Secretary-General, of the Special Envoy of the Secretary-General for Afghanistan and those of the United Nations Special Mission to Afghanistan;

12. *Supports* the intention of the Secretary-General to strengthen the United Nations Special Mission to Afghanistan with a view to assuring its primary role in conducting United Nations peacemaking activities in Afghanistan, in particular by appointing a new head of Mission, by progressively moving its head office to Kabul and by increasing its presence in neighbouring countries;

13. *Also supports* the intention of the Secretary-General to redouble the efforts of the United Nations Special Mission to Afghanistan to achieve a durable and equitable political settlement by facilitating an immediate and durable ceasefire and the resumption of a dialogue between the Afghan parties, by instituting a negotiating process leading to the formation of a broad-based, multi-ethnic and fully representative government of national unity and by continuing to work closely with all countries that are willing to help find a peaceful solution to the Afghan conflict, in particular with the members of the "six plus two" group, while continuing to monitor closely and encouraging the various peace initiatives of non-warring Afghan parties and personalities;

14. *Welcomes* the establishment of the Civil Affairs Unit within the United Nations Special Mission to Afghanistan, as approved by the General Assembly in its resolution 53/203 A, and the efforts of the Secretary-General and the United Nations High Commissioner for Human Rights to ensure that the ongoing process of deployment of a first group of civil affairs officers, including a coordinator for the Civil Affairs Unit, is completed as soon as possible;

15. *Also welcomes* the constitution of groups of interested States to coordinate their efforts as well as the activities of international organizations, in particular the Organization of the Islamic Conference, and encourages those organizations and States, in particular the "six plus two" group, to use their influence in a constructive manner in support of and in close coordination with the United Nations to promote peace in Afghanistan;

16. *Supports* the intention of the Secretary-General to continue to work with the "six plus two" group, to seek ways of improving the creativity and effectiveness of the group so as to ensure its more constructive and concrete involvement in a peaceful resolution of the conflict in Afghanistan and to consult other States on supplementary measures that could be taken in the search for peace;

17. *Calls upon* all Afghan parties, in particular the Taliban, and countries concerned to increase their level of cooperation within the framework of the peacemaking efforts of the United Nations with a view to enabling the Special Envoy of the Secretary-General for Afghanistan to renew his active involvement in these efforts as soon as possible;

18. *Calls upon* all signatories to the Tashkent Declaration on Fundamental Principles for a Peaceful Settlement of the Conflict in Afghanistan and the Afghan parties to implement the principles contained in the Declaration in support of the efforts of the United Nations towards a peaceful resolution of the Afghan conflict, in particular the agreement of members of the "six plus two" group not to provide military support to any Afghan party and to prevent the use of their territories for such purposes, and recalls their appeal to the international community to take identical measures to prevent the delivery of weapons to Afghanistan;

19. *Reiterates its strong condemnation* of the armed attacks against United Nations personnel in the summer of 1998 and the recent attacks against United Nations personnel and property following the imposition of sanctions against the Taliban by the Security Council;

20. *Expresses deep concern* at the lack of tangible progress in the Taliban's investigations of the death, serious injury or disappearance of international or national staff members and other persons employed by the United Nations, in particular the killing of the two Afghan staff members of the World Food Programme and of the Office of the United Nations High Commissioner for Refugees in Jalalabad and of the Military Adviser to the United Nations Special Mission to Afghanistan in Kabul, and once again urges the Taliban to proceed with the immediate and thorough investigation of these cases and to inform the United Nations about the progress of their investigation without further delay;

21. *Reiterates its strong condemnation* of the killing of the diplomatic and consular staff of the Consulate-General of the Islamic Republic of Iran in Mazar-e-Sharif and the correspondent of the Islamic Republic News Agency, expresses deep concern at the lack of progress in the Taliban's investigation of the murders, and once again urges the Taliban to carry out, without further delay, a credible investigation with a view to prosecuting the guilty parties and to inform the Government of the Islamic Republic of Iran and the United Nations about the results thereof;

22. *Urges* all Afghan parties to recognize, protect and promote all human rights and freedoms, including the right to life, liberty and security of persons, regardless of gender, ethnicity or religion;

23. *Calls upon* all Afghan parties, in particular the Taliban, to end discriminatory policies against women and girls, including policies regarding their rights to education, work and equal health care, and to recognize, protect and promote the equal rights and dignity of men and women;

24. *Condemns* the continuing widespread violations of international humanitarian law in Afghanistan, and urgently calls upon all Afghan parties to respect strictly all its provisions that provide essential protection for the civilian population in armed conflicts;

25. *Strongly demands* that all Afghan parties, in particular the Taliban, refrain from providing sanctuary or training for international terrorists and their organizations, cease the recruitment of terrorists, close down terrorist training camps inside Afghanistan, take effective measures to ensure that the territory under its control is not used for terrorist organizations and

camps and take the necessary steps to cooperate with efforts to bring indicted terrorists to justice without delay;

26. *Condemns* the acts of terrorists based in Afghanistan, including those in support of extremist groups operating against the interests of Member States and against their citizens, deplores the fact that the Taliban continues to provide safe haven to Usama bin Laden and to allow him and others associated with him to use Afghanistan as a base from which to sponsor international terrorist operations, recalls that the Security Council in its resolution 1267(1999) has demanded that the Taliban turn over Usama bin Laden without further delay, and urges the Taliban to comply;

27. *Reiterates its call* to all Afghan parties, in particular the Taliban, to halt all illegal drug activities and to support international efforts to ban illicit drug production and trafficking, and calls upon all Member States and all parties concerned to undertake concerted measures to stop the trafficking of illegal drugs from Afghanistan;

28. *Takes note* of the severe impact of the illicit drug production and trafficking on Afghanistan's immediate neighbours, and calls for further international cooperation in support of the efforts of the neighbouring States to stop the trafficking of illegal drugs from Afghanistan;

29. *Requests* the United Nations International Drug Control Programme to continue its crop monitoring and other work inside Afghanistan, including its alternative development pilot projects, and to further develop international measures against drug trafficking;

30. *Reiterates* that the cultural and historic relics and monuments of Afghanistan belong to the common heritage of mankind, calls upon all Afghan parties, in particular the Taliban, to protect the cultural and historic relics and monuments of Afghanistan from acts of vandalism, damage and theft, and requests all Member States to take appropriate measures to prevent the looting of cultural artifacts and to ensure their return to Afghanistan;

31. *Requests* the Secretary-General to report to the General Assembly every three months during its fifty-fourth session on the progress of the United Nations Special Mission to Afghanistan and to report to the Assembly at its fifty-fifth session on the progress made in the implementation of the present resolution;

32. *Decides* to include in the provisional agenda of its fifty-fifth session the item entitled "The situation in Afghanistan and its implications for international peace and security".

Also on 17 December, the Assembly adopted **resolution 54/189 B** on emergency international assistance for peace, normalcy and reconstruction of war-stricken Afghanistan (see PART THREE, Chapter III).

By **decision 54/465** of 23 December, the Assembly decided that the agenda item on the situation in Afghanistan and its implications for international peace and security would remain for consideration at its resumed fifty-fourth (2000) session.

Military and political developments

In his November report [A/54/536-S/1999/1145], the Secretary-General stated that fighting between the Taliban and UF ebbed and flowed during the year, with both ending roughly at the same positions they held in late 1998. The Taliban offensive of 28 July resulted only in further loss of lives, massive civilian displacement and suffering, and extensive physical destruction. Believed to have been reinforced by between 2,000 and 5,000 recruits from religious schools within Pakistan, including many non-Afghans and some under age 14, the offensive quickly overran most of the Shomali Plains, north of Kabul, up to the Panjshir Valley's entrance and areas near the Amu Darya (Oxus) River. A UF counter-attack, however, recaptured virtually all on 5 August.

On 11 August, the Taliban opened a new front line 50 kilometres north of Kabul that traversed the Kohi Safi Mountains to the vicinity of Nijrab. Through a similar move in the south-eastern region, UF made minor territorial gains. In Kandahar on 24 August, a large truck-bomb exploded outside the residential compound of the Taliban supreme leader, Mullah Mohammad Omar, killing at least 10 persons, including some of his close relatives. In September, the Taliban stepped up pressure on UF positions north of Kunduz and to the east of Khanabad in Takhar Province, while UF kept up diversionary attacks in the north-west and south-east. In a fresh offensive, the Taliban retook the territory lost to UF on 5 August, but by late October UF had once again driven the Taliban back to its starting positions. Intermittent fighting continued in the west. In early November, UF claimed to have made further advances in the northern provinces of Samangan and Sar-e-Pul.

Several events marked the political situation, starting with two rounds of intra-Afghan talks in Ashkabad, Turkmenistan, under UN auspices: the first (10-11 February) was held without a fixed agenda; the second (11-14 March) led to a framework agreement to form, in principle, a shared executive, legislature and judiciary. Shortly thereafter, however, the two sides lapsed into mutual recriminations. On 10 April, Mullah Omar suspended further talks, making clear they could be resumed only if UF accepted to join in a system of governance under an "Islamic Emirate of Afghanistan". That condition was unacceptable to President Rabbani's administration, which maintained that the Taliban had no popular or legal mandate to govern or impose an emirate system. The talks remained stalled, despite intense UN and diplomatic efforts to revive them, including President Rabbani's proposal to meet Mr. Omar under UN, Organization of the

Islamic Conference, or "six plus two" group auspices.

Apart from the July Tashkent Declaration (see p. 256), Pakistan, responding to the President's personal appeal, undertook several rounds of shuttle diplomacy between the parties in August and September, an initiative rejected by UF on the grounds that Pakistan's military and political support for the Taliban prevented it from acting as an honest broker. Another peace initiative, proposed on 29 April by the former King of Afghanistan, Zahir Shah, was to convene an emergency *loya jirgah* (grand assembly) as the most effective mechanism for resolving the Afghan conflict. Two preparatory meetings (Rome, 25 June and 22-25 November) were held for that purpose. Also in November, a parallel meeting with the same objective was held in Tehran, Iran.

In other developments, UF consolidated the anti-Taliban forces under a single command and established a 40-member Leadership Council, as well as a Supreme Military Council. It also announced the formation of a 10-member Political Committee and a ministerial cabinet reshuffle aimed at a broader representation of Afghanistan's four major ethnic groups: the Pashtun, Tajik, Hazara and Uzbek. On the Taliban side, Mr. Omar reshuffled his administration, appointing new foreign, interior and information ministers and replacing most of the governors and corps commanders. The Taliban continued to seek improved relations with certain regional States, including Kazakhstan, Pakistan, Turkmenistan and the United Arab Emirates, in addition to meeting representatives of the "six plus two" group at the Tashkent meeting. In February, senior Taliban and Iranian representatives met in Dubai, United Arab Emirates, which failed to satisfy Iran's continuing demand that the Taliban apprehend and bring to justice those responsible for the 1998 murder of its consular officials in Mazar-e Sharif.

UN activities

Special Envoy

The Secretary-General's Special Envoy for Afghanistan and head of UNSMA, Lakhdar Brahimi, undertook two missions to the region in 1999, in February and March visiting, in addition to Afghanistan, Saudi Arabia, Pakistan, Iran, the Russian Federation, Uzbekistan, Tajikistan and Turkmenistan. He met with the Taliban supreme leader in Kandahar and twice with the Taliban leadership in Kabul. He also held two meetings with UF Commander Ahmad Shah Massoud in Dushanbe (Tajikistan) and Taloqan (northern Afghanistan). He urged the parties to settle their differences by peaceful means through the resumption of the intra-Afghan talks. To facilitate those talks, he suggested that the parties pursue confidence-building measures, including agreement on a permanent ceasefire, the exchange of POWs and appointment of military liaison officers. He repeatedly underlined the importance for Afghanistan's neighbours, Iran and Pakistan in particular, to discuss their concerns more candidly and seriously.

The Special Envoy visited the region for the second time in July to represent the United Nations at the Tashkent meeting of the "six plus two" group, where he reiterated his confidence-building proposals to the Taliban and UF and helped bring them together in a private meeting. In a 22 July meeting with the Taliban in Kabul, he warned that its planned military offensive would prove costly to the Afghan people, negatively affect UN and international community efforts to broker peace, and never bring about lasting peace. He added that the hostile attitude of non-Afghan youths arriving from Pakistan in alarmingly large numbers posed a potential danger to the aid community in Kabul. In a last-minute attempt to avert the imminent offensive, he pleaded with Pakistani political, military and other leaders on his return to Islamabad on 25 July to exert their influence on the Taliban; no serious, sustained efforts were made to that end, however. The Special Envoy further pleaded with Afghanistan's neighbouring States for their constructive engagement, through the mechanism of the "six plus two" group, and made clear his disappointment at the continuous influx into Afghanistan of materiel and thousands of non-Afghan fighters, a trend contrary to their stated wish that the Afghans should resolve their own problems without outside interference.

Following a careful review of those developments, the Secretary-General and the Special Envoy concluded that, given the lack of progress so far, the Special Envoy's activities should be frozen until such time as circumstances justified his renewed intervention.

UN Special Mission to Afghanistan

Throughout 1999, the United Nations Special Mission to Afghanistan performed its mandated tasks: to support the Special Envoy in promoting peace through contact with the two warring parties and with the wider Afghan political and civil community; to monitor and report political and military developments in the country; and to coordinate activities with UNOCHA and with the indigenous and international humanitarian assistance community. UNSMA's mediation efforts early in the year with the Taliban and UF leaderships contributed greatly to the two rounds of talks between them in Ashkabad. Despite the Taliban's suspension of those talks, UNSMA endeavoured to promote confidence between the parties through a range of military, political and humanitarian measures, such as the establishment of an embryonic conflict-resolution centre, in addition to those suggested by the Special Envoy.

Although UNSMA's political and military monitoring were heavily circumscribed by the lack of security and cooperation from the Taliban military, it had maintained since March a rotational presence of a military officer in Kabul and visits by political officers to locations elsewhere in Afghanistan.

Establishment of the Civil Affairs Unit within UNSMA, proposed in 1998 [YUN 1998, p. 297], was set in motion by the dispatch of an assessment mission to Afghanistan in late April/early May. Following the agreement of both parties to the Unit's operation in the country, recruitment of the initial personnel began.

Reorganization

In his November report [A/54/536-S/1999/1145], the Secretary-General indicated that, in view of the freezing of the Special Envoy's activities, UNSMA would assume the primary role in conducting UN peacemaking activities in Afghanistan. To that end, he would appoint a substantive head of Mission at the Assistant Secretary-General level, to be assisted by a deputy director and four political affairs officers. The number of military advisers would be reduced from four to two owing to difficulties in fulfilling their monitoring and advisory functions. To increase the Organization's political effectiveness, UNSMA would progressively move its head office from Islamabad to Kabul, starting with the stationing of political affairs officers in Kabul and Kandahar when security conditions permitted. The closer proximity to both belligerents and non-belligerents should afford UNSMA more frequent contact with them. A sub-office would be opened in Tehran in early 2000 to increase regular contact with neighbouring States and with Afghan factions and individuals. Arrangements would be made to ensure effective liaison with representatives of Afghan factions in Dushanbe.

UNSMA would redouble efforts to bring about a durable and equitable political settlement. It would seek to persuade the two parties to agree to a ceasefire and resume dialogue while strengthening its links with Afghan civil society, and would closely monitor and encourage the various peace initiatives of non-UN actors, notably from within the Afghan diaspora, while continuing to work closely with the countries willing to help find a peaceful solution to the Afghan conflict, including those not represented in the "six plus two" group.

The new UNSMA Civil Affairs Unit, expected to be operational in early 2000, would work within Afghanistan primarily to promote respect for minimum humanitarian standards and deter massive and systematic violations of human rights.

Financing

Following the General Assembly's endorsement, in resolution 54/189 A, of the proposed reorganization of UNSMA as described above, the financial implications on the proposed programme budget for the 2000-2001 biennium, estimated by the Secretary-General at $3,407,600 [A/C.5/54/41], were considered by the Assembly. Based on the related ACABQ report [A/54/667] and the Fifth Committee's recommendation [A/54/671], that amount was to be charged against the $90,387,200 provided for in Assembly **resolution 54/251, section VIII**, on special political missions, of 23 December.

Humanitarian assistance

As presented in the 1999 Consolidated Appeal for Afghanistan, the common programme of humanitarian assistance undertaken in Afghanistan by UN agencies and the assistance community as a whole represented a significant step towards greater coherence and effectiveness (see also p. 837). The programme benefited from the Afghanistan Programming Body, which provided a forum for policy discussion and consensus-building on the direction of humanitarian activities, as well as from the biannual high-level policy discussions of the Afghanistan Support Group of donors. With the limited and phased return to the country of UN international staff in March 1999, the momentum of assistance increased from its restricted level stemming from their absence since 21 August 1998 [YUN 1998, p. 296]. Assistance delivery continued to be hampered, however, by security and access constraints arising from the fighting, as well as by the uneven receipt of funding against the Consolidated Appeal.

In 1999, UN programmes and agencies mounted emergency relief assistance jointly with ICRC, the International Federation of Red Cross and Red Crescent Societies, the American Red Cross Society and NGOs for some 16,000 families victims of an earthquake on 11 February (see

p. 838). Assistance was also being provided for over 30,000 households affected by the waves of fighting across the Hazarajat region in the central highlands, especially in Bamian, Shiber and Yakaolang. Of the estimated 65,000 displaced people who escaped to the Panjshir Valley from the July fighting in the Shomali Plains, where widespread burning of crops and destruction of homes reportedly occurred, about 50,000 were found to need food aid. A further 60,000 people forcibly displaced from the Shomali Plains were in Kabul, where, since August, WFP and NGOs had been providing food assistance for some 12,000 people housed in the former Soviet embassy compound, 90 per cent of whom were women and children.

With UNHCR assistance, 82,000 Afghan refugees voluntarily returned to Afghanistan from Pakistan and Iran between 1 January and 30 September. During the same period, some 70,000 Afghans were forcibly returned from Iran. Negotiations were under way between UNHCR and Iran for the orderly and voluntary return of refugees from that country.

Since its inception, the UNOCHA Mine Action Programme had cleared almost 400 square kilometres of mined areas, with a further 55 square kilometres already marked and surveyed for future clearance.

Human rights violations

Reported human rights violations in Afghanistan, largely attributable to the continuing war, had worsened, especially for civilians trapped in front-line areas. Abuses against civilians during the April/May fighting in the central highlands included the summary execution of women and children, forced displacement, looting and burning of homes, arbitrary detention and forced labour. Added to the same abuses perpetrated during the Taliban's July offensive in the Shomali Plains were the separation of men from families, the abduction and disappearance of women, the destruction and burning of agricultural assets and use of boy soldiers.

Report of UN investigation team. On 23 November [A/54/626], the Secretary-General submitted to the General Assembly a summary of the report of the UN investigation team for Afghanistan, submitted by the Office of the High Commissioner for Human Rights. Prepared in response to Assembly resolution 52/211 B [YUN 1997, p. 262] and Security Council presidential statement S/PRST/1997/55 [ibid., p. 261] and resolution 1193(1998) [YUN 1998, p. 296], the report summarized the results of an investigation into allegations of serious violations of international human rights or humanitarian law, including reported mass killings of POWs and civilians, incidents of rape in northern Afghanistan in 1997, and reports of atrocities alleged to have taken place in Mazar-e Sharif and Bamian in August 1998 [ibid., p. 301] in the wake of the Taliban conquests of those cities.

According to the findings, little information was forthcoming from the warring parties and neither extended meaningful cooperation, information provided by others and persons interviewed was patchy, site evidence was inconclusive and allegations against both parties were made at different times. Clearly, killings of civilians and serious violations of international humanitarian law and human rights had taken place, but for the foregoing reasons, the investigation team was unable to reach definitive conclusions.

(For the human rights situation in Afghanistan, see p. 704; for the situation of women and girls in Afghanistan, see pp. 670 and 1094.)

Communications. In a statement of 29 January [S/1999/109], Afghanistan described the inhumane and brutal conditions under which the detainees it visited, through facilitation by ICRC, in Taliban detention centres in Kandahar (15-20 January) and Kabul (21-23 January) were held, among whom were civilians detained on the basis of ethnicity and religion. By contrast, the Talibans detained by Afghanistan were treated humanely. Afghanistan appealed to the international community to urge the Taliban to respect the human dignity of detainees held by it and to end the suffering of those individuals.

Drug control

The annual survey by the United Nations International Drug Control Programme (UNDCP) estimated that opium production in Afghanistan would reach a record level of 4,600 metric tons in 1999, potentially convertible into 460 metric tons of heroin; an estimated 90,983 hectares were under opium poppy cultivation, representing a 43 per cent increase over 1998, with cultivation having spread from 73 to 104 districts. Those statistics put Afghanistan as the world's largest illicit producer of opium in 1999, with its output reaching up to 75 per cent of all illicit opium worldwide.

Such a large increase in available opium and heroin would weigh heavily on States bordering Afghanistan, which would have to counter the threat to their internal security from massive cross-border illicit-drug trafficking and associated criminal activity. To bolster their inadequate and under-resourced border security systems, Iran, Pakistan, Tajikistan, Turkmenistan and Uzbekistan agreed with UNDCP to implement border control and law enforcement programmes.

UNDCP approved two such programmes and concluded memoranda of understanding with all Central Asian countries for the improvement of coordination among their border control and law enforcement authorities. The UNDCP Executive Director was instructed by the Secretary-General to coordinate response to the growing drug problem in cooperation with the Department of Political Affairs and UNSMA. (See also PART THREE, Chapter XIV.)

Counter-terrorism measures

In his November report, the Secretary-General drew attention to the growing concern that Afghanistan was becoming a breeding ground for religious extremism and sectarian violence, as well as various types of international terrorism, whose scope far exceeded Afghanistan's boundaries. He pointed to a 7 October press conference at which Pakistan's former Prime Minister, Nawaz Sharif, claimed that Pakistan had evidence of the existence in Afghanistan of terrorist training camps, which had trained persons involved in terrorist activities in Pakistan. Most of Afghanistan's neighbours and other States beyond had made similar allegations.

The United States had earlier, on 5 July, imposed unilateral financial and economic sanctions against the Taliban until such time as Saudi national Usama bin Laden—whom it indicted for the 1998 bombings of its embassies in Nairobi, Kenya, and Dar es Salaam, United Republic of Tanzania, and for conspiring to kill United States nationals outside their country—was either expelled from Afghanistan or extradited to a country where he would be brought to justice. In August, the assets of Ariana Afghan Airlines held in United States banks were frozen. In September, India terminated the air link between Amritsar and Kabul, leaving the United Arab Emirates as that airline's only destination outside Afghanistan.

SECURITY COUNCIL ACTION

On 15 October [meeting 4051], the Security Council unanimously adopted **resolution 1267(1999)**. The draft [S/1999/1054] was sponsored by Canada, the Netherlands, the Russian Federation, Slovenia, the United Kingdom and the United States.

The Security Council,

Reaffirming its previous resolutions, in particular resolutions 1189(1998) of 13 August 1998, 1193(1998) of 28 August 1998 and 1214(1998) of 8 December 1998, and the statements by its President on the situation in Afghanistan,

Reaffirming its strong commitment to the sovereignty, independence, territorial integrity and national unity of Afghanistan, and its respect for Afghanistan's cultural and historical heritage,

Reiterating its deep concern over the continuing violations of international humanitarian law and of human rights, particularly discrimination against women and girls, and over the significant rise in the illicit production of opium, and stressing that the capture by the Taliban of the Consulate-General of the Islamic Republic of Iran and the murder of Iranian diplomats and a journalist in Mazar-e-Sharif constituted flagrant violations of established international law,

Recalling the relevant international counter-terrorism conventions and in particular the obligations of parties to those conventions to extradite or prosecute terrorists,

Strongly condemning the continuing use of Afghan territory, especially areas controlled by the Taliban, for the sheltering and training of terrorists and planning of terrorist acts, and reaffirming its conviction that the suppression of international terrorism is essential for the maintenance of international peace and security,

Deploring the fact that the Taliban continues to provide safe haven to Usama bin Laden and to allow him and others associated with him to operate a network of terrorist training camps from Taliban-controlled territory and to use Afghanistan as a base from which to sponsor international terrorist operations,

Noting the indictment of Usama bin Laden and his associates by the United States of America for, inter alia, the 7 August 1998 bombings of the United States embassies in Nairobi and Dar es Salaam and for conspiring to kill American nationals outside the United States, and noting also the request of the United States to the Taliban to surrender them for trial,

Determining that the failure of the Taliban authorities to respond to the demands in paragraph 13 of resolution 1214(1998) constitutes a threat to international peace and security,

Stressing its determination to ensure respect for its resolutions,

Acting under Chapter VII of the Charter of the United Nations,

1. *Insists* that the Afghan faction known as the Taliban, which also calls itself the Islamic Emirate of Afghanistan, comply promptly with its previous resolutions and in particular cease the provision of sanctuary and training for international terrorists and their organizations, take appropriate effective measures to ensure that the territory under its control is not used for terrorist installations and camps, or for the preparation or organization of terrorist acts against other States or their citizens, and cooperate with efforts to bring indicted terrorists to justice;

2. *Demands* that the Taliban turn over Usama bin Laden without further delay to appropriate authorities in a country where he has been indicted, or to appropriate authorities in a country where he will be returned to such a country, or to appropriate authorities in a country where he will be arrested and effectively brought to justice;

3. *Decides* that on 14 November 1999 all States shall impose the measures set out in paragraph 4 below, unless the Council has previously decided, on the basis of a report of the Secretary-General, that the Taliban has

fully complied with the obligation set out in paragraph 2 above;

4. *Decides also* that, in order to enforce paragraph 2 above, all States shall:

(a) Deny permission for any aircraft to take off from or land in their territory if it is owned, leased or operated by or on behalf of the Taliban as designated by the Committee established by paragraph 6 below, unless the particular flight has been approved in advance by the Committee on the grounds of humanitarian need, including religious obligation such as the performance of the Hajj;

(b) Freeze funds and other financial resources, including funds derived or generated from property owned or controlled directly or indirectly by the Taliban, or by any undertaking owned or controlled by the Taliban, as designated by the Committee established by paragraph 6 below, and ensure that neither they nor any other funds or financial resources so designated are made available, by their nationals or by any persons within their territory, to or for the benefit of the Taliban or any undertaking owned or controlled, directly or indirectly, by the Taliban, except as may be authorized by the Committee on a case-by-case basis on the grounds of humanitarian need;

5. *Urges* all States to cooperate with efforts to fulfil the demand in paragraph 2 above, and to consider further measures against Usama bin Laden and his associates;

6. *Decides* to establish, in accordance with rule 28 of its provisional rules of procedure, a Committee of the Security Council consisting of all the members of the Council to undertake the following tasks and to report on its work to the Council with its observations and recommendations:

(a) To seek from all States further information regarding the action taken by them with a view to effectively implementing the measures imposed by paragraph 4 above;

(b) To consider information brought to its attention by States concerning violations of the measures imposed by paragraph 4 above and to recommend appropriate measures in response thereto;

(c) To make periodic reports to the Council on the impact, including the humanitarian implications, of the measures imposed by paragraph 4 above;

(d) To make periodic reports to the Council on information submitted to it regarding alleged violations of the measures imposed by paragraph 4 above, identifying where possible persons or entities reported to be engaged in such violations;

(e) To designate the aircraft and funds or other financial resources referred to in paragraph 4 above in order to facilitate the implementation of the measures imposed by that paragraph;

(f) To consider requests for exemptions from the measures imposed by paragraph 4 above as provided for in that paragraph, and to decide on the granting of an exemption to these measures in respect of the payment by the International Air Transport Association to the aeronautical authority of Afghanistan on behalf of international airlines for air traffic control services;

(g) To examine the reports submitted pursuant to paragraph 10 below;

7. *Calls upon* all States to act strictly in accordance with the provisions of the present resolution, notwithstanding the existence of any rights or obligations conferred or imposed by any international agreement or any contract entered into or any licence or permit granted prior to the date of coming into force of the measures imposed by paragraph 4 above;

8. *Calls upon* States to bring proceedings against persons and entities within their jurisdiction that violate the measures imposed by paragraph 4 above and to impose appropriate penalties;

9. *Calls upon* all States to cooperate fully with the Committee established by paragraph 6 above in the fulfilment of its tasks, including supplying such information as may be required by the Committee in pursuance of the present resolution;

10. *Requests* all States to report to the Committee established by paragraph 6 above within thirty days of the coming into force of the measures imposed by paragraph 4 above on the steps they have taken with a view to effectively implementing paragraph 4 above;

11. *Requests* the Secretary-General to provide all necessary assistance to the Committee established by paragraph 6 above and to make the necessary arrangements in the Secretariat for this purpose;

12. *Requests* the Committee established by paragraph 6 above to determine appropriate arrangements, on the basis of recommendations of the Secretariat, with competent international organizations, neighbouring and other States, and parties concerned with a view to improving the monitoring of the implementation of the measures imposed by paragraph 4 above;

13. *Requests* the Secretariat to submit for consideration by the Committee established by paragraph 6 above information received from Governments and public sources on possible violations of the measures imposed by paragraph 4 above;

14. *Decides* to terminate the measures imposed by paragraph 4 above once the Secretary-General reports to the Security Council that the Taliban has fulfilled the obligation set out in paragraph 2 above;

15. *Expresses its readiness* to consider the imposition of further measures, in accordance with its responsibility under the Charter of the United Nations, with the aim of achieving the full implementation of the present resolution;

16. *Decides* to remain actively seized of the matter.

As the Taliban failed to comply with the Council's demand in paragraph 2 of the foregoing resolution, its sanctions provisions went into effect on 14 November. Ariana's flights to its only destination were discontinued, Afghan bank branches in Pakistan were closed and Taliban accounts were frozen. The Taliban, who had made some attempts to resolve the question, had earlier announced that the case against Mr. bin Laden had been closed for lack of evidence and that, as a guest of the Afghan people, he could not be forced to leave the country and, in any case, was prevented from acting on Afghan soil against any country.

Tajikistan

Implementation of the 1997 General Agreement on the Establishment of Peace and National Accord in Tajikistan (the General Agreement) [YUN 1997, p. 264] by the two parties to the Agreement, the Government and the United Tajik Opposition (UTO) was marked by two major achievements in 1999 that moved Tajikistan closer to its goal of national reconciliation and democratization: the proposed amendments to the Constitution were finally approved by referendum on 6 September; and the presidential elections were conducted without incident on 6 November, with the incumbent President, Emomali S. Rakhmonov, elected for a single seven-year term in accordance with the new Constitution. Those achievements were due in no small measure, the Secretary-General observed, to the extraordinary efforts of the United Nations Mission of Observers in Tajikistan (UNMOT), with the active support of the Contact Group of Guarantor States and International Organizations (Contact Group), as well as of the Organization for Security and Cooperation in Europe (OSCE) mission in Tajikistan. Following the presidential elections, preparations were under way for the forthcoming parliamentary elections.

On the recommendation of the Secretary-General, who deemed that international involvement in Tajikistan remained essential, the Security Council extended UNMOT's mandate twice during the year, the second time until 15 May 2000. UN system humanitarian operations involved mainly UNHCR, which assisted in the voluntary repatriation of Tajik refugees from neighbouring countries, the World Bank and UNDP, which were providing assistance to facilitate the reintegration into civilian life of former UTO combatants.

UN Mission of Observers in Tajikistan

The United Nations Mission of Observers in Tajikistan, established by Security Council resolution 968(1994) [YUN 1994, p. 596], continued to promote peace and national reconciliation and to assist in the implementation of the 1997 General Agreement. Its mandated tasks were to provide good offices and expert advice as stipulated in the General Agreement; cooperate with the joint Commission on National Reconciliation (CNR), the main implementation body, and its subcommissions, as well as with the Central Commission on Elections and Referendums (CCER); participate in the work of the Contact Group and serve as its coordinator; investigate reports of ceasefire violations and report on them to the United Nations and CNR; monitor the assembly of UTO fighters and their reintegration, disarmament and demobilization; assist ex-combatants in their reintegration into governmental power structures or in demobilization; coordinate UN assistance to Tajikistan during the transition period; and maintain close contacts with the parties, as well as cooperative liaison with the collective peacekeeping forces of the Commonwealth of Independent States (CIS), the Russian border forces and the OSCE mission in Tajikistan.

UNMOT, which had suspended its field activities following the July 1998 shooting of four members of its team in Garm [YUN 1998, p. 303], reopened its field offices in Khorog and Khujand on 1 and 21 June 1999, respectively. The three men accused of killing the four UNMOT personnel were found guilty of murder and related charges and sentenced to death by Tajikistan's Supreme Court on 26 March. The Secretary-General appealed to the President to consider commuting the sentence.

UNMOT maintained its headquarters in Dushanbe and three field offices: Kurgan-Tyube and the two reopened in June.

During the year, UNMOT continued to cooperate with OSCE on constitutional reform, democratization and elections. It maintained contact with the CIS collective peacekeeping forces regarding maintenance of the ceasefire and security, as well as with the Russian border forces on matters of mutual concern.

Composition

UNMOT was headed by the Special Representative of the Secretary-General for Tajikistan, Jan Kubis (Slovakia), until 21 June. He was succeeded by Ivo Petrov (Bulgaria), who was appointed by the Secretary-General with effect from 20 September through an exchange of letters with the Security Council on 13 and 17 September [S/1999/985, S/1999/986].

UNMOT's military component was under the command of the Chief Military Observer, Brigadier-General Tengku Ariffin Bin Tengku Mohammed (Malaysia), until 4 April. He was succeeded by Brigadier-General John Hvidegaard (Denmark), also appointed by the Secretary-General through an exchange of letters with the Council on 5 and 9 March [S/1999/254, S/1999/255].

As at October, UNMOT comprised 37 military observers from 13 contributing countries and 167 civilian staff (including 2 civilian police, four medical staff and 3 UN Volunteers), of whom 50 were internationally recruited.

UNMOT's mandate, which expired on 15 May, was extended by the Council for two six-month periods: the first ended on 15 November; the second was to end on 15 May 2000.

Financing

On 8 June 1999 [meeting 101], the General Assembly considered the Secretary-General's February reports on UNMOT's proposed budget for the 12-month period from 1 July 1999 to 30 June 2000 [A/53/816] and financial performance from 1 July 1997 to 30 June 1998 [A/53/784], together with ACABQ's related reports [A/53/895 & Add.5]. On the recommendation of the Fifth Committee [A/53/545/Add.1], the Assembly adopted **resolution 53/19 B** without vote [agenda item 136].

Financing of the United Nations Mission of Observers in Tajikistan

The General Assembly,

Having considered the reports of the Secretary-General on the financing of the United Nations Mission of Observers in Tajikistan and the related reports of the Advisory Committee on Administrative and Budgetary Questions,

Recalling Security Council resolution 968(1994) of 16 December 1994, by which the Council established the United Nations Mission of Observers in Tajikistan, and the subsequent resolutions by which the Council extended the mandate of the Mission of Observers, the latest of which was resolution 1240(1999) of 15 May 1999,

Recalling also Security Council resolution 1138(1997) of 14 November 1997, by which the Council authorized the Secretary-General to expand the size of the Mission of Observers,

Recalling further its resolution 49/240 of 31 March 1995 on the financing of the Mission of Observers and its subsequent resolutions and decisions thereon, the latest of which was resolution 53/19 A of 2 November 1998,

Reaffirming that the costs of the Mission of Observers are expenses of the Organization to be borne by Member States in accordance with Article 17, paragraph 2, of the Charter of the United Nations,

Recalling its previous decisions regarding the fact that, in order to meet the expenditures caused by the Mission of Observers, a different procedure is required from that applied to meet expenditures of the regular budget of the United Nations,

Taking into account the fact that the economically more developed countries are in a position to make relatively larger contributions and that the economically less developed countries have a relatively limited capacity to contribute towards such an operation,

Bearing in mind the special responsibilities of the States permanent members of the Security Council, as indicated in General Assembly resolution 1874(S-IV) of 27 June 1963, in the financing of such operations,

Noting with appreciation that voluntary contributions have been made to the Mission of Observers,

Mindful of the fact that it is essential to provide the Mission of Observers with the necessary financial resources to enable it to fulfil its responsibilities under the relevant resolutions of the Security Council,

1. *Takes note* of the status of contributions to the United Nations Mission of Observers in Tajikistan as at 30 April 1999, including the contributions outstanding in the amount of 3.7 million United States dollars, representing some 7 per cent of the total assessed contributions from the inception of the Mission of Observers to the period ending 15 May 1999, notes that some 15 per cent of the Member States have paid their assessed contributions in full, and urges all other Member States concerned, in particular those in arrears, to ensure payment of their outstanding assessed contributions;

2. *Expresses concern* about the financial situation with regard to peacekeeping activities, in particular as regards the reimbursement of troop contributors, which bear additional burdens owing to overdue payments by Member States of their assessments;

3. *Expresses its appreciation* to those Member States which have paid their assessed contributions in full;

4. *Urges* all other Member States to make every possible effort to ensure payment of their assessed contributions to the Mission of Observers in full and on time;

5. *Endorses* the observations and recommendations contained in the report of the Advisory Committee on Administrative and Budgetary Questions;

6. *Requests* the Secretary-General to take all necessary action to ensure that the Mission of Observers is administered with a maximum of efficiency and economy;

7. *Also requests* the Secretary-General, in order to reduce the cost of employing General Service staff, to continue efforts to recruit local staff for the Mission of Observers against General Service posts, commensurate with the requirements of the Mission;

8. *Decides* to appropriate to the Special Account for the United Nations Mission of Observers in Tajikistan the amount of 18,708,926 dollars gross (17,475,926 dollars net) for the maintenance of the Mission of Observers for the period from 1 July 1999 to 30 June 2000, inclusive of the amount of 930,639 dollars for the support account for peacekeeping operations and the amount of 182,487 dollars for the United Nations Logistics Base at Brindisi, Italy, for the period from 1 July 1999 to 30 June 2000, to be apportioned, as an ad hoc arrangement, among Member States at a monthly rate of 1,559,077 dollars gross (1,456,327 dollars net) in accordance with the composition of groups set out in paragraphs 3 and 4 of General Assembly resolution 43/232 of 1 March 1989, as adjusted by the Assembly in its resolutions 44/192 B of 21 December 1989, 45/269 of 27 August 1991, 46/198 A of 20 December 1991, 47/218 A of 23 December 1992, 49/249 A of 20 July 1995, 49/249 B of 14 September 1995, 50/224 of 11 April 1996, 51/218 A to C of 18 December 1996 and 52/230 of 31 March 1998 and its decisions 48/472 A of 23 December 1993 and 50/451 B of 23 December 1995, and taking into account the scale of assessments for the years 1999 and 2000, as set out in its resolution 52/215 A of 22 December 1997, subject to the decision of the Security Council to extend the mandate of the Mission of Observers beyond 30 June 1999;

9. *Decides also* that, in accordance with the provisions of its resolution 973(X) of 15 December 1955, there shall be set off against the apportionment among Member States, as provided for in paragraph 8 above, their respective share in the Tax Equalization Fund of

the estimated staff assessment income of 1,233,000 dollars approved for the period from 1 July 1999 to 30 June 2000;

10. *Decides further* that, for Member States that have fulfilled their financial obligations to the Mission of Observers, there shall be set off against the apportionment, as provided for in paragraph 8 above, their respective share of the unencumbered balance of 2,408,400 dollars gross (2,048,400 dollars net) in respect of the period from 1 July 1997 to 30 June 1998;

11. *Decides* that, for Member States that have not fulfilled their financial obligations to the Mission of Observers, their share of the unencumbered balance of 2,408,400 dollars gross (2,048,400 dollars net) in respect of the period from 1 July 1997 to 30 June 1998 shall be set off against their outstanding obligations;

12. *Invites* voluntary contributions to the Mission of Observers in cash and in the form of services and supplies acceptable to the Secretary-General, to be administered, as appropriate, in accordance with the procedure and practices established by the General Assembly;

13. *Decides* to include in the provisional agenda of its fifty-fourth session the item entitled "Financing of the United Nations Mission of Observers in Tajikistan".

By **decision 54/462 A** of 23 December, the Assembly decided that the Fifth Committee should continue its consideration of the agenda item on the financing of UNMOT at its resumed fifty-fourth (2000) session. By **decision 54/465** of the same date, the Assembly decided that the same item would remain for consideration during that session.

Activities

During the year, the Secretary-General submitted to the Security Council four reports bringing up to date the record of developments in Tajikistan and activities of UNMOT: the first two pursuant to Council resolution 1206(1998) [YUN 1998, p. 312] and the next two pursuant to resolution 1240(1999) (see p. 271).

Reports of Secretary-General (February and May). In his 8 February interim report [S/1999/124], the Secretary-General observed that progress in implementing the General Agreement remained slow. The first two stages foreseen in the military protocol had not been completed, as reflected in a 5 January CNR resolution, which acknowledged that UTO had not fully complied with the protocol's provisions and urged all UTO fighters, therefore, to return to their assembly sites and place their weapons in the designated storage areas, as well as stricter control over the carrying of weapons outside assembly sites. The Joint Central Review Commission, set up under stage III of the protocol, had so far reviewed only 225 fighters in Gorno-Badakshan and 1,084 in Kofarnikhon, Leninsky and Dushanbe, in addition to personnel of various government power structures.

At the beginning of the year, President Rakhmonov publicly announced the Government's intention to hold, in addition to a referendum on amendments to the Constitution, parliamentary and presidential elections in 1999, as his five-year term would end in November 1999 and the current Parliament's term in February 2000. Constitutional issues were still being debated, however, with the most contentious issue, namely, the retention of the constitutional provision describing the character of the State as "secular", held in abeyance. The Secretary-General, noting that, at the current stage, the referendum and elections remained uncertain, warned of the risk inherent in the slow pace, namely, the growing restlessness among the groups not direct parties to the General Agreement and to its power-sharing arrangements, as well as among UTO fighters awaiting demobilization or reintegration into the national army.

The Secretary-General remained concerned by the precarious security situation, characterized by an increase in crime, especially drug-related crime, and numerous violent incidents with possible political background. UNMOT thus continued to limit its activities to Dushanbe and to observe strict security precautions.

SECURITY COUNCIL ACTION (February)

On 23 February [meeting 3981], the Security Council President made statement **S/PRST/1999/8** on behalf of the Council:

The Security Council has considered the report of the Secretary-General of 8 February 1999 on the situation in Tajikistan, submitted pursuant to paragraph 11 of its resolution 1206(1998) of 12 November 1998.

The Council welcomes the regular contacts between the President of the Republic of Tajikistan and the leader of the United Tajik Opposition and the work of the Commission on National Reconciliation aimed at achieving further progress in the peace process. It regrets that progress has remained slow during the last three months and underlines the necessity for the parties to speed up the full and sequential implementation of the General Agreement on the Establishment of Peace and National Accord in Tajikistan, especially the protocol on military issues. The Council calls upon the parties to intensify their efforts to create conditions for the holding in 1999 of a constitutional referendum and presidential elections, as well as for the timely holding of parliamentary elections.

The Council notes with appreciation the work of the Special Representative of the Secretary-General and of all the personnel of the United Nations Mission of Observers in Tajikistan and encourages them to continue assisting the parties in the implementation of the General Agreement. It underlines the importance of the Mission playing a full and active role in the implementation of the General Agreement and requests the Secretary-General to continue to consider means of achieving this, taking into account the security situation.

The Council welcomes the continued contribution made by the collective peacekeeping forces of the Commonwealth of Independent States in assisting the parties in the implementation of the General Agreement in coordination with all concerned.

The Council welcomes also the contribution of the Contact Group of Guarantor States and International Organizations to the peace process and, in this context, considers that the holding of a meeting of the Contact Group at the level of Ministers for Foreign Affairs, in support of the peace process, could indeed be useful, if properly prepared.

The Council welcomes further the activities of various international organizations and humanitarian workers related to the implementation of the General Agreement and addressing the humanitarian, rehabilitation and development needs of Tajikistan. It calls upon Member States and others concerned to respond promptly and generously to the consolidated appeal for Tajikistan for 1999 launched in Geneva in December 1998.

The Council reiterates its concern that the security situation in some parts of Tajikistan remains precarious. It reiterates the importance of a full investigation into the murder in July 1998 of four members of the Mission and notes with appreciation the efforts of the Government of Tajikistan in this regard. The Council calls upon the United Tajik Opposition to contribute more effectively to the investigation in order to bring those responsible to justice. It acknowledges the efforts of the Government of Tajikistan to enhance the protection of international personnel and calls upon the parties to cooperate further in ensuring the security and freedom of movement of the personnel of the United Nations, the collective peacekeeping forces and other international personnel. The Council reminds both parties that the ability of the international community to mobilize and to continue assistance for Tajikistan is linked to the security of the personnel of the Mission and international organizations, and of humanitarian workers.

According to the Secretary-General's May report [S/1999/514], President Rakhmonov instructed his Cabinet and CNR on 2 March to expedite outstanding military and political issues, among them the pending UTO amnesty cases and nominations to high-level posts and incorporation of UTO representatives into regional governmental structures, discussion on constitutional amendments, reinstatement of UTO members and sympathizers to their former positions in the Government, as well as in the so-called power structures (army, police, security), the attestation process in Garm, Tajikabad and Jirgital, and the appointment of the Government's choice for the defence portfolio.

The CNR compromise proposals for constitutional reforms, hammered out after 14 months, were forwarded to the President, who rejected most of them, the notable exception being the proposed professional, bicameral parliament. Underlying much of the debate on constitutional reform was a dispute over the sequence of the forthcoming elections. The Government wanted the presidential election to take precedence, to ensure that a constitutionally elected executive was in place, bearing in mind that UTO retained its military capacity, whereas UTO wanted parliamentary elections first out of concern that an elected president might be emboldened to regard the power-sharing agreement as superseded.

Meanwhile the United Nations and OSCE had agreed on a joint effort to encourage preparations for holding credible elections acceptable to all. The Contact Group recommended that the media improve their credibility by including the views of every legitimately interested party and urged the inclusion of other parties in the political process to strengthen civil accord, in accordance with CNR's commitment to engage in a broad dialogue with all elements of the political spectrum.

The report provided CNR figures illustrating progress achieved in the demobilization and reintegration of ex-UTO fighters, noting at the same time that delays in that process and lack of support for the ex-fighters were creating discontent among them and their field commanders. To the two parties' request for international assistance for the fighters, the United Nations explained that, since UNMOT had exhausted its limited food and other assistance (meant to bridge only the first two of the six months envisaged for the quartering, registration and disarmament of the UTO fighters), it would renew efforts to obtain funds for reconstruction and other projects, such as food-for-work, food-for-training and land-lease projects, designed to create jobs and enable former fighters to return to civilian life.

On 5 May, the CNR Chairman and UTO leader wrote to the Special Representative, expressing the widespread dissatisfaction within UTO over the many unresolved problems, notably the President's rejection of the proposed constitutional amendments, the failure to grant amnesty to former UTO fighters and supporters, and the slow pace of power-sharing, including the Government's unwillingness to appoint a UTO representative to the defence portfolio.

Although security improved during the reporting period, the situation remained tense. Between March and April, a Parliament member was killed, a police post in Yavan, some 40 kilometres south-east of Dushanbe, was attacked, with six policemen taken hostage, and an NGO employee was stopped between Komsomolobad (Darband) and Obi-Garm by an armed group who threatened to kill all international persons entering the area. A ban on movement there remained in effect for all UN and related personnel.

Regarding UN humanitarian activities, at the time of reporting 1,800 housing units had been rebuilt or repaired, benefiting 15,000 refugees who had returned since the 1997 General Agreement. The World Bank earmarked $95 million for structural reforms, enhancement of the Government's organizational capabilities, educational reform, rehabilitation of private farms and disaster relief. UNDP, in conjunction with the World Bank, financed a survey of living conditions to enable the Government to review its poverty strategy and better focus on vulnerable groups. The 1999 consolidated inter-agency appeal for Tajikistan had so far generated only $617,045, or 2.5 per cent of the target funding (see also p. 841).

The Secretary-General stated that the peace process in Tajikistan continued to require direct international attention and support. He therefore recommended that UNMOT's mandate be extended for another six months, until 15 November.

SECURITY COUNCIL ACTION (May)

On 15 May [meeting 4004], the Security Council unanimously adopted **resolution 1240(1999)**. The draft [S/1999/557] was prepared in the course of the Council's prior consultations.

The Security Council,

Recalling all its relevant resolutions and the statements by its President,

Having considered the report of the Secretary-General of 6 May 1999 on the situation in Tajikistan,

Reaffirming its commitment to the sovereignty and territorial integrity of the Republic of Tajikistan and to the inviolability of its borders,

Welcoming progress in the peace process in Tajikistan and the effective maintenance of the ceasefire between the Government of Tajikistan and the United Tajik Opposition, while underlining the fact that more needs to be done to translate agreements and decisions into concrete actions and to deal with the many pending issues,

Welcoming also the renewed efforts of the President of the Republic of Tajikistan and the leadership of the Commission on National Reconciliation to advance and to expedite the implementation of the General Agreement on the Establishment of Peace and National Accord in Tajikistan, which have helped to achieve movement on both military and political issues,

Welcoming further the maintenance of close contact by the United Nations Mission of Observers in Tajikistan with the parties, as well as its cooperative liaison with the collective peacekeeping forces of the Commonwealth of Independent States, the Russian border forces and the mission in Tajikistan of the Organization for Security and Cooperation in Europe,

Noting with appreciation the continued contribution of the Contact Group of Guarantor States and International Organizations to the peace process, in particular through periodic joint plenary meetings with the Commission on National Reconciliation to review progress in the implementation of the General Agreement,

Welcoming the fact that the general situation in Tajikistan has remained relatively calm with better security than in earlier periods, while noting that the situation in some parts of the country has remained tense,

Recognizing that comprehensive international support remains crucial for achieving a positive outcome of the peace process in Tajikistan,

1. *Welcomes* the report of the Secretary-General of 6 May 1999;

2. *Calls upon* the parties to speed up the full and sequential implementation, in a balanced manner, of the General Agreement on the Establishment of Peace and National Accord in Tajikistan, especially the protocol on military issues, and to create conditions for the holding in 1999 of a constitutional referendum, as well as for the timely holding of presidential and parliamentary elections, and encourages the Commission on National Reconciliation to intensify its efforts aimed at the institution of a broad dialogue among the various political forces in the country in the interests of the restoration and strengthening of civil accord in Tajikistan;

3. *Notes with appreciation* the work of the Special Representative of the Secretary-General and of all the personnel of the United Nations Mission of Observers in Tajikistan, encourages them to continue assisting the parties in the implementation of the General Agreement, notes that the reopening of field offices should strengthen the Mission in this regard, underlines the need for the Mission to have the necessary personnel and financial support, and requests the Secretary-General to continue to consider means of ensuring a full and active role for the Mission in the implementation of the General Agreement;

4. *Encourages* the Organization for Security and Cooperation in Europe to continue its close cooperation with the United Nations on matters relating to constitutional reform, democratization and elections, as requested under the General Agreement;

5. *Supports* the active political work of the Contact Group of Guarantor States and International Organizations in promoting the implementation of the General Agreement, and considers that a meeting of the Contact Group at the level of Ministers for Foreign Affairs could lend further impetus to the peace process;

6. *Welcomes* the continued contribution made by the collective peacekeeping forces of the Commonwealth of Independent States in assisting the parties in the implementation of the General Agreement, in coordination with all concerned;

7. *Calls upon* the parties to cooperate further in ensuring the security and freedom of movement of the personnel of the United Nations, the collective peacekeeping forces and other international personnel, and reminds the parties that the ability of the international community to mobilize and to continue

assistance for Tajikistan is linked to the security of those personnel;

8. *Calls upon* Member States and others concerned to make voluntary contributions to launch projects for demobilization and to provide support for the elections, and to respond promptly and generously to the consolidated inter-agency appeal for Tajikistan for 1999;

9. *Decides* to extend the mandate of the Mission for a period of six months until 15 November 1999;

10. *Requests* the Secretary-General to keep the Council informed of all significant developments, and also requests him to report within three months of the adoption of the present resolution on its implementation;

11. *Decides* to remain actively seized of the matter.

By a 25 May statement [S/1999/614], the Government of Tajikistan, while appreciating UTO's role in advancing the peace process, objected to UTO's unwarranted demands and ultimatums, as well as its focus on securing posts and portfolios. Moreover, UTO had yet to honour fully its commitments under the military protocol. The Government said it was necessary to refrain from mutual recriminations and issuing ultimatums. It reaffirmed its determination to speed up the peace process as defined by the General Agreement but it had to proceed in strict compliance with the Constitution.

Reports of Secretary-General (August and November). The Secretary-General's August (interim) report [S/1999/872] recorded significant progress in the General Agreement's implementation, including agreement between the Government and UTO on the proposed amendments to the Constitution and the Parliament's 30 June decision to hold a referendum on the amendments on 26 September. On 3 August, UTO officially declared the disbandment of its armed forces; it was endorsed by a CNR resolution the same day, thus completing the second stage of the military protocol and opening the way for the legalization of the UTO political parties banned in 1993 and their participation in the political process.

On 14 May, Parliament adopted an Amnesty Act granting amnesty to over 5,000 UTO fighters registered in 1998 and subject to investigation for acts committed during the civil war. However, the new Act, which complemented the 1997 Law on Amnesty, did not meet UTO's demand for the amnesty of 93 UTO supporters imprisoned on criminal charges. UTO subsequently suspended its participation in CNR. Following the Contact Group's intervention, resulting in the signing of a formal protocol on 17 June on the completion of outstanding tasks within a specific time frame, CNR resumed its work with full UTO participation.

Progress was made thereafter on a number of key issues, including agreement on six constitutional amendments: replacement of the unicameral Parliament by a two-chamber one; the lower chamber members to be elected on the basis of equal, direct and secret vote and 75 per cent of upper chamber members to be elected by indirect vote through the local parliaments, with the remaining 25 per cent to be appointed by the President; the establishment of a judicial council; a clause permitting the functioning of religion-based political parties; and a single seven-year term for the President.

Twelve UTO members were appointed to government posts, bringing such appointments to 33. On 30 June, Parliament elevated the Committee on Emergency Situations to a full ministry. Appointed to head it was the UTO military chief of staff and commander of the Tavildara district, thus removing one of the most contentious appointment issues and paving the way for the completion, shortly thereafter, of the attestation and integration of opposition fighters in Tavildara and Darband (Komsomolobad).

In accordance with the 30 per cent quota and with the parties' agreement initially to allocate 22 towns and districts to UTO, the President appointed 11 UTO candidates as district chairmen. A two-member CNR panel, set up to review 58 of the 93 cases of UTO supporters in prison under criminal charges, recommended amnesty for 47. On 30 June, Parliament approved the nomination of four UTO candidates to CCER, in accordance with the 25 per cent quota stipulated in the General Agreement.

The previously reported dispute over the election's sequence was resolved with UTO's acceptance of holding the presidential before the parliamentary elections.

The CNR military subcommission chairman reported that 2,400 former opposition fighters had decided to return to civilian life, while 4,275 were being integrated into the armed forces and the police and security forces.

During the reporting period, UNOPS launched job-creation projects for ex-UTO fighters in six districts of the Karategin Valley: Darband, Tavildara, Garm, Tajikabad, Hoit and Jirgatal. Expansion of the projects into other areas was foreseen.

SECURITY COUNCIL ACTION (August)

On 19 August [meeting 4034], the Security Council President made statement **S/PRST/1999/25** on behalf of the Council:

The Security Council has considered the report of the Secretary-General of 12 August 1999 on the situation in Tajikistan, submitted pursuant to paragraph 10 of its resolution 1240(1999) of 15 May 1999.

The Council welcomes significant progress in the implementation of the General Agreement on the Establishment of Peace and National Accord in Tajikistan, achieved to a great extent owing to the renewed efforts of the President of the Republic of Tajikistan and the leadership of the Commission on National Reconciliation. It particularly welcomes the official declaration by the United Tajik Opposition of the disbandment of its armed units and the decision by the Supreme Court of Tajikistan lifting the bans and restrictions on activities by the political parties and movements of the United Tajik Opposition as important steps contributing to the democratic development of Tajik society. The Council reiterates its encouragement to the Commission on National Reconciliation to intensify its efforts aimed at the institution of a broad dialogue among the various political forces in the country in the interests of the restoration and strengthening of civil accord in Tajikistan.

The Council encourages the parties to undertake further concerted measures to ensure the full and sequential implementation, in a balanced manner, of the General Agreement, especially all the provisions of the protocol on military issues, including those related to the reintegration of former opposition fighters. It also encourages them to continue their active work in creating conditions for the timely holding of a constitutional referendum and presidential and parliamentary elections, underlines the importance of the involvement of the United Nations in this process, in continued close cooperation with the Organization for Security and Cooperation in Europe, and welcomes the intention of the Secretary-General to approach Member States with concrete proposals on voluntary contributions to support such involvement.

The Council notes with appreciation the work of the outgoing Special Representative of the Secretary-General, Mr. Ján Kubiš, and of all the personnel of the United Nations Mission of Observers in Tajikistan, and encourages the Mission to continue assisting the parties in the implementation of the General Agreement. It underlines the need for the Mission to operate throughout Tajikistan and to have the necessary personnel and financial support, and requests the Secretary-General to continue to consider means of ensuring a full and active role for the Mission in the implementation of the General Agreement up to the strength authorized by its resolution 1138(1997) of 14 November 1997, while continuing to observe stringent security measures. The Council urges the Secretary-General to appoint a successor to Mr. Kubiš as the Special Representative as soon as possible.

The Council supports the continued active involvement of the Contact Group of Guarantor States and International Organizations in the peace process.

The Council welcomes the continued contribution made by the collective peacekeeping forces of the Commonwealth of Independent States in assisting the parties in the implementation of the General Agreement in coordination with all concerned.

The Council expresses its concern at the precarious humanitarian situation in Tajikistan. It welcomes the activities of various international organizations and humanitarian workers related to the implementation of the General Agreement and addressing the humanitarian, rehabilitation and development needs of Tajikistan. The Council calls upon Member States and others concerned to respond promptly and generously to the mid-year review of the consolidated inter-agency appeal for Tajikistan for 1999.

The Secretary-General's November report [S/1999/1127] noted that the General Agreement's implementation reached two important benchmarks during the reporting period. The first was the Supreme Court's lifting, on 13 August, of the 1993 ban on UTO political parties, and the second was the referendum held on 26 September on the six amendments to the Constitution as outlined in the Secretary-General's August report [S/1999/872], which were approved by 72 per cent of votes cast.

Controversy arose, however, over the registration of candidates for the presidential election, prompting UTO to suspend again its participation in CNR on 18 October, and to threaten to boycott the election. Of the four presidential candidates—incumbent President Rakhmonov of the People's Democratic Party, Saifiddin Turayev of the Party of Justice in Tajikistan, Sulton Kuvvatov of the Democratic Party of Tajikistan (Tehran Platform) and Davlat Usmon of the Islamic Revival Party, representing UTO—only President Rakhmonov met the signatures requirement to be registered with CCER. Acting on the complaint by the other three candidates that they had been prevented from gathering the necessary signatures by intimidation from local-level officials, CCER, at a meeting with those candidates, attended by the Special Representative and the head of the OSCE mission in Tajikistan, extended the registration deadline to 11 October. Having failed again to collect the necessary signatures, the candidates could not be registered and appealed their case with the Supreme Court, which directed them to address their grievance to the local courts. The Court, however, ruled that CCER should allow the registration of UTO's candidate.

As scheduled, the presidential election took place on 6 November, with UTO participation. President Rakhmonov was re-elected for the new single seven-year term. On the eve of the election, the President and Abdullo Nuri, the UTO leader and CNR Chairman, signed a 22-point protocol on political guarantees during the preparation for and holding of the elections to the Majlis-i Oli (parliament) of Tajikistan. The text was transmitted to the Secretary-General on 11 November [S/1999/1159].

CNR, in which UTO resumed participation on 8 November, then took up the draft electoral law. The two most contentious issues were the number of seats in Parliament's lower house and the timing of the local elections, which had an impact on the composition of the upper house. On 3 December, the President and Mr. Nuri agreed that the

Assembly of Representatives (lower house) would comprise 63 seats and the National Assembly (upper house) 33 seats; and that the local elections would be held simultaneously with the elections for the Assembly of Representatives. On 10 December, Parliament adopted the new electoral law.

A UN/OSCE assessment mission visited Tajikistan (14-17 December) to determine whether the overall legislative, administrative and political framework for the election met standards to allow both organizations to observe the election. The mission found a number of shortcomings in the electoral law, but concluded that a level of political pluralism existed to allow the election to be contested by several political groups. The mission thus recommended that, despite the shortcomings, both organizations would deploy a joint observation mission.

Progress in the areas of amnesty, power-sharing and reintegration of former fighters were also recorded. During the reporting period, 40 of the 47 UTO supporters previously recommended for release from prison were granted amnesty; of the remaining 7, 3 were found ineligible for amnesty, 2 died before the amnesty decrees were issued and 2 were executed. Two UTO representatives were appointed to posts at the district and city levels, bringing such appointments to 14. CNR indicated that 2,309 former fighters had been integrated into the armed forces and police and security forces; another 2,370 had been demobilized. A nation-wide disarmament campaign (5-25 August), conducted after the official disarmament and disbandment of UTO, had disappointing results. It was believed that the majority of usable weapons remained in the hands of former UTO fighters and the population at large; none of the artillery pieces and weapons brought back by a UTO group from Afghanistan in 1998 were handed in. The job-creation projects for former fighters carried out by UNOPS in the Karategin Valley districts increased to 52, employing some 1,130 persons. Grants allocated through UNDP for those projects totalled $2 million ($350,000 from Canada, $500,000 from Norway and $1,150,000 from the United States).

Since January, UNHCR, in cooperation with the CNR Subcommission on Refugees, had assisted in the voluntary repatriation of 4,119 Tajik refugees from Afghanistan, Kazakhstan, Kyrgyzstan and Turkmenistan. The humanitarian operations of the UN system included life-saving interventions and programmes aimed at stabilizing populations at risk, complementing the job-creation projects for former fighters. In August and September, UNDP entered into final discussions with the Asian Development Bank and Tajikistan concerning the role of UNOPS as implementing partner of a $20 million social-sector grant to the Government.

Observing that close international involvement remained essential to see Tajikistan through the last steps towards national reconciliation and democratization, the Secretary-General recommended that the Security Council extend UNMOT's mandate for another six months, until 15 May 2000.

SECURITY COUNCIL ACTION (November)

On 12 November [meeting 4064], the Security Council unanimously adopted **resolution 1274 (1999)**. The draft [S/1999/1158] was prepared during prior Council consultations.

The Security Council,

Recalling all its relevant resolutions and the statements by its President,

Having considered the report of the Secretary-General of 4 November 1999 on the situation in Tajikistan,

Reaffirming its commitment to the sovereignty and territorial integrity of the Republic of Tajikistan and to the inviolability of its borders,

Welcoming significant progress made in the peace process in Tajikistan, particularly the holding of the constitutional referendum which followed the official declaration by the United Tajik Opposition of the disbandment of its armed units and the decision by the Supreme Court of Tajikistan lifting the bans and restrictions on activities by the political parties and movements of the United Tajik Opposition, and noting with satisfaction that these developments have set Tajikistan on the course of national reconciliation and democratization,

Welcoming also the renewed efforts of the President of the Republic of Tajikistan and the leadership of the Commission on National Reconciliation to advance and to expedite the implementation of the General Agreement on the Establishment of Peace and National Accord in Tajikistan, which have helped to contain emerging controversies and to reach the important milestones envisaged in the General Agreement,

Acknowledging the holding of the presidential elections on 6 November 1999 as a necessary and important step towards durable peace in Tajikistan,

Welcoming the maintenance of close contact by the United Nations Mission of Observers in Tajikistan with the parties, as well as its cooperative liaison with the collective peacekeeping forces of the Commonwealth of Independent States, the Russian border forces and the mission in Tajikistan of the Organization for Security and Cooperation in Europe,

Noting with appreciation the continued contribution of the Contact Group of Guarantor States and International Organizations to the peace process, in particular through periodic joint plenary meetings with the Commission on National Reconciliation to review progress and to help to overcome difficulties in the implementation of the General Agreement,

Welcoming the fact that the general situation in Tajikistan has remained relatively calm, with better security than in earlier periods, while noting that the situation in some parts of the country has remained tense,

Recognizing that comprehensive international support remains crucial for achieving a positive outcome of the peace process in Tajikistan,

1. *Welcomes* the report of the Secretary-General of 4 November 1999;

2. *Calls upon* the parties to undertake further concerted measures to implement fully the General Agreement on the Establishment of Peace and National Accord in Tajikistan, especially all the provisions of the protocol on military issues, and to create conditions for the timely holding of parliamentary elections, underlines the necessity for the full resumption of the work of the Commission on National Reconciliation, and reiterates its encouragement to the Commission to intensify its efforts to broaden a dialogue among the various political forces in the country in the interests of the restoration and strengthening of civil accord in Tajikistan;

3. *Welcomes* the signing on 5 November 1999 by the President of Tajikistan and the Chairman of the Commission on National Reconciliation of the protocol on political guarantees during the preparation for and holding of the elections to the Majlis-i Oli (the Parliament) of the Republic of Tajikistan, and, bearing in mind concerns expressed by the Secretary-General in his report, regards the strict implementation of the protocol as essential for the successful holding of free, fair and democratic parliamentary elections under international monitoring as foreseen in the General Agreement;

4. *Notes with appreciation* the work of the new Special Representative of the Secretary-General and of all the personnel of the United Nations Mission of Observers in Tajikistan, encourages them to continue assisting the parties in the implementation of the General Agreement, reiterates the need for the Mission to operate throughout Tajikistan and to have the necessary personnel and financial support, and requests the Secretary-General to continue to consider means of ensuring a full and active role for the Mission in the implementation of the General Agreement;

5. *Reiterates* the importance of the involvement of the United Nations, in continued close cooperation with the Organization for Security and Cooperation in Europe, in the preparations for and monitoring of the parliamentary elections in Tajikistan, which will be the last major event of the transitional period envisaged in the General Agreement;

6. *Supports* the continued active involvement of the Contact Group of Guarantor States and International Organizations in the peace process;

7. *Welcomes* the continued contribution made by the collective peacekeeping forces of the Commonwealth of Independent States in assisting the parties in the implementation of the General Agreement, in coordination with all concerned;

8. *Calls upon* the parties to cooperate further in ensuring the security and freedom of movement of the personnel of the United Nations, the collective peacekeeping forces and other international personnel, and reminds the parties that the ability of the international community to mobilize and to continue assistance for Tajikistan is linked to the security of those personnel;

9. *Expresses its deep concern* at the precarious humanitarian situation in Tajikistan, and welcomes the assistance provided by Member States, international organizations and humanitarian workers towards the implementation of the General Agreement and in addressing the humanitarian, rehabilitation and development needs of Tajikistan;

10. *Calls upon* Member States and others concerned to make voluntary contributions to launch projects for demobilization and reintegration and to provide support for the elections, and to continue to respond promptly and generously to the consolidated inter-agency appeal for Tajikistan for 1999, and welcomes the preparation of a new appeal for 2000 as a strategic document that will guide a gradual transition to a more development-oriented focus;

11. *Decides* to extend the mandate of the Mission for a period of six months until 15 May 2000;

12. *Requests* the Secretary-General to keep the Council informed of all significant developments, also requests him to submit after the parliamentary elections and within four months of the adoption of the present resolution an interim report on its implementation, and supports his intention to outline in that report the future political role for the United Nations in assisting Tajikistan to continue on the path of peace and national reconciliation and in contributing to the democratic development of Tajik society after the mandate of the Mission is concluded;

13. *Decides* to remain actively seized of the matter.

In a 16 November statement [S/1999/1191], the EU expressed its deep concern about the undemocratic events and procedures connected with the presidential elections, saying they were not compatible with democratic principles and values. It urged the Government to adopt and implement democratic rules and procedures for the upcoming parliamentary elections to ensure that they were fully free and fair. The EU strongly supported the peace process and linked it to the future development of contractual relations between it and Tajikistan.

Korea question

In Korea in 1999, the United Nations Command (UNC) continued to discharge its responsibilities in the maintenance of the 1953 Korean Armistice Agreement, thereby contributing to a stable environment conducive to the North-South dialogue and the ultimate goal of a durable peace on the Korean peninsula. The Democratic People's Republic of Korea (DPRK), however, did not comply with its obligations under that Agreement and continued to call for the dismantling of UNC. Nonetheless, it maintained its cooperation with the United States on the joint remains-recovery operation for Korean War and UNC soldiers.

DPRK cooperation with IAEA in respect of its obligations under its nuclear safeguards agreement remained limited and linked to its perception of progress in the implementation of the 1994 Agreed Framework between the DPRK and the United States.

Communications. The DPRK, in communications to the Security Council on its concept of national reconciliation and unity between it and the Republic of Korea, urged the latter to reject its dependence on foreign forces and ally itself with the North [S/1999/35]. It reaffirmed the agreed three principles of national reunification [YUN 1998, p. 313] and reiterated its five-point charter of national unity: to maintain national independence, achieve unity under the banner of patriotism, improve North-South relations, fight domination of foreign forces and promote visits, contacts and dialogue between them [S/1999/765]. It labelled as anti-reunification the so-called sunshine policy espoused by the Republic of Korea as a peaceful transition strategy towards reunification [S/1999/892].

In a 26 March statement [S/1999/486], the EU underlined its support for the policy of engagement pursued by the Republic of Korea, regarded the results of the recent DPRK-United States talks (New York, 27 February-15 March) as a reaffirmation of their commitment to the 1994 Agreed Framework (see p. 277), drew attention to the European Commission's agreement to provide the DPRK with a food aid and agricultural rehabilitation programme worth 30 million euro in 1999, and underscored its willingness to consider a second round of political dialogue subject to progress on the Korean peninsula.

Armistice Agreement

The United States, on behalf of the Unified Command established pursuant to Security Council resolution 84(1950) [YUN 1950, p. 230], submitted to the Council the UNC annual report [S/2000/1070] concerning the maintenance in 1998 of the 1953 Armistice Agreement contained in General Assembly resolution 725(VIII) [YUN 1953, p. 136]. Of the original 16 UN Member States represented in UNC, 9 remained: Australia, Canada, Colombia, France, New Zealand, the Philippines, Thailand, the United Kingdom and the United States.

The report noted that, in 1998, the Korean People's Army (KPA) continued to reject joint investigations of reported Agreement violations through the Military Armistice Commission, the joint body created to supervise the implementation of the Agreement and to settle violations of it through negotiations. KPA also routinely rejected meetings called by UNC on Agreement-related issues, meeting with it only selectively and informally. The Neutral Nations Supervisory Commission (NNSC), created to conduct independent inspections and investigations of Armistice Agreement violations outside the demilitarized zone (DMZ), continued to be represented by only two neutral nations in residence: Sweden and Switzerland. NNSC held weekly meetings in the DMZ's joint security area, commonly known as Panmunjom. The Polish member, forced to leave Panmunjom in 1995 [YUN 1995, p. 464], returned quarterly from Warsaw for meetings with the resident members, to demonstrate Poland's continuing support for NNSC and maintenance of the Armistice.

The 4-kilometre-wide DMZ that separated the North and the South and ran 151 miles across the entire width of the Korean peninsula remained relatively quiet throughout 1998. On 65 occasions, UNC dispatched joint observer/special investigative teams to its guard and observation posts along the DMZ to monitor Armistice compliance, as well as seven teams to investigate alleged violations. In addition to numerous sightings of KPA soldiers carrying unauthorized weapons within the DMZ and without the required distinctive civil police markings, UNC reported six major KPA incidents, including the defection of a KPA guard and infiltration into the Republic of Korea by a DPRK submarine and an armed agent [YUN 1998, p. 313].

A joint United States-KPA team conducted five separate recovery operations for Korean War remains in the DPRK, which resulted in the return of the remains of 22 UNC soldiers. UNC also returned to KPA the remains of the crew of nine recovered from the infiltrating submarine and of a drowned KPA soldier whose body had drifted into the South.

Communications. The DPRK continued to reiterate that UNC was not a UN organ but an instrument of the United States, stressing that country's refusal to consider replacing the Armistice Agreement with a DPRK-United States peace agreement [S/1999/167]. Claiming the United States maintained UNC for the purpose of igniting a second Korean war, preparations for which it said were under way through its annual joint military exercises with the South under the recently revised "Operation Plan 5027-98" [S/1999/677], the DPRK called on the United Nations to dismantle UNC [S/1999/1242].

In connection with the joint military exercises in June, the DPRK accused the Republic of Korea of having encroached on its territorial waters below the Northern Limit Line, which it claimed the United States and the Republic of Korea unilaterally established in violation of the Armistice Agreement [S/1999/693]. The Republic of Korea, on the other hand, protested against the repeated intrusion into its territorial waters by DPRK ships crossing the Northern Limit Line, asserting that that Line had been recognized by the North and the South since 1953 as a practical separation line off the peninsula's east and west coasts and reaffirmed by the 1992 South-North Basic Agreement; it warned that the unprovoked use of force against its vessels would be met with appropriate countermeasures [S/1999/695]. To resolve the issue, the DPRK proposed a redrawing of the maritime demarcation line based on the Armistice Agreement [S/1999/925]. Subsequently, the Republic of Korea categorically rejected a 2 September declaration by the DPRK military authority unilaterally to set up the so-called North Korean Military Demarcation Line in the West Sea (Yellow Sea) [S/1999/952].

The DPRK also transmitted its observations in connection with a recently published book entitled *The United States and Biological Warfare: Secrets from the Early Cold War and Korea* [S/1999/251].

IAEA safeguards inspections

Pursuant to the agreement between IAEA and the DPRK for the application of safeguards in connection with the 1968 Treaty on the Non-Proliferation of Nuclear Weapons, adopted by the General Assembly in resolution 2373(XXII) [YUN 1968, p. 17], which remained binding and in force since 1992 [YUN 1992, p. 73], IAEA continued to dispatch to the DPRK inspection teams from Vienna, in addition to two IAEA inspectors continuously present in Nyongbyon to monitor the freeze instituted by the DPRK in 1994 [YUN 1994, p. 442] of its graphite-moderated reactors and facilities. The IAEA Director General's yearly report on the safeguards implementation to the IAEA General Conference through its Board of Governors was also communicated to the Security Council through the Secretary-General.

In his report, transmitted to the Council on 20 December 1999 [S/1999/1268], the Director General repeated that the DPRK continued to accept IAEA monitoring activities solely within the context of the 1994 Agreed Framework [YUN 1994, p. 442] between the DPRK and the United States and not under its safeguards agreement with IAEA. He stated that, at the twelfth (Pyongyang, 10-12 March) and thirteenth (Vienna, 13-16 December) rounds of technical discussions with the DPRK, no progress was made on the long-standing issue related to the preservation of information necessary to verify the accuracy and completeness of the DPRK's initial, 1992 declaration [YUN 1992, p. 73] on its nuclear-material inventory or to methods for preserving such information in a verifiable manner to enable future verification of safeguards compliance—a requirement to be fulfilled under the Agreed Framework before any key nuclear components of the light-water reactors, foreseen in that document, could be delivered. Nor was there progress on the day-to-day activities related to monitoring of the freeze, including the DPRK's refusal to accept certain safeguards measures at its reprocessing plant and limitations on inspector access to technical support buildings at the 5-MW(e) Experimental Power Reactor.

The Director General reported again that the DPRK did not accept all the measures required, only ad hoc and routine inspections at facilities not subject to the freeze, and therefore was not in compliance with its safeguards agreement. He also concluded once again that its cooperation with IAEA was limited and remained linked to its perception of progress in the Agreed Framework's implementation.

In a 1 October resolution, the IAEA General Conference urged the DPRK to cooperate fully in the implementation of the safeguards agreement and to take the steps necessary to preserve all information relevant to verifying the accuracy and completeness of its initial nuclear declaration.

By **resolution 54/26** of 15 November (see p. 962), the General Assembly called on the DPRK to comply with the safeguards agreement and to cooperate fully with IAEA.

Cambodia

In response to a 1997 General Assembly request, the Secretary-General in 1999 dispatched a Group of Experts to Cambodia to evaluate existing evidence of past serious violations of Cambodian and international law and to propose measures to enable Cambodia to address that issue. Following its review of the Group's report, the Government decided to bring the top Khmer Rouge leaders to justice before Cambodia's court, rather than before an international court to be established for the purpose, as recommended by the Group, and welcomed the assistance of outside legal experts.

In December, the Assembly, in reaffirming that the most serious human rights violations in Cambodia in recent history had been committed by the Khmer Rouge, appealed to the Government to ensure that those responsible for the most serious violations were brought to account in accordance with international standards of justice, fairness and due process of law. It encouraged the Government to continue to cooperate with the United Nations in that regard.

(For the situation of human rights in Cambodia, see p. 584.)

Trial of Khmer Rouge leaders

Cambodia's Prime Minister, Samdech Hun Sen, in a 21 January aide-memoire [A/53/801-S/1999/67] transmitted to the Secretary-General and the Security Council, discussed the matter of working out a formula to bring top Khmer Rouge leaders to trial for crimes committed during Cambodia's civil war. Stating that the trial should mark the last stage of national reconciliation in Cambodia, the Prime Minister laid out the questions to be answered as to the appropriate court of law to conduct the trial, national, international or both, and the chargeable offences committed during the three distinct periods in the long conflict in Cambodia, namely, 1970 to 1975, 1975 to 1979 and 1979 to 1998. He said account should also be taken of the 1970 verdicts by the Martial Court of the former Khmer Republic, as well as the 1979 verdict of the Kampuchean People's Revolutionary Court.

Report of Group of Experts for Cambodia. On 15 March [A/53/850-S/1999/231], the Secretary-General transmitted to the General Assembly and the Council the report of the Group of Experts for Cambodia, established pursuant to Assembly resolution 52/135 [YUN 1997, p. 613]. The Group visited Cambodia and Thailand from 14 to 24 November 1998. On the basis of a review of the material and documents made available to it, the Group concluded that the evidence testified to serious crimes punishable by international and Cambodian laws and that existing physical and witness evidence were sufficient to justify legal proceedings against the Khmer Rouge leaders for crimes committed during 1975-1979, including those against humanity, genocide, war crimes, forced labour, torture and crimes against internationally protected persons, as well as crimes under Cambodian law. The Group analysed tribunal options to bring those leaders to justice: a Cambodian tribunal or an ad hoc international tribunal established by the Council or the Assembly; a Cambodian tribunal under UN administration; or an international tribunal established by multilateral treaty to conduct trials in third States. The Group further concluded that the Government had the ability to apprehend those leaders who were in known locations within Cambodia and were not physically protected from arrest. The Governments of Cambodia and Thailand expressed readiness to do so once formal charges were made.

The Group recommended that the Assembly or the Council should establish an ad hoc international tribunal to try Khmer Rouge officials for crimes against humanity and genocide committed from 17 April 1975 to 7 January 1979; and that the United Nations, in cooperation with the Government and non-governmental sector, should encourage a process of national reflection to determine the desirability of a truth-telling mechanism to provide a fuller picture of the Democratic Kampuchea atrocities.

The Secretary-General stated that the Prime Minister, having reviewed the report, cautioned on 3 March [A/53/851-S/1999/230] that any decision to bring Khmer Rouge leaders to justice had to take account of Cambodia's need for peace and national reconciliation and that, if improperly conducted, the trials would create panic among other former Khmer Rouge officers and rank and file and lead to a renewed guerrilla war. Cambodia's Foreign Minister conveyed to the Secretary-General, at their 12 March meeting, the Government's view that, on the basis of article 6 of the Convention on the Prevention and Punishment of the Crime of Genocide, contained in Assembly resolution 260 A (III) [YUN 1948-49, p. 959] and article 33 of the Cambodian Constitution, the national courts were fully competent to conduct the trials and had therefore decided to put on trial Ta Mok, the former Khmer Rouge military commander of the south-west region and a Standing Committee member, before a Cambodian court but would accept foreign assistance and expertise to that end. The Secretary-General reminded the Foreign Minister that the Group of Experts had concluded that the Cambodian judiciary, in its current state, was unlikely to meet minimal international standards of justice, even with external assistance.

The Secretary-General expressed confidence that the Assembly and the Council would take the Group's report fully into account in their determination of how to accommodate the principles of justice and national reconciliation in Cambodia. It was his view, however, that the trial of a single Khmer Rouge military leader that would leave the entire political leadership unpunished would not serve the cause of justice and accountability. Hence, the leaders responsible for the most serious crimes should be tried before a tribunal meeting the international standards of justice, fairness and due process of law; impunity was unacceptable in the face of genocide and other crimes against humanity. The Secretary-General stood ready to assist the Assembly or the Council and the Government in bringing about a process of judicial accountability, which alone could provide the basis for peace, reconciliation and development.

Communications. Cambodia, in a 12 March aide-memoire [A/53/866-S/1999/295] on the report of the Group of Experts, quoted the country's Constitution, which stipulated that Cambodian nationals should not, among other prohibitions, be exiled or arrested and extradited to any foreign country unless there was mutual agreement to do so. Cambodia reaffirmed on 19 March [A/53/867-S/1999/298] and 24 March [A/53/875-S/1999/324] that the existing national court would be responsible for the investigation, prosecution and trial of Khmer Rouge leader Ta Mok, as well as for the trial of other Khmer Rouge leaders charged with genocide, and welcomed assistance, including legal experts from various countries, in response to the concern that the national court did not meet international standards of justice. The Prime Minister, in an 18 April statement [A/53/916, S/1999/443] on his meeting with United States Senator John Kerry, affirmed that, to meet international standards, Cambodia would enact legislation to allow foreign judges and prosecutors to participate in the domestic trials, over which the judicial branch had sole competence and to which the Government could not give orders.

By **resolution 54/171**, the Assembly took note of the steps taken by the Cambodian Government to bring to justice the Khmer Rouge leaders responsible for the most serious human rights violations (see p. 585).

Office of Secretary-General's Personal Representative in Cambodia

On 31 December 1999, the political mandate of the Office of the Personal Representative of the Secretary-General in Cambodia, set up in Phnom Penh in March 1994 [YUN 1994, p. 450], ended and with it the term of Lakhan L. Mehrotra (India), who had served as Personal Representative since 8 June 1997 [YUN 1997, p. 284].

UNTAC financing and liquidation

In keeping with General Assembly decision 52/485 [YUN 1998, p. 325] on the combined financing of UN peacekeeping operations, the Assembly considered at its resumed fifty-third (1999) session a comprehensive analysis [ibid., p. 317] of the types and causes of UN asset losses during the period 1 January 1993-31 December 1995, in peacekeeping operations, among them the United Nations Transitional Authority in Cambodia (UNTAC), terminated in 1993 [YUN 1993, p. 371], as well as steps taken to prevent such losses. The related ACABQ report [A/53/895] was also before the Assembly. On the recommendation of the Fifth Committee [A/53/988], the Assembly, on 8 June [meeting 101], adopted **resolution 53/230** without vote [agenda item 126].

Financing and liquidation of the United Nations Transitional Authority in Cambodia

The General Assembly,

Recalling its resolution 52/239 of 26 June 1998,

Recalling also its decision 52/485 of 26 June 1998,

Having considered the report of the Secretary-General on the financing and liquidation of the United Nations Transitional Authority in Cambodia and the related report of the Advisory Committee on Administrative and Budgetary Questions,

1. *Notes with concern* that the provisions of its decision 52/485 have not been complied with, and reiterates that all reports on the final disposition of assets should contain detailed information on and justification of items written off and lost;
2. *Expresses its deep concern* regarding the losses of the United Nations property in this mission;
3. *Takes note* of the report of the Secretary-General relating to the losses of United Nations assets in peacekeeping operations;
4. *Endorses* the observations and recommendations of the Advisory Committee on Administrative and Budgetary Questions contained in paragraphs 49 to 55 of its report;
5. *Requests* the Secretary-General to provide an updated report in respect of the period 1 January 1996 to 31 December 1997 on losses of United Nations property in peacekeeping operations to the General Assembly at its fifty-fourth session;
6. *Also requests* the Secretary-General to ensure the safety of United Nations assets and the need to have accountability procedures in place to deter and penalize those responsible for the losses of United Nations property and to report thereon to the General Assembly at its fifty-fourth session.

As requested, the Secretary-General submitted, in December, a report [A/54/669 & Corr.1] updating information on property losses in UN peacekeeping operations (see p. 71).

On 23 December, the Assembly decided that the agenda item on the financing of UNTAC would remain for consideration at its resumed fifty-fourth (2000) session (**decision 54/465**), and that the Fifth Committee should continue consideration of the item at that session (**decision 54/462 A**).

East Timor

Negotiations on the political status of the Non-Self-Governing Territory (NSGT) of East Timor among Indonesia, Portugal (the administering Power) and East Timorese representatives, begun in 1982 under the Secretary-General's good offices, led to the signing on 5 May 1999 of an overall Agreement offering a constitutional framework for a special autonomy of East Timor within Indonesia. To ascertain its acceptance or rejection by the East Timorese, the Agreement called on the United Nations to conduct a popular consultation by direct ballot, the modalities and security arrangements for which were separately provided for in two supplementary Agreements concluded by the parties and the United Nations, also on 5 May.

The consultation, conducted on 30 August by the United Nations Mission in East Timor (UNAMET), created by the Security Council on 11 June for that purpose, resulted in the overwhelming rejection of the offer of autonomy in favour of a transition towards independence. Violence was immediately unleashed by those who refused to accept that choice, killing and forcibly displacing hundreds of thousands of people and engulfing East Timor in destruction and humanitarian disaster. That led the Council on 15 September to authorize the establishment of an international force under the unified command of Australia to restore law and order and support UNAMET in the continued discharge of the functions entrusted to it.

With the gradual normalization of conditions in the Territory and on the Secretary-General's recommendation, the Council, on 25 October, created the United Nations Transitional Administration in East Timor (UNTAET), for an initial period until 31 January 2000. Sergio Vieira de Mello, appointed Special Representative of the Secretary-General and Head of UNTAET, assumed that office on 16 November and began working for the orderly transition of East Timor towards independence, expected to take two to three years.

(For the consideration of the question of East Timor by the Special Committee on the Situation with regard to the Implementation of the Declaration of the Granting of Independence to Colonial Countries and Peoples, see PART ONE, Chapter VIII, under "Territories under review".)

Popular consultation on autonomy

Autonomy agreements

Tripartite negotiations among Indonesia, Portugal and East Timorese representatives to find an internationally acceptable solution to the question of the political status of East Timor, initiated by the Secretary-General as requested in General Assembly resolution 37/30 [YUN 1982, p. 1349], made rapid progress between January and April 1999. They culminated in the signing, in New York on 5 May, of an overall Agreement between Indonesia and Portugal. Appended to the Agreement was a proposed constitutional framework, based on a 1998 UN draft [YUN 1998, p. 572], which provided for a special autonomy for East Timor within the Republic of Indonesia. The Agreement entrusted the Secretary-General with organizing and conducting a popular consultation to ascertain the acceptance or rejection of the proposed framework by the East Timorese. It stipulated that, in case of its acceptance, Indonesia would initiate constitutional measures to implement the autonomy framework, while Portugal would initiate procedures for East Timor's removal from the list of NSGTs. In case of the proposal's rejection, Indonesia would take constitutional steps to terminate its links with East Timor, thus restoring its status prior to 17 July 1976; Indonesia and Portugal and the Secretary-General would agree on arrangements for a peaceful and orderly transfer of authority in East Timor to the United Nations, enabling East Timor to begin a process of transition to independence.

Two supplementary Agreements were also signed by the parties and the Secretary-General: one on the modalities for the consultation of the East Timorese through a direct ballot scheduled for 8 August, in and outside East Timor, and the other on security arrangements.

On 5 May [A/53/951-S/1999/513], the Secretary-General transmitted the Agreements to the Assembly and the Security Council. He also described the negotiations leading up to them and noted that, to enable him to proceed with the establishment of a UN presence in East Timor to execute the consultation, he had set up a trust fund to which Member States might channel voluntary contributions.

East Timor, which was added to the Assembly's list of NSGTs by General Assembly resolution 1542(XV) [YUN 1960, p. 513], was administered by Portugal, which, in 1974, sought to establish a provisional government and a popular assembly that would determine its status. Civil war broke out in 1975 [YUN 1975, p. 857], however, between those favouring independence and those advocating integration with Indonesia. Unable to control the situation, the Portuguese authorities in East Timor withdrew; Indonesia intervened militarily, abruptly altering the course of the decolonization process. Assembly resolution 3485(XXX) [ibid., p. 865] and Council resolution 384(1975) [ibid., p. 866] called for Indonesia's withdrawal from the Territory. Indonesia informed the Secretary-General that on 17 July 1976 [YUN 1976, p. 732] it had taken legislative action to integrate

East Timor as Indonesia's twenty-seventh province. Indonesia had since reiterated to the Assembly that the people of East Timor had completed the decolonization process by exercising their right to self-determination and choosing integration with Indonesia [YUN 1977, p. 868; YUN 1982, p. 1348; YUN 1998, p. 571]. That integration was never recognized by either the United Nations or Portugal.

SECURITY COUNCIL ACTION

The Security Council, on 7 May [meeting 3998], unanimously adopted **resolution 1236(1999)**. The draft [S/1999/520] was prepared during prior Council consultations.

The Security Council,

Recalling its previous resolutions on the situation in East Timor,

Recalling also General Assembly resolutions 1514(XV) of 14 December 1960, 1541(XV) of 15 December 1960 and 2625(XXV) of 24 October 1970 and Assembly resolutions on the question of East Timor, in particular resolution 37/30 of 23 November 1982,

Bearing in mind the sustained efforts of the Governments of Indonesia and Portugal since July 1983, through the good offices of the Secretary-General, to find a just, comprehensive and internationally acceptable solution to the question of East Timor,

Welcoming the progress made at the last round of talks between the Governments of Portugal and Indonesia, under the auspices of the Secretary-General, leading to the conclusion of a series of agreements in New York on 5 May 1999,

Commending in particular the efforts of the Personal Representative of the Secretary-General in this regard,

Taking note of the report of the Secretary-General,

Taking note also of the concerns expressed in the report of the Secretary-General regarding the security situation in East Timor,

1. *Welcomes* the concluding of the Agreement between Indonesia and Portugal on 5 May 1999 on the question of East Timor (the General Agreement);

2. *Welcomes also* the concluding of the Agreements between the United Nations and the Governments of Indonesia and Portugal also on 5 May 1999 regarding security arrangements and the modalities for the popular consultation of the East Timorese through a direct ballot;

3. *Welcomes further* the intention of the Secretary-General to establish as soon as practicable a United Nations presence in East Timor, with a view to assisting in the implementation of those Agreements, in particular by:

(*a*) Conducting a popular consultation of the East Timorese people on the acceptance or rejection of a constitutional framework for an autonomy for East Timor, scheduled for 8 August 1999, in accordance with the General Agreement;

(*b*) Making available a number of civilian police officers to act as advisers to the Indonesian Police in the discharge of their duties in East Timor and, at the time of the consultation, to supervise the escorting of ballot papers and boxes to and from the polling sites;

4. *Stresses* the importance of the requests made to the Secretary-General in the General Agreement to report the result of the popular consultation to the Security Council and the General Assembly, as well as to the Governments of Indonesia and Portugal and the East Timorese people, and, during the interim period between the conclusion of the popular consultation and the start of the implementation of either option, an autonomy within Indonesia or transition to independence, to maintain an adequate United Nations presence in East Timor;

5. *Stresses also* the responsibility of the Government of Indonesia to maintain peace and security in East Timor in order to ensure that the consultation is carried out in a fair and peaceful way and in an atmosphere free of intimidation, violence or interference from any side and to ensure the safety and security of United Nations and other international staff and observers in East Timor;

6. *Stresses further* the importance of the assistance of the Government of Indonesia in ensuring that the United Nations is able to carry out all the tasks entrusted to it for the implementation of the agreements;

7. *Welcomes* the establishment by the Secretary-General of a trust fund to enable Member States to make voluntary contributions to assist in the financing of the United Nations presence in East Timor, and urges all Member States in a position to do so to contribute without delay;

8. *Requests* the Secretary-General to keep the Security Council closely informed of the situation in East Timor, to report to it as soon as possible, and in any event by 24 May 1999, on the implementation of the present resolution and of the agreements referred to in paragraphs 1 and 2 above, inter alia, specifying the detailed modalities of the consultation process, to make detailed recommendations to the Council for decision on the mandate, size, structure and budget of the United Nations mission, including civilian police officers envisaged in paragraph 3 above, and to report to the Council thereafter every fourteen days;

9. *Expresses its intention* to take a prompt decision on the establishment of a United Nations mission on the basis of the report referred to in paragraph 8 above;

10. *Requests* the Secretary-General to inform the Council prior to the start of voter registration on whether, on the basis of the objective evaluation of the United Nations mission, the necessary security situation exists for the peaceful implementation of the consultation process;

11. *Decides* to remain seized of the matter.

UN Mission in East Timor

Report and communication by Secretary-General (May). Pursuant to Security Council resolution 1236(1999), the Secretary-General provided a detailed report in May [S/1999/595] on his proposal for a United Nations Mission in East Timor to organize and conduct the popular consultation called for by the 5 May General Agreement. In laying out the particulars of UNAMET's organization and the modalities for implementing the consultation, the Secretary-General pointed out that, to be effective, it was essential for UNAMET to have the confidence and backing of the Council, full cooperation of the Indonesian authorities and the required resources.

UNAMET would include political, electoral, civilian police, information and administrative/financial components, whose heads would report to the Special Representative for the East Timor Popular Consultation and Head of UNAMET. The political component would monitor the fairness of the political environment, ensure the freedom of all political and non-governmental organizations to carry out their activities and advise the Special Representative on all matters having political implications.

The electoral component would be responsible for all activities related to registration and voting under the direction of a Chief Electoral Officer. The external polling called for in the Agreements would be conducted on behalf of the United Nations by the Australian Election Commission and the International Organization for Migration (IOM), and coordinated through the IOM field coordinator, the UN Secretariat's Electoral Assistance Division and UNAMET's electoral component. An independent Electoral Commission of three eminent international experts, to be appointed by the Secretary-General, would be responsible for the overall assessment of the consultation process and for adjudicating complaints, challenges or disputes. It would have final decision-making authority. A status-of-mission agreement would be concluded between the United Nations and Indonesia.

Instructions and procedures on all aspects of the consultation process, including registration directives, documentation, appeals, codes of conduct, external polling and counting, were being drafted by the Electoral Assistance Division of the Secretariat's Department of Political Affairs.

UNAMET's civilian police component, to be headed by a Civilian Police Commissioner, would advise the Indonesian Police (responsible, under the security agreement, for maintaining law and order) and supervise the escort of ballot papers and boxes to and from the polling sites. Up to 280 experienced civilian police would be required for deployment in Dili, in the eight districts where electoral offices were to be set up and at the 200 registration/polling centres.

The information component would conduct a media campaign, with the cooperation of local media providers, to explain to the East Timorese the terms of the General Agreement and the proposed autonomy framework, the implications of a vote for or against the proposal and the voting procedure. The campaign would last for the duration of the Mission and be conducted in the Tetum, Bahasa Indonesia and Portuguese languages.

The Secretary-General was deeply concerned to learn from an assessment team that visited East Timor from 4 to 15 May that the situation there remained extremely tense and volatile. He underscored the measures required of the Indonesian authorities to ensure a free and secure environment for the peaceful implementation of the consultation process, namely, to bring armed civilian groups under strict control, arrest and prosecute those inciting or threatening to use violence, ban rallies by armed groups while ensuring freedom of association and expression of all political parties, redeploy Indonesian military forces and institute a process for disarming all armed groups well in advance of the holding of the ballot. He recommended that the Commission on Peace and Stability be brought into operation. Established on the recommendation of the Secretary-General's Personal Representative on 21 April, during the negotiations leading to the 5 May Agreements, the Commission was to elaborate a code of conduct governing the laying down of arms and to ensure the disarmament of both pro- and anti-integration groups, as envisaged in the supplementary Agreement on security.

The Secretary-General informed the Council on 21 May [S/1999/602] that preparations for establishing UNAMET had begun in earnest and that, following the necessary consultations, he had decided to appoint Ian Martin (United Kingdom) as his Special Representative for the East Timor Popular Consultation and Head of UNAMET. The Council took note of that decision on 25 May [S/1999/603].

SECURITY COUNCIL ACTION (11 June)

The Security Council met on 11 June [meeting 4013] to consider the Secretary-General's May report. It also had before it Indonesia's letter of 27 May [S/1999/612] objecting to the report's imbalanced depiction of the situation prevailing in East Timor, pointing to the fact that both pro- and anti-integration groups had perpetrated acts of violence and intimidation; to the unsubstantiated allegation that elements of the Indonesian army acquiesced in such acts; and, in view of the Government's support for a reconciliation meeting among all segments of East Timorese society, to the misleading portrayal of the inability of anti-integration groups to participate freely in the Commission on Peace and Stability. The Council also considered Portugal's 7 June letter [S/1999/652] advising of its appointment of the Reverend Victor Melícias as Portuguese Commissioner to coordinate Portugal's actions in the consultation process and in the transition towards self-determination for East Timor.

The Council unanimously adopted **resolution 1246(1999)**. The draft [S/1999/666] was prepared during prior Council consultations.

The Security Council,

Recalling its previous resolutions on the situation in East Timor, in particular resolution 1236(1999) of 7 May 1999,

Recalling the Agreement between Indonesia and Portugal of 5 May 1999 on the question of East Timor (the General Agreement) and the Agreements between the United Nations and the Governments of Indonesia and Portugal, of the same date, regarding the modalities for the popular consultation of the East Timorese through a direct ballot and regarding security arrangements (the Security Agreement),

Welcoming the report of the Secretary-General of 22 May 1999 on the question of East Timor,

Noting with concern the assessment by the Secretary-General in that report that the security situation in East Timor remains "extremely tense and volatile",

Taking note of the pressing need for reconciliation between the various competing factions within East Timor,

Welcoming the fruitful cooperation of the Government of Indonesia and the local authorities in East Timor with the United Nations,

Taking note of the letter dated 7 June 1999 from the Permanent Representative of Portugal to the United Nations addressed to the President of the Security Council,

Welcoming the conclusion of consultations between the Government of Indonesia and the United Nations on the deployment of military liaison officers within the mission established by paragraph 1 below,

Bearing in mind the sustained efforts of the Governments of Indonesia and Portugal since July 1983, through the good offices of the Secretary-General, to find a just, comprehensive and internationally acceptable solution to the question of East Timor,

Welcoming the appointment of the Special Representative of the Secretary-General for the East Timor Popular Consultation, and reiterating its support for the efforts of the Personal Representative of the Secretary-General for East Timor,

1. *Decides* to establish until 31 August 1999 the United Nations Mission in East Timor to organize and conduct a popular consultation, scheduled for 8 August 1999, on the basis of a direct, secret and universal ballot, in order to ascertain whether the East Timorese people accept the proposed constitutional framework providing for a special autonomy for East Timor within the unitary Republic of Indonesia or reject the proposed special autonomy for East Timor, leading to East Timor's separation from Indonesia, in accordance with the General Agreement and to enable the Secretary-General to discharge his responsibility under paragraph 3 of the Security Agreement;

2. *Authorizes* until 31 August 1999 the deployment within the Mission of up to 280 civilian police officers to act as advisers to the Indonesian Police in the discharge of their duties and, at the time of the consultation, to supervise the escorting of ballot papers and boxes to and from the polling sites;

3. *Also authorizes* until 31 August 1999 the deployment within the Mission of fifty military liaison officers to maintain contact with the Indonesian Armed Forces in order to allow the Secretary-General to discharge his responsibilities under the General Agreement and the Security Agreement;

4. *Endorses* the proposal of the Secretary-General that the Mission should also incorporate the following components:

(*a*) A political component responsible for monitoring the fairness of the political environment, for ensuring the freedom of all political and other non-governmental organizations to carry out their activities freely and for monitoring and advising the Special Representative on all matters with political implications;

(*b*) An electoral component responsible for all activities related to registration and voting;

(*c*) An information component responsible for explaining to the East Timorese people, in an objective and impartial manner without prejudice to any position or outcome, the terms of the General Agreement and the proposed autonomy framework, for providing information on the process and procedure of the vote, and for explaining the implications of a vote in favour or against the proposal;

5. *Notes* the intention of the Governments of Indonesia and Portugal to send an equal number of representatives to observe all the operational phases of the consultation process both inside and outside East Timor;

6. *Welcomes* the intention of the Secretary-General to conclude with the Government of Indonesia, as soon as possible, a status-of-mission agreement, and urges the early conclusion of negotiations with a view to the full and timely deployment of the Mission;

7. *Calls upon* all parties to cooperate with the Mission in the implementation of its mandate, and to ensure the security and freedom of movement of its staff in carrying out that mandate in all areas of East Timor;

8. *Approves* the modalities for the implementation of the popular consultation process scheduled for 8 August 1999 as set out in paragraphs 15 to 18 of the report of the Secretary-General of 22 May 1999;

9. *Stresses once again* the responsibility of the Government of Indonesia to maintain peace and security in East Timor, in particular in the present security situation referred to in the report of the Secretary-General, in order to ensure that the popular consultation is carried out in a fair and peaceful way and in an atmosphere free of intimidation, violence or interference from any side and to ensure the safety and security of United Nations and other international staff and observers in East Timor;

10. *Welcomes* in this regard the decision taken by the Government of Indonesia to establish a ministerial team to monitor and ensure the security of the popular consultation in accordance with article 3 of the General Agreement and paragraph 1 of the Security Agreement;

11. *Condemns* all acts of violence from whatever quarter, and calls for an end to such acts and the laying down of arms by all armed groups in East Timor, for the necessary steps to achieve disarmament and for further steps in order to ensure a secure environment devoid of violence or other forms of intimidation,

which is a prerequisite for the holding of a free and fair ballot in East Timor;

12. *Requests* all parties to ensure that conditions exist for the comprehensive implementation of the popular consultation, with the full participation of the East Timorese people;

13. *Urges* that every effort be made to make the Commission on Peace and Stability operative, and in particular stresses the need for the Indonesian authorities to provide security and personal protection for members of the Commission in cooperation with the Mission;

14. *Reiterates its request* to the Secretary-General to keep the Security Council closely informed of the situation, and to continue to report to it every fourteen days on the implementation of its resolutions and of the tripartite Agreements and on the security situation in East Timor;

15. *Decides* to remain seized of the matter.

Report of Secretary-General (June). The Secretary-General reported on 22 June [S/1999/705] that UNAMET's deployment had progressed markedly since his May report. By 15 June, four of the eight regional electoral offices were operational and the Chief Electoral Officer, Jeffrey Fischer, had arrived in Dili to lead the core electoral team already in place. The first United Nations Volunteers group to serve as field electoral officers were in training in Darwin, Australia. The Civilian Police Commissioner, Alan James Mills (Australia), appointed by a 15 June exchange of letters [S/1999/679, S/1999/680] between the Secretary-General and the Security Council, began working with the local police and with an advance team of 41 UN civilian police on 12 and 21 June, respectively. Indonesia had agreed to the deployment of 50 UN military liaison officers, to begin almost immediately. The public information campaign had been launched with the radio broadcast of the Secretary-General's statement outlining UNAMET's purpose and objectives and pointing to its impartiality with respect to the consultation's outcome, emphasizing the secrecy of the ballot and calling on all East Timorese to refrain from violence.

The Secretary-General noted that the relative calm in Dili and Baucau had not extended to the rest of the Territory, with the situation in the western districts remaining very serious. He highlighted the activities by pro-integration militias, believed by observers to be acting with the acquiescence of members of the Indonesian army, which continued to have a constricting effect on political freedom, silencing pro-independence activists and their supporters and forcing them into hiding. Militias involved in violence against civilians were reportedly being presented by some officials as civil defence forces. Complaints from pro-integration leaders of violent activity by the Armed Forces for the National Liberation of East Timor (Falintil) were also lodged with UNAMET, which was looking into the incidents cited.

Given the serious security situation throughout much of East Timor and the absence of a level playing field, which did not yet permit certification that the necessary conditions existed for the operational phases of the consultation process to begin, and in order to allow UNAMET to reach full deployment, the Secretary-General decided to postpone registration to 13 July (a three-week delay from the original starting date of 22 June), which in turn meant postponement of the ballot date.

Statement by Secretary-General. The Secretary-General, in a 29 June statement [SG/SM/7052], deplored in the strongest terms that day's attack on UNAMET's Maliana regional office by some 100 reportedly pro-integration militia. Several East Timorese taking refuge there were injured, a UNAMET staff member was hurt and the office was extensively damaged. He called on the Indonesian Police to investigate the incident and bring the perpetrators to justice.

SECURITY COUNCIL ACTION (29 June)

On 29 June [meeting 4019], the Security Council President made statement **S/PRST/1999/20** on behalf of the Council:

The Security Council has considered the report of the Secretary-General of 22 June 1999 on the question of East Timor.

The Council notes with understanding the decision of the Secretary-General to postpone for three weeks his determination, which he will base on the main elements identified in his report of 5 May 1999, of whether the necessary security situation exists for the start of the operational phases of the consultation process in accordance with the Agreement between the United Nations and the Governments of Indonesia and Portugal. The Council also endorses his intention not to start the operational phases of the popular consultation until the United Nations Mission in East Timor is fully deployed, and his decision to postpone the ballot date for two weeks.

The Council emphasizes that a popular consultation of the East Timorese people through a direct, secret and universal ballot represents an historic opportunity to resolve the question of East Timor peacefully. It concurs with the Secretary-General's assessment that this process must be transparent and that all parties must have the opportunity to express themselves freely.

In this regard, the Council expresses serious concern that the Secretary-General, in his assessment, concludes that the necessary conditions do not yet exist to begin the operational phases of the consultation process, given the security situation throughout much of East Timor and the absence of a "level playing field". It is especially concerned that the militias and other armed groups have carried out acts of violence against the local population and exercise an intimidating influence over them, and that these activities continue to constrict political freedom in East Timor, thus jeopardizing the necessary openness of the consultation process. The Council notes the Secretary-General's assessment that while the security situation has severely limited the opportunity for public expression by pro-independence activists, pro-autonomy campaigning has been actively pursued.

The Council stresses the need for all sides to put an end to all kinds of violence and for utmost restraint before, during and after the consultation. It calls upon the Mission to follow up reports of violent activity by both the pro-integration militias and Falintil (the Armed Forces for the National Liberation of East Timor). In this regard, it expresses grave concern at the attack on the Mission office in Maliana, East Timor, on 29 June 1999. The Council demands that the incident be thoroughly investigated and the perpetrators be brought to justice. The Council also demands that all parties respect the safety and security of Mission personnel. The Council supports the statement of the spokesman for the Secretary-General of 29 June 1999 and requests the Secretary-General to report further.

The Council welcomes the positive developments identified by the Secretary-General. The Council warmly welcomes the excellent channels of communication between the Mission and the Indonesian authorities, which have been facilitated by the establishment of a high-level Indonesian task force in Dili. The Council warmly welcomes the opening of the DARE II talks in Jakarta with representatives of all sides in East Timor, and the progress towards making the Commission on Peace and Stability operative.

The Council stresses once again the responsibility of the Government of Indonesia to maintain peace and security in East Timor. The Council emphasizes that all local officials in East Timor must abide by the provisions of the tripartite Agreements, in particular as regards the designated campaign period, the use of public funds for campaign purposes and the need to campaign only in their private capacity, without recourse to the pressure of office.

The Council is particularly concerned at the situation of internally displaced persons in East Timor and the implications which this may have for the universality of the consultation. It calls upon all concerned to grant full access and freedom of movement to humanitarian organizations for the delivery of humanitarian assistance, to cease immediately activities which may cause further displacement and to allow all internally displaced persons who wish to do so to return home.

The Council notes that full deployment of the Mission will not be possible before 10 July 1999. It urges the Secretary-General to take all necessary steps to ensure full deployment by that time, and urges all parties to cooperate fully with the Mission. It stresses the importance of allowing complete freedom of movement for the Mission within East Timor in order to carry out its tasks.

The Council urges the Indonesian Government and the pro-integration and pro-independence groups to continue to enhance cooperation with the Mission, to allow the popular consultation to go ahead in a timely manner.

The Council will remained seized of the matter.

Communications. In letter exchanges with the Security Council between 21 June and 6 July, the Secretary-General appointed Brigadier Rezaqui Haider (Bangladesh) as Chief Military Liaison Officer [S/1999/709, S/1999/710], who assumed his functions on 8 July; and named the 27 countries contributing civilian police personnel [S/1999/735, S/1999/736] and the 13 States contributing military liaison personnel [S/1999/750, S/1999/751].

On 10 July [S/1999/773], the Secretary-General informed the Council that preparations had been completed for UNAMET to begin registration on 13 July but that the security situation remained serious. Incidents at Maliana (29 June), Viqueque (30 June) and Liquica (3-4 July) involving UNAMET personnel highlighted the larger, continuing problem which militia impunity posed to a free consultation process. He thus shared with the Government a list of specific criteria towards which there should be meaningful, visible progress in security conditions to enable him to make a determination to proceed with the consultation process. To allow concrete steps to be taken by the Government, which reaffirmed its resolve to address the situation by the dispatch of a high-level government delegation to the Territory on 12 July, the Secretary-General, for a second time, rescheduled the start of the registration process, from 13 to 16 July. To set the record straight, Indonesia, on 9 July [S/1999/782], detailed what it claimed were the facts surrounding the incidents cited by the Secretary-General.

Although the security situation in the Territory as a whole continued to preclude a determination that the conditions existed for the peaceful implementation of the consultation, the Secretary-General wrote on 14 July [S/1999/786] that, in view of the assurances by the Indonesian authorities that they would take steps in the immediate future to fulfil the criteria he had provided, as well as of the need to adhere to the shortest possible time frame, the registration could begin on 16 July. He would make another assessment of conditions halfway through the registration period, based on UNAMET's objective evaluation. Indonesia replied on 16 July [S/1999/791] that it was obliged to draw attention to recent facts that would give the Council a more complete appreciation of the true situation on the ground.

On 26 July [S/1999/822], the Secretary-General reported that the 200 registration centres throughout East Timor had opened during the first 10 days of registration. In that period, 239,893 East Timorese had registered: 233,716 in East Timor itself, and the remainder at external registration centres. Security conditions remained inadequate, however. Intimidation by armed militia groups were particularly prevalent in the western districts, resulting in the continuing inability of tens of thousands of internally displaced persons to return to their homes in safety.

Voter registration and polling

Report and communication of Secretary-General (July). The Secretary-General reported on 20 July [S/1999/803] that voter registration which began on 16 July proceeded relatively peacefully, with a strong turnout. As called for by the Agreements, Indonesia and Portugal agreed to deploy up to 50 official observers at each registration and polling site in and outside East Timor, with more than 200 observers already accredited. UNAMET had arranged for the computerization of worldwide registration data in Australia. The three international electoral experts comprising the independent Electoral Commission, Patrick Bradley (United Kingdom), Johan Kriegler (South Africa) and Sohn Bong-Scuk (Republic of Korea), had assumed their responsibilities.

UNAMET was fully operational by the reporting date and the deployment of international personnel was virtually complete. By 19 July, 243 civilian police personnel and 47 military liaison officers were on duty, and the political affairs section was fully deployed. The public information component had intensified dissemination of information on the Agreements and of explanatory material to help voters understand the consultation process.

Noting no further attacks or serious threats against UNAMET, the Secretary-General stated that the serious efforts by the Indonesian authorities to provide the necessary security for UNAMET to discharge its responsibilities had contributed to that positive trend. Much remained to be done, however, to realize the Government's assurances on the ground. Militia activities, which had led to the displacement of many East Timorese and denied them basic security and freedom, with the clear intention of influencing political choice, continued to pose a fundamental challenge to a credible consultation process. Violent activities by Falintil also continued to be reported by Indonesian authorities.

The thousands of internally displaced persons, forcibly relocated or intimidated into fleeing their homes, remained a major concern. Besides its humanitarian dimensions, the problem had a direct bearing on the prospects for holding a free and fair ballot. According to some observers, a considerable number of such persons were either under militia control, in sanctuary in church compounds or in hiding in the Territory's remote areas. UNAMET was developing plans to assist them to participate in the consultation process.

The Secretary-General reported encouraging progress in bridging the deep divisions between the East Timorese parties. They included an agreement to end hostilities signed in Jakarta on 18 June between pro-independence and pro-integration leaders under the auspices of the Commission on Peace and Stability; an understanding, in principle, providing for a ceasefire and the cantonment of the pro-independence Falintil forces, pro integration armed groups and members of the Indonesian army, as well as for movement towards disarmament; and the reconciliation efforts of the Bishops of Dili and Baucau, which resulted in the Dare II Conference (Jakarta, 25-30 June) of leaders from inside and outside East Timor. The Conference issued a series of "points of convergence", including agreement to accept the outcome of the popular consultation. A meeting of senior Indonesian and Portuguese officials was also held under the Personal Representative's chairmanship (New York, 15-16 July) to begin discussions on arrangements for the period between the ballot and the implementation of its result.

The Secretary-General said he remained confident that Indonesia would take further determined measures to improve the security situation, in keeping with its undertakings under the 5 May Agreements.

On 28 July [S/1999/830], the Secretary-General informed the Council that, on UNAMET's advice, he had decided to postpone the popular consultation to 30 August to give UNAMET time to collate and to publicize adequately the list of voters, and to allow for a proper appeals procedure. Consequently, he requested the Council to extend UNAMET's mandate by one month, to 30 September.

SECURITY COUNCIL ACTION

The Security Council met on 3 August [meeting 4031] and unanimously adopted **resolution 1257 (1999)**. The draft [S/1999/843] was prepared during prior Council consultations.

The Security Council,

Recalling its previous resolutions on the situation in East Timor, in particular resolution 1246(1999) of 11 June 1999,

Taking note of the letter dated 28 July 1999 from the Secretary-General to the President of the Security Council which informs the Council of his decision to postpone the popular consultation in East Timor until 30 August 1999 and requests the authorization of a one-month extension to the mandate of the United Nations Mission in East Timor,

1. *Decides* to extend the mandate of the United Nations Mission in East Timor until 30 September 1999;
2. *Decides* to remain seized of the matter.

Report of Secretary-General (August). In a 9 August report [S/1999/862], the Secretary-General outlined modifications to UNAMET's composition and tasks in the interim phase between the conclusion of the popular consultation and the start of the implementation of its result, whether it was acceptance or rejection of the proposed autonomy. During that interim phase, UN efforts would focus on building confidence, fostering stability and reassuring all groups, particularly those in the minority in the ballot, that they had a role to play in East Timor's future political life.

Modifications would include reducing the electoral component to a unit that would plan and prepare for the monitoring of elections to the Regional Council, as foreseen in the autonomy plan, or for elections in case autonomy was rejected; increasing the civilian police to 460, including 50 to train a new East Timorese police force, and the military liaison personnel to 300, who would be deployed in all 13 districts to liaise with the Indonesian Armed Forces, the pro-integration militias and the pro-independence Falintil; replacing the political component with a civil affairs one to assist the Special Representative to foster reconciliation, help form a Representative Council, promote respect for the rule of law and human rights and coordinate humanitarian assistance; and maintaining the public information component to keep the East Timorese and the international community abreast of progress in the implementation of the consultation's outcome.

The Secretary-General recommended that the Council promptly consider and authorize the proposed adjustments to UNAMET and extend its mandate for a further three months, from 30 August until 30 November.

SECURITY COUNCIL ACTION

On 27 August [meeting 4038], the Security Council unanimously adopted **resolution 1262(1999)**. The draft [S/1999/904] was prepared during prior Council consultations.

The Security Council,

Recalling its previous resolutions on the situation in East Timor, in particular resolutions 1246(1999) of 11 June 1999 and 1257(1999) of 3 August 1999,

Recalling the Agreement between Indonesia and Portugal of 5 May 1999 on the question of East Timor and the Agreements between the United Nations and the Governments of Indonesia and Portugal of the same date regarding the modalities for the popular consultation of the East Timorese through a direct ballot and security arrangements,

Welcoming the report of the Secretary-General of 9 August 1999,

Taking note of the need for the United Nations to pursue its efforts in East Timor in the period following the ballot to build confidence and support stability and to reassure all groups, in particular those in the minority in the ballot, that they have a role to play in the future political life of East Timor,

Welcoming the proposal of the Secretary-General that the United Nations Mission in East Timor continue its operations in the interim phase between the conclusion of the popular consultation and the start of the implementation of its result and that its tasks and structure be adjusted accordingly,

Commending the Mission for the impartial and effective implementation of its mandate, and welcoming the confirmation in the report of the Secretary-General that the Mission will continue to do its utmost to fulfil its responsibility in this manner,

Welcoming the fruitful cooperation of the Government of Indonesia in East Timor with the United Nations,

1. *Decides* to extend the mandate of the United Nations Mission in East Timor until 30 November 1999, and endorses the proposal of the Secretary-General that in the interim phase the Mission should incorporate the following components:

(*a*) An electoral unit as set out in the report of the Secretary-General;

(*b*) A civilian police component of up to 460 personnel to continue to advise the Indonesian Police and to prepare for the recruitment and training of the new East Timorese police force;

(*c*) A military liaison component of up to 300 personnel as set out in the report of the Secretary-General to undertake the necessary military liaison functions, to continue to be involved in the work of the East Timorese bodies established to promote peace, stability and reconciliation, and to provide advice to the Special Representative for the East Timor Popular Consultation on security matters as required, pursuant to the implementation of the Agreements of 5 May 1999;

(*d*) A civil affairs component to advise the Special Representative for the East Timor Popular Consultation in monitoring the implementation of the Agreements of 5 May 1999, as set out in the report of the Secretary-General;

(*e*) A public information component to provide information on progress made towards implementation of the outcome of the ballot, and to disseminate a message promoting reconciliation, confidence, peace and stability;

2. *Calls upon* all parties to cooperate with the Mission in the implementation of its mandate, and to en-

sure the security and freedom of movement of its staff in carrying out that mandate in all areas of East Timor;

3. *Recalls* the continuing responsibility of Indonesia to maintain peace and security in East Timor in the interim phase;

4. *Decides* to remain seized of the matter.

Following the resolution's adoption, the President made a statement affirming, on the eve of the ballot, the Council's view, as set out in **S/PRST/1999/20** (see p. 284), that the popular consultation on 30 August represented a historic opportunity to resolve the East Timor question peacefully. In adopting the resolution mandating the UN presence until 30 November, the Council was demonstrating its readiness to continue to support the East Timorese after they had made their decision.

Consultation result

On 3 September [S/1999/944], the Secretary-General informed the Council that UNAMET had completed the popular consultation on the proposed autonomy. The ballot result, duly certified by the Electoral Commission, was 94,388 votes in favour and 344,580 against (or 21.5 per cent and 78.5 per cent, respectively, of total votes cast). The people of East Timor had thus rejected the proposed special autonomy and expressed their wish to begin a process of transition towards independence.

The Secretary-General observed that the orderly and peaceful transfer of authority in East Timor to the United Nations, called for by article 6 of the 5 May Agreement, would be complex and difficult, given the current insecurity in the Territory.

SECURITY COUNCIL ACTION

The Security Council met twice on 3 September [meetings 4041 & 4042]. At the second meeting, the President made statement **S/PRST/1999/27** on behalf of the Council:

The Security Council welcomes the successful popular consultation of the East Timorese people on 30 August 1999 and the letter dated 3 September 1999 from the Secretary-General to the President of the Security Council announcing the ballot result. The Council expresses its support for the courage of those who turned out in record numbers to express their views. It regards the popular consultation as an accurate reflection of the views of the East Timorese people.

The Council pays tribute to the extraordinary work of the Personal Representative of the Secretary-General. It also commends the courage and dedication of the Special Representative for the East Timor Popular Consultation and of the staff of the United Nations Mission in East Timor in organizing and conducting the popular consultation in extremely difficult conditions.

The Council calls on all parties, both inside and outside East Timor, to respect the result of the popular consultation. The Council urges the East Timorese people to work together to implement their decision as freely and democratically expressed in the ballot and to cooperate in the building of peace and prosperity in the territory. The Council now looks to the Indonesian Government to take the necessary constitutional steps to implement the result of the ballot, in accordance with the Agreements of 5 May 1999.

The Council recognizes that the Agreements of 5 May 1999 which led to the popular consultation of the East Timorese people would not have been possible without the timely initiative of the Government of Indonesia and the constructive attitude of the Government of Portugal. It commends the sustained efforts of the Governments of Indonesia and Portugal, through the good offices of the Secretary-General, to find a just, comprehensive and internationally acceptable solution to the question of East Timor, and expresses its appreciation to the Government of Indonesia for its cooperation with the United Nations in the process.

The Council condemns the violence in East Timor which both preceded and followed the ballot of 30 August 1999. It expresses its condolences to the families of United Nations local staff and others so tragically killed. It underlines the need for the result to be implemented in an atmosphere of peace and security without further violence and intimidation. In accordance with its responsibility for maintaining peace and security under the Agreements of 5 May 1999, it is for the Government of Indonesia to take steps to prevent further violence. It also looks to the Government of Indonesia to guarantee the security of Mission personnel and premises. The Council is ready to consider sympathetically any proposal from the Secretary-General to ensure the peaceful implementation of the popular consultation process.

The Council requests the Secretary-General to report as soon as possible on the implementation of the ballot result, including recommendations on the mandate, size and structure of the United Nations presence in East Timor in the implementation phase (phase III).

The Council will remain seized of the matter.

On 17 December, the General Assembly, by **resolution 54/194**, also welcomed the successful conduct of the popular consultation (see p. 535).

Post-consultation violence

In reports of 4 October [S/1999/1024] and 13 December [A/54/654], the Secretary-General recorded that, following announcement of the result of the 30 August consultation, pro-integration militias unleashed a campaign of violence, including killing, looting and arson, throughout most of the Territory. UNAMET local staff were targeted, killing at least four. Foreign observers, international relief workers and journalists were evacuated to Darwin, Australia, as were the majority of UNAMET personnel. Many East Timorese were killed and hundreds of thousands were displaced, often by force.

In the wake of the violence, most UNAMET facilities were found heavily damaged or destroyed. A UN inter-agency assessment team estimated that over 500,000 persons were displaced, including 150,000 to West Timor. Hardly any building in Dili was left undamaged. The towns of Ainaro and Cassa were completely destroyed, while about 70 per cent of Atsabe, Gleno, Lospalus, Maliana, Manatuto and Oecusoe was burned down or levelled, as was 20 per cent of Vineque. Suai and Liquica also sustained extensive damage. The Secretary-General was informed by the Indonesian authorities that the Indonesian Armed Forces had reduced their strength to about 1,200, all reportedly deployed in Dili. The withdrawing soldiers were observed by UNAMET setting fire to buildings and equipment, including their own facilities, and destroying infrastructure. The Indonesian Police also withdrew, leaving only a token presence in Dili, and the judicial and detention systems had ceased operating.

With the early departure of the Indonesian civil authorities, civil administration no longer functioned. The judiciary and court systems ceased to exist. Essential services, including water and electricity, were on the brink of collapse. Security conditions, which had begun to improve, remained precarious, with militia activity continuing to be reported throughout the Territory.

Subsequently, Indonesia lifted martial law (24 September) and the Indonesian Deputy Governor returned to Dili with a small staff (27 September), who informed UNAMET that Foreign Affairs officials would arrive shortly to oversee the transition on the Government's behalf. At a tripartite meeting (28 September) of the Secretariat and the Indonesian and Portuguese Foreign Ministers, it was agreed that ad hoc measures were required to fill the gap created by the early departure of Indonesian civil authorities. The two Governments reiterated their agreement for the transfer of authority in East Timor to the United Nations, in accordance with the 5 May Agreement.

UNAMET, which had operated with a skeleton staff of 12 at the former Australian consulate throughout the crisis period, re-established its headquarters in Dili on 28 September. By 4 October, its redeployed staff totalled 84, including 36 military liaison officers, 16 civilian police and 32 international staff. UNAMET resumed patrolling in Dili, overflying all districts and visiting all Falintil cantonments with the multinational force (INTERFET) (see p. 290). It accompanied multinational force-protected convoys to Manatuto and Baucau. Two military liaison officers were co-located with the INTERFET deployment in Baucau.

Communications. At the height of the violence in East Timor, Ireland wrote that, should Indonesia be unable to maintain security, it would support the deployment of an agreed peacekeeping force [S/1999/950]. Portugal requested an urgent meeting of the Council [S/1999/955], which it reiterated in view of Indonesia's inability to restore order and security to the Territory [S/1999/963]. Brazil also requested a Council meeting to debate the situation [S/1999/961], while Angola transmitted a declaration by the Community of Portuguese-speaking Countries calling on the international community and the Council, in particular, to do everything for the rapid re-establishment of security, including the deployment of peacekeeping forces [S/1999/956].

SECURITY COUNCIL ACTION

The Security Council, on 5 September [S/1999/946], informed the Secretary-General that it was dispatching a mission to Indonesia to discuss steps for the peaceful implementation of the ballot result in East Timor. The mission would be composed of the Permanent Representatives to the United Nations of Malaysia, Namibia (head of mission), Slovenia and the United Kingdom; the Deputy Permanent Representative of the Netherlands; and the Secretary-General's Deputy Personal Representative for East Timor [S/1999/972].

In view of the urgency of the situation, the Council requested that arrangements be made for the mission's departure for Indonesia on the evening of 6 September.

Security Council mission report. On 14 September [S/1999/976 & Corr.1], the Security Council mission reported on the results of its meetings in Jakarta and Dili from 8 to 12 September.

The mission concluded that government accounts of events in East Timor and of Indonesia's action to carry out its responsibilities under the 5 May Agreement tallied neither with the briefings provided by UN staff and senior diplomats in Jakarta and Dili, nor with the mission's observations on the ground. The involvement of large elements of the Indonesian military and police in organizing and backing the actions of the militias was acknowledged publicly by the Defence Minister on 11 September. The repeated failure of the defence forces to carry out the Government's obligations to provide security to UNAMET, international organizations and the population as a whole meant that the Indonesian authorities were either unable or unwilling to provide the proper environment for the peaceful implementation of the 5 May Agreement. The introduction of martial law on 7 September did not alter that state of affairs, nor did it adequately respond to the humanitarian crisis in East Timor, despite the authorities' assurances that that had been one of its aims. The humanitarian situation of the majority of the population in East Timor and of the refugee population in West Timor was extremely grave and needed to be addressed urgently. There was strong prima facie evidence of abuses of international humanitarian law committed since the announcement on 4 September of the ballot result. In that regard, the annexed UNAMET report on widespread destruction, forced displacement of the population and selective execution of students, intellectuals and activists was relevant.

In its recommendations, the mission called on the Council to welcome the Indonesian President's decision to invite an international peacekeeping force to cooperate with Indonesia in restoring peace and security in East Timor and to adopt a resolution providing a framework for its implementation; to authorize an advance party of the international security presence to undertake essential tasks in and around Dili related to UNAMET and to the delivery of humanitarian supplies; to hold Indonesia to its obligations under phase II of the 5 May Agreement, before and after the arrival of the international security presence, and insist on the proper care of internally displaced persons and on curtailing the role of the militias and preventing any clashes between them and Falintil; and to institute the investigation of apparent abuses of international humanitarian law in East and West Timor since 4 September.

The mission further called on the United Nations to give top priority to the grave humanitarian crisis in East Timor and insist on the Government's provision of access and security to UN and international humanitarian organizations. It called on the Secretary-General to reduce to a minimum or, if necessary, evacuate UNAMET staff from Dili before the arrival of an international security presence and to submit plans for the advance preparation of UN action in phase III so as to contribute to the effective implementation of phase II under the new circumstances. In the meantime, in response to the urgent calls for a meeting by Portugal and Brazil (see p. 289), the Council met on 11 September [meeting 4043] to debate the situation.

Deployment of International Force

On 4 October [S/1999/1024], the Secretary-General noted that, in addition to the activities of the Security Council mission above, numerous efforts were made on the diplomatic front to halt the violence in East Timor. He himself spoke directly with Indonesian President Habibie on several occasions. Given the failure of martial law to resolve the security situation, the Government, on 12 September, agreed to accept the offer of assistance from the international community to restore peace and security and to implement the consultation's result.

Following Indonesia's agreement and in response to a request from the Secretary-General, Australia, on 14 September [S/1999/975], indicated its willingness to accept the leadership of the proposed multinational force in East Timor, anticipated to be mandated by the Security Council.

SECURITY COUNCIL ACTION

On 15 September [meeting 4045], the Security Council unanimously adopted **resolution 1264 (1999)**. The draft [S/1999/977] was prepared during prior Council consultations.

The Security Council,

Recalling its previous resolutions and the statements by its President on the situation in East Timor,

Recalling also the Agreement between Indonesia and Portugal of 5 May 1999 on the question of East Timor and the Agreements between the United Nations and the Governments of Indonesia and Portugal, of the same date, regarding the modalities for the popular consultation of the East Timorese through a direct ballot and security arrangements,

Reiterating its welcome for the successful conduct of the popular consultation of the East Timorese people of 30 August 1999, and taking note of its outcome, which it regards as an accurate reflection of the views of the East Timorese people,

Deeply concerned by the deterioration in the security situation in East Timor, and in particular by the continuing violence against and large-scale displacement and relocation of East Timorese civilians,

Deeply concerned also at the attacks on the staff and premises of the United Nations Mission in East Timor, on other officials and on international and national humanitarian personnel,

Recalling the relevant principles contained in the Convention on the Safety of United Nations and Associated Personnel adopted on 9 December 1994,

Appalled by the worsening humanitarian situation in East Timor, particularly as it affects women, children and other vulnerable groups,

Reaffirming the right of refugees and displaced persons to return in safety and security to their homes,

Endorsing the report of the Security Council mission to Jakarta and Dili,

Welcoming the statement by the President of Indonesia on 12 September 1999 in which he expressed the readiness of Indonesia to accept an international peacekeeping force through the United Nations in East Timor,

Welcoming also the letter dated 14 September 1999 from the Minister for Foreign Affairs of Australia to the Secretary-General,

Reaffirming respect for the sovereignty and territorial integrity of Indonesia,

Expressing its concern at reports indicating that systematic, widespread and flagrant violations of international humanitarian and human rights law have been committed in East Timor, and stressing that persons committing such violations bear individual responsibility,

Determining that the present situation in East Timor constitutes a threat to peace and security,

Acting under Chapter VII of the Charter of the United Nations,

1. *Condemns* all acts of violence in East Timor, calls for their immediate end, and demands that those responsible for such acts be brought to justice;

2. *Emphasizes* the urgent need for coordinated humanitarian assistance and the importance of allowing full, safe and unimpeded access by humanitarian organizations, and calls upon all parties to cooperate with such organizations so as to ensure the protection of civilians at risk, the safe return of refugees and displaced persons and the effective delivery of humanitarian aid;

3. *Authorizes* the establishment of a multinational force under a unified command structure, pursuant to the request of the Government of Indonesia conveyed to the Secretary-General on 12 September 1999, with the following tasks: to restore peace and security in East Timor, to protect and support the United Nations Mission in East Timor in carrying out its tasks and, within force capabilities, to facilitate humanitarian assistance operations, and authorizes the States participating in the multinational force to take all necessary measures to fulfil this mandate;

4. *Welcomes* the expressed commitment of the Government of Indonesia to cooperate with the multinational force in all aspects of the implementation of its mandate, and looks forward to close coordination between the multinational force and the Government of Indonesia;

5. *Underlines* the continuing responsibility of the Government of Indonesia under the Agreements of 5 May 1999, taking into account the mandate of the multinational force set out in paragraph 3 above, to maintain peace and security in East Timor in the interim phase between the conclusion of the popular consultation and the start of the implementation of its result and to guarantee the security of the personnel and premises of the Mission;

6. *Welcomes* the offers by Member States to organize, lead and contribute to the multinational force in East Timor, calls upon Member States to make further contributions of personnel, equipment and other resources, and invites Member States in a position to contribute to inform the leadership of the multinational force and the Secretary-General;

7. *Stresses* that it is the responsibility of the Indonesian authorities to take immediate and effective measures to ensure the safe return of refugees to East Timor;

8. *Notes* that article 6 of the Agreement of 5 May 1999 states that the Governments of Indonesia and Portugal and the Secretary-General shall agree on arrangements for a peaceful and orderly transfer of authority in East Timor to the United Nations, and requests the leadership of the multinational force to cooperate closely with the United Nations to assist and support those arrangements;

9. *Stresses* that the expenses for the force will be borne by the participating Member States concerned, and requests the Secretary-General to establish a trust fund through which contributions could be channelled to the States or operations concerned;

10. *Agrees* that the multinational force should collectively be deployed in East Timor until replaced as soon as possible by a United Nations peacekeeping operation, and invites the Secretary-General to make prompt recommendations on a peacekeeping operation to the Security Council;

11. *Invites* the Secretary-General to plan and prepare for a United Nations transitional administration in East Timor, incorporating a United Nations peacekeeping operation, to be deployed in the implementation phase of the popular consultation (phase III) and to make recommendations as soon as possible to the Security Council;

12. *Requests* the leadership of the multinational force to provide periodic reports on progress towards the implementation of its mandate through the Secretary-General to the Council, the first such report to be made within fourteen days of the adoption of the present resolution;

13. *Decides* to remain actively seized of the matter.

The International Force, East Timor (INTERFET) began deployment on 20 September under the command of Major-General Peter Cosgrove (Australia). By 4 October, it consisted of 14 troop-contributing countries and expected to reach a troop strength of 8,000. The Indonesian Armed Forces undertook to cooperate with INTERFET in the implementation of Council resolution 1264(1999) through a Joint Consultative Security Group established in Dili, with UNAMET participation.

INTERFET reports and communications. In five periodic reports [S/1999/1025, S/1999/1072, S/1999/1106, S/1999/1169, S/1999/1248] submitted to the Security Council through the Secretary-General, INTERFET described its operations covering the 12-week period from inception to 9 December. In that time, it played a significant role in helping to establish peace and security through a credible and deterrent security presence throughout the Territory; to prevent armed violence by any group, including the militia; to develop, in cooperation with Indonesia, agreed procedures for border management along the border between East and West Timor; to create conditions and provide escort support for large numbers of displaced persons to return to their homes; to facilitate the transition from UNAMET to the United Nations Transitional Administration in East Timor (see p. 292); and to facilitate the conduct of humanitarian operations of increasing size and effectiveness across East Timor.

In addition, the reports noted that, by 10 November, INTERFET had a strength of over 9,400 troops (of whom some 5,300 were Australians) from 17 countries. It had marginalized the militias and their capacity to threaten the safety of the East Timorese. It had progressively established security to allow the return to Dili of 58 UNAMET staff and the re-establishment of UNAMET's offices in Baucau by 12 October. By 9 December, it had helped UNHCR repatriate more than 110,000 displaced persons.

By identical letters of 12 October [S/1999/1052] to the Secretary-General and the Security Council, Indonesia strongly deplored an incident on 10 October in the border village of Mato Ain in West Timor in which an exchange of fire between INTERFET and Indonesian military and police manning a border crossing point between East and West Timor resulted in three casualties on the Indonesian side. Also by identical letters of 13 October [S/1999/1055], Australia stated that the incident had occurred within East Timor's territory and that weapons were fired first by the Indonesian forces. On 8 November [S/1999/1146], Australia submitted the results of the joint investigation by INTERFET and the Indonesian Armed Forces, which found that the incident was attributable, at least in part, to conflicting maps.

UN Transitional Administration for East Timor

Reports of Secretary-General (October and December). Responding to Security Council resolution 1264(1999), the Secretary-General, on 4 October [S/1999/1024], set out his recommendations for a UN transitional administration in East Timor, incorporating a UN peacekeeping operation for deployment in the implementation phase (phase III) of the popular consultation. The United Nations Transitional Administration in East Timor (UNTAET), with overall responsibility for the administration of the Territory during its transition to independence, expected to take two to three years, would operate under the Council's authority, vested in the Secretary-General and exercised by the Special Representative, who would be responsible for all aspects of UN work in East Timor.

Under its mandate, UNTAET would provide security and maintain law and order throughout the Territory, establish an effective administration, assist in developing civil and social services, ensure coordination and delivery of humanitarian, rehabilitation and development assistance, support capacity-building for self-government, and assist in the establishment of conditions for sustainable development. That mandate was to be implemented in pursuit of a series of specific objectives, for which regular dialogue with representatives of East Timor was essential.

The Special Representative would establish advisory bodies at all levels to ensure East Timorese participation in the Territory's governance and administration.

UNTAET would have three main components: governance and public administration; humanitarian assistance and emergency rehabilitation; and military (including a UN force and a military observer group). The Special Representative, as the Transitional Administrator, would be responsible for all political, managerial and representational functions. He would be assisted by an Executive Committee composed of two Deputy Special Representatives, a Chief of Staff and the Force Commander and advised by offices for political, legal, constitutional and electoral and human rights affairs. He would facilitate the creation of an independent East Timorese human rights institution to investigate alleged violations of human rights, conduct public inquiries, provide guidance and assistance to nascent local governing institutions and develop curricula for human rights education. UNTAET would include a public information office and maintain liaison offices in Jakarta, Kupang (West Timor), Lisbon (Portugal) and Darwin.

UNTAET would continue to apply the existing law of East Timor to the extent of its compatibility with UNTAET's mandate and consistency with international human rights standards. It would be entrusted with rebuilding a structure of governance and administration capable of providing basic public services and a fully functioning administration of justice. It would focus on building local capacity to enable East Timorese to assume responsibility for their own governance. The United Nations would conclude such international agreements with States and international organizations as might be necessary for UNTAET to discharge its functions. UNTAET would also establish a mechanism for consultation with Portugal, given its special responsibilities.

The Secretary-General recommended Council approval of his recommendations and authorization for the timely deployment of UNTAET.

In his 13 December report [A/54/654], the Secretary-General stated that he had been informed by the Indonesian President that the Indonesian People's Consultative Assembly, at its meeting on 19 October, officially recognized the consultation result and revoked the law integrating East Timor within the Republic of Indonesia.

SECURITY COUNCIL ACTION

On 25 October [meeting 4057], the Security Council unanimously adopted **resolution 1272(1999)**. The draft [S/1999/1083] was sponsored by Brazil, Canada, France, Namibia, the Netherlands, Portugal, Slovenia, the United Kingdom and the United States.

The Security Council,

Recalling its previous resolutions and the statements by its President on the situation in East Timor, in particular resolutions 384(1975) of 22 December 1975, 389(1976) of 22 April 1976, 1236(1999) of 7 May 1999, 1246(1999) of 11 June 1999, 1262(1999) of 27 August 1999 and 1264(1999) of 15 September 1999,

Recalling also the Agreement between Indonesia and Portugal of 5 May 1999 on the question of East Timor and the Agreements between the United Nations and the Governments of Indonesia and Portugal of the same date regarding the modalities for the popular consultation of the East Timorese through a direct ballot and security arrangements,

Reiterating its welcome for the successful conduct of the popular consultation of the East Timorese people of 30 August 1999, and taking note of its outcome through which the East Timorese people expressed their clear wish to begin a process of transition under the authority of the United Nations towards independence, which it regards as an accurate reflection of the views of the East Timorese people,

Welcoming the decision of the Indonesian People's Consultative Assembly on 19 October 1999 concerning East Timor,

Stressing the importance of reconciliation among the East Timorese people,

Commending the United Nations Mission in East Timor for the admirable courage and determination shown in the implementation of its mandate,

Welcoming the deployment of a multinational force to East Timor pursuant to resolution 1264(1999), and recognizing the importance of continued cooperation between the Government of Indonesia and the multinational force in this regard,

Taking note of the report of the Secretary-General of 4 October 1999,

Noting with satisfaction the successful outcome of the trilateral meeting held on 28 September 1999, as outlined in the report of the Secretary-General,

Deeply concerned by the grave humanitarian situation resulting from violence in East Timor and the large-scale displacement and relocation of East Timorese civilians, including large numbers of women and children,

Reaffirming the need for all parties to ensure that the rights of refugees and displaced persons are protected, and that they are able to return voluntarily in safety and security to their homes,

Reaffirming respect for the sovereignty and territorial integrity of Indonesia,

Noting the importance of ensuring the security of the boundaries of East Timor, and noting in this regard the expressed intention of the Indonesian authorities to cooperate with the multinational force deployed pursuant to resolution 1264(1999) and with the United Nations Transitional Administration in East Timor,

Expressing its concern at reports indicating that systematic, widespread and flagrant violations of international humanitarian and human rights law have been committed in East Timor, stressing that persons committing such violations bear individual responsibility, and calling on all parties to cooperate with investigations into these reports,

Recalling the relevant principles contained in the Convention on the Safety of United Nations and Associated Personnel adopted on 9 December 1994,

Determining that the continuing situation in East Timor constitutes a threat to peace and security,

Acting under Chapter VII of the Charter of the United Nations,

1. *Decides* to establish, in accordance with the report of the Secretary-General, a United Nations Transitional Administration in East Timor, which will be endowed with overall responsibility for the administration of East Timor and will be empowered to exercise all legislative and executive authority, including the administration of justice;

2. *Decides also* that the mandate of the Transitional Administration shall consist of the following elements:

(a) To provide security and maintain law and order throughout the territory of East Timor;

(b) To establish an effective administration;

(c) To assist in the development of civil and social services;

(d) To ensure the coordination and delivery of humanitarian assistance, rehabilitation and development assistance;

(e) To support capacity-building for self-government;

(f) To assist in the establishment of conditions for sustainable development;

3. *Decides further* that the Transitional Administration will have objectives and a structure along the lines set out in section IV of the report of the Secretary-General, and in particular that its main components will be:

(a) A governance and public administration component, including an international police element with a strength of up to 1,640 officers;

(b) A humanitarian assistance and emergency rehabilitation component;

(c) A military component, with a strength of up to 8,950 troops and up to 200 military observers;

4. *Authorizes* the Transitional Administration to take all necessary measures to fulfil its mandate;

5. *Recognizes* that, in developing and performing its functions under its mandate, the Transitional Administration will need to draw on the expertise and capacity of Member States, United Nations agencies and other international organizations, including the international financial institutions;

6. *Welcomes* the intention of the Secretary-General to appoint a Special Representative who, as the Transitional Administrator, will be responsible for all aspects of the United Nations work in East Timor and will have the power to enact new laws and regulations and to amend, suspend or repeal existing ones;

7. *Stresses* the importance of cooperation between Indonesia, Portugal and the Transitional Administration in the implementation of the present resolution;

8. *Stresses* the need for the Transitional Administration to consult and cooperate closely with the East

Timorese people in order to carry out its mandate effectively with a view to the development of local democratic institutions, including an independent East Timorese human rights institution, and the transfer to these institutions of its administrative and public service functions;

9. *Requests* the Transitional Administration and the multinational force deployed pursuant to resolution 1264(1999) to cooperate closely with each other, with a view also to the replacement as soon as possible of the multinational force by the military component of the Transitional Administration, as notified by the Secretary-General following consultations with the leadership of the multinational force, taking into account conditions on the ground;

10. *Reiterates* the urgent need for coordinated humanitarian and reconstruction assistance, and calls upon all parties to cooperate with humanitarian and human rights organizations so as to ensure their safety, the protection of civilians, in particular children, the safe return of refugees and displaced persons and the effective delivery of humanitarian aid;

11. *Welcomes* the commitment of the Indonesian authorities to allow the refugees and displaced persons in West Timor and elsewhere in Indonesia to choose whether to return to East Timor, remain where they are or be resettled in other parts of Indonesia, and stresses the importance of allowing full, safe and unimpeded access by humanitarian organizations in carrying out their work;

12. *Stresses* that it is the responsibility of the Indonesian authorities to take immediate and effective measures to ensure the safe return of refugees in West Timor and other parts of Indonesia to East Timor, the security of refugees, and the civilian and humanitarian character of refugee camps and settlements, in particular by curbing the violent and intimidatory activities of the militias there;

13. *Welcomes* the intention of the Secretary-General to establish a trust fund to be available for, inter alia, the rehabilitation of essential infrastructure, including the building of basic institutions, the functioning of public services and utilities, and the salaries of local civil servants;

14. *Encourages* Member States and international agencies and organizations to provide personnel, equipment and other resources to the Transitional Administration as requested by the Secretary-General, including for the building of basic institutions and capacity, and stresses the need for the closest possible coordination of these efforts;

15. *Underlines* the importance of including in the Transitional Administration personnel with appropriate training in international humanitarian, human rights and refugee law, including child and gender-related provisions, negotiation and communication skills, cultural awareness and civilian-military coordination;

16. *Condemns* all violence and acts in support of violence in East Timor, calls for their immediate end, and demands that those responsible for such violence be brought to justice;

17. *Decides* to establish the Transitional Administration for an initial period until 31 January 2001;

18. *Requests* the Secretary-General to keep the Council closely and regularly informed of progress towards the implementation of the present resolution, including, in particular, with regard to the deployment of the Transitional Administration and possible future reductions of its military component if the situation in East Timor improves, and to submit a report within three months of the date of adoption of this resolution and every six months thereafter;

19. *Decides* to remain actively seized of the matter.

By two exchanges of letters with the Security Council, on 25 and 26 October [S/1999/1093, S/1999/1094] and on 29 and 30 December [S/1999/1294, S/1999/1295], the Secretary-General made known his intention to appoint Sergio Vieira de Mello as his Special Representative and Head of UNTAET and Major-General Jaime de los Santos (Philippines) as Force Commander, who was to be promoted to the rank of Lieutenant-General for that assignment.

Further report of Secretary-General. In his first progress report [S/2000/53] on developments since UNTAET was established, the Secretary-General stated that UNTAET had begun to set up operations throughout East Timor, developed consultative mechanisms with the East Timorese at all levels and established the basic elements of its administrative structure. In consultation with the East Timorese, it adopted a number of legislative measures (see below). At the initial stage, the Special Representative for the East Timor Popular Consultation and Head of UNAMET served as acting head of UNTAET until the arrival of the Transitional Administrator on 16 November. INTERFET assumed the functions of policing and justice, while the National Council of Timorese Resistance (CNRT), a coalition of pro-independence groups, and Falintil moved to fill the vacuum of local administrative authority and in some places asserted a security role. The situation improved as José Alexandre (Xanana) Gusmão, President of CNRT, who returned to East Timor on 22 October, began to play an effective leadership role.

Based on discussions with Mr. Gusmão and other East Timorese personalities, the Transitional Administrator established the National Consultative Council of East Timor (NCC) on 2 December through which the East Timorese could participate in the decision-making process. Composed of 15 members (7 from CNRT, 3 from political groups outside CNRT, 1 from the Catholic Church and 4 from UNTAET, including the Transitional Administrator who served as Chairman), NCC was authorized to create joint sectoral committees of East Timorese and international experts to provide advice on various areas of administration. The inclusion of pro-autonomy groups in NCC was an important step towards reconciliation. So was CNRT's meeting (Jakarta, 27 November-1 December) with President Abdurrahman Wahid (President since 20 October) and other senior government officials, who declared their determination to help ensure East Timor's stability, assist in the repatriation of East Timorese refugees in West Timor and control the militia there, release the remaining political prisoners, and assist post-secondary students to resume their studies at Indonesian institutions. A further step was Mr. Gusmão's meeting (12 December) with the principal commander of the pro-autonomy militias, who announced his intention to disband his militia in West Timor. Talks were under way towards concluding practical arrangements necessary for UNTAET, acting on East Timor's behalf, to replace Indonesia in treaty institutions.

The Secretary-General noted that the Transitional Administrator, in a meeting with President Wahid and other officials (Jakarta, 12-14 December), discussed official Indonesian representation in East Timor, UNTAET liaison arrangements in West Timor, resumption of air service to East Timor by Indonesian carriers, future commercial links and cooperation on banking and financial services, and measures to accelerate the return of refugees from West Timor and for the settlement in Indonesia of those choosing not to return.

Following five border incidents in October between INTERFET soldiers and armed militia groups, UN military observers deployed border liaison teams to West Timor for cross-border liaison and confidence-building. On 25 November, the Indonesian Armed Forces and INTERFET signed a memorandum on border management calling for the establishment of a joint border commission and of secure checkpoints for refugee border crossings.

UN humanitarian agencies, which maintained a small presence in Dili throughout the crisis, returned with NGOs to East Timor in late September to lay the groundwork for a comprehensive response. WFP and its NGO implementing partners distributed more than 10,500 metric tons of food to some 610,000 displaced persons. The return of refugees from West Timor and elsewhere in Indonesia was proceeding under UNHCR. However, pro-autonomy East Timorese militias had established control over the refugee camps in West Timor, impeding UN access to and free movement within the camps. UNTAET worked closely with three special rapporteurs of the Office of the United Nations High Commissioner for Human Rights to facilitate their mission in East Timor (4-10 November) and that of the International Commission of Inquiry on East Timor (25 November-8 December).

(For human rights violations in East Timor, see PART TWO, Chapter III; for assistance for humanitarian relief, rehabilitation and development for East Timor, see PART THREE, Chapter III.)

In a later addendum [S/2000/53/Add.1] to his report, the Secretary-General transmitted the texts of four regulations promulgated by the Transitional Administrator during 1999. The first laid down the scope of the Transitional Administrator's authority in East Timor; the second established NCC, defined its functions, membership and methods of work, and prescribed the text of the oath to be taken by appointees; the third established a Transitional Judicial Service Commission; and the fourth established the *Official Gazette of East Timor* to include: publication of all UNTAET regulations and directives; general and other acts of organs and institutions of East Timor, as required by law; and acts of public interest requiring public notification.

Financing of UN operations

UNAMET

The financing of UNAMET was considered by the General Assembly at its resumed fifty-third session under agenda item 113, entitled "Programme budget for the biennium 1998-1999". At the Secretary-General's request [A/54/231], it was included in the agenda of the Assembly's fifty-fourth (1999) session and allocated to the Fifth Committee.

Security Council resolution 1236(1999) (see p. 281), which welcomed the intention of the Secretary-General to establish a UN presence in East Timor as soon as practicable to conduct the consultation process, resulted in his need to enter into related commitments exceeding $10 million for the operation's initial requirements. Pursuant to General Assembly resolution 52/223 [YUN 1997, p. 1438], he presented for the Assembly's consideration, at its resumed fifty-third session, his report [A/C.5/53/61] requesting commitment authority for the estimated requirements of the operation and annexing a budget for the period 5 May-31 August 1999.

GENERAL ASSEMBLY ACTION

In May, following its consideration of the Secretary-General's request and of the related ACABQ report [A/53/7/Add.13], the General Assembly, on the recommendation of the Fifth Committee [A/53/485/Add.3], adopted **decision 53/472** without vote [agenda item 113].

Question of East Timor

At its 100th plenary meeting, on 25 May 1999, the General Assembly, on the recommendation of the Fifth Committee:

(*a*) Authorized the Secretary-General to enter into commitments up to 35 million United States dollars, from all sources of funds, for the initial requirements of United Nations activities related to East Timor, pending further action by the Security Council and the submission of a revised budget by the Secretary-General;

(*b*) Reaffirmed, in accordance with its resolution 45/248 B, section VI, of 21 December 1990, that the Fifth Committee is the appropriate Main Committee of the General Assembly entrusted with responsibilities for administrative and budgetary matters, and expressed its concern at the tendency of its substantive Committees and other intergovernmental bodies to involve themselves in administrative and budgetary matters.

Following Council resolution 1246(1999) establishing UNAMET until 31 August and in accordance with the Assembly decision above, the Secretary-General submitted a revised report on the 5 May–31 August 1999 budget for UNAMET [A/C.5/53/63], with a request for an increase in the existing commitment authority. Based on that report and ACABQ's related comments [A/53/7/Add.14], the Assembly, on 29 June [meeting 103], on the recommendation of the Fifth Committee [A/53/485/Add.5], adopted **resolution 53/240** without vote [agenda item 113].

Question of East Timor

The General Assembly,

Having considered the report of the Secretary-General on the United Nations Mission in East Timor and the related report of the Advisory Committee on Administrative and Budgetary Questions,

Recalling its decision 53/472 of 25 May 1999, wherein it authorized the Secretary-General to enter into commitments up to 35 million United States dollars, from all sources of funds, for the initial requirements of United Nations activities related to East Timor,

1. *Notes* that the budget proposed by the Secretary-General amounts to 52,531,100 United States dollars gross;

2. *Reiterates* that the expenses of the Organization shall be borne by Member States as apportioned by the General Assembly;

3. *Notes* that the contributions received so far for the Trust Fund for the Settlement of the Question of East Timor amount to 21,731,700 dollars and that further contributions may be received;

4. *Invites* voluntary contributions to the United Nations Mission in East Timor in cash and in the form of services and supplies acceptable to the Secretary-General, to be administered, as appropriate, in accordance with the financial regulations, rules, procedures and practices established by the General Assembly concerning such contributions;

5. *Expresses its appreciation* to all those Member States which have made voluntary contributions to the Mission;

6. *Decides* to appropriate an amount of 52,531,100 dollars for the Mission, and requests the Secretary-General to establish a special account for the Mission;

7. *Decides also* that the amount to be assessed will be determined after the review of the report which the Secretary-General will submit to the General Assembly at its fifty-fourth session, taking into account voluntary contributions received;

8. *Decides further* that such assessments as will be necessary shall be apportioned among Member States in accordance with the composition of groups set out in paragraphs 3 and 4 of General Assembly resolution 43/232 of 1 March 1989, as adjusted by the Assembly in its resolutions 44/192 B of 21 December 1989, 45/269 of 27 August 1991, 46/198 A of 20 December 1991, 47/218 A of 23 December 1992, 49/249 A of 20 July 1995, 49/249 B of 14 September 1995, 50/224 of 11 April 1996, 51/218 A to C of 18 December 1996 and 52/230 of 31 March 1998 and its decisions 48/472 A of 23 December 1993 and 50/451 B of 23 December 1995, and taking into account the scale of assessments for the year 1999, as set out in its resolution 52/215 A of 22 December 1997.

In the light of Security Council resolutions 1257(1999) and 1262(1999), extending UNAMET's mandate until 30 September (phase I) and 30 November (phase II), respectively, the Secretary-General submitted to the Assembly a report [A/54/380] on a revised proposed budget for phase I for the period 5 May–30 September 1999 and a preliminary estimate of requirements for phase II to implement resolution 1262(1999). On 29 October [meeting 43], following its consideration of that report and ACABQ's related observations [A/54/406], the Assembly, on the recommendation of the Fifth Committee [A/54/505], adopted **resolution 54/20 A** without vote [agenda item 169].

Financing of the United Nations Mission in East Timor

The General Assembly,

Having considered the report of the Secretary-General on the financing of the United Nations Mission in East Timor and the related report of the Advisory Committee on Administrative and Budgetary Questions,

Recalling its resolution 53/240 of 29 June 1999, wherein it appropriated an amount of 52,531,100 United States dollars gross for the Mission and decided that the amount to be assessed would be determined after the review of the report which the Secretary-General would submit to the General Assembly at its fifty-fourth session, taking into account voluntary contributions received,

Commending all United Nations missions for their continuing efforts to implement effectively their mandated activities,

Reaffirming the international character of the United Nations,

1. *Endorses* the observations and recommendations contained in the report of the Advisory Committee on Administrative and Budgetary Questions;

2. *Reiterates* that the expenses of the Organization shall be borne by Member States as apportioned by the General Assembly;

3. *Requests* the Secretary-General to ensure that staff in all United Nations missions continue to respect the relevant provisions of the Charter of the United Nations and the Staff Regulations and Rules of the United Nations;

4. *Urges* all Member States to make every possible effort to ensure payment of their assessed contributions to the United Nations Mission in East Timor in full and on time;

5. *Emphasizes* that all future and existing missions shall be given equal and non-discriminatory treatment in respect of financial and administrative arrangements;

6. *Also emphasizes* that all missions shall be provided with adequate resources for the effective and efficient discharge of their respective mandates;

7. *Requests* the Secretary-General to take all necessary action to ensure that the Mission is administered with a maximum of efficiency and economy;

8. *Encourages* the Secretary-General to continue to take additional measures to ensure the safety and security of all personnel under the auspices of the United Nations participating in the Mission;

9. *Notes* that voluntary contributions to the Trust Fund for the Settlement of the Question of East Timor paid and pledged so far amount to 43,834,700 dollars and in-kind contributions are valued at 3,438,700 dollars;

10. *Expresses its appreciation* to all those Member States that have made voluntary contributions to the Mission;

11. *Decides* to revise the level of appropriation to the Special Account for the United Nations Mission in East Timor for the period 5 May 1999 to 30 September 1999 (phase I) to a total amount of 54,428,400 dollars gross (52,941,100 dollars net);

12. *Also decides* to apportion the amount of 7,155,000 dollars gross (5,667,700 dollars net) among Member States, in accordance with the composition of groups set out in paragraphs 3 and 4 of General Assembly resolution 43/232 of 1 March 1989, as adjusted by the Assembly in its resolutions 44/192 B of 21 December 1989, 45/269 of 27 August 1991, 46/198 A of 20 December 1991, 47/218 A of 23 December 1992, 49/249 A of 20 July 1995, 49/249 B of 14 September 1995, 50/224 of 11 April 1996, 51/218 A to C of 18 December 1996 and 52/230 of 31 March 1998 and its decisions 48/472, A of 23 December 1993 and 50/451 B of 23 December 1995, and taking into account the scale of assessments for the year 1999, as set out in its resolution 52/215 A of 22 December 1997;

13. *Authorizes* the Secretary-General to enter into commitments up to 28,037,100 dollars gross (27,080,700 dollars net), in addition to the commitment authority up to 10 million dollars granted by the Advisory Committee on 9 September 1999, for the requirements of phase II of the Mission, pending the submission of a revised budget by the Secretary-General.

On 23 December, the Assembly decided that the agenda item on the financing of UNAMET would remain for consideration during its resumed fifty-fourth (2000) session (**decision 54/465**) and that the Fifth Committee should continue its consideration of the item at that session (**decision 54/462 A**).

UNTAET

By a 23 November note [A/54/236], the Secretary-General requested the inclusion in the agenda of the General Assembly's fifty-fourth (1999) session of an additional item entitled "Financing of the United Nations Transitional Administration in East Timor".

In a 29 November addendum [A/54/236/Add.1] to his note, the Secretary-General requested commitment authority with assessment for an amount of $205.4 million to cover the most immediate requirements for UNTAET, pending submission of detailed cost estimates to the Assembly.

GENERAL ASSEMBLY ACTION

On 23 December [meeting 88], following its consideration of the Secretary-General's request and of the related ACABQ report [A/54/653], the General Assembly, on the recommendation of the Fifth Committee [A/54/687], adopted **resolution 54/246 A** without vote [agenda item 173].

Financing of the United Nations Transitional Administration in East Timor

The General Assembly,

Having considered the report of the Secretary-General on the financing of the United Nations Transitional Administration in East Timor and the related report of the Advisory Committee on Administrative and Budgetary Questions,

Bearing in mind Security Council resolution 1272(1999) of 25 October 1999 regarding the establishment of the United Nations Transitional Administration in East Timor,

Recognizing that the costs of the Transitional Administration are expenses of the Organization to be borne by Member States in accordance with Article 17, paragraph 2, of the Charter of the United Nations,

Recognizing also that, in order to meet the expenditures caused by the Transitional Administration, a different procedure is required from that applied to meet expenditures of the regular budget of the United Nations,

Taking into account the fact that the economically more developed countries are in a position to make relatively larger contributions and that the economically less developed countries have a relatively limited capacity to contribute towards such an operation,

Bearing in mind the special responsibilities of the States permanent members of the Security Council, as indicated in General Assembly resolution 1874(S-IV) of 27 June 1963, in the financing of such operations,

Noting with appreciation that voluntary contributions have been made to the trust fund for the multinational force,

Inviting voluntary contributions to the Trust Fund for the United Nations Transitional Administration in East Timor,

Mindful of the fact that it is essential to provide the Transitional Administration with the necessary financial resources to enable it to fulfil its responsibilities under the relevant resolutions of the Security Council,

1. *Expresses concern* about the financial situation with regard to peacekeeping activities, in particular as regards the reimbursement of troop contributors, which bear additional burdens owing to overdue payments by Member States of their assessments;

2. *Urges* all Member States to make every possible effort to ensure payment of their assessed contributions to the United Nations Transitional Administration in East Timor in full and on time;

3. *Expresses concern* at the delay experienced by the Secretary-General in deploying and providing adequate resources to some recent peacekeeping missions, in particular those in Africa;

4. *Emphasizes* that all future and existing peacekeeping missions shall be given equal and non-discriminatory treatment in respect of financial and administrative arrangements;

5. *Also emphasizes* that all peacekeeping missions shall be provided with adequate resources for the effective and efficient discharge of their respective mandates;

6. *Requests* the Secretary-General to make the fullest possible use of facilities and equipment at the United Nations Logistics Base at Brindisi, Italy, in order to minimize the costs of procurement for the Transitional Administration, and for this purpose requests the Secretary-General to speed up the implementation of the asset management system at all peacekeeping missions in accordance with General Assembly resolution 52/1 of 15 October 1997;

7. *Endorses* the observations and recommendations contained in the report of the Advisory Committee on Administrative and Budgetary Questions;

8. *Requests* the Secretary-General to take all necessary action to ensure that the Transitional Administration is administered with a maximum of efficiency and economy;

9. *Also requests* the Secretary-General, in order to reduce the cost of employing General Service staff, to continue efforts to employ locally recruited staff for the Transitional Administration against General Service posts, commensurate with the requirements of the Transitional Administration;

10. *Authorizes* the Secretary-General to enter into commitments in an amount not exceeding 200 million United States dollars, inclusive of the amount of 50 million dollars authorized by the Advisory Committee, for the Transitional Administration under the terms of section IV of General Assembly resolution 49/233 A of 23 December 1994, and requests the Secretary-General to establish a special account for the Transitional Administration;

11. *Decides*, as an ad hoc arrangement, to apportion the amount of 200 million dollars among Member States in accordance with the composition of groups set out in paragraphs 3 and 4 of General Assembly resolution 43/232 of 1 March 1989, as adjusted by the Assembly in its resolutions 44/192 B of 21 December 1989, 45/269 of 27 August 1991, 46/198 A of 20 December 1991, 47/218 A of 23 December 1992, 49/249 A of 20 July 1995, 49/249 B of 14 September 1995, 50/224 of 11 April 1996, 51/218 A to C of 18 December 1996 and 52/230 of 31 March 1998 and its decisions 48/472 A of 23 December 1993, 50/451 B of 23 December 1995 and 54/456 to 54/458 of 23 December 1999, and taking into account the scale of assessments for the years 1999 and 2000, as set out in its resolutions 52/215 A of 22 December 1997 and 54/237 A of 23 December 1999;

12. *Emphasizes* that no peacekeeping mission shall be financed by borrowing funds from other active peacekeeping missions;

13. *Encourages* the Secretary-General to continue to take additional measures to ensure the safety and security of all personnel under the auspices of the United Nations participating in the Transitional Administration;

14. *Invites* voluntary contributions to the Transitional Administration in cash and in the form of services and supplies acceptable to the Secretary-General, to be administered, as appropriate, in accordance with the procedure and practices established by the General Assembly;

15. *Requests* the Secretary-General to submit to the General Assembly, as a matter of priority, a comprehensive report on the financing of the Transitional Administration, including full budget estimates and information on the utilization of resources until the time of the submission of the report, to enable the Assembly to take action on it at the first part of its resumed fifty-fourth session;

16. *Decides* to keep under review during its fifty-fourth session the item entitled "Financing of the United Nations Transitional Administration in East Timor".

On 23 December, the Assembly decided that the agenda item on the financing of UNTAET would remain for consideration during its resumed fifty-fourth (2000) session (**decision 54/465**), and that the Fifth Committee should continue consideration of the item at that session (**decision 54/462 A**).

Papua New Guinea

Bougainville

During 1999, Bougainville, a province of the South-East Asian country of Papua New Guinea, continued to implement the 1998 Lincoln Agreement on Peace, Security and Development on Bougainville (the Lincoln Agreement) [YUN 1998, p. 319], concluded between the Government of Papua New Guinea and the four Bougainville parties involved in the nine-year conflict that ended in the 1997 Burnham Truce [ibid.]. A UN presence in the form of the United Nations Political Office in Bougainville, requested under the terms of the Lincoln Agreement, continued to monitor and report on the Agreement's implementation by the parties and by the Peace Monitoring Group (Australia, Fiji, New Zealand and Vanuatu), which was also requested under the Agreement. The Bougainville People's Congress, the main body representing the Bougainville parties, elected Joseph Kabui as Congress President in April.

With Parliament's election in mid-July of Sir Mekere Morauta to the office of Prime Minister, left vacant by the previous incumbent's resignation the week before, a new Government was formed, which committed itself to pursuing a progressive political settlement. On 26 November, Papua New Guinea's Supreme Court reinstated the previously suspended Bougainville Provincial Government, following which John Momis, Member of Parliament, became Governor of Bougainville. On 14 December, the Congress President and the newly appointed Governor agreed jointly to negotiate Bougainville's political future with the Government.

UN Political Office in Bougainville

The Arawa-based United Nations Political Office in Bougainville (UNPOB), established in 1998 [YUN 1998, p. 320] in response to requests from the parties to the Lincoln Agreement and with the concurrence of the Security Council, continued to discharge its mandate as spelled out in the Agreement. Noel Sinclair (Guyana) remained Director of UNPOB.

Communication from Secretary-General. The Secretary-General, on 28 October [S/1999/1152], indicated to the Council that Papua New Guinea's new Government was committed to making the settlement of the Bougainville crisis a priority and that the Foreign Minister had reiterated the importance to the peace process of a continued UN presence in Bougainville. The Secretary-General stated that all the Bougainville parties had expressed their support for UNPOB's efforts to move the peace process forward. It was therefore his intention to extend UNPOB's mandate, due to expire on 31 December, by a further 12 months. The Council took note of the Secretary-General's intention on 10 November [S/1999/1153].

Financing

The costs associated with UNPOB's extension to December 2000 were estimated by the Secretary-General at $1,337,400 [A/C.5/54/39]. ACABQ recommended that the total requirements of $9,964,500 for eight political missions, including the estimate for UNPOB, should be charged against the provision for special political missions requested under section 3 (Political affairs) of the proposed programme budget for the 2000-2001 biennium [A/54/7/Add.10].

Other matters

India-Pakistan

The United Nations Military Observer Group in India and Pakistan (UNMOGIP) continued in 1999 to monitor the situation in Jammu and Kashmir. As at 31 December, UNMOGIP had a strength of 45 military observers under the command of Major-General Jozsef Bali (Hungary), appointed by an exchange of letters between the Secretary-General and the Security Council on 9 and 12 February [S/1999/148, S/1999/149]. UNMOGIP headquarters alternated between Srinagar, Kashmir, in the summer and Rawalpindi, Pakistan, in the winter.

Communications. On 27 May [A/54/118-S/1999/633], Pakistan drew attention to the recent sharp escalation of violations of the line of control in the Kargil and Drass sectors in Jammu and Kashmir, noting that, for the first time since the 1971 war [YUN 1971, p. 137], India had resorted to using its air force, in addition to long-range and heavy artillery. Pakistan urged the Secretary-General to initiate meaningful dialogue between the two countries to defuse the current situation. On 25 May, the Secretary-General expressed concern over the two-week-long heavy exchange of fire along the line of control and called on the parties to cease the fighting. On 28 May, he stated that he was encouraged by the direct contacts that had taken place between the Prime Ministers and other officials of the two parties and by their willingness to pursue dialogue on a number of issues, including Kashmir.

A 24 June statement by the EU Presidency [S/1999/732] reiterated the EU's deep concern over the continuing military confrontation and infiltration of armed intruders in violation of the line of control in the Kargil region.

Pakistan reported that, on the morning of 10 August [A/54/214-S/1999/867], Indian military aircraft shot down an unarmed Pakistan navy aircraft on a routine training flight inside Pakistani airspace, east of Karachi, killing all 16 persons aboard. The Secretary-General promptly issued a statement expressing his increasing concern at repeated incidents between the two countries and his hope for an early resumption of the bilateral dialogue. Pakistan, on 30 August [S/1999/937], stated that India admitted shooting down the aircraft but claimed the incident occurred over Indian airspace. To support that assertion, Pakistan alleged, Indian helicopters flew to the site of the wreckage 2 kilometres within Pakistani territory and removed parts of it to the Indian side of the border. Pakistan asked the Secretary-General to send a UN fact-finding mission to establish the truth of the incident and demanded appropriate compensation from India.

Iran complaints

In continued protest against violations of its territorial integrity, Iran on 11 May [S/1999/544] transmitted to the Secretary-General four notes verbales of 3 October and 7 December 1998 and 2 January and 2 February 1999 from its Ministry of Foreign Affairs to the Embassy of Afghanistan in Tehran, protesting numerous land and airspace intrusions from Afghanistan, as well as incidents of firings at Iranian sentry posts by light to heavy weapons, attacks on border guards, abduction of villagers by bandits—all resulting in injuries and some deaths—as well as damage to Iranian border installations. Iran expected the Embassy to take every possible measure to ensure respect for its territorial integrity.

On 21 December [S/1999/1274], Iran transmitted a recent note verbale to the United States Department of State protesting the intrusion into Iranian territorial waters by a United States warship, which, in disregard of Iran's warnings and radio communications, chased an Iranian commercial vessel. Iran demanded an end to such illegal actions.

Iran-Iraq

Throughout 1999, Iran and Iraq continued to communicate to the Secretary-General allegations of repeated violations of their 1988 ceasefire agreement [YUN 1988, p. 193] and of their 1991 Tehran agreements [YUN 1991, p. 163] concerning the area of separation between them. They also alleged cross-border attacks and terrorist activities in each other's territory.

Iran's communications covered previously unreported ceasefire violations for the periods 29 May–30 December 1997 [S/1999/265] and 21 January–3 July 1998 [S/1999/877]. Others concerned two separate 1998 incidents involving an Iraqi attack on an Iranian motorboat and theft of a fishing boat [S/1999/81], allegations rejected by Iraq as false [S/1999/280]; the seizure in September 1999 of an Iranian cargo boat and its crew of 11 by Iraqi forces [S/1999/125]; the interception and looting of Iranian commercial launches en route to Kuwait [S/2000/82]; and the seizure in September of 33 fishing boats and infiltration into Iranian territory by armed Iraqi bandits [S/2000/79].

Iran further protested against the assassination in April of the Deputy Chief of the Joint Staff Command of the Armed Forces of Iran by the Iraq-based terrorist group known as Mujahedin Khalq Organization (MKO) (also referred to as the People's Mujahedin Organization), claiming it could not have been accomplished without the involvement of Iraqi authorities [A/54/78-S/1999/420, A/54/81]. Iraq denied the accusation [A/54/90] and asserted that it was not responsible for MKO's actions [S/1999/455]. Iran also recalled drawing to the attention of the United Nations various 1994 incidents of transboundary terrorist activities by MKO [S/1999/536]. It reported that, on 25 November, four Iranian border guards, dispatched to the border to prevent the recurrence of a recent MKO infiltration into Iranian territory, were abducted by Iraqi forces and taken to Basrah [S/2000/78].

Iraq's communications on ceasefire violations by Iran covered the periods 22 June–7 December 1998 [S/1999/31], 11 April–28 July 1999 [S/1999/926], 23 June–4 October 1999 [S/1999/1101] and 5 October–27 November 1999 [S/1999/1271]. Iraq also requested the retention on the Security Council's agenda of its complaint concerning incidents on its frontier with Iran [S/1999/144]. In June, it reported that Iran fired three long-range ground-to-ground missiles at the MKO base camp, preceded by a bomb explosion that killed six MKO members along with several innocent Iraqis [S/1999/673]. Iran replied that MKO was responsible for many terrorist attacks and activities launched from Iraq, which could not take place without that country's collaboration and support. By providing sanctuary to MKO, Iraq was in violation of its obligations under the principles of international law [S/1999/781].

Saudi Arabia–Iraq

Saudi Arabia informed the Security Council on 4 January 1999 [S/1999/3] that, on 12 December 1998, an Iraqi patrol crossed the Saudi border and opened fire on a Saudi patrol, wounding one of them in the head, from which he later died. Replying on 9 January [S/1999/29], Iraq explained that the incident took place when three Saudi armoured cars, observed in the restricted area between two control posts 1 kilometre inside Iraqi territory, opened fire on the Iraqi patrol, which was obliged to return fire in self-defence. Saudi Arabia insisted on 1 March [S/1999/217] that the incident took place inside its borders and that the fire from the Iraqi patrol did not draw any return fire from the Saudi patrol.

In identical letters of 18 March to the Secretary-General and the Council [S/1999/297], Saudi Arabia protested the violation of its airspace on 16 and 17 March by Iraqi aircraft headed for Jeddah. While the authorities overlooked the earlier violation, as they had a similar 1997 violation, the 17 March aircraft ignored Saudi warnings and proceeded to land at the Jeddah international airport. Saudi Arabia warned that should an aircraft of any kind land illegally in its territory, it would be compelled to seize the aircraft and hand it and its crew over to the United Nations. (The 17 March incident was reported to the Sanctions Committee for Iraq; see p. 240.)

United Arab Emirates–Iran

Greater Tunb, Lesser Tunb and Abu Musa

The United Arab Emirates, on 5 January [S/1999/10] and again on 21 December [S/1999/1273], requested the Security Council to retain on its agenda the question of Iran's occupation of the Greater Tunb, Lesser Tunb and Abu Musa, three islands belonging to the United Arab Emirates. In a 7 February note verbale to the Embassy of Iran in Abu Dhabi, transmitted to the Secretary-General on 23 February [S/1999/191], the United Arab Emirates protested Iran's opening of a municipal office and an educational institution on Abu Musa to perpetuate its occupation of the island. That protest was rejected by Iran as interference in its internal affairs [S/1999/235], [S/1999/498]. On 17 March [S/1999/296], Iran transmitted eight notes verbales in response to complaints by the United Arab Emirates of 1996 and 1997 incidents relating to Abu Musa and to Iran's alleged interception of fishing boats belonging to the United Arab Emirates, all of which Iran said could be resolved through bilateral dialogue.

Additionally, the United Arab Emirates transmitted for circulation the March communiqué [S/1999/236] and press release [S/1999/305] issued by the Gulf Cooperation Council (GCC) rejecting Iran's occupation of the three islands; a September press communiqué by the GCC Ministerial Council [S/1999/974], which reviewed, among other matters, the work of the committee entrusted with promoting direct negotiations between the two countries on the issue of the islands' occupation; and an excerpt from the statement by the United Arab Emirates to the June/July session of the Islamic Conference of Foreign Ministers calling for a peaceful solution to that issue [S/1999/802].

A resolution adopted by the Council of the League of Arab States on 18 March denounced the measures taken by Iran to strengthen its occupation of the three islands, condemned Iran's military manoeuvres that extended to the occupied islands, called on Iran to end that occupation, and drew to the attention of the United Nations the importance of retaining the issue on its agenda until the United Arab Emirates regained its full sovereignty over the three islands [S/1999/395].

Chapter V

Europe and the Mediterranean

Peace and security in Europe were once again seriously jeopardized by the complicated and contentious political situation in the Balkans, as the crisis in the Kosovo province of the Federal Republic of Yugoslavia (Serbia and Montenegro) (FRY) reached critical proportions. That crisis and the air campaign by the North Atlantic Treaty Organization (NATO) against FRY dominated international attention for most of 1999, overshadowing the progress in reconciliation and reconstruction in other parts of the former Yugoslavia (Bosnia and Herzegovina, and the former Yugoslav Republic of Macedonia).

In Bosnia and Herzegovina, some progress was made towards implementing the pledges made at the Madrid Peace Implementation Conference in December 1998, but implementation of the General Framework Agreement for Peace in Bosnia and Herzegovina (also known as the Dayton-Paris Peace Agreement) and those pledges was affected by the events in Kosovo. In September, the members of the Presidency of Bosnia and Herzegovina adopted the New York Declaration, reaffirming their commitment to the Peace Agreement and pledging themselves to facing the remaining challenges. The Security Council, in June, extended the United Nations Mission in Bosnia and Herzegovina until June 2000.

No progress was made in the bilateral negotiations between Croatia and FRY regarding the disputed Prevlaka peninsula, although the parties responded positively to a package of confidence-building recommendations proposed by the Secretary-General following the cessation of NATO action against FRY.

In FRY, the conflict in Kosovo, characterized by gross human rights abuses on the part of the FRY forces and those of the Kosovo Liberation Army, intensified early in the year leading to a worsening humanitarian situation. Negotiations organized by the Contact Group on the Former Yugoslavia, which were held in Rambouillet, France, in February and continued in Paris in March, resulted in the Kosovo Albanian delegation signing the Rambouillet Accords: Interim Agreement for Peace and Self-Government in Kosovo. However, FRY did not sign and on 24 March NATO launched an air campaign against FRY. It was not until June that FRY accepted a peace plan proposed by the European Union and the principles set out by the Group of eight highly industrialized countries (G-8) Foreign Ministers to end the violence, which led to a cessation of the NATO air campaign. Subsequently, the Council on 10 June authorized the deployment in Kosovo, under UN auspices, of international civil and security presences—the international security force (KFOR) and the United Nations Interim Administration Mission in Kosovo. However, a resurgence of violence later in the year, directed mainly against Serbs and other non-Albanian minorities in Kosovo, again heightened tension and security concerns in the province.

In the former Yugoslav Republic of Macedonia, the mandate of the United Nations Protection Force ended in February and was not renewed, despite concerns about the possible spillover effects from neighbouring Kosovo.

In other parts of Europe, despite the continued efforts of the Secretary-General's Special Representative, the Russian Federation and the Friends of the Secretary-General (France, Germany, Russian Federation, United Kingdom, United States), the Abkhaz/Georgian peace process remained at an impasse at the end of 1999. The situation was further complicated by the holding by the Abkhaz side of "presidential elections", which were condemned as unacceptable and illegitimate by the Security Council. Georgia also held parliamentary elections on 31 October. The United Nations Observer Mission in Georgia continued to carry out its mandate, contributing to a lessening of tension and providing a climate in which negotiations could take place at the political level.

Armenia and Azerbaijan were also no nearer to settling the armed conflict between them over the Nagorny Karabakh region in Azerbaijan, despite continued efforts by the Minsk Group of the Organization for Security and Cooperation in Europe to reach a settlement.

However, a comprehensive settlement of the Cyprus issue took a small step forward in 1999 when Glafcos Clerides, President of Cyprus, and Rauf R. Denktas, leader of the Turkish Cypriot community, accepted the Secretary-General's 30 September invitation to enter into negotiations without preconditions and in a spirit of compromise. The first round of those proximity talks were held from 3 to 14 December in New York.

The United Nations Peacekeeping Force in Cyprus continued to assist in the restoration of normal conditions and in humanitarian functions. The Security Council twice extended its mandate, the second time until 15 June 2000.

The former Yugoslavia

UN operations

The United Nations continued its efforts in 1999 to restore peace and stability in the countries of the former Yugoslavia (Bosnia and Herzegovina, Croatia, the Federal Republic of Yugoslavia (Serbia and Montenegro) (FRY) and the former Yugoslav Republic of Macedonia (FYROM)) through its peacekeeping missions: the United Nations Preventive Deployment Force (UNPREDEP), whose mandate ended on 28 February; the United Nations Mission in Bosnia and Herzegovina (UNMIBH); the United Nations Mission of Observers in Prevlaka (UNMOP), which continued to monitor the demilitarization of the Prevlaka peninsula; and the United Nations Transitional Administration in the FRY province of Kosovo, established on 10 June to oversee the development of provisional democratic self-governing institutions. The Security Council extended the mandates of UNMIBH, which included the International Police Task Force, until 21 June 2000 and UNMOP to 15 January 2000.

Financing

In accordance with General Assembly decision 52/485 [YUN 1998, p. 325], the Fifth (Administrative and Budgetary) Committee, at the resumed fifty-third session, again considered the treatment of the unencumbered balance for the period 1 July 1996 to 30 June 1997 for the United Nations Protection Force (UNPROFOR), the United Nations Confidence Restoration Operation in Croatia (UNCRO) and UNPREDEP—known collectively as the United Nations Peace Forces (UNPF)—and UNPF headquarters (UNPF-HQ). Consideration had been deferred in 1998 pending the submission of the final performance report. In a February note [A/C.5/53/56], the Secretary-General stated that the performance report was not expected to be issued until the Assembly's fifty-fourth (1999) session, owing to various pending items. It was anticipated that the report would include a request to the Assembly for additional funds to settle amounts owed to Governments.

In April [A/53/895], the Advisory Committee on Administrative and Budgetary Questions (ACABQ) postponed consideration of the financial performance report for UNPREDEP for the period from 1 July 1997 to 30 June 1998 and the proposed budget for 1 July 1999 to 30 June 2000.

The Assembly, by **decision 53/477** of 8 June, took note of the Secretary-General's note and the relevant section of ACABQ's report. It requested the Secretary-General to address outstanding issues in connection with the preparation of the final performance report and included the item on the financing of UNPROFOR, UNCRO, UNPREDEP and UNPF-HQ in the provisional agenda of its fifty-fourth session.

The Assembly, on 23 December, decided that the item on the financing of UNPROFOR, UNCRO, UNPREDEP and UNPF-HQ would remain for consideration at the resumed fifty-fourth (2000) session (**decision 54/465**). It also decided that the Fifth Committee should continue to consider the item at the resumed session (**decision 54/462 A**).

(Details of the financing of the respective peacekeeping operations in the former Yugoslavia are described in the relevant sections below.)

UNTAES and UN Civilian Police Support Group

In a February report [A/53/838 & Corr.1], the Secretary-General provided information on the final disposition of the assets of the United Nations Transitional Administration for Eastern Slavonia, Baranja and Western Sirmium (UNTAES), whose mandate ended in January 1998 [YUN 1998, p. 347], and the UN Civilian Police Support Group, whose mandate ended in October of that year [ibid., p. 353]. As at 30 November 1998, the inventory of the two missions totalled $76.6 million, 67 per cent of which had been transferred to other peacekeeping operations or to the United Nations Logistics Base in Brindisi, Italy, for temporary storage.

ACABQ, in April [A/53/897], submitted its comments on the financial performance report for the two missions for the period 1 July 1997 to 30 June 1998 [YUN 1998, p. 350] and on the disposition of their assets.

GENERAL ASSEMBLY ACTION

On 8 June [meeting 101], the General Assembly, on the recommendation of the Fifth Committee [A/53/986], adopted **resolution 53/234** without vote [agenda item 139].

Financing of the United Nations Transitional Administration for Eastern Slavonia, Baranja and Western Sirmium and the Civilian Police Support Group

The General Assembly,

Having considered the reports of the Secretary-General on the financing of the United Nations Transitional Administration for Eastern Slavonia, Baranja and Western Sirmium and the Civilian Police Support Group and the related reports of the Advisory Committee on Administrative and Budgetary Questions,

Recalling Security Council resolution 1037(1996) of 15 January 1996, by which the Council established the United Nations Transitional Administration for Eastern Slavonia, Baranja and Western Sirmium for an initial period of twelve months, and resolution 1145(1997) of 19 December 1997, in which the Council noted the termination of the Transitional Administration on 15 January 1998 and established, with effect from 16 January 1998, the Civilian Police Support Group for a single period of up to nine months,

Recalling also its decision 50/481 of 11 April 1996 on the financing of the Transitional Administration and its subsequent resolutions thereon, the latest of which was resolution 52/244 of 26 June 1998,

Reaffirming that the costs of the Transitional Administration and the Support Group are expenses of the Organization to be borne by Member States in accordance with Article 17, paragraph 2, of the Charter of the United Nations,

Recalling its previous decisions regarding the fact that, in order to meet the expenditures caused by the Transitional Administration and the Support Group, a different procedure is required from that applied to meet expenditures of the regular budget of the United Nations,

Taking into account the fact that the economically more developed countries are in a position to make relatively larger contributions and that the economically less developed countries have a relatively limited capacity to contribute towards such an operation,

Bearing in mind the special responsibilities of the States permanent members of the Security Council, as indicated in General Assembly resolution 1874(S-IV) of 27 June 1963, in the financing of such operations,

Noting with appreciation that voluntary contributions have been made to the Transitional Administration,

Mindful of the fact that it is essential to continue to provide the account of the mission with the necessary financial resources to enable it to meet its outstanding liabilities,

1. *Takes note* of the status of contributions to the United Nations Transitional Administration for Eastern Slavonia, Baranja and Western Sirmium and the Civilian Police Support Group as at 30 April 1999, including the contributions outstanding in the amount of 36.3 million United States dollars, representing 7 per cent of the total assessed contributions from the inception of the Transitional Administration to the period ending 30 November 1998, notes that some 41 per cent of the Member States have paid their assessed contributions in full, and urges all other Member States concerned, in particular those in arrears, to ensure payment of their outstanding assessed contributions;

2. *Expresses concern* about the financial situation with regard to peacekeeping activities, in particular as regards the reimbursement of troop contributors, which bear additional burdens owing to overdue payments by Member States of their assessments;

3. *Expresses its appreciation* to those Member States which have paid their assessed contributions in full;

4. *Urges* all other Member States to make every possible effort to ensure payment of their assessed contributions to the mission in full and on time;

5. *Endorses* the observations and recommendations contained in the report of the Advisory Committee on Administrative and Budgetary Questions;

6. *Decides* that, on an exceptional basis, the special arrangements approved by General Assembly resolution 51/153 B of 13 June 1997 for the Transitional Administration with regard to the application of article IV of the financial regulations of the United Nations, whereby appropriations required in respect of obligations owed to Governments providing contingents and/or logistic support to the Transitional Administration shall be retained beyond the period stipulated under financial regulations 4.3 and 4.4, as set out in the annex to the present resolution, shall be applied to the Support Group;

7. *Decides also* to authorize the Secretary-General to utilize an amount of 601,200 dollars gross (541,500 dollars net) from the resources provided for the period ending 30 June 1998 in order to meet the cost of completing the liquidation of the mission as well as the final audit, inclusive of the amount of 553,400 dollars gross (493,700 dollars net) related to liquidation activities with which the Advisory Committee has already concurred;

8. *Decides further* that Member States that have fulfilled their financial obligations to the Transitional Administration and the Support Group shall be credited their respective share of the remaining unencumbered balance of 14,646,100 dollars gross (13,906,700 dollars net) in respect of the period ending 30 June 1998;

9. *Decides* that, for Member States that have not fulfilled their obligations to the Transitional Administration and the Support Group, their share of the remaining unencumbered balance of 14,646,100 dollars gross (13,906,700 dollars net) in respect of the period ending 30 June 1998 shall be set off against their outstanding obligations;

10. *Takes note* of the report of the Secretary-General on the final disposition of the assets of the Transitional Administration and the Support Group;

11. *Decides* to include in the provisional agenda of its fifty-fourth session the item entitled "Financing of the United Nations Transitional Administration for Eastern Slavonia, Baranja and Western Sirmium and the Civilian Police Support Group".

ANNEX

Special arrangements with regard to the application of article IV of the financial regulations of the United Nations

1. At the end of the twelve-month period provided for in financial regulation 4.3, any unliquidated obligations of the financial period in question relating to goods supplied and services rendered by Governments for which claims have been received or which are covered by established reimbursement rates shall be transferred to accounts payable; such accounts shall remain recorded in the Special Account for the Civilian Police Support Group until payment is effected.

2. *(a)* Any other unliquidated obligations of the financial period in question owed to Governments for goods supplied and services rendered, as well as other obligations owed to Governments, for which required claims have not yet been received shall remain valid for an additional period of four years following the end of the twelve-month period provided for in regulation 4.3;

(*b*) Claims received during this four-year period shall be treated as provided for under paragraph 1 of the present annex, if appropriate;

(*c*) At the end of the additional four-year period, any unliquidated obligations shall be cancelled and the then remaining balance of any appropriations retained therefor shall be surrendered.

On 23 December, the Assembly decided that the item on the financing of UNTAES and the Civilian Police Support Group would remain for consideration during the resumed fifty-fourth (2000) session (**decision 54/465**), and that the Fifth Committee should continue to consider the item at that session (**decision 54/462 A**).

State succession issues

As part of ongoing efforts to search for an agreement on State succession issues regarding the five successor States of the former Socialist Federal Republic of Yugoslavia (SFRY) (Bosnia and Herzegovina, Croatia, FRY, FYROM and Slovenia), the Special Negotiator on succession issues of the Office of the High Representative held bilateral meetings in Brussels, Belgium, in January, stated the High Representative in his May report [S/1999/524]. The meetings focused on a new, simplified approach, which emphasized the distribution of SFRY assets among the five States that were already in their respective territories or held abroad. Further discussions with the five States on such a "broad" settlement, which offered a more pragmatic way forward, were necessary, but were impractical in the current political circumstances.

Communications. On 22 November [A/54/638], FRY said that Croatia's Deputy Prime Minister and Minister for Foreign Affairs had blamed FRY, during the General Assembly's general debate on 25 September [A/54/PV.15], for the delay in finding a solution to the succession issues. FRY presented information to counter the charge, stating that the head of the Yugoslav Expert Group on Succession had asked the Special Negotiator for an explanation of the state of negotiations to remove blame from FRY; the head of the Expert Group had expressed surprise that there was no initiative to continue the negotiations since FRY had accepted, in principle, the Special Negotiator's last draft agreement on succession and the four other entities had not rejected it and had requested only additional explanations. The Yugoslav side had proposed that the Special Negotiator host the next meeting of the Working Group on Succession Issues if he considered that the last draft agreement necessitated a more specific declaration of other participants; and the head of the Expert Group had insisted that the Peace Implementation Council (PIC) give its opinion on the causes of the delay.

On 13 December [S/1999/1245], FRY said that the division of assets and liabilities was the subject of separate negotiations conducted in the framework of PIC, with the mediation of the Special Negotiator. FRY, Bosnia and Herzegovina, Croatia and FYROM had agreed to resolve the issue by agreement on the basis of the rules of international law on succession of States. FRY had assessed that the last draft agreement on succession proposed by the Special Negotiator was acceptable in principle and hoped that an agreement between the five States on that basis could be concluded quickly. Towards that end, the head of the Yugoslav Expert Group had proposed that negotiations continue.

UN status of FRY

Communications. Bosnia and Herzegovina, Croatia, Slovenia and FYROM, on 5 February [S/1999/120], drew attention to a 1 February statement by the FRY Minister for Foreign Affairs, in which he referred to FRY as a "State Member of the United Nations" [S/1999/107] . Citing Security Council resolution 777(1992) [YUN 1992, p. 138] and General Assembly resolution 47/1 [ibid., p. 139], they reiterated their common position that all five States that had emerged following the dissolution of SFRY were equal successor States, and until FRY was admitted to the United Nations in accordance with the relevant provisions of the Charter, it could not be considered a Member State.

In response, FRY, on 12 February [S/1999/152], explained that its current status in the United Nations was determined by General Assembly resolution 47/1, which, although it did not allow FRY to participate in the Assembly's work, did not, as advised by the United Nations Legal Counsel [YUN 1992, p. 139], terminate or suspend its membership in the Organization. Furthermore, FRY's Permanent Missions to the United Nations in New York and Geneva continued to function, FRY contributed to the UN regular budget and the Secretariat treated FRY as a Member State.

Bosnia and Herzegovina, Croatia, Slovenia and FYROM, on 25 February [S/1999/209], countered that the Legal Counsel's opinion dealt with practical, temporary arrangements for the United Nations to communicate with FRY as a party to disputes with which the United Nations was seized. The Legal Counsel had also concluded that the problem addressed in his opinion would be resolved after a new Yugoslavia was admitted to the United Nations, in accordance with the Charter. Therefore, FRY should submit an application for membership, as had been done by the other four equally legitimate successor States of SFRY. Their position was supported by the Organization of the Islamic Conference Contact Group [S/1999/266]. The four States, on 27 May [A/53/992], referring to a 25 April depositary notification to the International Court of Justice (ICJ) by FRY, by which FRY recognized the jurisdiction ipso facto of the Court, requested the Secretary-General to bring the issue to the attention of the ICJ Registry so that it could clarify in its *Yearbook* that the reference to Yugoslavia (original Member) in the list of United Nations Member States entitled to appear before the Court referred to the former SFRY and not to any of its successor States. On 3 June, they drew the Security Council President's attention to two instances in which FRY asserted that it was a current and founding UN Member State [S/1999/639].

On 15 December, the General Assembly postponed consideration of a draft text [A/54/L.62], by which the Assembly would have considered that SFRY had ceased to exist and that none of its five successor States could continue its membership.

FRY, on 27 December [S/1999/1282], said that the so-called Croatian initiative to challenge its UN membership contradicted the agreements on normalization of relations and the need for good-neighbourly relations and stabilization of the situation in the region, and ran counter to the principles of the Charter and international law. The initiative had failed and the position of a large number of countries had helped to protect FRY's rights and reaffirmed its international reputation and position.

FRY treaty status

Communications. On 27 May [A/53/975-S/1999/615], Bosnia and Herzegovina, Croatia, Slovenia and FYROM drew the Secretary-General's attention to a resolution adopted in May by the contracting parties to the 1971 Convention on Wetlands of International Importance especially as Waterfowl Habitat (the Ramsar Convention). The resolution, while noting that successor States in general continued to be bound by the treaty obligations of the predecessor State, called on Bosnia and Herzegovina and FRY to submit to the depositary (the Director-General of the United Nations Educational, Scientific and Cultural Organization) a notification of succession to the Convention as the other successor States had done. The four States asked the Secretary-General as depositary of international treaties to consider the position of the parties to the Convention on the status of the five successor States to a treaty to which that State had been a party before it was dissolved and ceased to exist.

FRY, on 6 August [A/53/1033-S/1999/858], said that it considered the resolution null and void and with no legal effect since the contracting parties had no authority to make a decision regarding its status in the Convention. FRY participated as a member in conferences of contracting parties and regularly paid its financial contributions. The Secretary-General had no authority to make decisions on the States' membership in international conventions.

Prevlaka peninsula

The United Nations continued in 1999 to assist Croatia and FRY in their search for a permanent solution to the disputed issue of the Prevlaka peninsula. The United Nations Mission of Observers in Prevlaka (UNMOP) continued to monitor the demilitarization of the peninsula and neighbouring areas in Croatia and FRY. The Security Council renewed its mandate until 15 January 2000.

During the year, both parties reiterated their commitment to a negotiated solution, in accordance with the Agreement on Normalization of Relations between them, signed in Belgrade in 1996 [YUN 1996, p. 340].

Pursuant to their 1998 agreement [YUN 1998, p. 358] to realize their commitments on delimitation and arranging their borders under the 1996 Agreement, the fourth meeting of the bilateral negotiations took place in May at the expert level but no substantive progress was made towards a settlement. Further meetings were affected by the events in the FRY province of Kosovo (see p. 333). However, the Secretary-General reported that the situation in the region remained stable and free of significant tension. In October, he proposed a package of confidence-building measures. One of those measures—the demilitarization of the demilitarized zone—was completed in December and discussions began on a regime for limited access to the UN-controlled zone.

Bilateral negotiations

The Secretary-General, in a 6 January report to the Security Council on UNMOP [S/1999/16], said that, despite three rounds of talks on the disputed issue of Prevlaka, the last of which was in December 1998 [YUN 1998, p. 358], FRY and Croatia had not made substantive progress on a settlement. They had, however, expressed their intention to continue their discussions through further meetings of their expert teams and other bilateral contacts. The Secretary-General urged the parties to take full advantage of the currently favourable conditions for progress on the issue and to pursue their negotiations towards securing a mutually acceptable and lasting solution. To enable him to keep the Council regularly informed of progress, he proposed that the Council request the parties to report their assessment of the negotiations to the Secretary-General on a monthly or bimonthly basis. If no substantial progress was made within the next six months, he suggested that the Council might wish to consider alternative mechanisms, such as international mediation or arbitration.

The Council, in **resolution 1222(1999)** of 15 January (see p. 309), requested that the parties report at least bimonthly and asked the Secretary-General to report by 15 April.

Communications. In a 7 January letter to the Council President [S/1999/19 & Corr.1], Croatia referred to FRY's negotiating position on Prevlaka, as stated in a memorandum to the December 1998 meeting of the negotiating teams [S/1998/1225]. FRY had stated that it considered Prevlaka its territory on the basis of the principle of *uti possidetis de facto*, adding that the fact that no delimitation in the disputed region had ever been carried out proved that Croatia's claim that FRY wished to change the international borders was not true. Croatia wished to demonstrate that FRY had not given up its territorial pretensions and was unwilling to engage in meaningful bilateral negotiations. FRY's claim of de facto control over Prevlaka was nothing more than a request for a change in the existing international borders, which were reconfirmed by the Arbitration Commission (established in 1991 by the European Community in the context of the International Conference on the Former Yugoslavia [YUN 1991, p. 214]) and by Council decisions. Croatia hoped that the Council would prevent UNMOP from being used by FRY as a mechanism for postponing full reintegration of the last part of Croatian territory and unequivocally state that Prevlaka was an integral part of Croatia. It should also press FRY to engage in constructive negotiations.

In accordance with Council resolution 1222(1999), Croatia and FRY submitted bimonthly reports to the Secretary-General in March. On 15 March [S/1999/291], Croatia reported that delegations from the two sides held their fourth meeting on 9 March in Belgrade. However, apart from establishing the rules of procedure and exchanging position papers, no substantive progress was made in the negotiations. Under the circumstances, Croatia's Foreign Minister had requested an urgent meeting with the FRY Foreign Minister to streamline and accelerate the negotiations. FRY, in its 23 March report [S/1999/313], informed the Secretary-General that at the 9 March meeting the two sides presented their ideas and arguments regarding where the inter-State border should extend. According to FRY, Croatia presented no arguments to negate the legal foundation of the Yugoslav arguments and demonstrated a lack of readiness for serious negotiations as testified by its proposal to call off the negotiations at that level and resume them at a higher one.

In a 25 June letter [S/1999/719], Croatia regretted that no progress had been made in bilateral negotiations and said that a recent letter of the FRY President presented a distorted picture of the current state of the negotiations. The Croatian delegation had submitted to the Yugoslav side clear evidence that Prevlaka lay within Croatia's international borders. Croatia remained prepared and willing to negotiate demilitarization in the Prevlaka area, as well as delimitation at sea, but could not tolerate any pretension towards its territory. Croatia was resolved to negotiate a permanent solution for Prevlaka's security and it was essential to build upon the results achieved so far at the local level.

However, on 27 April [S/1999/480], FRY had informed the Council President that to defend itself from the NATO aggression, it had declared a state of war and would resume the talks once NATO's criminal aggression against it had ceased (see p. 342). Croatia, on 3 May [S/1999/501], said it found that position disturbing, and the unilateral cessation of bilateral negotiations contravened Council resolutions. In response, FRY, on 10 May [S/1999/546], accused Croatia of taking a hostile position towards it by ceding its airspace to NATO for the aerial bombardment of FRY.

On 7 July [S/1999/760], FRY forwarded to the Council President a memorandum, which, it said, contained the facts to support its position that the Prevlaka peninsula was an integral part of Boka Kotorska Bay, an inalienable part of FRY territory. Croatia, on 13 July [S/1999/783 & Corr.1], stated that the intent of the FRY memorandum was to extend artificially the duration of its quest for a change of international borders in south-east Europe, and its selective approach to history did not deserve elaborate comment. The fact was that the borderline between the then Socialist Republics of Croatia and Montenegro in the Prevlaka area not only existed but was well known and recognized when Croatia proclaimed independence in June 1991 [YUN 1991, p. 214]. Croatia also drew attention to the official FRY map posted on the Yugoslav Government's official web site, showing the Croatian Prevlaka within the existing Croatian international borders. Croatia said that the Council should implement the decisions of the Arbitration Commission on the inviolability of international borders and other applicable international law.

On 19 July [S/1999/799], FRY informed the Council President that with the cessation of NATO's aggression impediments to the continuation of negotiations on a solution to the Prevlaka issue had been removed; it expressed its readiness to continue the negotiations without delay in Zagreb, Croatia.

On 4 October [S/1999/1027], FRY said that although Croatia had proposed that the next meeting be held in September, an invitation had not been received. The Yugoslav side expected that, at the fifth meeting, they would consider the arguments already exchanged. FRY had communicated to UNMOP on 15 September its readiness to resume negotiations and rejected Croatia's accusations of aggression and territorial aspirations before the General Assembly [A/54/PV.15]. Concerning Croatia's suggestion that UNMOP's mandate be terminated, FRY declared that any change to the 1996 Agreement on the Normalization of Relations would be a serious violation of the international obligations of both sides.

Croatia confirmed on 12 October [S/1999/1049] that it had proposed that the next meeting be held in Zagreb in September. However, that had been affected by FRY's delay in verifying the authenticity of the signatures of its former Prime Minister and the Head of the Joint Chiefs of Staff to a 1992 letter and map, indicating where the existing international border between Croatia and FRY existed and confirming FRY's intention to honour existing borders. The scheduling of the meeting was also affected by the absence of Montenegrin representatives from that delegation, which rendered the legitimacy of any outcome doubtful, and by the legacy of the Kosovo crisis.

FRY, in two letters of 24 December [S/1999/1278, S/1999/1280], maintained that Croatia had still not extended a concrete invitation to the fifth meeting of experts in Zagreb. To further the process and overcome objections raised in the Secretary-General's April report [S/1999/404], FRY had decided to replace the Yugoslav army units in the north-western part of the area (Bjelotina) with police as a goodwill gesture and a contribution to a speedier solution of the disputed issue. FRY expected UNMOP to abide by its mandate and that the Croatian side would carry out its obligations relative to the maintenance of the regimes of the "Yellow Zone" (a DMZ) and the "Blue Zone" (a UN-controlled zone), in particular the regime that Croatia had been violating. FRY pointed out that the Croatian side could not request that the status of the "Blue Zone" be modified or that UNMOP be withdrawn since that would be contrary to the Agreement on Normalization of Relations. Any change in UNMOP's regime without agreement on both sides would be contrary to the Agreement and would aggravate and complicate the negotiation process.

Report of Secretary-General. The Secretary-General, in a 31 December report on UNMOP [S/1999/1302], noted that 10 months had elapsed since the holding of the last round of bilateral negotiations between the parties in Belgrade. He expected the negotiations to resume as soon as possible, given the positive developments on the ground (see p. 312). However, the current pre-election period in Croatia might not be conducive to substantive negotiations, which he hoped could be held as soon as the elections were over.

UN Mission of Observers in Prevlaka (UNMOP)

During 1999, the United Nations Mission of Observers in Prevlaka, which became a separate mission in 1996 [YUN 1996, p. 330], continued to monitor the demilitarization of the disputed Prevlaka peninsula and of the neighbouring areas in Croatia and FRY by carrying out patrols on both sides of the border. The Mission, which comprised 27 military observers for most of the year, under the command of Chief Military Observer Colonel Graeme Williams (New Zealand), also maintained contacts with local authorities to strengthen liaison, reduce tension, improve safety and security, and promote confidence between the parties. UNMOP's area of responsibility consisted of two UN-designated zones: a DMZ (Yellow Zone) and a UN-controlled zone (Blue Zone). In the first quarter of the year, UNMOP headquarters was relocated from Dubrovnik, where the UN presence had been based since 1992, to Cavtat.

The Council authorized a six-month extension of UNMOP until 15 July and a further six-month extension until 15 January 2000.

Although an independent mission, UNMOP was treated for administrative and budgetary purposes as part of UNMIBH. (For details on the financing of UNMOP, see p. 320.)

Report of Secretary-General (January). The Secretary-General, in a January report on UNMOP [S/1999/16], stated that the most significant violation in the DMZ was the continued presence of Yugoslav troops in the north-eastern part. UNMOP remained unable to ascertain the exact strength and armament of those units because of constraints imposed by the Yugoslav authorities on the movement of UN military observers. The long-standing violations of the demilitarized regime in the UN-controlled zone continued, with some 30 Croatian Special Police located at three positions and one checkpoint and some 10 Yugoslav (Montenegrin) Border Police at one position and one checkpoint. The

Croatian authorities continued to allow unauthorized access to the UN zone by civilians, and the waters continued to be violated by Croatian and Yugoslav fishing boats and occasionally by Croatian police boats. The opening for the holiday period on 23 December 1998 [YUN 1998, p. 360] of the crossing point between Croatia and FRY (Montenegro) at Debeli Brijeg, in the DMZ, resulted in considerable civilian traffic in both directions; it was scheduled to remain open until 15 January 1999.

The Secretary-General said that the UNMOP area of operations remained stable and free of significant tension. The number of serious incidents had decreased and cooperation between the parties and the UN military observers had improved. He recommended a further six-month extension of UNMOP's mandate, until 15 July.

Communication. Croatia, on 7 January [S/1999/19], said that, following six extensions, the continuation of UNMOP's mandate without decisive impetus from the Security Council would be pointless, and appealed to the Council to provide the much-needed incentive. Otherwise, the Council would witness further needless use of UN resources, since the situation in Prevlaka was neither a threat to international peace and security nor a source of concern. By reducing the number of observers and indicating an impending end to the mandate, the Council would press FRY to engage in constructive negotiations.

SECURITY COUNCIL ACTION (January)

On 15 January [meeting 3966], the Security Council unanimously adopted **resolution 1222(1999)**. The draft [S/1999/39] was submitted by Canada, France, Germany, Italy, the Netherlands, the Russian Federation, the United Kingdom and the United States.

The Security Council,

Recalling all its earlier relevant resolutions, in particular resolutions 779(1992) of 6 October 1992, 981(1995) of 31 March 1995, 1147(1998) of 13 January 1998 and 1183(1998) of 15 July 1998,

Having considered the report of the Secretary-General of 6 January 1999 on the United Nations Mission of Observers in Prevlaka,

Recalling the letter dated 24 December 1998 from the Prime Minister of the Federal Republic of Yugoslavia and the letter dated 7 January 1999 from the Permanent Representative of Croatia to the United Nations, concerning the disputed issue of Prevlaka,

Reaffirming once again its commitment to the independence, sovereignty and territorial integrity of the Republic of Croatia within its internationally recognized borders,

Taking note once again of the Joint Declaration signed at Geneva on 30 September 1992 by the Presidents of the Republic of Croatia and the Federal Republic of Yugoslavia, in particular articles 1 and 3, the latter reaffirming their agreement concerning the demilitarization of the Prevlaka peninsula,

Noting with concern, however, that long-standing violations of the demilitarization regime by both parties continue, including the standing presence of Yugoslav military personnel and the occasional presence of Croatian military elements in the demilitarized zone, and limitations placed on the free movement of United Nations military observers by both parties,

Welcoming, in this regard, the recent lifting of certain restrictions on access for the Mission by Croatia, as well as the recent steps taken by the Croatian authorities to improve communication and coordination with the Mission to allow it to monitor more effectively the situation in its area of responsibility,

Welcoming also the Croatian willingness to open crossing points between Croatia and the Federal Republic of Yugoslavia (Montenegro) in the demilitarized zone, which has led to considerable civilian traffic in both directions and which represents a significant confidence-building measure in the normalization of relations between the two parties, and expressing the hope that further such openings will help to increase such civilian traffic,

Noting with approval the continuing bilateral negotiations between the parties pursuant to the Agreement on Normalization of Relations between the Republic of Croatia and the Federal Republic of Yugoslavia of 23 August 1996, but expressing serious concern that such negotiations have not yet resulted in any substantive progress towards a settlement of the disputed issue of Prevlaka,

Reiterating its call upon the parties urgently to put in place a comprehensive demining programme,

Noting that the presence of the United Nations military observers continues to be essential to maintain conditions that are conducive to a negotiated settlement of the disputed issue of Prevlaka,

1. *Authorizes* the United Nations military observers to continue monitoring the demilitarization of the Prevlaka peninsula, in accordance with resolutions 779(1992) and 981(1995) and paragraphs 19 and 20 of the report of the Secretary-General of 13 December 1995, until 15 July 1999;

2. *Welcomes* the improvement in cooperation between the Republic of Croatia and the Federal Republic of Yugoslavia and the United Nations military observers and the decrease in the number of serious incidents, and reiterates its calls upon the parties to cease all violations of the demilitarization regime in the United Nations designated zones, to take steps further to reduce tension and improve safety and security in the area, to cooperate fully with the United Nations military observers and to ensure their safety and full and unrestricted freedom of movement;

3. *Requests* the Secretary-General, in the light of the improved cooperation and reduction in tensions in Prevlaka as described in his report, to consider possible reductions, without prejudice to the main operational activities of the United Nations Mission of Observers in Prevlaka, focusing on the possibility of reducing the number of military observers to as few as twenty-two, in line with the reconsideration of the concept of operations of the Mission and the existing security regime and the desirability of closing the Mission when appropriate;

4. *Also requests* the Secretary-General to submit a report by 15 April 1999 on the progress of bilateral negotiations between the parties, as well as on possible ways to facilitate a negotiated settlement, should the parties require such assistance, and to this end requests the parties to report at least bimonthly to the Secretary-General on the status of the negotiations;

5. *Urges once again* that the parties abide by their mutual commitments and implement fully the Agreement on Normalization of Relations, and stresses in particular the urgent need for them to fulfil rapidly and in good faith their commitment to reach a negotiated resolution of the disputed issue of Prevlaka in accordance with article 4 of the Agreement;

6. *Requests* the United Nations military observers and the multinational Stabilization Force authorized by the Council in resolution 1088(1996) of 12 December 1996 and extended by resolution 1174(1998) of 15 June 1998 to cooperate fully with each other;

7. *Decides* to remain seized of the matter.

Communications. On 15 January [S/1999/42], Croatia informed the Council President of its decision to keep the border crossing points at Debeli Brijeg and Konfin between Croatia and FRY open permanently. FRY, on 27 January [S/1999/84], stated its opposition to the unilateral opening of any border crossing, since that presumed the existence of a joint agreement designating the location and regime of such crossings. In the absence of such an agreement with respect to Sector South, land border crossings could not legally be opened. FRY said that, on 20 January, Croatia had proposed that the 1997 agreement between FRY and Croatia designating border crossings [YUN 1997, p. 328] be amended to allow for the opening of border crossings in Sector South. Although FRY believed that the opening of land border crossings had to be resolved by bilateral agreement, it rejected the Croatian proposal because Croatia's attempt to open two border crossings, one of which was located on disputed territory, was tantamount to prejudging the solution of the disputed Prevlaka question and the outcome of ongoing negotiations.

Croatia, on 15 March [S/1999/291], said the two border crossing points had been opened permanently, in agreement with Montenegro, and were operational. In view of the approaching tourist season, it was essential to allow free movement of civilians and thus take another important step towards full normalization of relations.

Report of Secretary-General (April). The Secretary-General, in an April report [S/1999/404], said that, since 24 March, the commencement of NATO military action against FRY (see p. 342), tension had risen in the Prevlaka area, particularly in Montenegro. In the light of the security concerns arising from that action, UNMOP military observers in Herceg Novi were temporarily located to the Croatian side, but continued to carry out limited patrolling on the Yugoslav side. However, UNMOP had been unable to patrol the north-eastern part of the DMZ. An anti-aircraft gun was observed at Debeli Brijeg in violation of the UN security regime. In the northern part of the DMZ, Croatia prevented UNMOP from patrolling on two separate occasions. The Secretary-General said that, while the opening of the crossing point at Debeli Brijeg was not a violation of the DMZ, opening one in the UN-controlled zone on Cape Kobila constituted a violation of the security regime and seemed to be politically motivated. Croatia, as well as Montenegrin authorities, permitted civilians to enter the UN-controlled area and Croatia had established a manned checkpoint near the existing Montenegrin checkpoint. Both checkpoints were in violation of the security regime.

The Secretary-General urged the two countries to regularize the issue of the opening of the Debeli Brijeg crossing point in the context of their continuing bilateral negotiations or through other contacts. To resolve the issue of the crossing point on Cape Kobila, Croatia and FRY could conclude a bilateral agreement to redefine the security regime so that the opening of a crossing point in the UN-controlled zone did not result in a violation of the existing regime. The crossing point should therefore be closed until such an agreement had been reached.

Communications. On 20 April [S/1999/444], Croatia informed the Council President that, on that day, 200 to 300 FRY soldiers had entered the DMZ in the area of the border crossing points opened in agreement with Montenegro. That action nullified progress in establishing and maintaining security and stability in the Prevlaka area, and might affect international humanitarian assistance to the displaced populations of the FRY province of Kosovo. Croatia called on FRY to withdraw its forces immediately and on the Council to ensure strict compliance with its resolutions pertaining to Prevlaka.

FRY, on 22 April [S/1999/471], said that the Secretary-General's April report downplayed Croatia's continued violation of the UN-mandated regime of the DMZ, taking no account of data from the UNMOP Chief Military Observer's internal report, which contained some of the most evident instances of the violation, such as the construction of fortifications and bunkers and the presence of civilian vehicles and boats. Conversely, the report had singled out the presence of Yugoslav Army troops in the north-eastern part of the zone at Bjelotina as "the most significant violation of the demilitarized zone". Similarly, the presence of 25 Croatian Special Police in the Blue Zone was not condemned, nor was their withdrawal requested. The report did not mention that Croatia had blocked access to UN military observers to the area north of Dubravka, nor the statement in the internal report to the effect that FRY documents showed that Croatia had recognized in the past the Montenegrin jurisdiction in part of the disputed area and that Croatia had submitted only a copy of the 1992 UN map with the boundaries of the Blue Zone as proof of the extension of the border. In the light of NATO's aggression against FRY, openly supported by Croatia, the request that the anti-aircraft gun at Debeli Brijeg in FRY be removed was unacceptable.

On 27 April [S/1999/480], FRY informed the Council President that, to defend itself from NATO aggression, its Army had set up a checkpoint manned by 20 men in the Yellow Zone. The checkpoint did not threaten UNMOP members or any other person. Once the aggression against FRY ceased, the need for the checkpoint would also cease to exist. The Commander of the Yugoslav Army had advised the Chief Military Observer on 23 April of the checkpoint, and UNMOP's request that its office at Herceg Novi continue to work was positively resolved. The Yugoslav authorities agreed to establish a direct permanent connection between its Army command and UNMOP. Croatia's 20 April protest was therefore groundless and calculated to use NATO's aggression against FRY to achieve its own goals.

In response, Croatia stated on 3 May [S/1999/501] that FRY's proclaimed need to have a military checkpoint in the DMZ was disturbing; the Council should send a clear message to FRY that it would not tolerate Yugoslav Army checkpoints there, nor any other violations of the DMZ or its resolutions. Croatia rejected the assertion that it was using the current situation in the region to advance its own goals and expressed its continued support for NATO's humanitarian intervention in FRY. Croatia also brought to the Council's attention the fate of a journalist, Antun Masle, who had been apprehended by FRY military authorities. It called on the Council to demand Mr. Masle's immediate release.

Report of Secretary-General (July). In July [S/1999/764], the Secretary-General reported that the Yugoslav authorities had indicated that the restrictions that had applied to the movement of UN military observers in the northern part of the DMZ since 24 March had been lifted. However, since that date, heavier weapons, which had been introduced to the southern part of the zone by Yugoslav (Montenegrin) Border Police, remained there despite the suspension of NATO military action against FRY. Croatia had not completely removed restrictions placed on UNMOP's movements in the north-western part of the zone, requiring 24 hours' notice for foot patrols. In the southern DMZ, UNMOP was refused access to one position on two occasions. The DMZ and the UN-controlled zone were also violated by NATO during its military activity against FRY.

The Secretary-General said that, given the importance of ensuring that the situation on the ground remained stable and as free of tension as possible, and for political negotiations to have the greatest possible chance of success, UNMOP's mandate should be extended until 15 January 2000.

Communications. In view of the forthcoming Security Council consideration of the UNMOP mandate, Croatia and FRY transmitted communications to the Council President. FRY, on 18 June [S/1999/697], expressed its readiness to resume negotiations on Prevlaka without delay and requested the Council to extend UNMOP's mandate for another six months. Croatia, on 25 June [S/1999/719], conveyed its gratitude for UNMOP's contribution to the strengthening of peace and stability in the Prevlaka area during the preceding six months, during which time further progress was achieved in normalizing the situation. The permanent opening of the Debeli Brijeg and Konfin border crossing points had significantly contributed to confidence-building with the local population on both sides of the international border, as well as to lasting stability in the post-conflict period. UNMOP's presence also helped to deter attempts aimed at thwarting those practical measures. However, no progress had been made in bilateral negotiations on the Prevlaka issue.

SECURITY COUNCIL ACTION (July)

On 15 July [meeting 4023], the Security Council unanimously adopted resolution **1252(1999)**. The draft [S/1999/785] was prepared in consultations among Council members.

The Security Council,

Recalling all its earlier relevant resolutions, in particular its resolutions 779(1992) of 6 October 1992, 981(1995) of 31 March 1995, 1147(1998) of 13 January 1998, 1183(1998) of 15 July 1998 and 1222(1999) of 15 January 1999,

Having considered the report of the Secretary-General of 8 July 1999 on the United Nations Mission of Observers in Prevlaka,

Recalling the letter to the President of the Security Council dated 18 June 1999 from the Chargé d'affaires a.i. of the Permanent Mission of the Federal Republic of Yugoslavia to the United Nations and the letter dated 25 June 1999 from the Permanent Representative of Croatia to the United Nations, concerning the disputed issue of Prevlaka,

Reaffirming once again its commitment to the independence, sovereignty and territorial integrity of the Republic of Croatia within its internationally recognized borders,

Noting once again the Joint Declaration signed at Geneva on 30 September 1992 by the Presidents of the Republic of Croatia and the Federal Republic of Yugoslavia, in particular articles 1 and 3, the latter reaffirming their agreement concerning the demilitarization of the Prevlaka peninsula,

Reiterating its concern that long-standing violations of the demilitarization regime by both parties continue, including the standing presence of military personnel of the Federal Republic of Yugoslavia and the occasional presence of Croatian military elements in the demilitarized zone, and limitations placed on the free movement of United Nations military observers by both parties,

Expressing its concern about more recent, additional violations of the demilitarized zone, in particular the presence there of troops of the Federal Republic of Yugoslavia,

Noting with satisfaction that the opening of crossing points between Croatia and the Federal Republic of Yugoslavia (Montenegro) in the demilitarized zones continues to facilitate civilian and commercial traffic in both directions without security incidents and continue to represent a significant confidence-building measure in the normalization of relations between the two parties, and urging the parties to utilize these openings as a basis for further confidence-building measures to achieve the normalization of relations between them,

Reiterating its serious concerns about the lack of substantive progress towards a settlement of the disputed issue of Prevlaka in the continuing bilateral negotiations between the parties pursuant to the Agreement on Normalization of Relations between the Republic of Croatia and the Federal Republic of Yugoslavia of 23 August 1996, and calling upon the parties to resume discussions,

Reiterating its call upon the parties urgently to put in place a comprehensive demining programme,

Commending the role played by the Mission, and noting also that the presence of the United Nations military observers continues to be essential to maintain conditions that are conducive to a negotiated settlement of the disputed issue of Prevlaka,

1. *Authorizes* the United Nations military observers to continue monitoring the demilitarization of the Prevlaka peninsula, in accordance with resolutions 779(1992) and 981(1995) and paragraphs 19 and 20 of the report of the Secretary-General of 13 December 1995, until 15 January 2000;

2. *Reiterates its calls upon* the parties to cease all violations of the demilitarization regime in the United Nations designated zones, to take steps further to reduce tension and to improve safety and security in the area, to cooperate fully with the United Nations military observers and to ensure their safety and full and unrestricted freedom of movement;

3. *Requests* the Secretary-General to report by 15 October 1999 with recommendations and options further to develop confidence-building measures between the parties aimed, inter alia, at further facilitating freedom of movement of the civilian population;

4. *Urges once again* that the parties abide by their mutual commitments and implement fully the Agreement on Normalization of Relations, and stresses in particular the urgent need for them to fulfil rapidly and in good faith their commitment to reach a negotiated resolution of the disputed issue of Prevlaka in accordance with article 4 of the Agreement;

5. *Requests* the parties to continue to report at least bimonthly to the Secretary-General on the status of their bilateral negotiations;

6. *Requests* the United Nations military observers and the multinational Stabilization Force authorized by the Council in resolution 1088(1996) of 12 December 1996 and extended by resolution 1247(1999) of 18 June 1999 to cooperate fully with each other;

7. *Decides* to remain seized of the matter.

Further communication. On 16 July [S/1999/796], FRY, commenting on the Secretary-General's July report, stated that it had never accepted that the northern part of the area extending to the three-border junction between Bosnia and Herzegovina, Croatia (Bjelotina) and FRY did not belong to the DMZ, although it had allowed the area to be monitored as an expression of goodwill. That area therefore could not be the subject of a Secretary-General's report, in particular not as an area in which an alleged violation of the UN security system took place. FRY had always called for the preservation of the original concept of the UN security system in Prevlaka, on which the two sides had agreed in the Agreement on the Normalization of Relations [YUN 1996, p. 340].

Reports of Secretary-General (October and December). In October [S/1999/1051], the Secretary-General observed that a significant practical step that the parties could take in support of a peaceful solution to their dispute over Prevlaka would be to demonstrate full respect for the UN-monitored security regime. The DMZ was currently stable and free of heavy weapons. The parties had been provided, at his request, with a package of recommendations and options to develop confidence-building measures aimed at further facilitating the freedom of movement of the civilian population and covering basic elements of the disputed issue.

In December [S/1999/1302], the Secretary-General stated that the Yugoslav authorities had informed UNMOP in November of their intention to withdraw their Army units that had been in violation of the UN security regime from the DMZ. UNMOP confirmed that the withdrawal was completed on 11 December and that the zone was free of formed military units and heavy weapons for the first time since October 1992. Subsequently, FRY removed all restrictions on the movement of UN military observers. However, Croatia continued to impose restrictions in the northwestern part of the DMZ.

The Secretary-General observed that the fact that one of the confidence-building measures proposed in his package of recommendations—the demilitarization of the DMZ—had been implemented was an important step forward. It was now important to address the remaining permanent violations. FRY had indicated its willingness formally to demarcate the northern part of the border with Croatia, up to a point south of Debeli Brijeg, and to regularize the operation of the Debeli Brijeg crossing point. The Montenegrin authorities had also indicated that they would withdraw their Border Police from the UN-controlled zone if Croatia withdrew its Special Police simultaneously. Croatia had expressed an interest in a controlled access regime for local civilians wishing to enter that zone. Preliminary discussions on practical implementation had commenced.

The Secretary-General said that there were other elements of the October options package that had not been taken up by the parties and which, if implemented, could create a climate conducive to a peaceful resolution of the disputed Prevlaka issue. He urged the parties to study them further and devise an implementation strategy, including the regularization of the Debeli Brijeg crossing point, introduction of a limited access regime for local civilians to the UN-controlled zone and replacement of the Cape Kobila crossing point by that regime. The Secretary-General recommended that UNMOP's mandate be extended until 15 July 2000.

Bosnia and Herzegovina

The United Nations continued in 1999 to support efforts towards the full implementation of the 1995 General Framework Agreement for Peace in Bosnia and Herzegovina (the Peace Agreement) [YUN 1995, p. 544] through the Office of the High Representative responsible for the Agreement's civilian aspects [YUN 1996, p. 293] and the United Nations Mission in Bosnia and Herzegovina (UNMIBH) [ibid., p. 294], the key components of which were the International Police Task Force (IPTF) and the Mine Action Centre (MAC). Both those entities worked in cooperation with the multinational Stabilization Force (SFOR), led by NATO, which was responsible for the Agreement's military aspects.

The Steering Board of the Peace Implementation Council (PIC) continued to review the Peace Agreement's implementation, which was somewhat affected by events in the FRY province of Kosovo (see p. 333).

In November, the three members of the Joint Presidency of Bosnia and Herzegovina adopted the New York Declaration, in which they reaffirmed their commitment to the Agreement, noted the progress made and pledged themselves to facing the remaining challenges. They agreed that the future of Bosnia and Herzegovina—which consisted of two multi-ethnic entities, the Federation and Republika Srpska—was as a part of Europe.

The Security Council, in June, extended UNMIBH's mandate until June 2000.

Implementation of Peace Agreement

Progress in implementing the General Framework Agreement was reviewed by the PIC Steering Board, which met regularly at the level of political directors during the year in Brussels, Belgium (1 February, 11 May, 15 June, 12 July, 17 September and 30 November), and Sarajevo (17-18 March and 20 October). The Board, established in 1995 [YUN 1995, p. 511], comprised Canada, France, Germany, Italy, Japan, the Russian Federation, the United Kingdom, the United States, the European Union (EU) and the Organization of the Islamic Conference.

At its February meeting, the Steering Board focused on the handling of the situation in Republika Srpska and reviewed implementation of the Refugee and Reconstruction Task Force return plan for 1999, the functioning of common institutions and progress on the draft permanent election law. In March, it discussed the work of the Office of the High Representative relating to property legislation, the dismantling of parallel institutions and the conditions to be met before a donors' conference could be held. In May, it decided to proceed with the donors' conference, to extend the validity of Bosnia and Herzegovina passports until 30 September 1999 and to support the policy of refraining from any political action in Republika Srpska that might aggravate the situation there during the Kosovo crisis. In June, the Board decided to defer municipal elections and discussed the need for budgetary support to Republika Srpska, the creation of an economic space within Bosnia and Herzegovina and progress on the draft permanent election law. That law was approved at the Board's October meeting. At the September meeting, the new High Representative, Wolfgang Petritsch, outlined his overall strategy for his term.

The High Representative met with PIC Steering Board Ministers in New York on 22 September, when they endorsed his strategic concept of "ownership" for Bosnia and Herzegovina, whereby its citizens would become increasingly responsible for their own affairs.

New York Declaration

On 15 November [meeting 4069], the Security Council met to consider the situation in Bosnia and Herzegovina, during which it was briefed by Ante Jelavic, current Chair of the Presidency of Bosnia and Herzegovina, and Alija Izetbegovic and Zivko Radisic, members of the Presidency who also responded to questions from Council members.

During their appearance before the Council, on the eve of the fourth anniversary of the Peace Agreement, the members of the Presidency announced the adoption of the New York Declaration [S/1999/1179], in which they reaffirmed their commitment to the Agreement, noted the progress made towards fulfilling its goals and pledged themselves to facing the remaining challenges. The Presidency agreed that the future of Bosnia and Herzegovina was as a part of Europe, requiring full integration into European institutions and the creation of strong, functioning common institutions. The three Presidents agreed: to the establishment of a State Border Service; to the creation of a Permanent Secretariat for the Joint Presidency; that full funding of the State ministries should be a top priority for Bosnia and Herzegovina; and that the structure of the Council of Ministers should be rectified in an accelerated fashion in accordance with the Bosnia and Herzegovina Constituent Court decision and the Madrid decisions [YUN 1998, p. 329]. They agreed to secure full funding by 1 March 2000 of the Ministries of Foreign Affairs, Foreign Trade and Economic Relations, and Civil Affairs and Communications. They reaffirmed their support for the adoption of the permanent election law and expressed their intention to seek improved inter-entity military cooperation, including through the creation of joint units to participate in UN peacekeeping operations. The Presidents also agreed that the return of displaced persons and refugees should be the Government's highest priority and to press the Federation and Republika Srpska to provide additional staffing, funding and proper facilities to their ministries for refugees to accelerate urban returns. They endorsed the harmonized property laws announced by the High Representative in October and committed themselves to advocating strongly for their expeditious implementation. They agreed to create a joint commission of entities to establish refugee return priorities to urban areas and to report to the Security Council on progress made by 1 March 2000; that the State Government would serve as the central database and managing authority for Bosnia and Herzegovina passports and to propose to the Parliament the creation of a single national passport; and to support aggressive steps to combat corruption and lack of transparency. Annexed to the Declaration were Principles on the Establishment of a State Border Service.

Civilian aspects

The civilian aspects of the 1995 Peace Agreement [YUN 1995, p. 544] entailed a wide range of activities, including humanitarian aid, infrastructure rehabilitation, establishment of political and constitutional institutions, promotion of respect for human rights and the holding of free and fair elections. The High Representative, who chaired the PIC Steering Board and other key implementation bodies, was the final authority with regard to implementing the civilian aspects. UNMIBH, which comprised a UN civilian office, IPTF and MAC, reported to the Secretary-General through the United Nations Coordinator.

Appointment of High Representative. On 12 July, the PIC Steering Board designated Wolfgang Petritsch (Austria) as High Representative to succeed Carlos Westendorp (Spain).

SECURITY COUNCIL ACTION

On 3 August [meeting 4030], the Security Council unanimously adopted **resolution 1256(1999)**. The draft [S/1999/834] was prepared in consultations among Council members.

The Security Council,

Recalling its resolutions 1031(1995) of 15 December 1995, 1088(1996) of 12 December 1996 and 1112(1997) of 12 June 1997,

Recalling also the General Framework Agreement for Peace in Bosnia and Herzegovina and the annexes thereto (collectively the "Peace Agreement") and the conclusions of the Peace Implementation Conferences held in Bonn on 9 and 10 December 1997 and Madrid on 15 and 16 December 1998,

1. *Welcomes and agrees* to the designation by the Steering Board of the Peace Implementation Council on 12 July 1999 of Mr. Wolfgang Petritsch as High Representative in succession to Mr. Carlos Westendorp;

2. *Pays tribute* to the efforts of Mr. Westendorp in his work as High Representative;

3. *Reaffirms* the importance it attaches to the role of the High Representative in pursuing the implementation of the General Framework Agreement for Peace in Bosnia and Herzegovina and the annexes thereto (collectively the "Peace Agreement") and giving guidance to and coordinating the activities of the civilian organizations and agencies involved in assisting the parties to implement the Peace Agreement;

4. *Reaffirms also* the final authority of the High Representative in theatre regarding the interpretation of annex 10 on civilian implementation of the Peace Agreement.

Reports of High Representative. The High Representative reported on the implementation process during the year, covering the periods January to March [S/1999/524], April to June [S/1999/798] and June to October [S/1999/1115]. A later report [S/2000/376] covered activities during the remainder of the year. He described progress in the civilian implementation of the Peace Agreement, which he had been mandated to monitor, mobilize and coordinate. (For details, see below under specific subjects.)

In addition to the regular PIC Steering Board meetings at the political director level (see p. 313), the High Representative convened weekly meetings at the ambassadorial level in Sarajevo.

UN Mission in Bosnia and Herzegovina (UNMIBH)

Special Representative and Coordinator. On 2 August, Jacques Paul Klein (United States) succeeded Elisabeth Rehn (Finland) as the Secretary-General's Special Representative and Coordinator of United Nations Operations in Bosnia and Herzegovina [S/1999/774, S/1999/775]. On 6 April, Brigadier-General Detlef Buwitt (Germany) succeeded Richard Monk (United Kingdom) as Commissioner of IPTF [S/1999/287, S/1999/288].

Reports of Secretary-General (March and June). On 16 March [S/1999/284], the Secretary-General reported that IPTF continued efforts to restructure and reform the police services in the Federation of Bosnia and Herzegovina (the Federation). Progress was slow in Ljubuski and Livno cantons, where the inauguration of the police had still not taken place. UNMIBH made progress towards achieving minority quotas in the Federation. The cantonal working groups on minority police recruitment and return had identified and screened over 700 minority applicants and had begun to identify experienced minority officers for transfer within the Federation police service and between the two entities. In Republika Srpska, progress in police restructuring and reform was slow but significant. UNMIBH and Ministry of the Interior officials met weekly to ensure that the deadlines contained in the Framework Agreement on Police Restructuring, Reform and Democratization [YUN 1998, p. 333] were met. IPTF continued to expand its programme of co-location in the Federation and Republika Srpska with the goal of comprehensive coverage down to middle-management levels of the police administrations. Its advisers were deployed at police stations in both entities and in all nine public security centres in Republika Srpska and in the Federation's 10 cantonal Ministries of the Interior. An inter-entity advisory team on automobile theft was formed, as was an inter-entity planning effort to address organized crime along the inter-entity boundary line. In the area of police certification and training, UNMIBH established a Drug Control Unit, an Organized Crime Unit and a Public Order and Critical Incident Management Unit. It also assisted Federation authorities to assume greater responsibility and control over the police academy and was seeking funding to expand the academy's capacity from 120 to 500 places in each class. In Republika Srpska, it was working with the authorities to identify a site for a new police academy and was pursuing funding projects for its construction.

The Secretary-General observed that further progress in police reform would require tangible material support for the modernization of the country's police infrastructure from a donor community, whose support for police restructuring and reform had been relatively modest.

The Secretary-General noted that the establishment of self-sustaining political institutions continued to present a major challenge, and the prospects remained bleak for the return of refugees and displaced persons to their homes on any meaningful scale. It also appeared that the most significant progress came most frequently from initiatives by the High Representative, rather than from officials in the country itself. The continuing close cooperation of UNMIBH with the Office of the United Nations High Commissioner for Refugees (UNHCR), SFOR, the Office of the High Representative and the Organization for Security and Cooperation in Europe (OSCE) would be necessary to address those impediments to a sustainable peace. The Secretary-General emphasized that the support of SFOR would remain essential in providing adequate security arrangements for the successful implementation of UNMIBH's mandate. He appealed to Security Council members to extend their full diplomatic support to UNMIBH efforts to implement its core mandate of creating professional, multi-ethnic police services in the Federation and Republika Srpska.

In June [S/1999/670], the Secretary-General said that there was progress towards completing the provisional certification and training of existing officers by 31 December. A model identification card was agreed upon for issue to Republika Srpska officers upon their registration, and the Ministry of the Interior had created a division for the investigation of citizens' allegations of police misconduct and had drafted a code of ethics for police. However, the vacuum caused by the killing on 16 March of the Bosnian-Croat Deputy Minister of the Interior halted the reorganization of the Federation Ministry and impeded police restructuring throughout the Federation. Nevertheless, UNMIBH made progress in establishing a multi-ethnic police force in the Croat-majority community of Zepce and towards achieving minority quotas. Following reports of unregistered police officers in the Federation, IPTF acted to ensure that all 10,627 police officers serving in each canton were duly registered. A total of 10,808 officers in the Federation had completed human dignity training and 9,573 had completed transitional training, as well as 6,846 and 3,269, respectively, in Republika Srpska. In areas where training in the two basic courses was complete, IPTF training shifted to more specialized subjects, such as drug awareness and community policing. IPTF continued to implement its non-compliance policy, receiving between 28 February and 26 May some 90 reports of non-compliance of law enforcement agents with their obligations. During the reporting period, the IPTF Non-Compliance Unit recommended the decertification of 18 individuals responsible for 35 instances of non-compliance. Another 11 were recommended for decertification for human rights violations and six more were recommended following background checks by the International Tribunal for the Former Yugoslavia. UNMIBH was developing methods to compel authorities in the Federation and Republika Srpska to dismiss decertified officials promptly. IPTF worked with the UNMIBH Human Rights Office and Civil Affairs Unit, SFOR and UNHCR to establish a monitoring programme for incoming refugees from FRY.

Political developments in Bosnia and Herzegovina and in the wider region continued to challenge the establishment of the rule of law, the Secretary-General stated. Progress was difficult in Republika Srpska due to continuing opposition to multi-ethnic police among a significant part of the political forces there. There was also increasing insecurity associated with the popular response against the establishment of the Brcko District and the dismissal of Republika Srpska President Poplasen, as well as increasing tension and economic deprivation following the NATO air strikes in FRY. Progress in developing self-sustaining institutions in the Federation was complicated by the killing of the Deputy Minister of the Interior, by disappointing progress in sustaining the returns of minorities and by the possibility of revising fundamental principles of the Peace Agreement. On the other hand, broad sectors of the population were willing to use the mechanisms of integration, in particular the common licence plate and the common currency, to establish and deepen contacts between the two entities.

SECURITY COUNCIL ACTION

On 18 June [meeting 4014], the Security Council unanimously adopted **resolution 1247(1999)**. The draft [S/1999/688] was sponsored by Canada, France, Germany, Italy, the Netherlands, the Russian Federation, the United Kingdom and the United States.

The Security Council,

Recalling all its previous relevant resolutions concerning the conflicts in the former Yugoslavia, including resolutions 1031(1995) of 15 December 1995, 1035(1995) of 21 December 1995, 1088(1996) of 12 December 1996, 1144(1997) of 19 December 1997, 1168(1998) of 21 May 1998, 1174(1998) of 15 June 1998 and 1184(1998) of 16 July 1998,

Reaffirming its commitment to the political settlement of the conflicts in the former Yugoslavia, preserving the sovereignty and territorial integrity of all States there within their internationally recognized borders,

Underlining its commitment to supporting implementation of the General Framework Agreement for Peace in Bosnia and Herzegovina and the annexes thereto (collectively the "Peace Agreement"),

Emphasizing its appreciation to the High Representative, the Commander and personnel of the multinational Stabilization Force, the Special Representative of the Secretary-General and the personnel of the United Nations Mission in Bosnia and Herzegovina, including the Commissioner and personnel of the International Police Task Force, and the personnel of other international organizations and agencies in Bosnia and Herzegovina for their contributions to the implementation of the Peace Agreement,

Noting that the States in the region must play a constructive role in the successful development of the peace process in Bosnia and Herzegovina, and noting especially the obligations of the Republic of Croatia and the Federal Republic of Yugoslavia in this regard as signatories to the Peace Agreement,

Emphasizing that a comprehensive and coordinated return of refugees and displaced persons throughout the region continues to be crucial to lasting peace,

Taking note of the declaration of the Ministerial Meeting of the Peace Implementation Council in Madrid on 16 December 1998 and the conclusions of its previous meetings,

Noting the reports of the High Representative, including his latest report of 5 May 1999,

Having considered the report of the Secretary-General of 11 June 1999,

Determining that the situation in the region continues to constitute a threat to international peace and security,

Determined to promote the peaceful resolution of the conflicts in accordance with the purposes and principles of the Charter of the United Nations,

Acting under Chapter VII of the Charter,

I

1. *Reaffirms once again* its support for the General Framework Agreement for Peace in Bosnia and Herzegovina and the annexes thereto (collectively the "Peace Agreement"), as well as for the Dayton Agreement on implementing the Federation of Bosnia and Herzegovina of 10 November 1995, calls upon the parties to

comply strictly with their obligations under those Agreements, and expresses its intention to keep the implementation of the Peace Agreement, and the situation in Bosnia and Herzegovina, under review;

2. *Reiterates* that the primary responsibility for the further successful implementation of the Peace Agreement lies with the authorities in Bosnia and Herzegovina themselves and that the continued willingness of the international community and major donors to assume the political, military and economic burden of implementation and reconstruction efforts will be determined by the compliance and active participation by all the authorities in Bosnia and Herzegovina in implementing the Peace Agreement and rebuilding a civil society, in particular in full cooperation with the International Tribunal for the Prosecution of Persons Responsible for Serious Violations of International Humanitarian Law Committed in the Territory of the Former Yugoslavia since 1991, in strengthening joint institutions and in facilitating returns of refugees and displaced persons;

3. *Reminds* the parties once again that, in accordance with the Peace Agreement, they have committed themselves to cooperate fully with all entities involved in the implementation of this peace settlement, as described in the Peace Agreement, or which are otherwise authorized by the Security Council, including the International Tribunal for the Former Yugoslavia, as it carries out its responsibilities for dispensing justice impartially, and underlines the fact that full cooperation by States and entities with the International Tribunal includes the surrender for trial of all persons indicted by the Tribunal and provision of information to assist in Tribunal investigations;

4. *Emphasizes its full support* for the continued role of the High Representative in monitoring the implementation of the Peace Agreement and giving guidance to and coordinating the activities of the civilian organizations and agencies involved in assisting the parties to implement the Peace Agreement, and reaffirms that the High Representative is the final authority in theatre regarding the interpretation of annex 10 on civilian implementation of the Peace Agreement and that in case of dispute he may give his interpretation and make recommendations, and make binding decisions as he judges necessary on issues as elaborated by the Peace Implementation Council in Bonn on 9 and 10 December 1997;

5. *Expresses its support* for the declaration of the Ministerial Meeting of the Peace Implementation Council in Madrid on 16 December 1998;

6. *Recognizes* that the parties have authorized the multinational force referred to in paragraph 10 below to take such actions as required, including the use of necessary force, to ensure compliance with annex 1-A of the Peace Agreement;

7. *Reaffirms its intention* to keep the situation in Bosnia and Herzegovina under close review, taking into account the reports submitted pursuant to paragraphs 18 and 25 below, and any recommendations those reports might include, and its readiness to consider the imposition of measures if any party fails significantly to meet its obligations under the Peace Agreement;

II

8. *Pays tribute* to those Member States which participated in the multinational Stabilization Force established in accordance with its resolution 1088(1996), and welcomes their willingness to assist the parties to the Peace Agreement by continuing to deploy a multinational Stabilization Force;

9. *Notes* the support of the parties to the Peace Agreement for the continuation of the Stabilization Force, set out in the declaration of the Ministerial Meeting of the Peace Implementation Council in Madrid;

10. *Authorizes* the Member States acting through or in cooperation with the organization referred to in annex 1-A of the Peace Agreement to continue for a further planned period of twelve months the Stabilization Force as established in accordance with its resolution 1088(1996) under unified command and control in order to fulfil the role specified in annexes 1-A and 2 of the Peace Agreement, and expresses its intention to review the situation with a view to extending this authorization further as necessary in the light of developments in the implementation of the Peace Agreement and the situation in Bosnia and Herzegovina;

11. *Authorizes* the Member States acting under paragraph 10 above to take all necessary measures to effect the implementation of and to ensure compliance with annex 1-A of the Peace Agreement, stresses that the parties shall continue to be held equally responsible for compliance with that annex and shall be equally subject to such enforcement action by the Stabilization Force as may be necessary to ensure implementation of that annex and the protection of the Force, and takes note that the parties have consented to the Force taking such measures;

12. *Authorizes* Member States to take all necessary measures, at the request of the Stabilization Force, either in defence of the Force or to assist the Force in carrying out its mission, and recognizes the right of the Force to take all necessary measures to defend itself from attack or threat of attack;

13. *Authorizes* the Member States acting under paragraph 10 above, in accordance with annex 1-A of the Peace Agreement, to take all necessary measures to ensure compliance with the rules and procedures established by the Commander of the Stabilization Force, governing command and control of airspace over Bosnia and Herzegovina with respect to all civilian and military air traffic;

14. *Requests* the authorities in Bosnia and Herzegovina to cooperate with the Commander of the Stabilization Force to ensure the effective management of the airports of Bosnia and Herzegovina, in the light of the responsibilities conferred on the Force by annex 1-A of the Peace Agreement with regard to the airspace of Bosnia and Herzegovina;

15. *Demands* that the parties respect the security and freedom of movement of the Stabilization Force and other international personnel;

16. *Invites* all States, in particular those in the region, to continue to provide appropriate support and facilities, including transit facilities, for the Member States acting under paragraph 10 above;

17. *Recalls* all the agreements concerning the status of forces as referred to in appendix B to annex 1-A of

the Peace Agreement, and reminds the parties of their obligation to continue to comply therewith;

18. *Requests* the Member States acting through or in cooperation with the organization referred to in annex 1-A of the Peace Agreement to continue to report to the Council, through the appropriate channels and at least at monthly intervals;

* * *

Reaffirming the legal basis in the Charter of the United Nations on which the International Police Task Force was given its mandate in resolution 1035(1995),

III

19. *Decides* to extend the mandate of the United Nations Mission in Bosnia and Herzegovina, which includes the International Police Task Force, for an additional period terminating on 21 June 2000, and also decides that the Task Force shall continue to be entrusted with the tasks set out in annex 11 of the Peace Agreement, including the tasks referred to in the conclusions of the Peace Implementation Conferences held in London on 4 and 5 December 1996, Bonn on 9 and 10 December 1997, Luxembourg on 9 June 1998 and Madrid on 15 and 16 December 1998, and agreed by the authorities in Bosnia and Herzegovina;

20. *Requests* the Secretary-General to keep the Council regularly informed on the work of the International Police Task Force and its progress in assisting the restructuring of law enforcement agencies and the progress of the Mission in monitoring and assessing the court system, and to report every three months on the implementation of the mandate of the Mission as a whole;

21. *Reiterates* that the successful implementation of the tasks of the International Police Task Force rests on the quality, experience and professional skills of its personnel, and once again urges Member States, with the support of the Secretary-General, to ensure the provision of such qualified personnel;

22. *Reaffirms* the responsibility of the parties to cooperate fully with, and to instruct their respective responsible officials and authorities to provide their full support to, the International Police Task Force on all relevant matters;

23. *Reiterates its call upon* all concerned to ensure the closest possible coordination between the High Representative, the Stabilization Force, the Mission and the relevant civilian organizations and agencies so as to ensure the successful implementation of the Peace Agreement and of the priority objectives of the civilian consolidation plan, as well as the security of personnel of the International Police Task Force;

24. *Urges* Member States, in response to demonstrable progress by the parties in restructuring their law enforcement institutions, to intensify their efforts to provide, on a voluntary-funded basis and in coordination with the International Police Task Force, training, equipment and related assistance for local police forces in Bosnia and Herzegovina;

25. *Requests* the Secretary-General to continue to submit to the Council reports from the High Representative, in accordance with annex 10 of the Peace Agreement and the conclusions of the Peace Implementation Conference held in London, and later Peace Implementation Conferences, on the implementation of the Peace Agreement and in particular on compliance by the parties with their commitments under that Agreement;

26. *Decides* to remain seized of the matter.

Reports of Secretary-General (September and December). In September [S/1999/989], the Secretary-General reported that the return of normal security conditions in Bosnia and Herzegovina following the Kosovo crisis (see p. 333) had enabled progress in the implementation of UNMIBH's mandate. As of mid-September, UNMIBH resumed activities in all parts of Republika Srpska. Minority recruitment outside Brcko began in earnest when the Republika Srpska police academy was provisionally opened in July. The Republika Srpska police force still had only 182 minority officers, 110 of whom were in Brcko, well short of the first benchmark set by the Peace Agreement. In the Federation, the cantons and the Ministry of the Interior had yet to work out durable arrangements on cost sharing and employment contracts for minority officers. However, steps were taken to promote the establishment of cohesive police forces, particularly in cantons with substantial mixed populations, primarily in Central Bosnia and Mostar. The Anti-Terrorist Unit of the Federation Ministry of the Interior was still undergoing IPTF special training and selection procedures. However, no progress was made in the unification of the Unit, which remained ethnically divided. The size of the Unit was to be reduced from 242 to 123, but those efforts were contingent upon the reorganization and reallocation of positions within the Federation Ministry. IPTF and the UNMIBH judicial assessment programme instituted a Federation-wide court police force of 351 officers. UNMIBH intended to ensure that the force provided security for the court system, as confidence in the impartiality of the regular police forces was still open to question. The Secretary-General also reported that, with the phasing out of the IPTF-administered basic training, the training for cadets would increasingly be taken over by the Federation and Republika Srpska police academies, and efforts were under way to increase their capacity. UNMIBH was streamlining and concentrating support for the local police in Bosnia and Herzegovina to avoid duplication and parallel efforts by donors, and was completing the standardization of equipment.

The Secretary-General noted that, despite the progress achieved, in both entities the leadership of each of the ethnic communities continued to demonstrate a serious lack of political will to improve the functioning of the police and judiciary in line with international standards. UNMIBH faced constant difficulties in recruiting minority police officers and experienced inordinate delays due to the parties' failure to agree on and display neutral insignia. The difficulties posed by political obstructionism were compounded by a lack of employment and economic development opportunities in many areas, in particular with respect to areas of potential minority returns. During a time of increased calls for international resources for Kosovo and other parts of the world and when donor fatigue for Bosnia and Herzegovina was very real, the continued unwillingness of substantial parts of the local leadership to create conditions conducive to returns and to the integral implementation of the Peace Agreement could not be tolerated, the Secretary-General said. He reminded the leadership of each community that international economic and reconstruction support depended on compliance with their obligations and commitments, and they needed to reconfirm those commitments and pursue them more vigorously.

In December [S/1999/1260], the Secretary-General stated that intensified efforts in police registration, minority recruitment, exposing parallel police structures and the establishment of common institutions, such as the State Border Service, had begun to bear fruit. In November, UNMIBH commenced the establishment of the Law Enforcement Personnel Registry, which was expected to take at least two years and would result in the first-ever authoritative, comprehensive and transparent register of the approximately 20,000 authorized police officers in Bosnia and Herzegovina. The process would also assist in identifying parallel police structures by registering and checking any other personnel who currently had regular and free access to Interior Ministry facilities.

Despite limited space and facilities, the two recently established police academies commenced their second intakes of minority recruits. UNMIBH was pursuing several methods to accelerate the establishment of multi-ethnic police forces, including encouraging refugee former police officers to return to Bosnia and Herzegovina with the assistance of the International Organization for Migration, recruiting displaced former police officers and assisting them to return to their homes of origin, and arranging for the exchange of officers between Republika Srpska and the Federation.

Comprehensive and intrusive inspections and audits of police facilities continued to reveal grave deficiencies in supposedly unified police structures in ethnically mixed cantons of the Federation, further confirming the existence of parallel budgets and personnel systems, undeclared police personnel, separate crime databases and shortcomings in the chain of command that constituted major impediments to professional and democratic policing. UNMIBH was intensifying its use of intrusive audits and micro-audit mechanisms to examine, analyse and compare specific aspects of policing in different police administrations. It also expanded its co-location policy to enable closer scrutiny of police behaviour and provide on-the-job advice and training. In addition, civil affairs advisers were assigned to the Ministries of the Interior of both entities and of Mostar.

UNMIBH had begun to develop a more effective system of reporting on non-compliance and a more robust policy of decertification. Of particular concern was the refusal of several Bosnian Croat police administrations and judicial institutions to comply with the High Representative's decision on the removal of non-neutral and offensive insignia in the Federation. In cooperation with the High Representative, UNMIBH was pursuing a policy of targeted pressure to overcome political obstruction from the leaderships of certain cantons.

The Secretary-General stated that, during his visit to Bosnia and Herzegovina from 11 to 13 October, he noted that the substantial progress in physical reconstruction had not been matched by progress in political integration, social reconciliation and economic development. He had emphasized to the leaders of the country that they should make stronger efforts to breathe life into their common institutions and fully support the rule of law and the return of refugees and displaced persons. He therefore welcomed the November New York Declaration (see p. 314). However, in view of subsequent statements made by some members of the Joint Presidency, which appeared to detract from the Declaration and other commitments, the Secretary-General suggested that the Council might wish to reinforce the message that the people of Bosnia and Herzegovina expected their leaders to meet their responsibilities and commitments in full.

UNMIBH had made steady progress in laying the foundations for effective rule-of-law institutions. The gradual decline in the high national crime rate and an increased willingness of rank-and-file police officers and many judicial officials to perform their work in a professional manner were encouraging signs of new attitudes. They had to be supported by the people of Bosnia and Herzegovina and by the international community in order to overcome entrenched opposition from extremist political interests and criminals, the Secretary-General stated.

UNMIBH financing

The Secretary-General submitted to the General Assembly in January [A/53/800] the proposed budget for the maintenance of UNMIBH, including UNMOP (see p. 308) and the United Nations liaison offices in Belgrade and Zagreb, for the period 1 July 1999 to 30 June 2000. He proposed a total of $168,234,000 gross ($158,196,000 net) for the period.

ACABQ, in April [A/53/895/Add.6], made recommendations on the Secretary-General's proposed budget and on UNMIBH's financial performance for the period 1 July 1997 to 30 June 1998 [YUN 1998, p. 335]. The Committee was of the opinion that the budget for 1 July 1999 to 30 June 2000 should not exceed $167.6 million gross.

GENERAL ASSEMBLY ACTION

On 8 June [meeting 101], the General Assembly, on the recommendation of the Fifth Committee [A/53/985], adopted **resolution 53/233** without vote [agenda item 138].

Financing of the United Nations Mission in Bosnia and Herzegovina

The General Assembly,

Having considered the reports of the Secretary-General on the financing of the United Nations Mission in Bosnia and Herzegovina and the related reports of the Advisory Committee on Administrative and Budgetary Questions,

Recalling Security Council resolution 1035(1995) of 21 December 1995, by which the Council established the United Nations Mission in Bosnia and Herzegovina for an initial period of one year, and Council resolution 1174(1998) of 15 June 1998, by which the Council extended the mandate of the Mission until 21 June 1999,

Recalling also Security Council resolution 1222(1999) of 15 January 1999, in which the Council authorized the United Nations military observers to continue to monitor the demilitarization of the Prevlaka peninsula until 15 July 1999,

Recalling further its decision 50/481 of 11 April 1996 on the financing of the Mission and its subsequent resolutions and decisions thereon, the latest of which was resolution 52/243 of 26 June 1998,

Reaffirming that the costs of the Mission are expenses of the Organization to be borne by Member States in accordance with Article 17, paragraph 2, of the Charter of the United Nations,

Recalling its previous decisions regarding the fact that, in order to meet the expenditures caused by the Mission, a different procedure is required from that applied to meet expenditures of the regular budget of the United Nations,

Taking into account the fact that the economically more developed countries are in a position to make relatively larger contributions and that the economically less developed countries have a relatively limited capacity to contribute towards such an operation,

Bearing in mind the special responsibilities of the States permanent members of the Security Council, as indicated in General Assembly resolution 1874(S-IV) of 27 June 1963, in the financing of such operations,

Noting with appreciation that voluntary contributions have been made to the Mission,

Mindful of the fact that it is essential to provide the Mission with the necessary financial resources to enable it to fulfil its responsibilities under the relevant resolutions of the Security Council,

1. *Takes note* of the status of contributions to the United Nations Mission in Bosnia and Herzegovina as at 30 April 1999, including the contributions outstanding in the amount of 38 million United States dollars, representing 8 per cent of the total assessed contributions from the inception of the Mission to the period ending 21 June 1999, notes that some 42 per cent of the Member States have paid their assessed contributions in full, and urges all other Member States concerned, in particular those in arrears, to ensure payment of their outstanding assessed contributions;

2. *Expresses concern* about the financial situation with regard to peacekeeping activities, in particular as regards the reimbursement of troop contributors, which bear additional burdens owing to overdue payments by Member States of their assessments;

3. *Expresses its appreciation* to those Member States which have paid their assessed contributions in full;

4. *Urges* all other Member States to make every possible effort to ensure payment of their assessed contributions to the Mission in full and on time;

5. *Endorses* the observations and recommendations contained in the report of the Advisory Committee on Administrative and Budgetary Questions;

6. *Requests* the Secretary-General to take all necessary action to ensure that the Mission is administered with a maximum of efficiency and economy;

7. *Also requests* the Secretary-General, in order to reduce the cost of employing General Service staff, to continue efforts to recruit local staff for the Mission against General Service posts, commensurate with the requirements of the Mission;

8. *Takes note* of the fact that the amount of 10,608,000 dollars gross (9,987,600 dollars net) authorized by its decision 52/437 of 18 December 1997 was not utilized and, therefore, no appropriation or apportionment of this amount is required;

9. *Decides* to appropriate the amount of 178,204,381 dollars gross (168,191,981 dollars net) for the maintenance of the Mission for the period from 1 July 1999 to 30 June 2000, inclusive of the amount of 8,865,888 dollars for the support account for peacekeeping operations and the amount of 1,738,493 dollars for the United Nations Logistics Base at Brindisi, Italy, to be apportioned, as an ad hoc arrangement, among Member States at a monthly rate of 14,850,365 dollars gross (14,015,998 dollars net) in accordance with the composition of groups set out in paragraphs 3 and 4 of General Assembly resolution 43/232 of 1 March 1989, as adjusted by the Assembly in its resolutions 44/192 B of 21 December 1989, 45/269 of 27 August 1991, 46/198 A of 20 December 1991, 47/218 A of 23 December 1992, 49/249 A of 20 July 1995, 49/249 B of 14 September 1995, 50/224 of 11 April 1996, 51/218 A to C of 18 December 1996 and 52/230 of 31 March 1998 and its decisions 48/472 A of 23 December 1993 and 50/451 B of 23 December 1995, and taking into account the scale of assessments for the years 1999 and 2000, as set out in its

resolution 52/215 A of 22 December 1997, subject to the decision of the Security Council to extend the mandate of the Mission beyond 30 June 1999;

10. *Decides also* that, in accordance with the provisions of its resolution 973(X) of 15 December 1955, there shall be set off against the apportionment among Member States, as provided for in paragraph 9 above, their respective share in the Tax Equalization Fund of the estimated staff assessment income of 10,012,400 dollars approved for the Mission for the period from 1 July 1999 to 30 June 2000;

11. *Decides further* that, for Member States that have fulfilled their financial obligations to the Mission, there shall be set off against the apportionment, as provided for in paragraph 9 above, their respective share of the unencumbered balance of 21,752,900 dollars gross (19,524,600 dollars net) in respect of the period ending 30 June 1998;

12. *Decides* that, for Member States that have not fulfilled their financial obligations to the Mission, their share of the unencumbered balance of 21,752,900 dollars gross (19,524,600 dollars net) in respect of the period ending 30 June 1998 shall be set off against their outstanding obligations;

13. *Invites* voluntary contributions to the Mission in cash and in the form of services and supplies acceptable to the Secretary-General, to be administered, as appropriate, in accordance with the procedure and practices established by the General Assembly;

14. *Decides* to include in the provisional agenda of its fifty-fourth session the item entitled "Financing of the United Nations Mission in Bosnia and Herzegovina".

The Assembly, on 23 December, decided that the agenda item on the financing of UNMIBH should remain for consideration at its resumed fifty-fourth (2000) session (**decision 54/465**) and that the Fifth Committee should continue consideration of the item at that session (**decision 54/462 A**).

OIOS report. In December [A/54/683], the Secretary-General transmitted to the Assembly the report of the Office of Internal Oversight Services (OIOS) on the investigation into allegations of fraud in travel at UNMIBH, which caused the Organization to suffer an estimated loss of $800,000. Criminal prosecution of the officer involved was initiated in the United States District Court for the Southern District of New York and the investigation was proceeding in Croatia to secure the prosecution of the accomplices. The Department of Peacekeeping Operations concurred with the OIOS findings and recommendations, in particular the recommendation that the report be included in the Lessons Learned programmes, especially for the training of new Chief Administrative Officers and Chiefs of General Services, Finance and Travel before being sent on mission assignments.

International Police Task Force (IPTF)

During 1999, the authorized strength of UNMIBH's International Police Task Force remained at 2,057. However, its actual strength was reduced during the year, mainly due to redeployment to the United Nations Interim Administration in Kosovo (see p. 357). In December, IPTF's strength stood at 1,795.

IPTF continued to restructure and reform the police services in the Federation and Republika Srpska and to monitor the local police. Together with more specialized monitoring, such as co-location and support for local investigations, basic monitoring continued to be the core task of the majority of its officers. The training and certification programme continued to help promote the principles and practices of democratic policing and the depoliticization of the police. IPTF also continued, with SFOR support, to conduct weapons inspections in police facilities, which led to the confiscation of hidden weapons.

Following an incident in Foca in January, in which a crowd became violent and damaged the IPTF station, equipment and two vehicles and injured four IPTF monitors, UNMIBH began a Mission-wide assessment of the vulnerability of IPTF stations and was conducting threat assessments, as well as a review of communications equipment and training.

IPTF pursued its advisory programme rigorously through co-location at all command and functional levels in the Federation and the Republika Srpska police structures, identifying 800 co-location positions to provide advice on management, operational and specialized issues to the local police. It continued specialized training in traffic control, public order and major incident management, organized crime, drug control and dog handling. (See also p. 315 for further information on IPTF activities.)

Mine clearance

The High Representative reported that more than 500 houses, 1.8 million square metres of agricultural land and 26,000 square metres in urban areas were demined in 1999 [S/2000/376]. Nevertheless, he stated in his November report [S/1999/1115] that some 750,000 mines remained unaccounted for in Bosnia and Herzegovina and he estimated that it would take 25 to 30 years to clear most minefields, even if the current level of funding was maintained.

Through the Mine Action Centre and local civil defence organizations, UNHCR recruited six demining teams to survey and mark minefields and undertake demining in priority return areas, the Secretary-General reported in September [S/1999/989]. The Mine Action Board of Donors for Bosnia and Herzegovina concluded a comprehensive review of the entire framework for mine action in the country and made recommendations to strengthen mine action structures and reduce costs. Further financial support would be required to provide capacity-building and technical assistance to the local Demining Commission and mine-action centres, as recommended by the review team, the Secretary-General said.

Civil affairs

In his March report [S/1999/284], the Secretary-General stated that UNMIBH's Civil Affairs Unit had intensified efforts in support of the Mission's core tasks of police and judicial reform by participating in minority recruitment working groups and cooperating with IPTF advisers to cantonal ministries and public security centres. It represented UNMIBH in inter-agency and inter-regional working groups established to address common problems in the Travnik, Mostar, Ljubuski and Livno cantons and worked closely with IPTF and the judicial system assessment programme in developing the weekly report. Two officers were assigned to work wholly on implementation of the Republika Srpska restructuring agreement. The Civil Affairs Training Unit expanded its orientation programme to include all civilian staff and IPTF officials. In June [S/1999/670], the Secretary-General reported that the Civil Affairs Unit had worked closely with IPTF in monitoring border crossings during the recent influx of refugees from FRY. The Civil Affairs Project Unit worked with IPTF on the development of a multi-ethnic border service, minority police recruitment and community policing. It had begun to identify donors to win commitments for assistance in the retraining and employment of demobilized soldiers. Officers were increasingly assisting the UNMIBH judicial system assessment project as it focused on political interference in the judiciary and the monitoring of trials involving accusations of corruption among senior politicians.

Federation issues

The High Representative reported in May [S/1999/524] that the political scene in the Federation was dominated by increasing Croat complaints regarding the situation of the Bosnian Croat people within the Federation and by a deteriorating budget situation. The murder of the Deputy Minister of the Interior in March was a severe blow to the confidence, especially of the Bosnian Croat community. In early February, Bosnian Croat war veterans' organizations launched a campaign against the international community and promoted the concept of a Bosnian Croat "third entity".

In July [S/1999/798], the High Representative reported that the "third entity" discussion had disappeared from the agenda, although the distribution of leaflets in Mostar immediately after the start of the air strikes against FRY (see p. 342) was a sign that it could resurface at any time. Nevertheless, the Croat member of the Presidency, Ante Jelavic, was doing his best to demonstrate moderate behaviour. The Special Relations Agreement between Croatia and the Federation of Bosnia and Herzegovina was approved by the Federation Parliament on 7 May. Significant progress was achieved in developing the annexes to the Agreement, two of which had been signed by both parties, while the remaining proposed annexes had been exchanged and negotiations were nearing completion.

The functioning of the Federation's institutions continued to be a matter of concern. The obstructive behaviour of the Bosnian Croat hardliners in the Federation House of Peoples halted the work of Parliament for almost a month. A main issue in the Federation was corruption. The High Representative said he had taken action to accelerate anti-fraud activities, including the dismissal of the Tuzla canton Minister of the Interior for failure to act. Implementation of the Federation property laws continued to be slow and difficult. The administrative bodies responsible for resolving property claims were still subject to political pressure, often refusing to issue decisions or order the eviction of the current occupants of claimed housing. Only small numbers of double-occupancy cases were being resolved and there was little indication, outside Sarajevo canton, that the legal and administrative mechanisms for return could function without heavy international pressure. Creating conditions for sustainable returns continued to be a major challenge, requiring considerable effort and resources. Municipal authorities took little or no responsibility for providing basic services to returnees, particularly in Croat municipalities in Herzegovina. High-level non-implementation in the mixed cantons was a serious problem. In particular, the problem of filling positions in the Ministry of the Interior in Travnik canton had not been resolved. The situation in Mostar had not seen any significant improvement either, due to obstruction on both sides. Since early April, phase I returns (to empty and damaged private property) and assessment visits involving Bosniacs and Serbs had gathered pace, but Croats still showed a marked reluctance to return. Resolving double occupancy, which was particularly bad in the Mostar area and endemic in West Mostar, was the major stumbling block to the return process. While the legal framework to resolve double occupancy was in place, political obstruction and ineffective municipal housing offices made the issue a particularly difficult one to resolve.

In November [S/1999/1115], the High Representative said that the overall situation remained difficult and complicated. The Federation House of Peoples often found its work delayed by the inability of the Bosniac and Croat representatives to work together. The security situation remained stable, albeit with occasional incidents. In October, Radio Mostar's operations were suspended for three months after broadcasting calls for Bosnian Croat war veterans to mass during an SFOR operation seeking information on alleged illegal activities. Tensions in Drvar rose following Serb returns to the town, resulting in the duly-elected Serb mayor being unable to carry out his duties. The High Representative and the head of the OSCE mission replaced him and the Croat deputy mayor who had been a source of obstruction. Recognizing that the Drvar problem reflected much broader political circumstances, the High Representative also removed the cantonal Minister of Justice from office and strongly warned the cantonal Minister of the Interior that further obstruction of returns would lead to his dismissal also. On 20 July, the mayor of Sanski Most was suspended pending investigations into corruption charges. Mostar remained in serious deadlock; the persistent refusal of the Croats and Bosniacs to work together at the cantonal level reduced any possibility of a functional city administration and embodied the general dysfunction in the Federation structures.

In September, the education issue returned to the forefront. With more returns in the Federation, there were more minority communities that needed to provide education for their children and who could not or would not attend a local school run by another constituent people. The issue cut across all constituent peoples and had not been handled well by any of the municipalities. The Office of the High Representative was working with international experts to resolve the problem on a Federation-wide basis.

In a later report [S/2000/376], the High Representative said that, on 29 November, he and the OSCE head of mission had dismissed 22 public officials throughout Bosnia and Herzegovina for serious and persistent obstruction of the Peace Agreement; those officials were also barred by the Provisional Election Commission from running in future elections.

Republika Srpska issues

The High Representative reported during 1999 on issues related specifically to Republika Srpska, the entity of the Republic of Bosnia and Herzegovina where primarily Bosnian Serbs resided.

Reports of High Representative (February and May). In his February report [S/1999/139], the High Representative expressed concern that, over four months after the elections [YUN 1998, p. 339], the new President, Nikola Poplasen, had failed to nominate a candidate for Prime Minister who could command a majority in the National Assembly. The Assembly deputies had clearly expressed their support for the current Prime Minister, Milorad Dodik, but President Poplasen refused to nominate him, violating normal democratic procedures and damaging the process of implementation of the Peace Agreement.

In May [S/1999/524], the High Representative reported that, on 5 March, he had removed Mr. Poplasen from office because he had abused his power and blocked the will of the people by hindering the implementation of the election results, refusing to abide by the National Assembly's decisions, consistently impeding the formation of a legitimate government and attempting to trigger instability in Republika Srpska, putting peace at risk. That decision coincided with the Arbitral Tribunal's decision on Brcko (see p. 324). The NATO air campaign in FRY had a significant impact on implementation in Republika Srpska, bringing it to a standstill. Most international staff had to withdraw temporarily from the territory, and the buildings of several embassy offices, international organizations and non-governmental organizations (NGOs) were damaged or destroyed. Mr. Poplasen and other hardliners attempted to exploit the strength of feeling on the Brcko decision and the NATO action to reinforce their positions. The High Representative had urged a freeze on all major political developments, a policy supported by almost all political parties. The National Assembly adopted the Law on Amnesty, which the then-President Poplasen had refused to sign into law.

Communications. In a 5 March statement [S/1999/253], FRY declared Mr. Poplasen's removal an illegitimate and arbitrary act and a gross violation of the Peace Agreement and the Constitutions of Republika Srpska and Bosnia and Herzegovina. The High Representative's action should be considered null and void, as the legally elected President of Republika Srpska could be removed from office only by its citizens and not by international officers. On 11 March [A/53/861-S/1999/270], FRY said that the decisions dismissing President Poplasen and on the Brcko Arbitral Tribunal (see below) seriously devalued and threatened the stabilization of the peace process and the results and progress achieved in the establishment of Bosnia and Herzegovina. It called on the Steering Board to convene an emergency session of PIC to reverse those decisions and re-establish the situation in compliance with the Peace Agreement and the Constitutions of Bosnia and Herzegovina and Republika Srpska.

Reports of High Representative (July and November). In July [S/1999/798], the High Representative reported that although the NATO campaign against FRY had provoked a strong negative reaction, it did not destabilize Republika Srpska. All parties, except former President Poplasen's Radical Party, honoured the agreement to maintain the status quo, allowing the Dodik caretaker Government to continue to function. International assistance mitigated the economic impact of the crisis in FRY, which had done serious damage to Republika Srpska's economic and social situation. The process of return continued, despite the effect of the NATO campaign and concern about the security of returnees in Republika Srpska. There was a small but significant number of returns in eastern Republika Srpska.

The position of President remained vacant as Vice-President Sarovic remained reluctant to take over the office of President unless Mr. Poplasen resigned of his own accord. In the absence of a President capable of nominating a new Prime Minister, the Dodik Government would stay in power until a compromise could be reached. In order to speed up the legislative process in Republika Srpska, the High Representative decided that during the vacuum in the Presidency, the signature of the President would not be required for the publication of adopted laws in the official gazette.

In November [S/1999/1115], the High Representative reported on a number of important developments: the Revised Annex to the Brcko Final Award was announced on 18 August; there was increased pressure from the Federation-based coalition, KCD, on the SLOGA coalition (the three Serb government parties) to participate in the Republika Srpska Government; the Supreme Chief of the Armed Forces, General Talic, was arrested for alleged war crimes (see p. 1215); and deposed President Poplasen tried but failed to dismiss the National Assembly. Despite those events, and a generally unstable political situation, Republika Srpska remained calm. The SLOGA Government distanced itself from the Milosevic regime in FRY and radical notions of a "Greater Serbia". Vice-President Sarovic hinted his willingness to assume the Presidency, but the High Representative did not believe that that would serve the interests of Republika Srpska or political stability in Bosnia and Herzegovina in general. Failure of the two Serb parties to comply with requirements for certification for the April 2000 municipal elections by the 22 October deadline resulted in their not being allowed to participate in those elections.

Brcko and the inter-entity boundary line

Final Arbitral Award

On 5 March [S/1999/524], the Presiding Arbitrator for the Brcko Arbitral Tribunal announced the Final Award on Brcko, which stipulated that the pre-war Brcko municipality (or opstina), which the 1995 Peace Agreement [YUN 1995, p. 544] left divided between the two entities, would be reassembled as a self-governing "neutral district". While most Bosniac and Croat political leaders accepted the Final Award's provisions, virtually all Serb leaders resisted them. The Republika Srpska National Assembly passed a resolution denouncing the Final Award and Serb political parties held protest rallies in Brcko.

FRY, on 6 March [S/1999/243], pointed out that the decision of the Presiding Arbitrator to declare Brcko a district under the sovereignty of Bosnia and Herzegovina had no grounds under the Peace Agreement. FRY considered that the Tribunal's decisions might only refer to the disputed part of the inter-entity boundary line in the area of Brcko, and not to the status of the "Brcko opstina", which was not mentioned anywhere in the Agreement. The decision created in Bosnia and Herzegovina a de facto third entity and represented a flagrant violation of the Agreement and law in general. FRY said that the decision should be reconsidered to ensure unprejudiced deliberations and to bring back the proceedings within the framework of the mandate established by the Peace Agreement.

On 5 March [S/1999/263], the EU issued a statement, in which it welcomed the Arbitral Tribunal's decision and called on the authorities in Bosnia and Herzegovina and in neighbouring countries to live up to their commitment and seize the opportunity to build a self-sustaining peace.

On 11 March [A/53/861-S/1999/270], the FRY Federal Minister for Foreign Affairs called on the members of the Steering Board to convene an emergency session of PIC to reverse the decision.

On 18 August [S/1999/1115], following consultations between the Presiding Arbitrator and interested parties, the Revised Annex to the Brcko Final Award was issued, drawing to a close the arbitration process, which began in 1996 [YUN 1996, p. 293]. NATO air strikes over FRY delayed the

Brcko Supervisor's plans to implement the Final Award for over four months because the Bosnian Serbs refused to cooperate while the air campaign continued. However, as of mid-summer there seemed to be a growing acceptance of the Award among the Bosnian Serb inhabitants of the municipality, but the Bosnian Serb political parties continued to be grudging in their support.

On 7 December [S/2000/376], the Statute of the Brcko District of Bosnia and Herzegovina was made public.

Returns

Minority returns in Bosnia and Herzegovina took place in much greater numbers in 1999 (an estimated 80,000 to 90,000) compared to 1998 (35,000 to 40,000). Many of the returns were spontaneous and in defiance of political obstruction [S/2000/376]. The Property Law Implementation Plan, launched on 27 October, imposed harmonized property legislation in both entities and there was a marked increase in property repossession across the country. Progress was steady in the Bosniac areas of the Federation and in much of Republika Srpska. That progress was in large part due to concerted efforts by the key international agencies to systematize and depoliticize the process. However, obstruction remained at all levels. Problems of administrative integration following return remained, including reconnection to basic utilities, access to documentation, pensions, schooling or prior employment. The Refugee and Reconstruction Task Force would, as a priority, be working with the Economic Task Force to develop economic opportunities for sustaining minority returns.

The return of the displaced within Bosnia and Herzegovina remained inextricably linked to refugee movements elsewhere in the Balkans, particularly Croatia and FRY. Croatian Serbs in Republika Srpska, many of whom wished to return to Croatia and whose movement would free space for Bosniac and Croat return, were of particular concern. However, the procedures for return to Croatia remained obstructive and a complete overhaul was required to enable Croatian Serb refugees to exercise their right to return and instill confidence in the return process.

Human rights

In May [S/1999/524], the High Representative reported an increase in the number of assessment visits by potential returnees, which passed without incident across Bosnia and Herzegovina, but incidents of return-related violence continued to be reported. Attacks on representatives of the international community and minority returnees to Republika Srpska, particularly in Prijedor and Modrica, followed the commencement of NATO air strikes over FRY. IPTF, in January, placed all members of the Stolac Police Administration on three-month probation due to its inadequate response to more than 70 incidents of returnee-related violence and intimidation. IPTF also continued to monitor the investigation of the cantonal police into the murder by bombing of Bosnian Croat police officers in the Travnik area.

In July [S/1999/798], the High Representative reported improvements in the implementation of decisions of the Human Rights Chamber and recommendations of the Ombudsperson. The Federation and the Office of the High Representative agreed on legislative changes to eliminate human rights violations associated with military apartments. Investigation into the events surrounding the Mostar incident in February 1997 [YUN 1997, p. 307] finally took place, and the report of the investigation was transferred to the local prosecutor for action. Difficulties were anticipated in the implementation of decisions requiring the eviction of current occupants of previously abandoned accommodation.

On 1 July [S/1999/1115], the High Representative imposed certain amendments on the Federation's Law on Sale of Apartments with Occupancy Rights in order to implement the decisions of the Human Rights Chamber concerning former Yugoslav National Army apartments.

Implementation of the Textbook Review Project [YUN 1998, p. 340] progressed slowly. The Ministers of Education of both entities agreed to instruct their experts to draw up guidelines regarding the resolution of disputes over basic terminology and the removal of generally offensive material. By the autumn of 1999, the first phase of the textbook review had achieved mixed results. The best level of compliance with the terms of the Textbook Review Agreement was achieved in the Bosniac part of the Federation, followed by the Croat part and finally by Republika Srpska.

The High Representative was concerned by reports of persistent discrimination in economic and social rights. His Office established a Coordinating Group on Economic and Social Rights, which was considering, among many crucial issues, ways to address discrimination in employment.

Judicial reform

In March [S/1999/284], the Secretary-General reported that officers of the UNMIBH judicial system assessment programme, approved by Security Council resolution 1184(1998) [YUN 1998, p. 342], had been deployed to all seven UNMIBH regions to examine institutional, technical and political aspects of the judiciary, paying special attention to the application of new criminal legislation. The programme worked closely with the UNMIBH Human Rights Office and IPTF in developing a strategy on trial monitoring, improving the enforcement of court judgements and developing non-compliance procedures for judicial officials. The programme also developed a database on the Bosnia and Herzegovina judiciary and made proposals to the Office of the High Representative for strengthening the budgeting system, for enhancing administrative law and procedure, and for a pilot study on land registry in the Mostar area.

By June [S/1999/670], the programme's emphasis had changed to issues of special importance, including enforcement of court orders, the security of judges and witnesses, the early phase of the criminal process, planning the implementation of the Final Award on Brcko (see p. 324) and operational involvement in trial monitoring. The report on the first three months of the programme concluded that there were substantial institutional deficiencies, and although further legislative change was required, that alone would not remove the main impediments to the rule of law, which were rooted in the political environment of the court system. Following the completion of the first phase, the programme began to look at the broad, problematic areas of discrimination, the independence of the judiciary, inter-entity cooperation, delays in court proceedings and enforcement of court orders.

The Secretary-General stated in September [S/1999/989] that assessments by the programme had made local judicial officials sensitive to political factors affecting judicial performance, and its work had produced immediate and direct results in judicial administrative and institutional matters.

By December [S/1999/1260], UNMIBH had completed baseline assessments of the functioning of most of the judicial system in Bosnia and Herzegovina, which indicated a grave lack of judicial independence, overt political interference and intimidation of judicial officials and substantial court inefficiencies, all of which undermined public confidence and impeded the return of minorities to their pre-war homes of origin. UNMIBH experts were instrumental in improving court efficiency and practice in areas such as the appointment of judicial officials to long-vacant posts; helping to organize the first inter-entity judiciary meetings since the war to resolve some of the backlog of cases related to property and employment; supporting the prosecution of terrorism and corruption cases; improving the ethnic composition of courts in ethnically mixed cantons; promoting the transfer of the jurisdiction of minor offence courts to the appropriate level; and assisting with the drafting of laws and codes on criminal procedure, courts, and judicial and prosecutorial services.

The High Representative, in November [S/1999/1115], reported that the working groups in both entities responsible for proposing draft laws had completed the drafting of laws to establish an independent judiciary. The Federation Law on Judicial and Prosecutorial Service had been accepted by the Government and was pending action in Parliament. In Republika Srpska, the Law on Courts and Court Service was being reviewed by Council of Europe experts, following which it would be submitted to the National Assembly. The comprehensive judicial reform strategy was completed and presented to the PIC Steering Board in July. It was the road map to the international community's future efforts in judicial reform. In August, laws imposed by the Office of the High Representative regarding the investigation and prosecution of serious crime in the Federation came into effect. Those laws enhanced the authority of the Federation prosecutor in prosecuting Federation-level crimes and in directing and taking charge of prosecutions in cantonal courts.

Economic reform and reconstruction

In May [S/1999/524], the High Representative stated that despite the NATO strikes against FRY, donor commitment in Bosnia and Herzegovina had not faltered. Ongoing projects continued, although at a slower pace in Republika Srpska due to travel restrictions and the closure of international offices. Many reform initiatives and negotiations virtually came to a standstill in early March due to events in Republika Srpska and the Croatian moratorium following the death of the Federation Deputy Minister of the Interior (see p. 322). The reconstruction effort continued at a steady pace, with important projects under implementation in the transport, energy, water and housing sectors.

In July [S/1999/798], the High Representative reported that the Republika Srpska Government had estimated that, as a result of the NATO air strikes, some 30,000 jobs had been put at risk, principally by the disruption of Republika Srpska exports to FRY, its key trading partner before the crisis. The decline in production and trade affected public revenues and social services. Direct budgetary support (from the United States in particular, but also Denmark) had minimized the effects of the air strikes on the overall political and social situation, but the effect of the crisis would be difficult to overcome in the short term. The fifth donors' conference (Brussels, 20-21 May) pledged $1,052 million and met the target of $5.1 billion, under the Priority Reconstruction Programme. The funding requirement excluded the cost of the impact of the Kosovo crisis, estimated to be $90 million for both entities. On 21 June, the Central Bank of Bosnia and Herzegovina celebrated the first anniversary of the Konvertible Marka (KM). Increased use of the KM had expanded internal trade and bolstered economic activities. On 3 June, the Federation adopted amendments to the Law on the Internal Payment System, intended to abolish the monopoly position of the Payment Bureaux over domestic payment transactions. A team of experts developed a strategic plan for the transfer of the Payment Bureaux functions to the appropriate governmental institutions and commercial banks. As of 15 May, the customs policy of Bosnia and Herzegovina was being uniformly applied throughout the country. From 22 April, both entities ceased applying preferential customs treatment to imports from Croatia to the Federation and from FRY to Republika Srpska. A major step forward was the agreement on the harmonization of excise tax rates, signed by the entities on 8 June.

In November [S/1999/1115], the High Representative said that the International Monetary Fund had extended the standby arrangement for Bosnia and Herzegovina, increasing it by a further $23 million to assist the country in dealing with the economic repercussions of the Kosovo crisis. The World Bank approved two balance-of-payments support operations: the second public finance structural adjustment credit for $72 million; and the enterprise and bank privatization credit for $50 million.

The Secretary-General reported in June [S/1999/670] that the United Nations Development Programme (UNDP) continued to focus on capacity-building, mobilization of resources and implementation of projects for mine clearance, area-based reconstruction and development and short-term employment generation. UNDP was also implementing village employment and environmental programmes. It fielded a team of consultants to formulate an integrated recovery programme for Brcko, in support of the implementation of the Final Award (see p. 324).

Media issues

The High Representative reported in November [S/1999/1115] that, in response to the continued failure of the Bosnia and Herzegovina authorities to address deficiencies in the advancement of freedom of expression, he had issued on 30 July a decision on restructuring the public broadcasting system. It established a legal framework for public radio and television to serve the needs of all citizens and created a new Public Broadcasting Service to succeed the existing Radio and Television of Bosnia and Herzegovina. The High Representative also imposed the Law on the Radio-Television of the Federation of Bosnia and Herzegovina, based on the version of the law forwarded by the Federation Government.

A decision on freedom of information and decriminalization of libel and defamation, which sought to ensure full respect for freedom of expression, promote media freedom and allow citizens access to information about the work of governmental bodies, was also issued on 30 July. It required that, by the end of 1999, both entities adopt new legislation treating libel and defamation as civil offences. On 31 August, a decision was issued to ensure that the publicly funded radio and television served the interests of the citizens of Republika Srpska by amending the relevant law and requiring the National Assembly to adopt a new comprehensive law on the entity public broadcaster by February 2000.

Srebrenica

In response to General Assembly resolution 53/35 [YUN 1998, p. 343], the Secretary-General submitted a comprehensive report [A/54/549] on the events dating from the establishment of the safe area of Srebrenica on 16 April 1993 [YUN 1993, p. 451] until the endorsement of the Peace Agreement by the Security Council in resolution 1031(1995) [YUN 1995, p. 548].

The Secretary-General said the tragedy that occurred after the fall of Srebrenica was shocking for the magnitude of the crimes committed and because the enclave's inhabitants believed that the Council's authority, the presence of the United Nations Protection Force (UNPROFOR) peacekeepers and the might of NATO's air power would ensure their safety. Instead, the Bosnian Serb forces ignored the Council, pushed aside UNPROFOR troops and overran the safe area of Srebrenica, assessing correctly that air power would not be used against them. They proceeded to depopulate the territory within 48 hours and executed and buried thousands of men and boys within a matter of days, while their leaders negotiated with the international community.

The Secretary-General said that many of the errors the United Nations made flowed from its well-intentioned effort to keep the peace and apply the rules of peacekeeping when there was no peace to keep. Knowing that any other course of action would jeopardize the lives of the troops, the Council and Member States tried to create or imagine an environment in which the tenets of peacekeeping could be upheld, to stabilize the situation on the ground through ceasefire agreements and to eschew the use of force, except in self-defence. The international community's response to the war in Bosnia and Herzegovina, comprising an arms embargo, humanitarian aid and the deployment of a peacekeeping force, was a poor substitute for more decisive and forceful action to prevent the unfolding horror, the Secretary-General stated. None of the conditions for the deployment of peacekeepers had been met: there was no peace agreement, not even a functioning ceasefire, and there was no clear will to peace and no clear consent by the belligerents. It had become clear that the ability to adapt mandates to the reality on the ground was of critical importance to ensuring that the appropriate force under the appropriate structure was deployed. None of that flexibility was present in the management of UNPROFOR.

There was neither the will to use decisive air power against Serb attacks on the safe areas, nor the means on the ground to repulse them. Two of the safe areas, Srebrenica and Zepa, were demilitarized to a far greater extent than any of the others. However, instead of enhancing their security, it only made them easier targets for the Serbs. The failure to fully comprehend the extent of the Serb war aims might explain in part why the Secretariat and the peacekeeping mission did not react more quickly and decisively when the Serbs initiated their attack on Srebrenica. In fact, the Council was given the impression that the situation was under control and many believed that to be the case. Some instances of incomplete and inaccurate information being given to the Council could be attributed to problems with reporting from the field, but in other instances the reporting might have been illustrative of a more general tendency to assume that the parties were equally responsible for the transgressions that occurred. It was not clear, in any event, that the provision of more fully accurate information to the Council would have led to appreciably different results. In the end, the Bosnian Serb war aims were repulsed on the battlefield and not at the negotiating table, yet the Secretariat had convinced itself that the broader use of force by the international community was beyond its mandate and undesirable.

The fall of Srebrenica was replete with lessons for the Organization and its Member States: when peacekeeping operations were used as a substitute for political consensus they were likely to fail; and peacekeepers should never be deployed where there was no ceasefire or peace agreement, or told to use their peacekeeping tools—lightly armed soldiers in scattered positions—to impose the ill-defined wishes of the international community by military means. If the necessary resources were not provided, and the political, military and moral judgements were not made, the job simply could not be done. Protected zones and safe areas should be demilitarized and established by the agreement of the belligerents, as in the case of the "protected zones" and "safe havens" recognized by international humanitarian law, or they should be truly safe areas, fully defended by a credible military deterrent.

The responsibility for allowing that tragic course of events by its prolonged refusal to use force in the early stages of the war was shared by the Council, the Contact Group and other Governments, which contributed to that delay, as well as by the Secretariat and the mission in the field. Clearly, however, the primary and most direct responsibility lay with the architects and implementers of the attempted genocide in Bosnia. The cardinal lesson of Srebrenica was that a deliberate and systematic attempt to terrorize, expel or murder an entire people should be met decisively with all necessary means, and with the political will to carry the policy through to its logical conclusion.

The Secretary-General concluded that through error, misjudgement and an inability to recognize the scope of the evil, the United Nations failed to help save the people of Srebrenica from the Serb campaign of mass murder, crystallizing a truth understood only too late by the United Nations and the world at large: that Bosnia was as much a moral cause as a military conflict.

GENERAL ASSEMBLY ACTION

On 16 December [meeting 81], the General Assembly adopted **resolution 54/119** [draft: A/54/L.63/Rev.1 & Add.1] without vote [agenda item 42].

The situation in Bosnia and Herzegovina

The General Assembly,

Recalling its resolutions 46/242 of 25 August 1992, 47/1 of 22 September 1992, 47/121 of 18 December 1992, 48/88 of 20 December 1993, 49/10 of 3 November 1994, 51/203 of 17 December 1996, 52/150 of 15 December 1997, 53/35 of 30 November 1998 and all relevant resolutions of the Security Council regarding the situation in Bosnia and Herzegovina,

Reaffirming its support for the independence, sovereignty, legal continuity and territorial integrity of Bosnia and Herzegovina, within its internationally recognized borders,

Also reaffirming its support for the equality of the three constituent peoples and others in Bosnia and Herzegovina as a united country, with two multi-ethnic entities,

Welcoming the General Framework Agreement for Peace in Bosnia and Herzegovina and the annexes thereto (collectively the "Peace Agreement"), signed in Paris on 14 December 1995,

Also welcoming the efforts for the respect, promotion and protection of human rights and the strengthening of the rule of law in all of Bosnia and Herzegovina and for the development of the common institutions that will ensure that Bosnia and Herzegovina functions as an integrated modern State, accountable to its citizens,

Supporting those institutions and organizations of Bosnia and Herzegovina which are engaged in the implementation of the Peace Agreement and the process of reconciliation and reintegration, and noting, however, the insufficient progress by the common institutions of Bosnia and Herzegovina reported in the assessment of the High Representative for the Implementation of the Peace Agreement on Bosnia and Herzegovina before the Security Council on 1 November 1999,

Concerned by the continuing obstructions faced by refugees and displaced persons wishing to return to their pre-war homes, in particular in areas where they would be an ethnic minority, emphasizing the need for all parties and the relevant States and international organizations to create the conditions necessary to facilitate a secure and dignified return, particularly in urban areas such as Sarajevo, Banja Luka and Mostar, and stressing the need for a regional approach to the issue of refugees and displaced persons,

Supporting fully the efforts of the International Tribunal for the Prosecution of Persons Responsible for Serious Violations of International Humanitarian Law Committed in the Territory of the Former Yugoslavia since 1991, stressing the importance and urgency of the work of the International Tribunal as an element of the process of reconciliation and as a factor contributing to the maintenance of international peace and security in Bosnia and Herzegovina and in the region as a whole, demanding that States and parties to the Peace Agreement meet their obligations to cooperate fully with the Tribunal, as required by Security Council resolutions 827(1993) of 25 May 1993, 1022(1995) of 22 November 1995 and 1207(1998) of 17 November 1998, including with respect to surrendering persons sought by the Tribunal, and welcoming the efforts to secure compliance with the orders of the Tribunal, consistent with the Security Council mandate,

Having considered the sixth annual report of the International Tribunal, gravely concerned over the continued obstructionism of certain States and entities in the region with respect to execution of the Tribunal's orders and compliance with obligations under international law, as noted in the report, noting that thirty-five individuals named in public indictments still remain at large, most of them in the territory of the former Yugoslavia, and welcoming the efforts of the High Representative and the Commander of the multinational Stabilization Force in implementing the provisions of the Peace Agreement,

Welcoming the mutual recognition among all the successor States of the former Socialist Federal Republic of Yugoslavia within their internationally recognized borders, and stressing the importance of full normalization of relations, including the unconditional establishment of diplomatic relations among those States in accordance with the Peace Agreement and the settlement of all issues relating to the succession of the former Yugoslavia, in order to contribute to the achievement of lasting peace and stability in the area,

Also welcoming the successful summit meeting of heads of State and Government to launch the Stability Pact for South-Eastern Europe in Sarajevo on 29 and 30 July 1999, and stressing that the Stability Pact offers a broad regional framework for further progress in Bosnia and Herzegovina,

Noting that democratization in the region will enhance the prospects for a lasting peace and help to guarantee full respect for human rights in Bosnia and Herzegovina and in the region,

Stressing the importance of full respect for human rights and fundamental freedoms for the success of the peace efforts for the region, and calling upon the Governments and authorities in the region, as well as the relevant international organizations, to facilitate such full respect,

Welcoming the finalization of a draft of the permanent electoral law, expressing support for early adoption of the draft electoral law by the Parliament, noting that such adoption is a prerequisite for membership of the Council of Europe, and reaffirming the importance of genuine democratic representation of all three constituent peoples in all common institutions,

Noting the positive impact of the five previous pledging conferences, held on 21 December 1995, 13 and 14 April 1996, 25 July 1997, 8 and 9 May 1998 and 30 May 1999 and chaired by the World Bank and the European Union, on the peace process and reintegration of the country as well as the reconstruction effort, stressing the importance and urgency of providing the financial assistance and technical cooperation pledged for reconstruction efforts, and stressing the role of economic revitalization in the process of reconciliation, in the improvement of living conditions and in the maintenance of a durable peace in Bosnia and Herzegovina and in the region,

Stressing that the provision of reconstruction aid and financial assistance is conditional upon the parties meeting their obligations under the Peace Agreement,

Recognizing the importance of demining for the normalization of life and for the return of refugees and internally displaced persons,

Encouraging the efforts at reducing the military assets in line with the Agreement on Subregional Arms Control,

Welcoming the important efforts of the European Union and bilateral and other donors to provide humanitarian and economic assistance for reconstruction,

1. *Expresses its full support* for the General Framework Agreement for Peace in Bosnia and Herzegovina and the annexes thereto (collectively the "Peace Agreement"), which constitute the key mechanism for the achievement of a durable and just peace in Bosnia and Herzegovina, leading to stability and cooperation in the region and the reintegration of Bosnia and Herzegovina at all levels;

2. *Welcomes* the adoption on 15 November 1999 of the New York Declaration, in which the Joint Presidency of Bosnia and Herzegovina agreed to important steps for moving forward the process of fully implementing the Peace Agreement, including the establishment of a State border service, improved inter-entity military cooperation, steps to improve the functioning of common State institutions, including the creation of

a permanent secretariat for the Joint Presidency under one roof, the establishment of a joint commission on refugee returns and the creation of a single national passport;

3. *Demands* that all parties facilitate the full implementation of all aspects of the New York Declaration, including, in particular, the Principles on the Establishment of a State Border Service, in a timely manner;

4. *Notes* the progress that has been made towards the implementation of the Peace Agreement, and reiterates its demands for the full, comprehensive and consistent implementation thereof;

5. *Supports fully* the efforts of the High Representative for the implementation of the Peace Agreement on Bosnia and Herzegovina, in accordance with the Peace Agreement and subsequent Peace Implementation Council declarations, and calls upon all parties to cooperate fully and in good faith with him;

6. *Stresses* the importance of the summit meeting of heads of State and Government to launch the Stability Pact for South-Eastern Europe in Sarajevo on 29 and 30 July 1999;

7. *Endorses* the concept of "ownership" as presented by the High Representative, whereby the citizens of Bosnia and Herzegovina and, in particular, their political leaders, should assume more responsibility in the process of the implementation of the Peace Agreement;

8. *Recognizes* that the role of the international community remains essential, welcomes the readiness of the international community to continue its efforts towards a self-sustaining peace, and recalls that the responsibility for consolidating peace and security lies primarily with the authorities of Bosnia and Herzegovina;

9. *Welcomes* the vital contribution of the multinational Stabilization Force in providing a secure environment for the implementation of civilian aspects of the Peace Agreement, calls for the fullest cooperation by all parties in this regard, expresses its full support for the efforts of the United Nations International Police Task Force in carrying out its mandate, and commends its efforts in the establishment of the rule of law in Bosnia and Herzegovina;

10. *Underlines* the fact that the assistance provided by the international community remains strictly conditional upon compliance with the Peace Agreement and subsequent obligations, including, in particular, cooperation with the International Tribunal for the Prosecution of Persons Responsible for Serious Violations of International Humanitarian Law Committed in the Territory of the Former Yugoslavia since 1991 and facilitation of the return of refugees and displaced persons;

11. *Insists* upon the need to surrender all indictees to the International Tribunal for trial, notes that the Tribunal has the authority to address individual responsibility for the perpetration of the crime of genocide, crimes against humanity and other serious violations of international humanitarian law in Bosnia and Herzegovina, and demands that all the parties fulfil their obligations to hand over to the Tribunal all indicted persons in territories under their control and otherwise to comply fully with the orders of the Tribunal and to cooperate with the work of the Tribunal, including with exhumations and other investigative acts, in accordance with article 29 of the statute of the Tribunal, with all relevant Security Council resolutions and in accordance with the relevant provisions of the Peace Agreement, in particular the Constitution of Bosnia and Herzegovina;

12. *Welcomes* the support given by Member States so far, and urges Member States, taking into account the orders and requests of the International Tribunal, to offer the Tribunal their full support, including financial support, in order to ensure the achievement of the purpose of the Tribunal, and to carry out their obligations under the statute of the Tribunal and all relevant Security Council resolutions;

13. *Reaffirms once again* the right of refugees and displaced persons to return voluntarily to their homes of origin in accordance with the Peace Agreement, in particular annex 7, and the realization of the same in cooperation with the Office of the United Nations High Commissioner for Refugees and host countries, calls upon all parties to improve substantially their cooperation with the international community at the State, entity and local levels, in order to establish immediately the conditions necessary for the return of refugees and displaced persons to their homes and for the freedom of movement and communication of all the citizens of Bosnia and Herzegovina, and calls upon the relevant international organizations to enhance the conditions to facilitate return, in accordance with relevant provisions of the Peace Agreement, in particular the Constitution of Bosnia and Herzegovina, and welcomes continued and new efforts by the United Nations agencies, the European Union, bilateral and other donors and intergovernmental and non-governmental organizations to establish and implement projects designed to facilitate the early voluntary and orderly return of refugees and displaced persons to all regions of Bosnia and Herzegovina, including projects that would help to create a safe and secure environment with increased economic opportunity;

14. *Encourages* the acceleration of the peaceful, orderly and phased return of refugees and displaced persons, including in areas where they would be in the ethnic minority, strongly condemns all acts of intimidation, violence and killings, including those acts designed to discourage the voluntary return of refugees and displaced persons, and demands that such acts be investigated and prosecuted;

15. *Welcomes* the report of the Secretary-General pursuant to paragraph 18 of resolution 53/35, commends him for its thoroughness and candour, condemns the brutal acts described therein, deplores the appalling magnitude of the human tragedy that occurred before and after the fall of Srebrenica and Zepa, notes with deep concern the findings contained in the report, and therefore encourages the Secretary-General and Member States to address these concerns so as to prevent them from recurring in the future, as recommended in the report;

16. *Reaffirms* the previous conclusions of the Peace Implementation Council on the importance of reform of the media in Bosnia and Herzegovina, endorses the decision of the High Representative of 30 July 1999 on the restructuring of the public broadcasting system in Bosnia and Herzegovina, and calls upon the authorities of Bosnia and Herzegovina to implement that decision in full;

17. *Stresses* the importance of establishing, strengthening and expanding throughout all of Bosnia and Herzegovina free and pluralistic media, deplores any action that seeks to intimidate or restrict the freedom of the media, and condemns violent acts of intimidation against journalists;

18. *Supports* the efforts of the High Representative in accordance with the Peace Agreement and subsequent Peace Implementation Council declarations to counter obstructionist conduct against the Peace Agreement and reconciliation efforts, and notes in this regard the decision of the High Representative of 29 November 1999 to remove twenty-two Bosnian public officials;

19. *Reaffirms once again its support* for the principle that all statements and commitments made under duress, in particular those regarding land and property, are wholly null and void, in accordance with the relevant provisions of the Peace Agreement, and supports the effective engagement of the Commission for Real Property Claims of Displaced Persons and Refugees in compliance with its mandate;

20. *Endorses* the package of property law reforms imposed by the High Representative on 27 October 1999 aimed at harmonizing the laws in the two entities in order to enable refugees and displaced persons to return to their pre-war homes, as well as the subsequent action by the High Representative to ensure full implementation of the property implementation package, and calls upon the entity Parliaments to adopt those laws formally and to contribute actively to their speedy implementation;

21. *Emphasizes* the importance of economic revitalization and reconstruction for the successful consolidation of the peace process in Bosnia and Herzegovina, recognizes the important contribution of the international community in this regard, and invites it to continue its efforts;

22. *Notes* that corruption and the lack of transparency seriously hamper the economic development of Bosnia and Herzegovina, emphasizes the importance of combating corruption, welcomes the important contribution made in this regard by the Customs and Fiscal Assistance Office, and expresses its full support for the efforts of the Government of Bosnia and Herzegovina and its local bodies and others that are supportive in this regard;

23. *Supports* the efforts by the High Representative and the Commander of the multinational Stabilization Force, in accordance with the Peace Agreement and subsequent Peace Implementation Council declarations, to weaken the continued political and economic influence of remaining parallel nationalist structures obstructing the peace implementation;

24. *Stresses* the need for a more comprehensive approach to economic reform, which should contribute to the more homogeneous development of the economy and trade in the two entities and across the inter-entity boundary line;

25. *Stresses* the importance of establishing an economic programme that should include the creation of a framework for private-sector development, including privatizations and improvement of foreign investment conditions, the restructuring of banking and capital markets, the reform of the financial system and adequate social protection;

26. *Welcomes* the final arbitration award on Brcko, expresses its support for implementation of the final arbitration award in accordance with the Peace Agreement, and stresses that the obligation to cooperate fully with the Supervisor for Brcko is an essential obligation for the two entities;

27. *Also welcomes* the commitment made by the Joint Presidency of Bosnia and Herzegovina at the summit meeting on the Stability Pact for South-Eastern Europe to reduce unilaterally by 15 per cent the military budgets, equipment and personnel strength of the two entities, effective 31 December 1999, with a significant subsequent reduction thereafter, and calls for the full implementation of those commitments;

28. *Stresses* the need for timely information about the level of cooperation and compliance with the International Tribunal and its orders, the status and programme for the return of refugees and displaced persons to and within Bosnia and Herzegovina and the status and implementation of the Agreement on Subregional Arms Control;

29. *Welcomes* the efforts of international regional organizations, Member States and non-governmental organizations, including through the Board of Donors, and the Slovenian International Trust Fund for Demining and Mine Victims Assistance in Bosnia and Herzegovina, and invites Member States to continue to support the mine-action activities in Bosnia and Herzegovina;

30. *Commends* the efforts of the international community, including the Council of Europe, the European Union, the European Community Monitoring Mission, the European Bank for Reconstruction and Development, the International Committee of the Red Cross, the International Monetary Fund, the multinational Stabilization Force, non-governmental organizations, the Organization of the Islamic Conference, the Islamic Development Bank, the Islamic Chamber of Commerce and Industry, the Organization for Security and Cooperation in Europe, the Peace Implementation Council and the World Bank, in their roles in the implementation of the Peace Agreement;

31. *Commends* in particular the efforts of the International Tribunal for the Prosecution of Persons Responsible for Serious Violations of International Humanitarian Law Committed in the Territory of the Former Yugoslavia since 1991, the Office of the High Representative for the Implementation of the Peace Agreement on Bosnia and Herzegovina, the Office of the Special Rapporteur of the Commission on Human Rights on the situation of human rights in the territory of the former Yugoslavia, the Office of the United Nations High Commissioner for Refugees, the Office of the United Nations High Commissioner for Human Rights, the United Nations International Police Task Force, the United Nations Mission in Bosnia and Herzegovina, the United Nations Development Programme and the other United Nations agencies in the peace process, and encourages their further engagement in the peace process in Bosnia and Herzegovina;

32. *Decides* to include in the provisional agenda of its fifty-fifth session the item entitled "The situation in Bosnia and Herzegovina".

On 23 December, the Assembly, by **decision 54/465**, decided that the item on the situation in

Bosnia and Herzegovina would remain for consideration during its resumed fifty-fourth (2000) session.

Military aspects of Agreement

Stabilization Force

During 1999, the NATO Secretary-General reported 10 times to the Security Council, in accordance with resolution 1088(1996) [YUN 1996, p. 310], on the activities of SFOR, also known as Operation Joint Guard [S/1999/48, S/1999/212, S/1999/290, S/1999/419, S/1999/538, S/1999/642, S/1999/768, S/1999/864, S/1999/1041, S/1999/1237]. The strength of the Force, which operated under NATO's leadership, fell from 32,000 in January to 27,000 in December. The troops, which were deployed in Bosnia and Herzegovina and in Croatia, were contributed by all NATO members and 15 non-NATO countries. The Security Council, by **resolution 1247(1999)** of 18 June, authorized NATO member States to continue SFOR for a further period of 12 months (see p. 316). The SFOR Commander, in line with an October decision of the North Atlantic Council, began to implement the SFOR restructuring plan, which called for a gradual reduction in the size, role and profile of the Force. Military presence would be provided in critical areas and identified and emerging hot spots, and focused military support would be provided in areas critical to civil implementation. The restructuring would be accomplished in the spring of 2000.

During the year, SFOR continued to conduct surveillance and reconnaissance by ground and air patrols, and to monitor entity compliance with Security Council resolution 1160(1998) [YUN 1998, p. 369], prohibiting the transport of weapons and the movement of controlled petroleum products into FRY. It also supported IPTF by providing security for its inspection of local police stations and in conducting prison inspections, and provided assistance to international institutions in Bosnia and Herzegovina, including the Office of the High Representative.

In July, the Standing Committee on Military Matters (SCMM) agreed to establish a permanent secretariat for the Committee and two working groups to consider proposals for reducing the Republika Srpska and the Federation armed forces by 15 per cent by the end of the year, and to draw up proposals on a common security policy for Bosnia and Herzegovina. Final plans were announced in December for achieving the 15 per cent defence reduction. The weapons held by the 30 battalions to be disbanded would be stored centrally and subjected to joint monitoring and inspection by SFOR and the entity armed forces. A working group was established to verify the reductions and to agree on plans for storage of weapons. It would also initiate work on a further round of defence reductions for 2000. Concerning the development of a common security policy, the final release of the document agreed to at the 8 December meeting of SCMM was pending.

Communications. FRY, on 4 April [S/1999/372], informed the Council President that SFOR had dynamited the section of the Belgrade-Bar railroad passing through Republika Srpska. It requested an emergency meeting of the Council to condemn the use of SFOR in the aggression against FRY. In letters of 29 May [S/1999/626] and 30 May [S/1999/629], FRY informed the Council of the violations of its border by SFOR and asked the Council to take measures to prevent a repetition of the violation of its sovereignty and territorial integrity. On 7 May [S/1999/531], Bosnia and Herzegovina forwarded to the Council President a letter from Zivko Radisic, Chair of the Presidency of Bosnia and Herzegovina, alleging that NATO was using its territory for operations directed at FRY, and a letter from Alija Izetbegovic, a member of the Presidency, disputing that allegation. Also attached was a letter from the High Representative to Mr. Radisic, noting that it was incumbent upon political leaders to behave within the spirit and the letter of the law.

Federal Republic of Yugoslavia (FRY)

The situation in Kosovo, the southern province of the Republic of Serbia in the Federal Republic of Yugoslavia (Serbia and Montenegro) (FRY), deteriorated rapidly in early 1999 as the warring parties—the forces of FRY and those of the Kosovo Liberation Army (KLA)—failed to implement the agreements reached in 1998 for ending the conflict. Following negotiations in Rambouillet and Paris, France, convened by the Contact Group on the Former Yugoslavia, the Kosovo Albanian delegation signed an Interim Agreement for Peace and Self-Government on 18 March. However, FRY did not sign, claiming that it had not been discussed and agreed to between the parties, and further efforts to persuade FRY President Slobodan Milosevic to accept a ceasefire and a political solution also failed.

On 24 March, NATO launched an air campaign against FRY, an action that sparked a debate as to its validity, as several countries felt that the NATO countries had embarked on a course of action without Security Council authorization.

As the humanitarian situation deteriorated dramatically, the Secretary-General reported that the scale of the disaster was beyond the capacity of the United Nations. The Security Council, on 14 May, invited UNHCR and other international humanitarian relief organizations to extend assistance to all parts of FRY.

In June, FRY accepted a peace plan, proposed by the EU, and the principles set out by the G-8 Foreign Ministers to end the violence. That led to the Council on 10 June authorizing the deployment in Kosovo, under UN auspices, of international civil and security presences. The international security presence (KFOR), with substantial NATO participation, and the United Nations Interim Administration in Kosovo (UNMIK) assumed responsibility for creating and maintaining a secure environment and for the province's civil administration, rehabilitation and economic recovery. On the certification that FRY had complied with resolution 1244(1999) and the military-technical agreement, including withdrawal of its forces, NATO terminated its air campaign. UNMIK and the various UN agencies, together with other international organizations and NGOs, worked to put Kosovo back on a firm footing.

However, a resurgence of violence, directed mainly against Serbs and other non-Albanian minorities in Kosovo, again heightened tension and security concerns as the year progressed.

Situation in Kosovo

Communications. On 2 January [S/1999/2], FRY said that it was important that the Secretary-General's latest report on the situation in Kosovo [YUN 1998, p. 386] had noted the improvement in the humanitarian situation and the unhindered access of humanitarian agencies to the province. However, it did not mention the situation of the Serbian civilians who were under tremendous KLA pressure not to return to their homes. FRY objected to the reference to KLA as "paramilitary units", and said that terrorists calling themselves "the Kosovo Liberation Army" had not been, nor could they be, a military or political factor, that was to say any party to any conflict, since international law had accorded no terrorists any status whatsoever. FRY expected UN Member States to abide by Security Council resolution 1160(1998) [ibid., p. 369] and cut off all forms of assistance, especially financial, to terrorists in Kosovo and Metohija. Accusations about FRY's excessive use of force were unsubstantiated. FRY continued to implement the Holbrooke-Milosevic agreement [ibid., p. 380] and the agreement with OSCE [ibid., p. 381]. It had demonstrated its commitment to solving Kosovo's and Metohija's problems through political means by calling for an immediate and unconditional resumption of dialogue on many occasions. However, the Albanian political parties continued to obstruct all such efforts. It was therefore not appropriate to apportion equal blame for the impasse in the political dialogue.

Albania, on 12 January [S/1999/55], stated that the Holbrooke-Milosevic agreement was far from being implemented. The strong Serb military and police presence in Kosovo was a source of insecurity and of incidents that were of growing concern. The Belgrade authorities were trying to impose a *pax serba*, which was demonstrated by their punitive operations and the continuation of the scorched-earth policy. Albania was facing increasingly aggressive acts of the FRY military, especially at its border with FRY. That, together with FRY's allegations of the existence of terrorists' training camps in Albania, bore the danger of intensifying Serb violence and the potential spreading of the conflict into Albania.

FRY, on 9 January [S/1999/24], reported that the previous day terrorists had ambushed a police patrol near the village of Suva Reka, killing three officers and wounding four. On the same day, eight unarmed Yugoslav Army members were abducted by KLA, north-west of Kosovska Mitrovica, and continued to be held hostage. Those attacks, confirmed by the OSCE Kosovo Verification Mission (KVM), represented a rising aggressiveness of terrorists in recent months aimed at blocking a political solution, provoking retaliation and creating an excuse for foreign intervention. FRY requested the Council to condemn the terrorist acts and call on Member States to treat KLA as a terrorist organization and to take measures immediately to stop any external support to it.

Reports of Secretary-General (January and March). The Secretary-General, reporting on 30 January [S/1999/99], said that the humanitarian and human rights situation in Kosovo remained grave. The October 1998 ceasefire [YUN 1998, p. 380] had reduced the number of internally displaced persons and civilian casualties, the use of heavy weaponry and the destruction of property and means of livelihood. However, violence, including violations of the ceasefire, continued and the human rights situation had further deteriorated, culminating in the massacre of Kosovo Albanians in Racak (see p. 334). The most disturbing new elements were the spread and transformation of the nature of that violence. Calculated acts of violence followed by retaliatory measures now occurred frequently in cities that had been notably exempt from violence. The Office of the United Nations High Commissioner for Human Rights

(OHCHR) had observed that the transformation of the nature of the violence had reduced the geographic area of perceived safety. Assailants selectively fired directly on urban sidewalks and cafes, as well as civilian passenger vehicles, and influential individuals and localities known for open-mindedness and flexibility in community relations were also surgically targeted. The responsibility for targeted killings was increasingly a matter of attribution by one side or another, and the perpetrators had not been brought to justice, suggesting that acts were committed with impunity. The Secretary-General cited a number of incidents between 2 and 13 January, directed mostly at Kosovo Albanians, and the 15 January Racak massacre. He also reported that the 8 January attack on a Yugoslav Army convoy north-east of Kosovska Mitrovica by Kosovo Albanian paramilitary units led to the largest build-up of infantry, armour and artillery since KVM's deployment in October 1998 [YUN 1998, p. 381].

Reports of arbitrary detention and systematic ill-treatment of persons in police detention and under the jurisdiction of the Ministry of Justice continued, said the Secretary-General. OHCHR continued to monitor court proceedings on criminal charges of alleged terrorist and anti-State activity.

As to the humanitarian situation, UNHCR estimated that, as at 20 January, some 190,000 civilians remained displaced within Kosovo, the vast majority of whom were Kosovo Albanians, including some 5,000 displaced in late 1998. At least 20,000 were thought to have been moved to other parts of Serbia, and there were indications that the figure might be higher. Some 25,000 displaced were in the FRY Republic of Montenegro, 22,000 in Albania, 10,000 in Bosnia and Herzegovina, 3,000 in FYROM and an estimated 93,890 persons from FRY had sought asylum in other European countries, of whom 85 to 90 per cent were Kosovo Albanians.

The Secretary-General observed that violence since 24 December 1998, and in particular the Racak massacre on 15 January and subsequent events, had been a major setback for the humanitarian operation, just when KVM was beginning to help create and consolidate conditions for return of the internally displaced. Fear of fighting between the security forces and Kosovo Albanian paramilitary units and continued violence against civilians were the overriding obstacle to return and to its sustainability. He urged those in positions of public authority to put an end to the spiral of violence and seek the path of constructive dialogue.

In March [S/1999/293], the Secretary-General reported that, since 20 January, OHCHR had registered more than 65 cases of violent death, including one in custody. While clashes between Serbian security forces and Kosovo Albanian paramilitary units continued at a relatively lower level, civilians in Kosovo were increasingly becoming the main target of violent acts. Most violent incidents remained unclaimed, contributing to the climate of fear and insecurity, causing deep distrust among communities and adding to the humanitarian and social problems. Targeted violence against civilians was taking new and even more dangerous forms, such as increased terrorist acts against Serb and Albanian establishments in urban areas. The Secretary-General outlined major incidents occurring between 18 January and 17 February, including abductions.

Concerning detentions and trials, according to information released by the Serbian Public Prosecutor, 2,007 persons in Kosovo had been charged with criminal offences of terrorism, endangering the country's territorial integrity and seditious activity. Of those, 1,060 were in detention and 824 were under indictment.

The resumption of hostilities in January and February resulted in new displacements of population. Clashes in the Podujevo area prevented the return of some 15,000 displaced from about 17 villages. Serb and Albanian homes along the main Pristina-Podujevo road remained deserted, as intermittent fighting occurred 3 kilometres away, while in Drenica, Suva Reka, Stimlje, Prizren and Vucitrn, similar clashes led to new displacements of population. February was also marked by the continuing departure of the Serbian population from areas where they were in the minority or where clashes had occurred. According to information provided by the Serbian Commissioner for Refugees, 90 villages in central and western Kosovo had lost their entire Serbian population in recent months, while other towns had seen a reduction. Kosovo Albanians without identity documents were afraid to move from their villages for fear of harassment by the security forces. UNHCR was seeking to prevent further displacements.

Racak massacre

The Secretary-General, in his January report [S/1999/99], said that, between 15 and 18 January, fighting occurred in and around the village of Racak. On 15 January, Serb police and paramilitary units entered the village. On 16 January, KVM reported that the bodies of 45 Kosovo civilians, including three women, at least one child and several elderly men, were found. Many of the dead appeared to have been summarily executed, shot at close range in the head and neck.

On attempting to enter FRY to investigate the Racak deaths, the Chief Prosecutor of the International Tribunal for the Former Yugoslavia

(ICTY), Louise Arbour, was turned back at the border on 18 January. The FRY authorities continued to deny the Chief Prosecutor entry to Kosovo (see p. 336).

On 18 January, some autopsies were performed in the presence of KVM monitors. On 21 January, a Finnish forensic team performed autopsies on the remaining bodies and examined the autopsies done by Serb authorities before its arrival.

Communications. Responding to a statement by KVM head, William Walker, the Serbian President, in a 16 January statement [S/1999/51], said that when police attempted to arrest terrorists who had killed a police officer in the vicinity of Racak, terrorists attacked them with automatic weapons, portable launchers and mortars and the police responded. OSCE was immediately informed and an investigating team arrived at the scene but terrorists opened fire and prevented the on-site investigation. On 16 January, Mr. Walker, accompanied by foreign journalists and those from Albanian separatist newspapers, visited the scene and, in the absence of judicial and other State authorities, made a statement containing falsehoods and personal assessments that were totally baseless. The Serbian President accused Mr. Walker of deceiving world public opinion with fabrications to divert attention from terrorists, murderers and kidnappers and to once again protect them as he had been doing all along. It was another example not only of a one-sided approach but of protecting terrorism and the self-proclaimed terrorist KLA.

Albania, on 16 January [S/1999/52], said the incident showed Belgrade's unwillingness to cooperate with the international community. It was the latest in the chain of Serb carnages and was a well-planned and -executed policy of scorched land and ethnic cleansing. On the same date [S/1999/50], Albania requested an urgent meeting of the Security Council to consider the massacre.

On 18 January [S/1999/56], FRY informed the Secretary-General that it had declared Mr. Walker persona non grata and ordered him to leave the country within 48 hours. FRY said it had done so because of Mr. Walker's unacceptable, unprincipled and insulting behaviour towards the Yugoslav State and authorities. It was determined to continue cooperation with KVM in accordance with the October 1998 agreement [YUN 1998, p. 380]. Annexed to the letter were details regarding the police search and arrest operations in Racak on 15 January. Mr. Walker's expulsion was later unconditionally frozen.

SECURITY COUNCIL ACTION

On 19 January [meeting 3967], following consultations among Security Council members, the President made statement **S/PRST/1999/2** on behalf of the Council:

The Security Council strongly condemns the massacre of Kosovo Albanians in the village of Racak in southern Kosovo, Federal Republic of Yugoslavia, on 15 January 1999, as reported by the Kosovo Verification Mission of the Organization for Security and Cooperation in Europe. It notes with deep concern that the report of the Mission states that the victims were civilians, including women and at least one child. The Council also takes note of the statement by the head of the Mission that the responsibility for the massacre lay with security forces of the Federal Republic of Yugoslavia, and that uniformed members of both the armed forces of the Federal Republic of Yugoslavia and Serbian special police had been involved. The Council emphasizes the need for an urgent and full investigation of the facts and urgently calls upon the Federal Republic of Yugoslavia to work with the International Tribunal for the Prosecution of Persons Responsible for Serious Violations of International Humanitarian Law Committed in the Territory of the Former Yugoslavia since 1991 and the Mission to ensure that those responsible are brought to justice.

The Council deplores the decision by Belgrade to declare the head of the Mission, William Walker, persona non grata, and reaffirms its full support for Mr. Walker and the efforts of the Organization for Security and Cooperation in Europe to facilitate a peaceful settlement. It calls upon Belgrade to rescind this decision and to cooperate fully with Mr. Walker and the Mission.

The Council deplores the decision by the Federal Republic of Yugoslavia to refuse access to the Prosecutor of the International Tribunal for the Former Yugoslavia, and calls upon the Federal Republic of Yugoslavia to cooperate fully with the International Tribunal in carrying out an investigation in Kosovo, in line with the call for cooperation with the Tribunal in Council resolutions 1160(1998) of 31 March 1998, 1199(1998) of 23 September 1998 and 1203(1998) of 24 October 1998.

The Council notes that, against the clear advice of the Mission, Serb forces returned to Racak on 17 January 1999 and that fighting broke out.

The Council considers that the events in Racak constitute the latest in a series of threats to the efforts to settle this conflict through negotiation and peaceful means.

The Council condemns the shooting of Mission personnel on 15 January 1999 and all actions endangering Mission and international personnel. It reaffirms its full commitment to the safety and security of the Mission personnel. It reiterates its demands that the Federal Republic of Yugoslavia and the Kosovo Albanians cooperate fully with the Mission.

The Council calls upon the parties to cease immediately all acts of violence and to engage in talks on a lasting settlement.

The Council also strongly warns the Kosovo Liberation Army against actions which are contributing to tensions.

The Council considers all of these events to be violations of its resolutions and of relevant agreements and commitments calling for restraint. It calls upon all parties to respect fully their commitments under the relevant resolutions and affirms once again its full support for international efforts to facilitate a peaceful settlement on the basis of equality for all citizens and ethnic communities in Kosovo. The Council reaffirms its commitment to the sovereignty and territorial integrity of the Federal Republic of Yugoslavia.

The Council takes note with concern of the report of the United Nations High Commissioner for Refugees that five-and-a-half-thousand civilians fled the Racak area following the massacre, showing how rapidly a humanitarian crisis could again develop if steps are not taken by the parties to reduce tensions.

The Council will remain actively seized of the matter.

Further communications. Qatar, in its capacity as Chairman of the Islamic Group at the United Nations, conveyed to the Council and the General Assembly on 26 January [S/1999/76, A/53/807] the Group's condemnation of the massacre of innocent Muslim civilians at Racak and the ongoing Serbian policy of ethnic cleansing in Kosovo.

On 16 March [S/1999/383], the ICTY President reported continuing and additional instances of FRY's refusal to permit the ICTY Prosecutor to enter Kosovo to investigate alleged crimes committed in that territory pursuant to Council resolution 1160(1998), in particular its failure on 18 January to permit the entry of the Prosecutor and her team of investigators to investigate alleged criminal activity in Racak. The Prosecutor had requested the Tribunal President to notify the Council of FRY's failure to comply with its obligations under article 29 of the Tribunal's Statute [YUN 1993, p. 439]. The Tribunal President reported that, on 12 February, he had invited FRY to respond no later than 26 February, but had received no such response. He urged the Council to take measures to bring FRY into compliance with its obligations under international law.

Monitoring activities

Arms embargo

In its March report [S/1999/216], the Security Council Committee established pursuant to Council resolution 1160(1998) [YUN 1998, p. 369], which imposed an arms embargo on FRY, including Kosovo, expressed concern at the serious violations of the embargo, which had resulted in continuing military resupply and reinforcement of Kosovar Albanian armed groups. It also recognized that, owing to the lack of a comprehensive monitoring mechanism, its information was limited. It urged States, particularly those neighbouring FRY, to make every effort to prevent the sale or supply to FRY, including Kosovo, of arms and related materiel and to prevent the arming, training and financing of terrorist activities there. The Committee was apprised of the interception of arms and munitions worth $1 million at the end of December 1998 by Croatia. Switzerland had also informed the Committee that blocks on the Kosovo Foundation bank accounts were withdrawn, and Germany reported that, while making efforts to curb dubious fund-raising activities by Kosovar Albanians living in Germany, it had been unable to establish that the funds were intended to arm or train terrorists in Kosovo or to purchase weapons. Sweden informed the Committee that it was investigating mass media reports of the financing of KLA activities from Swedish territory.

The Secretary-General, in his March report on the situation in Kosovo [S/1999/293], recalled that he had stated in 1998 [YUN 1998, p. 387] that the United Nations Preventive Deployment Force (UNPREDEP) (see p. 370) would contribute towards providing a useful framework for reporting on violations and for assisting the Committee. However, the termination of UNPREDEP's mandate would affect efforts to monitor implementation of resolution 1160(1998). Accordingly, the Council might wish to reconsider the modalities for the monitoring regime.

OSCE/NATO Verification Missions

On 26 February, the Secretary-General transmitted to the Security Council the report [S/1999/214] of the OSCE Chairman-in-Office on the situation in Kosovo, covering mid-January to mid-February and submitted pursuant to Council resolutions 1160(1998) [YUN 1998, p. 369] and 1203(1998) [ibid., p. 382]. OSCE reported that the main areas of military tension remained the same: the Podujevo region in northern Kosovo, the Decani region in the west of the province and the area around Stimlje, south of Pristina. While the level of military conflict was reduced in February, KLA attacks on Serb police, isolated clashes and sporadic exchange of gunfire continued. Among the incidents reported by OSCE were serious breaches of the ceasefire towards the end of January in the Podujevo area. The continued KLA and security force stand-off in that area, with both sides digging trenches and preparing positions, had been a particular concern, and, though the fighting had subsided, neither side had withdrawn. On 29 January, 25 Kosovo Albanians and one Serb policeman were killed in the village of Rogovo. FRY authorities had agreed to a joint investigation of the incident by their specialists and the Finnish forensic team. Reports were received of KLA "policing" the Albanian community and administering punishments to those charged as collaborators with the Serbs. Several people said to be loyal to the Serbs were murdered in separate incidents in the area of Pec.

The OSCE presence in Albania, the OSCE Spillover Mission to Skopje, FYROM, and the OSCE Missions to Bosnia and Herzegovina and Croatia continued to follow closely the Kosovo conflict spillover potential. By mid-January, as the situation deteriorated in Kosovo, the activities of the Yugoslav forces along the border increased. Military planes and helicopters continuously patrolled the area, border posts and installations were reinforced and mines continued to be laid. Low KLA activity continued to take place in Albanian territory and crossing attempts by KLA units were reported, some of them resulting in deaths. There was little refugee movement across the border between Albania and FRY, although some cases of internal resettlement still occurred.

Albania had denied that it housed KLA bases and OSCE border monitoring confirmed lower levels of KLA presence, compared to the summer period. The FYROM northern border with FRY remained stable.

KVM continued to monitor the situation throughout Kosovo, verifying the maintenance of the ceasefire regime and investigating reports of violations, emplacement of roadblocks and checkpoints for purposes other than traffic control. It was also involved in activities to reduce tension, negotiating the release of hostages and engaging in confidence-building measures.

In March [S/1999/315], OSCE reported that the situation on the ground remained grave with localized clashes between KLA and Serb security forces. Unprovoked KLA attacks against the police continued and the number of casualties sustained by the security forces increased. A new area of military tension emerged at the border with FYROM. Military operations affecting the civilian population intensified in mid-March. Indiscriminate urban terrorist attacks against civilians continued and the number of security incidents involving OSCE personnel increased significantly. OSCE's ability to fulfil its task was seriously eroded. Intensive movement of Yugoslav Army convoys, including tanks and armoured personnel carriers, was observed within Kosovo since mid-February. The Yugoslav Army strengthened its positions in border areas and upgraded its defensive capabilities. KLA activity was also noted in certain areas of Kosovo. Due to the deteriorating security situation, the OSCE Chairman-in-Office, on 19 March, decided to temporarily withdraw the Mission from Kosovo to FYROM.

UNHCR reported that some 30,000 persons had fled their homes since 23 February and military operations in Prizren, Vucitrn and southern border areas had caused the displacement of as many as 18,000 people. There were at least 230,000 persons displaced within Kosovo, and the departure of Serbs and other minorities from Kosovo continued. The number of refugees from Kosovo had increased significantly; UNHCR and the International Committee of the Red Cross (ICRC) had registered 4,000 people since the beginning of March.

The NATO Secretary-General, in a January report to the UN Secretary-General [S/1999/99, annex II], said that NATO senior military authorities visited President Milosevic on 19 January to underline its concern and reinforce the need for him to honour his obligations. Regrettably, he had failed to do so. The North Atlantic Council was accordingly assessing the situation and considering how best to help the international community achieve a political solution to the crisis. NATO also provided an assessment of compliance trends, which showed that neither side in the conflict had respected the ceasefire and there had been a number of kidnappings and attacks by KLA elements. The response of the Yugoslav Army and Special Police was disproportionate and excessive, particularly the operations conducted from 10 to 16 January.

On 23 March [S/1999/338], the NATO Secretary-General reported that, following the withdrawal of KVM on 20 March, FRY had increased its military activities and was using excessive and wholly disproportionate force, thereby creating a further humanitarian catastrophe. He provided a further list of violations of Security Council resolutions 1199(1998) [YUN 1998, p. 377] and 1203(1998) [ibid., p. 382] during the period 16 January to 22 March 1999.

FRY, on 31 March [S/1999/367], said that the NATO Secretary-General's data citing instances of FRY's alleged non-compliance with Council resolutions were inaccurate, biased and malicious, and made no mention of the numerous instances of killings, kidnapping, mistreatment and other terrorist acts committed by the so-called KLA against civilians and members of the Yugoslav Army and security forces. KVM was withdrawn unilaterally. FRY had invested its best efforts to provide conditions for unhampered work by the Mission and had fulfilled its obligation towards it, including guarantees of full safety to its members.

Proposed framework for political settlement

Russian Federation/United States statement. On 26 January, the Russian Federation's Minister for Foreign Affairs, Igor S. Ivanov, and the United States Secretary of State, Madeleine K. Albright, following their meeting in Moscow, issued a statement [S/1999/77] urging the two sides in the Kosovo conflict to work harder to achieve an interim political settlement providing substantial autonomy for Kosovo and to engage in meaningful negotiations for that purpose. Such a settlement should respect FRY's territorial integrity and sovereignty. Backing the efforts of Christopher Hill (United States) and Wolfgang Petritsch (Austria) [YUN 1998, p. 386], they said that they would continue to press the two sides to agree on such a political settlement, and would collaborate in the Contact Group (see below) towards that end.

Secretary Albright and Foreign Minister Ivanov expressed their complete commitment to the unimpeded functioning of KVM under Mr. Walker's leadership. All attacks on and threats against KVM should cease immediately, and FRY authorities and the media should create a supportive atmosphere for the activities of KVM and its head.

FRY should comply fully with Security Council resolutions, particularly with regard to police and military units, and its agreements with OSCE and other international entities without delay. Its authorities should cooperate fully with ICTY and conduct a full investigation of the Racak events with the Tribunal's participation. Judge Louise Arbour and the Tribunal's investigators should be allowed to enter and work in Kosovo and participate in that investigation.

The United States and the Russian Federation urged the Kosovo Albanians to fulfil all their obligations and commitments. Noting that KLA provocations had contributed significantly to the renewed deep tensions in Kosovo, they condemned such provocations and demanded that they end immediately and that measures be developed to discourage such activity. They called on the Serbian authorities to carry out the commitments in their statement of principles of a political settlement [YUN 1998, p. 381], in particular to mitigate the sentences of persons detained in connection with the Kosovo conflict and to provide due process to all detainees. The two sides should avoid actions that affected the civilian population and facilitate the work of international organizations and NGOs providing humanitarian assistance.

Contact Group meeting (29 January). The Ministers of the Contact Group on the Former Yugoslavia (France, Germany, Italy, Russian Federation, United Kingdom, United States) (London, 29 January) issued a statement [S/1999/96], in which they called on both sides to commit themselves to negotiation of a political settlement. To that end, they insisted that the parties accept that the basis for a fair settlement should include the principles set out by the Contact Group; considered that the proposals drafted by the negotiators contained the elements for substantial autonomy for Kosovo, which should be refined further to serve as the framework for agreement between the parties; and recognized that the negotiators had identified those points requiring final negotiation between the parties. The Contact Group agreed to summon representatives from the Federal Yugoslav and Serbian Governments and the Kosovo Albanians to Rambouillet, France, by 6 February to begin negotiations. It recognized the legitimate rights of other communities within Kosovo and would ensure that their interests were fully reflected in a settlement. It agreed that the participants should work to conclude negotiations within seven days, after which the negotiators would report to Contact Group Ministers, who would assess whether the progress made justified a further period of less than one week to bring the negotiations to a successful conclusion.

In the meantime, the Contact Group demanded that FRY: stop all offensive actions/repression in Kosovo; comply fully with the OSCE/FRY and the NATO/FRY agreements and relevant Council resolutions; promote the safe return of all those forced to flee their homes; cooperate fully with OSCE and permit KVM and its Chief of Mission to continue to carry out their responsibilities unhindered; cooperate fully with ICTY; conduct a full investigation of the Racak massacre with ICTY participation, allowing the Chief Prosecutor and Tribunal investigators to enter and work in Kosovo; identify and suspend the Yugoslav Army/Serbian Special Police officers operating in Racak at the time of the massacre until the results of the investigation became available; and mitigate the sentences of those imprisoned in connection with the conflict and provide due process to all detainees.

The Contact Group emphasized that compliance with the Council's relevant resolutions applied equally to the Kosovo Albanians, condemned all KLA provocations and insisted that all hostages be released. The Group believed that its framework met the legitimate aspirations of the Kosovo Albanians and demanded that their leaders rally behind negotiations to reach a settlement and end provocative actions. It asked the United Kingdom Foreign Minister to transmit those messages to Belgrade and Pristina. Negotiations on a political settlement should be completed within 21 days.

SECURITY COUNCIL ACTION

On 29 January [meeting 3974], following consultations among members, the Security Council President made statement **S/PRST/1999/5** on behalf of the Council:

The Security Council expresses its deep concern at the escalating violence in Kosovo, Federal Republic of Yugoslavia. It underlines the risk of a further deterioration in the humanitarian situation if steps are not taken by the parties to reduce tensions. The Council reiterates its concern at attacks on civilians and underlines the need for a full and unhindered investigation of such actions. It calls once again upon the parties to respect fully their obligations under the relevant resolutions and to cease immediately all acts of violence and provocation.

The Council welcomes and supports the decisions of the Ministers for Foreign Affairs of France, Germany, Italy, the Russian Federation, the United Kingdom of Great Britain and Northern Ireland and the United States of America (the Contact Group), following their meeting in London on 29 January 1999, which aim at reaching a political settlement between the parties and establishing a framework and timetable for that purpose. The Council demands that the parties accept their responsibilities and comply fully with these decisions and requirements, as with its relevant resolutions.

The Council reiterates its full support for international efforts, including those of the Contact Group and the Kosovo Verification Mission of the Organization for Security and Cooperation in Europe, to reduce tensions in Kosovo and facilitate a political settlement on the basis of substantial autonomy and equality for all citizens and ethnic communities in Kosovo and the recognition of the legitimate rights of the Kosovo Albanians and other communities in Kosovo. It reaffirms its commitment to the sovereignty and territorial integrity of the Federal Republic of Yugoslavia.

The Council will follow the negotiations closely and would welcome members of the Contact Group keeping it informed about the progress reached therein.

The Council will remain actively seized of the matter.

Related developments

On 1 February [S/1999/107], FRY transmitted to the Security Council President a communication from its Foreign Minister regarding a 30 January letter from the NATO Secretary-General to the President of FRY. That letter attached "a final warning" from NATO, in which it expressed support for the Contact Group's negotiation strategy, which, it said, was intended to halt the violence and support completion of the negotiations on an interim political settlement for Kosovo. Steps to that end should include acceptance by both parties to begin negotiations in Rambouillet by 8 February and their completion within the specified time frame; full and immediate observance of the ceasefire by both parties and by FRY authorities of their commitments to NATO, including bringing Yugoslav Forces and Police/ Special Police force levels, posture and activities into strict compliance with the NATO/FRY October 1998 agreement [YUN 1998, p. 381]; and the ending of excessive and disproportionate use of force. If those steps were not taken, NATO was ready to take whatever measures were necessary. The North Atlantic Council had therefore agreed that the NATO Secretary-General might authorize air strikes against targets in FRY. A similar letter was sent to Ibrahim Rugova of the Democratic League of Kosovo.

FRY stated that the letter represented an open and clear threat of aggression and called on the President to inform Council members and to convene an emergency session of the Council to take appropriate measures under the Charter to prevent aggression against it.

On 4 February [S/1999/118], the National Assembly of the Republic of Serbia condemned NATO's threats. It reaffirmed its principles for resolving the Kosovo crisis: political means and dialogue; full respect for FRY's and Serbia's territorial integrity and sovereignty; full equality of all citizens, national communities and ethnic groups; solutions harmonized with Serbia's and FRY's Constitutions and international standards of human and civil rights and the rights of persons belonging to national communities; that Kosovo and Metohija would not be granted the status of a republic, but self-governance in line with international standards; non-acceptance of any measure that would attempt to secede Kosovo from Serbia; and non-acceptance of the presence of foreign soldiers in its territory under any pretext of implementing the achieved agreement. Serbia accepted the Contact Group's invitation for talks in France on 6 February and authorized the Government to designate its delegation to those talks.

The OSCE Chairman-in-Office, in his February report [S/1999/214], said that, after having accepted the invitations to the talks, representatives from both sides issued statements declaring that they would not abandon their stands or submit to dictates from the international community. They also announced that they would put forward their own plans and proposals.

On 9 February [S/1999/129], FRY reported attacks on two innocent civilians at the outskirts of Djakovica and the discovery of three other bodies in Kosovo and Metohija. Those acts, it said, demonstrated the opposition of the terrorists to a peaceful solution and their desire to undermine the talks in Rambouillet (see p. 340) and prevent an agreement from being achieved. On 18 February [S/1999/177], the President of the Republic of Serbia drew the attention of the Contact Group members, in the context of the talks in Rambouillet, to requests that FRY accept a document relating to foreign military troops on FRY territory. According to FRY, neither the document nor the issue had been discussed or approved by the Contact Group. While the Rambouillet meeting was proceeding, FRY was repeatedly subjected to threats of military aggression. The President was therefore seeking protection from any such requests and threats.

Belarus and Ukraine, in statements of 20 February [A/53/845-S/1999/208] and 19 February [S/1999/194], respectively, condemned the intention to use force to solve the problem of Kosovo and Metohija. Belarus said that it was important to preserve the negotiating process and to forestall any action that might jeopardize it.

Rambouillet Accords

Under the auspices of the Contact Group on the Former Yugoslavia, and as agreed in its 29 January statement [S/1999/96] (see p. 338), representatives from the Federal Yugoslav and Serbian Governments and representatives of the Kosovo Albanians met in Rambouillet, France, on 6 February under the co-chairmanship of France and the United Kingdom. The negotiations, which were suspended on 23 February, resumed in Paris on 15 March.

On 18 March, the Kosovo Albanian representatives signed the Rambouillet Accords: Interim Agreement for Peace and Self-Government in Kosovo, which was a three-year interim agreement providing for democratic self-government, and peace and security for everyone living in Kosovo. Security would be guaranteed by international troops deployed on the ground throughout Kosovo and an international meeting would be convened after three years to determine a mechanism for a final settlement.

However, the delegation of the Republic of Serbia refused to sign the Accords, signing instead its own text, "Agreement for Self-Government in Kosmet". The talks were adjourned on 19 March. On that day, OSCE withdrew KVM.

Rambouillet talks. The Security Council President, in a 23 February press statement [A/54/2], said that the Council took note of the conclusions of the Co-Chairmen of the Rambouillet Conference at the end of two weeks of intensive efforts aimed at reaching an agreement on substantial autonomy for Kosovo that respected FRY's national sovereignty and territorial integrity. The Council noted that, with the Rambouillet agreements, a political framework for substantial autonomy had been set out. It also noted the commitment of the parties to attend a conference covering all aspects of the implementation of those agreements, in Paris, on 15 March. It encouraged the parties to work constructively to that end and underlined that it was essential for them to refrain from any action that could jeopardize the achievements of the Rambouillet negotiations.

In a letter to the Contact Group Foreign Ministers [S/1999/177], Serbia's President Milan Milutinovic stated that in Rambouillet, Serbia had been asked to accept a military annex regarding foreign troops on FRY territory. That issue had not been discussed or approved by the Contact Group.

In his March report [S/1999/315], the OSCE Chairman-in-Office said that, on 3 March, the eight Kosovo Albanian political parties, including the Democratic League of Kosovo of Mr. Rugova, represented in a shadow "Parliament of the Republic of Kosova", called on Kosovo Albanians to support the Rambouillet Accords. On 5 March, Mr. Rugova told a press conference in Pristina that, despite difficulties on the ground, wide-ranging efforts to build support for the Accords across the whole spectrum of the Kosovo Albanian community were continuing.

In a 5 March statement [S/1999/245], the Serbian delegation, in its own review of the Rambouillet talks and preparations for their resumption on 15 March, assessed that initial success towards a peaceful settlement of the Kosovo and Metohija issue had been achieved. However, a lot still needed to be done. A political agreement had not been adopted and was far from being signed soon. Some key provisions had been put forth unilaterally, contravening the Contact Group's principles, and there was an attempt only a few hours before the close of the talks to deliver documents that had not even been discussed by the Contact Group (annexes 2 and 7 dealing with police issues and troops).

Unfortunately, the United States, as well as some other Contact Group members, was claiming that the political agreement was practically adopted and only needed to be signed on 15 March, to be followed by talks on its implementation.

Requests were being made for the signing of an agreement whose major part had not been discussed either within the Contact Group or in the Rambouillet talks, for an interim agreement, the holding of a referendum after three years, the granting of full equality to the ethnic Albanian community alone and not to all ethnic communities in Kosovo and Metohija, and accepting a quasi-State in Serbia and Yugoslavia. Ethnic Albanian separatist parties were being asked to accept something they had been asking for for years: independence with the assistance of their NATO allies. On the other hand, a theory had been advanced that if Serbia did not sign, it would be seen as the party opposing the political settlement.

Serbia had been requested to accept: the President of Kosovo, the Constitution of Kosovo and Metohija and legislative powers of the Kosovo and Metohija Assembly (Parliament); a special judicial system comprising the constitutional and supreme courts of Kosovo and Metohija; harmonization with the agreement, namely, a change of the Serbian and Yugoslav Constitutions; the need for obtaining Kosovo and Metohija's consent for changing the province's borders and declaring a state of emergency; and the entire agreement as interim and the holding of another international conference after three years to consider the will of the people, namely, a referendum, in only one part of the Serbian State. In short, it was a diktat that called for an international protectorate with a number of major requests, which the State delegation could not possibly accept.

Serbia was ready to resume talks wherever a political settlement could be reached, but would not give up Kosovo and Metohija, or allow its secession or transformation into a third republic. The Co-Chairmen of the Rambouillet meeting had given only a partial picture of the meeting, covering up the failure of the organizers and especially the behaviour and positions of the ethnic Albanian delegation.

On 6 March [S/1999/244], the Serbian Republic President said that the attention of the Foreign Ministers of the Contact Group member States had been drawn to the manipulations and campaign to have representatives of the Albanian separatists' political parties sign the non-existent "Agreement". Serbia's delegation and some members of the Contact Group had dissociated themselves from the Agreement. Serbia rejected attempts to impose a policy of fait accompli and demanded that the Contact Group member States and the international community prevent any manipulation and create appropriate conditions for the resumption of talks without pressure or blackmail.

Paris talks. The text of the Rambouillet Accords: Interim Agreement for Peace and Self-Government in Kosovo [S/1999/648], which was signed in Paris on 18 March by the Kosovo Albanian representatives, was forwarded to the Secretary-General by France on behalf of the Co-Chairmen of the Rambouillet Conference.

FRY forwarded to the Security Council President the text of the Agreement for Self-Government in Kosmet [S/1999/302] that was signed on the same day by the Serbian delegation, and a Serbian Government letter endorsing its delegation's stand at the talks. It said that the United States–ethnic Albanian agreement on separating a part of Serbian and Yugoslav territory constituted an unprecedented violation of all international rules. Also annexed to the letter was a statement by the Serbian President describing the document signed by the ethnic Albanian delegation as a fake that was never discussed, agreed or signed by the Contact Group as a whole.

FRY, in a 19 March statement on the Rambouillet talks [S/1999/301], maintained that the text signed by some Kosovo and Metohija Albanian representatives was only the draft text. The Serbia delegation could not be blamed for the failure of the talks as it had demonstrated its determination to achieve a political agreement by accepting the Contact Group's principles. FRY urged that the talks resume and supported its delegation in not accepting those provisions, bringing into question the equality of national communities and giving Kosovo and Metohija the status of a third federal unit or independent State. It also supported the position to first reach a political agreement before talking about implementation. FRY condemned the build-up of foreign troops at its borders and threats of aggression. It said that those threatening to use force against FRY had to face the responsibility for the consequences of humanitarian problems that might arise. It again called on the Security Council and the OSCE Permanent Council to rule out the use of force and military threats against FRY and to uphold a peaceful political settlement.

The Ministers for Foreign Affairs of the Countries of South-Eastern Europe Cooperation, on 19 March [S/1999/319], reiterated their full support for the international community's efforts for a political settlement of the Kosovo crisis. Emphasizing that the Paris talks might represent a last opportunity for a political settlement of the crisis, they welcomed the signing of the Interim Agreement, in its entirety, by the delegation of the Kosovar Albanians and urged FRY also to sign the Agreement at the earliest stage. Belarus, on 20 March [A/53/870-S/1999/309], also expressed regret that a constructive, mutually acceptable solution was not found during the negotiations in France. However, it did not believe that there were grounds for threats of the use of military force against FRY. It called for the continuation of joint international efforts to advance the peace process.

FRY President Milosevic, on 23 March [S/1999/314], repeated the position that two documents were signed in Paris, one by the representatives of all national communities in Kosovo and the other by representatives of the Albanian separatists and terrorists, who were not the representatives of Kosovo. The latter document was not the Rambouillet Agreement.

Serbia's National Assembly, in conclusions of the same date [S/1999/318], approved the Serbian delegation's report on the Rambouillet talks and regretted that the international mediators and the Co-Chairmen of the Rambouillet and Paris talks had not succeeded in bringing the delegation of the separatist movement to sit at the same table with the Serbian State delegation. The National Assembly declared that Serbia was still committed to a peaceful solution and was ready to continue direct negotiations. It authorized the State delegation to sign a political agreement on self-governance in Kosovo and Metohija to be agreed and signed by all national communities living there and to propose solutions so that it could be implemented as soon as possible.

On 17 March [S/1999/292], FRY informed the Security Council President of a build-up by NATO countries of troops and arms, including in FYROM, and called on the Council to convene a meeting to prevail upon NATO and its members to cease its use of force and stop a further build-up of troops.

On 23 March [S/1999/317], FRY declared a state of imminent danger of war. It forwarded to the Council President its National Assembly's decisions not to accept the presence of foreign troops in Kosovo and Metohija and its readiness after the signing of the political agreement on self-government to consider the scope and character of an international presence in Kosovo and Metohija with a view to implementing the agreement.

The European Council, on 25 March [S/1999/342], expressed concern about the failure of the mediation efforts of United States Ambassador Holbrooke and the three Rambouillet negotiators, Ambassadors Hill, Majorski and Petritsch, with President Milosevic to persuade him to accept a ceasefire and a political solution to the conflict to stop a humanitarian catastrophe in Kosovo. It urged the Yugoslav leadership to change radically its own policy and stressed that it was not too late to stop the internal repression and accept the international community's mediation efforts.

NATO air campaign

On 24 March, following FRY's refusal to sign the Rambouillet Accords, NATO started its air campaign against it. The main targets were military installations, communications facilities and government buildings. Meanwhile, Serbian security force operations aimed at destroying KLA were under way across the whole of Kosovo.

FRY declared a state of war on 24 March [S/1999/327]. In a letter to the Security Council President [S/1999/322], FRY said that by carrying out air strikes against military and civilian facilities, NATO's armed forces had committed an act of aggression in violation of the UN Charter. It requested him to convene an urgent meeting of the Council to condemn and stop the aggression and to protect FRY's sovereignty and territorial integrity. The request for convening the Council was supported by Belarus [S/1999/323] and the Russian Federation [S/1999/320].

SECURITY COUNCIL CONSIDERATION

The Security Council met on 24 March [meeting 3988] to consider the situation in Kosovo. The Russian Federation said that those involved in that unilateral use of force against FRY without the Council's authorization should realize the heavy responsibility they bore for subverting the Charter and international law. Attempts to justify the NATO strikes with arguments about preventing a humanitarian catastrophe in Kosovo were untenable. The decision was particularly unacceptable since the political and diplomatic methods had not been exhausted. The Russian Federation demanded the immediate cessation of the illegal military action. It added that, as a member of the Contact Group, it fully supported the document adopted in London that formed the basis of the draft political settlement. However, its partners in the Group had decided to discuss the military aspects of implementation in NATO and not within the Contact Group.

The United States said that NATO had begun military action with the greatest reluctance but it was necessary to respond to Belgrade's brutal persecution of Kosovar Albanians, violations of international law, excessive and indiscriminate use of force, refusal to negotiate and recent military build-up in Kosovo—all of which foreshadowed a humanitarian catastrophe of immense proportions. Some 40,000 Serb forces were in action in and around Kosovo, 30,000 Kosovars had left their homes since 19 March and the number of displaced persons was approaching 250,000. The continuing FRY offensive was threatening the stability of the region and had already resulted in cross-border activity in Albania, Bosnia and Herzegovina and FYROM. The United States believed that the NATO action was justified and necessary.

France observed that FRY had not respected the commitments and obligations contained in the agreements it had concluded with OSCE and

NATO in 1998 [YUN 1998, p. 381], and efforts to prompt the FRY Government to meet it obligations on the ground and to adhere to the Rambouillet agreements had been exhausted. Indeed, in recent weeks, the Yugoslav Army had massed a powerful offensive capacity, inspiring fears that there would be a new upsurge of massacres in a community of 2 million people. That community could not be abandoned to violent repression.

The United Kingdom stated that, in defiance of the international community, President Milosevic had refused to accept the Rambouillet agreements, observe the limits on security-force levels agreed in October 1998 [YUN 1998, p. 381], and end the excessive and disproportionate use of force in Kosovo. NATO was forced to take military action because all other means of preventing a humanitarian catastrophe had been frustrated by Serb behaviour. The action taken was to save lives and was legal and justified.

China said that the question of Kosovo, an internal FRY matter, should be resolved among the parties concerned. It opposed interference in the internal affairs of other States, under whatever pretext or in whatever form. It had always been China's position that, under the Charter, the Council bore the primary responsibility for the maintenance of peace and security and only the Council could take appropriate action. China was opposed to any act that violated that principle and that challenged the Council's authority.

Addressing the Council at the President's invitation, FRY stated that NATO had committed a unilateral act of the most brutal and unprovoked aggression against a sovereign and independent State and a founding Member of the United Nations. FRY had been attacked because it sought to solve an internal problem and used its sovereign right to fight terrorism and prevent the secession of part of its territory. NATO's blatant aggression was a flagrant violation of the basic principles of the Charter. FRY called on Council members to act swiftly and in accordance with the Charter to condemn the aggression and to take measures to stop it immediately and unambiguously so that all problems might be resolved by political means.

Albania, also addressing the Council at the President's invitation, said that the international community was intervening in Kosovo in order to stop the humanitarian catastrophe and the tragedy of a nation whose people had been tortured, killed and buried in common graves. Albania totally supported the NATO military action, considering it to be in support of peace and stability in the region. No country that committed genocide and crimes against humanity could expect to receive UN and Council protection.

Communications. In letters addressed to the Secretary-General between 24 and 26 March, several States, Parliaments and regional organizations expressed concern over NATO's recourse to the use of force without Council authorization and urged the parties to the conflict, as well as the international community, to consider urgently additional efforts to stop further escalation of the conflict. On 25 March [S/1999/353], FRY called on the OSCE Chairman-in-Office to convene a special session of the OSCE Permanent Council to consider the aggression against it and to take measures to stop it. FRY considered that OSCE's complete withdrawal of KVM was part of the orchestrated preparations for NATO's aggression, and by so doing OSCE had unilaterally broken the FRY-OSCE agreement [YUN 1998, p. 381].

On 26 March [S/1999/344], the Russian Federation protested the ban on flights by civil aviation in the airspace above Bosnia and Herzegovina, Croatia, FRY and FYROM by NATO, saying it was a gross violation of the 1944 Chicago Convention on International Civil Aviation. Such measures called for the active intervention of the International Civil Aviation Organization (ICAO). The Russian Federation had contacted the ICAO Secretary-General and was confident he would take measures to restore the freedom of civil aviation over those countries.

SECURITY COUNCIL ACTION

On 26 March [meeting 3989], the Security Council met to consider a draft resolution sponsored by Belarus, India and the Russian Federation [S/1999/328], by which the Council would have demanded an immediate cessation of the use of force against FRY and the urgent resumption of negotiations.

Canada, speaking against the draft resolution, said that those who supported it placed themselves outside the international consensus. Those countries might more usefully have directed their energies towards convincing the leaders in Belgrade to stop the violence and accept the Rambouillet Accords. Slovenia's representative argued that the text was an inadequate attempt to address the Kosovo situation, took a selective political view of it, lacked objectivity, and ignored the fact that several months earlier the Council had declared the situation in Kosovo to be one constituting a threat to peace and security in the region and had spelled out the requirements for the removal of that threat, which were flagrantly violated by FRY.

The United States said that Council resolutions 1199(1998) [YUN 1998, p. 377] and 1203(1998) [ibid., p. 382] had laid out the steps Belgrade had to take to resolve the crisis but it had chosen to defy repeatedly the will of the international community. The current draft resolution, if adopted, could only encourage President Milosevic to continue or even intensify military repression of Kosovo's civilian population, damage prospects for a negotiated settlement and make further bloodshed more likely. It did nothing to advance the cause of peace in the Balkans.

The draft resolution received 3 votes in favour and 12 against. Since the draft resolution did not obtain the required majority, it was not adopted and the Council continued its consideration of the matter.

Speaking after the vote at the President's invitation, FRY said that the NATO aggression and massive, reckless bombing campaign were not limited to so-called military targets, but brought death to hundreds of civilians and destroyed property. The Council was in a position to prevent NATO from robbing it of its rights and duties if it strongly condemned the aggression and requested NATO to stop it immediately and unconditionally. If the Council failed to do so, it would be responsible for the breakdown of the current system of international relations. It had to decide whether it would retain its responsibility under the Charter or cede it to NATO.

Further developments

The Organization of the Islamic Conference (OIC) Contact Group on Bosnia and Herzegovina and Kosovo, on 26 March [S/1999/363], noted that, due to the intransigence of the Belgrade authorities, a decisive international action was necessary to prevent humanitarian catastrophe and further violations of human rights in Kosovo. It would have preferred the Security Council to deal with the matter and regretted that the Council had been unable to discharge its responsibility.

The Russian Federation State Duma (Parliament), on 27 March [A/53/888-S/1999/358], supported the Russian President's decision to suspend all official relations with NATO until the end of NATO's military action, the recalling of the country's military representative to NATO, suspension of participation in the Partnership for Peace programme and the operation of NATO centres in the Russian Federation, and removal of the Russian contingent in the Stabilization Force in Bosnia and Herzegovina. It recommended that the Russian President put forward a peace initiative aimed at halting the attacks and resuming political negotiations and demand the holding of a special session of the General Assembly to consider the question of aggression against a UN Member State. In a 23 April statement [A/53/924-S/1999/475], the Russian Federation said that it expected NATO countries to assess the civilian casualties and damage to FRY's economy, and would like to know what measures they intended to take, and when, to stop the continuing violations of their obligations, and how they planned to compensate for the economic and other damage.

On 27 March [S/1999/360], the NATO Secretary-General informed the UN Secretary-General that in the circumstances he had directed the NATO Supreme Allied Command Europe to initiate a broader scope of operations to intensify action against FRY forces and compel them to desist from further attacks in Kosovo and to meet the demands of the international community. All allies were united in that action and in their determination to bring a halt to violence in Kosovo and to prevent a further humanitarian catastrophe.

On 29 March [S/1999/357], FRY said that NATO was increasingly targeting towns and cities, wreaking destruction primarily on civilians, which took a heavy toll in human lives. The devastation caused by the NATO air strikes throughout FRY had caused the largest humanitarian disaster in Europe since the Second World War. FRY listed the number of facilities destroyed or damaged by the air strikes. It called on the Secretary-General to use his influence to forestall serious humanitarian consequences of the aggression.

On the same day [S/1999/359], FRY appealed to international organizations, Governments, relevant political factors and the entire world to stop the senseless act of war aggression. It expressed to the Secretary-General on 31 March [S/1999/366] its disappointment that the Council had failed to act in accordance with its responsibilities under the Charter, and that the NATO aggression and air strikes continued unabated without any reaction from him. FRY called on the Secretary-General to act urgently to put an end to the aggression and the further endangerment of international peace and security. The FRY Army's Supreme Command warned of NATO plans for a land invasion from across its border and the recruitment of refugees towards that end [S/1999/412].

The OIC Contact Group on Bosnia and Herzegovina and Kosovo, in a 7 April declaration [S/1999/394], decided to establish contacts with all parties and further enhance cooperation with the Contact Group on the Former Yugoslavia and Kosovo's political leadership; urgently to mobilize humanitarian assistance for Kosovo victims; and to set up a coordination group to coordinate OIC assistance to Kosovo and interact with humanitarian agencies. The Movement of Non-Aligned Countries, on 9 April [S/1999/451], expressed concern over the deteriorating humanitarian situation in Kosovo and other parts of FRY and the displacement, both internal and to neighbouring countries, of vast numbers of the Kosovo civilian population. It urged the Secretary-General to intensify the UN role in alleviating the suffering of the displaced persons and refugees and to investigate all human rights abuses. It believed that the urgent resumption of diplomatic efforts constituted the only basis for a solution to the conflict.

The Council of Europe, on 26 April [A/54/91], declared its readiness to contribute to a peaceful settlement of the conflict and to redress human suffering and institutional damage.

The EU, on 26 April [S/1999/490], imposed on FRY a ban on the delivery of petroleum and petroleum products. It extended the existing EU sanctions regime and welcomed the European Commission's intention to introduce proposals, including a travel ban on President Milosevic, his family, and officials and persons close to the regime; extension of the freeze on funds held abroad by FRY and Serbia; prohibition of the provision of export finance by the private sector; extension of the investment ban; widening the export prohibitions; encouraging Member States and sporting organizations not to organize international sporting events with FRY participation; and a comprehensive flight ban between the EU countries and FRY. The EU agreed to start preparation of a stability pact for South-Eastern Europe (see p. 397), welcomed the international community's endorsement of the proposed pact and decided to convene a conference on the subject in Germany on 27 May. The Presidents of Central Europe also adopted a declaration supporting the elaboration of a stability pact [A/53/962- S/1999/574 & Corr.1].

OSCE report (April). The OSCE Chairman-in-Office, in an April report [S/1999/485], said that KVM had been temporarily withdrawn from Kosovo, following which the tempo of the Serbian security forces offensive began to quicken. Even during the NATO air campaign, Serbian security operations aimed at destroying KLA were under way across the whole of Kosovo. On 25 March, FRY suspended diplomatic relations with France, Germany, the United Kingdom and the United States. A number of Western countries closed their embassies in Belgrade and the Serbian Information Minister issued an order expelling all foreign journalists whose countries were taking part in the NATO air strikes. ICRC withdrew all its international personnel from Kosovo, and NGOs operating there were also withdrawn. Serbian resistance had shown no sign of weakening. Street lights in the majority of Serbian towns remained on and several thousand people gathered on 28 March for a rock concert in central Belgrade to protest the air strikes. Since then, concerts continued daily in other Serbian towns. In addition, human chains were formed on bridges to prevent NATO attacks. The Montenegrin authorities distanced themselves from a number of important decisions taken by Belgrade.

On 7 April, KLA's political director and leader of the Albanian delegation to Rambouillet, Hasim Thaci, revealed the composition of the transitional Kosovo "Government", with himself as Prime Minister and Foreign Minister, and including representatives of the United Democratic Front, led by Rexhep Qosja. The Democratic League of Kosovo, led by Ibrahim Rugova, had yet to name its representative.

The expulsion of vast numbers of Kosovo Albanian refugees was the most striking feature of the reporting period. Many thousands sought refuge in neighbouring countries, with Albania bearing the heaviest weight of numbers. By 17 April, UNHCR estimated that 340,000 refugees had fled Kosovo for Albania, 70,000 for Montenegro and 135,000 for FYROM. The exodus continued and showed no signs of abating.

The OSCE Human Rights Division had been monitoring and documenting violations committed against Kosovo's civilian population since the withdrawal of OSCE's international staff. Many people reported violations of humanitarian law committed by paramilitary groups and bands of armed civilians. The statements painted a picture of lawlessness and absence of any form of protection for ethnic Albanians. Yugoslav Army attacks targeted both civilians and their property and were most often followed by operations and raids by the Special Police, paramilitaries and armed civilians. Reports suggested that the absence of international representatives in Kosovo provided an opportunity for an increase in the frequency and intensity of violent acts.

The Kosovo crisis was dominating life in Albania, whose attention since 27 March was directed to the humanitarian dimension of the influx of refugees and the inability of its already weak economy and infrastructure to cope. Albania had welcomed the NATO air strikes and had formally approved the stationing of foreign troops on its territory. In FYROM, the crisis had put enormous burdens on the country, raising public anxiety, straining inter-ethnic relations and relations within the Government and with the international community, and greatly increasing the risk of destabilization. Following KVM's withdrawal and the emerging humanitarian crisis created by the exodus of Kosovo Albanian refugees to Albania and FYROM, two KVM task forces were established, one each in those countries, to assist

UNHCR, other international organizations and local authorities.

OSCE report (May). In a May report [S/1999/618], the OSCE Chairman-in-Office said that the refugee flow from Kosovo had remained constant. A disturbing development was the closure in early May of the FYROM border (see below). The Yugoslav Army Supreme Command announced a partial withdrawal of forces from Kosovo on 10 May. The head of the Kosovo Albanian delegation to the Rambouillet talks, Hasim Thaci, claimed that the withdrawal was a deception and the forces were regrouping to avoid NATO air strikes. KLA sources alleged that fighting continued, particularly near the towns of Junik and Djakovica, near the border with Albania, and remained a focus of conflict throughout May. On 20 April, media reports suggested that several hundred FRY soldiers entered three villages inside Montenegro close to Kosovo and fired on Kosovo Albanian refugees. New areas of conflict between Serbian security forces and KLA emerged, such as in Gnjilane, and, according to Albanian sources, fighting spread to other more central areas such as Prizren and Suva Reka, and Lipjan and Urosevac. The "interim Government" of the Kosovo Albanians reportedly issued a decree forming a National Guard.

The Kosovo Albanian leader, Ibrahim Rugova, met President Milosevic and other Serbian leaders on several occasions. A close aide to Mr. Rugova said that he was in FRY against his will and was under house arrest in Pristina. Criticism against him from across the Kosovo Albanian spectrum became more vociferous and, in a surprise move, FRY authorities allowed him to leave for Italy. Fehmi Agani, a Kosovo Albanian delegate to the Rambouillet talks, was allegedly taken into police custody and subsequently killed on his return from an unsuccessful attempt to cross the border into FYROM.

The refugee flow from Kosovo across the FRY-FYROM border maintained severe pressure on the already stretched resources of refugee camps. A new camp in Cegrane, south-west of Skopje, was filled in a matter of days. On 5 May, the number of refugees crossing the FYROM border led the Macedonian authorities to close their border with Kosovo. Following negotiations between UNHCR and Macedonian authorities, the border was re-opened on 6 May. However, the numbers crossing remained small. OSCE estimated there were some 232,000 refugees from Kosovo in Macedonian territory. The Albanian Government, NATO and other international partners initiated a plan to move large numbers of refugees from Kukes in the north of Albania, where the refugee population had grown from about 23,000 to 130,000 in nine camps and with host families. The plan had to be modified and the refugees were to be moved at a slower pace into previously planned camps nearing completion. OSCE estimated that there were 441,000 Kosovo refugees in Albania.

Communications. FRY complained of acts of aggression against it from Albanian territory [S/1999/406, S/1999/452] and accused the United States of a breach of the arms embargo established by Council resolution 1160(1998) [YUN 1998, p. 369] by maintaining contacts with, training and financing KLA via Albania [S/1999/453]. It also accused the EU of violating the Charter by imposing unilaterally a ban on the shipment of oil and oil derivatives to FRY [S/1999/497] and brought to the attention of the Council President or the Secretary-General the bombing of refugees by NATO on the Djakovica-Prizren road [S/1999/423], the destruction of the town of Surdulica [S/1999/496], and the bombing of civilian targets, including power plants and transmission lines and stations [S/1999/510]. FRY's Constitutional Court also sought to establish how NATO's action against the country violated international public law and the international legal order [S/1999/479]. Austria forwarded to the Secretary-General the Vienna Declaration on Peace and Tolerance in Kosovo, adopted at a conference in Vienna on 17 and 18 March, which brought together representatives from all major religions in Kosovo to discuss the crisis in the region [S/1999/405].

NATO bombing of diplomatic property

On 7 May [S/1999/523], China requested an urgent meeting of the Security Council to discuss NATO's attack on its Embassy in Belgrade. China later expressed its indignation and condemnation of the act and lodged the strongest protest [A/53/952-S/1999/535]. It said the action was a violation of Chinese sovereignty, the Vienna Convention on Diplomatic Relations [YUN 1961, p. 512] and the norms of international relations.

In its account of the incident [S/1999/529], FRY reported that at 11.45 p.m. on 7 May, China's Embassy was bombed by NATO. It said that the building was visibly marked and separated from other buildings in its vicinity, which indicated the clear intentions of the aggressors. FRY expected that the Council, as well as the entire international community, would strongly condemn that cruel act and demand that those who gave the orders would be appropriately punished. It also expected the Council to demand an immediate end to the aggression as the only way to eliminate those crimes.

South Africa, in an 8 May statement [S/1999/530], expressed concern about the NATO bombing raids, which it had predicted would exacerbate the humanitarian tragedy and lead to unfortunate incidents, such as the bombing of the Chinese Embassy and others. While it condemned the ethnic cleansing policies of the Milosevic Government, it believed that the only way to resolve the crisis was to support the current international diplomatic initiatives. The Sudan, on 10 May [S/1999/541], denounced the aggression against the Chinese Embassy.

SECURITY COUNCIL ACTION

On 14 May [meeting 4001], following consultations among Security Council members, the President made statement **S/PRST/1992/12** on behalf of the Council:

> The Security Council recalls the press statement by the President on 8 May 1999 and expresses its deep distress and concern over the bombing of the Embassy of the People's Republic of China in the Federal Republic of Yugoslavia on 7 May 1999, which has caused serious casualties and property damage. The Council expresses its deepest sympathy and profound condolences to the Chinese Government and families of the victims.
>
> The Council expresses profound regrets over the bombing and deep sorrow for the loss of lives, injuries and property damage caused by the bombing, and notes that regrets and apologies were expressed for this tragedy by members of the North Atlantic Treaty Organization. The Council, bearing in mind the Charter of the United Nations, reaffirms that the principle of the inviolability of diplomatic personnel and premises must be respected in all cases in accordance with internationally accepted norms.
>
> The Council stresses the need for a complete and thorough investigation of the bombing by the North Atlantic Treaty Organization. In this connection, it takes note of the fact that an investigation has been initiated by the North Atlantic Treaty Organization and awaits the results of the investigation.
>
> The Council will remain seized of this matter.

India informed the Council President that, on 20 May [S/1999/607], its Ambassador's residence in Belgrade was damaged by NATO. India said that it was unacceptable that diplomatic property and lives should continue to be put at risk in a war whose targets were increasingly indiscriminate and carried out without the Council's authority. FRY, in a 26 May aide-memoire [S/1999/619], reported damage to diplomatic and consular property of 18 other countries.

Humanitarian situation

On 3 April, FRY addressed letters to UNHCR [S/1999/376] and ICRC [S/1999/375] concerning the humanitarian catastrophe caused by the NATO aggression, stating that thousands of tons of NATO and United States bombs and explosives had hit towns, villages, refugee camps, cultural and historic monuments, religious shrines, schools, hospitals, bridges, factories and other civilian targets across Yugoslavia. Particularly tragic were the consequences of attacks in downtown areas of large cities, such as Belgrade, Pristina, Novi Sad, Cacak and others. Recently, NATO had destroyed a regional water system in Novi Sad supplying 600,000 people, and hit two shelters housing refugees from Bosnia and Herzegovina and Croatia, several hospitals, over 100 schools, cultural monuments and places of worship, telephone lines and other communications, private homes, farms and pharmaceutical plants. Some 11 refugees were killed in Kursumlija, and the destruction of chemical storages and other chemical industrial facilities had endangered the environment. FRY asked for assistance for refugees and the displaced. On 4 April [S/1999/371, S/1999/377], FRY informed the Secretary-General of the civilian destruction and destruction of its national heritage.

On 7 April [S/1999/391], the Council President circulated an exchange of letters between the NATO Secretary-General and the United Nations High Commissioner for Refugees. The NATO Secretary-General said that the North Atlantic Council had invited him to raise with the High Commissioner, as a matter of urgency, possible measures NATO could take to assist UNHCR in addressing the current humanitarian crisis in Albania and FYROM.

The High Commissioner informed the NATO Secretary-General that the scale of the crisis was such that UNHCR's capacity to respond had been overwhelmed, especially in Albania and FYROM, where over 270,000 people had arrived since 24 March and were continuing to arrive on an hourly basis. The High Commissioner, welcoming NATO's assistance, suggested that the operation should focus on those two countries where the need was greatest, and would welcome assistance with the management of the airlift operation to bring supplies into Tirana and Skopje airports; support in offloading and storage of aid; and logistical help in setting up refugee camps. UNHCR would provide the coordination, guidance and technical support. There was also need to relieve the pressure on FYROM, which otherwise risked destabilization. The High Commissioner requested that NATO members, particularly Greece, agree to accept some of the refugees in FYROM temporarily and welcomed offers of support from OSCE and OSCE/KVM, particularly in the processing of arrivals at critical border entry points.

In a 9 April statement [S/1999/402], the Secretary-General said that he was deeply distressed by the humanitarian tragedy in Kosovo and the region. He urgently called on the Yugoslav authorities to end immediately the campaign of intimidation and expulsion of civilians; cease all activities of military and paramilitary forces and withdraw them; accept unconditionally the return of all refugees and displaced persons; accept the deployment of an international military force to ensure a secure environment for their return and the unimpeded delivery of humanitarian aid; and permit the international community to verify compliance with those undertakings. Upon acceptance by the Yugoslav authorities of those conditions, he would urge NATO leaders to suspend immediately the air bombardments. The cessation of hostilities was a prelude to a lasting political solution to the crisis, which could only be achieved through diplomacy. He urged the resumption of talks among all parties concerned.

Responding to the Secretary-General's appeal, FRY, on 16 April [S/1999/436], denied that there was a campaign of intimidation or expulsion of the civilian population. NATO's aggression and bombing had caused enormous destruction and mass civilian casualties, resulting in an increased number of refugees and displaced persons. All FRY forces' activities against KLA had ceased on 6 April and the cessation was still in force. However, it was incomprehensible to request withdrawal of the legitimate forces of a sovereign State from its territory instead of calling for an end to foreign military aggression. The safe return of refugees and displaced persons was a Yugoslav policy priority, but it was hampered by the destruction of towns such as Pristina, Djakovica, Prizren, Decani and others. To resolve the humanitarian issues, its authorities were ready to cooperate with UNHCR and ICRC. FRY continued its efforts towards finding a peaceful solution through direct dialogue with the legitimate representatives of the national communities of Kosovo and Metohija.

On 8 April [S/1999/414], the EU Special General Council deplored the closure of FRY borders with Albania and FYROM to refugees. It supported the UNHCR regional refugee concept allowing them to return to their homes as soon as possible, but recognized the need to make the overwhelming task on the ground manageable by providing effective protection as extensively as possible. The EU would continue to assist the most affected countries to counter the destabilizing effects of the flow of deportees and urged the speedy implementation of the European Commission's assistance package for neighbouring Governments, in particular Albania and FYROM. The EU was working with international financial institutions to alleviate the exceptional burdens of the countries most affected. It welcomed FYROM's efforts to alleviate the plight of the deportees and urged it to intensify those efforts. It also welcomed Albania's stated readiness to accept, in addition to the huge numbers already admitted, additional deportees. It underlined its concern over the situation in the FRY Republic of Montenegro and reconfirmed its support for that Government and its readiness to help in coping with the flow of deportees. EU assistance would be directed to Montenegro for humanitarian and budgetary aid.

On 14 April [S/1999/417], Australia appealed to the Secretary-General to use his good offices to obtain the release of two Australians (Steve Pratt and Peter Wallace) working with the humanitarian organization CARE Australia, detained by FRY since 31 March. FRY, on 18 April [S/1999/439], confirmed the arrest of the two Australians, who, it said, had confessed to engaging in espionage. FRY said it found the Secretary-General's interest in the arrest of the two military spies completely out of step with the situation and his functions, especially since he had not condemned the aggression against FRY or the massacre of refugee convoys on 14 April on the Djakovica-Prizren road, in which NATO massacred 75 children, women and elderly people. On 19 April [S/1999/438], the Australian Special Envoy said CARE was concerned with maintaining its relationship with FRY to continue its humanitarian mission and assist in national reconstruction after the conflict. He appealed for the release of the two Australians at the earliest opportunity, with the undertaking that they would leave FRY.

FRY, in a 19 April aide-memoire [S/1999/437] on the humanitarian consequences of NATO aggression, further outlined the extent of the civilian casualties and listed the material damage caused by the bombings. It reported that both FRY and Serbia had issued a call to displaced persons and refugees to return safely to their homes. Its 6 April declaration of cessation of all anti-terrorist activities in Kosovo and Metohija was an important step for a successful solution of the humanitarian problems. It had also reached agreement with Ibrahim Rugova (one of the Kosovo Albanian leaders) on joint involvement in creating conditions for the return of refugees, as well as on the solution of other humanitarian issues, in cooperation with ICRC, UNHCR and Yugoslav humanitarian organizations. FRY and the Russian Federation complained also of the environmental consequences of NATO's aggression, particularly the bombing of environmentally hazardous targets [S/1999/458, A/53/921-S/1999/462, E/1999/46] and the destruction of FRY's agriculture [S/1999/511, A/53/941]. Both countries also drew attention to the destruction of civilian targets [S/1999/472, S/1999/592].

Iran, as Chairman of the OIC Contact Group, expressed concern on 22 April [S/1999/469] over the increasing number of Sandjak Muslims being forced to flee, mostly to Bosnia and Herzegovina. They were being victimized by an accelerated campaign of ethnic cleansing orchestrated by FRY, similar to that suffered by Albanian Kosovars. Iran urged the Council to address the situation and considered that the crimes perpetrated by regular Yugoslav Army and paramilitary forces deserved to be reviewed by ICTY.

Uruguay, on 22 April [S/1999/473], indicated its readiness to accept refugees from Kosovo. The Foreign Ministers of the G-8 group of highly industrialized countries, meeting on 6 May [S/1999/516], outlined a number of general principles designed to break the political deadlock, including the safe return of all refugees and displaced persons and unimpeded access to Kosovo by humanitarian aid organizations (see p. 352 for details).

SECURITY COUNCIL ACTION

On 14 May [meeting 4003], the Security Council adopted **resolution 1239(1999)** by vote (13-0-2). The draft [S/1999/517] was submitted by Argentina, Bahrain, Bosnia and Herzegovina, Brazil, Egypt, Gabon, the Gambia, Iran, Jordan, Kuwait, Malaysia, Morocco, Namibia, Pakistan, Qatar, Saudi Arabia, Senegal, Slovenia, Turkey, the United Arab Emirates and Yemen.

The Security Council,

Recalling its resolutions 1160(1998) of 31 March 1998, 1199(1998) of 23 September 1998 and 1203(1998) of 24 October 1998, and the statements by its President of 24 August 1998, 19 January 1999 and 29 January 1999,

Bearing in mind the provisions of the Charter of the United Nations, and guided by the Universal Declaration of Human Rights, the international covenants and conventions on human rights, the 1951 Convention and the 1967 Protocol relating to the Status of Refugees, the Geneva Conventions of 1949 and the Additional Protocols thereto of 1977, as well as other instruments of international humanitarian law,

Expressing grave concern at the humanitarian catastrophe in and around Kosovo, Federal Republic of Yugoslavia, as a result of the continuing crisis,

Deeply concerned by the enormous influx of Kosovo refugees into Albania, the former Yugoslav Republic of Macedonia, Bosnia and Herzegovina, and other countries, as well as by the increasing numbers of displaced persons within Kosovo, the Republic of Montenegro and other parts of the Federal Republic of Yugoslavia,

Stressing the importance of effective coordination of humanitarian relief activities undertaken by States, the Office of the United Nations High Commissioner for Refugees and international organizations in alleviating the plight and suffering of refugees and internally displaced persons,

Noting with interest the intention of the Secretary-General to send a humanitarian needs assessment mission to Kosovo and other parts of the Federal Republic of Yugoslavia,

Reaffirming the territorial integrity and sovereignty of all States in the region,

1. *Commends* the efforts that have been taken by Member States, the Office of the United Nations High Commissioner for Refugees and other international humanitarian relief organizations in providing urgently needed relief assistance to the Kosovo refugees in Albania, the former Yugoslav Republic of Macedonia and Bosnia and Herzegovina, and urges them and others in a position to do so to contribute resources for humanitarian assistance to the refugees and internally displaced persons;

2. *Invites* the Office of the United Nations High Commissioner for Refugees and other international humanitarian relief organizations to extend relief assistance to the internally displaced persons in Kosovo, the Republic of Montenegro and other parts of the Federal Republic of Yugoslavia, as well as to other civilians being affected by the ongoing crisis;

3. *Calls* for access for United Nations and all other humanitarian personnel operating in Kosovo and other parts of the Federal Republic of Yugoslavia;

4. *Reaffirms* the right of all refugees and displaced persons to return to their homes in safety and in dignity;

5. *Emphasizes* that the humanitarian situation will continue to deteriorate in the absence of a political solution to the crisis consistent with the principles adopted by the Ministers for Foreign Affairs of Canada, France, Germany, Italy, Japan, the Russian Federation, the United Kingdom of Great Britain and Northern Ireland and the United States of America on 6 May 1999, and urges all concerned to work towards this aim;

6. *Decides* to remain actively seized of the matter.

VOTE ON RESOLUTION 1239(1999):

In favour: Argentina, Bahrain, Brazil, Canada, France, Gabon, Gambia, Malaysia, Namibia, Netherlands, Slovenia, United Kingdom, United States.
Against: None.
Abstaining: China, Russian Federation.

In a 7 May letter concerning the draft text [S/1999/528], FRY had said that the Council's lack of readiness to condemn aggression continued to cause a humanitarian catastrophe all over Yugoslavia. FRY was ready to have humanitarian assistance distributed to all parts of the country, but those efforts had been rendered impossible by the continued NATO bombing, primarily of civilian targets. Dealing with the humanitarian issue in isolation diverted attention from the real cause, namely NATO's aggression. Speaking in the Council at the invitation of the President, FRY stated that NATO's 51-day campaign of terror and devastation was targeting civilians, infrastructure and the economy. More than 1,200 people had been killed and over 5,000 wounded. The Council's concern about the humanitarian situation was justified, but the attempt to legalize NATO's aggression by means of a so-called humanitarian resolution was not. The draft should contain a demand that the NATO aggression be stopped immediately and unconditionally.

Introducing the draft text in the Council, Bahrain said the text's goals were to draw the attention of the international community to the humanitarian catastrophe occurring in Kosovo, which had led to the displacement of 840,000 persons within FRY and more than 700,000 outside the country, and to make it possible for the Council to review the Kosovo situation from the humanitarian perspective and make humanitarian concerns fundamental to the consideration of the military and political aspects of the situation when it was ready to do so.

While expressing its sympathy for the Kosovars left homeless and separated from their loved ones, China said of equal concern was that, without the Council's authorization, NATO had launched military attacks against FRY and thus unleashed a regional war in the Balkans. China also referred to the attack on its Embassy (see p. 346). China had proposed amending the draft to include a reference to the need for an immediate cessation of all military activities. However, as that position was not accepted, China had no choice but to abstain.

The Russian Federation said that unless there was an immediate cessation to NATO's illegal military action, genuine progress would be impossible, either towards a political settlement or to overcome the humanitarian catastrophe. Since that fact was not reflected in the text, the Russian Federation could not support it.

The United States said it had contributed and would continue to contribute to humanitarian relief efforts, including building a camp in Albania to house 20,000 refugees. Also, the first of 20,000 Kosovar Albanians had recently arrived in the United States. However, it remained firm in its resolve to exert pressure on the FRY Government to stop its planned, systematic campaign of ethnic cleansing and to permit the return of all refugees and displaced persons.

On 14 May [S/1999/562], FRY informed the Council President that NATO planes had hit the refugee centre at Koriste near Suva Reka and Prizren, which accommodated refugees on their way back home from Albania, killing 79 of them, mostly women, children and the elderly. It accused NATO on 15 May [S/1999/564] of using banned military means and weapons, such as cluster bombs and depleted uranium, damaging and threatening the health and lives of the people. On 25 May [S/1999/620], it submitted a memorandum on the humanitarian consequences of the NATO aggression against it. FRY claimed that, since the onset of the aggression, over 10,000 tons of explosives were dropped with the destructive effect 10 times more than the nuclear bomb in the attack on Hiroshima, Japan. NATO had killed more than 1,700 civilians by 21 May, while over 10,000 people sustained injuries, many of whom had been crippled for life. At the same time, several thousand private homes and flats had been ruined. It had also embarked on a systematic destruction of FRY's power grid, bringing about a humanitarian catastrophe of unforeseen proportions, denying the entire population food, water and drugs and depriving its industry of power sources [S/1999/604].

FRY said on 3 June [S/1999/647] that it was open to accepting humanitarian aid from all countries, but was opposed to initiatives by some foreign Governments and NGOs to airdrop humanitarian relief to the inhabitants of Kosovo and Metohija, as that form of providing aid was fraught with great risks and could lead to undesired consequences. Furthermore, it was not necessary, since there were no obstacles to sending humanitarian dispatches over safer land routes. Humanitarian aid would have to be dispatched on the basis of cooperation with competent Yugoslav organs and institutions, with their full agreement and insight.

Inter-Agency Needs Assessment Mission

Against the background of the the grave humanitarian and human rights situation in Kosovo, the Secretary-General, with FRY's agreement, dispatched a United Nations Inter-Agency Needs Assessment Mission to FRY from 16 to 27 May [S/1999/662] to provide an initial assessment of the emergency needs of civilian populations and of the medium-term rehabilitation requirements, in the light of the approaching winter. That would be followed later by a more in-depth assessment, as well as sectoral evaluations by relevant agencies.

The Mission report stated that, in addition to immediate humanitarian needs of the refugees, internally displaced and other civilian populations, the socio-economic, environmental and physical toll of the conflict throughout FRY and beyond was immense and had created a new type of complex humanitarian emergency. The challenges presented by the emergency in a comparatively developed environment exceeded the humanitarian purview, the experience and capacity of any single agency. It would require, before and especially after a settlement of the Kosovo conflict was achieved, comprehensive action by the United Nations, the international financial institutions, regional organizations, ICRC, the International Federation of Red Cross and Red Crescent Societies and NGOs to address all the aspects of the crisis.

The Mission recommended a regional, integrated strategy, encompassing all south-eastern European countries and regions, and coordinated with and integrated into overall UN activities, including its peacekeeping and peacemaking efforts.

The United Nations, cooperating with intergovernmental organizations and NGOs, should urgently re-establish the necessary humanitarian and development presence in FRY, including in Belgrade, Pristina and Podgorica, to mount a comprehensive relief operation and to carry out more detailed sectoral assessments in FRY, particularly in Kosovo. In Kosovo, a clear distinction should be made between the pre-peace and post-peace scenarios. Prior to a peace settlement, the United Nations Kosovo office would be responsible for relief assistance in all accessible areas of the province, contingency planning and eventual implementation of operations to support the return and reintegration of refugees and internally displaced persons, preparations for the coming winter and other emergency and rehabilitation needs.

As part of a peace settlement, humanitarian, refugee and internally displaced person reintegration and rehabilitation activities should be given the highest priority under the leadership of a single entity as an integral component of an eventual unitary civilian implementation structure. A small operational inter-agency planning and coordination cell should be established in advance of its actual deployment, under the lead humanitarian agency and with support from the Office for the Coordination of Humanitarian Affairs, to be responsible for joint planning, coordination and allocation of tasks among all humanitarian organizations, as well as for coordination with other civilian components and the military contingents. The legal and administrative procedures to facilitate the work of NGOs within FRY needed to be established. An early and favourable resolution of the case of the Australian CARE staff detained by FRY authorities (see p. 348) was urgently required and the United Nations should continue to seek their release.

The report also made recommendations in relation to justice, including enabling ICTY to carry out its mandate, establishment of a substantial capacity for human rights monitoring, assistance to refugees and displaced persons, emergency assistance to civilians throughout FRY, women and children, winterization plans, budgetary support to Montenegro, a smooth transition from short-term to longer-term rehabilitation and reconstruction, preparation of reconstruction and development plans for Kosovo and ultimately FRY, employment promotion schemes, assessment of the full extent of the environmental impact of the NATO bombing, agriculture, health, mine action and small arms.

The Mission further recommended development of governance programmes for FRY and in particular Kosovo, in the context of a possible transitional administration as a priority area for the United Nations.

The General Assembly, on 15 December, adopted **resolution 54/96 F** on humanitarian assistance to FRY (see p. 844) and **resolution 54/96 G** on economic assistance to the Eastern European States affected by the developments in the Balkans (see p. 857).

Further peace proposals

On 6 April [S/1999/388], FRY and the Republic of Serbia announced that, proceeding from the joint statement signed on 1 April between FRY President Milosevic and Kosovo Albanian leader Ibrahim Rugova, and the 5 April agreement between Mr. Rugova and the FRY Vice-President to act jointly to achieve a political settlement and to work jointly on the return of refugees, all actions of the Yugoslav Army and police in Kosovo and Metohija against KLA should cease unilaterally beginning 6 April as a goodwill gesture in honour of the Easter holiday. They expected extreme elements to exercise restraint also. Government representatives should immediately, in cooperation with Mr. Rugova, prepare a political agreement, including an interim agreement to ensure the functioning of joint organs of self-government in Kosovo and Metohija of the Albanian and Serb national communities, which would eventually form the basis for lasting substantial autonomy in Kosovo and Metohija, within Serbia and FRY. They would also prepare a programme for the return of refugees and the establishment of self-government, with participation and assistance from UNHCR and ICRC.

Reacting to the FRY announcement of a unilateral ceasefire, Germany, in a 7 April statement [S/1999/413], agreed to by the Foreign Ministers of France, Italy, the United Kingdom and the United States, said that the ceasefire did not cover the activities of Serb police and paramilitaries, and was an insufficient basis for achieving the international community's objective of a peaceful, multi-ethnic, democratic Kosovo. Belgrade's proposal left unanswered questions relating to President Milosevic's preparedness for verification of combat activities; withdrawal of military, police and paramilitary forces; agreement to the deployment of an international security force; the unconditional return of all refugees and unimpeded access for humanitarian aid; and the putting in place of a political framework for Kosovo on the basis of the Rambouillet Accords. Belgrade's ceasefire proposal would be without significance unless accompanied by positive answers to those questions. The Foreign Ministers called for the release of Mr. Rugova and his family and for the international community to meet with him outside FRY under conditions free from intimidation.

The heads of State and Government of the EU (Brussels, 14 April) [S/1999/429] said they supported the Secretary-General's 9 April initiative [S/1999/402] (see p. 347). It was up to the Yugoslav authorities to accept fully the demands of the international community and begin immediately their implementation to permit a suspension of NATO military action and pave the way for a political solution. They agreed on the following elements of an interim arrangement for Kosovo, to be established directly after the end of the conflict: establishment of an international interim administration, which the EU could take over; creation of a police force reflecting the composition of the Kosovo population; holding of free and fair elections; and deployment of international military forces to guarantee protection for the whole Kosovo population. The EU would convene a Conference on South-Eastern Europe to decide further comprehensive measures for the long-term stabilization, security, democratization and economic reconstruction of the entire region.

On the same date [S/1999/428], Germany submitted to the Security Council a proposed solution to the Kosovo crisis, based on the results of a G-8 meeting of Political Directors in Dresden, Germany, setting out a list of demands to Belgrade, which should form the basis of a Council resolution (see p. 353).

Costa Rica, on 15 April [A/53/913-S/1999/435], welcomed the German and EU proposals and urged the parties to engage in effective negotiations with a view to formulating a peace accord acceptable to all involved. It appealed to the Council and the General Assembly to play a more active role in the solution of the conflict and the Secretary-General to intensify his efforts in that regard.

Ukraine President, Leonid Kuchma, in a 15 April press briefing [A/53/911-S/1999/431], revealed that he had proposed on 24 March a three-phase plan, which, in addition to providing for the cessation of FRY military action, the withdrawal of its armed forces, creation of conditions for the return of refugees and the end to NATO air strikes, envisaged the formation of a peacekeeping contingent under UN auspices, led by a Special Envoy or Representative of the Secretary-General and staffed from non-block and neutral States. The second phase would include the return of refugees under the supervision of peacekeeping forces, and the deployment of an OSCE humanitarian mission to ensure their return and housing, while the third phase could constitute the convening of a peace conference in the capital of one of the neutral States. Ukraine formally submitted its plan to the Council President and the Secretary-General on 17 April [S/1999/433]. Similar proposals were made by Yemen on 21 April [S/1999/465], Mexico on 21 April [A/53/929-S/1999/484] and the OIC Contact Group on 22 April [S/1999/468], which expressed support for the Secretary-General's initiatives and diplomatic efforts.

Special Envoys. On 6 May [S/1999/526], the Secretary-General appointed Carl Bildt (Sweden) and Eduard Kukan (Slovakia) as his Special Envoys for the Balkans to assist him in restoring peace and security and establishing conditions conducive to the voluntary return in safety of refugees and displaced persons to their homes, including maintaining contact with all parties concerned, facilitating a lasting political solution to the crisis, as well as interim arrangements, and helping to coordinate UN system efforts to ensure coherence and avoid duplication. The Council took note of his decision on 7 May [S/1999/527].

Peace agreement

On 6 May [S/1999/516], the G-8 Foreign Ministers, meeting in Bonn, Germany, adopted general principles on the political solution to the Kosovo crisis, and instructed their Political Directors to prepare elements of a UN resolution (see resolution 1244(1999), annex I, below) and draw up a roadmap of further concrete steps towards a political solution. The G-8 Presidency would inform the Government of China on the results of the meeting.

On 17 May [S/1999/589], the EU welcomed the adoption of the G-8 principles and supported Finnish President Martti Ahtisaari's willingness to work on its behalf, in cooperation with the Russian Federation and the United States, to ensure implementation of the international community's conditions to end the conflict. It also welcomed the Secretary-General's appointment of Special Envoys for the Kosovo crisis (see above). The EU stressed the need for an early Security Council resolution and confirmed its preparedness to bring such a resolution about. On 31 May [S/1999/650], the EU announced a mission to Belgrade, to be led by President Ahtisaari on its behalf, in close cooperation with the United States, the Russian Federation and the United Nations.

FRY, on 1 June [S/1999/631], indicated acceptance of the G-8 principles, including a UN presence, the mandate and other modalities which would be established by a Security Council resolution, with the precondition of an urgent cessation of the NATO aggression and the refocusing on political issues to achieve a stable and lasting political solution. It also conveyed to the Secretary-General, on 4 June [S/1999/646], its and Serbia's acceptance of the peace plan (principles) presented by President Ahtisaari and Victor Chernomyrdin, the Russian Federation President's personal envoy.

That peace plan, agreed to by the EU and brought to the Council President's attention on 7 June by Germany [S/1999/649], set out the terms and conditions and modalities to end the violence and echoed the principles established by the G-8 Foreign Ministers: withdrawal from Kosovo of military police and paramilitary forces; deployment in Kosovo, under UN auspices, of an international civil and security presence; deployment under unified command of an international security presence with substantial NATO participation; establishment of an interim administration for Kosovo; the return of a limited number of Yugoslav and Serbian personnel to perform specific identified functions; the return of refugees and displaced persons; a political process towards the establishment of an interim political framework agreement providing for substantial self-government for Kosovo; a comprehensive approach to economic development and stabilization of the crisis region; and acceptance of those principles and others previously identified. A military-technical agreement would then be concluded that would, among other things, specify additional modalities, including the roles and functions of Yugoslav/Serb personnel in Kosovo.

FRY said on 7 June [S/1999/655] that, having accepted the Ahtisaari-Chernomyrdin document on a peaceful solution for Kosovo and Metohija, it expected the Security Council to speed up the passing of its resolution. As negotiations of the military experts were being completed and the withdrawal of FRY's forces could begin immediately, FRY was of the view that the conditions had been created for a halt to the bombing. It wanted to be assured that a security vacuum would not be created between the period of its withdrawal and assumption of responsibility for the population's security by UN-sponsored forces. It expected the Council resolution to ensure respect for FRY's sovereignty and territorial integrity. However, on the same date [S/1999/658, S/1999/653], FRY complained that KLA, supported by Albanian armed forces and NATO, continued to carry out armed attacks against the Yugoslav Army defending the country's border. That followed earlier similar complaints to the Security Council President [S/1999/626, S/1999/628, S/1999/629, S/1999/637, S/1999/638].

SECURITY COUNCIL ACTION

On 10 June [meeting 4011], the Security Council adopted **resolution 1244(1999)** by vote (14-0-1). The draft [S/1999/661] was submitted by Bahrain, Canada, France, Gabon, Germany, Italy, Japan, the Netherlands, the Russian Federation, Slovenia, Ukraine, the United Kingdom and the United States.

The Security Council,

Bearing in mind the purposes and principles of the Charter of the United Nations, and the primary responsibility of the Security Council for the maintenance of international peace and security,

Recalling its resolutions 1160(1998) of 31 March 1998, 1199(1998) of 23 September 1998, 1203(1998) of 24 October 1998 and 1239(1999) of 14 May 1999,

Regretting that there has not been full compliance with the requirements of those resolutions,

Determined to resolve the grave humanitarian situation in Kosovo, Federal Republic of Yugoslavia, and to provide for the safe and free return of all refugees and displaced persons to their homes,

Condemning all acts of violence against the Kosovo population as well as all terrorist acts by any party,

Recalling the statement made by the Secretary-General on 9 April 1999, expressing concern at the humanitarian tragedy taking place in Kosovo,

Reaffirming the right of all refugees and displaced persons to return to their homes in safety,

Recalling the jurisdiction and the mandate of the International Tribunal for the Prosecution of Persons Responsible for Serious Violations of International Humanitarian Law Committed in the Territory of the Former Yugoslavia since 1991,

Welcoming the general principles on a political solution to the Kosovo crisis adopted on 6 May 1999, contained in annex I to the present resolution, and welcoming also the acceptance by the Federal Republic of Yugoslavia of the principles set forth in points 1 to 9 of the paper presented in Belgrade on 2 June 1999, contained in annex II to the present resolution, and the agreement of the Federal Republic of Yugoslavia to that paper,

Reaffirming the commitment of all Member States to the sovereignty and territorial integrity of the Federal Republic of Yugoslavia and the other States of the region, as set out in the Final Act of the Conference on Security and Cooperation in Europe, signed at Helsinki 1 August 1975, and in annex II to the present resolution,

Reaffirming the call in previous resolutions for substantial autonomy and meaningful self-administration for Kosovo,

Determining that the situation in the region continues to constitute a threat to international peace and security,

Determined to ensure the safety and security of international personnel and the implementation by all concerned of their responsibilities under the present resolution, and acting for these purposes under Chapter VII of the Charter of the United Nations,

1. *Decides* that a political solution to the Kosovo crisis shall be based on the general principles in annex I to the present resolution and as further elaborated in the principles and other required elements in annex II;

2. *Welcomes* the acceptance by the Federal Republic of Yugoslavia of the principles and other required elements referred to in paragraph 1 above, and demands the full cooperation of the Federal Republic of Yugoslavia in their rapid implementation;

3. *Demands* in particular that the Federal Republic of Yugoslavia put an immediate and verifiable end to violence and repression in Kosovo, and begin and complete verifiable phased withdrawal from Kosovo of all military, police and paramilitary forces according to a rapid timetable, with which the deployment of the international security presence in Kosovo will be synchronized;

4. *Confirms* that after the withdrawal, an agreed number of Yugoslav and Serb military and police personnel will be permitted to return to Kosovo to perform the functions in accordance with annex II;

5. *Decides* on the deployment in Kosovo, under United Nations auspices, of international civil and security presences, with appropriate equipment and personnel as required, and welcomes the agreement of the Federal Republic of Yugoslavia to such presences;

6. *Requests* the Secretary-General to appoint, in consultation with the Security Council, a Special Representative to control the implementation of the international civil presence, and further requests the Secretary-General to instruct his Special Representative to coordinate closely with the international security presence to ensure that both presences operate towards the same goals and in a mutually supportive manner;

7. *Authorizes* Member States and relevant international organizations to establish the international security presence in Kosovo as set out in point 4 of annex II with all necessary means to fulfil its responsibilities under paragraph 9 below;

8. *Affirms* the need for the rapid early deployment of effective international civil and security presences to Kosovo, and demands that the parties cooperate fully in their deployment;

9. *Decides* that the responsibilities of the international security presence to be deployed and acting in Kosovo will include:

(*a*) Deterring renewed hostilities, maintaining and where necessary enforcing a ceasefire, and ensuring the withdrawal and preventing the return into Kosovo of Federal and Republic military, police and paramilitary forces, except as provided for in point 6 of annex II;

(*b*) Demilitarizing the Kosovo Liberation Army and other armed Kosovo Albanian groups, as required in paragraph 15 below;

(*c*) Establishing a secure environment in which refugees and displaced persons can return home in safety, the international civil presence can operate, a transitional administration can be established, and humanitarian aid can be delivered;

(*d*) Ensuring public safety and order until the international civil presence can take responsibility for this task;

(*e*) Supervising demining until the international civil presence can, as appropriate, take over responsibility for this task;

(*f*) Supporting, as appropriate, and coordinating closely with the work of the international civil presence;

(*g*) Conducting border monitoring duties as required;

(*h*) Ensuring the protection and freedom of movement of itself, the international civil presence, and other international organizations;

10. *Authorizes* the Secretary-General, with the assistance of relevant international organizations, to establish an international civil presence in Kosovo in order to provide an interim administration for Kosovo under which the people of Kosovo can enjoy substantial autonomy within the Federal Republic of Yugoslavia and which will provide transitional administration while establishing and overseeing the development of provisional democratic self-governing institutions to ensure conditions for a peaceful and normal life for all inhabitants of Kosovo;

11. *Decides* that the main responsibilities of the international civil presence will include:

(*a*) Promoting the establishment, pending a final settlement, of substantial autonomy and self-government in Kosovo, taking full account of annex II and of the Rambouillet Accords;

(*b*) Performing basic civilian administrative functions where and as long as required;

(*c*) Organizing and overseeing the development of provisional institutions for democratic and autonomous self-government pending a political settlement, including the holding of elections;

(*d*) Transferring, as these institutions are established, its administrative responsibilities while overseeing and supporting the consolidation of Kosovo's local provisional institutions and other peace-building activities;

(*e*) Facilitating a political process designed to determine the future status of Kosovo, taking into account the Rambouillet Accords;

(*f*) In a final stage, overseeing the transfer of authority from Kosovo's provisional institutions to institutions established under a political settlement;

(*g*) Supporting the reconstruction of key infrastructure and other economic reconstruction;

(*h*) Supporting, in coordination with international humanitarian organizations, humanitarian and disaster relief aid;

(*i*) Maintaining civil law and order, including establishing local police forces and in the meantime through the deployment of international police personnel to serve in Kosovo;

(*j*) Protecting and promoting human rights;

(*k*) Assuring the safe and unimpeded return of all refugees and displaced persons to their homes in Kosovo;

12. *Emphasizes* the need for coordinated humanitarian relief operations, and for the Federal Republic of

Yugoslavia to allow unimpeded access to Kosovo by humanitarian aid organizations and to cooperate with such organizations so as to ensure the fast and effective delivery of international aid;

13. *Encourages* all Member States and international organizations to contribute to economic and social reconstruction as well as to the safe return of refugees and displaced persons, and emphasizes in this context the importance of convening an international donors conference, particularly for the purposes set out in paragraph 11 *(g)* above, at the earliest possible date;

14. *Demands* full cooperation by all concerned, including the international security presence, with the International Tribunal for the Prosecution of Persons Responsible for Serious Violations of International Humanitarian Law Committed in the Territory of the Former Yugoslavia since 1991;

15. *Demands* that the Kosovo Liberation Army and other armed Kosovo Albanian groups end immediately all offensive actions and comply with the requirements for demilitarization as laid down by the head of the international security presence in consultation with the Special Representative of the Secretary-General;

16. *Decides* that the prohibitions imposed by paragraph 8 of resolution 1160(1998) shall not apply to arms and related materiel for the use of the international civil and security presences;

17. *Welcomes* the work in hand in the European Union and other international organizations to develop a comprehensive approach to the economic development and stabilization of the region affected by the Kosovo crisis, including the implementation of a stability pact for South-Eastern Europe, with broad international participation, in order to further the promotion of democracy, economic prosperity, stability and regional cooperation;

18. *Demands* that all States in the region cooperate fully in the implementation of all aspects of the present resolution;

19. *Decides* that the international civil and security presences are established for an initial period of twelve months, to continue thereafter unless the Security Council decides otherwise;

20. *Requests* the Secretary-General to report to the Council at regular intervals on the implementation of the present resolution, including reports from the leadership of the international civil and security presences, the first reports to be submitted within thirty days of the adoption of this resolution;

21. *Decides* to remain actively seized of the matter.

ANNEX I

Statement by the Chairman on the conclusion of the meeting of the G-8 Foreign Ministers held at the Petersberg Centre on 6 May 1999

The G-8 Foreign Ministers adopted the following general principles on the political solution to the Kosovo crisis:

—Immediate and verifiable end of violence and repression in Kosovo;

—Withdrawal from Kosovo of military, police and paramilitary forces;

—Deployment in Kosovo of effective international civil and security presences, endorsed and adopted by the United Nations, capable of guaranteeing the achievement of the common objectives;

—Establishment of an interim administration for Kosovo to be decided by the Security Council of the United Nations to ensure conditions for a peaceful and normal life for all inhabitants in Kosovo;

—The safe and free return of all refugees and displaced persons and unimpeded access to Kosovo by humanitarian aid organizations;

—A political process towards the establishment of an interim political framework agreement providing for a substantial self-government for Kosovo, taking full account of the Rambouillet Accords and the principles of sovereignty and territorial integrity of the Federal Republic of Yugoslavia and the other countries of the region, and the demilitarization of the Kosovo Liberation Army;

—Comprehensive approach to the economic development and stabilization of the crisis region.

ANNEX II

Agreement should be reached on the following principles to move towards a resolution of the Kosovo crisis:

1. An immediate and verifiable end of violence and repression in Kosovo.

2. A verifiable withdrawal from Kosovo of all military, police and paramilitary forces according to a rapid timetable.

3. Deployment in Kosovo under United Nations auspices of effective international civil and security presences, acting as may be decided under Chapter VII of the Charter of the United Nations, capable of guaranteeing the achievement of common objectives.

4. The international security presence with substantial North Atlantic Treaty Organization participation must be deployed under unified command and control and authorized to establish a safe environment for all people in Kosovo and to facilitate the safe return to their homes of all displaced persons and refugees.

5. The establishment of an interim administration for Kosovo as a part of the international civil presence under which the people of Kosovo can enjoy substantial autonomy within the Federal Republic of Yugoslavia, to be decided by the Security Council of the United Nations. The interim administration would provide transitional administration while establishing and overseeing the development of provisional democratic self-governing institutions to ensure conditions for a peaceful and normal life for all inhabitants in Kosovo.

6. After withdrawal, an agreed number of Yugoslav and Serbian personnel will be permitted to return to perform the following functions:

—Liaising with the international civil mission and the international security presence;

—Marking/clearing minefields;

—Maintaining a presence at Serb patrimonial sites;

—Maintaining a presence at key border crossings.

7. The safe and free return of all refugees and displaced persons under the supervision of the Office of the United Nations High Commissioner for Refugees and unimpeded access to Kosovo by humanitarian aid organizations.

8. A political process towards the establishment of an interim political framework agreement providing for substantial self-government for Kosovo, taking full account of the Rambouillet Accords and the principles of sovereignty and territorial integrity of the Federal

Republic of Yugoslavia and the other countries of the region, and the demilitarization of the Kosovo Liberation Army. Negotiations between the parties for a settlement should not delay or disrupt the establishment of democratic self-governing institutions.

9. A comprehensive approach to the economic development and stabilization of the crisis region. This will include the implementation of a stability pact for South-Eastern Europe with broad international participation in order to further the promotion of democracy, economic prosperity, stability and regional cooperation.

10. The suspension of military activity will require acceptance of the principles set forth above in addition to agreement to other, previously identified, required elements, which are specified in the note below. A military-technical agreement will then be rapidly concluded that would, among other things, specify additional modalities, including the roles and functions of Yugoslav/Serb personnel in Kosovo:

Withdrawal

—Procedures for withdrawals, including the phased, detailed schedule and delineation of a buffer area in Serbia beyond which forces will be withdrawn;

Returning personnel

—Equipment associated with returning personnel;
—Terms of reference for their functional responsibilities;
—Timetable for their return;
—Delineation of their geographical areas of operation;
—Rules governing their relationship to the international security presence and the international civil mission.

Note

Other required elements

—A rapid and precise timetable for withdrawals, meaning, for example, seven days to complete withdrawal, and air defence weapons outside a 25-kilometre mutual safety zone to be withdrawn within 48 hours;
—The return of personnel for the four functions specified above will be under the supervision of the international security presence and will be limited to a small, agreed number (hundreds, not thousands);
—The suspension of military activity will occur after the beginning of verifiable withdrawals;
—The discussion and achievement of a military-technical agreement shall not extend the previously determined time for completion of withdrawals.

VOTE ON RESOLUTION 1244(1999):

In favour: Argentina, Bahrain, Brazil, Canada, France, Gabon, Gambia, Malaysia, Namibia, Netherlands, Russian Federation, Slovenia, United Kingdom, United States.
Against: None.
Abstaining: China.

China stated that it had great difficulty with the draft resolution. However, since FRY had already accepted the peace plan and NATO had suspended its bombing, China would not block the resolution's adoption.

Implementation of resolution 1244(1999)

End of NATO air operations and establishment of KFOR

On 9 June, NATO military authorities and FRY concluded the military-technical agreement (also known as the Kumanovo agreement) on the procedures and modalities for the withdrawal of FRY security forces from Kosovo [S/1999/682]. By that agreement, FRY and Serbia agreed to the deployment of the international security force (KFOR), which would operate without hindrance within Kosovo and establish and maintain a secure environment for all citizens of Kosovo. It also provided for a ceasefire and the phased withdrawal of FRY ground forces. KFOR would monitor and ensure compliance with the agreement and respond promptly to any violations, using military force if required; enforce withdrawals of FRY forces and compliance following the return of selected FRY personnel to Kosovo; assist other international entities involved in the implementation or otherwise authorized by the Security Council; establish liaison arrangements with local Kosovo authorities and FRY/Serbian civil and military authorities; and observe, monitor and inspect any and all facilities or activities in Kosovo that had or might have military or police capability.

On 10 June [S/1999/663], the NATO Secretary-General confirmed that FRY security forces had begun to withdraw from Kosovo in accordance with the military-technical agreement and NATO was monitoring its compliance closely. NATO air operations against FRY had therefore been suspended.

On the same date [S/1999/667], the Russian Federation said that NATO's decision to suspend the air strikes was a first step in the right direction, but not sufficient; the main task was to halt them completely. There was an urgent need to accelerate the process leading to a political settlement.

On 20 June [S/1999/702], the NATO Secretary-General confirmed that all uniformed FRY and Serbian security forces had withdrawn from Kosovo. As a result, NATO's limited air response and phased air campaign had been terminated.

KFOR activities

During the year, the NATO Secretary-General reported to the Security Council, in accordance with resolution 1244(1999), on the activities of KFOR, also known as Operation Joint Guardian [S/1999/692, S/1999/767, S/1999/868, S/1999/982, S/1999/1062, S/1999/1185, S/1999/1266], which began deployment in Kosovo on 12 June. By December, the force, which operated under NATO leadership, comprised 44,000 troops from 17 NATO countries, as well as from non-NATO countries. The deployment of troops from the Russian Federation in the town of Orahovac continued to be hampered by ongoing demonstrations and roadblocks set up by various groups of ethnic Albanians.

KFOR provided humanitarian assistance throughout Kosovo, focusing on transportation, distribution of food, medical support, re-establishment of support services and the protection and escorting of refugees and internally displaced persons. It also supported ICTY and guarded five detention centres for common law criminals, assisted in collecting and assessing applications for the Kosovar Police Service and helped with the construction and other preparatory work for the new Kosovo Police School. It deployed checkpoints on the main border-crossing points from Kosovo to FYROM and Albania to prevent illegal traffic in weapons and military equipment, and conducted helicopter-borne reconnaissance and quick reaction force missions in western Kosovo against smuggling and looting across the Albanian border.

KFOR strongly supported the United Nations Interim Administration Mission in Kosovo (see below) and was represented at all levels of civil administration and worked closely with its administrators. It also worked closely with the United Nations Mine Action Service and jointly established the United Nations Mine Action Coordination Centre to maintain visibility of mines and the unexploded ordnance threat in Kosovo.

KFOR attached the highest priority to the protection of minorities and some 50 per cent of its personnel was assigned to that task. Troops provided a permanent presence in Serb towns, villages and neighbourhoods and even in individual houses, and organized patrols and checkpoints in key areas to provide security and instil a feeling of confidence in the community. Simultaneously, KFOR followed an overall strategy to reduce the amount of ethnically motivated violence, including the establishment of joint security working groups, escorts for individuals and groups, humanitarian aid convoys, high-profile patrols and static checkpoints in and around ethnic minority pockets, and operations to find and confiscate illegal/unauthorized weapons and munitions throughout Kosovo. Its troops were also working to combat organized crime. KFOR's weapons destruction policy, which began on 15 October, resulted in the destruction of 2,053 weapons, 57 mines and explosive devices and 836 items of ammunition by mid-December.

UN Interim Administration in Kosovo

The Secretary-General, in a June report on the implementation of Security Council resolution 1244(1999) [S/1999/672], presented the preliminary operational concept for the overall organization of the civil presence in Kosovo, to be known as the United Nations Interim Administration Mission in Kosovo (UNMIK). The Mission would be headed by the Secretary-General's Special Representative, who would have overall authority to manage and coordinate activities and to facilitate a political process to determine Kosovo's future political status. The Special Representative would be supported by units for political and legal advice, military liaison, liaison with ICTY and relations with the mass media. The Mission would comprise four components, with an agency taking the lead role in each area: interim civil administration (United Nations); humanitarian affairs (UNHCR); institution-building (OSCE); and reconstruction (EU). The Special Representative would appoint an Executive Committee to assist him in fulfilling his responsibilities. Effective arrangements would be established for regular consultations between the Special Representative and the KFOR Commander, and the Military Liaison Unit would facilitate relations with KFOR and ensure effective liaison with it for all aspects of UNMIK's work. The Mission would also establish a system of advisory mechanisms and implementation committees to fully engage the local population.

Sergio Vieira de Mello, Under-Secretary-General for Humanitarian Affairs and Emergency Relief Coordinator was appointed interim Special Representative on 11 June [S/1999/675, S/1999/676]. On 2 July, the Secretary-General informed the Security Council of the appointment of Bernard Kouchner (France) as Special Representative [S/1999/748, S/1999/749].

The Council on 17 June approved UNMIK's concept of operations [S/1999/689].

Communications. On 18 June [S/1999/703], the FRY Government issued a statement announcing that it had duly and fully honoured all its commitments under resolution 1244(1999) and demanding that the UN security force do likewise regarding the security and safety of all inhabitants of Kosovo and Metohija, particularly the Serbs and Montenegrins who felt endangered by KLA aggression. In a further elaboration of its position regarding implementation of the resolution, issued on 22 June [S/1999/708], FRY offered its clarification of the coordination between the military and civilian aspects of the UN Mission: demilitarization and disarmament of all armed Albanian groups, in particular KLA, was a precondition for establishing secure conditions for all residents in Kosovo and Metohija; the international forces should act within the Council's mandate and be under the Special Representative's control; humanitarian assistance should be distributed without discrimination and equally to all residents, irrespective of ethnicity; the entire international presence was obliged to respect FRY's territorial integrity and sovereignty, including respect for its political, administrative, legal, economic and monetary system and unhindered functioning of public services in accordance with Yugoslav laws and regulations; and the role and mandate of international representatives vis-à-vis local organs should be clearly defined, as well as the modalities of their cooperation. An agreement between FRY and the United Nations should be signed.

In a later communication [S/1999/743], FRY complained to the Secretary-General of attempts to reinterpret the provisions of resolution 1244 (1999) relative to its territorial integrity and sovereignty. Statements by UN representatives on the need to introduce a separate currency for Kosovo and Metohija violated FRY's sovereignty and territorial integrity and the resolution. Regarding the establishment of a provisional and interim administration in the province, all measures and solutions would have to be taken in cooperation with, and with the agreement of, the legal authorities and in full respect for its unified legal, economic and monetary systems. That included FRY's right to control its international borders and to maintain Yugoslav customs and immigration services on its border crossings.

G-8 statement (June). In a 20 June statement [S/1999/711], the G-8 countries welcomed the decisive steps already taken and under way to end violence and repression in Kosovo, establish peace and provide for the safe and free return of all refugees and displaced persons. It reaffirmed support for the international civil and security presences in accordance with resolution 1244(1999) and pledged to cooperate closely to ensure UN success in carrying out its complex mission. They also welcomed the agreement reached between NATO and the Russian Federation on the international security presence and the military-technical agreement. The G-8 countries insisted that all parties respect the ceasefire and abide by the military-technical agreement and resolution 1244(1999) concerning the withdrawal of Yugoslav and Serb military, police and paramilitary forces from Kosovo and the demilitarization of KLA and other armed Kosovo Albanian groups. They would work cooperatively with each other, the United Nations, the EU, OSCE and other international organizations to facilitate the safe return of the refugees and displaced persons, as well as with ICTY. They affirmed their commitment to a meeting of the international donor community in July to address short-term humanitarian and other needs for Kosovo and a subsequent meeting in the autumn after a full assessment of needs.

Report of Secretary-General (July). The Secretary-General, in a July report on UNMIK [S/1999/779], said that, following the deployment of KFOR on 12 June and the completion of the withdrawal of FRY forces on 20 June (see p. 356), KLA, on 21 June, signed an undertaking, which established the modalities and the schedule for its demilitarization. The general situation in Kosovo had been tense but was stabilizing. KLA had rapidly moved back into all parts of Kosovo, in particular the south-west. A large number of Serbs had left for Serbia, due in part to an increasing number of incidents committed by Kosovo Albanians against them, including high-profile killings and abductions, looting, arson and forced expropriation of apartments. Cities, such as Prizren and Pec, were practically deserted by Kosovo Serbs and the towns of Mitrovica and Orahovac were divided along ethnic lines. The security problem was largely a result of the absence of law and order institutions and agencies, and criminal gangs competing for control of scarce resources were exploiting that void.

By 8 July, more than 650,000 of the estimated 800,000 refugees had returned to Kosovo, leaving an estimated 150,000 in neighbouring regions and countries, 90,000 in third countries and an unknown number of asylum-seekers. Many of the 500,000 internally displaced were in worse health than the refugees, having spent weeks in hiding without food or shelter. Kosovo's public service structures were largely inoperative due to a combination of neglect, war damage and the departure of trained staff, and the immediate economic outlook was precarious.

The bulk of UNMIK's advance team was deployed in Kosovo shortly after 13 June. It established working relations with KFOR and various international organizations, including ICTY, ICRC and NGOs. UNMIK also maintained contacts with local FRY representatives in Pristina. The first international police were deployed on 3 July. The interim Special Representative said he would appoint international administrators at the regional and municipal levels and had taken steps to re-establish a multi-ethnic and democratic judicial system. He appointed a Joint Advisory Council for judicial appointments, four prosecutors, two investigating judges and a three-judge panel.

At the functional level, UNMIK established joint civilian commissions, for health, universities, education and culture, municipalities and governance, post and telecommunications, and power, to facilitate a controlled transition to integrated public institutions and to address such contentious issues as administration and staffing of public facilities. At the political level, consultations continued on the formation of the Kosovo Transitional Council to provide a mechanism for enhancing cooperation between UNMIK and the people, restore confidence between the communities, identify candidates for the interim administration structures, and promote democratization and institution-building. Regional administrators were deployed to all five regions and links established with local leaders to ensure continuation of basic services and the reduction of tension.

UNMIK, in cooperation with KFOR, undertook various confidence-building measures aimed at restraining Kosovo Albanians and reassuring Kosovo Serbs. On 2 July, representatives from the two sides agreed on measures to enhance security and called for the creation of a joint crisis task force.

UNMIK cooperated with ICTY and provided support for its activities. Assisted by the United Nations Mine Action Service and the United Nations Office for Project Services, UNMIK's mine action team began setting up the mine action programme for Kosovo, the first step of which was the establishment of the United Nations Mine Action Coordination Centre. Principal UN humanitarian agencies, led by UNHCR, established representative offices in Pristina and were operating in all regions, while over 45 NGOs and major bilateral donors had committed personnel and resources to meet immediate relief needs.

The Secretary-General stated that UNMIK's work would be conducted in five integrated phases. The first would focus on the establishment and consolidation of UNMIK's authority and the creation of interim UNMIK administrative structures, including a phased plan for economic recovery and development and establishment and maintenance of a viable, self-sustaining economy. The second phase would be directed towards the administration of social services and utilities and consolidation of the rule of law, while the third would emphasize the finalization of preparations for elections for the Kosovo Transitional Authority. During the fourth phase, UNMIK would oversee and assist elected Kosovo representatives to organize and establish provisional institutions for democratic and autonomous self-government. A concluding fifth phase would depend on a final settlement, during which UNMIK would oversee the transfer of authority from Kosovo's provisional institutions to those established under a political settlement.

Communications. Commenting on the Secretary-General's report, FRY, on 16 July [S/1999/797], took exception to its presentation of the overall situation in Kosovo, considering it biased and tendentious and failing to address, or diluting, the true security situation following KFOR's deployment and UNMIK's arrival. It took exception especially to the definition of UNMIK's mandate and authority, particularly the authority and competencies of the Special Representative, which, it said, suspended, de facto, FRY sovereignty in Kosovo and Metohija. The Secretary-General's report interpreted UNMIK's mandate very broadly, outside the framework of resolution 1244(1999). Those views were further expanded in another communication of the same date [S/1999/800] and in a 27 July memorandum on the implementation of resolution 1244(1999) [S/1999/828 & Corr.1,2], in which FRY declared that it would not recognize KFOR and UNMIK decisions that were not in line with that resolution or which endangered FRY's sovereignty and territorial integrity. FRY, on 16 August, outlined a number of measures it expected the Security Council to take to ensure full and consistent implementation of resolution 1244(1999) [S/1999/887].

Report of Secretary-General (September). In September [S/1999/987], the Secretary-General reported that UNMIK had made significant progress. It had established structures at various levels, particularly the Kosovo Transitional Council. To broaden the Council's inclusiveness, the Special Representative proposed the creation within it of four directorates covering housing, health, education and public utilities, to involve the people of Kosovo in decision-making on those issues.

The level and nature of the violence in Kosovo, especially against minorities, remained a major concern (see p. 366). Measures to address the problem were having a positive effect, but continued vigilance was necessary, said the Secretary-General. Senior Kosovo Albanian personalities, including the KLA leadership, had voiced public positions on tolerance and security of minorities and had denied involvement in attacks, and called on non-Albanians to remain in Kosovo. However, that seemed to have had little effect in preventing attacks against minorities. Hardening Serb attitudes towards Kosovo Albanians were helping to radicalize Albanians in Mitrovica. Tensions also continued in Orahovac, where Albanian residents were blocking the deployment of KFOR troops. Around 4,000 of the 10,000 registered KLA combatants remained in assembly areas awaiting demilitarization. KFOR was developing a concept for demobilization, offering individual members an opportunity to participate in a disciplined, professional, multi-ethnic civilian emergency corps.

Significant problems had also resulted with respect to property rights, reinforcing ethnic divisions and complicating the process of return. As at 4 September, more than 770,000 refugees had returned to Kosovo. However, many non-Albanian groups, primarily Serbs and Roma, who had been the targets of harassment, intimidation and attacks, had left Kosovo.

Housing surveys conducted in 90 per cent of the affected villages revealed that an estimated 50,000 houses were beyond repair and another 50,000 severely damaged. However, it was estimated that the vast majority of the population would be housed, albeit temporarily, during the winter months. UNHCR, the United Nations Children's Fund and international and local NGOs were implementing projects under a "Kosovo Women's Initiative", while the International Federation of Red Cross Societies and the International Organization for Migration were working with the Kosovo Red Cross to support longer-term rehabilitation of health services, agriculture, village water systems, hospital training and psychological support. The World Health Organization was also involved in the rehabilitation of the health sector.

UNMIK's civil administration component, working in cooperation with KFOR and acting largely through joint civilian commissions, had achieved considerable progress in re-establishing public services and utilities, including post and telecommunications, sanitation services and restoration of the electricity system. With EU assistance, UNMIK had established, on an emergency basis, a customs system, and would begin issuing temporary identification cards to residents by 30 October. Under UNMIK's coordination, more than 400 schools, only two of which were ethnically mixed, reopened on 1 September. Some 263 schools were under repair and most were expected to be functional in October.

UNMIK's civilian police had expanded its presence in Kosovo, concentrating first on Pristina and its surrounding region. UNMIK police officers were also deployed at the major border crossings with Albania and FYROM. The full deployment of UNMIK civilian police was to be completed by 15 October. However, the Secretary-General noted that more international police would be needed until sufficient numbers of newly trained Kosovo Police Service officers were available. The development of that Service was proceeding rapidly. Its training school in Vucitrn inducted the first multi-ethnic class of 200 cadets in September.

An Advisory Judicial Commission was created to recommend suitable candidates for appointment as judges and prosecutors, as well as a Technical Advisory Commission to advise UNMIK on the structure and administration of the judiciary and prosecution services and to make recommendations for the establishment of the Kosovo Supreme Court. Kosovo's criminal codes, criminal procedures code and the laws on internal affairs and public peace and order were being reviewed to bring them in line with international human rights standards and regulations. An emergency judicial system was initiated on 30 June, with the opening of the District Court in Pristina. Other courts were established in Prizren, Pec, Gnijlane and Mitrovica.

A new public broadcasting service, known as Radio-Television Kosovo, was being developed. In the interim, Radio Pristina was operating under international supervision and was broadcasting in Albanian, Serbian and Turkish. To encourage the development of political parties, political party support centres were being established to provide services, on a shared basis, to all political parties. Human rights monitors, working with the humanitarian component and UNHCR, were active throughout Kosovo. The human rights training unit would coordinate with the Council of Europe and NGOs in training local human rights defenders in international standards and mechanisms. Work was continuing on the establishment of an ombudsman's office. A focal point for issues related to missing persons was also established within UNMIK's institution-building component. The matter was also being addressed by the Kosovo Transitional Council, which had established a subcommission for that purpose.

The Secretary-General observed that if the gains made were not to be eroded, the international community would have to continue to offer consistent and long-term political, material and financial support to UNMIK. Of critical importance to its success would be the provision of voluntary contributions to fund salaries of local public servants and other public activities. He appealed to Member States to contribute generously to the United Nations trust fund set up for that purpose.

In a later addendum [S/1999/987/Add.1], the Secretary-General, following a comprehensive review of UNMIK's requirements, recommended that the total number of UN civilian police officers be increased to 4,718 to ensure that the Mission had the capacity to establish and maintain civil law and order. That number would be gradually reduced as the force progressively fulfilled its parallel mandate of developing capable local police forces. The Security Council took note of the proposed increase in November [S/1999/1119].

Communications. On 22 September [S/1999/1001], FRY contested the description of the situation in Kosovo, as reflected in the Secretary-General's September report, and proposed that the Security Council dispatch a delegation there to ascertain the real situation. It claimed that KLA's disarmament had not been effected according to resolution 1244(1999), nor was KFOR determined to enforce it. Some of the measures taken by the Special Representative were instrumental in promoting Kosovo and Metohija's secession and some of the regulations (see p. 362) amounted to a flagrant violation of the resolution, as they disregarded or undermined FRY's sovereignty and territorial integrity, especially those on the establishment of customs and other related services. The report was silent on the Albanian terrorists' responsibility for acts of terrorism against Serbs and other non-Albanians following UNMIK's arrival. Of particular concern was the report's open support for the idea of creating a "Kosovo Corps" (see p. 366), which was just a change of name of the terrorist organization. FRY stated that, considering that no legal representatives of Kosovo and Metohija Serbs were on the Kosovo Transitional Council, it could not represent the interests of the Serbian population. FRY submitted a 3 November memorandum [S/1999/1124], in which it set out in further detail the systematic violations of its sovereignty and territorial integrity, of resolution 1244(1999) and of the military-technical agreement.

Report of Secretary-General (December). In December [S/1999/1250], the Secretary-General reported that UNMIK had made progress in involving the Kosovo population in the province's provisional administration through the establishment of a Kosovo-UNMIK Joint Interim Administrative Structure, agreed to on 15 December by the leaders of Kosovo's political parties. It would comprise an Interim Administrative Council, which would make recommendations for amendments to the Applicable Law and for new regulations and propose policy guidelines. At the municipal level, administration would be entrusted to an Administrative Board appointed and headed by the UNMIK Municipal Administrator. Under the 15 December agreement, the Kosovo Transitional Council would maintain its consultative role and would be enlarged to better reflect the pluralistic nature of the population. All parallel structures within Kosovo were to be transformed and progressively integrated into the Joint Administrative Structure.

Since September, the demilitarization of KLA was completed and the process of transforming former soldiers commenced. The establishment of the Kosovo Protection Corps (KPC) was instrumental in that regard (see p. 366).

At the political level, Kosovo Albanian and Kosovo Serb political parties had consolidated their representation. Two major parties dominated the political scene: the new Kosovo Democratic Progress Party, with Hasim Thaci as President; and the Democratic League of Kosovo, headed by Ibrahim Rugova. A Kosovo Serb National Council was established on 18 October.

Since September, a number of security incidents and crimes had taken place, reportedly involving former KLA members and potential KPC members (see p. 366), some of whom also attempted to exercise unauthorized and unacceptable police functions. UNMIK police arrested several of them and KFOR carried out raids on former KLA assembly areas and offices as part of a wider campaign to ensure that potential KPC leaders and members understood that there would be no tolerance for unauthorized weapons and criminal activities by Corps members.

By December, at least 810,000 refugees had returned to Kosovo. The total number of registered internally displaced persons from Kosovo in Serbia and Montenegro stood at some 243,000. The number of Kosovo Serbs returning from Serbia proper and Montenegro increased. Some visited temporarily to ascertain whether it was safe to return home, while others returned to monoethnic villages that were safer than their places of origin in areas of mixed ethnicity.

UNMIK administrators had been established in all 29 municipalities and five regions. The task of strengthening local administration at the municipal level was not easy owing to prevailing ethnic tensions, continued acts of violence, intimidation and extortion against minorities. UNMIK's limited presence in the regions and municipalities during the early stages of the Mission had allowed parallel local structures to take root in some areas. Those structures, mainly affiliated with the former KLA, were competing with UNMIK for interim administration authority through such illegal activities as tax collection and certification. The Special Representative made it known that UNMIK was the only legitimate authority in Kosovo. Additionally, an institutional framework common to all municipalities was established to carry out administrative tasks and execute policies, as well as a consultative body ensuring representation of as broad a spectrum of the population as possible. The objective was to incorporate individuals who participated in parallel structures into the municipal administration, as well as persons from other political parties and representatives of minorities.

UNMIK, in cooperation with the United Nations Centre for Human Settlements (Habitat), established a mechanism to regularize residential housing and property rights, including the establishment of an independent Housing and Property Directorate and a Housing and Property Claims Commission. At the same time, an inventory of all cadastral offices in Kosovo was being carried out to develop a new cadastral information system. Meanwhile, regional administrators were authorized temporarily to allocate vacant housing to homeless people on humanitarian grounds. The Special Representative repealed discriminatory legislation affecting housing and rights to property.

Concerning judicial matters, regulations were adopted on 12 December stating that applicable law in Kosovo would be the regulations promulgated by the Special Representative, including subsidiary rules, and the law in force on 22 March 1989. Federal law would continue to apply in any situation not governed by them, including the law of criminal procedure. Serbian law would apply only in rare cases where Federal law failed to cover a given situation.

With respect to human rights, the issue of Kosovo Albanians detained in Serbian prisons remained a major concern. An ICRC civilian prison census confirmed that 1,970 Kosovo Albanians were officially held. Some 300 Kosovo Albanian prisoners had been released by the Belgrade authorities since the summer. However, there was growing concern at reports that some prisoners were being released after paying prison officials or other intermediaries. On 6 December, the institution-building component (OSCE) released two reports documenting human rights violations in Kosovo before and after the arrival of KFOR and UNMIK, and organized on 10 and 11 December the first international human rights conference in Pristina.

A growing atmosphere of fear imperilled efforts to create the rule of law in Kosovo. Witnesses to human rights violations frequently refused to provide information to the police, or, if they did, later retracted their testimony or did not appear for court hearings. Judges and prosecutors had received threats. Impunity was emerging as a problem that undermined efforts to build an independent legal system and a police force that respected human rights.

The inaugural class of the future Kosovo Police Service graduated on 16 October. Among the 173 graduating officers were 156 Albanians, 8 Kosovo Serbs, 3 Muslim Slavs, 3 Roma and 3 Turks.

UNMIK had been studying the feasibility of holding municipal elections in Kosovo in 2000. It agreed to form a Registration Task Force, which should begin the registration process early in 2000, to be completed by June of that year. UNMIK's Department of Elections had also been addressing the procedural aspects of those elections, including residential criteria for enfranchisement. The timing of the elections would depend on a variety of factors, including the speed with which civil and voter registrations could be completed.

Radio-Television Kosovo transmitted its first television programme on 19 September. The transformation of public broadcasting was further advanced with the closing of Radio Pristina on 31 October and the opening of Radio Kosovo on 1 November. The Special Representative appointed a temporary Media Commissioner for Kosovo and the Kosovo Media Policy Advisory Board expanded its membership to seven. A Joint Consultative Committee was formed to discuss the advisability of codes of practice for the print and broadcast media and enforcement mechanisms.

UNMIK regulations

Pursuant to resolution 1244(1999), the Special Representative issued regulations relating to the functioning of the civil administration in Kosovo and establishing UNMIK's authority over all aspects of life there. Annexed to the Secretary-General's September report on UNMIK [S/1999/987] were seven regulations on: the establishment of UNMIK's authority in Kosovo; the prevention of access by individuals and their removal to secure public peace and order; the establishment of the customs and other related services in Kosovo; the currency to be used; the establishment of an ad hoc Court of Final Appeal and an ad hoc Office of the Public Prosecutor; the structure and administration of the judiciary and prosecution service; and the appointment and removal of judges and prosecutors. In December [S/1999/1250/Add.1], the Secretary-General submitted the texts of another 16 regulations issued by the Special Representative since 16 September concerning establishment of the Kosovo Protection Corps and budgetary, housing and banking matters, among others.

Communications. FRY, in a series of letters between 7 September and 15 December, protested, as being contrary to resolution 1244(1999), the introduction by UNMIK and the Special Representative of those regulations and actions [S/1999/953, S/1999/1143, S/1999/1165, S/1999/1190, S/1999/1247, S/1999/1255]. FRY also protested the opening of Pristina Airport to commercial flights and to the contracting of a number of air companies for that purpose [S/1999/1019, S/1999/1056] and UNMIK's decision to carry out a population registration in Kosovo [S/1999/1107]; permission to Albania to open a representative office in Kosovo [S/1999/1261]; and the participation of KFOR and UNMIK in staging the marking of Albania's national day in Kosovo [S/1999/1212].

On 17 December [S/1999/1262], FRY condemned the Special Representative's attitude in breach of the Charter, international law, Council resolution 1244(1999) and FRY's and Serbia's Constitutions and laws. It pointed to his systematic recourse to the policy of fait accompli and outright cooperation with ethnic Albanian separatists in the practice of ethnic cleansing, his issue of permits to foreign States to open representative offices in Kosovo and Metohija, and the establishment of the Joint Administrative Council. FRY inquired whether the Special Representative had the agreement of the Secretary-General and the Security Council for his acts.

In other communications, FRY protested the eviction of Serbian medical doctors from the medical centre in Gnjilane [S/1999/1164] and the maltreatment of Serbs by members of the United States KFOR contingent in the village of Cernica [S/1999/1090], and informed the Council President of UNMIK's practice of seizing FRY public and State property in Kosovo [S/1999/934]; it demanded restitution of the illegally seized property and its return and called on the Council to instruct UNMIK not to abuse its functions and abide by Council resolution 1244(1999).

It drew attention to the construction of military bases by the United States KFOR contingent in Urosevac, Podujevo and Pec, and urged the Council to take measures to prevent the violation of resolution 1244(1999) [S/1999/965, S/1999/1032].

In a statement of 6 July [S/1999/758] and a letter of 7 July [S/1999/766], FRY protested the joint statement signed on 2 July by Bishop Artemije of Pristina and Momcilo Trajkovic with Hasim Thaci, under the auspices of UNMIK and KFOR, on reconciliation and tolerance. FRY condemned the attempt by UN representatives to orchestrate a meeting between Serb and Kosovo Albanian representatives. The alleged representatives of the Serb people represented themselves and the Serbs had not delegated to the UN Representative the right to elect their representatives.

Concerning the contentious issue of the operation of customs facilities in Kosovo, FRY, on 6 July [S/1999/759], advised the Council that UNMIK and KFOR had shown no readiness to solve the question of the return of FRY customs authorities to the Kosovo border crossings with Albania and FYROM, and requested the Council to consider the issue urgently.

On 4 August [S/1999/850], FRY protested the manner in which UNMIK had established customs control at four border crossings on the FRY border with Albania and FYROM. It said that, despite meetings with UNMIK and KFOR at which no agreement was reached, and without the participation of competent Yugoslav authorities, UNMIK had set out to establish a separate customs service at the border crossings at Djeneral Jankovic, Globocica, Cafa Prusit and Vrbnica. On 20 August [S/1999/899], FRY drew the Council President's attention to the establishment of the customs service of Kosovo, of which the Federal Customs Administration was informed by the Customs Office in Pristina. FRY, on 3 September [S/1999/945], opposed that decision by the Special Representative, as well as the introduction of a foreign currency in Kosovo and Metohija. FRY requested that those services be disbanded, that its customs officers be allowed to return to the border crossings and that the customs service in Kosovo and Metohija be enabled to function undisturbed.

In a related communication [S/1999/1166], FRY conveyed its commiseration over the crash of a UN plane in Kosovo and Metohija. However, it pointed out that flights to the province were operated in violation of its sovereignty and territorial integrity and resolution 1244(1999), and in disregard for the air traffic norms and regulations for which FRY was responsible under relevant international agreements. It requested the UN civil and security presences to bring their flight operations into accord with FRY's international air traffic obligations and competencies.

UNMIK financing

By a 2 July note [A/53/238], the Secretary-General requested that the item "Financing of the United Nations Interim Administration Mission in Kosovo" be included in the agenda of the General Assembly's fifty-third (resumed) session. In an addendum [A/53/238/Add.1], he sought, following the adoption of Security Council resolution 1244(1999), authority to enter into commitments in an amount not exceeding $200 million to meet the most immediate requirements for carrying out the initial phase of UNMIK's implementation plan (see p. 357). ACABQ recommended that the Secretary-General be granted that authority, inclusive of the amount of $50 million it had already authorized [A/53/1019].

GENERAL ASSEMBLY ACTION (July)

On 28 July [meeting 105], the General Assembly, on the recommendation of the Fifth Committee [A/53/1025], adopted **resolution 53/241** without vote [agenda item 170].

Financing of the United Nations Interim Administration Mission in Kosovo

The General Assembly,

Having considered the report of the Secretary-General on the financing of the United Nations Interim Administration Mission in Kosovo and the related report of the Advisory Committee on Administrative and Budgetary Questions,

Bearing in mind Security Council resolution 1244(1999) of 10 June 1999 regarding the establishment of the United Nations Interim Administration Mission in Kosovo,

Acknowledging the complexity of the activities envisaged in the Mission,

Recognizing that the costs of the Mission are expenses of the Organization to be borne by Member States in accordance with Article 17, paragraph 2, of the Charter of the United Nations,

Recognizing also that, in order to meet the expenditures caused by the Mission, a different procedure is required from that applied to meet expenditures of the regular budget of the United Nations,

Taking into account the fact that the economically more developed countries are in a position to make relatively larger contributions and that the economically less developed countries have a relatively limited capacity to contribute towards such an operation,

Bearing in mind the special responsibilities of the States permanent members of the Security Council, as indicated in General Assembly resolution 1874(S-IV) of 27 June 1963, in the financing of such operations,

Mindful of the fact that it is essential to provide the Mission with the necessary financial resources to enable it to fulfil its responsibilities under the relevant resolutions of the Security Council,

1. *Expresses concern* about the financial situation with regard to peacekeeping activities, in particular as regards the reimbursement of troop contributors, which bear additional burdens owing to overdue payments by Member States of their assessments;

2. *Urges* all Member States to make every possible effort to ensure payment of their assessed contributions to the United Nations Interim Administration Mission in Kosovo in full and on time;

3. *Emphasizes* that all future and existing peacekeeping missions shall be given equal and non-discriminatory treatment in respect of financial and administrative arrangements;

4. *Also emphasizes* that all peacekeeping missions shall be provided with adequate resources for the effective and efficient discharge of their respective mandates;

5. *Deeply regrets* that the report of the Secretary-General does not contain adequate and precise information to substantiate fully the request submitted;

6. *Requests* the Secretary-General to take all necessary action to ensure that the Mission is administered with a maximum of efficiency and economy;

7. *Authorizes* the Secretary-General to enter into commitments in an amount not exceeding 200 million United States dollars, inclusive of the amount of 50 million dollars authorized by the Advisory Committee on Administrative and Budgetary Questions, for the operation of the Mission under the terms of section IV of General Assembly resolution 49/233 A of 23 December 1994, and requests the Secretary-General to establish a special account for the Mission;

8. *Decides,* as an ad hoc arrangement, to apportion the amount of 125 million dollars among Member States in accordance with the composition of groups set out in paragraphs 3 and 4 of General Assembly resolution 43/232 of 1 March 1989, as adjusted by the Assembly in its resolutions 44/192 B of 21 December 1989, 45/269 of 27 August 1991, 46/198 A of 20 December 1991, 47/218 A of 23 December 1992, 49/249 A of 20 July 1995, 49/249 B of 14 September 1995, 50/224 of 11 April 1996, 51/218 A to C of 18 December 1996 and 52/230 of 31 March 1998 and its decisions 48/472 A of 23 December 1993 and 50/451 B of 23 December 1995, and taking into account the scale of assessments for the year 1999, as set out in its resolution 52/215 A of 22 December 1997;

9. *Emphasizes* that no peacekeeping mission shall be financed by borrowing funds from other active peacekeeping missions;

10. *Encourages* the Secretary-General to continue to take additional measures to ensure the safety and security of all personnel under the auspices of the United Nations participating in the Mission;

11. *Invites* voluntary contributions to the Mission in cash and in the form of services and supplies acceptable to the Secretary-General, to be administered, as appropriate, in accordance with the procedure and practices established by the General Assembly;

12. *Requests* the Secretary-General to submit to the General Assembly, as a matter of priority, a comprehensive report on the financing of the Mission, including full budget estimates and information on the utilization of resources until the time of the submission of the report, to enable the General Assembly to take action on it at the earliest opportunity;

13. *Notes* the intention of the Secretary-General to submit the full budget to the General Assembly by the end of September or early October 1999;

14. *Decides* to include in the provisional agenda of its fifty-fourth session the item entitled "Financing of the United Nations Interim Administration Mission in Kosovo".

In October [A/54/494 & Corr.1], the Secretary-General submitted a comprehensive report on UNMIK's financing, containing the proposed budget for the period 10 June 1999 to 30 June 2000, inclusive of budgeted voluntary contributions in kind, and the commitment authority already authorized in resolution 53/241. The proposed budget supported a strength of 38 military liaison officers, 4,718 civilian police, 1,269 international staff, 3,566 local staff, 18 National Officers and 203 United Nations Volunteers. ACABQ's recommendations on the proposed budget were contained in its November report to the Assembly [A/54/622].

GENERAL ASSEMBLY ACTION (December)

On 23 December [meeting 88], the General Assembly, on the recommendation of the Fifth Com-

mittee [A/54/674], adopted **resolution 54/245 A** without vote [agenda item 166].

Financing of the United Nations Interim Administration Mission in Kosovo

The General Assembly,

Having considered the report of the Secretary-General on the financing of the United Nations Interim Administration Mission in Kosovo and the related report of the Advisory Committee on Administrative and Budgetary Questions,

Bearing in mind Security Council resolution 1244(1999) of 10 June 1999 regarding the establishment of the United Nations Interim Administration Mission in Kosovo,

Recalling its resolution 53/241 of 28 July 1999 on the financing of the Mission,

Acknowledging the complexity of the Mission,

Reaffirming that the costs of the Mission are expenses of the Organization to be borne by Member States in accordance with Article 17, paragraph 2, of the Charter of the United Nations,

Recalling its previous decisions regarding the fact that, in order to meet the expenditures caused by the Mission, a different procedure is required from that applied to meet expenditures of the regular budget of the United Nations,

Taking into account the fact that the economically more developed countries are in a position to make relatively larger contributions and that the economically less developed countries have a relatively limited capacity to contribute towards such an operation,

Bearing in mind the special responsibilities of the States permanent members of the Security Council, as indicated in General Assembly resolution 1874(S-IV) of 27 June 1963, in the financing of such operations,

Noting with appreciation that voluntary contributions have been made to the Mission,

Mindful of the fact that it is essential to provide the Mission with the necessary financial resources to enable it to fulfil its responsibilities under the relevant resolutions of the Security Council,

Recalling its resolutions 51/243 of 15 September 1997 and 52/234 of 26 June 1998,

1. *Takes note* of the status of contributions to the United Nations Interim Administration Mission in Kosovo as at 30 November 1999, including the contributions outstanding in the amount of 50.1 million United States dollars, representing 40 per cent of the total assessed contributions, notes that some 23 per cent of the Member States have paid their assessed contributions in full, and urges all other Member States concerned, in particular those in arrears, to ensure the payment of their outstanding assessed contributions;

2. *Expresses its appreciation* to those Member States which have paid their assessed contributions in full;

3. *Urges* all other Member States to make every possible effort to ensure payment of their assessed contributions to the Mission in full and on time;

4. *Expresses concern* at the delay experienced by the Secretary-General in deploying and providing adequate resources to some peacekeeping missions, in particular those in Africa;

5. *Emphasizes* that all future and existing peacekeeping missions shall be given equal and non-discriminatory treatment in respect of financial and administrative arrangements;

6. *Also emphasizes* that all peacekeeping missions shall be provided with adequate resources for the effective and efficient discharge of their respective mandates;

7. *Notes* the role of the specialized agencies in the implementation of humanitarian activities in the Mission under pillar II, including those related to technical cooperation, and requests the Secretary-General to finalize agreements with those agencies and to report thereon to the General Assembly in the context of the next budget proposal for the Mission;

8. *Requests* the Secretary-General to undertake the study called for by the Advisory Committee on Administrative and Budgetary Questions on the use of United Nations Volunteers in peacekeeping operations and to report to the General Assembly during the main part of its fifty-fifth session;

9. *Also requests* the Secretary-General to comply fully with the guidelines on the acceptance of gratis personnel approved by the General Assembly in its resolution 52/234;

10. *Further requests* the Secretary-General to make the fullest possible use of facilities and equipment at the United Nations Logistics Base at Brindisi, Italy, in order to minimize the costs of procurement for the Mission, and to this end requests the Secretary-General to speed up the implementation of the asset management system at all peacekeeping missions in accordance with General Assembly resolution 52/1 of 15 October 1997;

11. *Endorses* the observations and recommendations contained in the report of the Advisory Committee;

12. *Requests* the Secretary-General to take all necessary action to ensure that the Mission is administered with a maximum of efficiency and economy;

13. *Also requests* the Secretary-General, in order to reduce the cost of employing General Service staff, to continue efforts to employ locally recruited staff for the Mission against General Service posts, commensurate with the requirements of the Mission;

14. *Decides* to appropriate the amount of 427,061,800 dollars gross (410,091,700 dollars net) for the establishment and maintenance of the Mission for the period from 10 June 1999 to 30 June 2000, inclusive of the amount of 200 million dollars authorized by the General Assembly in its resolution 53/241;

15. *Decides also*, as an ad hoc arrangement, to apportion the amount of 302,061,800 dollars gross (285,091,700 dollars net) for the period from 10 June 1999 to 30 June 2000, taking into account the amount of 125 million dollars already apportioned among Member States in accordance with Assembly resolution 53/241 and in accordance with the composition of groups set out in paragraphs 3 and 4 of General Assembly resolution 43/232 of 1 March 1989, as adjusted by the Assembly in its resolutions 44/192 B of 21 December 1989, 45/269 of 27 August 1991, 46/198 A of 20 December 1991, 47/218 A of 23 December 1992, 49/249 A of 20 July 1995, 49/249 B of 14 September 1995, 50/224 of 11 April 1996, 51/218 A to C of 18 December 1996 and 52/230 of 31 March 1998 and its decisions 48/472 A of 23 December 1993, 50/451 B of 23 December 1995 and 54/456 to 54/458 of 23 December 1999, and taking into account the scale of assessments for the

years 1999 and 2000, as set out in its resolutions 52/215 A of 22 December 1997 and 54/237 A of 23 December 1999;

16. *Decides further* that, in accordance with the provisions of its resolution 973(X) of 15 December 1955, there shall be set off against the apportionment among Member States, as provided for in paragraph 15 above, their respective share in the Tax Equalization Fund of the estimated staff assessment income of 16,970,100 dollars approved for the Mission for the period from 10 June 1999 to 30 June 2000;

17. *Emphasizes* that no peacekeeping mission shall be financed by borrowing funds from other active peacekeeping missions;

18. *Encourages* the Secretary-General to continue to take additional measures to ensure the safety and security of all personnel under the auspices of the United Nations participating in the Mission;

19. *Invites* voluntary contributions to the Mission in cash and in the form of services and supplies acceptable to the Secretary-General, to be administered, as appropriate, in accordance with the procedure and practices established by the General Assembly;

20. *Regrets* that the report of the Secretary-General does not contain satisfactory explanations, and requests the Secretary-General to improve the presentation in his future reports on the budget of the Mission and to submit them in a timely manner;

21. *Decides* to keep under review during its fifty-fourth session the item entitled "Financing of the United Nations Interim Administration Mission in Kosovo".

On 23 December, the Assembly decided that the item on UNMIK's financing remained for consideration at its resumed fifty-fourth (2000) session (**decision 54/465**) and that the Fifth Committee should continue consideration of the item at that session (**decision 54/462 A**).

Further political developments

Creation of Kosovo Protection Corps

The Secretary-General, in his December report on implementation of resolution 1244(1999) [S/1999/1250] (see p. 369), reported that the demilitarization of KLA was completed on 20 September and the process of transforming former soldiers commenced with the establishment of the Kosovo Protection Corps. Consisting of up to 3,000 active and 2,000 reserve members, KPC would not have any role in law enforcement or the maintenance of law and order but would be used exclusively for civil emergencies, search and rescue, demining projects and rebuilding infrastructure and housing. Individuals from minority groups were to make up at least 10 per cent of both active and reserve members.

On 23 September [S/1999/1012], the EU welcomed KFOR's announcement that KLA had completed its disarmament obligations and the formation of the multi-ethnic KPC to assist UNMIK in civil emergencies.

On 23 and 24 [S/1999/999, S/1999/1002] September, FRY protested the signing on 20 September of the agreement between UNMIK and KLA on the establishment of KPC as a flagrant violation of resolution 1244(1999) and the concealed attempt to legalize a terrorist organization. FRY noted that KLA had not been disarmed or demilitarized. KFOR and UNMIK's arbitrariness and illegal decision constituted a substantial step towards Albanian separatist goals in Kosovo and Metohija and were unacceptable to FRY. FRY insisted that that decision and all those taken by KFOR and UNMIK violating resolution 1244(1999) be annulled.

Resurgence of violence

Communications. On 28 June [S/1999/729], FRY informed the Security Council President of a serious deterioration in the security situation in Kosovo since KFOR assumed responsibility there, and of a massive violation of basic human rights of the non-Albanian population, primarily Serbs, whose life and property had been threatened by KLA and other Albanian criminal groups. It accused KFOR of failing to close and establish full control over the border with Albania and FYROM, thereby enabling uncontrolled inroads by armed terrorists of KLA, Albanian regular military forces and criminal marauding gangs. The number of persons abducted continued to rise, private and State properties were threatened, home and apartment owners were evicted en masse, houses and villages burned and cultural and religious monuments destroyed. The goal of the ongoing violence was to complete the ethnic cleansing of the province of Serbs and the non-Albanian population in general.

FRY called on the Council to consider urgently the situation in Kosovo and Metohija and condemn, in the strongest terms, terrorism, violence and threats to human rights by KLA and criminal Albanian gangs; demand that KFOR and UNMIK take measures to eliminate further violence and threats to the security of persons and complete the demilitarization and disarmament of KLA; order restitution and rescission of all cases of illegal usurpation of private and State properties, illegal dismissals and employment of the use of force and intimidation; emphasize respect for FRY's sovereignty and territorial integrity, particularly in respect of the establishment of the interim and transitional administrations; call for the realization of the agreement on the return of Yugoslav and Serbian personnel; and establish, in cooperation with UNHCR, the framework of cooperation and procedures for the safe return of refugees and displaced citizens.

FRY considered it necessary, for the successful implementation of Council resolution 1244 (1999), to conclude an agreement on cooperation and on the status of the international presences in Kosovo and Metohija.

Attached to FRY's communication was an overview of terrorist and other acts of violence in Kosovo and Metohija between 12 and 27 June. On 24 July [S/1999/818], FRY repeated its call for an urgent meeting of the Council to discuss the massacre on the previous day of 14 Serbian farmers, including women and children, in the village of Staro Gradsko.

The Russian Federation, in a 17 August statement [S/1999/890], said it was disturbed at the slow process of disarming the Kosovo rebels and doubted that the agreement on complete demilitarization would be fulfilled within the 90 days. The activities of the Albanian extremists were challenging the international community, in violation of resolution 1244(1999). Outbreaks of violence were continuing in Kosovo and killings were on the rise, as were incidents of arson and looting against the non-Albanian population as a result of the policy of appeasement of Albanian separatism pursued by a number of Western countries. The international forces deployed in Kosovo were not coping with the wave of terror and it was necessary to speed up UNMIK's deployment. The international community should take steps to avert the dangerous trends in the developing situation in Kosovo and divert the process towards a political settlement, while fully respecting FRY's sovereignty and territorial integrity.

On 25 August [S/1999/914], FRY reported the discovery of a mass grave of 15 civilians of Serbian nationality in the village of Ugljare, near Gnjilane, including members of the Zdravkovic family, abducted on 10 July by KLA terrorists. It demanded, among other things, that the Council have KFOR and UNMIK effectively guarantee full personal and property security to Serbian, Montenegrin and other non-Albanian populations; put an end to the vandalism and terror; ensure the release of about 300 Serbs abducted; and allow a contingent of the Yugoslav Army and police to return to the province in accordance with resolution 1244(1999) and the military-technical agreement (see p. 356). The FRY leadership, in the light of the discovery of the 15 bodies in the United States zone of responsibility in Kosovo and Metohija, accused that country of responsibility for the massacre [S/1999/922]. On 29 August [A/53/300], FRY reported to the Secretary-General another incident involving the killing of 22 kidnapped Serbs in Klecka.

SECURITY COUNCIL CONSIDERATION (August/September)

The Security Council met on 30 August [A/55/2] to consider the situation in Kosovo and implementation of resolution 1244(1999). Council members, while noting the recent improvements in Kosovo, condemned violence against the civilian population, in particular against ethnic minorities, as well as against KFOR personnel, and demanded that such acts cease immediately. They reaffirmed the importance of full implementation of resolution 1244(1999) and reiterated the need to comply fully with the resolution's demands and cooperate fully with KFOR and UNMIK. On 7 September, the Under-Secretary-General for Peacekeeping Operations reported to the Council on the investigation by ICTY of mass graves with allegedly Serbian victims in Ugljare and Metohija. The Tribunal confirmed that the victims seemed to have been Serbs.

Further communications. On 1 September [S/1999/935], FRY, while welcoming the Council's 30 August statement, expressed surprise that no mention was made of all the massacres of Serbs and the systematic terror and ethnic cleansing that they and other non-Albanians had been exposed to in the presence of KFOR and UNMIK. It said that the Council had turned a blind eye to KLA's terrorism, towards which KFOR had taken a tolerant attitude. The tragedy of the Serbs and other non-Albanians was ignored and their brutalization took place with KFOR in attendance. Bearing in mind the gravity of the situation, urgent measures and actions were needed, including sanctions.

In letters of 9 and 12 [S/1999/962, S/1999/966] September, FRY protested the shelling of five Serbian villages near Gnjilane by KLA on 8 September, which, it said, was further proof that KLA had not disarmed, and reported the attack by ethnic Albanians on the northern part of Kosovska Mitrovica on 9 September. The latter incident was further proof of the very volatile situation in Kosovo and Metohija and the systematic pressure on Serbs to force them to leave localities in which they lived. Further, FRY reported a mortar attack on 28 September [S/1999/1018] on Serbian civilians at Kosovo Polje market, which killed two and wounded 42, seven of them seriously. It reiterated its demand that the Council annul the Special Representative's decision to transform KLA into KPC (see p. 366) and to effect its immediate disbandment.

FRY, on 5 October [S/1999/1031], requested that Yugoslav Army units and Serbian police personnel return to Kosovo and Metohija, in accordance with Council resolution 1244(1999), to avert the exodus of Serbs, Montenegrins and other non-

Albanians from the province, to facilitate their return and to help maintain its multi-ethnic, multicultural and multi-religious nature. It also brought to the Council's attention on 9 October [S/1999/1046] the dramatic situation of several thousand Serbs and a few hundred Roma in the town of Orahovac, where KLA had blocked humanitarian convoys for two months, preventing the delivery of food, while Albanian terrorists obstructed water and power supplies to the Serb-populated part of the town. In addition, over 1,000 Roma children were prevented from attending school. Instead of lifting the blockade, UN security and civil presences were organizing evacuation convoys to resettle Serbs and other non-Albanians from Orahovac. FRY accused KFOR of a double standard in doing nothing to remove the Albanian obstacles to the entry of Russian troops in Orahovac, while removing Serb roadblocks to protest various shortcomings.

On 28 October [S/1999/1103], FRY said that the situation was worsening dramatically with every passing day as Serbian villages were being shelled by KLA. The following day [S/1999/1104], it reported an attack on a convoy of Serbian refugees, protected by KFOR, by a large group of KLA on the road from Orahovac, near Pec, on 27 October. FRY placed responsibility for the latest atrocity on UN civil and security presences in Kosovo and especially on the Special Representative, who, it said, had only the previous day made statements that the situation in Kosovo and Metohija was stable and favourable for the Serbs. FRY called on the Council to exercise its authority and establish responsibility for the worsening security situation in Kosovo and Metohija.

EU statement (November). The EU, in a 4 November statement [S/1999/1157], said that it had learned with dismay of the recent acts of violence against the Serb population of Kosovo. It condemned, in particular, the 27 October incident near Pec, where a convoy of 155 Serbs, organized by UNHCR and under KFOR protection, was attacked and several people were injured, and the shooting against the President of the "Kosovo Serbian Resistance Movement" and co-chairman of the Serbian National Council, Momcilo Trajkovic, on 31 October, as well as the many other attacks against minorities and recent acts of violence. The EU expected full compliance with resolution 1244(1999) from all parties and full cooperation with UNMIK and KFOR.

The EU appealed to all the people of Kosovo to refrain from violence and to cooperate. It appealed, in particular, to the Kosovo Albanian community leaders to condemn violence and to use their influence and leadership to work with KFOR and UNMIK to stamp out violence and intimidation in Kosovo. It urged all parties to cooperate to quickly bring the perpetrators to justice, and called on all political forces in Kosovo to re-establish dialogue and stop threatening political opponents.

SECURITY COUNCIL CONSIDERATION (November)

The Security Council was briefed by the Special Representative on developments in Kosovo on 5 November [meeting 4061]. He reported that the protection of minorities was not fully provided for, but the number of murders per week was decreasing and the police were doing their best to prevent them. He appealed for more civilian police for UNMIK. He was also of the view that the international presence on the ground should aim to prevent an exodus of Serbs from Kosovo. For the time being, it was difficult to encourage them to return to the province, since security could not be fully guaranteed. He stressed the need to start working on the agenda for coexistence that would later be followed by the revitalization of a multi-ethnic society.

Council members expressed their support for UNMIK's efforts in Kosovo and supported the need for strengthening its civilian police component.

Further communications. In letters of 22 and 25 November [S/1999/1193, S/1999/1198], FRY protested the 21 November attack near Kursumlija, in which two members of the Serbian Ministry of the Interior were killed and six wounded.

On 8 December [S/1999/1229], FRY also protested the arbitrary arrest and detention by KFOR and UNMIK of 40 Serbs who had been prevented from choosing lawyers and from receiving visits from their families and doctors.

In an overview of the situation from 12 June to 7 December [S/1999/1240], FRY stated that 485 persons had been killed, 667 kidnapped or reported missing and 264 wounded, as well as 387 cases of physical assault, maltreatment and infliction of grievous bodily harm and 345 registered cases of threat. Many cities, towns and villages had been ethnically cleansed of Serbs and other non-Albanians. According to UNHCR data, 330,000 persons, of whom 250,000 were Serbs, had been expelled from Kosovo and Metohija. Over 50,000 houses had been burned and over 1,200 apartments broken into, looted or forcibly moved into. Over 30 Serbian villages had been sacked. Gorani and Muslims and Albanians loyal to FRY were also threatened and terrorized. Most of the predominantly Catholic Croatian population had left the villages of Letinice, Vrnez, Kolo and Sasare. Public institutions and companies had been unlawfully and forcibly taken over and in the process over 20,000 Serbs and Montenegrins had been dismissed and replaced.

Seventy-seven churches, monasteries and other religious shrines had been destroyed or damaged and looted and the clergy expelled. KFOR and UNMIK were responsible. They continued to disregard the mandate established by the Council and to infringe FRY's laws, sovereignty and territorial integrity. FRY again called on the Council to address the current dramatic situation in Kosovo and Metohija. In a 17 December letter [S/1999/1263], FRY further elaborated on the destruction of the Serbian cultural heritage and the demolition of churches, monasteries and other shrines of the Serbian Orthodox Church. It also protested the most recent attack, on 17 December, on a cafe in Orahovac [S/1999/1269].

FRY condemned the press conference given by Hasim Thaci at United Nations Headquarters on 17 September [S/1999/991]. According to FRY, it was under Mr. Thaci's leadership that KLA had intensified a relentless campaign of ethnic cleansing of Serbs and other non-Albanians. In another communication [S/1999/1075], FRY protested the visit of Albania's Foreign Minister to Kosovo and Metohija on 16 October, accusing Albania of providing active support to and arming KLA. Coming after the Secretary-General's visit to the province, it encouraged Albanian separatists and terrorists and was contrary to resolution 1244(1999). FRY also protested against the Secretary-General's failure, during that visit, to meet with its representatives in Pristina [S/1999/1074].

Report of Secretary-General. The Secretary-General, in his December report on the situation in Kosovo [S/1999/1250], confirmed that a number of serious incidents had heightened tension and security concerns. Both the local population and members of the international community had been targeted. The deteriorating situation was underlined by the murder on 11 October of Valentin Krumov, a newly arrived UNMIK international staff member, and the wounding of Momcilo Trajkovic, a member of the Kosovo Transitional Council on 1 November. The number of attacks on Kosovo Serbs and members of other ethnic minorities remained high and continued to be the overriding human rights issue in Kosovo. Serbs, Roma and, increasingly, Slavic Muslims were the victims of killings, abductions, illegal arrests, arbitrary detentions, beatings, threats and harassment. Ethnic Albanians were also targeted, on suspicion of collaborating with the Yugoslav authorities. The security situation of women in Kosovo also remained precarious, with an increasing number of abductions of young women. Members of ethnic minorities continued to suffer severe restrictions on their freedom of movement. In Pristina, the estimated remaining 300 to 600 Kosovo Serbs were frightened to go out and were mostly confined to their homes.

A growing number of juveniles had been suspected of committing serious crimes in Kosovo and there were signs that organized criminal elements were reinforcing their position and activities there.

To protect minorities, creative methods for increasing security were being implemented and particular attention was being paid to promoting unhindered and non-discriminatory access of minorities to food, health care, education and other public services. The humanitarian component had designed a special distribution network for needy minority groups, as well as interim systems for providing medical care to minority groups that were otherwise denied access. Other initiatives included facilitating contact between community leaders, organized "go and see" visits for displaced minorities to their home areas and the provision of satellite phones to minorities living in isolated enclaves. Freedom of movement improved with the commencement in October of a shuttle bus programme, with security provided by KFOR, between minority enclaves and to destinations outside Kosovo. The programme was temporarily suspended after the 27 October attack on a humanitarian convoy of 155 Kosovo Serbs leaving for Montenegro. UNHCR continued to evacuate minorities in life-threatening situations or particularly vulnerable circumstances to Serbia and Montenegro. Some 487 individuals had so far benefited from that protection measure. Since mid-September, Civil Affairs Minority Officers had been appointed to reside on a permanent basis in selected villages/communities in Kosovo to contribute to a further improvement of security in areas where minorities resided, to extend the provision of essential administrative services, and to facilitate access to essential public services and contacts with local and international actors in support of reconstruction and revitalization of the local economy.

The Secretary-General said that during his visit to Kosovo on 13 and 14 October, one of the most frequently raised concerns was the precarious security situation for Kosovo Serbs, Roma and other minority groups. Despite the concerted efforts of KFOR and UNMIK police, the level and nature of the violence, especially against vulnerable minorities, remained unacceptable. He had underlined that message in his meetings with political leaders and with the Kosovo Transitional Council. He urged all political leaders in Kosovo and the local population to stop the violence, intimidation and harassment. He said that the international community had to do better. KFOR and UNMIK police had redoubled their efforts, but more resources were needed. He emphasized the need to ensure the rapid deployment of international police to support the Kosovo Police Service, to have UNMIK's authority cemented and the judiciary and penal system strengthened. The involvement in criminal and unofficial law-enforcement activities of former KLA members and KPC members would not be tolerated. Unofficial law-enforcement structures had to be dismantled and authority had to rest only within legitimate bodies of the Joint Administrative Structure. All those efforts depended on the support of the Kosovo political leadership, which had to commit itself to peace, tolerance and respect for the rule of law.

The former Yugoslav Republic of Macedonia (FYROM)

At the beginning of 1999, the United Nations Preventive Deployment Force (UNPREDEP) continued its mandate of monitoring and reporting on developments along the borders of the former Yugoslav Republic of Macedonia that could affect its peace and stability. However, in February, a draft resolution by which the Security Council would have renewed the UNPREDEP mandate until 31 August was not adopted, owing to the negative vote of a permanent member. The mission's mandate, therefore, terminated on 28 February. UNPREDEP, which was established by Council resolution 983(1995) [YUN 1995, p. 597], was last extended by resolution 1186(1998) [YUN 1998, p. 362] when its troop strength was also increased.

Communication. In a 29 January letter to the Secretary-General [S/1999/108], FYROM presented arguments for the extension of UNPREDEP's mandate for another six months. UNPREDEP had so far functioned as a deterrent and had contributed greatly to the stabilization of the situation in the whole region. Peace in FYROM and other countries still depended on regional developments, particularly the spillover of the military conflicts from Kosovo, where the deteriorating situation suggested that, with the forthcoming spring, more open and intensive conflicts might be expected. That crisis had led also to an increase in the tensions at the Albanian-Yugoslav border and increased the sense of insecurity and distrust in the region, which burdened FYROM's efforts to prevent arms trafficking to Kosovo. Also, the FYROM-Yugoslav border was not yet demarcated, which, in the context of the current developments in Kosovo and the fact that part of that border extended in the direction of Kosovo, complicated the political and security situation in FYROM.

Report of Secretary-General. In a February report on UNPREDEP [S/1999/161], the Secretary-General said that FYROM's bilateral relations with its neighbours had strengthened and relations with Albania had improved significantly following the 1998 parliamentary elections in FYROM [YUN 1998, p. 363] and the inclusion in the new Government of a coalition of the ethnic Albanian Party for Democratic Prosperity of Albanians and the National Democratic Party. High-level bilateral visits and agreements on mutual cooperation between the two countries, as well as efforts to improve inter-ethnic relations, had a further positive impact on relations. The steady increase in trade and collaborative ventures with Greece reflected improved relations between those two countries, despite the still unresolved name-related dispute. Relations with Bulgaria were also strengthening, with both countries expressing determination to overcome the language dispute, while increasing economic and other forms of cooperation. However, relations with FRY were strained owing to FYROM's decision to authorize NATO deployment on its territory. There had also been no progress on the issue of the demarcation of the border between the two countries.

In keeping with the new Government's policy of inter-ethnic harmony, the newly constituted Parliament adopted on 4 February the law on amnesty, paving the way for the release of ethnic Albanian mayors and chairmen of the Gostivar and Tetovo municipal councils.

During the reporting period, UNPREDEP undertook the new tasks of monitoring and reporting on illicit arms flows and other activities prohibited under resolution 1160(1998) [YUN 1998, p. 369]. It enhanced its capacity to ascertain whether arms smuggling was taking place and established mobile reaction teams to respond to sighted smuggling activities. UNPREDEP was also effectively monitoring and reporting on developments that could affect peace and stability and working to implement the Special Representative's good offices mandate. It was also involved in programmes of good governance and the rule of law, strengthening national capacity and infrastructure, institution-building and human resources development. UNPREDEP continued its close cooperation with the OSCE Spillover Monitoring Mission to Skopje and the European Commission Monitoring Mission in the country and established a working relationship with NATO.

The Secretary-General observed that peace and stability in FYROM continued to depend largely on developments in other parts of the region, in particular Kosovo. Although FYROM had not been adversely affected so far by that conflict, the potential serious repercussions could not be ignored given the large proportion of ethnic Albanians in FYROM. UNPREDEP's presence had contributed successfully to preventing the spillover of conflicts elsewhere in the region to FYROM and continued to have a stabilizing effect, and had been useful in defusing tensions that could have arisen as a result of the continued crisis in Kosovo. The Secretary-General recommended an extension of UNPREDEP's mandate until 31 August, to be reviewed if discussions in the Contact Group on the Former Yugoslavia resulted in developments that could affect UNPREDEP's role and responsibilities.

SECURITY COUNCIL ACTION

On 25 February [meeting 3982], the Security Council considered a draft resolution [S/1999/201], sponsored by Canada, France, Germany, Italy, the Netherlands, Slovenia, the United Kingdom and the United States, by which the Council would have extended UNPREDEP's mandate until 31 August. The draft resolution received 13 votes in favour to 1 against, with 1 abstention. The draft was not adopted, owing to the negative vote of a permanent Council member.

China said that it had voted against the draft resolution because it had always maintained that UN peacekeeping operations, including preventive deployment missions, should not be open-ended. The situation in FYROM had stabilized, its relations with neighbouring countries had improved and peace and stability there had not been adversely affected by developments in the region. The Secretary-General had clearly indicated that the Council's original goal in establishing UNPREDEP had already been met, in which case there was no need to extend its mandate further.

Speaking before the vote, the Russian Federation said that it believed that UNPREDEP's function regarding monitoring compliance with the arms embargo should be the main component of its activities and be more clearly highlighted in its mandate. Although it had proposed corresponding amendments to the text, they were not duly reflected. Under those circumstances, the Russian Federation could not support the draft.

Communications. On 12 March [S/1999/275], FYROM's Minister for Foreign Affairs informed the Secretary-General that the reasons outlined in his January letter (see p. 370) requesting the extension of UNPREDEP's mandate remained, and the presence of the United Nations in the region was more than a necessity owing to the current and future developments in Kosovo. FYROM would appreciate the Secretary-General's suggestions for finding an acceptable way to fill the security gap created as a result of the non-extension of UNPREDEP's mandate. It was actively considering an arrangement, possibly led by NATO, but with a clear UN connection, which could be endorsed or noted by the Council. On the same date [S/1999/271], FYROM expressed its recognition of the UN contribution in preserving peace and security in FYROM and in the surrounding areas and stated that UNPREDEP had confirmed itself in the long term as a barrier to wider destabilization and was thus a very successful mission.

Financing of UNPREDEP

In January, the Secretary-General submitted to the General Assembly the UNPREDEP financial performance report for the period 1 July 1997 to 30 June 1998 [A/53/786], and the proposed budget for UNPREDEP's maintenance for the period 1 July 1999 to 30 June 2000 [A/53/812]. Following the termination of UNPREDEP's mandate, the Secretary-General, in May, submitted a revised budget for UNPREDEP's liquidation period from 1 July to 15 October [A/53/812/Add.1], and revised cost estimates for the period 1 July 1998 to 30 June 1999, including the liquidation of the Force during the period 1 March to 30 June 1999 [A/53/437/Add.1].

ACABQ's recommendations were contained in its May report to the Assembly [A/53/958].

GENERAL ASSEMBLY ACTION

On 8 June [meeting 101], the General Assembly, on the recommendation of the Fifth Committee [A/53/546/Add.1], adopted **resolution 53/20 B** without vote [agenda item 140].

Financing of the United Nations Preventive Deployment Force

The General Assembly,

Having considered the reports of the Secretary-General on the financing of the United Nations Preventive Deployment Force and the related reports of the Advisory Committee on Administrative and Budgetary Questions,

Recalling Security Council resolutions 983(1995) of 31 March 1995, by which the Council decided that the United Nations Protection Force within the former Yugoslav Republic of Macedonia should be known as the United Nations Preventive Deployment Force, and 1186(1998) of 21 July 1998, by which the Council extended the mandate of the Force until 28 February 1999,

Recalling also its decision 50/481 of 11 April 1996 on the financing of the Force and its subsequent resolutions thereon, the latest of which was resolution 53/20 A of 2 November 1998,

Reaffirming that the costs of the Force are expenses of the Organization to be borne by Member States in accordance with Article 17, paragraph 2, of the Charter of the United Nations,

Recalling its previous decisions regarding the fact that, in order to meet the expenditures caused by the Force, a different procedure is required from that applied to meet expenditures of the regular budget of the United Nations,

Taking into account the fact that the economically more developed countries are in a position to make relatively larger contributions and that the economically less developed countries have a relatively limited capacity to contribute towards such an operation,

Bearing in mind the special responsibilities of the States permanent members of the Security Council, as indicated in General Assembly resolution 1874(S-IV) of 27 June 1963, in the financing of such operations,

Noting with appreciation that voluntary contributions have been made to the Force by certain Governments,

Mindful of the fact that it is essential to provide the Force with the necessary financial resources to enable it to meet its outstanding liabilities,

1. *Takes note* of the status of contributions to the United Nations Preventive Deployment Force as at 30 April 1999, including the contributions outstanding in the amount of 12.2 million United States dollars, representing 8.2 per cent of the total assessed contributions from the inception of the Force to the period ending 28 February 1999, notes that some 26 per cent of the Member States have paid their assessed contributions in full, and urges all other Member States concerned, in particular those in arrears, to ensure payment of their outstanding assessed contributions;

2. *Expresses concern* about the financial situation with regard to peacekeeping activities, in particular as regards the reimbursement of troop contributors, which bear additional burdens owing to overdue payments by Member States of their assessments;

3. *Expresses its appreciation* to those Member States which have paid their assessed contributions in full;

4. *Urges* all other Member States to make every possible effort to ensure payment of their assessed contributions to the Force in full and on time;

5. *Endorses* the observations and recommendations contained in the report of the Advisory Committee on Administrative and Budgetary Questions;

6. *Requests* the Secretary-General to take all necessary action to ensure that the liquidation of the Force is administered with a maximum of efficiency and economy;

7. *Decides* to reduce the appropriation provided by the General Assembly in its resolutions 52/245 of 26 June 1998 and 53/20 A in the amount of 50,053,745 dollars gross (48,751,045 dollars net), inclusive of the amount of 1,053,745 dollars for the support account for peacekeeping operations, for the maintenance of the Force in respect of the period from 1 July 1998 to 30 June 1999, to the amount of 43,062,700 dollars gross (42,004,600 dollars net), inclusive of the amount of 1,053,745 dollars for the support account;

8. *Decides also* as an ad hoc arrangement, and taking into account the amount of 21,053,745 dollars gross (20,580,245 dollars net) already apportioned in accordance with its resolution 52/245 and the amount of 12,315,418 dollars gross (11,920,452 dollars net) apportioned in accordance with its resolution 53/20 A, to apportion among Member States the additional amount of 9,693,537 dollars gross (9,503,903 dollars net) for the period from 1 July 1998 to 30 June 1999 in accordance with the composition of groups set out in paragraphs 3 and 4 of General Assembly resolution 43/232 of 1 March 1989, as adjusted by the Assembly in its resolutions 44/192 B of 21 December 1989, 45/269 of 27 August 1991, 46/198 A of 20 December 1991, 47/218 A of 23 December 1992, 49/249 A of 20 July 1995, 49/249 B of 14 September 1995, 50/224 of 11 April 1996, 51/218 A to C of 18 December 1996 and 52/230 of 31 March 1998 and its decisions 48/472 A of 23 December 1993 and 50/451 B of 23 December 1995, and taking into account the scale of assessments for the years 1998 and 1999, as set out in its resolution 52/215 A of 22 December 1997;

9. *Decides further* that, in accordance with the provisions of its resolution 973(X) of 15 December 1955, there shall be set off against the apportionment among Member States, as provided for in paragraph 8 above, their respective share in the Tax Equalization Fund of the estimated additional staff assessment income of 189,634 dollars approved for the Force for the period from 1 July 1998 to 30 June 1999;

10. *Decides* that, for Member States that have fulfilled their financial obligations to the Force, there shall be set off against the apportionment, as provided for in paragraph 8 above, their respective share of the unencumbered balance of 6,895,700 dollars gross (6,310,400 dollars net) in respect of the period ending 30 June 1998;

11. *Decides also* that, for Member States that have not fulfilled their financial obligations to the Force, their share of the unencumbered balance of 6,895,700 dollars gross (6,310,400 dollars net) in respect of the period ending 30 June 1998 shall be set off against their outstanding obligations;

12. *Decides further* to appropriate the amount of 183,730 dollars gross (166,330 dollars net) for the liquidation of the Force for the period from 1 July to 15 October 1999, inclusive of the amount of 9,305 dollars for the support account for peacekeeping operations and the amount of 1,825 dollars for the United Nations Logistics Base at Brindisi, Italy;

13. *Invites* voluntary contributions to the Force in cash and in the form of services and supplies acceptable to the Secretary-General, to be administered, as appropriate, in accordance with the procedure and practices established by the General Assembly;

14. *Decides* to include in the provisional agenda of its fifty-fourth session the item entitled "Financing of the United Nations Preventive Deployment Force".

On 23 December, the Assembly decided that the item on the financing of UNPREDEP would remain for consideration at the resumed fifty-fourth (2000) session (**decision 54/465**), and that the item would be considered by the Fifth Committee at that session (**decision 54/462 A**).

Relations with Greece

In connection with FYROM's relations with Greece, the Secretary-General, in an exchange of letters [S/1999/1286, S/1999/1287], informed the Security Council of his intention to appoint Matthew Nimetz (United States) as his Personal Envoy, to replace Cyrus Vance who had resigned for personal reasons. The Secretary-General also reported that, pursuant to Council resolution 845(1993) [YUN 1993, p. 209], negotiations continued between the two countries concerning the differences between them, particularly the name-related dispute, the most recent meeting having been held on 6 December.

Georgia

Despite the continued efforts of the Secretary-General's Special Representative, of the Russian Federation and of the Group of Friends of the Secretary-General (France, Germany, Russian Federation, United Kingdom, United States), which led to positive developments on some issues, the Abkhaz/Georgian peace process remained at an impasse in 1999.

In April, in an attempt to reinvigorate the peace process, the Council of Heads of State of the Commonwealth of Independent States (CIS) had adopted and signed a draft agreement on peace and guarantees for the prevention of armed confrontation and a draft protocol on refugee return and economic rehabilitation. However, those measures remained largely unimplemented. Meanwhile, the Secretary-General's Special Representative convened a meeting on confidence-building measures in Turkey in July, which provided a forum for the development of direct bilateral ties at several levels and the elaboration of projects for cooperation in a variety of fields. That meeting also resulted in the revival of the Working Groups of the Coordinating Council. Those efforts continued to be supported by the United Nations Observer Mission in Georgia. The peace process was complicated by the holding of elections during the year. On 3 October, the Abkhaz side held "presidential elections" and a referendum on the Abkhaz "constitution". On 12 October, the Abkhaz de facto parliament adopted the "Act on State Independence of the Republic of Abkhazia". The Security Council condemned the elections as unacceptable and illegitimate. Georgia also held parliamentary elections on 31 October, except for the district of Abkhazia, whose parliamentarians retained their seats.

During the year, the security situation improved, in particular the reduction of tension along the line of separation of forces. However, the security forces of both sides remained unable to combat the criminal and terrorist elements operating in the area, particularly in the lower Gali region.

UN Observer Mission in Georgia

The United Nations Observer Mission in Georgia (UNOMIG), established by Security Council resolution 858(1993) [YUN 1993, p. 509], continued to monitor and verify compliance with the 1994 Agreement on a Ceasefire and Separation of Forces [YUN 1994, p. 583] and to fulfil other tasks as mandated by resolution 937(1994) [ibid., p. 584]. The Mission operated in close collaboration with the CIS collective peacekeeping force that had been in the zone of conflict, at the request of the parties, since 1994 [ibid., p. 583]. The Council extended the Mission's mandate twice during the year, the first time until 31 July 1999 and the second until 31 January 2000.

UNOMIG's main headquarters was located in Sukhumi (Abkhazia, Georgia), with administrative headquarters in Pitsunda, a liaison office in the Georgian capital of Tbilisi and team bases and a sector headquarters in each of the Gali and Zugdidi sectors. A team base in the Kodori Valley was manned by observers operating from Sukhumi. UNOMIG, as at October 1999, had a strength of 101 military officers.

The Mission was headed by Liviu Bota (Romania), who was also the Secretary-General's Special Representative. He was succeeded on 24 November by Dieter Boden (Germany) [S/1999/1079, S/1999/1080]. Major-General Tariq Waseem Ghazi (Pakistan) concluded his tour of duty as UNOMIG's Chief Military Observer on 31 December 1999 and was succeeded by Major-General Anis Ahmed Bajwa (Pakistan).

Activities

Report of Secretary-General (January). The Secretary-General, in response to resolution 1187(1998) [YUN 1998, p. 397], submitted a January report [S/1999/60] on the situation in Abkhazia, Georgia, including UNOMIG's operations. He observed that, while the political process towards a settlement had been slow, and at times seemed to be almost blocked, UNOMIG continued to contribute to a lessening of tensions, preventing an exacerbation of potentially serious incidents and providing a climate in which substantive political negotiations could take place. The measures taken by UNOMIG had enabled its military observers to conduct limited patrolling without serious security incidents during the past three months. Should that situation continue, and in view of the deployment of internationally recruited security personnel and the arrival of ballistic-protected vehicles, a return to the patrolling patterns in effect before February 1998 might reasonably be contemplated in the coming months. For that to happen, however, the two sides in the conflict would have to take substantive and tangible measures to curb criminal and terrorist activities.

The recent intensification of the peace process, the establishment of negotiation mechanisms and implementation of UNOMIG's mandate, together with the exercise of local good offices, highlighted the need for strengthening the Mission's civilian component, particularly in political and civil affairs and public information. An additional modest civil affairs capacity would allow UNOMIG to maintain better liaison with humanitarian agencies and NGOs. Public information activities were needed to promote a better understanding of UNOMIG's mandate and activities by the parties and within the population in the various sectors, as well as to provide impartial information for the better performance of the Mission and the advancement of the peace process. Those requirements were currently under review. The Secretary-General recommended that the Security Council extend UNOMIG's mandate until 31 July.

Communication. Georgia's President, Eduard Shevardnadze, said on 22 January [S/1999/71] that it was clear that the Abkhaz separatist regime was carrying out a well-planned obstruction of every peace initiative, creating insurmountable obstacles to the elaboration of documents to define measures for the return of refugees, the maintenance of peace and the region's economic rehabilitation, and preventing the holding of a meeting for the signing of those documents. The current situation demanded decisive steps: starting the process of return of refugees and displaced persons, with guaranteed security conditions; and definition of their international status. Georgia attached special importance to the 1998 meeting of the parties in Athens, Greece [YUN 1998, p. 400], and would actively support the development of that initiative. The development and promotion of UNOMIG's human rights activities could play an important role in establishing tolerance between the parties. Georgia hoped the Security Council would strengthen the Mission's joint investigative groups, which should define the direction of its investigative and political activities. Georgia was concerned about attacks on CIS peacekeepers and the damage they caused to the peace process. It was confident that, with the help of the Group of Friends of the Secretary-General, a plan of action could be worked out, but the international community should be aware of the consequences of the escalation of the conflict and that the elimination of that hotbed in the Caucasus required consideration of the use of force.

SECURITY COUNCIL ACTION

On 28 January [meeting 3972], the Security Council unanimously adopted **resolution 1225(1999)**. The draft [S/1999/79] was submitted by France, Germany, the Russian Federation, the United Kingdom and the United States.

The Security Council,

Recalling all its relevant resolutions, in particular resolution 1187(1998) of 30 July 1998, and the statement by its President of 25 November 1998,

Having considered the report of the Secretary-General of 20 January 1999,

Noting the letter dated 22 January 1999 from the President of Georgia to the President of the Security Council,

Deeply concerned at the continuing tense and unstable situation in the conflict zone and at the risk of resumed fighting,

Deeply concerned also at the continued deadlock in achieving a comprehensive settlement of the conflict in Abkhazia, Georgia,

Welcoming, in this context, the contribution that the United Nations Observer Mission in Georgia and the collective peacekeeping force of the Commonwealth of Independent States have made to stabilizing the situation in the zone of conflict, noting that the working relationship between the Mission and the collective peacekeeping force has been good at all levels, and stressing the importance of continued close cooperation and coordination between them in the performance of their respective mandates,

Recalling the conclusions of the Lisbon summit of the Organization for Security and Cooperation in Europe regarding the situation in Abkhazia, Georgia,

Reaffirming the necessity for the parties strictly to respect human rights, expressing its support for the efforts of the Secretary-General to find ways to improve their observance as an integral part of the work towards a comprehensive political settlement, and noting developments in the work of the United Nations Human Rights Office in Abkhazia, Georgia,

1. *Welcomes* the report of the Secretary-General of 20 January 1999;

2. *Expresses its concern* at the failure of the parties to conclude, after bilateral contacts and the Athens meeting of 16 to 18 October 1998 on confidence-building measures, agreements on security and the non-use of force, the return of refugees and displaced persons and economic reconstruction, and urges the parties to resume bilateral negotiations to this end;

3. *Demands* that both sides widen their commitment to the United Nations-led peace process, continue to seek and engage in dialogue, expand their contacts at all levels and display without delay the necessary will to achieve substantial results on the key issues of the negotiations, and underlines the necessity for the parties to achieve an early and comprehensive political settlement, which includes a settlement on the political

status of Abkhazia within the State of Georgia, which fully respects the sovereignty and territorial integrity of Georgia within its internationally recognized borders;

4. *Emphasizes,* in this context, that the readiness and ability of the international community to assist the parties depend on their political will to resolve the conflict through dialogue and mutual accommodation and on their acting in good faith to implement promptly concrete measures towards bringing about a comprehensive political settlement of the conflict;

5. *Strongly supports* the sustained efforts made by the Secretary-General and his Special Representative with the assistance of the Russian Federation, in its capacity as facilitator, as well as of the Group of Friends of the Secretary-General and the Organization for Security and Cooperation in Europe, to prevent hostilities and to give a new impetus to the negotiations within the United Nations–led peace process in order to achieve a comprehensive political settlement, and welcomes, in this context, the intention of the Secretary-General to propose a strengthening of the civilian component of the United Nations Observer Mission in Georgia;

6. *Demands* that both sides observe strictly the Agreement on a Ceasefire and Separation of Forces, signed in Moscow on 14 May 1994, and all their obligations to refrain from the use of force and to resolve disputed issues by peaceful means only, and calls upon them to display greater resolve and willingness to make the Joint Investigation Group functional;

7. *Expresses its continuing concern* at the situation of refugees and displaced persons, resulting most recently from the hostilities of May 1998, reaffirms the unacceptability of the demographic changes resulting from the conflict and the imprescriptible right of all refugees and displaced persons affected by the conflict to return to their homes in secure conditions in accordance with international law and as set out in the Quadripartite Agreement on the Voluntary Return of Refugees and Displaced Persons, of 4 April 1994, and calls upon the parties to address this issue urgently by agreeing and implementing effective measures to guarantee the security of those who exercise their unconditional right to return;

8. *Welcomes,* in this context, the efforts of the Special Representative of the Secretary-General to facilitate, as a first step, the safe return of refugees and displaced persons to the Gali region, and calls upon the parties to resume and intensify their bilateral dialogue to this end;

9. *Condemns* the activities by armed groups, including the continued laying of mines, which endanger the civilian population, impede the work of the humanitarian organizations and seriously delay the normalization of the situation in the Gali region, and deplores the lack of serious efforts by the parties to bring an end to those activities;

10. *Reiterates its demand* that both sides take immediate and determined measures to put a stop to such acts and ensure that the security environment of all international personnel improves significantly, and welcomes the first steps taken in this regard;

11. *Reiterates its deep concern* regarding the security of the Mission, welcomes the implementation of measures in this regard, and requests the Secretary-General to keep the security of the Mission under constant review;

12. *Decides* to extend the mandate of the Mission for a new period terminating on 31 July 1999, subject to a review by the Council of the mandate of the Mission in the event of any changes that may be made in the mandate or in the presence of the collective peacekeeping force of the Commonwealth of Independent States;

13. *Requests* the Secretary-General to continue to keep the Council regularly informed and to report after three months from the date of the adoption of the present resolution on the situation in Abkhazia, Georgia;

14. *Expresses its intention* to conduct a thorough review of the operation at the end of its current mandate, in the light of steps taken by the parties to achieve a comprehensive settlement;

15. *Decides* to remain actively seized of the matter.

On 19 February [S/1999/189], the Supreme Council of Abkhazia, Georgia, protested the participation of the delegation of the self-proclaimed "Republic of Abkhazia", headed by Vladislav Ardzinba, at the meeting of the Association for the Social and Economic Cooperation of the Republics and Regions of the North Caucasus (5-7 February), under the chairmanship of the Russian Federation's Deputy Prime Minister. The Supreme Council also demanded that the Russian Federation end the exercise of its jurisdiction in Georgia's territory occupied by the separatist regime.

Report of Secretary-General (April). The Secretary-General reported in April [S/1999/460] that his Special Representative, the Russian Federation and the Group of Friends of the Secretary-General had made a concerted effort to achieve an agreement on the return of refugees to the Gali district in its old boundaries and on Abkhazia's economic rehabilitation. On 12 January, the Special Representative and the Abkhaz leader, Mr. Ardzinba, discussed terms for the return of refugees and displaced persons to the Gali district and agreed on the extent of participation by returnees in the Gali district's local law enforcement organs; the role and deployment of the CIS peacekeeping force; normalization of the customs and border regime at the Psou River, including transportation; and that Mr. Ardzinba would formally outline those agreements to the Group of Friends of the Secretary-General. However, during a meeting on 23 January with the Special Representative and the Group of Friends, Mr. Ardzinba presented different proposals. On 27 January, the Friends of the Secretary-General expressed disappointment that an opportunity to take the first important step forward in the negotiation process had been lost.

The seventh session of the Coordinating Council of the Georgian and Abkhaz sides (Tbilisi, 11 February) discussed issues relating to the lasting non-resumption of hostilities and security problems, refugees and internally displaced persons, and economic and social problems. The Council decided that a meeting of the two sides, UNOMIG and the CIS peacekeeping force would be convened within two weeks to develop a mechanism for the Joint Investigation Group (see below); together, they would elaborate and implement measures for the non-resumption of hostilities, prevention of confrontation and separation of forces. Representatives of the force structures of the two sides would examine any information that could lead to a renewal of hostilities, and bilateral negotiations on a mechanism for the return of refugees and displaced persons to the Gali district should continue. The respective commissions of the two sides would report to the Council at its next session concerning missing-in-action cases from the 1992-1993 conflict [YUN 1993, p. 506]. Subsequently, active mediation efforts on the return of refugees to the Gali district led to agreement in principle on formulations for two of those issues. However, on 1 March, the Abkhaz side unilaterally began implementation of a refugee return programme to the Gali district, including registration of returnees. Because of lack of safety and security guarantees, the initiative elicited numerous reservations from the international community and the Georgian side. It was also feared that, because it would be implemented in a security vacuum, the return programme could prove fertile ground for an escalation of tensions.

UNOMIG continued limited patrolling within the security and restricted weapon zones, facilitated meetings between local commanders and monitored progress on the ground. The establishment of the Joint Investigation Group [YUN 1998, p. 399], as a mechanism for investigating violations of the 1994 Moscow Agreement [YUN 1994, p. 583], was still under negotiation. UNOMIG's legal experts produced draft guidelines for the Group's functioning but both sides requested more time to study them. Meanwhile, UNOMIG continued to arrange and monitor ad hoc joint investigations of alleged violations of the Moscow Agreement and acts of terrorism. While that approach was possible for incidents along the ceasefire line, the parties, particularly the Abkhaz side, did not permit joint investigations in other areas.

The Secretary-General also reported that, while the general situation in the conflict zone remained tense and unstable, the situation along the ceasefire line had become relatively calm and exchanges of fire had considerably diminished. However, activities by armed groups, particularly in the lower Gali area, had not ceased and the Abkhaz militia continued to be targeted. Criminal activities also increased. The situation in the Kodori Valley remained calm; however, the Abkhaz side repeatedly accused Georgia of undertaking a military build-up in the area. The team base at Ajara in the upper Kodori Valley remained closed.

The security and safety of UNOMIG personnel continued to receive the highest priority and consideration. Cases of theft of UNOMIG property occurred, mostly in Sukhumi at premises guarded by Abkhaz authorities. UNOMIG was pursuing better security arrangements.

UNHCR continued to protect and monitor activities in the parts of the Gali district where security conditions permitted access. Since 1 March, the start of the Abkhaz unilateral refugee return initiative, several displaced persons had returned, primarily to Gali town and some areas in the upper part of the district. The beginning of the agricultural season was expected to bring more returnees to lower Gali, in particular to those areas where the Abkhaz militia had limited presence. In other parts of western Georgia, UNHCR, in cooperation with its implementing partners and local authorities, completed emergency shelter repairs and school rehabilitation projects. Together with projects in the health, water and sanitation sectors, that assistance helped to improve basic living conditions in communal centres for the majority of internally displaced persons. The UN Human Rights Office in Abkhazia started projects in human rights training and education for schools. The security conditions, especially in the Gali region, as well as the rising level of poverty among the population as a whole, were responsible for numerous cases of violations of basic human rights.

The Secretary-General observed that the failure to reach agreement in January on the return of refugees and displaced persons and on Abkhazia's economic rehabilitation meant that a valuable opportunity was missed to take a major step forward in the peace process. The time for bargaining over formulations had long since passed. Each side had to demonstrate the political will to conclude an agreement. Pending such an agreement, direct bilateral contacts between the parties should continue, not only at the level of the Coordinating Council, but also in economic projects and confidence-building measures. In addition to measures to stabilize the security environment, the full separation of forces from the ceasefire line and the establishment of a joint investigation mechanism would significantly help to improve the situation on the ground.

The Secretary-General later reported that the eighth session of the Coordinating Council (Sukhumi, 29 April) decided to reinvigorate the activities of its three working groups; to discuss further the draft "Protocol concerning a Joint Group for Establishment of Facts concerning Violations of the Moscow Agreement of 14 May 1994 and Terrorist and Subversive Acts"; to continue bilateral talks on the creation of security conditions for returning refugees and internally displaced persons; and to support the activities of the Joint/Bilateral Coordination Commission of the two sides.

CIS peace proposals

The CIS Council of Heads of State (Moscow, 2 April) [S/1999/392] adopted further measures to settle the conflict in Abkhazia, Georgia, including consultations on ways in which other CIS States might participate, together with the Russian Federation, in the CIS peacekeeping operation. The Council also decided that, within one month, the sides should finalize and sign the draft agreement on peace and guarantees for the prevention of armed confrontation and the draft protocol on the return of refugees to the Gali district and measures for economic rehabilitation. It confirmed the mandate of the CIS peacekeeping force until 2 April and agreed in principle to extend its stay for six months, or until one of the parties requested that it cease operations. Should they fail to reach agreement within the designated period, the Council would reconsider the force's continued presence in the zone of conflict. It urged the parties to resolve the question of the establishment of temporary transitional administrations and instructed the CIS Councils of Ministers for Foreign Affairs and of Defence to establish, before 1 July, a task force to ensure their coordinating role in the implementation of its decisions.

SECURITY COUNCIL ACTION

On 7 May [meeting 3997], following consultations among Security Council members, the President made statement **S/PRST/1999/11** on behalf of the Council:

> The Security Council has considered the report of the Secretary-General of 21 April 1999 concerning the situation in Abkhazia, Georgia.
>
> The Council reiterates its demand that both sides widen their commitment to the United Nations-led peace process, continue to seek and engage in dialogue, expand their bilateral contacts and display without delay the necessary will to achieve substantial results on the key issues of the negotiations, and underlines the necessity for the parties to achieve an early and comprehensive political settlement, which includes a settlement on the political status of Abkhazia within the State of Georgia, which fully respects the sovereignty and territorial integrity of Georgia within its internationally recognized borders.
>
> The Council reaffirms the unacceptability of the demographic changes resulting from the conflict and the imprescriptible right of all refugees and displaced persons affected by the conflict to return to their homes in secure conditions, and calls upon the parties to address this issue urgently by agreeing and implementing effective measures to guarantee the security of those who exercise their unconditional right to return.
>
> The Council welcomes in this context the decision of the Council of Heads of State of the Commonwealth of Independent States of 2 April 1999 on further measures to settle the conflict in Abkhazia, Georgia. The Council notes the conclusions of the eighth session of the Coordinating Council of the Georgian and Abkhaz sides held on 29 April 1999.
>
> The Council expresses its deep concern at the failure of the parties to reach an agreement on the terms for the return of refugees and displaced persons to the Gali region and measures for economic rehabilitation. The Council stresses the need for them to conclude urgently such an agreement, which would make it possible for the international community to participate in this effort, as well as an agreement on peace and guarantees for the prevention of armed confrontation.
>
> The Council welcomes the improvements in the security situation, but notes that the general situation in the conflict zone still remains tense and unstable.
>
> The Council urges the parties to exercise great restraint in their responses to any incidents arising on the ground and to take concrete steps to improve their cooperation in this field. The Council demands that both sides take immediate and determined measures to put a stop to the activities by armed groups, including the continued laying of mines, and to establish a climate of confidence allowing refugees and displaced persons to return. The Council further demands that both sides ensure a full separation of forces from the ceasefire line, in accordance with the ceasefire protocol signed on 25 May 1998, and establish a joint investigation mechanism without further delay.
>
> The Council welcomes the continued contribution that the United Nations Observer Mission in Georgia and the collective peacekeeping force of the Commonwealth of Independent States have made to stabilizing the situation in the zone of conflict and notes that the working relationship between the Mission and the collective peacekeeping force has remained good.
>
> The Council reaffirms the importance it attaches to the security of the Mission and of all international personnel and recalls the obligations of both sides in this regard. The Council welcomes the steps taken to enhance the operations and security of the Mission.
>
> The Council strongly supports the sustained efforts made by the Secretary-General and his Special

Representative with the assistance of the Russian Federation, in its capacity as facilitator, as well as of the Group of Friends of the Secretary-General and the Organization for Security and Cooperation in Europe to prevent hostilities, to protect human rights and to advance a settlement.

Report of Secretary-General (July). In July [S/1999/805], the Secretary-General reported that his Special Representative convened a meeting of the Georgian and Abkhaz sides on confidence-building measures (Istanbul, Turkey, 7-9 June), focusing primarily on the return of refugees and displaced persons and economic issues. Agreement was reached to hold a meeting within one week to address the exchange of hostages and detainees; work with UNOMIG's Chief Military Observer in the joint investigation of potentially destabilizing incidents in the zone of conflict; revive the working groups within the framework of the Coordinating Council, including the convening of all three groups within one week after the Istanbul meeting; facilitate implementation of the Protocol concerning the stabilization of the situation along the line of separation of forces [YUN 1998, p. 400]; develop cooperation at the local level, particularly in the economic area; organize meetings between political and social figures of the two sides; create mechanisms for the regular exchange of information; exchange information and carry out consultations among the law enforcement organs for the prevention of illegal acts; and arrange a meeting among representatives of the respective missing-in-action commissions within one month.

Subsequently, the Coordinating Council's Working Group I dealing with security matters met on 25 June, after one and half years of deadlock. The Working Group decided: to hold monthly meetings, starting in early August; that the number of law enforcement personnel on both sides would be brought in line with agreed levels; that all fortifications and positions along the line of separation would be dismantled by 10 July and no new positions would be occupied; and that the sides would propose by 10 July measures for the withdrawal of forces and redeployment to rear positions. UNOMIG intended to pursue implementation vigorously, despite the fact that the initial deadlines had not been kept. In connection with the meeting of Working Group I, the Abkhaz leader's Personal Representative to the peace process met separately with the Georgian State Minister to discuss issues related to the return of refugees and internally displaced persons, and a mechanism for joint investigation and the exchange of hostages and detainees. That meeting made some progress on those issues.

The Secretary-General said that the meetings on confidence-building measures, held in Athens [YUN 1998, p. 400] and in Istanbul (see above), were successful in providing a forum for the development of direct bilateral ties at several levels and the elaboration of cooperation projects in a variety of fields. On 25 June, UNOMIG facilitated the travel to Tbilisi by the director of an Abkhaz wine-producing firm, who reached preliminary agreements with his Georgian counterparts on plans for business cooperation. The Joint/Bilateral Coordination Commission for Practical Questions continued to be instrumental in fostering economic cooperation between the sides.

Meanwhile, preparatory work continued on the political status of Abkhazia, Georgia. The Special Representative was working with academic institutions to elaborate proposals on the distribution of constitutional competences between Tbilisi and Sukhumi, which would be submitted to the two sides for consideration after consultations with the Russian Federation, OSCE and the Group of Friends of the Secretary-General.

On 4 June, the CIS Council of Foreign Ministers reviewed implementation of the 2 April decision on further measures to settle the conflict (see p. 377) and noted that the timetable envisaged for steps to be taken in the peace process remained unimplemented and therefore the mandate of the CIS peacekeeping force had not been extended. The Council decided that the Russian Federation and the Georgian side should consult before 1 August on measures for implementing those decisions.

Substantial progress was made towards the setting up of a joint investigation mechanism for violations of the 1994 Moscow Agreement [YUN 1994, p. 583], resulting in the acceptance of a modified UNOMIG draft as a basis for negotiations. Only the provision concerning the scope of incidents to be investigated remained contentious. While the final agreement was being negotiated, UNOMIG had undertaken initiatives to involve representatives from all parties in joint investigations of several incidents of violence and alleged acts of terrorism on an ad hoc basis. That effort contributed to keeping the situation under control and, more importantly, to preventing wider escalation.

The situation along the ceasefire line improved considerably and exchanges of fire were reduced even more as a result of UNOMIG's success in separating the opposing forces further. Despite apprehensions and widespread rumours of an impending escalation, the anniversary of the events of May 1998 [YUN 1998, p. 394] passed without any major incident. On the other hand, terrorist activities by so-called "uncontrolled" partisan groups, particularly in the lower Gali area, had not ceased and the Abkhaz militia continued to be targeted. The Moscow Agreement was violated by random acts of deployment of prohibited weapons, mine incidents and denial of access to patrols. During the spring season, a higher movement of refugees to the Gali region was observed and many internally displaced persons had taken up semi-permanent residence. The Abkhaz unilateral initiative to facilitate the return of refugees and displaced persons to the Gali region had met a fair response from the displaced population and an increased number of returnees had used the opportunity to cultivate their lands. However, that was assessed as a temporary phenomenon as the lack of security guarantees and absence of a supporting infrastructure inhibited their move on a permanent basis. Access to the upper Kodori Valley remained impossible by road because of the destroyed bridge on the route from Sukhumi and the closure of the mountain pass along the route from Zugdidi. An exploratory patrol along the latter route was robbed at gunpoint on 10 May. The local authorities in the Georgian-controlled part of the valley expressed displeasure with UNOMIG's efforts to report and pursue the perpetrators through the Zugdidi police. The situation in the valley had been calm; however, UNOMIG's efforts to facilitate a meeting between Abkhaz and Georgian military leaders had met with resistance.

The Secretary-General observed that, while progress in the negotiations process aimed at the comprehensive settlement of the conflict continued to be difficult, contacts between the sides at all levels continued to grow. The recent improvements in the security situation along the line of separation of forces and the efforts of the sides to produce those improvements were noted, but the full separation of forces, in accordance with the Moscow Agreement and the September 1998 Protocol [YUN 1998, p. 400], remained to be accomplished. The Secretary-General called on the sides to take immediate steps to implement Working Group I decisions towards that end. He recommended that the Security Council extend UNOMIG's mandate until 31 January 2000.

Communications. On 19 July [S/1999/801], Georgia informed the Security Council President that the Abkhaz separatist authorities intended to hold so-called presidential elections in the autumn in Abkhazia, Georgia. Georgia said that, at a time when two thirds of the Abkhazia population were disenfranchised and expelled from the region, the holding of elections was illegitimate and attempted to establish the demographic changes resulting from the conflict and to obstruct the peace process. The holding of free and fair elections would become possible only after agreement had been reached on Abkhazia's political status. Georgia expected the United Nations, the Friends of the Secretary-General and international organizations to condemn any attempt to subvert the process of the comprehensive settlement of the conflict in Abkhazia.

The Georgian President, on the same day [S/1999/809], expressed support for the NATO and Russian operation in the FRY province of Kosovo (see p. 356) and attempted to draw a parallel between the Kosovo and Abkhaz situations. He said that, while the United Nations might not be able to carry out an operation in Georgia similar to the one in Kosovo, he believed that it should assume a more firm and uncompromising position towards the separatists who blatantly disregarded all of the Council's resolutions. The Council should warn the separatist regime that more drastic measures would be taken against them if they continued their non-compliance with its demands and condemn the so-called elections, at any level, in Abkhazia, until the process of the return of refugees and displaced persons was complete. The Council should consider, as a matter of urgency, the full resumption of UNOMIG's functions, including reinforcing the monitoring of the human rights situation. Georgia requested that the Secretary-General renew consultations on his proposals for the introduction of self-protection units [YUN 1998, p. 393], and believed that the time was ripe to begin consultations on giving UNOMIG police functions as well.

The conflict in Abkhazia also merited the Council's attention in the context of its 8 July debate on the disarmament, demobilization and reintegration of ex-combatants in a peacekeeping environment, Georgia stated on 20 July [S/1999/806]. The continued availability of large amounts of armaments to the Abkhaz separatists had unleashed violence against returnees, claiming the lives of 1,500 people and displaying a consistent pattern of ethnic cleansing. The Abkhaz separatists were in possession of more than 124 units of heavy weaponry, as well as military aircraft, attack helicopters and military vessels, in violation of international treaties and Council resolutions. Georgia supported the commitment of Council members that all nations that exported arms and light weapons, or were involved in the traffic of those weapons, bore responsibility and that there was a need for concerted action to curb arms transfers to zones of conflict. It believed that presidential statement **S/PRST/1999/21** (see p. 50) offered sound ground for bringing strict implementation of resolution 876(1993) [YUN 1993, p. 510] into the focus of the

Council's forthcoming discussion on the situation in Abkhazia. Empowering UNOMIG to monitor arms transfers to Abkhazia could be one way to reinvigorate the process of the conflict settlement, which had been at an impasse for too long.

In that regard, Georgia, on 22 July [S/1999/813], submitted its basic principles for determining the status of Abkhazia within Georgia's new State structure. That status would be defined by the basic principles of the inviolability of Georgia's territorial integrity within the internationally recognized borders existing as at 21 December 1991, and of Abkhazia within the borders of the former Abkhaz Autonomous Republic as part of the Georgian Soviet Socialist Republic as at 21 December 1992; recognition of Abkhazia's right to exercise its competence within the federation as a component of the federal State of Georgia; and institutional incorporation, in the Constitutions of Abkhazia and Georgia, of the right of the Abkhaz people to develop their culture and long-standing traditions, and to integrate historical elements into the political and social life of the people, with full respect and guarantees for the human rights and freedoms of the entire multi-ethnic population of Abkhazia, and with the guarantee of active participation by its representatives in the work of the federal organs of power. Georgia also set out a number of specific principles and sovereign rights that the Republic of Abkhazia should enjoy.

Georgia also submitted to the Council President, on 22 July [S/1999/814], the text of President Shevardnadze's address to the International Conference-Seminar on the Policy of Genocide and Ethnic Cleansing in Abkhazia, Georgia: the Principal Weapon of Aggressive Separatism, together with the texts of the Conference's appeal to the Security Council and the world community, the statement of Georgia's Prosecutor General and statements by eyewitnesses of the Abkhaz tragedy.

SECURITY COUNCIL ACTION

On 30 July [meeting 4029], the Security Council unanimously adopted **resolution 1255(1999)**. The draft [S/1999/832] was prepared in consultations among Council members.

The Security Council,

Recalling all its relevant resolutions, in particular resolution 1225(1999) of 28 January 1999, and the statement by its President of 7 May 1999,

Having considered the report of the Secretary-General of 20 July 1999,

Taking note of the letter dated 19 July 1999 from the President of Georgia to the Secretary-General,

Stressing that, notwithstanding positive developments on some issues, the lack of progress on key issues of a comprehensive settlement of the conflict in Abkhazia, Georgia, is unacceptable,

Deeply concerned at the continuing volatile situation in the conflict zone, welcoming in this regard the important contributions that the United Nations Observer Mission in Georgia and the collective peacekeeping force of the Commonwealth of Independent States continue to make in stabilizing the situation in the zone of conflict, noting that the working relationship between the Mission and the collective peacekeeping force has been good at all levels, and stressing the importance of continuing and increasing close cooperation and coordination between them in the performance of their respective mandates,

Recalling the conclusions of the Lisbon summit of the Organization for Security and Cooperation in Europe regarding the situation in Abkhazia, Georgia,

Reaffirming the necessity for the parties strictly to respect human rights, and expressing its support for the efforts of the Secretary-General to find ways to improve their observance as an integral part of the work towards a comprehensive political settlement,

1. *Welcomes* the report of the Secretary-General of 20 July 1999;

2. *Demands* that the parties to the conflict widen and deepen their commitment to the United Nations-led peace process, continue to expand their dialogue and contacts at all levels and display without delay the necessary will to achieve substantial results on the key issues of the negotiations;

3. *Strongly supports* the sustained efforts of the Secretary-General and his Special Representative with the assistance of the Russian Federation, in its capacity as facilitator, as well as of the Group of Friends of the Secretary-General and the Organization for Security and Cooperation in Europe to promote the stabilization of the situation and to give new impetus to the negotiations within the United Nations-led peace process in order to achieve a comprehensive political settlement, and commends the tireless efforts of the retiring Special Representative of the Secretary-General, Mr. Liviu Bota, in carrying out his mandate;

4. *Emphasizes,* in this context, that the readiness and ability of the international community to assist the parties depend on their political will to resolve the conflict through dialogue and mutual accommodation and on their acting in good faith to implement promptly concrete measures towards bringing about a comprehensive political settlement of the conflict;

5. *Underlines* the necessity for the parties to achieve an early and comprehensive political settlement, which includes a settlement on the political status of Abkhazia within the State of Georgia, which fully respects the sovereignty and territorial integrity of Georgia within its internationally recognized borders, and supports the intention of the Secretary-General and his Special Representative, in close cooperation with the Russian Federation, in its capacity as facilitator, the Organization for Security and Cooperation in Europe and the Group of Friends of the Secretary-General, to continue to submit proposals for the consideration of the parties on the distribution of constitutional competences between Tbilisi and Sukhumi as part of a comprehensive settlement;

6. *Considers* the holding of self-styled elections in Abkhazia, Georgia, unacceptable and illegitimate;

7. *Expresses its continuing concern* at the situation of refugees and displaced persons, resulting, in particular, from the hostilities of May 1998, reaffirms the unacceptability of the demographic changes resulting from the conflict and the imprescriptible right of all refugees and displaced persons affected by the conflict to return to their homes in secure conditions in accordance with international law and as set out in the Quadripartite Agreement on the Voluntary Return of Refugees and Displaced Persons, of 4 April 1994, and calls upon the parties to address this issue urgently by agreeing and implementing effective measures to guarantee the security of those who exercise their unconditional right to return;

8. *Welcomes,* in this context, the efforts of the Special Representative of the Secretary-General to facilitate, as a first step, the safe return of refugees and displaced persons to the Gali region, and emphasizes, in this regard, that the lasting return of the refugees cannot be ensured without concrete results from the bilateral dialogue between the parties, which produce the necessary security and legal guarantees;

9. *Takes note with appreciation* of the agreements reached at the meetings of 16 to 18 October 1998 and 7 to 9 June 1999, hosted respectively by the Governments of Greece and Turkey, aimed at building confidence, improving security and developing cooperation, and calls upon the parties to enhance their efforts to implement those decisions in an effective and comprehensive manner, notably at the prospective meeting in Yalta at the invitation of the Government of Ukraine;

10. *Demands* that both sides observe strictly the Agreement on a Ceasefire and Separation of Forces, signed in Moscow on 14 May 1994, and takes note with appreciation, in this context, of the substantial progress reported towards setting up a joint investigation mechanism for violations of the Agreement, as well as of the greater restraint exercised by the parties along the line of separation of forces;

11. *Condemns* the ongoing activities by armed groups, which endanger the civilian population, impede the work of the humanitarian organizations and seriously delay the normalization of the situation in the Gali region, reiterates its concern regarding the security of the United Nations Observer Mission in Georgia, welcomes the implementation of measures in this regard, and requests the Secretary-General to keep the security of the Mission under constant review;

12. *Decides* to extend the mandate of the Mission for a new period terminating on 31 January 2000, subject to a review by the Council of the mandate of the Mission in the event of any changes that may be made in the mandate or in the presence of the collective peacekeeping force of the Commonwealth of Independent States;

13. *Requests* the Secretary-General to continue to keep the Council regularly informed and to report three months from the date of the adoption of the present resolution on the situation in Abkhazia, Georgia;

14. *Expresses its intention* to conduct a thorough review of the operation at the end of its current mandate, in the light of steps taken by the parties to achieve a comprehensive settlement;

15. *Decides* to remain actively seized of the matter.

Elections

On 27 August [A/54/284-S/1999/928], Georgia declared that, in accordance with a decree of 4 August, parliamentary elections would be held in Georgia on 31 October. The decree provided for the filing of the lists of political parties by 25 September, for the completion of the registration of candidates by 6 October and for the participation of foreign and local observers in the pre-election campaign and voting process.

The Secretary-General reported that the Abkhaz side held "presidential elections" on 3 October, in which Mr. Ardzinba ran unopposed, and a referendum on the Abkhaz November 1994 "Constitution" [YUN 1994, p. 586]. He recalled in that connection that the Security Council, in resolution 1255(1999) (see above), considered "unacceptable and illegitimate the holding of self-styled elections", in the absence of the majority of the population of Abkhazia, Georgia. On 12 October, the Abkhaz de facto parliament adopted a document entitled "Act on State Independence of the Republic of Abkhazia" [S/1999/1087].

The Security Council President, in a 4 October press statement [A/55/2], said that Council members regarded the 3 October self-styled elections and referendum as unacceptable and illegitimate and that such elections would be possible within the framework of a comprehensive political settlement, and with guaranteed full participation for all refugees and displaced persons.

The EU, on 6 October [S/1999/1040], regretted the 3 October elections and referendum and considered them null and void and detrimental to efforts to find a peaceful solution to the conflict.

The CIS Council of Ministers for Foreign Affairs, meeting in Yalta, Ukraine, on 8 October [S/1999/1156], considered those elections as flouting the will of the international community, particularly Council resolution 1255(1999), and that they were not conducive to the settlement of the conflict and complicated the search for mutually acceptable solutions regarding Abkhazia's status.

The Secretary-General later reported that, following the 3 October elections, an inauguration ceremony was held in Sukhumi for the Abkhaz leader on 6 December, who subsequently reshuffled his cabinet, replacing de facto Prime Minister Sergei Bagapsh with Viacheslav Tsugba [S/2000/39].

In the 31 October Georgian parliamentary elections, in which some 67.7 per cent of the eligible population took part, the ruling Citizens Union of Georgia won a clear majority in the 235-seat Parliament. Only two other parties, the Revival bloc and the Industry Will Save Georgia party, received the minimum 7 per cent of votes required to qualify for the 150 seats allocated by proportional representation. No elections were held for the districts of Abkhazia. The parliamentarians already representing those constituencies retained their seats.

Further developments

Report of Secretary-General (October). In October [S/1999/1087], the Secretary-General said that, on 20 September, he discussed important aspects of the peace process, including the political status of Abkhazia, Georgia, with President Shevardnadze in New York. The President welcomed the Special Representative's intention to submit later in the year, for the consideration of the two sides, proposals relating to the distribution of constitutional competences between Tbilisi and Sukhumi.

The ninth session of the Coordinating Council, which had originally been planned for 30 July, had been postponed indefinitely. Meanwhile, the intensity and scope of direct contacts between the Georgian and Abkhaz sides had accelerated, including a meeting in Moscow on 4 August and one in Tbilisi on 21 September. As a result, both sides reported progress on a draft agreement addressing the return of refugees and internally displaced persons to the Gali district in its old borders and on measures for Abkhazia's economic rehabilitation. In mid-September, Mr. Ardzinba expressed concern to President Shevardnadze about the possible deterioration of the security situation on the ground. As a result, the respective heads of the defence, internal affairs and security structures of the two sides met on 21 September in Tbilisi, with the participation of UNOMIG's Chief Military Observer and the Commander of the CIS peacekeeping force.

On the basis of the discussions held in June during the Istanbul meeting on confidence-building measures (see p. 378) and following numerous high-level direct telephone contacts, a number of detainees held by each side were exchanged on 8 September. The Special Representative continued to call on the two sides to effect a full exchange of detainees on an "all-for-all" basis. In the economic and cultural spheres, positive developments during the reporting period included the travel by a group of 20 Georgian and 20 Abkhaz children to summer camp in the United States; the convening of a meeting of Georgian and Abkhaz elders and war veterans and the restoration by the Georgiafilm studio of films shot in Abkhazia at various times during the century; and a meeting in September in Tbilisi, which brought winemakers from the Georgian and Abkhaz sides close to an agreement on cooperation in the production and sale of wine. Progress in the peace process was slow in part because of the campaign for the Georgian parliamentary elections held in October (see p. 381).

UNOMIG continued to take the lead in the joint investigations of violent incidents and pursued implementation of the agreements on the separation of forces reached at the June session of Working Group I (see p. 378). While the original deadline (10 July) for carrying out those measures had not been met, the main obligations had largely been fulfilled after significant pressure from UNOMIG. As a result, UNOMIG had noticed a steady improvement in mutual confidence between the sides, making direct bilateral contacts at the lower levels possible as well.

The strength of the forces directly confronting each other on both sides of the ceasefire line decreased noticeably during the reporting period. As a result, cross-border firing remained at a very low level in comparison to a year previously. The general level of calm along the line was also facilitated by agreements between lower-level force commanders and local administrators to maintain order.

During the reporting period, most of the violent incidents recorded were assessed to have been carried out by criminal elements motivated by economic gain. On the Abkhaz side, law enforcement structures remained unable to combat either the criminal or the terrorist elements operating in the area, especially in the lower Gali region. The Abkhaz authorities attempted to extend their authority in the security field by encouraging villages to form self-defence units of local residents armed with their own weapons, which were to be formally registered with the Gali administration. On the whole, the two sides had failed to check effectively, or to cooperate in preventing, the activities of criminals and armed groups. The establishment of effective law enforcement throughout the zone of conflict remained a priority task for both sides.

The situation in the Kodori Valley had been calm until the kidnapping for ransom by armed individuals of seven UNOMIG personnel on patrol in the Georgian-controlled part of the valley on 13 October. By 15 October, all seven were released unconditionally after negotiations led by senior Georgian government officials.

Late in August, Georgia supported the extension of the CIS peacekeeping force's mandate for six months. The Georgian side expressed its confidence that that step would encourage the peacekeeping force to carry out its mission with more vigour and determination.

Recent periods of calm on the ground in the Gali district had no fundamental effect on the human rights situation. There was no change in the language policy in the schools with predominantly Georgian-speaking students, where Georgian was taught a limited number of hours and the language of instruction in the first four grades continued to be Russian. The United Nations Human Rights Office in Abkhazia, Georgia, continued to monitor reports from local residents of apartment evictions and violations of the right of property. The Office was pursuing reported cases of harassment through local law enforcement authorities. Visiting Georgia from 4 to 7 September, the United Nations High Commissioner for Refugees expressed dismay about the politicization of the plight of persons displaced from Abkhazia, Georgia, many of whom lived in grim conditions. She urged President Shevardnadze and the Government of Georgia to do everything in their power to improve conditions for internally displaced persons and to provide them with the social and legal rights necessary to develop a capacity for self-reliance.

The socio-economic picture in Abkhazia remained bleak and without prospects for immediate change. Some of the region was affected again by a drought that had reduced the expected harvest. Wage-earning opportunities remained almost non-existent and the level of petty crime was high. Demographically, the population continued to dwindle, as those with any means or connections sought jobs or education elsewhere.

The Secretary-General said that his September meeting with President Shevardnadze had reinforced his conviction that, in the search for a comprehensive settlement of the Georgian/Abkhaz dispute, efforts should be strengthened to achieve progress on the core question of the conflict, namely, the political status of Abkhazia. In that regard, his Special Representative would work closely with the Russian Federation, OSCE and the Group of Friends of the Secretary-General before submitting proposals to both sides.

Communications. On 12 October [S/1999/1058], Georgia informed the Council President that it had issued a decree on 19 May on the Provisional Rules of Navigation to the Seaports of the Autonomous Republic of Abkhazia to prevent arms smuggling and other illegal shipments into Abkhazia and to ensure unimpeded access of humanitarian aid. On 12 November [S/1999/1173], Georgia said that, despite the positive developments reflected in the Secretary-General's October report (see above), it believed that the situation in Abkhazia remained tense as to merit more attention from the international community. The "Law on Independence" passed on 12 October constituted the only response of the separatist regime to the Council's efforts to consolidate a multilateral approach to determining Abkhazia's political status with Georgia. That regime had established a consistent pattern of behaviour against international efforts to defuse tensions and to secure positive developments in implementing confidence-building measures. Local criminal groups, abetted by the so-called Abkhazia militia, were appropriating the revenues from trading citrus and nuts of the returned peasants, depriving them of their only source of survival. Clashes between those groups and widespread violence against the population were becoming a normal sequence of life. By the same token, the intention of the separatist regime to encourage villages in the Gali region to form armed self-defence units was permeated by its desire to give the impression that formal registration of arms by the Georgian population was permitted to face the threat stemming from the negative reaction of "partisan" groups for doing so. Georgia welcomed UNOMIG's intensified efforts to enhance the flexibility of the Mission's access to remote and unvisited areas, thus strengthening its capability of monitoring and reporting on events in the conflict zone. It hoped that UNOMIG's operation in the Kodori Valley would be resumed soon.

SECURITY COUNCIL ACTION

On 12 November [meeting 4065], following consultations among Security Council members, the President made statement **S/PRST/1999/30** on behalf of the Council:

> The Security Council has considered the report of the Secretary-General of 22 October 1999 concerning the situation in Abkhazia, Georgia.
>
> The Council warmly welcomes the appointment of Mr. Dieter Boden as resident Special Representative of the Secretary-General, and hopes the parties will see this as an opportune moment to give renewed impetus to the search for a political settlement.
>
> The Council welcomes the acceleration of bilateral contacts at all levels between the Georgian and Abkhaz sides and calls upon them to continue to expand their contacts.
>
> The Council notes with grave concern that, notwithstanding positive developments on some issues, no progress has been made on the key issues of the settlement, particularly the core issue of the status of Abkhazia, Georgia. The Council therefore strongly supports the intention of the Special Representative to submit as soon as possible further proposals to both sides on the distribution of constitutional competences between Tbilisi and Sukhumi, as part of a comprehensive settlement, with full respect for the sovereignty and territorial integrity of Georgia within its internationally recognized borders, working in close cooperation with the Russian Federation, in its capacity as facilitator, the Group of

Friends of the Secretary-General, and the Organization for Security and Cooperation in Europe.

The Council reiterates its demand that the parties to the conflict widen and deepen their commitment to the United Nations–led peace process, in particular by resuming regular meetings of the Coordinating Council and of its working groups, and agrees with the Secretary-General that they must continue to meet regularly, regardless of the constraints of domestic politics. The Council calls upon the parties to agree upon and to take, in the nearest future, the first concrete steps towards the full return to Abkhazia, Georgia, of refugees and internally displaced persons in safe, secure and dignified conditions. The Council reminds the parties that this would enable the Office of the United Nations High Commissioner for Refugees to provide substantial material assistance. The Council reiterates its view on the unacceptability of any action by the Abkhaz leadership in contravention of the principles of the sovereignty and territorial integrity of Georgia.

The Council notes with satisfaction that the security situation has improved slightly, in particular in the reduction of tension along the line of separation of forces, while noting the persistent precariousness of the security of United Nations personnel. The Council reiterates its condemnation of the hostage-taking of seven United Nations personnel on 13 October 1999, welcomes the release of the hostages, and stresses that the perpetrators of this unacceptable act should be brought to justice. The Council welcomes the fact that the United Nations Observer Mission in Georgia is keeping its security arrangements under constant review in order to ensure the highest possible level of security for its staff.

The Council pays tribute to Mr. Liviu Bota for his valuable work while serving as Special Representative of the Secretary-General. The Council welcomes the important contributions that the Mission and the collective peacekeeping force of the Commonwealth of Independent States continue to make in stabilizing the situation in the zone of conflict, notes that the working relationship between the Mission and the collective peacekeeping force has been good at all levels, and stresses the importance of continuing and increasing close cooperation and coordination between them in the performance of their respective mandates.

Report of Secretary-General. The Secretary-General later reported that Georgia and the Russian Federation agreed in November that the Russian Federation would withdraw two of its four military bases in Georgia by 1 July 2001, including the base at Gudauta, in Abkhazia [S/2000/39]. Also in November, the Russian Federation decided to close the Russian-Georgian border at the Psou River to all crossings, including by UNOMIG personnel and vehicles. That decision had blocked a possible exit route from the zone of conflict and was seriously complicating the procurement of supplies for the Mission. Consultations were going on with the Russian Federation authorities to resolve the issue.

In November, Georgian Ministry of the Interior troops were withdrawn from their posts along the ceasefire line. On the Abkhaz side, there were currently no militia posts close to the ceasefire line. While undirected shooting across the line continued, incidents of targeted shooting were rare. The high level of criminal activity along the ceasefire line and the lack of effective action and mutual cooperation by the law enforcement agencies on both sides continued to be a cause for concern. In December, a series of tit-for-tat kidnappings occurred in the Gali and Zugdidi sectors. There was also a spate of criminal lootings by bandits in the Gali sector.

In December, OHCHR organized a human rights seminar for representatives of institutes of higher learning. A round table organized by the Office to address the situation of minorities in Abkhazia led to the establishment of a permanent public council on minority issues, which provided a forum for expressing views on the subject and for shaping public policy. The Office had begun drafting a plan of action for human rights education in schools, universities and law enforcement organs.

Financing

On 8 June [meeting 101], the General Assembly, having considered the Secretary-General's report on UNOMIG's financial performance for the period 1 July 1997 to 30 June 1998 [A/53/821], the proposed budget for the Mission's maintenance for the period 1 July 1999 to 30 June 2000 [A/53/844 & Corr.1,2], and ACABQ's comments and recommendations thereon [A/53/895/Add.4], adopted without vote, on the recommendation of the Fifth Committee [A/53/983], **resolution 53/232** [agenda item 131].

Financing of the United Nations Observer Mission in Georgia

The General Assembly,

Having considered the reports of the Secretary-General on the financing of the United Nations Observer Mission in Georgia and the related reports of the Advisory Committee on Administrative and Budgetary Questions,

Recalling Security Council resolution 854(1993) of 6 August 1993, by which the Council approved the deployment of an advance team of up to ten United Nations military observers for a period of three months and the incorporation of the advance team into a United Nations observer mission if such a mission was formally established by the Council,

Recalling also Security Council resolution 858(1993) of 24 August 1993, by which the Council decided to establish the United Nations Observer Mission in Georgia, and the subsequent resolutions by which the Council extended the mandate of the Observer Mission, the latest of which was resolution 1225(1999) of 28 January 1999,

Recalling further its decision 48/475 A of 23 December 1993 on the financing of the Observer Mission and its subsequent resolutions and decisions thereon, the latest of which was resolution 52/242 of 26 June 1998,

Reaffirming that the costs of the Observer Mission are expenses of the Organization to be borne by Member States in accordance with Article 17, paragraph 2, of the Charter of the United Nations,

Recalling its previous decisions regarding the fact that, in order to meet the expenditures caused by the Observer Mission, a different procedure is required from that applied to meet expenditures of the regular budget of the United Nations,

Taking into account the fact that the economically more developed countries are in a position to make relatively larger contributions and that the economically less developed countries have a relatively limited capacity to contribute towards such an operation,

Bearing in mind the special responsibilities of the States permanent members of the Security Council, as indicated in General Assembly resolution 1874(S-IV) of 27 June 1963, in the financing of such operations,

Noting with appreciation that voluntary contributions have been made to the Observer Mission,

Mindful of the fact that it is essential to provide the Observer Mission with the necessary financial resources to enable it to fulfil its responsibilities under the relevant resolutions of the Security Council,

1. *Takes note* of the status of contributions to the United Nations Observer Mission in Georgia as at 30 April 1999, including the contributions outstanding in the amount of 8.8 million United States dollars, representing 11 per cent of the total assessed contributions from the inception of the Observer Mission to the period ending 30 June 1999, notes that some 16 per cent of the Member States have paid their assessed contributions in full, and urges all other Member States concerned, in particular those in arrears, to ensure payment of their outstanding assessed contributions;

2. *Expresses concern* about the financial situation with regard to peacekeeping activities, in particular as regards the reimbursement of troop contributors, which bear additional burdens owing to overdue payments by Member States of their assessments;

3. *Expresses its appreciation* to those Member States which have paid their assessed contributions in full;

4. *Urges* all other Member States to make every possible effort to ensure payment of their assessed contributions to the Observer Mission in full and on time;

5. *Endorses* the observations and recommendations contained in the report of the Advisory Committee on Administrative and Budgetary Questions;

6. *Requests* the Secretary-General to take all necessary action to ensure that the Observer Mission is administered with a maximum of efficiency and economy;

7. *Also requests* the Secretary-General, in order to reduce the cost of employing General Service staff, to continue efforts to recruit local staff for the Observer Mission against General Service posts, commensurate with the requirements of the Mission;

8. *Decides* to appropriate the amount of 290,200 dollars gross (485,200 dollars net), for the maintenance of the Observer Mission for the period from 1 July 1997 to 30 June 1998, in addition to the amount of 18,580,500 dollars gross (17,582,100 dollars net) already appropriated under the terms of General Assembly resolution 51/236 of 13 June 1997 and inclusive of the amount of 290,200 dollars gross (485,200 dollars net) from the amount of 1,653,600 dollars authorized by the Advisory Committee under the terms of section IV of Assembly resolution 49/233 A of 23 December 1994;

9. *Decides also* to appropriate to the Special Account for the United Nations Observer Mission in Georgia the amount of 31,000,479 dollars gross (29,505,279 dollars net) for the maintenance of the Observer Mission for the period from 1 July 1999 to 30 June 2000, inclusive of the amount of 1,541,759 dollars for the support account for peacekeeping operations and the amount of 302,320 dollars for the United Nations Logistics Base at Brindisi, Italy;

10. *Decides further*, as an ad hoc arrangement, to apportion among Member States the amount of 2,583,373 dollars gross (2,458,773 dollars net) for the period from 1 to 31 July 1999, in accordance with the composition of groups set out in paragraphs 3 and 4 of General Assembly resolution 43/232 of 1 March 1989, as adjusted by the Assembly in its resolutions 44/192 B of 21 December 1989, 45/269 of 27 August 1991, 46/198 A of 20 December 1991, 47/218 A of 23 December 1992, 49/249 A of 20 July 1995, 49/249 B of 14 September 1995, 50/224 of 11 April 1996, 51/218 A to C of 18 December 1996, and 52/230 of 31 March 1998 and its decisions 48/472 A of 23 December 1993 and 50/451 B of 23 December 1995, and taking into account the scale of assessments for the year 1999, as set out in its resolution 52/215 A of 22 December 1997;

11. *Decides* that, in accordance with the provisions of its resolution 973(X) of 15 December 1955, there shall be set off against the apportionment among Member States, as provided for in paragraph 10 above, their respective share in the Tax Equalization Fund of the estimated staff assessment income of 124,600 dollars approved for the Observer Mission for the period from 1 to 31 July 1999;

12. *Decides also*, as an ad hoc arrangement, to apportion among Member States the amount of 28,417,103 dollars gross (27,046,503 dollars net) for the period from 1 August 1999 to 30 June 2000, at a monthly rate of 2,583,373 dollars gross (2,458,773 dollars net) in accordance with the scheme set out in the present resolution and taking into account the scale of assessments for the years 1999 and 2000, as set out in its resolution 52/215 A, subject to the decision of the Security Council to extend the mandate of the Observer Mission beyond 31 July 1999;

13. *Decides further* that, in accordance with the provisions of its resolution 973(X), there shall be set off against the apportionment among Member States, as provided for in paragraph 12 above, their respective share in the Tax Equalization Fund of the estimated staff assessment income of 1,370,600 dollars approved for the period from 1 August 1999 to 30 June 2000;

14. *Invites* voluntary contributions to the Observer Mission in cash and in the form of services and supplies acceptable to the Secretary-General, to be administered, as appropriate, in accordance with the procedure and practices established by the General Assembly;

15. *Decides* to include in the provisional agenda of its fifty-fourth session the item entitled "Financing of the United Nations Observer Mission in Georgia".

The Assembly, on 23 December, decided that the item on UNOMIG financing would remain for consideration at the resumed fifty-fourth (2000) session (**decision 54/465**). It also decided that the item would be considered by the Fifth Committee at that session(**decision 54/462 A**).

Armenia-Azerbaijan

Armenia and Azerbaijan, at the end of 1999, were no nearer to reaching a settlement of the armed conflict between them, which had erupted in 1992 [YUN 1992, p. 388] over the Nagorny Karabakh region in Azerbaijan, despite continued efforts by the Minsk Group of OSCE to reach a settlement. During the year, both countries addressed communications to the Secretary-General regarding developments in the conflict.

Communications. Azerbaijan said, on 29 January [S/1999/93], that military cooperation between the Russian Federation and Armenia and the Russian military presence in Armenia were a threat to its security, particularly since the Russian military base and personnel were being used to strengthen the Armenian armed forces in the context of the country's armed aggression against it. The strengthening of such cooperation, the continued delivery of military materiel to Armenia, and the inaction of the trilateral committee for the settlement of the problem of weapons deliveries pointed to the fact that there were certain forces in the Russian Federation plotting to nullify efforts to put an end to the arming of Armenia and to settle the conflict between Armenia and Azerbaijan by peaceful means. Azerbaijan was considering measures to guarantee the country's security and defend its independence and sovereignty.

Armenia, on 26 February [S/1999/211], described as unfounded the accusations relating to Armenian-Russian military cooperation, including the existence of a Russian military base in Armenia. Armenia reiterated that Armenia-Russia bilateral relations, including military cooperation, were regulated by internationally recognized legal documents and stressed that a nation's right to choose the means of ensuring its security was fully recognized within UN statutes and OSCE norms and principles. That cooperation was not directed at a third country. Armenia called on the Azerbaijani authorities to refrain from nonconstructive and provocative actions that endangered the peace and stability of the region and obstructed the peaceful settlement of the Nagorny Karabakh conflict.

In a further assessment of the situation, Armenia said, on 25 February [S/1999/210], that Azerbaijan's President had written to the Presidents of the three Co-Chair countries of the OSCE Minsk Group—France, the Russian Federation and the United States—expressing his dismay at the delays in finding a resolution to the Nagorny Karabakh conflict. That call on the three Presidents to promote constructive approaches came from the only party to the conflict that had rejected the most recent proposal presented by the three Co-Chairs. The main obstacle to the resolution of the conflict was Azerbaijan's counterproductive approach, which appeared to prefer a military solution. For Armenia, the "common state", a basic element of the latest proposal, was a promising concept for a true compromise, which might lead to a peaceful resolution of the conflict, and for that reason it had accepted it as a basis for negotiations. However, Azerbaijan had rejected the proposal, proving once again its unwillingness to compromise. Other Azerbaijan obstacles included its refusal to accept Nagorny Karabakh as a full party to the conflict and rejection of direct contact with the Nagorny Karabakh leadership; Azerbaijan's clear pattern of presenting the conflict in terms of the broader Russia/Turkey confrontation; the myth that the ongoing blockade of Armenia would eventually force it to make unilateral concessions; that the artificially inflated oil factor would help impose a resolution to the conflict advantageous to Azerbaijan; and the Azerbaijan leadership's belief that time was on their side and that they would eventually achieve military superiority over Armenia.

On 27 February [S/1999/222], Azerbaijan reported the violation of its airspace in the Kelbadjar district occupied by Armenian forces by a Russian air force fighter plane. Azerbaijan also drew attention to a statement by the Russian air force commander on 17 February referring to deliveries of C-300 surface-to-air missile systems to the Russian military base in Armenia in the light of the threat from a neighbouring State, and the fact that, as of 1 April, Armenia would be included in the roster of the unified anti-aircraft defence system. Azerbaijan hoped that the Russian side would take measures to prevent the recurrence of such incidents. It reiterated that developments in connection with Armenia's unilateral rearmament was fraught with unpredictable consequences for the region of the south Caucasus.

On 3 June [S/1999/643], Azerbaijan reported that it had sought clarification from China concerning the delivery of eight "Taifeng" missile systems to Armenia and which, according to information available, had already been deployed in the Azerbaijani region of Upper Karabakh, which was occupied by Armenian troops. The delivery of the missile systems was a matter of particular concern to Azerbaijan in that its people viewed China as a friendly State. Azerbaijan trusted that China would take measures to ensure the return to China of those weapons unlawfully delivered to Armenia, whose deployment had a negative impact on the process of settling the conflict, as well as the development of relations between Azerbaijan and China.

Azerbaijan reported on 14 June [S/1999/686] that its armed forces had repulsed three attempts by Armenian troops to capture Azerbaijani armed forces' positions in the vicinity of the town of Terter. Two Azerbaijani soldiers were killed and four injured.

The "Nagorny Karabakh Ministry of Foreign Affairs", on 15 June [S/1999/681], said that Azerbaijan had recently been disseminating reports of an alleged attack by Nagorny Karabakh armed forces in the Martakert sector of the line of contact between the two sides. In fact, on 14 June, Nagorny Karabakh defence forces had opposed the advance of Azerbaijani armed forces. After sustaining losses, the opposing side was compelled to withdraw to its initial position. Two Nagorny Karabakh soldiers were wounded. Nagorny Karabakh drew attention to Azerbaijani propaganda regarding the deliveries to Nagorny Karabakh of Chinese-manufactured "Typhoon" multiple rocket launchers. Azerbaijan's rejection of the latest proposals by the Co-Chairmen of the OSCE Minsk Group left no doubt as to its aim to resolve the Nagorny Karabakh problem by force. It called on Azerbaijan to refrain from propaganda and the policy of disinformation and to initiate constructive dialogue among all parties for a speedy and comprehensive settlement of the existing problems.

Cyprus

In 1999, efforts to bring about a negotiated settlement of the Cyprus problem between Cyprus President Glafcos Clerides and Turkish Cypriot leader Rauf R. Denktas continued. Progress towards a comprehensive settlement took a modest step forward in 1999 when the two leaders accepted the Secretary-General's 30 September invitation to enter into negotiations without preconditions and in a spirit of compromise. The first session of proximity talks was held from 3 to 14 December in New York. Meanwhile, the Secretary-General reported that the situation along the ceasefire lines remained essentially stable and the United Nations Peacekeeping Force in Cyprus (UNFICYP) continued to assist in the restoration of normal conditions and in humanitarian functions. The Security Council twice extended UNFICYP's mandate, the second time until 15 June 2000.

On 13 September (**decision 53/493**), the General Assembly included in the draft agenda of its fifty-fourth session the item entitled "Question of Cyprus". On 23 December (**decision 54/465**), it decided that the item would remain for consideration during its resumed fifty-fourth (2000) session.

Incidents

Communications. Throughout 1999, the Secretary-General received numerous letters from the Government of Cyprus and from the Turkish Cypriot authorities containing charges and countercharges, protests and accusations and explanations of position. The letters from the "Turkish Republic of Northern Cyprus" were transmitted by Turkey.

In communications dated between 13 January and 30 November [A/53/798-S/1999/57, A/53/824-S/1999/137, A/53/832-S/1999/164, A/53/842-S/1999/206, A/53/848-S/1999/218, A/53/864-S/1999/283, A/53/871-S/1999/310, A/53/874-S/1999/321, A/53/887-S/1999/355, A/53/933-S/1999/499, A/53/934-S/1999/502, A/53/949-S/1999/532, A/53/953-S/1999/537, A/53/956-S/1999/545, A/53/959-S/1999/565, A/53/965-S/1999/577, A/53/991-S/1999/632, A/53/1007-S/1999/744, A/53/1030-S/1999/835, A/53/1047-S/1999/932, A/54/446-S/1999/1034, A/54/522-S/1999/1120, A/54/642-S/1999/1211], Cyprus protested violations of its airspace and unauthorized intrusions into the flight information region of Nicosia by military aircraft of the Turkish Air Force. Turkey transmitted letters from the "Representative of the Turkish Republic of Northern Cyprus" refuting those allegations, stating that the flights took place within its sovereign airspace.

In letters of 8 March [A/53/858-S/1999/256], 20 May [A/53/973-S/1999/598], 30 June [A/53/1008-S/1999/745] and 13 October [A/54/463-S/1999/1059], the "Turkish Republic of Northern Cyprus" claimed that the "Greek Cypriot administration" was engaging in an unprecedented build-up of arms and armed forces, that its National Guard had sharply increased provocations along the borders and that the administration had held joint military manoeuvres with Greece in south Cyprus in October.

In several communications received during the year, Cyprus alleged that Turkey was methodically altering the demographic character of occupied Cyprus by plundering its religious, historical and cultural identity [A/53/836-S/1999/178], which was denied by the "Turkish Republic of Northern Cyprus" [A/53/852-S/1999/234], and each side accused the other of compulsory population transfers and the implantation of settlers [A/53/863-S/1999/282, A/53/903-S/1999/385].

Good offices mission

Negotiations on a comprehensive settlement

Communication (June). The G-8 countries (Canada, France, Germany, Italy, Japan, Russian Federation, United Kingdom, United States), in a 20 June statement [S/1999/711], said that the Cyprus problem had gone unresolved for too long and a resolution would benefit the people of Cyprus and have a positive impact on peace and security in the region. Both parties to the dispute had legitimate concerns that could and should be addressed in comprehensive negotiations covering all issues. They urged the Secretary-General to invite the two leaders to negotiations in the autumn of 1999. The leaders should commit themselves to the principles of no preconditions; all issues on the table; commitment in good faith to continue to negotiate until a settlement was reached; and full consideration of relevant UN resolutions and treaties.

Report of Secretary-General (June). Pursuant to Security Council resolution 1218(1998) [YUN 1998, p. 411], the Secretary-General submitted a June report [S/1999/707] stating that, in continuation of his 1998 initiative of on-island talks [ibid., p. 410], his Deputy Special Representative for Cyprus, Ann Hercus, had, over the preceding six months, held numerous meetings with Mr. Clerides and Mr. Denktas, both of whom continued to engage in them in a constructive manner. Those discussions, which remained confidential, confirmed the importance of the issue of political equality. In pursuing the mission of good offices, the Secretary-General had always dealt with the two sides on an equal footing and the work had been conducted on an equal and even-handed basis, said the report. However, the Turkish Cypriot side contended that other aspects of their situation placed them at a disadvantage and undermined the commitment to political equality. A major challenge of the negotiations was how to translate that commitment into clear, practical provisions to be agreed upon by both sides.

In the decades during which it had resisted efforts at settlement, the Cyprus problem had become overlain with legalistic abstractions and artificial labels, which were more difficult to disentangle and which appeared increasingly removed from the actual needs of both communities, the Secretary-General said. Based on past and current discussions and negotiations with and between the two leaders, the remaining core issues were: security, distribution of powers, property and territory. A compromise on those issues would remove the remaining obstacles towards a peaceful settlement, but it was essential that those core issues be addressed without preconditions in comprehensive negotiations.

The Secretary-General appreciated the call by the heads of State of the G-8 countries for holding comprehensive negotiations (see above). He was ready to invite both leaders to enter into a process of comprehensive negotiations without preconditions and in a spirit of compromise and cooperation. The Secretary-General would ask his Special Representative designate to continue the process of dialogue with the parties to that end.

SECURITY COUNCIL ACTION

On 29 June [meeting 4018], the Security Council unanimously adopted **resolution 1250(1999)**. The draft [S/1999/724] was prepared in consultations among Council members.

The Security Council,

Reaffirming all its earlier resolutions on Cyprus, particularly resolution 1218(1998) of 22 December 1998,

Reiterating its grave concern at the lack of progress towards an overall political settlement on Cyprus,

Appreciating the statement of the heads of State and Government of Canada, France, Germany, Italy, Japan, the Russian Federation, the United Kingdom of Great Britain and Northern Ireland and the United States of America on 20 June 1999 calling for comprehensive negotiations in the autumn of 1999 under the auspices of the Secretary-General,

1. *Expresses its appreciation* for the report of the Secretary-General of 22 June 1999 on his mission of good offices in Cyprus;

2. *Stresses its full support* for the Secretary-General's mission of good offices as decided by the Security Council and, in this context, for the efforts of the Secretary-General and his Special Representative;

3. *Reiterates its endorsement* of the initiative of the Secretary-General announced on 30 September 1998, within the framework of his mission of good offices, with the goal of reducing tensions and promoting progress towards a just and lasting settlement in Cyprus;

4. *Notes* that the discussions between the Special Representative of the Secretary-General and the two sides are continuing, and urges both sides to participate constructively;

5. *Expresses the view* that both sides have legitimate concerns that should be addressed through comprehensive negotiations covering all relevant issues;

6. *Requests* the Secretary-General, in accordance with the relevant Security Council resolutions, to invite

the leaders of the two sides to negotiations in the autumn of 1999;

7. *Calls upon* the two leaders, in this context, to give their full support to such a comprehensive negotiation, under the auspices of the Secretary-General, and to commit themselves to the following principles:

—No preconditions;

—All issues on the table;

—Commitment in good faith to continue to negotiate until a settlement is reached;

—Full consideration of relevant United Nations resolutions and treaties;

8. *Requests* the two sides in Cyprus, including military authorities on both sides, to work constructively with the Secretary-General and his Special Representative to create a positive climate on the island that will pave the way for negotiations in the autumn of 1999;

9. *Requests* the Secretary-General to keep the Security Council informed of progress towards the implementation of the present resolution and to submit a report to the Council by 1 December 1999;

10. *Decides* to remain actively seized of the matter.

In a November report [S/1999/1203], the Secretary-General stated that, on 14 November, in response to his invitation, Mr. Clerides and Mr. Denktas agreed to start proximity talks in New York on 3 December to prepare the ground for meaningful negotiations leading to a comprehensive settlement.

Proximity talks. On 14 December [A/55/2], the Special Adviser to the Secretary-General on Cyprus briefed the Security Council on the proximity talks held in New York from 3 to 14 December. Council members welcomed the fact that the talks had been conducted throughout in a positive and constructive atmosphere and without preconditions. They commended the commitment shown and encouraged all concerned to continue their efforts towards a comprehensive settlement of the Cyprus question. They looked forward to the continuation of the talks in early 2000.

UNFICYP

The United Nations Peacekeeping Force in Cyprus, established by Security Council resolution 186(1964) [YUN 1964, p. 165], continued in 1999 to monitor the ceasefire lines between the Turkish and Turkish Cypriot forces on the northern side and the Cypriot National Guard on the southern side; to maintain the military status quo and prevent a recurrence of fighting; and to undertake humanitarian and economic activities. In the absence of a formal ceasefire agreement, the military status quo, as recorded by UNFICYP in 1974, remained the standard by which the Force judged whether changes constituted violations of the status quo.

UNFICYP, under the overall authority of the Deputy Special Representative and Chief of Mission, continued to keep the area between the ceasefire lines, known as the buffer zone, under constant surveillance through a system of observation posts, and through air, vehicle and foot patrols.

On 20 June [S/1999/722], the Secretary-General informed the Council that he was considering the advantages in the longer term, including continuity and greater familiarity with events in Cyprus, of reverting to the previous practice of having a Special Representative of the Secretary-General resident on the island. In that connection, and following the resignation of Diego Cordovez as his Special Adviser on Cyprus on 22 April, he intended to appoint Ann Hercus as resident Special Representative and Chief of UNFICYP, with effect from 1 July. The Council, on 25 June [S/1999/723], noted the Secretary-General's intention. Ann Hercus relinquished her post as of 30 September and the Secretary-General appointed James Holger as Acting Special Representative and Chief of Mission for three months effective 1 October [S/1999/1043]. The Council noted that appointment on 11 October [S/1999/1044]. On 29 October, the Secretary-General informed the Council of his intention to appoint Alvaro de Soto as Special Adviser on Cyprus as of 1 November 1999, with the rank of Under-Secretary-General. Mr. de Soto would become Special Representative, resident in Cyprus, in the course of spring 2000 [S/1999/1111]. The Council noted the course of action proposed on 1 November [S/1999/1112].

As at November, UNFICYP, under the command of Major-General Evergisto Arturo de Vergara (Argentina), comprised 1,219 troops and 35 civilian police. The military personnel were from Argentina, Austria, Canada, Finland, Hungary, Ireland, the Netherlands, Slovenia and the United Kingdom. The civilian police were from Australia and Ireland. The civilian component comprised 37 international and 197 local staff.

On 10 December [S/1999/1234], the Council noted the Secretary-General's intention [S/1999/1233] to appoint Major-General Victory Rana (Nepal) as UNFICYP's Commander, replacing Major-General de Vergara who relinquished his post on 15 December.

Activities

Report of Secretary-General (June). The Secretary-General submitted a report covering developments and UNFICYP activities from 9 December 1998 to 9 June 1999 [S/1999/657 & Add.1]. He said that the situation along the ceasefire lines remained stable apart from small incidents, particularly in the area of Nicosia, where the positions of the opposing forces were in close proximity. Military construction along the ceasefire lines took place on both sides and there were also some overflights above the buffer zone from each side. UNFICYP continued to resist any challenge to the delineation of the ceasefire lines. The routine replacement by Turkish forces of marker buoys off the shore of Famagusta led to several days of tension in May, partly because of the wrong positioning of one buoy. UNFICYP continued to monitor the fenced area of Varosha; suggestions by the Turkish Cypriot side that they might open Varosha for settlement provoked a strong public reaction on the Greek Cypriot side. UNFICYP did not observe any significant change in the status quo in that area, for which the United Nations held the Government of Turkey responsible, said the report.

The suspension of bicommunal contacts imposed by the Turkish Cypriot authorities remained in effect and continued to limit on-island contacts between the two communities. However, trade unions on both sides continued to maintain regular contact, holding a forum on 26 and 29 May, which was attended by 300 Greek Cypriot and Turkish Cypriot trade union representatives. UNFICYP continued to facilitate civilian use of the buffer zone for manufacturing and agriculture and for the maintenance of public utilities and to act as intermediary between the two sides to facilitate cooperation on such matters as the distribution of water and electricity and the disposal of sewage. It also assisted in arranging pilgrimages to religious sites by members of both communities and was involved when police on either side detained members of the other community. UNFICYP also continued to carry out humanitarian tasks in respect of Greek Cypriots and Maronites residing in the northern part of the island and Turkish Cypriots in the southern part. Greek Cypriots on the Karpas Peninsula were being allowed to travel in the northern part of the island without first reporting to the local police, while first-degree relatives in the southern part of the island benefited from more flexible crossing regulations and could stay with relatives in the north beyond the previously imposed time limit. According to Turkish Cypriot authorities, the review of legislation prohibiting Greek Cypriots and Maronites in the northern part of the island from bequeathing their movable and immovable property to heirs that did not reside there had not been completed. The 310 Turkish Cypriots in the southern part of the island who had made themselves known to UNFICYP had made little use of the UNFICYP liaison office that was opened in Limassol in 1996; the office was therefore closed on 1 March 1999. However, UNFICYP had increased visits to the areas of residence of those Turkish Cypriots.

The Secretary-General recommended that the Security Council extend UNFICYP's mandate for a further period of six months, until 15 December 1999.

SECURITY COUNCIL ACTION

On 29 June [meeting 4018], the Security Council unanimously adopted **resolution 1251(1999)**. The draft [S/1999/725] was prepared in consultations among Council members.

The Security Council,

Welcoming the report of the Secretary-General of 8 June 1999 on the United Nations operation in Cyprus,

Noting that the Government of Cyprus has agreed that in view of the prevailing conditions in the island it is necessary to keep the United Nations Peacekeeping Force in Cyprus beyond 30 June 1999,

Reaffirming all its earlier resolutions on Cyprus, in particular resolutions 1217(1998) and 1218(1998), of 22 December 1998,

Calling once more upon all States to respect the sovereignty, independence and territorial integrity of the Republic of Cyprus, and requesting them, along with the parties concerned, to refrain from any action which might prejudice that sovereignty, independence and territorial integrity, as well as from any attempt at partition of the island or its unification with any other country,

Noting that the situation along the ceasefire lines is essentially stable, but expressing its grave concern at the increasing practice by both sides of engaging in provocative behaviour along the ceasefire lines, which heightens the risk of more serious incidents,

Reminding the parties that the package of measures of the Force aimed at reducing tensions along the ceasefire lines was designed to reduce incidents and tensions, without affecting the security of either side,

Reiterating the need to make progress on a comprehensive political solution,

1. *Decides* to extend the mandate of the United Nations Peacekeeping Force in Cyprus for a further period ending 15 December 1999;
2. *Reminds* both sides of their obligation to prevent any violence directed against Force personnel, to cooperate fully with the Force and to ensure its complete freedom of movement;
3. *Calls upon* the military authorities on both sides to refrain from any action, including acts of provocation in the vicinity of the buffer zone, which would exacerbate tensions;
4. *Requests* the Secretary-General and his Special Representative to continue to work intensively with the two sides with a view to early agreement on further specific tension-reducing steps, with full consideration of its resolution 1218(1998);
5. *Calls upon* the two sides to take measures that will build trust and cooperation and reduce tensions between them, including demining along the buffer zone;
6. *Urges* the Greek Cypriot side to agree to the implementation of the package of measures of the Force, and encourages the Force to continue its efforts

towards the rapid implementation of the package by both sides;

7. *Reiterates its grave concern* at the continuing excessive levels of military forces and armaments in the Republic of Cyprus and the rate at which they are being expanded, upgraded and modernized, including by the introduction of advanced weapon systems by either side, and at the lack of progress towards any significant reduction in the number of foreign troops in the Republic of Cyprus, which threaten to raise tensions both on the island and in the region and complicate efforts to negotiate an overall political settlement;

8. *Calls upon* all concerned to commit themselves to a reduction in defence spending, a reduction in the number of foreign troops in the Republic of Cyprus, and a staged process aimed at limiting and then substantially reducing the level of all troops and armaments in the Republic of Cyprus as a first step towards the withdrawal of non-Cypriot forces as described in the set of ideas, to help restore confidence between the sides, stresses the importance of eventual demilitarization of the Republic of Cyprus as an objective in the context of an overall comprehensive settlement, welcomes in this context any steps either side may take to reduce armaments and troops, and encourages the Secretary-General to continue to promote efforts in this direction;

9. *Calls upon* both sides to refrain from the threat or use of force or violence as a means to resolve the Cyprus problem;

10. *Reaffirms* that the status quo is unacceptable and that negotiations on a final political solution to the Cyprus problem have been at an impasse for too long;

11. *Reaffirms* its position that a Cyprus settlement must be based on a State of Cyprus with a single sovereignty and international personality and a single citizenship, with its independence and territorial integrity safeguarded, and comprising two politically equal communities as described in the relevant Security Council resolutions, in a bicommunal and bi-zonal federation, and that such a settlement must exclude union in whole or in part with any other country or any form of partition or secession;

12. *Welcomes* the ongoing efforts by the Force to implement its humanitarian mandate in respect of Greek Cypriots and Maronites living in the northern part of the island and Turkish Cypriots living in the southern part, as mentioned in the report of the Secretary-General;

13. *Reiterates its support* for the efforts of the United Nations and others concerned to promote the holding of bicommunal events so as to build cooperation, trust and mutual respect between the two communities, and calls upon the Turkish-Cypriot leadership to resume such activities;

14. *Requests* the Secretary-General to submit a report by 1 December 1999 on the implementation of the present resolution;

15. *Decides* to remain actively seized of the matter.

Report of Secretary-General (November). In his report covering the period 10 June to 29 November [S/1999/1203 & Corr.1 & Add.1], the Secretary-General said that the situation along the ceasefire lines remained stable. However, military construction continued along the lines on both sides, including minefield refurbishment and construction of anti-tank ditches by the National Guard. There were several violations by the National Guard in the area of Athienou. The annual National Guard exercise "Nikiforos" took place from 2 to 7 October. Its profile and duration were reduced from previous years. During the traditional National Guard parade on 1 October, the TOR-M1 low-to-medium-altitude surface-to-air missile system was publicly displayed for the first time. The annual Turkish Forces exercise "TOROS II" took place from 25 to 27 November, also on a smaller scale than in previous years. Some alterations of the status quo in the fenced area of Varosha were observed. Crossings of the eastern maritime security line by Greek Cypriot boats increased significantly, despite UNFICYP warnings, causing Turkish Forces to fire warning shots.

Despite the continuing Turkish Cypriot restrictions regarding on-island contact between the two communities, some 5,000 people, of whom 3,000 were Turkish Cypriots, attended an international open house organized by UNFICYP, and, on 12 November, a Turkish and a Greek television station organized and aired a debate attended by Greek Cypriot and Turkish Cypriot politicians, business personalities and journalists. In the buffer zone, new regulations relating to farming at night and burning of fields were introduced to increase safety. UNFICYP maintained close cooperation with both sides to resolve problems concerning water, electricity and sewage and continued to promote stability and the well-being of residents in the mixed village of Pyla. Religious pilgrimages by both sides were facilitated by UNFICYP. In the humanitarian area, the Turkish Cypriot practice of preventing the burial of Greek Cypriot residents in the Karpas Peninsula whenever their bodies had been temporarily brought to the southern part of the island for post mortem examinations remained unresolved. UNFICYP continued to press the Turkish Cypriot authorities to allow Greek Cypriots from the Peninsula to be buried there regardless of where and by whom the post mortem examinations were conducted. After an interruption of more than three years, the Committee on Missing Persons began its one hundred eighty-third session in November to discuss the possibility of resuming its investigative work.

UNDP, through the United Nations Office for Project Services, continued to implement its confidence-building programme in areas of mutual concern, notably public health, environment, sanitation, water, urban renovation, preservation of cultural heritage, natural resources and education.

The Secretary-General recommended a further extension of UNFICYP's mandate, until 15 June 2000.

SECURITY COUNCIL ACTION

On 15 December [meeting 4082], the Security Council unanimously adopted **resolution 1283(1999)**. The draft [S/1999/1249] was prepared in consultations among Council members.

The Security Council,

Welcoming the report of the Secretary-General of 29 November 1999 on the United Nations operation in Cyprus, and in particular the call to the parties to assess and address the humanitarian issue of missing persons with due urgency and seriousness,

Noting that the Government of Cyprus has agreed that in view of the prevailing conditions in the island it is necessary to keep the United Nations Peacekeeping Force in Cyprus beyond 15 December 1999,

1. *Reaffirms* all its relevant resolutions on Cyprus, in particular resolution 1251(1999) of 29 June 1999;

2. *Decides* to extend the mandate of the United Nations Peacekeeping Force in Cyprus for a further period ending 15 June 2000;

3. *Requests* the Secretary-General to submit a report by 1 June 2000 on the implementation of the present resolution;

4. *Decides* to remain actively seized of the matter.

Financing

On 8 June [meeting 101], the General Assembly, having considered the Secretary-General's report on UNFICYP's financial performance for the period 1 July 1997 to 30 June 1998 [A/53/783], the proposed budget for UNFICYP's maintenance for the period 1 July 1999 to 30 June 2000 [A/53/805] and ACABQ's comments and recommendations [A/53/895/Add.3], adopted, on the recommendation of the Fifth Committee [A/53/980], **resolution 53/231** without vote [agenda item 130].

Financing of the United Nations Peacekeeping Force in Cyprus

The General Assembly,

Having considered the reports of the Secretary-General on the financing of the United Nations Peacekeeping Force in Cyprus and the related reports of the Advisory Committee on Administrative and Budgetary Questions,

Recalling Security Council resolution 186(1964) of 4 March 1964, by which the Council established the United Nations Peacekeeping Force in Cyprus, and the subsequent resolutions by which the Council extended the mandate of the Force, the latest of which was resolution 1217(1998) of 22 December 1998,

Recalling also its resolution 52/241 of 26 June 1998 on the financing of the Force,

Reaffirming that the costs of the Force that are not covered by voluntary contributions are expenses of the Organization to be borne by Member States in accordance with Article 17, paragraph 2, of the Charter of the United Nations,

Noting with appreciation that voluntary contributions have been made to the Force by certain Governments,

Recalling its previous decisions regarding the fact that, in order to meet the expenditures caused by the Force, a different procedure is required from that applied to meet expenditures of the regular budget of the United Nations,

Taking into account the fact that the economically more developed countries are in a position to make relatively larger contributions and that the economically less developed countries have a relatively limited capacity to contribute towards such an operation,

Bearing in mind the special responsibilities of the States permanent members of the Security Council, as indicated in General Assembly resolution 1874(S-IV) of 27 June 1963, in the financing of such operations,

Expressing its appreciation to all those Member States and observer States which have made voluntary contributions to the Special Account established for the financing of the Force during the period prior to 16 June 1993,

Noting that voluntary contributions were insufficient to cover all the costs of the Force, including those incurred by troop-contributing Governments prior to 16 June 1993, and regretting the absence of an adequate response to appeals for voluntary contributions, including that contained in the letter dated 17 May 1994 from the Secretary-General to all Member States,

Mindful of the fact that it is essential to provide the Force with the necessary financial resources to enable it to fulfil its responsibilities under the relevant resolutions of the Security Council,

1. *Takes note* of the status of contributions to the United Nations Peacekeeping Force in Cyprus as at 30 April 1999, including the contributions outstanding in the amount of 17.7 million United States dollars, representing 12.7 per cent of the total assessed contributions from 16 June 1993 to the period ending 30 June 1999, notes that some 16 per cent of the Member States have paid their assessed contributions in full, and urges all other Member States concerned, in particular those in arrears, to ensure payment of their outstanding assessed contributions;

2. *Expresses concern* about the financial situation with regard to peacekeeping activities, in particular as regards the reimbursement of troop contributors, which bear additional burdens owing to overdue payments by Member States of their assessments;

3. *Expresses its appreciation* to those Member States which have paid their assessed contributions in full;

4. *Urges* all other Member States to make every possible effort to ensure payment of their assessed contributions to the Force in full and on time;

5. *Endorses* the observations and recommendations contained in the report of the Advisory Committee on Administrative and Budgetary Questions;

6. *Requests* the Secretary-General to take all necessary action to ensure that the Force is administered with a maximum of efficiency and economy;

7. *Also requests* the Secretary-General, in order to reduce the cost of employing General Service staff, to continue efforts to recruit local staff for the Force against General Service posts, commensurate with the requirements of the Force;

8. *Decides* to appropriate to the Special Account for the United Nations Peacekeeping Force in Cyprus an amount of 45,630,927 dollars gross (43,892,427 dollars net) for the maintenance of the Force for the period from 1 July 1999 to 30 June 2000, inclusive of an amount of 2,270,759 dollars for the support account for peacekeeping operations, and the amount of 445,268 dollars for the United Nations Logistics Base at Brindisi, Italy;

9. *Decides also,* as an ad hoc arrangement, taking into consideration the funding through voluntary contributions of one third of the cost of the Force, equivalent to 14,630,810 dollars, by the Government of Cyprus and the annual pledge of 6.5 million dollars from the Government of Greece, to apportion among Member States the amount of 24,500,117 dollars gross (22,761,617 dollars net), for the period from 1 July 1999 to 30 June 2000, at a monthly rate of 2,041,676 dollars gross (1,896,801 dollars net) in accordance with the composition of groups set out in paragraphs 3 and 4 of General Assembly resolution 43/232 of 1 March 1989, as adjusted by the Assembly in its resolutions 44/192 B of 21 December 1989, 45/269 of 27 August 1991, 46/198 A of 20 December 1991, 47/218 A of 23 December 1992, 49/249 A of 20 July 1995, 49/249 B of 14 September 1995, 50/224 of 11 April 1996, 51/218 A to C of 18 December 1996 and 52/230 of 31 March 1998 and its decisions 48/472 A of 23 December 1993 and 50/451 B of 23 December 1995, and taking into account the scale of assessments for the years 1999 and 2000 as set out in its resolution 52/215 A of 22 December 1997, subject to the decision of the Security Council to extend the mandate of the Force beyond 30 June 1999;

10. *Decides further* that, in accordance with the provisions of its resolution 973(X) of 15 December 1955, there shall be set off against the apportionment among Member States, as provided for in paragraph 9 above, their respective share in the Tax Equalization Fund of the estimated staff assessment income of 1,738,500 dollars approved for the Force for the period from 1 July 1999 to 30 June 2000;

11. *Decides* that, for Member States that have fulfilled their financial obligations to the Force, there shall be set off against the apportionment as provided for in paragraph 9 above, their respective share of the unencumbered balance of 178,500 dollars gross (6,300 dollars net) in respect of the period ending 30 June 1998;

12. *Decides also* that, for Member States that have not fulfilled their financial obligations to the Force, their share of the unencumbered balance of 178,500 dollars gross (6,300 dollars net) in respect of the period ending 30 June 1998 shall be set off against their outstanding obligations;

13. *Decides further* to continue to maintain as separate the account established for the period prior to 16 June 1993 for the Force, invites Member States to make voluntary contributions to that account, and requests the Secretary-General to continue his efforts in appealing for voluntary contributions to the account;

14. *Invites* voluntary contributions to the Force in cash and in the form of services and supplies acceptable to the Secretary-General, to be administered, as appropriate, in accordance with the procedure and practices established by the General Assembly;

15. *Decides* to include in the provisional agenda of its fifty-fourth session the item entitled "Financing of the United Nations Peacekeeping Force in Cyprus".

On 23 December, the Assembly decided that the item on UNFICYP's financing would remain for consideration at the resumed fifty-fourth (2000) session (**decision 54/465**). On the same date, it decided that the Fifth Committee would continue consideration of the item at that session (**decision 54/462 A**).

Other issues

Cooperation with OSCE

In response to General Assembly resolution 53/85 [YUN 1998, p. 419], the Secretary-General, in a November report [A/54/537 & Corr.1], described cooperation between the United Nations and the Organization for Security and Cooperation in Europe (OSCE).

He said that, during the year, contacts were maintained with the OSCE Chairman-in-Office, Secretary-General and representatives on a regular basis. The two organizations continued to face humanitarian and political challenges in the Balkans and in some countries of the former Soviet Union. Cooperation in the field had intensified and the two organizations continued to practice a division of labour based on their comparative advantages. Efforts to improve consultation and cooperation in the field and between the respective headquarters resulted in enhanced coordination that made better use of international resources in the interests of the countries being assisted.

In the context of the UNHCR/OSCE comprehensive strategic partnership, frequent consultations took place, particularly with the Chairman-in-Office, to share information and ensure coherence and complementarity of action. UNHCR was an active participant in the Implementation Meetings on the Human Dimension of the Office for Democratic Institutions and Human Rights (ODIHR), which covered issues directly relevant to UNHCR. Cooperation with the OSCE High Commissioner on National Minorities (HCNM) was also institutionalized and covered an ever larger range of topics, mainly on issues of citizenship and statelessness; the formerly deported peoples in Crimea, Ukraine; the problems faced by Meshketian Turks, another category of formerly deported peoples; and ethnic tolerance in Central Asia. As a follow-up to the Regional Conference to Address the Problems of Refugees, Displaced Persons, Other

Forms of Involuntary Displacement and Returnees in the Countries of the Commonwealth of Independent States and Relevant Neighbouring States [YUN 1996, p. 1117], UNHCR, together with the International Organization for Migration (IOM) and ODIHR, organized an annual steering group meeting in June to review progress made in implementing the Programme of Action adopted by the Conference. An international meeting sponsored by HCNM, UNHCR and the Open Society Institute was held in 1999 to address problems faced by Meshketian Turks. Significant progress was made towards developing a comprehensive approach to the issue with the participation of all concerned countries (Azerbaijan, Georgia, Russian Federation, Turkey, Uzbekistan).

The Economic Commission for Europe (ECE) continued its commitment to strengthening cooperation with OSCE. A new area for potential cooperation was the development of the UN special programme for the economies of Central Asia, in which ECE and the Economic and Social Commission for Asia and the Pacific played the leading role. Cooperation continued between UNDP and OSCE institutions at headquarters and at the field level, including the exchange of expertise and participation in meetings hosted by both organizations. UNDP worked closely with ODIHR in the area of human rights. Its focal point coordinated activities in support of democracy, good governance and participation with OSCE and ODIHR, with special attention to the Central Asian States and Estonia, Georgia and Ukraine. Additional cooperation with OSCE took place within the framework of the commemoration of the Universal Declaration of Human Rights adopted by General Assembly resolution 217 A (III) [YUN 1948-49, p. 535]. Partnership framework agreements were developed between UNDP and HCNM, including the establishment in April of a framework for close cooperation, with the nomination of focal points in each office.

The United Nations Mission in Bosnia and Herzegovina (UNMIBH) and OSCE worked together extensively in the field of human rights. In Bosnia and Herzegovina, the two organizations cooperated in the return of displaced persons and refugees. OSCE developed a support plan for the Return and Reconstruction Task Force led by OHCHR and UNHCR. In February, UNHCR, UNMIBH, OSCE and the European Commission Monitoring Mission signed an inter-agency memorandum of understanding on a returnee monitoring framework for Bosnia and Herzegovina to address national protection extended to returnees and displaced persons. Croatia and Bosnia and Herzegovina offered good examples of partnerships in fostering conditions conducive to return. UNHCR and OSCE cooperated on various levels in promoting and facilitating voluntary return, with UNHCR focusing on humanitarian activities and OSCE on monitoring elections, human rights and compliance with return agreements. There was close cooperation also with regard to cross-border returns of refugees from Croatia and Bosnia and Herzegovina (in particular Republika Srpska). In the context of the municipal elections in Bosnia and Herzegovina, OSCE and IOM concluded in 1999 a memorandum of understanding governing IOM's advisory and operational role with regard to Bosnians living abroad.

The establishment of an international civil presence in Kosovo to provide an interim administration required an integrated approach with a clear distribution of labour. At a 15 June meeting to discuss the allocation of responsibilities in Kosovo between the United Nations and OSCE, it was agreed that OSCE would take the lead role in human resources capacity-building, including training a new Kosovo police service, judicial personnel and civil administrators; media affairs; democratization and governance; the organization and supervision of elections; and the monitoring, protection and promotion of human rights, in cooperation with OHCHR and the Council of Europe.

GENERAL ASSEMBLY ACTION

On 15 December [meeting 80], the General Assembly adopted **resolution 54/117** [draft: A/54/L.64 & Add.1, amended by A/54/L.65], by recorded vote (124-0-2) [agenda item 30].

Cooperation between the United Nations and the Organization for Security and Cooperation in Europe

The General Assembly,

Recalling the framework for cooperation and coordination between the United Nations and the Conference on Security and Cooperation in Europe, signed on 26 May 1993, as well as its resolutions on cooperation between the two organizations,

Recalling also the declaration at the 1992 Helsinki Summit by the heads of State or Government of the participating States of the Conference on Security and Cooperation in Europe of their understanding that the Conference is a regional arrangement in the sense of Chapter VIII of the Charter of the United Nations and as such provides an important link between European and global security,

Acknowledging the increasing contribution of the Organization for Security and Cooperation in Europe to the establishment and maintenance of international peace and security in its region through activities in early warning and preventive diplomacy, including through the activities of the High Commissioner on National Minorities, crisis management and post-conflict rehabilitation, as well as arms control and disarmament,

Recalling the special ties between the Organization for Security and Cooperation in Europe and the Mediterranean Partners for Cooperation, as well as between that organization and the Asian Partners for Cooperation, Japan and the Republic of Korea, which have been further enhanced this year,

Underlining the continued importance of enhanced cooperation and coordination between the United Nations and the Organization for Security and Cooperation in Europe,

1. *Welcomes* the report of the Secretary-General;

2. *Notes with appreciation* the further improvement of cooperation and coordination between the United Nations and its agencies and the Organization for Security and Cooperation in Europe, including at the level of activities in the field;

3. *Welcomes,* in this context, the participation of the Secretary-General and high-level United Nations representatives in the meetings of the Permanent Council of the Organization for Security and Cooperation in Europe and the participation of the Secretary-General in the Summit of the Organization for Security and Cooperation in Europe, held in Istanbul in November 1999;

4. *Encourages* further efforts of the Organization for Security and Cooperation in Europe to foster security and stability in its region through early warning, conflict prevention, crisis management and post-conflict rehabilitation, as well as through continued promotion of democracy, the rule of law, human rights and fundamental freedoms;

5. *Welcomes* the adoption at the Istanbul Summit of the Charter for European Security, which reaffirms the Organization for Security and Cooperation in Europe as a primary organization for the peaceful settlement of disputes within its region and as a key instrument for early warning, conflict prevention, crisis management and post-conflict rehabilitation, which is aimed at strengthening security and stability in the region and improving the operational capabilities of that organization, inter alia, by enhancing the capability to deploy civilian expertise speedily through the Rapid Expert Assistance Teams Programme and which includes the establishment of the Platform for Cooperative Security as a basis for flexible and mutually supporting cooperation between organizations concerned with the promotion of comprehensive security within the region, whose members adhere to the principles embodied in the Charter of the United Nations and the principles and commitments of the Organization for Security and Cooperation in Europe as set out in the Platform;

6. *Welcomes also* the increasingly close cooperation between the Organization for Security and Cooperation in Europe and the United Nations High Commissioner for Refugees and the United Nations High Commissioner for Human Rights;

7. *Welcomes further* the participation of the Special Representative of the Secretary-General for Children and Armed Conflict in the Review Conference of the Organization for Security and Cooperation in Europe, held at Istanbul in November 1999, and notes with appreciation the commitment of that organization, as stated in the Declaration adopted by the heads of State or Government at the Istanbul Summit, to promote children's rights and interests, especially in conflict and post-conflict situations;

8. *Acknowledges* the work carried out by the Kosovo Verification Mission, prior to its withdrawal on 20 March 1999, in verifying the implementation of Security Council resolution 1199(1998) of 23 September 1998, in accordance with Council resolution 1203 (1998) of 24 October 1998, and the contribution of the Organization for Security and Cooperation in Europe to the implementation of Security Council resolution 1160(1998) of 31 March 1998, including the contribution of the Chairman-in-Office of that organization to the reports of the Secretary-General prepared pursuant to that resolution;

9. *Commends* the Organization for Security and Cooperation in Europe for its assistance to the United Nations High Commissioner for Refugees in handling the great influx of refugees from Kosovo, Federal Republic of Yugoslavia, to Albania and the former Yugoslav Republic of Macedonia in March-June 1999;

10. *Expresses its appreciation* for the contribution by the Organization for Security and Cooperation in Europe to the United Nations Interim Administration Mission in Kosovo in implementing Security Council resolution 1244(1999) of 10 June 1999, including the establishment pursuant to that resolution of the Organization for Security and Cooperation in Europe Mission in Kosovo as an essential part of the broader United Nations Interim Administration Mission in Kosovo, responsible for institution-building, including the training of a new Kosovo police service, judicial personnel and civil administrators, the development of free media, democratization and governance, the organization and supervision of elections and the monitoring, protection and promotion of human rights, in cooperation with, inter alia, the United Nations High Commissioner for Human Rights, and stresses the commitment of the United Nations and the Organization for Security and Cooperation in Europe to the full implementation of resolution 1244(1999);

11. *Welcomes* the readiness of the Organization for Security and Cooperation in Europe to continue to fulfil the role assigned to it in the General Framework Agreement for Peace in Bosnia and Herzegovina, in cooperation with the United Nations, in particular in the fields of human rights and judicial and police reform;

12. *Fully supports* the continued provision by the Organization for Security and Cooperation in Europe of advice and assistance within its field of experience to Albania in its continuing process of social, political and economic transition, including by furnishing the overall framework for the Group of Friends of Albania, which brings together countries and international institutions that actively wish to support Albania in its development efforts, and by co-chairing the Group together with the European Union at the international level;

13. *Commends* the Organization for Security and Cooperation in Europe for providing its assistance and expertise to Croatia in the field of human rights and the rights of persons belonging to national minorities, its role in Croatia in monitoring the implementation of commitments on the return of refugees and displaced persons, its monitoring of democratic institutions and means of promoting reconciliation and the rule of law and its continued provision of civilian police monitors in the Danubian region of Croatia;

14. *Welcomes* the decision of the Organization for Security and Cooperation in Europe to take under its auspices the Stability Pact for South-Eastern Europe, launched at the initiative of the European Union, adopted by the Cologne Ministerial Conference in June 1999 and endorsed by the Sarajevo Summit in July 1999, and to develop a regional strategy to support its aims;

15. *Notes* the principles embodied in the Helsinki Final Act;

16. *Fully supports* the activities of the Organization for Security and Cooperation in Europe to achieve a peaceful solution to the conflict in and around the Nagorny-Karabakh region of Azerbaijan, and welcomes cooperation between the United Nations and the Organization for Security and Cooperation in Europe in this regard;

17. *Applauds* the intensified dialogue between the President of Armenia and the President of Azerbaijan, whose regular contacts have created opportunities to dynamize the process of finding a lasting and comprehensive solution to the Nagorny-Karabakh conflict, firmly supports this dialogue and encourages its continuation, with the hope of resuming negotiations within the Minsk Group of the Organization for Security and Cooperation in Europe, and welcomes the fact that the Organization for Security and Cooperation in Europe and its Minsk Group, which remains the most appropriate forum for finding a solution, stand ready to advance further the peace process and its future implementation, including by providing all necessary assistance to the parties;

18. *Encourages* further close cooperation between the Organization for Security and Cooperation in Europe and the United Nations in the peace process in Tskhinvali region/South Ossetia and Abkhazia, Georgia, including through the Special Representative of the Secretary-General in Georgia and the United Nations Human Rights Office in Sukhumi, and fully supports that organization in its efforts aimed at the implementation of practical measures agreed at the Istanbul Summit and the decisions of the Oslo Ministerial Council Meeting;

19. *Fully supports* the efforts of the Organization for Security and Cooperation in Europe aimed at achieving a settlement of the problems in the Transdniestran region of the Republic of Moldova, welcomes the commitment of that organization to facilitate the implementation of the relevant decisions of the Budapest and Lisbon Summits, the Oslo Ministerial Council Meeting and the Istanbul Summit, and notes in this regard the commitment by the Russian Federation, undertaken at the Istanbul Summit, to complete within a specific timetable the withdrawal of the Russian forces from the territory of the Republic of Moldova;

20. *Welcomes* the increased presence of the Organization for Security and Cooperation in Europe in Central Asia and the readiness of that organization to contribute, inter alia, together with the United Nations, to strengthening cooperation in the region, as well as the commitment of that organization to promote democratic institutions and assist the Central Asian countries in addressing economic and environmental problems;

21. *Requests* the Secretary-General to continue exploring with the Chairman-in-Office and the Secretary-General of the Organization for Security and Cooperation in Europe possibilities for further enhancement of cooperation, information exchange and coordination between the United Nations and the Organization for Security and Cooperation in Europe;

22. *Decides* to include in the provisional agenda of its fifty-fifth session the item entitled "Cooperation between the United Nations and the Organization for Security and Cooperation in Europe", and requests the Secretary-General to submit to the General Assembly at its fifty-fifth session a report on cooperation between the United Nations and the Organization for Security and Cooperation in Europe in implementation of the present resolution.

RECORDED VOTE ON RESOLUTION 54/117

In favour: Afghanistan, Albania, Algeria, Andorra, Antigua and Barbuda, Argentina, Australia, Austria, Azerbaijan, Bahrain, Bangladesh, Barbados, Belarus, Belgium, Benin, Bhutan, Bolivia, Bosnia and Herzegovina, Botswana, Brazil, Brunei Darussalam, Bulgaria, Burkina Faso, Cambodia, Canada, Colombia, Costa Rica, Côte d'Ivoire, Croatia, Cyprus, Czech Republic, Denmark, Djibouti, Ecuador, Egypt, El Salvador, Eritrea, Estonia, Ethiopia, Finland, France, Georgia, Germany, Greece, Grenada, Guatemala, Haiti, Honduras, Hungary, Iceland, India, Indonesia, Iran, Ireland, Israel, Italy, Japan, Jordan, Kazakhstan, Kuwait, Latvia, Lebanon, Libyan Arab Jamahiriya, Liechtenstein, Lithuania, Luxembourg, Madagascar, Malaysia, Maldives, Malta, Mauritius, Mexico, Monaco, Morocco, Mozambique, Myanmar, Namibia, Nepal, Netherlands, New Zealand, Nigeria, Norway, Oman, Pakistan, Paraguay, Peru, Philippines, Poland, Portugal, Qatar, Republic of Korea, Republic of Moldova, Romania, Russian Federation, San Marino, Saudi Arabia, Senegal, Singapore, Slovakia, Slovenia, Solomon Islands, South Africa, Spain, Sri Lanka, Sudan, Swaziland, Sweden, Syrian Arab Republic, Tajikistan, Thailand, The former Yugoslav Republic of Macedonia, Togo, Trinidad and Tobago, Tunisia, Turkey, Turkmenistan, Ukraine, United Arab Emirates, United Kingdom, United States, Uruguay, Uzbekistan, Venezuela, Yemen.

Against: None.

Abstaining: Armenia, China.

Before the adoption of the resolution, a recorded vote (55-1-54) was taken on an amendment, adding paragraph 16, introduced by Azerbaijan [A/54/L.65], stating specifically that Nagorny Karabakh was a region of Azerbaijan.

Strengthening of security and cooperation in the Mediterranean region

In response to General Assembly resolution 53/82 [YUN 1998, p. 421], the Secretary-General submitted replies from Algeria, Finland, on behalf of the EU, and Qatar [A/54/261] to his note verbale requesting their views on ways to strengthen security and cooperation in the Mediterranean region.

GENERAL ASSEMBLY ACTION

On 1 December [meeting 69], the General Assembly, on the recommendation of the First (Disarmament and International Security) Committee [A/54/568], adopted **resolution 54/59** without vote [agenda item 81].

Strengthening of security and cooperation in the Mediterranean region

The General Assembly,

Recalling its previous resolutions on the subject, including resolution 53/82 of 4 December 1998,

Reaffirming the primary role of the Mediterranean countries in strengthening and promoting peace, security and cooperation in the Mediterranean region,

Bearing in mind all the previous declarations and commitments, as well as all the initiatives taken by the riparian countries at the recent summits, ministerial meetings and various forums concerning the question of the Mediterranean region,

Recognizing the indivisible character of security in the Mediterranean and that the enhancement of cooperation among Mediterranean countries with a view to promoting the economic and social development of all peoples of the region will contribute significantly to stability, peace and security in the region,

Recognizing also the efforts made so far and the determination of the Mediterranean countries to intensify the process of dialogue and consultations with a view to resolving the problems existing in the Mediterranean region and to eliminating the causes of tension and the consequent threat to peace and security, and their growing awareness of the need for further joint efforts to strengthen economic, social, cultural and environmental cooperation in the region,

Recognizing further that prospects for closer Euro-Mediterranean cooperation in all spheres can be enhanced by positive developments worldwide, in particular in Europe, in the Maghreb and in the Middle East,

Reaffirming the responsibility of all States to contribute to the stability and prosperity of the Mediterranean region and their commitment to respect the purposes and principles of the Charter of the United Nations, as well as the provisions of the Declaration on Principles of International Law concerning Friendly Relations and Cooperation among States in accordance with the Charter of the United Nations,

Noting the peace negotiations in the Middle East, which should be of a comprehensive nature and represent an appropriate framework for the peaceful settlement of contentious issues in the region,

Expressing its concern at the persistent tension and continuing military activities in parts of the Mediterranean that hinder efforts to strengthen security and cooperation in the region,

Taking note of the report of the Secretary-General,

1. *Reaffirms* that security in the Mediterranean is closely linked to European security as well as to international peace and security;

2. *Expresses its satisfaction* at the continuing efforts by Mediterranean countries to contribute actively to the elimination of all causes of tension in the region and to the promotion of just and lasting solutions to the persistent problems of the region through peaceful means, thus ensuring the withdrawal of foreign forces of occupation and respecting the sovereignty, independence and territorial integrity of all countries of the Mediterranean and the right of peoples to self-determination, and therefore calls for full adherence to the principles of non-interference, non-intervention, non-use of force or threat of use of force and the inadmissibility of the acquisition of territory by force, in accordance with the Charter and the relevant resolutions of the United Nations;

3. *Commends* the Mediterranean countries for their efforts in meeting common challenges through coordinated overall responses, based on a spirit of multilateral partnership, towards the general objective of turning the Mediterranean basin into an area of dialogue, exchanges and cooperation, guaranteeing peace, stability and prosperity, and encourages them to strengthen such efforts through, inter alia, a lasting multilateral and action-oriented cooperative dialogue among States of the region;

4. *Recognizes* that the elimination of the economic and social disparities in levels of development and other obstacles, as well as respect and greater understanding among cultures, in the Mediterranean area will contribute to enhancing peace, security and cooperation among Mediterranean countries through the existing forums;

5. *Calls upon* all States of the Mediterranean region that have not yet done so to adhere to all the multilaterally negotiated legal instruments related to the field of disarmament and non-proliferation, thus creating the necessary conditions for strengthening peace and cooperation in the region;

6. *Encourages* all States of the region to favour the necessary conditions for strengthening the confidence-building measures among them by promoting genuine openness and transparency on all military matters, by participating, inter alia, in the United Nations system for the standardized reporting of military expenditures and by providing accurate data and information to the United Nations Register of Conventional Arms;

7. *Encourages* the Mediterranean countries to strengthen further their cooperation in combating terrorism, in all its forms and manifestations, which poses a serious threat to peace, security and stability in the region and therefore to the improvement of the current political, economic and social situation;

8. *Invites* all States of the region to address, through various forms of cooperation, problems and threats posed to the region, such as terrorism, international crime and illicit arms transfers, as well as illicit drug production, consumption and trafficking, which jeopardize the friendly relations among States, hinder the development of international cooperation and result in the destruction of human rights, fundamental freedoms and the democratic basis of pluralistic society;

9. *Requests* the Secretary-General to submit a report on means to strengthen security and cooperation in the Mediterranean region;

10. *Decides* to include in the provisional agenda of its fifty-fifth session the item entitled "Strengthening of security and cooperation in the Mediterranean region".

Stability and development in South-Eastern Europe

On 17 May [S/1999/589], the EU, in its decision on the Kosovo crisis (see p. 345), agreed to begin preparatory work on the establishment of a stability pact for South-Eastern Europe and instructed the relevant working bodies to work towards the convening of a meeting of senior officials in Bonn, Germany, on 27 May. The stability pact, which would help ensure cooperation among the countries of the region towards comprehensive measures for the long-term stabilization, security, democratization and economic reconstruction and development of the region, and for the establishment of durable good-neighbourly relations among and between them and with the international community, would be founded on the UN Charter, OSCE principles and commitments and relevant Council of Europe treaties and conventions. The EU would play a key role in the stability pact, which should be developed and implemented in close association with OSCE.

The Stability Pact was adopted on 10 June in Cologne, Germany.

The G-8 countries, on 20 June [S/1999/711], welcomed the adoption of the Stability Pact and declared their readiness to take strong action to achieve its objectives. They called on the international donor community to give the countries of the region a strong signal of active international support and solidarity and to organize donor conferences as early as feasible. They also welcomed the progress through the European Commission and the World Bank towards establishing a donor coordination process to develop a coherent international assistance strategy for the region, which would be guided by the High-level Steering Group.

GENERAL ASSEMBLY ACTION

On 1 December [meeting 69], the General Assembly, on the recommendation of the First Committee [A/54/571], adopted **resolution 54/62** by recorded vote (155-0-2) [agenda item 84].

Maintenance of international security—stability and development of South-Eastern Europe

The General Assembly,

Recalling the purposes and principles of the Charter of the United Nations and the Final Act of the Conference on Security and Cooperation in Europe, signed at Helsinki on 1 August 1975,

Affirming its determination that all nations should live together in peace with one another as good neighbours,

Recalling its resolutions 48/84 B of 16 December 1993, 50/80 B of 12 December 1995, 51/55 of 10 December 1996, 52/48 of 9 December 1997 and 53/71 of 4 December 1998,

Mindful of the importance of national and international activities and activities by all relevant organizations aimed at the creation of peace, security, stability, democracy, cooperation, economic development, observance of human rights and good-neighbourliness of the South-Eastern European region,

Being aware of the crucial importance of the full implementation of Security Council resolution 1244(1999) of 10 June 1999 on Kosovo, Federal Republic of Yugoslavia, and stressing, inter alia, the role and responsibilities of the United Nations Interim Administration Mission in Kosovo, the Kosovo Force, the Organization for Security and Cooperation in Europe and the European Union in that regard,

Noting the direct negative repercussions of the Kosovo crisis on the economy of the region and, in particular, on the Republic of Albania and the former Yugoslav Republic of Macedonia as a consequence of the hosting of such a large number of refugees by them,

Welcoming the Stability Pact for South-Eastern Europe initiated by the European Union, adopted in Cologne, Germany, on 10 June 1999, and endorsed at the Sarajevo Summit of 30 July 1999, and stressing the crucial importance of its adequate and timely implementation,

Taking note of the Sarajevo Summit Declaration, in which the participants affirm their collective and individual readiness to give concrete meaning to the Pact by promoting political and economic reforms, development and enhanced security in the region and also their commitment to make every effort to assist countries in the region in making speedy and measurable progress along this road,

Noting, inter alia, the importance of the Process of Stability and Good-Neighbourliness in South-East Europe (Royaumont Initiative), the South-East European Cooperative Initiative, the South-East European Cooperation Process, the Central European Initiative and the Black Sea Economic Cooperation for the implementation of the Stability Pact for South-Eastern Europe,

1. *Affirms* the urgency of consolidating South-Eastern Europe as a region of peace, security, stability, democracy, cooperation, economic development, observance of human rights and good-neighbourliness, thus contributing to the maintenance of international peace and security and enhancing the prospects for sustained development and prosperity for all peoples in the region as an integral part of Europe;

2. *Calls upon* all participants in the Stability Pact for South-Eastern Europe, and all concerned international organizations, to support the efforts of South-Eastern European States to overcome the negative effects of the Kosovo crisis and to enable them to pursue sustainable development and integration of their economies into the European and global economy;

3. *Affirms* the need for full observance of the Charter of the United Nations and for strict compliance with the principles of sovereign equality, territorial integrity and inviolability of international borders of any State;

4. *Urges* the normalization of relations among the States of South-Eastern Europe and the strengthening of their mutual cooperation on the basis of respect of international law and agreements and within the principle of good-neighbourliness and mutual respect;

5. *Stresses* the importance of good-neighbourliness and the development of friendly relations among States, the solution of problems among States and the promotion of international cooperation in accordance with the Charter of the United Nations;

6. *Calls upon* all States to solve their disputes with other States by peaceful means, in accordance with the Charter of the United Nations;

7. *Calls upon* all States, the relevant international organizations and competent organs of the United Na-

tions to continue to take measures in accordance with the Charter of the United Nations, as appropriate, to eliminate threats to international peace and security and to help to prevent conflicts which can lead to the violent disintegration of States;

8. *Stresses* the importance of regional efforts aimed at preventing bilateral conflicts endangering the maintenance of international peace and security, and notes with satisfaction, in this regard, the establishment of the Multinational Peace Force for South-Eastern Europe, the headquarters of which, located at Plovdiv, Bulgaria, has become operational;

9. *Emphasizes* the importance of regional efforts in South-Eastern Europe on arms control, disarmament and confidence-building measures;

10. *Stresses* that closer engagement of the South-Eastern European States in furthering cooperation on the European continent will favourably influence the security, political and economic situation in the region, as well as the good-neighbourly relations among the Balkan States;

11. *Calls upon* all States and the relevant international organizations to communicate to the Secretary-General their views on the subject of the present resolution;

12. *Decides* to include in the provisional agenda of its fifty-fifth session an item entitled "Maintenance of international security—stability and development of South-Eastern Europe".

RECORDED VOTE ON RESOLUTION 54/62:

In favour: Albania, Algeria, Andorra, Angola, Antigua and Barbuda, Argentina, Armenia, Australia, Austria, Azerbaijan, Bahamas, Bahrain, Bangladesh, Barbados, Belgium, Belize, Benin, Bhutan, Bolivia, Bosnia and Herzegovina, Botswana, Brazil, Brunei Darussalam, Bulgaria, Burkina Faso, Cameroon, Canada, Cape Verde, Chad, Chile, Colombia, Congo, Costa Rica, Côte d'Ivoire, Croatia, Cuba, Cyprus, Czech Republic, Denmark, Djibouti, Dominica, Dominican Republic, Ecuador, Egypt, El Salvador, Equatorial Guinea, Eritrea, Estonia, Ethiopia, Fiji, Finland, France, Georgia, Germany, Ghana, Greece, Grenada, Guatemala, Guinea, Guyana, Haiti, Honduras, Hungary, Iceland, India, Iran, Ireland, Israel, Italy, Jamaica, Japan, Kazakhstan, Kenya, Kuwait, Latvia, Lebanon, Libyan Arab Jamahiriya, Liechtenstein, Lithuania, Luxembourg, Madagascar, Malawi, Malaysia, Maldives, Mali, Malta, Marshall Islands, Mauritius, Mexico, Micronesia, Monaco, Mongolia, Morocco, Mozambique, Myanmar, Namibia, Nepal, Netherlands, New Zealand, Nicaragua, Nigeria, Norway, Oman, Pakistan, Panama, Papua New Guinea, Paraguay, Peru, Philippines, Poland, Portugal, Qatar, Republic of Korea, Republic of Moldova, Romania, Russian Federation, Saint Kitts and Nevis, Saint Lucia, Saint Vincent and the Grenadines, Samoa, San Marino, Saudi Arabia, Senegal, Seychelles, Sierra Leone, Singapore, Slovakia, Slovenia, Solomon Islands, South Africa, Spain, Sri Lanka, Sudan, Suriname, Swaziland, Sweden, Tajikistan, Thailand, The former Yugoslav Republic of Macedonia, Togo, Trinidad and Tobago, Tunisia, Turkey, Turkmenistan, Uganda, Ukraine, United Arab Emirates, United Kingdom, United Republic of Tanzania, United States, Uruguay, Uzbekistan, Venezuela, Zambia, Zimbabwe.

Against: None.

Abstaining: Belarus, China.

Chapter VI

Middle East

In 1999, United Nations involvement in the Middle East peace process continued through its peacekeeping operations, the good offices of the Secretary-General and programmes of economic, social and other forms of assistance, as well as active participation in multilateral negotiations. During the first six months of the year, the peace process, which began in Madrid, Spain, in 1991, stagnated, due, among other things, to the accelerated establishment of new and the expansion of existing Israeli settlements in the occupied Palestinian territory. Following the election of a new Israeli Government in May, the peace process regained momentum in early September with the signing of the Sharm el-Sheikh Memorandum between Israel and the Palestine Liberation Organization (PLO). The Memorandum set out to resolve outstanding issues, such as those pertaining to the permanent status negotiations, and set a timetable for implementing previous commitments.

In February, the General Assembly resumed its tenth emergency special session, which first convened in 1997, to discuss the item "Illegal Israeli actions in Occupied East Jerusalem and the rest of the Occupied Palestinian Territory". It demanded, among other things, that Israel comply with the provisions of the resolutions adopted by the emergency session in 1997 and 1998 and the full cessation of all settlement activities, and recommended that the High Contracting Parties to the 1949 Geneva Convention relative to the Protection of Civilian Persons in Time of War (Fourth Geneva Convention) hold a conference on measures to enforce the Convention in the occupied Palestinian territory. The conference took place in Geneva on 15 July.

The Secretary-General appointed Terje Roed-Larsen as the new United Nations Special Coordinator for the Middle East Peace Process and as his Personal Representative to the PLO and the Palestinian Authority. In that position, the Special Coordinator would also serve as the focal point for overall UN assistance to the Middle East. The United Nations Relief and Works Agency for Palestine Refugees in the Near East (UNRWA) celebrated the fiftieth anniversary of its establishment and continued to provide a wide-ranging programme of education, health, relief and social services to over 3.6 million Palestinian refugees living both in and outside camps in the West Bank and the Gaza Strip, as well as in Jordan, Lebanon and the Syrian Arab Republic. Despite pledges of voluntary contributions, UNRWA continued to experience severe financial difficulties.

During the year, the Special Committee to Investigate Israeli Practices Affecting the Human Rights of the Palestinian People and Other Arabs of the Occupied Territories reported to the Assembly on the situation in the West Bank, including East Jerusalem, the Gaza Strip and the Golan Heights. The Committee on the Exercise of the Inalienable Rights of the Palestinian People continued to mobilize international support for the Palestinians. Among other activities, it organized, in cooperation with the Government of Italy, the Bethlehem 2000 International Conference, which, in its final document, the Rome Declaration, stressed the urgency of bringing economic recovery to the Palestinian people.

The situation in southern Lebanon remained tense and volatile in 1999. Nevertheless, a significant development occurred in May and June with the withdrawal of Israeli forces from Jezzin and the return of that town to Lebanese jurisdiction, thereby reducing the area under Israeli control for the first time since 1985. The United Nations Interim Force in Lebanon (UNIFIL) pursued efforts to limit the conflict and protect inhabitants from its consequences. The mandates of UNIFIL and of the United Nations Disengagement Observer Force in the Golan Heights were extended twice during the year, and the United Nations Truce Supervision Organization continued to assist both peacekeeping operations in their tasks. Some headway was made in Israel–Syrian Arab Republic relations with the resumption of negotiations in December 1999, under the auspices of the United States.

By **decision 54/425** of 9 December, the General Assembly deferred consideration of the agenda item "Armed Israeli aggression against the Iraqi nuclear installations and its grave consequences for the established international system concerning the peaceful use of nuclear energy, the non-proliferation of nuclear weapons and international peace and security" and included it in the provisional agenda of its fifty-fifth (2000) session. The item had been inscribed yearly on the Assembly's agenda since 1981, following the bombing by Israel of a nuclear research centre near Baghdad [YUN 1981, p. 275].

Peace process

Overall situation

The stalemate in the peace negotiations continued during the first six months of 1999. The escalation of Israeli settlement activities since the signing of the Wye River Memorandum [YUN 1998, p. 424], Israel's unilateral decision to halt its implementation of the Memorandum during the first six months of the year, the adoption in January 1999 by the Knesset of a new law that impeded the return of the occupied Syrian Arab Golan and Jerusalem to the Palestinian people, and the failure to hold a conference of the High Contracting Parties to the 1949 Geneva Convention relative to the Protection of Civilian Persons in Time of War (Fourth Geneva Convention), as recommended by the General Assembly at its tenth emergency special session in 1998, led to the reconvening of the emergency session in February 1999. The Assembly called once again for the convening of a conference by the High Contracting Parties on measures to enforce the Convention in the occupied Palestinian territory. A UN meeting on the convening of the conference was held in June. On 15 July, the High Contracting Parties met in Geneva.

A few months after the election in May 1999 of a new Israeli Government, led by Ehud Barak, peace negotiations resumed between Israel and the Palestine Liberation Organization (PLO). On 4 September, Prime Minister Barak and Palestinian Authority President Yasser Arafat signed the Sharm el-Sheikh Memorandum on Implementation Timeline of Outstanding Commitments of Agreements Signed and the Resumption of Permanent Status Negotiations. The agreement was a timetable for implementing the Wye River Memorandum. By the end of the five-month process laid down under the new agreement, Palestinians would control 41 per cent of the West Bank, some 350 Palestinian security prisoners would be released and negotiation teams would be established to begin intensive talks on a final peace accord. The target date for reaching the final-status deal was set for 13 September 2000. In addition, the southern "safe passage" route was to be opened and construction of the Gaza seaport was to commence on 1 October.

In an October report [A/54/457-S/1999/1050] on the question of Palestine (see p. 419) and the situation in the Middle East, the Secretary-General noted with cautious optimism that the signing of the Sharm el-Sheikh Memorandum had brought the peace process back on track. The new agreement contained a time line for implementation of all the commitments the two sides had made since the signing in 1993 of the Declaration of Principles on Interim Self-Government Arrangements [YUN 1993, p. 521]. It also stated that the two sides had reaffirmed their understanding that the negotiations on permanent status would lead to the implementation of Security Council resolutions 242(1967) [YUN 1967, p. 257] and 338(1973) [YUN 1973, p. 213], and that they had agreed to conclude a comprehensive agreement on all permanent status issues within one year from the resumption of those negotiations, i.e., September 2000.

In **resolution 54/42** of 1 December (see p. 420), the General Assembly, noting with satisfaction the signing of the Sharm el-Sheikh Memorandum, expressed its full support for the ongoing peace process, which began in Madrid in 1991 [YUN 1991, p. 221], and the Declaration of Principles on Interim Self-Government Arrangements, as well as the subsequent agreements, including the 1995 Israeli-Palestinian Interim Agreement on the West Bank and the Gaza Strip [YUN 1995, p. 626]. It also expressed the hope that the process would lead to the establishment of a comprehensive, just and lasting peace in the Middle East.

Committee on Palestinian Rights. In its annual report [A/54/35], the Committee on the Exercise of the Inalienable Rights of the Palestinian People (Committee on Palestinian Rights) welcomed the resumption in August 1999 of the Israeli-Palestinian negotiations followed by the signing of the Sharm el-Sheikh Memorandum. The Committee noted with satisfaction the beginning of the Memorandum's implementation and hoped that it would be completed in good faith and in strict compliance with the agreed timetable.

Occupied territories

Communications (February). On 1 February [S/1999/105], Israel informed the Secretary-General that it had implemented its end of the Wye River Memorandum by fulfilling its responsibilities according to the first two stages of the time line, as well as its other undertakings set forth in the agreement. Specifically, Israel stated that it had implemented the first stage of redeployment, transferring a total of 491.4 square kilometres; completed protocols on the Gaza Airport, which was opened in November 1998, and opened an industrial park in Gaza, planned to provide 20,000 jobs; and was ready to complete the opening of the southern route of safe passage. According to Israel, with the exception of the modification of the PLO Charter and the enactment of a partial anti-incitement law, the PLO had not fulfilled any of its obligations under the Memorandum. Those failures seriously elevated the security threat to Israel. Israel insisted on peace with reciprocity and would go forward if the Palestinians implemented their obligations as well.

Responding on 9 February [A/53/823-S/1999/136], the Permanent Observer of Palestine said that the content of Israel's letter was regrettable at a time when the international community was well aware of the reality of the state of the peace process and the responsibility the Israeli Government bore in that regard, especially the freezing of the Wye River Memorandum.

Emergency special session

In accordance with General Assembly resolution ES-10/5 [YUN 1998, p. 425] and at the request of Jordan [A/ES-10/31], on behalf of the Group of Arab States at the United Nations, supported by the Coordinating Bureau of the Movement of Non-Aligned Countries [A/ES-10/32], the tenth emergency special session of the Assembly resumed on 5 February 1999 to discuss "Illegal Israeli actions in Occupied East Jerusalem and the rest of the Occupied Palestinian Territory". The session was first convened in April 1997 [YUN 1997, p. 394] and resumed in July and November of that year, as well as in March 1998 [YUN 1998, p. 425].

GENERAL ASSEMBLY ACTION

On 9 February [meeting 12], the General Assembly adopted **resolution ES-10/6** by recorded vote (115-2-5) [draft: A/ES-10/L.5/Rev.1] [agenda item 5].

Illegal Israeli actions in Occupied East Jerusalem and the rest of the Occupied Palestinian Territory

The General Assembly,

Reaffirming the resolutions of its tenth emergency special session, namely, ES-10/2 of 25 April 1997, ES-10/3 of 15 July 1997, ES-10/4 of 13 November 1997 and ES-10/5 of 17 March 1998,

Determined to uphold the purposes and principles embodied in the Charter of the United Nations, international humanitarian law and all other instruments of international law, as well as relevant General Assembly and Security Council resolutions,

Reiterating the permanent responsibility of the United Nations towards the question of Palestine until it is solved in all its aspects,

Aware that Israel, the occupying Power, has not heeded the demands made in the resolutions of the tenth emergency special session and that it continues to carry out illegal actions in Occupied East Jerusalem and the rest of the Occupied Palestinian Territory, in particular settlement activity, including the construction of the new Israeli settlement at Jebel Abu Ghneim, the building of other new settlements and the expansion of existing settlements, the construction of bypass roads and the confiscation of lands,

Reaffirming that all illegal Israeli actions in Occupied East Jerusalem and the rest of the Occupied Palestinian Territory, especially settlement activities and the practical results thereof, remain contrary to international law and cannot be recognized, irrespective of the passage of time,

Expressing its appreciation to the Government of Switzerland, in its capacity as depositary of the four Geneva Conventions, and to the International Committee of the Red Cross for their efforts to uphold the integrity of the Conventions,

Increasingly concerned about the persistent violations by Israel, the occupying Power, of the provisions of the Fourth Geneva Convention relative to the Protection of Civilian Persons in Time of War, of 12 August 1949,

Conscious of the serious dangers arising from persistent violations and grave breaches of the Fourth Geneva Convention and the responsibilities arising therefrom,

Aware of the upcoming fiftieth anniversary of the four Geneva Conventions, which is an occasion for renewed determination to promote international humanitarian law further and to reaffirm the undertaking by the High Contracting Parties to respect and to ensure respect for the Conventions in all circumstances in accordance with common article 1,

Taking note of the measure taken by the Government of Switzerland to organize a meeting between the Palestinian and Israeli sides, in the presence of the International Committee of the Red Cross, which was held at Geneva from 9 to 11 June 1998 and was aimed at examining ways to contribute to the effective application of the Fourth Geneva Convention in the Occupied Palestinian Territory, and expressing disappointment that Israeli violations of the Convention continued unabated in spite of such a measure,

Taking note also of the meeting of experts of the High Contracting Parties, convened from 27 to 29 October 1998 at the invitation of the Government of Switzerland, in its capacity as the depositary of the Convention, on general problems concerning the Convention, in particular in occupied territories, as well as of the Chairman's report of the proceedings of that meeting,

Gravely concerned at the suspension, on 20 December 1998, by the Government of Israel of the implementation of the Wye River Memorandum, signed at the White House in Washington, D.C., on 23 October 1998, including the negotiations on the final settlement, which should be concluded by 4 May 1999,

Determined to persist in its work to bring about compliance by Israel, the occupying Power, with the terms of resolutions adopted by the tenth emergency special session,

Aware that, under the circumstances, it should continue to consider the situation with a view to making appropriate recommendations to the States Members of the United Nations in accordance with General Assembly resolution 377 A (V) of 3 November 1950,

1. *Reiterates its condemnation* of the failure of the Government of Israel to comply with the provisions of resolutions ES-10/2, ES-10/3, ES-10/4 and ES-10/5;

2. *Expresses its grave concern* at the adoption by the Knesset of the law of 26 January 1999 and the legislation of 27 January 1999, and reaffirms that all legislative and administrative measures and actions taken by Israel, the occupying Power, which have altered or purport to alter the character, legal status and demographic composition of Occupied East Jerusalem and the rest of the Occupied Palestinian Territory, are all null and void and have no validity whatsoever;

3. *Reiterates* in the strongest terms all the demands made of Israel, the occupying Power, in the above-mentioned resolutions of the tenth emergency special session, including the immediate and full cessation of the construction at Jebel Abu Ghneim and of all other Israeli settlement activities, as well as of all illegal measures and actions in Occupied East Jerusalem, the acceptance of the de jure applicability of the Fourth Geneva Convention and compliance with relevant Security Council resolutions, the cessation and reversal of all actions taken illegally against Palestinian Jerusalemites and the provision of information about goods produced or manufactured in the settlements;

4. *Reiterates also* its previous recommendations to Member States for the cessation of all forms of assistance and support for illegal Israeli activities in the Occupied Palestinian Territory, including Jerusalem, in particular settlement activities and actively to discourage activities that directly contribute to any construction or development of those settlements;

5. *Affirms* that, in spite of the actual deterioration of the Middle East peace process as a result of the lack of compliance by the Government of Israel with the existing agreements, increased efforts must be exerted to bring the peace process back on track and to continue the process towards the achievement of a just, comprehensive and lasting peace in the region on the basis of Security Council resolutions 242(1967) and 338(1973) and the principle of land for peace, as well as Security Council resolution 425(1978);

6. *Reiterates* its recommendation that the High Contracting Parties to the Fourth Geneva Convention convene a conference on measures to enforce the Convention in the Occupied Palestinian Territory, including Jerusalem, and to ensure respect thereof in accordance with common article 1, and further recommends that the High Contracting Parties convene the said conference on 15 July 1999 at the United Nations Office at Geneva;

7. *Invites* the Government of Switzerland, in its capacity as the depositary of the Geneva Convention, to undertake whatever preparations are necessary prior to the conference;

8. *Requests* the Secretary-General to make the necessary facilities available to enable the High Contracting Parties to convene the conference;

9. *Expresses its confidence* that Palestine, as a party directly concerned, will participate in the above-mentioned conference;

10. *Decides* to adjourn the tenth emergency special session temporarily and to authorize the President of the most recent General Assembly to resume its meeting upon request from Member States.

RECORDED VOTE ON RESOLUTION ES-10/6:

In favour: Algeria, Andorra, Angola, Antigua and Barbuda, Argentina, Armenia, Austria, Azerbaijan, Bahrain, Bangladesh, Barbados, Belarus, Belgium, Benin, Bhutan, Bolivia, Botswana, Brazil, Brunei Darussalam, Bulgaria, Burkina Faso, Canada, Chile, China, Colombia, Comoros, Costa Rica, Côte d'Ivoire, Croatia, Cuba, Cyprus, Czech Republic, Democratic People's Republic of Korea, Denmark, Egypt, Eritrea, Estonia, Finland, France, Gabon, Germany, Greece, Guatemala, Guyana, Hungary, Iceland, India, Indonesia, Iran, Ireland, Italy, Jamaica, Japan, Jordan, Kazakhstan, Kenya, Kuwait, Lao People's Democratic Republic, Latvia, Lebanon, Liechtenstein, Lithuania, Luxembourg, Malaysia, Maldives, Mali, Malta, Mexico, Monaco, Morocco, Mozambique, Myanmar, Namibia, Nepal, Netherlands, New Zealand, Nigeria, Norway, Oman, Pakistan, Paraguay, Peru, Philippines, Poland, Portugal, Qatar, Republic of Korea, Russian Federation, Saint Lucia, San Marino, Saudi Arabia, Senegal, Singapore, Slovakia, Slovenia, Solomon Islands, South Africa, Spain, Sri Lanka, Sudan, Suriname, Sweden, Syrian Arab Republic, Tajikistan, Thailand, Tunisia, Turkey, Ukraine, United Arab Emirates, United Kingdom, United Republic of Tanzania, Uruguay, Venezuela, Viet Nam, Zimbabwe.

Against: Israel, United States.

Abstaining: Australia, Bahamas, Cameroon, Romania, Swaziland.

Speaking before the vote [A/ES-10/PV.10], the Permanent Observer of Palestine said that Israel continued to construct settlements in Jerusalem and in the rest of the occupied Palestinian territory, to confiscate land and to build so-called bypass roads, separating the West Bank from the Gaza Strip. In addition, Israel had suspended implementation of the Wye River Memorandum on 20 December 1998 and froze the final status negotiations, which were scheduled to be completed by 4 May 1999, when the five-year transition period agreed upon by the two sides would come to an end. The Permanent Observer recalled that the Assembly, since 1997 in resolution ES-10/3 [YUN 1997, p. 402], had been recommending the convening of the High Contracting Parties to the Fourth Geneva Convention and, in resolution ES-10/5 [YUN 1998, p. 425], had requested Switzerland, in its capacity as the depositary of the Convention, to prepare for a conference on measures to enforce the Convention in the occupied territories. The Permanent Observer stressed that the time had come for the convening of the conference and hoped that the meeting would take place no later than 8 April.

Israel said that the High Contracting Parties had not met since 1949 to discuss the Fourth Geneva Convention or its application, even after wars of aggression against UN Member States. The calling for a conference of those Parties was an anti-Israel initiative that would be a precedent for selectively politicizing the application of the Geneva Conventions to any conflict and would compromise international humanitarian institutions that had remained neutral since 1949. Moreover, the Fourth Geneva Convention had been and continued to be applied in the West Bank and Gaza Strip and, in fact, Israel was the only country in the world to apply it at all.

The Chairman of the Committee on Palestinian Rights said that, after its suspension of the Wye River Memorandum, Israel imposed additional conditions on the Palestinian side, which could only result in delays and bring disillusionment to the Palestinian people. That decision re-attested to Israel's lack of good faith, since it always reneged on agreements it had entered into. In addition, on 26 January 1999, the Knesset adopted a law whose basic objective was to block future negotiations by tightening the conditions for the restoration of land to the Palestinians of East Jerusalem and to Syria in the occupied Syrian Golan. The Committee considered the convening of a conference of the High Contracting Parties at a specific date of crucial importance.

Egypt [A/ES-10/PV.12] said that, since the emergency special session adopted its first resolution in 1997 [YUN 1997, p. 395], Israel had continued to implement and intensify its settlement plans in the occupied Palestinian territory, including in particular East Jerusalem, and had confiscated more territory after signing of the Wye River Memorandum. By doing so, Israel was ignoring not only the requests embodied in the Assembly's resolutions on the matter, but also the consensus opinion expressed by the international community for 30 years regarding the applicability of the Fourth Geneva Convention to all the Arab and Palestinian territories occupied by Israel in June 1967. The continuing settlement activities, the confiscation of Palestinian and Arab land, the construction of bypass roads and the implementation of policies of closure of the areas under the control of the Palestinian Authority (PA) constituted serious violations of the Fourth Geneva Convention and justified the Assembly's recommendation to specify a date for convening the conference.

The United States said that the draft resolution's call for a meeting of all the High Contracting Parties would serve only to damage the climate necessary for productive and ultimately successful direct negotiations between the Palestinians and Israel. The draft's language and its proposed steps prejudged negotiations on permanent status issues and hampered the chances for eventually achieving peace. The United States remained concerned that the draft resolution, like similar ones in the past, constituted an unacceptable assault on the basic uses and meaning of the Fourth Geneva Convention. The United States wanted to see the Wye River Memorandum implemented in its entirety by both sides as soon as possible and progress in the permanent status negotiations.

The Observer of Switzerland, who participated in the debate at the Assembly's invitation, said his Government believed that the Convention was fully applicable to the occupied Palestinian territory, including Jerusalem. Major violations of the Convention had been noted that affected the development and rights of the civilian population. Switzerland, as the Convention's depositary, convened two meetings: one for the Palestinians and the Israelis with the participation of the International Committee of the Red Cross (ICRC) in June 1998 [YUN 1998, p. 427], and the other for experts of the High Contracting Parties in October 1998 [ibid.]. Convening such a conference, however, raised many questions that the Geneva Conventions and their additional protocols did not resolve, and which only the States parties could address. Since the October 1998 meeting, Switzerland had undertaken a new round of consultations with the States parties to the Conventions, ICRC and the organizations more directly concerned on the possible convening of conferences devoted to specific situations. Switzerland said that it could consider taking an active role in the convening and holding of a conference only if States parties first defined a solid basis for the implementation of such a measure.

Israel replied that the attempt to convene a conference of the signatories to the Fourth Geneva Convention with respect to the West Bank and Gaza was a distortion of international humanitarian law for political interests. Moreover, no conference intended to address the status of civilians in time of war could have any relevance whatsoever to the Israeli situation, since 97 per cent of the Palestinians in the West Bank and Gaza were under Palestinian rule.

Speaking after the vote, the Observer of Palestine said that the resolution constituted a step forward because it called for the High Contracting Parties to meet on 15 July 1999 in Geneva to consider measures to enforce the Convention in the occupied Palestinian territories, including Jerusalem.

Communications (March-November). By a 22 March letter [A/53/869-S/1999/308] to the Secretary-General, the United Arab Emirates transmitted a press release issued by the Ministerial Council of the Gulf Cooperation Council at its seventieth session (Riyadh, Saudi Arabia, 14-15 March) condemning Israel's policy of establishing settlements on occupied Arab land, its decision to extend its geographical borders to include "Al-Quds Al-Sharif" (Jerusalem), and its modification of the city's demographic structure. In that regard, the Council condemned the Israeli Parliament's 26 January decision on a new law impeding the return of the occupied Syrian Arab Golan to Syria and of Jerusalem to the Palestinian people, as well as the Israeli Government's decision to include the Lebanese village of Arnoun in the occupied border strip in southern Lebanon (see p. 442). The Council reaffirmed its belief that peace could not be achieved unless legitimate Arab rights were restored and a commitment made to relevant UN resolutions, the terms of reference of the Madrid conference and the principle of land for peace.

On 25 March [A/53/879-S/1999/334], the Permanent Observer of Palestine, responding to comments in the media and to the Israeli Foreign Minister's statement that General Assembly resolution 181(II) [YUN 1947-48, p.247] was "null and void", said that the resolution, among other things, provided the legal basis for the existence of both the Jewish and the Arab States in Mandated Palestine. The Israeli claim was therefore illegal and inadmissible.

Israel responded on 30 March [A/54/77-S/1999/365] that resolution 181(II) was made null and void by the Arab States and the Palestinian leadership in the aftermath of its adoption in November 1947. In addition, it had never been part of the agreed foundation for the peace process between Israel and the Palestinians. The letters of invitation to the 1991 Madrid peace conference [YUN 1991, p. 221] and the Oslo Agreements, which comprised the 1993 Declaration of Principles [YUN 1993, p. 521] and the 1995 Interim Agreement [YUN 1995, p. 626], signed between Israel and the PLO provided that permanent status negotiations were to be based only on Security Council resolutions 242(1967) [YUN 1967, p. 257] and 338(1973) [YUN 1973, p. 213].

The European Union (EU), on 25 March [A/54/76-S/1999/348], welcomed the decision by the Palestinian National Union and associated bodies to reaffirm the nullification of the provisions in the Palestinian National Charter which had called for the destruction of Israel and to reaffirm their commitment to recognize and live in peace with Israel. However, the EU remained concerned at the deadlock in the peace process and called on the parties to implement fully the Wye River Memorandum. The EU was convinced that the creation of a democratic, viable and peaceful sovereign Palestinian State on the basis of existing agreements and through negotiations would be the best guarantee of Israel's security and of Israel's acceptance as an equal partner in the region.

In a 19 April letter [A/54/83-S/1999/464] to the Secretary-General, Israel said that as 4 May 1999 approached, it was necessary to clarify the precise legal obligations of Israel and the PLO in the West Bank and the Gaza Strip with respect to the interim arrangements created by the Oslo Agreements, since repeated Palestinian arguments claimed that the transitional period would end on 4 May and the ensuing legal and political vacuum should be filled by a unilateral declaration of a Palestinian State. Israel noted that the original hope of the parties was indeed to reach agreement on permanent status arrangements by 4 May, while transitional interim agreements were being implemented. That, though, was only a suggested target date. The interim agreements were to continue until the permanent status negotiations had been concluded and the status of the disputed territories was not to be altered until those negotiations were completed. It was for that reason that the Interim Agreement contained a date for its entry into force but no date for its conclusion. Israel stressed that the Palestinians had refused to negotiate a permanent status agreement; therefore, they could not be permitted to rely on the absence of such an agreement to justify a unilateral declaration of statehood.

By a 23 April letter [A/53/923-S/1999/474], the Permanent Observer Mission of Palestine informed the Secretary-General that Israel, on 22 April, had decided to issue closure orders against PA offices at the Orient House in East Jerusalem in violation of international law and UN resolutions, as well as agreements reached between the two parties.

Israel contended on 3 May [A/54/92-S/1999/507] that PA governmental activity at the Orient House, or at any other location outside the areas under Palestinian territorial jurisdiction, constituted a clear violation of Israel-PLO agreements. Such activity was politically motivated and designed to change the legal status and character of the city with no legal validity whatsoever.

In identical letters of 11 May to the Secretary-General and the Security Council President [A/53/972-S/1999/597], the Permanent Observer of Palestine said that implementation of further closure orders issued on 10 May was delayed only as a result of a petition by an Israeli group to the Israeli High Court.

On 3 May [A/53/935-S/1999/505], the Permanent Observer of Palestine transmitted a 29 April letter by Yasser Arafat, PLO Chairman and PA President, and a copy of the final communiqué adopted by the Palestinian Central Council at its extraordinary session (Gaza, 27-29 April). Mr. Arafat said that the Council addressed all aspects of the political situation, the peace process, the options open to the Palestinian leadership with respect to the end of the interim period on 4 May, and the establishment of an independent State of Palestine with "Al-Quds Al-Sharif" as its capital. The Council also decided to form a number of working committees, including a special committee on the draft State constitution, and called on Israel to halt its policy of settlement and the expropriation of Palestinian land.

On 4 May [A/53/938-S/1999/512], the Chairman of the Committee on Palestinian Rights expressed the Committee's full support for the decisions taken by the extraordinary session of the Palestinian Central Council. The Committee was hopeful that the Council's statement would lead to the revitalization of the peace process and called on Israel to return to the negotiating table, without preconditions and in good faith, so as to allow the permanent status negotiations to proceed towards a comprehensive and lasting settlement of the question of Palestine.

In identical letters of 7 May to the Secretary-General and the Security Council President [A/53/946-S/1999/525], Algeria, on behalf of the members of the League of Arab States, referred to the fiftieth anniversary of the adoption by the General Assembly of resolution 273(III) [YUN 1948-49, p. 405], admitting Israel to UN to membership. The Arab States stressed that it was incumbent on Israel to discharge the obligations and fulfil the undertakings that it had assumed upon UN membership. They called on Israel to withdraw, without qualifications or conditions, from all the occupied Palestinian territories, including Jerusalem, from the occupied Syrian Golan back to the lines of 4 June 1967, and from the occupied zone in southern Lebanon. Israel also had to desist from its policy of settler colonialism and respect the national rights of the Palestinian people and principally its right to exercise self-determination and establish an independent Palestinian State.

On 11 May [A/53/972-S/1999/597], the Permanent Observer of Palestine said that Israel had funnelled in additional financial resources for settlement activity in Jerusalem. According to him, the Israeli Government had pledged to provide each settler who moved into a new neighbourhood in occupied East Jerusalem with $5,000. Settlement activities also continued in several locations throughout the occupied Palestinian territory, with the expansion of already existing settlements and the creation of new ones. On 20 May [A/53/968-S/1999/587], the Permanent Observer further informed the Secretary-General of resumed Israeli settlement activities in and around East Jerusalem, specifically at Jebel Abu-Ghneim and at Ras al-Amud. On 3 June [A/53/995-S/1999/640], the Permanent Observer informed the Secretary-General of the Israeli Government's decision the previous week to enlarge the Ma'ale Adumim settlement by approximately 12,000 dunums (3,250 acres). The settlement was located approximately 6 kilometres east of Jerusalem and, if implemented, the plan would link the settlement with the enlarged municipal boundaries of Jerusalem, thereby separating the northern half of the West Bank from its southern half, making it all the more difficult to apply international law and legitimacy with respect to Jerusalem.

On 5 August [A/53/1032-S/1999/854, A/ES-10/35], the Permanent Observer said that the Israeli army had announced its intention to allow 27 of the 31 settler encampments that were set near existing settlements since the signing of the Wye River Memorandum to remain intact. The Permanent Observer noted that that decision was the first Israeli reaction to the conference of the High Contracting Parties to the Fourth Geneva Convention (see p. 415). For the occupying Power, itself a High Contracting Party, to continue such serious violations of the Convention was a matter of grave concern; the recent Israeli actions, if not reversed, required serious consideration and follow-up by the High Contracting Parties.

On 21 October [A/54/485-S/1999/1081], the Permanent Observer informed the Secretary-General that the previous week the Israeli Government had taken a decision related to the so-called hilltop settlements, established by Jewish settlers after the signing of the Wye River Memorandum. That decision, while removing some of those settlements, effectively meant that Israel was proceeding with the establishment of 32 new settlements in the occupied Palestinian territory. Furthermore, the Israeli Government continued to issue tenders for the construction of additional housing units in existing settlements, including at Jebel Abu-Ghneim and in the Gaza Strip. Thousands of acres of land had also been confiscated by the Israeli army in the southern West Bank. The Permanent Observer noted that it was very unfortunate that all of the above was happening at a time when some hope had been emerging with regard to the implementation of the Sharm el-Sheikh Memorandum.

In related matters, on 20 July [A/54/173-S/1999/808], Israel's Foreign Minister said that the new Israeli Government was determined to advance the Middle East peace process on all fronts. On a practical level, the Government would accelerate diplomatic activities by focusing on the Wye River agreement, the renewal of the final status negotiations with the Palestinians and the advancement of negotiations between Israel, Syria and Lebanon. It would also restart the multilateral process, focusing on regional issues, such as the economy, water, environment, refugees and security. The Foreign Minister stressed that there could be no progress in the peace process against a background of terrorism and hostile political activity. He hoped that a solution would be found for the normalization of Israel's involvement in the UN system, since Israel's exclusion from any regional group had deprived it of its right to be an equal participant in the United Nations.

By an 8 November letter [A/54/538-S/1999/1150] to the Secretary-General, Israel said that on 6 November three pipe bombs exploded near the main shopping centre of Netanya, a coastal town in Israel. At least 14 people were wounded in the blast. The attack took place a day before the start of the permanent status negotiations between Israel and the PA. Israel affirmed that it would not allow acts of terror to weaken its resolve to advance the peace process.

Special Committee on Israeli Practices. In its thirty-first report [A/54/325], the Special Committee to Investigate Israeli Practices Affecting the Human Rights of the Palestinian People and Other Arabs of the Occupied Territories (Special Committee on Israeli Practices) stated that settlement activity had accelerated markedly after the signature of the Wye River Memorandum in 1998 and in particular subsequent to the unilateral suspension by Israel for six months of its implementation of the Memorandum. There were reportedly 194 Jewish settlements, although some Palestinian estimates placed that number at some 220. New settlements were established in 1999 in all parts of the West Bank, especially around Bethlehem, as well as in the occupied Syrian Golan. In the West Bank and Gaza, aside from East Jerusalem, the settler population had increased from 116,400 in 1993 to 175,000 in 1998. The Israeli Knesset had approved new funding for settlement expansion throughout the occupied territories. The Israeli army had assisted in the expropriation of land and, on occasion, had imposed curfews on the localities from which the land was to be confiscated. In general, Palestinians did not accept compensation for confiscated lands because they believed that the expropriations were political in nature and not due to any natural expansion. In addition, there were no legal procedures for confiscating land.

Report of Secretary-General. On 28 July [A/54/183], the Secretary-General informed the Assembly that Israel had not replied to his June request for information on steps taken or envisaged to implement the relevant provisions of resolution 53/55 [YUN 1998, p. 433], demanding that Israel, among other things, cease all construction of new settlements in the occupied Palestinian territory, including Jerusalem.

GENERAL ASSEMBLY ACTION

On 6 December [meeting 71], the General Assembly, on the recommendation of the Fourth (Special Political and Decolonization) Committee [A/54/576], adopted **resolution 54/78** by recorded vote (149-3-3) [agenda item 89].

Israeli settlements in the Occupied Palestinian Territory, including Jerusalem, and the occupied Syrian Golan

The General Assembly,

Guided by the principles of the Charter of the United Nations, and affirming the inadmissibility of the acquisition of territory by force,

Recalling its relevant resolutions, including those adopted at its tenth emergency special session, as well as relevant Security Council resolutions, including resolutions 242(1967) of 22 November 1967, 446(1979) of 22 March 1979, 465(1980) of 1 March 1980 and 497(1981) of 17 December 1981,

Reaffirming the applicability of the Geneva Convention relative to the Protection of Civilian Persons in Time of War, of 12 August 1949, to the Occupied Palestinian Territory, including Jerusalem, and to the occupied Syrian Golan,

Aware of the Middle East peace process started at Madrid and the agreements reached between the parties, in particular the Declaration of Principles on Interim Self-Government Arrangements of 13 September 1993 and the Israeli-Palestinian Interim Agreement on the West Bank and the Gaza Strip of 28 September 1995,

Expressing grave concern about the continuation by Israel of settlement activities, including the ongoing construction of the new settlement at Jebel Abu-Ghneim, in violation of international humanitarian law, relevant United Nations resolutions and the agreements reached between the parties,

Taking into consideration the detrimental impact of Israeli settlement policies, decisions and activities on the Middle East peace process,

Gravely concerned in particular about the dangerous situation resulting from actions taken by the illegal armed Israeli settlers in the occupied territory, as illustrated by the massacre of Palestinian worshippers by an illegal Israeli settler at Al-Khalil on 25 February 1994,

Taking note of the report of the Secretary-General,

1. *Reaffirms* that Israeli settlements in the Palestinian territory, including Jerusalem, and in the occupied Syrian Golan are illegal and an obstacle to peace and economic and social development;

2. *Calls upon* Israel to accept the de jure applicability of the Geneva Convention relative to the Protection of Civilian Persons in Time of War, of 12 August 1949, to the Occupied Palestinian Territory, including Jerusalem, and to the occupied Syrian Golan and to abide scrupulously by the provisions of the Convention, in particular article 49;

3. *Demands* complete cessation of the construction of the new settlement at Jebel Abu-Ghneim and of all Israeli settlement activities in the Occupied Palestinian Territory, including Jerusalem, and in the occupied Syrian Golan;

4. *Stresses* the need for full implementation of Security Council resolution 904(1994) of 18 March 1994, in which, among other things, the Council called upon Israel, the occupying Power, to continue to take and implement measures, including confiscation of arms, with the aim of preventing illegal acts of violence by Israeli settlers, and called for measures to be taken to guarantee the safety and protection of the Palestinian civilians in the occupied territory;

5. *Requests* the Secretary-General to report to the General Assembly at its fifty-fifth session on the implementation of the present resolution.

RECORDED VOTE ON RESOLUTION 54/78:

In favour: Albania, Algeria, Andorra, Angola, Antigua and Barbuda, Argentina, Armenia, Australia, Austria, Azerbaijan, Bahamas, Bahrain, Bangladesh, Barbados, Belarus, Belgium, Belize, Benin, Bhutan, Bolivia, Botswana, Brazil, Brunei Darussalam, Bulgaria, Burkina Faso, Cambodia, Canada, Cape Verde, Chad, Chile, China, Colombia, Congo, Côte d'Ivoire, Croatia, Cuba, Cyprus, Czech Republic, Democratic People's Republic of Korea, Denmark, Djibouti, Dominica, Ecuador, Egypt, El Salvador, Equatorial Guinea, Eritrea, Estonia, Ethiopia, Fiji, Finland, France, Gabon, Gambia, Georgia, Germany, Ghana, Greece, Grenada, Guatemala, Guinea, Guyana, Haiti, Hungary, Iceland, India, Indonesia, Iran, Ireland, Italy, Jamaica, Japan, Jordan, Kenya, Kuwait, Lao People's Democratic Republic, Latvia, Lebanon, Libyan Arab Jamahiriya, Liechtenstein, Lithuania, Luxembourg, Madagascar, Malaysia, Maldives, Mali, Malta, Mauritius, Mexico, Monaco, Mongolia, Morocco, Mozambique, Myanmar, Namibia, Nepal, Netherlands, New Zealand, Nicaragua, Nigeria, Norway, Oman, Pakistan, Panama, Papau New Guinea, Paraguay, Peru, Philippines, Poland, Portugal, Qatar, Republic of Korea, Republic of Moldova, Romania, Russian Federation, Saint Lucia, Saint Vincent and the Grenadines, Samoa, San Marino, Saudi Arabia, Senegal, Sierra Leone, Singapore, Slovakia, Slovenia, Solomon Islands, South Africa, Spain, Sri Lanka, Sudan, Suriname, Sweden, Syrian Arab Republic, Tajikistan, Thailand, The former Yugoslav Republic of Macedonia, Togo, Trinidad and Tobago, Tunisia, Turkey, Ukraine, United Arab Emirates, United Kingdom, United Republic of Tanzania, Venezuela, Viet Nam, Yemen, Zambia, Zimbabwe.

Against: Israel, Micronesia, United States.

Abstaining: Marshall Islands, Swaziland, Uruguay.

Jerusalem

East Jerusalem, where most of the city's Arab inhabitants lived, remained one of the most sensitive issues in the Middle East peace process. The construction and expansion of the Jebel Abu-Ghneim settlement to the south of East Jerusalem increased the level of hostilities and distrust in Israeli-Palestinian relations. The General Assembly's tenth emergency special session called once again for an end to Israel's settlement activities in and around East Jerusalem (see p. 402).

Special Committee on Israeli Practices. In its annual report [A/54/325], the Special Committee on Israeli Practices described restrictions imposed by the Israeli authorities on Jerusalem's Palestinian population and Israeli violations of their human rights.

The situation of Palestinians living in East Jerusalem had become more precarious since the Committee's last report [YUN 1998, p. 434]. Palestinian inhabitants continued to lose their residency rights when their identity cards were revoked and confiscated by Israeli authorities. More than 2,000 family identity cards were confiscated between 1996 and 1998 (700 in 1998), which affected some 8,000 persons. Palestinians who lost their identity cards since their "centre of life" was found not to be in Jerusalem were usually given 15 days to leave Israel. The Special Committee was informed that Palestinian identity cards were revoked in order to change the demographic composition of East Jerusalem with a view to reducing the Palestinian component. Additional difficulties for the Palestinian population were brought about by the alteration of the boundaries or city limits of East Jerusalem.

At the same time, the Israeli population in East Jerusalem had increased by tens of thousands in recent years, mainly as a consequence of the construction of new settlements around the city. The Committee was informed that 15 Israeli settlements with 45,000 housing units had been established in East Jerusalem since 1967, on 24 square kilometres of land confiscated for public use. The Israeli population in East Jerusalem stood at 170,000. Building in neighbourhoods such as Ras al-Amud and Silwan in East Jerusalem was exacerbating the trend. The Israeli policy concerning Jerusalem was to create and maintain that majority and remove any distinction between the eastern and western parts of the city.

Since the Israeli authorities considered Jerusalem a part of Israel, Palestinians from other parts of the occupied territories faced considerable difficulties in obtaining permits to enter the city. The lack of access to East Jerusalem had repercussions for the inhabitants of the West Bank as the principal Palestinian health, education, religious and cultural facilities were located there. Access of Palestinian health workers and patients to East Jerusalem had been restricted further during the period under review.

The Special Committee believed that the circumstances of East Jerusalem, because of their particular complexity, required special attention and emphasis in view of what seemed to be a very confusing environment in terms of residency rights, travel limitations, isolation from relatives and friends in other parts of the territories, disruption of family life and other aspects to which its attention was drawn.

Transfer of diplomatic missions

Report of Secretary-General. On 25 October [A/54/495], the Secretary-General reported that six Member States had replied to his request for information on steps taken or envisaged to implement General Assembly resolution 53/37 [YUN 1998, p. 436], which addressed the transfer by some States of their diplomatic missions to Jerusalem in violation of Security Council resolution 478(1980) [YUN 1980, p. 426] and called on them to abide by the relevant UN resolutions.

Committee on Palestinian Rights. In its annual report [A/54/35], the Committee on Palestinian Rights said that Israel continued to challenge and violate the internationally recognized status of Jerusalem. In a communiqué issued on 14 March 1999, the Israeli Cabinet challenged the legal status of the city by stating that Jerusalem's position as a *corpus separatum* was legally incorrect and unacceptable to Israel. It declared further that Israel would never accept the "division or internationalization" of the city. The Committee was particularly alarmed by the beginning of the actual Israeli construction work in May 1999 at Jebel Abu-Ghneim, south of East Jerusalem, and at the Ras al-Amud neighbourhood. The Committee stressed the illegality of the continued Israeli policy of "silent transfer" of Palestinians from East Jerusalem.

GENERAL ASSEMBLY ACTION

On 1 December [meeting 68], the General Assembly adopted **resolution 54/37** [draft: A/54/L.40 & Add.1] by recorded vote (139-1-3) [agenda item 43].

Jerusalem

The General Assembly,

Recalling its resolutions 36/120 E of 10 December 1981, 37/123 C of 16 December 1982, 38/180 C of 19 December 1983, 39/146 C of 14 December 1984, 40/168 C of 16 December 1985, 41/162 C of 4 December 1986, 42/209 D of 11 December 1987, 43/54 C of 6 December 1988, 44/40 C of 4 December 1989, 45/83 C of 13 December 1990, 46/82 B of 16 December 1991, 47/63 B of 11 December 1992, 48/59 A of 14 December 1993, 49/87 A of 16 December 1994, 50/22 A of 4 December 1995, 51/27 of 4 December 1996, 52/53 of 9 December 1997 and 53/37 of 2 December 1998, in which it, inter alia, determined that all legislative and administrative measures and actions taken by Israel, the occupying Power, which have altered or purported to alter the character and status of the Holy City of Jerusalem, in particular the so-called "Basic Law" on Jerusalem and the proclamation of Jerusalem as the capital of Israel, were null and void and must be rescinded forthwith,

Recalling also Security Council resolution 478(1980) of 20 August 1980, in which the Council, inter alia, decided not to recognize the "Basic Law" and called upon those States which had established diplomatic missions at Jerusalem to withdraw such missions from the Holy City,

Having considered the report of the Secretary-General,

1. *Determines* that the decision of Israel to impose its laws, jurisdiction and administration on the Holy City of Jerusalem is illegal and therefore null and void and has no validity whatsoever;

2. *Deplores* the transfer by some States of their diplomatic missions to Jerusalem in violation of Security Council resolution 478(1980) and their refusal to comply with the provisions of that resolution;

3. *Calls once more upon* those States to abide by the provisions of the relevant United Nations resolutions, in conformity with the Charter of the United Nations;

4. *Requests* the Secretary-General to report to the General Assembly at its fifty-fifth session on the implementation of the present resolution.

RECORDED VOTE ON RESOLUTION 54/37:

In favour: Afghanistan, Algeria, Andorra, Angola, Argentina, Armenia, Australia, Austria, Azerbaijan, Bahamas, Bahrain, Bangladesh, Belarus, Belgium, Benin, Bhutan, Bosnia and Herzegovina, Botswana, Brazil, Brunei Darussalam, Cambodia, Cameroon, Canada, Cape Verde, Chile, China, Colombia, Comoros, Congo, Côte d'Ivoire, Croatia, Cuba, Cyprus, Czech Republic, Democratic People's Republic of Korea, Denmark, Djibouti, Dominica, Ecuador, Egypt, Eritrea, Estonia, Ethiopia, Finland, France, Gabon, Georgia, Germany, Ghana, Greece, Grenada, Guatemala, Guinea, Guyana, Haiti, Honduras, Hungary, Iceland, India, Indonesia, Iran, Ireland, Italy, Jamaica, Japan, Jordan, Kenya, Kuwait, Lao People's Democratic Republic, Latvia, Lebanon, Libyan Arab Jamahiriya, Liechtenstein, Lithuania, Luxembourg, Madagascar, Malaysia, Maldives, Mali, Malta, Mauritius, Mexico, Monaco, Mongolia, Morocco, Mozambique, Myanmar, Namibia, Nepal, Netherlands, New Zealand, Nigeria, Norway, Oman, Pakistan, Panama, Paraguay, Peru, Philippines, Poland, Portugal, Qatar, Republic of Korea, Romania, Russian Federation, Saint Lucia, Saint Vincent and the Grenadines, Samoa, San Marino, Saudi Arabia, Senegal, Sierra Leone, Singapore, Slovakia, Slovenia, Solomon Islands, South Africa, Spain, Sri Lanka, Sudan, Sweden, Syrian Arab Republic, Tajikistan, Thailand, The former Yugoslav Republic of Macedonia, Togo, Trinidad and Tobago, Tunisia, Turkey, Ukraine, United Arab Emirates, United Kingdom, United Republic of Tanzania, Uruguay, Venezuela, Viet Nam, Yemen, Zambia, Zimbabwe.

Against: Israel.

Abstaining: Swaziland, United States, Uzbekistan.

Economic and social situation

A report on the economic and social repercussions of the Israeli occupation on the living conditions of Palestinians in the occupied territory, including Jerusalem, and of the Arab population of the occupied Syrian Golan [A/54/152-E/1999/92] was prepared by the Economic and Social Commission for Western Asia (ESCWA), in accordance with Economic and Social Council resolution 1998/32 [YUN 1998, p. 436] and General Assembly resolution 53/196 [ibid., p. 437]; it covered the period since its previous report [ibid., p. 436].

The repercussions of Israeli occupation on Palestinian health care had been severe. In education, movement restrictions continued to affect school attendance for those students who had to cross Israeli-controlled checkpoints. Economic development in Israeli settlements also had deleterious effects on the Palestinian community, and the numerous restrictions imposed by Israel for security reasons negatively affected Palestinians. The confiscation of lands declared by Israel as "State land" as a prelude to their transfer to Israeli control had a critical impact on the Palestinian community. Israeli occupation was also affecting and undermining the Palestinians' supply of drinking water as well as its quality, resulting in an increase of infectious diseases.

The unemployment situation among Palestinians in the occupied territories remained critical, owing in particular to closures and Israel's increased reliance on expatriate workers from outside the region. The number of Palestinian workers in Israel dropped from an average of 120,000 on a monthly basis in 1992 to 45,800 during the first half of 1998. Closures had an adverse effect on the continuity and regularity of production, marketing, income generation and employment of Palestinian workers. The macroeconomic impact of Israeli occupation on the occupied Palestinian territory inhibited investment and growth as a result of the continued ambiguity of the legal and political situation.

In the Syrian Golan, while incentives and investment continued to promote the Israeli presence, the Arab population faced further deterioration in living conditions due to Israel's restrictions on employment and education, as well as prohibitive levels of taxation. The employment available to the Syrian population in the Golan was limited to unskilled and semi-skilled daily wage labour, and, in most cases, those workers had no access to social benefits or health insurance.

ECONOMIC AND SOCIAL COUNCIL ACTION

On 29 July [meeting 45], the Economic and Social Council adopted **resolution 1999/53** [draft: E/1999/L.32] by roll-call vote (44-1-3) [agenda item 11].

Economic and social repercussions of the Israeli occupation on the living conditions of the Palestinian people in the occupied Palestinian territory, including Jerusalem, and the Arab population in the occupied Syrian Golan

The Economic and Social Council,

Recalling General Assembly resolution 53/196 of 15 December 1998,

Recalling also its resolution 1998/32 of 29 July 1998,

Guided by the principles of the Charter of the United Nations, affirming the inadmissibility of the acquisition of territory by force, and recalling relevant Security Council resolutions, including resolutions 242(1967) of 22 November 1967, 465(1980) of 1 March 1980 and 497(1981) of 17 December 1981,

Reaffirming the applicability of the Geneva Convention relative to the Protection of Civilian Persons in Time of War, of 12 August 1949, to the occupied Palestinian territory, including Jerusalem, and other Arab territories occupied by Israel since 1967,

Stressing the importance of the revival of the Middle East peace process on the basis of Security Council resolutions 242(1967), 338(1973) of 22 October 1973 and 425(1978) of 19 March 1978, and the principle of land for peace as well as the full and timely implementation of the agreements reached between the Government of Israel and the Palestine Liberation Organization, the representative of the Palestinian people,

Reaffirming the principle of the permanent sovereignty of peoples under foreign occupation over their natural resources,

Convinced that the Israeli occupation impedes efforts to achieve sustainable development and a sound economic environment in the occupied Palestinian territory, including Jerusalem, and the occupied Syrian Golan,

Gravely concerned about the deterioration of economic and living conditions of the Palestinian people in the occupied Palestinian territory, including Jerusalem, and of the Arab population of the occupied Syrian Golan, and the exploitation by Israel, the occupying Power, of their natural resources,

Aware of the important work being done by the United Nations and the specialized agencies in support of the economic and social development of the Palestinian people,

Conscious of the urgent need for the development of the economic and social infrastructure of the occupied Palestinian territory, including Jerusalem, and for the improvement of the living conditions of the Palestinian people as a key element of a lasting peace and stability,

1. *Stresses* the need to preserve the territorial integrity of all of the occupied Palestinian territory and to guarantee the freedom of movement of persons and goods in the territory, including the removal of restrictions on going into and from East Jerusalem, and the freedom of movement to and from the outside world;

2. *Also stresses* the vital importance of the construction and operation of the seaport in Gaza and safe passage to the economic and social development of the Palestinian people;

3. *Calls upon* Israel, the occupying Power, to cease its measures against the Palestinian people, in particular the closure of the occupied Palestinian territory, the enforced isolation of Palestinian towns, the destruction of homes and the isolation of Jerusalem;

4. *Reaffirms* the inalienable right of the Palestinian people and the Arab population of the occupied Syrian Golan to all their natural and economic resources, and calls upon Israel, the occupying Power, not to exploit, endanger or cause loss or depletion of these resources;

5. *Also reaffirms* that Israeli settlements in the occupied Palestinian territory, including Jerusalem, and the occupied Syrian Golan, are illegal and an obstacle to economic and social development;

6. *Stresses* the importance of the work of the organizations and agencies of the United Nations, and of the United Nations Special Coordinator in the Occupied Territories under the auspices of the Secretary-General;

7. *Urges* Member States to encourage private foreign investment in the occupied Palestinian territory, including Jerusalem, in infrastructure, job-creation projects and social development, in order to alleviate the hardship of the Palestinian people and improve living conditions;

8. *Requests* the Secretary-General to submit to the General Assembly at its fifty-fifth session, through the Economic and Social Council, a report on the implementation of the present resolution and to continue to include, in the report of the Special Coordinator, an update on the living conditions of the Palestinian people, in collaboration with relevant United Nations agencies;

9. *Decides* to include the item entitled "Economic and social repercussions of the Israeli occupation on the living conditions of the Palestinian people in the occupied Palestinian territory, including Jerusalem, and the Arab population in the occupied Syrian Golan" in the agenda of its substantive session of 2000.

ROLL-CALL VOTE IN COUNCIL AS FOLLOWS:

In favour: Algeria, Belarus, Belgium, Bolivia, Brazil, Bulgaria, Canada, Cape Verde, Chile, China, Colombia, Comoros, Cuba, Czech Republic, Denmark, Djibouti, France, Germany, Iceland, India, Indonesia, Italy, Japan, Latvia, Lesotho, Mauritius, Mexico, Morocco, Mozambique, New Zealand, Norway, Oman, Pakistan, Poland, Republic of Korea, Russian Federation, Saudi Arabia, Spain, Sri Lanka, Syrian Arab Republic, Turkey, United Kingdom, Venezuela, Viet Nam.

Against: United States.

Abstaining: El Salvador, Honduras, Zambia.

GENERAL ASSEMBLY ACTION

On 22 December [meeting 87], the General Assembly, on the recommendation of the Second (Economic and Financial) Committee [A/54/591], adopted **resolution 54/230** by recorded vote (145-3-6) [agenda item 103].

Permanent sovereignty of the Palestinian people in the Occupied Palestinian Territory, including Jerusalem, and of the Arab population in the occupied Syrian Golan over their natural resources

The General Assembly,

Recalling its resolution 53/196 of 15 December 1998 and taking note of Economic and Social Council resolution 1999/53 of 29 July 1999,

Reaffirming the principle of the permanent sovereignty of peoples under foreign occupation over their natural resources,

Guided by the principles of the Charter of the United Nations, affirming the inadmissibility of the acquisition of territory by force, and recalling the relevant Security Council resolutions, including resolutions 242(1967) of 22 November 1967, 465(1980) of 1 March 1980 and 497(1981) of 17 December 1981,

Reaffirming the applicability of the Geneva Convention relative to the Protection of Civilian Persons in Time of War, of 12 August 1949, to the Occupied Palestinian Territory, including Jerusalem, and other Arab territories occupied by Israel since 1967,

Expressing its concern at the exploitation by Israel, the occupying Power, of the natural resources of the Occupied Palestinian Territory, including Jerusalem, and other Arab territories occupied by Israel since 1967,

Aware of the additional, detrimental economic and social impact of the Israeli settlements on Palestinian and other Arab natural resources, especially the confiscation of land and the forced diversion of water resources,

Expressing the hope that the Middle East peace process, which started at Madrid on 30 October 1991, on the basis of Security Council resolutions 242(1967) of 22 November 1967, 338(1973) of 22 October 1973 and 425(1978) of 19 March 1978 and the principle of land for peace, will reach a final settlement within the agreed time-frame, and that final settlement will be reached on all tracks,

1. *Takes note* of the report transmitted by the Secretary-General;

2. *Reaffirms* the inalienable rights of the Palestinian people and the population of the occupied Syrian Golan over their natural resources, including land and water;

3. *Calls upon* Israel, the occupying Power, not to exploit, to cause loss or depletion of or to endanger the natural resources in the Occupied Palestinian Territory, including Jerusalem, and in the occupied Syrian Golan;

4. *Recognizes* the right of the Palestinian people to claim restitution as a result of any exploitation, loss or depletion of, or danger to, their natural resources, and expresses the hope that this issue will be dealt with in the framework of the final status negotiations between the Palestinian and Israeli sides;

5. *Requests* the Secretary-General to report to it at its fifty-fifth session on the implementation of the present resolution, and decides to include in the agenda of its fifty-fifth session the item entitled "Permanent sovereignty of the Palestinian people in the Occupied Palestinian Territory, including Jerusalem, and of the Arab population in the occupied Syrian Golan over their natural resources".

RECORDED VOTE ON RESOLUTION 54/230:

In favour: Afghanistan, Algeria, Andorra, Angola, Antigua and Barbuda, Argentina, Armenia, Austria, Azerbaijan, Bahamas, Bahrain, Bangladesh, Barbados, Belarus, Belgium, Belize, Benin, Bhutan, Bolivia, Botswana, Brazil, Brunei Darussalam, Bulgaria, Burkina Faso, Cambodia, Canada, Cape Verde, Chad, Chile, China, Colombia, Côte d'Ivoire, Croatia, Cuba, Cyprus, Czech Republic, Democratic People's Republic of Korea, Denmark, Djibouti, Ecuador, Egypt, Eritrea, Estonia, Ethiopia, Finland, France, Gabon, Gambia, Germany, Ghana, Greece, Grenada, Guinea, Guinea-Bissau, Guyana, Haiti, Hungary, Iceland, India, Indonesia, Iran, Ireland, Italy, Jamaica, Japan, Jordan, Kenya, Kuwait, Lao People's Democratic Republic, Latvia, Lebanon, Lesotho, Libyan Arab Jamahiriya, Liechtenstein, Lithuania, Luxembourg, Madagascar, Malaysia, Maldives, Mali, Malta, Mauritius, Mexico, Monaco, Mongolia, Morocco, Mozambique, Myanmar, Namibia, Nepal, Netherlands, New Zealand, Nigeria, Norway, Oman, Pakistan, Panama, Papua New Guinea, Paraguay, Peru, Philippines, Poland, Portugal, Qatar, Republic of Korea, Republic of Moldova, Romania, Russian Federation, Saint Lucia, Saint Vincent and the Grenadines, Samoa, San Marino, Saudi Arabia, Senegal, Seychelles, Sierra Leone, Singapore, Slovakia, Slovenia, Solomon Islands, South Africa, Spain, Sri Lanka, Sudan, Suriname, Swaziland, Sweden, Syrian Arab Republic, Tajikistan, Thailand, The former Yugoslav Republic of Macedonia, Togo, Trinidad and Tobago, Tunisia, Turkey, Uganda, Ukraine, United Arab Emirates, United Kingdom, United Republic of Tanzania, Uruguay, Venezuela, Viet Nam, Yemen, Zimbabwe.

Against: Israel, Marshall Islands, United States.

Abstaining: Australia, Cameroon, Georgia, Kazakhstan, Uzbekistan, Zambia.

Other aspects

Special Committee on Israeli Practices. On 8 September, the Special Committee on Israeli Practices, established in 1968 [YUN 1968, p. 556], reported for the thirty-first time to the General Assembly on events in the territories it considered to be occupied—the Golan Heights, the West Bank, including Jerusalem, and the Gaza Strip [A/54/325].

In addition to that annual report, the Special Committee, at the Assembly's request, submitted two periodic reports in 1999, one covering the period from 6 November 1998 to 31 January 1999 [A/54/73], and the other covering the period from 1 February to 31 August 1999 [A/54/73/Add.1]. The three reports contained information obtained from the Arab and Israeli press; testimony from persons from the occupied territories; and communications and reports from Governments, organizations and individuals. The Committee benefited from the cooperation of Egypt, Jordan, Syria, Palestinian representatives and the UN resident coordinator/United Nations Development Programme (UNDP) Resident Representative in Syria. As in the past, the Committee received no response from Israel to its requests for cooperation and was unable to obtain access to the occupied territories, which had been the case since 1968.

The Special Committee was informed that restrictions in the occupied territories of Gaza, the West Bank and East Jerusalem, with respect to land, housing and water, severely affected the Palestinians, and the confiscation of Palestinian-owned land continued, as well as the establishment of new and expansion of existing settlements.

In view of its natural scarcity and the manner of its utilization by the settlements, water was one of the most serious problems for the Palestinians. Israel controlled most of the West Bank aquifer, as well as the digging of artesian wells, and it had free use of some 80 per cent of water resources in the area, while the remaining 20 per cent was distributed by an Israeli State company. Some Palestinian villages had no water at all, while in others water shortages and cuts affected the cultivation of crops.

The general situation with respect to housing remained virtually unchanged. Severe housing shortages were reported in Gaza and the West Bank, including East Jerusalem, due, among other things, to the fact that the master plans for Palestinian towns and villages had not been modified since 1948, despite the increase in population; and to Israel's policy of not allowing the Palestinian population in Jerusalem to increase beyond 28 per cent. House demolitions continued throughout the period under review, and had been stepped up in East Jerusalem. It was estimated that some 30,000 persons had been left homeless since 1967 and 1,300 structures demolished since 1990. Palestinian families whose homes had been demolished had been living in abandoned buildings, buses and tents. Some Israeli human rights activist groups who cooperated with their Palestinian counterparts resisted demolitions of Palestinian houses and rebuilt structures that had been demolished, an illegal act in Israel since it was considered an act of resistance against the occupation.

Restrictions imposed by the Israeli authorities on the movement of Palestinians within and between parts of the occupied territories and departure for and return from travel abroad continued. In the West Bank, in particular, there were additional complications for travel between areas A, B and C established subsequent to the Oslo Accords. Requirements concerning identity cards and travel permits were complicated and there was a system of controls of movement through checkpoints and closures. The freedom of movement of Palestinians between the West Bank and East Jerusalem and the West Bank and Gaza remained severely restricted. The average number of work permits issued to Palestinians to work in Israel was about 55,000 in 1998. Restrictions were particularly visible at border crossings and checkpoints. Violence against Palestinian men at military checkpoints had resulted in killings on a number of occasions. According to representatives of Israeli organizations, reports of violence at checkpoints by the army or police were often not taken seriously by the Israeli judicial authorities.

The average number of Palestinian prisoners had been quite stable over the past years, averaging around 3,000. At the end of 1998, some 2,253 Palestinian political prisoners were in Israeli prisons. The conditions of detention of Palestinian prisoners had been described as very bad. Among the principal complaints were inadequate medical care and neglect, overcrowding, lack of hygiene, bad ventilation and bad and insufficient food. Allegations of psychological and physical torture by the Israeli General Security Service (GSS) against Palestinian prisoners were brought to the attention of the Special Committee. In May 1998, the Committee against Torture (the monitoring body of the 1984 Convention against Torture and Other Cruel, Inhuman or Degrading Treatment or Punishment, adopted by the General Assembly in resolution 39/46 [YUN 1984, p. 813]) concluded that some of the methods used by GSS constituted torture or cruel, inhuman or degrading treatment or punishment. Some members of the Knesset, civil rights activists, including doctors and lawyers, and human rights organizations had raised the issue of torture of Palestinian prisoners and had called for the establishment of ethics committees while trying to raise awareness of such issues among the Israeli public.

The prolonged Israeli occupation had affected the lives of all Palestinians in the occupied territories with respect to health, including access to medical care, psychological well-being, education and the economy. Numerous Palestinians had been killed, injured or permanently incapacitated as a result of violent incidents involving the Israeli army and security forces, as well as settlers. Many inhabitants, in particular former detainees and prisoners, had sustained permanent bodily and psychological disabilities. The integration of disabled persons into Palestinian society remained difficult, due to the general economic situation and to a lack of adequate rehabilitation centres. The Israeli Government had decided not to compensate those persons injured by the Israeli army during the intifada (the Palestinian uprising which started in 1987). The occupation had also engendered depression and pessimism not only among young people but also in Palestinian society as a whole.

The average unemployment rate in the occupied territories dropped to 14.5 per cent in 1998, owing to the creation of 25,000 additional jobs and to a reduction in the number of days workers were prevented from going to jobs in Israel. Nevertheless, the average in Gaza remained high, at around 20 per cent. It was estimated that the Palestinian labour force surpassed 600,000 in 1998, of whom some 400,000 were employed in the occupied territories. It was also estimated that more than 100,000 Palestinians made a living by working in Israel.

The Special Committee visited the Syrian Arab Republic and reported on the Israeli occupied Syrian Golan Heights (for details, see p. 450).

The Special Committee observed that the Israeli authorities had put in place a comprehensive and elaborate system of laws and regulations and administrative measures that affected all aspects of the lives of the Palestinian and Syrian peoples in the occupied territories. They were designed to meet the policy objectives of the Israeli Government and to enhance its control over the territories and their population. Though the Committee welcomed the resumption of dialogue in the peace process, it stressed that the sense of alienation, exclusion and separation from their homeland experienced by the Palestinians remained a matter of concern. The Committee called on the United Nations High Commissioner for Human Rights, in consultation with the Secretary-General, to establish a system of continuous communication with the Israeli authorities with a view to improving the difficult circumstances under which the Palestinian and Syrian peoples of the occupied territories lived.

In a later report [A/55/373], the Committee presented updated information on the human rights situation in the occupied territories during the last four months of 1999, providing details on restrictions relating to land, housing and water, as well as those affecting movement of Palestinians within and between the occupied territories, and the manner of implementation of restrictions and their economic, social and cultural effects on the Palestinian population. Also included was information on the occupied Syrian Arab Golan.

The report also provided information on the implementation of the Sharm el-Sheikh Memorandum (see p. 401). In accordance with the agreement, on 10 September 1999, the first stage of Israeli redeployment in the West Bank was completed. Seven per cent of Area C (Israeli control) was converted into the status of Area B (Palestinian civilian control), where Israel controlled security and the Palestinians exercised civilian control. That brought the total area under Palestinian civilian or civilian-security control to 36 per cent of the West Bank. The second redeployment, scheduled to take place on 15 November, was postponed due to disagreement between the two sides on the location of the withdrawal.

On 25 October, the first safe passage for Palestinians between Gaza and the West Bank was opened, a month after the target date outlined in the Sharm el-Sheikh Memorandum. On 9 September, Israel released 199 Palestinian security prisoners and, on 15 October, it fulfilled its commitment to the Memorandum by releasing another 151 Palestinian political prisoners. On 29 December, it was reported that Israel had released, as a goodwill gesture, 26 security prisoners, which represented the third group of prisoners Israel had agreed to free in accordance with the Memorandum.

Also, on 4 November, the Palestinian Civil Aviation and Airport Director-General announced that Gaza International Airport was to start operating 24 hours a day later in November.

Report of Secretary-General. On 28 July [A/54/185], the Secretary-General informed the Assembly that Israel had not replied to his June request for information on steps taken or envisaged to implement Assembly resolution 53/56 [YUN 1998, p. 440] demanding that Israel, among other things, cease all practices and actions which violated the human rights of the Palestinian people and accelerate the release of all remaining Palestinians arbitrarily detained or imprisoned.

GENERAL ASSEMBLY ACTION

On 6 December [meeting 71], following consideration of the Special Committee's annual and periodic reports and five reports of the Secretary-General on specific aspects of the situation in the occupied territories [A/54/181-185], the General Assembly, on the recommendation of the Fourth Committee [A/54/576], adopted **resolution 54/79** by recorded vote (150-2-3) [agenda item 89].

Israeli practices affecting the human rights of the Palestinian people in the Occupied Palestinian Territory, including Jerusalem

The General Assembly,

Recalling its relevant resolutions, including those adopted at its tenth emergency special session, and the resolutions of the Commission on Human Rights,

Bearing in mind the relevant resolutions of the Security Council, the most recent of which are resolutions 904(1994) of 18 March 1994 and 1073(1996) of 28 September 1996,

Having considered the reports of the Special Committee to Investigate Israeli Practices Affecting the Human Rights of the Palestinian People and Other Arabs of the Occupied Territories and the reports of the Secretary-General,

Aware of the responsibility of the international community to promote human rights and ensure respect for international law,

Reaffirming the principle of the inadmissibility of the acquisition of territory by force,

Reaffirming also the applicability of the Geneva Convention relative to the Protection of Civilian Persons in Time of War, of 12 August 1949, to the Occupied Palestinian Territory, including Jerusalem, and other Arab territories occupied by Israel since 1967,

Recalling the signing of the Declaration of Principles on Interim Self-Government Arrangements by the Government of the State of Israel and the Palestine Liberation Organization in Washington, D.C., on 13 September 1993, as well as the subsequent implementation agreements, including the Israeli-Palestinian Interim Agreement on the West Bank and the Gaza Strip signed in Washington, D.C., on 28 September 1995, and the signing of the Sharm el-Sheikh Memorandum on 4 September 1999,

Noting the withdrawal of the Israeli army, which took place in the Gaza Strip and the Jericho Area, and the subsequent Israeli redeployments in accordance with the agreements reached between the parties,

Concerned about the continuing violation of the human rights of the Palestinian people by Israel, the occupying Power, including the use of collective punishment, closure of areas, annexation and establishment of settlements and the continuing actions by it designed to change the legal status, geographical nature and demographic composition of the Occupied Palestinian Territory, including Jerusalem,

Convinced of the positive impact of a temporary international or foreign presence in the Occupied Palestinian Territory for the safety and protection of the Palestinian people,

Expressing its appreciation to the countries that participated in the Temporary International Presence in Hebron for their positive contribution,

Convinced of the need for the full implementation of Security Council resolutions 904(1994) and 1073(1996),

1. *Determines* that all measures and actions taken by Israel, the occupying Power, in the Occupied Palestinian Territory, including Jerusalem, in violation of the relevant provisions of the Geneva Convention relative to the Protection of Civilian Persons in Time of War, of 12 August 1949, and contrary to the relevant resolutions of the Security Council, are illegal and have no validity and that such measures should cease immediately;

2. *Demands* that Israel, the occupying Power, cease all practices and actions which violate the human rights of the Palestinian people;

3. *Stresses* the need to preserve the territorial integrity of all the Occupied Palestinian Territory and to guarantee the freedom of movement of persons and goods within the Palestinian territory, including the removal of restrictions on movement into and from East Jerusalem, and the freedom of movement to and from the outside world;

4. *Calls upon* Israel, the occupying Power, to accelerate the release of all remaining Palestinians arbitrarily detained or imprisoned, in line with agreements reached;

5. *Calls* for complete respect by Israel, the occupying Power, of all fundamental freedoms of the Palestinian people;

6. *Requests* the Secretary-General to report to the General Assembly at its fifty-fifth session on the implementation of the present resolution.

RECORDED VOTE ON RESOLUTION 54/79:

In favour: Albania, Algeria, Andorra, Angola, Antigua and Barbuda, Argentina, Armenia, Australia, Austria, Azerbaijan, Bahamas, Bahrain, Bangladesh, Barbados, Belarus, Belgium, Belize, Benin, Bhutan, Bolivia, Botswana, Brazil, Brunei Darussalam, Bulgaria, Burkina Faso, Cambodia, Canada, Cape Verde, Chad, Chile, China, Colombia, Congo, Côte d'Ivoire, Croatia, Cuba, Cyprus, Czech Republic, Democratic People's Republic of Korea, Denmark, Djibouti, Dominica, Ecuador, Egypt, El Salvador, Equatorial Guinea, Eritrea, Estonia, Ethiopia, Fiji, Finland, France, Gabon, Gambia, Georgia, Germany, Ghana, Greece, Grenada, Guatemala, Guinea, Guyana, Haiti, Hungary, Iceland, India, Indonesia, Iran, Ireland, Italy, Jamaica, Japan, Jordan, Kenya, Kuwait, Lao People's Democratic Republic, Latvia, Lebanon, Libyan Arab Jamahiriya, Liechtenstein, Lithuania, Luxembourg, Madagascar, Malaysia, Maldives, Mali, Malta, Mauritius, Mexico, Monaco, Mongolia, Morocco, Mozambique, Myanmar, Namibia, Nepal, Netherlands, New Zealand, Nicaragua, Nigeria, Norway, Oman, Pakistan, Panama, Papua New Guinea, Paraguay, Peru, Philippines, Poland, Portugal, Qatar, Republic of Korea, Republic of Moldova, Romania, Russian Federation, Saint Lucia, Saint Vincent and the Grenadines, Samoa, San Marino, Saudi Arabia, Senegal, Sierra Leone, Singapore, Slovakia, Slovenia, Solomon Islands, South Africa, Spain, Sri Lanka, Sudan, Suriname, Sweden, Syrian Arab Republic, Tajikistan, Thailand, The former Yugoslav Republic of Macedonia, Togo, Trinidad and Tobago, Tunisia, Turkey, Ukraine, United Arab Emirates, United Kingdom, United Republic of Tanzania, Uruguay, Venezuela, Viet Nam, Yemen, Zambia, Zimbabwe.

Against: Israel, United States.

Abstaining: Marshall Islands, Micronesia, Swaziland.

By **resolution 54/152**, the Assembly reaffirmed the right of the Palestinian people to self-determination, including the option of a State, and urged all States, as well as UN specialized agencies and organizations, to continue to support the Palestinian people in their quest for self-determination (see p. 622).

Work of Special Committee

In a July report [A/54/181], the Secretary-General stated that all necessary facilities were provided to the Special Committee on Israeli Practices, as requested in General Assembly resolution 53/53 [YUN 1998, p. 441]. Arrangements were made for it to meet in March, May and August, and a field mission was carried out to Egypt, Jordan and the Syrian Arab Republic in May. Two periodic reports [A/54/73 & Add.1] and the thirty-first annual report of the Special Committee [A/54/325] were circulated to Member States. The UN Department of Public Information continued to provide press coverage of Special Committee meetings and to disseminate information materials on its activities (see p. 426).

GENERAL ASSEMBLY ACTION

On 6 December [meeting 71], the General Assembly, on the recommendation of the Fourth Committee [A/54/576], adopted **resolution 54/76** by recorded vote (84-2-67) [agenda item 89].

Work of the Special Committee to Investigate Israeli Practices Affecting the Human Rights of the Palestinian People and Other Arabs of the Occupied Territories

The General Assembly,

Guided by the purposes and principles of the Charter of the United Nations,

Guided also by the principles of international humanitarian law, in particular the Geneva Convention relative to the Protection of Civilian Persons in Time of War, of 12 August 1949, as well as international standards of human rights, in particular the Universal Declaration of Human Rights and the International Covenants on Human Rights,

Recalling its relevant resolutions, including resolution 2443(XXIII) of 19 December 1968, and relevant resolutions of the Commission on Human Rights,

Recalling also relevant resolutions of the Security Council,

Aware of the lasting impact of the uprising (intifada) of the Palestinian people,

Convinced that occupation itself represents a gross violation of human rights,

Having considered the reports of the Special Committee to Investigate Israeli Practices Affecting the Human Rights of the Palestinian People and Other Arabs of the Occupied Territories and the relevant reports of the Secretary-General,

Recalling the signing of the Declaration of Principles on Interim Self-Government Arrangements by the Government of the State of Israel and the Palestine Liberation Organization in Washington, D.C., on 13 September 1993, as well as the subsequent implementation agreements, including the Israeli-Palestinian Interim Agreement on the West Bank and the Gaza Strip signed in Washington, D.C., on 28 September 1995, and the recent signing of the Sharm el-Sheikh Memorandum on 4 September 1999,

Expressing the hope that, with the progress of the peace process, the Israeli occupation will be brought to an end and therefore violation of the human rights of the Palestinian people will cease,

1. *Commends* the Special Committee to Investigate Israeli Practices Affecting the Human Rights of the Palestinian People and Other Arabs of the Occupied Territories for its efforts in performing the tasks assigned to it by the General Assembly and for its impartiality;

2. *Demands* that Israel cooperate with the Special Committee in implementing its mandate;

3. *Deplores* those policies and practices of Israel which violate the human rights of the Palestinian people and other Arabs of the occupied territories, as reflected in the reports of the Special Committee covering the reporting period;

4. *Expresses concern* about the situation in the Occupied Palestinian Territory, including Jerusalem, as a result of Israeli practices and measures;

5. *Requests* the Special Committee, pending complete termination of the Israeli occupation, to continue to investigate Israeli policies and practices in the Occupied Palestinian Territory, including Jerusalem, and other Arab territories occupied by Israel since 1967, especially Israeli lack of compliance with the provisions of the Geneva Convention relative to the Protection of Civilian Persons in Time of War, of 12 August 1949, to consult, as appropriate, with the International Committee of the Red Cross according to its regulations in order to ensure that the welfare and human rights of the peoples of the occupied territories are safeguarded, and to report to the Secretary-General as soon as possible and whenever the need arises thereafter;

6. *Also requests* the Special Committee to submit regularly to the Secretary-General periodic reports on the current situation in the Occupied Palestinian Territory, including Jerusalem;

7. *Further requests* the Special Committee to continue to investigate the treatment of prisoners in the Occupied Palestinian Territory, including Jerusalem, and other Arab territories occupied by Israel since 1967;

8. *Requests* the Secretary-General:

(*a*) To provide the Special Committee with all necessary facilities, including those required for its visits to the occupied territories, so that it may investigate the Israeli policies and practices referred to in the present resolution;

(*b*) To continue to make available such additional staff as may be necessary to assist the Special Committee in the performance of its tasks;

(*c*) To circulate regularly to Member States the periodic reports mentioned in paragraph 6 above;

(*d*) To ensure the widest circulation of the reports of the Special Committee and of information regarding its activities and findings, by all means available, through the Department of Public Information of the Secretariat and, where necessary, to reprint those reports of the Special Committee that are no longer available;

(*e*) To report to the General Assembly at its fifty-fifth session on the tasks entrusted to him in the present resolution;

9. *Decides* to include in the provisional agenda of its fifty-fifth session the item entitled "Report of the Special Committee to Investigate Israeli Practices Affecting the Human Rights of the Palestinian People and Other Arabs of the Occupied Territories".

RECORDED VOTE ON RESOLUTION 54/76:

In favour: Algeria, Angola, Azerbaijan, Bahrain, Bangladesh, Belarus, Belize, Benin, Bhutan, Botswana, Brazil, Brunei Darussalam, Burkina Faso, Cambodia, Cape Verde, Chad, Chile, China, Colombia, Congo, Côte d'Ivoire, Cuba, Cyprus, Democratic People's Republic of Korea, Djibouti, Dominica, Ecuador, Egypt, Eritrea, Gabon, Ghana, Guinea, Guyana, Haiti, India, Indonesia, Iran, Jordan, Kenya, Kuwait, Lao People's Democratic Republic, Lebanon, Libyan Arab Jamahiriya, Malaysia, Maldives, Mali, Malta, Mauritius, Mexico, Morocco, Mozambique, Myanmar, Namibia, Nepal, Nigeria, Oman, Pakistan, Panama, Papua New Guinea, Philippines, Qatar, Saint Lucia, Saudi Arabia, Senegal, Sierra Leone, Singapore, South Africa, Sri Lanka, Sudan, Suriname, Syrian Arab Republic, Thailand, Togo, Trinidad and Tobago, Tunisia, Turkey, United Arab Emirates, United Republic of Tanzania, Uruguay, Venezuela, Viet Nam, Yemen, Zambia, Zimbabwe.

Against: Israel, United States.

Abstaining: Albania, Andorra, Antigua and Barbuda, Argentina, Armenia, Australia, Austria, Bahamas, Barbados, Belgium, Bolivia, Bulgaria, Cameroon, Canada, Croatia, Czech Republic, Denmark, Equatorial Guinea, Estonia, Ethiopia, Fiji, Finland, France, Georgia, Germany, Greece, Grenada, Guatemala, Hungary, Iceland, Ireland, Italy, Jamaica, Japan, Kazakhstan, Latvia, Liechtenstein, Lithuania, Luxembourg, Madagascar, Marshall Islands, Micronesia, Monaco, Mongolia, Netherlands, New Zealand, Norway, Paraguay, Peru, Poland, Portugal, Republic of Korea, Republic of Moldova, Romania, Russian Federation, Saint Vincent and the Grenadines, Samoa, San Marino, Slovakia, Slovenia, Solomon Islands, Spain, Swaziland, Sweden, The former Yugoslav Republic of Macedonia, Ukraine, United Kingdom.

Fourth Geneva Convention

Conference of High Contracting Parties

The Conference of the High Contracting Parties to the Fourth Geneva Convention on Measures to Enforce the Convention in the Occupied Palestinian Territory, including Jerusalem, was held on 15 July in Geneva, pursuant to General Assembly resolution ES-10/6 (see p. 402). It was the first time in the history of the Geneva Conventions that a conference was convened to consider a specific case of violations of the 1949 Geneva

Convention relative to the Protection of Civilian Persons in Time of War.

The Conference was attended by the majority of States High Contracting Parties, a delegation from Palestine, ICRC, UN agencies and non-governmental organizations (NGOs). Australia, Canada, Israel and the United States announced that they would not participate.

The Permanent Observer Mission of Palestine to the United Nations presented a paper entitled "Israel's belligerent occupation of the Palestinian territory, including Jerusalem, and international humanitarian law".

In a statement adopted at the conclusion of the Conference, the participating High Contracting Parties reaffirmed the applicability of the Fourth Geneva Convention to the occupied Palestinian territory, including East Jerusalem, and reiterated the need for full respect for the Convention's provisions. The Conference adjourned on the understanding that it would convene again in the light of consultations on the development of the humanitarian situation in the field.

UN International Meeting

Prior to the Conference, the United Nations International Meeting on the Convening of the Conference on Measures to Enforce the Fourth Geneva Convention in the Occupied Palestinian Territory, including Jerusalem, (Cairo, Egypt, 14-15 June), organized under the auspices of the Committee on Palestinian Rights, was attended by international legal experts and representatives of the Secretary-General, intergovernmental organizations, the PA, Governments, UN system organizations and agencies, ICRC, NGOs and the media. The participants discussed Israeli violations of the Fourth Geneva Convention, enforcement of the Convention, and the conference of the High Contracting Parties and its possible outcomes. In its final document [A/ES-10/34, A/53/977], the participants expressed concern with regard to breaches and violations by Israel of the Convention, especially the continuing settlement activities, which included land confiscation and the transfer of Israeli civilians to the occupied Palestinian territory, including Jerusalem. The participants supported the convening by the High Contracting Parties of the conference on measures to enforce the Convention, on 15 July in Geneva. The participants called on the High Contracting Parties to strive for concrete results by the conference to be incorporated in a declaration or resolution or both. The conference should emphasize the responsibility of the High Contracting Parties to ensure respect for the Convention and live up to their obligations under it, affirm its de jure applicability in the occupied Palestinian territory, including Jerusalem, and establish a follow-up mechanism, in the form of a committee under the leadership of the depositary (Switzerland).

Report of Secretary-General. In July [A/54/182], the Secretary-General informed the General Assembly that Israel had not replied to his June request for information on steps taken or envisaged to implement Assembly resolution 53/54 [YUN 1998, p. 442] demanding that Israel accept the de jure applicability of the Convention in the occupied Palestinian territory, including Jerusalem, and that it comply scrupulously with its provisions. Also in June, the Secretary-General noted, he had drawn the attention of all States parties to paragraph 3 of resolution 53/54 calling on them to exert all efforts to ensure respect by Israel for the Convention's provisions.

GENERAL ASSEMBLY ACTION

On 6 December [meeting 71], the General Assembly, on the recommendation of the Fourth Committee [A/54/576], adopted **resolution 54/77** by recorded vote (154-2-1) [agenda item 89].

Applicability of the Geneva Convention relative to the Protection of Civilian Persons in Time of War, of 12 August 1949, to the Occupied Palestinian Territory, including Jerusalem, and the other occupied Arab territories

The General Assembly,

Recalling its relevant resolutions,

Bearing in mind the relevant resolutions of the Security Council,

Having considered the reports of the Special Committee to Investigate Israeli Practices Affecting the Human Rights of the Palestinian People and Other Arabs of the Occupied Territories and the relevant reports of the Secretary-General,

Considering that the promotion of respect for the obligations arising from the Charter of the United Nations and other instruments and rules of international law is among the basic purposes and principles of the United Nations,

Noting the convening of the meeting of experts of the high contracting parties to the Geneva Convention relative to the Protection of Civilian Persons in Time of War, of 12 August 1949, in Geneva from 27 to 29 October 1998, at the initiative of the Government of Switzerland in its capacity as the depositary of the Convention, concerning general problems of application of the Convention in general and, in particular, in occupied territories,

Noting also the convening on 15 July 1999 for the first time of a Conference of High Contracting Parties to the Fourth Geneva Convention, as recommended by the General Assembly in its resolution ES-10/6 of 9 February 1999, on measures to enforce the Convention in the Occupied Palestinian Territory, including Jerusalem, and to ensure respect thereof in accordance with article 1 common to the four Geneva Conventions, and aware of the statement adopted by the Conference,

Stressing that Israel, the occupying Power, should comply strictly with its obligations under international law,

1. *Reaffirms* that the Geneva Convention relative to the Protection of Civilian Persons in Time of War, of 12 August 1949, is applicable to the Occupied Palestinian Territory, including Jerusalem, and other Arab territories occupied by Israel since 1967;

2. *Demands* that Israel accept the de jure applicability of the Convention in the Occupied Palestinian Territory, including Jerusalem, and other Arab territories occupied by Israel since 1967, and that it comply scrupulously with the provisions of the Convention;

3. *Calls upon* all States parties to the Convention, in accordance with article 1 common to the four Geneva Conventions, to exert all efforts in order to ensure respect for its provisions by Israel, the occupying Power, in the Occupied Palestinian Territory, including Jerusalem, and other Arab territories occupied by Israel since 1967;

4. *Reiterates* the need for speedy implementation of the recommendations contained in its resolutions ES-10/3 of 15 July 1997, ES-10/4 of 13 November 1997, ES-10/5 of 17 March 1998 and ES-10/6 of 9 February 1999 with regard to ensuring respect by Israel, the occupying Power, for the provisions of the Convention;

5. *Requests* the Secretary-General to report to the General Assembly at its fifty-fifth session on the implementation of the present resolution.

RECORDED VOTE ON RESOLUTION 54/77:

In favour: Albania, Algeria, Andorra, Angola, Antigua and Barbuda, Argentina, Armenia, Australia, Austria, Azerbaijan, Bahamas, Bahrain, Bangladesh, Barbados, Belarus, Belgium, Belize, Benin, Bhutan, Bolivia, Botswana, Brazil, Brunei Darussalam, Bulgaria, Burkina Faso, Cambodia, Cameroon, Canada, Cape Verde, Chad, Chile, China, Colombia, Congo, Côte d'Ivoire, Croatia, Cuba, Cyprus, Czech Republic, Democratic People's Republic of Korea, Denmark, Djibouti, Dominica, Ecuador, Egypt, El Salvador, Equatorial Guinea, Eritrea, Estonia, Ethiopia, Fiji, Finland, France, Gabon, Gambia, Georgia, Germany, Ghana, Greece, Grenada, Guatemala, Guinea, Guyana, Haiti, Hungary, Iceland, India, Indonesia, Iran, Ireland, Italy, Jamaica, Japan, Jordan, Kazakhstan, Kenya, Kuwait, Lao People's Democratic Republic, Latvia, Lebanon, Libyan Arab Jamahiriya, Liechtenstein, Lithuania, Luxembourg, Madagascar, Malaysia, Maldives, Mali, Malta, Marshall Islands, Mauritius, Mexico, Monaco, Mongolia, Morocco, Mozambique, Myanmar, Namibia, Nepal, Netherlands, New Zealand, Nicaragua, Nigeria, Norway, Oman, Pakistan, Panama, Papua New Guinea, Paraguay, Peru, Philippines, Poland, Portugal, Qatar, Republic of Korea, Republic of Moldova, Romania, Russian Federation, Saint Lucia, Saint Vincent and the Grenadines, Samoa, San Marino, Saudi Arabia, Senegal, Sierra Leone, Singapore, Slovakia, Slovenia, Solomon Islands, South Africa, Spain, Sri Lanka, Sudan, Suriname, Swaziland, Sweden, Syrian Arab Republic, Tajikistan, Thailand, The former Yugoslav Republic of Macedonia, Togo, Trinidad and Tobago, Tunisia, Turkey, Ukraine, United Arab Emirates, United Kingdom, United Republic of Tanzania, Uruguay, Venezuela, Viet Nam, Yemen, Zambia, Zimbabwe.

Against: Israel, United States.

Abstaining: Micronesia.

Palestinian women

The Secretary-General, in a December report [E/CN.6/1999/2] to the Commission on the Status of Women on follow-up and progress in the implementation of the Beijing Declaration and Platform for Action [YUN 1995, p. 1170], reviewed, in response to Economic and Social Council resolution 1998/10 [YUN 1998, p. 444], the situation of Palestinian women and described assistance provided by UN organizations during the period September 1997 to September 1998. He stated that the daily life of women in the occupied territories continued to be adversely affected by the Israeli occupation, particularly the imposition of closures and other security-related measures, which had a detrimental impact on their socio-economic condition. As in the past, Palestinian women were experiencing the gender-specific impact of those measures, which was reinforced by existing inequalities in society between women and men. Women's average labour force participation rate declined from 13 per cent in 1996 to 12.3 per cent in 1997, a relative decline of 5.8 per cent for women compared with 1.5 per cent for men. Further, women's full employment rates and the total number of fully employed women also fell in 1997, while those for men rose considerably. Their average unemployment rate increased from 20.6 to 21.4 per cent. According to the 1997 Palestinian Population, Housing and Establishment Census, women represented 49.2per cent of the total Palestinian population. The census also showed that 20.1 per cent of women were illiterate, compared with 7.7 per cent of men, and that the fertility rate was 6.1 per cent.

The UN system continued to support Palestinian women and sought to mainstream a gender perspective in its programmes and funds. The four-year, $7.2 million programme of assistance to the Palestinian people of the United Nations Population Fund (UNFPA) focused on reproductive health including family planning, population and development strategies, and advocacy. The World Health Organization (WHO) assisted in the consolidation of the Women's Health Development Department at the PA's Ministry of Health, as well as with the implementation of two reproductive health projects in the West Bank and Gaza Strip. The United Nations Children's Fund (UNICEF) provided assistance to Palestinian women through its programmes in advocacy and capacity-building, health and nutrition, and basic education. The United Nations Volunteers were implementing the Community-based Youth Participation and Development Project, aimed at promoting the development of youth, in particular young women, to be participants in and contributors to the development of Palestinian society. The International Labour Organization (ILO), as part of its International Programme for More and Better Jobs for Women, formulated a draft Action Plan for the West Bank and Gaza Strip, which included the development of a gender-sensitive labour market information system to improve data collection, analysis and dissemination. Other ILO activities included the promotion and development of Palestinian women's entrepreneurship.

As part of its programme of assistance to the Palestinian people, UNDP supported the establishment of a Gender Statistics Unit within the Palestinian Central Bureau of Statistics. In conjunction with the PA's Inter-Ministerial Committee, UNDP created a Rural Girls Development Centre, which provided general education and comprehensive training in health and agriculture. The Office of the United Nations High Commissioner for Human Rights supported the establishment of a Women and Group Rights Unit within the Palestinian Centre for Human Rights in Gaza to work with the local community for the development of a favourable women's rights policy environment.

The United Nations Development Fund for Women (UNIFEM) implemented its empowerment agenda for women through three programme areas: strengthening women's economic capacity, engendering governance and leadership, and promoting women's human rights. UNIFEM's Global Campaign for the Eradication of Violence against Women was planning to raise public awareness among Palestinians on that particular issue. The United Nations Educational, Scientific and Cultural Organization (UNESCO) integrated Palestinian women's concerns in its assistance work, which included granting scholarships through the United Nations Relief and Works Agency for Palestine Refugees in the Near East (UNRWA). ESCWA supported the economic and social situation in the West Bank and Gaza Strip and provided advisory services and technical assistance.

Palestinian women refugees were direct or indirect beneficiaries of UNRWA's programmes. For example, in the education programme, women accounted for 62 per cent of all trainees enrolled in technical/semi-professional courses in 1997/98. Of the 1,055 scholarships granted during 1997/98 by UNRWA to refugee students, 46 per cent went to Palestinian women. As part of its income-generation programme, UNRWA granted loans valued at $2.7 million to 3,296 women who supported some 16,310 dependants.

The Secretary-General observed that the PA and civil society, with the assistance of the international community, had taken considerable steps to advance the situation of Palestinian women. However, further efforts and assistance were needed, particularly within the context of mainstreaming a gender perspective into all policies and programmes. A sound information basis was essential for gender mainstreaming; therefore the efforts of the Palestinian Central Bureau of Statistics to acquire and disseminate gender-disaggregated statistics had to be augmented by UN bodies in order to keep gender disaggregated data on their operations. That would aid the reporting process and enhance the effectiveness of support programmes.

ECONOMIC AND SOCIAL COUNCIL ACTION

On 28 July [meeting 43], the Economic and Social Council, on the recommendation of the Commission on the Status of Women [E/1999/27], adopted **resolution 1999/15** by roll-call vote (34-1-4) [agenda item 14 *(a)*].

Palestinian women

The Economic and Social Council,

Having considered with appreciation the section concerning the situation of Palestinian women and assistance provided by organizations of the United Nations system of the report of the Secretary-General on follow-up to and implementation of the Beijing Declaration and Platform for Action adopted by the Fourth World Conference on Women,

Recalling the Nairobi Forward-looking Strategies for the Advancement of Women, in particular paragraph 260 concerning Palestinian women and children, and the Beijing Platform for Action,

Recalling also its resolution 1998/10 of 28 July 1998 and other relevant United Nations resolutions,

Recalling further the Declaration on the Elimination of Violence against Women as it concerns the protection of civilian populations,

Gravely concerned at the suspension, on 20 December 1998, by the Government of Israel of the implementation of the Wye River Memorandum, signed in Washington, D.C., on 23 October 1998, including the negotiations on the final settlement which were to have been concluded by May 1999,

Concerned about the continuing difficult situation of Palestinian women in the Occupied Palestinian Territory, including Jerusalem, and about the severe consequences of continuous illegal Israeli settlement activities, as well as the harsh economic conditions and other consequences for the situation of Palestinian women and their families resulting from the frequent closures and isolation of the occupied territory,

1. *Stresses* its support for the Middle East peace process and the need for speedy and full implementation of the agreements already reached between the parties;

2. *Affirms* that in spite of the actual deterioration of the Middle East peace process as a result of the lack of compliance by the Government of Israel with the existing agreements, increased efforts must be exerted to bring the peace process back on track towards the achievement of a just, comprehensive and lasting peace in the region and the achievement of tangible results towards the improvement of the situation of Palestinian women and their families;

3. *Reaffirms* that the Israeli occupation remains a major obstacle for Palestinian women with regard to their advancement, self-reliance and integration into the development planning of their society;

4. *Demands* that Israel, the occupying Power, comply fully with the provisions and principles of the Universal Declaration of Human Rights, the Regulations annexed to The Hague Convention IV, of 18 October 1907, and the Geneva Convention relative to the Protection of Civilian Persons in Time of War, of 12 August

1949, in order to protect the rights of Palestinian women and their families;

5. *Calls upon* Israel to facilitate the return of all refugee and displaced Palestinian women and children to their homes and properties in the Occupied Palestinian Territory, in compliance with the relevant United Nations resolutions;

6. *Urges* Member States, financial organizations of the United Nations system, non-governmental organizations and other relevant institutions to intensify their efforts to provide financial and technical assistance to Palestinian women for the creation of projects responding to their needs, especially during the transitional period;

7. *Requests* the Commission on the Status of Women to continue to monitor and take action with regard to the implementation of the Nairobi Forward-looking Strategies for the Advancement of Women, in particular paragraph 260 concerning Palestinian women and children, and the Beijing Platform for Action;

8. *Requests* the Secretary-General to continue to review the situation and to assist Palestinian women by all available means and to submit to the Commission on the Status of Women at its forty-fourth session a report on the progress made in the implementation of the present resolution.

ROLL-CALL VOTE IN COUNCIL AS FOLLOWS:

In favour: Algeria, Belarus, Belgium, Bolivia, Brazil, Bulgaria, Chile, China, Colombia, Comoros, Cuba, Czech Republic, Denmark, El Salvador, France, Germany, Honduras, Indonesia, Italy, Latvia, Mauritius, Mexico, Morocco, Mozambique, Pakistan, Poland, Russian Federation, Rwanda, Spain, Syrian Arab Republic, Turkey, United Kingdom, Venezuela, Viet Nam.

Against: United States.

Abstaining: Canada, Japan, New Zealand, Norway.

Issues related to Palestine

General aspects

The General Assembly continued to consider the question of Palestine in 1999. Having discussed the annual report of the Committee on the Exercise of the Inalienable Rights of the Palestinian People (Committee on Palestinian Rights) [A/54/35], the Assembly adopted four resolutions, reaffirming, among other things, the necessity of achieving a peaceful settlement of the Palestine question—the core of the Arab-Israeli conflict—and stressing the need for the realization of the inalienable rights of the Palestinians, primarily the right to self-determination, for Israeli withdrawal from the Palestinian territory occupied since 1967 and for resolving the problem of the Palestine refugees.

In commemoration of the International Day of Solidarity with the Palestinian People, celebrated annually on 29 November, in accordance with Assembly resolution 32/40 B [YUN 1977, p. 304], the Committee held a solemn meeting and other activities. Under the Committee's auspices, an exhibit entitled "Follow the Star: Images from the Palestinian City of Bethlehem at the New Millennium" was presented by the Permanent Observer Mission of Palestine.

Report of Secretary-General. In an October report on the question of Palestine [A/54/457-S/1999/1050], the Secretary-General made observations on the Middle East peace process (see p. 401).

By a 28 July note verbale, the Secretary-General sought the positions of the Governments of Egypt, Israel, Jordan, Lebanon and the Syrian Arab Republic, as well as the PLO, regarding steps taken by them to implement the relevant provisions of resolution 53/42 [YUN 1998, p. 445]. As at 6 October, only Jordan and the PLO had responded.

Jordan stated that it was pursuing implementation of the provisions of the 1994 Jordanian-Israeli Treaty of Peace [YUN 1994, p. 614] and the agreements to which it gave rise. Jordan had also made use of its relations and contacts with all the parties to advance the negotiation process on the Palestinian-Israeli track. It was of the view that the outcome of the May 1999 Israeli elections and the assumption of office by the new Government constituted a plebiscite in which Israeli society voted in favour of peace. The new Government was urged to take decisive steps to honour the agreements and commitments that had been entered into and, in particular, to implement the 1998 Wye River Memorandum [YUN 1998, p. 424] and to resume negotiations on the Syrian and Lebanese tracks from the point at which they were suspended.

The PLO said that since the adoption of resolution 53/42, little progress was made in the implementation of the agreements reached; the situation on the ground, including the economic and living conditions of the Palestinian people, continued to deteriorate; and tension had increased in the region as a whole. However, with the new Israeli Government, the two parties, in September 1999, succeeded in reaching the Sharm el-Sheikh Memorandum. Initial steps in the implementation of the Memorandum had already begun. Moreover, the parties had agreed to reach the final settlement within a year from the signing of the Memorandum. The Palestinian side believed that the international community, represented by the General Assembly, had to uphold its positions related to the inalienable rights of the Palestinian people and should maintain its positions related to the elements of the final settlement (permanent status issues), including Jerusalem, settlements and refugees.

The PLO welcomed the work done by UNRWA and hoped that the United Nations would contribute to the efforts being undertaken to help push the peace process forward. For a peaceful settlement of the Palestine question to be achieved within the framework of the current peace process, it was necessary to respect the principle of the return of land for peace and the implementation of Council resolutions 242(1967) [YUN 1967, p. 257] and 338(1973) [YUN 1973, p. 213].

The Secretary-General observed that the signing of the Sharm el-Sheikh Memorandum brought with it cautious optimism that the Middle East peace process had been brought back on track. While the issues that remained to be resolved were difficult, five decades of conflict and unease should at least be brought to an end. It was hoped that progress on the Israeli-Palestinian track would soon lead to movement in the Syrian and Lebanese tracks so that peace, security and stability might be achieved for all peoples in the region.

Strengthening UN presence in the Middle East

On 10 September [S/1999/983], the Secretary-General informed the Security Council President of his intention to appoint Terje Roed-Larsen (Norway) as the new United Nations Special Coordinator for the Middle East Peace Process and his Personal Representative to the PLO and the Palestinian Authority (PA) as at 1 October 1999, replacing Chinmaya R. Gharekhan (India). The functions assigned to the new UN Special Coordinator took into account the resumption of Israeli-Palestinian negotiations and the prospect for renewed talks in other bilateral tracks. The Special Coordinator would act as a UN focal point on the ground, enabling the United Nations to respond in an integrated and coordinated manner to requests for assistance. On 16 September [S/1999/984], the Council took note of the Secretary-General's intention.

By a 9 November letter to the Council President [S/1999/1226], the Secretary-General said that the Prime Minister of Israel and the PLO Chairman, meeting in Oslo, Norway, on 1 and 2 November, had agreed that Israeli and Palestinian negotiating teams would start final status talks in Ramallah on 9 November, and that a deadline for a framework agreement would be set for 15 February 2000, prior to a final agreement to be reached by September 2000. With the Middle East peace process entering a new phase, the United Nations had to ensure that it was in a position to respond quickly and effectively to any requests from the parties as they made progress in their bilateral and multilateral negotiations. The Secretary-General had therefore decided that the United Nations should establish a unified structure in the region, with a clearly recognized focal point for the Organization's contributions to the implementation of the peace agreements and with overall responsibility for enhancing UN assistance. In that connection, the Secretary-General had asked the Special Coordinator to reconfigure the existing office based in Gaza, bearing in mind that he would likely require additional resources. On 8 December [S/1999/1227], the Council took note of the request to the Special Coordinator.

In a December report to the Fifth (Administrative and Budgetary) Committee [A/C.5/54/40], the Secretary-General stated that those additional requirements were estimated at $3,755,800, which would be charged against the $86.2 million proposed for special political missions under section 3, Political affairs, of the proposed programme budget for the biennium 2000-2001, as approved by Assembly resolution 53/206 [YUN 1998, p. 1284]. As the activities fell under the programme of political affairs, it was also proposed that the existing resources in the proposed 2000-2001 programme budget related to the activities of the Office of the Special Coordinator should be transferred from section 5, Peacekeeping operations, to section 3.

The Advisory Committee on Administrative and Budgetary Questions (ACABQ), in a December report [A/54/7/Add.11], stated that it had no objection to the Secretary-General's proposal.

On 23 December, by **resolution 54/251, section VII**, the Assembly approved the charge of total requirements of $3,755,800 against the provisions proposed for special political missions under section 3 of the proposed 2000-2001 programme budget, and concurred that the related provisions for the Office of the Special Coordinator should be transferred from section 5 to section 3.

GENERAL ASSEMBLY ACTION

On 1 December [meeting 68], the General Assembly adopted **resolution 54/42** [draft: A/54/L.45 & Add.1] by recorded vote (149-3-2) [agenda item 44].

Peaceful settlement of the question of Palestine

The General Assembly,

Recalling its relevant resolutions, including resolutions adopted at the tenth emergency special session,

Recalling also the relevant Security Council resolutions, including resolutions 242(1967) of 22 November 1967 and 338(1973) of 22 October 1973,

Aware that it has been more than fifty years since the adoption of resolution 181(II) of 29 November 1947 and thirty-two years since the occupation of Palestinian territory, including Jerusalem, in 1967,

Having considered the report of the Secretary-General submitted pursuant to the request made in its resolution 53/42 of 2 December 1998,

Reaffirming the permanent responsibility of the United Nations with regard to the question of Palestine until the question is resolved in all its aspects,

Convinced that achieving a final and peaceful settlement of the question of Palestine, the core of the Arab-Israeli conflict, is imperative for the attainment of a comprehensive and lasting peace in the Middle East,

Aware that the principle of equal rights and self-determination of peoples is among the purposes and principles embodied in the Charter of the United Nations,

Affirming the principle of the inadmissibility of the acquisition of territory by war,

Affirming also the illegality of the Israeli settlements in the territory occupied since 1967 and of Israeli actions aimed at changing the status of Jerusalem,

Affirming once again the right of all States in the region to live in peace within secure and internationally recognized borders,

Recalling the mutual recognition between the Government of the State of Israel and the Palestine Liberation Organization, the representative of the Palestinian people, and the signing by the two parties of the Declaration of Principles on Interim Self-Government Arrangements in Washington, D.C., on 13 September 1993, as well as the subsequent implementation agreements, including the Israeli-Palestinian Interim Agreement on the West Bank and the Gaza Strip, signed in Washington, D.C., on 28 September 1995,

Recalling also the withdrawal of the Israeli army, which took place in the Gaza Strip and the Jericho area in 1995 in accordance with the agreements reached by the parties, and the initiation of the Palestinian Authority in those areas, as well as the subsequent redeployments of the Israeli army in the rest of the West Bank,

Noting with satisfaction the successful holding of the first Palestinian general elections,

Noting with satisfaction also the signing of the Memorandum at Sharm el-Sheikh, Egypt, on 4 September 1999,

Noting the appointment by the Secretary-General of the United Nations Special Coordinator for the Middle East Peace Process and Personal Representative of the Secretary-General to the Palestine Liberation Organization and the Palestinian Authority, and its positive contribution,

Welcoming the convening of the Conference to Support Middle East Peace in Washington, D.C., on 1 October 1993, as well as all follow-up meetings and the international mechanisms established to provide assistance to the Palestinian people, including the donor meeting held at Tokyo on 14 October 1999,

Expressing the hope that the Sharm el-Sheikh Memorandum will be fully implemented towards full compliance with the existing agreements and the conclusion of the final settlement by the agreed time of September 2000,

1. *Reaffirms* the necessity of achieving a peaceful settlement of the question of Palestine, the core of the Arab-Israeli conflict, in all its aspects;

2. *Expresses its full support* for the ongoing peace process which began in Madrid and the Declaration of Principles on Interim Self-Government Arrangements of 1993, as well as the subsequent implementation agreements, including the Israeli-Palestinian Interim Agreement on the West Bank and the Gaza Strip of 1995 and the Sharm el-Sheikh Memorandum of 1999, and expresses the hope that the process will lead to the establishment of a comprehensive, just and lasting peace in the Middle East;

3. *Stresses* the necessity for commitment to the principle of land for peace and the implementation of Security Council resolutions 242(1967) and 338(1973), which form the basis of the Middle East peace process, and the need for the immediate and scrupulous implementation of the agreements reached between the parties, including the redeployment of the Israeli forces from the West Bank, and takes note with satisfaction of the commencement of the negotiations on the final settlement;

4. *Calls upon* the concerned parties, the co-sponsors of the peace process and other interested parties, as well as the entire international community to exert all the necessary efforts and initiatives to ensure the continuity and success of the peace process and its conclusion by the time agreed upon;

5. *Stresses* the need for:

(a) The realization of the inalienable rights of the Palestinian people, primarily the right to self-determination;

(b) The withdrawal of Israel from the Palestinian territory occupied since 1967;

6. *Also stresses* the need for resolving the problem of the Palestine refugees in conformity with its resolution 194(III) of 11 December 1948;

7. *Urges* Member States to expedite the provision of economic and technical assistance to the Palestinian people during this critical period;

8. *Emphasizes* the importance for the United Nations to play a more active and expanded role in the current peace process and in the implementation of the Declaration of Principles;

9. *Requests* the Secretary-General to continue his efforts with the parties concerned, and in consultation with the Security Council, for the promotion of peace in the region and to submit progress reports on developments in this matter.

RECORDED VOTE ON RESOLUTION 54/42:

In favour: Afghanistan, Algeria, Andorra, Angola, Antigua and Barbuda, Argentina, Armenia, Australia, Austria, Azerbaijan, Bahamas, Bahrain, Bangladesh, Belarus, Belgium, Benin, Bhutan, Bolivia, Bosnia and Herzegovina, Botswana, Brazil, Brunei Darussalam, Bulgaria, Burkina Faso, Cambodia, Cameroon, Canada, Cape Verde, Chile, China, Colombia, Comoros, Congo, Côte d'Ivoire, Croatia, Cuba, Cyprus, Czech Republic, Democratic People's Republic of Korea, Denmark, Djibouti, Dominica, Ecuador, Egypt, El Salvador, Eritrea, Estonia, Ethiopia, Finland, France, Gabon, Georgia, Germany, Ghana, Greece, Grenada, Guatemala, Guinea, Guinea-Bissau, Guyana, Haiti, Honduras, Hungary, Iceland, India, Indonesia, Ireland, Italy, Jamaica, Japan, Jordan, Kenya, Kuwait, Lao People's Democratic Republic, Latvia, Lebanon, Libyan Arab Jamahiriya, Liechtenstein, Lithuania, Luxembourg, Madagascar, Malaysia, Maldives, Mali, Malta, Mauritius, Mexico, Monaco, Mongolia, Morocco, Mozambique, Myanmar, Namibia, Nepal, Netherlands, New Zealand, Nicaragua, Nigeria, Norway, Oman, Pakistan, Panama, Papua New Guinea, Paraguay, Peru, Philippines, Poland, Portugal, Qatar, Republic of Korea, Republic of Moldova, Romania, Russian Federation, Saint Lucia, Saint Vincent and the Grenadines, Samoa, San Marino, Saudi Arabia, Senegal, Sierra Leone, Singapore, Slovakia, Slovenia, Solomon Islands, South Africa, Spain, Sri Lanka, Sudan, Suriname, Swaziland, Sweden, Syrian Arab Republic, Tajikistan, Thailand, The former Yugoslav Republic of Macedonia, Togo, Trinidad and Tobago, Tunisia, Turkey, Ukraine, United Arab Emirates, United Kingdom, United Republic of Tanzania, Uruguay, Venezuela, Viet Nam, Yemen, Zambia, Zimbabwe.

Against: Israel, Marshall Islands, United States.

Abstaining: Micronesia, Uzbekistan.

Speaking before the vote, the United States said that the text laid out the position of one party to the negotiations and, by adopting it, the Assembly would seek inappropriately to interject its views into those negotiations. The draft complicated United States efforts and those of the parties themselves to achieve a settlement.

Israel stated that all diplomatic breakthroughs in the Middle East were arrived at exclusively through direct negotiations between the parties. The draft resolution sought to predetermine the issues to be resolved by those negotiations, and it both violated existing agreements and undermined the integrity and the foundations of the peace process.

Speaking after the vote, the Observer of Palestine expressed the hope that Israel would abandon its current policy and positions and start complying with requirements of international legitimacy.

By **decision 54/465** of 23 December, the Assembly decided that the agenda items entitled "Question of Palestine" and "The situation in the Middle East" remained for consideration during its resumed fifty-fourth (2000) session.

Committee on Palestinian Rights

As mandated by General Assembly resolution 53/39 [YUN 1998, p. 450], the Committee on Palestinian Rights, established in 1975 by Assembly resolution 3376(XXX) [YUN 1975, p. 248], continued to review the situation relating to the Palestine question, reported on it and made suggestions to the Assembly or the Security Council.

The Committee, having restructured its NGO programme, including its programme of meetings, held consultations with NGO representatives during the Bethlehem 2000 International Conference (Rome, Italy, 18-19 February 1999). A second consultation meeting was held in New York on 26 November.

In response to Assembly resolution 53/27 [YUN 1998, p. 451], the Committee organized, in cooperation with Italy and the Holy See, the Bethlehem 2000 International Conference, which was attended by many high-level participants, including representatives of different religious denominations and the UN Under-Secretary-General for Political Affairs. At the conclusion of the Conference, the participants adopted the Rome Declaration, in which they promoted the Bethlehem 2000 Project launched by the PA and highlighted the urgency of bringing economic recovery and prosperity to the Palestinian people. The participants also expressed the view that freedom of movement and unhindered access to Holy Places in Bethlehem by all religions and nationalities were essential to the city's revival. The Committee Chairman submitted a report [A/54/416] to the Secretary-General on the Conference, in which he noted that the UN system had taken an early lead in offering support to the Bethlehem 2000 Project. Since 1997, UNDP had initiated a wide range of infrastructure improvements and the development of the tourist sector in close coordination with the Municipality of Bethlehem. The World Bank and UNESCO had, through their active involvement in specific projects on the ground, strengthened the viability of the initiative.

The Committee continued to follow the Palestine-related activities of intergovernmental bodies, such as the Organization of African Unity, and participated in a meeting celebrating the fiftieth anniversary of the Pontifical Mission for Palestine (New York, 25 October). Through its Bureau, the Committee continued its cooperation on the question of Palestine with the EU. The Committee took part in the United Nations African Meeting in Support of the Inalienable Rights of the Palestinian People (Windhoek, Namibia, 20-22 April). The Windhoek Declaration, the meeting's final document, focused on the role of African States in supporting the inalienable rights of the Palestinian people, as well as the international community's action in promoting the Bethlehem 2000 Project. The Committee supported the United Nations International Meeting on the Convening of the Conference on Measures to Enforce the Fourth Geneva Convention in the Occupied Palestinian Territory, including Jerusalem (see p. 416). Following that meeting, a Committee delegation visited Gaza from 16 to 18 June. During the visit, the first for the Committee, the delegation met with the Chairman of the PLO Executive Committee and PA President, Mr. Arafat, as well as with other high-ranking Palestinian officials and UN agencies' representatives, and visited, among other places, a number of UNDP projects in Gaza City.

In its annual report to the Assembly [A/54/35], covering the period from 4 November 1998 to 12 November 1999, the Committee expressed its regret that, for the greater part of 1999, the peace process remained stalled. At the same time, the Committee was encouraged by a series of important developments that had a positive effect on the peace process, including the decisions of the Palestinian Central Council at its extraordinary session from 27 to 29 April. It was also hopeful that the new Israeli Government would honour its obligations vis-à-vis the Palestinian side under the Wye River Memorandum, restore the spirit of confidence between the two parties, re-engage in the peace negotiations without preconditions and move forward towards the stage of permanent status negotiations. In that connection, the Committee noted the beginning of the implementation of the Sharm el-Sheikh Memorandum in September and hoped that it would be completed in strict compliance with the agreed timetable.

The Committee supported the convening of the Conference of the High Contracting Parties to the Fourth Geneva Convention on Measures to Enforce the Convention in the Occupied Palestinian Territory, including Jerusalem (see p. 415).

In the year under review, the Committee continued to follow closely the situation on the ground, including the illegal Israeli settlement activities. In May, the Knesset Finance Committee allocated $3 million for infrastructure work in 32 settlements in the West Bank and Gaza Strip, beyond the borders of existing settlements. According to Israeli press reports, more than 20 per cent of all land slated by Israel's Ministry of Construction and Housing for marketing in 1999 was located in the occupied Palestinian territory, including East Jerusalem. In February, the Israeli Government had approved its 1999 budget, adding $38 million for settlement construction. In spite of the stated position of the new Israeli Government not to build new settlements, the Ministry of Construction and Housing had since July reportedly issued tenders for the construction of over 2,500 new residential units slated for settlements around Jerusalem.

Another feature of the settlement drive had been the "grab and settle" policy targeting hilltops in the various parts of the West Bank, as well as the construction of bypass roads to service those settlements. Some 42 new hilltop settlements had been established since the signing of the Wye River Memorandum. The Committee also reported that, in the course of the year, groups of extremist settlers continued in their attempts to occupy Palestinian land and property, harassed Palestinian civilians and often engaged in violent confrontations with them. For the first time since 1967, a civilian guard was established in June 1999 in the West Bank settlements, intended to operate independently from the Israel Defence Forces.

The Committee expressed concern at Israel's detention of some 2,000 Palestinians, 350 of whom were released in September and October, in accordance with the Sharm el-Sheikh Memorandum. However, having noted the delay in the implementation of the second stage of the prisoner release, the Committee hoped that the release would be implemented on time and in compliance with the Memorandum. The Committee also noted the decision of Israel's High Court of Justice in September, stipulating that Israel's General Security Service was not authorized to employ certain investigation and interrogation methods involving the use of physical pressure against detainees.

Although the Palestinian economy showed signs of a slight growth in real terms during the year under review, it continued to suffer from structural imbalance due to the occupation and over-reliance on the Israeli economy. Israeli restrictions on the movement of goods and labour between the West Bank and East Jerusalem and between the West Bank and the Gaza Strip and the protracted lack of agreement on the safe passage routes had a negative impact on the Palestinian economy. The economic situation in the Gaza Strip, in particular, remained of great concern.

The Committee viewed continued UN system assistance to the Palestinian people as an important support for the peace process, as well as a crucial contribution to the development of a sustainable Palestinian economy and to Palestinian institution- and nation-building. It called on the international donor community to step up its assistance to the Palestinian people and hoped that contributions pledged towards the development of the Palestinian economy would be disbursed in full and as a matter of highest priority. In that regard, the Committee noted the signing at an Ad Hoc Liaison Committee meeting (Tokyo, 15 October) of a tripartite action plan aimed at assisting the peace process and accelerating the disbursement of commitments, to expedite implementation of essential development projects. The Committee stressed the crucial role played by UNRWA in assisting Palestine refugees through the provision of relief and social services, in spite of the worsening financial constraints faced by the Agency.

In making its recommendations, the Committee emphasized that after more than five decades of suffering and dispossession, the Palestinian people had yet to see its aspirations for self-determination and statehood realized. Despite breakthroughs in the peace process, millions of Palestinians were still forced to live in refugee camps, while the territory under the PA's jurisdiction represented a disjointed multitude of enclaves surrounded by a dense net of settlements, which restricted the Palestinians' freedom of movement and severely affected their livelihood. The Committee was of the view that the adjustments made to its programme of meetings had made the programme more effective and focused and had played a useful role in heightening international awareness of the question of Palestine and in achieving wider recognition for the exercise by the Palestinian people of its inalienable rights. The Committee would continue to review and assess that programme to make it more effective and responsive to the evolving situation on the ground and in the peace process. In its programme for the next year, the Committee intended to focus on the inalienable rights of the Palestinian people, Palestinian nation- and institution-building, socio-economic development and permanent status issues.

GENERAL ASSEMBLY ACTION

On 1 December [meeting 68], the General Assembly adopted **resolution 54/39** [draft: A/54/L.42 & Add.1] by recorded vote (105-3-48) [agenda item 44].

Committee on the Exercise of the Inalienable Rights of the Palestinian People

The General Assembly,

Recalling its resolutions 181(II) of 29 November 1947, 194(III) of 11 December 1948, 3236(XXIX) of 22 November 1974, 3375(XXX) and 3376(XXX) of 10 November 1975, 31/20 of 24 November 1976, 32/40 A of 2 December 1977, 33/28 A and B of 7 December 1978, 34/65 A of 29 November 1979 and 34/65 C of 12 December 1979, ES-7/2 of 29 July 1980, 35/169 A and C of 15 December 1980, 36/120 A and C of 10 December 1981, ES-7/4 of 28 April 1982, 37/86 A of 10 December 1982, 38/58 A of 13 December 1983, 39/49 A of 11 December 1984, 40/96 A of 12 December 1985, 41/43 A of 2 December 1986, 42/66 A of 2 December 1987, 43/175 A of 15 December 1988, 44/41 A of 6 December 1989, 45/67 A of 6 December 1990, 46/74 A of 11 December 1991, 47/64 A of 11 December 1992, 48/158 A of 20 December 1993, 49/62 A of 14 December 1994, 50/84 A of 15 December 1995, 51/23 of 4 December 1996, 52/49 of 9 December 1997 and 53/39 of 2 December 1998,

Having considered the report of the Committee on the Exercise of the Inalienable Rights of the Palestinian People,

Recalling the signing of the Declaration of Principles on Interim Self-Government Arrangements, including its Annexes and Agreed Minutes, by the Government of the State of Israel and the Palestine Liberation Organization, the representative of the Palestinian people, in Washington, D.C., on 13 September 1993, as well as the subsequent implementation agreements, in particular the Israeli-Palestinian Interim Agreement on the West Bank and the Gaza Strip, signed in Washington, D.C., on 28 September 1995, and the Memorandum signed at Sharm el-Sheikh, Egypt, on 4 September 1999,

Reaffirming that the United Nations has a permanent responsibility with respect to the question of Palestine until the question is resolved in all its aspects in a satisfactory manner in accordance with international legitimacy,

1. *Expresses its appreciation* to the Committee on the Exercise of the Inalienable Rights of the Palestinian People for its efforts in performing the tasks assigned to it by the General Assembly;

2. *Considers* that the Committee can continue to make a valuable and positive contribution to international efforts to promote the Middle East peace process and the full implementation of the agreements reached and to mobilize international support for and assistance to the Palestinian people during the transitional period;

3. *Endorses* the conclusions and recommendations of the Committee contained in chapter VII of its report;

4. *Requests* the Committee to continue to keep under review the situation relating to the question of Palestine and to report and make suggestions to the General Assembly or the Security Council, as appropriate;

5. *Authorizes* the Committee to continue to exert all efforts to promote the exercise of the inalienable rights of the Palestinian people, to make such adjustments in its approved programme of work as it may consider appropriate and necessary in the light of developments, to give special emphasis to the need to mobilize support and assistance for the Palestinian people and to report thereon to the General Assembly at its fifty-fifth session and thereafter;

6. *Requests* the Committee to continue to extend its cooperation and support to Palestinian and other non-governmental organizations in order to mobilize international solidarity and support for the achievement by the Palestinian people of its inalienable rights and for a peaceful settlement of the question of Palestine, and to involve additional non-governmental organizations in its work;

7. *Requests* the United Nations Conciliation Commission for Palestine, established under General Assembly resolution 194(III), and other United Nations bodies associated with the question of Palestine to continue to cooperate fully with the Committee and to make available to it, at its request, the relevant information and documentation which they have at their disposal;

8. *Requests* the Secretary-General to circulate the report of the Committee to all the competent bodies of the United Nations, and urges them to take the necessary action, as appropriate;

9. *Also requests* the Secretary-General to continue to provide the Committee with all the necessary facilities for the performance of its tasks.

RECORDED VOTE ON RESOLUTION 54/39:

In favour: Afghanistan, Algeria, Angola, Antigua and Barbuda, Azerbaijan, Bahamas, Bahrain, Bangladesh, Belarus, Benin, Bhutan, Bolivia, Bosnia and Herzegovina, Botswana, Brazil, Brunei Darussalam, Cambodia, Cameroon, Cape Verde, Chile, China, Colombia, Comoros, Congo, Costa Rica, Côte d'Ivoire, Cuba, Cyprus, Democratic People's Republic of Korea, Djibouti, Dominica, Ecuador, Egypt, El Salvador, Eritrea, Ethiopia, Gabon, Ghana, Grenada, Guinea, Guinea-Bissau, Guyana, Haiti, Honduras, India, Indonesia, Iran, Jamaica, Jordan, Kenya, Kuwait, Lao People's Democratic Republic, Lebanon, Libyan Arab Jamahiriya, Madagascar, Malaysia, Maldives, Mali, Malta, Mauritius, Mexico, Mongolia, Morocco, Mozambique, Myanmar, Namibia, Nepal, Nicaragua, Nigeria, Oman, Pakistan, Panama, Papua New Guinea, Paraguay, Peru, Philippines, Qatar, Republic of Korea, Saint Lucia, Saudi Arabia, Senegal, Sierra Leone, Singapore, Solomon Islands, South Africa, Sri Lanka, Sudan, Suriname, Swaziland, Syrian Arab Republic, Tajikistan, Thailand, Togo, Trinidad and Tobago, Tunisia, Turkey, Ukraine, United Arab Emirates, United Republic of Tanzania, Uruguay, Venezuela, Viet Nam, Yemen, Zambia, Zimbabwe.

Against: Israel, Marshall Islands, United States.

Abstaining: Andorra, Argentina, Armenia, Australia, Austria, Belgium, Bulgaria, Canada, Croatia, Czech Republic, Denmark, Estonia, Finland, France, Georgia, Germany, Greece, Guatemala, Hungary, Iceland, Ireland, Italy, Japan, Kazakhstan, Latvia, Liechtenstein, Lithuania, Luxembourg, Micronesia, Monaco, Netherlands, New Zealand, Norway, Poland, Portugal, Republic of Moldova, Romania, Russian Federation, Saint Vincent and the Grenadines, Samoa, San Marino, Slovakia, Slovenia, Spain, Sweden, The former Yugoslav Republic of Macedonia, United Kingdom, Uzbekistan.

The United States said that the draft resolution did not take into consideration achievements that had occurred in the Middle East peace process: the safe passage route between Gaza and the West Bank was operating, the Gaza seaport had been approved, further redeployments had been made, additional prisoners had been released and the parties had begun talks on a framework agreement for permanent status. It added that the Assembly should be in the business of supporting that process of negotiation and should not be issuing one-sided criticism or authorizing wasteful expenditure for anachronistic committees and reports.

Israel stated that the Committee on Palestinian Rights, as well as the UN Secretariat Division for Palestinian Rights, since their inception, had obstructed dialogue and understanding through a pre-set, one-sided portrayal of the Arab-Israeli conflict. They had been engaged in activities which hindered progress towards achieving a peaceful, negotiated and mutually acceptable solution.

Finland, on behalf of the EU, said that important progress had been made in the Middle East peace process over the years and welcomed the signing of the Sharm el-Sheikh Memorandum and the resumption of permanent status negotiations. It regretted that the mandate of the two UN entities in charge of the agenda item "Question of Palestine", the Committee on Palestinian Rights and the Division for Palestinian Rights, did not take into account the spirit of the peace process. The EU, nevertheless, welcomed the ongoing dialogue with the Committee on Palestinian Rights and stated that it would continue that exchange of views with the particular aim of adapting the Committee's mandate to the spirit of the Madrid and Oslo accords.

Division for Palestinian Rights

Under the guidance of the Committee on Palestinian Rights, the Division for Palestinian Rights of the UN Secretariat continued to function as a centre of research, monitoring, preparation of studies, and collection and dissemination of information on all issues related to the Palestine question. The Division continued to respond to requests for information and to prepare and disseminate the following publications: a monthly bulletin covering action by the Committee, UN bodies and agencies, and intergovernmental organizations concerned with Palestine; a periodic bulletin entitled "Developments related to the Middle East peace process"; a monthly chronology of events relating to the question of Palestine, based on media reports and other sources; reports of meetings organized under the auspices of the Committee; a special bulletin on the observance of the International Day of Solidarity with the Palestinian People (29 November); and an annual compilation of relevant General Assembly and Security Council resolutions, decisions and statements.

The Committee, in its annual report [A/54/35], noted that the Division had prepared publications for a number of related meetings and activities and, in cooperation with relevant technical services of the UN Secretariat, had continued to develop the electronic United Nations Information System on the Question of Palestine (UNISPAL), as mandated by Assembly resolution 46/74 B [YUN 1991, p. 228]. The Division also coordinated and supervised the electronic conversion of the records of the United Nations Conciliation Commission for Palestine, in accordance with Assembly resolution 51/129 [YUN 1996, p. 423].

The Committee requested the Division to continue its publications programme and other activities, including the completion of its work on the UNISPAL collection and on the project for the modernization of the records of the Conciliation Commission. It also requested that the annual training programme for staff members of the PA be continued.

GENERAL ASSEMBLY ACTION

On 1 December [meeting 68], the General Assembly adopted **resolution 54/40** [draft: A/54/L.43 & Add.1] by recorded vote (107-3-47) [agenda item 44].

Division for Palestinian Rights of the Secretariat

The General Assembly,

Having considered the report of the Committee on the Exercise of the Inalienable Rights of the Palestinian People,

Taking note in particular of the relevant information contained in chapter V.B of that report,

Recalling its resolutions 32/40 B of 2 December 1977, 33/28 C of 7 December 1978, 34/65 D of 12 December 1979, 35/169 D of 15 December 1980, 36/120 B of 10 December 1981, 37/86 B of 10 December 1982, 38/58 B of 13 December 1983, 39/49 B of 11 December 1984, 40/96 B of 12 December 1985, 41/43 B of 2 December 1986, 42/66 B of 2 December 1987, 43/175 B of 15 December 1988, 44/41 B of 6 December 1989, 45/67 B of 6 December 1990, 46/74 B of 11 December 1991, 47/64 B of 11 December 1992, 48/158 B of 20 December 1993, 49/62 B of 14 December 1994, 50/84 B of 15 December 1995, 51/24 of 4 December 1996, 52/50 of 9 December 1997 and 53/40 of 2 December 1998,

1. *Notes with appreciation* the action taken by the Secretary-General in compliance with its resolution 53/40;

2. *Considers* that the Division for Palestinian Rights of the Secretariat continues to make a useful and constructive contribution;

3. *Requests* the Secretary-General to continue to provide the Division with the necessary resources and to ensure that it continues to carry out its programme of

work as detailed in the relevant earlier resolutions, in consultation with the Committee on the Exercise of the Inalienable Rights of the Palestinian People and under its guidance, including, in particular, the organization of meetings in various regions with the participation of all sectors of the international community, the further development and expansion of the documents collection of the United Nations Information System on the Question of Palestine, the preparation and widest possible dissemination of publications and information materials on various aspects of the question of Palestine, the provision of assistance in completing the project on the modernization of the records of the United Nations Conciliation Commission for Palestine and the provision of the annual training programme for staff of the Palestinian Authority;

4. *Also requests* the Secretary-General to ensure the continued cooperation of the Department of Public Information and other units of the Secretariat in enabling the Division to perform its tasks and in covering adequately the various aspects of the question of Palestine;

5. *Invites* all Governments and organizations to extend their cooperation to the Committee and the Division in the performance of their tasks;

6. *Notes with appreciation* the action taken by Member States to observe annually on 29 November the International Day of Solidarity with the Palestinian People, requests them to continue to give the widest possible publicity to the observance, and requests the Committee and the Division to continue to organize, as part of the observance of the Day of Solidarity, an annual exhibit on Palestinian rights in cooperation with the Permanent Observer Mission of Palestine to the United Nations.

RECORDED VOTE ON RESOLUTION 54/40:

In favour: Afghanistan, Algeria, Angola, Antigua and Barbuda, Azerbaijan, Bahamas, Bahrain, Bangladesh, Belarus, Benin, Bhutan, Bolivia, Bosnia and Herzegovina, Botswana, Brazil, Brunei Darussalam, Burkina Faso, Cambodia, Cameroon, Cape Verde, Chile, China, Colombia, Comoros, Congo, Costa Rica, Côte d'Ivoire, Cuba, Cyprus, Democratic People's Republic of Korea, Djibouti, Dominica, Ecuador, Egypt, El Salvador, Eritrea, Ethiopia, Gabon, Ghana, Grenada, Guatemala, Guinea, Guinea-Bissau, Guyana, Haiti, Honduras, India, Indonesia, Iran, Jamaica, Jordan, Kenya, Kuwait, Lao People's Democratic Republic, Lebanon, Libyan Arab Jamahiriya, Madagascar, Malaysia, Maldives, Mali, Malta, Mauritius, Mexico, Mongolia, Morocco, Mozambique, Myanmar, Namibia, Nepal, Nicaragua, Nigeria, Oman, Pakistan, Panama, Papua New Guinea, Paraguay, Peru, Philippines, Qatar, Republic of Korea, Saint Lucia, Saudi Arabia, Senegal, Sierra Leone, Singapore, Solomon Islands, South Africa, Sri Lanka, Sudan, Suriname, Swaziland, Syrian Arab Republic, Tajikistan, Thailand, Togo, Trinidad and Tobago, Tunisia, Turkey, Ukraine, United Arab Emirates, United Republic of Tanzania, Uruguay, Venezuela, Viet Nam, Yemen, Zambia, Zimbabwe.

Against: Israel, Marshall Islands, United States.

Abstaining: Andorra, Argentina, Armenia, Australia, Austria, Belgium, Bulgaria, Canada, Croatia, Czech Republic, Denmark, Estonia, Finland, France, Georgia, Germany, Greece, Hungary, Iceland, Ireland, Italy, Japan, Kazakhstan, Latvia, Liechtenstein, Lithuania, Luxembourg, Micronesia, Monaco, Netherlands, New Zealand, Norway, Poland, Portugal, Republic of Moldova, Romania, Russian Federation, Saint Vincent and the Grenadines, Samoa, San Marino, Slovakia, Slovenia, Spain, Sweden, The former Yugoslav Republic of Macedonia, United Kingdom, Uzbekistan.

Special information programme

As requested in General Assembly resolution 53/41 [YUN 1998, p. 453], the UN Department of Public Information (DPI) in 1999 continued its special information programme on the question of Palestine, which included the convening of an international encounter on the theme "Prospects for Peace" (Madrid, Spain, 23-24 March) and the organization of a training programme for Palestinian broadcasters and journalists at UN Headquarters.

The DPI Public Inquiries Unit responded to 33 queries from the public on the question of Palestine, while the Dissemination and Communications Unit distributed material in hard copy and by electronic mail. DPI also provided press coverage of all meetings held at UN Headquarters, including those of the Committee on Palestinian Rights, as well as coverage of conferences and meetings held under the auspices of the Committee in Rome, Windhoek and Cairo. The quarterly publication *UN Chronicle* continued its coverage of the Palestine question, including articles on the establishment, 50 years earlier, of the United Nations Truce Supervision Organization and on the Bethlehem 2000 Project. The Radio and Central News Service covered all aspects of the Palestine question in daily news bulletins and current affairs radio programmes in various languages for regional and worldwide dissemination.

As in previous years, DPI cooperated in the media promotion of the International Day of Solidarity with the Palestinian People through extensive print and electronic media coverage. UN information centres (UNICs) organized briefings, media campaigns, press conferences, interviews, lectures, seminars and television programmes on the International Day. Also, throughout the year, many UNICs dealt with the Palestine question and organized special outreach activities related to the issue.

GENERAL ASSEMBLY ACTION

On 1 December [meeting 68], the General Assembly adopted **resolution 54/41** [draft: A/54/L.44 & Add.1] by recorded vote (151-3-2) [agenda item 44].

Special information programme on the question of Palestine of the Department of Public Information of the Secretariat

The General Assembly,

Having considered the report of the Committee on the Exercise of the Inalienable Rights of the Palestinian People,

Taking note in particular of the information contained in chapter VI of that report,

Recalling its resolution 53/41 of 2 December 1998,

Convinced that the worldwide dissemination of accurate and comprehensive information and the role of non-governmental organizations and institutions remain of vital importance in heightening awareness of and support for the inalienable rights of the Palestinian people,

Aware of the Declaration of Principles on Interim Self-Government Arrangements signed by the Government of the State of Israel and the Palestine Liberation Organization in Washington, D.C., on 13 September

1993, and of the subsequent implementation agreements, in particular the Israeli-Palestinian Interim Agreement on the West Bank and the Gaza Strip signed in Washington, D.C., on 28 September 1995, and the Sharm el-Sheikh Memorandum of 4 September 1999, and their positive implications,

1. *Notes with appreciation* the action taken by the Department of Public Information of the Secretariat in compliance with resolution 53/41;

2. *Considers* that the special information programme on the question of Palestine of the Department is very useful in raising the awareness of the international community concerning the question of Palestine and the situation in the Middle East in general, including the achievements of the peace process, and that the programme is contributing effectively to an atmosphere conducive to dialogue and supportive of the peace process;

3. *Requests* the Department, in full cooperation and coordination with the Committee on the Exercise of the Inalienable Rights of the Palestinian People, to continue, with the necessary flexibility as may be required by developments affecting the question of Palestine, its special information programme for the biennium 2000-2001, in particular:

(a) To disseminate information on all the activities of the United Nations system relating to the question of Palestine, including reports on the work carried out by the relevant United Nations organizations;

(b) To continue to issue and update publications on the various aspects of the question of Palestine in all fields, including materials concerning the recent developments in that regard, in particular the prospects for peace;

(c) To expand its collection of audio-visual material on the question of Palestine and to continue the production of such material, including the updating of the exhibit in the Secretariat;

(d) To organize and promote fact-finding news missions for journalists to the area, including the territories under the jurisdiction of the Palestinian Authority and the occupied territories;

(e) To organize international, regional and national seminars or encounters for journalists, aiming in particular at sensitizing public opinion to the question of Palestine;

(f) To continue to provide assistance to the Palestinian people in the field of media development, in particular to strengthen the training programme for Palestinian broadcasters and journalists initiated in 1995;

4. *Requests* the Department of Public Information to promote the Bethlehem 2000 Project, within existing resources and until the Bethlehem 2000 commemoration comes to a close, including the preparation and dissemination of publications, audio-visual material and the establishment of a "Bethlehem 2000" site on the United Nations Internet home page.

RECORDED VOTE ON RESOLUTION 54/41:

In favour: Afghanistan, Algeria, Andorra, Angola, Antigua and Barbuda, Argentina, Australia, Austria, Azerbaijan, Bahamas, Bahrain, Bangladesh, Belarus, Belgium, Benin, Bhutan, Bolivia, Bosnia and Herzegovina, Botswana, Brazil, Brunei Darussalam, Bulgaria, Burkina Faso, Cambodia, Cameroon, Canada, Cape Verde, Chile, China, Colombia, Comoros, Congo, Costa Rica, Côte d'Ivoire, Croatia, Cuba, Cyprus, Czech Republic, Democratic People's Republic of Korea, Denmark, Djibouti, Dominica, Ecuador, Egypt, El Salvador, Eritrea, Estonia, Ethiopia, Finland, France, Gabon, Georgia, Germany, Ghana, Greece, Grenada, Guatemala, Guinea, Guinea-Bissau, Guyana, Haiti, Honduras, Hungary, Iceland, India, Indonesia, Iran, Ireland, Italy, Jamaica, Japan, Jordan, Kazakhstan, Kenya, Kuwait, Lao People's Democratic Republic, Latvia, Lebanon, Libyan Arab Jamahiriya, Liechtenstein, Lithuania, Luxembourg, Madagascar, Malaysia, Maldives, Mali, Malta, Mauritius, Mexico, Monaco, Mongolia, Morocco, Mozambique, Myanmar, Namibia, Nepal, Netherlands, New Zealand, Nicaragua, Nigeria, Norway, Oman, Pakistan, Panama, Papua New Guinea, Paraguay, Peru, Philippines, Poland, Portugal, Qatar, Republic of Korea, Republic of Moldova, Romania, Russian Federation, Saint Lucia, Saint Vincent and the Grenadines, Samoa, San Marino, Saudi Arabia, Senegal, Sierra Leone, Singapore, Slovakia, Slovenia, Solomon Islands, South Africa, Spain, Sri Lanka, Sudan, Suriname, Swaziland, Sweden, Syrian Arab Republic, Tajikistan, Thailand, The former Yugoslav Republic of Macedonia, Togo, Trinidad and Tobago, Tunisia, Turkey, Ukraine, United Arab Emirates, United Kingdom, United Republic of Tanzania, Uruguay, Venezuela, Viet Nam, Yemen, Zambia, Zimbabwe.

Against: Israel, Marshall Islands, United States.

Abstaining: Micronesia, Uzbekistan.

Assistance to Palestinians

UN activities

Report of Secretary-General. In a July report [A/54/134-E/1999/85], the Secretary-General described UN assistance to the Palestinian people between June 1998 and May 1999, assessed ongoing programmes and needs still unmet and presented proposals for additional assistance.

Throughout the reporting period, the UN Special Coordinator in the Occupied Territories focused on ensuring better coordination between the relevant PA institutions and UN agencies, as well as the donor community; strengthening the rule of law and other institution-building programmes through better-targeted technical assistance; monitoring and documenting economic and social conditions in the occupied Palestinian territory and providing periodic analyses on those aspects and on specific issues relevant to the development effort; providing logistic and other assistance to the PA in the preparation of the Palestinian Development Plan, 1999-2003; and encouraging expeditious donor disbursements to facilitate its implementation. The Plan, which represented the PA's commitment to developing national capacity in medium-term development planning and in the implementation of development projects, was presented to the donor community at the sixth meeting of the Consultative Group for the West Bank and Gaza, convened by the World Bank (Paris, 4-5 February 1999). The Plan included over 170 projects with which the United Nations was associated that had a total value of about $286 million. Both in numerical and value terms, that amount represented an increase over the previous Plan [YUN 1998, p. 454], underscoring the deepening commitment of the UN system to the socio-economic development of the occupied Palestinian territory.

As part of his efforts to improve UN coordination, the Special Coordinator convened the fifth UN inter-agency meeting (Gaza, 7-8 October

1998), which assessed the role and contribution of UN agencies to Palestinian development. As in previous years, the meeting provided a forum for finalizing the document entitled "The United Nations and the Palestinian Development Plan", which surveyed some salient features of that relationship. The UN presence in the occupied Palestinian territory had increased from three organizations in 1993 to 13 in 1999, and an additional 16 UN organizations were providing the PA with technical assistance and expertise.

The Conference to Support Middle East Peace and Development (Washington, D.C., 30 November 1998) reaffirmed the international community's political commitment to the Middle East peace process and to continue the economic assistance required to give it momentum. Conference participants announced pledges totalling $3.36 billion to be disbursed over a two- to five-year period.

The Special Coordinator also gave an update on assistance provided to the Palestinian people in the occupied territories during the reporting period by UN departments, agencies and programmes. The update included information from the Department of Economic and Social Affairs, ESCWA, the International Atomic Energy Agency (IAEA), the International Civil Aviation Organization (ICAO), the International Fund for Agricultural Development (IFAD), ILO, the International Maritime Organization (IMO), the International Trade Centre, the International Telecommunication Union (ITU), the United Nations Centre for Human Settlements (Habitat), the Office of the United Nations High Commissioner for Human Rights, the United Nations Conference on Trade and Development (UNCTAD), the United Nations International Drug Control Programme, UNDP, UNESCO, UNFPA, UNICEF, the United Nations Development Fund for Women (UNIFEM), the United Nations Institute for Training and Research (UNITAR), UNRWA, the Office of the Special Coordinator, the World Food Programme (WFP) and WHO.

Living conditions in the West Bank and Gaza Strip

The Palestinian Ministry of Finance and the International Monetary Fund estimated real gross domestic product and gross national product growth rates of 3.0 and 5.5 per cent, respectively for 1998, as well as a marginal rise in annual per capita income levels in the occupied Palestinian territory for the first time since the beginning of the interim period in 1994. Such growth was mainly due to fewer comprehensive closures imposed by the Israeli authorities on the occupied territory. In fact, closures affected 5.2 per cent of working days in 1998, compared with 20.5 per cent of such days in 1997. That resulted in a 16.9 per cent increase in the number of Palestinian workers employed in Israel in 1998 and generally improved trade flows, as the nominal value of registered trade between Israel and the occupied Palestinian territory rose by 9.3 per cent.

Moderate growth was reported in the private investment sector. Construction licensing activity grew by 4.6 per cent in 1998, compared to over 13 per cent the previous year. Overall, new company registrations climbed by 12.6 per cent. While donor disbursements declined by 27.4 per cent in 1998 to a reported level of $399.8 million, total public investment spending rose by an estimated 11 per cent to $215 million. Public investment absorbed a higher share of total disbursement in 1998, in part because the PA achieved a balanced recurrent budget for the first time.

The labour force increased by an estimated 5.9 per cent to about 585,000 persons in 1998, and the number of fully employed persons increased by 18.9 per cent to 456,240. The standard unemployment rate fell from 20.9 per cent in 1997 to 15.6 per cent in 1998, the lowest rate recorded since 1995. An estimated 58,450 new jobs for Palestinian workers were created in 1998, a 13.4 per cent increase over the preceding year, with employment growth in every economic branch. However, women's labour force participation fell to 11.7 per cent of working-age women, as compared with 12.3 per cent in 1997. Under the impact of the sharp depreciation of the new shekel/United States dollar exchange rate in late 1998, the rate of inflation in the consumer price index rose 9.7 per cent, compared with 6.1 per ent in 1997. Food prices increased faster than the general price level, placing an additional burden on household budgets.

GENERAL ASSEMBLY ACTION

On 15 December [meeting 80], the General Assembly adopted **resolution 54/116** [draft: A/54/L.52 & Add.1] without vote [agenda item 20 *(e)*].

Assistance to the Palestinian people

The General Assembly,

Recalling its resolution 53/89 of 7 December 1998,

Recalling also previous resolutions on the question,

Welcoming the signing of the Declaration of Principles on Interim Self-Government Arrangements of 1993 between the Government of the State of Israel and the Palestine Liberation Organization, the representative of the Palestinian people, as well as the signing of the subsequent implementation agreements, including the Interim Agreement on the West Bank and the Gaza Strip of 1995, and the recent signing of the Sharm el-Sheikh Memorandum on 4 September 1999,

Gravely concerned about the difficult economic and employment conditions facing the Palestinian people throughout the occupied territory,

Conscious of the urgent need for improvement in the economic and social infrastructure of the occupied territory and the living conditions of the Palestinian people,

Aware that development is difficult under occupation and best promoted in circumstances of peace and stability,

Noting the great economic and social challenges facing the Palestinian people and their leadership,

Conscious of the urgent necessity for international assistance to the Palestinian people, taking into account the Palestinian priorities,

Noting the convening of the United Nations Seminar on Assistance to the Palestinian People, entitled "Facing the challenges of the year 2000: promoting Palestinian national development", held at Cairo on 27 and 28 April 1998,

Stressing the need for the full engagement of the United Nations in the process of building Palestinian institutions and in providing broad assistance to the Palestinian people, including assistance in the fields of elections, police training and public administration,

Noting the appointment by the Secretary-General of the United Nations Special Coordinator for the Middle East Peace Process and Personal Representative of the Secretary-General to the Palestine Liberation Organization and the Palestinian Authority,

Welcoming the results of the Conference to Support Middle East Peace, convened in Washington, D.C., on 1 October 1993, and the establishment of the Ad Hoc Liaison Committee and the work being done by the World Bank as its secretariat, as well as the establishment of the Consultative Group,

Welcoming also the work of the Joint Liaison Committee, which provides a forum in which economic policy and practical matters related to donor assistance are discussed with the Palestinian Authority,

Welcoming further the results of the Conference to Support Middle East Peace and Development, held in Washington, D.C., on 30 November 1998, and expressing appreciation for the pledges of the international donor community,

Welcoming the meeting of the Consultative Group at Frankfurt, Germany, on 4 and 5 February 1999, in particular the pledges of the international donor community and the presentation of the Palestinian Development Plan for the years 1999-2003,

Welcoming also the meeting of the Ad Hoc Liaison Committee held at Tokyo on 14 and 15 October 1999, the signing of the updated Tripartite Action Plan, and the proposal to hold the next meeting at Lisbon,

Having considered the report of the Secretary-General,

1. *Takes note* of the report of the Secretary-General;

2. *Expresses its appreciation* to the Secretary-General for his rapid response and efforts regarding assistance to the Palestinian people;

3. *Expresses its appreciation* to the Member States, United Nations bodies and intergovernmental, regional and non-governmental organizations that have provided and continue to provide assistance to the Palestinian people;

4. *Stresses* the importance of the work of the United Nations Special Coordinator for the Middle East Peace Process and Personal Representative of the Secretary-General to the Palestine Liberation Organization and the Palestinian Authority and of the steps taken under the auspices of the Secretary-General to ensure the achievement of a coordinated mechanism for United Nations activities throughout the occupied territories;

5. *Urges* Member States, international financial institutions of the United Nations system, intergovernmental and non-governmental organizations and regional and interregional organizations to extend, as rapidly and as generously as possible, economic and social assistance to the Palestinian people in close cooperation with the Palestine Liberation Organization and through official Palestinian institutions;

6. *Calls upon* relevant organizations and agencies of the United Nations system to intensify their assistance in response to the urgent needs of the Palestinian people in accordance with Palestinian priorities set forth by the Palestinian Authority, with emphasis on national execution and capacity-building;

7. *Urges* Member States to open their markets to exports of Palestinian products on the most favourable terms, consistent with appropriate trading rules, and to implement fully existing trade and cooperation agreements;

8. *Calls upon* the international donor community to expedite the delivery of pledged assistance to the Palestinian people to meet their urgent needs;

9. *Suggests* the convening in 2000 of a United Nations-sponsored seminar on the Palestinian economy;

10. *Requests* the Secretary-General to submit a report to the General Assembly at its fifty-fifth session, through the Economic and Social Council, on the implementation of the present resolution, containing:

(*a*) An assessment of the assistance actually received by the Palestinian people;

(*b*) An assessment of the needs still unmet and specific proposals for responding effectively to them;

11. *Decides* to include in the provisional agenda of its fifty-fifth session, under the item entitled "Strengthening of the coordination of humanitarian and disaster relief assistance of the United Nations, including special economic assistance", the sub-item entitled "Assistance to the Palestinian people".

UNRWA

In 1999, the revival of Middle East peace negotiations, amidst indications of a more vigorous pursuit of "final status" issues, which included the future of Palestinian refugees, affected the working environment of the United Nations Relief and Works Agency for Palestine Refugees in the Near East (UNRWA). Fifty years after its establishment by General Assembly resolution 302(IV) [YUN 1948-49, p. 211], the Agency was still providing vital education, health and relief and social services to a growing refugee population, but was facing increasing difficulty in mobilizing the financial resources to keep services at adequate levels.

By mid-1999, 3.62 million refugees were registered with UNRWA, an increase of 2.9 per cent over the 1998 figure of 3.52 million. The largest refugee population was registered in Jordan (1.5 million, or 41.4 per cent of the Agency-wide total), followed by the Gaza Strip (798,000, or 21.8 per cent), the West Bank (569,000, or 15.7 per cent), Lebanon (370,000, or 10 per cent) and the Syrian Arab Republic (374,000, or 10 per cent).

In his annual report on the work of the Agency (1 July 1998–30 June 1999) [A/54/13], the UNRWA Commissioner-General said that the reporting period was a time of challenges and some setbacks, but also of many achievements for the Agency. As it prepared to mark 50 years of operations, UNRWA could reflect on its significant contribution to educating new generations, maintaining the health of the Palestine refugee community and providing badly needed basic relief and social services to some of the poorest people in the region. The delivery of effective and efficient services remained UNRWA's top priority; by that measure, the Agency was successful during the reporting period, even though its financial difficulties seemed to overshadow its achievements.

The Palestine refugee community and host authorities in all fields of operation continued to express concern about the perceived reduction in UNRWA services. The Agency's financial difficulties were seen by many as politically motivated, signalling a weakening in the international community's commitment to the refugee issue, and a dereliction by UNRWA of its humanitarian duties. Austerity and other cost-reduction measures were rigorously maintained. Even with such measures in place and additional ad hoc contributions from donors, the Agency ended 1998 with a deficit and depleted cash and working capital reserves.

Advisory Commission. By a letter of 30 September to the Commissioner-General, included in his report [A/54/13], the Advisory Commission of UNRWA viewed the Agency's continuing difficult financial situation as extremely grave, for although some donors' annual contributions increased in absolute terms, UNRWA's resources were still constrained. The Commission noted with approval the Agency's decision to adjust and clarify its 2000-2001 budget format, which would hopefully increase transparency and improve programme management, and commended its continued commitment to internal restructuring. It also welcomed the findings contained in the report of the Office of Internal Oversight Services [A/54/367] on allegations of corruption at UNRWA's field office in Lebanon, which found no evidence of endemic corruption.

Peace Implementation Programme

In its sixth year of operation, UNRWA's Peace Implementation Programme (PIP) remained the main channel for project funding of activities associated with the Agency's education, health and relief and social services programmes, as well as income-generation. Since its inception in October 1993 [YUN 1993, p. 569], PIP had demonstrated the tangible benefits of the peace process by improving Palestine refugees' living conditions, creating employment opportunities and developing infrastructure. The latter focused on the construction and expansion of UNRWA facilities to meet the increasing demand for its services (especially in education), maintaining or upgrading existing facilities to adequate standards, and improving housing and environmental health conditions in camps. Against a background of insufficient funding for the Agency's regular programmes, PIP funds enabled UNRWA to meet some of the most pressing needs and helped to prevent a qualitative deterioration in programmes.

During the period under review, UNRWA received $7.8 million in pledges and contributions for PIP projects, a decline of $2.1 million or some 21 per cent in comparison to the $9.9 million received in its previous period. As at 30 June 1999, total pledges and contributions received over the life of the programme totalled $221.3 million. The number of projects funded under PIP as at that date was 347.

Between mid-1998 and mid-1999, with PIP funding, UNRWA completed construction of 10 schools, 39 additional classrooms, four specialized rooms (e.g., laboratories, libraries), two health centres, one health laboratory, one mother and child centre, two women's programme centres and three libraries at those centres, and two community rehabilitation centres. PIP funds also enabled the Agency to rehabilitate 334 shelters of special hardship families. Completed projects to improve camp infrastructure and services included a sewerage and drainage system for a refugee camp in Gaza; rehabilitation of a water supply system in Lebanon; construction of a central pharmacy, 11 water reservoirs and five latrines in refugee camps in Jordan; and upgrading a camp sewerage system and a mobile dental unit in Syria. Ongoing projects, as at mid-1999, included a feasibility study for sewerage and drainage in five refugee camps; reinstatement of stormwater drainage, roads and pathways; construction of a public health laboratory in the West Bank; several components of the sewerage and drainage scheme for the middle area camps in Gaza; a major sewerage and drainage project for eight refugee camps in Lebanon; and the construction of a polyclinic in Beirut. Other PIP-funded activities included a slow learners' programme in Jordan and Lebanon; integration of visually impaired children into the regular school system; care for the destitute aged; provision of prosthetic devices; and nurse training in Lebanon. PIP also helped to sustain regular Agency programmes by funding the routine maintenance of a number of schools in Gaza and the West Bank, the running costs of two health centres in Gaza and the cost of university scholarships for refugee students. Cash expenditure under PIP was $32 million between mid-1998 and mid-1999, excluding expenditures on the European Gaza Hospital project.

Lebanon appeal

Of the $11 million sought in additional contributions under the special emergency appeal, launched in July 1997 to support essential health, education, relief and social services activities for Palestine refugees in Lebanon, the Agency received $8.8 million and had expended $6.3 million by mid-1999. Ongoing projects included the construction of shelters and a secondary school; reconstruction of a health centre and an elementary/preparatory school; and the construction and operation of computer laboratories.

Major service areas

Education

During the 1998/99 school year, the 650 UNRWA schools across the region accommodated 458,716 pupils, mostly in the elementary and preparatory cycles, but also included 1,367 students at the three Agency secondary schools in Lebanon. Total enrolment increased by 2.6 per cent, or 11,448 pupils, over the 1997/98 school year. However, growth in enrolment was unevenly distributed, with rapid growth in the Gaza Strip (6 per cent), moderate growth in the West Bank and Lebanon (3.9 and 4.3 per cent, respectively), low growth in the Syrian Arab Republic (1.3 per cent) and negative growth in Jordan (-1.4 per cent). UNRWA's school system continued to maintain full gender balance, with 49.9 per cent of pupils being female. The education programme, which was run in cooperation with UNESCO, remained UNRWA's largest single area of activity, with the 13,915 education personnel representing more than two thirds of all Agency staff.

Financial constraints and steadily rising enrolment at UNRWA schools had obliged the Agency to continue hiring teachers on a contract basis at rates of pay lower than those of equivalent Agency posts, as well as on a daily-paid or temporary assistance basis in Jordan, Lebanon and Syria. The policy of operating schools on a double-shift basis (housing two schools in a single building) also continued.

The Agency's education infrastructure remained in need of major improvements. UNRWA sought to obtain funding for the improvement and expansion of its educational facilities and, between mid-1998 and mid-1999, it completed construction of four school buildings and 12 additional classrooms, upgraded five schools, and built seven toilet blocks, 12 water reservoirs and two canteens.

The eight UNRWA vocational and technical training centres had a total enrolment of 4,655 in the 1998/99 school year, an increase of 95 over the previous year. At the post-preparatory level, 22 two-year vocational training courses were offered to male trainees, and at the post-secondary level, 28 two-year technical/semi-professional courses were offered to male and female trainees in a variety of technical, paramedical and commercial skills. Women accounted for 30.5 per cent of all trainees and for 62.2 per cent of trainees in technical/semi-professional courses. In addition, at training centres in Jordan, Lebanon and the West Bank, 346 trainees were enrolled in 14 short-term courses, which included training in auto electrics, executive secretarial skills, building techniques, aluminium fabrication, numerical control systems in metal lathing, first aid, Hebrew and English language, computer software and technical drawing. The Agency also sponsored 25 Palestine refugee students in vocational training courses at private institutions in the West Bank, mainly with project funding.

The three branches of the Educational Sciences Faculty in Jordan and the West Bank continued to provide pre-service and in-service teacher training leading to a first university degree, as part of the process of upgrading the qualification of UNRWA teaching staff to meet revised standards set by the Government of Jordan and the PA. The Agency also provided in-service training to promote and improve the professional competence of its teachers, head-teachers and school supervisors, through the UNRWA/UNESCO Institute of Education. In 1998/99, the total number enrolled in such training was 1,119.

During the 1998/99 school year, UNRWA continued to contribute to a university scholarship programme through project funding. A total of 167 scholars graduated during the year, while the number of continuing scholars was 866, including 398 women.

Overall, the austerity measures in place since 1993 had restricted the education programme's ability to expand at a rate commensurate with growth in the beneficiary population. Financial constraints also curbed the Agency's efforts to keep up with education reforms introduced by the various host Governments, thereby widening the gap between their education systems and UNRWA's.

Health

UNRWA's health programme remained focused on comprehensive primary health care, including a full range of maternal and child health (MCH) and family planning services, school health services, health education and promotion activities, out-patient medical services, prevention and control of communicable diseases and non-communicable diseases, and specialist care, with emphasis on gynaecology and obstetrics, paediatrics and cardiology. Those services were provided through a network of 122 primary health-care facilities, including 89 health centres, 23 health points offering a wide range of health-care services on a part-time basis, and 10 MCH centres offering comprehensive family health services, backed up by basic services such as X-ray and laboratory facilities. During the reporting period, Agency outpatient facilities handled 5.4 million medical and 500,000 dental visits, as well as 1.1 million visits for nursing services.

The proposed health programme budget for the 1998-1999 biennium was $126 million. Owing to funding constraints, allocations had to be reduced below the 1996-1997 budget level, making average health expenditure per refugee a little more than $13.50 per year, a fraction of what other health-care providers in the area spent. Approximately 63 per cent of cash allocations to the health programme were devoted to the costs of 3,500 locally recruited health staff, who implemented all core programme activities. Workloads in UNRWA primary health-care facilities remained high, with an average of 100 patients seen by each doctor per day. WHO provided UNRWA with the services of the Agency's Director of Health and covered the cost of the four local posts of headquarters division chiefs.

Family health continued to be emphasized as an integral part of the Agency's regular health programme. Progress towards the development of a comprehensive maternal health and family planning strategy was reinforced through additional contributions under a three-year convention between UNRWA and the EU, which helped to meet staff costs, upgrade medical equipment in MCH clinics and procure contraceptive supplies.

UNRWA's health programme also sought to prevent and control communicable diseases. Special efforts were made to control vaccine-preventable diseases; prevent vector-borne diseases and newly emerging diseases, such as HIV/AIDS; control re-emerging infectious diseases, such as tuberculosis; and prevent and control other diseases, such as diabetes mellitus, hypertension, heart disease and cancer. As part of a WHO regional strategy, implemented in coordination with local health authorities and using poliomyelitis vaccines donated by UNICEF, the Agency immunized 214,115 refugee children under the age of five during two rounds of national immunization. UNRWA also joined with other health-care providers in the West Bank and Gaza in implementing the public health component of a brucellosis surveillance and control programme developed in 1997 by the PA, in cooperation with WHO and UNDP.

During the reporting period, UNRWA redefined its strategic approach to health education, integrating programmes within its health centres and within school educational activities. The youth-centred educational programme on the prevention of tobacco use resumed in 1998/99 and was expanded to include children in the sixth grade and above. With support from the Joint United Nations Programme on HIV/AIDS, the multisectoral school health education programme on the prevention of HIV/AIDS was maintained for schoolchildren in grades 9 and 10, and its scope was broadened to include UNRWA vocational and technical training centres, educational sciences faculties and women's programme centres.

The Agency provided assistance towards secondary care for Palestine refugees by partially reimbursing costs incurred for treatment at governmental or non-governmental hospitals or through contractual agreements with non-governmental or private hospitals. Secondary care was also provided directly at the Agency-run hospital in the West Bank. With project funding received mainly under PIP, UNRWA continued to rehabilitate or replace health facilities, which helped to improve service standards and patient flow.

More than 1.1 million Palestine refugees in 59 camps benefited from environmental health services provided by UNRWA, in cooperation with local municipalities, including sewage disposal, management of storm water run-off, provision of safe drinking water, collection and disposal of refuse, and control of insect and rodent infestation. The Agency continued to play an active role, particularly in the Gaza Strip, in planning and implementing large-scale projects to install sewerage, drainage and water networks in refugee camps.

UNRWA cooperated with the PA in the health sector and provided assistance to enhance the health infrastructure, including the implementation of a three-year maternal health and family planning project in Gaza. A close dialogue was maintained among UNRWA, the PA and the European Community to reach a common understanding on the commissioning and future operation of the European Gaza Hospital. The Agency cooperated with the PA and donors on the construction of a public health laboratory in the West Bank; the upgrading of UNRWA's Qalqilia Hospital in the West Bank; and improvements to environmental health infrastructure in the Gaza Strip. It also maintained close cooperation with health ministries in Jordan, Lebanon and Syria, including through the exchange of information, coordination of disease-control measures, and participation in national conferences and immunization campaigns.

Relief and social services

UNRWA assisted refugee families unable to meet basic needs for food, shelter and other essentials through food support, shelter rehabilitation, poverty alleviation initiatives (such as small loans for personal or business needs), higher hospitalization subsidies and preferential access to UNRWA training centres. The number of refugees in households meeting the stringent eligibility criteria—no male adult medically fit to earn an income and no other identifiable means of financial support above a defined threshold—increased by 2.3 per cent, from 195,616 in June 1998 to 200,078 a year later. The proportion of special hardship cases within the total registered refugee population decreased slightly, from 5.6 per cent to 5.5 per cent. The percentage of refugees enrolled in the programme continued to be highest in Lebanon (10.6 per cent) and the Gaza Strip (8.4 per cent) and lowest in Jordan (2.6 per cent). UNRWA's food support to 51,525 special hardship case families was a crucial safety net in areas subject to unexpected border closures or fluctuations in the price of commodities in local markets. However, the regular budget allocation for selective cash assistance, given to families who experienced distress as a result of emergency situations, remained frozen due to the Agency's continuing financial difficulties.

With extrabudgetary project funding, UNRWA rehabilitated 1,305 shelters of special hardship case families in 1998/99, compared with 505 in 1997/98. Shelter rehabilitation was carried out either on a self-help basis, with the Agency providing financial and technical assistance and beneficiary families arranging volunteer labour, or by small camp-based contractors, with the aim of creating employment within the local refugee community. Available resources for the programme continued to fall short of identified needs, especially in Lebanon, where a large number of special hardship case families lived in sub-standard shelters, and many families lived outside camps in terrible conditions.

Under its poverty alleviation programme, UNRWA assisted disadvantaged refugees, including women, youth and the physically and mentally disabled, to improve their socio-economic status. Soft loans and fully repayable loans for the establishment of micro-enterprises continued, and the number of grants increased from 58 in 1997/98 to 87 in 1998/99. The Agency increased cooperation with third-party partners in providing training in basic business skills to several centres and to families and social workers. A total of 1,526 participants benefited from the poverty alleviation programme, which was separate from the self-sustaining income-generating activities undertaken by the Agency in recent years (see next page).

Participation in UNRWA's community-based social development programmes for women, youth and persons with disabilities increased by 14.3 per cent, from 38,417 at mid-1998 to 43,918 at mid-1999. The focal point for the programmes was the network of 131 Agency-supported community centres, comprising 70 women's programmes centres, 27 youth activities centres and 34 community rehabilitation centres. Activities at women's centres included projects and training to establish income-generating micro-enterprises; lectures and workshops on issues of concern to women and the community, such as family health; training courses to enhance women's social development; and provision of support services for women, such as kindergartens and legal advice bureaux. Youth activities centres continued to offer sports and recreational and cultural activities to young men and women, while community rehabilitation centres focused on the rehabilitation and integration into schools and society of refugees with disabilities, as well as increasing public awareness of disability issues.

UNRWA's strategy for community-based organizations (CBOs) was to shift assistance away from direct financial and staff support towards skills training with a view to facilitating institution-building and self-sustainability in accordance with the five-year plan (1995-1999). The plan aimed to enhance and eventually achieve full administrative and financial sustainability for CBOs. The Agency provided technical assistance to develop the administrative structures of the centres, and continued to provide partial subsidies towards running costs until financial independence could be achieved.

Income generation

UNRWA's income-generation programme supported small and micro-enterprises within the refugee community by providing technical assistance, as well as capital investment and working capital through field-based revolving loan funds. The programme's objective was to create employment, generate income, reduce poverty and empower refugees, in particular women, through socio-economic growth.

The Agency's income-generation activities were concentrated in the Gaza Strip. During the reporting period, the programme achieved operational self-sufficiency. With 42 per cent of refugee camp dwellers and 51 per cent of the population of southern Gaza living below the poverty line, the programme continued to target formal business enterprises that had the capacity to provide jobs, as well as informal enterprises that could generate income for poor families. Credit to those target groups was provided through flexible collateral and guarantee mechanisms, including business plan-based lending and individual, group and cheque-guarantee methods. Although no additional donor funds were received, the number of loans disbursed increased from 6,193, valued at $7.3 million, in 1997/98, to 7,014 loans, valued at $8.3 million, in 1998/99. The income-generation programme in Gaza was composed of four subprogrammes: small-scale enterprise, which provided working capital and capital investment loans to new and established businesses in the industry and service sectors to promote job creation, exports and import substitution; solidarity group lending, which provided working capital loans solely to women micro-enterprise owners; micro-enterprise credit (MEC), which targeted the 20,432 micro-enterprises in Gaza; and small and micro-enterprise training, which contributed to employment generation and socio-economic development.

In the West Bank, small-scale enterprise lending methodology was restructured and the management information and loan-tracking system was improved and integrated with that in Gaza. By the end of June 1999, the programme had provided 197 loans valued at $2.5 million. The MEC subprogramme in the West Bank expanded rapidly through its Nablus branch office by concentrating on developing its credit delivery capacity. The programme was in the initial phase of opening two credit outreach units in the northern West Bank, where up to 28 per cent of the population lived below the poverty line. As at June 1999, MEC had provided 1,410 loans valued at $1.4 million and maintained an annual repayment rate of 96 per cent.

GENERAL ASSEMBLY ACTION

On 6 December [meeting 71], the General Assembly, on the recommendation of the Fourth Committee [A/54/575], adopted **resolution 54/69** by recorded vote (155-1-2) [agenda item 88].

Assistance to Palestine refugees

The General Assembly,

Recalling its resolution 53/46 of 3 December 1998 and all its previous resolutions on the question, including resolution 194(III) of 11 December 1948,

Taking note of the report of the Commissioner-General of the United Nations Relief and Works Agency for Palestine Refugees in the Near East covering the period from 1 July 1998 to 30 June 1999,

Welcoming the signature in Washington, D.C., on 13 September 1993 by the Government of the State of Israel and the Palestine Liberation Organization, the representative of the people of Palestine, of the Declaration of Principles on Interim Self-Government Arrangements and the subsequent implementation agreements, and also the signature of the Israeli-Palestinian Interim Agreement on the West Bank and the Gaza Strip in Washington, D.C., on 28 September 1995,

Welcoming also the signing of the Sharm el-Sheikh Memorandum on 4 September 1999,

Encouraging the Multilateral Working Group on Refugees of the Middle East peace process to continue its important work,

1. *Notes with regret* that repatriation or compensation of the refugees, as provided for in paragraph 11 of its resolution 194(III), has not yet been effected and that, therefore, the situation of the refugees continues to be a matter of concern;

2. *Also notes with regret* that the United Nations Conciliation Commission for Palestine has been unable to find a means of achieving progress in the implementation of paragraph 11 of General Assembly resolution 194(III), and requests the Commission to exert continued efforts towards the implementation of that paragraph and to report to the Assembly as appropriate, but no later than 1 September 2000;

3. *Expresses its thanks* to the Commissioner-General and to all the staff of the United Nations Relief and Works Agency for Palestine Refugees in the Near East, recognizing that the Agency is doing all it can within the limits of available resources, and also expresses its thanks to the specialized agencies and to private organizations for their valuable work in assisting refugees;

4. *Notes* the significant success of the Peace Implementation Programme of the Agency since the signing of the Declaration of Principles on Interim Self-Government Arrangements, and stresses the importance that contributions to this Programme not be at the expense of the General Fund;

5. *Welcomes* the increased cooperation between the Agency and international and regional organizations, States and relevant agencies and non-governmental organizations, which is essential to enhancing the contributions of the Agency towards improved conditions for the refugees and thereby the social stability of the occupied territory;

6. *Urges* all Member States to extend and expedite aid and assistance with a view to the economic and so-

cial development of the Palestinian people and the occupied territory;

7. *Reiterates its deep concern* regarding the persisting critical financial situation of the Agency, as outlined in the report of the Commissioner-General;

8. *Commends* the efforts of the Commissioner-General to move towards budgetary transparency and internal efficiency, and welcomes in this respect the new, unified budget structure for the biennium 2000-2001, which can contribute significantly to improved budgetary transparency of the Agency;

9. *Welcomes* the consultative process between the Agency, host Governments, the Palestinian Authority and donors on management reforms;

10. *Notes with profound concern* that the continuing shortfall in the finances of the Agency has a significant negative influence on the living conditions of the Palestine refugees most in need and that it therefore has possible consequences for the peace process;

11. *Calls upon* all donors, as a matter of urgency, to make the most generous efforts possible to meet the anticipated needs of the Agency, including the remaining costs of moving the headquarters to Gaza, encourages contributing Governments to contribute regularly and to consider increasing their contributions, and urges non-contributing Governments to contribute.

RECORDED VOTE ON RESOLUTION 54/69:

In favour: Albania, Algeria, Andorra, Angola, Antigua and Barbuda, Argentina, Armenia, Australia, Austria, Azerbaijan, Bahamas, Bahrain, Bangladesh, Barbados, Belarus, Belgium, Belize, Benin, Bhutan, Bolivia, Botswana, Brazil, Brunei Darussalam, Bulgaria, Burkina Faso, Cameroon, Canada, Cape Verde, Chad, Chile, China, Colombia, Congo, Costa Rica, Côte d'Ivoire, Croatia, Cuba, Cyprus, Czech Republic, Democratic People's Republic of Korea, Denmark, Djibouti, Dominica, Ecuador, Egypt, El Salvador, Equatorial Guinea, Eritrea, Estonia, Ethiopia, Fiji, Finland, France, Gabon, Gambia, Georgia, Germany, Ghana, Greece, Grenada, Guatemala, Guinea, Guyana, Haiti, Hungary, Iceland, India, Indonesia, Iran, Ireland, Italy, Jamaica, Japan, Jordan, Kazakhstan, Kenya, Kuwait, Lao People's Democratic Republic, Latvia, Lebanon, Libyan Arab Jamahiriya, Liechtenstein, Lithuania, Luxembourg, Madagascar, Malaysia, Maldives, Mali, Malta, Marshall Islands, Mauritius, Mexico, Monaco, Mongolia, Morocco, Mozambique, Myanmar, Namibia, Nepal, Netherlands, New Zealand, Nicaragua, Nigeria, Norway, Oman, Pakistan, Panama, Papua New Guinea, Paraguay, Peru, Philippines, Poland, Portugal, Qatar, Republic of Korea, Republic of Moldova, Romania, Russian Federation, Saint Lucia, Saint Vincent and the Grenadines, Samoa, San Marino, Saudi Arabia, Senegal, Seychelles, Sierra Leone, Singapore, Slovakia, Slovenia, Solomon Islands, South Africa, Spain, Sri Lanka, Sudan, Suriname, Swaziland, Sweden, Syrian Arab Republic, Tajikistan, Thailand, The former Yugoslav Republic of Macedonia, Togo, Trinidad and Tobago, Tunisia, Turkey, Ukraine, United Arab Emirates, United Kingdom, United Republic of Tanzania, Uruguay, Venezuela, Viet Nam, Yemen, Zambia, Zimbabwe.

Against: Israel.

Abstaining: Micronesia, United States.

The Assembly, on the same date [meeting 71] and also on the Fourth Committee's recommendation [A/54/575], adopted **resolution 54/73** by recorded vote (154-2-1) [agenda item 88].

Operations of the United Nations Relief and Works Agency for Palestine Refugees in the Near East

The General Assembly,

Recalling its resolutions 194(III) of 11 December 1948, 212(III) of 19 November 1948, 302(IV) of 8 December 1949 and all subsequent related resolutions,

Recalling also the relevant Security Council resolutions,

Having considered the report of the Commissioner-General of the United Nations Relief and Works Agency for Palestine Refugees in the Near East covering the period from 1 July 1998 to 30 June 1999,

Taking note of the letter dated 30 September 1999 from the Chairperson of the Advisory Commission of the United Nations Relief and Works Agency for Palestine Refugees in the Near East addressed to the Commissioner-General, contained in the report of the Commissioner-General,

Having considered the reports of the Secretary-General submitted in pursuance of its resolutions 48/40 E, 48/40 H and 48/40 J of 10 December 1993 and 49/35 C of 9 December 1994,

Recalling Articles 100, 104 and 105 of the Charter of the United Nations and the Convention on the Privileges and Immunities of the United Nations,

Affirming the applicability of the Geneva Convention relative to the Protection of Civilian Persons in Time of War, of 12 August 1949, to the Palestinian territory occupied since 1967, including Jerusalem,

Aware of the fact that Palestine refugees have, for over five decades, lost their homes, lands and means of livelihood,

Also aware of the continuing needs of Palestine refugees throughout the Occupied Palestinian Territory and in the other fields of operation, namely, in Lebanon, Jordan and the Syrian Arab Republic,

Further aware of the valuable work done by the refugee affairs officers of the Agency in providing protection to the Palestinian people, in particular Palestine refugees,

Deeply concerned about the continuing critical financial situation of the Agency and its effect on the continuity of provision of necessary Agency services to the Palestine refugees, including the emergency-related programmes,

Aware of the work of the new Peace Implementation Programme of the Agency,

Recalling the signing in Washington, D.C., on 13 September 1993 of the Declaration of Principles on Interim Self-Government Arrangements by the Government of the State of Israel and the Palestine Liberation Organization, and the subsequent implementation agreements, including the Israeli-Palestinian Interim Agreement on the West Bank and the Gaza Strip signed in Washington, D.C., on 28 September 1995, as well as the signing of the Sharm el-Sheikh Memorandum on 4 September 1999,

Taking note of the agreement reached on 24 June 1994, embodied in an exchange of letters between the Agency and the Palestine Liberation Organization,

Aware of the establishment of a working relationship between the Advisory Commission of the Agency and the Palestine Liberation Organization in accordance with General Assembly decision 48/417 of 10 December 1993,

1. *Expresses its appreciation* to the Commissioner-General of the United Nations Relief and Works Agency for Palestine Refugees in the Near East, as well as to all the staff of the Agency, for their tireless efforts and valuable work;

2. *Also expresses its appreciation* to the Advisory Commission of the Agency, and requests it to continue its efforts and to keep the General Assembly informed of its activities, including the full implementation of decision 48/417;

3. *Welcomes* the completion of the transfer of the headquarters of the Agency to Gaza and the signing of the Headquarters Agreement between the Agency and the Palestinian Authority;

4. *Acknowledges* the support of the host Governments and the Palestine Liberation Organization for the Agency in the discharge of its duties;

5. *Calls upon* Israel, the occupying Power, to accept the de jure applicability of the Geneva Convention relative to the Protection of Civilian Persons in Time of War, of 12 August 1949, and to abide scrupulously by its provisions;

6. *Also calls upon* Israel to abide by Articles 100, 104 and 105 of the Charter of the United Nations and the Convention on the Privileges and Immunities of the United Nations with regard to the safety of the personnel of the Agency, the protection of its institutions and the safeguarding of the security of the facilities of the Agency in the Occupied Palestinian Territory, including Jerusalem;

7. *Calls once again upon* the Government of Israel to compensate the Agency for damages to its property and facilities resulting from actions by the Israeli side;

8. *Requests* the Commissioner-General to proceed with the issuance of identification cards for Palestine refugees and their descendants in the Occupied Palestinian Territory;

9. *Notes* that the new context created by the signing of the Declaration of Principles on Interim Self-Government Arrangements by the Government of the State of Israel and the Palestine Liberation Organization and subsequent implementation agreements has had major consequences for the activities of the Agency, which is henceforth called upon, in close cooperation with the United Nations Special Coordinator for the Middle East Peace Process and Personal Representative of the Secretary-General to the Palestine Liberation Organization and the Palestinian Authority, the specialized agencies and the World Bank, to continue to contribute towards the development of economic and social stability in the occupied territory;

10. *Notes also* that the functioning of the Agency remains essential in all fields of operation;

11. *Notes further* the significant success of the Peace Implementation Programme of the Agency;

12. *Expresses concern* about the remaining austerity measures due to the financial crisis, which have affected the quality and level of some of the services of the Agency;

13. *Reiterates its request* to the Commissioner-General to consider the possibility of modernizing the archives of the Agency;

14. *Urges* all States, specialized agencies and non-governmental organizations to continue and to increase their contributions to the Agency so as to ease current financial constraints and to support the Agency in maintaining the provision of the most basic and effective assistance to the Palestine refugees.

RECORDED VOTE ON RESOLUTION 54/73:

In favour: Albania, Algeria, Andorra, Angola, Antigua and Barbuda, Argentina, Armenia, Australia, Austria, Azerbaijan, Bahamas, Bahrain, Bangladesh, Barbados, Belarus, Belgium, Belize, Benin, Bhutan, Bolivia, Botswana, Brazil, Brunei Darussalam, Bulgaria, Burkina Faso, Cambodia, Cameroon, Canada, Cape Verde, Chad, Chile, China, Colombia, Congo, Costa Rica, Côte d'Ivoire, Croatia, Cuba, Cyprus, Czech Republic, Democratic People's Republic of Korea, Denmark, Djibouti, Dominica, Ecuador, Egypt, El Salvador, Equatorial Guinea, Eritrea, Estonia, Ethiopia, Fiji, Finland, France, Gabon, Gambia, Georgia, Germany, Ghana, Greece, Grenada, Guatemala, Guinea, Guyana, Hungary, Iceland, India, Indonesia, Iran, Ireland, Italy, Jamaica, Japan, Jordan, Kenya, Kuwait, Lao People's Democratic Republic, Latvia, Lebanon, Libyan Arab Jamahiriya, Liechtenstein, Lithuania, Luxembourg, Madagascar, Malaysia, Maldives, Mali, Malta, Marshall Islands, Mauritius, Mexico, Monaco, Mongolia, Morocco, Mozambique, Myanmar, Namibia, Nepal, Netherlands, New Zealand, Nicaragua, Nigeria, Norway, Oman, Pakistan, Panama, Papua New Guinea, Paraguay, Peru, Philippines, Poland, Portugal, Qatar, Republic of Korea, Republic of Moldova, Romania, Russian Federation, Saint Lucia, Saint Vincent and the Grenadines, Samoa, San Marino, Saudi Arabia, Senegal, Seychelles, Sierra Leone, Singapore, Slovakia, Slovenia, Solomon Islands, South Africa, Spain, Sri Lanka, Sudan, Suriname, Swaziland, Sweden, Syrian Arab Republic, Tajikistan, Thailand, The former Yugoslav Republic of Macedonia, Togo, Trinidad and Tobago, Tunisia, Turkey, Ukraine, United Arab Emirates, United Kingdom, United Republic of Tanzania, Uruguay, Venezuela, Viet Nam, Yemen, Zambia, Zimbabwe.

Against: Israel, United States.

Abstaining: Micronesia.

UNRWA financing

In 1999, UNRWA continued to face a critical financial situation characterized by large funding shortfalls in the regular budget, depleted working capital and cash reserves, and cumulative deficits in certain project accounts. The structural deficit—representing the inability of income to keep pace with needs arising from natural growth in the refugee population and inflation, which increased the cost of maintaining a constant level of services—remained a problem. However, through a combination of ad hoc additional donor contributions and prudent financial management, including the retention of austerity and cost-reduction measures, UNRWA, by mid-1999, was making some progress in reducing the deficit.

UNRWA began 1999 with depleted working capital, low cash reserves and no expectation of a significant increase in overall income. Since expected cash income for 1999 fell far short of the $322.1 million regular budget for the year, the Agency was obliged to carry forward austerity measures previously implemented, including those announced in 1997 [YUN 1997, p. 453]. Expected cash expenditure was also reduced slightly by other factors, such as managed higher vacancy rates and delayed recruitment of all posts in the context of the general recruitment freeze; realization of benefits from previous and ongoing restructuring measures; and non-utilization of certain budget lines as a result of stricter financial controls. At mid-1999, those measures reduced expected 1999 cash expenditure below the $322.1 million level of the budget, which was then estimated at $251.5 million as compared to expected income of $251.8 million. However, the Agency's cash position remained weak and additional contributions were sought to overcome the difficult cash situation.

In an addendum to his report [A/54/13/Add.1], the Commissioner-General said that even if the core deficit were covered, the Agency would record an overall budget deficit of $67.1 million for

1999. The weak cash position underlined the need to restore the Agency's depleted working capital, eliminate cumulative deficits in certain extrabudgetary accounts ($11.6 million in the European Gaza Hospital account and $5.2 million in the headquarters relocation account) and secure payment of some $20 million owed by the PA. The addendum also contained the 2000-2001 budget estimates totalling $735.7 million, an increase of 6 per cent over the 1998-1999 budget of $695.7 million.

Working Group. The Working Group on the Financing of UNRWA held two meetings in 1999, on 10 September and 13 October. In its report to the General Assembly [A/54/477], the Working Group noted that UNRWA had ended the 1998 financial year with a core deficit of $1.9 million in its regular budget, representing the difference between actual expenditure of $254 million and the income of $252.1 million. However, the difference between cash income and the cash budget of $314 million for the year meant that the Agency had recorded a budget deficit of $61.9 million. The deficit in the cash budget was covered out of working capital, reducing it to a level of negative $4.8 million by the end of 1998.

The Agency's major donors had responded repeatedly and generously in recent years to special appeals from the Secretary-General and the Commissioner-General for special funding of UNRWA's General Fund budget, as well as of project funds. After consultations with donors in September 1998, April 1999 and September 1999, additional contributions were pledged to help the Agency with its cash-flow problem.

The Working Group noted that in 1999 UNRWA had adopted a more transparent budgeting methodology for the 2000-2001 biennium. By adopting a programme-based approach, UNRWA hoped to achieve full funding of its 2000-2001 budget and to move beyond the budget crisis of recent years. New policies were also adopted in 1999 for the engagement of area staff, beginning with teachers recruited for the 1999/2000 school year. Under those new policies, staff previously working on temporary contracts were being offered fixed-term contracts with an improved package of entitlements.

The Working Group expressed deep concern about UNRWA's financial prospects and emphasized that it was the responsibility of the international community to ensure the maintenance of UNRWA services at acceptable quantity and quality levels, as defined by the needs of the refugee community, and to ensure that service levels kept pace with the natural growth of the refugee population. It also expressed alarm at the continuing negative effect of seven years of austerity measures on the Agency's humanitarian operations, especially in the education and health-care sectors.

The Working Group appreciated that UNRWA had made significant progress towards eliminating the structural deficit problem through the use of contract teachers, reductions in international staffing and other reforms. It called for the early and complete fulfilment of pledges and other commitments to the Agency, in particular reimbursement of value-added tax and other charges paid to the PA, and of funds advanced by the Agency from its regular budget for the completion of the European Gaza Hospital and its headquarters relocation.

The Working Group noted the introduction of regularized conditions of employment for staff working on temporary contracts and the adoption of new staff policies that would facilitate the employment of fixed-term staff. Over the long run, that would make a significant contribution to reducing costs, particularly in its education programme. However, the Working Group appreciated that that action was not a long-term solution to securing funding of the Agency's regular activities on a sustainable basis. It was concerned that freezes on regular budget allocations for university scholarships, rehabilitation of shelters and selective cash assistance had not only reduced the Agency's activities in those areas, but made them dependent on extrabudgetary contributions. The Group feared that additional austerity cuts could cause severe social and economic hardships to an already suffering refugee population and put an increased burden on the authorities hosting the refugees.

The Working Group urged Governments, among other things, to consider making special contributions to cover the deficit and build up the working capital, so that UNRWA services could continue uninterrupted and the Agency could restore services cut as a result of the austerity measures, and to ensure that donor support of emergency-related and special programmes or capital projects did not in any way decrease or divert contributions to the Agency's regular programmes.

Pledging Conference. At a 1999 meeting of the Ad Hoc Committee of the General Assembly for the Announcement of Voluntary Contributions to UNRWA (New York, 8 December), 20 countries pledged $172 million for the Agency's 2000 programmes, about 61 per cent of what UNRWA needed to maintain its regular services. The largest pledges were made by the United States ($80 million), the European Community ($40 million), Sweden ($18.8 million), Norway ($12.5 million), the Netherlands ($5 million),

Switzerland ($4.9 million) and Germany ($4.5 million).

GENERAL ASSEMBLY ACTION

On 6 December [meeting 71], the General Assembly, on the Fourth Committee's recommendation [A/54/575], adopted **resolution 54/70** without vote [agenda item 88].

Working Group on the Financing of the United Nations Relief and Works Agency for Palestine Refugees in the Near East

The General Assembly,

Recalling its resolutions 2656(XXV) of 7 December 1970, 2728(XXV) of 15 December 1970, 2791(XXVI) of 6 December 1971, 53/47 of 3 December 1998 and the previous resolutions on this question,

Recalling also its decision 36/462 of 16 March 1982, by which it took note of the special report of the Working Group on the Financing of the United Nations Relief and Works Agency for Palestine Refugees in the Near East,

Having considered the report of the Working Group,

Taking into account the report of the Commissioner-General of the United Nations Relief and Works Agency for Palestine Refugees in the Near East covering the period from 1 July 1998 to 30 June 1999,

Deeply concerned about the continuing critical financial situation of the Agency, which has affected and affects the continuation of the provision of necessary Agency services to Palestine refugees, including the emergency-related programmes,

Emphasizing the continuing need for extraordinary efforts in order to maintain, at least at the current minimum level, the activities of the Agency, as well as to enable the Agency to carry out essential construction,

1. *Commends* the Working Group on the Financing of the United Nations Relief and Works Agency for Palestine Refugees in the Near East for its efforts to assist in ensuring the financial security of the Agency;

2. *Takes note with approval* of the report of the Working Group;

3. *Requests* the Working Group to continue its efforts, in cooperation with the Secretary-General and the Commissioner-General, to find a solution to the financial situation of the Agency;

4. *Welcomes* the new, unified budget structure for the biennium 2000-2001, which can contribute significantly to improved budgetary transparency of the Agency;

5. *Requests* the Secretary-General to provide the necessary services and assistance to the Working Group for the conduct of its work.

Displaced persons

In a September report [A/54/377] on compliance with General Assembly resolution 53/48 [YUN 1998, p. 468], which called for the accelerated return of all persons displaced as a result of the June 1967 and subsequent hostilities to their homes or former places of residence in the territories occupied by Israel since 1967, the Secretary-General said that since UNRWA was not involved in arrangements for the return of either refugees or displaced persons not registered with it, the Agency's information was based on requests by returning registered refugees for the transfer of their entitlements to their areas of return. Displaced refugees known by UNRWA to have returned to the West Bank and Gaza Strip since June 1967 numbered 18,380. Records indicated that, between 1 July 1998 and 30 June 1999, 1,022 refugees had returned to the West Bank and 257 to Gaza. Some of the refugees might not have been displaced in 1967, but might be family members of a displaced registered refugee whom they either had accompanied on return or had joined later.

GENERAL ASSEMBLY ACTION

On 6 December [meeting 71], the General Assembly, on the Fourth Committee's recommendation [A/54/575], adopted **resolution 54/71** by recorded vote (154-2-2) [agenda item 88].

Persons displaced as a result of the June 1967 and subsequent hostilities

The General Assembly,

Recalling its resolutions 2252(ES-V) of 4 July 1967 and 2341 B (XXII) of 19 December 1967 and all subsequent related resolutions,

Recalling also Security Council resolutions 237(1967) of 14 June 1967 and 259(1968) of 27 September 1968,

Taking note of the report of the Secretary-General submitted in pursuance of its resolution 53/48 of 3 December 1998,

Taking note also of the report of the Commissioner-General of the United Nations Relief and Works Agency for Palestine Refugees in the Near East covering the period from 1 July 1998 to 30 June 1999,

Concerned about the continuing human suffering resulting from the June 1967 and subsequent hostilities,

Taking note of the relevant provisions of the Declaration of Principles on Interim Self-Government Arrangements, signed in Washington, D.C., on 13 September 1993 by the Government of the State of Israel and the Palestine Liberation Organization, with regard to the modalities for the admission of persons displaced in 1967, and concerned that the process agreed upon has not yet been effected,

1. *Reaffirms* the right of all persons displaced as a result of the June 1967 and subsequent hostilities to return to their homes or former places of residence in the territories occupied by Israel since 1967;

2. *Expresses the hope* for an accelerated return of displaced persons through the mechanism agreed upon by the parties in article XII of the Declaration of Principles on Interim Self-Government Arrangements;

3. *Endorses,* in the meanwhile, the efforts of the Commissioner-General of the United Nations Relief and Works Agency for Palestine Refugees in the Near East to continue to provide humanitarian assistance, as far as practicable, on an emergency basis, and as a temporary measure, to persons in the area who are currently displaced and in serious need of continued

assistance as a result of the June 1967 and subsequent hostilities;

4. *Strongly appeals* to all Governments and to organizations and individuals to contribute generously to the Agency and to the other intergovernmental and non-governmental organizations concerned for the above-mentioned purposes;

5. *Requests* the Secretary-General, after consulting with the Commissioner-General, to report to the General Assembly before its fifty-fifth session on the progress made with regard to the implementation of the present resolution.

RECORDED VOTE ON RESOLUTION 54/71:

In favour: Albania, Algeria, Andorra, Angola, Antigua and Barbuda, Argentina, Armenia, Australia, Austria, Azerbaijan, Bahamas, Bahrain, Bangladesh, Barbados, Belarus, Belgium, Belize, Benin, Bhutan, Bolivia, Botswana, Brazil, Brunei Darussalam, Bulgaria, Burkina Faso, Cambodia, Cameroon, Canada, Cape Verde, Chad, Chile, China, Colombia, Congo, Costa Rica, Côte d'Ivoire, Croatia, Cuba, Cyprus, Czech Republic, Democratic People's Republic of Korea, Denmark, Djibouti, Dominica, Ecuador, Egypt, El Salvador, Equatorial Guinea, Eritrea, Estonia, Ethiopia, Fiji, Finland, France, Gabon, Gambia, Georgia, Germany, Ghana, Greece, Grenada, Guatemala, Guinea, Guyana, Haiti, Hungary, Iceland, India, Indonesia, Iran, Ireland, Italy, Jamaica, Japan, Jordan, Kenya, Kuwait, Lao People's Democratic Republic, Latvia, Lebanon, Libyan Arab Jamahiriya, Liechtenstein, Lithuania, Luxembourg, Madagascar, Malaysia, Maldives, Mali, Malta, Mauritius, Mexico, Monaco, Mongolia, Morocco, Mozambique, Myanmar, Namibia, Nepal, Netherlands, New Zealand, Nicaragua, Nigeria, Norway, Oman, Pakistan, Panama, Papua New Guinea, Paraguay, Peru, Philippines, Poland, Portugal, Qatar, Republic of Korea, Republic of Moldova, Romania, Russian Federation, Saint Lucia, Saint Vincent and the Grenadines, Samoa, San Marino, Saudi Arabia, Senegal, Seychelles, Sierra Leone, Singapore, Slovakia, Slovenia, Solomon Islands, South Africa, Spain, Sri Lanka, Sudan, Suriname, Swaziland, Sweden, Syrian Arab Republic, Tajikistan, Thailand, The former Yugoslav Republic of Macedonia, Togo, Trinidad and Tobago, Tunisia, Turkey, Ukraine, United Arab Emirates, United Kingdom, United Republic of Tanzania, Uruguay, Venezuela, Viet Nam, Yemen, Zambia, Zimbabwe.

Against: Israel, United States.

Abstaining: Marshall Islands, Micronesia.

Education, training and scholarships

In a September report [A/54/376], the Secretary-General transmitted responses received to the General Assembly's 1998 appeal in resolution 53/49 [YUN 1998, p. 469] for States, specialized agencies and NGOs to augment special allocations for scholarships and grants to Palestine refugees, for which UNRWA acted as recipient and trustee.

In the 1999 fiscal year, Japan awarded nine fellowships to Palestine refugees, of which five were for vocational training for staff employed by UNRWA, one was in vocational training administration and three were in community health. All the fellowships were for training in Japan. Under Japanese grants of $400,000 made annually between 1992 and 1994, $500,000 in 1995 and $600,000 in both 1996 and 1997, 437 students were participating in the UNRWA university scholarship programme during 1998/99. Contributions from Switzerland in 1997 totalling $338,000 enabled 19 scholars to continue pursuing their university studies in the 1998/99 academic year. Out of the 315 students who benefited from part of the 1997 Swiss contribution for one year only, 67 scholars graduated in 1998, seven failed and 87 were granted scholarships in 1998/99 from savings of previous Swiss contributions. UNESCO granted 13 scholarships to Palestinian students in 1998/99, while WHO provided 62 fellowships or study tours for candidates nominated by the PA.

GENERAL ASSEMBLY ACTION

On 6 December [meeting 71], the General Assembly, on the recommendation of the Fourth Committee [A/54/575], adopted **resolution 54/72** by recorded vote (158-0-1) [agenda item 88].

Offers by Member States of grants and scholarships for higher education, including vocational training, for Palestine refugees

The General Assembly,

Recalling its resolution 212(III) of 19 November 1948 on assistance to Palestine refugees,

Recalling also its resolutions 35/13 B of 3 November 1980, 36/146 H of 16 December 1981, 37/120 D of 16 December 1982, 38/83 D of 15 December 1983, 39/99 D of 14 December 1984, 40/165 D of 16 December 1985, 41/69 D of 3 December 1986, 42/69 D of 2 December 1987, 43/57 D of 6 December 1988, 44/47 D of 8 December 1989, 45/73 D of 11 December 1990, 46/46 D of 9 December 1991, 47/69 D of 14 December 1992, 48/40 D of 10 December 1993, 49/35 D of 9 December 1994, 50/28 D of 6 December 1995, 51/127 of 13 December 1996, 52/60 of 10 December 1997 and 53/49 of 3 December 1998,

Cognizant of the fact that the Palestine refugees have, for the last five decades, lost their homes, lands and means of livelihood,

Having considered the report of the Secretary-General,

Having also considered the report of the Commissioner-General of the United Nations Relief and Works Agency for Palestine Refugees in the Near East covering the period from 1 July 1998 to 30 June 1999,

1. *Urges* all States to respond to the appeal in its resolution 32/90 F of 13 December 1977 and reiterated in subsequent relevant resolutions in a manner commensurate with the needs of Palestine refugees for higher education, including vocational training;

2. *Strongly appeals* to all States, specialized agencies and non-governmental organizations to augment the special allocations for grants and scholarships to Palestine refugees, in addition to their contributions to the regular budget of the United Nations Relief and Works Agency for Palestine Refugees in the Near East;

3. *Expresses its appreciation* to all Governments, specialized agencies and non-governmental organizations that responded favourably to its resolutions on this question;

4. *Invites* the relevant specialized agencies and other organizations of the United Nations system to continue, within their respective spheres of competence, to extend assistance for higher education to Palestine refugee students;

5. *Appeals* to all States, specialized agencies and the United Nations University to contribute generously to the Palestinian universities in the Palestinian territory occupied by Israel since 1967, including, in due course,

the proposed University of Jerusalem "Al-Quds" for Palestine refugees;

6. *Appeals* to all States, specialized agencies and other international bodies to contribute towards the establishment of vocational training centres for Palestine refugees;

7. *Requests* the Agency to act as the recipient and trustee for the special allocations for grants and scholarships and to award them to qualified Palestine refugee candidates;

8. *Requests* the Secretary-General to report to the General Assembly at its fifty-fifth session on the implementation of the present resolution.

RECORDED VOTE ON RESOLUTION 54/72:

In favour: Albania, Algeria, Andorra, Angola, Antigua and Barbuda, Argentina, Armenia, Australia, Austria, Azerbaijan, Bahamas, Bahrain, Bangladesh, Barbados, Belarus, Belgium, Belize, Benin, Bhutan, Bolivia, Botswana, Brazil, Brunei Darussalam, Bulgaria, Burkina Faso, Cambodia, Cameroon, Canada, Cape Verde, Chad, Chile, China, Colombia, Congo, Costa Rica, Côte d'Ivoire, Croatia, Cuba, Cyprus, Czech Republic, Democratic People's Republic of Korea, Denmark, Djibouti, Dominica, Ecuador, Egypt, El Salvador, Equatorial Guinea, Eritrea, Estonia, Ethiopia, Fiji, Finland, France, Gabon, Gambia, Georgia, Germany, Ghana, Greece, Grenada, Guatemala, Guinea, Guyana, Haiti, Hungary, Iceland, India, Indonesia, Iran, Ireland, Italy, Jamaica, Japan, Jordan, Kazakhstan, Kenya, Kuwait, Lao People's Democratic Republic, Latvia, Lebanon, Libyan Arab Jamahiriya, Liechtenstein, Lithuania, Luxembourg, Madagascar, Malaysia, Maldives, Mali, Malta, Marshall Islands, Mauritius, Mexico, Micronesia, Monaco, Mongolia, Morocco, Mozambique, Myanmar, Namibia, Nepal, Netherlands, New Zealand, Nicaragua, Nigeria, Norway, Oman, Pakistan, Panama, Papua New Guinea, Paraguay, Peru, Philippines, Poland, Portugal, Qatar, Republic of Korea, Republic of Moldova, Romania, Russian Federation, Saint Lucia, Saint Vincent and the Grenadines, Samoa, San Marino, Saudi Arabia, Senegal, Seychelles, Sierra Leone, Singapore, Slovakia, Slovenia, Solomon Islands, South Africa, Spain, Sri Lanka, Sudan, Suriname, Swaziland, Sweden, Syrian Arab Republic, Tajikistan, Thailand, The former Yugoslav Republic of Macedonia, Togo, Trinidad and Tobago, Tunisia, Turkey, Ukraine, United Arab Emirates, United Kingdom, United Republic of Tanzania, United States, Uruguay, Venezuela, Viet Nam, Yemen, Zambia, Zimbabwe.

Against: None.

Abstaining: Israel.

Proposed University of Jerusalem "Al-Quds"

In response to General Assembly resolution 53/52 [YUN 1998, p. 470], the Secretary-General submitted a September report on the proposal to establish a university for Palestine refugees in Jerusalem [A/54/385]. First mentioned by the Assembly in resolution 35/13 B [YUN 1980, p. 443], the issue had been the subject of annual reports by the Secretary-General.

To assist in the preparation of a feasibility study and at the Secretary-General's request, the Rector of the United Nations University again asked expert Mihaly Simai to visit the area and meet with Israeli officials. In response to the Secretary-General's note verbale of 28 July, requesting Israel to facilitate the visit, Israel, in a 26 August reply, stated that it had consistently voted against the resolution on the proposed university and that its position remained unchanged. It charged that the resolution's sponsors sought to exploit higher education for political purposes extraneous to genuine academic pursuits. Accordingly, Israel was of the opinion that the proposed visit would serve no useful purpose. The Secretary-General reported that it had not been possible to complete the study as planned.

GENERAL ASSEMBLY ACTION

On 6 December [meeting 71], the General Assembly, acting on the Fourth Committee's recommendation [A/54/575], adopted **resolution 54/75** by recorded vote (155-2-1) [agenda item 88].

University of Jerusalem "Al-Quds" for Palestine refugees

The General Assembly,

Recalling its resolutions 36/146 G of 16 December 1981, 37/120 C of 16 December 1982, 38/83 K of 15 December 1983, 39/99 K of 14 December 1984, 40/165 D and K of 16 December 1985, 41/69 K of 3 December 1986, 42/69 K of 2 December 1987, 43/57 J of 6 December 1988, 44/47 J of 8 December 1989, 45/73 J of 11 December 1990, 46/46 J of 9 December 1991, 47/69 J of 14 December 1992, 48/40 I of 10 December 1993, 49/35 G of 9 December 1994, 50/28 G of 6 December 1995, 51/130 of 13 December 1996, 52/63 of 10 December 1997 and 53/52 of 3 December 1998,

Having considered the report of the Secretary-General,

Having also considered the report of the Commissioner-General of the United Nations Relief and Works Agency for Palestine Refugees in the Near East covering the period from 1 July 1998 to 30 June 1999,

1. *Emphasizes* the need for strengthening the educational system in the Palestinian territory occupied by Israel since 5 June 1967, including Jerusalem, and specifically the need for the establishment of the proposed university;

2. *Requests* the Secretary-General to continue to take all necessary measures for establishing the University of Jerusalem "Al-Quds", in accordance with General Assembly resolution 35/13 B of 3 November 1980, giving due consideration to the recommendations consistent with the provisions of that resolution;

3. *Calls once more upon* Israel, the occupying Power, to cooperate in the implementation of the present resolution and to remove the hindrances that it has put in the way of establishing the University of Jerusalem "Al-Quds";

4. *Requests* the Secretary-General to report to the General Assembly at its fifty-fifth session on the progress made in the implementation of the present resolution.

RECORDED VOTE ON RESOLUTION 54/75:

In favour: Albania, Algeria, Andorra, Angola, Antigua and Barbuda, Argentina, Armenia, Australia, Austria, Azerbaijan, Bahamas, Bahrain, Bangladesh, Barbados, Belarus, Belgium, Belize, Benin, Bhutan, Bolivia, Botswana, Brazil, Brunei Darussalam, Bulgaria, Burkina Faso, Cambodia, Cameroon, Canada, Cape Verde, Chad, Chile, China, Colombia, Congo, Côte d'Ivoire, Croatia, Cuba, Cyprus, Czech Republic, Democratic People's Republic of Korea, Denmark, Djibouti, Dominica, Ecuador, Egypt, El Salvador, Equatorial Guinea, Eritrea, Estonia, Ethiopia, Fiji, Finland, France, Gabon, Gambia, Georgia, Germany, Ghana, Greece, Grenada, Guatemala, Guinea, Guyana, Haiti, Hungary, Iceland, India, Indonesia, Iran, Ireland, Italy, Jamaica, Japan, Jordan, Kazakhstan, Kenya, Kuwait, Lao People's Democratic Republic, Latvia, Lebanon, Libyan Arab Jamahiriya, Liechtenstein, Lithuania, Luxembourg, Madagascar, Malaysia, Maldives, Mali, Malta, Marshall Islands, Mauritius, Mexico, Monaco, Mongolia, Morocco, Mozambique, Myanmar, Namibia, Nepal, Netherlands, New Zealand, Nicaragua, Nigeria, Norway, Oman, Pakistan, Panama, Papua New Guinea, Paraguay, Peru, Philippines, Poland, Portugal, Qatar, Republic of Korea, Republic of Moldova, Romania, Russian Federation, Saint Lucia, Saint Vincent and the Grenadines, Samoa, San Marino, Saudi Arabia, Senegal, Seychelles, Sierra Leone, Singapore, Slovakia, Slovenia, Solomon Islands, South Africa, Spain, Sri Lanka, Sudan, Suriname, Swaziland, Sweden, Syrian Arab Republic, Tajikistan, Thailand, The former Yugoslav Republic of Macedonia, Togo, Trinidad and Tobago, Tunisia, Turkey, Ukraine, United Arab Emirates, United Kingdom, United Republic of Tanzania, Uruguay, Venezuela, Viet Nam, Yemen, Zambia, Zimbabwe.

Against: Israel, United States.

Abstaining: Micronesia.

Property rights

In response to General Assembly resolution 53/51 [YUN 1998, p. 471], the Secretary-General submitted a September report [A/54/345] on steps taken to protect and administer Arab property, assets and property rights in Israel and to establish a fund for income derived therefrom, on behalf of the rightful owners. He indicated that he had transmitted the resolution to Israel and all other Member States, requesting information on any steps taken or envisaged with regard to its implementation.

In a 23 August reply, reproduced in the report, Israel stated that its position on the resolutions on Palestine refugees had been set forth in successive annual replies, the latest of which had been included in the Secretary-General's 1998 report on the subject [YUN 1998, p. 471]. Israel regretted that the resolutions regarding UNRWA remained rife with political issues irrelevant to the Agency's work and detached from the reality in the area. While Israel believed that UNRWA could play an important role in promoting the social and economic advancement foreseen in agreements between Israel and the Palestinians, it called on the Assembly to consolidate the resolutions on UNRWA into one directly related to the Agency's humanitarian tasks.

Report of Conciliation Commission. The United Nations Conciliation Commission for Palestine, in its fifty-third report covering the period from 1 September 1998 to 31 August 1999 [A/54/338], noted that, pursuant to Assembly resolution 51/129 [YUN 1996, p. 423], the project to preserve and modernize its records was nearing completion.

GENERAL ASSEMBLY ACTION

On 6 December [meeting 71], the General Assembly, on the recommendation of the Fourth Committee [A/54/575], adopted **resolution 54/74** by recorded vote (154-2-2) [agenda item 88].

Palestine refugees' properties and their revenues

The General Assembly,

Recalling its resolutions 194(III) of 11 December 1948, 36/146 C of 16 December 1981 and all its subsequent resolutions on the question,

Taking note of the report of the Secretary-General in pursuance of resolution 53/51 of 3 December 1998,

Taking note also of the report of the United Nations Conciliation Commission for Palestine for the period from 1 September 1998 to 31 August 1999,

Recalling that the Universal Declaration of Human Rights and the principles of international law uphold the principle that no one shall be arbitrarily deprived of his or her property,

Recalling in particular its resolution 394(V) of 14 December 1950, in which it directed the Conciliation Commission, in consultation with the parties concerned, to prescribe measures for the protection of the rights, property and interests of the Palestine Arab refugees,

Taking note of the completion of the programme of identification and evaluation of Arab property, as announced by the Conciliation Commission in its twenty-second progress report, and of the fact that the Land Office had a schedule of Arab owners and file of documents defining the location, area and other particulars of Arab property,

Recalling that, in the framework of the Middle East peace process, the Palestine Liberation Organization and the Government of Israel agreed, in the Declaration of Principles on Interim Self-Government Arrangements of 13 September 1993, to commence negotiations on permanent status issues, including the important issue of the refugees,

1. *Reaffirms* that the Palestine Arab refugees are entitled to their property and to the income derived therefrom, in conformity with the principles of justice and equity;

2. *Requests* the Secretary-General to take all appropriate steps, in consultation with the United Nations Conciliation Commission for Palestine, for the protection of Arab property, assets and property rights in Israel, expresses its appreciation for the work done to preserve and modernize the existing records of the Commission, and requests the Secretary-General to complete this task;

3. *Calls once more upon* Israel to render all facilities and assistance to the Secretary-General in the implementation of the present resolution;

4. *Calls upon* all the parties concerned to provide the Secretary-General with any pertinent information in their possession concerning Arab property, assets and property rights in Israel that would assist him in the implementation of the present resolution;

5. *Urges* the Palestinian and Israeli sides, as agreed between them, to deal with the important issue of Palestine refugees' properties and their revenues in the framework of the final status negotiations of the Middle East peace process;

6. *Requests* the Secretary-General to report to the General Assembly at its fifty-fifth session on the implementation of the present resolution.

RECORDED VOTE ON RESOLUTION 54/74:

In favour: Albania, Algeria, Andorra, Angola, Antigua and Barbuda, Argentina, Armenia, Australia, Austria, Azerbaijan, Bahamas, Bahrain, Bangladesh, Barbados, Belarus, Belgium, Belize, Benin, Bhutan, Bolivia, Botswana, Brazil, Brunei Darussalam, Bulgaria, Burkina Faso, Cambodia, Cameroon, Canada, Cape Verde, Chad, Chile, China, Colombia, Congo, Costa Rica, Côte d'Ivoire, Croatia, Cuba, Cyprus, Czech Republic, Democratic People's Republic of Korea, Denmark, Djibouti, Dominica, Ecuador, Egypt, El Salvador, Equatorial Guinea, Eritrea, Estonia, Ethiopia, Fiji, Finland, France, Gabon, Gambia, Georgia, Germany, Ghana, Greece, Grenada, Guatemala, Guinea, Guyana, Haiti, Hungary, Iceland, India, Indonesia, Iran, Ireland, Italy, Jamaica, Japan, Jordan, Kenya, Kuwait, Lao People's Democratic Republic, Latvia, Lebanon, Libyan Arab Jamahiriya, Liechtenstein, Lithuania, Luxembourg, Madagascar, Malaysia, Maldives, Mali, Malta, Mauritius, Mexico, Monaco, Mongolia, Morocco, Mozambique, Myanmar, Namibia, Nepal, Netherlands, New Zealand, Nicaragua, Nigeria, Norway, Oman, Pakistan, Panama, Papua New Guinea, Paraguay,

Peru, Philippines, Poland, Portugal, Qatar, Republic of Korea, Republic of Moldova, Romania, Russian Federation, Saint Lucia, Saint Vincent and the Grenadines, Samoa, San Marino, Saudi Arabia, Senegal, Seychelles, Sierra Leone, Singapore, Slovakia, Slovenia, Solomon Islands, South Africa, Spain, Sri Lanka, Sudan, Suriname, Swaziland, Sweden, Syrian Arab Republic, Tajikistan, Thailand, The former Yugoslav Republic of Macedonia, Togo, Trinidad and Tobago, Tunisia, Turkey, Ukraine, United Arab Emirates, United Kingdom, United Republic of Tanzania, Uruguay, Venezuela, Viet Nam, Yemen, Zambia, Zimbabwe.

Against: Israel, United States.

Abstaining: Marshall Islands, Micronesia.

Peacekeeping operations

Lebanon

Though the situation in southern Lebanon remained volatile and dangerous in 1999, the withdrawal of Israeli forces from Jezzin and the return of that town to the jurisdiction of the Lebanese Government was a positive development that could lead to the complete withdrawal of Israel from the occupied Lebanese zone, and thus remove a major obstacle to regional peace.

On 4 January [A/53/777-S/1999/6], Lebanon informed the Secretary-General that on 3 January Israeli military aircraft carried out an attack near the village of Nahlé, wounding seven civilians. Lebanon condemned that open assault on its sovereignty and urged the international community to take the necessary steps to halt Israeli military attacks and end the intimidation of its inhabitants. On 8 January [A/53/785-S/1999/23], Lebanon also reported that, the previous day, Israeli forces destroyed at least 14 homes in the township of Arnun and carried out a large-scale raid on the village of Shab'a, expelling 25 residents.

Responding on 26 January [A/53/809-S/1999/69], Israel said that Lebanon continued to be directly responsible for the volatile security situation along the Israeli-Lebanese border through its support for Hezbollah, an international terrorist organization, and its use of Lebanese territory for an elaborate military infrastructure. Lebanon had let itself become a launching pad for acts of aggression and terrorism against Israel and, in addition to Hezbollah, a number of Lebanese and Palestinian terrorist organizations had been given free rein to attack Israel from Lebanon. Israel reiterated its willingness to implement Security Council resolution 425(1978) [YUN 1978, p. 312] and called on the Lebanese Government to cooperate with Israel to restore peace along their common border.

On 11 February [A/53/825-S/1999/146], Lebanon transmitted to the Secretary-General a letter from the Follow-up Committee for the support of Lebanese detainees in Israeli prisons addressed to the Lebanese Prime Minister and Minister for Foreign Affairs. The letter recalled the decision of the Israeli Supreme Court granting the Israeli authorities permission to hold Lebanese detainees in Israeli prisons and detention camps without trial and to keep them as hostages.

Rejecting those statements, Israel, on 12 February [A/53/828-S/1999/150], reaffirmed that Lebanon had a clear duty under international law and the UN Charter not to allow its territory to be a base for attacks on Israel, to disarm all terrorist groups and to cease all aid and encouragement to them. As a result of Lebanon's failure to do so, Israel was compelled to take defensive measures against those terrorist activities, which were not only supported by Lebanon but directly aided, financially and otherwise, by the Syrian Arab Republic and Iran.

Responding on 24 March [A/53/876-S/1999/326] to the Israeli accusation, the Syrian Arab Republic said that it condemned terrorism as criminal and called for genuine cooperation among all States to prevent, combat and eliminate its causes. It had also called for the preparation of internationally agreed standards that clearly distinguished between terrorism, which had to be condemned and countered, and legitimate national struggles against foreign occupation, which had to be supported. Syria stated that the UN Charter enshrined the right of peoples to self-determination, freedom and independence and to liberate their territory from foreign occupation. On the other hand, Israeli State terrorism, as practised against the Lebanese people, the people of Palestine and Syrian citizens of the occupied Syrian Golan, had to be condemned. According to Syria, Israel had never ceased to carry out acts of terrorism in order to achieve its goal of extending its hegemony and intimidating the Arab people.

On 18 February [A/53/834-S/1999/172 & Corr.1], Lebanon said that Israel had expanded the area it occupied in southern Lebanon by incorporating the village of Arnun into its security zone. On 22 February [A/53/840-S/1999/185], Israel said Lebanon had deliberately misrepresented the facts on the ground, since Arnun had long been part of the security zone, which Israel had been compelled to maintain in response to the terrorist attacks emanating from Lebanese territory. Since the village was being exploited by Hezbollah as a forward staging area for terrorist attacks, Israeli forces had placed barbed wire on the outskirts of Arnun as an additional measure of self-defence. On 8 April [A/53/904-S/1999/399], Lebanon informed the Secretary-General that, on 6 April, Israeli occupation forces ejected 18 residents of Shab'a from the occupied zone, bringing the number of residents expelled from Shab'a since the beginning of the year to 70. On 15 April [A/53/909-S/1999/430], Lebanon said that Israeli armed forces, in a new attempt to include Arnun in the occupied southern zone, had entered and separated the village from the liberated area, arrested some residents and prevented inhabitants from entering it.

On 24 March [A/53/878-S/1999/333], Lebanon said that Israel's letters ignored the prime fact in southern Lebanon that had been the cause of the violence and abuse directed against Lebanese residents, namely the 21 years of Israeli occupation in violation of the UN Charter. Israel's leaders had repeatedly issued statements linking acceptance of resolution 425(1978) with measures and conditions that were alien to its letter and spirit and that, once admitted, would alter its legal and political character. The Lebanese resistance targeted only the Israeli occupation inside Lebanese territory and responded to Israel's targeting of Lebanese civilians in its assaults.

By a 19 April letter [A/54/82-S/1999/463], Israel said that Syria and Lebanon were engaging in an insidious form of complicity to terrorism in their letters and in their policies on the ground by trying to disguise terrorism as national resistance. In particular, the Lebanese claim that Hezbollah targeted only the Israeli forces that operated in Lebanon was false. The declared willingness of the Syrian and Lebanese Governments to host an elaborate terrorist infrastructure, permit its regular reinforcement and endorse its operations directed against a neighbouring country was incompatible with the provisions of resolution 425(1978). Israel added that the possibility of peace and security along its border with Lebanon was being sabotaged by Syria, which in effect was holding the implementation of that resolution hostage to its own bid for territorial gains with Israel.

On 24 June [A/53/1010-S/1999/714], Lebanon informed the Secretary-General that Israeli aircraft had launched that day a series of attacks against the area of Al-Joumhour on the Beirut heights and had bombed the local power station. At the same time, Israeli aircraft had launched a number of bombing attacks against an area south of Beirut and one in the northern Bekaa. Those attacks were part of a new series of Israeli incursions, which had left five people dead and 13 wounded and had caused destruction of civilian property. The next day [A/53/1011-S/1999/717], Lebanon said that Israeli aircraft had bombed an electric power station at Arb Salim, as well as several bridges connecting the southern region to Beirut and certain bridges linking the southern areas. Reports indicated that 13 people had been killed and about 84 civilians had been injured.

On 26 June [S/1999/734], the Secretary-General of the League of Arab States condemned those repeated Israeli assaults on Lebanon. He said that the League regarded Israel's practices as an escalation of tension and an indication that reflected negatively on efforts being made to revive the peace process. It requested that all necessary measures be taken to halt Israel's acts of aggression.

Explaining its version of the incidents, Israel, on 30 June [S/1999/740], said that Lebanon had presented only a selective and one-sided account of events, which disregarded the acts of terror that had precipitated Israel's response. Such acts were conducted by the Hezbollah group from within Lebanese territory against Israeli civilians and territory, with the support and active encouragement of the Lebanese Government. In an attempt to exercise maximum restraint, Israel had appealed to the monitoring group established by the 26 April 1996 understanding [YUN 1996, p. 428], with the hope that Lebanon and Hezbollah would honour commitments established by the understanding and refrain from further attacks. It was only after a 24 May Hezbollah attack on civilian areas in northern Israel, which caused the death of two civilians and injured several others, that Israel opted to respond.

On 9 July [A/53/1016-S/1999/771], Lebanon transmitted to the Secretary-General a letter by the Follow-up Committee for the support of Lebanese detainees in Israeli prisons on the occasion of Lebanese Detainee Day, commemorated on 14 July. The Committee called on the international community to intensify its efforts for the release of those Lebanese held in Khiam and other Israeli prisons. By a 15 July letter [A/53/1021] to the Secretary-General, Lebanon said that on the eve of Lebanese Detainee Day, Lebanese prisoners held at the Khiam prison declared a hunger strike to protest against their continued detention. According to the Committee for the Defence of Lebanese Detainees in Israeli Prisons, 130 Lebanese were being detained in Khiam, which was administered by the South Lebanon Army in collaboration with Israeli authorities, while 21 Lebanese were held in prisons inside Israel. Later, on 2 August [A/53/1031-S/1999/839], Lebanon informed the Secretary-General that Israeli military forces had been holding the people and village of Ayta under siege since 15 July. A number of villagers had been detained and taken to the Khiam detention centre. Lebanon called for an end to the siege there and other besieged villages and for the release of all those Lebanese citizens who were being held hostage.

On 9 August [A/53/1034-S/1999/861], Saudi Arabia affirmed that Israel was holding 170 Lebanese detainees in its prisons, 128 of them in the Khiam prison centre and 42 in prisons inside Israel, as well as 10 Palestinian residents of Lebanon. Saudi Arabia called on the international community to send an international commission of inquiry to the Khiam prison centre and to secure the immediate release of the sick, the young and the elderly. Responding on 22 August [A/53/1041-S/1999/906], Israel said that the detainees referred to by Lebanon and Saudi Arabia were all active members of terrorist organizations, such as Hezbollah. The detainees in Israel were not being held arbitrarily, but pursuant to Israeli law applicable to all detainees. With regard to the Khiam detention facility, it was common knowledge that the South Lebanon Army exercised independent authority and responsibility over the functioning of that centre and Israeli personnel were neither stationed there nor involved in its maintenance. Nonetheless, Israel had encouraged the establishment and enhancement of adequate conditions and improved standards for the detainees therein. An October 1998 ICRC report confirmed that the South Lebanon Army had taken steps towards improving the conditions at Khiam. Furthermore, that particular detention centre, according to Israel, was the only one of its kind in Lebanon, regularly visited and supervised by ICRC.

In a 28 October note verbale to the Secretary-General [A/54/516-S/1999/1105], the Syrian Arab Republic transmitted a statement issued by its Ministry of Foreign Affairs on the occasion of the International Day to Close the Khiam Detention Camp. Syria said that Khiam had become the symbol of the flagrant violation of the Universal Declaration of Human Rights [YUN 1948-49, p. 535] and all related international instruments, and that Israel had not allowed an international mission of inquiry or a human rights organization to enter the camp from the outset.

On 12 August [A/53/1035-S/1999/878], Israel said that an increasing number of roadside bombs had been placed along the main axes of movement in the central sectors of the security zone in southern Lebanon. On 22 July, Israel Defence Forces (IDF) units discovered a large store of weaponry, including roadside bombs for use by Hezbollah. Israel noted that the use by Hezbollah of Lebanese villages and population centres as launching points and staging areas for terror operations was yet a further violation of the April 1996 understanding. In that context, the allegations made by Lebanon on 2 August that Israel had been holding the people of Ayta under siege was baseless. Movement by residents of the village was unrestricted both within the security zone and outside.

On 6 December [A/54/656-S/1999/1224], Lebanon reported that Israeli military forces were maintaining their siege of Ayta and continued to harass and arrest its inhabitants. The town was completely cut off from the outside world owing to its continued encirclement by Israeli forces.

In a series of monthly communications [A/53/792-S/1999/33, A/53/831-S/1999/158, A/53/859-S/1999/257, A/53/918-S/1999/459, A/53/967-S/1999/586, A/53/999-S/1999/687, A/53/1024-S/1999/811, A/53/1050-S/1999/971, A/54/435-S/1999/1023, A/54/524-S/1999/1122, A/54/655-S/1999/1220, A/54/689-S/1999/1272], Lebanon detailed Israeli attacks on southern Lebanon and the Western Bekaa and its practices against the civilian inhabitants of those areas. Israel, on four occasions [A/54/74-S/1999/300, A/54/138-S/1999/704, A/54/351-S/1999/979, A/54/620-S/1999/1178], replied that Lebanon's monthly letters merely obscured the fact that the Lebanese Government was directly responsible for the volatile situation along its southern border, since it continued to encourage Hezbollah and other terrorist organizations to use Lebanese territory for their declared war against Israel.

UNIFIL

The Security Council twice extended the mandate of the United Nations Interim Force in Lebanon (UNIFIL) in 1999, in January and July, each time for a six-month period.

UNIFIL, which was established by Council resolution 425(1978) following Israel's invasion of Lebanon [YUN 1978, p. 296], was originally entrusted with confirming the withdrawal of Israeli forces, restoring international peace and security, and assisting the Lebanese Government in ensuring the return of its effective authority in southern Lebanon. Following a second Israeli invasion in 1982 [YUN 1982, p. 428], the Council, in resolution 511(1982) [ibid., p. 450], authorized the Force to carry out, in addition to its original mandate, the interim task of providing protection and humanitarian assistance to the local population, while maintaining its positions in the area of deployment.

The Force headquarters, based predominantly in Naqoura, provided command and control, as well as liaison with Lebanon and Israel, the United Nations Disengagement Observer Force, the United Nations Truce Supervision Organization (UNTSO) and a number of NGOs.

Composition and deployment

As at 31 December 1999, UNIFIL comprised 4,504 troops from: Fiji (600), Finland (494), France (245), Ghana (653), India (619), Ireland (612), Italy (46), Nepal (604) and Poland (631). The Force was assisted in its tasks by 51 military observers of UNTSO. In addition, UNIFIL employed 460 civilian staff, of whom 116 were recruited internationally and 344 locally. On 15 November [S/1999/1168], the Security Council took note of the Secretary-General's intention [S/1999/1167] to appoint Major-General Seth Kofi Obeng (Ghana) as Force Commander on 1 December, to replace Major-General Jioji Konousi Konrote (Fiji), who completed his tour of duty on 30 September.

Since the establishment of UNIFIL, 229 members of the Force had lost their lives: 77 as a result of firings or bomb explosions, 94 in accidents and 58 from other causes. A total of 341 were wounded by shooting or by mine or bomb explosions.

Activities

Report of Secretary-General (January). In a report on developments from 16 July 1998 to 15 January 1999 in the UNIFIL area of operation [S/1999/61], the Secretary-General said that hostilities continued between IDF and its local Lebanese auxiliary, the de facto forces (DFF), on the one hand, and armed elements who had proclaimed their resistance against the Israeli occupation, on the other.

During the reporting period, UNIFIL recorded 386 operations by armed elements against IDF/DFF, the highest number in a long time. Some 280 operations north of the Litani River were also reported, the vast majority of which were carried out by the Islamic Resistance, the military wing of the Shiite Muslim Hezbollah organization. The Shiite movement Amal took responsibility for some 30 operations; a few were attributed to other Lebanese groups. The armed elements employed small arms, mortars, rocket-propelled grenades, anti-tank missiles, recoilless rifles, rockets and explosive devices. IDF/DFF, in response to attacks or in operations they initiated, employed artillery, mortars, tanks, helicopter gunships, fixed-wing aircraft and explosive devices. IDF continued its practice of conducting pre-emptive artillery bombardments but reduced long-range patrols forward of its positions. UNIFIL recorded close to 18,000 rounds of artillery, mortar, tanks and missiles fired by IDF/DFF, an increase of 70 per cent over the last reporting period [YUN 1998, p. 476]. IDF conducted seven air raids in UNIFIL's area of operation and another 58 air raids were carried out against targets north of the Litani River. The Israeli navy patrolled the Lebanese territorial waters in the south and imposed restrictions on local fishermen.

UNIFIL continued its efforts to limit the conflict and to protect the inhabitants from the fighting through its network of checkpoints and observation posts and an active programme of patrolling, as well as continuous contacts with the parties. Nevertheless, civilians were again killed or injured in UNIFIL's area of operation. Serious incidents were also reported outside that area. Incidents of armed elements operating close to UN positions became more frequent and firings at or close to UN personnel increased to 98, compared to 72 during the last reporting period. The monitoring group set up in accordance with the 26 April 1996 understanding held 16 meetings at UNIFIL headquarters to consider complaints by Israel and Lebanon.

Within the Israeli-controlled area (ICA), Israel continued to maintain a civil administration and security service. The infrastructure in ICA continued to be improved with funds provided by the Lebanese Government. However, ICA remained economically dependent on Israel, where more than 2,500 of the inhabitants worked. IDF/DFF conducted search operations in some villages in ICA and made several arrests, while its security apparatus restricted the movement of the inhabitants on a number of occasions.

UNIFIL extended assistance to the civilian population in its area of operation and ICA in the form of medical care, harvest patrols and the distribution of educational material and equipment to poorer schools and orphanages. The Force also assisted the Government of Lebanon in transporting and distributing supplies to villages in ICA when they faced shortages owing to restrictions imposed by IDF/DFF. Throughout the period, UNIFIL cooperated on humanitarian matters with the Lebanese authorities, UN agencies, ICRC and other organizations and agencies operating in Lebanon. In addition, the Force carried out 41 controlled explosions of unexploded ordnance in its area of operation.

The Secretary-General observed that fighting in south Lebanon continued at an increased pace and the situation in the area remained volatile and dangerous, with a heightened risk of escalation. Although UNIFIL had been prevented from implementing the mandate contained in Security Council resolution 425(1978), its contribution to stability and the protection it was able to afford the population of the area remained important. Therefore, he recommended that the Council accede to Lebanon's request (see next page) and extend UNIFIL's mandate for another six months, until 31 July 1999.

Communication (January). By an 8 January letter to the Secretary-General [S/1999/22], Lebanon requested the Security Council to extend UNIFIL's mandate for a further interim period of six months. Lebanon called for the full implementation of resolution 425(1978), which called on Israel to cease its military action against Lebanese territorial integrity and to withdraw forthwith its forces from all Lebanese territory.

SECURITY COUNCIL ACTION (January)

On 28 January [meeting 3970], the Security Council unanimously adopted **resolution 1223(1999)**. The draft [S/1999/75] was prepared in consultations among Council members.

The Security Council,

Recalling its resolutions 425(1978) and 426(1978) of 19 March 1978, 501(1982) of 25 February 1982, 508(1982) of 5 June 1982, 509(1982) of 6 June 1982 and 520(1982) of 17 September 1982, as well as all its resolutions on the situation in Lebanon,

Having studied the report of the Secretary-General of 19 January 1999 on the United Nations Interim Force in Lebanon, and taking note of the observations expressed and the commitments mentioned therein,

Taking note of the letter dated 8 January 1999 from the Permanent Representative of Lebanon to the United Nations addressed to the Secretary-General,

Responding to the request of the Government of Lebanon,

1. *Decides* to extend the present mandate of the United Nations Interim Force in Lebanon for a further period of six months, that is, until 31 July 1999;
2. *Reiterates its strong support* for the territorial integrity, sovereignty and political independence of Lebanon within its internationally recognized boundaries;
3. *Re-emphasizes* the terms of reference and general guidelines of the Force as stated in the report of the Secretary-General of 19 March 1978, approved by resolution 426(1978), and calls upon all parties concerned to cooperate fully with the Force for the full implementation of its mandate;
4. *Condemns* all acts of violence committed in particular against the Force, and urges the parties to put an end to them;
5. *Reiterates* that the Force should fully implement its mandate as defined in resolutions 425(1978), 426(1978) and all other relevant resolutions;
6. *Encourages* further efficiency and savings provided they do not affect the operational capacity of the Force;
7. *Requests* the Secretary-General to continue consultations with the Government of Lebanon and other parties directly concerned with the implementation of the present resolution and to report to the Security Council thereon.

At the same meeting, the President made statement **S/PRST/1999/4** on behalf of the Council:

The Security Council has noted with appreciation the report of the Secretary-General of 19 January 1999 on the United Nations Interim Force in Lebanon, submitted in conformity with resolution 1188(1998) of 30 July 1998.

The Council reaffirms its commitment to the full sovereignty, political independence, territorial integrity and national unity of Lebanon within its internationally recognized boundaries. In this context, the Council asserts that all States shall refrain from the threat or use of force against the territorial integrity or political independence of any State, or in any other manner inconsistent with the purposes of the United Nations.

As the Council extends the mandate of the Force for a further interim period on the basis of resolution 425(1978), it again stresses the urgent need for the implementation of that resolution in all its aspects. It reiterates its full support for the Taif Agreement of 22 October 1989 and for the continued efforts of the Lebanese Government to consolidate peace, national unity and security in the country, while successfully carrying out the reconstruction process. The Council commends the Lebanese Government for its successful effort to extend its authority in the south of the country in full coordination with the Force.

The Council expresses its concern over the continuing violence in southern Lebanon, regrets the loss of civilian life and urges all parties to exercise restraint.

The Council takes this opportunity to express its appreciation for the continuing efforts of the Secretary-General and his staff in this regard. The Council notes with deep concern the high level of casualties the Force has suffered and pays a special tribute to all those who gave their lives while serving in the Force. It commends the troops of the Force and troop-contributing countries for their sacrifices and commitment to the cause of international peace and security under difficult circumstances.

Report of Secretary-General (July). In a report on developments from 16 January to 15 July [S/1999/807], the Secretary-General noted that there had been an increase in fighting between IDF/DFF and anti-Israeli armed elements. UNIFIL recorded 359 operations conducted by armed elements against IDF/DFF. There were also reports of some 200 operations north of the Litani River by the Islamic Resistance, 20 by Amal and a few by other Lebanese groups. The hostilities reached their peak on 24 June, when Israel carried out air raids against civilian targets in Lebanon and armed elements fired rockets into northern Israel.

A significant development was DFF's withdrawal from the town of Jezzin at the end of May and in the first days of June and its return under the full control of the Lebanese authorities, thereby reducing the area under Israeli control for the first time since 1985. The withdrawal complied with the April 1998 [YUN 1998, p. 472] decision by the Israeli Ministerial Committee for National Security to accept Security Council resolution 425(1978). Inside UNIFIL's area of operation, however, the situation was more volatile. Armed elements displayed an increasing tendency to operate in the vicinity of villages and UNIFIL positions. DFF showed signs of loosened control and, in some cases, vented their apparent frustration by firing into villages and targeting UNIFIL positions.

UNIFIL troops were deployed to provide a measure of protection to villages and farmers working in the fields, as part of its continued efforts to limit the conflict and protect the inhabitants from the fighting. Nevertheless, civilians were again killed or injured. In carrying out its functions, the Force encountered hostile reactions by both armed elements and IDF/DFF. On 31 May, a UNIFIL soldier was killed and two were wounded by a mortar round fired by IDF/DFF at a UN position. The number of firings at or close to UN positions and personnel was almost double that of the last reporting period, totalling 180—111 by IDF/DFF, 56 by armed elements and 13 unattributable.

The Secretary-General reported the death of five members of the Force during the period under review. In addition to the soldier killed by IDF/DFF fire, one member of the Force died due to the accidental discharge of a service rifle, while three others died of natural causes.

UNIFIL continued to assist in the delivery of humanitarian assistance to the civilian population and to cooperate on humanitarian matters with the Lebanese authorities, UN agencies, ICRC and other organizations. The disposal of unexploded ordnance also continued, with 117 explosions being carried out in UNIFIL's area of operation. The monitoring group set up in accordance with the April 1996 understanding held 15 meetings at UNIFIL headquarters to consider complaints by Israel and Lebanon.

The Secretary-General observed that, notwithstanding the escalation of hostilities, the return of Jezzin under the jurisdiction of the Lebanese Government had been a positive sign and it was hoped that the same would become possible for the part of Lebanon that was still under Israeli control. He reaffirmed his belief that UNIFIL's contribution to the stability and the protection it provided to the population of the area remained important. Therefore, he recommended that the Force's mandate be extended for another six months, until 31 January 2000, as requested by Lebanon on 25 June [S/1999/720].

On 2 June, the Security Council President issued a press statement in which the Council members noted the information provided by the Secretary-General on 1 June concerning a 31 May mortar attack on UN positions located in and around the edge of Brashit and the resulting casualties, including the death of an Irish soldier. Members of the Council expressed their deep sympathy and condolences to the families of the victims and condemned any action that violated UNIFIL's non-combatant status.

SECURITY COUNCIL ACTION (July)

On 30 July [meeting 4028], the Security Council adopted **resolution 1254(1999)** unanimously. The draft text [S/1999/826] had been prepared in consultations among Council members.

The Security Council,

Recalling its resolutions 425(1978) and 426(1978) of 19 March 1978, 501(1982) of 25 February 1982, 508(1982) of 5 June 1982, 509(1982) of 6 June 1982 and 520(1982) of 17 September 1982, as well as all its resolutions on the situation in Lebanon,

Having studied the report of the Secretary-General of 21 July 1999 on the United Nations Interim Force in Lebanon, and taking note of the observations expressed and the commitments mentioned therein,

Taking note of the letter dated 25 June 1999 from the Permanent Representative of Lebanon to the United Nations addressed to the Secretary-General,

Responding to the request of the Government of Lebanon,

1. *Decides* to extend the present mandate of the United Nations Interim Force in Lebanon for a further period of six months, that is, until 31 January 2000;
2. *Reiterates its strong support* for the territorial integrity, sovereignty and political independence of Lebanon within its internationally recognized boundaries;
3. *Re-emphasizes* the terms of reference and general guidelines of the Force as stated in the report of the Secretary-General of 19 March 1978, approved by resolution 426(1978), and calls upon all parties concerned to cooperate fully with the Force for the full implementation of its mandate;
4. *Condemns* all acts of violence committed in particular against the Force, and urges the parties to put an end to them;
5. *Reiterates* that the Force should fully implement its mandate as defined in resolutions 425(1978), 426(1978) and all other relevant resolutions;
6. *Encourages* further efficiency and savings provided they do not affect the operational capacity of the Force;
7. *Requests* the Secretary-General to continue consultations with the Government of Lebanon and other parties directly concerned with the implementation of the present resolution and to report to the Security Council thereon.

After the adoption of the resolution, the President made statement **S/PRST/1999/24**, which was identical to statement **S/PRST/1999/4** (see p. 446), except for the first paragraph:

> The Security Council has noted with appreciation the report of the Secretary-General of 21 July 1999 on the United Nations Interim Force in Lebanon, submitted in conformity with resolution 1223(1999) of 28 January 1999.

Further developments

In a report on developments during the second half of 1999 [S/2000/28], the Secretary-General noted that a significant political development for the region was the resumption, in December, of negotiations between Israel and the Syrian Arab Republic, under the auspices of the United States. Hostilities continued at a somewhat reduced level between IDF/DFF, on the one hand, and anti-Israeli armed elements, on the other. Nevertheless, the Secretary-General observed that the situation in the area remained volatile.

UNIFIL recorded 340 operations by armed elements against IDF/DFF from 16 July to 31 December. The Islamic Resistance continued to carry out operations north of the Litani River, while the Palestinian group Islamic Jihad, which had not been active in the area for two years, took responsibility for two operations. IDF/DFF, in response to attacks or in operations they initiated, relied more heavily on air raids as a retaliatory measure, though they continued their practice of conducting pre-emptive artillery bombardments. Incidents of armed elements operating from close to UN positions increased, reaching a high of 21 in December. Roughly half of those incidents were attributable to the Islamic Resistance and the other half to the Shiite movement Amal.

In the area where it was deployed, UNIFIL continued its efforts to limit the conflict, to protect the inhabitants from the fighting through its network of checkpoints and observations posts, and to assist the civilian population in the form of medical care, harvest patrols, water projects, services for schools and supplies to social services.

Financing

Reports of Secretary-General and ACABQ. In a January report [A/53/797], the Secretary-General submitted the financial performance report of UNIFIL for the period 1 July 1997 to 30 June 1998. Expenditures for the period totalled $125,027,300 gross ($121,704,700 net), resulting in additional requirements of $57,600 ($844,000 net), compared to the amount appropriated for the maintenance of UNIFIL by the General Assembly in its resolution 51/233 [YUN 1997, p. 463]. The report also provided updated information on expenditure in connection with the incident at Qana on 18 April 1996 [YUN 1996, p. 429], totalling $1,284,633 against the commitment authorization of $1,773,618 granted by the Assembly in resolution 51/233.

In February [A/53/819], the Secretary-General presented the proposed budget for UNIFIL for the period 1 July 1999 to 30 June 2000, in the amount of $140,044,200 gross ($136,014,800 net), inclusive of a $135,000 budgeted voluntary contribution.

The comments and recommendations of ACABQ were contained in an April report [A/53/895/Add.1].

GENERAL ASSEMBLY ACTION

On 8 June [meeting 101], the General Assembly, on the recommendation of the Fifth Committee [A/53/982], adopted **resolution 53/227** by recorded vote (119-2-1) [agenda item 122 *(b)*].

Financing of the United Nations Interim Force in Lebanon

The General Assembly,

Reaffirming its resolutions 51/233 of 13 June 1997 and 52/237 of 26 June 1998,

Having considered the reports of the Secretary-General on the financing of the United Nations Interim Force in Lebanon and the related reports of the Advisory Committee on Administrative and Budgetary Questions,

Bearing in mind Security Council resolution 425 (1978) of 19 March 1978, by which the Council established the United Nations Interim Force in Lebanon, and the subsequent resolutions by which the Council extended the mandate of the Force, the latest of which was resolution 1223(1999) of 28 January 1999,

Recalling its resolution S-8/2 of 21 April 1978 on the financing of the Force and its subsequent resolutions thereon, the latest of which was resolution 52/237,

Reaffirming that the costs of the Force are expenses of the Organization to be borne by Member States in accordance with Article 17, paragraph 2, of the Charter of the United Nations,

Recalling its previous decisions regarding the fact that, in order to meet the expenditures caused by the Force, a different procedure is required from that applied to meet expenditures of the regular budget of the United Nations,

Taking into account the fact that the economically more developed countries are in a position to make relatively larger contributions and that the economically less developed countries have a relatively limited capacity to contribute towards such an operation,

Bearing in mind the special responsibilities of the States permanent members of the Security Council, as indicated in General Assembly resolution 1874(S-IV) of 27 June 1963, in the financing of such operations,

Noting with appreciation that voluntary contributions have been made to the Force,

Mindful of the fact that it is essential to provide the Force with the necessary financial resources to enable it to fulfil its responsibilities under the relevant resolutions of the Security Council,

Concerned that the Secretary-General continues to face difficulties in meeting the obligations of the Force on a current basis, including reimbursement to current and former troop-contributing States,

Concerned also that the surplus balances in the Special Account for the United Nations Interim Force in Lebanon have been used to meet expenses of the Force in order to compensate for the lack of income resulting from non-payment and late payment by Member States of their contributions,

1. *Takes note* of the status of contributions to the United Nations Interim Force in Lebanon as at 30 April 1999, including the contributions outstanding in the amount of 119,646,994 United States dollars, representing 4 per cent of the total assessed contributions from the inception of the Force to the period ending 30 June 1999, notes that some 12 per cent of the

Member States have paid their assessed contributions in full, and urges all other Member States concerned, particularly those in arrears, to ensure payment of their outstanding assessed contributions;

2. *Expresses its deep concern* that Israel did not comply with General Assembly resolutions 51/233 and 52/237;

3. *Stresses once again* that Israel should strictly abide by General Assembly resolutions 51/233 and 52/237;

4. *Expresses concern* about the financial situation with regard to peacekeeping activities, in particular as regards the reimbursement of troop contributors, which bear additional burdens owing to overdue payments by Member States of their assessments;

5. *Expresses its appreciation* to those Member States which have paid their assessed contributions in full;

6. *Urges* all other Member States to make every possible effort to ensure payment of their assessed contributions to the Force in full and on time;

7. *Takes note* of the report of the Advisory Committee on Administrative and Budgetary Questions;

8. *Requests* the Secretary-General to take all necessary action to ensure that the Force is administered with a maximum of efficiency and economy;

9. *Also requests* the Secretary-General, in order to reduce the cost of employing General Service staff, to continue his efforts to recruit local staff for the Force against General Service posts, commensurate with the requirements of the Force;

10. *Decides* to revise the amount of the commitment authority granted in paragraph 7 of General Assembly resolution 51/233 in connection with the costs resulting from the incident at Qana on 18 April 1996 and, correspondingly, the amount to be borne by Israel as decided in paragraph 8 of the same resolution, from 1,773,618 dollars to 1,284,633 dollars;

11. *Reiterates its request* to the Secretary-General to take the necessary measures to ensure the full implementation of paragraph 8 of General Assembly resolution 51/233 and paragraph 5 of resolution 52/237, stresses once again that Israel shall pay the amount of 1,284,633 dollars resulting from the incident at Qana on 18 April 1996, and requests the Secretary-General to report on this matter to the Assembly at its fifty-fourth session;

12. *Takes note* of the additional requirements of 57,600 dollars gross (844,000 dollars net) for the period from 1 July 1997 to 30 June 1998, which will be covered by the liquidation of obligations no longer required for that period;

13. *Decides* to appropriate to the Special Account for the United Nations Interim Force in Lebanon the amount of 148,904,683 dollars gross (144,875,283 dollars net) for the maintenance of the Force for the period from 1 July 1999 to 30 June 2000, inclusive of the amount of 7,407,886 dollars for the support account for peacekeeping operations and the amount of 1,452,597 dollars for the United Nations Logistics Base at Brindisi, Italy;

14. *Decides also*, as an ad hoc arrangement, to apportion among Member States the amount of 12,397,474 dollars gross (12,061,690 dollars net) for the period from 1 to 31 July 1999, in accordance with the composition of groups set out in paragraphs 3 and 4 of General Assembly resolution 43/232 of 1 March 1989, as adjusted by the Assembly in its resolutions 44/192 B of 21 December 1989, 45/269 of 27 August 1991, 46/198 A of 20 December 1991, 47/218 A of 23 December 1992, 49/249 A of 20 July 1995, 49/249 B of 14 September 1995, 50/224 of 11 April 1996, 51/218 A to C of 18 December 1996 and 52/230 of 31 March 1998 and its decisions 48/472 A of 23 December 1993 and 50/451 B of 23 December 1995, and taking into account the scale of assessments for the years 1999 and 2000, as set out in its resolution 52/215 A of 22 December 1997;

15. *Decides further* that, in accordance with the provisions of its resolution 973(X) of 15 December 1955, there shall be set off against the apportionment among Member States, as provided for in paragraph 14 above, their respective share in the Tax Equalization Fund of the estimated staff assessment income of 335,784 dollars approved for the period from 1 to 31 July 1999;

16. *Decides*, as an ad hoc arrangement, to apportion among Member States the amount of 136,372,209 dollars gross (132,678,593 dollars net) for the period from 1 August 1999 to 30 June 2000, at a monthly rate of 12,397,474 dollars gross (12,061,690 dollars net) in accordance with the scheme set out in the present resolution and taking into account the scale of assessments for the years 1999 and 2000 as set out in its resolution 52/215 A, subject to the decision of the Security Council to extend the mandate of the Force beyond 31 July 1999;

17. *Decides also* that, in accordance with the provisions of its resolution 973(X), there shall be set off against the apportionment among Member States, as provided for in paragraph 16 above, their respective share in the Tax Equalization Fund of the estimated staff assessment income of 3,693,616 dollars approved for the period from 1 August 1999 to 30 June 2000;

18. *Invites* voluntary contributions to the Force in cash and in the form of services and supplies acceptable to the Secretary-General, to be administered, as appropriate, in accordance with the procedure and practices established by the General Assembly;

19. *Decides* to include in the provisional agenda of its fifty-fourth session, under the item entitled "Financing of the United Nations peacekeeping forces in the Middle East", the sub-item entitled "United Nations Interim Force in Lebanon".

RECORDED VOTE ON RESOLUTION 53/227:

In favour: Algeria, Andorra, Argentina, Armenia, Australia, Austria, Bahamas, Bahrain, Bangladesh, Barbados, Belarus, Belgium, Bhutan, Bolivia, Botswana, Brazil, Brunei Darussalam, Bulgaria, Burkina Faso, Canada, Chile, China, Colombia, Comoros, Congo, Costa Rica, Côte d'Ivoire, Croatia, Cuba, Cyprus, Czech Republic, Democratic People's Republic of Korea, Denmark, Djibouti, Dominican Republic, Ecuador, Egypt, Estonia, Finland, France, Georgia, Germany, Ghana, Greece, Guyana, Haiti, Hungary, Iceland, India, Indonesia, Ireland, Italy, Jamaica, Japan, Jordan, Kazakhstan, Kenya, Kuwait, Lao People's Democratic Republic, Lebanon, Libyan Arab Jamahiriya, Liechtenstein, Lithuania, Luxembourg, Madagascar, Malawi, Malaysia, Maldives, Mali, Malta, Mauritius, Mexico, Monaco, Morocco, Mozambique, Myanmar, Namibia, Nepal, Netherlands, New Zealand, Nicaragua, Nigeria, Norway, Oman, Pakistan, Panama, Papua New Guinea, Paraguay, Peru, Philippines, Poland, Portugal, Qatar, Republic of Korea, Romania, Russian Federation, Saudi Arabia, Senegal, Singapore, Slovakia, Slovenia, South Africa, Spain, Sri Lanka, Suriname, Sweden, Syrian Arab Republic, Thailand, Tunisia, Turkey, Uganda, Ukraine, United Arab Emirates, United Kingdom, United Republic of Tanzania, Uruguay, Viet Nam, Yemen, Zimbabwe.

Against: Israel, United States.

Abstaining: Iran.

The Assembly and the Committee adopted the first preambular paragraph and operative paragraphs 2, 3, 10 and 11 by a recorded vote of 74 to 2, with 42 abstentions, and 84 to 2, with 46 abstentions, respectively.

Speaking before the vote, Israel said that it bore no responsibility or blame for taking necessary measures in the legitimate exercise of self-defence, as it did in the case of the Qana incident. Israel could, however, negotiate a resolution to the conflict that would restore peace and security to the Israeli-Lebanese border and ultimately prevent those incidents.

Lebanon said that resistance against the Israeli forces in southern Lebanon would continue, along with political endeavours, until the implementation of Security Council resolution 425(1978), which called for the unconditional and immediate withdrawal of Israel from the Lebanese territories to internationally recognized boundaries.

By **decision 54/462 A** of 23 December, the Assembly decided that the Fifth Committee should continue consideration of UNIFIL's financing at the resumed fifty-fourth (2000) session.

Syrian Arab Republic

In 1999, the General Assembly again called for Israel's withdrawal from the Golan Heights in the Syrian Arab Republic, which it had occupied since 1967. The area was effectively annexed by Israel when it extended its laws, jurisdiction and administration to the territory towards the end of 1981 [YUN 1981, p. 309].

Israeli policies and measures affecting the human rights of the population in the Golan Heights and other occupied territories were monitored by the Special Committee to Investigate Israeli Practices Affecting the Human Rights of the Palestinian People and Other Arabs of the Occupied Territories (Committee on Israeli Practices) and were the subject of resolutions adopted by the Commission on Human Rights (see p. 736 to 738) and the Assembly.

Special Committee on Israeli Practices. In its annual report [A/54/325], the Committee on Israeli Practices stated that it had visited Damascus as well as Quneitra province, which bordered the occupied area, where it received information from witnesses on the current situation in the Syrian Arab Golan. The Committee was informed that there had been no change in Israeli policy regarding the occupied Golan, that the number of settlers had increased and existing settlements had expanded during the period under review, though no new ones were established.

The Committee was informed that the Golan was inhabited by some 23,000 Syrians who lived in five villages under Israeli occupation. The approximately 40 Israeli settlements in the Golan, the largest of which was Katzrin, were inhabited by 15,000 settlers. The Israeli authorities had set a target figure for 36,000 settlers and, accordingly, 2,500 new housing units were to be added to the settlements. The settlements competed with Syrians in economic terms regarding agriculture, and competition was rendered more uneven by the restricted access of the Syrian inhabitants to water resources. The Committee was informed that the main purpose of the Golan's occupation was control over those resources.

The Committee's attention was drawn in particular to three serious problems: the use of the educational curriculum by Israel to incite sectarian differences among the Arab population and the marginalization of the Arabic language; the separation of families living on either side of the valley constituting the demarcation line; and the danger posed by landmines, especially those laid close to villages and houses. The Committee called on the United Nations High Commissioner for Human Rights, in consultation with the Secretary-General, to establish a system of continuous communication with the Israeli authorities with a view to improving the living conditions of the Palestinian and Syrian peoples in the occupied territories.

Reports of Secretary-General. On 28 July [A/54/184], the Secretary-General reported that no reply had been received from Israel to his June request for information on steps taken to implement General Assembly resolution 53/57 [YUN 1998, p. 481], which called on Israel to desist from changing the physical character, demographic composition, institutional structure and legal status of the Golan, and from its repressive measures against the population.

By a 25 October report [A/54/495], the Secretary-General transmitted replies received from six Member States in response to his request for information on steps taken or envisaged to implement Assembly resolutions 53/38 [YUN 1998, p. 480], which dealt with Israeli policies in the Syrian territory occupied since 1967, and 53/37 [ibid., p. 436] on the transfer by some States of their diplomatic missions to Jerusalem (see p. 408).

GENERAL ASSEMBLY ACTION

On 1 December [meeting 68], the General Assembly adopted **resolution 54/38** [draft: A/54/L.41 & Add.1] by recorded vote (92-2-53) [agenda item 43].

The Syrian Golan

The General Assembly,

Having considered the item entitled "The situation in the Middle East",

Taking note of the report of the Secretary-General,

Recalling Security Council resolution 497(1981) of 17 December 1981,

Reaffirming the fundamental principle of the inadmissibility of the acquisition of territory by force, in accordance with international law and the Charter of the United Nations,

Reaffirming once more the applicability of the Geneva Convention relative to the Protection of Civilian Persons in Time of War, of 12 August 1949, to the occupied Syrian Golan,

Deeply concerned that Israel has not withdrawn from the Syrian Golan, which has been under occupation since 1967, contrary to the relevant Security Council and General Assembly resolutions,

Stressing the illegality of the Israeli settlement construction and activities in the occupied Syrian Golan since 1967,

Noting with satisfaction the convening at Madrid on 30 October 1991 of the Peace Conference on the Middle East, on the basis of Security Council resolutions 242(1967) of 22 November 1967, 338(1973) of 22 October 1973 and 425(1978) of 19 March 1978 and the formula of land for peace,

Expressing grave concern over the halt in the peace process on the Syrian and Lebanese tracks, and expressing the hope that peace talks will soon resume from the point they had reached,

1. *Declares* that Israel has failed so far to comply with Security Council resolution 497(1981);

2. *Declares also* that the Israeli decision of 14 December 1981 to impose its laws, jurisdiction and administration on the occupied Syrian Golan is null and void and has no validity whatsoever, as confirmed by the Security Council in its resolution 497(1981), and calls upon Israel to rescind it;

3. *Reaffirms its determination* that all relevant provisions of the Regulations annexed to the Hague Convention of 1907, and the Geneva Convention relative to the Protection of Civilian Persons in Time of War, of 12 August 1949, continue to apply to the Syrian territory occupied by Israel since 1967, and calls upon the parties thereto to respect and ensure respect for their obligations under those instruments in all circumstances;

4. *Determines once more* that the continued occupation of the Syrian Golan and its de facto annexation constitute a stumbling block in the way of achieving a just, comprehensive and lasting peace in the region;

5. *Calls upon* Israel to resume the talks on the Syrian and Lebanese tracks and to respect the commitments and undertakings reached during the previous talks;

6. *Demands once more* that Israel withdraw from all the occupied Syrian Golan to the line of 4 June 1967 in implementation of the relevant Security Council resolutions;

7. *Calls upon* all the parties concerned, the co-sponsors of the peace process and the entire international community to exert all the necessary efforts to ensure the resumption of the peace process and its success;

8. *Requests* the Secretary-General to report to the General Assembly at its fifty-fifth session on the implementation of the present resolution.

RECORDED VOTE ON RESOLUTION 54/38:

In favour: Afghanistan, Algeria, Angola, Antigua and Barbuda, Argentina, Armenia, Bahamas, Bahrain, Bangladesh, Belarus, Bhutan, Bosnia and Herzegovina, Botswana, Brunei Darussalam, Cambodia, Cameroon, Cape Verde, Chile, China, Colombia, Comoros, Congo, Costa Rica, Cuba, Cyprus, Democratic People's Republic of Korea, Djibouti, Dominica, Ecuador, Egypt, El Salvador, Ethiopia, Gabon, Ghana, Grenada, Guinea, Guyana, Haiti, Honduras, India, Indonesia, Iran, Jamaica, Jordan, Kuwait, Lao People's Democratic Republic, Lebanon, Libyan Arab Jamahiriya, Madagascar, Malaysia, Maldives, Mali, Malta, Mauritius, Mexico, Mongolia, Morocco, Mozambique, Myanmar, Namibia, Nepal, Nigeria, Oman, Pakistan, Panama, Papua New Guinea, Philippines, Qatar, Russian Federation, Saint Lucia, Saint Vincent and the Grenadines, Saudi Arabia, Senegal, Sierra Leone, Singapore, South Africa, Sri Lanka, Sudan, Syrian Arab Republic, Tajikistan, Thailand, Togo, Trinidad and Tobago, Tunisia, Turkey, United Arab Emirates, United Republic of Tanzania, Venezuela, Viet Nam, Yemen, Zambia, Zimbabwe.

Against: Israel, United States.

Abstaining: Andorra, Australia, Austria, Belgium, Brazil, Bulgaria, Canada, Croatia, Czech Republic, Denmark, Estonia, Finland, France, Georgia, Germany, Greece, Guatemala, Hungary, Iceland, Ireland, Italy, Japan, Kazakhstan, Kenya, Latvia, Liechtenstein, Lithuania, Luxembourg, Marshall Islands, Micronesia, Monaco, Netherlands, New Zealand, Norway, Paraguay, Peru, Poland, Portugal, Republic of Korea, Romania, Samoa, San Marino, Slovakia, Slovenia, Solomon Islands, Spain, Swaziland, Sweden, The former Yugoslav Republic of Macedonia, Ukraine, United Kingdom, Uruguay, Uzbekistan.

On 6 December [meeting 71], the Assembly, under the agenda item on the report of the Committee on Israeli Practices and on the Fourth Committee's recommendation [A/54/576], adopted **resolution 54/80** by recorded vote (150-1-5) [agenda item 89].

The occupied Syrian Golan

The General Assembly,

Having considered the reports of the Special Committee to Investigate Israeli Practices Affecting the Human Rights of the Palestinian People and Other Arabs of the Occupied Territories,

Deeply concerned that the Syrian Golan occupied since 1967 has been under continued Israeli military occupation,

Recalling Security Council resolution 497(1981) of 17 December 1981,

Recalling also its previous relevant resolutions, the last of which was resolution 53/57 of 3 December 1998,

Having considered the report of the Secretary-General submitted in pursuance of resolution 53/57,

Recalling its previous relevant resolutions in which, *inter alia*, it called upon Israel to put an end to its occupation of the Arab territories,

Reaffirming once more the illegality of the decision of 14 December 1981 taken by Israel to impose its laws, jurisdiction and administration on the occupied Syrian Golan, which has resulted in the effective annexation of that territory,

Reaffirming that the acquisition of territory by force is inadmissible under international law, including the Charter of the United Nations,

Reaffirming also the applicability of the Geneva Convention relative to the Protection of Civilian Persons in Time of War, of 12 August 1949, to the occupied Syrian Golan,

Bearing in mind Security Council resolution 237(1967) of 14 June 1967,

Welcoming the convening at Madrid of the Peace Conference on the Middle East on the basis of Security Council resolutions 242(1967) of 22 November 1967 and 338(1973) of 22 October 1973 aimed at the realization of a just, comprehensive and lasting peace, and expressing grave concern about the stalling of the peace process on the Syrian and Lebanese tracks,

1. *Calls upon* Israel, the occupying Power, to comply with the relevant resolutions on the occupied Syrian Golan, in particular Security Council resolution 497(1981), in which the Council, *inter alia*, decided that

the Israeli decision to impose its laws, jurisdiction and administration on the occupied Syrian Golan was null and void and without international legal effect, and demanded that Israel, the occupying Power, rescind forthwith its decision;

2. *Also calls upon* Israel to desist from changing the physical character, demographic composition, institutional structure and legal status of the occupied Syrian Golan and in particular to desist from the establishment of settlements;

3. *Determines* that all legislative and administrative measures and actions taken or to be taken by Israel, the occupying Power, that purport to alter the character and legal status of the occupied Syrian Golan are null and void, constitute a flagrant violation of international law and of the Geneva Convention relative to the Protection of Civilian Persons in Time of War, of 12 August 1949, and have no legal effect;

4. *Calls upon* Israel to desist from imposing Israeli citizenship and Israeli identity cards on the Syrian citizens in the occupied Syrian Golan, and to desist from its repressive measures against the population of the occupied Syrian Golan;

5. *Deplores* the violations by Israel of the Geneva Convention relative to the Protection of Civilian Persons in Timc of War, of 12 August 1949;

6. *Calls once again upon* Member States not to recognize any of the legislative or administrative measures and actions referred to above;

7. *Requests* the Secretary-General to report to the General Assembly at its fifty-fifth session on the implementation of the present resolution.

RECORDED VOTE ON RESOLUTION 54/80:

In favour: Albania, Algeria, Andorra, Angola, Antigua and Barbuda, Argentina, Armenia, Australia, Austria, Bahamas, Bahrain, Bangladesh, Barbados, Belarus, Belgium, Belize, Benin, Bhutan, Bolivia, Botswana, Brazil, Brunei Darussalam, Bulgaria, Burkina Faso, Cambodia, Cameroon, Canada, Cape Verde, Chad, Chile, China, Colombia, Congo, Costa Rica, Côte d'Ivoire, Croatia, Cuba, Cyprus, Czech Republic, Democratic People's Republic of Korea, Denmark, Djibouti, Dominica, Ecuador, Egypt, El Salvador, Equatorial Guinea, Eritrea, Estonia, Ethiopia, Fiji, Finland, France, Gabon, Gambia, Georgia, Germany, Ghana, Greece, Grenada, Guatemala, Guinea, Guyana, Haiti, Hungary, Iceland, India, Indonesia, Iran, Ireland, Italy, Jamaica, Japan, Jordan, Kenya, Kuwait, Lao People's Democratic Republic, Latvia, Lebanon, Libyan Arab Jamahiriya, Liechtenstein, Lithuania, Luxembourg, Madagascar, Malaysia, Maldives, Mali, Malta, Mauritius, Mexico, Monaco, Mongolia, Morocco, Mozambique, Myanmar, Namibia, Nepal, Netherlands, New Zealand, Nicaragua, Nigeria, Norway, Oman, Pakistan, Panama, Papua New Guinea, Paraguay, Peru, Philippines, Poland, Portugal, Qatar, Republic of Korea, Republic of Moldova, Romania, Russian Federation, Saint Lucia, Saint Vincent and the Grenadines, Samoa, San Marino, Saudi Arabia, Senegal, Sierra Leone, Singapore, Slovakia, Slovenia, Solomon Islands, South Africa, Spain, Sri Lanka, Sudan, Suriname, Sweden, Syrian Arab Republic, Tajikistan, Thailand, The former Yugoslav Republic of Macedonia, Togo, Trinidad and Tobago, Tunisia, Turkey, Ukraine, United Arab Emirates, United Kingdom, United Republic of Tanzania, Venezuela, Viet Nam, Yemen, Zambia, Zimbabwe.

Against: Israel.

Abstaining: Marshall Islands, Micronesia, Swaziland, United States, Uruguay.

UNDOF

The mandate of the United Nations Disengagement Observer Force (UNDOF), established by Security Council resolution 350(1974) [YUN 1974, p. 205], to supervise the observance of the ceasefire between Israel and Syria in the Golan Heights area and ensuring the separation of their forces, was renewed twice in 1999, in May and November, each time for a six-month period.

UNDOF maintained an area of separation, which was some 80 kilometres long and varied in width between approximately 10 kilometres in the centre to less than 1 kilometre in the extreme south. The area of separation was inhabited and policed by the Syrian authorities and no military forces other than UNDOF were permitted within it.

Composition and deployment

As at November 1999, UNDOF comprised 1,053 troops from Austria (368), Canada (189), Japan (45), Poland (358) and Slovakia (93). It was assisted by 78 UNTSO military observers. Major-General Cameron Ross (Canada) continued as Force Commander. The Force was entirely deployed within and close to the area of separation, with two base camps, 44 permanently manned positions and 11 observation posts. UNDOF's headquarters was located at Camp Faouar and an office was maintained in Damascus.

Thc Austrian battalion deployed in the northern part of the area of separation and the Polish battalion in the south conducted mine-clearing operations. The Canadian and Japanese logistic units, based in Camp Ziouani, with a detachment in Camp Faouar, performed second-line general transport tasks, rotation transport, control and management of goods received by the Force and maintenance of heavy equipment.

Activities

UNDOF continued in 1999 to supervise the area of separation between Israeli and Syrian troops in the Golan Heights, to ensure that no military forces of either party were deployed there, by means of fixed positions and patrols. The Force, accompanied by liaison officers from the party concerned, carried out fortnightly inspections of armament and force levels in the areas of limitation. As in the past, both sides denied inspection teams access to some of their positions and imposed some restrictions on the Force's freedom of movement.

UNDOF assisted ICRC with facilities for mail and the passage of persons through the area of separation. Within the means available, medical treatment was provided to the local population upon request.

Reports of Secretary-General. The Secretary-General reported to the Security Council on UNDOF activities between 15 November 1998 and 15 May 1999 [S/1999/575] and between 16 May and 15 November 1999 [S/1999/1175]. Both reports noted that UNDOF continued to perform its functions effectively, with the cooperation of the parties. In general, the ceasefire in the Israel-Syria sector was maintained without serious incident, and the UNDOF area of operation remained calm. On 1 April, two Austrian soldiers travelling in a UN vehicle were shot at near Damascus; Syrian authorities were investigating the incident. Minefields, especially in the area of separation, continued to be a concern.

The Secretary-General observed that, despite the quiet in the Israel-Syria sector, the situation in the Middle East continued to be potentially dangerous and was likely to remain so, unless and until a comprehensive settlement covering all aspects of the Middle East problem could be reached. He hoped for determined efforts by all concerned to tackle the problem in all its aspects, with a view to arriving at a just and durable peace settlement, as called for by Council resolution 338(1973) [YUN 1973, p. 213]. Stating that he considered the Force's continued presence in the area to be essential, the Secretary-General, with the agreement of both Syria and Israel, recommended that UNDOF's mandate be extended for a further six months, until 30 November 1999 in the first instance and 31 May 2000 in the second.

SECURITY COUNCIL ACTION

On 27 May [meeting 4009], the Security Council adopted **resolution 1243(1999)** unanimously. The draft [S/1999/609] was prepared during consultations among Council members.

The Security Council,

Having considered the report of the Secretary-General on the United Nations Disengagement Observer Force of 18 May 1999,

Decides:

(a) To call upon the parties concerned to implement immediately Security Council resolution 338(1973) of 22 October 1973;

(b) To renew the mandate of the United Nations Disengagement Observer Force for another period of six months, that is, until 30 November 1999;

(c) To request the Secretary-General to submit, at the end of this period, a report on the development in the situation and the measures taken to implement resolution 338(1973).

On 24 November [meeting 4071], the Council unanimously adopted **resolution 1276(1999)**. The draft [S/1999/1189] was prepared during consultations.

The Security Council,

Having considered the report of the Secretary-General of 15 November 1999 on the United Nations Disengagement Observer Force,

Decides:

(a) To call upon the parties concerned to implement immediately Security Council resolution 338(1973) of 22 October 1973;

(b) To renew the mandate of the United Nations Disengagement Observer Force for another period of six months, that is, until 31 May 2000;

(c) To request the Secretary-General to submit, at the end of this period, a report on the development in the situation and the measures taken to implement resolution 338(1973).

After the adoption of each resolution, the President made statements **S/PRST/1999/15** [meeting 4009] and **S/PRST/1999/33** [meeting 4071] on behalf of the Council:

> As is known, the report of the Secretary-General on the United Nations Disengagement Observer Force states, in paragraph 11 [10 in the November report]: "Despite the present quiet in the Israeli-Syrian sector, the situation in the Middle East continues to be potentially dangerous and is likely to remain so, unless and until a comprehensive settlement covering all aspects of the Middle East problem can be reached." That statement of the Secretary-General reflects the view of the Security Council.

Financing

Reports of Secretary-General and ACABQ. On 5 January, the Secretary-General presented a report [A/53/779 & Corr.1] on UNDOF's financial performance for the period 1 July 1997 to 30 June 1998. On 29 January, he also presented UNDOF's proposed budget for the period 1 July 1999 to 30 June 2000 [A/53/779/Add.1], totalling $33,247,500 gross ($32,514,600 net), which reflected a 1.2 per cent decrease in gross terms compared with the resources approved for the preceding 12 months.

ACABQ's comments and recommendations on the two reports were contained in an April report to the Assembly [A/53/895/Add.1].

GENERAL ASSEMBLY ACTION

On 8 June [meeting 101], the General Assembly, on the recommendation of the Fifth Committee [A/53/979], adopted **resolution 53/226** without vote [agenda item 122 *(a)*].

Financing of the United Nations Disengagement Observer Force

The General Assembly,

Having considered the reports of the Secretary-General on the financing of the United Nations Disengagement Observer Force and the related reports of the Advisory Committee on Administrative and Budgetary Questions,

Recalling Security Council resolution 350(1974) of 31 May 1974, by which the Council established the United Nations Disengagement Observer Force, and the subsequent resolutions by which the Council extended the mandate of the Force, the latest of which was Security Council resolution 1211(1998) of 25 November 1998,

Recalling also its resolution 3211 B (XXIX) of 29 November 1974 on the financing of the United Nations Emergency Force and of the United Nations Disengagement Observer Force and its subsequent resolutions thereon, the latest of which was resolution 52/236 of 26 June 1998,

Reaffirming that the costs of the United Nations Disengagement Observer Force are expenses of the Organization to be borne by Member States in accordance with Article 17, paragraph 2, of the Charter of the United Nations,

Recalling its previous decisions regarding the fact that, in order to meet the expenditures caused by the Force, a different procedure is required from that applied to meet expenditures of the regular budget of the United Nations,

Taking into account the fact that the economically more developed countries are in a position to make relatively larger contributions and that the economically less developed countries have a relatively limited capacity to contribute towards such an operation,

Bearing in mind the special responsibilities of the States permanent members of the Security Council, as indicated in General Assembly resolution 1874(S-IV) of 27 June 1963, in the financing of such operations,

Noting with appreciation that voluntary contributions have been made to the Force,

Mindful of the fact that it is essential to provide the Force with the necessary financial resources to enable it to fulfil its responsibilities under the relevant resolutions of the Security Council,

Concerned that the surplus balances in the Special Account for the United Nations Disengagement Observer Force have been used to meet expenses of the Force in order to compensate for the lack of income resulting from non-payment and late payment by Member States of their contributions,

1. *Takes note* of the status of contributions to the United Nations Disengagement Observer Force as at 30 April 1999, including the contributions outstanding in the amount of 17.6 million United States dollars, representing 1.4 per cent of the total assessed contributions from the inception of the Force to the period ending 31 May 1999, notes that some 15 per cent of the Member States have paid their assessed contributions in full, and urges all other Member States concerned, particularly those in arrears, to ensure payment of their outstanding assessed contributions;

2. *Expresses concern* about the financial situation with regard to peacekeeping activities, in particular as regards the reimbursement of troop contributors, which bear additional burdens owing to overdue payments by Member States of their assessments;

3. *Expresses its appreciation* to those Member States which have paid their assessed contributions in full;

4. *Urges* all Member States to make every possible effort to ensure payment of their assessed contributions to the Force in full and on time;

5. *Endorses* the observations and recommendations contained in the report of the Advisory Committee on Administrative and Budgetary Questions;

6. *Requests* the Secretary-General to take all necessary action to ensure that the Force is administered with a maximum of efficiency and economy;

7. *Also requests* the Secretary-General to expedite the process of improving the working conditions of the local staff in the Force, taking into account the difficulties arising from the relocation of Force headquarters from Damascus to Camp Faouar, and requests the Secretary-General to report thereon to the General Assembly at its fifty-fourth session;

8. *Further requests* the Secretary-General, in order to reduce the cost of employing General Service staff, to continue efforts to employ local staff for the Force against General Service posts, commensurate with the requirements of the Force;

9. *Decides,* as an ad hoc arrangement, to appropriate to the Special Account for the United Nations Disengagement Observer Force the amount of 35,351,308 dollars gross (34,618,408 dollars net) for the maintenance of the Force for the period from 1 July 1999 to 30 June 2000, inclusive of the amount of 1,758,908 dollars for the support account for peacekeeping operations and the amount of 344,900 dollars for the United Nations Logistics Base at Brindisi, Italy, to be apportioned among Member States at the monthly rate of 2,945,942 dollars gross (2,884,867 dollars net), in accordance with the composition of groups set out in paragraphs 3 and 4 of General Assembly resolution 43/232 of 1 March 1989, as adjusted by the Assembly in its resolutions 44/192 B of 21 December 1989, 45/269 of 27 August 1991, 46/198 A of 20 December 1991, 47/218 A of 23 December 1992, 49/249 A of 20 July 1995, 49/249 B of 14 September 1995, 50/224 of 11 April 1996, 51/218 A to C of 18 December 1996 and 52/230 of 31 March 1998 and its decisions 48/472 A of 23 December 1993 and 50/451 B of 23 December 1995, and taking into account the scale of assessments for the years 1999 and 2000, as set out in its resolution 52/215 A of 22 December 1997, subject to the decision of the Security Council to extend the mandate of the Force beyond 30 June 1999;

10. *Decides also* that, in accordance with the provisions of its resolution 973(X) of 15 December 1955, there shall be set off against the apportionment among Member States, as provided for in paragraph 9 above, their respective share in the Tax Equalization Fund of the estimated staff assessment income of 732,900 dollars approved for the period from 1 July 1999 to 30 June 2000;

11. *Decides further* that, for Member States that have fulfilled their financial obligations to the Force, there shall be set off against the apportionment, as provided for in paragraph 9 above, their respective share in the unencumbered balance of 1,085,300 dollars gross (887,600 dollars net) in respect of the period from 1 July 1997 to 30 June 1998;

12. *Decides* that, for Member States that have not fulfilled their financial obligations to the Force, their share of the unencumbered balance of 1,085,300 dollars gross (887,600 dollars net) in respect of the period from 1 July 1997 to 30 June 1998 shall be set off against their outstanding obligations;

13. *Requests* the Secretary-General to credit back to Member States in a phased manner not to exceed three years, beginning with 5.6 million dollars during the current session of the General Assembly, according to the procedures contained in paragraphs 9 to 12 above, the net surplus balance of 13,622,162 dollars held in the suspense account for the Force;

14. *Invites* voluntary contributions to the Force in cash and in the form of services and supplies acceptable to the Secretary-General, to be administered, as appropriate, in accordance with the procedure and practices established by the General Assembly;

15. *Decides* to include in the provisional agenda of its fifty-fourth session, under the item entitled "Financing of the United Nations peacekeeping forces in the Middle East", the sub-item entitled "United Nations Disengagement Observer Force".

On 23 December, the Assembly decided that the Fifth Committee would continue consideration of the item on the financing of UNDOF at the resumed fifty-fourth (2000) session (**decision 54/462 A**).

By **decision 54/465** of 23 December, the Assembly decided that agenda item "Financing of the United Nations peacekeeping forces in the Middle East" remained for consideration during its fifty-fourth session.

Chapter VII

Disarmament

During 1999, differences among Member States persisted on many disarmament issues. The Conference on Disarmament was unable to take action on any of the items on the agenda of its annual session due to continuing lack of agreement on what would constitute a balanced programme of work. The Disarmament Commission was not able to establish the objectives and agenda of a fourth special session of the General Assembly devoted to disarmament, but did agree on guidelines on establishing nuclear-weapon-free zones and on common guidelines for conventional arms control/limitation and disarmament.

The Preparatory Committee for the 2000 Review Conference of the Parties to the 1968 Treaty on the Non-Proliferation of Nuclear Weapons, at its third session, reviewed all aspects of the Treaty and finalized its consideration of organizational and procedural issues related to the Conference. However, no decisions were taken on substantive issues as divergences of views prevailed.

The Conference on Facilitating the Entry into Force of the 1996 Comprehensive Nuclear-Test-Ban Treaty (CTBT) in October called on signatory States to ratify the Treaty as soon as possible.

Efforts to strengthen the 1971 Convention on the Prohibition of the Development, Production and Stockpiling of Bacteriological (Biological) and Toxin Weapons and on Their Destruction, through the elaboration of a protocol to the Convention, were carried out within the Ad Hoc Group of the States Parties. The Organization for the Prohibition of Chemical Weapons, which marked its second full year of operation in 1999, continued its activities under the 1993 Convention on the Prohibition of the Development, Production, Stockpiling and Use of Chemical Weapons and on Their Destruction.

In December, the General Assembly decided to convene the United Nations Conference on the Illicit Trade in Small Arms and Light Weapons in All Its Aspects in June/July 2001. The United Nations Register of Conventional Arms and the standardized instrument of international reporting of military expenditures contributed to building transparency in military matters.

During the year, two legal instruments dealing with anti-personnel mines were strengthened. The 1997 Convention on the Prohibition of the Use, Stockpiling, Production and Transfer of Anti-personnel Mines and on Their Destruction (the Mine-Ban Convention, formerly known as the Ottawa Convention) entered into force on 1 March, followed by the First Meeting of the States Parties to the Mine-Ban Convention in May, when an inter-sessional work programme was developed. Also, the States parties to the 1996 amended Protocol on the Use of Mines, Booby Traps and Other Devices (Protocol II) to the 1980 Convention on Prohibitions or Restrictions on the Use of Certain Conventional Weapons Which May Be Deemed to Be Excessively Injurious or to Have Indiscriminate Effects held their first annual conference in December.

At the regional level, renewed efforts were made towards consolidating the existing nuclear-weapon-free zones, and negotiations on drafting the text of a treaty for a Central Asian nuclear-free zone continued. The issue of the illicit manufacturing and trafficking of small arms was addressed by various regional organizations. The Security Council emphasized the importance of regional cooperation in tackling that matter.

UN role in disarmament

UN machinery

Disarmament issues before the United Nations in 1999 were considered mainly through the General Assembly and its First (Disarmament and International Security) Committee, the Disarmament Commission (a deliberative body) and the Conference on Disarmament (a multilateral negotiating forum, which met in Geneva).

The Department for Disarmament Affairs (DDA) of the UN Secretariat continued to support the work of Member States and treaty bodies, to service the Advisory Board on Disarmament Matters and to administer the fellowship programme.

First Committee agenda items

In **decision 54/416** of 1 December, the General Assembly included in the provisional agenda of its fifty-sixth (2001) session the item entitled "Compliance with arms limitation and disarmament and non-proliferation agreements".

Fourth special session devoted to disarmament

Disarmament Commission action. Pursuant to General Assembly resolution 53/77 AA [YUN 1998, p. 487], the Disarmament Commission considered the question of the fourth special session of the Assembly devoted to disarmament. The Assembly, by resolution 51/45 C [YUN 1996, p. 447], had decided to convene the session in 1999, subject to the emergence of a consensus on its agenda and objectives. Working Group II of the Commission, entrusted to deal with the item, in an exchange of views held between 14 and 29 April, decided that the paper presented by its Chairman in 1998 [YUN 1998, p. 488], which was also annexed to its 1999 report to the Assembly [A/54/42], should serve as a basis for consideration of the subject. Following consideration of various proposals by delegations, the Chairman submitted two compromise proposals. Although, at its final meeting, the vast majority of delegations reiterated their agreement with the Chairman's proposals, the Group was not able to reach consensus on the fourth special session's objectives and agenda.

GENERAL ASSEMBLY ACTION

On 1 December [meeting 69], the General Assembly, on the recommendation of the First Committee [A/54/563], adopted **resolution 54/54 U** without vote [agenda item 76 *(s)*].

Convening of the fourth special session of the General Assembly devoted to disarmament

The General Assembly,

Recalling its resolutions 49/75 I of 15 December 1994, 50/70 F of 12 December 1995, 51/45 C of 10 December 1996, 52/38 F of 9 December 1997 and 53/77 AA of 4 December 1998,

Recalling also that, there being a consensus to do so in each case, three special sessions of the General Assembly devoted to disarmament were held in 1978, 1982 and 1988, respectively,

Bearing in mind the Final Document of the Tenth Special Session of the General Assembly, adopted by consensus at the first special session devoted to disarmament, which included the Declaration, the Programme of Action and the Machinery for disarmament,

Bearing in mind also the objective of general and complete disarmament under effective international control,

Taking note of paragraph 145 of the Final Document of the Twelfth Conference of Heads of State or Government of Non-Aligned Countries, held at Durban, South Africa, from 29 August to 3 September 1998, which supported the convening of the fourth special session of the General Assembly devoted to disarmament, which would offer an opportunity to review, from a perspective more in tune with the current international situation, the most critical aspects of the process of disarmament and to mobilize the international community and public opinion in favour of the elimination of nuclear and other weapons of mass destruction and of the control and reduction of conventional weapons,

Taking note also of the report of the 1999 substantive session of the Disarmament Commission and of the fact that no consensus was reached on the item entitled "Fourth special session of the General Assembly devoted to disarmament",

Desiring to build upon the substantive exchange of views on the fourth special session of the General Assembly devoted to disarmament during the 1999 substantive session of the Disarmament Commission,

Reiterating its conviction that a special session of the General Assembly devoted to disarmament can set the future course of action in the field of disarmament, arms control and related international security matters,

Emphasizing the importance of multilateralism in the process of disarmament, arms control and related international security matters,

Noting that, with the recent accomplishments made by the international community in the field of weapons of mass destruction as well as conventional arms, the following years would be opportune for the international community to start the process of reviewing the state of affairs in the entire field of disarmament and arms control in the post-cold-war era,

1. *Decides,* subject to the emergence of a consensus on its objectives and agenda, to convene the fourth special session of the General Assembly devoted to disarmament;

2. *Requests* the Secretary-General to seek the views of States Members of the United Nations on the objectives, agenda and timing of the special session and to report to the General Assembly at its fifty-fifth session;

3. *Decides* to include in the provisional agenda of its fifty-fifth session the item entitled "Convening of the fourth special session of the General Assembly devoted to disarmament".

Disarmament Commission

The Disarmament Commission, composed of all United Nations Member States, held six plenary meetings in 1999 (New York, 12-30 April) [A/54/42]; it also held organizational meetings on 19 March and on 2 December.

At its 1999 session, the Commission considered the establishment of nuclear-weapon-free zones on the basis of arrangements freely arrived at among the States of the region concerned (see p. 476); the fourth special session of the General Assembly devoted to disarmament (see above); and guidelines on conventional arms control/limitation and disarmament, with particular emphasis on consolidation of peace in the context of Assembly resolution 51/45 N [YUN 1996, p. 490] (see p. 493). The Commission adopted consensus texts on the items concerning nuclear-weapon-free zones and guidelines on conventional arms control/limitation and disarmament.

Those agenda items were dealt with by three working groups, which met between 14 and 29 April.

GENERAL ASSEMBLY ACTION

On 1 December [meeting 69], the General Assembly, on the recommendation of the First Committee [A/54/565], as orally amended by Mexico, adopted **resolution 54/56 A** without vote [agenda item 78 (a)].

Report of the Disarmament Commission

The General Assembly,

Having considered the report of the Disarmament Commission,

Recalling its resolutions 47/54 A of 9 December 1992, 47/54 G of 8 April 1993, 48/77 A of 16 December 1993, 49/77 A of 15 December 1994, 50/72 D of 12 December 1995, 51/47 B of 10 December 1996, 52/40 B of 9 December 1997 and 53/79 A of 4 December 1998,

Considering the role that the Disarmament Commission has been called upon to play and the contribution that it should make in examining and submitting recommendations on various problems in the field of disarmament and in the promotion of the implementation of the relevant decisions adopted by the General Assembly at its tenth special session,

Bearing in mind its decision 52/492 of 8 September 1998,

1. *Takes note* of the report of the Disarmament Commission;

2. *Commends* the Disarmament Commission for the successful conclusion of its consideration of the items entitled "The establishment of nuclear-weapon-free zones on the basis of arrangements freely arrived at among the States of the region concerned" and "Guidelines on conventional arms control/limitation and disarmament, with particular emphasis on consolidation of peace in the context of General Assembly resolution 51/45 N of 10 December 1996", and endorses the consensus texts adopted thereon;

3. *Notes with regret* that the Disarmament Commission was not able to reach a consensus on the item entitled "The fourth special session of the General Assembly devoted to disarmament";

4. *Reaffirms* the importance of further enhancing the dialogue and cooperation among the First Committee, the Disarmament Commission and the Conference on Disarmament;

5. *Also reaffirms* the role of the Disarmament Commission as the specialized, deliberative body within the United Nations multilateral disarmament machinery that allows for in-depth deliberations on specific disarmament issues, leading to the submission of concrete recommendations on those issues;

6. *Requests* the Disarmament Commission to continue its work in accordance with its mandate, as set forth in paragraph 118 of the Final Document of the Tenth Special Session of the General Assembly, and with paragraph 3 of Assembly resolution 37/78 H of 9 December 1982, and to that end to make every effort to achieve specific recommendations on the items of its agenda, taking into account the adopted "Ways and means to enhance the functioning of the Disarmament Commission";

7. *Recommends* that the Disarmament Commission, at its 1999 organizational session, adopt the following items for consideration at its 2000 substantive session:

(*a*) To be considered at the organizational session of the Disarmament Commission;

(*b*) To be considered at the organizational session of the Disarmament Commission;

8. *Requests* the Disarmament Commission to meet for a period not exceeding three weeks during 2000 and to submit a substantive report to the General Assembly at its fifty-fifth session;

9. *Requests* the Secretary-General to transmit to the Disarmament Commission the annual report of the Conference on Disarmament, together with all the official records of the fifty-fourth session of the General Assembly relating to disarmament matters, and to render all assistance that the Commission may require for implementing the present resolution;

10. *Also requests* the Secretary-General to ensure full provision to the Disarmament Commission and its subsidiary bodies of interpretation and translation facilities in the official languages and to assign, as a matter of priority, all the necessary resources and services, including verbatim records, to that end;

11. *Decides* to include in the provisional agenda of its fifty-fifth session the item entitled "Report of the Disarmament Commission".

Conference on Disarmament

The Conference on Disarmament, a multilateral negotiating body, held a three-part session in Geneva in 1999 (18 January–26 March, 10 May–25 June and 26 July–8 September) [A/54/27].

The Conference considered the cessation of the nuclear arms race and nuclear disarmament; prevention of nuclear war; prevention of an arms race in outer space; effective international arrangements to assure non-nuclear-weapon States against the use or threat of use of nuclear weapons; new types of weapons of mass destruction and new systems of such weapons; radiological weapons; a comprehensive programme of disarmament; and transparency in armaments.

During the session, successive Presidents of the Conference conducted intensive consultations with a view to reaching consensus on the programme of work. At the end of their respective terms of office, two Presidents tabled proposals for the programme of work [CD/1566, CD/1575]. Proposals in that regard were also submitted by the Group of 21 [CD/1570], and jointly by France, the United Kingdom and the United States [CD/1586]. Although those proposals had a number of common elements, they differed considerably on how the Conference should deal with nuclear disarmament and prevention of an arms race in outer space. As a result, none of them achieved consensus. The consultations conducted by the Presidents were inconclusive and, consequently, the Conference did not re-establish or establish any mechanism on any of its agenda items during the session.

Throughout the session, a number of Western and Eastern European States called for the re-establishment of the two ad hoc committees that had met in 1998 [YUN 1998, p. 489], so that they might continue their work on a ban on the production of fissile material for nuclear weapons or other nuclear explosive devices, and on effective international arrangements to assure non-nuclear-weapon States against the use or threat of use of nuclear weapons. Those calls were challenged by the non-aligned countries and China, which continued to insist that a comprehensive and balanced programme of work should be adopted as a whole. Chile made a proposal aimed at the intensification of informal consultations conducted by Presidents of the Conference, according to which the Presidents would organize open-ended consultations on each item of the agenda [CD/PV.834]. The proposal was favourably received by some Western and Eastern European States, but was not further developed.

Following consideration of a proposal by the President to expand the membership of the Conference [CD/1567], the Conference, on 5 August, decided to admit Ecuador, Ireland, Kazakhstan, Malaysia and Tunisia [CD/1588], bringing the membership to 66.

GENERAL ASSEMBLY ACTION

On 1 December [meeting 69], the General Assembly, on the recommendation of the First Committee [A/54/565], adopted **resolution 54/56 B** without vote [agenda item 78 *(b)*].

Report of the Conference on Disarmament

The General Assembly,

Having considered the report of the Conference on Disarmament,

Convinced that the Conference on Disarmament, as the single multilateral disarmament negotiating forum of the international community, has the primary role in substantive negotiations on priority questions of disarmament,

Recognizing, in this respect, the need for additional impetus to multilateral negotiations with the aim of reaching concrete agreements,

Noting that the Conference on Disarmament has a number of urgent and important issues to negotiate,

1. *Reaffirms* the role of the Conference on Disarmament as the single multilateral disarmament negotiating forum of the international community;
2. *Urges* the Conference on Disarmament to fulfil that role in the light of the evolving international situation, with a view to making early substantive progress on priority items of its agenda;
3. *Welcomes* the decision of the Conference on Disarmament on 5 August 1999 to admit five new members, and notes that the Conference recognizes the importance of continuing consultations on the question of the expansion of its membership;
4. *Also welcomes* the strong collective interest of the Conference on Disarmament in commencing substantive work as soon as possible during its 2000 session;
5. *Further welcomes* the undertaking by the current President of the Conference on Disarmament to conduct consultations jointly with the incoming President during the inter-sessional period to try to achieve this goal, as expressed in his statement contained in paragraph 38 of the report of the Conference;
6. *Encourages* the Conference on Disarmament to continue the ongoing review of its agenda and methods of work;
7. *Requests* the Secretary-General to continue to ensure the provision to the Conference on Disarmament of adequate administrative, substantive and conference support services;
8. *Requests* the Conference on Disarmament to submit a report on its work to the General Assembly at its fifty-fifth session;
9. *Decides* to include in the provisional agenda of its fifty-fifth session the item entitled "Report of the Conference on Disarmament".

Multilateral disarmament agreements

As at 31 December 1999, the following numbers of States had become parties to the multilateral agreements listed below (in chronological order, with the years in which they were initially signed or opened for signature).

(Geneva) Protocol for the Prohibition of the Use in War of Asphyxiating, Poisonous or Other Gases, and of Bacteriological Methods of Warfare (1925): 132 parties

The Antarctic Treaty (1959): 44 parties

Treaty Banning Nuclear Weapon Tests in the Atmosphere, in Outer Space and under Water (1963): 124 parties

Treaty on Principles Governing the Activities of States in the Exploration and Use of Outer Space, including the Moon and Other Celestial Bodies (1967) [YUN 1966, p. 41, GA res. 2222(XXI), annex]: 96 parties

Treaty for the Prohibition of Nuclear Weapons in Latin America and the Caribbean (Treaty of Tlatelolco) (1967): 38 parties

Treaty on the Non-Proliferation of Nuclear Weapons (1968) [YUN 1968, p. 17, GA res. 2373 (XXII), annex]: 187 parties

Treaty on the Prohibition of the Emplacement of Nuclear Weapons and Other Weapons of Mass Destruction on the Seabed and the Ocean Floor and in the Subsoil Thereof (1971) [YUN 1970, p. 18, GA res. 2660(XXV), annex]: 92 parties

Convention on the Prohibition of the Development, Production and Stockpiling of Bacteriological (Biological) and Toxin Weapons and on Their Destruction (1972) [YUN 1971, p. 19, GA res. 2826 (XXVI), annex]: 143 parties

Convention on the Prohibition of Military or Any Other Hostile Use of Environmental Modification Techniques (1977) [YUN 1976, p. 45, GA res. 31/72, annex]: 66 parties

Agreement Governing the Activities of States on the Moon and Other Celestial Bodies (1979) [YUN 1979, p. 111, GA res. 34/68, annex]: 9 parties

Convention on Prohibitions or Restrictions on the Use of Certain Conventional Weapons Which May Be Deemed to Be Excessively Injurious or to Have Indiscriminate Effects (1981): 75 parties

South Pacific Nuclear-Free Zone Treaty (Treaty of Rarotonga) (1985): 16 parties

Treaty on Conventional Armed Forces in Europe (CFE Treaty) (1990): 30 parties

Treaty on Open Skies (1992): 23 parties

Convention on the Prohibition of the Development, Production, Stockpiling and Use of Chemical Weapons and on Their Destruction (1993): 129 parties

Treaty on the South-East Asia Nuclear-Weapon-Free Zone (Bangkok Treaty) (1995): 9 parties

African Nuclear-Weapon-Free Zone Treaty (Pelindaba Treaty) (1996): 13 parties

Comprehensive Nuclear-Test-Ban Treaty (1996): 51 parties

Inter-American Convention against the Illicit Manufacturing of and Trafficking in Firearms, Ammunition, Explosives, and Other Related Materials (1997): 10 parties

Convention on the Prohibition of the Use, Stockpiling, Production and Transfer of Anti-personnel Mines and on Their Destruction (Mine-Ban Convention, formerly known as Ottawa Convention) (1997): 90 parties

Inter-American Convention on Transparency in Conventional Weapons Acquisitions (1999): 1 party

[*United Nations Disarmament Yearbook*, vol. 24: *1999*, Sales No. E.00.IX.1]

Nuclear disarmament

Conference on Disarmament

In 1999, the profound divergence of views on the possible role of the Conference on Disarmament in the field of nuclear disarmament was one of the reasons that prevented a comprehensive agreement on the establishment of subsidiary bodies to carry out substantive work on items on the Conference's agenda, despite the fact that new proposals were submitted by Egypt [CD/1563] and the Group of 21 [CD/1571] for the establishment of an ad hoc committee on nuclear disarmament, and by South Africa [CD/1564], Belgium, Germany, Italy, the Netherlands and Norway [CD/1565], and Canada [CD/1568, CD/1574, CD/1578]. In addition, certain international developments, particularly the stalling of the START process (see p. 462), attempts to define new roles for nuclear weapons and to strengthen deterrence doctrines, as well as proposals to amend the Anti-Ballistic Missile (ABM) Treaty (see p. 469), had adversely affected the international environment for advancing the multilateral arms limitation and disarmament agenda.

Fissile material

Although the re-establishment of the ad hoc committee on the prohibition of the production of fissile material for nuclear weapons or other nuclear explosive devices [YUN 1998, p. 492] was a non-controversial element of every proposal in 1999, the impasse with regard to the adoption of a comprehensive programme of work prevented the Conference on Disarmament from doing so. At the close of the annual session, Finland, on behalf of the European Union (EU), presented the EU declaration on the fissile material cut-off treaty negotiations [CD/1593], which emphasized that such a treaty would strengthen the international nuclear non-proliferation regime and constitute a significant step towards the effective implementation of article VI of the 1968 Treaty on the Non-Proliferation of Nuclear Weapons (NPT) [YUN 1968, p. 17]. In view of its agreement in 1998 to re-establish the ad hoc committee on fissile material, it was incumbent on the Conference to take an early decision to resume those negotiations.

Security assurances

The issue of security assurances for non-nuclear-weapon States against the use or threat of use of nuclear weapons was addressed in the Conference on Disarmament in the context of its programme of work. All proposals in that regard provided for the re-establishment of the ad hoc committee to negotiate with a view to reaching agreement on effective international arrangements to assure non-nuclear-weapon States against the use or threat of use of nuclear weapons. Those arrangements could take the form of an internationally legally binding instrument. However, due to the lack of consensus on a comprehensive programme of work, the ad hoc committee was not re-established.

GENERAL ASSEMBLY ACTION

On 1 December [meeting 69], the General Assembly, on the recommendation of the First Committee [A/54/561], adopted **resolution 54/52** by recorded vote (111-0-53) [agenda item 74].

Conclusion of effective international arrangements to assure non-nuclear-weapon States against the use or threat of use of nuclear weapons

The General Assembly,

Bearing in mind the need to allay the legitimate concern of the States of the world with regard to ensuring lasting security for their peoples,

Convinced that nuclear weapons pose the greatest threat to mankind and to the survival of civilization,

Welcoming the progress achieved in recent years in both nuclear and conventional disarmament,

Noting that, despite recent progress in the field of nuclear disarmament, further efforts are necessary towards the achievement of general and complete disarmament under effective international control,

Convinced that nuclear disarmament and the complete elimination of nuclear weapons are essential to remove the danger of nuclear war,

Determined strictly to abide by the relevant provisions of the Charter of the United Nations on the non-use of force or threat of force,

Recognizing that the independence, territorial integrity and sovereignty of non-nuclear-weapon States need to be safeguarded against the use or threat of use of force, including the use or threat of use of nuclear weapons,

Considering that, until nuclear disarmament is achieved on a universal basis, it is imperative for the international community to develop effective measures and arrangements to ensure the security of non-nuclear-weapon States against the use or threat of use of nuclear weapons from any quarter,

Recognizing that effective measures and arrangements to assure non-nuclear-weapon States against the use or threat of use of nuclear weapons can contribute positively to the prevention of the spread of nuclear weapons,

Bearing in mind paragraph 59 of the Final Document of the Tenth Special Session of the General Assembly, the first special session devoted to disarmament, in which it urged the nuclear-weapon States to pursue efforts to conclude, as appropriate, effective arrangements to assure non-nuclear-weapon States against the use or threat of use of nuclear weapons, and desirous of promoting the implementation of the relevant provisions of the Final Document,

Recalling the relevant parts of the special report of the Committee on Disarmament[a] submitted to the General Assembly at its twelfth special session, the second special session devoted to disarmament, and of the special report of the Conference on Disarmament submitted to the Assembly at its fifteenth special session, the third special session devoted to disarmament, as well as the report of the Conference on its 1992 session,

Recalling also paragraph 12 of the Declaration of the 1980s as the Second Disarmament Decade, contained in the annex to its resolution 35/46 of 3 December 1980, which states, inter alia, that all efforts should be exerted by the Committee on Disarmament urgently to negotiate with a view to reaching agreement on effective international arrangements to assure non-nuclear-weapon States against the use or threat of use of nuclear weapons,

Noting the in-depth negotiations undertaken in the Conference on Disarmament and its Ad Hoc Committee on Effective International Arrangements to Assure Non-Nuclear-Weapon States against the Use or Threat of Use of Nuclear Weapons, with a view to reaching agreement on this question,

Taking note of the proposals submitted under the item in the Conference on Disarmament, including the drafts of an international convention,

Taking note also of the relevant decision of the Twelfth Conference of Heads of State or Government of Non-Aligned Countries, held at Durban, South Africa, from 29 August to 3 September 1998, as well as the relevant recommendations of the Organization of the Islamic Conference,

Taking note further of the unilateral declarations made by all the nuclear-weapon States on their policies of non-use or non-threat of use of nuclear weapons against the non-nuclear-weapon States,

Noting the support expressed in the Conference on Disarmament and in the General Assembly for the elaboration of an international convention to assure non-nuclear-weapon States against the use or threat of use of nuclear weapons, as well as the difficulties pointed out in evolving a common approach acceptable to all,

Taking note of Security Council resolution 984(1995) of 11 April 1995 and the views expressed on it,

Recalling its relevant resolutions adopted in previous years, in particular resolutions 45/54 of 4 December 1990, 46/32 of 6 December 1991, 47/50 of 9 December 1992, 48/73 of 16 December 1993, 49/73 of 15 December 1994, 50/68 of 12 December 1995, 51/43 of 10 December 1996, 52/36 of 9 December 1997 and 53/75 of 4 December 1998,

1. *Reaffirms* the urgent need to reach an early agreement on effective international arrangements to assure non-nuclear-weapon States against the use or threat of use of nuclear weapons;

2. *Notes with satisfaction* that in the Conference on Disarmament there is no objection, in principle, to the idea of an international convention to assure non-nuclear-weapon States against the use or threat of use of nuclear weapons, although the difficulties with regard to evolving a common approach acceptable to all have also been pointed out;

3. *Appeals* to all States, especially the nuclear-weapon States, to work actively towards an early agreement on a common approach and, in particular, on a common formula that could be included in an international instrument of a legally binding character;

4. *Recommends* that further intensive efforts be devoted to the search for such a common approach or common formula and that the various alternative approaches, including, in particular, those considered in the Conference on Disarmament, be further explored in order to overcome the difficulties;

5. *Recommends also* that the Conference on Disarmament actively continue intensive negotiations with a view to reaching early agreement and concluding effective international arrangements to assure the non-nuclear-weapon States against the use or threat of use of nuclear weapons, taking into account the widespread support for the conclusion of an international convention and giving consideration to any other proposals designed to secure the same objective;

6. *Decides* to include in the provisional agenda of its fifty-fifth session the item entitled "Conclusion of ef-

fective international arrangements to assure non-nuclear-weapon States against the use or threat of use of nuclear weapons".

[a]Redesignated the Conference on Disarmament as from 7 February 1984.

RECORDED VOTE ON RESOLUTION 54/52

In favour: Algeria, Angola, Antigua and Barbuda, Armenia, Azerbaijan, Bahamas, Bahrain, Bangladesh, Barbados, Belarus, Belize, Benin, Bhutan, Bolivia, Botswana, Brazil, Brunei Darussalam, Burkina Faso, Cambodia, Cameroon, Cape Verde, Chad, Chile, China, Colombia, Congo, Costa Rica, Côte d'Ivoire, Cuba, Democratic People's Republic of Korea, Djibouti, Dominica, Dominican Republic, Ecuador, Egypt, El Salvador, Equatorial Guinea, Eritrea, Ethiopia, Fiji, Ghana, Grenada, Guatemala, Guinea, Guinea-Bissau, Guyana, Haiti, Honduras, India, Indonesia, Iran, Jamaica, Japan, Jordan, Kazakhstan, Kenya, Kuwait, Lao People's Democratic Republic, Lebanon, Libyan Arab Jamahiriya, Madagascar, Malaysia, Maldives, Mali, Mauritius, Mexico, Mongolia, Morocco, Mozambique, Myanmar, Namibia, Nepal, Nicaragua, Nigeria, Oman, Pakistan, Panama, Papua New Guinea, Paraguay, Peru, Philippines, Qatar, Saint Lucia, Saint Vincent and the Grenadines, Saudi Arabia, Senegal, Seychelles, Sierra Leone, Singapore, Sri Lanka, Sudan, Suriname, Swaziland, Syrian Arab Republic, Tajikistan, Thailand, Togo, Trinidad and Tobago, Tunisia, Turkmenistan, Uganda, Ukraine, United Arab Emirates, United Republic of Tanzania, Uruguay, Uzbekistan, Venezuela, Viet Nam, Yemen, Zambia, Zimbabwe.

Against: None.

Abstaining: Albania, Andorra, Argentina, Australia, Austria, Belgium, Bosnia and Herzegovina, Bulgaria, Canada, Croatia, Cyprus, Czech Republic, Denmark, Estonia, Finland, France, Georgia, Germany, Greece, Hungary, Iceland, Ireland, Israel, Italy, Latvia, Liechtenstein, Lithuania, Luxembourg, Malta, Marshall Islands, Micronesia, Monaco, Netherlands, New Zealand, Norway, Poland, Portugal, Republic of Korea, Republic of Moldova, Romania, Russian Federation, Samoa, San Marino, Slovakia, Slovenia, Solomon Islands, South Africa, Spain, Sweden, The former Yugoslav Republic of Macedonia, Turkey, United Kingdom, United States.

START and other bilateral agreements and unilateral measures

The United States and the Russian Federation continued to implement the 1991 Treaty on the Reduction and Limitation of Strategic Offensive Arms (START I) [YUN 1991, p. 34], which entered into force on 5 December 1994 [YUN 1994, p. 145], by reducing their nuclear-arms stockpiles. Although efforts continued in the Russian Federation to ratify the 1993 START II Treaty [YUN 1993, p. 117], concerns in the Russian Duma regarding strategic arms reductions, enlargement of the North Atlantic Treaty Organization (NATO) membership, the United States announcement of its intention to develop a national missile defence (NMD) system and NATO air strikes against the Federal Republic of Yugoslavia in March 1999 (see PART ONE, Chapter V) contributed to a pattern of postponement of votes, precluding the Treaty's ratification. At the summit of the Group of Eight (G-8) major industrialized countries (Cologne, Germany, 18-20 June), following discussions between Russian President Boris Yeltsin and United States President William J. Clinton, the two States issued a joint statement concerning strategic offensive and defensive arms and further strengthening of stability. They stated that strategic stability could be strengthened only through compliance with existing agreements between the parties on limitation and reduction of arms and that they would do everything to facilitate the successful completion of the START II ratification processes in both countries. They reaffirmed their readiness, expressed in Helsinki in 1997 [YUN 1997, p. 481], to conduct new negotiations on strategic offensive arms aimed at further reducing for each side the level of nuclear warheads and that they would strive to achieve results in those negotiations as soon as possible. In addition, they agreed to begin discussions on START III.

Following an agreement on 27 July between the Russian Federation and the United States, several rounds of talks on START III, as well as on ABM issues, took place. However, no progress was reported due to differences over warheads ceilings under START III. Questions also arose concerning tactical nuclear weapons, and whether to include sea-based cruise missiles and restrictions on anti-submarine warfare in the Treaty.

In June, a protocol to the Agreement between the Russian Federation and the United States concerning the Safe and Secure Transportation, Storage and Destruction of Weapons and the Prevention of Weapons Proliferation was signed by the two parties. The protocol continued the Cooperative Threat Reduction (CTR) programme in Russia until June 2006. Through the CTR programme, the United States provided equipment, services and technical support to assist Russia and other newly independent States in preventing proliferation and securing and dismantling weapons of mass destruction, related materials and production facilities inherited from the former Soviet Union. In July, the United States and Ukraine also extended the agreement to continue the CTR programme in Ukraine until December 2006. Earlier in the year, CTR achieved a major milestone: the complete elimination of the SS-9 intercontinental ballistic missile (ICBM) system, 130 missile silos and 13 launch control centres.

Under the 1996 "Trilateral Initiative" [YUN 1996, p. 465] among the United States, the Russian Federation and the International Atomic Energy Agency (IAEA)—established to address IAEA regulation of fissile material removed from weapons to ensure that, once withdrawn from weapons programmes, it would not be returned to the defence stockpile—further progress was made towards completing the model verification agreement that would serve as the basis for implementing the programme. Moreover, work was under way to develop the verification arrangements for specific facilities identified by Russia and the United States where the new agreement would apply. The model verification agreement could also be used by other NPT nuclear-weapon States for international verification of fissile material in conjunction with future arms control measures.

Communication. By a 15 October letter to the Secretary-General [A/54/469-S/1999/1063], South Africa, as Chairman of the Coordinating Bureau of the Movement of Non-Aligned Countries, transmitted a communiqué of the meeting of the Ministers for Foreign Affairs and Heads of Delegation of the Movement of Non-Aligned Countries (New York, 23 September). The Ministers, among other things, expressed concern at the updating of strategic defence doctrines that set out new rationales for the use of nuclear weapons. They called for an international conference, at the earliest possible date, to agree on a phased programme for the complete elimination of nuclear weapons with a specified time frame to eliminate all nuclear weapons, to prohibit their development and to provide for their destruction.

Report of Secretary-General. In a September report entitled "Towards a nuclear-weapon-free world: the need for a new agenda" [A/54/372], the Secretary-General presented observations on the implementation of General Assembly resolution 53/77 Y [YUN 1998, p. 501].

The Secretary-General said that global negotiations on nuclear disarmament remained at a standstill. The persistence of divergent views on the most pressing issues on the international disarmament agenda had affected, once again, the work of the Conference on Disarmament during 1999. The Secretary-General noted that the joint statement by the Russian Federation and the United States concerning strategic offensive and defensive arms and further strengthening of stability, signed at Cologne on 20 June (see p. 462), was an important development in revitalizing the START process. He also noted that a conference on facilitating the entry into force of the 1996 Comprehensive Nuclear-Test-Ban Treaty was to be held in Vienna in October 1999 (see p. 471).

In accordance with resolution 53/77 Y, a number of international organizations and bodies presented their views on possible elements for developing global verification arrangements. IAEA said that, from its perspective, the universal application of strengthened IAEA safeguards, and effective verification of compliance with agreements to eliminate existing nuclear arsenals, would provide a sound basis for a world free from nuclear weapons. The ability to verify the non-diversion of nuclear material to nuclear weapons and the absence of any undeclared nuclear material and activities would be conducive to an international environment that would discourage the pursuit of the nuclear weapons option. Additional views were expressed by the Organization for the Prohibition of Nuclear Weapons in Latin America and the Caribbean, Thailand, as depositary of the 1995 Treaty on the South-East Asia Nuclear-Weapon-Free Zone, the South Pacific Forum Secretariat, as depositary of the 1985 South Pacific Nuclear-Free Zone Treaty and the Provisional Technical Secretariat of the Preparatory Commission for the Comprehensive Nuclear-Test-Ban Treaty Organization.

GENERAL ASSEMBLY ACTION

On 1 December [meeting 69], the General Assembly, on the recommendation of the First Committee [A/54/563], adopted a series of resolutions related to nuclear disarmament.

The Assembly adopted **resolution 54/54 D** by recorded vote (153-0-12) [agenda item 76].

Nuclear disarmament with a view to the ultimate elimination of nuclear weapons

The General Assembly,

Recalling its resolutions 49/75 H of 15 December 1994, 50/70 C of 12 December 1995, 51/45 G of 10 December 1996, 52/38 K of 9 December 1997 and 53/77 U of 4 December 1998,

Bearing in mind the recent nuclear tests, as well as the regional situations, which pose a challenge to international efforts to strengthen the global regime of non-proliferation of nuclear weapons,

Noting the progress made in commencing the discussions between the United States of America and the Russian Federation on START III,

Welcoming the efforts to increase transparency in nuclear disarmament activities as a contribution towards building international confidence and security,

Also welcoming the international efforts to promote the entry into force of the Comprehensive Nuclear-Test-Ban Treaty at the conference convened at Vienna from 6 to 8 October 1999 in accordance with article XIV of the Treaty,

Taking note of the report of the Tokyo Forum for Nuclear Non-Proliferation and Disarmament,[a] bearing in mind the views of Member States on the report,

Recognizing that the enhancement of international peace and security and the promotion of nuclear disarmament mutually complement and strengthen each other,

Reaffirming the crucial importance of the Treaty on the Non-Proliferation of Nuclear Weapons as the cornerstone of the international regime for nuclear non-proliferation and as an essential foundation for the pursuit of nuclear disarmament,

Also reaffirming the conviction that further advancement in nuclear disarmament will contribute to consolidating the international regime for nuclear non-proliferation, ensuring international peace and security,

1. *Reaffirms* the importance of achieving the universality of the Treaty on the Non-Proliferation of Nuclear Weapons, and calls upon States not parties to the Treaty to accede to it without delay and without conditions;

2. *Also reaffirms* the importance for all States parties to the Treaty on the Non-Proliferation of Nuclear Weapons to fulfil their obligations under the Treaty;

3. *Calls* for the determined pursuit by the nuclear-weapon States of systematic and progressive efforts to reduce nuclear weapons globally, with the ultimate goal of eliminating those weapons, and by all States of general and complete disarmament under strict and effective international control;

4. *Stresses* that, in order to make advancements towards the ultimate goal of eliminating nuclear weapons, it is important and necessary to pursue such actions as:

(*a*) The early signature and ratification of the Comprehensive Nuclear-Test-Ban Treaty by all States, especially by those States whose ratification is required for its entry into force, with a view to its early entry into force, as well as the cessation of nuclear tests pending its entry into force;

(*b*) Intensive negotiations in the Conference on Disarmament on the early conclusion of a non-discriminatory, multilateral and internationally and effectively verifiable treaty banning the production of fissile material for nuclear weapons or other nuclear explosive devices, on the basis of the report of the Special Coordinator of 1995 and the mandate contained therein, and, pending its entry into force, a moratorium on the production of fissile material for nuclear weapons;

(*c*) Multilateral discussions on possible future steps on nuclear disarmament and nuclear non-proliferation;

(*d*) The early entry into force of the Treaty on Further Reduction and Limitation of Strategic Offensive Arms (START II) and the early commencement and conclusion of negotiations for START III by the Russian Federation and the United States of America, and the continuation of the process beyond START III;

(*e*) Further efforts by the five nuclear-weapon States to reduce their nuclear arsenals unilaterally and through their negotiations;

5. *Invites* the nuclear-weapon States to keep the States Members of the United Nations duly informed of the progress or efforts made towards nuclear disarmament;

6. *Welcomes* the ongoing efforts in the dismantlement of nuclear weapons, notes the importance of the safe and effective management of the resultant fissile material, and calls for continued efforts by States that possess fissile material no longer required for defence purposes to make such material available for safeguards by the International Atomic Energy Agency as soon as practicable;

7. *Calls upon* all States to redouble their efforts to prevent the proliferation of weapons of mass destruction, inter alia, nuclear weapons, confirming and strengthening if necessary their policies not to export equipment, materials or technology that could contribute to the proliferation of those weapons;

8. *Stresses* the importance of the Model Protocol Additional to the Agreement(s) between State(s) and the International Atomic Energy Agency for the Application of Safeguards for ensuring nuclear non-proliferation, and encourages all States that have not done so to conclude an additional protocol with the International Atomic Energy Agency as soon as possible;

9. *Underlines* the vital importance of the 2000 Review Conference of the Parties to the Treaty on the Non-Proliferation of Nuclear Weapons for the preservation and strengthening of the regime anchored in the Treaty, and calls upon all States parties to the Treaty to reaffirm the decisions and the resolution adopted at the 1995 Review and Extension Conference of the Parties to the Treaty and to intensify their efforts with a view to reaching an agreement on updated objectives for nuclear non-proliferation and disarmament, based on a review of the achievements since 1995;

10. *Encourages* the constructive role played by civil society in promoting nuclear non-proliferation and nuclear disarmament.

[a]A/54/205-S/1999/853

RECORDED VOTE ON RESOLUTION 54/54 D:

In favour: Albania, Andorra, Angola, Antigua and Barbuda, Argentina, Armenia, Australia, Austria, Azerbaijan, Bahamas, Bahrain, Bangladesh, Barbados, Belarus, Belgium, Belize, Benin, Bolivia, Bosnia and Herzegovina, Botswana, Brazil, Brunei Darussalam, Bulgaria, Burkina Faso, Cambodia, Cameroon, Canada, Cape Verde, Chad, Chile, Colombia, Congo, Costa Rica, Côte d'Ivoire, Croatia, Cyprus, Czech Republic, Denmark, Djibouti, Dominica, Dominican Republic, Ecuador, Egypt, El Salvador, Equatorial Guinea, Eritrea, Estonia, Ethiopia, Fiji, Finland, Georgia, Germany, Ghana, Greece, Grenada, Guatemala, Guinea, Guinea-Bissau, Guyana, Haiti, Honduras, Hungary, Iceland, Indonesia, Iran, Ireland, Italy, Jamaica, Japan, Jordan, Kazakhstan, Kenya, Kuwait, Lao People's Democratic Republic, Latvia, Lebanon, Libyan Arab Jamahiriya, Liechtenstein, Lithuania, Luxembourg, Madagascar, Malaysia, Maldives, Mali, Malta, Marshall Islands, Mexico, Micronesia, Monaco, Mongolia, Morocco, Mozambique, Namibia, Nepal, Netherlands, New Zealand, Nicaragua, Nigeria, Norway, Oman, Panama, Papua New Guinea, Paraguay, Peru, Philippines, Poland, Portugal, Qatar, Republic of Korea, Republic of Moldova, Romania, Saint Kitts and Nevis, Saint Lucia, Saint Vincent and the Grenadines, Samoa, San Marino, Saudi Arabia, Senegal, Seychelles, Sierra Leone, Singapore, Slovakia, Slovenia, Solomon Islands, South Africa, Spain, Sri Lanka, Sudan, Suriname, Swaziland, Sweden, Syrian Arab Republic, Tajikistan, Thailand, The former Republic of Macedonia, Togo, Trinidad and Tobago, Tunisia, Turkey, Turkmenistan, Uganda, Ukraine, United Arab Emirates, United Kingdom, United Republic of Tanzania, United States, Uruguay, Uzbekistan, Venezuela, Viet Nam, Yemen, Zambia, Zimbabwe.

Against: None.

Abstaining: Algeria, Bhutan, China, Cuba, Democratic People's Republic of Korea, France, India, Israel, Mauritius, Myanmar, Pakistan, Russian Federation.

In the First Committee, the second preambular paragraph and paragraphs 1 and 9 were adopted by recorded votes of 130 to 1, with 4 abstentions; 134 to 2, with 3 abstentions; and 103 to 1, with 27 abstentions, respectively. The text as a whole was adopted by a recorded vote of 128 to none, with 12 abstentions. Similarly, the Assembly retained the same paragraphs by recorded votes of 154 to 2, with 4 abstentions; 158 to 3, with 2 abstentions; and 132 to 1, with 22 abstentions, respectively.

Resolution 54/54 P was adopted by recorded vote (104-41-17) [agenda item 76 (*q*)].

Nuclear disarmament

The General Assembly,

Recalling its resolution 49/75 E of 15 December 1994 on a step-by-step reduction of the nuclear threat, and its resolutions 50/70 P of 12 December 1995, 51/45 O of 10 December 1996, 52/38 L of 9 December 1997 and 53/77 X of 4 December 1998 on nuclear disarmament,

Reaffirming the commitment of the international community to the goal of the total elimination of nuclear weapons and the establishment of a nuclear-weapon-free world,

Bearing in mind that the Convention on the Prohibition of the Development, Production and Stockpiling of Bacteriological (Biological) and Toxin Weapons and on Their Destruction of 1972 and the Convention on the Prohibition of the Development, Production, Stockpiling and Use of Chemical Weapons and on Their Destruction of 1993 have already established legal regimes on the complete prohibition of biological and chemical weapons, respectively, and determined to achieve a nuclear weapons convention on the prohibition of the development, testing, production, stockpiling, loan, transfer, use and threat of use of nuclear weapons and on their destruction, and to conclude such an international convention at an early date,

Recognizing that there now exist conditions for the establishment of a world free of nuclear weapons,

Bearing in mind paragraph 50 of the Final Document of the Tenth Special Session of the General Assembly, the first special session devoted to disarmament, calling for the urgent negotiation of agreements for the cessation of the qualitative improvement and development of nuclear-weapon systems, and for a comprehensive and phased programme with agreed time-frames, wherever feasible, for the progressive and balanced reduction of nuclear weapons and their means of delivery, leading to their ultimate and complete elimination at the earliest possible time,

Noting the reiteration by the States parties to the Treaty on the Non-Proliferation of Nuclear Weapons of their conviction that the Treaty is a cornerstone of nuclear non-proliferation and nuclear disarmament and the reaffirmation by the States parties of the importance of the decision on strengthening the review process for the Treaty, the decision on principles and objectives for nuclear non-proliferation and disarmament, the decision on the extension of the Treaty and the resolution on the Middle East, adopted by the 1995 Review and Extension Conference of the Parties to the Treaty on the Non-Proliferation of Nuclear Weapons,

Reiterating the highest priority accorded to nuclear disarmament in the Final Document of the Tenth Special Session of the General Assembly and by the international community,

Recognizing that the Comprehensive Nuclear-Test-Ban Treaty and any proposed treaty on fissile material for nuclear weapons or other nuclear explosive devices must constitute disarmament measures, and not only non-proliferation measures, and that these measures, together with an international legal instrument on the joint undertaking of no first use of nuclear weapons by the nuclear-weapon States and on adequate security assurances of non-use and non-threat of use of such weapons for non-nuclear-weapon States, respectively, and an international convention prohibiting the use of nuclear weapons, should be integral measures in a programme leading to the total elimination of nuclear weapons,

Welcoming the entry into force of the Treaty on the Reduction and Limitation of Strategic Offensive Arms (START I), to which Belarus, Kazakhstan, the Russian Federation, Ukraine and the United States of America are States parties,

Welcoming also the conclusion of the Treaty on Further Reduction and Limitation of Strategic Offensive Arms (START II) by the Russian Federation and the United States of America and the ratification of that Treaty by the United States of America, and looking forward to the full implementation of the START I and START II Treaties by the States parties, and to further concrete steps for nuclear disarmament by all the nuclear-weapon States,

Welcoming further the joint declaration of the Russian Federation and the United States of America to commence START III negotiations, regardless of the status of completion of the START II process,

Noting with appreciation the unilateral measures by the nuclear-weapon States for nuclear arms limitation, and encouraging them to undertake further such measures,

Recognizing the complementarity of bilateral, plurilateral and multilateral negotiations on nuclear disarmament, and that bilateral negotiations can never replace multilateral negotiations in this respect,

Noting the support expressed in the Conference on Disarmament and in the General Assembly for the elaboration of an international convention to assure non-nuclear-weapon States against the use or threat of use of nuclear weapons, and the multilateral efforts in the Conference on Disarmament to reach agreement on such an international convention at an early date,

Recalling the advisory opinion of the International Court of Justice on the *Legality of the Threat or Use of Nuclear Weapons*, issued on 8 July 1996, and welcoming the unanimous reaffirmation by all Judges of the Court that there exists an obligation for all States to pursue in good faith and bring to a conclusion negotiations leading to nuclear disarmament in all its aspects under strict and effective international control,

Mindful of paragraph 114 and other relevant recommendations in the Final Document of the Twelfth Conference of Heads of State or Government of the Non-Aligned Countries, held at Durban, South Africa, from 29 August to 3 September 1998, calling upon the Conference on Disarmament to establish, on a priority basis, an ad hoc committee to commence negotiations in 1998 on a phased programme of nuclear disarmament and for the eventual elimination of nuclear weapons with a specified framework of time,

Bearing in mind the proposal of twenty-eight delegations to the Conference on Disarmament that are members of the Group of 21 for a programme of action for the elimination of nuclear weapons, and expressing its conviction that this proposal will be an important input and will contribute to negotiations on this question in the Conference,

Commending the initiative by twenty-six delegations to the Conference on Disarmament that are members of the Group of 21 proposing a comprehensive mandate for an ad hoc committee on nuclear disarmament, which includes negotiations for, as a first step, a universal and legally binding multilateral agreement committing all States to the objective of the total elimination of nuclear weapons, an agreement on further steps required in a phased programme leading to the total elimination of these weapons and a convention on the prohibition of the production of fissile material for nuclear weapons or other nuclear explosive devices taking into account the report of the Special Coordinator on that item and the views relating to the scope of the treaty,

Recalling paragraphs 38 to 50 of the final communiqué of the meeting of Ministers for Foreign Affairs and Heads of Delegation of the Non-Aligned Countries, held in New York on 23 September 1999,

Taking note of the draft decision and mandate on the establishment of an ad hoc committee on nuclear disarmament proposed by the Group of 21,

1. *Recognizes* that, in view of recent political developments, the time is now opportune for all the nuclear-weapon States to undertake effective disarmament measures with a view to the total elimination of these weapons;

2. *Also recognizes* that there is a genuine need to de-emphasize the role of nuclear weapons and to review and revise nuclear doctrines accordingly;

3. *Urges* the nuclear-weapon States to stop immediately the qualitative improvement, development, production and stockpiling of nuclear warheads and their delivery systems;

4. *Also urges* the nuclear-weapon States, as an interim measure, to de-alert and deactivate immediately their nuclear weapons;

5. *Calls* for the conclusion, as a first step, of a universal and legally binding multilateral agreement committing States to the process of nuclear disarmament leading to the total elimination of nuclear weapons;

6. *Reiterates its calls upon* the nuclear-weapon States to undertake the step-by-step reduction of the nuclear threat and to carry out effective nuclear disarmament measures with a view to the total elimination of these weapons;

7. *Calls upon* the nuclear-weapon States, pending the achievement of the total elimination of nuclear weapons, to agree on an internationally and legally binding instrument on the joint undertaking not to be the first to use nuclear weapons, and calls upon all States to conclude an internationally and legally binding instrument on security assurances of non-use and non-threat of use of nuclear weapons against non-nuclear-weapon States;

8. *Urges* the nuclear-weapon States to commence plurilateral negotiations among themselves at an appropriate stage on further deep reductions of nuclear weapons as an effective measure of nuclear disarmament;

9. *Welcomes* the establishment in the Conference on Disarmament in 1998 of the Ad Hoc Committee on the prohibition of the production of fissile material for nuclear weapons or other nuclear explosive devices, urges a speedy conclusion of a universal and non-discriminatory convention thereon, welcomes the establishment in 1998 of the Ad Hoc Committee on effective international arrangements to assure non-nuclear-weapon States against the use or threat of use of nuclear weapons, and urges the pursuit of efforts in this regard as a matter of priority;

10. *Expresses its regret* that the Conference on Disarmament was unable to establish an ad hoc committee on nuclear disarmament at its 1999 session, as called for in General Assembly resolution 53/77 X;

11. *Reiterates its call upon* the Conference on Disarmament to establish, on a priority basis, an ad hoc committee on nuclear disarmament to commence negotiations early in 2000 on a phased programme of nuclear disarmament and for the eventual elimination of nuclear weapons, through a set of legal instruments, which may include a nuclear weapons convention;

12. *Calls* for the convening of an international conference on nuclear disarmament at an early date with the objective of arriving at an agreement or agreements on a phased programme of nuclear disarmament and for the eventual total elimination of nuclear weapons, through a set of legal instruments, which may include a nuclear weapons convention;

13. *Requests* the Secretary-General to submit to the General Assembly at its fifty-fifth session a report on the implementation of the present resolution;

14. *Decides* to include in the provisional agenda of its fifty-fifth session the item entitled "Nuclear disarmament".

RECORDED VOTE ON RESOLUTION 54/54 P:

In favour: Algeria, Angola, Antigua and Barbuda, Bahamas, Bahrain, Bangladesh, Barbados, Belize, Benin, Bhutan, Bolivia, Botswana, Brazil, Brunei Darussalam, Burkina Faso, Cambodia, Cameroon, Cape Verde, Chad, China, Colombia, Congo, Costa Rica, Côte d'Ivoire, Cuba, Democratic People's Republic of Korea, Djibouti, Dominica, Dominican Republic, Ecuador, Egypt, El Salvador, Equatorial Guinea, Eritrea, Ethiopia, Fiji, Ghana, Grenada, Guatemala, Guinea, Guinea-Bissau, Guyana, Haiti, Honduras, India, Indonesia, Iran, Jamaica, Jordan, Kenya, Kuwait, Lao People's Democratic Republic, Lebanon, Libyan Arab Jamahiriya, Madagascar, Malaysia, Maldives, Mali, Marshall Islands, Mauritius, Mexico, Mongolia, Morocco, Mozambique, Myanmar, Namibia, Nepal, Nicaragua, Nigeria, Oman, Pakistan, Panama, Papua New Guinea, Paraguay, Peru, Philippines, Qatar, Saint Kitts and Nevis, Saint Lucia, Saint Vincent and the Grenadines, Samoa, San Marino, Saudi Arabia, Senegal, Sierra Leone, Singapore, Solomon Islands, Sri Lanka, Sudan, Suriname, Swaziland, Syrian Arab Republic, Thailand, Togo, Trinidad and Tobago, Tunisia, United Arab Emirates, United Republic of Tanzania, Uruguay, Venezuela, Viet Nam, Yemen, Zambia, Zimbabwe.

Against: Albania, Andorra, Australia, Austria, Belgium, Bosnia and Herzegovina, Bulgaria, Canada, Croatia, Cyprus, Czech Republic, Denmark, Estonia, Finland, France, Germany, Greece, Hungary, Iceland, Israel, Italy, Latvia, Liechtenstein, Lithuania, Luxembourg, Malta, Micronesia, Monaco, Netherlands, Norway, Poland, Portugal, Republic of Moldova, Romania, Slovakia, Slovenia, Spain, The former Yugoslav Republic of Macedonia, Turkey, United Kingdom, United States.

Abstaining: Argentina, Armenia, Azerbaijan, Belarus, Chile, Georgia, Ireland, Japan, Kazakhstan, New Zealand, Republic of Korea, Russian Federation, South Africa, Sweden, Tajikistan, Ukraine, Uzbekistan.

The Assembly adopted **resolution 54/54 G** by recorded vote (111-13-39) [agenda item 76 *(r)*].

Towards a nuclear-weapon-free world: the need for a new agenda

The General Assembly,

Convinced that the existence of nuclear weapons is a threat to the survival of humanity,

Concerned at the prospect of the indefinite possession of nuclear weapons, believing that the contention that nuclear weapons can be retained in perpetuity and never used is not supported by the history of human experience, and convinced that the only complete defence is the elimination of nuclear weapons and the assurance that they will never be produced again,

Concerned also at the continued retention of the nuclear-weapons option by those three States that are nuclear-weapons-capable and that have not acceded to the Treaty on the Non-Proliferation of Nuclear Weapons, and concerned at their failure to renounce that option,

Concerned further that negotiations on nuclear arms reductions are currently stalled,

Bearing in mind that the overwhelming majority of States have entered into legally binding commitments not to receive, manufacture or otherwise acquire nuclear weapons or other nuclear explosive devices, and recalling that these undertakings were made in the context of the corresponding legally binding commitments by the nuclear-weapon States to the pursuit of nuclear disarmament,

Recalling the unanimous conclusion of the International Court of Justice in its 1996 advisory opinion that there exists an obligation to pursue in good faith and bring to a conclusion negotiations leading to nuclear disarmament in all its aspects under strict and effective international control,

Stressing that the international community must not enter the new millennium with the prospect that the possession of nuclear weapons will be considered legitimate for the indefinite future, and convinced of the imperative to proceed with determination to prohibit and eradicate them for all time,

Recognizing that the total elimination of nuclear weapons will require measures to be taken firstly by those nuclear-weapon States that have the largest arsenals, and stressing that these States must be joined in a seamless process by those nuclear-weapon States with lesser arsenals in the near future,

Welcoming the achievements to date and the future promise of the Strategic Arms Reduction Talks process and the possibility it offers for development as a plurilateral mechanism including all the nuclear-weapon States, for the practical dismantling and destruction of nuclear armaments undertaken in pursuit of the elimination of nuclear weapons,

Welcoming also the Trilateral Initiative between the United States of America, the Russian Federation and the International Atomic Energy Agency to ensure the irreversible removal of fissile materials from weapons programmes,

Believing that there are a number of practical steps that the nuclear-weapon States can and should take immediately before the actual elimination of nuclear arsenals and the development of requisite verification regimes take place, and in this connection noting certain recent unilateral and other steps,

Underlining that the Treaty on the Limitation of Anti-Ballistic Missile Systems remains a cornerstone of strategic stability,

Stressing that each article of the Treaty on the Non-Proliferation of Nuclear Weapons is binding on the respective States parties at all times and in all circumstances,

Stressing also the importance of pursuing negotiations in the Conference on Disarmament in the Ad Hoc Committee established under item 1 of its agenda entitled "Cessation of the nuclear arms race and nuclear disarmament", on the basis of the report of the Special Coordinator and the mandate contained therein, on a non-discriminatory, multilateral and internationally and effectively verifiable treaty banning the production of fissile material for nuclear weapons or other nuclear explosive devices, and considering that such a treaty must further underpin the process towards the total elimination of nuclear weapons,

Emphasizing that, for the total elimination of nuclear weapons to be achieved, effective international cooperation to prevent the proliferation of nuclear weapons is vital and must be enhanced through, inter alia, the extension of international controls over all fissile material for nuclear weapons or other nuclear explosive devices,

Emphasizing also the importance of existing nuclear-weapon-free-zone treaties and of the early signature and ratification of the relevant protocols to those treaties,

Noting the joint ministerial declaration of 9 June 1998 and its call for a new international agenda to achieve a nuclear-weapon-free world, through the pursuit, in parallel, of a series of mutually reinforcing measures at the bilateral, plurilateral and multilateral levels,

Acknowledging the report of the Secretary-General on the implementation of General Assembly resolution 53/77 Y of 4 December 1998,

Taking note of the observations of the Director General of the International Atomic Energy Agency contained in the report of the Secretary-General,

1. *Calls upon* the nuclear-weapon States to make an unequivocal undertaking to accomplish the speedy and total elimination of their nuclear arsenals and to engage without delay in an accelerated process of negotiations, thus achieving nuclear disarmament, to which they are committed under article VI of the Treaty on the Non-Proliferation of Nuclear Weapons;

2. *Calls upon* the United States of America and the Russian Federation to bring the Treaty on Further Reduction and Limitation of Strategic Offensive Arms (START II) into force without further delay and to commence negotiations on START III with a view to its early conclusion;

3. *Calls upon* the nuclear-weapon States to undertake the necessary steps towards the seamless integration of all five nuclear-weapon States into the process leading to the total elimination of nuclear weapons;

4. *Calls* for the examination of ways and means to diminish the role of nuclear weapons in security policies so as to enhance strategic stability, facilitate the process of the elimination of these weapons and contribute to international confidence and security;

5. *Calls upon* the nuclear-weapon States, in this context, to take early steps:

(a) To reduce tactical nuclear weapons with a view to their elimination as an integral part of nuclear arms reductions;

(b) To examine the possibilities for and to proceed to the de-alerting and removal of nuclear warheads from delivery vehicles;

(c) To examine nuclear weapons policies and postures further;

(d) To demonstrate transparency with regard to their nuclear arsenals and fissile material inventories;

(e) To place all fissile material for nuclear weapons declared to be in excess of military requirements under International Atomic Energy Agency safeguards in the framework of the voluntary safeguards agreements in place;

6. *Calls upon* those three States that are nuclear weapons capable and that have not yet acceded to the Treaty on the Non-Proliferation of Nuclear Weapons to reverse clearly and urgently the pursuit of all nuclear weapons development or deployment and to refrain from any action that could undermine regional and international peace and security and the efforts of the international community towards nuclear disarmament and the prevention of the proliferation of nuclear weapons;

7. *Calls upon* those States that have not yet done so to adhere unconditionally and without delay to the Treaty on the Non-Proliferation of Nuclear Weapons

and to take all the necessary measures which flow from adherence to that instrument as non-nuclear-weapon States;

8. *Calls upon* those States that have not yet done so to conclude full-scope safeguards agreements with the International Atomic Energy Agency and to conclude additional protocols to their safeguards agreements on the basis of the Model Protocol approved by the Board of Governors of the Agency on 15 May 1997;

9. *Calls upon* those States that have not yet done so to sign and ratify, unconditionally and without delay, the Comprehensive Nuclear-Test-Ban Treaty and, pending the entry into force of the Treaty, to observe a moratorium on nuclear tests;

10. *Calls upon* those States that have not yet done so to adhere to the Convention on the Physical Protection of Nuclear Material and to work towards its further strengthening;

11. *Urges* the development of the Trilateral Initiative between the United States of America, the Russian Federation and the International Atomic Energy Agency, and urges that similar arrangements be developed by the other nuclear-weapon States;

12. *Calls upon* the Conference on Disarmament to re-establish the Ad Hoc Committee under item 1 of its agenda entitled "Cessation of the nuclear arms race and nuclear disarmament", on the basis of the report of the Special Coordinator and the mandate contained therein, of a non-discriminatory, multilateral and internationally and effectively verifiable treaty banning the production of fissile material for nuclear weapons or other nuclear explosive devices, taking into consideration both nuclear non-proliferation and nuclear disarmament objectives, and to pursue and conclude these negotiations without delay, and, pending the entry into force of the treaty, urges all States to observe a moratorium on the production of fissile materials for nuclear weapons or other nuclear explosive devices;

13. *Also calls upon* the Conference on Disarmament to establish an appropriate subsidiary body to deal with nuclear disarmament and, to that end, to pursue as a matter of priority its intensive consultations on appropriate methods and approaches with a view to reaching such a decision without delay;

14. *Considers* that an international conference on nuclear disarmament and nuclear non-proliferation, which would effectively complement efforts being undertaken in other settings, could facilitate the consolidation of a new agenda for a nuclear-weapon-free world;

15. *Notes*, in this context, that the Millennium Summit of the United Nations in 2000 will consider peace, security and disarmament;

16. *Stresses* the importance of the full implementation of the decisions and the resolution adopted at the 1995 Review and Extension Conference of the Parties to the Treaty on the Non-Proliferation of Nuclear Weapons, and, in this connection, underlines the significance of the forthcoming Review Conference of the Parties to the Treaty on the Non-Proliferation of Nuclear Weapons, to be held in April/May 2000;

17. *Affirms* that the development of verification arrangements will be necessary for the maintenance of a world free from nuclear weapons, and requests the International Atomic Energy Agency, together with any other relevant international organizations and bodies, to continue to explore the elements of such a system;

18. *Calls* for the conclusion of an internationally legally binding instrument to effectively assure non-nuclear-weapon States parties to the Treaty on the Non-Proliferation of Nuclear Weapons against the use or threat of use of nuclear weapons;

19. *Stresses* that the pursuit, extension and establishment of nuclear-weapon-free zones, on the basis of arrangements freely arrived at, especially in regions of tension, such as the Middle East and South Asia, represent a significant contribution to the goal of a nuclear-weapon-free world;

20. *Affirms* that a nuclear-weapon-free world will ultimately require the underpinnings of a universal and multilaterally negotiated legally binding instrument or a framework encompassing a mutually reinforcing set of instruments;

21. *Requests* the Secretary-General, within existing resources, to compile a report on the implementation of the present resolution;

22. *Decides* to include in the provisional agenda of its fifty-fifth session the item entitled "Towards a nuclear-weapon-free world: the need for a new agenda", and to review the implementation of the present resolution.

RECORDED VOTE ON RESOLUTION 54/54 G:

In favour: Algeria, Angola, Antigua and Barbuda, Austria, Bahamas, Bahrain, Bangladesh, Barbados, Belarus, Belize, Benin, Bolivia, Botswana, Brazil, Brunei Darussalam, Burkina Faso, Cambodia, Cameroon, Cape Verde, Chad, Chile, Colombia, Congo, Costa Rica, Côte d'Ivoire, Croatia, Cuba, Cyprus, Djibouti, Dominica, Dominican Republic, Ecuador, Egypt, El Salvador, Equatorial Guinea, Eritrea, Ethiopia, Fiji, Ghana, Grenada, Guatemala, Guinea, Guinea-Bissau, Guyana, Haiti, Honduras, Indonesia, Iran, Ireland, Jamaica, Jordan, Kenya, Kuwait, Lao People's Democratic Republic, Lebanon, Libyan Arab Jamahiriya, Liechtenstein, Madagascar, Malaysia, Maldives, Mali, Malta, Marshall Islands, Mexico, Mongolia, Morocco, Mozambique, Namibia, Nepal, New Zealand, Nicaragua, Nigeria, Oman, Panama, Papua New Guinea, Paraguay, Peru, Philippines, Qatar, Saint Kitts and Nevis, Saint Lucia, Saint Vincent and the Grenadines, Samoa, San Marino, Saudi Arabia, Senegal, Seychelles, Sierra Leone, Singapore, Solomon Islands, South Africa, Sri Lanka, Sudan, Suriname, Swaziland, Sweden, Syrian Arab Republic, Tajikistan, Thailand, Togo, Trinidad and Tobago, Tunisia, Uganda, United Arab Emirates, United Republic of Tanzania, Uruguay, Venezuela, Viet Nam, Yemen, Zambia, Zimbabwe.

Against: Bulgaria, Estonia, France, Hungary, India, Israel, Monaco, Pakistan, Poland, Romania, Russian Federation, United Kingdom, United States.

Abstaining: Albania, Andorra, Argentina, Armenia, Australia, Azerbaijan, Belgium, Bhutan, Bosnia and Herzegovina, Canada, China, Czech Republic, Denmark, Finland, Georgia, Germany, Greece, Iceland, Italy, Japan, Kazakhstan, Latvia, Lithuania, Luxembourg, Mauritius, Micronesia, Myanmar, Netherlands, Norway, Portugal, Republic of Korea, Republic of Moldova, Slovakia, Slovenia, Spain, The former Yugoslav Republic of Macedonia, Turkey, Ukraine, Uzbekistan.

The First Committee adopted paragraphs 7 and 18 by separate recorded votes of 128 to 3, with 3 abstentions, and 128 to none, with 5 abstentions, respectively. The draft as a whole was adopted by a recorded vote of 90 to 13, with 37 abstentions. The Assembly retained those paragraphs by recorded votes of 150 to 3, with 2 abstentions, and 149 to none, with 4 abstentions, respectively.

Resolution 54/54 K was adopted by recorded vote (104-43-14) [agenda item 76 *(g)*].

Reducing nuclear danger

The General Assembly,

Bearing in mind that the use of nuclear weapons poses the most serious threat to mankind and to the survival of civilization,

Reaffirming that any use or threat of use of nuclear weapons would constitute a violation of the Charter of the United Nations,

Convinced that the proliferation of nuclear weapons in all its aspects would seriously enhance the danger of nuclear war,

Convinced also that nuclear disarmament and the complete elimination of nuclear weapons are essential to remove the danger of nuclear war,

Considering that until nuclear weapons cease to exist, it is imperative on the part of the nuclear-weapon States to adopt measures that assure non-nuclear-weapon States against the use or threat of use of nuclear weapons,

Considering also that the hair-trigger alert of nuclear weapons carries unacceptable risks of unintentional or accidental use of nuclear weapons, which would have catastrophic consequences for all mankind,

Emphasizing the imperative need to adopt measures to avoid accidental, unauthorized or unexplained incidents arising from computer anomaly or other technical malfunctions before the next millennium,

Conscious that limited steps relating to detargeting have been taken by the nuclear-weapon States and that further practical, realistic and mutually reinforcing steps are necessary to contribute to the improvement in the international climate for negotiations leading to the elimination of nuclear weapons,

Mindful that reduction of tensions brought about by a change in nuclear doctrines would positively impact on international peace and security and improve the conditions for the further reduction and the elimination of nuclear weapons,

Reiterating the highest priority accorded to nuclear disarmament in the Final Document of the Tenth Special Session of the General Assembly and by the international community,

Recalling that the advisory opinion of the International Court of Justice on the *Legality of the Threat or Use of Nuclear Weapons* states that there exists an obligation for all States to pursue in good faith and bring to a conclusion negotiations leading to nuclear disarmament in all its aspects under strict and effective international control,

1. *Calls* for a review of nuclear doctrines and, in this context, immediate and urgent steps to reduce the risks of unintentional and accidental use of nuclear weapons;

2. *Requests* the five nuclear-weapon States to undertake measures towards the implementation of paragraph 1 of the present resolution;

3. *Calls upon* Member States to take the necessary measures to prevent the proliferation of nuclear weapons in all its aspects and to promote nuclear disarmament, with the ultimate objective of eliminating nuclear weapons;

4. *Requests* the Secretary-General, within existing resources, to seek inputs from the Advisory Board on Disarmament Matters on information with regard to specific measures that would significantly reduce the risk of nuclear war and to report thereon to the General Assembly at its fifty-fifth session;

5. *Decides* to include in the provisional agenda of its fifty-fifth session the item entitled "Reducing nuclear danger".

RECORDED VOTE ON RESOLUTION 54/54 K:

In favour: Algeria, Angola, Antigua and Barbuda, Azerbaijan, Bahamas, Bahrain, Bangladesh, Barbados, Belize, Benin, Bhutan, Bolivia, Botswana, Brunei Darussalam, Burkina Faso, Cambodia, Cameroon, Cape Verde, Chad, Chile, Colombia, Congo, Costa Rica, Côte d'Ivoire, Cuba, Democratic People's Republic of Korea, Djibouti, Dominica, Dominican Republic, Ecuador, Egypt, El Salvador, Equatorial Guinea, Eritrea, Ethiopia, Fiji, Ghana, Grenada, Guatemala, Guinea, Guinea-Bissau, Guyana, Haiti, Honduras, India, Indonesia, Iran, Jamaica, Jordan, Kenya, Kuwait, Lao People's Democratic Republic, Lebanon, Libyan Arab Jamahiriya, Madagascar, Malaysia, Maldives, Mali, Marshall Islands, Mauritius, Mexico, Mongolia, Morocco, Mozambique, Myanmar, Namibia, Nepal, Nicaragua, Nigeria, Oman, Pakistan, Panama, Papua New Guinea, Peru, Philippines, Qatar, Saint Kitts and Nevis, Saint Lucia, Saint Vincent and the Grenadines, Samoa, Saudi Arabia, Senegal, Sierra Leone, Singapore, Solomon Islands, South Africa, Sri Lanka, Sudan, Suriname, Swaziland, Syrian Arab Republic, Thailand, Togo, Trinidad and Tobago, Tunisia, Turkmenistan, Uganda, United Arab Emirates, United Republic of Tanzania, Uruguay, Viet Nam, Yemen, Zambia, Zimbabwe.

Against: Albania, Andorra, Australia, Austria, Belgium, Bosnia and Herzegovina, Bulgaria, Canada, Croatia, Cyprus, Czech Republic, Denmark, Estonia, Finland, France, Germany, Greece, Hungary, Iceland, Ireland, Italy, Latvia, Liechtenstein, Lithuania, Luxembourg, Malta, Monaco, Netherlands, Norway, Poland, Portugal, Republic of Moldova, Romania, Russian Federation, San Marino, Slovakia, Slovenia, Spain, Sweden, The former Yugoslav Republic of Macedonia, Turkey, United Kingdom, United States.

Abstaining: Argentina, Armenia, Belarus, Brazil, China, Georgia, Israel, Japan, Kazakhstan, Paraguay, Republic of Korea, Tajikistan, Ukraine, Uzbekistan.

ABM Treaty and other missile issues

On 20 January, the United States announced that it would request a further $6.6 billion to finance its NMD and theatre missile defence (TMD) programmes. It also announced that the 1972 ABM Treaty might have to be amended in order to build an NMD system. On 23 July [CD/1589], President Clinton stated that he had signed the National Missile Defense Act of 1999, making it United States policy to deploy an NMD system as soon as technologically possible. The proposal to amend the ABM Treaty met with strong opposition from the Russian Federation [CD/1580].

In February, the United States and the Russian Federation discussed issues related to the ABM Treaty. Although they reaffirmed their belief that the Treaty was a cornerstone of strategic stability, they also recognized the serious differences between them regarding NMD and related ABM Treaty issues. Because of the NATO air strikes against the Federal Republic of Yugoslavia (see PART ONE, Chapter V), no consultations between the two sides took place until June. At the G-8 summit meeting in Cologne in June, Presidents Clinton and Yeltsin issued a joint statement reaffirming their commitment to the Treaty and affirming their obligations under the ABM Treaty to consider possible changes in the strategic situation that had a bearing on the Treaty and, as appropriate, possible proposals for further increasing the Treaty's viability. Although the parties continued to discuss those issues, no agreement was reached by the end of the year.

On 23 September [S/1999/996], the five permanent members of the Security Council called for, among other things, continued efforts to strengthen the ABM Treaty and to preserve its integrity and validity so that it would remain a cornerstone in maintaining global strategic stability and in promoting further strategic nuclear arms reduction.

On 2 October, the United States conducted a test of an anti-missile rocket. On 5 October [A/C.1/54/3], the Russian Federation criticized the action, stressing that the test was a step that ran counter to the ABM Treaty. China's reaction was reflected in a position paper, which stated that the development and deployment of an NMD system and eventual amendment of the ABM Treaty would have a severe negative impact on global strategic balance, hinder the nuclear disarmament process and disrupt international nonproliferation efforts [A/C.1/54/7].

GENERAL ASSEMBLY ACTION

On 1 December [meeting 69], the General Assembly, on the recommendation of the First Committee [A/54/563], adopted **resolution 54/54 A** by recorded vote (80-4-68) [agenda item 76].

Preservation of and compliance with the Treaty on the Limitation of Anti-Ballistic Missile Systems

The General Assembly,

Recalling its resolutions 50/60 of 12 December 1995 and 52/30 of 9 December 1997 on compliance with arms limitation and disarmament and nonproliferation agreements,

Recognizing the historical role of the Treaty on the Limitation of Anti-Ballistic Missile Systems of 26 May 1972 between the United States of America and the Union of Soviet Socialist Republics as a cornerstone for maintaining global peace and security and strategic stability, and reaffirming its continued validity and relevance, especially in the current international situation,

Stressing the paramount importance of full and strict compliance with the Treaty by the parties,

Recalling that the provisions of the Treaty are intended as a contribution to the creation of more favourable conditions for further negotiations on limiting strategic arms,

Mindful of the obligations of the parties to the Treaty under article VI of the Treaty on the Non-Proliferation of Nuclear Weapons,

Concerned that the implementation of any measures undermining the purposes and provisions of the Treaty affects not only the security interests of the parties, but also those of the whole international community,

Recalling the widespread concern about the proliferation of weapons of mass destruction and their means of delivery,

1. *Calls* for continued efforts to strengthen the Treaty on the Limitation of Anti-Ballistic Missile Systems and to preserve its integrity and validity so that it remains a cornerstone in maintaining global strategic stability and world peace and in promoting further strategic nuclear arms reductions;

2. *Calls also* for renewed efforts by each of the States parties to preserve and strengthen the Treaty through full and strict compliance;

3. *Calls upon* the parties to the Treaty, in accordance with their obligations under the Treaty, to limit the deployment of anti-ballistic missile systems and refrain from the deployment of anti-ballistic missile systems for the defence of the territory of their country and not to provide a base for such a defence, and not to transfer to other States or deploy outside their national territory anti-ballistic missile systems or their components limited by the Treaty;

4. *Considers* that the implementation of any measure undermining the purposes and the provisions of the Treaty also undermines global strategic stability and world peace and the promotion of further strategic nuclear arms reductions;

5. *Urges* all Member States to support efforts aimed at stemming the proliferation of weapons of mass destruction and their means of delivery;

6. *Supports* further efforts by the international community, in the light of emerging developments, towards safeguarding the inviolability and integrity of the Treaty, which is in the strongest interest of the international community;

7. *Decides* to include in the provisional agenda of its fifty-fifth session an item entitled "Preservation of and compliance with the Treaty on the Limitation of Anti-Ballistic Missile Systems".

RECORDED VOTE ON RESOLUTION 54/54 A:

In favour: Algeria, Angola, Antigua and Barbuda, Armenia, Bangladesh, Barbados, Belarus, Belize, Benin, Bhutan, Bolivia, Botswana, Brunei Darussalam, Burkina Faso, Cambodia, Cameroon, Cape Verde, Chad, China, Colombia, Congo, Côte d'Ivoire, Cuba, Cyprus, Democratic People's Republic of Korea, Dominica,* Ecuador, Egypt, Equatorial Guinea, Ethiopia, Fiji, France, Gabon, Grenada, Guinea-Bissau, Guyana, Haiti, Honduras, India, Indonesia, Iran, Ireland, Jamaica, Kazakhstan, Kenya, Lao People's Democratic Republic, Lebanon, Libyan Arab Jamahiriya, Madagascar, Malaysia, Mexico, Monaco, Mongolia, Mozambique, Myanmar, Namibia, Nepal, Pakistan, Papua New Guinea, Russian Federation, Saint Kitts and Nevis, Saint Lucia, Saint Vincent and the Grenadines, Senegal, Singapore, South Africa, Sri Lanka, Sudan, Suriname, Swaziland, Syrian Arab Republic, Tajikistan, Thailand, Togo, Turkmenistan, Uganda, United Republic of Tanzania, Viet Nam, Zambia, Zimbabwe.

Against: Albania, Israel, Micronesia, United States.

Abstaining: Andorra, Argentina, Australia, Austria, Bahamas, Bahrain, Belgium, Bosnia and Herzegovina, Brazil, Bulgaria, Canada, Chile, Costa Rica, Croatia, Czech Republic, Denmark, Djibouti, Dominican Republic, Eritrea, Estonia, Finland, Georgia, Germany, Ghana, Greece, Guatemala, Guinea, Hungary, Iceland, Italy, Japan, Jordan, Kuwait, Latvia, Liechtenstein, Lithuania, Luxembourg, Malta, Marshall Islands, Mauritius, Morocco, Netherlands, New Zealand, Nigeria, Norway, Paraguay, Peru, Poland, Portugal, Republic of Korea, Republic of Moldova, Romania, Samoa, San Marino, Sierra Leone, Slovakia, Slovenia, Solomon Islands, Spain, Sweden, The former Yugoslav Republic of Macedonia, Trinidad and Tobago, Turkey, Ukraine, United Kingdom, Uruguay, Uzbekistan, Venezuela.

*Later advised the Secretariat it had intended to abstain.

On the same date [meeting 69], the Assembly, also on the recommendation of the First Committee [A/54/563], adopted **resolution 54/54 F** by recorded vote (94-0-65) [agenda item 76].

Missiles

The General Assembly,

Reaffirming the role of the United Nations in the field of arms regulation and disarmament and the commitment of Member States to take concrete steps to strengthen that role,

Realizing the need to promote regional and international peace and security in a world free from the scourge of war and the burden of armaments,

Convinced of the need for a comprehensive approach towards missiles, in a balanced and non-discriminatory manner, as a contribution to international peace and security,

Bearing in mind that the security concerns of Member States at the international and regional levels should be taken into consideration in addressing the issue of missiles,

Underlining the complexities involved in considering the issue of missiles in the conventional context,

Expressing its support for the international efforts against the development and proliferation of all weapons of mass destruction,

1. *Requests* the Secretary-General to seek the views of all Member States on the issue of missiles in all its aspects, and to submit a report to the General Assembly at its fifty-fifth session;

2. *Decides* to include in the provisional agenda of its fifty-fifth session an item entitled "Missiles".

RECORDED VOTE ON RESOLUTION 54/54 F:

In favour: Algeria, Angola, Antigua and Barbuda, Bahamas, Bahrain, Bangladesh, Barbados, Belarus, Belize, Benin, Bhutan, Botswana, Brunei Darussalam, Burkina Faso, Cambodia, Cameroon, Cape Verde, Chad, Chile, China, Colombia, Congo, Costa Rica, Côte d'Ivoire, Cuba, Djibouti, Dominica, Dominican Republic, Ecuador, Egypt, El Salvador, Ethiopia, Fiji, Ghana, Grenada, Guinea, Guinea-Bissau, Guyana, Haiti, Honduras, India, Indonesia, Iran, Jamaica, Jordan, Kazakhstan, Kenya, Kuwait, Lao People's Democratic Republic, Libyan Arab Jamahiriya, Madagascar, Malaysia, Maldives, Mali, Mauritius, Mexico, Mongolia, Morocco, Mozambique, Myanmar, Namibia, Nepal, Nigeria, Oman, Pakistan, Panama, Papua New Guinea, Peru, Philippines, Qatar, Russian Federation, Saint Kitts and Nevis, Saint Lucia, Saint Vincent and the Grenadines, Saudi Arabia, Sierra Leone, Solomon Islands, South Africa, Sri Lanka, Sudan, Suriname, Swaziland, Tajikistan, Thailand, Trinidad and Tobago, Tunisia, Turkmenistan, Uganda, United Republic of Tanzania, Venezuela, Viet Nam, Yemen, Zambia, Zimbabwe.

Against: None.

Abstaining: Albania, Andorra, Argentina, Armenia, Australia, Austria, Azerbaijan, Belgium, Bolivia, Bosnia and Herzegovina, Brazil, Bulgaria, Canada, Croatia, Cyprus, Czech Republic, Denmark, Equatorial Guinea, Eritrea, Estonia, Finland, France, Georgia, Germany, Greece, Guatemala, Hungary, Iceland, Ireland, Israel, Italy, Japan, Latvia, Lebanon, Liechtenstein, Lithuania, Luxembourg, Malta, Marshall Islands, Micronesia, Monaco, Netherlands, New Zealand, Norway, Paraguay, Poland, Portugal, Republic of Korea, Republic of Moldova, Romania, Samoa, San Marino, Senegal, Singapore, Slovakia, Slovenia, Spain, Sweden, The former Yugoslav Republic of Macedonia, Togo, Turkey, Ukraine, United Kingdom, United States, Uruguay.

Comprehensive Nuclear-Test-Ban Treaty

Status

As at 31 December 1999, 155 States had signed the 1996 Comprehensive Nuclear-Test-Ban Treaty (CTBT), adopted by General Assembly resolution 50/245 [YUN 1996, p. 454], and 51 had ratified it.

During the year, the Treaty was ratified by Azerbaijan, Belgium, Bolivia, Bulgaria, Estonia, Finland, Greece, Hungary, Ireland, Italy, Lesotho, Luxembourg, Mali, Mexico, the Netherlands, New Zealand, Norway, Panama, Poland, the Republic of Korea, Romania, Senegal, Slovenia, South Africa and Switzerland.

In accordance with article XIV, CTBT was to enter into force 180 days after the 44 States possessing nuclear reactors, listed in annex 2 of the Treaty, had deposited their instruments of ratification. By year's end, 26 of those States had ratified the Treaty.

Conference on facilitating entry into force

The Conference on Facilitating the Entry into Force of CTBT (Vienna, 6-8 October) was convened in accordance with article XIV of the Treaty, which stipulated that if the Treaty had not entered into force three years after the date of its opening for signature, the depositary should convene a conference at the request of a majority of States that had already deposited their instruments of ratification to consider and decide by consensus the measures to facilitate early entry into force. Following informal consultations among the ratifying and signatory States in May, the ratifying States requested the Secretary-General, the depositary of CTBT, to convene the Conference. The Conference was attended by 92 ratifying and signatory States and 4 non-signatory States.

On 8 October, the Conference adopted a Final Declaration [A/54/514-S/1999/1102] in which it called on signatory States to ratify the Treaty as soon as possible, and urged the three States (Democratic People's Republic of Korea, India, Pakistan) whose ratifications were needed for entry into force, but had not yet signed, to do so. It also called on the remaining three nuclear-weapon States (China, Russian Federation, United States) to accelerate their ratification processes. It agreed that the ratifying States would select one of their number to lead informal consultations on the early entry into force.

GENERAL ASSEMBLY ACTION

On 1 December [meeting 69], the General Assembly, on the recommendation of the First Committee [A/54/572], adopted **resolution 54/63** by recorded vote (158-0-6) [agenda item 85].

Comprehensive Nuclear-Test-Ban Treaty

The General Assembly,

Recalling that the Comprehensive Nuclear-Test-Ban Treaty was adopted by its resolution 50/245 of 10 September 1996 and opened for signature on 24 September 1996,

Noting that the first Meeting of the States Signatories adopted resolution CTBT/MSS/RES/1 on 19 November 1996, thereby establishing the Preparatory Commission for the Comprehensive Nuclear-Test-Ban Treaty Organization,

Noting also that by decision 53/422 of 4 December 1998, it decided to include in the provisional agenda of its fifty-fourth session the item entitled "Comprehensive Nuclear-Test-Ban Treaty",

Encouraged by the signing of the Treaty by one hundred and fifty-five States, including forty-one of the forty-four needed for its entry into force, and welcoming also the ratification of fifty-one States, including twenty-six of the forty-four needed for its entry into force,

Welcoming the convening of the Conference on Facilitating the Entry into Force of the Comprehensive Nuclear-Test-Ban Treaty at Vienna from 6 to 8 October 1999 to promote the entry into force of the Treaty at the earliest possible date,

1. *Endorses* the Final Declaration of the Conference on Facilitating the Entry into Force of the Comprehensive Nuclear-Test-Ban Treaty and, in particular:

(*a*) Calls upon all States that have not yet signed the Treaty to sign and ratify it as soon as possible and to refrain from acts that would defeat its object and purpose in the meanwhile;

(*b*) Calls upon all States that have signed but not yet ratified the Treaty, in particular those whose ratification is needed for its entry into force, to accelerate their ratification processes with a view to their early successful conclusion;

2. *Urges* all States to sustain the momentum generated by the Conference by continuing to remain seized of the issue at the highest political level;

3. *Welcomes* the contributions by States signatories to the work of the Preparatory Commission for the Comprehensive Nuclear-Test-Ban Treaty Organization, in particular to its efforts to ensure that the Treaty's verification regime will be capable of meeting the verification requirements of the Treaty at entry into force, in accordance with article IV of the Treaty;

4. *Urges* States to maintain their moratoria on nuclear weapon test explosions or any other nuclear explosions;

5. *Decides* to include in the provisional agenda of its fifty-fifth session the item entitled "Comprehensive Nuclear-Test-Ban Treaty".

RECORDED VOTE ON RESOLUTION 54/63:

In favour: Albania, Algeria, Andorra, Angola, Antigua and Barbuda, Argentina, Armenia, Australia, Austria, Azerbaijan, Bahamas, Bahrain, Bangladesh, Barbados, Belarus, Belgium, Belize, Benin, Bolivia, Bosnia and Herzegovina, Botswana, Brazil, Brunei Darussalam, Bulgaria, Burkina Faso, Cambodia, Cameroon, Canada, Cape Verde, Chad, Chile, China, Colombia, Congo, Costa Rica, Côte d'Ivoire, Croatia, Cuba, Cyprus, Czech Republic, Denmark, Djibouti, Dominica, Dominican Republic, Ecuador, Egypt, El Salvador, Equatorial Guinea, Eritrea, Estonia, Ethiopia, Fiji, Finland, France, Georgia, Germany, Ghana, Greece, Grenada, Guatemala, Guinea, Guinea-Bissau, Guyana, Haiti, Honduras, Hungary, Iceland, Indonesia, Iran, Ireland, Israel, Italy, Jamaica, Japan, Jordan, Kazakhstan, Kenya, Kuwait, Lao People's Democratic Republic, Latvia, Liechtenstein, Lithuania, Luxembourg, Madagascar, Malawi, Malaysia, Maldives, Mali, Malta, Marshall Islands, Mexico, Micronesia, Monaco, Mongolia, Morocco, Mozambique, Myanmar, Namibia, Nepal, Netherlands, New Zealand, Nicaragua, Nigeria, Norway, Oman, Pakistan, Panama, Papua New Guinea, Paraguay, Peru, Philippines, Poland, Portugal, Qatar, Republic of Korea, Republic of Moldova, Romania, Russian Federation, Saint Kitts and Nevis, Saint Lucia, Saint Vincent and the Grenadines, Samoa, San Marino, Saudi Arabia, Senegal, Seychelles, Sierra Leone, Singapore, Slovakia, Slovenia, Solomon Islands, South Africa, Spain, Sri Lanka, Sudan, Suriname, Swaziland, Sweden, Tajikistan, Thailand, The former Yugoslav Republic of Macedonia, Togo, Trinidad and Tobago, Tunisia, Turkey, Turkmenistan, Uganda, Ukraine, United Arab Emirates, United Kingdom, United States, Uruguay, Uzbekistan, Venezuela, Viet Nam, Yemen, Zambia, Zimbabwe.

Against: None.

Abstaining: Bhutan, India, Lebanon, Mauritius, Syrian Arab Republic, United Republic of Tanzania.

Preparatory Commission for CTBT Organization

The Preparatory Commission for the Comprehensive Nuclear-Test-Ban Treaty Organization, established in 1996 [YUN 1996, p. 452], continued its efforts towards setting up an International Monitoring System (IMS), to detect and identify nuclear explosions prohibited under article I of CTBT, and an International Data Centre (IDC). IMS would comprise a network of 321 stations worldwide, including 50 primary and 120 auxiliary seismological stations equipped to detect nuclear explosions, and 80 radionuclide stations designed to identify radioactive particles released during a nuclear explosion. IMS would transmit data to IDC, located in Vienna. As at October 1999, IMS had completed about 55 per cent of the site surveys to select the most appropriate locations for the global network of stations and to assess the equipment they would need. About 45 per cent of the work to install the stations was under way or completed by that time, and the certification process for 16 stations had been initiated. The Preparatory Commission had also agreed to establish a database on chemical explosions, thereby creating the basic technical conditions for the implementation of confidence-building measures after the Treaty entered into force.

The Commission held its eighth (20-22 April) [CTBT/PC-8/1/Rev.1], ninth (24-26 August) [CTBT/PC-9/1] and tenth (15-19 November) [CTBT/PC-10/1] sessions, all in Vienna, to discuss organizational, budgetary and other matters. The Commission adopted a budget of $79.94 million for 2000, of which over half was earmarked for the continued establishment or upgrade of the global network of stations for IMS and the remainder for building up IDC, establishing the global communications infrastructure and developing procedures and guidelines to support on-site inspections once CTBT entered into force. The Commission also adopted a decision authorizing its Executive Secretary to enter into negotiations with the Secretary-General regarding an agreement to regulate the relationship between the two organizations [CTBT/PC-8/1/Annex IX].

GENERAL ASSEMBLY ACTION

On 6 December [meeting 70], the General Assembly adopted **resolution 54/65** [draft: A/54/L.48 & Add.1] without vote [agenda item 167].

Cooperation between the United Nations and the Preparatory Commission for the Comprehensive Nuclear-Test-Ban Treaty Organization

The General Assembly,

Noting that on 10 September 1996 the General Assembly, by its resolution 50/245, adopted the Comprehensive Nuclear-Test-Ban Treaty,

Noting also that the Comprehensive Nuclear-Test-Ban Treaty was opened for signature at United Nations Headquarters in New York on 24 September 1996,

Noting further that on 19 November 1996 the Meeting of States Signatories of the Comprehensive Nuclear-Test-Ban Treaty established the Preparatory Commission for the Comprehensive Nuclear-Test-Ban Treaty Organization, which has the status of an international organization, for the purpose of carrying out the necessary preparations for the effective implementation of the Treaty,

Reaffirming the decision on an agreement to regulate the relationship between the Preparatory Commission and the United Nations, adopted by the Preparatory Commission on 22 April 1999,

Invites the Secretary-General to take the appropriate steps to conclude with the Executive Secretary of the Preparatory Commission for the Comprehensive Nuclear-Test-Ban Treaty Organization an agreement to regulate the relationship between the United Nations and the Preparatory Commission, to be submitted to the General Assembly for its approval.

Non-Proliferation Treaty

In 1999, the number of States parties to the 1968 Treaty on the Non-Proliferation of Nuclear Weapons, adopted by the General Assembly in resolution 2373(XXII) [YUN 1968, p. 17], remained at 187. NPT entered into force on 5 March 1970.

Quinquennial review conferences, as called for under article VIII, paragraph 3, of the Treaty, were held in 1975 [YUN 1975, p. 27], 1980 [YUN 1980, p. 51], 1985 [YUN 1985, p. 56], 1990 [YUN 1990, p. 50] and 1995 [YUN 1995, p. 189].

At its third session (New York, 10-21 May) [NPT/CONF.2000/1], the Preparatory Committee for the 2000 NPT Review Conference considered all aspects of the Treaty, including the universality of NPT; nuclear non-proliferation and disarmament; negative security assurances; negotiations on a convention banning the production of fissile material for nuclear weapons; nuclear-weapon-free zones; IAEA safeguards; peaceful uses of nuclear energy; and the resolution on the Middle East adopted at the 1995 Review Conference [YUN 1995, p. 189].

The Committee finalized its consideration of organizational and procedural issues related to the Review Conference, scheduled to be held from 24 April to 19 May 2000 in New York. Regarding deliberations on substantive issues pertaining to the Treaty, significant differences persisted and no decisions on such matters were taken. The Chairman presented a working paper containing elements of draft recommendations to the Review Conference, which he later revised following consultations. However, the Committee was unable to agree on any substantive recommendations to the Conference. Both of the Chairman's working papers were annexed to the Committee's report.

On 8 December, the Committee held a brief resumed session in New York to decide on the presidency of the Conference. It unanimously endorsed the candidacy of Abdallah Baali (Algeria), the representative of the States parties members of the Movement of Non-Aligned Countries.

IAEA safeguards

As at 31 December, the Model Protocol Additional to Safeguards Agreements, approved by the IAEA Board of Governors in 1997 [YUN 1997, p. 486], had been signed by 45 States, including 4 nuclear-weapon States and Cuba, the first country outside NPT to do so. The Model Protocol, the first major change in the IAEA safeguards system in 25 years, provided the Agency with the legal authority to implement a more effective safeguards system to detect and verify possible non-peaceful nuclear activities in a State at an early stage. At year's end, Protocols were in force in Australia, the Holy See, Indonesia, Japan, Jordan, Monaco, New Zealand and Uzbekistan.

In October [GC(43)/RES/17], the IAEA General Conference again requested all concerned States and other parties to safeguards agreements that had not done so to sign additional protocols promptly. Those that had signed them were asked to bring them into force or to apply the protocols provisionally.

Regarding the implementation of the agreement between IAEA and the Democratic People's Republic of Korea (DPRK) for the application of safeguards in connection with NPT, the Director General stated in September that the Agency remained unable to verify that all nuclear material subject to safeguards in the DPRK had been declared to IAEA. The General Conference, on 1 October, again expressed its deep concern over the continuing non-compliance of the DPRK with the IAEA-DPRK safeguards agreements and called on the DPRK to comply fully with it [GC(43)/RES/3] (see also p. 277).

Middle East

In 1999, the General Assembly (see below) and the IAEA General Conference [GC(43)/RES/23] took action regarding the risk of nuclear proliferation in the Middle East. While the Assembly called on the non-party in the region to accede to NPT and to place all unsafeguarded nuclear facilities under full-scope safeguards, IAEA reaffirmed the urgent need for all States in the Middle East to accept forthwith the applications of full-scope Agency safeguards and invited the countries concerned to adhere to international non-proliferation regimes, including NPT.

Pursuant to Assembly resolution 53/80 [YUN 1998, p. 510], the Secretary-General reported in October [A/54/459] that, apart from the IAEA resolution on the application of IAEA safeguards in the Middle East, he had not received any additional information since his 1998 report on the subject [YUN 1998, p. 510]. The IAEA resolution was annexed to the Secretary-General's report.

GENERAL ASSEMBLY ACTION

On 1 December [meeting 69], the General Assembly, on the recommendation of the First Committee [A/54/566], adopted **resolution 54/57** by recorded vote (149-3-9) [agenda item 79].

The risk of nuclear proliferation in the Middle East

The General Assembly,

Bearing in mind its relevant resolutions,

Taking note of the relevant resolutions adopted by the General Conference of the International Atomic Energy Agency, the latest of which is resolution GC(43)/RES/23 adopted on 1 October 1999,

Cognizant that the proliferation of nuclear weapons in the region of the Middle East would pose a serious threat to international peace and security,

Mindful of the immediate need to place all nuclear facilities in the region of the Middle East under full-scope safeguards of the International Atomic Energy Agency,

Recalling the resolution on the Middle East adopted by the 1995 Review and Extension Conference of the Parties to the Treaty on the Non-Proliferation of Nuclear Weapons on 11 May 1995, in which the Conference noted with concern the continued existence in the Middle East of unsafeguarded nuclear facilities, reaffirmed the importance of the early realization of universal adherence to the Treaty and called upon all States in the Middle East that had not yet done so, without exception, to accede to the Treaty as soon as possible and to place all their nuclear facilities under full-scope International Atomic Energy Agency safeguards,

Recalling also the decision on principles and objectives for nuclear non-proliferation and disarmament adopted by the 1995 Review and Extension Conference of the Parties to the Treaty on the Non-Proliferation of Nuclear Weapons on 11 May 1995, in which the Conference urged universal adherence to the Treaty as an urgent priority and called upon all States not yet parties to the Treaty to accede to it at the earliest date, particularly those States that operate unsafeguarded nuclear facilities,

Noting that, since the adoption of General Assembly resolution 51/48 of 10 December 1996, Israel remains the only State in the Middle East that has not yet become party to the Treaty on the Non-Proliferation of Nuclear Weapons,

Concerned about the threats posed by the proliferation of nuclear weapons to the security and stability of the Middle East region,

Stressing the importance of taking confidence-building measures, in particular the establishment of a nuclear-weapon-free zone in the Middle East, in order to enhance peace and security in the region and to consolidate the global non-proliferation regime,

Noting the adoption of the Comprehensive Nuclear-Test-Ban Treaty and its signature by one hundred and fifty-five States, including a number of States in the region,

1. *Calls upon* the only State in the region that is not party to the Treaty on the Non-Proliferation of Nuclear Weapons to accede to the Treaty without further delay and not to develop, produce, test or otherwise acquire nuclear weapons, and to renounce possession of nuclear weapons, and to place all its unsafeguarded nuclear facilities under full-scope International Atomic Energy Agency safeguards as an important confidence-building measure among all States of the region and as a step towards enhancing peace and security;

2. *Requests* the Secretary-General to report to the General Assembly at its fifty-fifth session on the implementation of the present resolution;

3. *Decides* to include in the provisional agenda of its fifty-fifth session the item entitled "The risk of nuclear proliferation in the Middle East".

RECORDED VOTE ON RESOLUTION 54/57:

In favour: Albania, Algeria, Andorra, Angola, Antigua and Barbuda, Argentina, Armenia, Australia, Austria, Azerbaijan, Bahamas, Bahrain, Bangladesh, Belarus, Belgium, Belize, Benin, Bhutan, Bolivia, Bosnia and Herzegovina, Botswana, Brazil, Brunei Darussalam, Bulgaria, Burkina Faso, Cambodia, Cape Verde, Chad, Chile, China, Colombia, Congo, Costa Rica, Côte d'Ivoire, Croatia, Cuba, Cyprus, Czech Republic, Democratic People's Republic of Korea, Denmark, Djibouti, Dominica, Dominican Republic, Ecuador, Egypt, El Salvador, Equatorial Guinea, Eritrea, Estonia, Fiji, Finland, France, Georgia, Germany, Ghana, Greece, Grenada, Guatemala, Guinea, Guyana, Haiti, Honduras, Hungary, Iceland, Indonesia, Iran, Ireland, Italy, Jamaica, Japan, Jordan, Kuwait, Lao People's Democratic Republic, Latvia, Lebanon, Libyan Arab Jamahiriya, Liechtenstein, Lithuania, Luxembourg, Madagascar, Malawi, Malaysia, Maldives, Mali, Malta, Mauritius, Mexico, Monaco, Mongolia, Morocco, Mozambique, Myanmar, Namibia, Nepal, Netherlands, New Zealand, Nigeria, Oman, Pakistan, Panama, Papua New Guinea, Paraguay, Peru, Philippines, Poland, Portugal, Qatar, Republic of Korea, Republic of Moldova, Romania, Russian Federation, Saint Kitts and Nevis, Saint Lucia, Saint Vincent and the Grenadines, Samoa, San Marino, Saudi Arabia, Senegal, Seychelles, Sierra Leone, Slovakia, Slovenia, Solomon Islands, South Africa, Spain, Sri Lanka, Sudan, Suriname, Swaziland, Sweden, Syrian Arab Republic, Tajikistan, Thailand, The former Yugoslav Republic of Macedonia, Togo, Tunisia, Turkey, Turkmenistan, Uganda, Ukraine, United Arab Emirates, United Kingdom, United Republic of Tanzania, Uruguay, Venezuela, Viet Nam, Yemen, Zambia, Zimbabwe.

Against: Israel, Micronesia, United States.

Abstaining: Barbados, Cameroon, Canada, India, Kenya, Marshall Islands, Norway, Singapore, Trinidad and Tobago.

Prohibition of use of nuclear weapons

In 1999, the Conference on Disarmament was unable to carry out negotiations on a convention on the prohibition of the use of nuclear weapons, as requested in General Assembly resolution 53/78 D [YUN 1998, p. 512].

GENERAL ASSEMBLY ACTION

On 1 December [meeting 69], the General Assembly, on the recommendation of the First Committee [A/54/564], adopted **resolution 54/55 D** by recorded vote (104-42-17) [agenda item 77 *(d)*].

Convention on the Prohibition of the Use of Nuclear Weapons

The General Assembly,

Convinced that the use of nuclear weapons poses the most serious threat to the survival of mankind,

Bearing in mind the advisory opinion of the International Court of Justice of 8 July 1996 on the *Legality of the Threat or Use of Nuclear Weapons,*

Convinced that a multilateral, universal and binding agreement prohibiting the use or threat of use of nuclear weapons would contribute to the elimination of the nuclear threat and to the climate for negotiations leading to the ultimate elimination of nuclear weapons, thereby strengthening international peace and security,

Conscious that some steps taken by the Russian Federation and the United States of America towards a reduction of their nuclear weapons and the improvement in the international climate can contribute towards the goal of the complete elimination of nuclear weapons,

Recalling that, in paragraph 58 of the Final Document of the Tenth Special Session of the General Assembly, it is stated that all States should actively participate in efforts to bring about conditions in international relations among States in which a code of peaceful conduct of nations in international affairs could be agreed upon and that would preclude the use or threat of use of nuclear weapons,

Reaffirming that any use of nuclear weapons would be a violation of the Charter of the United Nations and a crime against humanity, as declared in its resolutions 1653(XVI) of 24 November 1961, 33/71 B of 14 December 1978, 34/83 G of 11 December 1979, 35/152 D of 12 December 1980 and 36/92 I of 9 December 1981,

Determined to achieve an international convention prohibiting the development, production, stockpiling and use of nuclear weapons, leading to their ultimate destruction,

Stressing that an international convention on the prohibition of the use of nuclear weapons would be an important step in a phased programme towards the complete elimination of nuclear weapons, with a specified framework of time,

Noting with regret that the Conference on Disarmament, during its 1999 session, was unable to undertake negotiations on this subject as called for in General Assembly resolution 53/78 D of 4 December 1998,

1. *Reiterates its request* to the Conference on Disarmament to commence negotiations, in order to reach agreement on an international convention prohibiting the use or threat of use of nuclear weapons under any circumstances;

2. *Requests* the Conference on Disarmament to report to the General Assembly on the results of those negotiations.

RECORDED VOTE ON RESOLUTION 54/55 D:

In favour: Algeria, Angola, Antigua and Barbuda, Bahamas, Bahrain, Bangladesh, Barbados, Belize, Benin, Bhutan, Bolivia, Botswana, Brazil, Brunei Darussalam, Burkina Faso, Cambodia, Cameroon, Cape Verde, Chile, Colombia, Congo, Costa Rica, Côte d'Ivoire, Cuba, Democratic People's Republic of Korea, Djibouti, Dominica, Dominican Republic, Ecuador, Egypt, El Salvador, Equatorial Guinea, Eritrea, Ethiopia, Fiji, Ghana, Grenada, Guatemala, Guinea, Guyana, Haiti, Honduras, India, Indonesia, Iran, Jamaica, Jordan, Kenya, Kuwait, Lao People's Democratic Republic, Lebanon, Libyan Arab Jamahiriya, Madagascar, Malawi, Malaysia, Maldives, Mali, Marshall Islands, Mauritius, Mexico, Mongolia, Morocco, Mozambique, Myanmar, Namibia, Nepal, Nicaragua, Nigeria, Oman, Pakistan, Panama, Papua New Guinea, Paraguay, Peru, Philippines, Qatar, Saint Lucia, Saint Vincent and the Grenadines, Samoa, Saudi Arabia, Senegal, Seychelles, Sierra Leone, Singapore, Solomon Islands, South Africa, Sri Lanka, Sudan, Suriname, Swaziland, Syrian Arab Republic, Thailand, Togo, Trinidad and Tobago, Tunisia, Uganda, United Arab Emirates, United Republic of Tanzania, Uruguay, Venezuela, Viet Nam, Yemen, Zambia, Zimbabwe.

Against: Albania, Andorra, Australia, Austria, Belgium, Bosnia and Herzegovina, Bulgaria, Canada, Croatia, Czech Republic, Denmark, Estonia, Finland, France, Germany, Greece, Hungary, Iceland, Ireland, Italy, Latvia, Liechtenstein, Lithuania, Luxembourg, Malta, Micronesia, Monaco, Netherlands, New Zealand, Norway, Poland, Portugal, Republic of Moldova, Romania, Slovakia, Slovenia, Spain, Sweden, The former Yugoslav Republic of Macedonia, Turkey, United Kingdom, United States.

Abstaining: Argentina, Armenia, Azerbaijan, Belarus, China, Cyprus, Georgia, Israel, Japan, Kazakhstan, Republic of Korea, Russian Federation, San Marino, Tajikistan, Turkmenistan, Ukraine, Uzbekistan.

Advisory opinion of International Court of Justice

Pursuant to General Assembly resolution 53/77 W [YUN 1998, p. 513], the Secretary-General presented information received from five States (Cuba, DPRK, India, Mexico, Saudi Arabia) on measures they had taken to implement the resolution and nuclear disarmament [A/54/161 & Add.1].

GENERAL ASSEMBLY ACTION

On 1 December [meeting 69], the General Assembly, on the recommendation of the First Committee [A/54/563], adopted **resolution 54/54 Q** by recorded vote (114-28-22) [agenda item 76 *(p)*].

Follow-up to the advisory opinion of the International Court of Justice on the *Legality of the Threat or Use of Nuclear Weapons*

The General Assembly,

Recalling its resolutions 49/75 K of 15 December 1994, 51/45 M of 10 December 1996, 52/38 O of 9 December 1997 and 53/77 W of 4 December 1998,

Convinced that the continuing existence of nuclear weapons poses a threat to all humanity and that their use would have catastrophic consequences for all life on Earth, and recognizing that the only defence against a nuclear catastrophe is the total elimination of nuclear weapons and the certainty that they will never be produced again,

Reaffirming the commitment of the international community to the goal of the total elimination of nuclear weapons and the creation of a nuclear-weapon-free world,

Mindful of the solemn obligations of States parties, undertaken in article VI of the Treaty on the Non-Proliferation of Nuclear Weapons, particularly to pursue negotiations in good faith on effective measures relating to cessation of the nuclear arms race at an early date and to nuclear disarmament,

Recalling the principles and objectives for nuclear non-proliferation and disarmament adopted at the 1995 Review and Extension Conference of the Parties to the Treaty on the Non-Proliferation of Nuclear Weapons, and in particular the objective of determined pursuit by the nuclear-weapon States of systematic and progressive efforts to reduce nuclear weapons globally, with the ultimate goal of eliminating those weapons,

Recalling also the adoption of the Comprehensive Nuclear-Test-Ban Treaty in its resolution 50/245 of 10 September 1996, and expressing its satisfaction at the increasing number of States that have signed and ratified the Treaty,

Recognizing with satisfaction that the Antarctic Treaty and the treaties of Tlatelolco, Rarotonga, Bangkok and Pelindaba are gradually freeing the entire southern hemisphere and adjacent areas covered by those treaties from nuclear weapons,

Noting the efforts by the States possessing the largest inventories of nuclear weapons to reduce their stockpiles of such weapons through bilateral agreements or arrangements and unilateral decisions, and calling for the intensification of such efforts to accelerate the significant reduction of nuclear-weapon arsenals,

Recognizing the need for a multilaterally negotiated and legally binding instrument to assure non-nuclear-weapon States against the threat or use of nuclear weapons,

Reaffirming the central role of the Conference on Disarmament as the single multilateral disarmament negotiating forum, and regretting the lack of progress in disarmament negotiations, particularly nuclear disarmament, in the Conference on Disarmament during its 1999 session,

Emphasizing the need for the Conference on Disarmament to commence negotiations on a phased programme for the complete elimination of nuclear weapons with a specified framework of time,

Desiring to achieve the objective of a legally binding prohibition of the development, production, testing, deployment, stockpiling, threat or use of nuclear weapons and their destruction under effective international control,

Recalling the advisory opinion of the International Court of Justice on the *Legality of the Threat or Use of Nuclear Weapons*, issued on 8 July 1996,

Taking note of the relevant portions of the note by the Secretary-General relating to the implementation of resolution 53/77 W,

1. *Underlines once again* the unanimous conclusion of the International Court of Justice that there exists an obligation to pursue in good faith and bring to a conclusion negotiations leading to nuclear disarmament in all its aspects under strict and effective international control;

2. *Calls once again upon* all States immediately to fulfil that obligation by commencing multilateral negotiations in 2000 leading to an early conclusion of a nuclear weapons convention prohibiting the development, production, testing, deployment, stockpiling, transfer, threat or use of nuclear weapons and providing for their elimination;

3. *Requests* all States to inform the Secretary-General of the efforts and measures they have taken on the implementation of the present resolution and nuclear disarmament, and requests the Secretary-General to apprise the General Assembly of that information at its fifty-fifth session;

4. *Decides* to include in the provisional agenda of its fifty-fifth session the item entitled "Follow-up to the advisory opinion of the International Court of Justice on the *Legality of the Threat or Use of Nuclear Weapons*".

RECORDED VOTE ON RESOLUTION 54/54 Q:

In favour: Algeria, Angola, Antigua and Barbuda, Argentina, Bahamas, Bahrain, Bangladesh, Barbados, Belize, Benin, Bhutan, Bolivia, Botswana, Brazil, Brunei Darussalam, Burkina Faso, Cambodia, Cameroon, Cape Verde, Chad, Chile, China, Colombia, Congo, Costa Rica, Côte d'Ivoire, Cuba, Democratic People's Republic of Korea, Djibouti, Dominica, Dominican Republic, Ecuador, Egypt, El Salvador, Equatorial Guinea, Eritrea, Ethiopia, Fiji, Ghana, Grenada, Guatemala, Guinea, Guinea-Bissau, Guyana, Haiti, Honduras, India, Indonesia, Iran, Ireland, Jamaica, Jordan, Kenya, Kuwait, Lao People's Democratic Republic, Lebanon, Libyan Arab Jamahiriya, Madagascar, Malaysia, Maldives, Mali, Malta, Marshall Islands, Mauritius, Mexico, Mongolia, Morocco, Mozambique, Myanmar, Namibia, Nepal, New Zealand, Nicaragua, Nigeria, Oman, Pakistan, Panama, Papua New Guinea, Paraguay, Peru, Philippines, Qatar, Saint Kitts and Nevis, Saint Lucia, Saint Vincent and the Grenadines, Samoa, San Marino, Saudi Arabia, Senegal, Seychelles, Sierra Leone, Singapore, Solomon Islands, South Africa, Sri Lanka, Sudan, Suriname, Swaziland, Sweden, Syrian Arab Republic, Thailand, Togo, Trinidad and Tobago, Tunisia, Uganda, Ukraine, United Arab Emirates, United Republic of Tanzania, Uruguay, Venezuela, Viet Nam, Yemen, Zambia, Zimbabwe.

Against: Albania, Andorra, Belgium, Bulgaria, Czech Republic, Denmark, Estonia, France, Germany, Greece, Hungary, Iceland, Israel, Italy, Lithuania, Luxembourg, Monaco, Netherlands, Poland, Portugal, Romania, Russian Federation, Slovakia, Slovenia, Spain, Turkey, United Kingdom, United States.

Abstaining: Armenia, Australia, Austria, Azerbaijan, Belarus, Bosnia and Herzegovina, Canada, Croatia, Cyprus, Finland, Georgia, Japan, Kazakhstan, Latvia, Liechtenstein, Norway, Republic of Korea, Republic of Moldova, Tajikistan, The former Yugoslav Republic of Macedonia, Turkmenistan, Uzbekistan.

The First Committee adopted paragraphs 1 and 2 by separate recorded votes of 137 to 2, with 3 abstentions, and 94 to 25, with 22 abstentions, respectively. The draft as a whole was adopted by a recorded vote of 98 to 27, with 21 abstentions. The Assembly retained those paragraphs by recorded votes of 156 to 3, with 3 abstentions, and 107 to 29, with 26 abstentions, respectively.

Nuclear-weapon-free zones

As decided at the 1998 organizational session of the Disarmament Commission [YUN 1998, p. 488] and in accordance with General Assembly resolution 53/79 A [ibid., p. 489], the Disarmament Commission continued to consider the agenda item "Establishment of nuclear-weapon-free zones on the basis of arrangements freely arrived at among the States of the region concerned" in Working Group I [A/54/42].

The Group based its discussion on a working paper submitted by the Chairman, which took into consideration working papers from previous Commission sessions. Following a discussion on specific elements contained in the Chairman's working paper and written and oral proposals made by delegations, the Chairman presented four revisions of his paper. The Group, by consensus, adopted its report and a text on the item. The text, which was annexed to the Commission's report, presented a general overview of developments and contained recommendations related to objectives and purpose of the zones, principles and guidelines on establishing them and future initiatives.

Africa

By year's end, 13 States had ratified the African Nuclear-Weapon-Free Zone Treaty (Treaty of Pelindaba) [YUN 1995, p. 203], which was opened for signature in 1996 [YUN 1996, p. 486]. China and France had ratified Protocols I and II thereto and France had also ratified Protocol III. The Russian Federation, the United Kingdom and the United States had signed Protocols I and II. The Treaty had 55 signatories.

GENERAL ASSEMBLY ACTION

On 1 December [meeting 69], the General Assembly, on the recommendation of the First Committee [A/54/557], adopted **resolution 54/48** without vote [agenda item 70].

African Nuclear-Weapon-Free Zone Treaty (Treaty of Pelindaba)

The General Assembly,

Recalling its resolution 52/46 of 9 December 1997 and all its other relevant resolutions, as well as those of the Organization of African Unity,

Recalling also the successful conclusion of the signing ceremony of the African Nuclear-Weapon-Free Zone Treaty (Treaty of Pelindaba) that was held in Cairo on 11 April 1996,

Recalling further the Cairo Declaration adopted on that occasion, which emphasized that nuclear-weapon-free zones, especially in regions of tension, such as the Middle East, enhance global and regional peace and security,

Noting the statement made by the President of the Security Council on behalf of the members of the Council on 12 April 1996, in which it was stated that the signature of the African Nuclear-Weapon-Free Zone Treaty constituted an important contribution by the African countries to the maintenance of international peace and security,

Considering that the establishment of nuclear-weapon-free zones, especially in the Middle East, would enhance the security of Africa and the viability of the African nuclear-weapon-free zone,

1. *Calls upon* African States that have not yet done so to sign and ratify the African Nuclear-Weapon-Free Zone Treaty (Treaty of Pelindaba) as soon as possible so that it may enter into force without delay;

2. *Expresses its appreciation* to the nuclear-weapon States that have signed the Protocols that concern them, and calls upon those that have not yet ratified the Protocols concerning them to do so as soon as possible;

3. *Calls upon* the States contemplated in Protocol III to the Treaty that have not yet done so to take all necessary measures to ensure the speedy application of the Treaty to territories for which they are, de jure or de facto, internationally responsible and which lie within the limits of the geographical zone established in the Treaty;

4. *Calls upon* the African States parties to the Treaty on the Non-Proliferation of Nuclear Weapons that have not yet done so to conclude comprehensive safeguards agreements with the International Atomic Energy Agency pursuant to the Treaty, thereby satisfying the requirements of article 9 *(b)* of and annex II to the Treaty of Pelindaba when it enters into force, and to conclude additional protocols to their safeguards agreements on the basis of the Model Protocol approved by the Board of Governors of the Agency on 15 May 1997;

5. *Expresses its gratitude* to the Secretary-General of the United Nations, the Secretary-General of the Organization of African Unity and the Director General of the International Atomic Energy Agency for the diligence with which they have rendered effective assistance to the signatories to the Treaty;

6. *Decides* to include in the provisional agenda of its fifty-sixth session the item entitled "African Nuclear-Weapon-Free Zone Treaty".

Asia

Central Asia

Negotiations on drafting the text of a treaty for a nuclear-weapon-free zone in Central Asia continued during the year. The UN-sponsored Expert Group, consisting of experts from each of the five States (Kazakhstan, Kyrgyzstan, Tajikistan, Turkmenistan, Uzbekistan), held three meetings (Tashkent, Uzbekistan, 1-3 February; Geneva, 27-30 April; and Sapporo, Japan, 5-8 October) with the assistance of the Regional Centre for Asia and the Pacific of DDA. It succeeded in narrowing differences on several key issues, but difficulties pertaining to transit and to the issue of other agreements remained unresolved.

At a number of meetings, the States of the region addressed issues related to the treaty. Thus, the heads of State of Kazakhstan, Kyrgyzstan, Tajikistan, Turkmenistan and Uzbekistan issued a joint statement (Ashgabat, Turkmenistan, 8-9 April) [A/54/80], in which they reaffirmed that the establishment of the zone was in keeping with the requirements and interests of national, regional and global security. Those efforts were supported by the heads of State of China, Kazakhstan, Kyrgyzstan, the Russian Federation and Tajikistan in the Bishkek (Kyrgyzstan) Declaration of 25 August [A/54/314]. The Ministers for Foreign Affairs of the member States of the Conference on Interaction and Confidence-Building Measures in Asia (Almaty, Kazakhstan, 14 September) [A/54/368- S/1999/993] expressed support for the establishment of zones free of nuclear weapons and other weapons of mass destruction in Asia.

On 1 December, the General Assembly decided to include in the provisional agenda of its fifty-fifth (2000) session the item entitled "Establishment of a nuclear-weapon-free zone in Central Asia" (**decision 54/417**).

Mongolia

On 1 September, Mongolia issued a memorandum on its international security and nuclear-weapon-free status [A/54/323-S/1999/951], in which it stated that it was consulting with the States concerned, especially the five nuclear-weapon States, on ways to implement General Assembly resolution 53/77 D [YUN 1998, p. 515], namely, defining its status and addressing its international security needs and interests. A regional disarmament meeting (Ulaanbaatar, Mongolia, 3-5 August), held under the auspices of the Government of Mongolia and DDA's Regional Centre for Asia and the Pacific, examined, among other things, questions pertaining to Mongolia's external security needs and its nuclear-weapon-free status.

South-East Asia

Consultations continued between the members of the Association of South-East Asian Nations (ASEAN) and various nuclear-weapon States regarding the adherence of the latter to the Protocol of the Treaty on the South-East Asia Nuclear-Weapon-Free Zone (Bangkok Treaty), but no further progress was made. The Treaty opened for signature in 1995 [YUN 1995, p. 207] and entered into force in 1997 [YUN 1997, p. 495]. With no new ratifications in 1999, the number of States that had ratified the Treaty remained at nine.

The Foreign Ministers of ASEAN convened for the first time the Commission of the Bangkok Treaty (Singapore, 23-24 July) as a step towards the implementation of the Treaty and urged the nuclear-weapon States to accede to the Protocol. The ASEAN Regional Forum made a similar appeal at their meeting in Singapore on 26 July.

Latin America and the Caribbean

The Agency for the Prohibition of Nuclear Weapons in Latin America and the Caribbean General Conference, at its sixteenth session (Lima, Peru, 30 November–1 December) [A/55/62], adopted the Lima Appeal, which called for, among other things, the creation of an international public awareness in order to advance a complete prohibition of the use and manufacture of nuclear weapons and other weapons of mass destruction.

GENERAL ASSEMBLY ACTION

On 1 December [meeting 69], the General Assembly, on the recommendation of the First Committee [A/54/569], adopted **resolution 54/60** without vote [agenda item 82].

Consolidation of the regime established by the Treaty for the Prohibition of Nuclear Weapons in Latin America and the Caribbean (Treaty of Tlatelolco)

The General Assembly,

Recalling that in its resolution 1911(XVIII) of 27 November 1963 it expressed the hope that the States of Latin America would take appropriate measures to conclude a treaty that would prohibit nuclear weapons in Latin America,

Recalling also that in the same resolution it voiced its confidence that, once such a treaty was concluded, all States, and in particular the nuclear-weapon States, would lend it their full cooperation for the effective realization of its peaceful aims,

Considering that in its resolution 2028(XX) of 19 November 1965 it established the principle of an acceptable balance of mutual responsibilities and obligations between nuclear-weapon States and those which do not possess such weapons,

Recalling that the Treaty for the Prohibition of Nuclear Weapons in Latin America and the Caribbean (Treaty of Tlatelolco) was opened for signature at Mexico City on 14 February 1967,

Noting with satisfaction the holding on 14 February 1997 of the eleventh special session of the General Conference of the Agency for the Prohibition of Nuclear Weapons in Latin America and the Caribbean in commemoration of the thirtieth anniversary of the opening for signature of the Treaty of Tlatelolco,

Recalling that in its preamble the Treaty of Tlatelolco states that military denuclearized zones are not an end in themselves but rather a means for achieving general and complete disarmament at a later stage,

Recalling also that in its resolution 2286(XXII) of 5 December 1967 it welcomed with special satisfaction the Treaty of Tlatelolco as an event of historic significance in the efforts to prevent the proliferation of nuclear weapons and to promote international peace and security,

Recalling further that in 1990, 1991 and 1992 the General Conference of the Agency for the Prohibition of Nuclear Weapons in Latin America and the Caribbean approved and opened for signature a set of amendments to the Treaty of Tlatelolco, with the aim of enabling the full entry into force of that instrument,

Recalling resolution C/E/RES.27 of the Council of the Agency for the Prohibition of Nuclear Weapons in Latin America and the Caribbean, in which the Council called for the promotion of cooperation and consultations with other nuclear-weapon-free zones,

Noting with satisfaction that the Treaty of Tlatelolco is now in force for thirty-two sovereign States of the region,

Also noting with satisfaction that on 18 January 1999 Colombia and on 20 January 1999 Costa Rica deposited their instruments of ratification of the amendments to the Treaty of Tlatelolco approved by the General Conference of the Agency for the Prohibition of Nuclear Weapons in Latin America and the Caribbean in its resolutions 267(E-V) of 3 July 1990, 268(XII) of 10 May 1991 and 290(E-VII) of 26 August 1992,

Further noting with satisfaction that the amended Treaty of Tlatelolco is fully in force for Argentina, Barbados, Brazil, Chile, Colombia, Costa Rica, Guyana, Jamaica, Mexico, Paraguay, Peru, Suriname, Uruguay and Venezuela,

1. *Welcomes* the concrete steps taken by some countries of the region during the past year for the consolidation of the regime of military denuclearization established by the Treaty for the Prohibition of Nuclear Weapons in Latin America and the Caribbean (Treaty of Tlatelolco);

2. *Urges* the countries of the region that have not yet done so to deposit their instruments of ratification of the amendments to the Treaty of Tlatelolco approved by the General Conference of the Agency for the Prohibition of Nuclear Weapons in Latin America and the Caribbean in its resolutions 267(E-V), 268(XII) and 290(E-VII);

3. *Decides* to include in the provisional agenda of its fifty-fifth session the item entitled "Consolidation of the regime established by the Treaty for the Prohibition of Nuclear Weapons in Latin America and the Caribbean (Treaty of Tlatelolco)".

Middle East

In response to General Assembly resolution 53/74 on the establishment of a nuclear-weapon-free zone in the Middle East [YUN 1998, p. 517], the Secretary-General reported in September on the implementation of that resolution [A/54/190 & Add.1]. He regretted that no positive developments had occurred and urged all concerned parties to review the situation to determine possible new approaches and to resume discussions. The report included information received from China, Egypt, Iraq and Saudi Arabia regarding measures to move towards the establishment of a nuclear-weapon-free zone.

GENERAL ASSEMBLY ACTION

On 1 December [meeting 69], the General Assembly, on the recommendation of the First Committee [A/54/560], adopted **resolution 54/51** without vote [agenda item 73].

Establishment of a nuclear-weapon-free zone in the region of the Middle East

The General Assembly,

Recalling its resolutions 3263(XXIX) of 9 December 1974, 3474(XXX) of 11 December 1975, 31/71 of 10 December 1976, 32/82 of 12 December 1977, 33/64 of 14 December 1978, 34/77 of 11 December 1979, 35/147 of 12 December 1980, 36/87 A and B of 9 December 1981, 37/75 of 9 December 1982, 38/64 of 15 December 1983, 39/54 of 12 December 1984, 40/82 of 12 December 1985, 41/48 of 3 December 1986, 42/28 of 30 November 1987, 43/65 of 7 December 1988, 44/108 of 15 December 1989, 45/52 of 4 December 1990, 46/30 of 6 December 1991, 47/48 of 9 December 1992, 48/71 of 16 December 1993, 49/71 of 15 December 1994, 50/66 of 12 December 1995, 51/41 of 10 December 1996, 52/34 of 9 December 1997 and 53/74 of 4 December 1998 on the establishment of a nuclear-weapon-free zone in the region of the Middle East,

Recalling also the recommendations for the establishment of such a zone in the Middle East consistent with paragraphs 60 to 63, and in particular paragraph 63 *(d)*, of the Final Document of the Tenth Special Session of the General Assembly,

Emphasizing the basic provisions of the above-mentioned resolutions, which call upon all parties directly concerned to consider taking the practical and urgent steps required for the implementation of the proposal to establish a nuclear-weapon-free zone in the region of the Middle East and, pending and during the establishment of such a zone, to declare solemnly that they will refrain, on a reciprocal basis, from producing, acquiring or in any other way possessing nuclear weapons and nuclear explosive devices and from permitting the stationing of nuclear weapons on their territory by any third party, to agree to place their nuclear facilities under International Atomic Energy Agency safeguards and to declare their support for the establishment of the zone and to deposit such declarations with the Security Council for consideration, as appropriate,

Reaffirming the inalienable right of all States to acquire and develop nuclear energy for peaceful purposes,

Emphasizing the need for appropriate measures on the question of the prohibition of military attacks on nuclear facilities,

Bearing in mind the consensus reached by the General Assembly since its thirty-fifth session that the establishment of a nuclear-weapon-free zone in the Middle East would greatly enhance international peace and security,

Desirous of building on that consensus so that substantial progress can be made towards establishing a nuclear-weapon-free zone in the Middle East,

Welcoming all initiatives leading to general and complete disarmament, including in the region of the Middle East, and in particular on the establishment therein of a zone free of weapons of mass destruction, including nuclear weapons,

Noting the peace negotiations in the Middle East, which should be of a comprehensive nature and represent an appropriate framework for the peaceful settlement of contentious issues in the region,

Recognizing the importance of credible regional security, including the establishment of a mutually verifiable nuclear-weapon-free zone,

Emphasizing the essential role of the United Nations in the establishment of a mutually verifiable nuclear-weapon-free zone,

Having examined the report of the Secretary-General on the implementation of General Assembly resolution 53/74,

1. *Urges* all parties directly concerned to consider seriously taking the practical and urgent steps required for the implementation of the proposal to establish a nuclear-weapon-free zone in the region of the Middle East in accordance with the relevant resolutions of the General Assembly, and, as a means of promoting this objective, invites the countries concerned to adhere to the Treaty on the Non-Proliferation of Nuclear Weapons;

2. *Calls upon* all countries of the region that have not done so, pending the establishment of the zone, to agree to place all their nuclear activities under International Atomic Energy Agency safeguards;

3. *Takes note* of resolution GC(43)/RES/23, adopted on 1 October 1999 by the General Conference of the International Atomic Energy Agency at its forty-third regular session, concerning the application of Agency safeguards in the Middle East;

4. *Notes* the importance of the ongoing bilateral Middle East peace negotiations and the activities of the multilateral Working Group on Arms Control and Regional Security in promoting mutual confidence and

security in the Middle East, including the establishment of a nuclear-weapon-free zone;

5. *Invites* all countries of the region, pending the establishment of a nuclear-weapon-free zone in the region of the Middle East, to declare their support for establishing such a zone, consistent with paragraph 63 *(d)* of the Final Document of the Tenth Special Session of the General Assembly, and to deposit those declarations with the Security Council;

6. *Also invites* those countries, pending the establishment of the zone, not to develop, produce, test or otherwise acquire nuclear weapons or permit the stationing on their territories, or territories under their control, of nuclear weapons or nuclear explosive devices;

7. *Invites* the nuclear-weapon States and all other States to render their assistance in the establishment of the zone and at the same time to refrain from any action that runs counter to both the letter and the spirit of the present resolution;

8. *Takes note* of the report of the Secretary-General;

9. *Invites* all parties to consider the appropriate means that may contribute towards the goal of general and complete disarmament and the establishment of a zone free of weapons of mass destruction in the region of the Middle East;

10. *Requests* the Secretary-General to continue to pursue consultations with the States of the region and other concerned States, in accordance with paragraph 7 of resolution 46/30 and taking into account the evolving situation in the region, and to seek from those States their views on the measures outlined in chapters III and IV of the study annexed to his report or other relevant measures, in order to move towards the establishment of a nuclear-weapon-free zone in the Middle East;

11. *Also requests* the Secretary-General to submit to the General Assembly at its fifty-fifth session a report on the implementation of the present resolution;

12. *Decides* to include in the provisional agenda of its fifty-fifth session the item entitled "Establishment of a nuclear-weapon-free zone in the region of the Middle East".

South Pacific

In 1999, the number of parties to the 1985 South Pacific Nuclear-Free Zone Treaty (Treaty of Rarotonga) [YUN 1985, p. 58] remained at 16. The total included nuclear-weapon States: China and the Russian Federation had ratified Protocols 2 and 3, and France and the United Kingdom had ratified all three Protocols.

Under Protocol 1, the States internationally responsible for territories situated within the zone would undertake to apply the relevant prohibitions of the Treaty to those territories; under Protocol 2, the five nuclear-weapon States would provide security assurances to parties or to territories within the same zone; and under Protocol 3, the five would not carry out nuclear tests in the zone.

Southern hemisphere and adjacent areas

On 1 December [meeting 69], the General Assembly, on the recommendation of the First Committee [A/54/563], adopted **resolution 54/54 L** by recorded vote (157-3-4) [agenda item 76 *(m)*].

Nuclear-weapon-free southern hemisphere and adjacent areas

The General Assembly,

Recalling its resolutions 51/45 B of 10 December 1996, 52/38 N of 9 December 1997 and 53/77 Q of 4 December 1998,

Welcoming the adoption by the Disarmament Commission at its 1999 substantive session of a text entitled "Establishment of nuclear-weapon-free zones on the basis of arrangements freely arrived at among the States of the region concerned",

Determined to continue to contribute to the prevention of the proliferation of nuclear weapons in all its aspects and to the process of general and complete disarmament under strict and effective international control, in particular in the field of nuclear weapons and other weapons of mass destruction, with a view to strengthening international peace and security, in accordance with the purposes and principles of the Charter of the United Nations,

Recalling the provisions on nuclear-weapon-free zones of the Final Document of the Tenth Special Session of the General Assembly, the first special session devoted to disarmament, as well as of the decision on principles and objectives for nuclear non-proliferation and disarmament of the 1995 Review and Extension Conference of the Parties to the Treaty on the Non-Proliferation of Nuclear Weapons,

Stressing the importance of the treaties of Tlatelolco, Rarotonga, Bangkok and Pelindaba, establishing nuclear-weapon-free zones, as well as the Antarctic Treaty, to, inter alia, the ultimate objective of achieving a world entirely free of nuclear weapons, and underlining also the value of enhancing cooperation among the nuclear-weapon-free zone treaty members by means of mechanisms such as joint meetings of States parties, signatories and observers to those treaties,

Recalling the applicable principles and rules of international law relating to the freedom of the high seas and the rights of passage through maritime space, including those of the United Nations Convention on the Law of the Sea,

1. *Welcomes* the continued contribution that the Antarctic Treaty and the treaties of Tlatelolco, Rarotonga, Bangkok and Pelindaba are making towards freeing the southern hemisphere and adjacent areas covered by those treaties from nuclear weapons;

2. *Calls* for the ratification of the treaties of Tlatelolco, Rarotonga, Bangkok and Pelindaba by all States of the region concerned, and calls upon all concerned States to continue to work together in order to facilitate adherence to the protocols to nuclear-weapon-free zone treaties by all relevant States that have not yet done so;

3. *Welcomes* the steps taken to conclude further nuclear-weapon-free zone treaties on the basis of arrangements freely arrived at among the States of the region concerned, and calls upon all States to consider all relevant proposals, including those reflected in General Assembly resolutions on the establishment of nuclear-weapon-free zones in the Middle East and South Asia;

4. *Reiterates* the important role of nuclear-weapon-free zones in strengthening the nuclear non-proliferation regime and in extending the areas of the world that are nuclear-weapon-free, and, with particular reference to the responsibilities of the nuclear-weapon States, calls upon all States to support the process of nuclear disarmament, with the ultimate goal of eliminating all nuclear weapons;

5. *Calls upon* the States parties and signatories to the treaties of Tlatelolco, Rarotonga, Bangkok and Pelindaba, in order to pursue the common goals envisaged in those treaties and to promote the nuclear-weapon-free status of the southern hemisphere and adjacent areas, to explore and implement further ways and means of cooperation among themselves and their treaty agencies;

6. *Encourages* the competent authorities of nuclear-weapon-free zone treaties to provide assistance to the States parties and signatories to such treaties so as to facilitate the accomplishment of these goals;

7. *Decides* to include in the provisional agenda of its fifty-fifth session the item entitled "Nuclear-weapon-free southern hemisphere and adjacent areas".

RECORDED VOTE ON RESOLUTION 54/54 L:

In favour: Albania, Algeria, Andorra, Angola, Antigua and Barbuda, Argentina, Armenia, Australia, Austria, Azerbaijan, Bahamas, Bahrain, Bangladesh, Barbados, Belarus, Belgium, Belize, Benin, Bhutan, Bolivia, Bosnia and Herzegovina, Botswana, Brazil, Brunei Darussalam, Bulgaria, Burkina Faso, Cambodia, Cameroon, Canada, Cape Verde, Chad, Chile, China, Colombia, Congo, Costa Rica, Côte d'Ivoire, Croatia, Cuba, Cyprus, Czech Republic, Democratic People's Republic of Korea, Denmark, Djibouti, Dominica, Dominican Republic, Ecuador, Egypt, El Salvador, Equatorial Guinea, Eritrea, Estonia, Ethiopia, Fiji, Finland, Georgia, Germany, Ghana, Greece, Grenada, Guatemala, Guinea, Guinea-Bissau, Guyana, Haiti, Honduras, Hungary, Iceland, Indonesia, Iran, Ireland, Italy Jamaica, Japan, Jordan, Kazakhstan, Kenya, Kuwait, Lao People's Democratic Republic, Latvia, Lebanon, Libyan Arab Jamahiriya, Liechtenstein, Lithuania, Luxembourg, Madagascar, Malaysia, Maldives, Mali, Malta, Marshall Islands, Mauritius, Mexico, Mongolia, Morocco, Mozambique, Myanmar, Namibia, Nepal, Netherlands, New Zealand, Nicaragua, Nigeria, Norway, Oman, Pakistan, Panama, Papua New Guinea, Paraguay, Peru, Philippines, Poland, Portugal, Qatar, Republic of Korea, Republic of Moldova, Romania, Saint Kitts and Nevis, Saint Lucia, Saint Vincent and the Grenadines, Samoa, San Marino, Saudi Arabia, Senegal, Seychelles, Sierra Leone, Singapore, Slovakia, Slovenia, Solomon Islands, South Africa, Spain, Sri Lanka, Sudan, Suriname, Swaziland, Sweden, Syrian Arab Republic, Tajikistan, Thailand, The former Yugoslav Republic of Macedonia, Togo, Trinidad and Tobago, Tunisia, Turkey, Turkmenistan, Uganda, Ukraine, United Arab Emirates, United Republic of Tanzania, Uruguay, Uzbekistan, Venezuela, Viet Nam, Yemen, Zambia, Zimbabwe.

Against: France, United Kingdom, United States.

Abstaining: India, Israel, Micronesia, Russian Federation.

The First Committee adopted paragraph 3 and its last three words, "and South Asia", by two separate recorded votes of 128 to 1, with 10 abstentions. The Assembly also retained the last three words and paragraph 3 by recorded votes of 147 to 2, with 9 abstentions, and 147 to 2, with 10 abstentions, respectively.

Other related issues

Nuclear safety and radioactive waste

The First Review Meeting of the Contracting Parties to the 1994 IAEA Convention on Nuclear Safety [YUN 1994, p. 925] (Vienna, 12-23 April) was convened to review States parties' national reports on steps and measures taken to implement the Convention. The meeting concluded that efforts to enhance nuclear safety were proceeding well, although certain improvements were necessary. The Convention entered into force in 1996.

In October, the IAEA General Conference adopted a series of resolutions on nuclear, radiation and waste safety. A resolution on the safety of radiation sources and the security of radiological materials [GC(43)/RES/10] endorsed an action plan developed and adopted by the IAEA Board of Governors [GOV/1999/46-GC(43)10]. Regarding the safety of transport of radioactive materials [GC(43)/RES/11], the General Conference asked States that shipped radioactive materials to provide assurances to potentially affected States that their national regulations took into account IAEA transport regulations. A resolution on the radiological protection of patients [GC(43)/RES/12] requested the UN Secretariat, in collaboration with the World Health Organization, to organize an international meeting on the subject.

GENERAL ASSEMBLY ACTION

On 1 December [meeting 69], the General Assembly, on the recommendation of the First Committee [A/54/563], adopted **resolution 54/54 C** without vote [agenda item 76 *(e)*].

Prohibition of the dumping of radioactive wastes

The General Assembly,

Bearing in mind resolutions CM/Res.1153(XLVIII) of 1988 and CM/Res.1225(L) of 1989, adopted by the Council of Ministers of the Organization of African Unity, concerning the dumping of nuclear and industrial wastes in Africa,

Welcoming resolution GC(XXXIV)/RES/530 establishing a Code of Practice on the International Transboundary Movement of Radioactive Waste, adopted on 21 September 1990 by the General Conference of the International Atomic Energy Agency at its thirty-fourth regular session,

Also welcoming resolution GC(XXXVIII)/RES/6, adopted on 23 September 1994 by the General Conference of the International Atomic Energy Agency at its thirty-eighth regular session, inviting the Board of Governors and the Director General of the Agency to commence preparations for a convention on the safety of radioactive waste management, and noting the progress that has been made in that regard,

Taking note of the commitment by the participants in the Summit on Nuclear Safety and Security, held in Moscow on 19 and 20 April 1996, to ban the dumping at sea of radioactive wastes,

Considering its resolution 2602 C (XXIV) of 16 December 1969, in which it requested the Conference of the Committee on Disarmament, inter alia, to consider effective methods of control against the use of radiological methods of warfare,

Recalling resolution CM/Res.1356(LIV) of 1991, adopted by the Council of Ministers of the Organization of African Unity, on the Bamako Convention on the Ban on the Import of Hazardous Wastes into Africa and on the Control of Their Transboundary Movements within Africa,

Aware of the potential hazards underlying any use of radioactive wastes that would constitute radiological warfare and its implications for regional and international security, in particular for the security of developing countries,

Recalling all its resolutions on the matter since its forty-third session in 1988, including its resolution 51/45 J of 10 December 1996,

Desirous of promoting the implementation of paragraph 76 of the Final Document of the Tenth Special Session of the General Assembly, the first special session devoted to disarmament,

1. *Takes note* of the part of the report of the Conference on Disarmament relating to a future convention on the prohibition of radiological weapons;

2. *Expresses grave concern* regarding any use of nuclear wastes that would constitute radiological warfare and have grave implications for the national security of all States;

3. *Calls upon* all States to take appropriate measures with a view to preventing any dumping of nuclear or radioactive wastes that would infringe upon the sovereignty of States;

4. *Requests* the Conference on Disarmament to take into account, in the negotiations for a convention on the prohibition of radiological weapons, radioactive wastes as part of the scope of such a convention;

5. *Also requests* the Conference on Disarmament to intensify efforts towards an early conclusion of such a convention and to include in its report to the General Assembly at its fifty-sixth session the progress recorded in the negotiations on this subject;

6. *Takes note* of resolution CM/Res.1356(LIV) of 1991, adopted by the Council of Ministers of the Organization of African Unity, on the Bamako Convention on the Ban on the Import of Hazardous Wastes into Africa and on the Control of Their Transboundary Movements within Africa;

7. *Expresses the hope* that the effective implementation of the International Atomic Energy Agency Code of Practice on the International Transboundary Movement of Radioactive Waste will enhance the protection of all States from the dumping of radioactive wastes on their territories;

8. *Welcomes* the adoption at Vienna on 5 September 1997 of the Joint Convention on the Safety of Spent Fuel Management and on the Safety of Radioactive Waste Management, as recommended by the participants in the Summit on Nuclear Safety and Security held in Moscow on 19 and 20 April 1996, and the signing of the Joint Convention by a number of States beginning on 29 September 1997, and appeals to all States to sign and subsequently ratify, accept or approve the Convention, so that it may enter into force as soon as possible;

9. *Decides* to include in the provisional agenda of its fifty-sixth session the item entitled "Prohibition of the dumping of radioactive wastes".

Weapons of mass destruction

Although the item "New types of weapons of mass destruction and new systems of such weapons; radiological weapons" was on the agenda of the Conference on Disarmament [A/54/27], the Conference did not establish an ad hoc committee on the subject.

On 1 December [meeting 69], the General Assembly, on the recommendation of the First Committee [A/54/552], adopted **resolution 54/44** without vote [agenda item 65].

Prohibition of the development and manufacture of new types of weapons of mass destruction and new systems of such weapons

The General Assembly,

Recalling its previous resolutions on the prohibition of the development and manufacture of new types of weapons of mass destruction and new systems of such weapons,

Recalling also its resolution 51/37 of 10 December 1996 relating to the prohibition of the development and manufacture of new types of weapons of mass destruction and new systems of such weapons,

Taking note of paragraph 77 of the Final Document of the Tenth Special Session of the General Assembly,

Determined to prevent the emergence of new types of weapons of mass destruction that have characteristics comparable in destructive effect to those of weapons of mass destruction identified in the definition of weapons of mass destruction adopted by the United Nations in 1948,

Noting the desirability of keeping the matter under review, as appropriate,

1. *Reaffirms* that effective measures should be taken to prevent the emergence of new types of weapons of mass destruction;

2. *Requests* the Conference on Disarmament, without prejudice to further overview of its agenda, to keep the matter under review, as appropriate, with a view to making, when necessary, recommendations on undertaking specific negotiations on identified types of such weapons;

3. *Calls upon* all States, immediately following any recommendations of the Conference on Disarmament, to give favourable consideration to those recommendations;

4. *Requests* the Secretary-General to transmit to the Conference on Disarmament all documents relating to the consideration of this item by the General Assembly at its fifty-fourth session;

5. *Requests* the Conference on Disarmament to report the results of any consideration of the matter in its annual reports to the General Assembly;

6. *Decides* to include in the provisional agenda of its fifty-seventh session the item entitled "Prohibition of the development and manufacture of new types of weapons of mass destruction and new systems of such weapons: report of the Conference on Disarmament".

Bacteriological (biological) and chemical weapons

Bacteriological (biological) weapons

Efforts continued in 1999 to strengthen the Convention on the Prohibition of the Development, Production and Stockpiling of Bacteriological (Biological) and Toxin Weapons and on Their Destruction (BWC), adopted by the General Assembly in resolution 2826(XXVI) [YUN 1971, p. 19]. The Ad Hoc Group of the States Parties to the Convention attempted to achieve that goal through the development of a protocol on verification and confidence-building measures. However, obstacles remained at the end of the year.

Ad Hoc Group

The Ad Hoc Group of the States Parties to BWC held its thirteenth (4-22 January) [BWC/AD HOC GROUP/44], fourteenth (29 March-9 April) [BWC/AD HOC GROUP/45], fifteenth (28 June-23 July) [BWC/AD HOC GROUP/46], sixteenth (13 September-8 October) [BWC/AD HOC GROUP/47] and seventeenth (22 November-10 December) [BWC/AD HOC GROUP/49 & Add. 1-3] sessions in 1999, all in Geneva.

The Group, as in 1998 [YUN 1998, p. 519], considered definitions of terms and objective criteria; measures to promote compliance; confidentiality; national implementation and assistance; measures related to article X (scientific exchange and technological cooperation); investigations; legal issues; and the seat of the organization. The work was conducted in groups, each led by a Friend of the Chair. At the sixteenth session, a Friend of the Chair was appointed for article I (general provisions) of the future protocol. The Chairman continued to steer discussions on issues relating to organization and implementation arrangements. As had been done previously, the results of discussions during the sessions were incorporated into the rolling text, with brackets reflecting sections of the text on which agreement was not yet possible. Although those proposals were annexed to the rolling text, it was reaffirmed that the rolling text was the only basis for negotiations in the Ad Hoc Group.

By year's end, the rolling text contained a preamble, 23 articles, 7 annexes and 6 appendices. The main articles, additional to the standard ones on legal issues, were: I. General provisions; II. [Definitions [and criteria]]; III. Compliance measures; IV. Confidentiality provisions; V. Measures to redress a situation and to ensure compliance; VI. Assistance and protection against biological and toxin weapons; VII. Scientific and technological exchange for peaceful purposes and technical cooperation; VIII. Confidence-building measures; IX. The Organization; and X. National implementation measures. The annexes, which provided detailed procedures for implementing the protocol's provisions, dealt with the following issues: A. Declarations; B. [Visits]; C. [Measures to strengthen the implementation of article III]; D. Investigations; E. Confidentiality provisions; F. Scientific and technological exchange for peaceful purposes and technical cooperation; and G. Confidence-building measures. The appendices covered the following areas: A. [Information to be provided in declarations of past biological and toxin offensive and/or defensive [programmes] [activities]]; B. Declaration of current biological defensive [programmes] [activities]; C. [Facilities]; D. [Listing of facilities participating in biological defensive activities]; E. [Information to be provided [in the declaration of implementation of article X of the Convention and article VII of the Protocol] [under section G of article VII]]; and F. [List of approved investigation/visit equipment].

At its December session, the Group decided that it would hold four sessions in 2000. In addition, it decided to reserve two periods of two weeks each in the latter part of 2000; by the end of the twentieth session, it would decide on whether a further session would be convened and, if so, in which of the two reserved periods.

Parallel to their efforts to develop a verification mechanism, States parties continued their information exchange in the agreed framework of politically binding confidence-building measures, exchanging information on, among other things, relevant research centres and laboratories; national biological defence research and development programmes; outbreaks of infectious diseases and similar occurrences caused by toxins; relevant legislation, regulations and other measures; past activities in offensive and/or defensive biological research and development programmes; and vaccine production facilities. In 1999, 36 States parties submitted reports to the United Nations, bringing the number of States that had submitted at least one report since 1987 to 82.

GENERAL ASSEMBLY ACTION

On 1 December [meeting 69], the General Assembly, on the recommendation of the First Committee [A/54/570], adopted **resolution 54/61** without vote [agenda item 83].

Convention on the Prohibition of the Development, Production and Stockpiling of Bacteriological (Biological) and Toxin Weapons and on Their Destruction

The General Assembly,

Recalling its previous resolutions relating to the complete and effective prohibition of bacteriological (biological) and toxin weapons and to their destruction,

Noting with satisfaction that there are one hundred and forty-three States parties to the Convention on the Prohibition of the Development, Production and Stockpiling of Bacteriological (Biological) and Toxin

Weapons and on Their Destruction, including all the permanent members of the Security Council,

Bearing in mind its call upon all States parties to the Convention to participate in the implementation of the recommendations of the Review Conferences, including the exchange of information and data agreed to in the Final Declaration of the Third Review Conference of the Parties to the Convention on the Prohibition of the Development, Production and Stockpiling of Bacteriological (Biological) and Toxin Weapons and on Their Destruction, and to provide such information and data in conformity with standardized procedure to the Secretary-General on an annual basis and no later than 15 April,

Recalling its resolution 49/86, adopted without a vote on 15 December 1994, in which it welcomed the final report of the Special Conference of the States Parties to the Convention, adopted by consensus on 30 September 1994, in which the States parties agreed to establish an ad hoc group, open to the participation of all States parties, whose objective should be to consider appropriate measures, including possible verification measures, and draft proposals to strengthen the Convention, to be included, as appropriate, in a legally binding instrument to be submitted for the consideration of the States parties,

Recalling also the provisions of the Convention related to scientific and technological cooperation and the related provisions of the final report of the Ad Hoc Group of Governmental Experts to Identify and Examine Potential Verification Measures from a Scientific and Technical Standpoint, the final report of the Special Conference of the States Parties to the Convention, and the final documents of the Review Conferences,

Recalling further the Final Document of the Twelfth Conference of Heads of State or Government of Non-Aligned Countries, held at Durban, South Africa, from 29 August to 3 September 1998, in which the heads of State or Government noted the progress achieved so far in the negotiation of a protocol, stressed the importance of achieving further substantive progress for the conclusion of a universally acceptable and legally binding instrument designed to strengthen the Convention and reaffirmed the decision of the Fourth Review Conference of the Parties to the Convention urging the conclusion of the negotiations by the Ad Hoc Group as soon as possible before the commencement of the Fifth Review Conference,

Welcoming the reaffirmation made in the Final Declaration of the Fourth Review Conference that under all circumstances the use of bacteriological (biological) and toxin weapons and their development, production and stockpiling are effectively prohibited under article I of the Convention,

Recalling the declaration of the informal ministerial meeting, held in New York on 23 September 1998, in which the participants and the co-sponsors affirmed their strong support for the Convention and for strengthening its effectiveness and improving its implementation,

Bearing in mind the forthcoming seventy-fifth anniversary of the signature of the Protocol for the Prohibition of the Use in War of Asphyxiating, Poisonous or Other Gases, and of Bacteriological Methods of Warfare, signed at Geneva on 17 June 1925, and the twenty-fifth anniversary of the entry into force of the Convention on the Prohibition of the Development, Production and Stockpiling of Bacteriological (Biological) and Toxin Weapons and on Their Destruction on 26 March 1975,

1. *Welcomes* the progress achieved so far in the negotiation of a protocol to strengthen the Convention on the Prohibition of the Development, Production and Stockpiling of Bacteriological (Biological) and Toxin Weapons and on Their Destruction, and reaffirms the decision of the Fourth Review Conference of the Parties to the Convention urging the conclusion of the negotiations by the Ad Hoc Group of Governmental Experts to Identify and Examine Potential Verification Measures from a Scientific and Technical Standpoint as soon as possible before the commencement of the Fifth Review Conference and urging it to submit its report, which shall be adopted by consensus, to the States parties to be considered at a special conference;

2. *Notes with satisfaction* the increase in the number of States parties to the Convention, and reaffirms the call upon all signatory States that have not yet ratified the Convention to do so without delay, and also calls upon those States that have not signed the Convention to become parties thereto at an early date, thus contributing to the achievement of universal adherence to the Convention, duly noting the forthcoming anniversary of the twenty-fifth year of the entry into force of the Convention;

3. *Calls upon* all States parties, in this context, to accelerate the negotiations and to redouble their efforts within the Ad Hoc Group to formulate an efficient, cost-effective and practical regime and to seek an early resolution of the outstanding issues through renewed flexibility in order to complete the protocol on the basis of consensus at the earliest possible date;

4. *Welcomes* the information and data provided to date, and reiterates its call upon all States parties to the Convention to participate in the exchange of information and data agreed to in the Final Declaration of the Third Review Conference;

5. *Requests* the Secretary-General to continue to render the necessary assistance to the depositary Governments of the Convention and to provide such services as may be required for the implementation of the decisions and recommendations of the Review Conferences, as well as the decisions contained in the final report of the Special Conference, including all necessary assistance to the Ad Hoc Group and the special conference that is to consider the report of the Ad Hoc Group, in accordance with its mandate, as confirmed by the Fourth Review Conference;

6. *Decides* to include in the provisional agenda of its fifty-fifth session the item entitled "Convention on the Prohibition of the Development, Production and Stockpiling of Bacteriological (Biological) and Toxin Weapons and on Their Destruction".

Chemical weapons

Chemical weapons convention

In 1999, Estonia, the Holy See, Liechtenstein, Micronesia, Nicaragua, Nigeria, San Marino and the Sudan ratified the Convention on the Prohibition of the Development, Stockpiling and Use of Chemical Weapons and on Their Destruction, bringing the total number of States parties to 129. The number of signatories stood at 165. The Convention was adopted by the Conference on Disarmament in 1992 [YUN 1992, p. 65] and entered into force in 1997 [YUN 1997, p. 499].

At the fourth session of the Conference of the States Parties to the Convention (see below), the Director-General of the Organization for the Prohibition of Chemical Weapons (OPCW) noted that 29 of the States parties had not submitted their initial declarations. (Under article III of the Convention, a State party was obligated to declare, 30 days after entry into force, whether or not chemical weapons or facilities existed on its territory, and to report on plans to destroy or convert existing chemical weapons and related facilities and on related laboratories and equipment that could be used to make chemical weapons. A State party was also obliged to declare all riot control agents.)

Organization for the Prohibition of Chemical Weapons

In 1999, the fourth session of the Conference of States Parties (The Hague, Netherlands, 28 June–2 July) [OPCW, C-IV/6] adopted the 2000 OPCW programme and budget, approved the draft relationship agreement between the United Nations and OPCW and authorized the Director-General to transmit it to the Secretary-General on the understanding that the Conference did not wish to reopen the text of the draft. With respect to inspections, the Conference approved model facility agreements for chemical weapons storage facilities and for chemical weapons production facilities.

The OPCW Executive Council considered a number of technical issues at its fourteenth (2-5 February), fifteenth (26-29 April), sixteenth (21-24 September) and seventeenth (30 November–3 December) sessions. It also held specially scheduled meetings on 23 June and 22 July. Among other things, it discussed requests for OPCW to provide more information about verification activities, including inspection results (a contentious issue because of the need to protect confidential information) and the issue of costs associated with inspections of old/abandoned chemical weapons.

GENERAL ASSEMBLY ACTION

On 1 December [meeting 69], the General Assembly, on the recommendation of the First Committee [A/54/563], adopted **resolution 54/54 E** without vote [agenda item 76 (*n*)].

Implementation of the Convention on the Prohibition of the Development, Production, Stockpiling and Use of Chemical Weapons and on Their Destruction

The General Assembly,

Recalling its previous resolutions on the subject of chemical weapons, in particular resolution 53/77 R of 4 December 1998, adopted without a vote, in which it noted with appreciation the ongoing work to achieve the objective and purpose of the Convention on the Prohibition of the Development, Production, Stockpiling and Use of Chemical Weapons and on Their Destruction,

Determined to achieve the effective prohibition of the development, production, acquisition, transfer, stockpiling and use of chemical weapons and their destruction,

Noting with satisfaction that, since the adoption of resolution 53/77 R, six additional States have ratified the Convention, bringing the total number of States parties to the Convention to one hundred and twenty-six,

1. *Notes with appreciation* the ongoing work of the Organization for the Prohibition of Chemical Weapons to achieve the objective and purpose of the Convention on the Prohibition of the Development, Production, Stockpiling and Use of Chemical Weapons and on Their Destruction, to ensure the full implementation of its provisions, including those for international verification of compliance with it, and to provide a forum for consultation and cooperation among States parties;

2. *Stresses* the importance of the Organization for the Prohibition of Chemical Weapons in verifying compliance with the provisions of the Convention as well as in promoting the timely and efficient accomplishment of all its objectives;

3. *Also stresses* the vital importance of full and effective implementation of and compliance with all provisions of the Convention;

4. *Urges* all States parties to the Convention to meet in full and on time their obligations under the Convention and to support the Organization for the Prohibition of Chemical Weapons in its implementation activities;

5. *Emphasizes* the necessity of universal adherence to the Convention, and calls upon all States that have not yet done so to become States parties to the Convention without delay;

6. *Stresses* the importance to the Convention that all possessors of chemical weapons, chemical weapons production facilities and chemical weapons development facilities, including previously declared possessor States, should be among the States parties to the Convention, and welcomes progress to that end;

7. *Welcomes* the cooperation between the United Nations and the Organization for the Prohibition of Chemical Weapons and efforts towards the prompt conclusion of a relationship agreement between the United Nations and the Organization, in accordance with the provisions of the Convention;

8. *Decides* to include in the provisional agenda of its fifty-fifth session the item entitled "Implementation of the Convention on the Prohibition of the Development, Production, Stockpiling and Use of Chemical Weapons and on Their Destruction".

Conventional weapons

In 1999, the United Nations continued to consider the question of small arms and light weapons. The General Assembly adopted nine resolutions dealing with conventional weapons, among them **resolution 54/54 V**, by which it decided to convene in 2001 the UN Conference on the Illicit Trade in Small Arms and Light Weapons in All Its Aspects.

While the Register of Conventional Arms remained the most well-known instrument of transparency for conventional weapons, the decrease in the number of replies for 1998 reflected the continuing differences among Member States regarding its future development. Some States, such as EU members and the United States, advocated the inclusion of additional information on procurement through national production and military holdings, while others, mostly non-aligned States, advocated inclusion of weapons of mass destruction. Participation by Member States in the standardized reporting instrument for military expenditures remained low. However, by the end of 1999, it appeared that military spending itself was on the rise.

Further progress was made in strengthening the two legal instruments dealing with anti-personnel mines. The 1997 Convention on the Prohibition of the Use, Stockpiling, Production and Transfer of Anti-personnel Mines and on Their Destruction [YUN 1997, p. 503] entered into force on 1 March and the first meeting of the States parties took place (Maputo, Mozambique, 3-7 May). Also, the First Annual Conference of the States Parties to Amended Protocol II to the 1980 Convention on Prohibitions or Restrictions on the Use of Certain Conventional Weapons Which May Be Deemed to Be Excessively Injurious or to Have Indiscriminate Effects [YUN 1980, p. 76] was held (Geneva, 15-17 December).

Small arms

Group of Governmental Experts. The Group of Governmental Experts on Small Arms, established by the Secretary-General in 1998 [YUN 1998, p. 524], completed its study [A/54/258] on progress made in implementing the 24 recommendations of the 1997 Panel of Governmental Experts on Small Arms [YUN 1997, p. 506] and recommended further actions. In 1999, the Group held its second and third sessions (Geneva, 22-26 February; New York, 21-30 July) and conducted regional workshops in Tokyo (31 May-3 June) and Geneva (18-20 February).

The Group reviewed the implementation of each of the 24 recommendations made in 1997, noting that progress was being made through the efforts of the United Nations, other international forums, regional and subregional organizations, and Member States. In general, they found that most of the recommendations were in the process of being implemented and a few had been almost completely implemented, while for a few others implementation had not yet begun.

In connection with the General Assembly's decision to convene an international conference on the illicit arms trade in all its aspects no later than 2001 (resolution 54/54 V), the Group recommended that the Conference's objective should be to develop and strengthen international efforts and that it should focus on small arms and light weapons that were manufactured to military specifications.

Disarmament Commission action. On 28 April [A/54/42], the Disarmament Commission adopted by consensus the report of its Working Group III on guidelines on conventional arms control/limitation and disarmament, with particular emphasis on consolidation of peace in the context of General Assembly resolution 51/45 N [YUN 1996, p. 490]. The Working Group had concluded that the excessive accumulation of small arms and light weapons could be best averted by a combination of reduction and prevention measures.

Other action. At the regional and subregional levels, the first Summit of the Heads of State and Government of Latin America and the Caribbean and the EU (Rio de Janeiro, Brazil, June) [A/54/448] adopted the Declaration of Rio de Janeiro and Priorities for Action, which welcomed the 1998 Joint Action on Small Arms adopted by the EU [A/54/374] aimed at combating the destabilizing accumulation and spread of small arms and light weapons. At its thirty-fifth ordinary session (Algiers, Algeria, 12-14 July) [A/54/424], the Assembly of Heads of State and Government of the Organization of African Unity (OAU) adopted a decision on the illicit proliferation, circulation and illicit trafficking of small arms and light weapons which, among other things, called for a coordinated African approach to the problems addressed by the decision and requested the OAU secretariat to organize a preparatory conference of continental experts on the matter.

The Second Oslo Meeting on Small Arms and Light Weapons (Oslo, Norway, 6-7 December) [A/54/739] discussed the humanitarian, developmental and security concerns raised by small arms and light weapons.

Issues related to small arms were also dealt with in the Coordinating Action on Small Arms

(CASA) mechanism, established in 1998 by DDA [YUN 1998, p. 525]. In 1999, CASA held three meetings (1 March, 25 May and 23 November) at which information was disseminated to participants within and outside the UN system via DDA's web site and press releases. At its May meeting, representatives of the International Action Network on Small Arms (IANSA), an initiative launched by over 200 organizations working to prevent the proliferation and misuse of small arms, briefed CASA on two broad categories of policy measures: controlling the availability and access to small arms and reducing the demand for small arms. They further noted that IANSA would act as a clearing house for information on small arms and, in particular, for the production and dissemination of educational materials on small arms to support NGOs in the field. CASA members shared the view that IANSA could make an important contribution in promoting advocacy and supporting the UN lead role in encouraging efforts to address the wide-ranging problems posed by small arms.

On 10 December, the Economic Community of West African States (ECOWAS) adopted a code of conduct for the implementation of the 1998 Moratorium on the Importation, Exportation and Manufacture of Small Arms and Light Weapons in West Africa [YUN 1998, p. 525].

Proposed conference on small arms trade. As requested in Assembly resolution 53/77 E [YUN 1998, p. 525], the Secretary-General, in an August report with later addenda [A/54/260 & Add.1-3], presented the views of 26 States on the objective, scope, agenda, dates and venue of and preparatory work for an international conference on the illicit arms trade in all its aspects.

GENERAL ASSEMBLY ACTION

On 15 December [meeting 80], the General Assembly, on the recommendation of the First Committee [A/54/563], adopted **resolution 54/54 V** by recorded vote (119-0-2) [agenda item 76 (*f*)].

Small arms

The General Assembly,

Recalling its resolutions 50/70 B of 12 December 1995, 52/38 J of 9 December 1997 and 53/77 E of 4 December 1998,

Reaffirming the role of the United Nations in the field of disarmament and the commitment of Member States to take concrete steps in order to strengthen that role,

Recognizing the importance of the role of civil society, including non-governmental organizations, in preventing and reducing the excessive and destabilizing accumulations of small arms and light weapons,

Convinced of the need for a comprehensive approach to promote, at the global and regional levels, the control and reduction of small arms and light weapons in a balanced and non-discriminatory manner as a contribution to international peace and security,

Bearing in mind Security Council resolution 1209(1998) of 19 November 1998 on illicit arms flows to and in Africa and the statement by the President of the Security Council of 24 September 1999 on behalf of the Council in connection with the Council's consideration of the item entitled "Small arms",

Taking note of the complementarity of the efforts to prevent and reduce the excessive and destabilizing accumulation and transfer of small arms and light weapons and the work of the Ad Hoc Committee on the Elaboration of a Convention against Transnational Organized Crime, including a protocol to combat illicit manufacturing of and trafficking in firearms, their parts and components and ammunition,

Reaffirming the inherent right to individual or collective self-defence recognized in Article 51 of the Charter of the United Nations, which implies that States also have the right to acquire arms with which to defend themselves,

Reaffirming also the right of self-determination of all peoples, in particular peoples under colonial or other forms of alien domination or foreign occupation, and the importance of the effective realization of this right, as enunciated, inter alia, in the Vienna Declaration and Programme of Action, adopted by the World Conference on Human Rights on 25 June 1993,

Concerned about the wide range of humanitarian and socio-economic consequences affecting, in particular, large segments of civilian populations, exacerbated by the illicit trafficking in and the ready availability of small arms and light weapons,

Also concerned about the close link between terrorism, organized crime and drug trafficking, on the one hand, and the uncontrolled spread of small arms and light weapons, on the other, and stressing the importance of international efforts aimed at combating them,

Welcoming the adoption by the Disarmament Commission of the "Guidelines on conventional arms control/limitation and disarmament, with particular emphasis on consolidation of peace in the context of General Assembly resolution 51/45 N",

Also welcoming the report of the Secretary-General on small arms, prepared with the assistance of the Group of Governmental Experts on Small Arms pursuant to General Assembly resolution 52/38 J,

Bearing in mind the note by the Secretary-General on the consultations held with a group of qualified experts to examine the feasibility of carrying out a study on restricting the manufacture and trade of small arms to manufacturers and dealers authorized by States and also his report on the broad-based consultations held by him pursuant to General Assembly resolution 53/77 T of 4 December 1998,

Noting the replies received to date to the request by the Secretary-General to Member States for their views on his report on small arms to the General Assembly at its fifty-second session and on the steps that they have taken to implement its recommendations, in particular, the recommendation concerning the convening of an international conference on the illicit arms trade in all its aspects,

Taking due note of the report of the Group of Experts on the problem of ammunition and explosives,

Welcoming with appreciation the recommendations of the Secretary-General on the international conference on the illicit trade in small arms and light weapons in all its aspects to be convened no later than 2001 and the relevant recommendations contained in his report on small arms,

Welcoming the offer by the Government of Switzerland to host at Geneva, no later than 2001, an international conference on the illicit arms trade in all its aspects,

1. *Decides* to convene the United Nations Conference on the Illicit Trade in Small Arms and Light Weapons in All Its Aspects in June/July 2001;

2. *Also decides* that the scope of the Conference shall be the illicit trade in small arms and light weapons in all its aspects;

3. *Further decides* to establish a preparatory committee open to participation by all States, which will hold no fewer than three sessions, the first session to be held in New York from 28 February to 3 March 2000;

4. *Decides* that the specialized agencies, other relevant intergovernmental organizations and relevant entities, having received a standing invitation to participate as observers in the sessions and in the work of the General Assembly, shall participate, as observers, in the Preparatory Committee, and requests the Committee to take a decision on the modalities of attendance of non-governmental organizations at its sessions;

5. *Requests* the Preparatory Committee to decide, at its first session, on the date and venue of the Conference in 2001 as well as on the dates and venue of its subsequent sessions;

6. *Stresses* the need to ensure the widest possible and effective participation in the Conference in 2001;

7. *Requests* the Preparatory Committee to make recommendations to the Conference on all relevant matters, including the objective, a draft agenda, draft rules of procedure and draft final documents, which will include a programme of action, and to decide on background documents to be made available in advance;

8. *Invites* all Member States, in particular those that have not yet done so, in response to the note verbale of the Secretary-General dated 20 January 1999, to communicate to the Secretary-General their views on the agenda and other relevant questions relating to the Conference;

9. *Requests* the Secretary-General to transmit the replies of Member States relevant to paragraph 8 above to the Preparatory Committee and to render to the Preparatory Committee and the Conference all necessary assistance, including the provision of essential background information, relevant documents and summary records;

10. *Endorses* the report of the Secretary-General on small arms, prepared with the assistance of the Group of Governmental Experts on Small Arms pursuant to General Assembly resolution 52/38 J, bearing in mind the views of Member States on the report;

11. *Calls upon* all Member States to implement the relevant recommendations contained in section IV of that report to the extent possible and where necessary in cooperation with appropriate international and regional organizations and/or through international and regional cooperation;

12. *Requests* the Secretary-General to seek the views of Member States on the report as well as on the implementation of the relevant recommendations contained therein;

13. *Also requests* the Secretary-General to implement the relevant recommendations contained in section IV of the report within available financial resources and with any other assistance provided by States in a position to do so and in cooperation with appropriate international and regional organizations where necessary;

14. *Further requests* the Secretary-General, in order to assist in preventing the illicit trafficking in and illicit circulation of small arms and light weapons:

(a) To carry out a study, within available financial resources and with any other assistance provided by Member States in a position to do so, and with the assistance of governmental experts appointed by him, on the basis of equitable geographical representation, while seeking the views of Member States, on the feasibility of restricting the manufacture and trade of such weapons to the manufacturers and dealers authorized by States, which will cover the brokering activities, particularly illicit activities, relating to small arms and light weapons, including transportation agents and financial transactions;

(b) To submit the study as one of the background documents for the Conference to be held in 2001;

15. *Decides* to include in the provisional agenda of its fifty-fifth session the item entitled "Small arms".

RECORDED VOTE ON RESOLUTION 54/54 V:

In favour: Albania, Algeria, Andorra, Antigua and Barbuda, Argentina, Armenia, Australia, Austria, Azerbaijan, Bahrain, Bangladesh, Barbados, Belgium, Benin, Bhutan, Bolivia, Bosnia and Herzegovina, Botswana, Brazil, Brunei Darussalam, Burkina Faso, Cambodia, Canada, Cape Verde, China, Colombia, Costa Rica, Côte d'Ivoire, Croatia, Cuba, Cyprus, Czech Republic, Denmark, Ecuador, Egypt, El Salvador, Eritrea, Estonia, Ethiopia, Finland, France, Gambia, Georgia, Germany, Greece, Guatemala, Haiti, Hungary, Iceland, India, Indonesia, Iran, Ireland, Israel, Italy, Japan, Jordan, Kazakhstan, Kenya, Kuwait, Lao People's Democratic Republic, Latvia, Libyan Arab Jamahiriya, Liechtenstein, Lithuania, Luxembourg, Madagascar, Malaysia, Malta, Mauritius, Mexico, Monaco, Morocco, Mozambique, Myanmar, Namibia, Nepal, Netherlands, New Zealand, Nigeria, Norway, Oman, Pakistan, Paraguay, Peru, Philippines, Poland, Portugal, Qatar, Republic of Korea, Republic of Moldova, Romania, San Marino, Saudi Arabia, Senegal, Singapore, Slovakia, Slovenia, Solomon Islands, South Africa, Spain, Sri Lanka, Sudan, Sweden, Tajikistan, Thailand, The former Yugoslav Republic of Macedonia, Togo, Trinidad and Tobago, Tunisia, Turkey, Turkmenistan, Ukraine, United Arab Emirates, United Kingdom, United States, Uzbekistan, Venezuela, Yemen.

Against: None.

Abstaining: Lebanon, Russian Federation.

In the First Committee, the eighth preambular paragraph was adopted by a recorded vote of 127 to 1, with 14 abstentions. The Assembly retained the paragraph by a recorded vote of 96 to 1, with 11 abstentions.

Ammunition and explosives

The Group of Experts appointed by the Secretary-General in 1998 [YUN 1998, p. 527] completed the study on the problems of ammunition and explosives in all their aspects [A/54/155], taking into account the work carried out by the Panel on Small Arms of 1997 [YUN 1997, p. 506]. The Group, which held its second and third sessions (New York, 11-15 January and 1-5 June), analysed information received on the manufacture of ammunition and explosives; legal transfers and illicit trafficking; stocks and surpluses; legislative control measures, with special reference to national legislation, and bilateral, regional and multilateral agreements; marking of ammunition and explosives; programmes for the reduction of ammunition stocks; and options for control measures on ammunition and explosives. The Group made recommendations concerning prevention and reduction measures, and proposed that the problem of ammunition and explosives be integrated into a number of UN activities.

Illicit traffic

In response to General Assembly resolution 53/77 E [YUN 1998, p. 525], the Secretary-General convened a consultative meeting of experts (New York, 20-21 May) [A/54/160] to ascertain the feasibility of undertaking a study for restricting the manufacture and trade of small arms and light weapons and ammunition to manufacturers and dealers authorized by States. After examining the scope of the proposed study, the experts concluded that a study on the subject was both feasible and desirable.

Regarding assistance to States to curb the illicit traffic in small arms and to collect them, the Secretary-General, in a September report [A/54/309] prepared in response to Assembly resolution 53/77 B [YUN 1998, p. 529], highlighted subregional, regional and international initiatives to address the issue. He also provided details on requests for assistance from four countries. In Albania, the collection of weapons in exchange for community development incentives took place through the Gramsh district pilot project, launched in January. Bolivia had presented to the Group of Interested States (see p. 493) a proposal for a programme on conflict prevention, negotiation and resolution within the framework of its strategy to fight drugs. DDA then requested Bolivia to prepare a project proposal with a clear disarmament dimension. The Government of Liberia, the United Nations and the Monitoring Group of ECOWAS (ECOMOG) agreed to dispose of all the weapons that were kept in a number of containers in Monrovia, with the United Nations Observer Mission in Liberia (UNOMIL) and ECOMOG in control of the keys. By August, 18,420 small arms, 2,870,910 rounds of ammunition and 606 heavy machine-guns had been destroyed. Consultations between the Government of the Niger and DDA resumed when the Niger submitted a project for collecting 5,000 weapons over an initial period of nine months.

In response to General Assembly resolution 53/77 T [YUN 1998, p. 528], the Secretary-General, in a September report with later addendum [A/54/404 & Add.1], presented the views of 10 Member States and the EU on the magnitude and scope of the phenomenon of illicit trafficking in small arms; possible measures to combat such trafficking, including those suited to indigenous regional approaches; and the role of the United Nations in collecting, sharing and disseminating information on illicit trafficking in small arms. The Secretary-General had held broad-based consultations on the issue of illicit small arms trafficking. In addition, DDA, through the UN Regional Centre for Peace, Disarmament and Development in Latin America and the Caribbean, organized a workshop on illicit trafficking issues in small arms in Latin America and the Caribbean (Lima, Peru, 23-25 June); and, through the UN Regional Centre for Peace and Disarmament in Africa, DDA organized a regional workshop on illicit trafficking in small arms in Africa (Lomé, Togo, 2-4 August).

Other action. In a 24 September statement [S/PRST/1999/28], the Security Council President, in reference to the implementation of arms embargoes, emphasized the importance of regional cooperation in tackling the issue of illicit trafficking in small arms (see p. 48).

The Council of Ministers at the nineteenth Summit of the Heads of State or Government of the Southern African Development Community (Maputo, Mozambique, 17-18 August) [A/54/488-S/1999/1082] adopted a decision on the prevention and combating of illicit trafficking in small arms and related crimes.

In June, the General Assembly of the Organization of American States (OAS) urged all member States that had not ratified the 1997 Inter-American Convention against the Illicit Manufacturing of and Trafficking in Firearms, Ammunition, Explosives, and Other Related Materials [YUN 1997, p. 509] to do so without delay. Also in June, OAS adopted a resolution on the proliferation of and illicit trafficking in small arms and light weapons, in which it requested its Inter-American Drug Abuse Control Commission to continue to provide assistance to OAS member States in order to facilitate compliance with the Inter-American Convention.

GENERAL ASSEMBLY ACTION

On 1 December [meeting 69], the General Assembly, on the recommendation of the First Committee [A/54/563], adopted **resolution 54/54 R** without vote [agenda item 76 *(o)*].

Illicit traffic in small arms

The General Assembly,

Recalling its resolution 53/77 T of 4 December 1998,

Expressing its appreciation to the Secretary-General for the report on the results of his broad-based consultations on the magnitude and scope of the phenomenon of illicit trafficking in small arms and light weapons, possible measures to combat illicit trafficking in and illicit circulation of small arms and light weapons, and the role of the United Nations in collecting, collating, sharing and disseminating information on illicit trafficking in small arms and light weapons,

Convinced of the importance of national, regional and international measures to combat illicit trafficking in and illicit circulation of small arms and light weapons, including those suited to indigenous regional approaches,

Welcoming in this regard the decision on the illicit proliferation, circulation and trafficking of small arms and light weapons, adopted by the Assembly of Heads of State and Government of the Organization of African Unity at its thirty-fifth ordinary session, held at Algiers from 12 to 14 July 1999, the entry into force of the Inter-American Convention against the Illicit Manufacturing of and Trafficking in Firearms, Ammunition, Explosives and Other Related Materials, the decision on prevention and combating of illicit trafficking in small arms and related crimes, adopted by the Council of Ministers at the nineteenth Summit of Heads of State or Government of the Southern African Development Community, held at Maputo on 17 and 18 August 1999, the initiative taken by States members of the Economic Community of West African States in declaring a moratorium on the importation, exportation and manufacture of small arms and light weapons in West Africa, and the adoption by the European Union of the Programme for Preventing and Combating Illicit Trafficking in Conventional Arms and the other initiatives it has taken, such as the Joint Action on Small Arms that has been endorsed by several Member States not members of the European Union,

Welcoming also the assistance provided by Member States in support of bilateral, regional and multilateral initiatives aimed at addressing illicit trafficking in small arms and light weapons,

Mindful of the impact of surplus small arms and light weapons on the illicit trade in these weapons, and welcoming the practical measures taken by Member States to destroy surplus weapons and confiscated or collected weapons, in accordance with the recommendations of the Secretary-General in his reports on small arms,

Recognizing the human suffering caused by illicit trafficking in small arms and that Governments bear the responsibility to intensify their efforts by developing an understanding of the issues and practical ways of addressing the problem,

Bearing in mind the interface between violence, criminality, drug trafficking and terrorism and illicit trafficking in small arms,

Stressing the importance of ongoing efforts to elaborate an international convention against transnational organized crime, including a protocol to combat the illicit manufacturing of and illicit trafficking in firearms, their parts and components and ammunition, within the framework of the Commission on Crime Prevention and Criminal Justice,

Considering that the United Nations could, through a coordinated approach, collect, share and disseminate information to Member States on useful and successful practices to prevent the illicit trafficking in small arms and light weapons, and mindful of the role of the mechanism for Coordinating Action on Small Arms in this regard,

Emphasizing the importance of increased cooperation and coordination both among the relevant United Nations intergovernmental bodies and within the Secretariat through the mechanism for Coordinating Action on Small Arms in its ongoing initiatives related to illicit trafficking in small arms and light weapons,

Noting with appreciation the workshops on illicit trafficking in small arms, held at Lomé and Lima, organized, respectively by the United Nations Regional Centre for Peace and Disarmament in Africa and the United Nations Regional Centre for Peace, Disarmament and Development in Latin America and the Caribbean,

Conscious of its decision to convene an international conference on the illicit trade in small arms and light weapons in all its aspects no later than 2001, and taking into consideration the recommendations of the Secretary-General in his report on small arms, prepared with the assistance of the Group of Governmental Experts on Small Arms, as well as the views of Member States on the objectives, scope, agenda, dates and venue of such an international conference,

1. *Requests* the Secretary-General to continue his broad-based consultations, within available financial resources and with any other assistance provided by Member States in a position to do so, and to submit to the international conference on the illicit trade in small arms and light weapons in all its aspects information on the magnitude and scope of illicit trafficking in small arms and light weapons, measures to combat illicit trafficking in and circulation of small arms and light weapons, and the role of the United Nations in collecting, collating, sharing and disseminating information on illicit trafficking in small arms and light weapons;

2. *Encourages* Member States to promote regional and subregional initiatives and requests the Secretary-General, within available financial resources, and States in a position to do so to assist States in taking such initiatives to address the illicit trafficking in small arms and light weapons in affected regions, and invites the Secretary-General to utilize these initiatives as part of his consultations;

3. *Encourages* Member States in a position to do so to take appropriate national measures to destroy surplus small arms and light weapons, confiscated or collected small arms and light weapons, and to provide, on a voluntary basis, information to the Secretary-General on the types and quantities destroyed;

4. *Invites* Member States in a position to do so to continue to provide assistance, bilaterally, regionally and through multilateral channels, such as the United Nations, in support of measures associated with combating illicit trafficking in small arms and light weapons;

5. *Requests* the Secretary-General to report to the General Assembly at its fifty-fifth session on the implementation of the present resolution;

6. *Decides* to include in the provisional agenda of its fifty-fifth session the item entitled "Illicit traffic in small arms".

Also on 1 December [meeting 69], the Assembly, on the recommendation of the First Committee [A/54/563], adopted **resolution 54/54 J** without vote [agenda item 76 *(d)*].

Assistance to States for curbing the illicit traffic in small arms and collecting them

The General Assembly,

Recalling its resolution 53/77 B of 4 December 1998,

Considering that the illicit proliferation and circulation of and traffic in small arms constitute an impediment to development, a threat to populations and to national and regional security and are a factor contributing to the destabilization of States,

Gravely concerned at the extent of the illicit proliferation and circulation of and traffic in small arms in the States of the Saharo-Sahelian subregion,

Welcoming the conclusions of the United Nations advisory missions sent to the affected countries of the subregion by the Secretary-General to study the best way of curbing the illicit circulation of small arms and ensuring their collection,

Welcoming also the designation of the Department for Disarmament Affairs of the Secretariat as the coordination centre for all United Nations activities concerning small arms,

Thanking the Secretary-General for his report on the causes of conflict and the promotion of durable peace and sustainable development in Africa, and bearing in mind the statement on small arms made by the President of the Security Council on 24 September 1999,

Welcoming the recommendations made at the meetings of the States of the subregion held at Banjul, Algiers, Bamako, Yamoussoukro and Niamey to establish close regional cooperation with a view to strengthening security,

Welcoming also the initiative taken by the Economic Community of West African States concerning the declaration of a moratorium on the importation, exportation and manufacture of small arms and light weapons in West Africa,

Recalling the Algiers Declaration adopted by the Assembly of Heads of State and Government of the Organization of African Unity at its thirty-fifth ordinary session, held at Algiers from 12 to 14 July 1999, and bearing in mind the report of the Secretary-General of the Organization of African Unity on the illicit proliferation and circulation of and traffic in small arms,

Bearing in mind the reports of the Panel of Governmental Experts on Small Arms,

Emphasizing the need to advance efforts towards wider cooperation and better coordination in the struggle against the accumulation, proliferation and widespread use of small arms through the common understanding reached at the meeting on small arms held at Oslo on 13 and 14 July 1998 and the Brussels Call for Action adopted by the International Conference on Sustainable Disarmament for Sustainable Development, held at Brussels on 12 and 13 October 1998,

1. *Encourages* the Secretary-General to continue his efforts, in the context of the implementation of resolution 49/75 G of 15 December 1994 and of the recommendations of the United Nations advisory missions, to curb the illicit circulation of small arms and to collect such arms in the affected States that so request, with the support of the United Nations Regional Centre for Peace and Disarmament in Africa and in close cooperation with the Organization of African Unity;

2. *Also encourages* the setting up in the countries of the Saharo-Sahelian subregion of national commissions against the proliferation of small arms, and invites the international community to support as far as possible the smooth functioning of the national commissions where they have been set up;

3. *Welcomes* the Declaration of a Moratorium on the Importation, Exportation and Manufacture of Small Arms and Light Weapons in West Africa, adopted by the Heads of State and Government of the Economic Community of West African States at Abuja on 31 October 1998, and urges the international community to give its support to the implementation of the moratorium;

4. *Takes note* of the conclusions of the meeting of Ministers for Foreign Affairs of the Economic Community of West African States, held at Bamako on 24 and 25 March 1999, on the modalities for the implementation of the Programme for Coordination and Assistance for Security and Development, and welcomes the adoption at the meeting of a plan of action;

5. *Expresses its full support* for the appeal launched by the Assembly of Heads of State and Government of the Organization of African Unity at its thirty-fifth ordinary session for a coordinated African approach, under the auspices of the Organization of African Unity, to the problems posed by the illicit proliferation and circulation of and traffic in small arms, bearing in mind the experiences and activities of the various regions in this regard;

6. *Also expresses its full support* for the convening of an international conference on the illicit arms trade in all its aspects no later than 2001, in accordance with General Assembly resolution 53/77 E of 4 December 1998;

7. *Requests* the Secretary-General to continue to examine the question and to submit to the General Assembly at its fifty-fifth session a report on the implementation of the present resolution;

8. *Decides* to include in the provisional agenda of its fifty-fifth session the item entitled "Assistance to States for curbing the illicit traffic in small arms and collecting them".

Convention on excessively injurious conventional weapons and Protocols

As requested in General Assembly resolution 53/81 [YUN 1998, p. 530], the Secretary-General reported on the status, as at 15 June 1999 [A/54/162], of the 1980 Convention on Prohibitions or Restrictions on the Use of Certain Conventional Weapons Which May Be Deemed to Be Excessively Injurious or to Have Indiscriminate Effects [YUN 1980, p. 76] and two of its four Protocols: the

1995 Protocol on Blinding Laser Weapons (Protocol IV) [YUN 1995, p. 221] and the 1996 amended Protocol on Prohibitions or Restrictions on the Use of Mines, Booby Traps and Other Devices (amended Protocol II) [YUN 1996, p. 484]. He stated that amended Protocol II had entered into force on 3 December 1998 and that 37 States had notified their consent to be bound by it. Regarding Protocol IV, which entered into force on 30 July 1998 [YUN 1998, p. 530], 39 States had notified their consent to be bound by it.

The accession of Senegal and Tajikistan in 1999 brought the number of States parties to the Convention as at 31 December to 75.

Pursuant to resolution 53/81, the First Annual Conference of the States Parties to Amended Protocol II met in Geneva from 15 to 17 December [CCW/AP.II/CONF.1/2].

The Conference had before it 31 national annual reports, containing information on: dissemination of information on the Protocol to armed forces and civilian populations; mine clearance and rehabilitation programmes; steps taken to meet technical requirements of the Protocol and any other relevant information pertaining thereto; legislation related to the Protocol; measures taken on international technical information exchange, on international cooperation on mine clearance, and on technical cooperation and assistance; and other relevant matters.

On 17 December, the Conference issued a declaration urging all States that had not done so to take all measures to accede to amended Protocol II as soon as possible.

The Conference recommended that the Secretary-General of the United Nations, as depositary of amended Protocol II, consider sending a communication to heads of State and/or Government of those States that had not acceded to the Protocol, urging them to do so at the earliest possible date. The Conference further requested the President of the Second Annual Conference to exercise his authority to achieve the goal of universality of the Protocol and, in that regard, requested him to consider reporting to the fifty-fifth session of the General Assembly. The Conference also called on the States parties to promote wider adherence to amended Protocol II in their respective regions and decided to convene the Second Annual Conference from 11 to 13 December 2000, in Geneva.

GENERAL ASSEMBLY ACTION

On 1 December [meeting 69], the General Assembly, on the recommendation of the First Committee [A/54/567], adopted **resolution 54/58** without vote [agenda item 80].

Convention on Prohibitions or Restrictions on the Use of Certain Conventional Weapons Which May Be Deemed to Be Excessively Injurious or to Have Indiscriminate Effects

The General Assembly,

Recalling its resolution 53/81 of 4 December 1998 and previous resolutions referring to the Convention on Prohibitions or Restrictions on the Use of Certain Conventional Weapons Which May Be Deemed to Be Excessively Injurious or to Have Indiscriminate Effects,

Recalling with satisfaction the adoption, on 10 October 1980, of the Convention, together with the Protocol on Non-Detectable Fragments (Protocol I), the Protocol on Prohibitions or Restrictions on the Use of Mines, Booby Traps and Other Devices (Protocol II) and the Protocol on Prohibitions or Restrictions on the Use of Incendiary Weapons (Protocol III), which entered into force on 2 December 1983,

Also recalling with satisfaction the adoption by the Review Conference of the States Parties to the Convention on Prohibitions or Restrictions on the Use of Certain Conventional Weapons Which May Be Deemed to Be Excessively Injurious or to Have Indiscriminate Effects, on 13 October 1995 of the Protocol on Blinding Laser Weapons (Protocol IV), and on 3 May 1996 of the amended Protocol on Prohibitions or Restrictions on the Use of Mines, Booby Traps and Other Devices (Protocol II),

Recalling that the States parties at the Review Conference declared their commitment to keeping the provisions of Protocol II under review in order to ensure that the concerns regarding the weapons it covers are addressed, and that they would encourage efforts of the United Nations and other organizations to address all problems of landmines,

Recalling also the role played by the International Committee of the Red Cross in the elaboration of the Convention and the Protocols thereto,

Welcoming the additional ratifications and acceptances of or accessions to the Convention, as well as the ratifications and acceptances of or accessions to amended Protocol II and Protocol IV,

Noting that, in conformity with article 8 of the Convention, conferences may be convened to examine amendments to the Convention or to any of the Protocols thereto, to examine additional protocols concerning other categories of conventional weapons not covered by existing Protocols or to review the scope and application of the Convention and the Protocols thereto and to examine any proposed amendments or additional protocols,

Welcoming the decision adopted by the Review Conference in its Final Declaration on 3 May 1996 to convene a Review Conference no later than 2001,

Noting that, in accordance with article 13 of amended Protocol II, a conference of States parties to that Protocol shall be held annually for the purpose of consultations and cooperation on all issues relating to the Protocol,

Noting also that the provisional rules of procedure of the First Annual Conference of the States Parties to Amended Protocol II provide for the invitation of States not parties to the Protocol, the International Committee of the Red Cross and interested non-governmental organizations to take part in the Conference,

I

1. *Expresses its satisfaction* that the Protocol on Blinding Laser Weapons (Protocol IV) entered into force on 30 July 1998, commends it to all States with a view to achieving the widest possible adherence to this instrument at an early date and calls, in particular, upon all States parties to the Convention on Prohibitions or Restrictions on the Use of Certain Conventional Weapons Which May Be Deemed to Be Excessively Injurious or to Have Indiscriminate Effects that have not yet done so to express their consent to be bound by the Protocol;

2. *Welcomes* the entry into force on 3 December 1998 of the amended Protocol on Prohibitions or Restrictions on the Use of Mines, Booby Traps and Other Devices (Protocol II), and calls, in particular, upon all States parties to the Convention that have not yet done so to express their consent to be bound by the Protocol;

3. *Notes* the convening, from 15 to 17 December 1999, of the First Annual Conference of States Parties to Amended Protocol II, in accordance with article 13 thereof, and welcomes in this context the successful Preparatory Meeting held by the States parties on 25 and 26 May 1999;

II

1. *Calls upon* all States parties that have not yet done so to notify the Secretary-General, in his capacity as depositary of the Convention on Prohibitions or Restrictions on the Use of Certain Conventional Weapons Which May Be Deemed to Be Excessively Injurious or to Have Indiscriminate Effects and the Protocols thereto, of their consent to be bound by the Protocol on Blinding Laser Weapons (Protocol IV), and by the amended Protocol on Prohibitions or Restrictions on the Use of Mines, Booby Traps and Other Devices (Protocol II);

2. *Welcomes* the convening, from 15 to 17 December 1999, of the First Annual Conference of States Parties to Amended Protocol II, in accordance with article 13 thereof;

3. *Calls upon* all States parties to amended Protocol II to address at the Conference, inter alia, the issue of holding the second annual conference in 2000;

4. *Requests* the Secretary-General to render the necessary assistance and to provide such services as may be required for the second annual conference of States parties to amended Protocol II and the preparatory committee for the conference;

III

1. *Recalls* the decision of States parties to the Convention on Prohibitions or Restrictions on the Use of Certain Conventional Weapons Which May Be Deemed to Be Excessively Injurious or to Have Indiscriminate Effects to convene the next review conference no later than 2001, preceded by the preparatory committee;

2. *Requests* the Secretary-General to render the necessary assistance and to provide such services, including summary records, as may be required for the second Review Conference of the States Parties to the Convention and the preparatory committee for the Review Conference;

3. *Urgently calls upon* all States that have not yet done so to take all measures to become parties, as soon as possible, to the Convention and the Protocols thereto, and in particular to the amended Protocol on Prohibitions or Restrictions on the Use of Mines, Booby Traps and Other Devices (Protocol II), with a view to achieving the widest possible adherence to this instrument at an early date, and calls upon successor States to take appropriate measures so that ultimately adherence to these instruments will be universal;

4. *Requests* the Secretary-General, in his capacity as depositary of the Convention and the Protocols thereto, to continue to inform the General Assembly periodically of ratifications and acceptances of and accession to the Convention and the Protocols thereto;

5. *Decides* to include in the provisional agenda of its fifty-fifth session the item entitled "Convention on Prohibitions or Restrictions on the Use of Certain Conventional Weapons Which May Be Deemed to Be Excessively Injurious or to Have Indiscriminate Effects".

Practical disarmament

The Group of Interested States, established in 1998 [YUN 1998, p. 531] to examine and, whenever possible, support concrete projects of practical disarmament, met four times during 1999 (27 January, 6 May, 10 September, 7 December) to discuss practical disarmament measures in Albania, Bolivia, South Africa–Mozambique and the Niger. It also reviewed projects that it had undertaken in Albania, Central Africa and Central America.

Representatives of 37 Member States and various UN departments and agencies met for the first time (New York, 26 January) to review and discuss the UN pilot project for weapons collection in Albania (see p. 489). During the year, in spite of the project's suspension for two months owing to the Kosovo crisis, 6,000 weapons and 100 tonnes of ammunition were voluntarily surrendered and stored for destruction. The project was overseen by a National Steering Committee, DDA and the United Nations Development Programme (UNDP).

Disarmament Commission action. In 1999 [A/54/42], the Disarmament Commission allocated to Working Group III the item entitled "Guidelines on conventional arms control/limitation and disarmament, with particular emphasis on consolidation of peace in the context of General Assembly resolution 51/45 N", using the Chairman's 1998 paper [YUN 1998, p. 531] as a basis for the deliberations. Following the Chairman's presentation of three revisions of his paper, the Group agreed on a set of guidelines, which the Commission adopted, consisting of practical disarmament measures in post-conflict situations; confidence-building in post-conflict situations; regional and international financial and technical assistance; other conventional arms control/limitation and disarmament measures; and the role of the United Nations. The Commission noted that the guidelines were primarily applicable to the consolidation of peace in post-conflict situations and should be applied on a voluntary basis and with the consent of the States concerned; the root causes of conflict and the specific conditions and characteristics of the region concerned should be taken into account; States within the region, as well as those outside, had a particular responsibility to promote arms control and disarmament measures; and the guidelines should not be used as a means to interfere in the internal affairs of other States.

GENERAL ASSEMBLY ACTION

On 1 December [meeting 69], the General Assembly, on the recommendation of the First Committee [A/54/563], adopted **resolution 54/54 H** without vote [agenda item 76 *(j)*].

Consolidation of peace through practical disarmament measures

The General Assembly,

Recalling its resolutions 51/45 N of 10 December 1996, 52/38 G of 9 December 1997 and 53/77 M of 4 December 1998,

Convinced that a comprehensive and integrated approach towards certain practical disarmament measures, such as, inter alia, arms control, particularly with regard to small arms and light weapons, confidence-building measures, demobilization and reintegration of former combatants, demining and conversion, often is a prerequisite to maintaining and consolidating peace and security and thus provides a basis for effective rehabilitation and social and economic development in areas that have suffered from conflict,

Noting with satisfaction that the international community is more than ever aware of the importance of such practical disarmament measures, especially with regard to the growing problems arising from the excessive and destabilizing accumulation and proliferation of small arms and light weapons, which pose a threat to peace and security and reduce the prospects for economic development in many regions, particularly in post-conflict situations,

Stressing that further efforts are needed in order to develop and effectively implement programmes of practical disarmament in affected areas,

Taking note of the report of the Secretary-General prepared with the assistance of the Group of Governmental Experts on Small Arms, and in particular the recommendations contained therein, as an important contribution to the consolidation of the peace process through practical disarmament measures,

1. *Welcomes* the adoption by consensus of the "Guidelines on conventional arms control/limitation and disarmament, with particular emphasis on consolidation of peace in the context of General Assembly resolution 51/45 N" at the 1999 substantive session of the Disarmament Commission;

2. *Stresses* the particular relevance of the guidelines in the context of the present resolution;

3. *Takes note* of the report of the Secretary-General on the consolidation of peace through practical disarmament measures, submitted pursuant to resolution 51/45 N, and once again encourages Member States, as well as regional arrangements and agencies, to lend their support to the implementation of recommendations contained therein;

4. *Welcomes* the activities undertaken by the group of interested States that was formed in New York in March 1998, and invites the group to continue to analyse lessons learned from previous disarmament and peace-building projects, as well as to promote new practical disarmament measures to consolidate peace, especially as undertaken or designed by affected States themselves;

5. *Encourages* Member States, including the group of interested States, to lend their support to the Secretary-General in responding to requests by Member States to collect and destroy small arms and light weapons in post-conflict situations;

6. *Decides* to include in the provisional agenda of its fifty-fifth session the item entitled "Consolidation of peace through practical disarmament measures".

Transparency

Conference on Disarmament. In 1999, the issue of transparency in armaments was addressed during plenary meetings of the Conference on Disarmament [A/54/27], mainly in connection with efforts to find a comprehensive agreement on the establishment of subsidiary bodies on the agenda items. All the proposals in that regard envisaged the reappointment of a special coordinator to seek the views of the members on the most appropriate way to deal with the question.

By a 29 July letter [CD/1591], Brazil and the United States transmitted the text of the Inter-American Convention on Transparency in Conventional Weapons Acquisitions, which was approved by the OAS General Assembly in Guatemala on 7 June.

UN Register of Conventional Arms

In response to General Assembly resolution 53/77 V [YUN 1998, p. 533], the Secretary-General submitted the seventh annual report on the United Nations Register of Conventional Arms [A/54/226 & Corr.1 & Add.1-6], which was established in 1992 [YUN 1992, p. 75] to promote enhanced levels of transparency regarding arms transfers.

The report presented information provided by 80 Governments on imports and exports during the 1998 calendar year in the seven categories of conventional arms (battle tanks, armoured combat vehicles, large-calibre artillery systems, attack helicopters, combat aircraft, warships, and missiles and missile launchers). Governments also provided information on procurement from national production and military holdings. The report indicated a decrease in the number of submissions.

The question of early expansion of the scope and further development of the Register was scheduled for examination in 2000 by a Group of Governmental Experts.

GENERAL ASSEMBLY ACTION

On 1 December [meeting 69], the General Assembly, on the recommendation of the First Committee [A/54/563], adopted **resolution 54/54 I** by recorded vote (97-48-15) [agenda item 76 *(b)*].

Transparency in armaments

The General Assembly,

Bearing in mind that, in accordance with the Charter of the United Nations, Member States have undertaken to promote the establishment and maintenance of international peace and security with the least diversion for armaments of the world's human and economic resources,

Considering the urgent need to accelerate efforts towards general and complete disarmament with a view to maintaining regional and international peace and security in a world free from the scourge of war and the burden of all types of armaments,

Considering also that openness and transparency relating to all types of armaments would contribute greatly to confidence-building and security among States,

Recognizing that an enhanced level of transparency relating to both conventional weapons and weapons of mass destruction and transfers of equipment and technologies directly related to the development and manufacture of such weapons, as well as to high technology with military applications, would promote stability, strengthen regional and international peace and security, and accelerate efforts towards general and complete disarmament,

Convinced that the principle of transparency should also apply to all weapons of mass destruction, in particular nuclear weapons, and to transfers of equipment and technology directly related to the development and manufacture of such weapons, as well as to high technology with military applications,

Recognizing that the United Nations Register of Conventional Arms, in its current form, constitutes an important first step towards the promotion of transparency in military matters on a comprehensive, universal and non-discriminatory basis,

Aware of the need to foster international efforts in this direction through, inter alia, the constant review of the operation of the Register with a view to its development,

Stressing the need to achieve universality of the Treaty on the Non-Proliferation of Nuclear Weapons, and of the Convention on the Prohibition of the Development, Production, Stockpiling and Use of Chemical Weapons and on Their Destruction and the Convention on the Prohibition of the Development, Production and Stockpiling of Bacteriological (Biological) and Toxin Weapons and on Their Destruction, with a view to realizing the goal of the total elimination of all weapons of mass destruction,

Recalling its earlier resolutions on transparency in armaments,

1. *Takes note* of the report of the Secretary-General on transparency in armaments;

2. *Recalls* the reports of the Group of Governmental Experts on the United Nations Register of Conventional Arms, which convened in 1994 and 1997 to consider the continuing operation of the Register and its development, and the views expressed and proposals presented therein;

3. *Recognizes* the importance of achieving greater progress in the development of the Register in order that it may truly enhance confidence-building and security among States and accelerate efforts towards attainment of general and complete disarmament;

4. *Requests* the Secretary-General, with the assistance of the Group of Governmental Experts to be convened in the year 2000 and taking into account the views submitted by Member States, to report to the General Assembly at its fifty-fifth session on:

(a) The early expansion of the scope of the Register;

(b) The elaboration of practical means for the development of the Register in order to increase transparency related to weapons of mass destruction, in particular nuclear weapons, and to transfers of equipment and technology directly related to the development and manufacture of such weapons;

5. *Decides* to include in the provisional agenda of its fifty-fifth session the item entitled "Transparency in armaments".

RECORDED VOTE ON RESOLUTION 54/54 I:

In favour: Algeria, Angola, Antigua and Barbuda, Bahamas, Bahrain, Bangladesh, Barbados, Belarus, Belize, Benin, Bhutan, Bolivia, Botswana, Brazil, Brunei Darussalam, Burkina Faso, Cambodia, Cameroon, Cape Verde, Chad, Chile, Colombia, Congo, Costa Rica, Côte d'Ivoire, Cuba, Djibouti, Dominica, Dominican Republic, Ecuador, Egypt, El Salvador, Equatorial Guinea, Eritrea, Ethiopia, Fiji, Ghana, Grenada, Guatemala, Guinea, Guinea-Bissau, Guyana, Haiti, Honduras, Indonesia, Iran, Jamaica, Jordan, Kenya, Kuwait, Lebanon, Libyan Arab Jamahiriya, Madagascar, Malaysia, Maldives, Mali, Mauritius, Mexico, Mongolia, Morocco, Mozambique, Myanmar, Namibia, Nepal, Nicaragua, Nigeria, Oman, Panama, Papua New Guinea, Paraguay, Peru, Philippines, Qatar, Saint Kitts and Nevis, Saint Lucia, Saint Vincent and the Grenadines, Saudi Arabia, Senegal, Sierra Leone, Solomon Islands, South Africa, Sri Lanka, Sudan, Suriname, Swaziland, Thailand, Togo, Trinidad and Tobago, Tunisia, Uganda, United Arab Emirates, United Republic of Tanzania, Venezuela, Viet Nam, Yemen, Zambia, Zimbabwe.

Against: Albania, Andorra, Australia, Austria, Belgium, Bosnia and Herzegovina, Bulgaria, Canada, Croatia, Cyprus, Czech Republic, Denmark, Estonia, Finland, France, Germany, Greece, Hungary, Iceland, Ireland, Israel, Italy, Latvia, Liechtenstein, Lithuania, Luxembourg, Malta, Marshall Islands, Micronesia, Monaco, Netherlands, New Zealand, Norway, Poland, Portugal, Republic of Moldova, Romania, Russian Federation, San Marino, Slovakia, Slovenia, Spain, Sweden, The former Yugoslav Republic of Macedonia, Turkey, Ukraine, United Kingdom, United States.

Abstaining: Argentina, Armenia, Azerbaijan, China, Georgia, India, Japan, Kazakhstan, Pakistan, Republic of Korea, Samoa, Singapore, Tajikistan, Uruguay, Uzbekistan.

The Committee adopted the eighth preambular paragraph and paragraph 4 *(b)* by separate recorded votes of 132 to 2, with 3 abstentions, and 77 to 45, with 16 abstentions, respectively. The Assembly retained the same paragraphs by recorded votes of 156 to 3, with 3 abstentions, and 93 to 50, with 17 abstentions, respectively.

Also on 1 December [meeting 69], the Assembly, on the recommendation of the First Committee

[A/54/563], adopted **resolution 54/54 O** by recorded vote (150-0-12) [agenda item 76 *(b)*].

Transparency in armaments

The General Assembly,

Recalling its resolutions 46/36 L of 9 December 1991, 47/52 L of 15 December 1992, 48/75 E of 16 December 1993, 49/75 C of 15 December 1994, 50/70 D of 12 December 1995, 51/45 H of 10 December 1996, 52/38 R of 9 December 1997 and 53/77 V of 4 December 1998 entitled "Transparency in armaments",

Continuing to take the view that an enhanced level of transparency in armaments contributes greatly to confidence-building and security among States and that the establishment of the United Nations Register of Conventional Arms constitutes an important step forward in the promotion of transparency in military matters,

Welcoming the consolidated report of the Secretary-General on the Register, which contains the returns of Member States for 1998,

Welcoming also the response of Member States to the request contained in paragraphs 9 and 10 of resolution 46/36 L to provide data on their imports and exports of arms, as well as available background information regarding their military holdings, procurement through national production and relevant policies,

Stressing that the continuing operation of the Register and its further development should be reviewed in order to secure a Register that is capable of attracting the widest possible participation,

1. *Reaffirms* its determination to ensure the effective operation of the United Nations Register of Conventional Arms, as provided for in paragraphs 7 to 10 of resolution 46/36 L;

2. *Calls upon* Member States, with a view to achieving universal participation, to provide the Secretary-General by 31 May annually with the requested data and information for the Register, including nil reports if appropriate, on the basis of resolutions 46/36 L and 47/52 L and the recommendations contained in paragraph 64 of the 1997 report of the Secretary-General on the continuing operation of the Register and its further development;

3. *Invites* Member States in a position to do so, pending further development of the Register, to provide additional information on procurement from national production and military holdings and to make use of the "Remarks" column in the standardized reporting form to provide additional information such as types and models;

4. *Reaffirms* its decision, with a view to further development of the Register, to keep the scope of and participation in the Register under review and, to that end, recalls:

(a) Its request to Member States to provide the Secretary-General with their views on the continuing operation of the Register and its further development and on transparency measures related to weapons of mass destruction;

(b) Its request to the Secretary-General, with the assistance of a group of governmental experts to be convened in 2000, on the basis of equitable geographical representation, to prepare a report on the continuing operation of the Register and its further development, taking into account the work of the Conference on Disarmament, the views expressed by Member States and his reports on the continuing operation of the Register and its further development, with a view to a decision at its fifty-fifth session;

5. *Requests* the Secretary-General to ensure that sufficient resources are made available for the Secretariat to operate and maintain the Register;

6. *Invites* the Conference on Disarmament to consider continuing its work undertaken in the field of transparency in armaments;

7. *Reiterates its call upon* all Member States to cooperate at the regional and subregional levels, taking fully into account the specific conditions prevailing in the region or subregion, with a view to enhancing and coordinating international efforts aimed at increased openness and transparency in armaments;

8. *Requests* the Secretary-General to report to the General Assembly at its fifty-fifth session on progress made in implementing the present resolution;

9. *Decides* to include in the provisional agenda of its fifty-fifth session the item entitled "Transparency in armaments".

RECORDED VOTE ON RESOLUTION 54/54 O:

In favour: Albania, Andorra, Angola, Antigua and Barbuda, Argentina, Armenia, Australia, Austria, Azerbaijan, Bahamas, Bahrain, Bangladesh, Barbados, Belarus, Belgium, Belize, Benin, Bhutan, Bolivia, Bosnia and Herzegovina, Botswana, Brazil, Brunei Darussalam, Bulgaria, Burkina Faso, Cambodia, Cameroon, Canada, Cape Verde, Chad, Chile, Colombia, Congo, Costa Rica, Côte d'Ivoire, Croatia, Cuba, Cyprus, Czech Republic, Denmark, Djibouti, Dominica, Dominican Republic, Ecuador, El Salvador, Equatorial Guinea, Eritrea, Estonia, Ethiopia, Fiji, Finland, France, Georgia, Germany, Ghana, Greece, Grenada, Guatemala, Guinea, Guinea-Bissau, Guyana, Haiti, Honduras, Hungary, Iceland, India, Indonesia, Ireland, Israel, Italy, Jamaica, Japan, Jordan, Kazakhstan, Kenya, Kuwait, Latvia, Libyan Arab Jamahiriya, Liechtenstein, Lithuania, Luxembourg, Madagascar, Malaysia, Maldives, Mali, Malta, Marshall Islands, Mauritius, Micronesia, Monaco, Mongolia, Mozambique, Namibia, Nepal, Netherlands, New Zealand, Nicaragua, Nigeria, Norway, Oman, Panama, Papua New Guinea, Paraguay, Peru, Philippines, Poland, Portugal, Qatar, Republic of Korea, Republic of Moldova, Romania, Russian Federation, Saint Kitts and Nevis, Saint Lucia, Saint Vincent and the Grenadines, Samoa, San Marino, Senegal, Seychelles, Singapore, Slovakia, Slovenia, Solomon Islands, South Africa, Spain, Sri Lanka, Sudan, Suriname, Swaziland, Sweden, Tajikistan, Thailand, The former Yugoslav Republic of Macedonia, Togo, Trinidad and Tobago, Tunisia, Turkey, Turkmenistan, Uganda, Ukraine, United Arab Emirates, United Kingdom, United Republic of Tanzania, United States, Uruguay, Uzbekistan, Venezuela, Yemen, Zambia, Zimbabwe.

Against: None.

Abstaining: Algeria, China, Democratic People's Republic of Korea, Egypt, Iran, Lebanon, Mexico, Morocco, Myanmar, Pakistan, Saudi Arabia, Syrian Arab Republic.

In the Committee, paragraphs 4 *(b)* and 6 were adopted by separate recorded votes of 121 to none, with 12 abstentions, and 120 to none, with 15 abstentions, respectively. The Assembly retained the paragraphs by recorded votes of 140 to none, with 16 abstentions, and 139 to none, with 17 abstentions, respectively.

Transparency of military expenditures

In response to General Assembly resolution 53/72 [YUN 1998, p. 535], the Secretary-General, in September [A/54/298], presented reports from 35 Member States on military expenditures for the latest fiscal year for which data were available. The reporting instrument used was that recommended by the Assembly in resolution 35/142 B [YUN 1980, p. 88].

Also pursuant to resolution 53/72, DDA continued consultations with international and regional organizations that received data on military expenditures from Member Governments and had received their views on the recommendations contained in the 1998 report of the Secretary-General [YUN 1998, p. 534].

GENERAL ASSEMBLY ACTION

On 1 December [meeting 69], the General Assembly, on the recommendation of the First Committee [A/54/551], adopted **resolution 54/43** without vote [agenda item 64 *(b)*].

Objective information on military matters, including transparency of military expenditures

The General Assembly,

Recalling its resolution 53/72 of 4 December 1998 on objective information on military matters, including transparency of military expenditures,

Also recalling its resolution 35/142 B of 12 December 1980, which introduced the United Nations system for the standardized reporting of military expenditures, and its resolutions 48/62 of 16 December 1993, 49/66 of 15 December 1994, 51/38 of 10 December 1996 and 52/32 of 9 December 1997, calling upon all Member States to participate in it, and its resolution 47/54 B of 9 December 1992, endorsing the guidelines and recommendations for objective information on military matters and inviting Member States to provide the Secretary-General with relevant information regarding their implementation,

Noting that since then national reports on military expenditures and on the guidelines and recommendations for objective information on military matters have been submitted by a number of Member States belonging to different geographic regions,

Welcoming the report of the Secretary-General on ways and means to implement the guidelines and recommendations for objective information on military matters, including, in particular, how to strengthen and broaden participation in the United Nations system for the standardized reporting of military expenditures,

Expressing its appreciation to the Secretary-General for providing Member States with the reports on military expenditures in standardized form reported by States and on the guidelines and recommendations for objective information on military matters,

Welcoming the decision of many Member States to exchange and to publish information annually on their military budgets and to implement the guidelines and recommendations for objective information on military matters, as appropriate,

Noting the efforts of several regional organizations to promote transparency of military expenditures, including standardized annual exchanges of relevant information among their member States,

Reaffirming its firm conviction that a better flow of objective information on military matters can help to relieve international tension and contribute to the building of confidence among States and to the conclusion of concrete disarmament agreements,

Convinced that the improvement of international relations forms a sound basis for promoting further openness and transparency in all military matters,

Recalling that the guidelines and recommendations for objective information on military matters recommended certain areas for further consideration, such as the improvement of the United Nations system for the standardized reporting of military expenditures,

1. *Recommends* the guidelines and recommendations for objective information on military matters to all Member States for implementation, fully taking into account specific political, military and other conditions prevailing in a region, on the basis of initiatives and with the agreement of the States of the region concerned;

2. *Welcomes* the continuation by the Secretary-General of consultations with relevant international bodies with a view to ascertaining the requirements for adjusting the present instrument to encourage wider participation;

3. *Expresses its appreciation* to the Secretary-General for providing Member States with a report on the outcome of those consultations, as well as for his intention to organize international and regional symposia and training seminars in the coming biennium, and notes his intention to encourage, inter alia, the United Nations regional centres for peace and disarmament in Africa, in Asia and the Pacific, and in Latin America and the Caribbean to assist Member States in their regions in enhancing their knowledge of the standardized reporting system;

4. *Calls upon* all Member States to report annually, by 30 April, to the Secretary-General their military expenditures for the latest fiscal year for which data are available, using, preferably and to the extent possible, the reporting instrument as recommended in its resolution 35/142 B or, as appropriate, any other format developed in conjunction with similar reporting on military expenditures to other international or regional organizations;

5. *Encourages* relevant international bodies and regional organizations to promote transparency of military expenditures and to enhance complementarity among reporting systems, taking into account the particular characteristics of each region, and to consider the possibility of an exchange of information with the United Nations;

6. *Requests* the Secretary-General:

(a) To continue the practice of sending an annual note verbale to Member States requesting the submission of data to the reporting system, together with the reporting format and related instructions, and to publish in a timely fashion in appropriate United Nations media the due date for transmitting data on military expenditures;

(b) To promote international and regional symposia and training seminars to explain the purpose of the United Nations system for the standardized reporting of military expenditures and to give relevant technical instructions;

(c) To circulate annually the reports on military expenditures as received from Member States;

7. *Also requests* the Secretary-General to continue consultations with relevant international bodies, within existing resources, with a view to ascertaining the requirements for adjusting the present instrument

to encourage wider participation, with emphasis on examining possibilities for enhancing complementarity among international and regional reporting systems, and to exchange related information with those bodies;

8. *Further requests* the Secretary-General to make recommendations, based on the outcome of those consultations and taking into account the views of Member States, on necessary changes to the content and structure of the United Nations system for the standardized reporting of military expenditures in order to strengthen and broaden participation, and to submit a report on the subject to the General Assembly at its fifty-sixth session;

9. *Calls upon* all Member States, in time for the deliberation by the General Assembly at its fifty-sixth session, to provide the Secretary-General with their views on the analysis and the recommendations contained in his report and with further suggestions to strengthen and broaden participation in the United Nations system for the standardized reporting of military expenditures, including necessary changes to its content and structure;

10. *Decides* to include in the provisional agenda of its fifty-sixth session the item entitled "Objective information on military matters, including transparency of military expenditures".

Verification

In response to General Assembly resolution 52/31 [YUN 1997, p. 515], the Secretary-General submitted a July report updating developments since 1997 on the verification of treaties [A/54/166]. He noted the activities undertaken by OPCW, the Preparatory Commission for CTBTO, the parties to the Biological Weapons Convention, and the parties to the Mine-Ban Convention.

GENERAL ASSEMBLY ACTION

On 1 December [meeting 69], the General Assembly, on the recommendation of the First Committee [A/54/555], adopted **resolution 54/46** without vote [agenda item 68].

Verification in all its aspects, including the role of the United Nations in the field of verification

The General Assembly,

Noting the critical importance of, and the vital contribution that has been made by, effective verification measures in arms limitation and disarmament agreements and other similar obligations,

Reaffirming its support for the sixteen principles of verification drawn up by the Disarmament Commission,

Recalling its resolutions 40/152 O of 16 December 1985, 41/86 Q of 4 December 1986, 42/42 F of 30 November 1987, 43/81 B of 7 December 1988, 45/65 of 4 December 1990, 47/45 of 9 December 1992, 48/68 of 16 December 1993, 50/61 of 12 December 1995 and 52/31 of 9 December 1997,

Recalling also the reports of the Secretary-General of 11 July 1986, 28 August 1990, 16 September 1992, 26 July 1993, 22 September 1995, 6 August 1997 and 9 July 1999, and the addenda thereto,

1. *Reaffirms* the critical importance of, and the vital contribution that has been made by, effective verification measures in arms limitation and disarmament agreements and other similar obligations;

2. *Requests* the Secretary-General to report to the General Assembly at its fifty-sixth session on further views received from Member States pursuant to resolutions 50/61 and 52/31;

3. *Decides* to include in the provisional agenda of its fifty-sixth session the item entitled "Verification in all its aspects, including the role of the United Nations in the field of verification".

On 1 December, the Assembly decided to include in the provisional agenda of its fifty-sixth (2001) session the item "Compliance with arms limitation and disarmament and non-proliferation agreements" (**decision 54/416**).

Anti-personnel mines

1997 Convention

The Convention on the Prohibition of the Use, Stockpiling, Production and Transfer of Anti-personnel Mines and on Their Destruction (Mine-Ban Convention, formerly known as the Ottawa Convention), adopted in 1997 [YUN 1997, p. 503], entered into force on 1 March 1999, six months following the deposit of the fortieth instrument of ratification. As at 31 December, 90 States had become parties to the Convention.

Pursuant to General Assembly resolution 53/77 N [YUN 1998, p. 536], the First Meeting of the States Parties to the Convention was convened in Maputo, Mozambique, from 3 to 7 May [APLC/MSP.1/1999/1]. Preparations were made during two rounds of open-ended informal consultations in Geneva, on 1 March, the day of the Convention's entry into force, and on 13 April.

The Meeting adopted the Maputo Declaration, in which the participants reaffirmed their commitment to the total eradication of anti-personnel mines, called on the international community to implement and universalize the new international standard and norm of behaviour that the Convention was establishing, committed themselves to mobilize resources and energies to that end, and established a programme of inter-sessional work.

It also considered a number of matters pertaining to specific articles of the Convention and agreed that the Second Meeting of the States Parties would be held from 11 to 15 September 2000 in Geneva.

During the course of the Meeting, the inter-sessional work programme was established, under which five Standing Committees of Experts (SCEs) would consider the themes of the general status and operation of the

Convention; mine clearance; victim assistance and mine-awareness; stockpile destructions; and technologies for mine action. Beginning in September, meetings of four of the SCEs were convened by the Geneva International Centre for Humanitarian Demining.

From May to the end of 1999, 34 States parties submitted their reports on transparency measures in accordance with article 7 of the Convention. With respect to stockpiles of anti-personnel landmines, many parties reported that they had none. Austria, Belgium, Canada, Germany and South Africa had destroyed their stocks prior to the entry into force of the Convention, with the exception of anti-personnel mines (APMs) retained for the development of and training in mine detection, mine clearance or mine destruction techniques, in accordance with article 3. On 21 December, the Government of France announced that it had completed the destruction of its stockpiles.

Several mine-affected countries—Croatia, Honduras, Jordan, Senegal, Thailand and Yemen—submitted their comprehensive reports, including detailed information on the type and quality of each type of APM in each detected mined area that contained, or was suspected to contain, APMs.

(For information on assistance in mine clearance, see p. 829.)

GENERAL ASSEMBLY ACTION

On 1 December [meeting 69], the General Assembly, on the recommendation of the First Committee [A/54/563], adopted **resolution 54/54 B** by recorded vote (139-1-20) [agenda item 76].

Implementation of the Convention on the Prohibition of the Use, Stockpiling, Production and Transfer of Anti-personnel Mines and on Their Destruction

The General Assembly,

Recalling its resolution 53/77 N of 4 December 1998,

Reaffirming its determination to put an end to the suffering and casualties caused by anti-personnel mines, which kill or maim hundreds of people every week, mostly innocent and defenceless civilians and especially children, obstruct economic development and reconstruction, inhibit the repatriation of refugees and internally displaced persons, and have other severe consequences for years after emplacement,

Believing it necessary to do the utmost to contribute in an efficient and coordinated manner to facing the challenge of removing anti-personnel mines placed throughout the world, and to assure their destruction,

Wishing to do the utmost in ensuring assistance for the care and rehabilitation, including the social and economic reintegration, of mine victims,

Welcoming the entry into force on 1 March 1999 of the Convention on the Prohibition of the Use, Stockpiling, Production and Transfer of Anti-personnel Mines and on Their Destruction,

Recalling the First Meeting of the States Parties to the Convention, held at Maputo from 3 to 7 May 1999, and the reaffirmation made in the Maputo Declaration of a commitment to the total eradication of anti-personnel mines,

Noting with satisfaction the addition of new States signatories to the Convention, the rapid ratification by many signatories, and the accession to the Convention by other States, bringing the total number of States that have signed to one hundred and thirty-three, and that eighty-nine States have ratified or acceded to the Convention in the two years since it was opened for signature,

Emphasizing the desirability of attracting the adherence of all States to the Convention, and determined to work strenuously towards the promotion of its universalization,

Noting with regret that anti-personnel mines continue to be used in conflicts around the world, causing human suffering and impeding post-conflict development,

1. *Invites* all States that have not signed the Convention on the Prohibition of the Use, Stockpiling, Production and Transfer of Anti-personnel Mines and on Their Destruction to accede to it without delay;

2. *Urges* all States that have signed but not ratified the Convention to ratify it without delay;

3. *Stresses* the importance of the full and effective implementation of, and compliance with, the Convention;

4. *Urges* all States parties to provide the Secretary-General with complete and timely information, as required in article 7 of the Convention in order to promote transparency and compliance with the Convention;

5. *Invites* all States that have not ratified the Convention or acceded to it to provide, on a voluntary basis, information to make global mine action efforts more effective;

6. *Renews its call upon* all States and other relevant parties to work together to promote, support and advance the care, rehabilitation and social and economic reintegration of mine victims, mine awareness programmes, and the removal of anti-personnel mines placed throughout the world and the assurance of their destruction;

7. *Invites and encourages* all interested States, the United Nations, other relevant international organizations or institutions, regional organizations, the International Committee of the Red Cross and relevant non-governmental organizations to participate in the programme of inter-sessional work established at the First Meeting of States Parties to the Convention;

8. *Requests* the Secretary-General, in accordance with article 11, paragraph 2, of the Convention, to undertake the preparations necessary to convene the Second Meeting of the States Parties to the Convention at Geneva, from 11 to 15 September 2000, and, on behalf of States parties and according to article 11, paragraph 4, of the Convention, to invite States not parties to the Convention, as well as the United Nations, other relevant international organizations or institutions, regional organizations, the International Committee of the Red Cross and relevant non-governmental organizations to attend the Meeting as observers;

9. *Decides* to include in the provisional agenda of its fifty-fifth session the item entitled "Implementation of the Convention on the Prohibition of the Use, Stockpiling, Production and Transfer of Anti-personnel Mines and on Their Destruction".

RECORDED VOTE ON RESOLUTION 54/54 B:

In favour: Albania, Algeria, Andorra, Angola, Antigua and Barbuda, Argentina, Armenia, Australia, Austria, Bahamas, Bahrain, Bangladesh, Barbados, Belarus, Belgium, Belize, Benin, Bhutan, Bolivia, Bosnia and Herzegovina, Botswana, Brazil, Brunei Darussalam, Bulgaria, Burkina Faso, Cambodia, Cameroon, Canada, Cape Verde, Chad, Chile, Colombia, Congo, Costa Rica, Côte d'Ivoire, Croatia, Cyprus, Czech Republic, Denmark, Djibouti, Dominica, Dominican Republic, El Salvador, Equatorial Guinea, Eritrea, Estonia, Ethiopia, Fiji, Finland, France, Georgia, Germany, Ghana, Greece, Grenada, Guatemala, Guinea, Guinea-Bissau, Guyana, Haiti, Honduras, Hungary, Iceland, Indonesia, Ireland, Italy, Jamaica, Japan, Jordan, Kenya, Latvia, Liechtenstein, Lithuania, Luxembourg, Madagascar, Malaysia, Maldives, Mali, Malta, Mauritius, Mexico, Monaco, Mongolia, Mozambique, Namibia, Nepal, Netherlands, New Zealand, Nicaragua, Nigeria, Norway, Oman, Panama, Papua New Guinea, Paraguay, Peru, Philippines, Poland, Portugal, Qatar, Republic of Moldova, Romania, Saint Kitts and Nevis, Saint Lucia, Saint Vincent and the Grenadines, Samoa, San Marino, Senegal, Seychelles, Sierra Leone, Singapore, Slovakia, Slovenia, Solomon Islands, South Africa, Spain, Sri Lanka, Sudan, Suriname, Swaziland, Sweden, Tajikistan, Thailand, The former Yugoslav Republic of Macedonia, Togo, Trinidad and Tobago, Tunisia, Turkey, Turkmenistan, Uganda, Ukraine, United Arab Emirates, United Kingdom, United Republic of Tanzania, Uruguay, Venezuela, Yemen, Zambia, Zimbabwe.

Against: Lebanon.

Abstaining: Azerbaijan, China, Cuba, Egypt, India, Iran, Israel, Kazakhstan, Libyan Arab Jamahiriya, Marshall Islands, Micronesia, Morocco, Myanmar, Pakistan, Republic of Korea, Russian Federation, Syrian Arab Republic, United States, Uzbekistan, Viet Nam.

By **resolution 54/191** of 17 December, the Assembly urged Member States to assist mine-affected countries in the establishment and development of national capacities in mine clearance, mine awareness and victim assistance (see p. 830).

Conference on Disarmament

In the Conference on Disarmament [A/54/27], a number of States presented documents on APMs: Argentina, Australia, Belgium, Bulgaria, Chile, Finland, France, Germany, Greece, Hungary, Italy, Japan, Poland, Romania, the Russian Federation, Slovakia, Spain, Turkey, Ukraine, the United Kingdom, the United States and Venezuela, in March, submitted a working paper concerning action by the Conference on an APM transfer ban [CD/1572]; Bulgaria and Turkey, also in March, an agreement signed in Sofia, Bulgaria, on 22 March, between the two Governments on non-use of APMs and their removal from or destruction in the areas of their common border [CD/1582]; Ukraine, in May, a decree issued on 22 March by its Government on the extension of the moratorium on the export of APMs [CD/1585]; and Norway, in June, the final report of the First Meeting of the States Parties to the Convention on the Prohibition of the Use, Stockpiling, Production and Transfer of Anti-personnel Mines and on Their Destruction [CD/1587] (see p. 498).

Regional and other approaches to disarmament

Africa

OAU continued to play a primary role in addressing the various political disputes and armed conflicts that had spread throughout the continent. The OAU Council of Ministers (Algiers, Algeria, 8-10 July) [A/54/424] urged the OAU Secretary-General to seek further the views of member States on illicit trafficking in small arms and appealed to the international community to assist affected countries in implementing programmes that would deal with such problems. At the thirty-fifth summit of OAU (Algiers, 12-14 July) [ibid.], member States adopted decisions on the illicit proliferation, circulation and trafficking of small arms and light weapons; on the First Meeting of the States Parties to the 1997 Mine-Ban Convention [YUN 1997, p. 503]; and on the UN Regional Centre for Peace and Disarmament in Africa.

On 10 December in Lomé, Togo, the ECOWAS heads of State and Government adopted a Code of Conduct to implement the 1998 Moratorium on the Importation, Exportation and Manufacture of Small Arms and Light Weapons in West Africa [YUN 1998, p. 525]. The Code of Conduct set out a stringent waiver procedure for ECOWAS member States wishing to import, export or manufacture light weapons during the Moratorium. In addition, the summit approved the implementation of the prototype of a regional arms register and database on light weapons. The UN Regional Centre for Peace and Disarmament in Africa would host the arms register and database.

Standing Advisory Committee

In response to General Assembly resolution 53/78 A [YUN 1998, p. 538], the Secretary-General submitted a September report on the activities of the United Nations Standing Advisory Committee on Security Questions in Central Africa, which held two summit meetings (Yaoundé, Cameroon, 25-26 February; Malabo, Equatorial Guinea, 25 June) [A/54/364]. At the first summit meeting [A/53/868-S/1999/303], the heads of State and Government decided to create the Council for Peace and Security in Central Africa (COPAX) to prevent, manage and settle conflicts in the subregion, as well as to promote, maintain and consolidate peace and security. It adopted the Yaoundé Declaration on Peace, Security and Stability in Central Africa, which, among other things, took note of the threat to stability and security posed by cross-border crime and by the trafficking in and illicit circulation and proliferation of weapons of war. At the second summit meeting [A/54/364], the heads of State and Government decided to incorporate COPAX into the Economic Community of Central African States (ECCAS).

The Standing Committee organized a high-level subregional seminar (Yaoundé, 19-21 July) [A/54/209-S/1999/859] on the implementation of the recommendations contained in the Secretary-General's 1998 report on the causes of conflict and the promotion of durable peace and sustainable development in Africa [YUN 1998, p. 66]. The participants adopted a number of recommendations, among them several measures to combat illicit trafficking in and proliferation of light weapons, including the establishment of national commissions; a request to the Secretary-General to establish an advisory mission on the proliferation of light weapons in the Central African subregion; the establishment of a subregional register of conventional arms; and revision and harmonization of national laws on the bearing of arms (see also p. 78). In addition, the Committee convened a subregional conference (N'Djamena, Chad, 25-27 October) [A/54/530-S/1999/1141], which reviewed the proliferation of and illicit traffic in small arms in Central Africa and discussed the development of an effective programme of action to combat the proliferation of small arms. The conference made a number of recommendations for practical measures at the national and subregional levels.

The Standing Committee held its eleventh (Yaoundé, 21-23 July) [A/54/210-S/1999/860] and twelfth (N'Djamena, 27-30 October) [A/54/530-S/1999/1141] ministerial meetings.

GENERAL ASSEMBLY ACTION

On 1 December [meeting 69], the General Assembly, on the recommendation of the First Committee [A/54/564], as amended [A/54/L.39], adopted **resolution 54/55 A** without vote [agenda item 77 *(a)*].

Regional confidence-building measures: activities of the United Nations Standing Advisory Committee on Security Questions in Central Africa

The General Assembly,

Bearing in mind the purposes and principles of the United Nations and its primary responsibility for the maintenance of international peace and security in accordance with the Charter of the United Nations,

Recalling its resolutions 43/78 H and 43/85 of 7 December 1988, 44/21 of 15 November 1989, 45/58 M of 4 December 1990, 46/37 B of 6 December 1991, 47/53 F of 15 December 1992, 48/76 A of 16 December 1993, 49/76 C of 15 December 1994, 50/71 B of 12 December 1995, 51/46 C of 10 December 1996, 52/39 B of 9 December 1997 and 53/78 A of 4 December 1998,

Considering the importance and effectiveness of confidence-building measures taken at the initiative and with the participation of all States concerned and taking into account the specific characteristics of each region, since such measures can contribute to regional stability and to international security,

Convinced that the resources released by disarmament, including regional disarmament, can be devoted to economic and social development and to the protection of the environment for the benefit of all peoples, in particular those of the developing countries,

Recalling the guidelines for general and complete disarmament adopted at its tenth special session, the first special session devoted to disarmament,

Convinced that development can be achieved only in a climate of peace, security and mutual confidence both within and among States,

Bearing in mind the establishment by the Secretary-General on 28 May 1992 of the United Nations Standing Advisory Committee on Security Questions in Central Africa, the purpose of which is to encourage arms limitation, disarmament, non-proliferation and development in the subregion,

Recalling the Brazzaville Declaration on Cooperation for Peace and Security in Central Africa, the Bata Declaration for the Promotion of Lasting Democracy, Peace and Development in Central Africa, and the Yaoundé Declaration on Peace, Security and Stability in Central Africa,

Bearing in mind resolutions 1196(1998) and 1197(1998), adopted by the Security Council on 16 and 18 September 1998 respectively, following its consideration of the report of the Secretary-General on the causes of conflict and the promotion of durable peace and sustainable development in Africa,

Emphasizing the need to strengthen the capacity for conflict prevention and peacekeeping in Africa,

Recalling the decision of the fourth meeting of the Standing Advisory Committee in favour of establishing, under the auspices of the United Nations High Commissioner for Human Rights, a subregional centre for human rights and democracy in Central Africa,

1. *Takes note* of the report of the Secretary-General on regional confidence-building measures, which deals with the activities of the United Nations Standing Advisory Committee on Security Questions in Central Africa in the period since the adoption by the General Assembly of resolution 53/78 A;

2. *Reaffirms its support* for efforts aimed at promoting confidence-building measures at regional and subregional levels in order to ease tensions and conflicts in the subregion and to further peace, stability and sustainable development in Central Africa;

3. *Also reaffirms its support* for the programme of work of the Standing Advisory Committee adopted at the organizational meeting of the Committee, held at Yaoundé from 27 to 31 July 1992;

4. *Notes with satisfaction* the progress made by the States members of the Standing Advisory Committee in implementing the programme of activities for the period 1998-1999, in particular by:

(a) Holding a joint meeting of ministers of defence and of the interior at Libreville from 28 to 30 April 1998 on questions of security in Central Africa;

(b) Organizing the Subregional Conference on Democratic Institutions and Peace in Central Africa, at Bata, Equatorial Guinea, from 18 to 21 May 1998;

(c) Holding a Seminar on the Training of Trainers in Practical Disarmament Measures for the Consolidation of Peace for Senior Military and Civilian Officials at Yaoundé, from 27 to 31 July 1998;

(d) Organizing the Subregional High-level Seminar on the Examination and Implementation of the Recommendations Contained in the Report of the Secretary-General of the United Nations on the Causes of Conflict and the Promotion of Durable Peace and Sustainable Development in Africa, at Yaoundé, from 19 to 21 July 1999;

(e) Holding the tenth ministerial meeting of the Standing Advisory Committee at Yaoundé from 26 to 30 October 1998;

(f) Holding the eleventh ministerial meeting of the Standing Advisory Committee at Yaoundé from 21 to 23 July 1999;

(g) Organizing a subregional conference on the proliferation of and illicit traffic in light weapons and small arms in Central Africa at N'Djamena from 25 to 27 October 1999;

(h) Holding the twelfth ministerial meeting of the Standing Advisory Committee at N'Djamena from 27 to 30 October 1999;

5. *Emphasizes* the importance of providing the States members of the Standing Advisory Committee with the essential support they need to carry out the full programme of activities which they adopted at the ninth and tenth ministerial meetings, in particular the organization of joint military exercises to simulate peacekeeping operations;

6. *Welcomes* the creation of a mechanism for the promotion, maintenance and consolidation of peace and security in Central Africa, to be known as the Council for Peace and Security in Central Africa, by the summit Conference of Heads of State and Government of the Central African countries, held at Yaoundé on 25 February 1999, and requests the Secretary-General to give his full support to the realization of that priority objective;

7. *Also welcomes* the decision of the heads of State and Government of the Economic Community of Central African States, meeting at Malabo on 24 June 1999, to integrate the Council into the Community and to establish a network of parliamentarians from the Community with a view to the eventual creation of a parliament of the Community;

8. *Emphasizes* the need to make the early-warning mechanism in Central Africa operational so that it will serve, on the one hand, as an instrument for analysing and monitoring political situations in the States members of the Standing Advisory Committee with a view to preventing the outbreak of future armed conflicts and, on the other hand, as a technical body through which the member States will carry out the work programme of the Committee, adopted at its organizational meeting held at Yaoundé in 1992, and requests the Secretary-General to provide it with the assistance necessary for it to function properly;

9. *Requests* the Secretary-General and the United Nations High Commissioner for Human Rights to lend their support to the establishment of a subregional centre for human rights and democracy in Central Africa;

10. *Requests* the Secretary-General, pursuant to Security Council resolution 1197(1998), to provide the States members of the Standing Advisory Committee with the necessary support in making operational the early-warning mechanism and the Council for Peace and Security in Central Africa;

11. *Also requests* the Secretary-General to support the establishment of a network of parliamentarians with a view to the creation of a subregional parliament in Central Africa;

12. *Requests* the Secretary-General and the Office of the United Nations High Commissioner for Refugees to continue to provide increased assistance to the countries of Central Africa for coping with the problems of refugees in their territories;

13. *Thanks* the Secretary-General for having established the Trust Fund for the United Nations Standing Advisory Committee on Security Questions in Central Africa;

14. *Appeals* to Member States and to governmental and non-governmental organizations to make additional voluntary contributions to the Trust Fund for the implementation of the programme of work of the Standing Advisory Committee, in particular the activities referred to in paragraphs 5, 6 and 7 above;

15. *Calls upon* the international community, non-governmental organizations and the mass media to support the dissemination of objective information on Central Africa;

16. *Requests* the Secretary-General to continue to provide the States members of the Standing Advisory Committee with assistance to ensure that they are able to carry on their efforts;

17. *Also requests* the Secretary-General to submit to the General Assembly at its fifty-fifth session a report on the implementation of the present resolution;

18. *Decides* to include in the provisional agenda of its fifty-fifth session the item entitled "Regional confidence-building measures: activities of the United Nations Standing Advisory Committee on Security Questions in Central Africa".

Asia and the Pacific

The Association of South-East Asian Nations (ASEAN), its Regional Forum (ARF) and the Council for Security Cooperation in the Asia Pacific continued to play important roles in maintaining regional security and stability. The United Nations Regional Centre for Peace and Disarmament in Asia and the Pacific also contributed to security and stability in the region through its activities (see p. 512).

At the thirty-second ASEAN ministerial meeting (Singapore, 23-24 July), the Foreign Ministers agreed to hasten the implementation of the 1998 Hanoi Plan of Action [YUN 1998, p. 539].

The sixth ministerial meeting of ARF (Singapore, 26 July) encouraged the further development of confidence-building measures and called on ARF countries to sign and ratify the global non-proliferation treaties. They also recognized that the illegal accumulation of small arms and light weapons posed a threat to peace and security in many regions and urged the international community to focus its attention on that problem. They endorsed the recommendations of the ARF Inter-sessional Support Group on Confidence-building Measures (Bangkok, 3-5 March).

At the bilateral level, on 30 July in Beijing, China and Japan signed a Memorandum of Understanding on the clean-up of chemical weapons abandoned in China by the Japanese Army, under which Japan would provide the necessary facilities, experts, expertise and funds, while China would provide appropriate cooperation for the destruction.

Europe

Developments that had an impact on security in Europe during 1999 included the Kosovo crisis and NATO air strikes against the Federal Republic of Yugoslavia (Serbia and Montenegro) (FRY) (see PART ONE, Chapter V); the approval of the 1997 Adaptation [YUN 1997, p. 518] of the 1990 Treaty on Conventional Armed Forces in Europe (CFE Treaty) [YUN 1990, p. 79] to the newly created security environment in the region; the adoption of the new NATO doctrine; and the adoption of the Vienna document on confidence- and security-building measures (CSBMs).

NATO continued its activities through various bodies and through the Euro-Atlantic Partnership Council, established in 1997 [YUN 1997, p. 519]. With regard to the 1997 Protocols of Accession of the New Members to NATO [ibid.], the Czech Republic, Hungary and Poland became members in March when they submitted their instruments of accession to the Alliance's depositary Power, the United States.

In accordance with the 1995 General Framework Agreement for Peace in Bosnia and Herzegovina (the Peace Agreement) [YUN 1995, p. 544] and under OSCE auspices, the States parties to the 1996 Agreement on Subregional Arms Control [YUN 1996, p. 493], signed by Bosnia and Herzegovina, Croatia, FRY, the Federation of Bosnia and Herzegovina and Republika Srpska, continued to destroy surplus weapons. However, owing to the escalation of violence in Kosovo, FRY temporarily suspended implementation of the Peace Agreement.

On 30 March, the CFE parties reached a preliminary agreement on the 1997 Adaptation of the Treaty [YUN 1997, p. 518], and the Agreement on the Adaptation of the CFE Treaty was signed on 18 November at the Istanbul Summit of OSCE. A CFE Final Act was also signed, containing a confirmation by the Russian Federation of its commitment to all Treaty provisions. The Adaptation Agreement updated the 1990 Treaty to create a new, transparent set of limitations on conventional forces and to bring it in line with the current European security environment. It replaced the Treaty's bloc-to-bloc structure with national based limits and a national ceiling for each State. Those States with territory in the CFE area of application would also have a territorial ceiling limiting the total amount of equipment that could be on their soil. The Agreement increased the quotas for mandatory on-site inspections and strengthened requirements for host nation consent to the presence of foreign forces, including notifications to all parties as to whether such consent had been granted.

The OSCE Forum for Security Cooperation adopted, on 16 November in Istanbul, the Vienna Document 1999 on the Negotiations on Confidence- and Security-Building Measures, which built upon and added to the CSBMs contained in previous documents. A major addition was a chapter on regional measures, which encouraged OSCE participating States to undertake measures of transparency and confidence in a bilateral, multilateral or regional context.

The EU continued, through its 1998 Joint Action on Small Arms [YUN 1998, p. 540], to contribute to combating the destabilizing accumulation and spread of small arms and light weapons and to cooperate with the United Nations, NATO and other regional organizations in promoting transparency, arms control and disarmament, and mine clearance.

Latin America

A major development in the Americas region was the adoption of the Inter-American Convention on Transparency in Conventional Weapons Acquisitions by the OAS General Assembly on 7 June [CD/1591], the main objective of which was to contribute to regional openness and transparency in the acquisition of conventional weapons through the exchange of information. States parties agreed to submit annual reports on imports and exports of conventional weapons and to exchange information on acquisitions through notification of imports, national production and "no activity".

In an effort to strengthen peace and security in the region, OAS members continued to promote the adoption and implementation of measures related to programmes such as mine-clearing, confidence-building and the prohibition of illicit trafficking in small arms. The OAS General Assembly also adopted a resolution on the 1997 Inter-American Convention against the Illicit Manufacturing of and Trafficking in Firearms (see p. 489).

A regional seminar on anti-personnel landmines, "Reaffirming our commitment" (Mexico City, 11-12 January), sponsored by Canada and Mexico, with the support of OAS and the Pan American Health Organization, discussed the future of the 1997 Mine-Ban Convention; the goal of the Americas as a landmine-free zone; the challenges of ratification, implementation and universality of the Convention; international cooperation for demining; and inter-American cooperation to rehabilitate mine victims.

In an effort to advance a strategic partnership between Latin America and Europe, the first Summit of the Heads of State and Government of Latin America and the Caribbean and the EU convened in Rio de Janeiro in June (see p. 486).

GENERAL ASSEMBLY ACTION

On 1 December [meeting 69], the General Assembly, on the recommendation of the First Committee [A/54/563], adopted **resolution 54/54 N** without vote [agenda item 76 *(k)*].

Regional disarmament

The General Assembly,

Recalling its resolutions 45/58 P of 4 December 1990, 46/36 I of 6 December 1991, 47/52 J of 9 December 1992, 48/75 I of 16 December 1993, 49/75 N of 15 December 1994, 50/70 K of 12 December 1995, 51/45 K of 10 December 1996, 52/38 P of 9 December 1997 and 53/77 O of 4 December 1998 on regional disarmament,

Believing that the efforts of the international community to move towards the ideal of general and complete disarmament are guided by the inherent human desire for genuine peace and security, the elimination of the danger of war and the release of economic, intellectual and other resources for peaceful pursuits,

Affirming the abiding commitment of all States to the purposes and principles enshrined in the Charter of the United Nations in the conduct of their international relations,

Noting that essential guidelines for progress towards general and complete disarmament were adopted at the tenth special session of the General Assembly,

Taking note of the guidelines and recommendations for regional approaches to disarmament within the context of global security adopted by the Disarmament Commission at its 1993 substantive session,

Welcoming the prospects of genuine progress in the field of disarmament engendered in recent years as a result of negotiations between the two super-Powers,

Taking note of the recent proposals for disarmament at the regional and subregional levels,

Recognizing the importance of confidence-building measures for regional and international peace and security,

Convinced that endeavours by countries to promote regional disarmament, taking into account the specific characteristics of each region and in accordance with the principle of undiminished security at the lowest level of armaments, would enhance the security of all States and would thus contribute to international peace and security by reducing the risk of regional conflicts,

1. *Stresses* that sustained efforts are needed, within the framework of the Conference on Disarmament and under the umbrella of the United Nations, to make progress on the entire range of disarmament issues;

2. *Affirms* that global and regional approaches to disarmament complement each other and should therefore be pursued simultaneously to promote regional and international peace and security;

3. *Calls upon* States to conclude agreements, wherever possible, for nuclear non-proliferation, disarmament and confidence-building measures at the regional and subregional levels;

4. *Welcomes* the initiatives towards disarmament, nuclear non-proliferation and security undertaken by some countries at the regional and subregional levels;

5. *Supports and encourages* efforts aimed at promoting confidence-building measures at the regional and subregional levels in order to ease regional tensions and to further disarmament and nuclear non-proliferation measures at the regional and subregional levels;

6. *Decides* to include in the provisional agenda of its fifty-fifth session the item entitled "Regional disarmament".

Also on 1 December [meeting 69], on the recommendation of the First Committee [A/54/563], the Assembly adopted **resolution 54/54 M** by recorded vote (159-1-1) [agenda item 76 *(l)*].

Conventional arms control at the regional and subregional levels

The General Assembly,

Recalling its resolutions 48/75 J of 16 December 1993, 49/75 O of 15 December 1994, 50/70 L of 12 December 1995, 51/45 Q of 10 December 1996, 52/38 Q of 9 December 1997 and 53/77 P of 4 December 1998,

Recognizing the crucial role of conventional arms control in promoting regional and international peace and security,

Convinced that conventional arms control needs to be pursued primarily in the regional and subregional contexts since most threats to peace and security in the post-cold-war era arise mainly among States located in the same region or subregion,

Aware that the preservation of a balance in the defence capabilities of States at the lowest level of armaments would contribute to peace and stability and should be a prime objective of conventional arms control,

Desirous of promoting agreements to strengthen regional peace and security at the lowest possible level of armaments and military forces,

Noting with particular interest the initiatives taken in this regard in different regions of the world, in particular the commencement of consultations among a number of Latin American countries and the proposals for conventional arms control made in the context of South Asia, and recognizing, in the context of this subject, the relevance and value of the Treaty on Conventional Armed Forces in Europe, which is a cornerstone of European security,

Believing that militarily significant States and States with larger military capabilities have a special responsibility in promoting such agreements for regional security,

Believing also that an important objective of conventional arms control in regions of tension should be to prevent the possibility of military attack launched by surprise and to avoid aggression,

1. *Decides* to give urgent consideration to the issues involved in conventional arms control at the regional and subregional levels;

2. *Requests* the Conference on Disarmament, as a first step, to consider the formulation of principles that can serve as a framework for regional agreements on conventional arms control, and looks forward to a report of the Conference on this subject;

3. *Decides* to include in the provisional agenda of its fifty-fifth session the item entitled "Conventional arms control at the regional and subregional levels".

RECORDED VOTE ON RESOLUTION 54/54 M:

In favour: Albania, Algeria, Andorra, Angola, Antigua and Barbuda, Argentina, Armenia, Australia, Austria, Azerbaijan, Bahamas, Bahrain, Bangladesh, Barbados, Belarus, Belgium, Belize, Benin, Bolivia, Bosnia and Herzegovina, Botswana, Brazil, Brunei Darussalam, Bulgaria, Burkina Faso, Cambodia, Cameroon, Canada, Cape Verde, Chad, Chile, China, Colombia, Congo, Costa Rica, Côte d'Ivoire, Croatia, Cyprus, Czech Republic, Denmark, Djibouti, Dominica, Dominican Republic, Ecuador, Egypt, El Salvador, Equatorial Guinea, Eritrea, Estonia, Ethiopia, Fiji, Finland, France, Georgia, Germany, Ghana, Greece, Grenada, Guatemala, Guinea, Guinea-Bissau, Guyana, Haiti, Honduras, Hungary, Iceland, Indonesia, Iran, Ireland, Israel, Italy, Jamaica, Japan, Jordan, Kazakhstan, Kenya, Kuwait, Latvia, Lebanon, Libyan Arab Jamahiriya, Liechtenstein, Lithuania, Luxembourg, Madagascar, Malaysia, Maldives, Mali, Malta, Marshall Islands, Mauritius, Mexico, Micronesia, Monaco, Mongolia, Morocco, Mozambique, Myanmar, Namibia, Nepal, Netherlands, New Zealand, Nicaragua, Nigeria, Norway, Oman, Pakistan, Panama, Papua New Guinea, Paraguay, Peru, Philippines, Poland, Portugal, Qatar, Republic of Korea, Republic of Moldova, Romania, Russian Federation, Saint Kitts and Nevis, Saint Lucia, Saint Vincent and Grenadines, Samoa, San Marino, Saudi Arabia, Senegal, Seychelles, Sierra Leone, Singapore, Slovakia, Slovenia, Solomon Islands, South Africa, Spain, Sri Lanka, Sudan, Suriname, Swaziland, Sweden, Syrian Arab Republic, Tajikistan, Thailand, The former Yugoslav Republic of Macedonia, Togo, Trinidad and Tobago, Tunisia, Turkey, Turkmenistan, Uganda, Ukraine, United Arab Emirates, United Kingdom, United Republic of Tanzania, United States, Uruguay, Uzbekistan, Venezuela, Yemen, Zambia, Zimbabwe.

Against: India.

Abstaining: Bhutan.

Other disarmament issues

Prevention of an arms race in outer space

In 1999, the Conference on Disarmament did not establish an ad hoc committee on the prevention of an arms race in outer space. The Third United Nations Conference on the Exploration and Peaceful Uses of Outer Space (UNISPACE III) was held from 18 to 30 July in Vienna (see p. 556).

GENERAL ASSEMBLY ACTION

On 1 December [meeting 69], the General Assembly, on the recommendation of the First Committee [A/54/562], adopted **resolution 54/53** by recorded vote (162-0-2) [agenda item 75].

Prevention of an arms race in outer space

The General Assembly,

Recognizing the common interest of all mankind in the exploration and use of outer space for peaceful purposes,

Reaffirming the will of all States that the exploration and use of outer space, including the Moon and other celestial bodies, shall be for peaceful purposes and shall be carried out for the benefit and in the interest of all countries, irrespective of their degree of economic or scientific development,

Reaffirming also the provisions of articles III and IV of the Treaty on Principles Governing the Activities of States in the Exploration and Use of Outer Space, including the Moon and Other Celestial Bodies,

Recalling the obligation of all States to observe the provisions of the Charter of the United Nations regarding the use or threat of use of force in their international relations, including in their space activities,

Reaffirming paragraph 80 of the Final Document of the Tenth Special Session of the General Assembly, in which it is stated that in order to prevent an arms race in outer space further measures should be taken and appropriate international negotiations held in accordance with the spirit of the Treaty,

Recalling its previous resolutions on this issue, and taking note of the proposals submitted to the General Assembly at its tenth special session and at its regular sessions, and of the recommendations made to the competent organs of the United Nations and to the Conference on Disarmament,

Recognizing that prevention of an arms race in outer space would avert a grave danger for international peace and security,

Emphasizing the paramount importance of strict compliance with existing arms limitation and disarmament agreements relevant to outer space, including bilateral agreements, and with the existing legal regime concerning the use of outer space,

Considering that wide participation in the legal regime applicable to outer space could contribute to enhancing its effectiveness,

Noting that the Ad Hoc Committee on the Prevention of an Arms Race in Outer Space, taking into account its previous efforts since its establishment in 1985 and seeking to enhance its functioning in qualitative terms, continued the examination and identification of various issues, existing agreements and existing proposals, as well as future initiatives relevant to the prevention of an arms race in outer space, and that this contributed to a better understanding of a number of problems and to a clearer perception of the various positions,

Noting also that there were no objections in principle in the Conference on Disarmament to the re-establishment of the Ad Hoc Committee, subject to re-examination of the mandate contained in the decision of the Conference on Disarmament of 13 February 1992,

Emphasizing the mutually complementary nature of bilateral and multilateral efforts in the field of preventing an arms race in outer space, and hoping that concrete results will emerge from those efforts as soon as possible,

Convinced that further measures should be examined in the search for effective and verifiable bilateral and multilateral agreements in order to prevent an arms race in outer space, including the weaponization of outer space,

Stressing that the growing use of outer space increases the need for greater transparency and better information on the part of the international community,

Recalling in this context its previous resolutions, in particular resolutions 45/55 B of 4 December 1990, 47/51 of 9 December 1992 and 48/74 A of 16 December 1993, in which, inter alia, it reaffirmed the importance of confidence-building measures as means conducive to ensuring the attainment of the objective of the prevention of an arms race in outer space,

Conscious of the benefits of confidence- and security-building measures in the military field,

Recognizing that negotiations for the conclusion of an international agreement or agreements to prevent an arms race in outer space remain a priority task of the Ad Hoc Committee and that the concrete proposals on confidence-building measures could form an integral part of such agreements,

1. *Reaffirms* the importance and urgency of preventing an arms race in outer space, and the readiness of all States to contribute to that common objective, in conformity with the provisions of the Treaty on Principles Governing the Activities of States in the Exploration and Use of Outer Space, including the Moon and Other Celestial Bodies;

2. *Reaffirms its recognition*, as stated in the report of the Ad Hoc Committee on the Prevention of an Arms Race in Outer Space, that the legal regime applicable to outer space by itself does not guarantee the prevention of an arms race in outer space, that this legal regime plays a significant role in the prevention of an arms race in that environment, that there is a need to consolidate and reinforce that regime and enhance its effectiveness, and that it is important to comply strictly with existing agreements, both bilateral and multilateral;

3. *Emphasizes* the necessity of further measures with appropriate and effective provisions for verification to prevent an arms race in outer space;

4. *Calls upon* all States, in particular those with major space capabilities, to contribute actively to the objective of the peaceful use of outer space and of the prevention of an arms race in outer space and to refrain from actions contrary to that objective and to the relevant existing treaties in the interest of maintaining international peace and security and promoting international cooperation;

5. *Reiterates* that the Conference on Disarmament, as the single multilateral disarmament negotiating forum, has the primary role in the negotiation of a multilateral agreement or agreements, as appropriate, on the prevention of an arms race in outer space in all its aspects;

6. *Invites* the Conference on Disarmament to complete the examination and updating of the mandate contained in its decision of 13 February 1992 and to establish an ad hoc committee as early as possible during the 2000 session of the Conference on Disarmament;

7. *Recognizes*, in this respect, the growing convergence of views on the elaboration of measures designed to strengthen transparency, confidence and security in the peaceful uses of outer space;

8. *Urges* States conducting activities in outer space, as well as States interested in conducting such activities, to keep the Conference on Disarmament informed of the progress of bilateral and multilateral negotiations on the matter, if any, so as to facilitate its work;

9. *Decides* to include in the provisional agenda of its fifty-fifth session the item entitled "Prevention of an arms race in outer space".

RECORDED VOTE ON RESOLUTION 54/53:

In favour: Albania, Algeria, Andorra, Angola, Antigua and Barbuda, Argentina, Armenia, Australia, Austria, Azerbaijan, Bahamas, Bahrain, Bangladesh, Barbados, Belarus, Belgium, Belize, Benin, Bhutan, Bolivia, Bosnia and Herzegovina, Botswana, Brazil, Brunei Darussalam, Bulgaria, Burkina Faso, Cambodia, Cameroon, Canada, Cape Verde, Chad, Chile, China, Colombia, Congo, Costa Rica, Côte d'Ivoire, Croatia, Cuba, Cyprus, Czech Republic, Democratic People's Republic of Korea, Denmark, Djibouti, Dominica, Dominican Republic, Ecuador, Egypt, El Salvador, Equatorial Guinea, Eritrea, Estonia, Ethiopia, Fiji, Finland, France, Georgia, Germany, Ghana, Greece, Grenada, Guatemala, Guinea, Guinea-Bissau, Guyana, Haiti, Honduras, Hungary, Iceland, India, Indonesia, Iran, Ireland, Italy, Jamaica, Japan, Jordan, Kazakhstan, Kenya, Kuwait, Lao People's Democratic Republic, Latvia, Lebanon, Libyan Arab Jamahiriya, Liechtenstein, Lithuania, Luxembourg, Madagascar, Malaysia, Maldives, Mali, Malta, Marshall Islands, Mauritius, Mexico, Monaco, Mongolia, Morocco, Mozambique, Myanmar, Namibia, Nepal, Netherlands, New Zealand, Nicaragua, Nigeria, Norway, Oman, Pakistan, Panama, Papua New Guinea, Paraguay, Peru, Philippines, Poland, Portugal, Qatar, Republic of Korea, Republic of Moldova, Romania, Russian Federation, Saint Kitts and Nevis, Saint Lucia, Saint Vincent and the Grenadines, Samoa, San Marino, Saudi Arabia, Senegal, Seychelles, Sierra Leone, Singapore, Slovakia, Slovenia, Solomon Islands, South Africa, Spain, Sri Lanka, Sudan, Suriname, Swaziland, Sweden, Syrian Arab Republic, Tajikistan, Thailand, The former Yugoslav Republic of Macedonia, Togo, Trinidad and Tobago, Tunisia, Turkey, Turkmenistan, Uganda, Ukraine, United Arab Emirates, United Kingdom, United Republic of Tanzania, Uruguay, Uzbekistan, Venezuela, Viet Nam, Yemen, Zambia, Zimbabwe.

Against: None.

Abstaining: Israel, United States.

Disarmament and development

In response to General Assembly resolution 53/77 K [YUN 1998, p. 545], the Secretary-General, in August [A/54/254], informed the Assembly that the high-level Steering Group on Disarmament and Development (consisting of the Under-Secretary-General for Disarmament Affairs, the Under-Secretary-General for Economic and Social Affairs, the UNDP Administrator and the Under-Secretary-General for Peacekeeping Operations) had been established to determine the short-, medium- and long-term priorities from a broadly defined mandate as contained in the action programme adopted at the 1987 International Conference on the Relationship between Disarmament and Development [YUN 1987, p. 83]. The Group reviewed disarmament and development issues, with particular reference to: conversion; conflict prevention; causes of conflict and arms acquisition; post-conflict practical disarmament measures; military expenditure; the role of other UN departments/agencies, as well as international organizations; relevant international events; the availability and dissemination of factual and analytical materials on disarmament and development; lessons learned by UNDP and the Department of Peacekeeping Operations (DPKO) in post-conflict situations; and the role of NGOs and their interaction with the United Nations.

The Steering Group adopted a forward-looking approach for revisiting disarmament and development and advocated a close interaction between the United Nations and civil society. It identified a series of programmes and activities.

The report contained the views of two States on the implementation of the action programme.

A symposium on disarmament and development (New York, 20 July), organized jointly by DDA, the Department of Economic and Social Affairs, DPKO and UNDP, in collaboration with Economists Allied for Arms Reduction, discussed military spending; conversion; small arms proliferation; disarmament; demobilization and reintegration; post-conflict peace-building; the peace dividend; and development assistance.

GENERAL ASSEMBLY ACTION

On 1 December [meeting 69], the General Assembly, on the recommendation of the First Committee [A/54/563], adopted **resolution 54/54 T** without vote [agenda item 76 *(i)*].

Relationship between disarmament and development

The General Assembly,

Recalling the provisions of the Final Document of the Tenth Special Session of the General Assembly concerning the relationship between disarmament and development,

Recalling also the adoption on 11 September 1987 of the Final Document of the International Conference on the Relationship between Disarmament and Development,

Recalling further its resolutions 49/75 J of 15 December 1994, 50/70 G of 12 December 1995, 51/45 D of 10 December 1996, 52/38 D of 9 December 1997 and 53/77 K of 4 December 1998,

Bearing in mind the Final Document of the Twelfth Conference of Heads of State or Government of Non-Aligned Countries, held at Durban, South Africa, from 29 August to 3 September 1998,

Taking note of the deliberations during the symposium on disarmament and development held at Headquarters on 20 July 1999,

Stressing the growing importance of the symbiotic relationship between disarmament and development in current international relations,

1. *Acknowledges* the report of the Secretary-General, and welcomes the establishment, as a first step by the Secretary-General, of the Steering Group on Disarmament and Development with the purpose of determining the short, medium and long-term priorities, according to the mandate set out in the action programme adopted at the International Conference on the Relationship between Disarmament and Development;

2. *Urges* the international community to devote part of the resources made available by the implementation of disarmament and arms limitation agreements to economic and social development, with a view to reducing the ever widening gap between developed and developing countries;

3. *Invites* all Member States to communicate to the Secretary-General, by 15 April 2000, their views and proposals for the implementation of the action programme adopted at the International Conference on the Relationship between Disarmament and Development, as well as any other views and proposals with a view to achieving the goals of the action programme, within the framework of current international relations;

4. *Requests* the Secretary-General to continue to take action, through appropriate organs and within available resources, for the implementation of the action programme adopted at the International Conference;

5. *Also requests* the Secretary-General to submit a report to the General Assembly at its fifty-fifth session;

6. *Decides* to include in the provisional agenda of its fifty-fifth session the item entitled "Relationship between disarmament and development".

Science and technology

In response to General Assembly resolution 53/73 [YUN 1998, p. 545], the Secretary-General submitted a July report [A/54/167] containing the view of one Member State (United States) on his 1998 report on scientific and technological developments and their impact on international security [YUN 1998, p. 545]. The Secretary-General stated that, in the absence of adequate information from Member States, he was not in a position to make recommendations on possible approaches to multilaterally negotiated, universally acceptable, non-discriminatory guidelines for international transfers of dual-use goods and technologies and high technologies with military applications. India submitted its views in October [A/54/167/Add.1].

GENERAL ASSEMBLY ACTION

On 1 December [meeting 69], the General Assembly, on the recommendation of the First Committee [A/54/559], adopted **resolution 54/50** by recorded vote (98-46-19) [agenda item 72].

Role of science and technology in the context of international security and disarmament

The General Assembly,

Recognizing that scientific and technological developments can have both civilian and military applications and that progress in science and technology for civilian applications needs to be maintained and encouraged,

Concerned that military applications of scientific and technological developments can contribute significantly to the improvement and upgrading of advanced weapon systems and, in particular, weapons of mass destruction,

Aware of the need to follow closely the scientific and technological developments that may have a negative impact on international security and disarmament and to channel scientific and technological developments for beneficial purposes,

Cognizant that the international transfers of dual-use as well as high-technology products, services and know-how for peaceful purposes are important for the economic and social development of States,

Also cognizant of the need to regulate such transfers of dual-use goods and technologies and high technology with military applications through multilaterally negotiated, universally applicable, non-discriminatory guidelines,

Expressing concern over the growing proliferation of ad hoc and exclusive export control regimes and arrangements for dual-use goods and technologies, which tend to impede the economic and social development of developing countries,

Recalling that in the Final Document of the Twelfth Conference of Heads of State or Government of Non-Aligned Countries, held at Durban, South Africa, from 29 August to 3 September 1998, it was noted with concern that undue restrictions on exports to developing countries of material, equipment and technology for peaceful purposes persist,

Emphasizing that internationally negotiated guidelines for the transfer of high technology with military applications should take into account the legitimate defence requirements of all States and the requirements for the maintenance of international peace and security, while ensuring that access to high-technology products and services and know-how for peaceful purposes is not denied,

1. *Affirms* that scientific and technological progress should be used for the benefit of all mankind to promote the sustainable economic and social development of all States and to safeguard international security and that international cooperation in the use of science and technology through the transfer and exchange of technological know-how for peaceful purposes should be promoted;

2. *Invites* Member States to undertake additional efforts to apply science and technology for disarmament-related purposes and to make disarmament-related technologies available to interested States;

3. *Urges* Member States to undertake multilateral negotiations with the participation of all interested States in order to establish universally acceptable, non-discriminatory guidelines for international transfers of dual-use goods and technologies and high technology with military applications;

4. *Takes note* of the report, including its addendum, submitted by the Secretary-General in pursuance of paragraph 4 of General Assembly resolution 53/73 of 4 December 1998;

5. *Encourages* United Nations bodies to contribute, within existing mandates, to promoting the application of science and technology for peaceful purposes;

6. *Decides* to include in the provisional agenda of its fifty-fifth session the item entitled "Role of science and technology in the context of international security and disarmament".

RECORDED VOTE ON RESOLUTION 54/50:

In favour: Algeria, Angola, Antigua and Barbuda, Bahamas, Bahrain, Bangladesh, Barbados, Belize, Benin, Bhutan, Bolivia, Botswana, Brunei Darussalam, Burkina Faso, Cambodia, Cameroon, Cape Verde, Chad, Chile, China, Colombia, Congo, Costa Rica, Côte d'Ivoire, Cuba, Democratic People's Republic of Korea, Djibouti, Dominica, Dominican Republic, Ecuador, Egypt, El Salvador, Equatorial Guinea, Eritrea, Ethiopia, Fiji, Ghana, Grenada, Guatemala, Guinea, Guinea-Bissau, Guyana, Haiti, Honduras, India, Indonesia, Iran, Jamaica, Jordan, Kenya, Kuwait, Lao People's Democratic Republic, Lebanon, Libyan Arab Jamahiriya, Madagascar, Malaysia, Maldives, Mali, Mauritius, Mexico, Mongolia, Morocco, Mozambique, Myanmar, Namibia, Nepal, Nicaragua, Nigeria, Oman, Pakistan, Panama, Papua New Guinea, Peru, Philippines, Qatar, Saint Kitts and Nevis, Saint Lucia, Saudi Arabia, Senegal, Sierra Leone, Singapore, Sri Lanka, Sudan, Suriname, Swaziland, Syrian Arab Republic, Thailand, Togo, Trinidad and Tobago, Tunisia, Uganda, United Arab Emirates, United Republic of Tanzania, Venezuela, Viet Nam, Yemen, Zambia, Zimbabwe.

Against: Albania, Andorra, Australia, Austria, Belgium, Bosnia and Herzegovina, Bulgaria, Canada, Croatia, Cyprus, Czech Republic, Denmark, Estonia, Finland, France, Germany, Greece, Hungary, Iceland, Ireland, Israel, Italy, Latvia, Liechtenstein, Lithuania, Luxembourg, Malta, Marshall Islands, Micronesia, Monaco, Netherlands, New Zealand, Norway, Poland, Portugal, Republic of Moldova, Romania, San Marino, Slovakia, Slovenia, Spain, Sweden, The former Yugoslav Republic of Macedonia, Turkey, United Kingdom, United States.

Abstaining: Argentina, Armenia, Azerbaijan, Belarus, Brazil, Georgia, Japan, Kazakhstan, Paraguay, Republic of Korea, Russian Federation, Samoa, Solomon Islands, South Africa, Tajikistan, Turkmenistan, Ukraine, Uruguay, Uzbekistan.

Arms limitation and disarmament agreements

Pursuant to General Assembly resolution 53/77 J [YUN 1998, p. 546], the Secretary-General submitted a July report with later addendum [A/54/163 & Add.1] containing information from four Member States on measures they had taken to ensure the application of scientific and technological progress in the context of international security, disarmament and related areas, without detriment to the environment or to its effective contribution to attaining sustainable development.

GENERAL ASSEMBLY ACTION

On 1 December [meeting 69], the General Assembly, on the recommendation of the First Committee [A/54/563], adopted **resolution 54/54 S** by recorded vote (159-0-4) [agenda item 76 (*h*)].

Observance of environmental norms in the drafting and implementation of agreements on disarmament and arms control

The General Assembly,

Recalling its resolutions 50/70 M of 12 December 1995, 51/45 E of 10 December 1996, 52/38 E of 9 December 1997 and 53/77 J of 4 December 1998,

Emphasizing the importance of the observance of environmental norms in the preparation and implementation of disarmament and arms limitation agreements,

Recognizing that it is necessary to take duly into account the agreements adopted at the United Nations Conference on Environment and Development, as well as prior relevant agreements, in the drafting and implementation of agreements on disarmament and arms limitation,

Mindful of the detrimental environmental effects of the use of nuclear weapons,

1. *Reaffirms* that international disarmament forums should take fully into account the relevant environmental norms in negotiating treaties and agreements on disarmament and arms limitation and that all

States, through their actions, should fully contribute to ensuring compliance with the aforementioned norms in the implementation of treaties and conventions to which they are parties;

2. *Calls upon* States to adopt unilateral, bilateral, regional and multilateral measures so as to contribute to ensuring the application of scientific and technological progress in the framework of international security, disarmament and other related spheres, without detriment to the environment or to its effective contribution to attaining sustainable development;

3. *Welcomes* the information provided by Member States on the implementation of the measures they have adopted to promote the objectives envisaged in the present resolution;

4. *Invites* all Member States to communicate to the Secretary-General information on the measures they have adopted to promote the objectives envisaged in the present resolution, and requests the Secretary-General to submit a report containing this information to the General Assembly at its fifty-fifth session;

5. *Decides* to include in the provisional agenda of its fifty-fifth session the item entitled "Observance of environmental norms in the drafting and implementation of agreements on disarmament and arms control".

RECORDED VOTE ON RESOLUTION 54/54 S:

In favour: Albania, Algeria, Andorra, Angola, Antigua and Barbuda, Argentina, Armenia, Australia, Austria, Azerbaijan, Bahamas, Bahrain, Bangladesh, Barbados, Belarus, Belgium, Belize, Benin, Bhutan, Bolivia, Bosnia and Herzegovina, Botswana, Brazil, Bulgaria, Burkina Faso, Cambodia, Cameroon, Canada, Cape Verde, Chad, Chile, China, Colombia, Congo, Costa Rica, Côte d'Ivoire, Croatia, Cuba, Cyprus, Czech Republic, Democratic People's Republic of Korea, Denmark, Djibouti, Dominica, Dominican Republic, Ecuador, Egypt, El Salvador, Equatorial Guinea, Eritrea, Estonia, Ethiopia, Finland, Georgia, Germany, Ghana, Greece, Grenada, Guatemala, Guinea, Guinea-Bissau, Guyana, Haiti, Honduras, Hungary, Iceland, India, Indonesia, Iran, Ireland, Italy, Jamaica, Japan, Jordan, Kazakhstan, Kenya, Kuwait, Lao People's Democratic Republic, Latvia, Lebanon, Libyan Arab Jamahiriya, Liechtenstein, Lithuania, Luxembourg, Madagascar, Malaysia, Maldives, Mali, Malta, Marshall Islands, Mauritius, Mexico, Micronesia, Monaco, Mongolia, Morocco, Mozambique, Myanmar, Namibia, Nepal, Netherlands, New Zealand, Nicaragua, Nigeria, Norway, Oman, Pakistan, Panama, Papua New Guinea, Paraguay, Peru, Philippines, Poland, Portugal, Qatar, Republic of Korea, Republic of Moldova, Romania, Russian Federation, Saint Kitts and Nevis, Saint Lucia, Saint Vincent and the Grenadines, Samoa, San Marino, Saudi Arabia, Senegal, Seychelles, Sierra Leone, Singapore, Slovakia, Slovenia, Solomon Islands, South Africa, Spain, Sri Lanka, Sudan, Suriname, Swaziland, Sweden, Syrian Arab Republic, Tajikistan, Thailand, The former Yugoslav Republic of Macedonia, Togo, Trinidad and Tobago, Tunisia, Turkey, Turkmenistan, Uganda, Ukraine, United Arab Emirates, United Republic of Tanzania, Uruguay, Uzbekistan, Venezuela, Viet Nam, Yemen, Zambia, Zimbabwe.

Against: None.

Abstaining: France, Israel, United Kingdom, United States.

Studies, information and training

Disarmament studies programme

Pursuant to General Assembly resolution 52/38 J [YUN 1997, p. 507], two studies were completed by groups of experts. The Group of Experts on the Problem of Ammunition and Explosives completed and submitted its report [A/54/155] to the Assembly in June (see p. 488). The Group of Governmental Experts on Small Arms, appointed by the Secretary-General to prepare a report on progress made in implementing the recommendations of the 1997 report on small arms [YUN 1997, p. 506], completed and submitted its report [A/54/258] to the Assembly in August (see p. 486).

In 1999, the Assembly, in **resolution 54/54 V**, requested the Secretary-General to carry out a study on the feasibility of restricting the manufacture and trade of small arms and light weapons to the manufacturers and dealers authorized by States, and to submit it as one of the background documents for the 2001 conference on illicit trade in small arms. By **resolution 54/54 I**, the Assembly requested the Secretary-General to carry out a study on the early expansion of the scope of the UN Register of Conventional Arms; and the elaboration of practical means to develop the Register in order to increase transparency related to weapons of mass destruction, in particular nuclear weapons, and to transfers of equipment and technology directly related to the development and manufacture of such weapons.

Disarmament Information Programme

The UN Disarmament Information Programme reflected the priorities of DDA. A continuing priority was in the area of weapons of mass destruction, especially nuclear weapons. Much of that activity centred on the third Preparatory Committee for the 2000 Review Conference of the Nuclear Non-Proliferation Treaty (NPT) (see above, under "Non-Proliferation Treaty"). Another priority area was that of conventional weapons, the excessive and destabilizing accumulation of small arms and light weapons, and the disarmament-development perspective, activities for which focused on preparations for the United Nations Conference on the Illicit Trade in Small Arms and Light Weapons in All Its Aspects, scheduled to take place in 2001 (see above, under "Conventional weapons"), and on events organized by the Secretary-General's newly established high-level Steering Group on Disarmament and Development (see above, under "Disarmament and development").

DDA expanded the volume of its publications output, establishing two new series: the quarterly *Update*, a newsletter containing accounts of UN activities in the area of disarmament, and *Occasional Papers*, collections of articles and presentations on topical subjects.

The DDA web site was expanded and incorporated into the "United Nations and Disarmament" web site (http://www.un.org, link to "Peace and security: Disarmament"), which provided access to the main disarmament bodies, to DDA and to a series of regularly updated materials, and to databases on disarmament resolutions and decisions.

The Disarmament Information Programme fostered cooperation between the UN and research institutes and educational institutions at various levels. In August, the UN Institute for Disarmament Research (UNIDIR) and DDA partnered a symposium in Geneva on developments in information and telecommunications in the context of international security, in partial response to General Assembly resolution 53/70 [YUN 1998, p. 38]. The aim of the meeting was to raise awareness among Member States of the possible negative potential of such technologies and to initiate multilateral discussions. The Department also organized a symposium on "Missile Development and Its Impact on Global Security" for the diplomatic community and NGOs on 22 April in New York.

In February, DDA, in collaboration with the Cooperative Monitoring Center of the Sandia National Laboratories of the United States Department of Energy, sponsored four workshops consisting of a portable demonstration of cooperative monitoring techniques. The Department cooperated with the NGO Committee on Disarmament and the UN Department of Public Information in conducting a number of panel discussions on issues related to weapons of mass destruction.

Advisory Board on Disarmament Matters

The Advisory Board on Disarmament Matters, which advised the Secretary-General on the disarmament studies programme and implementation of the Disarmament Information Programme and served as the Board of Trustees of UNIDIR, held its thirty-second and thirty-third sessions (Geneva, 20-22 January; New York, 28-30 June) [A/54/218 & Corr.1]. The Board also held a discussion away from headquarters (1-2 July) on disarmament and international security in the twenty-first century as a contribution to the report under preparation by the Secretary-General for the Millennium Summit in September 2000 (see PART ONE, Chapter VIII, and PART FIVE, Chapter IV).

At its two sessions, the Board formulated advice and recommendations to the Secretary-General on possible disarmament scenarios in Iraq; conventional disarmament in Europe; disarmament contributions to African security; tactical nuclear weapons; a ban on the production of fissile material for weapons purposes; biological weapons; missile defences; and the situation in the DPRK.

The Board continued to review its own mandate and functions and proposed that the language for the formal mandate of the Board, adopted by General Assembly resolution 37/99 K [YUN 1982, p. 150], be readjusted to reflect its actual functions as they had been performed for more than a decade. The thrust of the amendment would be to emphasize the Board's proactive advisory role on disarmament matters over its role to advise on various aspects of studies and research. Its function as the Board of Trustees of UNIDIR would remain unchanged. The Secretary-General endorsed the proposed mandate and recommended that the Assembly adopt it.

By **decision 54/418** of 1 December, the General Assembly requested the Secretary-General to adjust the language in the mandate of the Advisory Board.

UN Institute for Disarmament Research

The Secretary-General transmitted to the General Assembly the report of the UNIDIR Director covering the period from July 1998 to June 1999, as well as the report of the UNIDIR Board of Trustees on the proposed programme of work for 1999-2000 [A/54/201].

The Institute's research activities focused on global security, regional security and human security. The report described UNIDIR's cooperation with and among research institutes and contained a list of publications issued during the reporting period.

The Board of Trustees agreed that a subvention of $213,000 from the UN regular budget was necessary in order to cover the costs of the regular staff and to ensure the independence of the Institute.

By **resolution 54/251, section I**, of 23 December, the General Assembly approved the recommendation of a subvention to UNIDIR of $213,000 from the UN regular budget for 2000, on the understanding that no additional appropriation would be required under section 4, Disarmament, of the proposed programme budget for the 2000-2001 biennium.

Disarmament fellowship, training and advisory services

In 1999, 26 fellows participated in the UN disarmament fellowship, training and advisory programme, which began in Geneva on 30 August and ended in New York on 2 November. It included a study session in Geneva; study visits to Austria, Germany, Japan and the Netherlands; a seminar and a workshop in the United States; and a study session at Headquarters.

Regional centres for peace and disarmament

GENERAL ASSEMBLY ACTION

On 1 December [meeting 69], on the recommendation of the First Committee [A/54/564], the General Assembly adopted **resolution 54/55 E** without vote [agenda item 77 *(e)*].

United Nations regional centres for peace and disarmament

The General Assembly,

Recalling its resolution 53/78 F of 4 December 1998 regarding the maintenance and revitalization of the three United Nations regional centres for peace and disarmament,

Recalling also the reports of the Secretary-General on the United Nations Regional Centre for Peace and Disarmament in Africa, the United Nations Regional Centre for Peace and Disarmament in Asia and the Pacific and the United Nations Regional Centre for Peace, Disarmament and Development in Latin America and the Caribbean, and welcoming the appointment by the Secretary-General of the Director of the Centre for Africa and the Director of the Centre for Latin America and the Caribbean,

Reaffirming its decision, taken in 1982 at its twelfth special session, to establish the United Nations Disarmament Information Programme, the purpose of which is to inform, educate and generate public understanding and support for the objectives of the United Nations in the field of arms control and disarmament,

Bearing in mind its resolutions 40/151 G of 16 December 1985, 41/60 J of 3 December 1986, 42/39 D of 30 November 1987 and 44/117 F of 15 December 1989 on the regional centres for peace and disarmament in Nepal, Peru and Togo,

Recognizing that the changes that have taken place in the world have created new opportunities as well as posed new challenges for the pursuit of disarmament and, in this regard, bearing in mind that the regional centres for peace and disarmament can contribute substantially to understanding and cooperation among the States in each particular region in the areas of peace, disarmament and development,

Noting that in paragraph 146 of the Final Document of the Twelfth Conference of Heads of State or Government of Non-Aligned Countries, held at Durban, South Africa, from 29 August to 3 September 1998, the heads of State or Government welcomed the decision adopted by the General Assembly on maintaining and revitalizing the three regional centres for peace and disarmament in Nepal, Peru and Togo,

1. *Reiterates* the importance of the United Nations activities at the regional level to increase the stability and security of its Member States, which could be promoted in a substantive manner by the maintenance and revitalization of the three regional centres for peace and disarmament;

2. *Reaffirms* that, in order to achieve positive results, it is useful for the three regional centres to carry out dissemination and educational programmes that promote regional peace and security aimed at changing basic attitudes with respect to peace and security and disarmament so as to support the achievement of the principles and purposes of the United Nations;

3. *Appeals* to Member States in each region and those that are able to do so, as well as to international governmental and non-governmental organizations and foundations, to make voluntary contributions to the regional centres in their respective regions to strengthen their programmes of activities and implementation;

4. *Requests* the Secretary-General to provide all necessary support, within existing resources, to the regional centres in carrying out their programmes of activities;

5. *Also requests* the Secretary-General to report to the General Assembly at its fifty-fifth session on the implementation of the present resolution;

6. *Decides* to include in the provisional agenda of its fifty-fifth session the item entitled "United Nations regional centres for peace and disarmament".

Africa

Pursuant to General Assembly resolution 53/78 C [YUN 1998, p. 551], the Secretary-General described the activities of the United Nations Regional Centre for Peace and Disarmament in Africa [A/54/332], covering the period from July 1998 to August 1999. The Centre was established in Lomé, Togo, in 1986 [YUN 1986, p. 85].

The Secretary-General reported that, in accordance with Assembly resolution 52/220 [YUN 1997, p. 1421], he had appointed a new Director as a first step towards the Centre's revitalization. In February, the Director presented to the Group of African States at the United Nations a programme of work for the revitalization process. The programme, which was endorsed by the Group, comprised: support to peace initiatives in Africa; arms limitation and disarmament; and information, research and publications.

During the period under review, the Centre provided support for the implementation and realization of peace and security-related activities undertaken by African Governments, including the process of destruction of weapons in Liberia and observance of the peace talks between the Government of Sierra Leone and the Revolutionary United Front, which culminated in the signing of a peace agreement on 7 July (see PART ONE, Chapter II). The Centre provided support to DDA in organizing a workshop (Lomé, 2-4 August) for the African region on illicit trafficking in small arms. A workshop of experts (Accra, Ghana, 23-24 September) was organized to define the operational modalities and nature and type of an African arms register and database. The Centre also coordinated peace and disarmament activities and efforts of civil society organizations and research institutions.

While a number of Member States had made financial pledges in support of the implementation of its work programme, the Centre continued to experience financial and operational difficulties.

As at 30 June, the balance of the Centre's Trust Fund stood at $37,072 [A/54/332/Add.1].

GENERAL ASSEMBLY ACTION

On 1 December [meeting 69], the General Assembly, on the recommendation of the First Committee [A/54/564], adopted **resolution 54/55 B** without vote [agenda item 77 *(c)*].

United Nations Regional Centre for Peace and Disarmament in Africa

The General Assembly,

Mindful of the provisions of Article 11, paragraph 1, of the Charter of the United Nations stipulating that a function of the General Assembly is to consider the general principles of cooperation in the maintenance of international peace and security, including the principles governing disarmament and arms limitation,

Recalling its resolutions 40/151 G of 16 December 1985, 41/60 D of 3 December 1986, 42/39 J of 30 November 1987 and 43/76 D of 7 December 1988 on the United Nations Regional Centre for Peace and Disarmament in Africa, and its resolutions 46/36 F of 6 December 1991 and 47/52 G of 9 December 1992 on regional disarmament, including confidence-building measures,

Recalling also its resolutions 48/76 E of 16 December 1993, 49/76 D of 15 December 1994, 50/71 C of 12 December 1995, 51/46 E of 10 December 1996, 52/220 of 22 December 1997 and 53/78 C of 4 December 1998,

Aware of the widespread support for the revitalization of the Regional Centre and the important role that the Centre can play in the present context in promoting confidence-building and arms limitation measures at the regional level, thereby promoting progress in the area of sustainable development,

Taking into account the report of the Secretary-General on the causes of conflict and the promotion of durable peace and sustainable development in Africa,

Bearing in mind the efforts undertaken in the framework of the revitalization of the activities of the Regional Centre for the mobilization of the resources necessary for its operational costs,

Taking into account the need to establish close cooperation between the Regional Centre and the Mechanism for Conflict Prevention, Management and Resolution of the Organization of African Unity, in conformity with the decisions adopted by the Assembly of Heads of State and Government of the Organization of African Unity at its thirty-fifth ordinary session, held at Algiers from 12 to 14 July 1999,

1. *Takes note* of the report of the Secretary-General, and commends the activities carried out by the United Nations Regional Centre for Peace and Disarmament in Africa, in particular in support of the efforts made by the African States in the areas of peace and security;

2. *Reaffirms* its strong support for the revitalization of the Regional Centre, and emphasizes the need to provide it with resources to enable it to strengthen its activities and carry out its programmes;

3. *Appeals once again* to all States, as well as to international governmental organizations and foundations, to make voluntary contributions in order to strengthen the programmes of activities of the Regional Centre and facilitate their implementation;

4. *Requests* the Secretary-General to continue to provide the Regional Centre with all necessary support, within existing resources, for better achievements and results;

5. *Also requests* the Secretary-General to facilitate the establishment of close cooperation between the Regional Centre and the Organization of African Unity, in particular in the area of peace, security and development, and to continue to assist the Director of the Regional Centre in his efforts to stabilize the financial situation of the Centre and revitalize its activities;

6. *Further requests* the Secretary-General to report to the General Assembly at its fifty-fifth session on the implementation of the present resolution;

7. *Decides* to include in the provisional agenda of its fifty-fifth session the item entitled "United Nations Regional Centre for Peace and Disarmament in Africa".

Asia and the Pacific

As requested by the General Assembly in resolution 53/78 B [YUN 1998, p. 552], the Secretary-General reported in August on the activities of the United Nations Regional Centre for Peace and Disarmament in Asia and the Pacific from August 1998 to July 1999 [A/54/255]. The Centre was inaugurated in Kathmandu, Nepal, in 1989 [YUN 1989, p. 88].

During the reporting period, the Centre organized three major meetings. A UN conference on the theme "Towards a world free from nuclear weapons" (Nagasaki, Japan, 24-27 November 1998) considered, among other things, preventing further proliferation of nuclear weapons capability; improving and strengthening the existing nuclear non-proliferation regime; a multilateral approach towards nuclear disarmament; and immediate priorities to avoid accidental nuclear war. Participants adopted a resolution reaffirming their commitment to ensuring that Nagasaki would remain the last city to suffer from the calamity of nuclear weapons. The eleventh regional disarmament meeting in the Asia and Pacific region, on the theme "Security concerns and regional cooperation in Asia and the Pacific" (Kathmandu, 18-20 March 1999), focused on regional cooperation for confidence-building, stability and prosperity. A conference on the theme "Security concerns and disarmament strategy for the next decade" (Kyoto, Japan, 27-30 July 1999), organized in close cooperation with the Government of Japan, considered disarmament priorities for the next decade; nuclear disarmament and missile proliferation; the promotion of peace and security; and stability and cooperation in North-East Asia.

Pursuant to Assembly resolution 53/77 A [YUN 1998, p. 514], the Centre assisted five Central Asian

States in the drafting of a treaty to establish a nuclear-weapon-free zone in Central Asia (see p. 477).

The Secretary-General appealed to Member States to continue to contribute to the Centre in order to ensure its viability and enhance its effective functioning.

As at 30 June, the balance of the Centre's Trust Fund stood at $306,809 [A/54/255/Add.1].

GENERAL ASSEMBLY ACTION

On 1 December [meeting 69], the General Assembly, on the recommendation of the First Committee [A/54/564], adopted **resolution 54/55 C** without vote [agenda item 77 *(b)*].

United Nations Regional Centre for Peace and Disarmament in Asia and the Pacific

The General Assembly,

Recalling its resolutions 42/39 D of 30 November 1987 and 44/117 F of 15 December 1989, by which it established the United Nations Regional Centre for Peace and Disarmament in Asia and renamed it the United Nations Regional Centre for Peace and Disarmament in Asia and the Pacific, with headquarters at Kathmandu and with the mandate of providing, on request, substantive support for the initiatives and other activities mutually agreed upon by the Member States of the Asia-Pacific region for the implementation of measures for peace and disarmament, through appropriate utilization of available resources,

Welcoming the report of the Secretary-General, in which he expresses his belief that the mandate of the Regional Centre remains valid and that the Centre could be a useful instrument for fostering a climate of cooperation in the post-cold-war era,

Noting that trends in the post-cold-war era have emphasized the function of the Regional Centre in assisting Member States as they deal with new security concerns and disarmament issues emerging in the region,

Commending the useful activities carried out by the Regional Centre in encouraging regional and subregional dialogue for the enhancement of openness, transparency and confidence-building, as well as the promotion of disarmament and security through the organization of regional meetings, which has come to be widely known within the Asia-Pacific region as the "Kathmandu process",

Expressing its appreciation to the Regional Centre for its organization of substantive regional meetings at Nagasaki in 1998 and at Kathmandu, Kyoto and Ulaanbaatar in 1999,

Welcoming the idea of the possible creation of an educational and training programme for peace and disarmament in Asia and the Pacific for young people with different backgrounds, to be financed from voluntary contributions,

Noting the important role of the Regional Centre in assisting region-specific initiatives of Member States, including its assistance in the work related to the establishment of a nuclear-weapon-free zone in Central Asia,

Appreciating highly the important role that Nepal has played as the host nation of the headquarters of the Regional Centre,

1. *Reaffirms* its strong support for the continuing operation and further strengthening of the United Nations Regional Centre for Peace and Disarmament in Asia and the Pacific;

2. *Underscores* the importance of the Kathmandu process as a powerful vehicle for the development of the practice of region-wide security and disarmament dialogue;

3. *Expresses its appreciation* for the continuing political support and financial contributions to the Regional Centre, which are essential for its continued operation;

4. *Appeals* to Member States, in particular those within the Asia-Pacific region, as well as to international governmental and non-governmental organizations and foundations, to make voluntary contributions, the only resources of the Regional Centre, to strengthen the programme of activities of the Regional Centre and the implementation thereof;

5. *Requests* the Secretary-General, taking note of paragraph 6 of General Assembly resolution 49/76 D of 15 December 1994, to provide the Regional Centre with all necessary support, within existing resources, in carrying out its programme of activities;

6. *Invites* the Secretary-General to initiate consultations with the Government of the Kingdom of Nepal as well as with other Member States concerned and interested organizations to assess the possibility of enabling the Centre to operate effectively from Kathmandu;

7. *Requests* the Secretary-General to report to the General Assembly at its fifty-fifth session on the implementation of the present resolution;

8. *Decides* to include in the provisional agenda of its fifty-fifth session the item entitled "United Nations Regional Centre for Peace and Disarmament in Asia and the Pacific".

Latin America and the Caribbean

As requested by the General Assembly in resolution 53/78 F [YUN 1998, p. 550], the Secretary-General reported in September on the activities of the United Nations Regional Centre for Peace, Disarmament and Development in Latin America and the Caribbean from December 1998 to July 1999 [A/54/310]. The Centre was inaugurated in Lima, Peru, in 1987 [YUN 1987, p. 88].

The Secretary-General reported that he had appointed a Director as a first step towards the revitalization of the Centre, the activities of which had been suspended in July 1996 owing to lack of sufficient voluntary contributions to finance its operational and administrative costs. On assuming his post, the new Director undertook several missions within and outside the region with a view to securing funding and laying the groundwork for possible cooperation between the Regional Centre and Governments, regional entities, research institutes and NGOs. A programme of work drawn up by the Director addressed regional and subregional security issues, including training of national police forces and border patrol officers in combating trafficking in firearms, ammunition and explosives, the organization of seminars on awareness-building for existing regional agreements and the training of regional peacekeepers in implementing disarmament mandates. As the first such activity, the Centre organized a workshop (Lima, 23-25 June), on the theme "Illicit trafficking in small arms: Latin American and Caribbean issues", which provided a forum for regional experts to debate the role that the Centre could play as a UN entity. The Centre also launched a project entitled "Regional clearing house on illicit trafficking in firearms, ammunition and explosives", intended to serve as a tool for nurturing national and regional expertise in practical disarmament through workshops, training courses and preventive activities.

As at 30 June, the balance of the Trust Fund for the Centre stood at $59,939 [A/54/310/Add.1].

GENERAL ASSEMBLY ACTION

On 1 December [meeting 69], the General Assembly, on the recommendation of the First Committee [A/54/564], adopted **resolution 54/55 F** without vote [agenda item 77].

United Nations Regional Centre for Peace, Disarmament and Development in Latin America and the Caribbean

The General Assembly,

Recalling its resolutions 41/60 J of 3 December 1986, 42/39 K of 30 November 1987 and 43/76 H of 7 December 1988 on the United Nations Regional Centre for Peace, Disarmament and Development in Latin America and the Caribbean, with headquarters in Lima,

Recalling also its resolutions 46/37 F of 9 December 1991, 48/76 E of 16 December 1993, 49/76 D of 15 December 1994, 50/71 C of 12 December 1995, 52/220 of 22 December 1997 and 53/78 F of 4 December 1998,

Welcoming the report of the Secretary-General, in which he expresses his belief that the Regional Centre can make an important contribution to the exchange of information on peace, disarmament and development issues among Governments, non-governmental organizations, industry and various sectors of civil society in the region,

Noting that security and disarmament issues have always been recognized as transcendent topics in Latin America and the Caribbean, the first inhabited region in the world to be declared a nuclear-weapon-free zone,

Welcoming the revitalization of the Centre, the efforts made by the Government of Peru to that end and the appointment of the Director of the Centre by the Secretary-General,

Keeping in mind the important role the Centre can play in promoting confidence-building measures, arms control and limitation, disarmament and development at the regional level,

Expressing its appreciation to the Centre for organizing the international workshop on the theme "Illicit trafficking in small arms: Latin American and Caribbean issues", successfully held in Lima from 23 to 25 June 1999,

Bearing in mind the importance of information, research, education and training for peace, disarmament and development in order to achieve understanding and cooperation among States,

Recognizing the need to provide the three United Nations regional centres for peace and disarmament with sufficient financial resources for the planning and implementation of their programmes of activities,

1. *Reiterates* its strong support of the role of the United Nations Regional Centre for Peace, Disarmament and Development in Latin America and the Caribbean in the promotion of United Nations activities at the regional level to increase peace, stability, security and development among its Member States;

2. *Expresses its satisfaction* with the reinitiation of the activities of the Regional Centre, with headquarters in Lima;

3. *Expresses its appreciation* for the political support and financial contributions to the Regional Centre, which are essential for its continued operation;

4. *Urges* all the States of the region to make greater use of the potential of the Centre to meet the current challenges facing the international community, with a view to fulfilling the aims of the Charter of the United Nations regarding peace, disarmament and development;

5. *Appeals* to Member States, in particular those within the Latin American and Caribbean region, as well as to international governmental and non-governmental organizations and foundations, to make voluntary contributions to strengthen the programme of activities of the Regional Centre and the implementation thereof;

6. *Requests* the Secretary-General to provide the Centre with all necessary support, within existing resources, so that it may carry out its programme of activities and attain better results;

7. *Also requests* the Secretary-General to report to the General Assembly at its fifty-fifth session on the implementation of the present resolution;

8. *Decides* to include in the provisional agenda of its fifty-fifth session an item entitled "United Nations Regional Centre for Peace, Disarmament and Development in Latin America and the Caribbean".

Chapter VIII

Other political and security questions

The United Nations continued to consider in 1999 support for new or restored democracies, the promotion of self-determination of the remaining Non-Self-Governing Territories (NSGTs) and the peaceful uses of outer space. It also considered the activities of the United Nations Scientific Committee on the Effects of Atomic Radiation, the reform of UN information policies, and arrangements for the convening in 2000 of a special United Nations Millennium Assembly and Summit, under the theme "The United Nations in the twenty-first century".

During the year, preparations were under way for the convening of the Fourth (2000) International Conference of New or Restored Democracies. The General Assembly, in November, encouraged Member States to promote democratization and identify steps to support efforts of Governments to promote and consolidate new or restored democracies.

The Special Committee on the Situation with regard to the Implementation of the Declaration on the Granting of Independence to Colonial Countries and Peoples reviewed progress in implementing that 1960 Declaration, particularly the exercise of self-determination by the remaining NSGTs. By a popular consultation in August, the people of East Timor rejected a constitutional framework providing for special autonomy under Indonesian rule. In December, the Assembly concluded consideration of the item on the question of East Timor and decided to enter on its provisional agenda in 2000 the item "The situation in East Timor during its transition to independence".

The United Nations continued to reform its public information and communications activities through the development of a "communication culture", which aimed to ensure that information and communication priorities were featured prominently in all UN policies, programmes and projects.

The Third United Nations Conference on the Exploration and Peaceful Uses of Outer Space (UNISPACE III) took place in Vienna from 19 to 30 July, under the theme "Space benefits for humanity in the twenty-first century". The participants adopted a resolution entitled "The Space Millennium: Vienna Declaration on Space and Human Development" as a strategy to address global challenges in the future. In December, the Assembly endorsed the resolution and declared 4 to 10 October World Space Week to observe annually the contributions of space science and technology to the betterment of the human condition, bearing in mind that 4 October 1957 was the date of the launch of the first human-made satellite.

General aspects of international security

Implementation of 1970 Declaration

The General Assembly, by **decision 54/419** of 1 December, decided to include in the provisional agenda of its fifty-sixth (2001) session the item entitled "Review of the implementation of the Declaration on the Strengthening of International Security" [YUN 1970, p. 105].

Support for democracies

Report of Secretary-General. In response to General Assembly resolution 53/31 [YUN 1998, p. 555], the Secretary-General reported in October on UN support for the efforts of Governments to promote and consolidate new or restored democracies [A/54/492]. The report described the activities of the follow-up mechanism to the Third International Conference of New or Restored Democracies on Democracy and Development [YUN 1997, p. 530], preparations for the Fourth Conference, to be held in Benin in December 2000, and UN efforts to further democratization and governance.

The follow-up mechanism, comprising participants from interested countries, the UN system, academia and non-governmental organizations (NGOs), and chaired by Romania, continued to meet in 1999. A third "democracy forum" was held (New York, 22 March) on the theme of development of democracy in Albania. Romania hosted an expert meeting (Bucharest, 17-18 May), which discussed UN assistance to Governments, an analysis of indicators for evaluating national progress in strengthening democracy and preparations for the Fourth Conference. The meeting also considered the first draft of a code of democratic conduct, introduced by Romania, which was subsequently finalized [A/54/178].

The Fourth International Conference would be held on the theme "Democracy, Peace, Security and Development" and preceded by a forum for youth and a civil society forum. Four preparatory meetings would be held in Africa on the theme of the Conference and regional conferences or seminars would be organized on lessons learned about democratic transition in various parts of the world. The United Nations Development Programme (UNDP) was assisting Benin in the preparatory process.

An interim review of UN activities from 1994 to 1999 covered Assembly action, reports and documents, democracy forums, the establishment of inter-linked web sites on democratization and good governance by UNDP and the UN Departments of Political Affairs and of Economic and Social Affairs, and the creation of electronic networks of the "friends of democracy".

The report described initiatives outside the United Nations to promote democratization, such as the first conference of the Worldwide Movement for Democracy (New Delhi, India, February) and the Forum on Emerging Democracies (Sana'a, Yemen, 27-30 June), which adopted the Sana'a Declaration relating to democratic rights and principles [A/54/321].

The Secretary-General concluded that international conferences of new or restored democracies were part of a growing trend of the democratization process as a global phenomenon. New and fragile democracies still faced difficult challenges and periodic regressions, as did established democracies in their response to problems such as violent crime, discrimination, corruption, the manipulation of public opinion and inefficiencies in the public sector and in governance. Consequently, while assistance to new or restored democracies should continue and increase, debate about the measures to be taken by established democracies to address the multifaceted challenges of globalization and threats to security, progress and development in the coming decades should not be neglected.

GENERAL ASSEMBLY ACTION

On 29 November [meeting 64], the General Assembly adopted **resolution 54/36** [draft: A/54/L.33 & Add.1] without vote [agenda item 39].

Support by the United Nations system of the efforts of Governments to promote and consolidate new or restored democracies

The General Assembly,

Bearing in mind the indissoluble links between the principles enshrined in the Universal Declaration of Human Rights and the foundations of any democratic society,

Recalling the Manila Declaration adopted by the First International Conference of New or Restored Democracies in June 1988,

Considering the major changes taking place on the international scene and the aspirations of all peoples for an international order based on the principles enshrined in the Charter of the United Nations, including the promotion and encouragement of respect for human rights and fundamental freedoms for all and other important principles, such as respect for the equal rights and self-determination of peoples, peace, democracy, justice, equality, the rule of law, pluralism, development, better standards of living and solidarity,

Recalling its resolution 49/30 of 7 December 1994 in which it recognized the importance of the Managua Declaration and Plan of Action adopted by the Second International Conference of New or Restored Democracies in July 1994, as well as its resolutions 50/133 of 20 December 1995, 51/31 of 6 December 1996, 52/18 of 21 November 1997 and 53/31 of 23 November 1998,

Recalling also the document entitled "Progress Review and Recommendations", adopted by the Third International Conference of New or Restored Democracies on Democracy and Development, held at Bucharest from 2 to 4 September 1997, in which guidelines, principles and recommendations were addressed to Governments, civil society, the private sector, donor countries and the international community,

Noting in particular the recommendations contained in that document addressed to the United Nations system and the international financial organizations,

Taking note with satisfaction of the seminars, workshops and conferences on democratization and good governance organized in 1999, as well as those currently being planned, under the auspices of the International Conference of New or Restored Democracies,

Taking note of the views of Member States expressed in the debate on this question at its forty-ninth, fiftieth, fifty-first, fifty-second, fifty-third and fifty-fourth sessions,

Bearing in mind that the activities of the United Nations carried out in support of the efforts of Governments to promote and consolidate democracy are undertaken in accordance with the Charter of the United Nations and only at the specific request of the Member States concerned,

Also bearing in mind that democracy, development and respect for all human rights and fundamental freedoms are interdependent and mutually reinforcing and that democracy is based on the freely expressed will of the people to determine their own political, economic, social and cultural systems and on their full participation in all aspects of their lives,

Noting that a considerable number of societies have recently undertaken significant efforts to achieve their social, political and economic goals through democratization and the reform of their economies, pursuits that are deserving of the support and recognition of the international community,

Noting with satisfaction that the Fourth International Conference of New or Restored Democracies will be held at Cotonou, Benin, from 4 to 6 December 2000,

Stressing the importance of support by Member States, the United Nations system, the specialized agencies and other intergovernmental organizations for the holding of the Fourth International Conference of New or Restored Democracies,

Having considered the report of the Secretary-General,

1. *Welcomes* the report of the Secretary-General;

2. *Expresses its appreciation* for the activities carried out by the United Nations system, and endorses the recommendations contained in the report;

3. *Invites* the Secretary-General, Member States, the relevant specialized agencies and bodies of the United Nations system, as well as other intergovernmental and non-governmental organizations to continue to contribute actively to the follow-up process of the Third International Conference of New or Restored Democracies on Democracy and Development;

4. *Commends* the Secretary-General, and through him the United Nations system, for the activities undertaken at the request of Governments to support the efforts to consolidate democracy;

5. *Welcomes* the work carried out by the follow-up mechanism to the Third International Conference of New or Restored Democracies;

6. *Invites* the Secretary-General, Member States, the relevant specialized agencies and bodies of the United Nations system, as well as other intergovernmental organizations, to collaborate in the holding of the Fourth International Conference of New or Restored Democracies;

7. *Recognizes* that the Organization has an important role to play in providing timely, appropriate and coherent support to the efforts of Governments to achieve democratization within the context of their development efforts;

8. *Stresses* that the activities undertaken by the Organization must be in accordance with the Charter of the United Nations;

9. *Encourages* the Secretary-General to continue to improve the capacity of the Organization to respond effectively to the requests of Member States through coherent, adequate support of their efforts to achieve the goals of good governance and democratization;

10. *Encourages* Member States to promote democratization and to make additional efforts to identify possible steps to support the efforts of Governments to promote and consolidate new or restored democracies;

11. *Requests* the Secretary-General to submit a report to the General Assembly at its fifty-fifth session on the implementation of the present resolution;

12. *Decides* to include in the provisional agenda of its fifty-fifth session the item entitled "Support by the United Nations system of the efforts of Governments to promote and consolidate new or restored democracies".

Regional aspects of international peace and security

South Atlantic

As requested in General Assembly resolution 53/34 [YUN 1998, p. 557], the Secretary-General submitted an October report on the zone of peace and cooperation of the South Atlantic [A/54/447], declared in 1986 to promote cooperation among States of the region in political, economic, scientific, technical, cultural and other fields [YUN 1986, p. 369]. The Secretary-General stated that, as at 30 September 1999, two Governments and five UN organizations and bodies had responded to his request for views on the implementation of the declaration's objectives.

Algeria transmitted to the Assembly a decision on the illicit proliferation, circulation and trafficking of small arms and light weapons, adopted by the Assembly of Heads of State and Government of the Organization of African Unity (Algiers, 12-14 July) [A/54/424] (see preceding chapter). Also transmitted were decisions on the prevention and combating of illicit trafficking in small arms and related crimes, adopted by the Council of the Southern African Development Community at its nineteenth Summit of Heads of State or Government (Maputo, Mozambique, 17-18 August) [A/54/488-S/1999/1082]; the text of the Peace Agreement between the Government of Sierra Leone and the Revolutionary United Front concluded in Lomé, Togo, on 7 July [S/1999/777]; and the text of the Ceasefire Agreement on the conflict in the Democratic Republic of the Congo, signed in Lusaka, Zambia, on 10 July [S/1999/815] (see p. 87).

GENERAL ASSEMBLY ACTION

On 24 November [meeting 63], the General Assembly adopted **resolution 54/35** [draft: A/54/L.35 & Add.1, orally revised] by recorded vote (97-0-1) [agenda item 41].

Zone of peace and cooperation of the South Atlantic

The General Assembly,

Recalling its resolution 41/11 of 27 October 1986, in which it solemnly declared the Atlantic Ocean, in the region between Africa and South America, the zone of peace and cooperation of the South Atlantic,

Recalling also its subsequent resolutions on the matter, including resolution 45/36 of 27 November 1990, in which it reaffirmed the determination of the States of the zone to enhance and accelerate their cooperation in the political, economic, scientific, cultural and other spheres,

Reaffirming that the questions of peace and security and those of development are interrelated and inseparable and that cooperation for peace and development among States of the region will promote the objectives of the zone of peace and cooperation of the South Atlantic,

Aware of the importance that the States of the zone attach to the environment of the region, and recognizing the threat that pollution from any source poses to the marine and coastal environment, its ecological balance and its resources,

1. *Reaffirms* the importance of the purposes and objectives of the zone of peace and cooperation of the

South Atlantic as a basis for the promotion of cooperation among the countries of the region;

2. *Calls upon* all States to cooperate in the promotion of the objectives established in the declaration of the zone of peace and cooperation of the South Atlantic and to refrain from any action inconsistent with those objectives and with the Charter of the United Nations and relevant resolutions of the Organization, in particular actions that may create or aggravate situations of tension and potential conflict in the region;

3. *Takes note* of the report of the Secretary-General, submitted in accordance with its resolution 53/34 of 25 November 1998;

4. *Recalls* the agreement reached at the third meeting of the States members of the zone, held in Brasilia in 1994, to encourage democracy and political pluralism and, in accordance with the Vienna Declaration and Programme of Action adopted by the World Conference on Human Rights on 25 June 1993, to promote and defend all human rights and fundamental freedoms and to cooperate towards the achievement of those goals;

5. *Welcomes with satisfaction* the holding of the fifth meeting of the States members of the zone in Buenos Aires, on 21 and 22 October 1998, and takes note of the Final Declaration and Plan of Action adopted at the meeting;

6. *Welcomes* the progress towards the full entry into force of the Treaty for the Prohibition of Nuclear Weapons in Latin America and the Caribbean (Treaty of Tlatelolco) and of the African Nuclear-Weapon-Free Zone Treaty (Treaty of Pelindaba);

7. *Also welcomes* the entry into force of the Inter-American Convention against the Illicit Manufacturing of and Trafficking in Firearms, Ammunition, Explosives and Other Related Materials, adopted in November 1997, and the adoption of the Inter-American Convention on Transparency in Conventional Weapons Acquisitions by the General Assembly of the Organization of American States in June 1999;

8. *Further welcomes* the decision on the illicit proliferation, circulation and trafficking of small arms and light weapons taken by the Assembly of Heads of State and Government of the Organization of African Unity at its thirty-fifth ordinary session, held in Algiers in July 1999, as well as the decisions on the prevention and combating of illicit trafficking in small arms and related crimes taken by the Council of the Southern African Development Community at its nineteenth Summit of Heads of State or Government, held in Maputo in August 1999, and the initiatives taken by States members of the Economic Community of West African States to conclude their agreement on a moratorium on the importing, exporting and manufacture of light weapons;

9. *Welcomes* the restoration of democracy in Nigeria and the commitment of the present Nigerian Government to transparency and good governance;

10. *Also welcomes* the signing of the Peace Agreement between the Government of Sierra Leone and the Revolutionary United Front, in Lomé on 7 July 1999, calls upon the respective parties to implement the agreement fully, commends in this regard the President of Togo and the Economic Community of West African States, together with the Special Representative of the Secretary-General for Sierra Leone and all those involved in facilitating the negotiations in Lomé, on their contribution to this achievement, and welcomes the adoption by the Security Council of resolution 1270(1999) of 22 October 1999 on the establishment of the United Nations Mission in Sierra Leone;

11. *Further welcomes* the decision taken by the Government of Liberia to destroy arms and ammunition collected during the disarmament exercise and the completion in Liberia in October of 1999 of the weapons destruction programme, an important step in the fight against the proliferation of arms, which would promote peace, confidence and cooperation in the region;

12. *Welcomes* the signing of the Ceasefire Agreement on the conflict in the Democratic Republic of the Congo, in Lusaka on 10 July 1999, and the adoption by the Security Council of resolution 1258(1999) of 6 August 1999, commends in that context the Organization of African Unity and the Southern African Development Community and, in particular, the President of Zambia, for their efforts to find a peaceful settlement to the conflict, and also commends the Secretary-General, the Special Envoy of the Secretary-General for the peace process in the Democratic Republic of the Congo, the Representative of the Secretary-General to the Great Lakes Region and all those who contributed to the peace process;

13. *Calls* for the full implementation of the Lusaka Ceasefire Agreement, urges all the parties in the Democratic Republic of the Congo to engage in a process of political dialogue and negotiation without delay, and calls upon the international community to extend the necessary support to the Organization of African Unity, the United Nations and the Joint Military Commission to enable them to carry out their mandate without further delay;

14. *Reaffirms* the importance for Member States to contribute by all means at their disposal to an effective and lasting peace in Angola, and in that context reiterates that the primary cause of the present situation in Angola is the failure of the National Union for the Total Independence of Angola under the leadership of Jonas Savimbi to comply with its obligations under the Peace Accords, the Lusaka Protocol and relevant Security Council resolutions;

15. *Views with concern* the humanitarian effects on the civilian population of the present situation in Angola, commends in this regard the efforts of Member States, including the Government of Angola, and humanitarian organizations in rendering humanitarian assistance to Angola, and urges them to continue to provide and to increase such assistance;

16. *Notes* the commitment of the provisional Government of Guinea-Bissau to holding legislative and presidential elections on 28 November 1999, and calls upon the international community and the Government of Guinea-Bissau to support the economic reconstruction of, and to promote the consolidation of democracy in, Guinea-Bissau;

17. *Affirms* the importance of the South Atlantic to global maritime and commercial transactions and its determination to preserve the region for all peaceful purposes and activities protected by international law, in particular the United Nations Convention on the Law of the Sea;

18. *Calls upon* Member States to continue their efforts towards the achievement of appropriate regulation of maritime transport of radioactive and toxic

wastes, taking into account the interests of coastal States and in accordance with the United Nations Convention on the Law of the Sea and the regulations of the International Maritime Organization and the International Atomic Energy Agency;

19. *Views with concern* the increase in drug trafficking and related crimes, including drug abuse, and calls upon the international community and the States members of the zone to promote regional and international cooperation to combat all aspects of the problem of drugs and related offences;

20. *Recognizes,* in the light of the number, magnitude and complexity of natural disasters and other emergencies, the need to strengthen the coordination of humanitarian assistance by States members of the zone, so as to ensure a timely and effective response;

21. *Welcomes* the offer by Benin to host the sixth meeting of the States members of the zone;

22. *Requests* the relevant organizations, organs and bodies of the United Nations system to render all appropriate assistance that States members of the zone may seek in their joint efforts to implement the declaration of the zone of peace and cooperation of the South Atlantic;

23. *Requests* the Secretary-General to keep the implementation of resolution 41/11 and subsequent resolutions on the matter under review and to submit a report to the General Assembly at its fifty-fifth session, taking into account, inter alia, the views expressed by Member States;

24. *Decides* to include in the provisional agenda of its fifty-fifth session the item entitled "Zone of peace and cooperation of the South Atlantic".

RECORDED VOTE ON RESOLUTION 54/35:

In favour: Algeria, Andorra, Angola, Argentina, Armenia, Australia, Austria, Azerbaijan, Bahrain, Bangladesh, Belarus, Belgium, Benin, Botswana, Brazil, Brunei Darussalam, Burkina Faso, Cambodia, Cameroon, Canada, Cape Verde, China, Colombia, Costa Rica, Côte d'Ivoire, Cuba, Cyprus, Czech Republic, Denmark, Djibouti, Egypt, Eritrea, Estonia, Ethiopia, Finland, France, Germany, Ghana, Greece, Grenada, Guatemala, Haiti, Hungary, Iran, Ireland, Italy, Jamaica, Japan, Kazakhstan, Kuwait, Lao People's Democratic Republic, Libyan Arab Jamahiriya, Lithuania, Luxembourg, Malaysia, Maldives, Malta, Mauritius, Mexico, Myanmar, Namibia, Nepal, Netherlands, New Zealand, Nigeria, Norway, Oman, Pakistan, Paraguay, Philippines, Poland, Portugal, Qatar, Republic of Moldova, Romania, Russian Federation, San Marino, Saudi Arabia, Senegal, Seychelles, Slovakia, South Africa, Spain, Sri Lanka, Sudan, Sweden, Syrian Arab Republic, Thailand, Togo, Tunisia, United Arab Emirates, United Kingdom, United Republic of Tanzania, Uruguay, Uzbekistan, Venezuela, Yemen.

Against: None.

Abstaining: United States.

Indian Ocean

In 1999, the Ad Hoc Committee on the Indian Ocean (New York, 14 July) [A/54/29] continued to consider approaches to achieving the goals of the 1971 Declaration of the Indian Ocean as a Zone of Peace, adopted by the General Assembly in resolution 2832(XXVI) [YUN 1971, p. 34].

Following consultations with Committee members, permanent members of the Security Council and major maritime users of the Indian Ocean, the Chairman of the Committee concluded that there appeared to be a general sense among those Committee members consulted that there were complexities and difficulties in the way of implementation of the Declaration. As to the three permanent Council members that did not participate in the Committee's work (France, United Kingdom, United States), he concluded, after consulting them, that their earlier-stated views as to the Committee's work had not changed; hence, their continued non-participation.

The Ad Hoc Committee reaffirmed the conclusions of its 1994 [YUN 1994, p. 155], 1995 [YUN 1995, p. 182] and 1996 [YUN 1996, p. 512] sessions and emphasized the need to foster consensual, step-by-step approaches. It remained convinced that the participation of all permanent Council members and major maritime users in its work would assist the progress of a mutually beneficial dialogue to develop conditions of peace, security and stability in the region. The Chairman was requested to continue informal consultations with Committee members and to report to the Assembly in 2001.

GENERAL ASSEMBLY ACTION

On 1 December [meeting 69], the General Assembly, on the recommendation of the First (Disarmament and International Security) Committee [A/54/556], adopted **resolution 54/47** by recorded vote (120-3-41) [agenda item 69].

Implementation of the Declaration of the Indian Ocean as a Zone of Peace

The General Assembly,

Recalling the Declaration of the Indian Ocean as a Zone of Peace, contained in its resolution 2832(XXVI) of 16 December 1971, and recalling also its resolution 52/44 of 9 December 1997 and other relevant resolutions,

Recalling also the report of the Meeting of the Littoral and Hinterland States of the Indian Ocean held in July 1979,

Recalling further paragraph 148 of the Final Document of the Twelfth Conference of Heads of State or Government of Non-Aligned Countries, held at Durban, South Africa, from 29 August to 3 September 1998, in which it was noted, inter alia, that the Chairperson of the Ad Hoc Committee on the Indian Ocean would continue his informal consultations on the future work of the Committee,

Emphasizing the need to foster consensual approaches, in particular given the prevailing international climate, which is conducive to the pursuit of such endeavours,

Noting the initiatives taken by countries of the region to promote cooperation, in particular economic cooperation, in the Indian Ocean area and the possible contribution of such initiatives to overall objectives of a zone of peace,

Convinced that the participation of all the permanent members of the Security Council and the major maritime users of the Indian Ocean in the work of the Ad Hoc Committee is important and would assist the progress of a mutually beneficial dialogue to develop conditions of peace, security and stability in the Indian Ocean region,

Considering that greater efforts and more time are required to develop a focused discussion on practical measures to ensure conditions of peace, security and stability in the Indian Ocean region,

Having considered the report of the Ad Hoc Committee on the Indian Ocean,

1. *Takes note* of the report of the Ad Hoc Committee on the Indian Ocean;

2. *Reiterates its conviction* that the participation of all the permanent members of the Security Council and the major maritime users of the Indian Ocean in the work of the Ad Hoc Committee is important and would greatly facilitate the development of a mutually beneficial dialogue to advance peace, security and stability in the Indian Ocean region;

3. *Requests* the Chairman of the Ad Hoc Committee to continue his informal consultations with the members of the Committee and to report through the Committee to the General Assembly at its fifty-sixth session;

4. *Requests* the Secretary-General to continue to render, within existing resources, all necessary assistance to the Ad Hoc Committee, including the provision of summary records;

5. *Decides* to include in the provisional agenda of its fifty-sixth session the item entitled "Implementation of the Declaration of the Indian Ocean as a Zone of Peace".

RECORDED VOTE ON RESOLUTION 54/47:

In favour: Algeria, Angola, Antigua and Barbuda, Argentina, Armenia, Australia, Azerbaijan, Bahamas, Bahrain, Bangladesh, Barbados, Belarus, Belize, Bhutan, Bolivia, Botswana, Brazil, Brunei Darussalam, Burkina Faso, Cambodia, Cameroon, Cape Verde, Chad, Chile, China, Colombia, Congo, Costa Rica, Côte d'Ivoire, Cuba, Democratic People's Republic of Korea, Djibouti, Dominica, Dominican Republic, Ecuador, Egypt, El Salvador, Equatorial Guinea, Eritrea, Ethiopia, Fiji, Georgia, Ghana, Grenada, Guatemala, Guinea, Guinea-Bissau, Guyana, Haiti, Honduras, India, Indonesia, Iran, Jamaica, Japan, Jordan, Kazakhstan, Kenya, Kuwait, Lao People's Democratic Republic, Lebanon, Libyan Arab Jamahiriya, Madagascar, Malaysia, Maldives, Mali, Mauritius, Mexico, Mongolia, Morocco, Mozambique, Myanmar, Namibia, Nepal, New Zealand, Nicaragua, Nigeria, Oman, Pakistan, Panama, Papua New Guinea, Paraguay, Peru, Philippines, Qatar, Republic of Korea, Russian Federation, Saint Kitts and Nevis, Saint Lucia, Saint Vincent and the Grenadines, Samoa, San Marino, Saudi Arabia, Senegal, Seychelles, Sierra Leone, Singapore, Solomon Islands, South Africa, Sri Lanka, Sudan, Suriname, Swaziland, Syrian Arab Republic, Tajikistan, Thailand, Togo, Trinidad and Tobago, Tunisia, Turkmenistan, Uganda, Ukraine, United Arab Emirates, United Republic of Tanzania, Uruguay, Venezuela, Viet Nam, Yemen, Zambia, Zimbabwe.

Against: France, United Kingdom, United States.

Abstaining: Albania, Andorra, Austria, Belgium, Bosnia and Herzegovina, Bulgaria, Canada, Croatia, Cyprus, Czech Republic, Denmark, Estonia, Finland, Germany, Greece, Hungary, Iceland, Ireland, Israel, Italy, Latvia, Liechtenstein, Lithuania, Luxembourg, Malta, Marshall Islands, Micronesia, Monaco, Netherlands, Norway, Poland, Portugal, Republic of Moldova, Romania, Slovakia, Slovenia, Spain, Sweden, The former Yugoslav Republic of Macedonia, Turkey, Uzbekistan.

Antarctica

In response to General Assembly resolution 51/56 [YUN 1996, p. 515], the Secretary-General submitted a September report on the activities of the Antarctic Treaty system and international bodies and recent developments pertaining to the Antarctic environment [A/54/339 & Corr.1], based on reports of the Twenty-first Antarctic Treaty Consultative Meeting (Christchurch, New Zealand, 19-30 May 1997), the Twenty-second Meeting (Tromso, Norway, 25 May-5 June 1998) and the Twenty-third Meeting (Lima, Peru, 24 May-4 June 1999). The Antarctic Treaty was adopted in 1959 and entered into force on 23 June 1961 [UN Treaty Series, vol. 402, No. 5578]. At the Twenty-third Meeting, the Consultative Parties adopted the Lima Declaration on the occasion of the fortieth anniversary of the signing of the 1959 Treaty, reiterating their commitment to the principles of the Treaty and to the objectives of its 1991 Protocol on Environmental Protection (the Madrid Protocol).

Since the Twentieth Consultative Meeting in 1996 [YUN 1996, p. 514], Consultative Parties had carried out inspections in all areas of Antarctica to ensure observance of the Treaty's provisions. No infringements were observed. Strenuous efforts were being made at all stations to comply with the provisions of the Madrid Protocol, although operational practices varied and gaps in implementation were evident, notably with respect to environmental impact assessments. Although there was an agreement among Consultative Parties to establish a permanent secretariat, no consensus was reached on its location and modalities. Talks were being held between Argentina and the United Kingdom to help resolve the issue of location.

As at 21 May 1999, there were 28 parties to the Madrid Protocol. A Committee for Environmental Protection was established to, among other things, advise and formulate recommendations on the Protocol's implementation for consideration at the Consultative Meetings.

Fishing, sealing and whaling were regulated by the 1980 Convention on the Conservation of Antarctic Marine Living Resources. To reduce the risk of localized overfishing and augment the collection of data for stock assessment, a new regulation was introduced under the Convention for new fisheries of toothfish during the 1996/97 season. The Commission for the Conservation of Antarctic Marine Living Resources (CCAMLR) system of inspection was amended to increase its efficiency regarding illegal fishing activities. The Twenty-third Meeting recommended that the list of specifically protected species be reviewed by the Scientific Committee on Antarctic Research together with CCAMLR, Consultative Parties and other expert bodies, with a view to including new species and removing those no longer appropriate.

Developments relating to the Antarctic environment were reported in the areas of science and support activities, environmental monitoring and a possible state of the Antarctic environment report, environmental impact assessment, safety of operations, emergency response and contingency planning, waste disposal and management, prevention of marine pollution, ozone depletion, conservation of Antarctic fauna and flora, area protection and management, sea ice and ice sheets, the question of liability for damage arising from activities in the area, Antarctic tourism and other non-governmental operations, and the exchange of information on scientific and logistical activities in the Arctic and in Antarctica.

The Secretary-General stated that, with the entry into force of the Madrid Protocol, human activities in Antarctica were being regulated to protect the environment and its dependent and associated ecosystems. However, some issues of concern and possible challenges would have to be addressed, particularly unreported, unregulated and illegal fishing for toothfish in the Southern Ocean, which threatened not only the toothfish but also other dependent and related species. No agreement had been reached on one or more annexes to the Madrid Protocol concerning liability for environmental damage. As Antarctic tourism was increasing steadily, presenting risk to the marine and terrestrial environments, efforts by the Antarctic Treaty parties and the International Association of Antarctica Tour Operators to prevent and mitigate the environmental impacts of tourism should continue.

GENERAL ASSEMBLY ACTION

On 1 December [meeting 69], the General Assembly, on the recommendation of the First Committee [A/54/553], adopted **resolution 54/45** without vote [agenda item 66].

Question of Antarctica

The General Assembly,

Recalling its resolution 51/56 of 10 December 1996, in which it requested the Secretary-General to submit a report consisting of the information provided by the Antarctic Treaty Consultative Parties on their consultative meetings and on their activities in Antarctica, and on developments in relation to Antarctica,

Taking into account the debates on the question of Antarctica held since its thirty-eighth session,

Conscious of the particular significance of Antarctica to the international community, including for international peace and security, the global and regional environment, its effects on global and regional climate conditions, and scientific research,

Reaffirming that the management and use of Antarctica should be conducted in accordance with the purposes and principles of the Charter of the United Nations and in the interest of maintaining international peace and security and of promoting international cooperation for the benefit of mankind as a whole,

Recognizing that the Antarctic Treaty, which provides, inter alia, for the demilitarization of the continent, the prohibition of nuclear explosions and the disposal of nuclear wastes, the freedom of scientific research and the free exchange of scientific information, is in furtherance of the purposes and principles of the Charter,

Welcoming the entry into force of the Protocol on Environmental Protection to the Antarctic Treaty on 14 January 1998, under which Antarctica has been designated as a natural reserve, devoted to peace and science, and the provisions contained in the Protocol regarding the protection of the Antarctic environment and dependent and associated ecosystems, including the need for environmental impact assessment in the planning and conduct of all relevant activities in Antarctica,

Welcoming also the continuing cooperation among countries undertaking scientific research activities in Antarctica, which may help to minimize human impact on the Antarctic environment,

Welcoming further the increasing awareness of an interest in Antarctica shown by the international community, and convinced of the advantages to the whole of mankind of a better knowledge of Antarctica,

Reaffirming its conviction that, in the interest of all mankind, Antarctica should continue for ever to be used exclusively for peaceful purposes and that it should not become the scene or object of international discord,

1. *Takes note* of the report of the Secretary-General on the question of Antarctica and the role accorded by the Secretary-General to the United Nations Environment Programme in preparing his report and also of the Twenty-first, Twenty-second and Twenty-third Antarctic Treaty Consultative Meetings, which were held at Christchurch, New Zealand, from 19 to 30 May 1997, at Tromso, Norway, from 25 May to 5 June 1998, and at Lima, from 24 May to 4 June 1999, respectively;

2. *Recalls* the statement under chapter 17 of Agenda 21, adopted by the United Nations Conference on Environment and Development, that States carrying out research activities in Antarctica should, as provided for in article III of the Antarctic Treaty, continue:

(a) To ensure that data and information resulting from such research are freely available to the international community;

(b) To enhance the access of the international scientific community and the specialized agencies of the United Nations system to such data and information, including the encouragement of periodic seminars and symposia;

3. *Welcomes* the invitations to the Executive Director of the United Nations Environment Programme to attend Antarctic Treaty Consultative Meetings in order to assist such meetings in their substantive work, and urges the parties to continue to do so for future consultative meetings;

4. *Welcomes also* the practice whereby the Antarctic Treaty Consultative Parties regularly provide the Secretary-General with information on their consultative meetings and on their activities in Antarctica, and encourages the parties to continue to provide the Secretary-General and interested States with information on developments in relation to Antarctica, and requests the Secretary-General to submit a report which shall consist of that information to the General Assembly at its fifty-seventh session;

5. *Decides* to include in the provisional agenda of its fifty-seventh session the item entitled "Question of Antarctica".

Decolonization

The General Assembly's Special Committee on the Situation with regard to the Implementation of the Declaration on the Granting of Independence to Colonial Countries and Peoples (Special Committee on decolonization) held its annual session in New York in two parts—22 February and 31 March for the first part, and from 21 June to 21 July and on 28 July for the second. It considered various aspects of the implementation of the 1960 Declaration, adopted by the Assembly in resolution 1514(XV) [YUN 1960, p. 49], including general decolonization issues and the situation of individual Non-Self-Governing Territories (NSGTs). Pursuant to General Assembly resolution 53/68 [YUN 1998, p. 559], the Special Committee transmitted to the Assembly the report on its 1999 activities [A/54/23].

Decade for the Eradication of Colonialism

The Secretary-General, in response to General Assembly resolution 46/181 [YUN 1991, p. 777], submitted an August 1999 progress report [A/54/219] on implementation of the plan of action [YUN 1991, p. 777] for the International Decade for the Eradication of Colonialism (1990-2000), declared by the Assembly in resolution 43/47 [YUN 1988, p. 734]. He stated that the Special Committee on decolonization had encouraged the cooperation and participation of Member States, particularly the administering Powers, the UN system, intergovernmental organizations, the specialized agencies and international institutions to work towards achieving the Decade's objectives and to assist the peoples of NSGTs. The Special Committee had reviewed yearly the situation in each NSGT and held seminars in the Caribbean and Pacific regions in alternate years to review progress in implementing the plan of action.

The Economic and Social Council considered annually the Declaration's implementation by specialized agencies and other UN organizations. Also, in an ongoing effort to strengthen coordinated action, the Council President and the Special Committee Chairman had consulted on ways to strengthen international assistance for the economic and social development of NSGTs.

In the context of the International Decade, information on decolonization had been disseminated, including through the Internet, and was available at UN information centres and services worldwide.

The Secretary-General said he would present a detailed final report on the achievements of the Decade to the Assembly in 2000.

Caribbean regional seminar

As part of its activities to implement the plan of action for the Decade, the Special Committee on decolonization organized a Caribbean regional seminar (Castries, Saint Lucia, 25-27 May) to review the political, economic and social conditions in the small island NSGTs [A/54/23].

The seminar concluded that the implementation of the 1960 Declaration was not complete as long as there remained NSGTs that had yet to exercise their right to self-determination, a process in which the United Nations had a valid ongoing role. Participants supported closer cooperation between the Special Committee and the Economic and Social Council in providing UN economic and political assistance to NSGTs. Concerning proposed measures to be undertaken by the member States of the Organisation for Economic Cooperation and Development (OECD) in respect of offshore banking, participants emphasized the need for consultations between the administering Powers, OECD members and NSGT representatives to formulate appropriate laws and to ensure that the economic rights of NSGTs were not compromised by the administering Powers.

The seminar recommended that the Special Committee transmit to the General Assembly its conclusions and recommendations and that the Secretary-General prepare a consolidated report on the implementation of decolonization resolutions since the declaration of the International Decade. Participants supported the initiation, at the regional level, of a UN study on access of NSGTs to UN programmes and activities in furtherance of the decolonization process. They emphasized the desirability of holding future seminars in NSGTs, reconfirmed the need for periodic visiting missions to NSGTs, and requested the Special Committee to organize activities on the occasion of the fortieth anniversary of the Declaration and the last year of the Decade, particularly the dissemination of information on UN decolonization activities. Participants also recommended that the Special Committee formulate an updated plan of action to eradicate colonialism.

On 21 July, the Special Committee adopted the draft report of the seminar.

Status of remaining NSGTs

The Special Committee had before it a working paper by Chile on a conceptual framework for the review of the constitutional and juridical status of NSGTs and on progress in the implementation of the 1960 Declaration [A/AC.109/1999/20]. The paper contained a proposed set of guidelines to enable the Special Committee to decide on the status of the remaining NSGTs. A working paper by Saint Lucia [A/AC.109/1999/21] contained comments on Chile's submission.

GENERAL ASSEMBLY ACTION

On 6 December [meeting 71], the General Assembly adopted **resolution 54/91** [draft: A/54/L.50 & Add.1] by recorded vote (141-2-14) [agenda item 18].

Implementation of the Declaration on the Granting of Independence to Colonial Countries and Peoples

The General Assembly,

Having examined the report of the Special Committee with regard to the Implementation of the Declaration on the Granting of Independence to Colonial Countries and Peoples,

Recalling its resolution 1514(XV) of 14 December 1960, containing the Declaration on the Granting of Independence to Colonial Countries and Peoples, and all its subsequent resolutions concerning the implementation of the Declaration, most recently resolution 53/68 of 3 December 1998, as well as the relevant resolutions of the Security Council,

Recognizing that the eradication of colonialism is one of the priorities of the Organization for the decade that began in 1990,

Reconfirming the need to take measures to eliminate colonialism by 2000, as called for in its resolution 43/47 of 22 November 1988,

Reiterating its conviction of the need for the eradication of colonialism as well as racial discrimination and violations of basic human rights,

Noting with satisfaction the achievements of the Special Committee in contributing to the effective and complete implementation of the Declaration and other relevant resolutions of the United Nations on decolonization,

Stressing the importance of the participation of the administering Powers in the work of the Special Committee,

Noting with concern that the non-participation of certain administering Powers has adversely affected the implementation of the mandate and work of the Special Committee,

Noting with satisfaction the cooperation and active participation of some administering Powers in the work of the Special Committee, as well as their continued readiness to receive United Nations visiting missions in the Territories under their administration,

Noting that the other administering Powers have now agreed to work informally with the Special Committee,

Bearing in mind that the International Decade for the Eradication of Colonialism will end in the year 2000, and that it is necessary to examine ways to ascertain the wishes of the peoples of the Non-Self-Governing Territories on the basis of resolution 1514(XV) and other relevant resolutions on decolonization,

Taking note of the consultations and agreements between the parties concerned in some Non-Self-Governing Territories and the action undertaken by the Secretary-General in relation to certain Non-Self-Governing Territories,

Aware of the pressing need of newly independent and emerging States for assistance from the United Nations and its system of organizations in the economic, social and other fields,

Aware also of the pressing need of many of the remaining Non-Self-Governing Territories, including in particular small island Territories, for economic, social and other assistance from the United Nations and the organizations of its system,

Taking special note of the fact that the Special Committee held a Caribbean regional seminar to review the situation in the small island Non-Self-Governing Territories, particularly their political evolution towards self-determination for the year 2000 and beyond, at Castries, Saint Lucia, from 25 to 27 May 1999,

1. *Reaffirms* its resolution 1514(XV) and all other resolutions on decolonization, including its resolution 43/47, in which it declared the decade that began in 1990 as the International Decade for the Eradication of Colonialism, and calls upon the administering Powers, in accordance with those resolutions, to take all necessary steps to enable the peoples of the Non-Self-Governing Territories concerned to exercise fully as soon as possible their right to self-determination, including independence;

2. *Takes note* of the report of the Secretary-General on the International Decade for the Eradication of Colonialism;

3. *Reaffirms once again* that the existence of colonialism in any form or manifestation, including economic exploitation, is incompatible with the Charter of the United Nations, the Declaration on the Granting of Independence to Colonial Countries and Peoples and the Universal Declaration of Human Rights;

4. *Reaffirms its determination* to continue to take all steps necessary to bring about the complete and speedy eradication of colonialism and the faithful observance by all States of the relevant provisions of the Charter of the United Nations, the Declaration on the Granting of Independence to Colonial Countries and Peoples and the Universal Declaration of Human Rights;

5. *Affirms once again its support* for the aspirations of the peoples under colonial rule to exercise their right to self-determination, including independence;

6. *Approves* the report of the Special Committee on the Situation with regard to the Implementation of the Declaration on the Granting of Independence to Colonial Countries and Peoples covering its work during 1999, including the programme of work envisaged for 2000;

7. *Calls upon* the administering Powers to cooperate fully with the Special Committee to develop before the end of 2000 a constructive programme of work with respect to the Non-Self-Governing Territories to implement the resolutions on decolonization, including resolutions on specific Territories;

8. *Requests* the Special Committee to continue to seek suitable means for the immediate and full implementation of the Declaration and to carry out those actions approved by the General Assembly regarding the International Decade for the Eradication of Colonialism in all Territories that have not yet exercised their right to self-determination, including independence, and in particular:

(*a*) To formulate specific proposals to bring about an end to colonialism and to report thereon to the General Assembly at its fifty-fifth session;

(*b*) To continue to examine the implementation by Member States of resolution 1514(XV) and other relevant resolutions on decolonization;

(*c*) To continue to pay special attention to the small Territories, including through the dispatch of visiting missions, and to recommend to the General Assembly the most suitable steps to be taken to enable the populations of those Territories to exercise their right to self-determination, including independence;

(*d*) To develop a constructive programme of work on a case-by-case basis for the Non-Self-Governing Territories before the end of 2000 to facilitate the implementation of the mandate of the Special Committee and the relevant resolutions of the United Nations, including resolutions on specific Territories;

(*e*) To take all necessary steps to enlist worldwide support among Governments, as well as national and international organizations, for the achievement of the objectives of the Declaration and the implementation of the relevant resolutions of the United Nations;

(*f*) To conduct seminars, as appropriate, for the purpose of receiving and disseminating information on the work of the Special Committee, and to facilitate participation by the peoples of the Non-Self-Governing Territories in those seminars;

(*g*) To observe annually the Week of Solidarity with the Peoples of Non-Self-Governing Territories, beginning on 25 May;

9. *Calls upon* all States, in particular the administering Powers, as well as the specialized agencies and other organizations of the United Nations system, to give effect within their respective spheres of competence to the recommendations of the Special Committee for the implementation of the Declaration and other relevant resolutions of the United Nations;

10. *Calls upon* the administering Powers to ensure that all economic activities in the Non-Self-Governing Territories under their administration do not adversely affect the interests of the peoples but instead promote development, and to assist them in the exercise of their right to self-determination;

11. *Urges* the administering Powers concerned to take effective measures to safeguard and guarantee the inalienable rights of the peoples of the Non-Self-Governing Territories to their natural resources, including land, and to establish and maintain control over the future development of those resources, and requests the administering Powers to take all necessary steps to protect the property rights of the peoples of those Territories;

12. *Reiterates* that military activities and arrangements by administering Powers in the Non-Self-Governing Territories under their administration should not run counter to the rights and interests of the peoples of the Territories concerned, especially their right to self-determination, including independence, and calls upon the administering Powers concerned to terminate such activities and to eliminate the remaining military bases in compliance with the relevant resolutions of the General Assembly;

13. *Urges* all States, directly and through their action in the specialized agencies and other organizations of the United Nations system, to provide moral and material assistance to the peoples of the Non-Self-Governing Territories, and requests that the administering Powers take steps to enlist and make effective use of all possible assistance, on both a bilateral and a multilateral basis, in the strengthening of the economies of those Territories;

14. *Reaffirms* that the United Nations visiting missions to the Territories are an effective means of ascertaining the situation in the Territories as well as the wishes and aspirations of their inhabitants, and calls upon the administering Powers to continue to cooperate with the Special Committee in the discharge of its mandate and to facilitate visiting missions to the Territories;

15. *Calls upon* the administering Powers that have not participated formally in the work of the Special Committee to do so at its session in 2000;

16. *Requests* the Secretary-General, the specialized agencies and other organizations of the United Nations system to provide economic, social and other assistance to the Non-Self-Governing Territories and to continue to do so, as appropriate, after they exercise their right to self-determination, including independence;

17. *Requests* the Secretary-General to provide the Special Committee with the facilities and services required for the implementation of the present resolution, as well as of the other resolutions and decisions on decolonization adopted by the General Assembly and the Special Committee.

RECORDED VOTE ON RESOLUTION 54/91:

In favour: Albania, Algeria, Andorra, Angola, Antigua and Barbuda, Argentina, Armenia, Australia, Austria, Azerbaijan, Bahamas, Bahrain, Bangladesh, Barbados, Belarus, Belize, Benin, Bhutan, Bolivia, Botswana, Brazil, Brunei Darussalam, Bulgaria, Burkina Faso, Cambodia, Cameroon, Canada, Cape Verde, Chad, Chile, China, Colombia, Congo, Costa Rica, Côte d'Ivoire, Croatia, Cuba, Cyprus, Czech Republic, Democratic People's Republic of Korea, Denmark, Djibouti, Dominica, Dominican Republic, Ecuador, Egypt, El Salvador, Equatorial Guinea, Eritrea, Ethiopia, Fiji, Finland, Gabon, Gambia, Ghana, Greece, Grenada, Guatemala, Guinea, Guyana, Haiti, Iceland, India, Indonesia, Iran, Ireland, Italy, Jamaica, Japan, Kazakhstan, Kenya, Kuwait, Lao People's Democratic Republic, Lebanon, Libyan Arab Jamahiriya, Liechtenstein, Madagascar, Malaysia, Maldives, Mali, Malta, Marshall Islands, Mauritius, Mexico, Mongolia, Morocco, Mozambique, Myanmar, Namibia, Nepal, New Zealand, Nicaragua, Nigeria, Norway, Oman, Pakistan, Panama, Papua New Guinea, Paraguay, Peru, Philippines, Poland, Portugal, Qatar, Republic of Moldova, Romania, Russian Federation, Saint Lucia, Saint Vincent and the Grenadines, Samoa, San Marino, Saudi Arabia, Senegal, Sierra Leone, Singapore, Slovakia, Slovenia, Solomon Islands, South Africa, Spain, Sri Lanka, Sudan, Suriname, Swaziland, Sweden, Syrian Arab Republic, Tajikistan, Thailand, The former Yugoslav Republic of Macedonia, Togo, Trinidad and Tobago, Tunisia, Ukraine, United Arab Emirates, United Republic of Tanzania, Uruguay, Venezuela, Viet Nam, Yemen, Zambia, Zimbabwe.

Against: United Kingdom, United States.

Abstaining: Belgium, Estonia, France, Georgia, Germany, Hungary, Israel, Latvia, Lithuania, Luxembourg, Monaco, Netherlands, Republic of Korea, Turkey.

Implementation by international organizations

As requested by the General Assembly in resolution 53/62 [YUN 1998, p. 563], the Secretary-General reported, in June [A/54/119], that he had brought that resolution regarding implementation of the 1960 Declaration on decolonization to the attention of UN specialized agencies and organizations. Summaries of replies received, describing action taken to support NSGTs, were contained in a July report [E/1999/69].

Assistance to NSGTs was provided by UNDP, the Universal Postal Union, the Food and Agriculture Organization of the United Nations, the United Nations International Drug Control Programme, the World Health Organization regional office for the Western Pacific region and the United Nations Environment Programme.

In July [E/1999/SR.39], the Special Committee Chairman stated that the Committee had called for closer cooperation between the Economic and Social Council and itself in assisting the NSGTs. He said that, at the Committee's Caribbean regional seminar (see p. 522), a UNDP representative had stressed the importance of conducting analyses on governance, economic management and increasing resource mobilization to help those Territories, whose vulnerability persisted even as their graduated status precluded them from receiving aid and official development assistance.

The Chairman reported in August [A/AC.109/1999/L.16] that, in the context of resolution 53/62, he had held consultations in 1999 with the Council President. The Chairman emphasized the importance of cooperation between the Committee and the Council. UN programmes, specialized agencies and international organizations had to be mobilized to expand their activities and strengthen international assistance for economic and social development in respect of NSGTs. A joint meeting of the Committee and the Council devoted to NSGTs would provide an opportunity to discuss strategies to promote implementation of the 1960 Declaration. That could be done in the context of the International Decade, which would conclude in 2000, or as part of a new plan of action being developed by the Committee in consultation with administering Powers for the period beyond 2001.

ECONOMIC AND SOCIAL COUNCIL ACTION

On 29 July [meeting 45], the Economic and Social Council adopted **resolution 1999/52** [draft: E/1999/L.34] by roll-call vote (29-0-17) [agenda item 9].

Implementation of the Declaration on the Granting of Independence to Colonial Countries and Peoples by the specialized agencies and the international institutions associated with the United Nations

The Economic and Social Council,

Having examined the report of the Secretary-General and the information submitted by the specialized agencies and other organizations of the United Nations system on their activities with regard to the implementation of the Declaration on the Granting of Independence to Colonial Countries and Peoples,

Having heard the statement by the representative of the Special Committee on the Situation with regard to the Implementation of the Declaration on the Granting of Independence to Colonial Countries and Peoples,

Recalling General Assembly resolutions 1514(XV) of 14 December 1960 and 1541(XV) of 15 December 1960, the resolutions of the Special Committee and other relevant resolutions and decisions, including in particular Economic and Social Council resolution 1998/38 of 30 July 1998,

Bearing in mind the relevant provisions of the final documents of the successive Conferences of Heads of State or Government of Non-Aligned Countries and of the resolutions adopted by the Assembly of Heads of State and Government of the Organization of African Unity, the South Pacific Forum and the Caribbean Community,

Conscious of the need to facilitate the implementation of the Declaration,

Welcoming the participation, in the capacity of observer, of those Non-Self-Governing Territories that are associate members of the regional commissions in United Nations world conferences in the economic and social spheres, and in the special session of the General Assembly for the review and appraisal of the implementation of the Programme of Action of the International Conference on Population and Development, which convened at United Nations Headquarters from 30 June to 2 July 1999,

Noting that the large majority of the remaining Non-Self-Governing Territories are small island Territories,

Welcoming the assistance extended to Non-Self-Governing Territories by certain specialized agencies and other organizations of the United Nations system, in particular the United Nations Development Programme,

Stressing that, because the development options of small island Non-Self-Governing Territories are limited, there are special challenges to planning for and implementing sustainable development and that those Territories will be constrained in meeting the challenges without the continued cooperation and assistance of the specialized agencies and other organizations of the United Nations system,

Stressing also the importance of securing the necessary resources for funding expanded assistance programmes for the peoples concerned and the need to enlist the support of all major funding institutions within the United Nations system in that regard,

Reaffirming the mandates of the specialized agencies and other organizations of the United Nations system to take all the appropriate measures, within their respective spheres of competence, to ensure the full implementation of resolution 1514(XV) and other relevant resolutions,

Expressing its appreciation to the Organization of African Unity, the South Pacific Forum, the Caribbean Community and other regional organizations for the continued cooperation and assistance they have extended to the specialized agencies and other organizations of the United Nations system in this regard,

Expressing its conviction that closer contacts and consultations between and among the specialized agencies and other organizations of the United Nations system and regional organizations help to facilitate the effective formulation of assistance programmes to the peoples concerned,

Mindful of the imperative need to keep under continuous review the activities of the specialized agencies and other organizations of the United Nations system in the implementation of the various United Nations decisions relating to decolonization,

Bearing in mind the extremely fragile economies of the small island Non-Self-Governing Territories and their vulnerability to natural disasters, such as hurricanes, cyclones and sea-level rise, and recalling other relevant General Assembly resolutions,

Recalling General Assembly resolution 53/62 of 3 December 1998 entitled "Implementation of the Declaration on the Granting of Independence to Colonial Countries and Peoples by the specialized agencies and the international institutions associated with the United Nations",

1. *Takes note* of the information submitted by the specialized agencies and other organizations of the United Nations system on their activities with regard to the implementation of the Declaration on the Granting of Independence to Colonial Countries and Peoples, and endorses the observations and suggestions arising therefrom;

2. *Also takes note* of the report of the Secretary-General;

3. *Recommends* that all States intensify their efforts in the specialized agencies and other organizations of the United Nations system to ensure the full and effective implementation of the Declaration on the Granting of Independence to Colonial Countries and Peoples, contained in General Assembly resolution 1514(XV), and other relevant resolutions of the United Nations;

4. *Reaffirms* that the specialized agencies and other organizations and institutions of the United Nations system should continue to be guided by the relevant resolutions of the United Nations in their efforts to contribute to the implementation of the Declaration and all other relevant General Assembly resolutions;

5. *Also reaffirms* that the recognition by the General Assembly, the Security Council and other United Nations organs of the legitimacy of the aspirations of the peoples of Non-Self-Governing Territories to exercise their right to self-determination entails, as a corollary, the extension of all appropriate assistance to those peoples;

6. *Expresses its appreciation* to those specialized agencies and other organizations of the United Nations system that have continued to cooperate with the United Nations and the regional and subregional organizations in the implementation of resolution 1514(XV) and other relevant resolutions of the United Nations, and requests all the specialized agencies and other organizations of the United Nations system to implement the relevant provisions of those resolutions;

7. *Requests* the specialized agencies and other organizations of the United Nations system and international and regional organizations to examine and review conditions in each Territory so as to take appropriate measures to accelerate progress in the economic and social sectors of the Territories;

8. *Requests* the specialized agencies and the international institutions associated with the United Nations and regional organizations to strengthen existing measures of support and formulate appropriate programmes of assistance to the remaining Non-Self-Governing Territories, within the framework of their respective mandates, in order to accelerate progress in the economic and social sectors of those Territories;

9. *Recommends* that the executive heads of the specialized agencies and other organizations of the United Nations system formulate, with the active cooperation of the regional organizations concerned, concrete proposals for the full implementation of the relevant resolutions of the United Nations and submit the proposals to their governing and legislative organs;

10. *Also recommends* that the specialized agencies and other organizations of the United Nations system continue to review at the regular meetings of their governing bodies the implementation of resolution 1514(XV) and other relevant resolutions of the United Nations;

11. *Welcomes* the continued initiative exercised by the United Nations Development Programme in maintaining close liaison among the specialized agencies and other organizations of the United Nations system and in providing assistance to the peoples of Non-Self-Governing Territories;

12. *Encourages* Non-Self-Governing Territories to take steps to establish and/or strengthen disaster preparedness and management institutions and policies;

13. *Requests* the administering Powers concerned to facilitate the participation of appointed and elected representatives of Non-Self-Governing Territories in the relevant meetings and conferences of the specialized agencies and other organizations of the United Nations system so that the Territories may benefit from the related activities of the specialized agencies and other organizations;

14. *Recommends* that all Governments intensify their efforts in the specialized agencies and other organizations of the United Nations system of which they are members to accord priority to the question of providing assistance to the peoples of the Non-Self-Governing Territories;

15. *Draws the attention* of the Special Committee on the Situation with regard to the Implementation of the Declaration on the Granting of Independence to Colonial Countries and Peoples to the present resolution and to the discussion held on the subject at the substantive session of 1999 of the Economic and Social Council;

16. *Welcomes* the adoption by the Economic Commission for Latin America and the Caribbean of resolution 574(XXVII) of 16 May 1998 calling for the necessary mechanisms for its associate members, including small island Non-Self-Governing Territories, to participate in the special sessions of the General Assembly, subject to the rules of procedure of the Assembly, to review and assess the implementation of the plans of action of those United Nations world conferences in which the Territories originally participated in the capacity of observer, and in the work of the Economic and Social Council and its subsidiary bodies;

17. *Also welcomes* the adoption by the General Assembly of resolution 53/189 of 15 December 1998, in which, inter alia, the Assembly called for the participation of associate members of regional economic commissions in the special session on small island developing States, subject to the rules of procedure of the General Assembly, and in the preparatory process thereof, in the same capacity of observer that held for their participation in the 1994 Global Conference on the Sustainable Development of Small Island Developing States;

18. *Requests* the President of the Economic and Social Council to continue to maintain close contact on

these matters with the Chairman of the Special Committee and to report thereon to the Council;

19. *Requests* the Secretary-General to follow the implementation of the present resolution, paying particular attention to cooperation and integration arrangements for maximizing the efficiency of the assistance activities undertaken by various organizations of the United Nations system, and to report thereon to the Council at its substantive session of 2000;

20. *Decides* to keep these questions under continuous review.

ROLL-CALL VOTE IN COUNCIL AS FOLLOWS:

In favour: Algeria, Belarus, Bolivia, Brazil, Cape Verde, Chile, China, Colombia, Comoros, Cuba, Djibouti, El Salvador, Honduras, India, Indonesia, Mauritius, Mexico, Mozambique, New Zealand, Oman, Pakistan, Republic of Korea, Saudi Arabia, Sri Lanka, Syrian Arab Republic, Turkey, Venezuela, Viet Nam, Zambia.

Against: None.

Abstaining: Belgium, Bulgaria, Canada, Czech Republic, Denmark, France, Germany, Iceland, Italy, Japan, Latvia, Norway, Poland, Russian Federation, Spain, United Kingdom, United States.

GENERAL ASSEMBLY ACTION

On 6 December [meeting 71], the General Assembly, on the recommendation of the Fourth (Special Political and Decolonization) Committee [A/54/581], adopted **resolution 54/85** by recorded vote (101-0-52) [agenda items 94 & 12].

Implementation of the Declaration on the Granting of Independence to Colonial Countries and Peoples by the specialized agencies and the international institutions associated with the United Nations

The General Assembly,

Having considered the item entitled "Implementation of the Declaration on the Granting of Independence to Colonial Countries and Peoples by the specialized agencies and the international institutions associated with the United Nations",

Having also considered the reports submitted on the item by the Secretary-General and the Chairman of the Special Committee on the Situation with regard to the Implementation of the Declaration on the Granting of Independence to Colonial Countries and Peoples,

Having examined the chapter of the report of the Special Committee relating to the item,

Recalling its resolutions 1514(XV) of 14 December 1960 and 1541(XV) of 15 December 1960 and the resolutions of the Special Committee, as well as other relevant resolutions and decisions, including in particular Economic and Social Council resolution 1998/38 of 30 July 1998,

Bearing in mind the relevant provisions of the final documents of the successive Conferences of Heads of State or Government of Non-Aligned Countries and of the resolutions adopted by the Assembly of Heads of State and Government of the Organization of African Unity, the South Pacific Forum and the Caribbean Community,

Conscious of the need to facilitate the implementation of the Declaration on the Granting of Independence to Colonial Countries and Peoples, contained in resolution 1514(XV),

Noting that the large majority of the remaining Non-Self-Governing Territories are small island Territories,

Welcoming the assistance extended to Non-Self-Governing Territories by certain specialized agencies and other organizations of the United Nations system, in particular the United Nations Development Programme,

Also welcoming the participation in the capacity of observer of those Non-Self-Governing Territories which are associate members of regional commissions in the world conferences in the economic and social sphere, and in the special session of the General Assembly on the review and appraisal of the implementation of the Programme of Action of the International Conference on Population and Development, held at Headquarters from 30 June to 2 July 1999,

Noting that only some specialized agencies and other organizations of the United Nations system have been involved in providing assistance to Non-Self-Governing Territories,

Stressing that, because the development options of the small island Non-Self-Governing Territories are limited, there are special challenges to planning for and implementing sustainable development and that those Territories will be constrained in meeting the challenges without the continued cooperation and assistance of the specialized agencies and other organizations of the United Nations system,

Stressing also the importance of securing the necessary resources for funding expanded assistance programmes for the peoples concerned and the need to enlist the support of all major funding institutions within the United Nations system in that regard,

Reaffirming the mandates of the specialized agencies and other organizations of the United Nations system to take all appropriate measures, within their respective spheres of competence, to ensure the full implementation of General Assembly resolution 1514(XV) and other relevant resolutions,

Expressing its appreciation to the Organization of African Unity, the South Pacific Forum, the Caribbean Community and other regional organizations for the continued cooperation and assistance they have extended to the specialized agencies and other organizations of the United Nations system in this regard,

Expressing its conviction that closer contacts and consultations between and among the specialized agencies and other organizations of the United Nations system and regional organizations help to facilitate the effective formulation of programmes of assistance to the peoples concerned,

Mindful of the imperative need to keep under continuous review the activities of the specialized agencies and other organizations of the United Nations system in the implementation of the various United Nations decisions relating to decolonization,

Bearing in mind the extremely fragile economies of the small island Non-Self-Governing Territories and their vulnerability to natural disasters, such as hurricanes, cyclones and sea-level rise, and recalling its relevant resolutions,

Recalling its resolution 53/62 of 3 December 1998 on the implementation of the Declaration by the specialized agencies and the international institutions associated with the United Nations,

1. *Takes note* of the reports of the Secretary-General and the Chairman of the Special Committee on the Situation with regard to the Implementation of the

Declaration on the Granting of Independence to Colonial Countries and Peoples;

2. *Recommends* that all States intensify their efforts in the specialized agencies and other organizations of the United Nations system to ensure the full and effective implementation of the Declaration on the Granting of Independence to Colonial Countries and Peoples, contained in General Assembly resolution 1514(XV), and other relevant resolutions of the United Nations;

3. *Reaffirms* that the specialized agencies and other organizations and institutions of the United Nations system should continue to be guided by the relevant resolutions of the United Nations in their efforts to contribute to the implementation of the Declaration and all other relevant General Assembly resolutions;

4. *Reaffirms also* that the recognition by the General Assembly, the Security Council and other United Nations organs of the legitimacy of the aspirations of the peoples of the Non-Self-Governing Territories to exercise their right to self-determination entails, as a corollary, the extension of all appropriate assistance to those peoples;

5. *Expresses its appreciation* to those specialized agencies and other organizations of the United Nations system that have continued to cooperate with the United Nations and the regional and subregional organizations in the implementation of General Assembly resolution 1514(XV) and other relevant resolutions of the United Nations, and requests all the specialized agencies and other organizations of the United Nations system to implement the relevant provisions of those resolutions;

6. *Requests* the specialized agencies and other organizations of the United Nations system and international and regional organizations to examine and review conditions in each Territory so as to take appropriate measures to accelerate progress in the economic and social sectors of the Territories;

7. *Urges* those specialized agencies and organizations of the United Nations system which have not yet provided assistance to Non-Self-Governing Territories to do so as soon as possible;

8. *Requests* the specialized agencies and other organizations and institutions of the United Nations system and regional organizations to strengthen existing measures of support and formulate appropriate programmes of assistance to the remaining Non-Self-Governing Territories, within the framework of their respective mandates, in order to accelerate progress in the economic and social sectors of those Territories;

9. *Requests* the specialized agencies and other organizations of the United Nations system concerned to provide information on:

(*a*) Environmental problems facing the Non-Self-Governing Territories;

(*b*) The impact of natural disasters, such as hurricanes and volcanoes, and other environmental problems, such as beach and coastal erosion and droughts, on those Territories;

(*c*) Ways and means to assist the Territories in fighting drug trafficking, money-laundering and other illegal and criminal activities;

(*d*) The illegal exploitation of the marine resources of the Territories and the need to utilize those resources for the benefit of the peoples of the Territories;

10. *Recommends* that the executive heads of the specialized agencies and other organizations of the United Nations system formulate, with the active cooperation of the regional organizations concerned, concrete proposals for the full implementation of the relevant resolutions of the United Nations and submit the proposals to their governing and legislative organs;

11. *Also recommends* that the specialized agencies and other organizations of the United Nations system continue to review at the regular meetings of their governing bodies the implementation of General Assembly resolution 1514(XV) and other relevant resolutions of the United Nations;

12. *Welcomes* the continuing initiative exercised by the United Nations Development Programme in maintaining close liaison among the specialized agencies and other organizations of the United Nations system and in providing assistance to the peoples of the Non-Self-Governing Territories;

13. *Encourages* Non-Self-Governing Territories to take steps to establish and/or strengthen disaster preparedness and management institutions and policies;

14. *Requests* the administering Powers concerned to facilitate the participation of appointed and elected representatives of Non-Self-Governing Territories in the relevant meetings and conferences of the specialized agencies and other organizations of the United Nations system so that the Territories may benefit from the related activities of those agencies and organizations;

15. *Recommends* that all Governments intensify their efforts in the specialized agencies and other organizations of the United Nations system of which they are members to accord priority to the question of providing assistance to the peoples of the Non-Self-Governing Territories;

16. *Requests* the Secretary-General to continue to assist the specialized agencies and other organizations of the United Nations system in working out appropriate measures for implementing the relevant resolutions of the United Nations and to prepare for submission to the relevant bodies, with the assistance of those agencies and organizations, a report on the action taken in implementation of the relevant resolutions, including the present resolution, since the circulation of his previous report;

17. *Welcomes* the adoption by the Economic Commission for Latin America and the Caribbean of resolution 574(XXVII), in which the Commission called for the necessary mechanisms to permit its associate members, including small island Non-Self-Governing Territories, to participate, subject to the rules of procedure of the General Assembly, in the special sessions of the Assembly to review and appraise the implementation of the programmes of action of those United Nations conferences in which the Territories originally participated in the capacity of observer, and in the work of the Economic and Social Council and its subsidiary bodies;

18. *Recalls* its resolution 53/189 of 15 December 1998, in which, inter alia, it called for the participation of associate members of regional economic commissions in the special session of the General Assembly for the review and appraisal of the implementation of the Programme of Action for the Sustainable Development of Small Island Developing States, subject to the

rules of procedure of the Assembly, and in the preparatory process thereof, in the same capacity of observer that held for their participation in the Global Conference on the Sustainable Development of Small Island Developing States, held at Bridgetown from 25 April to 6 May 1994;

19. *Commends* the Economic and Social Council for its debate and resolution on this question, and requests it to continue to consider, in consultation with the Special Committee, appropriate measures for coordination of the policies and activities of the specialized agencies and other organizations of the United Nations system in implementing the relevant resolutions of the General Assembly;

20. *Requests* the specialized agencies to report periodically to the Secretary-General on the implementation of the present resolution;

21. *Requests* the Secretary-General to transmit the present resolution to the governing bodies of the appropriate specialized agencies and international institutions associated with the United Nations so that those bodies may take the necessary measures to implement it, and also requests the Secretary-General to report to the General Assembly at its fifty-fifth session on the implementation of the present resolution;

22. *Requests* the Special Committee to continue to examine the question and to report thereon to the General Assembly at its fifty-fifth session.

RECORDED VOTE ON RESOLUTION 54/85:

In favour: Algeria, Angola, Antigua and Barbuda, Armenia, Australia, Azerbaijan, Bahamas, Bahrain, Bangladesh, Barbados, Belarus, Belize, Benin, Bhutan, Bolivia, Botswana, Brazil, Brunei Darussalam, Burkina Faso, Cambodia, Cameroon, Cape Verde, Chad, Chile, China, Colombia, Congo, Costa Rica, Côte d'Ivoire, Cuba, Democratic People's Republic of Korea, Djibouti, Dominica, Dominican Republic, Ecuador, Egypt, Eritrea, Ethiopia, Fiji, Gambia, Ghana, Grenada, Guyana, Haiti, India, Indonesia, Iran, Jamaica, Kenya, Kuwait, Lao People's Democratic Republic, Lebanon, Libyan Arab Jamahiriya, Madagascar, Malaysia, Maldives, Mali, Mauritius, Mexico, Mongolia, Mozambique, Myanmar, Namibia, Nepal, New Zealand, Nigeria, Oman, Pakistan, Panama, Papua New Guinea, Paraguay, Peru, Philippines, Qatar, Saint Lucia, Saint Vincent and the Grenadines, Samoa, Saudi Arabia, Senegal, Seychelles, Sierra Leone, Singapore, Solomon Islands, South Africa, Sri Lanka, Sudan, Suriname, Swaziland, Syrian Arab Republic, Tajikistan, Thailand, Togo, Trinidad and Tobago, Tunisia, United Arab Emirates, United Republic of Tanzania, Uruguay, Venezuela, Viet Nam, Zambia, Zimbabwe.

Against: None.

Abstaining: Albania, Andorra, Argentina, Austria, Belgium, Bulgaria, Canada, Croatia, Cyprus, Czech Republic, Denmark, Estonia, Finland, France, Georgia, Germany, Greece, Guatemala, Hungary, Iceland, Ireland, Israel, Italy, Japan, Kazakhstan, Latvia, Liechtenstein, Lithuania, Luxembourg, Malta, Marshall Islands, Micronesia, Monaco, Netherlands, Norway, Poland, Portugal, Republic of Korea, Republic of Moldova, Romania, Russian Federation, San Marino, Slovakia, Slovenia, Spain, Sweden, The former Yugoslav Republic of Macedonia, Turkey, Ukraine, United Kingdom, United States, Uzbekistan.

Military activities and arrangements in colonial countries

The Special Committee on decolonization considered military activities and arrangements by colonial Powers in Territories under their administration. It had before it working papers containing, among other things, information on military activities and arrangements in Bermuda, Guam and the United States Virgin Islands [A/AC.109/1999/3, A/AC.109/1999/14, A/AC.109/1999/7 & Corr.1].

GENERAL ASSEMBLY ACTION

In December, the General Assembly, on the recommendation of the Fourth Committee [A/54/580], adopted **decision 54/421** by recorded vote (99-53-1) [agenda items 93 & 18].

Military activities and arrangements by colonial Powers in Territories under their administration

At its 71st plenary meeting, on 6 December 1999, the General Assembly, on the recommendation of the Special Political and Decolonization Committee (Fourth Committee), adopted the following text by a recorded vote of 99 to 53, with 1 abstention:

"1. The General Assembly, having considered the chapter of the report of the Special Committee on the Situation with regard to the Implementation of the Declaration on the Granting of Independence to Colonial Countries and Peoples relating to an item on the agenda of the Special Committee entitled 'Military activities and arrangements by colonial Powers in Territories under their administration', and recalling its resolution 1514(XV) of 14 December 1960 and all other relevant resolutions and decisions of the United Nations relating to military activities in colonial and Non-Self-Governing Territories, reaffirms its strong conviction that military bases and installations in the Territories concerned could constitute an obstacle to the exercise by the people of those Territories of their right to self-determination, and reiterates its strong views that existing bases and installations, which are impeding the implementation of the Declaration on the Granting of Independence to Colonial Countries and Peoples, should be withdrawn.

"2. Aware of the presence of such bases and installations in some of those Territories, the General Assembly urges the administering Powers concerned to continue to take all necessary measures not to involve those Territories in any offensive acts or interference against other States.

"3. The General Assembly reiterates its concern that military activities and arrangements by colonial Powers in Territories under their administration might run counter to the rights and interests of the colonial peoples concerned, especially their right to self-determination and independence. The Assembly once again calls upon the administering Powers concerned to terminate such activities and to eliminate such military bases in compliance with its relevant resolutions.

"4. The General Assembly reiterates that the colonial and Non-Self-Governing Territories and areas adjacent thereto should not be used for nuclear testing, dumping of nuclear wastes or deployment of nuclear or other weapons of mass destruction.

"5. The General Assembly deplores the continued alienation of land in colonial and Non-Self-Governing Territories, particularly in the small island Territories of the Pacific and Caribbean regions, for military installations. The large-scale utilization of local resources for this purpose could adversely affect the economic development of the Territories concerned.

"6. The General Assembly takes note of the decision of some of the administering Powers to close or downsize some of those military bases in the Non-Self-Governing Territories.

"7. The General Assembly requests the Secretary-General to continue to inform world public opinion of those military activities and arrangements in colonial and Non-Self-Governing Territories which constitute an obstacle to the implementation of the Declaration on the Granting of Independence to Colonial Countries and Peoples.

"8. The General Assembly requests the Special Committee on the Situation with regard to the Implementation of the Declaration on the Granting of Independence to Colonial Countries and Peoples to continue to examine this question and to report thereon to the Assembly at its fifty-fifth session."

RECORDED VOTE ON DECISION 54/421:

In favour: Algeria, Angola, Antigua and Barbuda, Argentina, Bahamas, Bahrain, Bangladesh, Barbados, Belize, Benin, Bhutan, Bolivia, Botswana, Brazil, Brunei Darussalam, Burkina Faso, Cambodia, Cameroon, Cape Verde, Chad, Chile, China, Colombia, Congo, Costa Rica, Côte d'Ivoire, Cuba, Cyprus, Democratic People's Republic of Korea, Djibouti, Dominica, Dominican Republic, Ecuador, Egypt, El Salvador, Eritrea, Ethiopia, Fiji, Gambia, Ghana, Grenada, Guinea, Guyana, Haiti, India, Indonesia, Iran, Jamaica, Kenya, Kuwait, Lao People's Democratic Republic, Lebanon, Libyan Arab Jamahiriya, Malaysia, Maldives, Mali, Mauritius, Mexico, Mongolia, Mozambique, Myanmar, Namibia, Nepal, Nigeria, Oman, Pakistan, Panama, Papua New Guinea, Paraguay, Peru, Philippines, Qatar, Saint Lucia, Saint Vincent and the Grenadines, Samoa, Saudi Arabia, Senegal, Seychelles, Sierra Leone, Singapore, Solomon Islands, South Africa, Sri Lanka, Sudan, Suriname, Swaziland, Syrian Arab Republic, Thailand, Togo, Trinidad and Tobago, Tunisia, United Arab Emirates, United Republic of Tanzania, Uruguay, Venezuela, Viet Nam, Yemen, Zambia, Zimbabwe.

Against: Albania, Andorra, Armenia, Australia, Austria, Belarus, Belgium, Bulgaria, Canada, Croatia, Czech Republic, Denmark, Estonia, Finland, France, Georgia, Germany, Greece, Guatemala, Hungary, Iceland, Ireland, Israel, Italy, Japan, Kazakhstan, Latvia, Liechtenstein, Lithuania, Luxembourg, Malta, Marshall Islands, Monaco, Netherlands, New Zealand, Norway, Poland, Portugal, Republic of Korea, Republic of Moldova, Romania, Russian Federation, San Marino, Slovakia, Slovenia, Spain, Sweden, The former Yugoslav Republic of Macedonia, Turkey, Ukraine, United Kingdom, United States, Uzbekistan.

Abstaining: Micronesia.

Economic and other activities affecting the interests of NSGTs

The Special Committee on decolonization continued consideration of economic and other activities that affected the interests of the peoples of NSGTs. It had before it working papers prepared by the Secretariat containing, among other things, information on economic conditions, with particular reference to foreign economic activities, in Bermuda, the Cayman Islands, the United States Virgin Islands and the British Virgin Islands [A/AC.109/1999/3, A/AC.109/1999/4, A/AC.109/1999/7 & Corr.1, A/AC.109/1999/9].

GENERAL ASSEMBLY ACTION

On 6 December [meeting 71], the General Assembly, on the recommendation of the Fourth Committee [A/54/580], adopted **resolution 54/84** by recorded vote (153-2-5) [agenda items 93 & 18].

Economic and other activities which affect the interests of the peoples of the Non-Self-Governing Territories

The General Assembly,

Having considered the item entitled "Economic and other activities which affect the interests of the peoples of the Non-Self-Governing Territories",

Having examined the chapter of the report of the Special Committee on the Situation with regard to the Implementation of the Declaration on the Granting of Independence to Colonial Countries and Peoples relating to the item,

Recalling its resolution 1514(XV) of 14 December 1960 and all its other relevant resolutions, including, in particular, resolution 46/181 of 19 December 1991,

Reaffirming the solemn obligation of the administering Powers under the Charter of the United Nations to promote the political, economic, social and educational advancement of the inhabitants of the Territories under their administration and to protect the human and natural resources of those Territories against abuses,

Reaffirming also that any economic or other activity that has a negative impact on the interests of the peoples of the Non-Self-Governing Territories and on the exercise of their right to self-determination in conformity with the Charter of the United Nations and General Assembly resolution 1514(XV) is contrary to the purposes and principles of the Charter,

Reaffirming further that the natural resources are the heritage of the peoples of the Non-Self-Governing Territories, including the indigenous populations,

Aware of the special circumstances of the geographical location, size and economic conditions of each Territory, and bearing in mind the need to promote the economic stability, diversification and strengthening of the economy of each Territory,

Conscious of the particular vulnerability of the small Territories to natural disasters and environmental degradation,

Conscious also that foreign economic investment, when done in collaboration with the peoples of the Non-Self-Governing Territories and in accordance with their wishes, could make a valid contribution to the socio-economic development of the Territories and could also make a valid contribution to the exercise of their right to self-determination,

Concerned about any activities aimed at exploiting the natural and human resources of the Non-Self-Governing Territories to the detriment of the interests of the inhabitants of those Territories,

Bearing in mind the relevant provisions of the final documents of the successive Conferences of Heads of State or Government of Non-Aligned Countries and of the resolutions adopted by the Assembly of Heads of State and Government of the Organization of African Unity, the South Pacific Forum and the Caribbean Community,

1. *Reaffirms* the right of peoples of Non-Self-Governing Territories to self-determination in conformity with the Charter of the United Nations and with General Assembly resolution 1514(XV), containing the Declaration on the Granting of Independence to Colonial Countries and Peoples, as well as their right to the enjoyment of their natural resources and their right to dispose of those resources in their best interest;

2. *Affirms* the value of foreign economic investment undertaken in collaboration with the peoples of the Non-Self-Governing Territories and in accordance with their wishes in order to make a valid contribution to the socio-economic development of the Territories;

3. *Reaffirms* the responsibility of the administering Powers under the Charter to promote the political, economic, social and educational advancement of the Non-Self-Governing Territories, and reaffirms the legitimate rights of their peoples over their natural resources;

4. *Reaffirms its concern* about any activities aimed at the exploitation of the natural resources that are the heritage of the peoples of the Non-Self-Governing Territories, including the indigenous populations, in the Caribbean, the Pacific and other regions, as well as their human resources, to the detriment of their interests, and in such a way as to deprive them of their right to dispose of those resources;

5. *Affirms* the need to avoid any economic or other activities that adversely affect the interests of the peoples of the Non-Self-Governing Territories;

6. *Calls once again upon* all Governments that have not yet done so to take, in accordance with the relevant provisions of General Assembly resolution 2621(XXV) of 12 October 1970, legislative, administrative or other measures in respect of their nationals and the bodies corporate under their jurisdiction that own and operate enterprises in the Non-Self-Governing Territories that are detrimental to the interests of the inhabitants of those Territories, in order to put an end to such enterprises;

7. *Reiterates* that the damaging exploitation and plundering of the marine and other natural resources of the Non-Self-Governing Territories, in violation of the relevant resolutions of the United Nations, is a threat to the integrity and prosperity of those Territories;

8. *Invites* all Governments and organizations of the United Nations system to take all possible measures to ensure that the permanent sovereignty of the peoples of the Non-Self-Governing Territories over their natural resources is fully respected and safeguarded;

9. *Urges* the administering Powers concerned to take effective measures to safeguard and guarantee the inalienable right of the peoples of the Non-Self-Governing Territories to their natural resources and to establish and maintain control over the future development of those resources, and requests the administering Powers to take all necessary steps to protect the property rights of the peoples of those Territories;

10. *Calls upon* the administering Powers concerned to ensure that no discriminatory working conditions prevail in the Territories under their administration and to promote in each Territory a fair system of wages applicable to all the inhabitants without any discrimination;

11. *Requests* the Secretary-General to continue, through all means at his disposal, to inform world public opinion of any activity that affects the exercise of the right of the peoples of the Non-Self-Governing Territories to self-determination in conformity with the Charter and General Assembly resolution 1514(XV);

12. *Appeals* to the mass media, trade unions and non-governmental organizations, as well as individuals, to continue their efforts to promote the economic well-being of the peoples of the Non-Self-Governing Territories;

13. *Decides* to follow the situation in the Non-Self-Governing Territories so as to ensure that all economic activities in those Territories are aimed at strengthening and diversifying their economies in the interest of their peoples, including the indigenous populations, and at promoting the economic and financial viability of those Territories;

14. *Requests* the Special Committee on the Situation with regard to the Implementation of the Declaration on the Granting of Independence to Colonial Countries and Peoples to continue to examine this question and to report thereon to the General Assembly at its fifty-fifth session.

RECORDED VOTE ON RESOLUTION 54/84:

In favour: Albania, Algeria, Andorra, Angola, Antigua and Barbuda, Argentina, Armenia, Australia, Austria, Azerbaijan, Bahamas, Bahrain, Bangladesh, Barbados, Belarus, Belgium, Belize, Benin, Bhutan, Bolivia, Botswana, Brazil, Brunei Darussalam, Bulgaria, Burkina Faso, Cambodia, Cameroon, Canada, Cape Verde, Chad, Chile, China, Colombia, Congo, Costa Rica, Côte d'Ivoire, Croatia, Cuba, Cyprus, Czech Republic, Democratic People's Republic of Korea, Denmark, Djibouti, Dominica, Dominican Republic, Ecuador, Egypt, El Salvador, Equatorial Guinea, Eritrea, Estonia, Ethiopia, Fiji, Finland, Gabon, Gambia, Germany, Ghana, Greece, Grenada, Guatemala, Guinea, Guyana, Haiti, Hungary, Iceland, India, Indonesia, Iran, Ireland, Italy, Jamaica, Japan, Jordan, Kazakhstan, Kenya, Kuwait, Lao People's Democratic Republic, Latvia, Lebanon, Libyan Arab Jamahiriya, Liechtenstein, Lithuania, Luxembourg, Madagascar, Malaysia, Maldives, Mali, Malta, Marshall Islands, Mauritius, Mexico, Mongolia, Mozambique, Myanmar, Namibia, Nepal, Netherlands, New Zealand, Nicaragua, Nigeria, Norway, Oman, Pakistan, Panama, Papua New Guinea, Paraguay, Peru, Philippines, Poland, Portugal, Qatar, Republic of Korea, Republic of Moldova, Romania, Russian Federation, Saint Lucia, Saint Vincent and the Grenadines, Samoa, San Marino, Saudi Arabia, Senegal, Seychelles, Sierra Leone, Singapore, Slovakia, Slovenia, Solomon Islands, South Africa, Spain, Sri Lanka, Sudan, Suriname, Swaziland, Sweden, Syrian Arab Republic, Tajikistan, Thailand, The former Yugoslav Republic of Macedonia, Togo, Trinidad and Tobago, Tunisia, Turkey, Ukraine, United Arab Emirates, United Republic of Tanzania, Uruguay, Uzbekistan, Venezuela, Viet Nam, Yemen, Zambia, Zimbabwe.

Against: Israel, United States.

Abstaining: France, Georgia, Micronesia, Monaco, United Kingdom.

Dissemination of information

In June [A/54/23], the Special Committee on decolonization held consultations with the UN Departments of Public Information (DPI) and Political Affairs on the dissemination of information on decolonization. Following consideration of a DPI report on its publicity activities on decolonization [A/AC.109/1999/19], the Committee, in July, approved a draft resolution for adoption by the General Assembly (see below).

In May, the Special Committee observed the Week of Solidarity with the Peoples of All Colonial Territories Fighting for Freedom, Independence and Human Rights, as had been done annually since 1972.

GENERAL ASSEMBLY ACTION

On 6 December [meeting 71], the General Assembly, on the recommendation of the Special Committee [A/54/23], adopted **resolution 54/92** by recorded vote (149-2-3) [agenda item 18].

Dissemination of information on decolonization

The General Assembly,

Having examined the chapter of the report of the Special Committee on the Situation with regard to the Implementation of the Declaration on the Granting of Independence to Colonial Countries and Peoples relating to the dissemination of information on decolonization and publicity for the work of the United Nations in the field of decolonization,

Recalling its resolution 1514(XV) of 14 December 1960, containing the Declaration on the Granting of Independence to Colonial Countries and Peoples, and other resolutions and decisions of the United Nations concerning the dissemination of information on decolonization, in particular General Assembly resolution 53/69 of 3 December 1998,

Recognizing the need for flexible, practical and innovative approaches towards reviewing the options of self-determination for the peoples of the Non-Self-Governing Territories with a view to achieving complete decolonization by 2000,

Reiterating the importance of dissemination of information as an instrument for furthering the aims of the Declaration, and mindful of the role of world public opinion in effectively assisting the peoples of the Non-Self-Governing Territories to achieve self-determination,

Recognizing the role played by the administering Powers in transmitting information to the Secretary-General in accordance with the terms of Article 73 *e* of the Charter of the United Nations,

Aware of the role of non-governmental organizations in the dissemination of information on decolonization,

1. *Approves* the activities in the field of dissemination of information on decolonization undertaken by the Department of Public Information and the Department of Political Affairs of the Secretariat;

2. *Considers it important* to continue its efforts to ensure the widest possible dissemination of information on decolonization, with particular emphasis on the options of self-determination available for the peoples of the Non-Self-Governing Territories;

3. *Requests* the Department of Political Affairs and the Department of Public Information to take into account the suggestions of the Special Committee on the Situation with regard to the Implementation of the Declaration on the Granting of Independence to Colonial Countries and Peoples to continue their efforts to take measures through all the media available, including publications, radio and television, as well as the Internet, to give publicity to the work of the United Nations in the field of decolonization and, inter alia:

(a) To continue to collect, prepare and disseminate, particularly to the Territories, basic material on the issue of self-determination of the peoples of the Non-Self-Governing Territories;

(b) To seek the full cooperation of the administering Powers in the discharge of the tasks referred to above;

(c) To maintain a working relationship with the appropriate regional and intergovernmental organizations, particularly in the Pacific and Caribbean regions, by holding periodic consultations and exchanging information;

(d) To encourage the involvement of non-governmental organizations in the dissemination of information on decolonization;

(e) To report to the Special Committee on measures taken in the implementation of the present resolution;

4. *Requests* all States, including the administering Powers, to continue to extend their cooperation in the dissemination of information referred to in paragraph 2 above;

5. *Requests* the Special Committee to follow the implementation of the present resolution and to report thereon to the General Assembly at its fifty-fifth session.

RECORDED VOTE ON RESOLUTION 54/92:

In favour: Albania, Algeria, Andorra, Angola, Antigua and Barbuda, Argentina, Armenia, Australia, Austria, Azerbaijan, Bahamas, Bahrain, Bangladesh, Barbados, Belarus, Belgium, Belize, Benin, Bhutan, Bolivia, Botswana, Brazil, Brunei Darussalam, Bulgaria, Burkina Faso, Cambodia, Cameroon, Canada, Cape Verde, Chad, Chile, China, Colombia, Congo, Côte d'Ivoire, Croatia, Cuba, Cyprus, Czech Republic, Democratic People's Republic of Korea, Denmark, Djibouti, Dominica, Dominican Republic, Ecuador, Egypt, El Salvador, Equatorial Guinea, Eritrea, Estonia, Ethiopia, Fiji, Finland, Gabon, Gambia, Georgia, Germany, Ghana, Greece, Grenada, Guatemala, Guinea, Guyana, Haiti, Hungary, Iceland, India, Indonesia, Iran, Ireland, Italy, Jamaica, Japan, Kazakhstan, Kenya, Kuwait, Lao People's Democratic Republic, Latvia, Lebanon, Libyan Arab Jamahiriya, Liechtenstein, Lithuania, Luxembourg, Madagascar, Malaysia, Maldives, Mali, Malta, Marshall Islands, Mauritius, Mexico, Mongolia, Mozambique, Myanmar, Namibia, Nepal, Netherlands, New Zealand, Nicaragua, Norway, Oman, Pakistan, Panama, Papua New Guinea, Paraguay, Peru, Philippines, Poland, Portugal, Qatar, Republic of Korea, Republic of Moldova, Romania, Russian Federation, Saint Lucia, Saint Vincent and the Grenadines, Samoa, San Marino, Saudi Arabia, Senegal, Sierra Leone, Singapore, Slovakia, Slovenia, Solomon Islands, South Africa, Spain, Sri Lanka, Sudan, Suriname, Swaziland, Sweden, Syrian Arab Republic, Tajikistan, Thailand, The former Yugoslav Republic of Macedonia, Togo, Trinidad and Tobago, Tunisia, Turkey, Ukraine, United Arab Emirates, United Republic of Tanzania, Uruguay, Venezuela, Viet Nam, Yemen, Zambia, Zimbabwe.

Against: United Kingdom, United States.

Abstaining: France, Israel, Monaco.

The United Kingdom stated that it viewed the obligation that the text placed on the Secretariat to publicize decolonization issues as a wholly unwarranted drain on the United Nations scarce resources.

Information on territories

In response to General Assembly resolution 53/60 [YUN 1998, p. 569], the Secretary-General submitted a September report on information received on economic, social and educational conditions in NSGTs, under article 73 *e* of the UN Charter [A/54/343]. The information covered the years from 1997 to 1999.

GENERAL ASSEMBLY ACTION

On 6 December [meeting 71], the General Assembly, on the recommendation of the Fourth Committee [A/54/579], adopted **resolution 54/83** by recorded vote (155-0-6) [agenda item 92].

Information from Non-Self-Governing Territories transmitted under Article 73 *e* of the Charter of the United Nations

The General Assembly,

Having examined the chapter of the report of the Special Committee on the Situation with regard to the Implementation of the Declaration on the Granting of Independence to Colonial Countries and Peoples relating to the information from Non-Self-Governing Territories transmitted under Article 73 *e* of the Charter of the United Nations and the action taken by the Special Committee in respect of that information,

Having also examined the report of the Secretary-General,

Recalling its resolution 1970(XVIII) of 16 December 1963, in which it requested the Special Committee to study the information transmitted to the Secretary-General in accordance with Article 73 *e* of the Charter and to take such information fully into account in examining the situation with regard to the implementation of the Declaration on the Granting of Independence to Colonial Countries and Peoples, contained in General Assembly resolution 1514(XV) of 14 December 1960,

Recalling also its resolution 53/60 of 3 December 1998, in which it requested the Special Committee to continue to discharge the functions entrusted to it under resolution 1970(XVIII),

Stressing the importance of timely transmission by the administering Powers of adequate information under Article 73 *e* of the Charter, in particular in relation to the preparation by the Secretariat of the working papers on the Territories concerned,

1. *Approves* the chapter of the report of the Special Committee on the Situation with regard to the Implementation of the Declaration on the Granting of Independence to Colonial Countries and Peoples relating to the information from Non-Self-Governing Territories transmitted under Article 73 *e* of the Charter of the United Nations;

2. *Reaffirms* that, in the absence of a decision by the General Assembly itself that a Non-Self-Governing Territory has attained a full measure of self-government in terms of Chapter XI of the Charter, the administering Power concerned should continue to transmit information under Article 73 *e* of the Charter with respect to that Territory;

3. *Requests* the administering Powers concerned to transmit or continue to transmit to the Secretary-General the information prescribed in Article 73 *e* of the Charter, as well as the fullest possible information on political and constitutional developments in the Territories concerned, within a maximum period of six months following the expiration of the administrative year in those Territories;

4. *Requests* the Secretary-General to continue to ensure that adequate information is drawn from all available published sources in connection with the preparation of the working papers relating to the Territories concerned;

5. *Requests* the Special Committee to continue to discharge the functions entrusted to it under resolution 1970(XVIII), in accordance with established procedures, and to report thereon to the General Assembly at its fifty-fifth session.

RECORDED VOTE ON RESOLUTION 54/83:

In favour: Albania, Algeria, Andorra, Angola, Antigua and Barbuda, Argentina, Armenia, Australia, Austria, Azerbaijan, Bahamas, Bahrain, Bangladesh, Barbados, Belarus, Belgium, Belize, Benin, Bhutan, Bolivia, Botswana, Brazil, Brunei Darussalam, Bulgaria, Burkina Faso, Cambodia, Cameroon, Canada, Cape Verde, Chad, Chile, China, Colombia, Congo, Costa Rica, Côte d'Ivoire, Croatia, Cuba, Cyprus, Czech Republic, Democratic People's Republic of Korea, Denmark, Djibouti, Dominica, Dominican Republic, Ecuador, Egypt, El Salvador, Equatorial Guinea, Eritrea, Estonia, Ethiopia, Fiji, Finland, Gabon, Gambia, Georgia, Germany, Ghana, Greece, Grenada, Guatemala, Guinea, Guyana, Haiti, Hungary, Iceland, India, Indonesia, Iran, Ireland, Italy, Jamaica, Japan, Jordan, Kazakhstan, Kenya, Kuwait, Lao People's Democratic Republic, Latvia, Lebanon, Libyan Arab Jamahiriya, Liechtenstein, Lithuania, Luxembourg, Madagascar, Malaysia, Maldives, Mali, Malta, Marshall Islands, Mauritius, Mexico, Mongolia, Morocco, Mozambique, Myanmar, Namibia, Nepal, Netherlands, New Zealand, Nicaragua, Nigeria, Norway, Oman, Pakistan, Panama, Papua New Guinea, Paraguay, Peru, Philippines, Poland, Portugal, Qatar, Republic of Korea, Republic of Moldova, Romania, Russian Federation, Saint Lucia, Saint Vincent and the Grenadines, Samoa, San Marino, Saudi Arabia, Senegal, Seychelles, Sierra Leone, Singapore, Slovakia, Slovenia, Solomon Islands, South Africa, Spain, Sri Lanka, Sudan, Suriname, Swaziland, Sweden, Syrian Arab Republic, Tajikistan, Thailand, The former Yugoslav Republic of Macedonia, Togo, Trinidad and Tobago, Tunisia, Turkey, Ukraine, United Arab Emirates, United Republic of Tanzania, Uruguay, Uzbekistan, Venezuela, Viet Nam, Yemen, Zambia, Zimbabwe.

Against: None.

Abstaining: France, Israel, Micronesia, Monaco, United Kingdom, United States.

Study and training

In response to General Assembly resolution 53/63 [YUN 1998, p. 569], the Secretary-General reported on offers by Member States of study and training facilities for inhabitants of NSGTs during the period from 7 August 1998 to 12 August 1999 [A/54/267]. Over the years, 47 Member States and one non-member State had made scholarship and training offers. During the reporting period, Austria, Finland and the United Kingdom informed the Secretary-General of their offers.

GENERAL ASSEMBLY ACTION

On 6 December [meeting 71], the General Assembly, on the recommendation of the Fourth Committee [A/54/582], adopted **resolution 54/86** without vote [agenda item 95].

Offers by Member States of study and training facilities for inhabitants of Non-Self-Governing Territories

The General Assembly,

Recalling its resolution 53/63 of 3 December 1998,

Having examined the report of the Secretary-General on offers by Member States of study and training facilities for inhabitants of Non-Self-Governing Territories, prepared pursuant to its resolution 845(IX) of 22 November 1954,

Conscious of the importance of promoting the educational advancement of the inhabitants of Non-Self-Governing Territories,

Strongly convinced that the continuation and expansion of offers of scholarships is essential in order to meet the increasing need of students from Non-Self-Governing Territories for educational and training assistance, and considering that students in those Territories should be encouraged to avail themselves of such offers,

1. *Takes note* of the report of the Secretary-General;

2. *Expresses its appreciation* to those Member States that have made scholarships available to the inhabitants of Non-Self-Governing Territories;

3. *Invites* all States to make or continue to make generous offers of study and training facilities to the inhabitants of those Territories that have not yet attained self-government or independence and, wherever possible, to provide travel funds to prospective students;

4. *Urges* the administering Powers to take effective measures to ensure the widespread and continuous dissemination in the Territories under their administration of information relating to offers of study and training facilities made by States and to provide all the necessary facilities to enable students to avail themselves of such offers;

5. *Requests* the Secretary-General to report to the General Assembly at its fifty-fifth session on the implementation of the present resolution;

6. *Draws the attention* of the Special Committee on the Situation with regard to the Implementation of the Declaration on the Granting of Independence to Colonial Countries and Peoples to the present resolution.

Visiting missions

The Special Committee on decolonization considered the question of sending visiting missions to Territories, particularly the specific Territories referred to it. In 1999, at the invitation of France, a mission visited New Caledonia from 23 to 28 August. In a report submitted by Papua New Guinea [A/54/921], the mission informed the Secretary-General of the results of its visit.

On 9 July [A/54/23], the Special Committee stressed the need to dispatch periodic visiting missions to NSGTs, called for the continued cooperation of the administering Powers and asked them to consider new approaches in the Committee's work. It asked its Chairman to enter into consultations with the administering Power of Guam (United States) to facilitate a mission there.

Puerto Rico

In accordance with the Special Committee's decision of 11 August 1998 concerning the self-determination and independence of Puerto Rico [YUN 1998, p. 570], the Committee's Rapporteur, in a June report [A/AC.109/1999/L.13], described recent constitutional and political developments in Puerto Rico, UN action on the question and the views of the parties concerned.

Based on its usual practice, the Committee acceded to requests for hearings from representatives of 21 organizations, who presented their views on 6 July. Subsequently, the Committee, by a roll-call vote (12-0-5), adopted a resolution that reaffirmed the inalienable right of Puerto Rico to self-determination and independence; expressed the hope that the United States would assume its responsibility to expedite a process to allow the full exercise of that right; and asked the Rapporteur to report in 2000 on the resolution's implementation.

Territories under review

East Timor

The Special Committee on decolonization in 1999 continued to consider the political status of the Territory of East Timor [A/54/23].

By resolution 32/34 [YUN 1977, p. 890], the General Assembly had rejected the claim, reaffirmed by Indonesia in 1977 [ibid., p. 868], that East Timor had been integrated into Indonesia, as the people of the Territory had not been able to exercise freely their right to self-determination and independence. In resolution 37/30 [YUN 1982, p. 1349], the Assembly had requested the Secretary-General to initiate consultations with the parties concerned to explore ways to achieve a compromise settlement. The Secretary-General, through his good offices, had since conducted tripartite talks involving Indonesia, Portugal (the administering Power) and East Timorese representatives. In October 1998, he had proposed to Indonesia and Portugal a draft constitutional framework for autonomy for East Timor within Indonesia, which did not prejudge the shape of a final settlement [YUN 1998, p. 572]. Negotiations between the two sides on that framework took place through the tripartite senior-officials meeting process.

The Special Committee examined a Secretariat working paper on political developments, the human rights situation, and economic, social and educational conditions in the Territory [A/AC.109/1999/10 & Corr.1]. Regarding political developments, on 27 January, prior to scheduled UN-sponsored talks between Indonesia and Portugal, Indonesia stated that it would be willing to grant East Timor independence if the East Timorese rejected an offer of autonomy. On the same day, the Secretary-General welcomed a report that Xanana Gusmão, the East Timorese resistance and pro-independence leader, imprisoned since 1992, would be transferred to residential detention. Following talks between the Secretary-General's Personal Representative for East Timor and the negotiator from Portugal, Portugal and Indonesia, on 11 March, agreed to a UN-supervised ballot involving Timorese living in the Territory and abroad (an estimated 600,000 of East Timor's population of 800,000 were eligible to vote, along with 20,000 to 30,000 living abroad). According to press reports, on 5 April, Mr. Gusmão ordered his supporters to take up arms, thus ending a four-month ceasefire, reportedly in reaction to the alleged killing of 17 civilians by Indonesian troops on that same day. Also on 5 April, two members of a six-person UN team that had been visiting East Timor to prepare for a consultative process on East Timor's future, met with the Portuguese Foreign Ministry official responsible for East Timor, as well as with the head of the International Organization for Migration, the representative of the National Resistance Council of Timor and other Timorese figures. In the meantime, a heated exchange had escalated between pro-integrationists and pro-independence supporters, resulting in numerous killings in and around Dili. A renewed ceasefire, signed in Dili on 21 April, called on all parties to cease the violence, to respect peacemaking efforts by the United Nations and the local Roman Catholic church, and to set up a peace and stability commission. The Governments of Indonesia and Portugal, on 5 May in New York, signed an Agreement entrusting the Secretary-General with the organization and conduct of a popular consultation to ascertain whether the East Timorese people would accept or reject a proposed constitutional framework providing for special autonomy for East Timor under Indonesian rule. The two parties also signed two supplementary Agreements with the United Nations on the modalities for the popular consultation of the East Timorese through a direct ballot and on security arrangements. The full texts of the Agreements were contained in a May report of the Secretary-General [A/53/951-S/1999/513].

A later Secretariat working paper [A/AC.109/2000/12] stated that the registration period for the vote, which was scheduled for 30 August, was marked by violence and intimidation carried out by pro-autonomy militias. Following the vote, in which 78.5 per cent voted to reject and 21.5 per cent voted to accept the proposed special autonomy, there was an eruption of violence, in which pro-integration militias and members of the Indonesian military and the police ransacked towns and forcibly displaced hundreds of thousands of East Timorese. Steps towards reconciliation were facilitated by the strong will on the part of the Government of Indonesia and the National Council of Timorese Resistance to establish good relations. In addition, the Special Representative of the Secretary-General and Transitional Administrator in East Timor, Sergio Vieira de Mello, visited Jakarta in December and met with the President of Indonesia, Abdurrahman Wahid, and other senior officials.

(See PART ONE, Chapter IV, for Security Council action, and PART TWO, Chapter III, for the Commission on Human Rights special session and action by the UN International Commission of Inquiry.)

General Assembly consideration. Portugal, on 2 June [A/54/121], said that since it continued to be de facto deprived from exercising its responsibilities for the administration of East Timor, it could not provide the information required under Article 73 *e* of the UN Charter. It drew the Secretary-General's attention to the Agreements of 5 May and provided information on the situation in East Timor and on the reaction of the international community to developments there.

The Secretary-General, in a 13 December progress report [A/54/654], described negotiations that led to the signing of the 5 May Agreements, the establishment of the United Nations Mission in East Timor, security concerns, the consultation process, post-consultation violence, the establishment of a multinational force and the establishment of the United Nations Transitional Administration in East Timor (see PART ONE, Chapter IV).

GENERAL ASSEMBLY ACTION

A report of the Fourth Committee [A/54/583] stated that on 17 September, the General Assembly, on the recommendation of the General Committee, decided to include in the agenda of its fifty-fourth session the item entitled "Question of East Timor" and to consider it in plenary, on the understanding that bodies and individuals having an interest in the question would be heard in the Committee.

The Assembly, by **decision 54/422** of 6 December, took note of the Committee's report.

On 17 December [meeting 84], the Assembly adopted **resolution 54/194** [draft: A/54/L.73] without vote [agenda item 96].

Question of East Timor

The General Assembly,

Recalling all relevant General Assembly resolutions on the question of East Timor,

Recalling also the relevant Security Council resolutions and decisions on the question of East Timor, in particular resolutions 1236(1999) of 7 May 1999, 1246(1999) of 11 June 1999, 1262(1999) of 27 August 1999, 1264(1999) of 15 September 1999 and 1272(1999) of 25 October 1999,

Recalling further the Agreement of 5 May 1999 between Indonesia and Portugal on the question of East Timor and the Agreements between the United Nations, Indonesia and Portugal of the same date regarding the modalities for the popular consultation of the East Timorese people through a direct ballot and security arrangements,

1. *Takes note* of the report of the Secretary-General;

2. *Welcomes* the successful conduct of the popular consultation of the East Timorese people on 30 August 1999, takes note of its outcome, which began a process of transition to independence under the authority of the United Nations, and welcomes the decision of the Indonesian People's Consultative Assembly on 19 October 1999 concerning East Timor in accordance with article 6 of the Agreement of 5 May 1999;

3. *Decides* to conclude its consideration of the item entitled "Question of East Timor" and to include in the provisional agenda of its fifty-fifth session a new item entitled "The situation in East Timor during its transition to independence".

Falkland Islands (Malvinas)

In July, during its consideration of the question of the Falkland Islands (Malvinas), the Special Committee on decolonization examined a Secretariat working paper on constitutional and political developments and the economic, social and educational conditions in the Territory [A/AC.109/1999/12]. The paper reported that, in his New Year's message, Prime Minister Tony Blair of the United Kingdom said that he had told Argentina's President, Carlos Menem, that the sovereignty of the islands was not for negotiation, nor was the right of the Falkland Islanders to determine their own future. Argentina's Ministry of Foreign Affairs, in a 2 January press communiqué, expressed its unwavering determination to regain, through diplomatic negotiations, the exercise of sovereignty over the Malvinas Islands, and reiterated its readiness to explore with the United Kingdom ways of consolidating mutual trust and cooperation in the South Atlantic. Argentina reaffirmed its belief that a resumption of negotiations on the substance of the question would contribute to a fair and definitive settlement of the dispute.

His Royal Highness Prince Charles visited Argentina from 9 to 11 March and held meetings with President Menem, at which they reportedly discussed the climate of reconciliation between the two countries. Argentina and the United Kingdom, at the end of talks on South Atlantic issues (London, 25-27 May), jointly agreed to continue to study air links and human contacts to and from the Falklands Islands, including access by Argentines; to exchange ideas for improving cooperation on the conservation of fish stocks in the South Atlantic, especially ways to tackle poaching; and to find ways of making progress over a range of South Atlantic issues of common interest.

In a 1 July resolution [A/54/23], the Special Committee reiterated that a peaceful and negotiated settlement of the sovereignty dispute between Argentina and the United Kingdom would put an end to the colonial situation of the Falkland Islands (Malvinas) and requested the two countries to resume negotiations.

The Foreign Ministers of the United Kingdom and Argentina issued a joint statement (London, 13-14 July) [A/54/229] regarding travel by Argentine citizens to the Falkland Islands on their own passports; the resumption of civil air services between Chile and the Falkland Islands, including stops in mainland Argentina; and the possibility of flights between the Falkland Islands and third countries, with the option from 16 October of making stops in mainland Argentina. They agreed on enhanced cooperation in the maintenance and conservation of fish stocks in the South Atlantic and on confidence-building measures, including landmine clearance in the Falkland Islands.

In an exchange of letters on 14 July, the United Kingdom informed Argentina that some of its commitments and responsibilities under the joint statement would be discharged by Her Majesty's Government of the Falkland Islands [A/54/230]. Argentina responded that, pursuant to their October 1989 joint statement issued in Madrid [YUN 1989, p. 766], any arrangements made by the United Kingdom with a view to their implementation were an internal affair of the United Kingdom and had no bearing on the nature of the controversy over sovereignty of the Falkland Islands (Malvinas), South Georgia and the South Sandwich Islands and surrounding maritime areas [A/54/253].

The President of Argentina, speaking during the Assembly's general debate on 21 September [A/54/PV.7], said that he was convinced the conditions existed for the two countries to begin a dialogue towards a definitive solution of the sovereignty dispute. Exercising its right of reply on 22 September [A/54/420], the United Kingdom said that nothing in the July agreement compromised the United Kingdom position in relation to its sovereignty over the Falkland Islands. Representatives of the Territory had asked the Special Committee on decolonization to recognize that they, like other democratic people, were entitled to exercise the right of self-determination and reiterated that the people of the Falkland Islands did not want to be part of Argentina.

On 13 October [A/54/472], Argentina rejected the United Kingdom's claim that the "wishes" of the inhabitants of the Malvinas should be respected. It had repeatedly proved its commitment to protect the interests of the islanders and Argentina's Constitution guaranteed strict respect for the lifestyle of the inhabitants of the islands. Argentina trusted that, in response to the numerous invitations by the international community and within the framework of bilateral relations, negotiations would be renewed.

By **decision 54/412** of 4 November, the General Assembly deferred consideration of the item on the Falkland Islands (Malvinas) and included it in the provisional agenda of its fifty-fifth (2000) session.

Gibraltar

The Special Committee on decolonization took up the question of Gibraltar on 21 June. It had before it a Secretariat working paper updating the overall situation in the Territory and setting forth the positions of the United Kingdom (the administering Power), Gibraltar and Spain concerning Gibraltar's future status [A/AC.109/1999/5]. The Committee heard statements by Spain, the Chief Minister of Gibraltar and a representative of the Self-Determination for Gibraltar Group, following which it decided to continue consideration of the question in 2000.

GENERAL ASSEMBLY ACTION

In December, the General Assembly, on the recommendation of the Fourth Committee [A/54/584], adopted **decision 54/423** without vote [agenda item 18].

Question of Gibraltar

At its 71st plenary meeting, on 6 December 1999, the General Assembly, on the recommendation of the

Special Political and Decolonization Committee (Fourth Committee), adopted the following text:

> "The General Assembly, recalling its decision 53/420 of 3 December 1998, and recalling at the same time that the statement agreed to by the Governments of Spain and the United Kingdom of Great Britain and Northern Ireland at Brussels on 27 November 1984 stipulates, inter alia, the following:
>
> > 'The establishment of a negotiating process aimed at overcoming all the differences between them over Gibraltar and at promoting cooperation on a mutually beneficial basis on economic, cultural, touristic, aviation, military and environmental matters. Both sides accept that the issues of sovereignty will be discussed in that process. The British Government will fully maintain its commitment to honour the wishes of the people of Gibraltar as set out in the preamble of the 1969 Constitution',
>
> takes note of the fact that, as part of this process, the Ministers for Foreign Affairs of Spain and the United Kingdom of Great Britain and Northern Ireland hold annual meetings alternately in each capital, the most recent of which was held in London on 10 December 1997, and urges both Governments to continue their negotiations with the object of reaching a definitive solution to the problem of Gibraltar in the light of relevant resolutions of the General Assembly and in the spirit of the Charter of the United Nations."

New Caledonia

The Special Committee on decolonization considered the question of New Caledonia on 29 June and 9 July. It had before it a Secretariat working paper describing political and economic developments and economic conditions in the Territory [A/AC.109/1999/6 & Corr.1]. The paper stated that the 1998 Nouméa Accord on the Territory's future status [YUN 1998, p. 574], signed by France (the administering Power) and the two main Caledonian political groupings—the Rassemblement pour la Calédonie dans la République (RPCR) and the Front de libération nationale kanake socialiste (FLNKS)—was ratified by New Caledonians on 8 November 1998, with 72 per cent of the electorate voting in favour. In keeping with the Accord, the French Parliament on 6 July 1998 passed a constitutional reform inserting two new articles, calling on the people of New Caledonia to express their views on the Accord before the end of the year (article 76), and providing that, following approval of the Accord, a Constitution would be voted on in Parliament in order to enable New Caledonia to move forward on the basis of the Accord (article 77). On 19 March 1999, the French Legislature ratified an organic law codifying the matters addressed in article 77, namely, the powers to be transferred to the newly created institutions and their organization, rules governing citizenship and the electoral regime and conditions and deadlines by which New Caledonians would determine their accession to full sovereignty; and an ordinary law dealing with social and economic matters covered under the Accord.

The governmental structure, created as a result of the entry into force of the organic law, provided for a 54-member Congress as New Caledonia's deliberative assembly, composed of 7 from the Provincial Assembly of the Loyalty Islands, 15 from the Provincial Assembly of the North Province and 32 from the Provincial Assembly of the South Province; and an executive (the Government), elected by the Congress and responsible to it and replacing the institution of the High French Commissioner for New Caledonia, which would cease to exist. The provincial assemblies were responsible for matters not directly attributed to the President of the Provincial Assembly, who would act as the executive of the province. A 28-member Economic and Social Council would be created to advise the Government on projects and possible economic and social laws. A parallel set of institutions was to be created in the eight areas that were designated as "customary" to accommodate the full political recognition of the Kanak identity. The uncertain legal status of the customary areas was to be revised, thereby enhancing their role. In particular, a Customary Council would be created in each customary area, whose composition would be determined by traditions proper to the area. In addition, a Territory-wide Customary Senate would be created, comprising 16 members (2 elected by each of the 8 customary councils). The Customary Senate would be represented in the Economic and Social Council, the Administrative Council, the Consultative Council on Mines and local development agencies. The Customary Senate and the councils were to be consulted by the executive and legislative organs on matters directly related to the Kanak identity. Elections were held on 9 May for the provincial assemblies and the Congress, which were in place by 14 May. The Government was to be elected by 18 June and the customary councils and the Customary Senate would be designated by 28 August.

The precondition for the talks leading to the Nouméa Accord, the exchange of nickel reserves from the French State-owned company, Eramet, to the Kanak-controlled Société minière du Sud Pacifique (SMSP), was realized, permitting SMSP to go ahead with the construction of a smelter in a joint venture with the Canadian company Falconbridge. In February, the French Government announced the acquisition of SIMA, an important producer of steel and nickel alloys. That acquisition strengthened the position of Eramet within its sector. Under the privatization agreement, 30 per cent of Eramet's New Caledonian nickel unit would be transferred to a public organization. Along with that organization, New Caledonia would take an 8 per cent stake in Eramet. In that way, New Caledonians would be shareholders in the management of the country's major source of economic wealth.

Regarding the 9 May elections, a later Secretariat report [A/AC.109/2000/4] stated that the campaign and the polling were conducted without incident, with 75 per cent of the electorate voting. RPCR obtained a majority of the 74 seats in the provincial assemblies in the South Province, while FLNKS obtained a majority in the other two provinces. Of those voted into the provincial assemblies, 54 of them became members of New Caledonia's Congress. Thus, RPCR obtained a relative majority of 24 seats in Congress and FLNKS, 18. Congress elected the new Government of Jean Lèques (RPCR) on 28 May, which comprised six members from RPCR, four from FLNKS and one from the Fédération des comités de coopération indépendantistes, a dissident offshoot of FLNKS currently allied with RPCR. The Customary Senate was formally constituted on 27 August.

However, following the elections, press reports noted considerable friction between RPCR and FLNKS due to differing interpretations of "collegiality" in government matters. They also disagreed on the interpretation of eligibility to vote in future elections to the Congress, provincial assemblies and, ultimately, to vote on accession to full sovereignty. The French National Assembly on 10 June and the Senate on 12 October passed legislation stipulating that the right to vote should be exercised by persons already on the electoral roll as at 8 November 1998 and who, at the time, had been residents for at least 10 years.

The Secretariat reported that 1999 was marked by high-level diplomatic visits to New Caledonia to explore commercial, economic and cultural partnerships. In August, the South Pacific Forum Ministerial Committee on New Caledonia completed a fact-finding mission on implementation of the Nouméa Accord. In October, the South Pacific Forum admitted New Caledonia as an official observer. Also, at the invitation of France, a three-member delegation of representatives of permanent missions to the United Nations visited New Caledonia from 23 to 28 August to observe implementation of the first phase of the Accord [A/54/921].

GENERAL ASSEMBLY ACTION

On 6 December [meeting 71], the General Assembly, on the recommendation of the Fourth Committee [A/54/584], adopted **resolution 54/88** without vote [agenda item 18].

Question of New Caledonia

The General Assembly,

Having considered the question of New Caledonia,

Having examined the chapter of the report of the Special Committee on the Situation with regard to the Implementation of the Declaration on the Granting of Independence to Colonial Countries and Peoples relating to New Caledonia,

Reaffirming the right of peoples to self-determination as enshrined in the Charter of the United Nations,

Recalling its resolutions 1514(XV) of 14 December 1960 and 1541(XV) of 15 December 1960,

Noting the importance of the positive measures being pursued in New Caledonia by the French authorities, in cooperation with all sectors of the population, to promote political, economic and social development in the Territory, including measures in the area of environmental protection and action with respect to drug abuse and trafficking, in order to provide a framework for its peaceful progress to self-determination,

Noting also, in this context, the importance of equitable economic and social development, as well as continuing dialogue among the parties involved in New Caledonia in the preparation of the act of self-determination of New Caledonia,

Noting with satisfaction the intensification of contacts between New Caledonia and neighbouring countries of the South Pacific region,

1. *Welcomes* the significant developments that have taken place in New Caledonia as exemplified by the signing of the Nouméa Accord of 5 May 1998 between the representatives of New Caledonia and the Government of France;

2. *Urges* all the parties involved, in the interest of all the people of New Caledonia, to maintain, in the framework of the Nouméa Accord, their dialogue in a spirit of harmony;

3. *Notes* the relevant provisions of the Nouméa Accord aimed at taking more broadly into account the Kanak identity in the political and social organization of New Caledonia, and also those provisions of the Accord relating to control of immigration and protection of local employment;

4. *Also notes* the relevant provisions of the Nouméa Accord to the effect that New Caledonia may become a member or associate member of certain international organizations, such as international organizations in the Pacific region, the United Nations, the United Nations Educational, Scientific and Cultural Organization and the International Labour Organization, according to their regulations;

5. *Further notes* the agreement between the signatories of the Nouméa Accord that the progress made in the emancipation process shall be brought to the attention of the United Nations;

6. *Welcomes* the fact that the administering Power invited to New Caledonia, at the time the new institutions were established, a mission of information which comprised representatives of countries of the Pacific region;

7. *Calls upon* the administering Power to transmit information regarding the political, economic and social situation of New Caledonia to the Secretary-General;

8. *Invites* all the parties involved to continue promoting a framework for the peaceful progress of the Territory towards an act of self-determination in which all options are open and which would safeguard the rights of all New Caledonians according to the letter and the spirit of the Nouméa Accord, which is based on the principle that it is for the populations of New Caledonia to choose how to control their destiny;

9. *Welcomes* measures that have been taken to strengthen and diversify the New Caledonian economy in all fields, and encourages further such measures in accordance with the spirit of the Matignon and Nouméa Accords;

10. *Also welcomes* the importance attached by the parties to the Matignon and Nouméa Accords to greater progress in housing, employment, training, education and health care in New Caledonia;

11. *Acknowledges* the contribution of the Melanesian Cultural Centre to the protection of the indigenous culture of New Caledonia;

12. *Notes* the positive initiatives aimed at protecting the natural environment of New Caledonia, notably the "Zonéco" operation designed to map and evaluate marine resources within the economic zone of New Caledonia;

13. *Acknowledges* the close links between New Caledonia and the peoples of the South Pacific and the positive actions being taken by the French and territorial authorities to facilitate the further development of those links, including the development of closer relations with the countries members of the South Pacific Forum;

14. *Welcomes,* in this regard, the accession by New Caledonia to the status of observer in the South Pacific Forum, continuing high-level visits to New Caledonia by delegations from countries of the Pacific region and high-level visits by delegations from New Caledonia to countries members of the South Pacific Forum;

15. *Decides* to keep under continuous review the process unfolding in New Caledonia as a result of the signing of the Nouméa Accord;

16. *Requests* the Special Committee on the Situation with regard to the Implementation of the Declaration on the Granting of Independence to Colonial Countries and Peoples to continue to examine this question and to report thereon to the General Assembly at its fifty-fifth session.

Tokelau

The Special Committee on decolonization on 29 June considered the question of Tokelau, three small atolls (Nukunonu, Fakaofo and Atafu) in the South Pacific, administered by New Zealand. It examined a Secretariat working paper detailing the Territory's constitutional development, economic and social conditions, and the positions of New Zealand and Tokelau concerning its future status [A/AC.109/1999/17].

In accordance with recommendations made in the "Modern House of Tokelau" report [YUN 1998, p. 575], a new electoral system was instituted for the General Fono (the national representative body of Tokelau), whose 27 members were chosen by each Taupulega (Council of Elders) to serve three-year terms. Only the Faipule (the representative of each village) and the Pulenuku (mayor of each village) were elected. In January, elections for the reformed General Fono, made up of six members from each village, were held on the basis of universal adult suffrage. The new arrangement was expected to promote continuity in administration and provide the basis for the development of a sense of professionalism. New Zealand said that Tokelau's decision to move from a system of selection and appointment to elections was significant in the wider context of preparation for self-determination.

The Tokelau Public Service was relocated from Samoa to the atolls and was restructured by devolving most public service functions to the villages and making all authorities accountable to Tokelau institutions. A draft of the restructuring plan was prepared, setting out the functions to be devolved to the villages (or corporatized or privatized).

The *Ulu-o-Tokelau* (the highest authority on Tokelau), speaking before the Special Committee, said that the current preference for free association did not mean that Tokelau dismissed any possibility of pursuing another option, particularly that of integration. Tokelau would wish to be more fully informed, in its dialogue with the administering Power, of what would be possible under integration, as well as under free association.

GENERAL ASSEMBLY ACTION

On 6 December [meeting 71], the General Assembly, on the recommendation of the Fourth Committee [A/54/584], adopted **resolution 54/89** without vote [agenda item 18].

Question of Tokelau

The General Assembly,

Having considered the question of Tokelau,

Having examined the chapter of the report of the Special Committee on the Situation with regard to the Implementation of the Declaration on the Granting of Independence to Colonial Countries and Peoples relating to the question of Tokelau,

Recalling the solemn declaration on the future status of Tokelau, delivered by the *Ulu-o-Tokelau* (the highest authority on Tokelau) on 30 July 1994, that an act of self-determination in Tokelau is now under active consideration, together with the constitution of a self-governing Tokelau, and that the present preference of Tokelau is for a status of free association with New Zealand,

Recalling also its resolution 1514(XV) of 14 December 1960, containing the Declaration on the Granting of Independence to Colonial Countries and Peoples, and all resolutions and decisions of the United Nations relating to Non-Self-Governing Territories, in particular General Assembly resolution 53/66 of 3 December 1998,

Recalling further the emphasis placed in the solemn declaration on the terms of Tokelau's intended free association relationship with New Zealand, including the expectation that the form of help Tokelau could continue to expect from New Zealand in promoting the well-being of its people, besides its external interests, would be clearly established in the framework of that relationship,

Noting with appreciation the continuing exemplary cooperation of New Zealand as the administering Power with regard to the work of the Special Committee relating to Tokelau and its readiness to permit access by United Nations visiting missions to the Territory,

Noting also with appreciation the collaborative contribution to the development of Tokelau by New Zealand and the specialized agencies and other organizations of the United Nations system, in particular the United Nations Development Programme and the International Telecommunication Union,

Recalling the dispatch in 1994 of a United Nations visiting mission to Tokelau,

Noting that, as a small island Territory, Tokelau exemplifies the situation of most remaining Non-Self-Governing Territories,

Noting also that, as a case study pointing to successful decolonization, Tokelau has wider significance for the United Nations as it seeks to complete its work in decolonization,

1. *Notes* that Tokelau remains firmly committed to the development of self-government and to an act of self-determination that would result in Tokelau assuming a status in accordance with the options on future status for Non-Self-Governing Territories contained in principle VI of the annex to General Assembly resolution 1541(XV) of 15 December 1960;

2. *Also notes* Tokelau's desire to move at its own pace towards an act of self-determination;

3. *Further notes* the inauguration in 1999 of a national Government based on village elections by universal adult suffrage;

4. *Commends* Tokelau's ongoing work in charting a distinctive constitutional course, reflecting its unique traditions and environment;

5. *Also commends* Tokelau for current initiatives and endeavours, based on wide consultation with its people, to construct a true "house of Tokelau", acknowledging the role of the village as the foundation of Tokelau, as well as the need to continue the process of strengthening the basis of national self-government and the aim of establishing the capacity for economic survival in a sustainable way;

6. *Acknowledges* the attention being given to broader matters of governance, including the upgrading of financial regulations, to establish clear local channels of responsibility in national and village government;

7. *Notes* that, responding to the desire of Tokelau, the Government of New Zealand has legislation in place to enable responsibility for the Tokelau Public Service to be passed from the State Services Commissioner in New Zealand to Tokelau, the timing to be set by mutual agreement when Tokelau has established a suitable local employment framework;

8. *Acknowledges* Tokelau's need for reassurance, given that local resources cannot adequately cover the material side of self-determination, and the ongoing responsibility of Tokelau's external partners to assist Tokelau in balancing its desire to be self-reliant to the greatest extent possible with its need for external assistance;

9. *Welcomes* the assurances of the Government of New Zealand that it will meet its obligations to the United Nations with respect to Tokelau and abide by the freely expressed wishes of the people of Tokelau with regard to their future status;

10. *Welcomes also* the statement on official development assistance cooperation between New Zealand and Tokelau, setting out the direction and broad structure of New Zealand official development assistance to Tokelau, to better meet new development and governance needs in the medium term;

11. *Calls upon* the administering Power and United Nations agencies to continue their assistance to Tokelau, as it further develops its economy and governance structures within the context of its ongoing constitutional evolution;

12. *Requests* the Special Committee on the Situation with regard to the Implementation of the Declaration on the Granting of Independence to Colonial Countries and Peoples to continue to examine this question and to report thereon to the General Assembly at its fifty-fifth session.

Western Sahara

The question of Western Sahara was considered by the Special Committee on 22 June [A/54/23]. A Secretariat working paper [A/AC.109/1999/11] provided detailed information on the exercise of the Secretary-General's good offices with the parties concerned and action taken by the Security Council and the General Assembly (see also PART ONE, Chapter II). The Special Committee transmitted the relevant documentation to the Assembly's fifty-fourth (1999) session to facilitate the Fourth Committee's consideration of the question.

Island Territories

The Special Committee on decolonization considered working papers prepared by the Secretariat on American Samoa [A/AC.109/1999/13], Anguilla [A/AC.109/1999/8], Bermuda [A/AC.109/1999/3], the British Virgin Islands [A/AC.109/1999/9], the Cayman Islands [A/AC.109/1999/4], Guam [A/AC.109/1999/14], Montserrat [A/AC.109/1999/15], Pitcairn [A/AC.109/1999/1 & Corr.1], St. Helena [A/AC.109/1999/16], the Turks and Caicos Islands [A/AC.109/1999/18] and the United States Virgin Islands [A/AC.109/1999/7 & Corr.1], describing political developments and economic and social conditions in each of those Territories. On 21 July, the Special Committee approved two draft resolutions for adoption by the General Assembly (see below).

GENERAL ASSEMBLY ACTION

On 6 December [meeting 71], the General Assembly, on the recommendation of the Fourth Committee [A/54/584], adopted **resolutions 54/90 A** and **B** without vote [agenda item 18].

Questions of American Samoa, Anguilla, Bermuda, the British Virgin Islands, the Cayman Islands, Guam, Montserrat, Pitcairn, St. Helena, the Turks and Caicos Islands and the United States Virgin Islands

A

General

The General Assembly,

Having considered the questions of American Samoa, Anguilla, Bermuda, the British Virgin Islands, the Cayman Islands, Guam, Montserrat, Pitcairn, St. Helena, the Turks and Caicos Islands and the United States Virgin Islands, hereinafter referred to as "the Territories",

Having examined the relevant chapter of the report of the Special Committee on the Situation with regard to the Implementation of the Declaration on the Granting of Independence to Colonial Countries and Peoples,

Recalling its resolution 1514(XV) of 14 December 1960, containing the Declaration on the Granting of Independence to Colonial Countries and Peoples, and all resolutions and decisions of the United Nations relating to those Territories, including, in particular, the resolutions adopted by the General Assembly at its fifty-third session on the individual Territories covered by the present resolution,

Recognizing that the specific characteristics and the sentiments of the peoples of the Territories require flexible, practical and innovative approaches to the options of self-determination, without any prejudice to territorial size, geographical location, size of population or natural resources,

Recalling its resolution 1541(XV) of 15 December 1960, containing the principles that should guide Member States in determining whether or not an obligation exists to transmit the information called for under Article 73 *e* of the Charter of the United Nations,

Expressing its concern that even thirty-nine years after the adoption of the Declaration there still remain a number of Non-Self-Governing Territories,

Acknowledging the significant achievements by the international community towards the eradication of colonialism in accordance with the Declaration, and conscious of the importance of continuing effective implementation of the Declaration, taking into account the target set by the United Nations to eradicate colonialism by the year 2000 and the plan of action for the International Decade for the Eradication of Colonialism,

Noting the positive constitutional developments in some Non-Self-Governing Territories about which the Special Committee has received information, while also acknowledging the need for recognition to be given to expressions of self-determination by the peoples of the Territories consistent with practice under the Charter,

Recognizing that in the decolonization process there is no alternative to the principle of self-determination as enunciated by the General Assembly in its resolutions 1514(XV), 1541(XV) and other resolutions,

Welcoming the stated position of the Government of the United Kingdom of Great Britain and Northern Ireland that it continues to take seriously its obligations under the Charter to develop self-government in the dependent Territories and, in cooperation with the locally elected Governments, to ensure that their constitutional frameworks continue to meet the wishes of the people, and the emphasis that it is ultimately for the peoples of the Territories to decide their future status,

Welcoming also the stated position of the Government of the United States of America that it supports fully the principles of decolonization and takes seriously its obligations under the Charter to promote to the utmost the well-being of the inhabitants of the Territories under United States administration,

Aware of the special circumstances of the geographical location and economic conditions of each Territory, and bearing in mind the necessity of promoting economic stability and diversifying and strengthening further the economies of the respective Territories as a matter of priority,

Conscious of the particular vulnerability of the Territories to natural disasters and environmental degradation and, in this connection, bearing in mind the programmes of action of the United Nations Conference on Environment and Development, the World Conference on Natural Disaster Reduction, the Global Conference on the Sustainable Development of Small Island Developing States and other relevant world conferences,

Aware of the usefulness both to the Territories and to the Special Committee of the participation of appointed and elected representatives of the Territories in the work of the Special Committee,

Convinced that the wishes and aspirations of the peoples of the Territories should continue to guide the development of their future political status and that referendums, free and fair elections and other forms of popular consultation play an important role in ascertaining the wishes and aspirations of the people,

Convinced also that any negotiations to determine the status of a Territory must not take place without the active involvement and participation of the people of that Territory,

Recognizing that all available options for self-determination of the Territories are valid as long as they are in accordance with the freely expressed wishes of the peoples concerned and in conformity with the clearly defined principles contained in resolutions 1514(XV), 1541(XV) and other resolutions of the General Assembly,

Mindful that United Nations visiting missions provide an effective means of ascertaining the situation in the Territories, and considering that the possibility of sending further visiting missions to the Territories at an appropriate time and in consultation with the administering Powers should be kept under review,

Noting that the Special Committee held a Caribbean regional seminar at Castries, Saint Lucia, from 25 to 27 May 1999 to hear the views of the representatives of the Territories, as well as Governments and organizations in the region, in order to review the political, economic and social conditions in the Territories,

Mindful that in order for the Special Committee to enhance its understanding of the political status of the peoples of the Territories and to fulfil its mandate effectively, it is important for it to be apprised by the administering Powers and to receive information from other appropriate sources, including the representatives of the Territories, concerning the wishes and aspirations of the peoples of the Territories,

Mindful also in this connection that the Special Committee regards the holding of regional seminars in the Caribbean and Pacific regions and at Headquarters and other venues, with the active participation of representatives of the Non-Self-Governing Territories, as a helpful means to fulfil its mandate, while recognizing the need for reviewing the role of those seminars in the context of a United Nations programme for ascertaining the political status of the Territories,

Mindful further that some Territories have not had any United Nations visiting mission for a long period of time and that no such visiting missions have been sent to some of the Territories,

Noting with appreciation the contribution to the development of some Territories by specialized agencies and other organizations of the United Nations system, in particular the United Nations Development Programme, and regional institutions such as the Caribbean Development Bank,

Noting the ongoing efforts of the Special Committee in carrying out a critical review of its work with the aim of making appropriate and constructive recommendations and decisions to attain its objectives in accordance with its mandate,

1. *Reaffirms* the inalienable right of the peoples of the Territories to self-determination, including, if they so wish, independence, in conformity with the Charter of the United Nations and with General Assembly resolution 1514(XV), containing the Declaration on the Granting of Independence to Colonial Countries and Peoples;

2. *Reaffirms also* that it is ultimately for the peoples of the Territories themselves to determine freely their future political status in accordance with the relevant provisions of the Charter, the Declaration and the relevant resolutions of the General Assembly, and in that connection calls upon the administering Powers, in cooperation with the territorial Governments, to facilitate programmes of political education in the Territories in order to foster an awareness among the people of their right to self-determination in conformity with the legitimate political status options, based on the principles clearly defined in Assembly resolution 1541(XV);

3. *Requests* the administering Powers to transmit to the Secretary-General information called for under Article 73 *e* of the Charter and other updated information and reports, including reports on the wishes and aspirations of the peoples of the Territories regarding their future political status as expressed in fair and free referendums and other forms of popular consultation, as well as the results of any informed and democratic processes consistent with practice under the Charter that indicate the clear and freely expressed wish of the people to change the existing status of the Territories;

4. *Stresses* the importance for the Special Committee on the Situation with regard to the Implementation of the Declaration on the Granting of Independence to Colonial Countries and Peoples to be apprised of the views and wishes of the peoples of the Territories and to enhance its understanding of their conditions;

5. *Reaffirms* that United Nations visiting missions to the Territories at an appropriate time and in consultation with the administering Powers are an effective means of ascertaining the situation in the Territories, and requests the administering Powers and the elected representatives of the peoples of the Territories to assist the Special Committee in this regard;

6. *Reaffirms also* the responsibility of the administering Powers under the Charter to promote the economic and social development and to preserve the cultural identity of the Territories, and recommends that priority continue to be given, in consultation with the territorial Governments concerned, to the strengthening and diversification of their respective economies;

7. *Requests* the administering Powers, in consultation with the peoples of the Territories, to take all necessary measures to protect and conserve the environment of the Territories under their administration against any environmental degradation, and requests the specialized agencies concerned to continue to monitor environmental conditions in those Territories;

8. *Calls upon* the administering Powers, in cooperation with the respective territorial Governments, to continue to take all necessary measures to counter problems related to drug trafficking, money laundering and other offences;

9. *Stresses* that the eradication of colonialism requires the full and constructive cooperation of all parties involved, and notes with concern that the plan of action for the International Decade for the Eradication of Colonialism cannot be concluded by the year 2000;

10. *Calls upon* the administering Powers to enter into constructive dialogue with the Special Committee before the fifty-fifth session of the General Assembly to develop a framework for the implementation of the provisions of Article 73 of the Charter and the Declaration on the Granting of Independence to Colonial Countries and Peoples for the period beyond 2000;

11. *Notes* the particular circumstances that prevail in the Territories concerned, and encourages the political evolution in them towards self-determination;

12. *Urges* Member States to contribute to the efforts of the United Nations to usher in the twenty-first century in a world free of colonialism, and calls upon them to continue to give their full support to the Special Committee in its endeavours towards that noble goal;

13. *Invites* the specialized agencies and other organizations of the United Nations system to initiate or to continue to take all necessary measures to accelerate progress in the social and economic life of the Territories, and calls for closer cooperation between the Special Committee and the Economic and Social Council in furtherance of the provision of assistance to the Territories;

14. *Requests* the Secretary-General to report to the General Assembly on the implementation of resolutions concerning decolonization adopted since the declaration of the International Decade for the Eradication of Colonialism;

15. *Requests* the Special Committee to continue to examine the question of the small Territories and to report thereon to the General Assembly at its fifty-fifth session.

B

Individual Territories

The General Assembly,

Referring to resolution A above,

I. *American Samoa*

Taking note of the report by the administering Power that most American Samoan leaders express satisfaction with the island's present relationship with the United States of America,

Taking note with interest of the statement made and the information on the political and economic situation in American Samoa provided by the Governor of American Samoa to the Pacific regional seminar held at Nadi, Fiji, from 16 to 18 June 1998,

Noting that the territorial Government continues to have significant financial, budgetary and internal control problems and that the Territory's deficit and financial condition are compounded by the high demand for government services from the rapidly growing population, a limited economic and tax base and recent natural disasters,

Noting also that the Territory, similar to isolated communities with limited funds, continues to experience a lack of adequate medical and other infrastructural facilities,

Aware of the efforts of the territorial Government to control and reduce expenditures, while continuing its programme of expanding and diversifying the local economy,

1. *Requests* the administering Power, bearing in mind the views of the people of the Territory ascertained through a democratic process, to keep the Secretary-General informed of the wishes and aspirations of the people regarding their future political status;

2. *Calls upon* the administering Power to continue to assist the territorial Government in the economic and social development of the Territory, including measures to strengthen the financial management capabilities and other functions of the territorial Government;

3. *Welcomes* the invitation extended by the Governor of American Samoa to the Special Committee on the Situation with regard to the Implementation of the Declaration on the Granting of Independence to Colonial Countries and Peoples to send a visiting mission to the Territory;

II. *Anguilla*

Conscious of the commitment of both the Government of Anguilla and the administering Power to a new and closer policy of dialogue and partnership through the Country Policy Plan for 1993-1997 and its successor,

Aware of the efforts of the Government of Anguilla to continue to develop the Territory as a viable and well-regulated offshore financial centre for investors, by enacting modern company and trust laws, as well as partnership and insurance legislation, and computerizing the company registry system,

Noting the need for continuing cooperation between the administering Power and the territorial Government in tackling the problems of drug trafficking and money laundering,

1. *Requests* the administering Power, bearing in mind the views of the people of the Territory ascertained through a democratic process, to keep the Secretary-General informed of the wishes and aspirations of the people regarding their future political status;

2. *Calls upon* the administering Power and all States, organizations and United Nations agencies to continue to assist the Territory in social and economic development;

3. *Welcomes* the country cooperation framework of the United Nations Development Programme for the period 1997-1999 currently being implemented following consultations with the territorial Government and key development partners in the United Nations system and the donor community;

4. *Also welcomes* the assessment by the United Nations Development Programme that the Territory has made considerable progress in the domain of sustainable human development and in its sound management and preservation of the environment, which has been incorporated into the National Tourism Plan;

5. *Further welcomes* the assessment by the Caribbean Development Bank in its 1998 report on the Territory that the medium- and long-term economic prospects for Anguilla were favourable;

III. *Bermuda*

Noting the results of the independence referendum held on 16 August 1995, and conscious of the different viewpoints of the political parties of the Territory on the future status of the Territory,

Noting also the functioning of the democratic process and the smooth transition of government in November 1998,

Noting further the comments made by the administering Power in its recently published White Paper on Partnership for Progress and Prosperity: Britain and the Overseas Territories,

1. *Requests* the administering Power, bearing in mind the views of the people of the Territory ascertained through a democratic process, to keep the Secretary-General informed of the wishes and aspirations of the people regarding their future political status;

2. *Calls upon* the administering Power to continue to work with the Territory for its socio-economic development;

3. *Requests* the administering Power to elaborate, in consultation with the territorial Government, programmes specifically intended to alleviate the economic, social and environmental consequences of the closure of the military bases and installations of the United States of America in the Territory;

IV. *British Virgin Islands*

Noting the completion of the constitutional review in the Territory and the coming into force of the amended Constitution, and noting also the results of the general elections held on 17 May 1999,

Noting also the results of the constitutional review of 1993-1994, which made it clear that a prerequisite to independence must be a constitutionally expressed wish by the people as a result of a referendum,

Taking note of the statement made in 1995 by the Chief Minister of the British Virgin Islands that the Territory was ready for constitutional and political advancement towards full internal self-government and that the administering Power should assist through the gradual transfer of power to elected territorial representatives,

Noting that the Territory is emerging as one of the world's leading offshore financial centres,

Noting also the need for continued cooperation between the administering Power and the territorial Government in countering drug trafficking and money laundering,

1. *Requests* the administering Power, bearing in mind the views of the people of the Territory ascertained through a democratic process, to keep the Secretary-General informed of the wishes and aspirations of the people regarding their future political status;

2. *Requests* the administering Power, the specialized agencies and other organizations of the United Nations system and all financial institutions to continue to provide assistance to the Territory for socio-economic development and the development of human resources, bearing in mind the vulnerability of the Territory to external factors;

V. *Cayman Islands*

Noting the constitutional review of 1992-1993, according to which the population of the Cayman Islands expressed the sentiment that the existing relations with the United Kingdom of Great Britain and Northern Ireland should be maintained and that the current status of the Territory should not be altered,

Aware that the Territory has one of the highest per capita incomes in the region, a stable political climate and virtually no unemployment,

Noting the actions taken by the territorial Government to implement its localization programme to promote increased participation by the local population in the decision-making process in the Cayman Islands,

Noting with concern the vulnerability of the Territory to drug trafficking, money laundering and related activities,

Noting the measures taken by the authorities to deal with those problems,

Noting also that the Territory has emerged as one of the world's leading offshore financial centres,

1. *Requests* the administering Power, bearing in mind the views of the people of the Territory ascertained through a democratic process, to keep the Secretary-General informed of the wishes and aspirations of the people regarding their future political status;

2. *Requests* the administering Power, the specialized agencies and other organizations of the United Nations system to continue to provide the territorial Government with all required expertise to enable it to achieve its socio-economic aims;

3. *Calls upon* the administering Power and the territorial Government to continue to cooperate to counter problems related to money laundering, smuggling of funds and other related crimes, as well as drug trafficking;

4. *Requests* the administering Power, in consultation with the territorial Government, to continue to facilitate the expansion of the current programme of securing employment for the local population, in particular at the decision-making level;

5. *Welcomes* the implementation of the country cooperation framework of the United Nations Development Programme for the Territory, which is designed to ascertain national development priorities and United Nations assistance needs;

VI. *Guam*

Recalling that, in a referendum held in 1987, the registered and eligible voters of Guam endorsed a draft Guam Commonwealth Act that would establish a new framework for relations between the Territory and the administering Power, providing for a greater measure of internal self-government for Guam and recognition of the right of the Chamorro people of Guam to self-determination for the Territory,

Recalling also its resolution 1514(XV) of 14 December 1960, containing the Declaration on the Granting of Independence to Colonial Countries and Peoples, and all resolutions and decisions of the United Nations relating to the Non-Self-Governing Territories, in particular General Assembly resolutions 52/77 A and B of 10 December 1997,

Recalling further the requests by the elected representatives and non-governmental organizations of the Territory that Guam not be removed from the list of the Non-Self-Governing Territories with which the Special Committee on the Situation with regard to the Implementation of the Declaration on the Granting of Independence to Colonial Countries and Peoples is concerned, pending the self-determination of the Chamorro people and taking into account their legitimate rights and interests,

Aware of the continuing negotiations between the administering Power and the territorial Government on the draft Guam Commonwealth Act and on the future status of the Territory, with particular emphasis on the question of the evolution of the relationship between the United States of America and Guam,

Cognizant that the administering Power continues to implement its programme of transferring surplus federal land to the Government of Guam,

Noting that the people of the Territory have called for reform in the programme of the administering Power with respect to the thorough, unconditional and expeditious transfer of land property to the people of Guam,

Conscious that immigration into Guam has resulted in the indigenous Chamorros becoming a minority in their homeland,

Aware of the potential for diversifying and developing the economy of Guam through commercial fishing and agriculture and other viable activities,

Noting the proposed closing and realigning of four United States Navy installations on Guam and the request for the establishment of a transition period to develop some of the closed facilities as commercial enterprises,

Recalling the dispatch in 1979 of a United Nations visiting mission to the Territory, and noting the recommendation of the 1996 Pacific regional seminar for sending a visiting mission to Guam,

Noting with interest the statements made and the information on the political and economic situation in Guam provided by the representatives of the Territory to the Caribbean regional seminar, held at Castries, Saint Lucia, from 25 to 27 May 1999,

1. *Requests* the administering Power to work with Guam's Commission on Decolonization for the Implementation and Exercise of Chamorro Self-Determination with a view to facilitating the decolonization of Guam, and to keep the Secretary-General informed of progress to that end;

2. *Calls upon* the administering Power to take into consideration the expressed will of the Chamorro people as endorsed by the people of Guam, encourages the

administering Power and the territorial Government of Guam to continue the negotiations on the matter, and requests the administering Power to inform the Secretary-General of progress to that end;

3. *Requests* the administering Power to continue to assist the elected territorial Government in achieving its political, economic and social goals;

4. *Also requests* the administering Power, in co-operation with the territorial Government, to continue to transfer land to the people of the Territory;

5. *Further requests* the administering Power to continue to recognize and respect the political rights and the cultural and ethnic identity of the Chamorro people of Guam, and to take all necessary measures to respond to the concerns of the territorial Government with regard to the question of immigration;

6. *Requests* the administering Power to cooperate in establishing programmes specifically intended to promote the sustainable development of economic activities and enterprises, noting the special role of the Chamorro people in the development of Guam;

7. *Also requests* the administering Power to continue to support appropriate measures by the territorial Government aimed at promoting growth in commercial fishing and agricultural and other viable activities;

VII. *Montserrat*

Taking note with interest of the statements made and the information on the political and economic situation in Montserrat provided by the elected representatives of the Territory to the Caribbean regional seminar, held at Castries, Saint Lucia, from 25 to 27 May 1999,

Taking note of the statement made by the Chief Minister of Montserrat on 22 May 1998 on the occasion of the observance of the Week of Solidarity with the Peoples of All Colonial Territories Fighting for Freedom, Independence and Human Rights,

Noting that the last visiting mission to the Territory was dispatched in 1982,

Noting also the functioning of a democratic process in Montserrat and that general elections were held in the Territory in November 1996,

Taking note of the reported statement of the Chief Minister that his preference was for independence within a political union with the Organization of Eastern Caribbean States and that self-reliance was more of a priority than independence,

Noting with concern the dire consequences of the eruptions of the Montsoufriere volcano, which led to the evacuation of three quarters of the population of the Territory to safe areas of the island and to areas outside the Territory, in particular Antigua and Barbuda and the United Kingdom of Great Britain and Northern Ireland, and which continues to have a negative impact upon the economy of the island,

Noting the efforts of the administering Power and the territorial Government to meet the emergency situation caused by the volcanic eruptions, including the implementation of a wide range of contingency measures for both the private and the public sectors in Montserrat,

Noting also the coordinated response measures taken by the United Nations Development Programme and the assistance of the United Nations disaster management team,

Noting with concern that a number of the inhabitants of the Territory continue to live in shelters because of volcanic activity,

1. *Requests* the administering Power, bearing in mind the views of the people of the Territory ascertained through a democratic process, to keep the Secretary-General informed of the wishes and aspirations of the people regarding their future political status;

2. *Calls upon* the administering Power, the specialized agencies and other organizations of the United Nations system as well as regional and other organizations to continue to provide urgent emergency assistance to the Territory in alleviating the consequences of the volcanic eruptions;

3. *Welcomes* the support of the Caribbean Community in the construction of housing in the safe zone to alleviate a shortage caused by the environmental and human crisis of the eruptions of the Montsoufriere volcano, as well as the material and financial support of the international community to help alleviate the suffering caused by the crisis;

VIII. *Pitcairn*

Taking into account the unique nature of Pitcairn in terms of population and area,

Expressing its satisfaction with the continuing economic and social advancement of the Territory, as well as with the improvement of its communications with the outside world and its management plan to address conservation issues,

1. *Requests* the administering Power, bearing in mind the views of the people of the Territory ascertained through a democratic process, to keep the Secretary-General informed of the wishes and aspirations of the people regarding their future political status;

2. *Also requests* the administering Power to continue its assistance for the improvement of the economic, social, educational and other conditions of the population of the Territory;

IX. *St. Helena*

Taking into account the unique character of St. Helena, its population and its natural resources,

Noting that a Commission of Inquiry into the Constitution appointed at the request of the Legislative Council of St. Helena reported its recommendations in March 1999, and that the Legislative Counsellors are currently considering its recommendations,

Also noting the administering Power's commitment to consider carefully suggestions for specific proposals for constitutional change from the territorial Governments as stated in its White Paper on Partnership for Progress and Prosperity: Britain and the Overseas Territories,

Aware of the establishment by the territorial Government of the Development Agency in 1995 to encourage private sector commercial development on the island,

Also aware of the efforts of the administering Power and the territorial authorities to improve the socio-economic conditions of the population of St. Helena, in particular in the sphere of food production, and the continuing negotiations to allow access to Ascension Island by civilian charter flights,

Noting with concern the problem of unemployment on the island, and noting the joint action of the administering Power and the territorial Government to deal with it,

1. *Notes* that the administering Power has taken note of various statements made by members of the Legislative Council of St. Helena about the Constitution and is prepared to discuss them further with the people of St. Helena;

2. *Requests* the administering Power, bearing in mind the views of the people of the Territory ascertained through a democratic process, to keep the Secretary-General informed of the wishes and aspirations of the people regarding their future political status;

3. *Requests* the administering Power and relevant regional and international organizations to continue to support the efforts of the territorial Government to address the socio-economic development of the Territory;

X. *Turks and Caicos Islands*

Taking note with interest of the statements made and the information on the political and economic situation in the Turks and Caicos Islands provided by the Cabinet Minister as well as a member of the legislature from the opposition of the Territory to the Caribbean regional seminar, held at St. John's, Antigua and Barbuda, from 21 to 23 May 1997,

Noting that the People's Democratic Movement was elected to power in the Legislative Council elections held in March 1999,

Also noting the efforts by the territorial Government to strengthen financial management in the public sector, including efforts to increase revenue,

Noting with concern the vulnerability of the Territory to drug trafficking and related activities, as well as its problems caused by illegal immigration,

Noting the need for continued cooperation between the administering Power and the territorial Government in countering drug trafficking and money laundering,

1. *Requests* the administering Power, bearing in mind the views of the people of the Territory ascertained through a democratic process, to keep the Secretary-General informed of the wishes and aspirations of the people regarding their future political status;

2. *Invites* the administering Power to take fully into account the wishes and interests of the Government and the people of the Turks and Caicos Islands in the governance of the Territory;

3. *Calls upon* the administering Power and the relevant regional and international organizations to continue to provide assistance for the improvement of the economic, social, educational and other conditions of the population of the Territory;

4. *Calls upon* the administering Power and the territorial Government to continue to cooperate to counter problems related to money laundering, smuggling of funds and other related crimes, as well as drug trafficking;

5. *Welcomes* the assessment by the Caribbean Development Bank in its 1998 report that the economy continued to expand with considerable output and low inflation;

6. *Also welcomes* the first country cooperation framework approved by the United Nations Development Programme for the period 1998-2002, which should, inter alia, assist in the development of a national integrated development plan that will put into place procedures for determining the national development priorities over ten years, with the focus of attention on health, population, education, tourism and economic and social development;

XI. *United States Virgin Islands*

Taking note with interest of the statements made and the information provided by the representative of the Governor of the Territory to the Caribbean regional seminar, held at Castries, Saint Lucia, from 25 to 27 May 1999,

Noting that although 80.4 per cent of the 27.5 per cent of the electorate that voted in the referendum on the political status of the Territory held on 11 October 1993 supported the existing territorial status arrangements with the administering Power, the law required the participation of 50 per cent of the registered voters for the results to be declared legally binding and therefore the status was left undecided,

Noting also the continuing interest of the territorial Government in seeking associate membership in the Organization of Eastern Caribbean States and observer status in the Caribbean Community and the Association of Caribbean States,

Noting further the necessity of further diversifying the economy of the Territory,

Noting the efforts of the territorial Government to promote the Territory as an offshore financial services centre,

Noting with satisfaction the interest of the Territory in joining the United Nations International Drug Control Programme as a full participant,

Recalling the dispatch in 1977 of a United Nations visiting mission to the Territory,

1. *Requests* the administering Power, bearing in mind the views of the people of the Territory ascertained through a democratic process, to keep the Secretary-General informed of the wishes and aspirations of the people regarding their future political status;

2. *Also requests* the administering Power to continue to assist the territorial Government in achieving its political, economic and social goals;

3. *Further requests* the administering Power to facilitate the participation of the Territory, as appropriate, in various organizations, in particular the Organization of Eastern Caribbean States, the Caribbean Community and the Association of Caribbean States;

4. *Expresses concern* that the Territory, which is already heavily indebted, had to borrow 21 million United States dollars from a commercial bank to carry out its year 2000 computer compliance programme, and calls for the United Nations year 2000 programme to be made available to the Non-Self-Governing Territories;

5. *Notes* that the general elections held in the Territory in November 1998 resulted in the orderly transfer of power;

6. *Expresses concern* that the territorial Government is facing severe fiscal problems, which has resulted in an accumulated debt of more than 1 billion dollars;

7. *Welcomes* the measures being taken by the newly elected territorial Government in addressing the fiscal

crisis, and calls upon the administering Power to provide every assistance required by the Territory to alleviate the crisis, including, inter alia, the provision of appropriate debt relief and loans.

Information

UN public information

The General Assembly's 93-member Committee on Information, at its twenty-first session (New York, 3-14 May (first part) and 1-5 November (resumed)) [A/54/21 & Add.1], continued to examine UN information policies and activities and to evaluate and follow up efforts made and progress achieved in information and communications. The Committee had before it reports on the reorientation of UN activities in public information and communications, the development of a UN international radio broadcasting capacity and the activities of the Joint United Nations Information Committee. It also considered reports on the integration of UN information centres (UNICs) with UNDP field offices and the allocation of resources for those centres, and the development of UN web sites.

The Committee recommended two draft resolutions to the Assembly—one on information in the service of humanity and the other on UN public information policies and activities—and a draft decision on increasing the Committee's membership, which were adopted by the Assembly in December.

By **decision 54/420** of 6 December, the Assembly increased the Committee's membership from 93 to 95.

Reorientation of information and communications activities

Pursuant to resolution 53/59 B [YUN 1998, p. 587], the Secretary-General submitted to the Committee on Information an April report on measures to reorient the public information and communications activities of the Department of Public Information (DPI) [A/AC.198/1999/2], particularly new measures to develop further the conceptual framework for policies of the new orientation, presented to the Committee in 1998 [YUN 1998, p. 583].

A more effective news gathering and delivery system, which the Secretary-General identified in his reorientation plan as one of the most immediate priorities of DPI, was entering into operation. DPI's immediate priority was the development of the UN News Service to transmit information via e-mail and facsimile directly to the media and other important opinion-making constituencies. The centrepiece of the Service would be a brief "Headline News Alert" on breaking news from the United Nations, which would be posted on the UN web site. The Service would also contain an expanded news feature service. In 1999, DPI began placement, on a worldwide basis, of op-ed articles by senior UN officials, who would also be able to brief senior journalists by telephone at the national and subregional levels on issues of pressing concern to them. Another priority was the development of a daily news page on the UN web site to provide breaking news on all major events and activities and information on upcoming meetings and events. DPI's press releases in English and French were currently disseminated worldwide, almost instantly, on the Internet.

In radio and television, efforts were under way to increase the provision of live feeds and other easy-to-assemble raw materials that could be quickly disseminated by establishing links with radio stations worldwide. An important breakthrough in that regard was the delivery of Chinese-language programmes to major broadcasting stations in China, as well as in the United States, by electronic audio transfer. Other important developments were the creation of the first audio-visual web page and the posting of brief audio news clips on the UN Radio web page for immediate use by broadcasters. Priority was also given to the development of the news content of programme production. To that end, DPI was engaged in staff training, strengthening cooperation with specialized agencies to generate more diverse programme material and setting up a network of field stringers to expand coverage and enrich programme content.

Similar changes were under way in the visual area to generate greater coverage for UN views and concerns. Finished video products, which were broadcast through cooperative arrangements with the Cable News Network International, were envisaged for posting as streaming video or digital files. The Department purchased equipment and upgraded technical facilities to change to digital television technology. A significant development was the introduction of web pages in all six UN official languages. Future plans for the web site included additions of audio and video elements, a larger volume of older documents and improved presentation and design.

In the context of DPI's reorientation, strengthening working relations with the thematic departments had become a key priority. Working arrangements with departments active in economic and social matters had been reinforced through a process of consultation with department heads. The effect of new technologies in the thematic areas was reflected in an improved capacity to produce better-quality information products more expeditiously and to design them simultaneously for issue in hard copy and on the Internet. DPI was engaged in revitalizing its publications programme and, although it retained its primary focus on the production of print, effective utilization of the electronic media was vital for the Department's outreach. The *Yearbook of the United Nations* was planning to launch a CD-ROM project incorporating the first 50 volumes, from 1946 to 1996. New web sites for the *UN Chronicle* and *Africa Recovery* were being further developed. *Development Business*, in cooperation with the World Bank, developed a web site version of the publication.

UN international radio broadcasting capacity

The Committee on Information had before it a March report of the Secretary-General on steps taken to design a small-scale pilot project in connection with DPI's direct international radio broadcasting capacity [A/AC.198/1999/5]. The main objective of the project would be to test the technical feasibility, programming capacity and listeners' interest in a UN international radio broadcasting capacity. It would emphasize the production and delivery of timely news packages and current affairs programmes on a daily and weekly basis to wider audiences, using more effective modes of transmission, including satellite distribution and the Internet. DPI had consulted regional and international radio broadcasting organizations on trends in national and international broadcasting, the most suitable programme design for target regions in different languages and the most cost-effective means for the timely delivery of UN radio programming to national and regional audiences. Member States and regional groups were contacted, but were unable to make a commitment regarding broadcasting facilities for the pilot project without consulting their respective broadcasting organizations.

The design and scope of the pilot project would link production capacity, linguistic diversity, telecommunications technology and target audiences. It would seek to provide a daily 5- to 15-minute package of news, interviews and features for broadcast to national and regional audiences in countries and regions where airtime might be made available for that purpose; weekly 10- to 15-minute regional magazines focusing on issues, activities and personalities of exclusive regional interest; special news bulletins covering Security Council and General Assembly meetings of particular interest to specific countries and regions; and a feature programme series on core issues of interest to national, regional and international audiences. The project would cover regions where the six official languages were used as principal languages and would use the most effective radio delivery system available in the target region. The duration of the pilot project would be one year, in two six-month periods, followed by an evaluation. The report described the broadcasting technology available in areas using the six languages.

The Secretary-General said that since no Member State or broadcast organization had made a commitment to provide the technical facilities or to contribute resources for the pilot project, and given the scale of extrabudgetary resources needed for the main project (some $4 million annually), DPI did not plan to initiate the project until there were clear indications of the availability of the resources required. In the meantime, it would continue to harness all affordable aspects of technological innovation in the ongoing modernization of UN Radio.

DPI activities

DPI continued the reorientation of its activities (see p. 547) with a view to projecting the United Nations as an open, transparent and public institution capable of meeting the objectives of the UN Charter, said the Secretary-General in a September report on questions relating to information [A/54/415]. Despite financial constraints, DPI made the UN web site available in all six official languages and increased the availability of audio and video elements on the web site; new elements were introduced, such as web pages on Kosovo and East Timor, the United Nations and civil society, and the United Nations and business.

The Office of the Spokesman of the Secretary-General used Internet technology to expand the audience for its products. Highlights of daily press briefings, information on the Secretary-General's appointments, the schedule of press conferences and other breaking developments were posted on the UN web site. DPI stepped up efforts to reach and establish links with journalists in as many Member States as possible through the web-based United Nations News Service (see p. 547). It produced a CD containing a special series of radio programmes on population and development. The Department continued to strengthen its relationship with television organizations worldwide. In cooperation with the United Nations Population Fund and the United Nations Children's Fund, it co-produced a five-part series of 45-minute documentaries with the German public broadcaster ZDF on the theme "Year of the six billion". DPI continued to enhance its cooperation with NGOs and held the fifty-second annual Conference for NGOs (New York, 15-17 September). Education outreach activities emphasized face-to-face contact, videoconferencing and student days at the United Nations. Other activities included workshops for teachers, briefing programmes for groups and special events. In October, in association with a coalition of NGOs active in distance learning, DPI launched a series of monthly videoconferences on UN issues.

DPI continued to develop thematically integrated information programmes, highlighting the Organization's role in furthering economic and social development, human rights and peace and security. It also focused on the follow-up to the global conferences held earlier in the decade. Publications remained an essential component of DPI's information and media strategy. While moving towards a greater use of electronic media, print remained its most widely accepted and authoritative method of communication. The *UN Chronicle*, *Africa Recovery* and *Development Business* continued to update their respective web pages, thus widening their outreach. Technological advances were also used to improve the timeliness of all four current publications, including the *Yearbook of the United Nations*.

Library services

The Dag Hammarskjöld Library continued efforts to become a virtual library with a worldwide outreach. New elements added to the Library's web page included the full text of current General Assembly resolutions in English and French, the electronic newsletter *Depository News Updates* and the "United Nations System Pathfinder", a guide to major references, sources and frequently requested UN and specialized agency reports. Parts of the web page became available in Arabic, Chinese and Russian. To facilitate multilingual subject access to UN databases, including the optical disk system, the Library had undertaken a project to translate the *UNBIS Thesaurus* (United Nations Bibliographic Information System) into the remaining official languages (Arabic, Chinese, Russian). With the launch of a specialized web page for maps, DPI cartographic services had been expanded significantly. DPI was also moving towards the Geographic Information Systems technology. DPI was cooperating with UN system organizations to develop a standard geographic database of the world using the new technology.

UN information centres

UNICs continued to develop networks with the media, NGOs and the business community to promote a greater understanding of UN priority issues. Some 24 centres thus far had increased their outreach considerably through web sites in local languages, while others made progress in the better use of new communications technology to develop and disseminate electronic news bulletins. Special consideration was given to youth outreach. The centres undertook numerous public information and communications activities geared to local audiences and concerns, and translated relevant information materials into local languages to promote issues relating to special events and observances.

At its 1999 session, the Committee on Information considered an April report of the Secretary-General on the status of the integration of UNICs with UNDP field offices [A/AC.198/1999/3]. The report stated that DPI's ongoing evaluations of UNICs had shown that, while the objectives of the integration exercise remained valid, problems had been encountered in implementation. The Secretary-General's Task Force on the Reorientation of United Nations Public Information Activities [YUN 1997, p. 567] recognized that the experience of integrating UNICs with UN offices under a resident coordinator had "not been uniformly productive".

DPI found that, in general, the integrated information centres had a lower level of programme delivery and a narrower range of activities than those that had not been integrated. Interaction with DPI at Headquarters and the frequency of reporting on activities were also often weaker. Some of the difficulties were the diminished availability of resources and the lack of familiarity on the part of some UNDP resident representatives/UN resident coordinators with DPI's mandate and the work of the UNICs. In terms of cost-effectiveness, integration with UNDP allowed all UNICs to be maintained, despite the abolition of a large number of director posts. Other savings relating to economies of scale or the sharing of common services were more difficult to discern. Benefits gained included a more central location, additional space and better possibilities for coordinating activities with other UN offices. Co-location also enhanced a unified image of the United Nations, one of the original objectives of integration. The sharing of communications networks with UNDP offices in common premises also had not been uniformly positive.

Future action included the development of guidelines, spelling out the operational framework for the integrated information centres; focal points in DPI, UNDP and the United Nations Development Group Office had been designated to do so. DPI would provide input into the performance evaluations of UNDP resident representatives/UN resident coordinators with regard to information functions and would be consulted in selecting them in countries where they served concurrently as centre directors or acting directors. DPI would strengthen its support structure at Headquarters to enhance its liaison with UNDP regarding the operations of the integrated UNICs. To enhance the calibre of the national information officers (local professionals), training opportunities should be increased and exchanges among UNICs in the same region encouraged. Measures to improve their conditions of service and career prospects should also be explored.

The Secretary-General called for a concerted effort to address the problems encountered in implementation of the integration exercise in a number of UNICs. To that end, he had asked DPI and UNDP to strengthen their cooperative relationship.

In a March report [A/AC.198/1999/4], the Secretary-General provided a breakdown of host government assistance to UNICs in 1998.

Development of UN web sites

In response to General Assembly resolution 53/208 C [YUN 1998, p. 1355], the Secretary-General submitted a March report on the continuous development, maintenance and enrichment of UN web sites [A/AC.198/1999/6].

The UN web site, which was coordinated, managed and maintained by DPI, currently received some 2.8 million accesses every week from over 140 countries. As the level of available technology developed and staff acquired skills, DPI, in cooperation with other departments and offices, embarked on a project aimed at making the web site available in all official languages.

The report presented three proposals to address the equitable treatment of official languages for consideration by Member States. Proposal A would accord all languages equal treatment on the UN web site regardless of the current availability of materials in other languages or the level of technology in those languages; differences in the availability of material among official languages should be overcome by the end of 2001, as long as the required funding was provided. Proposal B sought to establish the infrastructure to service and provide equitable coverage beginning on 1 January 2001, with the differences at that time addressed over a period of several bienniums, as staff and technological resources were made available. Under proposal C, certain modules would be made available in some languages, while addressing the issue of equality on an incremental basis over a period of several bienniums in accordance with the availability of the required resources.

The Secretary-General concluded that proposals A and B would require a prohibitive level of investment and recurrent maintenance costs. Thus, proposal C seemed to be the preferred option. Language materials in their conventional format would be included in the UN web site to the extent possible, and modules and audiovisual components would be included in accordance with priorities established by the Assembly. Additional activities for ongoing maintenance arrangements for all official languages would depend on available funding.

In October, the Secretary-General presented three further proposals for the multilingual development, maintenance and enrichment of UN web sites [A/AC.198/1999/9 & Corr.1,2], which were viewed as sub-options of proposal C. The first of those proposals entailed the translation and rendering of the contents of the current UN web site into all official languages on an incremental basis, with no time frame for achieving full parity. Under the second option, only selected basic modules, including the audio-visual module, would be translated and made available on an ongoing basis. The third proposal would establish a sound foundation for the current maintenance and enhancement activities of the web site, with provision of content in other languages related to the level of usage of the web site in those languages; additional monitoring of usage levels would be carried out and new modules made available on an ongoing basis as usage levels increased. Modules would not necessarily be translated in their entirety.

The Secretary-General recommended that, before enhancing the UN web site, the current ad hoc arrangements should be formalized so that at least the current status of the maintenance of the site in the six languages could be maintained. Also, minimum investment would need to be made to allow for an increase in web publishing and electronic distribution of adapted multilingual audio-visual products already available in the conventional format. He recommended pursuing the third proposal to ensure a realistic and cost-effective use of limited resources, achieve a balanced linguistic diversity on the web site and establish a sound foundation for its future expansion. Resource requirements were annexed to the report.

The Advisory Committee on Administrative and Budgetary Questions [A/54/7], during its consideration of the 2000-2001 proposed programme budget, requested that cost estimates with a Secretariat-wide plan for the development of the UN web site be submitted to the Assembly at its fifty-fourth (1999) session.

In an October note [A/C.5/54/27], the Secretary-General reported that the resource requirements for the recommended option were estimated at $13.5 million for 2000-2001.

The General Assembly, in **resolution 54/251, section XII**, of 23 December, took note of the Secretary-General's note.

OIOS review

In March [E/AC.51/1999/4], the Secretary-General transmitted to the Committee for Programme and Coordination (CPC) a report of the Office of Internal Oversight Services (OIOS) on the triennial review of the implementation of CPC recommendations made in 1996 [YUN 1996, p. 1349] on the evaluation of DPI. OIOS found that DPI had made an effort to follow through on a number of recommendations. However, progress was uneven and the effect of measures adopted in 1997 and 1998, following the reorientation of UN public information activities, needed to be reviewed at a later time, particularly progress in developing partnerships with important redisseminators of information.

CPC recommendations on the issuance of a Secretary-General's bulletin on disclosure of information and on the adoption of a policy for approving new UN publications, aimed at improving the quality of publications, were not implemented. Thus, OIOS recommended that the Secretary-General's bulletin be issued by September 1999 to facilitate prompt access to UN officials by media organizations. The bulletin should provide policy guidelines to encourage officials to speak informally to the media and to accept requests for formal interviews. Regarding improving the quality of publications, it recommended that the Publications Board adopt a policy by year's end that required departments to establish departmental reading committees, or a procedure for peer review of technical publications. Each author department should adopt arrangements adapted to the nature of its work.

CPC, at its thirty-ninth session (New York, 7 June–2 July) [A/54/16], recommended full implementation of the OIOS recommendation regarding the Secretary-General's bulletin. It endorsed the recommendation to improve the quality of publications.

JUNIC

The Joint United Nations Information Committee (JUNIC), the inter-agency Administrative Committee on Coordination (ACC) body on information activities within the UN system, held its twenty-fifth session in Vienna from 6 to 8 July [ACC/1999/11].

In its discussion of ways to promote better public understanding of the role and achievements of the United Nations, JUNIC members were informed of steps taken to promote a communication culture and the issuance of media guidelines for UN officials. In that regard, the need for training and guidance was stressed, possibly through the facilities offered by the United Nations Staff College, which might receive some funding from the host Government (Italy). JUNIC proposed that the Secretary-General bring the media guidelines to the attention of the executive heads of UN organizations. In view of the complexity and importance of communication issues in building support among UN constituencies, JUNIC reiterated its recommendation that a broad-based discussion on strengthening the information and communication capacity of the UN system be placed on the agenda of forthcoming ACC meetings. JUNIC agreed on the need to develop a joint vision of the common objectives of the UN system as a means of strengthening its sense of unified purpose. It was also agreed to consider further at future sessions the relationship of the organizations of the UN system with the business community.

JUNIC also discussed the work of the Non-Governmental Liaison Service and, in view of its continuing precarious financial situation, urged UN programmes, funds and specialized agencies to strengthen their support for the Service. In other action, the Committee considered a consolidated draft of the 1992 ACC guidelines on the joint participation of the UN system in international expositions and decided that suggestions for changes should be communicated to the Secretariat by 15 September to finalize the text in time for the meeting of the ACC Organizational Committee. JUNIC discussed the work of its Technical Advisory Group on the use of computer technology in public information, system-wide guidelines for posting information on the Internet and arrangements for joint participation in international film competitions, film festivals and media markets.

GENERAL ASSEMBLY ACTION

On 6 December [meeting 71], the General Assembly, on the recommendation of the Fourth Committee [A/54/578], adopted **resolutions 54/82 A** and **B** without vote [agenda item 91].

Questions relating to information

A

Information in the service of humanity

The General Assembly,

Taking note of the comprehensive and important report of the Committee on Information,

Also taking note of the report of the Secretary-General on questions relating to information,

Urges all countries, organizations of the United Nations system as a whole and all others concerned, reaffirming their commitment to the principles of the Charter of the United Nations and to the principles of freedom of the press and freedom of information, as well as to those of the independence, pluralism and diversity of the media, deeply concerned by the disparities existing between developed and developing countries and the consequences of every kind arising from those disparities that affect the capability of the public, private or other media and individuals in developing countries to disseminate information and communicate their views and their cultural and ethical values through endogenous cultural production, as well as to ensure the diversity of sources and their free access to information, and recognizing the call in this context for what in the United Nations and at various international forums has been termed "a new world information and communication order, seen as an evolving and continuous process":

(a) To cooperate and interact with a view to reducing existing disparities in information flows at all levels by increasing assistance for the development of communication infrastructures and capabilities in developing countries, with due regard for their needs and the priorities attached to such areas by those countries, and in order to enable them and the public, private or other media in developing countries to develop their own information and communication policies freely and independently and increase the participation of media and individuals in the communication process, and to ensure a free flow of information at all levels;

(b) To ensure for journalists the free and effective performance of their professional tasks and condemn resolutely all attacks against them;

(c) To provide support for the continuation and strengthening of practical training programmes for broadcasters and journalists from public, private and other media in developing countries;

(d) To enhance regional efforts and cooperation among developing countries, as well as cooperation between developed and developing countries, to strengthen communication capacities and to improve the media infrastructure and communication technology in the developing countries, especially in the areas of training and dissemination of information;

(e) To aim at, in addition to bilateral cooperation, providing all possible support and assistance to the developing countries and their media, public, private or other, with due regard to their interests and needs in the field of information and to action already adopted within the United Nations system, including:

(i) The development of the human and technical resources that are indispensable for the improvement of information and communication systems in developing countries and support for the continuation and strengthening of practical training programmes, such as those already operating under both public and private auspices throughout the developing world;

(ii) The creation of conditions that will enable developing countries and their media, public, private or other, to have, by using their national and regional resources, the communication technology suited to their national needs, as well as the necessary programme material, especially for radio and television broadcasting;

(iii) Assistance in establishing and promoting telecommunication links at the subregional, regional and interregional levels, especially among developing countries;

(iv) The facilitation, as appropriate, of access by the developing countries to advanced communication technology available on the open market;

(f) To provide full support for the International Programme for the Development of Communication of the United Nations Educational, Scientific and Cultural Organization, which should support both public and private media.

B

United Nations public information policies and activities

The General Assembly,

Reiterating its decision to consolidate the role of the Committee on Information as its main subsidiary body mandated to make recommendations to it relating to the work of the Department of Public Information of the Secretariat,

Concurring with the view of the Secretary-General that public information and communications should be placed at the heart of the strategic management of the United Nations, and that a culture of communications should permeate all levels of the Organization, as a means of fully informing the peoples of the world of the aims and activities of the United Nations,

1. *Reaffirms* its resolution 13(I) of 13 February 1946, in which it established the Department of Public Information of the Secretariat;

2. *Welcomes* Angola, the Republic of Moldova and Solomon Islands to membership in the Committee on Information;

3. *Calls upon* the Secretary-General, in respect of the public information policies and activities of the United Nations, to continue to implement fully the recommendations contained in paragraph 2 of its resolution 48/44 B of 10 December 1993 and other mandates as established by the General Assembly;

4. *Takes note* of the report of the Secretary-General on the reorientation of United Nations activities in the field of public information and communications and encourages him to continue the reorientation exercise, while stressing the need to take into account the views of Member States, and requests him to report thereon to the Committee on Information at its twenty-second session in May 2000;

5. *Emphasizes* that, through its reorientation, the Department of Public Information should maintain and improve its activities in the areas of special interest to developing countries and, where appropriate, other countries with special needs, including countries in transition, and that such reorientation should contribute to bridging the existing gap between the developing and the developed countries in the crucial field of public information and communications;

6. *Takes note* of the report of the Secretary-General on programme 23, Public information, of the proposed medium-term plan for the period 2002-2005 and, emphasizing that the implementation of the broad objec-

tives outlined in the proposal should be in accordance with the objectives set forth in relevant General Assembly resolutions regarding questions relating to information, requests the Secretary-General to proceed with the submission of the proposal to the Committee for Programme and Coordination for consideration, in accordance with section I of General Assembly resolution 53/207 of 18 December 1998;

7. *Requests* the Secretary-General also to focus in particular on educational institutions as key and indispensable partners of the United Nations in its efforts fully to inform the peoples of the world of its aims and activities;

8. *Takes note with appreciation* of the efforts of the Secretary-General to strengthen the public information capacity of the Department of Public Information for the formation and day-to-day functioning of the information components of peacekeeping and other field operations of the United Nations, and requests the Secretariat to continue to ensure the involvement of the Department from the planning stage of such future operations through interdepartmental consultations and coordination with other substantive departments of the Secretariat;

9. *Encourages* the Secretary-General further to strengthen consultative arrangements between the Department of Public Information and other substantive departments of the Secretariat, in particular those dealing with development issues;

10. *Recalls* its resolution 53/22 of 4 November 1998 concerning the proclamation of 2001 as the United Nations Year of Dialogue among Civilizations, and encourages the Secretary-General to strengthen the public information capacity of the Department of Public Information with a view to disseminating information on and drawing international attention to the dialogue among civilizations and the impact it could have on promoting mutual understanding, tolerance, peaceful coexistence and international cooperation;

11. *Also recalls* its resolution 53/202 of 17 December 1998 concerning the designation of the fifty-fifth session of the General Assembly as the Millennium Assembly of the United Nations and the convening, as an integral part of the Millennium Assembly, of the Millennium Summit of the United Nations, and encourages the Secretary-General to formulate and implement an effective public information strategy in this regard so as to ensure that the Summit will enjoy broad international support;

12. *Emphasizes* that all publications of the Department of Public Information should fulfil an identifiable need, should not duplicate other publications of the United Nations system and should be produced in a cost-effective manner;

13. *Takes note with appreciation* of the efforts of the Secretary-General to move the Dag Hammarskjöld Library in the direction of a virtual library, and requests him, at the same time, to enrich the stock of books and journals in the Library, including publications on peace and security and development-related issues, in order to ensure that it continues to be a broadly accessible resource for information about the United Nations and its activities;

14. *Urges* the Secretary-General to exert all efforts to ensure that publications and other information services of the Secretariat, including the United Nations Web site, contain comprehensive, objective and equitable information about the issues before the Organization and that they maintain editorial independence, impartiality, accuracy and full consistency with resolutions and decisions of the General Assembly;

15. *Notes* that the request made to the Secretary-General, in its resolution 53/59 B of 3 December 1998, to ensure full and direct access for the representatives of Member States to the briefings organized at Headquarters by the Office of the Spokesman for the Secretary-General and to ensure wider outreach of the outcome of such briefings has not been implemented, and therefore reiterates that request;

16. *Requests* the Secretary-General to ensure that information presented to the media is made available to delegations fully and in a timely fashion;

17. *Reaffirms* the importance attached by Member States to the role of United Nations information centres in effectively and comprehensively disseminating information in all parts of the world, in particular in developing countries and countries in transition, and especially in those countries where there is need for a better understanding of United Nations activities;

18. *Also reaffirms* the importance of all United Nations information centres meeting the primary objectives outlined by the Committee on Information in its report on its ninth session;

19. *Takes note* of the report of the Secretary-General on the integration of United Nations information centres with field offices of the United Nations Development Programme, in which he notes that the objectives of the integration exercise remain valid, and notes his intention to make a concerted effort to address the problems encountered in the implementation of the integration exercise in a number of information centres;

20. *Notes with concern* that, while the co-location of United Nations information centres with field offices of the United Nations Development Programme has, to some extent, been able to enhance the image of the United Nations, the integration of United Nations information centres with field offices of the Programme has, in general, resulted in a lower level of programme delivery and a narrower range of activities and, in cases of relocation of information centres to common premises with the Programme, has frequently resulted in higher maintenance costs and leadership and staff problems, and that, to a large extent, the policy of integration has not in all cases achieved its stated objective of performing functions efficiently, effectively and in a cost-effective manner;

21. *Requests* the Secretary-General to carry out a case-by-case review and submit his proposals on the functioning of the integrated centres on a priority basis, in full consultation with the host Governments, and to submit a report to the Committee on Information at its twenty-second session;

22. *Notes* that the Department of Public Information intends to prepare, in collaboration with the United Nations Development Programme, a set of guidelines indicating the operational framework for the integrated centres, and requests the Secretary-General to report on the guidelines, prior to their implementation, to the Committee on Information at its twenty-second session;

23. *Reaffirms* the role of the General Assembly in relation to the opening of new United Nations information centres, and invites the Secretary-General to make such recommendations as he may consider necessary regarding the establishment and location of such centres;

24. *Takes note* of the information provided by the Secretary-General in his report concerning the allocation of resources to United Nations information centres in 1998, and calls upon him to continue to study ways and means of rationalizing and effecting the equitable disbursement of available resources to all United Nations information centres and to report thereon to the Committee on Information at its twenty-second session;

25. *Welcomes* the action taken by some Member States with regard to providing financial and material support to United Nations information centres in their respective capitals, and invites the Secretary-General, through the Department of Public Information, to consult Member States, where appropriate, on the possibility of providing the centres with additional voluntary support on a national basis, bearing in mind that such support should not be a substitute for the full allocation of financial requirements for the United Nations information centres in the context of the programme budget of the United Nations;

26. *Welcomes also* the requests by Croatia, Gabon, Guinea, Haiti, Jamaica and Kyrgyzstan for information centres or information components;

27. *Recognizes* the continuing enhanced cooperation between the Department of Public Information and the University for Peace in Costa Rica as a focal point for promoting United Nations activities and disseminating United Nations information materials, and requests the Secretary-General to report on those activities;

28. *Expresses its full support* for wide, accurate, equal and prompt coverage of United Nations activities through the continuation and improvement of United Nations press releases, stresses the importance of having these press releases issued in all official languages of the United Nations, and requests other relevant bodies of the General Assembly to give due consideration to this matter;

29. *Stresses* that radio is one of the most cost-effective and far-reaching media available to the Department of Public Information and an important instrument in United Nations activities, such as development and peacekeeping, in accordance with General Assembly resolution 48/44 B;

30. *Encourages* further increasing the number of programmes of United Nations Radio, in all available languages, on the United Nations site on the Internet;

31. *Requests* the Secretary-General to implement fully the recommendations contained in paragraph 9 of General Assembly resolution 38/82 B of 15 December 1983 with regard to the introduction of full programming in French and Creole in the work programme of the Caribbean Unit of United Nations Radio;

32. *Takes note* of the report of the Secretary-General on the design and scope of a pilot project for the development of an international radio broadcasting capacity for the United Nations, and requests the Department of Public Information to start, as soon as possible, the implementation of the pilot project through, inter alia, contacts with interested Member States and specialized institutions, with a view to ensuring the assistance necessary for the success of the project, taking into account the need to enhance the existing resources and services, and requests the Secretary-General to submit a progress report on the implementation of this project to the Committee on Information at its twenty-second session;

33. *Underlines* the continuing importance of using traditional and mass media channels to disseminate information on the United Nations, and encourages the Secretary-General, through the Department of Public Information, to continue to take full advantage of recent developments in information technologies, including the Internet, in order to improve, in a cost-effective manner, the dissemination of information on the United Nations, in accordance with the priorities established by the General Assembly and taking into account the linguistic diversity of the Organization;

34. *Takes note* of efforts by some United Nations information centres to establish their own Web pages in local languages, and recommends that the Department of Public Information encourage other information centres to develop Web pages in the respective local languages of their host countries;

35. *Takes note with appreciation*, with reference to the report of the Secretary-General on the continuous development, maintenance and enrichment of United Nations Web sites and the report of the Secretary-General on the multilingual development, maintenance and enrichment of United Nations Web sites, of the efforts of the Secretary-General to develop and enhance the United Nations Web sites in all official languages of the Organization, requests him to pursue these efforts and to continue to develop proposals for consideration by the Committee on Information at its twenty-second session, having in mind the goal of achieving modular parity among official languages, stressing that this goal should be achieved in a cost-effective manner and with a focus on textual content;

36. *Welcomes* the establishment of the Geneva Diplomatic Community Network, which has improved the dissemination of information among the permanent missions, the United Nations Office at Geneva and the other international organizations based in Geneva, and requests the Secretary-General to continue providing his support to this important programme;

37. *Expresses its appreciation* for the ongoing programme for broadcasters and journalists from developing countries and countries in transition conducted by the Department of Public Information, and calls for its further expansion so as to include a larger number of trainees from developing countries;

38. *Acknowledges* the important work carried out by the United Nations Educational, Scientific and Cultural Organization and its collaboration with news agencies and broadcasting organizations in developing countries in disseminating information on priority issues;

39. *Requests* the Department of Public Information to continue to ensure the greatest possible access for United Nations guided tours, and to ensure that displays in public areas are kept as informative, up-to-date, relevant and technologically innovative as possible;

40. *Recalls* its resolutions concerning the consequences of the Chernobyl disaster, in particular resolutions 51/138 B of 13 December 1996 and 52/172 of 16 December 1997, and encourages the Department of Public Information, in cooperation with the countries concerned and with the relevant organizations and bodies of the United Nations system, to continue to take appropriate measures to enhance world public awareness of the consequences of that disaster;

41. *Recalls also* its resolution 53/1 H of 16 November 1998, concerning international cooperation and coordination for the human and ecological rehabilitation of the Semipalatinsk region of Kazakhstan, which has been affected by nuclear tests, and encourages the Department of Public Information, in cooperation with relevant organizations and bodies of the United Nations system, to take appropriate measures to enhance world public awareness of the problems and needs of the Semipalatinsk region;

42. *Recalls* its resolution 53/59 B of 3 December 1998 and urges the Department of Public Information to take the necessary measures, through the provision of relevant and objective information, with a view to achieving the major objectives set forth in the report of the Secretary-General on the causes of conflict and the promotion of durable peace and sustainable development in Africa;

43. *Requests* the Secretary-General to report to the Committee on Information at its twenty-second session and to the General Assembly at its fifty-fifth session on the activities of the Department of Public Information and on the implementation of the recommendations contained in the present resolution;

44. *Requests* the Committee on Information to report to the General Assembly at its fifty-fifth session;

45. *Decides* to include in the provisional agenda of its fifty-fifth session the item entitled "Questions relating to information".

Information and communications in the context of international security

Pursuant to General Assembly resolution 53/70 [YUN 1998, p. 38], the Secretary-General, in an August report [A/54/213], transmitted the views of 10 Member States on the general appreciation of the issues of international security; the definition of basic notions related to information security, including unauthorized interference with or misuse of information and telecommunications systems and information resources; and the advisability of developing international principles to enhance the security of global information and telecommunications systems and help combat information terrorism and criminality.

GENERAL ASSEMBLY ACTION

On 1 December [meeting 69], the General Assembly, on the recommendation of the First (Disarmament and International Security) Committee [A/54/558], adopted **resolution 54/49** without vote [agenda item 71].

Developments in the field of information and telecommunications in the context of international security

The General Assembly,

Recalling its resolution 53/70 of 4 December 1998,

Recalling also its resolutions on the role of science and technology in the context of international security, in which, inter alia, it recognized that scientific and technological developments could have both civilian and military applications and that progress in science and technology for civilian applications needed to be maintained and encouraged,

Noting that considerable progress has been achieved in developing and applying the latest information technologies and means of telecommunication,

Affirming that it sees in this process the broadest positive opportunities for the further development of civilization, the expansion of opportunities for cooperation for the common good of all States, the enhancement of the creative potential of mankind and additional improvements in the circulation of information in the global community,

Recalling in this connection the approaches and principles outlined at the Information Society and Development Conference, held at Midrand, South Africa, from 13 to 15 May 1996,

Taking note of the results of the Ministerial Conference on Terrorism, held in Paris on 30 July 1996, and of the recommendations it made,

Noting that the dissemination and use of information technologies and means affect the interests of the entire international community and that optimum effectiveness is enhanced by broad international cooperation,

Expressing concern that these technologies and means can potentially be used for purposes that are inconsistent with the objectives of maintaining international stability and security and may adversely affect the security of States in both civilian and military fields,

Considering that it is necessary to prevent the misuse or exploitation of information resources or technologies for criminal or terrorist purposes,

Noting the contribution of those Member States that have submitted their assessments on issues of information security to the Secretary-General pursuant to paragraphs 1 to 3 of resolution 53/70,

Taking note of the report of the Secretary-General containing those assessments,

Welcoming the timely initiative taken by the Secretariat and the United Nations Institute for Disarmament Research in convening an international meeting of experts at Geneva in August 1999 on developments in the field of information and telecommunications in the context of international security,

Considering that the assessments of Member States contained in the report of the Secretary-General and the international meeting of experts have contributed to a better understanding of the substance of issues of international information security, related notions and possible measures to limit the threats emerging in this field,

1. *Calls upon* Member States to promote further at multilateral levels the consideration of existing and potential threats in the field of information security;

2. *Invites* all Member States to continue to inform the Secretary-General of their views and assessments on the following questions:

(*a*) General appreciation of the issues of information security;

(*b*) Definition of basic notions related to information security, including unauthorized interference with or misuse of information and telecommunications systems and information resources;

(*c*) Advisability of developing international principles that would enhance the security of global information and telecommunications systems and help to combat information terrorism and criminality;

3. *Requests* the Secretary-General to submit a report to the General Assembly at its fifty-fifth session;

4. *Decides* to include in the provisional agenda of its fifty-fifth session the item entitled "Developments in the field of information and telecommunications in the context of international security".

Peaceful uses of outer space

UNISPACE III

In accordance with General Assembly resolution 52/56 [YUN 1997, p. 579], the Third United Nations Conference on the Exploration and Peaceful Uses of Outer Space (UNISPACE III) was held in Vienna from 19 to 30 July [A/CONF.184/6] as a special session of the Committee on the Peaceful Uses of Outer Space (Committee on Outer Space), under the theme "Space benefits for humanity in the twenty-first century".

The purpose of the Conference was to review the advances in space science and technology that had taken place since the Second Conference in 1982 [YUN 1982, p. 162], with a view to promoting their greater use, particularly by developing countries, in all areas of scientific, economic, social and cultural development.

On 30 July, the participants adopted a resolution entitled "The Space Millennium: Vienna Declaration on Space and Human Development", by which they declared a strategy to protect Earth's environment and manage its resources; use space applications for human security, development and welfare; advance scientific knowledge of space and protect the space environment; enhance education and training and ensure public awareness of the importance of space activities; and strengthen and reposition space activities in the UN system.

The Conference was attended by 98 Member States, Switzerland and the Holy See and the observer for Palestine. Also in attendance were the secretariats of UN regional commissions, several specialized agencies and UN programmes, intergovernmental organizations, international organizations having permanent observer status with the Committee on Outer Space and organizations not having permanent observer status, in addition to representatives of a large number of NGOs and space industries.

The Conference established two main committees and a Technical Forum. Committee I dealt with the status of the scientific knowledge of Earth and its environment; the benefits of basic space science and capacity-building; information needs; and the promotion of international cooperation [A/CONF.184/L.17]. Committee II considered the status and applications of space science and technology; and economic and societal benefits of space technology [A/CONF.184/L.18]. The Technical Forum, which examined issues of space science, technology and law, consisted of 38 seminars, workshops, symposia, scientific and technical forums, round tables and panel discussions. The conclusions and proposals emanating from the Technical Forum were annexed to the report of the Conference.

By an October note [A/54/476], the Secretary-General drew to the General Assembly's attention the report of the Conference.

Preparations for UNISPACE III

The Committee on Outer Space, at its forty-second session in Vienna from 14 to 16 July [A/54/20 & Corr.1], acting as the Preparatory Committee for UNISPACE III, continued to consider preparations for the Conference and reviewed the reports of the 1999 sessions of its Scientific and Technical and Legal Subcommittees on issues assigned to them by General Assembly resolution 53/45 [YUN 1998, p. 593]. The Preparatory Committee noted that the Advisory Committee (the Scientific and Technical Subcommittee) had convened the Working Group of the Whole to assist it in finalizing its preparatory work for UNISPACE III. The Working Group considered the revised draft text of the Conference's report and the revised draft text of the Vienna declaration on space and human development, as well as the recommendations of the regional preparatory conferences for UNISPACE III for Asia and the Pacific, Africa and the Middle East [A/CONF.184/PC/L.5] and for Latin America and the Caribbean and Eastern Europe [A/CONF.184/PC/L.5/Add.1]. In 1999, a regional preparatory conference for UNISPACE III for Eastern Europe took place (Bucharest, Romania, 25-29 January) [A/CONF.184/PC/5].

As part of the follow-up to UNISPACE III, the Preparatory Committee agreed that the executive secretariat should prepare a report on organizational matters relating to UNISPACE III to provide other entities of the UN system with guidelines on using existing resources to organize a conference on global issues. The report was submitted to the Assembly's Fourth Committee in October [A/C.4/54/9]. The Preparatory Committee recommended that the Working Group of the Whole be reconvened by the Scientific and Technical Subcommittee at its thirty-seventh (2000) session to assist the Subcommittee in considering its future work in the light of UNISPACE III recommendations.

GENERAL ASSEMBLY ACTION

On 6 December [meeting 71], the General Assembly, on the recommendation of the Fourth Committee [A/54/574], adopted **resolution 54/68** without vote [agenda item 87].

Third United Nations Conference on the Exploration and Peaceful Uses of Outer Space

The General Assembly,

Recalling its resolutions 51/123 of 13 December 1996, 52/56 of 10 December 1997 and 53/45 of 3 December 1998 concerning the preparations for and convening of the Third United Nations Conference on the Exploration and Peaceful Uses of Outer Space (UNISPACE III), held at Vienna from 19 to 30 July 1999,

Reaffirming the importance of international cooperation in the exploration and peaceful uses of outer space,

Expressing its satisfaction with the successful preparation of UNISPACE III through the Committee on the Peaceful Uses of Outer Space, as the Preparatory Committee, and its Scientific and Technical Subcommittee, as the Advisory Committee, as well as the Office for Outer Space Affairs of the Secretariat as the executive secretariat, and commending their efforts to organize UNISPACE III within existing resources,

Recognizing the contributions of the Technical Forum and the Space Generation Forum to UNISPACE III,

Having considered the report of the Third United Nations Conference on the Exploration and Peaceful Uses of Outer Space and the recommendations contained in the resolution entitled "The Space Millennium: Vienna Declaration on Space and Human Development",

Stressing the importance of promoting effective means of using space technology to assist in the solution of problems of regional or global significance and of strengthening the capabilities of Member States, in particular developing countries, to use the applications of space research for economic, social and cultural development,

Conscious of the need to expedite the use of space applications by Member States to promote sustainable development and to increase the awareness of the general public with regard to the benefits of space technology,

Desiring to enhance the opportunities for education, training and technical assistance in space science and technology and their applications aimed at the development of indigenous capabilities in all States,

Expressing its profound gratitude to the Government and people of Austria for the hospitality extended to the participants of UNISPACE III and for the facilities placed at their disposal,

1. *Takes note with satisfaction* of the report of the Third United Nations Conference on the Exploration and Peaceful Uses of Outer Space;

2. *Endorses* the resolution entitled "The Space Millennium: Vienna Declaration on Space and Human Development";

3. *Urges* Governments, organs, organizations and programmes within the United Nations system as well as intergovernmental and non-governmental organizations and industries conducting space-related activities to take the necessary action for the effective implementation of the Vienna Declaration;

4. *Calls upon* all concerned to implement the recommendations made by UNISPACE III as reflected in its report;

5. *Requests* all relevant organizations of the United Nations system to review and, where necessary, adjust their programmes and activities in line with the recommendations of UNISPACE III and to take appropriate measures to ensure their full and effective implementation, taking into account the needs of developing countries, in particular by further enhancing the coordination of their space-related activities through the Inter-Agency Meeting on Outer Space Activities;

6. *Invites* all relevant governing bodies of the organizations within the United Nations system responsible for space-related activities to establish an ad hoc intergovernmental advisory group to review interagency coordination of space-related activities with a view to increasing the effectiveness of the work of the Inter-Agency Meeting on Outer Space Activities;

7. *Declares* 4 to 10 October World Space Week to celebrate each year at the international level the contributions of space science and technology to the betterment of the human condition, bearing in mind that 4 October 1957 was the date of the launch into outer space of the first human-made Earth satellite, Sputnik 1, thus opening the way for space exploration, and that 10 October 1967 was the date of the entry into force of the Treaty on Principles Governing the Activities of States in the Exploration and Use of Outer Space, including the Moon and Other Celestial Bodies;

8. *Requests* the Secretary-General to modify the terms of reference of the Trust Fund for the United Nations Programme on Space Applications established pursuant to General Assembly resolution 37/90 of 10 December 1982 on the Second United Nations Conference on the Exploration and Peaceful Uses of Outer Space, to include implementation of the recommendations of UNISPACE III;

9. *Also requests* the Secretary-General to invite all States to contribute voluntarily to the Trust Fund for the United Nations Programme on Space Applications and, in his letter of invitation, to identify priority project proposals, on the basis of recommendations of the Committee on the Peaceful Uses of Outer Space, and requests the Office for Outer Space Affairs of the Secretariat to provide the Committee with a report listing those States which have responded to the invitation;

10. *Agrees* that the Committee on the Peaceful Uses of Outer Space and its secretariat should identify new and innovative funding sources for implementing the recommendations of UNISPACE III in order to supplement the resources to be provided through the Trust Fund for the United Nations Programme on Space Applications;

11. *Requests* the Secretary-General to recommend measures to ensure that the Office for Outer Space Affairs is provided with adequate resources to implement the following actions based on the recommendations of UNISPACE III:

(a) Providing the Scientific and Technical Subcommittee and the Legal Subcommittee of the Committee on the Peaceful Uses of Outer Space with necessary analytical documents, both on the substance and on the organization of work, to facilitate their consideration of new items called for in the agenda structures adopted by the Committee at its forty-second session;

(b) Organizing, in order to strengthen the partnership of the Scientific and Technical Subcommittee with industry, a one-day symposium during the thirty-seventh session of the Subcommittee to provide Member States with updated information on commercially available products, services and ongoing activities of the space-related industry;

(c) Identifying and promoting the use of appropriate space technologies to meet the needs of programmes and organizations within the United Nations system in carrying out activities that have not yet benefited from the use of space technology to enhance their effectiveness and efficiency;

(d) Strengthening the activities of the United Nations Programme on Space Applications to include the following:

(i) Facilitating and supporting the development and implementation of space-related projects that address the operational needs of Member States;

(ii) Providing support to the regional centres for space science and technology education affiliated with the United Nations, including the Network of Space Science and Technology Education and Research Institutions for Central, Eastern and South-Eastern Europe;

(iii) Reorienting the long-term fellowship programme;

(iv) Organizing workshops and conferences on advanced space applications and new system developments for programme managers and leaders of space technology development and applications activities;

(v) Organizing medium-term courses on remote-sensing education for university educators and on telecommunications and tele-health for professionals;

(vi) Providing technical advisory services to Member States, on request, on different aspects of space science and technology and related applications;

(vii) Promoting cooperation in space applications projects between government establishments, universities and research institutions and private industry;

(viii) Organizing an annual public forum to inform the general public of past, ongoing and planned space activities and the future direction of such activities;

(ix) Promoting activities for youth, so as to encourage interest among students and young scientists and engineers;

(x) Promoting cooperation in the development of educational programmes in space science and technology for primary and secondary school curricula;

(xi) Establishing a programme of visits by astronauts, cosmonauts and other space scientists and engineers to increase knowledge about space-related activities, in particular among young people;

(xii) Promoting the participation of scientists from developing countries in space science and planetary exploration;

(xiii) Initiating programmes to promote the use of satellite communications and Earth observation data for disaster management and to provide opportunities for professionals to put into practice the knowledge that they have acquired through training courses;

12. *Calls upon* the Secretary-General to ensure the availability of the report of UNISPACE III, including its proceedings, and to disseminate as widely as possible the results of UNISPACE III, in particular the Vienna Declaration and the summary of the background and recommendations of UNISPACE III;

13. *Notes* that, in response to a request made by the Preparatory Committee for UNISPACE III at its 1999 session, the executive secretariat has prepared for submission to the General Assembly a document on organizational matters relating to UNISPACE III, with the aim of providing other entities in the United Nations system with guidelines on using existing resources to organize a conference on global issues;

14. *Agrees* that the document prepared by the executive secretariat on organizational matters relating to UNISPACE III should be issued as a report to the General Assembly during its fifty-fourth session;

15. *Requests* the Secretary-General to report to the General Assembly at its fifty-fifth session on the implementation of the recommendations of UNISPACE III;

16. *Decides* to review and appraise, at its fifty-ninth session, the implementation of the outcome of UNISPACE III and to consider further actions and initiatives, and, in this context, requests the Committee on the Peaceful Uses of Outer Space to submit for consideration by the General Assembly at its fifty-seventh session recommendations on the format, scope and organizational aspects of the review.

Scientific and Technical Subcommittee

The Scientific and Technical Subcommittee of the Committee on Outer Space, at its thirty-sixth session (Vienna, 22-26 February) [A/AC.105/719], reviewed preparations for UNISPACE III, the United Nations Programme on Space Applications and space debris.

UN Programme on Space Applications

The United Nations Programme on Space Applications, as mandated by General Assembly resolution 37/90 [YUN 1982, p. 163], continued to focus on developing indigenous capability at the local level in space science and technology through long-range training fellowships, technical advisory services, regional and international training courses and conferences; acquiring and disseminating space-related information; and promoting cooperation between developed and developing countries.

As indicated by the UN Expert on Space Applications in his report to the Subcommittee [A/AC.105/730], pursuant to Assembly resolution 45/72 [YUN 1990, p. 99], the Programme continued to work with Member States to establish regional centres for space science and technology education in developing countries. Jordan, which was identified as the host country for a space science and technology education centre in western Asia, was asked to prepare a draft agreement to be entered into by all the countries of the region. Other centres were operating in Africa (Morocco and Nigeria); Asia and the Pacific (India); and Latin America and the Caribbean (Brazil). A meeting of national coordinators on the proposed network of space science and technology education and research institutions for Central, Eastern and South-Eastern Europe (Sofia, Bulgaria, 21-22 October) made progress towards finalizing a draft text of an agreement to establish the network. The Office for Outer Space Affairs would also prepare for signature a cooperation agreement between the Office and the network.

The Programme held six training courses, workshops and conferences in 1999, including one preparatory meeting for UNISPACE III. It received three fellowship offers from the European Space Agency for 1999-2000. Various technical advisory services were also provided under the Programme.

The Subcommittee, noting that the Programme was the priority activity of the Office for Outer Space Affairs, expressed concern over its limited financial resources and appealed for voluntary contributions from Member States.

The Assembly, in **resolution 54/67** (see p. 560), endorsed the 2000 UN Programme on Space Applications, as proposed by the Expert on Space Applications.

Scientific and technical issues

Space debris

In 1999, the Scientific and Technical Subcommittee agreed that international cooperation was needed to expand strategies to minimize the potential impact of space debris on future space missions. It considered information received from 14 States on their space programmes, including information on the spin-off benefits of space activities [A/AC.105/729 & Add.1], and noted the replies received from five States [A/AC.105/708 & Add.1,2] in response to its request for information on national research on space debris, the safety of nuclear-powered satellites and the problems of collisions of nuclear-powered sources with space debris. Further replies were received by December from six additional States [A/AC.105/731]. The Subcommittee adopted the final text of the technical report on space debris [A/AC.105/707]. In the Subcommittee, the view was expressed that there was a need to develop a common database for space debris that could serve as a clearing house of information for the international community for research.

The Committee on Outer Space agreed with the Subcommittee's recommendations that the Inter-Agency Space Debris Coordination Committee (IADC) should continue to brief the Subcommittee annually on space debris and that efforts should continue to model and characterize the debris environment. It also agreed that the Subcommittee in 2000 should review international application of the International Telecommunication Union (ITU) standards and IADC recommendations concerning the disposal of satellites at the end of their useful life. The Committee further recommended that the Secretariat should compile relevant data on space objects in geosynchronous orbit.

In response to that request, the Secretariat submitted a December report on the disposal of satellites in geosynchronous orbit [A/AC.105/734], which concluded that, because the ITU standards and IADC recommendations had been developed only recently and were not mandatory, it was difficult to evaluate their international application. Although most satellite operators were aware of the seriousness of the situation near the geostationary satellite orbit and had acknowledged the wisdom of taking some mitigation measures, because of technical and managerial problems even self-imposed guidelines were not being followed in many cases. For geostationary orbit-protection measures to become effective, a broad international consensus should be reached on the guidelines, and their implementation systematically monitored.

Legal Subcommittee

The Legal Subcommittee, at its thirty-eighth session (Vienna, 1-5 March) [A/AC.105/721], again considered, through its working group, the definition and delimitation of outer space and the character and utilization of the geostationary orbit, including ways to ensure its rational and equitable use, without prejudice to ITU's role. The Subcommittee agreed that a working paper submitted by the Czech Republic [A/AC.105/C.1/L.216] to the Scientific and Technical Subcommittee provided a scientific and technical basis for further discussions.

A working group established by the Subcommittee continued to review the status of the five legal instruments governing outer space: the 1966 Treaty on Principles Governing the Activities of States in the Exploration and Use of Outer Space, including the Moon and Other Celestial Bodies, adopted by the General Assembly in resolution 2222(XXI) [YUN 1966, p. 41]; the 1967 Agreement on the Rescue of Astronauts, the Return of Astronauts and the Return of Objects Launched into Outer Space, adopted in resolution 2345(XXII) [YUN 1967, p. 33]; the 1971 Convention on International Liability for Damage Caused by Space Objects, contained in resolution 2777(XXVI) [YUN 1971, p. 52]; the 1974 Convention on Registration of Objects Launched into Outer Space, contained in resolution 3235(XXIX) [YUN 1974, p. 63]; and the 1979 Agreement Governing the Activities of States on the Moon and Other Celestial Bodies, contained in resolution 34/68 [YUN 1979, p. 111].

The working group recommended a series of measures to achieve the fullest adherence to the five instruments: States not parties to them should be invited to consider ratifying or acceding to them; States should be invited to consider making a declaration, in accordance with Assembly resolution 2777(XXVI), thereby binding themselves on a reciprocal basis to the decisions of the Claims Commission, established in the event of a dispute in terms of the provisions of the 1971 Convention; and the issue of the strict compliance by States with the provisions of instruments governing outer space to which they were currently parties should be examined further to identify measures to encourage full compliance.

In response to a 1998 request of the Subcommittee [YUN 1998, p. 593], the Secretariat, in June [A/AC.105/724], submitted a list of international agreements and other available legal documents relevant to space-related activities. A revised version of the list, incorporating the comments of Member States, had been published in a booklet, *International Agreements and Other Available Legal Documents Relevant to Space-related Activities,* for reference during UNISPACE III.

In accordance with its 1998 recommendation [YUN 1998, p. 593], the Subcommittee suspended consideration of the 1992 Principles Relevant to the Use of Nuclear Power Sources in Outer Space [YUN 1992, p. 116], pending the results of deliberations in the Scientific and Technical Subcommittee.

GENERAL ASSEMBLY ACTION

On 6 December [meeting 71], the General Assembly, on the recommendation of the Fourth Committee [A/54/574], adopted **resolution 54/67** without vote [agenda item 87].

International cooperation in the peaceful uses of outer space

The General Assembly,

Recalling its resolutions 51/122 of 13 December 1996 and 53/45 of 3 December 1998,

Deeply convinced of the common interest of mankind in promoting the exploration and use of outer space for peaceful purposes and in continuing efforts to extend to all States the benefits derived therefrom, and also of the importance of international cooperation in this field, for which the United Nations should continue to provide a focal point,

Reaffirming the importance of international cooperation in developing the rule of law, including the relevant norms of space law and their important role in international cooperation for the exploration and use of outer space for peaceful purposes, and of the widest possible adherence to international treaties that promote the peaceful uses of outer space,

Concerned about the possibility of an arms race in outer space,

Recognizing that all States, in particular those with major space capabilities, should contribute actively to the goal of preventing an arms race in outer space as an essential condition for the promotion of international cooperation in the exploration and use of outer space for peaceful purposes,

Considering that space debris is an issue of concern to all nations,

Noting the progress achieved in the further development of peaceful space exploration and applications as well as in various national and cooperative space projects, which contributes to international cooperation, and the importance of further international cooperation in this field,

Taking note with satisfaction of the successful conclusion of the Third United Nations Conference on the Exploration and Peaceful Uses of Outer Space (UNISPACE III), held at Vienna from 19 to 30 July 1999 as a special session of the Committee on the Peaceful Uses of Outer Space open to all States Members of the United Nations,

Taking into account the recommendations contained in the resolution entitled "The Space Millennium: Vienna Declaration on Space and Human Development", adopted by UNISPACE III,

Having considered the report of the Committee on the Peaceful Uses of Outer Space on the work of its forty-second session,

1. *Endorses* the report of the Committee on the Peaceful Uses of Outer Space on the work of its forty-second session;

2. *Invites* States that have not yet become parties to the international treaties governing the uses of outer space to give consideration to ratifying those treaties or acceding to them;

3. *Notes* that, at its thirty-eighth session, the Legal Subcommittee of the Committee on the Peaceful Uses of Outer Space, in its working groups, continued its work as mandated by the General Assembly in its resolution 53/45;

4. *Welcomes* the new approach taken by the Committee in composing the agenda of the Legal Subcommit-

tee, and endorses the recommendation of the Committee that the Subcommittee, at its thirty-ninth session, taking into account the concerns of all countries, in particular those of developing countries:

(a) Consider the following as regular agenda items:

(i) General exchange of views;

(ii) Status of the international treaties governing the uses of outer space;

(iii) Information on the activities of international organizations relating to space law;

(iv) Matters relating to the definition and delimitation of outer space and to the character and utilization of the geostationary orbit, including consideration of ways and means to ensure the rational and equitable use of the geostationary orbit without prejudice to the role of the International Telecommunication Union;

(b) Continue its consideration of review and possible revision of the Principles Relevant to the Use of Nuclear Power Sources in Outer Space, as a single issue and item for discussion;

(c) Consider the following in accordance with the work plans adopted by the Committee:

(i) Review of the status of the five international legal instruments governing outer space;

(ii) Review of the concept of the "launching State";

5. *Notes* that the Legal Subcommittee, at its thirty-ninth session, will submit its proposals to the Committee for new items to be considered by the Subcommittee at its fortieth session, in 2001;

6. *Notes also* that, in the context of paragraph 4 *(a)* (iv) above, the Legal Subcommittee will reconvene its Working Group to consider the item;

7. *Endorses* the recommendation of the Committee that the Legal Subcommittee, at its thirty-ninth session, suspend consideration in its Working Group of the Principles Relevant to the Use of Nuclear Power Sources in Outer Space pending the results of the work in the Scientific and Technical Subcommittee, without prejudice to the possibility of reconvening its Working Group on that item if, in the opinion of the Legal Subcommittee, sufficient progress has been made in the Scientific and Technical Subcommittee at its thirty-seventh session, to warrant the reconvening of the Working Group;

8. *Also endorses* the recommendations and agreements concerning the organization of work in the Legal Subcommittee;

9. *Takes note* of the agreement reached by the Committee at its fortieth session on the composition of the bureaux of the Committee and its subsidiary bodies for the second term starting in 2000, in the context of the implementation of the measures relating to the working methods of those bodies, which were endorsed by the General Assembly in paragraph 11 of its resolution 52/56 of 10 December 1997, and notes that consultations among delegations and regional groups will be held concerning the members of the bureaux for the second term with a view to reaching consensus on the matter by the thirty-seventh session of the Scientific and Technical Subcommittee;

10. *Agrees* that the Committee should elect its officers at the beginning of its forty-third session, in accordance with consensus agreement to be reached among the members of the Committee on the members of the bureaux of the Committee and its subsidiary bodies for the second term, as an exceptional arrangement for that session of the Committee;

11. *Notes* that the Scientific and Technical Subcommittee of the Committee on the Peaceful Uses of Outer Space, at its thirty-sixth session, continued its work as mandated by the General Assembly in its resolution 53/45;

12. *Notes with satisfaction* that the Scientific and Technical Subcommittee at its thirty-sixth session continued to consider on a priority basis the agenda item on space debris and that the Subcommittee concluded its work according to the multi-year work plan adopted by the Subcommittee at its thirty-second session;

13. *Takes note with satisfaction* of the technical report on space debris submitted by the Scientific and Technical Subcommittee to the Committee, and agrees that the technical report should be widely distributed;

14. *Agrees* that the Scientific and Technical Subcommittee should assess the effectiveness of existing space debris mitigation practices and the extent to which they are being implemented and that efforts to model and characterize the debris environment should continue;

15. *Welcomes* the new approach taken by the Committee in composing the agenda of the Scientific and Technical Subcommittee, and endorses the recommendation of the Committee that the Subcommittee, at its thirty-seventh session, taking into account the concerns of all countries, in particular those of developing countries:

(a) Consider the following items:

(i) General exchange of views and introduction to reports submitted on national activities;

(ii) The United Nations Programme on Space Applications and the coordination of space activities within the United Nations system following the Third United Nations Conference on the Exploration and Peaceful Uses of Outer Space (UNISPACE III);

(iii) Matters relating to remote sensing of the Earth by satellites, including applications for developing countries and monitoring of the Earth's environment;

(b) Consider the item on the use of nuclear power sources in outer space in accordance with the work plan adopted by the Scientific and Technical Subcommittee at its thirty-fifth session;

(c) Consider the following single issues and items for discussion:

(i) International cooperation in human spaceflight;

(ii) Presentations on new launch systems and ventures;

(iii) Space debris, on a priority basis;

(iv) Examination of the physical nature and technical attributes of the geostationary orbit and of its utilization and applications, including, inter alia, in the field of space communications, as well as other questions relating to developments in space communications, taking particular account of the needs and interests of developing countries;

16. *Notes* that the Scientific and Technical Subcommittee, at its thirty-seventh session, will submit its proposal to the Committee for a draft provisional agenda for the thirty-eighth session of the Subcommittee, in 2001;

17. *Also notes* that the theme fixed for special attention at the thirty-seventh session of the Scientific and Technical Subcommittee will be "Space commercialization: an era of new opportunities" and that the Committee on Space Research and the International Astronautical Federation, in liaison with Member States, will be invited to arrange a symposium on that theme, with as wide a participation as possible, to be held during the first week of that session of the Subcommittee;

18. *Agrees* that, in the context of paragraphs 15 *(a)* (ii) and 16 above, the Scientific and Technical Subcommittee at its thirty-seventh session should reconvene the Working Group of the Whole to consider the future work of the Subcommittee in the light of the recommendations of UNISPACE III;

19. *Also agrees* that, in the context of paragraph 15 *(b)* above, the Scientific and Technical Subcommittee at its thirty-seventh session should reconvene its Working Group on the Use of Nuclear Power Sources in Outer Space;

20. *Endorses* the recommendation of the Committee that, in the context of paragraph 15 *(c)* (iii) above, the Scientific and Technical Subcommittee at its thirty-seventh session review international application of the standards of the International Telecommunication Union and recommendations of the Inter-Agency Space Debris Coordination Committee concerning the disposal of satellites in geosynchronous orbit at the end of their useful life;

21. *Also endorses* the United Nations Programme on Space Applications for 2000, as proposed to the Committee by the Expert on Space Applications;

22. *Notes with satisfaction* that, in accordance with paragraph 30 of General Assembly resolution 50/27 of 6 December 1995, the African regional centres for space science and technology education, in the French language and in the English language, were inaugurated in Morocco and Nigeria, respectively, that the Centre for Space Science and Technology Education in Asia and the Pacific continued its education programme in 1999 and that significant progress has been achieved in furthering the goals of the Network of Space Science and Technology Education and Research Institutions for Central, Eastern and South-Eastern Europe and establishing regional centres for space science and technology education in the other regions;

23. *Recommends* that Member States concerned in Asia and the Pacific hold further consultations, with the assistance of the Office for Outer Space Affairs of the Secretariat, with a view to making the Centre for Space Science and Technology Education in Asia and the Pacific grow into a network of nodes;

24. *Also recommends* that more attention be paid to all aspects related to the protection and the preservation of the outer space environment, especially those potentially affecting the Earth's environment;

25. *Considers* that it is essential that Member States pay more attention to the problem of collisions of space objects, including those with nuclear power sources, with space debris, and other aspects of space debris, calls for the continuation of national research on this question, for the development of improved technology for the monitoring of space debris and for the compilation and dissemination of data on space debris, also considers that, to the extent possible, information thereon should be provided to the Scientific and Technical Subcommittee, and agrees that international cooperation is needed to expand appropriate and affordable strategies to minimize the impact of space debris on future space missions;

26. *Urges* all States, in particular those with major space capabilities, to contribute actively to the goal of preventing an arms race in outer space as an essential condition for the promotion of international cooperation in the exploration and use of outer space for peaceful purposes;

27. *Emphasizes* the need to increase the benefits of space technology and its applications and to contribute to an orderly growth of space activities favourable to sustained economic growth and sustainable development in all countries, in particular in the developing countries, and mitigation of the consequences of natural disasters;

28. *Takes note* of the interest of some developing countries, as well as other countries, in becoming members of the Committee, and requests the continued examination of the subject of increasing the number of members of the Committee;

29. *Requests* the Committee to resume its consideration, at its forty-third session, as a matter of priority, of ways and means of maintaining outer space for peaceful purposes and to report thereon to the General Assembly at its fifty-fifth session;

30. *Also requests* the Committee to resume its consideration, at its forty-third session, of the item entitled "Spin-off benefits of space technology: review of current status";

31. *Requests* the specialized agencies and other international organizations to continue and, where appropriate, enhance their cooperation with the Committee and to provide it with progress reports on their work relating to the peaceful uses of outer space;

32. *Requests* the Committee to continue its work, in accordance with the present resolution, to consider, as appropriate, new projects in outer space activities and to submit a report to the General Assembly at its fifty-fifth session, including its views on which subjects should be studied in the future.

Effects of atomic radiation

The United Nations Scientific Committee on the Effects of Atomic Radiation held its forty-eighth session in Vienna from 12 to 16 April [A/54/46]. The Committee, responding to General Assembly resolution 53/44 [YUN 1998, p. 596], continued to review problems of radiation doses and effects. It reported that its deliberations focused on a review of documents prepared by the Secretariat on subjects that the Committee had selected as the most important topics for further study, including exposures from natural radiation sources; exposures from man-made sources of radiation; medical radiation exposures; occupational radiation exposures; dose assessment methodologies; epidemiological evaluation of radiation-induced cancer; DNA repair and mutagenesis; hereditary effects of radiation; combined effects of radiation and other agents; biological effects at low radiation doses—models, mechanisms and uncertainties; and exposures and effects of the Chernobyl accident. The Committee made suggestions for the further development of those topics.

The Committee expected to complete its current assessments and publish its findings in the year 2000.

GENERAL ASSEMBLY ACTION

On 6 December [meeting 71], the General Assembly, on the recommendation of the Fourth Committee [A/54/573], adopted **resolution 54/66** without vote [agenda item 86].

Effects of atomic radiation

The General Assembly,

Recalling its resolution 913(X) of 3 December 1955, by which it established the United Nations Scientific Committee on the Effects of Atomic Radiation, and its subsequent resolutions on the subject, including resolution 53/44 of 3 December 1998, in which, inter alia, it requested the Scientific Committee to continue its work,

Taking note with appreciation of the report of the United Nations Scientific Committee on the Effects of Atomic Radiation,

Reaffirming the desirability of the Scientific Committee continuing its work,

Concerned about the potentially harmful effects on present and future generations resulting from the levels of radiation to which mankind and the environment are exposed,

Noting the views expressed by Member States at its fifty-fourth session with regard to the work of the Scientific Committee,

Conscious of the continuing need to examine and compile information about atomic and ionizing radiation and to analyse its effects on mankind and the environment,

1. *Commends* the United Nations Scientific Committee on the Effects of Atomic Radiation for the valuable contribution it has been making in the course of the past forty-four years, since its inception, to wider knowledge and understanding of the levels, effects and risks of atomic radiation, and for fulfilling its original mandate with scientific authority and independence of judgement;

2. *Reaffirms* the decision to maintain the present functions and independent role of the Scientific Committee, including the present reporting arrangements;

3. *Requests* the Scientific Committee to continue its work, including its important activities to increase knowledge of the levels, effects and risks of ionizing radiation from all sources;

4. *Endorses* the intentions and plans of the Scientific Committee for its future activities of scientific review and assessment on behalf of the General Assembly, including publication of its next comprehensive report in 2000;

5. *Requests* the Scientific Committee to continue at its next session the review of the important problems in the field of radiation and to report thereon to the General Assembly at its fifty-fifth session;

6. *Requests* the United Nations Environment Programme to continue providing support for the effective conduct of the work of the Scientific Committee and for the dissemination of its findings to the General Assembly, the scientific community and the public;

7. *Expresses its appreciation* for the assistance rendered to the Scientific Committee by Member States, the specialized agencies, the International Atomic Energy Agency and non-governmental organizations, and invites them to increase their cooperation in this field;

8. *Welcomes*, in this context, the readiness of Member States to provide the Scientific Committee with relevant information on the effects of atomic radiation in affected areas, and invites the Scientific Committee to analyse and give due consideration to such information, particularly in the light of its own findings;

9. *Invites* Member States, the organizations of the United Nations system and non-governmental organizations concerned to provide further relevant data about doses, effects and risks from various sources of radiation, which would greatly help in the preparation of future reports of the Scientific Committee to the General Assembly.

Millennium Assembly

In accordance with the General Assembly's decision in resolution 53/202 [YUN 1998, p. 598] to designate its fifty-fifth (2000) session as the Millennium Assembly and to convene as part of the Assembly a Millennium Summit, the Secretary-General, in a May report with later addendum [A/53/948 & Add.1], proposed as the overall theme "The United Nations in the twenty-first century". He suggested that sub-topics of the Summit focus on peace and security, including disarmament; development, including poverty eradication; human rights; and strengthening the United Nations. The report contained other proposals submitted during informal consultations of the plenary.

By **resolution 53/239** of 8 June, the Assembly decided that the Millennium Summit should begin on Wednesday, 6 September 2000 (see p. 1269).

PART TWO

Human rights

blank page -- (566)

Chapter I

Promotion of human rights

In 1999, the United Nations continued its activities to promote and protect human rights through the Commission on Human Rights and its subsidiary body—the Subcommission on Prevention of Discrimination and Protection of Minorities, renamed in July the Subcommission on the Promotion and Protection of Human Rights. The Office of the High Commissioner for Human Rights proceeded with its increasing responsibilities in the United Nations system-wide, in national, regional and international coordination and implementation of human rights, and in the provision of advisory services and technical cooperation.

Human rights instruments and their monitoring bodies promoted civil, political, economic, social and cultural rights, and addressed racial discrimination, discrimination against women and migrants, the protection of children, and torture and other cruel, inhuman or degrading treatment or punishment. During the year, the tenth anniversary of the adoption of the Convention on the Rights of the Child was commemorated.

In September, the General Assembly adopted the Declaration and Programme of Action on a Culture of Peace to guide Governments, international organizations and civil society in promoting and strengthening a culture of peace in the new millennium.

UN machinery

Commission on Human Rights

The Commission on Human Rights held its fifty-fifth session in Geneva from 22 March to 30 April [E/1999/23], during which it adopted 82 resolutions and 13 decisions. The Commission recommended one draft resolution and 31 draft decisions for adoption by the Economic and Social Council. By **decision 1999/288** of 30 July, the Council took note of the Commission's report. In September, the Commission held a special session on the human rights situation in East Timor, convened in response to reports of widespread violence and serious human rights violations following the popular consultation on the future status of the country [E/1999/23/Add.1] (see PART TWO, Chapter III).

On 23 March [dec. 1999/101], the Commission invited special representatives, special rapporteurs, chairmen/rapporteurs of various working groups and experts to participate in its meetings.

In response to a 1998 Commission request [YUN 1998, p. 601], the Bureau reviewed the Commission's mechanisms to enhance their effectiveness [E/CN.4/1999/104 & Corr.1]. The Bureau presented 13 recommendations, supporting observations and related proposals for consideration by the United Nations High Commissioner for Human Rights or, in some cases, by the Secretary-General. On 26 February [E/CN.4/1999/120], Algeria, Bhutan, China, Cuba, Egypt, India, Iran, Malaysia, Myanmar, Nepal, Pakistan, Sri Lanka, the Sudan and Viet Nam transmitted their comments, observations and alternate recommendations on the report of the Bureau. On 9 March [E/CN.4/1999/124], the Asian Group transmitted a position paper on the Bureau's report. In a statement made by the Chairperson on behalf of the Commission on 29 April [E/1999/23], the Commission decided to establish an inter-sessional open-ended working group to continue to examine the Bureau report, as well as other contributions thereto. The Commission requested the chair of the group to report in 2000, including recommendations for endorsement by the Commission, and authorized the group to meet for 15 working days prior to its 2000 session. The Commission recommended that the Economic and Social Council include in its resumed organizational session consideration of proposals regarding special procedures mandates adopted at the Commission's annual session, and that the title of the Subcommission on Prevention of Discrimination and Protection of Minorities be changed to Subcommission on the Promotion and Protection of Human Rights. By **decision 1999/256** of 27 July, the Council endorsed the Commission's decisions and approved its recommendations.

The Subcommission, on 26 August [E/CN.4/2000/2 (dec. 1999/115)], expressing concern at the Bureau's view that the Subcommission was the most expensive of the Commission's subsidiary mechanisms, decided to ask the Secretary-General to submit to the working group and to the Commission in 2000 official data on all the respective estimated costs during the current biennium of the activities carried out by or programmed for the Subcommission, the Commission and all other mechanisms of the Commission mentioned by the Bureau.

The Working Group on Enhancing the Effectiveness of the Mechanisms of the Commission on Human Rights met twice in 1999 (Geneva, 28 September-1 October and 6-10 December) [E/CN.4/2000/112]. Further meetings were scheduled for 2000.

Organization of work in 2000

The Commission considered a January note by the Secretariat [E/CN.4/1999/109] containing statistical data regarding its 1998 session intended to assist it with the organization of its work in 1999.

On 28 April [dec. 1999/112], the Commission decided that its fifty-sixth session should take place from 20 March to 28 April 2000. On 27 July, by **decision 1999/254**, the Economic and Social Council approved that decision.

Also on 28 April [dec. 1999/113], the Commission recommended that the Council authorize 30 fully serviced additional meetings, to be utilized only if necessary, for the Commission's 2000 session, and requested its Chairperson to make every effort to organize the session's work within the times normally allotted. By **decision 1999/255** of 27 July, the Council authorized the additional meetings and approved the request to the Chairperson.

Thematic procedures

Pursuant to a 1998 Commission resolution [YUN 1998, p. 602], the Secretariat, in March [E/CN.4/1999/96], provided documentary references to the conclusions and recommendations of thematic special rapporteurs and working groups. Regarding the Commission's request to the Secretary-General to convene further periodic meetings of all thematic special rapporteurs, representatives, experts and chairpersons of working groups to enable them to continue to exchange views, cooperate and coordinate more closely and make recommendations, a meeting was held in 1998, the report of which [E/CN.4/1999/3 & Corr.1 & Add.1 & Add.1/Corr.1,2] was considered by the Commission in 1999.

On 28 April [dec. 1999/110], the Commission decided to consider human rights and thematic procedures in 2000.

Subcommission on the Promotion and Protection of Human Rights

1999 session

The Subcommission on the Promotion and Protection of Human Rights, formerly the Subcommission on Prevention of Discrimination and Protection of Minorities (see above), at its fifty-first session (Geneva, 2-27 August) [E/CN.4/2000/2], adopted 30 resolutions and 17 decisions, and recommended nine draft decisions for adoption by the Commission.

The Subcommission adopted decisions on voting by secret ballot whenever a vote was requested on proposals pertaining to allegations of violations of human rights [dec. 1999/104], and on the composition of its inter-sessional and pre-sessional working groups [dec. 1999/116]. The former decision was adopted by a roll-call vote of 23 to 1.

Review of Subcommission work

Report of Subcommission Chairman. The Commission on Human Rights had before it a report [E/CN.4/1999/84], submitted in response to its 1998 request [YUN 1998, p. 602] and prepared by the Subcommission's 1998 Chairperson, El-Hadji Guissé (Senegal), describing the steps taken to reform and improve the Subcommission's methods of work.

Commission action. On 28 April [res. 1999/81], the Commission, welcoming the steps taken by the Subcommission, asked it to continue to avoid duplication with Commission work, to improve further its methods of work and to devote sufficient time in 1999 to its working methods.

The Commission authorized the Subcommission to organize its 1999 four-week session so that it held not more than 30 public meetings and decided that the Subcommission should meet in closed session to consider the implementation of the present resolution; the Subcommission was asked to report in 2000 on the results of its consideration of its methods of work.

The Commission Chairperson was invited to address the Subcommission on the Commission's debate under the item. The Secretary-General was asked to ensure that documents were available in all UN official languages prior to each Subcommission session and, in responding to requests from the Subcommission to solicit information from Governments and intergovernmental and non-governmental organizations, to agree to the requests only after they were approved by the Commission. The Subcommission Chairperson was requested to report in 2000.

Subcommission action. On 3 August [dec. 1999/102], the Subcommission established a sessional working group on its methods of work. The working group met on 9, 11 and 13 August [E/CN.4/Sub.2/1999/22] to examine the working paper on rules of procedure, guidelines, decisions and practices applicable to the Subcommission [E/CN.4/Sub.2/1999/2], prepared by Ribot Hatano (Japan). Annexed to the working group's report were "Guidelines for the application by the Subcommission on the Promotion and Protection of Human Rights of the rules of procedure of the functional commissions of the Economic and Social Council and other decisions and practices related thereto", as revised by the group. On 26 August [dec. 1999/114], the Subcommission transmitted the guidelines to the Commission. It asked the High Commissioner for Human Rights to disseminate the guidelines in printed form in order to make them readily accessible to Subcommission participants.

In an August note [E/CN.4/Sub.2/1999/47], the Subcommission Chairperson stated that, as proposed by the Bureau of the Commission [E/CN.4/1999/104], the Subcommission held a discussion of its future functions and the consequences thereof for its working time, its methods of work, its composition and the election of its members. The Chairperson presented the conclusions agreed upon. Annexed to the report was a summary of discussions held by the Working Group on Communications concerning the procedure established under Economic and Social Council resolution 1503(XLVIII) [YUN 1970, p. 530] to deal with communications alleging denial or violation of human rights.

Areas of Subcommission work

Note by Secretary-General. In June [E/CN.4/Sub.2/1999/23], the Secretary-General reviewed developments between 1 June 1998 and 1 June 1999 in areas with which the Subcommission had been concerned. They related to the status and monitoring bodies of the 1965 International Convention on the Elimination of All Forms of Racial Discrimination [YUN 1965, p. 440, GA res. 2106 A (XX)], the 1966 International Covenants on Human Rights [YUN 1966, pp. 419 & 423, GA res. 2200 A (XXI)], the 1984 Convention against Torture and Other Cruel, Inhuman or Degrading Treatment or Punishment [YUN 1984, p. 813, GA res. 39/46], the 1989 Convention on the Rights of the Child [YUN 1989, p. 560, GA res. 44/25] and the 1990 International Convention on the Protection of the Rights of All Migrant Workers and Members of Their Families [YUN 1990, p. 594, GA res. 45/158].

ILO report. In July, the International Labour Organization (ILO) submitted a memorandum concerning ratifications of ILO conventions relating to the concerns of the Subcommission [E/CN.4/Sub.2/1999/24]. The conventions dealt with forced labour, discrimination, freedom of association, migrant workers, indigenous and tribal peoples, minimum age and vocational rehabilitation. The ILO Conference in June adopted the Convention and Recommendation on the elimination of the worst forms of child labour. ILO activities were described regarding the prevention of discrimination, action against discrimination based on HIV/AIDS and the situation of Arab workers of the occupied Arab territories.

Office of the High Commissioner for Human Rights

Reports of High Commissioner. In her annual report to the Commission on Human Rights [E/CN.4/1999/9], submitted in March, the United Nations High Commissioner for Human Rights, Mary Robinson (Ireland), summarized key areas of the human rights programme of particular interest to the Commission and presented the evolving orientations and trends in the Office of the High Commissioner (OHCHR). She stated that particular attention was being given to national strategies and systems, the integration of human rights in all areas of endeavour, the development of respect for human rights through education and promotional activities, efforts for human rights protection, universal implementation of the rights of the child, promoting equality and combating discrimination, responding to emerging problems affecting the enjoyment of human rights and harnessing the energies of new actors in the global quest to uphold respect for human rights. OHCHR was emphasizing professionalism and quality control, and arrangements and policies were developed to support field presences.

Areas dealt with in the report were: human rights violations; the rights of the child; gender and the human rights of women; the World Conference against Racism, Racial Discrimination, Xenophobia and Related Intolerance (see p. 602); the right to development; technical cooperation, national strategies, national institutions and education; field presences; civil society and non-governmental organizations (NGOs); the fiftieth anniversary of the Universal Declaration of Human Rights [YUN 1998, p. 615] and the five-year review of the implementation of the Vienna Declaration and Programme of Action [ibid., p. 626]; and strengthening UN machinery for the promotion and protection of human rights.

The High Commissioner concluded that the gap between human rights rhetoric and the reality of the lives of millions of human beings was the tragedy of the times. Genocide and mass killings were still part of the world and over 1 billion human beings were denied the basic material elements of life—food, shelter and access to health care. Similar large numbers were denied access to basic education and many were persecuted because of their race, religion or ethnic origin. Torture and arbitrary executions were commonplace and democratic participation in Government was denied to millions as corruption undermined the integrity of Government and the rule of law. Other challenges to human rights were scientific and technological developments in areas such as genetics, human cloning and biotechnology. The United Nations and the international community had much to contribute to overcome those challenges. However, the main responsibility was at the national level, with Governments, civil society and individuals.

In a July report [E/1999/96], the High Commissioner provided an overview of developments in the implementation of economic, social and cultural rights at the international level (see next chapter). By **decision 1999/288** of 30 July, the Economic and Social Council took note of that report.

In a September report [A/54/36], the High Commissioner presented an overview of the main activities of OHCHR to promote and protect human rights and information on specific areas, including widespread violations of human rights (East Timor, Kosovo, Sierra Leone (see PART TWO, Chapter III), civilians in armed conflict (see p. 647)); the implementation and protection of human rights (see next chapter); regional human rights cooperation (see p. 582); the right to development and economic, social and cultural rights (see p. 651); globalization and human rights (see p. 655); the World Conference against Racism, Racial Discrimination, Xenophobia and Related Intolerance (see p. 602); indigenous people (see p. 681); minorities (see p. 615); and gender issues and the human rights of women (see pp. 659 and 666).

On 17 December, the General Assembly took note of the September report (**decision 54/434**) and the report of the Third (Social, Humanitarian and Cultural) Committee [A/54/605/Add.5] regarding that report (**decision 54/436**).

Commission action. On 27 April [res. 1999/54], the Commission called on the High Commissioner to continue to emphasize the promotion and protection of the realization of the right to development in her Office and in that regard encouraged the High Commissioner to continue to strengthen her relationship with the appropriate UN bodies, funds and specialized organizations. It recommended that the Economic and Social Council and the General Assembly provide OHCHR with the means commensurate to its increasing tasks, as well as more resources for special rapporteurs; on 27 July, by **decision 1999/243**, the Council endorsed that recommendation.

The Commission called on the High Commissioner to continue to provide States with information on voluntary contributions. It invited her to continue to provide information on cooperation with other UN bodies and with Governments, and to make available information concerning agreements with States and other UN bodies and their implementation in an open and transparent manner. The Commission called on OHCHR to seek ways by which voluntary funds could be used to provide support to all of the Commission's mechanisms. The High Commissioner was asked to submit information pursuant to the current resolution in her annual report to the Commission.

Composition of staff

Report of High Commissioner. In response to a 1998 Commission request [YUN 1998, p. 606], the High Commissioner submitted a report on the composition of OHCHR staff reflecting grade, nationality and gender, as at 31 December 1998 [E/CN.4/1999/97].

Commission action. On 28 April [res. 1999/70], by a roll-call vote of 34 to 16, with 3 abstentions, the Commission requested the Secretary-General to pay particular attention to the recruitment of personnel from developing countries for existing vacancies and other OHCHR posts so as to ensure an equitable geographical distribution, giving priority to high-level and Professional posts and the recruitment of women. It asked the High Commissioner to report in 2000.

Strengthening UN action

Report of Secretary-General. In response to General Assembly resolution 53/149 [YUN 1998, p. 606], in August [A/54/216], the Secretary-General described approaches taken to strengthen UN action in human rights, including the promotion of international cooperation and the importance of non-selectivity, impartiality and objectivity. To promote transparency and the sharing of information with respect to mainstreaming technical cooperation in all areas of human rights, the Secretary-General suggested that OHCHR be invited to prepare and update a table, biennially, indicating the States that had received OHCHR assistance to establish or strengthen national institutions; OHCHR advisory services and technical cooperation assistance; or a mission under a special procedures mandate.

GENERAL ASSEMBLY ACTION

On 17 December [meeting 83], the General Assembly, on the recommendation of the Third Committee [A/54/605/Add.2], adopted **resolution 54/174** without vote [agenda item 116 (*b*)].

Strengthening United Nations action in the field of human rights through the promotion of international cooperation and the importance of non-selectivity, impartiality and objectivity

The General Assembly,

Bearing in mind that among the purposes of the United Nations are those of developing friendly relations among nations based on respect for the principle of equal rights and self-determination of peoples and taking other appropriate measures to strengthen universal peace, as well as achieving international cooperation in solving international problems of an economic, social, cultural or humanitarian character and in promoting and encouraging respect for human rights and fundamental freedoms for all without distinction as to race, sex, language or religion,

Desirous of achieving further progress in international cooperation in promoting and encouraging respect for human rights and fundamental freedoms,

Considering that such international cooperation should be based on the principles embodied in international law, especially the Charter of the United Nations, as well as the Universal Declaration of Human Rights, the International Covenants on Human Rights and other relevant instruments,

Deeply convinced that United Nations action in this field should be based not only on a profound understanding of the broad range of problems existing in all societies but also on full respect for the political, economic and social realities of each of them, in strict compliance with the purposes and principles of the Charter and for the basic purpose of promoting and encouraging respect for human rights and fundamental freedoms through international cooperation,

Recalling its previous resolutions in this regard,

Reaffirming the importance of ensuring the universality, objectivity and non-selectivity of the consideration of human rights issues, as affirmed in the Vienna Declaration and Programme of Action, adopted by the World Conference on Human Rights on 25 June 1993,

Affirming the importance of the objectivity, independence and discretion of the special rapporteurs and representatives on thematic issues and on countries, as well as of the members of the working groups, in carrying out their mandates,

Underlining the obligation that Governments have to promote and protect human rights and to carry out the responsibilities that they have undertaken under international law, especially the Charter, as well as various international instruments in the field of human rights,

1. *Reiterates* that, by virtue of the principle of equal rights and self-determination of peoples enshrined in the Charter of the United Nations, all peoples have the right freely to determine, without external interference, their political status and to pursue their economic, social and cultural development, and that every State has the duty to respect that right within the provisions of the Charter, including respect for territorial integrity;

2. *Reaffirms* that it is a purpose of the United Nations and the task of all Member States, in cooperation with the Organization, to promote and encourage respect for human rights and fundamental freedoms and to remain vigilant with regard to violations of human rights wherever they occur;

3. *Calls upon* all Member States to base their activities for the promotion and protection of human rights, including the development of further international cooperation in this field, on the Charter of the United Nations, the Universal Declaration of Human Rights, the International Covenant on Economic, Social and Cultural Rights, the International Covenant on Civil and Political Rights and other relevant international instruments, and to refrain from activities that are inconsistent with that international framework;

4. *Considers* that international cooperation in this field should make an effective and practical contribution to the urgent task of preventing mass and flagrant violations of human rights and fundamental freedoms for all and to the strengthening of international peace and security;

5. *Reaffirms* that the promotion, protection and full realization of all human rights and fundamental freedoms, as a legitimate concern of the world community, should be guided by the principles of non-selectivity, impartiality and objectivity and should not be used for political ends;

6. *Requests* all human rights bodies within the United Nations system, as well as the special rapporteurs and representatives, independent experts and working groups, to take duly into account the contents of the present resolution in carrying out their mandates;

7. *Expresses its conviction* that an unbiased and fair approach to human rights issues contributes to the promotion of international cooperation as well as to the effective promotion, protection and realization of human rights and fundamental freedoms;

8. *Stresses,* in this context, the continuing need for impartial and objective information on the political, economic and social situations and events of all countries;

9. *Invites* Member States to consider adopting, as appropriate, within the framework of their respective legal systems and in accordance with their obligations under international law, especially the Charter, and international human rights instruments, the measures that they may deem appropriate to achieve further progress in international cooperation in promoting and encouraging respect for human rights and fundamental freedoms;

10. *Requests* the Commission on Human Rights to take duly into account the present resolution and to consider further proposals for the strengthening of United Nations action in the field of human rights through the promotion of international cooperation and the importance of non-selectivity, impartiality and objectivity;

11. *Takes note* of the report of the Secretary-General, and further requests the Secretary-General to ask Member States to present practical proposals and ideas that should contribute to the strengthening of United

Nations action in the field of human rights, through the promotion of international cooperation based on the principles of non-selectivity, impartiality and objectivity, and to submit a comprehensive report on this question to the General Assembly at its fifty-fifth session;

12. *Decides* to consider this matter at its fifty-fifth session, under the item entitled "Human rights questions".

Promotion of dialogue on human rights issues

Commission action. On 28 April [res. 1999/68], the Commission called on States, intergovernmental organizations and specialized agencies to continue to carry out constructive dialogue and consultations to enhance understanding and the promotion and protection of all human rights and fundamental freedoms, and encouraged NGOs to contribute to the endeavour. It invited States and relevant UN human rights mechanisms and procedures to pay continued attention to the importance of mutual cooperation, understanding and dialogue in ensuring human rights promotion and protection. The High Commissioner was asked to report in 2001.

Subcommission action. On 26 August [res. 1999/25], the Subcommission, reiterating its commitment to international cooperation in human rights, invited governmental and non-governmental observers of the Subcommission to carry out constructive dialogue and consultations on human rights issues based on equality and mutual respect. It endorsed a cooperative approach in search of common understanding of divergent views.

GENERAL ASSEMBLY ACTION

On 17 December [meeting 83], the General Assembly, on the recommendation of the Third Committee [A/54/605/Add.2], adopted **resolution 54/181** without vote [agenda item 116 *(b)*].

Enhancement of international cooperation in the field of human rights

The General Assembly,

Recalling its resolution 53/154 of 9 December 1998, taking note of Commission on Human Rights resolution 1999/68 of 28 April 1999 on the enhancement of international cooperation in the field of human rights, and recalling also Assembly resolution 53/22 of 4 November 1998 on the United Nations Year of Dialogue among Civilizations,

Reaffirming its commitment to promoting international cooperation, as set forth in the Charter of the United Nations, in particular Article 1, paragraph 3, as well as relevant provisions of the Vienna Declaration and Programme of Action adopted by the World Conference on Human Rights on 25 June 1993, for enhancing genuine cooperation among Member States in the field of human rights,

Recognizing that the enhancement of international cooperation in the field of human rights is essential for the full achievement of the purposes of the United Nations, including the effective promotion and protection of all human rights,

Reaffirming the importance of ensuring the universality, objectivity and non-selectivity of the consideration of human rights issues, and underlining the importance of the promotion of dialogue on human rights issues,

Noting the adoption of resolution 1999/25 of 26 August 1999, entitled "Promotion of dialogue on human rights issues", by the Subcommission on the Promotion and Protection of Human Rights of the Commission on Human Rights at its fifty-first session, and noting the decision of the Subcommission to consider the question of a dialogue among civilizations at its fifty-second session,

1. *Welcomes* the decision of the Commission on Human Rights to continue to consider the enhancement of international cooperation in the field of human rights at its fifty-sixth session;

2. *Calls upon* Members States, specialized agencies and intergovernmental organizations to continue to carry out a constructive dialogue and consultations for the enhancement of understanding and the promotion and protection of all human rights and fundamental freedoms, and encourages non-governmental organizations to contribute actively to this endeavour;

3. *Invites* States and all relevant United Nations human rights mechanisms and procedures to continue to pay attention to the importance of mutual cooperation, understanding and dialogue in ensuring the promotion and protection of all human rights;

4. *Decides* to continue its consideration of this question at its fifty-fifth session.

Right to promote and protect human rights

Commission action. On 28 April [res. 1999/66], the Commission called on States to promote and give effect to the 1998 Declaration on the Right and Responsibility of Individuals, Groups and Organs of Society to Promote and Protect Universally Recognized Human Rights and Fundamental Freedoms, adopted by the General Assembly in resolution 53/144 [YUN 1998, p. 608]. Urging treaty bodies, special representatives, rapporteurs and working groups of the Commission and the Subcommission to give due regard to the Declaration within their mandates, the Commission asked the Secretary-General to report thereon in 2000. It also asked him to consider ways to promote and implement the Declaration and to report with proposals in 2000.

On the same date [dec. 1999/111], the Commission postponed until 2000 consideration of a draft text on human duties and responsibilities.

GENERAL ASSEMBLY ACTION

On 17 December [meeting 83], the General Assembly, on the recommendation of the Third Committee [A/54/605/Add.2], adopted **resolution 54/170** without vote [agenda item 116 *(b)*].

Declaration on the Right and Responsibility of Individuals, Groups and Organs of Society to Promote and Protect Universally Recognized Human Rights and Fundamental Freedoms

The General Assembly,

Reaffirming its resolution 53/144 of 9 December 1998, by which it adopted the Declaration on the Right and Responsibility of Individuals, Groups and Organs of Society to Promote and Protect Universally Recognized Human Rights and Fundamental Freedoms, annexed to that resolution,

Reiterating the importance of the Declaration,

Convinced of the important role of the Commission on Human Rights in following up the Declaration,

Noting with deep concern that, in many countries, persons and organizations engaged in promoting and defending human rights and fundamental freedoms are facing threats, harassment and insecurity as a result of those activities,

1. *Calls upon* Governments, specialized agencies and relevant intergovernmental and non-governmental organizations to submit, at the request of the Secretary-General, on the basis of Commission on Human Rights resolution 1999/66 of 28 April 1999, proposals and ideas that should contribute substantially to further work on the implementation of the Declaration on the Right and Responsibility of Individuals, Groups and Organs of Society to Promote and Protect Universally Recognized Human Rights and Fundamental Freedoms;

2. *Calls upon* the Commission on Human Rights to consider at its fifty-sixth session the report to be prepared by the Secretary-General pursuant to Commission resolution 1999/66;

3. *Requests* the Secretary-General to report to the General Assembly at its fifty-fifth session on measures to implement the Declaration;

4. *Decides* to consider this question at its fifty-fifth session, under the item entitled "Human rights questions".

Human rights instruments

General aspects

In 1999, seven UN human rights instruments were in force that required monitoring of their implementation by expert bodies. The instruments and their treaty bodies were: the 1965 International Convention on the Elimination of All Forms of Racial Discrimination [YUN 1965, p. 440, GA res. 2106 A (XX)] (Committee on the Elimination of Racial Discrimination); the 1966 International Covenant on Civil and Political Rights [YUN 1966, p. 423, GA res. 2200 A (XXI)] (Human Rights Committee); the 1966 International Covenant on Economic, Social and Cultural Rights [ibid., p. 419, GA res. 2200 A (XXI)] (Committee on Economic, Social and Cultural Rights); the 1973 International Convention on the Suppression and Punishment of the Crime of Apartheid [YUN 1973, p. 103, GA res. 3068(XXVIII)] (Group of Three, suspended in 1995) [YUN 1995, p. 693]; the 1979 Convention on the Elimination of All Forms of Discrimination against Women [YUN 1979, p. 895, GA res. 34/180] (Committee on the Elimination of Discrimination against Women); the 1984 Convention against Torture and Other Cruel, Inhuman or Degrading Treatment or Punishment [YUN 1984, p. 813, GA res. 39/46] (Committee against Torture); and the 1989 Convention on the Rights of the Child [YUN 1989, p. 560, GA res. 44/25] (Committee on the Rights of the Child).

Human rights treaty bodies

Pursuant to General Assembly resolution 49/178 [YUN 1994, p. 1060], the Secretary-General transmitted the report of the persons chairing the human rights treaty bodies on their eleventh meeting (Geneva, 31 May–4 June) [A/54/805]. The meeting reviewed recent developments relating to the work of the treaty bodies. Positive results were noted with respect to some treaty bodies as a consequence of modifications in their work methods. The chairpersons expressed concern over problems such as the large backlog of State reports to be examined, the unbalanced geographical and gender representation in their committees and inadequate meeting time and interpretation services. Ways to improve the work of treaty bodies and cooperation with other UN entities and NGOs were discussed. The chairpersons approved a Plan of Action for strengthening implementation of the International Covenant on Civil and Political Rights, the International Convention on the Elimination of All Forms of Racial Discrimination and the Convention against Torture and Other Cruel, Inhuman or Degrading Treatment on Punishment. On 2 June, a joint meeting was held between the chairpersons and the sixth meeting of special rapporteurs and representatives, experts and chairpersons of working groups of the special procedures system of the Commission on Human Rights and of the advisory services programme, which made suggestions to enhance cooperation between treaty bodies and the special procedures system.

The chairpersons made recommendations regarding their relationship with the Assembly, the Economic and Social Council and the Council's functional commissions; public information; HIV/AIDS; cooperation with NGOs; documents and publications; the recommendations of the joint meeting with the special procedures system; regional meetings; technical briefings; coordination among treaty bodies; the Plan of Action; human rights indicators; and corporate responsibility for human rights.

The chairpersons considered an April report [HRI/MC/1999/3] containing follow-up to the recommendations of the tenth meeting [YUN 1998, p. 611].

Reservations to human rights treaties

Pursuant to a 1998 Subcommission request [YUN 1998, p. 612], Françoise Jane Hampson (United Kingdom) submitted in June a working paper on reservations to human rights treaties [E/CN.4/Sub.2/1999/28 & Corr.1]. She concluded that the 1969 Vienna Convention on the Law of Treaties [YUN 1969, p. 730] was partly responsible for the difficulties posed by reservations since it did not contemplate the possibility of independent enforcement/monitoring bodies taking a view on the validity of reservations. The subject matter of human rights treaties, especially but not only non-derogable provisions, also contributed significantly to the nature and scale of the problem. There was a need for a comprehensive review of the reservations across different human rights treaties, to be carried out in cooperation with the enforcement/monitoring mechanisms and States and with NGO assistance. The study should gather together reservations and interpretative declarations on human rights treaty norms by norm, by treaty and by State. States and NGOs should comment on the provisions of domestic law which made the reservation necessary. States should be asked whether they envisaged removing the domestic impediment to withdrawing the reservation in due course and, where relevant, whether they regarded a statement as an interpretative declaration or a reservation. Ms. Hampson invited the Subcommission to recommend to the Commission that such a study be carried out. Annexed to the working paper was an analysis of reservations to certain human rights treaties.

Subcommission action. On 26 August [res. 1999/27], the Subcommission endorsed the conclusions made in the working paper. It appointed Ms. Hampson as Special Rapporteur to prepare a comprehensive study on reservations to human rights treaties based on the working paper, as well as comments made and discussions that took place at the Subcommission's 1999 session. She was requested to submit a preliminary report in 2000, a progress report in 2001 and a final report in 2002, and to seek the advice and cooperation of the relevant treaty bodies. The Secretary-General was asked to assist her.

Universal Declaration of Human Rights

In response to a 1998 Subcommission request [YUN 1998, p. 615], Vladimir Kartashkin (Russian Federation) submitted a working paper, in June [E/CN.4/Sub.2/1999/29], on ways in which the Subcommission could examine the observance of the human rights and fundamental freedoms contained in the 1948 Universal Declaration of Human Rights, adopted by the General Assembly in resolution 217 A (III) [YUN 1948-49, p. 535], by States not parties to UN human rights conventions. He proposed that the Subcommission establish for three years an inter-sessional working group to encourage efforts to observe those human rights and fundamental freedoms by States not parties to the International Covenants and other conventions that placed on States the obligation to observe the particular rights embodied in the Declaration. He suggested guidelines for the group's functions.

Subcommission action. On 26 August [res. 1999/28], the Subcommission asked Mr. Kartashkin to continue his work on the subject, without financial implications, and to submit an additional working paper in 2000.

Fiftieth anniversary of Geneva Conventions

On 12 August, the Secretary-General participated in a ceremony commemorating the fiftieth anniversary of the Geneva Conventions of 12 August 1949 on the protection of victims of war, sponsored by the International Committee of the Red Cross (ICRC). He signed, with others, an appeal to all peoples, nations and Governments, among other things, to reject the idea that war was inevitable and to work to eradicate its underlying causes.

On 26 August [dec. 1999/113], the Subcommission expressed gratitude and appreciation to ICRC on the fiftieth anniversary. It asked the Secretary-General to transmit the decision to ICRC.

Covenant on Civil and Political Rights and Optional Protocols

Accessions and ratifications

As at 31 December 1999, parties to the International Covenant on Civil and Political Rights and the Optional Protocol thereto, adopted by the General Assembly in resolution 2200 A (XXI) [YUN 1966, p. 423], totalled 144 and 95 States, respectively. During the year, Burkina Faso and Tajikistan acceded to the Covenant and the Optional Protocol.

In 1999, Azerbaijan, Bulgaria, Cyprus, Georgia, Slovakia and the United Kingdom became parties to the Second Optional Protocol, aiming at the abolition of the death penalty—adopted by the Assembly in resolution 44/128 [YUN 1989, p. 484]—bringing the total number of States parties to 41 at year's end.

The Secretary-General reported on the status of the Covenant and its Optional Protocols as at 1 August [A/54/277 & Corr.1] and 15 December [E/CN.4/2000/89].

Implementation

Monitoring body. The Human Rights Committee, established under article 28 of the Covenant, held three sessions in 1999: its sixty-fifth session from 22 March to 9 April in New York, and its sixty-sixth session from 12 to 30 July [A/54/40, vol. I] and its sixty-seventh from 18 October to 5 November [A/55/40, vol. I], both in Geneva.

In 1999, the Committee considered reports from 14 States—Cambodia, Cameroon, Canada, Chile, China (Hong Kong Special Administrative Region), Costa Rica, Lesotho, Mexico, Morocco, Norway, Poland, Portugal (Macau), Republic of Korea, Romania—under article 40 of the Covenant. It adopted views on communications from individuals claiming that their rights under the Covenant had been violated, and decided that other such communications were inadmissible. Those views and decisions were annexed to the Committee's reports [A/54/40, vol. II; A/55/40, vol. II].

On 18 October, the Committee adopted General Comment No. 27 concerning article 12 of the Covenant (freedom of movement).

Covenant on Economic, Social and Cultural Rights

Accessions and ratifications

As at 31 December 1999, the International Covenant on Economic, Social and Cultural Rights, adopted by the General Assembly in resolution 2200 A (XXI) [YUN 1966, p. 419], had 142 States parties. Burkina Faso, Tajikistan and Thailand acceded to the Covenant during the year.

The Secretary-General reported on the status of the Covenant as at 1 September [A/54/277 & Corr.1] and 15 December [E/CN.4/2000/89].

Draft optional protocol

In January and March [E/CN.4/1999/112 & Add.1], the Secretariat submitted comments received from States parties and NGOs on the draft optional protocol for the consideration of communications concerning non-compliance with the Covenant.

Commission action. On 26 April [res. 1999/25], the Commission requested the High Commissioner for Human Rights to urge all States to submit their comments on the draft optional protocol and to report in 2000 on options relating to the proposal for such a protocol.

Implementation

Monitoring body. The Committee on Economic, Social and Cultural Rights held its twentieth (26 April–14 May) and twenty-first (15 November–3 December) sessions, both in Geneva [E/2000/22]. The Committee's pre-sessional, five-member working group met in Geneva for five days prior to each of the sessions to identify issues that might most usefully be discussed with representatives of reporting States. In 1999, the Committee examined reports covering articles 16 and 17 of the Covenant submitted by Argentina, Armenia, Bulgaria, Cameroon, Denmark, Iceland, Ireland, Mexico, Solomon Islands and Tunisia. The Committee adopted General Comment No. 11 on plans of action for primary education, General Comment No. 12 on the right to adequate food (see p. 660) and General Comment No. 13 on the right to education (see p. 661).

In a draft decision for adoption by the Economic and Social Council [E/1999/L.19], the Committee sought approval to hold an additional regular session in New York beginning in 2000, as well as a pre-sessional working group for one week, to enhance the effectiveness and profile of its work. By **decision 1999/287** of 30 July, the Council approved the holding of two additional three-week extraordinary sessions of the Committee, as well as respective pre-sessional working groups for one week during 2000 and 2001, provided additional funding was made available. The Council requested that those sessions be used to reduce the backlog of reports and asked the Committee to consider ways to improve the efficiency of its working methods and to report in 2001.

GENERAL ASSEMBLY ACTION

On 17 December [meeting 83], the General Assembly, on the recommendation of the Third Committee [A/54/605/Add.1 & Corr.1], adopted **resolution 54/157** without vote [agenda item 116 *(a)*].

International Covenants on Human Rights

The General Assembly,

Recalling its resolution 52/116 of 12 December 1997 and Commission on Human Rights resolution 1998/9 of 3 April 1998,

Mindful that the International Covenants on Human Rights constitute the first all-embracing and legally binding international treaties in the field of human rights and, together with the Universal Declaration of Human Rights, form the core of the International Bill of Human Rights,

Taking note of the report of the Secretary-General on the status of the International Covenant on Economic, Social and Cultural Rights, the International Covenant on Civil and Political Rights and the Optional Protocols to the International Covenant on Civil and Political Rights,

Recalling the International Covenant on Economic, Social and Cultural Rights and the International Covenant on Civil and Political Rights, and reaffirming that all human rights and fundamental freedoms are universal, indivisible, interdependent and interrelated and that the promotion and protection of one category of rights should never exempt or excuse States from the promotion and protection of the other rights,

Recognizing the important role of the Human Rights Committee and the Committee on Economic, Social and Cultural Rights in examining the progress made by States parties in fulfilling the obligations undertaken in the International Covenants on Human Rights and the Optional Protocols to the International Covenant on Civil and Political Rights and in providing recommendations to States parties on their implementation,

1. *Reaffirms* the importance of the International Covenants on Human Rights as major parts of international efforts to promote universal respect for and observance of human rights and fundamental freedoms;

2. *Strongly appeals* to all States that have not yet done so to become parties to the International Covenant on Economic, Social and Cultural Rights and the International Covenant on Civil and Political Rights, as well as to accede to the Optional Protocols to the International Covenant on Civil and Political Rights and to make the declaration provided for in article 41 of the Covenant;

3. *Invites* the United Nations High Commissioner for Human Rights to intensify systematic efforts to encourage States to become parties to the International Covenants on Human Rights and, through the programme of advisory services in the field of human rights, to assist such States, at their request, in ratifying or acceding to the Covenants and to the Optional Protocols to the International Covenant on Civil and Political Rights;

4. *Emphasizes* the importance of the strictest compliance by States parties with their obligations under the International Covenant on Economic, Social and Cultural Rights and the International Covenant on Civil and Political Rights and, where applicable, the Optional Protocols to the International Covenant on Civil and Political Rights;

5. *Stresses* the importance of avoiding the erosion of human rights by derogation, and underlines the necessity of strict observance of the agreed conditions and procedures for derogation under article 4 of the International Covenant on Civil and Political Rights, bearing in mind the need for States parties to provide the fullest possible information during states of emergency so that the justification for the appropriateness of measures taken in those circumstances can be assessed;

6. *Encourages* States parties to consider limiting the extent of any reservations they lodge to the International Covenants on Human Rights, to formulate any reservations as precisely and narrowly as possible and to ensure that no reservation is incompatible with the object and purpose of the relevant treaty or otherwise incompatible with international treaty law;

7. *Also encourages* States parties to review regularly any reservations made in respect of the provisions of the International Covenants on Human Rights and the Optional Protocols to the International Covenant on Civil and Political Rights with a view to withdrawing them;

8. *Takes note with appreciation* of the annual report of the Human Rights Committee submitted to the General Assembly at its fifty-fourth session, and takes note of General Comments Nos. 25 and 26 adopted by the Committee;

9. *Also takes note with appreciation* of the reports of the Committee on Economic, Social and Cultural Rights on its sixteenth and seventeenth sessions and eighteenth and nineteenth sessions, and takes note of General Comments Nos. 8, 9, 10, 11 and 12 adopted by the Committee;

10. *Urges* States parties to fulfil in good time such reporting obligations under the International Covenants on Human Rights as may be requested and in their reports to make use of gender-disaggregated data;

11. *Stresses* the importance of taking fully into account a gender perspective in the implementation of the International Covenants on Human Rights at the national level, including in the national reports of States parties and in the work of the Human Rights Committee and the Committee on Economic, Social and Cultural Rights;

12. *Urges* States parties to take duly into account, in implementing the provisions of the International Covenants on Human Rights, the observations made at the conclusion of the consideration of their reports by the Human Rights Committee and by the Committee on Economic, Social and Cultural Rights, as well as the views adopted by the Human Rights Committee under the first Optional Protocol to the International Covenant on Civil and Political Rights;

13. *Invites* States parties to give particular attention to the dissemination at the national level of the reports they have submitted to the Human Rights Committee and the Committee on Economic, Social and Cultural Rights, the summary records relating to the examination of those reports by the Committees and the observations made by the Committees at the conclusion of the consideration of the reports;

14. *Once again encourages* all Governments to publish the texts of the International Covenant on Economic, Social and Cultural Rights, the International Covenant on Civil and Political Rights and the Optional Protocols to the International Covenant on Civil and Political Rights in as many local languages as possible and to distribute them and make them known as widely as possible in their territories;

15. *Invites* the Human Rights Committee and the Committee on Economic, Social and Cultural Rights, when considering the reports of States parties, to continue to identify specific needs that might be addressed by United Nations departments, funds and programmes and the specialized agencies, including through the advisory services and technical assistance programme of the Office of the United Nations High Commissioner for Human Rights;

16. *Stresses* the need for improved coordination between relevant United Nations mechanisms and bodies in supporting States parties, upon their request, in implementing the International Covenants on Human Rights and the Optional Protocols to the International

Covenant on Civil and Political Rights, and encourages continued efforts in this direction;

17. *Invites* States to continue to contribute, with practical proposals and ideas, to the dialogue on ways of improving the functioning of the Human Rights Committee and the Committee on Economic, Social and Cultural Rights;

18. *Welcomes* the continuing efforts of the Human Rights Committee and the Committee on Economic, Social and Cultural Rights to strive for uniform standards in the implementation of the provisions of the International Covenants on Human Rights, and appeals to other bodies dealing with similar human rights questions to respect those uniform standards, as expressed in the general comments of the Committees;

19. *Encourages* the Secretary-General to continue to assist States parties to the International Covenants on Human Rights in the preparation of their reports, including by convening seminars or workshops at the national level for the purpose of training government officials engaged in the preparation of such reports, and by exploring other possibilities available under the regular programme of advisory services in the field of human rights;

20. *Requests* the Secretary-General to ensure that the Office of the United Nations High Commissioner for Human Rights effectively assists the Human Rights Committee and the Committee on Economic, Social and Cultural Rights in the implementation of their respective mandates, including by the provision of adequate Secretariat staff resources;

21. *Welcomes* the initiative by the Secretary-General, taking into account the suggestions of the Human Rights Committee, to take determined steps, in particular through the Department of Public Information of the Secretariat, to give more publicity to the work of that Committee and, similarly, to the work of the Committee on Economic, Social and Cultural Rights;

22. *Requests* the Secretary-General to submit to the General Assembly at its fifty-sixth session, under the item entitled "Human rights questions", a report on the status of the International Covenant on Economic, Social and Cultural Rights, the International Covenant on Civil and Political Rights and the Optional Protocols to the International Covenant on Civil and Political Rights, including all reservations and declarations.

Convention against racial discrimination

Accessions and ratifications

As at 31 December 1999, there were 155 parties to the International Convention on the Elimination of All Forms of Racial Discrimination, adopted by the General Assembly in resolution 2106 A (XX) [YUN 1965, p. 440]. Georgia and Indonesia acceded to the Convention during the year.

On 28 April [res. 1999/78], the Commission appealed to States that had not done so to consider ratifying or acceding to the Convention and to consider making the declaration provided for in article 14 (see below).

Implementation

Monitoring body. The Committee on the Elimination of Racial Discrimination (CERD), set up under article 8 of the Convention, held its fifty-fourth and fifty-fifth sessions in Geneva from 1 to 19 March and from 2 to 27 August, respectively [A/54/18].

The Committee devoted its sessions mainly to examining reports submitted by States parties on measures taken to implement the Convention. It considered reports, comments and information submitted by 28 States parties and summarized its members' views on each country report and the statements made by the States parties concerned.

Under the item dealing with the prevention of racial discrimination, including early warning and urgent procedures, the Committee adopted decisions concerning situations in Australia, the Democratic Republic of the Congo, the Federal Republic of Yugoslavia (Kosovo), Rwanda and the Sudan. It adopted statements on the human rights of the Kurdish people and on Africa.

In conformity with article 14 of the Convention, CERD considered communications from individuals or groups of individuals claiming violation of their rights under the Convention by a State party recognizing CERD's competence to receive and consider such communications. Twenty-eight States parties (Algeria, Australia, Bulgaria, Chile, Costa Rica, Cyprus, Denmark, Ecuador, Finland, France, Hungary, Iceland, Italy, Luxembourg, Malta, Netherlands, Norway, Peru, Poland, Republic of Korea, Russian Federation, Senegal, Slovakia, South Africa, Spain, Sweden, Ukraine, Uruguay) had declared such recognition.

Under article 15, the Committee was empowered to consider copies of petitions, reports and other information relating to Trust and Non-Self-Governing Territories. CERD observed that it found it impossible to fulfil its functions under article 15 as documents received did not include copies of petitions. The Committee asked that the appropriate information be furnished.

In other action, the Committee decided to hold its fifty-eighth session in March 2001 in New York and asked the General Assembly to implement that decision. By **decision 54/433** of 17 December, the Assembly, while taking note of the Committee's report, decided to refer back to the Committee its decision for further consideration, in the light of a statement of programme budget implications submitted by the Secretary-General [A/54/18/Add.1].

In **resolution 54/154**, the Assembly urged States to limit the extent of any reservation they lodged to the Convention, to formulate any reservation as precisely and as narrowly as possible, to ensure that no reservations were incompatible with the Convention, to review their reservations regularly and to withdraw those that were contrary to the Convention's objective and purpose.

As at 31 December, 25 States parties had accepted a 1992 amendment to the Convention regarding the financing of CERD [YUN 1992, p. 714]. The amendment was to enter into force when accepted by a two-thirds majority of States parties.

Convention against torture

Accessions and ratifications

As at 31 December 1999, 118 States were parties to the 1984 Convention against Torture and Other Cruel, Inhuman or Degrading Treatment or Punishment, adopted by the General Assembly in resolution 39/46 [YUN 1984, p. 813]. During the year, Belgium, Bolivia, Burkina Faso, Japan, Mali, Mozambique and Turkmenistan became parties. Forty-one parties had made the required declarations under articles 21 and 22 (under which a party recognized the competence of the Committee against Torture to receive and consider communications to the effect that a party claims that another is not fulfilling its obligations under the Convention, and to receive communications from or on behalf of individuals claiming to be victims of a violation of the Convention by a State party) and three had made the declaration under article 21 only.

The Secretary-General reported on the status of the Convention as at 15 July [A/54/189 & Corr.1] and 1 November [E/CN.4/2000/50].

On 26 April [res. 1999/32], the Commission urged all States to become parties to the Convention, and invited States parties that had not done so to make the declaration provided for in articles 21 and 22 and to withdraw reservations to article 20.

Draft optional protocol

Commission action. On 26 April [res. 1999/30], the Commission requested the working group on the draft optional protocol to the Convention (intended to establish a preventive system of regular visits to places of detention) to meet prior to the Commission's 2000 session to complete the final and substantive text. It asked the Secretary-General to transmit the report of the working group to Governments, specialized agencies, chairpersons of human rights treaty bodies, intergovernmental organizations and NGOs and to invite them to submit their comments to the group. The Secretary-General was also requested to invite them, as well as the Chairperson of the Committee against Torture and the Special Rapporteur on the question of torture, to participate in working group activities.

By **decision 1999/237** of 27 July, the Economic and Social Council authorized the group to meet for two weeks and encouraged the group's Chairman/Rapporteur to hold informal inter-sessional consultations to facilitate the completion of a consolidated text.

Working group activities. The working group on the draft optional protocol held its eighth session in Geneva from 4 to 15 October [E/CN.4/2000/58]. Annexed to its report were the texts of the articles that constituted the outcome of the second reading and of those that constituted the basis for future work.

In response to the Commission's request that the group's Chairman/Rapporteur hold informal consultations during inter-sessional periods, the group, in April [E/CN.4/1999/59/Add.1], stated that its Chairman/Rapporteur at the seventh session would not be available to do so. On 29 April, the group met to elect someone as Chairperson until the group's eighth session.

Implementation

Monitoring body. The Committee against Torture, established as a monitoring body under the Convention, held its twenty-second session in Geneva from 26 April to 14 May [A/54/44]. Under article 19, it considered reports submitted by Bulgaria, Egypt, Italy, the Libyan Arab Jamahiriya, Liechtenstein, Luxembourg, Mauritius, Morocco, the former Yugoslav Republic of Macedonia and Venezuela.

The Committee held eight closed meetings during which, in accordance with article 20, it studied confidential information that appeared to contain well-founded indications that torture was systematically practised in a State party to the Convention. Under article 22, the Committee considered communications submitted by individuals who claimed that their rights, as enumerated in the Convention, had been violated by a State party and who had exhausted all available domestic remedies.

The Committee held its twenty-third session, also in Geneva, from 8 to 19 November [A/55/44], during which it reviewed reports submitted by Austria, Azerbaijan, Finland, Kyrgyzstan, Malta, Peru and Uzbekistan under article 19. In four closed meetings, the Committee examined communications from individuals claiming to be victims of violations by States parties. It also considered communications under article 22.

The seventh meeting of States parties to the Convention (Geneva, 24 November) [CAT/SP/23] elected five Committee members to replace those whose terms were to expire on 31 December 1999.

The General Assembly, in **resolution 54/156**, urged States that had not done so to become parties to the Convention and invited those becoming parties and those that were parties but had not done so to make the declarations provided for in articles 21 and 22 and to consider withdrawing reservations to article 20.

Convention on elimination of discrimination against women

On 17 December, the General Assembly, in **resolution 54/137**, urged States that had not ratified or acceded to the 1979 Convention on the Elimination of All Forms of Discrimination against Women to do so as soon as possible, so that universal ratification could be achieved by the year 2000. The Assembly noted its adoption of the Optional Protocol to the Convention (**resolution 54/4**).

(For details on the status of the Convention and on the Optional Protocol, see p. 1099.)

Convention on the Rights of the Child

Accessions and ratifications

As at 31 December 1999, there continued to be 191 States parties to the 1989 Convention on the Rights of the Child, adopted by the General Assembly in resolution 44/25 [YUN 1989, p. 560].

On 30 September and 1 October, the Committee on the Rights of the Child (CRC) held a special meeting entitled "The Convention on the Rights of the Child: a decade of achievements and challenges" to commemorate the tenth anniversary of the Convention's adoption. On 11 November, the Assembly commemorated the anniversary [A/54/PV.52].

The Secretary-General reported on the status of the Convention as at 1 August [A/54/265] and 30 November [E/CN.4/2000/70]; by **decision 54/432** of 17 December, the Assembly took note of the former report.

An amendment to the Convention that would expand CRC membership from 10 to 18, adopted by the Assembly in resolution 50/155 [YUN 1995, p. 706], had been accepted by 71 States parties in 1999. The amendment required acceptance by a two-thirds majority to enter into force.

Implementation

Monitoring body. In 1999, CRC held its twentieth (11-29 January) [CRC/C/84], twenty-first (17 May-4 June) [CRC/C/87] and twenty-second (20 September-8 October) [CRC/C/90] sessions, all in Geneva. Each session was preceded by a pre-sessional working group which facilitated the Committee's work by reviewing State party reports and identifying in advance the main questions that would need to be discussed with the representatives of the reporting States. It also provided an opportunity to consider technical assistance and international cooperation.

Under article 44 of the Convention, CRC considered reports from 17 States parties: Austria, Barbados, Belize, Benin, Chad, Guinea, Honduras, Mali, Mexico, Netherlands, Nicaragua, Russian Federation, Saint Kitts and Nevis, Sweden, Vanuatu, Venezuela, Yemen.

At its twenty-second session, CRC adopted a general recommendation on the administration of juvenile justice, by which it asked the High Commissioner to give priority to promoting the Convention's provisions and those of existing international standards relating to the subject; to consider steps to identify obstacles preventing their full implementation; and to design ways to overcome the obstacles.

The working group on the rights of children with disabilities, established as an outcome of the day of general discussion in 1997 [YUN 1997, p. 605], held its first and second meetings (London, 23-24 January, 29-30 May). The group developed a plan of action for its 18-month term.

On 18 and 19 November, a workshop on the child and the media, entitled "The Oslo Challenge", was held as a result of the Committee's day of general discussion in 1996 [YUN 1996, p. 581].

The seventh meeting of the States parties to the Convention met in New York on 16 February to elect five CRC members to replace those whose terms were to expire on 28 February.

Commission action. On 28 April [res. 1999/80], the Commission urged States that had not done so to sign and ratify or accede to the Convention. It called on States parties to implement the Convention; cooperate with CRC; ensure training for those involved in activities for children; ensure the registration of all children immediately after birth and improve national systems for the collection of comprehensive and disaggregated data for areas covered by the Convention; withdraw reservations incompatible with the purpose of the Convention and consider reviewing others; and accept the amendment that would increase CRC membership. The Commission asked the Secretary-General to ensure the provision of staff and facilities for CRC's effective performance; on 27 July, by **decision 1999/249**, the Economic and Social Council endorsed that request.

Children in armed conflict

Working group activities. At its fifth session (Geneva, 11 January and 24 March) [E/CN.4/

1999/73], the working group on a draft optional protocol to the Convention on the Rights of the Child on involvement of children in armed conflict held a general discussion on the draft. Annexed to the group's report was an informal working paper by the Chairperson, prepared pursuant to a 1998 Commission request [YUN 1998, p. 623].

Commission action. On 28 April [res. 1999/80], the Commission asked the Secretary-General to give the working group the necessary support to meet for a maximum of two weeks, and to transmit the group's report to Governments, relevant UN bodies and specialized agencies, CRC, the Special Representative on the question of the impact of armed conflict on children, intergovernmental organizations and NGOs, and to invite their comments thereon in time for circulation prior to the working group's next session. The Chairperson of the working group was asked to continue broad informal consultations to promote an early agreement on the optional protocol and to produce a report, including recommendations on how to finalize the formal negotiations. The working group was asked to meet early in 2000 to finalize its work before the tenth anniversary of the entry into force of the Convention and to report to the Commission in 2000. The Economic and Social Council, by **decision 1999/249** of 27 July, endorsed the Commission's requests.

(For further information on children in armed conflict, see p. 672.)

Sale of children, child prostitution and child pornography

Working group activities. At its fifth session (Geneva, 25 January-5 February and 24 March) [E/CN.4/1999/74], the working group for the elaboration of a draft optional protocol to the Convention on the Rights of the Child on the sale of children, child prostitution and child pornography held a general discussion on the draft protocol. Annexed to the report were texts resulting from the group's discussions.

Commission action. On 28 April [res. 1999/80], the Commission asked the Secretary-General to support the working group to meet for a maximum of two weeks, and to transmit the group's report to Governments, relevant UN bodies and specialized agencies, CRC, the relevant Special Rapporteur, intergovernmental organizations and NGOs, and to invite their comments thereon in time for circulation prior to the group's next session. The working group was requested to meet early in 2000 to finalize its work before the tenth anniversary of the entry into force of the Convention and to report to the Commission in 2000. The Chairperson was asked to conduct informal consultations. By **decision 1999/249** of 27 July, the Economic and Social Council endorsed the Commission's requests.

(For further information on the sale of children, child prostitution and child pornography, see p. 671.)

Convention on migrant workers

Status of convention

As at 31 December 1999, the International Convention on the Protection of the Rights of All Migrant Workers and Members of Their Families, adopted by the General Assembly in resolution 45/158 [YUN 1990, p. 594], had been ratified or acceded to by Azerbaijan, Bosnia and Herzegovina, Cape Verde, Colombia, Egypt, Mexico, Morocco, the Philippines, Senegal, Seychelles, Sri Lanka and Uganda, and signed by Bangladesh, Chile and Turkey.

The Secretary-General reported on the status of the Convention as at 31 August [A/54/346] and 1 November [E/CN.4/2000/77].

Commission action. On 27 April [res. 1999/45], the Commission called on all Member States to sign and ratify or accede to the Convention as a matter of priority. It asked the Secretary-General to provide all assistance necessary to promote the Convention through the World Public Information Campaign for Human Rights and the human rights programme of advisory services (see pp. 590 and 582), and to report in 2000 on the status of the Convention and on the Secretariat's efforts to promote it and the protection of the rights of migrant workers.

(For further information on migrant workers, see p. 612.)

GENERAL ASSEMBLY ACTION

On 17 December [meeting 83], the General Assembly, on the recommendation of the Third Committee [A/54/605/Add.1 & Corr.1], adopted **resolution 54/158** without vote [agenda item 116 *(a)*].

International Convention on the Protection of the Rights of All Migrant Workers and Members of Their Families

The General Assembly,

Reaffirming once more the permanent validity of the principles and norms set forth in the basic instruments regarding the international protection of human rights, in particular the Universal Declaration of Human Rights, the International Covenants on Human Rights, the International Convention on the Elimination of All Forms of Racial Discrimination, the Convention on the Elimination of All Forms of Discrimination against Women and the Convention on the Rights of the Child,

Bearing in mind the principles and norms established within the framework of the International Labour Organization and the importance of the work done in connection with migrant workers and members of their families in other specialized agencies and in various organs of the United Nations,

Reiterating that, despite the existence of an already established body of principles and norms, there is a need to make further efforts to improve the situation and to guarantee respect for the human rights and dignity of all migrant workers and members of their families,

Aware of the situation of migrant workers and members of their families and the marked increase in migratory movements that has occurred, especially in certain parts of the world,

Considering that, in the Vienna Declaration and Programme of Action adopted by the World Conference on Human Rights on 25 June 1993, all States are urged to guarantee the protection of the human rights of all migrant workers and members of their families,

Underlining the importance of the creation and promotion of conditions to foster greater harmony and tolerance between migrant workers and the rest of the society of the State in which they reside, with the aim of eliminating the growing manifestations of racism and xenophobia perpetrated in segments of many societies by individuals or groups against migrant workers,

Recalling its resolution 45/158 of 18 December 1990, by which it adopted and opened for signature, ratification and accession the International Convention on the Protection of the Rights of All Migrant Workers and Members of Their Families,

Bearing in mind that, in the Vienna Declaration and Programme of Action, States are invited to consider the possibility of signing and ratifying the Convention at the earliest possible time,

Recalling that, in its resolution 53/137 of 9 December 1998, it requested the Secretary-General to submit to it at its fifty-fourth session a report on the status of the Convention,

1. *Expresses its deep concern* at the growing manifestations of racism, xenophobia and other forms of discrimination and inhuman or degrading treatment directed against migrant workers in different parts of the world;

2. *Welcomes* the signature or ratification of or accession to the International Convention on the Protection of the Rights of All Migrant Workers and Members of Their Families by some Member States;

3. *Calls upon* all Member States to consider signing and ratifying or acceding to the Convention as a matter of priority, expresses the hope that it will enter into force at an early date, and notes that, pursuant to article 87 of the Convention, only eight ratifications or accessions are still needed for it to enter into force;

4. *Requests* the Secretary-General to provide all the facilities and assistance necessary for the promotion of the Convention through the World Public Information Campaign on Human Rights and the programme of advisory services in the field of human rights;

5. *Welcomes* the global campaign for the entry into force of the Convention, and invites the organizations and agencies of the United Nations system and intergovernmental and non-governmental organizations to intensify further their efforts with a view to disseminating information on and promoting understanding of the importance of the Convention;

6. *Also welcomes* the decision of the Commission on Human Rights, in its resolution 1999/44 of 27 April 1999, to appoint a Special Rapporteur on the human rights of migrants to examine ways and means to overcome the obstacles existing to the full and effective protection of the human rights of this vulnerable group;

7. *Takes note* of the report of the Secretary-General, and requests him to submit an updated report on the status of the Convention to the General Assembly at its fifty-fifth session;

8. *Decides* to consider the report of the Secretary-General at its fifty-fifth session under the sub-item entitled "Implementation of human rights instruments".

Convention on genocide

As at 31 December 1999, 130 States were parties to the 1948 Convention on the Prevention and Punishment of the Crime of Genocide, adopted by the General Assembly in resolution 260 A (III) [YUN 1948-49, p. 959]. In 1999, Portugal and Uzbekistan acceded to the Convention.

Commission action. On 28 April [res. 1999/67], by a roll-call vote of 48 to none, with 5 abstentions, the Commission stressed the importance of and the need to implement the Convention.

Convention against apartheid

As at 31 December 1999, there were 101 States parties to the 1973 International Convention on the Suppression and Punishment of the Crime of Apartheid, adopted by the General Assembly in resolution 3068(XXVIII) [YUN 1973, p. 103].

The Commission on Human Rights had suspended in 1995 both consideration of the item on the Convention's implementation [YUN 1995, p. 790] and meetings of the Group of Three [ibid., p. 693], the Convention's monitoring body.

Other activities

Follow-up to the 1993 World Conference

Report of High Commissioner. In March [E/CN.4/1999/9], the High Commissioner for Human Rights recalled that the Vienna Declaration and Programme of Action (VDPA), adopted by the 1993 World Conference on Human Rights [YUN 1993, p. 908], called on States to consider developing a national plan of action identifying steps to improve human rights promotion and protection. She stated that OHCHR had encouraged and supported State initiations for the creation of national plans as a means of translating commitments to human rights into concrete steps for action. Australia, Bolivia, Brazil, Ecuador, Indonesia, Latvia, Malawi, the Philippines, South Africa and Venezuela had developed such plans. In addition, a number of initiatives, many of them region-specific, were under way to facilitate the process by which national plans were developed and implemented, including specialized programmes and workshops in the African, Asian-Pacific, European, and Latin American and Caribbean regions.

Report of Secretary-General. In a June report [E/1999/83], the Secretary-General reviewed progress in the implementation of the 1998 agreed conclusions of the Economic and Social Council on the coordinated follow-up to and implementation of VDPA [YUN 1998, p. 626]. The Secretary-General stated that since the adoption of the agreed conclusions, new developments had given evidence that the processes initiated by the recognition of human rights as a cross-cutting challenge within the United Nations continued with the support of all sectors of the Organization. Progress was made in integrating human rights into policies of the UN system, as well as the willingness of its components to cooperate and coordinate activities; recognizing human rights as a vehicle of complementarity and consistency of UN system activities; integrating the human rights programme within the managerial structures of the United Nations at the Headquarters, regional and national levels; paying greater attention to the right to development and economic, social and cultural rights; mainstreaming a gender dimension and the human rights of women into the activities of the human rights machinery and the UN system; increasing the availability of technical cooperation in the area of human rights to States as a result of better programme coordination within the UN system; and intensifying human rights education and information campaigns. In spite of progress achieved, further efforts aimed at the optimal use of resources and capacities were necessary.

Note by High Commissioner. In an August note [E/CN.4/2000/5], the High Commissioner transmitted to the Commission the report of the meeting of special rapporteurs/representatives, experts and chairpersons of working groups of the Commission's special procedures and of its advisory services programme (Geneva, 31 May-3 June), as called for in VDPA. Participants discussed cooperation between special rapporteurs and UN departments, specialized agencies, funds, programmes and mechanisms; the future of the special procedures system and capacity-building to improve the effectiveness of extra-conventional mechanisms; and cooperation with the Commission and OHCHR. They adopted the "Manual for Special Rapporteurs".

By **decision 54/435** of 17 December, the General Assembly took note of the Third Committee's report on the comprehensive implementation of and follow-up to VDPA [A/54/605/Add.4].

ECONOMIC AND SOCIAL COUNCIL ACTION

On 28 July [meeting 44], the Economic and Social Council adopted **resolution 1999/35** [draft: E/1999/L.29] without vote [agenda item 6].

Implementation of agreed conclusions 1998/2 of the Economic and Social Council on the coordinated follow-up to and implementation of the Vienna Declaration and Programme of Action

The Economic and Social Council,

Recalling its agreed conclusions 1998/2 of 28 July 1998, on the coordinated follow-up to and implementation of the Vienna Declaration and Programme of Action in the United Nations system,

Recognizing that agreed conclusions 1998/2 provided an important contribution to the five-year review of the implementation of the Programme of Action,

1. *Takes note* of the report of the Secretary-General;
2. *Welcomes* the efforts of the United Nations High Commissioner for Human Rights and the relevant components of the United Nations system, within their respective mandates, towards the implementation of agreed conclusions 1998/2;
3. *Stresses* the need for further efforts for the full implementation by the relevant components of the United Nations system of agreed conclusions 1998/2;
4. *Decides* that the implementation of agreed conclusions 1998/2 shall be taken into account as part of the overall review by the Economic and Social Council in 2000 of progress made in an integrated and coordinated implementation of and follow-up to major United Nations conferences and summits.

Advisory services and technical cooperation

In 1999 [E/CN.4/2000/105 & Add.1], the UN technical cooperation programme in the field of human rights continued to assist Governments, at their request, in promoting and protecting human rights. Assistance included expert advisory services, training courses, workshops and seminars, fellowships, grants, the provision of information and documentation and assessment of domestic human rights needs. OHCHR assistance was provided for incorporating international human rights standards in national laws and policies, building and strengthening national institutions capable of promoting and protecting human rights and democracy under the rule of law, formulating national plans of action, training and education, and promoting a human rights culture. Priority was given to projects to be implemented in countries in transition and least developed countries, projects corresponding to national development objectives and integrated into broader UN strategies in the country concerned, and projects which facilitated broad participation of all elements of society and which offered sustainable institution-building benefits. Activities were funded partly by the UN regular budget and mainly by the Voluntary Fund for Technical Cooperation in the Field of Human Rights. During 1999, nine projects were completed and 45 were under way or approved.

During the year, a large number of countries received assistance to establish or strengthen national capacities and human rights institutions, including Armenia, Azerbaijan, Bhutan, Gabon, Georgia, Guatemala, Haiti, Indonesia, Latvia, Madagascar, Mongolia, Nepal, Somalia and Uganda. Other projects related to support for the rule of law and democratic processes (Burundi, Malawi, Palestine, Republic of Moldova); human rights education in schools (North-East Asia, Morocco, Russian Federation, Sierra Leone); and training for police (Southern African Regional Police Chiefs Cooperation Organization, El Salvador, Nicaragua). Technical cooperation activities were also carried out within the framework of OHCHR field presences in Abkhazia (Georgia), Afghanistan, Angola, Azerbaijan, Bosnia and Herzegovina, Burundi, Cambodia, Croatia, the Democratic Republic of the Congo, El Salvador, Guatemala, Indonesia, Liberia, Mongolia, Palestine, Sierra Leone, South Africa, Togo and Uganda.

The fellowship course for 1999 was facilitated by the United Nations Staff College project in Turin, Italy. Due to circumstances beyond the control of organizers, the training course was postponed and scheduled to take place from 7 to 18 February 2000. Twenty-six candidates were selected to attend the training representing 13 countries: Afghanistan, Democratic People's Republic of Korea, Ethiopia, Gambia, Indonesia, Kenya, Seychelles, Solomon Islands, Sri Lanka, Uganda, Viet Nam, Yemen and Zambia.

Commission action. On 28 April [res. 1999/73], by a roll-call vote of 27 to 19, with 7 abstentions, the Commission, welcoming the increase in the number of requests for advisory services and technical cooperation, called on the High Commissioner to take urgent measures to develop to the fullest extent the potential of advisory services and technical cooperation and to accord those activities the highest priority. It also called on her to include "exit strategies" based on the delivery of advisory services and technical cooperation as an integral part of all monitoring and preventive field operations; to offer advisory services to all countries irrespective of their economic status; and to examine ways to enhance the visibility and distinct identity of technical cooperation.

The Commission called on OHCHR to submit in 2000 a compendium of institutions and resource centres in developing countries specializing in human rights-related activities, with a view to promoting South-South cooperation; to make available annually to the Commission details of persons included on its roster of experts available for technical cooperation activities, to advertise widely in the media, especially in developing countries, its need for such experts and to invite States to nominate experts for inclusion on the roster; and to develop technical cooperation policy guidelines aimed at building national capacities and institutions. It invited OHCHR to institutionalize measures for the systematic follow-up of recommendations made by special rapporteurs and independent experts on the provision of advisory services and technical cooperation and for identifying resources required to implement them, and urged it to improve coordination with UN development agencies and to undertake an information campaign to publicize the importance of development for the promotion of human rights. The Commission asked the High Commissioner to report in 2000.

Workshop. On 27 April [E/CN.4/2000/163], Ecuador transmitted to the Commission the Conclusions and Framework of Technical Cooperation for the Promotion and Protection of Human Rights in Latin America and the Caribbean, adopted by a meeting of States of that region (Quito, 29 November–1 December).

Voluntary Fund Board

In 1999, the Board of Trustees of the Voluntary Fund for Technical Cooperation in the Field of Human Rights held its eleventh and twelfth sessions (Geneva, 14-17 June, 13-15 December) [E/CN.4/2000/105]. The Board considered 14 new project proposals; reviewed two completed and evaluated projects; examined the implementation status of nine current projects and activities; discussed project priorities, formats and procedures; and examined financial and administrative matters.

As part of a new fund-raising strategy, OHCHR developed a global Annual Appeal, beginning in 2000, to provide a thorough presentation of the planned activities and financial requirements to encourage more predictable and timely funding and permit longer-term planning.

Contributions received by the Fund in 1998/99 totalled $14.2 million.

Cambodia

Reports of Secretary-General. In three reports, the Secretary-General described the twelfth (9-21 January) [E/CN.4/1999/101], thirteenth (14-26 March), fourteenth (10-20 May) [A/54/353], fifteenth (21-26 August) and sixteenth (18-27 October) [E/CN.4/2000/109] missions of his Special Representative for human rights in Cambodia, Thomas Hammarberg (Sweden).

During his twelfth mission, the Special Representative visited the highland province of Ratanakiri where he focused on the economic, social and cultural rights of the indigenous peoples, in particular the aspects of logging and land use, as well as the difficulties faced by indigenous women in the areas of education, health and economic development. Major issues of concern were politically related violence, proceedings regarding Khmer Rouge crimes, impunity, the judicial system, torture and ill-treatment of arrested persons, prison conditions, labour rights, HIV/AIDS, women's and children's rights, the rights of ethnic minorities and of indigenous populations, and land rights.

In a review of the implementation of his previous recommendations, the Special Representative stated that, although the Government had recognized the need for major structural human rights reform, that work had not progressed very far. He presented the plans of various ministers of the new Government, stating that their implementation would go a long way towards addressing the problems he had raised. In an addendum to his report [E/CN.4/1999/101/Add.1], the Special Representative discussed the report of the Group of Experts on the crimes committed during the Khmer Rouge regime from 1975 to 1979 [A/53/850-S/1999/231] (see PART ONE, Chapter IV) and the 6 March arrest of Ta Mok, the former Khmer Rouge military commander of the south-west region.

The thirteenth mission focused on the question of bringing Khmer Rouge leaders to justice. The Special Representative sought clarifications concerning possible international assistance on the issue of the Khmer Rouge and, after detailed discussions with the Prime Minister, other Cambodian ministers and the diplomatic community, he received broad support to set up an international tribunal to bring former Khmer Rouge leaders to justice. The Special Representative also looked into the areas of the right to education, the protection of minorities and judicial reform.

The fourteenth mission continued discussions on the question of establishing a tribunal to try those most responsible for the most serious crimes committed under the Khmer Rouge regime. The Prime Minister indicated that work was under way to prepare a draft law which would enable foreign judges, prosecutors and lawyers to participate in the proceedings. He indicated Cambodia's interest in having the judges and prosecutors appointed by the Secretary-General and in receiving assistance in the drafting of the enabling law for submission to the National Assembly. The Special Representative stressed the importance of the entire process meeting international standards and outlined the legal issues that needed to be resolved before the undertaking of actual proceedings. He indicated his commitment to continue to facilitate international assistance to the Government and provide international expertise to assist with the preparation of the draft law. Other issues of concern were the right to health and the problem of torture. The Special Representative concluded that continued assistance to establish the rule of law was essential. The concern for civil and political rights was maintained, while at the same time economic, social and cultural rights would be given more attention. Priorities for the UN human rights programme were: assistance to the Government to monitor the human rights situation; greater integration of the human rights dimension into education, health and other development programmes; police, gendarmerie and armed forces training in support of government restructuring and reform; assistance to reform the administration of justice and the police; identifying assistance to combat impunity; strengthening the legislative process; provision of advice, on request, regarding Cambodia's submission of reports related to international human rights treaties; and provision of advice and assistance to the Government and its civil society partners on establishing an independent national human rights institution and the creation of a national plan of action on human rights. The priority areas were included in a draft memorandum of understanding (MOU) covering the work of the Cambodia Office of the High Commissioner for Human Rights (COHCHR) submitted for government consideration in August. The current MOU under which COHCHR operated was due to expire in March 2000. The report contained a review of COHCHR activities from September 1998 to June 1999.

During the fifteenth mission, the Special Representative discussed the continued cooperation of the Government with COHCHR. There was agreement that the MOU covering COHCHR activities would have a planning period of two years.

The last official mission stressed the functioning of the judicial system. The Special Representative raised the issue of prison conditions, including the diversion of daily allocations made for prisoners' subsistence to other purposes, overcrowding, special needs of women and prison reform. On the Khmer Rouge, he reiterated his conviction that the international community would support a trial in Cambodia provided that it met the standards of justice, fairness and due process of law and that it was fully independent. The Prime Minister stated that a new draft of the law to establish proceedings against the Khmer Rouge was in preparation with assistance from several foreign experts, and that the draft would be circulated for comment to the United Nations in November before it was submitted to the Council of Ministers in December. He expected the process to be under way in the first quarter of 2000. The Special Representative highlighted other areas of concern and reviewed the implementation of his recommendations.

Commission action. On 28 April [res. 1999/76], the Commission expressed grave concern about violations of human rights in Cambodia and called on the Government to investigate urgently and prosecute all those who had perpetrated human rights violations. It also expressed grave concern at the situation of impunity and appealed to the Government to ensure that those most responsible for the most serious human rights violations were brought to account in accordance with the international standards of justice, fairness and due process of law.

The Commission asked the Secretary-General, through his Special Representative, to assist the Government in ensuring the protection of human rights and to ensure adequate resources for the continued functioning of COHCHR and to enable the Special Representative to continue to fulfil his tasks. Those requests to the Secretary-General were approved by the Economic and Social Council in **decision 1999/247** of 27 July. The Secretary-General was requested to report in 2000.

Role of COHCHR

In a report on the 1999 activities and programmes of COHCHR [E/CN.4/2000/108], the Secretary-General provided an overview of the assistance provided for legislative reform, the administration of justice, national institutions for the promotion and protection of human rights, treaty reporting and international obligations, human rights NGOs, education and training programmes and curriculum development, information and documentation, monitoring and protection activities, the provincial office network and participation in UN system activities.

GENERAL ASSEMBLY ACTION

On 17 December [meeting 83], the General Assembly, on the recommendation of the Third Committee [A/54/605/Add.2], adopted **resolution 54/171** without vote [agenda item 116 *(b)*].

Situation of human rights in Cambodia

The General Assembly,

Guided by the purposes and principles embodied in the Charter of the United Nations, the Universal Declaration of Human Rights and the International Covenants on Human Rights,

Recalling the Agreement on a Comprehensive Political Settlement of the Cambodia Conflict, signed in Paris on 23 October 1991, including part III thereof, relating to human rights,

Recalling also its resolution 53/145 of 9 December 1998, taking note of Commission on Human Rights resolution 1999/76 of 28 April 1999, and recalling further previous relevant resolutions,

Recognizing that the tragic history of Cambodia requires special measures to assure the protection of the human rights of all people in Cambodia and the non-return to the policies and practices of the past, as stipulated in the Agreement signed in Paris on 23 October 1991,

Desiring that the international community continue to respond positively to assist efforts to investigate the tragic history of Cambodia, including responsibility for past international crimes, such as acts of genocide and crimes against humanity,

Bearing in mind the letter dated 15 March 1999 from the Secretary-General to the President of the General Assembly and the President of the Security Council and the report of the Group of Experts appointed by the Secretary-General in response to the request by the Cambodian authorities for assistance in responding to past serious violations of Cambodian and international law,

Recognizing the legitimate concern of the Government and people of Cambodia in the pursuit of internationally accepted principles of justice and of national reconciliation,

Recognizing also that accountability of individual perpetrators of grave human rights violations is one of the central elements of any effective remedy for victims of human rights violations and a key factor in ensuring a fair and equitable justice system and, ultimately, reconciliation and stability within a State,

Welcoming the continuing role of the United Nations High Commissioner for Human Rights in the promotion and protection of human rights in Cambodia,

1. *Requests* the Secretary-General, through his Special Representative for human rights in Cambodia, in collaboration with the office in Cambodia of the United Nations High Commissioner for Human Rights, to assist the Government of Cambodia in ensuring the protection of the human rights of all people in Cambodia and to ensure adequate resources for the continued functioning of the operational presence in Cambodia of the Office of the High Commissioner and to enable the Special Representative to continue to fulfil his tasks expeditiously;

2. *Takes note with appreciation* of the report of the Secretary-General, and notes in particular the concerns of the Special Representative about the problem

of impunity, the need to promote and protect the independence of the judiciary and to establish the rule of law and the need for the reform of police and the military;

3. *Welcomes* the agreement by the Government of Cambodia to extend the memorandum of understanding for the office at Phnom Penh of the High Commissioner until March 2002, enabling the office to continue its operations and to maintain its technical cooperation programmes, and encourages the Government to continue to cooperate with the office;

4. *Urges* the Government of Cambodia to continue to take the necessary measures to develop an independent, impartial and effective judicial system, including through the early adoption of the draft statute on magistrates, a penal code and a code on criminal procedures, and the reform of the administration of justice, and appeals to the international community to assist the Government to this end;

5. *Commends* the efforts by the Government of Cambodia with regard to the review and the stated commitment to the downsizing of the police and the military, urges the Government to take further measures to carry out effective reform aimed towards professional and impartial police and military forces, and invites the international community to assist the Government to this end;

6. *Also commends* the vital and valuable role played by non-governmental organizations in Cambodia, inter alia, in the development of civil society, and encourages the Government of Cambodia to continue to work with non-governmental organizations in efforts to strengthen and uphold human rights in Cambodia;

7. *Notes with interest* the activities undertaken by the governmental Cambodian Human Rights Committee, the National Assembly Commission on Human Rights and Reception of Complaints and the Senate Commission on Human Rights and Reception of Complaints, and welcomes preliminary efforts to establish an independent national human rights commission which should be based on international standards, such as the Paris principles, and requests the Office of the High Commissioner to provide advice and technical assistance in these efforts;

8. *Expresses grave concern* about numerous instances of violations of human rights, including extrajudicial executions, torture, illegal arrests and detention, as detailed in the reports of the Special Representative, and notes some progress made by the Government of Cambodia in addressing these issues;

9. *Expresses serious concern* about the situation of impunity in Cambodia, commends the commitment and efforts of the Government of Cambodia to tackle this question, such as amending article 51 of the 1994 Law on Civil Servants, and calls upon the Government to take further measures, as a matter of priority, to investigate urgently and prosecute, in accordance with due process of law and international human rights standards, all those who have perpetrated violations of human rights;

10. *Reaffirms* that the most serious human rights violations in Cambodia in recent history have been committed by the Khmer Rouge, welcomes the final collapse of the Khmer Rouge, which has paved the way for the investigation and prosecution of its leaders, and takes note with interest of the steps taken by the Government of Cambodia to bring to justice the Khmer Rouge leaders most responsible for the most serious violations of human rights;

11. *Strongly appeals* to the Government of Cambodia to ensure that those most responsible for the most serious violations of human rights are brought to account in accordance with international standards of justice, fairness and due process of law, welcomes the efforts of the Secretariat and actors of the international community in assisting the Government to this end, and encourages the Government to continue to cooperate with the United Nations with a view to reaching an agreement;

12. *Reaffirms* that ensuring the security of persons and rights of association, assembly and expression remain matters of critical priority;

13. *Also reaffirms* the importance of the upcoming communal elections being conducted in a free and fair manner, and urges the Government of Cambodia to prepare for the communal elections accordingly;

14. *Welcomes* the adoption of a five-year action plan by the Government of Cambodia, in particular by the Ministry of Women's Affairs and Veterans, as well as other measures taken by the Government to improve the status of women, and urges the Government to continue to take appropriate measures to eliminate discrimination against women, including in the political and public life of the country, to combat violence against women in all its forms and to take all steps to meet its obligations as a party to the Convention on the Elimination of All Forms of Discrimination against Women, including seeking technical assistance;

15. *Commends* the recent initiatives of and the progress made by the Government of Cambodia towards ensuring adequate health conditions, calls upon the Government to continue to take further measures to achieve this goal, with emphasis on ensuring adequate health conditions for women and children and minority groups and on the problem of the human immunodeficiency virus/acquired immunodeficiency syndrome, and encourages the international community to continue to support the Government to this end;

16. *Also commends* the continued efforts of the Government of Cambodia, together with non-governmental organizations and local authorities, to improve the quality of and access to education, and calls for further measures to be taken in order to ensure the right of Cambodian children to education, especially at the primary level, in accordance with the Convention on the Rights of the Child, and requests the international community to provide assistance for the achievement of this goal;

17. *Welcomes* the five-year national plan against child sexual exploitation in Cambodia, and encourages the Government of Cambodia to ensure the necessary law enforcement and other measures in support of the plan in order to tackle the problem of child prostitution and trafficking in Cambodia;

18. *Notes with serious concern* the problem of child labour, calls upon the Government of Cambodia to ensure adequate health and safety conditions for children and to outlaw, in particular, the worst forms of child labour, and invites the International Labour Organization to continue to extend the necessary assistance in this regard;

19. *Also notes with serious concern* the prison conditions in Cambodia, notes with interest the recent adoption of the Proclamation on Administration of Prisons and Prison Procedures, commends the continued international assistance to improve the material conditions of detention, and calls upon the Government of Cambodia to take the further measures necessary to improve prison conditions, especially with regard to providing the minimum standard of food and health care;

20. *Condemns* the use of racist rhetoric and acts of violence against ethnic minorities, urges an end to racial violence and vilification, and urges the Government of Cambodia to take all steps to meet its obligations as a party to the International Convention on the Elimination of All Forms of Racial Discrimination, including through seeking technical assistance;

21. *Welcomes,* in particular, the recent actions taken by the Government of Cambodia to combat illicit logging which has seriously threatened the full enjoyment of economic, social and cultural rights by many Cambodians, including indigenous people, expresses the hope that these efforts by the Government will continue, and notes with interest the current revision of the law on land;

22. *Also welcomes* the submission of the initial reports of Cambodia under the International Covenant on Civil and Political Rights, the International Convention on the Elimination of All Forms of Racial Discrimination and the Convention on the Rights of the Child, asks the Government of Cambodia to follow up the recommendations made by the Human Rights Committee regarding the report submitted under the International Covenant on Civil and Political Rights, calls upon the Government to meet its reporting obligations under all other international human rights instruments, and requests the office in Cambodia of the High Commissioner to continue to provide the necessary assistance in this regard;

23. *Expresses grave concern* at the devastating consequences and destabilizing effects of the use of anti-personnel landmines on Cambodian society, welcomes the ratification by Cambodia of the Convention on the Prohibition of the Use, Stockpiling, Production and Transfer of Anti-personnel Mines and on Their Destruction in July 1999, encourages the Government of Cambodia to continue its support and efforts for the removal of those mines and for victim assistance and mine awareness programmes, and commends donor countries for their contributions and assistance to mine action;

24. *Expresses concern* about the high number of small arms in society and commends the efforts by the Government of Cambodia to control the spread of weapons;

25. *Notes with appreciation* the use by the Secretary-General of the United Nations Trust Fund for a Human Rights Education Programme in Cambodia to finance the programme of activities of the office in Cambodia of the High Commissioner, as defined in resolutions of the General Assembly and the Commission on Human Rights, and invites Governments, intergovernmental and non-governmental organizations, foundations and individuals to consider contributing to the Trust Fund;

26. *Requests* the Secretary-General to report to the General Assembly at its fifty-fifth session on the role and achievements of the Office of the High Commissioner in assisting the Government and the people of Cambodia in the promotion and protection of human rights and on the recommendations made by the Special Representative on matters within his mandate;

27. *Decides* to continue its consideration of the situation of human rights in Cambodia at its fifty-fifth session under the item entitled "Human rights questions".

Chad

On 22 April [dec. 1999/102], the Commission requested the High Commissioner to report in 2000 on the establishment and implementation of a technical cooperation project based on a joint needs-assessment mission to Chad undertaken by OHCHR and the United Nations Development Programme (UNDP) in 1998.

In accordance with the Commission's decision, OHCHR and UNDP drew up a project document for technical cooperation with Chad in the areas of human rights and governance [E/CN.4/2000/107]. The project document was signed by the Government of Chad and UNDP on 6 and 13 August, respectively. It was also approved and signed by the High Commissioner.

Croatia

On 10 May, a technical cooperation agreement was signed between the Government of Croatia and OHCHR, with a view to building human rights capacity and human rights education. The agreement provided for capacity-building activities, including dissemination of documentation and training on human rights standards for military, police and prison officials; training and advice for government officials in reporting obligations; training and advice for NGOs; advice on developing human rights education curricula; advice and assistance to the Ombudsman's office; and establishment of a Human Rights Documentation Centre. As at December, OHCHR had conducted a human rights summer school for law students and had held seminars for the military on international human rights and humanitarian law standards, as well as for government representatives on reporting obligations. (For information on the human rights situation in Croatia, see p. 727.)

Haiti

Commission action. On 28 April [res. 1999/77], the Commission expressed concern at the lack of progress on judicial system reform and called upon the Government of Haiti to continue structural reforms in the police and justice sectors, to investigate politically motivated crimes properly and prosecute perpetrators of such crimes in accordance with Haitian law, and to eliminate continuing human rights violations. It urged Haiti to improve the overall conditions in prisons and to put in place measures to address violence against women. The Commission drew attention to the need for the Haitian National Police to continue receiving technical training to enable it to perform its functions efficiently, within the context of respect for human rights.

The Commission invited the High Commissioner to contribute to the strengthening of the Office of Protection of the Citizen, through a programme of technical cooperation. The Commission's independent expert was asked to report to the General Assembly in 1999 and to the Commission in 2000. The request to the expert was approved by Economic and Social Council **decision 1999/248** of 27 July.

Report of independent expert. In September, the Secretary-General transmitted to the General Assembly the report of the independent expert, Adama Dieng (Senegal) [A/54/366], who had visited Haiti (11-20 March) and met with high-level government officials, including the President. He observed that there had been significant advances in human rights since the return to constitutional legality; however, serious problems of governance, security and poverty remained as threats to the rule of law. The Haitian authorities were called on to ensure that the perpetrators of the crimes committed during and after the coup d'état were arrested, prosecuted and tried in accordance with the relevant human rights standards. Women's groups and other NGOs were taking action to combat violence against women; the Haitian National Police was committed to helping combat the violence as well. The situation of children working as servants was increasingly alarming. Access to education remained a major problem, despite government action. The independent expert reaffirmed that the renewal of the mandate of the International Civilian Mission in Haiti (MICIVIH) was necessary to improve the human rights situation.

GENERAL ASSEMBLY ACTION

On 17 December [meeting 83], the General Assembly, on the recommendation of the Third Committee [A/54/605/Add.3], adopted **resolution 54/187** without vote [agenda item 116 (*c*)].

Situation of human rights in Haiti

The General Assembly,

Guided by the principles embodied in the Charter of the United Nations, the Universal Declaration of Human Rights, the International Covenants on Human Rights and other international human rights instruments, including the Convention on the Elimination of All Forms of Discrimination against Women,

Recalling its resolution 53/159 of 9 December 1998, and taking note of Commission on Human Rights resolution 1999/77 of 28 April 1999,

Recognizing the interdependence and mutual reinforcement between democracy, development and respect for human rights and fundamental freedoms and the commitment of the international community to supporting, strengthening and promoting this principle,

Taking note with appreciation of the report of the independent expert of the Commission on Human Rights on the situation of human rights in Haiti, Adama Dieng, and encouraging active follow-up of the recommendations contained therein,

Recognizing the important contributions of the International Civilian Mission in Haiti, the United Nations Civilian Police Mission in Haiti and the National Commission for Truth and Justice to the task of restoring and strengthening democracy in Haiti and of establishing a climate of freedom and tolerance conducive to respect for human rights,

Commending the Organization of American States for its contribution to the Civilian Mission, and inviting that organization to pursue, as appropriate, its cooperation with the United Nations in Haiti,

Welcoming the establishment of the new Provisional Electoral Council and the decision taken to organize legislative and local elections on 19 March 2000 and in April 2000 as a step towards re-establishing a functional legislature,

Welcoming also the continued improvements in the situation of human rights in Haiti since the restoration of its democratic regime, and noting the declared commitment of the Government of Haiti to uphold human rights,

Expressing its concern at the security problems faced by Haitian society, some of which are due to the difficult social and economic conditions and which both account for and result from the limitations of the judicial and police systems, as indicated in the report of the independent expert,

Welcoming Economic and Social Council resolution 1999/11 of 27 July 1999, in which the Council, inter alia, emphasized the need to establish the necessary mechanisms to develop, on a priority basis, a long-term strategy and programme of support for Haiti,

1. *Expresses its gratitude* to the Secretary-General, his Special Representative for Haiti and the independent expert of the Commission on Human Rights on the situation of human rights in Haiti for their continuing efforts in favour of the consolidation of democratic institutions in Haiti and respect for human rights;

2. *Commends* the United Nations Civilian Police Mission in Haiti for its successful training and mentoring assistance to the Haitian National Police, as well as the efforts of the International Civilian Mission in Haiti in monitoring human rights and promoting democratic reform and assisting the Haitian authorities in the area of institution-building;

3. *Draws attention* to the need for the Haitian National Police to continue to receive technical assistance to enable it to perform its functions efficiently within a framework of respect for human rights;

4. *Commends* the United Nations Development Programme for its technical assistance to the Haitian National Police and the penitentiary system as well as in the organization of the forthcoming electoral process, also commends the international community for the provision of other assistance, including for judicial reform, and invites them to continue to provide appropriate assistance;

5. *Invites* the Government of Haiti to ratify the International Covenant on Economic, Social and Cultural Rights, the Convention against Torture and Other Cruel, Inhuman or Degrading Treatment or Punishment, and the Optional Protocols to the International Covenant on Civil and Political Rights;

6. *Strongly supports* the efforts made to enable the people of Haiti to express their political will in the forthcoming legislative and local elections, invites all the political leaders of the country to involve themselves in a constructive dialogue, and in this connection invites the Government of Haiti to ensure the necessary political and security environment for the holding of free and fair elections in accordance with the schedule recently announced by the Provisional Electoral Council;

7. *Calls upon* the Government of Haiti to continue structural reforms in the police and the judicial system and the improvement of the prison sector, to investigate properly politically motivated crimes and prosecute perpetrators of such crimes in accordance with Haitian law, to take vigorous action to eliminate any continuing human rights violations, including illegal arrests and detentions, and to ensure due process within a reasonable time;

8. *Reaffirms* the importance, for combating impunity and for the realization of a genuine and effective process of transition and national reconciliation, of the investigations undertaken by the National Commission for Truth and Justice, and once again calls upon the Government of Haiti to institute legal proceedings against the perpetrators of human rights violations identified by the National Commission and to create effective facilities for providing support to the victims, in particular women, children and members of their families, and in this specific context reiterates the recommendations contained in the report of the independent expert of the Commission on Human Rights on the situation of human rights in Haiti;

9. *Welcomes* the initiative of the Government of Haiti, in collaboration with the international community and women's groups, to put in place measures to address the human rights of women and, inter alia, violence against women, including the development of training programmes for judicial and legal personnel and the incorporation of the precept of the human rights of women at all levels of the education system;

10. *Encourages* the Government of Haiti to promote further the rights of children, in particular their right to education;

11. *Invites* the Secretary-General and the Government of Haiti to contribute to the strengthening of the Office for the Protection of Citizens through the establishment of a programme of technical cooperation, in close collaboration with the United Nations High Commissioner for Human Rights, and invites the international community to assist in this effort;

12. *Decides* to continue its consideration of the situation of human rights and fundamental freedoms in Haiti at its fifty-fifth session.

(See also p. 208)

Somalia

Commission action. On 28 April [res. 1999/75], with regard to Somalia, the Commission condemned the widespread violations and abuses of human rights and humanitarian law and violation of international law on armed conflicts, including hostage-taking and abduction. It expressed deep concern at reports of arbitrary and summary executions, torture and other cruel, inhuman or degrading treatment or punishment and violence, and at the absence of an effective judicial system. It strongly urged all parties in Somalia to respect human rights and international humanitarian law, to re-establish the rule of law and to protect UN personnel, humanitarian relief workers, and NGO and international media representatives.

The Commission welcomed the High Commissioner's decision to appoint a human rights officer within the office of the United Nations Resident Humanitarian Coordinator for Somalia. The Secretary-General was asked to continue to provide adequate resources to fund activities of the Commission's independent expert and the High Commissioner for the implementation of advisory services and technical cooperation. Governments and organizations were asked to respond positively to requests for assistance in implementing the Commission's resolution.

The Economic and Social Council approved the Commission's request to the Secretary-General to continue to provide resources to the expert by **decision 1999/246** of 27 July.

Report of independent expert. Independent expert Mona Rishmawi (Jordan) reported on the situation of human rights in Somalia following her visit to the country (14-24 November) [E/CN.4/2000/110 & Corr.1]. As to the security and political situations, during 1999, nearly half of the country had been peaceful, especially in the north. The powers of the warlords had declined and with their defeat in areas in the south much of the violence was criminal rather than political. A new power had emerged in parts of central and southern Somalia, with the institution of shariah courts that were supported by their own militia. Areas under the control of the courts experienced tranquillity and economic growth due to the deterrence of banditry. However, many acts that could be qualified as war crimes or crimes against humanity were being committed in Somalia, particularly in the south. The independent expert examined acts of violence, civilian attacks, recruitment of child soldiers, rape and other sexual violence, persecution of minorities, displacement of civilians and denial of due process. Regarding the mass graves in Hargeisa [YUN 1997, p. 617], she said that a technical committee for the investigation of war crimes continued to focus on identifying victims. The expert welcomed the placement by OHCHR of a human rights officer in Nairobi to serve as a focal point for human rights assistance to Somalia.

(See also p. 170.)

Public information

Commission action. On 28 April [res. 1999/60], the Commission urged OHCHR and the UN Department of Public Information (DPI) to cooperate closely to produce multimedia information programmes in the field of human rights; develop strategies to strengthen the role of the mass media to further human rights education and public information; utilize effectively UN information centres to disseminate information on human rights; and produce information material, in particular audio-visual material, on all aspects of human rights in connection with the World Public Information Campaign on Human Rights, launched by the General Assembly in resolution 43/128 [YUN 1988, p. 539], and the United Nations Decade for Human Rights Education (1995-2004), proclaimed by Assembly resolution 49/184 [YUN 1994, p. 1039]. The Commission asked the Secretary-General to report in 2001 on public information activities, emphasizing activities relating to the World Campaign.

Report of Secretary-General. The Secretary-General described, in September, public information activities in the area of human rights carried out by OHCHR and DPI [A/54/399 & Add.1]. He provided details of the OHCHR publications programme, the use of electronic means to maximize the impact of information and external relations, including briefings, exhibitions, human rights observances and fellowships. DPI continued to initiate and coordinate activities of the World Public Information Campaign, the United Nations Decade for Human Rights Education, the Third Decade to Combat Racism and Racial Discrimination (1993-2002), the International Decade of the World's Indigenous People (1995-2004) and the United Nations Decade for the Eradication of Poverty (1997-2006). Other DPI activities included the production of printed materials in various languages disseminated through UN information centres and services and other UN offices and electronically through the World Wide Web. Its multimedia approach entailed radio and television programmes, press conferences, press briefings and special events, exhibits, special media outreach activities, activities with educational organizations and NGOs, and public services for visitors. The Secretary-General presented a list of publications issued by OHCHR and human rights publications available from DPI.

Human rights education

Commission action. On 28 April [res. 1999/60], the Commission urged Members States to develop a comprehensive, effective and sustainable national plan of action for human rights education and public information in accordance with the guidelines for national plans of action for human rights education [YUN 1997, p. 618] and the Plan of Action for the United Nations Decade for Human Rights Education (1995-2004), proclaimed by the General Assembly in resolution 49/184 [YUN 1994, p. 1039]. OHCHR was encouraged, through its programme of advisory services and technical cooperation (see p. 582), to give priority and support for the development of national capacities in the areas of human rights education and public information.

Also on 28 April [res. 1999/64], the Commission asked the High Commissioner to accelerate implementation of the Plan of Action for the Decade and encourage and facilitate the establishment of national plans of action for human rights education in Member States in accordance with national conditions. It also asked her to continue to implement the Assisting Communities Together (ACT) project [YUN 1998, p. 635] and to consider other ways to support human rights education activities. The Secretary-General was asked to report on the implementation of the Commission's resolution in 2000.

Reports of Secretary-General. In September [A/54/399], the Secretary-General summarized activities taken to implement the Plan of Action for the Decade. OHCHR, in a joint effort with the United Nations Educational, Scientific and Cultural Organization (UNESCO), was carrying out a survey of existing programmes, materials and organizations for human rights education of Decade partners at all levels. A second round of ACT project grants would be awarded at year's end. Within the UN system, UNESCO held regional conferences on human rights education and publications were produced. Other international organizations, NGOs and human rights institutes initiated or continued projects for human rights education. The report summarized information on initiatives taken by 19 countries to strengthen human rights education. Work continued on the six training packages for human rights monitors, judges and lawyers, prison officials, primary and secondary schoolteachers, journalists and national and local NGOs.

In a later report [E/CN.4/2000/93], the Secretary-General provided supplementary information received in the period from September to mid-December 1999. In November, OHCHR launched the second phase of the ACT project, for which 16 countries/territories had been selected. In cooperation with the Government of the Republic of Korea and within the Asia-Pacific Framework for Regional Technical Cooperation, OHCHR organized a subregional training workshop on human rights education in North-East Asia (Seoul, 1-4 December). OHCHR was awarded the Guinness World Record for having collected, translated and disseminated the Universal Declaration of Human Rights into more than 300 languages and dialects, from Abkhaz to Zulu. The report described actions taken by human rights institutes, intergovernmental organizations and NGOs, and described the initiatives taken by 15 countries.

GENERAL ASSEMBLY ACTION

On 17 December [meeting 83], the General Assembly, on the recommendation of the Third Committee [A/54/605/Add.2], adopted **resolution 54/161** without vote [agenda item 116 *(b)*].

United Nations Decade for Human Rights Education, 1995-2004, and public information activities in the field of human rights

The General Assembly,

Guided by the fundamental and universal principles enshrined in the Charter of the United Nations and the Universal Declaration of Human Rights, article 26 of which states that "education shall be directed to the full development of the human personality and to the strengthening of respect for human rights and fundamental freedoms", and the provisions of other international human rights instruments, such as those of article 13 of the International Covenant on Economic, Social and Cultural Rights, article 10 of the Convention on the Elimination of All Forms of Discrimination against Women, article 7 of the International Convention on the Elimination of All Forms of Racial Discrimination, article 29 of the Convention on the Rights of the Child, article 10 of the Convention against Torture and Other Cruel, Inhuman or Degrading Treatment or Punishment and paragraphs 78 to 82 of the Vienna Declaration and Programme of Action adopted by the World Conference on Human Rights on 25 June 1993, which reflect the aims of the aforementioned article,

Recalling the relevant resolutions adopted by the General Assembly and the Commission on Human Rights concerning the United Nations Decade for Human Rights Education, 1995-2004, public information activities in the field of human rights, including the World Public Information Campaign on Human Rights, the project of the United Nations Educational, Scientific and Cultural Organization entitled "Towards a culture of peace", and the implementation of and follow-up to the Vienna Declaration and Programme of Action,

Believing that the World Public Information Campaign is a valuable complement to the activities of the United Nations aimed at the further promotion and protection of human rights, and recalling the importance attached by the World Conference on Human Rights to human rights education and information,

Convinced that every woman, man and child, in order to realize their full human potential, must be made aware of all their human rights and fundamental freedoms,

Convinced also that human rights education should involve more than the provision of information and should constitute a comprehensive, lifelong process by which people at all levels of development and in all societies learn respect for the dignity of others and the means and methods of ensuring that respect,

Recognizing that human rights education and information are essential to the realization of human rights and fundamental freedoms and that carefully designed training, dissemination and information programmes can have a catalytic effect on national, regional and international initiatives to promote and protect human rights and prevent human rights violations,

Convinced that human rights education and information contribute to a holistic concept of development consistent with the dignity of women and men of all ages, which takes into account particularly vulnerable segments of society such as children, young persons, older persons, indigenous people, minorities, the rural and urban poor, migrant workers, refugees, persons with the human immunodeficiency virus/acquired immunodeficiency syndrome and disabled persons,

Taking into account the efforts to promote human rights education made by educators and non-governmental organizations in all parts of the world, as well as by intergovernmental organizations, including the Office of the United Nations High Commissioner for Human Rights, the United Nations Educational, Scientific and Cultural Organization, the International Labour Organization, the United Nations Children's Fund and the United Nations Development Programme,

Recognizing the invaluable and creative role that non-governmental and community-based organizations can play in disseminating public information and engaging in human rights education, especially at the grass-roots level and in remote and rural communities,

Aware of the potential supportive role of the private sector in implementing at all levels of society the Plan of Action for the United Nations Decade for Human Rights Education, 1995-2004, and the World Public Information Campaign, through creative initiatives and financial support for governmental and non-governmental activities,

Convinced that the effectiveness of existing human rights education and public information activities would be enhanced by better coordination and co-operation at the national, regional and international levels,

Recalling that it is within the responsibility of the United Nations High Commissioner for Human Rights to coordinate relevant United Nations education and public information programmes in the field of human rights,

Taking note with appreciation of the increased efforts undertaken so far by the Office of the High Commissioner to disseminate human rights information through its web site and its publications and external relations programmes,

Welcoming the initiative of the Office of the High Commissioner to develop further the project entitled "Assisting Communities Together", launched in 1998, supported by voluntary funds and designed to provide small grants to grass-roots and local organizations carrying out practical human rights activities,

Recalling that, according to the Plan of Action, in 2000 a mid-term global evaluation of progress made towards the achievement of the objectives of the Decade shall be undertaken by the Office of the High Commissioner, in cooperation with all other principal actors in the Decade,

1. *Takes note with appreciation* of the report of the Secretary-General on the United Nations Decade for Human Rights Education, 1995-2004, and public information activities in the field of human rights, including the World Public Information Campaign on Human Rights;

2. *Welcomes* the steps taken by Governments and intergovernmental and non-governmental organizations to implement the Plan of Action for the United Nations Decade for Human Rights Education, 1995-2004, and to develop public information activities in the field of human rights, as indicated in the report of the Secretary-General;

3. *Urges* all Governments to contribute further to the implementation of the Plan of Action, in particular by establishing, in accordance with national conditions, broadly representative national committees for human rights education responsible for the development of comprehensive, effective and sustainable national plans of action for human rights education and information, taking into consideration the guidelines for national plans of action for human rights education developed by the Office of the United Nations High Commissioner for Human Rights within the framework of the Decade;

4. *Urges* Governments to encourage, support and involve national and local non-governmental and community-based organizations in the implementation of their national plans of action;

5. *Encourages* Governments to consider, within the national plans of action mentioned in paragraphs 3 and 4 above, the establishment of public access human rights resource and training centres capable of engaging in research, the gender-sensitive training of trainers, the preparation, collection, translation and dissemination of human rights education and training materials, the organization of courses, conferences, workshops and public information campaigns and assistance in the implementation of internationally sponsored technical cooperation projects for human rights education and public information;

6. *Encourages* States, where such national public access human rights resource and training centres already exist, to strengthen their capacity to support human rights education and public information programmes at the international, national, regional and local levels;

7. *Calls upon* Governments, in accordance with national conditions, to accord priority to the dissemination, in the relevant national and local languages, of the Universal Declaration of Human Rights, the International Covenants on Human Rights and other human rights instruments, human rights materials and training manuals, as well as reports of States parties under international human rights treaties, and to provide information and education in those languages on the practical ways in which national and international institutions and procedures may be utilized to ensure the effective implementation of those instruments;

8. *Encourages* Governments to support further, through voluntary contributions, the education and public information efforts undertaken by the Office of the High Commissioner within the framework of the Plan of Action;

9. *Requests* the High Commissioner to continue to coordinate and harmonize human rights education and information strategies within the United Nations system, including the implementation of the Plan of Action, and to ensure maximum effectiveness and efficiency in the use, processing, management and distribution of human rights information and educational materials, including through electronic means;

10. *Encourages* Governments to contribute to the further development of the web site of the Office of the High Commissioner, in particular with respect to the dissemination of human rights education materials and tools, and to continue and expand the publications and external relations programmes of the Office;

11. *Encourages* the Office of the High Commissioner to continue to support national capacities for human rights education and information through its technical cooperation programme in the field of human rights, including the organization of training courses and the development of targeted training materials for professional audiences, as well as the dissemination of human rights information materials as a component of technical cooperation projects;

12. *Urges* the Department of Public Information of the Secretariat to continue to utilize United Nations information centres for the timely dissemination, within their designated areas of activity, of basic information, reference and audio-visual materials on human rights and fundamental freedoms, including the reports of States parties under international human rights instruments and, to this end, to ensure that the information centres are supplied with adequate quantities of those materials;

13. *Stresses* the need for close collaboration between the Office of the High Commissioner and the Department of Public Information in the implementation of the Plan of Action and the World Public Information Campaign, and the need to harmonize their activities with those of other international organizations such as the United Nations Educational, Scientific and Cultural Organization with regard to its project entitled "Towards a culture of peace" and the International Committee of the Red Cross and relevant non-governmental organizations with regard to the dissemination of information on international humanitarian law;

14. *Invites* the specialized agencies and relevant United Nations programmes and funds to contribute, within their respective spheres of competence, to the implementation of the Plan of Action and the World

Public Information Campaign and to cooperate with the Office of the High Commissioner in that regard;

15. *Encourages* the human rights treaty bodies, when examining reports of States parties, to place emphasis on obligations of States parties in the area of human rights education and information and to reflect this emphasis in their concluding observations;

16. *Calls upon* international, national and regional non-governmental organizations and intergovernmental organizations, in particular those concerned with women, labour, development, food, housing, education, health care and the environment, as well as all other social justice groups, human rights advocates, educators, religious organizations and the media, to undertake specific activities of formal, non-formal and informal education, including cultural events, alone and in cooperation with the Office of the High Commissioner, in implementing the Plan of Action;

17. *Urges* Governments and intergovernmental and non-governmental organizations to contribute to the mid-term global evaluation of progress made towards the achievement of the objectives of the Decade to be undertaken by the Office of the High Commissioner in 2000, by providing appropriate information on steps taken in this regard;

18. *Requests* the Office of the High Commissioner to continue implementation of the "Assisting Communities Together" project and to consider other appropriate ways and means to support human rights education activities, including those undertaken by non-governmental organizations;

19. *Requests* the Secretary-General, through the High Commissioner, to bring the present resolution to the attention of all members of the international community and of intergovernmental and non-governmental organizations concerned with human rights education and public information, and to submit to the General Assembly at its fifty-fifth session the mid-term global evaluation of progress made towards the achievement of the objectives of the Decade for consideration under the item entitled "Human rights questions".

Culture of peace

Commission action. On 28 April [res. 1999/62], the Commission encouraged the General Assembly to conclude its deliberations on the adoption of a declaration and programme of action on a culture of peace and reiterated its invitation to States to promote a culture of peace based on the purposes and principles established in the UN Charter. It asked OHCHR to prepare a report in 2000, taking into consideration the comments and views of all Governments, intergovernmental organizations and NGOs, on the contribution of the promotion and protection of human rights to the further development of a culture of peace.

Report of OHCHR. In response to the above resolution, OHCHR invited Governments, intergovernmental organizations and NGOs to submit their comments and views. A December report summarized the views of two States [E/CN.4/2000/97].

Declaration and Programme of Action

On 13 September [meeting 107], the General Assembly adopted **resolutions 53/243 A and B** [draft: A/53/L.79] without vote [agenda item 31].

A

Declaration on a Culture of Peace

The General Assembly,

Recalling the Charter of the United Nations, including the purposes and principles embodied therein,

Recalling also the Constitution of the United Nations Educational, Scientific and Cultural Organization, which states that "since wars begin in the minds of men, it is in the minds of men that the defences of peace must be constructed",

Recalling further the Universal Declaration of Human Rights and other relevant international instruments of the United Nations system,

Recognizing that peace not only is the absence of conflict, but also requires a positive, dynamic participatory process where dialogue is encouraged and conflicts are solved in a spirit of mutual understanding and cooperation,

Recognizing also that the end of the cold war has widened possibilities for strengthening a culture of peace,

Expressing deep concern about the persistence and proliferation of violence and conflict in various parts of the world,

Recognizing the need to eliminate all forms of discrimination and intolerance, including those based on race, colour, sex, language, religion, political or other opinion, national, ethnic or social origin, property, disability, birth or other status,

Recalling its resolution 52/15 of 20 November 1997, by which it proclaimed the year 2000 as the "International Year for the Culture of Peace", and its resolution 53/25 of 10 November 1998, by which it proclaimed the period 2001-2010 as the "International Decade for a Culture of Peace and Non-Violence for the Children of the World",

Recognizing the important role that the United Nations Educational, Scientific and Cultural Organization continues to play in the promotion of a culture of peace,

Solemnly proclaims the present Declaration on a Culture of Peace to the end that Governments, international organizations and civil society may be guided in their activity by its provisions to promote and strengthen a culture of peace in the new millennium:

Article 1

A culture of peace is a set of values, attitudes, traditions and modes of behaviour and ways of life based on:

(a) Respect for life, ending of violence and promotion and practice of non-violence through education, dialogue and cooperation;

(b) Full respect for the principles of sovereignty, territorial integrity and political independence of States and non-intervention in matters which are essentially within the domestic jurisdiction of any State, in accordance with the Charter of the United Nations and international law;

(c) Full respect for and promotion of all human rights and fundamental freedoms;

(*d*) Commitment to peaceful settlement of conflicts;

(*e*) Efforts to meet the developmental and environmental needs of present and future generations;

(*f*) Respect for and promotion of the right to development;

(*g*) Respect for and promotion of equal rights and opportunities for women and men;

(*h*) Respect for and promotion of the right of everyone to freedom of expression, opinion and information;

(*i*) Adherence to the principles of freedom, justice, democracy, tolerance, solidarity, cooperation, pluralism, cultural diversity, dialogue and understanding at all levels of society and among nations;

and fostered by an enabling national and international environment conducive to peace.

Article 2

Progress in the fuller development of a culture of peace comes about through values, attitudes, modes of behaviour and ways of life conducive to the promotion of peace among individuals, groups and nations.

Article 3

The fuller development of a culture of peace is integrally linked to:

(*a*) Promoting peaceful settlement of conflicts, mutual respect and understanding and international cooperation;

(*b*) Complying with international obligations under the Charter of the United Nations and international law;

(*c*) Promoting democracy, development and universal respect for and observance of all human rights and fundamental freedoms;

(*d*) Enabling people at all levels to develop skills of dialogue, negotiation, consensus-building and peaceful resolution of differences;

(*e*) Strengthening democratic institutions and ensuring full participation in the development process;

(*f*) Eradicating poverty and illiteracy and reducing inequalities within and among nations;

(*g*) Promoting sustainable economic and social development;

(*h*) Eliminating all forms of discrimination against women through their empowerment and equal representation at all levels of decision-making;

(*i*) Ensuring respect for and promotion and protection of the rights of children;

(*j*) Ensuring free flow of information at all levels and enhancing access thereto;

(*k*) Increasing transparency and accountability in governance;

(*l*) Eliminating all forms of racism, racial discrimination, xenophobia and related intolerance;

(*m*) Advancing understanding, tolerance and solidarity among all civilizations, peoples and cultures, including towards ethnic, religious and linguistic minorities;

(*n*) Realizing fully the right of all peoples, including those living under colonial or other forms of alien domination or foreign occupation, to self-determination enshrined in the Charter of the United Nations and embodied in the International Covenants on Human Rights, as well as in the Declaration on the Granting of Independence to Colonial Countries and Peoples contained in General Assembly resolution 1514(XV) of 14 December 1960.

Article 4

Education at all levels is one of the principal means to build a culture of peace. In this context, human rights education is of particular importance.

Article 5

Governments have an essential role in promoting and strengthening a culture of peace.

Article 6

Civil society needs to be fully engaged in fuller development of a culture of peace.

Article 7

The educative and informative role of the media contributes to the promotion of a culture of peace.

Article 8

A key role in the promotion of a culture of peace belongs to parents, teachers, politicians, journalists, religious bodies and groups, intellectuals, those engaged in scientific, philosophical and creative and artistic activities, health and humanitarian workers, social workers, managers at various levels as well as to non-governmental organizations.

Article 9

The United Nations should continue to play a critical role in the promotion and strengthening of a culture of peace worldwide.

B

Programme of Action on a Culture of Peace

The General Assembly,

Bearing in mind the Declaration on a Culture of Peace adopted on 13 September 1999,

Recalling its resolution 52/15 of 20 November 1997, by which it proclaimed the year 2000 as the "International Year for the Culture of Peace", and its resolution 53/25 of 10 November 1998, by which it proclaimed the period 2001-2010 as the "International Decade for a Culture of Peace and Non-violence for the Children of the World",

Adopts the following Programme of Action on a Culture of Peace:

A. *Aims, strategies and main actors*

1. The Programme of Action should serve as the basis for the International Year for the Culture of Peace and the International Decade for a Culture of Peace and Non-violence for the Children of the World.

2. Member States are encouraged to take actions for promoting a culture of peace at the national level as well as at the regional and international levels.

3. Civil society should be involved at the local, regional and national levels to widen the scope of activities on a culture of peace.

4. The United Nations system should strengthen its ongoing efforts to promote a culture of peace.

5. The United Nations Educational, Scientific and Cultural Organization should continue to play its important role in and make major contributions to the promotion of a culture of peace.

6. Partnerships between and among the various actors as set out in the Declaration should be encouraged and strengthened for a global movement for a culture of peace.

7. A culture of peace could be promoted through sharing of information among actors on their initiatives in this regard.

8. Effective implementation of the Programme of Action requires mobilization of resources, including financial resources, by interested Governments, organizations and individuals.

B. *Strengthening actions at the national, regional and international levels by all relevant actors*

9. Actions to foster a culture of peace through education:

(a) Reinvigorate national efforts and international cooperation to promote the goals of education for all with a view to achieving human, social and economic development and for promoting a culture of peace;

(b) Ensure that children, from an early age, benefit from education on the values, attitudes, modes of behaviour and ways of life to enable them to resolve any dispute peacefully and in a spirit of respect for human dignity and of tolerance and non-discrimination;

(c) Involve children in activities designed to instil in them the values and goals of a culture of peace;

(d) Ensure equality of access to education for women, especially girls;

(e) Encourage revision of educational curricula, including textbooks, bearing in mind the 1995 Declaration and Integrated Framework of Action on Education for Peace, Human Rights and Democracy for which technical cooperation should be provided by the United Nations Educational, Scientific and Cultural Organization upon request;

(f) Encourage and strengthen efforts by actors as identified in the Declaration, in particular the United Nations Educational, Scientific and Cultural Organization, aimed at developing values and skills conducive to a culture of peace, including education and training in promoting dialogue and consensus-building;

(g) Strengthen the ongoing efforts of the relevant entities of the United Nations system aimed at training and education, where appropriate, in the areas of conflict prevention and crisis management, peaceful settlement of disputes, as well as in post-conflict peace-building;

(h) Expand initiatives to promote a culture of peace undertaken by institutions of higher education in various parts of the world, including the United Nations University, the University for Peace and the project for twinning universities and the United Nations Educational, Scientific and Cultural Organization Chairs Programme.

10. Actions to promote sustainable economic and social development:

(a) Undertake comprehensive actions on the basis of appropriate strategies and agreed targets to eradicate poverty through national and international efforts, including through international cooperation;

(b) Strengthen the national capacity for implementation of policies and programmes designed to reduce economic and social inequalities within nations through, inter alia, international cooperation;

(c) Promote effective and equitable development-oriented and durable solutions to the external debt and debt-servicing problems of developing countries through, inter alia, debt relief;

(d) Reinforce actions at all levels to implement national strategies for sustainable food security, including the development of actions to mobilize and optimize the allocation and utilization of resources from all sources, including through international cooperation, such as resources coming from debt relief;

(e) Undertake further efforts to ensure that the development process is participatory and that development projects involve the full participation of all;

(f) Include a gender perspective and empowerment of women and girls as an integral part of the development process;

(g) Include in development strategies special measures focusing on needs of women and children as well as groups with special needs;

(h) Strengthen, through development assistance in post-conflict situations, rehabilitation, reintegration and reconciliation processes involving all engaged in conflicts;

(i) Incorporate capacity-building in development strategies and projects to ensure environmental sustainability, including preservation and regeneration of the natural resource base;

(j) Remove obstacles to the realization of the right of peoples to self-determination, in particular of peoples living under colonial or other forms of alien domination or foreign occupation, which adversely affect their social and economic development.

11. Actions to promote respect for all human rights:

(a) Full implementation of the Vienna Declaration and Programme of Action;

(b) Encouragement of development of national plans of action for the promotion and protection of all human rights;

(c) Strengthening of national institutions and capacities in the field of human rights, including through national human rights institutions;

(d) Realization and implementation of the right to development, as established in the Declaration on the Right to Development and the Vienna Declaration and Programme of Action;

(e) Achievement of the goals of the United Nations Decade for Human Rights Education (1995-2004);

(f) Dissemination and promotion of the Universal Declaration of Human Rights at all levels;

(g) Further support to the activities of the United Nations High Commissioner for Human Rights in the fulfilment of her or his mandate as established in General Assembly resolution 48/141 of 20 December 1993, as well as the responsibilities set by subsequent resolutions and decisions.

12. Actions to ensure equality between women and men:

(a) Integration of a gender perspective into the implementation of all relevant international instruments;

(b) Further implementation of international instruments that promote equality between women and men;

(c) Implementation of the Beijing Platform for Action adopted at the Fourth World Conference on Women, with adequate resources and political will, and through, inter alia, the elaboration, implementation and follow-up of the national plans of action;

(d) Promotion of equality between women and men in economic, social and political decision-making;

(e) Further strengthening of efforts by the relevant entities of the United Nations system for the elimina-

tion of all forms of discrimination and violence against women;

(f) Provision of support and assistance to women who have become victims of any forms of violence, including in the home, workplace and during armed conflicts.

13. Actions to foster democratic participation:

(a) Reinforcement of the full range of actions to promote democratic principles and practices;

(b) Special emphasis on democratic principles and practices at all levels of formal, informal and non-formal education;

(c) Establishment and strengthening of national institutions and processes that promote and sustain democracy through, inter alia, training and capacity-building of public officials;

(d) Strengthening of democratic participation through, inter alia, the provision of electoral assistance upon the request of States concerned and based on relevant United Nations guidelines;

(e) Combating of terrorism, organized crime, corruption as well as production, trafficking and consumption of illicit drugs and money laundering, as they undermine democracies and impede the fuller development of a culture of peace.

14. Actions to advance understanding, tolerance and solidarity:

(a) Implement the Declaration of Principles on Tolerance and the Follow-up Plan of Action for the United Nations Year for Tolerance (1995);

(b) Support activities in the context of the United Nations Year of Dialogue among Civilizations in the year 2001;

(c) Study further the local or indigenous practices and traditions of dispute settlement and promotion of tolerance with the objective of learning from them;

(d) Support actions that foster understanding, tolerance and solidarity throughout society, in particular with vulnerable groups;

(e) Further support the attainment of the goals of the International Decade of the World's Indigenous People;

(f) Support actions that foster tolerance and solidarity with refugees and displaced persons, bearing in mind the objective of facilitating their voluntary return and social integration;

(g) Support actions that foster tolerance and solidarity with migrants;

(h) Promote increased understanding, tolerance and cooperation among all peoples through, inter alia, appropriate use of new technologies and dissemination of information;

(i) Support actions that foster understanding, tolerance, solidarity and cooperation among peoples and within and among nations.

15. Actions to support participatory communication and the free flow of information and knowledge:

(a) Support the important role of the media in the promotion of a culture of peace;

(b) Ensure freedom of the press and freedom of information and communication;

(c) Make effective use of the media for advocacy and dissemination of information on a culture of peace involving, as appropriate, the United Nations and relevant regional, national and local mechanisms;

(d) Promote mass communication that enables communities to express their needs and participate in decision-making;

(e) Take measures to address the issue of violence in the media, including new communication technologies, inter alia, the Internet;

(f) Increase efforts to promote the sharing of information on new information technologies, including the Internet.

16. Actions to promote international peace and security:

(a) Promote general and complete disarmament under strict and effective international control, taking into account the priorities established by the United Nations in the field of disarmament;

(b) Draw, where appropriate, on lessons conducive to a culture of peace learned from "military conversion" efforts as evidenced in some countries of the world;

(c) Emphasize the inadmissibility of acquisition of territory by war and the need to work for a just and lasting peace in all parts of the world;

(d) Encourage confidence-building measures and efforts for negotiating peaceful settlements;

(e) Take measures to eliminate illicit production and traffic of small arms and light weapons;

(f) Support initiatives, at the national, regional and international levels, to address concrete problems arising from post-conflict situations, such as demobilization, reintegration of former combatants into society, as well as refugees and displaced persons, weapon collection programmes, exchange of information and confidence-building;

(g) Discourage the adoption of and refrain from any unilateral measure, not in accordance with international law and the Charter of the United Nations, that impedes the full achievement of economic and social development by the population of the affected countries, in particular women and children, that hinders their well-being, that creates obstacles to the full enjoyment of their human rights, including the right of everyone to a standard of living adequate for their health and well-being and their right to food, medical care and the necessary social services, while reaffirming that food and medicine must not be used as a tool for political pressure;

(h) Refrain from military, political, economic or any other form of coercion, not in accordance with international law and the Charter, aimed against the political independence or territorial integrity of any State;

(i) Recommend proper consideration for the issue of the humanitarian impact of sanctions, in particular on women and children, with a view to minimizing the humanitarian effects of sanctions;

(j) Promote greater involvement of women in prevention and resolution of conflicts and, in particular, in activities promoting a culture of peace in post-conflict situations;

(k) Promote initiatives in conflict situations such as days of tranquillity to carry out immunization and medicine distribution campaigns, corridors of peace to ensure delivery of humanitarian supplies and sanctuaries of peace to respect the central role of health and medical institutions such as hospitals and clinics;

(l) Encourage training in techniques for the understanding, prevention and resolution of conflict for the concerned staff of the United Nations, relevant regional organizations and Member States, upon request, where appropriate.

ACC action. At an October meeting of the Organizational Committee of the Administrative Committee on Coordination (ACC) [ACC/1999/2/Add.1], it was proposed that the Consultative Committee on Programme and Operational Questions and the United Nations Development Group discuss the operational aspects of the Declaration and Programme of Action and issue guidance notes for the national coordination system. The Organizational Committee finalized the annotations to ACC along those lines.

Also in October [ACC/1999/20], ACC endorsed the proposal of the Director-General of UNESCO on the follow-up by organizations of the UN system to the Declaration and Programme of Action. The proposal included applying a "results-based" programming approach within a specified time frame. ACC endorsed the holding of an ad hoc meeting of the senior officials responsible for programme planning in their respective organizations to examine the feasibility of the proposed approach; UNESCO would host the meeting in 2000.

National institutions and regional arrangements

National institutions for human rights promotion and protection

Reports of Secretary-General. In response to General Assembly resolution 52/128 [YUN 1997, p. 623], the Secretary-General, in September, reported on OHCHR activities to strengthen national institutions and on the measures taken by Governments and national human rights institutions in those areas, as well as the work of the treaty monitoring bodies and the Commission's special mechanisms to consult further with established national institutions [A/54/336]. The report covered the period from 15 October 1997 to 15 August 1999.

OHCHR activities included the provision of information, advice or assistance at the request of Governments or entities in the process of establishing national institutions or contemplating doing so. It also responded to requests from Governments and NGOs seeking information on national institutions. The Special Adviser on National Institutions conducted missions to advise or assist Governments, among other things. OHCHR expanded its roster of consultants and experts on national human rights institutions, compiled legislation of such institutions, established a database on best practices of national institutions' work on thematic issues and was preparing a training manual for national institutions on economic, social and cultural rights. OHCHR had 11 field offices in Africa, a field office in Gaza and four others in the Asia and Pacific region, five in Europe, Central Asia and North America and three in Latin America and the Caribbean. The International Coordinating Committee of National Institutions, which constituted an international network promoting the establishment and strengthening of national human rights institutions, at its seventh session (Geneva, 20-22 April), considered the role of national institutions in promoting and protecting the rights of the child.

In December [E/CN.4/2000/103], the Secretary-General stated that in 1999 OHCHR emphasized facilitating the exchange of national institutions' practices in promotion and protection of the rights of women, children and human rights defenders, particularly in Asia and the Pacific. The fourth annual meeting of the Asia-Pacific Forum of National Human Rights Institutions (Manila, Philippines, September) addressed the problem of trafficking of persons in the region, including women, and discussed the results of a questionnaire distributed by the National Human Rights Commission of New Zealand to all established national institutions requesting information on their mandates, functions, methods of work, activities and programmes. In preparation for the "Beijing plus 5 review" (see PART THREE, Chapter X), OHCHR planned to organize in 2000 a series of meetings to review the implementation of the Platform for Action [YUN 1995, p. 1170], adopted at the 1995 Fourth World Conference on Women in Beijing, with international organizations, NGOs and national institutions. Regarding the tenth anniversary of the Convention on the Rights of the Child, related OHCHR initiatives included a preparatory workshop with national institutions of the Asia-Pacific region aimed at promoting the exchange of best practices in the promotion and protection of children's rights. The workshop was organized by OHCHR, in close consultation with the United Nations Children's Fund (UNICEF), in cooperation with the Philippines National Human Rights Commission and the Asia-Pacific Forum of National Human Rights Institutions, in Manila from 8 to 10 September.

In other action, the Special Adviser on National Institutions and/or the National Institutions Team sent advisory missions to Azerbaijan, Ecuador, Kazakhstan, Kyrgyzstan, Malawi, the Philippines, Rwanda, Sierra Leone and Zimbabwe. Advice on legislation for the establishment of a national institution was provided by the

Special Adviser in Sierra Leone and Zimbabwe; technical cooperation activities continued in Bolivia, Georgia, Guatemala, Indonesia, Latvia, Malawi, Palestine, the Republic of Moldova, South Africa and Uganda. Consultations on cooperating agreements continued with established institutions in Colombia, Ecuador, Fiji, Indonesia, Malawi, Peru and Rwanda and a new project for Ukraine was under consideration. At the regional level, OHCHR supported the fourth annual meeting of the Asia-Pacific Forum, the third Annual Congress of the Ibero-American Federation of Ombudsmen (Tegucigalpa, Honduras, September), the Central American Council of *Defensores* (Managua, Nicaragua, November) and the fifth UNDP International Workshop on Ombudsman and Human Rights Institutions (Almaty, Kazakhstan, November). OHCHR organized a governmental meeting in November on regional strategies for technical cooperation in the Latin American and Caribbean region. Cooperation on national technical cooperation projects continued with UNDP, the Organization for Security and Cooperation in Europe (OSCE), the Council of Europe, United Nations Volunteers and UNICEF. Joint initiatives between national institutions and NGOs, with OHCHR support, included a workshop, organized by the Asia-Pacific Forum, the Sri Lanka Human Rights Commission and the Asia-Pacific Consultative Group of NGOs (Kandy, Sri Lanka, 27-28 July), on early warning, public inquiries and promotional and educational activities.

Commission action. On 28 April [res. 1999/72], the Commission asked the Secretary-General to continue to provide assistance for the holding of Coordinating Committee meetings during its sessions; and to continue to provide, from within existing resources and the UN Voluntary Fund for Technical Cooperation in the Field of Human Rights, the necessary assistance for regional meetings of national institutions. Those requests were approved by the Economic and Social Council on 27 July by **decision 1999/245**.

The Secretary-General was asked to report in 2000.

GENERAL ASSEMBLY ACTION

On 17 December [meeting 83], the General Assembly, on the recommendation of the Third Committee [A/54/605/Add.2], adopted **resolution 54/176** without vote [agenda item 116 *(b)*].

National institutions for the promotion and protection of human rights

The General Assembly,

Recalling the relevant resolutions of the General Assembly and the Commission on Human Rights concerning national institutions for the promotion and protection of human rights,

Welcoming the rapidly growing interest throughout the world in the creation and strengthening of independent, pluralistic national institutions for the promotion and protection of human rights,

Convinced of the important role national institutions play and will continue to play in promoting and protecting human rights and fundamental freedoms and in developing and enhancing public awareness of those rights and freedoms,

Recognizing that the United Nations has played an important role and should continue to play a more important role in assisting the development of national institutions for the promotion and protection of human rights,

Recalling the Vienna Declaration and Programme of Action adopted by the World Conference on Human Rights on 25 June 1993, which reaffirmed the important and constructive role played by national human rights institutions, in particular in their advisory capacity to the competent authorities and their role in remedying human rights violations, in disseminating information on human rights and in education in human rights,

Recalling also the Platform for Action adopted by the Fourth World Conference on Women, in which Governments were urged to create or strengthen independent national institutions for the promotion and protection of human rights, including the human rights of women,

Noting the diverse approaches adopted throughout the world for the promotion and protection of human rights at the national level, emphasizing the universality, indivisibility and interdependence of all human rights, and emphasizing and recognizing the value of such approaches in promoting universal respect for and observance of human rights and fundamental freedoms,

Noting with satisfaction the constructive participation of representatives of national institutions for the promotion and protection of human rights in, and their positive contribution to, the deliberations of the World Conference on Human Rights and the Commission on Human Rights, as well as international seminars and workshops on human rights organized or sponsored by the United Nations,

Welcoming the strengthening of regional cooperation among national human rights institutions, including through the third annual meeting of the Asia-Pacific Forum of National Human Rights Institutions, held at Jakarta in September 1998, the second Regional Conference of African National Institutions for the Promotion and Protection of Human Rights, held at Durban, South Africa, in June and July 1998, the first meeting of Mediterranean National Institutions for the Promotion and Protection of Human Rights, held at Marrakesh, Morocco, in April 1998, the fourth annual meeting of the Asia-Pacific Forum of National Human Rights Institutions, held at Manila in September 1999, and the second session of the Coordinating Committee of African National Institutions for the Promotion and Protection of Human Rights, held at Algiers in October 1999,

1. *Welcomes* the report of the Secretary-General;

2. *Reaffirms* the importance of the development of effective, independent and pluralistic national institutions for the promotion and protection of human rights, in keeping with the principles relating to the status of national institutions for the promotion and protection of human rights contained in the annex to General Assembly resolution 48/134 of 20 December 1993;

3. *Recognizes* that, in accordance with the Vienna Declaration and Programme of Action, it is the right of each State to choose the framework for the national institutions that is best suited to its particular needs at the national level in order to promote human rights in accordance with international human rights standards;

4. *Encourages* Member States to establish or, where they already exist, to strengthen national institutions for the promotion and protection of human rights, as outlined in the Vienna Declaration and Programme of Action;

5. *Welcomes* the growing number of States establishing or considering the establishment of national institutions for the promotion and protection of human rights;

6. *Encourages* national institutions for the promotion and protection of human rights established by Member States to continue to play an active role in preventing and combating all violations of human rights as enumerated in the Vienna Declaration and Programme of Action and relevant international instruments;

7. *Reaffirms* the role of national institutions, where they exist, as appropriate agencies, inter alia, for the dissemination of human rights materials and other public information activities, including those of the United Nations, and in this context expresses its appreciation of the active role that national institutions have played in the celebrations marking the fiftieth anniversary of the Universal Declaration of Human Rights at the national and local levels;

8. *Urges* the Secretary-General to continue to give high priority to requests from Member States for assistance in the establishment and strengthening of national human rights institutions as part of the programme of advisory services and technical assistance in the field of human rights;

9. *Commends* the high priority given by the Office of the United Nations High Commissioner for Human Rights to work on national human rights institutions, and, in view of the expanded activities related to national institutions, encourages the High Commissioner to ensure that appropriate arrangements are made and budgetary resources provided to continue and further extend activities in support of national institutions, and invites Governments to contribute additional, earmarked funds to the United Nations Voluntary Fund for Technical Cooperation in the Field of Human Rights for that purpose;

10. *Notes with appreciation* the increasingly active and important role of the International Coordinating Committee of National Institutions, as recognized in Commission on Human Rights resolution 1994/54 of 4 March 1994, in close cooperation with the Office of the High Commissioner, in assisting Governments and national institutions, when requested, to follow up on relevant resolutions and recommendations concerning the strengthening of national institutions;

11. *Also notes with appreciation* the holding of regular meetings of the International Coordinating Committee of National Institutions and the arrangements for the participation of national human rights institutions in the annual sessions of the Commission on Human Rights;

12. *Requests* the Secretary-General to continue to provide the necessary assistance for holding meetings of the International Coordinating Committee of National Institutions during the sessions of the Commission on Human Rights, in cooperation with the Office of the High Commissioner;

13. *Also requests* the Secretary-General to continue to provide, including from the United Nations Voluntary Fund for Technical Cooperation in the Field of Human Rights, the necessary assistance for regional meetings of national institutions;

14. *Recognizes* the important and constructive role that non-governmental organizations may play, in cooperation with national institutions, for the better promotion and protection of human rights;

15. *Encourages* all Member States to take appropriate steps to promote the exchange of information and experience concerning the establishment and effective operation of national institutions for the promotion and protection of human rights;

16. *Encourages* all United Nations entities, funds and agencies to work in close cooperation with national institutions in the promotion and protection of human rights;

17. *Requests* the Secretary-General to report to the General Assembly at its fifty-sixth session on the implementation of the present resolution.

Regional arrangements

Report of Secretary-General. Pursuant to General Assembly resolution 53/148 [YUN 1998, p. 641], the Secretary-General reported on OHCHR regional strategies and developments [A/55/279] since the submission of his last report [YUN 1998, p. 640]. OHCHR had been developing close cooperation at the regional level with UN partners, particularly UNDP, UNICEF and UNESCO. It was continuing to explore possible areas in which to involve the regional commissions in the promotion of human rights. The High Commissioner had appointed four regional advisers who, among other things, stimulated government and public interest in the World Conference against Racism, Racial Discrimination, Xenophobia and Related Intolerance (see p. 602).

A concept of the subregional centre for human rights and democracy in Central Africa was in the implementation phase following the Assembly's request in December to the Secretary-General and the High Commissioner to establish the centre (**resolution 54/55 A**) (see p. 501). The decision to establish the centre originated at the fourth meeting of the Standing Advisory Committee on Security Questions in Central Africa. An appropriation of $1 million was to be made for the 2000-2001 biennium; the centre was to be established in Yaoundé, Cameroon, by the end of 2000. In Europe and Central Asia, OHCHR continued its cooperation with regional organizations, including the Council of Europe, OSCE and the European Union. A priority was the development of a regional strategy against trafficking in persons. In Latin America and the Caribbean, the Office organized a regional workshop that adopted the Quito Framework for Technical Cooperation in the Field of Human Rights (Quito, Ecuador, 29 November–1 December). (For information on the Asia and Pacific region, see below.)

Commission action. On 28 April [res. 1999/71], the Commission invited States in areas where regional arrangements in the field of human rights did not exist to consider concluding agreements with a view to establishing within their respective regions suitable regional machinery to promote and protect human rights. It asked OHCHR to continue to pay attention to ways of assisting, at their request, countries of the different regions under the programme of technical cooperation and to make, where necessary, relevant recommendations. The Secretary-General was asked to report in 2001.

Asia and the Pacific

As requested by the Commission in 1998 [YUN 1998, p. 641], the Secretary-General reported, in March, on regional arrangements to promote and protect human rights in Asia and the Pacific [E/CN.4/1999/94]. OHCHR organized the seventh workshop on regional arrangements for the promotion and protection of human rights in the Asia and Pacific region (New Delhi, India, 16-18 February). The workshop called on the High Commissioner to develop and implement the proposals made in the four areas of the framework for regional technical cooperation (national plans of action for the promotion and protection of human rights and the strengthening of national capacities; human rights education; national institutions for the promotion and protection of human rights; strategies for the realization of the right to development and economic, social and cultural rights) and to report to the next workshop on progress made. The workshop called on OHCHR to establish a bulletin board on the regional technical cooperation activities under the framework and decided that the annual regional workshop should take up a specific theme, pertaining to one of the four areas identified under the framework.

In later reports [A/55/279, E/CN.4/2000/102], the Secretary-General discussed inter-sessional workshops held to address issues covered by the framework, including the inter-sessional regional workshop on the role of national human rights commissions in the promotion and protection of economic, social and cultural rights (Manila, May), the inter-sessional regional workshop on national human rights action plans (Bangkok, Thailand, 5-7 July), the fourth annual meeting of the Asia-Pacific Forum of National Human Rights Institutions (Manila, September), the Seminar on the Role of National Institutions in the Protection and Promotion of the Human Rights of Children (Manila, September) and the inter-sessional subregional workshop on human rights education in North-East Asia (Seoul, Republic of Korea, 1-4 December).

Commission action. On 28 April [res. 1999/69], the Commission endorsed the conclusions of the seventh workshop and its decisions regarding the next steps to be taken to facilitate the process of regional cooperation in the Asia and Pacific region. It called on OHCHR to develop and implement the project proposals in the four areas identified under the regional framework. The Commission asked the Secretary-General to report in 2000 on the conclusions of the eighth workshop and on the progress achieved.

Cooperation with UN human rights bodies

In accordance with a 1998 Commission request [YUN 1998, p. 642], the Secretary-General, in January [E/CN.4/1999/27], summarized information covering situations in which persons were intimidated or suffered reprisals for having cooperated with UN human rights bodies; availed themselves of international procedures; provided legal assistance for that purpose; and/or were relatives of victims of human rights violations.

Commission action. On 23 April [res. 1999/16], the Commission urged Governments to refrain from acts of intimidation or reprisal against persons who sought to cooperate or had cooperated with representatives of UN human rights bodies, or who had provided testimony or information to them; individuals who availed themselves of UN procedures and those who had provided legal assistance to them for that purpose; those who submitted communications under procedures established by human rights instruments; and relatives of victims of human rights violations. It asked representatives of UN human rights bodies and treaty bodies monitoring the observance of human rights to help prevent the hampering of access to UN human rights procedures and to continue to take urgent steps to prevent the occurrence of intimidation or reprisal. It also asked them to include in their reports references to allegations of intimidation or reprisal, as well as an account of action taken. The Commission asked the Secretary-General to draw its resolution to the attention of UN human rights and treaty bodies and to report in 2000.

Chapter II

Protection of human rights

The protection of human rights—civil and political, as well as economic, social and cultural—continued to be a major focus of UN activities in 1999.

In an effort to protect children and other civilians in situations of armed conflict, the Security Council, in August and September, condemned the deliberate targeting of those groups. It called on all parties to end the practice and on States that had not done so to consider ratifying the major instruments of international humanitarian, human rights and refugee law.

The working group to review and formulate proposals for the World Conference against Racism, Racial Discrimination, Xenophobia and Related Intolerance, to be convened in 2001, held its first session. In December, the General Assembly welcomed the offer of South Africa to host the Conference. It reaffirmed the proclamation of the year 2001 as the International Year of Mobilization against Racism, Racial Discrimination, Xenophobia and Related Intolerance, aimed at drawing attention to the objectives of the Conference. In other action, a resolution adopted by the General Conference of the United Nations Educational, Scientific and Cultural Organization (UNESCO) proclaimed 23 August of every year International Day for the Remembrance of the Slave Trade and its Abolition.

Special rapporteurs, special representatives and independent experts of the Commission on Human Rights and its subsidiary body, the Subcommission on the Promotion and Protection of Human Rights, examined, among other issues, allegations of torture; extra-legal executions; impunity; mercenary activity; affirmative action; the rights of migrants; the independence of the judiciary; freedom of opinion and expression; religious intolerance; human rights and terrorism; internally displaced persons; globalization and its impact on human rights; extreme poverty; illicit practices related to toxic and dangerous products and wastes; sexual violence during armed conflict; violence against women; the sale of children, child prostitution and child pornography; and the situation of children affected by armed conflict.

Working groups considered arbitrary detention, enforced or involuntary disappearances, minorities, the right to development, structural adjustment policies, contemporary forms of slavery, and a draft declaration on the rights of indigenous peoples. The sessional working group on the working methods and activities of transnational corporations (TNCs), at its first session in August, decided to consider developing a code of conduct for TNCs based on human rights standards.

Racism and racial discrimination

Third Decade against racism

The General Assembly, in resolution 48/91 [YUN 1993, p. 853], had proclaimed the Third Decade to Combat Racism and Racial Discrimination (1993-2003) and adopted the Decade's Programme of Action. The Third Decade's goals and objectives were the same as those of the first Decade, which the Assembly had adopted in resolution 3057(XXVIII) [YUN 1973, p. 523]. The revised Programme of Action for the Third Decade was adopted by the Assembly in resolution 49/146 [YUN 1994, p. 988].

Implementation of Decade Programme

Commission action. On 28 April [E/1999/23 (res. 1999/78)], the Commission on Human Rights, regretting the lack of interest, support and financial resources for the Decade and Programme of Action and that few of the activities planned for 1994-1998 were carried out, recommended that the General Assembly, through the Economic and Social Council, ask the Secretary-General to assign high priority to the Programme's activities and earmark adequate resources to finance them. The Commission appealed to States, intergovernmental and non-governmental organizations (NGOs) and individuals in a position to do so to contribute to the Trust Fund for the Programme of Action for the Third Decade and asked the Secretary-General to encourage contributions to the Fund. States were asked to encourage the reporting of acts motivated by racism, racial discrimination, xenophobia or ethnic reasons and to give priority to education as the main means to prevent and eradicate racism and racial discrimination.

Reports of Secretary-General. In response to General Assembly resolution 53/132 [YUN 1998, p. 646], the Secretary-General submitted to the Economic and Social Council, in June [E/1999/61], his annual report describing activities to implement the Programme for the Decade. He concluded that contributions by the UN system, Governments, intergovernmental organizations and NGOs to the Third Decade continued to reflect global and concerted efforts to address the issues and provide long-lasting solutions. However, few of the activities planned for 1994-1998 could be carried out owing to lack of funds. Although there was strong support for holding the 2001 World Conference, it would require resources. Annexed to the report was a list of contributions received from Governments to the Trust Fund as at May 1999. By **decision 1999/288** of 30 July, the Economic and Social Council took note of the Secretary-General's report.

In a September report to the General Assembly on the same issue [A/54/299], the Secretary-General noted that the UN High Commissioner for Human Rights, pursuant to Assembly resolution 53/132, had sought the resources necessary to coordinate the Programme of Action, whose activities were to be oriented towards the objectives of the World Conference. Since the Programme of Action was scheduled to be completed in 2003, it would be possible to submit proposals to supplement it, if necessary, on the basis of the conclusions and recommendations of the Conference. Those proposals could serve as a basis for a possible programme of action to launch a fourth Decade. Annexed to the report was a list of contributions available in the Trust Fund as at 18 August.

In a December report to the Commission on Human Rights [E/CN.4/2000/15], the Secretary-General stated that activities under the Programme of Action included a seminar of experts on racism, refugees and multi-ethnic States (Geneva, 6-8 December); a study on economic factors contributing to racism and racial discrimination; and a study on the effects of racial discrimination on the children of minorities and of migrant workers. Reports on those activities would be submitted to the first (2000) session of the Preparatory Committee for the World Conference.

Subcommission action. On 25 August [E/CN.4/2000/2 (res. 1999/6)], the Subcommission on the Promotion and Protection of Human Rights, regretting the continued lack of interest, support and resources for the Decade and the Programme of Action, called on Governments, UN bodies, specialized agencies and interested NGOs to contribute fully to the Programme's implementation.

World Conference

As the General Assembly had decided in resolution 52/111 [YUN 1997, p. 629], the World Conference against Racism, Racial Discrimination, Xenophobia and Related Intolerance was scheduled to convene not later than 2001. The Conference would focus on practical measures to eradicate racism, including measures of prevention, education and protection and the provision of effective remedies. One of its aims would be to increase the effectiveness of UN programmes aimed at eradicating contemporary forms of racism and racial discrimination. The Commission on Human Rights was designated the Preparatory Committee for the Conference.

In December (**resolution 54/154**), the General Assembly welcomed the offer of South Africa to host the Conference in 2001.

Report of High Commissioner. Pursuant to a 1998 Commission request [YUN 1998, p. 644], the High Commissioner presented, in March [E/CN.4/1999/12], an analytical outline of the seven objectives of the World Conference as contained in General Assembly resolution 52/111: review progress made in the fight against racism, racial discrimination, xenophobia and related intolerance; consider ways to ensure respect for existing standards and instruments to combat the problem; increase awareness about the scourges of the problem; formulate recommendations on increasing the effectiveness of UN activities through programmes aimed at combating the problem; review the political, historical, economic, social, cultural and other factors leading to the problem; formulate recommendations for additional national, regional and international measures to combat all forms of racism, racial discrimination, xenophobia and related intolerance; and make recommendations for ensuring that the United Nations had the resources to combat the phenomenon. The report included a review of the views communicated to the Office of the High Commissioner for Human Rights (OHCHR) by States, UN bodies and NGOs.

The High Commissioner concluded that despite progress, racism and racial discrimination had not disappeared and were assuming new forms. Efforts should be intensified, especially through education and awareness-arousing as means of prevention. Universal and unconditional accession to the 1965 International Convention on the Elimination of All Forms of Racial Discrimination, adopted by the Assembly in resolution 2106 A (XX) [YUN 1965, p. 440] (see previous chapter), was vital. States were urged to adopt laws to prevent and eradicate racial discrimination and to abrogate and modify policies that had the effect of inciting or perpetuating racial hatred.

Working group activities. The open-ended working group to review and formulate proposals for the World Conference, established by the Commission in 1998 [YUN 1998, p. 644], held its first session (Geneva, 24-26 March) [E/CN.4/1999/16 & Corr.1,2]. It considered the seven objectives of the Conference by taking as a starting point proposals presented by the African Group, and discussed procedural matters. The discussions highlighted the organization of regional experts' seminars on recourse procedures and good practices; the creation of a web site on the Conference; and the preparation of questionnaires to evaluate measures taken by States, specialized agencies, international governmental organizations, NGOs and national institutions. Annexed to the report were the African Group's proposals and proposals by the Subcommittee on Racism, Racial Discrimination and Decolonization of the Special Committee of International NGOs on Human Rights.

Commission action. On 28 April [res. 1999/78], the Commission adopted recommendations regarding the Conference, as well as requests to the Secretary-General, the High Commissioner and the Subcommission that were either endorsed or approved by the Economic and Social Council (see below).

ECONOMIC AND SOCIAL COUNCIL ACTION

On 27 July [meeting 42], the Economic and Social Council, on the recommendation of the Commission on Human Rights [E/1999/23], as amended [E/1999/L.30], adopted **resolution 1999/12** without vote [agenda item 14 (h)].

Racism, racial discrimination, xenophobia and related intolerance

The Economic and Social Council,

Taking note of Commission on Human Rights resolution 1999/78 of 28 April 1999,

1. *Approves* the recommendation of the Commission on Human Rights that the General Assembly, through the Economic and Social Council, request the Secretary-General to assign high priority to the activities of the Programme of Action for the Third Decade to Combat Racism and Racial Discrimination and to earmark adequate resources to finance those activities;

2. *Also approves* the Commission's request to the United Nations High Commissioner for Human Rights to undertake research and consultations on the use of the Internet for purposes of incitement to racial hatred, racist propaganda and xenophobia, to study ways of promoting international cooperation in this area, and to draw up a programme of human rights education and exchanges over the Internet on experience in the struggle against racism, xenophobia and anti-Semitism;

3. *Further approves* the Commission's appeal to the High Commissioner to provide those countries which were visited by the Special Rapporteur on contemporary forms of racism, racial discrimination, xenophobia and related intolerance, at their request, with advisory services and technical assistance to enable them to implement fully the recommendations of the Special Rapporteur;

4. *Endorses* the Commission's decision, in accordance with General Assembly resolution 52/111 of 12 December 1997, which indicates that the Commission will act as the Preparatory Committee for the World Conference against Racism, Racial Discrimination, Xenophobia and Related Intolerance:

(a) That the sessions of the Preparatory Committee scheduled in 2000 and 2001 will be headed by the same bureau, composed of ten members, that is, two representatives per regional group, in order to ensure continuity and the adequate representation of all States Members of the United Nations;

(b) To recommend to the General Assembly, through the Economic and Social Council, that the World Conference and the sessions of the Preparatory Committee should be open to participation by:

(i) All States Members of the United Nations and States members of the specialized agencies;
(ii) Representatives of all regional organizations and regional commissions involved in the preparation of regional meetings;
(iii) Representatives of organizations that have received a standing invitation from the General Assembly to participate in the capacity of observers;
(iv) Representatives of the specialized agencies, the secretariats of the regional commissions and all United Nations bodies and programmes;
(v) Representatives of all United Nations mechanisms in the field of human rights;
(vi) Other interested governmental organizations, which shall be represented by observers;
(vii) Interested non-governmental organizations, which shall be represented by observers in accordance with Economic and Social Council resolution 1996/31 of 25 July 1996;

5. *Approves* the Commission's recommendations to the General Assembly, through the Economic and Social Council, that, if no offer is made to the United Nations High Commissioner for Human Rights for hosting the World Conference by the end of the first session of the Preparatory Committee to be held in 2000:

(a) The World Conference should be held in Geneva;

(b) The World Conference should be held in 2001, but after the session of the Commission on Human Rights and before that of the General Assembly;

6. *Also approves* the Commission's requests to the High Commissioner:

(a) To prepare, immediately following the fifty-fifth session of the Commission, the questionnaires referred to in the report of the open-ended Working Group to review and formulate proposals for the World Conference on Racism, Racial Discrimination, Xenophobia and Related Intolerance, with a view, on the one hand, to reviewing progress made in the fight

against racism, racial discrimination, xenophobia and related intolerance, particularly since the adoption of the Universal Declaration of Human Rights, and, on the other, to reappraise the obstacles to further progress in the field and ways to overcome them, and to send them as soon as possible to States, specialized agencies, international and non-governmental organizations and national institutions;

(b) To review and analyse the replies and submit a report to the Preparatory Committee, at its first session, six weeks before the beginning of its work;

(c) To open an Internet site on the preparations for the World Conference, in close cooperation with the Department of Public Information of the Secretariat;

(d) In her capacity as Secretary-General of the World Conference, to prepare and carry out, in close cooperation with the Department of Public Information, an effective world information campaign, with a view to mobilizing support for the objectives of the World Conference by all sectors of political, economic, social and cultural life, as well as other interested sectors;

(e) To include in her strategy for informing international public opinion and sensitizing it to the objectives of the World Conference:

(i) The appointment of renowned ambassadors from the entertainment, arts, culture, sports and musical worlds, and any other field, who might mobilize the attention of civil society;

(ii) An invitation to the sports world to cooperate actively as a partner in the World Conference;

(iii) Additional private-sector funding through sponsoring;

(iv) The need to ensure full coverage of preparatory activities and the World Conference by the media by making full use of the services of United Nations information centres;

(v) Sending to all Governments, international and non-governmental organizations and national institutions information handbooks and pamphlets that can be made available to the public and the media, as well as to United Nations information centres;

(f) To set up a voluntary fund designed specifically to cover all aspects of the preparatory process for the World Conference and the participation of non-governmental organizations, especially from developing countries, by requesting all Governments, international and non-governmental organizations and private individuals to contribute to this fund;

(g) To undertake appropriate consultations with non-governmental organizations on the possibility that they might hold a forum before and partly during the World Conference, and, in so far as possible, to provide them with technical assistance for that purpose;

(h) To undertake a study to be submitted to the Preparatory Committee at its first session on ways of improving coordination between the Office of the United Nations High Commissioner for Human Rights and all specialized agencies and international, regional and subregional organizations in the field of action to combat racism, racial discrimination, xenophobia and related intolerance;

(i) To help the Special Rapporteur of the Commission on contemporary forms of racism, racial discrimination, xenophobia and related intolerance to carry out a study on preventive measures relating to ethnic, racial, religious and xenophobically motivated conflicts and to formulate recommendations intended for the first session of the Preparatory Committee;

(j) To invite the Special Rapporteur on religious intolerance to participate actively in the preparatory process and in the World Conference by initiating studies on action to combat incitement to hatred and religious intolerance;

(k) To review progress made in the fight against racism, racial discrimination, xenophobia and related intolerance, in particular since the adoption of the Universal Declaration of Human Rights, and to reappraise the obstacles to further progress in the field and ways to overcome them, with a view to submitting her conclusions to the Preparatory Committee;

(l) To organize an international seminar of experts on the remedies available to the victims of acts of racism, racial discrimination, xenophobia and related intolerance and on good national practices in this field, which will be financed by voluntary contributions, to encourage other activities, particularly seminars forming part of the preparations for the World Conference, and to submit the recommendations of those seminars to the Preparatory Committee;

(m) To draw up a draft agenda for the first session of the Preparatory Committee;

7. *Approves* the Commission's appeals to the High Commissioner to help States and regional organizations, on request, to convene national and regional meetings or to undertake other initiatives, including at the expert level, to prepare for the World Conference, and also to the specialized agencies and the United Nations regional commissions, in coordination with the High Commissioner, to contribute to the holding of regional preparatory meetings;

8. *Also approves* the Commission's requests:

(a) To the Secretary-General, the United Nations specialized agencies and the regional commissions to provide financial and technical assistance for the organization of the regional preparatory meetings planned in the context of the World Conference, and stresses that such assistance should be supplemented by voluntary contributions;

(b) To the Subcommission on the Promotion and Protection of Human Rights to undertake a study on ways of making United Nations activities and mechanisms in the context of programmes aimed at combating racism, racial discrimination, xenophobia and related intolerance more effective;

(c) To the Secretary-General to submit a report to the Commission at its fifty-sixth session on the implementation of Commission resolution 1999/78 under the item entitled "Racism, racial discrimination, xenophobia and all forms of discrimination";

9. *Endorses* the recommendations of the Commission that the World Conference should adopt a declaration and a programme of action to combat racism, racial discrimination, xenophobia and related intolerance, that the particular situation of children should receive special attention during the preparations for and during the World Conference itself, especially in its outcome, and that the importance of systematically adopting a gender-based approach throughout the preparations for and in the outcome of the World Conference should be stressed;

10. *Decides* to extend the mandate of the Special Rapporteur on contemporary forms of racism, racial discrimination, xenophobia and related intolerance for a further period of three years.

Subcommission action. On 25 August [res. 1999/6], the Subcommission suggested that the World Conference focus on situations of racism, racial discrimination, xenophobia, related intolerance and ethnic conflict and other patterns of discrimination based on race, colour, descent, national or ethnic origin or gender, as well as a series of related topics. It recommended that the Conference prepare a declaration and a programme of action to combat racism, racial discrimination, xenophobia and related forms of intolerance and define a global and system-wide strategy to combat racism and racial discrimination. The Secretary-General was asked to provide for the participation in the Preparatory Committee, as the Subcommission's representative, of Paulo Sérgio Pinheiro (Brazil), who had been asked in 1998 to prepare proposals for the Conference's work [YUN 1998, p. 646]. The High Commissioner was called on to advance the regional preparatory processes.

In June [E/CN.4/Sub.2/1999/6], the secretariat had informed the Subcommission that Mr. Pinheiro was unable to prepare proposals for the Conference's work but would report orally on the subject. On 10 August [E/CN.4/Sub.2/1999/SR.9], he proposed that a working paper be prepared on proposals for the Conference based on the Subcommission's studies since the Second (1983) World Conference to Combat Racism and Racial Discrimination [YUN 1983, p. 802]. A preliminary version of the paper could be prepared for the Preparatory Committee in 2000.

CERD. On 26 August [A/54/18 (dec. 5(55))], the Committee on the Elimination of Racial Discrimination (CERD) proposed to the Preparatory Committee that it include in the Conference's agenda action by the international community to prevent or mitigate mass and flagrant human rights violations of persons belonging to ethnic and racial groups and minorities. It decided to make relevant information available to the Preparatory Committee and, with OHCHR assistance, to make an assessment of the best practices of States parties to the 1965 Convention in combating racial discrimination. CERD suggested elements for a plan of action for the Conference.

(For other CERD activities, see preceding chapter.)

GENERAL ASSEMBLY ACTION

On 17 December [meeting 83], the General Assembly, on the recommendation of the Third (Social, Humanitarian and Cultural) Committee [A/54/603], adopted **resolution 54/154** without vote [agenda item 114].

Third Decade to Combat Racism and Racial Discrimination and the convening of the World Conference against Racism, Racial Discrimination, Xenophobia and Related Intolerance

The General Assembly,

Reaffirming its objectives, as set forth in the Charter of the United Nations, of achieving international cooperation in solving problems of an economic, social, cultural or humanitarian character and in promoting and encouraging respect for human rights and fundamental freedoms for all without distinction as to race, sex, language or religion,

Reaffirming also its firm determination and its commitment to eradicate totally and unconditionally racism in all its forms and racial discrimination and its conviction that racism and racial discrimination constitute a total negation of the purposes and principles of the Charter and the Universal Declaration of Human Rights,

Recalling the Universal Declaration of Human Rights, the International Convention on the Elimination of All Forms of Racial Discrimination and the Convention against Discrimination in Education, adopted by the United Nations Educational, Scientific and Cultural Organization on 14 December 1960,

Noting the efforts of the Committee on the Elimination of Racial Discrimination since its establishment in 1970 to promote the implementation of the International Convention on the Elimination of All Forms of Racial Discrimination,

Recalling the outcome of the two World Conferences to Combat Racism and Racial Discrimination, held at Geneva in 1978 and in 1983,

Recalling also the outcome of the World Conference on Human Rights, held at Vienna from 14 to 25 June 1993, and, in particular, the attention given in the Vienna Declaration and Programme of Action to the elimination of racism, racial discrimination, xenophobia and other forms of intolerance,

Stressing the importance and sensitivity of the activities of the Special Rapporteur of the Commission on Human Rights on contemporary forms of racism, racial discrimination, xenophobia and related intolerance,

Recalling with satisfaction its resolutions 48/91 of 20 December 1993 and 49/146 of 23 December 1994, by which, respectively, it proclaimed the Third Decade to Combat Racism and Racial Discrimination, which began in 1993, and adopted the revised Programme of Action for the Third Decade to Combat Racism and Racial Discrimination,

Noting with grave concern that, despite the efforts of the international community, the principal objectives of the two previous Decades for Action to Combat Racism and Racial Discrimination have not been attained and that millions of human beings continue to the present day to be the victims of varied forms of racism and racial discrimination,

Noting with great concern that, despite the efforts undertaken by the international community at various levels, racism, racial discrimination, xenophobia and related forms of intolerance, ethnic antagonism and acts of violence are showing signs of increase in many parts of the world and that the number of associations established on the basis of racist and xenophobic platforms and charters is increasing, as reflected in the report of the Special Rapporteur,

Alarmed that technological developments in the field of communications, including the Internet, continue to be utilized by various groups engaged in violent activity to promote racist and xenophobic propaganda aimed at inciting racial hatred and to collect funds to sustain violent campaigns against multi-ethnic societies throughout the world,

Noting that the use of such technologies can also contribute to combating racism, racial discrimination, xenophobia and related intolerance,

Having considered the report submitted by the Secretary-General within the framework of the implementation of the Programme of Action,

Recalling its resolution 53/132 of 9 December 1998, in which it requested the Secretary-General to ensure the financial and personnel resources necessary for the implementation of the Programme of Action,

Recognizing the importance of strengthening national legislation and institutions for the promotion of racial harmony and for the effective enforcement of such legislation,

Remaining firmly convinced of the need to take more effective and sustained measures at the national and international levels for the elimination of all forms of racism and racial discrimination,

Deeply concerned that the phenomenon of racism and racial discrimination against migrant workers continues to increase, despite the efforts made by the international community to improve the protection of the human rights of migrant workers and members of their families,

Recalling the adoption at its forty-fifth session of the International Convention on the Protection of the Rights of All Migrant Workers and Members of Their Families,

Acknowledging that indigenous people are at times victims of particular forms of racism and racial discrimination,

I

Implementation of the Programme of Action for the Third Decade to Combat Racism and Racial Discrimination and coordination of activities

1. *Welcomes* the report submitted by the Secretary-General;

2. *Reaffirms* that racism and racial discrimination are among the most serious violations of human rights in the contemporary world, and expresses its firm determination and its commitment to eradicate, by all available means, racism in all its forms and racial discrimination;

3. *Urges* all Governments to take all necessary measures to combat new forms of racism, in particular by constantly adapting the means provided to combat them, especially in the legislative, administrative, education and information fields;

4. *Requests* the United Nations High Commissioner for Human Rights to assign a high priority to the follow-up to programmes and activities for combating racism and racial discrimination, consistent with the need to ensure the effective preparation of the World Conference against Racism, Racial Discrimination, Xenophobia and Related Intolerance;

5. *Requests* the Secretary-General in his reports on racism, racial discrimination, xenophobia and related intolerance to accord special attention to and provide information on the situation of migrant workers in this regard;

6. *Calls upon* all Member States to consider signing and ratifying or acceding to the International Convention on the Protection of the Rights of All Migrant Workers and Members of Their Families as a matter of priority;

7. *Commends* all States that have ratified or acceded to the international instruments to combat racism and racial discrimination, especially the International Convention on the Elimination of All Forms of Racial Discrimination and the Convention against Discrimination in Education;

8. *Urges* all States that have not yet done so to become parties to the International Convention on the Elimination of All Forms of Racial Discrimination in order to achieve its universal ratification;

9. *Urges* States to limit the extent of any reservation they lodge to the International Convention on the Elimination of All Forms of Racial Discrimination, to formulate any reservation as precisely and as narrowly as possible, to ensure that no reservations are incompatible with the objective and purpose of the Convention or otherwise incompatible with international treaty law, to review their reservations regularly with a view to withdrawing them and to withdraw reservations that are contrary to the objective and purpose of the Convention or that are otherwise incompatible with international treaty law;

10. *Encourages* the mass media to promote ideas of tolerance and understanding among peoples and different cultures;

11. *Requests* the Secretary-General to continue to draw attention to the effects of racial discrimination on minorities and migrant workers and members of their families, especially women and children, in the fields of education, training and employment and to submit in his report specific recommendations for the implementation of measures to combat such discrimination;

12. *Recognizes* the need for adequate support and financial resources for the Third Decade to Combat Racism and Racial Discrimination and the Programme of Action for the Third Decade to Combat Racism and Racial Discrimination, and requests the Secretary-General to include in his report to the General Assembly at its fifty-fifth session concrete proposals on how to ensure the financial and personnel resources required for the implementation of the Programme of Action, including through the regular budget of the United Nations and extrabudgetary sources;

13. *Expresses its appreciation* to those who have made contributions to the Trust Fund for the Programme of Action for the Third Decade to Combat Racism and Racial Discrimination, strongly appeals to all Governments, intergovernmental and non-governmental organizations and individuals in a position to do so to contribute generously to the Fund, and to this end requests the Secretary-General to continue to establish the appropriate contacts and undertake the appropriate initiatives;

14. *Requests* the Secretary-General to report to the Commission on Human Rights at its fifty-sixth session on the outcome of expert seminars held in connection with the activities of the Third Decade;

15. *Welcomes* the establishment of the racism project team in the Office of the United Nations High Commissioner for Human Rights with a view to coordinating all activities of the Third Decade;

16. *Urges* all Governments, the Secretary-General, United Nations bodies, the specialized agencies, intergovernmental organizations and relevant non-governmental organizations, in implementing the Programme of Action, to pay particular attention to the situation of indigenous people;

17. *Requests* States to consider the relevant decisions of the Economic and Social Council on the integrated follow-up to previous world conferences and the need to make optimum use of all available mechanisms in the struggle against racism;

18. *Strongly underlines* the importance of education as a significant means of preventing and eradicating racism and racial discrimination and of creating awareness of principles of human rights, in particular among young people, and in this regard requests the United Nations Educational, Scientific and Cultural Organization to continue its work on the preparation and dissemination of teaching materials and teaching aids to promote teaching, training and educational activities on human rights and against racism and racial discrimination, with particular emphasis on activities at the primary and secondary levels of education;

19. *Considers* that, in order to attain the objectives of the Third Decade, all parts of the Programme of Action should be given equal attention;

20. *Requests* the Secretary-General to accord high priority to the activities of the Programme of Action, and in this regard also requests the Secretary-General to ensure that the necessary financial resources are provided for the implementation of the activities of the Third Decade during the biennium 2000-2001;

21. *Also requests* the Secretary-General to continue to submit each year to the Economic and Social Council a detailed report on all activities of United Nations bodies and the specialized agencies containing an analysis of information received on activities to combat racism and racial discrimination;

22. *Invites* the Secretary-General to submit to the General Assembly proposals which would assist in the full implementation of the Programme of Action;

23. *Reiterates its calls upon* all Governments, United Nations bodies, the specialized agencies and intergovernmental and regional organizations and interested non-governmental organizations to contribute fully to the effective implementation of the Programme of Action;

II

World Conference against Racism, Racial Discrimination, Xenophobia and Related Intolerance

24. *Recalls* its resolutions 52/111 of 12 December 1997 and 53/132 of 9 December 1998, in which it established that the Commission on Human Rights would act as the Preparatory Committee for the World Conference against Racism, Racial Discrimination, Xenophobia and Related Intolerance, and takes note of Commission on Human Rights resolution 1999/78 of 28 April 1999 and Economic and Social Council resolution 1999/12 of 27 July 1999;

25. *Recommends* that the Preparatory Committee give consideration to the recommendations of the Special Rapporteur of the Commission on Human Rights on contemporary forms of racism, racial discrimination, xenophobia and related intolerance, including the recommendation contained in paragraph 41 *(b)* of his report to the General Assembly at its fifty-third session;

26. *Requests* the Secretary-General to continue to ensure that adequate financial resources are made available for the preparatory process for the World Conference, including from the regular budget of the United Nations;

27. *Requests* the Secretary-General and the United Nations High Commissioner for Human Rights to make every effort to ensure the mobilization of resources for the voluntary fund for the World Conference to cover the participation of the least developed countries in the preparatory process and in the Conference itself, and requests all Governments, international and non-governmental organizations and private individuals to contribute to the fund;

28. *Calls upon* the High Commissioner to help States and regional organizations, upon request, to convene national and regional meetings or to undertake other initiatives, including activities at the expert level, to prepare for the World Conference, and urges the specialized agencies and the regional commissions, in coordination with the High Commissioner, to contribute to the convening of regional preparatory meetings;

29. *Requests* the Secretary-General, the specialized agencies and the regional commissions to provide financial and technical assistance for the organization of the regional preparatory meetings planned in the context of the World Conference, and stresses that such assistance should be supplemented by voluntary contributions;

30. *Decides* that the World Conference and the sessions of the Preparatory Committee should be open to the participation of:

(a) All States Members of the United Nations and States members of the specialized agencies;

(b) Representatives of all regional organizations and regional commissions involved in the preparation of regional meetings, as well as associate members of the regional commissions;

(c) Representatives of organizations that have received a standing invitation from the General Assembly to participate in the capacity of observers;

(d) Representatives of the specialized agencies, the secretariats of the regional commissions and all United Nations bodies and programmes;

(e) Representatives of all United Nations mechanisms in the field of human rights;

(f) Other interested governmental organizations, which shall be represented by observers;

(g) Interested non-governmental organizations, which shall be represented by observers in accordance with Economic and Social Council resolution 1996/31 of 25 July 1996;

31. *Welcomes* the offer by the Government of South Africa to host the World Conference against Racism,

Racial Discrimination, Xenophobia and Related Intolerance in 2001;

32. *Requests* the High Commissioner:

(*a*) To undertake a study, to be submitted to the Preparatory Committee at its first session, on ways of improving coordination between her Office and all specialized agencies and international, regional and subregional organizations with regard to action to combat racism, racial discrimination, xenophobia and related intolerance;

(*b*) To continue to devise and implement, with the Department of Public Information of the Secretariat, a world information campaign aimed at sensitizing public opinion to the importance and the objectives of the World Conference, to publish in all the official languages of the United Nations an information pamphlet that is to be made available to non-governmental organizations, the media and the general public and to inform the Preparatory Committee of developments in this regard;

(*c*) To help States, upon request, and regional organizations to convene national and regional meetings or to undertake other initiatives, including activities at the expert level, to prepare for the World Conference;

(*d*) To draw up a draft agenda for the first session of the Preparatory Committee, taking into consideration, inter alia, the need to address in a comprehensive manner all forms of racism, racial discrimination, xenophobia and related contemporary forms of intolerance;

(*e*) To continue fund-raising activities in order to increase the resources for the voluntary fund established specifically to cover all aspects of the preparatory process for the World Conference and the participation of non-governmental organizations, in particular those from developing countries;

33. *Welcomes* the proposals on the themes for the World Conference made by the sessional open-ended working group to review and formulate proposals for the World Conference against Racism, Racial Discrimination, Xenophobia and Related Intolerance of the Commission on Human Rights;

34. *Decides* that the World Conference shall be action-oriented and shall focus on practical measures to eradicate racism, including measures of prevention, education and protection and through the provision of effective remedies, taking into full consideration the existing human rights instruments;

35. *Requests* the Preparatory Committee to begin drafting as soon as possible a final document on specific goals as well as objectives and timetables for their achievement;

36. *Appeals* to Member States to contribute generously to the voluntary fund for the World Conference to cover the preparatory process and the Conference and the participation of non-governmental organizations from developing countries;

37. *Requests* Governments, the specialized agencies, other international organizations, concerned United Nations bodies, regional organizations, non-governmental organizations, the Committee on the Elimination of Racial Discrimination, the Special Rapporteur of the Commission on Human Rights on contemporary forms of racism, racial discrimination, xenophobia and related intolerance, the Special Rapporteur of the Commission on Human Rights on the human rights of migrants and other human rights mechanisms to assist the Preparatory Committee and to undertake reviews and submit recommendations concerning the World Conference and the preparations therefor to the Preparatory Committee, through the Secretary-General, and to participate actively in the Conference;

38. *Calls upon* States and regional organizations to convene national and regional meetings or to undertake other initiatives, such as public information campaigns, to raise awareness of the World Conference as part of the preparation for the Conference, and requests regional preparatory meetings to submit reports to the Preparatory Committee, through the Secretary-General, on the outcome of their deliberations, including practical and action-oriented recommendations to combat racism, racial discrimination, xenophobia and related intolerance;

III

Proclamation of 2001 as the International Year of Mobilization against Racism, Racial Discrimination, Xenophobia and Related Intolerance

39. *Strongly reaffirms* the proclamation of 2001 as the International Year of Mobilization against Racism, Racial Discrimination, Xenophobia and Related Intolerance, and in this context calls upon Governments, the United Nations and non-governmental organizations to observe the International Year in a suitable manner, including through programmes of action;

IV

General

40. *Decides* to keep the item entitled "Elimination of racism and racial discrimination" on its agenda and to consider it as a matter of high priority at its fifty-fifth session.

Contemporary forms of racism

Reports of Special Rapporteur. In January [E/CN.4/1999/15], the Special Rapporteur on contemporary forms of racism, racial discrimination, xenophobia and related intolerance, Maurice Glélé-Ahanhanzo (Benin), presented information regarding activities of far right and neo-Nazi movements; discrimination against blacks; racism and racial discrimination against Arabs; anti-Semitism; discrimination against the Roma, Gypsies or travellers; and the untouchables in India. The report contained allegations of racism, racial discrimination and xenophobia transmitted to four Governments by the Special Rapporteur in 1998 and one reply. In conclusion, the Special Rapporteur regretted the rise of neo-fascism and neo-Nazism, continuing use of the Internet to spread racist ideologies, the rise in ethnonationalism, continuing discrimination against the Gypsies or travellers and manifestations of anti-Semitism. He recommended that OHCHR establish bodies and mechanisms to ensure that the World Conference was prepared for in a methodical manner, by organizing regional meetings of experts to assess work on the issue by reviewing studies and undertaking new ones on specific topics and contemporary situations; by involving UN specialized agencies and regional and subregional organizations and NGOs in the Conference preparatory process; and by establishing, within OHCHR and under the High Commissioner's authority, an observatory on neo-fascism, neo-Nazism and ethnonationalism.

In response to General Assembly resolution 53/133 [YUN 1998, p. 651], the Secretary-General transmitted, in September [A/54/347], an interim report of the Special Rapporteur describing his activities and follow-up to field missions, major trends in contemporary manifestations of racism, racial discrimination, xenophobia and related intolerance, and measures taken by Governments. The Special Rapporteur concluded that attention should be paid to the use of the Internet for purposes of incitation to racial hatred, racial discrimination and xenophobia. In preparation for the World Conference, measures should be taken to promote research and consultations on the use of the Internet to combat the phenomenon and to prepare an education programme on human rights, a culture for peace and non-violence in collaboration with, for example, UNESCO, NGOs and relevant governmental organizations. Collaboration should be established among the bodies and mechanisms of the Commission on Human Rights. A campaign should be launched to stimulate international awareness about the World Conference.

Commission action. On 28 April [res. 1999/78], the Commission asked the Special Rapporteur to continue his exchange of views with Member States and the UN system and to use all sources of information, including country visits and the mass media, and to elicit responses from Governments with regard to allegations. Governments of the States thus far visited were asked to consider implementing the Special Rapporteur's recommendations; any results would be included in his 2000 report. The High Commissioner was urged to provide the countries visited by the Special Rapporteur, at their request, with assistance to implement the recommendations. She was asked to conduct research and hold consultations on Internet use to incite racial hatred, racist propaganda and xenophobia, to study ways of promoting international cooperation thereon and to draw up a programme of human rights education over the Internet on the struggle against racism, xenophobia and anti-Semitism.

Regional mission. The Special Rapporteur visited the Czech Republic, Hungary and Romania (20-30 September) [E/CN.4/2000/16/Add.1] to consider allegations he had received of systematic discrimination, particularly in education, employment and housing, against the Roma citizens of those countries and frequent acts of violence against them by members of extreme right organizations and the police. Those countries were selected solely for illustrative and comparative purposes and owing to insufficient resources and time, and not because the situation of the Roma there was more unusual than in other countries. The Special Rapporteur observed that prejudice against the Roma was the same in the three countries but, whereas violence against them was under control in Romania, it persisted in the Czech Republic and Hungary. He stressed that in their common desire to become European Union members, the three Governments were committed to carrying out reforms to benefit the Roma. Recommendations were made to the three Governments. (For Subcommission action on the human rights of the Roma, see p. 616.)

Globalization and racism, racial discrimination and xenophobia

Working paper. In response to a 1998 Subcommission request [YUN 1998, p. 646], Joseph Oloka-Onyango (Uganda) submitted, in June [E/CN.4/Sub.2/1999/8], a working paper on globalization in the context of increased incidents of racism, racial discrimination and xenophobia, as a contribution to the World Conference. He stated that the issue required further study and action by the UN system, multilateral agencies and human rights organizations. CERD needed to encourage States parties to the 1965 International Convention on the Elimination of All Forms of Racial Discrimination to highlight the ways in which globalization had fostered increasing incidents of racism, racial discrimination and xenophobia, and their efforts to address those developments; examine ways that various international human rights instruments could be better applied to non-State actors having a critical role in the process of globalization; and urge countries to review methods of recruiting police and immigration officers, institute racially sensitive training systems, and encourage police and immigration forces to be more inclusive and diverse.

In the light of Commission resolution 1999/59 on globalization and its impact on the full enjoyment of all human rights (see below, under "Economic, social and cultural rights"), the Subcommission should cooperate with CERD in making a more comprehensive examination of the impacts of globalization on racism, racial discrimination and xenophobia.

GENERAL ASSEMBLY ACTION

On 17 December [meeting 83], the General Assembly, on the recommendation of the Third Committee [A/54/603], adopted **resolution 54/153** without vote [agenda item 114].

Measures to combat contemporary forms of racism, racial discrimination, xenophobia and related intolerance

The General Assembly,

Recalling its resolution 53/133 of 9 December 1998, and taking note of Commission on Human Rights resolution 1999/78 of 28 April 1999,

Stressing that the Vienna Declaration and Programme of Action adopted by the World Conference on Human Rights on 25 June 1993 attaches importance to the elimination of racism, racial discrimination, xenophobia and other forms of intolerance,

Convinced that racism, as one of the exclusionist phenomena plaguing many societies, requires resolute action and cooperation for its eradication,

Having examined the report of the Special Rapporteur of the Commission on Human Rights on contemporary forms of racism, racial discrimination, xenophobia and related intolerance, including its conclusions and recommendations,

Deeply concerned that, despite continued efforts, racism, racial discrimination, xenophobia and related intolerance, as well as acts of violence, persist and even grow in magnitude, incessantly adopting new forms, including tendencies to establish policies based on racial, religious, ethnic, cultural and national superiority or exclusivity,

Deeply concerned also that those advocating racism and racial discrimination misuse new communication technologies, including the Internet, to disseminate their repugnant views,

Noting that the use of such technologies can also contribute to combating racism, racial discrimination, xenophobia and related intolerance,

Conscious of the fundamental difference between, on the one hand, racism and racial discrimination as governmental policy or resulting from official doctrines of racial superiority or exclusivity and, on the other hand, other manifestations of racism, racial discrimination, xenophobia and related intolerance that are increasingly visible in segments of many societies and are perpetrated by individuals or groups, some of which manifestations are directed against migrant workers and members of their families,

Reaffirming, in this regard, the responsibility of Governments for safeguarding and protecting the rights of individuals residing in their territory against crimes perpetrated by racist or xenophobic individuals or groups,

Recognizing both the challenges and the opportunities in combating racism, racial discrimination, xenophobia and related intolerance in an increasingly globalized world,

Noting with concern that racism, racial discrimination, xenophobia and related intolerance may be aggravated by, inter alia, inequitable distribution of wealth, marginalization and social exclusion,

Deeply concerned that racism and racial discrimination against migrant workers continue to increase despite the efforts undertaken by the international community to protect the human rights of migrant workers and members of their families,

Noting that the Committee on the Elimination of Racial Discrimination, in its general recommendation XV(42) of 17 March 1993 concerning article 4 of the International Convention on the Elimination of All Forms of Racial Discrimination, holds that the prohibition of the dissemination of ideas based on racial superiority or racial hatred is compatible with the right to freedom of opinion and expression as outlined in article 19 of the Universal Declaration of Human Rights and in article 5 of the Convention,

Noting also that the reports that the States parties submit under the Convention contain, inter alia, information about the causes of as well as measures to combat contemporary forms of racism, racial discrimination, xenophobia and related intolerance,

Particularly alarmed at the rise of racist and xenophobic ideas in political circles, in the sphere of public opinion and in society at large,

Noting with appreciation that the Special Rapporteur will continue to pay attention to the rise of racist and xenophobic ideas in political circles, in the sphere of public opinion and in society at large,

Underlining the importance of urgently eliminating growing and violent trends of racism and racial discrimination, and conscious that any form of impunity for crimes motivated by racist and xenophobic attitudes plays a role in weakening the rule of law and democracy and tends to encourage the recurrence of such crimes, and requires resolute action and cooperation for its eradication,

Emphasizing the importance of creating conditions that foster greater harmony and tolerance within societies,

1. *Reaffirms* the proclamation of 2001 as the International Year of Mobilization against Racism, Racial Discrimination, Xenophobia and Related Intolerance;

2. *Calls upon* the relevant United Nations bodies, Member States and intergovernmental and non-governmental organizations to carry out, promote and disseminate activities and action within the framework of the commemorative year in order to strengthen its impact and ensure its success, in particular the outcome of the World Conference against Racism, Racial Discrimination, Xenophobia and Related Intolerance;

3. *Expresses its full support and appreciation* for the work of the Special Rapporteur of the Commission on Human Rights on contemporary forms of racism, racial discrimination, xenophobia and related intolerance, encourages its continuation, and takes note with appreciation of the report of the Special Rapporteur;

4. *Requests* the Special Rapporteur to continue his exchange of views with Member States, related United Nations organs and the specialized agencies, other relevant mechanisms and non-governmental organizations in order to further their effectiveness and mutual cooperation;

5. *Commends* the Committee on the Elimination of Racial Discrimination for its role in the effective implementation of the International Convention on the Elimination of All Forms of Racial Discrimination, which contributes to the fight against contemporary forms of racism, racial discrimination, xenophobia and related intolerance;

6. *Reaffirms* that acts of racist violence against others stemming from racism do not constitute expressions of opinion but rather offences;

7. *Declares* that racism and racial discrimination are among the most serious violations of human rights in the contemporary world and must be combated by all available means;

8. *Expresses its profound concern about and unequivocal condemnation* of all forms of racism, racial discrimination, xenophobia and related intolerance, in particular all racist violence, including related acts of random and indiscriminate violence;

9. *Also expresses its profound concern about and unequivocal condemnation* of all forms of racism and racial discrimination, including propaganda, activities and organizations based on doctrines of superiority of one race or group of persons that attempt to justify or promote racism and racial discrimination in any form;

10. *Expresses its profound concern about and condemnation* of manifestations of racism, racial discrimination, xenophobia and related intolerance against as well as stereotyping of migrant workers and members of their families, persons belonging to minorities and members of vulnerable groups in many societies;

11. *Expresses deep concern* about the increase in racial and xenophobic violence in many parts of the world, as well as the increasing number of associations established on the basis of racist and xenophobic platforms and charters, as reflected in the report of the Special Rapporteur;

12. *Encourages* all States to include in their educational curricula and social programmes at all levels, as appropriate, knowledge of and tolerance and respect for foreign cultures, peoples and countries;

13. *Recognizes* that the increasing gravity of different manifestations of racism, racial discrimination and xenophobia in various parts of the world requires a more integrated and effective approach on the part of the relevant mechanisms of United Nations human rights machinery;

14. *Encourages* Governments to take appropriate measures to eradicate all forms of racism, racial discrimination, xenophobia and related intolerance;

15. *Calls upon* all States to review and, where necessary, revise their immigration policies with a view to eliminating all discriminatory policies and practices against migrants which are inconsistent with relevant international human rights instruments;

16. *Condemns* the misuse of print, audio-visual and electronic media and new communication technologies, including the Internet, to incite violence motivated by racial hatred;

17. *Recognizes* that Governments should implement and enforce appropriate and effective legislation to prevent acts of racism, racial discrimination, xenophobia and related intolerance;

18. *Calls upon* all Governments and intergovernmental organizations, with the assistance of non-governmental organizations, as appropriate, to continue to supply relevant information to the Special Rapporteur to enable him to fulfil his mandate;

19. *Commends* non-governmental organizations for the action that they have taken against racism and racial discrimination and for the continuous support and assistance that they have provided to the victims of racism and racial discrimination;

20. *Urges* all Governments to cooperate fully with the Special Rapporteur with a view to enabling him to fulfil his mandate, including the examination of incidents of contemporary forms of racism and racial discrimination, inter alia, against blacks, Arabs and Muslims, xenophobia, Negrophobia, anti-Semitism and related intolerance;

21. *Requests* the Secretary-General to provide the Special Rapporteur with all the necessary human and financial assistance to carry out his mandate efficiently, effectively and expeditiously and to enable him to submit an interim report to the General Assembly at its fifty-fifth session.

Right to nationality

Report of Secretary-General. In response to a 1998 Commission request [YUN 1998, p. 652], the Secretary-General presented information received from 10 Governments on measures they had taken to prevent the arbitrary deprivation of nationality [E/CN.4/1999/56 & Add.1,2].

Commission action. On 26 April [res. 1999/28], the Commission called on States to refrain from taking measures that discriminated against persons on grounds of race, colour, gender, religion, or national or ethnic origin by nullifying or impairing the exercise, on an equal footing, of their right to a nationality, and to repeal such legislation if it existed. It urged the Commission's mechanisms and UN treaty bodies to continue to collect information and to report on the issue. The Secretary-General was also asked to continue to collect information and to make it available to the Commission.

Rights of non-citizens

Working paper. In response to a 1998 Subcommission request [YUN 1998, p. 652], David Weissbrodt (United States) presented, in May [E/CN.4/Sub.2/1999/7], a working paper on the rights of persons who were not citizens of the country in which they lived. It reviewed the development of the rights of non-citizens since the 1985 adoption by the General Assembly in resolution 40/144 of the Declaration on the Human Rights of Individuals Who are not Nationals of the Country in which They Live [YUN 1985, p. 850] and other issues not covered by the Declaration. It also examined the rights of non-citizens under the 1965 International Convention on the Elimination of All Forms of Racial Discrimination and other standards relevant to them. The paper recommended actions for CERD and proposed that the paper be transmitted to it for its advice and reactions. If CERD determined that a full study would be helpful, the Subcommission should transmit the paper, together with CERD's comments, to the Commission, along with a proposal for the study.

CERD should be encouraged to prepare a general recommendation on the rights of non-citizens.

An addendum to the report [E/CN.4/Sub.2/1999/7/Add.1] examined ways to overcome impediments to the ratification of the 1990 International Convention on the Protection of the Rights of All Migrant Workers and Members of Their Families, adopted by the Assembly in resolution 45/158 [YUN 1990, p. 594], and ways to contribute to the efforts of the working group of intergovernmental experts on the human rights of migrants. As the Commission had replaced the working group with a Special Rapporteur on the human rights of migrants, the paper should be transmitted to the Special Rapporteur. (For further information on the rights of migrants, see below.)

Subcommission action. On 25 August [res. 1999/7], the Subcommission recommended that the rights of non-citizens be addressed explicitly at the World Conference. It endorsed the conclusions contained in the working paper, including the importance of undertaking an updated study on the rights of non-citizens.

Migrant workers

Commission action. On 27 April [res. 1999/44], the Commission decided to appoint, for a three-year period, a special rapporteur on the human rights of migrants to examine ways to overcome obstacles to the protection of their human rights. The Special Rapporteur was asked to report in 2000 and the Secretary-General was asked to assist him/her.

ECONOMIC AND SOCIAL COUNCIL ACTION

In July, the Economic and Social Council, on the recommendation of the Commission on Human Rights [E/1999/23], adopted **decision 1999/239** without vote [agenda item 14 (*h*)].

Human rights of migrants

At its 42nd plenary meeting, on 27 July 1999, the Economic and Social Council, taking note of Commission on Human Rights resolution 1999/44 of 27 April 1999:

(*a*) Endorsed the Commission's decision to appoint, for a three-year period, a special rapporteur on the human rights of migrants to examine ways and means to overcome the obstacles existing to the full and effective protection of the human rights of that vulnerable group, including obstacles and difficulties for the return of migrants who are non-documented or in an irregular situation, with the following functions:

(i) To request and receive information from all relevant sources, including migrants themselves, on violations of the human rights of migrants and their families;

(ii) To formulate appropriate recommendations to prevent and remedy violations of the human rights of migrants, wherever they may occur;

(iii) To promote the effective application of relevant international norms and standards on the issue;

(iv) To recommend actions and measures applicable at the national, regional and international levels to eliminate violations of the human rights of migrants;

(v) To take into account a gender perspective when requesting and analysing information, as well as to give special attention to the occurrence of multiple discrimination and violence against migrant women;

(*b*) Approved the Commission's request to the Special Rapporteur, in carrying out his/her mandate, to give careful consideration to the various recommendations of the Working Group of intergovernmental experts aimed at the promotion and protection of the human rights of migrants, to take into consideration relevant human rights instruments of the United Nations to promote and protect the human rights of migrants and, in carrying out his/her mandate, to take into account bilateral and regional negotiations aimed at addressing, inter alia, the return and reinsertion of migrants who are non-documented or in an irregular situation;

(*c*) Also approved the Commission's invitation to the Special Rapporteur, in carrying out that mandate and within the framework of the Universal Declaration of Human Rights, and all other international instruments, to request, receive and exchange information on violations of the human rights of migrants from Governments, treaty bodies, specialized agencies, special rapporteurs for various human rights questions and from intergovernmental organizations, other competent organizations of the United Nations system and non-governmental organizations, including migrants' organizations, and to respond effectively to such information, and to contribute to the Preparatory Committee for the World Conference against Racism, Racial Discrimination, Xenophobia and Related Intolerance, within the framework of the objectives of the Conference, including by identifying major issues to be considered by the Conference;

(*d*) Further approved the Commission's request to:

(i) The Chairperson of the Commission, after consultations with the other members of the Bureau, to appoint as Special Rapporteur an individual of recognized international standing and experience in addressing the human rights of migrants;

(ii) The Special Rapporteur to submit a report on his/her activities to the Commission at its fifty-sixth session;

(iii) The Secretary-General to give the Special Rapporteur all necessary human and financial assistance for the fulfilment of his/her mandate.

On 6 August, the Chairperson of the Commission, following consultations with Bureau members, appointed Gabriela Rodríguez Pizarro (Costa Rica) as Special Rapporteur on the human rights of migrants.

GENERAL ASSEMBLY ACTION

On 17 December [meeting 83], the General Assembly, on the recommendation of the Third

Committee [A/54/605/Add.2], adopted **resolution 54/166** without vote [agenda item 116 *(b)*].

Protection of migrants

The General Assembly,

Considering that the Universal Declaration of Human Rights proclaims that all human beings are born free and equal in dignity and rights and that everyone is entitled to all the rights and freedoms set out therein, without distinction of any kind, in particular as to race, colour or national origin,

Reaffirming the provisions concerning migrants adopted by the World Conference on Human Rights, the International Conference on Population and Development, the World Summit for Social Development and the Fourth World Conference on Women,

Taking note of Commission on Human Rights resolution 1999/44 of 27 April 1999 on the human rights of migrants, and of its decision to appoint a Special Rapporteur on the human rights of migrants,

Recalling its resolution 40/144 of 13 December 1985, by which it approved the Declaration on the Human Rights of Individuals Who are not Nationals of the Country in which They Live,

Bearing in mind the situation of vulnerability in which migrants frequently find themselves, owing, inter alia, to their absence from their State of origin and to the difficulties they encounter because of differences of language, custom and culture, as well as the economic and social difficulties and obstacles for the return to their States of origin of migrants who are non-documented or in an irregular situation,

Deeply concerned at the manifestations of violence, racism, xenophobia and other forms of discrimination and inhuman and degrading treatment against migrants, especially women and children, in different parts of the world,

Encouraged by the increasing interest of the international community in the effective and full protection of the human rights of all migrants, and underlining the need to make further efforts to ensure respect for the human rights and fundamental freedoms of all migrants,

Taking note with appreciation of the recommendations on strengthening the promotion, protection and implementation of the human rights of migrants of the working group of intergovernmental experts on the human rights of migrants established by the Commission on Human Rights,

Noting the efforts made by States to penalize the international trafficking of migrants and to protect the victims of this illegal activity,

Taking note of the decisions of the relevant international juridical bodies on questions relating to migrants, in particular advisory opinion OC-16/99, issued by the Inter-American Court of Human Rights on 1 October 1999, regarding the right to information about consular assistance within the framework of due process guarantees,

1. *Requests* all Member States, in conformity with their respective constitutional systems, effectively to promote and protect the human rights of all migrants, in conformity with the Universal Declaration of Human Rights and the international instruments to which they are party, which may include the International Covenants on Human Rights, the Convention against Torture and Other Cruel, Inhuman or Degrading Treatment or Punishment, the International Convention on the Elimination of All Forms of Racial Discrimination, the International Convention on the Protection of the Rights of All Migrant Workers and Members of Their Families, the Convention on the Elimination of All Forms of Discrimination against Women, the Convention on the Rights of the Child and other applicable international human rights instruments;

2. *Strongly condemns* all forms of racial discrimination and xenophobia with regard to access to employment, vocational training, housing, schooling, health services and social services, as well as services intended for use by the public, and welcomes the active role played by governmental and non-governmental organizations in combating racism and assisting individual victims of racist acts, including migrant victims;

3. *Calls upon* all States to review and, where necessary, revise immigration policies with a view to eliminating all discriminatory policies and practices against migrants and to provide specialized training for government policy-making and law enforcement, immigration and other concerned officials, thus underlining the importance of effective action to create conditions that foster greater harmony and tolerance within societies;

4. *Reiterates* the need for all States to protect fully the universally recognized human rights of migrants, especially women and children, regardless of their legal status, and to provide humane treatment, in particular with regard to assistance and protection, including those under the Vienna Convention on Consular Relations, regarding the right to receive consular assistance from the country of origin;

5. *Welcomes* the decision of the Commission on Human Rights to appoint a Special Rapporteur on the human rights of migrants to examine ways and means to overcome the obstacles existing to the full and effective protection of the human rights of this vulnerable group, including obstacles and difficulties for the return of migrants who are non-documented or in an irregular situation, with the following functions:

(a) To request and receive information from all relevant sources, including migrants themselves, on violations of the human rights of migrants and their families;

(b) To formulate appropriate recommendations to prevent and remedy violations of the human rights of migrants, wherever they may occur;

(c) To promote the effective application of relevant international norms and standards on the issue;

(d) To recommend actions and measures applicable at the national, regional and international levels to eliminate violations of the human rights of migrants;

(e) To take into account a gender perspective when requesting and analysing information, as well as to give special attention to the occurrence of multiple discrimination and violence against migrant women;

6. *Requests* all Governments to cooperate fully with the Special Rapporteur in the performance of the tasks and duties mandated and to furnish all information requested, including by reacting promptly to his/her urgent appeals;

7. *Encourages* Member States that have not yet done so to enact domestic criminal legislation to combat in-

ternational trafficking of migrants, which should take into account, in particular, trafficking that endangers the lives of migrants or includes different forms of servitude or exploitation, such as any form of debt bondage, sexual or labour exploitation, and to strengthen international cooperation to combat such trafficking;

8. *Requests* the Secretary-General to submit to the General Assembly at its fifty-fifth session a report on the implementation of the present resolution under the sub-item entitled "Human rights questions, including alternative approaches for improving the effective enjoyment of human rights and fundamental freedoms".

The Assembly adopted the tenth preambular paragraph by a recorded vote of 134 votes to 1, with 14 abstentions. Similarly, the Committee adopted the paragraph by a recorded vote of 121 to 1, with 19 abstentions.

Freedom of travel

On 17 December [meeting 83], the Assembly adopted **resolution 54/169**, on the recommendation of the Third Committee [A/54/605/Add.2], by recorded vote (95-1-66) [agenda item 116 *(b)*].

Respect for the right to universal freedom of travel and the vital importance of family reunification

The General Assembly,

Reaffirming that all human rights and fundamental freedoms are universal, indivisible, interdependent and interrelated,

Recalling the provisions of the Universal Declaration of Human Rights,

Stressing that, as stated in the Programme of Action of the International Conference on Population and Development, family reunification of documented migrants is an important factor in international migration and that remittances by documented migrants to their countries of origin often constitute a very important source of foreign exchange and are instrumental in improving the well-being of relatives left behind,

Recalling its resolution 53/143 of 9 December 1998,

1. *Once again calls upon* all States to guarantee the universally recognized freedom of travel to all foreign nationals legally residing in their territory;

2. *Reaffirms* that all Governments, in particular those of receiving countries, must recognize the vital importance of family reunification and promote its incorporation into national legislation in order to ensure protection of the unity of families of documented migrants;

3. *Calls upon* all States to allow, in conformity with international legislation, the free flow of financial remittances by foreign nationals residing in their territory to their relatives in the country of origin;

4. *Also calls upon* all States to refrain from enacting, and to repeal if it already exists, legislation intended as a coercive measure that discriminates against legal migrants, whether individuals or groups, by adversely affecting family reunification and the right to send financial remittances to relatives in the country of origin;

5. *Decides* to continue its consideration of this question at its fifty-fifth session, under the item entitled "Human rights questions".

RECORDED VOTE ON RESOLUTION 54/169:

In favour: Afghanistan, Algeria, Angola, Antigua and Barbuda, Argentina, Armenia, Bangladesh, Barbados, Belize, Benin, Bhutan, Bolivia, Botswana, Brazil, Brunei Darussalam, Burkina Faso, Cambodia, Cameroon, Cape Verde, Chad, Chile, China, Colombia, Comoros, Congo, Costa Rica, Cuba, Democratic People's Republic of Korea, Djibouti, Dominica, Dominican Republic, Ecuador, Egypt, El Salvador, Eritrea, Ethiopia, Fiji, Gabon, Ghana, Grenada, Guinea, Guinea-Bissau, Guyana, Haiti, Honduras, India, Indonesia, Iran, Jamaica, Jordan, Kenya, Kuwait, Lao People's Democratic Republic, Lebanon, Libyan Arab Jamahiriya, Mali, Mauritius, Mexico, Morocco, Mozambique, Myanmar, Namibia, Nepal, Nicaragua, Nigeria, Oman, Pakistan, Panama, Papua New Guinea, Paraguay, Peru, Philippines, Qatar, Saint Lucia, Saudi Arabia, Senegal, Seychelles, Sierra Leone, Sri Lanka, Sudan, Suriname, Swaziland, Syrian Arab Republic, Tajikistan, Togo, Trinidad and Tobago, Tunisia, Turkey, United Arab Emirates, United Republic of Tanzania, Uruguay, Venezuela, Viet Nam, Yemen, Zimbabwe.

Against: United States.

Abstaining: Albania, Andorra, Australia, Austria, Azerbaijan, Bahamas, Bahrain, Belarus, Belgium, Bosnia and Herzegovina, Bulgaria, Canada, Côte d'Ivoire, Croatia, Cyprus, Czech Republic, Denmark, Estonia, Finland, France, Georgia, Germany, Greece, Hungary, Iceland, Ireland, Israel, Italy, Japan, Kazakhstan, Latvia, Liechtenstein, Lithuania, Luxembourg, Malawi, Malaysia, Maldives, Malta, Marshall Islands, Micronesia, Monaco, Mongolia, Netherlands, New Zealand, Norway, Poland, Portugal, Republic of Korea, Republic of Moldova, Romania, Russian Federation, Samoa, San Marino, Singapore, Slovakia, Slovenia, Solomon Islands, South Africa, Spain, Sweden, Thailand, The former Yugoslav Republic of Macedonia, Ukraine, United Kingdom, Uzbekistan, Zambia.

Affirmative action

Commission action. On 27 April [dec. 1999/107], the Commission endorsed the Subcommission's 1998 decision to appoint Marc Bossuyt (Belgium) as Special Rapporteur to undertake a study on the concept and practice of affirmative action [YUN 1998, p. 652]. By **decision 1999/253** of 27 July, the Economic and Social Council approved the Commission's decision.

Secretariat note. A June note by the secretariat [E/CN.4/Sub.2/1999/5] stated that the Special Rapporteur would report in 2000, owing to the fact that the collection of information for the report was not possible in the time available for the preparation of documents.

Subcommission action. On 25 August [dec. 1999/106], the Subcommission renewed its authorization to the Special Rapporteur to request the High Commissioner to send a questionnaire to Governments, international organizations and NGOs, inviting them to provide relevant national documentation on affirmative action. The Subcommission asked the Secretary-General to assist the Special Rapporteur.

Other forms of intolerance

Cultural prejudice

On 17 December [meeting 83], the General Assembly, on the recommendation of the Third

Committee [A/54/605/Add.2], adopted **resolution 54/160** without vote [agenda item 116 *(b)*].

Human rights and cultural diversity

The General Assembly,

Recalling the Universal Declaration of Human Rights and the relevant provisions of the International Covenant on Economic, Social and Cultural Rights, the International Convention on the Elimination of All Forms of Racial Discrimination and the Convention on the Rights of the Child,

Noting that numerous instruments within the United Nations system promote cultural diversity, as well as the conservation and development of culture, in particular the Declaration of the Principles of International Cultural Cooperation, proclaimed on 4 November 1966 by the General Conference of the United Nations Educational, Scientific and Cultural Organization at its fourteenth session,

Welcoming the designation by the General Assembly, in its resolution 53/22 of 4 November 1998, of the year 2001 as the United Nations Year of Dialogue among Civilizations,

Reaffirming that all human rights are universal, indivisible, interdependent and interrelated and that the international community must treat human rights globally in a fair and equal manner, on the same footing and with the same emphasis, and that, while the significance of national and regional particularities and various historical, cultural and religious backgrounds must be borne in mind, it is the duty of States, regardless of their political, economic and cultural systems, to promote and protect all human rights and fundamental freedoms,

Recognizing that cultural diversity and the pursuit of cultural development by all peoples and nations are a source of mutual enrichment for the cultural life of humankind,

Considering that tolerance of cultural, ethnic and religious diversities is essential for peace, understanding and friendship among individuals and people of different cultures and nations of the world,

Recognizing in each culture a dignity and value which deserves recognition, respect and preservation, and convinced also that in their rich variety and diversity, and in the reciprocal influences they exert on one another, all cultures form part of the common heritage belonging to all humankind,

Convinced that the promotion of cultural pluralism, tolerance towards and dialogue among various cultures and civilizations would contribute to the efforts of all peoples and nations to enrich their cultures and traditions by engaging in a mutually beneficial exchange of knowledge and intellectual, moral and material achievements,

1. *Affirms* the importance for all peoples and nations to hold, develop and preserve their cultural heritage and traditions in a national and international atmosphere of peace, tolerance and mutual respect;

2. *Recognizes* that respect for cultural diversity and the cultural rights of all enhances cultural pluralism, contributing to a wider exchange of knowledge and understanding of cultural background, advancing the application and enjoyment of universally accepted human rights across the world and fostering stable friendly relations among peoples and nations worldwide;

3. *Emphasizes* that the promotion of cultural pluralism and tolerance at the national and international levels is important for enhancing respect for cultural rights and cultural diversity;

4. *Calls upon* States, international organizations and United Nations agencies, and invites civil society, including non-governmental organizations, for the purpose of advancing the objectives of peace, development and universally accepted human rights, to recognize and respect cultural diversity;

5. *Requests* the Secretary-General, in the light of the present resolution, to prepare a report on human rights and cultural diversity, taking into account the views of Member States, relevant United Nations agencies and non-governmental organizations, and to submit it to the General Assembly at its fifty-fifth session;

6. *Decides* to continue consideration of this question at its fifty-fifth session under the sub-item entitled "Human rights questions, including alternative approaches for improving the effective enjoyment of human rights and fundamental freedoms".

Discrimination against minorities

Report of Secretary-General. In January [E/CN.4/1999/113], the Secretary-General provided an overview of the concluding observations of human rights treaty bodies relating to the rights of persons belonging to national or ethnic, religious and linguistic minorities; the 1997 visit to Germany of the Special Rapporteur on religious intolerance [YUN 1997, p. 637]; the work of the Working Group on Minorities in 1998 [YUN 1998, p. 654]; and the activities of the Special Rapporteurs on extrajudicial, summary or arbitrary executions [ibid., p. 670], on the situation of human rights in Bosnia and Herzegovina, Croatia and the Federal Republic of Yugoslavia (Serbia and Montenegro) [YUN 1997, p. 737], on the human rights situation in Iraq [ibid., p. 727] and on the human rights situation in Myanmar [ibid., p. 730].

Commission action. On 27 April [res. 1999/48], the Commission urged States and the international community to promote and protect the rights of persons belonging to national or ethnic, religious and linguistic minorities, as set out in the 1992 Declaration on the Rights of Persons Belonging to National or Ethnic, Religious and Linguistic Minorities, adopted by the General Assembly in resolution 47/135 [YUN 1992, p. 723]. The Secretary-General was called on to make available, at the request of Governments concerned, qualified expertise on minority issues. The High Commissioner for Human Rights was called on to promote the implementation of the Declaration and to engage in a dialogue with Governments to do so; to improve coordination and cooperation of UN programmes and agencies dealing with minority issues; and to seek voluntary contributions to facilitate participation by minority groups in the activities of the Working Group on Minorities. The Commission asked the Working Group to contribute to the preparations for the World Conference. The Secretary-General was asked to assist the Group and to report in 2000.

Working Group activities. The five-member Working Group on Minorities, at its fifth session (Geneva, 25-31 May) [E/CN.4/Sub.2/1999/21], reviewed the promotion of the 1992 Declaration, examined possible solutions to problems involving minorities, including the promotion of mutual understanding between and among minorities and Governments, and recommended further measures to promote and protect the rights of minorities.

The Working Group recommended that its members prepare a revised Commentary on the principles of the Declaration as part of a manual on the Declaration. The manual would also review procedures by which members of minorities could address regional and international organizations with their concerns. The Working Group considered the questions of effective participation by minorities, multicultural and intercultural education, and information presented by NGOs and minority representatives on situations where, in their opinion, the standards contained in the Declaration were not adequately implemented. It addressed the special case of the legacy of plantation slavery and the situation of African Americans generally in different parts of the Americas, and examined forcible displacement and the return of persons who had been forcefully displaced. The Group discussed a proposal to begin work on a definition of the concept of minority, and examined the feasibility of establishing a database containing a list of organizations and events, a bibliography of publications and a description of minorities. Recommendations included strengthening its secretariat and inviting the High Commissioner to call on Governments and others to provide voluntary contributions, with a view to facilitating participation by underrepresented minority groups in the Working Group's activities.

The Working Group and the European Centre for Minority Issues organized a regional Central and East European expert seminar on the effective participation of minorities (Flensburg, Germany, 30 April–2 May) [E/CN.4/2000/79]. The seminar focused on various mechanisms within States to enable the political participation of minorities in public life, and non-institutional conditions that provided an enabling environment for minorities to participate effectively.

The international seminar on intercultural and multicultural education (Montreal, Canada, 29 September–2 October), organized by the Centre d'études sur le droit et la mondialisation and the Working Group, considered the issue of intercultural and multicultural education in the light of the Declaration [E/CN.4/Sub.2/2000/27].

Subcommission action. On 26 August [res. 1999/23], the Subcommission, endorsing the conclusions and recommendations of the Working Group, decided to entrust Erika-Irene Daes (Greece) and Asbjørn Eide (Norway) with the preparation of a working paper on the relationship and distinction between the rights of persons belonging to minorities and those of indigenous peoples, for submission to the next sessions of the Working Group on Minorities and the Working Group on Indigenous Populations and to the Subcommission in 2000. It asked the Secretary-General to invite States, specialized agencies, other UN bodies, NGOs and scholars to provide comments to the Working Group in 2000 on the Commentary to the Declaration. He was asked to invite UN bodies and specialized agencies to provide information to the Working Group on their activities and programmes relating to minority protection. The Subcommission called for the report of the seminar on intercultural and multicultural education (see above) to be transmitted to the Working Group and the Preparatory Committee of the World Conference in 2000. It recommended that OHCHR be strengthened to support the Working Group's activities.

Also on 26 August [dec. 1999/109], the Subcommission decided to entrust Yeung Kam Yeung Sik Yuen (Mauritius) with preparing a working paper on the human rights problems and protection of the Roma, for submission to the Working Group in 2000 in order to enable the Subcommission to decide on the feasibility of a study on the subject.

Reports of Secretary-General. In September [A/54/303] and December [E/CN.4/2000/79], the Secretary-General described action taken to promote the 1992 Declaration. A number of projects had had an indirect impact on greater respect for minority rights, including assistance aimed at the effective functioning of the National Human Rights Office in Latvia; the provision of expertise to key institutions in South Africa; the organization of a seminar for human rights NGOs and workshops for governmental officials, NGOs, educators and the legal community in Armenia; human rights training for national police agencies in Eastern Slavonia, Croatia; practical assistance to promote human rights in Azerbaijan; and a national training workshop for human rights NGOs and the Government of the Russian Federation on the human rights treaty system. The reports described cooperation between OHCHR and the specialized agencies, action taken by human rights treaty bodies to monitor the observance by States parties of the minority-specific rights contained in the instruments, and the activities of special rapporteurs, special representatives and NGOs.

GENERAL ASSEMBLY ACTION

On 17 December [meeting 83], the General Assembly, on the recommendation of the Third Committee [A/54/605/Add.2], adopted **resolution 54/162** without vote [agenda item 116 *(b)*].

Effective promotion of the Declaration on the Rights of Persons Belonging to National or Ethnic, Religious and Linguistic Minorities

The General Assembly,

Recalling its resolution 47/135 of 18 December 1992, by which it adopted the Declaration on the Rights of Persons Belonging to National or Ethnic, Religious and Linguistic Minorities, and its subsequent resolutions thereon,

Considering that the promotion and protection of the rights of persons belonging to national or ethnic, religious and linguistic minorities contribute to political and social stability and peace and enrich the cultural heritage of society as a whole in the States in which such persons live,

Concerned by the frequency and severity of disputes and conflicts concerning minorities in many countries and their often tragic consequences, and concerned also that persons belonging to minorities are particularly vulnerable to displacement through, inter alia, population transfers, refugee flows and forced relocation,

Acknowledging that the United Nations has an increasingly important role to play regarding the protection of minorities by, inter alia, taking due account of and giving effect to the Declaration,

Noting that the Working Group on Minorities of the Subcommission on the Promotion and Protection of Human Rights of the Commission on Human Rights held its fourth and fifth sessions from 25 to 29 May 1998 and 25 to 31 May 1999, respectively,

1. *Takes note* of the report of the Secretary-General;

2. *Reaffirms* the obligation of States to ensure that persons belonging to minorities may exercise fully and effectively all human rights and fundamental freedoms without any discrimination and in full equality before the law, in accordance with the Declaration on the Rights of Persons Belonging to National or Ethnic, Religious and Linguistic Minorities;

3. *Urges* States and the international community to promote and protect the rights of persons belonging to national or ethnic, religious and linguistic minorities, as set out in the Declaration, including through the facilitation of their participation in all aspects of the political, economic, social, religious and cultural life of society and in the economic progress and development of their country;

4. *Urges* States to take, as appropriate, all the necessary constitutional, legislative, administrative and other measures to promote and give effect to the Declaration;

5. *Recognizes* that respect for human rights and the promotion of understanding and tolerance by Governments as well as between and among minorities are central to the promotion and protection of the rights of persons belonging to minorities;

6. *Appeals* to States to make bilateral and multilateral efforts, as appropriate, in order to protect the rights of persons belonging to national or ethnic, religious and linguistic minorities in their countries, in accordance with the Declaration;

7. *Calls upon* the Secretary-General to make available, at the request of Governments concerned, qualified expertise on minority issues, including the prevention and resolution of disputes, to assist in existing or potential situations involving minorities;

8. *Calls upon* the United Nations High Commissioner for Human Rights to promote, within her mandate, the implementation of the Declaration and to continue to engage in a dialogue with Governments concerned for that purpose;

9. *Requests* the High Commissioner to continue her efforts to improve the coordination and cooperation among United Nations programmes and agencies on activities related to the promotion and protection of the rights of persons belonging to minorities and to take the work of relevant regional organizations active in the field of human rights into account in her endeavours;

10. *Calls upon* the High Commissioner to resume inter-agency consultations with United Nations programmes and agencies on minority issues, and urges those programmes and agencies to contribute actively to this process;

11. *Encourages* intergovernmental and non-governmental organizations to continue to contribute to the promotion and protection of the rights of persons belonging to national or ethnic, religious and linguistic minorities;

12. *Calls upon* the Working Group on Minorities of the Subcommission on the Promotion and Protection of Human Rights of the Commission on Human Rights to implement further its mandate with the involvement of a wide range of participants;

13. *Invites* the High Commissioner to seek voluntary contributions to facilitate the effective participation, including through training seminars, in the work of the Working Group on Minorities of representatives of non-governmental organizations and persons belonging to minorities, in particular those from developing countries;

14. *Requests* the Secretary-General to report to the General Assembly at its fifty-sixth session on the implementation of the present resolution, including on good practices in the fields of education and the effective participation of minorities in decision-making processes;

15. *Decides* to continue consideration of this question at its fifty-sixth session, under the item entitled "Human rights questions".

Religious intolerance

Reports of Special Rapporteur. In January [E/CN.4/1999/58], the Special Rapporteur on religious intolerance, Abdelfattah Amor (Tunisia), described his examination of incidents and governmental action inconsistent with the provisions of the 1981 Declaration on the Elimination of All Forms of Intolerance and of Discrimination Based on Religion or Belief, contained in General Assembly resolution 36/55 [YUN 1981, p. 882]. He provided an analysis of: legislation as part of his efforts to create an international compendium of national enactments relating to freedom of religion or belief; initiatives taken by States and NGOs to combat intolerance and discrimination based on religion or belief; information on in situ visits and follow-up; and communications he had sent to and replies received from States since the Commission's 1998 session. The Special Rapporteur summarized 63 communications, including four urgent appeals, that he had sent to 46 States; he also summarized the responses of 22 States. An analysis of the communications revealed a decline in anti-religious State policies and the manipulation of religion in the interest of a political ideology, and yet the persistence of those policies in several countries and even the emergence of problems they had brought about. There was also an upsurge of State policies directed against minorities in matters of religion or belief; a growing number of policies and practices of intolerance and discrimination by non-State entities; and an increased number of policies and practices of intolerance and discrimination against women, deriving from interpretations and traditions attributed by men to religion.

A later report described the Special Rapporteur's visit (1-3 September) to the Holy See [E/CN.4/2000/65], which, the Special Rapporteur stated, provided an opportunity to see what was being done in the area of inter-religious dialogue from the point of view of the Holy See. The visit contributed to better knowledge of one religion in its relations with others and therefore to shared experience, as well as to dialogue between communities belonging to different religions and beliefs, and lastly to enhanced protection of freedom of religion and belief.

Commission action. On 26 April [res. 1999/39], the Commission, condemning all forms of intolerance and of discrimination based on religion or belief, urged States to: provide adequate constitutional and legal guarantees of freedom of thought, conscience, religion and belief; ensure that no one, because of religion or belief, was deprived of the rights to life, liberty and security of person, or was subjected to torture or arbitrary arrest or detention; combat hatred, intolerance and acts of violence, intimidation and coercion motivated by religious intolerance; recognize the right of all persons to worship or assemble in connection with a religion or belief and to establish and maintain places for those purposes; ensure that members of law enforcement bodies, civil servants, educators and other public officials respected different religions and beliefs; ensure that religious places, sites and shrines were respected and protected; and promote tolerance through education and other means. The Commission invited the Special Rapporteur to contribute to the 2001 World Conference against Racism, Racial Discrimination, Xenophobia and Related Intolerance by forwarding to the High Commissioner his recommendations on religious intolerance that had a bearing on the Conference. Noting the Special Rapporteur's request to change his title from Special Rapporteur on religious intolerance to Special Rapporteur on freedom of religion or belief, the Commission decided to consider the request in 2000. The Secretary-General was asked to assist the Special Rapporteur, submit an interim report to the Assembly in 1999 and report to the Commission in 2000.

On 30 April [res. 1999/82], the Commission urged States to take measures to combat hatred, discrimination, intolerance and acts of violence, intimidation and coercion motivated by religious intolerance, including attacks on religious places, and to encourage understanding, tolerance and respect in matters relating to freedom of religion or belief. It expressed concern at negative stereotyping of religions and that Islam was frequently and wrongly associated with human rights violations and with terrorism. The Commission invited the High Commissioner, in the context of preparations for the United Nations Year of Dialogue among Civilizations (2001) (see PART THREE, Chapter IX), to consider holding seminars to promote a dialogue among cultures. The Economic and Social Council approved that invitation on 27 July (**decision 1999/250**).

Interim reports of Special Rapporteur. Pursuant to General Assembly resolution 53/140 [YUN 1998, p. 657], the Secretary-General, in September [A/54/386], transmitted the Special Rapporteur's interim report. Since the submission of his last report, the Special Rapporteur had sent 65 communications (including two urgent appeals) to 49 States. The report contained summaries of his communications and the replies received.

Regarding the compendium of national enactments relating to freedom of religion and belief, 49 States had replied to the Special Rapporteur's requests to provide the text of constitutions or equivalent texts, legislation and regulations governing religious freedom and public worship. He recommended that research should be conducted on the status of women with regard to religion and human rights; proselytism, freedom of religion and poverty; and sects, new religious movements and communities of religion and belief and human rights. Referring to a questionnaire he had sent in 1994 to States on issues relating to freedom of religion and belief in primary and secondary schools [YUN 1995, p. 731], the Special Rapporteur stated that 77 States had replied, making it possible to formulate an international education strategy to combat intolerance and discrimination based on religion and belief. Lack of resources had delayed the analysis of replies. He had drawn up a plan to finalize the analysis by November 2001, the twentieth anniversary of the adoption of the 1981 Declaration. An international consultative conference would be held in November 2001 on the content of curricula and textbooks at institutions of primary or basic and secondary education relating to freedom of religion and belief. The Special Rapporteur described the initiatives of the Commission, States and NGOs.

Communications in 1999 revealed an increase in religious extremism, the continued existence of policies adversely affecting freedom of religion and belief and the persistence of discrimination against women. Religious extremism, the Special Rapporteur stressed, spared no society and no religion, and its most common victims were minorities and women. The report described where and by whom religious extremism and related policies were carried out.

The Special Rapporteur visited Turkey (30 November-9 December) [A/55/280/Add.1], where he examined legislation and policies relating to freedom of religion and beliefs, and the situation of the non-Muslim communities. He noted that Turkey's legislation, particularly its constitutional legislation, provided absolute guarantees of freedom of religion and belief and protected its manifestations, while imposing certain limitations. Those limitations were so vaguely worded as to lend themselves to very broad interpretation, which might lead to State intervention and excessive restrictions. The Special Rapporteur recommended the use of precise terminology and interpretation consistent with international human rights standards and with the jurisprudence of the Commission on Human Rights. While the constitution enshrined the principle of secularism in relations between the State and religion, secularism was apparently compromised by the optional mention of religion on identity cards and by compulsory religious and ethics instruction. Despite the proclaimed secular nature of the State, the treatment of Islam in Turkey tended to give a quasi-official status to Hanafi Islam.

The Special Rapporteur recommended that the authorities take steps to make education a vehicle for promoting human rights and building a culture of tolerance.

There had been violations against Muslim communities and non-Muslim minorities, arising mainly from a narrow interpretation and application of the principle of nationalism in the form of Turkization, which was not always compatible with the right to tolerance and to non-discrimination. The Special Rapporteur recommended that the authorities establish a principle whereby nationalism was not used against minority religious communities. The Criminal Code punished any attack on religion and religious manifestations and a law on public service and another on national education enshrined the constitutional principle of equal access to the public service and to national education, while a media law sought to ban any act of blasphemy. Other legislation, however, raised serious questions, such as a law permitting the authorities to reject any given or family name considered contrary to the national culture, which would appear to reflect limitations and bias against minority communities, inspired by a policy of Turkization. The Special Rapporteur recommended revision of the law on names.

Non-Muslims, with the exception of the Jewish minority, suffered as a result of State policies on secularism and nationalism. Representatives of the Christian, Greek Orthodox and Armenian (Orthodox, Catholic and Protestant) minorities said that they enjoyed freedom of religion and worship but that they faced problems affecting the religious affairs of their community. The Greek Orthodox community was slowly disappearing owing to Turkey's policy limiting the citizenship status of Orthodox Greeks. As to the Armenian minority, its position appeared fragile, despite the fact that numerically it was the most important Christian community. The Jewish minority insisted that its situation was satisfactory, explained in large part by the fact that, in contrast to the Armenians and the Greeks, the Jews had made no claim to lands in Turkey, and also by the close relations between Turkey and Israel. The Syriacs and the entire Assyro-Chaldean community were not recognized as a distinct religious and cultural community and seemed to be gradually disappearing. The impact of the armed conflict between the Turkish authorities and Kurdish insurrectionists had placed the community in a climate of constant fear from acts of terrorism and had provoked their massive departure from south-eastern Turkey. The Special Rapporteur made a series of recommendations regarding the Christian, Greek Orthodox and

Armenian minorities and general recommendations applicable to all religious communities in Turkey.

GENERAL ASSEMBLY ACTION

On 17 December [meeting 83], the General Assembly, on the recommendation of the Third Committee [A/54/605/Add.2], adopted **resolution 54/159** without vote [agenda item 116 *(b)*].

Elimination of all forms of religious intolerance

The General Assembly,

Recalling that all States have pledged themselves, under the Charter of the United Nations, to promote and encourage universal respect for and observance of human rights and fundamental freedoms for all without distinction as to race, sex, language or religion,

Reaffirming that discrimination against human beings on the grounds of religion or belief constitutes an affront to human dignity and a disavowal of the principles of the Charter,

Recalling article 18 of the Universal Declaration of Human Rights, and article 18 of the International Covenant on Civil and Political Rights,

Reaffirming its resolution 36/55 of 25 November 1981, by which it proclaimed the Declaration on the Elimination of All Forms of Intolerance and of Discrimination Based on Religion or Belief,

Emphasizing that the right to freedom of thought, conscience, religion and belief is far-reaching and profound and that it encompasses freedom of thought on all matters, personal conviction and the commitment to religion or belief, whether manifested individually or in community with others,

Reaffirming the call of the World Conference on Human Rights, held at Vienna from 14 to 25 June 1993, for all Governments to take all appropriate measures in compliance with their international obligations and with due regard to their respective legal systems to counter intolerance and related violence based on religion or belief, including practices of discrimination against women and the desecration of religious sites, recognizing that every individual has the right to freedom of thought, conscience, expression and religion,

Calling upon all Governments to cooperate with the Special Rapporteur of the Commission on Human Rights on religious intolerance to enable him to carry out his mandate fully,

Alarmed that serious instances of intolerance and discrimination on the grounds of religion or belief, including acts of violence, intimidation and coercion motivated by religious intolerance, occur in many parts of the world and threaten the enjoyment of human rights and fundamental freedoms,

Deeply concerned that, as reported by the Special Rapporteur, the rights violated on religious grounds include the right to life, the right to physical integrity and to liberty and security of person, the right to freedom of expression, the right not to be subjected to torture or other cruel, inhuman or degrading treatment or punishment and the right not to be arbitrarily arrested or detained,

Believing that further efforts are therefore required to promote and protect the right to freedom of thought, conscience, religion and belief and to eliminate all forms of hatred, intolerance and discrimination based on religion or belief,

1. *Reaffirms* that freedom of thought, conscience, religion and belief is a human right derived from the inherent dignity of the human person and guaranteed to all without discrimination;

2. *Urges* States to ensure that their constitutional and legal systems provide effective guarantees of freedom of thought, conscience, religion and belief, including the provision of effective remedies in cases where the right to freedom of religion or belief is violated;

3. *Also urges* States to ensure, in particular, that no one within their jurisdiction is, because of his or her religion or belief, deprived of the right to life or the right to liberty and security of person or subjected to torture or arbitrary arrest or detention;

4. *Further urges* States, in conformity with international standards of human rights, to take all necessary action to prevent such instances, to take all appropriate measures to combat hatred, intolerance and acts of violence, intimidation and coercion motivated by religious intolerance and to encourage, through the educational system and by other means, understanding, tolerance and respect in matters relating to freedom of religion or belief;

5. *Recognizes* that legislation alone is not enough to prevent violations of human rights, including the right to freedom of religion or belief;

6. *Emphasizes* that, as underlined by the Human Rights Committee, restrictions on the freedom to manifest religion or belief are permitted only if limitations are prescribed by law, are necessary to protect public safety, order, health or morals, or the fundamental rights and freedoms of others, and are applied in a manner that does not vitiate the right to freedom of thought, conscience and religion;

7. *Urges* States to ensure that, in the course of their official duties, members of law enforcement bodies, civil servants, educators and other public officials respect different religions and beliefs and do not discriminate against persons professing other religions or beliefs;

8. *Calls upon* all States to recognize, as provided for in the Declaration on the Elimination of All Forms of Intolerance and of Discrimination Based on Religion or Belief, the right of all persons to worship or assemble in connection with a religion or belief and to establish and maintain places for those purposes;

9. *Expresses its grave concern* at any attack upon religious places, sites and shrines, and calls upon all States, in accordance with their national legislation and in conformity with international human rights standards, to exert the utmost efforts to ensure that such places, sites and shrines are fully respected and protected;

10. *Recognizes* that the exercise of tolerance and non-discrimination by persons and groups is necessary for the full realization of the aims of the Declaration;

11. *Takes note with appreciation* of the interim report of the Special Rapporteur of the Commission on Human Rights on religious intolerance, who was appointed to examine incidents and governmental actions in all parts of the world that are incompatible with the provisions of the Declaration and to recommend remedial measures as appropriate, and encourages

the continued efforts on the part of the Special Rapporteur;

12. *Notes* the request by the Special Rapporteur that his title be changed from Special Rapporteur on religious intolerance to Special Rapporteur on freedom of religion or belief, which will be considered further by the Commission on Human Rights at its fifty-sixth session;

13. *Encourages* the Special Rapporteur to contribute effectively to the preparatory process for the World Conference against Racism, Racial Discrimination, Xenophobia and Related Intolerance to be held in 2001 by transmitting to the United Nations High Commissioner for Human Rights his recommendations on religious intolerance which have a bearing on the Conference;

14. *Encourages* Governments to give serious consideration to inviting the Special Rapporteur to visit their countries so as to enable him to fulfil his mandate even more effectively;

15. *Also encourages* Governments, when seeking the assistance of the United Nations Programme of Advisory Services and Technical Assistance in the Field of Human Rights, to consider, where appropriate, including requests for assistance in the field of the promotion and protection of the right to freedom of thought, conscience and religion;

16. *Welcomes and encourages* the continuing efforts of non-governmental organizations and religious bodies and groups to promote the implementation and dissemination of the Declaration;

17. *Requests* the Commission on Human Rights to continue its consideration of measures to implement the Declaration;

18. *Requests* the Special Rapporteur to submit an interim report to the General Assembly at its fifty-fifth session;

19. *Requests* the Secretary-General to ensure that the Special Rapporteur receives the necessary resources to enable him fully to discharge his mandate;

20. *Decides* to consider the question of the elimination of all forms of religious intolerance at its fifty-fifth session, under the item entitled "Human rights questions".

Civil and political rights

Right to self-determination

Pursuant to General Assembly resolution 53/134 [YUN 1998, p. 658], the Secretary-General, in September [A/54/327], summarized action taken by the Commission on Human Rights on the right of peoples to self-determination.

GENERAL ASSEMBLY ACTION

On 17 December [meeting 83], the General Assembly, on the recommendation of the Third Committee [A/54/604], adopted **resolution 54/155** without vote [agenda item 115].

Universal realization of the right of peoples to self-determination

The General Assembly,

Reaffirming the importance, for the effective guarantee and observance of human rights, of the universal realization of the right of peoples to self-determination enshrined in the Charter of the United Nations and embodied in the International Covenants on Human Rights, as well as in the Declaration on the Granting of Independence to Colonial Countries and Peoples contained in General Assembly resolution 1514(XV) of 14 December 1960,

Welcoming the progressive exercise of the right to self-determination by peoples under colonial, foreign or alien occupation and their emergence into sovereign statehood and independence,

Deeply concerned at the continuation of acts or threats of foreign military intervention and occupation that are threatening to suppress, or have already suppressed, the right to self-determination of sovereign peoples and nations,

Expressing grave concern that, as a consequence of the persistence of such actions, millions of people have been and are being uprooted from their homes as refugees and displaced persons, and emphasizing the urgent need for concerted international action to alleviate their condition,

Recalling the relevant resolutions regarding the violation of the right of peoples to self-determination and other human rights as a result of foreign military intervention, aggression and occupation adopted by the Commission on Human Rights at its thirty-sixth, thirty-seventh, thirty-eighth, thirty-ninth, fortieth, forty-first, forty-second, forty-third, forty-fourth, forty-fifth, forty-sixth, forty-seventh, forty-eighth, forty-ninth, fiftieth, fifty-first, fifty-second, fifty-third, fifty-fourth and fifty-fifth sessions,

Reaffirming its resolutions 35/35 B of 14 November 1980, 36/10 of 28 October 1981, 37/42 of 3 December 1982, 38/16 of 22 November 1983, 39/18 of 23 November 1984, 40/24 of 29 November 1985, 41/100 of 4 December 1986, 42/94 of 7 December 1987, 43/105 of 8 December 1988, 44/80 of 8 December 1989, 45/131 of 14 December 1990, 46/88 of 16 December 1991, 47/83 of 16 December 1992, 48/93 of 20 December 1993, 49/148 of 23 December 1994, 50/139 of 21 December 1995, 51/84 of 12 December 1996, 52/113 of 12 December 1997 and 53/134 of 9 December 1998,

Taking note of the report of the Secretary-General on the right of peoples to self-determination,

1. *Reaffirms* that the universal realization of the right of all peoples, including those under colonial, foreign and alien domination, to self-determination is a fundamental condition for the effective guarantee and observance of human rights and for the preservation and promotion of such rights;

2. *Declares its firm opposition* to acts of foreign military intervention, aggression and occupation, since these have resulted in the suppression of the right of peoples to self-determination and other human rights in certain parts of the world;

3. *Calls upon* those States responsible to cease immediately their military intervention in and occupation of foreign countries and territories and all acts of repression, discrimination, exploitation and maltreatment, in particular the brutal and inhuman methods report-

edly employed for the execution of those acts against the peoples concerned;

4. *Deplores* the plight of the millions of refugees and displaced persons who have been uprooted as a result of the aforementioned acts, and reaffirms their right to return to their homes voluntarily in safety and honour;

5. *Requests* the Commission on Human Rights to continue to give special attention to the violation of human rights, especially the right to self-determination, resulting from foreign military intervention, aggression or occupation;

6. *Requests* the Secretary-General to report on this question to the General Assembly at its fifty-fifth session under the item entitled "Right of peoples to self-determination".

Rights of Palestinians

On 27 April [res. 1999/55], the Commission, by a roll-call vote of 44 to 1, with 8 abstentions, reaffirmed the unqualified Palestinian right to self-determination, including the option of a State. It called on the Secretary-General to transmit its resolution to Israel and all other Governments, to distribute it as widely as possible, and to make available to the Commission, prior to its 2000 session, information pertaining to its implementation by the Government of Israel.

The Commission considered a report of the Secretary-General [E/CN.4/1999/10], which stated that he had received no reply to his request to Israel for information on implementation of its 1998 resolution on the situation in occupied Palestine [YUN 1998, p. 659].

GENERAL ASSEMBLY ACTION

On 17 December [meeting 83], the General Assembly, on the recommendation of the Third Committee [A/54/604], adopted **resolution 54/152** by recorded vote (156-2-1) [agenda item 115].

The right of the Palestinian people to self-determination

The General Assembly,

Aware that the development of friendly relations among nations, based on respect for the principle of equal rights and self-determination of peoples, is among the purposes and principles of the United Nations, as defined in the Charter,

Recalling the International Covenants on Human Rights, the Universal Declaration of Human Rights, the Declaration on the Granting of Independence to Colonial Countries and Peoples and the Vienna Declaration and Programme of Action adopted by the World Conference on Human Rights on 25 June 1993,

Recalling also the Declaration on the Occasion of the Fiftieth Anniversary of the United Nations,

Expressing hope for rapid progress in the peace process and the achievement of a final settlement between the Palestinian and Israeli sides by the agreed time of September 2000,

Affirming the right of all States in the region to live in peace within secure and internationally recognized borders,

1. *Reaffirms* the right of the Palestinian people to self-determination, including the option of a State;

2. *Expresses the hope* that the Palestinian people will soon be exercising their right to self-determination, which is not subject to any veto, in the current peace process;

3. *Urges* all States and the specialized agencies and the organizations of the United Nations system to continue to support and assist the Palestinian people in their quest for self-determination.

RECORDED VOTE ON RESOLUTION 54/152:

In favour: Afghanistan, Albania, Algeria, Andorra, Angola, Antigua and Barbuda, Argentina, Armenia, Australia, Austria, Azerbaijan, Bahamas, Bahrain, Bangladesh, Barbados, Belarus, Belgium, Belize, Benin, Bhutan, Bolivia, Bosnia and Herzegovina, Botswana, Brazil, Brunei Darussalam, Bulgaria, Burkina Faso, Cambodia, Cameroon, Canada, Cape Verde, Chad, Chile, China, Colombia, Comoros, Congo, Costa Rica, Côte d'Ivoire, Croatia, Cuba, Cyprus, Czech Republic, Democratic People's Republic of Korea, Democratic Republic of the Congo, Denmark, Djibouti, Dominica, Ecuador, Egypt, El Salvador, Eritrea, Estonia, Ethiopia, Finland, France, Gabon, Germany, Ghana, Greece, Grenada, Guinea, Guinea-Bissau, Guyana, Haiti, Honduras, Hungary, Iceland, India, Indonesia, Iran, Ireland, Italy, Jamaica, Japan, Jordan, Kazakhstan, Kenya, Kuwait, Lao People's Democratic Republic, Latvia, Lebanon, Libyan Arab Jamahiriya, Liechtenstein, Lithuania, Luxembourg, Malawi, Malaysia, Maldives, Mali, Malta, Mauritius, Mexico, Monaco, Mongolia, Morocco, Mozambique, Myanmar, Namibia, Nepal, Netherlands, New Zealand, Nigeria, Norway, Oman, Pakistan, Panama, Papua New Guinea, Paraguay, Peru, Philippines, Poland, Portugal, Qatar, Republic of Korea, Republic of Moldova, Romania, Russian Federation, Saint Lucia, Samoa, San Marino, Saudi Arabia, Senegal, Seychelles, Sierra Leone, Singapore, Slovakia, Slovenia, Solomon Islands, South Africa, Spain, Sri Lanka, Sudan, Suriname, Swaziland, Sweden, Syrian Arab Republic, Tajikistan, Thailand, The former Yugoslav Republic of Macedonia, Togo, Trinidad and Tobago, Tunisia, Turkey, Uganda, Ukraine, United Arab Emirates, United Kingdom, United Republic of Tanzania, Uruguay, Uzbekistan, Venezuela, Viet Nam, Yemen, Zambia, Zimbabwe.

Against: Israel, United States.

Abstaining: Georgia.

Western Sahara

On 23 April [res. 1999/4], the Commission, noting with satisfaction the agreements on the settlement plan reached between Morocco and the Frente Popular para la Liberación de Saguia el-Hamra y de Río de Oro, called on the two parties to cooperate fully with the Secretary-General, his Personal Envoy and his Special Representative in implementing the plan. It expressed support for further efforts of the Secretary-General for the organization and supervision by the United Nations, in cooperation with the Organization of African Unity, of a referendum for self-determination of the people of Western Sahara (see p. 176).

Mercenaries

Commission action. On 23 April [res. 1999/3], the Commission, by a roll-call vote of 35 to 12, with 6 abstentions, urged States to take legislative measures to ensure that their territories and those under their control were not used for the recruitment, assembly, financing, training and transit of mercenaries to plan activities designed to impede the right to self-determination. It called on States that had not done so to consider signing or ratifying the 1989 International Convention against the Recruitment, Use, Financing and Training of Mercenaries, adopted by the General Assembly in resolution 44/34 [YUN 1989, p. 825]. The Commission asked the Special Rapporteur to report in 2000 and the Secretary-General to invite Governments to make proposals towards a clearer legal definition of mercenaries. OHCHR was asked to publicize the adverse effects of mercenary activities on the right to self-determination and, when requested, to render advisory services to States that were so affected.

Reports of Special Rapporteur. Pursuant to General Assembly resolution 53/135 [YUN 1998, p. 661], the Secretary-General, in September [A/54/326], transmitted a report by the Special Rapporteur on the question of the use of mercenaries, Enrique Bernales Ballesteros (Peru).

The Special Rapporteur visited the United Kingdom (25-30 January), at the invitation of the Government. Meetings with high-level government officials, academic institutions, NGOs and individuals resulted in a concurrence of opinion on the treatment of mercenary activities, on the assessment of situations, and on procedures for better regulation of private companies offering security services and military assistance and advice.

Mercenary activities continued to be carried out through traditional recruitment and had taken on new forms, such as recruitment and hiring by private companies offering security services and military assistance and advice, and their hiring in turn by Governments to provide security, to maintain public order and safety and to engage in armed combat against rebel forces or organized crime. The growing tendency of such companies to hire mercenaries constituted a threat to the international human rights protection system. As recruitment and hiring had become more businesslike, the number of mercenaries had increased. The Special Rapporteur observed that the international rules to deal with and punish mercenary activities were inadequate. He made recommendations for action by the General Assembly.

In December [E/CN.4/2000/14 & Corr.1], the Special Rapporteur reported on his visit to Cuba (12-17 September), made at the invitation of the Government. He stated that the visit enabled him to confirm that attacks had been carried out on hotels and tourist facilities in Havana in 1997, that the attacks had been carried out by foreigners for financial gain and that the persons concerned had been recruited, trained, hired and funded by third parties of Cuban origin acting outside the country. He concluded that the attacks were designed to inflict high-profile damage on tourist flows to Cuba, thereby flouting the fundamental rights of the Cuban people and basic principles of international law. The Special Rapporteur recommended that the Commission condemn the incident in Cuba and recommend that judicial proceedings be initiated in each country whose territory had been used unlawfully. In more general recommendations, he called on the Commission to remind OHCHR of the need to carry out studies and disseminate information on the adverse effects of mercenary activities; suggest that Member States be extremely careful in their dealings with private military security companies; and, given the gaps in legislation that facilitated the use of mercenaries, reiterate its call to Member States to ratify or accede to the 1989 Convention. He also suggested that Member States should consider international and domestic rules on military security.

International Convention

As at 31 December, the International Convention against the Recruitment, Use, Financing and Training of Mercenaries had been ratified or acceded to by 19 States and had a total of 16 signatories. The Convention was to enter into force on the thirtieth day following the date of deposit with the Secretary-General of the twenty-second instrument of ratification or accession.

GENERAL ASSEMBLY ACTION

On 17 December [meeting 83], the General Assembly, on the recommendation of the Third Committee [A/54/604], adopted **resolution 54/151** by recorded vote (110-16-35) [agenda item 115].

Use of mercenaries as a means of violating human rights and impeding the exercise of the right of peoples to self-determination

The General Assembly,

Recalling its resolution 53/135 of 9 December 1998, and taking note of Commission on Human Rights resolution 1999/3 of 23 April 1999,

Recalling also all of its relevant resolutions, in which, inter alia, it condemned any State that permitted or tolerated the recruitment, financing, training, assembly, transit and use of mercenaries with the objective of overthrowing the Governments of States Members of the United Nations, especially those of developing countries, and recalling further the relevant resolutions of the Security Council and the Organization of African Unity,

Reaffirming the purposes and principles enshrined in the Charter of the United Nations concerning the strict observance of the principles of sovereign equality, political independence, the territorial integrity of States, the non-use of force or of the threat of use of force in international relations and the self-determination of peoples,

Reaffirming also that, by virtue of the principle of self-determination, as developed in the Declaration on

Principles of International Law concerning Friendly Relations and Cooperation among States in accordance with the Charter of the United Nations, all peoples have the right freely to determine, without external interference, their political status and to pursue their economic, social and cultural development and every State has the duty to respect this right in accordance with the provisions of the Charter,

Recognizing that mercenary activities continue to increase in many parts of the world and take on new forms, permitting mercenaries to operate in a better organized way, with increased pay, and that their numbers have grown and more persons are prepared to become mercenaries,

Alarmed and concerned about the danger that the activities of mercenaries constitute to peace and security in developing countries, in particular in Africa and in small States, and also elsewhere,

Deeply concerned about the loss of life, the substantial damage to property and the negative effects on the policy and economies of affected countries resulting from mercenary aggression and criminal activities,

Convinced that it is necessary for Member States to ratify the International Convention against the Recruitment, Use, Financing and Training of Mercenaries adopted by the General Assembly on 4 December 1989 and to develop and maintain international cooperation among States for the prevention, prosecution and punishment of mercenary activities,

Convinced also that, notwithstanding the way in which mercenaries or mercenary-related activities are used or the form they take to acquire some semblance of legitimacy, they are a threat to peace, security and the self-determination of peoples and an obstacle to the enjoyment of human rights by peoples,

1. *Takes note* of the report of the Special Rapporteur of the Commission on Human Rights on the question of the use of mercenaries as a means of violating human rights and impeding the exercise of the right of peoples to self-determination;

2. *Reaffirms* that the recruitment, use, financing and training of mercenaries are causes for grave concern to all States and violate the purposes and principles enshrined in the Charter of the United Nations;

3. *Recognizes* that armed conflict, terrorism, arms trafficking and covert operations by third Powers, inter alia, encourage the demand for mercenaries on the global market;

4. *Urges* all States to take the necessary steps and to exercise the utmost vigilance against the menace posed by the activities of mercenaries and to take the necessary legislative measures to ensure that their territories and other territories under their control, as well as their nationals, are not used for the recruitment, assembly, financing, training and transit of mercenaries for the planning of activities designed to destabilize or overthrow the Government of any State or threaten the territorial integrity and political unity of sovereign States, or to promote secession or to fight the national liberation movements struggling against colonial or other forms of alien domination or occupation;

5. *Calls upon* all States that have not yet done so to consider taking the necessary action to sign or to ratify the International Convention against the Recruitment, Use, Financing and Training of Mercenaries;

6. *Welcomes* the cooperation extended by those countries that have invited the Special Rapporteur;

7. *Also welcomes* the adoption by some States of national legislation that restricts the recruitment, assembly, financing, training and transit of mercenaries;

8. *Invites* States to investigate the possibility of mercenary involvement whenever criminal acts of a terrorist nature occur;

9. *Requests* the Secretary-General to provide the Special Rapporteur with all the necessary assistance, both professional and financial;

10. *Urges* all States to cooperate fully with the Special Rapporteur in the fulfilment of his mandate;

11. *Requests* the Office of the United Nations High Commissioner for Human Rights, as a matter of priority to be programmed in its immediate activities, to publicize the adverse effects of the activities of mercenaries on the right to self-determination and, when requested and where necessary, to render advisory services to States that are affected by the activities of mercenaries;

12. *Requests* the Secretary-General to invite Governments to make proposals towards a clearer legal definition of mercenaries, and, in this regard, requests the United Nations High Commissioner for Human Rights to convene expert meetings, as requested in previous General Assembly resolutions, to study and update the international legislation in force and to propose recommendations for a clearer legal definition of mercenaries that would allow for more efficient prevention and punishment of mercenary activities;

13. *Requests* the Special Rapporteur to report his findings on the use of mercenaries to undermine the right of peoples to self-determination, with specific recommendations, to the General Assembly at its fifty-fifth session;

14. *Decides* to consider at its fifty-fifth session the question of the use of mercenaries as a means of violating human rights and impeding the exercise of the right of peoples to self-determination under the item entitled "Right of peoples to self-determination".

RECORDED VOTE ON RESOLUTION 54/151:

In favour: Afghanistan, Algeria, Angola, Antigua and Barbuda, Argentina, Armenia, Azerbaijan, Bahamas, Bahrain, Bangladesh, Barbados, Belarus, Belize, Benin, Bhutan, Bolivia, Botswana, Brazil, Brunei Darussalam, Burkina Faso, Cambodia, Cameroon, Cape Verde, Chad, Chile, China, Colombia, Comoros, Costa Rica, Côte d'Ivoire, Cuba, Democratic People's Republic of Korea, Democratic Republic of the Congo, Djibouti, Dominica, Dominican Republic, Ecuador, Egypt, El Salvador, Eritrea, Ethiopia, Fiji, Gabon, Ghana, Grenada, Guinea, Guinea-Bissau, Guyana, Haiti, Honduras, India, Indonesia, Iran, Jamaica, Jordan, Kenya, Kuwait, Lao People's Democratic Republic, Lebanon, Libyan Arab Jamahiriya, Malawi, Malaysia, Maldives, Mali, Mauritius, Mexico, Mongolia, Morocco, Mozambique, Myanmar, Namibia, Nepal, Nicaragua, Nigeria, Oman, Pakistan, Panama, Papua New Guinea, Paraguay, Peru, Philippines, Qatar, Russian Federation, Saint Lucia, Samoa, Saudi Arabia, Senegal, Seychelles, Sierra Leone, Singapore, Solomon Islands, Sri Lanka, Sudan, Suriname, Swaziland, Syrian Arab Republic, Tajikistan, Thailand, Togo, Trinidad and Tobago, Tunisia, Turkey, United Arab Emirates, United Republic of Tanzania, Uruguay, Venezuela, Viet Nam, Yemen, Zambia, Zimbabwe.

Against: Belgium, Canada, Denmark, Finland, Georgia, Germany, Hungary, Iceland, Japan, Luxembourg, Micronesia, Netherlands, Norway, Sweden, United Kingdom, United States.

Abstaining: Albania, Andorra, Australia, Austria, Bosnia and Herzegovina, Bulgaria, Croatia, Cyprus, Czech Republic, Estonia, France, Greece, Ireland, Israel, Italy, Kazakhstan, Latvia, Liechtenstein, Lithuania, Malta, Marshall Islands, Monaco, New Zealand, Poland, Portugal, Republic of Korea, Republic of Moldova, Romania, San Marino, Slovakia, Slovenia, Spain, The former Yugoslav Republic of Macedonia, Ukraine, Uzbekistan.

Administration of justice

Although the Subcommission decided on 3 August [dec. 1999/103] not to establish a sessional working group on the administration of justice in 1999, papers were submitted in accordance with a 1998 Subcommission request [YUN 1998, p. 663]. A paper by Héctor Fix-Zamudio (Mexico) on the improvement and efficiency of the judicial instruments for the protection of human rights examined domestic instruments, notably *amparo* and habeas corpus, and analysed the impact of domestic legislation in the international sphere. Miguel Alfonso Martínez (Cuba) noted that an increasing trend towards the privatization of prisons could be identified in countries other than the United States. In a paper on the evolution of capital punishment, El Hadji Guissé (Senegal) stated that apart from Europe, where the use of the death penalty had diminished, not much progress had been made in abolishing the death penalty elsewhere.

Pursuant to a 1998 Subcommission request [YUN 1998, p. 662], the Secretary-General, in a January note [E/CN.4/1999/111], transmitted to the Commission the text of the draft international convention on the protection of all persons from enforced disappearance, as well as the comments thereon of the Subcommission and the sessional working group on the administration of justice. On 26 August [res. 1999/24], the Subcommission urged the Commission to give priority consideration to the draft convention.

Compensation for victims

Report of Secretary-General. Pursuant to a 1997 Commission request [YUN 1997, p. 650], the Secretary-General stated, in a January note [E/CN.4/1999/53], that he had received additional replies from Governments regarding legislation they had adopted or were in the process of adopting relating to the right to restitution, compensation and rehabilitation for victims of grave violations of human rights and fundamental freedoms. The replies were submitted to the independent expert on the right and their full texts were in the files of the Secretariat.

Report of independent expert. As requested by the Commission in 1998 [YUN 1998, p. 663], the independent expert on the right to restitution, compensation and rehabilitation for victims of grave violations of human rights and fundamental freedoms, M. Cherif Bassiouni (Egypt/United States), submitted a February report [E/CN.4/1999/65] in which he laid the groundwork for a revised version of the basic principles and guidelines on the right. He analysed previous versions of the guidelines proposed in 1993 [YUN 1993, p. 962], 1996 [YUN 1996, p. 623] and 1997 [YUN 1997, p. 649]. Based on the proposed guidelines, the 1985 Declaration of Basic Principles of Justice for Victims of Crime and Abuse of Power, contained in General Assembly resolution 40/34 [YUN 1985, p. 742], and the Statute of the International Criminal Court [YUN 1998, p. 1209], as well as the views of Governments, the expert observed that some areas needed clarification before a revised version could be prepared.

Commission action. On 26 April [res. 1999/33], the Commission asked the Secretary-General to invite States, intergovernmental organizations and NGOs to collaborate with the independent expert. The expert was asked to complete his work and submit to the Commission in 2000 a revised version of the basic principles and guidelines prepared in 1997, taking into account the views of States, intergovernmental organizations and NGOs.

Rule of law

On 28 April [res. 1999/74], the Commission, noting that the OHCHR programme of advisory services and technical cooperation did not have sufficient funds to provide substantial financial assistance to national projects on the realization of human rights and the maintenance of the rule of law in countries that were committed to those ends, but which faced economic hardship, welcomed the cooperation between OHCHR and the UN system, particularly between the United Nations Development Programme and OHCHR in providing technical assistance in the promotion of the rule of law. The High Commissioner was encouraged to pursue consultations with the UN system aimed at enhancing inter-agency cooperation in providing assistance for that purpose, as well as to explore support from financial institutions. She was asked to accord high priority to OHCHR technical cooperation activities regarding the rule of law.

(See p. 582 for further information on OHCHR technical cooperation activities.)

State of siege or emergency

As requested by the Commission in 1998 [YUN 1998, p. 664], OHCHR submitted, in July [E/CN.4/Sub.2/1999/31], a list of countries or territories in which a state of emergency had been proclaimed before June 1997 and extended thereafter. OHCHR stated that it had encountered difficulties in obtaining information on the imposition of states of emergency in countries not parties to the 1966 International Covenant on Civil and Political Rights, adopted by the General Assembly in resolution 2200 A (XXI) [YUN 1966, p. 423], and therefore had no obligation to notify the Secretary-General of such imposition. Furthermore, information could not be easily obtained on de facto states of emergency where various security laws and measures were imposed. In order to understand the implications of the proclamation, extension and termination of states of emergency for human rights, an analysis of legal instruments and States' practices affecting human rights and fundamental freedoms during states of emergency was essential. For those reasons, the list was not complete or comprehensive.

Humanitarian standards

The Commission considered a report of the Secretary-General [E/CN.4/1999/92] containing information received from Governments, UN bodies and NGOs on issues identified in his 1998 report on fundamental standards of humanity [YUN 1998, p. 664].

The Secretary-General stressed that fundamental standards of humanity were intended to ensure the protection of human beings at all times and in all circumstances, especially during international armed conflict and internal violence. Further means to ensure adequate protection of victims of abuses during situations of internal violence might be required, such as improved implementation of international law, better dissemination of information pertaining to existing human rights standards and humanitarian principles, and education and training programmes in international law.

Commission action. On 28 April [res. 1999/65], the Commission invited Governments, UN bodies, the human rights treaty bodies, mechanisms of the Commission, intergovernmental and regional organizations, the International Committee of the Red Cross (ICRC) and NGOs to comment on the Secretary-General's report, as well as on his 1998 report. The Secretary-General was requested to report in 2000 on fundamental standards of humanity.

Arbitrary detention

Commission action. On 26 April [res. 1999/37], the Commission, requesting the Governments concerned to take account of the views of the Working Group on Arbitrary Detention and to take steps to remedy the situation of persons arbitrarily deprived of their liberty, encouraged them to pay attention to the Group's recommendations and to ensure that their legislation was in conformity with the relevant international standards and legal instruments. Those Governments were requested to give attention to the Working Group's urgent appeals on a humanitarian basis. The Secretary-General was asked to assist Governments, special rapporteurs and working groups, with a view to ensuring observance of the guarantees on states of emergency embodied in international instruments. The Commission asked the Working Group to report in 2000.

Working Group activities. The Working Group on Arbitrary Detention held its twenty-fourth (17-21 May), twenty-fifth (13-17 September) and twenty-sixth (24 November-3 December) sessions in 1999 in Geneva [E/CN.4/2000/4]. During the year, the Working Group transmitted 30 communications concerning 116 new cases of alleged arbitrary detention to 19 Governments, of which 10 had provided information. The alleged cases were based on information submitted to the Group by NGOs and private sources. In 1999, the Group adopted 36 opinions regarding 115 persons in 24 countries. A description of the cases and the contents of the Governments' replies, as well as the complete text of 23 of the opinions, were contained in a separate report [E/CN.4/2000/4/Add.1]. The Group transmitted 101 urgent actions concerning 580 individuals to 39 Governments and to the Palestinian Authority. Of the 101 urgent actions, 56 appeals were issued by the Group jointly with other special rapporteurs. Replies to the appeals were received from 18 Governments.

The Group drew attention to the lack of protection for human rights defenders, who had become targets for repressive measures. In that regard, it urged States to implement the 1998 Declaration on the Right and Responsibility of Individuals, Groups and Organs of Society to Promote and Protect Universally Recognized Human Rights and Fundamental Freedoms, adopted by the General Assembly in resolution 53/144 [YUN 1998, p. 608]. It recommended that States make moderate use of so-called states of emergency.

The Working Group visited Indonesia (31 January–12 February) [E/CN.4/2000/4/Add.2], at the invitation of the Government, and was granted uninhibited access to detention facilities in Jakarta, Denpasar (Bali) and East Timor. The Group observed positive measures, such as the release of many political prisoners, notably those belonging to the former Indonesian Communist Party, decreased use of legislation that facilitated arbitrary deprivation of liberty, and the elimination of prolonged detention for political motives. On the other hand, the incidence of violence accompanying repressive activities had hardly diminished. Arrests were characterized by flaws that resulted in detentions being arbitrary. The majority of the situations were the responsibility of the former regime, while others resulted from deficiencies in legislation and from deficiencies of the authorities applying the law. The Working Group encouraged the Government to ratify international human rights instruments and recommended releasing political prisoners; separating the police from the armed forces; placing the judiciary under the authority of the Supreme Court instead of the Ministry of Justice in order to guarantee their independence; intensifying information and education efforts; reforming the Code of Criminal Procedure so that a detainee was presented before a judge promptly and in person; creating a central detention register; guaranteeing the independence of the National Commission for Human Rights; abrogating emergency laws and measures and replacing them with a legal system to be applied in times of national crisis; limiting the competence of military tribunals; and informing detained individuals of their rights and providing legal representation where needed.

(For further information on the human rights situation in East Timor and the Commission's special session held in that regard, see next chapter.)

Impunity

Report of Secretary-General. In January [E/CN.4/1999/57], the Secretary-General presented the views of Governments, UN agencies and programmes and NGOs on a report of the Special Rapporteur on the question of the impunity of perpetrators of violations of human rights (civil and political) and the revised set of principles for the protection of human rights through action to combat impunity annexed thereto [YUN 1997, p. 655], and information on steps they had taken to combat impunity and on remedies available to victims of human rights violations.

Commission action. On 26 April [res. 1999/34], the Commission asked all other States, international organizations and NGOs to provide the Secretary-General with their views on the Special Rapporteur's report, and asked the Secretary-General to provide information on steps they had taken to combat impunity for human rights violations and on remedies for victims. The Secretary-General was also asked to report in 2000. Special rapporteurs and other mechanisms of the Commission were invited to consider the issue of impunity in discharging their mandates.

On 28 April [res. 1999/58], by a roll-call vote of 21 to 9, with 22 abstentions, the Commission asked the Secretary-General to disseminate the final report of the Special Rapporteur on the question of impunity of perpetrators of violations of economic, social and cultural rights [YUN 1997, p. 655], and to invite States, intergovernmental organizations and NGOs to provide him with their views thereon. The Secretary-General was asked to report in 2000.

Independence of the judicial system

Reports of Special Rapporteur. In January, the Special Rapporteur on the independence of judges and lawyers, Param Cumaraswamy (Malaysia), submitted his annual report covering his activities in 1998 [E/CN.4/1999/60].

The Special Rapporteur transmitted 19 communications to 18 Governments and 11 urgent appeals to eight States. Replies to communications were received from eight countries and to urgent appeals from four countries. The report briefly summarized the communications and urgent appeals, as well as the replies received from Governments. The Special Rapporteur expressed concern over the possible proliferation of judicial standards. He appealed to Governments to respond promptly to his interventions and to his requests to visit the country. He called on Governments, national judiciaries, bar associations and NGOs to submit to him court judgements and legislation affecting the independence of the judiciary and the legal profession, and asked that OHCHR provide him with translation assistance.

The Special Rapporteur visited Guatemala (16-26 August) [E/CN.4/2000/61/Add.1] to inquire into allegations concerning threats, intimidation and harassment of lawyers, judges and prosecutors. He reported that the justice system, which was devastated during 34 years of armed conflict, was marginalized and had not recovered. Its neglect since had led to inefficiency and incompetence within the system, compounded by the fact that some of those who had allegedly committed human rights crimes were appointed to hold public office in the administration of justice and other related key public institutions, including the military. With regard to allegations of threats, harassment and intimidation of judges, the Special Rapporteur found those concerns to be real. The Supreme Court failed to respond to such concerns and instil public confidence in the judicial system. As for impunity, the Special Rapporteur regretted the unavailability of statistics, but, he stated, no one in the Government denied that impunity was prevalent. He found that there was no organized system of continued legal education for judges, prosecutors and lawyers, nor any statistics on court decisions. The Special Rapporteur was most concerned over juvenile justice, as the Government had not discharged its obligations to provide adequate shelter, welfare and justice for the country's 6,000 street children. He welcomed the appointment of the first woman in charge of matters relating to indigenous women, but expressed concern at the allegations of gender-based discriminatory provisions in the Criminal Procedure Code and the Labour Code. Recommendations were made regarding threats, harassment and intimidation of judges; impunity; the tenure of judges; reforms of the administration of justice; discipline and removal of judges; judicial corruption and influence peddling; human rights monitoring and capacity-building; the indigenous community; children; the status of women; lynching; and the media.

Commission action. On 26 April [res. 1999/31], the Commission, noting with concern the increasingly frequent attacks on the independence of judges, lawyers and court officers, encouraged Governments that faced difficulties to consult and to consider the Special Rapporteur's services, for instance by inviting him to their countries. It asked the High Commissioner to provide technical assistance to train judges and lawyers and to associate the Special Rapporteur in the development of a manual on human rights training of judges and lawyers. The Special Rapporteur was asked to report in 2000 and the Secretary-General was asked to assist him.

(For information on the privileges and immunities of the Special Rapporteur, see PART FOUR, Chapter I.)

Capital punishment

Report of Secretary-General. In response to a 1998 Commission request [YUN 1998, p. 669], the Secretary-General, in January, provided information received from States on changes in law and practice concerning the death penalty [E/CN.4/1999/52 & Corr.1]. As at 1 December 1998, 88 countries retained the death penalty for ordinary crimes; 65 were totally abolitionist; 16 were abolitionist for ordinary crimes only; and 26 were abolitionist de facto (they retained the death penalty for ordinary crimes but had not executed anyone in the preceding 10 years or more). The trend towards the abolition of the death penalty continued, with the number of totally abolitionist countries increasing from 61 to 65. There was also an increase in the number of countries ratifying international instruments that provided for the abolition of the death penalty. No abolitionist country made legal changes to reintroduce the death penalty and one retentionist country was reclassified as abolitionist de facto.

A March addendum [E/CN.4/1999/52/Add.1] summarized information received from Governments and intergovernmental organizations on the death penalty.

Commission action. By a roll-call vote of 30 to 11, with 12 abstentions, the Commission, on 28 April [res. 1999/61], called on States parties to the 1966 International Covenant on Civil and Political Rights that had not done so to consider acceding to or ratifying the Second Optional Protocol thereto, on the abolition of the death penalty, adopted by the General Assembly in resolution 44/128 [YUN 1989, p. 484]. States that maintained the death penalty were urged to comply with the Covenant and the Convention on the Rights of the Child, adopted by the Assembly in resolution 44/25 [ibid., p. 560], notably not to impose the death penalty for any but the most serious crimes, not to impose it for crimes committed by persons under the age of 18, to exclude pregnant women from capital punishment and to ensure the right to seek pardon or commutation of sentence; to ensure that the notion of most serious crimes did not go beyond international crimes with lethal or extremely grave consequences and that the death penalty was not imposed for non-violent financial crimes or for non-violent religious practice or expression of conscience; to observe the safeguards guaranteeing protection of the rights of those facing the death penalty, annexed to Economic and Social Council resolution 1984/50 [YUN 1984, p. 710]; not to impose the death penalty on a person suffering from any form of mental disorder; to restrict the number of offences for which the death penalty might be imposed; to establish a moratorium on executions, with a view to abolishing the death penalty; and to make available information on the imposition of the death penalty. The Secretary-General was asked to submit his sixth quinquennial report on capital punishment and implementation of the 1984 safeguards in 2000.

Communication. On 22 July [E/1999/113], Singapore, also on behalf of 49 other States, dissociated itself from the Commission's resolution.

Subcommission action. By a secret ballot vote of 14 to 5, with 5 abstentions, the Subcommission, on 24 August [res. 1999/4], condemning the imposition and execution of the death penalty on those aged under 18 at the time of the offence, called on States that did so to abolish the practice. It also called on States that retained the death penalty for refusal to undertake military service or for desertion not to apply it if the action was the result of conscientious objection to such service. States that retained the death penalty and did not apply a moratorium on executions were asked, in order to mark the millennium, to commute the sentences of those under sentence of death on 31 December 1999 to sentences of life imprisonment and to commit themselves to a moratorium on the imposition of the death penalty throughout 2000. The Commission was asked to reaffirm its resolution 1999/61 in 2000. The Secretary-General was asked to report in 2000 on the number of executions of juveniles carried out between the adoption of the Subcommission's resolution and the start of its next session and on the number of executions generally carried out in the same period.

Communication. On 27 August [E/CN.4/Sub.2/1999/52], Singapore, on behalf also of 25 other States, expressed concern that the recommendations in the Subcommission's resolution went beyond that body's mandate.

GENERAL ASSEMBLY ACTION

On 17 December [meeting 83], the General Assembly, on the recommendation of the Third Committee [A/54/605/Add.2], adopted **resolution 54/163** without vote [agenda item 116 *(b)*].

Human rights in the administration of justice

The General Assembly,

Bearing in mind the principles embodied in articles 3, 5, 8, 9 and 10 of the Universal Declaration of Human Rights and the relevant provisions of the International Covenant on Civil and Political Rights and the Optional Protocols thereto, in particular article 6 of the Covenant, which, inter alia, states that no one shall be arbitrarily deprived of his life and prohibits the imposition of the death penalty for crimes committed by persons below eighteen years of age, and article 10, which provides that all persons deprived of their liberty shall be treated with humanity and with respect for the inherent dignity of the human person,

Bearing in mind also the relevant provisions of the Convention against Torture and Other Cruel, Inhuman or Degrading Treatment or Punishment, the International Convention on the Elimination of All Forms of Racial Discrimination and the Convention on the Rights of the Child,

Recalling in particular article 37 of the Convention on the Rights of the Child, according to which every child deprived of liberty shall be treated in a manner which takes into account the needs of persons of his or her age,

Mindful of the Convention on the Elimination of All Forms of Discrimination against Women, in particular of the obligation of States to treat men and women equally in all stages of procedures in courts and tribunals,

Calling attention to the numerous international standards in the field of the administration of justice,

Aware of the need for special vigilance with regard to the vulnerable situation of children and juveniles, as well as women and girls, in detention,

Recalling the Guidelines for Action on Children in the Criminal Justice System and the establishment of a coordination panel on technical advice and assistance in juvenile justice,

Emphasizing that the right to access to justice as contained in applicable international human rights instruments forms an important basis for strengthening the rule of law through the administration of justice,

Mindful of the importance of establishing the rule of law and promoting human rights in the administration of justice, in particular in post-conflict situations, as a crucial contribution to building peace and justice,

Recalling its resolution 52/124 of 12 December 1997, and taking note of Commission on Human Rights resolution 1998/39 of 17 April 1998 and Economic and Social Council resolution 1999/28 of 28 July 1999 on the administration of juvenile justice,

1. *Reaffirms* the importance of the full and effective implementation of all United Nations standards on human rights in the administration of justice;

2. *Reiterates its call* to all Member States to spare no effort in providing for effective legislative mechanisms and procedures, as well as adequate resources, to ensure the full implementation of those standards;

3. *Invites* Governments to provide training, including gender-sensitive training, in human rights in the administration of justice, including juvenile justice, to all judges, lawyers, prosecutors, social workers, immigration and police officers, and other professionals concerned, including personnel deployed in international field presences;

4. *Stresses* the special need for national capacity-building in the field of the administration of justice in post-conflict situations, in particular through reform of the judiciary, the police and the penal system;

5. *Invites* States to make use of technical assistance offered by the relevant United Nations programmes in order to strengthen national capacities and infrastructures in the field of the administration of justice;

6. *Invites* the international community to respond favourably to requests for financial and technical assistance for the enhancement and strengthening of the administration of justice;

7. *Calls upon* the United Nations High Commissioner for Human Rights, as well as mechanisms of the Commission on Human Rights and its subsidiary bodies, including special rapporteurs, special representatives and working groups, to continue to give special attention to questions relating to the effective promotion of human rights in the administration of justice and to provide, where appropriate, specific recommendations in this regard, including proposals for measures to provide advisory services and technical assistance;

8. *Notes* the increased attention paid to the issue of juvenile justice by the High Commissioner, and encourages further activities, within her mandate, in this regard;

9. *Encourages* the regional commissions, the specialized agencies and United Nations institutes in the areas of human rights and crime prevention and criminal justice, and other organizations of the United Nations system, as well as intergovernmental and non-governmental organizations, including national professional associations concerned with promoting United Nations standards in this field, to continue to develop their activities in promoting human rights in the administration of justice;

10. *Calls upon* the coordination panel on technical advice and assistance in juvenile justice to increase cooperation among the partners involved, to share information and pool their capacities and interests in order to increase the effectiveness of programme implementation;

11. *Invites* the Commission on Human Rights and the Commission on Crime Prevention and Criminal Justice to coordinate closely their activities relating to the administration of justice;

12. *Underlines* the importance of rebuilding and strengthening structures for the administration of justice and respect for the rule of law and human rights in post-conflict situations, and requests the Secretary-General to ensure system-wide coordination and coherence of programmes and activities of the relevant parts of the United Nations system in the field of the administration of justice in post-conflict situations, including assistance provided through United Nations field presences;

13. *Decides* to consider the question of human rights in the administration of justice at its fifty-sixth session, under the item entitled "Human rights questions".

Right to democracy

By a roll-call vote of 51 to none, with 2 abstentions, the Commission, on 27 April [res. 1999/57], affirmed that the rights of democratic governance included, among other things, the rights to freedom of opinion and expression, of thought, conscience and religion, and of peaceful association and assembly; the right to freedom to seek, receive and impart information and ideas through any media ; the rule of law; the right of universal and equal suffrage, as well as periodic and free elections; the right of political participation; transparent and accountable government institutions; the right of citizens to choose their governmental system through constitutional or other democratic means; and the right to equal access to public service in one's country. Human rights treaty bodies, OHCHR and Commission and Subcommission mechanisms were asked to pay attention to those elements of democratic governance. The Commission requested OHCHR to give priority to its technical cooperation programmes to promote democracy and the rule of law and to promote democracy-related activities throughout the UN system. The High Commissioner was asked to reflect progress on implementation of the Commission's resolution in her report in 2000. The Secretary-General was asked to bring the Commission's resolution to the attention of Member States, UN organs, intergovernmental organizations and NGOs and to disseminate it widely.

Electoral processes

In response to General Assembly resolution 52/129 [YUN 1997, p. 644], the Secretary-General, in October [A/54/491], presented information on UN electoral assistance between 17 September 1997 and 30 September 1999. The number of requests for electoral assistance totalled 48 for 38 Member States.

During the biennium, the Electoral Assistance Division of the UN Secretariat assisted with two major missions: preparations for elections in the Central African Republic (see p. 118); and the popular consultation on the future status of East Timor (see p. 280). Other activities related primarily to coordinating international election observers and technical assistance.

Annexed to the report were summaries of the requests and action taken thereon.

GENERAL ASSEMBLY ACTION

On 17 December [meeting 83], the General Assembly, on the recommendation of the Third Committee [A/54/605/Add.2], adopted **resolution 54/173** by recorded vote (153-0-11) [agenda item 116 *(b)*].

Strengthening the role of the United Nations in enhancing the effectiveness of the principle of periodic and genuine elections and the promotion of democratization

The General Assembly,

Recalling its previous resolutions on the subject, in particular resolutions 49/190 of 23 December 1994, 50/185 of 22 December 1995 and 52/129 of 12 December 1997,

Reaffirming that United Nations electoral assistance and support for the promotion of democratization are provided only at the specific request of the Member State concerned,

Acknowledging that United Nations electoral assistance has facilitated the holding of successful elections in several Member States, which has resulted in the orderly and non-violent assumption of office by elected officials, recognizing that elections can be free and fair only if the secrecy of the ballot is protected and elections are held free of coercion and intimidation, and underlining the importance of respect for the results of elections that have been verified as free and fair,

Noting with satisfaction that increasing numbers of Member States are using elections as peaceful means of national decision-making and confidence-building, thereby contributing to greater national peace and stability,

Recalling the Universal Declaration of Human Rights, adopted on 10 December 1948, in particular the right freely to choose representatives through periodic and genuine elections which shall be by universal and equal suffrage and held by secret vote or by equivalent free voting procedures,

Taking note of Commission on Human Rights resolution 1999/57 of 27 April 1999, in which, inter alia, the Commission urged the continuation and expansion of activities carried out by the United Nations system, other intergovernmental and non-governmental organizations and Member States to promote and consolidate democracy within the framework of international cooperation and to build a democratic political culture through the observance of human rights, mobilization of civil society and other appropriate measures in support of democratic governance,

Recognizing the usefulness of a comprehensive and balanced approach in the activities carried out by the United Nations in this field in contributing to strengthening both democracy and all human rights within the country concerned,

Recognizing also the need for strengthening national capacity-building, electoral institutions and civic education in the requesting countries in order to consolidate and regularize the achievements of previous elections and support subsequent elections,

Recalling the Vienna Declaration and Programme of Action adopted by the World Conference on Human Rights on 25 June 1993, in particular the recognition therein that assistance provided upon the request of Governments for the conduct of free and fair elections is of particular importance in the strengthening of a pluralistic civil society,

Welcoming the support provided by States to the electoral assistance activities of the United Nations, inter alia, through the provision of electoral experts, including electoral commission staff, and observers, as well as through contributions to the United Nations Trust Fund for Electoral Observation,

Noting with appreciation the efforts of the Electoral Assistance Division of the Department of Political Affairs of the Secretariat, in collaboration with other electoral assistance organizations and United Nations agencies, to gather and make available through electronic means information on and for national election administrators, processes and institutions,

Noting the regional conference for Central Asian election administrators, held at Almaty, Kazakhstan, in November 1998, and the conference of the Global Electoral Organization Network, held at Ottawa in April 1999,

Welcoming the Fourth International Conference of the New or Restored Democracies, to be held at Cotonou, Benin, in December 2000, and calling upon the international community, including the United Nations Development Programme, the Electoral Assistance Division and other relevant organizations and institutions to render all possible assistance to ensure the successful outcome of the Conference,

Having considered the report of the Secretary-General on United Nations activities aimed at enhancing the effectiveness of the principle of periodic and genuine elections,

1. *Takes note with appreciation* of the report of the Secretary-General;

2. *Commends* the electoral assistance provided upon request to Member States by the United Nations, and requests that such assistance continue on a case-by-case basis in accordance with the evolving needs of requesting countries to improve and refine their electoral institutions and processes and with the guidelines on electoral assistance, recognizing that the fundamental responsibility of organizing free and fair elections lies with Governments;

3. *Requests* the Electoral Assistance Division of the Department of Political Affairs of the Secretariat, in its role as coordinator of United Nations electoral assistance, to continue to inform Member States on a regular basis about the requests received, responses given to those requests and the nature of the assistance provided;

4. *Requests* that the United Nations continue its efforts to ensure, before undertaking to provide electoral assistance to a requesting State, that there is adequate time to organize and carry out an effective mission for providing such assistance, that conditions exist to allow a free and fair election and that provisions can be made for adequate and comprehensive reporting of the results of the mission;

5. *Recommends* that the Electoral Assistance Division continue to provide technical advice before and after elections and post-election assistance, as appropriate, based on needs assessment missions, to requesting States and electoral institutions, in order to contribute to the sustainability of their electoral processes and the consolidation of the democratization process;

6. *Also recommends* that United Nations electoral assistance be geared towards comprehensive observation of the entire time-span of the electoral process in instances where more than technical assistance is required by the requesting State;

7. *Requests* the Secretary-General to take further steps to support States that request assistance by, inter alia, enabling the United Nations High Commissioner for Human Rights, in accordance with her mandate, to support democratization activities related to human rights concerns, including human rights training and education, assistance for human rights–related legislative reform, strengthening and reform of the judiciary, assistance to national human rights institutions and advisory services on treaty accession, reporting and international obligations as related to human rights;

8. *Requests* the United Nations Development Programme to continue its commendable programmes of assistance for governance in cooperation with other relevant organizations and institutions, as outlined in the report of the Secretary-General, in particular those for strengthening democratic institutions and participation and linkages between concerned sectors of society and Governments;

9. *Recalls* the establishment by the Secretary-General of the United Nations Trust Fund for Electoral Observation, and calls upon Member States to consider contributing to the Fund;

10. *Reiterates* the importance of reinforced coordination within the United Nations system, including cooperation with all relevant departments within the Secretariat, the Office of the United Nations High Commissioner for Human Rights, the United Nations Development Programme and the United Nations Volunteers, and encourages the Under-Secretary-General for Political Affairs, as the focal point for United Nations electoral assistance activities, supported by the Electoral Assistance Division, to continue to develop new and more effective mechanisms for cooperation and to strengthen collaboration with those entities, including through an exchange of personnel when appropriate;

11. *Notes with appreciation* additional efforts being made to enhance cooperation with other international, governmental and non-governmental organizations in order to facilitate more comprehensive and need-specific responses to requests for electoral assistance, and expresses appreciation to those Member States, regional organizations and non-governmental organizations that have provided observers or technical experts in support of United Nations electoral assistance efforts;

12. *Encourages* the Secretary-General, through the Electoral Assistance Division, to respond to the evolving nature of requests for assistance and the growing need for specific types of medium-term expert assistance aimed at supporting and strengthening the exist-

ing capacity of the requesting Government, in particular through enhancing the capacity of national electoral institutions;

13. *Requests* the Secretary-General to provide the Electoral Assistance Division with adequate human and financial resources to allow it to carry out its mandate, and to continue to ensure that the Office of the United Nations High Commissioner for Human Rights is able to respond, within its mandate and in close coordination with the Electoral Assistance Division, to the increasing number of requests from Member States for advisory services;

14. *Also requests* the Secretary-General to report to the General Assembly at its fifty-sixth session on the implementation of the present resolution, in particular on the status of requests from Member States for electoral assistance and verification, and on his efforts to enhance the Organization's support of the democratization process in Member States.

RECORDED VOTE ON RESOLUTION 54/173:

In favour: Afghanistan, Albania, Algeria, Andorra, Angola, Antigua and Barbuda, Argentina, Armenia, Australia, Austria, Azerbaijan, Bahamas, Bahrain, Bangladesh, Barbados, Belarus, Belgium, Belize, Benin, Bhutan, Bolivia, Bosnia and Herzegovina, Botswana, Brazil, Bulgaria, Burkina Faso, Cameroon, Canada, Cape Verde, Chad, Chile, Colombia, Comoros, Congo, Costa Rica, Côte d'Ivoire, Croatia, Cyprus, Czech Republic, Denmark, Djibouti, Dominica, Dominican Republic, Ecuador, Egypt, El Salvador, Eritrea, Estonia, Ethiopia, Fiji, Finland, France, Gabon, Georgia, Germany, Ghana, Greece, Grenada, Guatemala, Guinea, Guinea-Bissau, Guyana, Haiti, Honduras, Hungary, Iceland, India, Indonesia, Iran, Ireland, Israel, Italy, Jamaica, Japan, Jordan, Kazakhstan, Kenya, Kuwait, Latvia, Lebanon, Liechtenstein, Lithuania, Luxembourg, Malawi, Malaysia, Maldives, Mali, Malta, Marshall Islands, Mauritius, Mexico, Micronesia, Monaco, Mongolia, Morocco, Mozambique, Namibia, Nepal, Netherlands, New Zealand, Nicaragua, Nigeria, Norway, Oman, Pakistan, Panama, Papua New Guinea, Paraguay, Peru, Philippines, Poland, Portugal, Qatar, Republic of Korea, Republic of Moldova, Romania, Russian Federation, Saint Lucia, Samoa, San Marino, Senegal, Seychelles, Sierra Leone, Singapore, Slovakia, Slovenia, Solomon Islands, South Africa, Spain, Sri Lanka, Suriname, Swaziland, Sweden, Tajikistan, Thailand, The former Yugoslav Republic of Macedonia, Togo, Trinidad and Tobago, Tunisia, Turkey, Turkmenistan, Uganda, Ukraine, United Arab Emirates, United Kingdom, United Republic of Tanzania, United States, Uruguay, Uzbekistan, Venezuela, Yemen, Zambia, Zimbabwe.

Against: None.

Abstaining: Brunei Darussalam, Cambodia, China, Cuba, Democratic People's Republic of Korea, Lao People's Democratic Republic, Libyan Arab Jamahiriya, Myanmar, Sudan, Syrian Arab Republic, Viet Nam.

The Assembly retained paragraph 8 by a separate recorded vote of 136 to none, with 21 abstentions, as did the Committee by 120 votes to none, with 27 abstentions.

Also on 17 December [meeting 83], the Assembly, acting on the recommendation of the Third Committee [A/54/605/Add.2], adopted **resolution 54/168** by recorded vote (91-59-10) [agenda item 116 *(b)*].

Respect for the principles of national sovereignty and non-interference in the internal affairs of States in their electoral processes

The General Assembly,

Reaffirming the purpose of the United Nations to develop friendly relations among nations based on respect for the principle of equal rights and self-determination of peoples and to take other appropriate measures to strengthen universal peace,

Recalling its resolution 1514(XV) of 14 December 1960, containing the Declaration on the Granting of Independence to Colonial Countries and Peoples,

Recalling also its resolution 2625(XXV) of 24 October 1970, by which it approved the Declaration on Principles of International Law concerning Friendly Relations and Cooperation among States in accordance with the Charter of the United Nations,

Recalling further the principle enshrined in Article 2, paragraph 7, of the Charter, which establishes that nothing contained in the Charter shall authorize the United Nations to intervene in matters that are essentially within the domestic jurisdiction of any State or shall require the Members to submit such matters to settlement under the Charter,

Reaffirming the obligation of Member States to comply with the principles of the Charter and the resolutions of the United Nations regarding the right to self-determination, by virtue of which all peoples can freely determine, without external interference, their political status and freely pursue their economic, social and cultural development,

Recognizing that the principles of national sovereignty and non-interference in the internal affairs of any State should be respected in the holding of elections,

Recognizing also the richness and diversity of political systems and models for electoral processes in the world, based on national and regional particularities and various backgrounds,

Stressing the responsibility of States in ensuring ways and means to facilitate full and effective popular participation in electoral processes,

Welcoming the Vienna Declaration and Programme of Action, adopted by the World Conference on Human Rights on 25 June 1993, in which the Conference reaffirmed that the processes of promoting and protecting human rights should be conducted in conformity with the purposes and principles of the Charter,

1. *Reiterates* that, by virtue of the principle of equal rights and self-determination of peoples enshrined in the Charter of the United Nations, all peoples have the right, freely and without external interference, to determine their political status and to pursue their economic, social and cultural development and that every State has the duty to respect that right in accordance with the provisions of the Charter;

2. *Reaffirms* the right of peoples, without external interference, to determine methods and to establish institutions regarding electoral processes and that, consequently, States should ensure, in accordance with their constitutions and national legislation, the necessary mechanism and means to facilitate full and effective popular participation in those processes;

3. *Also reaffirms* that any activities that attempt, directly or indirectly, to interfere in the free development of national electoral processes, in particular in developing countries, or that are intended to sway the results of such processes, violate the spirit and letter of the principles established in the Charter and in the Declaration on Principles of International Law concerning Friendly Relations and Cooperation among States in accordance with the Charter of the United Nations;

4. *Further reaffirms* that electoral assistance to Member States should be provided by the United Nations at the request of interested States, or in special circumstances such as cases of decolonization, or in the context of regional or international peace processes;

5. *Strongly appeals* to all States to refrain from financing political parties or groups in other States and taking any other action that undermines their electoral processes;

6. *Condemns* any act of armed aggression or threat or use of force against peoples, their elected Governments or their legitimate leaders;

7. *Reaffirms* that all countries have the obligation under the Charter to respect the right of peoples to self-determination and to determine freely their political status and pursue their economic, social and cultural development;

8. *Decides* to consider this question at its fifty-sixth session, under the item entitled "Human rights questions".

RECORDED VOTE ON RESOLUTION 54/168:

In favour: Afghanistan, Algeria, Angola, Antigua and Barbuda, Bahamas, Bahrain, Bangladesh, Barbados, Belize, Benin, Bhutan, Bolivia, Botswana, Brunei Darussalam, Burkina Faso, Cambodia, Cameroon, Cape Verde, Chad, China, Colombia, Comoros, Congo, Côte d'Ivoire, Cuba, Democratic People's Republic of Korea, Democratic Republic of the Congo, Djibouti, Dominica, Ecuador, Egypt, El Salvador, Eritrea, Ethiopia, Fiji, Gabon, Ghana, Grenada, Guinea, Guinea-Bissau, Guyana, Haiti, Honduras, India, Indonesia, Iran, Jamaica, Jordan, Kenya, Kuwait, Lao People's Democratic Republic, Lebanon, Libyan Arab Jamahiriya, Malaysia, Maldives, Mali, Mauritius, Mexico, Mongolia, Morocco, Mozambique, Myanmar, Namibia, Nepal, Oman, Pakistan, Papua New Guinea, Paraguay, Peru, Philippines, Qatar, Saint Lucia, Saudi Arabia, Seychelles, Singapore, Sri Lanka, Sudan, Suriname, Swaziland, Syrian Arab Republic, Thailand, Trinidad and Tobago, Tunisia, United Arab Emirates, United Republic of Tanzania, Uruguay, Venezuela, Viet Nam, Yemen, Zambia, Zimbabwe.

Against: Albania, Andorra, Argentina, Armenia, Australia, Austria, Belgium, Bosnia and Herzegovina, Bulgaria, Canada, Chile, Croatia, Cyprus, Czech Republic, Denmark, Estonia, Finland, France, Georgia, Germany, Greece, Hungary, Iceland, Ireland, Israel, Italy, Japan, Kazakhstan, Latvia, Liechtenstein, Lithuania, Luxembourg, Malta, Marshall Islands, Micronesia, Monaco, Netherlands, New Zealand, Nigeria, Norway, Poland, Portugal, Republic of Korea, Republic of Moldova, Romania, Russian Federation, Samoa, San Marino, Sierra Leone, Slovakia, Slovenia, South Africa, Spain, Sweden, The former Yugoslav Republic of Macedonia, Turkey, Ukraine, United Kingdom, United States.

Abstaining: Belarus, Brazil, Costa Rica, Guatemala, Malawi, Nicaragua, Panama, Senegal, Solomon Islands, Tajikistan.

Other issues

Extra-legal executions

Reports of Special Rapporteur. A January report of the Special Rapporteur on extrajudicial, summary or arbitrary executions, Asma Jahangir (Pakistan) [E/CN.4/1999/39 & Add.1], updated activities since the submission of the last report on the subject [YUN 1998, p. 670]. Between 1 November 1997 and 31 October 1998, the Special Rapporteur transmitted to 40 Governments communications on allegations regarding the violation of the right to life of more than 2,300 individuals, as well as 63 urgent appeals regarding 158 individuals to prevent imminent loss of life. The report summarized the communications and the replies of Governments. Issues of special concern to the Special Rapporteur included capital punishment, impunity, child soldiers, traditional practices and customs affecting the right to life, and the right to life and sexual orientation. The Special Rapporteur concluded that there was no indication of a decrease in violations of the right to life. She made recommendations to Governments relating to capital punishment, death threats, deaths in custody, excessive use of force by law enforcement officials, violations of the right to life during armed conflict, the imminent expulsion of persons to countries where their lives were in danger, genocide, impunity and child soldiers.

The Special Rapporteur visited the former Yugoslav Republic of Macedonia (23-25 May) and Albania (25-28 May) [E/CN.4/2000/3/Add.2] to collect information regarding the situation in Kosovo, with a view to assessing and evaluating allegations of human rights violations relevant to her mandate. She observed that summary executions had taken place there in varying circumstances and situations: targeted, indiscriminate, individual and mass killings had been witnessed and recounted. Killings were mostly carried out by forces under direct or indirect State control. She had received notice of direct targeting and killing of activists, lawyers, intellectuals and others. Refugees described how groups of refugees were indiscriminately fired upon while trying to flee their homes and villages. Some of the most harrowing accounts described individual, random or group killings in connection with forced expulsion. The Special Rapporteur, stating that there could be no impunity for such crimes, encouraged the International Criminal Tribunal for the former Yugoslavia (see PART FOUR, Chapter II) to continue its investigations and to bring perpetrators to justice. She called for an end to the vicious circle of reprisals and restoration of confidence between ethnic groups.

At the invitation of the Government, the Special Rapporteur visited Mexico (12-24 July) [E/CN.4/2000/3/Add.3] in the light of repeated allegations of individual cases of extrajudicial killings, and reports of massacres in past years in the States of Guerrero and Chiapas. Despite the Government's initial steps to guarantee the right to life of all persons, extrajudicial killings and the impunity enjoyed by the perpetrators continued. The incidence of violence and killings remained widespread, although there had been a decrease in the last year. The ineffectiveness of the justice system had given rise to human rights violations. There was a reluctance on the part of the authorities to hold military personnel accountable for extrajudicial killings and other human rights violations. The Special Rapporteur recommended that the Government continue the reform process; invite international observers to elections in 2000; reopen talks with the Zapatista National Liberation Army; protect human rights defenders; avoid deputizing the armed forces to maintain law or to eradicate crime; strengthen the independence of the public prosecutors; grant the victims of human rights violations legal mechanisms to file criminal complaints; end impunity; strengthen its human rights commissions; and repeal capital punishment laws.

In a letter to OHCHR [E/CN.4/2000/126], Mexico stated that the Special Rapporteur had overstepped her mandate by bringing up the subject of the elections and the constitutional role of national bodies such as the armed forces.

Commission action. On 26 April [res. 1999/35], the Commission, strongly condemning all extrajudicial, summary or arbitrary executions, demanded that Governments end those practices. It appealed to them to ensure that all persons deprived of their liberty were treated with humanity and respect. The Commission asked the Special Rapporteur to continue her work and report annually; respond to information she received; enhance her dialogue with Governments and follow up on her recommendations after country visits; pay special attention to extrajudicial, summary or arbitrary executions of children and to allegations concerning violence against participants in peaceful public manifestations or against persons belonging to minorities; pay special attention to executions where the victims were carrying out peaceful activities in defence of human rights and fundamental freedoms; monitor the implementation of international standards on safeguards and restrictions relating to the imposition of capital punishment; and apply a gender perspective in her work. Governments were urged to cooperate with the Special Rapporteur and to respond to her communications. The Secretary-General was asked to assist her, particularly in cases where the minimum standard of legal safeguards provided for in articles 6, 9, 14 and 15 of the International Covenant on Civil and Political Rights, adopted by the General Assembly in resolution 2200 A (XXI) [YUN 1966, p. 423], appeared not to be respected, and to ensure that personnel specialized in human rights and humanitarian law issues formed part of UN missions, where appropriate, in order to deal with human rights violations, such as extrajudicial, summary or arbitrary executions.

On 27 September [E/1999/23/Add.1 (res. 1999/S-4/1)], the Commission asked the Special Rapporteur on extrajudicial, summary or arbitrary executions, among others, to carry out a mission to East Timor, to report to the Commission in 2000 and to submit an interim report to the Assembly in 1999.

The Special Rapporteur visited East Timor from 4 to 10 November [A/54/660] (see next chapter).

Disappearance of persons

Working Group on Enforced or Involuntary Disappearances

Commission action. On 26 April [res. 1999/38], the Commission encouraged the five-member Working Group on Enforced or Involuntary Disappearances to continue to promote communication between families of disappeared persons and the Governments concerned; to observe UN standards and practices regarding the handling of communications and the consideration of government replies; to continue to consider the question of impunity; to pay particular attention to cases of children subjected to enforced disappearance and children of disappeared persons; to pay particular attention to cases of ill-treatment, serious threats or intimidation of witnesses or relatives of disappeared persons; to pay particular attention to cases of disappearance of persons working for the promotion and protection of human rights and fundamental freedoms; to apply a gender perspective in its reporting process; to provide assistance to States in implementing the 1992 Declaration on the Protection of All Persons from Enforced Disappearance, adopted by the General Assembly in resolution 47/133 [YUN 1992, p. 744]; and to continue its deliberations on its working methods. The Commission asked the Group to report in 2000. The Secretary-General was asked to ensure that the Group received assistance and resources and to keep the Group and the Commission informed of action he had taken to disseminate and promote the 1992 Declaration. The Commission urged Governments to cooperate with the Group; to protect witnesses and the lawyers and families of disappeared persons against ill-treatment; to shed light on unresolved cases; and to provide mechanisms to seek reparation for victims or their families. States were asked to provide the Group with information on measures taken and obstacles encountered in preventing enforced, involuntary or arbitrary disappearances and in giving effect to the 1992 Declaration.

On 27 September [E/1999/23/Add.1 (res. 1999/S-4/1)], the Commission asked the Working Group on Enforced or Involuntary Disappearances, among others, to carry out a mission to East Timor, to report to the Commission in 2000 and to submit an interim report to the Assembly in 1999.

Working Group activities. The Working Group held three sessions in 1999: its fifty-seventh in New York (10-14 May) and its fifty-eighth and fifty-ninth in Geneva (30 August–3 September, 24 November–3 December) [E/CN.4/2000/64 & Corr.1,2]. In addition to its original mandate, which was to act as a channel of communication between families of disappeared persons and Governments concerned, with a view to ensuring that sufficiently documented individual cases were investigated and the whereabouts of the disappeared persons clarified, the Working Group monitored States' compliance with the 1992 Declaration. However, due to limitations in its resources and the requested reduction of its report, information regarding the Declaration was not included in the Group's report; nor did it include observations on the draft international convention on the prevention and punishment of enforced disappearances (see p. 625).

The number of cases under active consideration stood at 46,054 and the number of countries with outstanding cases of alleged disappearance was 69. During the period under review, up to 3 December, the Group received 300 new cases of disappearance in 23 countries. The Group regretted that out of the 69 countries with unclarified cases, the Governments of 34 countries had not communicated with the Group. The Group sent urgent action appeals to 19 Governments in respect of 125 cases.

The Group concluded that full implementation of the 1992 Declaration was crucial to prevent and end disappearances and emphasized the importance of cooperation with Governments and NGOs. It noted that since its establishment in 1980, it had transmitted more than 49,000 cases to Governments and, although 3,000 cases had been clarified, 46,000 remained outstanding. The Working Group stressed that impunity was one of the main causes of enforced disappearance and one of the major obstacles to clarifying past cases. In some cases, the Group was hindered because of the lack of cooperation on the part of Governments; it asked the Commission to appeal to them to cooperate. It urged the Commission to meet its need for resources. The report contained a separate opinion by two members of the Group objecting to the application of a 32-page limit on its report, in accordance with General Assembly resolution 47/202 B [YUN 1992, p. 1083].

A member of the Working Group visited Sri Lanka (25-29 October) [E/CN.4/2000/64/Add.1] to follow up on the Group's recommendations made during its visits in 1991 [YUN 1991, p. 560] and 1992 [YUN 1992, p. 742], as well as to follow up on the latest developments. The Group noted that since its inception in 1980, 12,258 cases of disappearance alleged to have occurred in the country had been reported to the Group.

The Group appreciated the measures that the current and previous Governments of Sri Lanka had taken, in compliance with the Group's earlier recommendations, to clarify cases of disappearances that occurred during the former Government, to provide justice to the families of disappeared persons and to prevent future disappearances. Notwithstanding those encouraging facts, the Group stressed that Sri Lanka remained the country with the second largest number of non-clarified cases of disappearances on its list. Although a considerable number of criminal investigations had been initiated in relation to disappearances that occurred some 10 years earlier, only very few of the suspected perpetrators had been convicted, and some of them had even been promoted. NGOs claimed that the current Government had not done enough to investigate disappearances that occurred after it took office and to prevent future disappearances. Regarding prevention, many of the Group's earlier recommendations had not been implemented. The Group recommended that the Government establish an independent body to investigate disappearances that had occurred since 1995; speed up efforts to bring the perpetrators to justice; make the act of enforced disappearance an independent offence under the criminal law of Sri Lanka punishable as stipulated in the 1992 Declaration; abolish the current Prevention of Terrorism Act and the Emergency Regulations or bring them into line with internationally accepted standards of personal liberty; dissolve unofficial places of detention; set up a central register of detainees; compensate families; apply equally the procedure for issuing death certificates; and respond to cases submitted by the Group on a case-by-case basis.

Torture and cruel treatment

Reports of Special Rapporteur. In January [E/CN.4/1999/61], the Special Rapporteur on torture, Nigel S. Rodley (United Kingdom), summarized his 1998 activities. He had sent 64 letters to 59 Governments on behalf of 400 individuals and 10 groups involving some 250 persons, and also transmitted 122 urgent appeals to 41 countries on behalf of some 380 individuals (30 known to be minors and 30 known to be women), as well as 20 groups of persons (one involving 190 women) involving about 1,500 persons with regard to whom fears had been expressed that they might be subjected to torture. In addition, 35 countries provided the Special Rapporteur with replies on 450 cases, whereas 17 did so regarding some 300 cases submitted in previous years. The Special Rapporteur provided brief summaries of general allegations and individual cases, as well as of the urgent appeals transmitted to Governments and their replies. His observations were presented where applicable. The Special Rapporteur recommended that States should ensure that prolonged incommunicado detention—any period beyond 24 to 48 hours—was not permitted; ratify the Rome Statute of the International Criminal Court [YUN 1998, p. 1209]; and enact legislation to permit them to take jurisdiction over perpetrators of human rights crimes, including torture, genocide, crimes against humanity and war crimes.

The Special Rapporteur visited Romania (19-29 April) [E/CN.4/2000/9/Add.3] to assess the situation with regard to the practice of torture and ill-treatment. Based on his observations, the Special Rapporteur concluded that such practices were not routine, but, as acknowledged by government officials, there were persistent, albeit sporadic, cases of police abuse. There was evidence that the Roma were more likely to be victims of police abuse than others. He expressed concern that military prosecutors lacked independence and impartiality and there was inadequate legal defence for indigent detainees. The establishment of the Office of the Ombudsman was a positive development but it did not receive the necessary cooperation from other government agencies. The Special Rapporteur recommended removing from confinement in detention centres on remand all persons detained in excess of the officially proclaimed capacity of existing institutions; using existing laws to release suspects on bail; repealing the 1974 order regulating conditions of detention in police lock-ups; ensuring regular inspection of places of detention; placing pre-trial detention centres under the authority of the Ministry of Justice; video- and audiotaping of proceedings in police interrogation rooms; transferring the power to investigate claims of police abuse and torture from military to civilian prosecutors; speeding up trials of public officials indicted for torture or ill-treatment and handing down sentences commensurate with the gravity of the crime; suspending public officials indicted for abuse or torture; prioritizing training of police officials; improving legal aid services; allowing the presence of legal counsel in the first 24 hours of detention prior to issuance of an arrest warrant; and granting the Ombudsman powers to sanction officials who refused to cooperate with the investigation of a complaint.

In Cameroon (12-20 May) [E/CN.4/2000/9/Add.2], the Special Rapporteur evaluated the situation regarding torture and ill-treatment. Torture was used to obtain information relevant to the maintenance of law and public order, to obtain confessions to crimes from suspects and to administer instant extrajudicial punishment. Neither youth nor age protected detained persons from being inhumanly treated. Contributing to the problem were corruption, a freeze on personnel recruitment, which led superiors to retain rather than dismiss undisciplined subordinates, and impunity. Prisons were overcrowded and lacked adequate health facilities and inmates were subjected to the arbitrariness of warders. Positive developments were the 1997 adoption of a law criminalizing torture and a decision to grant ICRC access to places of detention. The Special Rapporteur recommended proclaiming that torture and other ill-treatment committed by public officials would not be tolerated; establishing a corps of prosecutors, with specialized independent investigative personnel; endowing the National Commission on Human Rights with the authority to inspect any place of detention; granting detainees unmonitored access to families and lawyers; disbanding the anti-gang unit in Maroua, which had arbitrarily detained, tortured and summarily executed suspects; releasing non-violent first-time offenders, especially those under 18; and inviting the Special Rapporteurs on extrajudicial, summary or arbitrary executions and on the independence of judges and lawyers to visit the country.

At the invitation of the Government, the Special Rapporteur visited Kenya (20-29 September) [E/CN.4/2000/9/Add.4]. The internal state of affairs and the rule of law in the country lent itself to abuse, including abuse within the Special Rapporteur's mandate, he stated. Thus, in respect of any capital crime, which term included the crime of robbery with violence, the police were entitled to hold a suspect for up to 14 days, as compared with 24 hours for other crimes. Moreover, in practice, those time limits might not be respected. Legal aid was virtually unavailable for most of the suspects. In addition, not only were the police responsible for the forensic investigation of complaints against the police, but they sometimes refused to make available the form required for medical documentation of a complainant's physical state. The Special Rapporteur's official interlocutors acknowledged that there was a tradition in Kenya of physically rough treatment of suspects by the police. The prison system faced problems of extreme overcrowding and inadequate resources. Conscientious record-keeping in police stations, disbanding of the Special Branch, which dealt with political and public order cases and employed gruesome methods of torture, and a free and assertive press were encouraging signs. The Special Rapporteur recommended that the Government ensure independent and thorough investigation of torture and similar ill-treatment; grant compensation to victims; bring into line the period of police detention in capital cases with the normal 24-hour period applicable to persons suspected of other crimes; deem inadmissible confessions made in detention without a lawyer; provide legal aid to anyone held in police custody or on remand; inform family members of their relative's detention and grant access to them; abandon the police monopoly of issuing forms for detainees' medical examinations; abolish corporal punishment as a criminal penalty; and open up the prison system to better access by civil society.

Commission action. On 26 April [res. 1999/32], the Commission called on Governments to prohibit torture and other cruel, inhuman or degrading treatment or punishment and reminded them that prolonged incommunicado detention might facilitate the perpetration of torture and could constitute a form of cruel, inhuman or degrading treatment. Governments, the High Commissioner for Human Rights and UN bodies and agencies, as well as relevant intergovernmental organizations and NGOs, were called on to commemorate 26 June as the UN International Day in Support of Victims of Torture. States were urged to become parties to the 1984 Convention against Torture and Other Cruel, Inhuman or Degrading Treatment or Punishment contained in General Assembly resolution 39/46 [YUN 1984, p. 813]. The Commission invited the Special Rapporteur to continue to examine questions concerning torture and other cruel, inhuman or degrading treatment or punishment directed against women and to make recommendations concerning the prevention and redress of gender-specific forms of torture. It also asked him to continue to consider the torture of children. The Special Rapporteur was asked to present an interim report to the Assembly in 1999 and a full report to the Commission in 2000.

On 27 September [E/1999/23/Add.1 (res. 1999/S-4/1)], the Commission asked the Special Rapporteur on the question of torture, among others, to carry out a mission to East Timor, to report to the Commission in 2000 and to submit an interim report to the Assembly in 1999.

The Special Rapporteur visited East Timor from 4 to 10 November [A/54/660] (see next chapter).

Interim report of Special Rapporteur. In October, the Secretary-General transmitted to the Assembly the interim report of the Special Rapporteur [A/54/426]. The report covered the period from 15 December 1992 to 31 August 1999. Areas of special concern to the Special Rapporteur included gender-specific forms of torture, torture of children, corporal punishment, incommunicado detention, torture of human rights defenders, the question of non-refoulement, impunity, compensation and rehabilitation of torture victims, ratification of the 1984 Convention, the preparation of a manual on investigation of torture, and the International Criminal Court (see p. 1227).

The Special Rapporteur concluded that torture continued to plague all regions and it could be eradicated only if there was a genuine will on the part of Governments to prevent it. He recommended that States ratify the 1984 Convention and make the declaration provided for in articles 21 and 22 (see p. 578); enact legislation to ensure that torture was a punishable offence; prohibit incommunicado detention for more than 24 hours or, under special circumstances, 48 hours; ensure that education regarding the prohibition of torture was included in the training of law enforcement personnel and others involved in the custody, interrogation or treatment of those detained or imprisoned; carry out investigations whenever there were indications of torture; ensure that the victims obtained redress and had the right to compensation; and provide support to the UN Voluntary Fund for Victims of Torture. The General Assembly should consider endorsing the principles on the effective investigation and documentation of torture and other cruel, inhuman or degrading treatment or punishment, which were annexed to the Special Rapporteur's report.

Voluntary Fund for torture victims

Commission action. On 26 April [res. 1999/32], the Commission appealed to Governments, organizations and individuals to contribute annually to the United Nations Voluntary Fund for Victims of Torture. It called on the Fund's Board of Trustees to present in 2000 an updated assessment of the global need for international funding for rehabilitation services for torture victims. The Secretary-General was asked to continue to include the Fund among the programmes receiving donations at the annual UN Pledging Conference for Development Activities; transmit to Governments Commission appeals for contributions; ensure adequate staffing and technical facilities for the Fund; and inform the Commission of the Fund's operations annually.

Report of Secretary-General. The Secretary-General's annual report on the status of the Fund, submitted in July [A/54/177], stated that contributions received between 1 August 1998 and 2 July 1999 totalled $2,632,770 from 32 countries. Contributions from four private individuals totalled $3,881.

The Fund's Board of Trustees held its eighteenth session in Geneva (17-28 May). The total amount then available for grants to assist victims of torture came to some $5,100,000, of which $100,000 was earmarked for emergency grants falling between the Board's annual sessions and $200,000 for urgent grants to organizations that might face financial difficulties because of delayed payment of grants from the European Commission. During the year, $8.2 million was requested for 139 projects. On 11 June, the High Commissioner, on behalf of the Secretary-General, approved the Board's recommendations on grants to 133 projects submitted by 117 humanitarian organizations in 53 countries. The Fund also gave support to 14 other humanitarian organizations that provided medical, psychological and social assistance or trained health professionals. Annexed to the report was the Joint Declaration on the occasion of 26 June 1999, the International Day in Support of Victims of Torture—issued by the Committee against Torture, the Fund's Board of Trustees, the Special Rapporteur and the High Commissioner—and three press releases issued on that occasion.

In a December report [E/CN.4/2000/60], the Secretary-General stated that an additional $852,569 had been received since May for allocation at the nineteenth session of the Board in May 2000. Annexed to the report were the proceedings of the Eighth International Symposium on Torture (New Delhi, India, 22-25 September), which the Fund had helped to finance.

GENERAL ASSEMBLY ACTION

On 17 December [meeting 83], the General Assembly, on the recommendation of the Third Committee [A/54/605/Add.1 & Corr.1], adopted **resolution 54/156** without vote [agenda item 116 *(a)*].

Torture and other cruel, inhuman or degrading treatment or punishment

The General Assembly,

Recalling article 5 of the Universal Declaration of Human Rights, article 7 of the International Covenant on Civil and Political Rights, the Declaration on the Protection of All Persons from Being Subjected to Torture and Other Cruel, Inhuman or Degrading Treatment or Punishment and its resolution 39/46 of 10 December 1984, by which it adopted and opened for signature, ratification and accession the Convention against Torture and Other Cruel, Inhuman or Degrading Treatment or Punishment, and all its subsequent relevant resolutions,

Recalling that freedom from torture is a right that must be protected under all circumstances, including in times of internal or international disturbance or armed conflict,

Recalling also that the World Conference on Human Rights, held at Vienna from 14 to 25 June 1993, firmly declared that efforts to eradicate torture should, first and foremost, be concentrated on prevention and called for the early adoption of an optional protocol to the Convention against Torture and Other Cruel, Inhuman or Degrading Treatment or Punishment, which is intended to establish a preventive system of regular visits to places of detention,

Urging all Governments to promote the speedy and full implementation of the Vienna Declaration and Programme of Action, adopted by the World Conference on Human Rights on 25 June 1993, in particular the section relating to freedom from torture, in which it is stated that States should abrogate legislation leading to impunity for those responsible for grave violations of human rights, such as torture, and prosecute such violations, thereby providing a firm basis for the rule of law,

Recalling its resolution 36/151 of 16 December 1981, in which it noted with deep concern that acts of torture took place in various countries, recognized the need to provide assistance to the victims in a purely humanitarian spirit and established the United Nations Voluntary Fund for Victims of Torture,

Recalling also the recommendation in the Vienna Declaration and Programme of Action that high priority should be given to providing the necessary resources to assist victims of torture and effective remedies for their physical, psychological and social rehabilitation, inter alia, through additional contributions to the Fund,

Noting with satisfaction the existence of a considerable international network of centres for the rehabilitation of victims of torture, which plays an important role in providing assistance to victims of torture, and the collaboration of the Fund with the centres,

Mindful of the proclamation by the General Assembly in its resolution 52/149 of 12 December 1997 of 26 June as the United Nations International Day in Support of Victims of Torture,

1. *Welcomes* the work of the Committee against Torture, and takes note of the report of the Committee, submitted in accordance with article 24 of the Convention against Torture and Other Cruel, Inhuman or Degrading Treatment or Punishment;
2. *Notes with appreciation* that one hundred and eighteen States have become parties to the Convention;
3. *Urges* all States that have not yet done so to become parties to the Convention as a matter of priority;
4. *Invites* all States ratifying or acceding to the Convention and those States that are parties to the Convention and have not yet done so to consider joining the States parties that have already made the declarations provided for in articles 21 and 22 of the Convention and to consider the possibility of withdrawing their reservations to article 20;
5. *Urges* all States parties to the Convention to notify the Secretary-General of their acceptance of the amendments to articles 17 and 18 of the Convention as soon as possible;
6. *Urges* States parties to comply strictly with their obligations under the Convention, including their obligation to submit reports in accordance with article 19 of the Convention, in view of the high number of reports not submitted, and invites States parties to incorporate a gender perspective and information concerning children and juveniles when submitting reports to the Committee;
7. *Calls upon* the United Nations High Commissioner for Human Rights, in conformity with her mandate established in General Assembly resolution

48/141 of 20 December 1993, to continue to provide, at the request of Governments, advisory services for the preparation of national reports to the Committee and for the prevention of torture, as well as technical assistance in the development, production and distribution of teaching material for this purpose;

8. *Urges* States parties to take fully into account the conclusions and recommendations made by the Committee after its consideration of their reports;

9. *Emphasizes* the obligation of States parties under article 10 of the Convention to ensure education and training for personnel who may be involved in the custody, interrogation or treatment of any individual subjected to any form of arrest, detention or imprisonment;

10. *Stresses,* in this context, that States must not punish personnel referred to in paragraph 9 above for not obeying orders to commit or conceal acts amounting to torture or Other cruel, inhuman or degrading treatment or punishment;

11. *Welcomes* the progress made by the intersessional open-ended working group of the Commission on Human Rights on the development of a draft optional protocol to the Convention against Torture and Other Cruel, Inhuman or Degrading Treatment or Punishment, and urges the working group to complete as soon as possible a final text for submission to the General Assembly, through the Economic and Social Council, for consideration and adoption;

12. *Takes note with appreciation* of the interim report of the Special Rapporteur of the Commission on Human Rights on the question of torture and other cruel, inhuman or degrading treatment or punishment, describing the overall trends and developments with regard to his mandate, and encourages the Special Rapporteur to continue to include in his recommendations proposals on the prevention and investigation of torture;

13. *Invites* the Special Rapporteur to continue to examine questions of torture and other cruel, inhuman or degrading treatment or punishment directed against women, and conditions conducive to such torture, and to make appropriate recommendations for the prevention and redress of gender-specific forms of torture, including rape or any other form of sexual violence, and to exchange views with the Special Rapporteur on violence against women, its causes and consequences, with a view to enhancing further their effectiveness and mutual cooperation;

14. *Also invites* the Special Rapporteur to continue to consider questions relating to the torture of children and conditions conducive to such torture and other cruel, inhuman or degrading treatment or punishment and to make appropriate recommendations for the prevention of such torture;

15. *Calls upon* all Governments to cooperate with and to assist the Special Rapporteur in the performance of his task, in particular by supplying all necessary information requested by him, to react appropriately and expeditiously to his urgent appeals and to give serious consideration to his requests to visit their countries, and urges them to enter into a constructive dialogue with the Special Rapporteur with respect to the follow-up to his recommendations;

16. *Approves* the methods of work employed by the Special Rapporteur, in particular with regard to urgent appeals, reiterates the need for him to be able to respond effectively to credible and reliable information that comes before him, invites him to continue to seek the views and comments of all concerned, in particular Member States, and expresses its appreciation for the discreet and independent way in which he continues to carry out his work;

17. *Requests* the Special Rapporteur to continue to consider including in his report information on the follow-up by Governments to his recommendations, visits and communications, including progress made and problems encountered;

18. *Stresses* the need for the continued regular exchange of views between the Committee, the Special Rapporteur and other relevant United Nations mechanisms and bodies, as well as for the pursuance of cooperation with relevant United Nations programmes, notably the United Nations Crime Prevention and Criminal Justice Programme, with a view to enhancing further their effectiveness and cooperation on issues relating to torture, inter alia, by improving their coordination;

19. *Expresses its gratitude and appreciation* to the Governments, organizations and individuals that have already contributed to the United Nations Voluntary Fund for Victims of Torture;

20. *Appeals* to all Governments and organizations to contribute annually to the Fund, if possible with a substantial increase in the level of contributions, so that consideration may be given to the ever-increasing demand for assistance;

21. *Expresses its appreciation* to the Board of Trustees of the Fund for the work it has accomplished;

22. *Requests* the Secretary-General to transmit to all Governments the appeals of the General Assembly for contributions to the Fund;

23. *Also requests* the Secretary-General to continue to include the Fund on an annual basis among the programmes for which funds are pledged at the United Nations Pledging Conference for Development Activities;

24. *Further requests* the Secretary-General to assist the Board of Trustees of the Fund in its appeal for contributions and in its efforts to make better known the existence of the Fund and the financial means currently available to it, as well as in its assessment of the global need for international funding of rehabilitation services for victims of torture and, in this effort, to make use of all existing possibilities, including the preparation, production and dissemination of information materials;

25. *Requests* the Secretary-General to ensure the provision of adequate staff and facilities for the bodies and mechanisms involved in combating torture and assisting victims of torture, commensurate with the strong support expressed by Member States for combating torture and assisting victims of torture;

26. *Invites* donor countries and recipient countries to consider including in their bilateral programmes and projects relating to the training of armed forces, security forces, prison and police personnel, as well as health-care personnel, matters relating to the protection of human rights and the prevention of torture and to keep in mind a gender perspective;

27. *Calls upon* all Governments, the Office of the United Nations High Commissioner for Human

Rights and other United Nations bodies and agencies, as well as relevant intergovernmental and non-governmental organizations, to commemorate, on 26 June, the United Nations International Day in Support of Victims of Torture;

28. *Requests* the Secretary-General to submit to the Commission on Human Rights at its fifty-sixth session and to the General Assembly at its fifty-fifth session a report on the status of the Convention against Torture and Other Cruel, Inhuman or Degrading Treatment or Punishment and a report on the operations of the United Nations Voluntary Fund for the Victims of Torture;

29. *Decides* to consider at its fifty-fifth session the reports of the Secretary-General, including the report on the United Nations Voluntary Fund for Victims of Torture, the report of the Committee against Torture and the interim report of the Special Rapporteur of the Commission on Human Rights on the question of torture and other cruel, inhuman or degrading treatment or punishment.

Freedom of opinion and expression

Reports of Special Rapporteur. In January [E/CN.4/1999/64], the Special Rapporteur on the promotion and protection of the right to freedom of opinion and expression, Abid Hussain (India), described his 1998 activities and discussed issues that he considered important for the development of the right, including the right to seek and receive information, national security laws, criminal libel, new information technologies, and women and freedom of expression. He summarized the texts of communications he had sent to 25 States and replies received.

The Special Rapporteur encouraged States that had not ratified the International Covenant on Civil and Political Rights and the International Covenant on Economic, Social and Cultural Rights, adopted by the General Assembly in resolution 2200 A (XXI) [YUN 1966, pp. 423 & 419], to do so. Governments were urged to review their national security laws and ordinary criminal laws that might infringe on the rights to freedom of opinion and expression and information, and were encouraged to ensure the right to access to information. He recommended that reasonable steps be taken to promote access to the Internet and that on-line expression be guided by international standards and be guaranteed the same protection as other forms of expression. Governments were urged to remove obstacles to the exercise by women of their right to freedom of expression. The Special Rapporteur invited Governments, intergovernmental organizations, NGOs and specialized agencies to present submissions on the relationship between freedom of expression and violence against women, as he hoped to prepare a report with the Special Rapporteur on violence against women.

The Special Rapporteur visited the Sudan (20-26 September) [E/CN.4/2000/63/Add.1] where, owing to time constraints, his visit was confined to Khartoum. Thus, he was prevented from addressing the difficult situation in southern Sudan, where a state of emergency existed. The Special Rapporteur considered that the Government had made significant advances regarding political and civil rights in the past two years, particularly with the adoption of the new Constitution in 1998. However, the information he had received concerning the period following the Constitution's adoption, which was characterized by the violation of political freedoms and human rights abuses, failed to demonstrate a serious effort on the part of the Government to move in that direction. In addition, the Special Rapporteur noted that the majority of non-official persons he met did not have full confidence in the Government's intentions and considered the fundamental freedoms to be precarious. The Special Rapporteur was concerned at the State's monopoly and control of the national radio and television broadcasting system and of the major daily newspapers. Obstacles limited the use of satellite dishes and other restrictions hindered the circulation of information from abroad through the press or television. The Special Rapporteur was very disturbed by the number of cases of arbitrary detention, torture and harassment of persons who sought to express different opinions, especially journalists, political opponents, students and human rights advocates, and deplored the intimidation of journalists. Religious minorities continued to be discriminated against in law and practice. The Special Rapporteur welcomed some progress in the status of women but discriminatory legislation and practices against them remained in effect.

Recommendations to the Government included establishing an independent national human rights institution; accession to the 1979 Convention on the Elimination of All Forms of Discrimination against Women, adopted by the General Assembly in resolution 34/180 [YUN 1979, p. 895], and the two Optional Protocols to the International Covenant on Civil and Political Rights, adopted by the Assembly in resolutions 2200 A (XXI) and 44/128, respectively [YUN 1966, p. 423, & YUN 1989, p. 484] and ratification of the 1984 Convention against Torture and Other Cruel, Inhuman and Degrading Treatment or Punishment, contained in Assembly resolution 39/46 [YUN 1984, p. 813]; revising restrictive domestic laws; ensuring suppression of intimidation or harassment of persons who sought to exercise the right; removing unnecessary restrictions on freedom of expression and assembly; guaranteeing the independence of the media; avoiding restrictions on foreign newspapers and broadcasts; ending abuses against women committed by the security forces and militias; granting the media equal access to all parts of society, especially minorities and women; and wide dissemination of basic human rights instruments and information.

Regarding his visit to Ireland (18-22 October) [E/CN.4/2000/63/Add.2], the Special Rapporteur asserted that freedom of opinion and expression was widely apparent. However, he expressed concern at the use and implementation of certain laws to restrict the right. He was also concerned at the negative effects produced by libel and defamation suits, which could bring reluctance to report matters of public interest. The Freedom of Information Act, 1997, had been working well since it came into force in 1998. He noted with satisfaction that the Working Group on the Illegal and Harmful Use of the Internet recommended an approach of non-intervention by the State. The Government had made efforts to encourage women's participation in the political and public sectors and had taken measures to promote the right to freedom of opinion and expression of refugees and minorities. The Special Rapporteur recommended that journalists should not be compelled to reveal their sources except in the most limited and clearly defined circumstances. He also recommended the establishment of an independent press ombudsman and encouraged the preparation of a new Defamation Bill. The Government was urged to review or repeal the laws concerning the censorship of publications and of films and videos, and the adoption and implementation of the Equal Status Bill, 1999, to provide for temporary special measures to overcome systematic and indirect discrimination against women and members of the traveller community, were recommended.

The Special Rapporteur visited the United Kingdom (24-29 October) [E/CN.4/2000/63/Add.3], where he observed that freedom of opinion and expression was widely visible and that it was protected. However, he was concerned that the freedom had been hindered to some extent by certain laws. Emergency powers had eroded public confidence, not only in the criminal justice system but also in the free operation of the investigative press. The fact that anti-terrorism legislation had not been repealed was a matter of concern, as was the Government's decision to introduce permanent anti-terrorist legislation. The Special Rapporteur considered the use of the Official Secrets Act to prosecute journalists and writers, as well as the existence of the D-notice Committee, to be incompatible with media freedom. He noted with concern the attacks against the principle of the confidentiality of journalists' sources. The Special Rapporteur welcomed the appointment of a Police Ombudsman and the establishment of new institutions in Northern Ireland, especially the Human Rights Commission. He considered the enactment of the Human Rights Act, 1998, to be an important step. The Special Rapporteur urged the Government to amend certain restrictive domestic laws and to ensure that the law and practice governing public demonstrations complied with international standards. He called on the Government to disclose information to the victims of the conflict in Northern Ireland to the maximum extent, in order to restore confidence in the police system and to reinforce the peace process. Further efforts should be made to improve the media tone and attitude towards Northern Ireland.

In conclusions made following his visit to Tunisia (6-10 December) [E/CN.4/2000/63/Add.4], the Special Rapporteur noted that despite legislation to promote human rights, there existed a chasm between declaration of intent and reality. He expressed concern at the State's control of the national radio and television broadcasting system, and the major dailies. Government efforts to modernize the media and liberalize the right to information were inadequate in view of the censorship of the media and the fact that self-censorship was rooted in press organs and in the minds of journalists. The Government was encouraged to adopt additional measures to protect the right to freedom of opinion and expression, in particular by revising certain domestic laws, including the Press Code. It was urged to establish a press council, independent of State bodies and the judiciary, to which journalists and the public could submit complaints, request advice and obtain redress, and an independent body to deal with subjects of interest to the media. The Government was also urged to eliminate restrictions on foreign newspapers and broadcasts, abolish censorship, review cases of persons detained for exercising the right to freedom of expression, end alleged intimidation and harassment of persons who sought to exercise the right, and conduct an inquiry into the alleged cases of harassment of wives and kin of detained persons and persons suspected of unlawful political activities.

Commission action. On 26 April [res. 1999/36], the Commission expressed concern at the detention and extrajudicial killing, persecution and harassment of, as well as threats and acts of violence and discrimination directed at, persons who exercised the right to freedom of opinion and expression, the rights to freedom of thought, conscience and religion, of peaceful assembly and of association and the right to take part in the conduct of public affairs. It appealed to States to ensure respect and support for the rights of all persons who exercised those rights, to ensure than they were not discriminated against, and to cooperate with and assist the Special Rapporteur.

The Special Rapporteur was asked to draw the attention of the High Commissioner to situations of serious concern; to pay particular attention to the situation of women and the relationship between the promotion and protection of the right to freedom of opinion and expression and incidents of discrimination based on sex, in cooperation with the Special Rapporteur on violence against women; to cooperate with other UN human rights mechanisms and procedures; to develop further his commentary on the right to seek and receive information and to expand on his observations and recommendations arising from communications; and to provide his views on the advantages and challenges of new information technologies. The Commission decided to extend the Special Rapporteur's mandate for an additional three years and asked him to report in 2000. The Commission's decision on the mandate and request for a report were endorsed by the Economic and Social Council on 27 July in **decision 1999/238**.

Terrorism

Commission action. By a roll-call vote of 27 to none, with 26 abstentions, the Commission, on 26 April [res. 1999/27], condemning incitement of ethnic hatred, violence and terrorism, as well as violations of the right to live free from fear and of the right to life, liberty and security, called on States to take measures, in conformity with international law, to prevent, combat and eliminate terrorism. The Subcommission's Special Rapporteur on human rights and terrorism was asked, in her preliminary report, to give attention to the question of impunity.

Report of Special Rapporteur. In response to a 1998 Subcommission request [YUN 1998, p. 670], Kalliopi K. Koufa (Greece), the Special Rapporteur appointed to conduct a study on human rights and terrorism, presented, in June [E/CN.4/Sub.2/1999/27], a preliminary report. The Special Rapporteur provided a historical background on the subject and examined the link between terrorism and human rights, issues of definition and terminology regarding terrorism, international human rights law and the accountability of the non-State actor, and recent trends. She proposed that the legal accountability of non-State actors involved in human rights violations through acts of terrorism should be discussed further during the study, with a view to contributing a more balanced approach to the major divergences of opinion regarding the proper standard of accountability. Other trends and issues mentioned in her 1997 working paper [YUN 1997, p. 658] needed to be addressed at subsequent stages of the study.

Subcommission action. On 26 August [res. 1999/26], the Subcommission asked the Secretary-General to assist the Special Rapporteur by providing for visits to Geneva and New York and, in particular, the United Nations Centre for International Crime Prevention of the United Nations Office for Drug Control and Crime Prevention in Vienna, to hold consultations and complement her research. It asked the Secretary-General to transmit the preliminary report to Governments, specialized agencies and concerned intergovernmental organizations and NGOs for comments, information and data relating to the study.

Report of Secretary-General. In October [A/54/439], the Secretary-General, in response to General Assembly resolution 52/133 [YUN 1997, p. 658], reported on the views expressed by Member States on the implications of terrorism for the enjoyment of human rights and fundamental freedoms. The report summarized the replies received from the Governments that had responded to his request for their views, namely, Azerbaijan, Egypt, Nepal, Pakistan, Turkey and the Federal Republic of Yugoslavia (Serbia and Montenegro).

GENERAL ASSEMBLY ACTION

On 17 December [meeting 83], the General Assembly, on the recommendation of the Third Committee [A/54/605/Add.2], adopted **resolution 54/164** by recorded vote (106-0-58) [agenda item 116 *(b)*].

Human rights and terrorism

The General Assembly,

Guided by the Charter of the United Nations, the Universal Declaration of Human Rights, the Declaration on Principles of International Law concerning Friendly Relations and Cooperation among States in accordance with the Charter of the United Nations and the International Covenants on Human Rights,

Recalling the Declaration on the Occasion of the Fiftieth Anniversary of the United Nations,

Recalling also the Vienna Declaration and Programme of Action adopted by the World Conference on Human Rights on 25 June 1993, in which the Conference reaffirmed that terrorism is indeed aimed at the destruction of human rights, fundamental freedoms and democracy,

Recalling further its resolutions 48/122 of 20 December 1993, 49/185 of 23 December 1994, 50/186 of 22 December 1995 and 52/133 of 12 December 1997,

Recalling in particular its resolution 52/133, in which it requested the Secretary-General to seek the views of

Member States on the implications of terrorism, in all its forms and manifestations, for the full enjoyment of human rights and fundamental freedoms,

Recalling previous resolutions of the Commission on Human Rights, taking note, in particular, of resolution 1999/27 of 26 April 1999, and recalling also the relevant resolutions of the Subcommission on the Promotion and Protection of Human Rights,

Alarmed that acts of terrorism in all its forms and manifestations aimed at the destruction of human rights have continued despite national and international efforts,

Bearing in mind that the essential and most basic human right is the right to life,

Bearing in mind also that terrorism creates an environment that destroys the right of people to live in freedom from fear,

Reiterating that all States have an obligation to promote and protect all human rights and fundamental freedoms and that every individual should strive to secure their universal and effective recognition and observance,

Seriously concerned about the gross violations of human rights perpetrated by terrorist groups,

Profoundly deploring the increasing number of innocent persons, including women, children and the elderly, killed, massacred and maimed by terrorists in indiscriminate and random acts of violence and terror, which cannot be justified under any circumstances,

Noting with great concern the growing connection between the terrorist groups and other criminal organizations engaged in the illegal traffic in arms and drugs at the national and international levels, as well as the consequent commission of serious crimes such as murder, extortion, kidnapping, assault, the taking of hostages and robbery,

Emphasizing the importance of Member States taking appropriate steps to deny safe haven to those who plan, finance or commit terrorist acts, by ensuring their apprehension and prosecution or extradition,

Mindful of the need to protect the human rights of and guarantees for the individual in accordance with the relevant human rights principles and instruments, in particular the right to life,

Reaffirming that all measures to counter terrorism must be in strict conformity with the relevant provisions of international law including international human rights standards,

1. *Expresses its solidarity* with the victims of terrorism;

2. *Condemns* the violations of the right to live free from fear and of the right to life, liberty and security;

3. *Reiterates its unequivocal condemnation* of the acts, methods and practices of terrorism, in all its forms and manifestations, as activities aimed at the destruction of human rights, fundamental freedoms and democracy, threatening the territorial integrity and security of States, destabilizing legitimately constituted Governments, undermining pluralistic civil society and having adverse consequences for the economic and social development of States;

4. *Calls upon* States to take all necessary and effective measures in accordance with relevant provisions of international law, including international human rights standards, to prevent, combat and eliminate terrorism in all its forms and manifestations, wherever and by whomever committed;

5. *Urges* the international community to enhance cooperation at the regional and international levels in the fight against terrorism, in accordance with relevant international instruments, including those relating to human rights, with the aim of its eradication;

6. *Condemns* the incitement of ethnic hatred, violence and terrorism;

7. *Commends* those Governments that have communicated their views on the implications of terrorism in response to the note verbale by the Secretary-General dated 16 August 1999;

8. *Welcomes* the report of the Secretary-General, and requests him to continue to seek the views of Member States on the implications of terrorism, in all its forms and manifestations, for the full enjoyment of all human rights and fundamental freedoms, with a view to incorporating them in his report;

9. *Decides* to consider this question at its fifty-sixth session, under the item entitled "Human rights questions".

RECORDED VOTE ON RESOLUTION 54/164:

In favour: Afghanistan, Albania, Algeria, Angola, Antigua and Barbuda, Azerbaijan, Bahamas, Bahrain, Bangladesh, Barbados, Belarus, Belize, Bhutan, Bolivia, Bosnia and Herzegovina, Botswana, Brazil, Brunei Darussalam, Cambodia, Cameroon, Cape Verde, Chad, China, Colombia, Comoros, Costa Rica, Côte d'Ivoire, Cuba, Democratic People's Republic of Korea, Democratic Republic of the Congo, Djibouti, Dominica, Dominican Republic, Ecuador, Egypt, El Salvador, Eritrea, Fiji, Gabon, Georgia, Ghana, Grenada, Guatemala, Guinea-Bissau, Guyana, Haiti, Honduras, India, Indonesia, Iran, Jamaica, Jordan, Kazakhstan, Kenya, Kuwait, Lao People's Democratic Republic, Libyan Arab Jamahiriya, Malaysia, Maldives, Mali, Mauritius, Mongolia, Morocco, Mozambique, Myanmar, Namibia, Nepal, Nicaragua, Nigeria, Oman, Pakistan, Panama, Papua New Guinea, Paraguay, Peru, Philippines, Qatar, Republic of Moldova, Russian Federation, Saint Lucia, Saudi Arabia, Senegal, Seychelles, Sierra Leone, Singapore, Sri Lanka, Sudan, Suriname, Swaziland, Tajikistan, Thailand, The former Yugoslav Republic of Macedonia, Trinidad and Tobago, Tunisia, Turkey, Turkmenistan, Uganda, Ukraine, United Arab Emirates, United Republic of Tanzania, Uruguay, Uzbekistan, Viet Nam, Yemen, Zambia, Zimbabwe.

Against: None.

Abstaining: Andorra, Argentina, Armenia, Australia, Austria, Belgium, Benin, Bulgaria, Burkina Faso, Canada, Chile, Croatia, Cyprus, Czech Republic, Denmark, Estonia, Ethiopia, Finland, France, Germany, Greece, Hungary, Iceland, Ireland, Israel, Italy, Japan, Latvia, Lebanon, Liechtenstein, Lithuania, Luxembourg, Malawi, Malta, Marshall Islands, Mexico, Micronesia, Monaco, Netherlands, New Zealand, Norway, Poland, Portugal, Republic of Korea, Romania, Samoa, San Marino, Slovakia, Slovenia, Solomon Islands, South Africa, Spain, Sweden, Syrian Arab Republic, Togo, United Kingdom, United States, Venezuela.

Hostage-taking

On 26 April [res. 1999/29], the Commission, condemning hostage-taking, demanded that all hostages be released immediately and without preconditions. States were called on to take measures to prevent, combat and punish hostage-taking, and thematic special rapporteurs and working groups were urged to address the consequences of such acts in their reports.

Freedom of movement

Mass exoduses

Pursuant to General Assembly resolution 52/132 [YUN 1997, p. 661], the Secretary-General, in September [A/54/360], reported on human rights and mass exoduses, including UN efforts to avert new flows of refugees and to tackle the root causes of such flows. The Secretary-General said that much progress had been made regarding cooperation between the human rights and humanitarian communities in finding solutions to mass exoduses. However, more had to be done, including promoting accession to international law instruments; disseminating and advocating human rights and humanitarian principles to encourage compliance with prohibitions against arbitrary and forcible displacement and greater respect for the rights of those who fled; establishing mechanisms to ensure compliance with international law to end the culture of impunity; sharing responsibility with States that experienced the greatest political, economic and social impact of mass exoduses; improving security and access to humanitarian assistance; encouraging ratification of the 1994 Convention on the Safety of United Nations and Associated Personnel, adopted by the Assembly in resolution 49/59 [YUN 1994, p. 1289], and training humanitarian personnel in security procedures; and ensuring that the Security Council was informed of the human rights and humanitarian situation in cases of potential or actual conflict. In addition, various coordination and streamlining measures were needed.

GENERAL ASSEMBLY ACTION

On 17 December [meeting 83], the General Assembly, on the recommendation of the Third Committee [A/54/605/Add. 2], adopted **resolution 54/180** without vote [agenda item 116 *(b)*].

Human rights and mass exoduses

The General Assembly,

Deeply disturbed by the scale and magnitude of exoduses and displacements of people in many regions of the world and by the human suffering of refugees and displaced persons, a high proportion of whom are women and children,

Recalling its previous relevant resolutions, as well as those of the Commission on Human Rights, in particular Commission resolution 1998/49 of 17 April 1998, and the conclusions of the World Conference on Human Rights, held at Vienna from 14 to 25 June 1993, which recognized that gross violations of human rights, persecution, political and ethnic conflicts, famine and economic insecurity, poverty and generalized violence are among the root causes leading to mass exodus and displacements of people, and also recalling the second open debate that was held in the Security Council on the protection of civilians in armed conflict on 16 and 17 September 1999,

Recalling with satisfaction its endorsement, in its resolution 41/70 of 3 December 1986, of the call upon all States to promote human rights and fundamental freedoms and to refrain from denying these to individuals in their population because of nationality, ethnicity, race, religion or language,

Recalling all relevant human rights standards, including the Universal Declaration of Human Rights, the principles of international protection for refugees and the general conclusion of the Executive Committee of the Programme of the United Nations High Commissioner for Refugees on international protection and the fact that asylum applicants should have access to fair and expeditious status-determination procedures,

Stressing the importance of adherence to international humanitarian, human rights and refugee law in order to avert mass exoduses and to protect refugees and internally displaced persons, and expressing its deep concern at the lack of respect for those laws and principles, especially during armed conflict, including the denial of safe and unimpeded access to the displaced,

Noting, in this regard, the entry into force of the Convention on the Safety of United Nations and Associated Personnel of 9 December 1994, urging States to consider ratifying or acceding to the Convention, and condemning attacks and the use of force against United Nations and associated personnel, as well as personnel of international humanitarian organizations,

Reaffirming the primary responsibility of States to ensure the protection of refugees and internally displaced persons,

Recognizing the contribution of the establishment of the International Criminal Court to ending impunity for perpetrators of certain crimes, as defined in the Rome Statute of the International Criminal Court, which lead to or result from mass exoduses,

Noting with satisfaction the efforts by the United Nations system to develop a comprehensive approach to addressing the root causes and effects of movements of refugees and other displaced persons and the strengthening of emergency preparedness and response mechanisms,

Recognizing that the human rights machinery of the United Nations, including the mechanisms of the Commission on Human Rights and the human rights treaty bodies, has important capabilities to address human rights violations that cause movements of refugees and displaced persons or prevent durable solutions to their plight,

Recognizing also the complementarity between the systems for the protection of human rights and for humanitarian action, in particular the mandates of the United Nations High Commissioner for Human Rights and the United Nations High Commissioner for Refugees, as well as the work of the representative of the Secretary-General on internally displaced persons and the Special Representative of the Secretary-General for Children and Armed Conflict and that cooperation between them, in accordance with their respective mandates, as well as coordination between the human rights, political and security components of United Nations operations, make important contributions to the promotion and protection of human rights of persons forced into mass exodus and displacement,

1. *Takes note* of the report of the Secretary-General;

2. *Strongly deplores* ethnic and other forms of intolerance as one of the major causes of forced migratory movements, and urges States to take all necessary steps to ensure respect for human rights, especially the rights of persons belonging to minorities;

3. *Reaffirms* the need for all Governments, intergovernmental bodies and concerned international organizations to intensify their cooperation and assistance in worldwide efforts to address human rights situations that lead to, as well as the serious problems that result from, mass exoduses of refugees and displaced persons;

4. *Emphasizes* the responsibility of all States and international organizations to cooperate with those countries, in particular developing ones, affected by mass exoduses of refugees and displaced persons, and calls upon Governments, the United Nations High Commissioner for Human Rights, the United Nations High Commissioner for Refugees and other relevant parts of the United Nations system to continue to respond to assistance needs of countries hosting large numbers of refugees until durable solutions are found;

5. *Urges* the Secretary-General to give high priority to and to allocate the necessary resources within the regular budget of the United Nations for the consolidation and strengthening of emergency preparedness and response mechanisms, including early warning activities in the humanitarian area, for the purpose of ensuring, inter alia, that effective action is taken to identify all human rights abuses that contribute to mass exoduses of persons;

6. *Invites* the special rapporteurs, special representatives and working groups of the Commission on Human Rights and the United Nations human rights treaty bodies, acting within their mandates, to seek information, where appropriate, on human rights problems that may result in mass exoduses of populations or impede their voluntary return home and, where appropriate, to include such information, together with recommendations thereon, in their reports and to bring such information to the attention of the United Nations High Commissioner for Human Rights for appropriate action in fulfilment of her mandate, in consultation with the United Nations High Commissioner for Refugees;

7. *Requests* all United Nations bodies, acting within their mandates, the specialized agencies and governmental, intergovernmental and non-governmental organizations to cooperate fully with all mechanisms of the Commission on Human Rights and, in particular, to provide them with all relevant information in their possession on the human rights situations creating or affecting refugees and displaced persons;

8. *Requests* the United Nations High Commissioner for Human Rights, in the exercise of her mandate, as set out in General Assembly resolution 48/141 of 20 December 1993, to coordinate human rights activities throughout the United Nations system and, in cooperation with the United Nations High Commissioner for Refugees, to pay particular attention to situations that cause or threaten to cause mass exoduses or displacements and to contribute to efforts to address such situations effectively through promotion and protection measures, emergency preparedness and response mechanisms, early warning and information sharing, technical advice, expertise and cooperation in countries of origin as well as host countries;

9. *Welcomes* the efforts of the United Nations High Commissioner for Human Rights to contribute to the creation of an environment viable for return in post-conflict societies through initiatives such as the rehabilitation of the justice system, the creation of national institutions capable of defending human rights and broad-based programmes of human rights education and the strengthening of local non-governmental organizations through field presences and programmes of advisory services and technical cooperation;

10. *Welcomes with appreciation* the ongoing contributions of the United Nations High Commissioner for Refugees to the deliberations of the Commission on Human Rights and to other international human rights bodies and mechanisms, and also welcomes the invitation extended to her by the Commission to address the Commission at each of its future sessions;

11. *Encourages* States that have not already done so to consider acceding to the 1951 Convention and the 1967 Protocol relating to the Status of Refugees and to other relevant regional instruments concerning refugees, as applicable, and relevant international instruments of human rights and humanitarian law, and to take appropriate measures to disseminate and implement those instruments domestically to encourage compliance with provisions against arbitrary and forcible displacement and greater respect for the rights of those who flee;

12. *Notes with appreciation* that a number of States not parties to the 1951 Convention and the 1967 Protocol continue to maintain a generous approach to asylum;

13. *Encourages* States parties to the 1951 Convention to provide information to the Office of the United Nations High Commissioner for Refugees, in accordance with article 35 of the Convention;

14. *Calls upon* States to ensure effective protection of and assistance to refugees and internally displaced persons, consistent with international law, inter alia, by respecting the principle of non-refoulement, ensuring full, safe and unhindered access by humanitarian workers to displaced populations and ensuring the security and civilian and humanitarian nature of camps and settlements for refugees and internally displaced persons;

15. *Requests* the Secretary-General to prepare and submit to the General Assembly at its fifty-sixth session a report on the implementation of the present resolution as it pertains to all aspects of human rights and mass exoduses, including detailed information on the programmatic, institutional, administrative, financial and management efforts instituted to enhance the capacity of the United Nations to avert new flows of refugees and other displaced persons, to tackle the root causes of such flows, to protect those who have become displaced during mass exoduses and to facilitate their return and reintegration;

16. *Decides* to continue its consideration of this question at its fifty-sixth session.

Internally displaced persons

Report of Secretary-General's Representative. In January [E/CN.4/1999/79], the Secretary-General's Representative, Francis M. Deng (Sudan), updated developments regarding the Guiding Principles on Internal Displacement [YUN 1998, p. 675] and efforts to develop an institutional framework for internally displaced persons. He discussed country visits as a way to focus on specific situations of internal displacement. The Representative presented areas for further research, including strategies to approach the problem when it occurred in countries not acknowledging it, the issue of non-State actors, the needs of internally displaced women and children, and donor policies.

The Representative visited Colombia (20-27 May) [E/CN.4/2000/83/Add.1], where over a million persons were internally displaced, most of them uprooted from their homes because of the security situation. Displacement in Colombia was not merely incidental to the internal armed conflict but also a deliberate strategy of war. Overall, there appeared to be insufficient will on the part of the Government to put its laws into practice. Concerned by the deterioration of the situation of internal displacement, the Representative suggested components for a comprehensive strategy to clarify the role of the State and to integrate the work of intergovernmental and non-governmental actors.

Workshop. The Workshop on Implementing the Guiding Principles on Internal Displacement (Bogotá, Colombia, 27-29 May) [E/CN.4/2000/83/Add.2], sponsored by the Brookings Institution Project on Internal Displacement, the Grupo de Apoyo a Organizaciones de Desplazados and the United States Committee for Refugees, underlined the importance of enhanced coordination among the Government of Colombia, UN agencies and NGOs to improve protection of internally displaced persons and identified elements for successful return, resettlement or reintegration. The Workshop's Final Declaration reiterated the importance of applying the Guiding Principles to the situation, as well as to Colombian policies and legal norms.

Commission action. On 27 April [res. 1999/47], the Commission called on the High Commissioner to develop projects, in cooperation with Governments, international organizations and the Representative, to promote the human rights of internally displaced persons, as part of the programme of advisory services and technical cooperation (see p. 582), and to include in her report to the Commission information on their implementation. The Representative was asked to continue to report to the General Assembly and to the Commission, and the Secretary-General was asked to assist him.

On 27 September [E/1999/23/Add.1 (res. 1999/S-4/1], the Commission asked the Secretary-General's Representative, among others, to carry out a mission to East Timor, to report to the Commission in 2000 and to submit an interim report to the Assembly in 1999 (see p. 711).

Subcommission action. On 25 August [dec. 1999/108], the Subcommission, recalling its 1998 resolution on housing and property restitution in the context of the return of refugees and internally displaced persons [YUN 1998, p. 675], decided to consider the item in 2000.

Report of Secretary-General's Representative. In a September report [A/54/409], the Representative stated that since the creation of his mandate in 1992 [YUN 1992, p. 777], the international community's response to internal displacement had advanced. However, in view of the millions of internally displaced persons worldwide, there was a need to do much more in such areas as promoting the Guiding Principles, monitoring conditions on the ground, interceding on behalf of the internally displaced, and recommending collaborative action by the relevant agencies. For the mandate to address that challenge, it needed enhanced resources, which were currently dismally deficient.

GENERAL ASSEMBLY ACTION

On 17 December [meeting 83], the General Assembly, on the recommendation of the Third Committee [A/54/605/Add.2], adopted **resolution 54/167** without vote [agenda item 116 *(b)*].

Protection of and assistance to internally displaced persons

The General Assembly,

Deeply disturbed by the alarmingly high numbers of internally displaced persons throughout the world who receive inadequate protection and assistance, and conscious of the serious problem this is creating for the international community,

Conscious of the human rights and the humanitarian dimensions of the problem of internally displaced persons and the responsibilities this poses for States and the international community to explore methods and means better to address their protection and assistance needs,

Recalling the relevant norms of international human rights instruments, international humanitarian law and analogous refugee law, and emphasizing the need for their better implementation with regard to internally displaced persons,

Recalling also the emphasis in the Vienna Declaration and Programme of Action, adopted by the World Conference on Human Rights on 25 June 1993, on the need to develop global strategies to address the problem of internal displacement,

Deploring practices of forced displacement, in particular ethnic cleansing, and their negative consequences for the enjoyment of fundamental human rights by large groups of populations,

Noting the progress made thus far by the Representative of the Secretary-General on internally displaced persons in developing a legal framework, analysing institutional arrangements, undertaking dialogue with

Governments and issuing a series of reports on particular country situations, together with proposals for remedial measures,

Welcoming the cooperation established between the Representative of the Secretary-General and the United Nations and other international and regional organizations, in particular the participation of the Representative of the Secretary-General in the meetings of the Inter-Agency Standing Committee and its subsidiary bodies, and encouraging further strengthening of this collaboration in order to promote better assistance, protection and development strategies for internally displaced persons,

Welcoming also the publication and the wide dissemination of the compilation and analysis of legal norms prepared by the Representative of the Secretary-General, in particular the Guiding Principles on Internal Displacement,

Recalling its resolution 52/130 of 12 December 1997,

1. *Takes note with appreciation* of the report of the Representative of the Secretary-General on internally displaced persons;

2. *Commends* the Representative of the Secretary-General for the activities undertaken so far, despite the limited resources available to him, and for the catalytic role he continues to play in raising the level of consciousness about the plight of internally displaced persons;

3. *Encourages* the Representative of the Secretary-General to continue his analysis of the causes of internal displacement, the needs of those displaced, measures of prevention and ways to increase protection, assistance and solutions for internally displaced persons, including their safe return;

4. *Also encourages* the Representative of the Secretary-General to continue to pay specific attention in his review to the protection and assistance needs of women and children, bearing in mind the relevant strategic objective in the Beijing Declaration and the Platform for Action of the Fourth World Conference on Women;

5. *Welcomes* the study prepared by the Representative of the Secretary-General to promote a comprehensive strategy for better protection, assistance and development for internally displaced persons;

6. *Notes* the development by the Representative of the Secretary-General, on the basis of his compilation and analysis of legal norms, of a comprehensive framework for the protection of internally displaced persons, in particular the Guiding Principles on Internal Displacement;

7. *Welcomes* the fact that the Representative of the Secretary-General has made use of the Guiding Principles in his dialogue with Governments and intergovernmental and non-governmental organizations, and requests him to continue his efforts in that regard;

8. *Notes with appreciation* that the United Nations agencies, regional and non-governmental organizations are making use of the Guiding Principles in their work, and encourages the further dissemination and application of the Guiding Principles;

9. *Calls upon* all Governments to continue to facilitate the activities of the Representative of the Secretary-General, in particular Governments with situations of internal displacement, encourages them to give serious consideration to inviting the Representative to visit their countries so as to enable him to study and analyse more fully the issues involved, and thanks those Governments that have already done so;

10. *Invites* Governments to give due consideration, in dialogue with the Representative of the Secretary-General, to the recommendations and suggestions addressed to them, in accordance with his mandate, and to inform him of measures taken thereon;

11. *Urges* all relevant United Nations humanitarian assistance and development organizations concerned to enhance their collaboration with the Representative of the Secretary-General by developing frameworks of cooperation, especially through the Inter-Agency Standing Committee, to promote protection, assistance and development for internally displaced persons and to provide all possible assistance and support to him;

12. *Welcomes* the efforts to establish a global information system on internally displaced persons, as advocated by the Representative of the Secretary-General, and encourages the members of the Inter-Agency Standing Committee to continue to collaborate in those efforts;

13. *Requests* the Secretary-General to give all necessary assistance to the Representative to carry out his mandate effectively;

14. *Requests* the Representative of the Secretary-General to prepare, for consideration by the General Assembly at its fifty-sixth session, a report on the implementation of the present resolution;

15. *Decides* to continue its consideration of the question of protection of and assistance to internally displaced persons at its fifty-sixth session.

(For information on the situation of refugees and displaced person, see PART THREE, Chapter XII; see PART THREE, Chapter III for details on humanitarian assistance provided to internally displaced persons.)

Civilians in armed conflict

On 12 February [meeting 3977], the Security Council discussed the protection of civilians in armed conflict. On the same date [meeting 3978], its President made statement **S/PRST/1999/6** on behalf of the Council:

> The Security Council has considered the matter of protection of civilians in armed conflict.
>
> The Council expresses its grave concern at the growing civilian toll of armed conflict and notes with distress that civilians now account for the vast majority of casualties in armed conflict and are increasingly directly targeted by combatants and armed elements. The Council condemns attacks or acts of violence in situations of armed conflict directed against civilians, especially women, children and other vulnerable groups, including also refugees and internally displaced persons, in violation of the relevant rules of international law, including those of international humanitarian and human rights law.
>
> The Council is especially concerned about attacks on humanitarian workers, in violation of the rules of international law.

The Council notes that large-scale human suffering is a consequence and sometimes a contributing factor to instability and further conflict, whether due to displacement, violent assault or other atrocities. Bearing in mind its primary responsibility for the maintenance of international peace and security, the Council affirms the need for the international community to assist and protect civilian populations affected by armed conflict. The Council calls upon all parties concerned to ensure the safety of civilians and guarantee the unimpeded and safe access of United Nations and other humanitarian personnel to those in need. In this regard, the Council recalls the statement by its President of 19 June 1997 and also recalls its resolution 1208(1998) of 19 November 1998 on the status and treatment of refugees.

The Council expresses particular concern at the harmful impact of armed conflict on children and, in this regard, recalls the statement by its President of 29 June 1998.

The Council calls upon all parties concerned to comply strictly with their obligations under international law, in particular their relevant obligations under the Hague Conventions, the Geneva Conventions of 1949 and the Additional Protocols thereto, of 1977, and the United Nations Convention on the Rights of the Child of 1989, as well as with all decisions of the Council.

The Council strongly condemns the deliberate targeting by combatants of civilians in armed conflict and demands that all concerned put an end to such violations of international humanitarian and human rights law. The Council expresses its willingness to respond, in accordance with the Charter of the United Nations, to situations in which civilians, as such, have been targeted or humanitarian assistance to civilians has been deliberately obstructed.

The Council also condemns all attempts to incite violence against civilians in situations of armed conflict and calls upon States to fulfil their obligations to take action at the national level. The Council affirms the need to bring to justice, in an appropriate manner, individuals who incite or cause violence against civilians in situations of armed conflict or who otherwise violate international humanitarian and human rights law. In this regard, the Council reaffirms the importance of the work being done by the ad hoc Tribunals for the former Yugoslavia and Rwanda and calls upon all States to cooperate with the Tribunals, in accordance with the relevant Council resolutions. The Council acknowledges the historic significance of the adoption of the Rome Statute of the International Criminal Court.

The Council notes the deleterious impact of the proliferation of arms, in particular small arms, on the security of civilians, including refugees and other vulnerable populations. In this regard, it recalls its resolution 1209(1998) of 19 November 1998 which, inter alia, stressed the importance of all Member States, and in particular States involved in manufacturing and marketing of weapons, restricting arms transfers which could provoke or prolong armed conflicts or aggravate existing tensions or armed conflicts in Africa, and which urged international collaboration in combating illegal arms flows in Africa.

The Council expresses concern over the widening gap between the rules of international humanitarian law and their application. The Council welcomes the commemorative events planned to mark the fiftieth anniversary of the Geneva Conventions and the centenary of the first International Peace Conference, held at The Hague in 1899. These occasions provide an opportunity for a further exploration of ways and means by which the international community may enhance the compliance of parties to an armed conflict with the relevant rules of international law, including those of international humanitarian law.

The Council welcomes the continuing contribution to the implementation of international humanitarian law of the International Committee of the Red Cross.

The Council considers that a comprehensive and coordinated approach by Member States and international organizations and agencies is required in order to address the problem of the protection of civilians in situations of armed conflicts. To this end, the Council requests the Secretary-General to submit a report containing concrete recommendations to the Council by September 1999 on ways the Council, acting within its sphere of responsibility, could improve the physical and legal protection of civilians in situations of armed conflict. The report should also identify contributions the Council could make towards effective implementation of existing humanitarian law. The report should examine whether there are any significant gaps in existing legal norms, through the review of recent reports in this regard. The Council encourages the Secretary-General to consult the Inter-Agency Standing Committee in formulating his recommendations.

The Council affirms its intention to review the recommendations of the Secretary-General in accordance with its responsibilities under the Charter.

The Council met again on 22 February to discuss the protection of civilians in armed conflict [meeting 3980].

Report of Secretary-General. As requested by the Security Council (see above), the Secretary-General, in September [S/1999/957], submitted a report with recommendations on how the Council could improve the physical and legal protection of civilians in situations of armed conflict.

The Secretary-General described threats and violence against civilians in armed conflict and the role of the Council in their protection. He made recommendations aimed at identifying ways in which the Council could promote full respect for international humanitarian, human rights and refugee law, by States and non-State actors, and particularly by parties to conflicts. The recommendations concerned Member States' ratification of the major instruments of international humanitarian, human rights and refugee law; accountability and enforcement measures for war crimes; gaps in international law on protection of internally displaced persons, and the minimum age of recruitment for the armed forces; the safety of humanitarian personnel; conflict prevention; confidence-building; humanitarian access; special measures for children and women; targeted sanctions; small arms and anti-personnel landmines; peacekeeping; the separation of combatants and armed elements from civilians in camps; disarmament and demobilization; humanitarian zones, security zones and safe corridors; and intervention in cases of systematic and widespread violations of international law. Other recommendations were intended to permanently strengthen the capacity of the Council and the United Nations to protect civilians in armed conflict by strengthening the Organization's capacity to plan and deploy rapidly and establishing a technical review mechanism of sanctions. Other recommendations called for Council action upon receipt of information indicating the imminent outbreak of violence aimed at civilians, and proposals intended to alleviate the suffering of civilians in situations where conflict had already broken out and where civilians were being targeted.

SECURITY COUNCIL ACTION

On 16 and 17 September [meeting 4046], the Security Council discussed the Secretary-General's report. It unanimously adopted **resolution 1265 (1999)** on 17 September. The draft [S/1999/981] was prepared in consultations among Council members.

The Security Council,

Recalling the statement by its President of 12 February 1999,

Having considered the report of the Secretary-General of 8 September 1999 submitted to the Security Council in accordance with the above-mentioned statement,

Taking note of the reports of the Secretary-General on the causes of conflict and the promotion of durable peace and sustainable development in Africa and on the protection for humanitarian assistance to refugees and others in conflict situations, of 13 April and 22 September 1998, respectively, in particular their analysis related to the protection of civilians,

Noting that civilians account for the vast majority of casualties in armed conflicts and are increasingly targeted by combatants and armed elements, gravely concerned by the hardships borne by civilians during armed conflict, in particular as a result of acts of violence directed against them, especially women, children and other vulnerable groups, including refugees and internally displaced persons, and recognizing the consequent impact this will have on durable peace, reconciliation and development,

Bearing in mind its primary responsibility under the Charter of the United Nations for the maintenance of international peace and security, and underlining the importance of taking measures aimed at conflict prevention and resolution,

Stressing the need to address the causes of armed conflict in a comprehensive manner in order to enhance the protection of civilians on a long-term basis, including by promoting economic growth, poverty eradication, sustainable development, national reconciliation, good governance, democracy, the rule of law and respect for and protection of human rights,

Expressing its deep concern at the erosion in respect for international humanitarian, human rights and refugee law and principles during armed conflict, in particular by deliberate acts of violence against all those protected under such law, and expressing its concern also at the denial of safe and unimpeded access to people in need,

Underlining the importance of the widest possible dissemination of international humanitarian, human rights and refugee law and of relevant training for, inter alia, civilian police, armed forces, members of the judicial and legal professions, civil society and personnel of international and regional organizations,

Recalling the statement by its President of 8 July 1999, and emphasizing its call for the inclusion, as appropriate, within specific peace agreements and, on a case-by-case basis, within United Nations peacekeeping mandates, of clear terms for the disarmament, demobilization and reintegration of ex-combatants, including the safe and timely disposal of arms and ammunition,

Mindful of the particular vulnerability of refugees and internally displaced persons, and reaffirming the primary responsibility of States to ensure their protection, in particular by maintaining the security and civilian character of camps for refugees and internally displaced persons,

Underlining the special rights and needs of children in situations of armed conflict, including those of the girl child,

Recognizing the direct and particular impact of armed conflict on women as referred to in paragraph 18 of the report of the Secretary-General, and in this regard welcoming the ongoing work within the United Nations system on the implementation of a gender perspective in humanitarian assistance and on violence against women,

1. *Welcomes* the report of the Secretary-General of 8 September 1999, and takes note of the comprehensive recommendations contained therein;

2. *Strongly condemns* the deliberate targeting of civilians in situations of armed conflict as well as attacks on objects protected under international law, and calls upon all parties to put an end to such practices;

3. *Emphasizes* the importance of preventing conflicts which could endanger international peace and security, and, in this context, highlights the importance of implementing appropriate preventive measures to resolve conflicts, including the use of United Nations and other dispute-settlement mechanisms and of preventive military and civilian deployments, in accordance with the relevant provisions of the Charter of the United Nations, resolutions of the Security Council and relevant international instruments;

4. *Urges* all parties concerned to comply strictly with their obligations under international humanitarian, human rights and refugee law, in particular those contained in the Hague Conventions of 1899 and 1907 and in the Geneva Conventions of 1949 and the Additional Protocols thereto, of 1977, as well as with the decisions of the Security Council;

5. *Calls upon* States which have not already done so to consider ratifying the major instruments of international humanitarian, human rights and refugee law, and to take appropriate legislative, judicial and administrative measures to implement those instruments domestically, drawing on technical assistance, as appropriate, from relevant international organizations, including the International Committee of the Red Cross and United Nations bodies;

6. *Emphasizes* the responsibility of States to end impunity and to prosecute those responsible for genocide, crimes against humanity and serious violations of international humanitarian law, affirms the possibility, to this end, of using the International Fact-Finding Commission established by article 90 of Additional Protocol I to the Geneva Conventions, reaffirms the importance of the work being done by the ad hoc Tribunals for the former Yugoslavia and Rwanda, stresses the obligation of all States to cooperate fully with the Tribunals, and acknowledges the historic significance of the adoption of the Rome Statute of the International Criminal Court which is open for signature and ratification by States;

7. *Underlines* the importance of safe and unhindered access of humanitarian personnel to civilians in armed conflict, including refugees and internally displaced persons, and the protection of humanitarian assistance to them, and recalls in this regard the statements by its President of 19 June 1997 and 29 September 1998;

8. *Emphasizes* the need for combatants to ensure the safety, security and freedom of movement of United Nations and associated personnel, as well as personnel of international humanitarian organizations, and recalls in this regard the statements by its President of 12 March 1997 and 29 September 1998;

9. *Takes note* of the entry into force of the Convention on the Safety of United Nations and Associated Personnel of 1994, recalls the relevant principles contained therein, urges all parties to armed conflicts to respect fully the status of United Nations and associated personnel, and in this regard condemns attacks and the use of force against United Nations and associated personnel, as well as personnel of international humanitarian organizations, and affirms the need to hold accountable those who commit such acts;

10. *Expresses its willingness* to respond to situations of armed conflict where civilians are being targeted or humanitarian assistance to civilians is being deliberately obstructed, including through the consideration of appropriate measures at the disposal of the Council in accordance with the Charter, and notes, in that regard, the relevant recommendations contained in the report of the Secretary-General;

11. *Also expresses its willingness* to consider how peacekeeping mandates might better address the negative impact of armed conflict on civilians;

12. *Expresses its support* for the inclusion, where appropriate, in peace agreements and mandates of United Nations peacekeeping missions, of specific and adequate measures for the disarmament, demobilization and reintegration of ex-combatants, with special attention given to the demobilization and reintegration of child soldiers, as well as clear and detailed arrangements for the destruction of surplus arms and ammunition, and in this regard recalls the statement by its President of 8 July 1999;

13. *Notes* the importance of including in the mandates of peacemaking, peacekeeping and peace-building operations special protection and assistance provisions for groups requiring particular attention, including women and children;

14. *Requests* the Secretary-General to ensure that United Nations personnel involved in peacemaking, peacekeeping and peace-building activities have appropriate training in international humanitarian, human rights and refugee law, including child and gender-related provisions, negotiation and communication skills, cultural awareness and civilian-military coordination, and urges States and relevant international and regional organizations to ensure that appropriate training is included in their programmes for personnel involved in similar activities;

15. *Underlines* the importance of civilian police as a component of peacekeeping operations, recognizes the role of police in assuring the safety and well-being of civilians, and in this regard acknowledges the need to enhance the capacity of the United Nations for the rapid deployment of qualified and well-trained civilian police;

16. *Reaffirms its readiness,* whenever measures are adopted under Article 41 of the Charter, to give consideration to their impact on the civilian population, bearing in mind the needs of children, in order to consider appropriate humanitarian exemptions;

17. *Notes* that the excessive accumulation and destabilizing effect of small arms and light weapons pose a considerable impediment to the provision of humanitarian assistance and have a potential to exacerbate and prolong conflicts, endanger the lives of civilians and undermine security and the confidence required for a return to peace and stability;

18. *Takes note* of the entry into force of the Convention on the Prohibition of the Use, Stockpiling, Production and Transfer of Anti-personnel Mines and on Their Destruction, of 1997, and the amended Protocol on Prohibitions or Restrictions on the Use of Mines, Booby Traps and Other Devices (Protocol II) annexed to the Convention on Prohibitions or Restrictions on the Use of Certain Conventional Weapons Which May Be Deemed to Be Excessively Injurious or to Have Indiscriminate Effects, of 1980, recalls the relevant provisions contained therein, and notes the beneficial effect that their implementation will have on the safety of civilians;

19. *Reiterates its grave concern* at the harmful and widespread impact of armed conflict on children, recalls its resolution 1261(1999) of 25 August 1999, and reaffirms the recommendations contained therein;

20. *Stresses* the importance of consultation and cooperation between the United Nations, the International Committee of the Red Cross and other relevant organizations, including regional organizations, on follow-up to the report of the Secretary-General, and encourages the Secretary-General to continue consultations on this subject and to take concrete actions aimed at enhancing the capacity of the United Nations to improve the protection of civilians in armed conflict;

21. *Expresses its willingness* to work in cooperation with regional organizations to examine how these bod-

ies might better enhance the protection of civilians in armed conflict;

22. *Decides* to establish immediately an appropriate mechanism to review further the recommendations contained in the report of the Secretary-General and to consider appropriate steps by April 2000 in accordance with its responsibilities under the Charter;

23. *Decides* to remain actively seized of the matter.

Note by Council President. A November note [S/1999/1160] by the Council President stated that, pursuant to the Council's decision to establish a mechanism to review the recommendations contained in the Secretary-General's report, an informal 15-member working group had been established for a six-month period.

(For information on children in armed conflict, see p. 672.)

Weapons of mass destruction

A June note by the secretariat [E/CN.4/Sub.2/1999/26] stated that Clemencia Forero Ucros (Colombia) was unable to prepare a working paper assessing the utility, scope and structure of a study on weapons of mass destruction or with indiscriminate effect, or of a nature to cause superfluous injury or unnecessary suffering for the 1999 Subcommission session, as requested by the Subcommission in 1998 [YUN 1998, p. 682].

Economic, social and cultural rights

Right to development

Reports of Secretary-General. As requested by the Commission on Human Rights in 1998 [YUN 1998, p. 683], the Secretary-General presented replies received from four Governments [E/CN.4/1999/20] in response to his request for information on follow-up to the Declaration on the Right to Development, adopted by the General Assembly in resolution 41/128 [YUN 1986, p. 717].

In accordance with a 1998 Subcommission request [YUN 1998, p. 683], the Secretary-General presented, in June [E/CN.4/Sub.2/1999/30], replies received from UN bodies on steps they had taken to promote international cooperation in the context of the United Nations Decade for the Eradication of Poverty (1997-2006) (see PART THREE, Chapter I).

Pursuant to Assembly resolution 53/155 [YUN 1998, p. 684], which reaffirmed the importance of the right to development, the Secretary-General submitted a September report [A/54/319] on the resolution's implementation. He described UN efforts to promote human rights and the right to development within intergovernmental institutions. A workshop (Geneva, 8 July), organized jointly by the Office of the United Nations High Commissioner for Refugees, OHCHR and the Office for the Coordination of Humanitarian Affairs, at the invitation of the UN Development Group Office of the United Nations Development Programme (UNDP), held technical discussions on the common country assessment and the United Nations Development Assistance Framework (UNDAF) and their implementation (see also PART THREE, Chapter II). The programme for human rights strengthening, signed on 8 April by the High Commissioner for Human Rights and the UNDP Associate Administrator, provided for: support to five pilot countries in five regions to strengthen national capacity to promote, protect and realize human rights; support to five countries in five regions to design guidelines on mainstreaming human rights in UNDP sustainable human development country programmes; regional and subregional workshops to promote ratification of human rights instruments; a seminar on the impact of globalization on the enjoyment of human rights and issuing a publication thereon; and support to UNDP country office projects for human rights programming. OHCHR was preparing to participate in the pilot phase of a comprehensive development framework in sectors covering human rights issues, such as good governance, the justice system, social safety nets and programmes, education and health. OHCHR collaborated in the preparation of the *Human Development Report 2000*, which would be devoted to human rights.

Developments in the area of inter-agency coordination included the implementation of the Memorandum of Understanding signed in 1998 between OHCHR and UNDP [YUN 1998, p. 684]; completion of the first round of UNDAF; and the work of the ad hoc group on the right to development, which focused on preparing draft guidelines on human rights for resident coordinators and a training module on human rights for UN staff involved in the common country assessment/UNDAF process. An OHCHR workshop on the right to development (Geneva, 18-19 May) provided support to the study of the independent expert on the right to development (see next page). As part of the process of integrating human rights into the UN system, OHCHR and UNDP organized two training sessions (Abidjan, Côte d'Ivoire, and Colombo, Sri Lanka) to provide more human rights exposure to UNDP staff, as well as to their government counterparts.

Report of High Commissioner. Pursuant to a 1998 Commission request [YUN 1998, p. 683], the High Commissioner for Human Rights described activities of her Office to implement the right to development. She also provided information related to the implementation of General Assembly and Commission resolutions and inter-agency coordination within the UN system to implement relevant Commission resolutions.

Commission action. On 28 April [E/1999/23 (res. 1999/790)], the Commission reaffirmed the importance of the right to development for everyone in all countries, particularly developing countries, and urged States to eliminate obstacles to development by pursuing the promotion and protection of economic, social, cultural, civil and political rights and by implementing development programmes and promoting international cooperation. Welcoming Economic and Social Council decision 1998/269 [YUN 1998, p. 683], which authorized the Commission to establish a follow-up mechanism consisting of an open-ended working group and an independent expert, initially for a three-year period, the Commission invited the High Commissioner to report each year for the duration of the mechanism, to provide interim reports to the working group and to make the reports available to the independent expert. The Secretary-General was asked to report to the Assembly in 1999 and to the Commission in 2000.

Subcommission action. On 25 August [E/CN.4/2000/2 (res. 1999/9)], the Subcommission on the Promotion and Protection of Human Rights, taking note of the Secretary-General's June report [E/CN.4/Sub.2/1999/30] (see p. 651), asked him to invite UN bodies and specialized agencies to step up their action to promote international cooperation for the realization of the right to development in the context of the United Nations Decade for the Eradication of Poverty (1997-2006) and to transmit annually information received.

Working group activities. The open-ended working group on the right to development (Geneva, 13-14 September) [A/54/401] considered a report of independent expert Arjun Sengupta (India) on progress made in implementing the right. As his mandate called for developing a programme for realizing the right to development, he presented a preliminary plan for doing so, starting first with the right to food, primary health care and primary education, and combining international cooperation with the national obligations of States.

The group also considered an interim report of the High Commissioner on OHCHR activities to implement the right to development.

The group decided to suspend its deliberations and to resume again in Geneva from 13 to 17 December. However, it did not convene at that time and planned to meet early in 2000.

GENERAL ASSEMBLY ACTION

On 17 December [meeting 83], the General Assembly, on the recommendation of the Third Committee [A/54/605/Add.2], adopted **resolution 54/175** by recorded vote (119-10-38) [agenda item 116 *(b)*].

The right to development

The General Assembly,

Guided by the principles and purposes of the Charter of the United Nations, and expressing in particular the determination to promote social progress and better standards of life in larger freedom as well as to employ international mechanisms for the promotion of the economic and social advancement of all peoples,

Recalling its previous resolutions and those of the Commission on Human Rights relating to the right to development, including its resolution 53/155 of 9 December 1998, and taking note of Commission resolution 1999/79 of 28 April 1999,

Recalling also the Declaration on the Right to Development, and reaffirming the importance of its full implementation,

Reaffirming that the right to development, as established in the Declaration on the Right to Development, is universal and inalienable, and re-emphasizing that its promotion, protection and realization are an integral part of the promotion and protection of all human rights,

Noting that the human person is the central subject of development and that development policy should therefore make the human being the main participant in and beneficiary of development,

Stressing the importance of creating an economic, political, social, cultural and legal environment that will enable people to achieve social development at the national and international levels,

Emphasizing the fact that the realization of the right to development requires effective and efficient development policies at the national level, as well as equitable economic relations and a favourable economic environment at the international level,

Noting that sanctions often have a serious negative impact on the development capacity and activity of target countries, as well as third States, undermining their full realization of the right to development,

Recognizing that countries interact with the global economy from vastly different levels of development, and realizing that globalization affects all countries differently and makes them more susceptible to external developments, positive and negative, inter alia, in the field of human rights, in particular in the realization of the right to development,

Stressing the need for coordination and cooperation throughout the United Nations system for a more effective promotion and realization of the right to development,

Emphasizing that the Office of the United Nations High Commissioner for Human Rights has an important role to play in the promotion, protection and realization of the right to development, including through enhanced cooperation with the relevant bodies of the United Nations system for this purpose,

Affirming that developed countries have a major responsibility in the context of growing interdependence to create and sustain a global economic environment that is favourable to accelerated and sustainable development,

Emphasizing that measures should be taken to ensure that human rights are not exploited as a means of conditionality for loans, aid or trade, which then unduly results in the imposition of particular policies on recipient countries, thereby negatively affecting the full enjoyment of the right to development by the peoples of such countries,

Recognizing the importance of undertaking appropriate economic policies and creating an environment that is favourable and conducive to the enhancement of the realization of the right to development at the national and international levels,

Emphasizing the importance of strengthening good governance through the building of more effective and accountable institutions for promoting sustained growth and enabling all people to benefit equally from development,

Expressing its concern that the Declaration on the Right to Development is insufficiently disseminated, and noting that it should be taken into account, as appropriate, in bilateral and multilateral cooperation programmes, national development strategies and policies and activities of international organizations,

Having considered the report of the Secretary-General prepared pursuant to General Assembly resolution 53/155,

1. *Takes note* of the report of the Secretary-General;

2. *Reaffirms* the importance of the right to development for every human person and all people in all countries, in particular the developing countries, as an integral part of their fundamental human rights, as well as the potential contribution that its realization could make to the full enjoyment of all human rights and fundamental freedoms;

3. *Also reaffirms* that democracy, development and respect for all human rights and fundamental freedoms, including the right to development, are interdependent and mutually reinforcing, and in this context affirms that:

(a) The existence of widespread poverty inhibits the full and effective enjoyment of all human rights and renders democracy and popular participation fragile;

(b) For peace and stability to endure, national and international action and cooperation are required to promote a better life for all in larger freedom, a critical element of which is the eradication of poverty;

(c) The full realization of the right to development must be addressed within a global context through a constructive, dialogue-based approach, with objectivity, respect for national sovereignty and territorial integrity, impartiality, non-selectivity and transparency as the guiding principles, taking into account the political, historical, social, religious and cultural characteristics of each country;

(d) Effective popular participation is an essential component of successful and sustainable development;

(e) The participation of developing countries in the international economic decision-making process needs to be broadened and strengthened through its democratization;

4. *Expresses deep concern* that the gap between the developed and developing countries remains unacceptably wide and that developing countries continue to face difficulties in participating in the globalization process and may risk being marginalized and effectively excluded from its benefits;

5. *Notes with concern* that the realization of the right to development of many developing countries has been negatively affected as a result of severe economic and financial crises in many regions of the world, and recognizes that the international trade and financial conditions that caused the crises persist;

6. *Calls upon* Member States to take, individually and collectively, all relevant measures and policies to prevent the marginalization of the weak or vulnerable economies of developing countries and of countries with economies in transition and to enable them to participate fully in globalization and liberalization with a view to their full integration into the world economy;

7. *Calls upon* States to refrain from taking any unilateral measures that are not in accordance with international law and the Charter of the United Nations and that create obstacles to trade relations among States and impede the full realization of all human rights, including the right to development;

8. *Urges* States to eliminate all obstacles to development at all levels, inter alia, by pursuing the promotion and protection of economic, social, cultural, civil and political rights and implementing comprehensive development programmes at the national level, integrating those rights into development activities and promoting effective international cooperation;

9. *Reaffirms* that international cooperation is a necessity deriving from the recognized mutual interest of all countries and, therefore, that such cooperation should be strengthened in order to support the efforts of developing countries to solve their social and economic problems and to fulfil their obligations to promote and protect all human rights;

10. *Calls upon* the international community to address the deepening technological, financial and productive gaps between the developed and some developing countries, and among some developing countries themselves, as well as the widening inequalities between the rich and the poor;

11. *Affirms* the need to apply a gender perspective in the implementation of the right to development, inter alia, by ensuring that women play an active role in the development process, and emphasizes that the empowerment of women and their full participation on a basis of equality in all spheres of society is fundamental for development;

12. *Reaffirms* that, in the full realization of the right to development, inter alia:

(a) The rights to food and clean water are fundamental human rights and their promotion constitutes a moral imperative both for national Governments and for the international community;

(b) The right to shelter is a basic human right, and in this regard the Assembly emphasizes the urgent need for national Governments and the international community to develop urgently, where necessary, and implement national and international strategies to provide this right;

(c) Health is essential for sustainable development, and the Assembly calls upon all Governments to take reasonable legislative and other measures within their available resources to achieve the progressive realiza-

tion of the right to health-care services and urges the international community to support the efforts of Governments in this regard;

(*d*) Education is also an essential factor for the political, social, cultural and economic development of all people, and the Assembly recognizes that science and technology are important for ensuring growing levels of knowledge and must be put to use in the service of education;

13. *Recommends* proper consideration of the humanitarian effects of sanctions, in particular on women and children, which undermine and affect the right to development, with a view to minimizing those effects;

14. *Stresses* the need for the Secretary-General to continue to give high priority to the right to development, and urges all States to promote further the right to development, as a vital element in a balanced human rights programme;

15. *Welcomes* the high priority assigned by the United Nations High Commissioner for Human Rights to activities relating to the right to development, and urges the Office of the High Commissioner to continue to implement Commission on Human Rights resolution 1998/72 of 22 April 1998;

16. *Invites* the United Nations High Commissioner for Human Rights to continue to follow and review progress made in the promotion and implementation of the right to development and to submit annual reports to the General Assembly and the Commission on Human Rights and to provide interim reports to the open-ended working group and the independent expert on the right to development containing details on:

(*a*) The activities of her Office relating to the implementation of the right to development, as contained in her mandate;

(*b*) The implementation of resolutions of the General Assembly and the Commission on Human Rights with regard to the right to development;

(*c*) The coordination among the relevant entities of the United Nations system, within their respective mandates, in the implementation of relevant resolutions of the General Assembly and the Commission on Human Rights in this regard;

17. *Notes* the efforts undertaken by the Office of the United Nations High Commissioner for Human Rights, within its mandate, with relevant entities of the United Nations system to promote the realization of the right to development, and stresses the need for the Office of the High Commissioner to keep Governments fully informed of and involve them in those initiatives, as appropriate;

18. *Calls upon* Member States and the Office of the High Commissioner to ensure that the open-ended working group on the right to development convenes its first session, as a matter of urgency, no later than 17 December 1999;

19. *Urges* Member States, the Secretary-General and the United Nations system, in particular the Office of the High Commissioner, fully to support the follow-up mechanism established for the implementation of the right to development;

20. *Reaffirms* the need for the Office of the High Commissioner to take appropriate measures aimed at promoting universal public awareness of the right to development through, inter alia, the dissemination of the Declaration on the Right to Development;

21. *Invites* the open-ended working group, inter alia, to consider the question of elaborating a convention on the right to development;

22. *Calls upon* the independent expert on the right to development to submit comprehensive reports to the General Assembly at its fifty-fifth session and the Commission on Human Rights at its fifty-sixth session on, inter alia, the effects of poverty, structural adjustment, globalization, financial and trade liberalization and deregulation on the prospects of enjoyment of the right to development in developing countries;

23. *Invites* the open-ended working group to take note of the deliberations on the right to development held during the fifty-fourth session of the General Assembly;

24. *Takes note* of the report of the independent expert on the right to development, and encourages closer coordination with studies undertaken by other relevant experts established under the auspices of the Commission on Human Rights;

25. *Recognizes* the vital role of civil society, including non-governmental organizations and the private sector, in the implementation of the right to development, and in this regard encourages Member States and the United Nations system to foster partnerships and strengthen cooperation at the national level with civil society, as appropriate;

26. *Requests* the Secretary-General to continue to inform the Commission on Human Rights and the General Assembly of the activities of the organizations, funds, programmes and specialized agencies of the United Nations system relating to the implementation of the Declaration on the Right to Development, as well as obstacles identified in the realization of the right to development;

27. *Also requests* the Secretary-General to submit to the General Assembly at its fifty-fifth session and to the Commission on Human Rights at its fifty-sixth session a comprehensive report on the right to development, including obstacles identified in the realization of that right;

28. *Decides* to consider this question at its fifty-fifth session under the sub-item entitled "Human rights questions, including alternative approaches to improving the effective enjoyment of human rights and fundamental freedoms".

RECORDED VOTE ON RESOLUTION 54/175:

In favour: Afghanistan, Algeria, Angola, Antigua and Barbuda, Argentina, Azerbaijan, Bahamas, Bahrain, Bangladesh, Barbados, Belarus, Belize, Benin, Bhutan, Bolivia, Botswana, Brazil, Brunei Darussalam, Burkina Faso, Cambodia, Cameroon, Cape Verde, Chad, Chile, China, Colombia, Comoros, Congo, Costa Rica, Côte d'Ivoire, Croatia, Cuba, Democratic People's Republic of Korea, Democratic Republic of the Congo, Djibouti, Dominica, Dominican Republic, Ecuador, Egypt, El Salvador, Eritrea, Ethiopia, Fiji, Gabon, Ghana, Grenada, Guatemala, Guinea, Guinea-Bissau, Guyana, Haiti, Honduras, India, Indonesia, Iran, Jamaica, Jordan, Kazakhstan, Kenya, Kuwait, Lao People's Democratic Republic, Lebanon, Libyan Arab Jamahiriya, Malawi, Malaysia, Maldives, Mali, Mauritius, Mexico, Mongolia, Morocco, Mozambique, Myanmar, Namibia, Nepal, Nicaragua, Nigeria, Oman, Pakistan, Panama, Papua New Guinea, Paraguay, Peru, Philippines, Qatar, Russian Federation, Rwanda, Saint Lucia, Samoa, Saudi Arabia, Senegal, Seychelles, Sierra Leone, Singapore, Solomon Islands, South Africa, Sri Lanka, Sudan, Suriname, Swaziland, Syrian Arab Republic, Tajikistan, Thailand, The former Yugoslav Republic of Macedonia, Togo, Trinidad and Tobago, Tunisia, Turkey, Turkmenistan, Uganda, Ukraine, United Arab Emirates, United Republic of Tanzania, Uruguay, Venezuela, Viet Nam, Yemen, Zambia, Zimbabwe.

Against: Canada, Denmark, Germany, Hungary, Iceland, Japan, Liechtenstein, Netherlands, Sweden, United States.

Abstaining: Albania, Andorra, Armenia, Australia, Austria, Belgium, Bosnia and Herzegovina, Bulgaria, Cyprus, Czech Republic, Estonia, Finland, France, Georgia, Greece, Ireland, Israel, Italy, Latvia, Lithuania, Luxembourg, Malta, Marshall Islands, Micronesia, Monaco, New Zealand, Norway, Poland, Portugal, Republic of Korea, Republic of Moldova, Romania, San Marino, Slovakia, Slovenia, Spain, United Kingdom, Uzbekistan.

The Committee adopted the eighth preambular paragraph by a recorded vote of 90 to 39, with 2 abstentions; the thirteenth preambular paragraph, by 91 to 40; paragraph 3 *(c)*, by 94 to 38, with 2 abstentions; paragraph 3 *(e)*, by 96 to 36; paragraph 13, by 92 to 41; paragraph 21, by 90 to 41, with 2 abstentions; and paragraph 22, by 93 to 39.

The Assembly retained the eighth preambular paragraph by a recorded vote of 113 to 44, with 1 abstention; the thirteenth preambular paragraph, by 111 to 44, with 1 abstention; paragraph 3 *(c)*, by 113 to 42, with 3 abstentions; paragraph 3 *(e)*, by 121 to 39; paragraph 13, by 114 to 43, with 1 abstention; paragraph 21, by 112 to 43, with 2 abstentions; and paragraph 22, by 115 to 42.

Globalization

Commission action. By a roll-call vote of 30 to 2, with 20 abstentions, on 28 April [res. 1999/59], the Commission recognized that, while globalization, by its impact on the role of the State, might affect human rights, the promotion and protection of all human rights was the responsibility of the State. Underlining the need to analyse the consequences of globalization on the full enjoyment of all human rights, the Commission asked treaty bodies, special rapporteurs/representatives, independent experts and the Commission's working groups to take the issue into consideration in their reports. The Commission asked the Subcommission to undertake a study, based on those reports, for submission in 2001.

Subcommission action. On 25 August [res. 1999/8], the Subcommission decided to appoint Joseph Oloka-Onyango (Uganda) and Deepika Udagama (Sri Lanka) as Special Rapporteurs to prepare a study on globalization and its impact on the full enjoyment of all human rights and asked them to submit a preliminary report in 2000.

On 26 August [res. 1999/29], the Subcommission, noting the Commission's April request, decided to entrust Mr. Oloka-Onyango with preparing the study for submission in 2001.

GENERAL ASSEMBLY ACTION

On 17 December [meeting 83], the General Assembly, on the recommendation of the Third Committee [A/54/605/Add.2], adopted **resolution 54/165** by recorded vote (99-2-64) [agenda item 116 *(b)*].

Globalization and its impact on the full enjoyment of all human rights

The General Assembly,

Guided by the purposes and principles of the Charter of the United Nations, and expressing in particular the need to achieve international cooperation in promoting and encouraging respect for human rights and fundamental freedoms for all without distinction,

Recalling the Universal Declaration of Human Rights, as well as the Vienna Declaration and Programme of Action adopted by the World Conference on Human Rights on 25 June 1993,

Recalling also the International Covenant on Civil and Political Rights and the International Covenant on Economic, Social and Cultural Rights,

Reaffirming the Declaration on the Right to Development, adopted by the General Assembly in its resolution 41/128 of 4 December 1986,

Recognizing that all human rights are universal, indivisible, interdependent and interrelated and that the international community must treat human rights globally in a fair and equal manner, on the same footing and with the same emphasis,

Realizing that globalization affects all countries differently and makes them more susceptible to external developments, positive as well as negative, including in the field of human rights,

Realizing also that globalization is not merely an economic process, but also has social, political, environmental, cultural and legal dimensions which have an impact on the full enjoyment of all human rights,

Recognizing that multilateral mechanisms have a unique role to play in meeting the challenges and taking the opportunities presented by globalization,

Noting that human beings strive for a world that is respectful of cultures, identities and human rights and that, in that regard, they work to ensure that all activities, including those affected by globalization, are consistent with those aims,

1. *Recognizes* that, while globalization, by its impact on, inter alia, the role of the State, may affect human rights, the promotion and protection of all human rights is, first and foremost, the responsibility of the State;

2. *Underlines*, therefore, the need to analyse the consequences of globalization for the full enjoyment of all human rights;

3. *Takes note* of the request by the Commission on Human Rights to the Subcommission on the Promotion and Protection of Human Rights to undertake a study, based on the reports of the treaty bodies, special rapporteurs, independent experts and working groups of the Commission, on the issue of globalization and its impact on the full enjoyment of all human rights, for the consideration of the Commission at its fifty-seventh session;

4. *Requests* the Secretary-General, taking into account the different views of Member States, to submit a comprehensive report on globalization and its impact on the full enjoyment of all human rights to the General Assembly at its fifty-fifth session.

RECORDED VOTE ON RESOLUTION 54/165:

In favour: Afghanistan, Algeria, Angola, Antigua and Barbuda, Azerbaijan, Bahamas, Bahrain, Bangladesh, Barbados, Belarus, Belize, Benin, Bhutan, Botswana, Brazil, Burkina Faso, Cambodia, Cameroon, Cape Verde, Chad, China, Comoros, Congo, Costa Rica, Côte d'Ivoire, Croatia, Cuba, Democratic People's Republic of Korea, Democratic Republic of the Congo, Djibouti, Dominica, Dominican Republic, Ecuador, Egypt, El Salvador, Eritrea, Ethiopia, Fiji, Gabon, Ghana, Grenada, Guinea, Guinea-Bissau, Guyana, Haiti, Honduras, India, Indonesia, Iran, Jamaica, Jordan, Kazakhstan, Kenya, Kuwait, Lao People's Democratic Republic, Lebanon, Libyan Arab Jamahiriya, Malawi, Malaysia, Maldives, Malta,* Mauritius, Mexico, Mongolia, Morocco, Myanmar, Namibia, Nepal, Nigeria, Oman,

Pakistan, Papua New Guinea, Philippines, Qatar, Russian Federation, Rwanda, Saint Lucia, Samoa, Saudi Arabia, Senegal, Seychelles, Solomon Islands, South Africa, Sri Lanka, Sudan, Suriname, Swaziland, Syrian Arab Republic, Tajikistan, Trinidad and Tobago, Tunisia, Turkey, Turkmenistan, United Arab Emirates, United Republic of Tanzania, Venezuela, Viet Nam, Zambia, Zimbabwe.

Against: Togo,** United States.

Abstaining: Albania, Andorra, Argentina, Armenia, Australia, Austria, Belgium, Bolivia, Bosnia and Herzegovina, Brunei Darussalam,** Bulgaria, Canada, Chile, Colombia, Cyprus, Czech Republic, Denmark, Estonia, Finland, France, Georgia, Germany, Greece, Guatemala, Hungary, Iceland, Ireland, Israel, Italy, Japan, Latvia, Liechtenstein, Lithuania, Luxembourg, Marshall Islands, Micronesia, Monaco, Mozambique,** Netherlands, New Zealand, Nicaragua, Norway, Panama, Paraguay, Peru, Poland, Portugal, Republic of Korea, Republic of Moldova, Romania, San Marino, Sierra Leone, Singapore, Slovakia, Slovenia, Spain, Sweden, Thailand, The former Yugoslav Republic of Macedonia, Ukraine, United Kingdom, Uruguay, Uzbekistan, Yemen.**

*Later advised the Secretariat it had intended to abstain.

**Later advised the Secretariat it had intended to vote in favour.

In the Committee, an amendment to delete paragraph 4, proposed by Finland on behalf of the members of the European Union, was rejected by a recorded vote of 44 in favour to 92 against, with 22 abstentions.

Trade and investment

In accordance with a 1998 Subcommission request [YUN 1998, p. 690], Mr. Oloka-Onyango and Ms. Udagama, in June [E/CN.4/Sub.2/1999/11], submitted a working paper on integrating human rights concerns in international and regional trade, investment and financial policies, agreements and practices, and on how the UN human rights mechanisms could play a central role in that regard. The paper called for the establishment of mechanisms to carry out human rights impact assessments of the effects of policy decisions made in multilateral and intergovernmental organizations. According to the paper, there was a need to make accessible to all States and non-State actors the processes by which policy on international trade, investment and finance was discussed. The Subcommission should proceed to a more in-depth study on aspects of the relationship between trade, investment and finance policy and practice and human rights, and a preliminary report should be submitted to the Subcommission in 2000, to be followed in 2001 by a progress report.

Subcommission action. By a vote of 18 to none, with 4 abstentions, the Subcommission, on 26 August [res. 1999/30], requested Governments and economic policy forums to take into account international human rights obligations and principles in formulating international economic policy. It called on them to undertake studies, in consultation with UN and regional human rights mechanisms and relevant civil society organizations, of the human rights and social impacts of economic liberalization programmes, policies and laws. The High Commissioner was asked to intensify efforts at dialogue with the World Trade Organization (WTO) and its members on the human rights dimensions of trade and investment liberalization, and to ensure that human rights were fully integrated into future WTO negotiations. The United Nations Conference on Trade and Development was asked to include in its work programme a focus on ways to incorporate human rights principles in the process of international trade policy formulation.

Effects of debt

By a roll-call vote of 30 to 15, with 8 abstentions, the Commission, on 23 April [res. 1999/22], affirmed that the permanent solution to the foreign debt problem lay in the establishment of a just and equitable international economic order, which guaranteed developing countries better market conditions and commodity prices, stabilization of exchange rates and interest rates, easier access to financial and capital markets, adequate flows of financial resources and easier access to developed countries' technology. It also emphasized the need for initiatives on foreign debt and for new financial flows to debtor developing countries from all sources. Governments, international financial institutions and the private sector were called on to cancel or reduce the debt of heavily indebted poor countries. The Special Rapporteur was asked to report annually on the effects of foreign debt on the enjoyment of economic, social and cultural rights, and the Secretary-General was asked to assist him.

Structural adjustment policies

Pursuant to a 1998 Commission decision [YUN 1998, p. 688], the independent expert appointed to study the effects of structural adjustment policies on economic, social and cultural rights, Fantu Cheru (United States), in a February report [E/CN.4/1999/50], examined the roots of the third world development crises which, he said, manifested as debt, represented a fraction of a much deeper and systemic problem of underdevelopment. He described the links between structural adjustment programmes and the realization of economic, social and cultural rights and presented basic principles for "adjustment with transformation", which would emphasize sustainable economic growth combined with social justice.

Proposals for action at the international level included debt cancellation for the heavily indebted poor countries; instituting human rights conditionality in future lending; establishing international mechanisms to retrieve money stolen by corrupt leaders; reforming international economic, financial and trade systems; and natural resource preservation. Action at the regional level should emphasize stronger cooperation regarding economic development. At the national level, structural adjustment should focus on economic growth oriented towards human development. In post-conflict countries, growth that was oriented towards human development was most easily achieved by increasing the capacity of existing productive assets, massive investment in people, reconstruction and rehabilitation of neglected infrastructure through public works employment programmes, and democratic governance.

Working group activities. The open-ended working group on structural adjustment programmes, at its second session (Geneva, 1-3 March) [E/CN.4/1999/51], reviewed the independent expert's report and made recommendations to the Commission, which the Commission adopted (see below).

Commission action. By a roll-call vote of 33 to 15, with 4 abstentions, the Commission, on 26 April [dec. 1999/104], requested the Economic and Social Council to ask the Secretary-General to circulate the independent expert's report to and invite comments from Governments, UN bodies, academic institutions, NGOs and organizations representing disadvantaged and vulnerable groups. The Commission also asked the Council to take action regarding the work of the independent expert and of the working group, which were approved by the Council (see below).

ECONOMIC AND SOCIAL COUNCIL ACTION

In July, the Economic and Social Council, on the recommendation of the Commission on Human Rights [E/1999/23], adopted **decision 1999/251** by a roll-call vote of 25 to 17, with 4 abstentions [agenda item 14 *(h)*].

Effects of structural adjustment policies on the full enjoyment of human rights

At its 42nd plenary meeting, on 27 July 1999, the Economic and Social Council, taking note of Commission on Human Rights decision 1999/104 of 26 April 1999, decided:

(a) To extend for one year the mandate of the independent expert on structural adjustment policies to: (i) assist the Working Group on structural adjustment policies and economic, social and cultural rights in the fulfilment of its mandate, in particular by elaborating draft basic policy guidelines on structural adjustment policies; and (ii) monitor new developments, including actions and initiatives being taken by international financial institutions, other United Nations bodies and intergovernmental and non-governmental organizations with respect to structural adjustment policies and human rights, and submit a revised report to the Working Group at its third session;

(b) To authorize the Working Group to meet for two weeks well in advance of, but at least four weeks prior to, the fifty-sixth session of the Commission with the mandate to: (i) consider the updated report of the independent expert and comments received thereon; (ii) elaborate basic policy guidelines on structural adjustment programmes and economic, social and cultural rights which could serve as a basis for a continued dialogue between human rights bodies and the international financial institutions; and (iii) report to the Commission at its fifty-sixth session.

ROLL-CALL VOTE IN COUNCIL AS FOLLOWS:

In favour: Algeria, Bolivia, Brazil, Chile, China, Colombia, Comoros, Cuba, Djibouti, El Salvador, Honduras, India, Indonesia, Mauritius, Mexico, Morocco, Mozambique, Oman, Pakistan, Republic of Korea, Saudi Arabia, Sri Lanka, Syrian Arab Republic, Turkey, Viet Nam.

Against: Belgium, Bulgaria, Canada, Czech Republic, Denmark, France, Germany, Iceland, Italy, Japan, Latvia, New Zealand, Norway, Poland, Spain, United Kingdom, United States.

Abstaining: Belarus, Cape Verde, Russian Federation, Venezuela.

Income distribution

Commission action. On 27 April [res. 1999/53], the Commission decided that the Subcommission should further review the establishment of a forum on economic, social and cultural rights, to be called the Social Forum, with the following objectives: to exchange information on the enjoyment of those rights and its relationship to globalization; to follow up on the relationship between income distribution, the feminization of poverty and human rights; to follow up on situations of poverty; to discuss guidelines on violations of the rights; and to propose legal standards and initiatives, guidelines and recommendations for the consideration of the Commission, the open-ended working group on the right to development, the Committee on Economic, Social and Cultural Rights (see p. 575), the specialized agencies and other UN entities.

Subcommission action. On 25 August [res. 1999/10], the Subcommission decided to hold the Social Forum for three days during its session in 2000 with the agenda proposed by the Commission in resolution 1999/53 and with the participation of Subcommission members, government observers, intergovernmental organizations, NGOs in consultative status with the Economic and Social Council, international cooperation agencies, financial institutions, transnational corporations and other private international enterprises, and international labour associations and organizations. The Commission was asked to endorse the holding of the Social Forum in 2000 and to approve all Secretariat facilities for the preparation and servicing of the event.

OHCHR was asked to assemble a report including documents and studies on economic, social and cultural rights, and the High Commissioner was asked to issue invitations and an agenda, and publish the purpose of the meeting. The Subcommission suggested that the inaugural session emphasize extreme poverty and human rights, and asked the Secretariat to request possible participants to share their experiences and studies on situations of poverty and destitution.

Transnational corporations

Subcommission action. In accordance with its 1998 resolution [YUN 1998, p. 689], the Subcommission, on 3 August [dec. 1999/101], decided to establish a sessional working group to examine the working methods and activities of transnational corporations (TNCs).

Working group activities. The sessional working group on the working methods and activities of TNCs, at its first session (Geneva, 3, 6 and 10 August) [E/CN.4/Sub.2/1999/9], decided to consider developing a code of conduct for TNCs based on human rights standards. Subcommission member David Weissbrot (United States) volunteered to prepare a code in cooperation with relevant NGOs. Thc group also decided that, in its final report, it would identify a framework or definition of TNCs and the national and international legal standards applicable to them. A member of the group, Asbjørn Eide (Norway), volunteered to prepare a compilation and analysis of relevant human rights standards. The Chairman-Rapporteur proposed preparing a paper on the effects of TNC activities on the enjoyment of human rights, as well as on a draft mechanism for implementing the code of conduct. The group would address the issue of cultural rights and TNC activities in the context of globalization.

Coercive economic measures

Report of Secretary-General. Pursuant to a 1998 Commission request [YUN 1998, p. 689], the Secretary-General presented the views of three Governments on the implications and negative effects of unilateral coercive measures on their populations [E/CN.4/1999/44 & Add.1,2].

Commission action. On 23 April [res. 1999/21], by a roll-call vote of 37 to 10, with 6 abstentions, the Commission urged States to refrain from adopting or implementing unilateral measures not in accordance with international law and the UN Charter, particularly those of a coercive nature with extraterritorial effects, that created obstacles to trade relations among States. It rejected the application of such measures as tools for political or economic pressure against any country, particularly against developing countries. The Commission asked the open-ended working group on the right to development to consider human rights and the negative impact of unilateral coercive measures. The Commission asked the High Commissioner to give urgent consideration to its resolution. It requested the Secretary-General to bring its resolution to the attention of Member States and to seek their views and information on the implications and negative effects of unilateral coercive measures on their populations and to report thereon in 2000.

Subcommission action. On 26 August [dec. 1999/111], the Subcommission asked Marc Bossuyt (Belgium) to prepare a working paper on the adverse consequences of economic sanctions on human rights for 2000.

Report of Secretary-General. Pursuant to General Assembly resolution 53/141 [YUN 1998, p. 689], the Secretary-General, in an August report with later addendum [A/54/222 & Add.1], presented the replies of five Governments in response to his request for information on the implications and negative effects of unilateral coercive measures on their populations.

By **decision 54/434** of 17 December, the Assembly took note of the Secretary-General's report.

GENERAL ASSEMBLY ACTION

On 17 December [meeting 83], the General Assembly, on the recommendation of the Third Committee [A/54/605/Add.2], adopted **resolution 54/172** by recorded vote (109-48-7) [agenda item 116 *(b)*].

Human rights and unilateral coercive measures

The General Assembly,

Recalling its resolutions 51/103 of 12 December 1996, 52/120 of 12 December 1997 and 53/141 of 9 December 1998, as well as Commission on Human Rights resolution 1998/11 of 9 April 1998,

Reaffirming the pertinent principles and provisions contained in the Charter of Economic Rights and Duties of States proclaimed by the General Assembly in its resolution 3281(XXIX) of 12 December 1974, in particular article 32 thereof, in which it declared that no State may use or encourage the use of economic, political or any other type of measures to coerce another State in order to obtain from it the subordination of the exercise of its sovereign rights,

Recalling the report submitted by the Secretary-General, pursuant to Commission on Human Rights resolution 1995/45 of 3 March 1995, and the report of the Secretary-General on the implementation of General Assembly resolution 52/120,

Recognizing the universal, indivisible, interdependent and interrelated character of all human rights, and in this regard reaffirming the right to development as an integral part of all human rights,

Recalling that the World Conference on Human Rights, held at Vienna from 14 to 25 June 1993, called upon States to refrain from any unilateral coercive measure not in accordance with international law and the Charter of the United Nations that creates obstacles to trade relations among States and impedes the full realization of all human rights,

Bearing in mind all the references to this question in the Copenhagen Declaration on Social Development, adopted by the World Summit for Social Development on 12 March 1995, the Beijing Declaration and the Platform for Action, adopted by the Fourth World Conference on Women on 15 September 1995, and the Istanbul Declaration on Human Settlements and the Habitat Agenda, adopted by the second United Nations Conference on Human Settlements (Habitat II) on 14 June 1996,

Deeply concerned that, despite the recommendations adopted on this question by the General Assembly and recent major United Nations conferences and contrary to general international law and the Charter of the United Nations, unilateral coercive measures continue to be promulgated and implemented with all their extraterritorial effects, inter alia, on the economic and social development of targeted countries and peoples and individuals under the jurisdiction of other States,

Bearing in mind all the extraterritorial effects of any unilateral legislative, administrative and economic measures, policies and practices of a coercive nature against the development process and the enhancement of human rights in developing countries, which create obstacles to the full realization of all human rights,

Noting the continuing efforts of the Working Group on the Right to Development of the Commission on Human Rights, and reaffirming in particular its criteria according to which unilateral coercive measures are one of the obstacles to the implementation of the Declaration on the Right to Development,

1. *Urges* all States to refrain from adopting or implementing any unilateral measures not in accordance with international law and the Charter of the United Nations, in particular those of a coercive nature with all their extraterritorial effects, which create obstacles to trade relations among States, thus impeding the full realization of the rights set forth in the Universal Declaration of Human Rights and other international human rights instruments, in particular the right of individuals and peoples to development;

2. *Rejects* unilateral coercive measures with all their extraterritorial effects as tools for political or economic pressure against any country, in particular against developing countries, because of their negative effects on the realization of all the human rights of vast sectors of their populations, in particular children, women and the elderly;

3. *Calls upon* Member States that have initiated such measures to commit themselves to their obligations and responsibilities arising from the international human rights instruments to which they are party by revoking such measures at the earliest time possible;

4. *Reaffirms,* in this context, the right of all peoples to self-determination, by virtue of which they freely determine their political status and freely pursue their economic, social and cultural development;

5. *Urges* the Commission on Human Rights to take fully into account the negative impact of unilateral coercive measures, including the enactment of national laws and their extraterritorial application, in its task concerning the implementation of the right to development;

6. *Requests* the United Nations High Commissioner for Human Rights, in discharging her functions relating to the promotion, realization and protection of the right to development and bearing in mind the continuing impact of unilateral coercive measures on the population of developing countries, to give priority to the present resolution in her annual report to the General Assembly;

7. *Requests* the Secretary-General to bring the present resolution to the attention of all Member States, to continue to collect their views and information on the implications and negative effects of unilateral coercive measures on their populations and to submit an analytical report thereon to the General Assembly at its fifty-fifth session, highlighting the practical and preventive measures in this respect;

8. *Decides* to examine this question on a priority basis at its fifty-fifth session under the sub-item entitled "Human rights questions, including alternative approaches for improving the effective enjoyment of human rights and fundamental freedoms".

RECORDED VOTE ON RESOLUTION 54/172:

In favour: Afghanistan, Algeria, Angola, Antigua and Barbuda, Argentina, Bahamas, Bahrain, Bangladesh, Barbados, Belarus, Belize, Benin, Bhutan, Bolivia, Botswana, Brazil, Brunei Darussalam, Burkina Faso, Cambodia, Cameroon, Cape Verde, Chad, Chile, China, Colombia, Comoros, Congo, Costa Rica, Côte d'Ivoire, Cuba, Democratic People's Republic of Korea, Democratic Republic of the Congo, Djibouti, Dominica, Dominican Republic, Ecuador, Egypt, El Salvador, Eritrea, Ethiopia, Fiji, Gabon, Ghana, Grenada, Guatemala, Guinea, Guinea-Bissau, Guyana, Haiti, Honduras, India, Indonesia, Iran, Jamaica, Jordan, Kenya, Kuwait, Lao People's Democratic Republic, Lebanon, Libyan Arab Jamahiriya, Malawi, Malaysia, Mali, Mauritius, Mexico, Mongolia, Morocco, Mozambique, Myanmar, Namibia, Nepal, Nigeria, Oman, Pakistan, Panama, Papua New Guinea, Paraguay, Peru, Philippines, Qatar, Russian Federation, Saint Lucia, Samoa, Saudi Arabia, Senegal, Seychelles, Sierra Leone, Singapore, Solomon Islands, South Africa, Sri Lanka, Sudan, Suriname, Swaziland, Syrian Arab Republic, Tajikistan, Thailand, Togo, Trinidad and Tobago, Tunisia, Uganda, United Arab Emirates, United Republic of Tanzania, Uruguay, Venezuela, Viet Nam, Yemen, Zambia, Zimbabwe.

Against: Albania, Andorra, Australia, Austria, Belgium, Bosnia and Herzegovina, Bulgaria, Canada, Croatia, Cyprus, Czech Republic, Denmark, Estonia, Finland, France, Georgia, Germany, Greece, Hungary, Iceland, Ireland, Israel, Italy, Japan, Latvia, Liechtenstein, Lithuania, Luxembourg, Malta, Marshall Islands, Micronesia, Monaco, Netherlands, New Zealand, Norway, Poland, Portugal, Republic of Moldova, Romania, San Marino, Slovakia, Slovenia, Spain, Sweden, The former Yugoslav Republic of Macedonia, Turkey, United Kingdom, United States.

Abstaining: Armenia, Azerbaijan, Kazakhstan, Nicaragua, Republic of Korea, Ukraine, Uzbekistan.

Women and the right to development

On 25 August [res. 1999/15], the Subcommission urged Governments to amend or repeal laws and policies that inhibited women's economic rights and their right to development, and to promote the education of women, including education relating to their rights. International trade, investment and financial institutions were called on to take into account the human rights implications for women of their policies. The Committee on the Elimination of Discrimination against Women (see p. 1102) was invited to pay special attention to women's economic rights and to explore the possibility of a general recommendation on the subject. The High Commissioner was asked to promote women's economic rights and the right to development, and the Secretary-General was invited to provide information on women and the right to development.

Extreme poverty

Report of independent expert. In response to a 1998 Commission request [YUN 1998, p. 691], the independent expert to evaluate the relationship between the promotion of human rights and extreme poverty, Anne-Marie Lizin (Belgium), in a January report [E/CN.4/1999/48], discussed extreme poverty as a violation of human rights and described UN action to eradicate the problem, case studies where efforts to combat poverty had had positive results (Bulgaria, Portugal, Yemen), proposals for technical cooperation programmes and the situation of women in extreme poverty.

The expert concluded that extreme poverty denied the enjoyment of human rights to 1.3 billion people worldwide, a majority of them women. Poverty was the most massive cause of human rights violations, striking at the principles of equal dignity of all human beings and of non-discrimination. She recommended universal ratification of relevant human rights instruments; minimum guaranteed income; 0.7 per cent of national budgets earmarked for official development assistance; development of local social welfare facilities; occupational reintegration programmes; development and distribution of human rights information and education components for the very poor; aid to the poorest of the poor in prisons; legal aid to those living in extreme poverty; training for social workers as human rights agents; making available to Governments technical assistance to ensure the rights of the poorest of the poor; combating corruption; and according priority in State social policy to refugees and internally displaced persons. Regarding a draft declaration on human rights and extreme poverty, the expert stated that it should call on States to base their anti-poverty policy on human rights that aimed at the eradication, rather than the reduction, of poverty.

Commission action. On 26 April [res. 1999/26], the Commission, reaffirming that extreme poverty and exclusion from society constituted a violation of human dignity and that urgent action was required to eliminate them, called on: the General Assembly, specialized agencies, UN bodies and intergovernmental organizations to take into account the contradiction between the existence of situations of extreme poverty and the duty to guarantee enjoyment of human rights; States, intergovernmental organizations and NGOs to take into account the links between human rights and extreme poverty, as well as efforts to empower people living in poverty to participate in decision-making processes on policies that affected them; and the United Nations to strengthen poverty eradication as a priority throughout the UN system. Human rights treaty bodies were invited to take into account, when considering States parties' reports, the question of extreme poverty and human rights. The independent expert was asked to report in 2000, underlining the best practices observed during her country visits and making the report available to the Commission for Social Development and the Commission on the Status of Women (see PART THREE, Chapters IX and X, respectively); and to contribute to the Assembly's evaluation in 2000 of the 1995 World Summit for Social Development [YUN 1995, p. 1113] by making her final report and conclusions available to the preparatory committee for the Assembly's 2000 special session devoted to that evaluation. The High Commissioner was requested to consider holding a workshop with the independent expert and Subcommission members in 1999 with a view to consultations also involving the functional commissions of the Economic and Social Council on a possible draft declaration on human rights and extreme poverty. The Council approved the Commission's request to the High Commissioner in **decision 1999/236** of 27 July.

Workshop. In accordance with the Commission's request, the Workshop on Human Rights and Extreme Poverty (Geneva, 30-31 August) [E/CN.4/2000/52/Add.1], attended by the independent expert, Subcommission experts, the Chairman of the Commission on Population and Development, UN bodies and NGOs, proposed elements for inclusion in a draft declaration. Recommendations included the convening of a second consultation on a draft text, with the participation of interested Governments, the Council's functional commissions, the specialized agencies and NGOs. The Committee on Economic, Social and Cultural Rights and other interested human rights treaty bodies should be invited to participate in a future consultation. Due consideration should be given to the Council's global framework of initiatives on poverty eradication and the development of the declaration should be considered within the context of the United Nations Decade for the Eradication of Poverty (1997-2006) (see p. 754).

Right to food

Commission action. On 26 April [res. 1999/24], the Commission reaffirmed that hunger constituted a violation of human dignity and considered it intolerable that some 800 million people did not have enough food to meet their basic nutritional needs. It stressed the need to mobilize and optimize technical and financial resources to reinforce national actions to implement sustainable food security policies. The Committee on

Economic, Social and Cultural Rights was invited to draft and adopt a general comment as a contribution to the clarification of the rights related to food in the International Covenant on Economic, Social and Cultural Rights [YUN 1966, p. 419] (see p. 575). The High Commissioner was asked to transmit the Commission's resolution to Governments, relevant specialized agencies and programmes, treaty bodies and NGOs, and invited them to present suggestions to develop the implementation of the rights related to food. She was asked to report in 2000.

Study on the right to food. In June [E/CN.4/Sub.2/1999/12], Asbjørn Eide (Norway) submitted the final version of his updated study on the right to food. The study was first presented in 1987 [YUN 1987, p. 773] and a progress report submitted in 1998 [YUN 1998, p. 694].

The final report described the dimensions, consequences and emerging issues surrounding malnutrition and hunger. It discussed follow-up to commitments made at the 1996 World Food Summit [YUN 1996, p. 1129] and action for States to ensure freedom from hunger and to implement the right. The treatment of the right to food and nutrition by relevant treaty bodies, the Commission and its special rapporteurs was reviewed. Examination of the evolving roles of those bodies on the issue revealed increased support for a human rights approach. Globalization had created new challenges and dangers regarding the right to food, as well as new opportunities; action was needed to prevent negative consequences.

The report concluded that since 1987 there was a better and more widely shared understanding of the impact of hunger and malnutrition; there was a broader recognition of the rights to be free from hunger and to adequate food as human rights; and international institutions broadly endorsed the human rights approach. Recommendations were made to States, the High Commissioner, treaty bodies, the Commission, specialized agencies, NGOs, professional organizations and academic institutions, many of which were based on consultations convened by the High Commissioner [YUN 1998, p. 693] and on a symposium on a human rights approach to food policies and programmes, held in the context of the twenty-sixth session (Geneva, 12-15 April) of the Subcommittee on Nutrition of the Administrative Committee on Coordination [ACC/1999/9]. Among the recommendations, the High Commissioner was called on to develop a strategy to implement the right to food and nutrition as a human right; organize a consultation on a UN strategy to implement freedom from hunger and the enjoyment of the right to food; strengthen OHCHR capacity to deal with the right; promote a coordinated approach in the UN system through UNDAF; organize a third expert consultation; prepare a study on the impact of globalization on the food and nutritional situation of vulnerable groups; organize a consultation involving treaty bodies, relevant agencies and humanitarian organizations and international financial and trade institutions; and initiate a study on the joint and separate responsibility of States in ensuring access to food for all in emergencies, especially during armed conflicts.

Subcommission action. On 25 August [res. 1999/12], the Subcommission endorsed the study's recommendation to the High Commissioner to organize a third expert consultation following those in 1997 and 1998, focusing on implementation mechanisms at the country level, inviting government experts to bring experiences from their countries as a contribution to the operationalization at the national level of the right to food, including the drawing up of a framework law. The Subcommission endorsed other recommendations made to her, including the organization of a consultation involving treaty body and relevant agency and humanitarian organization representatives and international financial and trade institutions. It asked the Commission to endorse the study's conclusions and recommendations.

Right to education

Reports of Special Rapporteur. The Commission considered a January report [E/CN.4/1999/49] of the Special Rapporteur on the right to education, Katarina Tomasevski (Croatia), covering the first four months of her work (August-December 1998). She provided an overview of UN efforts to enhance access to primary education, highlighting the financial obstacles, outlining strategies to achieve universal primary education, and stressing the need for data to monitor the right to education. She presented a scheme for governmental obligations corresponding to the right, denoting the four essential features that primary schools should exhibit: availability, accessibility, acceptability and adaptability (the 4-A scheme). The Special Rapporteur discussed compulsory education laws and provided a table of compulsory education categorizing countries in which primary education had been made compulsory according to its duration from 3 to 12 years.

The Special Rapporteur visited Uganda (26 June–2 July) [E/CN.4/2000/6/Add.1], at the invitation of the Government, to assess the realization of the right to education, especially experiences with universal primary education, introduced in

1997. Applying the 4-A scheme, she noted the huge challenge the country faced in ensuring the availability of schools and teachers. Securing access to school for girls had been prioritized, while the shift to inclusive education promised to improve access to school for children with disabilities. She highlighted aspects of the acceptability criterion, ranging from the absence of all internationally prohibited grounds of discrimination to school discipline, evidenced by corporal punishment or making pregnant schoolgirls leave school. Regarding adaptability, the Special Rapporteur emphasized the need for education to equip learners with income-generating abilities and thus contribute to poverty eradication. The Special Rapporteur was concerned about the absence of legislation that would specify rights and duties, freedoms and obligations in education. She recommended ensuring sustainability of primary education, formulating a human rights strategy based on Uganda's existing commitments, paying attention to the full recognition of teacher's trade union freedoms and soliciting the collective voice of teachers in educational planning and policy-making.

The Special Rapporteur visited the United Kingdom (18-22 October) [E/CN.4/2000/6/Add.2], inspired by the country's rights-based education, which had just been introduced. Following a review of educational changes from 1944 to 1996, the Special Rapporteur stated that she supported the Government's conceptual shift to rights-based education. However, that approach was promoted at the international level, while silence prevailed with regard to the right to education and rights in education at the domestic level. She was also concerned about the inherited legal status of the child as the object of a legally recognized relationship between the school and the child's parents, rather than the subject of the right to education and of human rights in education. Compulsory education left few categories of children without access to school, but closing the gap deserved priority, particularly with regard to children deprived of their liberty and traveller children. The Special Rapporteur was concerned about access to university education for those who could not afford it and urged the Government to prioritize its commitment to utilize funds generated within education to improve accessibility for disadvantaged categories. The cumulation of different grounds of discrimination, reinforced by class, required unravelling the causes and contributing factors at the structural rather than at only the individual level.

Commission action. On 26 April [res. 1999/25], the Commission asked the Special Rapporteur to report in 2000 and the Secretary-General to assist her. The High Commissioner was asked to consider organizing, in collaboration with relevant UN agencies, particularly the United Nations Children's Fund and UNESCO, a workshop to identify progressive developmental benchmarks and indicators related to the right to education that might be informative to the Committee on Economic, Social and Cultural Rights, the Committee on the Rights of the Child and other human rights treaty bodies and human rights mechanisms, UN specialized agencies, funds and programmes; by **decision 1999/235** of 27 July, the Economic and Social Council endorsed the Commission's request to the High Commissioner. The Commission asked the Secretary-General to report in 2000.

Working paper. As requested by the Subcommission in 1998 [YUN 1998, p. 694], Mustapha Mehedi (Algeria) presented, in July [E/CN.4/Sub.2/1999/10], a working paper on the realization of the right to education, including education in human rights. He analysed the objectives of education, as reflected in international and regional human rights instruments, and considered the expressions used in the instruments as a basis for the rights of each individual to receive education. Discussing responsibility for implementing the right, he provided information on the right to education as a social right, as a free and freedom-forming act and as a collective or solidarity right.

Subcommission action. On 25 August [res. 1999/11], the Subcommission asked Mr. Mehedi to prepare a final paper for 2000.

Scientific concerns

Human rights and the environment

In response to a 1997 Commission request [YUN 1997, p. 677], the Secretary-General submitted a report containing replies received from two UN bodies [E/CN.4/1999/89 & Add.1] in response to his request for comments on his 1996 and 1997 reports on human rights and the environment [YUN 1996, p. 652, & YUN 1997, p. 677]. The Secretary-General provided an analysis of subjects of common interest and concern in respect of human rights, environmental issues and sustainable development, as reflected in discussions at the General Assembly's 1997 special session on Agenda 21 [YUN 1997, p. 790].

Toxic wastes

Reports of Special Rapporteur. In January [E/CN.4/1999/46], the Special Rapporteur on the adverse effects of the illicit movement and dumping of toxic and dangerous products and wastes on the enjoyment of human rights, Fatma-Zohra Ksentini (Algeria), described her activities in 1998 and summarized comments she had received from three countries, as well as information submitted by intergovernmental organizations. She reviewed five incidents of illicit movement and dumping of toxic wastes and presented replies from the Governments concerned.

The Special Rapporteur expressed concern that a number of confirmed cases of illegal traffic in toxic wastes had not been solved satisfactorily and recommended the provision of international assistance more rapidly and on a larger scale. She favoured the development of a legal instrument restricting trade in dangerous chemical substances, as well as the ratification and amendment of the 1989 Basel Convention on the Control of Transboundary Movements of Hazardous Wastes and Their Disposal [YUN 1989, p. 420], which prohibited the export of dangerous wastes from industrialized to developing countries. Noting that the public at large, NGOs and local bodies responsible for environmental problems and human rights were not sufficiently familiar with her mandate, the Special Rapporteur asked OHCHR to publicize her mandate to a greater extent.

The Special Rapporteur visited Germany and the Netherlands (18-29 October) [E/CN.4/2000/50/Add.1] to hold consultations, study their laws and learn more about their policies. She also wished to exchange views with the authorities regarding allegations of illicit exports of toxic and dangerous products to developing countries and intended to study national and regional measures to prevent and punish the illicit activities.

Government representatives of the two countries stressed their commitment to sustainable development and measures to counteract the illicit trade in toxic and dangerous products and wastes, which was backed by international obligations and specific national measures. Both Governments believed that the illicit trade was a diminishing problem of limited scale. Steps had been taken to enforce the principle of the return of unwanted products and wastes to the country of origin at the expense of the initial shipper. The Special Rapporteur recommended greater information-sharing and more focal points to enhance the early warning systems. She raised the legal, economic, social, human and environmental problems caused by the export of contaminated ships destined for scrap in developing countries. Both Governments regarded such ships as hazardous wastes as defined under the Basel Convention, and accordingly they intended to ban their export to countries not members of the Organisation for Economic Cooperation and Development. She wished to see the issue examined in the relevant international forums to arrive at a satisfactory solution.

Commission action. By a roll-call vote of 36 to 16, with 1 abstention, on 26 April [res. 1999/23], the Commission, reaffirming that illicit traffic and dumping of toxic and dangerous products and wastes constituted a threat to the human rights to life, health and a sound environment, urged Governments to prevent the illegal trafficking. The Commission urged the Special Rapporteur to continue the study of existing problems of and solutions to the illicit trafficking, in particular in developing countries, with a view to making recommendations to control, reduce and eradicate the problem. The Special Rapporteur was asked to include in her reports information on persons killed or injured in developing countries through illicit movement and dumping of toxic and dangerous products and wastes.

Water and sanitation services

Commission action. On 27 April [dec. 1999/108], the Commission, taking note of a 1998 Subcommission resolution and the working paper on the right of access of everyone to drinking-water supply and sanitation services, prepared by El Hadji Guissé (Senegal) [YUN 1998, p. 696], noted that the right remained undefined and therefore asked the Subcommission to consider that aspect in preparing a study on the realization and promotion of the right.

Subcommission action. On 25 August [dec. 1999/107], the Subcommission asked Mr. Guissé to supplement his 1998 working paper for submission in 2000.

Bioethics

In response to a 1997 Commission request [YUN 1997, p. 678], the Secretary-General, in a January report [E/CN.4/1999/90], described developments in international bioethics law. The UNESCO General Conference in 1997 had adopted the Universal Declaration on the Human Genome and Human Rights [YUN 1997, p. 1530], which contained human rights standards and established an ethical framework for activities in that area. The Declaration and the Convention for the Protection of Human Rights and Dignity of the Human Being with regard to the Application of Biology and Biomedicine, adopted in 1996 by the Council of Ministers of the Council of Europe, demonstrated that the rapid development of science and its technological applications had been accompanied by the emergence of specific international principles aimed at ensuring that scientific advances benefited human rights and protected human dignity. Based on information received from Governments, the Secretary-General concluded that a positive development at the national level was the establishment of ethics committees to supervise scientific activity, to foresee and prevent possible excesses, to alert authorities and public opinion, and to act in an advisory capacity to assist public authorities, as well as scientific researchers and their professional organizations. Further standards were likely to be developed and mechanisms established at the international level.

Commission action. On 28 April [res. 1999/63], the Commission invited UNESCO, the World Health Organization, OHCHR and other UN bodies and specialized agencies to report to the Secretary-General on activities to ensure that the principles in the 1997 Declaration were taken into account. Based on those contributions, the Secretary-General was asked to draw up proposals for consideration by the General Assembly in 1999 concerning ways to ensure the coordination of bioethics activities throughout the UN system. The High Commissioner was asked to pay due attention to the issue, and Governments were invited to consider establishing ethics committees. The Commission asked the Subcommission to consider the contribution it could make to the reflections of the International Bioethics Committee on the follow-up to the 1997 Declaration and to report in 2001. It also asked the Secretary-General to report in 2001.

Computerized files

Pursuant to a 1997 Commission request [YUN 1997, p. 678], the Secretary-General submitted a report [E/CN.4/1999/88] containing information received from four UN entities and one NGO on follow-up to the guidelines for the regulation of computerized personal data files, adopted by the General Assembly in resolution 45/95 [YUN 1990, p. 621].

Commission action. On 28 April [dec. 1999/109], the Commission decided to remove the item from its agenda, since the guidelines were being taken into consideration by States. It asked the Secretary-General to entrust the competent inspection bodies with ensuring the implementation of the guidelines by the concerned organizations of the UN system.

Slavery and related issues

Commission action. By a roll-call vote of 36 to none, with 17 abstentions, the Commission, on 27 April [res. 1999/46], expressing grave concern at manifestations of contemporary forms of slavery, called on States to review, amend and enforce existing laws or enact new ones to prevent the use of the Internet for trafficking and sexual exploitation of women and children; protect particularly vulnerable groups against exploitation of the prostitution of others and other slavery-like practices; develop national plans of action taking into account the Programme of Action for the Prevention of the Traffic in Persons and the Exploitation of the Prostitution of Others [YUN 1995, p. 766]; and ratify the relevant international instruments relating to slavery, the slave trade and slavery-like practices.

The Secretary-General was asked to designate the High Commissioner as the focal point to coordinate activities and disseminate information in the UN system on the suppression of contemporary forms of slavery; to reassign to the Working Group on Contemporary Forms of Slavery an OHCHR staff member to ensure continuity of the implementation of Commission and Subcommission resolutions; and to appeal to Governments for contributions to the United Nations Voluntary Trust Fund on Contemporary Forms of Slavery (see p. 666).

Working Group activities. The five-member Working Group on Contemporary Forms of Slavery, at its twenty-fourth session (Geneva, 23 June–2 July) [E/CN.4/Sub.2/1999/17], reviewed developments in contemporary forms of slavery and measures to prevent and repress all its forms, including the economic exploitation of domestic and migrant workers, bonded labour, child labour, forced labour and the sexual exploitation of children. Other forms of exploitation examined were the illegal activities of certain religious and other sects, illegal and pseudo-legal adoptions aimed at exploiting children, traffic in human organs and tissues, and slavery-like practices in armed conflicts.

The Group concluded that despite the progress made in human rights protection and the preservation of human dignity, various forms of slavery still existed and new insidious forms were emerging. The Group made a series of recommendations on the issues it considered during the session.

Documents considered by the Group included May notes by the Secretary-General updating the status of the slavery conventions (1956 Supplementary Convention on the Abolition of Slavery, the Slave Trade, and Institutions and Practices Similar to Slavery [YUN 1956, p. 228] and the 1949 Convention for the Suppression of the Traffic in Persons and of the Exploitation of the Prostitution of Others, adopted by the General Assembly in resolution 317(IV) [YUN 1948-49, p. 613]) [E/CN.4/Sub.2/AC.2/1999/2 & E/CN.4/Sub.2/AC.2/

1999/3]; a June report of the Secretary-General containing proposals regarding the Group's future work received from Governments, UN bodies and intergovernmental organizations [E/CN.4/Sub.2/AC.2/1999/5]; and an executive summary of a working paper prepared by David Weissbrodt (United States) and Anti-Slavery International on a comprehensive review of existing treaty and customary law covering all the traditional and contemporary slavery-related practices and relevant monitoring mechanisms [E/CN.4/Sub.2/AC.2/1999/6].

Subcommission action. On 26 August [res. 1999/17], the Subcommission addressed the prevention of traffic in persons and exploitation of the prostitution of others; the prevention of transborder traffic in children; the role of corruption in perpetuating slavery and slavery-like practices; misuse of the Internet for sexual exploitation; implementation of the slavery conventions; migrant workers; child domestic workers; child labour; the eradication of bonded labour and elimination of child labour; and the sale of children, child prostitution and child pornography.

The Subcommission recommended that the General Assembly declare a UN year against trafficking in persons and asked OHCHR to draft guidelines for developing national plans of action against such trafficking. The Subcommission decided to consider the extent of corruption and its relationship to slavery and slavery-like practices, as well as the role of international debt in perpetuating slavery. The Working Group was asked to focus each of its annual sessions on an important issue for the abolition of slavery and to designate that issue two years prior to the annual session. The Secretary-General was asked to invite States to inform the Group of measures adopted to implement the 1993 Programme of Action for the Elimination of the Exploitation of Child Labour [YUN 1993, p. 965] and to report thereon to the Subcommission and Commission in 2000. He was also asked to invite States to continue to inform the Group of measures adopted to implement the 1992 Programme of Action for the Prevention of the Sale of Children, Child Prostitution and Child Pornography [YUN 1992, p. 814]. The Subcommission invited the Special Rapporteur on the sale of children, child prostitution and child pornography and the Special Rapporteur on violence against women to address the problem of trafficking and related practices and to make recommendations to strengthen the regime against those practices. The Secretary-General was asked to designate OHCHR as the focal point for the coordination of activities and the dissemination of information within the UN system for the suppression of contemporary forms of slavery.

UNESCO action. By a June note [A/54/137], the Secretary-General transmitted to the General Assembly a resolution adopted by the UNESCO General Conference, which proclaimed 23 August of every year International Day for the Remembrance of the Slave Trade and its Abolition.

Traffic in human organs and tissues

A January note by the Secretariat [E/CN.4/1999/75] stated that, pursuant to the Commission's 1997 request to the Secretary-General to continue to examine the reliability of allegations regarding the removal of organs and tissues of children and adults for commercial purposes [YUN 1997, p. 678], he had asked Governments, relevant UN agencies, the International Criminal Police Organization and relevant NGOs for information on the issue. As at 29 December 1998, no replies had been received.

Commission action. By a roll-call vote of 36 to none, with 17 abstentions, the Commission, on 27 April [res. 1999/46], noting that the Secretary-General had not received any information, asked him again to seek information and to report in 2000.

Sexual exploitation during armed conflict

On 26 April [dec. 1999/105], the Commission, taking note of a 1998 Subcommission resolution [YUN 1998, p. 698], approved the Subcommission's decision to extend the mandate of the Special Rapporteur on systematic rape, sexual slavery and slavery-like practices during armed conflict for an additional year, to enable her to submit an update of developments in 1999. The Commission recommended that the final report be transmitted to Governments, UN bodies, specialized agencies, regional intergovernmental organizations, the established international tribunals (see PART FOUR, Chapter II) and the secretariat of the Preparatory Commission for the Establishment of an International Criminal Court (see PART FOUR, Chapter III).

A June note by the Secretariat [E/CN.4/Sub.2/1999/16] stated that the Special Rapporteur was not in a position to submit her written report in 1999, as requested by the Subcommission in 1998. She would report orally at the Subcommission's August 1999 session and the report would be available in 2000.

By **decision 1999/252** of 27 July, the Economic and Social Council endorsed the Commission's decision to approve the extension of the Special Rapporteur's mandate.

On 16 August [E/CN.4/Sub.2/1999/SR.17], the Special Rapporteur, Gay J. McDougall (United States), informed the Subcommission that the most effective deterrent to the use of sexual violence during armed conflicts was to hold the perpetrators responsible for their crimes. In order to combat the atrocities still occurring, States should adopt legislation to allow for their prosecution of international crimes, and ensure that their legal systems conformed to internationally accepted norms and were capable of adjudicating international crimes without gender bias. Since the International Criminal Court and the established tribunals could address only a small fraction of the violations committed in armed conflicts, it was imperative that all perpetrators of sexual violence be prosecuted at the national level.

Subcommission action. By a vote of 15 to 2, with 5 abstentions, the Subcommission, on 26 August [res. 1999/16], called on States to enact and enforce legislation allowing for prosecution in national courts of sexual violence committed during armed conflict and to provide criminal penalties and compensation for unremedied violations in order to end the cycle of impunity. It also called on them to adopt instructions for and to train their armed forces; set up mechanisms to investigate and prosecute such offences committed by their armed forces; and seek technical assistance from the ICRC International Humanitarian Law Advisory Service. The Commission was asked to endorse in 2000 the principles contained in the Subcommission's resolution. The Subcommission called on the High Commissioner to monitor the implementation of its resolution and to report in 2000, and asked the Special Rapporteur to report in 2000.

1992 Programme of Action

In a June report with later addendum [E/CN.4/Sub.2/1999/15 & Add.1], the Secretary-General presented information received from two Governments on action they had taken to implement the 1992 Programme of Action for the Prevention of the Sale of Children, Child Prostitution and Child Pornography [YUN 1992, p. 814]. A November note by the Secretariat [E/CN.4/2000/72] drew the Commission's attention to the Secretary-General's report.

Trust fund on slavery

Reports of Secretary-General. In September [A/54/348], the Secretary-General reported on the status of the United Nations Voluntary Trust Fund on Contemporary Forms of Slavery, established by the General Assembly in resolution 46/122 [YUN 1991, p. 563].

The Fund's Board of Trustees, at its fourth session (Geneva, 24-26 March), recommended 10 travel grants, amounting to $13,505, to enable NGO representatives to participate, during three working days, in the deliberations of the 1999 session of the Working Group on Contemporary Forms of Slavery, and five humanitarian assistance project grants amounting to $27,000. Taking into consideration the fact that requests received in 1999 amounted to some $900,000, the Fund, in order to meet at least one third of requests expected in 2000, would need $300,000 in contributions, according to the Board. As at 31 August 1999, the contributions available to the Board in 2000 stood at approximately $38,000.

In December [E/CN.4/2000/80], the Secretary-General stated that, as at 26 November, the balance of funds available for 2000 amounted to $129,000.

Subcommission action. On 26 August [res. 1999/18], the Subcommission emphasized the need for regular contributions to enable the Board of Trustees to recommend grants to assist representatives of organizations to participate in the Working Group's deliberations in 2000 and to finance humanitarian assistance projects by NGOs.

Vulnerable groups

Women

Violence against women

Reports of Special Rapporteur. In March [E/CN.4/1999/68], the Special Rapporteur on violence against women, its causes and consequences, Radhika Coomaraswamy (Sri Lanka), reported on States' compliance with their international obligations with respect to domestic violence, specifically in terms of her 1996 report on violence in the family [YUN 1996, p. 654]. Information provided by States indicated that they were failing in their international obligations to prevent, investigate and prosecute violence against women in the family. While there were encouraging moves to implement new policies, procedures and laws, such violence did not appear to command Governments' attention. NGOs had the burden of pressuring Governments to fulfil their obligations. Annexed to the report was a table of States and their response mechanisms to domestic violence, covering the period 1995 to 1997. An addendum [E/CN.4/1999/68/Add.1] to the Special Rapporteur's report summarized 13 communications she had sent to Governments and five replies regarding cases of alleged violence against women.

A further addendum [E/CN.4/1999/68/Add.4] examined policies and practices that impacted women's reproductive rights and contributed to, caused or constituted violence against women. The Special Rapporteur pointed out that serious repercussions for women's reproductive health resulted from rape, domestic violence, trafficking and forced prostitution and cultural practices. State policies that diminished women's ability to make reproductive choices included forced abortions, forced sterilization, forced contraception or the provision of unsafe or inappropriate contraception methods and the denial of contraception.

The Special Rapporteur recommended that States ratify international human rights instruments; demonstrate respect for women's rights in reproductive health and family planning programmes; draw up specific laws to combat rape, domestic violence, trafficking and forced prostitution, female genital mutilation, sex-selective abortions and female infanticide; enforce a minimum legal age limit for marriage; eradicate discrimination and violence against women using public health-care services; provide increased education to health workers and ensure availability of information about the human rights implications of reproductive health; implement training programmes for those who worked in minority communities; monitor reproductive health services; support the creation of support groups, shelters, crisis centres and women-only police stations with trained workers and 24-hour hotlines; support research on the regulation of fertility, protection against sexually transmitted diseases (STDs) and confidential testing for STDs; and support organizations promoting women's reproductive and sexual health.

The Special Rapporteur visited Cuba (7-12 June) [E/CN.4/2000/68/Add.2], at the invitation of the Government, to study the situation of violence against women and its causes and consequences. She stated that it was hard to determine the scope and prevalence of violence against women in Cuba because of the lack of statistics. Efforts were being made to remedy the situation. As no specific domestic violence legislation existed, sentences were determined by the level of physical violence. The Penal Code provided for sanctions against rape and sexual abuse, although the law did not discriminate in cases of marital rape. Regarding sexual harassment, it was considered that adequate measures were in place and that specific legislation was not warranted. Most of the Special Rapporteur's interlocutors held that, as a result of the 1959 revolution, prostitution was virtually eliminated. However, she was informed that, with the increase of tourism, prostitution was on the rise, mostly in tourist destinations. Women who were found in prostitution repeatedly were committed by the judicial authorities to rehabilitation centres. The Federation of Cuban Women (FMC), the women's national umbrella organization working towards the full integration of women in economic, political, social and cultural life in conditions of equal opportunity, collaborated closely with government authorities. FMC had 175 "houses of family orientation" programmes to respond to the particular situation of women in a given community, which were managed with the participation of various professionals, including psychologists, social workers and health professionals. In addition to various assistance services, FMC disseminated information materials. As shelters did not exist, the Special Rapporteur urged FMC to establish them. The Special Rapporteur called on the Government to accede to human rights instruments to which it was not a party; urged it to invite thematic mechanisms of the Commission that had requested to visit Cuba; recommended that it cooperate with OHCHR; and called on the United States to terminate its economic embargo against Cuba, which had a negative impact on the economic and social conditions of women in Cuba. She also urged the Government to give FMC the maximum available resources; adopt domestic violence and sexual harassment legislation; sensitize its police, judiciary and prosecutors regarding violence against women; dismantle the special rehabilitation centres for prostitutes, as the centres violated their due process rights; permit organizations to monitor prison conditions regularly; and ensure the independence of the judiciary.

In a note verbale to OHCHR [E/CN.4/2000/131], Cuba presented its comments on the Special Rapporteur's report, stating, among other things, that the Special Rapporteur used sources that were poorly informed, or of doubtful credibility. Other comments related to alleged violations of civil and political rights of women in Cuba, and the alleged limitation on the independence of the judiciary. Cuba regarded her recommendations as unacceptable and did not feel obliged to comply with them. Annexed to the comments was a list of some women killed or disabled as a result of the United States policy against Cuba. In response, a note by the Secretariat stated that OHCHR maintained scrupulous objectivity regarding all Member States, including Cuba [E/CN.4/2000/151]. OHCHR had sought legal advice from the United Nations Office of Legal Affairs over the acquisition of internal correspondence.

Cuba, presenting its comments [E/CN.4/2000/165] on the note, stated that the Secretariat should be concerned about the principles of universality, objectivity and non-selectivity in the consideration of human rights issues. The legal advice being sought did not apply to Cuba, which was not subject to internal Secretariat regulations and had the right to defend itself.

The Special Rapporteur visited Haiti (14-17 June) [E/CN.4/2000/68/Add.3], where she focused on the situation of violence against women and the available response mechanisms, including the law enforcement and judicial institutions, and on the political rape committed against women during the military regime from 1991 to 1994. Most of her interlocutors characterized Haiti as an inherently and structurally violent society, in which violence against women was manifest in all its forms. The Minister for Social Affairs and Labour held that the root cause of the persisting violence against women was largely financial, and estimated that 90 per cent of Haitian women were victims of violence. Her Ministry had initiated workshops to increase women's independence. The Minister of Justice said that national legislation was discriminatory against women and that he was working with a commission on legal reform in general. The Ministry for the Status of Women had launched a radio/television campaign denouncing rape as a crime, and initiated a pilot project to provide legal assistance and representation to women victims. The Chief of Police recognized that, in addition to improved training courses on violence against women, the system for victims to lodge complaints needed revision. No special domestic violence legislation existed in Haiti and rape was not recognized as a serious crime. The Special Rapporteur expressed concern that recommendations made by the Truth and Justice Commission in the light of its factual and legal analysis of the acts of political rape had not been implemented. She was impressed by the work of NGOs and human rights organizations that had kept the issue of violence against women alive. Recommendations to Haiti included ratification of human rights instruments; taking steps to punish perpetrators and compensate victims; amending rape laws to meet international standards and introducing legislation on domestic violence and sexual harassment; strengthening the Ministry for the Status of Women; and establishing detention facilities where women would be held separately from men.

At the invitation of their Governments, the Special Rapporteur visited Pakistan and Afghanistan (1-13 September) [E/CN.4/2000/68/ Add.4] to study the issue of violence against Afghan women. During the Special Rapporteur's visit, civil war and political instability continued unabated in Afghanistan (see p. 255). She found official, widespread and systematic violation of women's human rights in Taliban-controlled areas. Women were subjected to grave indignities in their physical security and the rights to education, health, freedom of movement and freedom of association. As a result of pressure from the international community and the local population, some minor changes had taken place since 1997; for example, there were primary schools for girls aged 6 to 10, and women were allowed to work in the health sector. An estimated 1.2 million Afghans were living in Pakistan, where the rise in violence against women among the refugee population, including child abuse, prostitution and trafficking, was cause for concern.

Recommendations included withholding international recognition of the Taliban until it met its international obligations regarding women's rights; halting the arms flow into Afghanistan; increasing humanitarian aid to the Afghan population and to refugees in Pakistan; ceasing non-humanitarian aid to Taliban-controlled areas; ending the human rights violations of women and girls; and involving women in the peace process. The Special Rapporteur urged UN agencies in Afghanistan and Pakistan to initiate and fund programmes to rehabilitate women. The United Nations and other international organizations should employ more female international staff and should employ educated Afghan women for their projects, where possible. The United Nations should lift its travel ban on United Kingdom and United States nationals as soon as the security situation permitted, and UN staff members had to be recognized as international civil servants.

(See p. 670 for additional information on the situation of women and girls in Afghanistan.)

Commission action. On 26 April [res. 1999/42], the Commission condemned all acts of gender-based violence against women, violence in the family and violations of the human rights of women in situations of armed conflict. Stressing the Special Rapporteur's conclusions that States had a duty to promote and protect women's human rights, the Commission called on them to ratify and implement relevant international human rights instruments; report on violence against women and measures taken to implement the 1993 Declaration on the Elimination of Violence against Women, adopted by the General Assembly in resolution 48/104 [YUN 1993, p. 1046], and the 1995 Beijing Platform for Action [YUN 1995, p. 1170]; condemn violence against women and not invoke custom, tradition or religious practices to avoid obligations to eliminate such violence; enact, reinforce or amend penal, civil, labour and administrative sanctions in domestic legislation to punish and redress the wrongs done to women and girls; investigate and punish perpetrators of violence against women; conduct information campaigns about the problem; establish relations with NGOs, community-based organizations, and public and private sector institutions; create, develop and fund training programmes for judicial, legal, medical, social, educational, police, correctional service, military, peacekeeping and immigration personnel; and sensitize persons to the causes and effects of violence against women and highlight men's role in its prevention. The Secretary-General was asked to assist the Special Rapporteur and to ensure that her reports were brought to the attention of the Commission on the Status of Women and of the Committee on the Elimination of Discrimination against Women.

On 27 September [E/1999/23/Add.1 (res. 1999/S-4/1)], the Commission asked the Special Rapporteur on violence against women, its causes and consequences, among others, to carry out a mission to East Timor, to report to the Commission in 2000 and to submit an interim report to the Assembly in 1999.

The Special Rapporteur visited East Timor from 4 to 10 November (see p. 711).

Traditional practices affecting the health of women and girls

Report of Special Rapporteur. In response to a 1998 Subcommission request [YUN 1998, p. 701], the Special Rapporteur on traditional practices affecting the health of women and the girl child, Halima Embarek Warzazi (Morocco), in her third report submitted in July [E/CN.4/Sub.2/1999/14], presented a brief survey of the subject and of action taken, nationally and internationally, to combat the practices. She noted the yearly increase in the numbers among the general public in countries particularly affected by the phenomenon who were taking an interest in it, welcomed the initiatives taken within the communities concerned and commended NGO efforts to combat such practices. The Special Rapporteur called on countries with large inflows of immigrants to develop and implement programmes to combat the practices, showing due respect for the cultural values of the migrant population groups. Annexed to the report was the Ouagadougou (Burkina Faso) Declaration, adopted at the regional workshop on the fight against female genital mutilation in the member countries of the West African Economic and Monetary Union (4-6 May).

Subcommission action. On 25 August [res. 1999/13], the Subcommission appealed to States to intensify public awareness of the harmful effects of female genital mutilation and to the international community to provide support to NGOs and groups working to eliminate the practice. It called on Governments to implement the 1994 Plan of Action on the practice [YUN 1994, p. 1123] and asked the Secretary-General to invite them to submit information regularly on the situation regarding the practice. The Subcommission proposed that three seminars be held, in Africa, Asia and Europe, to review progress achieved since 1985 and ways to overcome the obstacles encountered in implementing the Plan of Action.

Traffic in women and girls

Commission action. On 26 April [res. 1999/40], the Commission called on Governments of origin, transit and destination, and regional and international organizations, to implement the Platform for Action of the Fourth World Conference on Women [YUN 1995, p. 1170] and the Vienna Declaration and Programme of Action of the World Conference on Human Rights [YUN 1993, p. 908]. It also called on Governments to criminalize trafficking in women and girls and to condemn and penalize offenders, and encouraged them to strengthen cooperation to combat the problem and rehabilitate victims. OHCHR was encouraged to continue to include the issue of traffic in women and girls in its advisory, training and information activities. The Secretary-General was asked to report in 2000.

Mainstreaming women's rights

Reports of Secretary-General. In accordance with a 1998 Commission request [YUN 1998, p. 707], the Secretary-General, in January [E/CN.4/1999/67 & Add.1], summarized steps taken by OHCHR, human rights treaty-monitoring bodies and human rights mechanisms to integrate gender perspectives fully into the UN human rights system. He noted that progress had been made in implementing the recommendations of the 1995 expert group meeting on the development of guidelines for the integration of gender perspectives into human rights activities [YUN 1995, p. 767]. He recommended that Governments ratify the Convention on the Elimination of All Forms of Discrimination against Women, adopted by the General Assembly in resolution 34/180 [YUN 1979, p. 895], and the Convention on the Rights of the Child, adopted in resolution 44/25 [YUN 1989, p. 561]. Treaty bodies were urged to clarify State parties' obligations to protect and promote human rights; develop a gender analysis of each article of every treaty, cross-referenced to the Convention on the Elimination of All Forms of Discrimination against Women, and develop gender-sensitive model questions for use in reviewing States parties' reports; ensure that attention was paid to gender dimensions in the consideration of States parties' reports; and incorporate a gender perspective in their concluding observations so that they delineated the strengths and weaknesses of each State party on women's enjoyment of the rights guaranteed by the treaty in question.

The Secretary-General presented to the Commission on the Status of Women in March [E/CN.6/1999/2] the joint work plan for the UN Division for the Advancement of Women and OHCHR for 1999. The plan emphasized continued cooperation between the Division and OHCHR on the work of treaty bodies; integrating a gender perspective in the work of the treaty bodies; support of the Special Rapporteurs on violence against women, on extrajudicial, summary or arbitrary executions, and on education; the issue of trafficking in women and girls; the development of a gender strategy for OHCHR; and national machineries for the advancement of women and national human rights institutions. The information exchange between the Division and OHCHR on planned and ongoing research and study projects would be improved. The two entities would hold a workshop as follow-up to the 1995 expert group meeting (see below).

Commission action. On 26 April [res. 1999/41], the Commission called for further strengthening of cooperation between the Commission on Human Rights and the Commission on the Status of Women and between OHCHR and the Division for the Advancement of Women. It asked the human rights treaty bodies, special procedures and other human rights mechanisms of the Commission and Subcommission to take a gender perspective into account when implementing their mandates, and to include in their reports information on and qualitative analysis of women's and girls' human rights. The Secretary-General was asked to report in 2000.

Workshop. The workshop on gender integration into the human rights system (Geneva, 26-28 May), convened by OHCHR, the Division for the Advancement of Women and the United Nations Development Fund for Women, was organized as a follow-up to the 1995 expert group meeting. Sources of information available to independent experts, the particularities of different mandates, issues of normative clarity and consistency, and cooperation and coordination were identified as areas where further progress was needed. The workshop adopted recommendations on the sources of information and methods of work of the treaty bodies and special procedures.

The girl child

On 28 April [res. 1999/80], the Commission approved the Subcommission's 1998 decision to extend the mandate of the Special Rapporteur on traditional practices affecting the health of women and the girl child [YUN 1998, p. 701]. It called on States to institute legal reforms to ensure the enjoyment by girls of all human rights and fundamental freedoms; to eliminate discrimination against girls and the causes of son preference; and to eradicate traditional or customary practices, particularly female genital mutilation, that were harmful to or discriminatory against women and girls. States, international organizations and NGOs were asked to set goals and to develop and implement gender-sensitive strategies to address the rights and needs of children, especially the particular needs of girls in education, health and nutrition.

Women in Afghanistan

Commission action. On 23 April [res. 1999/9], the Commission, condemning the continuing grave human rights violations of women and girls in Afghanistan, particularly in Taliban-controlled areas, urged all Afghan parties, particularly the Taliban, to end those violations and to ensure: the repeal of measures that discriminated against women; women's participation in civil, cultural, economic, political and social life; respect for women's right to work; the right of women and girls to education without discrimination, and the admission of women and girls to all levels of education; respect for women's right to security of person and ensuring that those responsible for physical attacks on women were brought to justice; and respect for women's freedom of movement and equal access to facilities necessary to protect their right to physical and mental health.

Report of Secretary-General. In response to a 1998 Subcommission request [YUN 1998, p. 707], the Secretary-General, in July [E/CN.4/Sub.2/1999/13], reported on the situation of women and girls in Afghanistan, which, he stated was extremely serious, owing to the undeclared policy of gender discrimination. UN work to promote women's and girls' human rights had been reasonably successful. Nevertheless, opportunities for constructive engagement at the community level through community-level projects should be pursued. The Secretary-General made recommendations to all Afghan parties, particularly the Taliban.

He stated that the Special Rapporteur on violence against women should be invited to undertake a mission to Afghanistan (see p. 668).

The Economic and Social Council, by **resolution 1999/14** of 28 July, condemned the grave violations of women's and girls' human rights in Afghanistan and urged States to continue to give special attention to the promotion and protection of women's human rights and to mainstream a gender perspective into all aspects of their policies and actions related to the country.

Subcommission action. On 25 August [res. 1999/14], the Subcommission, condemning all forms of discrimination and violation of the fundamental rights of women and girls in Afghanistan, considered it essential that the international community follow the situation very closely and bring maximum pressure to bear so that all restrictions imposed on women were removed.

(See also next chapter and PART THREE, Chapter X.)

Children

Sale of children, child prostitution and child pornography

Reports of Special Rapporteur. In a January report [E/CN.4/1999/71], the Special Rapporteur on the sale of children, child prostitution and child pornography, Ofelia Calcetas-Santos (Philippines), focused on the sale and trafficking of children. A basic problem faced in addressing the situation, she stated, was the lack of clear definitions, which resulted in difficulty in drafting legislation and in weak enforcement mechanisms. Problems were further compounded by constantly changing recruitment strategies and varying modes of deception, coercion and force employed in the process. Most countries of destination lacked response mechanisms to extricate children from exploitative situations arising from sale or trafficking. There was no comprehensive gathering of data on the extent of sale and/or trafficking. The Special Rapporteur expressed support for actions of the Working Group on Trafficking in Women and Children [YUN 1998, p. 709] and recommended condemning those who engaged in the sale and trafficking of persons; setting international standards; monitoring hospitals, clinics and care institutions to reduce the risk of abduction, sale and trafficking from such places; establishing international and regional registers for children adopted internationally and for missing children; training for law enforcement agents, border police, customs and immigration officials and members of the judiciary in the countries affected; guaranteeing victims freedom from persecution or harassment by the authorities; prosecution of perpetrators by States; developing procedures to distinguish between victims of trafficking and illegal immigrants; sanctions to deter the sale and/or trafficking of children; victim and witness protection; disseminating information on the practice; and government identification and removal of corrupt public officials acting as accomplices.

The Special Rapporteur visited Guatemala (19-30 July) [E/CN.4/2000/73/Add.2], where the sale and/or trafficking of children out of the country mainly occurred for the purpose of intercountry adoption, but there were also reports of trafficking of children into Guatemala for prostitution. Guatemala had a very high rate of adoptions, of which 95 per cent were intercountry; it was reported that Guatemala was the fourth largest "exporter" of children in the world. According to information obtained, legal adoption appeared to be the exception rather than the rule. It appeared that international adoption involved criminal offences such as the buying and selling of children, falsifying documents, kidnapping children, and housing babies awaiting private adoption. As a result of armed conflict and the violence of the 1970s and 1980s, thousands of Guatemalan children were deprived of one or both parents, and many orphans had ended up in refugee camps or on the streets. Child prostitution was visible in Guatemala City, where police estimated that over 2,000 children were being exploited in over 600 brothels. Among the Special Rapporteur's recommendations were adopting an adoption law; carrying out adoptions only by State bodies; making education available to all children; monitoring places where street children congregated; addressing the problem of drug addiction; creating courts for minors; instituting rehabilitation programmes for child victims of sexual offences; establishing a focal point to eradicate the commercial sexual exploitation of children; and government commitment to eradicate the trafficking of children.

At the invitation of the Government of Fiji, the Special Rapporteur visited Suva and Nadi (11-16 October) [E/CN.4/2000/73/Add.3] and then travelled to Australia, where a large percentage of all tourists originated, for meetings on 18 October with government and NGO representatives. The Special Rapporteur had received allegations that Fiji was a popular destination for child sex tourists—adults who travelled to certain countries where they sexually abused children. Few incidents involving the sale of a child had been reported, other than for prostitution. The primary causes for children entering prostitution were attributed to family abuse, poverty and the availability of few recreational activities. In the absence of hard data and statistics, the Special Rapporteur cited strong indicators pointing to child exploitation, such as the escalating number of street children; drug, alcohol and substance abuse by children; sexual violence suffered by children; and a dependence on tourism. She recommended legislative reform and policies to protect children; mainstreaming child protection throughout government programmes and activities; educating the public about the Convention on the Rights of the Child, adopted by the General Assembly in resolution 44/25 [YUN 1989, p. 561]; providing children with wholesome recreational facilities; providing sex education in schools; police training; designating a national focal point for children; and enhanced cooperation between government agencies and NGOs concerned with children.

Expert meeting. UNESCO organized an expert meeting entitled "Sexual abuse of children, child pornography and paedophilia on the Internet: an international challenge" (Paris, 18-19 January) [E/CN.4/2000/73], which dealt with the promotion of the free flow of information in a manner that would not place children at greater risk of sexual exploitation; making the Internet safe for children to use; and the need for research, information-monitoring and sensitization of the public. Participants put forward a declaration and an action plan that proposed measures for UNESCO, Governments, international agencies, NGOs, industry, educators, parents, law enforcement agencies and the media. Subsequently, UNESCO set up "Innocence in danger", an international Internet education and safety programme.

Commission action. On 28 April [res. 1999/80], the Commission called on States to prevent the abduction of, the sale of, or traffic in children. States and UN bodies and agencies were called on to allocate resources for programmes to rehabilitate child victims of sale, trafficking, abduction and any form of sexual exploitation and abuse. The Commission welcomed the UNESCO expert meeting and its declaration and action plan, and encouraged follow-up in cooperation with the Special Rapporteur. The Commission asked the Secretary-General to assist the Special Rapporteur to enable her to submit an interim report to the General Assembly in 1999 and a report to the Commission in 2000.

Interim report of Special Rapporteur. Pursuant to the Commission's request, the Special Rapporteur submitted, in September [A/54/411], an interim report updating developments relating to her mandate and country-specific and regional developments.

Child labour

Commission action. On 28 April [res. 1999/80], the Commission called on States to ratify the conventions of the International Labour Organization (ILO) relating to child labour; eliminate all forms of child labour contrary to accepted international standards; support an ILO convention and recommendation on the elimination of the worst forms of child labour (see p. 1388); assess and examine the nature and causes of the exploitation of child labour and develop strategies for combating such practices; promote education to prevent child labour; and strengthen international coordination and cooperation.

Children and armed conflict

Commission action. On 28 April [res. 1999/80], the Commission called on States and other parties to armed conflict to respect international humanitarian law; to end the use of child soldiers; to cooperate with the Secretary-General's Special Representative on the situation of children in armed conflict and to implement commitments they had undertaken; to provide training for armed forces and civilian police to address the needs of children in armed conflict; and to address the impact on children of the use of weapons in armed conflict. It decided to recommend that the Special Representative and relevant UN bodies develop a concerted approach on the rights, protection and welfare of children affected by armed conflict, and to increase cooperation among their respective mandates and with NGOs. It asked the Secretary-General to ensure support to the Special Representative and called on institutions and States to provide voluntary contributions to him. The Secretary-General was also asked, in cooperation with States, international organizations and relevant NGOs, to encourage regional training programmes for the armed forces relating to the protection of children and women during armed conflicts.

(For information on a draft optional protocol to the Convention on the Rights of the Child on the involvement of children in armed conflict, see p. 579.)

SECURITY COUNCIL ACTION

On 25 August [meeting 4037], the Security Council unanimously adopted **resolution 1261(1999)**. The draft [S/1999/911] was prepared during consultations among Council members.

The Security Council,

Recalling the statements by its President of 29 June 1998, 12 February 1999 and 8 July 1999,

Noting recent efforts to bring to an end the use of children as soldiers in violation of international law, in International Labour Organization Convention

No. 182 on the Prohibition and Immediate Action for the Elimination of the Worst Forms of Child Labour, which prohibits forced or compulsory labour, including the forced or compulsory recruitment of children for use in armed conflict, and in the Rome Statute of the International Criminal Court, in which conscripting or enlisting children under the age of fifteen into national armed forces or using them to participate actively in hostilities is characterized as a war crime,

1. *Expresses its grave concern* at the harmful and widespread impact of armed conflict on children and the long-term consequences this has for durable peace, security and development;

2. *Strongly condemns* the targeting of children in situations of armed conflict, including killing and maiming, sexual violence, abduction and forced displacement, recruitment and use of children in armed conflict in violation of international law, and attacks on objects protected under international law, including places that usually have a significant presence of children, such as schools and hospitals, and calls on all parties concerned to put an end to such practices;

3. *Calls upon* all parties concerned to comply strictly with their obligations under international law, in particular the Geneva Conventions of 12 August 1949 and the obligations applicable to them under the Additional Protocols thereto of 1977 and the United Nations Convention on the Rights of the Child of 1989, and stresses the responsibility of all States to bring an end to impunity, as well as their obligation to prosecute those responsible for grave breaches of the Geneva Conventions of 12 August 1949;

4. *Expresses its support* for the ongoing work of the Special Representative of the Secretary-General for Children and Armed Conflict, the United Nations Children's Fund, the Office of the United Nations High Commissioner for Refugees, other parts of the United Nations system and other relevant international organizations dealing with children affected by armed conflict, and requests the Secretary-General to continue to develop coordination and coherence among them;

5. *Welcomes and encourages* efforts by all relevant actors at the national and international level to develop more coherent and effective approaches to the issue of children and armed conflict;

6. *Supports* the work of the open-ended intersessional working group of the Commission on Human Rights on a draft optional protocol to the Convention on the Rights of the Child on the involvement of children in armed conflicts, and expresses the hope that it will make further progress with a view to finalizing its work;

7. *Urges* all parties to armed conflicts to ensure that the protection, welfare and rights of children are taken into account during peace negotiations and throughout the process of consolidating peace in the aftermath of conflict;

8. *Calls upon* parties to armed conflicts to undertake feasible measures during armed conflicts to minimize the harm suffered by children, such as "days of tranquillity", to allow the delivery of basic necessary services, and further calls upon all parties to armed conflicts to promote, implement and respect such measures;

9. *Urges* all parties to armed conflicts to abide by concrete commitments made to ensure the protection of children in situations of armed conflict;

10. *Also urges* all parties to armed conflicts to take special measures to protect children, in particular girls, from rape and other forms of sexual abuse and gender-based violence in situations of armed conflict and to take into account the special needs of the girl child throughout armed conflicts and their aftermath, including in the delivery of humanitarian assistance;

11. *Calls upon* all parties to armed conflicts to ensure the full, safe and unhindered access of humanitarian personnel and the delivery of humanitarian assistance to all children affected by armed conflict;

12. *Underscores* the importance of the safety, security and freedom of movement of United Nations and associated personnel to the alleviation of the impact of armed conflict on children, and urges all parties to armed conflicts to respect fully the status of United Nations and associated personnel;

13. *Urges* States and all relevant parts of the United Nations system to intensify their efforts to ensure an end to the recruitment and use of children in armed conflict in violation of international law, through political and other efforts, including promotion of the availability of alternatives for children to their participation in armed conflict;

14. *Recognizes* the deleterious impact of the proliferation of arms, in particular small arms, on the security of civilians, including refugees and other vulnerable populations, particularly children, and in this regard recalls resolution 1209(1998) of 19 November 1998, in which, inter alia, the Council stresses the importance of all Member States, and in particular States involved in manufacturing and marketing of weapons, restricting arms transfers which could provoke or prolong armed conflicts or aggravate existing tensions or armed conflicts, and in which it urges international collaboration in combating illegal arms flows;

15. *Urges* States and the United Nations system to facilitate the disarmament, demobilization, rehabilitation and reintegration of children used as soldiers in violation of international law, and calls upon in particular the Special Representative of the Secretary-General for Children and Armed Conflict, the United Nations Children's Fund and the Office of the United Nations High Commissioner for Refugees and other relevant agencies of the United Nations system to intensify their efforts in this regard;

16. *Undertakes*, when taking action aimed at promoting peace and security, to give special attention to the protection, welfare and rights of children, and requests the Secretary-General to include in his reports recommendations in this regard;

17. *Reaffirms its readiness* when dealing with situations of armed conflict:

(*a*) To continue to support the provision of humanitarian assistance to civilian populations in distress, taking into account the particular needs of children, including the provision and rehabilitation of medical and educational services to respond to the needs of children, the rehabilitation of children who have been maimed or psychologically traumatized, and child-focused mine-clearance and mine-awareness programmes;

(b) To continue to support the protection of displaced children, including their resettlement by the Office of the High Commissioner and others as appropriate;

(c) Whenever adopting measures under Article 41 of the Charter of the United Nations, to give consideration to their impact on children, in order to consider appropriate humanitarian exemptions;

18. *Also reaffirms its readiness* to consider appropriate responses whenever buildings or sites which usually have a significant presence of children are specifically targeted in situations of armed conflict, in violation of international law;

19. *Requests* the Secretary-General to ensure that personnel involved in United Nations peacemaking, peacekeeping and peace-building activities have appropriate training in respect of the protection, rights and welfare of children, and urges States and relevant international and regional organizations to ensure that appropriate training is included in their programmes for personnel involved in similar activities;

20. *Also requests* the Secretary-General to submit to the Council by 31 July 2000 a report on the implementation of the present resolution, consulting all relevant parts of the United Nations system and taking into account other relevant work;

21. *Decides* to remain actively seized of the matter.

Communication. At a 29 August meeting in Egilsstardir, Iceland, the Foreign Ministers of the five Nordic countries (Denmark, Finland, Iceland, Norway and Sweden) signed the Declaration against the Use of Child Soldiers [A/54/419].

Report of Special Representative. In response to General Assembly resolution 53/128 [YUN 1998, p. 712], the Secretary-General's Special Representative, Olara A. Otunnu (Côte d'Ivoire), submitted, in October [A/54/430], his second annual report on the situation of children affected by armed conflict. He stated that currently over 20 million children were displaced by war and some 300,000 young persons under the age of 18 were being exploited as soldiers. Children were maimed and killed, uprooted from home and community, faced with survival issues, orphaned, separated from their parents, subjected to sexual abuse and exploitation, traumatized, deprived of their education and made perpetrators of violence when used as combatants.

The Special Representative described his field missions during the preceding year and initiatives for children in Rwanda (21-24 February), Burundi (24-28 February), the Sudan (2-9 March), Kosovo refugees in Albania and the former Yugoslav Republic of Macedonia (FYROM) (10-13 April), Mozambique (18-22 April), Colombia (30 May- 6 June) and Sierra Leone and Guinea (30 August-4 September).

Regarding Rwanda, the Special Representative said that among the estimated 800,000 people massacred during the genocide of 1994, 300,000 were children. Over 84 per cent of children had experienced death in their family and over 95 per cent had directly witnessed violence. An estimated 20 per cent of the child population was severely traumatized. In view of the estimated 45,000 households headed by children, 90 per cent of them girls, the Special Representative had urged the Government to adopt legislation allowing girls to inherit farms and other properties, which was passed and due to come into force. The Government announced a policy to demobilize all child soldiers; in that regard, the Special Representative urged the Government to raise the age limit for recruitment from 17 to 18. While in Rwanda, the Special Representative met with the chairman of the principal insurgency group in the Democratic Republic of the Congo, who accepted a temporary cessation of hostilities to immunize children against polio and deliver emergency food to malnourished children. The chairman accepted a proposal to adopt the age limit of 18 for recruitment, observe the Convention on the Rights of the Child and refrain from using the media and public rallies to incite ethnic and racial hatred.

During his visit to Burundi, the Government agreed to raise the minimum age for recruitment from 16 to 18 and include the protection and welfare of children in the Arusha peace process (see p. 98). The Special Representative obtained commitments from the Government of the Sudan and from the Sudan People's Liberation Movement (SPLM) regarding the use of landmines; placing the protection and welfare of children on the peace agenda; the abduction and kidnapping of children in southern Sudan; repatriation of abducted Ugandan children (see next page); access to the SPLM-held areas in the Nuba mountains; and support for a "neighbourhood initiative" that would bring together a group of eastern African countries linked by cross-border issues affecting children.

The Special Representative visited FYROM and Albania to assess the impact on children of the Kosovo crisis (see p. 333). Children, who were the most traumatized by the violence, constituted over 65 per cent of those expelled from Kosovo. The Special Representative put forward an agenda for action for the children of Kosovo, which included ensuring basic survival needs; reunification of families; trauma counselling; schooling for refugee children; support to host families of refugees; television and radio programmes devoted to the needs of refugee children; relocation to third countries; preventing recruitment and participation of children in hostilities; protection of young women against sexual exploitation; and access by the international community to children remaining in Kosovo.

The Special Representative visited Mozambique to assess the situation of children in the aftermath of the protracted armed conflict, which ended in 1992. He found that children seemed to have adjusted relatively well, although they still faced many problems. He called for such measures as including children's welfare on peace agendas and providing resources for post-conflict arrangements and demining.

In Colombia, the Special Representative assessed the impact of the conflict on children, who had suffered for over 40 years as victims, witnesses and perpetrators of violence. He was pleased that both the Government and the opposition had agreed to place the needs and protection of children as a high priority in the peace process. The Special Representative undertook a mission to Sierra Leone and Guinea to assess the conditions of children following the signing of the Lomé Peace Agreement (see p. 152); to review progress since his 1998 visit [YUN 1998, p. 710]; to assess the situation of Sierra Leonean refugee children in Guinea; and to identify initiatives to ensure the protection, rights and welfare of children in the aftermath of the war. He put forward a special agenda for action for the children of Sierra Leone to ensure their rehabilitation and welfare, including a national commission for children's welfare, provisions for child protection in the mandate of the United Nations Observer Mission in Sierra Leone, rehabilitation of amputees, a programme for sexually abused children, access to and release of abducted children, demobilization of child combatants, provision of basic education and medical services and a special fund for war victims.

The Special Representative made general recommendations regarding launching an era of application for international norms; promoting and strengthening local value systems; reinforcing commitments made by parties to a conflict; deepening the engagement of the Security Council; government protection of children as a feature of domestic and international policy; a voluntary code of conduct to be developed by the business community to monitor and control the flow of arms and the exploitation of natural resources in conflict areas; placing child protection and welfare on peace agendas; making child protection and welfare a central concern in post-conflict programmes; integrating child protection into UN peace operations; providing for children in periods of "imperfect peace"; providing protection and relief for internally displaced communities; signing and ratifying new international instruments; concluding work on an optional protocol to the Convention on the Rights of the Child on involvement of children in armed conflict; protecting children from the impact of sanctions; building local capacities for protection and advocacy; and demonstrating equal concern for the plight of all children affected by armed conflict.

Abduction of children from northern Uganda

Report of Secretary-General. In January [E/CN.4/1999/69 & Corr.1], the Secretary-General summarized the situation of children abducted from northern Uganda and presented information received from the Sudan and Uganda, his Special Representative on the impact of armed conflict on children, and international and non-governmental sources. The Secretary-General stated that the armed conflict in Uganda had lasted for 12 years, with Gulu and Kitgum districts on the border with the Sudan being the worst affected. The United Nations Children's Fund (UNICEF) and NGO sources stated that the Lord's Resistance Army (LRA), an armed opposition group, had abducted up to 10,000 children, mostly teenagers and more boys than girls, to carry military equipment and supplies to LRA camps in Uganda and southern Sudan. At the camps, the children were taught how to use weapons and were forced to fight. Smaller children might be given chores to do and girls as young as 12 were given to commanders as "wives". Children who disobeyed orders were beaten or killed, and other abducted children were often forced to do the killing. Uganda stated that, since the adoption of the Commission's 1998 resolution on the subject [YUN 1998, p. 712], it had continued to encourage a political solution to the conflict and it remained open to seeking bilateral negotiations with the Sudan. The Sudan stated that it would continue to honour its commitments as stipulated in the Convention on the Rights of the Child and any other obligations concerning the protection, safety and welfare of the child.

Commission action. By a roll-call vote of 28 to 1, with 24 abstentions, the Commission, on 26 April [res. 1999/43], condemning all parties involved in the abduction, torture, killing, rape, enslavement and forceful recruitment of children in northern Uganda, particularly LRA, called for their unconditional release and safe return. It asked the United Nations Voluntary Fund for Victims of Torture (see p. 637) to assist victims and their families, and demanded that parties external to the conflict in northern Uganda supporting the continued abduction and detention of children by LRA cease all such assistance and collaboration. The Special Representative,

UNICEF, UNHCR, OHCHR and other UN system entities were asked to address the situation as a matter of priority. The Secretary-General was asked to report in 2000.

Refugee and internally displaced children

On 28 April [res. 1999/80], the Commission called on States to increase protection of refugee and internally displaced children. While calling on States and other parties to armed conflicts to recognize the risks to which refugee and internally displaced children were exposed, the Commission called on Governments and UN bodies to give those situations urgent attention. States and UN bodies and agencies were asked to ensure the early identification and registration of unaccompanied refugee and internationally displaced children, to give priority to programmes for family tracing and reunification and to develop programmes for voluntary repatriation, local integration and resettlement.

Children with disabilities

The Commission, on 28 April [res. 1999/80], welcomed the establishment of a working group on children with disabilities aimed at developing a plan of action in respect of the recommendations of the Committee on the Rights of the Child (see p. 579). It called on States to adopt measures to ensure the enjoyment of all human rights and fundamental freedoms by children affected by disabilities and to develop and enforce anti-discriminatory legislation. States parties to the Convention on the Rights of the Child were called on to report on the situation and the needs of children with disabilities.

Children's rights to health and education

On 28 April [res. 1999/80], the Commission called on States to adopt measures to ensure the enjoyment of human rights and fundamental freedoms by children affected by disease and malnutrition. States and UN bodies were called on to ensure training of health professionals in human rights and to pay attention to the development of sustainable health systems and social services to ensure the prevention of diseases, malnutrition, disabilities and infant and child mortality.

Regarding a child's right to education, the Commission called on States to make primary education compulsory and free of charge, and to ensure that education was directed, among other things, towards respect for human rights and fundamental freedoms and to the preparation of the child for responsible life in a free society. It also called on them to make education accessible to children living in poverty, children living in remote areas, children with special education needs and children requiring special protection. States, educational institutions and the UN system were called on to develop and implement gender-sensitive strategies to address the particular needs of the girl child in education.

Juvenile justice

On 28 April [res. 1999/80], the Commission called on States to ensure compliance with the principle that depriving children of their liberty should be used only as a measure of last resort and to ensure that, if they were arrested, detained or imprisoned, children were separated from adults. It also asked them to ensure that no child detained was deprived of the access to and provision of health-care services, hygiene and environmental sanitation, education and basic instruction.

Street children

On 28 April [res. 1999/80], the Commission called on States to seek solutions to problems that caused children to work and/or live on the street; provide services for children to divert them from involvement in harmful, exploitative and abusive activity; and take urgent measures to prevent the killing of street children and combat torture and violence against them. States and the international community were called on to support the efforts of States to improve the situation of street children.

Rights of the child

On 17 December [meeting 83], the General Assembly, following consideration of a broad range of issues relating to children's rights and acting on the recommendation of the Third Committee [A/54/601], adopted **resolution 54/149** without vote [agenda item 112].

The rights of the child

The General Assembly,

Recalling its resolutions 53/127 and 53/128 of 9 December 1998, and taking note of Commission on Human Rights resolution 1999/80 of 28 April 1999,

Bearing in mind the Convention on the Rights of the Child, emphasizing that the provisions of the Convention and other relevant human rights instruments must constitute the standard in the promotion and protection of the rights of the child, and reaffirming that the best interest of the child shall be the primary consideration in all actions concerning children,

Reaffirming the World Declaration on the Survival, Protection and Development of Children and the Plan of Action for Implementing the World Declaration on the Survival, Protection and Development of Children in the 1990s adopted by the World Summit for Children, held in New York on 29 and 30 September 1990, notably the solemn commitment to give high priority to the rights of children, to their survival and to their protection and development, and reaffirming also the Vienna Declaration and Programme of Action adopted by the World Conference on Human Rights, held at Vienna from 14 to 25 June 1993, which, inter alia, states that national and international mechanisms and programmes for the defence and protection of children, in particular those in especially difficult circumstances, should be strengthened, including through effective measures to combat exploitation and abuse of children, such as female infanticide, harmful child labour, sale of children and organs, child prostitution and child pornography, and which reaffirms that all human rights and fundamental freedoms are universal,

Profoundly concerned that the situation of girls and boys in many parts of the world remains critical as a result of poverty, inadequate social and economic conditions in an increasingly globalized world economy, pandemics, natural disasters, armed conflict, displacement, exploitation, illiteracy, hunger, intolerance, discrimination and inadequate legal protection, and convinced that urgent and effective national and international action is called for,

Underlining the need for mainstreaming a gender perspective in all policies and programmes relating to children,

Recognizing the need for the realization of a standard of living adequate for the child's physical, mental, spiritual, moral and social development, as well as the provision of universal and equal access to primary education,

Recognizing also that partnership between Governments, international organizations and all sectors of civil society, in particular non-governmental organizations, is important to realizing the rights of the child,

Emphasizing the importance of the tenth anniversary of the Convention on the Rights of the Child for mobilizing and taking further action towards the full realization of the rights of the child,

Welcoming the preparations for the special session of the General Assembly on the follow-up to the World Summit for Children in 2001,

I

Implementation of the Convention on the Rights of the Child

1. *Once again urges* the States that have not yet done so to sign and ratify or accede to the Convention on the Rights of the Child as a matter of priority, with a view to reaching the goal of universal adherence by the tenth anniversary, in 2000, of the World Summit for Children and of the entry into force of the Convention;

2. *Reiterates its concern* at the great number of reservations to the Convention, and urges States parties to withdraw reservations incompatible with the object and purpose of the Convention and to review regularly any reservations with a view to withdrawing them;

3. *Calls upon* States parties to implement fully the Convention, and stresses that the implementation of the Convention contributes to the achievement of the goals of the World Summit for Children;

4. *Urges* States to involve children and youth in their efforts to implement the goals of the World Summit for Children and the Convention;

5. *Calls upon* States parties to cooperate closely with the Committee on the Rights of the Child and to comply in a timely manner with their reporting obligations under the Convention, in accordance with the guidelines elaborated by the Committee, and encourages States parties to take into account the recommendations made by the Committee in the implementation of the provisions of the Convention;

6. *Also calls upon* States parties to encourage training on the rights of the child for those involved in activities concerning children, for example, through the programme of advisory services and technical cooperation in the field of human rights;

7. *Requests* the Secretary-General to ensure the provision of appropriate staff and facilities for the effective and expeditious performance of the functions of the Committee, notes the temporary support given by the plan of action of the United Nations High Commissioner for Human Rights to strengthen the important role of the Committee in advancing the implementation of the Convention, and also requests the Secretary-General to make available information on the follow-up to the plan of action;

8. *Calls upon* States parties urgently to take appropriate measures so that acceptance of the amendment to paragraph 2 of article 43 of the Convention by a two-thirds majority of States parties can be reached as soon as possible, in order for the amendment to enter into force, increasing the membership of the Committee from ten to eighteen experts;

9. *Invites* the Committee to continue to enhance its constructive dialogue with the States parties and its transparent and effective functioning;

10. *Welcomes* the attention given by the Committee to the realization of the highest attainable standards of health and access to health care, and to the rights of children affected by human immunodeficiency virus/acquired immunodeficiency syndrome, and urges Governments, in cooperation with relevant United Nations bodies and organizations, to adopt all appropriate measures with a view to the realization of all their rights;

11. *Calls upon* States to protect all human rights of migrant children, in particular unaccompanied migrant children, and to ensure that the best interest of the child shall accordingly be a primary consideration, and encourages the Committee, the United Nations Children's Fund and other relevant United Nations bodies, within their respective mandates, to pay particular attention to the conditions of migrant children in all States and, as appropriate, to make recommendations to strengthen their protection;

12. *Recommends* that, within their mandates, all relevant human rights mechanisms and all other relevant organs and mechanisms of the United Nations system and the supervisory bodies of the specialized agencies pay attention to particular situations in which children are in danger and in which their rights are violated and that they take into account the work of the Committee, and encourages the further development of the rights-based approach adopted by the United Nations Children's Fund and further steps to increase system-wide coordination and inter-agency cooperation for the promotion and protection of the rights of the child;

13. *Encourages* the Committee, in monitoring the implementation of the Convention, to continue to pay

attention to the needs of children in especially difficult circumstances;

14. *Encourages* Governments and relevant United Nations bodies, as well as relevant non-governmental organizations and child rights advocates, to contribute, as appropriate, to the Web-based database launched by the United Nations Children's Fund, so as to continue the provision of information on laws, structures, policies and processes adopted at the national level to translate the Convention into practice;

II

Prevention and eradication of the sale of children and of their sexual exploitation and abuse, including child prostitution and child pornography

1. *Welcomes* the interim report of the Special Rapporteur of the Commission on Human Rights on the sale of children, child prostitution and child pornography, and expresses its support for her work;

2. *Requests* the Secretary-General to provide the Special Rapporteur with all necessary human and financial assistance to enable her to discharge her mandate fully;

3. *Invites* further voluntary contributions through the Office of the United Nations High Commissioner for Human Rights and support for the work of the Special Rapporteur for the effective fulfilment of her mandate;

4. *Strongly supports* the work of the open-ended inter-sessional working group of the Commission on Human Rights on the elaboration of a draft optional protocol to the Convention on the Rights of the Child related to the sale of children, child prostitution and child pornography, and urges the working group to finalize its work before the tenth anniversary of the entry into force of the Convention in 2000;

5. *Reaffirms* the obligation of States parties to prevent the abduction of, the sale of or trafficking in children for any purpose or in any form and to protect children from all forms of sexual exploitation and abuse, in accordance with articles 35 and 34 of the Convention;

6. *Calls upon* States to criminalize and to penalize effectively all forms of sexual exploitation and abuse of children, including within the family or for commercial purposes, child pornography and child prostitution, including child sex tourism, while ensuring that the children victims of such practices are not penalized, and to take effective measures to ensure the prosecution of offenders, whether local or foreign, by the competent national authorities, either in the country of origin of the offender or in the country of destination, in accordance with due process of law;

7. *Also calls upon* States, in cases of child sex tourism, to enhance international cooperation among all relevant authorities, in particular law enforcement authorities, including the sharing of relevant data, in order to eradicate this practice;

8. *Requests* States to increase cooperation and concerted action at the national, regional and international levels, including in the context of the United Nations, by all relevant authorities and institutions, in order to adopt and implement effective measures for the prevention and eradication of the sale of children and of their sexual exploitation and abuse and to prevent and dismantle networks trafficking in children;

9. *Stresses* the need to combat the existence of a market that encourages such criminal practices against children, including through preventive and enforcement measures targeting customers or individuals who sexually exploit or abuse children;

10. *Calls upon* States to enact and enforce, review and revise, as appropriate, laws and to implement policies, programmes and practices to protect children from and to eliminate all forms of sexual exploitation and abuse, including commercial sexual exploitation, taking into account the particular problems posed by the use of the Internet in this regard;

11. *Encourages* Governments to facilitate the active participation of child victims of sexual exploitation and abuse in the development and implementation of strategies to protect children from sexual exploitation and abuse;

12. *Encourages* continued regional and interregional efforts, with the objective of identifying best practices and issues requiring particularly urgent action, to follow up the implementation of the measures in line with those outlined in the Declaration and Agenda for Action of the World Congress against Commercial Sexual Exploitation of Children, held at Stockholm from 27 to 31 August 1996;

13. *Invites* States and relevant United Nations bodies and agencies to allocate appropriate resources for the rehabilitation of child victims of sexual exploitation and abuse and to take all appropriate measures to promote their full recovery and social reintegration;

III

Protection of children affected by armed conflict

1. *Welcomes* the report of the Special Representative of the Secretary-General on the impact of armed conflict on children;

2. *Expresses its support* for the work of the Special Representative, in particular in raising worldwide awareness and mobilizing official and public opinion for the protection of children affected by armed conflict, in order to promote respect for the rights and needs of children in conflict and post-conflict situations, and recommends that the Secretary-General extend his mandate, as established in paragraphs 35 to 37 of General Assembly resolution 51/77 of 12 December 1996, for a further period of three years;

3. *Urges* the Secretary-General and all relevant parts of the United Nations system, including the Special Representative and the United Nations Children's Fund, to intensify their efforts to develop a concerted approach to the rights, protection and welfare of children affected by armed conflict, including, as appropriate, in the preparations for the field visits of the Special Representative and in the follow-up to such visits;

4. *Calls upon* all States and other parties concerned to continue to cooperate with the Special Representative, to implement the commitments they have undertaken and to consider carefully all the recommendations of the Special Representative and address the issues identified;

5. *Welcomes* the continued support for and voluntary contributions to the work of the Special Representative;

6. *Urges* all States and other parties to armed conflict to respect international humanitarian law and to put an end to any form of targeting of children and to

attacking sites that usually have a significant presence of children, calls upon States parties to respect fully the provisions of the Geneva Conventions of 12 August 1949 and the Additional Protocols thereto, of 1977, and calls upon all parties to armed conflict to take all measures required to protect children from acts constituting violations of international humanitarian law, including prosecution by States, within their national legal framework, of those responsible for such violations;

7. *Recognizes,* in this regard, the contribution of the establishment of the International Criminal Court to ending impunity for perpetrators of certain crimes committed against children, as defined in the Statute of the Court, which include, inter alia, those involving sexual violence or child soldiers, and thus to the prevention of such crimes;

8. *Condemns* the abduction of children in situations of armed conflict and into armed conflict, urges States, international organizations and other concerned parties to take all appropriate measures to secure the unconditional release of all abducted children, and urges States to bring the perpetrators to justice;

9. *Notes* the importance of the second open debate, held in the Security Council on 25 August 1999, on children and armed conflict and the undertaking by the Council to give special attention to the protection, welfare and rights of children when taking action aimed at maintaining peace and security, and reaffirms the essential role of the General Assembly and the Economic and Social Council in the promotion and protection of the rights and welfare of children;

10. *Calls upon* all parties to armed conflict to ensure the full, safe and unhindered access of humanitarian personnel and the delivery of humanitarian assistance to all children affected by armed conflict;

11. *Welcomes* the decision of the Economic and Social Council to call for systematic, concerted and comprehensive inter-agency efforts on behalf of children, as well as adequate and sustainable resource allocation, to provide both immediate emergency assistance to and long-term measures for children throughout all the phases of an emergency;

12. *Urges* States and all other parties to armed conflict to end the use of children as soldiers and to ensure their demobilization and effective disarmament, and to implement effective measures for the rehabilitation, physical and psychological recovery and reintegration into society of all child victims in cases of armed conflict, invites the international community to assist in this endeavour, and emphasizes that no support that enables or contributes to the use of child soldiers should be given to those who use child soldiers;

13. *Calls upon* States and relevant United Nations bodies to continue to support national and international mine action efforts, including by financial contributions, mine awareness programmes, victim assistance and child-centred rehabilitation, and welcomes the positive effects on children of concrete legislative measures with respect to anti-personnel mines;

14. *Notes with concern* the impact of small arms and light weapons on children in situations of armed conflict, in particular as a result of their illicit production and traffic, and calls upon States to address this problem;

15. *Recommends* that, whenever sanctions are imposed, their impact on children be assessed and monitored and that humanitarian exemptions be child-focused and formulated with clear guidelines for their application;

16. *Calls upon* States, relevant United Nations bodies and agencies and regional organizations to integrate the rights of the child into all activities in conflict and post-conflict situations, including training programmes and emergency relief operations, country programmes and field operations aimed at promoting peace and preventing and resolving conflict, as well as negotiating and implementing peace agreements, and, given the long-term consequences for society, underlines the importance of including specific provisions for children, including resourcing, in peace agreements and in arrangements negotiated by parties;

17. *Welcomes* the ongoing efforts by, inter alia, regional organizations, intergovernmental organizations and non-governmental organizations to bring to an end the use of children as soldiers in armed conflict, and reaffirms the urgent need to raise the current minimum age limit set by article 38 of the Convention on the Rights of the Child on the recruitment and participation of any person in armed conflict with the aim of ending the use of child soldiers;

18. *Strongly supports* the work of the open-ended inter-sessional working group of the Commission on Human Rights on the elaboration of a draft optional protocol to the Convention on the Rights of the Child related to the involvement of children in armed conflict and the consultations conducted by the chairperson of the working group in order to make further progress with the aim of finalizing its work before the tenth anniversary of the entry into force of the Convention;

IV

Refugee and internally displaced children

1. *Urges* Governments to improve the implementation of policies and programmes for the protection, care and well-being of refugee and internally displaced children, with the necessary international cooperation, in particular with the Office of the United Nations High Commissioner for Refugees, the United Nations Children's Fund and the Representative of the Secretary-General on internally displaced persons, in accordance with the obligations of States under the Convention on the Rights of the Child;

2. *Calls upon* all States and other parties to armed conflict, as well as United Nations bodies and organizations, to give urgent attention, in terms of protection and assistance, to the fact that refugee and internally displaced children are particularly exposed to risks in connection with armed conflict, such as being forcibly recruited or subjected to sexual violence, abuse or exploitation;

3. *Expresses its deep concern* about the growing number of unaccompanied refugee and internally displaced children, and calls upon all States and United Nations bodies and agencies and other relevant organizations to give priority to programmes for family tracing and reunification and to continue to monitor the care arrangements for unaccompanied refugee and internally displaced children;

V

Progressive elimination of child labour

1. *Reaffirms* the right of the child to be protected from economic exploitation and from performing any work that is likely to be hazardous or to interfere with the child's education or to be harmful to the child's health or physical, mental, spiritual, moral or social development;

2. *Welcomes* the adoption by the International Labour Organization, at the eighty-seventh session of the International Labour Conference, held at Geneva from 1 to 17 June 1999, of the Convention concerning the Prohibition and Immediate Action for the Elimination of the Worst Forms of Child Labour, Convention No. 182, and encourages all States to consider ratifying it as a matter of priority with a view to its entry into force as soon as possible;

3. *Calls upon* all States that have not yet done so to consider ratifying the conventions of the International Labour Organization relating to child labour, in particular the Convention concerning Forced or Compulsory Labour, 1930, Convention No. 29, and the Convention concerning Minimum Age for Admission to Employment, 1973, Convention No. 138, and to implement those Conventions;

4. *Calls upon* all States to translate into concrete action their commitment to the progressive and effective elimination of child labour contrary to accepted international standards, and urges them, inter alia, to eliminate immediately the worst forms of child labour as set out in the new International Labour Organization Convention No. 182;

5. *Also calls upon* all States to assess and examine systematically the magnitude, nature and causes of child labour and to elaborate and implement strategies for the elimination of child labour contrary to accepted international standards, giving special attention to specific dangers faced by girls, as well as to the rehabilitation and social reintegration of the children concerned;

6. *Recognizes* that primary education is one of the main instruments for reintegrating child workers, calls upon all States to recognize the right to education by making primary education compulsory and to ensure that all children have access to free primary education as a key strategy to prevent child labour, and recognizes, in particular, the important role of the United Nations Educational, Scientific and Cultural Organization and the United Nations Children's Fund in this regard;

7. *Calls upon* all States and the United Nations system to strengthen international cooperation as a means of assisting Governments in preventing or combating violations of the rights of the child and in attaining the objective of the elimination of child labour contrary to accepted international standards;

8. *Calls upon* all States to strengthen cooperation and coordination at the national and the international levels to address effectively the problem of child labour, in close cooperation, inter alia, with the International Labour Organization and the United Nations Children's Fund;

VI

The plight of children working and/or living on the streets

1. *Calls upon* Governments to seek comprehensive solutions to the problems causing children to work and/or live on the streets and to implement appropriate programmes and policies for the protection and the rehabilitation and reintegration of those children, bearing in mind that such children are particularly vulnerable to all forms of violence, abuse, exploitation and neglect;

2. *Calls upon* all States to ensure that services are provided for children to divert them from and to address the economic imperatives for involvement in harmful, exploitative and abusive activity;

3. *Strongly urges* all Governments to guarantee respect for all human rights and fundamental freedoms, in particular the right to life, to take urgent and effective measures to prevent the killing of children working and/or living on the streets, to combat torture and abusive treatment and violence against them and to bring the perpetrators to justice;

4. *Calls upon* the international community to support, through effective international cooperation, including technical advice and assistance, the efforts of States to improve the situation of children working and/or living on the streets;

VII

Children with disabilities

1. *Welcomes* the establishment of a working group, following the decision of the Committee on the Rights of the Child, with the aim of elaborating a plan of action on children with disabilities, in close cooperation with the Special Rapporteur of the Commission for Social Development on disability and other relevant parts of the United Nations system;

2. *Calls upon* all States to take all necessary measures to ensure the full and equal enjoyment of all human rights and fundamental freedoms by children with disabilities and to develop and enforce legislation against their discrimination;

3. *Also calls upon* all States to promote for children with disabilities a full and decent life, in conditions that ensure dignity, promote self-reliance and facilitate the child's active participation in the community, including effective access to education and health services;

VIII

Decides:

(a) To request the Secretary-General to submit to the General Assembly at its fifty-fifth session a report on the rights of the child containing information on the status of the Convention on the Rights of the Child and the problems addressed in the present resolution;

(b) To request the Special Representative of the Secretary-General on the impact of armed conflict on children to submit to the General Assembly and the Commission on Human Rights reports containing relevant information on the situation of children affected by armed conflict, bearing in mind existing mandates and reports of relevant bodies;

(c) To continue its consideration of this question at its fifty-fifth session under the item entitled "Promotion and protection of the rights of the child".

Indigenous populations

Commission action. On 27 April [res. 1999/51], the Commission, urging the Subcommission's Working Group on Indigenous Populations to continue its review of developments and of the diverse situations of the world's indigenous people, recommended that the Economic and Social Council authorize the Group to meet for five working days prior to the Subcommission's 1999 session. It welcomed the Group's proposal to highlight specific themes of the International Decade of the World's Indigenous People (1995-2004), proclaimed by the General Assembly in resolution 48/163 [YUN 1993, p. 865], in its future sessions, including the theme of indigenous peoples and their relationship to land in 1999. The Commission invited the Group to continue to consider ways in which the expertise of indigenous people could contribute to its work. The Secretary-General was asked to assist the Group and to transmit its reports to Governments, organizations of indigenous people, intergovernmental organizations and NGOs for comments and suggestions.

By **decision 1999/241** of 27 July, the Council authorized the Working Group to meet for five days prior to the Subcommission's 1999 session and approved the Commission's request to the Secretary-General.

Working Group activities. The Working Group on Indigenous Populations, at its seventeenth session (Geneva, 26-30 July) [E/CN.4/Sub.2/1999/19], reviewed developments regarding the promotion and protection of human rights and fundamental freedoms of indigenous populations, giving attention to the evolution of standards concerning their rights. The Group also considered indigenous peoples and their relationship to land, together with information received thereon from indigenous organizations [E/CN.4/Sub.2/AC.4/1999/7], a permanent forum for indigenous people, indigenous peoples and health, the final report of the Special Rapporteur of the Subcommission on treaties, agreements and other constructive arrangements between States and indigenous populations (see p. 686), the International Decade of the World's Indigenous People and the 2001 World Conference against Racism, Racial Discrimination, Xenophobia and Related Intolerance (see p. 602).

The Group decided to highlight in 2000 the theme of indigenous children and youth. Regarding standard-setting activities, it invited OHCHR, in collaboration with ILO, WTO and the United Nations Conference on Trade and Development (UNCTAD), to convene a workshop on indigenous peoples, private sector natural resource, energy and mining companies, and human rights. The Special Rapporteur on the study on treaties, agreements and other constructive arrangements between States and indigenous populations was asked to submit his final report to the Commission in 2000. The Working Group recommended that the Subcommission ask OHCHR to organize, not later than June 2000, a seminar on treaties, agreements and other legal instruments between indigenous peoples and States, to discuss possible follow-up to the Special Rapporteur's study, and to explore ways of implementing the recommendations of his final report (see p. 686). The High Commissioner was encouraged to consider organizing a follow-up workshop to the UN workshop on research and higher education institutions and indigenous peoples (see next page). The Working Group proposed to the Subcommission and the Commission that a world conference on indigenous issues be held during the last year of the International Decade (2004). It recommended the appointment of a special rapporteur on indigenous issues to obtain information from Governments, indigenous peoples and NGOs relating to the promotion and protection of the human rights of indigenous peoples.

Subcommission action. On 26 August [res. 1999/20], the Subcommission asked the Secretary-General to transmit the Working Group's report on its 1999 session to the High Commissioner, indigenous organizations, Governments, intergovernmental organizations and NGOs concerned, as well as to thematic rapporteurs, special representatives, independent experts and working groups, and make it available to the Commission in 2000. The High Commissioner was asked to encourage studies on the rights to food and adequate nutrition of indigenous peoples and indigenous peoples and poverty. The Subcommission recommended that the Group's Chairperson/Rapporteur prepare a working paper on indigenous peoples and racism and racial discrimination for consideration at the preparatory meetings for the 2001 World Conference against Racism, Racial Discrimination, Xenophobia and Related Intolerance. It asked Miguel Alfonso-Martínez (Cuba) to submit in 2000 a working paper on principles and guidelines for private sector energy and mining concerns that might affect indigenous lands. The Subcommission recommended the appointment by the Commission of a special rapporteur on indigenous issues to obtain information from Governments, indigenous peoples, intergovernmental organizations and NGOs relating to indigenous peoples' human rights. The Commission was asked to request the Economic and Social Council to authorize the Group to meet for eight days prior to the Subcommission's 2000 session. The Secretary-General was requested to prepare an annotated agenda for the Group's 2000 session.

Voluntary Fund

A June note by the secretariat [E/CN.4/Sub.2/AC.4/1999/6] contained the recommendations adopted by the Board of Trustees of the UN Voluntary Fund for Indigenous Populations at its twelfth session (Geneva, 12-14 April). The recommendations were approved by the High Commissioner on the Secretary-General's behalf on 22 April. The Board recommended travel grants for 62 representatives of indigenous communities and organizations to allow them to attend meetings of the Working Group, for a total of some $192,640; travel grants to allow 14 representatives to attend the working group on the draft UN declaration on the rights of indigenous peoples, totalling some $56,000; and that sufficient funds be allocated for grants for up to 30 indigenous representatives to attend the second session of the working group on a permanent forum for indigenous peoples in February 2000. (See also p. 683.)

Subcommission action. On 26 August [res. 1999/20], the Subcommission asked the Working Group on Indigenous Populations to inform the Fund's Board of Trustees that the Working Group in 2000 would highlight indigenous children and youth. It appealed to Governments, organizations and individuals to contribute to the Fund.

Also on 26 August [res. 1999/19], the Subcommission recommended that the Coordinator for the Decade hold a fund-raising meeting to encourage financial contributions to the Voluntary Fund for the Decade (see next page) and the Voluntary Fund for Indigenous Populations.

International Decade of the World's Indigenous People

Commission action. On 27 April [res. 1999/51], the Commission asked the Working Group to continue its review of activities undertaken during the International Decade of the World's Indigenous People (1995-2004). The High Commissioner for Human Rights, in her capacity as coordinator of the Decade, was asked to update in 2000 her annual report on activities within the UN system under the Decade's programme of activities. The Commission also asked her to submit a mid-term report to the General Assembly and a preliminary report to the Economic and Social Council, and to ensure that the OHCHR indigenous people's unit was adequately staffed and resourced; it recommended that she give due regard to developing human rights training for indigenous people. The Working Group was asked to submit its views on the activities of the Decade to the High Commissioner.

UN financial and development institutions, operational programmes and specialized agencies were requested to: give increased priority and resources to improve the conditions of indigenous peoples; launch special projects to strengthen their community-level initiatives and facilitate the exchange of information and expertise among indigenous people and other relevant experts; and designate focal points or other mechanisms to coordinate with OHCHR activities relating to the Decade.

Workshop. In response to a 1997 Commission request [YUN 1997, p. 693], OHCHR and the Ministry of Foreign Affairs and Religion of Costa Rica supported the holding of the Workshop on Higher Education and Indigenous Peoples (San José, 28 June-2 July) [E/CN.4/Sub.2/AC.4/1999/5]. Recommendations to indigenous peoples included encouraging the exchange of students, teachers and experience between their own higher education and research establishments, promoting models of education by setting up their own institutions and searching for a decolonized process and outcome within all teaching establishments. States should support the establishment of educational institutions run by indigenous peoples and finance them adequately, guarantee young indigenous persons the opportunity to study at all levels and in all disciplines and to work as qualified professionals in their communities, and support curricula that were relevant to indigenous peoples. The United Nations should transmit the conclusions and recommendations of the Workshop to the Special Rapporteur on the right to education and consider supporting the establishment of an international indigenous university. OHCHR should consider holding annual workshops and seminars relating to indigenous peoples and higher education and compile a list of experts and institutions for indigenous higher education and research. UNESCO should hold a meeting of indigenous peoples to draw up a code of ethics for research.

Subcommission action. On 26 August [res. 1999/19], the Subcommission recommended that the International Day of the World's Indigenous People be held on the fourth day of the Working Group's 2000 session to ensure as great a participation of indigenous peoples as possible. It also recommended that the coordinator of the Decade consider holding a fund-raising meeting to encourage financial contributions to the Voluntary Fund for the Decade and the Voluntary Fund for Indigenous Populations, as well as the appointment of qualified staff, including indigenous persons, to assist OHCHR in work relating to the indigenous programme. Governments, intergovernmental organizations, NGOs and individuals were urged to contribute to the Voluntary Fund for the Decade, as were indigenous organizations. The Subcommission asked the High Commissioner to consider ways by which she might support the World Indigenous Nations Games, and recommended that she organize meetings and other activities in Africa and Asia in order to raise public awareness about indigenous issues. It also recommended that the High Commissioner organize a workshop, in collaboration with UNCTAD, ILO, WTO and other relevant organizations, on indigenous peoples, private sector natural resource, energy and mining companies and human rights. The Commission was invited to consider organizing a world conference on indigenous issues during the last year of the Decade (2004) to evaluate the Decade and consider future policies and programmes that would contribute to the reconciliation of Governments with indigenous peoples.

Report of Secretary-General. In October [A/54/487 & Add.1], the Secretary-General discussed action taken by the UN system to implement the programme of activities for the Decade, adopted by the General Assembly in resolution 50/157 [YUN 1995, p. 774]. He observed that several UN organizations had specific programmes and projects that were being implemented during the Decade and that an increasing number of them were organizing consultations with indigenous peoples to help them as they developed internal guidelines on indigenous issues and outlined an overall strategy. The observance of the International Day of the World's Indigenous People on 9 August had become a well-attended and effective event in New York and Geneva. Preliminary work had been done to improve the flow of information about UN programmes to indigenous communities through the workshop on indigenous media [YUN 1998, p. 719] and its follow-up. Problems faced in implementing the Decade's activities were the limited human and financial resources available. Only a quarter of the UN organizations for which information was available had a designated focal point or unit for indigenous people or for the Decade. The Secretary-General recommended that Governments consider holding a meeting in 2000 to develop practical and realizable projects.

Report of High Commissioner. In December [E/CN.4/2000/85], the High Commissioner reviewed implementation of the programme of activities for the Decade. OHCHR had implemented the Indigenous Fellowship Programme for four candidates from 1 June to 30 November. Under the Voluntary Fund for the Decade, the Advisory Group held its fourth session in April and an inter-sessional consultation began in October to evaluate the Fellowship Programme and to select candidates for 2000. On the Group's recommendation, in the light of the few new contributions received in 1999, it had been possible to finance the Programme from within the regular OHCHR budget. The total cost of activities for 2000 amounted to some $530,000, whereas contributions available as at 23 November 1999 totalled $65,273.

The Board of Trustees of the UN Voluntary Fund for Indigenous Populations considered applications for travel grants from representatives of indigenous communities and organizations to enable them to participate in the second session of the open-ended inter-sessional ad hoc working group on a permanent forum (see p. 685). The Board recommended the allocation of 34 travel grants totalling $149,380. As at 25 November, contributions amounted to $71,054. The Fund needed an additional $500,000 to meet the increasing requests from indigenous populations. The coordinator of the Decade appealed for new contributions on 1 October.

The High Commissioner summarized information received from three Governments on action they had taken to implement the programme of activities for the Decade.

Voluntary Fund for International Decade

By a June note [E/CN.4/Sub.2/AC.4/1999/4], the Secretariat transmitted the report of the Advisory Group of the United Nations Voluntary Fund for the International Decade on its fourth session (Geneva, 15-16 April), including its recommendations for grants from the Fund that had been approved by the coordinator of the Decade. Contributions available to the Group as at 6 April totalled $125,377.

On 27 April [res. 1999/51], the Commission encouraged Governments to support the Decade by contributing to the Fund.

Draft declaration

Commission action. On 27 April [res. 1999/50], the Commission recommended that the working group to elaborate a draft UN declaration on the rights of indigenous peoples meet for 10 working days prior to the Commission's 2000 session, and asked the group to submit a progress report. It encouraged indigenous peoples' organizations to participate in the group.

By **decision 1999/240** of 27 July, the Economic and Social Council approved the recommendation.

Subcommission action. On 26 August [res. 1999/19], the Subcommission recommended that, in accordance with General Assembly resolution

50/157 [YUN 1995, p. 772], the draft UN declaration on the rights of indigenous peoples be adopted as early as possible and not later than the end of the Decade. It appealed to the working group and others concerned to accelerate its preparation.

Working group activities. The working group established to consider a draft declaration on the rights of indigenous peoples, at its fifth session (Geneva, 18-29 October) [E/CN.4/2000/84], continued its discussion of articles 15 to 18. The articles related to the right to education, the right of indigenous peoples to establish their own media and rights established under labour law.

By **decision 1999/216** of 7 May, the Economic and Social Council had approved the participation of two indigenous peoples' organizations not in consultative status with the Council to participate in the working group.

GENERAL ASSEMBLY ACTION

On 17 December [meeting 83], the General Assembly, on the recommendation of the Third Committee [A/54/602], adopted **resolution 54/150** without vote [agenda item 113].

International Decade of the World's Indigenous People

The General Assembly,

Recalling its resolution 53/129 of 9 December 1998 and previous resolutions on the International Decade of the World's Indigenous People,

Recalling also that the goal of the Decade is to strengthen international cooperation for the solution of problems faced by indigenous people in such areas as human rights, the environment, development, education and health and that the theme of the Decade is "Indigenous people: partnership in action",

Recognizing the importance of consultation and cooperation with indigenous people in planning and implementing the programme of activities of the International Decade of the World's Indigenous People, the need for adequate financial support from the international community, including support from within the United Nations system, and the need for adequate coordination and communication channels,

1. *Takes note* of the report of the Secretary-General on the implementation of the programme of activities of the International Decade of the World's Indigenous People;

2. *Affirms its conviction* of the value and diversity of the cultures and forms of social organization of indigenous people and its conviction that the development of indigenous people within their countries will contribute to the socio-economic, cultural and environmental advancement of all the countries of the world;

3. *Emphasizes* the importance of strengthening the human and institutional capacity of indigenous people to develop their own solutions to their problems, welcomes in this context the holding of the Workshop on Higher Education and Indigenous Peoples at San José, Costa Rica, from 28 June to 2 July 1999, and requests the Commission on Human Rights to consider the recommendations of the Workshop;

4. *Takes note* of the mid-term report of the United Nations High Commissioner for Human Rights, in her capacity as coordinator of the International Decade of the World's Indigenous People, reviewing the implementation of the programme of activities of the Decade, and of the information contained therein about the activities of the United Nations system, including the specialized agencies and other intergovernmental organizations, relating to indigenous people, and urges all parties concerned to intensify their efforts to achieve the goals of the Decade;

5. *Requests* the High Commissioner, as coordinator of the Decade:

(*a*) To continue to promote the objectives of the Decade, taking into account, in the fulfilment of her functions, the special concerns of indigenous people;

(*b*) To give due regard to the dissemination, from within existing resources and voluntary contributions, of information on the situation, cultures, languages, rights and aspirations of indigenous people and, in that context, to consider the possibility of organizing projects, special events, exhibitions and other activities addressed to the public, in particular to young people;

(*c*) To submit, through the Secretary-General, an annual report to the General Assembly on the implementation of the programme of activities of the Decade;

6. *Reaffirms* the adoption of a declaration on the rights of indigenous people as a major objective of the Decade, and underlines the importance of effective participation by indigenous representatives in the open-ended inter-sessional working group of the Commission on Human Rights charged with developing a draft declaration on the rights of indigenous people, established pursuant to Commission resolution 1995/32 of 3 March 1995;

7. *Also reaffirms*, among the objectives of the Decade listed in the programme of activities, the consideration of the establishment of a permanent forum for indigenous people in the United Nations system;

8. *Urges* Governments to participate actively in the open-ended inter-sessional ad hoc working group that the Commission on Human Rights in its resolution 1999/52 of 27 April 1999 decided to re-establish from within existing overall United Nations resources, which is to meet for eight working days prior to the fifty-sixth session of the Commission to submit, with a view to completing its task, one or more concrete proposals on the possible establishment of a permanent forum for indigenous people in the United Nations system;

9. *Decides* that the United Nations Voluntary Fund for Indigenous Populations, established pursuant to General Assembly resolution 40/131 of 13 December 1985 and modified by Commission on Human Rights resolution 1995/32 and Assembly resolutions 50/156 of 21 December 1995 and 53/130 of 9 December 1998, should also be used to assist representatives of indigenous communities and organizations in participating in the deliberations of the open-ended inter-sessional ad hoc working group of the Commission on Human Rights re-established in accordance with Commission resolution 1999/52;

10. *Expresses its appreciation* to the Board of Trustees of the United Nations Voluntary Fund for Indigenous Populations for the work it has accomplished;

11. *Encourages* Governments to support the Decade by:

(*a*) Preparing relevant programmes, plans and reports in relation to the Decade, in consultation with indigenous people;

(*b*) Seeking means, in consultation with indigenous people, of giving indigenous people greater responsibility for their own affairs and an effective voice in decisions on matters that affect them;

(*c*) Establishing national committees or other mechanisms involving indigenous people to ensure that the objectives and activities of the Decade are planned and implemented on the basis of full partnership with indigenous people;

(*d*) Contributing to the United Nations Trust Fund for the International Decade of the World's Indigenous People;

(*e*) Contributing, together with other donors, to the United Nations Voluntary Fund for Indigenous Populations in order to assist indigenous representatives in participating in the Working Group on Indigenous Populations of the Subcommission on the Promotion and Protection of Human Rights, the open-ended inter-sessional working group charged with developing a draft declaration on the rights of indigenous people and the re-established open-ended inter-sessional ad hoc working group on the possible establishment of a permanent forum for indigenous people in the United Nations system;

(*f*) Considering contributing, as appropriate, to the Fund for the Development of Indigenous Peoples in Latin America and the Caribbean, in support of the goals of the Decade;

(*g*) Identifying resources for activities designed to implement the goals of the Decade, in cooperation with indigenous people and intergovernmental and non-governmental organizations;

12. *Welcomes* the offer of the Government of Spain to host at Seville in February 2000 the first meeting of the open-ended inter-sessional ad hoc working group on article 8 (*j*) of the Convention on Biological Diversity regarding the traditional knowledge, innovations and practices of indigenous and local communities, and encourages Governments to include representatives of indigenous and local communities in their delegations to the meeting;

13. *Invites* United Nations financial and development institutions, operational programmes and the specialized agencies, as well as other regional and international organizations, in accordance with the existing procedures of their governing bodies:

(*a*) To give increased priority and resources to improving the conditions of indigenous people, with particular emphasis on the needs of those people in developing countries, including through the preparation of specific programmes of action for the implementation of the goals of the Decade, within their areas of competence;

(*b*) To launch special projects, through appropriate channels and in cooperation with indigenous people, to strengthen their community-level initiatives and to facilitate the exchange of information and expertise among indigenous people and other relevant experts;

(*c*) To designate focal points for the coordination of activities related to the Decade with the Office of the United Nations High Commissioner for Human Rights;

and commends those institutions, programmes, agencies and regional and international organizations that have already done so;

14. *Recommends* that the Secretary-General ensure coordinated follow-up to the recommendations concerning indigenous people of relevant United Nations conferences, namely, the World Conference on Human Rights, held at Vienna from 14 to 25 June 1993, the United Nations Conference on Environment and Development, held at Rio de Janeiro, Brazil, from 3 to 14 June 1992, the International Conference on Population and Development, held at Cairo from 5 to 13 September 1994, the Fourth World Conference on Women, held at Beijing from 4 to 15 September 1995, the World Summit for Social Development, held at Copenhagen from 6 to 12 March 1995, the second United Nations Conference on Human Settlements (Habitat II), held at Istanbul, Turkey, from 3 to 14 June 1996, and the World Food Summit, held at Rome from 13 to 17 November 1996, and other relevant international conferences;

15. *Requests* the United Nations High Commissioner for Human Rights to submit, through the Secretary-General, a report on the implementation of the programme of activities of the Decade to the General Assembly at its fifty-fifth session;

16. *Decides* to include in the provisional agenda of its fifty-fifth session the item entitled "Programme of activities of the International Decade of the World's Indigenous People".

Permanent forum for indigenous people

Working Group activities. In accordance with a 1998 Commission resolution [YUN 1998, p. 723], the ad hoc working group on a permanent forum for indigenous people in the UN system (Geneva, 15-19 February) [E/CN.4/1999/83] considered proposals for the establishment of such a forum in the UN system. The group discussed the forum's mandate, terms of reference, membership and participation. Participants expressed the view that the forum should be linked in some way to the Economic and Social Council, taking into account the responsibilities and views of other bodies and organs.

Commission action. On 27 April [res. 1999/52], the Commission decided to re-establish the open-ended inter-sessional ad hoc working group to meet for eight working days prior to the Commission's session in 2000, and asked the working group to submit proposals on the establishment of a permanent forum for the Commission's consideration. It asked the group's Chairman/Rapporteur to submit a working paper to Member States and other group participants containing suggestions and possible alternatives on all aspects of the matter. The Secretary-General was asked to transmit the group's report to Governments, UN organizations and bodies, specialized agencies, indigenous peoples' organizations and the Working Group on Indigenous Populations and to invite their comments.

By **decision 1999/242** of 27 July, the Economic and Social Council endorsed the Commission's decision to re-establish the group and to request the group to submit proposals on the establishment of a permanent forum.

Subcommission action. On 26 August [res. 1999/19], the Subcommission recommended that the permanent forum be established as soon as possible in the course of the Decade with functions that did not duplicate those already conferred on the Working Group on Indigenous Populations. It endorsed the view expressed by indigenous participants at the Working Group's session in 1999 that the establishment of the permanent forum should not be understood as a justification for abolishing the Working Group.

Study on treaties, agreements and other constructive arrangements

In June, the Special Rapporteur on the study on treaties, agreements and other constructive arrangements between States and indigenous populations, Miguel Alfonso-Martínez (Cuba), submitted his final report [E/CN.4/Sub.2/1999/20]. The Special Rapporteur stated that indigenous peoples who had entertained treaty relationships with non-indigenous settlers and their continuators strongly argued that those instruments not only continued to be valid and applicable to their current situation but were a key element for their survival as distinct peoples. Nonetheless, he had been able to ascertain a large number of serious violations of the legal obligations undertaken by State parties to those instruments. His research revealed that treaties, in particular those concluded with indigenous nations, had frequently played a negative role with respect to indigenous rights. He stated that, according to the evidence available to him, there was no acceptance by the affected indigenous parties of the obligations included in the provisions of, nor any participation by them in the implementation of, treaties between States affecting indigenous peoples as third parties. Regarding the situation of indigenous peoples who had never been formally recognized as nations by means of negotiated formal international juridical instruments with non-indigenous States, attention should be paid to the issue of whether or not they continued to retain their status as nations in the light of contemporary international law.

Recommendations included the establishment within States with a sizeable indigenous population of a new, special jurisdiction to deal exclusively with indigenous issues, and State application and construction of provisions of national legislation and international standards and instruments in the most favourable way for indigenous peoples. States should not take part in development projects that might impair the environment of indigenous lands and/or adversely affect their traditional economic activities, religious ceremonies or cultural heritage, without previously commissioning ecological studies. OHCHR should increase its staff assigned to indigenous affairs-related activities. A section within the United Nations Treaty Registry should be established to locate, compile, register, number and publish treaties concluded between indigenous peoples and States. Workshops should be convened on the establishment of an international conflict-resolution mechanism on indigenous issues, modalities for redressing the effects of the historical process of land dispossession suffered by indigenous peoples, and the implementation/observance of indigenous treaty rights. An Internet page should be created on indigenous issues and UN activities relating to indigenous interests.

Subcommission action. On 26 August [res. 1999/22], the Subcommission endorsed the conclusions and recommendations of the Special Rapporteur and requested him to submit, not later than 15 November 1999, any corrections and additions he might consider necessary to the English, French and Spanish versions of his final report, including addenda concerning organizations and individuals in Africa and Asia, as mentioned in the report of the Working Group on Indigenous Populations [E/CN.4/Sub.2/1999/19]. It asked him to present to the Commission in 2000 the revised version of his final report. The High Commissioner was asked to organize, not later than June 2000, a seminar on treaties, agreements and other legal instruments between indigenous peoples and States to discuss follow-up to the study and explore ways to implement his recommendations. The Secretary-General was requested to transmit the final report to Governments, indigenous peoples and organizations, intergovernmental organizations and NGOs. The Working Group was asked to remain seized of the topic during its annual sessions for the remainder of the Decade.

Indigenous land rights

Commission action. On 27 April [dec. 1999/106], the Commission, taking note of a 1998 Subcommission resolution [YUN 1998, p. 723], decided to approve the Subcommission's request to the Secretary-General to transmit the Special Rapporteur's progress report on the working paper on indigenous people and their relationship to land [ibid.] and the preliminary working paper on the topic [YUN 1997, p. 698] to Governments, indigenous peoples, intergovernmental organizations and NGOs for their comments, data and suggestions, and to assist the Special Rapporteur.

Report of Special Rapporteur. In June, the Special Rapporteur on indigenous people and their relationship to land, Erica-Irene A. Daes (Greece), submitted a second progress report [E/CN.4/Sub.2/1999/18] based on a working paper she had submitted in 1997 [YUN 1997, p. 698] and the suggestions received from Governments, indigenous peoples, intergovernmental organizations and NGOs. She stated that the very survival of indigenous peoples was at risk owing to the continuing threats to their lands, territories and resources. States had failed to recognize the existence of indigenous land use, occupancy and ownership, and failed to accord legal status and legal rights to protect that use, occupancy or ownership. In countries with laws concerning indigenous peoples, problems arose because of discriminatory laws and legal doctrines applied to indigenous peoples, their lands and resources. In certain countries, claims processes were improper, grossly unfair or fraudulent for indigenous peoples.

The Special Rapporteur recommended that States enact legislation to recognize, demarcate and protect indigenous peoples' lands and resources. Governments should renounce discriminatory legal policies and consider impartial mechanisms to oversee and facilitate equitable resolution of indigenous land and resource claims and the implementation of land agreements. The United Nations should provide technical assistance to States and to indigenous peoples to resolve land claims and resource issues and assure the protection of indigenous peoples' cultural diversity, traditional values and ways of life. The High Commissioner should collect examples of indigenous land agreements to facilitate the promotion of technical cooperation in that area. Indigenous peoples should participate in decision-making and policy-making regarding land, resources and development.

Subcommission action. On 26 August [res. 1999/21], the Subcommission asked the Secretary-General to transmit the Special Rapporteur's second progress report to Governments, indigenous peoples, intergovernmental organizations and NGOs for their comments, data and suggestions. The Special Rapporteur was asked to submit her final working paper to the Working Group on Indigenous Populations and to the Subcommission in 2000. The Secretary-General was asked to assist her.

People with HIV/AIDS

Report of Secretary-General. In January [E/CN.4/1999/76], the Secretary-General, in response to the Commission's 1997 request [YUN 1997, p. 639], provided an overview of comments received from Governments, UN bodies, specialized agencies and NGOs on the Guidelines recommended by the experts participating in the Second International Consultation on HIV/AIDS and Human Rights [YUN 1996, p. 617], and their dissemination and implementation. The report also addressed the issue of technical cooperation for the promotion and protection of human rights in the context of HIV/AIDS.

Commission action. On 27 April [res. 1999/49], the Commission asked States to establish coordinated, participatory, transparent and accountable national policies and programmes for HIV/AIDS response and to translate national policies to district level and local action; develop and support services to educate people infected and affected by HIV/AIDS about their rights and to assist them in realizing their rights; combat discrimination and prejudice and ensure the full enjoyment of all rights by people with or affected by HIV/AIDS; ensure that codes of professional conduct, responsibility and practice respected human rights and dignity, including access to care for people with and affected by HIV/AIDS; and develop and support mechanisms to monitor and enforce HIV/AIDS-related human rights.

The Commission asked its special representatives, special rapporteurs and working groups, including the special rapporteurs on the right to education, on the promotion and protection of freedom of opinion and expression, on violence against women, its causes and consequences, and on the sale of children, child prostitution and child pornography, to integrate the protection of HIV-related human rights within their mandates. The Secretary-General was asked to invite UN bodies and Member States to integrate HIV-related human rights into their policies, programmes and activities, and to involve NGOs and community-based organizations in all phases of development and implementation, to help ensure a system-wide approach, stressing the coordinating and catalytic role of the Joint United Nations Programme on HIV/AIDS (UNAIDS) (see p. 1148). He was also asked to solicit comments from Governments, UN organs, programmes and specialized agencies, international organizations and NGOs on steps taken to promote and implement the Guidelines on HIV/ AIDS and human rights, and to report in 2001.

Subcommission action. On 26 August [dec. 1999/112], the Subcommission decided to entrust Alberto Diaz Uribe (Colombia) with preparing a working paper, in consultation with UNAIDS, OHCHR, NGOs and other interested parties, on the implementation of the Guidelines, for submission in 2000.

Chapter III

Human rights violations

Alleged violations of human rights and international humanitarian law in a number of countries were examined in 1999 by the General Assembly, the Economic and Social Council, the Commission on Human Rights and its Subcommission on the Promotion and Protection of Human Rights (formerly the Subcommission on Prevention of Discrimination and Protection of Minorities), as well as by special rapporteurs, special representatives of the Secretary- General and independent experts appointed to examine the allegations. In September, the Commission held a special session to discuss the situation in East Timor.

General aspects

Under a procedure established by Economic and Social Council resolution 1503(XLVIII) [YUN 1970, p. 530] to deal with communications alleging denial or violation of human rights, the Working Group on Situations of the Commission on Human Rights, established by Council resolution 1990/41 [YUN 1990, p. 648], in closed meetings, considered the human rights situations in Chad, the Gambia, Nepal, Saudi Arabia, Sierra Leone and Yemen [E/1999/23]. The Commission discontinued consideration of the situations in the Gambia, Nepal, Saudi Arabia and Yemen and concluded consideration of the situations in Chad and Sierra Leone.

In a July note with a later addendum [E/CN.4/Sub.2/1999/4 & Add.1], the Secretariat, pursuant to a 1998 Subcommission request [YUN 1998, p. 726], provided information about the security situation of eight human rights defenders. In August [E/CN.4/Sub.2/1999/42], Indonesia presented information regarding one of those individuals, an Indonesian national who had left the country.

On 20 August [E/CN.4/2000/4 (res. 1999/3)], the Subcommission, by a secret ballot of 18 to 6, with 1 abstention, expressing deep concern at the increasing number of cases of which it had been informed concerning human rights defenders, strongly condemned the murders of 14 human rights activists and called on the Governments concerned to carry out investigations to identify the perpetrators and bring them to justice. It also called on them to ensure that the crimes committed against human rights defenders did not go unpunished, to allow and facilitate inquiry and to ensure judgement by a civil tribunal and punishment of the perpetrators, as well as compensation to victims' families. The United Nations High Commissioner for Human Rights was asked to inquire about the security of 11 persons listed in an annex to the Subcommission's resolution and to report thereon in 2000. She was also asked to transmit the resolution to all States.

On the same date [res. 1999/2], the Subcommission, by a secret ballot of 15 to 7, with 3 abstentions, expressing concern at efforts to develop the concept of an alleged duty or right of certain States to carry out "humanitarian interventions", including through armed force, in situations unilaterally identified by themselves, called on States to step up measures to achieve international cooperation in search of peaceful solutions to international humanitarian problems. It also called on them to comply strictly with the basic principles and norms of general international law and standards of international human rights law and international humanitarian law, particularly those governing the main UN bodies, accountability for war crimes, the realization and protection of the rights of national or ethnic minorities, and the protection of civilian populations and installations in cases of military operations.

Africa

Burundi

Report of Special Rapporteur. A February note by the Secretariat [E/CN.4/1999/43] stated that during his last mission to Burundi [YUN 1998, p. 726], Special Rapporteur Paulo Sérgio Pinheiro (Brazil) had had a serious car accident and would report only orally to the Commission in 1999.

On 1 April [E/CN.4/1999/SR.13], the Special Rapporteur noted the efforts made by authorities in Burundi to promote the peace process. The adoption of a constitutional act had made it possible to reduce hostility and restore a modicum of trust between the parties. The lifting of sanctions imposed on Burundi by nine East African countries would help alleviate the suffering of the bulk of the population. Agents of both the State and rebel groups had committed human rights violations, including massacres, summary executions, forced or involuntary disappearances, arbitrary detention, rape and other forms of sexual abuse, and mistreatment of prisoners. On 7 April [E/CN.4/1999/SR.20], the Special Rapporteur stated that, while the war continued with very serious violations of human rights and international humanitarian law, some degree of security had returned in large parts of the country. Improvements were occurring in the cost of living and in health services and education; however, a great deal remained to be done before a State based on the rule of law was established.

Commission action. On 23 April [E/1999/23 (res. 1999/10)], the Commission on Human Rights, expressing appreciation for the mediation efforts of the United Nations, the Organization of African Unity (OAU) and the European Union (EU) (see PART ONE, Chapter II), noted progress in: security and public order in some areas; efforts by the Government to ensure respect for established legal safeguards for human rights and international human rights standards; and the struggle against impunity and for human rights promotion. It adjured the parties to the conflict in Burundi to abstain from action liable to hamper activities of the International Committee of the Red Cross (ICRC) and other humanitarian assistance operations and to work constructively with international mediators in the search for a lasting peace.

The Commission urged all parties to the conflict to end the cycle of violence and killings and condemned the illegal sale and distribution of weapons and related materials. It asked States not to allow their territories to be used as bases for incursions or attacks against another State. The international community was urged to resume economic cooperation with Burundi and to provide humanitarian assistance needed by displaced persons and returnees in Burundi (see p. 832). The Commission decided to extend the Special Rapporteur's mandate for an additional year and asked him to submit an interim report to the General Assembly in 1999 and a report to the Commission in 2000, giving his work a gender-specific dimension. By **decision 1999/227** of 27 July, the Economic and Social Council endorsed the Commission's decision and its requests to the Special Rapporteur.

Following the resignation of the Special Rapporteur, the Commission appointed, in August, Marie-Thérèse Kéita-Bocoum (Côte d'Ivoire).

Report of Special Rapporteur. The Special Rapporteur's first report, based on her visit to Burundi (8-22 October), covered the period from 15 August to 15 November [E/CN.4/2000/34].

The Special Rapporteur presented a brief analysis of the impact of history on the development of the conflict in Burundi, and of the current political and economic and social conditions, and examined the country's human rights situation. On the whole, the human rights situation had deteriorated, as shown by the increase in violations of the right to life and physical integrity, allegedly committed by State agents, armed rebel groups and unidentified gangs. The displacement of the population to regroupment camps not only took place under coercion, but also had led to gross violations of the rights to life, liberty and security of person, freedom of movement and residence, property ownership, housing, work and the free choice of employment, health, education, adequate food and a decent living. The civil war, large-scale displacements, the regroupment of persons and increasing poverty had led to the violation of children's rights, as provided for in the 1989 Convention on the Rights of the Child, adopted by the General Assembly in resolution 44/25 [YUN 1989, p. 560]. Poverty had also affected the human rights situation.

The Special Rapporteur recommended that the parties to the conflict end attacks on civilians and respect the lives of civilians and representatives of humanitarian organizations; participate fully in negotiations to reach a ceasefire; and resolve conflicts without resort to weapons and support the new facilitator of the peace negotiations in Arusha, United Republic of Tanzania. The Special Rapporteur launched an appeal to guarantee the safety and free access of representatives of humanitarian and human rights organizations to those in need. The authorities in Burundi were asked to suspend the policy of population displacement and guarantee human rights; combat poverty and insecurity; combat regional disparities and the exploitation of ethnic differences; disseminate and implement the new Code of Criminal Procedure; set up a police force separate from the armed forces; ensure the advancement and fulfilment of women; support efforts by civil society to improve the status of women; combat exclusion and impunity; and guarantee the safety of convoys and the persons delivering and distributing assistance in emergency situations. The international community was asked to assist the peace process in Arusha; provide access to microcredit and development assistance; take measures to combat impunity and irregularities in the judiciary; support human rights education and promotion; support women's programmes; increase resources to maintain security for emergency humanitarian assistance; step up efforts against the illicit traffic in weapons and munitions and ensure that refugee camps were kept strictly civilian; and bring about an end to human rights violations. The Special Rapporteur advocated the holding of an international conference on peace and security in the Great Lakes region.

Burundi suggested corrections to sections of the Special Rapporteur's report relating to the impact of history on the situation in the country [E/CN.4/ 2000/141].

(For political details, see PART ONE, Chapter II.)

Congo

Subcommission action. By a secret ballot of 20 to 3, with 2 abstentions, the Subcommission, on 20 August [res. 1999/1], called on the Government of the Republic of the Congo to ensure respect for human rights in the country and to ratify the 1984 Convention against Torture and Other Cruel, Inhuman or Degrading Treatment or Punishment, adopted by the General Assembly in resolution 39/46 [YUN 1984, p. 813], the Rome Statute of the International Criminal Court [YUN 1998, p. 1209] and the draft optional protocol to the African Charter of Human and People's Rights, establishing the African Court on Human and People's Rights. The African Charter was adopted by OAU in 1981 [YUN 1981, p. 942]. The Subcommission asked all parties to the conflict to respect their obligations under international humanitarian law. It asked the Secretary-General to report on the situation of human rights in the Congo in 2000 and recommended that the Commission consider the matter in 2000.

Report of Secretary-General. In December [E/CN.4/2000/30], the Secretary-General summarized developments in the Congo during the period 1997-1999, mainly the wars of 1997 [YUN 1997, p. 112] and 1998, and described improvements in security conditions and the recent national reconciliation process. Currently, some 580,000 people were internally displaced; according to the Office of the United Nations High Commissioner for Refugees (UNHCR), nearly 24,000 Congolese were still refugees in the Democratic Republic of the Congo and about 20,000 in Gabon. The Congo was host to refugees from the Cabinda enclave (21,000) and Rwanda (7,000) (see PART THREE, Chapter XII, for information on refugees). The main human rights violations, as communicated to the Secretary-General by non-governmental organizations (NGOs), were summary or extrajudicial executions; arbitrary arrest and detention; torture and rape; forced or involuntary disappearances; and violations of the freedom of expression, opinion and assembly. The sources emphasized that most violations were allegedly committed for political or ethnic reasons by all parties to the conflict, and that those responsible had never been prosecuted or brought to justice following an inquiry ordered by the authorities.

On 3 September, the Special Rapporteur sent a communication to the Government regarding information received concerning 7 allegations of rape and 15 of torture and other cruel, inhuman or degrading treatment, said to have taken place between October 1997 and November 1998. On 12 November, the Government replied that it had no knowledge of any such events.

The Office of the United Nations High Commissioner for Human Rights (OHCHR) had prepared a programme for the Congo which included training courses for NGOs on human rights; human rights teaching programmes at various school levels; and the provision of human rights documents to government authorities and NGOs. OHCHR wished to recruit a national human rights coordinator to implement the programme and collect information on human rights violations.

Democratic Republic of the Congo

Communication. On 6 April [E/CN.4/1999/148], the Democratic Republic of the Congo (DRC) submitted an overview of how human rights were promoted and protected in the country, and its response to the report of the Special Rapporteur in 1998 [YUN 1998, p. 729].

Commission action. On 27 April [res. 1999/56], the Commission welcomed the commitment of the DRC to a process of democratization; the Government's intention to hold a national debate as a precursor to elections; the recognition by the authorities that massacres were committed against refugees and internally displaced persons in 1996 and 1997; the appointment of a Minister for Human Rights; the release of prisoners whose arrest was irregular or politically motivated, and improvements in the prison system; the Government's decision to establish a national commission of inquiry to investigate alleged human rights violations and breaches of international humanitarian law between 1996 and 1997; the Government's intention to ratify Additional Protocol II to the Geneva Conventions of 12 August 1949 for the protection of war victims, adopted in 1977 [YUN 1977, p. 706]; and the setting up of human rights education programmes for the military and the police. It expressed concern at the human rights situation, particularly in the east of the country, and at the continuing violations of human rights and fundamental freedoms; at the large numbers of refugees and displaced persons in the DRC who disappeared between 1994 and 1997; and at arms trafficking in the region. The Commission welcomed the Secretary-General's appointment of his Special Envoy for the DRC peace process. It called on the DRC to promote and protect human rights and fundamental freedoms; reform and restore the judiciary; implement its commitment to democratization and the rule of law; hold free and fair elections; remove restrictions on political parties; ensure respect for freedom of opinion and expression; and promote human rights awareness.

The Commission decided to extend the Special Rapporteur's mandate for an additional year and asked him to submit an interim report to the General Assembly in 1999, to report to the Commission in 2000 and to maintain a gender perspective in seeking and analysing information. It also decided to ask the Special Rapporteurs on the situation of human rights in the DRC and on extrajudicial, summary or arbitrary executions and a member of the Working Group on Enforced or Involuntary Disappearances to carry out, immediately after the signing of a ceasefire agreement or as soon as security considerations permitted, and, where appropriate, in cooperation with the National Commission of Inquiry, an investigation of alleged human rights violations and breaches of international humanitarian law in the DRC between 1996 and 1997, and a joint mission to investigate massacres carried out in the DRC, with a view to bringing to justice those responsible, and to report to the Assembly in 1999 and to the Commission in 2000. The Economic and Social Council endorsed the Commission's decisions and requests to the Special Rapporteurs and the Working Group member by **decision 1999/244** of 27 July. The Commission also asked the Secretary-General to assist the Special Rapporteur on the situation of human rights in the DRC and the joint mission, and asked the High Commissioner to provide technical expertise to the mission.

Reports of Special Rapporteur. In September [A/54/361], the Secretary-General transmitted to the General Assembly the report of Special Rapporteur Roberto Garretón (Chile), based on his visits to the DRC (16-23 February and 27 August-6 September).

A ceasefire of 10 July, agreed upon in Lusaka, Zambia, by representatives of the DRC, the Congo, Namibia, Rwanda, Uganda, Zimbabwe and Angola, was not signed by the rebel groups, Rassemblement congolais pour la démocratie (RCD) and the Mouvement de libération du Congo (MLC). The latter signed on 1 August and, on 31 August, RCD had it signed by 50 of its founding members, thereby revealing deep-seated internal differences.

The Special Rapporteur had transmitted to the Government two communications containing allegations of human rights violations of 2,375 individuals. He also sent 19 urgent actions on cases regarding 218 individuals. Government replies for the most part consisted of denials of the allegations and of accusations against the other side in the war.

In Government-controlled territory, the Special Rapporteur examined violations of the rights to life, physical and psychological integrity, security of person, liberty of person, due process, freedom of expression and opinion, a nationality, freedom of association, freedom of assembly, as well as economic, social and cultural rights, women's rights and children's rights. In territory controlled by RCD and MLC, similar violations had occurred. The principal violations of international humanitarian law by the Government were attacks on civilians in five locations and murders in Moba, where some 300 civilians were killed. RCD forces were responsible for attacks on civilians, property destruction, deportations, mutilation, and rape of women as a means of warfare.

The Special Rapporteur called for support to the work of the Ministry of Human Rights; restoration of human rights; support for human rights advocates and their organizations; respect for the human right to justice; abolition of the death penalty; an end to discretionary authority, impunity and illegal acts of the so-called security forces; observation of the peace agreements; trial and sentencing for war crimes and crimes against humanity; suspension of military assistance to all parties to the conflict; and an end to the recruitment of children. RCD had to stop viewing any dissident as a person guilty of acts of genocide or as an instigator of ethnic hatred.

In a later report describing human rights violations [E/CN.4/2000/42], the Special Rapporteur stated that the Government continued to apply the death penalty; the Military Court did not guarantee the rights of the accused; and the independent press continued to be attacked. The systematic use of torture, enforced disappearances and summary executions were also among the most serious violations. On the positive side, the Minister of Human Rights had tried to make some improvements and a solution was found to the problem of persons at risk—those of Tutsi appearance who needed protection to prevent reprisals by the population. In RCD-controlled territory, there reigned a climate of terror, humiliation and rejection of those in power. The right to life was constantly being violated, as were all the public liberties, such as the right to freedom of association, assembly, expression and opinion. There were no independent news media, and the few that did exist were banned. Any dissent or opposition was presented as attempted genocide. The deportation of prisoners to Rwanda and Uganda was a serious matter. One positive aspect was that the death penalty, which was provided for by law, was not being applied. The situation of human rights advocates was serious. There was no form of democracy under the Government as all powers were vested in the President, Laurent Désiré Kabila, nor was there any right to democracy under RCD. The Special Rapporteur reiterated his previous recommendations.

Joint mission. A December note issued by the Secretariat [E/CN.4/2000/43] stated that, although a ceasefire agreement had been signed on 10 July, the insecurity prevailing in the DRC, and in the province of South Kivu in particular, had prevented the deployment of the joint mission of inquiry, as called for by the Commission in resolution 1999/56.

(For political details, see PART ONE, Chapter II.)

GENERAL ASSEMBLY ACTION

On 17 December [meeting 83], the General Assembly, on the recommendation of the Third (Social, Humanitarian and Cultural) Committee [A/54/605/Add.3], adopted **resolution 54/179** by recorded vote (91-10-54) [agenda item 116 *(c)*].

Situation of human rights in the Democratic Republic of the Congo

The General Assembly,

Guided by the Charter of the United Nations, the Universal Declaration of Human Rights, the International Covenants on Human Rights and other human rights instruments,

Reaffirming that all Member States have an obligation to promote and protect human rights and fundamental freedoms and to fulfil the obligations they have undertaken under the various international instruments in this field,

Mindful that the Democratic Republic of the Congo is a party to the International Covenant on Civil and Political Rights, the International Covenant on Economic, Social and Cultural Rights, the Convention against Torture and Other Cruel, Inhuman or Degrading Treatment or Punishment, the Geneva Conventions of 12 August 1949 for the protection of victims of war, the International Convention on the Elimination of All Forms of Racial Discrimination, and the Convention on the Rights of the Child, as well as to the African Charter on Human and Peoples' Rights,

Recalling its previous resolutions on this subject, including the most recent, resolution 53/160 of 9 December 1998, taking note of Commission on Human Rights resolution 1999/56 of 27 April 1999, as well as Security Council resolution 1234(1999) of 9 April 1999, and mindful of Security Council resolutions 1258(1999) of 6 August 1999 and 1273(1999) of 5 November 1999,

Recognizing that the promotion and protection of human rights for all are essential for achieving stability and security in the region and will contribute to the creation of the necessary environment for cooperation among States in the region,

Taking into account the regional dimension of the human rights issues in the Great Lakes region, while underlining the primary responsibility of States for the promotion and protection of human rights, and stressing the importance of technical cooperation with a view to strengthening regional cooperation for the promotion and protection of human rights,

Bearing in mind the decision of the Commission on Human Rights to request the special rapporteurs of the Commission on the situation of human rights in the Democratic Republic of the Congo and on extrajudicial, summary or arbitrary executions and a member of the Working Group on Enforced or Involuntary Disappearances to carry out a joint mission to the Democratic Republic of the Congo,

Noting the stated intention of the Government of the Democratic Republic of the Congo progressively to abolish the death penalty, and, with that in view, encouraging the Government to fulfil its commitment to reform and restore the judicial system in conformity with the provisions of the International Covenant on Civil and Political Rights,

1. *Welcomes*:

(a) The report of the Special Rapporteur on the situation of human rights in the Democratic Republic of the Congo;

(b) The two visits of the Special Rapporteur to the Democratic Republic of the Congo in February and August/September 1999 at the invitation of the Government and the cooperation of the Government in this regard;

(c) The activities of the human rights field office in the Democratic Republic of the Congo, while encouraging the Government of the Democratic Republic of the Congo to work closely and to strengthen further its cooperation with the field office;

(d) The Ceasefire Agreement, which was signed at Lusaka on 10 July 1999 by all parties involved in the conflict in the Democratic Republic of the Congo;

(e) The appointment by the Secretary-General of a special envoy for the peace process for the Democratic Republic of the Congo;

(f) The appointment by the Secretary-General of a special representative for the Democratic Republic of the Congo;

(g) The appointment of the Minister of Human Rights within the Government of the Democratic Republic of the Congo, and expresses the hope that that appointment will contribute to an improvement of the situation of human rights;

(h) The commitment by the Government of the Democratic Republic of the Congo to cooperate with United Nations agencies and non-governmental organizations in ensuring the demobilization, rehabilitation and reintegration of child soldiers, and encourages the Government to implement fully its commitment;

2. *Expresses its concern* at:

(a) The adverse impact of the conflict on the situation of human rights and its severe consequences for the security and well-being of the civilian population throughout the territory of the Democratic Republic of the Congo;

(b) The preoccupying situation of human rights in the Democratic Republic of the Congo, in particular in the eastern parts of the country, and the continuing violations of human rights and international humanitarian law committed throughout the territory of the Democratic Republic of the Congo, often with impunity, and, with that in view, condemns:

(i) The perpetration of massacres, in the course of the conflicts, including, more recently, in 1998 and 1999, those in Kasika, Makobola, Kamituga, Kavumu, Kilungutwe, Kasanga, Kazima, Mboko, Kabare, Mwenga, Libenge and Kasala;

(ii) The occurrence of cases of summary or arbitrary execution, disappearance, torture, beating, harassment, arbitrary arrest and detention without trial, including of journalists, opposition politicians, human rights defenders and people who have cooperated with the United Nations mechanisms, and reports of sexual violence against women and children and the continuing recruitment and use of child soldiers;

(iii) The trial of civilians and the imposition of the death penalty by the Military Court;

(c) The excessive accumulation and spread of small arms and light weapons and the illicit distribution, circulation and trafficking of arms in the region and their negative impact on human rights;

3. *Urges* all parties to the conflict in the Democratic Republic of the Congo:

(a) To work for the full and timely implementation of the provisions of the Ceasefire Agreement and to re-establish the authority of the Government of the Democratic Republic of the Congo throughout its territory, stressing, in the context of a lasting peaceful settlement, the need for the engagement of all Congolese in an all-inclusive process of political dialogue with a view to achieving national reconciliation and the holding of democratic, free, transparent and fair elections;

(b) To protect human rights and to respect international humanitarian law, in particular, as applicable to them, the Geneva Conventions of 12 August 1949 for the protection of victims of war, the Additional Protocols thereto, of 1977, and the Convention on the Prevention and Punishment of the Crime of Genocide, especially with regard to respect for the rights of women and children, and to ensure the safety of all civilians, including refugees and internally displaced persons within the territory of that country regardless of their origin;

(c) To ensure the safety, security and freedom of movement of United Nations and associated personnel within the Democratic Republic of the Congo and, in this regard, to ensure safe and unhindered access of humanitarian personnel to all affected populations;

(d) To bring an end to all violations of human rights and to ensure that there is no impunity for human rights violators;

(e) To cooperate fully with the National Commission of Inquiry on the alleged massacres of a large number of refugees and displaced persons in the Democratic Republic of the Congo, and also with the Secretary-General and the United Nations High Commissioner for Human Rights in addressing these allegations, with a view to the submission of a further report by the National Commission of Inquiry to the Secretary-General on the progress of its investigations into this question;

4. *Calls upon* the Government of the Democratic Republic of the Congo:

(a) To comply with its obligations under international human rights law and to promote and protect human rights and fundamental freedoms throughout its entire territory;

(b) To take a leading part in efforts to prevent conditions that might lead to further flows of internally displaced persons and refugees within the Democratic Republic of the Congo and across its borders;

(c) To uphold its commitment to reform and restore the judicial system and in particular to reform military justice in conformity with the provisions of the International Covenant on Civil and Political Rights, and encourages provisional assistance to this end;

(d) To implement fully its commitment to the democratization process, in particular the national dialogue, as set out in the Ceasefire Agreement, and to create, in this context, conditions that would allow for a democratization process that is genuine and all-inclusive and that fully reflects the aspirations of all people of the country;

(e) To fulfil its responsibility to ensure that those responsible for human rights violations are brought to justice;

(f) To remove the remaining administrative restrictions on the activities of political parties and to prepare for the holding of democratic, free, transparent and fair elections;

(g) To promote human rights awareness, inter alia, by strengthening cooperation with civil society, including all human rights organizations, and to remove the restrictions that still affect the work of non-governmental organizations;

(h) To ensure full respect for freedom of opinion and expression, including freedom of the press in all types of mass media, as well as freedom of association and assembly;

(i) To cooperate fully with the International Criminal Tribunal for the Prosecution of Persons Responsible for Genocide and Other Serious Violations of International Humanitarian Law Committed in the Territory of Rwanda and Rwandan Citizens Responsible for Genocide and Other Such Violations Committed in the Territory of Neighbouring States between 1 January and 31 December 1994 in ensuring that all those responsible for the crime of genocide, crimes against humanity and other grave violations of human rights are brought to justice in accordance with international principles of due process;

5. *Decides* to continue to examine the situation of human rights in the Democratic Republic of the Congo, and requests the Special Rapporteur to report to the General Assembly at its fifty-fifth session.

RECORDED VOTE ON RESOLUTION 54/179:

In favour: Albania, Andorra, Argentina, Armenia, Australia, Austria, Azerbaijan, Bahamas, Barbados, Belarus, Belgium, Belize, Bolivia, Bosnia and Herzegovina, Brazil, Bulgaria, Canada, Chile, Colombia, Costa Rica, Croatia, Cyprus, Czech Republic, Denmark, Dominica, Dominican Republic, Ecuador, El Salvador, Estonia, Finland, France, Georgia, Germany, Greece, Grenada, Guatemala, Guyana, Haiti, Hungary, Iceland, Ireland, Israel, Italy, Jamaica, Japan, Kazakhstan, Kuwait, Latvia, Liechtenstein, Lithuania, Luxembourg, Maldives, Malta, Marshall Islands, Mauritius, Mexico, Micronesia, Monaco, Mongolia, Netherlands, New Zealand, Nicaragua, Norway, Panama, Paraguay, Peru, Poland, Portugal, Republic of Korea, Republic of Moldova, Romania, Russian Federation, Samoa, San Marino, Saudi Arabia, Slovakia, Slovenia, Solomon Islands, South Africa, Spain, Sweden, Tajikistan, Trinidad and Tobago, Turkey, Ukraine, United Arab Emirates, United Kingdom, United States, Uruguay, Uzbekistan, Venezuela.

Against: Angola, Burkina Faso, Chad, China, Cuba, Democratic Republic of the Congo, Iran, Myanmar, Sudan, Zimbabwe.

Abstaining: Afghanistan, Algeria, Antigua and Barbuda, Bahrain, Bangladesh, Benin, Bhutan, Botswana, Brunei Darussalam, Cambodia, Cameroon, Cape Verde, Congo, Côte d'Ivoire, Democratic People's Republic of Korea, Djibouti, Egypt, Eritrea, Ethiopia, Fiji, Ghana, Guinea, Guinea-Bissau, India, Indonesia, Jordan, Kenya, Lao People's Democratic Republic, Libyan Arab Jamahiriya, Malawi, Malaysia, Mali, Morocco, Mozambique, Namibia, Nepal, Nigeria, Pakistan, Papua New Guinea, Philippines, Rwanda, Saint Lucia, Senegal, Sierra Leone, Singapore, Sri Lanka, Suriname, Swaziland, Thailand, Togo, Tunisia, Uganda, United Republic of Tanzania, Zambia.

Equatorial Guinea

Commission action. On 23 April [res. 1999/19], the Commission encouraged the Government of Equatorial Guinea and OHCHR, in conjunction and with the support of the United Nations Development Programme (UNDP), to develop a human rights technical assistance programme, and called on the international community to contribute to the fund for that purpose. It decided to appoint a special representative for one year and asked him to monitor the human rights situation and to report in 2000, keeping in mind a gender perspective in the reporting process. The Economic and Social Council endorsed the Commission's decision and the requests to the Special Representative by **decision 1999/233** of 27 July. The Commission also asked the Special Representative to make recommendations on the implementation of the technical assistance programme, emphasizing human rights, the administration of justice and the legislative reforms and the strengthening of the capacity of NGOs, as well as other groups of civil society.

In August, the Commission appointed Gustavo Gallón (Colombia) as Special Representative.

Report of Special Representative. Special Representative Gallón submitted his first report based on his visit to the country (7-21 November) [E/CN.4/2000/40].

The Special Representative stated that the human rights situation in Equatorial Guinea was grave. There was no sustained rule of law; rather, power was concentrated in the hands of the executive, with the support of a government party that controlled employment in Government and private enterprise. The executive was also reinforced by the dominance of the military, which exercised jurisdiction over civilians. Violations of the rights to equality were seen in various forms of daily harassment against the Bubi ethnic group by the Fang majority, which held power. Press activity was almost non-existent and Government-controlled radio and television operated more as propaganda tools than as information carriers. During his visits to several prisons, the Special Representative observed ill-treatment of prisoners and deplorable sanitary conditions. Other violations of civil and political rights related to freedom of movement and the right to due process. The Special Representative observed that the enjoyment of economic, social and cultural rights was seriously limited to a minority of the population. The health-care system was inadequate, restrictions affected the right to work, no recognized trade union existed and only 1.8 per cent of the country's income was earmarked for education. The growing number of female dropouts from school was caused by the persistence of women's inferior role and discrimination within the family. There were high rates of infant mortality and child labour. Nevertheless, account should be taken of the progress made through accession to some international human rights conventions and acceptance, since 1992, of the legal existence of political parties other than the governing party.

Regarding human rights technical assistance, the Special Representative stated that in the last 20 years successive rapporteurs and experts had agreed on technical assistance activities to strengthen the capacity of the national authorities and the local population to protect human rights and prevent violations. Some progress had been achieved, but most of the repeated recommendations in the last 20 years had yet to be acted upon, including the suggestion that an OHCHR staff member be appointed to provide human rights technical assistance while living in Equatorial Guinea. The Special Representative outlined a cooperation strategy that would include immediate implementation of recommendations not requiring technical assistance; proof of the Government's willingness to implement the remaining recommendations; and preparation of a detailed programme of activities, defining how and when each recommendation would be put into practice. The resident official should have the capacity to provide technical assistance to organizations from civil society and the Commission and its Special Representative with technical support in monitoring the human rights situation; the strategy should be jointly coordinated by the Special Representative and the High Commissioner. Recommendations applied to civil rights, freedom of opinion, the principle of legality, the right to justice, equality of women, political rights and economic, social and cultural rights, many of which could be carried out directly by the Government without assistance. The Special Representative recommended that the Commission continue to monitor the human rights situation, concentrating on the implementation of the recommendations repeatedly made to the country.

Nigeria

On 23 April [res. 1999/11], the Commission, commending the Government of Nigeria for measures it had taken to promote, protect and enhance the enjoyment of human rights and fundamental freedoms, decided to conclude consideration of the situation of human rights in Nigeria. It asked OHCHR to respond positively to any request by the Government for human rights technical assistance and advisory services.

Rwanda

Report of Special Representative. Special Representative Michel Moussalli (Switzerland) visited Rwanda (11-23 January) [E/CN.4/1999/33], where he noted with satisfaction the adoption of a bill by the National Assembly establishing the National Human Rights Commission (NHRC), as provided for in the Arusha Accords [YUN 1993, p. 284] and as enshrined in the Basic Law of Rwanda. It was expected to enter into force in February. The security situation in Rwanda was complex and intertwined with the situation in the DRC, and was most fragile in the north-west along the border. Observers reported that the level of violence and human rights violations had abated since mid-1998, partly due to some punitive and preventive measures of the Government. At collective resettlement camps, the Government offered material assistance and protection from raiding forces. The Government estimated that at the end of 1998, the total number of persons in detention was just under 125,000 and the number of persons in communal detention centres was around 36,000. Those figures reflected a slight decrease in the total detainee population over the previous year. Conditions of detention remained deplorable. General progress in all areas of the justice sector had been recorded throughout 1998, with genocide and other trials progressing in all prefectures despite continued problems of insufficient resources for legal assistance, training and functioning of the courts. Regarding economic, social and cultural rights, the situation of women was of particular concern. Many were sexually abused and injured, or even killed. Many survivors contracted AIDS from rape; others lost their husbands and were left having to support many children. Children had also suffered immeasurably from the genocide.

In his conclusions and recommendations, the Special Representative regretted that it was not possible for an understanding to be reached in 1998 between the Government and OHCHR with respect to the mandate of the United Nations Human Rights Field Operation in Rwanda, which was closed in 1998 [YUN 1998, p. 737]. He urged the long-term provision of technical and material assistance to promote human rights; improvement in conditions in detention centres; strengthening the judicial system; alleviating the plight of survivors of the genocide; and provision of assistance by the international community in the area of housing. The international community was urged to promote a peaceful resolution of the conflict in the DRC, and to adopt a comprehensive approach to providing financial and technical assistance to Rwanda.

Commission action. On 23 April [res. 1999/20], the Commission, welcoming the efforts of the Government of Rwanda to build a State based on the rule of law and the guarantee of respect for human rights and fundamental freedoms, strongly condemned the crime of genocide and the crimes against humanity that were committed in Rwanda in 1994 and expressed concern at continued violations of human rights and international humanitarian law. Noting the efforts that the International Criminal Tribunal for Rwanda (ICTR) (see p. 1221) had made to improve its performance, the Commission expressed concern over the effectiveness of the Tribunal's witness protection programme and called for improvements in that regard. It asked States to cooperate with ICTR.

The Commission decided to extend the Special Representative's mandate for a further year and asked him to report to the General Assembly in 1999 and to the Commission in 2000. The High Commissioner was asked to assist him. The Economic and Social Council endorsed the Commission's decision and approved its requests to the Special Representative and the High Commissioner by **decision 1999/234** of 27 July. The Commission called for close regular consultation between the Special Representative, the Government and NHRC and other national institutions regarding the functions of NHRC.

Reports of Special Representative. In September [A/54/359], the Special Representative updated information on the human rights situation in Rwanda based on further missions he had taken to the country in April, June and August. He observed that Rwanda was stepping out of the shadow of genocide, as the Rwandan people were taking steps to ensure that it no longer impeded the development of their nation. Positive developments over the past year included: successful local elections; the establishment of two national commissions (on human rights and on unity and reconciliation); the first steps towards drafting a new constitution; a plan to professionalize the civilian police force; a revision of the press law; the adoption of a law allowing women to inherit property; a growing commitment to good governance; and a proposal to use traditional justice (*gacaca*) to speed up genocide trials. In spite of the progress, there was not yet a culture of human rights in Rwanda. Areas needing further improvement included prison administration and detention centre and prison conditions, freedom of movement, and freedom of opinion and expression. Efforts to eradicate ethnic tension needed to be increased. In addition, a lasting regional solution was needed to conflicts in the Great Lakes area. The Special Representative recommended improved and better coordinated human rights assistance from donors; assistance by the UN system; complementarity of the efforts of NHRC and the National Commission for Unity and Reconciliation; and assistance by the international community to the newly established Commissions.

In a later report [E/CN.4/2000/41], the Special Representative pointed out that as fighting diminished in the eastern part of the DRC in 1999, the number of incursions of armed infiltrators into north-west Rwanda diminished, which in turn led to a decline in alleged abuses by the Rwandan armed forces. The humanitarian emergency was receding as a result of good harvests and improved security. Bilateral donors discussed partnership rather than aid. In 1999, 32,087 Rwandans returned voluntarily from the DRC, and the number of Rwandans in exile had fallen from 3 million to less than 100,000. The reintegration of refugees inside the country had improved steadily. The National Assembly (parliament) had emerged as an independent body, and NHRC, which became operational in May, developed a work plan up to 2002. Although some 120,000 detainees were still crowded into jails five years into the transition (many without being charged), a new law on prisons had been drafted, and new prison regulations were scheduled for adoption. Regarding the genocide trials, by 30 November, 2,406 persons had been tried before a special genocide court, of the 121,500 in detention. Of those, 14.4 per cent (348) were sentenced to death, 30.3 per cent to life imprisonment, 34 per cent to jail terms between 1 and 20 years, and 19 per cent were acquitted. The Special Representative stated that efforts to improve justice and speed up trials would enter a new phase with the introduction of *gacaca* for genocide suspects. Trials would take place in public before the entire community. The most widely voiced concerns were that due legal process would be compromised and the rights of the defendants ignored, and that *gacaca* could be inconsistent with international standards. The Special Representative applauded the UNDP initiative to establish a Justice and Human Rights Unit in Kigali, but expressed concern that the unit remained severely underfunded and understaffed. He called for efforts in the area of economic and social rights, including protection for children from sexual violence and HIV/AIDS; land and settlement reform; and education. The Special Representative made a series of recommendations regarding prison conditions, the administration of justice, NGOs, the media, NHRC and bilateral donors. He appealed to all countries in the region, OAU and the United Nations to ensure that a lasting and comprehensive peace was agreed upon by all the affected countries.

(For political details, see PART ONE, Chapter II.)

GENERAL ASSEMBLY ACTION

On 17 December [meeting 83], the General Assembly, on the recommendation of the Third Committee [A/54/605/Add.3], adopted **resolution 54/188** without vote [agenda item 116 (*c*)].

Situation of human rights in Rwanda

The General Assembly,

Guided by the Charter of the United Nations, the International Bill of Human Rights, the Convention on the Prevention and Punishment of the Crime of Genocide and other applicable human rights and humanitarian law standards,

Recalling its resolution 53/156 of 9 December 1998 and previous relevant resolutions, and taking note of Commission on Human Rights resolution 1999/20 of 23 April 1999,

Reaffirming that the promotion and protection of human rights are necessary for sustaining the process of national reconstruction and reconciliation in Rwanda,

Welcoming the commitment of the Government of Rwanda to promote and protect respect for human rights and fundamental freedoms and to eliminate impunity, the progress made towards the development of a State governed on the basis of the rule of law and the efforts undertaken to consolidate peace and stability and promote unity and reconciliation,

Recognizing that the promotion and protection of human rights for all are essential for achieving stability and security in the region,

1. *Takes note with appreciation* of the report of the Special Representative of the Commission on Human Rights on the situation of human rights in Rwanda;
2. *Reiterates its strong condemnation* of the crime of genocide and the crimes against humanity committed in Rwanda in 1994;
3. *Reaffirms* that all persons who committed or authorized acts of genocide or other grave violations of human rights and international law are individually responsible and accountable for those violations;

4. *Expresses concern* that most of the perpetrators of the genocide and other gross violations of human rights continue to evade justice;

5. *Also expresses concern* that, despite the imposition by the Security Council of an arms embargo which has remained in force since the genocide of 1994, the *Interahamwe* militias and the former members of the Rwandan armed forces continue to receive military, financial and logistical support, and in this regard calls upon the international community to take urgent measures to enable the disarmament of those groups in accordance with the letter and spirit of the Ceasefire Agreement, signed at Lusaka on 10 July 1999;

6. *Reiterates its request* that all States cooperate fully, without delay, with the International Criminal Tribunal for the Prosecution of Persons Responsible for Genocide and Other Serious Violations of International Humanitarian Law Committed in the Territory of Rwanda and Rwandan Citizens Responsible for Genocide and Other Such Violations Committed in the Territory of Neighbouring States between 1 January and 31 December 1994 in ensuring that all those responsible for the crime of genocide, crimes against humanity and other grave violations of human rights are brought to justice in accordance with international principles of due process;

7. *Encourages* the International Tribunal for Rwanda to adopt further measures to enhance its efficiency and effectiveness;

8. *Notes* improvements in the situation of human rights in Rwanda since the fifty-third session of the General Assembly, expresses concern at those violations of human rights that are reported, and urges the Government of Rwanda to continue to investigate and prosecute such violations;

9. *Welcomes* the continuation of domestic trials of those suspected of genocide and crimes against humanity and the improvements that have been made in the trial process, and encourages the Government of Rwanda, with the support of the international community, to strengthen the capacity of the independent judicial system in accordance with international human rights standards;

10. *Encourages* the International Tribunal for Rwanda and the Government of Rwanda to continue to prosecute crimes of sexual violence committed against women during the genocide of 1994;

11. *Welcomes* the deliberations currently being conducted in Rwanda to determine new mechanisms to handle the large caseload of detainees awaiting trial on genocide and related charges in a more expeditious manner, notes in this regard the proposal of the Government of Rwanda to establish a complementary system of participatory justice, urges the Government of Rwanda to ensure that any such system is in conformity with the law and international human rights standards, and encourages the international community to assist in this area;

12. *Reiterates its appeal* to the international community to provide financial and technical assistance to the Government of Rwanda within a mutually agreed framework of cooperation to help to strengthen the protection of genocide survivors and witnesses and the administration of justice, including adequate access to legal representation to prosecute those responsible for genocide and other violations of human rights and to promote the rule of law in Rwanda, and notes with appreciation the assistance already provided by some members of the donor community;

13. *Welcomes* the continuing efforts of the Government of Rwanda to build a State based on the rule of law and the guarantee of respect for human rights and fundamental freedoms in accordance with the Universal Declaration of Human Rights and other relevant international human rights instruments;

14. *Notes* that in July 1999 the transitional Government mandate was extended for a further four years, commends the Government of Rwanda for holding elections at the cell and sector levels in a peaceful and successful manner, and supports the Government in the continuation of its democratization process;

15. *Commends* the Government of Rwanda for its continued efforts to improve the situation of children, and encourages it to continue with these efforts, guided by a concern for the best interests of children, as specified in the Convention on the Rights of the Child;

16. *Welcomes* the establishment by legislation of the National Human Rights Commission, encourages the Government of Rwanda and the international community to provide their full support to the Commission to enable it to carry out its mandate to monitor human rights in the country effectively and independently, in accordance with internationally recognized norms, notes the convening of a Commission round-table meeting in October 1999, and urges the Government of Rwanda to pursue its recommendations;

17. *Encourages* the United Nations High Commissioner for Human Rights, the Government of Rwanda, other Governments, international organizations and non-governmental organizations to provide, within a mutually agreed framework of cooperation, support for the reconstruction of a human rights infrastructure, including a strong civil society;

18. *Notes with appreciation* the continuing assistance provided to the National Human Rights Commission by the High Commissioner;

19. *Welcomes* the commitment of the Government of Rwanda to continue to promote national unity and reconciliation, and also welcomes the establishment by legislation of the National Unity and Reconciliation Commission as a basis for the promotion of tolerance and non-discrimination;

20. *Encourages* the National Unity and Reconciliation Commission and the National Human Rights Commission to work together closely to ensure the complementarity of their efforts;

21. *Reiterates its concern* at the conditions in many communal detention centres and some prisons in Rwanda, calls upon the Government of Rwanda to continue its efforts to ensure that persons in detention are treated in a manner that respects their human rights, emphasizes the need for greater attention and resources to be directed to this problem, and again urges the international community to assist the Government of Rwanda in this area;

22. *Encourages* the continuing efforts of the Government of Rwanda to reduce the prison population by releasing minors, elderly prisoners, prisoners suffering from terminal illnesses and suspects with incomplete files who were detained for their alleged involvement in genocide and other abuses of human rights, and re-

affirms the urgent need to complete a dossier for every detainee with a view to identifying those who should be formally charged and those who should be released immediately, early or conditionally;

23. *Encourages* the Government of Rwanda, in cooperation with the Office of the United Nations High Commissioner for Refugees, to continue to provide protection and assistance to returnees to Rwanda;

24. *Notes* the initiative by the Government of Rwanda to regroup scattered rural populations in the country under a programme of villagization in order to facilitate community development infrastructure, and urges the Government of Rwanda to ensure that the human rights and fundamental freedoms of all are respected in the implementation of this programme;

25. *Calls* for close regular consultation between the Special Representative and the Government of Rwanda, the National Human Rights Commission and all relevant national institutions regarding the functioning of the Commission;

26. *Decides* to keep the situation of human rights in Rwanda under consideration at its fifty-fifth session, in the light of additional elements provided by the Commission on Human Rights and the Economic and Social Council.

Sierra Leone

Commission action. On 6 April [res. 1999/1], the Commission, appealing to all factions and forces in Sierra Leone to respect human rights and abide by applicable international humanitarian law, reminded them that hostage-taking, wilful killing and torture or inhuman treatment of persons taking no active part in the hostilities constituted grave breaches of international humanitarian law, and that all countries were obligated to bring persons alleged to have committed such grave breaches before their own courts. It decided to discontinue consideration of the human rights situation in Sierra Leone in closed meetings under Economic and Social Council resolution 1503(XLVIII) [YUN 1970, p. 530] and to consider the matter under the public procedure provided for by the Commission in 1967 [YUN 1967, p. 508] and by the Council in resolution 1235(XLII) [ibid., p. 512]. The High Commissioner was asked to apprise the Commission in 2000 of the reports of the Secretary-General about violations of human rights and international humanitarian law in Sierra Leone, including, to the extent possible, references contained in reports submitted to the Commission.

OHCHR activities. OHCHR, in cooperation with the United Nations Mission in Sierra Leone (see PART ONE, Chapter II) and the Sierra Leone authorities, was working to create a truth and reconciliation commission, a renewed National Human Rights Commission and a commission of inquiry [E/CN.4/2000/31]. OHCHR's work was inspired by the Human Rights Manifesto, a moral and political commitment signed by the High Commissioner, the Secretary-General's Special Representative in Sierra Leone, the President of the country and others during the High Commissioner's visit in June.

Sudan

Commission action. On 23 April [res. 1999/15], the Commission expressed deep concern at continued serious violations of human rights, fundamental freedoms and humanitarian law in the Sudan by all parties to the conflict (see PART ONE, Chapter II). It called on the Government to comply with applicable international human rights instruments; ensure the rule of law; bring its legislation into accord with the instruments to which the Sudan was a party; end acts of torture and cruel, inhuman or degrading treatment and ensure that all accused persons were held in ordinary custody and received fair trials; investigate reports of the abduction of women and children; cease the indiscriminate aerial bombardment of civilian and humanitarian targets; ensure respect for freedom of opinion, expression, thought, conscience and religion, as well as freedom of association; and comply with the commitment made to the Secretary-General's Special Representative for children and armed conflict not to recruit children under the age of 18 as soldiers (see p. 674). Parties to the conflict were urged to respect and protect human rights, fundamental freedoms and international humanitarian law; stop the use of weapons against civilians; grant safe and unhindered access to international agencies and humanitarian organizations; cooperate with the peace efforts of the Intergovernmental Authority on Development; and not use children under the age of 18 as soldiers and refrain from forced conscription.

The Commission decided to extend the Special Rapporteur's mandate for an additional year and asked him to report to the General Assembly in 1999 and to the Commission in 2000, keeping a gender perspective in mind in the reporting process; the Economic and Social Council endorsed the Commission's decision and approved its request to the Special Rapporteur by **decision 1999/230** of 27 July. The Commission also asked the Secretary-General to assist the Special Rapporteur. OHCHR was asked to urgently consider requests for assistance by the Government, including with a view to establishing a permanent representation of the High Commissioner in Khartoum.

Reports of Special Rapporteur. Special Rapporteur Leonardo Franco (Argentina) visited the Sudan (13-24 February) [E/CN.4/1999/38/Add.1], where serious human rights violations continued to be committed, including summary executions, extrajudicial killings, arbitrary arrests, detention without due process of law, displacement of persons, systematic torture, and restriction or denial of the freedoms of religion, expression, association and peaceful assembly. In particular, his mission addressed human rights violations relating to the adoption in April 1998 of a new Constitution and the transition to democracy, respect for human rights and humanitarian law in the conflict, women's rights and the rights of the child, and other reported human rights violations, including arbitrary detention, the military trial of 27 southerners accused of participating in the Khartoum bombings, torture and extrajudicial killings, and the persecution of non-Muslims.

The Special Rapporteur noted that the new Constitution was not a product of a political consensus among the main political parties and, moreover, the procedure leading to its adoption was highly questionable. He regretted that the period following the Constitution's adoption was overshadowed by the violation of political freedoms and the perpetration of human rights abuses, such as the harassment or arbitrary arrest of human rights advocates and political, religious and student leaders; torture was inflicted on victims and arrests were conducted without due process of law. The Security Act, as well as other emergency laws, was being revised in conformity with the new Constitution, which the Special Rapporteur hoped would bring the executive and the various security organs under jurisdictional control. Violations of human rights and humanitarian law by the parties to the conflict were evident in forced displacement, killings, rape and abduction of women and children, and slavery. However, the Special Rapporteur was encouraged by developments promoting respect for human rights and humanitarian law during the conflict, the construction of peace, the improvement of humanitarian assistance, post-conflict national development and confidence-building. The Special Rapporteur recommended that the Government adopt the legal, political and administrative measures required to ensure the transition from an emergency regime to a political system based on the rule of law. All parties had to ensure that civilians were not targeted by military operations. He called for the punishment of transgressors for raids, burning and looting and physical attacks on civilians, as well as a ban on: reprisal against the unarmed population in response to military attacks; forced population displacement and arbitrary or discriminatory restriction of freedom of movement; recruiting child soldiers; hampering access to civilians by humanitarian aid workers and aid delivery; and the use of anti-personnel mines. The Government should ensure that raids by Murahaleen or other militia against civilians were prohibited and the perpetrators punished, and should cease aerial bombing of civilians and humanitarian sites. The Special Rapporteur outlined measures for the Government to end slavery-like practices and to prevent torture. He recommended that the Sudan consider accepting a UN human rights field presence.

In October [A/54/467], the Special Rapporteur reported a number of positive measures taken by the Government, including authorization for the United Nations to undertake a needs assessment mission to the Nuba Mountains; the creation of the Committee for the Eradication of Abduction of Women and Children; and the fielding of an OHCHR needs assessment mission to determine priority areas for human rights assistance. The 17-year conflict, however, had been aggravated during 1999 by developments in the oil zones. The economic, political and strategic implications of the oil zones had exacerbated the conflict, resulting in further deterioration of the human rights situation. Furthermore, government strategies for the control of oil production were causing tribal fragmentation. There were reports that government forces had attacked and burned villages to the ground in the oil-producing areas, causing civilian displacement. Other abuses against civilians, mostly by Matiep forces but with the government army allegedly playing a role, included abduction of young boys to use as soldiers, abduction of girls and women for sexual abuse, and a number of summary executions of women, never recorded prior to 1999. The Special Rapporteur concluded that the Government still needed to adopt the legal, political and administrative measures required to ensure the transition from an emergency regime to a political system based on the rule of law.

(For information on the visit to the Sudan by the Special Rapporteur on the right to freedom of opinion and expression, and by the Secretary-General's Special Representative on children and armed conflict regarding the abduction and kidnapping of children in southern Sudan, see pp. 640 and 674. For political details, see PART ONE, Chapter II.)

GENERAL ASSEMBLY ACTION

On 17 December [meeting 83], the General Assembly, on the recommendation of the Third Committee [A/54/605/Add.3], adopted **resolution 54/182** by recorded vote (89-30-39) [agenda item 116 *(c)*].

Situation of human rights in the Sudan

The General Assembly,

Reaffirming that all Member States have an obligation to promote and protect human rights and fundamental freedoms as stated in the Charter of the United Nations, the Universal Declaration of Human Rights, the International Covenants on Human Rights and other applicable human rights instruments and to fulfil the obligations that they have undertaken under the various international instruments in this field,

Mindful that the Sudan is a party to the International Covenant on Civil and Political Rights, the International Covenant on Economic, Social and Cultural Rights, the Convention on the Rights of the Child, the African Charter on Human and Peoples' Rights and the Geneva Conventions of 12 August 1949,

Recalling its previous resolutions on the situation of human rights in the Sudan, and taking note of Commission on Human Rights resolution 1999/15 of 23 April 1999,

Aware of the urgent need to implement effective measures in the field of human rights and humanitarian relief to protect the civilian population from the effects of armed conflicts,

Welcoming the Peace Agreement of 1997, the acceptance of the Declaration of Principles as a basis for negotiations, the declaration by the Government of the Sudan of a comprehensive ceasefire on 5 April 1999 and the decision made by the Sudanese People's Liberation Army to extend the ceasefire in the Bahr el-Ghazal region in southern Sudan for a further three months, while at the same time deeply concerned at the impact of the continuing conflict in the Sudan between the Government of the Sudan and the Sudanese People's Liberation Movement/Army on the situation of human rights and at the disregard by all parties to the conflict of relevant rules of international humanitarian law,

Expressing its firm belief that progress towards a peaceful settlement of the conflict in southern Sudan within the peace initiative of the Intergovernmental Authority on Development will greatly contribute to the creation of a better environment to encourage respect for human rights in the Sudan,

Condemning the murder of four Sudanese relief workers in April 1999 while in the custody of the Sudanese People's Liberation Army,

1. *Welcomes:*

(*a*) The interim report of the Special Rapporteur of the Commission on Human Rights on the situation of human rights in the Sudan;

(*b*) The visit by the Special Rapporteur to the Sudan in February 1999 at the invitation of the Government of the Sudan and the excellent cooperation extended by the Government in this regard, as well as the stated willingness of the Government to continue to cooperate with the Special Rapporteur and the invitation extended to the Special Rapporteur;

(*c*) The visit by the Special Representative of the Secretary-General for Children and Armed Conflict to the Sudan in March 1999 and the cooperation extended by the Government of the Sudan in this regard;

(*d*) The cooperation extended by the Government of the Sudan to the needs assessment mission of the Office of the United Nations High Commissioner for Human Rights, which took place from 14 to 26 September 1999;

(*e*) The fact-finding mission by the Special Rapporteur of the Commission on Human Rights on the promotion and protection of the right to freedom of opinion and expression in September 1999, pursuant to the invitation extended by the Government of the Sudan;

(*f*) The cooperation extended by the Government of the Sudan and the Sudanese People's Liberation Movement/Army to the humanitarian needs assessment mission of the Office for the Coordination of Humanitarian Affairs of the Secretariat, the United Nations Children's Fund and the World Food Programme to the Nuba Mountains, which took place from 21 to 24 June 1999;

(*g*) The expressed commitment of the Government of the Sudan to respect and promote human rights and the rule of law and its expressed commitment to a process of democratization with a view to establishing a representative and accountable government, reflecting the aspirations of the people of the Sudan;

(*h*) The stipulation of basic human rights and freedoms in the Constitution of the Sudan, which entered into force on 1 July 1998;

(*i*) The establishment of the Constitutional Court, which has been in operation since April 1999;

(*j*) The creation of the Committee for the Eradication of Abduction of Women and Children as a constructive response on the part of the Government of the Sudan and the cooperation extended to the Committee by the local communities and the support of the international community and non-governmental organizations;

(*k*) The efforts to implement the right to education;

(*l*) The commitments made by the Government of the Sudan to the Special Representative of the Secretary-General for Children and Armed Conflict, in particular the commitment not to use or recruit children under the age of 18 as soldiers;

(*m*) The efforts to address the problem of internally displaced persons;

2. *Expresses its deep concern:*

(*a*) At the impact of the current armed conflict on the situation of human rights and its adverse effect on the civilian population, in particular women and children, and continuing serious violations of human rights and international humanitarian law by all parties, in particular:

(i) The occurrence of cases of extrajudicial, summary or arbitrary execution resulting from conflict between members of the armed forces and their allies, and armed insurgent groups, including the Sudanese People's Liberation Army;

(ii) The occurrence, within the framework of the conflict in southern Sudan, of cases of enforced or involuntary disappearance, the use of children as soldiers and combatants, forced conscription, forced displacement, arbitrary detention, torture and ill-treatment of civilians;

(iii) The abduction of women and children to be subjected to forced labour or similar conditions;

(iv) The use of weapons, including landmines, against the civilian population;

(*b*) At violations of human rights in areas under the control of the Government of the Sudan, in particular:

(i) The widespread use of torture and arbitrary detention affecting, inter alia, human rights defenders, journalists and political opponents, as well as the lack of due process of law and acts of intimidation and harassment of the population, in particular by the security organs;

(ii) Cases of restriction on freedom of religion and peaceful assembly;

3. *Urges* all parties to the continuing conflict in the Sudan:

(*a*) To respect and protect human rights and fundamental freedoms, to respect fully international humanitarian law, thereby facilitating the voluntary return, repatriation and reintegration of refugees and internally displaced persons to their homes, and to ensure that those responsible for violations of human rights and international humanitarian law are brought to justice;

(*b*) To stop immediately the use of weapons, including landmines, against the civilian population, which runs counter to principles of humanitarian law, and urges in particular the Sudanese People's Liberation Army to stop immediately the use of civilian premises for military purposes;

(*c*) To grant safe and unhindered access to international agencies and humanitarian organizations in order to facilitate by all means possible the delivery of humanitarian assistance to all civilians in need of protection and assistance, in particular in Bahr el-Ghazal, the Nuba Mountains and the Western Upper Nile, and to continue to cooperate in this regard with the Office for the Coordination of Humanitarian Affairs and Operation Lifeline Sudan in the delivery of such assistance;

(*d*) To continue to cooperate with the peace efforts of the Intergovernmental Authority on Development;

(*e*) Not to use or recruit children under the age of 18 as soldiers, and urges the Sudanese People's Liberation Army to undertake a commitment similar to that made by the Government of the Sudan to the Special Representative of the Secretary-General for Children and Armed Conflict in this regard and to refrain from the practice of forced conscription;

(*f*) To fulfil their commitments concerning the protection of children affected by war, such as to cease the use of anti-personnel landmines, the abduction and exploitation of children and the recruitment of children as soldiers, to advance the demobilization and reintegration of child soldiers and to ensure access to displaced and unaccompanied minors;

(*g*) To allow for an independent investigation of the case of the four Sudanese nationals who were abducted on 18 February 1999 while accompanying a team from the International Committee of the Red Cross on a humanitarian mission and subsequently killed while in the custody of the Sudanese People's Liberation Movement/Army, and urges the Sudanese People's Liberation Movement/Army to return the bodies to their families;

4. *Calls upon* the Government of the Sudan:

(*a*) To comply fully with its obligations under the international human rights instruments to which the Sudan is a party and to promote and protect human rights and fundamental freedoms, as well as to respect its obligations under international humanitarian law;

(*b*) To continue its efforts to ensure the rule of law by bringing legislation into line with the Constitution and the practice of law enforcement more into line with legislation;

(*c*) To continue its efforts to bring its national legislation into conformity with the applicable international human rights instruments to which the Sudan is a party and to ensure that all individuals in its territory enjoy fully the rights recognized in those instruments;

(*d*) To take all effective measures to end and to prevent all acts of torture and cruel, inhuman or degrading treatment, to ensure that all accused persons are held in ordinary custody and receive prompt, just and fair trials under internationally recognized standards and to investigate all reported acts of torture brought to its attention;

(*e*) To ensure full respect for freedom of expression, opinion, thought, conscience and religion, as well as freedom of association and assembly;

(*f*) To continue to investigate reports of the abduction of women and children taking place within the framework of the conflict in southern Sudan, to bring to trial any persons suspected of supporting or participating in such activities, to facilitate the safe return of affected children to their families as a matter of priority and to take further measures, in particular through the Committee for the Eradication of Abduction of Women and Children;

(*g*) To stop immediately the indiscriminate aerial bombardment of civilian and humanitarian targets, which runs counter to fundamental principles of human rights and humanitarian law;

(*h*) To make further efforts to address the problem of internally displaced persons;

(*i*) To continue to implement its commitment to the democratization process and the rule of law and to create, in this context, conditions that would allow for a democratization process that is genuine and wholly reflects the aspirations of the people of the country and ensures their full participation;

(*j*) To continue efforts to implement the commitment made to the Special Representative of the Secretary-General for Children and Armed Conflict not to recruit children under the age of 18 as soldiers;

(*k*) To implement the Standard Minimum Rules for the Treatment of Prisoners and to give special consideration to imprisoned women and juveniles;

5. *Encourages* the Government of the Sudan to continue to pursue its dialogue with the Office of the United Nations High Commissioner for Human Rights with a view to establishing a permanent representation of the High Commissioner;

6. *Encourages* the Office of the High Commissioner to continue to take into consideration requests for assistance by the Government of the Sudan, inter alia, with a view to establishing a permanent representation of the High Commissioner as a matter of priority;

7. *Calls upon* the international community to expand its support for activities, in particular those of the Committee for the Eradication of Abduction of Women and Children, aimed at improving respect for human rights and humanitarian law during the conflict;

8. *Decides* to continue its consideration of the situation of human rights in the Sudan at its fifty-fifth session under the item entitled "Human rights questions", in the light of further elements provided by the Commission on Human Rights.

RECORDED VOTE ON RESOLUTION 54/182:

In favour: Andorra, Angola, Argentina, Armenia, Australia, Austria, Bahamas, Barbados, Belarus, Belgium, Belize, Bolivia, Bosnia and Herzegovina, Botswana, Brazil, Bulgaria, Canada, Chile, Colombia, Costa Rica, Croatia, Cyprus, Czech Republic, Denmark, Dominica, Dominican Republic, Ecuador, El Salvador, Eritrea, Estonia, Finland, France, Georgia, Germany, Ghana, Greece, Grenada, Guatemala, Guyana, Haiti, Hungary, Iceland, Ireland, Israel, Italy, Jamaica, Japan, Kazakhstan, Latvia, Liechtenstein, Lithuania, Luxembourg, Malta, Mauritius, Mexico, Micronesia, Monaco, Mongolia, Namibia, Netherlands, New Zealand, Nicaragua, Norway, Panama, Paraguay, Peru, Poland, Portugal, Republic of Korea, Republic of Moldova, Romania, Russian Federation, Samoa, San Marino, Slovakia, Slovenia, Solomon Islands, South Africa, Spain, Sweden, Tajikistan, Thailand, The former Yugoslav Republic of Macedonia, Trinidad and Tobago, Uganda, United Kingdom, Uruguay, Venezuela, Zimbabwe.

Against: Afghanistan, Algeria, Bahrain, Chad, China, Comoros, Cuba, Democratic People's Republic of Korea, Democratic Republic of the Congo, Djibouti, Egypt, Fiji, India, Indonesia, Iran, Jordan, Kuwait, Lebanon, Libyan Arab Jamahiriya, Morocco, Myanmar, Oman, Pakistan, Qatar, Saudi Arabia, Sudan, Suriname, Syrian Arab Republic, United Arab Emirates, Viet Nam.

Abstaining: Albania, Antigua and Barbuda, Bangladesh, Benin, Bhutan, Brunei Darussalam, Burkina Faso, Cambodia, Cameroon, Cape Verde, Congo, Côte d'Ivoire, Gabon, Guinea, Guinea-Bissau, Kenya, Lao People's Democratic Republic, Malawi, Malaysia, Maldives, Mali, Marshall Islands, Mozambique, Nepal, Nigeria, Papua New Guinea, Philippines, Saint Lucia, Senegal, Sierra Leone, Singapore, Sri Lanka, Swaziland, Togo, Tunisia, Ukraine, United Republic of Tanzania, United States, Zambia.

Togo

A note by the Secretary-General [E/CN.4/Sub.2/2000/8] stated that the Subcommission had before it a report issued on 5 May by Amnesty International on the human rights situation in Togo, based on a fact-finding mission conducted in November and December 1998. It told of torture and extrajudicial execution of several hundred victims in Togo in 1998 and of enforced disappearances, arrests, arbitrary detention, ill-treatment and deaths in detention caused by the poor conditions in which detainees were kept. The Subcommission Chairman, in a statement on 20 August, took note of the controversy as to whether, or the extent to which, those allegations were true, and welcomed Togo's proposal to agree to an international commission of inquiry, to be set up by the UN and OAU Secretaries-General.

Americas

Colombia

Report of High Commissioner. A report of the High Commissioner described the activities of OHCHR in Colombia in 1999 [E/CN.4/2000/11].

During the year, 1,376 complaints were received, 211 communications were sent to the authorities and many direct representations were made. OHCHR members visited various parts of the country, making 56 on-site visits outside of Bogotá. The Office increased its legal advisory activities and attended many working meetings of committees and other bodies in order to promote the investigation of violations of human rights and international humanitarian law and to identify action to protect such rights. Regarding advisory and technical assistance activities, OHCHR intensified talks with Colombian institutions responsible for human rights promotion and protection, as well as with NGOs and academic institutions.

Serious violations of civil and political rights occurred in 1999 throughout the territory, including violations of the right to life, personal integrity, liberty and security of person, freedom of movement and residence, and due process. The main concerns of OHCHR were the seriousness of internal displacement, the problem of impunity and the weakening of government agencies. The armed conflict worsened and had serious consequences for civilians as the paramilitary groups intensified their activities by killing civilians and the guerrillas increased hostage-taking, at times on a large scale. The Government had not prioritized human rights, and none of the parties to the hostilities had made any obvious effort to respect minimum humanitarian standards that would alleviate the suffering of civilians. The State bore responsibility for the complexity of the paramilitary problem, and had taken insufficient action on displacement. The problem of impunity persisted, and no changes had been made in the context of economic, social and cultural rights that would encourage their equitable exercise. The High Commissioner urged parties to the armed conflict to respect international humanitarian law, and encouraged government efforts to achieve a negotiated solution to the armed conflict. Colombia was urged to combat paramilitarism, to respond adequately to the serious problem of displacement and to assume responsibility for protecting the life and integrity of prosecutors, judges, judicial police officials, victims and witnesses, without violating the fundamental rights of the accused. Other recommendations dealt with impunity, the new Military Penal Code, the right of habeas corpus, reform of the prison system and improved conditions of detention, bringing domestic legislation into line with the 1989 Convention on the Rights of the Child, adopted by the General Assembly in resolution 44/25 [YUN 1989, p. 560], the adoption of domestic legislation on racial discrimination, and freedom of association and protection of the right to organize.

Communications. Colombia submitted its comments [E/CN.4/2000/117] on the High Commissioner's report. Regarding the ongoing peace process, Colombia claimed that the report understated the high degree of political will that had been mobilized and sustained, with a view to building a climate of confidence between the parties. There was also no mention of the countrywide popular movement calling for peace and an end to the crimes committed by irregular armed groups. Other comments referred to the lack of information on the impact of drug trafficking and the illicit drug economy, the report's description of self-defence groups and its appraisal of the legal status of such groups.

In April [E/CN.4/1999/141], Colombia had submitted comments on the High Commissioner's report describing activities in 1998 [YUN 1998, p. 739].

Commission action. On 27 April [E/1999/23], the Chairperson, on behalf of the Commission, welcomed the renewal of the agreement between the Government of Colombia and the High Commissioner to extend the mandate of the permanent office in Bogotá until 30 April 2000. The Commission acknowledged the steps taken by the Government for the application of humanitarian standards in the conflict. It deplored the fact that its recommendations, as well as those made by thematic mechanisms and other UN bodies, had not been fully implemented. It also deplored the prolonged occurrence of serious and massive violations of human rights and of international humanitarian law, condemned the high rates of judicial impunity in cases of serious crime and expressed profound concern over the attacks against human rights defenders. The High Commissioner was asked to report in 2000 on OHCHR activities in Colombia.

(See pp. 646 and 675 for information regarding the visit to Colombia of the Secretary-General's representative on internally displaced persons and of the Secretary-General's Special Representative on children and armed conflict.)

Cuba

Commission action. On 23 April [res. 1999/8], by a roll-call vote of 21 to 20, with 12 abstentions, the Commission called on Cuba to ensure respect for human rights and fundamental freedoms, and to guarantee the rule of law through democratic institutions and the independence of the judicial system. It expressed concern about the repression of political opposition members and the detention of dissidents, most recently the four members of the Internal Dissidence Working Group (see communication below), and called on the Government to release those imprisoned for peacefully expressing their political, religious and social views and for exercising their rights to full and equal participation in public affairs. Cuba was called on to consider acceding to human rights instruments to which it was not a party and to cooperate with other mechanisms of the Commission. The Commission welcomed steps that the Government had taken to open society for religious institutions and expected that citizens would be granted the right to freedom of religion and belief. It recommended that the Government take advantage of the technical cooperation programmes under OHCHR auspices (see pp. 582-590).

Communication. On 19 March [A/53/872], the EU regretted that its repeated appeals for the unconditional release of the four members of the Internal Dissidence Working Group had been ignored. The EU stated that the group had exercised the freedom of expression and could not accept that citizens who did so were criminalized by State authorities. It expressed concern about the events surrounding the trial of the four and disappointment that neither diplomats nor international media representatives were allowed to attend the trial.

(See pp. 623 and 667 for information on the visit to Cuba by the Special Rapporteur to examine the question of the use of mercenaries as a means of violating human rights and impeding the exercise of the right of peoples to self-determination and by the Special Rapporteur on violence against women.)

Mexico

On 25 August [E/CN.4/2000/2], the Subcommission welcomed positive developments in Mexico in the past year, including the ratification of the International Convention on the Protection of the Rights of All Migrant Workers and Members of their Families, adopted by the General Assembly in resolution 45/158 [YUN 1990, p. 594], as well as ratification of the Inter-American Convention on the Prevention, Punishment and Eradication of Violence against Women and the establishment of the National Programme for the Defence and Promotion of Human Rights. The Subcommission noted that on 6 June the Federal Congress approved a constitutional amendment providing for the complete autonomy of the National Commission of Human Rights, but expressed concern over the persistent allegations of torture, extrajudicial executions (see p. 633) and disappearances, as well as violations perpetrated against indigenous communities. The Government was asked to implement urgently the National Programme for the Defence and Promotion of Human Rights, as well as to investigate human rights violations and to take steps to bring the perpetrators to justice.

Asia and the Pacific

Afghanistan

Report of Special Rapporteur. Special Rapporteur Kamal Hossain (Bangladesh) visited Afghanistan (16-18 March) [E/CN.4/1999/40] to examine the human rights situation in the country. He also visited Pakistan on 15, 16 and 18-20 March.

The Special Rapporteur noted the continuation of the armed conflict (see p. 255). A daunting challenge was presented by the economic and social factors and the political realities on the ground. The economic and social factors included widespread loss of life, destruction of social and economic infrastructure, environmental degradation, food insecurity and malnutrition, high unemployment and poverty, and further increases in illicit drug production (see p. 1174). The political context was defined by a lull in the fighting as possibilities of a transition towards a negotiated peace were explored. The Special Rapporteur outlined a strategy to enable the international community to meet the urgent humanitarian needs of the Afghan people, while adhering to the commitment to establish a framework for peace based on a realization of the human rights of all Afghans.

Commission action. On 23 April [res. 1999/9], the Commission condemned the widespread violations and abuses of human rights and humanitarian law, the continuing grave human rights violations of women and girls (see pp. 670 and 1094) and the frequent practice of arbitrary arrest and detention and of summary trials, which had resulted in summary executions. It urged all Afghan parties to cease hostilities, reaffirm publicly their commitment to international human rights and principles, protect civilians, provide remedies to victims of grave violations of human rights and accepted humanitarian rules and bring perpetrators to trial, provide ICRC access to prisoners, and repeal discriminatory legislation and other measures against women. The Commission asked the parties to continue to cooperate with the Special Rapporteur. The High Commissioner was asked to ensure a human rights presence in Afghanistan to provide advice and human rights training to all the parties, as well as to intergovernmental organizations and NGOs. The Commission decided to extend the Special Rapporteur's mandate for another year, and asked him to report to the General Assembly in 1999 and to the Commission in 2000.

ECONOMIC AND SOCIAL COUNCIL ACTION

On 27 July, the Economic and Social Council, on the recommendation of the Commission on Human Rights [E/1999/23], adopted **decision 1999/226** without vote [agenda item 14 *(h)*].

Situation of human rights in Afghanistan

At its 42nd plenary meeting, on 27 July 1999, the Economic and Social Council, taking note of Commission on Human Rights resolution 1999/9 of 23 April 1999:

(a) Approved the Commission's invitation to the Secretary-General:

(i) To implement promptly, security conditions permitting, the decision to investigate fully reports of mass killings of prisoners of war and civilians, rape and other cruel treatment in Afghanistan;

(ii) To ensure that the deployment of the civilian affairs observers in Afghanistan took place as soon as possible, security conditions permitting, and that gender issues were fully incorporated into their mission;

(b) Also approved the Commission's request to the United Nations High Commissioner for Human Rights to ensure a human rights presence in the context of the United Nations activities in Afghanistan in order to provide advice and training in the field of human rights to all the Afghan parties, as well as to the intergovernmental and non-governmental organizations active in the field;

(c) Endorsed the Commission's decision to extend the mandate of the Special Rapporteur on the situation of human rights in Afghanistan for one year, and to request the Special Rapporteur to report on the situation of human rights in Afghanistan to the General Assembly at its fifty-fourth session and to the Commission on Human Rights at its fifty-sixth session.

Reports of Special Rapporteur. The Special Rapporteur visited Pakistan and Afghanistan in May and from 8 to 13 September [A/54/422].

In reaction to an uprising by the local population, Taliban forces, on 28 March, reportedly destroyed and burned houses and villages located on the road between Shiber and Bamian city (Bamian city had been the stronghold of Hezb-e-Wahdat forces up to September 1998). They also burned houses in Surkh Qul and other villages located in the Kalu valley. Hezb-e-Wahdat forces secured control of Bamian for three weeks, and the Taliban retook the city on 9 May. Following the receipt of allegations of serious human rights violations in the central highlands of Afghanistan, particularly in Bamian, the Special Rapporteur decided to seek first-hand information through interviews with newly arrived refugees from Hazarajat. Credible eyewitnesses described human rights violations, including forced displacement of civilians; deliberate burning of houses; summary executions of non-combatants, including women and children; arbitrary detentions; and forced labour. On 23 May, the Special Rapporteur met with the Special Adviser to the Taliban leadership to review with him the allegations, which were recorded in an aide-mémoire, with the request that the Taliban take action to halt the pattern of violations described therein. The text of the aide-mémoire and a letter dated 8 June received in response, as well as a series of letters of the Special Rapporteur, were appended to the Special Rapporteur's report. On 28 July, a large-scale offensive was launched by the Taliban across the Shomali Plains (see p. 261), resulting in massive displacement of civilians. Reports indicated that there were house and crop burnings, forced deportations, family separations, the separation and deportation of women, and arbitrary killings in southern Shamali. Officials in Kabul denied reports that the Taliban had systematically destroyed property and agriculture.

In September, together with the Special Rapporteur on violence against women (see preceding chapter), the Special Rapporteur visited Kabul. In discussions with the Taliban, the Special Rapporteur covered two areas: ending the externally supported military conflict and establishing a broad-based, multi-ethnic and fully representative Government; and compliance with international human rights norms, particularly with regard to women's and girls' access to education, health and employment, and measures to prevent human rights abuses, such as deliberate and arbitrary killing, abduction, torture, infliction of inhuman and degrading punishment and breaches of humanitarian law. The Special Rapporteur recommended that a human rights-based programme of humanitarian assistance should be given the highest priority to meet the basic needs essential for survival and the right to life. In that regard, he outlined a number of principles to develop and implement such a programme.

In a later report [E/CN.4/2000/33], the Special Rapporteur described actions taken in 1999 to promote the peace process, the armed conflict between the United Front and the Taliban from August to November, and grave breaches of international humanitarian law resulting from resumption of the conflict. Internally displaced persons reported that the right to the freedom of movement of women continued to be severely curtailed, with little access to employment or education; women were imprisoned without official reason in various regions; women and girls were abducted and kidnapped; and women entered into forced marriages to Taliban members. There were also reports of non-Afghans involved in the fighting; the forcible evacuation of Shia and Tajik families from Kandahar and surrounding areas; and the separation of families from central Afghanistan (Tajiks and Hazaras) and the Shomali Plains. The Special Rapporteur concluded that Afghanistan should be restored to all of its people, through reviving and sustaining a peace process, a process to fill the constitutional and political vacuum in which externally supported armed groups had imposed arbitrary rule without the consent or participation of the Afghan people, violating their human rights.

GENERAL ASSEMBLY ACTION

On 17 December [meeting 83], the General Assembly, on the recommendation of the Third Committee [A/54/605/Add.3], adopted **resolution 54/185** without vote [agenda item 116 *(c)*].

Question of human rights in Afghanistan

The General Assembly,

Guided by the Charter of the United Nations, the Universal Declaration of Human Rights, the International Covenants on Human Rights and accepted humanitarian rules, as set out in the Geneva Conventions of 12 August 1949 and the Additional Protocols thereto, of 1977,

Reaffirming that all Member States have an obligation to promote and protect human rights and fundamental freedoms and to fulfil the obligations they have freely undertaken under the various international instruments,

Recalling that Afghanistan is a party to the Convention on the Prevention and Punishment of the Crime of Genocide, the International Covenant on Civil and Political Rights, the International Covenant on Economic, Social and Cultural Rights, the Convention against Torture and Other Cruel, Inhuman or Degrading Treatment or Punishment, the Convention on the Rights of the Child and the Geneva Convention relative to the Protection of Civilian Persons in Time of War and that it has signed the Convention on the Elimination of All Forms of Discrimination against Women,

Recalling also all its relevant resolutions, as well as the resolutions and presidential statements of the Security Council, the decisions of the Economic and Social Council and the resolutions and decisions of the Commission on Human Rights,

Recalling further that the United Nations continues to play its central and impartial role in international efforts towards a peaceful resolution of the Afghan conflict, and encouraging all efforts at the national, regional and international levels aimed at finding a solution to the continuing conflict through a broad-based dialogue involving all concerned actors,

1. *Takes note with appreciation* of the interim report of the Special Rapporteur of the Commission on Human Rights on the situation of human rights in Afghanistan

and of the conclusions and recommendations contained therein;

2. *Strongly condemns* the mass killings and systematic human rights violations against civilians and prisoners of war, including in the areas of Mazar-e Sharif and Bamian, and notes with alarm the resumption by the Taliban of the wider conflict during the past summer, especially in the Shamali Valley, resulting in the massive, forced displacement of the civilian population, in particular of women and children;

3. *Condemns* the widespread violations and abuses of human rights and humanitarian law, including the rights to life, liberty and security of person, freedom from torture and from other forms of cruel, inhuman or degrading treatment or punishment, freedom of opinion, expression, religion, association and movement, the forced or compulsory recruitment of children for use in armed conflict and, in particular, the grave human rights violations against women and girls;

4. *Reiterates its condemnation* of the killings of Iranian diplomats and the correspondent of the Islamic Republic News Agency by the Taliban, which constituted flagrant violations of established international law, as well as of the attacks on and killing of United Nations personnel in Taliban-held territories of Afghanistan, and calls upon the Taliban to fulfil their stated commitment to cooperate in urgent investigations of these heinous crimes with a view to bringing those responsible to justice;

5. *Notes with deep concern*:

(*a*) The persisting pattern of human rights violations in Afghanistan;

(*b*) The continuing and substantiated reports of human rights violations against women and girls, including all forms of discrimination against them, notably in areas under the control of the Taliban;

(*c*) The intensification of armed hostilities in Afghanistan and the complex nature of the conflict, including its ethnic, religious and political aspects, which have resulted in extensive human suffering and forced displacement, including on the grounds of ethnicity;

(*d*) The continued displacement of millions of Afghan refugees to the Islamic Republic of Iran, Pakistan and other countries;

(*e*) The lack of major reconstruction in Afghanistan;

6. *Also notes with deep concern* the sharp deterioration of the humanitarian situation in several areas of Afghanistan, in particular in the Shamali and Panjshir valleys, and calls for the full implementation of the agreement on the security of United Nations personnel in Afghanistan;

7. *Urges* all States to respect the sovereignty, independence, territorial integrity and national unity of Afghanistan, to refrain from interfering in its internal affairs and to end immediately the supply of arms, ammunition, military equipment, training or any other military support, including the provision of foreign military personnel, to all parties to the conflict;

8. *Urges* all the Afghan parties:

(*a*) To respect fully all human rights and fundamental freedoms, regardless of gender, ethnicity or religion, in accordance with international human rights instruments;

(*b*) To cease hostilities immediately, to work and cooperate fully with the Special Envoy of the Secretary-General for Afghanistan and the United Nations Special Mission to Afghanistan with a view to achieving a ceasefire and to implement the Tashkent Declaration on Fundamental Principles for a Peaceful Settlement of the Conflict in Afghanistan of 19 July 1999, thus laying the foundation for a comprehensive political solution leading to the voluntary return of displaced persons to their homes in safety and with dignity and to the establishment of a broad-based, multi-ethnic, fully representative Government through the full exercise of the Afghan people of the right to self-determination;

(*c*) To reaffirm publicly their commitment to international human rights and principles and to recognize, promote and protect all human rights and fundamental freedoms;

(*d*) To respect fully international humanitarian law, to protect civilians, to halt the use of weapons against the civilian population, to refrain from the wanton destruction of food crops and civilian property, in particular homes, to stop the laying of landmines, especially anti-personnel mines, to prohibit conscripting or enlisting children or using them to participate in hostilities in violation of international law and to ensure the disarmament, demobilization and reintegration of children into society;

(*e*) To provide efficient and effective remedies to the victims of grave violations and abuses of human rights and of international humanitarian law and to bring the perpetrators to trial;

(*f*) To treat all suspects and convicted or detained persons in accordance with relevant international instruments and to refrain from arbitrary detention, including detention of civilian foreign nationals, and urges their captors to release them as well as noncriminal civilian prisoners;

9. *Demands* that all the Afghan parties fulfil their obligations regarding the safety of all personnel of diplomatic missions, the United Nations and other international organizations, as well as their premises in Afghanistan, and to cooperate fully and without discrimination on grounds of gender, nationality or religion with the United Nations and associated bodies and with other humanitarian organizations, agencies and non-governmental organizations;

10. *Urges* all the Afghan parties, in particular the Taliban, to bring to an end without delay all violations of human rights against women and girls and to take urgent measures to ensure:

(*a*) The repeal of all legislative and other measures that discriminate against women and girls and those that impede the realization of all their human rights;

(*b*) The effective participation of women in civil, cultural, economic, political and social life throughout the country;

(*c*) Respect for the right of women to work and their reintegration into employment;

(*d*) The right of women and girls to education without discrimination, the reopening of schools and the admission of women and girls to all levels of education;

(*e*) Respect for the right of women to security of person, and that those responsible for physical attacks on women are brought to justice;

(*f*) Respect for the freedom of movement of women and their effective and equal access to the facilities necessary to protect their right to the highest attainable standard of physical and mental health;

11. *Notes with appreciation* the visit of the Special Rapporteur of the Commission on Human Rights on violence against women, its causes and consequences, and looks forward to her conclusions and recommendations;

12. *Also notes with appreciation* the activities carried out by the International Committee of the Red Cross throughout the territory of Afghanistan;

13. *Invites* the Secretary-General and the United Nations High Commissioner for Human Rights to proceed without delay to investigate fully reports of mass killings of prisoners of war and civilians, rape and cruel treatment in Afghanistan, and calls upon the United Front and the Taliban to fulfil their stated commitment to cooperate with such investigations;

14. *Also invites* the Secretary-General and the High Commissioner to ensure that the ongoing process of deployment of the civilian affairs observers in Afghanistan is completed as soon as possible and that gender issues and the rights of children are fully taken into account in their mission;

15. *Appeals* to all States, organizations and programmes of the United Nations system, specialized agencies and other international organizations to provide humanitarian assistance to all in need as soon as the situation on the ground permits and as part of an overall effort to achieve peace;

16. *Expresses its deep concern* at reports of attacks on and looting of cultural artifacts in Afghanistan, emphasizes that all parties share the responsibility to protect their common heritage, and requests all Member States to take appropriate measures to prevent the looting of cultural artifacts and to ensure their return to Afghanistan;

17. *Urges* all the Afghan parties to extend their cooperation to the Commission on Human Rights and its Special Rapporteur on the situation of human rights in Afghanistan and to all those special rapporteurs who are seeking invitations;

18. *Requests* the Secretary-General to give all necessary assistance to the Special Rapporteur;

19. *Decides* to keep the situation of human rights in Afghanistan under consideration at its fifty-fifth session, in the light of additional elements provided by the Commission on Human Rights and the Economic and Social Council.

Bhutan-Nepal

In a statement by its Chairman, the Subcommission, on 27 August [E/CN.4/2000/2], regretted that no progress had been made in the resolution of the human rights situation of persons mainly of Nepalese ethnicity who had claimed to be refugees from Bhutan and who, during the past seven or eight years, had been living in camps in Nepal administered by UNHCR. It expressed satisfaction that negotiations between the two Governments were scheduled to take place in September to seek a solution to the problem. It suggested that the two Governments avail themselves of technical assistance from OHCHR and UNHCR.

Cambodia

For information on the human rights situation in Cambodia, see p. 584.

China

On 23 April [E/1999/23], China made a motion that no action be taken on a draft text introduced in the Commission by the United States, which, among other things, called on China to ensure the observance of all human rights, improve the impartial administration of the rule of law, release political prisoners, preserve and protect the cultural, ethnic, linguistic and religious identity of Tibetans and others, and cooperate with the Commission's thematic special rapporteurs and working groups and engage in a dialogue with the High Commissioner. A roll-call vote on the motion was carried by 22 to 17, with 14 abstentions.

East Timor

On the basis of the Agreement between Indonesia and Portugal on the question of East Timor of 5 May 1999 (the General Agreement) and the Agreements between the United Nations and the Governments of Indonesia and Portugal of the same date regarding the modalities for the popular consultation of the East Timorese through a direct ballot and on security arrangements [A/53/951-S/1999/513], the people of East Timor participated in a popular consultation on the future of the territory on 30 August. The agreements stressed that the responsibility for ensuring a secure environment devoid of violence or other forms of intimidation would rest with the appropriate Indonesian security authorities. Further, they underscored that the absolute neutrality of the Indonesian Armed Forces (TNI) and the Indonesian Police would be essential. On 11 June, the United Nations Mission in East Timor (UNAMET) was established to organize and conduct the popular consultation. Despite several incidents, particularly violence and threats at the time of voter registration, the preparations prior to the consultation, as well as the voting itself, proceeded satisfactorily. In announcing the results of the ballot, in which over 78 per cent of voters opted for an independent East Timor, the Secretary-General asked all parties to bring an end to the violence that, for 24 years, had caused untold suffering to East Timor and to begin a process of dialogue and reconciliation through the East Timor Consultative Commission. His call, however, was not heeded and violence by different militia groups, in which elements of the security forces were also involved, targeting those who supported independence, as well as UN and other international staff, led to grave human rights violations. Thousands of East Timorese were expelled or fled the territory, many were killed and property was destroyed.

(For political details, see PART ONE, Chapters IV and VIII, and for information on humanitarian assistance and on refugees and displaced persons, see PART THREE, Chapters III and XII, respectively.)

Report of Secretary-General. In March [E/CN.4/1999/28], the Secretary-General stated that in the preceding year significant progress had been achieved, through the good offices of the Secretary-General, towards a solution to the question of East Timor. Agreement had been reached between Indonesia and Portugal to consult the East Timorese people to determine whether they would accept a proposed plan to give East Timor an autonomous status within the unitary State of Indonesia or opt for a transition to independence. In February, in response to the Secretary-General's repeated appeals for the release of the East Timorese resistance leader, Xanana Gusmão, who was serving a 20-year prison term in Jakarta, the Government of Indonesia transferred him to a residence in Jakarta, with a view to facilitating his participation in the efforts to resolve the question of East Timor. The Secretary-General described relevant actions taken by the Commission's thematic special rapporteurs and working groups, notably a visit in 1999 to Indonesia by the Working Group on Arbitrary Detention (see p. 626) and a visit in 1998 by the Special Rapporteur on violence against women, its causes and consequences [YUN 1998, p. 700]. Annexed to the report was information on human rights issues in East Timor provided by Indonesia and by Portugal.

Subcommission action. On 25 August [E/CN.4/2000/2], the Subcommission Chairman stated that the Subcommission was encouraged by significant improvements towards the protection of human rights in Indonesia, but remained concerned at the persistent reports of human rights violations.

Commission action. The Commission on Human Rights held its fourth special session in Geneva on 23, 24 and 27 September [E/1999/23/Add.1], pursuant to a request by Portugal and agreement by the majority of Commission members to convene to discuss the situation in East Timor.

On 27 September [res. 1999/S-4/1], the Commission welcomed Indonesia's decision to allow the exercise by the East Timorese of their right of self-determination and their participation in the free and fair popular consultation of 30 August, as well as Indonesia's announcement on 4 September of its intention to honour the result of the popular consultation. It also welcomed the Secretary-General's efforts to promote the consultation and to implement the General Agreement; Indonesia's invitation for an international force in East Timor; the High Commissioner's efforts to address the situation, including her visit to Darwin, Australia, and Jakarta (see below); the assurances by the Indonesian authorities that displaced persons had the freedom to exercise their right to return voluntarily, assurances regarding the activities of UNHCR and other international humanitarian organizations, including the security of UNHCR personnel, and further assurances regarding free access to all displaced persons, particularly in West Timor; the humanitarian response to the current crisis (see p. 840); and the establishment on 22 September of the independent Fact-Finding Commission for Post-Ballot Human Rights Violations in East Timor by the Indonesian National Commission on Human Rights (NCHR).

The Commission condemned the widespread, systematic and gross violations of human rights and international humanitarian law in East Timor; widespread violations and abuses of the right to life, personal security, physical integrity and the right to property; and the activities of the militias in terrorizing the population. Expressing deep concern at the widespread forced removal and dislocation of persons to West Timor and other nearby areas, the serious humanitarian situation of the displaced East Timorese, the violence and intimidation directed against international agencies, as well as the independent media, and the lack of effective measures to prevent militia violence and the reported collusion between the militias and members of the Indonesian armed forces and police in East Timor, the Commission called on Indonesia to: ensure, in cooperation with NCHR, that the persons responsible for acts of violence and systematic human rights violations were brought to justice; ensure full respect for human rights and international humanitarian law regarding all persons within its jurisdiction or under its control; continue to implement its obligations under the General Agreement; guarantee the voluntary return of all refugees and displaced persons, including those forcibly displaced to camps in West Timor; ensure immediate access by humanitarian agencies to displaced persons, and guarantee the security and free movement of international personnel; continue to allow the deployment of emergency humanitarian assistance; and cooperate fully with the High Commissioner and the Commission's special procedures and with OHCHR in Jakarta.

The Secretary-General was called on to establish an international commission of inquiry, with adequate representation of Asian experts, in cooperation with NCHR and thematic rapporteurs, in order to gather and compile information on possible human rights violations and acts that might constitute breaches of international humanitarian law committed in East Timor since the announcement in January 1999 of the consultation and to provide the Secretary-General with its conclusions in order for him to make recommendations, and to report to the Security Council, the General Assembly and the Commission in 2000. The Commission decided to request the Special Rapporteur on extrajudicial, summary or arbitrary executions, the Representative of the Secretary-General on internally displaced persons, the Special Rapporteur on the question of torture, the Special Rapporteur on violence against women, its causes and consequences, and the Working Group on Enforced or Involuntary Disappearances to carry out missions to East Timor and report to the Commission in 2000 and, on an interim basis, to the Assembly in 1999. It also decided to ask the High Commissioner to facilitate the activities of the mechanism of the Commission, to prepare a comprehensive programme of human rights technical cooperation, in cooperation with other UN activities, focusing on capacity-building and reconciliation with a view to a durable solution to the problems in East Timor, and to keep the Commission informed of developments.

In previous action, on 23 April [E/1999/23], the Commission Chairperson, on behalf of the Commission, expressed concern at the serious human rights situation and at the outbreaks of violence in East Timor and asked the Secretary-General to report in 2000.

ECONOMIC AND SOCIAL ACTION

On 15 November, the Economic and Social Council, on the recommendation of the Commission on Human Rights [E/1999/23/Add.1], adopted **decision 1999/293** by recorded vote (27-10-11) [agenda item 14 *(h)*].

Situation of human rights in East Timor

At its 50th plenary meeting, on 15 November 1999, the Economic and Social Council:

(a) Took note of Commission on Human Rights resolution 1999/S-4/1 of 27 September 1999, and endorsed the Commission's call upon the Secretary-General to establish an international commission of inquiry, with adequate representation of Asian experts, in order, in cooperation with the Indonesian National Commission on Human Rights and thematic rapporteurs, to gather and compile systematically information on possible violations of human rights and acts that might constitute breaches of international humanitarian law committed in East Timor since the announcement in January 1999 of the vote and to provide the Secretary-General with its conclusions with a view to enabling him to make recommendations on future actions, and to make the report of the commission of inquiry available to the Security Council, the General Assembly and the Commission on Human Rights at its fifty-sixth session;

(b) Also took note of the decision of the Commission to request the Special Rapporteur on extrajudicial, summary or arbitrary executions, the Representative of the Secretary-General on internally displaced persons, the Special Rapporteur on the question of torture, the Special Rapporteur on violence against women, its causes and consequences, and the Working Group on Enforced or Involuntary Disappearances to carry out missions to East Timor and report on their findings to the Commission at its fifty-sixth session and, on an interim basis, to the General Assembly at its fifty-fourth session, and to request the United Nations High Commissioner for Human Rights to prepare a comprehensive programme of technical cooperation in the field of human rights, in cooperation with other United Nations activities, focusing especially on capacity-building and reconciliation with a view to a durable solution to the problems in East Timor.

RECORDED VOTE ON DECISION 1999/293:

In favour: Belgium, Bolivia, Brazil, Bulgaria, Canada, Cape Verde, Chile, Colombia, Czech Republic, Denmark, El Salvador, France, Germany, Guinea-Bissau, Honduras, Iceland, Italy, Latvia, Lesotho, Mauritius, Mozambique, New Zealand, Norway, Poland, Spain, United Kingdom, United States.

Against: China, India, Indonesia, Oman, Pakistan, Russian Federation, Saudi Arabia, Sri Lanka, Syrian Arab Republic, Viet Nam.

Abstaining: Algeria, Belarus, Cuba, Djibouti, Japan, Mexico, Morocco, Republic of Korea, Sierra Leone, Turkey, Venezuela.

Report of High Commissioner. The High Commissioner visited Darwin and Jakarta from 10 to 13 September, to assess the situation in East Timor, discuss with the authorities involved actions necessary to protect the human rights of civilians and gather information that might assist the Commission, the Secretary-General, the Security Council and others [E/CN.4/2000/44].

Since the results of the popular consultation were announced on 3 September 1999, there was a breakdown of law and order. Martial law, declared on 7 September, did not stabilize the situation. Armed members of pro-integration militias had erected roadblocks throughout the capital, Dili, and controlled the streets, and militia members terrorized and murdered unarmed civilians, burned houses, displaced large numbers of people, and intimidated, threatened and attacked personnel of international organizations. UN staff in East Timor witnessed militia members perpetrating acts of violence in full view of heavily armed police and military personnel, who either stood by and watched or actively assisted the militias. Many pro-independence activists and other community leaders, including the clergy, were reported to have been killed for their support of independence. There were also reports of mass killings at various locations, including in Dili, where 15 Catholic priests and the director of a humanitarian organization, Caritas, together with many of his staff, had reportedly been summarily executed. In an attack at the residence of Nobel Peace Prize laureate Bishop Carlos Belo, militiamen reportedly hacked to death some 40 persons in the courtyard while TNI soldiers fired into the bishop's residence from the street. On 30 August, a UNAMET local staff member was killed in Atsabe, and on 1 September, at least two persons were killed while seeking refuge in UNAMET headquarters. Journalists and international humanitarian workers, as well as displaced persons, had reportedly been assaulted at displaced person camps, possibly by militia members. On 8 September, the Chairman-Rapporteur of the Working Group on Arbitrary Detention, the Representative of the Secretary-General on internally displaced persons, the Special Rapporteur on extrajudicial, summary or arbitrary executions and the Special Rapporteur on the question of torture sent an urgent appeal to the Government of Indonesia following information received concerning attacks by regular and irregular armed elements, which had resulted in over 100 individuals being killed.

Reports were received that 120,000 to 200,000 persons had been forcibly displaced—nearly one fourth of the entire population. Plans for systematic attacks on villages and the forced displacement of East Timorese were said to have been leaked as early as July. Those reports were denied by the authorities. On 6 September, UNAMET was forced to evacuate all eight of its regional offices and to evacuate a large number of international staff from its headquarters in Dili. Also on 6 September, armed militiamen carried out attacks against the ICRC office in Dili where some 2,000 displaced people had sought refuge. ICRC evacuated its expatriate staff to Darwin. According to reports from Kalyanamitra, women were raped and sexually harassed by militia and Indonesian military in Dili between 7 and 10 September. Sexual violence also allegedly occurred during the forced movement of people to West Timor. OHCHR received reports of thousands of involuntary or enforced disappearances. UNHCR was alarmed by cases of men being separated from their women and children. Media reports indicated that the militia were preventing men from leaving East Timor. Those displaced by the violence, in both East Timor and West Timor, faced the threat of malnutrition and disease as domestic and international humanitarian efforts were hampered by militia and military activity that blocked access to camps for displaced persons. They had no access to food, water, urgently needed medicine, shelter, sanitation and human security. Many were barely surviving on roots and leaves.

In West Timor, armed militia were reportedly operating with official support. Many of those displaced into West Timor stated that their identification documents were confiscated by the militia. The Indonesian military and police had reportedly prevented international aid workers, journalists and observers from visiting camps in West Timor and from interviewing East Timorese. UNHCR staff were assaulted and foreign aid workers sustained injuries after being stoned in the Nolebake camp. In Dili, reliable sources said that hundreds of houses had been burned, the entire business district completely destroyed and almost all houses emptied of their valuable contents. In all cases, those involved had acted with impunity and been given protection by the Indonesian police and military. Journalists and observers were reportedly forced at gunpoint by Indonesian police to evacuate their hotels and residences in East Timor and West Timor on 5 and 6 September and were driven to the airport. A small number of journalists refused to leave and took refuge at UNAMET headquarters.

The High Commissioner condemned those responsible in the strongest possible terms. She urged the Indonesian authorities to cooperate in the establishment of an international commission of inquiry into the violations so that those responsible were brought to justice. A multinational force to assist in restoring peace and security in East Timor was vital to protect the human rights of East Timorese. It would help stop systematic killings, displacement, destruction of property and intimidation carried out by militia groups and elements of the security forces. The High Commissioner also recommended that the Indonesian authorities should facilitate the immediate access of aid agencies to those in need; secure conditions to ensure the safety of humanitarian aid workers; and airdrops should be deployed to assist the displaced. The cooperation of Indonesia with the United Nations was vital to ensure human rights protection for the East Timorese during the transition process to the implementation of the agreements of 5 May 1999. The High Commissioner intended to keep the Commission informed of developments and efforts to bring the perpetrators of gross violations to justice.

Joint mission. Pursuant to Commission resolution 1999/S-4/1 (see p. 708), the Special Rapporteur on extrajudicial, summary or arbitrary executions, Asma Jahangir (Pakistan), the Special Rapporteur on the question of torture, Nigel Rodley (United Kingdom), and the Special Rapporteur on violence against women, its causes and consequences, Radhika Coomaraswamy (Sri Lanka), visited East Timor (4-10 November) [A/54/660]. The report on the mission focused on human rights abuses committed since January 1999. Many of the observations presented were not conclusive and were aimed at highlighting issues that required further attention, including criminal and forensic investigation.

The Special Rapporteur on extrajudicial, summary or arbitrary executions stated that, according to information provided by the International Force, East Timor (INTERFET)—an international intervention force deployed on 20 September to provide security, facilitate the distribution of humanitarian aid and re-establish law and order in East Timor—extrajudicial killings up to 10 November 1999 totalled 1,093 persons. NGOs had received information of killings of over 1,500 people. As more than 400,000 people had been displaced and many had lost contact with relatives in the process, it was difficult to ascertain the number of missing persons. There were reports of continuing abuses by militia elements directed against displaced East Timorese civilians in camps in West Timor. INTERFET military police and UN civilian police officers in charge of investigating alleged crimes and human rights violations complained of the lack of forensic and other facilities for investigating crime scenes and exhuming bodies of persons alleged to have been extrajudicially killed.

The Special Rapporteur on the question of torture observed that the bulk of allegations of torture and ill-treatment related to such treatment either as a prelude to murder or as taking the form of sexual violence. He had received numerous allegations from NGOs that in early 1999 persons were seized by militia groups, sometimes acting in collaboration with TNI, and subjected to torture, such as beatings and woundings with sticks, machetes, spears, knives and rifle butts. The Special Rapporteur found the allegations sufficiently substantiated and consistent to transmit them to Indonesia for its observations.

The Special Rapporteur on violence against women received many reports of such violence, allegedly committed by the Indonesian armed forces in East Timor. Relatives of political opponents were raped by the military as a form of revenge or to force their relatives out of hiding. At the time of the Special Rapporteur's visit, rape of Timorese women reportedly continued; however, the Regional Army Commander in Dili assured the Special Rapporteur that he would not tolerate violence against women by the armed forces. There were cases of sexual slavery, sexual violence as a means of intimidation and sexual violence as a result of the climate of impunity, as well as reports of violence against women in refugee camps in West Timor. The Special Rapporteur was concerned that INTERFET did not include any expertise in cases of sexual violence.

As to State responsibility, the joint mission concluded that, while most of the atrocities in East Timor were attributable to pro-integration militias, there was evidence of the direct and indirect involvement of TNI and police in supporting, planning, assisting and organizing the pro-integration militia groups, thus incurring the responsibility of the Indonesian Government. Credible information received during the joint mission indicated that, as at the end of 1998, at least 22 new militia groups had been formed in East Timor, reportedly armed and paid by Indonesian army intelligence to unleash terror and violence in East Timor. Under the 5 May agreements, the Government of Indonesia assumed responsibility for maintaining peace and security in East Timor to ensure that the popular consultation was carried out in an atmosphere free from intimidation, violence or interference. The Government had not disclosed any security arrangements, despite widespread reports of violence by militia groups acting in collusion with TNI and the police.

The Special Rapporteurs recommended that Indonesia secure unimpeded access of UNHCR to the camps in West Timor and comply with the call of NCHR to disband the militias. The most pressing needs of the United Nations Transitional Administration in East Timor (UNTAET), established by the Security Council on 25 October to support the Territory's transition to independence (see p. 293), should be met. Those needs included expertise in forensic anthropology and pathology, autopsy facilities, medical professionals, criminal investigation and relevant staff for an effective information storage and retrieval system. They also recommended: making available psychiatric services, counselling and rehabilitation to victims of human rights violations; UNTAET efforts to involve the East Timorese in institution-building and governance, including economic development; Security Council action to establish an international criminal tribunal to bring perpetrators of the atrocities to justice; investigation of State, institutional and individual responsibility for the crimes over the past year; support by the international community to UNTAET; and special attention by UNTAET and the international community to support NGOs and other civil society institutions.

(For information on a visit by the Working Group on Arbitrary Detention to Indonesia, see p. 626.)

International Commission of Inquiry. In accordance with Commission resolution 1999/S-4/1 (see p. 708), the Secretary-General transmitted the report of the International Commission of Inquiry on East Timor (ICI) [A/54/726-S/2000/59], established by him to compile information on possible human rights violations and acts that might have constituted breaches of international humanitarian law committed since January 1999.

The five-member Commission convened its first meetings (Geneva, 18-20 November) to meet with the High Commissioner and hold briefings with the ICI secretariat. On 23 and 24 November, ICI met in Darwin to finalize its working methods and to meet with the former Special Representative of the Secretary-General, the UNAMET Commissioner of Police and representatives of the Indonesian National Commission of Inquiry on East Timor.

ICI visited East Timor from 25 November to 3 December where, over the nine-day period, it received detailed testimonies from 170 victims and witnesses. As the number of victims who wished to testify became overwhelming, the Commission was unable to interview them all. ICI also considered the reports of experts, information provided by the United Nations in East Timor and INTERFET, reports of other organizations, as well as information and views provided by the Government of Indonesia and by the Indonesian Commission of Inquiry.

The evidence gathered clearly demonstrated a pattern of serious violations of fundamental human rights and humanitarian law in East Timor, which took the form of systematic intimidation and terror, destruction of property, violence against women and displacement of people. Intimidation and terror, particularly aimed at pro-independence groups and individuals, prevented people from freely exercising their political choice. There was evidence of threats of violence, violence resulting in injuries and brutal killings in large numbers. Because men fled to the mountains, the women were targeted for sexual assault in a cruel and systematic way. UNAMET and other agencies' staff, as well as journalists and others, were evacuated, apparently to prevent them from witnessing violent acts and destruction of property. Prior to the popular consultation, the destruction of property was selective, involving properties of individuals known to support independence, but, following the announcement of the results, the destruction became widespread and systematic, with damage to property ranging from 60 to 80 per cent in the whole country. Most hospitals, health centres and school buildings were destroyed, and public utilities damaged.

Before the popular consultation ballot, intimidation and terror, including killings in places of refuge, denial of access to humanitarian agencies, and denial of necessities, such as water, resulted in internal displacement. Following the popular consultation, thousands of people were forcibly assembled and moved to camps in West Timor, where they were subjected to intimidation and terror, including abduction of children. There was a systematic attempt to destroy evidence, including removal of corpses from the sites of killings. Evidence showed that militia groups were responsible for the intimidation and terror before and after the popular consultation, and that the policy of engaging militias was implemented by the Kopassus (Special Forces Command of TNI) and other units of the Indonesian army. In certain cases, Indonesian army personnel, in addition to directing the militias, were involved in acts of intimidation and terror. The Indonesian police, who were responsible for security under the 5 May agreement, appeared to have been involved in those acts as well.

ICI called for the rapid return of displaced persons; the disarming of militias in West Timor to enable the East Timorese to return home safely and the demobilization of all non-regular forces in East Timor; and respect for victims' basic human rights to justice, compensation and the truth. As the actions violating human rights and international humanitarian law in East Timor were directed against a decision of the Security Council (see PART ONE, Chapter IV) and were contrary to agreements reached by Indonesia with the United Nations to carry out that decision, a specific international response was required. The United Nations had a vested interest in participating in the process of investigation, establishing responsibility and punishing those responsible, and in promoting reconciliation. ICI recommended that the United Nations establish an independent investigation and prosecution body to: conduct further investigations of violations of human rights and of international humanitarian law in East Timor from January 1999; identify those responsible for the violations; ensure reparations for the violations from those responsible; prosecute those guilty of serious human rights violations; and consider the issues of truth and reconciliation. In addition, the United Nations should establish an international human rights tribunal consisting of UN-appointed judges, preferably with the participation of members from East Timor and Indonesia. The tribunal would sit in Indonesia, East

Timor and any other relevant territory to receive the complaints and to try and sentence those accused.

Communication. In response to the ICI report, the Minister for Foreign Affairs of Indonesia stated that, having rejected Commission resolution 1999/S-4/1 (see p. 708), which established ICI, Indonesia was bound neither by the resolution nor by the ICI conclusions and recommendations [A/54/727-S/2000/65]. In its view, the ICI report consisted of uncorroborated allegations and was one-sided. The report concentrated on violations allegedly perpetrated by pro-integration groups without cross-checking with members of those groups. Indonesia asserted that the pro-integration groups also suffered many human rights violations, and outlined reasons why the recommendation to establish an international human rights tribunal was unacceptable. It welcomed the establishment by NCHR of the National Commission of Inquiry on Human Rights Violations in East Timor (KPP-HAM). KPP-HAM had sent a fact-finding mission to East Timor, which was expected to submit a report on its findings and recommendations. The report would be transmitted to the Attorney-General to decide on legal action to be taken through the national judicial mechanism. Indonesia placed utmost confidence in the independence, credibility and competence of KPP-HAM members in accomplishing their mission.

(See also pp. 279-298.)

Iran

Commission action. On 23 April [res. 1999/13], the Commission, by a roll-call vote of 23 to 16, with 14 abstentions, noted positive statements by the Government of Iran about the need to review discriminatory measures against women, the reported elimination of discrimination against Baha'i youth in education, the increasing focus of the Islamic Human Rights Commission on the human rights situation in the country and the beginnings of a public discussion on the appropriateness of the death penalty for drug-related offences. However, it expressed concern at the continued human rights violations in Iran as reported by the Special Representative on the human rights situation in Iran [YUN 1998, p. 745]. It called on the Government, among other things, to continue its positive efforts to consolidate respect for the rule of law and to abide by its obligations under international human rights instruments; ensure that capital punishment would not be imposed for other than the most serious crimes; end discrimination against the Baha'is and other minority religious groups; end the use of torture; end discriminatory measures against women; and make use of human rights technical cooperation programmes.

The Commission decided to extend the Special Representative's mandate for a further year and asked him to submit an interim report to the General Assembly in 1999 and to report to the Commission in 2000, keeping in mind a gender perspective. The Economic and Social Council, by **decision 1999/228** of 27 July, endorsed the Commission's decision.

Reports of Special Representative. In September [A/54/365], Special Representative Maurice Copithorne (Canada) reported on the human rights situation in Iran, based on information from the Government of Iran, other Governments, the UN system, NGOs, individuals and media reports.

Tension increased markedly in July and August in the aftermath of a series of brutal murders of intellectuals and political dissidents that had occurred in November and December 1998. Efforts to consolidate freedom of expression were being challenged more vigorously, culminating in the closure of prominent reformist newspapers and the introduction of new repressive press legislation. Those and other developments played a large part in the peaceful student-initiated demonstrations that subsequently turned violent, resulting in the arrests of some 1,200 persons. As there had been little change with regard to women's rights, the Special Representative called on the Government to introduce changes in law and in practice affecting the status of women. The reform of the legal system remained an urgent matter, and the Special Representative recommended that the Government publish statistics on executions by category of offence and ensure that punishment was in accordance with international standards, as well as the laws of Iran. The status of religious minorities remained precarious and, in that regard, the Special Representative recommended that the Government address the matter of the Baha'is. Terrorism by Iranians against Iranians was on the rise within and outside the country. There continued to be progress in the development of democracy in Iran; the arrangements made to ensure open and fair elections for the sixth Majlis (Islamic Consultative Assembly) in February 2000 would be critical in that regard.

In a later report [E/CN.4/2000/35], the Special Representative covered developments that occurred between 1 July and 15 December.

Although there were improvements in the human rights situation in Iran, by international standards serious human rights violations continued to occur, particularly regarding the judiciary and the law enforcement agencies. There had been significant progress in the area of freedom of expression, except with respect to the press, where reformist-minded newspapers were susceptible to arbitrary discipline by various tribunals. The situation of women had improved in education, health and the integration of a gender dimension into government planning. However, little progress was made regarding remaining systemic barriers to equality. The Special Representative, concluding that there was insufficient political will to accord priority to the status of minorities, recommended that the Government publicly acknowledge the need for change and commit itself to addressing the human rights problems in that area. The machinery to address other areas, such as disappearance and suspicious deaths and student demonstrations, seemed inadequate. The Special Representative recommended that the announced reform of the legal system be prioritized.

GENERAL ASSEMBLY ACTION

On 17 December [meeting 83], the General Assembly, on the recommendation of the Third Committee [A/54/605/Add.3], adopted **resolution 54/177** by recorded vote (61-47-51) [agenda item 116 *(c)*].

Human rights situation in the Islamic Republic of Iran

The General Assembly,

Guided by the Charter of the United Nations, the Universal Declaration of Human Rights, the International Covenants on Human Rights, and other human rights instruments,

Reaffirming that all Member States have an obligation to promote and protect human rights and fundamental freedoms and to fulfil the obligations they have undertaken under the various international instruments in this field,

Mindful that the Islamic Republic of Iran is a party to the International Covenants on Human Rights,

Recalling its previous resolutions on this subject, including the most recent, resolution 53/158 of 9 December 1998, and taking note of Commission on Human Rights resolution 1999/13 of 23 April 1999,

1. *Welcomes* the interim report of the Special Representative of the Commission on Human Rights on the situation of human rights in the Islamic Republic of Iran;

2. *Also welcomes* the stated commitment of the Government of the Islamic Republic of Iran to promote the rule of law, including the elimination of arbitrary arrest and detention, and to reform the legal and penitentiary system and bring it into line with international human rights standards in this field;

3. *Further welcomes* the continued public debate in the Islamic Republic of Iran on issues of governance and human rights, encourages further efforts to ensure freedom of opinion, of the press and of cultural activities, and also welcomes the support given by the Government to the development of non-governmental organizations;

4. *Welcomes* the progress in democracy achieved by the holding of local elections in the Islamic Republic of Iran in February 1999, trusts that the forthcoming elections to the Majlis will be held with full respect for due democratic process, and calls upon the Government to continue its efforts towards strengthening democracy and the holding of free and fair elections;

5. *Also welcomes* the needs assessment mission undertaken by the Office of the United Nations High Commissioner for Human Rights to the Islamic Republic of Iran at the invitation of the Government, as well as the invitation by the Government to the Working Group on Enforced or Involuntary Disappearances to visit the country, and expresses the hope that the visit will take place soon;

6. *Further welcomes* the efforts undertaken by the Government of the Islamic Republic of Iran to investigate the cases of disappearances and killings of intellectuals and political activists, and calls upon the Government to continue its efforts to investigate the cases fully in due process of law and to bring the perpetrators to justice;

7. *Takes note with interest* of the gradual increase in the presence of women in public life in the Islamic Republic of Iran and the efforts made by the Government in this regard, expresses its concern at the continued discrimination in law and in practice against women, and calls upon the Government to take further measures to ensure the full and equal enjoyment by women of their human rights;

8. *Also takes note with interest* of the focus of the Islamic Human Rights Commission on the human rights situation in the Islamic Republic of Iran, and expresses the hope that the Commission will align itself with the 1993 principles relating to the status of national institutions for the promotion and protection of human rights;

9. *Expresses its concern* at continuing threats by the 15 Khordad Foundation to the life of Salman Rushdie, including the increase in the bounty announced by the Foundation after the assurance given by the Government of the Islamic Republic of Iran in New York in September 1998, and welcomes the assurance given by the Government that it has no intention of taking any action whatsoever to threaten the life of Mr. Rushdie and those associated with his work or of encouraging or assisting anyone to do so, and that it dissociates itself from any reward offered in this regard and does not support it;

10. *Also expresses its concern* that, since 1996, no invitation has been extended by the Government of the Islamic Republic of Iran to the Special Representative to visit the country, and calls upon the Government to resume its full cooperation with the Special Representative and to extend an invitation to him to visit the country;

11. *Expresses its serious concern* at the continuing violations of human rights in the Islamic Republic of Iran, as reported by the Special Representative, in particular executions in the apparent absence of respect for internationally recognized safeguards, the use of national security laws as a basis for derogating from the rights of the individual, cases of torture and cruel, inhuman or degrading treatment or punishment as well as the fail-

ure to meet international standards in the administration of justice and the absence of due process of law, and calls upon the Government of the Islamic Republic of Iran to take all necessary steps to end the use of torture and the practice of amputation, stoning and other forms of cruel, inhuman and degrading punishment;

12. *Expresses its concern* at the restrictions on freedom of expression, opinion, thought and the press and at the interference with the work of writers and journalists and the closure of publications, as well as at the circumstances surrounding the arrests of individuals based on involvement in student demonstrations and at reports that some of them may be subject to death sentences, or other harsh sentences, and calls upon the Government of the Islamic Republic of Iran to take further measures to secure freedom of expression, opinion, thought and the press;

13. *Also expresses its concern* at the discrimination against religious minorities, in particular the Baha'is, and remains gravely concerned at the unabated pattern of persecution against the Baha'is, including death sentences, arrests and the closure of the Baha'i Institute of Higher Education, and calls upon the Government of the Islamic Republic of Iran to implement fully the conclusions and recommendations of the Special Rapporteur of the Commission on Human Rights on religious intolerance relating to the Baha'is and other religious minorities until they are completely emancipated;

14. *Calls upon* the authorities of the Islamic Republic of Iran to make further efforts to ensure for all the application of due process of law by the judiciary in all instances and, in this context, to ensure a fair and transparent trial for the group of people detained early in 1999, which includes thirteen members of the Iranian Jewish community, and notes the stated commitments of the Government of the Islamic Republic of Iran in this regard;

15. *Calls upon* the Government of the Islamic Republic of Iran to continue its efforts and to abide by its freely undertaken obligations under the International Covenants on Human Rights and other international instruments on human rights, and to ensure that all individuals within its territory and subject to its jurisdiction, including persons belonging to religious minorities, enjoy the rights enshrined in those instruments;

16. *Also calls upon* the Government of the Islamic Republic of Iran to ensure that capital punishment will not be imposed for crimes other than the most serious, for apostasy or otherwise in disregard of the provisions of the International Covenant on Civil and Political Rights and United Nations safeguards, and to provide the Special Representative with relevant statistics on this matter;

17. *Decides* to continue the examination of the situation of human rights in the Islamic Republic of Iran, including the situation of minority groups such as the Baha'is, at its fifty-fifth session under the item entitled "Human rights questions", in the light of additional elements provided by the Commission on Human Rights.

RECORDED VOTE ON RESOLUTION 54/177:

In favour: Andorra, Australia, Austria, Bahamas, Barbados, Belgium, Belize, Bolivia, Brazil, Bulgaria, Canada, Chile, Costa Rica, Croatia, Czech Republic, Denmark, Dominica, Ecuador, El Salvador, Estonia, Finland, France, Germany, Greece, Grenada, Guatemala, Haiti, Honduras, Hungary, Iceland, Ireland, Israel, Italy, Japan, Latvia, Liechtenstein, Lithuania, Luxembourg, Malta, Marshall Islands, Mauritius, Micronesia, Monaco, Mongolia, Netherlands, New Zealand, Norway, Paraguay, Poland, Portugal, Romania, Samoa, San Marino, Slovakia, Slovenia, Solomon Islands, Spain, Sweden, Trinidad and Tobago, United Kingdom, United States.

Against: Afghanistan, Armenia, Azerbaijan, Bahrain, Bangladesh, Belarus, Bhutan, Brunei Darussalam, Burkina Faso, Chad, China, Colombia, Comoros, Côte d'Ivoire, Cuba, Democratic People's Republic of Korea, Democratic Republic of the Congo, Djibouti, Egypt, Ghana, India, Indonesia, Iran, Jordan, Kuwait, Lebanon, Libyan Arab Jamahiriya, Malaysia, Maldives, Morocco, Myanmar, Nepal, Oman, Pakistan, Philippines, Qatar, Saudi Arabia, Senegal, Sri Lanka, Sudan, Syrian Arab Republic, Tajikistan, Tunisia, Turkmenistan, United Republic of Tanzania, Venezuela, Viet Nam.

Abstaining: Albania, Algeria, Angola, Antigua and Barbuda, Argentina, Benin, Botswana, Cambodia, Cameroon, Cape Verde, Congo, Cyprus, Eritrea, Ethiopia, Fiji, Gabon, Georgia, Guinea, Guinea-Bissau, Guyana, Jamaica, Kenya, Lao People's Democratic Republic, Malawi, Mali, Mexico, Mozambique, Namibia, Nicaragua, Nigeria, Panama, Papua New Guinea, Peru, Republic of Korea, Republic of Moldova, Russian Federation, Saint Lucia, Sierra Leone, Singapore, South Africa, Suriname, Swaziland, Thailand, The former Yugoslav Republic of Macedonia, Togo, Uganda, Ukraine, United Arab Emirates, Uruguay, Zambia, Zimbabwe.*

*Later advised the Secretariat it had intended to vote against.

Iraq

Commission action. By a roll-call vote of 35 to none, with 18 abstentions, the Commission, on 23 April [res. 1999/14], strongly condemned the systematic, widespread and extremely grave violations of human rights and international humanitarian law by the Government of Iraq, which had resulted in an all-pervasive repression and oppression sustained by broad-based discrimination and widespread terror. It called on the Government to: abide by its obligations under international human rights treaties and international humanitarian law; conform its military and security forces to standards of international law; cooperate with UN human rights mechanisms; establish the independence of the judiciary and abrogate laws granting impunity; ensure that torture and cruel punishment and treatment no longer occurred; abrogate laws and procedures that penalized free expression; cease repressive practices aimed at ethnic and religious groups; cooperate to resolve the fate of missing persons, including victims of the Iraqi occupation of Kuwait; release detained Kuwaitis and other nationals; cooperate with aid agencies and NGOs to provide humanitarian assistance; facilitate the work of UN humanitarian personnel; ensure equitable distribution of humanitarian supplies purchased with the proceeds of Iraqi oil; and cooperate in identifying minefields in the country.

The Commission decided to: extend the Special Rapporteur's mandate for another year; ask him to submit an interim report to the General Assembly in 1999 and to report to the Commission in 2000; and request the Secretary-General to approve the allocation of resources to send human rights monitors to locations that would facilitate improved information on the human rights situation in Iraq. By **decision 1999/229** of 27 July, the Economic and Social Council endorsed the Commission's decision.

Subcommission action. On 26 August [dec. 1999/109], the Subcommission appealed to the international community, and to the Security Council in particular, for the embargo provisions affecting the humanitarian situation of the Iraqi population to be lifted and urged the international community and all Governments, including that of Iraq, to alleviate the suffering of Iraqis, particularly by facilitating the delivery of food, medical supplies and the wherewithal to meet their basic needs.

In other action, the Subcommission circulated, at Iraq's request, a study on the economic sanctions imposed on Iraq [E/CN.4/Sub.2/1999/33] and another on the use of depleted uranium and its impact on man and the environment in Iraq [E/CN.4/Sub.2/1999/32].

Report of Special Rapporteur. In October [A/54/466], Special Rapporteur Max van der Stoel (Netherlands) presented information on the human rights situation in Iraq based on information he had received up until 20 September. He had received persistent allegations of: violations of the right to life; arbitrary arrest; detention; torture and other cruel, inhuman or degrading treatment or punishment; disappearances; and violations of the rights to due process of law and freedom of movement. According to reports and testimonies, the allegations related to governmental tactics, including indiscriminate bombardment of civilian settlements and arbitrary killings; arbitrary arrest and detention of suspected traitors and criminals; and forced displacement. The situation regarding economic, social and cultural rights continued to deteriorate, as all available resources had not been used to ensure the enjoyment of those rights. The Special Rapporteur concluded that the political-legal order in the country was not compatible with respect for human rights but entailed systematic and systemic violations throughout the country, affecting the whole population. The President exercised executive and legislative power, with judges and magistrates answerable to him; the armed forces, the police and Ba'ath Party agents were in the service of the President. The courts were subject to the executive branch; political parties were banned, except for the Ba'ath Party, which was identified with the State; and there was neither freedom of speech or action nor freedom of information on radio or television. Regarding Iraq's failure to resolve the outstanding cases of the over 600 persons of Kuwaiti and third-country nationality who disappeared during or subsequent to Iraq's illegal occupation of Kuwait and who were still missing, the Special Rapporteur recommended that the Government release all those being held, reveal the names of those who had died in its custody and review the outstanding case files of the missing. He reiterated his proposal that a human rights monitoring mechanism composed of UN staff be established throughout Iraq.

Following the resignation of the Special Rapporteur, the Commission, on 22 December, appointed Andreas Mavrommatis (Cyprus) as Special Rapporteur on the situation of human rights in Iraq.

(For political details, see PART ONE, Chapter IV.)

GENERAL ASSEMBLY ACTION

On 17 December [meeting 83], the General Assembly, on the recommendation of the Third Committee [A/54/605/Add.3], adopted **resolution 54/178** by recorded vote (100-3-53) [agenda item 116 (c)].

Human rights situation in Iraq

The General Assembly,

Guided by the Charter of the United Nations, the Universal Declaration of Human Rights, the International Covenants on Human Rights, and other human rights instruments,

Reaffirming that all Member States have an obligation to promote and protect human rights and fundamental freedoms and to fulfil the obligations they have undertaken under the various international instruments in this field,

Mindful that Iraq is a party to the International Covenants on Human Rights, to other international human rights instruments and to the Geneva Conventions of 12 August 1949 for the protection of victims of war,

Recalling its previous resolutions and those of the Commission on Human Rights on the subject, and taking note of the most recent, Commission resolution 1999/14 of 23 April 1999,

Recalling also Security Council resolution 686(1991) of 2 March 1991, in which the Council called upon Iraq to release all Kuwaitis and nationals of other States who might still be held in detention, Council resolutions 687(1991) of 3 April 1991, 688(1991) of 5 April 1991, in which the Council demanded an end to repression of the Iraqi civilian population and insisted that Iraq cooperate with humanitarian organizations and that the human rights of all Iraqi citizens be respected, and Council resolutions 986(1995) of 14 April 1995, 1111(1997) of 4 June 1997, 1129(1997) of 12 September 1997, 1143(1997) of 4 December 1997, 1153(1998) of 20 February 1998, 1175(1998) of 19 June 1998, 1210 (1998) of 24 November 1998, 1242(1999) of 21 May 1999 and 1266(1999) of 4 October 1999, by which the Council authorized States to permit imports of Iraqi oil in order to allow Iraq to purchase humanitarian supplies,

Taking note of the concluding observations of the Human Rights Committee, the Committee on the Elimination of Racial Discrimination, the Committee on Economic, Social and Cultural Rights and the Committee on the Rights of the Child on the recent reports submitted to them by Iraq, in which these treaty-monitoring bodies point to a wide range of human rights problems and hold the view that the Government of Iraq remains bound by its treaty obligations, while pointing to the adverse effect of sanctions on the daily life of the population, including children,

Taking note also of the reports of the Secretary-General concerning the implementation of Security Council resolutions 986(1995), 1111(1997), 1143(1997), 1175(1998), 1210(1998), 1242(1999) and, in particular, his report of 19 August 1999 concerning the implementation of Council resolution 1242(1999),

Reaffirming that it is the responsibility of the Government of Iraq to ensure the well-being of its entire population and the full enjoyment of all human rights and fundamental freedoms, concerned about the dire humanitarian situation in Iraq, which particularly affects certain vulnerable groups, such as children, inter alia, as stated in the reports of several United Nations human rights treaty bodies, and appealing to all concerned to fulfil their mutual obligations in the management of the humanitarian programme established by the Security Council in its resolution 986(1995),

1. *Welcomes* the interim report of the Special Rapporteur of the Commission on Human Rights on the situation of human rights in Iraq and the observations, conclusions and recommendations contained therein, and notes with dismay that there has been no improvement in the situation of human rights in the country;

2. *Strongly condemns:*

(a) The systematic, widespread and extremely grave violations of human rights and of international humanitarian law by the Government of Iraq, resulting in an all-pervasive repression and oppression sustained by broad-based discrimination and widespread terror;

(b) The suppression of freedom of thought, expression, information, association, assembly and movement through fear of arrest, imprisonment, executions and other sanctions;

(c) The widespread use of the death penalty in disregard of the provisions of the International Covenant on Civil and Political Rights and the United Nations safeguards;

(d) Summary and arbitrary executions, including political killings and the continued, so-called clean-out of prisons, as well as enforced or involuntary disappearances, routinely practised arbitrary arrests and detention, and consistent and routine failure to respect due process and the rule of law, for example, in the execution of delinquents for minor property offences and customs violations;

(e) Widespread, systematic torture and the enactment and implementation of decrees prescribing cruel and inhuman punishment as a penalty for offences;

3. *Calls upon* the Government of Iraq:

(a) To abide by its freely undertaken obligations under international human rights treaties and international humanitarian law and to respect and ensure the rights of all individuals, irrespective of their origin, ethnicity, gender or religion, within its territory and subject to its jurisdiction;

(b) To bring the actions of its military and security forces into conformity with the standards of international law, in particular those of the International Covenant on Civil and Political Rights;

(c) To cooperate with United Nations human rights mechanisms, in particular by receiving a return visit by the Special Rapporteur to Iraq and allowing the stationing of human rights monitors throughout Iraq pursuant to the relevant resolutions of the General Assembly and the Commission on Human Rights;

(d) To establish independence of the judiciary and abrogate all laws granting impunity to specified forces or persons killing or injuring individuals for any purpose beyond the administration of justice under the rule of law as prescribed by international standards;

(e) To abrogate all decrees that prescribe cruel and inhuman punishment or treatment, including mutilation, and to ensure that torture and cruel punishment and treatment no longer occur;

(f) To abrogate all laws and procedures, including Revolution Command Council Decree No. 840 of 4 November 1986, that penalize free expression, and to ensure that the genuine will of the people shall be the basis of authority of the State;

(g) To respect the rights of all ethnic and religious groups and to cease immediately its repressive practices aimed at the Iraqi Kurds, Assyrians and Turkmen, in particular their deportation from the regions of Kirkuk and Khanaqin, and at the population of the southern marsh areas, where drainage projects have provoked environmental destruction and a deterioration of the situation of the civilian population, and to ensure the personal integrity and freedom, including the full freedom of belief, of the Shi'a and their religious establishment;

(h) To cooperate with the Tripartite Commission and its Technical Subcommittee to establish the whereabouts and resolve the fate of the remaining several hundred missing persons, including prisoners of war, Kuwaiti nationals and third-country nationals, victims of the illegal Iraqi occupation of Kuwait, to cooperate with the Working Group on Enforced or Involuntary Disappearances of the Commission on Human Rights for that purpose, and to pay compensation to the families of those who died or disappeared in the custody of the Iraqi authorities, through the mechanism established by the Security Council in its resolution 692(1991) of 20 May 1991, and to release immediately all Kuwaitis and nationals of other States who may still be held in detention;

(i) To cooperate fully with international aid agencies and non-governmental organizations in providing humanitarian assistance and monitoring in the northern and southern areas of the country;

(j) To continue to cooperate in the implementation of Security Council resolutions 986(1995), 1111(1997), 1143(1997), 1153(1998), 1210(1998), 1242(1999) and 1266(1999) so as to ensure fully the equitable distribution, without discrimination, to the Iraqi population, including members of the population in remote areas, of the humanitarian supplies purchased under the oil for food programme and to continue to facilitate the work of United Nations humanitarian personnel in Iraq by ensuring the free and unobstructed movement of observers throughout the country;

(k) To cooperate in the identification of minefields existing throughout Iraq with a view to facilitating their marking and eventual clearing;

4. *Requests* the Secretary-General to provide the Special Rapporteur with all necessary assistance in carrying out his mandate, and decides to continue the examination of the situation of human rights in Iraq at its fifty-fifth session under the item entitled "Human

rights questions", in the light of additional elements provided by the Commission on Human Rights.

RECORDED VOTE ON RESOLUTION 54/178:

In favour: Albania, Andorra, Angola, Antigua and Barbuda, Argentina, Armenia, Australia, Austria, Bahamas, Barbados, Belarus, Belgium, Belize, Bhutan, Bolivia, Bosnia and Herzegovina, Botswana, Brazil, Bulgaria, Canada, Chile, Colombia, Costa Rica, Croatia, Cyprus, Czech Republic, Denmark, Dominica, Dominican Republic, Ecuador, El Salvador, Estonia, Ethiopia, Finland, France, Georgia, Germany, Greece, Grenada, Guatemala, Guyana, Haiti, Hungary, Iceland, Ireland, Israel, Italy, Jamaica, Japan, Kazakhstan, Kuwait, Latvia, Liechtenstein, Lithuania, Luxembourg, Malawi, Maldives, Malta, Marshall Islands, Mauritius, Mexico, Micronesia, Monaco, Mongolia, Netherlands, New Zealand, Nicaragua, Norway, Panama, Paraguay, Peru, Poland, Portugal, Republic of Korea, Republic of Moldova, Romania, Russian Federation, Samoa, San Marino, Saudi Arabia, Senegal, Sierra Leone, Slovakia, Slovenia, Solomon Islands, South Africa, Spain, Swaziland, Sweden, Tajikistan, The former Yugoslav Republic of Macedonia, Trinidad and Tobago, Turkey, Ukraine, United Kingdom, United States, Uruguay, Uzbekistan, Zambia, Zimbabwe.

Against: Iran,* Libyan Arab Jamahiriya, Sudan.

Abstaining: Afghanistan, Algeria, Bahrain, Bangladesh, Benin, Brunei Darussalam, Burkina Faso, Cambodia, Cameroon, Cape Verde, Chad, China, Congo, Côte d'Ivoire, Cuba, Democratic People's Republic of Korea, Djibouti, Egypt, Eritrea, Fiji, Gabon, Ghana, Guinea, Guinea-Bissau, India, Indonesia, Jordan, Kenya, Lao People's Democratic Republic, Lebanon, Malaysia, Mali, Morocco, Mozambique, Myanmar, Namibia, Nepal, Nigeria, Pakistan, Papua New Guinea, Philippines, Saint Lucia, Singapore, Sri Lanka, Suriname, Syrian Arab Republic, Thailand, Togo, Tunisia, United Arab Emirates, United Republic of Tanzania, Venezuela, Viet Nam.

*Later advised the Secretariat it had intended not to participate.

In the Committee, paragraphs 2 *(a)* and 3 *(g)*, *(i)* and *(j)* were adopted jointly by a recorded vote of 91 to 1, with 54 abstentions. The Assembly retained the paragraphs by a recorded vote of 94 to none, with 56 abstentions.

Myanmar

Commission action. On 23 April [res. 1999/17], the Commission welcomed the accession by Myanmar to the 1979 Convention on the Elimination of All Forms of Discrimination against Women, adopted by the General Assembly in resolution 34/180 [YUN 1979, p. 895]; the pardoning and release of two political prisoners, noting at the same time an increase in the number of political prisoners during 1998; and the efforts being made by the Special Envoy of the Secretary-General to visit the country [YUN 1998, p. 751]. It expressed grave concern at the continued closure of higher education institutions for political reasons; that the National Convention did not permit members of Parliament-elect or representatives of ethnic minorities to express their views freely; at the use of forced labour; and that the Government had not yet agreed to a visit by the Special Rapporteur. The Commission deplored the continued human rights violations in Myanmar; disrespect for the rule of law; violations of the rights of minorities, women and children; the persecution of the democratic opposition; and severe restrictions on the freedoms of opinion, expression, assembly and association and on freedom of movement. It called on Myanmar to establish a constructive dialogue with the UN system; to continue to cooperate with the Secretary-General or his representative; and to consider becoming a party to human rights instruments. The Government was urged to implement the Special Rapporteur's recommendations; ensure full respect for human rights and fundamental freedoms; ensure the establishment of democracy; allow all citizens to participate freely in the political process; release political detainees; improve conditions of detention; ensure the well-being of all political leaders; fulfil its obligations under the Convention on the Rights of the Child, contained in Assembly resolution 44/25 [YUN 1989, p. 560], and under the Convention on the Elimination of All Forms of Discrimination against Women; end forced labour and allow freedom of association; cease laying landmines; end enforced displacement of persons; and end impunity.

The Commission decided to extend the Special Rapporteur's mandate for a further year and asked him to report to the Assembly in 1999 and to the Commission in 2000; the Economic and Social Council endorsed the Commission's decision on 27 July (**decision 1999/231**). The Commission also asked the Secretary-General to ensure that the Special Rapporteur would be authorized to visit Myanmar, and to continue his discussions with the Government and others who could assist in implementing Assembly resolution 53/162 [YUN 1998, p. 752], as well as its current resolution. It also asked the High Commissioner to cooperate with the Director-General of the International Labour Organization in identifying ways in which their offices might collaborate to improve the human rights situation in Myanmar.

Report of Special Rapporteur. In accordance with Economic and Social Council decision 1999/231, the Secretary-General transmitted, in October [A/54/440], the interim report of Special Rapporteur Rajsoomer Lallah (Mauritius) on the human rights situation in Myanmar as at 30 August. He reported that there had been no progress in the human rights situation, except for the resumption of work by ICRC and the cooperation of the Government in that regard. Repression of civil and political rights continued. The rule of law did not exist, as the judicial system was subject to a military regime and served only as handmaiden to a policy of repression. No effective measures had been taken to restrain forced labour. Regarding ethnic issues, the policy of establishing absolute political and administrative control resulted in killings, brutality, rape and other human rights violations. The Special Rapporteur renewed his previous recommendations [YUN 1998, p. 752].

Report of Secretary-General. Pursuant to General Assembly resolution 53/162 [YUN 1998,

p. 752], the Secretary-General, in October, submitted a report on the progress of discussions on the human rights situation in Myanmar and the restoration of democracy [A/54/499]. His Special Envoy, Alvaro de Soto, had visited the country (14-18 October), where he had held consultations with high-level government officials, leaders of political parties (the National League for Democracy (NLD) and the Shan Nationalities League for Democracy) and representatives of minority groups. Discussions with the Government focused on the restoration of democracy and human rights; a dialogue involving the Government, political parties—particularly NLD—and ethnic groups; freedom for political parties to conduct normal political activities; the release of political prisoners; a visit of the Special Rapporteur; access to prisoners by ICRC; and forced labour practices. In a departure from previous missions, an official of the World Bank accompanied the Special Envoy to explain the cooperation that might be available to Myanmar from international financial institutions. The Secretary-General welcomed ICRC visits to prisons and places of detention but reported no other progress.

Communications. On 15 March [E/CN.4/1999/129], Myanmar submitted to the Commission a memorandum concerning the human rights situation in the country, in the hope that Commission members would judge the situation objectively and understand the challenges the Government faced in preserving the unity and perpetuation of the nation, and in building a democratic State.

A similar memorandum to the General Assembly in October [A/C.3/54/4] concerned Assembly resolution 53/162, which, Myanmar claimed, had totally ignored the steps that the Government had taken to improve the country's situation. It stated that the Government was committed to establishing a democratic political system and to improving the overall situation in the country in the face of various obstacles and undue political pressures.

Report of Special Rapporteur. The Special Rapporteur reported on the human rights situation in Myanmar based on information received up to 15 December [E/CN.4/2000/38]. No concrete progress was reported on the general situation of human rights. Repression of political and civil rights continued, comprising summary or arbitrary executions, abuse of women and children by soldiers and the imposition of oppressive measures directed at ethnic and religious minorities, including the continued use of forced labour and relocation. Persecution of the democratic opposition continued, including long prison sentences and the use of intimidation and harassment.

GENERAL ASSEMBLY ACTION

On 17 December [meeting 83], the General Assembly, on the recommendation of the Third Committee [A/54/605/Add.3], adopted **resolution 54/186** without vote [agenda item 116 *(c)*].

Situation of human rights in Myanmar

The General Assembly,

Reaffirming that all Member States have an obligation to promote and protect human rights and fundamental freedoms as stated in the Charter of the United Nations and elaborated in the Universal Declaration of Human Rights, the International Covenants on Human Rights and other applicable human rights instruments,

Aware that, in accordance with its Charter, the United Nations promotes and encourages respect for human rights and fundamental freedoms for all and that the Universal Declaration of Human Rights states that the will of the people shall be the basis of the authority of government, and therefore expressing its grave concern that the Government of Myanmar still has not implemented its commitment to take all necessary steps towards democracy in the light of the results of the elections held in 1990,

Recalling its resolution 53/162 of 9 December 1998,

Recalling also Commission on Human Rights resolution 1992/58 of 3 March 1992, in which the Commission, inter alia, decided to nominate a special rapporteur with a given mandate, and taking note of Commission resolution 1999/17 of 23 April 1999, in which the Commission decided to extend for one year the mandate of its Special Rapporteur on the situation of human rights in Myanmar,

Recalling further the observation made by the Special Rapporteur that the absence of respect for the rights pertaining to democratic governance is at the root of all major violations of human rights in Myanmar,

Gravely concerned at the continuing and intensified repression of civil and political rights in Myanmar, as reported by the Special Rapporteur,

Deeply regretting the failure of the Government of Myanmar to cooperate fully with the relevant United Nations mechanisms, in particular the Special Rapporteur, while noting the recent increased contacts between the Government of Myanmar and the international community,

Noting that the Government of Myanmar, as a State party to the Convention on the Elimination of All Forms of Discrimination against Women, has submitted its initial report to the Committee on the Elimination of Discrimination against Women for its consideration,

1. *Expresses its appreciation* to the Special Rapporteur of the Commission on Human Rights on the situation of human rights in Myanmar for his interim report, and calls upon the Government of Myanmar to implement fully the recommendations made by the Special Rapporteur;

2. *Urges* the Government of Myanmar to cooperate fully and without further delay with the Special Rap-

porteur and to allow him, without preconditions, to conduct a field mission and to establish direct contacts with the Government and all other relevant sectors of society, thus enabling him fully to discharge his mandate, and, in this context, notes with interest that the Government has expressed its willingness to give serious consideration to a visit by the Special Rapporteur;

3. *Welcomes* the resumption of cooperation with the International Committee of the Red Cross, allowing the Committee to communicate with and visit prisoners in accordance with its standard working rules, and encourages continued cooperation in that regard;

4. *Expresses its appreciation* to the Secretary-General for his report, and notes with deep concern his conclusion that he is unable to report concrete progress, with the exception of the visit by the International Committee of the Red Cross, on issues that the international community has raised time and again in successive resolutions of the General Assembly and the Commission on Human Rights;

5. *Deplores* the continuing violations of human rights in Myanmar, including extrajudicial, summary or arbitrary executions, enforced disappearances, rape, torture, inhuman treatment, mass arrests, forced labour, including the use of children, forced relocation and denial of freedom of assembly, association, expression and movement, as reported by the Special Rapporteur;

6. *Expresses its grave concern* at the increased repression of any form of public political activity and the arbitrary detention and arrest of those exercising their rights to freedom of thought, expression, assembly and association, as well as the harassment of their families;

7. *Strongly urges* the Government of Myanmar to release immediately and unconditionally detained political leaders and all political prisoners, to ensure their physical integrity and to permit them to participate in the process of national reconciliation;

8. *Expresses its grave concern* at the escalation in the persecution of the democratic opposition, notably over the past year, in particular members and supporters of the National League for Democracy, at the harsh long-term prison sentences imposed and the use by the Government of intimidatory measures against elected representatives and members of the National League for Democracy, which forced them to resign from their positions and to dissolve their party offices;

9. *Expresses its concern* that the composition and working procedures of the National Convention do not permit either members of Parliament-elect or representatives of the ethnic minorities to express their views freely, and urges the Government of Myanmar to seek new and constructive means to promote national reconciliation;

10. *Strongly urges* the Government of Myanmar, taking into account the assurances it has given on various occasions, to take all necessary steps towards the restoration of democracy in accordance with the will of the people as expressed in the democratic elections held in 1990 and, to this end and without delay, to engage in a substantive political dialogue with political leaders, including Aung San Suu Kyi, and representatives of ethnic groups, and, in this context, notes the existence of the Committee representing the People's Parliament;

11. *Notes with grave concern* that the Government of Myanmar has failed to review its legislation, to cease to inflict the practice of forced labour on its people and to punish those exacting forced labour, which has forced the International Labour Conference to exclude further cooperation with the Government until such time as it has implemented the recommendations of the Commission of Inquiry of the International Labour Organization regarding the implementation of the Forced Labour Convention, 1930, Convention No. 29, of the International Labour Organization;

12. *Strongly urges* the Government of Myanmar to cease the widespread and systematic use of forced labour and to implement the recommendations of the Commission of Inquiry, while noting the order by the Government of Myanmar issued in May 1999 directing that the power to requisition forced labour under the Towns Act and the Village Act not be exercised, as well as the invitation to visit addressed to the International Labour Organization in October 1999;

13. *Deplores* the continued violations of human rights, in particular those directed against persons belonging to ethnic and religious minorities, including summary executions, rape, torture, forced labour, forced portering, forced relocations, destruction of crops and fields and dispossession of land and property, which deprives those persons of all means of subsistence;

14. *Also deplores* the continuing violations of the human rights of women, especially women who are refugees, are internally displaced or belong to ethnic minorities or the political opposition, in particular forced labour, sexual violence and exploitation, including rape, as reported by the Special Rapporteur;

15. *Strongly urges* the Government of Myanmar to ensure full respect for all human rights and fundamental freedoms, including economic and social rights, to fulfil its obligation to end the impunity of perpetrators of human rights violations, including members of the military, and to investigate and prosecute alleged violations committed by government agents in all circumstances;

16. *Urges* the Government of Myanmar to end the enforced displacement of persons and other causes of refugee flows to neighbouring countries and to create conditions conducive to their voluntary return and full reintegration in conditions of safety and dignity;

17. *Notes with interest* the recent visit to Myanmar by the Special Envoy of the Secretary-General for the purpose of holding discussions with the Government and with political leaders, including Aung San Suu Kyi and representatives of some ethnic minority groups, and calls upon the Government of Myanmar to enter into a constructive dialogue with the Secretary-General in order to make better use of his good offices;

18. *Requests* the Secretary-General to continue his discussions on the situation of human rights and the restoration of democracy with the Government of Myanmar, to submit additional reports to the General Assembly during its fifty-fourth session on the progress of those discussions and to report to the Assembly at its fifty-fifth session and to the Commission on Human Rights at its fifty-sixth session on the progress made in the implementation of the present resolution;

19. *Decides* to continue its consideration of this question at its fifty-fifth session.

Europe and the Mediterranean

Belarus

On 20 August [E/CN.4/2000/2], a draft text regarding Belarus, sponsored by 13 members, was withdrawn from the Subcommission. By the draft, the Subcommission would have expressed its concern at alleged reports that authorities continued to harass Belarusian political leaders, journalists and human rights defenders; at the concentration of legislative power in the executive branch of government and a weak judiciary, such that the rule of law had not been preserved; and at the lack of meaningful democratic process.

Based on a statement by Belarus following the withdrawal of the draft text, the Subcommission Chairman made a statement that was adopted by consensus [ibid.]. It was the Chairman's understanding that the Government would invite the Special Rapporteur on the independence of judges and lawyers and the Working Group on Arbitrary Detention to visit the country, and that one of the visits would take place prior to the Subcommission's session in 2000. In addition, the Government would make efforts to join the Council of Europe and sign and ratify the 1950 Convention for the Protection of Human Rights and Fundamental Freedoms; to withdraw its reservation to article 20 of the 1984 Convention against Torture and Other Cruel, Inhuman or Degrading Treatment or Punishment (see p. 578) prior to the Subcommission's 2000 session; to undertake legislative reforms to improve human rights protection and democracy; and to report in 2000 to the Subcommission on the steps it had taken.

In view of the Chairman's statement, the Subcommission, on 20 August [dec. 1999/105], decided to adjourn the debate on the draft resolution on the human rights situation in Belarus.

Cyprus

As requested by the Commission on Human Rights in 1998 [YUN 1998, p. 754], the Secretary-General, in a March report on the question of human rights in Cyprus [E/CN.4/1999/25], described activities taken under his good offices mission, the United Nations Peacekeeping Force in Cyprus and the Committee on Missing Persons in Cyprus (see p. 387).

On 23 April [dec. 1999/103], the Commission decided to retain the item on its agenda, on the understanding that action required by previous resolutions would continue to remain operative, including its request to the Secretary-General to report on their implementation.

The former Yugoslavia

Kosovo province of FRY

Commission action. By a roll-call vote of 44 to 1, with 6 abstentions, the Commission, on 13 April [res. 1999/2], strongly condemned the widespread and systematic practice of ethnic cleansing perpetrated by the Belgrade and Serbian authorities against the Kosovars, and the risk of destabilization of neighbouring countries. It demanded an immediate halt to repressive actions in Kosovo by the Serbian authorities, which had led to further ethnic cleansing and massive criminal violations of international human rights and humanitarian law inflicted against the Kosovars, and that the Serbian authorities immediately sign and implement the Rambouillet Accords (see PART ONE, Chapter V). The Commission called on the international community and the International Tribunal for the Former Yugoslavia (ICTY) (see PART FOUR, Chapter II) to bring to justice the perpetrators of international war crimes and crimes against humanity, and appealed to the international community, including UNHCR, to extend urgently humanitarian assistance to refugees from Kosovo and those internally displaced. Welcoming the High Commissioner's decision to dispatch human rights monitors to the region to assess the human rights and humanitarian crisis, the Commission asked her to report urgently on the human rights situation and the humanitarian crisis relating to Kosovo and on the implementation of its current resolution.

On 23 April [res. 1999/18], by a roll-call vote of 46 to 1, with 6 abstentions, the Commission condemned the grave, horrendous and ongoing war crimes and human rights abuses in Kosovo, including violent repression of the non-violent expression of political views, systematic terrorization of ethnic Albanians and others, torture, deaths in detention, summary executions and widespread destruction of homes and property. It also condemned the escalation of the Serbian military offensive against civilians in Kosovo in recent weeks and abuses by elements of the Kosovo Liberation Army (KLA), in particular killings, enforced disappearances and the abduction of Serbian police and Serb and Albanian civilians. It called on the authorities of the Federal Republic of Yugoslavia (Serbia and Montenegro) (FRY) to stop all military action and end the violence and repression against civilians; ensure the withdrawal from Kosovo of all military, Ministry of Interior police and paramilitary forces; agree to the stationing of an international military peacekeeping presence; agree to the voluntary, unconditional return of internally displaced persons and refugees and to provide unhindered access to them by humanitarian aid organizations; and to work, on the basis of the Rambouillet Accords, on establishing a political framework agreement for Kosovo, in conformity with international law and the UN Charter. The Commission insisted that the FRY authorities and the ethnic Albanian leadership in Kosovo condemn acts of terrorism, refrain from violence, encourage the pursuit of political ends through peaceful means, act with respect for the rights of minorities, and respect international human rights standards and international humanitarian law. It also insisted that FRY implement a ceasefire; demilitarize the province; respect the democratic process; ensure all residents were guaranteed equal treatment and protection; release political detainees; guarantee the right to voluntary return in safety and dignity of all refugees and displaced persons to Kosovo and respect fully all human rights and fundamental freedoms; allow the establishment of democratic institutions in Kosovo; abide by its obligations under the 1949 Geneva Conventions for the protection of victims of war; and cooperate with international humanitarian organizations regarding missing persons in Kosovo and ensure that NGOs could cooperate freely.

Communication. On 16 April [E/CN.4/1999/155], FRY claimed that the Commission's resolution of 13 April was an example of politicization of the Commission's work. It stated that the sole goal of those who suggested its adoption was to justify and get further support for the barbaric North Atlantic Treaty Organization (NATO) aggression against FRY. Similarly, on 26 April [E/CN.4/1999/159], FRY stated that the Commission's resolution of 23 April was based on falsehoods and deliberately launched disinformation to justify what it called the barbarian aggression against FRY by NATO.

Following air strikes by NATO in FRY, which began on 24 March, FRY transmitted to the Commission on Human Rights a series of communications denouncing them.

Reports of High Commissioner. On 16 April [E/CN.4/1999/SR.39], the High Commissioner updated the Commission on developments in the Kosovo crisis over the past week. Over half a million people had fled Kosovo. The number of internally displaced persons within Kosovo was estimated at several hundred thousand. Detailed accounts of serious human rights violations, allegedly perpetrated by Serbian police and paramilitary forces, continued to be received. Over the past few days, there had been alarming reports of large-scale summary executions of ethnic Albanians in Djakovica, Orahovac, Ljubenic and Kotlina. There was widespread reporting of the separation of family members, particularly young males, who had not subsequently been traced. A significant number of civilians had been killed in the course of military action. The High Commissioner called on FRY authorities and on the international community to take steps to end the human rights violations against the people of Kosovo.

On 19 April [E/CN.4/1999/164], FRY stated that the High Commissioner's report was based solely on media reports from countries that were taking part in what it called the brutal aggression against it, including NATO, Pentagon (United States), and Foreign and Commonwealth Office (United Kingdom) briefings. It put forward a list of events and consequences related to the NATO bombings launched against FRY on 24 March, on which the High Commissioner, in its view, should have based the report in order to make it credible and impartial.

In May [E/CN.4/2000/7], the High Commissioner presented information gathered by the OHCHR Kosovo Emergency Operation (KEO) and information she had obtained during her mission to the region (2-13 May). The objectives of KEO were to establish a human rights presence as close as possible to the actual developments in Kosovo; to interview refugees and seek impartial verification about alleged human rights violations; to seek to identify patterns and trends in human rights violations; to consult and help coordinate among international partners the assembling and analysis of information relating to human rights violations in Kosovo; to assemble information in reports to the High Commissioner, the Special Rapporteur and other UN mechanisms, including ICTY; and to explore opportunities for technical cooperation. Nine additional human rights officers had been deployed to Tirana, Albania, and to Skopje, the former Yugoslav Republic of Macedonia (FYROM), to join OHCHR staff there. Two data-processing experts had initiated a database to manage information gathered by the three OHCHR field presences in Tirana, Skopje and Montenegro (FRY).

Accounts received by the High Commissioner and OHCHR staff in those locations provided substantial evidence of gross human rights violations committed in Kosovo, including summary executions, forcible displacement, rape, physical abuse and the destruction of property and identity documents. As at 20 May, more than 750,000 Kosovars were refugees or displaced persons, while an unknown, reportedly large number of internally displaced persons remained in the region. OHCHR had documented cases of persons who had been taken away by Serbian authorities and whose whereabouts were unknown. Refugees had witnessed or confirmed accounts of summary executions, while others reported having seen mass graves. Women had experienced and witnessed the same violations as men, such as forced expulsion from their homes and ill-treatment by the paramilitary and police. Refugees also had experienced ill-treatment (beatings, shootings, mutilation, rape, threats) by Serbian paramilitary and police. Newly arrived refugees had reported that ethnic Albanians were being used as human shields to protect military convoys from NATO air strikes. The High Commissioner described the impact of the armed conflict on civilians, noting that, according to the Serbian authorities, more than 1,200 civilians had died in FRY as a result of the NATO air strikes and some 4,500 had been seriously injured. In addition, bridges had been damaged and communications disrupted, and schools, hospitals and places of worship had been destroyed or damaged. The air strikes had caused serious environmental damage, and the destruction of petrochemical installations and the bombing of warehouses storing chemical products raised serious health concerns. The destruction of private radio and television stations had seriously impeded freedom of expression and freedom of information. The use of graphite bombs by NATO had caused short circuits on power lines, leaving areas without water and electricity. NATO was also using cluster bombs, which could leave unexploded ordnance across wide areas, capable of detonation on contact.

Regarding the humanitarian situation, Albania estimated that, as at 20 May, it was hosting more than 400,000 Kosovo refugees. Security for refugees was an increasing concern; major issues included trafficking and prostitution, abduction of children, recruitment and training for KLA and illegal immigration. According to government sources, FYROM harboured more than 200,000 Kosovo refugees, who were at risk due to poor hygiene, inadequate medical attention and overcrowding. There was also concern about the presence of KLA members in the camps and the possible forced recruitment of refugees into KLA. Montenegro hosted more than 60,000 internally displaced persons from Kosovo; a blockade by the federal authorities on humanitarian assistance arriving through the port of Bar had placed their well-being at risk. In Serbia, according to the findings of the United Nations Needs Assessment Mission (see p. 350), which travelled throughout FRY from 16 to 28 May, the situation was so grave that in each republic and province, people, regardless of their ethnicity, political affiliation, socio-economic status, gender or age, feared for their survival.

The High Commissioner called on the FRY authorities to end human rights violations. She urged the Government to withdraw immediately and unconditionally all army and police units from Kosovo, as well as federal police and paramilitary forces responsible for gross human rights violations, and called on it to allow humanitarian agencies to bring aid to internally displaced persons in FRY. NATO was called on to respect the principles of international humanitarian law, including the principle of proportionality, in its military actions against FRY. She advocated the inclusion of a key human rights component in any future UN presence in Kosovo to monitor and promote respect for human rights and the rule of law; follow up individual cases of violations and determine patterns of continuing violations; investigate complaints of human rights abuses, in cooperation with international civilian police; and provide support to UN human rights mechanisms. The High Commissioner stressed the need to strengthen democracy and the rule of law, economic and social development and respect for human rights and fundamental freedoms throughout the region.

In September [E/CN.4/2000/10], the High Commissioner provided an update of the findings of KEO. She described the displacement and deportation of more than 1 million ethnic Albanians from Kosovo, including from the municipalities of Pristina, Podujevo, Mitrovica, Orahovac, Lipljan, Urosevac, Suva Reka, Glogovac, Srbica, Kacanik and Djakovica. The High Commissioner presented information regarding killings and executions, violence against women and children, arbitrary arrest and detention, torture and mistreatment, the destruction and confiscation of property, the role played by KLA during the NATO campaign and the impact of the armed conflict on civilians. Following confirmation on 10 June by NATO of the withdrawal of FRY security forces from Kosovo and the subsequent suspension of NATO air operations against FRY, the Security Council authorized the Secretary-General to establish an international civil presence in Kosovo in order to provide an interim administration and the establishment of an international security presence. Following those developments, and in the light of the return of refugees to Kosovo, KEO was terminated and OHCHR-FRY staff returned to Kosovo with the advance team of the United Nations Interim Administration Mission in Kosovo (UNMIK) (see

p. 357). In June and July, the High Commissioner convened two informal meetings of international organizations to discuss long-term strategies to promote and protect human rights in the region; met in Pristina with the commander of the international security force in Kosovo (KFOR), the acting Special Representative of the Secretary-General and other UN representatives; and chaired a meeting there with representatives of the Council for the Defence of Human Rights and Freedoms and the Centre for the Protection of Women and Children. As at 24 August, OHCHR had 12 international officers in Pristina and had reopened offices in Belgrade and Podgorica.

The High Commissioner chronicled the human rights situation in Kosovo following the establishment of UNMIK. According to UNHCR, as at 24 August, more than 761,000 Kosovars had returned to Kosovo while 6,800 remained in Albania, 19,000 in FYROM, 8,000 in Montenegro and 11,400 in Bosnia and Herzegovina. It estimated that some 50,000 refugees in the region were awaiting repatriation. Yugoslav sources estimated that as many as 165,000 Serbs and Montenegrins had left Kosovo since the arrival of the international force, while more than half of Kosovo's estimated 120,000 to 150,000 Roma population had fled since mid-June. UNHCR reported that, as at mid-August, there were only 50,000 non-Albanians left in Kosovo. The exodus was rooted in fear, killings, kidnapping, looting, evictions, widespread burning of villages, as well as cultural, historical and religious monuments, and other forms of intimidation. In Kosovo, minority ethnic groups had become victims of human rights abuses, including murders, which KFOR, as at 14 August, confirmed at 280 since 15 June; eviction of Kosovar Serbs and other minorities; rape; and kidnapping, primarily of ethnic Serbs and some Roma. Reports were received daily by KFOR, the Organization for Security and Cooperation in Europe (OSCE), UNHCR and ICRC of discovered bodies. In response to the arrest and detention of persons by KFOR, and in the absence of a functioning judiciary in Kosovo, the Secretary-General's Special Representative issued emergency decrees establishing a Joint Advisory Council on Provisional Judicial Appointments (JAC). The Council was composed of four national judges, including two Albanians, one Serb and one Turk, and three international lawyers. JAC advised the Special Representative on the provisional appointment of judges, judicial personnel and prosecutors in order to re-establish an independent and multi-ethnic judiciary. As at mid-August, the judges and prosecutors had conducted hearings in 144 cases involving 263 individuals, 120 of whom had been released. Allegedly, some 5,000 detainees were held by Serbian authorities on terrorism charges. In July, the Government of Serbia provided the names of over 2,000 individuals who had been transferred from Kosovo prisons to prisons in Serbia. Family members in Kosovo had difficulty visiting detainees in Serbia given the fears for the security of Albanians in some parts of Serbia.

The High Commissioner concluded that Serb forces committed shocking crimes during the NATO air campaign. Following the withdrawal of Serb forces, gross violations of human rights continued to take place at an alarming rate, particularly targeting the non-Albanians (Serb, Roma and other communities) in Kosovo. The High Commissioner urged Member States to support ICTY, and called on ICTY, ICRC and OSCE to continue to investigate the fate and whereabouts of missing persons. She recommended the rapid deployment of UN police; the re-establishment of customs control at borders; support by the international community for UNHCR and other agencies engaged in assisting the estimated 500,000 Kosovars without adequate housing before the onset of winter; investigation of allegations of KLA detention centres, killings, rape, torture, arson, expulsion, looting, theft and other violations of the rights of Kosovo inhabitants; and the complete demilitarization and disarmament of KLA by UNMIK. The High Commissioner called on the Government of Serbia to provide a list of all detainees transferred from Kosovo, specifying the charges under which they were held, and to guarantee their families access to them. She also called on the Kosovo population to refrain from violence and end attacks against minority groups, and on Albanian leaders to condemn the violence. She invited KLA to cooperate with UNMIK and KFOR in investigating the crimes.

In a later report [E/CN.4/2000/32], the High Commissioner stated that in September a Senior Human Rights Adviser was appointed in the Office of the Special Representative of the Secretary-General in Pristina to ensure a proactive approach on human rights in all UNMIK activities and the compatibility of UNMIK regulations with human rights standards. The deployment of the large international presence in Kosovo was followed by the resumed activities of OHCHR-FRY. In September, the Special Representative apppointed OHCHR-FRY to organize and chair the Commission on Prisoners and Detainees. It was important, the High Commissioner said, to recognize the role of the Stability Pact for South-Eastern Europe, established in June (see p. 397), which represented the collective effort of the EU, the Group of Eight industrialized countries (G-8), the countries of the region and key international organizations to address the challenges of the region in a coordinated and strategic manner.

During the final months of the year, grave human rights violations, mostly but not only of persons belonging to minorities, persisted in Kosovo. Dozens of killings were reported. Minorities continued to face serious restrictions on freedom of movement and difficulties in obtaining employment. Access to basic services, including health and education, on an equitable basis needed improvement. On 21 September, UNMIK established the Commission on Prisoners and Detainees in the framework of the Kosovo Transitional Council, under the chairmanship of the OHCHR Chief of Mission. The Commission gathered information on the circumstances of detention to support interventions and advocacy on behalf of detainees, prisoners and their families. Commission members were drawn from all parts of Kosovo and represented a broad spectrum of social and ethnic origins. In mid-December, in the context of the Commission, OHCHR brought representatives of Kosovo Serbs and Kosovo Albanians together for the first time with KFOR and UNMIK representatives to discuss the fate and whereabouts of detainees. OHCHR regularly visited places of detention in Serbia and Montenegro and monitored trials in various court districts. According to Kosovo Albanians recently released, detainees had suffered mistreatment while in Serbian custody, especially in Kosovo during the NATO campaign, while poor health conditions and overcrowding were common in almost all detention centres. OHCHR and ICRC had not obtained access to places of detention of persons kidnapped or abducted in Kosovo. The High Commissioner welcomed the Special Representative's recommendations made in December on the establishment of a Kosovo Court that would prosecute persons suspected of having committed war crimes or serious crimes committed on the basis of a person's ethnicity, religion or political beliefs. The Kosovo Human Rights Conference (Pristina, 10 and 11 December) was marked by the participation of persons representing different ethnic groups who had the opportunity to express their views in a free and democratic context. The High Commissioner welcomed the adoption of a final declaration calling for the promotion of peaceful coexistence, tolerance, establishment of the rule of law and a strengthened judiciary in a human rights-oriented society.

(See also below, under "Bosnia and Herzegovina, Croatia and FRY", for further details on the human rights situation in Kosovo. For information on the visit of the Special Rapporteur on extrajudicial, summary or arbitrary executions to FYROM and Albania regarding the situation in Kosovo, see p. 633.)

GENERAL ASSEMBLY ACTION

On 17 December [meeting 83], the General Assembly, on the recommendation of the Third Committee [A/54/605/Add.3], adopted **resolution 54/183** by recorded vote (108-4-45) [agenda item 116 *(c)*].

Situation of human rights in Kosovo

The General Assembly,

Guided by the Charter of the United Nations, the Universal Declaration of Human Rights, the International Covenants on Human Rights and other human rights instruments,

Bearing in mind Security Council resolutions 1160(1998) of 31 March 1998, 1199(1998) of 23 September 1998, 1203(1998) of 24 October 1998, 1239(1999) of 14 May 1999 and 1244(1999) of 10 June 1999, and the general principles annexed to that resolution, as well as the statement made on 24 March 1998 by the Chairman of the Commission on Human Rights at the fifty-fourth session of the Commission, Commission on Human Rights resolutions 1998/79 of 22 April 1998 and 1999/2 of 13 April 1999 and the report of the United Nations High Commissioner for Human Rights to the Bureau of the Commission on the situation of human rights in Kosovo of 7 September 1999,

Recalling, against the background of years of repression, intolerance and violence in Kosovo, the challenge to build a multi-ethnic society on the basis of substantial autonomy, respecting the sovereignty and territorial integrity of the Federal Republic of Yugoslavia (Serbia and Montenegro), pending final settlement in accordance with Security Council resolution 1244 (1999),

Taking fully into account the regional dimensions of the crisis in Kosovo, in particular with regard to the human rights and humanitarian situation and the continuing problems in that regard, and noting that the return of refugees to their homes has contributed to the easing of this crisis,

Taking note with concern of the report of the Special Rapporteur of the Commission on Human Rights on the situation of human rights in Bosnia and Herzegovina, the Republic of Croatia and the Federal Republic of Yugoslavia (Serbia and Montenegro), which describes the persistent and grave violations and abuses of human rights and international humanitarian law in Kosovo,

Condemning the grave violations of human rights in Kosovo that affected ethnic Albanians prior to the arrival of personnel of the United Nations Interim Administration Mission in Kosovo and troops of the international security presence, the Kosovo Force, as demonstrated in the many reports of torture, indiscriminate and widespread shelling, mass forced displacement of civilians, summary executions and illegal detention of ethnic Albanians in Kosovo by the Yugoslav police and military,

Deeply concerned, in spite of the efforts of the Mission and the Force, about the frequent instances of harassment, periodic kidnapping and murder of ethnic Serb, Roma and other minorities of Kosovo by ethnic Albanian extremists,

Expressing concern that the entire population of Kosovo has been affected by the conflict, and stressing that all of the national minorities there must benefit from their full and equal rights,

Stressing, in this context, the importance of the International Tribunal for the Prosecution of Persons Responsible for Serious Violations of International Humanitarian Law Committed in the Territory of the Former Yugoslavia since 1991,

Distressed by the lack of due process in the trials in Serbia of the ethnic Albanians who have been detained, charged or brought to trial in relation to the crisis in Kosovo in violation of international human rights standards,

Stressing the urgent need to implement effective measures to stop trafficking in women and children,

1. *Underlines* the obligation of the authorities of the Federal Republic of Yugoslavia (Serbia and Montenegro) to abide by the terms of Security Council resolution 1244(1999) and the general principles on the political solution to the Kosovo crisis adopted on 6 May 1999 and annexed to that resolution;

2. *Reaffirms* that the human rights and humanitarian crisis in Kosovo shall be addressed within the framework of a political solution based upon the general principles annexed to Security Council resolution 1244(1999);

3. *Welcomes* the establishment of the United Nations Interim Administration Mission in Kosovo and the Kosovo Force, and calls upon all parties in Kosovo and the authorities of the Federal Republic of Yugoslavia (Serbia and Montenegro) to cooperate fully with the Mission and the Force in the fulfilment of their respective mandates;

4. *Also welcomes* the work of the Office of the United Nations High Commissioner for Human Rights in Kosovo and the Office of the United Nations High Commissioner for Refugees and the efforts of the Organization for Security and Cooperation in Europe;

5. *Calls upon* all parties in Kosovo to cooperate with the Mission in ensuring full respect for all human rights and fundamental freedoms and democratic norms in Kosovo;

6. *Calls upon* all authorities in the Federal Republic of Yugoslavia (Serbia and Montenegro), the local Serb leaders in Kosovo and the leaders of the Albanian community in Kosovo to condemn all acts of terrorism, sequestration or kidnapping and forced eviction from homes or places of work of any resident of Kosovo, whatever the ethnic background of the victim and whoever the perpetrators, to refrain from all acts of violence and to use their influence and leadership to cooperate with the Force and the Mission in stopping these incidents and in bringing the perpetrators to justice;

7. *Expresses its concern* about the forced division of any part of Kosovo into ethnic cantons or ethnically based divisions of any type, which is counter to Security Council resolution 1244(1999) and to the guiding principles of Rambouillet, and stresses the need for all parties in Kosovo to take all necessary measures to stop or reverse any action that de facto or *de jure* permits such ethnic cantonization;

8. *Calls upon* all parties, in particular the authorities and representatives of the Federal Republic of Yugoslavia (Serbia and Montenegro) and the Kosovar Serb and Albanian leaderships, to cooperate with the Mine Action Coordination Centre;

9. *Demands* that the Government of the Federal Republic of Yugoslavia (Serbia and Montenegro) provide an updated list of all persons detained and transferred from Kosovo to other parts of the Federal Republic of Yugoslavia (Serbia and Montenegro), specifying the charge, if any, under which each individual is detained, and that it guarantee their families and non-governmental organizations and international observers unimpeded and regular access to those who remain in detention and release all individuals detained and transferred from Kosovo prior to July 1999 in violation of international humanitarian and human rights standards;

10. *Calls upon* the authorities of the Federal Republic of Yugoslavia (Serbia and Montenegro) to open to public observation trials or criminal prosecutions against all those charged in relation to the conflict in Kosovo;

11. *Calls upon* the authorities of the Federal Republic of Yugoslavia (Serbia and Montenegro) and ethnic Kosovar Serb and Albanian representatives to allow for and to facilitate the free and unhindered return to their homes, in safety and with dignity, of all displaced persons and refugees, of whichever ethnic background, and expresses its concern about reports of continuing harassment or other impediments in this regard;

12. *Calls upon* the authorities of the Federal Republic of Yugoslavia (Serbia and Montenegro) to return or to facilitate the fair, unbiased and accurate restoration or reconstruction of Kosovar documentation and legal records taken or destroyed during the conflict;

13. *Stresses* the importance of and the responsibility of all parties to create a secure environment in Kosovo that will allow refugees and displaced persons to return and allow all those who wish to remain in Kosovo a genuine possibility to do so, irrespective of their ethnic origin;

14. *Requests* the Secretary-General to pursue his humanitarian efforts in Kosovo through the Office of the United Nations High Commissioner for Refugees, the World Food Programme, the United Nations Children's Fund, other appropriate humanitarian organizations and the Office of the United Nations High Commissioner for Human Rights and to continue to take the urgent practical steps to meet the critical needs of the people in Kosovo and to assist in the voluntary return of displaced persons to their homes in conditions of safety and dignity;

15. *Encourages* the Office of the Prosecutor of the International Tribunal for the Prosecution of Persons Responsible for Serious Violations of International Humanitarian Law Committed in the Territory of the Former Yugoslavia since 1991 to continue investigations at all levels concerning official individuals or private citizens with regard to serious violations of international humanitarian law committed in Kosovo, and reaffirms that the investigation of such crimes falls within the jurisdiction of the Office;

16. *Demands* that the authorities of the Federal Republic of Yugoslavia (Serbia and Montenegro) and the Kosovar Serb and Albanian leaderships and all others concerned cooperate fully with the International Tribunal for the Former Yugoslavia and honour all obligations towards it;

17. *Reiterates its call upon* the authorities of the Federal Republic of Yugoslavia (Serbia and Montenegro) to live up to their commitment to provide financial and material assistance to those residents of Kosovo whose homes have been damaged;

18. *Calls upon* the authorities of the Federal Republic of Yugoslavia (Serbia and Montenegro) to provide information on the fate and the whereabouts of the high number of missing persons from Kosovo, and encourages the International Committee of the Red Cross to pursue its clarification efforts in this regard, in cooperation with other organizations such as the Organization for Security and Cooperation in Europe;

19. *Encourages* the ongoing cooperation provided by the Federal Republic of Yugoslavia (Serbia and Montenegro) regarding the visits to some two thousand prisoners, mainly of Kosovar Albanian origin, carried out by the International Committee of the Red Cross and held under the authority of the Ministry of Justice of Serbia;

20. *Welcomes* the efforts made by the international community, and calls for continuing support for the Office of the United Nations High Commissioner for Refugees and other agencies engaged in the effort to provide those in need in Kosovo with proper accommodation, in particular with a view to facilitating the preparation and provision of adequate winter accommodation;

21. *Urges* all parties involved in Kosovo to support the efforts of the United Nations Children's Fund to ensure that all children in Kosovo return to school as soon as possible and to contribute to the rebuilding and repair of schools destroyed or damaged during the conflict in Kosovo;

22. *Calls* for the most rapid and full deployment of United Nations police and for the creation of a multiethnic local police force throughout Kosovo, as a key step towards guaranteeing respect for law and order and for creating a safe environment for all inhabitants of Kosovo;

23. *Condemns* any effort, on behalf of any ethnic group, to create any sort of parallel institutions for Kosovar Serb and Albanian populations, be they police, school, administrative or other institutions, and calls upon the Mission and the Force to prevent any such institutions from being formed;

24. *Requests* the Special Rapporteur of the Commission on Human Rights on the situation of human rights in Bosnia and Herzegovina, the Republic of Croatia and the Federal Republic of Yugoslavia (Serbia and Montenegro) to continue to monitor closely the situation of human rights in Kosovo, to pay special attention to Kosovo in his reporting and to report his findings to the Commission on Human Rights at its fifty-sixth session and to the General Assembly at its fifty-fifth session.

RECORDED VOTE ON RESOLUTION 54/183:

In favour: Afghanistan, Albania, Algeria, Andorra, Argentina, Australia, Austria, Azerbaijan, Bahamas, Bahrain, Bangladesh, Barbados, Belgium, Bolivia, Bosnia and Herzegovina, Botswana, Brazil, Brunei Darussalam, Bulgaria, Canada, Cape Verde, Chile, Colombia, Comoros, Costa Rica, Croatia, Cyprus, Czech Republic, Denmark, Djibouti, Dominican Republic, Ecuador, Egypt, El Salvador, Estonia, Finland, France, Georgia, Germany, Ghana, Greece, Guatemala, Guyana, Haiti, Hungary, Iceland, Indonesia, Ireland, Israel, Italy, Japan, Jordan, Kazakhstan, Kuwait, Latvia, Liechtenstein, Lithuania, Luxembourg, Malawi, Malaysia, Maldives, Malta, Marshall Islands, Mauritius, Mexico, Micronesia, Monaco, Mongolia, Morocco, Netherlands, New Zealand, Nicaragua, Nigeria, Norway, Oman, Pakistan, Papua New Guinea, Paraguay, Philippines, Poland, Portugal, Qatar, Republic of Korea, Republic of Moldova, Romania, Samoa, San Marino, Saudi Arabia, Senegal, Sierra Leone, Slovakia, Slovenia, Solomon Islands, South Africa, Spain, Sri Lanka, Sudan, Sweden, Thailand, Tunisia, Turkey, United Arab Emirates, United Kingdom, United States, Uruguay, Uzbekistan, Zambia, Zimbabwe.

Against: Belarus, India, Iran,* Russian Federation.

Abstaining: Angola, Antigua and Barbuda, Belize, Benin, Bhutan, Burkina Faso, Cambodia, Cameroon, Chad, China, Congo, Côte d'Ivoire, Cuba, Democratic People's Republic of Korea, Democratic Republic of the Congo, Dominica, Eritrea, Ethiopia, Gabon, Grenada, Guinea, Jamaica, Kenya, Lao People's Democratic Republic, Libyan Arab Jamahiriya, Mali, Mozambique, Myanmar, Namibia, Nepal, Panama, Peru, Saint Lucia, Singapore, Suriname, Swaziland, Tajikistan, The former Yugoslav Republic of Macedonia, Togo, Trinidad and Tobago, Uganda, Ukraine, United Republic of Tanzania, Venezuela, Viet Nam.

*Later advised the Secretariat it had intended to vote in favour.

Bosnia and Herzegovina, Croatia and FRY

Commission action. On 23 April [res. 1999/18], by a roll-call vote of 46 to 1, with 6 abstentions, the Commission expressed grave concern at the serious human rights violations and the deteriorating human rights and humanitarian situation in FRY and condemned the continued repression of the independent media. It called on FRY authorities to comply with the Commission's resolutions and the Special Rapporteur's recommendations and to cooperate with other relevant Commission mechanisms; cooperate with ICTY (see PART FOUR, Chapter II); institutionalize democratic norms of governance; end torture and other cruel, inhuman or degrading treatment or punishment of detainees; repeal the 1989 Serbian Law on Special Conditions for Real Property Transactions and the 1998 Serbian Law on Public Information; and respect the rights of minority groups. The Commission welcomed positive developments in Montenegro regarding the democratic process and the selection by OHCHR of nine civil society organizations in the Assisting Communities Together Programme.

Taking note of Croatia's request for technical cooperation and assistance programmes and the positive response thereto by the High Commissioner, the Commission urged the Government and OHCHR to conclude an agreement (see p. 587). The Government was called on to adhere to democratic principles and to continue efforts to comply with international norms and standards of human rights and fundamental freedoms. The Commission called on the international community to support the High Commissioner's involvement in human rights monitoring in Eastern Slavonia and to continue to provide for an international presence.

Taking note of progress made in some areas of Bosnia and Herzegovina (composed of Republika Srpska and the Federation of Bosnia and Herzegovina) to implement the 1995 General Framework Agreement for Peace in Bosnia and Herzegovina (the Peace Agreement) [YUN 1995, p. 544] and improve respect for human rights, the Commission expressed serious concern about continuing human rights violations within Bosnia and Herzegovina and continuing obstruction of full implementation of the Peace Agreement's human rights provisions. It condemned the intimidation and perpetration of violence against minority refugees and internally displaced persons returning to their homes, the destruction of their homes and all other acts designed to discourage their voluntary return, and called for the authorities to determine responsibility for those acts and to ensure that perpetrators were brought to justice.

The Commission called on States to cooperate with ICTY and welcomed the decision by the Prime Minister of Republika Srpska to allow the Tribunal to open an office in Banja Luka. Noting with dismay that the large majority of those indictees still at large were known to be present in FRY, the Commission called on all indicted persons to surrender voluntarily.

Welcoming increased cooperation in the joint exhumation process in Bosnia and Herzegovina with the Office of the High Representative and the International Commission on Missing Persons in the Former Yugoslavia, the Commission urged that the cooperation continue and insisted that FRY authorities and Kosovar Albanians cooperate with international humanitarian organizations in dealing with the issue of missing persons in Kosovo.

The Commission asked the High Commissioner and the Secretary-General to develop early-warning procedures in the area of human rights to identify situations that could lead to conflict or humanitarian tragedy, and asked them to report in 2000.

The Commission decided to renew for one year the mandate of the Special Rapporteur on the situation of human rights in Bosnia and Herzegovina, Croatia and FRY and asked him to carry out missions to Bosnia and Herzegovina, including Republika Srpska; Croatia, including Eastern Slavonia, Baranja and Western Sirmium; and FRY, including Kosovo, as well as Sandjak and Vojvodina. It asked him to report in 2000 and to submit interim reports about his work in support of the Kosovo initiative of the High Commissioner, and to present interim reports to the General Assembly at its fifty-fourth (1999) session. The Secretary-General was asked to make his reports available to the Security Council, OSCE and other international human rights and humanitarian organizations. By **decision 1999/232** of 27 July, the Economic and Social Council endorsed the Commission's decision to renew the Special Rapporteur's mandate and approved its request that he carry out missions to the designated areas. It also endorsed the Commission's decisions regarding the submission of reports and its requests to the Secretary-General.

Reports of Special Rapporteur. In September [A/54/396-S/1999/1000], Special Rapporteur Jiri Dienstbier (Czech Republic) described his visits to Bosnia and Herzegovina, Croatia and FRY. In Bosnia and Herzegovina (15-20 May), mainly in Republika Srpska, he stopped in Banja Luka, Brcko, Bijeljina and other towns to assess the impact of the Kosovo crisis on human rights. Regarding civil and political rights, he found that there were still major problems surrounding the role of the police, although some progress had been made. The police remained mono-ethnic in most areas and general effectiveness in crime detection remained low, which had led to impunity. The political will to create a multi-ethnic police continued to be lacking and the number of women police was alarmingly low. The lack of a functioning and independent judiciary remained a major concern. Judges and prosecutors, unlike police, were never subjected to a recertification process after the war. Substantial numbers of judicial personnel were either incompetent or inadequately trained, and corruption and political influence tainted the judicial system. In the Federation, several war crimes proceedings were under way. Minority returns continued, but the numbers remained insignificant compared with the number of displaced persons. Returnees were often not provided with the most basic services. While joint institutions existed at the State level, they did not work effectively. As to economic, social and cultural rights, property laws in both the Federation and Republika Srpska had been amended. A major barrier to the implementation of the laws was the non-execution of eviction orders against temporary occupants of property belonging to someone else. There were reports of discrimination in employment. The education system remained divided along ethnic lines, and it lacked material resources. Pensioners experienced major difficulties receiving and surviving on their pensions, authorities failed to adequately address the rights of persons with disabilities and women faced particular obstacles to realizing their economic rights. The Special Rapporteur concluded that minimal progress had been made regarding respect for human rights and freedoms and the development of a tolerant, multi-ethnic society. The Kosovo crisis and the NATO operations against FRY (see p. 342) had slowed progress. The Special Rapporteur emphasized the need to continue reform of the police and the judicial system; to end discriminatory practices in the areas of economic and social rights; and to better coordinate international and national human rights mechanisms.

The Special Rapporteur visited Croatia (25 July–4 August), with stops in Opatija, Istria, Rijeka, Knin, Split and Zagreb. In Eastern Slavonia, there had been a series of ethnically motivated violent incidents, with increasingly serious cases of intimidation, threat and arson against minority ethnic Serbs. In central and southern Croatia, the security situation had been generally calm, although there had been a slight increase in ethnically related incidents in Petrinja, Hrvatska Kostajnica, Karlovac and Kistanje. There was little improvement in the Government's protection of the right to return to one's place of origin. The slow implementation of the Programme for the Return and Accommodation of Displaced Persons, Refugees and Exiled Persons [YUN 1998, p. 347] seemed to be rooted in a lack of will on the part of the central and local authorities, the Government Commission on Return and local housing commissions. The Government reported that, as at 14 July, 22 per cent of the 6,613 filed claims for property repossession had been completed. The Special Rapporteur noted that reconstruction of war-damaged houses and infrastructure continued according to ethnic priorities. The administration of justice was held up by vacant posts in all branches of the judiciary. Government control of the electronic media, as well as indirect pressure on press freedom, remained major concerns. The Special Rapporteur called on the Government to continue to actively address the issue of missing persons in Croatia. He advocated the investigation and trial of all war crimes with international monitors to ensure transparency and the bringing of perpetrators to justice. Regarding gender issues, he commended the initiatives of the State Commission on Issues of Equality regarding legislative changes and supported its efforts to integrate gender issues into the country's public agenda.

The Special Rapporteur visited FRY (26-30 April, Montenegro, including part of Sandzak; 8-12 June, Vojvodina and central Serbia; 7-12 July, Kosovo). In April, he had conducted a special mission to FYROM to inquire into the situation of Kosovo refugees. He reported on the period from mid-March through mid-August, including the period of the NATO air campaign against FRY until the signing of the military agreement on 9 June (see p. 356), and subsequent developments. The scope of the human and material tragedy sparked by the Kosovo crisis, but caused by systemic failures to respect or protect human rights throughout FRY, was still being calculated. From the perspective of human rights, it was difficult to assess what 78 days of war had achieved. There had been mass expulsion and ethnic cleansing of hundreds of thousands of Kosovo Albanians; killings of civilians; arrest and arbitrary detention of several thousand Kosovo Albanians, held in prisons in Serbia; systematic destruction of villages, neighbourhoods, means of livelihood and homes of selected individuals; rape as an instrument of terror; use of landmines and depleted uranium ammunition; forced mobilization; destruction of civilian transport, communications and public utilities infrastructure; mass unemployment and impoverishment; suppression of civil freedoms, including freedom of expression; targeted killings of journalists; martial law; deliberate destruction of religious and cultural monuments; and ethnic cleansing of nearly 200,000 non-Albanians from Kosovo. As a result of his inquiries, the Special Rapporteur concluded that most of the deaths and damage inside Kosovo resulted from a systematic campaign of ethnic cleansing and terror waged by FRY and Serbian forces against Kosovo Albanians. Human rights violations were also attributed to KLA. Given the magnitude of the FRY and Serbian operations, and NATO's massive bombing of Kosovo, the number of persons killed within Kosovo during the war was unlikely ever to be accurately known. The Special Rapporteur stated that the first casualty of the war was the rule of law. Many legal protections of the accused were removed, and substituted expedited procedures allowed for searches without warrants and police investigations without prior legal requests. Other casualties of the war were freedom of expression and access to information. The NATO air campaign was especially intensive in the densely populated centres of Vojvodina, southern Serbia and Belgrade. The damage done to industrial centres in Pancevo, Kragujevac, Bor and Pristina, as well as to national parks, raised environmental concerns. Civilians were killed in Aleksinac, Nis, Novi Pazar, Surdulica and Kursumlija. Strikes on bridges and means of transportation resulted in deaths, and large convoys moving through Kosovo were attacked from the air, resulting in the deaths of 87 internally displaced persons at Korisa on 14 May. All three bridges in Novi Sad were destroyed, as well as the water pipes that supplied potable water to nearly half the city. Following NATO attacks on fuel reserves, restrictions on fuel brought civilian Serbia to a standstill, with many areas often without electricity and water. In

Montenegro, the large number and pervasive presence of the Yugoslav army, army reservists and military police gave rise to internal tensions and human rights violations. The human rights violation in Kosovo most often described to the Special Rapporteur was forced expulsion. Accounts from persons who remained in Kosovo during the war agreed that the period from 24 March to 10 April saw a rampage of killing, burning, looting, forced expulsion and terror. All civilian accounts agreed that paramilitaries often accompanied police and army forces. In mid-May, the large cities of Kosovo saw sweeping mass arrests of men of military age. FRY had the largest refugee caseload in Europe, estimated before the war at 500,000 persons from Bosnia and Herzegovina and Croatia (see PART THREE, Chapter XII). The war slowed or completely stopped refugee returns to Croatia, halted the integration of refugees into Yugoslav society, interrupted the resettlement of refugees to third countries, and prevented the regular flow of humanitarian aid to refugees in FRY. Following the war in Kosovo, human rights violations in Kosovo occurred with virtual impunity despite UNMIK efforts to create a temporary judiciary. Killings, abductions, destruction of property and continued displacements of non-Albanians and politically suspect Kosovo Albanians reflected the failure of the international community to bring the territory under control. Many human rights violations perpetrated by non-State actors were not dissimilar to those that preceded the NATO intervention in March. UNHCR and FRY sources agreed that some 200,000 non-Albanians had left Kosovo. From 15 June to 14 August, according to KFOR statistics, 280 persons were murdered in Kosovo, at a rate of 30 to 40 murders per week. The killings of Serbs, Kosovo Albanians, Roma, Muslim Slavs and others were attributed to Kosovo Albanian paramilitaries. The issue of detainees remained unresolved at the time of the report. Groups representing detainees had called for their release or, at a minimum, their transfer to UNMIK custody in Kosovo. Although the KLA commander denied the continued existence of detention centres, KFOR located several within Kosovo, including at least two, in Prizren and Gnjilane, described as containing instruments of torture. The Special Rapporteur noted that KFOR not only had failed to locate and arrest KLA "police" and "military police" associated with detentions and abductions, but had also reportedly relied on information provided by KLA on persons whom KFOR should have arrested.

In his concluding observations, the Special Rapporteur noted that there had been no initiatives for a political settlement. He recommended that ICTY should investigate violations that had occurred in Kosovo after the signing of the Kumanovo agreement (see p. 356) and the undertaking with KLA in June; under UN agency leadership, studies should continue on the long-term consequences for public health of damage done by NATO bombing of industrial centres; the international community should launch winterization programmes for the whole of FRY, which was threatened with another humanitarian catastrophe; FRY should provide ICRC and the High Commissioner with the names, whereabouts and status of charges against persons arrested in Kosovo and detained in FRY; detainees held outside Kosovo should be guaranteed access to defence counsel of their choice, as well as visits by family and physicians; UNMIK and FRY should discuss the return of detainees to Kosovo and their release to UNMIK; KLA should release information on detainees held since March 1998, release detainees to UNMIK and shut down its detention operations; UNMIK should establish a full, permanent court system in Kosovo; UNMIK and KFOR should protect the rights of all Kosovo citizens against violence, intimidation and other unlawful acts by members of the same or other ethnic groups; and attention should be paid to the social rights of the elderly, the handicapped and children, and reports of trafficking in women or children should be investigated.

FRY, on 9 November [A/C.3/54/10], presented its comments on the Special Rapporteur's report, stating that it was highly politicized and that the Special Rapporteur was unable to fulfil his mandate impartially and independently. FRY charged that alleging that the source of all problems was systemic failure to respect or protect human rights throughout FRY, while tiptoeing around massive NATO human rights violations in Kosovo and Metohija and keeping silent about NATO violations in the rest of FRY, was morally suspect. FRY contended that the Special Rapporteur's concluding observations and recommendations had been simplified and did not correspond with the gravity of the situation in the reporting period. It claimed that, in its entirety, the report diverted attention from, or was completely silent about, the persecution and ethnic cleansing of over 330,000 Serbs, Montenegrins, Roma, Turks, Gorani, Muslims, Croats and other non-Albanians from Kosovo and Metohija, which continued unabated in the presence of KFOR and UNMIK.

The Special Rapporteur updated information as at 2 November [A/54/396/Add.1-S/1999/1000/Add.1]. In Bosnia and Herzegovina, there was a near-total absence of the rule of law regarding property rights, which had led to very few returns. Insufficient progress was made to eliminate discriminatory practices relating to social and economic rights. The Special Rapporteur called for the implementation of the Peace Agreement and individual decisions affecting property.

The Special Rapporteur expressed concern with respect to the legality of the election of judges by the Croatian Parliament to the Croatian Constitutional Court as a package of eight and not individually, as was the usual practice. He recommended that Croatian Serbs who wished to return should be enabled to do so and the authorities should establish conditions that would make their return possible. All returnees should have access to an effective legal remedy for the restitution of their property. Harassment of independent media should be stopped. The fairness of elections scheduled for December would be evaluated, among other factors, by the equality of access of all competing parties to the media.

The Special Rapporteur visited FRY (1-9 October), where he travelled to Belgrade, Nis, Kraljevo, Novi Pazar, Rozaje, Kosovska, Mitrovica, Gnjilane and Pristina. He reported that the Kosovo crisis had not ended: the spring ethnic cleansing of Albanians had been replaced by the fall ethnic cleansing of non-Albanians. As at the end of October, some 250,000 persons had been displaced since mid-June from Kosovo, a region that had lost most of its non-Albanian population. Since July, the international presence in Kosovo had grown, as had the UNMIK staff and its police forces. UNMIK institutions of civil administration had not supplanted parallel institutions, which were controlled by KLA. Regional courts had started to prosecute some common criminal cases and, in two districts, had initiated domestic war crime proceedings. New collective and individual graves continued to be discovered daily, but many victims remained unidentified. Efforts to address the situation of several thousand detainees in Kosovo moved forward with the creation by UNMIK in late September of the Commission on Prisoners and Detainees, chaired by OHCHR-FRY. KLA had created a de facto government, appointed mayors, directors of enterprises and other officials, pursued a policy of ethnic cleansing in jobs, and supported the confiscation of property of non-Albanians and even of some Albanians. The Special Rapporteur recommended that, in Kosovo, UNMIK should appoint to posts in the provisional multi-ethnic administration only persons who had demonstrated their democratic beliefs. Elections for all levels of administration should be postponed until stability had been achieved. Property rights of all citizens should be respected and violators of laws should be arrested and punished. Arms should be registered and confiscated. The borders with Albania and FYROM should be controlled to prevent free access to Kosovo by criminals, drug traffickers and other undesirable elements. Member States should send to Kosovo the necessary personnel they had promised. All sanctions and embargoes against FRY (except for the arms embargo) should be terminated and humanitarian aid should be delivered.

A further report [E/CN.4/2000/39] by the Special Rapporteur covered developments until the first week of December and was based on information gathered by OHCHR field offices. He noted that there had been little change in the human rights situation in Bosnia and Herzegovina. The number of minority returns was still exceedingly low, despite large numbers of refugees and displaced persons who had expressed their wish to return to their pre-war homes. The Special Rapporteur urged that combating discriminatory practices, including in the areas of economic and social rights, be accorded the highest priority. The number of refugee returns in Croatia was also small. The Special Rapporteur urged Croatia to devise a system of compensation to resolve the problem raised by the wartime law abolishing occupancy rights and to repeal or amend discriminatory property legislation. He urged the Government to undertake a more earnest campaign to foster returns of ethnic Serb refugees and to undertake reconstruction and economic revitalization projects to benefit all ethnic communities. He recommended that it increase resources allocated to the judiciary; guarantee employees their salaries or effective legal remedies through which salaries could be claimed; identify the fate of 1,668 persons officially registered as missing; and, with the participation of international representatives, undertake investigations and trials of all war crimes. In Kosovo, the ethnic cleansing of Serbs and "undesirable" non-Albanians was being followed by threats, intimidation and episodic acts of violence directed against Albanians who did not share the view of the "parallel administration" controlled by KLA. OHCHR had noted new abductions of Montenegrin citizens from parts of Montenegro that bordered Kosovo and had received several reports weekly of harassment, searches, and confiscation of goods and personal funds at police checkpoints in Serbia. The Special Rapporteur repeated recommendations made in his previous reports and added that the Government of FRY, including the authorities of the republics of Serbia and Montenegro, should: permit OHCHR and ICRC access to places of detention and allow court proceedings to be accessible to monitors; improve its performance in the administration of justice; end torture and ill-treatment of those in prison and other detention facilities and bring perpetrators to justice; expand the competence of local government bodies; ensure fair government representation of national minorities ; and pay attention to the social and economic rights of the most vulnerable. Detainees, except those suspected of human rights violations, should be released; UNMIK and KFOR should investigate reports of trafficking of women and children from Kosovo; FRY should agree to the formal establishment of OHCHR sub-offices in Pristina and Podgorica; Serbia should repeal the Law on Public Information and the Law on Universities; UNMIK should adopt a "rules of the road" protocol with ICTY regarding domestic war-crimes prosecutions; and the international community should cease isolating the people of FRY.

FRY transmitted its comments on the Special Rapporteur's report [E/CN.4/2000/154], stating, among other things, that the report was selective in its subject matter, which, FRY claimed, had served to cover up the massive crimes against the Serbs in Kosovo and Metohija and the serious human rights abuses, and the plight, of internally displaced persons. Comments were also presented on freedom of the media and access to information; arrest, detention and missing persons; the rule of law and the right to a fair trial; and freedom of association.

GENERAL ASSEMBLY ACTION

On 17 December [meeting 83], the General Assembly, on the recommendation of the Third Committee [A/54/605/Add.3], adopted **resolution 54/184** by recorded vote (123-2-34) [agenda item 116 *(c)*].

Situation of human rights in Bosnia and Herzegovina, the Republic of Croatia and the Federal Republic of Yugoslavia (Serbia and Montenegro)

The General Assembly,

Bearing in mind all relevant resolutions on this subject, in particular Commission on Human Rights resolution 1999/18 of 23 April 1999, as well as all Security Council resolutions and statements,

Bearing in mind also General Assembly resolution 54/183 of 17 December 1999 on the situation of human rights in Kosovo,

Reaffirming the obligations of all Member States under the Charter of the United Nations and the Universal Declaration of Human Rights, the obligations of States parties under the International Covenants on Human Rights and all other human rights instruments and the obligation of all to respect international humanitarian law, including the Geneva Conventions of 12 August 1949 for the protection of victims of war and the Additional Protocols thereto, of 1977, as well as the principles and commitments undertaken by participating States of the Organization for Security and Cooperation in Europe,

Reaffirming also the territorial integrity of all States in the region, within their internationally recognized borders, taking fully into account all relevant Security Council resolutions,

Expressing its full support for the General Framework Agreement for Peace in Bosnia and Herzegovina and the annexes thereto (collectively the "Peace Agreement"), which, inter alia, committed the parties of Bosnia and Herzegovina, the Republic of Croatia and the Federal Republic of Yugoslavia (Serbia and Montenegro) to respect human rights fully, and for the Basic Agreement on the Region of Eastern Slavonia, Baranja and Western Sirmium (the "Basic Agreement"),

Expressing its deep concern at the continuing evidence of violations of human rights and fundamental freedoms taking place to varying degrees in Bosnia and Herzegovina, the Republic of Croatia and the Federal Republic of Yugoslavia (Serbia and Montenegro) and, in particular, the failure of the Federal Republic of Yugoslavia (Serbia and Montenegro) to follow the recommendations made in 1996 by the personal representative of the Chairman-in-Office of the Organization for Security and Cooperation in Europe,

Welcoming all contributions of the Office of the High Representative, the Office of the United Nations High Commissioner for Human Rights, the Office of the United Nations High Commissioner for Refugees and other parts of the United Nations, the Organization for Security and Cooperation in Europe, the Council of Europe, the European Community Monitoring Mission, Governments and intergovernmental and non-governmental organizations in the area in 1999,

1. *Reiterates its call* for the full and consistent implementation of the General Framework Agreement for Peace in Bosnia and Herzegovina and the annexes thereto (collectively the "Peace Agreement") and the Basic Agreement on the Region of Eastern Slavonia, Baranja and Western Sirmium (the "Basic Agreement") by all parties to those agreements;

2. *Stresses* the crucial role of human rights in the successful implementation of the Peace Agreement, and underlines the obligations of the parties under the Peace Agreement to secure for all persons within their jurisdiction the highest level of international norms and standards of human rights and fundamental freedoms;

3. *Also stresses* the need to direct international human rights efforts in the region to the core issues of the lack of full respect for the human rights and fundamental freedoms of all individuals without distinction, the rule of law and effective administration of justice at all levels of government, the freedom and independence of the media, freedom of expression, freedom of association, including with respect to political parties, freedom of religion and freedom of movement;

4. *Further stresses* the need for enhanced international human rights efforts to foster and effect the prompt and voluntary return of displaced persons and refugees in safety and with dignity;

5. *Reiterates its call upon* all parties and States in the region to ensure that the promotion and protection of human rights and effective, functioning democratic institutions will be central elements in developing civilian structures, as reaffirmed at the meetings of the

Steering Board of the Peace Implementation Council and the Peace Implementation Conference;

6. *Urges* all States and parties to the Peace Agreement that have not done so to meet their obligations to cooperate fully with the International Tribunal for the Prosecution of Persons Responsible for Serious Violations of International Humanitarian Law Committed in the Territory of the Former Yugoslavia since 1991, as required by Security Council resolution 827 (1993) of 25 May 1993 and all subsequent relevant resolutions, and, in particular, to comply with their obligations to arrest and transfer to the custody of the Tribunal those indicted persons present in their territories or in territories under their control;

7. *Continues to call upon* all parties to the Peace Agreement to take immediate steps to determine the identity, whereabouts and fate of missing persons in their territories, including through close cooperation with the United Nations as well as with humanitarian organizations and independent experts, and stresses the importance of coordination in this area;

8. *Notes* that varying degrees of progress have been made in the human rights situation in several areas, but that substantial efforts remain to be made;

I. Bosnia and Herzegovina

9. *Notes* the progress made in Bosnia and Herzegovina with regard to the increase in political pluralism and freedom of expression, through the participation of all groups and individuals, which represents another step towards democracy in Bosnia and Herzegovina, but remains concerned that freedom of speech and the media are still curtailed by political influence, notably through the selective and intimidating application of slander laws;

10. *Expresses its continued serious concern* about continuing human rights violations within Bosnia and Herzegovina and delays in the full implementation of the human rights provisions of the Peace Agreement, notably the delay in bringing legislation into compliance with the human rights provisions of the national Constitution of the country, and the failure of local authorities and groups to comply with the obligations of the Peace Agreement;

11. *Condemns in the strongest terms* the complicity by local governments in the perpetration of violence against minority refugees and internally displaced persons returning to their homes and in the destruction of their homes, including acts of intimidation and all those acts designed to discourage the voluntary return of refugees and internally displaced persons, and calls for the removal from office of implicated local government officials as well as the immediate arrest and bringing to justice of those responsible for such acts;

12. *Calls upon* all the authorities of Bosnia and Herzegovina to adjudicate claims for and implement decisions on property rights made by local authorities and/or by the Commission for Real Property Claims of Displaced Persons and Refugees without further delay;

13. *Reiterates its demand* that all parties in Bosnia and Herzegovina immediately create conditions conducive to the voluntary return, in safety and with dignity, of refugees and internally displaced persons to their homes, with equal emphasis on the rights of persons belonging to minorities, pass immediately and enforce legislation on property rights in conformity with recommendations made by the Office of the High Representative and end practices of discrimination on ethnic or political grounds;

14. *Notes with satisfaction* the decline in violence against returning refugees and displaced persons, while remaining concerned that all ethnic groups continue to report harassment;

15. *Welcomes* the adoption of a new criminal code and of codes of ethics by the judges and prosecutors of both entities and the increased strength of the prosecutor's office of the Federation of Bosnia and Herzegovina as a result of laws imposed by the High Representative, but notes that the judicial processes still do not sufficiently protect the rights of the accused;

16. *Notes* that implementation of the decisions of the Human Rights Chamber has begun, while reminding both State- and entity-level governments to pay increased attention to decisions of the Chamber;

17. *Calls upon* the authorities of Bosnia and Herzegovina and, in particular, the authorities of the Republika Srpska to increase their cooperation with the Commission on Human Rights for Bosnia and Herzegovina, to cooperate fully with the International Tribunal for the Former Yugoslavia and to intensify their efforts in this regard;

18. *Notes* that police standards and protection have improved, while remaining concerned about continuing indications among the police of unprofessional conduct, political influence and instances of interference with the return of refugees and the use of excessive force;

19. *Urges* the authorities of Bosnia and Herzegovina, in particular those of the Republika Srpska, to ensure full and free access to their territories for all institutions and organizations concerned with the implementation of the present resolution, including non-governmental organizations, and to provide for the protection of those organizations, especially those providing humanitarian assistance;

20. *Stresses* the importance of the implementation of the programme proposed by the High Representative in coordination with the United Nations Mission in Bosnia and Herzegovina, the Council of Europe and the Organization for Security and Cooperation in Europe for a comprehensive judicial reform;

21. *Calls upon* the authorities of both entities to cooperate closely with the Office of the United Nations High Commissioner for Refugees in matters relating to the return of refugees and to ensure that local authorities and groups permit and encourage the return of displaced persons to their homes of origin;

22. *Calls upon* the authorities of Bosnia and Herzegovina urgently to consider, with a view to its early adoption and full implementation, the draft permanent election law designed by the Organization for Security and Cooperation in Europe to strengthen ties between constituents and representatives, strengthen democratic accountability and encourage pluralistic, multi-ethnic political parties;

23. *Notes* the importance of the work of the Human Rights Ombudsman in bringing to light many cases of human rights violations and in resolving several of them, and urges the authorities of Bosnia and Herzegovina to implement the recommendations of the Ombudsman;

24. *Condemns* recurrent instances of religious discrimination and violence and the denial to religious minorities of their rights to reclaim and rebuild their religious sites;

25. *Expresses its concern* that trafficking in women is a growing problem, and calls upon the authorities of Bosnia and Herzegovina to act vigorously to combat this problem;

II. Republic of Croatia

26. *Notes with interest* the initiatives taken by the Republic of Croatia to improve the legislative and economic framework for the return of refugees, in particular steps to eliminate discriminatory provisions of Croatian laws;

27. *Notes with satisfaction* the cooperation between the Police Monitoring Group of the Organization for Security and Cooperation in Europe and the local police forces in Eastern Slavonia, while also noting continued instances of ethnically based problems in Eastern Slavonia;

28. *Welcomes* the continuing efforts by the Republic of Croatia to train and to guarantee the professionalism and impartiality of the Croatian police and military forces, and notes, in particular, the commitment on the part of the Ministry of the Interior to maintain an ethnically diverse police force in the Danube region;

29. *Also welcomes* the actions of the Government of the Republic of Croatia related to the return of significant numbers of persons to their places of origin since 1995 and the steps being taken by the Government to eliminate discriminatory provisions of Croatian laws, while noting that the pace of minority returns from third countries has been disappointing, and expresses concern that protection of the rights of persons belonging to minorities has not met the level of Croatia's legal obligations;

30. *Notes* that the Government of the Republic of Croatia has continued its efforts to codify democratic norms, including the independence of its judiciary and freedom of association and assembly, while also noting that the application by the Government of those laws and principles has lagged behind its stated intentions;

31. *Expresses deep concern* about the fact that commitments by the Government to improve the freedom of the press have remained unfulfilled, and reaffirms the need for free and independent media and the need to provide to all political parties equal access to all forms of media during the forthcoming electoral campaign;

32. *Notes* the passage of a new telecommunications law as a positive step, but urges the Government of the Republic of Croatia to comply with international recommendations, in particular those of the mission of the Organization for Security and Cooperation in Europe in the areas of electoral and media reform, regrets that until now those recommendations have been only partially fulfilled, and stresses the importance of the full application of the citizenship law of 1991;

33. *Expresses deep concern* about the reported extensive campaign of wiretapping against the independent media and opposition political figures, and calls upon the Government of the Republic of Croatia to ensure that the media and opposition political figures and parties are not harassed or hindered in their actions or intimidated by actions of the Government and are guaranteed the same protections as representatives of the media or political establishment who are favourable to the Government;

34. *Welcomes* the signing on 10 May 1999 by the Government of the Republic of Croatia of the programme of technical assistance of the Office of the United Nations High Commissioner for Human Rights, with a view to building national human rights capacity and human rights education, and looks forward to the implementation of the programme in December 1999;

35. *Notes* the efforts of the Republic of Croatia to codify and incorporate the impartial application of the law, but urges the swift and complete implementation of judicial decisions for all citizens, irrespective of ethnicity, religion or political affiliation, while noting with concern that due process, the rule of law, the treatment of ethnic minorities and press freedoms fall short of the standards of the Organization for Security and Cooperation in Europe, notably that lengthy judicial processes plague the Croatian judiciary and that cases of interest to the ruling party are processed more expeditiously than others;

36. *Also notes* the formal steps taken by the Republic of Croatia to guarantee the rights of persons belonging to minorities and the ratification of the Framework Convention for the Protection of National Minorities and the European Charter for Regional or Minority Languages, but continues to remind the Government of its primary responsibility to restore the multi-ethnic character of Croatia, in fact as well as in law, including the pledge to guarantee the representation of national minorities, including Serbs, at various levels of local, regional and national government;

37. *Further notes* outstanding letters from the President of the International Tribunal for the Prosecution of Persons Responsible for Serious Violations of International Humanitarian Law Committed in the Territory of the Former Yugoslavia since 1991 to the Security Council, and calls upon the Republic of Croatia to cooperate fully with the Tribunal and to comply, in particular, with its obligation to arrest and transfer to the custody of the Tribunal those indicted persons known to be present in its territory and, when prosecuting war crimes, to ensure that domestic prosecution complies with international standards and the obligations of the Republic of Croatia to the Tribunal;

III. Federal Republic of Yugoslavia
(Serbia and Montenegro)

38. *Condemns* the Federal Republic of Yugoslavia (Serbia and Montenegro) for its gross violations of the human rights of the ethnic Albanians of Kosovo and its violent campaign to expel or deport ethnic Albanian Kosovars from their homes and communities in the Federal Republic of Yugoslavia (Serbia and Montenegro);

39. *Calls upon* the Government of the Federal Republic of Yugoslavia (Serbia and Montenegro) and all authorities and representatives of ethnic groups in Kosovo to implement Security Council resolution 1244(1999) of 10 June 1999 and consequently to cooperate fully with and support the United Nations Interim Administration Mission in Kosovo in the fulfilment of its mandate;

40. *Strongly condemns* the presence of indicted war criminals in the hierarchy of the Government of the

Federal Republic of Yugoslavia (Serbia and Montenegro) and of the Government of the Republic of Serbia or those who are fugitives in the territory of the Federal Republic of Yugoslavia (Serbia and Montenegro), and calls for them to be removed from office and transferred to the custody of the International Tribunal for the Former Yugoslavia as one of the first steps towards reinstating the Federal Republic of Yugoslavia (Serbia and Montenegro) in the community of law-abiding States;

41. *Demands* that the Government of the Federal Republic of Yugoslavia (Serbia and Montenegro) hand over to the International Tribunal for the Former Yugoslavia all government officials of the Federal Republic of Yugoslavia (Serbia and Montenegro) and of the Government of the Republic of Serbia indicted as war criminals and repudiate the leadership of anyone so indicted as a first step towards establishing a democratic government and becoming a full and respected member of the international community, and reminds the Government of the Federal Republic of Yugoslavia (Serbia and Montenegro) of its obligations to cooperate fully with the Tribunal;

42. *Also demands* that the Government of the Federal Republic of Yugoslavia (Serbia and Montenegro) immediately bring to justice any persons, in particular those among its personnel, who have authorized or engaged in breaches of international humanitarian law and violations of human rights, including summary executions, indiscriminate attacks on civilians, indiscriminate destruction of property, mass forced displacement of civilians, the taking of civilian hostages, torture and other cruel, inhuman or degrading treatment or punishment, and, in this context, reminds the Government of the Federal Republic of Yugoslavia (Serbia and Montenegro) of its obligations to cooperate fully with the International Tribunal for the Former Yugoslavia and the United Nations High Commissioner for Human Rights;

43. *Further demands* an immediate end to illegal and/or hidden detention by the Federal Republic of Yugoslavia (Serbia and Montenegro), as well as by paramilitary groups in Kosovo, and requests the Special Rapporteur of the Commission on Human Rights on the situation of human rights in Bosnia and Herzegovina, the Republic of Croatia and the Federal Republic of Yugoslavia (Serbia and Montenegro) to investigate any and all allegations of hidden detentions, including detentions of ethnic Serbs, Albanians and others;

44. *Demands* that the Government of the Federal Republic of Yugoslavia (Serbia and Montenegro) institutionalize democratic norms by holding free and fair elections at all levels of government, respecting the rule of law and the administration of justice and fully respecting human rights and fundamental freedoms;

45. *Also demands* that the Government of the Federal Republic of Yugoslavia (Serbia and Montenegro) promote and protect free and independent media and that the authorities of the Federal Republic of Yugoslavia (Serbia and Montenegro) repeal any law that hinders the full and free exercise of the democratic rights of the citizens of the Federal Republic of Yugoslavia (Serbia and Montenegro), cease any harassment and hindrance of journalists, wherever within the Federal Republic of Yugoslavia (Serbia and Montenegro) they may be practising their profession, and repeal repressive laws on universities and the media which suppress any and all internal dissent or expression of independent views, and concomitantly respect the right of free speech;

46. *Emphasizes* that the subversion of the fundamental democratic rights of the citizens of the Federal Republic of Yugoslavia (Serbia and Montenegro) extends to the Federal Republic of Yugoslavia (Serbia and Montenegro) as a whole, calls upon the Government of the Federal Republic of Yugoslavia (Serbia and Montenegro) to respect the rights of all persons belonging to minority groups, especially in the Sandjak and Vojvodina, and of persons belonging to the Bulgarian minority, and supports the unconditional return of the long-term missions of the Organization for Security and Cooperation in Europe, as called for by the Security Council in its resolutions;

47. *Expresses its concern* at the continued grave infringements upon freedom of expression in the Federal Republic of Yugoslavia (Serbia and Montenegro), in particular with regard to the exploitation of the crisis in Kosovo as a means to stifle and suppress views opposing the Government in power, a violation of the basic right of free speech;

48. *Denounces* the Government of the Federal Republic of Yugoslavia (Serbia and Montenegro) for its legal and physical intimidation of peaceful political opposition and of individuals who express views that differ from those of the Government, and demands that the Federal Republic of Yugoslavia (Serbia and Montenegro) respect the fundamental rights of individuals to free assembly and free speech;

49. *Insists* that the Government of the Federal Republic of Yugoslavia (Serbia and Montenegro) support the activities of the international community and the United Nations Interim Administration Mission in Kosovo to rebuild and facilitate the multi-ethnic society in Kosovo that the policy of ethnic cleansing, intimidation and discrimination largely destroyed, in particular by using the influence of the Government of the Federal Republic of Yugoslavia (Serbia and Montenegro) among the local Serb representatives in Kosovo and by working in good faith with the local Albanian representatives to that end;

50. *Calls upon* the authorities of the Federal Republic of Yugoslavia (Serbia and Montenegro) to implement fully, with dispatch and in good faith, their obligations under the Peace Agreement, notably to cooperate fully with the Office of the United Nations High Commissioner for Refugees and other humanitarian organizations to alleviate the suffering of refugees and internally displaced persons and to assist in their safe and voluntary return to their homes;

51. *Calls upon* States to consider additional voluntary contributions to meet the pressing human rights and humanitarian needs in the area, and underlines the need for continued coordination among States, international organizations and non-governmental organizations of initiatives and programmes with the aim of avoiding duplication, overlap and working at cross-purposes;

52. *Decides* to continue its examination of this question at its fifty-fifth session under the item entitled "Human rights questions".

RECORDED VOTE ON RESOLUTION 54/184:

In favour: Afghanistan, Albania, Algeria, Andorra, Antigua and Barbuda, Argentina, Australia, Austria, Azerbaijan, Bahamas, Bahrain, Bangladesh, Barbados, Belgium, Belize, Bhutan, Bolivia, Bosnia and Herzegovina, Botswana, Brazil, Brunei Darussalam, Bulgaria, Canada, Cape Verde, Chile, Colombia, Comoros, Costa Rica, Cyprus, Czech Republic, Denmark, Djibouti, Dominica, Dominican Republic, Ecuador, Egypt, El Salvador, Estonia, Finland, France, Georgia, Germany, Greece, Grenada, Guatemala, Guinea-Bissau, Guyana, Haiti, Hungary, Iceland, Indonesia, Iran, Ireland, Italy, Jamaica, Japan, Jordan, Kazakhstan, Kuwait, Latvia, Lebanon, Libyan Arab Jamahiriya, Liechtenstein, Lithuania, Luxembourg, Malawi, Malaysia, Maldives, Malta, Marshall Islands, Mauritius, Micronesia, Monaco, Mongolia, Morocco, Mozambique, Nepal, Netherlands, New Zealand, Nicaragua, Nigeria, Norway, Oman, Pakistan, Panama, Papua New Guinea, Paraguay, Peru, Philippines, Poland, Portugal, Qatar, Republic of Korea, Republic of Moldova, Romania, Samoa, San Marino, Saudi Arabia, Senegal, Sierra Leone, Slovakia, Slovenia, Solomon Islands, South Africa, Spain, Sri Lanka, Sudan, Sweden, Syrian Arab Republic, Thailand, The former Yugoslav Republic of Macedonia, Trinidad and Tobago, Tunisia, Turkey, Ukraine, United Arab Emirates, United Kingdom, United States, Uruguay, Uzbekistan, Venezuela, Zambia, Zimbabwe.

Against: Belarus, Russian Federation.

Abstaining: Angola, Benin, Burkina Faso, Cambodia, Cameroon, Chad, China, Congo, Côte d'Ivoire, Croatia, Cuba, Democratic People's Republic of Korea, Democratic Republic of the Congo, Eritrea, Ethiopia, Fiji, Gabon, Ghana, Guinea, India, Kenya, Lao People's Democratic Republic, Mali, Mexico, Myanmar, Namibia, Saint Lucia, Singapore, Suriname, Swaziland, Tajikistan, Togo, Uganda, United Republic of Tanzania.

The Assembly adopted sections I and II by a separate recorded vote of 119 to none, with 34 abstentions, and section III by 120 votes to 3, with 31 abstentions.

In the Committee, sections I and II were adopted by a separate recorded vote of 107 to none, with 28 abstentions, and section III by 105 to 3, with 26 abstentions. The draft as a whole was adopted by a recorded vote of 112 to 2, with 26 abstentions.

Middle East

Lebanon

Commission action. By a roll-call vote of 49 to 1, with 3 abstentions, the Commission, on 23 April [res. 1999/12], deplored continued Israeli violations of human rights in the occupied zone in southern Lebanon and Western Bekaa and called on Israel to end those practices. Israel was also called on to comply with the Geneva Conventions of 1949, particularly the Geneva Convention relative to the Protection of Civilian Persons in Time of War (Fourth Geneva Convention), and to release all Lebanese who had been detained, as well as others arbitrarily detained. The Commission asked the Secretary-General to bring its resolution to Israel's attention and to invite Israel to provide information on its implementation. He was also asked to report to the General Assembly in 1999 and to the Commission in 2000.

Reports of Secretary-General. As requested by the Commission in 1998 [YUN 1998, p. 767], the Secretary-General stated that he had asked Israel for information on the extent of the implementation of the Commission's resolution on the situation of human rights in southern Lebanon, but had received no response [E/CN.4/1999/26]. In July [A/54/188], the Secretary-General reported that he had asked Israel for information on the implementation of the Commission's 1999 resolution and had received no reply to his request.

Territories occupied by Israel

During the year, the question of human rights violations in the territories occupied by Israel as a result of the 1967 hostilities in the Middle East was again considered by the Commission on Human Rights. Political and other aspects were considered by the General Assembly, its Special Committee to Investigate Israeli Practices Affecting the Human Rights of the Palestinian People and Other Arabs of the Occupied Territories (Committee on Israeli Practices) and other bodies (see PART ONE, Chapter VI).

Reports of Secretary-General. In accordance with Commission resolution 1998/2 [YUN 1998, p. 768], the Secretary-General reported that he had brought the Commission's resolution concerning the occupied Syrian Golan to the attention of all Governments, the Committee on Israeli Practices, the Committee on the Exercise of the Inalienable Rights of the Palestinian People (Committee on Palestinian Rights), the United Nations Relief and Works Agency for Palestine Refugees in the Near East (UNRWA), regional intergovernmental organizations and international humanitarian organizations [E/CN.4/1999/22]. The UN Department of Public Information provided press coverage for all meetings of the Committee on Israeli Practices and distributed information through documents, press releases, briefings and UN information centres and services.

In response to Commission resolution 1998/1 [YUN 1998, p. 768], the Secretary-General reported that he had brought the resolution on the violation of human rights in the occupied Arab territories to the attention of Israel and all other Governments, the specialized agencies, regional intergovernmental organizations, international humanitarian organizations, the Committee on Israeli Practices, the Committee on Palestinian Rights and UNRWA [E/CN.4/1999/21]. He had received no reply from Israel regarding efforts to implement the Commission's resolution.

The Secretary-General submitted to the Commission in January a list of all General Assembly and other reports issued since 24 April 1998 on the situation of the population living in the occupied Arab territories [E/CN.4/1999/23].

Report of Special Rapporteur. In January [E/CN.4/1999/24], Special Rapporteur Hannu Halinen (Finland) discussed the human rights situation in the occupied Palestinian territories. He had visited the occupied Palestinian territories, Israel and Egypt (3-12 January).

The Special Rapporteur stated that human rights violations in the occupied Palestinian territories had continued, to a large extent along the same lines as in the past. Human rights concerns among the Palestinian population had been exacerbated by the unilateral suspension by Israel in December of the implementation of the Wye River Memorandum [YUN 1998, p. 424]. Several interlocutors told the Special Rapporteur that human rights violations actually stemmed from the peace agreements and that the Palestinian population was currently living in a vacuum as far as human rights protection was concerned. He was told that Israel was violating human rights in the name of security. The expansion of Israeli settlements and the building of new ones, as well as bypass roads connecting the settlements to each other and with Israel, was the greatest concern in the occupied territories. The increased rate of demolition of Palestinian houses had given rise to serious concern. The Special Rapporteur was informed that, in addition to constituting collective punishment, house demolitions were considered by Palestinians as sources of extreme provocation and incitement. The situation of the Arab inhabitants in Jerusalem continued to be precarious. The issue of Palestinian prisoners who remained detained in Israeli prisons and detention centres continued to be a serious source of concern. The Special Rapporteur was informed that more than 2,200 Palestinians continued to be detained in Israel, in conditions not meeting international standards, especially regarding medical care and sanitation. Palestinian detainees lacked access to their lawyers and family visits owing to the travel restrictions placed on Palestinians by Israel. The number of administrative detainees had declined considerably and stood at fewer than 100 persons. Among those detainees were persons who had served their prison terms and had been transferred to administrative detention instead of being released. Administrative detentions by the Palestinian Authority continued to increase sharply at the end of 1998, with many cases related to the right to freedom of expression. Torture methods used by the Israeli General Security Service (GSS) had become less dramatic and violent, mostly consisting of hooding and position abuse. The Special Rapporteur was informed that closures of the occupied territories as a form of collective punishment were fewer than in the past. Palestinian workers required a permit to work in Israel, and permits were limited in number. Restrictions on the freedom of movement of the population of the occupied territories affected their social and economic well-being. The economic and social situation had also affected children's health. The number of violent clashes between Palestinians and Israelis declined owing to the few opportunities for direct physical contact in comparison to the intifada period.

The Special Rapporteur made a series of recommendations regarding administrative detention, the peace process and women's and children's rights.

The report contained a letter from Israel stating the Government's position regarding cooperation with the Special Rapporteur, in which Israel termed the Special Rapporteur's mandate biased and one-sided, and called for its revision. According to the 1993 mandate [YUN 1993, p. 958], the Special Rapporteur was "to investigate Israel's violations of the principles and bases of international law, international humanitarian law and the Geneva Convention relative to the Protection of Civilian Persons in Time of War, of 12 August 1949, in the Palestinian territories occupied by Israel since 1967". The Special Rapporteur believed that the mandate should not be the obstacle to cooperation and had proposed its revision.

Communication. On 12 April [E/CN.4/1999/152], Palestine stated that the Special Rapporteur had exceeded his mandate when he discussed matters relating to the peace process and allegations concerning Palestinian justice. It rejected the request made by Israel and the Special Rapporteur to change his mandate.

Commission action. By a roll-call vote of 31 to 1, with 21 abstentions, the Commission, on 23 April [res. 1999/5], condemned the continued human rights violations in the occupied Palestinian territories, and called on Israel to cease those acts immediately. It also condemned the expropriation of Palestinian homes in Jerusalem and the revocation of identity cards and called on Israel to end those practices. The Commission also called on Israel to abolish the use of torture against Palestinians during interrogation; cease its policy of enforcing collective punishments; desist from all forms of human rights violations in the Palestinian and other occupied Arab territories and respect the bases of international law, the principles of international humanitarian law and its international commitments and agreements; and withdraw from the Palestinian territories. The Secretary-General was asked to bring the Commission's resolution to the attention of

Israel and all other Governments, competent UN organs, the specialized agencies, regional intergovernmental organizations and international humanitarian organizations, to disseminate it as widely as possible and to report in 2000 on its implementation by Israel. He was also asked to provide the Commission with all UN reports issued between its sessions that dealt with conditions in which the Palestinians were living under Israeli occupation.

Also on 23 April [res. 1999/6], by a roll-call vote of 32 to 1, with 20 abstentions, the Commission called on Israel to comply with UN resolutions on the occupied Syrian Golan and demanded that it rescind its decision to impose its laws, jurisdiction and administration on that occupied territory. It also called on Israel to desist from changing the physical character, demographic composition, institutional structure and legal status of the occupied Syrian Golan and to desist from imposing Israeli citizenship and identity cards on the Syrian citizens in the Syrian Golan and from its repressive measures against them. The Secretary-General was asked to bring the Commission's resolution to the attention of all Governments, UN organs, specialized agencies, regional intergovernmental organizations and international humanitarian organizations, to give the resolution wide publicity and to report in 2000.

On the same date [res. 1999/7], by a roll-call vote of 50 to 1, with 2 abstentions, the Commission expressed grave concern at the Israeli settlement activities and their increase since the signing of the Wye River Memorandum in 1998 [YUN 1998, p. 424], which were illegal and constituted a violation of the relevant provisions of the Fourth Geneva Convention. It condemned all acts of terrorism and called on all parties not to allow those acts to affect negatively the ongoing peace process. The Commission urged Israel to comply with the Commission's previous resolutions; to cease its policy of expanding the settlements and related activities in the occupied territories; and to forgo and prevent any new installation of settlers.

PART THREE

Economic and social questions

blank page -- (740)

Chapter I

Development policy and international economic cooperation

In 1999, the world economy began to show signs of recovery from the aftermath of the financial crises in Asia and the Russian Federation and the uncertainties related to Brazil. Overall, world growth expanded by 2.6 per cent, a notable improvement over the 1.8 per cent of 1998. The rate of growth in the developing countries—which had borne the brunt of the previous year's economic slowdown—increased from 1.3 per cent in 1998 to over 3 per cent in 1999. However, on a per capita basis, growth in output was marginal and considerably less than in the industrialized economies, where the strong performance of North America was a critical factor underlying the global acceleration.

In September, the General Assembly held its twenty-second special session at which it adopted a Declaration and review document on the state of progress and initiatives for the future implementation of the Programme of Action for the Sustainable Development of Small Island Developing States (SIDS), a comprehensive plan resulting from a Global Conference on the subject in 1994. The Commission on Sustainable Development, which served as preparatory body for the special session, held high-level discussions at its April session on issues of special concern to SIDS, focusing in particular on sustainable tourism development.

In May, the Commission on Science and Technology marked the twentieth anniversary of the United Nations Conference on Science and Technology for Development by adopting a common vision statement on the future contribution of science and technology to development.

International economic relations

Development and international economic cooperation

A number of UN bodies addressed development and international economic cooperation issues during 1999, including the General Assembly and the Economic and Social Council.

The Assembly, by **decision 54/428** of 9 December, deferred consideration of the launching of global negotiations on international economic cooperation for development and included the item in the provisional agenda of its fifty-fifth (2000) session.

On 22 December, the Assembly took note of the reports of the Second (Economic and Financial) Committee on its discussions of macroeconomic policy questions [A/54/585] (**decision 54/440**) and on sustainable development and international economic cooperation [A/54/587] (**decision 54/442**). By **decision 54/465** of 23 December, the Assembly decided that those agenda items would remain for consideration during its resumed fifty-fourth (2000) session.

Economic and Social Council consideration. On 29 April, the Economic and Social Council held its second special high-level meeting with the Bretton Woods institutions (the World Bank Group and the International Monetary Fund) [A/54/3/Rev.1]. It had before it a note by the Secretary-General identifying issues related to the functioning of international financial markets and stability in financing for development [E/1999/42 & Corr.1] (see PART THREE, Chapter IV).

Development through partnership

High-level dialogue

As requested by the General Assembly in resolution 53/181 [YUN 1998, p. 772], the Secretary-General submitted a September note on the themes for the second high-level dialogue on strengthening international economic cooperation for development through partnership [A/54/328]. The first dialogue was held in 1998 [YUN 1998, p. 772]. Based on his consultations with Governments, bodies of the UN system and intergovernmental organizations, the Secretary-General proposed that the theme for the second dialogue—scheduled for 2000—should be "Responding to the challenges of globalization: strengthening regional cooperation and building new partnerships for development". He suggested that preparations for the dialogue employ a bottom-up approach that would allow the traditional intergovernmental process to benefit from an infusion of ideas and policy advice from those directly involved in and affected by globalization.

GENERAL ASSEMBLY ACTION

On 22 December [meeting 87], the General Assembly, on the recommendation of the Second Committee [A/54/587/Add.7], adopted **resolution 54/213** without vote [agenda item 99 *(g)*].

Renewal of the dialogue on strengthening international economic cooperation for development through partnership

The General Assembly,

Recalling its resolutions 48/165 of 21 December 1993, 49/95 of 19 December 1994, 50/122 of 20 December 1995, 51/174 of 16 December 1996, 52/186 of 18 December 1997 and 53/181 of 15 December 1998,

Recalling also the adoption of the Agenda for Development and the relevant provisions on its follow-up and implementation, and the need to give impetus to international economic cooperation for development so as to follow up on the Agenda effectively,

Reaffirming the importance of continuing the dialogue to be conducted in response to the imperative of solidarity, mutual interests and benefits, genuine interdependence, shared responsibility and the partnership in promoting international economic cooperation for development,

Recognizing, in this context, the importance of an enabling environment and sound economic policy at both the national and the international levels,

Recognizing also the role of regional cooperation in promoting complementarity and in creating synergies and partnerships at the subregional, regional, interregional and global levels in the process of globalization and thereby furthering multilateral economic cooperation,

Emphasizing the importance of recognizing and addressing the specific concerns of countries with economies in transition so as to help them to benefit from globalization, with a view to their full integration into the world economy,

Noting the need to ensure the integrated and coordinated follow-up and implementation by the United Nations system of major United Nations conferences and summits,

Noting also the past experience of the high-level dialogue on strengthening international economic cooperation for development through partnership,

1. *Reaffirms* the importance of continued constructive dialogue and genuine partnership to promote further international economic cooperation for development in the twenty-first century;

2. *Decides* that the theme of the second high-level dialogue on strengthening international economic cooperation for development through partnership will be "Responding to globalization: facilitating the integration of developing countries into the world economy in the twenty-first century";

3. *Also decides,* without changing the biennial nature of the high-level dialogue, to defer the holding of the second two-day high-level dialogue to the fifty-sixth session of the General Assembly;

4. *Requests* the President of the General Assembly to begin consultations with Member States so as to arrive at an early decision on the date, modalities, nature of the outcome and focus of the discussions of the second high-level dialogue, taking into account past experience and the contributions to be provided by Member States as well as regional institutions and the United Nations system, and commends the continuing use of interactive panel discussions, including with the participation of non-governmental actors, to facilitate the dialogue in accordance with relevant regulations and rules;

5. *Requests* the Secretary-General, in close cooperation with Governments, all relevant parts of the United Nations system, relevant organizations and other development agencies, to make initial preparations for the dialogue, while also taking into account the results of major United Nations conferences and summits;

6. *Decides* to include in the provisional agenda of its fifty-fifth session, under the item entitled "Sustainable development and international economic cooperation", the sub-item entitled "High-level dialogue on strengthening international economic cooperation for development through partnership", and requests the Secretary-General to submit to it at that session a consolidated report on the implementation of the present resolution.

Also on 22 December, the Assembly took note of the Secretary-General's note on the themes for the second high-level dialogue (**decision 54/444**).

Globalization and interdependence

In response to General Assembly resolution 53/169 [YUN 1998, p. 773], the Secretary-General submitted a September report on the role of the United Nations in promoting development in the context of globalization and interdependence [A/54/358]. The report was prepared in the wake of the high-level dialogue on the social and economic impact of globalization and interdependence and their policy implications [YUN 1998, p. 727], in collaboration with the United Nations Conference on Trade and Development (UNCTAD) and in consultation with other organizations of the UN system. It focused on the core issues of finance and trade and explored ways to enhance the coherence of the UN system's response to the challenges of globalization and interdependence. Analysis at the global level was supplemented by a review of country-level trends based on responses to a questionnaire from a number of resident coordinators.

From a development perspective, the challenge posed by globalization was not internationalization of production, the telecommunications revolution or the emergence of "uncivil" society, but rather the cumulative impact of all those processes on policy-making and policy implementation. UN development activities needed to bring coherence to national and international policy-making in interrelated areas of trade and finance, economic, social and environmental issues, and other ramifications of globalization, such as the loss of cultural diversity, new patterns of labour migration, challenges and opportunities for health and new opportunities for criminal activity. Perhaps the most important catalyst for bringing about increasing globalization was the spread of information technology. Full and effective participation in the emerging information network was crucial for a country to benefit from globalization and to avoid being marginalized. UN operational activities for development should aim to increase national capacity to manage globalization; create an enabling environment for investment; facilitate the diversification of production, trade and technology transfer; expand capacities to deal with external debt management; and address the social dimensions in the globalization process.

UNCTAD action. The UNCTAD Trade and Development Board, at its twentieth executive session (Geneva, 5 February) [A/54/15/Rev.1], decided to include in the substantive agenda for the tenth session of the Conference (UNCTAD X), to be held in 2000, an item addressing developmental strategies in an increasingly interdependent world: applying the lessons of the past to make globalization an effective instrument for the development of all countries and all people (see PART THREE, Chapter IV).

ECONOMIC AND SOCIAL COUNCIL ACTION

On 30 July, by **decision 1999/281**, the Economic and Social Council decided that the theme of the high-level segment of its 2000 substantive session would be "Development and international cooperation in the twenty-first century: the role of information technology in the context of a knowledge-based global economy".

GENERAL ASSEMBLY ACTION

On 22 December [meeting 87], the General Assembly, on the recommendation of the Second Committee [A/54/592], adopted **resolution 54/231** without vote [agenda item 104].

Role of the United Nations in promoting development in the context of globalization and interdependence

The General Assembly,

Recalling its resolution 53/169 of 15 December 1998,

Recognizing the challenges and opportunities of globalization and interdependence,

Expressing its serious concern over the increasing risks of marginalization of a large number of developing countries from the globalization process, including in the finance, trade and technology sectors, and the additional vulnerability of those developing countries that are in the process of integrating into the world economy, resulting in particular from the volatility of short-term capital flows and the accentuation of income disparities within and among countries,

Recognizing that globalization and interdependence are opening new opportunities through trade, investment and capital flows, and advancements in technology, including information technology, for the growth of the world economy, for development and for the improvement of living standards around the world,

Emphasizing that the international systems dealing with development, finance, trade and transfer of technology should further address the negative impacts of globalization on developing countries,

Expressing its grave concern over the generally widening technological gap between the developed and developing countries, particularly in the area of information and communication technology, which is shaping the contours of globalization,

Mindful, in the process of trade liberalization, of the diminution of trade preferential margins for developing countries, particularly the least developed countries and small island developing States, and of the need for countries to take measures, as appropriate, in accordance with the rules of the World Trade Organization, to address that diminution with a view to offsetting it,

Underlining the need to continue to work on a wide range of reforms in order to create a strengthened international financial system,

Recognizing the importance of appropriate policy responses at the national level by all countries to the challenges of globalization, in particular by pursuing sound macroeconomic and social policies, noting the need for support from the international community for the efforts of the least developed countries, in particular, to improve their institutional and management capacities, and also recognizing that all countries should pursue policies conducive to economic growth and to promoting a favourable global economic environment,

Underlining the importance of promoting the integration of developing countries into the world economy in order to enable them to take the fullest possible advantage of the trading opportunities arising from globalization and liberalization,

Underscoring the urgent need to mitigate the negative consequences of globalization and interdependence for all developing countries, including landlocked developing countries, small island developing States and, in particular, African countries and the least developed countries,

Convinced of the need, in the context of globalization and interdependence, to develop and to implement policies to promote equity, transparency and inclusion, with the goal of promoting development, particularly of developing countries,

Reiterating that the United Nations, as a universal forum, is in a unique position to achieve international cooperation in addressing the challenges of promoting development in the context of globalization and interdependence,

Convinced that the United Nations has a key role to play in fostering greater coherence, complementarity and coordination in addressing economic and development issues at the global level,

Taking note of the report of the Secretary-General,

Taking note also of the *Human Development Report, 1999*, which focuses on globalization with a human face,

Taking note further, in the context of globalization and interdependence, of the ongoing work of the Commonwealth Secretariat/World Bank Joint Task Force on Small States,

Noting with appreciation that the United Nations Conference on Trade and Development, at its tenth session, to be held at Bangkok from 12 to 19 February 2000, will focus on "Development strategies in an increasingly interdependent world: applying the lessons of the past to make globalization an effective instrument for the development of all countries and all people",

Welcoming the decision of the Economic and Social Council to devote the high-level segment of its substantive session of 2000 to the theme "Development and international cooperation in the twenty-first century: the role of information technology in the context of a knowledge-based global economy",

1. *Reaffirms* that the United Nations has a central role to play in promoting international cooperation for development and in promoting greater policy coherence on global development issues, including in the context of globalization and interdependence;

2. *Strongly stresses* that the United Nations, the Bretton Woods institutions and the World Trade Organization should intensify their collaboration, as appropriate, in promoting policy coherence, complementarity and coordination on economic, financial, trade and development issues at the global level, which should aim at optimizing the benefits and minimizing the negative consequences of globalization, liberalization and interdependence, taking into account the specific vulnerabilities, concerns and needs of developing countries;

3. *Calls* for increased international cooperation to address the challenges of globalization through the enhanced participation of developing countries in the international economic policy decision-making process; integrated consideration of trade, finance, technology transfer and development issues by the relevant international institutions; and the continuation of a wide range of reforms of the international financial system;

4. *Calls upon* all countries, in particular the major developed economies, to enhance coherence among their financial, trade and development cooperation policies, with a view to creating an enabling international economic environment supportive of development, in particular of developing countries;

5. *Stresses* the importance, at the national level, of maintaining sound macroeconomic policies and developing effective institutional and regulatory frameworks and human resources, so as to realize the mutually reinforcing objectives of poverty eradication and development, including through national poverty reduction strategies and enhanced policy coherence;

6. *Urges* the international community to promote international development cooperation aimed at enhancing the participation of developing countries in the globalizing world economy;

7. *Also urges* the international community to adopt policies that promote equity in finance, trade and transfer of technology and address the problems of developing countries in the areas of external debt and transfer of resources, financial vulnerability, declining terms of trade and market access;

8. *Welcomes* the efforts of the United Nations Conference on Trade and Development and the International Trade Centre and other multilateral and bilateral efforts to help developing countries, including landlocked developing countries, small island developing States and, in particular, African countries and the least developed countries, in addressing their specific concerns within the globalizing economy, in particular through technology-related assistance in the fields of trade and policy, in the improvement of trade efficiency and policies and trade in services, and in electronic commerce;

9. *Emphasizes* the importance of recognizing and addressing the specific concerns of countries with economies in transition so as to help them to benefit from globalization with a view to their full integration into the world economy;

10. *Strongly underlines* the importance of an enabling environment for investment, in particular foreign direct investment, and of market access, governance responsive to the needs of the people based on efficient, participatory, transparent and accountable public service, policy-making processes and administration, an increase in the volume and effectiveness of official development assistance, tackling unsustainable debt burdens, including debt conversion measures and flexibility in the implementation of the enhanced Heavily Indebted Poor Countries Debt Initiative and, as recommended in the report of the Secretary-General, support for regional cooperation and integration as priority areas that need to be addressed in order to achieve sustainable development in African countries and to encourage the participation of all African countries in the global economy;

11. *Emphasizes* the technology-led dimension of globalization and the importance of facilitating access to and transfer of information and communication technology and corresponding knowledge, in particular to developing countries, on favourable terms, including concessional and preferential terms, as mutually agreed, taking into account the need to protect intellectual property rights, as well as the special needs of developing countries, to enable them to benefit from globalization through full and effective integration into the emerging global information network;

12. *Strongly emphasizes* the need for the regional and national capacity-building programmes of the United Nations system, the regional commissions, United Nations funds and programmes and the specialized agencies to have a strong component oriented towards assisting developing countries, as well as countries with economies in transition, in the area of information and communication technology;

13. *Requests* the Secretary-General to prepare, in close collaboration with the United Nations Conference on Trade and Development and in consultation with other relevant organizations, a comprehensive report containing action-oriented recommendations on promoting further the role of the United Nations system in the transfer of information and communication technology to developing countries and also on its role in promoting policy coherence, complementarity and coordination on economic, financial, trade, technol-

ogy and development issues at the global level in order to optimize the benefits of globalization;

14. *Also requests* the Secretary-General to convene, if possible, from extrabudgetary resources, a meeting of a high-level panel of experts on information and communication technology, taking into account equitable geographical representation, and in consultation with Member States, to prepare a report, to be made available in early June 2000, containing recommendations on the role of the United Nations in enhancing the integration of developing countries in the emerging global information network, facilitating access for developing countries to information and communication technology, including access on preferential and concessional terms, where appropriate, and promoting the participation of developing countries, including through infrastructure facilities, in knowledge-intensive sectors of the global economy;

15. *Invites* countries, and other relevant entities in a position to do so, to provide the necessary extrabudgetary resources for the convening of the high-level panel;

16. *Decides* to include in the provisional agenda of its fifty-fifth session the item entitled "Globalization and interdependence".

Implementation of the Declaration on International Economic Cooperation and the International Development Strategy

In response to General Assembly resolution 53/178 [YUN 1998, p. 775], the Secretary-General submitted a report [A/54/389] on the implementation of the Declaration on International Economic Cooperation, in particular the Revitalization of Economic Growth and Development of the Developing Countries, adopted by the Assembly in resolution S-18/3 [YUN 1990, p. 337], and of the International Development Strategy for the Fourth United Nations Development Decade (the 1990s), adopted by the Assembly in resolution 45/199 [ibid., p. 343]. The report was also prepared in accordance with the need for a quinquennial review of the Charter of Economic Rights and Duties of States, adopted by the Assembly in resolution 3281(XXIX) [YUN 1974, p. 403], as successful implementation of the Declaration and the Strategy was considered a major contribution to the fulfilment of the Charter's provisions.

Progress was assessed in relation to six interrelated goals singled out in the Strategy: economic growth in the developing countries; international financial matters, including foreign direct investment, debt and official development assistance; world trade; science and technology, industry and agriculture; human resources development, including education and health; and the situation of the least developed countries.

The achievements of the Decade, particularly in relation to those goals, had been mixed, the report concluded. Although there had been some improvement during the 1990s from both a social and an economic perspective, there had also been major setbacks, especially as a result of recent financial crises. There was also an increasing danger for marginalization of the weaker members of the world community. Major challenges faced by the world economy at the end of the 1990s included poverty alleviation and sustainability. Because economic growth was no longer considered a sufficient indicator of development, the focus had shifted from macroeconomic challenges to a number of institutional preconditions for development, including good governance, transparency and accountability, decentralization and participation, and social security.

GENERAL ASSEMBLY ACTION

On 22 December [meeting 87], the General Assembly, on the recommendation of the Second Committee [A/54/587/Add.1], adopted **resolution 54/206** without vote [agenda item 99 *(a)*].

Implementation of the commitments and policies agreed upon in the Declaration on International Economic Cooperation, in particular the Revitalization of Economic Growth and Development of the Developing Countries, and implementation of the International Development Strategy for the Fourth United Nations Development Decade

The General Assembly,

Reaffirming the importance and continued validity of the Declaration on International Economic Cooperation, in particular the Revitalization of Economic Growth and Development of the Developing Countries, contained in the annex to its resolution S-18/3 of 1 May 1990, and of the International Development Strategy for the Fourth United Nations Development Decade, contained in the annex to its resolution 45/199 of 21 December 1990,

Recalling its resolutions 45/234 of 21 December 1990, 46/144 of 17 December 1991, 47/152 of 18 December 1992, 48/185 of 21 December 1993, 49/92 of 19 December 1994, 51/173 of 16 December 1996 and 53/178 of 15 December 1998 on the implementation of the Declaration and the Strategy, and the Agenda for Development,

Recalling also the results, as agreed, of all the major United Nations conferences and summit meetings held since the beginning of the 1990s,

1. *Takes note* of the report of the Secretary-General;

2. *Recognizes* the efforts made to implement the Declaration on International Economic Cooperation, in particular the Revitalization of Economic Growth and Development of the Developing Countries, and the International Development Strategy for the Fourth United Nations Development Decade in the 1990s, and stresses the need to strengthen such actions in collaboration with, *inter alia,* efforts taken in the context of the United Nations New Agenda for the Development of Africa in the 1990s and its implementing arm, the United Nations System-wide Special Initiative on Africa, and the Programme of Action for the Least Developed Countries for the 1990s;

3. *Requests* the Secretary-General, in consultation with all concerned organs and organizations of the United Nations system, including the Bretton Woods institutions, as well as other relevant international organizations, to submit to the General Assembly, for consideration at its fifty-fifth session, an update of the report of the Secretary-General;

4. *Also requests* the Secretary-General, in collaboration with all concerned organs and organizations of the United Nations system, in particular the Committee for Development Policy, to submit to the General Assembly for consideration at its fifty-fifth session, through the Economic and Social Council, a draft text of an international development strategy for the first decade of the new millennium, with the aim of giving further impetus to international cooperation for development and of monitoring long-term trends in the global economy as well as the attainment of internationally agreed targets:

(*a*) Building on the outcomes, *inter alia*, of the major United Nations conferences and summit meetings held during the 1990s, the Agenda for Development and any other relevant ongoing processes related to international cooperation for development;

(*b*) Taking into account the dynamic changes to the world economy resulting from, *inter alia*, globalization, interdependence and liberalization and the rapid advances in science and technology;

5. *Requests* the President of the General Assembly at its fifty-fourth session to initiate consultations with all Member States with a view to establishing the modalities for the consideration and conclusion of the proposal of the Secretary-General called for in paragraph 4 above at the fifty-fifth session of the General Assembly;

6. *Decides* to include in the provisional agenda of its fifty-fifth session the sub-item entitled "Sustainable development and international cooperation: implementation of the commitments and policies agreed upon in the Declaration on International Economic Cooperation, in particular the Revitalization of Economic Growth and Development of the Developing Countries, and implementation of the International Development Strategy for the Fourth United Nations Development Decade".

Business and development

In response to General Assembly resolution 52/209 [YUN 1997, p. 788], the Secretary-General submitted his third biennial report on business and development [A/54/451]. He provided information on UN activities in promoting an enabling environment for the business sector, as well as on the increasing efforts for a partnership with business to realize the norms and goals established in the various UN conferences in the 1990s.

The Secretary-General stated that the private sector could play a very important role in fostering economic growth and development, and the UN system was actively facilitating the private sector's involvement in the development process through a twofold approach. On the one hand, it was developing a supportive international "soft infrastructure" for the orderly interaction of business—including legal and fiscal frameworks, privatization policies and processes, liberalization of financial flows, regulation of capital markets, adoption of competition policies and laws, deregulation or simplification of regulations and processes applicable to business, and development of entrepreneurship. On the other, it was facilitating private sector participation in pursuing the goals of the global conferences, in embracing universal principles and norms, including those relating to environment, human rights and gender, as well as in promoting economic growth, fighting poverty and rebuilding nations after conflict or crisis.

GENERAL ASSEMBLY ACTION

On 22 December [meeting 87], the General Assembly, on the recommendation of the Second Committee [A/54/586], adopted **resolution 54/204** without vote [agenda item 98 (*b*)].

Business and development

The General Assembly,

Reaffirming its resolutions 52/209 of 18 December 1997 on business and development and 51/191 of 16 December 1996 on the United Nations Declaration against Corruption and Bribery in International Commercial Transactions,

Noting the adoption of relevant conventions by the International Labour Organization relating to labour,

Recalling the successful outcome of the World Summit for Social Development, including the commitments contained in the Copenhagen Declaration on Social Development and the Programme of Action of the World Summit, and calling for the implementation of those commitments,

Noting the important efforts of the United Nations system to facilitate the active and constructive involvement of the private sector in the development process and the efforts of the Secretary-General to create partnerships with the private sector in this regard,

Recognizing the sovereign right of each State to decide on the development of its private and public sectors in accordance with its priorities,

Emphasizing that business and industry, including corporations engaged in international business activities, can contribute substantially to a country's economic and social development and environmental protection, and are important generators of employment and economic growth,

Reaffirming the importance, in the context of national development efforts, of promoting appropriate privatization, competition, entrepreneurship and a supportive legal and fiscal framework for business so as to increase efficiency, economic growth and sustainable development,

Recognizing the important role of small and medium-sized enterprises and micro-financing in supporting economic and social development,

Recognizing also that a dynamic business sector is essential to economic growth, job creation, trade expansion and technology development,

Recognizing further the link among effective, accountable and transparent administration of the public sector, financial transparency in the private sector, investor confidence and the stability of financial systems,

1. *Takes note* of the report of the Secretary-General;

2. *Encourages* Governments, multilateral institutions and the private sector, including corporations engaged in international business activities, to strengthen partnerships so as to advance sustainable development through, *inter alia,* supporting the stable functioning of the international finance and trade system and investment flows, particularly in support of the development efforts of developing countries, as well as countries with economies in transition;

3. *Encourages* Governments to create an environment that enables businesses to conduct their activities in a humane, sustainable and socially responsible way;

4. *Urges* all Governments to create an enabling environment for business and investment, including through sound macroeconomic, fiscal and development policies, the rule of law, anti-corruption and anti-bribery efforts, and transparent business practices that promote efficiency, fairness and competitiveness in international commercial transactions, taking into account the needs of developing countries;

5. *Urges* the private sector, including corporations engaged in international business activities, to pursue orderly and fair business practices while adhering to and promoting the principles of honesty, transparency and accountability in international commercial transactions, with a view to contributing to efforts to create an enabling environment for business and investment;

6. *Requests* the international community, including the business community and relevant international bodies, to consider ways and means of promoting such principles and practices and respect for those practices by multinational companies in their operations in all countries;

7. *Emphasizes* the importance of a supportive international economic environment, including investment and trade, for the promotion of entrepreneurship and privatization;

8. *Strongly stresses* the need for adequate resources, including the provision of new and additional resources from all sources, and transfer of technology on favourable terms, *inter alia,* on concessional and preferential terms as mutually agreed, to developing countries, particularly to Africa and the least developed countries, for developing appropriate infrastructure and business services to promote entrepreneurship;

9. *Recognizes* the special development priorities and concerns of developing countries, and in this regard calls for international support for the realization of their development goals, *inter alia,* through the promotion of business and entrepreneurship;

10. *Stresses* the importance of micro-finance, including micro-credit, to people living in poverty, in allowing them to undertake the establishment of micro-enterprises, which in turn generate self-employment and contribute to the achievement of empowerment, particularly of women, and calls for the strengthening of institutions supportive of micro-financing, in particular micro-credit;

11. *Values* the promotion of entrepreneurship, *inter alia,* through the informal sector and micro-enterprises, in the development of small and medium-sized enterprises and industries by various actors throughout civil society, and of privatization, demonopolization and the simplification of administrative procedures;

12. *Stresses* the importance, in the context of establishing and maintaining adequate social safety nets, including assistance to workers, of encouraging investment in human resources through programmes devoted to health, education and job training, and recognizes that such efforts are an integral part of overall poverty reduction strategies;

13. *Encourages* the United Nations Conference on Trade and Development to continue to provide a forum for intergovernmental discussions concerning issues related to private sector development and international flows of investment, with input from representatives of the private sector;

14. *Invites* the United Nations Industrial Development Organization and other relevant United Nations bodies to strengthen further their activities, in particular those concerning Africa and the least developed countries, in the promotion of entrepreneurship development, especially with respect to small and medium-sized enterprises, and calls upon the international community to lend its support, where appropriate, to the United Nations Industrial Development Organization in this regard;

15. *Calls upon* the United Nations funds and programmes, in accordance with their mandates, to continue to strengthen support for the promotion of entrepreneurship and, in their work in implementing the present resolution, to give due consideration to the role of the business sector in development, taking into account the priorities set by each country, while ensuring a gender perspective;

16. *Calls upon* the relevant bodies of the United Nations system, within their respective mandates and agreed work programmes, to continue to assist Member States, at their request, in implementing national programmes to create an enabling environment for business, investment and development;

17. *Stresses* the need to continue to assist developing countries and countries with economies in transition, at their request, in strengthening their capacity to encourage wider participation of the private sector in their economies;

18. *Invites* relevant United Nations organizations, within their mandates and in consultation with Governments, to promote meaningful contributions by business, in both the public and the private sectors, in support of economic growth and sustainable development;

19. *Decides* to include in the provisional agenda of its fifty-sixth session the item entitled "Business and development", and requests the Secretary-General, in cooperation with the relevant United Nations organizations, to submit at that session a report on the implementation of the present resolution.

Coercive economic measures

In response to General Assembly resolution 52/181 [YUN 1997, p. 789], the Secretary-General submitted an October 1999 report on unilateral economic measures as a means of political and economic coercion against developing countries [A/54/486]. The report contained summaries of information received from 13 Governments and on action on the subject taken by relevant UN bodies.

The report also contained a summary of an ad hoc expert group meeting (New York, 14-16 June), which was convened by the UN Department of Economic and Social Affairs to seek the views of internationally recognized experts on the impact of coercive economic measures, particularly on trade and development in the affected countries. The expert group discussed current concepts, recent developments, available case studies and emerging policy issues pertaining to the unilateral versus multilateral application of economic sanctions. From a legal perspective, the experts agreed that unilateral measures of coercion were increasingly at odds with the evolving principles and rules of international economic and social cooperation embodied in the Charter of the United Nations and the constituent treaties of multilateral trade and financial institutions, such as the World Trade Organization (WTO).

Regarding policy options and alternatives, current approaches to minimizing the adverse effects of coercive economic measures on the general population, particularly its most vulnerable groups, were reviewed. One alternative that had recently attracted wide attention was the concept of "smart" or targeted sanctions designed to penalize directly those individuals or policy makers responsible for an objectionable action. International cooperation—including bilateral and multilateral negotiations on contentious issues, engagement strategies and positive economic measures involving adequate incentives and reward systems to induce policy changes—was considered a more rational and viable alternative to unilateral coercive economic measures.

GENERAL ASSEMBLY ACTION

On 22 December [meeting 87], the General Assembly, on the recommendation of the Second Committee [A/54/585/Add.3 & Corr.1], adopted **resolution 54/200** by recorded vote (107-3-46) [agenda item 97 *(c)*].

Unilateral economic measures as a means of political and economic coercion against developing countries

The General Assembly,

Recalling the relevant principles set forth in the Charter of the United Nations,

Reaffirming the Declaration on Principles of International Law concerning Friendly Relations and Cooperation among States in accordance with the Charter of the United Nations, which states, *inter alia,* that no State may use or encourage the use of unilateral economic, political or any other type of measures to coerce another State in order to obtain from it the subordination of the exercise of its sovereign rights,

Bearing in mind the general principles governing the international trading system and trade policies for development contained in relevant resolutions, rules and provisions of the United Nations and the World Trade Organization,

Recalling its resolutions 44/215 of 22 December 1989, 46/210 of 20 December 1991, 48/168 of 21 December 1993, 50/96 of 20 December 1995 and 52/181 of 18 December 1997,

Gravely concerned that the use of unilateral coercive economic measures adversely affects the economy and development efforts of developing countries in particular and has a general negative impact on international economic cooperation and on worldwide efforts to move towards a non-discriminatory and open multilateral trading system,

1. *Takes note* of the report of the Secretary-General;
2. *Urges* the international community to adopt urgent and effective measures to eliminate the use of unilateral coercive economic measures against developing countries that are not authorized by relevant organs of the United Nations or are inconsistent with the principles of international law as set forth in the Charter of the United Nations and that contravene the basic principles of the multilateral trading system;
3. *Requests* the Secretary-General to continue to monitor the imposition of measures of this nature and to study the impact of such measures on the affected countries, including the impact on trade and development;
4. *Also requests* the Secretary-General to submit a report to the General Assembly at its fifty-sixth session on the implementation of the present resolution.

RECORDED VOTE ON RESOLUTION 54/200:

In favour: Afghanistan, Algeria, Angola, Antigua and Barbuda, Argentina, Armenia, Bahamas, Bahrain, Bangladesh, Barbados, Belarus, Belize, Benin, Bhutan, Botswana, Brazil, Brunei Darussalam, Burkina Faso, Cambodia, Cameroon, Cape Verde, Chad, Chile, China, Colombia, Costa Rica, Côte d'Ivoire, Cuba, Democratic People's Republic of Korea, Djibouti, Dominican Republic, Ecuador, Egypt, Eritrea, Ethiopia, Fiji, Gabon, Ghana, Grenada, Guatemala, Guinea, Guinea-Bissau, Guyana, Haiti, India, Indonesia, Iran, Jamaica, Jordan, Kazakhstan, Kenya, Kuwait, Lao People's Democratic Republic, Lebanon, Lesotho, Libyan Arab Jamahiriya, Madagascar, Malaysia, Maldives, Mali, Mauritius, Mexico, Mongolia, Morocco, Mozambique, Myanmar, Namibia, Nepal, Nicaragua, Nigeria, Oman, Pakistan, Panama, Papua New Guinea, Paraguay, Peru, Philippines, Qatar, Russian Federation, Saint Lucia, Saint Vincent and the Grenadines, Saudi Arabia, Senegal, Seychelles, Singapore, Solomon Islands, South Africa, Sri Lanka, Sudan, Suriname, Swaziland, Syrian Arab Republic, Tajikistan, Thailand, Togo, Trinidad and Tobago, Tunisia, Turkmenistan, Uganda, United Arab Emirates, United Republic of Tanzania, Uruguay, Venezuela, Viet Nam, Yemen, Zambia, Zimbabwe.

Against: Germany, Marshall Islands, United States.

Abstaining: Andorra, Australia, Austria, Azerbaijan, Belgium, Bulgaria, Canada, Croatia, Cyprus, Czech Republic, Denmark, Estonia, Finland, France, Georgia, Greece, Hungary, Iceland, Ireland, Israel, Italy, Japan, Latvia, Liechtenstein, Lithuania, Luxembourg, Malta, Monaco, Netherlands, New Zealand, Norway, Poland, Portugal, Republic of Korea, Republic of Moldova, Romania, San Marino, Slovakia, Slovenia, Spain, Sweden, The former Yugoslav Republic of Macedonia, Turkey, Ukraine, United Kingdom, Uzbekistan.

Sustainable development

Commission on Sustainable Development

The Commission on Sustainable Development held the second part of its seventh session in New York from 19 to 30 April [E/1999/29]; it had held two organizational meetings on 1 May and 27 July 1998. The session included a multi-stakeholder dialogue on tourism (see below) and a high-level segment, which addressed tourism and a plan of action for small island developing States (see below, under "Developing countries"). Other issues considered related to oceans and seas (see PART THREE, Chapter VII), changing consumption and production patterns and challenges for the future.

The Commission adopted decisions on: education, public awareness and training; exchange of national experience; voluntary initiatives and agreements on sustainable development; the proposed programme of work in sustainable development for 2000-2001; matters related to the Commission's inter-sessional work; and preparations for the review of Agenda 21, adopted by the 1992 United Nations Conference on Environment and Development (UNCED) [YUN 1992, p. 672] (see below). Two draft resolutions—on preparations for the Commission's consideration at its ninth (2001) session of matters related to energy (see PART THREE, Chapter VI) and on guidelines for consumer protection (see PART THREE, Chapter IV)—were recommended for adoption by the Economic and Social Council.

By a vote of 33 to 4, with 8 abstentions, the Commission adjourned debate without action on a draft resolution on sustainable development in the region of the Balkans. By that text, the Commission would have expressed grave concern at the unfolding environmental crisis in the Balkans as a result of the destruction of chemical, oil and other industries in the Federal Republic of Yugoslavia (FRY) (see PART ONE, Chapter V) and urged the UN system to undertake immediate measures to address the sustainable development problems of FRY and neighbouring countries.

By **decision 1999/222** of 26 July, the Economic and Social Council took note of the Commission's report on its seventh session [E/1999/29] and approved the provisional agenda for the eighth (2000) session.

In an April report [E/CN.17/1999/9], the Secretary-General outlined the main challenges on the agenda for future Commission sessions—including energy, land and agriculture—as well as policy options related to ocean governance. In **resolution 1999/48** of 28 July, the Council decided on issues to be considered during the preparatory process for the Commission's eighth session in relation to the sectoral theme of integrated planning and management of land resources and agriculture (see PART THREE, Chapter VI).

Tourism

During the multi-stakeholder dialogue on tourism (19-21 April), the Commission met with representatives of business and industry, workers and trade unions, local authorities and non-governmental organizations (NGOs) to discuss four themes related to sustainable tourism: industry initiatives for sustainable tourism; influencing consumer behaviour; promoting broad-based sustainable development while safeguarding the integrity of local cultures and protecting the environment; and the coastal impact of tourism.

The Commission had before it a January report of the Secretary-General [E/CN.17/1999/5], which discussed policy challenges for the tourism industry, national Governments and the international community in the areas of tourism and economic development, tourism and social development and tourism and environmental protection. Three addenda covering tourism and economic development [E/CN.17/1999/5/Add.1], tourism and social development [E/CN.17/1999/5/Add.2] and tourism and environmental protection [E/CN.17/1999/5/Add.3], were prepared by the World Tourism Organization, the International Labour Organization and the United Nations Environment Programme, respectively.

The session also had before it the report of the Inter-sessional Ad Hoc Working Group on Consumption and Production Patterns and on Tourism (New York, 22-26 February) [E/CN.17/1999/16], which suggested possible elements for action by the Commission in relation to those issues.

On 30 April [E/1999/29 (dec. 7/3)], the Commission adopted an international work programme on sustainable tourism development and decided that its implementation would be reviewed in 2002 at the time of the 10-year review of progress achieved since UNCED. The work programme outlined action to be taken by Governments, the tourism industry and other major groups involved in the development of tourism, including organizations of the UN system. Governments were urged to adopt policies and strategies for sustainable tourism development based on Agenda 21, which would encourage their tourism industries, assist in attracting foreign direct investment and appropriate environmentally sound technologies, and provide direction for the active participation of major groups, including national tourism councils, tourism agencies and the private sector, as well as indigenous and local communities. The tourism industry was called on to develop environmentally, socially and culturally compatible forms of tourism and to continue to develop and implement voluntary initiatives in support of sustainable tourism development.

Among other elements of the work programme were those aiming to: encourage more responsible behaviour among tourists; promote integrated planning approaches to tourism development at the local level; support preparations for the International Years of Ecotourism and of Mountains, both in 2002; develop indicators and guiding principles for sustainable tourism development; and encourage industry to implement eco-efficiency approaches to reduce environmental impacts of travel and tourism activities. The World Tourism Organization and the UN Secretariat were asked jointly to facilitate establishment of an ad hoc informal open-ended working group on tourism to assess financial leakages and determine how to maximize benefits for indigenous and local communities, as well as address other matters relevant to the work programme's implementation.

Education, public awareness and training

In a January report [E/CN.17/1999/11], the Secretary-General described progress made in implementing the international work programme on education, public awareness and training for sustainability, launched by the Commission in 1996 and expanded in 1998 [YUN 1998, p. 786]. Prepared by the United Nations Educational, Scientific and Cultural Organization (UNESCO), as task manager for chapter 36 of Agenda 21, the progress report focused on seven long-term initiatives: clarifying and communicating the concept and key messages of education for sustainable development; reviewing national education policies and reorienting formal educational systems; incorporating education strategies and action plans for sustainable development; educating to promote sustainable consumption and production patterns; promoting investments in education; identifying and sharing innovative practices; and raising public awareness. Integrated follow-up to UN conferences and conventions, strategic issues concerning the work programme and UNESCO action to promote its implementation were also addressed.

On 30 April [dec. 7/4], the Commission called for intensified collaborative efforts by UNESCO, Governments, relevant UN bodies and NGOs in implementing the work programme. Priority was to be given to the integration of aspects of sustainable development in educational policies.

Voluntary initiatives

In an April report [E/CN.17/1999/12], the Secretary-General presented to the Commission the conclusions of a multi-stakeholder consultative meeting on voluntary initiatives and agreements (Toronto, Canada, 10-12 March), which included the participation of industry, trade unions and NGOs. The meeting examined the lessons learned about voluntary initiatives and agreements in order to come up with the key elements for a review of their effectiveness. A number of case studies were presented on different aspects of voluntary initiatives, and the elements that worked or did not work in relation to each initiative's stated goals and objectives were discussed. It was noted that voluntary initiatives and agreements increased direct action for sustainable development by business and other major groups. Those that were participatory in design and delivery helped to build partnerships and generate a renewed sense of commitment to long-term sustainability among the parties involved. There was broad agreement on the main elements for a review of voluntary initiatives and agreements, but further consultation was required on how such reviews might be structured.

The Commission, on 30 April [dec. 7/6], encouraged all relevant major groups and other stakeholders, in cooperation with UN bodies, to continue generating information about voluntary initiatives and agreements, including the most appropriate means for possible reviews, and to report periodically on steps taken or progress made in assisting developing countries in understanding and making use of the lessons learned from the use of such initiatives and agreements. The Secretary-General was asked to report in 2000 on progress and developments.

National reporting

In a March note [E/CN.17/1999/10], the Secretary-General summarized activities related to national reporting on the implementation of Agenda 21 subsequent to the Commission's sixth (1998) session [YUN 1998, p. 779]. Activities focused on: facilitating national reporting to the seventh session; preparation of an analytical report of national information on the sustainable development of oceans and seas (see PART THREE, Chapter VII); maintenance and updating of the UN system-wide sustainable development web site; and early preparations to facilitate reporting to the Commission's eighth (2000) session.

On 30 April [dec. 7/5], the Commission emphasized the need to draw more fully on the information contained in national reports and other voluntary submissions. Governments were encouraged to continue providing such reports and information with the broad involvement of all sectors of society. The efforts of developing countries in that regard were to be supported by the international community and the United Nations Development Programme (UNDP). The Commission secretariat was asked to invite Governments to submit proposals on improving the guidelines for elaboration of national reports and to prepare a new version of the country profiles complementing those presented during the five-year review in 1997 [YUN 1997, p. 790] for submission to the General Assembly for the comprehensive review of the implementation of Agenda 21 in 2002.

Inter-Agency Committee

The Inter-Agency Committee on Sustainable Development (IACSD) of the Administrative Committee on Coordination (ACC) met twice in 1999. At its thirteenth meeting (New York, 8-9 March) [ACC/1999/1], it discussed follow-up to meetings of ACC and matters related to the work of the Commission on Sustainable Development and the General Assembly. Regarding its work in support of the implementation of Agenda 21, IACSD considered expanding the task manager system in order to avoid multiple inter-agency mechanisms of policy coordination at the global level in any given thematic area.

In addition to reviewing the reports of the ACC Subcommittees on Water Resources and on Oceans and Coastal Areas, the Committee addressed: cooperation in the energy area, in preparation for consideration of energy issues by the Commission in 2001; strengthening of UN system coverage of waste management issues; the status of the UNDP Development Watch mechanism; and work related to guidelines for national action.

At its fourteenth meeting (Vienna, 9-10 September) [ACC/1999/12], IACSD again considered expanding the task manager system, follow-up to meetings of intergovernmental bodies, cooperation in the area of energy, and a report from the Subcommittee on Oceans and Coastal Areas. It also discussed preparations for the Commission's eighth (2000) session.

Follow-up to UNCED and to nineteenth special session

Commission on Sustainable Development. On 30 April [E/1999/29 (dec. 7/9)], the Commission asked the Secretary-General to submit in 2000 suggestions for the form, scope and nature of the preparatory process for the next comprehensive review of the implementation of Agenda 21, adopted by UNCED in 1992 [YUN 1992, p. 672]. The first such review was carried out by the General Assembly at its nineteenth special session, when it adopted the Programme for the Further Implementation of Agenda 21 by resolution S/19-2 [YUN 1997, p. 792].

Report of Secretary-General. In a June report [A/54/131-E/1999/75], the Secretary-General reviewed the work under way in the UN system to accelerate the implementation of Agenda 21 and the Programme for the Further Implementation of Agenda 21. Constraints to their implementation included a lack of additional resources, institutional capacity and clearly defined priorities for both individual organizations and the system as a whole. Some constraints were related to inconsistent decisions in various governing bodies of UN organizations. Other difficulties were related to fostering progress in intersectoral aspects of sustainable development, such as health.

The Secretary-General recommended a more coordinated approach to the follow-up of all recent major UN conferences in order to achieve synergies for sustainable development and ensure more efficient and effective use of resources.

The Economic and Social Council on 30 July (**decision 1999/286**) and the General Assembly on 22 December (**decision 54/447**) took note of the Secretary-General's report.

GENERAL ASSEMBLY ACTION

On 22 December [meeting 87], the General Assembly, on the recommendation of the Second Committee [A/54/588/Add.1], adopted **resolution 54/218** without vote [agenda item 100 *(a)*].

Implementation of and follow-up to the outcome of the United Nations Conference on Environment and Development and the nineteenth special session of the General Assembly

The General Assembly,

Recalling the United Nations Conference on Environment and Development, held at Rio de Janeiro from 3 to 14 June 1992, and the nineteenth special session of the General Assembly for the purpose of an overall review and appraisal of the implementation of Agenda 21, held in New York from 23 to 28 June 1997,

Reaffirming that Agenda 21 is the fundamental programme of action for achieving sustainable development and that the Programme for the Further Implementation of Agenda 21, adopted by the General Assembly at its nineteenth special session, will enhance the full implementation of the outcome of the United Nations Conference on Environment and Development,

Recognizing that the Programme for the Further Implementation of Agenda 21 includes a statement of commitment to Agenda 21 and the goals of sustainable development, an assessment of progress made since the United Nations Conference on Environment and Development in all main areas of Agenda 21 and other outcomes of the Conference, and recommendations on the future methods of work of the Commission on Sustainable Development and the programme of work of the Commission for the period 1998-2002,

Recognizing also that mutually supportive efforts at the national and international levels are needed in the pursuit of sustainable development and that the gap between developed and developing countries points to the continuing need for a dynamic and enabling national and international economic environment that is supportive of international cooperation, in particular in the fields of finance, transfer of technology, debt and trade, if the momentum for global progress towards sustainable development is to be maintained and increased,

Noting with concern that, during the assessment and review of progress made at its nineteenth special session, the General Assembly concluded that although some progress had been made, especially at the local level, the overall trends with respect to the global environment had not improved, and emphasizing that the implementation of Agenda 21 in a comprehensive manner remains vitally important and is now more urgent than ever,

Noting that the next review of the implementation of Agenda 21 is to be carried out by the General Assembly in 2002,

Noting also the need for early substantive preparations for the ten-year review of the implementation of the outcome of the United Nations Conference on Environment and Development in order to attain meaningful results,

Recalling General Assembly resolution 53/188 of 15 December 1998 and Commission on Sustainable Development decision 7/9, on preparations for the review of the implementation of Agenda 21 and the Programme for the Further Implementation of Agenda 21,

1. *Stresses* the need to accelerate the full implementation of Agenda 21 and the Programme for the Further Implementation of Agenda 21;

2. *Recognizes* that the Commission on Sustainable Development, within its mandate as specified in General Assembly resolution 47/191 of 22 December 1992 and in the Programme for the Further Implementation of Agenda 21, will continue to provide the central forum for reviewing progress on and urging further implementation of Agenda 21, the Programme for the Further Implementation of Agenda 21 and other commitments made at the United Nations Conference on Environment and Development or as a result of it, for conducting a high-level policy debate aimed at building consensus on sustainable development and for catalysing action on and long-term commitment to sustainable development at all levels;

3. *Calls upon* the Commission on Sustainable Development to continue to undertake these tasks in complementing and providing interlinkages to the work of other United Nations organs, organizations and bodies active in the field of sustainable development, to play its role in assessing the opportunities and challenges of globalization as they relate to sustainable development and to perform its functions in coordination with other subsidiary bodies of the Economic and Social Council and with related organizations and institutions, including making recommendations, within its mandate, to the Council, bearing in mind the interrelated outcomes of recent United Nations conferences;

4. *Emphasizes* that the achievement of more substantive results by the next review of the implementation of Agenda 21 in 2002 will require concerted efforts at all levels, including by Governments, calls upon all countries to fulfil their commitments to Agenda 21, and in this context calls upon developed countries to fulfil the commitments that they have undertaken with respect to financial resources and the transfer of environmentally sound technology;

5. *Reaffirms,* in this context, the necessity of providing adequate and predictable financial resources, transferring environmentally sound technologies and providing capacity-building and technical assistance to developing countries for the implementation of Agenda 21 and for the achievement of the long-term goals of sustainable development, and calls for the preparations for the ten-year review of the implementation of the outcome of the United Nations Conference on Environment and Development, without prejudice to other priority areas that may be identified during the preparatory process, to address the challenges and constraints in the implementation of the commitments of the Conference at all levels and to identify ways and means of accelerating the implementation of Agenda 21, including the development of measures to remedy the slow rate of progress of the international community in implementing Agenda 21;

6. *Notes* the need for assistance to be provided by the international community to countries with economies in transition in their efforts to achieve the objectives of Agenda 21 and the long-term goals of sustainable development;

7. *Emphasizes* the importance of the continued active and collaborative involvement of all relevant bodies of the United Nations system in the implementation of Agenda 21 and the Programme for the Further Implementation of Agenda 21, and requests the Secretary-General, in close collaboration with all relevant bodies of the United Nations system and taking into account the outcome of the deliberations in the Commission on Sustainable Development, to submit to the General Assembly for consideration at its fifty-fifth session, through the Economic and Social Council in view of its coordination function, an analytical report on the measures taken within the United Nations system to accelerate the implementation of Agenda 21 and the Programme for the Further Implementation of Agenda 21, including the identification of constraints and recommendations on how to address those constraints;

8. *Recognizes* the importance, for the effective implementation of Agenda 21 and the Programme for the Further Implementation of Agenda 21, of a multifaceted approach at the local, national, regional and global levels, as well as of the continued involvement of major groups, as defined in Agenda 21, and calls for the preparations for the ten-year review to facilitate continued involvement and input from those various levels and from major groups;

9. *Stresses,* in this connection, the importance of high-quality preparations for the forthcoming ten-year review of Agenda 21 and the Programme for the Further Implementation of Agenda 21, requests the Secretary-General to include the views of Member States in the preliminary report requested by the Commission on Sustainable Development in its decision 7/9, and invites Member States to submit their views to the Secretariat by February 2000;

10. *Renews its request* to the secretariat of the Commission on Sustainable Development to invite Governments to submit proposals on how to improve the guidelines for the elaboration of national reports and,

based on the information received, to prepare a report to be submitted to the Commission as part of the preparations for the comprehensive review of the implementation of Agenda 21;

11. *Invites*, as part of the preparations for the ten-year review:

(*a*) The regional commissions to provide reports, through the Economic and Social Council in view of its coordination function, on how their activities are contributing to the implementation of Agenda 21 and the Programme for the Further Implementation of Agenda 21, for the consideration of the General Assembly at its fifty-fifth session;

(*b*) The relevant functional commissions that are implementing chapters of Agenda 21 to submit reports, through the Economic and Social Council in view of its coordination function, on how their activities are contributing to the implementation of Agenda 21 and the Programme for the Further Implementation of Agenda 21, for the consideration of the General Assembly at its fifty-fifth session;

(*c*) The Governing Council of the United Nations Environment Programme to consider how the activities of the Programme are contributing to the implementation of Agenda 21 and the Programme for the Further Implementation of Agenda 21, and to submit its views to the General Assembly at the earliest opportunity;

(*d*) The Global Environment Facility, in the course of its regular work, to provide a report on how its activities are contributing to the implementation of Agenda 21 and the Programme for the Further Implementation of Agenda 21, for the consideration of the General Assembly at its fifty-fifth session;

(*e*) The secretariats of the United Nations Framework Convention on Climate Change, the Convention on Biological Diversity and the United Nations Convention to Combat Desertification in those Countries Experiencing Serious Drought and/or Desertification, particularly in Africa, to provide reports on how their activities are contributing to the implementation of Agenda 21 and the Programme for the Further Implementation of Agenda 21, for the consideration of the General Assembly at its fifty-fifth session;

12. *Invites* the Secretary-General, while preparing the report requested by the General Assembly in paragraph 6 of its resolution 53/188, to take into account the preliminary discussions held by the Commission on Sustainable Development at its eighth session and by the Economic and Social Council, and to include in that report proposals for the analytical reports to be prepared for the review process.

Eradication of poverty

Economic and Social Council consideration. At the high-level segment of its 1999 substantive session (Geneva, 5-7 July) [A/54/3/Rev.1], the Economic and Social Council addressed the role of employment and work in poverty eradication, particularly in relation to the empowerment and advancement of women (see PART THREE, Chapter X). At its operational activities segment, the Council discussed poverty eradication and capacity-building (see next chapter).

Poverty eradication and capacity-building

In May [E/1999/55], the Secretary-General reported to the Council on poverty eradication and capacity-building in relation to UN operational activities for international development (see also next chapter). The report provided an assessment of the country-level role of operational activities for development in poverty eradication and recommended practical steps to help achieve the goal of poverty eradication as agreed at the World Summit for Social Development [YUN 1995, p. 1113] and in General Assembly resolution 51/178 [YUN 1996, p. 743] on the first United Nations Decade on the Eradication of Poverty (1997-2006) (see below). The evolution of the issue of capacity-building over 30 years was also reviewed, as were the relevant decisions of General Assembly resolution 53/192 on the triennial comprehensive policy review of operational activities for development of the UN system [YUN 1998, p. 802]. According to the report, the organizations of the UN system had translated global mandates regarding poverty eradication into operational action at the country level by strengthening national capacities to define policies, giving a pro-poor orientation to development policies and enhancing the capacities of the poor through direct assistance initiatives. The concept of capacity-building had gradually evolved from a primary focus on institution-building to a broader process involving policy and programme formulation, budgeting and financial management, development planning, programme implementation, coordination and performance monitoring and evaluation. Capacity-building efforts had come to involve larger-scale, complex, multisectoral issues—such as urban development, HIV/AIDS, poverty and environmental management—which posed new challenges for the UN system whose technical capacity was for the most part organized on a sectoral basis.

Among its recommendations, the report suggested that the Council address the sustainability and adaptability of capacity-building in a variety of development contexts and in response to a range of sectoral, cross-sectoral and technical requirements of recipient countries. In two addenda, the Secretary-General reported on progress in implementing General Assembly resolution 53/192 [E/1999/55/ Add.1] and provided detailed statistical data on operational activities for development during 1997 [E/1999/55/Add.2].

In an annual report on operational activities for development [E/1999/47], the UNDP Administrator stated that the advancement of women was an integral part of UNDP work in poverty eradication and sustainable livelihoods for the poor. Empowerment of the poor, particularly poor women, was a key dimension of the UNDP approach to poverty eradication. Future work by UNDP and its partners needed to focus on strengthening gender-aware macroeconomic planning and policy-making as well as on community efforts to address their own poverty, especially the poverty of women.

UN Decade for Eradication of Poverty

In response to General Assembly resolution 53/198 [YUN 1998, p. 783], the Secretary-General submitted a September 1999 progress report [A/54/316] on the implementation of the measures, themes, recommendations and activities related to the first United Nations Decade for the Eradication of Poverty (1997-2006), proclaimed by the Assembly in resolution 50/107 [YUN 1995, p. 844]. The report, in addition to recommending possible actions and initiatives and proposals for better coordination of UN system action, highlighted progress made and challenges remaining in global poverty reduction. The need for poverty alleviation strategies that encompassed a comprehensive mix of policies and programmes and included all interacting development sectors impacting on the poor was stressed. Emphasis was also placed on the issues of gender inequalities and poverty, and the importance of public policy in reducing poverty and mitigating vulnerability during crisis.

GENERAL ASSEMBLY ACTION

On 22 December [meeting 87], the General Assembly, on the recommendation of the Second Committee [A/54/593], adopted **resolution 54/232** without vote [agenda item 105].

Implementation of the first United Nations Decade for the Eradication of Poverty

The General Assembly,

Recalling its resolutions 50/107 of 20 December 1995 and 53/198 of 15 December 1998 regarding the first United Nations Decade for the Eradication of Poverty (1997-2006) and all of its other resolutions relating to international cooperation for the eradication of poverty in the developing countries,

Recalling also the declarations and programmes of action of the major United Nations conferences and summits in the 1990s as they relate to the eradication of poverty,

Taking note of the report of the Secretary-General,

Expressing its deep concern that the number of people living in extreme poverty continues to increase, with women and children constituting the majority and the most affected group,

Expressing its deep concern also that efforts to reduce poverty have been severely constrained because of the slowing down of economic growth in developing countries, as a result of, *inter alia,* and, in particular, the 1997-1998 financial crisis and declining commodity prices, and noting that while some of the most visible effects of the crisis are being overcome in some regions and sectors, there is a need to sustain and to expand the momentum of recovery,

Recognizing that, while the process of globalization brings with it opportunities, it poses new challenges and risks for developing countries, in particular the least developed among them, at a time when they are intensifying their efforts to achieve sustained economic growth and directing their national policies towards the eradication of poverty through the implementation of comprehensive strategies, policies and programmes, including those with a long-term perspective,

Recognizing also that, while the rate of poverty in some countries has been reduced, some developing countries and disadvantaged groups are being marginalized, others are at risk of being marginalized and effectively excluded from the benefits of globalization, and there is increased income disparity among and within countries, thereby constraining efforts to eradicate poverty,

Recognizing further that the combined effects of natural disasters, conflicts, entrenched poverty, disease, especially malaria and the human immunodeficiency virus/acquired immunodeficiency syndrome epidemic, and lack of proper education affect the economic prospects of, and efforts to eradicate poverty in, the most severely affected countries, especially in Africa,

Recognizing that, while it is the primary responsibility of States to attain social development, the international community should support the efforts of the developing countries to eradicate poverty and to ensure basic social protection,

Expressing its appreciation to the developed countries that have agreed to and have reached the target of 0.7 per cent of their gross national product for overall official development assistance,

Emphasizing the need to strengthen further the efforts of international organizations, agencies, funds, programmes and bodies of the United Nations system, including the World Bank and the International Monetary Fund within their respective mandates, as well as the efforts of civil society, including non-governmental organizations, to implement measures and to take action to eradicate poverty within the framework of the first United Nations Decade for the Eradication of Poverty,

Noting with appreciation the debt initiative launched by the Group of Seven major industrialized countries at its meeting held at Cologne, Germany, from 18 to 20 June 1999, the decisions taken by the international community to assign priority to the eradication of poverty in the programmes and policy advice of the Bretton Woods institutions and the enhancement to the Heavily Indebted Poor Countries Debt Initiative introduced with a view to achieving deeper, broader and faster debt relief for the heavily indebted poor countries,

1. *Reiterates* that the main objective of the first United Nations Decade for the Eradication of Poverty is to achieve the goal of eradicating absolute poverty and reducing overall poverty substantially in the world through decisive national action and international cooperation;

2. *Reiterates also* the call for strengthened efforts at all levels to implement fully and effectively the relevant

resolutions and decisions of the United Nations and all agreements and commitments adopted at major United Nations conferences and summits organized since 1990 as they relate to the eradication of poverty, and, in this context, calls for specific action aimed at achieving tangible results through an output-oriented approach to attaining the objectives of the Decade as soon as possible;

3. *Reaffirms* that, within the context of overall action for the eradication of poverty, special attention should be given to the multidimensional nature of poverty and the national and international conditions and policies that are conducive to its eradication by fostering, *inter alia*, the social and economic integration of people living in poverty, thus empowering them to participate in decision-making with regard to the policies that affect them, to the promotion and protection of all human rights and fundamental freedoms for all, including the right to development, and to an efficient, transparent and accountable public service and administration;

4. *Stresses* the importance of tackling the root causes of poverty and the necessity of meeting the basic needs of all, and, in this context, emphasizes the fundamental role in the eradication of poverty of strong and sustained economic growth that favours the poor, creates substantive expansion in productive opportunities and employment, increases incomes, promotes equitable income distribution and minimizes environmental degradation;

5. *Recognizes* the importance of adopting appropriate policy responses to the challenges of globalization at the national level, in particular by pursuing sound and stable domestic policies, including sound macroeconomic and social policies, in order to realize the objective of eradicating poverty;

6. *Calls upon* all Governments to incorporate, as they deem appropriate, the recommendations made by the Secretary-General for possible action and initiatives for poverty eradication towards the new millennium in the design and implementation of their national poverty alleviation strategies and to explore policies best suited to their national circumstances with a view to maximizing efforts aimed at poverty reduction and eradication;

7. *Reaffirms* that the causes of poverty should be addressed in the context of sectoral strategies, such as those on environment, food security, population, migration, health, shelter, the development of human resources, including education, fresh water, rural development and productive employment, and of the specific needs of disadvantaged and vulnerable groups in such a way as to increase opportunities and choices for people living in poverty and to enable them to build and to strengthen their assets so as to achieve social and economic integration;

8. *Urges* the strengthening of international assistance to developing countries in their efforts to alleviate poverty, including by creating an enabling environment that would facilitate the integration of developing countries into the world economy, improving their market access, facilitating the flow of financial resources and implementing fully and effectively all initiatives already launched regarding debt relief for developing countries, and emphasizes that the international community should consider further measures that would lead to effective, equitable, development-oriented and durable solutions to the external debt and debt-servicing problems of developing countries so that they can share equally in the benefits of globalization, cope with its negative effects, avoid being marginalized in the process of globalization and achieve full integration into the world economy;

9. *Calls upon* all countries to formulate and to implement outcome-oriented national strategies and programmes, including setting time-bound targets for poverty reduction, and, in this context, notes the efforts being made to achieve the target of reducing by one half, by 2015, the proportion of people living in extreme poverty, which requires strengthened national action and international assistance;

10. *Reaffirms* that all Governments and the United Nations system should promote an active and visible policy of mainstreaming a gender perspective in all policies and programmes aimed at the eradication of poverty, at both the national and international levels, and encourages the use of gender analysis as a tool for the integration of a gender dimension into planning the implementation of policies, strategies and programmes for the eradication of poverty;

11. *Calls upon* the developed countries to strengthen their efforts to achieve, as soon as possible, the agreed target of 0.7 per cent of their gross national product for overall official development assistance and, where agreed, within that target, to earmark 0.15 to 0.20 per cent of their gross national product for the least developed countries;

12. *Emphasizes* the importance of increasing the control of the poor over resources, including land, skills, knowledge, capital and social connections;

13. *Emphasizes also* the role of microcredit as an important anti-poverty tool that promotes the generation of productive self-employment and empowers people living in poverty, especially women, and therefore encourages Governments to adopt policies that support the development and capacity of microcredit institutions, and calls upon the international community, in particular the relevant organs, organizations and bodies of the United Nations system and international and regional financial institutions involved in the eradication of poverty, to support and to explore the incorporation of the microcredit approach into their programmes and the further development, as appropriate, of other microfinancing instruments;

14. *Calls upon* the developed countries, by means of intensified and effective cooperation with developing countries, to promote capacity-building and to facilitate access to and transfer of technologies and corresponding knowledge, in particular to developing countries, on favourable terms, including concessional and preferential terms, as mutually agreed, taking into account the need to protect intellectual property rights, as well as the special needs of developing countries, by identifying and implementing practical steps to ensure the achievement of progress in this regard and to assist developing countries in their efforts to eradicate poverty in an era influenced in large measure by technology;

15. *Emphasizes* the critical role of both formal and non-formal education and training and basic education in the empowerment of those living in poverty, notes the importance of the world forum on education to be held at Dakar in April 2000, and invites the

United Nations system, in particular the United Nations Educational, Scientific and Cultural Organization and the United Nations Children's Fund, to propose measures aimed at enhancing the role of the United Nations system, including the World Bank, in helping Member States to provide effective and equitable education for all;

16. *Welcomes* the efforts made by the United Nations system to assign priority to the eradication of poverty and to enhance coordination, and, in this regard, encourages those agencies of the United Nations system, including the Bretton Woods institutions, and other partners in development to continue to support all Member States in carrying forward their own strategy for the achievement of the objectives of the Decade;

17. *Reaffirms* the importance of agreeing on a mutual commitment of interested developed and developing country partners to allocate, on average, 20 per cent of official development assistance and 20 per cent of the national budget, respectively, to basic social programmes, and welcomes the efforts made to implement the 20/20 initiative, which emphasizes that promoting access for all to basic social services is essential for sustainable and equitable development and is an integral part of the strategy for the eradication of poverty;

18. *Welcomes* the Cologne debt initiative, launched in June 1999, which called for substantial additional financing, and recognizes the importance of fair burden-sharing among creditors and the recent decisions of the International Monetary Fund and the World Bank on the enhanced Heavily Indebted Poor Countries Debt Initiative, which should provide deeper, broader and faster debt relief that will contribute to the reduction of poverty in a sustainable manner in those countries;

19. *Recognizes* the difficulties of highly indebted middle-income developing countries and other highly indebted middle-income countries in meeting their external debt and debt-servicing obligations, and notes the worsening situation in some of them in the context, *inter alia*, of higher liquidity constraints, which may require debt treatment including, as appropriate, debt-reduction measures that will assist them in their efforts effectively to combat poverty;

20. *Encourages* the continued examination in all relevant intergovernmental forums of ways and means to integrate poverty reduction objectives and strategies into discussions on international financial and development issues;

21. *Requests* the Secretary-General to report to it at its fifty-fifth session on the progress made in the implementation of measures, recommendations and activities relating to the first United Nations Decade for the Eradication of Poverty, including a thorough examination of the impact of globalization on the eradication of poverty, recommendations for possible action and initiatives for the eradication of poverty and proposals for better coordination of action taken by the United Nations system, as well as on the implementation of the present resolution;

22. *Decides* to include in the provisional agenda of its fifty-fifth session the item entitled "Implementation of the first United Nations Decade for the Eradication of Poverty (1997-2006)".

Science and technology for development

Commission on Science and Technology for Development

The Commission on Science and Technology for Development, at its fourth session (Geneva, 17-21 May) [E/1999/31], marked the twentieth anniversary of the United Nations Conference on Science and Technology for Development [YUN 1979, p. 635], by adopting a vision statement on the future of science and technology for development, to be delivered at the UNESCO World Conference on Science (Budapest, Hungary, 26 June-1 July) (see PART SIX, Chapter IV).

The session had as its main substantive theme "Science and technology partnerships and networking for national capacity-building". Other issues considered included: the report of a panel meeting on biotechnology (see below); activities related to the coordination of science and technology for development [E/CN.16/1999/8]; promotion of a coalition of resources to support science and technology in developing countries [E/CN.16/1999/6]; technical cooperation activities by the UN system in information and communication technologies [E/CN.16/1999/Misc.3]; action arising from the Commission's third session [YUN 1997, p. 826] [E/CN.16/1999/7]; and inter-sessional and budget activities [E/CN.16/1999/5]. Two draft decisions and a draft resolution were recommended to the Economic and Social Council for adoption.

Partnerships and networking for capacity-building

For its main substantive theme, the Commission had before it a report on the work of the Working Group on Science and Technology Partnerships and Networking for National Capacity-Building (Sliema, Malta, 28-30 September 1998) [E/CN.16/1999/2]. The Working Group discussed whether developments in the world economy, such as globalization, had opened up new opportunities for developing countries and countries in transition to build up indigenous capacity and technological capability, especially at the enterprise level. It also considered whether the success of newly industrialized countries in forging alliances and partnerships and using them to enhance technological upgrading and improve competitiveness could be replicated in other countries. Particular attention was given to partnerships and networking in energy and biotechnology, industries considered vital to economic growth and development in developing countries. The meeting was divided into three substantive sessions, focusing on: recent trends in partnerships for capacity-building in all sectors of the global economy; energy partnerships and their contribution to the provision of energy supplies and services; and biotechnology, an issue considered to be at the forefront of new forms of strategic alliances and partnerships.

The Working Group recommended that Governments create and maintain a stable macroeconomic and policy environment that included incentives and support mechanisms to encourage investment and foster technological capabilities and industrial development; prepare the ground for inter-firm cooperation by creating a forum for dialogue with private and public sector bodies; identify priority areas for developing technological capacity where international partnerships and networking could play an essential role, the major needs of local firms in terms of technology, expertise and know-how, and useful services that could be provided to foreign firms interested in forming partnerships with domestic companies; provide a stable legal and regulatory framework for business and inter-firm agreements and transactions; provide support to foster partnerships between public and private institutions; support partnerships and networking between academic institutions and provide the means and infrastructure for basic research; and increase partnerships and collaboration in energy technologies.

Panel on biotechnology

Discussions of the Panel Meeting on Biotechnology for Food Production and Its Impact on Development (Geneva, 21-22 January) [E/CN.16/1999/3], which was convened in accordance with Economic and Social Council resolution 1997/62 [YUN 1997, p. 827], focused on three thematic areas: issues related to plant and animal species and their traits, as well as to some biotechnology techniques and their applications at the local level; endogenous capacity-building for biotechnology development and transfer, including mechanisms for incorporating biotechnology into mainstream agricultural research; and other critical issues related to biotechnology that had an impact on food production, particularly those that needed to be addressed at the international level.

The Panel recommended that Governments: identify, develop and disseminate balanced information on biotechnology, intellectual property rights and biosafety; undertake studies on the relationships between intellectual property rights and technology transfer; encourage networking and linkages between the public and private sectors and encourage interaction between industry, investors and the scientific community; and build endogenous capacity and strengthen research capability in biotechnology through training skilled manpower and providing incentives for research and development personnel. It recommended that the international community: support developing countries in their efforts to develop and diffuse biotechnology to provide food for their populations; encourage private sector participation by educating industry and investors on the potential benefits of biotechnology; support mechanisms encouraging private firms to adapt and apply new technologies and find new ways to finance firm development; and establish strategic alliances and networking with centres of excellence in developed countries and encourage interaction with pioneering initiatives to develop and apply genomic technologies and computational tools to the conservation, evaluation and utilization of plant genetic resources worldwide. The Commission, through UNCTAD, should identify and initiate dialogues involving the private and public sectors and NGOs with a view to fostering the exchange of information and ideas among scientists, policy makers, industry and end-users. It should also address the need for regulatory capacity-building in biosafety for all countries, disseminate the results of other efforts already under way and support initiatives that had proved useful in designing national biosafety programmes suitable to local needs and priorities.

Twentieth anniversary of Vienna Conference

On 21 May, the Commission approved the text of "A Common Vision", a statement on the future contribution of science and technology to development [E/1999/31], which was formulated in response to Economic and Social Council resolution 1995/4 [YUN 1995, p. 850] as a way to commemorate the twentieth anniversary of the United Nations Conference on Science and Technology for Development [YUN 1979, p. 635]. The Commission had before it a note by the UNCTAD secretariat [E/CN.16/1999/4 & Corr.1] containing the draft vision statement, which had resulted from a series of panel and expert group meetings on the subject.

The approved text called for science and technology to be considered the common heritage of mankind and went on to outline the challenges facing science and technology if it was to serve the goal of sustainable development. They included capacity-building in developing countries; ensuring an enabling political and economic environment; more transparent, participatory and innovative government policies; close cooperation among actors at all levels to strengthen systems of innovation and ensure that their outcomes enhanced general welfare; and new policies and services to bring women into the mainstream of technological change. In the area of education, the text called for priority to be given to increased investment in engineering and science education, promotion of vocational training and improvement of the scope and methodology of scientific and technological education.

A proper balance was needed between providing an incentive to invest in knowledge creation and maintaining the tradition of openness and free exchange of scientific information. Links beyond national borders were also crucial to the acquisition of knowledge and information for development and it was important that technological innovation be assessed in terms of its economic, social and environmental impact with the participation of all those concerned. The Commission could serve as a forum in the process of finding new ways to ensure that science and technology improved, through development, the well-being of all peoples as well as of future generations.

ECONOMIC AND SOCIAL COUNCIL ACTION

On 30 July [meeting 46], the Economic and Social Council, on the recommendation of the Commission on Science and Technology for Development [E/1999/31], adopted **resolution 1999/61** without vote [agenda item 13 *(b)*].

Science and technology for development

The Economic and Social Council,

Recognizing the role of the Commission on Science and Technology for Development as a forum for the examination of science and technology questions, for improving understanding of science and technology policies for development and for the formulation of recommendations and guidelines on science and technology matters within the United Nations system, all in relation to development,

Recognizing also that the Commission, in carrying out its work, should pay special attention to the needs and requirements of developing countries, in particular the least developed countries and landlocked and small island developing States, and that it should take into consideration the relevant problems of countries with economies in transition,

Taking note with appreciation of the reports of the Commission's Working Group on Science and Technology Partnerships and Networking for National Capacity-Building and its Panel Meeting on Biotechnology for Food Production and Its Impact on Development,

Recognizing that the economic potential of science and technology partnerships and networking is enormous and that those without the capabilities to form equitable partnerships and participate in networks risk being marginalized from active participation in the global economy,

Aware of the extremely precarious situation of science and technology in some countries, in particular those in Africa, and of the need for these countries to overcome the constraints that have adverse effects on the well-being of people, the development of nations and the competitiveness of their economies,

Taking note with satisfaction of the notes by the secretariat on a common vision on science and technology for development, on budget and inter-sessional activities of the Commission and on the coalition of resources, and other relevant documentation submitted to the Commission for consideration at its fourth session,

Recognizing the importance of science, technology and innovation policies, and noting with satisfaction that two such reviews, for Colombia and Jamaica, have been completed and that others are under way or awaiting financing,

Noting that the fourth session of the Commission was taking place twenty years after the United Nations Conference on Science and Technology for Development, held in Vienna from 20 to 31 August 1979, and reaffirming the increasing importance of science and technology in effectively addressing development challenges, and the role that the United Nations can play in this area,

Recalling its resolutions 1997/62 of 25 July 1997 on science and technology for development and 1998/46 and 1998/47 of 31 July 1998 concerning the restructuring and revitalization of the United Nations in the economic, social and related fields,

Recognizing that enhanced transparency and accountability are essential for the efficient and effective functioning of the Commission,

Welcoming the initiative taken by the United Nations Educational, Scientific and Cultural Organization in holding the World Conference on Science in Budapest from 26 June to 1 July 1999,

Activities as follow-up to the earlier work of the Commission

A. *Science and technology partnerships and networking for national capacity-building*

1. *Recommends* that developing countries and countries with economies in transition identify, in cooperation with all stakeholders:

(a) Priority areas for the development of technological capacity, where international partnerships and networking could play an essential role;

(b) The major needs of domestic firms in terms of technology, expertise and know-how, in order to map out clear objectives, expected output and monitoring tools;

(c) Useful services that could be provided to foreign public and private institutions interested in forming partnerships with domestic public and private institutions and that could help in establishing more equitable and balanced partnerships;

2. *Also recommends* that Governments explore ways and means of fostering partnerships among public and private institutions, *inter alia*, by creating an enabling policy, regulatory and legal environment, and by contributing information and knowledge, financing the development of research and development activities and infrastructure, and raising public awareness of the role and benefits of partnerships and networking in science and technology, and, where such processes already exist, that they should be updated;

3. *Further recommends* that Governments support partnerships and networking for both basic and ap-

plied research, with a view to enhancing national capacity-building;

4. *Requests* the secretariat of the Commission on Science and Technology for Development, using the resources it can mobilize:

(*a*) To identify and analyse best practices in partnering and networking;

(*b*) To build an inventory of opportunities for international science and technology partnerships and networking;

5. *Invites* Governments, the public and business sectors, academia and non-governmental organizations in industrialized countries to engage in partnerships and networking in science and technology with their counterparts in developing countries and countries with economies in transition in order to facilitate access to and the use and adaptation of new technologies, and to improve their technological capability and build national capacity;

6. *Recommends* that, given the extent of the burgeoning energy demand and the financial constraints in developing countries, partnerships and collaboration on renewable as well as on conventional sources of energy, such as those envisaged in the clean development mechanism and the joint implementation arrangements envisioned in the context of the Kyoto Protocol to the United Nations Framework Convention on Climate Change, should be increased in order to:

(*a*) Promote capacity-building in developing countries;

(*b*) Provide modern energy services to rural and unserved urban populations;

(*c*) Encourage private sector participation in the provision of electricity supplies under innovative arrangements such as build-operate-transfer or build-operate-own schemes;

7. *Also recommends* that the Commission collaborate more closely with United Nations bodies and specialized agencies of the United Nations system, in particular the United Nations Conference on Trade and Development, the United Nations Development Programme, the Food and Agriculture Organization of the United Nations, the United Nations Educational, Scientific and Cultural Organization, the World Health Organization, the World Bank, the World Intellectual Property Organization and the United Nations Industrial Development Organization, to promote science and technology partnerships;

8. *Further recommends* that the least developed countries, in particular those in Africa, support their effective integration into the global process of mobilization of scientific knowledge and available technology, especially by:

(*a*) Supporting all initiatives aimed at the subregional regrouping of resources in the area of science and technology for development;

(*b*) Identifying equitable partnerships and placing due value on their scientists;

(*c*) Creating centres of excellence in priority areas and enhancing local education in science and technology skills;

B. *Biotechnology for food production*

9. *Recommends* that the Commission, through its secretariat, initiate a dialogue that involves the private and the public sectors, non-governmental organizations and specialized biotechnology centres and networks, such as the Global Forum on Agricultural Research, with a view to fostering the exchange of information and ideas among scientists, policy makers, representatives of industry and end-users. Such a dialogue can also provide a forum in which to raise issues concerning global developments in biotechnology, such as intellectual property rights, biosafety, bioethics, "pharma-foods" and "terminator genes", and to raise public awareness and create a better understanding of the potential benefits of biotechnology and other critical issues;

10. *Also recommends* that Governments in developing countries and countries with economies in transition undertake, with the cooperation of the international community, the following strategies:

(*a*) Strengthen research capability, build national capacity in biotechnology and undertake training programmes to provide a skilled workforce;

(*b*) Identify and encourage the development of centres of competence in biotechnology in each country;

(*c*) Develop and maintain partnerships with centres of excellence and networks in all countries;

(*d*) Encourage linkages and interaction among the public and private sectors and research and development institutions;

(*e*) Encourage the participation of the scientific community in policy discussions on biotechnology, biosafety and bioethics and in increasing public understanding of the risks and benefits of this new technology;

11. *Requests* the secretariat of the Commission:

(*a*) To assist in identifying and disseminating balanced information on biotechnology, intellectual property rights and biosafety;

(*b*) To examine case studies of approaches to address issues related to technology, intellectual property rights and biosafety issues in a practical, understandable and concrete way;

12. *Requests* the Commission to collaborate with the United Nations Conference on Trade and Development in preparing the next issue of the *Advanced Technology Assessment System Bulletin* on biotechnology for food production;

13. *Recommends* that the Commission and its secretariat cooperate with other international and regional organizations active in biotechnology, such as the regional commissions, the United Nations Environment Programme, the Food and Agriculture Organization of the United Nations, the World Bank, the United Nations Industrial Development Organization, the International Centre for Genetic Engineering and Biotechnology, non-governmental organizations and other international institutions such as the Consultative Group on International Agricultural Research, in particular to build understanding and to exchange information on biosafety regulation and capacity-building, including through case studies on (*a*) partnerships in biotechnology, (*b*) biosafety, (*c*) bioethics and (*d*) approaches to biotechnology and intellectual property rights issues;

C. *Coalition of resources*

14. *Requests* the secretariat of the Commission, using the extrabudgetary resources already allocated for this purpose, to finalize the publication of the reports

on the coalition of resources for the application of information and communications technologies in transmissions infrastructure, education and health, and to ensure the widest possible dissemination of the final report;

D. *Science, technology and innovation policy reviews*

15. *Recommends* that the Commission continue to liaise with the United Nations Conference on Trade and Development on science, technology and innovation policy reviews with interested countries in order to identify options for national action, especially those that foster technological capability and innovation and the transfer and diffusion of technology;

E. *New substantive theme and other activities*

16. *Decides* that the substantive theme for the inter-sessional period 1999-2001 shall be "National capacity-building in biotechnology", with particular attention being paid to agriculture and the agro-industry, health and the environment. The theme shall include human resource development through basic science education, research and development, as well as their inter-disciplinary aspects; the transfer, commercialization and diffusion of technology; increasing public awareness and participation in science policy-making; and bioethics, biosafety, biodiversity and the legal and regulatory matters affecting these issues to ensure equitable treatment;

F. *Coordination of science and technology for development in the United Nations system*

Mindful of the need to continue to strengthen the functioning of the Commission in the context of its restructuring, including its role regarding the coordination of science and technology for development,

Welcoming the steps taken by the secretariat of the United Nations Conference on Trade and Development to establish a web site for the dissemination of information regarding the activities of the Commission,

17. *Urges* the secretariat of the Commission to continue efforts, in collaboration with other United Nations bodies, including the regional commissions and the Ad Hoc Open-ended Working Group on Informatics, to establish an electronic network linking information on their activities in science and technology for development and to build awareness of scientific developments that are particularly important for fostering economic and social development;

18. *Requests* the secretariat of the Commission to continue to issue the regular newsletter updating activities in the United Nations system pertaining to science and technology for development, including information on plans for and the results of the inter-sessional activities of the Commission itself;

19. *Calls upon* the secretariat and Bureau of the Commission to identify and take advantage of opportunities to interact closely with bodies of the United Nations system in order to promote greater information exchange and coordination of activities in science and technology for development; such interaction should include participation by the secretariat in the relevant coordination meetings of the Consultative Committee on Programme and Operational Questions;

20. *Recommends* that every other year one panel meeting should be held in Geneva, following which the Bureau shall meet the Geneva-based delegations of member States and observers for one day to discuss with the delegations the status of the inter-sessional activities of the Commission and its efforts to coordinate activities of the United Nations system pertaining to science and technology for development;

21. *Agrees* to include in its agenda the item entitled "Functioning of the Commission on Science and Technology for Development, including its role in coordinating science and technology for development", and requests the secretariat of the Commission to prepare a succinct analytical report on relevant activities within the United Nations system, including the outcome of the World Conference on Science, for consideration under this item.

In other action, on 28 July, the Council took note of the Commission's report on its fourth session, endorsed the resolutions and decisions adopted and approved the provisional agenda and documentation for the Commission's fifth (2001) session (**decision 1999/274**). On the same date, by **decision 1999/275**, the Council extended the mandate of the Gender Advisory Board (an expert group established by the Commission in 1995 [YUN 1995, p. 850] to facilitate its discussions on the gender implications of science and technology for developing countries) until 30 June 2001. The Council further decided that two vacancies on the Board should be filled by Commission members, in order to ensure continued linkages between the two bodies, and that the Commission should assess the desirability of continuing the work of the Board—and the potential for obtaining external resources to do so—at its fifth session.

Report of Secretary-General. In an August report on science and technology for development [A/54/270 & Corr.1], submitted in response to General Assembly resolution 52/184 [YUN 1997, p. 829], the Secretary-General described action taken by the Commission on Science and Technology for Development on the issues before it: science and technology partnerships and networking for national capacity-building; biotechnology and its impact on development, with particular emphasis on food production; the formulation of a common vision regarding the future contribution of science and technology for development; the coalition of resources; information and communication technologies; science, technology and innovation policy reviews; gender, science and technology; and coordination of the science and technology-related activities within the UN system.

GENERAL ASSEMBLY ACTION

On 22 December [meeting 87], the General Assembly, on the recommendation of the Second Committee [A/54/585/Add.4], adopted **resolution 54/201** without vote [agenda item 97 *(d)*].

Science and technology for development

The General Assembly,

Reaffirming the continuing validity of the Vienna Programme of Action on Science and Technology for Development, adopted in 1979, its resolution 52/184 of 18 December 1997 and all other relevant United Nations resolutions and decisions, as well as the outcomes of major United Nations conferences and their five-year reviews concerning science and technology for development,

Taking note of those outcomes, including the Science Agenda—Framework for Action, adopted by the World Conference on Science, held at Budapest from 26 June to 1 July 1999,

Noting that issues related to utilizing science and technology for development were dealt with in the "Partners for Development" summit held at Lyon, France, from 9 to 12 November 1998 under the auspices of the United Nations Conference on Trade and Development,

Reaffirming the Common Vision on the future of science and technology for development as approved by the Commission on Science and Technology for Development at its fourth session, which stated that science and technology should be considered the common heritage of mankind and should be shared,

Stressing that the pace of globalization is influenced in large measure by the development of science and technology and that developing countries should be assisted in becoming well equipped with the knowledge of science and technology as well as the practical skills associated with technology management so as to enable them to benefit from the opportunities offered by globalization and to avoid the risk of their marginalization in the process of globalization,

Recognizing the importance of establishing and strengthening partnership and networking among public and private sectors and academic institutions from the South and the North to build and strengthen the technological capabilities and skills needed for developing countries to compete in the international markets,

Recognizing also that information technologies are important requisites for research, planning, development and decision-making in science and technology and that they have far-reaching implications for society,

Noting the work being undertaken by the Commission in its work programme for Member States, especially the developing countries, and its work with some countries with economies in transition, and reaffirming its unique role as a global forum for examining science and technology questions, improving the understanding of science and technology policies and formulating recommendations and guidelines on science and technology matters within the United Nations system in relation to development,

Recognizing the need for adequate resources, including through provision of new and additional resources from all sources, to be devoted to fostering science and technology for development,

Recognizing also the need to address the obstacles faced by developing countries in accessing new technologies, while taking into account the need to protect intellectual property rights and the special needs of developing countries,

Recognizing further the need for dissemination of research knowledge and sharing of technologies and expertise in the field of biotechnology, in particular in the areas of agriculture, pharmaceuticals and health care, that could benefit mankind,

Taking note of the report of the Secretary-General,

1. *Reaffirms* the important role that the United Nations should play in the promotion of cooperation in science and technology, as one of its priorities, and in the enhancement of support and assistance to developing countries in their efforts to achieve sustainable development, and emphasizes the need to enhance the capability of the relevant United Nations organizations, including the United Nations Conference on Trade and Development, to address relevant issues in the field of science and technology;

2. *Takes note* of Economic and Social Council resolution 1999/61 of 30 July 1999 and Council decision 1999/274 of 28 July 1999 in which the Council approved the provisional agenda and substantive theme for the fifth session of the Commission on Science and Technology for Development;

3. *Recognizes* the role of the Commission in coordinating the activities of the United Nations system in the area of science and technology for development, emphasizes the importance of the activities that are to be pursued within the framework of the Commission, including a broad spectrum of new global challenges in science and technology, and encourages support to these undertakings;

4. *Also recognizes* the importance for developing countries of having access to science and technology so as to enhance their productivity and competitiveness in the world market, and stresses the need to promote, facilitate and finance, as appropriate, access to and transfer of environmentally sound technologies and the corresponding know-how, in particular to the developing countries, on concessional, preferential and favourable terms, as mutually agreed, taking into account the need to protect intellectual property rights and the special needs of developing countries;

5. *Further recognizes* the role of Governments in science and technology for development, in particular in providing appropriate regulatory frameworks and incentives for the development of science and technology;

6. *Stresses* the role of Governments and international development institutions in facilitating the transfer of privately owned technologies on concessional terms, as mutually agreed, to developing countries, especially the least developed countries;

7. *Recognizes* the role of partnership among the public and private sectors, academic research centres and international funding agencies in science and technology for development, in particular in the transfer, creation and development of science and technology capabilities;

8. *Reaffirms* that capacity-building in science and technology in developing countries should remain a priority issue in the United Nations agenda, and urges that international cooperation efforts be intensified and strengthened towards endogenous capacity-building in developing countries in science and technology, including their capacity to utilize scientific and technological developments from abroad as well as to modify and adapt them to suit local conditions;

9. *Recognizes* the role of the public and private sectors, industry and academia in science and technology for development, in particular in the transfer and development of science and technology capabilities;

10. *Stresses* the importance of facilitating the transfer of technology to developing countries, in particular in knowledge-intensive sectors, with the objective of enhancing technological capacities, capabilities and skills in developing countries;

11. *Recognizes* the need for Governments and regional and international bodies to take measures to ensure better access to and participation in scientific and technological areas for women, especially where they are not represented or are under-represented, bearing in mind the important role that they can play in further developing innovation and methodologies for science and technology;

12. *Emphasizes* the role of partnership and networking mechanisms for the integration of developing countries and countries with economies in transition into the world economy, in particular by strengthening national capacity-building, promoting market access across a large number of sectors and industries, disseminating new business and management cultures, especially among small and medium-sized enterprises, and expanding opportunities for them to leverage their own research and development activities;

13. *Reaffirms* the need to fulfil the commitments on the provision of financial resources and transfer of technology contained in chapter 34 of Agenda 21, the outcome of the nineteenth special session of the General Assembly and the Agenda for Development;

14. *Recognizes* that, while applications of agricultural biotechnology in developing countries, if associated with the capacity to ensure their compatibility with human health and ecosystems, provide viable opportunities for improving productivity and increasing production capacity in the agricultural sector, a large number of developing countries have limited access to such technologies and face a number of impediments to their development of biotechnology;

15. *Also recognizes* the need for studying the impact of new biotechnologies on human health, the welfare and livelihood of the farmers, and poverty in developing countries;

16. *Calls* for safe biotechnology that will, *inter alia*, foster crop reproduction and enhance the development of developing countries;

17. *Reaffirms* that the substantive theme for the work of the Commission on Science and Technology for Development during the inter-sessional period 1999-2001 will be "National capacity-building in biotechnology", with particular attention to agriculture and the agro-industry, health and the environment; the theme will include human resource development through basic science education, research and development, as well as their interdisciplinary aspects; the transfer, commercialization and diffusion of technology; increasing public awareness and participation in science policy-making; and bioethics, biosafety, biodiversity and the legal and regulatory matters affecting these issues to ensure equitable treatment;

18. *Stresses* the necessity of promoting linkages and partnership among public and private sectors and centres of excellence and networks in developed and developing countries and countries with economies in transition with the objective of strengthening national research capability and capacity in biotechnology in developing countries;

19. *Also stresses* the need to establish science and technology as a cross-cutting theme within the work of the United Nations, particularly through effective and better coordination, including of international cooperation in technology assessment, monitoring and forecasting, information and communication technologies, partnership and networking for innovative and new technologies, biotechnology and providing an environment conducive to the development of new environmentally sound technologies, and calls upon United Nations organizations, funds and programmes to work in a coordinated manner to develop a catalogue of proven technologies to enable developing countries to make effective choices in state-of-the-art technologies;

20. *Encourages* the United Nations system to ensure, where appropriate in its operational activities, the provision for the transfer of appropriate technical know-how and technological skills to developing countries;

21. *Reaffirms* the need for adequate financial resources on a continuous and assured basis to foster science and technology for development, in particular to promote endogenous capacity-building in developing countries in accordance with their priorities;

22. *Emphasizes* the need to reduce regulatory limitations on the transfer of technology, particularly to developing countries, and stresses the importance of identifying barriers to and unjustifiable restrictions on the transfer of technologies, with a view to addressing such constraints while creating specific incentives, fiscal and otherwise, for the transfer of new and innovative technologies;

23. *Recognizes* the importance of cooperation among developing countries in the field of science and technology, building on their complementarities, and the need to advance further such cooperation through the establishment or strengthening of national technology and information centres in developing countries and their networking on subregional, regional, interregional and global levels to promote technology research, training and dissemination as well as joint projects in developing countries, urges the organizations and bodies of the United Nations system and other relevant international, regional and subregional organizations and programmes to provide continued and enhanced support through technical assistance and financing for such efforts, calls for further cooperation between centres of excellence, universities and research institutions, and urges the international community to support such initiatives, where appropriate, through financial and technical assistance;

24. *Also recognizes* the importance of maintaining mutually beneficial scientific and technological cooperation between and among developing countries and countries with economies in transition;

25. *Invites* the relevant bodies of the United Nations system to provide assistance and to promote cooperation in the areas of partnership and networking, biotechnology, and information and communication technologies, including in the design and implementation of national strategies on such technologies or mechanisms;

26. *Requests* the Secretary-General to submit to the General Assembly for consideration at its fifty-fifth ses-

sion, through the Economic and Social Council, without prejudice to the periodicity of this item, proposals for strengthening the coordination of mechanisms on the Commission on Science and Technology for Development within the United Nations Conference on Trade and Development in order to ensure coordination of the various efforts and activities in the area of new and innovative technologies, in particular information and communication technologies, and their applications, such as in electronic commerce, with the objective of promoting complementarity of activities within the United Nations system;

27. *Also requests* the Secretary-General to submit to the General Assembly at its fifty-fifth session a report on the progress made in the implementation of the present resolution.

Economic and social trends

Economic surveys and trends

The *World Economic and Social Survey 1999* [Sales No. E.99.II.C.1], prepared in mid-1999 by the UN Department of Economic and Social Affairs (DESA), stated that, following two years of financial turbulence and a marked slowdown in global economic growth, the world economy was no longer weakening. Most of the countries affected by the financial crises of 1997 and 1998—which spread from East Asia to the Russian Federation and then Latin America—were moving towards recovery. Led by the easing of monetary policy in major developed economies, economic prospects had improved and global financial markets had stabilized. Commodity prices had also stabilized, including oil prices, which had rebounded since early 1999, and inflation was expected to remain subdued in most developing and transition economies.

Nevertheless, economic growth in 1999 was markedly lower than at mid-decade, particularly for the majority of developing and transition economies. Gross world output was expected to increase by just 2 per cent in 1999, a minor improvement over 1998 and far short of the growth necessary to improve living standards and reduce the number of people living in poverty. While 39 developing countries attained a 3 per cent growth of output per capita in 1996, only 23 did so in 1998 and just 13 were expected to meet that level in 1999.

With output per capita increasing faster in the developed economies than in the rest of the world, the gap between rich and poor countries was widening. Furthermore, without successful systemic reforms of the international financial and monetary systems, the world economy would remain highly vulnerable to future economic crises. The issue of financing for development—including a review of the major changes that had taken place in recent decades in banking and financial systems around the world—was addressed in the second half of the report (see PART THREE, Chapter IV).

All of the developed countries—apart from Japan and New Zealand—maintained or slightly increased their output in 1998, with growth in the United States exceeding expectations, making it the main engine of growth in the world economy. By 1999, the United States economy had experienced sustained expansion for more than eight years—the longest period of continuous peacetime growth—nurtured by sound macroeconomic policy, major technological innovations, and increasing global integration, in which the benefits for the United States outweighed the costs. Canada also continued to grow at a fast pace, despite weak consumption caused in part by the depreciation of the Canadian dollar at the end of 1998. In 1999, consumer confidence was rebounding. Unemployment figures and inflation levels remained low in both countries.

By contrast, Japan's economy descended into severe recession during 1998, dampening prospects throughout the East Asia region. There were signs that the Japanese economy was reviving during the first quarter of 1999, due in part to the Government's fiscal stimulus measures and restructuring of the banking sector.

In Europe, economic activity slowed in late 1998 and early 1999, particularly in Germany and Italy, both of which were harder hit than other countries by the slowdown in trade with East Asia, Latin America and the transition economies. However, growth in the Continental European economies was expected to resume in the second half of 1999 and into 2000, supported by improvement in emerging markets, subdued inflation, low interest rates and the more competitive exchange rate of the euro, as well as by policies aimed at employment stimulation and removing obstacles to full exploitation of the opportunities afforded by the single market. Despite improvements, unemployment in most European countries remained high. In the United Kingdom, growth was expected to accelerate, following interest rate cuts and increased government spending on infrastructure projects and public services.

In Australia, despite close links with Asian economies, an eight-year trend of economic expansion continued, with growth accelerating, unemployment continuing to fall and inflation remaining low. Several years of structural reforms had also strengthened the Australian economy's resilience to external events.

In 1999, the outlook for the economies in transition was discouraging. The decline was mainly the result of a financial crisis in the Russian Federation, triggered in August 1998 by a drop in commodity prices, particularly oil. The slow pace of market reforms and high public debt contributed to the crisis. By the end of the year, Russia's formal banking system had almost ceased to operate and gross domestic product (GDP) fell by more than 4 per cent.

The other countries of the Commonwealth of Independent States (CIS) and the Baltic countries were affected by the Russian economic collapse. In Ukraine, GDP fell by 1.7 per cent in 1998 and was expected to decline a further 3 per cent in 1999, with inflation as high as 50 per cent. Aggregate GDP in the CIS region as a whole contracted by 3.4 per cent. Although the Baltic countries had the lowest inflation of all the transition economies, growth slowed from 4 per cent in 1998 to less than 2 per cent in 1999. Only Armenia, Azerbaijan, Tajikistan and Turkmenistan had rising growth rates. The economies of Central and Eastern Europe, including those that were doing well, such as Poland, were also expected to stagnate. Output was likely to fall in the Czech Republic and Romania; recession was possible in Croatia and Slovakia.

Economic growth in the developing countries decelerated sharply from 5.5 per cent in 1997 to 1.7 per cent in 1998, mainly due to the spillover effects of the Asian crisis. For the developing countries overall, growth was expected to recover only gradually, achieving rates of 2.5 per cent in 1999 and 4.5 per cent in 2000. In contrast, rapid growth was forecast to continue in China and India, which augured well for the large proportion of the world's poorest who lived in those countries.

Growth in African developing countries was expected to increase from a weak 2.5 per cent in 1998 to about 3 per cent in 1999 and 3.5 per cent in 2000. However, substantial per capita gains were unlikely due to relatively fast population growth. Africa's exports were expected to remain depressed in 1999, though they could sharply increase in 2000 if oil prices recovered. Many African countries still suffered under the heavy burden of debt servicing, with total external debt well over 400 per cent of GDP in some economies.

In Asia and the Pacific, the countries of East Asia experienced the worst economic performance in decades during 1998: GDP growth contracted by more than 4 per cent, after having grown by 5.2 per cent in 1997 and by an annual average of 7 per cent during the period 1980-1996. The sharpest contractions following the regional financial crisis of mid-1997 were experienced in Indonesia—where GDP declined by more than 13 per cent in 1998—Malaysia, the Republic of Korea and Thailand. Growth also decelerated markedly in Singapore and Taiwan Province of China. Output declined in the Philippines, despite impressive growth in electronics exports to countries outside the region. The Asian crisis also had severe social consequences as unemployment rates soared.

By early 1999, however, there were signs of improvement in an increasing number of Asian countries, including Malaysia, the Republic of Korea and Thailand. Recovery in Indonesia continued to lag behind because of political and social tensions, as well as delays in implementing stabilization and restructuring measures. In the region as a whole, growth was expected to recover slowly to about 2.5 per cent in 1999.

In China, GDP grew by 7.8 per cent in 1998, in marked contrast to the poor economic performance of many neighbouring countries. However, it was China's lowest rate of growth since the early 1990s, reflecting a weakening of domestic demand due to the restructuring of State-owned enterprises, a severe flood and the impact of the Asian economic crisis. The adoption of economic policies to stimulate domestic demand resulted in GDP growth of 8.3 per cent during the first quarter of 1999, with growth forecast at about 7.5 per cent for the year.

The financial crisis had limited impact on South Asia, where GDP growth exceeded or was close to 5 per cent in1998 in all countries of the region, except Nepal. A regional growth rate of 5.6 per cent was forecast for 1999. In Western Asia, growth contracted in 7 out of 15 countries during 1998. The regional outlook for 1999 depended in large part on the demand for oil, which was forecast to be sluggish. Other significant factors for economic growth in the region included the Middle East peace process and the situation of Iraq.

Latin America as a whole was plunged into recession in 1999 due to contagion from the Asian crisis and the measures adopted to address it. Economic difficulties intensified in early 1999 with a currency crisis in Brazil—a country accounting for 40 per cent of the region's GDP—and the impact of adverse natural phenomena, including floods, drought, hurricanes and earthquakes. While several Latin American countries were expected to register a recession or no growth in GDP for 1999, growth was expected to return to the region in 2000. Economic prospects were better for 1999 in the Caribbean countries, due in part to improving agricultural production, particularly in Cuba. Mexico and the economies of Central America were expected to perform better than the South American countries.

The *Trade and Development Report, 1999* [Sales No. E.99.II.D.1] observed that while the developed countries had suffered little and even derived some benefit from the aftermath of the Asian crisis, the impact on the rest of the world had been dramatic. Virtually all developing countries and transition economies were affected. For the first time in 10 years, developing countries grew at a lower rate than industrialized countries, a shift that wiped out the fruits of decades of economic growth and poverty reduction in the most seriously affected countries, and had serious repercussions for international trade (see PART THREE, Chapter IV).

Regarding the impact on the developing countries of their rapid integration into the world economy, the *Report* noted that in the face of deep-seated imbalances in economic power and systemic biases in international trading and financial systems, their expectations of the gains from such integration in terms of faster growth, greater employment opportunities and reduced levels of poverty had been disappointed. The vulnerability of even the strongest developing economies to the forces of globalization was revealed by the humbling of the Asian tigers, stated the *Report*. The downside risks of integration had been further demonstrated by the effects of the crisis on Latin America and Eastern Europe. In spite of the return to stability in the Asian economies and the apparent confinement of the impact of the Brazilian crisis to neighbouring countries, potential instability remained inherent in the dependence of so many developing countries on foreign capital inflows that were so volatile.

According to a report on the world economic situation and prospects, prepared jointly by DESA and UNCTAD, gross world product expanded by an estimated 2.6 per cent in 1999, a notable improvement over the 1.8 per cent of 1998 and 0.6 per cent higher than anticipated in mid-1999. Much of the improvement stemmed from a faster and stronger recovery than foreseen in the Asian crisis countries, particularly the Republic of Korea, and an unexpected spurt of growth in Japan. Although Brazil experienced a recession, with negative effects on neighbouring economies, the setback was less than expected. Similarly, instead of the anticipated further decline in output following the rouble devaluation in August 1998, the Russian Federation grew by 2 per cent in 1999. A critical factor underlying the global acceleration was the continued strong performance of North America, while the slower growth in Western Europe was broadly in line with expectations. The economies in transition continued to perform poorly, but at widely differing growth rates. Following a decline in output in 1998, growth for the group in 1999 was about 0.6 per cent, stemming largely from developments in the Russian Federation.

The developing economies, which bore the brunt of the slowdown in 1998, registered the largest improvement in output in 1999, with growth recovering to over 3 per cent. On a per capita basis, however, output growth was marginal and considerably less than in the developed economies. By the end of the year, the developing countries had still not returned to the growth of over 5 per cent per year that had prevailed for some years prior to the crisis, nor made up the loss in per capita output in 1998.

Human Development Report 1999

The *Human Development Report 1999*, prepared by UNDP, addressed human development in the context of globalization, calling for a much bolder agenda of global and national reforms to achieve globalization with a human face. While globalization offered great opportunities for human advance, stronger governance was needed, the *Report* stated. Seven key challenges to securing human development in an era of globalization were outlined: adapting policies to the realities of the global economy; reducing the threats and human costs of financial volatility; tackling global threats to human security; developing technologies for human development and poverty eradication; reversing the marginalization of the poor; remedying structural imbalances; and building a more coherent and democratic architecture for global governance.

The *Report* ranked 174 countries in its human development index by combining indicators of life expectancy, educational attainment and adjusted per capita income, among other factors. In 1999, the methodology and data used for computing the index were improved, affecting the ranking of almost all countries compared to the previous year. However, that did not necessarily reflect deterioration or improvement in their state of human development. Of the 174 countries listed, 45 were in the high human development category, 94 were in the medium category and 35 were in the low category. Sixteen countries had experienced reversals in human development since 1990 due to the HIV/AIDS pandemic (mostly in sub-Saharan Africa) or economic stagnation (in sub-Saharan Africa and Eastern Europe and CIS). Wide disparities in global human development persisted both between and within regions. The speed of human progress was also uneven, most often being determined by the policy measures taken by countries to enhance people's well-being.

Development policy and public administration

The Committee for Development Policy—formerly the Committee for Development Planning, which was renamed by the Economic and Social Council in resolution 1998/46 [YUN 1998, p. 1262]—held its first session in April to discuss the theme of the role of employment and work in poverty eradication in the context of globalization: the empowerment and advancement of women (see PART THREE, Chapter X).

The Meeting of Experts on the United Nations Programme in Public Administration and Finance did not convene in 1999; the Fifteenth Meeting was scheduled for the first quarter of the year 2000.

Committee for Development Policy

In a January note [E/1999/4], the Secretary-General discussed issues for consideration by the Committee for Development Policy at its 1999 session. The Secretary-General noted that two issues had been retained for further work by the Committee: refinement of the criteria for inclusion in and graduation from the list of least developed countries (LDCs); and a vulnerability index and how a measure of vulnerability might affect the designation of LDCs. In addition, the Secretary-General proposed three further issues for consideration: the coherence of economic policy-making in the context of globalization; parameters of the global environment; and the impact, including the social dimensions, of advances in technology and the information revolution on developing countries, particularly LDCs.

ECONOMIC AND SOCIAL COUNCIL ACTION

On 5 February [meeting 4], the Economic and Social Council adopted **resolution 1999/2** [draft: E/1999/L.8] without vote [agenda item 7].

Work programme for the Committee for Development Policy

The Economic and Social Council,

Recalling its resolutions 1998/39 of 30 July 1998 and 1998/46 of 31 July 1998,

1. *Stresses* the crucial importance of the completion of the work of the Committee for Development Policy on the vulnerability index;

2. *Requests* the Committee to continue, and to make all possible efforts to complete, its work in this regard during its forthcoming session and to report thereon to the Economic and Social Council at its substantive session of 1999;

3. *Also requests* the Committee to consider the theme of the role of employment and work in poverty eradication in the context of globalization: the empowerment and advancement of women, and, in this regard, requests the Secretariat to make available to the Committee its work in preparing for the substantive session of 1999 of the Economic and Social Council.

1999 session

In accordance with Economic and Social Council **decision 1999/204** of 2 February, the first session of the Committee for Development Policy was held in New York from 26 to 30 April [E/1999/33]. The Committee considered the theme of the role of employment and work in poverty eradication in the context of globalization: the empowerment and advancement of women (see PART THREE, Chapter X). The Committee concluded that if globalization was to proceed smoothly, the major imbalance between short-term adjustment and long-term development needed to be addressed. Preventive strategies should be developed and policies adopted to create employment and reduce inequalities in income, in opportunity and in capabilities at the domestic and international levels. The Committee also addressed the increased vulnerability and inequality that accompanied the globalization process. In particular, the usefulness of a vulnerability index as a criterion for designating LDCs was considered (see below).

ECONOMIC AND SOCIAL COUNCIL ACTION

On 30 July, by **decision 1999/286**, the Economic and Social Council took note of the Committee's report on its first session.

On 16 December [meeting 51], the Council adopted **resolution 1999/67** [draft: E/1999/L.62] without vote [agenda item 13 *(a)*].

Report of the Committee for Development Policy

The Economic and Social Council,

Recalling section B of annex I to its resolution 1998/46 of 31 July 1998, in which it decided that the Council should decide on an appropriate programme of work for the Committee for Development Policy,

Recalling also its resolution 1998/39 of 30 July 1998 on the status of the least developed countries and its decision 1999/290 of 26 October 1999 on consideration of the graduation of the Republic of Maldives from the list of the least developed countries,

Recalling further General Assembly resolutions 46/206 of 20 December 1991 and 52/210 of 18 December 1997 on the report of the Committee for Development Planning,

1. *Welcomes* the report of the Committee for Development Policy on its first session, the views contained therein regarding the criteria for the identification of the least developed countries and the recognition that vulnerability should be explicitly taken into account in

the identification criteria for the least developed countries;

2. *Requests* the Secretary-General to facilitate an expert group meeting of members of the Committee in January/February 2000 in order to enable them to carry out the necessary diagnostic testing and simulations of the proposed criteria for the designation of least developed country status, in particular the economic vulnerability index, as contained in annex II to the report of the Committee, and to report to the Committee at its second session in April 2000;

3. *Requests* the expert group to review and analyse the format and content of the "vulnerability profiles" developed by the United Nations Conference on Trade and Development, as identified in chapter III, section F, of the report of the Committee;

4. *Requests,* in this context, the Committee to continue its dialogue with other international organizations working on vulnerability issues, and encourages those organizations to communicate their views on the proposed economic vulnerability index to the Committee;

5. *Also requests* the Committee, on the basis of the report of the expert group, to recommend, as appropriate, revised criteria for the identification of the least developed countries for the consideration of the Council as soon as possible, but no later than its substantive session of 2000, so that the review and decision on the list of the least developed countries can be completed by the end of 2000;

6. *Further requests* the Committee to include in its report to be submitted to the Council in 2000 its views on the theme for the high-level segment of the Council in 2000, namely "Development and international cooperation in the twenty-first century: the role of information technology in the context of a knowledge-based global economy";

7. *Requests* the Committee to collaborate in the preparation of a draft text of an international development strategy for the first decade of the new millennium, in accordance with the General Assembly resolution on implementation of the commitments and policies agreed upon in the Declaration on International Economic Cooperation, in particular the Revitalization of Economic Growth and Development of the Developing Countries, and implementation of the International Development Strategy for the Fourth United Nations Development Decade.

Developing countries

Least developed countries

The Least Developed Countries 1999 Report [Sales No. E.99.II.D.2], issued by UNCTAD, assessed the main trends in the socio-economic development of LDCs, particularly in relation to the ongoing processes of liberalization and globalization. As an input to the preparatory process for the Third United Nations Conference on LDCs, to be held in 2001, the *Report* examined the relevance of the Programme of Action for the Least Developed Countries for the 1990s in the light of the globalizing world economy (see below). The domestic and international policy measures required for the improvement of LDCs' productive capacities and competitiveness, taking into account the nature of their export trade and the challenges they faced, were also reviewed.

The *Report* noted that the average GDP growth rate for LDCs suffered its third successive decline, falling from a peak of 6 per cent in 1995 to 3.8 per cent in 1998, due in large part to the world economic deceleration resulting from the Asian financial crisis. Regionally, between 1996 and 1998, real GDP growth rates decreased from 5.8 to 4 per cent in Asian LDCs and from 4.3 to 3.6 per cent in African LDCs. The Pacific island LDCs were hardest hit, with the 3.4 per cent GDP growth of 1996 falling to -4.6 per cent in 1998. Prospects for LDC economic growth would continue to be dependent on external economic conditions and the flow of external resources, as well as domestic weather and internal conflict situations.

Trade issues. A Coordinating Workshop for Senior Advisers to Ministers of Trade in LDCs (Sun City, South Africa, 21-25 June) [UNCTAD/LDC/106] adopted proposals for a comprehensive new plan of action for integrating LDCs into the global economy in the context of the third WTO Ministerial Conference (see PART SIX, Chapter XVII). The meeting, which was jointly sponsored by South Africa, UNCTAD and UNDP, reviewed the experiences and problems faced by LDCs in implementing the agreements resulting from the Uruguay Round of multilateral trade negotiations [YUN 1994, p. 1474] and the impact of the agreements on their trade and development prospects. The question of enhancing the participation of LDCs in global trade rule-making and ways of maximizing the benefits of globalization to LDCs, while minimizing the risks, were also discussed. Measures were called for to overcome the marginalization of LDCs, as reflected in their low and declining share in world trade, investment and output. The report of the workshop—including a strategy of collective bargaining to further the interests of LDCs—would be part of the formal input from LDCs to the third WTO Ministerial Conference, to be held later in 1999, and to UNCTAD X (2000) and the third United Nations Conference on LDCs (2001).

LDC list

The number of officially designated LDCs remained at 48 in 1999. They were: Afghanistan, Angola, Bangladesh, Benin, Bhutan, Burkina Faso, Burundi, Cambodia, Cape Verde, Central

African Republic, Chad, Comoros, Democratic Republic of the Congo, Djibouti, Equatorial Guinea, Eritrea, Ethiopia, Gambia, Guinea, Guinea-Bissau, Haiti, Kiribati, Lao People's Democratic Republic, Lesotho, Liberia, Madagascar, Malawi, Maldives, Mali, Mauritania, Mozambique, Myanmar, Nepal, Niger, Rwanda, Samoa, Sao Tome and Principe, Sierra Leone, Solomon Islands, Somalia, Sudan, Togo, Tuvalu, Uganda, United Republic of Tanzania, Vanuatu, Yemen, Zambia.

Communication. By a 22 July letter [E/1999/118 & Corr.1], Maldives transmitted to the Economic and Social Council President a letter from its President expressing concern at the 1997 recommendation of the Committee for Development Planning that Maldives be graduated from the LDC list after a review in 2000.

On 26 October, the Council, by **decision 1999/290**, postponed consideration of the graduation of Maldives from the LDC list until submission of a report of the Committee for Development Policy and completion of the review of the vulnerability index (see below).

Committee for Development Policy. In accordance with Economic and Social Council resolution 1998/39 [YUN 1998, p. 793], at its 1999 session [E/1999/33], the Committee for Development Policy reviewed the usefulness of a vulnerability index as a criterion to designate LDCs, proposing that the existing economic diversification index be replaced by a composite economic vulnerability index, giving equal weight to five indicators: export concentration; instability of export earnings; instability of agricultural production; share of manufacturing and modern services in GDP; and population size. A document—to be called "a country vulnerability profile"—should be prepared for some countries to provide a more detailed assessment of the impact of external economic and natural shocks on their economic performance and structure. Regarding other LDC criteria, the Committee proposed replacing the three-year average of per capita GDP by per capita GDP for a benchmark year (the same year for all countries), converted to United States dollars at the country's average exchange rates over three years and taking into account inflation. It also proposed two changes to the Augmented Physical Quality of Life Index: using the average calorie intake per capita as a percentage of average calorie requirements per capita; and using data on child mortality under five years of age instead of life expectancy at birth.

The Committee, which was responsible for adding countries to or graduating them from the list, would be conducting the next triennial review of the LDC list in 2000.

Programme of Action for the 1990s

The ninth annual review of progress in implementing the Programme of Action for the Least Developed Countries for the 1990s, adopted by the Second (1990) United Nations Conference on the Least Developed Countries [YUN 1990, p. 369] and endorsed by the General Assembly in resolution 45/206 [ibid., p. 373], was carried out by the UNCTAD Trade and Development Board (TDB) in October. The background document was *The Least Developed Countries 1999 Report* [Sales No. E.99.II.D.2] (see above).

On 29 October [A/54/15/Rev.1 (agreed conclusions 457(XLVI))], the Board highlighted the need for more vigorous debt relief, increased flows of official development assistance (ODA) and improved productive capacity, as well as unencumbered market access for LDCs. Immediate action was called for to improve export opportunities and to assist the integration of LDCs into the multilateral trading system, especially by improving trade-related technical cooperation.

Report of Secretary-General. In August, the Secretary-General submitted to the General Assembly an update on the implementation of the Programme of Action, including an overview of the recent economic performance of LDCs [A/54/269 & Corr.1]. The policies and measures adopted by LDCs in line with the recommendations of the Programme of Action and those of the mid-term global review of progress towards its implementation, conducted in 1995 [YUN 1995, p. 863], were also reviewed, as were the overall arrangements for implementation, follow-up and monitoring of the Programme of Action at the national, regional and global levels. In addition, the report described measures taken by the UN system and provided information on international support related to external resources, debt and trade.

The Secretary-General concluded that, in most LDCs, progress in realizing the overall objectives of the Programme of Action had not been made during the 1990s. Their precarious socio-economic situation and the structural weaknesses inherent in their economies continued unabated. At the same time, globalization and liberalization had exposed additional supply-side constraints to improving the position of LDCs in the global economy. The challenges facing LDCs were beyond their capacity to overcome on their own. Financial, technical and commercial international support measures—including reversing the decline in ODA flows—were of critical importance to their future growth and development.

On 23 December, by **decision 54/453**, the General Assembly took note of the Secretary-General's report. In **resolution 54/235** of the same date, which dealt mainly with preparations for the Third Conference (see below), the Assembly decided that the Programme of Action would continue to provide the framework for national and international action for LDCs until the adoption of the next programme of action at that Conference.

Third UN Conference on LDCs (2001)

In July, the preparatory process for the Third United Nations Conference on the Least Developed Countries, scheduled for 2001, was officially launched with the convening of the first inter-agency meeting (Geneva, 20 July) [A/CONF.191/IPC/7] and the first meeting of the consultative forum (Geneva, 21-22 July) [A/CONF.191/IPC/6]. The meetings were convened in accordance with resolution 53/182 [YUN 1998, p. 794], by which the General Assembly had also designated the UNCTAD Secretary-General as Secretary-General of the Conference.

The purpose of the inter-agency meeting was to ensure the full mobilization and coordination of all relevant organs, organizations and bodies of the UN system, as well as other relevant institutions, in preparations for and follow-up to the Conference. The consultative forum served as a consensus-building medium between the UN system and other stakeholders, including NGOs and the private sector, discussing and exchanging views on the conceptual framework of the objectives of the Conference, as well as on the intergovernmental preparatory process. Both meetings considered various aspects and steps of the preparatory process based on a note by the UNCTAD secretariat [UNCLDC/III/1]. The Conference—which was to assess the results of the Programme of Action and formulate a new action plan for sustainable development of LDCs up to the year 2010—would include some 2,000 participants, including heads of State and other high-level delegates, according to the note. During the Conference, analysis of past performance would shed light on the most critical constraints on the effective realization of the goals of the previous Programmes of Action and suggest new strategies to reverse them. Domestic and external constraints, which had limited the performance of LDCs, could be useful in determining the range of issues to be addressed by the Conference.

ECONOMIC AND SOCIAL COUNCIL ACTION

On 28 July [meeting 44], the Economic and Social Council, on the recommendation of the Economic Commission for Africa [E/1999/14/Add.3], adopted **resolution 1999/40** without vote [agenda item 10].

Third United Nations Conference on the Least Developed Countries

The Economic and Social Council,

Recalling General Assembly resolution 52/187 of 18 December 1997 and resolution 53/182 of 15 December 1998, in which the Assembly decided to convene the Third United Nations Conference on the Least Developed Countries in the first semester of the year 2001 and accepted the offer of the European Union to host the Conference,

Recognizing the important role played by the Economic Commission for Africa in the preparatory process for the First and Second United Nations Conferences on the Least Developed Countries,

Noting that the mandate of the Conference is to assess the results of the Programme of Action for the Least Developed Countries for the 1990s at the country level, to review the implementation of international support measures, in particular in the areas of official development assistance, debt, investment and trade, and to consider the formulation and adoption of appropriate national and international policies and measures for the sustainable development of the least developed countries and their progressive integration into the world economy,

1. *Requests* the Executive Secretary of the Economic Commission for Africa to provide, in collaboration with the Secretary-General of the United Nations Conference on Trade and Development in his capacity as the Secretary-General of the Third United Nations Conference on the Least Developed Countries, support to African least developed countries in their preparation for the Conference at the country, regional and global levels;

2. *Invites* the Executive Secretary to ensure that the Commission makes substantive technical contributions to the Conference and its preparatory process;

3. *Invites* the bilateral, regional and multilateral development partners of the least developed countries, the host of the Conference and the United Nations Development Programme to provide adequate technical and financial assistance to the least developed countries to ensure a substantive and effective preparatory process for the Conference at the country level;

4. *Requests* the Secretary-General of the Third United Nations Conference on the Least Developed Countries to intensify his efforts to mobilize resources for the participation of representatives of the least developed countries in the envisaged regional expert-level meetings, the meetings of the intergovernmental preparatory committee and the Conference itself.

Report of Secretary-General. In an August report [A/54/271], the Secretary-General reviewed the state of preparations for the Third Conference, describing the official launch of the preparatory process and various meetings held so far. As a result of consultations with the European Union, it had been agreed that the Conference would be held in Brussels, Belgium, at a date to be decided upon between April and June 2001. Activities at the regional and country levels, the involvement of the private sector and NGOs, and the participation of LDCs were also outlined. The General Assembly, on 23 December, took note of the report (**decision 54/453**).

TDB action. On 29 October [A/54/15/Rev.1 (agreed conclusions 457(XLVI))], TDB welcomed the launching of the preparatory process for the Conference and called for its linkage with other relevant upcoming global meetings and conferences, including the third WTO Ministerial Conference, UNCTAD X, reviews of major global conferences, the Millennium Assembly and the high-level international intergovernmental consideration of financing for development (see also PART THREE, Chapter IV).

GENERAL ASSEMBLY ACTION

On 23 December [meeting 88], the General Assembly, on the recommendation of the Second Committee [A/54/487/Add.6], adopted **resolution 54/235** without vote [agenda item 99 (*f*)].

Implementation of the Programme of Action for the Least Developed Countries for the 1990s

The General Assembly,

Recalling its resolution 52/187 of 18 December 1997, in which it decided to convene the Third United Nations Conference on the Least Developed Countries at a high level in 2001, as well as its resolution 53/182 of 15 December 1998,

Noting the progress made in the preparatory process for the Third United Nations Conference on the Least Developed Countries,

Taking note of the Ministerial Declaration and Ministerial Statement on the South Summit adopted at the twenty-third annual meeting of Ministers for Foreign Affairs of the Group of 77, held in New York on 24 September 1999, and the Declaration adopted by the Ninth Annual Ministerial Meeting of the Least Developed Countries, held in New York on 29 September 1999,

1. *Recalls* that the Third United Nations Conference on the Least Developed Countries will convene in 2001, welcomes the offer of the European Union to host the Conference in Brussels, and decides to accept the offer;

2. *Decides* that the meeting of the intergovernmental preparatory committee envisaged in paragraph 4 of its resolution 53/182 will be held in New York in two parts, in the third quarter of 2000 and the first quarter of 2001, each for five working days;

3. *Also decides* that the Secretary-General of the Conference will organize the three expert-level preparatory meetings provided for in paragraph 4 of its resolution 53/182 at the venues and for the durations deemed most appropriate in consultation with Member States;

4. *Requests* the Secretary-General of the Conference to organize regional-level preparatory events in collaboration with the regional commissions and other relevant regional and subregional organizations, as appropriate;

5. *Reiterates* its request to the Secretary-General of the Conference, in consultation with Member States and in cooperation with relevant organizations and agencies, to organize well-focused sectoral, thematic and country-specific round-table meetings, as appropriate, during the Conference to contribute to its work;

6. *Emphasizes* the importance of country-level preparations;

7. *Notes with appreciation,* in this regard, the initiative of the European Union to assist the least developed countries in their preparations at the country level through the assistance of their representatives in those countries, invites the World Bank, the United Nations Development Programme and all other relevant bodies and agencies of the United Nations system to provide support to country-level preparations through their field offices in the least developed countries, and calls upon the development partners to support this preparatory process;

8. *Urges* the organizations involved in the implementation of the Integrated Framework for Trade-related Technical Assistance, including for Human and Institutional Capacity-building, to Support Least Developed Countries in their Trade and Trade-related Activities to intensify their support for efforts to assist those countries in enhancing their export supply capacity and trade opportunities and to integrate them into the multilateral trading system, and requests the Secretary-General of the Conference to ensure that information on progress in the implementation of the Integrated Framework is included in the reports submitted to the preparatory committee and to the Conference itself;

9. *Calls upon* the least developed countries, together with their development partners, in particular the United Nations Development Programme and the World Bank, as appropriate, to link the forthcoming round-table and consultative group meetings to the country-level preparatory process for the Conference and to ensure that those meetings make substantive contributions to the Conference;

10. *Requests* the Administrator of the United Nations Development Programme, in his capacity as convenor of the United Nations Development Group, to ensure the full involvement of United Nations resident coordinators and country teams in the least developed countries in the preparations for the Conference, in particular at the country level;

11. *Calls upon* the Secretary-General, in consultation with the Secretary-General of the Conference, to convene inter-agency meetings, as necessary, to ensure the full mobilization and coordination of all relevant organs, organizations and bodies of the United Nations system, as well as other relevant institutions, for the purpose of carrying out preparations for and providing follow-up to the Conference;

12. *Invites* the Secretary-General of the Conference to make arrangements, on the basis of consultations with Member States, to facilitate the broad-based involvement of civil society, including non-governmental organizations and the private sector, in the preparatory process and in the Conference and its follow-up;

13. *Requests* the Secretary-General, with the assistance of concerned organizations and bodies of the United Nations system, including the Department of Public Information of the Secretariat, to take the necessary measures to intensify their public information efforts and other appropriate initiatives to enhance pub-

lic awareness in favour of the Conference, including by highlighting its objectives and significance;

14. *Decides* to defray the cost of the participation of two government representatives from each least developed country in the meetings of the preparatory committee and the Conference itself through the use of extrabudgetary resources, and, in the event that those resources prove to be insufficient, requests the Secretary-General to consider all other options, including the use of unspent balances from the regular budget for the biennium 1996-1997 as an exceptional measure;

15. *Calls upon* donor countries to provide financial support for the participation of the least developed countries in both the preparatory process and the Conference itself, and welcomes efforts already made to that effect;

16. *Requests* the Secretary-General, in consultation with the Secretary-General of the United Nations Conference on Trade and Development and Member States, to make the necessary arrangements, through redeployment and the use of other resources at their disposal, for the substantial strengthening of the Office of the Special Coordinator for Least Developed, Landlocked and Island Developing Countries, through the provision of sufficient staff and resources, with a view to enabling it to organize effectively and efficiently the Third United Nations Conference on the Least Developed Countries and the follow-up to its outcome, while satisfactorily carrying out its mandates relating to the least developed, landlocked and small island developing countries;

17. *Also requests* the Secretary-General to submit a report to the General Assembly at its fifty-fifth session on the state of preparations for the Third United Nations Conference on the Least Developed Countries, taking into account the consideration of the matter at the forty-seventh session of the Trade and Development Board;

18. *Decides* that the Programme of Action for the Least Developed Countries for the 1990s will continue to provide the framework for national and international action for the least developed countries until the adoption of the next programme of action at the Third United Nations Conference on the Least Developed Countries, and requests the Secretary-General to continue to give high priority to the implementation of the present and future programmes of action for the least developed countries on a system-wide basis and in the context of the follow-up to all major United Nations conferences and summits as well as all forthcoming events, including the tenth session of the United Nations Conference on Trade and Development, and the high-level international intergovernmental consideration of financing for development, including the preparatory process, and the Millennium Assembly;

19. *Decides* to include in the provisional agenda of its fifty-fifth session an item entitled "Third United Nations Conference on the Least Developed Countries".

Island developing countries

In September, the General Assembly held its twenty-second special session to review and appraise the implementation of the Programme of Action for the Sustainable Development of Small Island Developing States (SIDS), an integrated and comprehensive framework for the sustainable development of SIDS, adopted in 1994 at a Global Conference on the subject in Barbados [YUN 1994, p. 783]. The special session culminated in the adoption of a Declaration and a text on the state of progress and initiatives for the future implementation of the Programme of Action. The Declaration called for efforts to improve financial resources, capacity-building, institutional arrangements and technology transfer for the sustainable development of SIDS. The accompanying text presented a series of broad initiatives for the further implementation of the Programme of Action, including recommendations for urgent action in six sectoral areas: climate change, natural disasters, freshwater resources, coastal and marine resources, energy and tourism.

The Commission on Sustainable Development held preparatory discussions for the special session during its seventh session in April and at a resumed preparatory meeting in September.

Twenty-second special session

A special session of the General Assembly to review and appraise the implementation of the Programme of Action for the Sustainable Development of Small Island Developing States was held in New York on 27 and 28 September, as decided by the Assembly on 7 April in **resolution 53/189 B**. The special session was convened in accordance with resolution S-19/2 [YUN 1997, p. 792], adopted in 1997 at the conclusion of the nineteenth special session of the Assembly, which reviewed the implementation of Agenda 21, adopted by the United Nations Conference on Environment and Development in 1992 [YUN 1992, p. 672]. The twenty-second special session concluded with the adoption of a Declaration and a document on the state of progress and initiatives for the future implementation of the Programme of Action.

In other action, the Assembly, on 27 September, approved a number of organizational arrangements for the session (**decision S-22/21**), adopted the agenda (**decision S-22/22**), elected the Chairman of the Ad Hoc Committee of the Whole of the Twenty-second Special Session, which discussed the text of the draft declaration (**decision S-22/15**) and decided on the NGOs that might make statements in the debate in plenary (**decision S-22/23**). On 28 September, the Assembly approved the Credentials Committee's report (**resolution S-22/1**) and transmitted to its fifty-fourth session a draft resolution on promoting an integrated management approach to the Caribbean Sea, contained in a 24 September letter from Canada [A/S-22/6] (**decision S-22/24**). The Assembly took action on that draft by **resolution 54/225** (see p. 995).

Among the documents before the special session were the report of the Commission on Sustainable Development acting as the preparatory body for the session [A/S-22/2 & Add.1], a Ministerial Declaration on Agriculture in SIDS, adopted by a Special Ministerial Conference (Rome, Italy, 12 March), and a Plan of Action on Agriculture in SIDS [A/S-22/3], and the report of a meeting of representatives of donors and SIDS (New York, 24-26 February) [A/S-22/4].

Preparatory meetings. Acting as preparatory body for the twenty-second special session, the Commission on Sustainable Development convened two meetings (23 and 30 April) and a number of informal working groups during its seventh session (see above) [A/S-22/2]. The provisional agenda and other organizational arrangements for the special session were approved and recommended to the General Assembly for adoption. The Commission also recommended authorization of a resumed preparatory session for two days in September. In addition, the list of speakers and accreditation of NGOs for the special session were approved.

At its seventh session [E/1999/29 (dec. 7/7)], the Commission requested that budget deliberations for the biennium 2000-2001 by the Committee for Programme and Coordination, the Advisory Committee on Administrative and Budgetary Questions and the Fifth (Administrative and Budgetary) Committee take into account relevant outcomes of the special session.

As authorized in a 24 August letter from the Chairman of the Committee on Conferences to the President of the General Assembly [A/53/1043] and noted by the Assembly on 2 September (**decision 53/486**), the Commission held a two-day resumed preparatory session on 9 and 10 September in order to complete its work [A/S-22/2/Add.1]. On 10 September, the preparatory body transmitted a draft declaration and a draft text on the state of progress and initiatives for the future implementation of the Programme of Action for the Sustainable Development of SIDs to the special session for further consideration.

GENERAL ASSEMBLY ACTION

On 28 September [meeting 5], the General Assembly, on the recommendation of the Ad Hoc Committee of the Whole of the Twenty-second Special Session [A/S-22/9/Rev.1], adopted **resolution S/22-2** without vote [agenda item 8].

Declaration and state of progress and initiatives for the future implementation of the Programme of Action for the Sustainable Development of Small Island Developing States

The General Assembly

Adopts the Declaration and the text entitled "State of progress and initiatives for the future implementation of the Programme of Action for the Sustainable Development of Small Island Developing States" contained in the annex to the present resolution.

ANNEX

Declaration and state of progress and initiatives for the future implementation of the Programme of Action for the Sustainable Development of Small Island Developing States

Declaration

We, the States participating in the special session of the General Assembly for the review and appraisal of the implementation of the Programme of Action for the Sustainable Development of Small Island Developing States,

Having met at United Nations Headquarters on 27 and 28 September 1999,

Reaffirming the principles of and commitments to sustainable development embodied in the Rio Declaration on Environment and Development, Agenda 21, the Declaration of Barbados and the Programme of Action for the Sustainable Development of Small Island Developing States,

Recalling resolution S-19/2 of 28 June 1997, adopted by the General Assembly at its nineteenth special session, as well as the decisions adopted by the Commission on Sustainable Development at its fourth, sixth and seventh sessions,

Recognizing that small island developing States share a common aspiration for economic development and improved living standards and remain strongly committed to conserving the natural and cultural heritage upon which their future depends, and considering that the review of the further implementation of the Programme of Action aims to build on agreements already reached by the small island developing States and the international community concerning sustainable development, and that it provides a measure of progress towards sustainable development among those States and their regions and identifies where special attention is required to advance further the implementation of sustainable development,

Recalling that small island developing States are recognized as a special case for both environment and development because they are ecologically fragile and economically vulnerable, they face particular constraints in their efforts to achieve sustainable development and their specific physical circumstances often make it difficult for them to benefit from global economic development and thus achieve sustainable development,

Reaffirming that the Global Conference on the Sustainable Development of Small Island Developing States translated Agenda 21 into specific policies, actions and measures to be taken at the international, national and regional levels to enable small island developing States to address those constraints and achieve sustainable development,

Recognizing that communities of small island developing States are custodians of large areas of the world's oceans and have a high share of global biodiversity, that they are at the forefront in the fight against climate change and that their exposure and predicament underline the urgent need to take action to implement the Programme of Action,

Recognizing also that solutions found in this regard may provide examples beneficial to other countries around the world,

Recognizing further that considerable efforts have been made at all levels to implement the Programme of Action, and that there is a need for these efforts to be further supplemented by effective support from the international community, including financial support, by institutional strengthening and improved coordination, by targeted capacity-building and by facilitating the transfer of environmentally sound technologies in accordance with paragraph 34.14 *(b)* of Agenda 21,

Having considered progress reports on the implementation of the Programme of Action and the views expressed by delegations at the special session,

Convinced that the implementation of the Programme of Action must be accelerated by progress in the cross-cutting and interlinked areas of capacity-building, financing and technology transfer, and that institutional arrangements should be strengthened for its successful implementation,

1. *Welcome* the efforts by small island developing States to implement the commitments of the Programme of Action for the Sustainable Development of Small Island Developing States and the support of the international community, and note that these efforts have been affected by financial and other resource constraints and by global economic and environmental factors;

2. *Welcome also* the continued efforts of small island developing States to formulate national sustainable development strategies;

3. *Encourage* the efforts of all parties to foster an enabling environment to assist small island developing States in addressing overarching issues so as to achieve sustainable development;

4. *Call upon* the international community to provide effective means, including adequate, predictable, new and additional financial resources, in accordance with chapter 33 of Agenda 21 and paragraphs 91 to 95 of the Programme of Action, to support efforts to achieve the full implementation of the Programme of Action, particularly in tackling complex issues, such as poverty, as highlighted in paragraph 6 of the text entitled "State of progress and initiatives for the future implementation of the Programme of Action for the Sustainable Development of Small Island Developing States", which appears below;

5. *Also call upon* the international community to provide support for capacity- and institution-building programmes and projects in small island developing States and, where appropriate, to support the establishment of training centres and other relevant capacity-building efforts;

6. *Call* for increased efforts to assist small island developing States in obtaining the transfer of environmentally sound technology, as set forth in the Programme of Action, needed for them to achieve sustainable development and implement the Programme of Action;

7. *Call upon* the Secretary-General to improve the existing institutional arrangements in the United Nations effectively to support small island developing States so that the United Nations system becomes more proactive in promoting and assisting sustainable development in those States;

8. *Welcome* the continued efforts of the Alliance of Small Island States in promoting the interests and concerns of small island developing States, including in the implementation of the Programme of Action;

9. *Endorse* the series of broad initiatives for the further implementation of the Programme of Action as outlined in the recommendations of the Commission on Sustainable Development acting as the preparatory body for the twenty-second special session, as set forth below.

State of progress and initiatives for the future implementation of the Programme of Action for the Sustainable Development of Small Island Developing States

I. Introduction

1. Since its adoption in 1994 at the Global Conference for the Sustainable Development of Small Island Developing States, all chapters of the Programme of Action for the Sustainable Development of Small Island Developing States, which contain an integrated and comprehensive basis for the sustainable development of small island developing States, have been reviewed by the Commission on Sustainable Development at its fourth session, in 1996, and at its sixth session, in 1998. At its seventh session, in 1999, the Commission, in preparation for the special session of the General Assembly for the review and appraisal of the implementation of the Programme of Action, further reviewed the progress made in the implementation of the Programme of Action and identified the following areas for priority action, including the means for their implementation: climate change, including climate variability and sea level rise; natural disasters; freshwater resources; coastal and marine resources; energy; and tourism. The Commission recognized that the sectoral focus of its review should not detract from the need for a full and comprehensive implementation of all chapters of the Programme of Action. The Commission emphasized that the Programme of Action remained a valuable and living framework for the sustainable development efforts being undertaken by small island developing States, and noted the actions taken by Governments, regional commissions and organizations, organizations of the United Nations system and intergovernmental and non-governmental organizations in support of activities relating to its implementation. The special session of the General Assembly reaffirms the commitment of the international community to the continued implementation of the Programme of Action.

2. The Commission on Sustainable Development, at its seventh session, also took note of the results of the meeting of representatives of donors and small island developing States, from 24 to 26 February 1999, which, *inter alia,* considered a compendium of national and regional project proposals. The meeting underscored the strong sense of commitment to and ownership of the Programme of Action by small island developing States, and was welcomed as contributing towards strengthening and enriching the partnership between small island developing States and the international community. It also noted that, in accordance with their responsibility, considerable efforts had been made by

small island developing States at the national and regional levels to meet the priorities and objectives of the Programme of Action, especially the elaboration of national sustainable development strategies. Consistent with their special concerns, and bearing in mind that small island developing States are custodians of a significant portion of the world's oceans and seas and their resources, small island developing States have been actively and constructively engaged in international negotiations in pursuing integrated approaches in such areas as climate change, biodiversity, law of the sea, sustainable fisheries and marine pollution, and have undertaken efforts to meet their commitments under related international agreements.

3. At the nineteenth special session of the General Assembly, held in 1997, the international community reiterated its recognition of the specific constraints faced by small island developing States and the need for particular support in their efforts to advance sustainable development owing to their small size and remoteness, ecological fragility, vulnerability to climate change and economic vulnerabilities. Small island developing States share many concerns and constraints with regard to sustainable development and are affected by them in varying degrees. The specificity of the situation and needs of small island developing States in relation to sustainable development were acknowledged in Agenda 21 and further articulated in the Programme of Action. Constraints to the sustainable development of small island developing States include a narrow resource base, which does not allow those States to benefit from economies of scale; small domestic markets and heavy dependence on a few external and remote markets; high costs of energy, infrastructure, transportation, communication and servicing; long distances from export markets and import sources; low and irregular international traffic volumes; little resilience to natural disasters; rising populations; high volatility of economic growth; limited opportunities for the private sector and a disproportionately large reliance of their economies on the public sector; and fragile natural environments.

4. At its seventh session, the Commission on Sustainable Development also noted that since the holding of the Global Conference in 1994, the pace of globalization and trade liberalization had affected the economies of small island developing States by presenting new problems and opportunities for them and increasing the need for focused implementation of the Programme of Action. As a result of globalization, national policy frameworks and external factors, including trade impacts, have become critical in determining the success or failure of small island developing States in their national efforts. These States are particularly concerned that the specific problems and vulnerabilities confronting them exacerbate the difficulties encountered in their efforts to integrate into the world economy, particularly in the areas of trade, investment, commodities and capital markets. In order to address these challenges, small island developing States are undertaking domestic reforms in the area of macroeconomic policy to facilitate integration into the global economy. At the regional level, they have also begun to put in place appropriate policy frameworks and arrangements to integrate their economic, social and environmental approaches to sustainable development in order to maximize opportunities available to them and minimize the constraints they face. A mutually supportive balance between the international and national environment is needed so as to achieve sustainable development.

5. The General Assembly recognizes that, while it is up to small island developing States to pursue sustainable development and all partners should foster an enabling environment, the international community is committed to taking further measures to support those States in this regard. The Commission on Sustainable Development recognized that the further successful implementation of the Programme of Action would require action by all partners in the following areas: fostering of an enabling environment for investment and external assistance; resource mobilization and financing; transfer of environmentally sound technologies as set forth in the Programme of Action; and capacity-building, including education, training, awareness-raising and institutional development. The Commission assessed the progress made since the Global Conference by the international community in responding to the financial provisions of the Programme of Action, including through mobilization of resources, initiation of discussions on financing for development, work on a vulnerability index, donor coordination, strengthened and expanded partnerships, mainstreaming sustainable development activities and working to ensure a better response from institutions to efforts of small island developing States to achieve sustainable development, especially through capacity-building. The Commission reiterated the need for more focused action at all levels, including the international level, to strengthen support, including financial support from all sources, to small island developing States for programmes and projects targeted towards capacity- and institution-building, facilitating the access of those States to, and the transfer and use of, environmentally sound technology, as set forth in the Programme of Action. In order to facilitate targeted action in these areas, there is a need for Governments of small island developing States to develop or strengthen an effective policy framework along with national and regional sustainable development strategies or plans of action.

6. Poverty remains a major problem affecting the capacity of many small island developing States to achieve sustainable development. The complexity, pervasiveness and persistence of poverty has compromised the ability of States to provide basic social services, including basic education, health care, nutrition, clean water and sanitation, and to undertake effective land and coastal area management and urban planning and development. Poverty in small island developing States has been exacerbated by increasing levels of unemployment; the two problems need to be addressed in tandem in order to deal effectively with the crippling effect of poverty on sustainable development capacity. Eradication of poverty is therefore a serious issue and an objective of high priority for small island developing States, and requires the integration of economic, environmental and social components of action to achieve sustainable development.

7. At its seventh session, the Commission on Sustainable Development concluded that, among other things, the full, effective, and long-term implementation of the Programme of Action required a strong and

committed partnership between small island developing States and the international community. The Commission encouraged the continuation and strengthening of the partnership between small island developing States and their private sector. It also encouraged the private sector of other countries to develop further partnerships with small island developing States.

II. Sectoral areas requiring urgent action

A. *Climate change*

8. Small island developing States are among those States most at risk from the adverse effects of climate change. The capacities and means to adapt to this phenomenon are an absolute necessity for them. The involvement and committed support of the international community are critical complements to small island developing States' own efforts in any response and long-term planning by those States. International support is particularly required for identifying adaptation options and linking efforts to reduce vulnerability with the best available information.

9. In the context of actions being undertaken to address these issues and on the basis of a strong and committed partnership between small island developing States and the international community, the international community and small island developing States should pursue and support the following goals, objectives and activities, including through specific modalities, to assist in the continued implementation of the Programme of Action:

(a) Improvement of the capacity of small island developing States to respond adequately and adapt to climate change and to participate in and make the necessary linkages to other international activities, such as the study of climate variability;

(b) Improvement of work on capabilities for climate prediction;

(c) Closer collaboration between the Small Island Developing States Unit of the Department of Economic and Social Affairs of the Secretariat and the secretariat of the United Nations Framework Convention on Climate Change so that information can be readily incorporated into the overall planning for long-term adaptation.

B. *Natural and environmental disasters and climate variability*

10. Small island developing States are prone to extremely damaging natural disasters, primarily in the form of cyclones, volcanic eruptions and earthquakes, and are subject to effects of climate variability. In some islands, the range of these disasters and phenomena includes storm surges, landslides, extended droughts and extensive floods. During 1997-1998, the El Niño phenomenon had its strongest impact on record on the sustainable development of many small island developing States.

11. In the context of actions being undertaken to address these issues and on the basis of a strong and committed partnership between small island developing States and the international community, the international community and small island developing States should pursue and support the following goals, objectives and activities, including through specific modalities, to assist in the continued implementation of the Programme of Action:

(a) Greater effort to improve the scientific understanding of severe weather events, such as those associated with the El Niño/Southern Oscillation phenomenon, and the development of long-term strategies for prediction and reduction of their impact;

(b) Improvement of work on capabilities for natural disaster reduction and early warning systems, including in-depth assessment and consideration of effective means of natural disaster reduction;

(c) Development of partnerships between small island developing States and the private sector consistent with responsible business practices to implement schemes that spread out risks, reduce insurance premiums, expand insurance coverage and thereby increase financing for post-disaster reconstruction and rehabilitation.

C. *Freshwater resources*

12. The issue of freshwater availability is crucial for small island developing States in all regions. Surface water and groundwater resources are limited by the small watershed and aquifer-recharge areas, and urban expansion has further affected the availability and quality of water resources. The geophysical characteristics of many small islands leave them vulnerable to extreme climatological, seismic and volcanic events and, more critically, to periods of drought, low recharge and adverse environmental impacts, including pollution, saline intrusion and soil erosion, among others, and they require increased attention to watershed management and land and water use planning.

13. In the context of actions being undertaken to address these issues and on the basis of a strong and committed partnership between small island developing States and the international community, the international community and small island developing States should pursue and support the following goals, objectives and activities, including through specific modalities, to assist in the continued implementation of the Programme of Action:

(a) Implementation of Commission on Sustainable Development decision 6/1, relating to its programme of work on freshwater issues in the special context of small island developing States;

(b) Improvement of assessment, planning and integrated management of freshwater resources in the special context of small island developing States;

(c) Coordination and refocusing of aid and other programmes and projects designed to assist small island developing States, as and where appropriate, in developing or implementing national policies, strategies and legal frameworks, as well as coherent plans and actions, within an integrated water resources management approach.

D. *Coastal and marine resources*

14. The health, protection and preservation of coastal and marine resources are fundamental to the well-being and sustainable development of small island developing States. Improved coastal and ocean management as well as conservation of the coasts, oceans and seas and the sustainable use of coastal and marine resources and arrangements and initiatives, including efforts aimed at reducing land- and sea-based pollution, are critical both in support of regional fisheries organizations and in maintaining the oceans as a

source of food and a principal factor in tourism development.

15. In the context of actions being undertaken to address these issues and on the basis of a strong and committed partnership between small island developing States and the international community, the international community and small island developing States should pursue and support the following goals, objectives and activities, including through specific modalities, to assist in the continued implementation of the Programme of Action:

(a) Establishment and/or strengthening of programmes to build capacity and assess and manage the vast oceanic resources of small island developing States, and establishment and/or strengthening of specific regional or subregional arrangements for addressing issues concerning oceans and small island developing States;

(b) Establishment and/or strengthening of programmes within the framework of the Global Programme of Action for the Protection of the Marine Environment from Land-based Activities and the regional seas programme to assess the impact of planning and development on the coastal environment, including coastal communities, wetlands, coral reef habitats and the areas under the sovereignty or national jurisdiction of small island developing States and to implement the Programme of Action;

(c) Strengthening of national capacity for the development of a methodology or guidelines for sound practices and techniques suitable for small island developing States, for achieving the integrated management and sustainable development of the coastal and marine areas under the sovereignty or national jurisdiction of small island developing States, building on existing experience in that area;

(d) Scientific research and analysis relevant to the conservation and management of highly migratory and straddling fish stocks on the high seas and in the marine areas under the sovereignty or national jurisdiction of small island developing States;

(e) Enhancement of the conservation and sustainable management and utilization of coastal zone ecosystems and resources of the marine areas under the sovereignty or national jurisdiction of small island developing States;

(f) Ratification of or accession by States to the 1995 United Nations Agreement for the Implementation of the Provisions of the United Nations Convention on the Law of the Sea of 10 December 1982 relating to the Conservation and Management of Straddling Fish Stocks and Highly Migratory Fish Stocks, and the 1993 Agreement to Promote Compliance with International Conservation and Management Measures by Fishing Vessels on the High Seas, of the Food and Agriculture Organization of the United Nations, and active participation by small island developing States in emerging and existing regional fisheries management organizations in order for these agreements to be fully implemented;

(g) Formulation of policies, strategies and measures to address the needs of fisheries, including the urgent need to address illegal, unregulated and unreported fishing in the marine areas under the sovereignty or national jurisdiction of small island developing States, to ensure essential sources of food supplies for island populations and economic development;

(h) Strengthening of national, regional and subregional capacity for negotiating fishing agreements;

(i) Strengthening of national, regional and subregional capacity for the promotion, assessment and monitoring of commercial investment in sustainable fisheries, including in catching, processing and marketing, as well as, where appropriate, in environmentally sound methods of aquaculture to increase ownership and improve management of commercial fisheries by communities within small island developing States and to promote national activities in the context of the Code of Conduct for Responsible Fisheries, keeping in mind the International Plan of Action on Management of Fishing Capacity adopted in 1999 by the Food and Agriculture Organization of the United Nations;

(j) Greater regional coordination in management and monitoring, control and surveillance, including vessel monitoring systems and enforcement, consistent with international agreements between coastal countries and fishing countries, in the marine areas under the sovereignty or national jurisdiction of small island developing States, including the management of straddling fish stocks and highly migratory fish stocks;

(k) Assistance to small island developing States in assessing the impact of land-based sources of marine pollution, in developing mechanisms to eliminate or minimize pollution sources and in participating in the implementation of the Programme of Action;

(l) Recalling the provisions of paragraph 24 C (iii) of the Programme of Action, and reaffirming that the implementation of that paragraph shall be consistent with international law, including the United Nations Convention on the Law of the Sea and other relevant existing international legal instruments, in particular those mentioned in paragraph 67 of the Programme of Action;

(m) Taking into account the views and concerns of small island developing States that the transboundary movement of hazardous and radioactive wastes is not adequately covered in the existing international legal regimes, in particular regarding safety measures, disclosure, liability and compensation in relation to accidents and remedial measures in relation to contamination from such wastes, calling upon States and relevant international organizations to continue to address these concerns in a specific and comprehensive manner, and calling upon the Secretary-General to report to the General Assembly no later than at its fifty-sixth session on the efforts and measures undertaken and progress achieved;

(n) Continuation of efforts to implement the Basel Convention on the Control of Transboundary Movements of Hazardous Wastes and their Disposal.

16. Action is needed to sustain healthy reefs. Such action will build on the International Coral Reef Initiative and global reef assessments to ensure food security and fish stock replenishment, and will provide a focus for implementation of the Jakarta Mandate on the Conservation and Sustainable Use of Marine and Coastal Biological Diversity, including in marine-protected areas, and the Global Programme of Action for the Protection of the Marine Environment from Land-based Activities.

17. In the context of actions being undertaken to address these issues and on the basis of a strong and committed partnership between small island developing States and the international community, the international community and small island developing States should pursue and support the following goals, objectives and activities, including through specific modalities, to assist in the continued implementation of the Programme of Action:

(a) Encouragement of national and regional community-based reef conservation and management;

(b) Initiatives related to alternative livelihoods, such as aquaculture and ecotourism;

(c) Post-harvest technology and management initiatives;

(d) Integrated reef management initiatives;

(e) Research, monitoring and transfer of technology, as set forth in the Programme of Action, to assess the impact of the exploration of non-living resources on the coastal and marine environments;

(f) Further implementation of coral reef action plans as part of the International Coral Reef Initiative and its "call to action", "renewed call to action" and "framework for action".

E. *Energy*

18. In view of the dependency of small island developing States on conventional energy sources, there is a need for mobilization of resources from all sources, including from the private sector, for the provision of technical, financial and technological assistance, as appropriate, to small island developing States, in order to encourage energy efficiency and to accelerate and maximize the development and utilization of environmentally sound renewable energy sources.

19. In the context of actions being undertaken to address these issues and on the basis of a strong and committed partnership between small island developing States and the international community, the international community and small island developing States should pursue and support the following goals, objectives and activities, including through specific modalities, to assist in the continued implementation of the Programme of Action:

(a) Establishment of renewable energy initiatives at the regional level so as to avoid duplication of efforts and to achieve economies of scale;

(b) Development of human resources for the planning and sustainable management needs of a renewable energy sector;

(c) Promotion of research and development and private sector investment in priority renewable energy projects;

(d) Financing of renewable energy applications, including standards and guidelines for energy efficiency and conservation;

(e) Implementation in small island developing States of the best practices to achieve clean, sustainable energy resources and encouragement of private sector involvement in the utilization of renewable energy resources and innovative financing schemes with a view to longer-term self-sufficiency in energy resources.

F. *Tourism*

20. The development and promotion of sustainable tourism will require efforts by small island developing States undertaken at the national and regional levels. In this regard, there is a need for continued international support and cooperation. Particular attention will be required to coordinate ecotourism ventures at the regional level and to facilitate the sharing of information and experiences and the integration of the private sector within official development assistance-supported ecotourism projects. Specific actions have been identified in the report of the United Nations Environment Programme and the World Tourism Organization on sustainable tourism development for small island developing States. In this regard, the special session took note of decision 7/3 on tourism and sustainable development adopted by the Commission on Sustainable Development at its seventh session, and called for its application, as appropriate, to small island developing States.

21. In the context of actions being undertaken to address these issues and on the basis of a strong and committed partnership between small island developing States and the international community, the international community and small island developing States should pursue and support the following goals, objectives and activities, including through specific modalities, to assist in the continued implementation of the Programme of Action:

(a) Establishment of regional and national environmental assessment programmes to address the carrying capacity of natural resources, including the social, economic and cultural implications of tourism development;

(b) Strengthening of institutional capacity-building in the tourism sector and promotion of environmental protection and the preservation of cultural heritage through local community awareness and participation;

(c) Encouragement of the use of modern technologies and communications systems that effectively maximize the use of global, regional and national information in support of sustainable tourism development;

(d) Improvement of the collection and use of tourism data as a means to facilitate the development of sustainable tourism;

(e) Establishment of partnerships for sustainable tourism to conserve and utilize limited resources effectively, based on consumer and market demand and the development of community-based initiatives. Destination marketing should preserve local culture and a healthy environment;

(f) Building of institutional capacity, further development of human resources at all levels of the tourism industry, with particular emphasis on small- and medium-sized enterprises, and improvement of the capacity to utilize modern technologies.

22. In the context of actions being undertaken to address these issues and on the basis of a strong and committed partnership between small island developing States and the international community, the international community and small island developing States should pursue and support the following goals, objectives and activities, including through specific modalities, to assist in the continued implementation of the Programme of Action:

(a) Enhancement of sustainable tourism and sustainably managed tourism operations through the adoption of appropriate regulations, a voluntary code

of conduct, criteria for best practices and other innovative measures;

(b) Mobilization of adequate resources from all sources to assist small island developing States in strengthening institutional capacity, human resources and environmental protection;

(c) Improvement of the capacity of small island developing States to implement treaty requirements of the International Civil Aviation Organization and the International Maritime Organization.

23. The linkages between sustainable tourism, energy and transport are of considerable importance to developing countries, in particular the least developed countries and the small island developing States among them. This should be borne in mind in preparation for the consideration of the agenda item on energy and transport at the ninth session of the Commission on Sustainable Development.

III. Means of implementation

A. *Sustainable development strategies*

24. National and regional sustainable development strategies allow for a more effective use of national and regional human, institutional, financial and natural resources, as well as cooperation at the regional and interregional levels. Comprehensive and collaborative strategies can also provide a solid basis for the more efficient and cost-effective implementation of donor-assisted programmes and projects. This is especially the case if these strategies are conceived as action-oriented, allowing for a process of step-by-step improvements and adjustments, and as an instrument to promote broader participation of all relevant groups and civil society.

25. In the context of actions being undertaken to address these issues and on the basis of a strong and committed partnership between small island developing States and the international community, the international community and small island developing States should pursue and support the following goals, objectives and activities, including through specific modalities, to assist in the continued implementation of the Programme of Action:

(a) Renewed commitment by small island developing States to the completion of national sustainable development strategies and, as appropriate, of regional and subregional strategies, ideally before the target date of 2002 as agreed at the nineteenth special session of the General Assembly, so as to enable the earliest possible implementation of those strategies;

(b) Exchange of experience among different island regions in the implementation of their national sustainable development strategies;

(c) Formulation of sustainable development strategies through transparent and participatory approaches and, to the extent possible, establishment of clear indicators and benchmarks of progress which, while reflecting individual country circumstances, will also reflect wider goals, including regional objectives. Such indicators should also provide a framework for measuring and evaluating the effectiveness of national implementation strategies and international cooperation in this regard;

(d) Strengthening of national and regional statistical and analytical services so that they can adequately record and measure progress, including changes in the vulnerability and fragility of the economic and environmental conditions of small island developing States. Data collection should be gender- and age-disaggregated;

(e) Consistency with the goals of the programmes and plans of action of the international sustainable development strategies, adopted at successive global conferences of the 1990s.

B. *Capacity-building*

26. Capacity-building remains critical to the long-term sustainable development of small island developing States. Those States are determined to continue their efforts at capacity-building. Concern remains in respect of the levels of external assistance for capacity-building. Mobilization of resources from all sources is essential to enable small island developing States to continue their commitment to sustainable development at all levels, in particular to build capacity for the implementation of the Programme of Action.

27. In the context of actions being undertaken to address these issues and on the basis of a strong and committed partnership between small island developing States and the international community, the international community and small island developing States should pursue and support the following goals, objectives and activities, including through specific modalities, to assist in the continued implementation of the Programme of Action:

(a) Continued development and implementation of sustainable development strategies to strengthen institutional capacity;

(b) Promotion of education for sustainable development, including training in demographic issues and gender balance in the delivery of all education and public-awareness programmes;

(c) Building, as appropriate, with international support to sectoral agencies, of the capacities of small island developing States for operationalizing sustainable development management concepts, including, where appropriate, the ecosystem approach;

(d) Increased use of traditional and indigenous skills-training and awareness-raising approaches, use of local languages in the development and presentation of resource material and involvement of local communities in education, training and awareness programmes;

(e) Continued development and strengthening of public-private partnerships involving the full range of potential partners to promote and support sustainable development;

(f) Strengthening of regional technical training and scientific research centres, scientific research, including the improvement of data and data collection, and centres of excellence in tourism and sustainable development.

C. *Resource mobilization and finance*

28. Resource mobilization is clearly one of the main challenges for small island developing States, and while their concern with resource constraints is by no means new, small island developing States believe it must be addressed with a new resolve by all partners if the special session is to provide the needed impetus to implement the Programme of Action. Adequate financial resources at all levels remain crucial to the continued implementation of the Programme of Action.

Availability of and access to appropriate and current technology and improved baseline information and environmental data to address technical issues are also crucial. The successful implementation of the Programme of Action will thus require the provision of effective means, including adequate, predictable, new and additional financial resources, in accordance with chapter 33 of Agenda 21, paragraphs 91 to 95 of the Programme of Action and paragraphs 76 to 87 of the Programme for the Further Implementation of Agenda 21. The mobilization of resources will also be necessary for the transfer of environmentally sound technology, as set forth in the Programme of Action, and for science and technology and capacity-building, including education, awareness-raising and institutional development.

29. Many small island developing States find it increasingly difficult to access concessional development finance owing to the application of criteria by some members of the international community which focus on their relatively higher per capita gross national product levels without taking full account of their actual levels of development, vulnerability or standard of living in real terms. Financial requirements and technical support remain as critical as ever if the implementation of the Programme of Action is to progress further, and will depend ultimately on the resources that small island developing States can mobilize from internal and external sources to meet the great challenges of sustainable development in general and capacity-building in particular. Recognizing that small island developing States are among the most environmentally vulnerable, the Commission on Sustainable Development urged the international community to give special priority to their situations and needs, including through access to grants and other concessional resources.

30. Statistics provided through the Commission on Sustainable Development indicate that the overall decline in official development assistance has also affected small island developing States, for which net bilateral and multilateral disbursements have decreased from US$ 2,366.2 million in 1994 to $1,966.2 million in 1997.

31. It is recognized that financial resources for sustainable development need to be further mobilized at the national level, in accordance with national priorities and capacity. Small island developing States must also intensify their search for new modalities for resource mobilization, particularly for regional initiatives. Donors and small island developing States should make more efficient use of existing resources, including through better coordination. Action should be initiated to optimize the role of existing regional coordinating mechanisms. Possibilities for encouraging private sector cooperation with partners in small island developing States should be an area for further attention in the follow-up to the Programme of Action. Resources could also be mobilized through the adoption of a regional approach to issues of policy, legislation and technical development.

32. The responsiveness of such international funding sources as the Global Environment Facility to issues concerning small island developing States has been welcomed, particularly in relation to the implementation of the commitments of those States under the relevant conventions, and the Facility will remain an important channel for financial resources to assist those States. Overall, access by small island developing States to multilateral financial institutions and the responsiveness of those institutions should be improved.

33. In the context of actions being undertaken to address these issues and on the basis of a strong and committed partnership between small island developing States and the international community, the international community and small island developing States should pursue and support the following goals, objectives and activities, including through specific modalities, to assist in the continued implementation of the Programme of Action:

(*a*) Identification of programmes and projects, with particular reference to the areas identified for urgent action which could be financed by the Global Environment Facility and other multilateral financial mechanisms;

(*b*) Improvement of the effectiveness of bilateral and multilateral development assistance, including by streamlining and harmonizing procedures, indicators and reporting methods, and by promoting coordination among donors;

(*c*) Building on the recent meeting of representatives of donors and small island developing States, with special consideration from the international community for new and additional financial commitments and disbursements of resources, as well as better and more efficient use of official development assistance and other existing external sources of finance, taking into account the specific development needs and priorities of small island developing States;

(*d*) Evaluation of project proposals submitted by small island developing States by competent authorities, taking into account the specific development needs and priorities of those States and paying particular attention to the areas of the Programme of Action which have not yet received adequate resources;

(*e*) Inviting international financial institutions to continue their commitment to sustainable development projects and programmes in small island developing States.

D. *Globalization and trade liberalization*

34. Small island developing States face new challenges and opportunities from globalization and have diverse capacities to adapt. Thus, the potential benefits to small island developing States from globalization and trade liberalization will be severely constrained unless their limitations and vulnerabilities are further recognized by the international community, including the relevant international organizations. There is therefore an urgent need to facilitate the integration of the economies of those States into the world economy in a sustainable manner, including through specific provisions and measures. This should be given due consideration in the ongoing work being done by the United Nations Conference on Trade and Development and by the World Trade Organization, taking into account, among other considerations, within the context of trade liberalization, the effects on the economies of small island developing States of the erosion of trade preferences, as well as difficulties faced with diversification and access markets.

35. In the context of actions being undertaken to address these issues and on the basis of a strong and committed partnership between small island developing States and the international community, the international community and small island developing States should pursue and support the following goals, objectives and activities, including through specific modalities, to assist in the continued implementation of the Programme of Action:

(*a*) Addressing, as appropriate, the disadvantages and the vulnerabilities of small island developing States in the context of international trade, including market access, taking into account the consequences, positive and negative, of globalization and trade liberalization on small island developing States, and the need to facilitate their integration into the global market;

(*b*) Addressing the adverse consequences and benefits, existing and potential, of globalization and trade liberalization for the economies of small island developing States, and assisting those States, as appropriate, in improving their competitiveness, including through provisions and specific measures. In this regard the multilateral trading system is encouraged to consider, as appropriate, the grant of special and differential treatment;

(*c*) Calling upon the United Nations Conference on Trade and Development, in consultation with small island developing States, to address the economic situation and trading prospects of those States in its ongoing comprehensive examination of the impact of globalization and trade liberalization on their economies during the fifty-fourth session of the General Assembly;

(*d*) Calling upon the international community to provide support to small island developing States, as necessary, towards the improvement and strengthening of their capabilities in trade policy, trade efficiency policies and trade in services, including in electronic commerce, to assist them in coping with the challenge posed by the globalization of markets;

(*e*) Calling upon the international community to provide support and technical assistance, as necessary, to small island developing States, including in capacity-building, to enhance their effective participation in multilateral trade negotiations, activities and dispute settlement, including the dispute settlement mechanism of the World Trade Organization, and formulating a positive agenda for future trade negotiations;

(*f*) Addressing, as appropriate, the difficulties of diversification in the economies of small island developing States.

E. *Transfer of environmentally sound technology*

36. Small island developing States have special characteristics and concerns in such areas as the environment. The development and application of new approaches and technologies to mitigate greenhouse gas emissions and to adapt to the effects of climate change are critical to them. In order to enhance their effectiveness, these technologies should be modified, if necessary, to take into account the special needs of small island developing States, and emphasis should be placed on technologies that are low in cost and proven in terms of environmental benefit and security, such as renewable energy and conservation technologies. Small island developing States have devoted considerable time, effort and resources to work on technologies and technology information. Continued financial and technical support from all sources is needed.

37. Small island developing States are at different stages in assessing nationally their vulnerabilities and ways of adapting to climate change. They recognize that further study, research and analysis are required to assess the effects of climate change. One particular urgency is to identify appropriate technology to meet the needs of low-lying small island developing States whose national freshwater supplies are already contaminated by saline intrusion. International efforts in studying the problems, conducting research and developing adaptation technologies could usefully complement and strengthen the work begun by small island developing States.

38. In the context of actions being undertaken to address these issues and on the basis of a strong and committed partnership between small island developing States and the international community, the international community and small island developing States should pursue and support the following goals, objectives and activities, including through specific modalities, to assist in the continued implementation of the Programme of Action:

(*a*) Development, with the participation of small island developing States, of clean technology initiatives, including the identification of investment opportunities in environmentally sound technologies and environmental management practices;

(*b*) Promotion of access by small island developing States to information on the availability of environmentally sound technologies and terms of their transfer, in particular in areas identified for priority action;

(*c*) Capacity-building of small island developing States for science and technology needs assessment and technology assessment;

(*d*) Provision of support to small island developing States in the development of networking technology-related institutional support structures, including information systems and sources, technology centres, enterprise development centres and research and development institutions;

(*e*) Provision of multilateral and bilateral support to small island developing States and their institutions involved in technologies and technology information;

(*f*) Encouragement of private sector participation, *inter alia*, through the use of partnership arrangements, including public-private partnerships, in developing cooperation between small island developing States and other countries in order to facilitate the transfer and use of environmentally sound technology and environmentally sound technology-related investments to those States as set forth in the Programme of Action;

(*g*) Encouragement of strategic alliances between research and development institutions and potential technology users to harness the creative capabilities of the scientific communities in the development of new, proven and innovative adaptation strategies and relevant technologies suitable to the particular circumstances of small island developing States, for example, in the context of the United Nations Framework Convention on Climate Change.

F. *Vulnerability index*

39. At its sixth session, the Commission on Sustainable Development recalled that a vulnerability index that takes account of the constraints arising from small size and environmental fragility, as well as the incidence of natural disasters on a national scale, and the consequent relationship of those constraints to economic vulnerability, would assist in defining the vulnerability of small island developing States and in identifying the challenges to their sustainable development. It has also been recognized that a vulnerability index of environmental as well as socio-economic parameters, which takes fully into account the special circumstances and vulnerabilities of small island developing States, could be useful. The widespread use of a vulnerability index as a potential supplement to other criteria used in decision-making on cooperation with small island developing States, including concessional treatment, is strongly encouraged.

40. The need for a vulnerability index of socio-economic and environmental parameters is highlighted in the Programme of Action. Small island developing States have set a high priority on the development of the vulnerability index and support the process of defining the concept of vulnerability as it applies to small island developing States and the identification of common elements of vulnerability, which render them susceptible to economic and ecological exogenous shocks. The coordination of efforts by the United Nations and other international organizations to develop an index is essential.

41. In the context of actions being undertaken to address these issues and on the basis of a strong and committed partnership between small island developing States and the international community, the international community and small island developing States should pursue and support the following goals, objectives and activities, including through specific modalities, to assist in the continued implementation of the Programme of Action:

(a) Completion of the quantitative and analytic work on a vulnerability index for small island developing States, preferably by the year 2000;

(b) Capacity-building at all levels for the long-term monitoring and evaluation of vulnerability;

(c) Welcoming of the inclusion of small island developing States in the global environment outlook process, which will provide better environmental baseline data.

G. *Information management: Small Island Developing States Network*

42. The Small Island Developing States Network is a tangible outcome of the Programme of Action. Along with other information technology programmes, it holds significant potential for the effective and successful implementation of the Programme of Action. In collaboration with the United Nations Development Programme, small island developing States, through their Alliance of Small Island States, have been closely involved in the development of the Network. In order to strengthen the Network concept, it is important that small island developing States enhance their ownership of it.

43. In the context of actions being undertaken to address these issues and on the basis of a strong and committed partnership between small island developing States and the international community, the international community and small island developing States should pursue and support the following goals, objectives and activities, including through specific modalities, to assist in the continued implementation of the Programme of Action:

(a) Facilitation of the transfer, as set forth in the Programme of Action, of modern technology and communication systems in order to promote their use;

(b) Addressing the constraints to Internet connectivity;

(c) Improvement of information packaging in relation to sustainable development;

(d) Encouragement of private sector opportunities and involvement;

(e) Provision of necessary human resources support and training;

(f) Establishment of links to existing clearing house and similar network mechanisms and to relevant conventions;

(g) Invitation of appropriate international cooperation for the aforementioned purposes;

(h) Strengthening of the Network as an important source of information on best practices in environmental management.

H. *International cooperation and partnership*

44. The effective implementation of the Programme of Action requires that the United Nations system make more effective use of existing resources, seek possibilities for mobilizing new resources and improve coordination mechanisms for the focused and harmonized delivery of support for priorities relevant to small island developing States. In this respect, ongoing efforts undertaken by the United Nations system to enhance coordination could be useful. The existing institutional arrangements within the United Nations system would also require strengthening in order for the Programme of Action to be implemented fully. The United Nations should continue to play its catalytic and supportive role, particularly through the regional commissions, which play an integral role in the overall implementation of the Programme of Action, especially in the provision of assistance for capacity-building in small island developing States. Consequently, the efforts to reform the institutional arrangements within the United Nations system must take these concerns into account for future actions.

45. Ongoing monitoring and review is an important aspect of measuring performance and needs to continue by way of reports of the Secretary-General and the work of the Commission on Sustainable Development and its agreed programme of work. United Nations bodies need to focus further on their areas of expertise and agreed mandates, as well as build upon regional or national strategies, conventions and programmes that are country-driven. Moreover, there are important linkages with the Commission's review of oceans and seas and recommendations on international coordination and cooperation.

46. In addition to improving coordination, United Nations bodies should be more proactive in seeking the views of small island developing States across the full range of sustainable development issues in order to ensure that they take due account of both national differ-

ences and local sensitivities, in particular, sensitivities in relation to such areas as traditional knowledge and the special place of local and indigenous communities.

47. Increased international support for regional monitoring and assessment will be required and the participation of small island developing States in the global environment outlook will be welcomed. It will be essential to develop benchmarks and improve performance indicators, including time-frames for measuring and assessing the implementation of the Programme of Action and decisions by governing bodies of United Nations agencies. Although periodic reviews of certain aspects of the Programme of Action are envisaged within the context of the work of the Commission on Sustainable Development, a full and comprehensive review of these decisions and the implementation of the Programme of Action will be useful and required in 2004.

48. In the context of actions being undertaken to address these issues and on the basis of a strong and committed partnership between small island developing States and the international community, the international community and small island developing States should pursue and support the following goals, objectives and activities, including through specific modalities, to assist in the continued implementation of the Programme of Action:

(a) Strengthening of the existing institutional arrangements through more efficient use of resources in the United Nations to maximize support for small island developing States and so that the United Nations, its bodies and regional commissions may become more effective in promoting and assisting sustainable development in island States;

(b) Facilitating the development of partnerships among all stakeholders, in particular local communities, non-governmental organizations and the private sector;

(c) Recognizing the role and function of the Alliance of Small Island States and encouraging and supporting the efforts of the Alliance in promoting the interests and concerns of those States and their sustainable development;

(d) Ensuring that United Nations bodies and Member States take into consideration national and regional sustainable development strategies and mechanisms, such as regional conventions, treaties and other regional agreements and/or arrangements adopted by small island developing States, as the umbrella for programme design, in close consultation with the small island developing States of the regions concerned, thereby ensuring that the activities of the United Nations bodies are increasingly aligned with the strategies, work plans and coordination mechanisms of the regional organizations of small island developing States;

(e) Support by United Nations bodies of the efforts of small island developing States to accede to and implement relevant international conventions. In the event that some small island developing States are unable, on account of financial or human resource constraints, to accede to international conventions, their partners in sustainable development should consult with them to seek their views on the issues addressed by such conventions in order that they may be able to take account of their positions during meetings of the conferences of parties to those conventions;

(f) Support to other regional and subregional organizations belonging to or operating in regions of small island developing States in continuing and strengthening their efforts to implement the Programme of Action, and support to the national implementation effort of the Governments of small island developing States.

Implementation of the Programme of Action

Commission on Sustainable Development. The Commission, at its seventh session [E/1999/29], carried out a comprehensive review of the 1994 Programme of Action for the Sustainable Development of SIDS [YUN 1994, p. 783], in accordance with Assembly resolution S-19/2 [YUN 1997, p. 792]. It had before it a February report of the Secretary-General [E/CN.17/1999/6], which contained an assessment of progress achieved, as well as the constraints encountered in implementing the Programme of Action. Recent trends in external resource flows in support of SIDS were outlined and emerging problems and issues of particular concern to SIDS were highlighted. In addition, the report set out priority issues for future action as identified by SIDS through regional and subregional expert and ministerial meetings and provided recommendations for the Commission's work programme for the next five years.

The report was complemented by 16 addenda [E/CN.17/1999/6/Add.1-16]—each focusing on a major theme of the Programme of Action—which updated reports previously submitted to the Commission. The addenda addressed the following issues in relation to SIDS: climate change and sea-level rise; waste management; fresh water; land resources; biodiversity; national institutions and administrative capacity; regional institutions and technical cooperation; science and technology; human resource development; management of coastal and marine resources; sustainable tourism development; sustainable development of energy resources; management of natural and environmental disasters; telecommunications development; sustainable development of air transport; and maritime transport. On 30 April, the Commission took note of the report [E/1999/29 (dec. 7/10)].

The Commission also considered a report of the Secretary-General providing updated information on donor activities in support of the implementation of the Programme of Action [E/CN.17/1999/7] and the report of a donor meeting (New York, 24-26 February) [E/CN.17/1999/18], which considered ways to assist SIDS in mobilizing resources to implement a range of sustainable development projects and to build momentum at the international level for the continued implementation of the Programme of Action. The Commission also had before it the report of the Ad Hoc Working Group on Oceans and Seas and on the Sustainable Development of SIDS (New York, 1-5 March) [E/CN.17/1999/17 & Corr.1] (see PART THREE, Chapter VII).

Alliance of Small Island States. By a 26 September letter [A/54/402], Samoa transmitted to the Secretary-General the communiqué of the Third Summit Meeting of the Heads of State and Government of the Alliance of Small Island States (New York, 25 September). The participants noted that little was being done at the international level to assist SIDS to overcome their unique problems and expressed concern about, among other things, the non-provision of financial resources to implement the Programme of Action; the decline in concessionary financial assistance to SIDS; the need for the international community to assist SIDS to advance their sustainable development strategies; the effect of the pace and terms of globalization and trade liberalization on the economies of SIDS; the protection of marine resources; climate change; the increasing incidence and magnitude of natural disasters; the transportation of hazardous and nuclear materials through the exclusive economic zones of SIDS; and the need for further capacity-building measures in support of SIDS.

GENERAL ASSEMBLY ACTION

On 22 December [meeting 87], the General Assembly, on the recommendation of the Second Committee [A/54/588/Add.6], adopted **resolution 54/224** without vote [agenda item 100 (*f*)].

Implementation of the outcome of the Global Conference on the Sustainable Development of Small Island Developing States

The General Assembly,

Recalling its resolution 49/122 of 19 December 1994 on the Global Conference on the Sustainable Development of Small Island Developing States,

Recalling also its resolutions 51/183 of 16 December 1996, 52/202 of 18 December 1997 and 53/189 of 15 December 1998,

Recognizing that small island developing States face special challenges and vulnerabilities of both an environmental and an economic nature in their efforts to achieve sustainable development,

Recalling the Declaration and review document adopted at the twenty-second special session of the General Assembly,

Noting the significant efforts being made at the national and regional levels and the need for them to be supplemented by effective financial support from the international community,

Bearing in mind the over three hundred projects that were presented for financing within the context of the implementation of the Programme of Action for the Sustainable Development of Small Island Developing States at the meeting of representatives of donors and small island developing States held in New York from 24 to 26 February 1999,

1. *Reiterates* the significance of the effective implementation of the Declaration and review document adopted at the twenty-second special session of the General Assembly;

2. *Requests* the Secretary-General to transmit the Declaration and review document to the various organs of the United Nations system and the regional commissions and organizations, taking into account the areas identified in the review document for priority action, and urges them to take the action necessary for further implementation and effective follow-up;

3. *Calls upon* Governments, the regional commissions and organizations and other intergovernmental organizations to support the efforts of the small island developing States, taking into account those areas identified in the review document for priority action, and urges them to take the action necessary for the further implementation of and effective follow-up to the Programme of Action for the Sustainable Development of Small Island Developing States;

4. *Calls upon* all stakeholders, in particular local communities, non-governmental organizations and the private sector, to take the action necessary for the further implementation of and effective follow-up to the Programme of Action;

5. *Emphasizes* the need for the provision of resources for the further implementation of the Programme of Action;

6. *Urges* all relevant organizations to finalize, preferably before the end of 2000, the work on the development of a vulnerability index, in particular for the small island developing States, which would assist in defining the vulnerability of those States and in identifying the challenges to their sustainable development, for consideration by the Economic and Social Council and the General Assembly at the appropriate time;

7. *Welcomes* the acknowledgement by the Committee for Development Policy that the concept of vulnerability should be included explicitly in the identification criteria for the least developed countries, and notes the ongoing discussions on the new criteria proposed by the Committee;

8. *Calls upon* the United Nations Conference on Trade and Development to give substantive consideration in its work to the Declaration and review document, including in its preparations for its tenth session;

9. *Invites* the Commission on Sustainable Development to consider in its work programme, as appropriate, matters relating to the further implementation of the Programme of Action, bearing in mind the outcome of the twenty-second special session of the General Assembly;

10. *Decides* to include in the provisional agenda of its fifty-fifth session, under the item entitled "Environment and sustainable development", a sub-item entitled "Further implementation of the Programme of Action for the Sustainable Development of Small Island Developing States";

11. *Requests* the Secretary-General to submit to it at its fifty-fifth session a report on the implementation of the present resolution.

Landlocked developing countries

In response to resolution 52/183 [YUN 1997, p. 842], the Secretary-General, in November [A/54/529], transmitted to the General Assembly a progress report by the UNCTAD secretariat on specific actions related to the particular needs and problems of landlocked developing countries.

The report presented the conclusions and recommendations of the fourth Meeting of Governmental Experts from Landlocked and Transit Developing Countries and Representatives of Donor Countries and Financial and Development Institutions (New York, 24-26 August), which addressed problems related to physical infrastructure and non-physical barriers in lowering transit costs. UNCTAD activities with regard to developing transport systems in the landlocked and transit developing countries—including assistance in drafting or negotiating bilateral or regional agreements and efforts to extend the computerization of transport and customs information systems—were also described. In addition, the report contained information provided by landlocked and transit developing countries and other countries, as well as by international organizations, on activities related to improvement of transit transport systems.

GENERAL ASSEMBLY ACTION

On 22 December [meeting 87], the General Assembly, on the recommendation of the Second Committee [A/54/585/Add.3 & Corr.1], adopted **resolution 54/199** without vote [agenda item 97 *(c)*].

Specific actions related to the particular needs and problems of landlocked developing countries

The General Assembly,

Recalling the provisions of its resolutions 44/214 of 22 December 1989, 46/212 of 20 December 1991, 48/169 of 21 December 1993, 50/97 of 20 December 1995 and 52/183 of 18 December 1997 and the Global Framework for Transit Transport Cooperation between Landlocked and Transit Developing Countries and the Donor Community, as well as the relevant parts of the Agenda for Development,

Recognizing that the lack of territorial access to the sea, aggravated by remoteness and isolation from world markets, and prohibitive transit costs and risks impose serious constraints on the overall socio-economic development efforts of the landlocked developing countries,

Recognizing also that sixteen of the landlocked developing countries are also classified by the United Nations as least developed countries and that their geographical situation is an added constraint on their overall ability to cope with the challenges of development,

Recognizing further that most transit countries are themselves developing countries facing serious economic problems, including the lack of adequate infrastructure in the transport sector,

Noting the importance of continuing to strengthen the existing international support measures with a view to addressing further the problems of landlocked developing countries,

Emphasizing the importance of further strengthening effective and close cooperation and collaboration between landlocked developing countries and their transit neighbours, at regional, subregional and bilateral levels, *inter alia,* through cooperative arrangements in developing efficient transit transport systems in landlocked and transit developing countries, and noting the important role of the activities of the regional commissions in this regard,

Welcoming the holding of the fourth Meeting of Governmental Experts from Landlocked and Transit Developing Countries and Representatives of Donor Countries and Financial and Development Institutions, in New York from 24 to 26 August 1999,

Expressing its appreciation to donor partners for participating in the fourth Meeting of Governmental Experts and for the generous contribution that facilitated the participation of landlocked developing countries,

1. *Welcomes* the note by the Secretary-General transmitting the progress report of the secretariat of the United Nations Conference on Trade and Development on specific actions related to the particular needs and problems of landlocked developing countries;

2. *Also welcomes* the agreed conclusions and recommendations for future action adopted by the fourth Meeting of Governmental Experts from Landlocked and Transit Developing Countries and Representatives of Donor Countries and Financial and Development Institutions;

3. *Reaffirms* the right of access of landlocked countries, including landlocked developing countries, to and from the sea and freedom of transit through the territory of transit States by all means of transport, in accordance with international law;

4. *Also reaffirms* that transit countries, in the exercise of their full sovereignty over their territory, have the right to take all measures necessary to ensure that the rights and facilities provided for landlocked countries, including landlocked developing countries, in no way infringe upon their legitimate interests;

5. *Calls upon* the landlocked developing countries and their transit neighbours to implement measures to strengthen further their cooperative and collaborative efforts to deal with transit transport issues, including bilateral and, as appropriate, subregional cooperation, *inter alia,* by improving the physical infrastructure and non-physical aspects of transit transport systems, strengthening and concluding, where appropriate, bilateral and subregional agreements to govern transit transport operations, developing joint ventures in the area of transit transport and strengthening institutions and human resources dealing with transit transport, and, in this respect, notes that South-South cooperation also plays an important role in this field;

6. *Appeals once again* to all States, international organizations and financial institutions to implement, as a matter of urgency and priority, the specific actions related to the particular needs and problems of landlocked developing countries agreed upon in the resolutions and declarations adopted by the General Assembly, the outcomes of recent major United Nations conferences relevant to landlocked developing

countries and the Global Framework for Transit Transport Cooperation between Landlocked and Transit Developing Countries and the Donor Community and to take fully into account the agreed recommendations and conclusions of the fourth Meeting of Governmental Experts from Landlocked and Transit Developing Countries and Representatives of Donor Countries and Financial and Development Institutions;

7. *Welcomes* the continuing efforts being made by the Secretary-General of the United Nations Conference on Trade and Development, in collaboration with donor countries and institutions, in particular the United Nations Development Programme, the regional commissions and relevant subregional institutions, to organize specific consultative groups, as appropriate, when requested by the landlocked and transit developing countries concerned, to identify priority areas for action at the national and subregional levels and draw up action programmes;

8. *Invites* donor countries, the United Nations Development Programme and multilateral financial and development institutions to provide landlocked and transit developing countries with appropriate financial and technical assistance in the form of grants or concessional loans for the construction, maintenance and improvement of their transport, storage and other transit-related facilities, including alternative routes and improved communications, and to promote subregional, regional and interregional projects and programmes, and, in this regard, also to consider, *inter alia*, improving the availability and optimal use of the different transport modes and intermodal efficiency along transport corridors;

9. *Emphasizes* that assistance for the improvement of transit transport facilities and services should be integrated into the overall economic development strategies of the landlocked and transit developing countries and that donor assistance should consequently take into account the requirements for the long-term restructuring of the economies of the landlocked developing countries;

10. *Notes* the important role that the simplification, harmonization and standardization of transit procedures and documentation as well as the application of information technologies have played in enhancing the efficiency of transit systems, and calls upon the United Nations Conference on Trade and Development, in cooperation with other relevant organizations of the United Nations system, to continue to assist landlocked and transit developing countries in these areas, in accordance with their mandates;

11. *Requests* the Secretary-General of the United Nations to convene in 2001, within the overall level of resources for the biennium 2000-2001, another meeting of governmental experts from landlocked and transit developing countries and representatives of donor countries and financial and development institutions, including relevant regional and subregional economic organizations and commissions, to review progress in the development of transit transport systems, including sectoral aspects and transit transportation costs, with a view to exploring the possibility of formulating necessary action-oriented measures;

12. *Requests* the fifth Meeting of Governmental Experts from Landlocked and Transit Developing Countries and Representatives of Donor Countries and Financial and Development Institutions to consider a proposal made at the fourth Meeting to convene in 2003 a ministerial meeting on transit transport issues so as to give appropriate emphasis to the problems of landlocked and transit developing countries;

13. *Requests* the Secretary-General of the United Nations Conference on Trade and Development to seek voluntary contributions to ensure the participation of representatives of landlocked and transit developing countries at the meeting referred to in paragraph 11 above;

14. *Notes with appreciation* the contribution of the United Nations Conference on Trade and Development to formulating international policies and measures dealing with the special problems of landlocked developing countries, *inter alia*, through technical cooperation programmes, and urges the Conference, *inter alia*, to keep under constant review the evolution of transit transport infrastructure facilities, institutions and services, monitor the implementation of agreed measures, *inter alia*, by means of a case study as necessary, promote regional and subregional cooperation, build up consensus on cooperative arrangements, mobilize international support measures, collaborate in all relevant initiatives, including those of the private sector and non-governmental organizations, and serve as a focal point for cross-regional issues of landlocked developing countries;

15. *Invites* the Secretary-General of the United Nations, in consultation with the Secretary-General of the United Nations Conference on Trade and Development, to take appropriate measures for the effective implementation of the activities called for in the present resolution, and to provide, in accordance with resolution 52/183, the Office of the Special Coordinator for Least Developed, Landlocked and Island Developing Countries of the Conference with adequate resources so as to allow it to implement effectively its mandate to continue to support landlocked developing countries;

16. *Requests* the Secretary-General of the United Nations, together with the Secretary-General of the United Nations Conference on Trade and Development, to prepare a report on the implementation of the present resolution and submit it to the Trade and Development Board and to the General Assembly at its fifty-sixth session.

Chapter II

Operational activities for development

In 1999, the income of the United Nations Development Programme (UNDP), the central United Nations funding body for technical assistance to developing countries, totalled $2,608 million, as compared with $2,704 million in 1998. The total expenditure for all programme activities plus support costs decreased slightly, from $2,713 million in 1998 to $2,681 million in 1999.

Throughout the UN system, efforts were made to implement the new policy guidelines on operational activities for development, as set out by the General Assembly in its 1998 resolution on the triennial policy review of those activities. In response to the guidelines, reforms in UN activities were made in such areas as poverty eradication and capacity-building, funding modalities of operational activities, policy coordination and programming frameworks, strengthening field representation, and cooperation between the United Nations and the Bretton Woods institutions (the World Bank and the International Monetary Fund).

UNDP activities in 1999 concentrated on six goals: creating an enabling environment for sustainable human development; reduction of poverty; protection of the environment and use of natural resources; gender equality and advancement of women; providing support to countries in special development situations; and providing support to UN activities.

In April, the Secretary-General appointed Mark Malloch Brown as Administrator of UNDP for a four-year term beginning on 1 July. The new Administrator continued the work of his predecessor in reorganizing the UNDP programming and reporting procedures. In 1999, the first multi-year funding framework was adopted to provide a more predictable funding plan, integrating programme objectives, resources, budget and outcomes. Together with that plan, a new reporting procedure was introduced, the results-oriented annual report, which presented programme results by goal. UNDP also introduced its Business Plan for 2000-2003, which outlined a new vision and goals for UNDP to ensure that it had the capacity to deliver its services effectively.

The United Nations Office for Project Services continued to operate in accordance with the self-financing principle, without assessed budget financing. Total delivery continued to increase, reaching $764 million in 1999, compared to $713 million in 1998.

The United Nations Volunteers (UNV) programme also continued to expand. The total value of UNV activities carried out in 1998-1999 was $150.8 million.

The High-level Committee on the Review of Technical Cooperation among Developing Countries (TCDC), in June, reviewed progress in implementing the 1978 Buenos Aires Plan of Action for Promoting and Implementing TCDC. In December, the General Assembly recognized the significant role of economic and technical cooperation between developing countries and countries with economies in transition in promoting implementation of South-South programmes and projects.

System-wide activities

Operational activities segment of the Economic and Social Council

The Economic and Social Council, at its 1999 substantive session (New York, 23 June; Geneva, 5-30 July; New York, 16 September, 26 October, 15 November, 16 December), considered the question of UN operational activities for international development cooperation at meetings on 8, 9, 12, 13 and 23 July. A high-level meeting on operational activities was held on 8 July. The Council held an informal dialogue with the heads of UN funds and programmes on 9 July, and with the UN system country teams from Indonesia and Mali on 12 July. The next day, the Council considered follow-up to policy recommendations of the General Assembly on implementation of Assembly resolution 53/192 [YUN 1998, p. 802].

Implementation of resolution 53/192

Describing action taken by the UN system to implement General Assembly resolution 53/192 on the 1998 policy review of UN operational activities, the Secretary-General's May report [E/1999/55/Add.1] focused on the common country assessment and the United Nations Development Assistance

Framework (UNDAF); the resident coordinator system; planning, programming and implementation; humanitarian assistance, peace-building and development; the regional dimension; South-South cooperation/technical cooperation and economic cooperation among developing countries (TCDC-ECDC); national execution; and monitoring and evaluation. The issues of resources and action by the executive boards of the funds and programmes were dealt with in the main report [E/1999/55], together with the themes of the 1999 operational activities segment, "Poverty eradication and capacity-building".

The Secretary-General stated that significant progress was being made with the implementation of UNDAF as a tool for promoting goal-oriented collaboration, programmatic coherence and mutual reinforcement. The UNDAF guidelines were revised and modalities were shaped for the gradual extension of the exercise to other countries. Common country assessment guidelines were also elaborated and common country assessments undertaken and/or updated by some 18 pilot countries. However, a number of challenges remained for the entire UN system, including rationalization and simplification of programming procedures, linkages with other UN core missions, the optimal interface between the common country assessment/UNDAF and World Bank instruments, and the UNDAF impact on development activities. The common country assessment and revised UNDAF provided a means of articulating support to national efforts through enhanced collaborative programming of UN system activities, and in some cases the UNDAF process provided a platform for the formulation of issue papers on the follow-up to major world conferences. The revised UNDAF guidelines were endorsed in the statement by the Administrative Committee on Coordination (ACC) on implementation of resolution 53/192 and in the ACC guidance note on the implementation of the common country assessment and UNDAF processes, both adopted by the Consultative Committee on Programme and Operational Questions (CCPOQ) in March [ACC/1999/7].

The resident coordinator system was strengthened, in particular through improvement of the selection process, the appraisal system and training. A priority concern was ensuring that all UN system staff in programme countries were fully aware of their responsibility for the effective functioning of the system, including support for their dual responsibility as representatives of their own organization and as members of the UN system. Also, as part of efforts to strengthen the system, guidelines on the functioning of the resident coordinator system were finalized and adopted by CCPOQ, at its fifteenth session (New York, 21-24 September) [ACC/1999/15], on behalf of ACC for inclusion in the CCPOQ operational activities reference manual.

In terms of planning, programming and implementation, the Secretary-General reported that, building on significant growth of relations among the United Nations, Governments and other development partners, CCPOQ, at its fourteenth session (Geneva, 10-12 March) [ACC/1999/7], adopted, on ACC's behalf, a guidance note on the principles underpinning the UN system's operational collaboration with civil society organizations, entitled "The partnership approach". ACC also agreed to pursue a "compact" or understanding with the private sector to stress the development dimension.

In terms of the simplification, harmonization and rationalization of programme procedures, specific measures and timetables, through country-specific action plans, had been put in place to advance the harmonization of programming cycles of UN funds and programmes. That had so far been achieved in 86 countries and the United Nations Development Group (UNDG) was working on an overall action plan to increase that number to 99 by 2003. However, programming cycles discrepancies, different degrees of decentralization and delegation of authority for decision-making at the country level and varying levels of commitment at Headquarters hindered a more effective and coordinated UN system response to national development needs and discouraged joint activities with Governments. The Secretary-General recommended that funds and programmes accord high priority to the issue of simplification and harmonization and take steps to reduce, simplify and harmonize their procedures and reporting requirements.

Concerning humanitarian assistance, peace-building and development, the UN system had taken several steps to implement resolution 53/129, including adoption of a strategic framework for Afghanistan as a basic reference for UN development activities; approval of guidelines for a strategic framework approach for response to and recovery from crisis for use in selected countries; establishment of a UNDP-led reference group to explore issues of post-conflict reintegration, with the aim of providing greater support to the field in addressing operational aspects of improving UN performance; and convening of a round table to make recommendations on institutional arrangements and financing strategies. The UNDAF and common country assessment guidelines also included references to the comprehensive approach sought by the General Assembly. Despite those efforts, the mechanisms for strategic coordination remained somewhat disaggregated, incompletely understood and not widely known, especially outside the UN system. More attention was needed to develop a "tool kit" of responses in which country teams would be encouraged to experiment, in partnership with national authorities and with support from headquarters. Difficulties persisted in obtaining support for the transition from relief to development.

Progress towards a more coordinated and integrated follow-up to major global conferences was being facilitated by a number of ACC initiatives. Thematic groups continued to be the main UN system instruments in that regard, particularly the group on human immunodeficiency virus/acquired immunodeficiency syndrome (HIV/AIDS). In terms of regional cooperation, CCPOQ developed common principles on how better to use the UN system's comparative advantage in bringing the regional dimension to bear on operational activities at the country level. In March [ACC/1999/7], it approved, on behalf of ACC, a guidance note on regional and subregional development cooperation, which identified responsibilities throughout the UN system.

Funds and programmes reported progress in national execution, but evaluations of the system revealed signs of possible tension between the accountability and the capacity-building aspects of national execution. As for monitoring and evaluation, the Secretary-General said that it would be necessary for the system to take further steps to strengthen aspects of the evaluation dimension of its operational activities, including those outlined in the management process. The UN Department of Economic and Social Affairs would continue to conduct impact evaluations. The United Nations Children's Fund (UNICEF) was involved in strengthening national capacity in evaluation, and steps were being initiated to promote greater collaboration on evaluation at the country level.

In the main report [E/1999/55], the Secretary-General stated that the financial stability of the UN development system continued to be of serious concern and suggested that the issue needed to be addressed in the broader framework of the UN system's presence, profile and programming at the country level. The steady decline in UNDP's core contributions carried important policy implications, for which a strategic decision was needed, not only for UNDP's future but also for the entire UN system. There were indications that the new funding strategy based on the multi-year funding framework [YUN 1998, p. 825] might help to stop the declining trend in the core resources situation (see p. 794). A review of resource trends in operational activities for development within the UN system from 1993 to 1997 was provided in an addendum to the report [E/1999/55/Add.2].

Management process. Annexed to the report on the implementation of resolution 53/192 [E/1999/55/Add.1] was the text of the management process for the implementation of that resolution and related resolutions, which identified action the UN system could take at all levels. Appended to the annex was an ACC statement, expressing its commitment to implement the provisions of that resolution in a coordinated manner as outlined in the management process.

ECONOMIC AND SOCIAL COUNCIL ACTION

On 23 July [meeting 38], the Economic and Social Council adopted **resolution 1999/6** [draft: E/1999/L.24] without vote [agenda item 3 *(b)*].

Progress on the implementation of General Assembly resolution 53/192

The Economic and Social Council,

Recalling General Assembly resolution 53/192 of 15 December 1998 on the triennial policy review of operational activities for development of the United Nations system,

1. *Takes note* of the report of the Secretary-General and of the consolidated list of issues related to the coordination of operational activities, 1999;

2. *Reiterates* that the fundamental characteristics of the operational activities of the United Nations system should be, inter alia, their universal, voluntary and grant nature, their neutrality, impartiality and multilateralism and their ability to respond to the development needs of developing countries in a flexible manner, and that all operational activities must be country-driven, in response to and in accordance with the national development plans, policies and priorities of the recipient Governments concerned;

3. *Stresses* the primary responsibility of national Governments for their country's development, and recognizes the importance of national ownership of development programmes;

4. *Reaffirms* that untied core resources are the bedrock of the operational activities of the United Nations system, and, in this context, calls on Governments to take steps to address the urgent and immediate need for a substantial increase in their funding on a predictable, continuous and assured basis, reflecting the increasing needs of developing countries, taking into account the development of multi-year funding frameworks;

5. *Requests* the Secretary-General to prepare documentation for its substantive session of 2000 on the subject of resources and funding, highlighting, inter alia, the following:

(a) Voluntary contributions by Governments to resources for operational activities for development of the programmes, funds and agencies of the United Nations system, including the relationship to official development assistance, over the past decade, and the relationship between core and non-core resources;

(b) Reasons for the decline in core resources to the operational activities of the United Nations system;

(*c*) An evaluation of the effects of such decline, including, as appropriate, on the effectiveness and impact of the operational activities of the United Nations system on the level of economic growth and sustainable development in developing and other recipient countries;

(*d*) Linkages between structural and managerial changes within the United Nations programmes and funds and resource mobilization, including the introduction of the multi-year funding frameworks that integrate programme objectives, resources, budgets and outcomes, with a view to improving effectiveness and increasing core resources;

6. *Takes note* of the progress made in the introduction of the United Nations Development Assistance Framework and the common country assessment in accordance with the provisions of General Assembly resolution 53/192, paragraphs 17 to 22, and calls for further progress on the harmonization of programming cycles as well as steps to simplify and harmonize relevant programming procedures of the United Nations programmes, funds and agencies, bearing in mind their mandates, within specified target dates for the accomplishment of these prescribed actions;

7. *Takes note* of the progress and challenges with the common country assessment and the Framework, as highlighted in the reports of the programmes and funds, and encourages the programmes and funds to try to achieve a Framework that promotes a country-driven, collaborative and coherent response by the United Nations system to achieve greater impact at the country level fully consistent with and in support of national priorities;

8. *Calls upon* the programmes, funds and agencies of the United Nations system, and the resident coordinator system in particular, to ensure continued sharing of the common country assessment and the Framework experiences and to give special attention to the involvement, in the preparation of the common country assessment and the Framework, of United Nations agencies without representation at the country level, as well as of the regional commissions, and to take into account the regional development dimension;

9. *Welcomes* the progress made to strengthen the resident coordinator system, to broaden the base for the recruitment of resident coordinators and to continue to increase the number of women resident coordinators;

10. *Takes note* of the efforts already made to strengthen field-level coordination and the role of the resident coordinator system, and encourages further steps towards greater collaboration, at the field level, by ensuring well-functioning, highly participatory and active country teams, and full consultation with the Governments concerned, while respecting the specific identities and mandates of United Nations operational activities;

11. *Calls* for rapid progress to improve the self-assessment process of the resident coordinator system and to measure the performance against the work plans established;

12. *Requests* the programmes, funds and agencies of the United Nations system to examine ways to simplify further their programming procedures and instruments, and, in this context, to accord the issue of simplification and harmonization high priority and to take concrete steps to reduce, simplify and harmonize their programming, operational and administrative procedures and the reporting requirements placed on recipient countries, particularly in regard to programme development, approval and implementation, while ensuring appropriate accountability, and to report on the progress made to the Economic and Social Council in 2000, and urges further progress towards the full harmonization of programme cycles in all countries;

13. *Notes* the progress made by the United Nations system to support a coordinated follow-up to major United Nations conferences, and encourages the system to continue efforts to ensure a more integrated approach;

14. *Re-emphasizes* the central importance of thematic or theme groups within the resident coordinator system as a tool to address the cross-cutting issues identified in the follow-up to global conferences and the need to include in the annual report of the resident coordinator feedback on United Nations operational activities relating to conference follow-up;

15. *Requests* the programmes and funds to submit to the Council through their executive boards information and analyses of the extent to which the cross-cutting themes and goals emerging from global conferences have been integrated into their programme priorities in a coherent manner, as well as on specific steps taken to develop complementary and collaborative approaches with other United Nations organizations in promoting the implementation of global targets;

16. *Encourages* States Members and the entities and agencies of the United Nations system to contribute to the effective five-year review of conferences, with special attention to promoting the linkages among them and the timely implementation of the outcomes emanating from the reviews;

17. *Calls* for continued promotion and support for broad-based partnerships at the national level in support of conference outcomes;

18. *Encourages* States Members and the entities and agencies of the United Nations system to give special attention to providing coherent support for national capacity-building in accordance with the priority needs of developing countries in the area of data collection, indicators, monitoring and evaluation, recognizing that these activities are the basis for all other aspects of development planning;

19. *Notes* the need for better assessment of national capacity and the development of consistent approaches to strengthening such capacity within the United Nations Development Group and the broader United Nations system in order to strengthen significantly national capacity-building in programme countries;

20. *Encourages* greater cooperation between the World Bank, regional development banks and all funds and programmes, with a view to increased complementarity and better division of labour as well as enhanced coherence in their sectoral activities, building on the existing arrangements and fully in accordance with the priorities of the recipient Government;

21. *Welcomes* the progress made in pursuing common premises and services, and requests the members of the United Nations Development Group to consult their respective governing bodies, as appropriate, on issues related to their further involvement in the devel-

opment of common premises and services, bearing in mind that those arrangements should not impose additional burdens on developing countries;

22. *Urges* the United Nations system to use to the fullest extent possible and practicable available national expertise and indigenous technologies, and to report to the Council at its substantive session of 2000 on the use of the recently agreed guidelines of the Consultative Committee on Programme and Operational Questions on national execution, with a view to resolving the issues identified in those guidelines;

23. *Calls upon* the United Nations system to make full use of national capacity in the formulation, implementation and evaluation of programmes and projects, including through the use of national execution as provided by General Assembly resolution 53/192;

24. *Takes note* of the lessons learned by the programmes and funds in the implementation of their gender-balance policy and calls for further efforts to retain women at mid-career and to actively promote their career advancement;

25. *Calls* for further efforts, based on lessons learned, to strengthen the adoption of an effective approach to gender mainstreaming for women's empowerment and gender equality, and programming for women and girls;

26. *Also calls* for the involvement of men and the education and sensitization of boys in the creation of an environment conducive to the realization of the rights of women and girls;

27. *Requests* the United Nations system to take appropriate measures to improve the effective incorporation of technical cooperation among developing countries into their programmes and projects and to intensify efforts towards mainstreaming the modality of the cooperation, including through support to the activities of the Special Unit for Technical Cooperation among Developing Countries, and encourages other relevant international institutions to take similar measures, bearing in mind the catalytic role of technical cooperation among developing countries;

28. *Stresses* that South-South cooperation, including technical and economic cooperation among developing countries, offers viable opportunities for the development of developing countries, and in this context requests the executive boards of the programmes and funds to review the allocation of resources for activities involving technical cooperation among developing countries, with a view to considering an increase therein;

29. *Recommends* that the practice of holding joint meetings of the bureau of the Economic and Social Council and the bureaux of the Executive Boards of the United Nations Development Programme and the United Nations Population Fund, the United Nations Children's Fund and the World Food Programme be continued, and requests the respective bureaux to report on the meetings to their governing bodies;

30. *Invites* the governing bodies of the agencies of the United Nations to encourage greater and more active participation, as appropriate, in the United Nations Development Group initiatives in which they have been invited to take part, in keeping with their respective mandates;

31. *Requests* the United Nations entities, in their future reporting to the Council, to assess whether coordination mechanisms result in improved, timely and effective programmes and increased resource mobilization;

32. *Reaffirms* the importance of independent, transparent and impartial joint and periodic evaluations of operational activities at the country level, under the leadership of recipient Governments, and with the support of the resident coordinator system, to enhance the efficiency, effectiveness and impact, particularly on poverty-eradication programmes, and encourages the programmes and funds to increase collaboration in monitoring and evaluation within the framework of the United Nations Development Group and in consultation with all relevant partners, in accordance with the provisions of paragraph 55 of General Assembly resolution 53/192;

33. *Calls upon* the United Nations entities to promote further national capacity-building for effective programme, project and financial monitoring, as well as impact evaluations, in their programme activities.

By **decision 54/465** of 23 December, the General Assembly decided that the agenda item on operational activities for development remained for consideration at its resumed fifty-fourth (2000) session.

Poverty eradication and capacity-building

In response to resolution 53/192 [YUN 1998, p. 802], the Secretary-General submitted a May report [E/1999/55], which examined poverty eradication and capacity-building, the theme chosen for the 1999 operational activities segment of the Economic and Social Council, in terms of UN operational activities.

The report, in assessing the country-level role of operational activities for development in poverty eradication, noted that poverty eradication was the principal challenge of the international community and a global objective of the UN system, which provided direct assistance to the poor in a wide range of areas: advocacy initiatives, policy dialogue, information activities, support to formulation of national policies or programmes, analytical activities and measures of direct support to the poor.

Individual organizations had evaluated poverty-focused projects to assess their effectiveness and conducted studies on the effectiveness of specific poverty reduction instruments and measures. More comprehensive assessments of poverty reduction activity were promoted by UNDP and the World Bank. However, the effectiveness of UN system initiatives to support poverty eradication could not be easily measured. Country studies focused on the assessment of poverty situations or strategies and needed to go beyond the distribution of financial resources and look instead at household welfare.

Among the recommendations contained in the report was that further progress should be made in harmonizing UN system support to national poverty eradication programmes through the UNDP country strategy notes, common country assessments and UNDAF, and that full use should be made of thematic groups and other coordination mechanisms within the resident coordinator system to provide a coordinated and collaborative response to national priorities for poverty eradication.

The Secretary-General said that capacity-building should be increasingly an explicit objective of all technical cooperation. Efforts were underway within CCPOQ to develop a shared understanding of capacity-building with the aim of combining effectively specific goals of cooperation within capacity-building objectives. Impact evaluations conducted in the context of the 1998 triennial comprehensive policy review showed that a major factor for achieving positive and sustainable results in capacity-building was the availability of financial resources. However, national capacity created successfully with UN system support remained vulnerable to resource constraints. It was clear that the notion of sustainability of capacity needed a fresh look. The UN system approach might need to move towards codifying a body of sound basic principles, reflected in solid practical guidance. One of the lessons learned from the evaluations was that capacity-building might be too broad a term to have sufficient operational significance and more attention should be paid to analysing specific types of capacity-building and codifying best practices for each kind. It was important for all relevant UN system entities, as well as Member States, to monitor their support to capacity-building much more closely to detect required changes and take appropriate measures. The Council should maintain an interest in and monitor the development of a systematic and system-wide approach.

As follow-up to resolution 53/192, the Department of Economic and Social Affairs was disseminating the six pilot impact evaluations of capacity-building, which would be used to develop a draft guidance note to the UN system to ensure that capacity-building and its sustainability were explicitly articulated as a goal of the operational activities at the country level. The Secretary-General recommended that the Council call on the UN system to ensure that all programmes had a capacity-building objective and explicit indicators of performance, as well as baseline data built into such programmes before they were approved. The Council might also point out to donors and recipients the necessity of ensuring the financial viability of capacity created in priority areas.

ECONOMIC AND SOCIAL COUNCIL ACTION

On 23 July [meeting 38], the Economic and Social Council adopted **resolution 1999/5** [draft: E/1999/L.23] without vote [agenda item 3 *(a)*].

Poverty eradication and capacity-building

The Economic and Social Council,

Recalling General Assembly resolutions 51/178 of 16 December 1996 on the first United Nations Decade for the Eradication of Poverty and 53/192 of 15 December 1998 on the triennial policy review of operational activities for development of the United Nations system,

1. *Takes note* of the report of the Secretary-General;

2. *Recognizes* that investment in human resources and domestic and international policies supportive of economic and social development are essential prerequisites for the eradication of poverty;

3. *Calls upon* the programmes, funds and agencies of the United Nations system to continue to give priority and to further enhance support to developing countries in their efforts to eradicate poverty;

4. *Recognizes* that formulating, coordinating, implementing, monitoring and assessing integrated poverty eradication strategies, including through capacity-building initiatives, is the primary responsibility of the Governments of recipient countries, and calls upon the United Nations system to support these efforts upon the request of national Governments;

5. *Calls upon* the United Nations development system organizations to support the strengthening of the capacity of Governments to establish data banks and to carry out poverty assessments at the country level;

6. *Calls upon* the United Nations system, upon the request of Governments, to support policy analysis activities at the national and international levels, in particular regarding indicators relating to poverty eradication and human development strategies;

7. *Requests* the organizations of the United Nations system to continue to support, in a coherent and coordinated manner, national efforts to empower people living in poverty, in particular women, through, inter alia, education, sustainable livelihoods, health services, in particular health care, and employment-creation policies;

8. *Reaffirms* the importance of mainstreaming gender perspectives into all poverty eradication policies, including through gender-impact analyses, as women constitute the majority of persons living in poverty;

9. *Stresses* that national Governments have the primary responsibility for their country's development and for coordinating development assistance, as well as enhancing its effectiveness;

10. *Urges,* in this context, further progress in harmonizing United Nations system support to national poverty eradication programmes through mechanisms such as the common country assessment and the United Nations Development Assistance Framework, fully consistent with and in support of national priorities as expressed in the country strategy notes or rele-

vant national development plans, as appropriate, as well as full use of thematic groups and other coordination mechanisms within the resident coordinator system, in order to provide an integrated, coordinated and collaborative response by the United Nations system to national priorities for poverty eradication;

11. *Calls upon* the United Nations system to strengthen cooperation with all development partners in supporting national development priorities and policies, reflecting the cross-cutting nature of poverty eradication and capacity-building, including by increased collaboration with multilateral financial institutions, particularly the World Bank, taking note of its new initiatives, the International Monetary Fund, regional banks, as well as other donors, the private sector and other civil society organizations, as appropriate;

12. *Encourages* the United Nations system to take further steps to enhance the efficiency, effectiveness and impact of its support to poverty eradication programmes, including by undertaking impartial, transparent and independent joint evaluations under the overall leadership and with the full and effective involvement of the Government;

13. *Underlines* the importance of the interdependence and the interlinkage between development assistance and national capacity-building;

14. *Stresses* that the United Nations system should adopt flexible responses to specific capacity-building needs as articulated by the recipient countries in accordance with their national development plans and priorities;

15. *Takes note* of the steps being taken to implement General Assembly resolution 53/192, paragraph 37, dealing with capacity-building, particularly the development of United Nations system guidance on capacity-building, with a view to making it an explicit objective of programmes and projects supported by the system, within the context of the 1998 triennial comprehensive policy review, including by revising, inter alia, relevant programming guidelines of the United Nations programmes and funds;

16. *Encourages* the Governments of recipient countries to work towards ensuring that all programmes have capacity-building components;

17. *Calls upon* the United Nations system to take further steps to collect and disseminate relevant information on capacity-building, including best practices;

18. *Stresses* the need to address the subject of sustainability and adaptability of capacity-building in different development contexts and in response to a range of sectoral, cross-sectoral and technical requirements of recipient countries, and in particular to take appropriate steps to ensure the sustainability of capacity-building created in priority areas;

19. *Requests* the Secretary-General, in preparing documentation on resources for the operational activities for development segment of the Council's substantive session of 2000, as stated in paragraph 5 of its resolution 1999/6 of 23 July 1999 on the implementation of General Assembly resolution 53/192, to give consideration to the effect of the decline in core resources for operational activities on the capacity of the United Nations system to implement effective development programmes that support poverty eradication and capacity-building.

Economic and Social Council oversight role

The Secretary-General, in his May report on operational activities for development [E/1999/55], drew the attention of the Economic and Social Council to issues arising from the executive boards of the UN funds and programmes where the Council might want to provide policy guidance. He suggested that the Council assess whether the division of responsibilities between it and the boards was functioning as mandated, particularly on issues in which both had roles to play, such as funding and programming. The Council had largely left the initiative to the boards and the funds and programmes to raise issues requiring the Council's attention, but it would be useful if the Council indicated the kinds of issues that the boards should consider for eventual transmission to the Council for appropriate action. Those might include funding, target setting, resource mobilization and allocation, which had policy, programmatic and development implications extending beyond a single organization. Given the interrelatedness of issues and the converging mandates of funds and programmes, the Council might consider the issue of collective coherence and how to reverse shrinking core funding and identify measures to ensure coordinated programming at the country level. The boards might identify areas of convergence, complementarity and contradictions and bring specific issues before the Council.

In 1999 [E/1999/35], the joint meetings of the Executive Boards of UNDP/United Nations Population Fund (UNFPA) and UNICEF addressed major areas of concerted action for 1999: resource flows, follow-up to international conferences, the resident coordinator system, monitoring and evaluation, use of common indicators, harmonization of programme cycles, common premises and services, UNDAF and the common country assessments, and the link between development and humanitarian operations.

In April 1999, the bureaux of the Council and the UNDP/UNFPA and UNICEF Boards for the first time held joint meetings to review how the Boards took into account the work of functional commissions as regards coordinated follow-up to global conferences and on cross-cutting issues. It was agreed that one possible tool for facilitating future collaboration could be joint meetings of the bureaux, and that the Council should identify cross-cutting areas not adequately addressed and provide feedback to funds and programmes.

Internal oversight mechanisms

The General Assembly, by **decision 53/474** of 8 June, deferred consideration of the Secretary-General's 1997 report [YUN 1997, p. 855] on enhancing the internal oversight mechanisms in operational funds and programmes until its fifty-fourth (1999) session.

Common premises and services

The UNDP Assistant Administrator, reporting to the UNDP/UNFPA Executive Board at its April session [E/1999/35], described progress made to date in pursuit of the United Nations house programme and the required financial resources allocations. She said that the programme was progressing faster than anticipated. The Secretary-General had formally designated UN houses in 31 countries and there were a number of potential UN houses where relocation to new premises was scheduled to take place in the near future. In countries where UN houses were not an immediate prospect, separate offices were connected through a country-based intranet that facilitated the sharing of information, practices and expertise. A survey of common services at the country-level was under way and would provide a basis for a strategy to achieve more efficiency in the management of administrative and financial resources.

On 16 April [E/1999/35 (dec. 99/7)], the Executive Board took note of the report on the UN house programme.

In his May report on progress in the implementation of resolution 53/192 [E/1999/55/Add.1], the Secretary-General said that the UNDG Management Group on Services and Premises was developing tools and guidance on the development and implementation of common and shared services by collecting information on the current status of and experience with those services in field offices. It intended to develop prototype service agreements, standards for services provision, measures of service performance and suggested governance arrangements for common and shared services.

In September [dec. 99/23], the Executive Board, in the context of the 2000-2001 biennial budget, approved the Administrator's proposals for funding the UN house programme: the formula for sharing costs (one third from UNDP and from UNICEF, and one sixth from UNFPA and from the World Food Programme (WFP)) would apply strictly to the evaluation planning and management costs. Relocation costs would be funded through the establishment of a capital reserve from UNDP general resources in the amount of $3.8 million.

In a later report [DP/2000/11], the Administrator indicated that, as at November 1999, the number of UN houses had risen to 36. It was expected that 10 more would be designated each year.

Financing of operational activities

Expenditures by the UN system on operational activities, excluding loans and grants through the World Bank Group, reached $5.3 billion in 1998 [E/2000/46/Add.2], the most recent year for which complete figures were available, compared with $4.8 billion in 1997 and $4.3 billion in 1996. Of the total amount, $2,131 million was distributed in development grants through UNDP or UNDP-administered funds, $1,238 million by WFP, $645 million by UNICEF, $217 million by UNFPA, $297 million by specialized agencies and other organizations (mainly the World Health Organization (WHO)) from regular budgets, and $738 million by specialized agencies and other organizations from extrabudgetary sources.

In addition, concessional loans of $299 million were disbursed by the International Fund for Agricultural Development (IFAD), and $150 million was made available for management service agreements through the United Nations Office for Project Services (UNOPS).

By region, 34.4 per cent of grant expenditures went to Africa, 30.4 per cent to the Americas, 24.3 per cent to Asia and the Pacific, 7.5 per cent to Western Asia and 3.4 per cent to Europe.

Contributions from Governments and other sources for operational activities, including IFAD but excluding the World Bank Group, totalled $5.8 billion in 1998, compared with $5.54 billion in 1997 and $5.5 billion in 1996.

The 1999 United Nations Pledging Conference for Development Activities (New York, 2-3 November) [A/CONF.190/3] received pledges from Governments to UN programmes and funds concerned with development. The Conference heard the announcement of pledges by a number of Governments and took note of the fact that several Governments were not in a position to announce their contributions but proposed to communicate their announcement of such contributions to the Secretary-General as soon as they were in a position to do so.

The Secretary-General provided a statement of contributions pledged or paid at the 1998 Pledging Conference, as at 30 June 1999, to 22 funds and programmes [A/CONF.185/2]. The total came to some $1.2 billion, with an estimated $606 million designated for UNDP.

Technical cooperation through UNDP

The UNDP Administrator, in his annual report covering 1999 [DP/2000/23 & Add.1,2], stated that throughout 1999 the Executive Board was engaged in intensive dialogue on restoring growth and enhanced predictability to UNDP's regular funding base, and specifically in developing and negotiating a sustainable funding strategy. The Board's decisions on the multi-year funding framework (MYFF) (see p. 806) embodied the results of those efforts. Provisional data so far indicated that total net regular (core) resources income for 1999 was $682 million, some 8.5 per cent below the 1998 figure of $750 million. Other resources (non-core resources) increased to approximately $1.5 billion, including $970 million for country cost-sharing, $244.65 million for third-party cost sharing and $329 million mobilized through trust funds.

The Administrator said that in response to the far-reaching changes taking place in the development arena, UNDP embarked on a major programme of reform and renewal focusing on articulating a new vision for the organization in the form of the Administrator's Business Plans (see p. 802), to be presented to the Board in 2000.

The first MYFF provided a more predictable core-funding framework for the organization, integrating programme objectives, resources, budget and outcomes. MYFF showed that the greatest demand for UNDP services was as an adviser and advocate, indicating that the organization could maximize its impact only by moving upstream. Policy was being realigned to make UNDP a stronger global advocate for human development, to align capacity with demand, and to make the organization more highly networked and field-based. To remain a trusted partner of programme countries in developing policies and institutions, UNDP was gearing itself to provide services in response to demand, to assist programme countries in the crafting of pro-poor policies, and to help build the institutional capacity to sustain and implement them, including in crisis and post-conflict situations. UNDP was building on its advocacy work through the *Human Development Report* and other publications to ensure that it stayed abreast of new development trends. It intended to be more responsive to country office needs, strengthen the offices in the thematic areas where demand was greatest and ensure that knowledge was accessible to the partners and clients. The shifting emphasis of UNDP towards upstream activities demanded a stronger presence on the ground, and key personnel and functions were being relocated to the field, with headquarters staff to be reduced by 26 per cent by the end of 2001.

As part of its commitment to strengthening partnerships, progress was made in: promoting relationships within the UN operational system, particularly with the specialized agencies; cooperation with the Bretton Woods institutions, and with civil society organizations and the private sector; and promoting aid coordination.

UNDP/UNFPA Executive Board

In 1999, the UNDP/UNFPA Executive Board held three regular sessions (New York, 25-29 January, 12-16 April and 13-17 September) and an annual session (New York, 14-22 June) [E/1999/35].

At the first regular session, the Board adopted three decisions, including one that gave an overview of the Board's action taken at that session [E/1999/35 (dec. 99/3)]. The other decisions dealt with MYFF and successor programming arrangements (see p. 807).

The Board, at its second regular session, adopted four decisions, including one presenting an overview of the decisions taken at that session [dec. 99/7]. The others dealt with matters relating to UNFPA (see p. 1022).

At the annual session, the Executive Board adopted seven decisions. In addition to an overview of decisions [dec. 99/14], other decisions dealt with UNFPA, an expression of thanks to the outgoing Administrator, a review of the operational reserve, UNDP corporate communication and advocacy strategy, technical cooperation among developing countries, and the annual report of UNOPS (see p. 812).

At its third regular session, the Executive Board adopted 11 decisions, one of which was an overview of action at the session [dec. 99/25]. Three decisions dealt with population matters. Others concerned the United Nations Revolving Fund for Natural Resources Exploration (see PART THREE, Chapter VI), the United Nations Capital Development Fund, budget estimates for 2000-2001 and the funding structure, and UNOPS financial matters.

Appointment of Administrator

By a 21 April note [A/53/237], the Secretary-General informed the General Assembly of the resignation of James Gustave Speth as UNDP Administrator. He requested that the Assembly confirm his appointment of Mark Malloch Brown (United Kingdom) to that position for a four-year term beginning on 1 July. The Assembly confirmed the appointment on 23 April (**decision 53/323**). The UNDP/UNFPA Executive Board, on 15 June [dec. 99/8], expressed its appreciation and gratitude to Mr. Speth for his effective management of UNDP from 1993 to 1999.

UNDP/UNFPA reports

Annual report to Economic and Social Council

The Executive Board, on 16 April [dec. 99/7], took note of the annual report of the UNDP Administrator to the Economic and Social Council [DP/1999/10].

Results-oriented annual report

In 1999, UNDP initiated a new reporting procedure, the results-oriented annual report (ROAR), with the first one covering 1999 UNDP activities [DP/2000/23/Add.1]. An integral part of MYFF, ROAR, based on the intended results outlined in MYFF, was a systematic analysis of the results achieved and showed how those results related to the goals and sub-goals of the organization. In that process, the strategic results framework (SRF) was a key management tool for UNDP to report and improve on results. It represented a critical opportunity to test and streamline the application of results-based management in UNDP; by providing a comprehensive picture of the results achieved, it afforded an opportunity to identify problems and challenges in a more simplified and strategic manner that responded to the specific operational concerns of the organization, particularly those of the country offices. The 1999 ROAR was both a performance analysis and strategic document, emphasizing not only results but how to measure them.

The methodology used assessed progress in relation to intended outcomes. An overall percentage of progress was calculated based on the number of outcomes where progress was demonstrated in relation to the total number of outcomes contained in SRF. Those percentage figures were then aggregated at the levels of strategic areas of support, sub-goals and goals. As in MYFF, results covered both outcomes and outputs. SRF identified specific goals in six major areas of interest to UNDP: creating an enabling environment for sustainable human development; eliminating extreme poverty and reducing overall poverty; protecting the environment and natural resources; achieving gender equality and the advancement of women; preventing or reducing the effects of emergencies and natural disasters; and providing UNDP support to the United Nations Agenda for Development.

The performance analysis for the 1999 ROAR was presented in three main segments. The first reviewed performance and analysed trends for each of the six goals covered by MYFF; the second segment covered the three sub-goals chosen for more detailed analysis and the third segment presented an update of the integrated resource framework with some analysis of the 1999 budgetary and resources performance. In each category or goal, an analysis was made by providing: a summary quantitative picture of performance; an identification of broad trends; the highlights of key issues with reference to clusters of countries, including reasons underlying levels of performance; and some implications of the analysis for the future work of the organization. The ROAR analysis updated the UNDP profile as presented in MYFF and assessed its continuing validity by looking at 1999 expenditures and generic outcomes. The 1999 expenditures were presented in ROAR at the level of goals.

According to the analysis, the first goal, an enabling environment for sustainable human development, was the most significant in terms of overall resources, representing 52 per cent of total expenditures and 38 per cent of core resources. The second most important goal, poverty and sustainable livelihoods, accounted for 32 per cent and nearly 40 per cent of core expenditures, followed by the environment and natural resources (13 per cent), and gender equality and special development situations, less than 2 per cent each. Seven sub-goals (promoting livelihoods of the poor; efficient public sector; dialogue for equitable growth; governance institutions and social cohesion; pro-poor policies and monitoring; decentralization and local governance; equity and global and regional environment) accounted for 89.7 per cent of the total UNDP estimated expenditure for 1999 of $1,681 million. Most of the non-core expenditure was in Latin America and the Caribbean, where there was a higher proportion of higher-income countries than other regions. In terms of performance trends, there was considerable variation across goals within the same region. Sub-Saharan Africa, for example, was heavily involved in governance and poverty reduction, but less so in environment, gender and special development situations. Latin America and the Caribbean, while focusing on poverty and governance issues, was also achieving results in environment. Variations in focus and in rates of progress might reflect different country and regional circumstances.

ROAR findings confirmed that UNDP was moving upstream and was performing well at that level; however, the analysis pointed to the lack of strong links between UNDP policy work and its direct interventions. Most of the micro-interventions were focused on community interventions, especially in Africa. There was some evidence of a shift towards linking project-specific work and its results to policy frameworks; for instance, in microfinance, where UNDP worked mostly at the downstream level. Outcomes of the policy work carried out by UNDP did not have the same development value. Outcomes dealing with advocacy and awareness-building could be seen as initial outcomes, with outcomes relating to the formulation and implementation of policies being more indicative of actual development change. The ROAR analysis pointed out that the link between governance programmes and poverty reduction was not well established and it affirmed that the UNDP policy work was focused on promoting pro-poor policies across the board. In capacity-building, data collection pointed to considerable emphasis by UNDP on promoting civil society and public-private partnerships, emerging as a strong feature in its work. About 50 per cent of the governance category still went to public sector improvement activities. Data collection improved, especially with the development of the national human development reports (NHDRs) as major vehicles for developing new data frontiers, such as developing gender-disaggregated data at the provincial levels and advocating their use for policy-setting.

The integrated resource framework encapsulated the resources allocated for programmes, UN operational activities, programme support and management/administration within one framework, which allowed a clearer link with results. Overall, most of the estimates presented were in line with MYFF targets.

As follow-up to the first ROAR exercise, the Administrator said that the next challenge was to ensure that the notion of results and SRF in particular drove management decisions throughout the organization. At the country level, each management team had to make its SRF more strategic, concentrating on a limited number of key outcomes with reporting on progress backed up by relevant indicators. At the corporate level, the analysis undertaken by regional bureaux and units, such as the Bureau for Development Policy and the Evaluation Office, had to identify and promote the key lessons learned from the exercise. UNDP might need to select a limited number of key outcomes, stemming from the global conferences, in which it wished to take global leadership, and purse a coordinated effort, jointly with key development partners, to track and evaluate progress in achieving global goals and targets.

UNDP operational activities

Country programmes

The UNDP/UNFPA Executive Board approved first country cooperation frameworks for Kenya, Madagascar, the Niger, Suriname and Tajikistan on 29 January [dec. 99/3], and for Aruba on 16 April [dec. 99/7]. By the latter decision, the Board took note of the report on assistance to Somalia [DP/1999/11] and authorized the Administrator to continue to approve projects for that country on a case-by-case basis. It also took note of the report on assistance to Montserrat [DP/1999/12 & Corr.1]. On 22 June [dec. 99/14], the Board took note of the Administrator's note on assistance to Myanmar [DP/1999/18]. On 17 September [dec. 99/25], it approved first country cooperation frameworks for Antigua and Barbuda, the Central African Republic, Ecuador and Haiti, and took note of the first extension of the first country cooperation framework for Eritrea. It also took note of the Administrator's note on assistance to the Democratic Republic of the Congo [DP/1999/36] and authorized the Administrator to approve assistance for that country on a project-by-project basis.

UNDP performance analysis by goal

Creating an enabling environment for sustainable human development

Of the six main goals identified by UNDP, creating an enabling environment for sustainable human development (SHD) was the most significant in terms of expenditure, accounting for 38 per cent of estimated 1999 core budget expenditures and 57 per cent of all expenditures ($790 million), including core and non-core resources. In terms of the sub-goals of that category, expenditures were: the promotion of an efficient and accountable public sector ($323 million); promoting national, regional and global dialogue on SHD ($240 million); strengthening the capacity of key governance institutions ($240 million); and the promotion of decentralization ($167 million).

From the reports of country offices, average performance appeared to be good as a whole with a 72 per cent rate of progress against intended outcomes. The results were overwhelmingly of an upstream nature, mainly in capacity-building with a focus on policy, regulatory or legal frameworks and support to institutional capacity. Advocacy on SHD matters and related policy formulation was also a key result area. Justice and human rights were growing in importance, with an emphasis on institutional development and civil society awareness, particularly in Europe, Latin America and the Caribbean, and in some conflict-stricken countries, such as Afghanistan, Angola, Burundi, the Democratic Republic of the Congo and the Sudan. At the country level, UNDP was a partner in expanding participation in governance; a facilitator in consultative processes; a technical adviser on legal and institutional aspects of decentralization; and a source of assistance in empowering civil society, local governments and communities to become more active in decision-making.

At the sub-goal level, NHDRs emerged as a useful tool in raising awareness on SHD issues and as a springboard for policy advocacy. In 1999, some 75 NHDRs were produced, focusing on a wide array of development concerns. NHDRs led to innovative approaches in monitoring human development conditions in Brazil, Kyrgyzstan, Poland and the Russian Federation. In Uganda, the report led to the establishment of a human development policy-making forum, while in Senegal it contributed to the formulation of a national long-term development plan. Provincial and regional-level HDRs, and the creation of SHD centres in Argentina and Tajikistan brought about a new, broader policy dialogue on SHD concerns. In China, the 1999 NHDR focused on the transition and the role of the State in correcting market failures, including poverty and strengthening health, education and protecting the environment.

In human rights, UNDP was active in strengthening governance institutions in the Commonwealth of Independent States (CIS), Europe and Latin America and the Caribbean through awareness-raising and legislative improvements.

UNDP's work was also aimed at the decentralization of government in support of local governance and empowering communities. It provided assistance in Cambodia, Samoa and Thailand for policy and legislation on decentralization and for the creation of additional funding mechanisms at the local level in Bhutan, Cambodia, Indonesia, Mongolia and Nepal. Progress in decentralization was complemented by strengthening the capacity of local authorities in Asia and the Pacific and in Africa. However, results were limited, underlining the need for more strategic intervention and expanded partnerships.

Public sector reform was a key area of UNDP support in 1999. In Africa, the results targeted were the development of plans, laws, regulations and new organizational structures to strengthen macroeconomic or public finance management. The Asia and Pacific and the Arab States regions shared a focus on administrative reform and improved human resources. Institutional strengthening in information technology was a specific dimension of results in Latin American and Caribbean countries. Promoting increased transparency levels and combating corruption were of particular significance for Asian and Pacific and Latin American and Caribbean countries. National bodies to fight corruption were established in Bolivia, Colombia and Georgia. In both African and Asian countries, results focused on improved and more transparent management systems in areas relating to national accounts, audit and revenue.

ROAR data indicated that UNDP was not yet systematically incorporating its insights on poverty reduction into its approaches to governance. UNDP support across a wide range of enabling environment issues, from decentralization to public sector reform, or support to the judicial system, needed to be connected to the needs of the poor. Decentralization did not appear to have been prioritized by the regional bureaux, other than the Regional Bureau for Asia and the Pacific. ROAR highlighted the significance of NHDRs as a powerful tool to stir development debate, particularly in countries where civil society was weak and reliable data scarce, and noted the need to have NHDRs produced by all country offices to promote focused attention on key development issues at the national and regional levels. ROAR data also suggested the need to review linkages between global, regional and country office programming, as country office ROARs often omitted to report progress realized through global or regional initiatives.

Poverty eradication and sustainable livelihoods

Over $195 million of estimated UNDP expenditures from core resources was spent on poverty eradication and supporting sustainable livelihoods. That accounted for 40 per cent of UNDP core resources or 31.6 per cent when cost-sharing contributions were taken into account.

All country offices in Latin America and the Caribbean reported on poverty eradication activities, with high levels of reporting from other regions. The Asia and Pacific region showed the highest rate of progress against intended outcomes, (74 per cent), followed closely by Europe and CIS, but with sub-Saharan Africa (64 per cent) and Latin America and the Caribbean (58 per cent) at somewhat lower levels.

ROAR data revealed good progress in capacity-building. UNDP made headway in all regions in advocacy and awareness-raising, and there was evidence of a correlation between UNDP achievements in advocacy and the development of policy and legal frameworks. UNDP helped to review existing legislation and to prepare recommendations for changes. The involvement of civil society and the promotion of a broad national dialogue were key dimensions of UNDP work that was yielding positive results. Downstream expenditures for poverty eradication were about double those for upstream, particularly in Africa. Strategic support relating to health epidemics, social services, employment, microfinance and self-organization of the poor covered UNDP results for empowerment, participatory approaches and targeted/pilot interventions at the local community level. UNDP's downstream interventions yielded positive results in terms of actual changes occurring and the number of beneficiaries. Knowledge dissemination and networking through information technology was an emerging area for UNDP. Global and regional programmes contributed to the development of networks and exchange of experience. A limited number of UNDP results included a specific gender component. Progress in terms of benefits to women was mostly reported in employment promotion and access to microfinance services.

ROARs confirmed the trends highlighted in the MYFF document. In terms of frequency of UNDP anti-poverty interventions, by number of country offices reporting, UNDP intended results focused on: national pro-poor policies and anti-poverty plans (84); entrepreneurship promotion and access of the poor to microfinance services (74); employment promotion among the poor (67); and self-organization of civil society and the poor (59). UNDP made strong advocacy efforts in countries in transition (in Europe, CIS and Mongolia) and those emerging from financial crisis (Indonesia, Thailand). Indicators demonstrated a meaningful increase in media coverage of poverty issues and more references to those issues by senior government officials. In the prevention and reduction of health epidemics, particularly HIV/AIDS, UNDP was involved in raising awareness, supporting national programmes and making community-level interventions. There was a wide discrepancy in results and frequency of interventions. Little evidence was found of positive results in direct interventions translating into change at the policy-making level. Only 15 country offices, mostly from Asia, were active in strengthening national capacity for monitoring the labour market and the development of pro-poor employment policies. In Bhutan and Sri Lanka, a skills development fund was instituted by the Government and the private sector. In the promotion of employment of the poor, reports from 53 country offices showed progress against intended outcomes at 62 per cent. UNDP provided support through direct training or advisory centres providing support to the poor. A high rate of success was registered for micro-enterprise start-up and expansion with 82 per cent of the 23 reporting country offices showing progress. A total of 76 per cent of active country offices saw improvements at the policy level for microfinance development, such as amendment of regulations, including banking regulations in Cambodia, Kazakhstan, Mongolia and the Philippines, among other countries.

Securing access of the poor to basic services, particularly health and education, was an important goal in most regions. Two thirds of the country offices reported positive results through participatory approaches and local partnership-building. However, results were strikingly modest in structural reforms in the rights of the poor to access to land and natural resources, with only 13 country offices providing reports and only one third of those reporting positive changes in that area. Interventions for food security were concentrated in Africa and Asia, with 13 countries reporting in each of the two regions, and almost all reporting progress with an emphasis on rural areas and training of farmers. Efforts to promote the self-organization of the poor were reported on from all regions and yielded positive results with progress against intended outcomes averaging 66 per cent.

Environment and natural resources

Environment was the third largest beneficiary of estimated UNDP expenditures in 1999. The category absorbed 14 per cent of total expenditures ($240 million), of which non-core resources amounted to $170 million, a third of which came from the UNDP/Global Environment Facility (GEF). Downstream activities absorbed more than one third of total expenditures.

Reporting by country offices was generally concentrated in the priority areas identified in MYFF. Progress reported by those offices against intended outcomes averaged 67 per cent. Performance for downstream activities was significantly lower than the average rate of progress for that category; those included micro or targeted programmes, awareness-raising and technology development. Results were more visible for upstream activities aiming at developing policy and regulatory frameworks, including the follow-up to global agreements, data collection and analysis and capacity-building. The main focus of action was on climate change, biodiversity and, to a lesser extent, desertification. GEF funding was a critical determinant in shaping UNDP activities.

Strategic support was provided in: ratification of, and national follow-up to, international conventions and agreements (67 countries); legal/regulatory frameworks and policy implementation (52 countries); management capacity of national environmental agencies (49 countries); local participation in programme design/implementation (45 countries); programmes for sustainable environmental management (43 countries); and capacity for data collection, analysis and dissemination (42 countries).

UNDP offices in all regions reported progress in the formulation, discussion and official endorsement of environmental strategies and/or action plans, for the sector as well as for goals specifically geared towards biodiversity and desertification. All regions, with the Arab States to a lesser extent, reported progress in the drafting and/or adoption of policy, legislation or regulation on a mix of environmental issues, such as authority and responsibilities in environmental management, land/water use, environmental or energy conservation, social forestry and waste management. All regions, with Africa to a lesser extent, reported progress in the compilation of national greenhouse gas inventories, formulation of action plans and legislation on climate change and preparation of national reports to the 1992 United Nations Framework Convention on Climate Change [YUN 1992, p. 681], which entered into force in 1994 [YUN 1994, p. 938].

Capacity development was targeted at improving capabilities in environmental management, data collection and analysis, mostly in Asia and the Pacific and Latin America and the Caribbean. The estimated rate of progress against intended outcomes was below the average for that thematic category at approximately 56 per cent and there were pockets of particularly weak performance, for example, with regard to technology development where Asia and the Pacific, Latin America and the Caribbean, and the Arab States reported rates of progress between 40 and 50 per cent. The most important strategic area of support concerned interventions for specific geographic areas and target groups, but performance was mixed. Examples of area-based rehabilitation and conservation schemes, such as adoption of sustainable farming practices and alternative energy options and the recovery of degraded or marginal land, included a management plan for a national park in Cambodia; construction of a waste-water treatment plant in Pakistan; pilot projects in Panama on the sustainable use of wild resources; and training of 400 trainers and 12,000 farmers on forest fire prevention and control in Brazil. Initiatives were made to promote the adoption of sustainable natural resources management and livelihood models by target groups at the community level, for example, in the Niger, leading to the establishment of 130 firewood stoves owned by local communities, enabling the sustainable exploitation of 400,000 hectares of savannah forest. In Bangladesh, preparatory work on the adoption of alternative livelihoods had started in 30 villages.

The ROAR analysis called for improved management of the UNDP environment and natural resources portfolio. A review of the portfolio to identify and either phase out or tackle low-performing activities was proposed so that future efforts could be concentrated on a few key areas of intervention.

Gender equality and advancement of women

At $30 million, the gender category represented the smallest portion of resources distributed by goal. It accounted for 3.4 per cent of UNDP core expenditures for 1999 and only 1 per cent of non-core expenditures. Overall reporting for the gender category was lower than for other SRF categories. However, Asia and the Pacific and Europe and CIS provided more comprehensive information on their interventions and results than the other three regions. Progress was significant in Asia and the Pacific with a rate of 75 per cent progress against intended outcomes.

Among its findings, ROAR reported that the new reporting system under-represented the emphasis UNDP placed on gender, as did MYFF. Policy and legal frameworks on gender were key types of results targeted by UNDP and an area of progress for all five regions. Results were more limited for the integration of gender concerns into development policies. UNDP was active in promoting networking for regional and cross-regional exchanges of knowledge, with a growing use of information technology. Partnerships involved non-governmental organizations (NGOs), civil society and media organizations, with support from the global and regional gender programmes. Interventions were focused chiefly on employment promotion for women. The main strategic areas of support and the number of countries offices reporting were: strengthening entrepreneurial and technical skills, knowledge and capacities (37); providing capacity-building support for gender mainstreaming in policies, plans and programmes (37); strengthening the capacity of organizations that represented women's interests and promoted advocacy, networking and partnerships for the advancement of women (35); and supporting the implementation of national action plans for the advancement of women (32).

UNDP was actively involved in the promotion of women's leadership and involvement in the decision-making process, with both Governments and parliaments, through training, international exposure and sensitization. Positive changes were measured in the form of increased media attention towards women's representation in political life, gender-based salary gaps in the economy and political commitment to increase women's participation.

Progress in policy and legislation for gender equality ranged from gender-policy frameworks in Estonia and the Gambia and an implementation strategy in Malawi to legislative changes, with a draft law on gender equality submitted in Haiti and passed in Lithuania, legislation against gender discrimination passed in the Republic of Korea and a bill of rights of spouses adopted in Samoa. In Nepal, UNDP supported the creation of a women's committee in Parliament for gender sensitivity and representation in the civil service. In Estonia, it sponsored a radio/television programme on women's representation in elections and monitored its impact. In Pakistan, the unequal portrayal of women in the media was highlighted, with progress measured through a media-watch system. In El Salvador, 400 women, including municipal counsellors, were trained in political leadership, and in Papua New Guinea, 50 women officials received UNDP training. Women candidates received training in Albania, Botswana and Viet Nam.

Support was provided to national action plans and follow-up on the Fourth World Conference on Women [YUN 1995, p. 1169]. Of 32 country offices reporting, 26 indicated progress. All regions reached tangible results, although there were fewer in Africa, in the formulation and adoption of national action plans, with notable examples in Cambodia, Eritrea, Guyana and the Sudan.

Other activities were aimed at promoting women's equal access to and control over economic and social assets and resources. A total of 37 country offices mentioned interventions in that area and 20 registered progress. Support was given to women's associations, business centres and vocational training, resulting in increased employment opportunities in Albania, Bangladesh and Mexico, which focused on indigenous women. UNDP also sought to ensure the full exercise of human rights, including security and freedom from violence. Concerning the latter goal, Latin America and the Caribbean, Europe and CIS and Asia and the Pacific reported progress. Activities included media campaigns in Jamaica, Kenya and Trinidad and Tobago, and legislative work in Haiti and the Republic of Korea. In Jamaica, 3,000 people received training on women's rights, existing legislation and skills to cope with domestic violence. Police officers were sensitized to gender issues in Kenya, and in the Sudan UNDP held workshops with local leaders and officials on harmful traditional practices for women's health. UNDP also concentrated on integrating gender concerns into development policies; of reports received from 32 country offices in all regions, only half described some progress.

Overall, under-representation highlighted the need for a strengthened effort to mainstream gender concerns into UNDP interventions, particularly those relating to an enabling environment for SHD and poverty.

Special development situations

Under the special development situations (SDS) goal, UNDP supported recovery from natural disasters and the consolidation of peace and stability. Results under SDS accounted for only a small share of 1999 core expenditures ($20 million or 4.1 per cent, and $16 million or 1.1 per cent of all cost-sharing expenditures). Those figures, however, were considered to be the result of under-reporting because SDS results were often reported under other goals. Overall performance was generally good, with country offices reporting an average rate of progress against intended outcomes of 75 per cent.

Eighty-one per cent of all outcomes for SDS related to capacity-building. UNDP's priority was on strengthening the link between development activity and disaster mitigation, planning and reduction, as well as support for sustainable livelihoods in the post-conflict phase. Its activities affected populations, such as demobilized soldiers, who were provided with new opportunities for civilian life in Angola, Guatemala, Nicaragua, the Philippines, Rwanda and Tajikistan.

As part of its activities to mainstream disaster reduction capacity-building, including policy-making, planning and investment, UNDP gave institutional support for improved disaster-management arrangements in five European countries, and helped to establish the National Disaster Management Committee in the Lao People's Democratic Republic and a national task force in Afghanistan. In Angola, the Democratic Republic of the Congo and Sierra Leone, the focus was on government knowledge on disaster management and prevention. Legislation and regulations in those Central American countries most affected by hurricane Mitch (see p. 868) were revised with UNDP assistance.

Restoring the capacity of national institutions and civil society organizations was another focus of such activities through community-level confidence-building and conflict resolution in Burundi, Colombia, the Democratic Republic of the Congo, Georgia, Guatemala and Tajikistan. In Rwanda, a successful reintegration programme allowed some 10,000 child soldiers to be reunited with their families (see also p. 674). In Somalia, the rehabilitation of a centre in the north-west had allowed the training of 800 cadets and the establishment of a functional police force in both the north-west and the north-east of the country. Support for affected populations, refugees and the displaced was provided through the resettlement of distressed and/or conflict-affected populations and access to new productive activities in Angola, Armenia, Azerbaijan, Bosnia and Herzegovina, Burundi, the Democratic Republic of the Congo, Guinea-Bissau, Rwanda, Sierra Leone and the former Yugoslav Republic of Macedonia (FYROM). In Ukraine, where an estimated 250,000 of those who had been deported had returned to the Crimea, some 50,000 benefited from the UNDP integration and development programme. Other results concerned improved access to basic social services by communities affected by conflict through reconstruction/rehabilitation. UNDP also provided technical assistance for the formulation of national demining plans, such as in Bosnia and Herzegovina, and played a role in post-conflict assistance coordination in Albania, Armenia, Azerbaijan, Georgia, Kazakhstan and FYROM.

An area of growth potential for UNDP was supporting institutions during crisis situations, leading to faster progress from rehabilitation to sustained recovery. To meet that challenge, UNDP needed to improve its ability to intervene and strengthen its response. Finding additional resources was critical for SDS activities, particularly with regard to recovery programmes, such as reintegration and demining.

UNDP support to the United Nations

UNDP support to the United Nations was the most heavily reported of all thematic categories. Progress achieved against intended outcomes for that category was almost 80 per cent, with estimated 1999 core budget expenditures totalling $73 million.

The principal focus of UNDP direct support for the follow-up to global conferences was on the World Summit for Social Development [YUN 1995, p. 1113], the United Nations Conference on Environment and Development [YUN 1992, p. 670] and the Fourth World Conference on Women [YUN 1995, p. 1169]. Follow-up to the World Conference on Education for All [YUN 1990, p. 763] was also notable. Results of aid coordination efforts were mixed. UNDP was actively managing the round-table mechanism and supporting the Consultative Group process, with activities in about 40 countries, mostly in Africa, Asia and the Pacific and Latin America and the Caribbean. Country offices were raising the profile of UNDP and the UN system with good coverage through the media, as well as the Internet. At the corporate level, progress was made in developing common positions on development issues and field operations. The situation was less encouraging with regard to special development situations. Overall, ROARs indicated that a useful role was being played by UNDP in generating momentum within the UN system, especially at the country level, on a common development vision based on the global conferences to facilitate change in programme countries.

In terms of strategic support, within the resident coordinator system, UNDP's role focused on increased use of the common country assessment (CCA) and UNDAF, and adopting programming and operational modalities to improve the coherence and cost-effectiveness of UN system development operations. Progress was made in the formulation and adoption of CCA and UNDAF. A diverse group of countries reported the integration of global conference follow-up in their CCA and/or UNDAF, especially on issues of poverty, basic social services, gender and human rights. Joint initiatives, from advocacy to joint development of cross-sectoral strategies and programmes, to a coordinated response in special development situations, increased. Those included joint assessments with UNICEF on the 20/20 initiative in Lebanon, Morocco, the Niger, Sri Lanka, Togo and Viet Nam; reports on national follow-up to the global conferences in Bangladesh, Bulgaria, Ethiopia, Fiji, Kyrgyzstan and Pakistan; joint evaluations and review exercises in Nigeria; and collaborative planning on post-hurricane Mitch rehabilitation and recovery in Central America. Other results included the harmonization of programme cycles; needs assessment and agreement on common services and UN houses; and the formation or restructuring of thematic groups. A number of offices reported progress towards focusing on fewer thematic groups and/or using them for substantive analysis, advocacy, planning and technical support, as in Indonesia, Kenya, Malaysia, Myanmar, Pakistan and the Republic of Moldova. HIV/AIDS emerged as a key priority for thematic groups.

UNDP's work in support of aid coordination was closely related to its role as funder and manager of the resident coordinator system. Three quarters of country offices active in that area reported progress. Analysis of data by income group indicated that country offices in the net-contributor countries were doing best, followed by those in low- and middle-income countries, and country offices in the least developed countries in the bottom tier.

Country offices were making considerable efforts in communication and outreach to a wide variety of target groups on the mission and the work of the UN system, especially that of non-representated agencies, by contributing to joint information/communication strategies for the UN system; the establishment or development of UN information centres (UNICs); the organization of special events; the preparation of press releases, briefings and newspaper supplements;

and the production of public relations materials. Particularly noteworthy was the development of UNDP and UN web sites in more than 30 countries.

The strong performance in that category could be seen as both a strength and a weakness for UNDP. It reflected United Nations strength in internalizing its reforms, yet it pointed to a weakness in that progress was measured by the number of UNDAFs and CCAs under way rather than by what they had achieved. That indicated the need for a substantial revision of the SRF structure and content with greater emphasis on outcomes to be pursued in collaboration with other UN organizations.

The issue of process also raised questions. The sharp rise in transaction costs (the cost of doing business with the UN) was a consequence of the lack of progress on streamlining agency-specific programming processes. Second, the uniform methodology for preparing CCA and UNDAF penalized those regions with limited capacities, either in the country offices or the host Governments. Therefore, it might not be meaningful to pursue such a standardized approach. The findings of the analysis supported a stronger role for UNDP in seeking a reduction in transaction costs with the UN system; mobilizing UN partners to achieve concrete development outcomes at the country level; and defining and pursuing its own niche in direct support to conference follow-up.

Programme planning and management

Reform measures

The UNDP Administrator, in a February report to the Executive Board [DP/1999/10], commented that the Secretary-General's reform programme (see p. 1269) had provided a strong boost to the implementation of General Assembly resolutions 50/120 [YUN 1995, p. 883] and 53/192 [YUN 1998, p. 802] on the triennial policy review of operational activities for development. The reform programme and legislation had provided for a coherent coordination structure at headquarters and the country level; where the UNDP Administrator chaired UNDG, UNDP managed and funded the resident coordinator system and the UNDP resident representative was normally the resident coordinator. At the same time, UNDG had taken the lead on a number of initiatives to enhance coordination of operational activities such as UNDAF, common premises and the resident coordinator system.

On 16 April [E/1999/35 (dec. 99/7)], the Executive Board took note of the Administrator's report.

A March report to the Executive Board on UNDP and UN reform [DP/1999/16] highlighted developments within UNDP in the context of the Secretary-General's programme of reform. It stated that the creation of UNDG had boosted implementation of General Assembly resolutions on operational activities, particularly resolution 53/192. UNDG had achieved rapid progress on specific provisions of the legislation in operational activities. The main challenge remaining was to achieve effective outreach to the UN system as a whole since operational activities coordinated under the resident coordinator system concerned the system as a whole. Annexed to the report was an update by the UNDG Office of overall progress on the UNDG initiative.

Concerning funding, the Executive Board had paved the way for a new era in UNDP core funding, with its 1998 [YUN 1998, p. 825] and 1999 [dec. 99/1] decisions on MYFF (see p. 806). UNDP was developing MYFF, integrating programme objectives, resources, budget and outcomes. The transfer to UNDP of technical cooperation support functions in natural disaster mitigation had been effected. The Emergency Response Division had already initiated new capacity-building activities in developing countries to promote comprehensive disaster reduction approaches. UNDP also supported a coordinated inter-agency approach within the UN system and with other development partners, including NGOs.

The proposal for the establishment of a UN enterprise liaison service with the private sector had been redefined. UNDP continued to strengthen its operational relations with the World Bank and both were engaged in discussions on issues that had arisen out of the change processes being undertaken by their respective organizations, particularly the issue of grant-based funding for technical cooperation.

In June [dec. 99/14], the Executive Board took note of the March report.

In a later report [DP/2000/11], the Administrator stated that, in 1999, the UNDG Executive Committee decided to proceed with a thorough review of UNDG with a view to rationalizing the number of subsidiary bodies and introducing sunset clauses in all subgroups. Where possible, standing groups would be replaced by ad hoc task-oriented meetings of limited duration.

UNDP Business Plans (2000-2003)

In December [DP/2000/8], the UNDP Administrator submitted to the Executive Board the UNDP Business Plans for 2000-2003, aimed at ensuring that UNDP responded effectively to the growing demand for upstream activities and complemented those activities with strong global advocacy and direct support to programme countries through aid coordination and resource mobilization. The Plans, which emanated from the seventh goal of MYFF, outlined a new vision and goals for UNDP. A key priority would be to ensure also that UNDP had the policy expertise, key partnerships and internal capacity to deliver its services effectively. The Administrator explained that the starting place should be the needs of the programme countries, where the unprecedented pace of global change had created tremendous demand for new kinds of support. MYFF reflected the force of those new demands by showing a clear trend towards upstream activities, such as policy and institutional support. Those kinds of activities played to UNDP strengths. They leveraged the trust it enjoyed from programme countries, and built upon its roles in advocacy, UN development coordination and country-level resource mobilization. However, helping those countries implied considerable change in UNDP operations, policies, partnerships and culture.

The Administrator said that programmes would remain country-driven but UNDP would be much more effective at policy dialogue and institution-building than at directly supporting isolated poverty-alleviation projects. Project work would continue and even increase as resources grew but would be aligned behind policies. They would be designed to sustain policy change by incorporating policy dialogue, pilot approaches and institutional support, with a special emphasis on South-South knowledge transfer.

Through the ROAR process, the areas of high priority to programme countries would be reviewed and checked against current institutional processes and expertise; the shortfalls and gaps that emerged would be signposts for where capacities needed to be built up. The new global and regional programmes that began in 2001 would be designed with a clear view to high-demand areas. By the same token, low-demand areas would point to activities that might be undertaken more effectively by others. UNDP would be rigorous in identifying partners in all areas where there was duplication, where others clearly had a comparative advantage or where it was not feasible to build in-house expertise. The discussions that had already begun with the United Nations Development Fund for Women (UNIFEM) were an example of that.

At the same time, the overall trend towards policy support, institution-building and other upstream activities was clear. The Administrator intended to redesign the Bureau for Development Policy to focus on applied policy support; strengthen the link between policy and operations; enhance capacity to advocate for more equitable global and national policies; re-engineer activities to provide more effective support to countries in special development situations; strengthen capacity to capture and leverage global best practices by investing in networking and knowledge management capability; and prioritize TCDC in all activities, including global and regional programmes. He intended to strengthen reforms already begun within UNDG and the resident coordinator system. At the corporate level, to increase the coherence of overall partnership activities, he intended to group a number of key activities into a new Bureau of Resources and Strategic Partnerships to increase UNDP's capacity for resource mobilization. A true culture of performance would also be created, including reducing the overall size of headquarters by 25 per cent, partly through shifts of staff to the field.

The Administrator also intended to pursue vigorously the core and non-core MYFF resource targets and believed that the successful implementation of the Business Plans would be a major step in that direction. At the same time, he was committed to maximizing resources for programming and would therefore fund the estimated $25 million short-term additional costs associated with those Plans through savings or extrabudgetary contributions. In that regard, he had instructed managers to target an additional $12 million of savings to be redeployed towards change projects. The 2000-2001 budget proposals also included implementation of a strategy relating to improvement of government contributions to local office costs performance and proposals for strengthening cost-recovery mechanisms.

Those initiatives should lead to a revitalized, dynamic UNDP that could respond effectively to the increasing demands of its programme-country clients for upstream services, playing a leading role in the struggle for human development and poverty eradication worldwide.

Change management: UNDP 2001

In January, the UNDP Administrator reported to the Executive Board on the implementation of the UNDP 2001 change management process [E/1999/35], observing that there had been progress in all the key strategic issues since the launching of the programme [YUN 1997, p. 871]. Referring to decentralization as the central theme of UNDP 2001, the Administrator cited examples of several initiatives that were contributing to that outcome, including the subregional resource facilities, new streamlined programme and finance manuals, and new guidelines on national execution, collaboration with the private sector and decentralized cost-sharing agreements. Human resource policies were having a positive impact on the effectiveness of country offices, including the national staff career management policy to enhance the professional capabilities of national staff, and a gender balance policy that was contributing to enhancing the number of women staff members at all levels; the number of women resident representatives had risen from 14 in 1996 to 30 in 1998. The Administrator reported that UNDP was using a fast-track mechanism for placing staff in country offices in countries in special development circumstances and was going to introduce competency-based approaches for staff in other offices. He assured the Board that the 2000-2001 budget strategy would include measures for managing staff growth at headquarters. The Administrator also discussed systems improvements, problems in carrying out the five-day response mandate for requests from country offices, building an accountability culture and UNDP's contribution to the overall UN reform process through UNDG and UNDAF. On 29 January [dec. 99/3], the Executive Board took note of the progress report on the implementation of change management.

In December [DP/2000/3], UNDP issued a comprehensive assessment of the UNDP 2001 change process. The assessment found that the impact of the change management process had been limited by the prevalence of restructuring over re-engineering, which should have provided the context for organizational restructuring and determined the core competencies necessary to accomplish the organization's mission. There had been much tinkering with processes and procedures to improve efficiencies without questioning whether certain activities should be done. A more systematic approach was required for the optimization of the organization. Moreover, the change management process had not fostered closer bonds between corporate spheres and operations; in fact, the traditional divide might have grown wider. There was an urgent need to redefine the headquarters structure to ensure that it was more closely knit, and to streamline decision-making functions at the highest levels of the organization.

The report also found that a culture supportive of learning had not been achieved because of a lack of leadership incentives and career rewards for results-based learning accomplishments. While evidence of learning was visible in many areas, there was no systematic means of assessing its overall organizational impact. The report suggested that UNDP elevate the Learning Advisory Board to play a central role in organizational learning, bringing together strategic organizational initiatives and resource commitments.

The idea of setting a finite date for the end of the change management process in December 1999 was unrealistic, after only two years of operation, since organizational change required continuous commitment with adequate resources. In attempting to overcome the challenges, it was necessary to recognize the deeply rooted, complacent culture of an organization based on entitlement that carried out a central coordinating and funding role within the UN system. The centrifugal tendencies or diverse power centres in headquarters became points of resistance, and negotiations on change were often defensive and parochial, protecting unit positions while trying to stave off budget cuts. It was premature to disband the Change Management Committee and the idea of building a coalition for change across the organization still merited consideration. Greater attention should be paid to re-engineering that would adapt general principles to the circumstances. The entrepreneurial spirit needed to be unleashed to take advantage of the changing environment, and the organization needed to become less risk-averse, seizing opportunities to experiment. However, despite the difficulties, UNDP was better positioned to appreciate the challenges of and opportunities for change. The positive aspects of change management would be exploited to allow the organization to over come those challenges in the twenty-first century.

Communications and advocacy strategy

In an oral report to the Executive Board's first regular session in January [E/1999/35], the Director of the Division of Public Affairs reviewed progress in implementing UNDP's communications and advocacy strategy during the period June to December 1998 in key communications areas. He noted that substantial efforts were being made to develop a communications culture at all levels and locations of the organization. UNDP had shifted its work in public affairs to advance an active radio and television strategy in addition to its work with the print media. Advocacy and constituency-building, special events and helping to shape the media agenda were other areas of focus. A major effort was made to update key public information materials and data to reflect UNDP reform, its leadership role in UNDG and action in pursuit of its main goals, as well as monitoring the use of UNDP's information material. The Division of Public Affairs worked closely with the UN Department of Public Information in sharing information and providing guest experts for press briefings. UNDP also made special efforts to get the organization's viewpoint heard through opinion pages and interviews with its senior management by mass media.

The main challenge in implementing the strategy was the overall shrinking of development assistance in donor countries and the competition among funds and programmes for limited resources. Specifically, additional resources were needed for sharpening messages, expanding media consciousness and outreach, increasing language translation and expanding monitoring, evaluation and audience-targeting.

On 29 January [dec. 99/3], the Board took note of the oral presentation on key areas of communications needs and the comments made thereon by delegations.

In response to the Board's 1998 request [YUN 1998, p. 823], UNDP reported in May on its corporate communications and advocacy strategy [DP/1999/19], which was aimed at increasing understanding of what UNDP did and increasing support and resources for the organization. The report reviewed the 10-point strategic action plan on which the strategy was based and presented results achieved since its introduction in 1995; problems encountered in promoting a culture of communications and advocacy; and action to be taken in 2000-2001 to profile UNDP more effectively and to demonstrate the organization's distinctive value-added activities when compared to other providers of development services. The public affairs and advocacy activities of all bureaux at UNDP headquarters, including the associated funds and programmes, and UNDP country and liaison offices were taken into consideration in the report's analyses.

In his annual report covering 1999 [DP/2000/23], the Administrator said that UNDP had refined its communications strategy to target more effectively the donor country media that influenced policy and decision makers. At the same time, to support the organization's shifting emphasis towards the field, UNDP expanded its support to communications efforts at the country level through special public affairs training for resident representatives and senior managers and the preparation of a public affairs manual for media and advocacy outreach. UNDP stepped up its promotional efforts for specialized publications, such as the *Poverty Report* and the book *Global Public Goods*, and for its flagship monthly magazine *Choices*. Media attention on the cause of poverty eradication was generated by UNDP with the launch of netaid.org in 1999, with three simultaneous concerts in New York, London and Geneva broadcast live over the new web site, radio and television, including the youth-oriented cable television networks MTV and VH1. Other special events included trips of UNDP Goodwill Ambassadors, generating media attention.

The Board, on 22 June [dec. 99/10], noted that elaboration of the UNDP corporate communications and advocacy strategy continued as a work in progress and welcomed the emphasis of the strategy on results and progress towards a clearer demonstration of the UNDP development achievements. The Board requested further elaboration of the results-based strategy to strengthen the linkage with MYFF and to report on budgetary and staffing implications. It invited the Administrator to report in 2000 on the strategy, taking into account the results of the discussion on MYFF.

Evaluation

The Administrator, in his annual report on evaluation in UNDP for 1998 [DP/1999/17], described the work of the Evaluation Office, which was built on three strategic directions: supporting UNDP in becoming a results-oriented organization; strengthening substantive accountability; and promoting organizational learning. It reported progress in applying results-based management and the Office also provided technical leadership and support in designing and implementing the results framework, specifically SRFs, which formed part of MYFF. Concerning substantive accountability, efforts were undertaken to connect evaluations and their findings to decision-making and enhanced organizational practices, primarily through tracking and compliance systems, which revealed a rate of 71 per cent compliance at the end of 1998 for projects approved in 1988-1989. The Office emphasized the systematic sharing of the lessons learned from empirical evidence by introducing products that provided timely, relevant lessons for practitioners and decision makers.

In 1998, the Evaluation Office and UNDP-associated funds and programmes had carried out strategic and thematic evaluations. Two strategic evaluations were initiated, one on refugees and internally displaced persons and the other on the relationship between UNDP and UNOPS. Among thematic evaluations, one covered activities in governance in Latin America and the Caribbean, and in the Arab States. At the request of the Regional Bureau for Europe and CIS, the Evaluation Office provided a review on the role of NGOs and the promotion of human rights, which covered five countries in the region. The Office continued to monitor evaluations at the country level and the recommendations made as a result of them. The Office received a total of 85 reports in 1998 against 79 the previous year. Partnership development was an essential dimension of the work of the Office, which developed dialogue with its partners for evaluation cooperation.

In June [dec. 99/14], the Executive Board took note of the report on evaluation.

Funding strategy

Multi-year funding framework

As requested by the Executive Board in 1998 [YUN 1998, p. 825], the UNDP Administrator submitted to the Board's first regular session in January his proposals for a multi-year funding framework [DP/1999/CRP.4]. He explained that the process would include a four-year funding framework, encompassing programme goals, sub-goals, areas for UNDP support, expected outcomes and outputs and a resource framework integrating all financial allocations; a results-oriented annual report (ROAR) (see p. 795) to provide the Board at its second regular session each year with a comprehensive assessment of results and a review of the use of resources; and the MYFF report, containing a more in-depth assessment every four years of performance relating to outcomes and outputs.

MYFF would consist of a strategic results framework and an integrated resource framework. The strategic results framework would provide a broad frame of reference of UNDP development goals in the categories of sustainable human development, poverty eradication and sustainable livelihood, environment, gender, special development situations, UNDP support to the United Nations and management. Within each category, broad goals, sub-goals and strategic areas would be identified to provide a frame of reference for operating units in the definition of outcomes and outputs. The framework would also identify outcomes and outputs at the operating unit level (country office). Each operating unit would define the expected outcomes and outputs to enable an assessment of results achieved. The strategic results framework would provide a frame of reference for the regional bureaux, country offices and other operating units.

The integrated resource framework would relate the overall framework to the allocation of programme, programme support, support to the United Nations and management and administrative costs. Resource allocations would be provided within three broad groupings, consistent with the strategic-results framework—the five programme/thematic categories, UNDP support to the United Nations, and management and administration. Within the programme/thematic category, allocations would be differentiated between least developed countries (LDCs), middle-income countries, net contributor countries and other countries.

The Administrator stated that MYFF represented a major step forward for UNDP since it would for the first time provide a comprehensive framework for assessing results together with an integrated resource framework. It would replace the overall framework provided by the current successor programming arrangements, starting in January 2000. MYFF would lead to a redefinition of budgetary expenditures and provide a mechanism for capturing "soft results", a critical dimension of UNDP's work. The Administrator also presented preliminary proposals for the overall timing and linkages between the funding system and MYFF and ROAR, the April special funding session, the required documentation and the decisions to be taken, emphasizing that MYFF would become the main vehicle for mobilizing core resources for UNDP.

In terms of reporting, ROAR would report on actual performance against expected outcomes and outputs, provide information on the use of resources in each of the seven categories in MYFF and include reference to situational indicators.

The Executive Board, on 29 January [dec. 99/1], reaffirmed the need to reverse the decline in core resources and to place UNDP core funding on a predictable and continuous basis and to reach, as soon as possible, the target of $1.1 billion, while recognizing the risk of over-dependence on a limited number of donors. It also reaffirmed the importance of developing MYFF as an integral element of the funding strategy. It took note of the development of a reporting system comprising an annual ROAR and a four-yearly assessment of MYFF and requested the Administrator to continue to develop MYFF and the reporting system. The Board decided to hold the first funding session in April 1999. It requested all UNDP member States to communicate to the secretariat their voluntary core contributions and a schedule of payments by early April, and the Administrator to provide a record of actual core contributions and payment of government contributions to local office costs. The Administrator should continue to consult with member States on the further development and implementation of MYFF, and submit in 1999 an interim report on the implications of the funding strategy for the funds and programmes associated with UNDP and, in 2000, a report on the proposed timing, format and content of MYFF, including a clear indication of how lessons learned in one MYFF cycle would be fed into the next.

In response to that decision, the Board held the first funding session during its second regular session in April at which the Administrator reported on core funding commitments to UNDP for 1999 and onwards.

On 16 April [dec. 99/7], the Board took note of the Administrator's report with the comments made thereon, including the revised tables setting out commitments/estimates of contributions to UNDP core resources for 1999-2000 and income to UNDP core resources and government local office costs for 1997-1998, as at 30 April 1999; and the schedule of payments confirmed for 1999 commitments to UNDP core resources.

Responding to the Board's January decision, the Administrator submitted in April an interim report on the implications of the funding strategy for UNDP-associated funds and programmes (the United Nations Capital Development Fund (UNCDF), the United Nations Volunteers and UNIFEM) [DP/1999/20]. He stated that UNDP had initiated dialogue with those funds and programmes to ensure that their future programme reporting and budgetary processes would be aligned with the requirement of the funding strategy. While concrete arrangements would be worked out in 1999 to ensure that their reporting of results and resource allocations were integrated in the new UNDP MYFF cycle, due regard needed to be given to the fact that those entities had their own organizational policies and priorities and that their activities were subject to their established business plans and strategies.

On 22 June [dec. 99/14], the Executive Board took note of the interim report.

In August, the Administrator submitted to the Board his proposals for the first MYFF, covering 2000-2003 [DP/1999/30], and the strategic results framework [DP/1999/CRP.12].

In September [dec. 99/23 A], the Executive Board took note of MYFF 2000-2003 and the strategic results framework. It requested the Administrator to develop and refine MYFF as a strategic management tool and to consult with the Board on its further implementation, including the development of indicators for measuring outcomes and results, the scope and content of the reporting system for reporting on results and priority areas of the UNDP mandate, such as eradication of poverty, to define the outcomes and results of UNDP programmes. The Administrator should enable full participation of programme countries in the elaboration, monitoring and reporting of the strategic results framework and submit in 2000 proposals for revising and updating MYFF, indications of how lessons learned from one MYFF would be taken into account in the subsequent cycle, and proposals for the structure and timing of the MYFF report. The Administrator should submit every year an updated resources allocation framework on the basis of a table included in the integrated resources framework presented in the 2000-2003 MYFF; and strategic results and integrated resources frameworks for the funds administered by UNDP, incorporating them into MYFF.

As called for by the Board, the Administrator issued the first ROAR covering 1999 [DP/2000/23/Add.1], which provided a comprehensive picture of where UNDP had focused its efforts and assessed progress made against intended outcomes for each of the six goals covered by MYFF (see p. 806).

Successor programming arrangements

As requested by the Executive Board in 1998 [YUN 1998, p. 827], the Administrator presented in January information on successor programming arrangements [E/1999/35]. He stated that it was imperative that the Board resolve the difficulties that had arisen in applying the approved target for resource assignment from the core (TRAC) distribution model, so that countries could proceed with future programme planning. Of the various options he presented, the Administrator stated that adjusting the gross national product (GNP) per capita breakpoint between low- and middle-income countries from $750 to $900 most closely adhered to the main principles of UNDP's programme resource allocation. That option ensured enhanced focus on low-income and least developed countries where UNDP had always concentrated the bulk of its resources and safeguarded the principle of a gradual move to net contributor country (NCC) status for countries that achieved a higher GNP per capita, since it allowed floor provisions for the middle-income group to be met.

The Administrator underlined the important role that UNDP played in NCCs through the resident coordinator system and participation in self-financed development activities. He expected that involvement to lead to a more significant level of voluntary contributions from NCCs and invited the Board to provide guidance on the issue of NCC thresholds.

On 29 January [dec. 99/2], the Board reaffirmed the basic principles for the allocation of programme resources as outlined in 1995 [YUN 1995, p. 895]: the focus on low-income countries and LDCs; progressivity in favour of low-income countries; and a gradual move to net contributor status and graduation for countries that achieved higher levels of GNP. It adjusted the GNP per capita breakpoint delineating low- and middle-income countries from $750 to $900. Expressing concern that unless there was early attainment of the $1.1 billion target, the focus on low-income countries and LDCs in terms of impact would not be attained, the Board asked the Administrator to propose ways to redress any shortfall in the target. It decided that UNDP should consider NCCs as a separate group of programme countries outside the TRAC distribution model and endorsed the proposal to eliminate the system of reimbursable TRAC earmarkings with effect from 2001, subject to certain provisions, among them that first-time NCCs would continue to receive, for a grace period of three years, a TRAC-1 (TRAC under line 1.1.1 of the budget) calculated at 60 per cent of the earmarking of the previous period. The Board maintained the current GNP per capita thresholds for NCCs at $4,700 and requested the Administrator to proceed with the calculation of TRAC-1 earmarkings, using 1997 or the latest available GNP and population data, and to proceed with programme planning and implementation for 2001-2003. It requested the Administrator to report in 2002 on possible improvements of the current TRAC resource distribution model, including a review of thresholds. The Board endorsed the proposed establishment in all interested NCCs of a locally reimbursed revolving TRAC.

UNDP reported in March on preliminary TRAC-1 and TRAC-2 (budget line 1.1.2) earmarkings for 2001-2003 totalling $1,738.8 million, broken down by category of country and region; preliminary TRAC-1 earmarkings by country for the same period; and TRAC-1 earmarkings for new NCCs for 2001-2003 and reimbursable TRAC-1 for 2000 [DP/1999/27].

On 16 April [dec. 99/7], the Executive Board took note of the preliminary TRAC earmarkings for 2001-2003.

Risk management

The Administrator, in a February report on UNDP financial risk management [DP/1999/5/Rev.1], reviewed the Operational Reserve, established in 1970 to guarantee the financial liquidity and integrity of UNDP [YUN 1970, p. 346], and analysed the nature of the financial risks UNDP faced. The report also defined and discussed the concepts of risk management, liquidity, working capital, the Operational Reserve and other contingency reserves and made recommendations regarding liquidity, working capital and reserve levels.

The Administrator explained that the Operational Reserve was initially established at the level of $150 million, with a shift in policy from full funding to a partial funding system. In 1980 [YUN 1980, p. 587], the then Governing Council established the Reserve for the third programming cycle (1982-1986) at 25 per cent of anticipated contributions and expenditures for each year, which was reduced to 20 per cent in 1990 under a modified formula [YUN 1990, p. 391]. If that formula were retained, the Reserve would be set at $180 million for 1998 and 1999.

By definition, the Operational Reserve was limited to providing reserves for regular resources activities. However, based on trends in the growth of "other resources", particularly cost-sharing and trust funds, which under the Financial Regulations and Rules were required to be fully funded, the Administrator believed that a contingency reserve was also needed for risks associated with those activities. The Operational Reserve should continue to be a reserve for risks associated with regular resources activities.

The most significant financial risks faced by UNDP for regular resources and other resources activities were income related, due to unpredictable fluctuations in contributions pledged from year to year, their variable value as a result of currency exchange rates, and unknown timing of payments of contributions. Other risks related to expenditures, cash and investment assets, liability and business interruption. Based on those risk elements, the Administrator recommended that the formula for the calculation of the Operational Reserve be amended.

The proposed formula would be the sum of the income component (the equivalent of 10 per cent of the average annual voluntary contributions over the most recent three years); the expenditure component (the equivalent of 2 per cent of the average total expenditure over the most recent three years); the liability and structural component (the equivalent of 25 per cent of the sum of the income and expenditure components); and the cash-flow component (the equivalent of cash needed for one month, calculated as one twelfth of total expenditure of the most recent year). Based on the amended formula, the level of the Reserve would be set at $206 million for the current biennium, an increase of $26 million over the current formula. He also recommended the establishment of a reserve for other resources activities of $49 million funded through a transfer from the extrabudgetary account.

In discussing the implication of liquidity for the Operational Reserve, the Administrator believed that UNDP should manage its liquidity to fall within the range of the equivalent of 6 to 12 months' expenditure as a prudent level.

The Advisory Committee on Administrative and Budgetary Questions (ACABQ), in March [DP/1999/26], stated that the Administrator's report did not provide a satisfactory review of actual experience with the risk elements identified, nor did it address adequately the impact that the increase in the Operational Reserve might have on the resources available for programmes. ACABQ agreed with the proposal to establish a reserve for other resources activities at the level of $49 million.

In June [dec. 99/9], the Executive Board supported the establishment of a reserve for other resources activities and the mechanism for its funding. It approved the recommended formula for the calculation of the level of the Operational Reserve for regular resources, annexed to its decision, and decided to reduce the factor used to calculate the liability and structural risk component of the Reserve from 25 per cent of the sum of the income and expenditure components to 10 per cent.

Financing

In his annual review of the financial situation for 1999 [DP/2000/29 & Add.1], the Administrator presented an overview of UNDP's financial condition at the end of 1999, as well as the comparative figures for 1998.

While UNDP continued to attract other resources, the organization was greatly affected by the decline in voluntary contributions. Contributions to UNDP regular resources (i.e., core resources) in 1999 represented 28 per cent of the aggregate contributions received during the year ($2,370 million) compared to 46 per cent in 1995. The report thus emphasized the serious financial crisis that UNDP was facing in its regular resource base. Reductions in voluntary contributions since 1992 had led to continuous erosion of the amount of financial assistance that programme countries received from UNDP through the TRAC system. Tight spending controls in the interests of financial discipline were being introduced to prevent problems of liquidity. The unpredictability in voluntary contributions gave rise to stop-go programming of the kind that MYFF, as a mechanism for more predictable contributions, was designed to avoid.

Compared to 1998, total income, including those of the Special Measures Fund for the Least Developed Countries (SMF/LDC) decreased by 8.4 per cent to $719 million and total expenditure went down by 8 per cent to $811 million. Overall, there was a 49.6 per cent decline in the available resource balance. Voluntary contributions to the regular resources (inclusive of SMF/LDC) fell by 8.6 per cent ($64 million) to $681 million in 1999. Contributions received from the top 15 non-programme country donors (Austria, Canada, Denmark, Finland, France, Germany, Italy, Japan, Netherlands, Norway, Spain, Sweden, Switzerland, United Kingdom, United States) amounted to $1 billion or 96 per cent of total contributions received from non-programme countries, the same level received in the previous two years. As at 31 December 1999, some $38 million in pledges remained unpaid, compared to $21 million at the end of the previous year.

Total expenditure under regular resources declined to $811 million from $882 million in 1998, reflecting an adjustment to the lower level of contributions. Programme expenditures in 1999 decreased by 16.6 per cent to $490 million against $558 million in 1998. Expenditure for nationally executed projects also decreased. The percentage share of programme expenditure among the regions remained stable. The largest regions, Africa and Asia and the Pacific, were severely impacted by the decrease in core resources. Compared to 1998, delivery dropped in the Africa region from $244 million to $206 million and in the Asia and Pacific region from $169 million to $145 million. In the Arab States, there was a significant decrease from $53 million in 1998 to $25 million in 1999. In Europe and CIS, there was a slight decrease from $44 million in 1998 to $41 million in 1999, while in the Latin America and Caribbean region the delivery dropped from $46 million in 1998 to $23 million in 1999.

Programme support to implementing agents increased to $51 million, compared to $38.9 million in 1998, owing to claims of prior years for implementing projects under national execution.

As at 31 December 1999, the balance of unexpended resources for regular resource activities amounted to $107 million, a decline of some 50 per cent compared to $212 million a year earlier. The level of investments for regular resources decreased 77 per cent to $45.5 million from $197 million in 1998, due mainly to the drop in unexpended resources by $105.1 million.

The other resources activities, which comprised mainly government cost-sharing, third-party cost-sharing, government cash counterpart contributions, trust funds, management services agreements and the Junior Professional Officer programme, represented the bulk of all activities managed by UNDP. The overall income and expenditure in 1999 remained stable and the resource balance at the end of the year comprised 85 per cent of UNDP's aggregate resources from all sources. Contributions for government cost-sharing activities decreased by almost 8 per cent to $1.2 billion.

In September [dec. 99/24], the Executive Board noted with concern the continuing and significant decline in core contributions to UNDP, particularly resources available for programme activities, and the impact that such resource shortfalls had on UNDP's capacity to meet the needs of programme countries. The Board requested the Administrator to bring the situation to the attention of the Secretary-General with a view to mobilizing the support of world political leaders to reverse the trend of declining contributions.

In a related decision [dec. 99/25], the Board took note of the Administrator's report on the annual review of the 1998 financial situation [YUN 1998, p. 827].

Audit reports

In January, the Executive Board considered the Administrator's report [DP/1999/3] on follow-up to recommendations of the report of the Board of Auditors for the 1996-1997 biennium [YUN 1998, p. 1288], which provided a tabular summary of recommendations by area of audit, together with the status of follow-up action and target date for implementation. The Administrator said that progress was achieved in many areas and efforts were being made to address outstanding issues.

On 29 January [dec. 99/3], the Board took note of the Administrator's report. In a further report submitted in October [DP/2000/6], the Administrator updated the information provided in his earlier report.

In March [DP/1999/23], the Administrator submitted a report on UNDP internal audit and oversight activities conducted by the UNDP Office of Audit and Performance Review (OAPR) for 1998. OAPR issued 189 audit, investigation and related reports. Some of those were carried out with the UN Office of Internal Oversight Services (OIOS) and the UNICEF internal audit group. In addition, the results of 764 national execution audit reports were evaluated and feedback was provided to country offices. OAPR provided internal audit and related services to 45 of the 134 country offices and five headquarters or functional units during the year. A total of 94 internal audit reports were issued. Of the recommendations made in those reports, 91 per cent were accepted by auditees and were being implemented. Regarding special audits and investigations, 33 new cases were initiated during 1998, ranging from allegations of fraud and serious misconduct to inadequate performance and potential conflicts of interest. Several cases were being dealt with in cooperation with OIOS, including a case involving legal action against two individuals. In the report, the Administrator also commented on six recommendations made by the Joint Inspection Unit in a 1998 report entitled "More coherence for enhanced oversight in the United Nations system" [YUN 1998, p. 1257].

On 22 June [dec. 99/14], the Board took note of the Administrator's report.

Budget estimates 2000-2001

In June [DP/1999/31], the Administrator submitted to the Executive Board the support budget estimates for the 2000-2001 biennium. He proposed a zero nominal growth budget in net terms of $518.2 million, which was $0.3 million less than the budget approved for 1998-1999 [YUN 1997, p. 879]. The Administrator's proposals resulted in a decrease of the gross budget from $590.6 million for 1998-1999 to $585.4 million for 2000-2001.

The proposals incorporated total net reductions of $24.5 million, which included $16.8 million in real reductions and $7.7 million relating to the shift of the allocation for development support services to the programme. The proposals also incorporated a net increase of $19.2 million relating to cost increases. The estimates also took into account more realistic income projections relating to contributions by host country Governments towards local costs of UNDP country presence. Those income projections resulted in a net decrease of $5 million in 2000-2001 compared to the 1998-1999 projections.

In an August report [DP/1999/33], ACABQ recommended that the Executive Board authorize the biennial support budget as proposed by the Administrator, on the understanding that a revised budget would be submitted to the Board after the new Administrator and his Transition Team had completed the review of the UNDP management processes. That review should take into account such matters as charging other resources a fair share for administrative, management and other services provided by UNDP to activities funded by other resources. If little improvement was made in core income, ACABQ believed that a hard look would have to be taken on how to curtail programmes and activities.

In September [E/1999/35 (dec. 99/23)], the Executive Board took note of the report on the support budget for 2000-2001, which was an integral part of the MYFF integrated resources framework. It approved the proposal on programme support for country offices and headquarters, as well as those on government contributions towards local office costs, including the mechanism for calculating such contributions. The Administrator was asked to consult with programme countries on other modalities of meeting local office costs obligations.

The Board approved the proposal on the UN house programme to establish common premises and common services, ensuring that there would be no additional burden on the host countries. It requested the Administrator to consult with the Board as to whether a revised 2000-2001 budget was required.

The Board approved the proposals on the separation reserve (relating to post reductions) amounting to $7 million, $1.5 million for the transitional measures reserve (support to the new Administrator in priority areas), gross appropriations in the amount of $585,371,600 for the biennial support budget, and gross appropriations for the 2000-2001 biennial support budgets of UNCDF, the United Nations Revolving Fund for Natural Resources Exploration and UNIFEM, in the amounts of $13,594,000, $740,000 and $11,612,100, respectively. It requested the Administrator to consult with the Board on cost-recovery practices in the light of the current review by UNDP and any comments provided by ACABQ.

Revision of financial regulations and rules

The Administrator, in a November report [DP/2000/4], submitted to the Executive Board for approval the revised UNDP Financial Regulations and Rules and provided information about the objectives pursued and the process followed during their revision. An annex to the report contained the text of the revised regulations and rules.

The comprehensive revision was intended to reflect the new framework of authority and accountability over financial management arising out of the UNDP 2001 change process (see p. 803), the results of the financial risk assessment completed in 1998 (see p. 808), the impact of the Secretary-General's reform proposals being implemented by UNDP and other necessary adjustments. Substantive changes included both updates incorporated to reflect past decisions made by the Executive Board and policy changes already introduced by the Administrator, as well as new policies for which no clear mandate or policies existed and for which the Administrator was seeking the Board's endorsement. They dealt with such issues as: a new mechanism for voluntary contributions to UNDP regular resources; resource planning frameworks; execution modalities; framing of the delegation of authority within UNDP management; a simplified resource-assignment process for selected countries; cost recovery; NGO execution and payment of execution fees to NGOs; expenditure control; a new procurement framework; the other resources reserve; increased dollar limits on payments; a new type of partnership through grant modality; limited authority to advance regular resources; and authority to establish credit facilities. Once approved, the revisions would be followed by the release of a revised Finance Manual and supported by learning instruments for staff.

Procurement

The Administrator, in his report on the activities of the UNDP Inter-Agency Procurement Services Office (IAPSO) [DP/2000/33], stated that the volume of procurement handled by IAPSO was $71.3 million in 1998 and $66.5 million in 1999, an increase of 15 per cent over the previous biennium. In 1998 and 1999, IAPSO conducted 11 regional procurement training workshops in Armenia, Bolivia, China, Côte d'Ivoire, Kazakhstan, Mozambique, Nepal, Paraguay, Switzerland, Turkey and the United Republic of Tanzania. Those courses covered both local and international procurement and were designed to strengthen local capacity, manage procurement in a cost-effective manner and identify the benefits of effective and transparent procurement. Additional courses were provided by IAPSO in New York, specifically for the staff of UNDP and other UN organizations. It also provided support to UNDP activities under the oil-for-food programme in Iraq (see p. 269) in the order of $5 million, primarily for the procurement of electric power generators, and assisted the United Nations Administration Mission in Kosovo, Federal Republic of Yugoslavia, in setting up procurement procedures and practices and advice and guidance to government ministries. The procurement volume in 1999 was some $5 million.

In 1999, IAPSO undertook a survey of clients to assess the specific needs of the various client groups, determine the quality of service it provided and identify additional requirements from its clients. The survey found that there was a considerable lack of awareness among potential clients regarding the range of services offered by IAPSO. Those clients aware of the services offered in the traditional hard-copy catalogues indicated that its services were not always available when required. To address those issues, IAPSO improved services by providing on-line access to collective price agreements. Details of all products available under those agreements were posted on the IAPSO web site and IAPSO currently had Internet catalogues available for motor vehicles, office equipment and software.

On 17 September [dec. 99/25], the Executive Board took note of the 1998 statistical report [YUN 1998, p. 829], including procurement of goods and services.

Other technical cooperation

UN activities

The UNDP Administrator provided information on UN system technical cooperation expenditure for 1999 [DP/2000/39] provided by UNDP, the executing and specialized agencies, UNFPA,

UNICEF and WFP, but excluding the World Bank/ International Development Association.

In 1999, technical cooperation expenditure reached $6 billion, up 5.8 per cent from $5.7 billion in 1998.

UNDP remained the largest source for technical cooperation, with its share standing at 34 per cent in 1999, slightly lower than the 37.6 per cent reached in 1998. UNDP disbursed $2,044 million in technical cooperation in 1999, a decrease of 4.1 per cent from 1998. That was the first contraction of overall expenditure from UNDP since 1993. Expenditure by WFP, after contracting from 1993 to 1997, recovered in 1998 and 1999; both years experienced growth of over 15 per cent, reaching $1,431 million in 1999. Six countries (Angola, Ethiopia, Rwanda, Democratic People's Republic of Korea, Federal Republic of Yugoslavia (FRY), Sudan) absorbed 55 per cent of the value of all assistance supplied by WFP in 1999. Seven other countries received over $25 million in assistance (Afghanistan, Bangladesh, China, India, Kenya, Liberia, Nicaragua).

The executing and specialized agencies' expenditure rose 5.6 per cent in 1999 to $1,525 million, providing about a quarter of total technical cooperation expenditure. Of the 23 contributing agencies, WHO and the Food and Agriculture Organization of the United Nations were jointly responsible for 30 per cent of the expenditure. Four other agencies provided significant amounts of technical cooperation expenditure: the United Nations Educational, Scientific and Cultural Organization, the International Labour Organization, the United Nations Industrial Development Organization and the United Nations Centre for Human Settlements.

On 17 September [dec. 99/25], the Executive Board took note of the Administrator's report on UN system technical cooperation expenditure in 1998 [YUN 1998, p. 830].

DESA activities

The Department of Economic and Social Affairs (DESA)—responsible for UN technical cooperation activities—had more than 1,100 technical cooperation projects under execution during 1999 in a dozen sectors, with a total project expenditure of some $67.3 million. Projects financed by UNDP represented $43.4 million; those by trust funds, $21.6 million; and those by UNFPA, $2.3 million.

On a geographical basis, the DESA-executed programme included expenditures of $25.1 million in the Middle East, $17.6 million in interregional and global programmes, $15.6 million in Africa, $5.7 million in Asia and the Pacific, $1.8 million in Europe and $1.5 million in the Americas. Project delivery in the Middle East, which included expenditures of $17.6 million for the Iraq Programme, was the largest, with a 37 per cent share of total delivery.

Distribution of expenditure by substantive sectors was as follows: energy, $21.1 million; economic policy, $14 million; Associate Expert Programme, $13.4 million; public administration, $6.2 million; water, $4.2 million; statistics, $2.5 million; social policy, $2 million; infrastructure, $1.9 million; minerals, $0.6 million; programme support, $0.5 million; public finance, $0.5 million; and advancement of women, $0.4 million. Of the total delivery of $67.3 million, energy (including the Iraq Programme) comprised 31 per cent, economic policy, 21 per cent, and the Associate Expert Programme, 20 per cent.

On a component basis, DESA delivery in 1999 included $38.8 million for project personnel, $15.4 million for equipment, $8 million for subcontracts, $3.5 million for training and $1.6 million for miscellaneous expenses.

UN Office for Project Services

The United Nations Office for Project Services (UNOPS) continued to respond to specific demands of the UN system for project services, ranging from the management of multidisciplinary projects to specialized services in implementation of project components. In 1999, UNOPS fulfilled its financial targets as set in the 1999-2000 UNOPS Business Plan, operating in accordance with the self-financing principle with no assessed budget funding.

1999 activities

The UNOPS Executive Director, in his annual report to the Executive Board for 1999 [DP/2000/25], said that the 1999-2000 Business Plan established the targets against which performance was assessed in the report.

The targets for delivery were set at $807 million for 1999, $550 million for the project portfolio and $257 million in authorized disbursements on the services only portfolio. Total delivery for the year stood at $764 million, comprising $568 million in expenditures on the project portfolio and $196 million in disbursement authorizations processed for IFAD-funded projects, under the services only portfolio. That represented an overall increase of 7 per cent in 1999 over the previous year. Projects under national execution continued an upward trend in 1999, although sharply less than in 1998. Delivery within projects under national execution reached $39.4 million in 1999, compared to $44.8 million in 1998. Projects funded from UNDP core resources decreased, by $111 million or 36 per cent as compared to the previous year. New projects funded by the UNDP trust funds and UNDP-administered funds acquired in 1999 returned close to the 1997 value. However, new acquired management services agreements, under arrangements signed by UNDP with international financial institutions, grew from $50 million in 1998 to $73 million in 1999, including a new project in Tajikistan utilizing loan resources from the Asian Development Bank. In the services only sector, the total value of new projects funded by IFAD and assigned to UNOPS supervision and loan administration in 1999 increased by 129 per cent, from $284 million in 1998 to $652 million in 1999. In total, the portfolio acquisition with clients other than UNDP more than doubled, rising from nearly $49 million in 1998 to $101 million in 1999. The value of the total UNOPS portfolio grew from $3.5 billion in 1998 to $3.7 billion in 1999, an increase of 5.7 per cent, of which $566 million was in new acquisitions for the project portfolio and $652 million for the services only portfolio.

While the target for income was set at $51.1 million, actual UNOPS income for 1999 amounted to $51.5 million distributed as follows: $43 million came from delivery of the project portfolio, $5.8 million from loan-administration and project-supervision services, and $2.7 million in other income. Income derived from sources other than UNDP rose from over $8 million in 1998, or 16 per cent of total income, to $11 million in 1999, or 21 per cent of total UNOPS income.

Recurrent administrative expenditure, projected at $48.1 million for 1999, stood at $48.6 million by the end of the year, while non-recurring expenditure stood at $16.7 million. The gap between total income and total administrative expenditure had required a drawdown from the operational reserve in the amount of $13.8 million. The amount paid by UNOPS to UNDP for all central services fell to $2.8 million in 1999.

The Executive Director reported that UNOPS financial performance in 1999 came close to the targets that had been set for the year in the 1999-2000 Business Plan. Due to the high value of the new services only portfolio acquired in 1999, the $1 billion mark for acquisition was crossed again, and the $700 million mark for delivery and the 100 per cent for the income target were surpassed again.

UNOPS activities in 1999 included the management of mine-action projects on behalf of the Department of Peacekeeping Operations (DPKO), the Office of the Iraq Programme and UNDP. In Kosovo province of FRY, UNOPS used its implementation model to help to orchestrate mine action through the establishment and operation of the United Nations Mine Action Coordinating Centre. Acting on behalf of a number of clients such as UNDP, DPKO, the Department of Political Affairs, the Office for the Coordination of Humanitarian Affairs and the Office of the United Nations High Commissioner for Refugees (UNHCR), UNOPS provided a variety of management and other services to more than 20 countries in post-conflict situations. Specialized management services were provided to support modernization and strengthening of democratic processes, for example, in organizing elections, recruitment of experienced parliamentarians and jurists to advise legislators, and the procurement of software to track cases in the courts. UNOPS took over the supervision of 14 agricultural investment projects, at IFAD's request, in addition to 44 new projects already planned for assignment to UNOPS in 1999. The portfolio of IFAD-funded projects under UNOPS supervision and related loan administration amounted to over $2.2 billion at the end of 1999.

UNOPS provided support to UNDP-funded projects in Asia. For community-based poverty-alleviation programmes, the UNOPS approach was to improve project delivery and performance, as well as national capacity in project design and management. In other cases, such as in Bangladesh, where UNOPS implemented the nationally executed parliament- and governance-related programmes, UNOPS provided an operational management support package that ensured government substantive ownership of project processes and results. In other situations, UNOPS provided customized procurement services, particularly when complex international or national bidding processes were required.

The Executive Board, on 22 June [E/1999/35 (dec. 99/12)], took note of the 1998 annual report of the UNOPS Executive Director [YUN 1998, p. 831]. The Board took note of the ongoing evaluation by UNDP of the UNDP/UNOPS relationship to be submitted in 2000, and requested the Administrator to ensure that UNOPS was fully consulted in that process. The Board requested the UNOPS Executive Director, in collaboration with the Administrator, to present in 1999 a proposal on UNOPS's responsibility in personnel matters (see p. 815).

Comments on JIU report. The UNOPS Executive Director, in an April report [DP/1999/25], submitted his comments on the JIU review of UNOPS activities for 1997 and 1998 entitled "UNOPS: Broader engagement with UN system organizations" [YUN 1998, p. 832]. According to the Executive Director, in his comments on the JIU recommendations, UNOPS welcomed the overall focus of the report, which it found to be supportive of the intent of the Secretary-General and the Executive Board to build an effective division of labour between itself and the other organizations and agencies of the United Nations. UNOPS viewed the JIU report as a constructive addition to the dialogue on how to move forward on the objectives of offering its services to a wider range of UN system clients and endeavouring to find ways of making better use of the expertise available in other organizations, as called for in the report.

On 22 June [dec. 99/14], the Executive Board took note of the Executive Director's report.

Budget estimates

The Executive Director, in July [DP/1999/39], issued revised 1998-1999 budget estimates and 2000-2001 budget estimates for UNOPS. The revised 1998-1999 budget estimates proposed a decrease from $89.6 million to $88.5 million for recurring activities and an increase from $11.4 million to $14 million for extraordinary, non-recurring activities. The budget estimates for 2000-2001 included a total of $110.9 million for recurring activities (mainly personnel costs) and $2.9 million for non-recurring activities. The budget estimates were based on the expectation that UNOPS would continue to operate in accordance with the self-financing principle for recurring expenditures and that extraordinary, non-recurring expenditures would be funded by the UNOPS operational reserve if income generated during 1999 or the 2000-2001 biennium was insufficient.

The revised budget was based on actual delivery and income performance in 1998 and on the projections of operations divisions as put forward in the business planning process for 1999. In planning for project delivery and income, account was taken of the estimated impact on overall UNOPS performance resulting from relocation of headquarters, as well as the systems projects for implementing the Integrated Management Information System (IMIS) and upgrades to the computer system due to year 2000 computer compliance (Y2K) problems. The portfolio, delivery and income for 2000-2001 were based on the targets of the divisional business plans. The projected delivery of $620 million in 2000 was $70 million higher (13 per cent) than the projection for 1999. It would support the expansion of staff (36 additional posts) and increases in related administrative expenditures. In 2000, it was anticipated that total income would again cover all UNOPS recurring expenditures and make a significant contribution towards covering non-recurring expenditures. Projections for 2001 indicated an amount of income over expenditure, which would be the first step towards rebuilding the UNOPS reserve to its required level.

ACABQ, in an August report [DP/1999/41], recommended that the Executive Board accept the Executive Director's proposals.

In September [dec. 99/15], the Executive Board approved the 1998-1999 revised budget in the amount of $102.6 million and the 2000-2001 budget estimates of $113.8 million. The Board also approved the staffing level as proposed for 1998-1999, including the relocation of four posts from New York to Rome and one post from New York to Geneva, and the establishment of the post of Chief of the Division for Special Programme Development at the D-1 level.

Operational reserve

The Executive Director, as requested by the Board in 1997 [YUN 1997, p. 885], reported in July [DP/1999/40] on the level of the operational reserve established at 4 per cent of the combined expenditure on administrative and project budgets of the previous year. Due to exceptional circumstances in 1998 and 1999 (headquarters relocation, Y2K compliance, implementation of IMIS), it was projected that drawdowns from the operational reserve of $9.5 million in 1999 and $1.5 million in 2000 would be necessary. The Executive Director expected that restoration of the reserve to the prescribed level would begin in 2001 and would be completed in the 2002-2003 biennium. While sharing the concern that the 4 per cent level of the reserve might be too low, he said that once the operational reserve was restored, an analysis of the appropriateness of that reserve level would be a meaningful exercise in 2003. In the meantime, he proposed that the current reserve level remain in effect through the current and next bienniums.

The Executive Director, in his revised 1998-1999 budget and proposed 2000-2001 budget estimates [DP/1999/39], stated that, in the approved budget for 1998-1999, it was anticipated that the operational reserve would be reduced to $11.2 million, or 2 per cent of the delivery and income of the prior year, but by July 1999 the projected balance of the reserve by the end of the year was $19.9 million, or a reserve rate of 3.25 per cent. For 2000, the reserve was expected to be reduced to $18.4 million, while at the end of 2001, it was forecast at $22.6 million, or 3.1 per cent.

ACABQ, in August [DP/1999/41], recommended that the Executive Board accept the Executive Director's proposal.

The Executive Board, in September [dec. 99/16], took note of the Executive Director's report on the operational reserve and decided that the level and rate of replenishment of the reserve established in 1997 remained in effect through the 1998-1999 and 2000-2001 bienniums. It requested the Executive Director to submit in 2001 a report on the appropriateness of that level.

Audit reports

In March [DP/1999/24], the Executive Director reported to the Executive Board on follow-up to recommendations by the Board of Auditors contained in the UNOPS financial report and audited financial statements for the 1996-1997 biennium [A/53/5/Add.10]. Those recommendations covered areas such as procurement procedures, receipt and inspection reports, evaluation of consultants by measurable objectives, staff appraisal, financial reporting, year 2000 compliance and a process for reporting fraud. The Executive Director described efforts to implement the recommendations and said that those efforts to address all issues continued.

In April [DP/1999/22/Add.2], the Executive Director issued his annual report on internal oversight of UNOPS activities. The oversight framework included an external audit performed by the UN Board of Auditors; an internal audit performed by the UNDP Office of Audit and Performance Review (OAPR) under an agreement between the two organizations; and internal management oversight.

OAPR conducted audits and management reviews of both headquarters and field activities. A report on UNOPS administration of the activities of limited duration contractual mechanism was also completed. Three cases relating to alleged conflict of interest and one case of attempt to defraud were reviewed. In 1998, a total of 33 audit reports were issued. Of the 289 recommendations contained in those reports, 115 were in the area of finance, 25 in personnel, 41 in administration (including contracts and procurement), 45 in programme and 63 in management. UNOPS agreed with 273 of the recommendations and provided its response on the action taken or contemplated to implement them.

Major issues identified in the audit reports included: weaknesses in the overall managerial oversight of some projects that contributed to serious shortcomings in project operations; the need to reassess procedures for reviewing and approving implementation of sub-project activities by government entities, taking into consideration the potential added value of those arrangements; shortcomings in the approval and management of micro-projects in one of the "Africa 2000 Network" projects; and the need to strengthen the guidelines on imprest account operations and the timely submission of the monthly imprest accounts to headquarters. UNOPS continued to address the issues raised.

On 22 June [dec. 99/14], the Executive Board took note of the Executive Director's report on follow-up to the recommendations of the Board of Auditors and requested him to provide in 2000 an updated overview of the implementation of those recommendations. It also took note of the UNOPS internal oversight report.

Personnel matters

In June [dec. 99/12], the Executive Board, recognizing that changes in the current UNOPS personnel regime were necessary, requested the UNOPS Executive Director, in collaboration with the UNDP Administrator and in consultation with all interested parties on all relevant legal, budgetary, staff and policy implications, to present a proposal on UNOPS responsibility in personnel matters, as envisioned in its 1994 decisions on the delegation of authority in the areas of personnel [YUN 1994, p. 806].

In response to that request, the Executive Director issued a report on the subject in July [DP/1999/38]. He recalled that in the 1994 proposals establishing UNOPS as a separate entity, the basic framework of UNOPS personnel arrangements were outlined. It provided for authority in all personnel matters, except those retained by the Secretary-General, to be vested in the Executive Director. It was also brought to the attention of the Executive Board at that time that additional proposals intended to further the UNOPS ability to respond to evolving client needs would be submitted for approval in due course. The Executive Director was, therefore, asking the Executive Board to endorse his request that the delegation of authority in personnel matters be issued by the Secretary-General to UNOPS, including the authority for UNOPS to issue its own letters of appointment.

A new delegation of authority would cover the administration of the UN Staff Regulations and Rules in respect of UNOPS staff members, and would formalize many functions already carried out by UNOPS, allocating the authority and accountability directly to the Executive Director. Specifically, the Executive Director would be authorized to appoint, promote and terminate appointments of staff members. Since approximately one third of the volume of UNOPS services related to the hiring of individuals, either as independent contractors or as staff members, it was essential for UNOPS to be able to develop a dedicated personnel regime, involving changes to the current arrangements. It was anticipated that the proposed dedicated personnel regime, established within the framework of the UN system, would provide for a single, comprehensive system of personnel authority and accountability, covering all categories of personnel. Annexed to the report were the legislative and institutional grounds on which the personnel regime would be based, as well as operational modalities under which the Executive Director would exercise his authority.

In September [dec. 99/17], the Board reaffirmed that appropriate authority and accountability for personnel matters should be vested in the Executive Director, including the authority to issue UNOPS letters of appointment. As a first step, the UNDP Administrator would delegate to the Executive Director authority to issue letters of appointment and to administer the staff in accordance with the UN Staff Regulations and Rules. The Executive Director was requested to report to the Board in 2000 on implementation of its decision.

UN Volunteers

The United Nations Volunteers (UNV) programme, administered by UNDP, continued to grow, reflecting its ability to respond to the changing global environment. The number of volunteers increased from 3,643 in 1998 to 4,383 in 1999, an increase of more than 20 per cent, comprising 141 nationalities serving in 148 countries. The number of assignments carried out also increased, by 17.5 per cent to 4,755, compared to 4,047 in 1998.

The UNDP Administrator, in a report to the Executive Board [DP/2000/24], provided an overview of the key features and achievements of the programme during 1998-1999. With UNDP's introduction of the first multi-year funding framework (see p. 806), including SRF, a part of the results-based management was put in place. For UNV, the framework provided an instrument through which it could provide a clear picture of the areas, outcomes and results to which the UNV programme and the volunteers contributed.

The 1998-1999 review of programme activities was presented along the main categories of generic outcomes and related goals that were identified in the corporate SRF of UNDP (see p. 806). Thirty per cent of all UNV assignments supported activities in promoting sustainable human development, including strengthening, at the community level, key governance institutions and supporting decentralization processes, as well as assisting in electoral exercises. A total of 861 volunteers assisted in elections in Cambodia, the Central African Republic, East Timor, Haiti, Indonesia, Mozambique, Nepal, the Niger, Nigeria and South Africa. At the request of DPKO, 500 UNVs were mobilized to support the United Nations Assistance Mission in East Timor. In Kyrgyzstan, UNVs contributed to the decentralization process by strengthening local planning and project-implementation capacity, increasing access to information and improving resource allocation to communities.

UNV regional activities included strengthening institutional capacity for governance. In Central America and the Caribbean, UNV collaborated with UNICEF and local partners to implement the Convention of the Rights of the Child, adopted by General Assembly resolution 44/25 [YUN 1989, p. 561], by drafting new national legislation on the Child and Adolescent Code and, where such a code existed, assisting in its implementation. Issues of concern, such as child labour and sexual exploitation, the juvenile criminal justice system and national registry, were addressed through local, national and regional networks established with UNV involvement. In Peru, national UNVs contributed to strengthening human rights institutions by dealing with complaints and requests for intervention and mediation, acted on undue delays in court processes, set up education programmes for human rights and mounted public information campaigns.

In poverty eradication and sustainable livelihoods, some 30 per cent of UNV assignments were carried out in over 40 countries. Activities included baseline surveys of poverty levels, linking communities and institutions at intermediate and national levels, disseminating information on services, assisting in the management of natural resources, and providing access to micro-credit. Support was provided to women's agricultural centres in rural areas in Yemen, national volunteer organizations dealing with poverty eradication were strengthened in Mali, and indigenous communities in Ecuador were assisted through environmental management and the establishment of micro-enterprises. With other partners, UNV supported community efforts in responding to the HIV/AIDS epidemic. Efforts were also made to promote employment and foster skills among youth. In collaboration with UNDP, UNV initiated a project in Egypt to assist "information poor" communities by providing access to information technologies and connectivity to the Internet.

UNV support to countries in special development situations encompassed peace-building and reconciliation, and humanitarian and emergency operations, as well as relief activities linked to rehabilitation and reconstruction. During 1998-1999, 34 per cent of UNV assignments related to those areas. Specific activities in support of relief operations included assistance and protection of refugees and internally displaced persons, human rights monitoring, field coordination, food distribution and logistics. UNV was involved in humanitarian and relief operations in over 60 countries, the largest being in the Balkans, the Great Lakes region and the Horn of Africa. With UNHCR, UNVs were engaged in all aspects of refugee assistance and, with WFP, in food distribution. UNVs also supported UNICEF and WHO in emergency activities, particularly focusing on children and health. In response to hurricane Mitch, which hit Central America in late 1998 (see p. 868), UNV mobilized volunteers for emergency operations in Honduras, Nicaragua and El Salvador. UNVs in Georgia assisted in building up national capacity for conflict resolution through training representatives of civil society groups and supported local NGOs in establishing links with international bodies. In Kosovo, UNV mobilized volunteer civil administration support officers to work in such areas as rehabilitation, regional and municipal administration and civil registration.

In a report on the review of the financial situation in 1999 [DP/2000/29], the UNDP Administrator stated that direct contributions to the UNV programmme, including the Special Voluntary Fund, increased slightly in 1999 ($21.3 million) compared to 1998 ($17.6 million). Programme expenditure increased significantly, $23.9 million, compared to $19.8 million in 1998.

UNV, the designated focal point for the International Year of Volunteers, 2001, as proclaimed by the General Assembly in resolution 52/17 [YUN 1997, p. 889], continued work to ensure that the Year was successful in terms of global coverage and impact. A team was assembled in UNV headquarters in Bonn, Germany, to assist in preparations.

The ACC Consultative Committee on Programme and Operational Questions, at its fifteenth session (New York, 21-24 September) [ACC/1999/15], approved, on behalf of ACC, the ACC guidance note on the UN system and International Year of Volunteers, 2001. ACC recommended that UN system organizations should review the involvement of volunteers in their activities, as well as their priorities and procedures towards the use of that resource; and consider the activities they might wish to undertake in 2001 to mark the Year to enhance the involvement of volunteers in their work. The resident coordinator system in all member countries should explore ways of associating the United Nations collectively and through the sectoral perspectives of individual agencies in the work of national committees, steering groups, or whatever structure might be put in place for preparing for and implementing the Year at the country level. That should be specifically geared to determining how UN organizations and volunteer groups could enhance their partnership to mutual benefit.

Economic and technical cooperation among developing countries

The UNDP Administrator reported in April on the activities supported by the Special Unit for Technical Cooperation among Developing Countries (TCDC) [DP/1999/21] with the resources provided by the Executive Board for the 1997-1998 period. The report highlighted the Unit's role in fostering South-South exchanges of expertise and practical experiences, policy dialogue and partnership-building, the broadening of South-South channels of communication, including Internet connectivity, the sharing of best practices to achieve sustainable human development, and efforts to promote policy coherence and a coordinated approach to TCDC in the UN system.

Introducing the report to the Executive Board, the Associate Administrator noted that the Board had allocated 0.5 per cent of its core resources (approximately $15 million) for the programming period 1997-2000 to the Special Unit.

In June [E/1999/35 (dec. 99/11)], the Executive Board took note of the report and requested the Administrator to prepare a report to enable the Board to respond, in the context of the MYFF and the United Nations Development Assistance Framework (UNDAF) processes when the budget was being discussed in 2000, to the General Assembly's request in resolution 53/192 [YUN 1998, p. 802] for a review of the allocation of resources for TCDC activities, taking into account the Special Unit's mandate.

High-level Committee on TCDC

The High-level Committee on the Review of Technical Cooperation among Developing Countries, at its eleventh session (New York, 1-4 June) [A/54/39], reviewed progress in implementing the 1978 Buenos Aires Plan of Action for Promoting and Implementing TCDC [YUN 1978, p. 467], the decisions of the Committee and the recommendations of the South Commission [TCDC/11/1]. It also considered progress made in the implementation of the new directions strategy for TCDC [TCDC/11/2] and reports of the UNDP Administrator on implementation of the guidelines for the review of policies and procedures by the UN development system concerning TCDC and on organizational and supportive arrangements for TCDC [TCDC/11/3].

The Committee adopted three substantive decisions. In the first [A/54/39 (dec. 11/1 A)], the Committee urged developing countries to continue to elaborate national policies and strategies for TCDC, to establish national TCDC focal points and, where they had been established, to ensure their effective and efficient functioning. It stressed the need for UN organizations and agencies to integrate further TCDC into their programmes, policies and procedures. The Committee invited the international community to increase financial resources for increased interregional TCDC by both developing countries and the UN system and urged international organizations and donor countries to increase the use of the TCDC modality and financial and other support for TCDC activities. The Committee requested the UNDP Administrator to submit to the Committee's twelfth (2001) session a comprehensive biennial report on the progress made in implementing the Buenos Aires Plan of Action, as well as on the implementation of the current de cision.

In the second decision [dec. 11/1 B], the Committee recognized that progress had been made by Member States and UN organizations in implementing the new directions strategy for TCDC, and commended the Special Unit for TCDC for orienting its activities in line with that strategy. It recognized that further progress could be achieved through the availability of adequate resources, strengthening participating institutions and enhancing awareness of and the commitment to the TCDC modality. It stressed the need for additional financial resources to assist the Special Unit to further implement and operationalize the strategy. The Committee requested the UN organizations to improve the incorporation of TCDC into their programmes and projects and to mainstream the TCDC modality, including through support to the Special Unit's activities. The Committee welcomed the broad criteria, highlighted in the report on progress made in implementing the new directions strategy, for identifying future pivotal countries, and requested the Special Unit to refine those criteria for wider application. The Committee urged countries to contribute to the Trust Fund for South-South Cooperation and the Perez-Guerrero Trust Fund for Economic and Technical Cooperation among Developing Countries, and requested the Special Unit to report on the management and use of the former. The Special Unit should also document and disseminate information on efforts to utilize TCDC and economic cooperation among developing countries (ECDC), as well as on triangular cooperation arrangements to encourage greater use of such cooperation modality. The Committee welcomed the launching of the TCDC home page by some developing countries, as well as the Special Unit's expansion of the Information Referral System into a multidimensional web of information for development, and, in that regard, encouraged the Special Unit to establish focal points of developing countries. The Special Unit should ensure implementation of the new directions strategy in Africa. The UNDP Administrator was asked to ensure that the Special Unit's separate identity within UNDP was maintained, and to include in his biennial report to the Committee at its twelfth session information on progress made in implementing the new directions strategy for TCDC, with emphasis on implementing the current decision.

In its decision on the overall framework for the promotion and application of TCDC [dec. 11/2], the Committee decided to review the revised Guidelines for the Review of Policies and Procedures concerning Technical Cooperation among Developing Countries, which had been applied on an experimental basis since 1993 and revised in 1997 [YUN 1997, p. 891]. The Committee stressed that South-South cooperation, including TCDC/ECDC, offered viable opportunities for the development of developing countries, and recalled the General Assembly's request in resolution 53/192 for a review of, and possible increase in, allocation of resources by funds and programmes for TCDC activities. The UNDP Administrator was requested to ensure that the Special Unit, in view of its increasing responsibilities, was adequately staffed, and to report on the implementation of the decision to the Committee at its twelfth session.

The Economic and Social Council, by **decision 1999/221** of 23 July, and the General Assembly, by **decision 54/448** of 22 December, took note of the report of the High-level Committee on its eleventh session.

South-South cooperation

The Secretary-General, in response to the General Assembly's request in resolution 52/205 [YUN 1997, p. 892], reported in October on the state of South-South cooperation [A/54/425]. The report reviewed recent developments and trends in South-South cooperation, with particular attention to regional and subregional cooperation, trade, investment and finance, industry, technology and enterprise development. Multilateral system support to South-South cooperation was also examined to the extent that it had contributed to broadening global partnerships and enhancing collective capacities and knowledge networking for such cooperation.

The report noted that the new economic environment was marked by globalization and the integration of the world market fuelled by liberalization and technological advancement. Rapid international mobility of factors of production, except labour, was taking place. However, there remained enormous disparities in experiences across countries and regions.

To deal with the challenges of globalization, many developing countries had embarked on bold economic reforms, liberalized trade, eliminated or reduced price controls, cut down State interventions and brought inflation under control, thus leading to a convergence of economic policies among them. In that context, South-South cooperation, premised on the need for developing countries to strengthen collective and individual capacities to deal with the opportunities and challenges of globalization, was pursued through trade expansion, investment diversification, industrial complementation and technology transfer. South-South cooperation had gained new momentum and developing countries were increasingly exploiting special links derived from shared resources, geographic proximity and cultural and economic convergence, as well as improved transport and communication links. Regional and subregional cooperation arrangements had increased from 39 in the 1970s to 82 by 1996. New cooperation arrangements had been formed and existing cooperation arrangements had experienced an upsurge in activity, contributing to increased South-South cooperation in trade, investment and finance, and providing new scope for cooperation in industry, technology and enterprise development. South-South investment and financial flows had also increased, especially in the Asian and Latin American regions. Despite such progress, the lack of adequate funding for South-South cooperation remained a formidable challenge.

The UN development system continued to support South-South cooperation, particularly through strengthening broad-based partnerships for such cooperation, enhancing the collective capacities of developing countries, facilitating the South-South information flow, and integrating South-South cooperation into operational activities. Orienting operational activities for development towards the support of South-South cooperation constituted an important element of the UN development system strategy. While progress had been registered in recent years, more efforts were needed to increase the level of financial support for such cooperation. Senior managers at headquarters and country levels should be oriented to supporting South-South cooperation while UNDAF, the UNDP regional and country frameworks and the regular technical assistance programmes of all UN organization and agencies, including the regional commissions, should give concrete expression to the support of collaborative initiatives among developing countries.

The Secretary-General concluded that while external support remained crucial and needed to be increased, the realization of the full potential of such cooperation depended largely on the South's own efforts. In that regard, he suggested that more efforts be made to strengthen the collective self-reliance of the South. Regional and subregional economic arrangements should seek regional integration more rapidly, and develop and coordinate common positions on global economic issues and be transformed into strong platforms of common interest; their bargaining capacity through the building and consolidation of regional and global organizations and the support of Southern think tanks should be strengthened. Innovative regional mechanisms for dealing with financial and monetary matters should be explored to attract external capital flows, provide early warning of financial crisis, mobilize international rescue operations and formulate structural adjustment programmes suited to the economic and financial systems and social conditions of the countries concerned. The international community, and especially the multilateral system, should work together to develop and support more results-oriented and self-sustaining South-South initiatives.

The issue of South-South cooperation was addressed by the twenty-third annual meeting of the Foreign Ministers of the Group of 77 (New York, 24 September) in a declaration forwarded to the General Assembly on 29 September by Guyana [A/54/432].

GENERAL ASSEMBLY ACTION

On 22 December [meeting 87], the General Assembly, on the recommendation of the Second (Economic and Financial) Committee [A/54/589], adopted **resolution 54/226** without vote [agenda item 101 *(b)*].

Economic and technical cooperation among developing countries

The General Assembly,

Stressing that South-South cooperation, as an important element of international cooperation for development, offers viable opportunities for developing countries in their individual and collective pursuit of sustained economic growth and sustainable development in accordance with relevant General Assembly resolutions and recent United Nations conferences and for ensuring their effective and meaningful participation in the newly emerging global economic system,

Recognizing the fact that developing countries have the primary responsibility for promoting and implementing economic and technical cooperation among themselves, and reiterating the need for the international community to support the efforts of the developing countries to expand South-South cooperation through the modality of economic and technical cooperation among developing countries,

Reaffirming its resolutions 33/134 of 19 December 1978, in which it endorsed the Buenos Aires Plan of Action for Promoting and Implementing Technical Cooperation among Developing Countries, 46/159 of 19 December 1991 on technical cooperation among developing countries, 49/96 of 19 December 1994 on a United Nations conference on South-South cooperation and 50/119 of 20 December 1995 and 52/205 of 18 December 1997 on economic and technical cooperation among developing countries and a United Nations conference on South-South cooperation, as well as other relevant resolutions of the General Assembly and the Economic and Social Council on economic and technical cooperation among developing countries,

Welcoming the San José Declaration and Plan of Action adopted by the Group of 77 at the South South Conference on Trade, Investment and Finance, held at San José from 13 to 15 January 1997, which outlined concrete modalities on sectoral issues relating to trade, finance and investment and enterprise cooperation,

Taking note of the Ministerial Declaration on the South Summit adopted by the Ministers for Foreign Affairs of the Group of 77 at their twenty-third annual meeting, held in New York on 24 September 1999, in which the increased importance and relevance of South-South cooperation was emphasized,

Recognizing the important contribution that the forthcoming South Summit, to be held at Havana in April 2000, could provide for the strengthening of South-South cooperation,

1. *Endorses* the report of the High-level Committee on the Review of Technical Cooperation among Developing Countries on its eleventh session and the decisions adopted by the High-level Committee at that session;

2. *Takes note with appreciation* of the report of the Secretary-General on the state of South-South cooperation;

3. *Reiterates* that South-South cooperation should be viewed not as a substitute for but rather as a complement to North-South cooperation, and in that connection emphasizes the need to promote effectively, inter alia, triangular approaches to facilitate South-South programmes and projects;

4. *Recognizes* the significant role of economic and technical cooperation between developing countries and countries with economies in transition in promoting implementation of South-South programmes and projects;

5. *Welcomes* the significant increase in South-South cooperation among developing countries, both in number and in sectoral coverage, reported by developing countries and the United Nations system;

6. *Notes with appreciation* the recent expansion in the scope of economic cooperation among developing countries, with increasing cooperation among business sectors and enterprises in different countries, including through the Trade Point Programme of the United Nations Conference on Trade and Development, the buyers and sellers meetings of the International Trade Centre and the business forums and Enterprise Forums of the International Labour Organization, and encourages those United Nations organizations to document and to disseminate their experiences, lessons and operational methodologies for future application;

7. *Also notes with appreciation* the growing economic cooperation among developing countries with increasing mutual trade and investment, as well as industrial and technical cooperation, including in the context of small and medium-sized enterprises;

8. *Welcomes* the successful conclusion of the second round of negotiations on the Global System of Trade Preferences among Developing Countries, and invites participating countries to join in efforts towards deepening, accelerating and expanding the Global System to enhance its impact;

9. *Recognizes* the progress achieved in a number of developing countries in strengthening human and institutional capacities, inter alia, in such areas as education, health, biotechnology, information and communications technology, space technology, financial sector management and microfinance, the sharing of which would be beneficial to enhancing growth and development in other developing countries, and urges the international community, particularly bilateral and multilateral donors, to continue to assist the capacity-building efforts of developing countries in these areas;

10. *Notes with appreciation* the growing number of developed countries participating in triangular cooperation, encourages the use of such cooperation by other countries, and in this context requests the Special Unit for Technical Cooperation among Developing Countries of the United Nations Development Programme, in collaboration with the countries that have been supporting such cooperation, to seek innovative ways to document and disseminate relevant lessons learned on the basis of progress achieved and problems encountered and to identify options for the exploitation of the full potential of such cooperation;

11. *Also notes with appreciation* the contribution made by some countries to the Voluntary Trust Fund for the Promotion of South-South Cooperation and to the Perez-Guerrero Trust Fund for Economic and Technical Cooperation among Developing Countries, and invites all countries, in particular developed countries, to contribute to the Trust Funds;

12. *Calls upon* all Governments and all relevant United Nations organizations and multilateral and regional financial institutions to consider increasing allocations of financial resources for economic and technical cooperation among developing countries and to strengthen funding modalities to promote South-South cooperation, such as triangular cooperation and private sector funding;

13. *Encourages* developing countries and relevant organizations and agencies of the United Nations system, as well as other partners in development efforts, in the practice of technical and economic cooperation among developing countries, to develop and to support innovative mechanisms to foster South-South cooperation in science and technology, with particular

emphasis on the development and the sharing of high technologies and appropriate technologies, with a view to their better utilization for the growth and the development of developing countries;

14. *Stresses,* in this context, that South-South cooperation in science and technology is not a replacement for but a complement to traditional North-South cooperation in science and technology, in particular appropriate North-South technology transfer;

15. *Emphasizes* the need for concerted action by developing countries and their development partners, including relevant international organizations, with a view to strengthening cooperation and collaboration among developing countries at the subregional, regional and interregional levels;

16. *Reiterates its invitation* to the United Nations Conference on Trade and Development and the Special Unit for Technical Cooperation among Developing Countries, as well as other relevant organizations, taking into account their agreed mandates, work programmes and priorities, to undertake jointly further work on formulating concrete recommendations on the implementation of and follow-up to the Caracas Programme of Action, adopted at the High-level Conference on Economic Cooperation among Developing Countries, held at Caracas in May 1981, as an important mechanism for economic cooperation among developing countries, and the San José Declaration and Plan of Action adopted by the Group of 77 at the South-South Conference on Trade, Investment and Finance, as well as on the Bali Declaration on Regional and Subregional Economic Cooperation of the Developing Countries and the Bali Plan of Action on Regional and Subregional Economic Cooperation of the Developing Countries adopted by the Group of 77 High-level Conference on Regional and Subregional Economic Cooperation of the Developing Countries, held on Bali, Indonesia, from 2 to 5 December 1998, within the context of South-South cooperation;

17. *Requests* the United Nations system to take appropriate measures to improve the effective incorporation of technical cooperation among developing countries into its programmes and projects and to intensify efforts towards mainstreaming the modality of technical cooperation among developing countries, including through support to the activities of the Special Unit for Technical Cooperation among Developing Countries, and encourages other relevant international institutions to take similar measures;

18. *Reiterates its request* to the Administrator of the United Nations Development Programme to ensure that the separate identity of the Special Unit for Technical Cooperation among Developing Countries is maintained and that the Unit is supported so that it may fully implement its mandate and system-wide responsibilities for promoting, monitoring and coordinating technical cooperation among developing countries;

19. *Stresses* the need, with reference to decision 11/3 adopted by the High-level Committee on the Review of Technical Cooperation among Developing Countries at its eleventh session and the provisional agenda for the twelfth session of the High-level Committee approved therein, to take appropriate measures to ensure the necessary level of attendance of all member States in the meeting of the High-level Committee, including through discussions of country experiences at the field level, in terms of progress achieved, problems encountered and lessons learned;

20. *Decides* to include in the provisional agenda of its fifty-sixth session the sub-item entitled "Economic and technical cooperation among developing countries", and in that context requests the Secretary-General, in collaboration with the Special Unit for Technical Cooperation among Developing Countries and the United Nations Conference on Trade and Development, to submit to it at that session a report on the state of South-South cooperation and a comprehensive report on the implementation of the present resolution.

UN Capital Development Fund

In 1999, the core contributions to the United Nations Capital Development Fund (UNCDF) totalled $27.4 million, a 10 per cent decrease from $30.5 million in 1998. A total of 13 new projects were approved, worth some $56.3 million. Programme expenditure totalled $44.1 million, representing an overall project delivery of 84 per cent, compared to $43.7 million or 78 per cent in 1998.

In July, the Administrator submitted a report on UNCDF [DP/1999/37], which referred to the 1995 challenge to donors to give it three years to deliver on the goals contained in its 1995 policy paper [YUN 1995, p. 903], after which the Executive Board would recommend closure of the entity if it was not successful. The report outlined events that had taken place since that challenge and presented the results of the 1999 donor-led evaluation of UNCDF.

The evaluation clearly showed that UNCDF had responded to the challenge of corporate change in a positive way. It had enhanced its distinctive identity by developing competence in decentralization, local governance and microfinance. The institution's capacity had improved and its new approaches had had a positive effect on field operations. The number of programme objectives had been reduced, making programmes more strategic and targeted and corporate key performance indicators were established for microfinance projects and were being finalized for local development programmes. UNCDF was well placed to become a centre of excellence in the planning and implementation of local governance and microfinance programmes. It had developed innovative participatory methods, improving its relevance, targeting and efficiency. At the corporate level, it was crucial for UNDP and UNCDF to focus on how a future UNCDF could further advance UNDP corporate goals in governancc.

The evaluation team concluded that donors should continue to support UNCDF, but funding should be linked to performance targets and results performance, with arrangements for objective verification and monitoring. It recommended that UNCDF should reduce the current portfolio, which would allow staff to concentrate further on the newer projects, intensify the knowledge content of programming and free technical resources to build strategic alliances with key partners, such as UNDP and the World Bank.

UNCDF had already begun to implement many of the evaluation's recommendations. It was taking steps to improve: the quality of its programme and project documents; its ability to collect and disseminate lessons learned; and structure the organization to respond better to the technical needs of the programmes.

In his annual report for 1999 [DP/2000/23], the UNDP Administrator said that UNCDF had ensured the maximum operational impact of its investments with the poor in the poorest countries, to produce results in piloting local governance programmes and microfinance operations that could be replicated on a larger scale and provide a basis for pro-poor policy decisions. The year marked the end of an internal programme review with the publication of new UNCDF policies on local governance and microfinance. UNCDF had moved to ensure that new programming reflected those policies and had realigned ongoing programming. In September, the Special Unit on Microfinance was fully integrated into UNCDF. The Unit managed the UNCDF-funded microfinance portfolio and the UNDP-funded Microstart programme and continued to provide UNDP with microfinance advisory services.

The Executive Board, in a September decision [E/1999/35 (dec. 99/22)], welcomed UNCDF's work in policy review and development, as well as in strengthening the focus of its programme activities, and endorsed its efforts to establish innovative microfinance and local development programmes, including in local governance. It also welcomed the positive assessment of the Fund's work summarized in the Administrator's report. The Board encouraged the Fund to implement the recommendations contained in the evaluation and to report to the Board on its performance in 2000. The Board encouraged the Fund and UNDP to intensify collaboration, particularly in local governance and microfinance, and to report in the 2000 ROAR on those efforts. It urged UNCDF to strengthen alliances with partners and invited all countries in a position to do so to make voluntary contributions to the Fund in order to secure adequate funding of its programmes. The Board requested the Administrator to carry out an independent evaluation of the impact of UNCDF programmes and projects and to report in 2003.

Chapter III

Humanitarian and special economic assistance

In 1999, the United Nations, through the Office for the Coordination of Humanitarian Affairs, continued to coordinate the collective efforts of the international community, in particular those of the UN system, to provide humanitarian and special economic assistance to States and population groups stricken by complex emergencies and natural disasters. Attention was devoted to reducing vulnerability, promoting solutions to root causes and strengthening the coordination of emergency humanitarian assistance, especially in the context of the transition from relief to rehabilitation, reconstruction and development. Consolidated inter-agency appeals were launched or ongoing in Afghanistan, Angola, the Democratic People's Republic of Korea, East Timor, the Great Lakes region and Central Africa, Guinea-Bissau, the northern Caucasus, Sierra Leone, Somalia, South-Eastern Europe, the Sudan and Tajikistan. The amount sought for the appeals totalled $2,382 million, of which $1,715 million was received, meeting 72.4 per cent of the requirements.

During the year, some of the most intractable conflicts, such as those in Afghanistan, Angola, Burundi and the Democratic Republic of the Congo, deteriorated further, and in other parts of the world, such as Kosovo and East Timor, new emergencies erupted and the fragile situation in the northern Caucasus was aggravated further. In addition to complex emergencies, the world witnessed natural disasters, especially floods and earthquakes, of unprecedented devastation.

The International Decade for Natural Disaster Reduction (1990-2000) came to a close in December.

Humanitarian assistance

Coordination

Humanitarian affairs segment of the Economic and Social Council

An April note of the Secretariat [E/1999/45] presented suggestions by Member States on the organization of the humanitarian affairs segment of the Economic and Social Council, established pursuant to General Assembly resolution 52/12 B [YUN 1997, p. 1392]. It also contained their views on strengthening the Council's coordination and policy guidance role in humanitarian affairs. Subsequently, the Council, by **decision 1999/214** of 7 May, decided on the programme of work for the humanitarian affairs segment of its 1999 substantive session.

During the segment held from 13 to 15 July (**decision 1999/211**) and on 23 July under the theme "International cooperation and coordinated responses to the humanitarian emergencies, in particular in the transition from relief to rehabilitation, reconstruction and development" (**decision 1999/208**), the Council considered special economic, humanitarian and disaster relief assistance. It had before it, in addition to reports on individual States, a June report of the Secretary-General on strengthening coordination of UN emergency humanitarian assistance [A/54/154-E/1999/94], submitted pursuant to requests by the Assembly in resolutions 46/182 [YUN 1991, p. 421] and 52/168 [YUN 1997, p. 897], and by the Council in resolution 1995/56 [YUN 1995, p. 927]. The report covered the coordination of humanitarian assistance and further progress of the Inter-Agency Standing Committee (IASC) in strengthening UN capacity in humanitarian assistance. It also documented the implementation of the Council's agreed conclusions 1998/1 [YUN 1998, p. 841] in the context of the UN programme of reform endorsed by the Assembly in resolution 52/12 A [YUN 1997, p. 1391], in particular those measures aimed at strengthening the Office of the Emergency Relief Coordinator (ERC).

The Secretary-General stated that a particularly striking phenomenon of the past year had been the extraordinary rise in the number and scale of natural disasters, and of their human and financial cost. Estimated economic losses exceeded $90 billion, compared with $30 billion in 1997. Indications were that the increase was linked to factors such as rapid population growth and urbanization, environmental degradation, global climatic changes and other causes. In many cases, man-made elements exacerbated the impact of disasters, highlighting the need for intensive disaster-reduction/prevention activities as part of relief and development strategies.

Regarding complex emergencies, conflicts intensified and internal wars took on a larger regional dimension, as in the Democratic Republic of the Congo and West Africa. In 1999, new violence broke out and attacks on civilians led to massive forced displacement and increases of internally displaced persons and refugees. In many emergency situations, humanitarian agencies were denied access to the affected areas, not only by conditions of insecurity but also by Governments and parties to conflicts. Attacks on humanitarian personnel continued, and the HIV/AIDS pandemic, especially in Africa, had major humanitarian implications. Difficulties in responding to the numerous challenges were exacerbated by uneven levels of funding to consolidated appeals. While the overall response for 1999 was 30 per cent as at 31 May, compared to 15 per cent in 1998, it was uneven in geographical and sectoral distribution and threatened to undermine the principle that aid was provided irrespective of political and other considerations.

The Secretary-General reported that ERC and IASC—the principal inter-agency policy coordination, consultation and decision-making forum for addressing humanitarian issues—had responded by trying to improve the environment for humanitarian action and strengthening coordination mechanisms. Humanitarian agencies sought to improve the environment for action through negotiation with parties to conflicts over issues of access and security; reinforcement of the principles of humanitarian action; strengthening of the legal framework; and advocacy with the Security Council and other bodies. Progress had been made in strengthening the consolidated appeal process, particularly by enhancing the capacity of country teams to manage and implement the process, and IASC, which was reinforced by the admission of the World Bank into its membership in March, planned to build on improvements in the appeal process, including through the development of monitoring systems. IASC efforts to enhance field coordination included effective preparedness and multisectoral planning for emergencies; efforts to promote follow-up through monitoring and evaluation; and efforts to improve the coordination of responses to internally displaced person situations.

As to coordination in natural disasters, the Secretary-General stated that they should be considered on a par with complex emergencies in terms of their impact and long-lasting economic consequences. The United Nations Development Programme (UNDP) strengthened the responsiveness of in-country coordination systems, and the Office for the Coordination of Humanitarian Affairs (OCHA) allocated priority status to response preparedness. However, evaluations drew attention to areas that needed improvement, such as response preparedness and capacity-building, access to resources for emergency relief, and bridging the gap between emergency relief and early recovery. A newly established inter-agency reference group was preparing recommendations to strengthen IASC response mechanisms. In addition, the International Emergency Response Consultative Mechanism was established to improve linkage between the donor community and disaster-prone countries.

With regard to international cooperation and coordination in response to the humanitarian emergencies, particularly in the transition from relief to rehabilitation, reconstruction and development, whether related to conflict or disaster, a number of common themes emerged in developing comprehensive approaches. They included the need for early joint planning and prioritization, the central role of capacity-building, the importance of a clearly agreed division of labour in relief efforts through inter-agency collaboration and the inflexible and discretionary nature of existing financing systems for transitional programming.

In the agreed conclusions of its humanitarian affairs segment [A/54/3/Rev.1 (agreed conclusions 1999/1)], the Council recognized that efforts were needed to ensure a coherent approach to relief, rehabilitation, reconstruction and development, as well as to enhance disaster preparedness and local capacities for disaster response. It called on all parties to conflicts to respect humanitarian and human rights law and to ensure the safety of humanitarian personnel. Noting the need to strengthen the consolidated appeal process and regretting low and uneven funding of the appeals, the Council called on the international community to increase its contributions.

Recognizing the need for a comprehensive approach to both natural disasters and complex emergencies, the Council stressed the need for early joint planning, the central role of capacity-building and the importance of an agreed division of labour through inter-agency collaboration, as well as the need for more flexible financing systems for transitional programming. It emphasized that the planning for rehabilitation should begin at a very early stage, local actors should be involved and existing local capacities integrated. A more systematic evaluation was needed. Consideration should be given to the issue of the humanitarian impact of sanctions.

As to natural disasters, the Council emphasized the need for measures to reduce the vulnerability of societies, particularly in developing countries, small island developing States and landlocked countries, and reaffirmed that disaster preparedness and early warning systems should be strengthened through better coordination among UN bodies and cooperation with Governments of affected countries and regional and other relevant organizations. At the field level, the Council called on the resident coordinator and relevant agencies to improve response preparedness and capacity-building; at the inter-agency level, it encouraged ERC, IASC and other UN system members to promote response preparedness at the international, regional and national levels. Rehabilitation funds should be released rapidly to prevent dependence on relief funding. With regard to transitions from complex humanitarian emergencies, the Council affirmed that early reconstruction and development activities could support the implementation of peace agreements, and it stressed that humanitarian agencies should integrate a development perspective in their planning. Stressing the importance of strategic frameworks to countries in crisis, the Council requested the Secretary-General to submit recommendations on their preparation, scope and applicability. It called on the Secretary-General and ERC to ensure a high degree of coherence between assistance and the political and human rights aspects of the UN response, while maintaining their separate and mutually reinforcing nature. The Council encouraged enhanced inter-linkages between the consolidated appeal process and the United Nations Development Assistance Framework (UNDAF), and requested ERC to intensify efforts in that respect. Cooperation between all actors, including UN bodies and non-governmental organizations (NGOs), should be strengthened.

With respect to the financial mechanisms available for transitional activities, donor countries were called on to ensure that their funding systems facilitated early, integrated approaches for recovery and to provide an adequacy of funding from assistance through transition activities to development cooperation. The Council urged the Secretary-General and ERC to ensure that priority was given to demobilization, reintegration and rehabilitation, which were major areas where gaps between relief and development occurred. It stressed the importance of addressing the needs of returning refugees, called on States to apply internationally recognized norms to internally displaced persons, called for inter-agency efforts on behalf of children, underlining their vulnerabilities in armed conflict, and asserted the need to integrate a gender perspective in the planning and implementation of activities.

Report of UNDP Administrator. In a report to the Economic and Social Council [DP/2000/11], the UNDP Administrator stated that the agreed conclusions adopted by the humanitarian segments of the Council in 1998 [YUN 1998, p. 841] and in 1999, as well as General Assembly resolution 53/192 [ibid., p. 802], provided a legislative basis for the interaction of operational activities and humanitarian assistance. In following up on the agreed conclusions, UNDP and its UN partners ensured a coherent approach to relief, rehabilitation, reconstruction and development. As chair of the IASC Reference Group on Post-Conflict Reintegration—a body whose task was to seek solutions for a smooth transition from relief to development—UNDP took part in other efforts to ensure coherent approaches to transitional situations. The United Nations Development Group (UNDG) promoted linkages between UNDAF and the consolidated appeal process through joint meetings with the other executive committees. The crises of Kosovo and East Timor (see PART ONE, Chapters V and VIII, respectively), in particular, demonstrated to UNDP and other UNDG members the difficulties of linking development to relief, rehabilitation and recovery. The UNDP Administrator recommended that the Council take note of the efforts within the UN Secretariat to achieve a closer integration of relief, reconstruction, rehabilitation and development and to encourage progress in line with the agreed conclusions. He also recommended that the Council recognize the common country assessment as the building block for both the consolidated appeal process and UNDAF; invite the Security Council and call on the Secretariat to include a development perspective to eradicate the cause of a crisis and to promote human development; and encourage UNDP and other UNDG members to develop further their dialogue with the Bretton Woods institutions.

GENERAL ASSEMBLY ACTION

On 8 December [meeting 73], the General Assembly adopted **resolution 54/95** [draft: A/54/L.54 & Add.1] without vote [agenda item 20 *(a)*].

Strengthening of the coordination of emergency humanitarian assistance of the United Nations

The General Assembly,

Recalling its resolution 46/182 of 19 December 1991 and the guiding principles contained in its annex, other relevant General Assembly and Economic and Social Council resolutions and agreed conclusions 1998/1 of the humanitarian affairs segment of the substantive session of 1998 of the Council,

Noting the decision by the Economic and Social Council to hold further consultations on ways and means to strengthen its role by enhancing its work in the humanitarian field,

Taking note of the report of the Secretary General,

Welcoming the progress made by the Emergency Relief Coordinator and the Office for the Coordination of Humanitarian Affairs in strengthening the coordination of humanitarian assistance of the United Nations,

Noting the efforts made by the Emergency Relief Coordinator and the members of the Inter-Agency Standing Committee to implement fully the recommendations set forth in agreed conclusions 1998/1,

1. *Welcomes* the holding of the second humanitarian affairs segment by the Economic and Social Council during its substantive session of 1999 and agreed conclusions 1999/1 adopted at that session;

2. *Calls upon* relevant organizations of the United Nations system, other relevant international organizations, Governments and non-governmental organizations to cooperate with the Secretary-General and the Emergency Relief Coordinator to ensure timely implementation of and follow-up to agreed conclusions 1999/1;

3. *Emphasizes* the importance of discussion of humanitarian policies and activities in the General Assembly and the Economic and Social Council;

4. *Invites* the Economic and Social Council to continue to consider ways to enhance further the humanitarian affairs segment of its future sessions;

5. *Requests* the Secretary-General to submit to the General Assembly, in early 2000, concrete proposals on how to enhance the functioning and utilization of the Central Emergency Revolving Fund, including, as necessary, amendments to its terms of reference;

6. *Also requests* the Secretary-General to report to the General Assembly at its fifty-fifth session, through the 2000 substantive session of the Economic and Social Council, on the strengthening of the coordination of emergency humanitarian assistance of the United Nations, including the implementation of and follow-up to agreed conclusions 1999/1.

On 22 December [meeting 87], the General Assembly adopted **resolution 54/233** [draft: A/54/L.74 & Add.1] without vote [agenda item 20].

International cooperation on humanitarian assistance in the field of natural disasters from relief to development

The General Assembly,

Reaffirming its resolution 46/182 of 19 December 1991, which contains in its annex the guiding principles for the strengthening of the coordination of emergency humanitarian assistance of the United Nations system, and its resolutions 52/12 B of 19 December 1997 and 54/219 of 22 December 1999, and recalling Economic and Social Council agreed conclusions 1999/1, which addressed the theme "International cooperation and coordinated responses to the humanitarian emergencies, in particular in the transition from relief to rehabilitation, reconstruction and development", and Council resolution 1999/63 of 30 July 1999,

Noting with appreciation the report of the Secretary-General on strengthening of the coordination of emergency humanitarian assistance of the United Nations, in particular in the context of the transition from relief to rehabilitation, reconstruction and development,

Recognizing the importance of the principles of neutrality, humanity and impartiality for the provision of humanitarian assistance,

Emphasizing that the affected State has the primary responsibility in the initiation, organization, coordination and implementation of humanitarian assistance within its territory and in the facilitation of the work of the humanitarian organizations in mitigating the consequences of natural disasters,

1. *Expresses deep concern* at the increasing number and scale of natural disasters, resulting in massive losses of life and property worldwide, in particular in vulnerable societies lacking adequate capacity to mitigate effectively long-term negative social, economic and environmental consequences of natural disasters;

2. *Stresses* that humanitarian assistance for natural disasters should be provided in accordance with and with due respect for the guiding principles contained in the annex to resolution 46/182 and should be determined on the basis of the human dimension and needs arising out of the particular natural disaster;

3. *Calls upon* States to adopt, where required, and to continue to implement effectively necessary legislative and other appropriate measures to mitigate the effects of natural disasters, inter alia, by disaster prevention, including building regulations, as well as disaster preparedness and capacity-building in disaster response, and requests the international community in this context to continue to assist developing countries, where appropriate;

4. *Stresses* the need to strengthen efforts at all levels, inter alia, at the domestic level, to improve natural disaster awareness, prevention, preparedness and early warning systems, as well as international cooperation, in response to emergencies from relief to rehabilitation, reconstruction and development, bearing in mind the overall negative impact of natural disasters, the resulting humanitarian needs and requests from affected countries, as appropriate;

5. *Encourages* further efforts by the Under-Secretary-General for Humanitarian Affairs and Emergency Relief Coordinator, Inter-Agency Standing Committee members and other members of the United Nations system in promoting preparedness for response at the international, regional and national levels and strengthening the mobilization and coordination of humanitarian assistance of the United Nations system in the field of natural disasters, inter alia, through the effective deployment in all regions of the world and expansion of the United Nations Disaster Assessment and Coordination roster appropriately to include more representatives from countries of Africa, Asia and the Pacific and Latin America and the Caribbean, bearing in mind that these representatives are funded by the participating countries;

6. *Also encourages* further efforts by the United Nations Development Programme to strengthen operational activities and capacity-building in natural disaster mitigation, prevention and preparedness, taking due account of the evolving comprehensive strategy to maximize international cooperation in the field of natural disasters;

7. *Invites* the Office for the Coordination of Humanitarian Affairs of the Secretariat and concerned organizations, taking due account of the evolving comprehensive strategy to maximize international cooperation in the field of natural disasters, to strengthen their support to the United Nations disaster management teams which are dispatched upon re-

quest by host Governments and steered by the United Nations resident coordinator;

8. *Recalls* the consideration of natural disasters contained in the report of the Third United Nations Conference on the Exploration and Peaceful Uses of Outer Space, held in Vienna from 19 to 30 July 1999, and encourages further use of space-based technologies for the prevention, mitigation and management of natural disasters, noting in this regard, the establishment of the Global Disaster Information Network;

9. *Takes note* of the Tampere Convention on the Provision of Telecommunication Resources for Disaster Mitigation and Relief Operations, adopted at Tampere, Finland, on 18 June 1998, and encourages States that have not signed the Convention to consider doing so;

10. *Welcomes* innovative efforts to link various phases of international assistance from relief to rehabilitation, such as the joint Office for the Coordination of Humanitarian Affairs, United Nations Development Programme, United Nations Children's Fund and World Health Organization and Pan American Health Organization Disaster Response and Recovery Mission undertaken in all countries affected by hurricane Mitch, and stresses the need to ensure adequate assessment of and follow-up to these approaches with a view to further developing and applying them in other disasters;

11. *Encourages* Governments, in particular through their disaster response agencies, relevant organizations of the United Nations system and non-governmental organizations, to continue to cooperate appropriately with the Secretary-General and the Under-Secretary-General for Humanitarian Affairs and Emergency Relief Coordinator to maximize the effectiveness of the international response to natural disasters, based, inter alia, on humanitarian need, from relief to development;

12. *Recalls,* in this regard, its request to the Secretary-General to solicit the required input further to optimize and disseminate listings of organizations of civil protection and emergency response at all levels with updated inventories of available resources to help in natural disasters, as well as information, including handbooks, that guide the international cooperation in responding to natural disasters;

13. *Stresses* that particular international cooperation efforts should be undertaken to enhance and broaden further the utilization of national and local capacities and, where appropriate, regional and subregional capacities of developing countries for disaster preparedness and response, which may be made available in closer proximity to the site of a disaster, more efficiently and at lower cost;

14. *Notes* that the transition phase after natural disasters is often excessively long and characterized by a number of gaps, and that Governments, in cooperation with relief agencies, as appropriate, when planning for meeting immediate needs, should place these needs in the perspective of sustainable development whenever such an approach is possible;

15. *Stresses* the need to continue to provide adequate funds and to release funds quickly for natural disasters in order to contribute to a comprehensive recovery in the shortest time possible;

16. *Also stresses,* in this regard, that contributions for humanitarian assistance for natural disasters should be provided in a way that is not to the detriment of resources made available for international cooperation for development or complex humanitarian emergencies;

17. *Reiterates its request* to the Secretary-General, contained in resolution 54/95 of 8 December 1999, to submit to the General Assembly, early in 2000, concrete proposals in order to enhance the functioning and utilization of the Central Emergency Revolving Fund, and, in this regard, invites the Secretary-General to consider more active use of the Fund for timely and adequate natural disaster response;

18. *Invites* the Secretary-General further to consider innovative means for timely and adequate natural disaster response, inter alia, through mobilization of additional resources from the private sector;

19. *Invites* the Economic and Social Council, at its substantive session of 2000, in the context of the follow-up to its agreed conclusions 1999/1, to consider ways to enhance further the effectiveness of international cooperation and coordination in respect of the provision of timely and adequate humanitarian assistance in response to natural disasters;

20. *Invites* the Secretary-General to continue to consider innovative mechanisms to improve the international response to natural disasters and other emergencies, inter alia, through addressing any geographical and sectoral imbalances in such a response where they exist, as well as more effective use of national emergency response agencies, taking into account their comparative advantages and specialization, as well as existing arrangements, and to report thereon to the General Assembly at its fifty-fifth session under the item entitled "Strengthening of the coordination of humanitarian and disaster relief assistance of the United Nations, including special economic assistance" with a view, inter alia, to contributing towards the comprehensive report on the implementation of the international strategy for disaster reduction to be submitted to the Assembly at its fifty-sixth session under the item entitled "Environment and sustainable development".

By **decision 54/465** of 23 December, the Assembly decided that the item on strengthening the coordination of humanitarian and disaster relief assistance of the United Nations, including special economic assistance, would remain for consideration during its resumed fifty-fourth (2000) session.

Humanitarian and UN personnel

In an October addendum [A/54/154/Add.1-E/1999/94/Add.1] to his report on strengthening of the coordination of emergency humanitarian assistance of the United Nations (see p. 823), the Secretary-General updated information related to the safety and security of UN and humanitarian personnel. The report stated that killings and threats against UN and humanitarian personnel were daily occurrences, which impeded the implementation of UN programmes and the freedom of humanitarian organizations to access vulnerable populations. Steps taken by the

United Nations to address the problem included the establishment of training mechanisms, the adoption of resolutions by the Assembly and the entry into force of international instruments. However, those measures fell short of providing the protection intended, owing to a lack of respect by armed elements for UN personnel, but also to a lack of resources. The Secretary-General called on States that had not done so to ratify the 1994 Convention on the Safety of United Nations and Associated Personnel, adopted by the Assembly in resolution 49/59 [YUN 1994, p. 1289], which entered into force in January 1999. They were also asked to contribute to the Trust Fund for Security of personnel of the UN system. It was recommended that the Assembly pursue the development of a protocol to the 1994 Convention, which would extend the scope of legal protection to all UN and associated personnel.

In December, by **resolution 54/192**, the General Assembly called on Governments and parties in complex humanitarian emergencies to ensure the safe and unhindered access of humanitarian personnel (see p. 1336).

OCHA review

In accordance with General Assembly resolution 48/218 B [YUN 1994, p. 1362], the Secretary-General, on 9 September, transmitted a report of the Office of Internal Oversight Services (OIOS) [A/54/334] on a review of OCHA management strategies aimed at strengthening its capacity to respond to humanitarian crises. Action taken to focus on core functions, as contained in Assembly resolution 46/182 [YUN 1991, p. 421], were assessed. OIOS concluded that the streamlining and reorganization within OCHA in 1998 [YUN 1998, p. 842] had enhanced its capabilities to respond to crises and strengthened its coordination with other departments of the Secretariat, UN funds and programmes, other humanitarian agencies and NGOs. OCHA established an open dialogue with donors, displayed sensitivity to the mandates of other humanitarian agencies and took measures to reduce the incidence of duplication of responsibilities, competition and disagreement over areas of operation. The OIOS inspection also confirmed that the working of IASC and the consolidated appeal process had improved. Additional efforts were required, however, to enforce a more action-oriented approach in addressing coordination issues within the Executive Committee on Humanitarian Affairs, and there was need for a strategic management framework to enhance the appeals process. OIOS recommended that OCHA enhance the functioning of the Executive Committee, make new institutional arrangements in the elaboration and implementation of sanctions regimes regarding UN efforts to minimize the humanitarian impact of sanctions, establish more effective monitoring of the consolidated appeals process, implement a strategic management framework and strengthen its advocacy role with the general public.

On 30 September [A/54/334/Add.1], the Secretary-General transmitted to the Assembly the comments of the Joint Inspection Unit (JIU) on the OIOS report, stating that JIU concurred with the thrust of the report. It recommended that the issue of coordination be better analysed in the case of complex emergencies where a military component was present on the ground; that more attention be devoted to the human rights component in complex emergencies and to lessons learned from humanitarian operations; and that the concern about the decreasing funds collected through the consolidated appeals process be examined in parallel with the reasons for the increasing preference of donors for bilateral interventions. JIU suggested that the Secretary-General issue a bulletin describing OCHA's functions.

Resource mobilization

Central Emergency Revolving Fund

In 1999 [A/55/649], the Central Emergency Revolving Fund, established in 1992 [YUN 1992, p. 584] as a cash-flow mechanism for the initial phase of humanitarian emergencies, granted 15 advances, amounting to $22.1 million. The decline in the Fund's use was the result of the availability within operational organizations of their own emergency funds and other sources of financing for start-up requirements.

Consolidated appeals

The consolidated appeals process continued to coordinate and facilitate the capacity of the UN system to meet its emergency resource requirements. In 1999, inter-agency consolidated appeals were prepared and issued for the following countries or regions: Afghanistan, Angola, the Democratic People's Republic of Korea, East Timor, the Great Lakes region and Central Africa, Guinea-Bissau, the northern Caucasus, Sierra Leone, Somalia, South-Eastern Europe, the Sudan and Tajikistan.

White Helmets

Pursuant to General Assembly resolution 52/171 [YUN 1997, p. 899], the Secretary-General submitted an August report on the "White Helmets" initiative [A/54/217], which was established by Argentina to provide expertise on a standby team basis from various national volunteer corps to support immediate relief, rehabilitation, reconstruction and development activities. The report, which covered the period from January 1998 to June 1999, provided an overview of progress made in collaboration with various partners, particularly with the Government of Argentina, through its Secretariat for International Humanitarian Assistance, also known as the White Helmets Commission for Argentina. The report incorporated findings emanating from the United Nations Volunteers/White Helmets Commission programme review covering the period 1995-1999. During the reporting period, a total of $4.7 million was expended for assistance to countries.

GENERAL ASSEMBLY ACTION

On 8 December [meeting 73], the General Assembly adopted **resolution 54/98** [draft: A/54/L.34/Rev.1 & Add.1] without vote [agenda item 20 *(d)*].

Participation of volunteers, "White Helmets", in activities of the United Nations in the field of humanitarian relief, rehabilitation and technical cooperation for development

The General Assembly,

Reaffirming its resolutions 49/139 B of 20 December 1994, 50/19 of 28 November 1995 and 52/171 of 16 December 1997,

Reaffirming also its resolutions 46/182 of 19 December 1991, 47/168 of 22 December 1992, 48/57 of 14 December 1993, 49/139 A and B of 20 December 1994, 50/57 of 12 December 1995 and 51/194 of 17 December 1996 and Economic and Social Council resolutions 1995/56 of 28 July 1995 and 1996/33 of 25 July 1996,

Recognizing that recent events emphasize the need for the international community, in addressing the growing magnitude and complexity of natural disasters and other humanitarian emergencies, to rely not only on the formulation of a well-coordinated global response within the framework of the United Nations but also on the promotion of a smooth transition from relief to rehabilitation, reconstruction and development,

Recalling that prevention, preparedness and contingency planning for emergencies at the global level depend, for the most part, on the strengthened local and national response capacities as well as on the availability of financial resources, both domestic and international,

1. *Takes note* of the report of the Secretary-General, prepared in pursuance of its resolution 52/171 on the participation of volunteers, "White Helmets", in activities of the United Nations in the field of humanitarian relief, rehabilitation and technical cooperation for development;

2. *Encourages* voluntary national and regional actions aimed at making available to the United Nations system, through the United Nations Volunteers, national volunteer corps such as the White Helmets on a standby basis, in accordance with accepted United Nations procedures and practices, in order to provide specialized human and technical resources for emergency relief and rehabilitation;

3. *Expresses its appreciation* for the commendable progress of the White Helmets initiative as a singular voluntary international effort to provide the United Nations system with volunteer expertise to respond, in a quick and coordinated manner, to humanitarian relief, rehabilitation, reconstruction and development, while preserving the non-political, neutral and impartial character of humanitarian action;

4. *Recognizes with appreciation* that the White Helmets, in close cooperation with the Office for the Coordination of Humanitarian Affairs of the Secretariat and as an operational partner of the United Nations Volunteers, are an efficient and viable mechanism for making pre-identified and trained homogeneous teams available to the United Nations system, in support of immediate relief, rehabilitation, reconstruction and development activities, in the light of the increasing number, growing magnitude and complexity of natural disasters and other emergencies;

5. *Calls upon* Member States to promote the facilitation of cooperative actions between the United Nations system and the civil society, through national volunteer corps, in order to strengthen the United Nations capacities for early and effective response to humanitarian emergencies, and invites them to make the commensurate financial resources available through the special financing window of the Special Voluntary Fund of the United Nations Volunteers;

6. *Encourages* Member States to identify and support their respective national focal points for the White Helmets in order to continue to provide the United Nations system with an accessible global network of rapid response facilities in case of humanitarian emergencies;

7. *Invites* Member States, international financial institutions, regional organizations and the United Nations system to consider ways and means to ensure the integration of the White Helmets initiative into their programme activities, particularly those related to humanitarian and disaster relief assistance;

8. *Invites* the Secretary-General, on the basis of the experience acquired, to consider further the potential use of White Helmets as a resource for preventing and mitigating the effects of emergencies and post-conflict humanitarian emergencies and, in this context, to maintain an adequate structure for the White Helmets liaison functions, taking into account the ongoing reforms process;

9. *Requests* the Secretary-General to conclude his consideration of the possible strengthening and broadening of consultative mechanisms to promote further and operationalize the concept, as referred to in paragraph 14 of his report, and to report to the General Assembly at its fifty-sixth session, under the item entitled "Strengthening of the coordination of humanitarian and disaster relief assistance of the United Nations, including special economic assistance", on the actions taken in conformity with the present resolution.

Mine clearance

In an October report on assistance in mine action [A/54/445], submitted pursuant to General

Assembly resolution 53/26 [YUN 1998, p. 844], the Secretary-General provided information on the activities of UN organizations, as well as those of other bodies and NGOs. He reviewed mine-action programmes in Afghanistan, Angola, Azerbaijan, Bosnia and Herzegovina, Cambodia, Chad, Croatia, Iraq, Kosovo province of the Federal Republic of Yugoslavia, the Lao People's Democratic Republic, Mozambique, Nicaragua, Somalia and Sri Lanka.

Annexed to the report was a table listing contributions by donor, totalling $60.3 million as at 7 October, to the Voluntary Trust Fund for Assistance in Mine Action, established by the Assembly in resolution 49/215 [YUN 1994, p. 173] as the Voluntary Trust Fund for Assistance in Mine Clearance and renamed by the Assembly in resolution 53/26.

GENERAL ASSEMBLY ACTION

On 17 December [meeting 84], the General Assembly adopted **resolution 54/191** [draft: A/54/L.71] without vote [agenda item 35].

Assistance in mine action

The General Assembly,

Recalling its resolutions 48/7 of 19 October 1993, 49/215 of 23 December 1994, 50/82 of 14 December 1995, 51/149 of 13 December 1996 and 52/173 of 18 December 1997 on assistance in mine clearance and its resolution 53/26 of 17 November 1998 on assistance in mine action, all adopted without a vote,

Considering mine action to be an important component of United Nations humanitarian and development activities,

Reaffirming its deep concern at the tremendous humanitarian problem caused by the presence of mines and other unexploded devices that have serious and lasting social and economic consequences for the populations of mine-infested countries and constitute an obstacle to the return of refugees and other displaced persons, to humanitarian aid operations and to reconstruction and economic development, as well as to the restoration of normal social conditions,

Bearing in mind the serious threat that mines and other unexploded devices pose to the safety, health and lives of personnel participating in humanitarian, peacekeeping and rehabilitation programmes and operations,

Reiterating its dismay at the high number of victims of mines, especially among civilian populations, particularly children, and recalling in this context Commission on Human Rights resolutions 1995/79 of 8 March 1995, 1996/85 of 24 April 1996, 1997/78 of 18 April 1997, 1998/76 of 22 April 1998 and 1999/80 of 28 April 1999 on the rights of the child and resolutions 1996/27 of 19 April 1996 and 1998/31 of 17 April 1998 and decision 1997/107 of 11 April 1997 on the human rights of persons with disabilities,

Deeply alarmed by the number of mines that continue to be laid each year, as well as the presence of a large number of mines and other unexploded devices as a result of armed conflicts, and thus convinced of the necessity and urgency of a significant increase in mine-clearance efforts by the international community with a view to eliminating the threat of landmines to civilians as soon as possible,

Noting the decisions taken at the Review Conference of the States Parties to the Convention on Prohibitions or Restrictions on the Use of Certain Conventional Weapons Which May Be Deemed to Be Excessively Injurious or to Have Indiscriminate Effects, particularly with respect to Protocol II to the Convention and the inclusion in the Amended Protocol of a number of provisions of importance for mine-clearance operations, notably the requirement of detectability,

Noting the entry into force of the Amended Protocol II to the Convention on 3 December 1998,

Recalling that the States parties at the Review Conference declared their commitment to keep the provisions of Protocol II under review in order to ensure that the concerns regarding the weapons it covers are addressed, and that they would encourage efforts of the United Nations and other organizations to address all the problems of landmines,

Noting the entry into force on 1 March 1999 of the Convention on the Prohibition of the Use, Stockpiling, Production and Transfer of Anti-personnel Mines and on Their Destruction and that the Convention has been signed by over one hundred and thirty-five States, that the First Meeting of the States Parties to the Convention was held at Maputo in May 1999 and that measures were taken at that meeting to, among other things, provide assistance for mine clearance and rehabilitation, the social and economic reintegration of mine victims and mine-awareness programmes,

Stressing the need to convince mine-affected States to halt new deployments of anti-personnel mines in order to ensure the effectiveness and efficiency of mine-clearance operations,

Recognizing the important role that the international community, particularly States involved in the deployment of mines, can play in assisting mine clearance in mine-affected countries through the provision of necessary maps and information and appropriate technical and material assistance to remove or otherwise render ineffective existing minefields, mines and booby traps,

Concerned about the limited availability of safe and cost-effective mine-detection and mine-clearance equipment as well as the need for effective global coordination in research and development to improve the relevant technology, and conscious of the need to promote further and more rapid progress in this field and to foster international technical cooperation to this end,

Recognizing that, in addition to the primary role of States, the United Nations has an important role in the field of assistance in mine action,

Welcoming in this regard the mine-action coordination centres already established under the auspices of the United Nations as well as the creation of international trust funds for mine clearance and mine assistance,

Noting with satisfaction the inclusion in the mandates of several peacekeeping operations of provisions relating to mine-action work carried out under the direction of the Department of Peacekeeping Operations of the Secretariat, in the context of such operations,

Commending the action already taken by the United Nations system, donor and recipient Governments, the International Committee of the Red Cross and non-governmental organizations to coordinate their efforts and seek solutions to the problems related to the presence of mines and other unexploded devices, as well as their assistance to victims of mines,

Also commending the role of the Secretary-General in increasing public awareness of the problem of landmines,

1. *Welcomes* the report of the Secretary-General concerning the activities of the United Nations in assistance in mine action, in particular the emphasis on the lessons learned, and the recommendation to improve the emergency preparedness capability of the Organization;

2. *Calls*, in particular, for the continuation of the efforts of the United Nations, with the assistance of States and institutions as appropriate, to foster the establishment of mine-action capacities in countries where mines constitute a serious threat to the safety, health and lives of the local population, also calls for the extension of these efforts to countries where mines are an impediment to social and economic development efforts at the national and local levels, emphasizes the importance of developing national mine-action capacities, and urges all Member States, particularly those that have the capacity to do so, to assist mine-affected countries in the establishment and development of national capacities in mine clearance, mine awareness and victim assistance;

3. *Invites* Member States to develop national programmes, in cooperation with the relevant bodies of the United Nations system where appropriate, to promote awareness of landmines, especially among children;

4. *Expresses its appreciation* to Governments, regional organizations and other donors for their financial and in-kind contributions to mine action, including contributions for emergency operations and for national capacity-building programmes;

5. *Appeals* to Governments, regional organizations and other donors to continue their support to mine action through further contributions, including contributions through the Voluntary Trust Fund for Assistance in Mine Action to allow for the timely delivery of mine-action assistance in emergency situations;

6. *Encourages* all relevant multilateral and national programmes and bodies to include, in coordination with the United Nations, activities related to mine action in their humanitarian, rehabilitation, reconstruction and development assistance activities, where appropriate, bearing in mind the need to ensure national ownership, sustainability and capacity-building;

7. *Stresses* the importance of international support for emergency assistance to victims of mines and for the care and rehabilitation, and social and economic reintegration, of the victims, and also stresses that such assistance should be integrated into broader public health and socio-economic strategies;

8. *Encourages* Governments, relevant United Nations bodies and other donors to take further action to promote gender- and age-appropriate mine-awareness programmes, victim assistance and child-centred rehabilitation, thereby reducing the number of child victims and relieving their plight;

9. *Emphasizes again* the important role of the United Nations in the effective coordination of mine-action activities, including those by regional organizations, and especially the role of the Mine Action Service of the Department of Peacekeeping Operations of the Secretariat on the basis of the policy on mine action and effective coordination developed by the Secretary-General in annex II to his report;

10. *Emphasizes* in this regard the role of the Mine Action Service as the focal point for mine action within the United Nations system and its ongoing collaboration with and coordination of all the mine-related activities of the United Nations agencies, funds and programmes;

11. *Encourages* the Secretary-General to develop further a comprehensive mine-action strategy, taking into consideration the impact of the landmine problem on rehabilitation, reconstruction and development, with a view to ensuring the effectiveness of assistance in mine action by the United Nations, and emphasizes in this respect the importance of further multisectoral assessments and surveys;

12. *Emphasizes* in this respect the importance of developing a comprehensive information management system for mine action, under the overall coordination of the Mine Action Service and with the support of the Geneva International Centre for Humanitarian Demining, in order to facilitate the setting of priorities and the coordination of field activities;

13. *Welcomes* recent approaches with regard to the establishment of mine-action coordination centres, encourages the further establishment of such centres, especially in emergency situations, and also encourages States to support the activities of mine-action coordination centres and trust funds established to coordinate assistance in mine action under the auspices of the Mine Action Service;

14. *Urges* Member States, regional, governmental and non-governmental organizations and foundations to continue to extend full assistance and cooperation to the Secretary-General and, in particular, to provide him with information and data as well as other appropriate resources that could be useful in strengthening the coordination role of the United Nations in mine action, particularly in the fields of mine awareness, training, surveying, detection and clearance, scientific research on mine detection and clearance technology and information on and distribution of medical equipment and supplies;

15. *Emphasizes* in this regard the importance of recording the location of mines, of retaining all such records and making them available to concerned parties upon cessation of hostilities, and welcomes the strengthening of the relevant provisions in international law;

16. *Calls upon* Member States, especially those that have the capacity to do so, to provide the necessary information and technical and material assistance, as appropriate, and to locate, remove, destroy or otherwise render ineffective minefields, mines, booby traps and other devices in accordance with international law, as soon as possible;

17. *Urges* Member States and regional, intergovernmental and non-governmental organizations and foundations that have the ability to do so to provide, as appropriate, technological assistance to mine-infested

countries and to promote scientific research and development on humanitarian mine-action techniques and technology so that mine-action activities may be carried out more effectively at lower costs and through safer means and to promote international collaboration in this regard;

18. *Encourages* Member States and regional, intergovernmental and non-governmental organizations and foundations to continue to support ongoing activities to promote appropriate technology, as well as international operational and safety standards for humanitarian mine-action activities, and in this context welcomes the initiation of the revision of international mine-clearance standards and the development of guidelines for the use of mine-detection dogs and mechanical mine-clearance equipment, as well as the development of an international test and evaluation programme;

19. *Requests* the Secretary-General to submit to the General Assembly at its fifty-fifth session a report on the progress achieved on all relevant issues outlined both in his previous reports to the Assembly on assistance in mine clearance and mine action and in the present resolution, including progress made by the International Committee of the Red Cross and other international and regional organizations as well as national programmes, and on the operation of the Voluntary Trust Fund for Assistance in Mine Action and other mine-action programmes;

20. *Decides* to include in the provisional agenda of its fifty-fifth session the item entitled "Assistance in mine action".

Humanitarian activities

Africa

Angola

The United Nations consolidated inter-agency appeal for Angola launched in 1998, which initially sought $66.7 million for programmes for the period January to December 1999, was revised to $106 million by July given the magnitude of the crisis in the country. The donor community covered 71.7 per cent, or $82.1 million, of the revised appeal by October.

The consequences of renewed civil war in Angola (see p. 102) exceeded the 1999 appeal's worst case scenario in terms of human suffering. The number of new internally displaced persons rose to nearly 1 million between April 1998 and September 1999; and, not including vulnerable persons from non-accessible areas, there were 2 million war-affected people who required immediate assistance. Insecurity impeded the continuous delivery of humanitarian assistance and the lack of regular secure access to farms and markets gave rise to competition for scarce resources. In November, OCHA launched a UN consolidated inter-agency appeal covering January to December 2000 for a total of $258.5 million.

Eritrea

In Eritrea, tension along the border with Ethiopia remained high (see p. 130), preventing displaced people from returning to their places of origin. Attacks on civilians drove additional waves of people from their homes to rural and urban centres. Displaced persons stretched the capacity of public services, facilities and infrastructure. Adding to the humanitarian crisis, Ethiopia started to deport people of Eritrean origin, and a severe drought in the Sahel area of Anseba region and the northern and southern Red Sea regions led to widespread crop failure.

A 1998 Flash Appeal [YUN 1998, p. 848], outlining requirements through February 1999, was followed by a UN Country Team Appeal requesting $31.4 million to cover the most urgent needs for the period April-September. To respond to humanitarian needs, UN agencies worked closely with the Eritrean Relief and Refugee Commission, which, in January, issued an appeal requesting $58.9 million for 1999 and, following the resumption of hostilities in February, issued an "Urgent Appeal for Humanitarian Assistance" for $31.4 million. As at 31 December, UN agencies had received $14.4 million or 46 per cent of the Country Team Appeal.

Great Lakes region and Central Africa

The humanitarian situation in the Great Lakes region and Central Africa (Burundi, Democratic Republic of the Congo (DRC), Rwanda, Uganda, United Republic of Tanzania) worsened during the year. The fragility of the peace process was apparent as violence against civilians continued and the number of people forced to leave their homes increased (see p. 80). The number of affected population rose by 59 per cent since the beginning of the year, stressing the humanitarian community to meet the population's most basic needs.

In November, a UN consolidated inter-agency appeal sought $163 million covering the period January to December 2000 for assistance to Burundi, the Congo, the DRC, Uganda and the United Republic of Tanzania.

Burundi

The suffering which had plagued Burundi since 1993 remained unabated in 1999. More than half a million people continued to live in 300 sites away from their homes and nearly 300,000 remained refugees, mainly in the United Republic of Tanzania. Insecurity increased during the latter half of the year, forcibly moving some 250,000 additional people, thus raising the number of displaced to over 800,000. Although the embargo imposed in 1996 was suspended in January 1999, the economy weakened further. In October, an attack on a humanitarian mission in Rutana province caused the massacre of several members of the mission, including two UN officials (see p. 100).

In November, OCHA issued a UN consolidated inter-agency appeal, seeking $70.6 million for January to December 2000.

Congo (Republic of the)

As a result of the civil war in the Republic of the Congo, of the 810,000 persons who were displaced since December 1998, 580,000 remained internally displaced. Some 200,000 urban dwellers had returned to Brazzaville and the towns of Dolisie and Nkayi, while another 30,000 remained refugees in the DRC and Gabon. Access for the delivery of humanitarian assistance up until the second half of 1999 was mainly restricted to Brazzaville and Pointe Noire. In May, following the improvement of the security situation, President Sassou Nguesso announced that internally displaced persons could return to the southern districts of the country, and by mid-June, over 60,000 persons had already returned. In July, OCHA launched a UN consolidated inter-agency appeal covering the period from July to December, which sought $14.7 million for the implementation of 12 emergency interventions. By 30 September, the donor community had responded to the appeal with $7.8 million, or 53 per cent. The majority of pledges ($6 million) were received for food assistance.

In November, OCHA launched a UN consolidated inter-agency appeal covering January to December 2000 for a total of $17.1 million.

Uganda

In Uganda, the Allied Democratic Forces carried out violent attacks from January to July in Bundibugyo, causing massive and rapid displacement. Attacks in the Rwenzoli mountains continued. Attention focused on Karamoja, which experienced its worst insecurity in years. In July and August, violent attacks erupted amongst the Karamojong and between Karamojong and the Uganda People's Defence Force. Moreover, a prolonged drought threatened the food security in some western, central and northern (Karamoja) districts. Refugees continued to seek asylum in Uganda from neighbouring wars, with inflows largely from the Sudan and the DRC.

In November, OCHA issued a UN consolidated inter-agency appeal seeking $56.1 million for January to December 2000.

United Republic of Tanzania

The United Republic of Tanzania continued to receive substantial influxes of refugees, particularly from the DRC, but also from Burundi. The refugees went to the remote Kigoma and Kagera regions, a poverty-stricken part of the country where social services such as health and education were minimal and the physical infrastructure was poor.

In November, OCHA launched a UN consolidated inter-agency appeal covering January to December 2000 for a total of $59.7 million.

Guinea-Bissau

The outbreak of fighting in Guinea-Bissau between January and May 1999 ended with the ouster of the country's President and an alteration of the political landscape. The UN consolidated inter-agency appeal for January to December 1999, launched in 1998, was revised downward from $28.6 million to $17.3 million. The downward revision was due to sufficient in-country food to meet the requirements until year's end. In addition, some of the bilaterally funded developmental programmes which were frozen during the conflict were reactivated, responding to needs in the water/sanitation, health and education sectors.

Sierra Leone

In 1999, the civil war in Sierra Leone saw rebel forces in control of the northern province and parts of the east, and exposed all Sierra Leoneans to brutality and destruction (see p. 152). The implementation of 1999 humanitarian objectives was hampered by the combined effects of resource and security constraints. As at 12 October, response to the 1999 appeal of $25.1 million, revised downward from $27.9 million, remained low at $11.4 million or 40.7 per cent of requirements, despite a dire humanitarian situation. As a result of the periods of instability that followed the January 1999 invasion of Freetown by rebels of the Revolutionary United Front/Armed Forces Revolutionary Council, most humanitarian activities were curtailed or not undertaken. Displaced populations and refugees delayed returning to their communities due to lack of adequate security, social services and productive activities.

The humanitarian context of Sierra Leone changed with the signing on 7 July of the Lomé Peace Accord (see p. 159), which ended the war, provided a framework for the resolution of hostilities and bound the parties to the principle of immediate humanitarian access. Progress made in the implementation of the Accord provided the opportunity for the international community to address the dire humanitarian situation of hundreds of thousands of war-affected Sierra Leoneans.

A UN consolidated inter-agency appeal issued in November sought $71 million to implement 34 projects in the year 2000.

Somalia

In an August report [A/54/296], submitted pursuant to General Assembly resolution 53/1 M [YUN 1998, p. 853], the Secretary-General described assistance provided to Somalia by the United Nations and its partners from August 1998 to July 1999. Although insecurity was a constant feature and an obstacle to the provision of humanitarian assistance, especially in urban areas and much of rural central and southern Somalia, the UN agencies and their humanitarian partners were able to gain intermittent access to a significant proportion of the most affected areas. Sudden humanitarian emergencies in Somalia were met by a substantial response from the donor community; however, the decline in general donor support resulted in the loss of operational capacity, the Secretary-General stated.

The UN consolidated inter-agency appeal for Somalia launched in December 1998, which initially solicited $65.7 million for the period January to December 1999, was revised to $64.1 million. As at 14 October, the appeal had received $39.2 million or 55.4 per cent of the requirements. In November, a UN consolidated inter-agency appeal was issued, seeking $124.3 million for January to December 2000.

GENERAL ASSEMBLY ACTION

On 8 December [meeting 73], the General Assembly adopted **resolution 54/96 D** [draft: A/54/L.57 & Add.1] without vote [agenda item 20 *(b)*].

Assistance for humanitarian relief and the economic and social rehabilitation of Somalia

The General Assembly,

Recalling its resolutions 43/206 of 20 December 1988, 44/178 of 19 December 1989, 45/229 of 21 December 1990, 46/176 of 19 December 1991, 47/160 of 18 December 1992, 48/201 of 21 December 1993, 49/21 L of 20 December 1994, 50/58 G of 20 December 1995, 51/30 G of 13 December 1996, 52/169 L of 16 December 1997 and 53/1 M of 8 December 1998 as well as the resolutions and decisions of the Economic and Social Council on emergency assistance to Somalia,

Recalling also Security Council resolution 733(1992) of 23 January 1992 and all subsequent relevant resolutions, in which the Council, inter alia, urged all parties, movements and factions in Somalia to facilitate the efforts of the United Nations, its specialized agencies and humanitarian organizations to provide urgent humanitarian assistance to the affected population in Somalia, and reiterated the call for the full respect of the security and safety of the personnel of those organizations and guarantee of their complete freedom of movement in and around Mogadishu and other parts of Somalia,

Noting the cooperation between the United Nations, the Organization of African Unity, the League of Arab States, the European Union, the Organization of the Islamic Conference, the countries members of the Intergovernmental Authority on Development, the Movement of Non-Aligned Countries and others in their efforts to resolve the humanitarian, security and political crisis in Somalia,

Noting with appreciation the continued efforts made by the Secretary-General to assist the Somali people in their efforts to promote peace, stability and national reconciliation,

Noting with concern that the absence of central authority and effective civil institutions that characterizes Somalia continues to impede sustained comprehensive development, and that, while the environment has become conducive to some reconstruction and development-oriented work in certain parts of the country, the humanitarian and security situation has remained fragile in other parts,

Welcoming the joint strategy for targeted assistance of the United Nations system focusing on rehabilitation and reconstruction of infrastructure and on sustainable community-based activities, and reaffirming the importance it attaches to the need for effective coordination and cooperation among the United Nations agencies and their partners,

Taking note of the report of the Secretary-General,

Deeply appreciative of the humanitarian assistance and rehabilitation support rendered by a number of States to alleviate the hardship and suffering of the affected Somali population,

Recognizing that, while the humanitarian situation remains fragile in some parts of Somalia, there is a need to continue the ongoing rehabilitation and reconstruction process, in those parts of the country where peace and security prevail, alongside the national reconciliation process, without prejudice to the provision of emergency relief assistance wherever and whenever required, as security allows,

Noting with appreciation that the prospects for humanitarian, rehabilitation and development activities have been more favourable in some parts of the country, owing to the formation of stronger local administrative structures which are able to take responsibility for meeting humanitarian needs, with the presence and support of the United Nations system,

Noting also with appreciation the efforts of the United Nations system aimed at working directly with Somali communities, whenever possible, in the absence of a recognized national Government, and welcoming the continued focus of the United Nations, in partnership with Somali elders, other local leaders and skilled local counterparts at the grass-roots level and non-governmental organizations, on a programme of assistance combining humanitarian and developmental approaches, given the varying conditions in different areas,

Re-emphasizing the importance of implementing further its resolution 47/160 to rehabilitate basic social and economic services at local and regional levels throughout the country,

1. *Expresses its gratitude* to all States and the intergovernmental and non-governmental organizations that have responded to the appeals of the Secretary-General and others by extending assistance to Somalia;

2. *Expresses its appreciation* to the Secretary-General for his continuing and tireless efforts to mobilize assistance to the Somali people;

3. *Welcomes* the ongoing efforts of the United Nations, the Organization of African Unity, the League of Arab States, the European Union, the Organization of the Islamic Conference, the countries members of the Intergovernmental Authority on Development, the Movement of Non-Aligned Countries and others to resolve the situation in Somalia;

4. *Also welcomes* the strategy of the United Nations focusing on the implementation of community-based interventions aimed at rebuilding local infrastructures and increasing the self-reliance of the local population, and the ongoing efforts by the United Nations agencies, their Somali counterparts and their partner organizations to establish and maintain close coordination and cooperation mechanisms available for the implementation of relief, rehabilitation and reconstruction programmes;

5. *Notes with appreciation* the holistic and prioritized approach of the United Nations system to addressing the continuing crisis in some parts of Somalia, while making long-term commitments to rehabilitation, recovery and development activities in more stable parts;

6. *Emphasizes* the principle that the Somali people, in particular at the local level, have the primary responsibility for their own development and for the sustainability of rehabilitation and reconstruction assistance programmes, and reaffirms the importance it attaches to the creation of workable arrangements for collaboration between the United Nations system and its partner organizations and their Somali counterparts for the effective execution of rehabilitation and development activities in those parts of the country where peace and security prevail;

7. *Urges* all States and intergovernmental and non-governmental organizations concerned to continue to implement further its resolution 47/160 in order to assist the Somali people to embark on the rehabilitation of basic social and economic services, as well as institution building aimed at the restoration of civil administration at the local level in all those parts of the country where peace and security prevail;

8. *Appeals* to all the Somali parties concerned to seek peaceful means for resolving differences and to redouble their efforts to achieve national reconciliation that allows for transition from relief to reconstruction and development;

9. *Calls upon* all parties, movements and factions in Somalia to respect fully the security and safety of personnel of the United Nations and the specialized agencies and of non-governmental organizations, and to guarantee their complete freedom of movement throughout the country;

10. *Calls upon* the Secretary-General to continue to mobilize international humanitarian, rehabilitation and reconstruction assistance for Somalia;

11. *Calls upon* the international community to provide continuing and increased assistance in response to the United Nations Consolidated Inter-Agency Appeal for relief, rehabilitation and reconstruction assistance for Somalia covering the period from October 1999 to December 2000;

12. *Requests* the Secretary-General, in view of the critical situation in Somalia, to take all necessary measures for the implementation of the present resolution and to report thereon to the General Assembly at its fifty-fifth session.

Sudan

During 1999, conflict continued unabated in southern Sudan, the Nuba Mountains, the southern Blue Nile region and eastern Sudan along the border with Eritrea. Despite progress in food security in some areas, others remained affected by the fighting, which caused disruption of livelihood and displacement of civilians. In eastern Sudan, insecurity provoked massive displacements and relocations of civilians to Khartoum. The operational environment for humanitarian workers deteriorated, particularly in the Upper Nile area, where the shooting and detaining of aid staff made relief work unsafe and difficult.

A UN consolidated inter-agency appeal seeking $198.4 million for January to December 1999, issued in January, was revised upward to $204.2 million in June. As at 18 October, total financial resources amounted to $204.4 million, representing new contributions of $187.6 million and carry-over funding from 1998 of $16.9 million.

In November, OCHA issued a UN consolidated inter-agency appeal for the Sudan, seeking $125.6 million for 24 projects for January to December 2000.

In response to General Assembly resolution 53/1 O [YUN 1998, p. 855], the Secretary-General, in an August report on emergency assistance to the Sudan [A/54/295], covering the period August 1998 to July 1999, described the situation in the country, emergency operations and the work of Operation Lifeline Sudan (OLS), and action taken by Member States. During the reporting period, OLS remained the only viable instrument for humanitarian policy with donor support and a commitment from the Government and the Sudan People's Liberation Movement/Army (SPLM/A). OLS concentrated on expanding access to all war-affected populations and provided life-saving food and non-food emergency assistance. However, the crisis was exacerbated by a ban on OLS flights in an area marked by a resurgence of fighting. The Secretary-General emphasized that the principles and instruments defining cooperation within OLS should be respected, and that humanitarian action in areas of crisis in southern Sudan should benefit from further extensions and a geographical broadening of the ceasefire applicable in Bahr Al Ghazal. He stated that the UN humanitarian assessment mission to the SPLM-controlled areas of the Nuba Mountains had taken place in late June.

Communications. In a 5 April letter [A/54/84], the Sudan informed the Secretary-General that on that date the country's President announced a ceasefire in all the southern states effective 15 April, with a view to enabling UN humanitarian agencies to deliver relief to the affected population.

In a 21 May letter [A/54/113], the Sudan announced that, on 18 May, SPLA had carried out an attack against a boat operated under OLS authority, which resulted in the death of one person and injury to three others who worked for the World Food Programme (WFP). The Government reiterated its call to the international community to bring pressure to bear on SPLA to respect the current ceasefire so as to allow the delivery of relief supplies and achieve durable peace.

On 25 August [A/54/282], Finland transmitted to the Secretary-General a statement on the humanitarian ceasefire in the Sudan, issued on 19 August by the Presidency of the European Union (EU). The EU called on the Sudan and SPLM to implement their commitments to a ceasefire and to cover all areas of humanitarian needs and activities of OLS, as well as to agree to a permanent humanitarian ceasefire.

GENERAL ASSEMBLY ACTION

On 17 December [meeting 84], the General Assembly adopted **resolution 54/96 J** [draft: A/54/L.72/Rev.1] without vote [agenda item 20 *(b)*].

Emergency assistance to the Sudan

The General Assembly,

Recalling its resolution 53/1 O of 17 December 1998 and its previous resolutions on emergency assistance to the Sudan,

Bearing in mind its resolution 54/192 of 17 December 1999 on the safety and security of humanitarian personnel and protection of United Nations personnel,

Welcoming agreed conclusions 1998/1 of the Economic and Social Council, adopted by the Council at the humanitarian segment of its substantive session of 1998, in which, among other things, the Council reaffirmed that international cooperation to address emergency situations should be provided in accordance with international law and national laws, and that the affected State has the primary role in the initiation, organization, coordination and implementation of humanitarian assistance within its territory,

Welcoming also agreed conclusions 1999/1 of the Economic and Social Council, in which the Council addressed the theme of "International cooperation and coordinated responses to humanitarian emergencies, in particular in the transition from relief to rehabilitation, reconstruction and development" in its second humanitarian segment,

Taking note of the report of the Secretary-General,

Welcoming the decision of the Government of the Sudan to provide access to the Nuba Mountains, noting in that regard the results of the inter-agency needs assessment mission undertaken by the United Nations, and calling upon all parties to continue to cooperate with the United Nations in meeting the needs identified in that assessment,

Noting the occasional obstacles to the delivery of humanitarian assistance, welcoming the agreements reached by the parties to Operation Lifeline Sudan, among them the Rome protocol, aiming at facilitating delivery of relief assistance to affected populations, as well as the progress made by the Emergency Relief Coordinator and the Office for the Coordination of Humanitarian Affairs of the Secretariat in strengthening the coordination of the Operation,

Urging United Nations agencies, non-governmental organizations and donor countries to continue channelling their humanitarian assistance to all affected populations in the Sudan through Operation Lifeline Sudan,

Expressing concern over the continued conflict in the Sudan and its negative impact on the humanitarian situation,

Taking note of the ongoing peace efforts taking place under the auspices of the Intergovernmental Authority on Development and the initiative of Egypt and the Libyan Arab Jamahiriya for achieving a negotiated and lasting peace in the Sudan,

Noting with appreciation the contributions for the inter-agency appeal for Operation Lifeline Sudan and the progress made in the Operation, and noting also that considerable relief needs still remain to be addressed, including assistance to combat diseases such as malaria and assistance for logistic needs, emergency recovery, rehabilitation and development,

Expressing concern over the damaging consequences of floods that have occurred in various parts of the Sudan lately,

Calling for an early resolution to the conflict, and expressing concern that its continuation further increases the suffering of the civilian population and undermines the effectiveness of international, regional and national humanitarian assistance,

Reaffirming the need for all parties to continue to facilitate the work of humanitarian organizations in implementing emergency assistance, in particular the supply of food, medicine, shelter and health care, and to ensure safe and unhindered access to all affected populations,

Recognizing the need in emergency situations to ensure the smooth transition from relief to rehabilitation and development so as to reduce dependence on external food aid and other relief services,

1. *Expresses its appreciation* to the donor community, United Nations agencies and governmental and non-governmental organizations for the contributions so far made to the humanitarian needs of the Sudan, and calls upon them to continue their assistance, in particular by responding to the consolidated appeal and providing support for programmes in the Nuba Mountains;

2. *Acknowledges with appreciation* the cooperation by the Government of the Sudan with the United Nations, including the agreements and arrangements achieved to facilitate relief operations with a view to improving United Nations assistance to the affected areas, encourages the continuation of that cooperation, and

calls upon all parties to the conflict to respect the current humanitarian ceasefire, in order to ensure the delivery of relief assistance;

3. *Stresses* the need for Operation Lifeline Sudan to be operated and managed with a view to ensuring its efficiency, transparency and effectiveness, with the full involvement and cooperation of the Government of the Sudan, taking cognizance of the relevant Operation Lifeline Sudan agreements reached by the parties, as well as consultations in the preparation of the consolidated annual inter-agency appeal for the Operation;

4. *Recognizes* the need for Operation Lifeline Sudan to be conducted in strict adherence to the principles of neutrality and impartiality and within the principles of national sovereignty and territorial integrity of the Sudan, and within the framework of international cooperation, in accordance with the relevant provisions of international law;

5. *Calls upon* the international community to continue to contribute generously to the emergency needs, recovery and development of the Sudan;

6. *Urges* the international community to give assistance for the rehabilitation of transportation means and infrastructure vital for the provision of relief supplies in the Sudan and their cost-effectiveness, and in this context stresses the importance of continued cooperation by all the parties involved so as to facilitate and improve the delivery of relief supplies;

7. *Calls upon* the donor community and the organizations of the United Nations system to provide financial, technical and medical assistance, guided by the actions called for by the General Assembly in its relevant resolutions, to combat such diseases as malaria and other epidemics in the Sudan;

8. *Urges* the international community to continue to support national programmes of rehabilitation, voluntary resettlement and reintegration of returnees and internally displaced persons, as well as assistance to refugees;

9. *Stresses* the imperative of ensuring the safety and security of humanitarian personnel, as well as safe and unhindered access for providing relief assistance to all affected populations, and the importance of strict observance of the principles and guidelines of Operation Lifeline Sudan, and of international humanitarian law reaffirming the necessity for humanitarian personnel to respect the national laws of the Sudan;

10. *Welcomes* the decision of the Government of the Sudan to extend for a further period of three months the ceasefire for all the areas of military operation in the country and the announcement by the Sudan People's Liberation Movement and Army of the continuation of the humanitarian ceasefire within the same period for Bahr al Ghazal and parts of the Upper Nile, strongly appeals for a comprehensive ceasefire and appeals to the parties and the revitalized mediation structure to work to this end as part of a negotiated solution to the conflict;

11. *Urges* all parties involved to continue to offer all feasible assistance, including facilitating the movement of relief supplies and personnel, so as to guarantee the success of Operation Lifeline Sudan in all affected parts of the country, with especial emphasis on national capacity-building in the humanitarian field for governmental and non-governmental organizations, as well as on meeting emergency relief needs;

12. *Calls upon* all parties to respect international humanitarian law on the protection of civilians during times of war and, in this connection, condemns attacks against civilians and humanitarian personnel, including the case of four Sudanese nationals who were abducted on 18 February 1999 while accompanying a humanitarian mission of an International Committee of the Red Cross team and subsequently killed while in the custody of the Sudan People's Liberation Movement and Army, and urges the Sudan People's Liberation Movement and Army to return the bodies to their families;

13. *Condemns* the detention of humanitarian personnel, and calls for appropriate investigations into all allegations of such incidents, including into the whereabouts of the eleven personnel of the sub-Saharan international development organizations last seen in rebel-held areas;

14. *Welcomes* the signing by the Government of the Sudan of the Convention on the Prohibition of the Use Stockpiling, Production and Transfer of Anti-personnel Mines and on Their Destruction, urges all parties to the conflict to desist from using them, calls upon the international community to refrain from supplying mines to the region, and urges the international community and United Nations agencies to provide appropriate assistance related to mine action in the Sudan;

15. *Requests* the Secretary-General to continue to mobilize and coordinate resources and support for Operation Lifeline Sudan and to report to the General Assembly at its fifty-sixth session on the emergency situation in the affected areas and the recovery, rehabilitation and development of the Sudan.

Special assistance to Central and East Africa

In September [A/54/421], the Secretary-General described the activities of the United Nations and other organizations relating to special assistance to Central and East African countries hosting refugees, returnees and displaced persons, and areas where large numbers of refugees had repatriated. Activities consisted of providing emergency relief and assistance to refugees in Burundi, the Central African Republic, the Congo, the DRC, Gabon, Kenya, Rwanda, Uganda, the United Republic of Tanzania and Zambia. The Secretary-General concluded that lack of funding remained a great concern. In view of the continuing instability in the region, providing protection and assistance for uprooted populations would continue to be given priority by the UN system (see p. 1140).

Asia

Afghanistan

In Afghanistan, the peace process had collapsed, external support to warring parties continued unabated, and the fighting between the Taliban and opposition forces (see p. 255) brought deliberate targeting of civilians, large-scale displacement and attendant humanitarian needs. Security constraints, restricted access and inadequate funding limited the potential of the assistance community. Emergency relief interventions were undertaken, such as those for persons displaced by conflict in Kabul, the Panjshir and Hazarajat, and for the February earthquake in Logar and Wardak provinces, while work continued to support social infrastructure development at the community level. During the year, the assistance community strengthened its capacity to address the human rights concerns and, since April, the gender adviser to the UN system in Afghanistan had been engaged in working with UN agencies and the authorities to widen women's access to employment and basic social services.

As at 11 November, only $78.3 million, or 44 per cent of requirements, was available in response to a January UN consolidated inter-agency appeal for Afghanistan of $184.7 million for 1999.

A UN consolidated inter-agency appeal for $220.8 million was issued for the period January to December 2000.

Pursuant to General Assembly resolution 53/203 B [YUN 1998, p. 857], the Secretary-General, in an August report covering the period from 4 September 1998 to 1 July 1999 [A/54/297], reviewed the major humanitarian and socio-economic developments in Afghanistan and described assistance provided by the United Nations and its partners and by Member States. He stated that the condition of the country had worsened during the first half of 1999, owing to the enduring instability, conflict and natural disasters, in particular the February earthquake in Logar and Wardak provinces that affected 16,000 families. Moreover, the combatants still denied most humanitarian agencies access to many areas, and the absence of UN international staff from August 1998 until March 1999, owing to security concerns, limited the capacity of the aid community to provide assistance. However, starting in early 1999, progress was made on security issues and towards the implementation of the 1998 Memorandum of Understanding between the Taliban and the United Nations governing humanitarian operations in Taliban-held areas [YUN 1998, p. 300].

Regarding the refugee situation, there were still 2.6 million refugees in the two main neighbouring countries (1.4 million in Iran and 1.2 million in Pakistan). During 1999, the increase in the number of refugees returning from Iran was a concern both to the Taliban authorities and the humanitarian agencies, which were faced with the challenge of supporting resettlement and ensuring that the returnees' rights were protected. Assistance programmes remained affected by the lack of access of women to health, education and employment opportunities. The country remained affected by landmines and unexploded ordnance, and the OCHA Mine Action Programme for Afghanistan undertook activities, including clearance of areas contaminated. The Secretary-General concluded that the failure of the peace talks and the resumption of fighting between the Taliban and the Northern Alliance resulted in the implementation of international assistance activities in an insecure environment, providing temporary relief until a sustained peace prevailed. A durable political settlement remained the key to resolving the crisis and securing a stable future for Afghanistan's people.

GENERAL ASSEMBLY ACTION

On 17 December [meeting 84], the General Assembly adopted **resolution 54/189 B** [draft: A/54/L.58] without vote [agenda items 20 (*f*) & 50].

Emergency international assistance for peace, normalcy and reconstruction of war-stricken Afghanistan

The General Assembly,

Recalling its resolutions 50/88 A of 19 December 1995, 51/195 A of 17 December 1996, 52/211 A of 19 December 1997 and 53/203 B of 18 December 1998,

Expressing its grave concern about the continuation of the military confrontation in Afghanistan, threatening regional peace and security and causing massive loss of life and extensive human suffering, further destruction of property, serious damage to the economic and social infrastructure, refugee flows and other forcible displacements of large numbers of people,

Noting with deep concern that the people of Afghanistan continue to suffer from a serious loss of their human rights, which can be largely attributed to the effects of decades of warfare that continues to create a worsening humanitarian crisis,

Remaining deeply concerned about the problem of millions of anti-personnel landmines and unexploded ordnance as well as the continued laying of new anti-personnel landmines in Afghanistan, which continue to prevent many Afghan refugees and internally displaced persons from returning to their villages and working in their fields,

Deeply disturbed by the continuing security threat to United Nations personnel and other humanitarian personnel, including locally engaged staff, and by various impediments to their access to affected populations,

Expressing its grave concern at the serious violations of human rights and international humanitarian law, in particular by the Taliban, in Afghanistan and at the inadequacy of measures taken by the warring factions to reverse the situation,

Deeply concerned by the continuing and substantiated reports of violations of human rights, in particular of women and girls, including all forms of discrimination against them, notably in areas under the control of the Taliban,

Welcoming the ongoing work of gender and human rights advisers appointed by the United Nations, who form an integral part of the office of the United Nations resident and humanitarian coordinator in Afghanistan,

Welcoming the visit of the Special Rapporteur of the Commission on Human Rights on violence against women, its causes and consequences to Afghanistan in September 1999, and looking forward to her conclusions and recommendations,

Expressing its grave concern for the well-being of internally displaced persons, particularly in Kabul and in the Panjshir, Bamian and Kunduz regions, and the civilian population of Afghanistan living without shelter, who face a long winter possibly deprived of basic foods as a result of the recent fighting, as well as the denial by the warring factions of adequate conditions for the delivery of aid by humanitarian organizations,

Distressed by the loss of life caused by earthquakes and epidemics, and expressing its appreciation to all States, international agencies and non-governmental organizations that have provided emergency relief,

Affirming the urgent need to continue international humanitarian assistance to Afghanistan for the restoration of basic services, as well as the need for the conflicting parties to guarantee the safety and security of the personnel of all international organizations,

Welcoming the principle-centred approach towards humanitarian assistance and rehabilitation in Afghanistan as outlined in the Strategic Framework for Afghanistan and in the document entitled "Next Steps for the United Nations in Afghanistan", and the common programming mechanisms introduced by the United Nations, and also welcoming the initiative to establish an independent strategic monitoring unit,

Expressing its gratitude to all Governments that have rendered assistance to Afghan refugees, and, at the same time, calling on all parties to continue to honour their obligations for the protection of refugees and internally displaced persons and to allow international access for their protection and care,

Recognizing the need for continuing international assistance for the maintenance abroad and the voluntary repatriation and resettlement of refugees and internally displaced persons, and welcoming the voluntary return of refugees to rural districts in Afghanistan that are relatively stable and secure,

Expressing its appreciation to the United Nations system, to all States and international and non-governmental organizations that have responded positively and continue to respond, where conditions permit, to the humanitarian needs of Afghanistan, as well as to the Secretary-General for his efforts in mobilizing and coordinating the delivery of appropriate humanitarian assistance,

1. *Takes note* of the report of the Secretary-General, and endorses the observations contained therein;

2. *Stresses* that the responsibility for the humanitarian crisis lies with all warring parties, in particular with the Taliban;

3. *Strongly condemns* the recent fighting in the Shomali Plains and the forced displacement of civilian populations, the torching of residential houses, the burning of crops, the cutting of fruit trees and the deliberate destruction of infrastructure;

4. *Calls upon* all relevant organizations of the United Nations system to continue to coordinate closely their humanitarian assistance to Afghanistan on the basis of the Strategic Framework for Afghanistan, in particular to assure a consistent approach on matters of principle, human rights and security, and appeals to donor countries as well as other humanitarian organizations to cooperate closely with the United Nations, taking into account the inter-agency consolidated appeal for emergency humanitarian and rehabilitation assistance to Afghanistan for 2000;

5. *Calls upon* the leaders of all Afghan parties to place the highest priority on national reconciliation, acknowledging the desire of the Afghan people for rehabilitation, reconstruction and economic and social development;

6. *Urges* all Afghan parties to respect international humanitarian law and to ensure the safety, security and free movement of all United Nations and humanitarian personnel and the protection of the property of the United Nations and of humanitarian organizations, including non-governmental organizations, so as to facilitate their work;

7. *Demands* that all Afghan parties cooperate fully with the United Nations and associated bodies as well as with other agencies and humanitarian organizations in their efforts to respond to the humanitarian needs of the people of Afghanistan, and urges them to secure the uninterrupted supply of humanitarian aid to all in need of it;

8. *Condemns* all blockades or other interference in the delivery of humanitarian relief supplies to the Afghan people as a violation of international humanitarian law, and notes the recent lifting of the blockade in central Afghanistan by the Taliban;

9. *Strongly condemns* the recent acts of violence in Kabul, Farah, Kandahar, Mazar-e Sharif, Kunduz and Jalalabad directed against United Nations offices and personnel;

10. *Urges* all Afghan parties, in particular the Taliban, to ensure safe and unimpeded access for and to facilitate the delivery of humanitarian assistance, in particular the supply of food, medicine, shelter and health care, especially in the Panjshir Valley;

11. *Takes note* of the Supplementary Protocol to the Memorandum of Understanding of 13 May 1998, signed by the United Nations and the Taliban, on the security of United Nations personnel in Afghanistan, and urges the Taliban to take the necessary steps for its full implementation;

12. *Denounces* the continuing discrimination against girls and women as well as ethnic and religious groups, including minorities, and other violations of human rights and international humanitarian law in Afghanistan, notably in areas under the control of the Taliban, notes with deep concern their adverse effects on international relief and reconstruction programmes in Afghanistan, and calls upon all parties within Afghanistan to respect fully the human rights and fundamental freedoms of all, regardless of gender, ethnicity or religion, in accordance with international human rights instruments, inter alia, the International Covenants on Human Rights;

13. *Strongly urges* all of the Afghan parties to end discriminatory policies and to recognize, protect and promote the equal rights and dignity of women and men, including their rights to full and equal participation in the life of the country, freedom of movement, access to education and health facilities, employment outside the home, personal security and freedom from intimidation and harassment, in particular with respect to the implications of discriminatory policies for the distribution of aid, notwithstanding some progress made with respect to access to education and health care for girls and women;

14. *Urges* all Afghan parties to prohibit conscripting or enlisting children or using them to participate in hostilities in violation of international law;

15. *Appeals* to all States and to the international community to ensure that all humanitarian assistance to the people of Afghanistan integrates a gender perspective, that it actively attempts to promote the participation of both women and men and that women benefit equally with men from such assistance;

16. *Expresses its appreciation* to those Governments that continue to host Afghan refugees, appeals to the Governments concerned to reaffirm their commitment to international refugee law on the rights of asylum and protection, and calls upon the international community to do so and to consider providing further assistance to Afghan refugees;

17. *Expresses concern* over the continued laying of anti-personnel landmines, and urges all Afghan parties to put a complete halt to the use of landmines, which continues to take a heavy toll on civilians and seriously impedes the delivery of humanitarian assistance;

18. *Urgently appeals* to all States, the United Nations system and international and non-governmental organizations to continue to provide, when conditions on the ground permit, all possible financial, technical and material assistance for the Afghan population and the voluntary, safe and secure return of refugees and internally and forcibly displaced persons;

19. *Calls upon* the international community to respond to the inter-agency consolidated appeal for emergency humanitarian and rehabilitation assistance for Afghanistan, launched by the Secretary-General on 23 November 1999 for the period from 1 January to 31 December 2000, bearing in mind the availability also of the Afghanistan Emergency Trust Fund;

20. *Requests* the Secretary-General to submit to the General Assembly at its fifty-fifth session a report on the actions taken pursuant to the present resolution;

21. *Decides* to include in the provisional agenda of its fifty-fifth session, under the cluster of items on coordination of humanitarian assistance, the sub-item entitled "Emergency international assistance for peace, normalcy and reconstruction of war-stricken Afghanistan".

East Timor

During the violence that followed the 30 August popular consultation in East Timor (see p. 280), more than 75 per cent of the population was displaced (see p. 1144) and 70 per cent of private residences, public buildings and utilities were destroyed. The crisis was deepened when all government functions collapsed with the departure of Indonesian authorities. The vacuum was filled by humanitarian agencies and by the deployment, on 20 September, of the International Force for East Timor, which established a security presence throughout the province. During the first month of the operation, humanitarian intervention in Dili included the creation of camps for displaced persons, a distribution of rice and non-food assistance for more than 64,000 people, the reopening of health facilities and repairs to infrastructure systems. In addition, food and non-food assistance was dispatched to displaced populations in conjunction with humanitarian and military reconnaissances and convoys. Agencies worked together to develop a programme strategy that covered the emergency and initial reconstruction needs of more than 650,000 displaced persons and returnees, and to provide basic services to people while a new civil administration was established under the auspices of the United Nations Transitional Administration for East Timor.

Some 290,000 people fled to West Timor during the violence. While voluntary repatriation remained the best option for a resolution of the situation, assistance was provided to refugees in temporary camps. However, a number of constraints prevented the Government and the aid community from organizing an effective approach, particularly the presence of hostile armed elements among the refugees, which limited access to many camps until the end of 1999. In West Timor, the United Nations provided assistance to displaced persons, and agencies worked with authorities to create an environment enabling displaced East Timorese to make a free decision regarding their future, help reintegration, enhance the coping strategies of communities in West Timor hosting East Timorese and support reconciliation.

In October, a UN consolidated inter-agency appeal covering emergency and transitional programmes sought $199 million for the period October 1999 to June 2000. The appeal contained 48 projects for $183.1 million for East Timor and 16 projects for $16 million for West Timor.

GENERAL ASSEMBLY ACTION

On 15 December [meeting 80], the General Assembly adopted **resolution 54/96 H** [draft: A/54/L.68 & Add.1] without vote [agenda item 20 *(b)*].

Assistance for humanitarian relief, rehabilitation and development for East Timor

The General Assembly,

Recalling all its relevant resolutions on the situation in East Timor,

Recalling also the relevant Security Council resolutions and decisions on the situation in East Timor, in particular resolution 1272(1999) of 25 October 1999,

Recalling further agreed conclusions 1998/1 and 1999/1 of the humanitarian affairs segment of the substantive session of the Economic and Social Council,

Recalling its resolution 46/182 of 19 December 1991 and the guiding principles contained in the annex to that resolution,

Recalling also the agreements of 5 May 1999 between Indonesia and Portugal, and between the United Nations, Indonesia and Portugal, on modalities and security arrangements for the popular consultation, welcoming the successful conduct of the popular consultation of the East Timorese people on 30 August 1999, taking note of its outcome, which began a process of transition under the authority of the United Nations towards independence, and welcoming the decision of the Indonesian People's Consultative Assembly on 19 October 1999 concerning East Timor,

Emphasizing the urgent need for humanitarian assistance to overcome the grave humanitarian situation resulting from violence and damage to property in East Timor and the large-scale displacement of East Timorese civilians, including large numbers of women and children,

1. *Welcomes* the contribution of Member States, the United Nations system, international organizations and non-governmental organizations in addressing the humanitarian assistance needs of the people of East Timor;

2. *Welcomes also* the establishment by Security Council resolution 1272(1999) of the United Nations Transitional Administration in East Timor, whose mandate includes the coordination and delivery of humanitarian, rehabilitation and development assistance, as well as the appointment of the Under-Secretary-General for Humanitarian Affairs and Emergency Relief Coordinator as the Special Representative of the Secretary-General in East Timor and Transitional Administrator of the United Nations Transitional Administration in East Timor;

3. *Emphasizes* the importance of close consultation and collaboration with the East Timorese people and organizations in the planning and delivery of humanitarian, rehabilitation and development assistance to East Timor;

4. *Requests* all Member States to respond urgently to meet fully the requirements of the United Nations consolidated inter-agency appeal for the East Timor crises, which was launched on 27 October 1999;

5. *Urges* Member States to respond fully to meet the identified needs of the Transitional Administration, including in such areas as the provision of civil and social services, institutions and capacity;

6. *Welcomes* the Joint Assessment Mission of the World Bank, United Nations agencies, the donor community, the Asian Development Bank and the East Timorese to assess the immediate and long-term rehabilitation, reconstruction and development needs of East Timor, within the United Nations arrangements for East Timor and in close cooperation with immediate relief and rehabilitation efforts, and requests all Member States to respond to meet the needs identified fully;

7. *Welcomes also,* in this regard, the convening of the Donors Meeting for East Timor in Tokyo on 16 and 17 December 1999;

8. *Calls upon* Member States, United Nations agencies, other international organizations and non-governmental organizations to continue to collaborate to ensure the safe and unhindered access and provision of humanitarian, rehabilitation and development assistance to all those in need in East Timor, including internally displaced persons;

9. *Calls upon* Member States, United Nations agencies and other international organizations to continue to collaborate, in full cooperation with the Indonesian Government, to ensure safe and unimpeded access for humanitarian assistance to the East Timorese in western Timor and other parts of Indonesia, including those who do not wish to return to East Timor, in accordance with national and international law;

10. *Welcomes* the assurances given by the Indonesian authorities regarding the activities of the Office of the United Nations High Commissioner for Refugees and other humanitarian organizations, including the security of the personnel of the Office of the High Commissioner, and assurances regarding free access to all East Timorese in western Timor;

11. *Calls upon* Member States to ensure the voluntary, safe and unimpeded return of refugees and displaced persons to East Timor, emphasizes the responsibility of States to ensure the civilian and humanitarian character of refugee and displaced persons camps and settlements, and, in this regard, welcomes the policy of the Indonesian Government to ensure that the East Timorese have the freedom to exercise their right to return voluntarily, to remain in western Timor or to relocate within other parts of Indonesia or other countries;

12. *Welcomes,* in this regard, the memorandum of technical understanding of 22 November 1999 establishing a joint border monitoring group to ensure safe conditions in the border area and to facilitate the efficient and safe flow of returning East Timorese refugees;

13. *Urges* the United Nations to continue to address the humanitarian, rehabilitation and development needs of East Timor;

14. *Requests* the Secretary-General to report to the General Assembly at its fifty-fifth session on the implementation of the present resolution.

Tajikistan

The aim of UN humanitarian operations in Tajikistan continued to be to support the country's two-year peace process (see p. 267) through a three-pronged strategy designed to meet the basic needs of at-risk populations during the critical post-conflict period. The strategy included life-saving interventions, programmes aimed at stabilizing at-risk populations and projects designed to facilitate the reintegration of demobilized combatants and civilian returnees.

The UN consolidated inter-agency appeal for Tajikistan, launched in December 1998 and requesting $24.8 million for 1999, was revised to

$30.2 million, of which $17.6 million, accounting for 56 per cent of requirements, was received as at 14 October.

In November, OCHA launched a UN consolidated inter-agency appeal for January to December 2000, which sought $34.8 million.

In response to General Assembly resolution 53/1 K [YUN 1998, p. 860], the Secretary-General, in an August report [A/54/294], described the situation in Tajikistan and the humanitarian operations during the period December 1998 to mid-July 1999. Despite progress in the peace process and economic reform and improvements in security, significant humanitarian needs continued to exist. The level of need was so great that it would be premature to halt relief assistance, stated the Secretary-General. The United Nations would re-evaluate the humanitarian assistance required following parliamentary elections, scheduled for 2000. In the meantime, humanitarian programmes would continue to serve as a bridge to help at-risk populations to meet their basic needs. In stable areas, UN agencies and NGOs were engaged in rehabilitation projects aimed at revitalizing communities and promoting self-sufficiency.

GENERAL ASSEMBLY ACTION

On 8 December [meeting 73], the General Assembly adopted **resolution 54/96 A** [draft: A/54/L.49 & Add.1] without vote [agenda item 20 (*b*)].

Emergency international assistance for peace, normalcy and rehabilitation in Tajikistan

The General Assembly,

Recalling its resolutions 51/30 J of 25 April 1997, 52/169 I of 16 December 1997 and 53/1 K of 7 December 1998,

Recalling also Security Council resolutions 1113(1997) of 12 June 1997, 1128(1997) of 12 September 1997, 1138(1997) of 14 November 1997, 1167(1998) of 14 May 1998, 1206(1998) of 12 November 1998, 1240(1999) of 15 May 1999 and 1274(1999) of 12 November 1999,

Having considered the report of the Secretary-General,

Welcoming the significant progress made by the parties in the implementation of the General Agreement on the Establishment of Peace and National Accord in Tajikistan,

Commending the efforts of the United Nations, in particular those of the Special Representative of the Secretary-General for Tajikistan and of the personnel of the United Nations Mission of Observers in Tajikistan, in assisting the parties in the implementation of the General Agreement,

Bearing in mind the close interrelationship between ensuring peace and achieving national reconciliation in Tajikistan and the ability of the country to meet the humanitarian needs of its people and to take effective steps towards the rapid revitalization of the economy, and reaffirming the urgent need to assist Tajikistan in its efforts to restore basic services and the infrastructure of the country,

Noting that, despite progress in both the peace process and economic reform and improvements in security, significant humanitarian needs continue to exist throughout Tajikistan,

Recognizing that until the economy is able to support the Tajik population and the peace process has been fully consolidated, humanitarian operations will remain a critical factor in ensuring stability in Tajikistan,

Expressing regret that, despite the importance of humanitarian operations for contributing to peace and stability, donor response to both the 1998 and the 1999 consolidated inter-agency appeals has been disappointing,

Stressing that international funding for humanitarian operations is particularly important since such operations remain the principal means by which hundreds of thousands of Tajiks meet their basic needs,

Noting with concern the lack of support for food assistance and health programmes, which aim to save lives and must receive immediate funding if social catastrophe is to be avoided in Tajikistan,

1. *Takes note* of the report of the Secretary-General, and endorses the observations and recommendations set out therein;

2. *Welcomes* the efforts aimed at achieving peace and national reconciliation in Tajikistan, encourages the parties to ensure the full implementation of the General Agreement on the Establishment of Peace and National Accord in Tajikistan, and encourages the Commission on National Reconciliation to continue its efforts, in particular those aimed at the institution of a broad dialogue among the various political forces in the country in the interest of restoration and strengthening of civil accord in Tajikistan;

3. *Recognizes* that comprehensive international support remains essential to ensuring that Tajikistan can continue on the path of peace and national reconciliation;

4. *Welcomes with appreciation* the efforts undertaken by the Secretary-General in drawing the attention of the international community to the acute humanitarian problems of Tajikistan and in mobilizing assistance for the implementation of the General Agreement and the rehabilitation and reconstruction of the country;

5. *Expresses its appreciation* to the States, the United Nations, the World Bank and other intergovernmental organizations and all relevant humanitarian organizations, agencies and non-governmental organizations, including the International Committee of the Red Cross, that have responded and continue to respond positively to the humanitarian needs of Tajikistan;

6. *Encourages* Member States and others concerned to continue assistance to alleviate the urgent humanitarian needs of Tajikistan and to offer support to that country for the rehabilitation and reconstruction of its economy;

7. *Warmly welcomes* the intention of the Secretary-General to continue the United Nations humanitarian programme in Tajikistan by issuing a consolidated inter-agency appeal for humanitarian assistance to Tajikistan for 2000 as a strategic document that will guide a gradual transition to a more development-

oriented focus, and invites Member States to fund programmes included in the appeal;

8. *Calls upon* the Secretary-General to re-evaluate in 2000 all humanitarian assistance activities with a view to addressing longer-term developmental issues;

9. *Urges* the parties to ensure security and freedom of movement of humanitarian personnel and United Nations and associated personnel, as well as the safety and security of their premises, equipment and supplies;

10. *Requests* the Secretary-General to continue to give special attention, in the dialogue with the multilateral lending institutions, to the humanitarian implications of their adjustment programmes in Tajikistan;

11. *Also requests* the Secretary-General to continue to monitor the humanitarian situation in Tajikistan and to report to the General Assembly at its fifty-fifth session on the progress made in the implementation of the present resolution;

12. *Decides* to consider at its fifty-fifth session the question of the situation in Tajikistan under the item entitled "Strengthening of the coordination of humanitarian and disaster relief assistance of the United Nations, including special economic assistance".

Europe

Northern Caucasus (Russian Federation)

The humanitarian situation in the northern Caucasus had been aggravated since conflict erupted anew in August 1999. The economy of the region remained one of the Russian Federation's poorest. Hundreds of thousands of persons were displaced, mostly from the Republic of Chechnya into the Republic of Ingushetia, but also within Chechnya and the Republic of Dagestan. Some displaced persons moved to other regions of the Russian Federation. In October, the Russian Government and the United Nations signed a Memorandum on Consultations to establish a framework for cooperation. An assessment team went to Ingushetia and Dagestan in November to assess the possibility of conducting rehabilitation and reconstruction activities, as well as the emergency relief needs of internally displaced persons.

In November, OCHA launched a UN inter-agency flash appeal for the northern Caucasus in order to deliver relief supplies, start initial rehabilitation programmes and address protection issues. It sought $16.2 million for the period 1 December 1999 to 29 February 2000.

South-Eastern Europe (Albania and the former Yugoslavia)

In 1999, developments in South-Eastern Europe—Albania, Bosnia and Herzegovina, Croatia, the Federal Republic of Yugoslavia (FRY) and the former Yugoslav Republic of Macedonia (FYROM)—reflected the volatility of the ongoing complex emergency in the region. Assistance on a regional basis was expanded many times following the escalation of fighting and human displacement connected with the Kosovo crisis in late March (see p. 332). Albania absorbed the bulk of the Kosovo refugee outflow from March to June. But the spontaneous repatriation of Kosovo refugees occurred earlier and much more rapidly than expected. By the end of August, all but about 6,000 out of an original 480,000 refugees in Albania had returned to Kosovo, resulting in agency budgets allocated to support refugees in Albania that exceeded requirements. Several agencies adjusted by transferring staff and resources to Kosovo. In Bosnia and Herzegovina, implementation of the 1995 General Framework Agreement for Peace (Dayton Accords) [YUN 1995, p. 544] was made more difficult by the new arrival of refugees from Kosovo and other areas of FRY from April to June, and the shifting of donor attention away from Bosnia and Herzegovina.

The agencies operating in Croatia strengthened coordination and cooperation mechanisms with the Government, its respective ministries and institutes, and other partners. Some, however, were seriously underfunded while others reported late pledges, which had a detrimental effect on the commencement of planned projects. In FRY, the Kosovo crisis mobilized a high level of donor contributions for activities within Kosovo. In other parts of FRY, slow pledging and provision of funds in the first part of 1999 gave way to a situation of donor reticence in the second half of the year. In contrast, resource needs grew faster than in other parts of the region. The humanitarian situation in FRY by late summer was worse than planned for. Additionally, humanitarian agencies needed to re-staff and replace confiscated equipment and supplies following the summer's evacuation and North Atlantic Treaty Organization military action. In that environment, and given the reduced NGO presence, some agencies were forced to scale back their programme goals. Health monitoring was lacking, urgent mental health needs had not been fully addressed, many refugees went without food rations in July and August, and concerns were rising about the achievement of necessary winterization measures for refugees, internally displaced persons and vulnerable groups. A 20 September Internet report [www.reliefweb.int], prepared by OCHA, summarized electricity and heating in FRY in winter 1999/2000: it predicted winter shortages, recommended humanitarian measures and assessed energy needs for the winter.

In FYROM, refugees were given asylum and protection, and received emergency relief as well as repatriation assistance. After the massive, spontaneous repatriation to Kosovo in summer

1999, agencies continued assistance to remaining refugees but also reoriented their programmes to new circumstances and reallocated part of the material and human resources to Kosovo operations.

The UN consolidated inter-agency appeal for South-Eastern Europe, launched in December 1998, which sought $359.4 million for the period January to December 1999, was revised to $929 million in July, following revisions necessary to meet needs related to the crisis, as well as a review of agency programmes concerning post-Dayton implementation. As at 29 October, $720.9 million, or 77.5 per cent, was received.

In November, OCHA launched a UN consolidated inter-agency appeal for South-Eastern Europe for the period January to December 2000, for a total of $660 million.

(For details of an Inter-Agency Needs Assessment Mission dispatched to Kosovo, see p. 350.)

GENERAL ASSEMBLY ACTION

On 15 December [meeting 80], the General Assembly adopted **resolution 54/96 F** [draft: A/54/L.66 & Add.1] without vote [agenda item 20 *(b)*].

Humanitarian assistance to the Federal Republic of Yugoslavia

The General Assembly,

Recalling its resolution 46/182 of 19 December 1991 and reaffirming that humanitarian assistance should be provided in accordance with and with due respect for the guiding principles contained in the annex to that resolution,

Recalling also agreed conclusions 1999/1 of the Economic and Social Council adopted at the humanitarian affairs segment of its substantive session of 1999, in particular the relevant paragraphs thereof,

Stressing the importance of an adequate United Nations presence in the Federal Republic of Yugoslavia,

Noting the efforts by the United Nations system to assess the situation in the Federal Republic of Yugoslavia, starting with the Inter-Agency Needs Assessment Mission dispatched by the Secretary-General to the Federal Republic of Yugoslavia from 16 to 27 May 1999,

Taking note of the report prepared by the Office for the Coordination of Humanitarian Affairs of the Secretariat, entitled "Electricity and heating in the Federal Republic of Yugoslavia: winter 1999-2000",

Also taking note of the report entitled "The Kosovo conflict: consequences for the environment and human settlements", prepared by the joint United Nations Environment Programme and United Nations Centre for Human Settlements Balkans task force on environment and human settlements,

Taking further note of the report of the Special Rapporteur of the Commission on Human Rights on the situation of human rights in Bosnia and Herzegovina, the Republic of Croatia and the Federal Republic of Yugoslavia (Serbia and Montenegro),

Stressing, in this context, the need to prevent attacks on ethnic minorities which may lead to additional humanitarian needs,

Aware of the humanitarian requirements of the Federal Republic of Yugoslavia,

Bearing in mind that the Federal Republic of Yugoslavia has been affected by the problems caused by refugee flows from neighbouring countries and has a large number of internally displaced persons,

Deeply appreciative of the humanitarian assistance, and noting the rehabilitation support rendered by a number of States, international agencies and organizations and non-governmental organizations to alleviate the humanitarian needs of the affected population in the Federal Republic of Yugoslavia,

1. *Calls upon* all States and intergovernmental and non-governmental organizations to provide humanitarian assistance to alleviate the humanitarian needs of the affected population in the Federal Republic of Yugoslavia, especially during winter months, in particular bearing in mind the special situation of women, children and other vulnerable groups;

2. *Urges* the relevant authorities and the international community to support programmes to ensure that the humanitarian needs of refugees and internally displaced persons in the Federal Republic of Yugoslavia are met and to support durable solutions to their plight, in particular voluntary repatriation and reintegration, and stresses the need to create conditions conducive for their safe return;

3. *Calls upon* the Secretary-General to continue to mobilize international humanitarian assistance for the Federal Republic of Yugoslavia;

4. *Requests* the Secretary-General to submit to it at its fifty-fifth session, under the agenda item entitled "Strengthening of the coordination of humanitarian and disaster relief assistance of the United Nations, including special economic assistance", a report on the implementation of the present resolution.

Special economic assistance

African economic recovery and development

During its coordination segment, held from 16 to 20 July (**decision 1999/211**) and on 28 July, the Economic and Social Council discussed coordination of the policies and activities of the specialized agencies and other UN bodies related to the development of Africa. It had before it a letter of 1 July from the United States [E/1999/104-S/1999/754], transmitting the text of the Blueprint for a United States–Africa Partnership for the Twenty-first Century, that emanated from a ministerial meeting (Washington, D.C., 15-18 March) and was based on an agreement between the United States and 46 sub-Saharan nations to foster economic development, trade, investment and political reform. The Council also considered a June report of the Secretary-General on development of Africa: implementation and coordinated follow-up by the UN system of initiatives on Africa [A/54/133-E/1999/79], submitted pursuant to General Assembly resolution 53/92 [YUN 1998, p. 77]. The report dealt with measures taken relating to the recommendations in the Secretary-General's 1998 report on the causes of conflict and the promotion of peace and sustainable development in Africa [ibid., p. 66] (see p. 846), priority areas under the current initiatives on Africa and possible priorities in partnership, and coordinated follow-up by the UN system of initiatives on Africa. It was based on information provided by the UN system and donor countries.

The Secretary-General stated that financing Africa's development was crucial. Improving education and infrastructure, providing adequate health care, reducing poverty, reintegrating refugees and displaced persons from conflicts and catalysing structural transformation required massive investment. However, domestic resource mobilization remained limited by low savings ratios, and Africa's external debt continued to be a drag on its potential. Beyond domestic resources, other sources of external finance, including foreign direct investment (FDI) and official development assistance (ODA), had to increase to the levels required to transform African economies. A wide range of actions had been taken to implement the recommendations of the Secretary-General's 1998 report, including strengthening good governance; enhancing social development through activities to create an enabling environment for enhancing the effectiveness of the informal sector in both rural and urban areas; intensified action by the Joint United Nations Programme on HIV/AIDS and other health programmes; malaria prevention and control; by the UN Department of Economic and Social Affairs, support to over 100 projects in the areas of social policy, poverty eradication and management of social change; and measures to eliminate discrimination against women. Efforts were made to improve trade flows and financial resource flows. UN organizations continued to support activities aimed at strengthening regional cooperation and integration.

Regarding priority areas, the report described various initiatives, and although they differed in specificity, they could be grouped under the broader priorities established by the Organization of African Unity (OAU) Assembly of Heads of State and Government in the 1995 Cairo Agenda for Action [YUN 1995, p. 989], namely, democracy, governance, peace, security, stability and sustainable development; food security; capacity-building and human resources development; structural transformation of African economies; mobilization and utilization of resources; and regional cooperation and integration. The Secretary-General suggested that the Council might wish to ask the UN system, multilateral and regional organizations and bilateral donors to collaborate with African Governments and among themselves to ensure consistency of the various coordination mechanisms. In an effort to harmonize non-UN initiatives, the United Nations could organize selected thematic consultations.

The Council, in agreed conclusions adopted at its coordination segment [A/54/3/Rev.1 (agreed conclusions 1999/2)], reaffirmed the importance of UN participation in the development of Africa and underscored its intention to ensure that all initiatives on Africa were maximized. It reiterated the importance of a stable political and economic environment for local and foreign investment, and urged the international community to improve access to markets and to continue to assist African countries in making better use of market opportunities already available while facilitating FDI, ensuring adequate flows of ODA in tandem with agreed targets, and providing deeper relief from external debt. The Council called for a more concerted effort towards faster debt relief under the Heavily Indebted Poor Countries Initiative and through other means, and urged that any International Monetary Fund (IMF) gold reserve sales should be undertaken in a limited manner so as to minimize any adverse effect on African gold-producing countries. The Council stressed the need to strengthen administrative and institutional capacity and the financial systems.

Relevant components of the UN system were called on to strengthen their support in the areas of governance, poverty eradication and social development, and the creation of an enabling environment to expand trade and investment, and towards regional integration and cooperation. Recognizing the need to take note of the variety of country-specific situations and needs, the Council stated that prioritization for partnership should be based on an Africa-driven agenda and on ownership by the African countries, and should take place in cooperation with development partners and civil society.

The Council called on the international community to support the efforts of the African Governments in the implementation of national and international strategies to prevent the spread and mitigate the impact of HIV/AIDS, which threatened the economic and social development of many African countries. Continued efforts were needed to enhance market access for products of export interest to Africa and to support economies to diversify and to build supply capacity; the international community was called on to support broad-based trade liberalization and to address issues that could hinder the ability of African economies to be more competitive. The Council called for support to implement the Second Industrial Development Decade for Africa (1993-2002) [YUN 1993, p. 597] and the Alliance for Africa's Industrialization and to foster industrial production and development. It encouraged the strengthening of technology development and facilitating technology transfer.

The Council called for more effective coordination and harmonization of the implementation of all initiatives, better funding and stronger ownership by recipient countries. The UN system was encouraged to build coherence among initiatives aimed at increasing the effectiveness of activities at the field level and to consolidate the initiatives. Donor countries were urged to give priority to increasing their core contributions. The Council called for the strengthening of the existing coordination arrangements at the global and regional levels and for clarification of the UN system role in support of the priority areas identified in various UN-sponsored initiatives to support Africa's overall development.

Regarding regional coordination meetings, the Council recommended thematic consultations among development partners held under the chairmanship of the UN Deputy Secretary-General, with OAU involvement and African regional and subregional economic communities. It also recommended the establishment of a linkage between the conclusions on coordination and the preparatory work for its high-level segment on African development, to be scheduled before 2002, and the final review of the United Nations New Agenda for the Development of Africa in the 1990s (see p. 847); it requested the Secretary-General to commission an independent evaluation of the performance of the New Agenda, and to submit a report outlining the progress achieved in strengthening African capacity to coordinate international development assistance and in developing coordination mechanisms. International coordination efforts should be designed under the leadership of recipient countries, add coherence among international initiatives and utilize simple yet effective coordination mechanisms.

By **decision 1999/270** of 28 July, the Council, having considered the Secretary-General's report, recommended that the agreed conclusions arising from its coordination segment become an integral part of the reports and issues to be considered by the open-ended working group to be established by the General Assembly at its fifty-fourth session.

On 25 October [A/54/513], the Council President drew to the attention of the Assembly President the agreed conclusions.

Report of Secretary-General. In a September report [S/1999/1008], the Secretary-General described progress in the implementation of the recommendations contained in his 1998 report on the causes of conflict and the promotion of durable peace and sustainable development in Africa [YUN 1998, p. 66]. The report contained follow-up actions taken in the areas of peace and security (see p. 78), as well as in development and related areas. With regard to humanitarian assistance, the Secretary-General stated that UN efforts focused on holding combatants financially liable to their victims under international law, ensuring adherence to humanitarian and human rights norms by all parties to a conflict, and funding special human rights missions from assessed contributions. Commitments were obtained from various Governments and insurgency groups to end the recruitment of children under age 18 (see p. 672), demobilize and reintegrate child soldiers and ensure humanitarian access to protect children. In the light of increasing difficulties in delivering assistance, the Inter-Agency Standing Committee carried out studies on strategic coordination in the Great Lakes region and made recommendations aimed at increasing system-wide accountability and ownership of humanitarian action. As to refugees and internally displaced persons, new policy tools were developed for their protection; the Office of the United Nations High Commissioner for Refugees (UNHCR) assisted several countries in relocating refugees away from the borders, and in dealing with security in refugee camps (see p. 1139). Measures were taken to ensure that the UN humanitarian coordinator in the field would operate under the authority of the representative of the Secretary-General, to coordinate humanitarian action consistent with broader UN peace and development activities, and to deliver relief efforts aimed at promoting long-term development objectives.

Security Council consideration. The Security Council, on 29 and 30 September [S/PV.4049], discussed the situation in Africa with regard to the Secretary-General's September report. The Secretary-General stated that access for humanitarian relief to victims of crises must be ensured, but should not be a substitute for the political and military engagement needed to bring stability and address the root causes of the upheavals. Each crisis situation was different, and UN and Council commitment to peacekeeping, humanitarian assistance and other such action should be applied fairly and consistently, irrespective of region or nation.

GENERAL ASSEMBLY ACTION

On 22 December [meeting 87], the General Assembly adopted **resolution 54/234** [draft: A/54/L.75 & Add.1] without vote [agenda item 46].

The causes of conflict and the promotion of durable peace and sustainable development in Africa

The General Assembly,

Recalling its resolution 46/151 of 18 December 1991, the annex to which contains the United Nations New Agenda for the Development of Africa in the 1990s, its resolutions 48/214 of 23 December 1993, 49/142 of 23 December 1994 and 51/32 of 6 December 1996, on the mid-term review of the New Agenda, as well as its resolution 53/90 of 7 December 1998 on the implementation of the New Agenda,

Recalling also its resolution 53/92 of 7 December 1998 on the causes of conflict and the promotion of durable peace in Africa,

Mindful of agreed conclusions 1999/2 adopted by the Economic and Social Council at its substantive session of 1999, on coordination of the policies and activities of the specialized agencies and other bodies of the United Nations system related to the theme "Development of Africa: implementation and coordinated follow-up by the United Nations system of initiatives on African development", and of Council decision 1999/270,

Taking note of the deliberations of the Security Council at its meeting on the situation in Africa, held on 29 and 30 September 1999, on the report of the Secretary-General on the implementation of the recommendations contained in the report on the causes of conflict and the promotion of durable peace and sustainable development in Africa and of the work of the Security Council on the follow-up to the report of the Secretary-General,

Taking note with appreciation of the report of the Secretary-General to the General Assembly and the Economic and Social Council on the development of Africa: implementation of the recommendations in the report of the Secretary-General to the Security Council and the General Assembly, specifically the implementation and coordinated follow-up by the United Nations system of initiatives on Africa,

1. *Welcomes* agreed conclusions 1999/2 adopted by the Economic and Social Council at its substantive session of 1999, on coordination of the policies and activities of the specialized agencies and other bodies of the United Nations system related to the theme "Development of Africa: implementation and coordinated follow-up by the United Nations system of initiatives on African development", and Council decision 1999/270;

2. *Requests* all Governments and intergovernmental and non-governmental organizations in their respective areas and sectors to work towards the implementation of agreed conclusions 1999/2;

3. *Welcomes* the decision of the Economic and Social Council to hold a high-level segment on Africa in 2001;

4. *Stresses* the paramount importance for the final review and appraisal of the United Nations New Agenda for the Development of Africa in the 1990s, to be held in 2002, of an independent evaluation of the New Agenda that should include a thorough review of existing initiatives on Africa;

5. *Decides* to consider at its fifty-sixth session the modalities for undertaking the final review and appraisal of the New Agenda, taking into account the mid-term review of the New Agenda, agreed conclusions 1999/2 and decision 1999/270;

6. *Requests* the President of the General Assembly to establish the open-ended ad hoc working group to monitor the implementation of the recommendations made by the Secretary-General in his report to the General Assembly and the Security Council on the causes of conflict and the promotion of durable peace and sustainable development in Africa, to prepare for discussions at the fifty-fifth session of the General Assembly;

7. *Requests* that, in addition to monitoring the recommendations referred to in paragraph 6 above, the ad hoc working group monitor the implementation of agreed conclusions 1999/2 and of decision 1999/270, as well as poverty eradication, debt relief, the human immunodeficiency virus/acquired immunodeficiency syndrome (HIV/AIDS) and support to countries in post-conflict situations;

8. *Requests* the President of the General Assembly at its fifty-fourth session to establish the ad hoc working group, to serve as its ex officio chairman, to designate, in close consultation with Member States, two vice-chairpersons and to convene an organizational meeting of the ad hoc working group not later than March 2000 to decide on modalities and develop arrangements for the effective functioning of the ad hoc working group;

9. *Requests* the Secretary-General to provide the ad hoc working group with all necessary assistance to ensure the accomplishment of its mandate;

10. *Also requests* the Secretary-General to report to the General Assembly at its fifty-fifth session on the implementation of the present resolution.

New Agenda for the Development of Africa

The United Nations New Agenda for the Development of Africa in the 1990s, adopted by the General Assembly in resolution 46/151 [YUN 1991, p. 402], continued to be implemented by the United Nations Conference on Trade and Development (UNCTAD), among other UN bodies.

UNCTAD action. The twenty-first executive session of the UNCTAD Trade and Development Board (TDB) (Geneva, 1 July) [A/54/15/Rev.1] considered an April report by the UNCTAD Secretary-General [TD/B/EX(21)/2], which contained information on UNCTAD's contribution towards implementing the New Agenda. The report covered UNCTAD activities regarding policy research and analysis, post-conflict rehabilitation and development in Rwanda and Somalia and sectoral issues, including international trade; services development; debt, debt management and financial flows; international investment and enterprise development; and the UN System-wide Special Initiative on Africa (see p. 848).

At its forty-sixth session (Geneva, 18-29 October) [A/54/15/Rev.1], TDB considered an August report by the UNCTAD secretariat [TD/B/46/10], which assessed the extent to which transport problems had adverse effects on African trade and balance of payments, analysed the underlying factors which accounted for key problems, and explored policy issues to resolve them. Emphasis was given to policy options for financing transport infrastructure and the need for regional and subregional cooperation.

In its agreed conclusions of 29 October [A/54/15/Rev.1 (agreed conclusions 458(XLVI))], TDB recognized that a problem preventing Africa from achieving sustainable development was the lack of investment in infrastructure, of which the transport sector was among the most important elements. The high cost of transport undermined export competitiveness and increased prices of key imports, adversely affecting African balance-of-payments positions, which were particularly high for sub-Saharan countries. High transaction costs were also contributing factors. Poor rural transport systems had an adverse influence on specialization and market development, as well as on international tradeability of goods. Multilateral financial institutions could provide long-term finance and credit guarantees to enable countries to tap capital markets, and Governments could facilitate market forces by adopting a strategic perspective on infrastructure rehabilitation and development. There was a need to adopt principles of cost recovery, which should be enhanced by measures aiming to reduce infrastructure financing cost. There was an important role for ODA in infrastructure financing, including as a catalyst to attract foreign investment and as a means of promoting rural development. A heavy debt burden and lower export earnings from falling commodity prices limited the possibility of Governments to raise capital for investments in transport. Better access to markets for products of export interest was required to generate income for investment. Multilateral financial institutions were invited to increase their share of financing of regional and subregional projects. The Board encouraged the secretariat to continue its analysis of the development problems of African countries, as well as its technical activities aimed at reducing transaction costs.

UN System-wide Special Initiative on Africa

CPC action. The Committee for Programme and Coordination (CPC), at its thirty-ninth session (New York, 7 June–2 July), considered an April report of the Secretary-General updating progress on the United Nations System-wide Special Initiative for the Implementation of the New Agenda [E/AC.51/1999/6], submitted in response to a 1998 request of the Committee [YUN 1998, p. 865]. The report described activities undertaken by the UN system from June 1998 to May 1999 to implement the priority areas of the Initiative, addressed coordination issues and described measures taken in response to CPC recommendations. Progress was achieved in the areas of governance, information technology for development, education, health, and population and gender and was emerging in poverty eradication, trade access and opportunities, diversification of African economies, regional cooperation and integration, water, environment and South-South cooperation. There was improvement in macroeconomic policies, with greater emphasis on social development in many African countries, where the private sector played an increasingly greater role. A resource mobilization strategy for the implementation of the Special Initiative was under way, involving the Special Initiative secretariat and the World Bank. The UN system had taken initiatives to enhance coordination among its organizations at the country level. Feedback received from resident coordinators in 18 countries indicated that the collaboration had given momentum to implementation.

At the subregional level, the development centres of the Economic Commission for Africa (ECA) aimed to foster cooperation and integration between member States and intergovernmental organizations. However, their efforts were limited because of the absence of a general coordinating mechanism that would allow agencies to interact on a periodic and sustained basis and take a long-term view of issues in the region. The case for programmatic coordination was strongest in areas where cross-border effects were significant, such as transportation, health and social issues, and trade and regional integration issues. In response to Economic and Social Council resolution 1998/46 [YUN 1998, p. 1262], the first annual coordination meeting of the UN system in Africa, attended by representatives of 23 organizations, was held in March in Nairobi, Kenya, to discuss enhanced coordination of UN system activities at the regional level and ascertain whether there was adequate coordination among organizations on African issues. Annexed to the report were a note by the UNCTAD secretariat on a programme for economic diversification in Africa and a note by ECA on a programme for regional cooperation and integration.

On 10 June [A/54/16], CPC recommended expanding the number of countries covered by the Initiative. It endorsed the elaboration of the programmes annexed to the Secretary-General's report. CPC requested that a resource mobilization strategy together with the concrete action plan be submitted in 2000 and that activities be implemented on opportunities to access markets. It asked that a progress report be submitted in 2000, and that its comments be reported to the Council's July 1999 coordination segment on Africa.

ACC action. At its first regular session of 1999 (Geneva, 9-10 April) [ACC/1999/4], the Administrative Committee on Coordination (ACC) reviewed progress achieved by the Special Initiative and agreed that reporting should capture all relevant information from the UN system on actions in Africa, to be used for other reporting requirements. At its second regular session (New York, 29-30 October) [ACC/1999/20], ACC reviewed the coordination of UN activities in Africa and endorsed the thrust of the recommendations made at the first inter-agency meeting for Africa (Nairobi, March), which concluded that other relevant UN system activities could be brought under the umbrella of the Special Initiative.

In **resolution 1999/57**, the Economic and Social Council welcomed the closer collaboration among UN entities in implementing the Special Initiative (see p. 1351).

Democratic Republic of the Congo

Although a ceasefire was observed across the Democratic Republic of the Congo (DRC) following the signing of the Lusaka Ceasefire Agreement (see p. 81), the humanitarian conditions in the country remained appalling. Almost 14 million persons were in need of assistance. Indispensable to the peace architecture in the DRC were the return of internally displaced persons and refugees, representing over 1 million persons; reintegration schemes for the demobilized militia, including child soldiers; and the enhancement of ethnic cohabitation.

A UN consolidated inter-agency appeal, covering January to December 1999, which sought $26.1 million, was revised in July to $60.3 million. More than half of that new budget represented costs for food purchase and shipment for 500,000 vulnerable persons, including refugees. As at November, only 20 per cent of requirements was pledged for that sector. For other emergency interventions by various UN agencies, $21.4 million was requested, but only $3.3 million, or 15.5 per cent, was received. The inadequate international response and the severe underfunding diminished coverage and quality of assistance. An inter-agency appeal issued in November sought $71.4 million for January to December 2000.

Report of Secretary-General. Pursuant to General Assembly resolution 53/1 L [YUN 1998, p. 866], the Secretary-General presented an August report on special assistance for the economic recovery and reconstruction of the DRC [A/54/278], which described assistance provided by UNDP, WFP, UNHCR, the United Nations Children's Fund (UNICEF), the World Health Organization (WHO), the United Nations Population Fund (UNFPA), the Food and Agriculture Organization of the United Nations (FAO), the Office for the Coordination of Humanitarian Affairs and the Office of the United Nations High Commissioner for Human Rights. The Secretary-General stated that the Government and the UN system were in agreement with regard to recovery and reconstruction needs. The UN system operating in Kinshasa had agreed to harmonize its cooperation programmes, whose execution should coincide with the Government's 1997 Triennial Minimum Programme, which identified the reconstruction needs and outlined medium-term priorities. The Secretary-General concluded that to end the economic crisis, appeals should be made to the international community for assistance; the establishment of a framework of peace and reconciliation was a sine qua non for the creation of an environment conducive to rehabilitation; assistance should be provided to the Government to prepare a strategy comprising financial stabilization, reform, reconstruction and development; and an agreement should be reached to stabilize payment arrears owed to IMF.

UNDP action. In order to promote economic recovery and reconstruction in the DRC, UNDP continued to shift the focus of its activities to sustainable human development and poverty alleviation. In a July note on assistance to the DRC [DP/1999/36], the UNDP Administrator stated that, as a result of the crisis, it had not been possible for the Government to prepare a cooperation framework; he requested the UNDP/UNFPA Executive Board to authorize him to continue to provide support to the country on a project-by-project basis until the situation improved. On 17 September [E/1999/35 (dec. 99/25)], the Board took note of the Administrator's note and authorized him to continue to approve assistance to the DRC on a project-by-project basis.

GENERAL ASSEMBLY ACTION

On 8 December [meeting 73], the General Assembly adopted **resolution 54/96 B** [draft: A/54/L.53 & Add.1] without vote [agenda item 20 *(b)*].

Special assistance for the economic recovery and reconstruction of the Democratic Republic of the Congo

The General Assembly,

Recalling its resolutions 52/169 A of 16 December 1997 and 53/1 L of 7 December 1998,

Recalling also Security Council resolutions 1234 (1999) of 9 April 1999, 1258(1999) of 6 August 1999,

1273(1999) of 5 November 1999 and 1279(1999) of 30 November 1999 on the situation in the Democratic Republic of the Congo,

Welcoming the signing in Lusaka of the Ceasefire Agreement on the conflict in the Democratic Republic of the Congo by all parties involved, which represents a viable basis for a resolution of the conflict in the country,

Expressing its concern at the alleged violations of the Ceasefire Agreement, and urging all parties to refrain from any declarations or action that could jeopardize the peace process,

Alarmed at the plight of the civilian population throughout the country, and calling for its protection,

Gravely concerned at the deteriorating economic and social situation in the Democratic Republic of the Congo, in particular in the eastern Congo, and at the effect of the continued fighting on the inhabitants of the country,

Reaffirming the sovereignty, territorial integrity and political independence of the Democratic Republic of the Congo and all States in the region,

Urging all parties to respect and protect human rights and respect international humanitarian law, in particular the Geneva Conventions of 1949 and the additional Protocols thereto, of 1977,

Deeply concerned about the continued extensive destruction of life and property as well as the severe damage to infrastructure and the environment suffered by the Democratic Republic of the Congo,

Bearing in mind that the Democratic Republic of the Congo also suffers from the problems encountered by a country that has received thousands of refugees from neighbouring countries,

Recalling that the Democratic Republic of the Congo is a least developed country with severe economic and social problems arising from its weak economic infrastructure and aggravated by the ongoing conflict,

Bearing in mind the close interrelationship between ensuring peace and security and the ability of the country to meet the humanitarian needs of its people and to take effective steps towards the rapid revitalization of the economy, and reaffirming the urgent need to assist the Democratic Republic of the Congo in the rehabilitation and reconstruction of its damaged economy and in its efforts to restore basic services and the infrastructure of the country,

1. *Takes note* of the report of the Secretary-General;

2. *Calls* for the full implementation of the Ceasefire Agreement on the conflict in the Democratic Republic of the Congo by all its signatories;

3. *Calls upon* all parties concerned in the region to create the conditions necessary for the speedy and peaceful resolution of the crisis, and urges all parties to engage in a process of political dialogue and negotiation without delay;

4. *Encourages* the Government of the Democratic Republic of the Congo to pursue sound macroeconomic policies and to promote good governance and the rule of law, and urges the Government and the people of the Democratic Republic of the Congo to exert all efforts for economic recovery and reconstruction despite the ongoing armed conflict;

5. *Renews its invitation* to the Government of the Democratic Republic of the Congo to cooperate with the United Nations, the specialized agencies and other organizations in addressing the need for rehabilitation and reconstruction, stresses the need for the Government to assist and protect the civilian population, including refugees and internally displaced persons within the territory of that country regardless of their origin, and reaffirms the need for respect for the provisions of international humanitarian law, in particular the safety of humanitarian personnel, and safe and unhindered access to all affected populations;

6. *Renews its urgent appeal* to the executive boards of the United Nations funds and programmes to continue to keep under consideration the special needs of the Democratic Republic of the Congo, and in that regard welcomes, inter alia, the authorization given to the Administrator of the United Nations Development Programme by the Executive Board of the United Nations Development Programme and the United Nations Population Fund to continue to approve assistance to the Democratic Republic of the Congo on a project-by-project basis;

7. *Invites* Governments to continue to provide support to the Democratic Republic of the Congo and to respond in a timely manner to the United Nations consolidated appeal for the Great Lakes region for 2000;

8. *Requests* the Secretary-General:

(a) To continue to consult urgently with regional leaders, in coordination with the Secretary-General of the Organization of African Unity, about ways to bring about a peaceful and durable solution to the conflict;

(b) To continue to consult with regional leaders in coordination with the Secretary-General of the Organization of African Unity in order to convene, when appropriate, an international conference on peace, security and development in the Great Lakes region, under the auspices of the United Nations and the Organization of African Unity, to address the problems of the region in a comprehensive manner;

(c) To keep under review the economic situation in the Democratic Republic of the Congo with a view to promoting participation in and support for a programme of financial and material assistance to the country in order to enable it to address its urgent need for economic recovery and reconstruction;

(d) To submit to the General Assembly at its fifty-fifth session a report on the actions taken pursuant to the present resolution.

Djibouti

Pursuant to General Assembly resolution 53/1 J [YUN 1998, p. 868], the Secretary-General, in a June report [A/54/153-E/1999/93], described the situation in Djibouti and progress made in providing assistance for reconstruction and development. Djibouti's difficulties were related to the economic and financial crisis, which resulted from the civil strife and the change in the international and subregional situation. In addition, recurring emergency situations had increased the need for emergency and humanitarian assistance, and a large refugee population from neighbouring countries had strained the meagre resources available. The rehabilitation process already initiated needed to be strengthened. The Secretary-General proposed the rebuilding of rural infrastructure, the implementation of microcredit programmes and the promotion of income-generating activities. Assistance was needed in the areas of governance, administrative reform and economic management. Djibouti should find a way to enable refugees and displaced persons from neighbouring countries to return to their countries of origin, with the support of the Intergovernmental Authority on Development and UNHCR. The Secretary-General called on the international community to provide financial support for technical assistance to meet urgent socio-economic programmes.

GENERAL ASSEMBLY ACTION

On 8 December [meeting 73], the General Assembly adopted **resolution 54/96 C** [draft: A/54/L.56 & Add.1] without vote [agenda item 20 (*b*)].

Assistance for the reconstruction and development of Djibouti

The General Assembly,

Recalling its resolution 53/1 J of 7 December 1998 and its previous resolutions on economic assistance to Djibouti,

Recalling also the Paris Declaration and the Programme of Action for the Least Developed Countries for the 1990s, adopted by the Second United Nations Conference on the Least Developed Countries on 14 September 1990, as well as the mutual commitments undertaken on that occasion and the importance attached to the follow-up to that Conference,

Recalling further agreed conclusions 1999/1 adopted by the Economic and Social Council at the humanitarian segment of its substantive session of 1999,

Conscious that Djibouti is included in the list of least developed countries and that it is ranked 157th out of the 174 countries studied in the *Human Development Report 1999,*

Noting that the economic and social development efforts of Djibouti are constrained by the extremes of the local climate, in particular cyclical droughts and torrential rains and floods, such as those that occurred in October and November 1997, and that the implementation of reconstruction and development programmes requires the deployment of substantial resources which exceed the capacity of the country,

Emphasizing that there is an urgent need to provide financial support in the areas of demobilization, reconstruction and rehabilitation of the regions affected by civil strife, with a view to strengthening peace and stability in the country,

Noting that the situation in Djibouti has been made worse by the deteriorating situation in the Horn of Africa, in particular in Somalia, and noting also the presence of tens of thousands of refugees and persons displaced from their countries, which has placed serious strains on the fragile economic, social and administrative infrastructure of Djibouti and caused security problems in the country, in particular in the city of Djibouti,

Noting with satisfaction that the Government of Djibouti is continuing to implement a structural adjustment programme, and convinced of the necessity to support that financial recovery programme and to take effective measures to alleviate the consequences, in particular the social consequences, of that adjustment policy, so that the country may achieve lasting economic results,

Noting with gratitude the support provided to relief and rehabilitation operations by various countries and by intergovernmental and non-governmental organizations,

1. *Takes note* of the report of the Secretary-General;

2. *Declares its solidarity* with the Government and the people of Djibouti, who continue to face critical challenges owing, in particular, to the scarcity of natural resources, harsh climatic conditions and the continuing critical situation in the Horn of Africa;

3. *Notes with concern* the cyclical drought phenomenon in Djibouti, including the current severe drought that is wreaking a major humanitarian disaster upon tens of thousands of people, particularly those who are vulnerable, and requests the international community to respond urgently to the appeal launched by the Government;

4. *Encourages* the Government of Djibouti, despite difficult economic and regional situations, to continue its serious efforts towards the consolidation of democracy;

5. *Notes with satisfaction* the implementation of a structural adjustment programme by Djibouti and, in that context, appeals to all Governments, international financial institutions, the specialized agencies and non-governmental organizations to respond adequately to the financial and material needs of the country;

6. *Considers* that the process of demobilization, reintegration and employment of demobilized soldiers is essential not only for national rehabilitation, but also for the success of agreements with the international financial institutions and for the consolidation of peace, and that it requires substantial resources which exceed the capacity of the country;

7. *Expresses its gratitude* to the States and intergovernmental organizations that have already fulfilled their pledges at the round table on Djibouti, held in Geneva on 29 and 30 May 1997;

8. *Also expresses its gratitude* to the intergovernmental organizations and especially to the United Nations Development Programme, as well as the other funds and programmes of the United Nations system, for their contributions to the national rehabilitation of Djibouti, and invites them to continue their efforts;

9. *Expresses its appreciation* to the Secretary-General for his continued efforts to make the international community aware of the difficulties faced by Djibouti;

10. *Requests* the Secretary-General to continue, in close cooperation with the Government of Djibouti, his efforts to mobilize resources necessary for an effective programme of financial, technical and material assistance to Djibouti;

11. *Also requests* the Secretary-General to report to the General Assembly at its fifty-sixth session on the progress made with regard to economic assistance to Djibouti and the implementation of the present resolution.

Other economic assistance

Central America

Report of Secretary-General. Pursuant to General Assembly resolution 52/169 G [YUN 1997, p. 921], the Secretary-General, in September [A/54/350], described the activities of UNDP and other UN organs, organizations and programmes, carried out between July 1997 and July 1999 in support of the efforts of the Central American countries to implement a new sustainable development programme. He stated that two UNDP regional initiatives concluded in 1999—the state of the region project and support to processes of dialogue and consensus-building for the consolidation of peace in Central America—coupled with the regional programme for sustainable human development at the local level, constituted the backbone of UNDP support to the Alliance for the Sustainable Development of Central America (ALIDES). The Economic Commission for Latin America and the Caribbean (ECLAC) supported ALIDES priorities in the economic sphere and produced reports on issues related to ALIDES, including the reform of the institutional framework for Central American integration; liberalization of agricultural trade; transformation of the industrial sector; the productive use of family remittances; and social infrastructure and natural disasters. El Fondo Centroamericano para el Desarrollo Sostenible (FOCADES), a private entity created by the Governments of the region to facilitate the financing of the environmental component of ALIDES, would enable communities, private sector firms, NGOs and other interested groups to incorporate environmental aspects into their economic development activities. With estimates that between 6 and 12 per cent of the world's biodiversity was contained within the Meso-American region, which extended from Darién, Colombia, to Tehuantepec, Mexico, efforts were being made to create a system of biological corridors to link the region. The UNDP Global Environment Facility had assigned some $25 million in seed capital to build the system and to create a sustainable development fund.

Communication. On 17 November, Belize, Costa Rica, the Dominican Republic, El Salvador, Guatemala, Honduras, Nicaragua and Panama transmitted the Declaration of Guatemala II, signed by the Central American Presidents (Guatemala City, 19 October) [A/54/630]. Among other things, they reaffirmed the importance of implementing ALIDES.

GENERAL ASSEMBLY ACTION

On 15 December [meeting 80], the General Assembly adopted **resolution 54/96 E** [draft: A/54/L.29/Rev.1 & Add.1] without vote [agenda item 20 *(b)*].

International assistance to and cooperation with the Alliance for the Sustainable Development of Central America

The General Assembly,

Reaffirming the resolutions in which it emphasizes and acknowledges the importance of international, bilateral and multilateral economic, financial and technical support, cooperation and assistance for peacekeeping and peace-building in Central America following the armed conflicts in the region, in particular its resolutions 49/21 I of 20 December 1994, 50/58 B of 12 December 1995, 50/132 of 20 December 1995 and 52/169 G of 16 December 1997, which provide a frame of reference for international assistance to and cooperation with the Alliance for the Sustainable Development of Central America, in support of national efforts to make the region a zone of peace, freedom, democracy and development,

Noting that, as the century draws to a close, the Central American countries have achieved significant progress towards the consolidation of democracy and good governance, the strengthening of civilian Governments, respect for human rights and the rule of law and the promotion of State and economic reforms, sustainable development and regional integration, reflecting the desire of the Central American peoples to live and prosper in a climate of peace and solidarity,

Stressing the importance and effectiveness of the commitments undertaken by the Central American Presidents at various regional presidential summits, in particular those which constitute the global framework for promoting and consolidating peace, democracy and sustainable human development in Central America,

Recognizing that hurricane Mitch, the worst disaster to strike the Central American region in this century, underscored the extreme vulnerability of the poorest sectors of the population, in particular women and children, which were the most severely affected, and the inadequacy of existing local and national institutions to deal with natural disasters,

Noting that the various natural phenomena which have affected the region are one of the factors that have put at risk the biodiversity of Central America,

Taking into consideration that, at the second Consultative Group Meeting for the Reconstruction and Transformation of Central America, co-hosted by the Inter-American Development Bank and the Government of Sweden and held in Stockholm from 25 to 28 May 1999, the Governments of the region, the principal donors and representatives of civil society renewed their commitment to democratic change and sustainable human development as the best means of reducing economic, social and ecological vulnerability to disasters, and looking forward to the next round of Consultative Group Meetings, to be held in Nicaragua and Honduras in February 2000,

Taking into account that the Governments of the region have designated the period 2000-2004 as the Quinquennium for the Reduction of Vulnerability to and the Impact of Natural Disasters in Central America and have adopted a strategic framework for the reduction of vulnerability and disasters in Central America, which contain guidelines for the elaboration, updating, improvement and development of regional plans for the reduction of vulnerability to and the impact of natural disasters, the integrated management and conservation of water resources and the prevention and control of forest fires,

Stressing that the achievement of the national priorities in the political, economic, social, cultural, environmental, public safety and regional integration fields, which are set out in the programme of the Alliance for the Sustainable Development of Central America, is essential for reducing the region's vulnerability to natural disasters and for promoting sustainable human development,

Considering the necessity of ensuring the elimination of anti-personnel mines from Central American territory as well as the rehabilitation and reintegration of mine victims in their communities in order to restore normal conditions for the integral development of the region,

Recognizing the valuable and effective contribution made by the organs, organizations and programmes of the United Nations system and by the various governmental and non-governmental mechanisms, the donor community and the Consultative Group for the Reconstruction and Transformation of Central America and the importance of the political dialogue and cooperation taking place between the European Union and Central America and the joint initiative of the industrialized countries of the Group of Twenty-four and the Group of Three (Colombia, Mexico and Venezuela) in the progress made towards consolidating peace, democracy and the implementation of the Alliance for the Sustainable Development of Central America,

Reaffirming the need to continue focusing attention on the situation in Central America with a view to overcoming the underlying causes of the armed conflicts which have impeded the region's development and avoiding a reversal of the achievements,

1. *Takes note with satisfaction* of the reports of the Secretary-General on international assistance to and cooperation with the Alliance for the Sustainable Development of Central America and on collaborative efforts to assist Belize, Costa Rica, El Salvador, Guatemala, Honduras, Nicaragua and Panama and progress made with the relief, rehabilitation and reconstruction efforts of the affected countries, in particular their recommendations and conclusions;

2. *Emphasizes* the importance of supporting and strengthening the efforts of the Central American countries to implement the Strategic Framework for the Reduction of Vulnerability and Disasters in Central America, adopted by their Presidents in the Declaration of Guatemala II on 19 October 1999, and the projects and programmes of the Quinquennium for the Reduction of Vulnerability to and the Impact of Natural Disasters in Central America, in accordance with the process of transformation and sustainable development for the region for the next millennium, which contain basic guidelines for the prevention and mitigation of damage, with special emphasis on the most vulnerable groups and sectors, as identified by gender-based levels of poverty and marginality;

3. *Notes* the efforts and achievements relating to mine clearance in Central America, despite the negative impact of hurricane Mitch, and appeals to the organs of the United Nations system, in particular the Mine Action Service of the Department of Peacekeeping Operations of the Secretariat, and the Organization of American States as well as the international community to continue providing the material, technical and financial support needed by the Central American Governments to complete mine-clearance, mine-awareness and victim assistance activities in the region, in conformity with the relevant resolutions of the United Nations and with the provisions of the Convention on the Prohibition of the Use, Stockpiling, Production and Transfer of Anti-personnel Mines and on Their Destruction that relate to international cooperation and assistance;

4. *Stresses* the need for the international community to maintain its cooperation and assistance, including provision of financial resources, both bilateral and multilateral, with the Central American countries, to support the promotion of sustainable development and the consolidation of peace, freedom and democracy in the region;

5. *Notes with satisfaction* the progress achieved towards the implementation of the subregional cooperation programme in Central America of the United Nations Development Programme focusing on peace and democratic governance, strengthening of the rule of law, economic and social development and sustainable development, which was established in 1996;

6. *Recognizes* the importance for the subregion of the studies being undertaken by the United Nations Development Programme, in collaboration with its national and regional partners and with donors, in particular in the preparation of the forthcoming meeting of the Inter-American Development Bank Consultative Group on the regional aspects of the reconstruction and transformation of Central America, to be hosted by the Government of Spain in Madrid in 2000, which will seek to establish new relations of cooperation in pursuit of the objectives of the Alliance for the Sustainable Development of Central America;

7. *Notes with satisfaction* the initiative to introduce the new and innovative approach of a Meso-American Biological Corridor, which is being developed with assistance from the United Nations Development Programme's own funds, the World Bank, the Inter-American Development Bank, the German Agency for Technical Cooperation and the United States Agency for International Development, as an initiative with an innovative approach that seeks to conserve biodiversity, mitigate the effects of climate change and promote the sustainable development of rural communities, which will facilitate the establishment of a network of protected areas throughout Central America that will help to reduce vulnerability to natural disasters;

8. *Supports* the decision of the Central American Governments to concentrate their efforts on the implementation of updated programmes with strategies to achieve sustainable human development in previously determined priority areas, which help to consolidate peace and resolve social inequalities, extreme poverty and social explosion;

9. *Requests* the Secretary-General, the organs, organizations and programmes of the United Nations system and all States, international financial institutions and regional and subregional organizations to continue providing the support needed to attain the objectives of the programme for the sustainable development of Central America, in particular those which

are being pursued within the framework of the Quinquennium for the Reduction of Vulnerability to and the Impact of Natural Disasters in Central America;

10. *Requests* the Secretary-General to report to the General Assembly at its fifty-sixth session on the implementation of the present resolution;

11. *Decides* to consider at its fifty-sixth session the question of international assistance to and cooperation with the Alliance for the Sustainable Development of Central America.

El Salvador

In accordance with General Assembly resolution 52/169 C [YUN 1997, p. 922], the Secretary-General submitted an October report on assistance for the reconstruction and development of El Salvador [A/54/462], which described the economic and social situation of the country and the state of its democratic institutions, and examined the advances and obstacles during 1998-1999 in the efforts to make the transition from peace-building to sustainable development. Regarding the integration of outstanding issues (land transfer programme; rural settlements programme; Fund for the Protection of the Wounded and War-Disabled; transfer of lands in excess of 245 hectares) into a national development agenda, UNDP and the Secretariat had developed a strategy to ensure that the process of peace-building received support from the United Nations, the international community and El Salvador, with a view to strengthening progress in democratization and promoting the resolution of the pending issues. During the period under review, UNDP had worked on all of the outstanding issues and had achieved results in the land transfer programme and the rural settlements programme. Unfortunately, there had been a clear lack of will even to open a dialogue on the issue of lands exceeding the constitutional limit of 245 hectares. With regard to the families of fallen combatants, despite the addition of some new beneficiaries to the programmes under the Fund for the Protection of the Wounded and War-Disabled, most of those who were entitled to those benefits had not received them, owing to difficulties in obtaining the required legal documents. UNDP took steps to incorporate the themes of reintegration and human rights into its programme, and its institutional strategy provided for intervention in local development and democratic governance. From 1996 to 1998, international cooperation with El Salvador declined from $514.7 million to $308.4 million, which represented an annual reduction in cooperation resources of 22.6 per cent.

Haiti

Communications. In response to a 16 February letter addressed to him from the President of the Economic and Social Council [E/1999/7-S/1999/170], seeking advice on the interpretation of paragraph 8 of resolution 1212(1998) [YUN 1998, p. 229], the President of the Security Council, in a 7 April letter [E/1999/12-S/1999/403], confirmed that the Security Council had invited the Economic and Social Council to contribute to designing a long-term programme of support for Haiti. The Security Council would continue to follow the matter and might have suggestions as to how the two Councils could cooperate in that regard.

ECONOMIC AND SOCIAL COUNCIL ACTION (May)

On 7 May [meeting 9], the Economic and Social Council adopted **resolution 1999/4** [draft: E/1999/L.15] without vote [agenda item 2].

Long-term programme of support for Haiti

The Economic and Social Council

1. *Recalls* paragraph 17 of its agreed conclusions 1998/1 of 17 July 1998, in which the Council noted the need to develop, through a strategic framework, when appropriate, a comprehensive approach to countries in crisis, in which key aspects of durable recovery, peace-building, all human rights, sustained economic growth and sustainable development, in accordance with the relevant resolutions of the General Assembly and recent United Nations conferences, were included. The development of such a comprehensive approach must involve national authorities as well as the United Nations system, donors and intergovernmental and non-governmental organizations. National authorities must take a leading role in all aspects of the recovery plan;

2. *Affirms* the leading role of the Government of Haiti in all aspects of the recovery plans for Haiti;

3. *Takes note* of paragraph 8 of Security Council resolution 1212(1998) of 25 November 1998, in which the Economic and Social Council was invited to contribute to the elaboration of a long-term programme of support for Haiti, and of the exchange of letters between the Presidents of the Economic and Social Council and the Security Council;

4. *Decides* to create an Ad Hoc Advisory Group on Haiti, composed of representatives of five Economic and Social Council members, designated by the President of the Council on the basis of equitable geographical distribution and in consultation with regional groups and the Government of Haiti;

5. *Also decides* that the Ad Hoc Advisory Group on Haiti should submit to the Economic and Social Council at its substantive session of 1999, for its consideration, its recommendations on how to ensure that international community assistance to the efforts to support the Government of Haiti in achieving sustainable development is adequate, coherent, well coordinated and effective;

6. *Requests* the Group to ensure that the Government of Haiti is fully involved in its work;

7. *Encourages* other interested Member States, including in particular the Friends of Haiti, to contribute to the work of the Group, and requests the Group to consider ways and means to facilitate their doing so;

8. *Requests* the Secretary-General and his Special Representative for Haiti, relevant United Nations funds and programmes and the specialized agencies, including the World Bank, to provide all necessary assistance to the Group;

9. *Invites* other relevant multilateral institutions, in particular the Inter-American Development Bank, regional organizations and bilateral donors, to cooperate fully with the Group.

Report of Ad Hoc Advisory Group. The Secretary-General, on 2 July, transmitted to the Council the report of the newly established Ad Hoc Advisory Group on Haiti [E/1999/103]. As noted in a May report of the Secretary-General to the Security Council (see p. 210), the country had been slowly recovering from its political crisis since April 1997, and continued to be a least developed country, the only one in the western hemisphere. The UN agencies in Haiti worked with the Government and NGOs in assisting the population at the grass-roots level. Excluding the World Bank and IMF, the UN system's disbursements in support of socio-economic development stood at $127.8 million since the return of the constitutional Government. External assistance since then had sought to respond to development needs identified by the Government and the international community within the framework of the emergency recovery programme to which donors pledged funds. A factor affecting aid was the concentration of donor resources on humanitarian activities, and there was a need to shift it towards support for sustainable development, including capacity- and institution-building. Strengthening the role of the Government in aid coordination was key to making Haiti's cooperation with its partners more effective. The consultative group process facilitated by the World Bank remained the framework for inter-donor coordination and donor-government consultations on development priorities and policies, as well as on issues of funding.

The Group recommended that the Council request the Secretary-General to establish, in consultation with the Government, mechanisms to develop a long-term strategy and programme of support in areas such as education, peace-building, poverty eradication, durable recovery and sustainable development, aimed at reinforcing capacity-building in governmental and civil society institutions. It also recommended that the UN specialized agencies, funds and programmes, the World Bank, the Inter-American Development Bank, other multilateral institutions, regional organizations, bilateral donors and NGOs continue support and work in collaboration with the Government and the donor community to develop the programme. Coordination should take place through the resident coordinator mechanism. The Group proposed that the Council urge the UN system to continue to support the preparations for legislative, local and presidential elections, and invite the General Assembly to renew the mandate of the International Civilian Mission in Haiti. Recognizing the importance of a stable environment as a precondition for free and fair elections and of its link with sustainable development efforts, as well as of a functioning national police for the consolidation of democracy and the revitalization of the system of justice, the Group recommended that the Council urge the UN system to continue to work in the areas of consolidation of democracy, training and professionalization of the national police force. It also recommended that it request the Secretary-General to submit an annual report on the long-term programme of support.

ECONOMIC AND SOCIAL COUNCIL ACTION (July)

On 27 July [meeting 41], the Economic and Social Council adopted **resolution 1999/11** [draft: E/1999/L.35] without vote [agenda item 7].

Long-term strategy and programme of support for Haiti

The Economic and Social Council,

Recalling paragraph 17 of its agreed conclusions 1998/1 of 17 July 1998, in which the Council noted the need to develop, through a strategic framework, when appropriate, a comprehensive approach to countries in crisis, in which key aspects of durable recovery, peace-building, all human rights, sustained economic growth and sustainable development, in accordance with the relevant resolutions of the General Assembly and recent United Nations conferences, were included,

Recalling also that the development of such a comprehensive approach must involve national authorities as well as the United Nations system, donors and intergovernmental and non-governmental organizations, and that national authorities must take a leading role in all aspects of the recovery plan,

Recalling further its resolution 1999/4 of 7 May 1999, by which it created an Ad Hoc Advisory Group on Haiti, with the mandate of submitting to the Council, at its substantive session of 1999, for its consideration, its recommendations on how to ensure that international community assistance to the efforts to support the Government of Haiti in achieving sustainable development is adequate, coherent, well coordinated and effective,

Reaffirming the leading role of the Government of Haiti in all aspects of the recovery plans for Haiti,

Having examined the report of the Ad Hoc Advisory Group on Haiti,

Emphasizing the need to develop a strategic framework and a comprehensive approach for a long-term United Nations programme of support for Haiti,

Emphasizing also that capacity-building is a key element to enable Governments and civil society to manage their affairs and effectively absorb international assistance in post-conflict situations,

Stressing the vital link between national stability and economic and social development,

Taking note of the request by the Government of Haiti for international electoral assistance for its plans to organize and hold the forthcoming legislative, local and presidential elections,

Bearing in mind the importance of the role of the United Nations High Commissioner for Human Rights with regard to human rights issues in Haiti and of the work of the independent expert on Haiti of the Commission on Human Rights,

1. *Takes note with appreciation* of the report of the Ad Hoc Advisory Group on Haiti, and welcomes its recommendations;

2. *Requests* the Secretary-General, in consultation with the Government of Haiti and making use of the existing United Nations presence in Haiti, to take the necessary steps to develop on a priority basis a long-term strategy and programme of support for Haiti in such areas as education, peace-building, poverty eradication, social integration, productive employment, trade, durable recovery and sustainable development, aimed particularly at reinforcing capacity-building objectives in both governmental and civil society institutions;

3. *Requests* the programmes, funds and agencies of the United Nations system, the World Bank, the Inter-American Development Bank, other multilateral institutions and regional organizations, bilateral donors, including within the Consultative Group meetings led by the World Bank, non-governmental organizations and the rest of the donor community to continue to support and to work in close collaboration with the Government of Haiti for the purpose of elaborating and supporting the long-term strategy and programme for Haiti, including prioritizing sustainable development and capacity-building objectives;

4. *Urges* that the coordination of the work of the organizations of the United Nations system in Haiti continue to function through the resident coordinator mechanism, since it has proved to be an adequate means for effective coordination, and that such coordination should be further strengthened through the completion of the common country assessment and subsequent preparation of a United Nations Development Assistance Framework for Haiti, which will provide the elements to define an effective long-term United Nations development assistance programme for the country;

5. *Recommends* that the long-term programme of support for Haiti address the issues of capacity-building of governmental institutions, especially in areas such as governance, the promotion of human rights, the administration of justice, the electoral system, law enforcement, police training and other areas of social and economic development, which would enable the Government of Haiti to adequately and effectively coordinate, manage, absorb and utilize international assistance and development aid;

6. *Also recommends* that the long-term strategy and programme of support for Haiti also address the issue of capacity-building in civil society institutions, particularly community-based organizations, labour unions and professional associations;

7. *Urges* the United Nations system to continue to support the preparations for legislative, local and presidential elections in Haiti, including supporting financially the ongoing efforts of the Government of Haiti to organize those elections;

8. *Recommends* to the General Assembly to review all aspects of the mandate and operations of the International Civilian Mission in Haiti in the light of the situation in Haiti and to consider renewing the mandate of the United Nations component of the Mission;

9. *Requests* the Secretary-General to coordinate with the Government of Haiti other modalities under which reinforced support from the international community can be ensured for the electoral processes;

10. *Urges* the United Nations system to continue to work in the areas of consolidation of democracy and training and professionalization of the national police force of Haiti, and, to that end, recommends to the General Assembly to consider devising a United Nations special training and technical assistance programme for the Haitian National Police;

11. *Recommends* to the General Assembly to consider requesting the Secretary-General to continue his good offices in Haiti through his Representative and to maintain the existence of the office there, which would also have the responsibility of managing any new civilian mission mandated by the United Nations;

12. *Requests* the Secretary-General to submit to the Economic and Social Council, at its substantive session of 2000, and to the appropriate United Nations intergovernmental bodies, an integrated synthesis report on the elaboration and implementation of the long-term programme of support for Haiti, including observations and recommendations on the work of the relevant United Nations bodies in their respective areas of competence.

Third States affected by sanctions

In a May note on assistance to third States affected by the application of sanctions [E/1999/51], the Secretary-General, recalling General Assembly resolution 53/107 [YUN 1998, p. 1236], stated that a summary of the deliberations and main findings of the ad hoc expert group meeting on developing a methodology for assessing the consequences incurred by third States as a result of preventive or enforcement measures, and on exploring innovative measures of international assistance to the affected third States, as contained in the Secretary-General's 1998 report [ibid., p. 1235], would be made available to the Economic and Social Council at its substantive session of 1999 (see also p. 1252).

ECONOMIC AND SOCIAL COUNCIL ACTION

On 30 July [meeting 46], the Economic and Social Council adopted **resolution 1999/59** [draft: E/1999/L.52] without vote [agenda item 13].

Assistance to third States affected by the application of sanctions

The Economic and Social Council,

Recalling General Assembly resolution 53/107 of 8 December 1998 on the implementation of the provisions of the Charter of the United Nations related to assistance to third States affected by the application of sanctions,

Taking note of the note by the Secretary-General,

1. *Takes note* of the summary of the deliberations and main findings of the ad hoc expert group meeting on developing a methodology for assessing the consequences incurred by third States as a result of preventive or enforcement measures and on exploring innovative and practical measures of international assistance to the affected third States, as contained in section IV of the report of the Secretary-General on implementation of the provisions of the Charter related to assistance to third States affected by the application of sanctions;

2. *Reaffirms* the important role of the General Assembly, the Economic and Social Council and the Committee for Programme and Coordination in mobilizing and monitoring, as appropriate, the economic assistance efforts of the international community and the United Nations system to States confronted with special economic problems arising from the carrying out of preventive or enforcement measures imposed by the Security Council and, as appropriate, in identifying solutions to the special economic problems of those States;

3. *Decides* to continue consideration of this question, taking into account the relevant decisions of the General Assembly.

States affected in the Balkans

In response to General Assembly resolution 52/169 H [YUN 1997, p. 925], the Secretary-General submitted a November report on economic assistance to States affected by the consequences of severing their economic relations with the Federal Republic of Yugoslavia during the period when sanctions had been in force and during the period following the lifting of the sanctions [A/54/534]. The report contained information provided by Governments on action they had taken to assist the affected States. It also described UN assistance activities, regional initiatives and assistance arrangements, humanitarian assistance programmes, and procurements for UN peacekeeping missions. Regarding reconstruction and development efforts, the international community, including all countries of the region, pledged to mobilize funds or in-kind assistance. The Kosovo crisis had produced an overwhelming impact on the fragile economies of several neighbouring countries. The affected countries of South-Eastern Europe continued to face adjustment problems, which, the Secretary-General stressed, needed to be addressed in the context of the rehabilitation effort and through enhancing regional cooperation. Donor support for the reconstruction process in the former Yugoslavia and other regional cooperation programmes had already yielded a positive impact on the most seriously affected countries.

Although the UN system continued to implement financial and technical assistance programmes, new resources were needed in support of reconstruction and recovery efforts. Specific concerns in the areas of transport and infrastructure development as well as trade and investment promotion were pursued through regional initiatives and assistance arrangements under the auspices of the EU and in cooperation with other regional organizations, but additional resources were needed to support a long-term approach to the consolidation of the Balkans. Affected countries should be encouraged to participate in the international support for rehabilitation efforts. Mobilization and coordination of assistance and co-financing of projects under the auspices of multilateral agencies should facilitate regional allocation of resources and increase transparency in procurement of products and services. Moreover, in follow-up to the Stability Pact for South-Eastern Europe—adopted in Cologne, Germany, on 10 June—activities of its Economic Table, aimed at reconstruction assistance, sustainable investment and structural reforms in the subregion, would help promote further intraregional cooperation and integration of South-East Europe into the European mainstream as an important contribution to stability in the Balkans and beyond.

GENERAL ASSEMBLY ACTION

On 15 December [meeting 80], the General Assembly adopted **resolution 54/96 G** [draft: A/54/L.67 & Add.1] without vote [agenda item 20 (*b*)].

Economic assistance to the Eastern European States affected by the developments in the Balkans

The General Assembly,

Taking note of the report of the Secretary-General on the implementation of resolution 52/169 H of 16 December 1997 and the conclusions contained therein,

Recalling agreed conclusions 1999/1 of the humanitarian affairs segment of the Economic and Social Council, in particular the relevant paragraphs thereof,

Stressing the importance of the regional cooperation initiatives and assistance arrangements, such as the Process of Stability and Good-Neighbourliness in South-East Europe (Royaumont Initiative), the South-East European Cooperative Initiative, the South-East European Cooperation Process, the Central European Initiative and the Black Sea Economic Cooperation,

Welcoming the Stability Pact for South-Eastern Europe, adopted in Cologne, Germany, on 10 June 1999,

Taking note of issue number 2 of the *Economic Survey of Europe, 1999*, in particular the relevant chapters thereof,

Recalling its resolution 54/62 of 1 December 1999,

1. *Expresses concern* at the special economic problems confronting the Eastern European States affected by the developments in the Balkans, in particular their impact on regional trade and economic relations and on navigation along the Danube and on the Adriatic Sea;

2. *Welcomes* the support already provided by the international community, in particular by the European Union and other donors, to the affected States to assist them in coping with their special economic problems during the transition period following the lifting of the sanctions pursuant to Security Council resolution 1074(1996) of 1 October 1996, as well as in the process of economic adjustment following the developments in the Balkans;

3. *Stresses* the importance of the effective implementation of the Stability Pact for South-Eastern Europe, the objective of which is to strengthen countries in South-Eastern Europe in their efforts to foster peace, democracy, respect for human rights and economic prosperity, in order to achieve stability in the whole region, and of its follow-up activities aimed, inter alia, at economic reconstruction, development and cooperation, including economic cooperation in the region and between the region and the rest of Europe;

4. *Invites* all States and the relevant international organizations, both within and outside the United Nations system, in particular the international financial institutions, to continue to take into account the special needs and situations of the affected States in providing support and assistance to their efforts for economic recovery, structural adjustment and development;

5. *Encourages* the affected States of the region to continue the process of multilateral regional cooperation in such fields as transport and infrastructure development, including the resumption of navigation on the Danube, as well as to foster conditions favourable to trade and investment in all the countries of the region;

6. *Invites* the relevant international organizations to take appropriate steps, consistent with the principle of efficient and effective procurement and with resolution 54/14 of 29 October 1999 on procurement reform, in order to broaden access for interested local and regional vendors and to facilitate their participation in the efforts for reconstruction, recovery and development of the region;

7. *Requests* the Secretary-General to report to the General Assembly at its fifty-fifth session on the implementation of the present resolution.

Disaster relief

In 1999, the world witnessed natural disasters of unprecedented devastation, causing extraordinary human and financial losses. Floods were the most frequent natural disasters, affecting hundreds of thousands of people in the Gambia, Ghana, the Sudan and Togo and some 100 million people in China. In December, unprecedented floods and mud slides hit Venezuela, killing about 30,000 people and affecting hundreds of thousands: it was Latin America's worst disaster of the century. The combined destructive forces of gale winds and high seas of the cyclone in Orissa, India, killed 9,500 people and affected 12.6 million others. Major earthquakes were also recorded. Afghanistan suffered a strong earthquake at the beginning of the year and Turkey was hit in August and November by two devastating events causing the death of 18,000 people and affecting more than 600,000. Between those two events, a severe earthquake hit Greece. In September, 2,300 people lost their lives in Taiwan after a strong earthquake hit the island.

In most cases, national efforts were complemented by assistance from the international community. During the year, the Office for the Coordination of Humanitarian Affairs (OCHA), through its Disaster Response Branch (DRB), responded to 75 natural disasters, helped to mobilize more than $200 million in contributions from the international community for disaster-affected countries and led the international response to the earthquakes in Turkey. In coordination with key regional players, DRB supported 12 United Nations Disaster Assessment and Coordination (UNDAC) missions and participated in UNDAC training in Asia and the Pacific, Latin America and Europe. It made emergency cash grants for a total of $765,000 to Governments of disaster-stricken countries so that they could meet the most pressing needs of the affected populations, and channelled $7 million in voluntary cash and in-kind contributions from donors. OCHA maintained a permanent stock of donated disaster relief items at its warehouse in Pisa, Italy. Between January and August, it shipped some 2,624 tons of relief goods to 20 countries.

International Decade for Natural Disaster Reduction

In response to General Assembly resolution 53/185 [YUN 1998, p. 873], the Secretary-General submitted a July report [A/54/132-E/1999/80] on the activities of the International Decade for Natural Disaster Reduction (IDNDR) (1990-2000), proclaimed by the Assembly in resolution 44/236 [YUN 1989, p. 355]. The activities focused on the implementation of the 1998-1999 action plan, presented to the Scientific and Technical Committee of IDNDR in 1997 [YUN 1997, p. 926].

The report discussed the outcome of the 1994 World Conference on National Disaster Reduction [YUN 1994, p. 851], the substantive platform for the mid-term review of the Decade, and natural disaster reduction activities and UN reform. It summarized the Decade's achievements in the areas of advocacy, policy development and coordination, and described selected activities at the regional level, as well as those carried out by UN agencies. A two-tiered closing event for the Decade consisted of the legislative platform provided by the 1999 substantive session of the Economic and Social Council and the IDNDR programme forum (Geneva, 5-9 July). Within the forum, all partners of the IDNDR Framework had exchanged information on 10 years of achievements, as well as emerging trends and challenges for the future. They also exchanged views on how best to tackle those challenges through a concerted programme of action towards a safer world in the twenty-first century.

The report contained a summary of the results of the various thematic sessions organized within the IDNDR programme forum, which reflected the conclusions emanating from the implementation of the Decade's 10-year programme of disaster reduction. The thematic topics emphasized poverty reduction, mega-cities and urban areas, community-based actions, public awareness, improvements in warning systems, communications technology, education and training for disaster reduction, partnerships involving public and private organizations, integrating risk management into developmental and environmental planning, health consequences of natural disasters, climate variability, environmental protection, research, land-use planning, modifications to building codes and practices, ensuring reliable data on losses, and the international and regional framework provided by IDNDR. The final declaration adopted by the IDNDR programme forum focused on guaranteeing a safer world for future generations, with the 1994 Yokohama Strategy [YUN 1994, p. 851] and the strategy "A safer world in the twenty-first century: risk and disaster reduction" (1999) charting the course.

The Scientific and Technical Committee of IDNDR, at its eleventh meeting (Canberra, Australia, 15-19 February) [A/54/132/Add.1-E/1999/80/Add.1], assessed progress made during the Decade and outlined the major challenges for the twenty-first century. The Committee observed that mitigation and prevention practices were achieving a priority approaching that previously reserved for contingent emergency management activities associated with relief and recovery during the acute phase of individual disasters. There was a need to ensure UN inter-agency coordination, possibly through an intergovernmental panel or commission.

IDNDR successor arrangements

Pursuant to General Assembly resolution 53/185, the Secretary-General, in June [A/54/136-E/1999/89], discussed an IDNDR secretariat proposal for future arrangements following the closure of the Decade. It proposed the establishment, on 1 January 2000, of an inter-agency secretariat for disaster reduction, composed of an international team of experts and funded by voluntary contributions from Member States and other sources. The secretariat recognized the need for an inter-agency task force for natural disaster reduction, composed of representatives from within and outside the UN system, to provide a platform for the realization of disaster reduction in a concerted manner. Its main functions would be to: serve as the main forum within the UN system for devising strategies and policies for the reduction of natural hazards; identify gaps in disaster reduction policies and programmes and recommend remedial action; ensure complementarity of action by agencies; provide policy guidance to the secretariat; and convene ad hoc expert meetings.

ACC action. At its first regular session (Geneva, 9-10 April) [ACC/1999/4], ACC underlined the importance of an inter-agency approach to the follow-up to IDNDR. It noted that the United Nations would prepare a proposal which would be the subject of consultations with agencies concerned prior to its submission to the General Assembly through the Economic and Social Council.

ECONOMIC AND SOCIAL COUNCIL ACTION

On 30 July [meeting 46], the Economic and Social Council adopted **resolution 1999/63** [draft: E/1999/L.44] without vote [agenda item 13 *(h)*].

International Decade for Natural Disaster Reduction: successor arrangements

The Economic and Social Council,

Recalling its resolution 1995/47 B of 27 July 1995 and General Assembly resolutions 44/236 of 22 December 1989 and 49/22 A of 2 December 1994 on the International Decade for Natural Disaster Reduction, as well as Assembly resolutions 49/22 B of 20 December 1994 on early warning capacities of the United Nations system with regard to natural disasters, 52/12 A of 12 November 1997 and 52/12 B of 19 December 1997 entitled "Renewing the United Nations: a programme for reform" and 53/185 of 15 December 1998 on international cooperation to reduce the impact of the El Niño phenomenon,

Recalling also the programme forum on the Decade, held at Geneva from 5 to 9 July 1999, and the Geneva mandate on disaster reduction adopted by the forum, together with the strategy document entitled "A safer world in the twenty-first century: risk and disaster reduction",

Having considered the reports of the Secretary-General concerning the activities of the International Decade for Natural Disaster Reduction and on the recommendations on institutional arrangements for disaster reduction activities of the United Nations system after the conclusion of the Decade,

Expressing concern that the world is increasingly being threatened by large-scale natural disasters which will have long-term negative social, economic and environmental consequences for vulnerable societies worldwide, in particular in developing countries,

Reiterating that the promotion of economic growth and sustainable development cannot be achieved without adequate measures to prevent and reduce the impact of natural disasters and that there are close linkages between losses owing to natural disasters and environmental degradation, as emphasized in Agenda 21 and in the Programme for the Further Implementation of Agenda 21, adopted by the General Assembly at its nineteenth special session,

Emphasizing the multisectoral, interdisciplinary and cross-cutting nature of natural disaster reduction, and stressing that continued interaction, cooperation and partnerships among the institutions concerned are considered essential to accomplish jointly agreed objectives and priorities,

Recognizing the necessity for the international community to demonstrate the strong political determination required to use existing scientific and technical knowledge to reduce vulnerability to natural disasters and environmental hazards, bearing in mind the particular needs of developing countries,

Reiterating in that regard that regard that natural disasters damage the social and economic infrastructure of all countries, although the long-term consequences of natural disasters are especially severe for developing countries, including the least developed countries, and landlocked and small island developing States, as well as for countries with economies in transition, thus hampering their sustainable development processes,

Stressing the importance of developing and strengthening regional approaches dedicated to disaster reduction in order to take into account regional and local specificity and needs,

Stressing also that the United Nations has a special role as well as considerable experience in the disaster prevention and reduction fields, in view of its universal character, its broad policy agenda and its vital role as a forum for global dialogue,

Recalling the forward-looking platform for international concerted disaster reduction as developed by the World Conference on Natural Disaster Reduction, held at Yokohama, Japan, from 23 to 27 May 1994, and as expressed in the Yokohama Strategy for a Safer World: Guidelines for Natural Disaster Prevention, Preparedness and Mitigation and its Plan of Action,

Recognizing the importance of early warning as an integrated process at all levels, including hazard monitoring and impact prediction, technology development and transfer, capacity-building for the detection of hazards, as well as the issuance and communication of early warnings, education and professional training, public information and awareness-raising, and interface between the public and private sectors in order to ensure adequate action to warnings,

1. *Takes note with appreciation* of the reports of the Secretary-General concerning the activities of the International Decade for Natural Disaster Reduction and on the recommendations on institutional arrangements for disaster reduction activities of the United Nations system after the conclusion of the Decade;

2. *Recognizes* the success achieved since 1990 in meeting the goals and objectives of the Decade, as expressed in General Assembly resolution 44/236 and in the Yokohama Strategy for a Safer World: Guidelines for Natural Disaster Prevention, Preparedness and Mitigation and its Plan of Action;

3. *Also recognizes* the increased emphasis being given to natural disaster prevention and the need for taking comprehensive measures with regard to natural disaster reduction as an integral part of sustainable development strategies and an essential element of government policy;

4. *Reiterates* the importance of fully integrating natural disaster reduction into the sustainable development strategies of the United Nations and of other international organizations;

5. *Decides,* therefore, that the international cooperative framework for natural disaster reduction, as recommended in the report of the Secretary-General, should draw on the success of the functional and organizational arrangements that were put in place for the implementation of the Decade;

6. *Requests* the Secretary-General to establish, as of January 2000, an inter-agency task force, with representation from all relevant United Nations bodies and members of the scientific and technical community, including regional representation, to serve as the main forum within the United Nations for continued and concerted emphasis on natural disaster reduction, in particular for defining strategies for international cooperation at all levels in this field, while ensuring complementarity of action with other agencies;

7. *Also requests* the Secretary-General, in this respect, to maintain the existing inter-agency secretariat function for natural disaster reduction as a distinct focal point for the coordination of the work of the inter-agency task force, to place the inter-agency task force and inter-agency secretariat under the direct authority of the Under-Secretary-General for Humanitarian Affairs and to finance it from extrabudgetary resources through a specific trust fund;

8. *Calls upon* all Governments to maintain and strengthen established national and multisectoral platforms for natural disaster reduction in order to achieve sustainable development goals and objectives, with the full utilization of scientific and technical means;

9. *Emphasizes,* in this respect, the need for the international community to support appropriate initiatives and mechanisms for strengthening regional, subregional, national and local capabilities for natural disaster prevention and reduction, making early warning a key element within these efforts;

10. *Requests* the Secretary-General to submit a report to the General Assembly at its fifty-fourth session on the implementation of the present resolution, under the item entitled "Environment and sustainable development".

Report of Secretary-General. In response to the Council's resolution, the Secretary-General, in a November report [A/54/497], presented the international strategy for disaster reduction (ISDR), which would serve as a framework for UN system activities. He described the organizational measures to be taken to implement the Council's resolution, including the establishment of an inter-agency task force and a secretariat. ISDR, which would succeed the programme for the Decade, was contained in the document entitled "A safer world for the twenty-first century: risk and disaster reduction", adopted at the programme forum for the Decade held in July (see p. 859). Its main objectives were to enable communities to become resilient to the effects of natural, technological and environmental hazards, and to proceed from protection against hazards to the management of risk, by integrating risk prevention strategies into sustainable development activities. The strategy was structured around the goals of increasing public awareness of the risks to societies; obtaining commitments by public authorities to reduce risks; engaging public participation to create disaster-resistant communities; and reducing economic and social losses caused by disasters. The task force and secretariat, aimed at facilitating the implementation of the ISDR goals, would function under the authority of the Under-Secretary-General for Humanitarian Affairs from 1 January 2000. The provisions of Council resolution 1999/46 on international cooperation to reduce the impact of the El Niño phenomenon (see p. 863) should be taken into account in the establishment of the task force. The successor arrangements for IDNDR should be flexible in the initial period and adapted as experience was gained. Therefore, they would be reviewed after one year in consultation with key stakeholders. The Secretary-General appealed to all Governments to increase their support to national, regional and international programmes and to establish a better balance between their expenditures on relief and those on prevention activities.

GENERAL ASSEMBLY ACTION

On 22 December [meeting 87], the General Assembly, on the recommendation of the Second (Economic and Financial) Committee [A/54/588/Add.2], adopted **resolution 54/219** without vote [agenda item 100 *(b)*].

International Decade for Natural Disaster Reduction: successor arrangements

The General Assembly,

Recalling its resolutions 44/236 of 22 December 1989, 49/22 A of 2 December 1994, 49/22 B of 20 December 1994 and 53/185 of 15 December 1998, and taking note of Economic and Social Council resolution 1999/63 of 30 July 1999 on the successor arrangements for the International Decade for Natural Disaster Reduction,

Recalling also the results of the programme forum on the International Decade, held at Geneva from 5 to 9 July 1999, and the Geneva mandate on disaster reduction adopted by the forum, together with the strategy document entitled "A safer world in the twenty-first century: risk and disaster reduction",

Recalling further the forward-looking platform for international concerted disaster reduction as developed by the World Conference on Natural Disaster Reduction and as expressed in the Yokohama Strategy for a Safer World: Guidelines for Natural Disaster Prevention, Preparedness and Mitigation and its Plan of Action,

Reiterating that natural disasters damage the social and economic infrastructure of all countries, although the long-term consequences of natural disasters are especially severe for developing countries and hamper their sustainable development,

Recognizing the need for the international community to demonstrate the firm political determination required to utilize scientific and technical knowledge to reduce vulnerability to natural disasters and environmental hazards, taking into account the particular needs of developing countries,

Having considered the report of the Secretary-General on the implementation of Economic and Social Council resolution 1999/63,

Noting the Declaration on Technical Cooperation for the Prevention and Relief of Natural Disasters, adopted by the Rio Group at its thirteenth summit meeting, held in Mexico on 28 and 29 May 1999, as well as the results of the first summit meeting of heads of State and Government of Latin America and the Caribbean and the European Union, held at Rio de Janeiro on 28 and 29 June 1999,[a]

Taking into account the consideration of natural disasters contained in the report of the Third United Nations Conference on the Exploration and Peaceful Uses of Outer Space, held at Vienna from 19 to 30 July 1999,

1. *Takes note with appreciation* of the reports of the Secretary-General concerning the activities of the International Decade for Natural Disaster Reduction and on the recommendations on institutional arrangements for disaster reduction activities of the United Nations system after the conclusion of the Decade;

2. *Expresses deep concern* at the increasing number and scale of natural disasters, which have resulted in massive losses of life and long-term negative social, economic and environmental consequences for vulnerable societies worldwide, in particular in developing countries;

3. *Endorses* the proposals put forward in the report of the Secretary-General to ensure the swift establishment of future arrangements for disaster reduction as well as functional continuity for the effective implementation of the international strategy for disaster reduction;

4. *Also endorses* the proposal of the Secretary-General to establish an inter-agency task force and inter-agency secretariat for disaster reduction, under the direct authority of the Under-Secretary-General for Humanitarian Affairs, in a flexible manner, for the initial period of the biennium 2000-2001, and to undertake a review of these arrangements after the first year of operations with a view to submitting proposals on adjustments;

5. *Decides* to maintain the observance of the International Day for Natural Disaster Reduction on the second Wednesday of October;

6. *Requests* the Secretary-General to establish, from voluntary contributions, a trust fund for disaster reduction to enable the funding of the inter-agency secretariat for disaster reduction and to transfer all as-

sets of the Trust Fund for the International Decade for Natural Disaster Reduction to the new trust fund for disaster reduction, effective 1 January 2000;

7. *Calls upon* Governments to continue to cooperate and coordinate their efforts with the Secretary-General and the Under-Secretary-General for Humanitarian Affairs, the United Nations system, non-governmental organizations and other partners, as appropriate, to implement and to develop further a comprehensive strategy to maximize international cooperation in the field of natural disasters, based upon an effective division of labour, from prevention to early warning, response, mitigation, rehabilitation and reconstruction, including through capacity-building at all levels, and the development and strengthening of global and regional approaches that take into account regional, subregional, national and local circumstances and needs, as well as the need to strengthen coordination of national emergency response agencies in natural disasters;

8. *Requests* the Secretary-General to solicit the required inputs from Governments, the relevant organizations of the United Nations system and non-governmental organizations in order to optimize further and disseminate listings of organizations of the United Nations system as well as non-governmental organizations that provide civil protection and emergency response at all levels, with updated inventories of available resources, to help during natural disasters;

9. *Also requests* the Secretary-General to optimize further and disseminate through all available channels, including handbooks, the information necessary to guide the international community at large in the effective management of international cooperation in the fields of disaster prevention, early warning, response, mitigation, rehabilitation and reconstruction;

10. *Emphasizes* the urgent need to develop further and make use of the existing scientific and technical knowledge to reduce vulnerability to natural disasters, bearing in mind the particular needs of developing countries, and, in this regard, calls upon all countries to strengthen scientific research and training of experts in universities and specialized institutions and to promote the exchange of information;

11. *Recognizes* the importance of early warning as an essential element in the culture of prevention, and encourages renewed efforts at all levels to contribute to natural hazard monitoring and impact prediction, the development and transfer of technology, capacity-building for disaster preparedness, the detection of natural hazards and the issuance and communication of early warnings, as well as education and professional training, public information and awareness-raising activities, such as the International Conference on Early-Warning Systems for the Reduction of Natural Disasters, held at Potsdam, Germany, from 7 to 11 September 1998, to ensure adequate action warnings;

12. *Reaffirms* the need for strengthening an international framework for the improvement of early warning systems and disaster preparedness by developing an effective international mechanism for early warning, including the transfer of technology related to early warning to developing countries, under the auspices of the United Nations, as an integral part of future strategies and frameworks or any arrangements for natural disaster reduction;

13. *Requests* the Secretary-General to submit to the General Assembly at its fifty-sixth session, through the Economic and Social Council, a report on the implementation of the international strategy for disaster reduction, under the agenda item entitled "Environment and sustainable development".

[a]A/54/448.

El Niño

In response to General Assembly resolutions 52/200 [YUN 1997, p. 927] and 53/185 [YUN 1998, p. 873], the Secretary-General submitted a June report on international cooperation to reduce the impact of the El Niño phenomenon [A/54/135-E/1999/88], a disruption of the ocean-atmosphere system in the tropical Pacific that had important consequences for weather and climate worldwide. He reported that international activity towards the reduction of El Niño–related natural disasters had intensified since the first Intergovernmental Meeting of Experts on El Niño held in 1998 in Guayaquil, Ecuador [YUN 1998, p. 873], and the Assembly decision in resolution 52/200 to intensify inter-agency collaboration. In accordance with its lead role on science and technology in the Inter-Agency Task Force on El Niño, the World Meteorological Organization (WMO) embarked on a feasibility study for an international centre for research on El Niño in Guayaquil. The proposed centre would promote and undertake research on the El Niño/Southern Oscillation (ENSO) phenomenon and mathematical modelling to permit downscaling of global climate predictions to regional and national scales; and provide outreach services to the community of users of ENSO data and predictions. A progress report on the feasibility study was annexed to the report. In parallel with the study, WMO acted as the executing agency for an Inter-American Development Bank–funded study on the prediction and amelioration of socio-economic impacts of ENSO in Latin America and the Caribbean.

El Niño concerns with regard to disaster reduction were discussed at various IDNDR conferences, including an IDNDR–Economic and Social Commission for Asia and the Pacific regional conference for Asia (Bangkok, Thailand, 13-17 February) and an IDNDR–United Nations Environment Programme conference for Africa (Nairobi, 18-21 May). A second intergovernmental meeting of experts, to be held in Lima, Peru, in September, would focus on institutional arrangements, the role of decision makers and the application of scientific and technological knowledge in prevention (see p. 863). As a further follow-up to the Guayaquil meeting, the Commission on Sustainable Development, in its segment on oceans and seas of its seventh session [E/1999/29], requested the Secretary-General to gather information on the impact of ENSO and provide it to the Task Force in order to contribute to the development of the strategy towards the assessment, prevention, mitigation and rehabilitation of the damage caused by ENSO.

The Secretary-General concluded that efforts should be made to intensify observations of climate oscillation systems in the three large ocean basins (Indian, Atlantic, Pacific) and to develop ENSO prediction skills, based on improved modelling. Underscoring the value of inter-agency collaboration among disaster reduction constituencies at the regional and national levels, both within and outside the UN system, he stressed that efforts should be made to ensure that action would continue after the conclusion of IDNDR at the end of 1999. In view of the global hazards posed by climate variability and extremes, including ENSO events, it was crucial that, within the framework of the successor arrangements for IDNDR proposed by the Secretary-General (see p. 859), the institutional connections between the Inter-Agency Committee on the Climate Agenda and the UN system-wide disaster prevention constituency were retained.

ECONOMIC AND SOCIAL COUNCIL ACTION

On 28 July [meeting 44], the Economic and Social Council adopted **resolution 1999/46** [draft: E/1999/L.40] without vote [agenda item 13 *(e)*].

International cooperation to reduce the impact of the El Niño phenomenon

The Economic and Social Council,

Recalling General Assembly resolutions 52/200 of 18 December 1997 and 53/185 of 15 December 1998,

Concerned about the extreme force and severe impact of the El Niño phenomenon during the period 1997-1998 and the subsequent La Niña episode in many regions of the world,

Having considered the report of the Secretary-General concerning the implementation of the mandates contained in General Assembly resolution 53/185 and the report of the Commission on Sustainable Development on its seventh session,

Bearing in mind agreed conclusions 1999/1 of the Council adopted on 23 July 1999 at the humanitarian affairs segment of its substantive session of 1999,

Noting with appreciation the concerted international efforts made, in particular through the Inter-Agency Task Force on El Niño, in close cooperation with member agencies of the Inter-Agency Committee on the Climate Agenda, to reduce the impact of natural disasters related to the El Niño phenomenon through improved scientific understanding, close monitoring and the dissemination of timely forecasts to communities affected,

Recognizing the importance of regional and subregional cooperation for the development of effective measures to reduce the negative impacts caused by the El Niño and La Niña phenomena,

1. *Welcomes* the conclusions and recommendations contained in the report of the Secretary-General on international cooperation to reduce the impact of the El Niño phenomenon;

2. *Requests* the Secretary-General to continue to assess the feasibility of establishing an international research centre on the El Niño phenomenon at Guayaquil, Ecuador;

3. *Welcomes* the recommendations, contained in the report of the Commission on Sustainable Development on its seventh session, concerning how to deal with the El Niño phenomenon;

4. *Reiterates* its coordination role of providing guidance to its functional commissions on the reduction of natural disasters within the overall context of sustainable development strategies;

5. *Calls* for strengthened interregional cooperation, in particular in the scientific and technical fields, inter alia, to consider existing interregional opportunities as identified at the Asia-Europe Foreign Ministers meeting, held in Berlin on 29 March 1999, and the first Summit of Heads of State and Government of Latin America and the Caribbean and the European Union, held in Rio de Janeiro, Brazil, on 28 and 29 June 1999, and by the Asia-Pacific Economic Cooperation Forum;

6. *Welcomes* the outcome and conclusions of the first Intergovernmental Meeting of Experts on El Niño, held in Guayaquil from 9 to 13 November 1998, and the convening of a second Intergovernmental Meeting of Experts on El Niño, which will be held in Lima from 20 to 24 September 1999;

7. *Calls* for the continued and full implementation of General Assembly resolutions 52/200 and 53/185 as an integral function of the successor arrangements to be made following the conclusion of the International Decade for Natural Disaster Reduction.

Report of Secretary-General. The Secretary-General reported that, in September, the Inter-American Development Bank and WMO signed an agreement for a study on the prediction and amelioration of socio-economic impacts of ENSO in Latin American and Caribbean countries, which would begin in March 2000 and run for 18 months [A/55/99-E/2000/86].

Communication. On 4 November [A/C.2/54/7], Ecuador transmitted a study assessing the feasibility of establishing an international centre for research of the El Niño phenomenon in Guayaquil.

GENERAL ASSEMBLY ACTION

On 22 December [meeting 87], the General Assembly, on the recommendation of the Second Committee [A/54/588/Add.2], adopted **resolution 54/220** without vote [agenda item 100 *(b)*].

International cooperation to reduce the impact of the El Niño phenomenon

The General Assembly,

Recalling its resolutions 52/200 of 18 December 1997 and 53/185 of 15 December 1998 on international cooperation to reduce the impact of the El Niño phenomenon, and taking note of Economic and Social Council resolutions 1999/46 of 28 July 1999, on the same subject, and 1999/63 of 30 July 1999 on the successor arrangements for the International Decade for Natural Disaster Reduction,

Recalling also paragraph 20 of the report of the Secretary-General on successor arrangements for the Decade,

Having considered the report of the Secretary-General on international cooperation to reduce the impact of the El Niño phenomenon and the report of the Commission on Sustainable Development on its seventh session,

Having also considered the report on the conclusions and recommendations of the first Intergovernmental Meeting of Experts on El Niño, held at Guayaquil, Ecuador, from 9 to 13 November 1998, and the feasibility study for the establishment of an international research centre on the El Niño/Southern Oscillation,

Reaffirming the importance of developing strategies at the national, subregional, regional and international levels that aim to prevent, mitigate and rehabilitate the damage caused by natural disasters resulting from the El Niño phenomenon,

Taking into account the considerations in relation to the use of tele-observation systems on weather forecast and climate contained in the report of the Third United Nations Conference on the Exploration and Peaceful Uses of Outer Space, held at Vienna from 19 to 30 July 1999,

1. *Takes note with satisfaction* of the report of the Secretary-General, and endorses the conclusions and recommendations contained therein;

2. *Welcomes* the 1999 retrospective report on the El Niño/Southern Oscillation prepared by the World Meteorological Organization;

3. *Reiterates* its invitation to Member States in paragraphs 8 and 9 of resolution 52/200 in relation to the technical and financial assistance needed to strengthen the national capacity of developing countries to support observation and research systems at the global and regional levels to prevent, mitigate and repair the damage caused by the El Niño/Southern Oscillation;

4. *Welcomes* the recommendations of the Commission on Sustainable Development at its seventh session regarding the approach that the United Nations system and the international community should take in dealing with the El Niño/Southern Oscillation, and reiterates its invitation to Member States to cover the impact of the El Niño/Southern Oscillation in their annual national reports;

5. *Calls upon* the Secretary-General, the relevant United Nations organizations and the international community to take the necessary measures, as appropriate, to establish an international research centre on El Niño at Guayaquil, Ecuador, invites the international community to provide financial, technical and scientific assistance and cooperation for this purpose, and encourages the centre, once established, to strengthen its links with other relevant regional and global climate-study organizations and to focus on the practical application of information regarding El Niño in such areas as disaster preparedness, agriculture, health, tourism, water and energy;

6. *Requests* the Secretary-General to continue to promote the full implementation of its resolutions 52/200 and 53/185 as an integral part of the agreed arrangements after the conclusion of the International Decade for Natural Disaster Reduction;

7. *Also requests* the Secretary-General to submit to the General Assembly at its fifty-fifth session, through the Commission on Sustainable Development at its eighth session and the Economic and Social Council at its substantive session of 2000, a report on the implementation of the present resolution, under the agenda item entitled "Environment and sustainable development".

Disaster assistance

Asia

Democratic People's Republic of Korea

While food shortages and malnutrition in children persisted in the Democratic People's Republic of Korea (DPRK) in 1999, there had been improvements in the food situation since the peak of the crisis in 1996/97. However, agencies continued to report the presence of malnourished children, and the health situation remained fragile, affected by the decline in the economy, resource shortages, lack of drugs and medical supplies and a health care system in crisis. The humanitarian strategy focused on targeted food aid, improvements in health services and programmes to support water purification and improved sanitation. However, the absence of a peace accord on the Korean peninsula led to special security concerns resulting in restrictions on access and mobility of international humanitarian personnel in-country. In late July and early August, the DPRK was hit by typhoons Neil and Olga, which caused severe but localized damage along the south-west and south-east coastal areas, including damage to property and infrastructure and loss of life.

A UN consolidated inter-agency appeal covering January to December 1999, which sought $274.8 million, was revised to $292.1 million in July. As at 4 October, $186.4 million, or 51.5 per cent, was pledged or contributed.

In November, OCHA launched a UN consolidated inter-agency appeal for January to December 2000, which sought $331.7 million.

India

In October, the Indian State of Orissa, situated on the east coast, was hit by two violent cyclones, whose devastating combination resulted in physical destruction, flooding and saline inundation. About 10,000 people died during the cyclones, and those who survived were threatened with disease, epidemics and malnutrition. Fourteen of the State's 30 districts were devastated, agricultural land was destroyed and infrastructure was rendered inoperative.

The Government of India and the State Government of Orissa, the national Red Cross and NGOs implemented a massive relief operation. The UN system, bilateral donors and international NGOs supported the national response with relief and rehabilitation initiatives. The response of the in-country UN system was coordinated by the Resident Coordinator through the UN Disaster Management Team (UNDMT). An UNDAC team was dispatched by OCHA to strengthen UNDMT. A UN office consisting of staff from UNICEF, WFP, WHO and OCHA was set up to facilitate the delivery of assistance. Of the international assistance of $23 million (excluding in-kind contributions and services) reported to OCHA, UN assistance amounted to $15 million.

Viet Nam

Record floods devastated the central provinces of Viet Nam in early November and then four weeks later in early December. In the combined tragedy, 793 people were killed, 55,000 families were left homeless, and hundreds of thousands of others lost all their property and livestock.

On 9 November, the Vietnamese Ministry of Foreign Affairs issued an appeal for international assistance, which was disseminated by OCHA. Governments, international organizations and private enterprises responded rapidly and, by the time the December floods hit, the rescue and logistics system was working well. OCHA kept the international community informed, provided cash grants for immediate relief assistance and served as a channel for funds. Total international assistance reported to OCHA amounted to $7.6 million.

Europe

Greece

In Greece, an earthquake measuring 5.9 on the Richter scale hit the northern suburbs of Athens on 7 September. According to official figures, 138 people died, 74,053 houses were affected (homes for 209,842 people) and some 8,388 enterprises that had employed 28,116 people were completely or partially destroyed. OCHA closely monitored the situation in cooperation with the General Secretariat for Civil Protection of the Ministry of Interior and Decentralization.

On 17 September [A/54/357], Ukraine transmitted a statement of the participants attending the International Conference on "Baltic and Black Sea Cooperation: To the Integrated Europe of the 21st Century without Dividing Lines" (Yalta, 10-11 September), welcoming the humanitarian assistance provided to the victims of the earthquakes in Greece and Turkey (see below) and appealing for continued relief efforts.

Turkey

On 17 August, a major earthquake measuring 6.7 on the Richter scale hit north-western Turkey. The epicentre was located close to the city of Izmit on the Sea of Marmara. The earthquake, one of the most powerful in the last 20 years, was followed by a wave of aftershocks. On 13 and 20 September, earthquakes of magnitude 5.8 and 5.0 respectively hit the same region, and another major earthquake hit the country on 14 November. The casualties were close to 18,000 dead and 25,000 injured; over 43,500 housing units collapsed or were heavily damaged; and a fire broke out at the Tupras oil refinery, near Izmit, endangering the population.

As soon as the alert was received on 17 August, OCHA activated its Disaster Response System, including mobilization and deployment of the UNDAC team, dispatch of disaster management experts to support the UN Resident Coordinator in Ankara, activation of the International Search and Rescue Advisory Group and establishment of an On-Site Operations Coordination Centre. OCHA also coordinated information-sharing with relevant organizations. A team from the UN system in Turkey, including UNDP, UNICEF, UNFPA and FAO, conducted a needs assessment in the affected area and worked with the OCHA team. OCHA allocated a $50,000 cash grant for immediate relief needs and served as a channel for cash contributions. The international community, as at September, had provided humanitarian assistance totalling $60.7 million.

GENERAL ASSEMBLY ACTION

On 22 November [meeting 60], the General Assembly adopted **resolution 54/30** [draft: A/54/L.17/Rev.1 & Add.1] without vote [agenda item 20 *(a)*].

Emergency response to disasters

The General Assembly,

Recalling its resolution 44/236 of 22 December 1989 on the International Decade for Natural Disaster Reduction and agreed conclusions 1999/1 of the humanitarian affairs segment of the substantive session of 1999 of the Economic and Social Council,

Deeply regretting the great number of casualties and the unprecedented devastation caused by one of the most powerful earthquakes of the century, which struck the north-west region of Turkey on 17 August 1999,

Expressing its deep sorrow at the loss of lives and devastation caused by the earthquake on 7 September 1999 in the north of Athens,

Noting with appreciation the prompt response of Governments, international agencies and organizations, non-governmental organizations and individuals throughout the world in providing search and rescue and emergency relief assistance to the victims of the earthquake in Turkey,

Expressing its satisfaction for the timely assistance provided by Governments, international agencies and organizations, non-governmental organizations and individuals throughout the world to the search and rescue and relief efforts undertaken by Greece in the aftermath of the 7 September earthquake,

Welcoming the efforts of the Secretary-General as regards the urgent steps he has taken to mobilize humanitarian assistance and to coordinate activities of agencies of the United Nations system in the field for purposeful and unified assistance by the international community,

Deeply concerned about the fact that natural disasters in every corner of the globe continue to claim high numbers of casualties and cause immense material damage and that the frequency and magnitude of these catastrophes place an ever-increasing material and moral burden on nations,

Reiterating the importance of mounting prompt and effective rescue operations in the aftermath of such deadly calamities in the future, as evidenced by the exemplary response of the international community to the earthquakes in Turkey and Greece,

1. *Expresses its solidarity* with the Governments and the peoples of Greece and Turkey as they cope with the consequences of the disasters;

2. *Expresses its appreciation* to all States of the international community, international agencies and organizations and non-governmental organizations and individuals that are providing emergency relief to the affected areas;

3. *Notes with satisfaction* the decision taken by the Governments of Greece and Turkey to establish a joint standby disaster relief unit comprising contingents drawn from governmental and non-governmental organizations and agencies of both countries to reinforce and expand existing standby arrangements of the United Nations system with no financial implications to the programme budget of the United Nations;

4. *Requests* the Secretary-General, through the Office for the Coordination of Humanitarian Affairs of the Secretariat, to formulate the modalities for the utilization of the standby disaster relief unit by the relevant agencies of the United Nations system;

5. *Requests* the Secretary-General to report to the General Assembly at its fifty-fifth session on the progress made in the implementation of the present resolution.

Latin America and the Caribbean

Colombia

On 25 January, an earthquake measuring 6.0 on the Richter scale struck central Colombia. More than 30 aftershocks occurred. The Government declared a state of emergency in the Quindío, Risaralda and Valle del Cauca departments; 20 municipalities were considered disaster zones. Some 425,000 people were affected and 45,000 houses were destroyed or damaged.

On 29 January, an UNDAC team was deployed by OCHA to Colombia. The team supported the UN Resident Coordinator, UNDMT and the national authorities in assessing needs and coordinating relief activities. Contributions from the international community amounted to over $32 million.

Hurricane Georges

In response to General Assembly resolution 53/1 B [YUN 1998, p. 875], the Secretary-General, in September [A/54/129/Rev.1-E/1999/73/Rev.1], reported on progress made in the relief, rehabilitation and reconstruction efforts of Antigua and Barbuda, Cuba, the Dominican Republic, Haiti and Saint Kitts and Nevis following hurricane Georges in 1998 [YUN 1998, p. 875].

The Secretary-General stated that, together with UN resident coordinators and disaster management teams, the Emergency Relief Coordinator/OCHA issued situation reports to highlight unmet emergency requirements in order to mobilize international assistance and sum up international response; channelled contributions for relief and immediate rehabilitation; deployed UNDAC teams to assist the resident coordinators in the Dominican Republic and Haiti; and facilitated shipments of emergency relief supplies to some of the affected countries. The resident coordinator played a key role in coordinating the international assistance and in designing the rehabilitation and reconstruction programmes. In many cases, UNDP and the country team heightened the importance of disaster preparedness, prevention and mitigation. OCHA mobilized $100,000 for relief and immediate rehabilitation. In addition, UNDP provided $100,000 for emergency response coordination for Saint Kitts and Nevis and $50,000 for Antigua and Barbuda for emergency response coordination through the Caribbean Disaster Emergency Response Agency.

In the Dominican Republic, where economic damage was estimated at $2.2 billion, the objective of the UNDP/UN programme was to support the Government in the implementation of a transition process from the initial emergency situation towards integrated and sustainable development. Programme activities, initially focused on direct emergency relief to refugees and the provision of equipment to the central governmental institutions, were subsequently directed at the rehabilitation process, emergency preparedness, housing reconstruction and access to safe water, the beneficiaries of which totalled 110,000 persons. In February, a national seminar was organized and co-financed by the programme to prepare an integrated national evaluation report of hurricane Georges, which was released within the framework of a regional seminar on disaster preparedness and mitigation in the Americas (Santo Domingo, 16-19 February).

In Haiti, where high population density, subsistence living standards, widespread soil erosion and lack of disaster management magnified the hurricane's impact, the office of the Resident Coordinator played an important coordination role during the emergency and rehabilitation phases. In order to strengthen national capacities in disaster preparedness, mitigation and management, UNDP and WHO/Pan American Health Organization launched longer-term capacity-building programmes.

Regarding Cuba, an information meeting for member States and UN system organizations was co-chaired by OCHA and UNDP (Geneva, 26 February) to update the emergency situation and the appeal. Some $15 million of the $87 million of required support identified in the consolidated appeal was mobilized. About $13 million was used for emergency supplies, and the remaining $2 million was allocated to recovery and rehabilitation programmes.

Hurricanes Jose and Lenny

In October and November, several small island developing States and territories of the eastern Caribbean were struck by hurricanes Jose and Lenny, at a time when several of the countries were still rebuilding from previous hurricane strikes. Hurricane Jose moved over the northern Leeward Islands on 20 October with wind speeds of between 90 and 100 miles per hour, striking the island of Antigua, followed by milder impacts on Barbuda, Saint Kitts and Nevis, Anguilla, Dominica, Montserrat and the British Virgin Islands. The storm lost strength on 21 October. In Antigua and Barbuda, more than 500 persons were forced to seek shelter, with 2,000 severely affected, and major roads were flooded. Flooding also affected Saint Kitts and Nevis. Hurricane Lenny moved towards the northern Leeward Islands on 14 November with winds of 100 miles per hour, disrupting life in Antigua and Barbuda, Saint Kitts and Nevis, Dominica, Saint Lucia, Grenada, Saint Vincent and the Grenadines and Saint Martin; other islands affected were Anguilla and Montserrat. It was downgraded to a tropical depression on 20 November, as it moved away from the Caribbean, leaving limited loss of life but extensive damage. In each case, damage was largely economic, affecting tourism infrastructure, electricity and telephones.

A rapid needs assessment team was deployed to Anguilla, Antigua and Barbuda, Dominica, Grenada, Saint Kitts and Nevis and Saint Vincent and the Grenadines on 21 and 22 November, following hurricane Lenny. However, the ability to carry out initial damage assessments was made difficult owing to the heavy toll on physical infrastructure, in particular roads, ports and bridges. Disaster planning and mitigation had been singled out as a particularly critical aspect of the UNDP strategy for the Caribbean subregion, and it would work closely with multilateral agencies, bilateral donors and the Governments of the region.

GENERAL ASSEMBLY ACTION

On 15 December [meeting 80], the General Assembly adopted **resolution 54/96 I** [draft: A/54/L.69 & Add.1] without vote [agenda item 20 *(b)*].

Emergency assistance to countries affected by hurricanes Jose and Lenny

The General Assembly,

Recalling its resolution 53/1 B of 5 October 1998 and other relevant resolutions under the agenda item entitled "Strengthening of the coordination of emergency humanitarian assistance of the United Nations",

Deeply distressed at the damage caused by hurricanes Jose and Lenny and the grave effects on the people, infrastructure and productive sectors of the economies of Anguilla, Antigua and Barbuda, the Bahamas, Grenada, the Netherlands Antilles, Saint Kitts and Nevis, Saint Lucia, Saint Vincent and the Grenadines and several other countries and territories of the region,

Deeply concerned at the frequency and unpredictability in the recurrence of these natural disasters, which seriously undermine the capacity of these countries to achieve sustained development,

Also concerned that hurricanes and other natural disasters exacerbate the effect of sea level rise, loss of biodiversity and the destruction of land resources and marine and coastal zones,

Mindful of the vulnerability of the natural environment and infrastructure of these countries to the effects of these disasters and the new challenges which they present to the efforts of the affected countries and territories to preserve their economic viability and insurability,

Conscious of the efforts of the Governments and the peoples of Anguilla, Antigua and Barbuda, the Bahamas, Grenada, the Netherlands Antilles, Saint Kitts and Nevis, Saint Lucia, Saint Vincent and the Grenadines and several other countries and territories of the region to restore infrastructure and rehabilitate productive sectors, particularly agriculture and tourism,

Also conscious of the efforts of the Governments and the peoples of the affected countries and territories of the region to save lives and alleviate the sufferings of the victims of the hurricanes,

Noting the enormous effort that will be required to rebuild the affected areas and to alleviate the grave situation caused by these natural disasters,

Recognizing that the magnitude of the disasters and the medium-term and long-term effects will require, as a complement to the efforts being made by the peoples and the Governments of the affected countries, a demonstration of international solidarity and humanitarian concern to ensure broad multilateral cooperation in order to meet the immediate emergency situation in the affected areas and to initiate the process of reconstruction and rehabilitation,

1. *Notes* the efforts of the Governments of Anguilla, Antigua and Barbuda, the Bahamas, Grenada, the Netherlands Antilles, Saint Kitts and Nevis, Saint Lucia, Saint Vincent and Grenadines and several other countries and territories of the region;

2. *Expresses its appreciation* to all States of the international community, international agencies and non-governmental organizations that are providing emergency relief to the affected countries;

3. *Urges* all States of the international community, as a matter of urgency, to contribute generously to the relief, rehabilitation and reconstruction efforts in the affected countries and to provide financing for the national and regional relief, rehabilitation and reconstruction efforts being undertaken by the affected countries;

4. *Urges* the bodies and agencies of the United Nations system and the international financial institutions to assist Governments in their rehabilitation and redevelopment efforts, taking into account their vulnerability to natural disasters;

5. *Calls upon* the relevant organizations and agencies of the United Nations system and other multilateral organizations to assist in the strengthening of national and regional capacity for disaster preparedness, planning, mitigation and reconstruction, including early warning systems;

6. *Calls upon* the relevant agencies and bodies of the United Nations system as well as regional bodies to assist the States and territories of the Caribbean region in convening, when possible, a workshop for building national and regional capacity in disaster preparedness and disaster management;

7. *Requests* the Secretary-General to report to it at its fifty-fifth session, under the agenda item entitled "Strengthening of the coordination of humanitarian and disaster relief assistance of the United Nations, including special economic assistance", on the collaborative effort referred to in the present resolution, and on the progress made in the relief, rehabilitation and reconstruction efforts of the affected countries;

8. *Also requests* that the Secretary-General include in his report to the General Assembly information on the linkages between implementation of the present resolution and implementation of the Programme of Action for the Sustainable Development of Small Island Developing States and the outcome of the twenty-second special session of the General Assembly on the review and appraisal of the implementation of the Programme of Action.

Hurricane Mitch

In response to Assembly resolution 53/1 C [YUN 1998, p. 877], the Secretary-General, in September, reported on efforts to assist Belize, Costa Rica, El Salvador, Guatemala, Honduras, Nicaragua and Panama, affected by hurricane Mitch, which struck in 1998 [ibid., p. 876], and progress made with regard to relief, rehabilitation and reconstruction [A/54/130/Rev.1-E/1999/72/Rev.1]. He stated that hurricane Mitch had aggravated pre-existing social conditions and showed how little progress had been made in factoring disaster risk considerations into development in Central America. It affected most of the population of Honduras and Nicaragua, large tracts of El Salvador and Guatemala, and to a lesser extent Belize and Costa Rica. Damage in the four most affected countries reached over $5 billion. Honduras demonstrated an unparalleled degree of damage that constituted a threat to its economic viability. Damage was concentrated in the infrastructure sector in Nicaragua and in the agricultural sector in El Salvador and Guatemala. ECLAC assessment missions were mobilized immediately after the hurricane. The UN system took advantage of its field presence and available stocks of medicines, food and materials. The availability of WFP food stocks ensured immediate food delivery. OCHA organized missions to El Salvador, Honduras and Nicaragua, while locally based assessment coordination experts supported the management team in Guatemala. As at September, response to the December 1998 consolidated appeal for relief and rehabilitation, which had requested $153 million [YUN 1998, p. 877], stood at 64 per cent. The UN system supported rehabilitation efforts while focusing on the root causes of the disaster. The Secretary-General stressed the need to ensure that disaster reduction was mainstreamed into rehabilitation and reconstruction activities; to improve accessibility to early warning information; to develop multisectoral legislative and administrative systems; to ensure that information on disaster risks was available to decision makers; and to strengthen regional cooperation and increase investment in human resource development.

In a later report [A/55/125-E/2000/91], the Secretary-General provided information on specific assistance to Nicaragua. He stated that hurricane Mitch had killed more than 3,000 people, affected 800,000, and swept crops away and destroyed infrastructure, with the total destruction amounting to $1.5 billion. The work of the UN system had focused on the basic needs of the population. Several meetings were held with the donor community to coordinate assistance; the UN Resident Coordinator promoted a meeting with NGOs and established a working group of emergency focal points of the UN disaster management team to strengthen coordination mechanisms during the emergency. Under the coordination of an inter-agency working group, the coordinator and the team prepared a transitional appeal for relief and immediate rehabilitation to cover needs during the period December 1998–May 1999. In a consultative group meeting for the reconstruction and transformation of Central America (Stockholm, Sweden, 25-28 May), Nicaragua presented a five-year plan, defining needs of $2.5 billion and focusing on the social sectors, infrastructure, rural development and governance.

Venezuela

Weeks of torrential rains in Venezuela reached a record level on 15 and 16 December, causing landslides and severe flooding in the northern states that washed away thousands of homes and devastated coastal regions. Over 270,000 persons were affected, 200,000 of whom were in Vargas State, 64,500 houses were damaged and 24,500 destroyed. An in-country UNDAC team was deployed at the onset of the disaster to assist the UN Resident Coordinator, UNDMT and the national authorities. From December 1999 to March 2000, OCHA's Regional Disaster Response Advisor would carry out four missions to Caracas to support the Resident Coordinator and UNDMT in coordinating disaster response and facilitating the transition from relief to rehabilitation.

GENERAL ASSEMBLY ACTION

On 22 December [meeting 87], the General Assembly adopted **resolution 54/96 K** [draft: A/54/L.76 & Add.1] without vote [agenda item 20 *(b)*].

Assistance to Venezuela following the devastating floods and landslides

The General Assembly,

Deeply concerned at the loss of human lives and the unprecedented destruction of property and infrastructure caused in recent days by the worst floods and landslides Venezuela has ever suffered,

Recognizing that natural disasters constitute a major problem for development whose solution requires considerable resources and calls for efforts at the national level to be supplemented by international financial and technical assistance,

Recognizing also the large-scale relief and emergency assistance efforts being made by the Government and the people of Venezuela in order to alleviate the suffering of the disaster victims,

Aware that to mitigate and prevent the consequences of this disaster, international emergency assistance is required,

Taking note of the appeal by the Secretary-General to the international community for aid and assistance to Venezuela in dealing with the effects of the floods and landslides,

Taking note also of the appeal to the international community by the Government of Venezuela to provide emergency humanitarian aid, and of the need for assistance in rehabilitation and reconstruction of the areas affected by the disastrous floods and landslides,

1. *Expresses its solidarity,* at this difficult time, with the Government and the people of Venezuela in their efforts to cope with the serious humanitarian and material consequences of the disaster;

2. *Appeals* to all Member States, the specialized agencies and other organizations and bodies of the United Nations system, as well as to international financing institutions and non-governmental organizations, to respond urgently and provide generous assistance to Venezuela in its relief, rehabilitation and reconstruction efforts and programmes following the unprecedented calamity it has suffered;

3. *Expresses its gratitude* to the Member States, international organizations and non-governmental organizations and private individuals and groups that are with such great generosity providing assistance to the Government of Venezuela in the initial immediate relief work;

4. *Expresses its deep gratitude* to the Secretary-General for the urgent steps he has taken to mobilize emergency humanitarian assistance;

5. *Requests* the Secretary-General to make all necessary arrangements to continue mobilizing and coordinating humanitarian assistance from the specialized agencies and other organizations and bodies of the United Nations system with a view to supporting the efforts of the Government of Venezuela.

Chernobyl aftermath

In an October report [A/54/449], submitted in response to General Assembly resolution 52/172 [YUN 1997, p. 931], the Secretary-General described the action undertaken in 1998-1999 by the UN system and other entities to mitigate the effects of the 1986 Chernobyl disaster [YUN 1986, p. 584]. The report provided an overview of the strategy and coordination activities, as well as the role of the UN Coordinator of International Cooperation on Chernobyl. It documented the difficulty of mobilizing resources to a disaster whose effects would span generations. Thirteen years after the catastrophe, Chernobyl remained a major environmental and humanitarian problem. The long-term consequences continued to call for international assistance, particularly regarding health effects, environmental problems, psychological impact on the population, and social and economic rehabilitation of the affected areas. Significant needs remained in the areas of health and environment in Belarus, the Russian Federation and Ukraine, the three most affected countries. During the reporting period, the Coordinator defined a new strategy based on a better-prioritized assistance programme, increased local coordination and a more targeted approach to public information and resource mobilization.

The Coordinator carried out a mission to Belarus, the Russian Federation and Ukraine in October 1998, when three high-priority projects were selected per country, using the criteria of acuteness of the problems, prospects for donor funding and support from the national authorities.

The nine projects, totalling $9.51 million, were the basis for the 1999 UN Appeal for International Cooperation on Chernobyl, which was circulated to the donor missions and embassies in Geneva, New York, Minsk, Moscow and Kiev in May. To coordinate the work of UN field offices, national authorities and donor representatives, the Chernobyl Coordinator promoted the establishment of UN country team core groups, supported by the United Nations Educational, Scientific and Cultural Organization, UNDP and OCHA. The office of the WHO International Thyroid Project in Minsk was also involved. Programmes and projects addressed problems in the key sectors of health, socio-psychological and environmental rehabilitation, economic recovery, nuclear safety and employment. However, limited financial support from the Chernobyl Trust Fund and the voluntary contributions to the Fund, which amounted to $600,000 during 1998-1999, did not allow the most critical needs to be addressed. Consequently, many were underfunded and lacked the resources to cope with the residual consequences of the accident.

In his concluding observations, the Secretary-General stated that the UN programmes aimed at addressing the human consequences of the disaster had been chronically underfunded for many reasons. The Chernobyl accident was difficult to classify since it was neither a traditional emergency nor a developmental issue. Subsequently, budgetary constraints were faced by some donor States as Chernobyl fell into a budgetary gap. Donors questioned whether health, environmental, social and economic hardship were the sole results of Chernobyl. Moreover, the many natural disasters and complex emergencies that had occurred over the past two years made it difficult for Chernobyl to remain perceived as a priority. The Group of Seven expected to complete the Chernobyl site rehabilitation in 2007. Member States, multilateral institutions and private donors were urged to support the highly prioritized projects presented in the 1999 Appeal for International Cooperation by contributing to the Chernobyl Trust Fund.

GENERAL ASSEMBLY ACTION

On 8 December [meeting 73], the General Assembly adopted **resolution 54/97** [draft: A/54/L.22/Rev.1 & Add.1] without vote [agenda item 20 *(c)*].

Strengthening of international cooperation and coordination of efforts to study, mitigate and minimize the consequences of the Chernobyl disaster

The General Assembly,

Reaffirming its resolutions 45/190 of 21 December 1990, 46/150 of 18 December 1991, 47/165 of 18 December 1992, 48/206 of 21 December 1993, 50/134 of 20 December 1995 and 52/172 of 16 December 1997, and taking note of the decisions adopted by the organs, organizations and programmes of the United Nations system in the implementation of those resolutions,

Recalling Economic and Social Council resolutions 1990/50 of 13 July 1990, 1991/51 of 26 July 1991 and 1992/38 of 30 July 1992 and Council decision 1993/232 of 22 July 1993,

Noting with appreciation the contribution made by States and by organizations of the United Nations system to the development of cooperation to mitigate and minimize the consequences of the Chernobyl disaster, and the activities of regional and other organizations, in particular the Commission of the European Communities, as well as bilateral activities and those of non-governmental organizations,

Welcoming the commitments made by Member States in the Programme for the Further Implementation of Agenda 21 to intensify cooperation, inter alia, in the prevention and reduction of major technological and other disasters with an adverse impact on the environment and in disaster relief and post-disaster rehabilitation in order to enhance the capabilities of affected countries to cope with such situations, as well as commitments made in response to the appeal of the Secretary-General on the occasion of the tenth anniversary of the Chernobyl nuclear power plant accident,

Conscious of the long-term nature of the consequences of the disaster at the Chernobyl nuclear power plant, which was a major technological catastrophe in terms of its scope and created humanitarian, environmental, social, economic and health consequences and problems of common concern, requiring for their solution wide and active international cooperation and coordination of efforts in this field at the international and national levels,

Stressing that the Governments of the affected countries have a primary role to play in facilitating efforts to mitigate the humanitarian consequences of the Chernobyl catastrophe, including the efforts of non-governmental organizations in providing humanitarian assistance,

Expressing profound concern about newly emerged signs of the effects on the lives and health of people, in particular children, in the affected areas of Belarus, the Russian Federation and Ukraine, as well as in other countries affected by the Chernobyl disaster,

Taking into consideration the findings and outcome of the visit of the Under-Secretary-General for Humanitarian Affairs to the affected areas in Belarus, the Russian Federation and Ukraine in October 1998,

Taking note of the report of the Secretary-General concerning the implementation of resolution 52/172,

Noting the readiness of Ukraine to close the Chernobyl nuclear power plant by 2000, in accordance with the memorandum of understanding between the Governments of the members of the Group of Seven and the Commission of the European Communities and the Government of Ukraine on the closure of the Chernobyl nuclear power plant, and bearing in mind the support already provided by a number of countries and international organizations for that purpose and the need for further support from relevant countries and international organizations,

1. *Requests* the Secretary-General to continue his efforts in the implementation of the relevant General Assembly resolutions and, through existing coordination mechanisms, in particular the United Nations Coordinator of International Cooperation on Chernobyl, to continue to maintain close cooperation with the agencies of the United Nations system, as well as with regional and other relevant organizations, with a view to encouraging the regular exchange of information, cooperation and coordination of multilateral and bilateral efforts in those areas, while implementing programmes and specific projects, inter alia, in the framework of relevant agreements and arrangements;

2. *Invites* States, in particular donor States, relevant multilateral financial institutions and other concerned parties of the international community, including non-governmental organizations, to continue to provide support to the ongoing efforts made by Belarus, the Russian Federation and Ukraine to mitigate the consequences of the Chernobyl disaster and to pay special attention to the United Nations Appeal for International Cooperation on Chernobyl, launched in April 1999;

3. *Emphasizes* the importance of full cooperation and assistance by the authorities of the affected countries in facilitating the work of humanitarian organizations, including non-governmental organizations, to mitigate the humanitarian consequences of the Chernobyl catastrophe, notes the measures already taken by the Governments of the affected countries in this regard, and encourages them to take further measures to simplify their relevant internal procedures and to identify ways in which to make their systems of granting exemption from customs and other duties more effective with regard to goods provided free of charge as humanitarian assistance by humanitarian organizations, including non-governmental organizations;

4. *Welcomes* the efforts made by the United Nations, in cooperation with the Governments of Belarus, the Russian Federation and Ukraine, to promote the Inter-Agency Programme of International Assistance to Areas Affected by the Chernobyl Disaster;

5. *Welcomes also* the convening by the United Nations of a number of special international meetings on Chernobyl to generate further support to the populations of Belarus, the Russian Federation and Ukraine affected by the Chernobyl nuclear power plant disaster, and urges the international community and the Governments of the affected countries to continue to contribute towards the implementation of the projects specified in the above-mentioned inter-agency programme;

6. *Expresses its appreciation* for the contributions made to the shelter implementation plan aimed at securing the environmental safety of the sarcophagus covering the remains of the destroyed Chernobyl reactor, and urges further contributions to the plan;

7. *Welcomes* the decision of the heads of State and Government of the seven major industrial States and the European Union, adopted at Cologne, Germany, in June 1999, to help to ensure the continued financing and progress in work under the shelter implementation plan and, in this regard, welcomes the convening of the pledging conference in Germany in May 2000;

8. *Takes note with satisfaction* of the activities of the International Chernobyl Centre established in Ukraine, with the active participation of Belarus and the Russian Federation, as an important contribution towards enhancement of the capabilities of the international community to study, mitigate and minimize the consequences of such accidents, and invites all interested parties to take part in the activities of the Centre;

9. *Urges* the United Nations Coordinator of International Cooperation on Chernobyl to continue his efforts aimed at strengthening international cooperation to overcome the health, social, economic and ecological consequences of the Chernobyl disaster in the most affected areas of Belarus, the Russian Federation and Ukraine, based on the Inter-Agency Programme of International Assistance to Areas Affected by the Chernobyl Disaster;

10. *Calls upon* the Secretary-General to continue the regular exchange of information with the countries concerned, relevant organizations and bodies of the United Nations system, with a view to enhancing world public awareness of the consequences of such disasters;

11. *Requests* the Secretary-General to submit to the General Assembly at its fifty-sixth session, under a separate sub-item, a report containing a comprehensive assessment of the implementation of the present resolution and proposals for innovative measures for optimizing the effectiveness of the response of the international community to the Chernobyl disaster.

Chapter IV

International trade, finance and transport

International trade grew very slowly in the first half of 1999, with significant declines in some regions as many economies, especially in Asia and Latin America but also among the economies in transition, continued their adjustment to the 1997 Asian crisis and its aftermath by cutting import demand. However, as the recovery strengthened and more economies began to move towards positive growth, trade began to rebound, rather strongly in the second half of the year.

The *Trade and Development Report, 1999*—produced by the United Nations Conference on Trade and Development (UNCTAD)—focused on the fragile recovery of the world economy and its downside risks, and on trade, external financing and economic growth in developing countries. The Trade and Development Board (TDB), UNCTAD's governing body, considered interdependence and global economic issues from a trade and development perspective, focusing on globalization and the global financial system. It stressed that the benefits of globalization were not shared equally, and that some countries were becoming increasingly marginalized.

With regard to developments in the multilateral trading system, the General Assembly, in December, emphasized the importance of the expansion of international trade and of continued trade liberalization. It recognized that the reduction or removal of tariff and non-tariff barriers should be a priority for multilateral trade negotiations, and stressed the need to ensure that anti-dumping and countervailing measures were subjected to multilateral surveillance and were not used for protectionist purposes. Also in December, the Assembly adopted the United Nations Guidelines for Consumer Protection, as expanded to include elements of sustainable consumption.

In action on financial issues, the Assembly stressed the importance of an enabling international environment through cooperative efforts by all countries and institutions to promote global economic development. Recognizing that equitable and development-oriented solutions to external debt and debt-service burdens of developing countries could strengthen the global economy, it encouraged the international creditor community to consider appropriate measures in the case of countries with a high level of debt overhang, and called for concerted national and international action to address debt problems of middle-income developing countries. With regard to financing for development, the Assembly decided to convene in 2001 a high-level intergovernmental event on the subject, at least at the ministerial level.

The International Trade Centre supported the national capacity of developing countries and transition economies to integrate into the global trading system; during the year, 98 countries benefited directly from its services.

In the area of transport, the International Convention on Arrest of Ships, 1999 was adopted by the United Nations/International Maritime Organization Diplomatic Conference in March.

Preparations for the tenth session of UNCTAD, to be held in February 2000, began with TDB's approval of the draft provisional agenda. The Conference, to be held in Bangkok, Thailand, was to have the unifying theme "Developmental strategies in an increasingly interdependent world: applying the lessons of the past to make globalization an effective instrument for the development of all countries and all people".

International trade

The *Trade and Development Report, 1999* [Sales No. E.99.II.D.1] noted that in 1998 growth in the volume of world trade, which had begun to slow with the onset of the Asian crisis in mid-1997, decelerated abruptly, but trade performance differed widely among regions. While the developed world suffered little, and even derived some benefits from the crisis, virtually all developing countries and transition economies were affected. In the wake of the crisis, growth in the developing world slowed from almost 6 per cent in 1996 to under 2 per cent in 1998. The two largest developing countries, China and India, were the striking exceptions. Notably, both countries had resisted the temptation to pursue premature trade liberalization and rapid integration into the global financial system.

The situation in the developing countries had serious repercussions for international trade. The substantial swing in trade balances in the Asian countries through massive import cuts played an important role in the re-emergence of major trade imbalances in the world economy not experienced since the 1980s. It was also the main factor in the slowdown of world trade, which suffered in value terms its strongest decline since 1982, and in the dramatic and widespread fall in commodity prices.

A fall by one third in world oil prices was responsible for approximately 86 per cent of the overall decline in the value of world trade. Oil exporters as a whole lost more than 6 per cent of their gross national product (GNP) and non-oil developing countries also suffered terms-of-trade declines and income losses. At 12 per cent, the drop in non-oil commodity prices was unprecedented since the mid-1970s.

By contrast, industrial countries gained from the collapse in commodity prices and cheaper manufactured imports from countries that suffered currency devaluations.

The *World Economic and Social Survey 1999* [Sales No. E.99.II.C.1], produced by the UN Department of Economic and Social Affairs (DESA), observed that world trade grew by about 3.5 per cent in 1998, the smallest increase of the decade. The value of world trade in dollars fell, and the fact that commodity prices, particularly of oil, plunged during the year negatively affected the export earnings, and therefore the import demand, of many economies. Africa's exports declined by 15 per cent in nominal terms, while in Western Asia the value of merchandise exports shrank by about 25 per cent. The slowdown in the growth of world output, especially the contraction in South-East and East Asia, reduced the demand for imports to such an extent that the growth of world merchandise trade (in terms of export volume) was only 3.6 per cent. The setback was most pronounced for the developing countries, whose volume of trade decreased in 1998. Measured in dollars, the value of world exports of goods declined by 2.3 per cent and exports of services dropped by 2 per cent. The international crisis also changed the pattern of international trade flows, with imports of developing countries dropping by 10 per cent in value terms and 5 per cent in volume terms in 1998. In South-East and East Asia, total imports fell by more than 20 per cent in value and 13 per cent in volume; many economies in West Asia also registered a decline in imports as the drop in the oil price reduced their export revenues and capacity to import. Conversely, imports by the Latin America and the Caribbean region increased, although by substantially less than during the previous few years. Imports into Mexico and the Central American economies continued to grow strongly. Imports into Africa also grew, but at a slower rate. Except for Japan, which had a fall in import volume of 10 per cent, most developed economies maintained a strong import growth. Imports into North America grew by 10 per cent in volume and into Western Europe by 6 per cent. Economies in transition as a group maintained their 1997 import levels, but the situation varied within the group; the imports of Central and Eastern European economies grew by 10 per cent in volume, but the volume of imports into the Russian Federation and other Commonwealth of Independent States (CIS) economies declined 15 per cent.

Export performance also differed across countries. In Latin America and the Caribbean, export volume grew by almost 8 per cent. However, the export growth of the Asian developing economies was almost zero. The collapse of regional markets and the recession in Japan resulted in a deceleration in the growth of Chinese exports to about 4 per cent in 1998, from 26 per cent in the previous year. A marked feature for developing economies was the decline in export revenues, largely because of the drop in commodity prices. The value of merchandise exports measured in dollars declined by 7 per cent. The worst-hit region was Western Asia, where it dropped by almost a quarter during the year. Africa also experienced a significant decline in export earnings.

Most developed economies registered moderate export growth. Western European exports grew by over 5 per cent, and although North American exports decelerated, they were expected to register a positive growth. Japan's export volume, however, shrank by 4 per cent. The export performance of economies in transition differed across two sub-groups. Central and Eastern European economies grew in both volume and value, while the value of exports of the CIS economies fell by about one sixth, even though their volume was almost unchanged.

In a joint report on the world economic situation and prospects issued at the end of 1999 by DESA and UNCTAD, it was observed that, although world trade had slackened in 1999, it embodied the beginnings of a recovery that was expected to become more visible in 2000. Over the course of 1999, prices of many commodities, especially oil and related energy products, either stabilized or started to recover. As the recovery process strengthened and more economies began to move towards positive growth, international trade began to rebound, rather strongly in the second half of 1999.

Report of Secretary-General. In response to General Assembly resolution 53/170 [YUN 1998, p. 882], the Secretary-General submitted a September report [A/54/304], prepared in collaboration with UNCTAD, on international trade and development. It discussed the implementation of the ministerial communiqué on market access adopted by the Economic and Social Council in 1998 [YUN 1998, p. 881], developments in the multilateral trading system and elements of a positive trade agenda. Other issues discussed in the report that arose from resolution 53/170 included: coherence, complementarity and coordination of global economic policy-making; investment agreements; landlocked countries; small island developing States; and UNCTAD's contribution to the implementation of the United Nations New Agenda for the Development of Africa in the 1990s (see p. 847).

The report stated that peak tariffs barriers continued to have a substantial constraining effect on market access for both agricultural and industrial products from developing countries. In agriculture, tariffication of non-tariff barriers, under the agreement reached at the Uruguay Round of multilateral trade negotiations, resulted in extremely high rates; developing countries' trade remained hampered by the massive domestic support and export subsidy programmes in developed countries, peak tariffs and difficulties in the implementation of the tariff quota system. In textiles and clothing, United States, European Union (EU) and Canadian industries continued to enjoy double protection from high tariffs and stringent quantitative restrictions on imports from developing countries. In other industrial sectors, relatively high most-favoured-nation peak tariffs were applied to major exporters of certain technologically advanced products and the major developing country exporters of those products were frequently excluded from Generalized System of Preferences schemes. Tariff escalation decreased, but nevertheless continued, after the Uruguay Round, affecting trade in sectors of export interest to developing countries, such as metals, textiles and clothing, leather, rubber and wood products and furniture.

With the entry into force in 1995 of the World Trade Organization (WTO) Agreement [YUN 1995, p. 1515], some non-tariff measures lost their importance, prompting domestic industries to seek other measures to protect domestic production, notably contingent protection measures, in particular anti-dumping duties. The majority of anti-dumping cases were directed against exporters from developing countries. Developing country exporters were also increasingly affected by scientific non-tariff measures (sanitary and phytosanitary measures). Countries required that domestically produced and imported goods conformed to regulations on quality, health and safety, and possibly adhered to standards. The number of technical regulations and standards was constantly increasing, with the risk that they might become new tools for disguised non-tariff protection. Despite considerable improvements achieved under the General Agreement on Trade in Services (GATS), one of the limitations to market access in services trade was the economic needs test, the discretionary nature of which left considerable uncertainty as to the level of market access commitment. Another area in which developing countries faced market access barriers in countries members of the Organisation for Economic Cooperation and Development (OECD) was related to the movement of business visitors, whereby delays or unreasonable criteria associated with the issuance of visas where no work permits or economic needs tests were required presented a barrier to the movement of business persons.

The Secretary-General stated that the removal of high tariff protection in industrial countries should be given priority and seen as an integral part of future liberalization measures and that duty-free access should be extended to all imports from the least developed countries (LDCs). In the area of trade in services, it was important to ensure that the GATS architecture remained intact; in most service sectors, the benefits from liberalization could only be derived by developing countries if accompanied by supportive capacity-building measures. Ways should be found to enable developing countries to participate more effectively in the formulation of international standards and gain access to mutual recognition agreements, as well as to meet sanitary and phytosanitary regulations.

With regard to developments in the multilateral trading system, the report stated that, despite the financial crisis, there were no major trade policy reversals in 1998 and the first part of 1999; protectionist tendencies gained strength, however, particularly in some major developed countries. The preparatory process pursued by WTO since September 1998 was aimed at defining the future work programme of the organization, which included further trade liberalization objectives and the preparation of recommendations to the third WTO Ministerial Conference (Seattle, United States, 30 November–3 December 1999) (see p. 1422).

GENERAL ASSEMBLY ACTION

On 22 December [meeting 87], the General Assembly, on the recommendation of the Second (Economic and Financial) Committee [A/54/585/Add.3 & Corr.1], adopted **resolution 54/198** without vote [agenda item 97 (c)].

International trade and development

The General Assembly,

Reaffirming its resolutions 50/95 and 50/98 of 20 December 1995, 51/167 of 16 December 1996, 52/182 of 18 December 1997 and 53/170 of 15 December 1998, as well as relevant international agreements concerning trade, economic growth, development and interrelated issues,

Reaffirming also the outcome of the ninth session of the United Nations Conference on Trade and Development, held at Midrand, South Africa, which provides an important framework for promoting a partnership for growth and development,

Emphasizing that a favourable and conducive international economic and financial environment and a positive investment climate are necessary for the economic growth of the world economy, including the creation of employment, in particular for the growth and development of developing countries, and emphasizing also that each country is responsible for its own economic policies for sustainable development,

Noting the need for multilateral trade liberalization, and noting also that a large number of developing countries have assumed the rights and obligations of the World Trade Organization without being able to reap the full benefits of, and participate fully in, the multilateral trading system, and that there is a need for progress towards liberalization and enhanced market access, including in areas and products of particular interest to developing countries,

Noting also the importance of assisting developing countries in building their capacity to engage effectively in international trade,

Stressing that full and faithful implementation of the commitments and obligations in multilateral trade agreements is important to the equitable and sustainable development and stability of the world economy,

Strongly emphasizing the importance of providing all members of the World Trade Organization with the opportunity to engage fully and effectively in the process of multilateral trade negotiations and in other activities within the multilateral trading system, in order to facilitate the attainment of balanced results with respect to the interests of all members,

Taking note of the report of the Trade and Development Board on its forty-sixth session, and the report of the Secretary-General of the United Nations Conference on Trade and Development on specific actions related to the particular needs and problems of land-locked developing countries,

Noting, in the context of international trade and development, the ongoing work of the Commonwealth Secretariat/World Bank Joint Task Force on Small States,

Taking note of the report of the Secretary-General,

1. *Recognizes* the importance of the expansion of international trade as an engine of growth and development and, in this context, the need for expeditious and complete integration of developing countries and countries with economies in transition into the international trading system, in full cognizance of the opportunities and challenges of globalization and liberalization and taking into account the circumstances of individual countries, in particular the trade interests and development needs of developing countries;

2. *Renews its commitment* to uphold and strengthen an open, rule-based, equitable, secure, non-discriminatory, transparent and predictable multilateral trade system, which contributes to the economic and social advancement of all countries and peoples by promoting the liberalization and expansion of trade, employment and stability and by providing a framework for the conduct of international trade relations;

3. *Expresses concern* at the declining terms of trade in primary commodities, in particular for net exporters of such commodities, as well as the lack of progress in many developing countries in diversification, and in this regard strongly emphasizes the need for actions at both the national and international levels, inter alia, through improved market access conditions and support for capacity-building;

4. *Recognizes* that the substantial improvement of market access for exports of goods and services from developing countries through, inter alia, the reduction or removal of tariff and non-tariff barriers should be a high priority for multilateral trade negotiations, and in this regard notes the needs and concerns of some countries with economies in transition;

5. *Deplores* any attempt to bypass or undermine multilaterally agreed procedures on the conduct of international trade by unilateral actions inconsistent with the multilateral trade rules and regulations, including those agreed upon in the Uruguay Round of multilateral trade negotiations;

6. *Expresses concern* about the proliferation of anti-dumping and countervailing measures, and stresses that they should not be used as protectionist measures;

7. *Reaffirms* the role of the United Nations Conference on Trade and Development as the focal point within the United Nations for the integrated treatment of development and related issues in the areas of trade, finance, technology, investment and sustainable development;

8. *Welcomes* the progress made so far in the preparations for the tenth session of the United Nations Conference on Trade and Development, to be held at Bangkok from 12 to 19 February 2000, by the Trade and Development Board and the host Government, considers that the tenth session of the Conference will provide, inter alia, an important opportunity for the United Nations system and the international community to engage in a collective reflection on development so as to reach a consensus on development strategies in an increasingly interdependent world by applying lessons of the past to making globalization an effective instrument for the development of all countries and all people, through which the international community should undertake a rigorous and balanced review of the policy and institutional framework for global trade and finance, and that, in this context, the Conference will provide member States with an opportunity to take stock of and review the major international economic initiatives and developments, in particular those that have taken place since the ninth session of the Conference, and urges the Conference to consider the strate-

gies and policies that are most likely to ensure the successful integration of all countries concerned, particularly the developing countries, into the world economy on an equitable basis and to avoid the risk of further marginalization;

9. *Reiterates* the importance of continued trade liberalization in developed and developing countries, including in sectors of export interest to developing countries, through, inter alia:

(*a*) Substantial reductions of tariffs, the rolling back of tariff peaks and the removal of tariff escalation;

(*b*) The elimination of trade-distorting policies, protectionist practices and non-tariff barriers in international trade relations;

(*c*) Ensuring that resort to anti-dumping duties, countervailing duties, phytosanitary regulations and technical standards is subjected to effective multilateral surveillance so that such measures respect and are consistent with multilateral rules and obligations and are not used for protectionist purposes;

(*d*) The improvement and renewal, by preference-giving countries, of their Generalized System of Preferences schemes with the objective of integrating developing countries, especially the least developed countries, into the international trading system and of finding ways and means to ensure more effective utilization of the Generalized System of Preferences schemes, and in this context reiterates its original principles, namely, non-discrimination, universality, burden-sharing and non-reciprocity;

10. *Also reiterates* that it is an ethical imperative for the international community to arrest and reverse the marginalization of the least developed countries and to promote their expeditious integration into the world economy and that all countries should work together towards further enhanced market access for exports from the least developed countries within the context of supporting their own efforts at capacity-building; welcomes the initiatives taken by the World Trade Organization in cooperation with other organizations in the implementation of the Plan of Action for the Least Developed Countries adopted at its first Ministerial Conference, held at Singapore from 9 to 13 December 1996, including through effective follow-up to the High-level Meeting on Integrated Initiatives for Least Developed Countries' Trade Development, held at Geneva on 27 and 28 October 1997, taking note of the proposals adopted by the Least Developed Countries' Coordinating Workshop held at Sun City, South Africa, from 21 to 25 June 1999; recognizes that the full implementation of the Plan of Action requires further and expeditious progress towards duty-free imports from the least developed countries; invites the relevant international organizations to provide the enhanced technical assistance required to help to strengthen the supply capacity of the least developed countries so as to help them to take the fullest possible advantage of trading opportunities arising from globalization and liberalization; and welcomes the holding of the Third United Nations Conference on the Least Developed Countries at Brussels in 2001;

11. *Stresses* the urgent need to facilitate the integration of the countries of Africa into the world economy, and in this context welcomes the action-oriented agenda for the development of Africa contained in the report of the Secretary-General on the causes of conflict and the promotion of durable peace and sustainable development in Africa, and endorses the call, contained in the ministerial communiqué adopted by the Economic and Social Council on 8 July 1998, for continued efforts to enhance market access for products of export interest to African economies and support for their efforts at diversification and building of supply capacity, and in this context requests the United Nations Conference on Trade and Development to continue to enhance its contribution to the United Nations New Agenda for the Development of Africa in the 1990s, taking into account the agreed conclusions of the Trade and Development Board on Africa;

12. *Requests* the Secretary-General to ensure the initiation by the United Nations Conference on Trade and Development, in the areas falling within its mandate, of the preparatory process for the final review and appraisal of the implementation of the New Agenda to be held in 2002, in particular focusing on market access, diversification and supply capacity, resource flows and external debt, foreign direct and portfolio investment and access to technology, and in this context also requests the Secretary-General to submit a report, based on the recommendations of the Trade and Development Board on Africa, on measures taken in this regard, with a special emphasis on African trade issues, for the consideration of the General Assembly at its fifty-sixth session under the agenda item entitled "International trade and development";

13. *Stresses* the need to give special attention, within the context of international cooperation on trade and development issues, to the implementation of the many international development commitments geared to meeting the special development needs and problems of small island developing States and of landlocked developing countries and to recognize that those developing countries that provide transit services need adequate support in maintaining and improving their transit infrastructure;

14. *Endorses* the relevant provisions adopted at the twenty-second special session of the General Assembly for the review and appraisal of the implementation of the Programme of Action for the Sustainable Development of Small Island Developing States, and in this context reiterates the need for the United Nations Conference on Trade and Development to enhance its contribution to the implementation of the Programme of Action;

15. *Reiterates* the importance of the effective application by all members of the World Trade Organization of all provisions of the Final Act Embodying the Results of the Uruguay Round of Multilateral Trade Negotiations, taking into account the specific interests of developing countries so as to maximize economic growth and development benefits for all, and the need for the effective implementation of the special provisions in the multilateral trade agreements and related ministerial decisions in favour of developing countries, particularly making operational the previously agreed special and differential provisions, including the strengthening of these concepts, taking into account the changing realities of world trade and of globalization, and urges Governments and concerned international organizations to apply effectively the Ministerial Decisions on Measures in Favour of Least Developed Countries and on Measures Concerning the Possible

Negative Effects of the Reform Programme on Least Developed and Net Food-importing Developing Countries;

16. *Recognizes* that it is important that the momentum towards increased trade liberalization, particularly as regards areas and products of interest to developing countries, be maintained and that further liberalization be sufficiently broad-based to respond to the range of interests and concerns of all members, within the framework of the World Trade Organization, and in this regard welcomes the activities of the United Nations Conference on Trade and Development aimed at assisting developing countries in developing a positive agenda for future multilateral trade negotiations, and invites the Conference to continue to provide analytical support and technical assistance, including capacity-building activities, to those countries for their effective participation in the negotiations;

17. *Invites* members of the international community to consider the interests of non-members of the World Trade Organization in the context of trade liberalization;

18. *Invites* the international financial institutions to ensure that, in their development cooperation activities with developing countries, the obligations of the latter with regard to their development policies, strategies and programmes in trade and trade-related areas are consistent with their commitments under the framework of rules agreed upon within the multilateral trading system;

19. *Emphasizes* the importance of the strengthening of, and the attainment of greater universality by, the international trading system and of accelerating the process directed towards accession to the World Trade Organization of developing countries and countries with economies in transition, and also emphasizes the necessity for Governments that are members of the World Trade Organization and relevant international organizations to assist non-members of the World Trade Organization so as to facilitate their efforts with respect to accession in an expeditious and transparent manner, on the basis of undertaking balanced World Trade Organization rights and obligations, and for the United Nations Conference on Trade and Development and the World Trade Organization to provide the technical assistance, within their mandates, that will contribute to the rapid and full integration of those countries into the multilateral trading system;

20. *Stresses* the need for improved measures to address the volatility of short-term capital flows as well as the effects of financial crisis on the international trading system and the development prospects of developing countries and the countries affected by such crisis, emphasizing that keeping all markets open and maintaining continued growth in world trade are key elements in overcoming such a crisis, and in this context rejects the use of any protectionist measures; at a broader level, there is a need for greater coherence between the development objectives agreed to by the international community and the functioning of the international trading and financial system, and in this context calls for close cooperation between the organizations of the United Nations system and the multilateral trade and financial institutions, with the participation of their secretariats and the States Members of the United Nations and observer States;

21. *Requests* the Secretary-General, in scheduling and organizing mandated events on trade and trade-related issues, to promote complementarity in the work of the relevant bodies of the United Nations system and with other international organizations, with the participation of their secretariats and the States Members of the United Nations and observer States, as appropriate, bearing in mind the mandate of the United Nations Conference on Trade and Development;

22. *Recognizes* the importance of open regional economic integration in the creation of new opportunities for expanding trade and investment, stresses the importance of those initiatives being in conformity with World Trade Organization rules, where applicable, and, bearing in mind the primacy of the multilateral trading system, affirms that regional trade agreements should be outward-oriented and supportive of the multilateral trading system, and in this context invites Governments and intergovernmental and multilateral institutions to continue to provide support to economic integration among developing countries as well as among countries with economies in transition;

23. *Requests* the United Nations Conference on Trade and Development to continue to identify and analyse the implications for development of issues relevant to investment, as well as to identify ways and means to promote foreign direct and portfolio investment directed to all developing countries, taking into account their interests, in particular to those most in need, as well as to those countries with economies in transition with similar needs, and bearing in mind the work undertaken by other organizations, including the regional commissions;

24. *Emphasizes* that the dispute settlement mechanism of the World Trade Organization is a key element with regard to the integrity and credibility of the multilateral trading system and the full realization of the benefits anticipated from the conclusion of the Uruguay Round of multilateral trade negotiations;

25. *Strongly emphasizes* the need for technical assistance, including legal assistance, to developing countries, through, inter alia, the newly established Advisory Centre on World Trade Organization Law and other mechanisms, to enable those countries to take the fullest possible advantage of the dispute settlement mechanism of the World Trade Organization, based on multilaterally agreed rules and regulations, and also in this context emphasizes that it is important for the United Nations Conference on Trade and Development to strengthen its technical assistance to developing countries, in particular the least developed countries, landlocked developing countries and small island developing States in this area;

26. *Notes* the increasing importance and application of electronic commerce in international trade and the need to strengthen the capacities of developing countries to participate effectively in electronic commerce, and urges the organizations of the United Nations system, within their mandates and in cooperation with other relevant bodies, with the participation of their secretariats and the States Members of the United Nations and observer States, the United Nations Conference on Trade and Development, the International Telecommunication Union, the International Trade Centre and the regional commissions, to continue to assist developing countries and countries with econo-

mies in transition, and, in this regard, emphasizes the need for analysis of the fiscal, legal and regulatory aspects of electronic commerce as well as its implications for the trade and development prospects of developing countries;

27. *Stresses* the importance of assisting developing countries and interested countries with economies in transition in improving the efficiency of trade-supporting services, inter alia, through the elimination of procedural barriers and by greater use of trade facilitating mechanisms, particularly in the areas of transport, customs, banking and insurance, and business information, especially in the case of small and medium-sized enterprises, and in this respect invites the United Nations Conference on Trade and Development, within its mandate, in collaboration with other relevant bodies of the United Nations, including the regional commissions, to continue to assist these countries in these areas;

28. *Requests* the Secretary-General of the United Nations Conference on Trade and Development to provide, in collaboration with other relevant bodies, substantive input on the role of information and communications technology in trade, finance, investment and related areas to the Economic and Social Council at the high-level segment of its substantive session of 2000;

29. *Requests* the Secretary-General of the United Nations, in collaboration with the secretariat of the United Nations Conference on Trade and Development, to report to the General Assembly at its fifty-fifth session on the implementation of the present resolution and the developments in the multilateral trading system.

Trade policy

Trade in goods and services, and commodities

The Commission on Trade in Goods and Services, and Commodities held its fourth session in Geneva from 11 to 14 October [TD/B/46/14].

Commodities. The Commission had before it an UNCTAD secretariat report [TD/B/COM.1/27 & Add.1] on the world commodity economy: recent evolution, financial crises and changing market structures. The report provided an overview of the evolution of world commodity trade since the 1970s, emphasizing the loss of market shares by developing countries, in particular African countries and LDCs; presented information on the declining trends and current collapse of commodity prices, making reference to increasing productivity in both agriculture and metals and minerals; analysed the implications of recent crises on the supply of and demand for commodities, focusing particularly on the impact of devaluations and the links between financial and commodity markets; and reviewed the changes in distribution and market structures, emphasizing the twin trends of concentration in global markets and liberalization in producing countries, and examined the impact of those trends on commodity-exporting countries.

The report offered some policy proposals, including the elimination of agricultural support and protectionism in developed countries; measures to make international markets more competitive; filling the void in developing countries created by the withdrawal of the State from the commodity sector; improved skills in the enterprise sector of those countries; and renewed producer-consumer dialogue involving all stakeholders.

In agreed conclusions, the Commission noted that many developing countries continued to be dependent on commodities for their export earnings. Also, their share in the major segment of world commodity exports—agricultural commodities—had declined as a result of agricultural production, processing and export support policies in developed countries. Moreover, the recent financial crises had illustrated the vulnerability of commodity-dependent economies to external shocks and the need for their competitive position to be improved towards diversification and broader-based economic development. The Commission adopted a series of recommendations addressed to Governments, the international community and UNCTAD.

Services. For its analysis of certain services sectors, including successful experiences in those sectors, particularly those that enhanced the export capacity of developing countries (such as professional and business services and access to transport services), including the development implications of electronic commerce, the Commission had before it an UNCTAD secretariat report on the subject [TD/B/COM.1/28]. The report examined successful experiences in service strategies, both in strengthening the domestic services sector and in increasing exports of services; identified barriers faced by developing countries in expanding their participation in the world market for services; and described how the growth of electronic commerce had provided new challenges and opportunities for developing countries. The report stated that for developing countries, exports of services could be crucial in diversifying away from dependence on one or two primary commodities. Attracting investment to the service sectors and acquiring technologies so as to strengthen the positions of services producers in developing countries were key to success. Strategies had to address fiscal and other institutional disincentives to services exports.

The Commission adopted agreed conclusions addressed to Governments, the international community and UNCTAD.

Subsidiary bodies. The Commission had before it the reports of the following expert meetings: the Expert Meeting on Examining Trade in the Agricultural Sector, with a view to Expanding the Agricultural Exports of Developing Countries, and to Assisting Them in Better Understanding the Issues at Stake in the Upcoming Agricultural Negotiations (Geneva, 26-28 April) [TD/B/COM.1/23]; the Expert Meeting on Air Transport Services: clarifying issues to identify the elements of the positive agenda of developing countries regarding both GATS and specific sector negotiations of interest to them (Geneva, 21-23 June) [TD/B/COM.1/25]; the Expert Meeting on the Impact of Changing Supply-and-Demand Market Structures in Commodity Prices and Exports of Major Interest to Developing Countries (Geneva, 7-9 July) [TD/B/COM.1/26] (for its consideration of the item, the Expert Meeting had before it an UNCTAD secretariat report on the same subject [TD/B/COM.1/EM.10/2]); and the Ad Hoc Expert Meeting on Applications of Structured Commodity Finance Techniques for Commodity-Dependent Countries (Rio de Janeiro, Brazil, 19-21 May) [UNCTAD/ITCD/COM/Misc.39]. The Commission endorsed the agreed conclusions and recommendations of the expert meetings, and recommended that UNCTAD's Trade and Development Board (TDB) also endorse them.

Implementation of recommendations. The Commission had before it an UNCTAD secretariat progress report on the implementation of agreed conclusions and recommendations adopted at its third (1998) session [YUN 1998, p. 884] [TD/B/COM.1/29]. The Commission recognized that the issues in the areas of international trade in goods and services, as identified in the final document adopted at UNCTAD IX [YUN 1996, p. 845], had been addressed at its four sessions and relevant expert meetings, and that the issues of competition law and policy had been addressed within the Commission on Investment, Technology and Related Financial Issues and the Intergovernmental Group of Experts on Competition Law and Policy. It also recognized that it had made a positive contribution to the integration of developing countries into the international trading system and expressed its satisfaction with the work undertaken by its expert meetings. It emphasized the need, however, for a more meaningful interface between the Commission and its expert meetings and for strengthening the work in the areas of international trade in goods and services, and commodities.

At its twenty-second executive session in October [A/54/15/Rev.1], TDB endorsed the Commission's agreed conclusions.

Interdependence and global economic issues

TDB, at its forty-sixth session (Geneva, 18-29 October) [A/54/15/Rev.1], considered interdependence and global economic issues from a trade and development perspective. Discussions focused on globalization, more specifically the multilateral trading system and, to a lesser extent, the global financial system. There was broad agreement that an equitable sharing of costs and benefits of globalization was essential for sustaining the momentum of global integration. However, it was stressed that the benefits of globalization were not shared equally and that some countries ran the risk of becoming increasingly marginalized (for information on globalization and human rights, see p. 655). The Board expressed concern over the widening income gaps between rich and poor nations and argued that integration into the world economy could not be left to markets alone: neither the State nor the market on its own was capable of creating and distributing wealth efficiently and equitably. For most developing countries, the problem was not globalization per se, but its regulation and management.

There was wide agreement that trade liberalization could bring substantial benefits to all countries; that trade should be used for development; and that market access was essential for that purpose. There was also consensus on the benefits of a rules-based multilateral trading system, particularly for developing countries. However, there was some disagreement over the future direction of the multilateral trading system.

Speakers from developing countries stressed that the trading system lacked a development component and observed that little progress had been made since the Uruguay Round in areas of export interest to developing countries. New non-tariff measures had been introduced, anti-dumping provisions had been abused, the special agreements had not been applied, and built-in biases had impeded exports and transfer of technology. Speakers from developed countries stressed the benefits to developing as well as developed countries from the Uruguay Round, and underlined the importance of appropriate policies and good governance in developing countries.

Trade promotion and facilitation

In 1999, United Nations bodies continued to assist developing countries to promote their exports and to facilitate the movement of their goods in international commerce. The International Trade Centre was the main originator of technical cooperation projects in that area.

The TDB Commission on Enterprise, Business Facilitation and Development held its fourth session in July.

International Trade Centre

During 1999, the International Trade Centre (ITC), under the joint sponsorship of WTO and UNCTAD, focused on capacity-building for trade development in partner countries [ITC/AG (XXXIII)/180 & Add.1,2]. It made headway in applying new technical assistance tools, in focusing and improving its technical cooperation activities, and in contributing to multi-agency trade development efforts. ITC's principal programme targets were: facilitating understanding of and response to the rules of the multilateral trading system; better export strategy formulation; raising the competitiveness of export enterprises and the effectiveness of their support institutions; and identifying and exploiting new export opportunities. It applied its product-potential analytical processes and its product and market expertise to contribute to export strategy formulation in various countries. For example, initial decisions on sectoral priorities in several African countries were taken as a result of high-level, public-private sector consultation and debate under the Joint ITC/UNCTAD/WTO Integrated Technical Assistance Programme in Selected Least Developed and Other African Countries (JITAP). To help businesses address the implications of WTO agreements, the Centre concentrated on developing national networks of trainers and advisers, forming a critical mass of expertise from business, academia and the public sector on multilateral trading systems rules and issues. The key to ITC's capacity-building, "product network" strategy was the country-level adaptation of generic technical assistance tools to minimize costs, cut the application lead time, and maximize reach, feedback and sustainability.

Under ITC's transaction-oriented activities, the South-South trade programme intensified within the Arab and African regions; substantial volumes of new business were reported to have resulted from several buyers-sellers meetings. The programme was extended to the regions covered by the Economic Cooperation Organization and the Inter-State Council where trade flow analyses were initiated, and to Asia where preparations were made for a buyers-sellers meeting on pharmaceuticals, to be held in 2000 on the occasion of UNCTAD X.

New programme initiatives were undertaken in all geographic areas. ITC implemented 47 national projects in 1999, in addition to 17 regional and 24 interregional projects. Altogether, 98 countries were active partners and benefited directly and substantially from ITC services. Within the Centre's evolving export-led poverty reduction strategy, export production village activities continued in India; feasibility studies of export schemes for microproducer groups were undertaken elsewhere in Asia, and in Africa and Latin America and the Caribbean; and a new programme was launched in Ghana. Implementation of projects in economies in transition also continued and a number of new projects were proposed. New activities were initiated or proposed in all other regions, for example, in Bolivia, Romania, Saudi Arabia, South Africa and Viet Nam. The ITC programme to expand trade among developing countries intensified with activities within the Arab and African regions. ITC placed special emphasis on technical cooperation activities addressing the needs of LDCs and to the pressing need to help them to integrate into the global trading system. Those countries accounted for 36 per cent of project delivery from extrabudgetary resources in 1999.

ITC's first Executive Forum on National Export Strategies (Annecy, France, 26-29 September) highlighted the theme "Redefining trade promotion—the need for a strategic response". It was attended by senior trade officials from 16 developing and transition economies and experts from the World Bank, UNCTAD, WTO, the Commonwealth Secretariat and OECD.

ITC technical meeting. The ITC technical meeting (Geneva, 3 November) [ITC/AG(XXXIII)/179] considered the report of the evaluation of the ITC programme: trade information [ITC/AG (XXXIII)/177], and discussed the ITC strategy proposed in the report on ITC strategy for trade information services [ITC/AG(XXXIII)/178]. Overall, the technical meeting expressed its support for the new trade information strategy.

JAG action. The ITC Joint Advisory Group (JAG) held its thirty-second session in Geneva from 19 to 23 April [ITC/AG(XXXII)/173]. JAG had before it the report on ITC activities in 1998 [YUN 1998, p. 886] and the report of the ITC Global Trust Fund's Consultative Committee [ITC/AG(XXXII)/174].

The Group expressed appreciation for the completion of ITC's institutional reform, as a result of which the Centre was now better equipped to contribute to the development of the national export and import capacities of developing and transition economies. The Group reaffirmed the relevance of ITC's contribution to poverty reduction and gender equality, and stressed that high priority should continue to be given to LDCs. It encouraged ITC to continue to use and promote the new information technologies as a way of accessing trade-related information. JITAP and the

Integrated Framework for LDCs were cited as good examples of improved coherence among participating institutions and of opportunities for optimal use of human and financial resources; and the importance of ensuring an adequate balance between interregional, regional and national programmes and projects was stressed. The Group expressed satisfaction with the Global Trust Fund, which had proved to be a useful funding mechanism enabling ITC to prepare generic technical assistance tools.

Pledges of trust fund contributions to ITC were announced by Canada, China, Denmark, Finland, France, Germany, India, the Netherlands, Norway, Sweden, Switzerland and the United Kingdom. Earlier pledges had been made by Belgium, Côte d'Ivoire, Greece, Ireland and Italy.

TDB, at its twenty-first executive session in July [A/54/15/Rev.1], took note of the JAG report and of the statements made.

ITC administrative arrangements

In accordance with the arrangements approved by the General Assembly in decision 53/411 B [YUN 1998, p. 888], the Secretary-General, in June, submitted an outline of the proposed programme budget for ITC for the 2000-2001 biennium [A/54/127]. The outline contained the ITC budget for the first year of activities for the biennium and a projection of requirements for the second year. The ITC requirements, expressed in Swiss francs at 2000-2001 rates, were estimated at SwF 29,516,000 for 2000 and SwF 29,688,600 for 2001. It was projected that an amount of SwF 405,000, representing income from various sources, would be available to ITC annually. On that basis, the annual contribution of each organization (the United Nations and WTO) was estimated at SwF 14,555,500 and SwF 14,641,800 for 2000 and 2001, respectively.

Having considered the Secretary-General's report, the Advisory Committee on Administrative and Budgetary Questions (ACABQ), in June [A/53/7/Add.15], recommended that the Assembly approve the amount of SwF 59,204,600 for the 2000-2001 biennium.

By **decision 53/485** of 28 July, the Assembly took note of the Secretary-General's report on the outline of the proposed programme budget for the 2000-2001 biennium for ITC and of the report of ACABQ.

ACABQ, having considered the proposed programme budget for 2000-2001 for ITC [A/54/6/Rev.1/Add.1], submitted to the Assembly a December report [A/54/7/Add.6], in which it noted that the proposed programme budget amounted to $19,980,000 (SwF 29,170,800), representing an increase of 1.3 per cent over the 1998-1999 appropriation.

Enterprise, business facilitation and development

The Commission on Enterprise, Business Facilitation and Development held its fourth session in Geneva from 19 to 23 July [TD/B/46/11].

Small and medium-sized enterprises. The Commission had before it an UNCTAD secretariat assessment of policies and non-fiscal measures for upgrading small and medium-sized enterprise (SME) clusters [TD/B/COM.3/22]. The report stressed the importance for policy makers to focus on technological capability-building as an essential element for the sustained competitiveness and productivity of SMEs in an increasingly technology-intensive global economy. It noted that foreign direct investment could accelerate the process of technological upgrading, but not substitute for local technological capabilities. The increasing knowledge-intensity of production in a globalizing world economy required structural change that should be addressed by long-term policy measures. The report stated that, since the bulk of the world's technology was in the hands of transnational corporations (TNCs), creating TNC-SME linkages was a key element of innovation policy, as was building and strengthening networks between SMEs and local research institutions, including North-South networks between researchers in order to facilitate knowledge creation in the South.

The Commission recognized that SME clusters and networks were among the most effective ways of delivering technical assistance to SMEs in order to upgrade technology, increase participation in domestic and international trade, and strengthen entrepreneurship and management and marketing skills. It adopted a series of agreed conclusions addressed to Governments, the international community and UNCTAD.

Electronic commerce. For its consideration of electronic commerce and the integration of developing countries and countries with economies in transition in international trade, the Commission had before it an UNCTAD secretariat note on the subject [TD/B/COM.3/23], which observed that the Internet had evolved into a commercial mass medium of over 100 million users worldwide. However, it stressed that most rural areas in developing countries were still unconnected, and even in countries listed as "electronic-commerce enabled", the cost of access to the Internet remained beyond the means of most SMEs. The report proposed two areas of priority for future work: the production of data, analyses and scenarios relevant to electronic commerce and development; and the examination of emerging trends in the global information economy and their possible impact on developing countries' participation in electronic commerce.

The Commission adopted a series of agreed conclusions addressed to Governments, the international community and UNCTAD.

Subsidiary bodies. The Commission had before it the report of the Expert Meeting on Sustainable Financial and Non-Financial Services for SME Development (Geneva, 2-4 June) [TD/B/COM.3/26]. The Expert Meeting on Capacity-building in the Area of Electronic Commerce: Legal and Regulatory Dimensions met in Geneva from 14 to 16 July [TD/B/COM.3/28].

Other matters. The Commission considered an UNCTAD secretariat note [TD/B/COM.3/24] that provided an in-depth evaluation of the Trade Point Programme, in follow-up to a decision adopted by the Working Party on the Medium-term Plan and the Programme Budget at its thirty-third session (see p. 910). It also had before it two progress reports on the implementation of the Commission's agreed conclusions and recommendations, prepared in accordance with a 1998 TDB decision on guidelines on the efficiency and functioning of UNCTAD's intergovernmental machinery [YUN 1998, p. 913]. They reviewed the impact and relevance of electronic commerce on trade growth and development [TD/B/COM.3/25], and analysed issues related to enterprise development [TD/B/COM.3/27].

At its twenty-second executive session in October [A/54/15/Rev.1], TDB endorsed the Commission's agreed conclusions.

Commodities

The *Trade and Development Report, 1999* [Sales No. E.99.II.D.1] stated that commodity markets had weakened considerably since the outbreak of the Asian financial crisis in 1997. The more than 12 per cent price decline in 1998 for non-oil commodities as a whole was the largest since the mid-1970s and embraced all major commodity groups. Declines were particularly pronounced for commodities such as coffee, sugar, maize and wheat; hides and skins, and rubber; and aluminium, copper, nickel, lead and zinc. In early 1999, the price decline continued, also affecting cocoa.

Although many of the fast-growing economies in Asia were major suppliers of commodities to world markets, it was the decline in their consumption, either directly (in the case of foodstuffs) or indirectly (in the case of industrial inputs and construction materials), that was the main channel through which the impact of the Asian crisis was felt. On the other hand, prices of natural rubber, rice and timber—commodities exported primarily by countries in South-East Asia—were hit by increases in supply associated with sharp currency devaluations and by slower demand growth in the region. Since developing countries as a whole were highly dependent on commodities for their export earnings, they suffered losses of real income on account of worsened terms of trade. Many sub-Saharan African countries nevertheless fared relatively well in 1998, since their major exports were of products such as cocoa and tea, the prices of which increased in both 1997 and 1998. The collapse in Asian demand reinforced the cyclical decline in commodity prices, reflecting a combination of supply and demand factors, including reduced raw material and energy intensity of production, substitution by other materials and the fall in production costs of commodities themselves. Technological changes in production and economies of scale brought about major productivity increases in metal mining, smelting and refining. At the same time, advances in agronomic and genetic research increased yields in agriculture. For many agricultural commodities, large price declines since mid-1997 were also a reflection more of record world production than of reduced consumption.

World supplies of metals and minerals rose in lagged response to the high prices of 1994-1996, and also as a result of substantial investments in mining and refining over the decade. Prices of most non-oil commodities continued to decline up to March 1999, due in part to the continued effects of the Brazilian devaluation on the markets for coffee, soybeans (soybean oil) and sugar. On average, metals and minerals prices stabilized in early 1999, with higher nickel and silver prices offsetting the continued decline in those of aluminium and copper.

The world oil market was highly unstable in 1998. There was a large build-up of crude oil inventories on account of low demand in Asia and an unseasonably warm winter in the northern hemisphere, combined with an abundance of supply resulting from buoyant production by the Organization of Petroleum Exporting Countries (OPEC), increased exports from Iraq and resilient net exports from the CIS countries. Prices remained depressed during much of 1998 and early 1999. In 1998, the average price of crude oil was $12.3 a barrel, or 40 per cent lower than in 1996. The one-third drop in oil price in 1998 reduced the value of international oil trade by about $86 billion and accounted for an estimated 86 per cent of the decline in the value of world trade. It also contributed to the 7 per cent fall in the total export revenue of developing countries.

The *World Economic and Social Survey 1999* [Sales No. E.99.II.C.1] stated that the price of oil had begun to rebound since early 1999. The international prices of other commodities, which experienced a sharp decline in 1997-1998 and were an economic setback to many developing countries, also stabilized. However, prospects for commodity prices in 1999 were not encouraging. The plunge to record lows for the majority of commodities in 1998 stemmed from a number of developments that coincided in most markets. Weak demand in Japan and in the South-East and East Asian economies in crisis was a critical factor, exacerbated by the direct and indirect effects of the slowdown in the world economy. The speed of the decline was accelerated by oversupply in many markets: in general, producers were reluctant to cut back production, preferring to build up stocks. The purchasing power of the commodity export revenues of developing countries in terms of their imports of manufactures from industrial countries fell by almost 10 per cent, leading to a deterioration in the external and fiscal balances of the many developing countries heavily dependent on commodity-export revenues.

The collapse in prices applied to all groups of commodities except vegetable oilseeds and oils, which gained 7 per cent. Supply gluts and weak demand pushed down prices of food products by an average of 13 per cent; prices for beef and sugar fell more sharply, dropped to very low levels for the grain sub-group, and fell 17 per cent for tropical beverages. Prices of some agricultural raw materials were hit by supply shocks and declined by 11 per cent; prices of cotton, rubber, timber and wool dropped by even more; and, with some exceptions, including iron ore, phosphates, silver and tin, gold, metals and minerals suffered large declines.

Individual commodities

Natural rubber. According to the *World Economic and Social Survey 1999*, the falling price for natural rubber led to the virtual collapse of the International Natural Rubber Agreement, 1995 [YUN 1995, p. 964], the last remaining international commodity agreement with a price-stabilization clause. At the beginning of 1999, Thailand, the world's biggest producer of rubber, left the organization and withheld its contribution to the group's buffer stocks. That decision followed the withdrawal in 1998 by Malaysia, which was trying to create its own buffer-stock system and was encouraging Indonesia and Thailand to do likewise. The three countries together produced around 80 per cent of the world's natural rubber.

Common Fund for Commodities

The 1980 Agreement Establishing the Common Fund for Commodities [YUN 1980, p. 621], a mechanism intended to stabilize the commodities market by helping to finance buffer stocks of specific commodities, as well as commodity development activities such as research and marketing, entered into force in 1989 and the Fund became operational later that year.

As at 31 December 1999, the number of parties to it remained at 106 States, plus the European Community (EC), the Common Market for Eastern and Southern Africa and the Organization of African Unity (OAU).

Structured commodity finance

The ad hoc expert meeting on applications of structured commodity finance techniques for commodity-dependent countries was held in Rio de Janeiro from 19 to 21 May [UNCTAD/ITCD/COM/Misc.39]. The experts discussed how structured commodity finance, particularly in the agricultural sector, could enhance development and alleviate poverty, which policies and practices hindered the use of such finance and what measures could enhance it. They agreed that structured commodity finance could unlock much of the growth potential of commodity production and processing, while enabling the less powerful links in the marketing chain (farmers and small traders) to improve their bargaining power, and developing countries to compete in a global market place. The experts identified the major obstacles to the use of structured commodity finance, and addressed recommendations to the private sector (including farmers' associations and non-governmental organizations (NGOs)), Governments and the international community.

Consumer protection

Commission on Sustainable Development. The Commission on Sustainable Development, at its seventh session (19-30 April) [E/1999/29] (see PART THREE, Chapter I), had before it a report by the Secretary-General on the comprehensive review of changing consumption and production patterns [E/CN.17/1999/2]. The report discussed progress in implementing the work programme on the subject, adopted by the Commission in 1995 [YUN 1995, p. 837]. It also reviewed work by the United Nations, other international organizations, Governments, business and industry, and NGOs, with a focus on activities since the nineteenth special session of the General Assembly in 1997 [YUN 1997, p. 790], and proposed some refocusing of the work for the period 1999-2002 and beyond.

With regard to consumer guidelines for sustainable consumption, the report noted that the Commission had before it a draft text of extended guidelines. It recalled that the Assembly, by resolution 39/248 [YUN 1985, p. 571], had adopted the guidelines for consumer protection, which provided an internationally accepted framework for the development of national consumer protection policies. Extension of the guidelines to include elements of sustainable consumption was recommended by the Commission on Sustainable Development in 1995 and endorsed by the Economic and Social Council in resolution 1995/53 [YUN 1995, p. 966]. The process of extending the guidelines began in 1998 at an interregional expert group meeting [YUN 1998, p. 893], which proposed a set of new elements for inclusion in the guidelines.

In a decision on changing consumption and production patterns [dec. 7/2], the Commission stated that developed countries should continue to take the lead in efforts to reverse unsustainable trends in consumption and production, especially those threatening the global environment. Developing countries' priorities were to eradicate poverty and improve standards of living, including meeting basic needs and lessening the burden of external debt, while taking all possible steps to avoid environmental damage and social inequity, for the furtherance of sustainable development; countries with economies in transition faced the challenge of integrating policies to make consumption and production patterns more sustainable into the reform process. Developed countries should therefore fulfil the commitments undertaken to reach the accepted UN official development assistance (ODA) target of 0.7 per cent of GNP as soon as possible. That would require a reversal in the downward trend of ODA as a percentage of GNP. The Commission considered priorities for future work and recommended action to be taken by Governments, in cooperation with relevant international organizations and in partnership with major groups, in the areas of effective policy development and implementation; natural resource management and cleaner production; and globalization and urbanization and their impacts on consumption and production patterns. Annexed to the decision was a summary of the discussions at the Inter-sessional Ad Hoc Working Group on Consumption and Production Patterns and on Tourism (New York, 22-26 February) [E/CN.17/1999/16].

The Commission recommended to the Council for adoption a draft resolution on the expansion of the UN guidelines for consumer protection to include sustainable consumption.

ECONOMIC AND SOCIAL COUNCIL ACTION

On 26 July [meeting 39], the Economic and Social Council, on the recommendation of the Commission on Sustainable Development [E/1999/29], adopted **resolution 1999/7** without vote [agenda item 13 *(a)*].

Expansion of the United Nations guidelines for consumer protection to include sustainable consumption

The Economic and Social Council,

Recalling General Assembly resolution 39/248 of 9 April 1985, in which the Assembly adopted the guidelines for consumer protection,

Noting that the Commission on Sustainable Development, at its third session, recommended that the guidelines be expanded to include guidelines for sustainable consumption,

Recalling its resolutions 1995/53 of 28 July 1995 and 1997/53 of 23 July 1997, in which it requested the Secretary-General, inter alia, to elaborate guidelines in the area of sustainable consumption patterns,

Taking note of the report of the Secretary-General and the recommendations of the Interregional Expert Group Meeting on Consumer Protection and Sustainable Consumption, held at São Paulo, Brazil, from 28 to 30 January 1998,

Noting with appreciation the organization by the Bureau of the seventh session of the Commission on Sustainable Development of open-ended consultations among member States, as requested by the Council in its decision 1998/215 of 23 July 1998,

Aware that the need remains great for assistance in the area of consumer protection, particularly in developing countries and countries with economies in transition,

Recognizing the impact that the guidelines have had in many countries in promoting just, equitable and sustainable economic and social development through their implementation by Governments,

Recognizing also the important role of civil society, in particular of non-governmental organizations, in promoting the implementation of the guidelines,

1. *Decides* to transmit to the General Assembly, for consideration, with a view to their adoption, the draft guidelines for consumer protection expanded to include sustainable consumption, as contained in the annex;

2. *Urges* Member States, other entities of the United Nations system and relevant intergovernmental and non-governmental organizations to continue their efforts to implement effectively the United Nations guidelines for consumer protection.

[For annex, see General Assembly decision 54/449 below.]

GENERAL ASSEMBLY ACTION

In December, the General Assembly, on the recommendation of the Second Committee [A/54/594], adopted **decision 54/449** without vote [agenda item 12].

United Nations Guidelines for Consumer Protection (as expanded in 1999)

At its 87th plenary meeting, on 22 December 1999, the General Assembly, on the recommendation of the Second Committee, decided to adopt the United Nations Guidelines for Consumer Protection (as expanded in 1999), as set out in the annex to the present decision.

ANNEX

United Nations Guidelines for Consumer Protection (as expanded in 1999)

I. Objectives

1. Taking into account the interests and needs of consumers in all countries, particularly those in developing countries, recognizing that consumers often face imbalances in economic terms, educational levels and bargaining power, and bearing in mind that consumers should have the right of access to non-hazardous products, as well as the right to promote just, equitable and sustainable economic and social development and environmental protection, these guidelines for consumer protection have the following objectives:

(a) To assist countries in achieving or maintaining adequate protection for their population as consumers;

(b) To facilitate production and distribution patterns responsive to the needs and desires of consumers;

(c) To encourage high levels of ethical conduct for those engaged in the production and distribution of goods and services to consumers;

(d) To assist countries in curbing abusive business practices by all enterprises at the national and international levels which adversely affect consumers;

(e) To facilitate the development of independent consumer groups;

(f) To further international cooperation in the field of consumer protection;

(g) To encourage the development of market conditions which provide consumers with greater choice at lower prices;

(h) To promote sustainable consumption.

II. General principles

2. Governments should develop or maintain a strong consumer protection policy, taking into account the guidelines set out below and relevant international agreements. In so doing, each Government should set its own priorities for the protection of consumers in accordance with the economic, social and environmental circumstances of the country and the needs of its population, bearing in mind the costs and benefits of proposed measures.

3. The legitimate needs which the guidelines are intended to meet are the following:

(a) The protection of consumers from hazards to their health and safety;

(b) The promotion and protection of the economic interests of consumers;

(c) Access of consumers to adequate information to enable them to make informed choices according to individual wishes and needs;

(d) Consumer education, including education on the environmental, social and economic impacts of consumer choice;

(e) Availability of effective consumer redress;

(f) Freedom to form consumer and other relevant groups or organizations and the opportunity of such organizations to present their views in decision-making processes affecting them;

(g) The promotion of sustainable consumption patterns.

4. Unsustainable patterns of production and consumption, particularly in industrialized countries, are the major cause of the continued deterioration of the global environment. All countries should strive to promote sustainable consumption patterns; developed countries should take the lead in achieving sustainable consumption patterns; developing countries should seek to achieve sustainable consumption patterns in their development process, having due regard to the principle of common but differentiated responsibilities. The special situation and needs of developing countries in this regard should be fully taken into account.

5. Policies for promoting sustainable consumption should take into account the goals of eradicating poverty, satisfying the basic human needs of all members of society and reducing inequality within and between countries.

6. Governments should provide or maintain adequate infrastructure to develop, implement and monitor consumer protection policies. Special care should be taken to ensure that measures for consumer protection are implemented for the benefit of all sectors of the population, particularly the rural population and people living in poverty.

7. All enterprises should obey the relevant laws and regulations of the countries in which they do business. They should also conform to the appropriate provisions of international standards for consumer protection to which the competent authorities of the country in question have agreed. (Hereinafter, references to international standards in the guidelines should be viewed in the context of the present paragraph.)

8. The potential positive role of universities and public and private enterprises in research should be considered when developing consumer protection policies.

III. Guidelines

9. The following guidelines should apply both to home-produced goods and services and to imports.

10. In applying any procedures or regulations for consumer protection, due regard should be given to ensuring that they do not become barriers to international trade and that they are consistent with international trade obligations.

A. Physical safety

11. Governments should adopt or encourage the adoption of appropriate measures, including legal systems, safety regulations, national or international standards, voluntary standards and the maintenance of safety records to ensure that products are safe for either intended or normally foreseeable use.

12. Appropriate policies should ensure that goods produced by manufacturers are safe for either intended or normally foreseeable use. Those responsible for bringing goods to the market, in particular suppliers, exporters, importers, retailers and the like (hereinafter referred to as "distributors"), should ensure that while in their care these goods are not rendered unsafe through improper handling or storage and that while in their care they do not become hazardous through

improper handling or storage. Consumers should be instructed in the proper use of goods and should be informed of the risks involved in intended or normally foreseeable use. Vital safety information should be conveyed to consumers by internationally understandable symbols wherever possible.

13. Appropriate policies should ensure that if manufacturers or distributors become aware of unforeseen hazards after products are placed on the market, they should notify the relevant authorities and, as appropriate, the public without delay. Governments should also consider ways of ensuring that consumers are properly informed of such hazards.

14. Governments should, where appropriate, adopt policies under which, if a product is found to be seriously defective and/or to constitute a substantial and severe hazard even when properly used, manufacturers and/or distributors should recall it and replace or modify it, or substitute another product for it; if it is not possible to do this within a reasonable period of time, the consumer should be adequately compensated.

B. Promotion and protection of consumers' economic interests

15. Government policies should seek to enable consumers to obtain optimum benefit from their economic resources. They should also seek to achieve the goals of satisfactory production and performance standards, adequate distribution methods, fair business practices, informative marketing and effective protection against practices which could adversely affect the economic interests of consumers and the exercise of choice in the market place.

16. Governments should intensify their efforts to prevent practices which are damaging to the economic interests of consumers through ensuring that manufacturers, distributors and others involved in the provision of goods and services adhere to established laws and mandatory standards. Consumer organizations should be encouraged to monitor adverse practices, such as the adulteration of foods, false or misleading claims in marketing and service frauds.

17. Governments should develop, strengthen or maintain, as the case may be, measures relating to the control of restrictive and other abusive business practices which may be harmful to consumers, including means for the enforcement of such measures. In this connection, Governments should be guided by their commitment to the Set of Multilaterally Agreed Equitable Principles and Rules for the Control of Restrictive Business Practices adopted by the General Assembly in its resolution 35/63 of 5 December 1980.

18. Governments should adopt or maintain policies that make clear the responsibility of the producer to ensure that goods meet reasonable demands of durability, utility and reliability, and are suited to the purpose for which they are intended, and that the seller should see that these requirements are met. Similar policies should apply to the provision of services.

19. Governments should encourage fair and effective competition in order to provide consumers with the greatest range of choice among products and services at the lowest cost.

20. Governments should, where appropriate, see to it that manufacturers and/or retailers ensure adequate availability of reliable after-sales service and spare parts.

21. Consumers should be protected from such contractual abuses as one-sided standard contracts, exclusion of essential rights in contracts and unconscionable conditions of credit by sellers.

22. Promotional marketing and sales practices should be guided by the principle of fair treatment of consumers and should meet legal requirements. This requires the provision of the information necessary to enable consumers to take informed and independent decisions, as well as measures to ensure that the information provided is accurate.

23. Governments should encourage all concerned to participate in the free flow of accurate information on all aspects of consumer products.

24. Consumer access to accurate information about the environmental impact of products and services should be encouraged through such means as product profiles, environmental reports by industry, information centres for consumers, voluntary and transparent eco-labelling programmes and product information hotlines.

25. Governments, in close collaboration with manufacturers, distributors and consumer organizations, should take measures regarding misleading environmental claims or information in advertising and other marketing activities. The development of appropriate advertising codes and standards for the regulation and verification of environmental claims should be encouraged.

26. Governments should, within their own national context, encourage the formulation and implementation by business, in cooperation with consumer organizations, of codes of marketing and other business practices to ensure adequate consumer protection. Voluntary agreements may also be established jointly by business, consumer organizations and other interested parties. These codes should receive adequate publicity.

27. Governments should regularly review legislation pertaining to weights and measures and assess the adequacy of the machinery for its enforcement.

C. Standards for the safety and quality of consumer goods and services

28. Governments should, as appropriate, formulate or promote the elaboration and implementation of standards, voluntary and other, at the national and international levels for the safety and quality of goods and services and give them appropriate publicity. National standards and regulations for product safety and quality should be reviewed from time to time, in order to ensure that they conform, where possible, to generally accepted international standards.

29. Where a standard lower than the generally accepted international standard is being applied because of local economic conditions, every effort should be made to raise that standard as soon as possible.

30. Governments should encourage and ensure the availability of facilities to test and certify the safety, quality and performance of essential consumer goods and services.

D. Distribution facilities for essential consumer goods and services

31. Governments should, where appropriate, consider:

(a) Adopting or maintaining policies to ensure the efficient distribution of goods and services to consum-

ers; where appropriate, specific policies should be considered to ensure the distribution of essential goods and services where this distribution is endangered, as could be the case particularly in rural areas. Such policies could include assistance for the creation of adequate storage and retail facilities in rural centres, incentives for consumer self-help and better control of the conditions under which essential goods and services are provided in rural areas;

(b) Encouraging the establishment of consumer co-operatives and related trading activities, as well as information about them, especially in rural areas.

E. Measures enabling consumers to obtain redress

32. Governments should establish or maintain legal and/or administrative measures to enable consumers or, as appropriate, relevant organizations to obtain redress through formal or informal procedures that are expeditious, fair, inexpensive and accessible. Such procedures should take particular account of the needs of low-income consumers.

33. Governments should encourage all enterprises to resolve consumer disputes in a fair, expeditious and informal manner, and to establish voluntary mechanisms, including advisory services and informal complaints procedures, which can provide assistance to consumers.

34. Information on available redress and other dispute-resolving procedures should be made available to consumers.

F. Education and information programmes

35. Governments should develop or encourage the development of general consumer education and information programmes, including information on the environmental impacts of consumer choices and behaviour and the possible implications, including benefits and costs, of changes in consumption, bearing in mind the cultural traditions of the people concerned. The aim of such programmes should be to enable people to act as discriminating consumers, capable of making an informed choice of goods and services, and conscious of their rights and responsibilities. In developing such programmes, special attention should be given to the needs of disadvantaged consumers, in both rural and urban areas, including low-income consumers and those with low or non-existent literacy levels. Consumer groups, business and other relevant organizations of civil society should be involved in these educational efforts.

36. Consumer education should, where appropriate, become an integral part of the basic curriculum of the educational system, preferably as a component of existing subjects.

37. Consumer education and information programmes should cover such important aspects of consumer protection as the following:

(a) Health, nutrition, prevention of food-borne diseases and food adulteration;

(b) Product hazards;

(c) Product labelling;

(d) Relevant legislation, how to obtain redress, and agencies and organizations for consumer protection;

(e) Information on weights and measures, prices, quality, credit conditions and availability of basic necessities;

(f) Environmental protection;

(g) Efficient use of materials, energy and water.

38. Governments should encourage consumer organizations and other interested groups, including the media, to undertake education and information programmes, including on the environmental impacts of consumption patterns and on the possible implications, including benefits and costs, of changes in consumption, particularly for the benefit of low-income consumer groups in rural and urban areas.

39. Business should, where appropriate, undertake or participate in factual and relevant consumer education and information programmes.

40. Bearing in mind the need to reach rural consumers and illiterate consumers, Governments should, as appropriate, develop or encourage the development of consumer information programmes in the mass media.

41. Governments should organize or encourage training programmes for educators, mass media professionals and consumer advisers, to enable them to participate in carrying out consumer information and education programmes.

G. Promotion of sustainable consumption

42. Sustainable consumption includes meeting the needs of present and future generations for goods and services in ways that are economically, socially and environmentally sustainable.

43. Responsibility for sustainable consumption is shared by all members and organizations of society, with informed consumers, Government, business, labour organizations, and consumer and environmental organizations playing particularly important roles. Informed consumers have an essential role in promoting consumption that is environmentally, economically and socially sustainable, including through the effects of their choices on producers. Governments should promote the development and implementation of policies for sustainable consumption and the integration of those policies with other public policies. Government policy-making should be conducted in consultation with business, consumer and environmental organizations, and other concerned groups. Business has a responsibility for promoting sustainable consumption through the design, production and distribution of goods and services. Consumer and environmental organizations have a responsibility for promoting public participation and debate on sustainable consumption, for informing consumers, and for working with Government and business towards sustainable consumption.

44. Governments, in partnership with business and relevant organizations of civil society, should develop and implement strategies that promote sustainable consumption through a mix of policies that could include regulations; economic and social instruments; sectoral policies in such areas as land use, transport, energy and housing; information programmes to raise awareness of the impact of consumption patterns; removal of subsidies that promote unsustainable patterns of consumption and production; and promotion of sector-specific environmental-management best practices.

45. Governments should encourage the design, development and use of products and services that are safe and energy and resource efficient, considering their

full life-cycle impacts. Governments should encourage recycling programmes that encourage consumers to both recycle wastes and purchase recycled products.

46. Governments should promote the development and use of national and international environmental health and safety standards for products and services; such standards should not result in disguised barriers to trade.

47. Governments should encourage impartial environmental testing of products.

48. Governments should safely manage environmentally harmful uses of substances and encourage the development of environmentally sound alternatives for such uses. New potentially hazardous substances should be evaluated on a scientific basis for their long-term environmental impact prior to distribution.

49. Governments should promote awareness of the health-related benefits of sustainable consumption and production patterns, bearing in mind both direct effects on individual health and collective effects through environmental protection.

50. Governments, in partnership with the private sector and other relevant organizations, should encourage the transformation of unsustainable consumption patterns through the development and use of new environmentally sound products and services and new technologies, including information and communication technologies, that can meet consumer needs while reducing pollution and depletion of natural resources.

51. Governments are encouraged to create or strengthen effective regulatory mechanisms for the protection of consumers, including aspects of sustainable consumption.

52. Governments should consider a range of economic instruments, such as fiscal instruments and internalization of environmental costs, to promote sustainable consumption, taking into account social needs, the need for disincentives for unsustainable practices and incentives for more sustainable practices, while avoiding potential negative effects for market access, in particular for developing countries.

53. Governments, in cooperation with business and other relevant groups, should develop indicators, methodologies and databases for measuring progress towards sustainable consumption at all levels. This information should be publicly available.

54. Governments and international agencies should take the lead in introducing sustainable practices in their own operations, in particular through their procurement policies. Government procurement, as appropriate, should encourage development and use of environmentally sound products and services.

55. Governments and other relevant organizations should promote research on consumer behaviour related to environmental damage in order to identify ways to make consumption patterns more sustainable.

H. Measures relating to specific areas

56. In advancing consumer interests, particularly in developing countries, Governments should, where appropriate, give priority to areas of essential concern for the health of the consumer, such as food, water and pharmaceuticals. Policies should be adopted or maintained for product quality control, adequate and secure distribution facilities, standardized international labelling and information, as well as education and research programmes in these areas. Government guidelines in regard to specific areas should be developed in the context of the provisions of the present document.

Food

57. When formulating national policies and plans with regard to food, Governments should take into account the need of all consumers for food security and should support and, as far as possible, adopt standards from the Food and Agriculture Organization of the United Nations and the World Health Organization Codex Alimentarius or, in their absence, other generally accepted international food standards. Governments should maintain, develop or improve food safety measures, including safety criteria, food standards and dietary requirements and effective monitoring, inspection and evaluation mechanisms.

58. Governments should promote sustainable agricultural policies and practices, conservation of biodiversity and protection of soil and water, taking into account traditional knowledge.

Water

59. Governments should, within the goals and targets set for the International Drinking Water Supply and Sanitation Decade, formulate, maintain or strengthen national policies to improve the supply, distribution and quality of water for drinking. Due regard should be paid to the choice of appropriate levels of service, quality and technology, the need for education programmes and the importance of community participation.

60. Governments should assign high priority to the formulation and implementation of policies and programmes concerning the multiple uses of water, taking into account the importance of water for sustainable development in general and its finite character as a resource.

Pharmaceuticals

61. Governments should develop or maintain adequate standards, provisions and appropriate regulatory systems for ensuring the quality and appropriate use of pharmaceuticals through integrated national drug policies which could address, inter alia, procurement, distribution, production, licensing arrangements, registration systems and the availability of reliable information on pharmaceuticals. In so doing, Governments should take special account of the work and recommendations of the World Health Organization on pharmaceuticals. For relevant products, the use of that organization's Certification Scheme on the Quality of Pharmaceutical Products Moving in International Commerce and other international information systems on pharmaceuticals should be encouraged. Measures should also be taken, as appropriate, to promote the use of international non-proprietary names (INNs) for drugs, drawing on the work done by the World Health Organization.

62. In addition to the priority areas indicated above, Governments should adopt appropriate measures in other areas, such as pesticides and chemicals, in regard, where relevant, to their use, production and storage, taking into account such relevant health and environmental information as Governments may require producers to provide and include in the labelling of products.

IV. International cooperation

63. Governments should, especially in a regional or subregional context:

(a) Develop, review, maintain or strengthen, as appropriate, mechanisms for the exchange of information on national policies and measures in the field of consumer protection;

(b) Cooperate or encourage cooperation in the implementation of consumer protection policies to achieve greater results within existing resources. Examples of such cooperation could be collaboration in the setting up or joint use of testing facilities, common testing procedures, exchange of consumer information and education programmes, joint training programmes and joint elaboration of regulations;

(c) Cooperate to improve the conditions under which essential goods are offered to consumers, giving due regard to both price and quality. Such cooperation could include joint procurement of essential goods, exchange of information on different procurement possibilities and agreements on regional product specifications.

64. Governments should develop or strengthen information links regarding products which have been banned, withdrawn or severely restricted in order to enable other importing countries to protect themselves adequately against the harmful effects of such products.

65. Governments should work to ensure that the quality of products, and information relating to such products, does not vary from country to country in a way that would have detrimental effects on consumers.

66. To promote sustainable consumption, Governments, international bodies and business should work together to develop, transfer and disseminate environmentally sound technologies, including through appropriate financial support from developed countries, and to devise new and innovative mechanisms for financing their transfer among all countries, in particular to and among developing countries and countries with economies in transition.

67. Governments and international organizations, as appropriate, should promote and facilitate capacity-building in the area of sustainable consumption, particularly in developing countries and countries with economies in transition. In particular, Governments should also facilitate cooperation among consumer groups and other relevant organizations of civil society, with the aim of strengthening capacity in this area.

68. Governments and international bodies, as appropriate, should promote programmes relating to consumer education and information.

69. Governments should work to ensure that policies and measures for consumer protection are implemented with due regard to their not becoming barriers to international trade, and that they are consistent with international trade obligations.

Finance

Financial policy

The depth and global ramifications of the East Asian financial crisis, which broke out in 1997, were a major cause of periods of extreme volatility in international financial markets in 1998, said the *Trade and Development Report, 1999* [Sales No. E.99.II.D.1]. By the middle of the year, the crisis was reducing growth rates not only in the directly affected countries, but also in most other developing and transition economies. The political unrest in Indonesia provoked large capital outflows and focused attention on the political risks inherent in the policies introduced in a number of emerging markets in response to the crisis.

The decline in commodity prices (see p. 882) reduced not only foreign-exchange earnings, but also fiscal revenues in countries where commodity earnings constituted a source of government income through direct ownership in the commodity sector or taxation. The response was to introduce expenditure cuts for fear that failure to do so would jeopardize capital inflows and currency stability.

The problems in Indonesia touched off an outbreak of financial turbulence in mid-1998 that spread rapidly, first from Asia to the Russian Federation and then to South Africa and Latin America. The greatest impact was in Russian financial markets, where overnight interest rates were raised to 200 per cent to avoid a collapse of the currency. In August, the Russian Federation announced the first long-term bond default by a major sovereign debtor in the post-war period. The value of the Russian bonds used as the collateral for the dollar funds borrowed by investors in those bonds dropped to zero. The United States Federal Reserve organized a private sector recapitalization and lowered interest rates three times to support the international financial system. That move was followed by a similar monetary relaxation in Europe. The effects of the financial turbulence of 1998 were also evident from other indicators: in the United States, there was a more than doubling of long-term corporate debt defaults, and global stock markets went into a decline in the summer. Investors sought refuge in only the most liquid and safest securities, causing sales to be made not only in the emerging-market and high-yield sectors, but also in less liquid treasury obligations; as a result, new issues of both bonds and equity virtually ground to a halt. The Russian moratorium produced large losses for major Western financial institutions and led them to sell assets to raise funds to cover their losses; many of those sales were in emerging markets, thus creating an outflow of capital. A second impact involved the banks, which increased their collateral requirements and cut back lending to emerging markets. One of the first economies to feel the impact of the Russian crisis was Brazil. The markets for Brazilian equities and

Brady bonds were among the largest and most liquid of emerging markets, and played important roles in global arbitrage strategies. The equities were sold both to close arbitrage positions and to cover losses linked to Russian investment positions, and they fell by nearly 40 per cent. Although Brazil, unlike Russia, had large foreign-exchange reserves that were used to provide for an orderly exit of foreign investors, the country was forced to allow its currency to float in January 1999, when it became evident that foreign lenders would not return until the exchange rate had been adjusted. However, additional effects on global financial markets were more limited and emerging-market borrowers returned to international capital markets in the early spring. Thus, some two years after the outbreak of the Asian crisis, international capital markets came full circle and there were again predictions of relatively rapid recovery.

The *World Economic and Social Survey 1999* [Sales No. E.99.II.C.1] stated that developments in international financial markets in 1998 had an unfavourable impact on developing countries. In particular, the South and East Asian region was faced with a massive withdrawal of funds and financial transfers to the region declined to a net outflow of over $110 billion in 1998. Until the third quarter of the year, monetary policies worldwide were restrictive and did not provide a stimulus to the global economy. Policy makers in the United States focused on the inflationary potential from stronger-than-expected growth, and most European Governments and central banks concentrated on achieving the convergence criteria, notably for inflation, interest rates and fiscal deficits, for entry of their economies into the monetary union, which was inaugurated in early 1999. Interest rates in many emerging economies surged in a fruitless attempt to retain foreign capital and thus stabilize their currencies. The exchange rates of many Asian developing economies stabilized in 1998, and countries hit by renewed turbulence in early 1999 succeeded in stabilizing their currency more quickly than anticipated. However, exchange rates for a majority of countries remained at values far below their pre-crisis levels.

Developing countries made a net transfer of $11 billion abroad in 1997, which soared to $60 billion in 1998. A counterpart to that adjustment was the increase in net financial transfer to the United States; there was also an increase in the net outward transfer by Japan.

In a joint report on the world economic situation and prospects, issued at the end of 1999 by DESA and UNCTAD, it was observed that the international financial crises of 1997-1998 led not only to a slowdown in world trade growth but also to a sharp and uneven shift in external balances across countries. Capital flows into emerging economies dropped sharply during the crises, and although investor confidence was gradually restored after the Brazilian devaluation at the beginning of 1999, net private capital flows to emerging economies remained low. Corresponding to the net transfer of financial resources out of the developing countries, the net inflows to them of investment, credit and grants were smaller in aggregate than their net payment of interest and dividends.

High-level meeting of Economic and Social Council and Bretton Woods institutions. In accordance with General Assembly resolution 53/172 [YUN 1998, p. 898] and as decided by the Economic and Social Council on 2 February (**decision 1999/204**), the second special high-level meeting between the Council and the Bretton Woods institutions (the World Bank Group and the International Monetary Fund (IMF)) took place on 29 April. The first such meeting was held in 1998 [ibid.]. An informal summary of the meeting was circulated to the Council on 14 June [E/1999/78]. The meeting had before it a note by the Secretary-General on the functioning of international financial markets and stability in financing for development [E/1999/42 & Corr.1], identifying some of the questions that the meeting might wish to address: measures to promote recovery in the developing and transition economies; financial architecture and financial flows for development; international policy on external debt; economic crisis and social policy initiatives; and opportunities for further cooperation between the United Nations and the Bretton Woods institutions. The debate at the high-level meeting, which brought together senior policy makers in the areas of development cooperation, foreign affairs and finance, focused on six main subjects: measures to promote recovery and sustained economic growth; financial architecture and financial flows for development; increasing participation and cross-sectoral coherence; international policy on external debt; economic crisis and social policy initiatives; and further cooperation between the United Nations and the Bretton Woods institutions.

In concluding remarks, the President of the World Bank said that the discussion had highlighted the prevalence of poverty issues and the need for unifying efforts. There was no significant distinction between the establishing of principles by the United Nations and the attempt of the World Bank to determine financial policies. What was critical was ensuring that the two institutions worked together. There was a consensus on the link among the macroeconomic, structural, social and human issues, which needed to be taken together. The Bank had set forth some ideas in that regard in its Comprehensive Development Framework (see p. 1398). The Heavily Indebted Poor Countries Debt Initiative (the HIPC Initiative), which was part of the development process, had made substantial progress, and reduction in debt services had been agreed upon for a total of about $6 billion. However, although the world was paying attention to debt issues, they should be viewed in context. Good governance, capacity-building and human development were critical.

The Managing Director of IMF stated that preventing crises remained an essential objective; some countries had been warned by the Fund of impending crisis in their economies, but little action had been taken before the crisis erupted. The HIPC Initiative could not deliver what it promised without reform in the beneficiary countries and efforts by some countries to open their markets to them. Also, ODA should be strengthened, and it was necessary to properly marry debt relief and social relief. While member countries supported deepening debt relief for the poorest countries, no interest or readiness had been shown to include middle-income countries in the cancellation of debt. He stated that it was important to make sure that countries adopted, in advance of crisis, minimal social safety nets; and reiterated the need for a better integration of the United Nations and Bretton Woods families [A/54/3/Rev.1].

By **decision 1999/279** of 29 July, the Economic and Social Council took note of the Secretariat's informal summary of the special high-level meeting [E/1999/78].

International financial system

Report of Secretary-General. In response to General Assembly resolution 53/172 [YUN 1998, p. 898], the Secretary-General submitted an October report on the financial crisis and its impact on growth and development, especially in the developing countries [A/54/471]. The report stated that in 1998 the negative transfer of financial resources was an indicator of economic weakness, reflecting the sharp economic contractions in East Asia. Most of the swing in financial flows was accounted for by changes in private foreign lending, particularly short-term lending. The shift was concentrated in Asia, although flows to Latin America were curtailed by the end of the year. The large changes in the financial transfers of Latin America in 1998 (which continued into 1999) were the result of international financial contagion; there continued to be large financial flows into Latin America for much of the year, but there was also increasing uncertainty in the international community about some Latin American economies, especially after the Russian crisis of August. In response, the monetary authorities in several of those countries increased domestic interest rates.

The interest costs faced by developing and transition economies that were able to borrow on international markets remained high since the Russian crisis. The foreign direct investment (FDI) pace eased only slightly during the year, mainly as a result of lower foreign investment in South and East Asian countries. Flows of official financing rose, reflecting large commitments to crisis-affected countries both in 1998 and in preceding years. In 1998 alone, IMF committed almost $30 billion to developing countries and $3 billion to economies in transition for disbursement over a number of years. Commitments of concessional funds also rose. Despite the overall decline in ODA, there was a steady net inward transfer of financial resources to low-income countries in the 1990s, in particular to LDCs. However, resource transfers to them remained inadequate; moreover, the net transfer included some inflows that flowed out again as debt-servicing payments, leaving no net gain in terms of imports or investment.

In reviewing progress in strengthening global financial arrangements, the report stated that the international economic and financial environment was a central determinant of the contagion that might follow a crisis and could be instrumental in the recovery process. Action taken by national and international policy makers in response to the financial volatility of 1997-1998 included: strengthening the financial sector in developing and transition economies; improved information flows and standards and regulations; the introduction of additional means to cope with the volatility of international financial markets; increased availability of emergency external financing; more effective and equitable policy responses to financial crises; and new institutional arrangements.

The Secretary-General suggested that avenues for further action might include: attuning financial regulations to financial systems; confronting international financial volatility; meeting the need for international financing during crises; focusing the content of adjustment programmes; and democratizing governance of the international financial system.

UNCTAD note. Also in response to resolution 53/172, the Secretary-General transmitted an October note by UNCTAD on the same subject [A/54/512 & Add.1], which described trends and perspectives in external financing for developing countries, addressed financial instability and crises, and suggested possible policy responses as a defence against financial crises. It stated that IMF estimates of net flows of private capital to developing and transition economies in 1998 showed a fall of 50 to 70 per cent. The incidence and scale of the declines in 1996-1998 varied significantly among different regions: those for Asian economies were larger than elsewhere and began earliest, while those for Latin America were more moderate, but were expected to begin their recovery later. Net inflows of FDI were relatively little affected by recent financial crises; by contrast, net debt inflows fell very sharply. Since the breakdown of the Bretton Woods arrangements, increased global capital mobility was accompanied by greater frequency of financial crises in both developed and developing countries; there were, however, important differences between them in the nature and effects of financial instability and crises. In developing countries, reversal of external capital flows and sharp declines in the currency often threatened domestic financial stability, and domestic crises usually translated into currency turmoil, payments difficulties and external debt crises. By contrast, currency turmoil in industrialized countries did not usually spill into domestic financial markets, nor did domestic disruptions lead to currency and payment crises. The report stated that possible policy responses at the national level included domestic macroeconomic policies, and hedging by keeping sufficient foreign exchange reserves and credit lines. However, reliance on those policies was likely to be costly and to afford, at best, partial protection. As a result, attention had turned increasingly to structural and institutional weaknesses in the global financial architecture. The resulting debate had concentrated on five issues: transparency, disclosure and early warning systems; financial regulation and supervision; surveillance of national policies; an international lender of last resort; and orderly debt workouts.

Regional meeting. By a 20 September letter [A/54/384], Mexico transmitted to the Secretary-General the report of the High-Level Regional Meeting "Towards a stable and predictable international financial system and its relationship to social development" (Mexico City, 5-7 September), which was held under the auspices of the Government of Mexico and in collaboration with the Economic Commission for Latin America and the Caribbean (ECLAC), as a contribution to the discussions initiated by resolution 53/172.

GENERAL ASSEMBLY ACTION

On 22 December [meeting 87], the General Assembly, on the recommendation of the Second Committee [A/54/585/Add.2], adopted **resolution 54/197** by recorded vote (155-1) [agenda item 97 *(b)*].

Towards a stable international financial system, responsive to the challenges of development, especially in the developing countries

The General Assembly,

Reaffirming its resolution 53/172 of 15 December 1998 on the financial crisis and its impact on growth and development, especially in the developing countries,

Taking note of the high-level regional meeting on the theme "Towards a stable and predictable international financial system and its relationship to social development", held at Mexico City from 5 to 7 September 1999, in collaboration with the Economic Commission for Latin America and the Caribbean, in order to contribute to the process launched by the General Assembly in its resolution 53/172,

Recognizing that the increasing globalization of financial markets and capital flows has presented Governments, the multilateral financial institutions and the international community at large with new challenges and opportunities for the mobilization of adequate and more stable resources for promoting economic development and social welfare,

Stressing the importance of the provision of adequate financial resources for the development of all countries, in particular developing countries, inter alia, through public and private financial flows, international trade, official development assistance and an adequate level of funding support for debt relief, in particular the agreement for an overall financing plan for the enhanced Heavily Indebted Poor Countries Debt Initiative, as well as mobilization of domestic resources, and that the comprehensive and integrated consideration of those issues should continue in the framework of the dialogue and collaboration between the United Nations system and the Bretton Woods institutions,

Deeply concerned at the overall declining trend in official development assistance, which is a significant external resource for financing development and an important source of support for the efforts of developing countries, in particular the least developed countries, to create an enabling environment for eradicating poverty and tackling basic social needs, especially where private capital flows may be either inadequate or unavailable,

Emphasizing the importance of finding a durable solution to the problem of developing countries in meeting their external debt and debt-servicing obligations in order to release resources for financing their development efforts, welcoming, in this context, the Cologne debt initiative launched in June 1999 and the recent decisions of the International Monetary Fund and the World Bank on the enhanced Heavily Indebted Poor Countries Debt Initiative, which should provide deeper, broader and faster relief, and in this regard stressing the need for fair, equitable and transparent burden-sharing among the international public creditor community and other donor countries,

Noting the establishment of credit contingency lines by the International Monetary Fund and the efforts to create and to strengthen the regional reserves in some regions,

Expressing the need for future multilateral trade negotiations to result, inter alia, in increased access to markets for goods and services that are of export interest to developing countries, in particular the least developed countries, as trade is an important source of financial resources for their development efforts,

Mindful of the need for the benefits of the increasing integration of global markets to be extended to all nations and peoples, in particular to developing countries, especially the least developed among them, noting that, while a number of developing countries have been able to take advantage of globalization of finance, not all of them have benefited from such flows, as they may be unavailable, inadequate or too concentrated to satisfy their needs, especially the least developed among them, and, therefore, noting the need to expand private capital flows while reducing the risks of volatility and to broaden access by developing countries to those flows,

Noting the desirability of having financial regulatory frameworks so that capital mobility may benefit developing economies rather than undermine their development efforts, and noting in particular that short-term speculative capital flows, owing to their highly volatile nature, can often have negative impacts on the long-term goals of developing countries,

Regretting that the recent financial crises led to a significant slowdown in the economic growth of many developing countries and other affected countries and had negative impacts in terms of social development, with the gravest impact on the most vulnerable, and in this context noting that, while some of the most visible effects of the crises are being overcome in some regions and sectors, continued action on a wide range of reforms needs to be taken so as to strengthen the international financial system and to adopt as well as to implement economic and legal frameworks, while reaffirming the need for continued efforts by individual economies to avoid the repetition of those crises,

Recognizing that the recent financial crises have exposed weaknesses in the international financial system, and underlining the urgent need to continue to work on a wide range of reforms for a strengthened and more stable international financial system with a view to enabling it to deal more effectively and in a timely manner with the new challenges of development in the context of global financial integration,

Emphasizing that the United Nations, in fulfilling its role in the promotion of development, in particular of developing countries, plays an important role in the international efforts to build up the necessary international consensus on the continuation of a wide range of reforms needed for a strengthened and more stable international financial system that is responsive to the challenges of development, especially in the developing countries, and to the promotion of economic and social equity in the global economy,

1. *Takes note with appreciation* of the report of the Secretary-General, and the note by the United Nations Conference on Trade and Development on the financial crisis and its impact on growth and development, especially in the developing countries, the report of the Task Force of the Executive Committee on Economic and Social Affairs of the United Nations Secretariat entitled "Towards a new international financial architecture", the *World Economic and Social Survey 1999* and the *Trade and Development Report, 1999;*

2. *Emphasizes* the need to renew national, regional and international efforts to promote international financial stability and, to this end, to improve early warning, prevention and response capabilities for dealing with the emergence and spread of financial crises in a timely manner, taking a comprehensive and long-term perspective while remaining responsive to the challenges of development and the protection of the most vulnerable countries and social groups;

3. *Stresses* the importance of having an enabling international environment through strong cooperative efforts by all countries and institutions to promote global economic development, and to this end calls upon all countries, in particular major industrialized countries, which have significant weight in influencing world economic growth, to adopt and pursue coordinated policies conducive to world economic growth and international financial stability and the promotion of an external economic environment favourable to a widespread economic recovery, including the full recovery of crisis-affected countries;

4. *Recognizes* the importance of international financial stability, and in this context invites developed countries, in particular major industrialized countries, when formulating their macroeconomic policies, to take into account the priorities of growth and development, in particular of developing countries;

5. *Stresses* the importance at the national level of strong domestic institutions to promote the achievement of growth and development, inter alia, through sound macroeconomic policies and policies aimed at strengthening the regulatory and supervisory systems of the financial and banking sectors, including appropriate institutional arrangements in the countries of both origin and destination of international capital flows;

6. *Recognizes* the importance of accelerating the growth and development prospects of the least developed countries, which remain the poorest and most vulnerable of the international community, and calls upon development partners to carry on with their efforts to increase official development assistance and their efforts aimed at strengthening debt relief, improving market access and enhancing balance-of-payments support;

7. *Stresses* the need for a continued and constructive dialogue, in the relevant institutions and forums, among developed and developing countries at the regional and subregional levels, among others, on the need for the international community to continue to work together in formulating approaches to promoting financial stability and on issues related to strengthening and reforming the international financial system, and in this context reiterates the need for broadening and strengthening the participation of developing countries in the international economic decision-making process in order to promote more efficient international financial institutions and arrangements in which all relevant interests can be effectively represented;

8. *Encourages* the deepening of the dialogue between the Economic and Social Council and the Bretton Woods institutions in order to promote the wide range of reforms needed in an international financial architecture that reflects the global interests of the international community, and in this regard recommends that their next high-level meeting give priority to the consideration of the modalities needed to achieve a strengthened and more stable international financial system responsive to the challenges of development, especially in the developing countries, and to the promotion of economic and social equity in the global economy;

9. *Emphasizes* that the international financial institutions, in providing policy advice and supporting adjustment programmes, should ensure that they are sensitive to the specific circumstances of concerned countries and to the special needs of developing countries and should work towards the best possible outcomes in terms of growth and development, including poverty eradication, inter alia, through the protection of effective social expenditure determined by each country in accordance with its national economic and social development strategies;

10. *Stresses* the need further to define the role and improve the capacities of the international, regional and subregional financial institutions with regard to the prevention, management and resolution in a timely and effective manner of international financial crises, encourages efforts to enhance the stabilizing role of regional and subregional financial institutions and arrangements in supporting the management of monetary and financial issues, in accordance with the mandate of each institution, and requests the regional commissions to provide their views on this matter to the General Assembly at its fifty-fifth session through their regular reports to the Economic and Social Council;

11. *Emphasizes* the need to develop further early warning capacities and modalities to prevent or, as the case may be, to take timely action to address the threat of financial crisis, and in this regard encourages the International Monetary Fund and other relevant international and regional institutions to continue their efforts to contribute to this process;

12. *Underscores* the need for the enhancement of worldwide financial stability, *inter alia,* through the provision to the international financial institutions, in particular the International Monetary Fund, of adequate resources to provide emergency financing in a timely manner to countries affected by financial crises;

13. *Stresses* that the opening of capital accounts must be carried out in an orderly, gradual and well-sequenced manner, at a pace that is in line with the strengthening of the ability of countries to cope with its consequences, underscores the crucial importance of solid domestic financial systems and of an effective prudential framework, invites the International Monetary Fund, the World Bank and relevant international regulatory bodies to contribute to this process, and in this context recognizes that all countries have autonomy in the management of capital accounts in accordance with their own national priorities and needs;

14. *Reaffirms* the need to strengthen international and national financial systems through more effective national, regional and international surveillance of both the public and private sectors, based, inter alia, on the improved availability and transparency of information, as appropriate, and possible additional regulatory and voluntary disclosure measures concerning financial market participants, including international institutional investors, in particular concerning highly leveraged operations, and in this context also reaffirms the importance of continuing to work in the relevant forums on questions related to surveillance, transparency and disclosure, regulation and supervision;

15. *Stresses* the importance of strengthened collaboration between the World Bank and the International Monetary Fund in specific areas where collaboration is needed, such as the financial sector, while recognizing the specific mandates of the two institutions, and also stresses the need for institutions dealing with financial crises to keep in mind the overall objective of facilitating long-term development;

16. *Calls* for the renewal of national, regional and international efforts to promote the greater involvement of the private sector in the prevention and resolution of financial crises, underscores in this context the importance of a more equitable distribution of the cost of adjustments between the public and private sectors and among debtors, creditors and investors, and requests the United Nations Conference on Trade and Development to provide information to the General Assembly at its fifty-fifth session about the work it has undertaken on this matter;

17. *Reiterates its call* upon the international community to pursue national, regional and international efforts to contribute to minimizing the negative impacts of excessive volatility of global financial flows, reiterates in this context the need to consider the establishment of regulatory frameworks for short-term capital flows and trade in currencies, and invites the International Monetary Fund and the relevant regulatory bodies to contribute to this process;

18. *Emphasizes* that it is important for sovereign risk assessments made by private sector agencies to be based on objective and transparent parameters, and in this regard invites the relevant national, regional and international regulatory bodies to contribute to the development of appropriate standards to ensure that risk-assessment agencies provide complete and accurate information on a timely and regular basis;

19. *Encourages* the continuing efforts of the World Bank and regional development banks to help Governments to address the social consequences of crises, in particular through the strengthening of social safety nets in developing countries, particularly for the most vulnerable groups, without losing sight of the long-term goals of development;

20. *Requests* the Secretary-General to support, inter alia, through collaboration with the regional commissions and regional and subregional initiatives, the ongoing work on the identification of measures that will contribute to a more stable and predictable international financial system that is responsive to the challenges of development, in particular of developing countries, and in this regard requests the Secretary-General to make available the results of those exercises to the General Assembly at its fifty-fifth session;

21. *Also requests* the Secretary-General, in close cooperation with all relevant entities of the United Nations, including the United Nations Conference on Trade and Development and the regional commis-

sions, within their respective mandates, and in consultation with the Bretton Woods institutions, to report to the General Assembly at its fifty-fifth session on the implementation of the present resolution under the sub-item entitled "Financing of development, including net transfer of resources between developing and developed countries", with an analysis of the current trend in global financial flows and recommendations for an agenda for a strengthened and more stable international financial system that is responsive to the priorities of growth and development, in particular of developing countries, and to the promotion of economic and social equity in the global economy;

22. *Requests* the President of the General Assembly to transmit the present resolution to the Board of Executive Directors of the World Bank and the Executive Board of the International Monetary Fund, in order to bring it to their attention as an input to their discussions on the matters addressed herein.

RECORDED VOTE ON RESOLUTION 54/197:

In favour: Afghanistan, Algeria, Andorra, Angola, Antigua and Barbuda, Argentina, Armenia, Australia, Austria, Azerbaijan, Bahamas, Bahrain, Bangladesh, Barbados, Belarus, Belgium, Belize, Benin, Bhutan, Botswana, Brazil, Brunei Darussalam, Bulgaria, Burkina Faso, Cambodia, Cameroon, Canada, Cape Verde, Chad, Chile, China, Colombia, Costa Rica, Côte d'Ivoire, Croatia, Cuba, Cyprus, Czech Republic, Democratic People's Republic of Korea, Denmark, Djibouti, Dominican Republic, Ecuador, Egypt, Eritrea, Estonia, Ethiopia, Fiji, Finland, France, Gabon, Georgia, Germany, Ghana, Greece, Grenada, Guatemala, Guinea, Guinea-Bissau, Guyana, Haiti, Hungary, Iceland, India, Indonesia, Iran, Ireland, Israel, Italy, Jamaica, Japan, Jordan, Kazakhstan, Kenya, Kuwait, Lao People's Democratic Republic, Latvia, Lebanon, Lesotho, Libyan Arab Jamahiriya, Liechtenstein, Lithuania, Luxembourg, Madagascar, Malaysia, Maldives, Mali, Malta, Marshall Islands, Mauritius, Mexico, Monaco, Mongolia, Morocco, Mozambique, Myanmar, Namibia, Nepal, Netherlands, New Zealand, Nigeria, Norway, Oman, Pakistan, Panama, Papua New Guinea, Paraguay, Peru, Philippines, Poland, Portugal, Qatar, Republic of Korea, Republic of Moldova, Romania, Russian Federation, Saint Lucia, Saint Vincent and the Grenadines, Samoa, San Marino, Saudi Arabia, Senegal, Seychelles, Singapore, Slovakia, Slovenia, Solomon Islands, South Africa, Spain, Sri Lanka, Sudan, Suriname, Swaziland, Sweden, Syrian Arab Republic, Tajikistan, Thailand, The former Yugoslav Republic of Macedonia, Togo, Trinidad and Tobago, Tunisia, Turkey, Turkmenistan, Uganda, Ukraine, United Arab Emirates, United Kingdom, United Republic of Tanzania, Uruguay, Uzbekistan, Venezuela, Viet Nam, Yemen, Zambia, Zimbabwe.

Against: United States.

In the Second Committee, the United States said that it could not support the draft resolution because its recommendations surpassed the Assembly's mandate and prejudged the work of the international financial institutions regarding the strengthening of the international financial system.

Debt problems of developing countries

In response to General Assembly resolution 53/175 [YUN 1998, p. 902], the Secretary-General submitted a September report on recent developments in the debt situation of developing countries [A/54/370]. The report analysed new initiatives introduced by the international community to tackle the debt problems of developing countries, and stressed that the debt problems of HIPCs, which were structurally rooted, remained largely unresolved. In the middle-income countries, the worst phase of the liquidity crisis had been overcome, and recovery had timidly redressed the economies of Asian countries, which were, however, still struggling with problems of corporate sector debt.

Discussing recent trends in external debt, the Secretary-General stated that the total external debt of developing countries and countries in transition at the end of 1998 was estimated at nearly $2.5 trillion, an increase of 6 per cent over 1997. Short-term debt was reduced and represented less than 17 per cent of the total. As a result of a reduction in exports and a slowing down of gross domestic product (GDP) growth, there was an increase in the ratios of debt to exports and debt to GDP. Measures taken in the wake of the Asian crisis contributed to reducing the reliance on short-term debt, which in 1998 took about 59 per cent of the stock of foreign exchange reserves. The amount of total paid debt service remained almost unchanged, while arrears on interest and principal payments increased slightly. The distribution of debt among the different developing and transition country regions did not change: Latin America accounted for 30 per cent of the total, Asia increased its share to 35 per cent, and Africa together with the Middle East and Eastern Europe and Central Asia maintained their respective shares of 17 and 18 per cent. The group of 41 HIPCs had a total amount of debt equivalent to $201 billion at the end of 1997, 28 per cent of which represented multilateral debt; the ratio of debt to exports, at 345 per cent, was the highest ever reached by any group of developing country debtor countries.

As to international debt strategies, the Secretary-General stated that between July 1998 and July 1999, important initiatives were taken by the international community to bring about changes. Most noticeable were efforts to make the HIPC Initiative more effective and efforts by the Paris Club creditors to involve the private sector in a comparable treatment of developing countries' debt. The renegotiation of official bilateral debts took place within the Paris Club framework. Activities in the second half of 1998 and the first of 1999 were marked by continued restructuring of the debts of the poorest countries in the context of the HIPC Initiative; the return of middle-income countries to reschedule their official bilateral debts; and special measures taken in support of countries affected by conflict or natural disaster. Under the HIPC Initiative, seven of those countries restructured their debt for a total amount of $4.5 billion. The Central African Republic, Honduras, Rwanda and Zambia obtained Naples terms, with a 67 per cent reduction of the flow of debt service falling due during three-year consolidation periods following new Enhanced Structural Adjustment Facility (ESAF) agreements with IMF. Having reached their HIPC completion points, Bolivia, Guyana and Mozambique also concluded new agreements with the Paris Club.

The East Asian financial crisis affected the debt-servicing capacity of some middle-income debtor countries, and some of them sought new arrangements with their commercial, as well as official bilateral creditors. Thus, Indonesia met with its group of official creditors in September 1998 to reschedule principal payments following an Extended Funding Facility arrangement with IMF, and in January 1999, Pakistan rescheduled its non-concessional and ODA debts. In May, Jordan sought additional debt relief from the Paris Club and, at the end of July, the Russian Federation negotiated a rescheduling of some $8 billion of arrears and payments falling due between July 1999 and December 2000 on debts contracted by or guaranteed on behalf of the Government of the former USSR.

With regard to Paris Club support to countries affected by conflict and natural disasters, Bosnia and Herzegovina obtained a restructuring on Naples terms of its external debt service obligations, resulting from debt incurred by the former Yugoslavia; all payments by Honduras and Nicaragua were deferred following hurricane Mitch; and exceptional treatment was extended to specially affected countries—Albania and the former Yugoslav Republic of Macedonia.

Relief on official debts for the poorest countries was complemented by buy-backs of private creditor debt undertaken since 1991 under the World Bank/International Development Association (IDA) Debt Reduction Facility for IDA-only countries. The programme involved buying back commercial debt, primarily from banks, at substantial discount. Eighteen operations were carried out under the Facility and through them $3.7 billion of principal and more than $2.7 billion of associated interest arrears were extinguished.

By mid-1999, 12 countries had had their debt sustainability reviewed under the HIPC Initiative. Only one new country, Mali, reached the decision point, and three additional countries attained the completion point: Bolivia, Guyana and Mozambique. In June 1999, the Group of Seven (G-7) major industrialized countries at their summit in Cologne, Germany, made recommendations for the enhancement of the HIPC Initiative, known as the Cologne debt initiative, making debt relief faster.

The report concluded that the Cologne debt initiative allowed a deeper debt relief through lower debt sustainability targets and larger debt reductions. Debt sustainability targets should realistically reflect HIPCs' capacity to pay, and HIPC debt relief should seek to remove the binding constraint, be it scarcity of foreign exchange or lack of budgetary resources. Debt relief for the poorest countries should not be provided at the expense of ODA funding for development programmes and projects, but it should be financed by resources additional to budgetary ODA allocations. In addition to enhancing HIPCs' external viability, reducing fiscal pressure and creating room for transferring resources to social expenditures should also be key concerns under the HIPC Initiative. Besides HIPCs, middle-income debtor countries also needed additional liquidity for economic recovery. In the cases of lower middle-income countries, some degree of debt relief might be necessary; in the framework of the Paris Club, for example, some relief to those countries was provided only through debt conversions.

With specific regard to the official debt relief for HIPCs, the *World Economic and Social Survey 1999* stated that the initiative for HIPCs was the focus of international efforts to address debt problems, and emphasized the need to address the special conditions of post-conflict HIPCs. In response to the proposals for change in the Initiative, IMF and the World Bank undertook a review of the options and suggested a general approach, including: lowering key target ratios; earlier provision of relief; a tighter link between debt relief and poverty reduction and social policy in the debtor countries; increased bilateral debt relief and official bilateral assistance; and commitment by member countries to seeking prompt solutions to fund the relief.

GENERAL ASSEMBLY ACTION

On 22 December [meeting 87], the General Assembly, on the recommendation of the Second Committee [A/54/585/Add.5], adopted **resolution 54/202** without vote [agenda item 97 *(e)*].

Enhancing international cooperation towards a durable solution to the external debt problem of developing countries

The General Assembly,

Recalling its resolutions 51/164 of 16 December 1996, 52/185 of 18 December 1997 and 53/175 of 15 December 1998 on enhancing international cooperation towards a durable solution to the external debt problems of developing countries,

Reaffirming the urgent need for further implementation in an effective, equitable and development-oriented way of existing mechanisms for the treatment of the external debt and debt-servicing problems of developing countries in order to help them to exit from the rescheduling process and unsustainable debt burdens,

Welcoming and emphasizing the importance of the efforts of debtor countries, despite the great social cost often involved, in pursuing economic reform, stabilization and structural adjustment programmes aimed at achieving stability, raising domestic savings and investments, attaining competitiveness to take advantage of market access opportunities where available, reducing inflation, improving economic efficiency and addressing the social aspects of development, including the eradication of poverty as well as the development of social safety nets for the vulnerable and poorer strata of their populations, and encouraging them to continue in these efforts,

Welcoming the debt initiative launched by the Group of Seven major industrialized countries at its meeting held in Cologne, Germany, from 18 to 20 June 1999, and the recent decisions of the International Monetary Fund and the World Bank on the enhanced Heavily Indebted Poor Countries Debt Initiative, which should provide deeper, broader and faster debt relief,

Noting with great concern that one of the major obstacles to the speedy implementation of the enhanced Heavily Indebted Poor Countries Debt Initiative is financial constraints, stressing the need for fair, equitable and transparent burden-sharing among the international public creditor community and other donor countries and in this regard stressing that the Heavily Indebted Poor Countries Trust Fund must be adequately funded,

Welcoming the actions taken by creditor countries within the framework of the Paris Club and by some creditor countries through the cancellation and equivalent relief of bilateral debts,

Noting with concern the continuing debt and debt-servicing problems of heavily indebted developing countries as constituting an element adversely affecting their development efforts and economic growth, and stressing the importance of alleviating once and for all, where applicable, the onerous debt and debt-service burden with the aim of attaining a sustainable level of debt and debt service on the basis of an effective, equitable, development-oriented and durable approach, and, where appropriate, addressing the full stock of debt of the poorest and most indebted developing countries as a matter of priority,

Noting with great concern the continuing high debt burden borne by most African countries and least developed countries as exacerbated, inter alia, by the declining trend in many commodity prices,

Noting also with great concern that the recent financial crisis has aggravated the debt-service burdens of many developing countries, including low-income and middle-income countries, particularly in the context of meeting their international debt and debt-servicing obligations in a timely fashion despite serious external and domestic financial constraints,

Noting with concern that a growing number of highly indebted middle-income developing countries are facing difficulties in meeting their external debt-servicing obligations, owing, inter alia, to liquidity constraints,

Stressing that effective management of the debt of developing countries, including middle-income countries, is an important factor, among others, in their sustained economic growth and in the smooth functioning of the world economy,

Noting with great concern that the debt overhang of the heavily indebted poor countries still constitutes a problem hampering their development, and in this context emphasizing the importance of the full and speedy implementation of the enhanced Heavily Indebted Poor Countries Debt Initiative,

Stressing the need for evolving debt strategies to continue to address the debt sustainability of developing countries, and in this connection stressing also the urgent need for full and swift implementation of initiatives that will further assist developing countries, in particular the poorest and most heavily indebted countries, especially in Africa, in their efforts to improve their debt situation, in view of their continued very high levels of total debt stock and debt-service burdens,

Stressing also the need for continuing global economic growth and a continuing supportive international economic environment with regard to, inter alia, terms of trade, commodity prices, improved market access, trade practices, access to technology, exchange rates and international interest rates, and noting the continued need for resources for sustained economic growth and sustainable development of the developing countries, in accordance with the relevant General Assembly resolutions and the outcomes of recent United Nations conferences,

Noting that mechanisms such as debt rescheduling and debt conversions alone are not sufficient to resolve all the problems relating to long-term debt sustainability,

Stressing the importance of a sound enabling environment for effective debt management,

Recognizing those efforts of the international community that contribute to effective, equitable, development-oriented and durable solutions to the external debt and debt-servicing problems of developing countries, and emphasizing that the international community should consider further appropriate measures to that end,

1. *Takes note* of the report of the Secretary-General on recent developments in the debt situation of developing countries;

2. *Recognizes* that effective, equitable, development-oriented and durable solutions to external debt and debt-service burdens of developing countries can contribute substantially to the strengthening of the global economy and to the efforts of developing countries to achieve sustained economic growth and sustainable development, in accordance with the relevant General Assembly resolutions and the outcomes of recent United Nations conferences;

3. *Also recognizes* that the Cologne debt initiative and the recent decisions of the World Bank and the International Monetary Fund on the enhanced Heavily Indebted Poor Countries Debt Initiative contribute to achieving durable solutions to the external debt and debt-service burdens of the heavily indebted poor developing countries;

4. *Reiterates* the call for industrialized countries that have not yet contributed to the Enhanced Structural Adjustment Facility (now renamed Poverty Reduction and Growth Facility) and the Heavily Indebted Poor Countries Trust Fund to come forward immediately with their contribution;

5. *Notes* the agreement on the elements of a financing plan for multilateral development banks, and in this regard stresses the urgency of providing new and additional resources to secure adequate funding for an overall financing plan for the enhanced Heavily Indebted Poor Countries Debt Initiative, including in

particular the Heavily Indebted Poor Countries Trust Fund in the context of equitable and transparent burden-sharing that would permit the Initiative to be launched and the delivery of debt relief to begin for those countries requiring retroactive relief and those expected to reach their decision points over the near term, without compromising the financing made available through concessional windows such as the International Development Association, and in this regard stresses the importance of applying the enhanced Initiative in those eligible countries that have already reached their decision and completion points within the framework of the previous Initiative;

6. *Also notes* that the so-called floating completion points approach offers the opportunity to shorten the time frame for implementation of the Heavily Indebted Poor Countries Debt Initiative to countries that meet the necessary conditions so that debt relief can be provided faster than under the original heavily indebted poor countries framework, and in this regard urges speedy implementation of the approach and welcomes the flexibility that the enhanced Initiative provides in terms of interim assistance and front-loading of the delivery of debt to qualifying eligible countries;

7. *Stresses* the importance of implementing the Heavily Indebted Poor Countries Debt Initiative flexibly, including shortening the interval between the decision and completion points, taking due account of the policy performance of the countries concerned in a transparent manner and with the full involvement of the debtor countries;

8. *Notes* that there is now a possibility of expanding eligibility under the Heavily Indebted Poor Countries Debt Initiative to thirty-six countries, and in this regard looks forward to an early review of the list of heavily indebted poor countries;

9. *Stresses* the importance of considering increased flexibility with regard to Heavily Indebted Poor Countries Debt Initiative eligibility criteria, including continuously evaluating and actively monitoring the implication of existing terms of the eligibility criteria so as to ensure sufficient coverage of heavily indebted poor countries, increased flexibility being, in this context, particularly important for known borderline cases and countries in post-conflict situations, in respect of, inter alia, avoiding delays in the establishment of a track record of economic performance caused by temporary setbacks due to external shocks in order to help them to exit from the rescheduling process and from unsustainable debt burdens;

10. *Invites* the International Monetary Fund and the World Bank to continue to strengthen the transparency and integrity of debt sustainability analysis, and encourages the further commissioning of relevant independent studies on the debt problem of developing countries;

11. *Welcomes* the proposed framework for strengthening the link between debt relief and poverty eradication, and stresses the need for its flexible implementation, recognizing that, while the poverty reduction strategy paper should be in place by the decision point, on a transitional basis the decision point could be reached without agreement on a poverty paper, but that in all cases demonstrable progress in implementing a poverty reduction strategy would be required by the completion point;

12. *Emphasizes* that poverty reduction programmes as linked to the implementation of the enhanced Heavily Indebted Poor Countries Debt Initiative must be country-driven and in accordance with the priorities and programmes of countries eligible under the Initiative, and stresses the role of civil society in this regard;

13. *Stresses* the need for debt-relief initiatives to be guided by enhanced transparency and predictability, involving debtor countries in any review and analysis that is conducted during the adjustment period;

14. *Welcomes* the decision of those countries that have cancelled bilateral official debt, and urges creditor countries that have not done so to consider full cancellation of bilateral official debts of countries eligible under the Heavily Indebted Poor Countries Debt Initiative and, as appropriate, action to address the needs of post-conflict countries, in particular those with protracted arrears, developing countries affected by serious natural disasters and poor countries with very low social and human development indicators, including the possibility of debt-relief measures through, inter alia, the cancellation and equivalent relief of bilateral official debt, and stresses the importance of building coalitions with civil society organizations and non-governmental organizations in all countries to ensure in the shortest possible time the implementation of pronouncements on debt forgiveness in order that countries eligible under the Initiative may quickly benefit from such pronouncements;

15. *Notes* that the multilateral debt-relief funds can have a positive impact in respect of assisting Governments in safeguarding or increasing expenditures on priority social sectors, and encourages donors to continue efforts in this regard in the context of the enhanced Heavily Indebted Poor Countries Debt Initiative;

16. *Stresses* the principle that funding of any debt relief should not affect adversely the support for other development activities in favour of developing countries, including the level of funding for the United Nations funds and programmes, and in this regard welcomes the decision of the Joint Ministerial Committee of the Boards of Governors of the World Bank and the International Monetary Fund on the Transfer of Real Resources to Developing Countries (Development Committee) that financing of debt relief should not compromise the financing made available through concessional windows such as the International Development Association, and expresses its appreciation that certain developed countries have reached or even gone beyond the agreed target for official development assistance of 0.7 per cent of their gross national product, while at the same time calling upon other developed countries to fulfil this target for official development assistance as soon as possible;

17. *Expresses its appreciation* for the action taken by creditor countries of the Paris Club in December 1998 with regard to the debts of countries affected by hurricane Mitch, and in this regard reiterates the need for relief promises to come to fruition within the shortest possible time-frames in order to free the requisite resources for national reconstruction efforts, welcomes the decision of various countries to address the debt situation of Honduras and Nicaragua, including through cancellation of their bilateral official debt, and invites others to take similar action;

18. *Encourages* the international creditor community to consider appropriate measures in the case of countries with a very high level of debt overhang, including in particular low-income African countries, in order to make an appropriate and consistent contribution to the common objective of debt sustainability;

19. *Recognizes* the difficulties of highly indebted middle-income developing countries and other highly indebted middle-income countries in meeting their external debt and debt-servicing obligations, and notes the worsening situation in some of them in the context, inter alia, of higher liquidity constraints, which may require debt treatment including, as appropriate, debt-reduction measures;

20. *Calls* for concerted national and international action to address effectively debt problems of middle-income developing countries with a view to resolving their potential long-term debt-sustainability problems through various debt-treatment measures, including, as appropriate, orderly mechanisms for debt reduction, and encourages all creditor and debtor countries to utilize to the fullest extent possible, where appropriate, all existing mechanisms for debt reduction;

21. *Recognizes* the efforts made by indebted developing countries with regard to fulfilling their debt-servicing commitments despite the high social cost incurred, and in this regard encourages private creditors and, in particular, commercial banks to continue their initiatives and efforts to address the commercial debt problems of middle-income developing countries, in particular those affected by the financial crisis;

22. *Also recognizes* the need to continue to work with all creditors in order to facilitate continued access to international capital markets, and, in the event that extraordinary circumstances preclude a country from temporarily meeting its debt-servicing commitments, urges Governments to work with creditors in a transparent and timely fashion towards a workable resolution of the repayment problem;

23. *Further recognizes* the need to make the maximum use of existing debt-relief measures, including existing facilities to provide relief through various debt-conversion programmes, such as debt-equity swaps, debt-for-nature swaps, debt-for-child-development swaps and other debt-for-development efforts, as well as to support measures in favour of the most vulnerable segments of the societies of those countries and to develop techniques of debt conversion to be applied to social development programmes and projects, in conformity with the priorities of the World Summit for Social Development;

24. *Stresses* that debt relief should contribute to development objectives, including poverty reduction, and in this regard urges countries to direct those resources freed through debt relief, in particular through debt cancellation and reduction, towards these objectives;

25. *Notes,* while recognizing the benefits of the liberalization of international capital flows, the adverse impact of the volatility of short-term capital flows on exchange rates, interest rates and the debt situation of developing countries, and stresses the need for coherence in implementing policies and for the liberalization of capital accounts in an orderly, gradual and well-sequenced manner to keep pace with the strengthening of the ability of countries to sustain its consequences so as to mitigate the adverse impact of such volatility;

26. *Also notes* that debt relief alone will not lead to poverty reduction, and in this regard emphasizes the need for an enabling environment as well as for an efficient, transparent and accountable public service and administration, and also emphasizes the urgency of securing an adequate level of funding support for debt relief, in particular the agreement for an overall financing plan for the enhanced Heavily Indebted Poor Countries Debt Initiative;

27. *Stresses* the need to strengthen the institutional capacity of developing countries in debt management, calls upon the international community to support the efforts towards this end, and in this regard stresses the importance of initiatives such as the Debt Management and Financial Analysis System and the debt-management capacity-building programme;

28. *Reaffirms* the Mid-term Global Review of Progress towards the Implementation of the Programme of Action for the Least Developed Countries for the 1990s, in particular the actions required in favour of those countries concerning their official bilateral, commercial and multilateral debts;

29. *Stresses* the need for new financial flows to debtor developing countries from all sources, in addition to debt-relief measures that include debt and debt-service reduction, and urges creditor countries and multilateral financial institutions to continue to extend concessional financial assistance, in particular to the least developed countries, in order to support the implementation by the developing countries of economic reforms and stabilization and structural adjustment programmes that will enable them to extricate themselves from the debt overhang and attract new investment and to assist them in achieving sustained economic growth and sustainable development, in accordance with the relevant General Assembly resolutions and the outcomes of recent United Nations conferences, and the eradication of poverty;

30. *Notes* the importance of providing adequate resources for debt-relief measures in the light of the adverse effects of the international financial crisis on the mobilization of both domestic and external resources for the development of the developing countries, including those in Africa and the least developed countries;

31. *Stresses* the importance of trade to development, poverty alleviation and sustained global economic recovery, and in this regard emphasizes that multilateral trade negotiations should deliver early and substantial benefits to developing countries, in particular the least developed countries, as well as improve market access and further reduce barriers to trade;

32. *Also stresses* the importance for developing countries of continuing their efforts to promote a favourable environment for attracting foreign investment, thereby promoting economic growth and sustainable development, so as to favour their exit from debt and debt-servicing problems, and further stresses the need for the international community to promote a conducive external environment through, inter alia, improved market access, stabilization of exchange rates, effective stewardship of international interest rates, increased resource flows, access to international financial mar-

kets, flow of financial resources and improved access to technology for developing countries;

33. *Calls upon* the international community, including the United Nations system, and invites the Bretton Woods institutions, as well as the private sector, to take appropriate measures and actions for the implementation of the commitments, agreements and decisions of the major United Nations conferences and summits organized since the beginning of the 1990s on development, as well as of the outcomes of review processes, in particular those related to the question of the external debt problem of developing countries;

34. *Requests* the Secretary-General to report to the General Assembly at its fifty-fifth session on the implementation of the present resolution and to include in his report a comprehensive and substantive analysis of the external debt and debt-servicing problems of the developing countries.

Financing for development

High-level intergovernmental event (2001). In accordance with General Assembly resolutions 52/179 [YUN 1997, p. 954] and 53/173 [YUN 1998, p. 906], the Ad Hoc Open-ended Working Group of the General Assembly on Financing for Development was established to undertake an in-depth examination of inputs received with regard to high-level intergovernmental consideration of financing for development [A/53/470, A/53/479], which had been submitted to the Assembly in 1998 [YUN 1998, pp. 905 & 906]. The Group's mandate was to make recommendations on the form, scope and agenda of a high-level international intergovernmental forum on financing for development, to be held not later than 2001, and its preparatory process.

The Working Group held four sessions in 1998 and 1999 (17 December 1998; 9-11 February 1999; 4 May 1999; 28 May 1999). It also held two informal sessions (16-19 March; 5-8 April) [A/54/28]. The Bureau of the Second Committee hosted two panels in support of the work of the Working Group (15 March and 1 April). With regard to the scope and agenda of the high-level intergovernmental event, the Working Group stated that it would address national, international and systemic issues relating to financing for development in the context of globalization and interdependence. It recommended that the items to be discussed should include: domestic financial resources; international resources: trade, foreign direct investments and other private flows; international financial cooperation for development, including ODA and debt relief; enhancing coherence and consistency of the international monetary, financial and trading systems in support of development and avoidance of financial crisis and volatility, and enhancing participation and integration of developing and transition countries in the global economic system, including through capacity-building; and the special needs of Africa, LDCs, small island developing States, landlocked developing countries and other developing countries with special difficulties in attracting financing for development. Annexed to its report was an elaboration of ideas discussed in the following areas: mobilizing domestic resources and international private financial flows for development; international financial cooperation for development; external debt; financing for development and trade; innovative sources of financing; governance of the international monetary, financial and trade systems; and the interrelationship between major elements and other special topics.

As to the form of the event, the Working Group recommended that: it should be a high-level intergovernmental meeting of political decision makers, at least at the ministerial level; it should have a comprehensive agenda that would attract the attention of diverse national departments and ministries, for example of finance, commerce, development and foreign affairs; both the event and the preparatory process should involve participation by all relevant stakeholders, involve IMF and the World Bank as active partners, and include participation by all other relevant parts of the UN system; the final event could be self-standing, linked with the Assembly, including a high-level segment of three to four days' duration; the high-level segment should be preceded by an effective and participatory preparatory stage; and both the event and preparatory process should have a high level of public and media visibility and public awareness.

The Working Group felt that, in order to prepare for the event in 2001, it would be desirable to establish a substantive preparatory process that would draw on the successful experiences of the Group itself. It should be open to all States Members, members of specialized agencies and observers and report to the Assembly at its fifty-fifth (2000) session.

GENERAL ASSEMBLY ACTION

On 22 December [meeting 87], the General Assembly, on the recommendation of the Second Committee [A/54/585/Add.1], adopted **resolution 54/196** without vote [agenda item 97 *(a)*].

High-level international intergovernmental consideration of financing for development

The General Assembly,

Recalling its resolutions 52/179 of 18 December 1997 and 53/173 of 15 December 1998,

Taking note of the report of the Ad Hoc Open-ended Working Group of the General Assembly on Financing for Development,

Taking note also of Economic and Social Council resolution 1999/51 of 29 July 1999 on the restructuring and revitalization of the United Nations in the economic, social and related fields and cooperation between the United Nations and the Bretton Woods institutions,

1. *Endorses* the report of the Ad Hoc Open-ended Working Group of the General Assembly on Financing for Development, as an important input for the continuation of the process, as it provides the framework and reference for the scope, agenda and form of the final event of the high-level international intergovernmental consideration of financing for development, as well as for the preparatory process;

2. *Decides* to convene in 2001 a high-level intergovernmental event of political decision makers, at least at the ministerial level, on financing for development, in the context of paragraph 20 of the report of the Working Group;

3. *Also decides* that the high-level intergovernmental event in 2001 will address national, international and systemic issues relating to financing for development in a holistic manner in the context of globalization and interdependence, and, by so doing, will also address development through the perspective of finance; within this overall context, the event should also address the mobilization of financial resources for the full implementation of the outcome of major conferences and summits organized by the United Nations during the 1990s and the implementation of the Agenda for Development, in particular with regard to poverty eradication;

4. *Reiterates* that, as identified in the report of the Working Group, both the preparatory process and the high-level intergovernmental event should involve the participation of all relevant stakeholders;

5. *Decides* to establish an intergovernmental Preparatory Committee, open to all States, to carry out the substantive preparations for the high-level intergovernmental event;

6. *Also decides* that the Preparatory Committee, at its resumed organizational session, based on the results of consultations to be held with all relevant stakeholders in a flexible manner, should consider innovative ways and mechanisms to facilitate the active involvement of all relevant stakeholders in both the preparatory process and the high-level intergovernmental event;

7. *Requests* the Secretary-General, in consultation with Member States and in the context of paragraphs 20 and 21 of the report of the Working Group and paragraphs 17 and 18 of Economic and Social Council resolution 1999/51, to initiate as soon as possible preliminary consultations with all relevant stakeholders, in particular the World Bank, the International Monetary Fund and the World Trade Organization, on the potential modalities for their participation in both the substantive preparatory process and the high-level intergovernmental event, and also requests the Secretary-General to provide the results of those consultations to the Preparatory Committee for consideration at the first part of its organizational session;

8. *Decides* to constitute a Bureau of the Preparatory Committee, which will consist of fifteen representatives of Member States to the United Nations selected according to the principle of equitable geographical representation and will be presided over by two co-chairmen;

9. *Also decides* that the first organizational session of the Preparatory Committee should be held as soon as possible and no later than the end of January 2000 to elect the Bureau, and in this regard requests the President of the General Assembly to begin consultations with Member States as soon as possible;

10. *Requests* the Bureau, inter alia, in the context of paragraphs 20 and 21 of the report of the Working Group and paragraphs 17 and 18 of Economic and Social Council resolution 1999/51 and with the further assistance of the Secretary-General, to continue consultations with all relevant stakeholders on the modalities for their participation, including the possibility of creating a joint task force, in both the substantive preparatory process and the high-level intergovernmental event, and also requests the Bureau to submit proposals to the Preparatory Committee at its resumed organizational session on the modalities of participation of all relevant stakeholders;

11. *Decides* that the resumed organizational session of the Preparatory Committee should be held as soon as possible and no later than March 2000, and, on the basis of the report of the Working Group and the proposals on modalities to be submitted by the Bureau, and taking into account the outcome of the consultations of the Secretary-General, will consider the following questions:

(*a*) The form of the final event, including a possible summit, international conference, special session of the General Assembly or other high-level international intergovernmental forum on financing for development;

(*b*) The venue of the final event;

(*c*) The timing, duration and format of the final event;

(*d*) Clarification of the agenda;

(*e*) Modalities for the participation of institutional stakeholders in both the preparatory process and the high-level intergovernmental event, notably:

(i) The World Bank, the International Monetary Fund and the World Trade Organization, including, in the last case, participation at the secretariat level and by member and observer States;

(ii) The United Nations Conference on Trade and Development and the regional commissions;

(*f*) Modalities for the participation of other stakeholders, notably non-governmental organizations and the private sector, in both the preparatory process and the high-level intergovernmental event;

(*g*) The programme of work of the Preparatory Committee;

12. *Also decides* that the first substantive session of the Preparatory Committee should be held in May 2000;

13. *Invites* Member States to consider sending experts to participate in the preparatory process, and encourages bilateral and multilateral donors to facilitate the participation of developing countries in both the preparatory process and the high-level intergovernmental event;

14. *Calls upon* the relevant entities of the United Nations system, including the United Nations Conference on Trade and Development and the regional commissions, as well as the regional development banks

and all other relevant stakeholders, to provide inputs for consideration during the preparatory process;

15. *Requests* the relevant entities of the United Nations system, in accordance with their respective mandates, to take into account the schedule of the Preparatory Committee and meetings of the regional commissions in assisting countries, in particular developing countries and countries with economies in transition, in preparing for the discussion on financing for development;

16. *Requests* the United Nations Conference on Trade and Development to take into account the schedule of the Preparatory Committee and meetings of the regional commissions in assisting developing countries and countries with economies in transition in preparing for the discussion on financing for development;

17. *Requests* the Secretary-General, in close consultation with all Member States, to provide the Preparatory Committee and the high-level intergovernmental event with a secretariat commensurate with the level of the event and adequate staff and other resources, further invites the Secretary-General in this context to explore, in consultation with all relevant institutional stakeholders, the possibility of utilizing, in that secretariat, staff from among the stakeholders, as appropriate, and also requests the Secretary-General to make proposals in this regard to the Preparatory Committee at its resumed organizational session in accordance with the rules and procedures of the United Nations;

18. *Also requests* the Secretary-General to report to the General Assembly at its fifty-fifth session on the implementation of the present resolution and on the overall work undertaken with regard to the high-level international intergovernmental consideration of financing for development;

19. *Decides* to include in the provisional agenda of its fifty-fifth session the item entitled "High-level international intergovernmental consideration of financing for development".

Investment, technology and related financial issues

The UNCTAD Commission on Investment, Technology and Related Financial Issues held its fourth session in Geneva from 4 to 8 October [TD/B/46/12]. For its consideration of FDI trends, it had before it an UNCTAD secretariat report on recent trends and ways and means of enhancing FDI flows to and among developing countries, in particular LDCs and countries receiving relatively low FDI inflows, with a view to increasing the benefits they entailed, and taking into account the factors that played a part in private sector firms' choices of investment location [TD/B/COM.2/21]. In addition to presenting an overview of trends in FDI flows, with particular emphasis on LDCs, the report contained an overview of the differences and complementarities between FDI and foreign portfolio investment flows, and an analysis of FDI determinants. It stated that in 1998 global FDI inflows increased by 39 per cent over 1997, a growth fuelled by a 70 per cent increase in flows to developed countries, which more than offset the decline of 4 per cent in flows to developing countries, with Asia and Latin America receiving $85 billion and $72 billion, respectively, and Africa $8 billion. Total 1998 FDI inflows into LDCs increased by 13.5 per cent, totalling $2.4 billion; Central and Eastern Europe received $18 billion.

The Commission also had before it the reports of two expert meetings, one on international investment agreements (IIAs): concepts allowing for a certain flexibility in the interest of promotion growth and development (Geneva, 24-26 March) [TD/B/COM.2/17], and the other on portfolio investment flows and FDI (Geneva, 28-30 June) [TD/B/COM.2/20]. The Commission also considered the *World Investment Report 1999* [Sales No. E.99.II.D.3], which focused on FDI and the challenge of development.

For its consideration of investment policy and science, technology and innovation policy reviews: methodology and experiences, the Commission discussed an UNCTAD report on the subject [TD/B/COM.2/23], which introduced the UNCTAD secretariat investment policy reviews undertaken in Egypt, Peru, Uganda and Uzbekistan and science, technology and innovation policy reviews undertaken for Colombia and Jamaica. It complemented the individual country reviews by drawing common policy implications with respect to determinants of FDI, privatization, policy coherence, economic linkages, inter-firm collaboration, infrastructure and support institutions.

In agreed conclusions, the Commission recognized the contribution that FDI could make to development, the work undertaken in the area of capacity-building in developing countries to enable them to attract FDI to their economies, and the importance of the development dimension in IIAs. It agreed that adequate policies and institutions were important to attracting investment flows. Recognizing the importance of country examinations as a novel form of intergovernmental discussions at UNCTAD for understanding the diversity of development experiences and contributing to the deliberations and the dissemination of best practices in investment policy and in science, technology and innovation policy, the Commission commended the work carried out by the UNCTAD secretariat on the policy reviews; expressed appreciation to the countries that participated in the round of reviews, to the senior officials from capitals who shared valuable experience with other Governments, and to the international private sector; encouraged follow-up on the findings of the policy reviews and assistance to countries seeking to implement the recommendations contained in the reviews; and invited donor countries and institutions to support the preparation of the policy reviews.

The Commission endorsed the report of the Intergovernmental Group of Experts on Competition Law and Policy and took note of the report of the Intergovernmental Working Group of Experts on International Standards of Accounting and Reporting (see below). It also considered the progress report on the implementation of its agreed conclusions and recommendations [TD/B/COM.2/22], prepared in accordance with a 1998 TDB decision on guidelines on the efficiency and functioning of the UNCTAD intergovernmental machinery [YUN 1998, p. 913].

At its twenty-second executive session in October [A/54/15/Rev.1], TDB took note of the Commission's report and endorsed its agreed conclusions. It also reviewed the functioning of the Commission's subsidiary bodies, the Working Groups of Experts on Competition Law and Policy and on International Standards of Accounting and Reporting, and decided to extend the mandate of the informal consultations with a view to receiving a report on the outcome of the consultations at its forty-sixth session. At its forty-sixth session (18-29 October) [ibid.], TDB agreed that the status of the two Groups of Experts should remain unchanged; that greater participation of all member States of UNCTAD in the work of both Groups should be encouraged; and that their work programmes should be brought under the auspices of the competent Commission.

Competition law and policy

The Intergovernmental Group of Experts on Competition Law and Policy held its second session in Geneva from 7 to 9 June [TD/B/COM.2/19]. It considered the consultations on competition law and policy, including the model law and studies related to the provisions of the set of principles and rules; and the work programme, including technical assistance, advisory and training programmes and preparations for the fourth United Nations conference to review all aspects of the set of principles and rules.

In agreed conclusions, the Group of Experts, reaffirming the fundamental role of competition law and policy for sound economic development and stressing the importance of the creation of a competition culture, recommended that UNCTAD X, to be held in 2000, take into account the work carried out within the UNCTAD intergovernmental machinery on competition law and policy issues. It recognized the need for strengthened international cooperation in the area of competition law and policy and invited UNCTAD to continue cooperation with WTO and other organizations working in that area. The Group recommended that the Fourth Review Conference to Review All Aspects of the Set of Multilaterally Agreed Equitable Principles and Rules for the Control of Restrictive Business Practices (known as the Set), to be held in 2000, consider the following issues related to the better implementation of the Set: experience gained with the establishment of competition laws and competition authorities and enforcement of the law and competition advocacy in developing countries, countries with economies in transition, and relevant regional organizations; organization and powers of competition authorities; treatment of confidential information in competition law and policy; the role of competition policy in economic development; competition policy issues in telecommunications; and competition policy and its implications for regulatory and legislative reforms. It requested the UNCTAD secretariat to prepare for consideration by the Fourth Review Conference a revised report on experiences gained with international cooperation on competition policy issues and the mechanisms used; an updated review of technical assistance; a report on how competition policy addressed the exercise of intellectual property rights; and an updated version of the model law, taking into account recent trends in competition legislation and its enforcement.

International standards of accounting and reporting

The Intergovernmental Working Group of Experts on International Standards of Accounting and Reporting (ISAR) held its sixteenth session in Geneva from 17 to 19 February [TD/B/COM.2/16].

In recommendations to Governments and related organizations regarding the requirements for the qualification of professional accountants, ISAR reaffirmed the fundamental need to harmonize national requirements and adopted a guideline for national systems in that regard. The guideline contained recommendations concerning general education; professional education other than education for professional knowledge; the model curriculum for education for professional knowledge; assessment of professional competence (examinations); practical experience; a programme of continuing education; and adherence to a code of professional ethics.

Taxation

In accordance with Economic and Social Council decision 1998/218 [YUN 1998, p. 908], the ninth meeting of the Ad Hoc Group of Experts on International Cooperation in Tax Matters was held in New York from 3 to 7 May 1999 [E/1999/84 & Corr.1]. The Group of Experts' focus group on revising and updating the United Nations Model Double Taxation Convention between Developed and Developing Countries [YUN 1980, p. 531] met in New York in December 1998 and Amsterdam, Netherlands, in March 1999.

The Group of Experts discussed exchange of information; transfer pricing; revision and updating of the United Nations Model Convention; and technical training. It adopted in principle the United Nations Model Double Taxation Convention between Developed and Developing Countries (revised version), subject to editorial changes to be recommended by the Group via correspondence, and decided to keep it under a biennial revision process.

By **decision 1999/225** of 26 July, the Economic and Social Council deferred consideration of the recommendations contained in the report of the Secretary-General on the ninth meeting of the Ad Hoc Group of Experts on International Cooperation in Tax Matters [E/1999/84 & Corr.1].

Transport

Maritime transport

The *Review of Maritime Transport 1999* [Sales No. E.99.II.D.21] stated that world seaborne trade recorded its thirteenth consecutive annual increase in 1998, reaching a record high of 5.064 billion tons. The annual growth rate, however, turned downwards, registering 2.2 per cent, which was the lowest since 1987. That relatively lower rate of growth was expected to continue in 1999, owing to the downward trade in the dry bulk cargo sector. World maritime activities measured in ton-miles in global trade decreased by 1.1 per cent to 21,425 billion ton-miles in 1998, compared to 21,672 billion ton-miles in the previous year.

The world merchant fleet expanded to 788.7 million deadweight tons (dwt) at the end of 1998, representing a 1.6 per cent increase over 1997. The slower rate of expansion was attributable primarily to new-building deliveries of 35.5 million dwt, while tonnage broken up and lost was registered at 23.5 million dwt, leaving a net gain of 12 million dwt. The developing countries' share of tonnage registered in major open-registry countries increased slowly, reaching nearly one third in 1998. On the other hand, the developed market-economy countries' share was on a downward trend, representing two thirds of the total tonnage registered in the major open-registry countries.

Arrest of ships

In accordance with General Assembly resolution 52/182 [YUN 1997, p. 935], the United Nations/International Maritime Organization Diplomatic Conference on Arrest of Ships was convened in Geneva from 1 to 12 March [A/CONF.188/5]. The Conference adopted its Final Act and established the text of the International Convention on Arrest of Ships, 1999 [A/CONF.188/6], a legal instrument establishing international uniformity in the field of arrest of ships, which took account of developments in related fields. The Convention gave definitions of the terms used therein and contained articles on: powers and exercise of right of arrest; release from arrest and right of rearrest and multiple arrest; protection of owners and demise charterers from arrested ships; jurisdiction on the merits of the case; application; non-creation of maritime liens; reservations; the depositary (Secretary-General of the United Nations); signature, ratification, acceptance, approval and accession; States with more than one system of law; entry into force; revision and amendment; denunciation; and languages.

The Convention was opened for signature in New York on 1 September. It was to remain open until 31 August 2000.

Transport of dangerous goods

In response to Economic and Social Council resolution 1997/3 [YUN 1997, p. 957], the Secretary-General submitted an April report on the work during 1997-1998 of the Committee of Experts on the Transport of Dangerous Goods [E/1999/43]. The Committee finalized step 2 in the reformatting of the *Recommendations on the Transport of Dangerous Goods* into model regulations; developed detailed packing instructions for the transport of individual substances and articles on the list of dangerous goods most commonly carried and guidelines for the assignment of portable tank requirements; and adopted new provisions for inclusion in the model regulations and amendments to the existing provisions. In order to give effective follow-up to chapter 19, on environmentally sound management of toxic chemicals, of Agenda 21, adopted by the United Nations Conference on Environment and Development in 1992 [YUN 1992, p. 672], the Committee continued to cooperate with other organizations concerned with the development of a globally harmonized system for the classification and labelling of chemicals, in particular the International Labour Office and OECD, and almost finalized its work in the area of physical hazards. On the basis of a proposal made by the Inter-Organization Programme for the Sound Management of Chemicals Coordinating Group for the Harmonization of Chemical Classification Systems, the Committee considered possible future arrangements for the implementation of the globally harmonized classification system and agreed that its reconfiguration into a Committee of Experts on the Transport of Dangerous Goods and on the Globally Harmonized System of Classification and Labelling of Chemicals, with two subcommittees, would be an appropriate solution. With respect to future policy regarding the cycle of amendments to the *Recommendations*, it considered that no firm decision could be taken on the model regulations during the period of alignment of the various international instruments dealing with the transport of dangerous goods and pending the implementation of the globally harmonized system for the classification and labelling of chemicals in accordance with Agenda 21 objectives. The Committee adopted a programme of work for the 1999-2000 biennium, with an item on the future evolution of the model regulations, including the rationalized development of the regulations and the periodicity of amendments thereto.

In 1999, the Committee's Subcommittee of Experts on the Transport of Dangerous Goods held its sixteenth (Geneva, 5-14 July) [ST/SG/AC.10/C.3/32 & Add.1,2] and seventeenth (Geneva, 6-15 December) [ST/SG/AC.10/C.3/34 & Add.1,2] sessions, while the Committee itself was scheduled to meet again in 2000.

ECONOMIC AND SOCIAL COUNCIL ACTION

On 30 July [meeting 46], the Economic and Social Council, on the recommendation of the Committee of Experts on the Transport of Dangerous Goods [E/1999/43], adopted **resolution 1999/62** without vote [agenda item 13 *(g)*].

Work of the Committee of Experts on the Transport of Dangerous Goods

The Economic and Social Council,

Recalling its resolutions 1995/6 of 19 July 1995 and 1997/3 of 18 July 1997,

Bearing in mind the increasing volume of dangerous goods in worldwide commerce and the rapid expansion of technology and innovation,

Bearing in mind also the continuing need to meet the growing concern for the protection of life, property and the environment through the safe transport of dangerous goods, while facilitating trade,

Aware that, in order to achieve internationally harmonized laws, the Economic Commission for Europe, the International Civil Aviation Organization, the International Maritime Organization and other specialized agencies and international organizations involved in activities related to the transport of dangerous goods and interested Member States have responded positively to the various resolutions adopted by the Council since 15 April 1953, and that, being committed to taking the recommendations of the Committee of Experts on the Transport of Dangerous Goods as a basis for the formulation of their requirements and regulations, including those concerning labelling and classification, those organizations therefore rely on the work of the Committee,

A. Work of the Committee of Experts during the biennium 1997-1998

1. *Takes note* of the report of the Secretary-General on the work of the Committee of Experts on the Transport of Dangerous Goods during the biennium 1997-1998, in particular regarding:

(a) The adoption of new and amended provisions for inclusion in the *Recommendations on the Transport of Dangerous Goods;*

(b) The completion of the second step in the reformatting of the existing *Recommendations* into model regulations annexed to a basic recommendation, in particular:

(i) The revision of provisions for the transport of dangerous goods in multimodal portable tanks;

(ii) The inclusion of detailed packing instructions for transport in packagings, including intermediate bulk containers and large packagings;

(iii) The inclusion, in cooperation with the International Atomic Energy Agency, of detailed provisions for the transport of radioactive material;

(c) The completion, pursuant to resolution 1995/6, of proposals for criteria for the classification of flammable, explosive and reactive materials, except for flammable aerosols, globally harmonized for various regulatory purposes, in cooperation with the International Labour Organization in the context of the implementation of chapter 19 of Agenda 21;

2. *Commends* the Secretary-General for the publication of the tenth revised edition of the *Recommendations on the Transport of Dangerous Goods* in all the official languages of the United Nations and for the publication of the second revised edition of the *Manual of Tests and Criteria* in Arabic and Chinese;

3. *Requests* the Secretary-General:

(a) To circulate the new and amended recommendations to the Governments of Member States, the specialized agencies, the International Atomic Energy Agency and other international organizations concerned;

(b) To publish an eleventh revised version of the *Recommendations on the Transport of Dangerous Goods*, as amended, and a third revised edition of the *Manual of Tests and Criteria*, in all the official languages of the United Nations, in the most cost-effective manner, no later than the end of 1999;

(c) To envisage means of publishing the *Recommendations* on CD-ROM, if possible as a navigable version, for example, by commercial arrangement with external contractors;

4. *Invites* all Governments, the specialized agencies, the International Atomic Energy Agency and the other international organizations concerned to transmit to the Secretary-General their views on the work of the

Committee, together with any comments that they may wish to make on the amended recommendations;

5. *Invites* all interested Governments, regional commissions and specialized agencies and the international organizations concerned, when developing or updating appropriate codes and regulations, to take full account of the recommendations of the Committee, in particular those referred to in paragraph 1 *(b)* above, including as regards the structure and format of such codes and regulations;

B. Programme of work for the biennium 1999-2000

6. *Approves* the programme of work of the Committee and its Subcommittee of Experts on the Transport of Dangerous Goods for the biennium 1999-2000, as follows:

(a) Development of provisions for the transport of gases in gas cylinders and multiple-element gas containers;

(b) Review of provisions concerning documentation on the transport of dangerous goods;

(c) Follow-up to chapter 19 of Agenda 21 as regards harmonization of classification and labelling of chemicals, including development of criteria for the classification of flammable aerosols, in cooperation with the International Labour Organization, and implementation of already agreed criteria through the model regulations on the transport of dangerous goods;

(d) Miscellaneous amendments to the model regulations (listing and classification, explosives, lithium batteries, limited quantities, packaging issues, portable tank issues, consignment procedures, segregation) and to the *Manual of Tests and Criteria;*

(e) Development of new provisions for the transport of solid substances in bulk in tanks and freight containers;

(f) Evolution of the model regulations (rationalized development of the model regulations and periodicity of amendments);

C. Periodicity of amendments to the *Recommendations on the Transport of Dangerous Goods*

7. *Takes note* of the advice of the Committee that:

(a) No firm decision as regards a possible future four-year periodicity of amendments should be taken during the period of alignment of the format of the various legal instruments concerning modal aspects of the transport of dangerous goods on that of the model regulations, and pending decisions regarding the implementation of the globally harmonized system of classification and labelling of chemicals in accordance with the objectives of Agenda 21;

(b) A new revised version of the *Recommendations on the Transport of Dangerous Goods* should be published in 2001 after the session of the Committee in 2000;

8. *Notes with satisfaction* that this issue has been included in the programme of work of the Committee for the next biennium, for discussion, together with the question of the evolution of the model regulations in the long term;

D. Report to the Council

9. *Requests* the Secretary-General to submit a report to the Council in 2001 on the implementation of the present resolution.

Committee membership

By a February note [E/1999/5], the Secretary-General informed the Economic and Social Council that he had received an application from the Czech Republic for full membership in the Committee of Experts on the Transport of Dangerous Goods. He approved the application and requested the Council's endorsement.

By **decision 1999/217** of 6 May, the Council endorsed the Secretary-General's approval of the application of the Czech Republic for full membership in the Committee.

Reconfiguration of Committee of Experts

By a June note [E/1999/90], the Secretary-General brought to the Economic and Social Council's attention a 12 January letter from the President of the Intergovernmental Forum on Chemical Safety on the reconfiguration of the Committee of Experts on the Transport of Dangerous Goods. The reconfiguration had been discussed in the Committee of Experts (see p. 905), which had recommended to the Council a draft resolution on the matter.

ECONOMIC AND SOCIAL COUNCIL ACTION

By **decision 1999/286** of 30 July, the Economic and Social Council took note of the June note by the Secretary-General on the reconfiguration of the Committee of Experts. On the same date, the Council, by **decision 1999/289**, deferred to a subsequent session consideration of the draft resolution on the reconfiguration of the Committee of Experts contained in the report of the Secretary-General on the work of the Committee of Experts [E/1999/43].

On 26 October [meeting 48], the Council, on the recommendation of the Committee of Experts on the Transport of Dangerous Goods [E/1999/43], adopted **resolution 1999/65** without vote [agenda item 13 *(g)*].

Reconfiguration of the Committee of Experts on the Transport of Dangerous Goods into a Committee of Experts on the Transport of Dangerous Goods and on the Globally Harmonized System of Classification and Labelling of Chemicals

The Economic and Social Council,

Recalling its resolution 1995/6 of 19 July 1995 on the role of the Committee of Experts on the Transport of Dangerous Goods in the development of a harmonized system of classification and labelling of chemicals for implementing the recommendations of the United Nations Conference on Environment and Development contained in chapter 19 of Agenda 21,

Recalling also section B of its resolution 1997/3 of 18 July 1997 whereby global harmonization of systems of classification and labelling of chemicals, inter alia, was given priority in the work programme of the Committee for the biennium 1997-1998,

Noting with satisfaction that the Committee, in cooperation with the International Labour Organization, has completed the elaboration of proposals for classification criteria for physical hazards, except for the flammability of aerosols, on which work will continue into the next biennium,

Aware that the Organisation for Economic Cooperation and Development, as focal point for health hazards and hazards to the environment, has also completed most of its tasks with respect to the classification criteria and has established a working group for criteria on mixtures, and that the International Labour Organization has established a working group for harmonization of chemical hazard communication systems,

Aware also that the Committee, the International Labour Organization and the Organisation for Economic Cooperation and Development, as focal points designated by the Coordinating Group for the Harmonization of Chemical Classification Systems of the Inter-Organization Programme for the Sound Management of Chemicals, are expected to make available, through their cooperative efforts, by the year 2000, a globally harmonized hazard classification and compatible labelling system, including material safety data sheets and easily understandable symbols, in accordance with the objectives of paragraph 19.27 of chapter 19 of Agenda 21,

Noting that the Coordinating Group has prepared proposals for the implementation of the globally harmonized system, consisting in reconfiguring the present Committee and extending its mandate to cover not only transport of dangerous goods but also implementation and updating of the globally harmonized system,

Noting also that those proposals were endorsed by the Inter-sessional Group of the Intergovernmental Forum on Chemical Safety at its third meeting, held at Yokohama, Japan, from 1 to 4 December 1998, at which it requested that the Coordinating Group develop draft terms of reference, in cooperation with the Committee,

Noting further that the Committee agreed to the proposals of the Coordinating Group, subject to certain conditions, and that draft terms of reference have been developed, accordingly, by the Group,

Recognizing that reconfiguring the Committee in accordance with those proposals would be the most cost-effective and efficient option for the implementation of the globally harmonized system, ensuring at the same time cooperation between various authorities and organizations concerned with the sound management of chemicals, harmonization between various regulatory systems and facilitation of trade,

1. *Decides* to reconfigure, as from 2001, the Committee of Experts on the Transport of Dangerous Goods and its Subcommittee into a Committee of Experts on the Transport of Dangerous Goods and on the Globally Harmonized System of Classification and Labelling of Chemicals, with one Subcommittee of Experts on the Transport of Dangerous Goods and a second Subcommittee of Experts on the Globally Harmonized System of Classification and Labelling of Chemicals, with terms of reference and arrangements as described in the annex to the present resolution, and provided that the total meeting time does not exceed that currently allocated to the work of the Committee in a biennium;

2. *Invites* the reconfigured Committee and the Subcommittee on the Globally Harmonized System to endeavour, whenever possible, to work on a consensus basis;

3. *Invites* Member States interested in participating in the Subcommittee on the Globally Harmonized System to apply for membership at the latest by the end of 2000 so that the composition of the Subcommittee and of the reconfigured Committee may be decided at the organizational session for 2001 of the Council;

4. *Requests* the Secretary-General to provide, not later than 1 January 2001, adequate resources to the Transport Division of the Economic Commission for Europe and plan sessions of the Subcommittees and the reconfigured Committee for 2001 and 2002, as appropriate, in accordance with the arrangements outlined in the annex to the present resolution.

ANNEX

Draft terms of reference and working arrangements for the biennium 2001-2002 of the Committee of Experts on the Transport of Dangerous Goods and on the Globally Harmonized System of Classification and Labelling of Chemicals and the Subcommittee of Experts on the Transport of Dangerous Goods and the Subcommittee of Experts on the Globally Harmonized System of Classification and Labelling of Chemicals

1. Draft terms of reference

1.1 Committee of Experts on the Transport of Dangerous Goods and on the Globally Harmonized System of Classification and Labelling of Chemicals

The Committee of Experts on the Transport of Dangerous Goods and on the Globally Harmonized System of Classification and Labelling of Chemicals shall deal with strategic issues rather than technical issues. It is not envisaged that it will review, change or revisit technical recommendations of the Subcommittee of Experts on the Transport of Dangerous Goods and the Subcommittee of Experts on the Globally Harmonized System of Classification and Labelling of Chemicals. Accordingly, its main functions shall be:

(a) To approve the programmes of work for the Subcommittees in the light of available resources;

(b) To coordinate strategic and policy directions in areas of shared interests and overlap;

(c) To give formal endorsement to the recommendations of the Subcommittees and provide the mechanism for channelling them to the Economic and Social Council;

(d) To facilitate and coordinate the smooth running of the Subcommittees.

1.2 Subcommittee of Experts on the Globally Harmonized System of Classification and Labelling of Chemicals

The functions of the Subcommittee of Experts on the Globally Harmonized System of Classification and Labelling of Chemicals shall be:

(a) To act as custodian of the globally harmonized system of classification and labelling of chemicals, managing and giving direction to the harmonization process;

(b) To keep the system up to date, as necessary, considering the need to introduce changes to ensure its continued relevance and practical utility, and deter-

mining the need for and timing of the updating of technical criteria, while working with existing bodies, as appropriate;

(c) To promote understanding and use of the system and encourage feedback;

(d) To make the system available for worldwide use and application;

(e) To make guidance available on the application of the system and on the interpretation and use of technical criteria to support consistency of application;

(f) To prepare programmes of work and submit recommendations to the Committee.

1.3 Subcommittee of Experts on the Transport of Dangerous Goods

The Subcommittee of Experts on the Transport of Dangerous Goods replaces the existing Committee and its Subcommittee of Experts on the Transport of Dangerous Goods with the same terms of reference.

2. Working arrangements for the biennium 2001-2002

The total number of meeting days shall not exceed that currently allocated to the Committee and its Subcommittee of Experts on the Transport of Dangerous Goods, namely, thirty-eight, with a maximum of three days for the Committee of Experts on the Transport of Dangerous Goods and on the Globally Harmonized System of Classification and Labelling of Chemicals and ten days for the Subcommittee of Experts on the Globally Harmonized System of Classification and Labelling of Chemicals (to be arranged by the secretariat after consultation with the Committee and the Coordinating Group for the Harmonization of Chemical Classification Systems of the Inter-Organization Programme for the Sound Management of Chemicals).

UNCTAD institutional and organizational questions

UNCTAD programme

In 1999, the Trade and Development Board (TDB)—the executive body of UNCTAD—held five sessions, all in Geneva: the twentieth (5 February), twenty-first (1 July) and twenty-second (15 October) executive sessions and the forty-sixth regular session (18-29 October) [A/54/15/Rev.1], as well as the first part of the twenty-third executive session (17 December) [A/55/15 (Part I)]. In February, the Board discussed the draft provisional agenda for UNCTAD X (2000) (see p. 912); the report of the Working Party on the Medium-term Plan and the Programme Budget on its thirty-third session [TD/B/46/2]; and the outcome of the 1998 "Partners for Development" summit [YUN 1998, p. 882]. In July, it considered UNCTAD's contribution to the United Nations New Agenda for the Development of Africa in the 1990s (NADAF): UNCTAD's activities in favour of Africa (see p. 847); preparations for UNCTAD X; and the report of the Joint Advisory Group on ITC on its thirty-second session (see p. 880). In October, TDB took note of the reports of its subsidiary bodies, and of an UNCTAD report on financing and on the participation of experts in UNCTAD expert meetings (see p. 909). It discussed the preparations for the review by UNCTAD X of the lists of States annexed to General Assembly resolution 1995(XIX) [YUN 1964, p. 210], and the designation of NGOs for the purposes of rule 77 of TDB's rules of procedure. It also reviewed the functioning of the Intergovernmental Groups of Experts on International Standards of Accounting and Reporting and on Competition Law and Policy (see p. 903).

In October, the Board discussed interdependence and global economic issues from a trade and development perspective: trade, growth and external financing in developing countries; and adopted agreed conclusions on progress in the implementation of the Programme of Action for LDCs for the 1990s and the status of the preparatory process for the Third United Nations Conference on LDCs [agreed conclusions 457(XLVI)] (see p. 770); and on UNCTAD's contribution to the implementation of NADAF: African transport infrastructure, trade and competitiveness [458(XLVI)] (see p. 848). It also took action on the preparatory process for UNCTAD X: establishment of the Committee of the Whole; on technical cooperation activities; and on other trade and development issues. In December, the Board noted that the Preparatory Committee of the Whole for UNCTAD X had not completed its work. The Board would therefore reconvene in January 2000.

By **decision 54/441** of 22 December, the General Assembly took note of TDB's report on its nineteenth [YUN 1998, p. 909], twentieth, twenty-first and twenty-second executive sessions.

UNCTAD activities 1998-1999

The *Report on UNCTAD Activities 1998-1999* [UNCTAD/EDM/15], the first of its kind, provided member States and other stakeholders with a comprehensive account of the organization's activities. The report covered issues relating to: UNCTAD and UN reform; working with UN partners and other multilateral agencies; working with civil society and the private sector; development strategies; international trade; investment, technology and enterprise development; assisting LDCs and weak and vulnerable economies; helping economies in transition join the global system; services infrastructure for development and trade efficiency; and international transport.

Technical cooperation activities

In an August report [TD/B/46/3 & Add.1,2], the UNCTAD Secretary-General gave an overview of technical cooperation activities in 1998, when UNCTAD's expenditures amounted to $21.8 million, a decrease of some 7 per cent from the previous year. Of that amount, $6 million was financed by UNDP, $15.2 million was from trust fund contributions and $0.6 million was from the regular programme of technical cooperation. Funding provided by UNDP and trust funds declined in 1998, in roughly similar proportions.

By region, approximately $5.9 million went to Africa, $4.2 million to Asia and the Pacific, $3.2 million to Europe and $0.9 million to Latin America and the Caribbean. Some $7.6 million went to the interregional programme. The LDCs' share of technical cooperation expenditures in 1998 was 37.6 per cent, down from about 40 per cent in 1997.

By programme, the Division for Services Infrastructure for Development and Trade Efficiency accounted for 52.1 per cent of total expenditures; the three other divisions, on International Trade in Goods and Services, and Commodities, on Globalization and Development Strategies and on Investment, Technology and Enterprise Development, represented respectively 13.6, 14.1 and 13.4 per cent of total expenditures. The balance (6.9 per cent) was represented by the Office of the Special Coordinator for Least Developed, Landlocked and Island Developing Countries (2 per cent) and by activities reported for the secretariat as a whole (4.9 per cent).

In October [A/54/15/Rev.1], TDB took note of the overview of technical cooperation activities, of the oral report of the Chairperson of the Working Party on the Medium-term Plan and the Programme Budget (see p. 910), and of the fact that technical cooperation issues not resolved by the Working Party should be taken up by the Committee of the Whole.

As requested by the Working Party on the Medium-term Plan and the Programme Budget at its thirty-third session (see p. 910), the UNCTAD secretariat, in February, submitted the revised technical cooperation plan for 1999-2001 [TD/B/EX(20)/3]. The plan was intended to implement the UNCTAD Technical Cooperation Strategy [YUN 1997, p. 959]; inform delegations, cooperating organizations and other interested parties of the UNCTAD operational activities in 1998, of those approved for 1999 and subsequent years, and of those proposed by the secretariat for 1999-2001; facilitate discussions with potential donors on the mobilization of the necessary extrabudgetary resources to implement the plan; and serve as the secretariat's monitoring tool. On 5 February [A/54/15/Rev.1], TDB took note of the revised plan.

Participation of developing country experts in UNCTAD meetings

In response to a 1998 TDB request [YUN 1998, p. 911], the UNCTAD Secretary-General submitted a September report on the financing and participation of experts in UNCTAD expert meetings [TD/B/EX(22)/2 & Corr.1]. The report stated that the main objective of the financing was to enhance the deliberations of expert meetings by increasing the participation of developing country experts, and that $1,088,000 had been allocated for that purpose from a trust fund that was partly financed from savings resulting from improved cost-effectiveness [YUN 1998, p. 911]. In its financial summary, the report stated that, against that allocation, total expenditures amounted to $511,000. It concluded that the positive impact of the increased participation of developing country experts in UNCTAD expert meetings was confirmed by the experience under the "savings" exercise, and that the secretariat had made the utmost efforts to ensure satisfactory geographical balance; however, representation of LDCs could be improved.

TDB, in October [A/54/15/Rev.1], took note of the report and requested its President to undertake consultations on financing the participation of experts in UNCTAD meetings and on the use of the unspent balance of the funds allocated for that purpose.

Savings resulting from improved cost-effectiveness

In response to General Assembly resolution 53/3 [YUN 1998, p. 912], the Secretary-General submitted an October report on the status of implementation by UNCTAD of the activities financed from the unspent balance from the regular budget for the 1996-1997 biennium, and of the extent to which those activities and the related resources contributed to strengthening UNCTAD [A/54/501]. He also provided an analysis of savings resulting from the improved overall cost-effectiveness achieved pursuant to UNCTAD IX [YUN 1996, p. 845], as requested in Assembly resolutions 51/167 [ibid., p. 847], 52/220 [YUN 1997, p. 1421] and 53/3 [YUN 1998, p. 912]. The report indicated that expenditures of $3,988,800, out of the total authorized allocation of $5,526,600, had been incurred as at 30 September. Regarding the notional reduction of $2 million in conference-servicing requirements attributable to the restructuring of the intergovernmental machinery, it stated that changes introduced by UNCTAD IX resulted in a reduction of

526 meeting units in 1998-1999, which would amount to a reduction of $2 million for that biennium compared to 1994-1995.

ACABQ, in December [A/54/7/Add.3], stated that expenditures as at 15 November totalled $4,403,135, and that further funds would be committed between 16 November and 31 December, leaving an unspent balance of approximately $1 million in the special account set up to handle those funds. The Committee recommended that, on an exceptional basis, the special account be maintained and the unspent balance retained until all the activities and programmes outlined in the Secretary-General's May 1998 report [YUN 1998, p. 911] and approved by resolution 53/3 were completed.

By **resolution 54/251, section XIV**, of 23 December, the Assembly took note of the information provided in the report of the Secretary-General and concurred with ACABQ's recommendations.

Publications policy

In its progress report on the implementation of UNCTAD's publication policy [TD/B/WP/114] since its first such report in 1998 [YUN 1998, p. 912], the UNCTAD secretariat stated that the Publications Committee, which was charged with implementing the policy, had launched the preparatory process for the 2000-2001 programme. The draft programme had been distributed to member States in the form of a questionnaire. By making the proposed publications programme available in advance of the January 1999 session of the Working Party on the Medium-term Plan and the Programme Budget (see below), the questionnaire had facilitated the task of that body by allowing experts located in capitals to be consulted. During the preparatory process, programme managers were informed about the new UN guidelines on attribution of authorship; some progress was made in the area of electronic publishing; and the use of the Internet for dissemination of documentation was enhanced.

Medium-term plan and programme budget

The UNCTAD Working Party on the Medium-term Plan and the Programme Budget held two sessions in 1999, both in Geneva.

At its thirty-third session (25-29 January) [TD/B/46/2], the Working Party reviewed the draft programme of work for the 2000-2001 biennium [UNCTAD/ISS/Misc.200/Rev.1] and recommended that UNCTAD strengthen the capacity to provide timely global macroeconomic analysis, if necessary through redeploying resources; ensure that the financial and human resources available to the Office of the Special Coordinator for the Least Developed, Landlocked and Island Developing Countries were identical to those in the 1998-1999 programme budget, and that LDCs had priority in UNCTAD assistance; ensure that poverty alleviation and employment generation were fully taken into account; ensure that the gender dimension of development was included; and enable the Working Party to meet in resumed session to examine section 11A (on UNCTAD) of the proposed programme budget of the Secretary-General of the United Nations for the 2000-2001 biennium (see p. 1288).

The Working Party considered the implementation of UNCTAD's publications policy and encouraged the secretariat to ensure timely dissemination of the flagship reports in all official languages; devise additional methods to ensure participation and feedback from member States; and improve the use of electronic dissemination of publications. It also stressed the need for suitable pricing of sales publications in order to ensure wide dissemination, and the monitoring of sales and requests in order to assess their usefulness.

In accordance with a 1998 TDB decision [YUN 1998, p. 910], the Working Party reviewed proposals for partial cost recovery for selected UNCTAD technical cooperation programmes (ACIS, ASYUDA and DMFAS) and adopted conclusions on their financial sustainability, which, it agreed, would be based on: programme budget resources; programme support resources; extrabudgetary resources from donors; and annual maintenance fees. It also agreed that the arrangements for annual maintenance fees required further consideration prior to their introduction and, to that end, the secretariat was asked to refine the calculations on which the level of maintenance fees would be based, by undertaking, on a pilot basis, cost accounting for each programme in order to assess the actual level and composition of central costs incurred by the secretariat, including in the provision of maintenance services. The Working Party requested the UNCTAD Secretary-General to provide TDB with an evaluation of possibilities for increasing the budgetary resources allocated to those programmes, as well as information on the percentage of programme support resources to be allocated to them. It also agreed to review arrangements for annual maintenance fees three years after their introduction, and that such arrangements should not create any precedent for other technical cooperation activities. It appealed to donors that had supported the central support teams to continue and invited other potential donors to consider providing similar support.

In agreed conclusions on the in-depth evaluation of the Trade Point Programme [TD/B/WP/110 & Add.1], the Working Party invited the secretariat to prepare a strategy for its further consideration. The strategy should contain proposals on the financial and technical feasibility of the implementation of the recommendations contained in the evaluation and, in that context, the secretariat should prepare a comprehensive report detailing the activities undertaken to implement various mandates entrusted to it since the inception of the Programme. The UNCTAD Secretary-General was invited to convene a meeting of Trade Point managers and end-users on the proposals to be made by the secretariat regarding the implementation of the evaluation's recommendations, and to advise on future actions aimed at enhancing programme delivery, especially with regard to assistance to be provided to the Trade Points.

The Working Party also took note of UNCTAD's technical cooperation plan for 1999-2001 [YUN 1998, p. 910], and requested the secretariat to revise it, taking into account comments made by delegations, for transmission to TDB in February.

In February [A/54/15/Rev.1], TDB took note of the Working Party's proposals for the draft programme of work for 2000-2001 and invited the UNCTAD Secretary-General to take them into account. It also endorsed the Working Party's agreed conclusions on financial sustainability of selected technical cooperation programmes and its conclusions on the in-depth evaluation of the Trade Point Programme. In July, TDB took note of the information provided on annual maintenance fees for selected UNCTAD technical cooperation programmes, and requested the Working Party to consider the matter at its thirty-fourth session.

At its thirty-fourth session (27 September-1 October) [TD/B/46/9], the Working Party had before it a review of UNCTAD technical cooperation activities [TD/B/46/3 & Add.1,2]; an evaluation of the programme of technical cooperation activities on competition law and policy [TD/B/WP/119 & Add.1]; the follow-up to the evaluation of the Trade Point Programme: Trade Point Programme strategy [TD/B/WP/120 & Add.1]; a report on activities undertaken to implement various mandates for the Trade Point Programme since its inception [TD/B/WP/121 & Corr.1]; and information on follow-up action pursuant to the recommendations in the evaluation and implementation of the agreed conclusions of its thirty-third session [TD/B/WP/122]. With regard to the evaluation of the programme of technical cooperation activities on competition law and policy, the Working Party requested the secretariat to implement the recommendations contained therein, taking into consideration the comments made by the Working Party. Regarding the follow-up to the evaluation of the Trade Point Programme, it invited the secretariat to explore options for a suitable non-profit organization to manage the Electronic Trade Opportunity system, and to implement the Trade Point Programme strategy in close cooperation with ITC, taking into consideration the comments made by the Working Party; it also agreed that the implementation of the strategy would be reviewed annually within UNCTAD's intergovernmental machinery.

OIOS investigation

In response to General Assembly resolution 48/218 B [YUN 1994, p. 1362], the Secretary-General submitted a September report by the Office of Internal Oversight Services (OIOS) on its investigation into allegations concerning an electronic commerce project at UNCTAD [A/54/413]. OIOS had received reports of illegal exportation and improper retention of intellectual property by a Melbourne (Australia)-based project of UNCTAD responsible for Trade Points and related electronic commerce initiatives, known as the United Nations Trade Point Development Centre (UNTPDC). Investigators uncovered serious problems with the project, including unauthorized solicitation of funds and resources; the entering of unauthorized commercial agreements with private sector interests; private sector interests engaged in unauthorized activities for the UN-sponsored project; a failure of supervision of the project; and its expansion into commercial agreements and electronic transactions without notification of or authorization by UNCTAD senior management.

The investigation concluded that, while the aim of involving the private sector in the UNTPDC project to assist in the development of secured electronic commercial transactions for developing countries was a sound concept, it had been sabotaged by the utilization of unauthorized foundations and the involvement of non-UN staff.

It was recommended that UNCTAD management evaluate the goals and status of UNTPDC and set forth clear goals and responsibilities, and that the United Nations decide how it would interact with the private sector, mindful of competing interests.

The Secretary-General took note of the findings and concurred with the recommendations, also noting that measures were already being initiated to correct the issues addressed.

Preparations for UNCTAD X

In February [A/54/15/Rev.1], TDB approved the substantive agenda item, and the annotation to it, for UNCTAD X, to be held in Bangkok, Thailand, in February 2000: "Developmental strategies in an increasingly interdependent world: applying the lessons of the past to make globalization an effective instrument for the development of all countries and all people". It requested the UNCTAD Secretary-General to complete the draft provisional agenda for UNCTAD X with the normal procedural items and issue it to all delegations. In a May note [TD/379] containing the provisional agenda and annotations, the UNCTAD secretariat stated that UNCTAD X should provide member States with an opportunity to review the major international economic initiatives and developments, particularly those that had taken place since UNCTAD IX [YUN 1996, p. 844]. UNCTAD should consider the strategies and policies that were most likely to ensure the successful integration of all countries, particularly the developing countries, into the world economy on an equitable basis and to avoid the risk of further marginalization.

At its twenty-second executive session in October [A/54/15/Rev.1], TDB, discussing the preparations for the review by UNCTAD X of the lists of States annexed to General Assembly resolution 1995(XIX) [YUN 1964, p. 210], noted that nine UNCTAD member States had not yet applied for inclusion in any of those lists. It further noted that Kiribati, Nauru and Tonga had been admitted to UN membership and therefore automatically became UNCTAD members. At its forty-sixth session, also in October, TDB established an open-ended Committee of the Whole to elaborate the substantive pre-Conference text for transmittal to UNCTAD X and to consider other relevant matters necessary as part of the preparatory process. It took note of the fact that the Committee had set a timetable of work with a view to reporting to the Board in December. In December, TDB was informed that the Preparatory Committee of the Whole had not been able to complete its work on the pre-Conference text for UNCTAD X.

The Ninth Ministerial Meeting of the Group of 77 developing countries and China convened in Marrakesh, Morocco, from 13 to 16 September [A/54/392] in preparation for UNCTAD X, and adopted the Marrakesh Declaration. In October, the UNCTAD secretariat transmitted to TDB the Plan of Action [TD(X)/PC/4] and the draft Bangkok Consensus [TD(X)/PC/5], as reviewed by the Preparatory Committee of the Group of 77 in the light of the Marrakesh ministerial decision, to be transmitted to the Preparatory Committee of the Whole for consideration as the basis for the pre-Conference text of UNCTAD X. The secretariat also circulated the guidelines for the participation of the EU in UNCTAD X [TD(X)/PC/6], which outlined the basic position to be followed by the EU at the Conference.

Among meetings held in preparation for UNCTAD X during 1999 were: the Pre-UNCTAD X Seminar on the Role of Competition Policy for Development in Globalizing World Markets (Geneva, 14-15 June) [TD(X)/PC/1]; the Pre-UNCTAD X Workshop on Exchange of Experiences among Enterprises in the Area of Electronic Commerce (Geneva, 17-18 June) [TD(X)/PC/3]; the Pre-UNCTAD X Expert Workshop on Trade, Sustainable Development and Gender (Geneva, 12-13 July) [TD(X)/PC/2]; and the Pre-UNCTAD X Seminar on Making FDI Work for Sustainable Development (Geneva, 15 November) [TD(X)/PC/7].

UNCTAD Secretary-General

By **decision 53/321** of 18 February, the General Assembly, on the proposal of the Secretary-General [A/53/799], confirmed the extension of the appointment of Rubens Ricupero as Secretary-General of UNCTAD for another term of office of four years, beginning on 15 September 1999 and expiring on 14 September 2003.

Chapter V

Regional, economic and social activities

In 1999, the five UN regional commissions continued efforts to promote the economic and social development of the countries in their areas. Four of them met for regular sessions during the year at their headquarters: the Economic Commission for Africa (ECA) (Addis Ababa, Ethiopia); the Economic and Social Commission for Asia and the Pacific (ESCAP) (Bangkok, Thailand); the Economic Commission for Europe (ECE) (Geneva); and the Economic and Social Commission for Western Asia (ESCWA) (Beirut, Lebanon). The Economic Commission for Latin America and the Caribbean (ECLAC), located in Santiago, Chile, did not meet in 1999, having held its most recent session in 1998. In observance of its twenty-fifth anniversary, ESCWA adopted the Beirut Declaration as a new vision of the Commission's role and tasks, which was endorsed by the Economic and Social Council in July.

Each regional commission held hearings in preparation for the Millennium Assembly and Summit in 2000 and made proposals for strengthening the United Nations and ensuring its continued relevance in the twenty-first century.

The Council endorsed ECA's programme of work for 2000-2001 and adopted agreed conclusions on the coordinated follow-up by the UN system of initiatives on African development. It urged the UN system, among others, to participate in the International Partnership against AIDS in Africa to achieve its goals and objectives.

The Council also endorsed the changes to ESCWA's 1998-1999 programme of work and the action taken for the transfer of its permanent headquarters to Beirut.

Regional cooperation

Efforts continued in 1999 to strengthen the regional commissions within the context of the restructuring of the United Nations in the economic, social and related fields and as part of the programme of reform. On 2 February (**decision 1999/203**), the Economic and Social Council decided to consider at its substantive session, under the item entitled "Regional cooperation", the question of "Economic and social issues arising out of the Asian economic crisis: regional perspective".

Meeting of executive secretaries. The executive secretaries of the regional commissions, meeting in New York on 14 January and in Beirut, Lebanon, on 29 May, reviewed development issues as they related to their respective regions and that warranted cooperation among the commissions and with other bodies and programmes. They took stock of progress achieved and measures taken at the secretariat level to coordinate the work of the regional commissions with that of other parts of the Organization. The executive secretaries noted that their representation at the United Nations Development Group (UNDG) facilitated the active involvement of the commissions in the common country assessment and United Nations Development Assistance Framework process (see PART THREE, Chapter II). As to the regional commissions' relations with the United Nations Development Programme (UNDP), the executive secretaries believed that although UNDP's role as a funder had been de-emphasized, new opportunities should be sought for a closer working relationship and cooperation on establishing regional and subregional priorities, joint initiatives on core issues at the regional level, jointly undertaking flagship projects, and interregional projects involving UNDP and two or more regional commissions with UNDP funding.

The executive secretaries suggested that the Economic and Social Council might further consider ways to improve interaction with the intergovernmental bodies of the regional commissions. They suggested the participation of chairpersons or members of the bureaux of the regional commissions at Council sessions whenever the commissions' agendas were relevant to its deliberations, and the participation of executive secretaries at the Council's organizational sessions.

On 21 July, the Council held a dialogue with the executive secretaries of the regional commissions.

Review and reform of the regional commissions

Reports of Secretary-General. In a June report [E/1999/14], the Secretary-General updated the Economic and Social Council on action taken by the regional commissions with respect to the guidance given for improving the commissions' contributions to and relevance in the UN reform process as contained in Council resolution 1998/46 [YUN 1998, p. 1262]. The report discussed the role of the regional commissions as UN outposts and as the regional expression of the United Nations, as well as measures undertaken by them to consolidate reform and achieve greater effectiveness and efficiency. It also examined trends and activities, interregional cooperation and the report of the executive secretaries (see p. 913).

In an addendum to his report [E/1999/14/Add.1], the Secretary-General reviewed cooperation between the regional commissions and other regional bodies in their respective regions. A second addendum [E/1999/14/Add.2] provided information on the work of the regional commissions in normative and operational activities and follow-up activities to global conferences. A third addendum [E/1999/14/Add.3] contained resolutions and decisions adopted at recent sessions of the regional commissions calling for action by the Council.

Communication. On 17 May [A/54/97-E/1999/52], Armenia transmitted the Yerevan Declaration on Decentralization, adopted at the international conference on the theme "Decentralization in Eastern and Central Europe and the Commonwealth of Independent States (CIS): conditions of success" (Yerevan, Armenia, 26-28 April).

ECONOMIC AND SOCIAL COUNCIL ACTION

By decision **1999/273** of 28 July, the Economic and Social Council took note of the Secretary-General's reports on regional cooperation (see above) and the summaries of the survey of the economic and social situation in Africa, 1998 [E/1999/16]; the economic survey of Europe, 1998 [E/1999/15]; the economic survey of Latin America and the Caribbean, 1998 [E/1999/18]; the economic and social survey of Asia and the Pacific, 1999 [E/1999/17]; the survey of economic and social developments in the ESCWA region, 1998-1999 [E/1999/19]; and the Secretary-General's note on the project for a Europe-Africa permanent link through the Strait of Gibraltar [E/1999/20].

The Council also adopted resolutions on the programme of work and priorities of ECA for the 2000-2001 biennium (1999/39); change of name of Macau to Macau, China, in the terms of reference of ESCAP (1999/38); frequency of sessions of the sectoral committees of ESCWA (1999/41); redesignation of ESCWA's Technical Committee (1999/42); changes in ESCWA's programme of work and priorities for the 1998-1999 biennium (1999/43); ESCWA's relocation to its permanent headquarters in Beruit (1999/44); and the Beirut Declaration on Western Asia preparing for the twenty-first century (1999/45). (The summaries of the surveys and the resolutions are covered in the relevant sections of this chapter.)

Africa

The Economic Commission for Africa (ECA) held its thirty-third session/twenty-fourth meeting of the Conference of Ministers/Seventh Conference of African Ministers of Finance (Addis Ababa, Ethiopia, 6-8 May), with the theme "The challenges of financing development in Africa" [E/1999/38].

Panel discussions were held on policy reforms and aid effectiveness, and on the African debt situation. In addition, a ministerial policy debate took place on the economic and social situation and challenges of financing development in Africa, based on the *Economic Report on Africa, 1999* [E/ECA/CM.24/3]. At the end of the meeting, the Joint Conference adopted a Ministerial Statement.

The Conference was preceded by the nineteenth meeting of the Technical Preparatory Committee of the Whole/seventh Meeting of the Intergovernmental Group of Experts (Addis Ababa, 30 April–4 May) [E/ECA/CM.24/9], which discussed the Conference theme, the current economic and social situation in Africa, the report on the work of the Commission 1996-1998 [E/ECA/CM.24/4], coordination and collaboration among UN agencies at the regional and subregional levels in Africa, rationalization and harmonization of ECA-sponsored institutions [E/ECA/CM.24/6] and the proposed 2000-2001 work programme of ECA [E/ECA/CM.24/7].

The Conference of Ministers adopted the Technical Preparatory Committee's report [E/ECA/CM.24/8], including the resolutions contained therein.

ECA organized the African regional hearings (Addis Ababa, 24-25 June) for the Millennium Assembly of the United Nations in 2000 [A/54/281] (see p. 563). The hearings reviewed and assessed UN institutional weaknesses in order to identify challenges to the region that should form part of the overall vision of the United Nations in the twenty-first century.

Economic and social trends

Economic trends

According to the summary of the ECA survey of the economic and social situation in Africa, 1999 [E/2000/12], Africa's economy grew an estimated 3.2 per cent, barely improving the previous year's modest performance of 3.1 per cent. However, at the country level, in contrast to previous experience, no country posted negative gross domestic product (GDP) in 1999 and only one economy grew at a rate of less than 1 per cent. GDP growth rates ranged between 1 and 10 per cent, with Mozambique and Equatorial Guinea having the strongest economic performance. At the subregional level, East and Southern Africa enjoyed higher growth in 1999 than in 1998, while the other three subregions experienced lower growth rates. East Africa's aggregate growth rate rose from 2.6 per cent in 1998 to 4.1 per cent in 1999, while Southern Africa improved its performance from 1.7 to 2.2 per cent. In North Africa, average growth declined from 4.4 to 3.6 per cent and in West and Central Africa from 3.6 to 3.3 per cent and from 5 to 4.5 per cent, respectively. The five largest economies in Africa (Algeria, Egypt, Morocco, Nigeria, South Africa) posted a growth rate of 2.8 per cent, while the 11 oil-exporting economies marginally improved their 1998 performance by 0.1 per cent, reaching 3.7 per cent in 1999. The least developed African countries showed dynamic GDP growth, increasing the 1998 rate by 0.2 percentage points, to reach 4.5 per cent.

At the sectoral level, growth rates declined in agriculture (from 3.5 per cent in 1998 to 2.1 per cent in 1999) and in the industrial sector (from 3.2 per cent to 2.8 per cent). On the other hand, the growth rate in the service sector increased by 1 percentage point, to reach 4 per cent in 1999, with the financial and communications services the lead performers.

Agricultural performance was mixed across the region; growth decelerated in North Africa but increased in West Africa. In Central Africa, performance was restrained due to civil unrest, political instability and pest infestation, while output declined in East and Southern Africa as a result of erratic rainfall, war and uncontrolled crop pests. The poor performance of agriculture, aggravated by population displacements due to political instability, exposed nearly 20 million people to critical food shortages, requiring emergency food assistance.

The terms of trade declined by nearly 6 per cent in 1999, as the unit value of exports fell by more than 3 per cent and the unit price of imports rose by more than 2 per cent. The value of exports increased by 2.4 per cent, due to a 6 per cent increase in the volume of goods exported. Imports increased in value by 4 per cent and in volume by 1.4 per cent.

The balance of trade registered export earnings of $101 billion, an increase of 2.4 per cent over 1998. The current account balance deteriorated further, increasing to $21 billion, a 13 per cent increase from 1998. External resource flows rose from $16 billion in 1998 to $22 billion in 1999. Foreign direct investment amounted to about $6 billion, while $7 billion came in as transfers. Borrowing totalled $8.4 billion, an increase of nearly 45 per cent over 1998. The volume of debt rose from $351 billion in 1998 to $359 billion in 1999. Debt servicing increased from $35.7 billion in 1998 to $39.4 billion in 1999.

Policy implications

Following a long period of experimentation, the policy community seemed to be gravitating towards a consensus on development policies for Africa. The World Bank's Comprehensive Development Framework (see PART SIX, Chapter VI) exemplified the new consensus. Africa's development strategy should be based on and target a participating approach; broad-based and equitable growth; savings and investment; investment in human capital; technological development; a trade and industrialization strategy; agriculture and rural development; environmental protection; integration into the global economy; aid and external debt; institutional structure and good governance; and the role of Governments and public policy.

Social trends

According to the summary of the economic and social situation, Africa was the poorest and least developed region of the world, the most technologically backward, the most indebted and the most ravaged by civil conflicts. Half of Africa's population lived in poverty, on an average of $0.83 per person per day. Malnutrition, disease, inadequate housing and unemployment were rampant. War and conflicts had affected 61 per cent of the African population since 1963, with East, Central and West Africa showing the highest percentage of affected populations. Poorer countries showed a considerably higher risk of civil war than richer countries. African countries tended to be the least free in the world, with repressive regimes still common and democracy still fragile.

Africa's population was neither healthy nor sufficiently schooled. More than 23 million Africans lived with HIV/AIDS, and almost 14 million had died. With more than 70 per cent of the world's total number of people living with HIV/AIDS, Africa's economy was seriously threatened by the pandemic. AIDS had reduced life expectancy by as much as 20 years in some hard-hit countries. Infant mortality rates were also higher due to AIDS, reversing the progress made in infant and child survival in many countries. In East and Southern Africa, those rates were nearly 70 per cent higher than normal. Other preventable diseases were all too prevalent, such as malaria and tuberculosis, further straining already depleted health budgets. The health disadvantages of African countries had a negative impact on wages and productivity.

As for the brain drain, thousands of African doctors, engineers and scientists were leaving the continent to search for better opportunities elsewhere.

On 8 May [E/1999/38 (dec. 832(XXXIII))], the Conference of Ministers, concerned with the devastating impact of the AIDS pandemic on Africa's socio-economic development prospects, requested the ECA Executive Secretary to work closely with the Joint United Nations Programme on HIV/AIDS and co-sponsors of other institutions to gather, analyse and disseminate data on the economic impact of HIV to facilitate policy development and programme planning. It called on member States to increase efforts in the fight against AIDS, to make available adequate resources and involve all concerned sectors of the economy, interested parties and governmental and non-governmental organizations (NGOs) and to be more open and intensify efforts in educating the general public about the pandemic.

The Economic and Social Council, in resolution **1999/36** of 28 July, endorsed the International Partnership against HIV/AIDS in Africa and urged Governments, the UN system and intergovernmental and non-governmental organizations to participate in the programme's activities.

Activities in 1999

In 1999, ECA's work was carried out under five subprogrammes: facilitating economic and social analysis; ensuring food security and sustainable development; strengthening development management; harnessing information for development; and promoting regional cooperation for development. The cross-cutting themes of promoting the advancement of women and capacity-building underpinned those subprogrammes.

Development policy and regional economic cooperation

African recovery and development

ECA continued to monitor implementation of the United Nations New Agenda for the Development of Africa in the 1990s, adopted by the General Assembly in resolution 46/151 [YUN 1991, p. 397], and the United Nations System-wide Special Initiative on Africa, launched in 1996 [YUN 1996, p. 832] (see pp. 847 and 848, respectively). It undertook several initiatives to promote economic cooperation and integration and to strengthen Africa's position in the global economy.

The key message from the Joint Conference of African Ministers of Finance and Ministers of Economic Development and Planning (Addis Ababa, 6-8 May), which discussed "The challenges of financing development in Africa", was that African countries needed to intensify efforts to mobilize domestic resources and boost economic efficiency and productivity in the utilization of scarce resources, not just to offset possible reduction in external resource flows but also to enhance Africa's attractiveness as a destination for international financial resource flows. At the same time, development partners had to support the region's political and economic reforms and maintain adequate flows of complementary external financial resources that were necessary to sustain Africa's recovery, growth, transformation and sustainable development.

On 8 May [E/1999/38 (dec. 831(XXXIII))], the Conference of Ministers, having considered the *Economic Report on Africa, 1999* [E/ECA/CM.24/3], commended the secretariat on developing a set of indicators for measuring and evaluating short- and long-term economic performance and sustainability, and requested the Executive Secretary to provide member States with an explanatory note on the methodology and technical approaches used, to enable them to study the *Report's* findings and the proposed economic performance indicators, as well as refine and internalize them in their assessments, analysis and policy-making. He was asked to continue to refine the indicators developed in the report, in collaboration with member countries and the region's development partners. ECA called on other development partners to collaborate with member States and ECA on furthering the development of strategies to address Africa's socio-economic challenges, including those generated by conflicts and economic integration.

The Economic and Social Council, following consideration of the item "Development of Africa: implementation and coordinated follow-up by the UN system of initiatives on African development", adopted **agreed conclusions 1999/2** on the subject (see p. 845).

Third Conference on LDCs (2001)

On 8 May [E/1999/38 (dec. 834(XXXIII))], the Conference of Ministers requested the Executive Secretary, in collaboration with the Secretary-General of the United Nations Conference on Trade and Development (UNCTAD), to support African LDCs in preparing for the Third United Nations Conference on the Least Developed

Countries, to be held in 2001 (see p. 769), at the country, regional and global levels. He was asked to ensure that ECA made substantive technical contributions to the Conference and its preparatory process. LDCs' bilateral, regional and multilateral development partners and UNDP were requested to provide assistance to LDCs to ensure a substantive and effective preparatory process at the country level. The Conference Secretary-General was asked to intensify efforts to mobilize resources for the participation of LDC representatives in the regional expert-level meetings, as well as those of the Intergovernmental Preparatory Committee and the Conference itself.

Information technology

ECA carried out a number of activities in the area of information and communication technologies for development, including implementation of the African Information Society Initiative (AISI), adopted by ECA in 1996 [YUN 1996, p. 880]. Advisory services were provided on AISI, electronic technology and, to a limited extent, on statistics, geographical information systems and database management. Through the Partnership for Information and Communication Technologies in Africa, ECA developed partnerships with other institutions to ensure effective implementation of AISI. It worked with the global telecommunications private sector in organizing the Global Connectivity for Africa Conference (Marrakech, Morocco, May). Activities undertaken in statistical development were: an ad hoc expert group meeting on measures to improve intra-African trade statistics (4-8 October), and workshops for national census personnel (1-5 November) and on environmental statistics, indicators and accounting (5-11 November), all in Addis Ababa.

The ninth meeting of the Coordinating Committee of African Statistical Development (Addis Ababa, 24-26 June) reviewed ECA secretariat activities and considered the reports of the task force on monitoring the implementation of the Addis Ababa Plan of Action for Statistical Development in Africa in the 1990s [YUN 1991, p. 304]. ECA began a major study in 1999 entitled "ICT-SCAN", on the status of information and communication technologies for Africa. It organized the first African Development Forum (Addis Ababa, 24-28 October) on the theme "The challenge to Africa of globalization and the information age". Initiatives arising out of the meeting included a plan for a regional School Net Africa and African Distance Learning Programme; a telecentre network; the formation of a business-to-business network, the Alliance for African Business; and the formation of national action groups with the aim of preparing for the Global Knowledge Information Infrastructure.

The first meeting of the Committee on Development Information (Addis Ababa, 28 June–2 July), held under the theme "Harnessing information for development", made recommendations to enhance Africa's socio-economic development.

Transportation and communications

In the area of transport, ECA organized a special regional meeting of African Ministers Responsible for Civil Aviation (Yamoussoukro, Côte d'Ivoire, 9-14 November) to review and evaluate progress in implementing the Yamoussoukro Declaration on a New African Air Transport Policy [YUN 1988, p. 273]. Several studies were undertaken to address the impact of improved rural transport on women; liberalization of air traffic rights and the development of African air services; and privatization of ports and railways in selected countries. The three subregional port management associations were assisted in establishing in November the Pan African Association for Port Cooperation, a regional organization responsible for the development of port programmes and activities in Africa. ECA collaborated with the International Maritime Organization in introducing and implementing maritime port State and flag systems in Africa.

Europe-Africa permanent link

In response to Economic and Social Council resolution 1997/48 [YUN 1997, p. 970], the Secretary-General submitted an April report from the Executive Secretaries of ECA and ECE on a Europe-Africa permanent link through the Strait of Gibraltar [E/1999/20], which reviewed studies and activities carried out during 1997 and 1998. The Executive Secretaries reported that in 1997, stage two of the feasibility phase, "F2. Feasibility 2", began, which focused on deep drilling, construction cost estimates and traffic projections. A new stage, designated "F3. Investigation", was based on clarifying the geological problems encountered and extending knowledge of the Europe-Africa traffic system related to the project, with a view to better consolidating long-term traffic projections.

Activities in 1999 included a workshop on tunnel-boring costs (Rabat, Morocco, 22-24 April).

ECONOMIC AND SOCIAL COUNCIL ACTION

On 28 July [meeting 44], the Economic and Social Council adopted **resolution 1999/37** without vote [draft: E/1999/L.27] [agenda item 10].

Europe-Africa permanent link through the Strait of Gibraltar

The Economic and Social Council,

Recalling its resolutions 1982/57 of 30 July 1982, 1983/62 of 29 July 1983, 1984/75 of 27 July 1984, 1985/70 of 26 July 1985, 1987/69 of 8 July 1987, 1989/119 of 28 July 1989, 1991/74 of 26 July 1991, 1993/60 of 30 July 1993, 1995/48 of 27 July 1995 and 1997/48 of 22 July 1997,

Recalling also General Assembly resolution 43/179 of 20 December 1988, by which the Assembly declared the period 1991-2000 the Second Transport and Communications Decade in Africa,

Referring to resolution 912(1989) adopted on 1 February 1989 by the Parliamentary Assembly of the Council of Europe regarding measures to encourage the construction of a major traffic artery in south-western Europe and to study thoroughly the possibility of a permanent link through the Strait of Gibraltar,

Referring also to the Barcelona Declaration adopted at the Euro-Mediterranean Conference, held at Barcelona, Spain, in November 1995, and to the work programme annexed thereto, aimed at connecting the Mediterranean transport networks to the trans-European transport network so as to ensure their interoperability,

Referring further to the Lisbon Declaration adopted at the Conference on Transport in the Mediterranean, held at Lisbon in January 1997, and to the conclusions of the Pan-European Transport Conference, held at Helsinki in June 1997, on corridors in the Mediterranean incorporating the permanent link,

Taking note of the follow-up report prepared jointly by the Economic Commission for Africa and the Economic Commission for Europe in accordance with resolution 1997/48,

Taking note also of the conclusions of the second and third meetings of the Western Mediterranean Transport Group, held at Rabat in September 1995 and at Madrid in January 1997, respectively, which included the permanent link among the priority corridors in the extension of the trans-European network,

1. *Welcomes* the cooperation on the project for the link through the Strait of Gibraltar established between the Economic Commission for Africa, the Economic Commission for Europe, the Governments of Morocco and Spain and specialized international organizations;

2. *Also welcomes* the organization, under the auspices of the Economic Commission for Africa and the Economic Commission for Europe, by the International Tunnelling Association, of the workshop held at Rabat in April 1999 on costs of tunnels bored with tunnel-boring machines;

3. *Further welcomes* the progress achieved with project studies and especially the deep-sea drilling work, which has provided a decisive impetus to geological and geotechnical knowledge of undersea formations;

4. *Commends* the Economic Commission for Africa and the Economic Commission for Europe on the work done in preparing the project follow-up report requested by the Council in its resolution 1997/48, even though the necessary resources were not forthcoming from the General Assembly;

5. *Renews its invitation* to the competent organizations of the United Nations system, and to non-governmental organizations, including in particular the International Tunnelling Association and the International Union of Railways, to participate in the studies and work on the permanent link through the Strait of Gibraltar;

6. *Also renews its invitation* to the European Commission to consider the possibility of participating in the consolidation of the studies and the development of the project both institutionally and financially;

7. *Requests* the Executive Secretaries of the Economic Commission for Africa and the Economic Commission for Europe to continue to take an active part in the follow-up to the project and to report to the Council at its substantive session of 2001;

8. *Requests* the Secretary-General to provide formal support and, to the extent that priorities permit, the necessary resources, within the regular budget, to the Economic Commission for Africa and the Economic Commission for Europe to enable them to carry out the activities mentioned above.

Industrial development

Second Industrial Development Decade

Report of Secretary-General. In response to General Assembly resolution 52/208 [YUN 1997, p. 968], the Secretary-General submitted a September report on the implementation of the Second Industrial Development Decade for Africa (1993-2002) (IDDA-II) [A/54/320], endorsed by the Economic and Social Council in resolution 1992/44 [YUN 1992, p. 468]. The report examined economic and industrial development trends in Africa, including the challenges of globalization for African industries, and described specific action by the United Nations Industrial Development Organization (UNIDO) and ECA to support IDDA goals and objectives during the 1998-1999 biennium. It also examined progress in implementing the 1997 Plan of Action of the Alliance for Africa's Industrialization, which was endorsed by the Assembly in resolution 52/208 [YUN 1997, p. 968]. The Secretary-General further reported that the first meeting of the Patrons Group of Heads of State and Government of the Alliance for Africa's Industrialization (Algiers, Algeria, 13 July) had issued a communiqué, in which they expressed the intention to intensify implementation of the Alliance as an African strategy for ensuring the continent's industrial development and to reverse the decline of direct investment flows to Africa.

The Secretary-General said that the Africa region needed to be integrated into the global economy, and that the production and trade of products with a high value-added content was key. The region needed to shift to improving the productivity of its labour, effectively transforming its static comparative advantages to dynamic competitive advantages. Effective public and private investments in industrial infrastructure, strengthening technological capabilities through human resource development, institution-building and effective economic governance were required to close the income and technological gap between the region and the rest of the world. Poverty alleviation and employment creation required a strategic focus on enhancing manufacturing value added, promotion of rural industrialization and stronger sectoral linkages between industry and agriculture.

UNIDO's IDDA programme was refocused, emphasizing more effective country-level programming and alignment of country programmes to the United Nations Development Assistance Framework (see p. 786). UNIDO launched the new integrated approach, which promoted capacity-building, in seven countries in 1998, and by June 1999 had finalized programmes in 15 African countries, including eight LDCs, valued at $103 million. It had contributed $10.47 million from its programmable resources to implement those programmes, and had received significant support from UNDP, as well as $20 million in donor support. However, further financial support was urgently needed. The Secretary-General asked the donor community to support the funds mobilization effort to be launched at the Conference on Industrial Partnership and Investment (Dakar, Senegal, 20-21 October), in response to Assembly resolution 52/208.

To complement industrial development technical assistance provided by UNIDO and other UN agencies, the Secretary-General proposed: strengthening the complementarity between aid and investment to create an enabling environment for private sector-led industrial development and provide more entry points for foreign investment and industrial partnership in Africa; investment concessions for private sector venture capitalists; debt-for-industrial-development swaps as a financing mechanism for industrial projects; and enhancing investments in small and medium-sized enterprises (SMEs) engaged in manufacturing, including the combination of venture capital funds with technical and managerial support to enterprises to facilitate start-ups and increase the survival rate of SMEs.

Conference of African Ministers of Industry. The fourteenth meeting of the Conference of African Ministers of Industry (Dakar, 22-23 October) [E/ECA/CAMI.14/99/10] considered the theme "Industrialization and poverty eradication". In their conclusions and recommendations, participants stated that to promote industrial development, African countries should improve the business environment, particularly by combating corruption. To manage globalization and enhance competitiveness, they should improve infrastructure to reduce transaction costs, strengthen industrial development, promote technological progress, strengthen training and skills development, create comparative and competitive advantages by means of industrial policy, strengthen the private sector, create an enabling environment for private sector development, facilitate foreign direct investment and foster public/private sector dialogue and cooperation.

Challenges facing the manufacturing sector could be met by increasing accessibility of scientific and technological information; eliminating bottlenecks due to infrastructural inadequacies; restoring links between large enterprises and SMEs; introducing new financial instruments and mechanisms more suitable for financing, in particular of SMEs; reviewing parameters for the adoption by African enterprises of the requisite environmental standards for cleaner production; and optimizing utilization of human resources through training policies and a more systematic use of modern technologies to increase the productivity of labour.

The Ministers adopted an African common position for the eighth session of the UNIDO General Conference (Vienna, November/December), which, among other things, noted that the implementation of World Trade Organization (WTO) rules might have adverse implications for Africa's economic development, particularly its industrialization in terms of capacity-building for industrial competitiveness. It invited African countries to support and reinforce current trade negotiations to ensure a favourable environment for the development of African industry; assess and review the impact of existing international rules, agreements and efforts to remove obstacles to accelerating industrial takeoff; and solicit international support for establishing conditions for successful industrialization in terms of infrastructure and services and enhancing political stability.

GENERAL ASSEMBLY ACTION

On 22 December [meeting 87], the General Assembly, on the recommendation of the Second (Economic and Financial) Committee [A/54/586], adopted **resolution 54/203** without vote [agenda item 98 *(a)*].

Second Industrial Development Decade for Africa

The General Assembly,

Recalling the Declaration on International Economic Cooperation, in particular the Revitalization of Economic Growth and Development of the Developing Countries, the International Development Strategy for the Fourth United Nations Development Decade, the United Nations New Agenda for the Development of

Africa in the 1990s and its resolutions 52/208 of 18 December 1997 and 53/177 of 15 December 1998, and taking note of Economic and Social Council decision 1999/270 of 28 July 1999 concerning the implementation and coordinated follow-up by the United Nations system of initiatives on African development,

Recalling also the Declaration on Africa's Industrialization, adopted by the Assembly of Heads of State and Government of the Organization of African Unity at its thirty-third ordinary session, held at Harare from 2 to 4 June 1997, and the Plan of Action for the Alliance for Africa's Industrialization, adopted by the Conference of African Ministers of Industry at its thirteenth meeting, held at Accra in May 1997, and taking note of the final communiqué of the first meeting of the Patrons Group of Heads of State and Government of the Alliance for Africa's Industrialization, adopted at Algiers on 13 July 1999, and the Conference on Industrial Partnerships and Investment in Africa, held at Dakar on 20 and 21 October 1999,

Taking note of the statement of the Conference of African Ministers of Trade, held at Algiers in September 1999, to the Third Ministerial Conference of the World Trade Organization and resolution 2(XIV) on the African common position on globalization, adopted by the fourteenth meeting of the Conference of African Ministers of Industry, held at Dakar on 22 and 23 October 1999, both of which recognize the critical need for support for African countries in addressing the supply-side constraints on their integration into the world economy,

Recognizing the importance of industrialization as a key element in promoting sustained economic growth and sustainable development in Africa, in accordance with relevant General Assembly resolutions, as well as the outcomes of major United Nations conferences, and also its role in facilitating efforts for the eradication of poverty through, inter alia, promotion of competitiveness, productive employment, capacity-building, gender-mainstreaming and effective and efficient management systems,

Recognizing also the commendable efforts of African countries to engage their respective private sectors in policy dialogue at the highest levels and to improve further the capacity of the private sector, including small and medium-sized enterprises,

Recognizing further the need for African countries to continue their efforts to create a climate favourable to private sector development and foreign direct investment and also the commitment of African countries to using both human and financial resources more efficiently in the process of industrialization, and emphasizing the continuing need for the mobilization of adequate resources through domestic initiatives and international support, inter alia, through enhanced official development assistance, investment guarantees, debt-for-industrial development swaps, as appropriate, and enhanced market access,

Welcoming the reform and revitalization of the United Nations Industrial Development Organization, as well as its new approach of providing comprehensive packages of integrated services to promote sustainable industrial development in African countries and its approach to field activities through joint programming with the United Nations resident coordinator system in the United Nations Development Assistance Framework, where appropriate, and commending the United Nations Industrial Development Organization for initiating closer collaboration with the World Trade Organization, with the participation of their secretariats and the States Members of the United Nations and observer States, with a view to, inter alia, contributing to efforts towards enhancing market access, as appropriate, for African industrial products,

1. *Takes note* of the report of the Secretary-General on the implementation of the programme for the Second Industrial Development Decade for Africa (1993-2002);

2. *Reaffirms* the need for the African countries that have yet to do so to integrate the objectives of the Alliance for Africa's Industrialization, as appropriate, into their national plans for the establishment of institutional capacity for monitoring programmes and related projects;

3. *Invites* the international community, the African Development Bank and other relevant regional institutions to support the implementation of the programme for the Second Industrial Development Decade for Africa and the Plan of Action for the Alliance for Africa's Industrialization, including the outcome of the Conference on Industrial Partnerships and Investment in Africa;

4. *Appeals* to the international community, the World Bank, the African Development Bank and United Nations funds and programmes, in accordance with their respective mandates, to support the efforts of the African countries to intensify and to expand industrial cooperation among themselves;

5. *Calls upon* the United Nations Industrial Development Organization to strengthen its close working relationship with the World Trade Organization and other relevant multilateral institutions, with the participation of their secretariats and the States Members of the United Nations and observer States, for the provision of technical assistance to African countries, particularly the least developed among them, so as to enhance their capacity to overcome technical barriers to trade in industrial and other products, including improving quality standards to alleviate supply-side constraints, and to promote industrial competitiveness within the context of the integrated framework initiative in order to enable them to integrate fully into the world economy;

6. *Requests* the United Nations Industrial Development Organization and the Economic Commission for Africa, in accordance with their respective mandates, and in coordination with the United Nations system, to support African countries in the implementation of the relevant recommendations contained in the report of the Secretary-General;

7. *Requests* the Secretary-General to submit to the General Assembly at its fifty-sixth session a report on the implementation of the present resolution.

Energy and natural resources

During 1999, ECA provided secretariat support to the Inter-agency Group on Water in Africa and collaborated on various issues with member agencies of the Working Group on Water of the United Nations Special Initiative on Africa. It prepared studies on the contribution of transnational corporations in the mining and energy sectors in

Africa; on modalities for accessing new sources of capital for the development of Africa's mineral resources; on assessing the adequacy of policy, legal and regulatory frameworks for sustained development of mineral resources; and on reviewing projection models for Africa's energy and power requirements.

The Committee on Natural Resources and Science and Technology met from 15 to 18 November, in Addis Ababa.

Food security and sustainable development

ECA activities to ensure food security and sustainable development were aimed at promoting a better understanding of the interrelationship among agricultural productivity, population growth and environment sustainability, as well as promoting strategies for integrating those concerns into development policies and planning. Studies were prepared on best practices; interregional trade in agriculture; the scope for joint food security schemes in Africa; sustainable food production and food security in the Sahelian countries; agricultural development in the West African subregion; and soil erosion and destruction of land resources. The secretariat organized policy workshops, meetings and training, including the first meeting of the Advisory Board on Population, Agriculture and the Environment (Addis Ababa, 20-21 September); and a workshop on women's reproductive health and household food security in Africa (Addis Ababa, 11-13 October).

The secretariat collaborated with other UN agencies and regional and subregional organizations by exchanging data and information. It also participated in or jointly organized meetings, including the first francophone and lusophone mayors' seminar on the problems of street food in Africa (Praia, Cape Verde, 7-9 June) and a regional consultative meeting on sustainable development (Abidjan, Côte d'Ivoire, 7-9 September).

The first meeting of the Committee on Sustainable Development (Addis Ababa, 25-29 January) [ECA/FSSD/CSD/99/9], a technical and legislative body of experts on food security, population and the environment, focused on the five-year review of the 1994 International Conference on Population and Development [YUN 1994, p. 955] (see p. 1005). It also considered the population, environmental development and agriculture model and the review and appraisal of the implementation in Africa of plans of action of the 1992 United Nations Conference on Environment and Development [YUN 1992, p. 672], the Second (1996) United Nations Conference on Human Settlements [YUN 1996, p. 993] and the 1996 World Food Summit [ibid., p. 1129].

The General Assembly, in **resolution 54/214** of 22 December, encouraged the countries of Central Africa to implement the undertakings set out in the Declaration on the Conservation and Sustainable Management of Tropical Forests [A/C.2/54/5], adopted by the Summit of Central African Heads of State (Yaoundé, Cameroon, 12-17 March) (see p. 992).

Development management

ECA activities in support of strengthening development management emphasized fostering public-private sector partnership; promoting public sector reforms; advancing sound public sector policies and practices; and enhancing the capacity of civil society organizations. Public sector management activities were aimed at enhancing the capacity of central and local government institutions for efficient service delivery. To that end, the secretariat undertook a study to analyse government policy on financing local development and administrative structures to support policy implementation, which recommended measures to accelerate the decentralization of financial authority to the local level and strengthen local government structures. A number of technical comparative studies were undertaken in the area of civil service reforms with the aim of promoting efficiency, accountability and transparency in African civil services.

In private sector development, ECA emphasized promoting enterprise formation, privatization, microfinancing and the development of capital markets in Africa. Other activities included the preparation of comprehensive case studies on experiences and strategies to promote privatization in Africa; the role of microfinancing in the sustainable development of SMEs in Africa; and the promotion and strengthening of capital markets in Africa.

Integration of women in development

ECA activities to promote the advancement of women focused on mainstreaming gender issues into policies and programmes of its member States and promoting the economic and social empowerment of women.

The Sixth African Regional Conference on Women (Addis Ababa, 22-26 November), organized by ECA, reviewed and evaluated progress made in formulating and implementing gender-sensitive policies and programmes in the priority areas of concern identified in the 1995 Beijing Platform for Action [YUN 1995, p. 1171], adopted at the Fourth World Conference on Women [ibid., p. 1169]. It adopted an African Plan of Action for accelerating the implementation of the 1994 Dakar [YUN 1994, p. 696] and Beijing Platforms for

Action over the period 2000-2004 at the national, subregional and regional levels. An East and Southern Africa subregional follow-up meeting on the implementation of the global and regional platforms for action was held in the Seychelles in February.

Other ECA activities to foster the economic and social empowerment of women centred on the establishment of two subregional development centres to provide training and information and enhance networking among African women entrepreneurs. Those activities were supported by a forum held in Bujumbura, Burundi, in June and field missions to West and East Africa in November.

The ECA African Centre for Women was given the mandate to build the capacity of the secretariat's substantive divisions in mainstreaming gender concerns in their programmes to ensure gender-sensitive responses. Several sensitization workshops for ECA staff were held and a capacity-building needs assessment was undertaken in August.

Social development

ECA organized subregional follow-up conferences to the 1995 World Summit for Social Development [YUN 1995, p. 1113] for Central and West Africa (Ouagadougou, Burkina Faso, January); for East and Southern Africa (Nairobi, Kenya, March); for North Africa (Marrakech, Morocco, March); and for Central and West Africa (Ouagadougou, September). The conferences monitored progress in implementing the Copenhagen Declaration on Social Development and the Programme of Action of the World Summit [ibid., p. 1115] in order to achieve social sector objectives in education, health and poverty. It also held an ad hoc expert group meeting on analytical and conceptual tools for poverty management (Addis Ababa, 12-13 October).

The Committee on Human Development and Civil Society held its first meeting (Addis Ababa, 21-23 June) on the theme "Popular participation for sustainable social and human development in Africa". The Committee discussed issues from the subregional follow-up conferences and capacity-building of indigenous African civil society organizations. It reviewed ECA activities on human and social development, as well as civil society, and previewed the 2000-2001 work plan.

Programme, administrative and organizational questions

The ECA Technical Preparatory Committee of the Whole reviewed the proposed programme of work and ECA priorities for the 2000-2001 biennium [E/ECA/CM.24/7]. The Conference of Ministers recommended a resolution on the subject [E/1999/38 (dec. 833(XXXIII))] for adoption by the Economic and Social Council (see below).

ECONOMIC AND SOCIAL COUNCIL ACTION

On 28 July [meeting 44], the Economic and Social Council, on the recommendation of ECA [E/1999/14/Add.3], adopted **resolution 1999/39** without vote [agenda item 10].

Programme of work and priorities of the Economic Commission for Africa for the biennium 2000-2001

The Economic and Social Council,

Recalling General Assembly resolution 41/203 of 19 December 1986 and subsequent relevant resolutions on programme planning,

Recalling also resolution 809(XXXI) of 8 May 1996 of the Conference of Ministers of the Economic Commission for Africa on new directions for the Commission, and in particular the programme structure, which was characterized by congruence between substantive organizational charts and programmes to foster synergy and achieve greater efficiency and impact in the delivery of service,

Taking note of General Assembly resolution 53/207 of 18 December 1998 on programme planning, by which the Assembly adopted the proposed revisions to the medium-term plan for the period 1998-2001 submitted by the Secretary-General, as amended by the Committee for Programme and Coordination,

Having taken note of the report on the work of the Commission, 1996-1998, and having examined the proposed programme of work and priorities for the biennium 2000-2001,

Convinced that the proposals contained in the proposed programme of work and priorities for the biennium 2000-2001 will enhance the role of the Commission as an important contributor in the process of Africa's economic and social rebirth,

Recognizing, however, that the economic development of Africa and the reduction of poverty are severely affected by, among other factors, the socio-economic impact of conflicts and the resulting large-scale population displacements, and realizing that the challenge of post-conflict reconciliation, rehabilitation and reconstruction require reorientation of development strategies and resource arrangements,

1. *Commends* the Executive Secretary of the Economic Commission for Africa and the staff of the Commission for the considerable work that has been undertaken in the past three years to advance institutional reforms and renewal at the Commission to enable it to remain at the forefront of policy innovations for the socio-economic development of Africa;

2. *Endorses* the programme of work and priorities of the Commission for the biennium 2000-2001, taking into account the discussion and related recommendations made at the thirty-third session of the Commission;

3. *Requests* the Executive Secretary and member States, in collaboration with bilateral and multilateral partners, to undertake a special initiative to examine issues related to the socio-economic impact of conflicts on the region's development, based on a research project, and to organize a meeting to discuss the findings

and make recommendations aimed at defining appropriate post-conflict assistance programmes and financing strategies;

4. *Also requests* the Executive Secretary and member States, in collaboration with development partners, to undertake the necessary studies that would provide a better appreciation of and response to the World Trade Organization agreements and of globalization on the region's economies;

5. *Requests* the Secretary-General, in making his proposals for the programme budget for the biennium 2000-2001, to give special consideration to the development needs of the African region by providing the Commission with adequate resources to enable it to respond adequately to the new development challenges facing Africa;

6. *Calls upon* the General Assembly and its Second and Fifth Committees to ensure that adequate resources are made available to the Commission for the implementation of its programme of work.

Subregional Development Centres

The Subregional Development Centres (SRDCs), based in Central, Eastern, North, Southern and West Africa, played a vital role in improving ECA's capacity to support regional cooperation and integration efforts. The work of SRDCs focused on providing technical support to, and strengthening cooperation with, the regional economic communities; facilitating development networking and information exchange among governments, civil society and the private sector at the subregional level; facilitating coordination services for UN system operational programmes, in collaboration with the resident coordinator system at the national level; and strengthening ECA's outreach in the subregions.

Cooperation between SADC and the United Nations

In response to General Assembly resolution 52/204 [YUN 1997, p. 980], the Secretary-General, in August [A/54/273], summarized information received from Member States and UN organizations and bodies on measures they had taken to cooperate with the Southern African Development Community (SADC).

GENERAL ASSEMBLY ACTION

On 22 December [meeting 87], the General Assembly, on the recommendation of the Second Committee [A/54/589], adopted **resolution 54/227** without vote [agenda item 101 *(b)*].

Cooperation between the United Nations and the Southern African Development Community

The General Assembly,

Reaffirming its resolution 37/248 of 21 December 1982 and all other relevant General Assembly resolutions on the promotion of cooperation between the United Nations and the Southern African Development Community,

Commending States members of the Community for demonstrating continued commitment to deeper and more formal arrangements for cooperation among themselves towards regional integration,

Noting the signing of Community protocols on wildlife conservation, law enforcement and health and the establishment of the Association of Southern African Development Community National Chambers of Commerce, as well as the adoption of a declaration on productivity, which are further steps towards enhancing regional cooperation,

Recognizing the strengthening of democratic governance and other positive developments, including the consolidation of peace, the enhancement of democracy and the respect for the rule of law in the region, through the creation of institutions to further regional integration, such as the Parliamentary Forum, the Electoral Forum and the Lawyers Association of the Community,

Reaffirming that the successful implementation of the development programmes of the Community can be achieved only if the Community has adequate resources at its disposal,

Noting that the effects of armed conflict, resulting in the loss of life and the destruction of economic and social infrastructures in southern Africa, demand the continuation and the strengthening of rehabilitation and reconstruction programmes to regenerate the economies of the countries of the region,

Welcoming the Community's efforts to make southern Africa a landmine-free zone,

Noting with grave concern that adverse weather conditions have created a regional cereal deficit in 1999-2000, with a risk of increased poverty, in particular in rural areas,

Recognizing the valuable and effective economic and financial contribution that some organs, organizations and bodies of the United Nations system and the international community have made to complementing national and subregional efforts to advance the process of democratization, rehabilitation and development in southern Africa,

Reiterating that the primary cause of the present situation in Angola is the failure of the National Union for the Total Independence of Angola, under the leadership of Jonas Savimbi, to comply with its obligations under the Peace Accords, the Lusaka Protocol and the relevant Security Council resolutions,

Expressing its grave concern at the serious deterioration of an already dire humanitarian situation in Angola caused by the current conditions in the country, which is also hampering efforts towards economic rehabilitation and national reconstruction as well as regional development projects,

Expressing its satisfaction over the initiatives to bring peace to the Democratic Republic of the Congo, launched by the Community under the leadership of President F. J. T. Chiluba of Zambia, in collaboration with the Organization of African Unity, the United Nations and other entities,

Welcoming with satisfaction the signing at Lusaka, on 10 July 1999, of the Ceasefire Agreement by all parties involved in the conflict in the Democratic Republic of the Congo as a step forward towards a durable peace in that country,

Noting with concern the high prevalence in the region of human immunodeficiency virus/acquired immunodeficiency syndrome, which has far-reaching social and economic consequences,

Reaffirming the recognition of the important role that women play in the development of the region,

1. *Takes note* of the report of the Secretary-General;

2. *Expresses its appreciation* to the international community for the financial, technical and material support given to the Southern African Development Community;

3. *Appeals* to the international community and to relevant organizations and bodies of the United Nations system to continue providing, where appropriate, financial, technical and material assistance to the Community in order to enable it to implement fully its programme of action and to meet the reconstruction and rehabilitation needs of the region and to advance further the process of regional economic integration;

4. *Calls upon* the States Members of the United Nations and organs, organizations and bodies of the United Nations system that have not yet established contact and relationships with the Community to explore the possibility of so doing;

5. *Appeals* to the United Nations, its related bodies and the international community to assist and to support the Community in its efforts against landmines, and calls upon the States members of the Community to continue to strengthen their efforts in this regard;

6. *Also appeals* to the United Nations, its related bodies and the international community to assist the Community, with the appropriate resources, in implementing the programmes and decisions adopted by various United Nations world conferences, with specific emphasis on the enhancement of the role of women in the development process, and in this regard welcomes the establishment of the Southern African Development Community Women in Business Network, aimed at empowering women through, inter alia, facilitating and enhancing their access to credit and to training in business and technical skills;

7. *Appeals* to the international community to support the measures being taken by the Community in addressing human immunodeficiency virus/acquired immunodeficiency syndrome, including proposals for key future actions for the further implementation of the Programme of Action of the International Conference on Population and Development;

8. *Appeals* to the international community and to the United Nations system to continue to extend much-needed assistance to those countries of the Community that are engaged in the process of national reconstruction so as to enable them to consolidate democracy and to enhance the implementation of their national development programmes;

9. *Appeals* to the international community to comply with all relevant Security Council resolutions on Angola pertaining to sanctions imposed on the National Union for the Total Independence of Angola, which, together with other efforts, would help to bring peace and to facilitate the process of rehabilitation and reconstruction of the Angolan economy;

10. *Urges* the international community to take appropriate action, especially by providing humanitarian assistance, to prevent the suffering of the Angolan people, in particular children, women and the elderly, urges the Angolan authorities to continue to facilitate the assistance and the delivery of such assistance, and urges all other relevant parties to the conflict to do their utmost in this regard;

11. *Calls upon* the international community, in particular the United Nations, to continue to contribute to the promotion of peace and stability in the Democratic Republic of the Congo and to assist in the rehabilitation and economic reconstruction of that country;

12. *Urges* all parties to the Lusaka Ceasefire Agreement to work towards its full implementation and to cooperate in this regard with the United Nations and the Organization of African Unity;

13. *Urges* the international community to continue to assist those countries receiving refugees in coping with the resulting economic, social, humanitarian and environmental challenges;

14. *Appeals* to the United Nations and the international community to assist in the strengthening of the region's capacity for sustainable water resource management and to respond generously with respect to the drought situation in southern Africa by supporting the region in its drought preparedness and management strategies;

15. *Calls upon* the international community to consider supporting the creation of special economic zones and development corridors in the Community, with the active participation of the private sector, while recognizing the responsibilities and the ongoing efforts of the countries concerned to create the necessary environment, including the appropriate legal and economic framework for such activities;

16. *Also calls upon* the international community to support the efforts of the Community to address the consequences, new challenges and opportunities presented to the economies of the region arising from the process of globalization and liberalization;

17. *Requests* the Secretary-General, in consultation with the Executive Secretary of the Southern African Development Community, to continue to intensify contacts aimed at promoting and harmonizing cooperation between the United Nations and the Community;

18. *Also requests* the Secretary-General to report to the General Assembly at its fifty-sixth session on the implementation of the present resolution.

Asia and the Pacific

The Economic and Social Commission for Asia and the Pacific (ESCAP), at its fifty-fifth session (Bangkok, Thailand, 22-28 April) [E/1999/39], had as its theme "Asia and the Pacific into the twenty-first century: information technology, globalization, economic security and development". The Commission also reviewed the implications of recent economic and social developments and emerging issues and developments at the regional level, including regional economic cooperation; environment and natural resources development;

socio-economic measures to alleviate poverty in rural and urban areas; transport, communications, tourism and infrastructure development; statistics; and least developed, landlocked and island developing countries. In addition, it considered technical cooperation activities and programme and organizational questions.

The Commission decided to hold its fifty-sixth session in April 2000 with the theme "Development through globalization and partnership in the twenty-first century: an Asia-Pacific perspective for integrating developing countries and economies in transition into the international trading system on a fair and equitable basis".

Economic trends

According to the summary of the economic and social survey of Asia and the Pacific [E/2000/13], developments in the economy of the ESCAP region in 1999 showed a resurgence of growth in an environment of substantially improved macroeconomic stability. The improved growth performance had been broad-based, cutting across all subregions, with the exception of South and South-West Asia, and pulling up the average growth rate of the developing countries of the region from nearly 0 per cent in 1998 to 5.6 per cent in 1999. The major contribution to the dramatic upturn in GDP growth came from the economies of East and South-East Asia that were hit by the financial crisis in 1997.

By early 1999, exchange rates had appreciated considerably in the countries affected by the crisis and had stabilized. Domestic supply conditions improved as a consequence of falling interest rates, easing of the credit crunch and rising imports. In several countries, better weather conditions led to higher agricultural output. However, private consumption demand remained muted, particularly in the countries that had fallen victim to the 1997 crisis. A noteworthy aspect was that the substantial reduction in inflation, averaging only 4 per cent for developing economies of the region in 1999, was shared by all subregions. Among the 25 developing economies of the region, as many as 19 recorded lower inflation rates.

Fiscal stimulus and export performance provided a significant boost to growth in many economies, helping to increase capacity utilization and containing a rise in unemployment. Several economies in the region also benefited from external capital inflows, including official flows, and a return of some private financial flows, which in the first eight months of 1999 exceeded the amount channelled to the region during the whole of 1998. Although many countries had undertaken structural reforms, the region was not free from some downside risks. Financial sectors in many countries remained plagued with serious problems, such as large volumes of non-performing loans, inadequate capital and insufficient loan loss provisions. In addition, reliance on external demand as a primary stimulus for growth was fraught with some degree of risk. In that context, enhancing export competitiveness assumed critical significance, as did improving agricultural productivity. There were also limits to the degree of reliance that could be put on fiscal stimulus for improved economic performance.

As far as social safety net mechanisms were concerned, large numbers of people, especially in the unorganized sector, remained virtually excluded from social security coverage. The design and operation of existing schemes needed to be improved in such areas as the financing modalities, the levels of benefits provided, the standards and cost-effectiveness of delivered services, and transparency and accountability in supervision and control. In addition, targeted safety nets for basic social protection needed to be introduced in favour of social groups so far excluded.

Policy issues

ESCAP, in a February report [E/ESCAP/1119 & Corr.1] on the current economic situation in Asia and the Pacific and policy issues, analysed recent economic performance and problems and the social impact of the 1997 economic crisis. According to the report, policies at the national, regional and international levels were needed to overcome the problems that the economic crisis had brought in its wake. The most immediate of those was to revive economic activity by overcoming the credit crunch, strengthening the financial sector and restructuring the corporate sector. Over the longer term, consideration needed to be given to reforming the international financial architecture so as to minimize the likelihood of a recurrence of such crises in the future. Governments had to play a critical role in ensuring social protection, including through the establishment of a "social fund".

On 28 April, the Commission, in a resolution on economic and financial monitoring and surveillance in the ESCAP region [E/1999/39 (res. 55/2)], requested the Executive Secretary to analyse the financial and economic crisis, paying particular attention to the role of financial markets, and to present options to be used as inputs in the formulation of relevant national policies for ensuring the attraction of a steady inflow of private capital. He should study the social and economic consequences of the crisis, paying particular attention to disadvantaged groups, and enhance the exchange of information on policies and measures adopted to address the impact of the crisis. The Executive Secretary should also study possible regional mechanisms for the exchange of information and early warning systems in relation to the financial and economic situation, with a focus on crisis prevention and reduction of the vulnerability of countries to economic and financial turmoil. The Executive Secretary should pay special attention to the implications of the financial crisis for the developing countries, particularly the least developed, landlocked and island developing countries, as well as economies in transition, by providing them with advisory services and technical assistance; and cooperate with the Bretton Woods institutions (the World Bank Group and the International Monetary Fund (IMF)) and other relevant international and regional institutions in undertaking those analyses and studies.

Activities in 1999

ESCAP activities in 1999 were carried out under thematic sub-programmes approved by the Commission in 1994 [YUN 1994, p. 720]: regional economic cooperation; environment and sustainable development; poverty alleviation through economic and social development; transport and communications; statistics; and least developed, landlocked and island developing countries.

Development policy and regional economic cooperation

ESCAP's fifty-fifth session had before it the report of the Committee for Regional Economic Cooperation on its seventh session (Bangkok, 10-12 March) [E/ESCAP/1121]; a secretariat note that reviewed trade and investment developments [E/ESCAP/1122]; and another on the implications of the Asian economic crisis for sustained industrial and technological development in the region [E/ESCAP/1123]. The Commission noted that the meetings of the Committee for Regional Economic Cooperation and its steering group had been decisive in shaping the regional agenda in trade, investment and technology. The steering group held its eleventh meeting in Bangkok from 27 to 29 September [E/ESCAP/1160].

With regard to trade and investment, the Commission acknowledged that ESCAP had an important role to play in consensus-building around policy responses, mobilizing new forms of technical and economic assistance, and linking regional thinking to the global search for more coherent macroeconomic and microeconomic policies. It requested the secretariat to promote preventive measures to safeguard against market failures concomitant with the liberalization process, continue providing detailed analysis of the economic situation in the ESCAP region, explore ways to improve access by the developing countries to more current information on short-term private capital flows and analyse the risks associated with those flows, and examine the viability of WTO for regulating international investment and financial flows.

The economic crisis notwithstanding, the Commission accorded particular importance to maintaining open trade and investment regimes. It supported the universality of WTO membership and endorsed the requests for secretariat assistance in removing obstacles to accession to WTO, as well as in improving transparency in the whole WTO process. The Commission directed the secretariat to continue addressing trade barriers affecting the exports of the developing countries, particularly non-tariff measures, government procurement practices and the effective implementation of the rules of origin. Stressing the importance of trade in services for long-term sustainable economic development, the Commission requested the secretariat to conduct studies on the impact of liberalization of such trade. It should also conduct a study to assist developing countries in addressing impediments to "quality" investment inflows in Asia and the Pacific.

The Commission recommended that the secretariat study the impact of information technology and electronic commerce on economic activity and trade to ensure that market access and trade opportunities for developing countries were not eroded. It expressed concern over the volatility of commodity prices and the resulting adverse terms of trade for commodity-dependent developing economies. The Commission stressed the importance of access to timely and quality information on trade and investment flows, supported the secretariat's efforts to upgrade and restructure its Regional Trade and Investment Information Network, and endorsed the convening of an expert group meeting for that purpose.

Concerning the implications of the Asian economic crisis for sustained industrial and technological development in the region, the Commission endorsed the recommendations contained in the secretariat note on the subject, in particular the importance of skills development, upgrading of infrastructure, strengthening the private sector, development of SMEs, technology transfer and promotion of industrial complementarities. It recommended greater regional cooperation in human resources development and that a study on skills development in the light of emerging and new technologies especially relevant to developing countries be undertaken. The Commission also stressed the importance of the transfer, development and application of environmentally sound technology for the sustainable economic and social development of the region's economies and for the very survival of some Pacific island countries.

The Commission endorsed the findings and policy recommendations contained in a secretariat note on Asia and the Pacific into the twenty-first century: information technology, globalization, economic security and development [E/ESCAP/ 1120]. It recognized that the application of information technology could play an important role in promoting social development, in working towards more equitable distribution of income and of social services, particularly education and health, and in preserving the environment. However, increased use of information technology brought new and difficult risks to the economic security of countries, which became increasingly exposed to the vagaries of international market volatility. The Commission observed that Governments should be at the forefront of the new information age and develop a vision of how to harness the full potential of information technology. It noted that regional cooperation could play an important role in supporting national efforts, particularly in the development of infrastructure and in narrowing disparities between countries.

The Commission suggested that the international community should devise a code of conduct for the use of the information superhighway, including formulating modalities and policy frameworks for the regulation of the global cyberspace electronic commerce market, for Internet banking and for the trading of securities. It urged the secretariat and other international and regional organizations to continue to assist developing countries in information technology through technical assistance and policy advice, as well as by raising the awareness of businesses, including SMEs, of the modalities of the use and advantages of the applications of electronic commerce, and by providing training for related human resources development. It was recommended that an ESCAP working group should be set up to formulate a regional policy on information technology. The Commission welcomed Pakistan's offer to host an Asian-Pacific centre for information and communications technology for the ESCAP region and asked the secretariat to work out the procedures for its establishment and donors to provide technical assistance.

Least developed, landlocked and island developing countries

Special Body on Pacific Island Developing Countries

Having considered the report of the Special Body on Least Developed and Landlocked Developing Countries on its fourth session (Bangkok, 20-21 April) [E/ESCAP/1140], the Commission endorsed its recommendations on the effective utilization of development assistance, and multi-agency integrated initiatives for the development of exports. In view of the need for capital, technology and skills in the least developed, landlocked and island developing countries, the Commission urged the secretariat to explore innovative modalities for strengthening capacity in such areas as managing capital inflows, technology transfer and industrial development strategies. It welcomed the offers of economic and technical cooperation by several developing countries in such areas as agriculture, family planning, public health and urban development for the benefit of least developed, landlocked and island developing countries.

Economic and technical cooperation

In 1999, ESCAP received $15.9 million in contributions for technical cooperation activities, of which $6.02 million was received from within the UN system, $9.5 million from bilateral donors and developing and associate members, and $375,000 from other intergovernmental or non-governmental organizations [E/2000/39]. The total was a decrease of about $500,000 from the previous year. Japan remained the largest bilateral donor, followed by Germany and the Netherlands. Other contributors from developed nations included Australia, France, New Zealand, Norway and Sweden. Twenty-three developing members and associate members contributed to ESCAP's technical cooperation programme, the largest being the Republic of Korea, followed by China. In addition to cash contributions, donors and developing countries provided about 285 work-months of services by experts recruited on a non-reimbursable loan basis in 1999. During the year, 71 technical assistance projects were initiated, with a value of $6 million.

Technical cooperation among developing countries

The Commission considered a secretariat note [E/ESCAP/1145] on ESCAP's technical cooperation activities, including technical cooperation among developing countries (TCDC) and economic cooperation among developing countries (ECDC), and the constraints on those activities.

In 1999, the secretariat developed and implemented about 100 promotional TCDC/ECDC-related activities within the framework of its various subprogrammes [E/ESCAP/1189]. It also promoted and facilitated the participation of approximately 120 officials in 41 TCDC activities. Those activities included training courses, seminars, workshops and study visits. Officials, particularly from the least developed, landlocked and island developing countries, and economies in transition, enhanced their management and technical capabilities over a wide range of areas.

In order to sensitize TCDC national focal points to the benefits of TCDC, exchange experience on their important role in that regard and disseminate up-to-date information on the available opportunities within the TCDC programme of the more advanced developing countries, the secretariat, in collaboration with China, organized the Workshop on TCDC National Focal Points in Beijing in September. It also carried out in-country consultations with TCDC national focal points of the Cook Islands, Fiji, Kiribati, Samoa, Tonga and Vanuatu to advise them on assistance they could obtain from ESCAP. The secretariat continued to promote TCDC activities through third-country training programmes.

The Commission urged that sensitization workshops aimed at strengthening TCDC national focal points should be organized annually to promote opportunities for beneficiary countries and to facilitate exchange of experience and expertise on a regular basis. In that regard, it suggested that networking of TCDC national focal points through the Internet could contribute to more cost-effective virtual TCDC workshops.

Transport, communications, tourism and infrastructure development

The Commission had before it the Executive Secretary's report on progress in the implementation of resolutions and major decisions of the Commission in transport, communications, tourism and infrastructure development [E/ESCAP/1136], and the report of the first session (1998) of the Committee on Transport, Communications, Tourism and Infrastructure Development [YUN 1998, p. 934], which it endorsed.

The second session of the Committee on Transport, Communications, Tourism and Infrastructure Development (Bangkok, 24-26 November 1999) [E/ESCAP/1178] expressed strong commitment to the 1995 New Delhi Action Plan on Infrastructure Development in Asia and the Pacific, 1997-2006 [YUN 1995, p. 1012] and recommended that a review of the regional action programme for phase I (1997-2001) of the Plan should be undertaken before the third session of the Committee in 2000. The Committee recommended that further work should be carried out on assisting countries to establish a legislative and regulatory framework that was conducive to private-sector development. Concerning the development of infrastructure in the power section, the Committee called for the enhancement of cooperation in strengthening regulatory frameworks and the integration of electricity networks at the subregional level.

Infrastructure development

The Commission expressed satisfaction with progress in implementing the New Delhi Action Plan on Infrastructure Development in Asia and the Pacific [YUN 1995, p. 1012], noting that work had commenced on 27 of the Plan's 64 operational activities. It requested the secretariat to prioritize the remaining activities. The Commission noted with concern the inadequate funding for the regional action programme and urged donors, as well as intergovernmental and non-governmental organizations, to provide additional financial and technical support for its implementation. It endorsed the convening of a ministerial conference on infrastructure in 2001.

While appreciating the secretariat's work in developing regional transport networks and facilitating cross-border movement of vehicles, goods and passengers, the Commission expressed concern about related issues that needed to be addressed urgently, including the vulnerability of vehicle drivers and crews to HIV/AIDS, and the role of the transport sector in the spread of the virus and its potential negative impact on productivity within the industry. It requested the secretariat to hold seminars on HIV/AIDS and the transport industry and to produce publications on the issues and responses that were appropriate to the ESCAP region.

The Commission noted progress made in implementing the Asian land transport infrastructure development (ALTID) project at the national and subregional levels. It stressed that, as the formulation of the Asian Highway and Trans-Asian Railway networks covering the whole of Asia would be completed soon, more emphasis should be placed on improving the operational efficiency of the routes. It also stressed the need to give increased attention to maintenance and private-sector participation, as well as to safety and environmental protection, in the development of land transport; and the importance of the further promotion of the integrated approach to the development of the transport system in Asia, with the transport corridor from Europe through the Caucasus to Asia routes constituting an integral part of the ALTID networks.

The Commission noted the involvement of member countries in the water transport sector programmes and requested the secretariat to develop training materials and information for wide dissemination and as the basis for ongoing training activities and advisory services in freight forwarding and multimodal transport and the formulation of shipping policies. Recognizing the increasing importance of private sector involvement in the financing and management of ports, the Commission requested the secretariat to assist countries in establishing a favourable climate in which stakeholders, including Governments, the private sector and port workers, could collaborate in creating a suitable environment for attracting investment. The secretariat should also undertake a comparative study of regional port charges and tariff structures as the basis for developing guidelines to assist countries in streamlining tariff-setting and establishing key indicators for port performance and update its study on medium- and long-term demands for container shipping and port development, taking into account the impact of the regional economic crisis on capacity requirements. The Commission asked the secretariat to place high priority on establishing a consultative mechanism to discuss matters of crucial concern and mutual interest in the maritime sector.

The Commission welcomed the establishment of the maritime information network (MARINET) and urged further work in promoting usage of the standard web site software developed by the secretariat for ports and shipping companies. It reaffirmed the high priority assigned to inland water transport within the regional action programme for implementation of the New Delhi Action Plan.

By a 28 April resolution [E/1999/39 (res. 55/1)], the Commission urged concerned members and associate members to integrate inland water transport within intermodal transport systems; examine technical and administrative issues related to bringing national waterways into operation; accord priority to inland water transport in policy, planning and investment; enhance cooperation between national agencies responsible for inland water transport and water resources management; and increase the public sector resources allocated to inland water transport.

The Executive Secretary was asked to: assist riverine members and associate members to formulate policies and strategies to foster inland water transport development; promote technological advancement of the inland water transport sector; assist in increasing the awareness of policy makers and the public of the advantages of inland water transport; promote human resources development in the inland water transport sector; organize an international conference/exhibition on inland water transport; and report in 2001 on the implementation of the resolution.

Tourism

The Commission reaffirmed the important role of tourism in the socio-economic development of Asian and Pacific countries and adopted the Plan of Action for Sustainable Tourism Development in the Asian and Pacific Region [E/ESCAP/1137]. It suggested additional issues that should receive the special attention of Governments and international organizations in implementing the Plan and urged ESCAP, the World Tourism Organization and other organizations concerned to assist countries in assessing the economic and social impact of tourism, cultural preservation and facilitation of travel through improved intermodal and intramodal transport.

The Commission requested the secretariat further to strengthen activities related to the environmental management of tourism, the preservation of cultural heritage and the promotion of ecotourism, and to promote tourism in the Greater Mekong subregion and in the Bangladesh-India-Myanmar-Sri Lanka-Thailand Economic Cooperation and the Economic Cooperation Organization member countries.

Science and technology

The Governing Board of the Asian and Pacific Centre for the Transfer of Technology (APCTT) held its fourteenth session in Kish Island, Iran, on 24 and 25 November [E/ESCAP/1163 & Corr.1].

In 1999, APCTT organized a wide range of technology transfer activities, including training programmes, regional workshops, exhibitions, seminars and expert group meetings in 13 countries. Over 750 business meetings of prospective technology suppliers with technology seekers were arranged and APCTT was facilitating more than 270 technology transfer negotiations per month. Efforts were made to strengthen the Centre's institutional framework, its financial base and personnel infrastructure, with assistance from Germany, India and the Netherlands.

The Commission endorsed the report of the APCTT Governing Board's thirteenth session [YUN 1998, p. 937], urged the Centre to continue facilitating the networking of technology transfer institutions to promote intreregional cooperation and directed it to expand its technology management programme, focusing on technological capacity-building and human resources development and to strengthen its activities in community-enterprise cooperation in research and development and in specialized fields, such as innovation management, technology acquisition and pricing and technology assessment.

Environment and sustainable development

The Commission endorsed the recommendations of the first session of the Committee on Environment and Natural Resources Development

(Bangkok, 21-23 October 1998) [E/ESCAP/1126]. It called on the secretariat to continue its efforts in the four areas discussed at the session: subregional cooperation for environmental programmes; the transfer and adoption of environmentally sound technology; integrated development and management of water resources and economical use of water; and the promotion of the development of remote sensing and special information systems and other space technology applications for environmental monitoring, natural resources development and natural disaster reduction. The Commission considered it imperative to strengthen regional and subregional cooperation to cope with environmental problems in the region. It noted that the Regional Action Programme for Environmentally Sound and Sustainable Development, 1996-2000 [YUN 1996, p. 908] was beneficial as a guide for the regional implementation of Agenda 21 [YUN 1992, p. 672].

The Commission recognized the importance of assisting developing countries in building the requisite capacity to adopt, develop and transfer environmentally sound technologies and to implement environmental management systems. It felt that a separate research and development fund to support the indigenous development of environmentally sound technologies, along with a special credit line to facilitate switching from polluting technologies to environmentally sound technologies, merited further consideration. It encouraged developed countries to support developing countries in acquiring such technologies on favourable terms and emphasized the catalytic role of ESCAP and APCTT in that regard. The Commission endorsed the Committee's recommendations on the adoption of a holistic approach to water resources development and management, including surface and groundwater resources.

The Commission called on the secretariat to strengthen further the activities in the integration of environmental considerations in its overall programme of work, and requested it to develop policy guidelines for the environmental impact assessment of development projects and develop programmes on the integration of population, resources, environment and development, including the role of women in environmental management.

The second session of the Committee on Environment and Natural Resources Development (Bangkok, 13-15 October) [E/ESCAP/1165] reviewed policy issues in integrating environmental considerations into economic decision-making; efficient utilization of energy in supply-side facilities and demand-side management; and integrated assessment, development and management of land and mineral resources for sustainable economic development.

The Committee recognized the challenges faced by policy makers in the region in addressing sustainable energy development. It emphasized the importance of developing regulatory frameworks for improved energy efficiency and the need to promote market-driven policy instruments and facilitate the transfer of technology on both the supply and demand side, as well as access to low-cost international funds.

The Second Ministerial Conference on Space Applications for Sustainable Development in Asia and the Pacific (New Delhi, India, 15-20 November) [E/ESCAP/1166] endorsed the Strategy and Action Plan on Space Technology Applications for Sustainable Development in Asia and the Pacific for the New Millennium, and adopted the Delhi Declaration on Space Technology Applications in Asia and the Pacific for Improved Quality of Life in the New Millennium.

Natural resources development

Energy and mineral resources

Having considered a secretariat note on the impact of the economic crisis on the energy sector [E/ESCAP/1128], the Commission observed with concern the impact on energy prices, the demand/supply gap, reductions in energy demand, financial difficulties and the slowing down of energy infrastructure development. It noted the various national policy efforts and other measures planned or undertaken by affected countries to cope with the impact of the crisis on the energy sector and to achieve long-term sustainable energy development. The Commission encouraged regional and subregional cooperation in the utilization of natural gas and intercountry power exchange, including the exchange of national experience, as well as technical and economic advisory services and exchange visits of multidisciplinary expert teams.

It emphasized the importance of Agenda 21 [YUN 1992, p. 672] in achieving a sustainable energy future for all. In that context, the importance of the transfer of environmentally sound energy technologies was reiterated, in particular technologies related to clean coal, the harnessing of renewable sources of energy and increased levels of efficiency in energy-intensive end-use sectors.

The Forum on Urban Geology in Asia and the Pacific, which held its fourth session in January, agreed that, to promote the integration of geology in urban planning effectively, a series of ESCAP meetings on geology for urban planning should be convened in and hosted by participating countries. Countries should prepare and submit proposals to ESCAP regarding hosting such meetings.

Water resources

Mekong River basin development. In 1999, important achievements and progress were made by the Mekong River Commission (MRC), established by the 1995 Mekong Agreement [YUN 1995, p. 1017], including the adoption of its first strategic plan for 1999-2003, the streamlining of its programmes and strengthening of its technical capacity, including improved coordination of its work with other partners in the region. Particular progress was made in MRC's water utilization, environmental, fisheries, agriculture and irrigation and human resources development/capacity-building programmes and in the formulation of the Basin Development Plan. Eight studies and projects were completed in 1999, and MRC shifted its approach from projects to programmes that focused more on its core functions.

The MRC report on its 1998 activities was transmitted to the Commission by a March secretariat note [E/ESCAP/1148].

Agriculture and development

The Commission had before it the report on the Regional Coordination Centre for Research and Development of Coarse Grains, Pulses, Roots and Tuber Crops in the Humid Tropics of Asia and the Pacific [E/ESCAP/1131]. Major developments in 1998 were summarized, as were issues requiring action by the Commission. Implementation of programmes in 1998, planned activities for 1999 and the financial status of the Centre were discussed.

The Commission recommended that the Centre should continue to strengthen collaborative research and development projects, covering a broad range of issues concerning the effect of trade liberalization and agriculture, the sustainable development of upland agriculture and poverty alleviation. It urged the Centre to focus further on enhancing and stabilizing regional agricultural and rural economies in the region. The Commission expressed concern over the continuing unstable condition of institutional support resources for which a substantial increase in contributions and early allocation by member and associate members were needed. It called for the further strengthening of programme resources, their timely allocation and provision of the services of experts, so as to ensure the effective implementation of programme activities.

The Commission endorsed the report on the Regional Network for Agricultural Machinery (RNAM) [E/ESCAP/1125] and its recommendations. It directed the secretariat to continue seeking extrabudgetary assistance for RNAM's approved activities for 1999-2001 and urged donor countries, and others in a position to do so, to provide programme support for RNAM projects.

In endorsing RNAM's work programme, the Commission welcomed the expansion of its activities in human resources development in post-harvest technologies, especially in food, fruit and vegetable processing and preservation. It recommended that RNAM promote better working conditions for rural women affected by agricultural mechanization.

At its nineteenth session (Kathmandu, Nepal, 17-19 November) [E/ESCAP/1164], the RNAM Governing Body recommended that the Network's name be changed to Regional Network for Agricultural Engineering and Machinery.

Social development

The Commission noted that poverty remained a serious challenge in the ESCAP region and the situation had deteriorated as a result of the economic crisis. It had before it the report of the Committee on Socio-economic Measures to Alleviate Poverty in Rural and Urban Areas on its first (1998) session [YUN 1998, p. 931], as well as a secretariat note on progress in implementing resolutions and decisions relating to socio-economic measures to alleviate poverty in rural and urban areas [E/ESCAP/1130].

The Commission recommended that Governments ensure that adjustment programmes in response to the crisis did not result in the worsening of the economic and social conditions of the poor, women, disabled persons, older persons and other disadvantaged groups. Policies and programmes should be designed to strengthen social safety nets, including implementation of labour-intensive public works for infrastructure maintenance, and other employment-creation programmes targeted at the poorest and the unemployed. It requested the secretariat to provide technical assistance to support national efforts, with an emphasis on organizing special safety nets for vulnerable groups, implementing community-based initiatives, strengthening decentralization and promoting partnerships among NGOs and the private and public sectors. It should also assist in implementing the people-centred development approach, self-help initiatives and the strengthening of family support.

The Senior Officials' Meeting on the Agenda for Action on Social Development in the ESCAP region (Bangkok, 1-5 November) [E/ESCAP/1173] reviewed progress made and constraints encountered in implementing the 1994 Agenda for Action on Social Development in the ESCAP region [YUN 1994, p. 714] and considered development trends and emerging challenges to the full implementation of the Agenda. It adopted a Regional Perspective and Recommendations for the Global Review of the Follow-up to the World Summit for Social Development by the General Assembly at its Special Session in 2000.

The secretariat continued to implement its technical assistance project on the establishment of national social development management information systems (SOMIS). Pilot projects were carried out to test the framework in three selected countries and a regional seminar was organized to discuss findings in order to further refine SOMIS for eventual dissemination to ESCAP members.

At its second session (Bangkok, 1-3 December) [E/ESCAP/1169], the Committee on Socio-economic Measures to Alleviate Poverty in Rural and Urban Areas focused on social safety net programmes, in particular their implementation at the community level. It recommended that the secretariat undertake a comprehensive assessment of such programmes in countries in the region affected by the recent economic crisis.

Disabled persons

ESCAP convened the regional forum on education for children and youth with disabilities into the twenty-first century (Bangkok, 15-19 November). A joint regional inter-organizational initiative, the forum focused on the need for early intervention and the largely unaddressed right of children and youth with disabilities to participate in education programmes. ESCAP also convened a major forum on meeting the targets of the Asian and Pacific Decade of Disabled Persons [YUN 1993, p. 621] and equalization of opportunities for persons with disabilities in the ESCAP region (Bangkok, 22-24 November). The forum reviewed and revised the 73 Decade targets [YUN 1995, p. 1021] into a framework of 107 strengthened targets with a common implementation time frame (January-December 2002). ESCAP also organized an exhibition on art and technology to promote equalization of opportunities by and for disabled persons.

International Year of Older Persons

In 1999, within the context of the observance of the International Year of Older Persons (see PART THREE, Chapter XI), proclaimed by the General Assembly in resolution 47/5 [YUN 1992, p. 889], the Commission endorsed, on 28 April [E/1999/39 (res. 55/4)], the Macau Declaration and Plan of Action on Ageing for Asia and the Pacific, adopted in 1998 by the Regional Meeting on a Plan of Action on Ageing for Asia and the Pacific [YUN 1998, p. 942]. The Commission urged ESCAP members and associate members to take early and effective action to implement the Plan; called on those who had not yet done so to set up and strengthen national mechanisms on ageing to enable them, among other things, to coordinate the observance of the International Year of Older Persons and to set specific time-bound targets on ageing and related issues; and urged them to pay attention to older persons in severe poverty and enable them to access basic health services. The Commission called on civil society, NGOs and private organizations to assist in the implementation of the Plan and their respective national plans of action on older persons.

It requested the secretariat to support and assist members and associate members in implementing the Plan; to report in 2000 on the observance of the Year and the implementation of the Plan; to recommend further action and initiatives to achieve the goal and targets contained therein; and to report on a five-year basis on the review and appraisal of the Plan.

In observance of the International Year of Older Persons in the ESCAP region, national agencies and mechanisms, as well as national focal points for the Year, were established in many countries. They initiated activities at the national and local levels to generate greater awareness of issues relating to ageing and to older persons. Cooperation between government agencies and NGOs and other organizations, and the contribution of the mass media, were distinctive features of the observance of the Year, which also provided an opportunity to review and strengthen existing policies and programmes for older persons and for adopting such measures in countries where they were not yet established. India, the Philippines and Thailand took action in 1999. The ESCAP secretariat organized seminars, workshops and consultations on preparations for the Year, including the International Symposium on Planning Attainable Targets for Societies for All Ages (Macau, China, October), which developed guidelines on the implementation of the Plan of Action, and a Regional Seminar on Support and Protection of Older Persons as Consumers (Shanghai, China, October).

Women in development

The Commission had before it a secretariat note [E/ESCAP/1133] that examined recent trends in the economic and social empowerment of women in Asia and the Pacific and some critical challenges, and described ESCAP initiatives.

The Commission observed that considerable progress had been achieved in promoting women's participation in the economic and social fields in the region, but expressed concern at the continuing disproportionate burden being borne by them during the current economic crisis. It recommended that social safety nets and projects and schemes be implemented for women at the grass-roots levels to promote community-based well-being and urged the secretariat to carry out comprehensive analyses of the impact of the current economic crisis on the poor, the vast majority of whom were women. The Commission felt that continued efforts should be directed at improving the access of women in poverty to productive resources, particularly in the rural sector.

Noting with concern that women were still being exposed to many forms of exploitation and discrimination, the Commission urged the countries of the region to make a concerted effort to remove such exploitation. It considered that overall progress in promoting the participation of women in the decision-making process was still far from satisfactory and urged the countries of the region to adopt effective measures to increase women's participation in that process.

The High-level Intergovernmental Meeting to Review Regional Implementation of the Beijing Platform for Action (Bangkok, 26-29 October) [E/ESCAP/1177] reviewed progress made and obstacles encountered in implementing the 12 critical areas of the 1995 Platform for Action [YUN 1995, p. 1170] and reiterated the region's commitment to its fundamental objectives and principles for achieving gender equality.

The Meeting urged countries to take measures to counter the effects of the slowdown in growth rates in many countries of the region, to adopt measures to protect migrant workers and to alleviate the economic plight of poor female-headed households. It recommended that countries be encouraged to ratify the Convention on the Elimination of All Forms of Discrimination against Women, adopted by General Assembly resolution 34/180 [YUN 1979, p. 895], and urged that they review and amend laws to ensure that they were in line with the Convention and other human rights treaties. It urged countries to ratify the Optional Protocol to the Convention, adopted by the General Assembly on 6 October in resolution 54/4 (see PART THREE, Chapter X), keeping in view national needs, priorities and other considerations.

Natural disasters

The Commission, having considered a secretariat note on emerging issues and developments related to natural and man-made disasters [E/ESCAP/1127 & Corr.1], reiterated the importance of natural disaster reduction for economic and social development and called on Governments to attach priority to continuing national efforts in that area, particularly in the five priority areas identified in the note: realistic integrated planning for disaster prevention and mitigation; enhancement of disaster preparedness, including real-time information exchange; community participation throughout the natural disaster reduction and management process; more effective transfer of disaster reduction and management technology; and exchange of experiences and information on institutional arrangements for disaster reduction and management. The Commission endorsed the three common goals for regional cooperation in natural disaster reduction: realistic reduction of damage; increased disaster awareness; and improvement of forecasting systems. It requested the secretariat to give priority to the development of an integrated regional strategy for better coordination of national and international efforts.

The Commission also considered the report of the Typhoon Committee [E/ESCAP/1149]. It urged UNDP and other donors to support the Committee's work and the secretariat to continue to support the Committee within its own programme of work.

Statistics

The Commission took note of the major conclusions and recommendations contained in the report of the Committee on Statistics on its eleventh session [YUN 1998, p. 944]. It endorsed the secretariat's programme of work for 2000-2001 and the priority areas identified by the Committee, including the 1993 System of National Accounts (SNA), poverty statistics and gender statistics. The Commission also considered a report on the Statistical Institute for Asia and the Pacific [E/ESCAP/1139] and endorsed the decisions and recommendations of the fourth session of its Governing Board (Bangkok, 18-19 November 1998).

The Commission noted that, as a result of the Asian financial crisis, many national statistical agencies had suffered budget cuts. Cooperation from data providers, especially in the business sector, had also deteriorated. In order to meet the challenge of providing more data with limited resources, the Commission urged national statistical offices in the region to find ways to strengthen technical cooperation with each other. Also, recognizing the need to strengthen census-taking capacities in the countries of the region, the Commission urged the United Nations Population Fund (UNFPA) to increase its level of funding for the coming census decade.

The Commission noted that awareness about the year 2000 (Y2K) problem had grown significantly in the region and that many Governments had launched remedial efforts. It agreed that strengthening regional cooperation could contribute to the resolution of the problem.

In a resolution on cooperation and support in addressing the year 2000 problem [E/1999/39 (res. 55/3)], the Commission urged all members and associate members to take early and effective action to bring their countries to the highest possible level of Y2K readiness, enhance the sharing of information across borders and forge regional and global cooperation to ensure a timely and effective response to the challenge, expedite the remediation of their systems to guarantee continued availability of basic infrastructure services, urge the private sector to become Y2K compliant and develop contingency plans and address the possibility of large-scale failures in the public and private sectors.

The Executive Secretary was asked to report annually until the fifty-seventh (2001) session on progress achieved and difficulties encountered, monitor closely actual and potential sources of funding to support the efforts of developing countries, in particular least developed and landlocked countries and the economies in transition, continue to facilitate the exchange of national experience and to collaborate with UN bodies and specialized agencies, intergovernmental and non-governmental organizations in providing support to ESCAP countries finding difficulty in addressing the Y2K problem.

Programme and organizational questions

The Commission reviewed the implementation of ESCAP's 1998-1999 programme of work [E/ESCAP/1141] and endorsed changes to that programme for 1999 [E/ESCAP/1142 & Corr.1]. It expressed satisfaction that, in spite of the reduction in both regular and extrabudgetary resources, the secretariat had managed to implement a substantial number of programmed activities.

The Commission emphasized the importance of regular monitoring and evaluation of secretariat activities and, in that connection, recommended that the advisory services and group training conducted by the secretariat be reviewed to enhance their cost-effectiveness and ensure that the specific needs of the concerned member and associate member Governments were met.

The Commission endorsed the proposed programme of work for 2000-2001 [E/ESCAP/1143 & Corr.1]. It welcomed the anticipated shift from input-based to results-based budgeting and noted the proposal to establish a formal mechanism for identifying performance indicators and evaluation criteria for the monitoring and review of performance. The Commission urged donors and international agencies, particularly UNDP, to provide extrabudgetary resources to facilitate the implementation of the 2000-2001 programme of work.

ESCAP reform

The Commission had before it a secretariat note [E/ESCAP/1152] that reviewed reform measures undertaken in ESCAP in response to Commission resolution 53/1 [YUN 1997, p. 993] and another on the restructuring of the Commission's conference structure [E/ESCAP/1159].

The Commission welcomed the measures taken so far regarding the reform of the secretariat to bring it in line with the revised conference structure [YUN 1997, p. 993]. It stressed that the reform measures should be considered as ongoing and be pursued more vigorously to ensure that the secretariat's work was responsive to the needs of the member States. It supported the proposal to reconvene the Open-ended Informal Working Group of the Advisory Committee of Permanent Representatives and Other Representatives Designated by Members of the Commission (ACPR) to define priorities for the programme of work and advise on the strategic directions for the secretariat's future activities. It also adopted the recommendations contained in a report on ACPR activities [E/ESCAP/1151] regarding improving the mechanism within the secretariat for appraising the timely and full implementation of Commission resolutions; reviewing existing mandates to ascertain their continuing relevance; strengthening the secretariat's capacity to review ESCAP activities; and further strengthening cooperation with other UN bodies.

A regional hearing in preparation for the Millennium Assembly of the United Nations (2000) for the ESCAP region was held in Tokyo on 9 and 10 September [A/54/754]. Proposals were made for strengthening the role of the United Nations and ensuring its continued relevance in the twenty-first century.

Change of name of Macau

In an April note [E/ESCAP], the ESCAP secretariat drew to the Commission's attention China's resumption of sovereignty over Macau with effect from 20 December 1999 and its request that Macau continue its associate member status in ESCAP under the name "Macau, China". The Commission approved a draft resolution for submission to the Economic and Social Council regarding amending ESCAP's terms of reference to reflect the change.

ECONOMIC AND SOCIAL COUNCIL ACTION

On 28 July [meeting 44], the Economic and Social Council, on the recommendation of ESCAP [E/1999/39], adopted **resolution 1999/38** without vote [agenda item 10].

Change of the name of Macau to "Macau, China" in the terms of reference of the Economic and Social Commission for Asia and the Pacific

The Economic and Social Council,

Noting that the Economic and Social Commission for Asia and the Pacific has recommended that the name "Macau" in paragraphs 2 and 4 of the terms of reference of the Commission should be changed to "Macau, China", effective from 20 December 1999, with the objective of enabling Macau to continue thereafter as an associate member of the Commission,

Decides to amend paragraphs 2 and 4 of the terms of reference of the Economic and Social Commission for Asia and the Pacific accordingly.

Subregional activities

Cooperation between the United Nations and the Economic Cooperation Organization

In response to General Assembly resolution 53/15 [YUN 1998, p. 946], the Secretary-General reported in September [A/54/168] on cooperation between the United Nations and the Economic Cooperation Organization (ECO). The report described the cooperation activities with ECO of UNDP, UNCTAD, UNFPA, the United Nations International Drug Control Programme and the Food and Agriculture Organization of the United Nations (FAO).

GENERAL ASSEMBLY ACTION

On 9 December [meeting 75], the General Assembly adopted **resolution 54/100** [draft: A/54/L.55] without vote [agenda item 28].

Cooperation between the United Nations and the Economic Cooperation Organization

The General Assembly,

Recalling its resolution 48/2 of 13 October 1993, by which it granted observer status to the Economic Cooperation Organization,

Recalling also its resolutions 50/1 of 12 October 1995, 51/21 of 27 November 1996, 52/19 of 21 November 1997 and 53/15 of 29 October 1998, in all of which it urged the specialized agencies and other organizations and programmes of the United Nations system and invited international financial institutions to extend their assistance to the Economic Cooperation Organization in the attainment of its objectives,

Recalling further that one of the main objectives of the United Nations and of the Economic Cooperation Organization is to promote international cooperation in solving international problems of an economic, social, cultural or humanitarian character,

Mindful of the role of the Economic Cooperation Organization as a regional organization, which, after having restructured itself, is now better prepared to play an enhanced role as a regional economic grouping for all-round socio-economic development of its member States,

Welcoming the recent developments concerning the increased interaction between the various entities of the United Nations system and the Economic Cooperation Organization towards promoting the economic and social development of the States members of that organization,

Taking note of the communiqué issued at the ninth meeting of the Council of Ministers of the Economic Cooperation Organization, held in Baku on 21 May 1999, which stressed the importance of, and the renewed resolve of the States members of the Economic Cooperation Organization with regard to, socio-economic development and enhanced trade exchanges in the Economic Cooperation Organization region,

Recognizing the risks and challenges posed as well as the opportunities offered by the process of globalization and liberalization to the economies of the States members of the Economic Cooperation Organization, and emphasizing the need to address the concerns of those States in order to mitigate the negative consequences of globalization and enable them to benefit from the process,

Expressing grave concern over the heavy human casualties caused by natural disasters and their devastating impact on the socio-economic situation of some States members of the Economic Cooperation Organization,

1. *Takes note with appreciation* of the report of the Secretary-General on the implementation of resolution 53/15, and expresses satisfaction at the enhanced pace of mutually beneficial interaction between the United Nations and the Economic Cooperation Organization;

2. *Notes with satisfaction* the ongoing cooperation between the Economic Cooperation Organization and the United Nations Development Programme through the project "Capacity-building of the Economic Cooperation Organization secretariat", and invites the two organizations to continue to enhance and strengthen their ongoing cooperation;

3. *Notes* the keen participation of the Economic Cooperation Organization in various events sponsored by the specialized agencies and programmes of the United Nations system such as the United Nations Development Programme, the Economic and Social Commission for Asia and the Pacific, the United Nations Conference on Trade and Development, the United Nations International Drug Control Programme and the United Nations Population Fund during the past year, and calls for further contacts and active participation, as appropriate, of the Economic Cooperation Organization and the specialized agencies in each other's meetings and activities;

4. *Welcomes* the ongoing cooperation between the Economic Cooperation Organization and the United Nations Conference on Trade and Development in-

cluding the trade efficiency action programme and the development of a multimodal transport and transit transport system in the Economic Cooperation Organization region;

5. *Appreciates* the ongoing cooperation between the Economic Cooperation Organization and the United Nations International Drug Control Programme including, inter alia, the implementation of the Economic Cooperation Organization and United Nations International Drug Control Programme project for the establishment of a drug control coordination unit within the Economic Cooperation Organization secretariat and other activities contributing towards curtailment of the drug abuses and drug trafficking in the Economic Cooperation Organization region;

6. *Welcomes* the recommendations of the Economic and Social Commission for Asia and the Pacific at its fifty-fifth session, held in Bangkok from 22 to 28 April 1999, on promoting cooperation with the Economic Cooperation Organization in the identified areas of mutual concern, and invites the Commission to enhance the mutual collaboration with that organization, focusing on implementable projects in the priority areas of the Economic Cooperation Organization, namely, transport and communications, trade, investment, energy, environment, industry and agriculture, for the overall benefit of the entire region;

7. *Also welcomes* the continuation of efforts towards further consolidation of interregional consultations and exchange of views on issues of common concern through such useful forums as the fourth Consultative Meeting among Executive Heads of Subregional Organizations and the Economic and Social Commission for Asia and the Pacific, held in Kathmandu in October 1998;

8. *Further welcomes* the enhanced contacts between the Economic Cooperation Organization and the World Bank pursuant to resolution 53/15, and reiterates its invitation addressed to the relevant international financial institutions to initiate, maintain and increase consultations in order to extend their assistance to the Economic Cooperation Organization and its associated institutions towards the realization of their objectives;

9. *Requests* the United Nations system and the international community to continue assisting in the strengthening of the capacity of the States members of the Economic Cooperation Organization as well as its secretariat to meet the challenges, and benefit from the opportunities, of globalization;

10. *Invites* the United Nations system, its relevant bodies and the international community to provide technical and other assistance, as appropriate, to the States members of the Economic Cooperation Organization and its secretariat in strengthening their early warning system, preparedness, timely response and reconstruction with a view to reducing human casualties and mitigating the socio-economic impact of natural disasters;

11. *Requests* the Secretary-General to submit to the General Assembly at its fifty-fifth session a report on the implementation of the present resolution;

12. *Decides* to include in the provisional agenda of its fifty-fifth session the item entitled "Cooperation between the United Nations and the Economic Cooperation Organization".

Europe

The Economic Commission for Europe (ECE), at its fifty-fourth session (Geneva, 4-6 May) [E/1999/37], focused on strengthening cooperation within the ECE region and implementation of ECE reform.

As called for in the Plan of Action on strengthening economic cooperation in Europe, endorsed by the Economic and Social Council in decision 1997/224 [YUN 1997, p. 1002], the ECE secretariat organized a debate on a major economic theme, which concentrated on the consequences of the financial crisis on the ECE region. Discussions focused on the impact of the global financial and economic crisis for the ECE region, with special emphasis on western and central Europe; overcoming the crisis of the Russian economy; and threats to the transition process in other economics.

With regard to operational activities, the Commission invited the Executive Secretary to respond to requests for technical assistance in a geographically balanced manner, paying special attention to requests from those countries most in need. In view of the limited resources available, the Executive Secretary and ECE member States should explore possibilities for providing additional financing for ECE's operational activities, in close cooperation with relevant financial institutions and donor organizations, in support of various types of activities, such as advisory missions, seminars, training workshops and for developing projects within the framework of subregional groupings and initiatives. To maximize the impact of ECE technical assistance, each principal subsidiary body (PSB) of the Commission was requested to identify the needs for operational activities within its field of competence and financing for them. A synthesis of the conclusions should be prepared for consideration at the fifty-fifth (2000) session.

The Commission, having considered the report of the Group of Experts on the Programme of Work on the prioritization process [E/ECE/1372], endorsed the new system of prioritization of PSBs' work programmes proposed by the Group of Experts.

The Commission reviewed progress made in the integration of the two cross-sectoral concerns, namely sustainable development and gender mainstreaming, into the ECE work programme (see also below). The Commission invited the Committee on Environmental Policy to review all activities related to sustainable development and make suggestions to each PSB and to the Commission on a more systematic approach at the ECE level. It also expressed its desire to see further efforts made in gender mainstreaming. In response to a General Assembly request contained in resolution 53/120 [YUN 1998, p. 1063], the Commission endorsed the convening of an intergovernmental expert meeting to review economic issues, problems and policies relating to the situation of women in ECE countries, in order to provide a regional assessment for the 2000 review of the implementation of the 1995 Beijing Platform for Action [YUN 1995, p. 1170]. It commended recent developments in intersectoral cooperation, particularly in transport and the environment, as well as environment and health, and urged that further advances be made in that direction.

The Commission invited the ECE secretariat to continue to participate in UN management coordinating mechanisms and urged it to strengthen its cooperation with other European institutions and pan-European and subregional organizations, paying due regard to the comparative advantages of each organization and ensuring the most efficient use of resources. It endorsed the recommendation that the Meeting of Officials on Land Administration (MOLA) be granted a standing character, in recognition of its work in promoting land privatization and land registration systems in the ECE region and the need for such work to continue, in particular for the benefit of countries with economies in transition that were moving from traditional to modern systems of land administration. That endorsement was noted by the Economic and Social Council by **decision 1999/272** of 28 July.

The Commission agreed that the question of the biennialization of its sessions would be reconsidered by the Group of Experts on the Programme of Work, as agreed at the fifty-third session [YUN 1998, p. 948], and that the Group would report back to an ad hoc informal meeting of the Commission.

Economic trends

According to the summary of the economic survey of Europe, 1999 [E/2000/11], the negative effects of the financial crises in Asia in 1997 and the Russian Federation in 1998 were still depressing real economic activity in much of the ECE region, including international trade, until the early months of 1999. However, by the middle of the year, the situation in most parts of the world economy had stabilized and in the second half business confidence, real activity and expectations for 2000 were all improving steadily. In Western Europe, economic growth received a strong boost from exports to the rest of the world, not least from the strong import demand of the United States economy, and by the third quarter GDP was rising at its highest annual rate since before the Asian crisis. In the transition economies of Central Europe, the worst effects of the Russian financial crisis of 1998 were receding in the second half of 1999 and they were starting to benefit from the revival of domestic demand in Western Europe. In the Russian Federation, there was a significant recovery in output for the first time in a decade, and although the extent to which underlying factors provided a basis for sustainable growth was uncertain, that had nevertheless had a positive effect on most other members of the Commonwealth of Independent States (CIS).

The widespread improvements in the economic situation were not reflected in the 1999 annual performance figures, which for the most part showed a marked deterioration on those for 1998, but could be seen in the quarterly and monthly indicators for late 1999.

Eastern Europe, Baltic States and CIS

Economic growth slowed very sharply in virtually all the 27 transition economies of the ECE region and the outcomes were generally much lower than the forecasts made at the start of the year. Instead of growing by some 3 per cent as forecast, Eastern Europe only managed 1.4 per cent, while the Baltic States plunged into a sharp recession. Only the CIS moved in the opposite direction, partly under the influence of the Russian Federation, where GDP increased unexpectedly by more than 3 per cent when most forecasts had been predicting another large fall in output.

The weak performance in 1999 to a large extent reflected the carry-over from the second half of 1998 of the after-effects of the general turmoil created by the Asian and Russian crises, aggravated for some economies by the crisis in Kosovo, Federal Republic of Yugoslavia (FRY) (see p. 332), and by the slowdown in West European import demand. The Russian crisis had particularly severe consequences for the Baltic economies with massive cuts in their exports to the Russian Federation, leading to a severe deterioration in output and employment. Central Europe, however, showed a marked improvement in the second half of the year and the Baltic States a more moderate one. Economic growth in three of the leading reformers (Hungary, Poland and Slovenia) was least affected by the various shocks of 1998 and 1999: all three reported GDP growth for 1999 of more than 4 per cent. The recovery of output in the Russian Federation was due to the sharp rise in oil prices, a real depreciation of the exchange rate by nearly 50 per cent since the August 1998 crisis and a fall in real wages. Recovery in the Russian economy had a favourable impact on the other CIS members, with output continuing to fall only in Ukraine and the Republic of Moldova.

The economies of South-East Europe were greatly affected by the Kosovo conflict and its aftermath for much of the year, although direct impact on neighbouring economies appeared to have been less than feared. Reconstruction work in Kosovo itself helped to raise industrial production in the region, as did the recovery in West European import demand. However, Romania remained in severe recession, with GDP falling over 3 per cent. In FRY, with its severely damaged infrastructure, GDP and industrial output were estimated to have fallen by some 20 per cent and more. There was modest growth in Bulgaria and the former Yugoslav Republic of Macedonia (some 2.5 per cent), although in the former, industry remained in severe recession.

Western Europe and North America

In the second half of 1999, Western Europe finally shook off the sluggishness of activity that had marked 1998 and early 1999, and by the third quarter GDP was growing at an annual rate of about 3.5 per cent. The improvement in output led to rising levels of employment, by some 1.5 per cent on average between the fourth quarters of 1998 and 1999. Unemployment in Western Europe fell from 9.1 per cent at the end of 1998 to 8.4 per cent in the last quarter of 1999. Nevertheless, unemployment remained the greatest blot on the West European economic landscape and the major challenge for policy makers. The rise in import prices in 1999, due to the higher oil prices and weakness of the euro, had a modest impact on West European rates of inflation. Intense competition forced absorption of higher producer prices in lower margins, but there were also offsetting price falls for other products and services. Labour cost pressures also remained mild. A major concern of analysts and policy makers in Western Europe remained the relatively weak performance of the European economies over the past decade in comparison with the United States economy; the question being asked was whether the "new economy" of the United States could be replicated in Europe. The contrast between the two sides of the Atlantic was highlighted by the fact that after eight years of sustained growth, the increase in United States GDP in 1999 was still double the West European average; at the same time, inflation was just 2.2 per cent. In addition, unemployment was 4.2 per cent, compared to 9.2 per cent in the European Union (EU). The process of convergence between the two economies had been slowing down since the early 1960s, and by 1990 real incomes in Western Europe were some 35 per cent lower than in the United States. In the 1990s, Western Europe had actually fallen behind rather than continuing to close the gap. Thus, the potential for Western Europe to "catch up" with the United States was still significant.

The underlying argument for a "new economy" in the United States was that a microeconomic combination of new information technology and market liberalization had transformed the key macroeconomic relationships between the growth of output and productivity, inflation and employment. Since the mid-1990s, there had been a sharp acceleration in United States productivity growth and a major boom in fixed investment. Thus, one reason for more labour productivity in the United States was that it had more and better capital to work with. However, the interesting feature of the more rapid growth of United States labour productivity was that it reflected to a large degree a stronger growth of total factor productivity rather than of capital intensity, which pointed to a more general and efficient use of all resources in the economy. Plus, the investment boom in the United States was largely driven by the growth of business expenditure on information and communication technology.

There were two problems, however, that Western Europe had to face that differentiated its situation from the United States experience of the 1990s. First, the massive United States investment in fixed assets and new technology was financed, despite the low domestic savings rate, by large inflows of foreign capital. Second, the long United States upswing was also assisted by the boom in stock prices, which fuelled domestic spending and lowered the cost of equity capital for enterprises. If the risks of a premature tightening of monetary policy and of a disruptive fall in stock prices could be avoided, Western Europe could be on the threshold of a period of sustained growth of 3 per cent or more.

Activities in 1999

Trade, industry and enterprise development

The Committee for Trade, Industry and Enterprise Development (third session, Geneva, 7-10 June) [ECE/TRADE/231] considered how it could contribute to post-conflict recovery in South-East Europe. It endorsed the conclusions of the May 1999 international workshop "Implementation and Use of International Standards", which contained recommendations for reducing divergencies between international, regional and national standards that could create barriers to trade, and approved the establishment of an ad hoc team of specialists to study the relationship between international standardization and regulations as a means of reducing technical barriers to trade. The Committee approved new terms of reference and changed the name of the Working Party on International Contract Practices in Industry to the Working Party on International Legal and Commercial Practice. It also approved the establishment of an advisory group on the protection and implementation of intellectual property rights for promoting investment and an expert advisory group to consider possible revisions to the 1961 European Convention on International Commercial Arbitration [YUN 1961, p. 272]. It adopted its programme of work for 1999-2001 and agreed to organize a major round table prior to its next meeting in June 2000 on "Electronic Commerce and its Implications for International Trade in the UN/ECE Region".

The Committee endorsed the report of the fourth session of the UN Centre for the Facilitation of Procedures and Practices for Administration, Commerce and Transport (CEFACT) and requested the secretariat to prepare a working document on the possibilities for closer linkages between UN/CEFACT and the Committee's other subsidiary bodies. It noted the decisions taken by the Working Party on Technical Harmonization and Standardization Policies at its ninth session (17-19 May) and approved its proposal to establish an ad hoc team of specialists to examine the relationship between international standardization and regulations. The Committee endorsed the report of the Working Party on Standardization of Perishable Produce and Quality Development.

Transport

The Inland Transport Committee (sixty-first session, Geneva, 8-11 February) [ECE/TRANS/128] discussed, among other things, the transport situation in ECE member countries, assistance to countries in transition, the status of UN/ECE transport agreements and conventions, transport trends and policy and transport economics, road transport, road traffic safety, regulations for the construction of vehicles, rail transport and inland water transport, combined transport, customs questions, transport of dangerous and perishable goods and transport statistics.

As follow-up to the 1997 Regional Conference on Transport and the Environment [YUN 1997, p. 1005], the Committee endorsed the report of the first joint meeting on Transport and the Environment (July 1998) and underlined the importance of good cooperation and coordination among international organizations in the effective implementation of the Joint Programme of Action adopted at the 1997 Conference [ibid.].

The Committee asked member Governments to become contracting parties to the legal instruments developed under its auspices and to take all necessary measures to implement them. It also underscored ECE's role in the follow-up to the third Pan-European Transport Conference (Helsinki, Finland, 1997). The Committee amended and adopted a draft resolution (No. 248) inviting ECE member Governments to seek a solution to limit overall waiting times to 60 minutes for shuttle trains at borders.

The Committee also adopted a resolution (No. 247) inviting ECE Governments to take a census of traffic on the E Roads on their national territory in line with the 2000 Combined Census of Motor Traffic and Inventory of Standards and Parameters on Main International Traffic Arteries in Europe (E Road Census and Inventory) and to supply the results before 31 March 2002. It also recommended that Governments take a census of motor traffic on other non-urban roads and inform the ECE Executive Secretary by 31 December 1999 whether they agreed to implement the resolution.

Energy

The Committee on Sustainable Energy (ninth session, Geneva, 9-11 November) [ECE/ENERGY/41] noted progress achieved in applying the UN Framework Classification for Reserves/Resources [YUN 1997, p. 1006] to the energy and mineral sectors in Europe and Asia. It recommended that the Framework Classification be extended to gas, oil and uranium reserves/resources in the evaluation of world energy reserves/resources.

It invited participants to communicate to the secretariat the situation and experience of their respective countries in the development of mining legislation and regulations and requested the secretariat to consolidate and publish that information. The Committee agreed to hold a High-level Multi-Stakeholder Forum on Sustainable Energy in a Competitive Market: Forging Partnerships, in conjunction with its tenth session in 2000. It requested the secretariat to disseminate the initial strategy for the Energy Efficiency 21 Project and incorporate additional information and guidance provided by delegations for the preparation of a draft Project Plan (2000-2002).

The Committee reviewed ECE's provision of technical assistance and support to the Southeast European Cooperative Initiative (SECI) and Special Programme for the Economies of Central Asia [YUN 1996, p. 915]. It took note of the work done, recognized the difficult economic situation confronted by many economies in transition and invited the Executive Secretary to examine the possibilities of providing additional resources to meet their needs for technical assistance.

Agriculture

The Meeting of the Specialized Section on Standardization of Dry and Dried Produce (Fruit) (forty-sixth session, Geneva, 7-10 June) [TRADE/WP.7/GE.2/1999/12] discussed a draft revision of the standard layout for UN/ECE standards and agreed to finalize it at its next session. It also recommended a revision of standards for cashew kernels and in-shell walnuts and reached a compromise on quality classes and the colour chart for walnut kernels. It decided not to elaborate a standard for pitted dates for the time being.

The Timber Committee (fifty-seventh session, Geneva, 27-30 September) [ECE/TIM/93] reviewed its operational activities and cross-sectoral concerns relating to countries in transition and participation of the business community. It endorsed the general direction of ECE/FAO activities in support of sustainable forest management and welcomed the contributions of ECE/FAO to the Lisbon Ministerial Conference on the Protection of Forests in Europe [YUN 1998, p. 952] and the follow-up to it.

The session's special topic was "trade and environment issues in the forest and forest products sector". With regard to future work in that area, the need for objective monitoring and analysis was emphasized, especially where ECE/FAO had a comparative advantage. It was also suggested that in view of ECE's special role with regard to countries in transition, the possibility should be examined of approaching trade/environment issues from their perspective.

Environment

The Committee on Environmental Policy (sixth session, Geneva, 20-24 September) [ECE/CEP/69] discussed preparations for the Fifth Ministerial Conference "Environment for Europe", to be held in Kiev, Ukraine, in 2002, and established an ad hoc preparatory group of senior officials. The Committee stressed that integrating environmental concerns into sectoral policies would play a major role in the Kiev Conference and endorsed a draft decision for submission to the Commission in 2000.

The Committee reviewed the environmental performance of Croatia and Ukraine and adopted recommendations for strengthening environmental policy and management in those countries. An open-ended informal consultation on the experience gained in countries in transition in integrating environmental considerations into sectoral policies was held on 20 September, as was a round table on environmental policy and management in Ukraine. The Committee urged countries to make further contributions to the Trust Fund for Assistance to Countries in Transition to allow activities to continue and for the participation of delegations from countries in transition. It gave the Ad Hoc ECE Expert Group on Environmental Performance Reviews (EPR Expert Group) a new mandate for a period of two years.

The Committee approved holding the second meeting of the signatories to the Convention on Access to Information, Public Participation in Decision-making and Access to Justice in Environmental Matters (Århus Convention) [YUN 1998, p. 952] in 2000 and noted that the links between the convention and other ECE conventions should be looked at in the framework of the Committee's round table on cooperation between ECE and multilateral agreements.

The Committee endorsed a two-step approach to the project on cooperation between the ECE multilateral environmental agreements to improve their effectiveness and cooperation among them; a background paper would be prepared for a round table to be held at the Committee's seventh session in 2000.

Human settlements

The Committee on Human Settlements (sixtieth session, Geneva, 13-15 September) [ECE/HBP/114] discussed the draft ECE strategy for sustainable quality of life in human settlements in the twenty-first century and agreed to adopt it at a ministerial meeting to be organized in conjunction with its 2000 session.

The Committee noted the report of the ECE focal point on land administration in the Balkan region on the effects of the conflict there and agreed that the Working Party on Land Administration should decide on further work based on a long-term strategy for the subregion at its first session in November.

The Committee agreed that the organizational set-up of the Housing and Urban Management Advisory Network was appropriate for cooperation with the business community and that guidelines on relations with the business community should be developed.

The Committee invited the Conference of European Statisticians to organize a joint meeting on housing and building statistics. It reviewed its operational activities and invited the secretariat and its Bureau to further promote expert missions on land administration and spatial planning to supplement similar operational activities on country profiles on the housing sector and sectoral case studies.

Statistics

The Conference of European Statisticians (forty-seventh session, Neuchâtel, Switzerland, 14-16 June) [ECE/CES/56] considered the implications of meetings of the Conference's parent bodies—the May session of ECE and the March session of the Statistical Commission (see PART THREE, Chapter XV). The Conference requested its Bureau to consider prioritizing the Conference's work programme for review in 2000. It noted the Bureau's initiative in establishing a task force to look into the possible role statistics could play in a wide-ranging programme of recovery and reconstruction of Southern Europe after the end of the Kosovo conflict.

The Conference agreed to review the integrated presentation of the international statistical work in the ECE region, especially labour and health statistics and the hidden economy. In labour statistics, it agreed that more attention should be given to relevant policy indicators for monitoring the effectiveness of labour programmes, structural changes in the labour market and other areas. Support was expressed for making health statistics a priority and coordination encouraged in international health work and data collection. It was agreed that a health monitoring system capable of supporting policy analysis and decision-making in health should be the long-term goal of the Conference's work.

The Conference also considered joint data collection and assistance to countries in transition and the involvement of national statistical offices in analysis and forecasting. It discussed performance indicators for statistical offices and recommended that the Bureau discuss at its next meeting how to take the issue forward and whether to constitute a small working group.

Strengthening cooperation

The Commission had before it a note by the Executive Secretary [E/ECE/1368 & Add.1] on strengthening cooperation within the ECE region, including operational activities and cooperation with regional and subregional groupings, initiatives and organizations. The Executive Secretary said that there was an increasing need for member States to explore possibilities for providing additional financing in support of various types of activities, such as advisory missions, seminars and training workshops, enabling countries in transition to implement the norms and standards adopted by ECE. Additional funding was also needed for developing projects within the framework of subregional groupings and initiatives, in particular the Southeast European Cooperative Initiative and the Special Programme for the Economies of Central Asia. ECE also recognized the specific problems of the countries of the Mediterranean area, which comprised developing countries, economies in transition and advanced market economies.

ECE had witnessed a diminishing level of resources with respect to funding and staffing for the Regional Advisory Programme in 1999. Consequently, activities of the Regional Advisers had been considerably reduced. To maximize the impact of its technical assistance, the Executive Secretary suggested that the Commission request each PSB to look at operational activities within its field of competence and mandate and provide its views on the directions they should take, including the activities of the Regional Advisers. A synthesis of the conclusions of those reviews would be submitted to the Commission in 2000 to enable it to provide guidance for the technical assistance programme and its financing.

The Executive Secretary also submitted a February note [E/ECE/1371] on cooperation with European institutions and pan-European organizations and subregional organizations. By **resolution 54/5** of 8 October, the General Assembly invited the Black Sea Economic Cooperation Organization to participate in the sessions and work of the Assembly in the capacity of observer (see p. 1360).

The Commission also had before it a note by the Secretary-General on regional hearings in preparation for the Millennium Assembly of the United Nations [A/54/503]. The hearings were convened by the executive secretaries of the five regional commissions for a representative segment of civil society, with the participation of members of the commissions. The ECE regional hearing was held in Geneva on 7 and 8 July.

Cross-sectoral concerns

The Commission had before it a note by the secretariat on cross-sectoral concerns, including intersectoral linkages [E/ECE/1369]. It dealt with progress made in respect of two cross-sectoral issues—sustainable development and gender mainstreaming—that were identified under the Plan of Action on the Strengthening of Economic Cooperation in Europe [YUN 1997, p. 1002].

The note stated that the ECE Committee on Environmental Policy played the key policy role in furthering pan-European cooperation on the environmental component of sustainability. Its work was organized around three pillars: the "Environment for Europe" process; the environmental performance reviews; and the environmental conventions. The report outlined activities undertaken under the "Environment for Europe" process, as well as in the areas of environmental reviews, environmental conventions, transport, statistics, human settlements, timber, industry and enterprise development and sustainable energy. It described the development of intersectoral activities in transport and the environment as a follow-up to the 1997 Regional Conference on Transport and the Environment [YUN 1997, p. 1005].

Gender-mainstreaming concerns as they related to the environment were expressed within the framework of the Convention on Access to Information, Public Participation in Decision-making and Access to Justice in Environmental Matters (Århus Convention) [YUN 1998, p. 952]. The note also described gender-mainstreaming efforts in the areas of transportation; statistics; economic analysis; trade, industry and enterprise development; timber; and human settlements. The outcome of the 1998 Seminar on Implementing Economic and Social Rights of Women in Countries in Transition was summarized.

Restructuring and revitalization

As follow-up to Economic and Social Council resolution 1998/46 [YUN 1998, p. 1262] on further measures for the restructuring and revitalization of the United Nations in the economic, social and related fields, the Executive Secretary submitted to the Commission a note [E/ECE/1370] describing actions that had been taken in response to the guidance provided by that resolution.

The first Regional Inter-agency Coordination Meeting for the ECE region (Geneva, 9 February) reviewed cooperation mechanisms and arrangements at the regional level and exchanged views on areas of cooperation to improve UN system response to the region's needs. It was agreed that dialogue at the regional level needed to be further developed for all organizations collectively to improve their common understanding of the needs, trends and challenges that would lead to a joint assessment of the economic and social situation. The meeting also underlined the rationale for developing regional consultations and activities, recognizing that there were problems inherently regional in nature that could not be solved at the country level, such as air pollution and border crossing. It further agreed that a common assessment of the regional situation should be carried out, which should lead to further defining priority areas for cooperative efforts in the region.

The report also examined cooperation with a number of UN agencies and programmes.

Latin America and the Caribbean

The Economic Commission for Latin America and the Caribbean (ECLAC) did not meet in 1999. The Commission's twenty-eighth session was to be held in Mexico City from 3 to 7 April 2000.

Economic trends

According to the 1999 summary of the economic survey of Latin America and the Caribbean [E/2000/14], the region's economic performance was weak, with almost zero growth and downturns in investment and consumption. The slowdown in economic growth was due to a sharp decrease in capital inflows, together with the high volume of interest and dividend payments abroad; low commodity prices, except for oil; and the downturn in intraregional trade experienced by the South American countries. Regional growth stagnated at 0.3 per cent and per capita GDP declined by 1.3 per cent. The regional average, however, masked sharp differences across countries. Mexico and much of Central America and the Caribbean grew at moderate or even high rates. Costa Rica, Cuba, the Dominican Republic, Nicaragua and Trinidad and Tobago were particularly notable, with GDP growth of between 6 and 8 per cent. The South American countries, by contrast, with their concentration in commodity exports and their significant level of intraregional industrial trade, fared poorly. Declines of 3 per cent or more were posted in Argentina, Colombia, Ecuador and Venezuela, while Brazil's growth was a modest 0.8 per cent.

The regional inflation rate, which, at 9.5 per cent, was the lowest in half a century, remained under control despite the depreciation of a number of currencies. Of 22 countries for which information was available, 17 had single-digit inflation rates. Brazil and Ecuador were the only countries where the inflation rate increased significantly, from 2.5 per cent in 1998 to about 8.5 per cent in 1999, and from 43 per cent to 61 per cent, respectively.

Regional exports rose by nearly 5 per cent in 1999, but that result was largely due to Mexico, as half of the countries posted lower export values. Export growth, without Mexico, would have been negative (-3 per cent). The slump in export earnings in the region was due to weak commodity prices of agricultural products and industrial commodities in the world market and the fact that the bulk of sales were made in the regional market, where they were hurt by the weakness of economic activity and demand.

The total value of the region's merchandise imports fell for the first time in 15 years, by more than 4 per cent; excluding Mexico, it fell by 15 per cent. That was brought about by slack domestic demand and currency devaluations.

The regional current account deficit narrowed from $87.5 billion in 1998 to $56.5 billion in 1999, due to the slump in imports triggered by the stagnation of income levels and the depreciation of local currencies. Nominal interest rates were lowered, and a number of countries shifted towards flexible exchange rates. The most prominent was Brazil, but similar steps were also taken in Chile, Colombia and Ecuador.

Sluggish economic growth rates led to the worsening of labour market problems. For the region as a whole, employment slipped from 53.7 per cent of the working-age population in 1998 to 52.5 per cent in 1999, while unemployment climbed from 8 to 8.7 per cent, the highest rate registered since records began to be kept for a significant number of countries. However, employment levels in Mexico and some Central American and Caribbean countries were boosted by higher growth rates. The largest increases in unemployment were in Argentina, Chile, Colombia, Ecuador and Venezuela.

External debt

In 1999, the region's total external debt expanded slightly to just under $750 billion from $700 billion the previous year, a 0.5 per cent nominal increase, the lowest rate for the 1990s. Jamaica, Peru and Venezuela saw a reduction in their external debt in nominal terms, while Argentina, Chile, Costa Rica and Uruguay saw their gross external liabilities increase by between 4 and 7 per cent. Paraguay registered a spectacular increase of nearly 40 per cent due to an unprecedented $400 million government bond issue. Indicators of the region's external debt burden remained the same as those for 1998. The ratio of interest due to exports of goods and services held steady at 17 per cent, while the ratio of external debt to exports of goods and services eased slightly to 216 per cent. Over half of the countries continued to display satisfactory debt burden indicators, while in some countries those indicators remained cause for concern. Ecuador defaulted on interest payments on its collateralized Brady bonds and on other government liabilities with private sector creditors. However, the international financial community appeared to see those events as being confined to Ecuador.

Activities in 1999

Development policy and regional economic cooperation

The biennial report on ECLAC activities covering May 1998 to April 2000 [E/2000/40] stated that the Economic Development Division continued to monitor and analyse the region's national macroeconomic policies in order to supply the regional and international communities with information on the state of the regional economy. It also assessed the effects of structural changes and institutional reforms on patterns of economic growth and social equity. Due to the disturbances of the Asian crisis in 1997, which turned into a global financial crisis in 1998, the region's economies went through economic difficulties that revealed the external fragility of their economic growth patterns, particularly international capital movements. The *Economic Survey of Latin America and the Caribbean* and the *Preliminary Overview of the Economies of Latin America and the Caribbean* analysed the state of the regional economy and fuelled a regional debate on the most appropriate monetary and exchange-rate policy and on the modalities of capital account openness. The Division focused its research programme on the linkages between the results seen in the region in terms of growth and equity, on the one hand, and the macroeconomic policies and structural and institutional reforms executed in the countries of the region and the international context, on the other. Priority issues included the study of macroeconomic and fiscal policies aimed at restoring macroeconomic stability; strengthening domestic capacity to generate financial resources for investment and facilitating the working of institutions and instruments to channel those resources toward capital accumulation; productivity trends and job creation; and social spending. The Division carried out operational activities that sought to promote a multidisciplinary approach to the evaluation of development policies in the region during the preceding 15 years. Activities were also carried out in fiscal policy and public sector decentralization and institutional requirements for market-led structures in the region. In addition to numerous technical documents and studies prepared for those projects, a number of seminars, workshops and training courses were organized, particularly in fiscal policy, decentralization, and the relation between growth, employment and equity. The Division also participated in activities supporting negotiations for the Free Trade Area of the Americas (FTAA).

The Latin American Centre for Economic and Social Documentation, which focused on the management of information and information technologies for development, directed its activities towards enhancing knowledge, reflection and dissemination of new information management and information technology standards that conditioned the performance and functioning of Latin American and Caribbean societies. Training seminars were held on the design of information projects (Santiago, Chile, 11-15 January); knowledge management with information science researchers (Medellín, Columbia, 18-21 March); and knowledge management via Internet web sites (Santiago, 23-27 August, 29 November–3 December).

The Latin American and Caribbean Institute of Economic and Social Planning worked to satisfy the concerns and priorities expressed by member Governments on the central issue of strategic management and reform of the State. It organized a high-level seminar on basic planning functions (Santiago, 7-8 October) and organized 11 international, 4 subregional and 3 national courses, involving nearly 500 participants from the region, as well as the first international distance education course supported by the Internet on local management of solid household waste and environmental impact. A cycle of conferences in Argentina was held on knowledge, globalization and territory.

The International Trade Unit, the main body responsible for integration, open regionalism and regional cooperation, continued to analyse the evolution of the main Latin American and Caribbean regional integration schemes and their prospects. An expert meeting (Santiago, 17-18 November) was held on open regionalism: evolution and outlook—comparing experiences between Latin America and the Caribbean and the Asia-Pacific region. There was also a meeting of the Integration and Cooperation Secretariats of Latin America and the Caribbean (Lima, Peru, 12 November). A workshop was held in conjunction with the Andean Community to identify measures affecting trade in services (Lima, 20-22 September).

Productive, technological and entrepreneurial development

The Division of Production, Productivity and Management continued to work with countries on analysing and implementing policies and actions to enhance the technological dimension of productive activities; increase competitiveness; overcome bottlenecks in the markets for key factors of production; and stimulate entrepreneurial development.

A project on mining clusters in Latin America, consisting of comparative studies with mining clusters in developed countries, was started, and implementation began on a project funded by the German Agency for Technical Cooperation (GTZ) on a natural reserve cluster development strategy.

ECLAC/GTZ seminars were held on education and training to meet the challenges of economic openness and company restructuring (Mexico City, 15-16 July) and land markets (La Paz, Bolivia, 10 September; Lima, 1 December). Workshops dealt with concepts and methodologies in cluster analysis (Santiago, 17-18 May) and the promotion of small and medium-sized enterprises (Santiago, 10 September). An international seminar on globalization and new business strategies in Latin America took place in Santiago on 20 and 21 December.

International trade and development finance

The International Trade Unit, the main ECLAC body in charge of linkages with the world economy, competitiveness and productive specialization, focused on changes in the international economy and their effect on the demand for the region's exports, the international organization of production and the capacity to adapt. The Fifth Meeting of Trade Policy Officials of Latin America and the Caribbean was held in Lima on 11 and 12 November to foster interchange of opinions and develop approaches to define negotiating stances among countries in the region with respect to FTAA and the World Trade Organization negotiations. A workshop was also held (Santiago, November) on the need for research and the training of negotiators on multilateral negotiation issues, and a regional meeting took place on international trade research and training needs in Latin America and the Caribbean (Santiago, 4-5 November).

Environmental and land resource sustainability

In 1999, the ECLAC Environment and Development Division was restructured into two divisions, the Environment and Human Settlements Division and the Division on Natural Resources and Infrastructure. The subprogramme organized the second meeting of the Inter-Agency Technical Committee of the Forum of Ministers of the Environment of Latin America and the Caribbean (Santiago, 7-8 April); workshops on the identification of an international agenda for research into water resources in the Altiplano (Arica, Chile, 26-28 May) and on policy, law and administration of biosafety in Latin America and the Caribbean (Santiago, 29-30 November); and seminars on the concession of public services and the protection and promotion of foreign investments (Buenos Aires, Argentina, 1-2 July), innovative cases of local management for the protection of the air and climate in Latin America (Santiago, 4-6 November), and urban management strategies and tools for sustainable development in Latin America and the Caribbean (Santiago, 6-7 December).

The subprogramme coordinated several exhibitions on different themes, including: decentralization and the environment (Validivia, Chile, 20-22 June); openness, sustainability and FTAA (Ottawa, Canada, 4-5 October); and institutional cooperation trade and the environment (Miami, United States, 28-29 October).

In human settlements, support was provided to the fourth meeting of the Forum for Consultation and Coordination among the Ministers and High-level Authorities of the Housing and Urban Development Sector in Latin America and the Caribbean and its eighth regional meeting (Havana, Cuba, 10-17 October). Activities began under a project that assisted urban management in countries of the region, with emphasis on poverty alleviation and the pursuit of social equity, efficiency of public services and urban renewal.

In response to emergencies caused by various natural disasters, a project was launched on improving damage assessment methodology to promote natural disaster mitigation and risk-reduction awareness and preparedness in the region.

Social development and equity

ECLAC's programme of work in social development and equity was carried out in four sectors: designing and implementing social policies, programmes and projects; intensifying and keeping up to date the social diagnosis of the countries in the region; examining the effects of socio-economic development policies on welfare and social equity; and analysing the social, economic and institutional effects of the cultivation, traffic and consumption of drugs, and strategies to deal with them. Seminars, meetings, workshops and round tables were organized, in most cases co-sponsored with other organizations. Several publications were issued dealing with topics related to equity trends in education and employment, youth and rural development, comparative experiences in health care, the management of social policies and programmes, and citizen safety. The 1999 edition of *Social Panorama of Latin America* was also published and included a study on the living conditions of older adults, especially their family arrangements.

Integration of women in development

ECLAC activities for the integration of women in development in 1999 continued to focus on the follow-up to the Regional Programme of Action for the Women of Latin America and the Caribbean, 1995-2001 [YUN 1994, p. 739], the Platform for Action of the Fourth World Conference on Women [YUN 1995, p. 1170], the Santiago Consensus [YUN 1997, p. 1012] and preparations for the eighth session of the Regional Conference on Women in Latin America and the Caribbean, to be held in Lima in February 2000.

Two meetings of the Presiding Officers of the Regional Conference were held (Curaçao, Netherlands Antilles, 3-4 June; Santiago, 11-12 November). The Third Caribbean Ministerial Conference on Women: Review and Appraisal of the Fourth World Conference on Women Platform for Action (Port of Spain, Trinidad and Tobago, 5-7 October) assessed progress achieved, decided on future action and adopted the Port of Spain Consensus. At the Central American meeting in preparation for the eighth session of the Regional Conference (San Salvador, El Salvador, 11-12 October), participants formulated a subregional contribution to the Conference in the form of a 19-point proposal.

Population and development

The Population Division-Latin American and Caribbean Demographic Centre (CELADE) assigned high priority to monitoring demographic trends relating to fertility, mortality and international migration in the countries of the region. It published the *Demographic Bulletin*, which included estimates and projections at the national level. The database on spatial distribution of the population and urbanization was updated and improved, as was the databank of the project on investigation of international migration in Latin America. Work continued on updating the RADATAM-Plus software (retrieval of data for small areas by microcomputer), developed to facilitate the management of large amounts of data from different sources in combination with geographical data systems and related tools.

Several analytical studies were made of the socio-economic situation of older persons in some countries of the region, with special emphasis on social vulnerability. They were discussed at the Latin American and Caribbean Symposium on Older Persons (Santiago, 8-10 September) in the context of the International Year of Older Persons (see p. 1124).

Regarding international migration, the Division supported the activities of the Regional Advisory Group on Migration and worked with the International Organization for Migration in supporting the Andean Community countries (Bolivia, Colombia, Ecuador, Peru, Venezuela) in the design and application of an integrated information system on international migration. A report was prepared on the use of remittances from migrants to their place of origin.

Economic statistics and projections

The ECLAC Economic Statistics and Projections Division continued to carry out activities to expand the regional framework of statistical information; develop and disseminate statistical information; promote regional cooperation on statistical matters; and produce forward-looking studies on development. A workshop was held on the technology of electronic commerce in statistical data via the Internet (Santiago, 24-28 May). In the household survey area, the Division extensively participated in the activities of the MECOVI programme to improve surveys on living conditions in the region by providing technical assistance to countries in training local technical staff, holding regional workshops and designing databases. Improvements were made to methods for estimating income distribution and poverty and in calculating new indices of unit value for international trade. A system was put into practice for the retrieval and analysis of data from the External Trade Data Bank for Latin America and the Caribbean, from the Balance-of-Payments Data Bank and from the Regional Short-term Indicators Database.

The meeting of Directors of Statistics of the Americas (Santiago, 24-26 March) approved the establishment of a new institutional framework involving the creation of the Statistical Conference of the Americas as an ECLAC subsidiary body. Several projects were under way in relation to the formation of statistical databases, household surveys, improvements to national accounts, the production of basic statistics and social programmes and policies. A technical seminar on consumer price indices was held (Santiago, 21-23 April).

Technical cooperation and assistance

During 1999, ECLAC's Programme Planning and Operations Division completed 71 regional, subregional and national projects, financed from extrabudgetary funds. It launched 32 new projects, 15 of which were completed in 1999.

ECLAC continued to promote technical cooperation among developing countries (TCDC) through the new operational guidelines for the triennium 1997-1999, adopted by the UNDP/UNFPA Executive Board [YUN 1997, p. 891], and to build TCDC elements into the execution of projects financed from extrabudgetary resources. That involved strengthening national institutions; setting up cooperation networks and supporting their operation; strengthening information systems to better communicate the demand and supply of technical cooperation between the countries; holding seminars and technical meetings to facilitate an exchange of experiences of interest to the countries; preparing studies and reports specifically aimed at identifying cooperation possibilities; and facilitating the provision of horizontal cooperation services from experts and local consultants linked to projects.

The ECLAC web site became the main information tool, producing gains in terms of coverage and in the timeliness of information relating to TCDC activities in technical cooperation projects being executed. It replaced the bulletin *Cooperation and Development*, which was published until mid-1997.

Subregional activities

Caribbean

The ECLAC subregional headquarters for the Caribbean—the secretariat of the Caribbean Development and Cooperation Committee (CDCC) (Port of Spain)—focused on the analysis of issues relevant to the economic and social development of the subregion. CDCC, in its capacity as provisional joint secretariat, continued its activities relating to the Global Conference on the Sustainable Development of Small Island Developing States [YUN 1994, p. 783], in cooperation with the secretariat of the Caribbean Community (CARICOM). Meetings were held to assist member countries in preparing for the General Assembly's special session for an assessment and appraisal of the implementation of the Programme of Action for the Sustainable Development of Small Island Developing States (see p. 771). Project proposals relating to the Programme of Action were submitted to a meeting of potential donors and representatives of small island developing States (New York, 24-26 February).

CDCC also assisted member States with preparations for the Assembly's special session for the review and appraisal of the Programme of Action of the International Conference on Population and Development [YUN 1994, p. 956] (see PART THREE, Chapter VIII).

CDCC convened a Caribbean subregional meeting (Port of Spain, 2 September), which reviewed the implementation of the Programme of Action of the World Summit for Social Development [YUN 1995, p. 1115]. To commemorate the International Year of Older Persons (see p. 1124), a special meeting (Port of Spain, 3 September) was held to consider strategies and programmes relating to ageing and older persons in the Caribbean.

As a follow-up to the Fourth World Conference on Women [ibid., p. 1170], several technical workshops were held to assist countries in preparing their country reports, which were included in the Caribbean report on the review and appraisal of the Platform for Action adopted by the Conference. That report was adopted at the Third Caribbean Ministerial Conference on Women (Port of Spain, 5-7 October).

CDCC supported the secretariats of CARICOM and the Association of Caribbean States on issues relating to trade agreements, new information technologies, transfer of technologies and other subjects of interest to the subregion. It also cooperated with the Organization of Eastern Caribbean States and other regional and subregional institutions.

Mexico and Central America

During 1999, the ECLAC subregional headquarters in Mexico City continued to expand its studies on regional and hemisphere-wide integration, macroeconomic policies and growth, sustainable technological development in agricultural production, industrial competitiveness, new modalities of participation on the international market, policies on social development and equity, and integration in energy.

The subregional headquarters organized a seminar on "The Fiscal Covenant" (Guatemala City, Guatemala, 22 January), as well as the Guatemalan national seminar on the same topic (Guatemala City, 12 January).

At an international symposium of economists on globalization and the problems of development (Havana, 18-22 January), ECLAC presented a paper on the myths and realities of financial modernization in Central America. It also participated in preparatory meetings organized by the General Secretariat of the Central American Integration System (San Salvador, El Salvador, 13 April and 26-27 April) for the Second Meeting of the Consultative Group for the Reconstruction and Transformation of Central America (Stockholm, Sweden, 23-29 May).

Cooperation between the United Nations and the Latin American Economic System

In accordance with decision 53/408 [YUN 1998, p. 966], the General Assembly considered the Secretary-General's 1998 report on cooperation between the United Nations and the Latin American Economic System [ibid., p. 965].

GENERAL ASSEMBLY ACTION

On 25 October [meeting 38], the General Assembly adopted **resolution 54/8** [draft: A/54/L.13 & Add.1] without vote [agenda item 32].

Cooperation between the United Nations and the Latin American Economic System

The General Assembly,

Recalling its resolution 52/3 of 22 October 1997 on cooperation between the United Nations and the Latin American Economic System,

Having considered the report of the Secretary-General on cooperation between the United Nations and the Latin American Economic System,

Bearing in mind the Agreement between the United Nations and the Latin American Economic System, in which the parties agree to strengthen and expand their cooperation in matters that are of common concern in the field of their respective competence pursuant to their constitutional instruments,

Considering that the Economic Commission for Latin America and the Caribbean has intensified its ties of cooperation with the Latin American Economic System,

Bearing in mind that the Permanent Secretariat of the Latin American Economic System has carried out programmes with the support of the United Nations Development Programme in areas that are considered of priority for the economic and social development of the region,

Considering that the Latin American Economic System is developing joint activities with the specialized agencies and other organizations and programmes of the United Nations system, such as the United Nations Conference on Trade and Development, the United Nations Educational, Scientific and Cultural Organization, the Food and Agriculture Organization of the United Nations and the World Intellectual Property Organization,

Welcoming the continued monitoring of changes in the treatment of topics relating to the United Nations system, in close contact with the delegations of the Member States participating in such deliberations,

1. *Takes note with satisfaction* of the report of the Secretary-General;

2. *Urges* the Economic Commission for Latin America and the Caribbean to continue deepening its coordination and mutual support activities with the Latin American Economic System;

3. *Urges* the United Nations Development Programme, within its new overall framework and high-priority development objectives in support of sustainable human development, to renew its financial and technical cooperation with the programmes that the Permanent Secretariat of the Latin American Economic System is carrying out in areas of mutual interest and concern, aimed at complementing the technical assistance activities conducted by the Latin American Economic System;

4. *Urges* the specialized agencies and other organizations, funds and programmes of the United Nations system to continue and intensify their support for, and cooperation in the activities of, the Latin American Economic System;

5. *Requests* both the Secretary-General of the United Nations and the Permanent Secretary of the

Latin American Economic System to assess, at the appropriate time, the implementation of the Agreement between the United Nations and the Latin American Economic System and to report thereon to the General Assembly at its fifty-sixth session;

6. *Requests* the Secretary-General to submit to the General Assembly at its fifty-sixth session a report on the implementation of the present resolution.

Programme and organizational questions

Millennium Assembly

The hearings for the ECLAC region (Santiago, 1-2 September) held in preparation for the UN Millennium Assembly in 2000 were conducted under the theme "The United Nations in the twenty-first century: a view from Latin America and the Caribbean"[A/54/718].

Implementation of pilot projects on budgetary practices and procedures

In a May report [A/53/947], submitted in response to General Assembly decision 53/456 [YUN 1998, p. 1274], the Secretary-General stated that the Department of Management team had carried out an April assessment of the results of the implementation of the pilot project by which authority had been extended to ECLAC in several areas of human resources management and limited aspects of financial management. The team concluded that the project had been implemented without any impact on budgetary practices and procedures; regular monitoring had ensured the proper application of the rules and regulations and overall policies of the Organization. The Secretary-General would continue close monitoring of ECLAC's delegation of authority at the current level (see PART FIVE, Chapter II).

Western Asia

The Economic and Social Commission for Western Asia (ESCWA) held its twentieth session in Beirut, Lebanon, on 27 and 28 May [E/1999/41/Rev.1 & Corr.1]. On 28 May, it held a special session to commemorate its twenty-fifth anniversary and adopt the Beirut Declaration. The session was preceded by the eleventh session of the Technical Committee (Beirut, 25-26 May) [E/ESCWA/20/4]. ESCWA adopted resolutions relating to: changes introduced in the programme of work and priorities for the 1998-1999 biennium; the frequency of sessions of its subsidiary bodies and summaries of their reports; the draft programme of work and priorities for the 2000-2001 biennium; the redesignation of the Technical Committee to Preparatory Committee; and the relocation of its permanent headquarters to Beirut.

Economic and social trends

Economic trends

Economic growth accelerated in the ESCWA region in 1999, according to the summary of the survey of economic and social developments in the region [E/2000/15]. Provisional estimates indicated that the combined real GDP of ESCWA members, excluding Iraq, grew by 3.12 per cent, compared with 2.31 per cent in 1998. Real GDP growth rates differed significantly between the Gulf Cooperation Council (GCC) countries (Bahrain, Kuwait, Oman, Qatar, Saudi Arabia, United Arab Emirates) and the countries with more diversified economies (Egypt, Iraq, Jordan, Lebanon, Syrian Arab Republic, Yemen, the West Bank and Gaza Strip) and among countries within each group. The combined real GDP growth rate for the GCC countries was 2.63 per cent, while those countries with more diversified economies, excluding Iraq, achieved a 4.1 per cent growth rate.

Estimates indicated that among the GCC countries, the higher growth rates in 1999 were registered in the United Arab Emirates (6 per cent), Bahrain (4.5 per cent) and Oman (3.7 per cent), and the lower rates in Saudi Arabia (1.8 per cent), Qatar (1.3 per cent) and Kuwait (0.5 per cent). Important factors affecting economic growth in the GCC countries were higher oil prices and revenues, oil production cutbacks, fiscal and monetary policies and economic diversification and reform.

The United Arab Emirates real growth rate of 6 per cent was achieved because the Government was able to maintain planned expenditures, despite tumbling oil prices and revenues, by drawing on its earnings from overseas investments. Oman—not a member of the Organization of Petroleum Exporting Countries (OPEC)—reduced its oil production only marginally in 1999 and benefited from the economic and structural reforms undertaken in previous years. Bahrain, also not an OPEC member, did not curtail its oil production in 1999 and continued State expenditures on planned projects. Its tourism and banking sectors performed well. The improvement of Saudi Arabia's real GDP over 1998 was due to the considerable increase in government expenditures and investment by the private sector as a result of the sharp rise in oil prices and revenues. Real growth in the non-oil sector, which accounted for 64 per cent of GDP in 1999, was estimated to have more than offset the 4.7 per cent decline in oil production and reductions in capital spending in the energy sector. Qatar maintained its austere spending plans in 1999, which hampered growth in the non-oil sectors. Moreover, the exodus of expatriates from the country continued to depress overall market activity, particularly in the real estate, trade and services sectors. Kuwait's positive, though low, growth rate of 0.5 per cent in 1999 was a result of a cut in oil production by 12.02 per cent and the slow increase in government expenditures after oil revenues rebounded sharply from 1998 levels.

Among ESCWA members with diversified economies, estimates of real GDP growth rates differed widely. Egypt, Jordan, Yemen and the West Bank and Gaza Strip achieved rates of 2 per cent or higher, while Lebanon and the Syrian Arab Republic registered rates of 1 per cent or lower. Egypt's real GDP grew by 6 per cent in 1999, the highest rate not only among that group of countries but within the region as a whole. That was a result mainly of its economic reform and structural adjustment programme, the surge in foreign direct investment inflows, booming tourism and a rejuvenated private sector. Yemen's real GDP growth rose from 3.2 to 4.2 per cent due to a 5 per cent increase in oil production and a sharp rise in prices. In the West Bank and Gaza Strip, real GDP was estimated to have grown from 4.1 per cent in 1998 to 4.6 per cent in 1999. Its economy benefited from the services of the international airport and the Gaza port, surging tourism and soft loans for economic development. Estimates indicated that Jordan's real GDP grew from 1.7 per cent in 1998 to 2.1 per cent in 1999, owing to a notable increase in private investment and higher growth in the services sector, particularly tourism. Lebanon's real GDP growth declined from 3 per cent in 1998 to 0.8 per cent in 1999 and was brought about by the continued crisis in the construction sector, sustained mostly by high interest rates. The Syrian Arab Republic's real GDP grew by 7.8 per cent in 1998 but only 0.5 per cent in 1999. The reversal was due to the decline in agricultural output, a major contributor to the country's economy. Economic conditions in Iraq remained very poor, despite an increase in economic growth due to the effects of significantly higher oil revenues. The economic sanctions imposed by the United Nations (see p. 240) remained in force.

Labour market conditions remained generally unfavourable for job seekers in most of the countries with more diversified economies in 1999. However, Egypt's unemployment rate dropped from 8.3 per cent in 1998 to 7.9 per cent in 1999 due to economic reforms, gigantic development projects, surging foreign direct investment and the booming tourism sector. Labour market conditions improved in Yemen and the West Bank and Gaza in 1999, compared to the previous year. In GCC countries, the indigenization of the labour force, which had been a declared policy for many years and was enforced strictly in 1998, continued in 1999.

Estimated 1999 inflation rates were marginally higher than in the previous year in four of the six GCC countries. It was highest in the United Arab Emirates, while Qatar was the only GCC country to have witnessed a decline from the previous year's level. Except for Qatar, tight monetary policies, higher government expenditures and the partial removal of subsidies on goods and services provided by the Government were responsible for the increased inflation rates. Bahrain registered a 0.5 per cent inflation rate, the lowest among all ESCWA members. Among the countries with more diversified economies, Lebanon and the Syrian Arab Republic had the lowest estimated inflation rate, at 1 per cent. The sharpest decline in inflation among ESCWA members was estimated to have taken place in Yemen, where it dropped from 12.2 per cent in 1998 to 2 per cent in 1999 due to the strengthening of the Yemeni rial as a result of higher oil revenues and a significant increase in foreign aid.

In 1999, budget deficits as a percentage of GDP decreased in most countries of the region to about 3 per cent or less. The largest declines were registered in the GCC countries, which based their respective 1999 budgets on the assumption that oil prices would average about $11 per barrel. To reduce their dependence on oil revenue, GCC countries introduced policies aimed at raising non-oil revenues and reducing expenditures. Those member countries with more diversified economies resorted increasingly to domestic resources mobilization, such as improving tax collection, introducing new taxes and raising the rates of existing ones, as well as increasing the use of financial instruments, such as bonds and treasury bills. Both groups of member countries sought to reduce budget deficits either by raising the prices and user fees of public utilities and services or by reducing subsidies and granting lower increases in public sector wages and salaries.

Oil

The region's oil production averaged 17.74 million barrels per day in 1999, a decline of some 3.3 per cent compared with the 18.35 million barrels per day in 1998. That reduction, which was a result of OPEC's March decision to cut production, was offset by the rise in prices. The annual average price of the OPEC crude-oil basket was estimated at $17.47 per barrel for 1999, which was about $5 per barrel higher than the average for the preceding year, representing an increase of over 40 per cent. The region's oil revenues totalled some $93.94 billion in 1999, a 35.8 per cent increase over the 1998 level of $69.15 billion.

Trade

Overall trade performance in the region in 1999 was largely determined by oil export levels. In the first half of the year, when oil prices were depressed, GCC exports remained almost 11 per cent below their 1998 level, but they accelerated as the full impact of increased oil prices became apparent. Total exports for GCC countries were estimated to have increased by 21 per cent and those of the more diversified economies by 12 per cent. The value of ESCWA's total exports in 1999 was estimated at $117.5 billion, compared to $98 billion in 1998. Export revenues for the GCC countries were estimated at $104.8 billion in 1999, with Saudi Arabia and the United Arab Emirates achieving the highest levels, while the smallest were registered by Bahrain. The value of exports of the more diversified economies, excluding Iraq and the West Bank and Gaza Strip, was $12.7 billion, led by Egypt and the Syrian Arab Republic.

ESCWA's total imports in the first half of 1999 dropped by about 6 per cent compared to the same period in 1998, due mainly to a 12 per cent drop in the imports of GCC countries, which accounted for more than 65 per cent of the region's imports. In the second half of the year, as export revenues rose, imports began to increase. Overall, imports of GCC countries rose by an estimated average of 4 per cent in 1999 compared with 1998. The more diversified economies achieved import growth of nearly 4 per cent between the first half of 1998 and the first half of 1999, owing primarily to the increase in the Syrian Arab Republic's imports. For the year as a whole, the more diversified economies registered an estimated negative growth in imports of nearly 2 per cent over 1998.

In November, the GCC countries, after two decades of debate, agreed to establish a customs union by 2005. The unification of tariffs would be an important step forward for GCC countries in their negotiations to establish a free trade area with the EU.

Social trends

ESCWA's population continued to grow at an estimated rate of 2.9 per cent, and high fertility combined with low mortality had led to an imbalance in the age structure of the population, creating a population momentum phenomenon. Therefore, an early stabilization of population would make a crucial contribution to realizing the objective of sustainable economic development. Unless comprehensive macro-level measures targeting women at various micro- and household levels were taken at the regional level, the total fertility rate would remain well above the stabilization level of 2.1 children per women until 2015. High fertility rates were often associated with a low level of female participation in the labour force.

At the dawn of the new millennium, the imbalance between social and economic development, which was initially created by the sudden upsurge in oil revenues in the 1970s, had not yet been totally eliminated in the region, despite significant improvements during the past few decades. The shortfalls of social development were more pronounced, if the data were presented for each gender separately.

The ESCWA region had made a substantial increase in primary school enrolment rate for both sexes and the gender gap had been minimized, except in Yemen, where it was still significant. The primary school dropout rate was still relatively high in some member countries. In 1998, it was 28 per cent in Iraq and 53 per cent in Yemen. Despite the improvement in total enrolment rates at the regional level, especially for the GCC countries, those rates remained significantly lower than those registered in countries with similar GDP per capita. In all levels of education, the female-to-male ratio had been constantly increasing during the past few decades, and at the university level, in a few Gulf countries, more women were enrolled in university than men. However, almost all member countries had female enrolment rates that were significantly lower than those registered in countries with similar GDP per capita. Also, the quality of education, particularly higher education, in the region was cause for great concern.

To meet the challenges of globalization, the skills of labour in the region needed to be upgraded and improved. The ratio of technical training compared to formal secondary training was very low in most member countries, in particular in the GCC countries and Lebanon.

Activities in 1999

During 1999, ESCWA activities under the 1998-1999 work programme [E/ESCWA/2000/1] focused on the management of energy, natural resources and the environment; improvement of the quality of life; economic development and global changes; social development issues; coordination of policies and harmonization of norms and regulations for sectoral development; and development, coordination and harmonization of statistics and information.

Economic development and cooperation

The first session of the Technical Committee on Liberalization of Foreign Trade and Economic Globalization in the Countries of the ESCWA region, established by Economic and Social Council resolution 1997/12 [YUN 1997, p. 1021], was held in Abu Dhabi, United Arab Emirates, on 15 and 16 May. It examined current issues of trade liberalization and globalization and their possible impact on the countries of the region.

On 27 May [E/1999/41/Rev.1 (res. 219(XX))], the Commission decided that sessions of the Technical Committee would be held biennially rather than annually.

To track and assess economic and social trends, the *Survey of Economic and Social Developments, 1998-1999* was published. It was a special issue covering economic and social developments in the region over the past 25 years and served to commemorate the Commission's twenty-fifth anniversary. The *Preliminary Overview of Economic Developments in the ESCWA Region, 1999* provided the business community and policy makers with an early forecast of the region's economic performance and highlighted the direction of economic change.

ESCWA organized the Expert Group Meetings on the Assessment of Economic and Social Developments in the ESCWA Region during the Last Twenty-five Years and Regional Priorities for the Next Decade (2000-2009) (Beirut, 4-6 May); and an expert group meeting on Environment and Trade Issues: The Impact of WTO Environment Committee Decisions on ESCWA Member States (Beirut, 2-4 November). In the globalization area, including the WTO Agreements and their impact on the region, studies were completed on the implications of issues negotiated in the WTO Committee on Trade and Environment for ESCWA member countries: the cases of Egypt, Jordan and Lebanon; and challenges and opportunities of WTO regarding services in selected ESCWA member countries: tourism. Other studies examined developments in the economic and financial systems and the effects of globalization. They dealt with inflation in the ESCWA region: causes and effects; development of financial markets in the region; the role of foreign direct investment in economic development in ESCWA countries; Arab economic integration efforts; and consumer protection under a liberalized trade system in Egypt, Lebanon, Saudi Arabia and the Syrian Arab Republic.

Transport

The first session of the Committee on Transport (Beirut, 9-10 February) [E/ESCWA/C.1/20/7/Add.6], established by Economic and Social Council resolution 1997/11 [YUN 1997, p. 1022], adopted for approval by the Commission the Declaration on the Adoption and Development of an Integrated Transport System in the Arab Mashreq. The Declaration recommended, among other things, the numbering of road and railway network routes. The Committee recommended that the ESCWA secretariat prepare a convention on the cooperation and harmonization of maritime transport policies, the development of national fleets and the facilitation of intraregional commercial traffic.

ESCWA organized two expert group meetings to support member States' efforts to harmonize sectoral policies and globalization trends in transport: one on the WTO Agreement on Maritime and Air Transport Services in the Arab Region (Beirut, 9-11 June), and the other on Harmonization of Transport Norms and Legislative Instruments for Regional Cooperation, including UN/Electronic Data Interchange for Administration, Commerce and Transportation (EDIFACT) (Beirut, 16-18 November).

The Commission undertook a study on the harmonization of environmental standards in the transport sector in ESCWA member countries, which examined the issue of environmental pollution caused by land transport from the regional and global points of view, finalized a preliminary assessment of transport and related infrastructure in the GCC region, and organized a workshop on land transport policy in Lebanon (Beirut, 6-8 July).

Statistics

The Statistical Committee, at its third session (Beirut, 16-18 March) [E/ESCWA/C.1/20/7/Add.7], examined ways to achieve greater coordination of and support for cooperation between the countries of the region and the Statistical Division in statistical activities and programmes; reviewed the ESCWA statistical programme for 2000-2001; examined the status of the 1993 System of National Accounts; and discussed the participation of ESCWA members in the International Comparison Programme (see also PART THREE, Chapter XV). It also considered technical cooperation programmes, the Regional Household Survey Project, the impact of UN global conferences on social statistics, the general system for the publication of statistical data and the strategy of the 2000 Round of Population and Housing Censuses.

Among other action, the Committee encouraged the adoption of the General Data Dissemination System, prepared by IMF; requested ESCWA members to link that System to the basic principles of official statistics established by the UN Statistical Commission and the ESCWA Statistical Committee; and asked IMF to offer technical and financial support.

The ESCWA Statistics Division organized regional workshops on vital statistics and civil registration systems in ESCWA member States (Cairo, Egypt, 16-21 October); industrial and construction statistics (Beirut, 29 November–4 December); and gender statistics in the Arab countries (Amman, Jordan, 8-11 November).

A number of publications were issued on statistical issues, including the *Statistical News Letter*, *Statistical Abstract of the ESCWA Region*; *External Trade Bulletin of the ESCWA Region; National Accounts Studies of the ESCWA Region; Bulletin on Vital Statistics in the ESCWA Region;* and *Bulletin of Industrial Statistics for the Arab Countries, 1990-1998*. For the first time, ESCWA produced a publication on gender statistics, entitled *Women and Men in the Arab Region: A Statistical Portrait.*

Natural resources, energy and environment

The Committee on Water Resources, at its third session (Beirut 21-22 April) [E/ESCWA/C.1/20/7/Add.3], adopted "The Commission's View of the Future of the Field of Water Resources", in which it set out action to be taken by ESCWA to assist States in water resources development, management and conservation. It also adopted a Declaration on the water situation in the ESCWA region, in which it appealed to States to take action to ward off the danger threatened by the decline in surface water and ground-water resources.

On 27 May [E/1999/41/Rev.1 (res. 219(XX))], the Commission decided that future sessions of the Committee would be held biennially rather than annually.

To contribute to the development of sustainable sources of water and raise public awareness about the rational use and conservation of water, ESCWA convened the Expert Group Meeting on Updating the Assessment of Water Resources in the ESCWA Member Countries (Beirut, 20-23 April) to discuss the assessment, development, utilization and management of water resources at the national and regional levels. It completed studies on the development of freshwater resources in ESCWA's rural areas by using non-conventional techniques and on current water policies and practices in selected ESCWA countries.

The Committee on Energy held its second session in Beirut on 3 and 4 November. It followed up on progress made in implementing the work programme for 1998-1999; examined the planned work programme for 2000-2001; discussed the medium-term plan for 2002-2005; and reviewed the advisory services provided by ESCWA in the field of energy.

ESCWA completed a study on the promotion of new and renewable sources of energy with particular emphasis on remote areas, which presented a proposal for a regional programme on the dissemination of renewable energy services to rural communities. Three projects were identified for implementation, two on village electrification in Yemen and the third on the gasification of agricultural waste for energy production in Egypt. The Expert Group Meeting on the Privatization of the Electric Power Sector (Beirut, 1-4 November) discussed prospects for privatization of the power sector, particularly in electricity generation.

In the environment area, the Expert Group Meeting on the Adequacy of Environmental Legislation and the Promotion of Enforcement (Beirut, 7-9 June) assessed the status and adequacy of environmental laws and regulations and recommended enforcement mechanisms. ESCWA organized a study and expert group meeting on the harmonization of environmental standards in the water sector in ESCWA countries (Beirut, 28 September–1 October). A study on the harmonization of environmental standards in the energy sector of ESCWA member States was also undertaken and an expert group meeting organized on the subject (Cairo, 29 June–1 July).

Quality of life

The second session of the Committee on Social Development (Beirut, 7-8 April) [E/ESCWA/C.1/20/7/Add.4] focused on policy issues, the ESCWA subprogramme on improvement of the quality of life and the integrated follow-up to UN global conferences held in the 1990s. The Committee issued a Declaration setting out its objectives and commitments with regard to achieving sustainable human development and comprehensive development.

ESCWA continued work on developing guidelines for applying the concept of sustainable human development in four main areas: poverty alleviation; sustainable human development; the role of NGOs; and persons with disabilities. Preparatory meetings held in 1998 [YUN 1998, p. 971] in follow-up to UN global conferences culminated in the Arab Conference on Integrated Regional

Follow-up to Global Conferences (Beirut, 29 November-1 December). Under the ESCWA/UNDP Flagship Project, ESCWA serviced the first meeting of the Project's Steering Committee; disseminated information on the recommendations of the global conferences; convened the Roundtable Discussion on Partnership between Government and Civil Society (Beirut, 4-5 October); created a web site on the Project; and prepared a brochure on cross-cutting issues.

Work began on the formulation of poverty alleviation policies for consideration by policy makers. Two studies on poverty alleviation were completed: "Feasibility and operationalization of microcredit finance facilities targeting poor women in urban and rural areas in selected Arab countries: theoretical perspectives and practical considerations"; and "Urban settlements and poverty".

In the context of its focus on persons with disabilities, ESCWA convened simultaneously an international seminar on environmental accessibility and a training workshop on a barrier-free environment (Beirut, 30 November-3 December). Further activities were carried out under the project on enhancing the accessibility of disabled persons in the ESCWA region.

Population issues were addressed in a study entitled "Five years after the Cairo Conference: Population policies in Arab countries" and in the Expert Group Meeting on Migration and Population Policies in the ESCWA Member Countries (Beirut, 23-24 November). A workshop on population policies and sustainable development was organized in conjunction with that meeting (Beirut, 15-17 November).

With respect to human settlements, an Expert Group Meeting on Urban Management: Follow-up of National Strategies in the ESCWA Member States was convened (Dubai, United Arab Emirates, 8-12 November).

The database on social policies was expanded to include information on human development, women and human settlements and was renamed the ESCWA Integrated Information System on Policies, Measures and Indicators.

Programme and organizational questions

Redesignation of Technical Committee

On 27 May [E/1999/41/Rev.1 (res. 223(XX))], the Commission decided to change the name of the Technical Committee to the Preparatory Committee and recommended a resolution to the Economic and Social Council for adoption.

ECONOMIC AND SOCIAL COUNCIL ACTION

On 28 July [meeting 44], the Economic and Social Council, on the recommendation of ESCWA [E/1999/14/Add.3], adopted **resolution 1999/42** without vote [agenda item 10].

Redesignation of the Technical Committee of the Economic and Social Commission for Western Asia

The Economic and Social Council,

Recalling its resolution 1982/64 of 30 July 1982, by which it established, within the Economic Commission for Western Asia, a Standing Committee for the Programme of the Commission, and its resolution 1984/80 of 27 July 1984 on the general policy-making structure of the Commission, in which it designated the Standing Committee as the Technical Committee,

Recalling also Commission resolution 114(IX) of 12 May 1982, in which the Commission entrusted to the Committee the task of reviewing programming issues and presenting recommendations in that regard, as a preparatory committee, to the sessions of the Commission held at the ministerial level,

Recalling further the successive establishment of six technical committees of the Commission during the period from 1992 to 1997,

Wishing to avoid possible confusion between the name of the present Technical Committee and the names of the sectoral technical committees,

Decides to change the name of the Technical Committee to Preparatory Committee.

Programme of work, 1998-1999

The Commission had before it a report on progress made between 1 January 1998 and 30 April 1999 in implementing the programme of work for the 1998-1999 biennium [E/ESCWA/C.1/20/4 (Part I)].

The major problems faced by programme managers in carrying out the 1998-1999 work programme included the loss of most of the local staff because of the move of ESCWA's headquarters from Amman to Beirut and the high vacancy rate, which resulted in the delivery of a number of 1998 outputs being delayed until 1999. A limited number of departures from programmed activities were effected, mainly for programmatic reasons or pursuant to legislative mandates.

On 27 May [E/1999/41/Rev.1 (res. 218(XX))], the Commission approved the changes introduced in the programme of work and recommended a resolution for adoption by the Economic and Social Council.

ECONOMIC AND SOCIAL COUNCIL ACTION

On 28 July [meeting 44], the Economic and Social Council, on the recommendation of ESCWA, [E/1999/14/Add.3], adopted **resolution 1999/43** without vote [agenda item 10].

Changes introduced in the programme of work and priorities of the Economic and Social Commission for Western Asia for the biennium 1998-1999

The Economic and Social Council,

Noting with satisfaction the progress made in the implementation of the programme of work and priorities of the Economic and Social Commission for Western Asia for the biennium 1998-1999,

Cognizant of the changes introduced by the secretariat of the Commission in programme activities,

Having studied the reasons and justifications for those changes, which relate to the cancellation, reformulation, addition or postponement of activities or outputs,

Aware of the need for a certain degree of flexibility in the implementation of the programme of work of the Commission in order that it may include new issues directly related to it,

Approves the changes introduced in the programme of work of the Economic and Social Commission for Western Asia as they appear in the annex to the report of the Executive Secretary on progress made during 1998 in the implementation of the programme of work for the biennium 1998-1999.

Programme of work, 2000-2001

The Commission had before it the draft programme of work and priorities for the 2000-2001 biennium [E/ESCWA/C.1/20/8]. Among the main features were the maintenance of the multidisciplinary approach through the development of clusters of outputs around regional follow-up to global conferences, as well as issues relating to the environment, poverty, civil society institutions, gender, WTO and related concerns, globalization of the world economy, electronic commerce and free trade in the region, as well as gender mainstreaming and human rights.

On 27 May [E/1999/41/Rev.1 (res. 222(XX))], the Commission adopted the draft programme of work and priorities for the 2000-2001 biennium.

Draft medium-term plan, 2002-2005

The Technical Committee (eleventh session, Beirut, 25-26 May) [E/ESCWA/20/4] considered the ESCWA draft medium-term plan for 2002-2005, programme 18. Economic and social development in Western Asia [E/ESCWA/C.1/20/9]. The Committee discussed the need to grant representatives sufficient time to study the plan and consult with their Governments. A number of additions to the Plan were proposed, relating to Arab economic integration, the encouragement of investment in the region, the Arab common market, assistance and support to member countries desirous of joining WTO or entering into future multilateral trade negotiations, and postal services.

Permanent headquarters

Having considered the Executive Secretary's note on the relocation of ESCWA to its permanent headquarters in Beirut [E/ESCWA/20/7/Rev.1], the Commission on 27 May [E/1999/41/Rev.1 (res. 224(XX))] endorsed the transfer of the permanent headquarters to United Nations House in Beirut and submitted a resolution for adoption by the Economic and Social Council.

ECONOMIC AND SOCIAL COUNCIL ACTION

On 28 July [meeting 44], the Economic and Social Council, on the recommendation of ESCWA [E/1999/14/Add.3], adopted **resolution 1999/44** without vote [agenda item 10].

Relocation of the Economic and Social Commission for Western Asia to its permanent headquarters at Beirut

The Economic and Social Council,

Recalling resolution 197(XVII) of 31 May 1994 of the Economic and Social Commission for Western Asia, in which the Commission decided to submit a recommendation to the Economic and Social Council that the permanent headquarters of the Commission be relocated to Beirut,

Recalling also its resolution 1994/43 of 29 July 1994 on the permanent headquarters of the Commission, in which the Council requested the Secretary-General to take all steps necessary to effect the transfer of the permanent headquarters of the Commission to Beirut and to ensure that the transfer was financed within existing resources and primarily from extrabudgetary contributions,

Recalling further Commission resolution 207(XVIII) of 25 May 1995 on facilitating the relocation of the Commission to its permanent headquarters at Beirut, in which the Commission called on member States to take measures to support the Secretary-General in his efforts to secure the necessary resources for the implementation of resolution 197(XVII),

Recalling Commission resolution 215(XIX) of 7 May 1997 on progress made in facilitating the relocation of the Commission to its permanent headquarters at Beirut, in which the Commission requested the authorities concerned within the Secretariat to examine the possibility of utilizing the skills of local Commission staff at Amman in other areas within the United Nations or of finding ways to compensate them,

Cognizant of the note by the Executive Secretary of the Economic and Social Commission for Western Asia on the relocation of the Commission to its permanent headquarters at Beirut, which deals with all the legal, administrative, logistic and financial aspects of the transfer,

Commending the measures adopted by the Commission secretariat for the implementation of the relocation plan in accordance with a timetable that did not affect the implementation of its programmes and took into account the needs of the staff,

Commending also the measures adopted by the Secretariat to utilize the skills of the local staff at Amman in other areas within the United Nations or determine ways to compensate them,

1. *Endorses* the action taken by the secretariat of the Economic and Social Commission for Western Asia for the transfer of the permanent headquarters of the Commission to United Nations House at Beirut by 31 December 1997, in particular the conclusion of the agreement between the United Nations and the Government of Lebanon concerning the headquarters of the Commission, signed on 27 August 1997, and the supplementary agreement between the United Nations and the Government of Lebanon relating to the occupancy and use of United Nations premises at Beirut, signed on 9 October 1997;

2. *Also endorses* the action taken by the Commission secretariat to facilitate the transfer of other United Nations offices and agencies at Beirut to United Nations House on 1 December 1998, and to devise internal mechanisms for the sharing of common services and related costs;

3. *Endorses with satisfaction* the financial arrangements related to the move, made by the Commission secretariat in compliance with Council resolution 1994/43, in which the Council requested the Secretary-General to ensure that the transfer was financed within existing resources and primarily from extrabudgetary contributions;

4. *Reiterates its expression of gratitude* to the Government of Lebanon for its financial contributions and its efforts to provide a headquarters that satisfies the requirements and needs of the United Nations and for its cooperation in complying with the provisions of the Headquarters Agreement signed on 27 August 1997;

5. *Expresses its gratitude* to the Government of Kuwait for its financial contribution towards the transfer of the headquarters of the Commission, and to the Government of Saudi Arabia for the contribution which it made to supporting the activities of the Commission following its transfer to its permanent headquarters;

6. *Reiterates its thanks* to the Governments of Iraq and Jordan for the facilities offered to the Commission during its stay at Baghdad and Amman, respectively, and to the Government of the Syrian Arab Republic for facilitating the movement of staff and equipment through its territory.

Twenty-fifth anniversary of ESCWA

ESCWA, in considering the agenda item "Celebration of the twenty-fifth anniversary of the Commission", had before it a note by the Executive Secretary [E/ESCWA/20/8], to which were annexed summaries of studies on: peace and security in the ESCWA countries; economic developments; social developments; the development of institutions; and ESCWA (1974-1999): twenty-five years of service to the region's development.

The morning session of 28 May was devoted to the celebrations, which took the form of panel discussions of the studies mentioned above.

On 27 May [E/1999/41/Rev.1 (res. 220(XX))], the Commission adopted the Beirut Declaration as a new vision that defined its role and tasks in line with regional and world developments in the coming century. It submitted the declaration to the Economic and Social Council for adoption.

ECONOMIC AND SOCIAL COUNCIL ACTION

On 28 July [meeting 44], the Economic and Social Council, on the recommendation of ESCWA [E/1999/14/Add.3], adopted **resolution 1999/45** without vote [agenda item 10].

Beirut Declaration

The Economic and Social Council,

Recalling resolution 217(XIX) of 7 May 1997 of the Economic and Social Commission for Western Asia concerning the celebration of the twenty-fifth anniversary of the Commission, in particular paragraph 3, in which the Commission invited the Governments of member States to take the opportunity to formulate a new vision for the region in line with regional and world developments in the coming century,

Recalling also the call by the Commission for the issuance of a declaration embodying the Commission's vision of the future and its role in coordinating the policies of member States in the economic and social spheres and broadening cooperation between them,

1. *Decides* to take note of the Beirut Declaration, annexed hereto, as a new vision that defines the role and tasks of the Economic and Social Commission for Western Asia in line with regional and world developments in the coming century;

2. *Invites* member States to take inspiration from elements of the Declaration in formulating their national policies and programmes and in strengthening international and regional cooperation between themselves;

3. *Requests* the Executive Secretary of the Economic and Social Commission for Western Asia to ensure that in future the activities of the Commission take into account the content of the Declaration.

ANNEX

Beirut Declaration: Western Asia preparing for the twenty-first century

We, the representatives of the Governments of the member States of the Economic and Social Commission for Western Asia, meeting at Beirut on 27 and 28 May 1999 at the twentieth session of the Commission and gathered here today to celebrate its twenty-fifth anniversary,

Acting in accordance with the desire of our Governments to assume their responsibilities towards their peoples in their aspiration towards integrated, sustainable development, stressing their originality and their contributions to civilization, believing in the principles and purposes of the Charter of the United Nations, aware of the development of international relations and partnership, and acting on the experience and lessons of the past, understanding the present and its dimensions and looking with confidence to the future,

Taking the opportunity offered by the celebration of the twenty-fifth anniversary of the Economic and Social Commission for Western Asia,

Present our vision of the role and tasks of the Commission in line with regional and world developments in the coming century, as set out below.

1. The growth of globalism does not diminish or detract from the extreme importance of acting at the regional level. Nor does the global nature of problems

preclude area-specific solutions and policies. In the trend towards globalism, with full respect for the sovereignty of States, regionalism cannot be bypassed. Cooperative arrangements within homogeneous groups, especially of small and medium-sized countries, represent a bridge between national and global interests. Moreover, development trends and requirements do not materialize all at once throughout the world, but rather do so in the form of regional waves, in which the conditions and situations peculiar to each area must be taken into account.

2. The role and functions of the Economic and Social Commission for Western Asia are based primarily on development and economic and social cooperation, the objective being to raise the level of economic activity in Western Asia and to maintain and strengthen economic relations between its member countries and other countries of the world. Such development can be achieved only to the extent that it is comprehensive, integrated and sustainable in both the economic and social spheres.

3. Recognition of the sovereignty, independence and territorial integrity of States, non-interference in their internal affairs and settlement of disputes by peaceful means in accordance with the Charter of the United Nations and the principles of international law constitute the basis of a sound international community. However, the State is not capable by itself of achieving comprehensive, sustainable development unless there exists international cooperation in the economic and social fields that is based, on the one hand, on a just and comprehensive peace, security on equal terms, and respect for the principles of justice and international law, and on the other hand, on international relations that are balanced in all areas and based on effective international cooperation and a genuine sense of partnership on the part of donor States and international donor institutions.

4. The increasing importance of regional cooperation in the economic and social fields places a great responsibility on the Commission. As part of the United Nations system, the Commission is the natural place for dealing with issues related to such cooperation, for it is not merely a regional arrangement for expressing the needs and particularities of the region to which it belongs, but also the embodiment, at the regional level, of the universal purposes and principles set forth in the Charter and resolutions of the United Nations.

5. The future of the region, on the threshold of the twenty-first century, requires its transformation into a zone of economic and social cooperation and mutual respect of all for the rights and interests of the peoples of the region in an atmosphere of a just and comprehensive peace, security on a basis of equality, and economic and social stability. These goals can be achieved only if cooperation is strengthened between the members of the Commission, the United Nations and international financial institutions and the following objective conditions are met:

(*a*) The achievement of a just and comprehensive peace, security on equal terms and stability in the region of Western Asia through the implementation of relevant United Nations resolutions, and full respect for international legitimacy and the foundations and principles of the peace process, foremost among them being the principle of land for peace and respect for the rights of peoples and their legitimate aspirations;

(*b*) The creation of an environment that will stimulate economic and social cooperation and development in all domains, including cooperation between the countries of the region in the areas of water, environment and energy, which calls for a comprehensive view that takes into account the balancing of national needs and global requirements and is based on integration of the various aspects of sustainable human development, with recognition of the mutually supportive roles of an effective state administration, an efficient private sector and a sound civil society;

(*c*) The exertion of efforts to integrate member States of the Economic and Social Commission for Western Asia into the international economic and trading system, by assisting them in dealing with the rules and principles on which it is based and heightening the advantages and at the same time limiting the drawbacks that might be involved, and by the establishment of a dialogue with the international organizations concerned;

(*d*) The promotion of democracy and respect for human rights, including the right to life, the right of self-determination and the right to development, and fundamental freedoms within a context of respect for national and regional characteristics and different religious, cultural and historical values. Achieving complementarity between freedom and responsibility at all levels in a State based on institutions and law constitutes a fundamental guarantee for enabling the region to continue its creative participation in the civilization of humankind;

(*e*) The development of the role of the Commission through support for its technical bodies and the obtainment of adequate support from the United Nations system, including the financial and human resources needed to enable the Commission to carry out its activities in the best possible way in order to be able to bolster the efforts of member States and become a basic forum in the economic and social fields with a view to promoting regional economic cooperation on a sound basis that will help to strengthen development and progress among the Commission's member States.

Reports of subsidiary bodies

The Executive Secretary submitted to the Commission in May summaries of the reports of its subsidiary bodies [E/ESCWA/C.1/20/7], namely, the Committees on Energy, Water Resources, Social Development, Transport, and Statistics, and the Technical Committee on Liberalization of Foreign Trade and Economic Globalization in the Countries of the ESCWA region.

On 27 May [E/1999/41/Rev.1 (res. 221(XX))], the Commission, having examined the reports, amended the titles of the annexes to some of them to read "statements issued by the subsidiary bodies" instead of "declarations issued by the subsidiary bodies".

On the same date [res. 219(XX)], the Commission decided that the session of the Committee on Water Resources and the Technical Committee on Liberalization of Foreign Trade and Economic Globalization in the Countries of the ESCWA region should be held biennially rather than annually. It emphasized that the sessions of all it subsidiary bodies should be held once every two years. A draft resolution on the subject was recommended to the Economic and Social Council for approval.

ECONOMIC AND SOCIAL COUNCIL

On 28 July [meeting 44], the Economic and Social Council, on the recommendation of ESCWA [E/1999/14/Add.3], adopted **resolution 1999/41** without vote [agenda item 10].

Frequency of sessions of the sectoral committees of the Economic and Social Commission for Western Asia

The Economic and Social Council,

Conscious of the need for uniform frequency of the sessions of all the sectoral committees of the Economic and Social Commission for Western Asia,

Recalling Commission resolution 212(XIX) of 7 May 1997, in which the Commission decided that the Committee on Water Resources should hold its meetings annually,

Recalling also Commission resolution 214(XIX) of 7 May 1997, in which the Commission decided to establish a technical committee on liberalization of foreign trade and economic globalization in the countries of the region of the Economic and Social Commission of Western Asia, the meetings of which would be held annually,

Recalling further that the Commission secretariat can provide support and advice to member States, on request, during years in which no sessions of the sectoral committees are held,

Realizing that the sectoral committees can hold special sessions, as needed, in accordance with the provisions of the rules of procedure of the Commission,

1. *Approves* the amendment of resolutions 212(XIX) and 214(XIX) of the Economic and Social Commission for Western Asia to the effect that the sessions of the Committee on Water Resources and of the Technical Committee on Liberalization of Foreign Trade and Economic Globalization in the Countries of the Region of the Economic and Social Commission for Western Asia shall be held biennially rather than annually;

2. *Emphasizes* that the sessions of all the sectoral committees shall be held once every two years.

Millennium Assembly

In an October note [A/54/280 & Corr.1], the Secretary-General reported on the hearings (Beirut, 23-24 May) held for ESCWA's region in preparation for the Millennium Assembly in 2000, which produced proposals aimed at strengthening the role of the United Nations and ensuring its relevance in the twenty-first century. The issues selected for discussion were peace and security, economic and social development, and human rights and governance.

Chapter VI

Natural resources, energy and cartography

The conservation, development and use of natural resources and energy were considered by several UN bodies in 1999, including the Committee on Energy and Natural Resources for Development, which held its first session in April. The Committee, established in 1998, paid particular attention to the issue of energy in the context of sustainable development and the impact of agriculture and land management on the water resource base. The Committee drafted contributions to reports of the Secretary-General on water-related matters, on which the Economic and Social Council took action in July.

The General Assembly, in December, calling for further action to ensure that the World Solar Programme 1996-2005 was fully integrated into UN efforts towards attaining the objective of sustainable development, encouraged the Secretary-General to continue efforts to mobilize technical assistance and funding for the effective implementation of national and regional projects in renewable sources of energy.

The report of the International Atomic Energy Agency was presented to the Assembly in November by its Director General; the Assembly welcomed the Agency's measures to strengthen and fund its technical cooperation activities, which would contribute to achieving sustainable development in developing countries.

Energy and natural resources

The Committee on Energy and Natural Resources for Development, which was established by the Economic and Social Council by resolution 1998/46 [YUN 1998, p. 1262] through the merger of the Committee on Natural Resources and the Committee on New and Renewable Sources of Energy and on Energy for Development, held its first session in New York from 5 to 16 April [E/1999/32], as decided by the Council on 2 February (**decision 1999/204**). The Committee comprised two sub-groups—one on energy and one on water resources.

The Committee recommended to the Council for adoption draft resolutions on: its contributions to the preparation of the Secretary-General's report on progress made in providing safe water supply and sanitation for all during the 1990s and to the preparatory process for the eighth (2000) session of the Commission on Sustainable Development (CSD) on integrated planning and management of land resources and agriculture; and the Secretary-General's report on the spatial planning of land (including minerals) and water resources (see p. 967).

It also recommended two draft decisions on procedural matters. On 28 July, the Council decided that the dates for the Committee's second session should be brought forward to 14 to 25 August 2000, after which the Committee would continue to meet biennially, with its third session to be held in 2002, and that provisions should be made for the Committee's two sub-groups to hold parallel meetings (**decision 1999/276**). By **decision 1999/277** of the same date, the Council took note of the report on the Committee's first session and transmitted it to CSD. It also approved the provisional agenda and documentation for the second session.

In other action, the Committee brought to the Council's attention a decision on its contribution to the preparatory process for the ninth (2001) session of CSD [E/1999/32 (dec. 1/1)] and another suggesting the convening of a meeting on the environmental effects of small-scale and artisanal mining operations, including but not limited to pollution of surface water and groundwater [dec. 1/2].

Energy

At the first session of the Committee on Energy and Natural Resources for Development [E/1999/32], the Sub-group on Energy considered the Committee's contribution to the preparatory process for the ninth session of CSD; reviewed salient trends and issues of energy development and use in the context of sustainable development; and met with the Inter-Agency Task Force on Energy in a dialogue session to determine how to contribute to CSD's ninth session in a mutually supportive way.

For its review of salient trends, the Committee had before it documents prepared for the third session of the Committee on New and Renewable Sources of Energy and on Energy Development, which had been scheduled for 1998, but did not take place due to the termination of its mandate [YUN 1998, p. 972]. Those reports covered: follow-up to the previous sessions of the Committee on New and Renewable Sources of Energy and on Energy for Development [E/C.13/1998/2]; environmentally sound and efficient fossil energy technologies [E/C.13/1998/3]; renewable sources of energy, with special emphasis on wind energy [E/C.13/1998/4]; development and implementation of rural energy policies [E/C.13/1998/5]; energy and transportation [E/C.13/1998/6]; and coordination of activities of the organizations of the UN system in the field of energy [E/C.13/1998/7].

On 30 July, the Economic and Social Council, bearing in mind the nature and purposes of the Ad Hoc Open-ended Intergovernmental Group of Experts on Energy and Sustainable Development, which would meet in conjunction with the inter-sessional ad hoc working groups of CSD at its eighth (2000) and ninth (2001) sessions, decided that States not members of the Commission would be allowed to nominate their nationals to the Bureau of the Group (**decision 1999/285**).

Contribution to CSD (ninth session). The Committee decided to submit to the ninth session of CSD, in accordance with Economic and Social Council resolution 1998/46 [YUN 1998, p. 1262], its contribution to the preparatory process for that session [dec. 1/1]. The sectoral theme of the session would be "Atmosphere/energy", while in the economic sector "Energy/transport" would be considered. The Committee identified seven critical issues requiring urgent attention during the preparatory process, particularly by the Open-ended Intergovernmental Group of Experts on Energy and Sustainable Development and by CSD: accessibility of energy; energy and atmospheric emissions; sustainable energy technology development; energy and transportation; the impact of liberalization and privatization; adequate financing; and formulation and implementation of sustainable energy policies. The Committee also identified six options that should be given special attention for a sustainable energy future: improving energy and materials efficiency; speeding up development and use of renewable energy technologies; cleaner production and use of fossil fuels; the role of nuclear power in a sustainable energy future; cleaner alternative fuels and new technologies for the transportation sector; and extension and interconnection of energy transportation grids. As to policy and measures for a sustainable energy future, the Committee found the following to be of crucial importance: development and implementation of national sustainable energy policies; a regulatory framework for the implementation of energy policies; financing and investment, including research and development funding; economic instruments to facilitate a sustainable energy future; capacity-building; and international cooperation.

ECONOMIC AND SOCIAL COUNCIL ACTION

On 30 July [meeting 46], the Economic and Social Council, on the recommendation of the Commission on Sustainable Development [E/1999/29], adopted **resolution 1999/60** without vote [agenda item 13 *(a)*].

Preparations for the ninth session of the Commission on Sustainable Development, on energy issues

The Economic and Social Council,

Recalling the Programme for the Further Implementation of Agenda 21 adopted by the General Assembly at its nineteenth special session, in which the Assembly, inter alia, decided that preparations for the ninth session of the Commission on Sustainable Development, on energy issues, should utilize an open-ended intergovernmental group of experts on energy and sustainable development, to be convened in conjunction with inter-sessional meetings of the eighth and ninth sessions of the Commission,

Recalling also the multi-year programme of work of the Commission on Sustainable Development, 1998-2002, and paragraph 46 of the Programme for the Further Implementation of Agenda 21,

1. *Decides* that the first session of the Ad Hoc Open-ended Intergovernmental Group of Experts on Energy and Sustainable Development shall be held in New York in the first quarter of 2000 for a duration of one work week, immediately before or after the meetings of the inter-sessional ad hoc working groups of the Commission on Sustainable Development, and that the session shall have the following provisional agenda:
    1. Election of officers.
    2. Adoption of the agenda and other organizational matters.
    3. Preparations for the ninth session of the Commission on Sustainable Development, on energy issues.
    4. Provisional agenda of the second session of the Group of Experts.
    5. Adoption of the report of the Group of Experts on its first session.

2. *Also decides* that the Bureau of the Group of Experts shall consist of five members, one from each of the five regional groups of the United Nations, and shall include two co-chairmen, one from a developed country and one from a developing country, and invites the regional groups to nominate their candidates expeditiously and to inform the Bureau of the eighth session of the Commission so that they can be involved in the preparations;

3. *Requests* the Group of Experts to report to the Commission at its eighth session on progress made on its work at its first session and to recommend to the Commission the agenda, timing and duration of its second session, to be held in 2001;

4. *Decides* to transmit the report of the Committee on Energy and Natural Resources for Development on its first session to the Commission at its eighth session, as

well as to the Group of Experts at its first session, as an input to the preparatory process for the ninth session of the Commission;

5. *Invites* the Secretary-General, on the basis of submissions and information provided by Governments and working in close collaboration with entities within the United Nations as well as with other relevant international organizations, to prepare analytical reports and other documentation, as appropriate, for consideration at the first session of the Group of Experts;

6. *Calls upon* Governments to participate actively and contribute to the preparatory process;

7. *Encourages* the participation of civil society and other major groups, including the private sector, in particular from developing countries, in the preparatory process;

8. *Decides* that the participation of non-governmental organizations in the work of the Group of Experts should be in accordance with the rules of procedure of the functional commissions of the Economic and Social Council;

9. *Recognizes* that funding to support the participation of representatives, in particular from developing countries, in the meetings of the Group of Experts is essential, and should be provided in accordance with the provisions of paragraph *(d)* of Council decision 1993/207 of 12 February 1993, and urges additional voluntary contributions to support the participation of representatives from developing countries that are not members of the Commission.

World Solar Programme (1996-2005)

In response to General Assembly resolution 53/7 [YUN 1998, p. 976], the Secretary-General submitted an August report on the World Solar Programme 1996-2005 [A/54/212]. With regard to international coordination and cooperation in implementing the Programme, which was endorsed by the Assembly in resolution 53/7, the Secretary-General stated that the Director-General of the United Nations Educational, Scientific and Cultural Organization (UNESCO) had written to the heads of relevant UN organizations and programmes inviting their cooperation. Also, a letter signed by the UNESCO Director-General and the Administrator of the United Nations Development Programme (UNDP) had been sent to all UNDP resident representatives and directors/heads of UNESCO field offices instructing them to assist Member States in implementing the projects included in the Programme. Initiatives had also been taken by UNDP, the Global Environment Facility, the UN Department of Economic and Social Affairs, the World Solar Commission and the United Nations Environment Programme.

The Secretary-General reported that, over the preceding two years, the World Solar Commission had mobilized some $500 million of international assistance for the execution of projects included in the Programme. In addition, a number of countries had taken legislative action favouring the development and deployment of renewable energy technologies.

GENERAL ASSEMBLY ACTION

On 22 December [meeting 87], the General Assembly, on the recommendation of the Second (Economic and Financial) Committee [A/54/588/Add.7], adopted **resolution 54/215** without vote [agenda item 100].

World Solar Programme 1996-2005

The General Assembly,

Recalling its resolution 53/7 of 16 October 1998, by which it, inter alia, endorsed the World Solar Programme 1996-2005 as a contribution to the overall sustainable development agenda and invited all States Members of the United Nations to contribute to its successful implementation,

Recalling also resolution 29 C/14 concerning the World Solar Programme 1996-2005, adopted by the General Conference of the United Nations Educational, Scientific and Cultural Organization in November 1997,

Reaffirming that the convening at Harare on 16 and 17 September 1996 of the World Solar Summit, at which the Harare Declaration on Solar Energy and Sustainable Development was adopted and the preparation of the World Solar Programme 1996-2005 approved, was a step in pursuance of the implementation of Agenda 21, which is a multifaceted and, at the same time, fundamental programme of action for achieving sustainable development,

Recognizing that mutually supportive efforts at the national and international levels are imperative in the pursuit of sustainable development, which includes, inter alia, the provision of financial resources and the transfer of technology for the application of cost-effective energy systems and wider use of environment-friendly, renewable energies,

Acknowledging the important role of the General Assembly in promoting the World Solar Programme 1996-2005,

Acknowledging also the role of the Commission on Sustainable Development and the Economic and Social Council as forums for the discussion of new and renewable sources of energy and sustainable development,

Expressing its appreciation of the efforts of the Secretary-General in bringing the World Solar Programme 1996-2005 to the attention of relevant sources of funding and technical assistance,

Noting the establishment of the Inter-agency Working Group on Energy with a view to ensuring the coordination of the activities of all relevant organizations of the United Nations system in the preparations for the ninth session of the Commission on Sustainable Development in 2001, and to contributing to sustainable development, taking into account the recommendations of the World Solar Programme 1996-2005,

Noting also that the Global Renewable Energy Education and Training Programme 1996-2005 constitutes one of the major programmes of universal value of the World Solar Programme 1996-2005,

Calling for further action to ensure that the World Solar Programme 1996-2005 is fully integrated into and brought into the mainstream of the efforts of the United Nations system towards attaining the objective of sustainable development,

Emphasizing that the achievement of more substantive results in the implementation of the World Solar Programme 1996-2005, as part of the promotion of new and renewable sources of energy, will require the more active and collaborative involvement of all concerned parties, including Governments, multilateral funding agencies and relevant parts of the United Nations system,

1. *Takes note with appreciation* of the report of the Secretary-General, including measures taken by the various entities of the United Nations system for the implementation of the World Solar Programme 1996-2005;

2. *Notes with appreciation* the role of the United Nations Educational, Scientific and Cultural Organization in promoting, within its mandate, the implementation of the World Solar Programme 1996-2005, in particular its education and training programmes in the field of new and renewable sources of energy, and, in this context, also notes with appreciation the initiative undertaken by the United Nations Educational, Scientific and Cultural Organization of inviting the competent organs and programmes of the United Nations system to cooperate in the implementation of the Programme;

3. *Notes* the role that the World Solar Commission has so far played in the mobilization of international support and assistance for the implementation of many of the national high-priority projects on renewable sources of energy included in the World Solar Programme 1996-2005, many of which are being executed with national funding;

4. *Commends highly* the efforts of many Member States in taking concrete national actions, including legislative measures, that have resulted in the wider use of renewable sources of energy in their countries;

5. *Notes with appreciation* the financial support that has been provided by some developed countries that are Members of the United Nations and some intergovernmental organizations, within and outside the United Nations system, in the implementation of the World Solar Programme 1996-2005;

6. *Calls upon* all relevant funding institutions and bilateral and multilateral donors, as well as regional funding institutions and non-governmental organizations, to support, as appropriate, the efforts being made for the development of the renewable energy sector in developing countries on the basis of environment-friendly, renewable sources of energy of demonstrated viability, while taking fully into account the development structure of energy-based economies of developing countries, and to assist in the attainment of the levels of investment necessary to expand energy supplies beyond urban areas;

7. *Takes note* of the decision of the General Conference of the United Nations Educational, Scientific and Cultural Organization regarding the strategic importance of the Global Renewable Energy Education and Training Programme 1996-2005 in attaining the objective of sustainable development, and encourages the Director-General of the United Nations Educational, Scientific and Cultural Organization to make efforts to promote public awareness in all Member States in this regard, with the support of international, regional and national institutions, both public and private;

8. *Invites* all Governments to encourage the involvement of all relevant stakeholders, including the private sector, in the promotion of research on and the development of renewable sources of energy, in particular, within this context, in the implementation of the World Solar Programme 1996-2005, in accordance with their respective national policies;

9. *Encourages* the Secretary-General to continue his efforts to promote the mobilization of adequate technical assistance and funding and the full utilization of existing international funds for the effective implementation of national and regional high-priority projects in the area of renewable sources of energy;

10. *Invites* the Inter-agency Working Group on Energy to facilitate the contribution of the work under the World Solar Programme 1996-2005 to the consideration of the theme of energy by the Commission on Sustainable Development at its ninth session, to be held in 2001;

11. *Requests* the Secretary-General, in consultation with the United Nations Educational, Scientific and Cultural Organization and in cooperation with the United Nations Environment Programme and other relevant organizations, to submit to the General Assembly at its fifty-fifth session a report on concrete action being taken for the effective implementation of the World Solar Programme 1996-2005, including promotion for mobilization of resources;

12. *Also requests* the Secretary-General to include in his report on energy and sustainable development to the Commission on Sustainable Development a report on action to be taken to implement the present resolution, including further recommendations on appropriate modalities to promote new and renewable sources of energy;

13. *Decides* to include in the provisional agenda of its fifty-fifth session, under the item entitled "Environment and sustainable development", a sub-item entitled "Promotion of new and renewable sources of energy, including the implementation of the World Solar Programme 1996-2005".

Nuclear energy

By an August note [A/54/215], the Secretary-General transmitted to the General Assembly the 1998 report of the International Atomic Energy Agency (IAEA). Presenting and updating the report in the Assembly on 4 November [A/54/PV.46], the IAEA Director General stated that nuclear power was one of the few energy options that could provide large-scale electricity generation and do so without greenhouse gas emissions. He noted that, despite its environmental advantage, nuclear power was at a standstill in Western Europe and North America, although it continued to expand in a few rapidly developing countries in Asia and in parts of Eastern Europe. In the Director General's view, a resurgence of nuclear power depended on action on three crucial fronts: further improvement in economic competitiveness, continued improvement in the global safety record, including waste management, and the restoration of public confidence. He went on to describe various areas of the Agency's work, including nuclear techniques in human health, nuclear safety, managing water resources and radioactive waste disposal (see p. 1385). He also discussed the difficulties regarding IAEA's nuclear inspection activities in the Democratic People's Republic of Korea (see p. 277) and in Iraq (see p. 228).

GENERAL ASSEMBLY ACTION

On 15 November [meeting 53], the General Assembly adopted **resolution 54/26** [draft: A/54/L.21/Rev.1 & Add.1, orally amended] by recorded vote (122-1-6) [agenda item 14].

Report of the International Atomic Energy Agency

The General Assembly,

Having received the report of the International Atomic Energy Agency for the year 1998,

Noting the statement of the Director General of the International Atomic Energy Agency, in which he provided additional information on the main developments in the activities of the Agency during 1999,

Recognizing the importance of the work of the Agency in promoting the further application of nuclear energy for peaceful purposes as envisaged in the statute of the Agency and in accordance with the inalienable right of States parties to the Treaty on the Non-Proliferation of Nuclear Weapons and other relevant internationally legally binding agreements that have concluded relevant safeguards agreements with the Agency to develop research, production and use of nuclear energy for peaceful purposes without discrimination and in conformity with articles I and II and other relevant articles of the Treaty, and with the objectives and purposes thereof,

Conscious of the importance of the work of the Agency in the implementation of the safeguards provisions of the Treaty on the Non-Proliferation of Nuclear Weapons and other international treaties, conventions and agreements designed to achieve similar objectives, as well as in ensuring, as far as it is able, that the assistance provided by the Agency or at its request or under its supervision or control is not used in such a way as to further any military purpose, as stated in article II of its statute,

Reaffirming that the Agency is the competent authority responsible for verifying and assuring, in accordance with the statute and the safeguards system of the Agency, compliance with its safeguards agreements with States parties undertaken in fulfilment of their obligations under article III, paragraph 1, of the Treaty on the Non-Proliferation of Nuclear Weapons, with a view to preventing diversion of nuclear energy from peaceful uses to nuclear weapons or other nuclear explosive devices, and also reaffirming that nothing should be done to undermine the authority of the Agency in this regard and that States parties that have concerns regarding non-compliance with the safeguards agreement of the Treaty by the States parties should direct such concerns, along with supporting evidence and information, to the Agency to consider, investigate, draw conclusions and decide on necessary actions in accordance with its mandate,

Stressing the need for the highest standards of safety in the design and operation of nuclear installations and in peaceful nuclear activities so as to minimize risks to life, health and the environment, and recognizing that a good safety record relies on good technology, good regulatory practices and well-qualified and trained staff, as well as international cooperation,

Considering that an expansion of technical cooperation activities relating to the peaceful uses of nuclear energy will contribute to the well-being of the peoples of the world, recognizing the special needs of the developing countries for technical assistance from the Agency and the importance of funding in order to benefit effectively from the transfer and application of nuclear technology for peaceful purposes as well as from the contribution of nuclear energy to their economic development, and desiring that the resources of the Agency for technical cooperation activities be assured, predictable and sufficient to meet the objectives mandated in article II of its statute,

Recognizing the importance of the work of the Agency on nuclear energy, applications of nuclear methods and techniques, nuclear safety, radiological protection and radioactive waste management, including its work directed towards assisting developing countries in all these fields,

Taking note of the report of the Director General to the General Conference of the International Atomic Energy Agency on the implementation of Security Council resolutions relating to Iraq, of his reports to the Security Council of 15 January, 9 April, 27 July, 7 October and 14 December 1998, of 7 April 1999, and of resolution GC(43)/RES/22 of 1 October 1999 of the General Conference and of his letter to the President of the Security Council of 6 October 1999,

Welcoming the convening of the second Scientific Forum, on "Sustainable development: a role for nuclear power?", during the forty-third regular session of the General Conference of the Agency,

Taking note of resolutions GOV/2711 of 21 March 1994 and GOV/2742 of 10 June 1994 of the Board of Governors and GC(43)/RES/3 of 1 October 1999 of the General Conference of the Agency in connection with the implementation of the Agreement between the Government of the Democratic People's Republic of Korea and the International Atomic Energy Agency for the application of safeguards in connection with the Treaty on the Non-Proliferation of Nuclear Weapons, the statements by the President of the Security Council of 31 March, 30 May and 4 November 1994 and the authorization of the Board of Governors, on 11 November 1994, to the Director General, to carry out all the tasks requested of the Agency in the statement by the President of the Security Council of 4 November 1994,

Taking note also of resolutions GC(43)/RES/8 on the amendment of article XIV.A of the statute of the Agency, GC(43)/RES/10 on the safety of radiation sources and the security of radioactive materials, GC(43)/RES/11 on the safety of transport of radioactive materials, GC(43)/RES/12 on the radiological protection of patients, GC(43)/RES/13 on measures to strengthen international cooperation in nuclear, radiation and waste safety, GC(43)/RES/14 on the strengthening of the Agency's technical cooperation activities, GC(43)/RES/15 on the plan for producing potable water economically, GC(43)/RES/16 on the extensive use of isotope hydrology for water resources management, GC(43)/RES/17 on strengthening the effectiveness and improving the efficiency of the safeguards system and application of the Model Protocol, GC(43)/RES/18 on measures against illicit trafficking in nuclear materials and other radioactive sources and GC(43)/RES/23 on the application of Agency safeguards in the Middle East, adopted on 1 October 1999 by the General Conference of the Agency at its forty-third regular session,

Taking note further of resolution GC(43)/RES/20 of 1 October 1999 on the staffing of the Agency's secretariat, in which the General Conference called on developing and under-represented member States to encourage well-qualified candidates to apply for vacant posts in the Agency, and considering the related resolution GC(43)/RES/21 of 1 October 1999 on women in the secretariat, in which the General Conference called on the Director General to integrate further the Platform for Action of the Fourth World Conference on Women into the Agency's relevant policies and programmes and noted the intention of the Agency's secretariat to participate in the forthcoming review at the Fifth World Conference on Women, to be held in 2000,

Recalling resolution GC(43)/RES/19 on the amendment to article VI of the statute and the statement by the President of the forty-third regular session of the General Conference of the Agency with respect to article VI, adopted on 1 October 1999 by the General Conference,

Noting the statement by the President of the forty-third regular session of the General Conference of the Agency, which was endorsed by the General Conference at its tenth plenary meeting and issued under the item concerning Israeli nuclear capabilities and threat, that:

> "The General Conference recalls the statement by the President of the thirty-sixth session of the General Conference in 1992 concerning the item entitled 'Israeli nuclear capabilities and threat'. That statement considered it desirable not to consider that item at the thirty-seventh session. The General Conference also recalls the statement by the President of the forty-second session, in 1998, concerning the same agenda item. At the forty-third session, the item was, at the request of certain member States, included again in the agenda. The item was discussed. The President notes that certain member States intend to include the item in the provisional agenda of the forty-fourth regular session of the General Conference",

1. *Takes note* of the report of the International Atomic Energy Agency;

2. *Affirms its confidence* in the role of the Agency in the application of nuclear energy for peaceful purposes;

3. *Takes note* of the adoption by the General Conference of the Agency of resolution GC(43)/RES/19 on the amendment to article VI of the statute and the accompanying statement by the President of the forty-third regular session of the General Conference relating to the expansion of the membership of the Board of Governors of the Agency from thirty-five to forty-three following the allocation of each member State to one of the areas listed in article VI, and recalls that the report by the Board of Governors as contained in document GC(43)/12 includes criteria and indicators to be used as guidelines in designating members to the Board of Governors, after article VI, as amended, has entered into force, on the understanding that they will serve as a reference;

4. *Welcomes* the adoption by the General Conference of the Agency of resolution GC(43)/RES/8 on the amendment of article XIV.A of the statute, which will provide for biennial budgeting by the Agency;

5. *Also welcomes* the measures and decisions taken by the Agency to maintain and strengthen the effectiveness and cost-efficiency of its integrated safeguards system in conformity with the statute of the Agency, in particular, stressing the importance of the Model Additional Protocol approved on 15 May 1997, affirms that strengthening the effectiveness and improving the efficiency of the safeguards system with a view to detecting undeclared nuclear activities must be implemented rapidly and universally by all concerned States and other parties in compliance with their respective international commitments, and requests all concerned States and other parties to safeguards agreements to conclude additional protocols without delay;

6. *Urges* all States to strive for effective and harmonious international cooperation in carrying out the work of the Agency, pursuant to its statute, in promoting the use of nuclear energy and the application of the necessary measures to strengthen further the safety of nuclear installations and to minimize risks to life, health and the environment, in strengthening technical assistance and cooperation for developing countries and in ensuring the effectiveness and efficiency of the safeguards system of the Agency;

7. *Welcomes* the measures and decisions taken by the Agency to strengthen and fund its technical cooperation activities, which should contribute to achieving sustainable development in developing countries, and calls upon States to cooperate in contributing to and in implementing the measures and decisions pursuant thereto;

8. *Commends* the Director General and the secretariat of the Agency for their continuing, impartial efforts to implement the safeguards agreement still in force between the Agency and the Democratic People's Republic of Korea, recognizes the important role of the Agency in monitoring the freeze of nuclear facilities in the Democratic People's Republic of Korea as requested by the Security Council, expresses deep concern about the continuing non-compliance of the Democratic People's Republic of Korea with the safeguards agreement, in spite of repeated calls by the international community for such compliance, calls upon the Democratic People's Republic of Korea to comply fully with that safeguards agreement and, to this end, urges it to cooperate fully with the Agency in the implementation of the safeguards agreement and to take all steps the Agency may deem necessary to preserve all information relevant to verifying the accuracy and completeness of the initial report of the Democratic People's Republic of Korea on the inventory of nuclear material subject to safeguards, until the Democratic People's Republic of Korea comes into full compliance with the safeguards agreement;

9. *Also commends* the Director General of the Agency and his staff for their strenuous efforts to implement Security Council resolutions 687(1991) of 3 April 1991, 707(1991) of 15 August 1991, 715(1991) of 11 October 1991, 1051(1996) of 27 March 1996, 1060(1996) of 12 June 1996, 1115(1997) of 21 June 1997, 1154(1998) of

2 March 1998, 1194(1998) of 9 September 1998 and 1205(1998) of 5 November 1998, stresses the need for full implementation by Iraq of all relevant Security Council resolutions, stresses also that the Agency's ongoing monitoring and verification activities should be resumed without delay, and stresses further that it is essential that, although the Agency is satisfied that the remaining questions which were unanswered as of mid-December 1998 do not prevent the full implementation of the ongoing monitoring and verification plan, the basis for this resumption preserve the Agency's rights specified in its ongoing monitoring and verification plan, including the full exercise of rights of access as enshrined therein and the necessary cooperation of Iraq, and that greater transparency by Iraq in its dealings with the Agency would contribute greatly to the resolution of the few remaining questions and concerns in the framework of the plan;

10. *Welcomes* the entry into force on 24 October 1996 of the Convention on Nuclear Safety, appeals to all States to become parties to it so that it obtains the widest possible adherence, expresses its satisfaction with the outcome of the first review meeting of the contracting parties to the Convention, held in April 1999, and looks forward to the report from the second review meeting, expecting safety improvements, in particular in all areas where the first review meeting found that there was room for such improvements;

11. *Also welcomes* the measures taken by the Agency in support of efforts to prevent illicit trafficking in nuclear materials and other radioactive sources and, in this context, decides to bear in mind, while drafting an international convention on the suppression of acts of nuclear terrorism, the activities of the Agency in the prevention and combating of illicit trafficking in nuclear material and other radioactive materials;

12. *Requests* the Secretary-General to transmit to the Director General of the Agency the records of the fifty-fourth session of the General Assembly relating to the activities of the Agency.

RECORDED VOTE ON RESOLUTION 54/26:

In favour: Algeria, Andorra, Angola, Argentina, Armenia, Australia, Austria, Bahrain, Bangladesh, Belarus, Belgium, Bhutan, Botswana, Brazil, Brunei Darussalam, Bulgaria, Burkina Faso, Cameroon, Canada, Chile, China, Colombia, Congo, Costa Rica, Côte d'Ivoire, Cuba, Cyprus, Czech Republic, Democratic Republic of the Congo, Denmark, Djibouti, Ecuador, Egypt, El Salvador, Equatorial Guinea, Estonia, Ethiopia, Finland, France, Gabon, Georgia, Germany, Ghana, Greece, Guatemala, Guinea, Guinea-Bissau, Guyana, Honduras, Hungary, Iceland, India, Indonesia, Iran, Ireland, Israel, Italy, Jamaica, Japan, Kazakhstan, Kuwait, Libyan Arab Jamahiriya, Liechtenstein, Lithuania, Luxembourg, Madagascar, Malaysia, Maldives, Mali, Malta, Mauritius, Mexico, Monaco, Morocco, Mozambique, Myanmar, Namibia, Netherlands, New Zealand, Nicaragua, Nigeria, Norway, Oman, Pakistan, Paraguay, Peru, Philippines, Poland, Portugal, Qatar, Republic of Korea, Republic of Moldova, Romania, Russian Federation, Saint Lucia, San Marino, Saudi Arabia, Senegal, Seychelles, Singapore, Slovakia, Slovenia, South Africa, Spain, Sri Lanka, Sudan, Suriname, Swaziland, Sweden, Tajikistan, Thailand, The former Yugoslav Republic of Macedonia, Togo, Tunisia, Turkey, Ukraine, United Arab Emirates, United Kingdom, United States, Venezuela, Yemen, Zambia.

Against: Democratic People's Republic of Korea.

Abstaining: Benin, Lao People's Democratic Republic, Lebanon, Syrian Arab Republic, United Republic of Tanzania, Viet Nam.

Natural resources

Water resources

The key issues in water management linked to poverty alleviation and sustainable development—the provision of water supply and sanitation and the impact of agriculture and land management on the water resource base—were considered by the Sub-group on Water Resources of the Committee on Energy and Natural Resources for Development at its April session [E/1999/32].

By **decision 54/450** of 22 December, the General Assembly took note of Economic and Social Council **decision 1999/277** (see p. 958) and requested CSD to consider, at its eighth (2000) session, those parts of the Committee's report that were relevant to its agreed programme of work for that year, bearing in mind the recommendations contained in Council **resolutions 1999/47, 1999/48** and **1999/49** (see below), and Assembly resolution 50/126 [YUN 1995, p. 1059], and to submit to the Assembly at its fifty-fifth (2000) session, through the Council, a report for its consideration.

Water supply and sanitation

The Committee on Energy and Natural Resources for Development reviewed the outline of the report of the Secretary-General on water supply and sanitation, to be prepared by the Subcommittee on Water Resources of the Administrative Committee on Coordination (ACC) (see p. 969) and submitted to the eighth session of CSD. The Committee noted that the report would provide up-to-date information on both water supply and sanitation coverage around the world; evaluate the progress made in attaining the ultimate goal of providing safe water supply and sanitation for all; and provide proposals for further action, particularly in developing countries and countries with economies in transition.

ECONOMIC AND SOCIAL COUNCIL ACTION

On 28 July [meeting 44], the Economic and Social Council, on the recommendation of the Committee on Energy and Natural Resources for Development [E/1999/32], adopted **resolution 1999/47** without vote [agenda item 13 *(k)*].

Contribution to the preparation of the report of the Secretary-General on progress made in providing safe water supply and sanitation for all during the 1990s

The Economic and Social Council,

Recalling General Assembly resolution 50/126 of 20 December 1995, in which the Assembly requested the Secretary-General to submit a report, through the Commission on Sustainable Development and the Economic and Social Council, to the General Assembly at its fifty-fifth session, containing an assessment of the water supply and sanitation situation in developing countries, including proposals for action for the ensuing decade at the national and international levels,

Recalling also the progress that has been made in water supply and sanitation,

Recalling further the importance given to integrated water resources management in Agenda 21,

Noting the need for progress in the alleviation of poverty and the links between poverty and the lack of drinking water and adequate sanitation;

Noting also the lack of adequate progress that has been made in providing sanitation and the negative impacts on human health and the health of ecosystems,

1. *Requests* the Secretary-General, in the preparation of his report:

(*a*) To ensure that the connections between water supply and sanitation and other sectors are explored;

(*b*) To focus the report on an analysis of the shortfalls in progress in providing water supply and sanitation, including an analysis of the barriers thereto;

(*c*) To explore how inadequate attention to an integrated approach to water and land management can exacerbate problems of water supply and sanitation and vice versa;

(*d*) To emphasize the analysis of issues;

(*e*) To explore topics where adequate progress has not been made and identify actions and examples of efforts that have been successful;

2. *Requests* that the following issues, as elaborated in the annex to the present resolution, be included in the analysis:

(*a*) Mobilization of political will;

(*b*) Economic sustainability and private-sector involvement in water supply and sanitation;

(*c*) Community participation and social mobilization;

(*d*) Sanitation, sewage treatment and wastewater recycling;

(*e*) Communication and awareness-training;

(*f*) Gender issues;

(*g*) Protection of water sources;

(*h*) Water conservation efforts.

ANNEX

Issues for inclusion in the report of the Secretary-General on progress made in providing safe water supply and sanitation for all during the 1990s

1. The need to mobilize political will to accomplish water supply and sanitation objectives and integrated land and water resources management, including:

(*a*) The need for a clear policy framework for water supply and sanitation which recognizes the fundamental role of water supply and sanitation in socio-economic development and incorporates these considerations into basic development planning, including a commitment to the mobilization of public and private funding for this effort;

(*b*) The need to incorporate water supply and sanitation in a broader integrated land and water resources management strategy;

(*c*) The need to pay attention to the most vulnerable groups in society;

(*d*) The need to give priority to addressing sanitation issues where they are lagging;

2. The need for economic sustainability and private-sector involvement in water supply and sanitation, including:

(*a*) The need for a clear and transparent policy and management framework which facilitates private-sector involvement, while protecting environmental and social concerns through transparent regulatory and administrative guidelines;

(*b*) The need for a commitment of public funding to assist in the provision of water supply and sanitation to the most vulnerable groups;

(*c*) Community participation and social mobilization, including:

(i) The need for a national policy framework which facilitates community participation in decision-making and contributions by beneficiaries;

(ii) The need for a policy framework that encourages, as appropriate, community participation in the construction, management and operations of water supply and sanitation projects;

(iii) The need to include socio-economic studies as a part of the initial planning process for water supply and sanitation projects;

(iv) The need to link the provision of water supply and sanitation service to demonstrated needs;

(v) The need to link community education and awareness-raising efforts to community participation efforts and to encourage the use of local inputs;

(vi) The need to promote public sector–private sector partnerships;

(vii) The need to strengthen local capacity and participation in monitoring and assessing water resources, including water quality;

(viii) The need to strengthen the capacity of the most vulnerable in society to participate in water supply and sanitation planning and decision-making;

(ix) The need to review various models of basin management and participation, including basin agencies and organizations, catchment councils, integrated watershed management efforts and international cooperation;

(*d*) Sanitation, sewage treatment and wastewater recycling, including:

(i) The chronic underfunding of these issues;

(ii) The costs, benefits and trade-offs of various treatment levels and the extent of coverage considering limited financial resources;

(iii) The problems of mixed domestic/industrial/storm-water systems;

(iv) The potential of industrial water recycling and pre-treatment before transfer to municipal systems;

(v) The potential for wastewater use for agricultural purposes;

(*e*) Communication and awareness-raising, including:

(i) The need to set aside support for water and hygiene education and communication efforts associated with technical and construction projects;

(ii) The need to use all appropriate existing and emerging communication channels (e.g., radio, television, newspapers, Internet and public information campaigns);

(iii) The need to use local networks (e.g., religious leaders, health and extension workers, women's groups, youth associations and sports clubs);

(iv) The need to use the education system at all levels, with special emphasis on youth and women;

(v) The need to identify target populations to maximize the benefits of education outreach;
(vi) The need to assess existing data-collection and information management to ensure that it meets management and decision-making requirements;
(*f*) Gender issues, including:
(i) The need to ensure full participation by women in all aspects of land and water resources management, including decision-making;
(ii) The need for gender-disaggregated data in water supply and sanitation planning, monitoring and evaluation;
(*g*) Protection of water sources, including:
(i) The need to examine the extent to which water supply programmes can be linked to protection of the catchment which is the source of the water (e.g., the Quito water supply);
(ii) The need for protection of headwater forests and wetlands to moderate stream flow and facilitate groundwater recharge;
(iii) The need for an ecosystem approach to water supply and sanitation planning;
(iv) The need for water quality monitoring and dissemination of information, including on manufactured and natural contaminants, such as harmful trace elements and heavy metals (e.g., arsenic in South Asia), and for the identification of sources of contaminants;
(v) The need to protect water sources and their catchments from pollution, examining the potential for incentives, regulation, administrative measures and intersectoral coordination;
(vi) The need regularly to update and disseminate hydrological information;
(*h*) Water conservation efforts, including:
(i) The need to examine leakage in water distribution and sewage lines;
(ii) The need to examine demand management programmes to moderate demand and wasting of water;
(iii) The need to encourage the adoption of water-saving devices;
(iv) The need to give high priority to water conservation in national land and water policies;
(v) The need to develop and transfer appropriate water conservation technologies and to encourage the use of local resources in their application;
(vi) The need to include water conservation efforts in water balance calculations for basin management.

Land and water

Agriculture and water

The Committee considered the interrelationship between agriculture and water as a contribution to the preparatory process for CSD's eighth (2000) session, the sectoral theme of which would be integrated planning and management of land resources and agriculture. The Committee noted the dependency of agriculture on water resources for both rain-fed and irrigated agriculture, but also stressed the impact of agriculture on the water resource base through high levels of consumptive use and degradation of water quality. It stressed the scope for improving the productive use of water in agriculture through improved technologies, outreach and community participation and clear economic and environmental regulation, but noted that that would need to occur in the appropriate catchment, basin or aquifer framework.

ECONOMIC AND SOCIAL COUNCIL ACTION

On 28 July [meeting 44], the Economic and Social Council, on the recommendation of the Committee on Energy and Natural Resources for Development [E/1999/32], as amended [E/1999/L.42], adopted **resolution 1999/48** without vote [agenda item 13 (*k*)].

Contribution to the preparatory process for the eighth session of the Commission on Sustainable Development: integrated planning and management of land resources and agriculture

The Economic and Social Council,

Recalling its resolution 1998/46 of 31 July 1998, in the annex to which it directed the Committee on Energy and Natural Resources for Development, in formulating its programme of work, to take into full account the multi-year programme of work of the Commission on Sustainable Development, so as to ensure that its own work would be structured to contribute to the work of the Commission,

Recalling also that, in the multi-year programme of work of the Commission, the sectoral theme for the eighth session of the Commission, to be held in 2000, is integrated planning and management of land resources and that the economic sector focus will be agriculture,

Noting the inextricable interrelationship between agriculture and water,

Recalling that the Food and Agriculture Organization of the United Nations is the task manager for the implementation of the chapters of Agenda 21 relating to land management and agriculture,

1. *Invites* the Food and Agriculture Organization of the United Nations, in preparing documentation for the eighth session of the Commission on Sustainable Development, to take account of the interrelationship of agriculture and water, examine the use of water for agriculture, recognizing the scarce and vulnerable nature of water and also recognizing that agriculture is one of many users and that it is the sector that is primarily responsible for the consumptive use of water on a global basis, and also examine, as appropriate, the following issues, analyse their importance and recommend actions or alternatives, citing case studies, where possible:

(*a*) Overarching issues

The water crisis and the role of agriculture as water-dependent and highly vulnerable to water deficiencies, and also with regard to its impact on both water quality and water quantity;

Conciliation of water availability and agricultural planning within or without transboundary agreements between States to allocate water and guarantee availability;
Extension and promotion of technology and information on water and agriculture;
Demand management;
Integrated approaches to soil and water conservation;
Interrelationship of agriculture and water quality;
Importance of community participation in decisions affecting shared water sources;
Importance of the availability of agro-meteorological, hydrological and hydrogeological data;
Need for a re-evaluation of the concept of food security, taking into account water shortages, and consideration of meeting nutritional needs through trade and crop diversification, taking into account customs and marketing, as appropriate;
Consideration in programme planning, policy and reviews of relevant international conventions, treaties and agreements relating to water management or agriculture;

(*b*) Irrigation and drainage
Use of fossil water for crop production and unsustainable use of groundwater, threatening drinking-water supplies;
Agricultural drainage and long-term agricultural yield;
Soil and aquifer salinization;
River depletion problems (for example, the Yellow River and the Aral Sea);
Development of environmental guidelines for irrigation and drainage;

(*c*) Rain-fed agriculture
Need to emphasize the non-irrigated sub-optimal producers, who are also the most vulnerable and among the poorest producers;
Need for varieties that are drought-tolerant, flood-tolerant and more water-efficient;
Need to catalogue and disseminate new and traditional water-saving technologies and integrated soil and water conservation techniques;
Need to consider rainwater harvesting techniques and ponds or water-holding areas for dry-season agricultural production and for livestock and fish production;
Soil and water conservation;
Importance of soil and water conservation techniques, including contour ploughing, conservation tillage and buffer strips;
Consideration of the type of soil, crop and water quality in relation to the availability of land and water resources;
Protection of wetlands;
Use of an ecosystem approach to development and planning;
Control of chemical pollution;
Promotion of integrated pest and integrated nutrient management systems;
Encouragement of organic food production;
Monitoring of groundwater and surface water for nutrient loads and pesticides (for example, nitrate contamination of groundwater in Europe and persistent problems from pesticide misuse in El Salvador);
Opportunities for organic production;

2. *Also invites* the Food and Agriculture Organization of the United Nations to include the consideration of water in all of its preparations and discussions for the preparatory meeting that it is co-sponsoring with the Government of the Netherlands.

Spatial planning

The Committee had before it a report of the Secretary-General on issues related to the spatial planning of land (including minerals) and water resources [E/C.7/1998/5], which had been prepared for the 1998 session of the Committee on Natural Resources that did not take place because of the termination of its mandate [YUN 1998, p. 972]. Noting that CSD would focus on integrated planning and management of land resources in 2000, the Committee recognized a need to take an integrated approach to the protection and sustainable management of land and soil resources. Accordingly, it recommended revisions to the Secretary-General's report.

ECONOMIC AND SOCIAL COUNCIL ACTION

On 28 July [meeting 44], the Economic and Social Council, on the recommendation of the Committee on Energy and Natural Resources for Development [E/1999/32], as amended [E/1999/L.42], adopted **resolution 1999/49** without vote [agenda item 13 (*k*)].

Report of the Secretary-General on issues related to the spatial planning of land (including minerals) and water resources

The Economic and Social Council

1. *Takes note with appreciation* of the report of the Secretary-General on issues related to the spatial planning of land (including minerals) and water resources;

2. *Requests* the Secretary-General to prepare a report based on the above-mentioned report and taking into account the suggested revisions contained in the annex to the present resolution, and to make it available to the Commission on Sustainable Development at its eighth session as a background document on integrated land management.

ANNEX

Suggested revisions to the report of the Secretary-General on issues related to the spatial planning of land (including minerals) and water resources

I. Introduction

A paragraph should be added to address the concerns expressed in the inter-sessional strategy paper of the Committee on Natural Resources on future water resources management issues and appropriate strategies and policies about the serious implications for society as a whole and the life-support systems on which it is based if the looming water crisis with its four basic components—water quality, water quantity, urbanization and land degradation—is allowed to develop into a full-scale crisis. Such a crisis, owing to the close interrelationship between freshwater and land use, would be felt in many different societal sectors, including human health, food security, economic production and biological diversity.

A summary of the recommendations of major international meetings on the integration of land and water management, such as the United Nations Water Conference, the International Conference on Water and the Environment, and the United Nations Conference on Environment and Development, should be included.

II. Current and emerging management issues

References to the finite nature of water and the water crisis should be included to balance paragraphs 7 to 9 on land limitations.

Land-use planning and development need to take into consideration the finite nature of water and apportion projected needs in a coherent manner; this should be discussed.

A reference to forest resources should be included.

In paragraph 7, the following could be considered: Forests in the main help to provide a balance between life-support systems within the ecosystem. Deforestation tilts this balance and exposes the ecosystem to ever-increasing degradation. The role of forestry in land use and in land management techniques should therefore not be underestimated. The interdependency of forestry and agriculture in the lives of rural people is now becoming an issue which Governments must resolve in an integrated manner.

In paragraph 9, a stronger reference to the misuse of agricultural chemicals should be considered.

Between paragraphs 10 and 11, the following text should be inserted:

"The allocation of scarce water resources among competing uses has fundamental effects on human welfare, socio-economic development and the protection of ecosystems. The provision of adequate amounts of water for basic human needs should be incorporated into the formulation and implementation of policies for water resources development and allocation. In this context, the equitable and sustainable allocation of water resources is an essential element of rural and urban development strategies aimed at poverty alleviation through generation of employment, income and productivity. Such strategies should be based as much as possible upon community participation at the lowest appropriate levels, taking into particular account the role of women in rural and urban communities as ultimate managers of water resources in both household and agricultural use. Such approaches require specific policies to improve local institutional capacity and promote human resources development.

Economic evaluations need to consider positive and negative impacts on both human and ecosystem health. To the extent that subsidies are required to maintain public health and equitable access, they should be clearly targeted to the intended beneficiaries and aligned with rural development strategies. Additional funding, targeted mainly to peri-urban and rural areas, may also be required to implement such strategies. The integration of water resources development and management with land-use planning is also essential to promote stabilization of rural populations through the alleviation of rural poverty and promotion of local employment opportunities in the productive use of water and land."

III. Actions to improve and enhance the spatial planning of land and water resources

A paragraph should be added to address the following concern:

While water moves through the landscape from the watershed to the mouth of the river according to natural laws, climate and topography, the societal sectors in the river basin depend on access to water and at the same time influence the quality and quantity of the water accessible to those downstream. As stressed at the Expert Group Meeting on Strategic Approaches to Freshwater Management, held at Harare from 27 to 30 January 1998, integrated water resources management is therefore essential for integrating and reconciling interests in the river basin—whether national or international—with regard to water quality and quantity and the aquatic ecosystems. A constructive dialogue needs to be made possible at the basin level to develop consensus between land and water users and stakeholders. Strategies should be specific about methods of pollution avoidance to ensure sequential water use downstream. The integration between management and use of land and water and waste management should be reflected in the approach to human health, nutrition, employment, poverty alleviation and ecosystem integrity.

A. Integration of land and water resources management into national socio-economic strategies

The inclusion of an additional box on the Murray-Darling basin land and water management initiative in Australia is recommended.

Greater attention should be paid, possibly in an additional paragraph, to grass-roots participatory approaches and gender issues in this section.

B. Land, water and food security

The concept of food security needs to be re-evaluated to take into account water shortages and to focus on meeting nutritional needs through crop diversification and trade, as appropriate; the concept of long-term sustainability of the food production system should incorporate soil and water conservation, and should not focus on production level only.

Traditional practices relating to agriculture need to be acknowledged and appropriately addressed.

Extension services to facilitate the adoption of water-saving practices in agriculture need to be strengthened.

Small-scale irrigation efforts (for example, the use of groundwater) need to be reviewed.

C. Land, water and health

The need for measures to encourage sustainable approaches to agricultural production, including organic agriculture, should be discussed.

An analysis of the contamination of land and water by harmful trace elements and heavy metals, such as mercury used for the amalgamation of gold in artisanal and small-scale mining, should be included.

Up-to-date information about health risks posed by contaminated land and water resources should be provided.

The disposal of solid, liquid and toxic wastes and their impacts on basin hydrology should be considered.

D. Protection of land and water ecosystems

The first half of the paragraph should be retained. The relationship between land and water development and its implications for the ecosystem may be summarized as discussed in paragraphs 60 to 66 of the report of the Harare Expert Group Meeting.

The paragraph could be divided into two paragraphs, one focusing on international agreements (several more need to be added, including the United Nations Framework Convention on Climate Change, the Convention to Combat Desertification in Those Countries Experiencing Serious Drought and/or Desertification, Particularly in Africa, and the Global Programme of Action for the Protection of the Marine Environment from Land-based Activities), and one dealing with an evolution of the potential need for policy and institutional re-evaluation in the light of treaty obligations.

International cooperation needs to be evaluated in the cases of shared watercourses, and cooperation between upstream and downstream countries needs to be encouraged; the relevance of Convention on the Law of the Non-Navigational Uses of International Watercourses to land use as well as to access to water and sanitation and environmental questions needs to be examined; successful cooperation examples, such as the Zambezi River Authority, might be considered.

E. Information management and monitoring systems

Hydrological and hydrogeological information needs to be made available between neighbouring countries in the same manner that meteorological information is made available through the World Meteorological Organization.

Hydrologic, meteorologic and hydrogeologic data need to be accessible to the public on a timely basis, especially for flood and drought management.

F. Institutional and legal framework and capacity-building

The section could be divided, placing paragraphs 32 to 34 in a section on capacity-building and paragraph 35 in a section on gender.

The different strategies for local participation and basin-wide integration need to be clarified in paragraphs 27 and 28.

The potential for local participation in the construction, operation, maintenance and management of waterworks should be evaluated.

Paragraph 30 is a general paragraph, and any specific reference to water, soil or minerals is unhelpful and should therefore be deleted.

In paragraph 31, the channelling of financial resources through basin management organizations should be examined.

Economic analysis of river basin management should be encouraged.

G. Mobilization of financial resources

The importance of streamlining regulatory and institutional structures and making them transparent so as to mobilize all available resources needs to be evaluated.

In paragraph 38, after the words "Developing countries", the words "and countries with economies in transition" should be added.

Inter-agency action

The ACC Subcommittee on Water Resources, at its twentieth session (Geneva, 4-8 October) [ACC/1999/18], reviewed its methods of work and discussed reports of the Secretary-General to be submitted to CSD's eighth (2000) session (on progress made in providing safe water and sanitation for all during the 1990s and on issues related to the spatial planning of land (including minerals) and water resources) and plans to produce the World Water Development Report.

The Subcommittee also discussed the briefing given to CSD's seventh (1999) session; its contribution to the development and implementation of the World Water Vision of the World Water Forum; public information, with particular reference to the World Day for Water (22 March); the water quality initiative; an international network for information management; and water supply and sanitation.

Exploration

At its first regular session of 1999, the Executive Board of UNDP and of the United Nations Population Fund considered the Administrator's report on activities of the UNDP special funds and programmes [DP/1999/4], including the United Nations Revolving Fund for Natural Resources Exploration (UNRFNRE) [YUN 1998, p. 975]. The Board took note of the report on 29 January [E/1999/35 (dec. 99/3)]. During the discussion of the report, the Board asked the Administrator to provide an analysis of the Fund's usefulness and the rationale for its continuation.

In response to that request, the Administrator submitted a report on UNRFNRE [DP/1999/42] to the Board's September session. He provided background information on the Fund and its financial status and outlined UNDP plans to phase out its activities by the end of 2000. The Administrator stated that, since its establishment by Economic and Social Council resolution 1762(LIV) [YUN 1973, p. 406] and General Assembly resolution 3167(XXVIII) [ibid., p. 408], UNRFNRE had received $91 million in voluntary contributions and other income from 26 countries. The voluntary contributions declined from $3 million in 1991 to $1.6 million in 1998 (provided by China, Indonesia and Japan). It was estimated that some $2.48 million would be available for programming and administration at the end of 2000 if current commitments were fulfilled, no new initiatives were undertaken and no additional contributions were made.

In phasing out UNRFNRE activities, UNDP was ensuring that all existing project and contractual commitments were fulfilled in a responsible manner; ensuring that all usable information compiled by the Fund was archived electronically and made available to all programme countries; and addressing the issue of the utilization of the balance of funds. With regard to the last matter, UNDP planned to use the balance for capacity-building for natural resources management in programme countries in consultation with the major donor, Japan.

On 17 September [E/1999/35 (dec. 99/20)], the Board endorsed the plans to phase out UNRFNRE activities by the end of 2000.

Cartography

By a 2 March letter [E/1999/68], Germany, referring to Economic and Social Council decision 1998/221 [YUN 1998, p. 979], by which it was decided that the Eighth United Nations Conference on the Standardization of Geographical Names should be held in 2002, offered to host the Conference.

ECONOMIC AND SOCIAL COUNCIL ACTION

On 26 July [meeting 39], the Economic and Social Council adopted **resolution 1999/9** [draft: E/1999/L.28] without vote [agenda item 13 (*c*)].

Eighth United Nations Conference on the Standardization of Geographical Names

The Economic and Social Council,

Recalling its decision 1998/221 of 23 July 1998 and General Assembly resolution 40/243 of 18 December 1985,

1. *Welcomes* the generous offer of the Government of Germany to host the Eighth United Nations Conference on the Standardization of Geographical Names in 2002,

2. *Decides* that the Eighth United Nations Conference on the Standardization of Geographical Names will be held in Germany from 27 August to 5 September 2002.

By **decision 1999/286** of 30 July, the Council took note of the report of the Seventh United Nations Conference on the Standardization of Geographical Names, held in 1998 [YUN 1998, p. 978].

Chapter VII

Environment and human settlements

In 1999, the United Nations and the international community continued efforts to protect the environment through legally binding instruments and the activities of the United Nations Environment Programme (UNEP).

In September, UNEP presented the second report in the Global Environment Outlook series, the key finding of which was that the continued poverty of the majority of the world's inhabitants and excessive consumption by the minority were the major causes of environmental degradation. Areas of concern were the world water supply, the impact of land degradation on agricultural productivity, air pollution, the overexploitation of tropical forests and marine fisheries, and the loss of plant and animal species, as well as stretches of coral reef.

The Conference of the Parties to the 1992 United Nations Framework Convention on Climate Change (Bonn, October/November) took action to bring the 1997 Kyoto Protocol into force as early as possible. The Protocol aimed to reduce industrialized countries' collective emissions of carbon dioxide and five other greenhouse gases.

The combined meeting of the Conference of the Parties to the 1985 Vienna Convention for the Protection of the Ozone Layer and the Eleventh Meeting of the Parties to the 1987 Montreal Protocol on Substances that Deplete the Ozone Layer (Beijing, China, November/December) agreed on a funding package to enable developing countries to maintain the momentum of their efforts to phase out chlorofluorocarbons and other ozone-destroying chemicals. The meeting adopted a further amendment to the Protocol that banned trade in hydrochlorofluorocarbons (HCFCs) with countries that had not ratified the Protocol's 1992 Amendment, which had introduced the HCFC phase-out. Parties to the 1979 Convention on Long-Range Transboundary Air Pollution adopted an additional protocol to abate acidification, eutrophication and ground-level ozone, which opened for signature on 30 November. The Conference of the Parties to the 1994 United Nations Convention to Combat Desertification in those Countries Experiencing Serious Drought and/or Desertification, particularly in Africa, adopted the Recife (Brazil) Initiative, which called for the drafting in 2000 of a declaration to enhance implementation of the obligations accepted by States parties. The Basel Protocol on Liability and Compensation for Damage resulting from Transboundary Movements of Hazardous Wastes and their Disposal was adopted in December.

United Nations human settlements activities were guided by follow-up to the 1996 United Nations Conference on Human Settlements (Habitat II), which focused on shelter for all. The Commission on Human Settlements (Nairobi, Kenya, 5-14 May) adopted a number of resolutions dealing with the implementation of Habitat II. The Commission, acting as the Preparatory Committee for the Assembly's special (2001) session for an overall review and appraisal of the implementation of the 1996 Habitat Agenda, adopted its provisional agenda and agreed that the Committee's first session would be held in May 2000. Regarding the revitalization of the United Nations Centre for Human Settlements (UNCHS), the Commission mandated the UNCHS Executive Director to implement a new strategic vision through subprogrammes on adequate shelter for all and through the global campaigns on secure tenure and on urban governance.

Environment

UN Environment Programme

Governing Council

The Governing Council of the United Nations Environment Programme (UNEP) held its twentieth session at UNEP headquarters in Nairobi, Kenya, from 1 to 5 February [A/54/25]. The Council, which held a high-level segment on 4 and 5 February [UNEP/GC.20/48], decided to hold its twenty-first session in Nairobi from 5 to 9 February 2001. It elected the members of the High-level Committee of Ministers and Officials. The Committee of the Whole considered the programme, the Environment Fund and administrative and other budgetary matters [UNEP/GC.20/48].

By **decision 1999/286** of 30 July, the Economic and Social Council took note of the Council's report on its twentieth session.

Subsidiary bodies

The 36-member High-level Committee of Ministers and Officials, a subsidiary organ of the Council established in 1997 [YUN 1997, p. 1040], held its fourth meeting (Bonn, Germany, 1 November) [UNEP/HLC/4/4]. The Committee considered a September report [UNEP/HLC/4/INF/1] of the Executive Director summarizing UNEP activities in its five focus areas (environmental information, assessment and research; coordination of environmental conventions and development of environmental policy instruments; fresh water; technology transfer and industry; and support to Africa). In addition, the report covered communications and public information, as well as the status of the Environment Fund and other sources of funding. A further report contained UNEP's contribution to the UN medium-term plan for 2002-2005 [UNEP/HLC/4/2]; the European Union (EU) and the United States submitted separate submissions thereon. The Committee had before it a report of the Executive Director on the implementation of General Assembly resolution 53/242 (see p. 975) regarding the environment and human settlements [UNEP/HLC/4/INF/2] and a statement by the Nairobi Chapter of the Group of 77 and China thereon [UNEP/HLC/4/INF/4].

During a panel discussion on globalization, agriculture and the environment, the Executive Director drew attention to his September report on the environmental and social impacts of globalized agriculture [UNEP/HLC/4/3]. A separate submission by Japan stated that the report explained only destructive environmental impacts of government subsidies for agriculture. Japan presented a series of amendments to the report, as proposed by the EU. Separate notes of the Executive Director contained the reports of the Committee's first, second and third meetings [UNEP/GC.20/INF/14] and reviewed the status of the 1997 Governing Council decision [YUN 1997, p. 1040] that established the Committee [UNEP/GC.20/12]. On 4 February, the Council took note of the reports [A/54/25 (dec. 20/14)].

The Executive Director reported in January [UNEP/GC.20/12] that the Committee of Permanent Representatives, comprising representatives of all UN Member States and members of specialized agencies, and the European Community, established a working group that held 18 meetings to prepare the draft decisions for the Council's current session. He also presented information on strengthening the Committee, in accordance with a 1997 Council decision [YUN 1997, p. 1040]. The Council had before it a note of the Executive Director transmitting a report on the assessment of the functioning of the UNEP secretariat [UNEP/GC.20/13]. The Committee recommended that UNEP continue to strengthen, restructure and revitalize the secretariat and endorsed the UNEP reform process. Regarding the United Nations Office at Nairobi (UNON), it recommended defining its roles and tasks; enhancing the contribution of the UN regular budget to UNON; improving communication and document distribution; and strengthening the regional offices.

Welcoming the Committee's recommendations on the functioning of the secretariat, the Governing Council, on 4 February [dec. 20/15], urged the Executive Director to take them into account and asked him to keep the Committee informed of progress made.

GENERAL ASSEMBLY ACTION

On 22 December [meeting 87], the General Assembly, on the recommendation of the Second (Economic and Financial) Committee [A/54/588/Add.7], adopted **resolution 54/216** without vote [agenda item 100].

Report of the Governing Council of the United Nations Environment Programme

The General Assembly,

Recalling its resolution 2997(XXVII) of 15 December 1972, by which it decided to establish the Governing Council of the United Nations Environment Programme,

Recalling also its resolutions 53/187 of 15 December 1998 on the report of the Governing Council of the United Nations Environment Programme and 53/242 of 28 July 1999 on the report of the Secretary-General on environment and human settlements,

Recalling further the results and decisions of the nineteenth special session of the General Assembly, convened for the purpose of the overall review and appraisal of the implementation of Agenda 21 and, in particular, paragraphs 119 and 122 to 124 of the Programme for the Further Implementation of Agenda 21,

Recalling the Nairobi Declaration on the Role and Mandate of the United Nations Environment Programme, adopted by the Governing Council of the United Nations Environment Programme at its nineteenth session,

Having considered the report of the Governing Council of the United Nations Environment Programme on its twentieth session,

1. *Welcomes* the report of the Governing Council of the United Nations Environment Programme on its twentieth session and the decisions contained therein;

2. *Takes note,* in particular, of Governing Council decision 20/31 of 4 February 1999, entitled "Proposed programme budget of the United Nations Environment Programme: revised requirements for the biennium 1998-1999 and proposed requirements for the biennium 2000-2001", in which the Governing Council gives concrete support to the integrated work programme of the Programme and endorsement of its new functional organizational structure, and anticipates an increased level of funding to the Environment Fund for the biennium 2000-2001;

3. *Supports* the proposals for the facilitation of and support for enhancing linkages and coordination within and among environmental and environment-

related conventions, inter alia, by the United Nations Environment Programme, with full respect for the status of the respective convention secretariats and the autonomous decision-making prerogatives of the conferences of the parties to the conventions concerned;

4. *Notes with appreciation* the contribution of the United Nations Environment Programme to the Commission on Sustainable Development at its seventh session, and encourages the Governing Council at future sessions to provide its scientific, technical and policy information and analysis of and advice on global environmental issues to the Commission at future sessions and, in particular, to contribute to the preparation of the ten-year review of the United Nations Conference on Environment and Development in 2002;

5. *Welcomes* the progress in the negotiation of an international legally binding instrument for implementing international action on certain persistent organic pollutants with a view to its earlier conclusion;

6. *Encourages* the supporting role of the United Nations Environment Programme for developing countries, particularly in Africa, through the development of policy support and capacity-building for international environmental negotiation, inter alia, through the revitalization of the African Ministerial Conference on the Environment;

7. *Stresses* the importance of strengthening the United Nations Office at Nairobi in its capacity as the only United Nations Office located in a developing country, and encourages the increased utilization of its facilities;

8. *Notes* the increased cooperation and collaboration between the United Nations Environment Programme and the United Nations Centre for Human Settlements (Habitat), within the framework of their respective mandates and separate programmatic, budgetary and organizational identities, with a view to improving the effectiveness of their work;

9. *Calls upon* all countries to ensure the provision of sufficient financial resources, on a stable and predictable basis, for the successful implementation of the work programme for the biennium 2000-2001;

10. *Requests* the Secretary-General to provide the necessary resources from the regular budget of the United Nations to the United Nations Environment Programme for the biennium 2000-2001, in accordance with current budgetary practices, and to consider ways to support further the revitalization of the Programme.

Policy and advisory services

Institution-building

The Governing Council reviewed a report of the Executive Director describing UNEP activities aimed at providing Governments and other institutions with policy and advisory services, particularly technical, legal and policy advice [UNEP/GC.20/6]. The institution-building activities focused on areas identified by the Governing Council in 1998 (environmental information, assessment and research; enhanced coordination of environmental conventions and development of environmental policy instruments; fresh water; technology transfer and industry; and support to Africa) [YUN 1998, p. 982].

On 5 February [A/54/25 (dec. 20/6)], the Council asked the Executive Director to strengthen the UNEP secretariat to provide policy and advisory services and to enhance cooperation with Governments, other relevant organizations and entities in activities related to those services.

Economics, trade and financial services

The Executive Director provided a brief account of UNEP activities in the area of economics, trade and financial services, in particular policy guidance and technical support to enhance the capacities of countries to develop and apply integrated environment and economic analysis, policies and instruments for environmental management and sustainable development [UNEP/GC.20/43].

On 4 February [dec. 20/29], the Governing Council asked the Executive Director to assist countries, particularly developing countries and countries with economies in transition, to enhance their capacities to integrate environmental considerations with development planning and decision-making. It also asked him to continue to examine policy options to address the challenges of integrating environmental considerations with trade and trade policies and to continue to assist countries, particularly developing countries and countries with economies in transition, to improve their understanding of the environmental effects of trade. He was asked to continue to carry out studies on the effectiveness of market-based incentives in achieving the objectives of environmental conventions and on the relationship between trade measures contained in the conventions and international trade policy; cooperate with other international organizations dealing with the relationship between the environment and trade, particularly the World Trade Organization (see PART SIX, Chapter XVII) and the United Nations Conference on Trade and Development (see PART THREE, Chapter IV); and collaborate with the private sector to enhance their contribution to sustainable development activities through the integration of environmental considerations into their operations. He was asked to strengthen the secretariat's capacities to carry out the tasks identified by the Council.

Coordination and cooperation

Environment and human settlements

A January report of the Executive Director [UNEP/GC.20/15] outlined the status of the consideration of recommendations contained in the Secretary-General's 1998 report on the environment and human settlements [YUN 1998, p. 981]. The report summarized the General Assembly's November 1998 debate on the item but noted that no formal action was taken. However, the Secretary-General expressed support for the recommendations requiring intergovernmental action, stating that their implementation would go a long way to enhance policy coherence and coordination.

The Governing Council provided its views on the Secretary-General's report on 5 February [dec. 20/17]. It agreed with the proposal to consider, particularly in the light of the recommendation to establish an annual ministerial-level forum, the role of the High-level Committee of Ministers and Officials, and supported the institution of an annual ministerial-level global environmental forum, with the Council's regular biennial sessions constituting the forum in the years that the Council met, and in alternate years taking the form of a special session of the Council, meeting in different regions as a ministerial-level forum. The Council welcomed proposals at the secretariat level relating to inter-agency coordination; linkages among and support to environmental and environment-related conventions; UNEP, the United Nations Centre for Human Settlements (Habitat) and UNON; information, monitoring, assessment and early warning; involvement of major groups; future initiatives; facilitation and support by UNEP of coordination among the bureaux and secretariats of environment and environment-related conventions; and enhancing UNEP's role in providing environmental advocacy, analysis and advice in shaping the priorities and programmes of the Global Environment Facility consistent with UNEP's envisaged role in the Instrument for the Establishment of the Restructured Global Environment Facility. It also welcomed the recommendations on the Council's future action-oriented agendas and the structure and timing of its meetings to enhance coordination with the Commission on Sustainable Development and the conferences of the parties to environmental and environment-related conventions. It took note of the recommendations intended for action by intergovernmental bodies relating to linkages among and support to such conventions, intergovernmental forums and the involvement of major groups, and welcomed the call to engage non-governmental organizations (NGOs) and civil society in UN work. It took note of the proposal concerning universal membership of the Council.

Environment management group

In accordance with two 1997 Governing Council decisions [YUN 1997, p. 1041], the Executive Director updated developments on the Inter-Agency Environment Coordination Group (IAEG)—an advisory body set up to coordinate UN system activities in addressing the major challenges in the UNEP work programme—and on the UN system-wide environment strategy for 1998-2002 [UNEP/GC.20/7]. He noted that both the UN Task Force on Environment and Human Settlements and the Secretary-General, in 1998, had recommended the establishment of an inter-agency environmental management group (EMG) to improve inter-agency policy coherence and collaboration [YUN 1998, p. 981]. EMG would replace IAEG and create a process for reviewing planned activities and modification of goals regarding the environment and human settlements. The group would supersede IAEG and the need for a system-wide strategy in the area of the environment.

The most important goal of EMG would be to achieve effective coordination and joint action in key areas related to the environment and human settlements. It would assist intergovernmental bodies, particularly the Governing Council and the Commission on Human Settlements, in the preparation of coordinated inputs to intergovernmental forums, notably the Commission on Sustainable Development. It was recommended that the group report on an informational basis to the Administrative Committee on Coordination (ACC) and bring an environmental perspective into the work of the Inter-Agency Committee on Sustainable Development (IACSD). EMG should establish time-bound task forces or working groups covering clusters of issues and should include convention secretariats among its participants when needed. The Secretary-General would hold consultations with ACC to ensure the participation of the entire UN system and to decide on the formal establishment of EMG.

Noting the proposal to establish EMG, the Governing Council, on 5 February [A/54/25 (dec. 20/13)], asked the Executive Director to consider the need for an inter-agency coordination group and system-wide strategy for the environment and to report thereon in 2001. On the same date [dec. 20/17], the Council expressed support for the establishment of EMG.

ACC action. Following consideration of IACSD recommendations regarding the establishment of EMG, ACC, at its first regular session of 1999 (Geneva, 9-10 April) [ACC/1999/4], agreed that further consultations, to be conducted by the UNEP Executive Director with ACC members regarding the proposed group's terms of reference, criteria for membership and methods of work, should take into account the views expressed by IACSD.

GENERAL ASSEMBLY ACTION

On 28 July [meeting 105], the General Assembly adopted **resolution 53/242** [draft: A/53/L.78] without vote [agenda item 30].

Report of the Secretary-General on environment and human settlements

The General Assembly,

Recalling its resolution 52/12 A of 12 November 1997, entitled "Renewing the United Nations: a programme for reform",

Reaffirming its determination to strengthen the role, capacity, effectiveness and efficiency of the United Nations, including in the field of environment and human settlements, and thus improve its performance in order to realize the full potential of the Organization,

Taking note of the report of the Secretary-General on environment and human settlements and the report of the United Nations Task Force on Environment and Human Settlements annexed thereto, which contain recommendations on reforming and strengthening the activities of the United Nations in the field of environment and human settlements,

Expressing its appreciation to the Chairman and members of the Task Force for their commendable work,

Conscious of the continued deterioration of the global environment and the state of human settlements, despite some positive achievements, as well as of the need to strengthen the institutions of the United Nations charged with responsibility for environment and human settlements, to improve their performance and to promote coordination in the implementation of the environmental and human settlements dimension of sustainable development within the United Nations system,

Emphasizing the importance of strengthening the capacity of the United Nations Environment Programme and the United Nations Centre for Human Settlements (Habitat) in their Nairobi location and of ensuring the provision of requisite support and stable, adequate and predictable financial resources necessary to both organizations for the fulfilment of their mandates, as contained in General Assembly resolutions 2997 (XXVII) of 15 December 1972 and 32/162 of 19 December 1977, as well as in the Nairobi Declaration on the Role and Mandate of the United Nations Environment Programme, adopted by the Governing Council of the United Nations Environment Programme in its decision 19/1 of 7 February 1997, and the Istanbul Declaration on Human Settlements, adopted by the United Nations Conference on Human Settlements (Habitat II) on 14 June 1996, including by seeking additional financial resources through broadening the range of sources of funding for both organizations, in accordance with the Financial Regulations and Rules of the United Nations,

Taking into account the views of Member States on the report of the Secretary-General on environment and human settlements,

Taking into account also the views contained in decision 20/17, adopted on 5 February 1999 by the Governing Council of the United Nations Environment Programme, and Commission on Human Settlements resolution 17/6 of 14 May 1999, concerning the report of the Secretary-General on environment and human settlements,

1. *Welcomes* the efforts undertaken to strengthen the United Nations in the field of environment and human settlements, and in that context takes note of the general thrust of the recommendations contained in the report of the Secretary-General on environment and human settlements, proposing actions to be taken by the Secretary-General, the Executive Director of the United Nations Environment Programme and the Executive Director of the United Nations Centre for Human Settlements (Habitat), and takes note also of the recommendations outlined in section IV of the report;

2. *Requests* the Secretary-General to strengthen the United Nations Office at Nairobi, in its capacity as the only United Nations headquarters located in a developing country, through the provision of requisite support and stable, adequate and predictable financial resources, including by proposing additional regular budget resources, as envisaged by the General Assembly in its resolution 52/220 of 22 December 1997, for the consideration of the Assembly, with due regard for proper United Nations budgetary procedures;

3. *Encourages* the Director-General of the United Nations Office at Nairobi to take steps to increase the level of utilization of the Office, and in this regard encourages other agencies, funds and programmes to consider increasing their utilization of its facilities for their activities;

4. *Calls upon* the United Nations Environment Programme and the United Nations Centre for Human Settlements (Habitat) to increase cooperation in and strengthen coordination of their activities, within the framework of their respective mandates and separate programmatic and organizational identities, as well as their separate Executive Directors;

5. *Supports* the proposal of the Secretary-General regarding the establishment of an environmental management group for the purpose of enhancing inter-agency coordination in the field of environment and human settlements, and requests the Secretary-General to develop, in consultation with the Member States and members of the Administrative Committee on Coordination, the mandate, terms of reference, appropriate criteria for membership and flexible, cost-effective working methods of the proposed environmental management group and to submit them to the General Assembly for consideration at its fifty-fourth session;

6. *Welcomes* the proposal to institute an annual, ministerial-level, global environmental forum, with the Governing Council of the United Nations Environment Programme constituting the forum in the years that it meets in regular session and, in alternate years, with the forum taking the form of a special session of the Governing Council, in which participants can gather to review important and emerging policy issues in the field of the environment, with due consideration for the need to ensure the effective and efficient functioning of the governance mechanisms of the United Nations Environment Programme, as well as possible financial implications, and the need to maintain the role of the Commission on Sustainable Development as the main forum for high-level policy debate on sustainable development;

7. *Supports* the proposals for the facilitation of and support for enhancing linkages and coordination within and among environmental and environment-related conventions, including by the United Nations Environment Programme, with full respect for the status of the respective convention secretariats and the autonomous decision-making prerogatives of the conferences of the parties to the conventions concerned, and emphasizes in this regard the need to provide the United Nations Environment Programme with adequate resources to perform this task;

8. *Welcomes* the proposals for the involvement, participation and constructive engagement of major groups active in the field of environment and human settlements, with due consideration for the relevant rules, regulations and procedures of the United Nations;

9. *Reiterates* the importance of strengthening the capacity and capability of the United Nations Environment Programme and the United Nations Centre for Human Settlements (Habitat), within the framework of their existing mandates, in the areas of information, the monitoring and assessment of global and regional environmental and human settlements trends and early warning information on environmental threats, so as to catalyse and promote international cooperation and action, and in this context emphasizes the importance of strengthening the system-wide Earthwatch as an effective, accessible and strictly non-political science-based system;

10. *Reaffirms* that, in accordance with its mandate, the United Nations Environment Programme should not become involved in conflict identification, prevention or resolution;

11. *Stresses* the need to ensure that capacity-building and technical assistance, in particular with respect to institutional strengthening in developing countries, as well as research and scientific studies in the field of environment and human settlements, must remain important components of the work programmes of both the United Nations Environment Programme and the United Nations Centre for Human Settlements (Habitat), within their existing mandates, and also stresses, in this regard, the need for adequate financial resources as well as the need to avoid duplication of efforts;

12. *Also stresses* the need to enhance further the role of the United Nations Environment Programme as an implementing agency of the Global Environment Facility, consistent with its role as defined in the Instrument for the Establishment of the Restructured Global Environment Facility;

13. *Reaffirms* the role of the Commission on Human Settlements in the implementation of the Habitat Agenda, emphasizes the need for it to take steps to prepare for the review of its implementation in 2001, and welcomes the proposals that the United Nations Centre for Human Settlements (Habitat) should strengthen its core activities and develop into a centre for excellence with regard to human settlements;

14. *Welcomes* the proposal to continue ongoing work in the development of indicators in the field of environment and human settlements, and in this regard stresses the importance of the need to avoid duplication of efforts;

15. *Requests* the Secretary-General to submit to the General Assembly at its fifty-fourth session a report on the implementation of the present resolution.

In a September note to the High-level Committee of Ministers and Officials [UNEP/HLC/4/INF/2], the Executive Director provided an overview of the implementation of Assembly resolution 53/242. Preliminary action had been taken regarding increasing resources to UNON; the utilization of UNON conference facilities; strengthened coordination between UNEP and Habitat; the draft terms of reference for EMG; the convening of the first ministerial-level forum in June 2000; the development of interlinkages among the conventions and the promotion of their implementation, with priority given to the revitalization of the regional seas conventions and action plans; the establishment of a Civil Society and NGO Liaison Unit within UNEP; and initiatives to develop a strategy for the UNEP information, assessment and monitoring role. The report proposed capacity-building and technical assistance activities, and stated that work on environmental indicators would be strengthened. Considerable progress had been made regarding enhancing UNEP's role as an implementing agency of the Global Environment Facility (GEF) (see next page). In an October addendum [UNEP/HLC/4/INF/2/Add.1], the Executive Director reported on plans to upgrade the conference facilities at UNON (see also p. 1366).

The High-level Committee considered an October note by the secretariat [UNEP/HLC/4/INF/4] containing a statement by the Nairobi Chapter of the Group of 77 and China calling for the effective and speedy implementation of the resolution. Annexed to the note was the Ministerial Declaration of the twenty-third annual meeting of Ministers for Foreign Affairs of the Group of 77 (New York, 24 September).

Environmental emergencies

A report of the Executive Director discussed the joint project on environmental emergencies carried out by UNEP and the UN Office for the Coordination of Humanitarian Affairs (OCHA) (the Joint UNEP/OCHA Environment Unit) [UNEP/GC.20/9], which provided international assistance to countries facing environmental emergencies. The Executive Director said that the Unit, which was staffed and financed by UNEP, provided support, including development of core response services, the facilitation of initial assessment and post-emergency analysis to improve environmental emergency services to Governments upon request. The Unit had established a network of designated national focal points as conduits for information and assistance that covered more than 100 countries. Guidelines and a questionnaire for environmental assessment following chemical emergencies had been elaborated, as had guidelines for developing national environmental contingency plans.

On 5 February [A/54/25 (dec. 20/8)], the Governing Council asked the Executive Director to enhance collaboration between UNEP and OCHA by strengthening the activities of the Joint Environment Unit. It also asked him to further focus and strengthen the contribution of UNEP's environmental expertise to the coordination of UN system-wide responses to natural disasters or natural phenomena coupled with effects of human actions; to develop linkages between UNEP's work on environmental emergencies and its overall work on environmental assessment and early warning; and to report to Governments on progress made in the Unit's activities. Governments and international organizations were urged to contribute to the Trust Fund for Environmental Emergencies.

Regional cooperation

On 5 February [dec. 20/11], the Governing Council, recalling its 1995 decision requesting support of the goals of the Council of Arab Ministers Responsible for the Environment and the UNEP Regional Office for West Asia [YUN 1995, p. 1090] and expressing appreciation for the results achieved owing to the cooperation between UNEP and the Council of Arab Ministers, asked the Executive Director to support the goals of the Council and the regional offices for West Asia and Africa and to establish a mechanism to support the implementation and coordination of programmes in the Arab region.

Global Environment Facility

The Global Environment Facility (GEF), a joint programme of the United Nations Development Programme (UNDP), UNEP and the World Bank, was established in 1991 [YUN 1991, p. 505] to help solve global environmental problems. In January [UNEP/GC.20/8], the UNEP Executive Director reported on the participation of UNEP in the Facility during 1997 and 1998 and outlined a new UNEP profile in GEF. He proposed three areas of strategic partnership between UNEP and GEF. First, the GEF-UNEP assessment programme would monitor and assess global environmental status, developments and scientific links between global environmental issues; develop early warning systems and identify global environmental hot spots and disasters; and identify progress and the contributing factors thereto. Secondly, the GEF-UNEP environment knowledge management programme, consisting of an up-to-date searchable information system, available online, could collect, disseminate and share experiences from actors and stakeholders on implementation efforts. Lastly, the GEF-UNEP outreach programme would implement elements of the GEF strategy for greater outreach and communications.

In response to a 1998 GEF Council request [YUN 1998, p. 982], the Executive Director proposed in January [UNEP/GC.20/44] an action plan on complementarity between the activities carried out by UNEP under GEF and its regular work programme. The draft plan identified three elements to achieve complementarity: ensuring that GEF activities would be additional to the UNEP work programme; ensuring synergy between UNEP's GEF activities and its work programme; and integrating GEF objectives and activities with UNEP's overall management and programming. In addition, UNEP proposed the following strategic objectives for its GEF work programme: contributing to the ability of GEF and countries to make informed strategic and operational decisions on scientific and technical issues in the GEF focal areas; relating national and regional environmental priorities to the GEF global environmental objectives; promoting regional and multi-country cooperation to achieve global environmental benefits; catalysing responses to environmental emergencies in the GEF focal areas through short-term measures; and supporting the GEF Scientific and Technical Advisory Panel, as the interface between GEF and the scientific and technical community at all levels. The Executive Director outlined measures to achieve complementarity. He concluded that implementation of the action plan would enhance UNEP's GEF work programme over the period 2000-2001.

On 5 February [dec. 20/7], the Governing Council welcomed the Executive Director's proposal to establish a strategic partnership between UNEP and GEF, as well as the suggested action plan on complementarity. It invited the GEF Council to support the Executive Director's efforts to strengthen UNEP's role in the Facility. The Executive Director was asked to submit the action plan to the GEF Council in May and to report in 2001 on the implementation of its decision.

The GEF Council, at its thirteenth meeting (Washington, D.C., 5-7 May), took note of the action plan and welcomed the recognition of additionality, synergy and integration to best contribute to promoting complementarity. It asked UNEP to report annually on progress made in its efforts to strengthen complementarity.

The first meeting of the UNEP/GEF Programme Coordination Committee (Nairobi, 24 June) on the operational modalities to implement the action plan for 2000-2001—comprising UNEP senior management—designated focal points in UNEP's regular programme for biodiversity, international waters and climate change.

UN entities

In April [UNEP/GC.21/INF/7], UNEP concluded a memorandum of understanding (MOU) with the United Nations Population Fund aimed at strengthening cooperation between the two programmes in areas of technical guidance and research; advocacy, public awareness, environment and population-related education and training; and consultation within coordination mechanisms and initiatives.

UNEP and the World Health Organization, by an MOU signed in August, agreed to strengthen their cooperation in the area of environmental health as an essential factor in achieving sustainable development.

General Assembly issues

The Executive Director provided information on issues arising from resolutions adopted by the General Assembly in 1997 and 1998 that called for action by UNEP [UNEP/GC.20/14]. The resolutions included those adopted at the nineteenth special session in 1997 [YUN 1997, p. 790] to review and appraise the implementation of Agenda 21, adopted at the 1992 United Nations Conference on Environment and Development [YUN 1992, p. 672].

On 3 February [dec. 20/16], the Governing Council took note of the report.

Issues related to information

In 1999, the Governing Council considered a report describing UNEP communications and public information services [UNEP/GC.20/INF/2]. As limited resources made it difficult to reach the general public directly, communication efforts focused on current and potential partners and identifiable target groups.

A January report of the Executive Director [UNEP/GC.20/45] highlighted the need for international action to promote access to information, public participation in decision-making and access to justice in environmental matters as a critical element for UNEP to discharge its mandate. Although the Convention on Access to Information, Public Participation in Decision-making and Access to Justice in Environmental Matters (Arhus Convention) [YUN 1998, p. 1000], developed under the auspices of the UN Economic Commission for Europe (ECE), covered the main issues, it pertained to only one region. Therefore, there was no truly global mechanism that provided an overall institutional setting and response to the need to involve and empower all sectors of civil society and relevant segments of Governments to discharge their rights and responsibilities to protect the environment and achieve sustainable development. Furthermore, many countries lacked the legal and institutional modalities to enhance public participation in environmental decision-making and access to justice in environmental matters. It was proposed that UNEP initiate, in consultation with Governments and in collaboration with ECE and other relevant organizations, a process to examine ways to improve access to environmental information, public participation in decision-making and access to justice in environmental matters and the need for and feasibility of legally binding instruments at the regional and global levels.

The Governing Council, on 4 February [dec. 20/4], asked the Executive Director, in consultation with Governments and relevant international organizations, to build capacity in and enhance access to environmental information, public participation in decision making and access to justice in environmental matters; to study various models of related national legislation, policies and guidelines related thereto; and to report in 2001.

Another January report of the Executive Director [UNEP/GC.20/46] summarized recommendations made by the UNEP global environmental information exchange network (INFOTERRA) Advisory Committee (Washington, D.C., November 1998) [UNEP/GC.20/INF.17] on the reform of the network. The proposed reform consisted of a new network structure and a set of recommendations under four headings—political, organizational, operational and technological—to design, develop and implement the new structure globally. The Committee unanimously agreed on INFOTERRA's new role as UNEP's advocate of the public's right to know about environmental issues. It was suggested that the network should operate at the national level, the regional level and UNEP headquarters.

The Governing Council, on 4 February [dec. 20/5], taking note of those recommendations, asked the Executive Director to develop a plan to establish a restructured INFOTERRA, in cooperation with relevant partners; to consult with Governments on the launching in 2000 of the revitalized INFOTERRA at a global conference of senior government officials and representatives of relevant organizations and to seek extrabudgetary resources for it; and to report in 2001.

In response to a 1997 Governing Council request [YUN 1997, p. 1043], the Executive Director presented a review and cost-benefit analysis of the Mercure satellite communications system since April 1998 when it became fully operational [UNEP/GC.20/30]. The system was designed by the

European Space Agency (ESA) in response to the call in Agenda 21 to utilize modern electronic telecommunications to improve access to, and the exchange of, environmental data and information for responsible decision-making concerning the environment. ESA handed over the system to UNEP in 1997. The cost-benefit analysis showed that the potential savings for UNEP from the use of the network of the 15 Mercure installations worldwide, which delivered data, Internet, videoconference and facsimile services, and UNEPnet (Internet mechanisms for environmental information access and exchange) were substantially greater than the costs of operating the network.

The Council, on 4 February [dec. 20/30], asked the Government of Kenya, in consultation with the Executive Director, to facilitate the implementation of voice telephony on Mercure to UNEP and other UN agencies based in Nairobi. It called on the Executive Director to examine ways to improve communications between the secretariat and permanent missions in Nairobi, with UNON assistance, and authorized him to discuss with other donors the expansion of the existing UNEPnet/ Mercure infrastructure through extrabudgetary support. Noting that, despite the impression conveyed in reports of the UN Board of Auditors and the Advisory Committee on Administrative and Budgetary Questions (ACABQ), UNEP had the authority to sign the agreement on the Mercure project with ESA on behalf of the United Nations, and that the system provided cost-effective services, the Council urged the Executive Director to bring his report to the attention of those bodies, with a view to rectifying those errors. The Executive Director was asked to ensure that a comprehensive review and cost-benefit analysis of the UNEPnet/ Mercure system was presented to the Council in 2001 and was brought to the attention of ACABQ, the Office of Internal Oversight Services (OIOS) and the Board of Auditors.

Global Environment Outlook

In September, UNEP presented the second report in the Global Environment Outlook series (GEO-2), which assessed the state of the environment. The key finding was that the continued poverty of the majority of the world's inhabitants and excessive consumption by the minority were the major causes of environmental degradation; the present course was unsustainable and postponing action was not an option. Areas of concern were the world water supply, the impact of land degradation on agricultural productivity, air pollution, the overexploitation of tropical forests and marine fisheries, and the loss of plant and animal species, as well as stretches of coral reef. GEO-1 was launched in 1997 [YUN 1997, p. 1043].

The Governing Council considered a progress report of the Executive Director on GEO-2 [UNEP/GC.20/3] and a report summarizing its highlights [UNEP/GC.20/INF/8].

On 4 February [dec. 20/1], the Council asked the Executive Director to submit in 2001 a GEO user profile and qualitative analysis of the actual use of the GEO reports and the GEO process, with a proposal for an optimal frequency and production schedule for future GEO and related reports. It also asked him to produce a third GEO report in 2002 in the form of a "30 years after Stockholm" report, referring to the 1972 United Nations Conference on the Human Environment held in Stockholm, Sweden [YUN 1972, p. 318]; and to collaborate with UNDP, the World Bank, the World Resources Institute and other institutions in preparing the next report in the *World Resources* series, to be published in December 2000, which would focus on global ecosystems' conditions and trends, and to produce simultaneously an expert report on policy issues and responses to changes in the ecosystems dealt with in the 2000 report. Major actors in data compilation and in global report production were urged to collaborate in the production and use of a common data and knowledge base, comprising indicators, models, scenarios and expert systems, in order to avoid duplication, save costs and ensure that global reports were mutually supportive.

Women in environment and development

Taking note of the Executive Director's report on UNEP efforts to improve the collection, dissemination and use of gender-disaggregated data related to women and the environment [UNEP/ GC.20/10] and of his decision to refocus the institutional arrangements for gender in the UNEP secretariat by hiring a Professional-level staff member to deal with action related to the role of women in environment and development, the Governing Council, on 5 February [dec. 20/9], asked him to continue to fulfil UNEP's commitments contained in its contribution to the Fourth (1995) World Conference on Women [YUN 1995, p. 1169]; to strengthen efforts to assist Governments in empowering women's participation in the decision-making process on environmental matters and in providing them with information on the environment; and to extend the network of gender focal points to cover all Governments, particularly those of developing countries and countries with economies in transition, and also relevant NGOs.

Support to Africa

The Governing Council reviewed a January report of the Executive Director that highlighted UNEP activities regarding support to Africa since

1997 and contained priority areas for UNEP action in Africa [UNEP/GC.20/34]. It also considered a report of the Secretary-General on the causes of conflict and the promotion of durable peace and sustainable development in Africa [UNEP/GC.20/INF/11], as submitted to the Security Council and the General Assembly in 1998 [YUN 1998, p. 66].

The Council, on 4 February [dec. 20/27], asked the Executive Director to continue to support the African Ministerial Conference on the Environment to facilitate the integration of global and African environmental agendas, and to strengthen cooperation with African regional and subregional organizations. It also asked him to enhance UNEP's coordinating role, particularly the Regional Office for Africa, in promoting programmatic coherence among activities regarding the implementation of environmental conventions, as well as in enhancing African countries' participation in international environmental negotiations.

The Council asked the Executive Director to assist African countries upon their request and provide them with technical, legal and policy advice to develop environmental legislation and institutions. He was also asked to explore ways to assist them in developing GEF projects, and to collaborate with GEF in strengthening their capacity through training and information so that they could better participate in developing and implementing global environmental conventions. The Executive Director was asked to give high priority to assisting African countries in implementing their commitments under the 1994 United Nations Convention to Combat Desertification in those Countries Experiencing Serious Drought and/or Desertification, particularly in Africa [YUN 1994, p. 944]; to strengthen UNEP's role in environmental assessment and monitoring in Africa; and to take into account the Council's priorities in revising the 1999 work programme. The Council asked him to report in 2001.

Environment and sustainable development

On 5 February [dec. 20/19], the Governing Council adopted a decision on UNEP's contribution to the seventh (1999) session of the Commission on Sustainable Development (see p. 748). The Council asked the Executive Director to ensure that it had the required information to prepare UNEP's views for all Commission sessions scheduled to occur before its own next session. He was also asked to submit to the Commission, at its seventh session, decisions, recommendations and reports regarding oceans and seas, the Global Programme of Action for the Protection of the Marine Environment from Land-based Activities, sustainable tourism, small island developing States (SIDS) and changing production and consumption patterns (see below, under "Environmental activities").

Regarding SIDS [dec. 20/19 D], the Council asked the Executive Director to promote integrated island management programmes to improve resource protection and use of their terrestrial environment, coastline and adjacent exclusive economic zones; strengthen and expand research, monitoring and assessment activities; promote the transfer of, and facilitate access to, scientific information and advice on technologies; prepare guidelines and programmes for waste minimization, reduction, treatment and disposal; promote principles for sustainable tourism; and promote public education activities on the need for the sustainable development and use of natural resources of SIDS.

As to sustainable tourism, the Council considered a report of the Executive Director describing UNEP activities regarding tourism and containing draft principles for sustainable tourism [UNEP/GC.20/19/Add.2]. On 5 February [dec. 20/19 C], the Council asked him to further develop the draft guiding principles and, in cooperation with relevant partners, to continue the preparation of voluntary initiatives and codes of conduct for the tourism sector. The Commission on Sustainable Development was asked to call on Governments to integrate sustainable tourism in their national development strategies, as well as in relevant multilateral environment conventions. (See also p. 749.)

The Council had before it a report of the Executive Director on promoting interlinkages among global environmental issues and human needs [UNEP/GC.20/40]. An interlinkages assessment report, *Protecting Our Planet: Securing Our Future* [Sales No. E.99.III.D.75], a collaborative effort of UNEP and the World Bank, with additional support from the United States National Aeronautics and Space Administration, showed that environmental degradation was accelerating and the human condition deteriorating in many parts of the world, and the two were driven by population size, the level of consumption and the choice of technologies. The report pointed to the need to address global environmental issues holistically and in an integrated manner; for new institutional partnerships to achieve a sustainable world, involving Governments, the private sector, academia, NGOs and civil society; and for the adoption by decision makers of cost-effective and adaptive management approaches.

On 4 February [dec. 20/28], the Council urged Governments to consider the conclusions and recommendations of *Protecting Our Planet: Securing Our Future* in preparing their national environment and sustainable development strategies and plans. It asked the Executive Director to address global environmental issues within a more holistic and synergistic policy context. He was also asked to recognize that policy implementation that linked global environmental issues and sustainable development required scientific understanding of the links among environmental issues and their relationships to meeting human needs; identification of combinations of policies that were effective and cost-efficient, and that encouraged the public and private sectors to work together; political will and public commitment; and improved coordination among national and international institutions charged with developing measures to meet human needs, without undermining the environmental foundation for development. The World Bank and other organizations concerned were urged to collaborate with UNEP.

The Council, on 5 February [dec. 20/12], invited the Executive Director to intensify work on the integration of the environmental dimension of sustainable development into UN programmes and asked him to report in 2001.

By **decision 54/446** of 22 December, the General Assembly took note of the report of the Second Committee on environment and sustainable development [A/54/588].

Freshwater issues

Regarding freshwater issues, the Governing Council, on 4 February [dec. 20/25], took note of the Executive Director's report containing a proposal for UNEP's freshwater strategy [UNEP/GC.20/31] and welcomed UNEP's focus on the environmental aspects of assessment and sustainable integrated management in accordance with national needs. It decided that UNEP should accord high priority to the identification of expertise and knowledge resident in countries regarding freshwater quality, the establishment of partnerships between those countries and countries in need of the expertise and knowledge, and the promotion of intergovernmental collaboration. The Council asked the Executive Director to identify key policy issues for freshwater quality and to propose policy options for debate and endorsement by the Council in 2001. It also asked him to take into account the work carried out by other UN agencies and international organizations, as well as Governments, in order to avoid duplication; to promote the transfer of environmentally sound technologies for freshwater management through the International Environmental Technology Centre; and to report in 2001.

UNEP assessment strategy

The Executive Director, in January [UNEP/GC.20/INF/18], presented a draft strategy working paper prepared by an expert team of external consultants, on the development of a UNEP-wide assessment strategy. The paper gave a general overview of the direction that UNEP might take in the area of environmental assessment and reporting, the tasks ahead and the scope of activities. UNEP considered that the paper was innovative and strategic enough to be used in consultations with major stakeholders. However, it did not cover in depth the management and dissemination of scientific and technical information or existing commitments and cooperative relationships with global assessment stakeholders, including UN partner organizations.

UNEP secretariat

In response to a 1997 Governing Council decision [YUN 1997, p. 1042], the Executive Director examined the functions of UNEP's regional offices and their common mandates and responsibilities, and proposed measures to strengthen regionalization and decentralization through the involvement of regional ministerial and other forums [UNEP/GC.20/28]. The six regional offices covered Africa, Asia and the Pacific, Europe, Latin America and the Caribbean, North America and West Asia. The Forum of Environment Ministers of Latin America and the Caribbean, for which the UNEP regional office in Latin America and the Caribbean served as secretariat, could be used as a model by UNEP and its other regional offices to strengthen regionalization and decentralization through the involvement of regional ministerial and other forums.

On 4 February [dec. 20/39], the Governing Council asked the Executive Director to continue to strengthen regionalization and decentralization, while maintaining the central coordinating role of UNEP headquarters in Nairobi.

The Governing Council considered the Executive Director's report describing the activities of UNEP's specialized offices, namely the Industry and Environment Programme Activity Centre (Paris) (IE/PAC) and the International Environment Technology Centre (Osaka and Shiga, Japan) (IETC) [UNEP/GC.20/29]. He stated that IE/PAC had always adopted a collaborative approach to integrating environmental criteria into industrial development, based on a broad participation of industry and government specialists, as well as NGOs, while IETC had adopted a collaborative approach with other partners and UN agencies, particularly Habitat (Sustainable Cities Programme) and the United Nations University. He concluded that the need for building synergies between the two centres and other UNEP units under one umbrella had become apparent.

On 4 February [dec. 20/40], the Governing Council endorsed the Executive Director's steps to bring greater efficiency through synergies between the main units of the UNEP secretariat addressing technology transfer, environmental issues related to industrial and urban activities, energy and the related economic and trade aspects. It asked him to give priority to issues of trade and environment and to the promotion of cleaner production and transfer of environmentally sound technologies through the specialized offices.

Management issues

The Governing Council had before it a report on the status of implementation of recommendations [UNEP/GC.20/20] made in 1997 by OIOS on the review of UNEP and the administrative practices of its secretariat [YUN 1997, p. 1044]. Among the measures taken by UNEP were the introduction of results management and performance indicators for its 1998-1999 work programmme; the integration of the economics and trade subprogrammes; the establishment of the Division of Environmental Conventions; and a new organizational structure for UNEP, based on functions rather than subject areas. The report included the status of implementation of recommendations made by ACABQ on the Environment Fund.

On 4 February [dec. 20/38], the Council took note of the implementation of the OIOS and ACABQ recommendations. Regarding the Ombudsman Unit, the Council, on 4 February [dec. 20/41], endorsed a proposal by the Executive Director to increase budget allocations to the Unit in 2000-2001. It invited him to submit all annual reports on the Unit still pending and to extend the Unit's services to other UN entities if they so requested. The Executive Director was asked to prepare an evaluation report on the Unit.

UNEP Fund

Following consideration of the Executive Director's report on the proposed programme budget, revised requirements for 1998-1999 and proposed requirements for 2000-2001 [UNEP/GC.20/22 & Add.1], the related ACABQ report [UNEP/GC.20/21] and his comments on ACABQ recommendations [UNEP/GC.20/47], the Governing Council, on 4 February [dec. 20/31], approved the revised appropriations of Environment Fund resources in 1998-1999 of $25.83 million for the management and administrative support costs budget, and reconfirmed the appropriation of $75 million for Fund programme activities and $5 million for the Fund programme reserve. It also approved Fund resources in 2000-2001 of $14.23 million for the management and administrative support costs budget, $100 million for Fund programme activities and $5 million for the Fund programme reserve. The Council noted that the $14.23 million for 2000-2001 management and administrative support costs was contingent upon an increase in funding from the UN regular budget for UNON of some $2 million for administrative services provided to UNEP and Habitat. It noted with concern the large discrepancy in the funding provided from the UN regular budget to UNON, in relation to that provided to the United Nations Office at Vienna and the United Nations Office at Geneva, and appealed to the General Assembly to consider a substantial increase in the regular budget allocation to UNON. The Executive Director was authorized to approve costed work plans for implementation of specific subprogrammes and activities and to prepare a 2002-2003 work programme consisting of Fund programme activities of $120 million. It further authorized him to enter into commitments not exceeding $20 million for 2002-2003 Fund programme activities. The Council approved the programmatic restructuring set out in the proposed 2000-2001 programme of work consisting of seven subprogrammes and 26 subprogramme elements that integrated all elements previously contained in the programme activity centres, and noted the resulting dissolution of the following programme activity centres: Dryland Ecosystems and Desertification Control, Environmental Law and Institutions, Global Environment Monitoring System, Industry and Environment, International Register for Potentially Toxic Chemicals, INFOTERRA, Global Resource Information Database, and Oceans and Coastal Areas.

Noting the ACABQ recommendations on the proposed programme budget, the revised requirements for 1998-1999 and the proposed requirements for 2000-2001 [UNEP/GC.20/21] and the Executive Director's comments thereon [UNEP/GC.20/47], the Governing Council, on 4 February [dec. 20/32], asked him to address all recommendations and to report to the Committee of Permanent Representatives.

In October [A/C.5/54/20], the Secretary-General presented revisions to the narrative of the proposed 2000-2001 programme budget for the environment, in accordance with a recommendation made by the Committee for Programme and Coordination [A/54/16].

On 4 February [dec. 20/33], the Council took note of efforts to define the outline of a strategy concerning stable, adequate and predictable funding for UNEP, based on a January report of the Executive Director [UNEP/GC.20/23]. The Council asked him to initiate consultations with

Governments and others to develop a strategy for such funding for UNEP and to report in 2001.

The Council, on 4 February [dec. 20/36], took note of ACABQ's observations on the report of the Board of Auditors on the financial report and audited financial statements of the Fund for 1996-1997 and of the Executive Director's comments on ACABQ's observations [UNEP/GC.20/24]. On the same date [dec. 20/37], the Council took note of the Executive Director's report on the revision of the Financial Rules of the Fund and of the General Procedures Governing the Operation of the Environment Fund [UNEP/GC.20/27].

Trust funds

Following consideration of the Executive Director's report on the management of trust funds [UNEP/GC.20/25], the Governing Council, on 4 February [dec. 20/34], approved the establishment of 22 trust funds and the extension of 26 others.

Taking note of the Executive Director's report on the cost of administering trust funds [UNEP/GC.20/26], the Council, on 4 February [dec. 20/35], asked him to take action to reduce the cost of programme-support services provided to trust funds and related activities, with a view to containing such costs within the programme support charges levied. He was asked to report in 2001.

International conventions and mechanisms

Implementation of conventions related to sustainable development

In response to General Assembly resolution 53/186 [YUN 1998, p. 987], the Secretary-General, in October [A/54/468], provided an overview of progress made in the scientific understanding of ecological linkages among environmental and environment-related conventions, and in the development of responses by the UN system, as well as developments at the intergovernmental level, that had given guidance to enhancing coordination among those conventions. The report concluded that considerable progress had been made, which was reflected in increased scientific understanding and the concerted action taken by various UN entities. While the work on providing hard scientific evidence of linkages continued to evolve, consideration could be given to developing coherent and planned interventions for implementation at the national level and to identifying the specific issues that each convention could address with the other conventions.

GENERAL ASSEMBLY ACTION

On 22 December [meeting 87], the General Assembly, on the recommendation of the Second Committee [A/54/588/Add.7], adopted **resolution 54/217** without vote [agenda item 100].

Enhancing complementarities among international instruments related to environment and sustainable development

The General Assembly,

Recalling the Programme for the Further Implementation of Agenda 21 adopted at its nineteenth special session, in particular part IV thereof, entitled "International institutional arrangements",

Recalling also its resolutions 53/186 of 15 December 1998, on international institutional arrangements related to environment and development, and 53/242 of 28 July 1999, on the report of the Secretary-General on environment and human settlements,

Taking note with appreciation of the report of the Secretary-General on international institutional arrangements related to environment and development,

Taking note of decision 20/28 on promoting interlinkages among global environmental issues and human needs, adopted on 4 February 1999 by the Governing Council of the United Nations Environment Programme,

Emphasizing that policy decisions under the respective conventions are taken by the conferences of the parties thereto, which are autonomous governing bodies,

Noting that various conventions related to environment and sustainable development are at different stages of implementation, and recognizing the role of the General Assembly in fostering progress in the implementation of environmental and environment-related conventions and of the commitments contained therein,

Noting with appreciation the relevant ongoing work on the implementation of environmental and environment-related conventions at the national, bilateral, regional and international levels,

Reaffirming the need, as stipulated in part IV of the Programme for the Further Implementation of Agenda 21, for greater coherence in various intergovernmental organizations and processes by means of better policy coordination at the intergovernmental level, as well as for continued and more concerted efforts to enhance collaboration among the secretariats of relevant decision-making bodies,

Emphasizing the need for environmental conventions to continue to pursue sustainable development objectives that are consistent with their provisions and to be fully responsive to Agenda 21,

1. *Encourages* the conferences of the parties to, and the permanent secretariats of, the United Nations Framework Convention on Climate Change, the Convention on Biological Diversity and the United Nations Convention to Combat Desertification in those Countries Experiencing Serious Drought and/or Desertification, particularly in Africa, to examine further appropriate opportunities and measures to strengthen their complementarities and to improve scientific assessments of ecological linkages among the three conventions;

2. *Stresses* the need for the integrated consideration of linkages, both among sectors and between sectoral and cross-sectoral aspects of Agenda 21;

3. *Emphasizes* the importance of facilitating and supporting the enhancement of linkages and coordination

within and among environmental and environment-related conventions, inter alia, by the United Nations Environment Programme, with full respect for the status of the secretariats of the conventions and the autonomous decision-making prerogatives of the conferences of the parties to the conventions concerned, and, in this regard, supports the proposal of the Secretary-General concerning the establishment of an environmental management group for the purpose of enhancing inter-agency coordination in the areas of environment and human settlements, as stipulated in resolution 53/242;

4. *Notes with appreciation* all the progress made in the implementation of resolution 53/186;

5. *Encourages* the secretariats of the various environmental and environment-related conventions and international organizations, with full respect for the status of the secretariats of the conventions and the autonomous decision-making prerogatives of the conferences of the parties to the conventions concerned, to strengthen cooperation with a view to facilitating progress in the implementation of those conventions at the international, regional and national levels by:

(*a*) Identifying opportunities for complementarity of activities undertaken to facilitate the implementation of commitments made by the parties to the various conventions;

(*b*) Encouraging the carrying out of further scientific analyses by relevant international organizations, such as the United Nations Environment Programme, the secretariats of the conventions, their subsidiary bodies, the United Nations Secretariat and relevant international scientific bodies, in order to identify possible activities with potential multiple benefits and to bring them to the attention of the conferences of the parties;

(*c*) Promoting more effective and coherent support from international organizations and financial institutions and mechanisms for national action aimed at the implementation of the conventions, in particular in the area of capacity-building;

(*d*) Addressing practical issues, such as more effective exchange of information, enhanced awareness-raising and streamlining of national reporting;

(*e*) Supporting, upon request, efforts being made at the national level towards adopting an integrated and holistic approach to the implementation of environmental and environment-related conventions;

(*f*) Bringing relevant issues to the attention of the General Assembly and relevant intergovernmental bodies for the consideration of Member States and the formulation of agreed policy recommendations, with a view to promoting a more holistic approach;

6. *Requests* the Secretary-General, in consultation with the Executive Director of the United Nations Environment Programme and the executive secretaries of the conventions, to prepare a report on the implementation of the present resolution and to submit it to the General Assembly at its fifty-fifth session for consideration under the item entitled "Environment and sustainable development".

UNEP and environmental conventions

Taking note of the Executive Director's report on developments in and changes to the status of international conventions and protocols related to the environment from 11 December 1996 to 10 November 1998 [UNEP/GC.20/18], the Governing Council, on 4 February [dec. 20/18 A], authorized him to transmit the report to the General Assembly, together with comments made by delegations and relevant information received by UNEP by 31 May. Additional information was transmitted to the Assembly in October [A/54/25/Add.1].

Following consideration of the Executive Director's reports on strengthening UNEP's role in promoting collaboration among environmental conventions [UNEP/GC.20/16], UNEP support to environmental conventions [UNEP/GC.20/17] and promoting interlinkages among global environmental issues and human needs [UNEP/GC.20/40] (see p. 980), the Council, on 4 February [dec. 20/18 B], called on Governments parties to multilateral environmental conventions and their conferences to consider ways to strengthen interlinkages among the conventions. It asked the Executive Director to explore with the conventions' secretariats areas of cooperation and modalities in support of the implementation of the work programmes of the respective conventions, and to make available UNEP technical, scientific and legal expertise to assist the conventions in achieving their objectives. He was also asked to assist developing countries and countries with economies in transition in strengthening their legal capacities in implementing the conventions and to report in 2001.

Climate change convention

As at 31 December, 181 States were parties to the United Nations Framework Convention on Climate Change, which was opened for signature in 1992 [YUN 1992, p. 681] and entered into force in 1994 [YUN 1994, p. 938]. During the year, the Libyan Arab Jamahiriya, Madagascar and Sao Tome and Principe ratified the Convention, and Palau acceded to it.

Conference of Parties

The fifth session of the Conference of the Parties to the UN Framework Convention on Climate Change (Bonn, 25 October–5 November) [FCCC/CP/1999/6 & Add.1] took action to bring the 1997 Kyoto Protocol [YUN 1997, p. 1048] into force as early as possible. It decided that the sixth session of the Conference would be held in The Hague, Netherlands, from 13 to 24 November 2000, and empowered the Conference President to take steps to intensify the negotiating process on all issues. The Kyoto Protocol, which was opened for signature from 16 March 1998 to 15 March 1999 at UN Headquarters, had received 84 signatures and 21

States had become parties. The Protocol would enter into force 90 days after countries, including developed countries accounting for at least 55 per cent of the total carbon dioxide emissions for 1990 from that group, had deposited their instruments of ratification, acceptance, approval or accession.

The Conference reached agreement on how to improve the national reports from industrialized countries and strengthen the guidelines for measuring their greenhouse gas emissions, endorsed a work programme and elements of a decision-making framework to address the conclusions of land-use change and forestry adopted by the Subsidiary Body for Scientific and Technological Advice (SBSTA), and adopted reporting guidelines on global climate observing systems [FCCC/CP/1999/7]. Other decisions dealt with the development and transfer of technologies, capacity-building in developing countries and in countries with economies in transition, the pilot phase of activities implemented jointly by SBSTA and the Subsidiary Body for Implementation (SBI), continuation of the work of the Joint Working Group on Compliance on the development of procedures and mechanisms for a compliance system under the Kyoto Protocol, the relationship between protecting the stratospheric ozone layer and safeguarding the global climate system, emissions based on fuel sold to ships and aircraft engaged in international transport, and cooperation with the Intergovernmental Panel on Climate Change.

SBSTA held its tenth (31 May–11 June) [FCCC/SBSTA/1999/6] and eleventh (25 October–5 November) [FCCC/SBSTA/1999/14] sessions, both in Bonn, as did SBI [FCCC/SBI/1999/8, FCCC/SBI/1999/14].

GENERAL ASSEMBLY ACTION

On 22 December [meeting 87], the General Assembly, on the recommendation of the Second Committee [A/54/588/Add.4], adopted **resolution 54/222** without vote [agenda item 100 *(d)*].

Protection of global climate for present and future generations of mankind

The General Assembly,

Recalling its resolutions 50/115 of 20 December 1995, 51/184 of 16 December 1996 and 52/199 of 18 December 1997 and other resolutions relating to the protection of global climate for present and future generations of mankind,

Noting with satisfaction that most States and one regional economic integration organization have ratified or acceded to the United Nations Framework Convention on Climate Change,

Noting that, to date, the Kyoto Protocol to the United Nations Framework Convention on Climate Change has attracted sixteen ratifications, and encouraging necessary action to facilitate the entry into force of the Kyoto Protocol at the earliest possible date,

Expressing its deep appreciation to the Government of Argentina for hosting the fourth session of the Conference of the Parties to the United Nations Framework Convention on Climate Change, held from 2 to 14 November 1998, which culminated in the adoption of the Buenos Aires Plan of Action,

Noting that the fifth session of the Conference of the Parties to the United Nations Framework Convention on Climate Change was held at Bonn, Germany, from 25 October to 5 November 1999,

Taking note of decision 1/CP.5 adopted by the Conference of the Parties to the Convention at its fifth session, stressing the importance of a successful outcome to the sixth session of the Conference of the Parties, in particular in reaching decisions on the early and full implementation of the Buenos Aires Plan of Action, and welcoming, in that decision, the agreement to an intensified negotiating process leading to the sixth session of the Conference of the Parties,

Welcoming the generous offer of the Government of the Netherlands to host the sixth session of the Conference of the Parties, and urging the Parties to undertake thorough preparations to advance progress at that session,

Taking note of the decision of the Conference of the Parties at its fifth session to approve the continuation of the institutional linkage of the Convention secretariat to the United Nations, subject to review not later than 31 December 2001, in consultation with the Secretary-General, with a view to making such modifications as may be desirable by both parties,

Taking note also of the decision of the Conference of the Parties whereby the General Assembly is invited to decide, at its fifty-fourth session, on the issue of meeting the Convention's conference-servicing expenses from its regular budget, taking into account the views expressed by Member States,

Noting the oral report of the Secretary-General and the advice on the continuation of the institutional linkage of the Convention secretariat to the United Nations,

Noting also that, by paragraph 9 of resolution 50/115, the Secretary-General was requested to make the necessary arrangements to include in the calendar of conferences and meetings for the biennium 1998-1999 those sessions of the Conference of the Parties and its subsidiary bodies that the Conference may need to convene in that period,

1. *Encourages* Member States that have not ratified or acceded to the Kyoto Protocol to the United Nations Framework Convention on Climate Change to do so with a view to bringing it into force;

2. *Calls upon* all States parties to continue to take effective steps to implement their commitments under the United Nations Framework Convention on Climate Change, in accordance with the principle of common but differentiated responsibilities;

3. *Encourages* all countries to work constructively towards advancing the work necessary for the timely entry into force of the Kyoto Protocol and its implementation;

4. *Approves* the continuation of the institutional linkage of the Convention secretariat to the United Nations, as advised by the Secretary-General and ap-

proved by the Conference of the Parties at its fifth session;

5. *Encourages* the conferences of the parties to the United Nations Framework Convention on Climate Change, the Convention on Biological Diversity and the United Nations Convention to Combat Desertification in those Countries Experiencing Serious Drought and/or Desertification, particularly in Africa, to examine further appropriate opportunities and measures to strengthen their complementarities and to improve scientific assessments of ecological linkages between the three conventions;

6. *Encourages* the secretariats of various environmental and environment-related conventions and other international organizations, with full respect for the status of the respective convention secretariats and the autonomous decision-making prerogatives of the conferences of the parties of the conventions concerned, to strengthen cooperation with a view to facilitating progress in their implementation at the international, regional and national levels;

7. *Requests* the Secretary-General to review the functioning of this institutional linkage not later than 31 December 2001, in consultation with the Conference of the Parties to the United Nations Framework Convention on Climate Change, with a view to making such modifications as may be considered desirable by both parties, and to report thereon to the General Assembly;

8. *Decides* to include in the calendar of conferences and meetings for the biennium 2000-2001 the sessions of the Conference of the Parties and its subsidiary bodies envisaged for that biennium, in accordance with the decisions adopted by the Conference of the Parties;

9. *Also decides* to include in the provisional agenda of its fifty-fifth session the sub-item entitled "Protection of global climate for present and future generations of mankind".

Vienna Convention and Montreal Protocol

As at 31 December, 172 States and the European Community (EC) were parties to the 1985 Vienna Convention for the Protection of the Ozone Layer [YUN 1985, p. 804], which entered into force in 1988 [YUN 1988, p. 810]. In 1999, Albania, Armenia, Djibouti and Oman acceded to the Convention. Related to the Convention, 171 States and the EC were parties to the 1987 Montreal Protocol on Substances that Deplete the Ozone Layer [YUN 1987, p. 686], 137 States and the EC were parties to the 1990 Amendment to the Protocol [YUN 1990, p. 522], and 104 States and the EC were parties to the 1992 Amendment [YUN 1992, p. 684]. On 10 November 1999, the 1997 Amendment [YUN 1997, p. 1050] entered into force, having received the requisite 20 ratifications; at year's end, there were 33 parties to the Amendment. In 1999, an additional amendment was adopted (see below).

The combined fifth meeting of the Conference of the Parties to the Vienna Convention and the Eleventh Meeting of the Parties to the Montreal Protocol (Beijing, 29 November–3 December) [UNEP/OzL.Pro.11/10] agreed on a funding package to enable developing countries to maintain the momentum of their efforts to phase out chlorofluorocarbons and other ozone-destroying chemicals. The funding, which included $440 million in new contributions for the period 2000-2002, plus $35.7 million carried over from the previous period, constituted the fourth replenishment of the Montreal Protocol's Multilateral Fund. The funds were used to support the adoption of more ozone-friendly technologies for refrigerators, air conditioners, and other consumer products and industrial processes. The meeting adopted a further amendment to the Protocol and adjustments regarding controlled substances in annexes to the Protocol. The amendment banned trade in hydrochlorofluorocarbons (HCFCs) with countries that had not ratified the 1992 Amendment, which had provided for an HCFC phase-out. It required developed countries to freeze HCFC production in 2004 at 1989 levels and developing countries to do so in 2016 with a similar baseline of 2015. Production of 15 per cent above baseline was permitted to meet the basic domestic needs of developing countries. In addition, the production of bromochloromethane was to be phased out in all countries by 2002. The Beijing amendment was to enter into force on 1 January 2001, provided that at least 20 instruments of ratification, acceptance or approval were deposited by States or regional economic organizations that were parties to the Montreal Protocol. The meeting adopted the Beijing Declaration on Renewed Commitment to the Protection of the Ozone Layer.

The fifth meeting of the Conference of the Parties to the Vienna Convention [UNEP/OzL.Conv.5/6] noted the adjustments and Amendment to the Montreal Protocol, took note of the reports of the Scientific, Environmental Effects and Technology and Economic Assessment Panels and the Technical Options Committees, endorsed the recommendations of the fourth meeting of the Ozone Research Managers and decided to hold its sixth meeting in 2002, in conjunction with the Fourteenth Meeting of the Parties to the Montreal Protocol.

Convention on air pollution

As at 31 December, there were 45 parties to the 1979 Convention on Long-Range Transboundary Air Pollution [YUN 1979, p. 710], which entered into force in 1983 [YUN 1983, p. 645]. A protocol to the Convention to abate acidification, eutrophication and ground-level ozone opened for signature in Gothenburg, Sweden, on 30 November and later at UN Headquarters until 30 May 2000. As at 31 December, the protocol had 27 signatories.

Convention on Biological Diversity

In 1999, Palau and Sao Tome and Principe became parties to the Convention on Biological Diversity, bringing the total number of parties to 176. The Convention opened for signature in 1992 [YUN 1992, p. 683] and entered into force in 1993 [YUN 1993, p. 810].

The first extraordinary meeting of the Conference of the Parties to the Convention (Cartagena, Colombia, 22-24 February) [UNEP/CBD/ExCOP/1/3] was convened to adopt a protocol on biosafety. The meeting was preceded by the sixth meeting of the open-ended ad hoc working group on biosafety (Cartagena, 14-22 February) [UNEP/CBD/ExCOP/1/2], which adopted a number of draft articles and annexes. As the Conference of Parties was unable to reach consensus on the draft submitted by the working group, on 24 February, at its third session, the Conference suspended its meeting and decided to hold a resumed session. The essential core issues that remained were the scope of the protocol, and the application of the advanced informed agreement procedure and its relationship with other international agreements. The resumed session was scheduled for January 2000.

The Subsidiary Body on Scientific, Technical and Technological Advice (Montreal, Canada, 21-25 June) [UNEP/CBD/SBSTTA/4/14] considered the Global Taxonomy Initiative; the conservation and sustainable use of terrestrial biological diversity (drylands, Mediterranean, arid, semi-arid, grassland and savannah ecosystems); development of guiding principles for the prevention of impacts of alien species; consequences of the new technology for the control of plant gene expression for the conservation and sustainable use of biological diversity; the incorporation of biological diversity considerations into environmental impact assessment; and the development of approaches and practices for the sustainable use of biological resources, including tourism (see also below and p. 749).

Taking note of the development and implementation on an interim basis of the 1995 UNEP International Technical Guidelines for Safety in Biotechnology [UNEP/Global Consultation/Biosafety/4] and the Executive Director's report [UNEP/GC.20/33] on the implementation of its 1997 decision on biosafety [YUN 1997, p. 1056], the Governing Council, on 4 February [dec. 20/26], asked him to assist Governments in implementing the forthcoming biosafety protocol. He was also asked to mobilize resources to support developing countries and countries with economies in transition to prepare national biosafety frameworks in the context of the proposed protocol, and to support subregional and regional biosafety risk-assessment capabilities in collaboration with the Convention secretariat and other relevant organizations.

Pursuant to General Assembly resolution 53/190 [YUN 1998, p. 990], the Secretary-General transmitted, in October [A/54/428], a report of the Executive Secretary of the Convention summarizing action taken by the Conference of the Parties and the Subsidiary Body.

GENERAL ASSEMBLY ACTION

On 22 December [meeting 87], the General Assembly, on the recommendation of the Second Committee [A/54/588/Add.3], adopted **resolution 54/221** without vote [agenda item 100 *(c)*].

Convention on Biological Diversity

The General Assembly,

Recalling its resolution 53/190 of 15 December 1998 on the Convention on Biological Diversity and other relevant resolutions,

Recalling also the provisions of the Convention on Biological Diversity,

Reaffirming that the conservation of biological diversity is a common concern of humankind,

Recalling that States have, in accordance with the Charter of the United Nations and the principles of international law, the sovereign right to exploit their own resources pursuant to their own environmental policies and the responsibility to ensure that activities within their jurisdiction or control do not cause damage to the environment of other States or of areas beyond the limits of national jurisdiction,

Recalling Agenda 21, in particular its chapter 15 on the conservation of biological diversity and related chapters,

Having considered the report of the Executive Secretary of the Convention on Biological Diversity as submitted by the Secretary-General to the General Assembly,

Deeply concerned about the continued loss of the world's biological diversity, and, on the basis of the provisions of the Convention, reaffirming the commitment to the conservation of biological diversity, the sustainable use of its components and the fair and equitable sharing of benefits arising out of the utilization of genetic resources, including by appropriate access to genetic resources and appropriate transfer of relevant technologies, taking into account all rights over those resources and technologies, and by appropriate funding,

Recognizing the contribution of indigenous and local communities, and women within those communities, to the conservation and sustainable use of biological resources,

Recalling the decisions adopted by the Conference of the Parties to the Convention on Biological Diversity at its fourth meeting relating to intellectual property rights, traditional knowledge and the relationship of the Convention with other international agreements,

Noting the continuing dialogue taking place in the Committee on Trade and Environment of the World Trade Organization on the provisions of the Agreement on Trade-related Aspects of Intellectual Property Rights,

Encouraged by the work carried out to date under the Convention, and satisfied that most States and one regional economic integration organization have ratified the Convention,

Taking note with appreciation of the generous offer of the Government of Kenya to host the fifth meeting of the Conference of the Parties, which will be held at Nairobi from 15 to 26 May 2000,

Recalling its invitation to the Executive Secretary of the Convention on Biological Diversity to report to the General Assembly on the results of future meetings of the Conference of the Parties,

1. *Takes note* of the results of the fourth meeting of the Conference of the Parties to the Convention on Biological Diversity, held at Bratislava from 4 to 15 May 1998;

2. *Recognizes* the importance of the inter-sessional efforts of the Conference of the Parties since its fourth meeting to improve the effectiveness of the operations of the Convention;

3. *Reaffirms* the importance of the decision of the fourth meeting of the Conference of the Parties on the adoption of the programmes of work and the thematic approach to guide its work in the development of the Convention for the foreseeable future, including its in-depth consideration of ecosystems;

4. *Calls upon* Governments, in cooperation with the Conference of the Parties, to use science-based analysis to study and monitor closely the evolution of new technologies to prevent possible adverse effects on the conservation and sustainable use of biological diversity, which might have an impact on farmers and local communities;

5. *Recognizes* the importance of the adoption of a protocol on biosafety at the resumed session of the first extraordinary meeting of the Conference of the Parties, to be held at Montreal, Canada, from 24 to 28 January 2000, and calls upon States participating in the negotiations on a protocol on biosafety to work constructively to bring this process to a satisfactory conclusion;

6. *Welcomes* decision IV/15, adopted by the Conference of the Parties at its fourth meeting, in which it stressed the need to ensure consistency in implementing the Convention and World Trade Organization agreements, including the Agreement on Trade-related Aspects of Intellectual Property Rights, with a view to promoting increased mutual supportiveness and integration of biological diversity concerns and the protection of intellectual property rights;

7. *Reaffirms* paragraph 10 of decision IV/15, in which the Conference of the Parties emphasized that further work is required to help develop a common appreciation of the relationship between intellectual property rights and the relevant provisions of the Agreement on Trade-related Aspects of Intellectual Property Rights and the Convention on Biological Diversity, in particular on issues relating to technology transfer and conservation and sustainable use of biological diversity and the fair and equitable sharing of benefits arising out of the use of genetic resources, including the protection of knowledge, innovations and practices of indigenous and local communities embodying traditional lifestyles relevant for the conservation and sustainable use of biological diversity;

8. *Takes note* of the fourth meeting of the Subsidiary Body on Scientific, Technical and Technological Advice of the Conference of the Parties, including its recommendation IV/5 on the consequences of the use of the new technology for the control of plant gene expression for the conservation and sustainable use of biological diversity;

9. *Stresses* the importance of the implementation of the Convention at all levels, including through the preparation and implementation of national strategies, plans and programmes, taking into account the need for financial resources to support the implementation activities, in particular those of developing countries, in accordance with the provisions of the Convention and the decisions of the Conference of the Parties;

10. *Encourages* those States that have not yet ratified the Convention to do so as soon as possible;

11. *Takes note* of the meeting of the Panel of Experts on Access and Benefit-sharing, established in accordance with decision IV/8, adopted by the Conference of the Parties at its fourth meeting;

12. *Recognizes* the importance of national action to conserve biological diversity in many habitats, including forests, wetlands and coastal areas, in accordance with the relevant provisions of the Convention, in particular article 8, and the need to mobilize national and international support for such national actions;

13. *Welcomes* the offer of Spain to host, at Seville in March 2000, the first meeting of the Ad Hoc Open-ended Inter-sessional Working Group on article 8 *(j)* of the Convention regarding the traditional knowledge, innovations and practices of indigenous and local communities, and encourages Governments to include representatives of indigenous and local communities on their delegations to that meeting;

14. *Recognizes* the utility of information exchange, and encourages the development of biodiversity information networks at the national, regional and international levels by way of the clearing-house mechanism;

15. *Encourages* the conferences of the parties to the United Nations Framework Convention on Climate Change, the Convention on Biological Diversity and the United Nations Convention to Combat Desertification in those Countries Experiencing Serious Drought and/or Desertification, particularly in Africa, to examine further appropriate opportunities and measures to strengthen their complementarities and improve scientific assessments of ecological linkages between the three conventions;

16. *Encourages* the secretariats of various environmental and environment-related conventions and other international organizations, with full respect for the status of the respective convention secretariats and the autonomous decision-making prerogatives of the conferences of the parties to the conventions concerned, to strengthen cooperation with a view to facilitating progress in their implementation at the international, regional and national levels;

17. *Invites* all funding institutions and bilateral and multilateral donors, as well as regional funding institutions and non-governmental organizations, to cooperate with the secretariat of the Convention in the implementation of the programme of work;

18. *Calls upon* States parties to the Convention to settle urgently any arrears and to pay their contributions in full and in a timely manner so as to ensure continuity in the cash flows required to finance the ongoing work

of the Conference of the Parties, the subsidiary bodies and the Convention secretariat;

19. *Invites* the Executive Secretary of the Convention on Biological Diversity to report to the General Assembly on the ongoing work regarding the Convention;

20. *Decides* to include in the provisional agenda of its fifty-fifth session the sub-item entitled "Convention on Biological Diversity".

Convention to combat desertification

In 1999, an additional 15 States became parties to the United Nations Convention to Combat Desertification in those Countries Experiencing Serious Drought and/or Desertification, particularly in Africa, which was adopted in 1994 [YUN 1994, p. 944] and entered into force in 1996 [YUN 1996, p. 958], bringing the number of parties to 160.

The Conference of the Parties, at its third session (Recife, Brazil, 15-26 November) [ICCD/COP(3)/20 & Add.1], adopted the Recife Initiative, which called for the drafting, in 2000, of a declaration on the commitments under the Convention to enhance implementation of the obligations accepted by States parties. The declaration would set a time frame for making progress on priority thematic and sectoral issues and focus on integrating anti-desertification activities into the development strategies of affected countries, as well as of all developed States parties and multilateral and other development institutions. It would also emphasize the development of benchmarks and indicators to evaluate progress against desertification.

The Conference focused on national reports submitted by 41 African countries, which represented over 75 per cent of the continent's land area. Reports were also submitted by four African subregional organizations, 11 developed country Governments and 17 UN and other international organizations. It was decided to establish an ad hoc working group to follow up on the national reports process and its evaluation. Consultations on a new annex to the Convention continued, with the aim of adopting a regional implementation annex V for Central and Eastern Europe to complement the existing annexes for Africa, Asia, Latin America and the Caribbean, and the northern Mediterranean. Other decisions dealt with the Global Mechanism, traditional knowledge, a survey of existing networks, institutions, agencies and bodies, early warning systems, a roster of independent experts, the 2000-2001 budget and the Conference work programme. The Conference decided that its fourth session would be held from 16 to 27 October 2000 in Bonn, which became the site of the Convention's permanent secretariat at the end of January.

The Committee on Science and Technology, a subsidiary body of the Conference (Recife, 16-19 November) [ICCD/COP(3)/20 & Add.1], mainly adopted decisions similar to those of the Conference. It also adopted its work programme for 2000.

Governing Council action. Following consideration of the Executive Director's report on the implementation of the Convention [UNEP/GC.20/11], the Governing Council, on 5 February [dec. 20/10], asked him to maintain UNEP's capability to respond to global land-degradation issues; accord priority to promoting action to combat desertification; assist African countries in the development and strengthening of action plans; enhance GEF support for land degradation; strengthen collaboration with relevant UN bodies and other organizations; assist affected countries in land-degradation projects; involve UNEP in the activities of the Convention's Global Mechanism; and report in 2001.

Report of Secretary-General. In response to General Assembly resolution 53/191 [YUN 1998, p. 991], the Secretary-General reported, in May [A/54/96], on the headquarters agreement for the Convention's secretariat, the Global Mechanism, an additional regional implementation annex to the Convention for the countries of Eastern and Central Europe, the status of the Convention and arrangements for the third session of the Conference of the Parties.

GENERAL ASSEMBLY ACTION

On 22 December [meeting 87], the General Assembly, on the recommendation of the Second Committee [A/54/588/Add.5], adopted **resolution 54/223** without vote [agenda item 100 *(e)*].

Implementation of the United Nations Convention to Combat Desertification in those Countries Experiencing Serious Drought and/or Desertification, particularly in Africa

The General Assembly,

Recalling its resolution 53/191 of 15 December 1998 and other resolutions relating to the United Nations Convention to Combat Desertification in those Countries Experiencing Serious Drought and/or Desertification, particularly in Africa,

Noting with satisfaction that, as indicated in paragraph 19 of its resolution 52/198 of 18 December 1997, the second session of the Conference of the Parties to the Convention was held at Dakar from 30 November to 11 December 1998,

Expressing its deep appreciation to the Government of Senegal for the generous manner in which it hosted and provided facilities for the second session of the Conference of the Parties,

Expressing its deep appreciation also to the Government of Brazil for the generous offer to host the third session of the Conference of the Parties,

Welcoming the allocation of additional resources to the Global Mechanism by the Conference of the Parties at its third session,

Looking forward to the continued efforts of the Conference of the Parties and its subsidiary bodies in addressing desertification, land degradation and drought issues,

Acknowledging that desertification and drought are problems of a global dimension in that they affect all regions of the world and that joint action of the international community is needed to combat desertification and to mitigate the effects of drought,

Stressing the need, inter alia, to integrate strategies for poverty eradication into efforts to combat desertification and to mitigate the effects of drought,

Noting with satisfaction that an increasing number of countries and one regional economic integration organization have ratified or acceded to the Convention,

Having considered the report of the Secretary-General on the outcome of the second session of the Conference of the Parties and on the implementation of resolution 53/191,

1. *Welcomes* the convening of the third session of the Conference of the Parties to the United Nations Convention to Combat Desertification in those Countries Experiencing Serious Drought and/or Desertification, particularly in Africa, at Recife, Brazil, from 15 to 26 November 1999;

2. *Calls upon* all States and other actors to contribute effectively to the successful outcome of the third session of the Conference of the Parties;

3. *Also calls upon* all remaining countries that are not yet parties to the Convention to ratify or accede to the Convention as soon as possible;

4. *Emphasizes* the importance of implementing the provisions of the Convention at all levels, including the general provisions and obligations of affected and developed countries;

5. *Notes with satisfaction* that the Convention secretariat was relocated to Bonn, Germany, at the end of January 1999 and that it has begun functioning as the permanent secretariat of the Convention;

6. *Notes* that the Global Mechanism started its activities early in 1999, that it has not yet begun to support fully, inter alia, enabling activities under the Convention, and that resources have been made available to it, and invites the Global Mechanism to develop effectively all its activities and support under the Convention;

7. *Also notes* the decision of the Conference of the Parties at its third session related to the first review of policies, operational modalities and activities of the Global Mechanism, and, in this context, urges donors, international organizations and the Global Mechanism, within its mandate, to support the preparation of national reports;

8. *Welcomes* the steps being taken by affected developing country parties to the Convention, with the assistance of international organizations, to implement the Convention and the efforts being made to promote the participation of all actors of society in the elaboration of national, subregional and regional action programmes to combat desertification;

9. *Also welcomes* the efforts made by affected African country parties, developed country parties, international organizations and non-governmental organizations to produce and to submit reports for consideration by the Conference of the Parties at its third session;

10. *Requests* the Global Mechanism, in conformity with the provisions of the Convention and the relevant decisions taken by the Conference of the Parties at its first, second and third sessions, to carry out effectively its mandate of assisting affected developing country parties in the implementation of the Convention;

11. *Calls upon* the secretariat of the Convention and the Global Mechanism to cooperate fully in carrying out their activities, as provided for in their respective mandates;

12. *Welcomes* the financial support already provided on a voluntary basis by some countries, and urges Governments, the private sector and all relevant organizations, including non-governmental organizations, to make or to continue to make voluntary contributions to the Global Mechanism to enable it to implement effectively and fully its mandate;

13. *Also welcomes* the contributions paid by some country parties, and calls upon all parties that have not done so to pay promptly and in full the contributions required for the core budget of the Convention envisaged in the financial rules of the Conference of the Parties, so as to ensure continuity in the cash flow required to finance the ongoing work of the Conference, the subsidiary bodies, the permanent secretariat and the Global Mechanism;

14. *Further welcomes* the initial contribution made by the International Fund for Agricultural Development to the Special Resources for the Convention to Combat Desertification Finance Account, and invites the Fund to make available as soon as possible the remaining balance to the Account, in conformity with its pledge made at the first session of the Conference of the Parties in Rome;

15. *Invites* all other relevant organizations and programmes, in particular the United Nations Development Programme, the World Bank and other members of the Facilitation Committee of the Global Mechanism, also to make contributions to enable the Global Mechanism to support successfully the implementation of the Convention;

16. *Notes with satisfaction* that the Secretary-General, in conformity with paragraph 11 of resolution 52/198, closed, on 31 December 1998, the Trust Fund and the Special Voluntary Fund established under the provisions of General Assembly resolution 47/188 of 22 December 1992 and transferred the amounts remaining in the Trust Fund and in the Special Voluntary Fund, respectively, to the Supplementary Fund and the Special Fund established on 1 January 1999, in accordance with the relevant paragraphs of the financial rules of the Conference of the Parties;

17. *Calls upon* Governments, multilateral financial institutions, regional development banks, regional economic integration organizations and all other interested organizations, as well as non-governmental organizations and the private sector, to contribute generously to the General Fund, the Supplementary Fund and the Special Fund, in accordance with the relevant paragraphs of the financial rules of the Conference of the Parties;

18. *Decides* to include in the calendar of conferences and meetings for the biennium 2000-2001 the sessions of the Conference of the Parties and its subsidiary bodies, including the fourth and fifth ordinary sessions of the Conference of the Parties and the meetings of its subsidiary bodies;

19. *Notes with appreciation* that some affected developing countries and one region have adopted their na-

tional and regional action programmes, and therefore calls upon the international community to contribute to the implementation of those programmes through, inter alia, the conclusion of partnership agreements, relevant bilateral and multilateral cooperation programmes that are available to implement the Convention and contributions from non-governmental organizations and the private sector;

20. *Invites* affected developing countries that have not yet adopted their national action programmes, and, where appropriate, regional and subregional action programmes, to accelerate the process of elaboration and adoption of their action programmes with a view to finalizing them no later than the end of 2000;

21. *Calls upon* the international community, in particular the developed countries and the United Nations system, and invites the multilateral financial institutions, the private sector and all other interested actors to support the efforts of affected developing countries in the processes of elaborating and implementing action programmes to combat desertification, including, as appropriate, interregional programmes and platforms of cooperation, by providing them with financial resources and other forms of assistance;

22. *Welcomes* the progress made in producing a draft additional regional implementation annex to the Convention for the countries of Eastern and Central Europe with a view to adopting it at the fourth session of the Conference of the Parties, and invites those countries to continue their efforts towards acceding to the Convention;

23. *Encourages* the conferences of the parties to the United Nations Framework Convention on Climate Change, the Convention on Biological Diversity and the United Nations Convention to Combat Desertification in those Countries Experiencing Serious Drought and/or Desertification, particularly in Africa, to examine further appropriate opportunities and measures to strengthen the complementarities and to improve scientific assessments of ecological linkages among the three conventions;

24. *Also encourages* the secretariats of various environmental and environment-related conventions and other international organizations, with full respect for the statutes of the respective convention secretariats and the autonomous decision-making prerogatives of the conferences of the parties to the conventions concerned, to strengthen cooperation with a view to facilitating progress in their implementation at the international, regional, subregional and national levels;

25. *Requests* the Secretary-General to report to the General Assembly at its fifty-fifth session on the implementation of the present resolution, as well as on the outcome of the third session of the Conference of the Parties;

26. *Reminds* the States parties to the Convention that, in accordance with General Assembly decision 52/445 of 18 December 1997, beginning in 2000, the conferences of the parties to the conventions signed at the United Nations Conference on Environment and Development or established as a result of the Conference, as well as other conventions relating to sustainable development, shall take all appropriate measures to avoid convening their sessions and those of their subsidiary bodies during the sessions of the General Assembly;

27. *Decides* to include in the provisional agenda of its fifty-fifth session the sub-item entitled "Implementation of the United Nations Convention to Combat Desertification in those Countries Experiencing Serious Drought and/or Desertification, particularly in Africa".

Environmental activities

The atmosphere

In an effort to combat the recurring forest-fire/smog problem in South-East Asia, UNEP, in collaboration with the secretariat of the Association of South-East Asian Nations (ASEAN), was helping to establish a legally binding agreement on transboundary haze pollution in the region. The eighth ASEAN Ministerial Meeting on Haze concluded on 26 August in Singapore.

On 16 September, the International Day for the Preservation of the Ozone Layer was observed.

On 17 November, UNEP cautioned that the ozone hole in the Antarctic covered an area of 22 million square kilometres, an expanse more than twice the size of mainland China. The ozone layer over different parts of the world was monitored systematically. According to the Scientific Assessment Panel of the Montreal Protocol on Substances that Deplete the Ozone Layer, the ozone layer was projected to recover to pre-1980 levels in the year 2050, provided the Protocol was implemented and all countries completely phased out the use of ozone-depleting chemicals.

Intergovernmental Panel on Climate Change

The Intergovernmental Panel on Climate Change, at its fifteenth session (San José, Costa Rica, 15-18 April), among other things, reviewed work on vulnerabilities to climate change in SIDS, Asia, Africa and Latin America, and special reports on technology transfer, emissions scenarios and land use, and land-use change and forestry.

In June, the Panel released a report, "Aviation and the global atmosphere", which assessed the impact of aircraft engine emissions on climate and atmospheric ozone.

Terrestrial ecosystems

Deforestation and forest degradation

Intergovernmental Forum on Forests

The Intergovernmental Forum on Forests (IFF), established in 1997 [YUN 1997, p. 1057] under the aegis of the Commission on Sustainable Development to work towards a legally binding instrument on the management, conservation and sustainable development of all types of forests, held its third session (Geneva, 3-14 May) [E/CN.17/IFF/1999/25]. IFF continued to consider promoting and facilitating the implementation of the proposals for action of the Intergovernmental Panel on Forests (IPF) [YUN 1997, p. 1057] and reporting on progress in the management, conservation and sustainable development of all types of forests; matters left pending and other issues arising from IPF programme elements; and international arrangements to promote the management, conservation and sustainable development of all types of forests.

The Forum had before it a series of communications transmitting the texts of various reports: from Austria, the report on the International Consultation on Research and Information Systems in Forestry (Gmunden, 7-10 September 1998) [E/CN.17/IFF/1999/17]; from Costa Rica, the final report of the Global Workshop on Addressing the Underlying Causes of Deforestation and Forest Degradation (San José, 18-22 January) [E/CN.17/IFF/1999/18] and the report of the meeting of experts of the Costa Rica–Canada Initiative on forests in support of the IFF work programme (San José, 22-26 February) [E/CN.17/IFF/1999/23]; from Germany, the report of the Chairman of the International Cooperation Programme on the Assessment and Monitoring of Air Pollution Effects on Forests [E/CN.17/IFF/1999/19]; from Australia, an executive summary of a report on international forest conservation: protected areas and beyond [E/CN.17/IFF/1999/20] and of a study on the global outlook for plantations [E/CN.17/IFF/1999/24]; from Chile, Denmark, India, New Zealand and Portugal, the sponsors of an international expert meeting on the role of planted forests in sustainable forest management (Santiago, Chile, 6-10 April), the final report of the meeting [E/CN.17/IFF/1999/21]; and from Brazil, the final report of the Brazil–United States international experts' meeting on protected forest areas (San Juan, Puerto Rico, 15-19 March) [E/CN.17/IFF/1999/22].

Central African forest ecosystems

On 12 October [A/C.2/54/5], Cameroon transmitted to the Secretary-General the Declaration of the Summit of Central African Heads of State on the Conservation and Sustainable Management of Tropical Forests (Yaoundé, 12-17 March). By the Declaration, the heads of State of Cameroon, the Central African Republic, Chad, the Congo, Equatorial Guinea and Gabon undertook to accelerate the setting up of protected transborder zones lying between Central African States; develop a forestry tax system and attendant implementation measures; adopt harmonized national forestry policies; involve the rural population in the planning and sustainable management of ecosystems; involve economic operators in the sustainable management and conservation of forest ecosystems; make efforts to stamp out large-scale poaching and other non-sustainable exploitation; promote and increase the pace of industrialization in the sector; promote national and subregional forums; establish lasting mechanisms for financing forest development; organize summits on the conservation and sustainable management of forest ecosystems; and revive the Organization for Wildlife Conservation in Central Africa.

GENERAL ASSEMBLY ACTION

On 22 December [meeting 87], the General Assembly, on the recommendation of the Second Committee [A/54/588/Add.7], adopted **resolution 54/214** without vote [agenda item 100].

Conservation and sustainable development of Central African forest ecosystems

The General Assembly,

Recalling the United Nations Conference on Environment and Development, held at Rio de Janeiro from 3 to 14 June 1992, and General Assembly resolutions 47/190 of 22 December 1992, on the report of the Conference, and 47/191 of 22 December 1992, establishing the institutional arrangements for the follow-up to the Conference,

Recalling also its resolution 53/188 of 15 December 1998 on the implementation of and follow-up to the outcome of the United Nations Conference on Environment and Development and the nineteenth special session of the General Assembly,

Recalling further the work of the Intergovernmental Forum on Forests within the context of the Commission on Sustainable Development,

Noting with appreciation the Summit of Central African Heads of State on the Conservation and Sustainable Management of Tropical Forests, held at Yaoundé from 12 to 17 March 1999,

Mindful of the need for the conservation and sustainable management of the forest ecosystems of Central Africa, which constitute an important natural asset for present and future generations,

Convinced that the sustainable management of forest resources can contribute significantly to the economic, social and cultural development of the States that border on forests,

Convinced also of the important role of subregional and international cooperation in the management of forest ecosystems and combating desertification, in keeping with the international commitments entered into by the international community,

Considering that a synergy of international and national efforts is essential in order to achieve sustainable development,

1. *Recognizes* the importance of the forests of the Central African subregion, the natural characteristics of which play an essential role in the equilibrium of the biosphere of the entire planet;

2. *Welcomes* the Declaration adopted by the Summit of Central African Heads of State on the Conservation and Sustainable Management of Tropical Forests, held

at Yaoundé from 12 to 17 March 1999, encourages the countries of Central Africa to implement to the fullest extent possible the undertakings set out in the Declaration, and recognizes the efforts made by those countries in this respect, in particular with regard to policy coherence and coordination, with a view to the sustainable management and conservation of the forest ecosystems of the Central African subregion;

3. *Invites* the international community to support the countries of Central Africa in these efforts, including through the provision of financial and technical assistance on a regional basis;

4. *Encourages* the international community, including the Global Environment Facility and the Intergovernmental Forum on Forests, when considering ways and means of achieving the conservation and sustainable management of all types of forests, to take into account, inter alia, the forests of the Central African subregion;

5. *Requests* the Secretary-General to report to the General Assembly at its fifty-fifth session on the implementation of the present resolution, within the context of the reporting emanating from the Intergovernmental Forum on Forests and taking into account other reporting requests under the item entitled "Environment and sustainable development".

Marine ecosystems

Oceans and seas

The Commission on Sustainable Development considered February reports of the Secretary-General on the current state of the ocean and main trends of ocean matters [E/CN.17/1999/4] and on national trends and progress made towards sustainable development within oceans and seas [E/CN.17/1999/4/Add.1].

Deterioration of the coastal and marine environment had been caused by land-based activities of humans, as well as natural phenomena, such as climate change, floods and storms, which together threatened the sustainability of coastal resources. Coral reefs were particularly vulnerable to human activities, including coastal development, overexploitation and destructive fishing practices, impacts from inland pollution and erosion, and marine-based pollution. As to living marine resources, it was estimated that 35 per cent of major marine fisheries were subjected to severe overfishing, 25 per cent were fully exploited and 40 per cent still offered scope for development. With regard to the prevention and control of marine pollution from shipping and related activities, there was a reduction in pollution incidents and the near elimination of the dumping of industrial wastes and other matter at sea. However, there were serious weaknesses in the international regulatory regime, such as polluting ships that had not acceded to relevant agreements or ships that flew non-party flags of convenience. In addition, there was no international instrument to regulate offshore oil and gas exploration and production activities as a source of marine pollution. Areas requiring further attention were the Global Programme of Action for the Protection of the Marine Environment from Land-based Activities (see p. 996), fisheries management and international cooperation and coordination.

An analysis of general trends in national implementation indicated achievements in the improvement of decision-making, particularly the strengthening of legal and administrative frameworks; respect for the rights of indigenous and local people; improved information for decision-making and public awareness; the use of financial incentives that promoted sustainability; and increased collaboration at international, regional and bilateral levels. The report highlighted developments in integrated coastal zone management, marine environment protection, sustainable use and conservation of marine living resources and regional trends in Africa, Asia, Europe, the Mediterranean and the Americas.

In February [E/CN.17/1999/15], South Africa transmitted to the Commission the conclusions and recommendations of the regional Conference on Cooperation for Development and Protection of the Coastal and Marine Environment in Sub-Saharan Africa (Cape Town, 30 November-4 December 1998. Also in February [E/CN.17/1999/14], the United Kingdom transmitted the report of the Second London Oceans Workshop, hosted jointly by the Governments of Brazil and the United Kingdom (London, 10-12 December 1998).

The UNEP Governing Council had before it a report of the Executive Director [UNEP/GC.20/19/Add.1] on UNEP activities regarding oceans management, which was submitted to the Commission.

Commission action. In April, the Commission on Sustainable Development called on Governments to strengthen national, regional and international action to develop integrated approaches to oceans and coastal area management [E/1999/29 (dec. 7/1)]. It emphasized the importance of international cooperation in ensuring that the oceans and seas remained sustainable through integrated management. The Commission supported the need to strengthen the UNEP regional seas programme and to enhance cooperation with other regional seas and intergovernmental organizations. The UN system and Governments were asked to review the priority given to building capacities needed to manage regional seas organizations, intergovernmental regional fisheries organizations and arrangements and regional monitoring systems. The Commission brought to the attention of the international community areas of particular concern relating to marine resources, the effects of land-based activities, marine science and other marine activities such as navigation, pollution by dumping at sea, and offshore oil and gas operations.

The Commission recommended that the General Assembly establish a process to promote improved cooperation and coordination on oceans and seas. It proposed that the process function under the Assembly's aegis to facilitate consideration of matters within the Assembly's mandate, as contained in its resolution 49/28 [YUN 1994, p. 1314].

GENERAL ASSEMBLY ACTION

On 24 November [meeting 62], the General Assembly adopted **resolution 54/33** [draft: A/54/L.32 & Add.1] without vote [agenda item 40 *(c)*].

Results of the review by the Commission on Sustainable Development of the sectoral theme of "Oceans and seas": international coordination and cooperation

The General Assembly,

Recalling its resolutions 49/28 of 6 December 1994 on the law of the sea and 53/32 of 24 November 1998 on oceans and the law of the sea,

Mindful of the importance of the oceans and seas for the earth's ecosystem and for providing the vital resources for food security and for sustaining economic prosperity and the well-being of present and future generations,

Convinced that all aspects of oceans and seas are closely interrelated and need to be considered as a whole,

Recalling that the United Nations Convention on the Law of the Sea sets out the legal framework within which all activities in the oceans and seas must be carried out, and with which these activities should be consistent, as recognized also by the United Nations Conference on Environment and Development in chapter 17 of Agenda 21,

Recognizing the importance of maintaining the integrity of the Convention,

Convinced of the importance of the annual consideration and review of ocean affairs and the law of the sea by the General Assembly, as the global institution having the competence to undertake such a review,

Convinced also of the need, building on existing arrangements, for an integrated approach to all legal, economic, social, environmental and other relevant aspects of oceans and seas and the need to improve coordination and cooperation at both the intergovernmental and inter-agency levels,

Bearing in mind the necessity of strengthening existing structures and mandates within the United Nations system and the need to avoid duplication or overlapping of debates that take place in other forums,

Recognizing the important role that international organizations have in relation to ocean affairs and in promoting sustainable development of the oceans and seas and their resources,

Recognizing also the significant contribution that major groups, as identified in Agenda 21, can make to this goal,

Welcoming the review of the sectoral theme of "Oceans and seas" by the Commission on Sustainable Development, in particular those aspects related to international coordination and cooperation,

1. *Endorses* the recommendations made by the Commission on Sustainable Development through the Economic and Social Council under the sectoral theme of "Oceans and seas" regarding international coordination and cooperation;

2. *Decides,* consistent with the legal framework provided by the United Nations Convention on the Law of the Sea and the goals of chapter 17 of Agenda 21, to establish an open-ended informal consultative process in order to facilitate the annual review by the General Assembly, in an effective and constructive manner, of developments in ocean affairs by considering the Secretary-General's report on oceans and the law of the sea and by suggesting particular issues to be considered by it, with an emphasis on identifying areas where coordination and cooperation at the intergovernmental and inter-agency levels should be enhanced;

3. *Also decides* that the meetings within the framework of the consultative process will be organized as follows:

(a) The meetings will be open to all States Members of the United Nations, States members of the specialized agencies, all parties to the Convention, entities that have received a standing invitation to participate as observers in the work of the General Assembly pursuant to its relevant resolutions, and intergovernmental organizations with competence in ocean affairs;

(b) The meetings will take place for one week each year; in 2000 they will be held from 30 May to 2 June;

(c) The meetings will deliberate on the Secretary-General's report on oceans and the law of the sea, with due account given to any particular resolution or decision of the General Assembly, any relevant special reports of the Secretary-General and any relevant recommendations of the Commission on Sustainable Development;

(d) The meetings should, in identifying areas where coordination and cooperation are to be enhanced, bear in mind the differing characteristics and needs of the different regions of the world, and should not pursue legal or juridical coordination among the different legal instruments;

(e) The meetings will be coordinated by two co-chairpersons, who will be appointed by the President of the General Assembly in consultation with Member States and taking into account the need for representation from developed and developing countries;

(f) The co-chairpersons will elaborate, in consultation with delegations, a format for the discussions that best facilitates the work of the consultative process, in accordance with the rules of procedure and practices of the General Assembly;

(g) In accordance with the rules of procedure and practices of the General Assembly, the format of this informal consultative process should ensure the opportunity to receive input from representatives of the major groups as identified in Agenda 21, in particular through the organization of discussion panels;

(*h*) The meetings may propose elements for the consideration of the General Assembly, including, as appropriate, in relation to Assembly resolutions under the agenda item entitled "Oceans and the law of the sea";

4. *Further decides* to review the effectiveness and utility of the consultative process at its fifty-seventh session;

5. *Highlights* the importance of the participation of developing countries, including least developed countries and small island developing States, in the consultative process, and encourages States and international organizations to support efforts in this regard;

6. *Requests* the Secretary-General to provide the consultative process with the necessary facilities for the performance of its work and to arrange for support to be provided by the Division for Ocean Affairs and the Law of the Sea of the Office of Legal Affairs of the Secretariat, in cooperation with other relevant parts of the Secretariat, including the Division for Sustainable Development of the Department of Economic and Social Affairs, as appropriate;

7. *Also requests* the Secretary-General, working in cooperation with the heads of relevant organizations of the United Nations, to include in his annual comprehensive report to the General Assembly on oceans and the law of the sea, suggestions on initiatives that could be undertaken to improve coordination and cooperation and achieve better integration on ocean affairs, and requests the Secretary-General to make the report available at least six weeks in advance of the meeting of the consultative process;

8. *Further requests* the Secretary-General, working through appropriate United Nations bodies and in cooperation with the heads of relevant organizations, funds or programmes of the United Nations, to undertake measures aimed at:

(*a*) Ensuring more effective collaboration and coordination between relevant parts of the Secretariat and the United Nations system as a whole on ocean affairs and the law of the sea;

(*b*) Improving the effectiveness, transparency and responsiveness of the Subcommittee on Oceans and Coastal Areas of the Administrative Committee on Coordination;

and to include information on progress in this regard in his next report on oceans and the law of the sea;

9. *Notes* the importance of coordination and cooperation at the national level in order to promote an integrated approach on ocean affairs so as, inter alia, to facilitate the effective participation of States in the consultative process and other international forums;

10. *Requests* the Secretary-General to bring the present resolution to the attention of heads of intergovernmental organizations, the specialized agencies and funds and programmes of the United Nations engaged in activities relating to ocean affairs and the law of the sea, and the Subcommittee on Oceans and Coastal Areas of the Administrative Committee on Coordination, and underlines the importance of their participation in the consultative process and of their input to the report of the Secretary-General on oceans and the law of the sea;

11. *Invites* Member States, as part of their participation in relevant competent bodies of intergovernmental organizations engaged in activities relating to ocean affairs and the law of the sea, to encourage their participation in the consultative process and their contribution to the report of the Secretary-General on oceans and the law of the sea.

On 22 December [meeting 87], the General Assembly, on the recommendation of the Second Committee [A/54/588/Add.6], adopted **resolution 54/225** without vote [agenda item 100 (*f*)].

Promoting an integrated management approach to the Caribbean Sea area in the context of sustainable development

The General Assembly,

Reaffirming the principles and commitments enshrined in the Rio Declaration on Environment and Development, adopted by the United Nations Conference on Environment and Development in 1992, and the principles embodied in the Declaration of Barbados and the Programme of Action for the Sustainable Development of Small Island Developing States, adopted by the Global Conference on the Sustainable Development of Small Island Developing States in 1994, as well as other relevant declarations and international instruments,

Recalling the Declaration and review document adopted by the General Assembly at its twenty-second special session,

Recalling also the relevant work done by the International Maritime Organization,

Taking into account all other relevant resolutions adopted by the General Assembly,

Reaffirming the United Nations Convention on the Law of the Sea and emphasizing the fundamental character of the Convention,

Recalling the Convention for the Protection and Development of the Marine Environment of the Wider Caribbean Region, signed at Cartagena de Indias, Colombia, on 24 March 1983, which contains the definition of the wider Caribbean region of which the Caribbean Sea is part,

Considering that the Caribbean Sea area includes a large number of States, countries and territories, most of which are developing countries and small island developing States which are ecologically fragile and economically vulnerable and also affected, inter alia, by their limited capacity, narrow resource base, need for financial resources, social problems, high levels of poverty and the challenges and opportunities of globalization,

Considering also that the Caribbean Sea area, nearly all of which is separated from the open ocean by either continental or insular land masses, is characterized by a unique biodiversity and highly fragile ecosystems, such as the second largest coral reef system in the world, the heavy reliance of most States, countries and territories on their coastal areas and the marine environment in general to achieve their sustainable development needs and goals, the number and interlocking character of the maritime areas under national sovereignty and jurisdiction, which present a challenge to the effective management of resources, the intensive use of the Caribbean Sea area for maritime transportation and, notwithstanding the increase in the number of regulatory measures, the threat of pollution from ship-generated waste and from the release of hazardous and noxious substances in violation of relevant international rules and standards,

Emphasizing that the Caribbean countries have a high degree of vulnerability occasioned by climate change and variability, associated phenomena, such as the rise in sea level, the El Niño/Southern Oscillation phenomenon and the increase in the frequency and intensity of natural disasters caused by hurricanes, floods and droughts and that they are also subject to natural disasters, such as those caused by volcanoes, tsunamis and earthquakes,

Mindful of the strong interaction and competition among socio-economic activities in the countries of the region for the use of the coastal areas and the marine environment and their resources,

Mindful also of the efforts made by the Caribbean countries to address, in a more holistic manner, the sectoral issues relating to the management of the Caribbean Sea and in so doing to promote an integrated management approach to the Caribbean Sea in the context of sustainable development,

Noting the efforts of Caribbean countries, within the framework of the Association of Caribbean States, to develop further and seek recognition of the concept of the Caribbean Sea as an area of special importance in the context of sustainable development,

Cognizant of the importance of the Caribbean Sea area to present and future generations and its importance to the heritage, the continuing economic well-being and the sustenance of people living in the area and the urgent need for the countries of the region to take appropriate steps for its preservation and protection, with the support of the international community,

Noting the problem of marine pollution caused, inter alia, by land-based sources in the Caribbean Sea area,

1. *Recognizes* the importance of adopting an integrated management approach to the Caribbean Sea area in the context of sustainable development;

2. *Encourages* the further development of the integrated management approach to the Caribbean Sea area in the context of sustainable development, which will include environmental, economic, social, legal and institutional elements and will take into account the experience gained, as well as the provisions of Agenda 21, the Programme of Action for the Sustainable Development of Small Island Developing States, the outcome of the twenty-second special session of the General Assembly and the work of the Commission on Sustainable Development, in conformity with relevant international law, including the United Nations Convention on the Law of the Sea;

3. *Calls upon* the Caribbean countries to develop further an integrated management approach to the Caribbean Sea area in the context of sustainable development;

4. *Also calls upon* the international community and the United Nations system, in particular the relevant agencies, actively to support efforts to develop further and implement the above-mentioned approach;

5. *Further calls upon* Member States to give priority to improving their emergency response capabilities and to increasing their participation in existing mechanisms so as to allow for a timely, effective and coordinated response to natural disasters and for the containment of environmental damage in the Caribbean Sea area in the event of an accident or incident relating to maritime transport;

6. *Invites* all parties concerned to take action, as appropriate, to address land-based sources of marine pollution;

7. *Requests* the Secretary-General to report to the General Assembly at its fifty-fifth session, under a sub-item entitled "Further implementation of the Programme of Action for the Sustainable Development of Small Island Developing States" of the item entitled "Environment and sustainable development", on the implementation of the present resolution, taking into account the views expressed by relevant regional organizations.

Global Programme of Action

A report of the Executive Director [UNEP/GC.20/32 & Corr.1] discussed UNEP's progress, as secretariat of the Global Programme of Action for the Protection of the Marine Environment from Land-based Activities [YUN 1995, p. 1081], in support of implementation of the Programme. It described the establishment of the Global Programme of Action Coordination Office in The Hague, regional implementation, inter-agency and international cooperation, the clearing-house mechanism and Programme of Action–related assessments.

On 5 February [A/54/25 (dec. 20/19 B)], the Governing Council urged the Executive Director to complete the establishment of the Hague Coordination Office and, in cooperation with Governments, UN bodies and other relevant organizations, to explore the feasibility for UNEP to convene, by 2000, a global conference to address sewage as a major land-based source of pollution affecting human and ecosystem health. It decided to undertake the first intergovernmental review of the implementation of the Global Programme of Action in 2001, and invited the Executive Director to organize, by the end of 1999, an expert group meeting to facilitate preparations for the review, with the participation of Governments, international organizations and NGOs. The Council recommended the creation of technical working groups in regional seas programmes and that national and regional meetings be held to create implementation partnerships with donor organizations, the private sector, NGOs, local government and all other stakeholders. It called on the Executive Director to improve the functioning of the Steering Committee of the Global Programme of Action.

Coral reefs

Recalling its 1997 decision [YUN 1997, p. 1064] on the International Coral Reef Initiative [YUN 1995, p. 1084], the Governing Council, on 4 February [dec. 20/21], endorsed proposed UNEP collaborative activities with organizations both within and outside the UN system for the protection and conservation of coral reef ecosystems. It asked the Executive Director to assess UNEP experience in implementing the Initiative, to circulate to the Council in 2001 the Renewed Call to Action of the International Tropical Marine Ecosystems Management Symposium (Townsville, Australia, 23-26 November 1998), and to seek funding to implement the Initiative's activities.

The Council reviewed the Executive Director's report on UNEP activities in support of the International Coral Reef Initiative and the Global Coral Reef Monitoring Network [UNEP/GC.20/36] and, on 5 February [dec. 20/19 A], endorsed UNEP's enhanced cooperation with the Intergovernmental Oceanographic Commission of the United Nations Educational, Scientific and Cultural Organization, the World Bank, UNDP and other international organizations, and decided to assess the Initiative in 2001.

Regional seas programme

The Governing Council considered the status report of the Executive Director on the establishment of a regional seas programme for the East Central Pacific [UNEP/GC.20/35] and, on 4 February [dec. 20/20], endorsed action taken to establish the proposed programme. It noted wide support by Governments for the draft action plan and corresponding legal instrument, and invited Costa Rica, El Salvador, Guatemala, Honduras, Mexico, Nicaragua and Panama to endorse the proposed Meeting of High-level Government-designated Experts to Review the Proposals for a Convention and Plan of Action for the Protection of the Marine and Coastal Environment of the East Central Pacific Region.

Conservation of wildlife

As at 31 December, the 1994 Lusaka Agreement on Cooperative Enforcement Operations Directed at Illegal Trade in Wild Fauna and Flora [YUN 1994, p. 951], which entered into force in 1996 [YUN 1996, p. 970], had been ratified or acceded to by six States (Congo, Kenya, Lesotho, Uganda, United Republic of Tanzania, Zambia). The Agreement aimed to reduce, and ultimately eliminate, illegal trafficking in African wildlife.

Protection against harmful products and wastes

Chemical safety

As at 31 December, 73 States had signed and 2 had ratified (El Salvador and Slovenia) the 1998 Convention on the Prior Informed Consent Procedure for Certain Hazardous Chemicals and Pesticides in International Trade (the Rotterdam Convention) [YUN 1998, p. 997]. The Convention was to enter into force following the deposit of the fiftieth instrument of ratification. The sixth session of the Intergovernmental Negotiating Committee (INC) for an International Legally Binding Instrument for the Application of the Prior Informed Consent (PIC) Procedure (Rome, 12-16 July) [UNEP/FAO/PIC/INC.6/7] adopted decision guidance documents for already identified chemicals, established an Interim Chemical Review Committee and adopted the interim PIC regional lists of countries for the application of the PIC procedure. It discussed preparations for the first meeting of the Conference of the Parties to the Convention.

Following consideration of the Executive Director's report on the outcome of the 1998 Conference of Plenipotentiaries on the Convention [UNEP/GC.20/39 & Corr.1], the Governing Council, on 4 February [dec. 20/22], called on States and regional economic integration organizations to become party to the Convention, and recommended that the General Assembly endorse the institutional linkage between UNEP and the Convention, through which the Executive Director provided secretariat services jointly with the Director-General of the Food and Agriculture Organization of the United Nations (FAO). The Executive Director was authorized, together with the FAO Director-General, to convene further INC sessions, until the opening of the first meeting of the Conference of the Parties to the Convention, to oversee the operation of the interim PIC procedure and to prepare for and service the Conference until the end of the fiscal year in which the first meeting took place. States and regional economic integration organizations were asked to contribute to the trust fund to support the interim arrangements and operation of the Conference, and to ensure the participation of developing countries and countries with economies in transition in further INC work. States and regional economic integration organizations with more advanced programmes for regulating chemicals were asked to provide technical assistance to others in developing their infrastructure and capacities to manage chemicals. The Council requested the Executive Director to report in 2001.

Having considered the Executive Director's reports on the outcome of the 1998 Conference of Plenipotentiaries, on reducing risks from a limited number of hazardous chemicals [UNEP/GC.20/37], on reducing discharges of persistent organic pollutants [UNEP/GC.20/41] (see next page) and on enhanced coherence and efficiency among international activities related to chemicals [UNEP/GC.20/INF/20], the Council, on 4 February [dec. 20/23], invited him to consider preparing for a general policy discussion on chemicals management in 2001.

Persistent organic pollutants

The second session of the Intergovernmental Negotiating Committee for an International Legally Binding Instrument for Implementing International Action on Certain Persistent Organic Pollutants (POPs) took place in Nairobi from 25 to 29 January [UNEP/POPS/INC.2/6]. The 12 initially identified POPs were aldrin, chlordane, DDT, dieldrin, dioxins, endrin, furans, heptachlor, hexachlorobenzene, mirex, PCBs and toxaphene. The Committee considered a draft expanded outline of a legally binding instrument for implementing international action on certain POPs. Annexed to its report was a preliminary draft text of the instrument. The Committee, at its third session (Geneva, 6-11 September) [UNEP/POPS/INC.3/4], considered individual draft articles. At its second session (Vienna, 14-18 June), the Criteria Expert Group, established in 1998 [YUN 1998, p. 999], had continued to consider information requirements and criteria for the proposal and screening of proposed POPs, and had proposed three options for the definition of the term "long-range environmental transport".

On 4 February [dec. 20/24], the Governing Council, having reviewed the Executive Director's report on international action to protect human health and the environment through measures which would reduce and/or eliminate emissions and discharges of POPs, including the development of an international legally binding instrument [UNEP/GC.20/41], invited the Committee to continue its work with a view to concluding a legally binding instrument by 2000. The Executive Director was asked to report in 2001.

Hazardous wastes

The fifth meeting of the Conference of the Parties to the 1989 Basel Convention on the Control of Transboundary Movements of Hazardous Wastes and their Disposal [YUN 1989, p. 420] (Basel, Switzerland, 6-10 December) [UNEP/CHW.5/29] adopted the Basel Protocol on Liability and Compensation for Damage resulting from Transboundary Movements of Hazardous Wastes and their Disposal. The text of the Protocol was annexed to the report of the Conference. The Conference also adopted the Basel Declaration on Environmentally Sound Management, as well as decisions relating to regional centres for training and technology transfer; capacity-building activities; cooperation with UNEP on POPs and with the Rotterdam Convention, the World Customs Organization, the Organisation for Economic Cooperation and Development, UN bodies, specialized agencies, regional systems and organizations, environmental NGOs and industry and business sectors; information management; monitoring of implementation and compliance with the Basel Convention; the dispute settlement mechanism; illegal traffic in hazardous and other wastes; the classification and hazard characterization of wastes; guidelines to identify and manage plastic waste and its disposal; hazardous waste minimization; and the dismantling of ships. The Conference decided that its sixth meeting would be held in Geneva in May 2002.

Cleaner and safer production

Following a review of a January report summarizing UNEP activities to promote sustainable production and consumption [UNEP/GC.20/42], the Governing Council, on 5 February [dec. 20/19 E], encouraged Governments, industries and institutions to promote and implement preventive strategies, such as cleaner production, green productivity and pollution prevention, as preferred options to address environmental problems, and asked those that had not already done so to sign the 1998 International Declaration on Cleaner Production [YUN 1998, p. 1000]. It encouraged UNEP and the Commission on Sustainable Development to develop, in partnership with the UNEP Youth Advisory Council, a sustainable strategy for youth. The Executive Director was encouraged to promote more sustainable production and consumption patterns in industry and the wider community, and to further develop draft guidelines to evaluate environmentally sound technologies, including guidelines for exporters of potentially hazardous or outdated technologies, and submit them in 2001.

Other matters

Environmental law

The Governing Council reviewed a report of the Executive Director [UNEP/GC.20/5] describing progress made in implementing the Programme for the Development and Periodic Review of Environmental Law for the 1990s (Montevideo II) [YUN 1993, p. 820], and proposing a process for the preparation of a new strategic UNEP programme on environmental law for the 2000s and the following decade. The Council also considered a report on emerging policy issues, including a study on dispute avoidance and dispute settlement in international environmental law [UNEP/GC.20/INF/16].

On 3 February [dec. 20/3], the Council asked the Executive Director to prepare a new programme for the development and periodic review of environmental law and, as part of the process, to convene in 2000 a meeting of senior government experts in environmental law. It authorized him to use the current Programme until a new one was adopted and to assist Governments and organizations in developing international environmental agreements. The Executive Director was asked to assist developing countries and countries with economies in transition in strengthening national environmental legislation and institutions and to report in 2001.

Occupied Palestinian and other Arab territories

The Governing Council, having considered the Executive Director's updates on the environmental situation in the occupied Palestinian and other Arab territories [UNEP/GC.20/4, UNEP/GC.20/INF/9], on 4 February [dec. 20/2], asked him to continue participating in the activities of the multilateral working groups of the Middle East peace process, as well as those of the United Nations Special Coordinator in the Occupied Territories. Expressing concern regarding the continued environmental degradation in the territories, it asked the Executive Director to report in 2001.

Human settlements

Follow-up to 1996 UN Conference on Human Settlements (Habitat II)

2001 General Assembly special session

Report of Secretary-General. In September [A/54/322], the Secretary-General, in response to General Assembly resolution 53/180 [YUN 1998, p. 1021], reported on preparations for the Assembly's special (2001) session for an overall review and appraisal of the implementation of the Habitat Agenda, adopted by the 1996 United Nations Conference on Human Settlements (Habitat II) [YUN 1996, p. 992]. The Commission on Human Settlements acting as the Preparatory Committee for the special session held its organizational session in Nairobi on 13 May. The Committee adopted its provisional agenda based on the provisions of resolution 53/180 and agreed that its first session would be held in Nairobi in May 2000. It also adopted its rules of procedure.

Commission action. The Commission on Human Settlements considered a February report of the Executive Director of the United Nations Centre for Human Settlements (UNCHS) on the Assembly's special session [HS/C/17/3/Add.1].

On 12 May [A/54/8 (res. 17/14)], the Commission called on the Preparatory Committee to devise a framework for the exchange of information and knowledge of effective policies and alternative solutions to problems for the Assembly's special session, and asked it to ensure that the session elaborated on the key items of the Habitat Agenda. The Commission recommended a number of items to the Committee for consideration at its organizational session, including the provisional agenda for the first session, the scope to be covered by the review and appraisal process, issues for consideration by the Economic and Social Council in 2000 and issues to be addressed by the Commission in 2001.

GENERAL ASSEMBLY ACTION

On 22 December [meeting 87], the General Assembly, on the recommendation of the Second Committee [A/54/587/Add.2], adopted **resolution 54/207** without vote [agenda item 99 *(b)*].

Preparations for the special session of the General Assembly for an overall review and appraisal of the implementation of the Habitat Agenda

The General Assembly,

Recalling its resolution 53/180 of 15 December 1998, in which, inter alia, it decided that the special session for an overall review and appraisal of the implementation of the outcome of the United Nations Conference on Human Settlements (Habitat II) would be held in June 2001 for a period of three working days, and that the Commission on Human Settlements should serve as the Preparatory Committee for the special session,

Having considered the report of the Commission on Human Settlements acting as Preparatory Committee for the special session on its organizational session,

1. *Endorses* the decisions of the Commission on Human Settlements acting as the Preparatory Committee for the special session, in particular regarding its rules of procedure and the dates, venue and provisional agenda for its first substantive session;

2. *Decides* to include in the provisional agenda of its fifty-fifth session the sub-item entitled "Implementation of the outcome of the United Nations Conference on Human Settlements (Habitat II)".

Implementation

A February report of the Executive Director on the implementation of the Habitat Agenda [HS/C/17/3] documented significant developments at the local, national, regional and global levels, as well as gaps and weaknesses that needed to be overcome. In other reports, the Executive Director focused on international cooperation to implement the Habitat Agenda [HS/C/17/6] and local implementation of the Habitat Agenda, with particular attention to local Agenda 21s [HS/C/17/5], referring to Agenda 21 adopted by the 1992 United Nations Conference on Environment and Development [YUN 1992, p. 672].

On 14 May [res. 17/17], the Commission recommended that Governments and development agencies mobilize resources to promote participatory mechanisms to implement the Habitat Agenda and related national plans of action, called on them to support the revitalization of the UNCHS monitoring mandate to follow up on the progress of international assistance to the human settlements sector, and also called on them to support the global campaigns on secure tenure and on urban governance (see below), key elements of the UNCHS 2000-2001 work programme [HS/C/17/8]. The Executive Director was asked to pursue an increase in resources from the international community; to support regional and subregional forums; to work with the UN system to support systematic coordinated approaches addressing urban poverty; and to prepare a theme paper on international cooperation for the implementation of the Habitat Agenda for presentation at the Assembly's special session.

Considering that innovative measures needed to be adopted to accelerate the work leading to the special session, the Commission, on 14 May [res. 17/18], asked the Executive Director to establish a committee of local authorities as an advisory body to strengthen dialogue with local authorities worldwide involved in the implementation of the Habitat Agenda. It decided that the committee would be composed of not more than 20 members, selected by the Executive Director from UN Member States and members of the specialized agencies or of the International Atomic Energy Agency. He was also asked to convene the constituting meeting of the committee, if possible in 1999, and to report in 2001.

Also on 14 May [res. 17/16], the Commission called on Governments to increase awareness of the Habitat Agenda and the local Agenda 21s; to revise legal and institutional frameworks in order to facilitate partnerships at the local level; and to develop training for locally elected representatives, community leaders and local-level partners in how to establish and manage local-level partnerships within the context of the Habitat Agenda and the local Agenda 21s. The Executive Director was asked to assist countries in the local-level implementation of the Habitat Agenda and Agenda 21, and to ensure that increasing awareness of the two was an integral part of the two global campaigns, for secure tenure and for urban governance, as proposed in the UNCHS 2000-2001 work programme.

GENERAL ASSEMBLY ACTION

On 22 December [meeting 87], the General Assembly, on the recommendation of the Second Committee [A/54/587/Add.2], adopted **resolution 54/208** without vote [agenda item 99 *(b)*].

Implementation of the outcome of the United Nations Conference on Human Settlements (Habitat II)

The General Assembly,

Recalling its resolution 51/177 of 16 December 1996, in which it endorsed the Istanbul Declaration on Human Settlements and the Habitat Agenda, adopted by the United Nations Conference on Human Settlements (Habitat II) at Istanbul on 14 June 1996,

Recalling also its resolutions 52/190 and 52/192 of 18 December 1997 on the follow-up to the United Nations Conference on Human Settlements (Habitat II) and the future role of the Commission on Human Settlements,

Recalling further its resolution 53/242 of 28 July 1999 concerning environment and human settlements,

Having considered the report of the Commission on Human Settlements on the work of its seventeenth session,

1. *Takes note with appreciation* of the report of the Commission on Human Settlements on the work of its seventeenth session;

2. *Welcomes* the steps taken by the Acting Executive Director of the United Nations Centre for Human Settlements (Habitat) to strengthen the capacity of the Centre, in particular the normative area, and to improve the linkages between the normative and operational activities of the Centre so as to enable it to exercise effectively its vital role as focal point for the implementation of the Habitat Agenda;

3. *Also welcomes* the progress made by the Acting Executive Director in the revitalization of the Centre, and encourages the Executive Director to implement fully, as a matter of urgency, all administrative and financial management reforms, as part of the ongoing revitalization process;

4. *Requests* the Secretary-General to ensure that the staffing of the new organizational structure is completed as a matter of urgency in accordance with the principle of equitable geographical representation and gender balance, including, in particular, improving the status of women in the Secretariat, and bearing in mind the need for recruitment of qualified staff in accordance with the relevant United Nations regulations and rules;

5. *Also requests* the Secretary-General as a matter of urgency to appoint a full-time Executive Director for the Centre in accordance with resolution 53/242;

6. *Takes note* of the increased cooperation and collaboration between the United Nations Centre for Human Settlements (Habitat) and the United Nations Environment Programme within the framework of their respective mandates and separate programmatic, budgetary and organizational identities with a view to improving the effectiveness of their work;

7. *Stresses* the importance of strengthening the United Nations Office at Nairobi as the only United Nations headquarters located in a developing country;

8. *Calls upon* all countries to ensure the provision of sufficient financial resources, on a stable and predictable basis, for the successful implementation of the work programme for the biennium 2000-2001, and reiterates the recognition by the Commission on Human Settlements at its seventeenth session that this implementation will require substantial additional funding and its request to the Executive Director to raise more funds from all sources and to broaden the donor base;

9. *Calls upon* the Secretary-General to provide the necessary resources from the regular budget to the Centre for the biennium 2000-2001 in accordance with current budgetary practices and procedures;

10. *Welcomes* the decision by the Economic and Social Council to discuss human settlements issues at its coordination segment in 2000 and to have as its sectoral theme the coordinated implementation by the United Nations system of the Habitat Agenda, and requests the Secretary-General to ensure that the report submitted to the Council on the question, along with the recommendations of the Council thereon, be made available to the General Assembly for its consideration under the sub-item entitled "Implementation of the outcome of the United Nations Conference on Human Settlements (Habitat II)";

11. *Requests* the Secretary-General to submit to the General Assembly at its fifty-fifth session a report on the implementation of the present resolution;

12. *Decides* to include in the provisional agenda of its fifty-fifth session the sub-item entitled "Implementation of the outcome of the United Nations Conference on Human Settlements (Habitat II)".

Also on 22 December [meeting 87], the Assembly, on the recommendation of the Second Committee [A/54/587/Add.2], adopted **resolution 54/209** without vote [agenda item 99 *(b)*].

Follow-up to the United Nations Conference on Human Settlements (Habitat II)

The General Assembly,

Bearing in mind its resolutions 52/192 of 18 December 1997 on the follow-up to the United Nations Conference on Human Settlements (Habitat II) and the future role of the Commission on Human Settlements and 53/180 of 15 December 1998 on the special session of the General Assembly for an overall review and appraisal of the implementation of the Habitat Agenda,

Noting that the work programme for the biennium 2000-2001 approved by the Commission on Human Settlements at its seventeenth session, in line with resolution 52/192, is organized according to the structure of the Habitat Agenda,

Noting also that the two subprogrammes of the work programme for the biennium 2000-2001 correspond to the goals of the Habitat Agenda of adequate shelter for all and sustainable human settlements development in an urbanizing world,

Recognizing that the overall thrust of the new strategic vision for the United Nations Centre for Human Settlements (Habitat) and its emphasis on two global campaigns, concerning secure tenure and urban governance, are strategic points of entry for effective implementation of the Habitat Agenda,

Reaffirming the role of the Centre as focal point for the implementation of the Habitat Agenda and the need for the Centre adequately to perform this role through the active mobilization and broadening of its network of United Nations, governmental and non-governmental partners,

Stressing the need to provide strategic support to the efforts of local authorities and partners from civil society in the global, regional and local implementation of the Habitat Agenda,

1. *Calls upon* all relevant United Nations organizations and specialized agencies to take initiatives and continue with their specific actions towards the implementation of the Habitat Agenda;

2. *Also calls upon* relevant United Nations organizations and specialized agencies that have not yet done so to identify specific initiatives and actions to be undertaken in preparation for the special session of the General Assembly for an overall review and appraisal of the implementation of the Habitat Agenda;

3. *Invites* the United Nations coordinator system to strengthen its support to the implementation of the Habitat Agenda through, inter alia, assistance in the implementation of national local plans of action based on the full involvement of local authorities and partners from civil society;

4. *Calls upon* all Member States to initiate preparations for reporting on in-country implementation of the Habitat Agenda, in line with the recommendations by the Commission on Human Settlements as described in its resolution 17/1 of 14 May 1999, with a view to contributing fully to the preparatory process for the special session of the General Assembly to be held in the year 2001 for an overall review and appraisal of the implementation of the Habitat Agenda, including the strengthening and activation, wherever necessary, of national coordination mechanisms, inclusive of local authorities and civil society partners, along the models pioneered at the United Nations Conference on Human Settlements (Habitat II);

5. *Invites* all Member States in a position to do so to provide financial resources for the preparatory process for the special session, in particular to enable least developed countries and their national civil-society partners to prepare adequately for, and be fully involved in, the preparatory process and the special session itself.

Commission on Human Settlements

The Commission on Human Settlements, at its seventeenth session (Nairobi, 5-14 May) [A/54/8], adopted 23 resolutions and one decision. By the first resolution [res. 17/1], the Commission proposed a draft resolution for adoption by the General Assembly on the follow-up to Habitat II (see p. 999). It adopted a resolution on assistance for human settlements reconstruction to Latin America and the Caribbean and other regions following recent natural catastrophes and asked the Executive Director to report on the subject in 2001 [res. 17/2]. By a vote of 25 to 1, with 23 abstentions, the Commission adopted a resolution on illegal human settlements in the occupied Palestinian territory [res. 17/9], in which it called on the Executive Director to organize a meeting on the establishment of a human settlements fund for the Palestinian people in the occupied Palestinian territory. The Executive Director was requested to clarify the status of the Committee of Permanent Representatives, to explore the possibilities for its future status and role, and to report thereon in 2001 [res. 17/5]. The Commission asked that urban-rural interdependence be taken into consideration in executing the Centre's work programme for the next biennium [res. 17/10]. Other resolutions dealt with the human settlements needs of countries with economies in transition [res. 17/3] and the elimination of lead in petrol [res. 17/12].

On 14 May [res. 17/20], the Commission approved the 2000-2001 draft work programme [HS/C/17/8] and approved an allocation of $22.8 million for the revised 1998-1999 budget and $23 million for 2000-2001, as presented by the Executive Director in March [HS/C/17/9 & Corr.1], and following comments by ACABQ on the 2000-2001 budget [HS/C/17/9/Add.1].

By **decision 1999/286** of 30 July, the Economic and Social Council took note of the Commission's report.

Global Strategy for Shelter to the Year 2000

The Commission on Human Settlements had before it a February report [HS/C/17/3] containing a review of the implementation during 1997-1998 of the Global Strategy for Shelter to the Year 2000, which was adopted by the General Assembly in resolution 43/181 [YUN 1988, p. 478].

The report stated that, despite the fact that a majority of countries adopted shelter policies in concurrence with the recommendations of the Global Strategy and the Habitat Agenda, progress in carrying out programmes to improve the shelter conditions in low-income groups, particularly in developing countries, had been slow and not facilitated in a sustainable way and on a sufficient scale. The problem was compounded by forced evictions, demolition of informally built settlements and upgrading schemes that often resulted in depriving slum and squatter dwellers of affordable accommodation.

In Africa, rapid urbanization continued to place heavy demands on shelter and services; consequently, shelter conditions continued to deteriorate. Governments in the region focused on the provision of serviced land for shelter production, as well as on upgrading existing informal settlements. In addition to establishing new institutions and improving existing ones in the shelter sector, South Africa established subsidy programmes to cater for the most vulnerable groups and initiated activities in regard to the right to housing. In other African countries (Ghana, Morocco, Namibia, Senegal, Uganda, Zambia, Zimbabwe), there were activities to promote participation and empower communities in shelter provision and upgrading. Shelter-upgrading was initiated in Egypt, Morocco and Senegal.

Provision of serviced land and upgrading activities was a priority in the South-East Asia and the Pacific region, with increased involvement of community-based and non-governmental organizations. Although China continued its extensive housing construction and improvement programmes and developed new housing financing, there was still a serious need for housing, particularly in rapidly growing urban centres. The housing shortage in India by 2000 was estimated to be some 41 million units, with more than 15 million needed in urban areas. The Government was working with UN organizations and the Asian Development Bank to implement the shelter-related recommendations of the Habitat Agenda. In Japan, improvements in residential standards were accomplished. The participation of citizens' movements and of civil-society organizations in shelter-development processes increased in Nepal and the Republic of Korea. In Pakistan, the Philippines and Thailand, communities and civil-society organizations contributed to shelter and environmental development with new initiatives. Saudi Arabia continued its massive low-income housing construction programme to settle new urban residents.

Western Europe and other highly industrialized regions focused on improving residential standards, and revitalization and modernization of inner-city housing. Facilitating reforms in the housing, building and financial sectors had been the main thrust of activities in Eastern and Central Europe. In Latin America and the Caribbean, actions related to shelter development focused on rehabilitation, the link between poverty reduction and housing programmes, and measures to address the needs of the lowest-income groups. Several countries initiated new financial and regulatory mechanisms. The regional commissions initiated a variety of activities related to human settlements and shelter development and the UN system continued activities to support Member States in improving shelter and services.

Commission action. In May [res. 17/13], the Commission reconfirmed that in 2001 it would carry out the final review of the Global Strategy and decided to report the results of the review to the General Assembly at its special session on the Habitat Agenda in June 2001. It asked Governments to prepare final reports on the Strategy. The Executive Director was requested to conduct a review of the Strategy and to incorporate the results into the Commission's report on its 2001 session.

Follow-up to Agenda 21

On 14 May [res. 17/15], the Commission on Human Settlements, following consideration of a January report of the UNCHS Executive Director on follow-up to the General Assembly's special session to review Agenda 21 [HS/C/17/4], asked him to assist Governments by intensifying research and monitoring and evaluating progress in the Programme for the Further Implementation of Agenda 21 [YUN 1997, p. 792] at the local level; promoting information exchange and the transfer of expertise regarding sustainable human-settlements development; and building capacity and mobilizing support to strengthen the means of implementation of developing countries and countries with economies in transition. He was asked to report in 2001.

On the same date [res. 17/19], the Commission decided to include in the agenda of its session in 2001 the item "Role of youth in the implementation of the Habitat Agenda and Agenda 21".

UN Centre for Human Settlements

Activities

UNCHS operational activities in 1999 were focused on supporting Governments in developing policies and strategies to create and strengthen a self-reliant management capacity at the national and local levels. Technical and managerial expertise was provided to assess human settlements development, constraints and opportunities; identify and analyse policy options; design and implement housing and urban development projects; and mobilize national resources, as well as external support to improve human settlements conditions. The national capacity-building process involved not only central government institutions but also other stakeholders, such as community-based and non-governmental organizations, universities and research institutions, as well as local governments and municipalities. Emphasis was also placed on strengthening the monitoring capacities of Governments in human settlements management.

In accordance with the 1998-1999 work programme, UNCHS focused on promoting housing for all, improving urban governance, reducing urban poverty, improving the living environment and managing disaster mitigation and post-conflict rehabilitation. Acting as a catalyst in the mobilization of technical cooperation, the Centre supported the implementation of the Habitat Agenda at local, national and regional levels.

As at the fourth quarter of 1999 [HS/C/18/INF/3], UNCHS had 217 technical programmes and projects under execution in 80 countries, of which 62 were in the least developed countries. Approximately 59 per cent of the financing for those projects came from funds-in-trust with UNCHS, 25 per cent from UNDP and 14 per cent from government and third-party cost-sharing.

Cooperation with UNEP

A joint progress report of the UNEP and UNCHS Executive Directors [HS/C/17/10] highlighted cooperation between the two entities in the assessment of environmental conditions in human settlements; the environmental aspects of policies, planning and management of rural and urban human settlements; environmentally sound and appropriate human settlements technology; and research, training and information dissemination on environmentally sound human settlements planning and management. The report outlined future prospects for cooperation.

Welcoming the Secretary-General's 1998 report on environment and human settlements [YUN 1998, p. 981], the Commission on Human Settlements, on 14 May [res. 17/6], supported his proposal to establish an environmental management group to coordinate the environmental and human settlements activities of the UN system. It also supported proposals to strengthen the Nairobi location and welcomed the proposal that the Centre should strengthen its normative core activities consistent with the new strategic vision (see below), which would allow it to develop into a centre of excellence on adequate shelter for all and sustainable urban development. The Commission recommended that the Centre maintain its operational support within the framework of the Habitat Agenda and the Centre's strategic vision, agreed with the proposal that the Commission should devote particular attention to its own role in monitoring the Agenda's implementation, and welcomed the recommendations concerning the need to engage constructively NGOs and civil society in UN work.

Also on 14 May [res. 17/23], the Commission asked the Executive Director to explore and possibly enter into an inter-agency agreement for UNEP to extend the services of its Ombudsman Unit to UNCHS until the Commission's eighteenth (2001) session. It decided to review in 2001 the Ombudsman services and the financial implications to the Centre of continuing the services.

On the same date [res. 17/22], the Commission requested the Executive Director to expand cooperation between UNCHS and UNEP, particularly in the Sustainable Cities Progamme, the project on managing water for Africa cities and the Urban Environment Forum. He was also asked to strengthen cooperation between the two organizations in media outreach on public information and awareness-building activities.

Revitalization

The Commission on Human Settlements considered reports of the Executive Director on the revitalization of UNCHS. The revitalization team, which was appointed in 1998 to assist him with UNCHS reform, established two working groups—one on a strategic vision for the Centre [HS/C/

17/2/Add.2] and the second on management and administrative matters [HS/C/17/2].

Working group one proposed that the aim of the Centre should be to identify global priorities and lead campaigns that would improve the quality of life and give meaning to the notion of sustainable cities. It was recommended that UNCHS confirm its status as the UN agency for cities, adopt the style and profile of the global advocacy agency in its field of operations, and make clear that its efforts would be measured by the positive impact on the poor, their integration into city-wide policies and strategies, and its focus on reducing urban poverty. A further suggestion was that equity and social justice would be used as basic principles underpinning the work of UNCHS and that women would be the primary indicator of the success of its interventions and an explicit focus for its policy work. The working group recommended that two issues should form the basis for two global campaigns: a global campaign for secure tenure and a global campaign on urban governance.

The main recommendations of working group two were the establishment of a planning and coordination office; the rationalization of funding and resource mobilization; identification of potential joint synergies with UNEP and UNON; and regularization of particular contracts. In response to the recommendations, a new Planning and Coordination Office was established. An inter-agency working group was set up to address recommendations dealing with services shared jointly by UNEP and UNON, and to develop proposals for consideration by the revitalization team.

Commission action. On 14 May [res. 17/7], the Commission mandated the Executive Director to implement the new strategic vision, through the subprogrammes on adequate shelter for all and on sustainable urban development and through the global campaigns on secure tenure and on urban governance. It called on him to seek States' views on catch-phrases that could assist in the mobilization of support for the Habitat Agenda and to report in 2001. The Bureau of the Commission was asked to monitor the revitalization process and its results in implementing the prioritized UNCHS work programme and to report in 2001. On the same date [dec. 17/24], the Commission decided that it would consider the themes of security of tenure and urban governance at its eighteenth (2001) session. It also decided that the draft outlines for the proposed themes [HS/C/17/13] would be presented to it in 2001.

Taking note of the UNCHS revitalization and reform and following consideration of a report of the Executive Director [HS/C/17/2], the Commission, on 14 May [res. 17/4], asked him to develop a strategy for representation of the Centre in the regions, its decentralized functions and its offices other than in Nairobi. Noting the offer made by Turkey to host a UNCHS office in Istanbul, it asked the Executive Director to consult with the Government and to report in 2001.

In related action [res. 17/11], the Commission asked the Executive Director to develop by 2000 a gender action plan to implement General Assembly resolution 53/119 on improvement of the status of women in the Secretariat [YUN 1998, p. 1316], and urged him to use the revitalization process to implement it. He was also asked to report in 2001.

State of the world's cities

In 1999, the Commission on Human Settlements had before it a March report of the Executive Director entitled *The State of the World's Cities* [HS/C/17/2/Add.1], which represented a new approach to the way the UN system gathered, managed, analysed and disseminated information about the world's cities. The report summarized information on global trends, their urban impacts and policy responses.

On 14 May [res. 17/8], the Commission called on UNCHS to continue, in cooperation with capacity-building partners, the implementation of an Internet-based urban information and knowledge system to strengthen the ability of Governments, local authorities and key partners to gain access to and make use of information in order to monitor and assess urban conditions and trends. The Executive Director was asked to synthesize information and knowledge from the system in a summary report entitled *The State of the World's Cities* prior to the Commission's biennial sessions and to produce a report on the state of the world's cities for the Assembly to review in 2001. He was also asked to facilitate a process to establish universal urban information standards and protocols and to produce an urban classification system. The Commission invited the Executive Director to consider consolidating the report *The State of the World's Cities: 2001* with the third edition of the *Global Report on Human Settlements.*

Chapter VIII

Population

In 1999, the General Assembly held its twenty-first special session to consider progress in implementing the Programme of Action adopted by the 1994 International Conference on Population and Development. The year of that five-year review, known as ICPD+5, also saw the day of 6 billion—12 October—when it was estimated that the 6 billionth baby was born. A third population milestone in 1999 was the thirtieth anniversary of the founding of the United Nations Population Fund (UNFPA), the largest internationally funded source of population assistance and the lead United Nations organization for advancing the ICPD Programme of Action.

On 2 July, the special session adopted key actions for the further implementation of the Programme of Action, which called for intensified efforts in the areas of reproductive and sexual health; maternal mortality; the reproductive health needs of adolescents; reducing abortion and addressing the health consequences of unsafe abortion; prevention of HIV/AIDS; gender issues; and education. It recommended new benchmarks in a number of areas. The Commission on Population and Development acted as the preparatory committee for the special session.

In addition to organizing round tables and technical symposiums as inputs into ICPD+5, UNFPA carried out a field inquiry of 114 developing and 18 developed countries to assess progress made since 1994. The year also saw a major effort by UNFPA to develop a multi-year funding framework. The Fund's expenditures on country and intercountry programmes in 1999 totalled $187.1 million.

At its thirty-second session, the Commission on Population and Development considered the central theme of population growth, structure and distribution, with special emphasis on sustained economic growth and sustainable development, including education. On the Commission's recommendation, the Economic and Social Council adopted a resolution on that subject in July. In December, the General Assembly adopted a resolution on international migration and development, in which it urged Member States and the United Nations system to strengthen international cooperation in order to address the root causes of migration, especially those related to poverty.

During the year, the United Nations Population Division continued to analyse demographic trends and population policies and to prepare and publish population estimates and projections.

Follow-up to the 1994 Conference on Population and Development

Twenty-first special session (ICPD+ 5)

The General Assembly held its twenty-first special session from 30 June to 2 July to review and appraise the implementation of the Programme of Action adopted by the International Conference on Population and Development (ICPD), which was held in Cairo, Egypt, in 1994 [YUN 1994, p. 955]. The 16-chapter Programme of Action identified a range of demographic and social goals, to be achieved over a 20-year period, for population growth and sustainable development, poverty eradication, gender equality and the family, among other issues. The special session, which was held in accordance with Assembly resolution 52/188 [YUN 1997, p. 1075], culminated in the adoption of key actions for the further implementation of the Programme of Action. The key actions made a number of noteworthy advances, calling attention to population and development concerns and noting the linkages between population, economic growth and environment. The Assembly recognized the implications of changing age structure and the ageing of the population, and underscored the urgent need for policies and programmes to deal with the causes of international migration, internal migration and urbanization, and the resultant dislocations. Governments were called on to ensure that the human rights of women and girls, particularly the freedom from coercion, discrimination and violence, including harmful practices and sexual exploitation, were respected, protected and promoted through the development, implementation and effective enforcement of gender-sensitive policies and legislation. The special session called for intensified action in the following areas: reproductive and sexual health;

maternal mortality; the reproductive health needs of adolescents; reducing abortion and addressing the health consequences of unsafe abortion; prevention of HIV/AIDS; gender issues; and education. It recommended new benchmarks for education, primary health care and family planning facilities, maternal mortality, contraception and HIV/AIDS prevention (see full text below).

Preparations for the session were discussed by the Commission on Population and Development in March/April and June (see below).

The twenty-first special session—known as ICPD+5—was addressed by 152 Member States, 10 observers and three non-governmental organizations (NGOs). Addressing the session, the Secretary-General emphasized the connection between population and development and praised ICPD for promoting a fuller understanding of those interactions. He underscored the linkage between sexual and reproductive health and human rights and urged that efforts be made to implement the Programme of Action fully, particularly the financial resource levels agreed to in Cairo.

In a decision on organizational arrangements for the session, the Assembly established an Ad Hoc Committee of the Whole to discuss the overall review and appraisal of the implementation of the Programme of Action (**decision S-21/21**). In other action, the Assembly appointed the members of the Credentials Committee (**decision S-21/11**); approved the report of the Credentials Committee (**resolution S-21/1**); elected the President of the Assembly (**decision S-21/12**); elected the Vice-Presidents of the Assembly (**decision S-21/13**); elected the Chairmen of the Main Committees (**decision S-21/14**); and elected the officers of the Ad Hoc Committee (**decision S-21/15**) (see APPENDIX III for details). The Assembly also adopted the agenda for the special session (**decision S-21/22**) and decided that three NGOs might make statements in the debate in plenary (**decision S-21/23**).

Preparatory meetings. The Commission on Population and Development acting as the preparatory committee for the twenty-first special session of the General Assembly met in New York from 24 March to 1 April [A/S-21/2]. As authorized by the Assembly in **decision 53/482** of 8 June, the Commission held a resumed session from 24 to 29 June to finalize its work [A/S-21/2/Add.1]. The Commission took action on the accreditation of NGOs and transmitted the text on proposals for key actions for the further implementation of the Programme of Action to the special session [A/S-21/2/Add.2].

The International Forum for the Operational Review and Appraisal of the Implementation of the Programme of Action of the International Conference on Population and Development (known as the Hague Forum) (The Hague, Netherlands, 8-12 February) [E/CN.9/1999/PC/3] drew on the outcomes of the technical and regional meetings held in 1998 [YUN 1998, p. 1002] in preparation for ICPD+5 to formulate operational recommendations for the next phases of implementing the Programme of Action. The Forum was preceded by three meetings of partner groups, namely, the International Forum of Parliamentarians on the International Conference on Population and Development Review (The Hague, 4-6 February) [E/CN.9/1999/PC/5], the NGO Forum (6-7 February) and the Youth Forum (6-7 February).

GENERAL ASSEMBLY ACTION

On 2 July [meeting 9], the General Assembly, on the recommendation of the Ad Hoc Committee of the Whole [A/S-21/5/Rev.1], adopted **resolution S-21/2** without vote [agenda items 8 & 9].

Key actions for the further implementation of the Programme of Action of the International Conference on Population and Development

The General Assembly

Adopts the key actions for the further implementation of the Programme of Action of the International Conference on Population and Development annexed to the present resolution.

ANNEX

Key actions for the further implementation of the Programme of Action of the International Conference on Population and Development

I. Preamble

1. The Programme of Action of the International Conference on Population and Development, approved by consensus on 13 September 1994, as contained in the report of the Conference and as endorsed by the General Assembly in its resolution 49/128 of 19 December 1994, marked the beginning of a new era in population and development. The objective of the landmark agreement reached at the Conference was to raise the quality of life and the well-being of human beings and to promote human development by recognizing the interrelationships between population and development policies and programmes aiming to achieve poverty eradication, sustained economic growth in the context of sustainable development, education, especially for girls, gender equity and equality, infant, child and maternal mortality reduction, the provision of universal access to reproductive health services, including family planning and sexual health, sustainable patterns of consumption and production, food security, human resources development and the guarantee of all human rights, including the right to development as a universal and inalienable right and an integral part of fundamental human rights.

2. The Programme of Action acknowledges that the goal of the empowerment and autonomy of women and the improvement of their political, social, economic and health status is a highly important end in itself and

is essential for the achievement of sustainable development. Greater investments in health and education services for all people, in particular women, to enable the full and equal participation of women in civil, cultural, economic, political and social life are essential to achieving the objectives of the Programme of Action.

3. The Programme of Action emphasizes that everyone has the right to education, which shall be directed to the full development of human resources, and human dignity and potential, with particular attention to women and the girl child, and therefore everyone should be provided with the education necessary to meet basic human needs and to exercise human rights. It calls for the elimination of all practices that discriminate against women, and affirms that advancing gender equality and equity and the empowerment of women, the elimination of all kinds of violence against women and ensuring women's ability to control their own fertility are cornerstones of population and development-related programmes. It affirms that the human rights of women and the girl child are an inalienable, integral and indivisible part of universal human rights. It further affirms that reproductive rights embrace certain human rights that are already recognized in national laws, international human rights documents, and other consensus documents. These rights rest on the recognition of the basic right of all couples and individuals to decide freely and responsibly the number, spacing and timing of their children and to have the information and means to do so, and the right to attain the highest standard of sexual and reproductive health. It also includes their right to make decisions concerning reproduction free of discrimination, coercion and violence, as expressed in human rights documents. In the exercise of this right, they should take into account the needs of their living and future children and their responsibilities towards the community. The promotion of the responsible exercise of those rights for all people should be the fundamental basis for government- and community-supported policies and programmes in the area of reproductive health, including family planning.

4. The International Conference on Population and Development and its implementation must be seen as being closely related to the outcome of and coordinated follow-up to the other major United Nations conferences held in the 1990s. Progress in the implementation of the Programme of Action should be supportive of and consistent with the integrated follow-up to all major United Nations conferences and summits.

5. The implementation of the recommendations contained in the Programme of Action and those contained in the present document is the sovereign right of each country, consistent with national laws and development priorities, with full respect for the various religious and ethical values and cultural backgrounds of its people, and in conformity with universally recognized international human rights.

6. The Programme of Action recommended a set of interdependent quantitative goals and objectives. These included universal access to primary education, with special attention to closing the gender gap in primary and secondary school education, wherever it exists; universal access to primary health care; universal access to a full range of comprehensive reproductive health-care services, including family planning, as set out in paragraph 7.6 of the Programme of Action; reductions in infant, child and maternal morbidity and mortality; and increased life expectancy. The Programme of Action also proposed a set of qualitative goals that are mutually supportive and of critical importance to achieving the quantitative goals and objectives.

7. The Programme of Action articulates a comprehensive approach to issues of population and development, identifying a range of demographic and social goals to be achieved over a 20-year period. While the Programme of Action does not quantify goals for population growth, structure and distribution, it reflects the view that an early stabilization of world population would make a crucial contribution to realizing the overarching objective of sustainable development.

8. According to the United Nations estimates and projections, the world's population will exceed 6 billion for the first time in 1999, of which nearly 80 per cent will be living in developing countries. Depending on the quality and the magnitude of the actions taken over the next five to ten years in the areas of population policy and reproductive health, including the provision of family planning services, world population will total somewhere between 6.9 billion and 7.4 billion in 2015. The majority of the world's countries are converging in a pattern of low birth and death rates, but since these countries are proceeding at different speeds, the emerging picture is that of a world facing increasingly diverse demographic situations. The world's reproductive age population continues to grow at a slightly higher rate than the world's population as a whole, reflecting the large number of young people entering their childbearing years. The Programme of Action rightly emphasizes the need to integrate population concerns fully into development strategies and planning, taking into account the interrelationship of population issues with the goals of poverty eradication, food security, adequate shelter, employment and basic social services for all, with the objective of improving the quality of life of present and future generations through appropriate population and development policies and programmes.

9. The five-year review of progress shows that the implementation of the recommendations of the Programme of Action has shown positive results. Many countries have taken steps to integrate population concerns into their development strategies. Mortality in most countries has continued to fall in the five years since the adoption of the Programme of Action. The Conference's broad-based definition of reproductive health is being accepted by an increasing number of countries and steps are being taken to provide comprehensive services in many countries, with increasing emphasis being given to quality of care. The rising use of family planning methods indicates that there is greater accessibility to family planning and that more and more couples and individuals are able to choose the number and spacing of their children. Many countries, both countries of origin and countries of destination, have taken important steps, including, inter alia, at the regional level, aimed at better managing international migration flows through bilateral and multinational agreements. In addition, many civil society organizations are contributing to the formulation and implementation of policies, programmes and projects on

their own or in partnerships with governmental and intergovernmental organizations as well as the private sector.

10. However, for some countries and regions, progress has been limited and, in some cases, setbacks have occurred. Women and the girl child continue to face discrimination. The human immunodeficiency virus/acquired immunodeficiency syndrome (HIV/AIDS) pandemic has led to rises in mortality in many countries, in particular in sub-Saharan Africa. Mortality and morbidity among adults and children from infectious, parasitic and water-borne diseases, such as tuberculosis, malaria and schistosomiasis, continue to take their toll. Maternal mortality and morbidity remain unacceptably high. Adolescents remain particularly vulnerable to reproductive and sexual risks. Millions of couples and individuals still lack access to reproductive health information and services. An increase in adult mortality, especially among men, is a matter of special concern for countries with economies in transition and some developing countries. The impact of the financial crises in countries of Asia and elsewhere, as well as the long-term and large-scale environmental problems in Central Asia and other regions, is affecting the health and well-being of individuals and limiting progress in implementing the Programme of Action. Despite the goal of the Programme of Action of reducing pressures leading to refugee movements and displaced persons, the plight of refugees and displaced persons remains unacceptable.

11. Achieving the goals and objectives of the Programme of Action will require sufficient domestic and external resources, committed government action and effective, transparent partnerships. In order to implement further the Programme of Action, a number of financial, institutional and human-resource constraints must be overcome. Implementing the key actions of the present document and addressing the full range of recommendations of the Programme of Action will require greater political commitment, development of national capacity, increased international assistance and increased domestic resources. Effective priority-setting, within each national context, is an equally critical factor for the successful implementation of the Programme of Action.

12. In implementing and taking forward the Programme of Action, an integrated approach should be adopted towards policy design, development planning, service delivery, research and monitoring to utilize scarce resources for greater added value and to promote intersectoral coordination.

13. The present document draws on the results and findings of intergovernmental reviews under the auspices of the United Nations, including the annual and quinquennial review and appraisal by the Commission on Population and Development and meetings and reports of the United Nations regional commissions regarding progress made and constraints faced in the implementation of the Programme of Action.

14. In recommending the key actions contained in the present document, Governments affirm their renewed and sustained commitment to the principles, goals and objectives of the Programme of Action. Governments and civil society at the national level, in partnership with the international community, should join in efforts to ensure that the goals and objectives of the International Conference on Population and Development are accomplished as soon as possible, with special attention to those that should be met within the twenty-year time frame of the Programme of Action.

II. Population and development concerns

A. *Population, economic development and the environment*

15. Governments should:

(a) Intensify efforts to equip planners and decision makers with a better understanding of the relationships among population, poverty, gender inequity and inequality, health, education, the environment, financial and human resources, and development; and re-examine recent research concerning the relationships among reductions in fertility and economic growth and its equitable distribution;

(b) Draw attention to and promote linkages among macroeconomic, environmental and social policies through increased dialogue among finance ministries and other relevant ministries;

(c) Intensify efforts to implement legislative and administrative measures as well as to promote public education, with special attention to youth, about the need for sustainable production and consumption patterns; foster sustainable natural resource use; and work concertedly to prevent environmental degradation within their countries;

(d) Increase investments in the social sector, especially health and education, as an effective strategy for development;

(e) Develop and expand integrated community-based approaches to sustainable development.

16. Governments, in cooperation with the international community, should reaffirm their commitment to promoting an enabling environment to achieve sustained economic growth in the context of sustainable development and to eradicating poverty, with a special emphasis on gender, including by promoting an open, equitable, secure, non-discriminatory and predictable trading system; stimulating direct investment; reducing the debt burden; and ensuring that structural adjustment programmes are responsive to social, economic and environmental concerns. Population-related goals and policies outlined in the Programme of Action need to be reflected, as appropriate, in international agreements in such areas as environment and trade.

17. Governments of developing countries and countries with economies in transition, with the assistance of the international community, especially donors, including through bilateral and multilateral financial support, should ensure that social safety nets are implemented, especially in those countries most affected by the recent global financial crisis, and ensure that they are adequately funded.

18. Governments of developing countries and countries with economies in transition, with the assistance of the international community, especially donors, should:

(a) Continue to support declines in infant and child mortality rates by strengthening infant and child health programmes that emphasize improved prenatal care and nutrition, including breastfeeding, unless it is medically contraindicated, universal immunization, oral rehydration therapies, clean water sources, infectious disease prevention, reduction of exposure to toxic substances, and improvements in household sanita-

tion; and by strengthening maternal health services, quality family-planning services to help couples to time and space births, and efforts to prevent transmission of HIV/AIDS and other sexually transmitted diseases;

(b) Strengthen health-care systems to respond to priority demands on them, taking into account the financial realities of countries and the need to ensure that resources are focused on the health needs of people in poverty;

(c) Determine the causes of the stagnation or increase in mortality levels among adult populations and develop special policies and programmes on health promotion where such stagnation or increase is observed, especially among women in reproductive age groups and males in productive age groups;

(d) Ensure that poverty eradication programmes are targeted particularly at females and that priority is given to female-headed households;

(e) Develop innovative ways to provide more effective assistance to strengthen families in extreme poverty, such as providing micro-credit for poor families and individuals;

(f) Undertake policies and programmes that seek to ensure a level of consumption that meets the basic needs of the poor and disadvantaged.

19. Measures should be taken to strengthen food, nutrition and agricultural policies and programmes, and fair trade relations, with special attention to the creation and strengthening of food security at all levels.

20. Governments should promote and protect the rights of indigenous people with particular regard to their cultures, resources, belief systems, land rights and languages.

B. *Changing age structure and ageing of the population*

21. Governments should:

(a) Continue to examine the economic and social implications of demographic change and how they relate to development planning concerns and the needs of individuals;

(b) Meet the needs of youth, especially young women, with the active support, guidance and participation, as appropriate, of parents, families, communities, non-governmental organizations and the private sector, by investing in the development and implementation of national, regional and local plans. In this context, priority should be given to programmes such as education, income-generating opportunities, vocational training, and health services, including those related to sexual and reproductive health. Youth should be fully involved in the design, implementation and evaluation of such programmes and plans. These policies, plans and programmes should be implemented in line with the commitments made at the International Conference on Population and Development and in conformity with the relevant international conventions and agreements. Emphasis should be placed on fostering intergenerational dialogue through better communication and mutual support;

(c) Support research and develop comprehensive strategies at the national, regional and local levels to meet, where appropriate, the challenges of population ageing. Invest more resources in gender-sensitive research as well as in training and capacity-building in social policies and health care of older persons, especially the elderly poor, paying special attention to the economic and social security of older persons, in particular older women; affordable, accessible and appropriate health-care services; the human rights and dignity of older persons and the productive and useful roles that they can play in society; support systems to enhance the ability of families and communities to care for older family members; the ability of the elderly to care for family members and community victims of HIV/AIDS; and generational solidarity with the goal of maintaining and improving social cohesion.

22. Governments and civil society, including non-governmental organizations and the private sector, should create opportunities and remove barriers that hinder elderly women and men from continuing to contribute their skills to their families, to the workforce and to their communities, in order to help to foster intergenerational solidarity and enhance the well-being of society. This will require life-long education and opportunities for retraining.

23. The United Nations system should, provided that additional resources are made available, document the positive experience of policies and programmes in the area of ageing of men and women and disseminate information and recommendations about those practices. Countries should be enabled, through adequate training and capacity-building, to evolve their own policies appropriate to their cultures, traditions and socio-economic circumstances.

C. *International migration*

24. Governments in both countries of origin and countries of destination, including through international cooperation, are urged:

(a) To intensify efforts to protect the human rights and dignity of migrants irrespective of their legal status; provide effective protection for migrants; provide basic health and social services, including sexual and reproductive health and family-planning services; facilitate family reunification of documented migrants; monitor violations of the human rights of migrants; effectively enforce the laws applicable to the protection of human rights; and ensure the social and economic integration of documented migrants, especially of those who have acquired the right to long-term residence in the country of destination, and their equal treatment before the law. Non-governmental organizations should play a valuable role in meeting the needs of migrants;

(b) To prevent trafficking in migrants, in particular women and children subjected to forced labour or sexual or commercial exploitation; to develop clear penalties for such trafficking and migrant smuggling, backed by effective administrative procedures and laws, ensuring punishment of those who commit such crimes; and to finalize as soon as possible the trafficking and smuggling protocols which are currently being negotiated by the Commission on Crime Prevention and Criminal Justice;

(c) To support and ensure effective follow-up to bilateral and multilateral initiatives, including regional and subregional consultation processes, where appropriate, to develop national policies and cooperative strategies to maximize the benefits and manage the challenges posed by international migration;

(d) To conduct public information campaigns on migration in both countries of origin and countries of

destination so that racist and xenophobic attitudes in countries of destination are combated and so that potential migrants fully understand the implications of the decisions to move;

(e) To consider ratifying or acceding to the International Convention on the Protection of the Rights of All Migrant Workers and Members of Their Families, if they have not already done so.

25. The international community should extend assistance and support to programmes in developing countries that host the majority of refugees and displaced persons. Assistance should also be extended to programmes in countries lacking the capacity to manage large flows of migrants and displaced persons.

26. All States are encouraged to become parties to the 1951 Convention and the 1967 Protocol relating to the Status of Refugees and put in place effective asylum procedures.

27. Governments, with the assistance of the international community, should intensify their efforts to improve data collection and analysis, including gender-based analysis, in the areas of international migration and, in this context, promote the implementation of the United Nations recommendations on statistics of international migration; encourage studies designed to assess the causes of international migration and displacement and the positive contribution that migration makes to both countries of origin and countries of destination; and improve understanding of the links between relevant factors that have an impact on international migration.

28. The international community should channel adequate support to effective programmes to address the causes of movement of refugees and displaced persons.

29. In planning and implementing refugee assistance activities, special attention should be given to the specific needs of refugee women and children and elderly refugees. Adequate and sufficient international support should be extended to meet the basic needs of refugee populations, including the provision of access to adequate accommodation, education, protection from violence, health services, including reproductive health and family planning, and other basic social services, including clean water, sanitation, and nutrition. Refugees should respect the laws and regulations of their countries of asylum. Governments are urged to abide by international law concerning refugees, inter alia, by respecting the principle of non-refoulement. In acknowledging refugees' rights to repatriation, their return and integration should be facilitated in cooperation with relevant international organizations.

D. *Internal migration, population distribution and urban agglomerations*

30. Governments should carry out research to strengthen the understanding of the factors, trends and characteristics of internal migration and geographical distribution of the population in order to provide grounds for the formulation of effective population distribution policy.

31. Governments should improve the management and delivery of services for the growing urban agglomerations and put in place enabling legislative and administrative instruments and adequate financial resources to meet the needs of all citizens, especially the urban poor, internal migrants, older persons and the disabled.

32. Governments should strongly reaffirm the call in the Programme of Action that population distribution policies should be consistent with such international instruments as the Geneva Convention relative to the Protection of Civilian Persons in Time of War, of 12 August 1949, including article 49 thereof.

33. Governments should strongly reaffirm the call in the Programme of Action that countries should address the causes of internal displacement, including environmental degradation, natural disasters, armed conflict and forced resettlement, and establish the necessary mechanisms to protect and assist displaced persons, including, where possible, compensation for damages, especially for those who are not able to return to their normal place of residence in the short term and, where appropriate, facilitate their return and reintegration, with special attention to the needs of women and children.

E. *Population, development and education*

34. Governments and civil society, with the assistance of the international community, should, as quickly as possible, and in any case before 2015, meet the goal of the International Conference on Population and Development of achieving universal access to primary education, eliminate the gender gap in primary and secondary education by 2005 and strive to ensure that by 2010 the net primary school enrolment ratio for children of both sexes will be at least 90 per cent, compared with an estimated 85 per cent in 2000. Special efforts should be made to increase the retention rates of girls in primary and secondary school. Parents should be sensitized to the value of education of children, particularly of girls, so that the girls do achieve their full potential.

35. Governments, in particular of developing countries, with the assistance of the international community, should:

(a) Expand youth and adult education and lifelong culture- and gender-sensitive learning policies and programmes, with particular attention to migrants, indigenous people and people with disabilities;

(b) Include at all levels, as appropriate, of formal and non-formal schooling, education about population and health issues, including sexual and reproductive health issues, in order to implement further the Programme of Action in terms of promoting the well-being of adolescents, enhancing gender equality and equity as well as responsible sexual behaviour, and protecting them from early and unwanted pregnancy, sexually transmitted diseases, including HIV/AIDS, and sexual abuse, incest and violence; and ensure the active involvement and participation of parents, youth, community leaders and organizations for the sustainability, increased coverage and effectiveness of such programmes;

(c) Reduce the rate of illiteracy of women and men, at least halving it for women and girls by 2005, compared with the rate in 1990;

(d) Promote the achievement of functional literacy for adults as well as children, where schooling remains unavailable;

(e) Continue to give high priority to investments in education and training in development budgets;

(f) Provide adequately equipped facilities by rehabilitating existing schools and building new ones.

36. The Programme of Action recognized that greater public knowledge, understanding and commitment at all levels, from the individual to the international, are vital to the achievement of its goals and objectives. To this end, ensuring access to and use of modern communication technology, including satellite transmission and other communication mechanisms, should be studied and appropriate action taken as a means to address the barriers to education in developing countries, in particular, the least developed countries, with assistance from the international community.

F. *Data systems, including indicators*

37. Governments, in collaboration with research institutions and non-governmental organizations, as well as with the assistance of the international community, including donors, should strengthen national information systems to produce reliable statistics on a broad range of population, environment and development indicators in a timely manner. The indicators should include, inter alia, poverty rates at the community level; women's access to social and economic resources; enrolment and retention of girls and boys in schools; access to sexual and reproductive health services disaggregated by population sub-groups, including indigenous people; and gender sensitivity in sexual and reproductive health services, including family planning. In addition, in consultation with indigenous people, Governments should establish and strengthen national statistics and data collection concerning the health of indigenous people, including sexual and reproductive health and their determinants. All data systems should ensure availability of age- and sex-disaggregated data, which are crucial for translating policy into strategies that address age and gender concerns and for developing appropriate age- and gender-impact indicators for monitoring progress. Governments should also collect and disseminate the quantitative and qualitative data needed to assess the status of male and female reproductive health, including in urban areas, and to design, implement, monitor and evaluate action programmes. Special attention should be given to maternal mortality and morbidity, as this database remains inadequate. Health and reproductive health data should be disaggregated by income and poverty status to identify the specific health profile and needs of people living in poverty and as a basis for focusing resources and subsidies on those who need them most.

38. The United Nations system and donors should be specifically urged to strengthen the capacity of developing countries, particularly the least developed countries, and those with economies in transition, to undertake censuses and surveys on a regular basis so as to improve vital registration systems, and to develop innovative and cost-effective solutions for meeting data requirements, especially for regular monitoring of the implementation of the goals of the International Conference on Population and Development, including improved estimates of maternal mortality.

III. Gender equality, equity and empowerment of women

A. *Promotion and protection of women's human rights*

39. Governments should ensure that the human rights of women and girls are respected, protected and promoted through the development, implementation and effective enforcement of gender-sensitive policies and legislation. All Governments are encouraged to sign, ratify and implement the Convention on the Elimination of All Forms of Discrimination against Women and are also encouraged to promote consideration by the Economic and Social Council and the General Assembly of the Optional Protocol thereto, and interested States parties are encouraged to work towards removing all existing reservations that are incompatible with the objective and purpose of the Convention. In the implementation of the goals of the Programme of Action and those of other United Nations conferences, measures aimed at promoting and achieving gender equality and equity in a systematic and comprehensive manner should be coordinated and harmonized.

40. The implementation of population and development policies by Governments should continue to incorporate reproductive rights in accordance with paragraphs 1.15, 7.3 and 8.25 of the Programme of Action. Governments should take strong measures to promote the human rights of women. Governments are encouraged to strengthen, as appropriate, the reproductive and sexual health as well as the reproductive rights focus on population and development policies and programmes. The work of relevant United Nations bodies on indicators for the promotion and protection of the human rights of women should incorporate issues related to sexual and reproductive health. Governments should ensure the protection and promotion of the rights of adolescents, including married adolescent girls, to reproductive health education, information and care. Countries should establish mechanisms for consultation with all relevant groups, including women's organizations. In this context, Governments are urged to incorporate human rights into both formal and informal education processes.

41. Governments, civil society and the United Nations system should advocate for the human rights of women and the girl child. Governments, in reporting to the human rights treaty bodies, are encouraged to consult, as appropriate, with civil society on and promote civil society awareness of the reporting process, to ensure the broadest representation in the area of human rights, including reproductive rights.

42. Governments should promote and protect the human rights of the girl child and young women, which include economic and social rights as well as freedom from coercion, discrimination and violence, including harmful practices and sexual exploitation. Governments should review all legislation and amend and revoke that which discriminates against the girl child and young women.

B. *The empowerment of women*

43. Governments should establish mechanisms to accelerate women's equal participation and equitable representation at all levels of the political process and public life in each community and society and enable women to articulate their concerns and needs and ensure the full and equal participation of women in decision-making processes in all spheres of life. Governments and civil society should take actions to eliminate attitudes and practices that discriminate against and subordinate girls and women and that reinforce gender inequality.

44. Governments should take measures to promote the fulfilment of girls' and women's potential through education, skills development and the eradication of illiteracy for all girls and women without discrimination of any kind, giving paramount importance to the elimination of poverty and ill health. Governments, in collaboration with civil society, should take the necessary measures to ensure universal access, on the basis of equality between women and men, to appropriate, affordable and quality health care for women throughout their life cycle.

45. Governments should take every possible action to remove all gender gaps and inequalities pertaining to women's livelihoods and participation in the labour market through the creation of employment with secure incomes, which has been shown to advance women's empowerment and enhance their reproductive health. Legislation ensuring equal pay for equal work or for work of equal value should be instituted and enforced.

C. *Gender perspective in programmes and policies*

46. A gender perspective should be adopted in all processes of policy formulation and implementation and in the delivery of services, especially in sexual and reproductive health, including family planning. In this regard, the institutional capacity and expertise of staff in Government, civil society, including non-governmental organizations, and the United Nations system should be strengthened in order to promote gender mainstreaming. This should be done by sharing tools, methodologies and lessons learned in order to develop and strengthen their capacity and institutionalize effective strategies for gender-based analysis and gender mainstreaming. This includes the development and availability of gender-disaggregated data and appropriate indicators for monitoring progress at the national level.

47. The differential impact on women and men of globalization of the economy and the privatization of basic social services, particularly reproductive health services, should be monitored closely. Special programmes and institutional mechanisms should be put in place to promote and protect the health and well-being of young girls, older women and other vulnerable groups. The provision of services to meet men's reproductive and sexual health needs should not prejudice reproductive and sexual health services for women.

48. Governments should give priority to developing programmes and policies that foster norms and attitudes of zero tolerance for harmful and discriminatory attitudes, including son preference, which can result in harmful and unethical practices such as prenatal sex selection, discrimination and violence against the girl child and all forms of violence against women, including female genital mutilation, rape, incest, trafficking, sexual violence and exploitation. This entails developing an integrated approach that addresses the need for widespread social, cultural and economic change, in addition to legal reforms. The girl child's access to health, nutrition, education and life opportunities should be protected and promoted. The role of family members, especially parents and other legal guardians, in strengthening the self-image, self-esteem and status and in protecting the health and well-being of girls should be enhanced and supported.

D. *Advocacy for gender equality and equity*

49. Governments, parliamentarians, community and religious leaders, family members, media representatives, educators and other relevant groups should actively promote gender equality and equity. These groups should develop and strengthen their strategies to change negative and discriminatory attitudes and practices towards women and the girl child. All leaders at the highest levels of policy- and decision-making should speak out in support of gender equality and equity, including empowerment of women and protection of the girl child and young women.

50. All leaders at all levels, as well as parents and educators, should promote positive male role models that make it easier for boys to become gender-sensitive adults and enable men to support, promote and respect women's sexual and reproductive health and reproductive rights, recognizing the inherent dignity of all human beings. Men should take responsibility for their own reproductive and sexual behaviour and health. Research should be undertaken on men's sexuality, their masculinity and their reproductive behaviour.

51. Governments, donors and the United Nations system should encourage and support expansion and strengthening of women's grass-roots, community-based and advocacy groups.

IV. Reproductive rights and reproductive health

The present section is especially guided by the principles of the Programme of Action.

A. *Reproductive health, including family planning and sexual health*

52. Governments, in collaboration with civil society, including non-governmental organizations, donors and the United Nations system, should:

(*a*) Give high priority to reproductive and sexual health in the broader context of health-sector reform, including strengthening basic health systems, from which people living in poverty in particular can benefit;

(*b*) Ensure that policies, strategic plans and all aspects of the implementation of reproductive and sexual health services respect all human rights, including the right to development, and that such services meet health needs over the life cycle, including the needs of adolescents, address inequities and inequalities due to poverty, gender and other factors and ensure equity of access to information and services;

(*c*) Engage all relevant sectors, including non-governmental organizations, especially women's and youth organizations and professional associations, through ongoing participatory processes in the design, implementation, quality assurance, monitoring and evaluation of policies and programmes, in ensuring that sexual and reproductive health information and services meet people's needs and respect their human rights, including their right to access to good-quality services;

(*d*) Develop comprehensive and accessible health services and programmes, including sexual and reproductive health, for indigenous communities, with their full participation, that respond to the needs and reflect the rights of indigenous people;

(*e*) Increase investments designed to improve the quality and availability of sexual and reproductive health services, including establishing and monitoring clear standards of care; ensuring the competence, particularly the technical and communication skills, of service providers; ensuring free, voluntary and informed choices, respect, privacy, confidentiality and client comfort; establishing fully functioning logistical systems, including efficient procurement of necessary commodities; and ensuring effective referral mechanisms across services and levels of care, taking care that services are offered in conformity with human rights and with ethical and professional standards;

(f) Ensure that sexual and reproductive health programmes, free of any coercion, provide pre-service and in-service training and supervision for all levels of health-care providers to ensure that they maintain high technical standards, including for hygiene; respect the human rights of the people they serve; are knowledgeable and trained to serve clients who have been subjected to harmful practices, such as female genital mutilation and sexual violence; and are able to provide accurate information about the prevention and symptoms of reproductive tract diseases, as well as about personal hygiene and other factors in reproductive tract infections, in order to minimize adverse physical consequences such as pelvic inflammatory disease, infertility and ectopic pregnancy, as well as psychological consequences;

(g) Promote men's understanding of their roles and responsibilities with regard to respecting the human rights of women; protecting women's health, including supporting their partners' access to sexual and reproductive health services; preventing unwanted pregnancy; reducing maternal mortality and morbidity; reducing transmission of sexually transmitted diseases, including HIV/AIDS; sharing household and child-rearing responsibilities; and promoting the elimination of harmful practices, such as female genital mutilation, and sexual and other gender-based violence, ensuring that girls and women are free from coercion and violence;

(h) Strengthen community-based services, social marketing and new partnerships with the private sector while working to ensure that safety, ethical and other relevant standards are met; and provide subsidies from public resources and donor funds, as appropriate, to ensure availability and access for those otherwise unable to access services.

53. Governments, with assistance from the international community, should develop and use indicators that measure access to and choice of family-planning and contraceptive methods and indicators that measure trends in maternal mortality and morbidity and HIV/AIDS and use them to monitor progress towards the goal of the International Conference on Population and Development of universal access to reproductive health care. Governments should strive to ensure that by 2015 all primary health-care and family planning facilities are able to provide, directly or through referral, the widest achievable range of safe and effective family planning and contraceptive methods; essential obstetric care; prevention and management of reproductive tract infections, including sexually transmitted diseases; and barrier methods, such as male and female condoms and microbicides if available, to prevent infection. By 2005, 60 per cent of such facilities should be able to offer this range of services, and by 2010, 80 per cent of them should be able to offer such services.

54. The United Nations system and donors should support Governments in the building of national capacity to plan, manage, implement, monitor and evaluate reproductive and sexual health services, including ensuring that all refugees and all other persons in emergency humanitarian situations, particularly women and adolescents, receive appropriate health care, including sexual and reproductive health care and information, and greater protection from sexual and gender-based violence. They should also ensure that all health workers in relief and emergency situations are given basic training in sexual and reproductive health-care information and services.

55. Increased efforts are needed by the United Nations system, with support from the international community, to develop and agree upon common key indicators on reproductive health programmes, including, inter alia, family planning, maternal health, sexual health, sexually transmitted diseases, HIV/AIDS, and information, education and communication for appropriate consideration in the relevant intergovernmental process. Bearing in mind the efforts made by national Governments, the World Health Organization is invited to take the lead role in this area, in coordination with the United Nations Children's Fund, the United Nations Population Fund, the United Nations Development Programme, the Joint and Co-sponsored United Nations Programme on Human Immunodeficiency Virus/Acquired Immunodeficiency Syndrome, the Department of Economic and Social Affairs of the Secretariat and other relevant United Nations entities, drawing on other expertise and knowledge as appropriate. Indicators on maternal and neonatal mortality, maternal morbidity and maternal health programmes should be given a prominent place, in order to monitor progress effectively and ensure that priority is given to reproductive health care in the provision of general health services. The international community is encouraged to provide financial and technical assistance to developing countries to improve their capacity-building in terms of indicators, data collection, monitoring, and evaluation in this field.

B. *Ensuring voluntary quality family-planning services*

56. Governments, in accordance with the Programme of Action, should take effective action to ensure the basic right of all couples and individuals to decide freely and responsibly the number, spacing and timing of their children and to have the information, education and means to do so.

57. The United Nations system and donors should, upon request, support Governments in:

(a) Mobilizing and providing sufficient resources to meet the growing demand for access to information, counselling, services and follow-up on the widest possible range of safe, effective, affordable and acceptable family planning and contraceptive methods, including new options and underutilized methods;

(b) Providing quality counselling services and ensuring ethical, professional and technical standards of care, as well as voluntary, free and informed choices in an atmosphere of privacy, confidentiality and respect;

(c) Strengthening programme management capacity, including logistical systems, to make services safer,

more affordable and more convenient and accessible to clients and to ensure the availability and continuous supply of safe and effective contraceptives and other sexual and reproductive health supplies and, as appropriate, the raw material for them;

(d) Adequately strengthening social safety nets using resources and funds and, in the context of primary health care, ensuring the availability of and access to reproductive health services, including family planning, particularly for people most affected by poverty, the adverse impact of structural adjustment policies and financial crises, or otherwise unable to access services.

58. Where there is a gap between contraceptive use and the proportion of individuals expressing a desire to space or limit their families, countries should attempt to close this gap by at least 50 per cent by 2005, 75 per cent by 2010 and 100 per cent by 2050. In attempting to reach this benchmark, demographic goals, while legitimately the subject of government development strategies, should not be imposed on family planning providers in the form of targets or quotas for the recruitment of clients.

59. Governments, with the increased participation of the United Nations system, civil society, donors and the private sector, are urged to pursue the research and development of new, safe, low-cost and effective family-planning and contraceptive methods, for both men and women, including female-controlled methods that both protect against sexually transmitted diseases, including HIV/AIDS, and prevent unwanted pregnancy. All actors must abide by internationally accepted ethical, technical and safety standards in all research and development as well as, where appropriate, by applicable standards in manufacturing practices, quality control and product design, production and distribution.

60. The international community and the private sector should also take the necessary measures, particularly in the transfer of technology, as appropriate, to enable countries, in particular developing countries, to produce, store and distribute safe and effective contraceptives and other supplies essential for reproductive health services in order to strengthen the self-reliance of those countries.

61. The United Nations Population Fund is urged to continue to strengthen its leadership role within the United Nations system in assisting countries to take the strategic action necessary to ensure availability of reproductive health services and choice of reproductive health products, including contraceptives.

C. *Reducing maternal mortality and morbidity*

62. Governments, with the increased participation of the United Nations system, civil society, including non-governmental organizations, donors and the international community, should:

(a) Recognize the linkages between high levels of maternal mortality and poverty and promote the reduction of maternal mortality and morbidity as a public health priority and reproductive rights concern;

(b) Ensure that the reduction of maternal morbidity and mortality is a health sector priority and that women have ready access to essential obstetric care, well-equipped and adequately staffed maternal health-care services, skilled attendance at delivery, emergency obstetric care, effective referral and transport to higher levels of care when necessary, post-partum care and family planning. In health sector reform, the reduction of maternal mortality and morbidity should be prominent and used as an indicator for the success of such reform;

(c) Support public health education to create awareness of the risks of pregnancy, labour and delivery and to increase the understanding of the respective roles and responsibilities of family members, including men, as well as of civil society and Governments, in promoting and protecting maternal health;

(d) Develop appropriate interventions, beginning at birth, to improve the nutritional, health and educational status of girls and young women, so that they are better able to make informed choices at maturity about childbearing and obtain access to health information and services;

(e) Implement programmes to address the negative impact of environmental degradation, in some regions, on the high levels of maternal mortality and morbidity.

63. (i) In no case should abortion be promoted as a method of family planning. All Governments and relevant intergovernmental and non-governmental organizations are urged to strengthen their commitment to women's health, to deal with the health impact of unsafe abortion as a major public-health concern and to reduce the recourse to abortion through expanded and improved family planning services. Prevention of unwanted pregnancies must always be given the highest priority and every attempt should be made to eliminate the need for abortion. Women who have unwanted pregnancies should have ready access to reliable information and compassionate counselling. Any measures or changes related to abortion within the health system can be determined only at the national or local level according to the national legislative process. In circumstances where abortion is not against the law, such abortion should be safe. In all cases, women should have access to quality services for the management of complications arising from abortion. Post-abortion counselling, education and family planning services should be offered promptly, which will also help to avoid repeat abortions;

(ii) Governments should take appropriate steps to help women to avoid abortion, which in no case should be promoted as a method of family planning, and in all cases provide for the humane treatment and counselling of women who have had recourse to abortion;

(iii) In recognizing and implementing the above, and in circumstances where abortion is not against the law, health systems should train and equip health-service providers and should take other measures to ensure that such abortion is safe and accessible. Additional measures should be taken to safeguard women's health.

64. In order to monitor progress towards the achievement of the goals of the International Conference on Population and Development for maternal

mortality, countries should use the proportion of births assisted by skilled attendants as a benchmark indicator. By 2005, where the maternal mortality rate is very high, at least 40 per cent of all births should be assisted by skilled attendants; by 2010 this figure should be at least 50 per cent and by 2015, at least 60 per cent. All countries should continue their efforts so that globally, by 2005, 80 per cent of all births should be assisted by skilled attendants, by 2010, 85 per cent, and by 2015, 90 per cent.

65. In order to have a basis for cost-benefit analysis for interventions aimed at reducing maternal mortality, the societal costs of maternal deaths should be calculated. This should be done in cooperation with Governments, United Nations agencies and development banks, and the research community.

66. The World Health Organization, in cooperation with other relevant United Nations bodies, is urged to fulfil its leadership role within the United Nations system in assisting countries, in particular developing countries, to put in place standards for the care and treatment for women and girls that incorporate gender-sensitive approaches and promote gender equality and equity in health-care delivery and to advise on functions that health facilities should perform to help guide the development of health systems to reduce the risks associated with pregnancy, taking into consideration the level of development and the economic and social conditions of countries. At the same time, United Nations agencies, including the United Nations Population Fund and the United Nations Children's Fund, and multilateral development banks, such as the World Bank, should intensify their role in promoting, supporting, advocating for and investing in action to improve maternal health.

D. Prevention and treatment of sexually transmitted disease, including human immunodeficiency virus/acquired immunodeficiency syndrome

67. Governments, from the highest political levels, should take urgent action to provide education and services to prevent the transmission of all forms of sexually transmitted diseases and HIV and, with the assistance, where appropriate, of the Joint and Co-sponsored United Nations Programme on Human Immunodeficiency Virus/Acquired Immunodeficiency Syndrome, develop and implement national HIV/AIDS policies and action plans, ensure and promote respect for the human rights and dignity of persons living with HIV/AIDS, improve care and support for people living with HIV/AIDS, including support services for home-based care, and take steps to mitigate the impact of the AIDS epidemic by mobilizing all sectors and segments of society to address the social and economic factors contributing to HIV risk and vulnerability. Governments should enact legislation and adopt measures to ensure non-discrimination against people living with HIV/AIDS and vulnerable populations, including women and young people, so that they are not denied the information needed to prevent further transmission and are able to access treatment and care services without fear of stigmatization, discrimination or violence.

68. Governments should ensure that prevention of and services for sexually transmitted diseases and HIV/AIDS are an integral component of reproductive and sexual health programmes at the primary health-care level. Gender, age-based and other differences in vulnerability to HIV infection should be addressed in prevention and education programmes and services. Governments should develop guidelines for HIV treatment and care, emphasizing equitable access, and for wide provision of and access to voluntary HIV testing and counselling services, and should ensure wide provision of and access to female and male condoms, including through social marketing. Advocacy and information, education and communication campaigns developed with communities and supported from the highest levels of Government should promote informed, responsible and safer sexual behaviour and practices, mutual respect and gender equity in sexual relationships. Special attention needs to be given to preventing sexual exploitation of young women and children. Given the enhanced susceptibility to HIV/AIDS of individuals infected by conventional and treatable sexually transmitted diseases and the high prevalence of such diseases among young people, priority must be given to the prevention, detection, diagnosis and treatment of such infections. Governments should immediately develop, in full partnership with youth, parents, families, educators and health-care providers, youth-specific HIV education and treatment projects, with special emphasis on developing peer-education programmes.

69. While one of the most important interventions to reduce HIV infections in infants is primary prevention of infection, Governments should also scale up, where appropriate, education and treatment projects aimed at preventing mother-to-child transmission of HIV. Anti-retroviral drugs, where feasible, should be made available to women living with HIV/AIDS during and after pregnancy as part of their ongoing treatment of HIV/AIDS and provide infant-feeding counselling for mothers living with HIV/AIDS so that they can make free and informed decisions.

70. Governments, with assistance from the Joint and Co-sponsored United Nations Programme on Human Immunodeficiency Virus/Acquired Immunodeficiency Syndrome and donors, should, by 2005, ensure that at least 90 per cent, and by 2010 at least 95 per cent, of young men and women aged 15 to 24 have access to the information, education and services necessary to develop the life skills required to reduce their vulnerability to HIV infection. Services should include access to preventive methods such as female and male condoms, voluntary testing, counselling and follow-up. Governments should use, as a benchmark indicator, HIV infection rates in persons 15 to 24 years of age, with the goal of ensuring that by 2005 prevalence in this age group is reduced globally, and by 25 per cent in the most affected countries, and that by 2010 prevalence in this age group is reduced globally by 25 per cent.

71. The private and public sectors should increase investments in research on the development of microbicides and other female-controlled methods, simpler and less expensive diagnostic tests, single-dose treatments for sexually transmitted diseases and vaccines. Governments, in particular of developing countries, with the support of the international community, should strengthen measures to improve generally the

quality, availability and affordability of care of people living with HIV/AIDS.

72. In accordance with its mandate, the Joint and Co-sponsored United Nations Programme on Human Immunodeficiency Virus/Acquired Immunodeficiency Syndrome should be provided with financial resources in order to do the utmost to ensure a well-coordinated response from the United Nations system to the HIV/AIDS pandemic and to provide support to national programmes, particularly in developing countries.

E. *Adolescents*

73. Governments, with the full involvement of young people and with the support of the international community, should, as a priority, make every effort to implement the Programme of Action in regard to adolescent sexual and reproductive health, in accordance with paragraphs 7.45 and 7.46 of the Programme of Action, and should:

(a) In order to protect and promote the right of adolescents to the enjoyment of the highest attainable standards of health, provide appropriate, specific, user-friendly and accessible services to address effectively their reproductive and sexual health needs, including reproductive health education, information, counselling and health promotion strategies. These services should safeguard the rights of adolescents to privacy, confidentiality and informed consent, respecting their cultural values and religious beliefs and in conformity with relevant existing international agreements and conventions;

(b) Continue to advocate for the protection and promotion of and support for programmes for adolescent health, including sexual and reproductive health; identify effective and appropriate strategies to achieve this goal; and develop gender- and age-based indicators and data systems to monitor progress;

(c) Develop at national and other levels, as appropriate, action plans for adolescents and youth, based on gender equity and equality, that cover education, professional and vocational training and income-generating opportunities. Such programmes should include support mechanisms for the education and counselling of adolescents in the areas of gender relations and equality, violence against adolescents, responsible sexual behaviour, responsible family planning practices, family life, reproductive health, sexually transmitted diseases, HIV infection and AIDS prevention, in accordance with paragraph 7.47 of the Programme of Action. Adolescents and youth themselves should be fully involved in the design and implementation of such information and services, with proper regard for parental guidance and responsibilities. Special attention should be devoted to vulnerable and disadvantaged youth;

(d) Acknowledge and promote the central role of families, parents and other legal guardians in educating their children and shaping their attitudes and ensure that parents and persons with legal responsibilities are educated about and involved in providing sexual and reproductive health information, in a manner consistent with the evolving capacities of adolescents, so that they can fulfil their rights and responsibilities towards adolescents;

(e) With due respect for the rights, duties and responsibilities of parents and in a manner consistent with the evolving capacities of the adolescent and their right to reproductive health education, information and care, and respecting their cultural values and religious beliefs, ensure that adolescents, both in and out of school, receive the necessary information, including information on prevention, education, counselling and health services to enable them to make responsible and informed choices and decisions regarding their sexual and reproductive health needs, in order, inter alia, to reduce the number of adolescent pregnancies. Sexually active adolescents will require special family planning information, counselling and health services, as well as sexually transmitted diseases and HIV/AIDS prevention and treatment. Those adolescents who become pregnant are at particular risk and will require special support from their families, health-care providers and the community during pregnancy, delivery and early childcare. This support should enable these adolescents to continue their education. Programmes should involve and train all who are in a position to provide guidance to adolescents concerning responsible sexual and reproductive behaviour, particularly parents and families, and also communities, religious institutions, schools, the mass media and peer groups. These policies and programmes must be implemented on the basis of commitments made at the International Conference on Population and Development and in conformity with relevant existing international agreements and conventions;

(f) Countries should ensure that programmes and attitudes of health-care providers do not restrict the access of adolescents to appropriate services and the information they need, including for the prevention and treatment of sexually transmitted diseases, HIV/AIDS and sexual violence and abuse. Countries should, in this context, and in the context of paragraph 73 *(e)* of the present document, where appropriate, remove legal, regulatory and social barriers to reproductive health information and care for adolescents.

74. Recognizing the growing and special needs of youth and adolescents, including reproductive and sexual health issues, and taking into account the special situations they face, the United Nations system and donors should complement Governments' efforts to mobilize and provide adequate resources to respond to those needs.

75. Governments, in consultation with national non-governmental organizations, including youth organizations where applicable, and with the required assistance of United Nations agencies, international non-governmental organizations and the donor community, should evaluate programmes and document experiences and develop data-collection systems to monitor progress, and widely disseminate information about the design and functioning of programmes and their impact on young people's sexual and reproductive health. United Nations agencies and donor countries should support regional and international mechanisms for sharing those experiences among all countries, especially among developing countries.

V. Partnerships and collaborations

76. Governments are encouraged, in dialogue with non-governmental organizations and local community

groups, and in full respect for their autonomy, to facilitate, as appropriate, the involvement of civil society at the national level in policy discussions and in the formulation, implementation, monitoring and evaluation of strategies and programmes to achieve Programme of Action objectives. Partnerships between Governments and multilateral and donor agencies and civil society need to be based, as appropriate, on delivering agreed outcomes that bring benefits to poor people's health, including reproductive and sexual health.

77. Governments, where appropriate, should include representatives of non-governmental organizations and local community groups in country delegations to regional and international forums where issues related to population and development are discussed.

78. Governments, civil society at the national level and the United Nations system should work towards enhancing and strengthening their collaboration and cooperation, with a view to fostering an enabling environment for partnerships for the implementation of the Programme of Action. Governments and civil society organizations should develop systems for greater transparency and information-sharing, so as to improve their accountability.

79 Governments are encouraged to recognize and support the important and complementary role that civil society at the national level can play towards changing attitudes and actions for further implementation of the Programme of Action.

80. Governments are also encouraged to recognize and support the important and complementary role that civil society at the national level can play in helping communities to articulate and meet their needs for health care, including reproductive health care.

81. Governments and international organizations should create and support mechanisms to build and sustain partnerships with community-based organizations and non-governmental organizations committed to assisting women to establish and realize their rights, including those that relate to reproductive and sexual health, as well as other relevant organizations, the research community and professional organizations. Governments, civil society at the national level and the international community should together focus on human resources development and on building and strengthening national capacity to implement sustainable population and reproductive health programmes.

82. Governments and civil society organizations, where appropriate, are encouraged to design innovative approaches and build partnerships with, among others, the media, the commercial sector, religious leaders, local community groups and leaders, as well as youth, which can serve as effective advocates for the achievement of the goals and objectives of the Programme of Action.

83. With reference to paragraph 15.10 of the Programme of Action, Governments, international organizations and donors are encouraged to provide, in accordance with national laws and regulations and national development priorities, adequate financial and technical resources and information to build the human resources, institutional capacity and sustainability of civil society organizations, particularly women's and youth groups, in a manner not compromising their full autonomy, to facilitate their active involvement in the research, design, implementation, monitoring and evaluation of national population and development policies, programmes and activities. Like Governments, civil society organizations should also put in place transparency and accountability mechanisms to ensure that programme implementation is directly targeted to, and funds are used effectively for, national population and development programmes, as well as activities, services and evaluation procedures.

84. Governments, international organizations and civil society organizations at the national level, including non-governmental organizations, should encourage partnerships with the private and, where appropriate, the informal sector to strengthen their engagement and collaboration in the implementation of the Programme of Action. The private sector may assist the efforts of Governments, but it cannot substitute for the Government's responsibility to ensure and provide quality, full, safe, accessible, affordable and convenient health services, including reproductive health, family planning and sexual health services. Governments are encouraged to review relevant national laws, standards and regulations, as appropriate, to facilitate private-sector involvement and to seek to ensure that all health-care products and services, including reproductive health products and services, meet internationally accepted standards.

85. Implementation of key elements of the Programme of Action must be tied closely to a broader strengthening of health systems. The public sector plays an important role in this regard and should be encouraged to define its role and to work more closely with the private and informal sectors to monitor and improve standards and to ensure that services are available and that their delivery is of good quality and affordable.

86. Recognizing its increasing role in providing reproductive health information, education, services and commodities, the private sector should ensure that its services and commodities are of high quality and meet internationally accepted standards; that its activities are conducted in a socially responsible, culturally sensitive, acceptable and cost-effective manner; that it fully respects various religions, ethical values and cultural backgrounds of each country's people; and that it adheres to basic rights recognized by the international community and recalled in the Programme of Action.

87. Parliamentarians and members of national legislatures are invited to ensure the legislative reform and expanded awareness-raising necessary for implementing the Programme of Action. They are encouraged to be advocates for the implementation of the Programme of Action, including through the allocation, as appropriate, of financial resources. There should be regular exchanges of experiences among parliamentarians at the subregional, regional, interregional and international levels, where appropriate.

88. External funding and support, from donor countries as well as the private sector, should be provided to promote and sustain the full potential of South-South cooperation, including the South-South initiative "Partners in Population and Development", in order to bolster the sharing of relevant experiences, and the mobilization of technical expertise and other resources among developing countries. Updated information on institutions and expertise available within developing countries in the area of population and de-

velopment, including reproductive health, should be compiled and disseminated.

89. All relevant bodies and entities of the United Nations system should continue to clarify, within existing mechanisms, their specific leadership roles and responsibilities and continue to strengthen their efforts to promote system-wide coordination and collaboration, especially at the country level. The intergovernmental work of the Commission on Population and Development should be reinforced, as should also the inter-agency coordination role of the United Nations Population Fund, in the field of population and reproductive health.

90. Governments, civil society organizations at the national level and the United Nations system are urged to consult youth organizations in the design, implementation and evaluation of policies and programmes for youth.

VI. Mobilizing resources

91. Increased political will from all Governments and reaffirmation of the commitment for mobilization of international assistance, as was agreed at Cairo, are urgently needed to accelerate the implementation of the Programme of Action which, in turn, will contribute to the advancement of the broad population and development agenda.

92. All developed countries are urged to strengthen their commitment to the goals and objectives of the Programme of Action, in particular its cost estimates, and to make every effort to mobilize the agreed estimated financial resources required for its implementation; in so doing, the needs of least developed countries should receive priority.

93. All developing countries and countries with economies in transition are urged to strengthen their commitment to the goals and objectives of the Programme of Action, in particular its cost estimates, and to continue to make efforts to mobilize domestic resources. Developing and developed countries and countries with economies in transition are urged to promote international cooperation and to increase technical cooperation and transfer of technology through South-South cooperation, in order to implement fully the Programme of Action.

94. Donor countries and international funding agencies are urged to support the inclusion of South-South components in development cooperation programmes and projects so as to promote cost-effectiveness and sustainability.

95. Translation of commitment to the goals of the International Conference on Population and Development into commensurate levels of donor funding has not been forthcoming, and there is an urgent need for donor countries to renew and intensify efforts to meet the need for complementary external resources required to implement the costed elements of the Programme of Action, namely, in 1993 United States dollars, $5.7 billion in 2000, $6.1 billion in 2005, $6.8 billion in 2010 and $7.2 billion in 2015. Donor countries are also urged to increase significantly official development assistance funding for other elements of the Programme of Action as contained in chapter XIII thereof, in particular, improvement in the status and empowerment of women, basic health care and education, emerging and continued health challenges, such as malaria and other diseases identified by the World Health Organization as having a major impact on health, including those having the highest mortality and morbidity rates; and to intensify efforts to help countries to eradicate poverty. Donor countries are therefore urged to take the necessary action to reverse the current decline in overall official development assistance and should strive to fulfil the agreed target of 0.7 per cent of gross national product for overall official development assistance as soon as possible.

96. With full regard to their respective jurisdiction and mandates, legislators and other decision makers are encouraged to undertake measures to increase support for achieving the goals and objectives of the Programme of Action through legislation, advocacy and expanded awareness-raising and resource mobilization. Advocacy efforts should be increased at all levels, both national and international, to ensure that the resource goals are met.

97. Since the HIV/AIDS pandemic is having a more severe impact than was originally projected, special attention should be given to providing promptly the necessary resources, as has been called for in the Programme of Action, for the prevention of sexually transmitted diseases and HIV. Particular attention should be given to vulnerable populations, especially children and young people. All countries affected by the pandemic must continue to make efforts to mobilize domestic resources from all sources in order to combat it. The international community is called upon to assist developing countries and countries with economies in transition in their efforts. Additionally, Governments and the donor community should intensify efforts to provide resources for care and support to those affected by HIV/AIDS and for specialized prevention needs.

98. The international community should provide the necessary financial and technical assistance to support developing countries and countries with economies in transition committed to implementing the goals and objectives of the Programme of Action. Special attention should be paid to the needs of Africa and the least developed countries, countries facing or suffering from emergency humanitarian situations and financial and economic crises, and those developing countries suffering from low commodity prices, as well as countries facing long-term and large-scale environmental problems.

99. Donor countries and international funding agencies, including the World Bank and the regional development banks, are urged to complement, at the request of countries, the domestic efforts made to meet the growing and urgent basic health and reproductive health needs, including reproductive health commodities, of the developing and the least developed countries, countries facing increasing demands for such commodities and a diminishing share of international assistance and countries with economies in transition.

100. Governments and the international community should encourage and promote additional ways and mechanisms to increase funding for population and development programmes, including sexual and reproductive health programmes, in order to ensure their sustainability. These could include, as appropriate: *(a)* advocacy for increased funding from international financial institutions and regional development banks; *(b)* selective use of user fees, social marketing,

cost-sharing and other forms of cost recovery; and *(c)* increased involvement of the private sector. These modalities should facilitate access to services and should be accompanied by adequate social safety net measures to promote access to services by those living in poverty and other members of vulnerable groups. Consideration should also be given to more efficient and coordinated mechanisms to address the debt problem, including the reduction of the burden of external debt through various measures such as debt cancellation and debt swaps for population, health and other social sector investment to promote sustainable development.

101. Governments of recipient countries are encouraged to ensure that public resources, subsidies and assistance received from international donors for the implementation of the goals and objectives of the Programme of Action are invested to maximize benefits to the poor and other vulnerable population groups, including those who suffer disproportionately from reproductive ill health.

102. Utilizing existing coordinated mechanisms at the national level, as appropriate, donor countries, international agencies and recipient countries should continue to strengthen their efforts and their collaboration, so as to avoid duplication, identify funding gaps and ensure that resources are used as effectively and efficiently as possible.

103. Governments, in cooperation with the United Nations Population Fund as appropriate, should seek to ensure full and regular monitoring of resource flows, paying particular attention to transparency and accountability for the costed population and reproductive health package included in the Programme of Action. Non-governmental organizations may provide the necessary information, as appropriate, in this regard.

104. Countries, especially developed countries, are urged to increase substantially their voluntary contribution to the United Nations Population Fund, as well as to other relevant United Nations programmes and specialized agencies, so that they will be in a better position to assist countries to implement further the goals and objectives of the Programme of Action, including reproductive health programmes.

105. Governments of developed and developing countries are encouraged to give thorough consideration to the implementation of the 20/20 initiative, a voluntary compact between interested donor and recipient countries, which can provide increased resources for broader poverty eradication objectives, including population and social sector objectives.

106. Governments should implement policies that facilitate increased access to basic health services, including high-quality and affordable reproductive health and family planning services; promote effective interventions and support services, including private sector services, as appropriate; set standards for service delivery; and review legal, regulatory and import policies to identify and eliminate those policies that unnecessarily restrict or prevent the greater involvement of the private sector. Public sector resources and subsidies should have as a priority people living in poverty, underserved populations and low-income sectors of the population.

Executive Board action. On 17 September [E/1999/35 (dec. 99/18)], the United Nations Development Programme (UNDP)/UNFPA Executive Board requested the UNFPA Executive Director to present in 2000 a report on UNFPA's strategic role in supporting countries' implementation of relevant key actions adopted at the special session.

Report of Secretary-General. In response to General Assembly resolution 53/183 [YUN 1998, p. 1003], the Secretary-General submitted an October report on the twenty-first special session [A/54/442]. He described the review and appraisal process, in which there was close collaboration between the United Nations Population Division and UNFPA, including the technical and regional meetings held in preparation for the session, the Hague Forum and the UNFPA field inquiry [YUN 1998, p. 1006]; the action taken by the special session; and the next steps to be taken.

By **decision 54/445** of 22 December, the Assembly took note of the Secretary-General's report.

Follow-up by Population Commission

The Commission on Population and Development, the principal body responsible for reviewing the follow-up to and implementation of the ICPD Programme of Action, considered as the central theme of its thirty-second session (New York, 22, 23 and 26 March) [E/1999/25] population growth, structure and distribution.

Under the item on follow-up to ICPD, the Commission considered three reports (one of which was on the 1998 Technical Symposium on International Migration and Development [YUN 1998, p. 1005]) and recommended a draft resolution to the Economic and Social Council for adoption.

Population growth, structure and distribution

The Commission on Population and Development had before it the concise report on world population monitoring, 1999: population growth, structure and distribution [E/CN.9/1999/2]. It noted that since the 1974 United Nations World Population Conference [YUN 1974, p. 550], world population size had increased from 4 billion persons to nearly 6 billion and was growing at a rate of 1.3 per cent annually (it was estimated that the population reached 6 billion on 12 October 1999).

The report noted that about 96 per cent of the total annual increase occurred in the less developed regions; the proportion of people living in the more developed regions had declined and was projected to continue to decline significantly. Although world total fertility had fallen by 39 per cent since the early 1970s, variations in fertility among the regions persisted, with fertility rates ranging from 1.4 births per woman in Europe to 5.1 in Africa. The reduction of mortality continued to progress as the level of life expectancy at birth continued to increase, from 58 years prior to 1974 to 65 years. Infant mortality had also declined, from 93 deaths per 1,000 live births to 57. However, there had been a devastating toll from AIDS in a number of countries, particularly in sub-Saharan Africa.

Due to the shift to lower fertility and mortality rates, developed countries had attained older age structures than were ever seen in the past, while developing countries were undergoing rapid shifts in respect of the share of children, youth and adults. The world child population (those under 15) had increased to 1.8 billion from 1.4 billion in 1970. Although the population of older persons was considerably smaller, it was growing at a much faster rate, with 580 million persons aged 60 or over in the world in 1998, constituting 10 per cent of the global population. The changing age structure was likely to have wide-ranging economic and social consequences through such factors as economic growth, savings and investment, labour supply and employment, pension schemes, health and long-term care, intergenerational transfers, family composition and living arrangements. While once limited to developed countries, concern for ageing's consequences had spread to developing countries.

As to population distribution, urbanization and internal migration, the report stated that the urban population was growing three times faster than its rural counterpart, with 47 per cent of the world population living in urban areas in mid-1998. In many developing countries, population distribution policies were largely synonymous with measures to reduce or even reverse rural-urban migration.

The report observed that poverty reduction, food provision and environmental maintenance were integrally linked with demographic, economic and political change. Cumulatively worsening performance in the two latter areas might be exacerbated by rapid population growth; breaking that interaction could be facilitated by government policies to promote income growth, empower the poor with education and health, and provide incentives for the prudent allocation of resources.

ECONOMIC AND SOCIAL COUNCIL ACTION

On 26 July [meeting 39], the Economic and Social Council, on the recommendation of the Commission on Population and Development [E/1999/25], adopted **resolution 1999/10** without vote [agenda item 13 (*i*)].

Population growth, structure and distribution

The Economic and Social Council,

Reaffirming the commitment of Member States to the implementation of the Programme of Action of the International Conference on Population and Development,

Recalling the recommendations of the Programme of Action relating to population growth, structure and distribution,

Recalling also that the theme for the thirty-second session of the Commission on Population and Development was population growth, structure and distribution, with special emphasis on sustained economic growth and sustainable development, including education, and noting the importance of the issues related to, inter alia, youth, ageing and migration, as well as the need for data collection,

Requests the Population Division of the Secretariat to continue its research on population growth, structure and distribution, including levels, trends, determinants, consequences and policies, while giving due attention to issues related to, inter alia, youth, ageing, migration and data collection, so that Governments may benefit by comparing experiences and by understanding the factors underlying changing demographic circumstances, and calls upon Governments to continue to facilitate the work of the Population Division in this regard.

Financial resources

In response to General Assembly resolutions 49/128 [YUN 1994, p. 963] and 50/124 [YUN 1995, p. 1094], the Secretary-General submitted to the Commission on Population and Development a report on the flow of financial resources for assisting in the implementation of the ICPD Programme of Action [E/CN.9/1999/4]. He observed that external assistance for population activities increased 54 per cent from the immediate pre-Conference period, from $1.3 billion in 1993 to slightly over $2 billion in 1996. That figure represented roughly 35 per cent of the $5.7 billion target agreed on at ICPD as the international community's share in financing the Programme of Action by the year 2000. Preliminary indications were that in 1997 total assistance for population activities decreased to just under $1.9 billion. Difficult economic circumstances, resulting in budget cuts and declining official development assistance, had translated into stagnating or decreasing funding for population programmes. The report concluded that donors and developing countries should re-examine priorities and increase allocations for population and related sectors.

International migration

In response to General Assembly resolution 52/189 [YUN 1997, p. 1072], the Secretary-General submitted an August report [A/54/207], in which he presented the views of 76 Governments on convening a UN conference on international migration and development. Of the total responses, 45 were generally in favour of and 26 expressed reservations about holding such a conference. The remaining five Governments expressed only partial support for convening a conference and considered that other options should first be pursued to address the issue of international migration and development. The number of responses received was relatively small and represented only 39 per cent of the full membership of the United Nations. Although the majority of the responding Governments appeared to be in favour of holding a conference, there was a lack of consensus on its objectives, its funding and the composition of its secretariat. Furthermore, a number of Governments expressed serious reservations about convening such a conference, given the current financial constraints of the United Nations. Generally, those Governments appeared more in favour of adopting a regional or subregional approach in considering the issue. Taking all those elements into account, the prospects for holding an international conference on international migration and development remained uncertain.

The Secretary-General went on to describe the work carried out on issues of international migration and development by mechanisms both within the UN system (Commission on Population and Development; twenty-first special session of the General Assembly; Commission on Human Rights; Administrative Committee on Coordination; Committee for Development Policy; Office of the United Nations High Commissioner for Refugees; United Nations Educational, Scientific and Cultural Organization; International Labour Organization) and outside it (International Organization for Migration; Organisation for Economic Cooperation and Development).

By an 8 October letter [A/C.2/54/2], Thailand transmitted to the President of the General Assembly the text of the "Bangkok Declaration on Irregular Migration", which was adopted at the International Symposium on Migration, held in Bangkok, from 21 to 23 April.

GENERAL ASSEMBLY ACTION

On 22 December [meeting 87], the General Assembly, on the recommendation of the Second (Economic and Financial) Committee [A/54/587/Add.5], adopted **resolution 54/212** without vote [agenda item 99 *(e)*].

International migration and development

The General Assembly,

Recalling the Programme of Action of the International Conference on Population and Development adopted at Cairo, in particular chapter X on international migration, and the key actions for the further implementation of the Programme of Action, set out in the annex to General Assembly resolution S-21/2 of 2 July 1999, in particular section II.C on international migration, as well as the relevant provisions contained in the Copenhagen Declaration on Social Development and the Programme of Action of the World Summit for Social Development and in the Platform for Action adopted by the Fourth World Conference on Women,

Recalling also its resolutions 49/127 of 19 December 1994, 50/123 of 20 December 1995 and 52/189 of 18 December 1997 on international migration and development, as well as Economic and Social Council decision 1995/313 of 27 July 1995,

Reaffirming the continuing validity of the principles set forth in the international instruments regarding the protection of human rights and fundamental freedoms, in particular the Universal Declaration of Human Rights, the International Convention on the Elimination of All Forms of Racial Discrimination, the Convention on the Elimination of All Forms of Discrimination against Women and the Convention on the Rights of the Child,

Recalling that the General Assembly and the Economic and Social Council should carry out their respective responsibilities as entrusted to them in the Charter of the United Nations, as well as by the relevant United Nations conferences of the 1990s, in the formulation of policies and the provision of guidance to and coordination of United Nations activities in the field of population and development, including activities on international migration,

Noting the need for the relevant United Nations organizations and other international organizations to enhance their technical support to developing countries to ensure that migration contributes to development,

Recognizing the diversity of views expressed by the respondents to the survey regarding the question of convening a United Nations conference on international migration, its scope, form and agenda, which represented 39 per cent of the full United Nations membership, and that forty-five respondents were in favour of convening a conference, five were partially in favour and twenty-six were against,

Noting in particular the need for more migration data, a coherent theory to explain international migration and a better understanding of the complex interrelationships between migration and development,

Noting the critical role of the existing forums within the United Nations system in addressing the issues of international migration and development, including through the Commission on Population and Development, the Commission on Human Rights, the Committee for Development Policy, the International Labour Organization and other relevant key organizations,

Noting with appreciation the numerous meetings and conferences convened relating to migration and development, in particular in the context of regional cooperation,

Noting the establishment of the International Migration Policy Programme in May 1998 by the United Nations Institute for Training and Research, the International Organization for Migration and the United Nations Population Fund, to be implemented in partnership with the International Labour Office, the Office of the United Nations High Commissioner for Refugees, the Office of the United Nations High Commissioner for Human Rights and other relevant international and regional institutions, with a view to strengthening the capacity of Governments in different regions to manage migration flows at national and regional levels and thus to foster cooperation among States towards orderly migration,

Aware that, among other factors, the process of globalization and liberalization, including the widening economic and social gap between and among many countries and the marginalization of some countries in the global economy, has contributed to large flows of peoples between and among countries and to the intensification of the complex phenomenon of international migration,

Aware also that, in spite of the existence of an already established body of principles, there is a need to make further efforts to ensure that the human rights and dignity of all migrants and their families are respected and protected and that it is desirable to improve the situation of all documented migrants and their families,

Recognizing the importance, from an analytical and operational point of view, of identifying the existing linkages among the social, economic, political and cultural factors related to international migration and development and of the need for comprehensive, coherent and effective policies on international migration based on the spirit of genuine partnership and common understanding,

1. *Takes note* of the report of the Secretary-General;

2. *Urges* Member States and the United Nations system to strengthen international cooperation in the area of international migration and development in order to address the root causes of migration, especially those related to poverty, and to maximize the benefits of international migration to those concerned;

3. *Encourages,* where relevant, interregional, regional and subregional mechanisms to continue to address the question of migration and development;

4. *Calls upon* all relevant bodies, agencies, funds and programmes of the United Nations system and other relevant intergovernmental, regional and subregional organizations, within their continuing mandated activities, to continue to address the issue of international migration and development and to provide appropriate support for interregional, regional and subregional processes and activities on international migration and development;

5. *Also calls upon* the international community to seek to make the option of remaining in one's country viable for all people, to which end efforts to achieve sustainable economic and social development, ensuring a better economic balance between developed and developing countries, should be strengthened;

6. *Requests* the Secretary-General, whenever feasible, to solicit more views from Member States, particularly those that have not responded to the survey requested in pursuance of resolution 52/189, as well as from the International Labour Organization, the International Organization for Migration and other relevant organizations, both within and outside the United Nations system, on the report of the Secretary-General submitted to the General Assembly at its fifty-second session, bearing in mind various regional processes, and to recommend ways and means to address the problems related to migration and development;

7. *Also requests* the Secretary-General to initiate appropriate action in consultation with regional commissions in order to ensure the carrying out of interregional activities, with the contribution of the relevant actors on issues relating to international migration and development, taking into account, inter alia, the report of the Secretary-General, and encourages the United Nations bodies and other appropriate international organizations to provide support to such activities;

8. *Further requests* the Secretary-General to submit to the General Assembly at its fifty-sixth session a report that will, inter alia, summarize the lessons learned, as well as best practices on migration management and policies, from the various activities relating to international migration and development that have been carried out at the regional and interregional levels, and recommend for the consideration of the Assembly policy actions that could be pursued at the international level, taking into account, inter alia, the following:

(a) The report of the Committee for Development Policy on its examination of the issue of migration and development;

(b) The work of the relevant bodies, agencies, funds and programmes of the United Nations system and other international organizations in the field of international migration and development;

(c) The possible mechanisms within the United Nations system to examine international migration and development in a comprehensive and integrated manner;

(d) The need to provide, in consultation with relevant United Nations bodies, an analysis of data relating to migration within and between the various regions;

9. *Decides* to include in the provisional agenda of its fifty-sixth session the sub-item entitled "International migration and development, including the question of the convening of a United Nations conference on international migration and development to address migration issues".

UN Population Fund

On 27 October, the General Assembly devoted a plenary meeting to commemorating the thirtieth anniversary of the operations of UNFPA, in accordance with decision 53/443 [YUN 1998, p. 1009]. In a message to the meeting, the Secretary-General stated that the Fund (originally the United Nations Fund for Population Activities), which began operations in 1969 [YUN 1969, p. 419] with a small amount of money provided by a few donors, was one of the leading success stories of the United Nations. The meeting was also addressed by the Assembly President, representatives of the regional groups and the United States, the host country.

GENERAL ASSEMBLY ACTION

On 27 October [meeting 40], the General Assembly adopted **resolution 54/11** [draft: A/54/L.18 & Add.1] without vote [agenda item 99 *(h)*].

Thirtieth anniversary of the operations of the United Nations Population Fund

The General Assembly,

Recalling its resolution 2211(XXI) of 17 December 1966, in response to which a trust fund, subsequently named the United Nations Fund for Population Activities, was established in 1967 by the Secretary-General,

Noting that the United Nations Fund for Population Activities, renamed in 1987 as the United Nations Population Fund, began operations in 1969,

Recalling its resolutions 3019(XXVII) of 18 December 1972, 31/170 of 21 December 1976 and 34/104 of 14 December 1979, in which it, inter alia, recognized the leading role and effectiveness of the Fund in the United Nations system in the population field and affirmed the Fund as a subsidiary body of the General Assembly,

Reaffirming Economic and Social Council resolutions 1763(LIV) of 18 May 1973 and 1986/7 of 21 May 1986 stating the aims and purposes of the Fund,

1. *Congratulates* the United Nations Population Fund on the occasion of the thirtieth anniversary of its operations;

2. *Notes with appreciation* the positive contributions the Fund and its dedicated staff have made during its thirty years in promoting better understanding and awareness of population and development issues, in improving the quality of human life and in extending systematic and sustained assistance to developing countries and countries with economies in transition, at their request, in undertaking appropriate national programmes to address their population and development needs.

1999 activities

In her report for 1999 [DP/FPA/2000/8 (Part I)] to the UNDP/UNFPA Executive Board, the UNFPA Executive Director stated that the most significant event for UNFPA was ICPD+5, the culmination of the review of the accomplishments and constraints that had been experienced in the five years since the International Conference on Population and Development (ICPD) had taken place in 1994 [YUN 1994, p. 955] (see p. 1005). The Fund had organized some ICPD+5 events and worked with the secretariat of the Commission on Population and Development in its role as preparatory committee for the General Assembly's twenty-first special session.

The Executive Director focused on two of those aspects of UNFPA's work in 1999 that figured prominently in the key future actions recommended by the special session: the importance of addressing the reproductive health needs of adolescents through the provision of information and services; and the need for all organizations concerned with population and reproductive health to work together more closely if ICPD's goals were to be achieved. The other major issue addressed in the report was the Fund's effort to develop a multi-year funding framework (MYFF).

During the year, the Fund worked to document experiences in adolescent reproductive health from various countries, using a joint programme strategy developed with the World Health Organization (WHO) and the United Nations Children's Fund (UNICEF). Efforts were made, for example, to identify countries that had developed national youth policies or had integrated youth and adolescent reproductive health concerns into existing population, education, gender and other development policies. Reviews of UNFPA country programmes and other studies that were conducted as part of the ICPD+5 process revealed the serious challenges faced by developing countries in addressing adolescent sexual and reproductive health issues. The high rate of abortions among adolescents and the spread of HIV/AIDS throughout the world had highlighted the risks posed by the lack of reproductive health information and services for young people. Approximately half of all people who contracted HIV became infected before they turned 25.

In order to address those challenges, UNFPA was working in three major areas: supporting information, education and communication programmes both in and out of schools; providing greater access by young people to youth-friendly reproductive health information, counselling and services; and advocating relevant youth policies that recognized the rights of young people and promoted their reproductive health. A key factor was the prevention of HIV infection.

With regard to partnerships, the Executive Director noted that the ICPD Programme of Action had identified the expanding number and configuration of development partners in the field of population and development as a shortcoming that had to be addressed and had cited the need to clarify the reciprocal responsibilities of development partners and improve coordination of their efforts as one of its key objectives. The key actions document of the special session (see p. 1006) noted the importance of effective, transparent partnership and called on Governments and civil society at the national level, in partnership with the international community, to join in efforts to ensure that the goals and objectives of ICPD were accomplished as soon as possible. It also mentioned the role of the relevant UN bodies, including UNFPA, throughout the document.

In carrying out its coordination role within the UN system, UNFPA depended on the work of partner agencies in a number of fields. An inter-agency meeting of the Basic Social Services for All Task Force, of which UNFPA was the chair, met in October 1999 and discussed the roles of all UN partners in the follow-up to the ICPD review. As a result, the Task Force was updating and simplifying a series of guidelines and guidance notes to the field on the implementation of the goals of the major international conferences that had taken place over the last decade and of their five-year follow-ups, including ICPD+5. Among the large number of mechanisms by which UNFPA co-operated with its partner agencies and organizations within the system were: the United Nations Development Group and its Executive Committee, made up of UNICEF, UNDP, UNFPA and the World Food Programme; the resident coordinator system, both at the country and UN system levels; UNFPA's Technical Advisory Programme; the WHO/UNICEF/UNFPA Coordinating Committee on Health; and the Inter-Agency Committee on Women and Gender Equality. An important result of UNFPA's cooperation with other UN and multilateral agencies in emergency situations was the *Inter-Agency Field Manual for Reproductive Health in Refugee Situations*, published in 1999 by UNFPA, WHO and the Office of the United Nations High Commissioner for Refugees. The manual provided guidance for reproductive health assistance in crisis situations, which was too often given short shrift even though the assistance focused on such vital matters as safe birth and helping women who were victims of violence. UNFPA also participated fully in the inter-agency assessments for the consolidated appeals process (see PART THREE, Chapter III) and was a co-sponsor of the Joint United Nations Programme on HIV/AIDS (see PART THREE, Chapter XIII).

The Executive Director went on to describe UNFPA's cooperation with the international financial institutions; civil society organizations, including NGOs; professional groups and mass organizations; South-South partnerships; parliamentarians; religious groups; foundations; and the private sector.

In its continuing efforts to improve performance, UNFPA accelerated the shift towards a results-based approach in 1999 by developing its first MYFF, for the years 2000-2003. The framework built on clearly defined organizational results and a set of indicators to track progress towards achieving them. It also included resource requirements to achieve the expected results. Noting that a three-year decline in the Fund's general resources was adversely affecting country-level efforts to achieve ICPD goals, the Executive Director said that MYFF, with its emphasis on results, on organizational effectiveness and on tracking and reporting on performance, was designed to improve programme management, performance and accountability. That should better position UNFPA to attract predictable and stable funding.

In another section of her annual report for 1999 [DP/FPA/2000/8 (Part II)], the Executive Director provided information on the Global Initiative on Reproductive Health Commodity Management (see p. 1027), the Global Contraceptive Commodity Programme (see p. 1028), and implementation of the UNFPA country programmes in Algeria, China, Egypt, Nicaragua and Paraguay, and in the Pacific subregion.

By **decision 1999/219** of 23 July, the Economic and Social Council took note of the annual reports of the UNDP Administrator and the UNFPA Executive Director to the Council [E/1999/47].

Sector-wide approaches

The UNDP/UNFPA Executive Board had before it in April a conference room paper on sector-wide approaches (SWAps) [DP/FPA/1999/CRP.1], which referred to integrated, sector-wide development programmes calling for a new type of partnership among Governments, donors, development banks, the private sector and wider civil society. The paper stated that UNFPA field offices were active partners in national dialogues around both health-sector reform and the introduction of SWAps in several countries in Africa and, in some of them, where SWAp implementation was more advanced, such as Ethiopia, Ghana and Zambia, UNFPA had developed close working partnerships with the Government and other donors. However, it had not yet contributed to common funding mechanisms. It was advisable, said the paper, for UNFPA to proceed proactively but cautiously with regard to the SWAp process, documenting and building on its own in-country experiences, as well as on the experiences shared by other donors and Governments. It would benefit from continued dialogue with other donors in order to develop joint strategies for more effective partnerships in SWAp implementation.

On 16 April [E/1999/35 (dec. 99/4)], the Executive Board encouraged UNFPA to take an active part in the policy-making and planning stages in SWAps in programme countries, with the concurrence and overall guidance of Governments, and to take an important advocacy role regarding reproductive and sexual health services and reproductive rights in such processes. The Fund was asked to strengthen the competencies needed to secure full and active participation in the policy-making and planning stages in SWAps, and to strengthen arrangements to access a full range of technical expertise. The Executive Director was asked to present a conference room paper on UNFPA's involvement in SWAps in 2000.

Reproductive health in emergency situations

The Executive Director submitted to the UNDP/UNFPA Executive Board a February report on UNFPA support for reproductive health in emergency situations [DP/FPA/1999/6]. She stated that, since 1994, 52 UNFPA-supported emergency reproductive health projects had been carried out in 33 countries in collaboration with 24 executing agencies, at a cost of $6.4 million. Countries assisted included Afghanistan, Albania, Bosnia and Herzegovina, Eritrea, Guinea-Bissau, Rwanda and the United Republic of Tanzania. All activities emphasized reproductive health, including the need for particular attention to the treatment and prevention of sexual violence and sexually transmitted diseases, including the prevention of HIV/AIDS. UNFPA had developed a number of manuals, kits and training materials and had provided important support for developing demographic and other databases needed in emergency situations. However, its efforts and impact were constrained by its programming and administrative procedures and by the limited success in mobilizing outside funds for projects included in consolidated appeals. To improve its work in reproductive health in emergency/crisis situations, UNFPA would develop mechanisms and strengthen the management of emergency requests through close cooperation with the Emergency Relief Adviser in Geneva. Appropriate staff training would also be provided. UNFPA proposed making more flexible use of a limited amount of programme funds to provide immediate support for reproductive health and data provision needs in emergencies.

On 16 April [dec. 99/6], the Executive Board requested the Executive Director to submit to its third regular session in 1999 a report containing concrete proposals on UNFPA emergency programming procedures. Submission of that report was delayed until 2000.

Country and intercountry programmes

UNFPA's provisional project expenditures for country and intercountry (regional and interregional) programmes in 1999 totalled $187.1 million, compared to $216.6 million in 1998, according to the Executive Director's statistical overview report covering 1999 [DP/FPA/2000/8 (Part I, Add.1)]. The 1999 figure included $150.7 million for country programmes and $36.4 million for intercountry programmes. In accordance with criteria defined by the UNDP/UNFPA Executive Board in 1996 [YUN 1996, p. 989], total expenditures in 1999 to those countries most in need amounted to $96 million, compared to $109.3 million in 1998. Country population assessments (CPAs) were completed in 12 countries—Azerbaijan, Chad, Indonesia, Kazakhstan, Kyrgyzstan, Pakistan, the Philippines, Tajikistan, Turkmenistan, Uzbekistan and Zimbabwe. In the case of Viet Nam, a common country assessment, rather than a CPA, was carried out.

The overarching objective of the intercountry programme, 1996-1999, was to build country capacity to implement the ICPD Programme of Action in the Fund's three programme priority areas: reproductive health, including family planning and sexual health; population and development strategies (PDS); and advocacy, with gender concerns mainstreamed into each of those areas.

Africa. Provisional expenditures for UNFPA programmes in sub-Saharan Africa totalled $59.4 million in 1999, compared to $70.8 million in 1998. Most of the resources (65 per cent) went to reproductive health and family planning, followed by PDS (27.1 per cent) and advocacy (4.9 per cent).

Training was the predominant function in the reproductive health and PDS sectors. Of eight reproductive health initiatives, five were training projects in English, French and Portuguese dealing with information, education and communication (two), reproductive health among refugees (two) and integrated community-based delivery of services (one). Special efforts were made to attract female participants in all training projects. Four PDS training and research projects were taking place. Capacity-building for advocacy was undertaken at the Organization of African Unity; an African Population Commission was established; and projects were launched with parliamentarians, national-level networks of women ministers and youth-related organizations. The programme also began cooperation with new implementing partners and strengthened collaboration with other UN organizations and agencies. Tangible results were also evident in the advocacy sector, especially with respect to two projects dealing with African political leaders. Eleven national-level networks of women ministers and parliamentarians were established and all undertook advocacy, lobbying and sensitization activities. Some 15 regional meetings were organized, contributing significantly to moving the reproductive health agenda forward.

In January [E/1999/35 (dec. 99/3)], the UNDP/UNFPA Executive Board approved assistance to Burundi and Madagascar; in April [dec. 99/7], it approved assistance to Benin.

Arab States and Europe. Provisional expenditures for UNFPA programmes in the Arab States and Europe totalled $21.8 million in 1999, compared to $24.4 million in 1998. Most of the resources (67 per cent) went to reproductive health and family planning, followed by PDS (26.6 per cent) and advocacy (2.8 per cent).

Reproductive health activities in the Arab States addressed the improvement of management and quality of services and supported research and information dissemination. In Europe, projects concentrated on training in service delivery and contraceptive technology and on improving data collection and analysis in family planning and reproductive health.

PDS projects in the Arab States included policy-oriented research, NGO management training and the dissemination of information on population and development. In Europe, interrelated projects supported policy-oriented research on fertility decline, ageing and migration. In the advocacy sector, assistance in the Arab States was directed to studies and information activities on women's reproductive health, the role of Arab women, empowerment of youth, and post-ICPD advocacy concerns. In Europe, projects worked to raise awareness of reproductive health among youth and to mobilize donors for the year 2000 round of population censuses.

Programmes for both subregions made some advances in broadening the numbers of dedicated partner agencies and organizations. Among the noteworthy achievements were advances in promoting the adoption of a comprehensive approach to reproductive health, broadening the scope of a new regional survey, and including advocacy and peer counselling in a major regional reproductive health project for youth. Advocacy projects surpassed their expected outcomes; that was attributed to the use of a wide range of media to reach target audiences.

Asia and the Pacific. Provisional expenditures for UNFPA programmes in Asia and the Pacific totalled $63.1 million in 1999, compared to $69.9 million in 1998. Most of the resources (67.7 per cent) went to reproductive health and family planning, followed by PDS (23.3 per cent) and advocacy (6 per cent).

The regional Asia programme comprised 32 projects in the areas of reproductive health, PDS and advocacy. Training projects in reproductive health focused on community-based service-delivery models and strengthening and promoting collaboration between the Government and NGOs. Assistance was provided for research in four countries on gender relationships among Muslim women, the development of reproductive health indicators, sexual abuse among children and an assessment of reproductive health care. Two projects supported information, education and communication. PDS projects supported research on female migration and employment, problems of ageing and support for the elderly, and the effects of the economic crisis in Asian countries. Other PDS initiatives aimed to improve the quality of population data and technologies for data collection and dissemination and to develop information networks to improve coordination among national and subregional centres. Advocacy projects promoted awareness and networking among parliamentarians.

The regional projects were executed by 15 partner agencies, including NGOs, UN agencies and academic institutions, all of which played leading roles in the areas of population and development in the region. The regional programme impact was limited because of the absence of means for transferring tools, methods, experience and technology from global to regional and from regional to national levels. It was noted that in project execution it was crucial to involve multiple agencies that could complement skills and experiences to build a multidisciplinary sense into the project implementation process.

On 17 September [E/1999/35 (dec. 99/25)], the UNDP/UNFPA Executive Board approved country programmes for Azerbaijan, Kazakhstan, Kyrgyzstan, Pakistan, the Philippines, Tajikistan, Turkmenistan and Uzbekistan.

Latin America and the Caribbean. Provisional expenditures for UNFPA programmes in Latin America and the Caribbean totalled $19 million in 1999, compared to $24.7 million in 1998. Most of the resources (53.7 per cent) went to reproductive health and family planning, followed by PDS (31 per cent) and advocacy (6.8 per cent).

Reproductive health initiatives were undertaken to improve conditions for poorer women, adolescents and indigenous groups in the region, while advocacy campaigns promoted access to services and efforts to prevent violence against women. Knowledge was exchanged among NGOs and the governmental sector, and research on existing patterns of surgical contraception supported the concept of ensuring an adequate mix of contraceptives. Training in reproductive health and population in schools of health was funded, while supportive advocacy efforts brought population, reproductive health and rights and gender concerns to regional forums to influence political decision-making. PDS projects included support for the development of population databases, provision of new technologies for census activity, dissemination of socio-demographic data and demographic training.

Noticeable progress was made with respect to planned objectives, including advances in promoting reproductive health and rights. Considerable activity in the PDS sector was recorded, especially in assistance to countries in improving methodologies and technologies for upcoming census rounds. In the advocacy area, efforts focused in particular on increasing awareness of the concept of reproductive health. Regional meetings were conducted for professionals, policy makers and parliamentarians, and there was a major regional workshop for NGOs on the topic of reproductive health awareness. Much effort was also made to support the participation of key nationals to speak up for ICPD goals in regional forums on economic and social issues.

By a September decision [E/1999/35 (dec. 99/25)], the UNDP/UNFPA Executive Board approved the extension of and additional resources for the country programme for Haiti.

Interregional programmes. Provisional expenditures for UNFPA's interregional and global programmes in 1999 totalled $23.8 million, compared to $26.8 million in 1998. Of the total, 47.9 per cent went to PDS, 38 per cent to reproductive health/family planning, 11.1 per cent to advocacy and 3.3 per cent to multisectoral activities.

The interregional reproductive health programme continued to promote the development of new methods of fertility regulation and to collect information on contraceptive safety. UNFPA strengthened its cooperation with UNDP, the World Bank and WHO, supporting the latter in providing countries with appropriate technical guidance in operationalizing reproductive health by furnishing technical orientation on specific aspects, such as adolescent reproductive health. A major focus was the Centres of Excellence Initiative that offered training within South-South cooperative settings, and the 12-country Partners in Population and Development Initiative that provided training, research and networking on ICPD Programme of Action issues. A major thrust of the intercountry programme was the Global Initiative on Contraceptive Requirements and Logistics Management Needs (see below). Through that Initiative, studies on contraceptive requirements and logistics management needs were completed in 11 countries, followed by expanded publication of the UNFPA contraceptive commodity database on donor-supported contraceptives. Technical assistance and training in logistics management and forecasting were provided through six regional workshops. The monthly injectable Cyclofem became widely available in three countries as a result of a 16-country market and needs assessment, and the Thailand-based Concept Foundation became self-sustaining through private-sector sales. Investing in adolescents was an important goal of UNFPA. In Egypt, Uganda and Zambia, efforts were made to promote the reproductive health of adolescent refugees. Another important area of the Fund's work was that of violence against women. UNFPA developed a programme advisory note on the reproductive health effects of gender-based violence to guide country-level programmatic efforts.

In the PDS sector, emphasis was placed on increasing the attention of policy makers to the links between population and development planning. The most significant undertaking was the large-scale strengthening of the Global Training Programme in Population and Sustainable Development. Five regional training centres became fully operational, meeting training demands from all regions. UNFPA continued to receive increased requests from countries to monitor their own policies, programme implementation and progress in achieving ICPD goals, as well as the goals of other major UN conferences. Among the principal research areas supported by the interregional programme were sociocultural research methodologies, which sought to provide frameworks for the study of the impact of social and cultural factors on fertility behaviour, and of the role and status of women. The information dissemination projects included the Population Information Network (POPIN), the *Annual Review of Population Law*, the UNFPA *Inventory of Population Projects in Developing Countries Around the World*, and demographic software such as *DemoTables* and *PopMap*. Special attention was given to mainstreaming gender concerns into population and development policy and programme activities.

The Fund's interregional advocacy efforts were carried out mainly through the production, distribution and dissemination of publications, computer software and audio-visual materials. The annual *State of World Population* report, which was central to the Fund's advocacy efforts, continued to be produced and distributed. The Fund improved the flow of information to NGOs and helped them to be more effective advocates for mobilizing resources and achieving ICPD goals. It also increased its activities with NGOs, especially in Europe and Japan, through its programme of block grants. With regard to media outreach, UNFPA sponsored many regional meetings of print and television representatives from the developing and industrialized world to create a nucleus of informed journalists. Its advocacy resources were teamed with those of the UN Department of Public Information and the specialized agencies for the production of films, radio programmes and brochures.

Global Initiative on Reproductive Health Commodity Management

The Global Initiative on Reproductive Health Commodity Management (formerly the Global Initiative on Contraceptive Requirements and Logistics Management Needs) played a crucial role in UNFPA's efforts to strengthen reproductive health commodity security and management as part of its country programmes. Its work emphasized building national capacity in order to make safe, high-quality reproductive health commodities accessible and available at affordable prices. At the headquarters level, it coordinated with donors to help countries meet shortfalls in the supply of those commodities.

During 1999, the Global Initiative conducted in-depth studies in Kazakhstan, Mongolia and Uzbekistan and organized workshops in logistics management training strategy development, involving two participants from each of five to six countries in a region. Since 1997, it had operated a pilot project, the UNFPA Private-Sector Initiative, to expand the commercial market share of contraceptive supply in selected countries. The Private-Sector Initiative sponsored studies of relevant countries that emphasized a systematic, coordinated and cohesive approach to the total contraceptive market and carried out follow-up missions in Ghana, India and Zimbabwe.

Global Contraceptive Commodity Programme

The UNFPA Global Contraceptive Commodity Programme continued to provide essential buffer stocks of contraceptives and other reproductive health supplies to developing countries. In 1999, it supplied over 20 million condoms to nine countries and 12 emergency destinations and expanded its stock holdings to include oral contraceptive pills and intrauterine devices. It also supplied 1,200 emergency reproductive health kits with a value of $1.3 million to 19 destinations.

Financial and administrative questions

UNFPA's General Fund income for 1999 totalled $254.2 million, a decrease of $24.5 million (9 per cent) from 1998 [DP/FPA/2000/15]. Expenditures totalled $279.6 million, resulting in an excess of expenditure over income of $25.4 million. After adjusting for excess expenditure in 1998 [YUN 1998, p. 1013] and the reduction in the level of the operational reserve of $6 million, UNFPA was required to draw down from the operational reserve to finance a regular resource deficit of $26 million. That deficit, along with a $2.4 million balance of unexpended cost-sharing resources, comprised the negative $23.6 million in unspent General Fund resources at the end of 1999. Contributions, including additions and adjustments to pledges during 1999, totalled $249.5 million, a decrease of $21.5 million from 1998. The cumulative outstanding balance of unpaid pledges for 1999 and prior years was $1.5 million.

In a 17 September decision [E/1999/35 (dec. 99/24)], the Executive Board noted with concern the significant decline in core contributions to UNFPA. It requested the Executive Director to bring the critical resource situation to the Secretary-General's attention with a view to mobilizing the support of world political leaders in order to reverse the declining trend.

2000-2001 budget

The UNFPA Executive Director submitted to the Executive Board a July report on estimates for the 2000-2001 biennial support budget [DP/FPA/1999/11]. She requested appropriations of $149.4 million gross ($127.4 million net) for the biennium to cover the cost of staff and support resources. The proposed net budget reflected a slight decrease of 0.1 per cent, or $0.2 million in absolute terms, from the budget for 1998-1999. The biennial support budget for 2000-2001 accounted for 18.7 per cent of total expenditure; in the 1998-1999 budget, the corresponding figure was 16.5 per cent. Although it appeared that the 2000-2001 biennial support budget was larger than the 1998-1999 budget, the increase in percentage was due to declining resources, not to an increase in the size of the support budget.

The Advisory Committee on Administrative and Budgetary Questions (ACABQ) issued an August report containing its comments on the support budget estimates [DP/FPA/1999/14], noting that it had been prepared in accordance with the common format and guidelines approved by the Executive Board in its decisions on the harmonized presentation of budgets of UNDP, UNFPA and UNICEF. The Committee welcomed the additional information submitted to it with the budget estimates. However, it believed that the report still required some further refinements.

The Executive Board, in September [E/1999/35 (dec. 99/21)], took note of the UNFPA 2000-2001 support budget estimates and of the ACABQ report and urged the Executive Director to continue to make efforts to contain both the administrative and programme support costs at headquarters, as well as in the field. It approved gross appropriations of $149.4 million for the support budget and resolved that income estimates of $22 million should be used to offset the gross appropriations, resulting in estimated net appropriations of $127.4 million. The Executive Director was asked to report to the Executive Board in 2000 on any significant increases or shortfalls in estimated income and to suggest proposals on how to deal with the new situation.

Audit reports

A November report [DP/FPA/2000/4] described action taken in response to the recommendations contained in the report of the United Nations

Board of Auditors for the 1996-1997 biennium [A/52/5/Add.7], including: showing the value of contributions-in-kind; establishing procedures for accurately recording non-expendable project equipment held by Governments and NGOs and disclosing the value of the inventory; amending the financial regulations to require exchange losses, other than those arising from voluntary contributions, to be charged as expenditure; taking action to recover overdue travel advances; expediting the receipt of outstanding disbursement reports in respect of Government- and NGO-executed projects; reviewing inactive projects and closing them if appropriate; negotiating with Governments the issue of cost-free premises; and undertaking a comprehensive staff review.

In an April report [DP/FPA/1999/8], the Executive Director described UNFPA internal audit and oversight activities in 1998. They included: management audits in eight field offices; compliance audits in 15 countries in the Africa region; compliance audits in seven countries in the Asia and Pacific region; and a review of one division at UNFPA headquarters. In general, the country offices in the Africa and Asia and Pacific regions were rated as satisfactory based on the audits. Of 43 reports issued in 1998 (including 1997 audits for which reports were issued during 1998), the level of internal controls and compliance with financial and administrative requirements were found to be satisfactory in most offices, with two offices receiving a good rating. However, one office was rated seriously deficient; two offices were rated deficient in at least one area of the operations; nine offices were rated marginally deficient; and five offices were rated marginally deficient in at least one area of the operations.

Policy application reviews were conducted in five countries in 1998—three in Latin America and the Caribbean region and one each in the Africa and Asia and Pacific regions.

2000-2003 work plan

In an April report [DP/FPA/1999/9], the Executive Director outlined the 2000-2003 UNFPA work plan and put forward a request for programme expenditure authority. The report reviewed UNFPA 1998 resource utilization; described the work plan for 2000-2003, including information about projected resources and the proposed utilization of programmable resources among country categories; and presented the Executive Director's proposed programme expenditure authority for 2000 from regular resources, the estimates for new programmable regular resources for 2001-2003 and the estimates of new programme resources from multi-bilateral funding.

The income from regular resources for 1998 decreased to $278 million from $289.7 million in 1997. The income assumption for 1999 was $280 million from regular resources, about the same level as the actual income of 1998. With that income assumption, the need to replenish the operational reserve by $5 million utilized in 1998 and the absence of carry-forwards from 1998, UNFPA was obliged to allocate a lower level of resources for programme areas in 1999—$220 million compared to $248 million in 1998. That would slow down programme implementation, losing the momentum gained since ICPD in 1994. In view of the decrease in regular resources, including the non-contribution of one of the major traditional donors, the importance of multi-bilateral and other resources became greater.

The UNFPA work plan was a rolling four-year plan based on income projections, prior commitments and foreseeable needs. The proposed work plan for 2000-2003 estimated programmable resources based on an income assumption of $280 million in 1999, minus the necessary support budget and additions to the operational reserve. The Executive Director, in line with the Executive Board's approval of the work plan for 1999-2002 [YUN 1998, p. 1016], assumed a constant 7 per cent income growth rate for the current work-plan period. Thus, income projections for 2000-2003 of $1,331 million from regular resources represented a decrease compared to the 1999-2002 work-plan period of $1,474 million. The estimated income from multi-bilateral resources was $35 million per year, yielding a total combined income of $1,471 million. The programmable resources from regular resources were projected to increase from $220 million for 1999 to $234 million for 2000, $250 million for 2001, $269 million for 2002 and $288 million for 2003. That yielded a total of $1,041 million for the four-year period, compared to the estimated $1,174 million for the period 1999-2002. Since multi-bilateral income was fully used for programmes, the total combined programmable resources from regular and multi-bilateral resources were estimated at $1,181 million for the period, or an annual average of $295 million, compared to $319 million estimated for the previous work-plan period. Regrettably, that would compel UNFPA to scale back future programming considerably.

While programmable resources were 11 per cent lower than the level foreseen in the previous year's work plan, the Executive Director proposed to distribute the absolute amount of $758 million for country activities, an average reduction of 10 per cent compared to what was previously foreseen. In addition, a new cycle of technical support services was estimated to require $97 million, 9 per cent less than the amount approved by the Board for the 1996-1999 cycle. Administrative and operational services costs for UN agency-executed projects and other projects were estimated at $36 million from regular resources for 2000-2003, or $4 million less than for 1999-2002.

The new work plan reflected the 1996 Board decision to use a new system of allocation of UNFPA resources [YUN 1996, p. 989] by categorizing developing countries in three groups. The share for Group A countries (those with low level of development) was expected to increase to 67 per cent for the period 2000-2003; the share for Group B countries (those with considerable progress in achieving ICPD goals) was planned to average 24 per cent; the share of resources for Group C countries (those that had met the thresholds of all seven ICPD goal indicators) to average 5 per cent; and for other countries and countries with economies in transition the share would be an average of 4 per cent for the same period.

By a June decision [E/1999/35 (dec. 99/13)], the Executive Board approved the request for 2000 programme expenditure authority for expected new programmable resources at an estimated level of $224 million and asked the Executive Director to report on any significant increases or shortfalls in estimated income for 2000. It noted the Executive Director's annual estimates of new programmable resources for 2001-2003 and asked her to reconsider them in preparing MYFF. The Board endorsed the use of new programmable resources for multi-bilateral funding at $35 million per year for 2000-2003 and asked the Executive Director to report on progress in developing MYFF in 2000.

Technical Advisory Programme

In response to a 1998 Executive Board decision [YUN 1998, p. 1016], the Executive Director submitted a July report on the UNFPA Technical Advisory Programme (TAP) (formerly the Technical Support Services (TSS) system) for 2000-2003 [DP/FPA/1999/12]. It stated that TAP was continuously evolving in response to the changing needs and priorities of countries, the availability of new technologies for supporting and delivering technical assistance, as well as in relation to changing cost structures and resource considerations. TAP maintained a multidisciplinary and inter-agency approach with its primary purpose being to improve national capacity to plan and implement population programmes that would help achieve the goals and objectives of the ICPD Programme of Action. Having considered other options for the provision of technical assistance, UNFPA proposed to retain the existing arrangements but with stronger emphasis on national capacity-building and technical backstopping of the Country Advisory Teams (CATs).

During the 2000-2003 cycle, increased development and use of national expertise would be actively pursued as a strategy to strengthen national capacity, reduce the current workload of CAT specialists and decrease overall costs. Local hiring resulted in substantial savings to programmes, and resources spent on the training of national consultants were a sound developmental investment. UNFPA would also adopt additional measures to improve the cost-effectiveness of the programme.

The Fund proposed a total of 152 Professional posts (134 CAT specialists' posts plus 18 Technical Advisory Services (TAS) specialists' posts) for 2000-2003, compared with the current 154 posts. Based on an analysis of the expected demand for the services of the CAT specialists, the Fund needed to increase the number of CAT specialists' posts to 134, as compared with 130 for 1996-1999. However, if sufficient resources were not available, the Fund proposed 113 CAT posts as a second option. Under both options in the new TAP arrangements, the Fund also proposed 18 TAS specialists' posts, as well as backstopping from NGOs.

In another report [DP/FPA/1999/4], submitted in accordance with a 1998 Executive Board request [YUN 1998, p. 1016], the Executive Director submitted a brief progress report on the effectiveness of the improvements that had been implemented in the operation of the TSS system.

By a September decision [E/1999/35 (dec. 99/19)], the Executive Board supported the increased emphasis on national capacity-building under TAP. It expressed concern that the Executive Director's report did not fully respond to its request for a detailed strategic analysis of options for ensuring that country programmes received high-quality technical and strategic support; that it did not adequately describe the value added by TAP to the overall work of UNFPA; and about the high cost of the arrangements proposed. The Executive Director was authorized to commit $56.5 million over the two-year period 2000-2001 to implement the TAP arrangements, with $47.5 million being made available from regular resources, and $9 million from multi-bilateral and/or other resources, including regular resources, should income levels increase. The Executive Director was asked to: give priority to category A countries; base the implementation on an analysis of programme country needs in terms of access to local expertise; and not interrupt ongoing programmes. She was also asked to submit a report in 2000 on progress made in implementing the

TAP arrangements and to report in 2001 on further options to ensure that UNFPA country programmes received the strategic and technical assistance they needed. The Board requested the Executive Director to elaborate further on the proposal to establish a country support team office to cover countries with economies in transition and submit the information to the Board for approval in 2000.

Funding strategy

On 16 April [dec. 99/5], the Executive Board, having considered the Executive Director's conference room paper on the multi-year planning, management and funding framework [DP/FPA/1999/CRP.2], reaffirmed its 1998 decision on the UNFPA funding strategy [YUN 1998, p. 1016], in which it decided that the Fund should develop a multi-year funding framework (MYFF) that integrated programme objectives, resources, budget and outcomes, with the objective of increasing core resources. It welcomed the steps that UNFPA had taken to implement its 1998 decision and asked the Executive Director to continue to develop the multi-year planning, management and funding framework, taking into account the Executive Board's views and fully respecting the principles contained in the 1998 decision. The Executive Director was asked to submit in 2000 the first MYFF, 2000-2003; the Board decided to hold the first funding session at its second regular session of 2000. It requested the Executive Director to ensure that in future the funding session and the annual reporting on the framework were both held at the second regular session. It also asked her to continue to hold regular open-ended informal consultations with States members of UNFPA on the further development and implementation of MYFF.

Evaluation activities

In a periodic report on evaluation [DP/FPA/2000/10], the Executive Director stated that a total of 316 projects in 103 countries were evaluated during the period 1998-1999. On average, 46 per cent of all operationally completed projects were evaluated. In addition to formal evaluations, all components of UNFPA-funded country programmes were subject to internal reviews as part of the country programme mid-term review process. The new policies and procedures introduced in 1997 required that all UNFPA-assisted country programmes be evaluated at the end of the programme cycle. Of the 29 country programmes that ended during 1998 and 1999, 9 were evaluated. UNFPA was in the process of analysing the root causes of the relatively low compliance rate of country programme evaluations and would recommend measures to address them. Unlike country programmes, end-of-cycle evaluations of intercountry programmes were not required. Nevertheless, a fair number of intercountry projects were assessed.

UN Population Award

The 1999 United Nations Population Award was presented to Dr. Seyed Alireza Marandi of Iran in the individual category and the National Committee for Population and Family Planning of Viet Nam in the institutional one. Dr. Marandi was selected for his almost single-handed change of Iranian population policy. As Deputy Minister of Health in 1983, and Minister of Health in 1985, he championed reproductive health activities and encouraged breastfeeding, longer child spacing and raising the age at which women should give birth to their first child to 20 years. The National Committee was selected for its significant contributions to achievements in the areas of population and family planning in Viet Nam. Established in 1984, the Committee played a key role in the coordination, management and monitoring of population and family planning policy, programmes and strategies. The award was established by the General Assembly in resolution 36/201 [YUN 1981, p. 792], to be presented annually to individuals or institutions for outstanding contributions to increased awareness of population problems and to their solutions.

In September, the Secretary-General transmitted to the General Assembly the report of the UNFPA Executive Director on the Population Award [A/54/407]. By **decision 54/451** of 22 December, the Assembly took note of that report.

Other population activities

Commission on Population and Development

The Commission on Population and Development, at its thirty-second session (New York, 22, 23 and 26 March) [E/1999/25], considered as its central theme population growth, structure and distribution, with special emphasis on sustained economic growth and sustainable development, including education. The Commission also met in open-ended session as the preparatory committee for the General Assembly's special session for the review and appraisal of the implementation of the ICPD Programme of Action (see p. 1006). Both the central theme and the issue of the flow of financial resources for assisting in the implementation of the Programme of Action were considered as follow-up to the recommendations of ICPD (see p. 1019). The Commission also discussed a report on world demographic trends as at 1998 [E/CN.9/1999/5]; the work of the United Nations Population Division in 1998 [YUN 1998, p. 1018]; and the proposed programme of work in population for the 2000-2001 biennium.

The Commission reaffirmed its 1998 decision [ibid.] that the special theme for the thirty-third (2000) session should be "Gender, population and development" and that the special theme for the thirty-fourth (2001) session should be "Population, environment and development" [dec. 1999/1]. It recommended to the Economic and Social Council for adoption a draft resolution on population growth, structure and distribution, which was adopted by the Council as resolution 1999/10 (see p. 1020), and a draft decision on its thirty-second session report and provisional agenda for its thirty-third session. The Council took note of the report and approved the draft agenda by **decision 1999/224** of 26 July.

1999 UN activities

In a report on programme implementation and progress of work of the UN Population Division in 1999 [E/CN.9/2000/6], the Secretary-General described the activities dealing with the analysis of demographic variables at the world level; world population estimates and projections; population policy and socio-economic development; monitoring, coordination and dissemination of population information; and technical cooperation.

The report entitled "Levels and Trends of Contraceptive Use as Assessed in 1998" was completed and issued as a working paper. Its findings showed that worldwide contraceptive prevalence had reached 58 per cent, up from 50 per cent in 1983. Average levels of use were higher in the more developed regions than in the less developed regions, at 70 and 55 per cent, respectively. Data for the report were compiled from national sample surveys from 142 countries representing 92 per cent of the world's population and pertained on average to the year 1993. It was estimated that, by 2025, contraceptive prevalence for the world as a whole would need to be at least 66 per cent in order to attain the projected decline in fertility to 2.2 children per woman. To achieve that goal, the number of contraceptive users among married women of reproductive age would need to be nearly 60 per cent higher in 2025 than in 1993. Globally, female sterilization was the single most-used method of contraception, accounting for one third of all contraceptive use. The intrauterine device was a distant second (22 per cent), followed by the pill (14 per cent).

The Population Division issued a wall chart on marriage patterns, "World Marriage Patterns 1999", which showed the most recent data available from censuses and surveys on patterns of marriage for 197 countries or areas. The data shown included the proportions of men and women aged 15-19, 20-24 and 45-49 who were ever married, and the average age at first marriage for men and women.

Work continued on the preparation of the manual on the estimation of adult mortality, which presented census survival methods, methods utilizing intercensal deaths (extinct generations), estimations of adult deaths derived from the survivorship of parents, and estimations derived from the survivorship of siblings. It was expected that the manual would be published in 2000. The proceedings of the Symposium on Health and Mortality (Brussels, Belgium, 19-22 November 1997) were published as *Health and Mortality: Issues of Global Concern.* An updated "United Nations DataBase on Mortality in Childhood" was completed, with data for 92 countries of Africa, Asia and Latin America and the Caribbean. Each country file contained estimates of infant mortality, child mortality and under-five mortality, based on all the sources of data available since 1960.

The report of the 1998 Technical Symposium on International Migration and Development [YUN 1998, p. 1005] was issued in February 1999 and the Population Division prepared the Secretary-General's report on international migration and development [A/54/207] (see p. 1020). A database on trends in migrant stock by sex, completed in June, was a revised version of a first set issued in 1994, with a considerably more comprehensive collection of census data. It presented estimates of international migrants, by sex, for each country and major region, as at early 1965, 1975, 1985 and 1990, and the annual growth rate of the stock of international migrants for 1965-1975, 1975-1985, 1985-1990 and 1965-1990.

The results of the 1998 revision of world population estimates and projections, which were officially announced in 1998 [YUN 1998, p. 1019], were published in two volumes: *World Population Prospects: The 1998 Revision, vol. I, Comprehensive Tables;* and *vol. II, Sex and Age.* A third volume, entitled *Analytical Report,* had been completed and was available in draft form. It contained a detailed analysis of levels, trends and future prospects of fertility, mortality, international migration and population size and growth in the world's major areas, regions and countries. A set of diskettes presenting the results of the 1998 revision in digital form had also been issued. A new set of population estimates and projections over the medium term (1950 to 2050) was expected to be completed by the end of 2000. Work on the 2000 revision was under way, with concentration on the updating of population estimates so that the base year for all projection variants could be set to 2000.

An updated set of estimates and projections of the urban and rural populations of all countries and of all cities with a population of 750,000 inhabitants or more in 1995 was completed and announced in December. A report on the results obtained would be issued in 2000. As the date of completion of those estimates and projections was usually one year later than that of national population estimates and projections, the series was being renamed to coincide with the year of completion. Thus, the 1998 revision was being issued under the title *World Urbanization Prospects: The 1999 Revision.* According to that revision, as at mid-1999, 47 per cent of the world population lived in urban areas and half of the world population was expected to live in urban centres by 2007. By 2030, over three fifths of the world population would be urban. The world urban population was growing at a rate of 2.1 per cent per year, more than three times that of the rural population (0.7 per cent per year). As a result, urban areas were absorbing 57 million persons each year, compared with the 21 million absorbed annually by rural areas. By 2025-2030, urban areas would be growing at a projected rate of 1.5 per cent per year, gaining 71 million persons annually.

A major activity of the work programme in 1999 was the completion of the report on the Eighth United Nations Inquiry among Governments on Population and Development, the first Inquiry to be carried out since the convening of ICPD. As at 1 October 1999, 90 countries had replied to the Inquiry, corresponding to an overall response rate of 47 per cent. The seventh edition of the Global Population Policy Database, 1999 (GRIPP: 1999) was completed, along with the accompanying diskette and diskette documentation. In the area of emerging issues in population policy, the ongoing project on abortion policies was significantly expanded. In addition to the wall chart entitled "World Abortion Policies, 1999", the first volume of a three-volume series—*Abortion Policies: A Global Review*—was completed (vol. I, *Afghanistan to France*) and the second and third volumes were under preparation. The publication aimed to provide objective information about the nature of abortion law and policy in all countries at the end of the twentieth century. For each country, there was a fact sheet containing information on the grounds on which abortions were performed, additional requirements and key indicators on reproductive health. Included in the background text was information on the social and political setting of changes in abortion laws and policies, the ways in which those laws and policies had been formulated and how they had evolved over time.

As part of its ongoing work on the demographic, economic and social aspects of population ageing, the first UN wall chart on population ageing was issued in 1999 to coincide with the International Year of Older Persons and the special session of the General Assembly for the overall review and appraisal of the implementation of the ICPD Programme of Action. According to the 1998 revision of population estimates and projections, 1 of every 10 persons was aged 60 years or over; by 2050, 1 person of every 5 and, by 2150, 1 of every 3 would be aged 60 years or over. Although the percentage of older persons was currently much higher in the more developed than in the less developed regions, the pace of ageing in less developed regions was more rapid, and their transition from a young to an old age structure would be faster. The majority of older persons were women. Among those aged 60 years or over, 55 per cent were women. In addition, among the oldest old (aged 80 years or over), 65 per cent were women.

During 1999, the Population Division completed the fifth edition of the *World Population Monitoring Report.* Following the Assembly's special session, the Division prepared and issued a special publication, *Review and Appraisal of the Progress Made in Achieving the Goals and Objectives of the Programme of Action of the International Conference on Population and Development: 1999 report* [Sales No. E.99.XIII.16], to make the Assembly's substantive review of ICPD and resulting recommendations easily available to the international community.

During the year, the Division's Global Population Information Network (POPIN) project continued to use the Internet as a tool to stimulate and facilitate global, regional and national networking for the dissemination and utilization of population information. A primary POPIN focus was on increasing access to substantive population information and data to better enable implementation of the Programme of Action and to provide information support for informed decision-making. In partnership with the UN regional commissions and specialized agencies, the Global POPIN focused on strengthening the regional POPIN networks and building interregional, regional and national population information capacities in Africa, Asia and the Pacific, Europe and Latin America and the Caribbean. Regional capacity-building workshops combined discussion of demographic and reproductive health topics and training in the use of the Internet, including web site creation. Collaboration between the Global POPIN and the regional commissions also resulted in the creation of regional Internet web sites for the display and dissemination of information about the regional implementation of the Programme of Action and a global web site for the Assembly's special session.

Other web sites created during 1999 included one produced in collaboration with the League of Arab States Population Research Unit for the dissemination of Arabic population information and data; a bilingual (French/English) web site designed to enhance the flow of population information within the Africa region (created in collaboration with the Union for African Population Studies); a web site for POPIN-Africa, created by the Economic Commission for Africa; and a Spanish-English web site, created by the Economic Commission for Latin America and the Caribbean, to encourage regional sharing of population information and data and to make information on regional events and population-related news known to a wider public. In 1999, the first two issues of *Africa's Population and Development Bulletin*, an electronic/hard-copy journal, which incorporated contributions from regional African population research institutes, were published. The global and regional POPIN web sites were accessed over 5 million times in 1999.

As to technical cooperation, the Interregional Adviser in Population formulated a programme to build capacity among population research centres in developing countries in the effective use of new technologies of information and communication—particularly the Internet—for population research. As part of that programme, a training workshop on "Internet for population research" was held in Ouagadougou, Burkina Faso, in October, organized in collaboration with the University of Ouagadougou. The workshop marked the launching of a subregional network of francophone population research centres in western Africa, with its own web site and electronic discussion forum. Planning for follow-up activities and similar training workshops for other groups of countries was undertaken.

Chapter IX

Social policy, crime prevention and human resource development

During 1999, the United Nations continued to promote the advancement of social, cultural and human resource development, and to strengthen its crime prevention and criminal justice programme.

In February, the Commission for Social Development, the body responsible for follow-up to the 1995 World Summit for Social Development focused on the priority themes: "Social services for all", and "Initiation of the overall review of the implementation of the outcome of the World Summit for Social Development"; and on the review of relevant United Nations plans and programmes of action pertaining to the situation of social groups.

The Preparatory Committee for the 2000 Special Session of the General Assembly on the Implementation of the Outcome of the World Summit for Social Development and Further Initiatives held its first session in May and July, and a resumed session in September. In October, the Assembly decided that the title of the special session would be: "World Summit for Social Development and beyond: achieving social development for all in a globalizing world".

Other social issues addressed by the Assembly included follow-up to the 1994 International Year of the Family and implementation of the 1982 World Programme of Action concerning Disabled Persons. Regarding cultural development, the Assembly took action on the questions of the return and restitution of cultural property, the United Nations Year of Dialogue among Civilizations in 2001, the Olympic truce and the Bethlehem 2000 project.

The Commission on Crime Prevention, in April/May, continued to consider preparations for the Tenth United Nations Congress on the Prevention of Crime and Treatment of Offenders (Tenth Crime Congress), scheduled for April 2000, and prepared for the Congress a preliminary draft of the Vienna Declaration on Crime and Justice: Meeting the Challenges of the Twenty-first Century. In other action, the intergovernmental process for establishing a convention against transnational organized crime and three additional legal instruments was launched when the Ad Hoc Committee on its elaboration met for the first time in January. In December, the Assembly decided to convene a high-level conference in Palermo, Italy, in 2000 to finalize and adopt the Convention and its Protocols.

Human resources development remained the focus of the United Nations Institute for Training and Research and the United Nations University.

Social policy and cultural issues

Social aspects of development

Commission for Social Development

The Commission for Social Development, at its thirty-seventh session (New York, 9-19 February) [E/1999/26], considered several topics in the context of the follow-up to the 1995 World Summit for Social Development [YUN 1995, p. 1113]: the priority themes "Social services for all", and "Initiation of the overall review of the implementation of the outcome of the World Summit for Social Development"; and the review of UN plans and programmes of action pertaining to the situation of social groups (see below). It adopted agreed conclusions on action to promote the efficient and effective delivery of social services for all, and a resolution inviting Governments to provide additional input for the review of the implementation of the outcome of the 1995 World Summit in 2000. The Commission also adopted a resolution on the International Year of Older Persons (1999) (see PART THREE, Chapter XI), as well as five decisions. It recommended for adoption by the Economic and Social Council a resolution on policies and programmes involving youth (see PART THREE, Chapter XI) and a decision on the Commission's 1999 report and the provisional agenda and documentation for its 2000 session. A decision calling for action by the Council dealt with the nomination of Commission members. In other action, the Commission took note of a Secretariat note [E/CN.5/1999/L.2] containing the 2000-2001 proposed programme of work in social policy and development [dec. 37/105].

By **decision 1999/259** of 28 July, the Council took note of the Commission's report on its thirty-seventh session and endorsed its resolutions and decisions. It also approved the provisional agenda and documentation for the Commission's thirty-eighth (2000) session.

Follow-up to 1995 World Summit for Social Development

In 1999, the UN system continued to carry out activities at the national and international levels to implement the Copenhagen Declaration on Social Development and the Programme of Action [YUN 1995, p. 1114], adopted at the 1995 World Summit for Social Development.

In February, the Commission for Social Development considered follow-up to the 1999 World Summit and the Preparatory Committee for the Special Session of the General Assembly on the Implementation of the Outcome of the World Summit for Social Development and Further Initiatives (2000) held its first substantive session in May and July and a resumed session in September. In accordance with Assembly resolution 53/28 [YUN 1998, p. 1026], the special session was scheduled to take place from 26 to 30 June in Geneva.

On 2 February, the Council decided to invite those non-governmental organizations (NGOs) that had been accredited to the World Summit for Social Development to attend the thirty-seventh session of the Commission, provided that they had started the process of applying for consultative status in accordance with Council decision 1996/315 [YUN 1996, p. 1368] (**decision 1999/206**).

On 15 November, the Council adopted a similar decision with regard to NGOs attending the Commission's thirty-eighth (2000) session (**decision 1999/294**).

Commission action. In February, the Commission for Social Development, the body responsible for Summit follow-up and implementation of the Copenhagen Declaration and Programme of Action, focused on the priority themes: "Social services for all" and "Initiation of the overall review of the implementation of the outcome of the World Summit for Social Development"; and the review of relevant UN plans and programmes of action pertaining to the situation of social groups.

In a January report [E/CN.5/1999/2], the Secretary-General presented recommendations with regard to meeting the Summit's target of quality basic social services for all, focusing on social service availability and coverage; establishing partnerships among providers and users; generating adequate resources to support the services; and improving access to information for all. The report suggested guidelines to ensure that external resources contributed effectively to extending and improving social services.

The Commission also had before it the reports of the Expert Workshop on Innovations in the Delivery and Financing of Social Services (New York, 13-16 October 1998) [E/CN.5/1999/7] and of the Workshop on Ensuring Access to Social Services of Under-served Populations (Bangkok, Thailand, 2-6 November 1998) [E/CN.5/1999/6]. Germany transmitted the report of the International Expert Meeting on Social Services for All (Frankfurt, Germany, 14-16 October 1998) [E/CN.5/1999/11].

On 19 February, the Commission adopted a resolution [E/1999/26 (res. 37/1)] containing agreed conclusions on social services for all, which presented recommendations for action to promote the efficient and effective delivery of social services for all, as a contribution to overall social development. The agreed conclusions set out general principles and goals, suggested priorities for delivery and provision of social services, discussed the need for partnership between Governments and other social actors, stressed the importance of information, encouraged the mobilization of resources and established parameters for international cooperation for social services. The Commission decided to transmit the agreed conclusions to the Economic and Social Council in 1999 and to the Preparatory Committee for the Assembly's special session. Also on 19 February [dec. 37/102], the Commission decided to include in its report the Chairman's summary of the expert panel discussion on social services for all, held during the session.

Regarding the initiation of the overall review of the implementation of the outcome of the 1995 World Summit, the Commission had before it a report of the Secretary-General containing proposals on further initiatives to be addressed by the special session [E/CN.5/1999/3]. The report described criteria for the selection of issues for the special session's agenda and identified issues under each of the 10 commitments for action contained in the Copenhagen Declaration. Another report of the Secretary-General, which provided a preliminary assessment of the implementation of the outcome of the Summit [E/CN.5/1999/4], stated that, although most countries had taken some steps towards fulfilling the commitments made at the Summit, much more needed to be achieved. Several of the targets specified in the Programme of Action would not be met within the period agreed, and in some instances there had been severe setbacks.

In February, the Commission adopted a resolution on the initiation of the overall review of the implementation of the outcome of the Summit [res. 37/3], by which it invited Governments to provide additional inputs, in particular proposals concerning possible further initiatives, to the Preparatory Committee to facilitate its work. It asked the Secretary-General to update the reports on further initiatives and preliminary assessments.

The Commission's review of relevant UN plans and programmes of action pertaining to the situation of social groups focused on the International Year of Older Persons (1999) (see p. 1124).

A report of the Secretary-General [A/54/220], submitted to the General Assembly in August, updated information on the implementation of the outcome of the Summit by intergovernmental bodies and on preparations for the special session.

Special session of General Assembly (2000)

The Preparatory Committee for the Special Session of the General Assembly on the Implementation of the Outcome of the World Summit for Social Development and Further Initiatives held its first session (New York, 17-29 May and 15 July) [A/54/45 & Corr.1] and a resumed session on 21 September, also in New York [A/54/45/Add.1]. In accordance with General Assembly resolution 53/28 [YUN 1998, p. 1026], the Preparatory Committee established an in-session open-ended working group to facilitate consultations on organizational matters for the special session, which met from 24 to 28 May. The Committee had before it contributions prepared by entities of the UN system [A/AC.253/9 & Adds. 1-10] and Secretariat notes on the participation of NGOs [A/AC.253/10/Add.1] and the status of preparations for the special session [A/AC.253/6]. Annexed to the Committee's report was a working draft by the Chairman of the Committee on the proposed outcome of the first substantive session.

In May, the Committee recommended three decisions for adoption by the Assembly relating to arrangements for the special session, the session's title and the provisional agenda of the Preparatory Committee's second (2000) session. Decisions that were brought to the Assembly's attention dealt with the role of the UN system; further preparations for the special session; and accreditation and modalities for the participation of NGOs.

On 7 July [A/54/1015], the Preparatory Committee Chairman requested the Assembly to authorize the Committee to hold a half-day resumed session during the week beginning 12 July to conclude negotiations on proposals relating to the review and appraisal and further initiatives. The Committee had also decided to continue to examine arrangements for the participation of NGOs in informal consultations to be held between 30 August and 3 September, with a view to adopting decisions at a resumed session before year's end.

The Assembly authorized the resumed half-day session by **decision 53/484** of 12 July.

At that session on 15 July, the Committee took note of two reports of the Secretary-General (see below).

By **decision 54/403 C** of 20 September, the Assembly, on the recommendation of the Committee on Conferences [A/54/313/Add.1], decided that the Preparatory Committee should be authorized to meet in New York during the main part of the Assembly's fifty-fourth (1999) session.

At the resumed first session on 21 September [A/54/45/Add.1], the Preparatory Committee adopted decisions on arrangements regarding the participation of NGOs at the the special session for adoption by the Assembly and on NGO accreditation.

GENERAL ASSEMBLY ACTION

On 8 October, the General Assembly adopted a series of decisions on the recommendation of the Preparatory Committee. It decided that the special session should have an ad hoc committee of the whole and agreed on arrangements for the participation of observers, States members of the specialized agencies that were non-United Nations members, associate members of the regional commissions and representatives of the UN system (**decision 54/404**). The Assembly decided that the special session would be entitled "World Summit for Social Development and beyond: achieving social development for all in a globalizing world" (**decision 54/405**), approved the provisional agenda for the Preparatory Committee's second session (3-14 April 2000) (**decision 54/406**) and decided on arrangements regarding the participation of NGOs (**decision 54/407**).

By **decision 54/465** of 23 December, the Assembly decided that the item "Implementation of the outcome of the World Summit for Social Development" would remain for consideration during its resumed fifty-fourth (2000) session.

Reports of Secretary-General. The Preparatory Committee considered April reports of the Secretary-General on the preliminary assessment of the implementation of the World Summit outcome [A/AC.253/7] and on further initiatives for the implementation of the World Summit outcome [A/AC.253/8]. Both reports updated his reports on the subject to the Commission (see above).

An August report to the Secretary-General summarized preparations made for the special session [A/54/220].

Meetings and symposiums. In May [A/AC.253/11], Spain transmitted the report of the second

Tripartite Meeting of Representatives of Parliaments, Governments and Intergovernmental Organizations on follow-up to the World Summit for Social Development (New York, 30-31 March). The meeting was organized by the Inter-Parliamentary Union, in cooperation with the UN Division for Social Policy and Development and the United Nations Development Programme (UNDP).

The Secretariat organized a symposium on States, markets and social progress: roles and cooperation of the public and private sectors, in cooperation with the State Development Planning Commission of the People's Republic of China (Beijing, 11-13 October) [A/AC.253/14].

The UN Department of Economic and Social Affairs, in cooperation with UNDP and the Government of Turkmenistan, organized a regional symposium on socio-economic policies during macroeconomic stabilization in countries with economies in transition (Ashgabat, Turkmenistan, 9-11 November) [A/AC.253/15].

GENERAL ASSEMBLY ACTION

On 10 November [meeting 51], the General Assembly adopted **resolution 54/23** [draft: A/54/L.16 & Add.1] without vote [agenda item 37].

Implementation of the outcome of the World Summit for Social Development

The General Assembly,

Recalling its resolutions 46/139 of 17 December 1991, 47/92 of 16 December 1992, 48/100 of 20 December 1993, 50/161 of 22 December 1995, 50/227 of 24 May 1996, 51/202 of 17 December 1996, 52/25 of 26 November 1997 and 53/28 of 19 November 1998,

Recalling also Economic and Social Council decision 1991/230 of 30 May 1991, resolutions 1992/27 of 30 July 1992, 1995/60 of 28 July 1995, 1996/7 of 22 July 1996, 1996/36 of 26 July 1996, 1997/56 of 23 July 1997, 1998/44 and 1998/46 of 31 July 1998 and 1999/55 of 30 July 1999 and agreed conclusions 1995/1 of 28 July 1995, 1996/1 of 26 July 1996 and 1997/1 of 25 July 1997,

1. *Reaffirms* the commitments adopted by heads of State and Government at the World Summit for Social Development, contained in the Copenhagen Declaration on Social Development and the Programme of Action, and their pledge to give the highest priority to national, regional and international policies and actions for the promotion of social progress, social justice, the betterment of the human condition and social integration, based on full participation by all;

2. *Emphasizes* the urgency of placing the goals of social development as contained in the Copenhagen Declaration and the Programme of Action at the centre of economic policy-making, including policies influencing domestic and global market forces and the global economy;

3. *Also emphasizes* the need for revitalized economic and social development everywhere within a framework that places people at the centre of development and aims to meet human needs rapidly and more effectively by, inter alia, enhancing positive interaction between economic and social policies, and stresses the need for strong, sustained political will at the national, regional and international levels to invest in people and their well-being in order to achieve the objectives of social development;

Special session of the General Assembly and its preparatory process

4. *Recalls* its resolution 50/161, in which it decided to hold a special session in 2000 for an overall review and appraisal of the implementation of the outcome of the Summit and to consider further actions and initiatives;

5. *Reiterates its invitation* to Member States to participate in the special session at the highest political level possible and in the meantime to continue to extend support to the preparatory process;

6. *Also reiterates its invitation* to the regional commissions, in accordance with their mandates and in cooperation with the regional intergovernmental organizations and banks, to continue to be involved in and to support the implementation of the objectives of the Summit, and welcomes in this context the holding of regional meetings for the preparation of the special session;

7. *Reiterates once again* that the objectives of the special session will be to reaffirm the Declaration and the Programme of Action agreed at the Summit and not to renegotiate them, to identify progress made and constraints therein, as well as lessons learned, in the implementation of the Declaration and the Programme of Action at the national, regional and international levels and to recommend concrete actions and initiatives to further efforts towards full and effective implementation of the Declaration and the Programme of Action;

8. *Reaffirms* the need for effective partnership and cooperation between Governments, international organizations, the relevant actors of civil society, including the private sector, social partners and non-governmental organizations, in the implementation of and follow-up to the Declaration and the Programme of Action and in the preparatory process of the special session;

9. *Takes note* of the report on the first session of the Preparatory Committee for the Special Session, established by the General Assembly in its resolution 52/25;

10. *Reiterates its invitation* to all relevant organs, funds and programmes, as well as the specialized agencies of the United Nations system, including the Bretton Woods institutions and the World Trade Organization, to continue to contribute to and be actively involved in the preparatory process and the special session, and in this regard takes note in particular of the decision of the Preparatory Committee on the role of the United Nations system, in which it invited all relevant organs and specialized agencies of the United Nations system and other concerned organizations, within their mandates, to elaborate and submit review reports and proposals for further action and initiatives, and of its decision on further preparations for the special session;

11. *Takes note* of the decision adopted by the Preparatory Committee at its resumed first session on accreditation and modalities for participation of non-governmental organizations at the special session, and

recalls General Assembly decision 54/407 of 8 October 1999 on arrangements regarding participation of non-governmental organizations in the special session;

12. *Recalls* the provisional agenda of the second session of the Preparatory Committee as adopted by the General Assembly in its decision 54/406 of 8 October 1999;

13. *Also recalls* the arrangements for the special session as recommended by the Preparatory Committee and adopted by the General Assembly in its decision 54/404 of 8 October 1999;

14. *Further recalls* General Assembly decision 54/405 of 8 October 1999, by which the special session will be entitled "World Summit for Social Development and beyond: achieving social development for all in a globalizing world";

15. *Recalls* the recommendation by the Preparatory Committee at its organizational session that the Commission for Social Development be entrusted with the responsibility of acting as the forum for national reporting, benefiting from the sharing of experiences gained and thus identifying areas where further initiatives are needed for consideration by the Preparatory Committee;

16. *Takes note* of resolution 37/1 of the Commission for Social Development, entitled "Social services for all", and the agreed conclusions contained therein, and its resolution 37/3 entitled "Initiation of the overall review of the implementation of the outcome of the World Summit for Social Development";

17. *Recalls* that in accordance with the Commission's multi-year programme of work, as approved by the Economic and Social Council in its resolution 1996/7, the priority theme for its thirty-eighth session in February 2000 will be "Contribution of the Commission to the overall review of the implementation of the outcome of the Summit", and in this connection also recalls the invitation by the Preparatory Committee at its first session to the Commission to undertake the overall review of the implementation of the outcome of the Summit, and to transmit the results of its deliberations to the Preparatory Committee at its second session;

18. *Takes note* of the ministerial communiqué adopted by the Economic and Social Council at the high-level segment of its substantive session of 1999, entitled "The role of employment and work in poverty eradication: the empowerment and advancement of women";

19. *Reaffirms* in this context the decision of the Preparatory Committee at its organizational session that its substantive activities should take into account the results of other major United Nations conferences and contributions by other relevant organs and specialized agencies of the United Nations system;

20. *Recalls* its decision in its resolution 53/28 to hold the special session at the United Nations Office at Geneva from 26 to 30 June 2000;

21. *Expresses its appreciation* to the Government of Switzerland for initiating and making arrangements for the special session;

22. *Takes note* of the report of the Secretary-General on the implementation of the outcome of the World Summit for Social Development;

23. *Requests* the Secretary-General to submit to the General Assembly at its fifty-fifth session a report on the special session;

24. *Decides* to include in the provisional agenda of its fifty-fifth session the item entitled "Implementation of the outcome of the World Summit for Social Development and of the special session of the General Assembly in this regard".

Role of cooperatives

In response to General Assembly resolution 51/58 [YUN 1996, p. 1016], the Secretary-General submitted a report on the status and role of cooperatives in the light of new economic and social trends [A/54/57]. The report contained information on legislative and administrative initiatives taken by States regarding cooperatives. The Secretary-General, in cooperation with the Committee for the Promotion and Advancement of Cooperatives, an inter-agency committee comprising an ongoing partnership between three UN agencies and four international NGOs, had sought to ascertain the positions of Governments and national cooperative organizations on the desirability and feasibility of elaborating UN guidelines aimed at creating a supportive environment for the development of cooperatives. Based on information received from 94 governmental agencies and national cooperative organizations in 65 countries, the Secretary-General concluded that no Government was explicitly opposed to such an exercise or had stated explicitly its unwillingness to participate. The cooperative organizations noted that they could not specify their Government's position, but many indicated that, based on current policy, they believed that their Governments would support and contribute to developing the guidelines. Annexed to the report were draft guidelines aimed at creating a supportive environment for the development of cooperatives submitted to the Secretary-General by the Committee.

In February, the Commission on Social Development took note of the Secretary-General's report [dec. 37/104].

GENERAL ASSEMBLY ACTION

On 17 December [meeting 83], the General Assembly, on the recommendation of the Third (Social, Humanitarian and Cultural) Committee [A/54/595], adopted **resolution 54/123** without vote [agenda item 106].

Cooperatives in social development

The General Assembly,

Recalling its resolutions 47/90 of 16 December 1992 and 49/155 of 23 December 1994 and its resolution 51/58 of 12 December 1996 in which it requested the Secretary-General to ascertain, in cooperation with the Committee for the Promotion and Advancement of Cooperatives, the desirability and feasibility of elaborating United Nations guidelines aimed at creating a supportive environment for the development of cooperatives,

Welcoming the report of the Secretary-General on the status and role of cooperatives in the light of new economic and social trends and the draft guidelines aimed at creating a supportive environment for the development of cooperatives annexed thereto,

Recognizing that cooperatives, in their various forms, are becoming a major factor of economic and social development by promoting the fullest possible participation in the development process of women and all population groups, including youth, older persons and people with disabilities, and are increasingly providing an effective and affordable mechanism for meeting people's needs for basic social services,

Recognizing also the important contribution and potential of all forms of cooperatives to the follow-up to the World Summit for Social Development, held at Copenhagen from 6 to 12 March 1995, the Fourth World Conference on Women, held at Beijing from 4 to 15 September 1995, the second United Nations Conference on Human Settlements (Habitat II), held at Istanbul, Turkey, from 3 to 14 June 1996, and the World Food Summit, held at Rome from 13 to 17 November 1996, including their five-year reviews,

1. *Takes note with appreciation* of the report of the Secretary-General on the status and role of cooperatives in the light of new economic and social trends;

2. *Welcomes* the elaboration of the draft guidelines aimed at creating a supportive environment for the development of cooperatives;

3. *Requests* the Secretary-General to seek views from Governments on the draft guidelines and provide, if necessary, a revised version for adoption;

4. *Urges* Governments, relevant international organizations and specialized agencies, in collaboration with national and international cooperative organizations, to give due consideration to the role and contribution of cooperatives in the implementation of and follow-up to the outcomes of the World Summit for Social Development, the Fourth World Conference on Women, the second United Nations Conference on Human Settlements (Habitat II) and the World Food Summit, including their five-year reviews, by, inter alia:

(a) Utilizing and developing fully the potential and contribution of cooperatives for the attainment of social development goals, in particular the eradication of poverty, the generation of full and productive employment and the enhancement of social integration;

(b) Encouraging and facilitating the establishment and development of cooperatives, including taking measures aimed at enabling people living in poverty or belonging to vulnerable groups to engage on a voluntary basis in the creation and development of cooperatives;

(c) Taking appropriate measures aimed at creating a supportive and enabling environment for the development of cooperatives by, inter alia, developing an effective partnership between Governments and the cooperative movement;

5. *Invites* Governments, relevant international organizations, specialized agencies and local, national and international cooperative organizations to continue to observe the International Day of Cooperatives annually, on the first Saturday of July, as proclaimed by the General Assembly in its resolution 47/90;

6. *Requests* the Secretary-General, in cooperation with the relevant United Nations and other international organizations, to render support to Member States, as appropriate, in their efforts to create a supportive environment for the development of cooperatives, including through the organization of workshops and seminars at the national, subregional and regional levels;

7. *Also requests* the Secretary-General to prepare, in consultation with Member States and the relevant United Nations organizations and international organizations, a report on the implementation of the present resolution and to submit it, through the Economic and Social Council, to the General Assembly at its fifty-sixth session.

UN Research Institute for Social Development

During 1999, the United Nations Research Institute for Social Development (UNRISD) continued to conduct research into the social dimensions of development problems. While its main objectives continued to be the promotion of cross-country comparative research on critical problems and issues of social development, UNRISD had diversified its role in response to the changing demands of the 1990s, becoming more involved in applied research that responded directly to the concerns of policy makers and the international development community. Through workshops, seminars and conferences, the Institute promoted dialogue among policy makers, donors, scholars, NGOs and grass-roots activists. A report on the Institute's activities in 1999 [E/CN.5/2001/3] stated that UNRISD had undertaken five projects related to the special session of the General Assembly to consider implementation of the World Summit for Social Development (see p. 1037). The largest project evaluated progress towards fulfilling the first commitment of the Copenhagen Declaration: to create an enabling environment for social development. Findings were presented in the report *Visible hands: Taking Responsibility for Social Development*.

The Institute also contributed to preparatory work for the five-year review of the implementation of the Beijing Declaration and Platform for Action [YUN 1995, p. 1170], adopted at the 1995 Fourth World Conference on Women [ibid., p. 1169] (see p. 1075). Papers were commissioned to assess how contemporary debates on rights and democracy had strengthened women's struggles for greater gender justice. At the same time, research continued within six UNRISD projects initiated during the previous biennium: information technologies and social development; gender, poverty and well-being; business responsibility for sustainable development; public sector reform and crises-ridden States; grass-roots initiatives for land reform; and urban governance.

As a result of a consultative meeting of 25 third world scholars (Thailand, May), the UNRISD research programme was regrouped under the areas of social policy and development; democracy, governance and human rights; identities, conflict and cohesion; civil society and social movements; and technology and society.

Although it was part of the UN system, all UNRISD activities were financed by voluntary contributions from Governments, international development agencies and foundations.

Commission action. In February [dec. 37/105], the Commission on Social Development took note of the report of the UNRISD Board covering the period 1997-1998 [YUN 1997, p. 1113; YUN 1998, p. 1029]. Following consideration of a note by the Secretary-General [E/CN.5/1999/10], the Commission renominated five members of the UNRISD Board whose terms would expire on 30 June and nominated one new replacement member for confirmation by the Economic and Social Council [dec. 37/101]. The Commission also took note of the Secretary-General's note [dec. 37/105].

By **decision 1999/260** of 28 July, the Council confirmed the five renominations and one new nomination to the UNRISD Board.

Follow-up to International Year of the Family

In response to General Assembly resolution 50/142 [YUN 1995, p. 1128] and decision 53/434 [YUN 1998, p. 1333], the Secretary-General submitted an August report [A/54/256], in which he summarized the activities of Governments, the UN system, research centres and NGOs to follow up the International Year of the Family (1994), proclaimed by the Assembly in resolution 44/82 [YUN 1989, p. 612].

The Secretary-General observed that follow-up to the Year had been hampered by a lack of consensus on terminology and basic definitions. Also, since the Year did not result in a global instrument setting standards and a plan of action, the process of follow-up was more complex, as there was no clear set of objectives against which to assess and review progress.

The Secretary-General concluded that there was a need to improve the knowledge base through research, data collection and collaboration among Governments and research institutions. To that end, the UN system should play a supporting role, including the provision of technical cooperation to Governments. Priority should be given to building local capacity in developing countries and in countries with economies in transition and to training personnel to formulate, implement, monitor and evaluate policies and programmes related to families. Attention needed to be given to the most appropriate way of observing the tenth anniversary of the Year in 2004. In that regard, the Commission for Social Development might be invited to undertake in 2004 a comprehensive review of the global situation of families, based on information made available by the Secretary-General in collaboration with other UN system entities. In order to meet the requests from Governments for assistance in formulating and implementing family-related policies and programmes and to strengthen the family component of development projects when requested, the resources of the United Nations Trust Fund on Family Activities needed to be increased.

GENERAL ASSEMBLY ACTION

On 17 December [meeting 83], the General Assembly, on the recommendation of the Third Committee [A/54/595], adopted **resolution 54/124** without vote [agenda item 106].

Follow-up to the International Year of the Family

The General Assembly,

Recalling its resolutions 44/82 of 8 December 1989, 46/92 of 16 December 1991, 47/237 of 20 September 1993, 50/142 of 21 December 1995 and 52/81 of 12 December 1997 concerning the proclamation, preparations for and observance of the International Year of the Family,

Recognizing that the basic objective of the follow-up to the International Year of the Family should be to strengthen and support families in performing their societal and developmental functions and to build upon their strengths, in particular at the national and local levels,

Noting that the family-related provisions of the outcomes of the world conferences of the 1990s continue to provide policy guidance on ways to strengthen family-centred components of policies and programmes as part of an integrated comprehensive approach to development,

Emphasizing that equality between women and men and respect for the rights of all family members is essential to family well-being and to society at large,

Noting with concern that the contributions to the United Nations Trust Fund on Family Activities have steadily decreased, reducing its resource base, and that, unless this trend is reversed and the Fund strengthened, many priority concerns relating to family issues will not be met,

Having considered the report of the Secretary-General on the follow-up to the International Year of the Family,

1. *Takes note* of the report of the Secretary-General and the recommendations contained therein;

2. *Invites* Governments to continue their actions to build family-friendly societies, inter alia, by promoting the rights of individual family members, in particular gender equality and the rights of the child;

3. *Urges* Governments to continue to take sustained action at all levels concerning family issues, including studies and applied research, to promote the role of families in development and to develop concrete meas-

ures and approaches to address national priorities to deal with family issues;

4. *Recommends* that all relevant actors, including Governments, research and academic institutions and civil society, contribute to developing strategies and programmes aimed at strengthening the economic and sustainable livelihood of families;

5. *Requests* the Secretary-General to continue to play an active role in facilitating international cooperation within the framework of the follow-up to the International Year of the Family, to facilitate the exchange of experiences and information among Governments on effective policies and strategies, to facilitate technical assistance, with a focus on least developed and developing countries, and to encourage the organization of subregional and interregional meetings and relevant research;

6. *Invites* the Commission for Social Development, when adopting its next multi-year programme of work, to consider undertaking a review of the global situation of the family in 2004, bearing in mind that, in different cultural, political and social systems, various forms of the family exist;

7. *Requests* the Secretary-General to report to the General Assembly at its fifty-sixth session, through the Commission for Social Development and the Economic and Social Council, on the appropriate ways and means to observe the tenth anniversary of the International Year of the Family in 2004.

Persons with disabilities

In response to General Assembly resolution 52/82 [YUN 1997, p. 1117], the Secretary-General submitted to the Commission on Social Development a January report [E/CN.5/1999/5] on the implementation of the World Programme of Action concerning Disabled Persons, adopted by the Assembly in resolution 37/52 [YUN 1982, p. 981]. The report described progress to equalize opportunities for persons with disabilities in the areas of accessible information resources and environmental accessibility; social services and social safety nets; and employment and sustainable livelihoods. Within the context of the Asian and Pacific Decade of Disabled Persons (1993-2002), proclaimed in 1992 by the Economic and Social Commission for Asia and the Pacific (ESCAP) [YUN 1992, p. 490], ESCAP issued eight volumes of technical material relating to assistive devices, legislation, community-based rehabilitation and self-help organizations. Topics were being developed on education and technology for disabled children and youth. The report discussed the implementation of international norms and standards relating to persons with disabilities.

In February, the Commission on Social Development took note of the Secretary-General's report [dec. 37/104].

A September report of the Secretary-General [A/54/388], submitted in response to Assembly resolution 52/82, summarized information received from 24 countries on their social and economic policies related to equalization of opportunities for persons with disabilities, particularly regarding accessibility, social services and social safety nets, and employment and sustainable livelihoods. Information provided suggested that much governmental action centred around formulation of national plans of action and the establishment and strengthening of national coordinating bodies, legislative measures and cultural activities, both to promote awareness of disability issues and to engage persons with disabilities in cultural and social life.

Within the UN system, the Department of Public Information and United Nations Information Centres organized exhibitions, lectures, seminars and special events to publicize UN activities to promote equalization of persons with disabilities. The UN Radio Service produced more than 11 radio magazines on selected disability issues. ESCAP had created a web page on the Asian and Pacific Decade of Disabled Persons (1993-2002). In May, the Food and Agriculture Organization of the United Nations launched a database to provide users with access to selected information on rural disability issues. The World Bank had identified 11 projects that benefited persons with disabilities. On 15 and 16 June, UNDP convened an inter-agency consultation in Geneva on disability.

The report also described the activities of NGOs, international norms and standards, the improvement of statistical concepts, methods and data collection by the UN Statistics Division and the accessibility of Headquarters.

An addendum to the Secretary-General's report [A/54/388/Add.1], also submitted in September, presented an analytical review of progress in equalization of opportunities by, for and with persons with disabilities.

It also provided information on the United Nations Voluntary Fund on Disability, which from 1 January 1998 to 31 August 1999 provided nearly $1 million to 35 disability-related projects, mainly grass roots-based and locally focused activities. In terms of regional distribution, Africa accounted for 40 per cent of the projects supported and received 30 per cent of the grants disbursed. Asia and the Pacific and Latin America and the Caribbean accounted for 17 per cent of the projects supported, followed by the Central and Eastern European region with 14 per cent of projects supported. The report described cooperation between the Fund and the Arab Gulf Programme for United Nations Development Organizations.

GENERAL ASSEMBLY ACTION

On 17 December [meeting 83], the General Assembly, on the recommendation of the Third

Committee [A/54/595], adopted **resolution 54/121** without vote [agenda item 106].

Implementation of the World Programme of Action concerning Disabled Persons: towards a society for all in the twenty-first century

The General Assembly,

Recalling its resolutions 37/52 of 3 December 1982, by which it adopted the World Programme of Action concerning Disabled Persons, 48/96 of 20 December 1993, by which it adopted the Standard Rules on the Equalization of Opportunities for Persons with Disabilities, 49/153 of 23 December 1994, 50/144 of 21 December 1995 and 52/82 of 12 December 1997,

Recalling also Economic and Social Council resolutions 1997/19, on equalization of opportunities for persons with disabilities, and 1997/20, on children with disabilities, of 21 July 1997 and Commission on Human Rights resolution 1998/31, on the human rights of persons with disabilities, of 17 April 1998,

Recalling further the purposes and principles of the Charter of the United Nations, and reaffirming the obligations contained in relevant human rights instruments, including the Convention on the Elimination of All Forms of Discrimination against Women and the Convention on the Rights of the Child,

Reaffirming the outcomes of the major United Nations conferences and summits and their respective follow-up reviews, in particular as they pertain to the promotion of the rights and well-being of persons with disabilities,

Noting with appreciation the important contributions of subregional, regional and international seminars and conferences related to persons with disabilities, such as the Fifth World Assembly of Disabled Peoples' International, held at Mexico City from 1 to 7 December 1998, on the theme "Towards an inclusive twenty-first century",

Expressing grave concern that situations of armed conflict have especially devastating consequences for the human rights of persons with disabilities,

Mindful of the need to adopt and implement effective policies and strategies to promote the rights and the full and effective participation of persons with disabilities in economic, social, cultural and political life, on the basis of equality, to achieve a society for all,

Concerned that improvement of disability awareness and sensitivity to disability issues has not been significant enough to improve the quality of life of persons with disabilities worldwide,

Recognizing the importance of timely and reliable data on disability-sensitive policies, programme planning and evaluation and the need for further development of practical statistical methodology for the collection and compilation of data on populations with disabilities,

Realizing that technology, in particular information technology, provides new possibilities for improving accessibility and employment for persons with disabilities and facilitating their full participation and equality, and welcoming the initiatives of the United Nations in promoting information technology as a means of achieving the universal goal of a society for all,

1. *Takes note with appreciation* of the report of the Secretary-General on the implementation of the World Programme of Action concerning Disabled Persons;

2. *Welcomes* the initiatives of Governments to enhance the rights of persons with disabilities and for the further equalization of opportunities by, for and with persons with disabilities, and also welcomes the contribution of the United Nations system and non-governmental organizations, as appropriate, in this regard;

3. *Notes with appreciation* the valuable work undertaken by the Special Rapporteur for monitoring the implementation of the Standard Rules on the Equalization of Opportunities for Persons with Disabilities of the Commission for Social Development under his second mandate for the period 1997-2000;

4. *Encourages* Governments, non-governmental organizations and the private sector, as appropriate, to take concrete measures to promote the implementation of relevant United Nations resolutions and agreed international standards concerning persons with disabilities, in particular the Standard Rules on the Equalization of Opportunities for Persons with Disabilities, and for the further equalization of opportunities for persons with disabilities by focusing on accessibility, health, social services, including training and rehabilitation, safety nets, employment and sustainable livelihoods, in the design and implementation of strategies, policies and programmes to promote a more inclusive society;

5. *Calls upon* Governments to undertake all necessary measures to advance beyond the adoption of national plans for people with disabilities through, inter alia, the creation or reinforcement of arrangements for the promotion and awareness of disability issues and the allocation of sufficient resources for the full implementation of existing plans and initiatives, and emphasizes the importance of supporting national efforts through international cooperation in this regard;

6. *Encourages* Governments and intergovernmental and non-governmental organizations to take practical actions, including public information campaigns, by, for and with persons with disabilities, with a view to increasing disability awareness and sensitivity to disability issues and to combating and overcoming discrimination against persons with disabilities and in order to further their full and effective participation in society;

7. *Encourages* Governments to continue their support to non-governmental organizations contributing to the fulfilment of the implementation of the World Programme of Action concerning Disabled Persons;

8. *Also encourages* Governments to involve persons with disabilities in the formulation of strategies and plans aimed at eradicating poverty, promoting education and enhancing employment;

9. *Urges* relevant bodies and organizations of the United Nations system, including relevant human rights treaty bodies and the regional commissions, as well as intergovernmental and non-governmental organizations and institutions, to work closely with the programme on disability of the Division for Social Policy and Development of the Secretariat in the promotion of the rights of persons with disabilities, including activities at the field level, by sharing experiences, findings and recommendations on persons with disabilities;

10. *Urges* Governments to cooperate with the Statistics Division of the Secretariat in the continued development of global statistics and indicators on disability,

and encourages them to avail themselves of the technical assistance of the Division to build national capacities for national data-collection systems, as needed;

11. *Also urges* Governments, in collaboration with the United Nations system, to give special attention to the rights, needs and well-being of children with disabilities and their families in the development of policies and programmes;

12. *Encourages* Governments, concerned non-governmental organizations and the private sector to continue to support the United Nations Voluntary Fund on Disability with a view to implementing fully the World Programme of Action and the Standard Rules, including the work of the Special Rapporteur, and to support activities to build national capacities, with emphasis on priorities identified in resolution 52/82;

13. *Requests* the Secretary-General to continue to support initiatives of relevant bodies and organizations of the United Nations system, as well as those of regional, intergovernmental and non-governmental organizations and institutions, for the promotion of the human rights of persons with disabilities and the further implementation of the World Programme of Action and in their efforts to integrate persons with disabilities in technical cooperation activities, both as beneficiaries and as decision makers;

14. *Also requests* the Secretary-General to include, in his assessments of the implementation of the outcome of major United Nations conferences and summits to be considered at the forthcoming special sessions of the General Assembly, the contribution of these meetings to the promotion of the rights and well-being of persons with disabilities;

15. *Expresses its appreciation* to the Secretary-General for his efforts in improving the accessibility of the United Nations for persons with disabilities, and urges him to continue to implement plans to provide a barrier-free environment, as well as information in an accessible format and communication services;

16. *Requests* the Secretary-General to submit to the General Assembly at its fifty-sixth session, through the Commission for Social Development at its thirty-ninth session, a report on the implementation of the present resolution.

Cultural development

International Year of Dialogue among Civilizations

In response to General Assembly resolution 53/22 [YUN 1998, p. 1031], the Secretary-General, in November [A/54/546], presented a provisional report of his Personal Representative for the United Nations Year of Dialogue among Civilizations (2001), proclaimed by the Assembly in resolution 53/22.

The Personal Representative, appointed by the Secretary-General in August, stated that the dialogue should be between those that perceived diversity as a threat and those that perceived it as an integral component of growth. He stated that it would be fitting if the spirit of dialogue among civilizations could open the door to a major process of reconciliation in one or more parts of the world. The Personal Representative would translate into action the conceptual underpinnings of the dialogue, the admission of reality and the goals of the Year.

Communications. During 1999, Iran submitted a series of communications describing activities it had undertaken regarding dialogue among civilizations, some of which were in accordance with General Assembly resolution 53/22.

Iran transmitted a report on the establishment of the Center for Dialogue Among Civilizations, which was set up in December 1998 to engage in in-depth analysis of the concept of dialogue among civilizations and to coordinate the activities of various government agencies [A/54/291]. It also transmitted the Teheran Declaration on Dialogue among Civilizations, adopted by the Islamic Symposium on Dialogue among Civilizations (Teheran, 3-5 May) [A/54/116]. In collaboration with Columbia University (New York), Iran sponsored a panel discussion on "Dialogue among civilizations: a new paradigm" (New York, 6 May) [A/54/263 & Corr.1]. It also transmitted a statement by its President on his conception of dialogue among civilizations, which was made at the General Conference of the United Nations Educational, Scientific and Cultural Organization (UNESCO) in October [A/54/539].

GENERAL ASSEMBLY ACTION

On 10 December [meeting 78], the General Assembly adopted **resolution 54/113** [draft: A/54/ L.60 & Add.1] without vote [agenda item 34].

United Nations Year of Dialogue among Civilizations

The General Assembly,

Recalling its resolution 53/22 of 4 November 1998 entitled "United Nations Year of Dialogue among Civilizations",

Reaffirming the purposes and principles embodied in the Charter of the United Nations, which, inter alia, call for collective effort to strengthen friendly relations among nations, remove threats to peace and foster international cooperation in resolving international issues of economic, social, cultural and humanitarian character and in promoting and encouraging universal respect for human rights and fundamental freedoms for all,

Bearing in mind the valuable contribution that dialogue among civilizations can make to an improved awareness and understanding of the common values shared by all humankind,

Recognizing the diverse civilizational achievements of mankind, crystallizing cultural pluralism and creative human diversity,

Aware that positive and mutually beneficial interaction among civilizations has continued throughout human history despite impediments arising from disputes and wars,

Underlining the fact that tolerance and respect for diversity facilitate universal promotion and protection of human rights and constitute sound foundations for civil society, social harmony and peace,

Emphasizing the indispensable role of dialogue as a means to reach understanding, promote a culture of peace, remove threats to peace and strengthen interaction and exchange among and within civilizations,

Reaffirming that civilizational achievements constitute the collective heritage of mankind, providing a source of inspiration and progress for humanity at large,

Welcoming the collective endeavour of the international community to enhance understanding through constructive dialogue among civilizations on the threshold of the third millennium,

Encouraged by the positive reception of Governments, international organizations, civil society organizations and international public opinion to the proclamation of the United Nations Year of Dialogue among Civilizations, and welcoming the initiatives undertaken by governmental and non-governmental actors to promote dialogue,

Expressing its firm determination to facilitate and promote dialogue among civilizations,

1. *Takes note with interest* of the report of the Secretary-General;

2. *Welcomes* the decision of the Secretary-General to appoint his personal representative for the United Nations Year of Dialogue among Civilizations;

3. *Invites* Governments, the United Nations system, including the United Nations Educational, Scientific and Cultural Organization, and other relevant international and non-governmental organizations, to continue and further intensify planning and organizing appropriate cultural, educational and social programmes to promote the concept of dialogue among civilizations, including through organizing conferences and seminars and disseminating information and scholarly material on the subject, and to inform the Secretary-General of their activities;

4. *Calls upon* Governments to encourage all members of society to take part in promoting dialogue among civilizations and to provide them with an opportunity to make contributions to the United Nations Year of Dialogue among Civilizations;

5. *Notes with interest* the activities undertaken and proposals made by Member States, the United Nations Educational, Scientific and Cultural Organization and international and regional organizations, including the Organization of the Islamic Conference and non-governmental organizations, for the preparation of the United Nations Year of Dialogue among Civilizations;

6. *Requests* the Secretary-General to submit to the General Assembly at its fifty-fifth session a further substantive report on preparations for the United Nations Year of Dialogue among Civilizations;

7. *Decides* to include in the provisional agenda of its fifty-fifth session the item entitled "United Nations Year of Dialogue among Civilizations".

Cultural property

In response to General Assembly resolution 52/24 [YUN 1997, p. 1119], the Secretary-General transmitted a report of the UNESCO Director-General on action taken by the organization on the return and restitution of cultural property to the countries of origin [A/54/436]. The report contained the recommendations of the Intergovernmental Committee for Promoting the Return of Cultural Property to its Countries of Origin or its Restitution in Case of Illicit Appropriation at its tenth session (Paris, 25-28 January).

The Committee adopted a recommendation in which member States decided to establish an international fund to facilitate the restitution of stolen or illicitly exported cultural objects to countries of origin. The Fund would be used to finance training and education projects. The Committee invited the Director-General to convene a working group of governmental experts to consider the question of the return of cultural property displaced during and after the Second World War. It endorsed "Object-ID", an international standard intended to simplify and rationalize the description of art objects and antiquities with a view to finding stolen property.

GENERAL ASSEMBLY ACTION

On 17 December [meeting 84], the General Assembly adopted **resolution 54/190** [draft: A/54/L.47/Rev. 1 & Add.1] without vote [agenda item 24].

Return or restitution of cultural property to the countries of origin

The General Assembly,

Reaffirming the relevant provisions of the Charter of the United Nations,

Recalling its resolutions 3026 A (XXVII) of 18 December 1972, 3148(XXVIII) of 14 December 1973, 3187(XXVIII) of 18 December 1973, 3391(XXX) of 19 November 1975, 31/40 of 30 November 1976, 32/18 of 11 November 1977, 33/50 of 14 December 1978, 34/64 of 29 November 1979, 35/127 and 35/128 of 11 December 1980, 36/64 of 27 November 1981, 38/34 of 25 November 1983, 40/19 of 21 November 1985, 42/7 of 22 October 1987, 44/18 of 6 November 1989, 46/10 of 22 October 1991, 48/15 of 2 November 1993, 50/56 of 11 December 1995 and 52/24 of 25 November 1997,

Recalling the Convention for the Protection of Cultural Property in the Event of Armed Conflict, adopted at The Hague on 14 May 1954,

Recalling also the Convention on the Means of Prohibiting and Preventing the Illicit Import, Export and Transfer of Ownership of Cultural Property, adopted on 14 November 1970 by the General Conference of the United Nations Educational, Scientific and Cultural Organization,

Recalling further the Convention on Stolen or Illegally Exported Cultural Objects, adopted at Rome on 24 June 1995 by the International Institute for the Unification of Private Law,

Recalling the Medellin Declaration for Cultural Diversity and Tolerance and the Plan of Action on Cultural Cooperation, adopted at the first Meeting of the Ministers of Culture of the Movement of Non-Aligned Countries, held at Medellin, Colombia, on 4 and 5 September 1997,

Taking note with interest of the report of the Secretary-General submitted in cooperation with the Director-General of the United Nations Educational, Scientific and Cultural Organization,

Aware of the importance attached by the countries of origin to the return of cultural property which is of fundamental spiritual and cultural value to them, so that they may constitute collections representative of their cultural heritage,

Expressing concern about the loss, destruction, damage, removal, theft, pillage or misappropriation of and any acts of vandalism directed against cultural property in areas of armed conflict and territories that are occupied,

Also expressing concern about the illicit traffic in cultural property and its damages on the cultural heritage of nations,

1. *Commends* the United Nations Educational, Scientific and Cultural Organization and the Intergovernmental Committee for Promoting the Return of Cultural Property to its Countries of Origin or its Restitution in Case of Illicit Appropriation on the work they have accomplished, in particular through the promotion of bilateral negotiations, for the return or restitution of cultural property, the preparation of inventories of movable cultural property, the reduction of illicit traffic in cultural property and the dissemination of information to the public;

2. *Reaffirms* the importance of the provisions of the Convention for the Protection of Cultural Property in the Event of Armed Conflict, and invites Member States which have not already done so to become parties to the Convention and facilitate its implementation;

3. *Welcomes* the adoption of the Second Protocol to the Convention, adopted at The Hague on 26 March 1999, and invites all States Parties to the Convention to consider becoming parties to the Second Protocol to the Convention;

4. *Reaffirms* the importance of the provisions of the Convention on Stolen or Illegally Exported Cultural Objects, invites those Member States which have not already done so to consider becoming parties to the Convention;

5. *Calls upon* all relevant bodies, agencies, funds and programmes of the United Nations system and other relevant intergovernmental organizations to work in coordination with the United Nations Educational, Scientific and Cultural Organization, within their mandates and in cooperation with Member States, in order to continue to address the issue of return or restitution of cultural property to the countries of origin, and to provide appropriate support accordingly;

6. *Invites* Member States to continue drawing up, in cooperation with the United Nations Educational, Scientific and Cultural Organization, systematic inventories of their cultural property;

7. *Commends* the efforts of the United Nations Educational, Scientific and Cultural Organization to encourage the linking of existing databases and identification systems, taking into account the one developed by the International Criminal Police Organization, to allow for electronic transmission of information in order to reduce illicit trafficking in cultural property, and encourages the United Nations Educational, Scientific and Cultural Organization to make further efforts in this regard in cooperation with Member States, where appropriate;

8. *Requests* the Secretary-General to cooperate with the United Nations Educational, Scientific and Cultural Organization in its efforts to develop all possibilities, including any further initiatives, for bringing about the attainment of the objectives of the present resolution;

9. *Also requests* the Secretary-General, in cooperation with the Director-General of the United Nations Educational, Scientific and Cultural Organization, to submit to the General Assembly at its fifty-sixth session a report on the implementation of the present resolution;

10. *Decides* to include in the provisional agenda of its fifty-sixth session the item entitled "Return or restitution of cultural property to the countries of origin".

Olympic truce

On 24 November [meeting 63], the General Assembly adopted **resolution 54/34** [draft: A/54/L.26 & Add.1] without vote [agenda item 22].

Building a peaceful and better world through sport and the Olympic ideal

The General Assembly,

Recalling its resolution 52/21 of 25 November 1997, in which it decided to include in the provisional agenda of its fifty-fourth session the item entitled "Building a peaceful and better world through sport and the Olympic ideal" and to consider this item every two years in advance of each Summer and Winter Olympic Games,

Recalling also its resolution 48/11 of 25 October 1993, which, inter alia, revived the ancient Greek tradition of the *ekecheiria*, or "Olympic Truce", calling for all hostilities to cease during the Games, thereby mobilizing the youth of the world in the cause of peace,

Taking into account resolution CM/Res. 1608(LXII), adopted by the Council of Ministers of the Organization of African Unity at its sixty-second ordinary session, held at Addis Ababa from 21 to 23 June 1995, and endorsed by the Assembly of Heads of State and Government of that organization, which supports the appeal for an Olympic Truce,

Recognizing the valuable contribution that the appeal launched by the International Olympic Committee for an Olympic Truce, with which the National Olympic Committees of the Member States are associated, could make towards advancing the purposes and principles of the Charter of the United Nations,

Reaffirming that the Olympic ideal promotes international understanding, particularly among the youth of the world, through sport and culture in order to advance the harmonious development of mankind,

Noting with satisfaction the flying of the United Nations flag at all competition sites of the Olympic Games and the increasing number of joint endeavours of the International Olympic Committee and the United Nations system, for example in the fields of development, humanitarian assistance, protection of the environment, health promotion, education, eradication of poverty, the fight against AIDS, drug abuse, violence and juvenile delinquency,

Noting also with satisfaction the joint organization by the International Olympic Committee and the United Nations Educational, Scientific and Cultural Organization of the World Conference on Education and Sport for a Culture of Peace in Paris from 5 to 7 July 1999, in accordance with General Assembly resolution 52/13 of 20 November 1997, and their initiation of a programme of action pursuant to Assembly resolution 53/243 of 13 September 1999,

1. *Urges* Member States to observe the Olympic Truce during the games of the XXVII Olympiad, to be held at Sydney, Australia, from 15 September to 1 October 2000, the vision of which, at the dawn of the new millennium, is to be a highly harmonious, athlete-oriented and environmentally committed Olympic Games;

2. *Also urges* Member States to take the initiative to abide by the Olympic Truce, individually and collectively, and to pursue, in conformity with the purposes and principles of the Charter of the United Nations, the peaceful settlement of all international conflicts through diplomatic solutions;

3. *Calls upon* all Member States to cooperate with the International Olympic Committee in its efforts to use the Olympic Truce as an instrument to promote peace, dialogue and reconciliation in areas of conflict, beyond the Olympic Games period;

4. *Reaffirms* the Declaration and Programme of Action on a Culture of Peace, adopted in its resolution 53/243, and in this context welcomes the decision of the International Olympic Committee to mobilize all international sports organizations and National Olympic Committees of the Member States to undertake concrete action at the local, national, regional and world levels to promote and strengthen a culture of peace based on the spirit of the Olympic Truce;

5. *Welcomes* the setting up by the International Olympic Committee of an International Olympic Forum for Development, a platform for consultation between intergovernmental and non-governmental organizations on issues related to the development of physical education and sport for all, and an International Centre for the Olympic Truce to promote peace and human values through sport and the Olympic ideal;

6. *Requests* the Secretary-General to promote the observance of the Olympic Truce among Member States, drawing the attention of world public opinion to the contribution such a truce would make to the promotion of international understanding and the preservation of peace and goodwill, and to cooperate with the International Olympic Committee in the realization of this objective;

7. *Decides* to include in the provisional agenda of its fifty-sixth session the item entitled "Building a peaceful and better world through sport and the Olympic ideal" and to consider this item before the XIX Olympic Winter Games, to be held at Salt Lake City, United States of America, in 2002.

By **decision 54/465** of 23 December, the Assembly decided that the item "Building a peaceful and better world through sport and the Olympic ideal" would remain for consideration during its resumed fifty-fourth (2000) session.

Bethlehem 2000

On 10 November [meeting 51], the General Assembly adopted **resolution 54/22** [draft: A/54/L.20 & Add.1] without vote [agenda item 36].

Bethlehem 2000

The General Assembly,

Recalling the fact that the Palestinian city of Bethlehem is the birthplace of Jesus Christ and one of the most historic and significant sites on earth,

Noting that the world will celebrate in Bethlehem, a city of peace, the onset of the new millennium in a global vision of hope for all peoples,

Stressing the monumental importance of the event for the Palestinian people, for the peoples of the region and for the international community as a whole, as it comprises significant religious, historical and cultural dimensions,

Aware of the Bethlehem 2000 project as a multifaceted undertaking for commemoration of the event, which will begin at Christmas, 1999, and conclude at Easter, 2001,

Aware also of the needed assistance with regard to the above-mentioned project, and expressing appreciation for the steps taken towards increasing the engagement and participation of the international community, including donor countries, and organizations of the United Nations system, in particular the United Nations Educational, Scientific and Cultural Organization, the United Nations Development Programme and the World Bank, as well as the European Commission, religious institutions and others,

Welcoming the convening of the Bethlehem 2000 International Conference in Rome, on 18 and 19 February 1999, and the participation of many high-level individuals and institutions from governmental, religious, intergovernmental, academic, cultural, non-governmental and private sectors in that important Conference,

Expressing the need for immediate change in the situation on the ground in the vicinity of Bethlehem, especially with regard to ensuring freedom of movement,

Stressing the need for ensuring free and unhindered access to the holy places in Bethlehem to the faithful of all religions and the citizens of all nationalities,

Expressing the hope for rapid progress in the Middle East peace process and the achievement of the final settlement between the Palestinian and Israeli sides by September 2000, as agreed by the parties, so that the millennium may be celebrated most appropriately in an atmosphere of peace and reconciliation,

1. *Welcomes* the impending arrival of this global, historic celebration in Bethlehem of the birth of Jesus Christ and the onset of the third millennium as a symbol of the shared hope for peace among all peoples of the world;

2. *Expresses support* for the Bethlehem 2000 project and commends the efforts undertaken by the Palestinian Authority in this regard;

3. *Notes with appreciation* the assistance given by the international community in support of the Bethlehem 2000 project, and calls for the acceleration of assistance and engagement by the international community as a whole, including private sector participation, to ensure the success of the Bethlehem 2000 project and the fruition of this monumental commemoration;

4. *Requests* the Secretary-General to continue to mobilize the pertinent organizations and agencies of the United Nations system to increase their efforts to ensure the success of the Bethlehem 2000 project;

5. *Decides* to include in the provisional agenda of its fifty-fifth session the item entitled "Bethlehem 2000"

so that the General Assembly may have a renewed opportunity to reaffirm its further support for the project until the commemoration comes to a close at Easter, 2001.

Crime prevention and criminal justice

Commission on Crime Prevention and Criminal Justice

The Commission on Crime Prevention and Criminal Justice, at its eighth session (Vienna, 27April–6 May) [E/1999/30], recommended the adoption of four draft resolutions by the General Assembly and six draft resolutions and three draft decisions by the Economic and Social Council. Pursuant to Council decision 1997/232 [YUN 1997, p. 1121], the theme of the session was crime prevention.

ECONOMIC AND SOCIAL COUNCIL ACTION

The Economic and Social Council, by **decision 1999/262** of 28 July, took note of the Commission's report on its eighth session and approved the provisional agenda and documentation for the ninth (2000) session. On the same date, by **decision 1999/263**, the Council endorsed the Commission's appointment of three members of the Board of Trustees of the United Nations Interregional Crime and Justice Research Institute.

Preparations for Tenth (2000) UN Crime Congress

The Commission on Crime Prevention and Criminal Justice had before it a February report of the Secretary-General on preparations for the Tenth United Nations Congress on the Prevention of Crime and the Treatment of Offenders [E/CN.15/1999/6 & Corr.1], to be held in Vienna from 10 to 17 April 2000, with pre-congress consultations on 9 April, in accordance with General Assembly resolution 53/110 [YUN 1998, p. 1032]. Also pursuant to that resolution, the theme of the Congress would be "Crime and justice: meeting the challenges of the twenty-first century". Since 1955, UN crime congresses had been held quinquennially.

The Secretary-General described substantive and organizational preparations for and planning aspects of the Congress and annexed to the report a draft programme of work for the Congress. Preparations had been made for four workshops scheduled to take place during the Congress on combating corruption, crimes related to the computer network, community involvement in crime prevention, and women in the criminal justice system. A regional preparatory meeting for Latin America and the Caribbean was held (San José, Costa Rica, 22-24 February) [A/CONF.187/RPM.4/1]. Three other regional meetings were held in 1998 [YUN 1998, p. 1033].

Working papers prepared for the Congress by the Secretariat dealt with promoting the rule of law and strengthening the criminal justice system [A/CONF.187/3]; international cooperation in combating transnational crime [A/CONF.187/6]; and offenders and victims: accountability and fairness in the criminal justice process [A/CONF.187/8]. Background papers were prepared for the workshops on combating corruption [A/CONF.187/9] and on community involvement in crime prevention [A/CONF.187/11]. In accordance with Assembly resolution 52/91 [YUN 1997, p. 1176], the Secretary-General prepared an overview of the state of crime and criminal justice worldwide [A/CONF.187/5] for presentation at the opening of the Congress. The report described major crime trends and developments since the Ninth (1995) Crime Congress [YUN 1995, p. 1132]. It also contained preliminary results of the sixth UN survey on crime trends and operations of criminal justice systems, as well as the global programme against corruption, the global programme against trafficking in human beings and the global study on transnational organized crime.

ECONOMIC AND SOCIAL COUNCIL ACTION

On 28 July [meeting 43], the Economic and Social Council, on the recommendation of the Commission on Crime Prevention and Criminal Justice [E/1999/30], adopted **resolution 1999/19** without vote [agenda item 14 *(c)*].

Tenth United Nations Congress on the Prevention of Crime and the Treatment of Offenders

The Economic and Social Council

Recommends to the General Assembly the adoption of the following draft resolution:

[For text, see General Assembly resolution 54/125 below.]

On the same date, the Council, also on the recommendation of the Commission [E/1999/30], adopted **decision 1999/261** without vote [agenda item 14 *(c)*].

Preliminary draft of the Vienna Declaration on Crime and Justice: Meeting the Challenges of the Twenty-first Century

At its 43rd plenary meeting on 28 July 1999, the Economic and Social Council, recalling General Assembly resolutions 52/91 of 12 December 1997 and 53/110 of 9 December 1998, decided to transmit to the Tenth United Nations Congress on the Prevention of Crime and the Treatment of Offenders a preliminary draft of the Vienna Declaration on Crime and Justice: Meeting the Challenges of the Twenty-first Century, annexed to the present decision.

ANNEX

Preliminary draft of the Vienna Declaration on Crime and Justice: Meeting the Challenges of the Twenty-first Century

We the States Members of the United Nations,

Concerned about the impact on our societies of the commission of serious crimes of a global nature, and convinced of the need for bilateral, regional and international cooperation in crime prevention and criminal justice,

Concerned in particular about transnational organized crime and the relationships between its various forms,

Stressing that a fair, responsible, ethical and efficient criminal justice system is at the very core of economic and social development and of human security,

Having assembled at the Tenth United Nations Congress on the Prevention of Crime and the Treatment of Offenders in Vienna from 10 to 17 April 2000 to decide to take more effective concerted action, in a spirit of cooperation, to combat the world crime problem,

Declare as follows:

1. We note with appreciation the results of the regional preparatory meetings for the Tenth United Nations Congress on the Prevention of Crime and the Treatment of Offenders.

2. We reaffirm the goals of the United Nations in the field of crime prevention and criminal justice, specifically the reduction of criminality, more efficient and effective law enforcement and administration of justice, respect for human rights and fundamental freedoms, and promotion of the highest standards of fairness, humanity and professional conduct.

3. We emphasize the responsibility of each State to establish and maintain a fair, responsible, ethical and efficient criminal justice system in accordance with the principles of the Charter of the United Nations and international law.

4. We recognize the necessity of closer coordination and cooperation among States in combating the world crime problem, bearing in mind that action against it is a common and shared responsibility. In this regard, we acknowledge the need to develop and promote technical cooperation activities to assist countries in their efforts to strengthen their domestic criminal justice systems and their capacity for international cooperation.

5. We shall accord high priority to the expeditious adoption and entry into force of the United Nations Convention against Transnational Organized Crime and the protocols thereto. We shall undertake to take early steps for the signature of the Convention and the protocols thereto and shall endeavour to ratify those instruments within two years of their adoption.

6. We request the Centre for International Crime Prevention of the Office for Drug Control and Crime Prevention of the Secretariat to carry out, in cooperation with interested countries, regional assessments of the needs of Member States concerning legislation, capacity-building, expertise, training and resources with a view to ensuring a rapid ratification and implementation of the Convention and the protocols thereto.

7. We commit ourselves to the implementation of the Convention and the protocols thereto and undertake:

(a) To incorporate a crime prevention component into national and international development strategies;

(b) To intensify bilateral and multilateral cooperation, including technical cooperation, in the areas covered by the Convention and the protocols thereto;

(c) To enhance donor cooperation in areas with crime prevention aspects;

(d) To strengthen the capability of the Centre for International Crime Prevention, as well as the United Nations Crime Prevention and Criminal Justice Programme network, to assist Member States, at their request, in building capacity in areas covered by the Convention and the protocols thereto.

8. We welcome the efforts being made by the Centre for International Crime Prevention to develop, in cooperation with the United Nations Interregional Crime and Justice Research Institute, a comprehensive global overview of organized crime as a reference tool and to assist Governments in policy and programme development.

9. We reaffirm our continued support for and commitment to the United Nations and to the United Nations Crime Prevention and Criminal Justice Programme, especially the Commission on Crime Prevention and Criminal Justice and the Centre for International Crime Prevention, the United Nations Interregional Crime and Justice Research Institute and the institutes of the Programme network, and resolve to strengthen the Programme further through sustained funding, as appropriate.

10. We shall undertake to incorporate a gender perspective into the United Nations Crime Prevention and Criminal Justice Programme, as well as into national crime prevention and criminal justice strategies.

11. We commit ourselves to the development of action-oriented policy recommendations based on the special needs of women as criminal justice practitioners, victims, prisoners and offenders.

12. We emphasize that effective action for crime prevention and criminal justice requires the involvement, as partners and actors, of Governments, national, regional, interregional and international institutions, intergovernmental and non-governmental organizations and various segments of civil society, including the mass media and the private sector, as well as the recognition of their respective roles and contributions.

13. We commit ourselves to the development of more effective ways of collaborating with one another with a view to eradicating the scourge of trafficking in human beings, especially women and children, and the smuggling of migrants, in line with the provisions of the two protocols under negotiation supplementary to the United Nations Convention against Transnational Organized Crime. We shall also consider supporting the global programme against trafficking in human beings developed by the Centre for International Crime Prevention and the United Nations Interregional Crime and Justice Research Institute, and we establish the year 2005 as the target year for achieving a significant decrease in the incidence of those crimes worldwide.

14. We also commit ourselves to the enhancement of international cooperation to curb illicit trafficking in firearms, in line with the provisions of the protocol under negotiation against the illicit manufacturing of and trafficking in firearms, their parts and components and ammunition, supplementary to the United Nations Convention against Transnational Organized

Crime, and we establish the year 2005 as the target year for achieving a significant decrease in the incidence of illicit manufacturing of and trafficking in firearms worldwide.

15. We further commit ourselves to taking enhanced international action against corruption, building on the United Nations Declaration against Corruption and Bribery in International Commercial Transactions, the International Code of Conduct for Public Officials and relevant regional conventions, and we request the Secretary-General to submit to the Commission on Crime Prevention and Criminal Justice, at its tenth session, a report containing concrete proposals to this effect. We shall consider supporting the global programme against corruption developed by the Centre for International Crime Prevention and the United Nations Interregional Crime and Justice Research Institute.

16. We decide to develop action-oriented policy recommendations on the prevention and control of computer-related crime, and we invite the Commission on Crime Prevention and Criminal Justice to undertake work in this regard in an expeditious manner.

17. We note that acts of violence and terrorism are on the increase. We shall together, in conjunction with our other efforts to prevent and to combat terrorism, take effective, resolute and speedy measures with respect to preventing and combating criminal activities carried out for the purpose of furthering terrorism in all its forms and manifestations.

18. We also note that racial discrimination, xenophobia and related forms of intolerance continue and we recognize the importance of taking steps to incorporate into international crime prevention strategies and norms measures to prevent and combat crime associated with racism, racial discrimination, xenophobia and related forms of intolerance.

19. We affirm our determination to combat violence stemming from intolerance on the basis of ethnicity, resolve to make a strong contribution, in the area of crime prevention and criminal justice, to the planned World Conference against Racism, Racial Discrimination, Xenophobia and Related Intolerance, and we invite the Centre for International Crime Prevention to prepare proposals for the World Conference.

20. We recognize that the United Nations standards and norms in crime prevention and criminal justice contribute to efforts to deal with crime effectively, in particular transnational organized crime. We also recognize the importance of prison reform, independence of the judiciary and the International Code of Conduct for Public Officials. We commit ourselves to the promotion of the United Nations standards and norms in crime prevention and criminal justice, and shall make every effort to use and apply those standards and norms in national law and practice by the year 2002. To that end, we shall review relevant legislation and administrative procedures, provide the necessary education and training to the officials concerned and ensure the necessary strengthening of institutions entrusted with the administration of criminal justice.

21. We also recognize the value of the model treaties on international cooperation in criminal matters as important tools for the development of international cooperation.

22. We further recognize with great concern that juveniles in difficult circumstances are often at risk of becoming delinquent or easy candidates for recruitment by criminal groups, including groups involved in transnational organized crime, and we commit ourselves to undertaking countermeasures to prevent this growing phenomenon and to including, where necessary, provisions for juvenile justice in national development plans and international development strategies and to including the administration of juvenile justice in our funding policies for development cooperation.

23. We acknowledge the crucial importance of applying successful strategies to reduce the opportunities for the commission of crimes (situational crime prevention) as well as social development-oriented crime prevention strategies to address all forms of crime, including transnational organized crime, and we pledge to foster and support the sharing of best practices and success stories in that area.

24. We commit ourselves to according priority to containing the growth and overcrowding of pre-trial and detention prison populations, as appropriate, by promoting safe and effective alternatives to incarceration.

25. We decide to introduce, where appropriate, national, regional and international action plans in support of victims of crime, including mechanisms for mediation and restorative justice, and we establish the year 2002 as a target date for States to review their relevant practices, to develop further victim support services and awareness campaigns on victims' rights and to consider the establishment of funds for victims, in addition to developing and implementing witness protection programmes.

26. We invite the Commission on Crime Prevention and Criminal Justice to design specific measures for the implementation and monitoring of and follow-up to the commitments that we have undertaken in the present Declaration.

GENERAL ASSEMBLY ACTION

On 17 December [meeting 83], the General Assembly, on the recommendation of the Third Committee [A/54/596], adopted **resolution 54/125** without vote [agenda item 107].

Tenth United Nations Congress on the Prevention of Crime and the Treatment of Offenders

The General Assembly,

Recalling its resolutions 52/91 of 12 December 1997 and 53/110 of 9 December 1998 on preparations for the Tenth United Nations Congress on the Prevention of Crime and the Treatment of Offenders,

Recalling also Economic and Social Council resolution 1993/32 of 27 July 1993 and the rules of procedure for United Nations congresses on the prevention of crime and the treatment of offenders,

Emphasizing the role of the Tenth Congress as a consultative body of the United Nations Crime Prevention and Criminal Justice Programme, in accordance with paragraph 29 of the statement of principles and programme of action of the Programme annexed to General Assembly resolution 46/152 of 18 December 1991,

Welcoming the recommendations made by the Commission on Crime Prevention and Criminal Justice at its seventh and eighth sessions on the organizational and substantive preparations for the Tenth Congress,

Stressing the importance of undertaking all the preparatory activities for the Tenth Congress in a timely and concerted manner,

1. *Takes note* of the report of the Secretary-General on progress made in the preparations for the Tenth United Nations Congress on the Prevention of Crime and the Treatment of Offenders;

2. *Also takes note* of the reports of the four regional preparatory meetings for the Tenth Congress, and invites Member States and other entities involved to take into account the conclusions and recommendations contained in those reports;

3. *Reiterates its request* to the Secretary-General to ensure, in collaboration with Member States, a wide and effective programme of public information related to the preparations for the Tenth Congress, to the Congress itself and to the follow-up to and implementation of its conclusions;

4. *Requests* the Secretary-General to assist least developed countries and consider ways to assist developing countries in need to participate in the Tenth Congress by providing the necessary resources for the travel and per diem of delegations from least developed countries, within available resources, and by exploring the possibility of obtaining contributions for that purpose from governmental, intergovernmental and relevant non-governmental organizations and donors;

5. *Calls upon* the specialized agencies and other relevant United Nations bodies and institutes and other intergovernmental and non-governmental organizations to participate effectively in the Tenth Congress and to contribute to the formulation of regional and international measures aimed at preventing crime and ensuring justice;

6. *Requests* the Secretary-General to ensure that the substantive and organizational arrangements for the Tenth Congress are adequate in relation to its expected outcome and to provide the required resources for that purpose in the proposed programme budget for the biennium 2000-2001;

7. *Approves* the documentation and the draft programme of work for the Tenth Congress, as proposed by the Secretary-General in his report on progress made in the preparations for the Congress, taking into account the recommendations of the Commission on Crime Prevention and Criminal Justice related thereto;

8. *Decides* that the high-level segment of the Tenth Congress shall be held on 14 and 15 April 2000 to allow heads of State or Government or government ministers to focus on the main theme of the Congress;

9. *Encourages* States, other entities concerned and the Secretary-General to work together in order to ensure that the four workshops to be held during the Tenth Congress focus clearly on the respective issues and achieve practical results, and invites interested Governments to follow up with concrete technical cooperation projects or activities;

10. *Invites* donor countries to cooperate with developing countries to ensure their full participation in the workshops;

11. *Encourages* Governments to make preparations for the Tenth Congress at an early stage and by all necessary means, including, where appropriate, by establishing national preparatory committees, with a view to contributing to a focused and productive discussion of the topics and to participating actively in the organization of and follow-up to the workshops, the submission of national position papers on different agenda items and the encouragement of contributions from the academic community and relevant scientific institutions;

12. *Reiterates its invitation* to Member States to be represented at the Tenth Congress at a high political level, for example, by heads of State or Government, government ministers or attorneys-general;

13. *Requests* the Secretary-General to invite prominent personalities with acknowledged expertise in the topics of the Tenth Congress, on the basis of equitable geographical distribution, to participate in panels under each topic of the Congress at the expense of the United Nations, with a view to ensuring a more focused discussion and action-oriented conclusions;

14. *Decides* that the Tenth Congress, within the framework of the provisional agenda approved by the General Assembly in its resolution 53/110, should devote particular attention to ways and means of making operational the provisions of the United Nations convention against transnational organized crime, especially taking into account the needs of developing countries in the area of capacity-building;

15. *Requests* the Tenth Congress to submit, through the Commission on Crime Prevention and Criminal Justice and the Economic and Social Council, its declaration to the Millennium Assembly for consideration and action;

16. *Requests* the Commission on Crime Prevention and Criminal Justice to give priority attention at its ninth session to the conclusions and recommendations of the Tenth Congress, with a view to recommending, through the Economic and Social Council, appropriate follow-up by the General Assembly at its fifty-fifth session;

17. *Requests* the Secretary-General to appoint a Secretary-General and an Executive Secretary of the Tenth Congress, in accordance with past practice, to perform their functions under the rules of procedure for United Nations congresses on the prevention of crime and the treatment of offenders;

18. *Decides* to consider this question at its fifty-fifth session.

UN Programme on Crime Prevention and Criminal Justice

An August report of the Secretary-General [A/54/289] reviewed progress made in implementing General Assembly resolutions 53/110 and 53/114 [YUN 1998, pp. 1032 & 1034] on preparations for the Tenth Crime Congress and on strengthening the United Nations Crime Prevention and Criminal Justice Programme, respectively. The report updated information contained in the Secretary-General's report on preparations for the Congress (see p. 1048) and in the report of the Executive Director on the work of the Centre for International Crime Prevention of the Office for Drug Control and Crime Prevention [E/CN.15/1999/2]. Upon completion of its proposed reform

[YUN 1998, p. 1035], the Centre had established coordinated provision of technical expertise and effective operational assistance as its core objective, reflected in its newly launched global programmes against transnational organized crime, trafficking in human beings and corruption. A gender perspective, including enabling the criminal justice system in efforts to eliminate gender-based discrimination and violence against women, was being integrated into its work. Closer operational synergy between the Centre and the United Nations International Drug Control Programme (UNDCP) had been enhanced through common management of both entities under the Executive Director.

The Centre was advancing substantive preparations for the Congress. A guide had been prepared containing information for Governments, intergovernmental and non-governmental organizations, as well as the professional community to assist in preparing for the Congress.

The report described progress made by the Ad Hoc Committee on the Elaboration of a Convention against Transnational Organized Crime in drafting the Convention and the three additional international legal instruments against illicit manufacturing of and trafficking in firearms, their parts and components and ammunition; illegal transporting of and trafficking in migrants; and trafficking in human beings, especially women and children (see p. 1057).

Regarding the Centre's technical cooperation activities, steps were being taken to formulate and implement projects under the global programme against corruption in Guatemala, Hungary, Lebanon and South Africa. In June, a memorandum of understanding was signed between Hungary, the Centre and the United Nations Interregional Crime and Justice Research Institute (UNICRI) regarding the launching of a joint pilot project against corruption. A scientific expert meeting was held (Budapest, Hungary, 8-9 June) to identify the methodology and tools for rapid assessment in the area of corruption. In Lebanon, the Centre was reorienting an ongoing project on support for the national anti-corruption plan to align it with the global programme. Under the global programme on trafficking in human beings, a pilot project in the Philippines sought to assess the involvement of organized crime and identify the main routes and patterns of trafficking from and to the country. Another pilot project, on inter-agency coalitions against trafficking in human beings, addressed two levels of action to harmonize law enforcement, criminal justice and social welfare responses in a number of European countries.

The Centre was finalizing a transnational organized crime assessment survey and designing a project to assess and analyse the threat posed by Nigerian organized crime groups with criminal networks in the region of the Economic Community of West African States and outside it. Another project in the pipeline aimed at establishing a database on organized crime in the Russian Federation and the Commonwealth of Independent States. In 1999, the Centre supported country projects totalling $5 million in Bosnia and Herzegovina, Lebanon, Romania, the Russian Federation, South Africa and the former Yugoslav Republic of Macedonia. New projects in 1999 were formulated for the Caribbean, on prison reform; for Senegal, on urban crime prevention; for South Africa, on organized crime, corruption, money-laundering and proliferation of firearms; and for the Russian Federation, on establishing a database and assessment of organized crime. In collaboration with UNDCP, the Centre formulated a project for Guatemala on developing a multi-sectoral programme of crime prevention and drug control. Implementation of those projects depended on funding from donors.

An outline of contributions and pledges made to the United Nations Crime Prevention and Criminal Justice Fund indicated an upward trend in resource mobilization, but the high proportion of contributions for special purposes restricted the Centre's flexibility in handling technical cooperation projects.

GENERAL ASSEMBLY ACTION

On 17 December [meeting 83], the General Assembly, on the recommendation of the Third Committee [A/54/596], adopted **resolution 54/131** without vote [agenda item 107].

Strengthening the United Nations Crime Prevention and Criminal Justice Programme, in particular its technical cooperation capacity

The General Assembly,

Recalling its resolution 46/152 of 18 December 1991 on the creation of an effective United Nations crime prevention and criminal justice programme, in which it approved the statement of principles and programme of action annexed to that resolution,

Emphasizing the role of the United Nations in the field of crime prevention and criminal justice, specifically the reduction of criminality, more efficient and effective law enforcement and administration of justice, respect for human rights and promotion of the highest standards of fairness, humanity and professional conduct,

Convinced of the desirability of closer coordination and cooperation among States in combating crime, including drug-related crimes such as money-laundering, illicit arms trade and terrorist crimes, bearing in mind the role that could be played by both the United Nations and regional organizations in this respect,

Recognizing the urgent need to increase technical cooperation activities to assist countries, in particular developing countries and countries with economies in transition, with their efforts in translating United Nations policy guidelines into practice,

Recalling its relevant resolutions in which it requested the Secretary-General, as a matter of urgency, to provide the United Nations Crime Prevention and Criminal Justice Programme with sufficient resources for the full implementation of its mandate, in conformity with the high priority attached to the Programme,

1. *Takes note with appreciation* of the report of the Secretary-General on the progress made in the implementation of General Assembly resolution 53/114 of 9 December 1998;

2. *Reaffirms* the importance of the United Nations Crime Prevention and Criminal Justice Programme in promoting effective action to strengthen international cooperation in crime prevention and criminal justice, in responding to the needs of the international community in the face of both national and transnational criminality and in assisting Member States in achieving the goals of preventing crime within and among States and improving the response to crime;

3. *Also reaffirms* the role of the Centre for International Crime Prevention of the Office for Drug Control and Crime Prevention of the Secretariat in providing to Member States, upon request, technical cooperation, advisory services and other forms of assistance in the field of crime prevention and criminal justice, including in the area of prevention and control of organized crime;

4. *Notes* the programme of work of the Centre, including the launching of three global programmes addressing, respectively, trafficking in human beings, corruption and organized crime, formulated on the basis of close consultations with Member States and review by the Commission on Crime Prevention and Criminal Justice, and calls on the Secretary-General to strengthen further the Centre by providing it with the resources necessary for the full implementation of its mandate;

5. *Supports* the high priority given to technical cooperation and advisory services in the field of crime prevention and criminal justice, including in the area of prevention and control of transnational organized crime, and stresses the need to enhance the operational activities of the Centre to assist, in particular, developing countries and countries with economies in transition;

6. *Welcomes* the increased number of technical assistance projects in the field of juvenile justice, reflecting an increased awareness among Member States of the importance of juvenile justice reform in establishing and maintaining stable societies and the rule of law;

7. *Invites* all States to support, through voluntary contributions to the United Nations Crime Prevention and Criminal Justice Fund, the operational activities of the United Nations Crime Prevention and Criminal Justice Programme;

8. *Encourages* relevant programmes, funds and organizations of the United Nations system, in particular the United Nations Development Programme, international financial institutions, in particular the World Bank, and regional and national funding agencies to support the technical operational activities of the Centre;

9. *Urges* States and funding agencies to review, as appropriate, their funding policies for development assistance and to include a crime prevention and criminal justice component in such assistance;

10. *Welcomes* the efforts undertaken by the Commission on Crime Prevention and Criminal Justice to exercise more vigorously its mandated function of resource mobilization, and calls upon the Commission to strengthen further its activities in this direction;

11. *Expresses its appreciation* to non-governmental organizations and other relevant sectors of civil society for their support to the United Nations Crime Prevention and Criminal Justice Programme;

12. *Welcomes* the efforts of the Executive Director of the Office for Drug Control and Crime Prevention to enhance the synergies between the United Nations International Drug Control Programme and the Centre for International Crime Prevention, in conformity with the reform proposals of the Secretary-General;

13. *Requests* the Secretary-General to take all necessary measures to assist the Commission on Crime Prevention and Criminal Justice, as the principal policy-making body in this field, in performing its activities, including cooperation and coordination with other relevant bodies, such as the Commission on Narcotic Drugs, the Commission on Human Rights, the Commission on the Status of Women and the Commission for Social Development;

14. *Reaffirms* the high priority attached to the elaboration of a comprehensive convention against transnational organized crime and additional international instruments addressing trafficking in persons, especially women and children, combating the illicit manufacturing of and trafficking in firearms, their parts and components and ammunition, and smuggling of migrants by land, air and sea, notes the progress achieved by the Ad Hoc Committee on the Elaboration of a Convention against Transnational Organized Crime in this regard, and calls upon Member States to make all possible efforts to ensure the rapid development and conclusion of the convention and the protocols thereto;

15. *Welcomes* the decision of the Commission on Crime Prevention and Criminal Justice to mainstream a gender perspective into its activities and its request to the Secretariat that a gender perspective be integrated into all activities of the Centre;

16. *Requests* the Secretary-General to submit a report on the implementation of the present resolution to the General Assembly at its fifty-fifth session.

Programme and administrative questions

A March note of the Secretary-General [E/CN.15/1999/9] summarized the proposed 2000-2001 programme of work in crime prevention and criminal justice for consideration by the Commission. The programme's objectives included promoting international cooperation and the fundamental principles of the rule of law; improving States' capacity to prevent crime, particularly organized crime, corruption, trafficking in human beings and terrorism; enhancing the capacity of Governments to reform legislation and strengthen their criminal justice systems, establish institutions and mechanisms and upgrade the skills of crime prevention and criminal justice personnel; mobilizing resources for technical cooperation; ensuring improved coordination within the UN system and with other relevant organizations; and providing substantive support to the Commission and to the Tenth Crime Congress. Noting that the convention against transnational organized crime was expected to be finalized in 2000, the Centre would support the development of additional protocols to it or other international conventions, should the General Assembly decide to do so. The note outlined activities for 2000-2001, such as support for the final drafting of the convention; technical assistance and advisory services; monitoring the use of UN crime prevention and criminal justice legal instruments; collection and analysis of relevant data and information; and development of research to prevent terrorism. Attention would focus on transnational organized crime, terrorism and economic crime, particularly corruption.

An April note by the Secretariat contained a preliminary outline of the programme narrative on crime prevention and criminal justice for the medium-term plan for 2002-2005 [E/CN.15/1999/11]. The overall orientation of the programme was to promote effective international cooperation in crime prevention and criminal justice issues and assist Governments in addressing them.

In April [E/CN.15/1999/8 & Add.1], the Secretary-General circulated the curricula vitae of candidates to fill three vacancies on the UNICRI Board of Trustees.

Coordination

In accordance with Economic and Social Council resolutions 1992/22 [YUN 1992, p. 842] and 1994/21 [YUN 1994, p. 1174], the Secretary-General submitted a February report [E/CN.15/1999/4] highlighting activities conducted in 1997 and 1998 by the institutes comprising the United Nations Crime Prevention and Criminal Justice Programme network, which included UNICRI, the affiliated regional institutes and associate institutes and centres. The report also covered activities of the International Scientific and Professional Advisory Council.

ECONOMIC AND SOCIAL COUNCIL ACTION

On 28 July [meeting 43], the Economic and Social Council, on the recommendation of the Commission on Crime Prevention and Criminal Justice [E/1999/30], adopted **resolution 1999/23** without vote [agenda item 14 (*c*)].

Work of the United Nations Crime Prevention and Criminal Justice Programme

The Economic and Social Council,

Recalling General Assembly resolution 53/114 of 9 December 1998 on strengthening the United Nations Crime Prevention and Criminal Justice Programme, in particular its technical cooperation capacity,

Recalling also the statement of principles and programme of action of the United Nations Crime Prevention and Criminal Justice Programme, annexed to General Assembly resolution 46/152 of 18 December 1991, in which it is stated that the Commission on Crime Prevention and Criminal Justice should have certain functions, including facilitating and helping to coordinate the activities of the United Nations interregional and regional institutes for the prevention of crime and the treatment of offenders, and that, given the important role of the institutes, their contributions to policy development and implementation and their resource requirements should be fully integrated into the overall United Nations Crime Prevention and Criminal Justice Programme,

Recalling further General Assembly resolution 48/103 of 20 December 1993, in which the Assembly, inter alia, requested the Secretary-General to provide from existing resources adequate funds to build and maintain the institutional capacity of the United Nations Crime Prevention and Criminal Justice Programme to respond to requests from Member States for assistance in the field of crime prevention and criminal justice, if necessary through the reallocation of resources,

Recalling its resolution 1992/22 of 30 July 1992,

Recalling also its agreed conclusions 1997/2 on mainstreaming a gender perspective into all policies and programmes of the United Nations system, adopted at the coordination segment of its substantive session of 1997, and the need to maintain a balance between the different priority issues within the United Nations Crime Prevention and Criminal Justice Programme,

1. *Notes* the new structure of the United Nations Crime Prevention and Criminal Justice Programme as laid out in the Secretary-General's bulletin on the organization of the Office for Drug Control and Crime Prevention of the Secretariat;

2. *Takes note* of the report of the Executive Director on the work of the Centre for International Crime Prevention and the report of the Secretary-General on the activities of the institutes comprising the United Nations Crime Prevention and Criminal Justice Programme network;

3. *Welcomes* Commission on Crime Prevention and Criminal Justice resolution 7/1 of 30 April 1998, in section I of which the Commission decided to mainstream a gender perspective into all its activities and requested the Secretariat to integrate a gender perspective into all the activities of the Centre for International Crime Prevention of the Office for Drug Control and Crime Prevention;

4. *Notes* the initiative of the Centre, in cooperation with the United Nations Interregional Crime and Justice Research Institute, in developing the global programme against trafficking in human beings, the global programme against corruption and the global studies on transnational organized crime, but stresses that the programmes promoted by the Centre should

be formulated on the basis of close consultation with Member States and review by the Commission on Crime Prevention and Criminal Justice;

5. *Calls upon* the Centre to reinforce its efforts to focus its technical cooperation activities on priority issues and concerns in crime prevention and criminal justice, to pursue a comprehensive approach in carrying out its operational activities, to coordinate more fully its activities with recipient and donor countries and to interact with other relevant United Nations entities and with the United Nations Crime Prevention and Criminal Justice Programme network;

6. *Urges* States and funding agencies to review, as appropriate, their funding policies for development assistance and to include a crime prevention and criminal justice component in such assistance;

7. *Calls upon* States to make every effort to contribute to the United Nations Crime Prevention and Criminal Justice Fund;

8. *Encourages* States to provide the Centre with information on best practices and lessons learned from technical cooperation projects executed by the Centre;

9. *Takes note with appreciation* of the report of the Thirteenth Joint Programme Coordination Meeting of the United Nations Crime Prevention and Criminal Justice Programme Network, held in Courmayeur, Italy, on 23 and 24 September 1998;

10. *Welcomes* the unique contribution of the institutes of the United Nations Crime Prevention and Criminal Justice Programme network, individually and collectively, to the implementation of the mandate of the Secretary-General in crime prevention and criminal justice, as reflected in the annex to the report of the Thirteenth Joint Programme Coordination Meeting;

11. *Requests* the Secretary-General to ensure that the expertise and resources of the institutes of the United Nations Crime Prevention and Criminal Justice Programme network are utilized effectively in the implementation of the Programme;

12. *Invites* interested Member States to explore the possibility of cooperative projects with the institutes of the United Nations Crime Prevention and Criminal Justice Programme network;

13. *Invites* the workshop on women in the criminal justice system, to be held at the Tenth United Nations Congress on the Prevention of Crime and the Treatment of Offenders at Vienna in April 2000, to consider the desirability of conducting an international victimization survey on violence against women that will enable Member States and the international community to develop action-oriented policies to eliminate violence against women;

14. *Requests* the Secretary-General, taking into account the activities of the workshop on crimes related to the computer network, to be held at the Tenth Congress, to conduct a study on effective measures that could be taken at the national and international levels to prevent and control computer-related crime, which would include an examination of the desirability of preparing manuals, guidelines and recommendations, and to report on the conclusions of the study to the Commission on Crime Prevention and Criminal Justice at its tenth session.

On the same date [meeting 43], the Council, also on the recommendation of the Commission [E/1999/30], adopted **resolution 1999/24** without vote [agenda item 14 *(c)*].

Action to promote cooperation and the functioning of the clearing house on international projects in the field of crime prevention and criminal justice

The Economic and Social Council,

Recalling General Assembly resolution 46/152 of 18 December 1991, in which the Assembly decided that the United Nations Crime Prevention and Criminal Justice Programme should be devoted to providing States with practical assistance to achieve the goals of preventing crime and improving the response to crime,

Recalling also its resolution 1994/22 of 25 July 1994, in which it requested the Secretary-General to establish a database on technical assistance, integrating needs of Member States, in particular developing countries, as well as on existing collaborative arrangements and funding, taking into account regional concerns,

Recalling further its resolution 1995/12 of 24 July 1995, in which it requested the Secretary-General to initiate a pilot project to establish a regional database on international training and technical assistance projects, with a view to considering additional regional databases or a global database,

Expressing its appreciation to the European Institute for Crime Prevention and Control, affiliated with the United Nations, for the establishment, in close cooperation with the National Institute of Justice of the United States of America, of such a regional centralized clearing house for central and eastern Europe aimed at facilitating the exchange of information to assist policy makers in all Member States in better allocating resources, identifying potential partners in cooperative projects and opportunities for collaborative action and improving support for an incremental approach to preventing crime and ensuring criminal justice,

Recognizing that this clearing house is also operational and available to interested parties via the Internet and that its structure is also applicable to other regions,

Concerned about the duplication and lack of evaluation of technical assistance and training projects, which may result in wastage of scarce resources for technical cooperation,

Noting that Member States, international organizations and other entities engaged in collaborative training and technical assistance have made insufficient use of the clearing house,

Aware of the operation of other databases on cooperation in specific fields, including the database of the United Nations International Drug Control Programme,

1. *Requests* the Secretary-General to collect information from Member States and relevant international organizations and other entities on their projects involving international technical assistance and training in the field of crime prevention and criminal justice, in close cooperation with the institutes of the United Nations Crime Prevention and Criminal Justice Programme network;

2. *Invites* all Member States, international organizations and other entities to utilize the existing central clearing house either by submitting information to the Secretary-General or to the manager of the clearing

house or by making direct use of the clearing house via the Internet;

3. *Recommends* that, in order to avoid duplication and to ensure transparency, entities with national or specialized clearing houses cooperate with the central clearing house by providing contact points for information or direct electronic linkages;

4. *Also recommends* that Member States consider the establishment of central contact points for information on their technical assistance and training projects in the field of crime prevention and criminal justice, as appropriate;

5. *Further recommends* that the Secretary-General explore the possibility of expanding this pilot phase as a standing activity;

6. *Requests* the Secretary-General to report on the functioning of the pilot phase to the Commission on Crime Prevention and Criminal Justice at its tenth session.

UN African crime prevention institute

Pursuant to General Assembly resolution 53/113 [YUN 1998, p. 1038], the Secretary-General submitted, in September, a report on the African Institute for the Prevention of Crime and the Treatment of Offenders (UNAFRI) [A/54/340], describing the Institute's programme activities, operations and funding, and proposals to enhance the Institute's capacity to implement its programmes and activities, thus strengthening crime prevention and criminal justice systems in Africa. The report outlined possible strategies to sustain the Institute.

During 1999, UNAFRI emphasized collaborative activities and joint action to combat crime, particularly transnational offences, and intensified efforts to make African Governments aware that crime impeded economic sustainability and poverty alleviation. It also encouraged senior officials of the criminal justice systems in African countries to use the Internet to exchange information.

UNAFRI implemented projects on developing regional legal instruments on extradition and mutual legal assistance, and on illegal trafficking in firearms and ammunition. Other activities included a proposal to address widespread corruption by public officials in Africa, studies on penal reform and strategies to assist African countries to implement UN legal instruments on juvenile justice. The Institute continued to implement a crime victimization study. UNAFRI's resources for 1999 amounted to $403,407, which came from assessed contributions from its 29 member States, a UN grant and a specific project grant, and income generated by the rental of its premises and facilities, and other sources. However, member States' outstanding balances stood at more than $2.2 million. Only 14 members had paid their contributions, while 15 had never done so.

Noting that UNAFRI's mission was becoming increasingly important as organized crime, economic crimes and crimes against the environment were committed more frequently in the region, the Secretary-General said that criminal justice systems were ill-prepared to tackle their incidence. Therefore, technical assistance in crime prevention and criminal justice should be an integral part of country programmes. The Institute's operational resources continued to decrease because of major economic transformations of African member States. In addition to conventional sources of funding, new resource mobilization strategies were needed to ensure that adequate financial requirements were met. Therefore, UNAFRI had reoriented its programmes to bring them in line with the new strategic direction of the United Nations Crime Prevention and Criminal Justice Programme network, as well as the development programme priorities of donor agencies.

GENERAL ASSEMBLY ACTION

On 17 December [meeting 83], the General Assembly, on the recommendation of the Third Committee [A/54/596], adopted **resolution 54/130** without vote [agenda item 107].

United Nations African Institute for the Prevention of Crime and the Treatment of Offenders

The General Assembly,

Recalling its resolution 53/113 of 9 December 1998 and all other relevant resolutions,

Taking note of the report of the Secretary-General,

Bearing in mind the urgent need to establish effective crime prevention strategies for Africa, as well as the importance of law enforcement agencies and the judiciary at the regional and subregional levels,

Noting that the financial situation of the United Nations African Institute for the Prevention of Crime and the Treatment of Offenders has greatly affected its capacity to deliver its services to African Member States in an effective and comprehensive manner,

1. *Commends* the United Nations African Institute for the Prevention of Crime and the Treatment of Offenders for its efforts to promote and coordinate regional technical cooperation activities related to crime prevention and criminal justice systems in Africa;

2. *Reiterates* the need to strengthen further the capacity of the Institute to support national mechanisms for crime prevention and criminal justice in African countries;

3. *Urges* the States members of the Institute to make every possible effort to meet their obligations to the Institute;

4. *Calls upon* all Member States and non-governmental organizations to adopt concrete practical measures to support the Institute in the development of the requisite capacity and implement its programmes and activities aimed at strengthening crime prevention and criminal justice systems in Africa;

5. *Requests* the Secretary-General to intensify efforts to mobilize all relevant entities of the United Nations

system to provide the necessary financial and technical support to the Institute to enable it to fulfil its mandate;

6. *Also requests* the Secretary-General to deploy his efforts to mobilize the financial resources necessary to provide the Institute with the core professional staff required to enable it to function effectively in the fulfilment of its mandated obligations;

7. *Calls upon* the United Nations Crime Prevention and Criminal Justice Programme and the United Nations International Drug Control Programme to work closely with the Institute;

8. *Requests* the Secretary-General to enhance the promotion of regional cooperation, coordination and collaboration in the fight against crime, especially in its transnational dimension, which cannot be dealt with adequately by national action alone;

9. *Also requests* the Secretary-General to make concrete proposals, including the provision of additional core professional staff, in order to strengthen the programmes and activities of the Institute and to report to the General Assembly at its fifty-fifth session on the implementation of the present resolution.

Transnational crime

As a central element of the implementation of the Naples Political Declaration and Global Action Plan against Organized Transnational Crime, adopted in 1994 by the World Ministerial Conference on Organized Transnational Crime [YUN 1994, p. 1160], the intergovernmental process was launched in 1999 to elaborate a convention against transnational organized crime and three additional legal instruments. In accordance with General Assembly resolutions 53/111 and 53/114 [YUN 1998, pp.1034 & 1039], the Ad Hoc Committee on the Elaboration of a Convention against Transnational Organized Crime began its work, holding six sessions during the year. A conference of plenipotentiaries was foreseen for 2000.

International convention

The Ad Hoc Committee on the Elaboration of a Convention against Transnational Crime held six sessions in Vienna in 1999 to elaborate a convention and three additional legal instruments against illicit manufacturing of and trafficking in firearms, their parts and components and ammunition; illegal transporting of and trafficking in migrants; and trafficking in human beings, especially women and children: 19-29 January [A/AC.254/9]; 8-12 March [A/AC.254/11]; 28 April–3 May [A/AC.254/14]; 28 June–9 July [A/AC.254/17]; 4-15 October [A/AC.254/19 & Add.1]; 6-17 December [A/AC.254/23]. Pursuant to General Assembly resolution 53/111 [YUN 1998, p. 1039], the Ad Hoc Committee submitted an April report [E/CN.15/1999/5] to apprise the Commission of progress achieved in the implementation of its mandate. In order to eliminate inconsistencies and to ensure specificity, a November note by the Secretariat provided an overview of provisions common to the draft convention and to its draft protocols [A/AC.254/21].

A symposium for policy makers on the convention (Rome, Italy, 26-27 February), attended by ministers of justice from around the world, raised awareness of the convention's necessity and of the UN role in its preparation and implementation. In October, an Asia-Pacific ministerial seminar on building capacities for fighting transnational organized crime was convened in Bangkok, Thailand.

Note by Secretary-General. A March note by the Secretary-General [E/CN.15/1999/3/Add.1] contained preliminary observations on the conduct of a study, in accordance with Economic and Social Council resolution 1998/17 [YUN 1998, p. 1052], on illicit manufacturing of and trafficking in explosives by criminals and on the abuse and misuse of explosives for criminal purposes.

ECONOMIC AND SOCIAL COUNCIL ACTION

On 28 July [meeting 43], the Economic and Social Council, on the recommendation of the Commission on Crime Prevention and Criminal Justice, [E/1999/30], adopted **resolution 1999/21** without vote [agenda item 14 *(c)*].

Activities of the Ad Hoc Committee on the Elaboration of a Convention against Transnational Organized Crime: illicit manufacturing of and trafficking in firearms, their parts and components and ammunition, as well as consideration of the need to develop an instrument on the illicit manufacturing of and trafficking in explosives

The Economic and Social Council

Recommends to the General Assembly the adoption of the following draft resolution:

[For text, see General Assembly resolution 54/127 below.]

On 30 July [meeting 46], the Council, on the recommendation of the Commission [E/1999/30], adopted **resolution 1999/20** without vote [agenda item 14 *(c)*].

Draft United Nations Convention against Transnational Organized Crime and the draft protocols thereto

The Economic and Social Council

Recommends to the General Assembly the adoption of the following draft resolution:

[For text, see General Assembly resolution 54/126 below.]

GENERAL ASSEMBLY ACTION

On 17 December [meeting 83], the General Assembly, on the recommendation of the Third Committee [A/54/596], adopted **resolution 54/127** without vote [agenda item 107].

Activities of the Ad Hoc Committee on the Elaboration of a Convention against Transnational Organized Crime: illicit manufacturing of and trafficking in firearms, their parts and components and ammunition, as well as consideration of the need to develop an instrument on the illicit manufacturing of and trafficking in explosives

The General Assembly,

Recalling its resolution 53/111 of 9 December 1998 on transnational organized crime,

Recalling also Economic and Social Council resolutions 1998/17 on the regulation of explosives for the purpose of crime prevention and public health and safety and 1998/18 on measures to regulate firearms for the purpose of combating illicit trafficking in firearms, of 28 July 1998,

Taking into account the work of the Panel of Governmental Experts on Small Arms, established pursuant to General Assembly resolution 50/70 B of 12 December 1995,

Recognizing the need for effective coordination between the Ad Hoc Committee on the Elaboration of a Convention against Transnational Organized Crime and the different United Nations bodies involved in the field of small arms,

Taking note of the *United Nations International Study on Firearm Regulation* and of the note by the Secretary-General on the illicit manufacturing of and trafficking in explosives by criminals and the abuse and misuse of explosives for criminal purposes,

Concerned by the increase, at the international level, in the illicit manufacturing of and trafficking in firearms, their parts and components and ammunition and by the seriousness of the problems arising from them, as well as by their links with transnational organized crime,

Aware of the urgent need to prevent, combat and eradicate the illicit manufacturing of and trafficking in firearms, their parts and components and ammunition,

Aware also that the illicit manufacturing of, trafficking in and criminal misuse of explosives have a harmful effect on the security of States and endanger the well-being of peoples and their social and economic development,

Deeply concerned that effective action against transnational organized crime is hampered by the easy access that criminals have to explosives,

Convinced that combating the illicit manufacturing of and trafficking in firearms, their parts and components and ammunition, as well as combating the illicit manufacturing of and trafficking in explosives, requires international cooperation, the exchange of information and other appropriate measures at the national, regional and global levels,

Aware of the importance of bilateral and multilateral instruments and arrangements in the furtherance of international cooperation in the matter, including guidelines and model regulations,

Stressing the need for all States, especially those States which produce, export or import arms, to take the necessary measures to prevent, curb, combat and eradicate the illicit manufacturing of and trafficking in firearms, their parts and components and ammunition, as well as explosives,

Reaffirming the principles of sovereignty, non-intervention and the sovereign equality of all States and the rights and obligations enshrined in the Charter of the United Nations,

1. *Welcomes* the work of the Ad Hoc Committee on the Elaboration of a Convention against Transnational Organized Crime, and encourages it to continue the negotiation of an international legal instrument dealing with the illicit manufacturing of and trafficking in firearms, their parts and components and ammunition;

2. *Recommends* that, in negotiating the international legal instrument, the Ad Hoc Committee take into account, when appropriate and pertinent, the Inter-American Convention against the Illicit Manufacturing of and Trafficking in Firearms, Ammunition, Explosives, and Other Related Materials, adopted by the General Assembly of the Organization of American States at its twenty-fourth special session, held in Washington, D.C., on 13 and 14 November 1997, as well as other existing international instruments and ongoing initiatives;

3. *Calls upon* States to consider the adoption of such legislative or other measures as may be necessary to establish as criminal offences under their domestic law the illicit manufacturing of and trafficking in firearms, their parts and components and ammunition, as well as explosives;

4. *Encourages* States to consider ways to enhance cooperation and the exchange of data and other information with a view to preventing, curbing, combating and eradicating the illicit manufacturing of and trafficking in firearms, their parts and components and ammunition, as well as explosives;

5. *Requests* the Secretary-General, from within existing or extrabudgetary resources, to convene an expert group of no more than twenty members, with equitable geographical representation, to prepare a study on the illicit manufacturing of and trafficking in explosives by criminals and their use for criminal purposes, taking fully into consideration the issues listed in paragraph 2 of Economic and Social Council resolution 1998/17;

6. *Also requests* the Secretary-General to facilitate the participation of experts from developing countries in the meeting of the expert group by providing, from within existing or extrabudgetary resources, for the travel of experts from such countries;

7. *Invites* Member States to make voluntary contributions in order to support the study to be prepared by the expert group and to ensure the participation of experts from developing countries;

8. *Requests* the Secretary-General to report, as early as possible, to the Commission on Crime Prevention and Criminal Justice on the results of the study, and directs the Ad Hoc Committee, following the completion of the study, to consider the possible elaboration of an international instrument on the illicit manufacturing of and trafficking in explosives.

Also on 17 December [meeting 83], the Assembly, on the recommendation of the Third Committee [A/54/596], adopted **resolution 54/126** without vote [agenda item 107].

Draft United Nations Convention against Transnational Organized Crime and the draft protocols thereto

The General Assembly,

Recalling its resolution 49/159 of 23 December 1994, in which it approved the Naples Political Declaration and Global Action Plan against Organized Transnational Crime, adopted by the World Ministerial Conference on Organized Transnational Crime, held at Naples, Italy, from 21 to 23 November 1994,

Recalling also its resolution 52/85 of 12 December 1997, in which it decided to establish an inter-sessional open-ended intergovernmental group of experts for the purpose of elaborating a preliminary draft of a possible comprehensive international convention against organized transnational crime, which met at Warsaw from 2 to 6 February 1998,

Recalling further the Buenos Aires Declaration on Prevention and Control of Organized Transnational Crime, adopted by the Regional Ministerial Workshop on Follow-up to the Naples Political Declaration and Global Action Plan against Organized Transnational Crime, held at Buenos Aires from 27 to 30 November 1995, the Dakar Declaration on the Prevention and Control of Organized Transnational Crime and Corruption, adopted by the African Regional Ministerial Workshop on Organized Transnational Crime and Corruption, held at Dakar from 21 to 23 July 1997, and the Manila Declaration on the Prevention and Control of Transnational Crime, adopted by the Asian Regional Ministerial Workshop on Organized Transnational Crime and Corruption, held at Manila from 23 to 25 March 1998,

Recalling its resolution 53/111 of 9 December 1998, in which it decided to establish an open-ended intergovernmental ad hoc committee for the purpose of elaborating a comprehensive international convention against transnational organized crime and of discussing the elaboration, as appropriate, of international instruments addressing trafficking in women and children, combating the illicit manufacturing of and trafficking in firearms, their parts and components and ammunition, and illegal trafficking in and transporting of migrants, including by sea,

Convinced of the need to ensure the rapid development and conclusion of the convention and the protocols thereto,

Bearing in mind the report of the Ad Hoc Committee on the Elaboration of a Convention against Transnational Organized Crime on its second session, held at Vienna from 8 to 12 March 1999,

1. *Takes note* of the report of the Ad Hoc Committee on the Elaboration of a Convention against Transnational Organized Crime submitted to the Commission on Crime Prevention and Criminal Justice at its eighth session, and expresses its appreciation of the results achieved by the Ad Hoc Committee during its first, second and third sessions, held at Vienna from 19 to 29 January, 8 to 12 March and 28 April to 3 May 1999, respectively, in the development of the draft United Nations Convention against Transnational Organized Crime and the draft protocols thereto, addressing trafficking in women and children, combating the illicit manufacturing of and trafficking in firearms, their parts and components and ammunition, and smuggling of migrants by land, air and sea;

2. *Expresses its appreciation* to the Government of Argentina for acting as host to the informal preparatory meeting of the Ad Hoc Committee, held at Buenos Aires from 31 August to 4 September 1998;

3. *Decides* that the additional international instrument being prepared by the Ad Hoc Committee addressing trafficking in women and children should address trafficking in all persons, but especially women and children, and requests the Ad Hoc Committee to make any corresponding changes to the draft instrument;

4. *Requests* the Ad Hoc Committee to continue its work, in accordance with resolutions 53/111 and 53/114 of 9 December 1998, and to intensify its work in order to complete it in 2000;

5. *Decides* that the Ad Hoc Committee shall be convened in 2000 as required in order to complete its tasks, holding no fewer than four sessions of two weeks each, according to a schedule to be drawn up;

6. *Requests* the Ad Hoc Committee to schedule sufficient time, subject to the availability of funds from the regular budget or extrabudgetary resources, for the negotiation of the draft protocols addressing trafficking in persons, especially women and children, the illicit manufacturing of and trafficking in firearms, their parts and components and ammunition, and smuggling of migrants by land, air and sea, in order to enhance the possibility of their completion at the same time as the draft Convention;

7. *Welcomes* the offer of the International Institute of Higher Studies in Criminal Sciences to host informal meetings as deemed appropriate to assist the work of the Ad Hoc Committee;

8. *Encourages* Member States to convene informal regional or interregional meetings to assist the work of the Ad Hoc Committee;

9. *Welcomes* the offer of the Government of Japan to host an international seminar on the illicit manufacturing of and trafficking in firearms;

10. *Decides* that the Ad Hoc Committee shall submit the final text of the Convention and the protocols thereto to the General Assembly for early adoption prior to a high-level signing conference;

11. *Notes with appreciation* the offer by the Government of Italy to host a high-level political signing conference at Palermo;

12. *Requests* the Secretary-General to provide the Ad Hoc Committee with the required facilities and resources to support its work;

13. *Invites* donor countries to cooperate with developing countries to ensure their full participation in the ongoing negotiating process and in the implementation of the Convention through appropriate means of technical assistance;

14. *Requests* the Secretary-General to continue to provide to Member States, upon request, technical cooperation, advisory services and other forms of assistance in the field of crime prevention and criminal justice, including in the area of prevention and control of transnational organized crime;

15. *Requests* the Ad Hoc Committee to submit a report to the Commission on Crime Prevention and Criminal Justice at its ninth session on the progress achieved in its work.

On the same date [meeting 83], the Assembly, also on the recommendation of the Third Committee [A/54/596], adopted **resolution 54/129** without vote [agenda item 107].

High-level Political Signing Conference for the United Nations Convention against Transnational Organized Crime

The General Assembly,

Recalling its resolution 53/111 of 9 December 1998, in which it decided to establish an open-ended intergovernmental ad hoc committee for the purpose of elaborating a comprehensive international convention against transnational organized crime and of discussing the elaboration, as appropriate, of international instruments addressing trafficking in women and children, combating the illicit manufacturing of and trafficking in firearms, their parts and components and ammunition, and illegal trafficking in and transporting of migrants, including by sea,

Bearing in mind that in resolution 54/126 of 17 December 1999 it requested the Ad Hoc Committee on the Elaboration of a Convention against Transnational Organized Crime to schedule sufficient time, subject to the availability of funds from the regular budget or from extrabudgetary resources, for the negotiation of the draft protocols addressing trafficking in persons, especially women and children, the illicit manufacturing of and trafficking in firearms, their parts and components and ammunition, and smuggling of migrants by land, air and sea, in order to enhance the possibility of their completion at the same time as the draft Convention,

Acknowledging the progress made thus far by the Ad Hoc Committee towards the goal of completing negotiations in 2000,

Mindful that substantive negotiations on the Convention and the protocols thereto continue in Vienna in accordance with General Assembly resolutions 40/243 of 18 December 1985 and 53/111 and 53/114 of 9 December 1998,

Recalling that in its resolution 54/126 it decided that the Ad Hoc Committee should submit the final text of the Convention and the protocols thereto to the General Assembly for early adoption prior to a high-level signing conference,

Recalling also the Naples Political Declaration and Global Action Plan against Organized Transnational Crime, adopted by the World Ministerial Conference on Organized Transnational Crime, held in Naples, Italy, from 21 to 23 November 1994, in which the Commission on Crime Prevention and Criminal Justice was requested to initiate the process of elaborating international instruments, such as a convention or conventions against organized transnational crime,

Recognizing the initiating role and the contribution of the Government of Poland to the development of a draft convention against transnational organized crime,

Recognizing also the historic and symbolic importance of associating the first international convention against transnational organized crime with the city of Palermo, Italy,

1. *Accepts with appreciation* the offer of the Government of Italy to host a high-level political signing conference in Palermo for the purpose of signing the United Nations Convention against Transnational Organized Crime (Palermo Convention) and the protocols thereto;

2. *Decides* to convene the High-level Political Signing Conference in Palermo;

3. *Requests* the Secretary-General to schedule the Conference for a period of up to one week before the end of the Millennium Assembly in 2000, with the Conference to be organized in accordance with resolution 40/243;

4. *Requests* the Centre for International Crime Prevention of the Office for Drug Control and Crime Prevention of the Secretariat to work with the Government of Italy, in consultation with Member States, to propose the agenda for and the organization of the Conference, including opportunities for high-level delegates to discuss matters related to the Convention and the protocols thereto, in particular the follow-up activities, for their effective implementation and future work;

5. *Invites* all States to be represented at the High-level Political Signing Conference at the highest possible levels of government.

Strategies for crime prevention

Crime prevention and trends

In March [E/CN.15/1999/3], the Secretary-General stated that the level of conventional crime in most countries was still unacceptably high. Victimization by crime was highest in cities in Latin America and sub-Saharan Africa, but people in cities elsewhere also were at risk. While crime in the developed world seemed to be levelling off, in several developed countries, violent crime was on the increase. In less developed countries, more people tended to regard criminal activity as a means of economic survival and to engage in such activity. Transnational organized crime exacerbated existing crime problems. There was an enormous annual turnover in markets for illegal goods, such as drugs, protected wildlife, stolen works of art, firearms and nuclear and/or toxic waste, as well as for trafficking in human beings. A rapidly growing body of knowledge of crime prevention indicated not only that special preventive measures resulted in lower crime rates, but also that such measures were often more cost-effective than conventional punitive ones. Crime prevention implied close cooperation between police, prosecutors, courts and probation offices with other State agencies, such as those involved in education, health care, social services, housing and urban development, as well as non-governmental organizations, local communities and other elements of civil society. The report noted that the meeting of the expert group on community involvement in crime prevention (Buenos Aires, Argentina, 8-10 February) had discussed a two-pronged approach to crime prevention, comprising long-term strategies dealing with economic, social and cultural causes of crime through economic, social, health-care and educational policies, and broad comprehensive programmes with a public health perspective aimed at assisting vulnerable families.

In an addendum to his report [E/CN.15/1999/3/Add.1], the Secretary-General stated that, regarding a study on the illicit and manufacturing of and trafficking in explosives by criminals, and abuse and misuse of explosives for criminal purposes, as called for by Economic and Social Council resolution 1998/17 [YUN 1998, p. 1052], the Centre for International Crime Prevention had conducted a preliminary review of the information available concerning the issues to be covered by the study. The review indicated that there were neither globally and firmly agreed upon definitions of terms for use in the study, nor comprehensive statistics on the criminal incidents in which explosive substances were involved worldwide. Thus, an effort to carry out the study could benefit from the assistance of a group of experts, as requested by the Council. As soon as the required funds were made available, the Centre would begin to prepare the study.

The attention of the Commission was drawn to the UNDCP publication, *Global Report on Crime and Justice*, which contained a comprehensive presentation of global crime trends, statistics and developments, including new and emerging issues, drawn from various sources, including the periodic UN surveys of crime trends and operations of criminal justice systems.

ECONOMIC AND SOCIAL COUNCIL ACTION

On 28 July [meeting 43], the Economic and Social Council, on the recommendation of the Commission on Crime Prevention and Criminal Justice [E/1999/30], adopted **resolution 1999/25** without vote [agenda item 14 *(c)*].

Effective crime prevention

The Economic and Social Council,

Bearing in mind its resolution 1996/16 of 23 July 1996, in which the Council requested the Secretary-General to continue to promote the use and application of United Nations standards and norms in crime prevention and criminal justice matters,

Recalling the preliminary draft elements of responsible crime prevention annexed to its resolution 1997/33 of 21 July 1997, in particular those on community involvement in crime prevention, contained in paragraphs 14 to 23 of that annex,

Recognizing that effective crime prevention is increasingly being regarded as a development issue in the international arena and that a viable criminal justice system is at the core of economic growth and social stability,

1. *Takes note* of the conclusions of the Expert Group Meeting on Community Involvement in Crime Prevention, held at Buenos Aires from 8 to 10 February 1999, and of the report of that meeting to the Commission on Crime Prevention and Criminal Justice at its eighth session;

2. *Requests* the Commission to urge Member States to recognize that effective crime prevention is the result of mobilizing local, national and international actors, stakeholders and partners;

3. *Requests* the Secretary-General to convene an interregional expert group meeting, with the extrabudgetary support of interested Governments, bearing in mind the preliminary draft elements of responsible crime prevention contained in the annex to Economic and Social Council resolution 1997/33, in order to analyse possible mechanisms for applying successful crime prevention strategies that are both situational and oriented towards social development to forms of crime such as urban crime, domestic violence and juvenile crime and, where appropriate, to new and emerging forms of crime such as organized crime, trafficking in persons, especially women and children, and corruption;

4. *Also requests* the Secretary-General, with the extrabudgetary support of interested Governments, to conduct a study on possible cultural and institutional differences in effective crime prevention and to make the study available to the Commission on Crime Prevention and Criminal Justice;

5. *Requests* the Commission to explore the possibility of preparing guidelines on crime prevention for policy makers and a handbook on crime prevention for practitioners;

6. *Requests* Member States to use the occasion of the workshop on community involvement in crime prevention that will be organized at the Tenth United Nations Congress on the Prevention of Crime and the Treatment of Offenders, to be held at Vienna from 10 to 17 April 2000, as an opportunity for Governments with technical assistance needs to form partnerships with interested donor Governments and with United Nations entities for the express purpose of developing practical technical cooperation projects aimed at addressing common problems of crime prevention;

7. *Takes note with appreciation* of the initiative of the Governments of Canada, France and the Netherlands to convene a conference in collaboration with the Centre for International Crime Prevention on the theme "Putting crime prevention knowledge to work", to be held at Montreal from 3 to 6 October 1999, which will assist in the preparations for the Tenth Congress workshop on community involvement in crime prevention;

8. *Invites* Member States to hold regional meetings of government experts on community involvement in crime prevention in order to study and develop differentiated models of crime prevention strategies that are both situational and oriented towards social development in countries with similar cultural and legal traditions;

9. *Urges* the Centre for International Crime Prevention of the Office for Drug Control and Crime Prevention of the Secretariat to promote projects that contribute to the exchange of information and experience in crime prevention for the purpose of encouraging new forms of collaboration between countries at the levels of government, the community and non-governmental organizations;

10. *Requests* the Secretary-General to ensure broad professional and geographical participation at the

workshop of, inter alia, policy advisers, law enforcement, prosecutorial and judicial authorities, academics, social workers, health workers and educators, relevant United Nations bodies, including the United Nations Development Programme, relevant non-governmental organizations, members of the private security industry, the business community, the media, local government officials and crime prevention coordinators.

Corruption and bribery

The Expert Group Meeting on Corruption and its Financial Channels (Paris, 30 March-1 April) [E/CN.15/1999/10], convened in accordance with Economic and Social Council resolution 1998/16 [YUN 1998, p. 1045], considered issues such as improving international cooperation in combating corruption, national efforts to strengthen international cooperation, and measures to improve the detection of financial flows resulting from corruption.

The experts submitted a number of recommendations for combating and controlling the phenomenon. In that regard, they proposed that Member States consider elaborating a universal instrument on the subject, taking into account relevant international best practices, international legal instruments and the ongoing negotiations on drafting the international convention against transnational organized crime. In that context, special attention should be paid to technical cooperation and assistance for developing countries or appropriate regional organizations through implementation of the global programme against corruption developed by UNDCP.

The experts were of the opinion that the international community needed to equip itself with effective international tools to control corruption and curb its detrimental effects on economic and financial systems.

Regarding measures to be taken at the national level, the experts encouraged ratification of existing anti-corruption instruments and enactment of appropriate legislation to combat different forms of corruption and laundering of the proceeds of corruption. They also considered that international cooperation involving all States would aid in prosecuting bribe-givers and -takers worldwide.

In other action, participants at the Global Forum on Fighting Corruption (Washington, D.C., 24-26 February) called on their 90 Governments to cooperate in regional and global bodies to adopt effective anti-corruption principles and practices and to create ways to assist each other through mutual evaluation.

ECONOMIC AND SOCIAL COUNCIL ACTION

On 28 July [meeting 43], the Economic and Social Council, on the recommendation of the Commission on Crime Prevention and Criminal Justice [E/1999/30], adopted **resolution 1999/22** without vote [agenda item 14 *(c)*].

Action against corruption

The Economic and Social Council

Recommends to the General Assembly the adoption of the following draft resolution:

[For text, see General Assembly resolution 54/128 below.]

GENERAL ASSEMBLY ACTION

On 17 December [meeting 83], the General Assembly, on the recommendation of the Third Committee [A/54/596], adopted **resolution 54/128** without vote [agenda item 107].

Action against corruption

The General Assembly,

Noting the corrosive effect that corruption has on democracy, development, the rule of law and economic activity,

Recognizing that corruption is a primary tool of organized crime in its efforts, often conducted on an international basis, to subvert Governments and legitimate commerce,

Drawing attention to the increasing number of regional conventions and other regional instruments recently developed to fight corruption, including the Convention on Combating Bribery of Foreign Public Officials in International Business Transactions of the Organisation for Economic Cooperation and Development adopted on 21 November 1997, the Inter-American Convention against Corruption adopted by the Organization of American States on 29 March 1996, the Principles to Combat Corruption in African Countries of the Global Coalition for Africa, the Criminal Law Convention on Corruption and the Agreement Establishing the Group of States against Corruption adopted by the Council of Europe on 27 January and 1 May 1999, respectively, the conventions and related protocols on corruption of the European Union and recommendation 32 of the Senior Experts Group on Transnational Organized Crime endorsed by the Political Group of Eight at Lyon, France, on 29 June 1996, as well as to best practices, such as those compiled by the Financial Action Task Force on Money Laundering, the Basel Committee on Banking Supervision and the International Organization of Securities Commissions,

Commending the efforts in the United Nations to address corruption concerns in a global forum, including the United Nations Declaration against Corruption and Bribery in International Commercial Transactions and the International Code of Conduct for Public Officials, the ongoing development of a comprehensive international convention against transnational organized crime and protocols thereto by the Ad Hoc Committee on the Elaboration of a Convention against Transnational Organized Crime, established pursuant to General Assembly resolution 53/111 of 9 December 1998, and the manual prepared by the Secretariat on practical measures against corruption,

Noting the holding of the Expert Group Meeting on Corruption and its Financial Channels in Paris from 30 March to 1 April 1999, pursuant to Economic and Social Council resolution 1998/16 of 28 July 1998,

Noting also the holding of the first Global Forum on Fighting Corruption in Washington, D.C., from 24 to 26 February 1999, at the invitation of the Vice-President of the United States of America, at which participants from ninety Governments called upon their Governments to cooperate in regional and global bodies to adopt effective anti-corruption principles and practices and to create ways to assist one another through mutual evaluation,

1. *Takes note with appreciation* of, and subscribes to, the conclusions and recommendations of the Expert Group Meeting on Corruption and its Financial Channels, held in Paris from 30 March to 1 April 1999, which are contained in the report of the Expert Group Meeting;

2. *Also takes note with appreciation* of the Declaration made by the first Global Forum on Fighting Corruption, held in Washington, D.C., from 24 to 26 February 1999, and notes that the second Global Forum is to be held in the Netherlands in 2000 as a follow-up to the first Global Forum;

3. *Invites* Member States to examine, at the national level, as appropriate, taking into account the above-mentioned documents, the adequacy of their domestic legal regimes in terms of guarding against corruption and providing for forfeiture of the proceeds of corruption, drawing upon international assistance available for that purpose, with a view, where necessary:

(*a*) To strengthening national laws and regulations in order to criminalize corruption in all its forms, amending provisions against money-laundering so that they cover bribes and the proceeds of corruption, as well as provisions concerning the prevention and detection of acts of corruption and money-laundering;

(*b*) To improving the transparency, vigilance and monitoring of financial transactions and limiting bank and professional secrecy in cases involving criminal investigation;

(*c*) To promoting both inter-agency coordination and international administrative and judicial cooperation in matters involving corruption;

(*d*) To enacting legislation and establishing programmes promoting the full involvement of civil society in efforts to fight corruption;

(*e*) To providing, in accordance with relevant international instruments and domestic legislation, for the possibility of providing extradition and mutual assistance in cases involving corruption or money-laundering;

4. *Stresses* the need to develop a global strategy to strengthen international cooperation aimed at the prevention and punishment of corruption, including the links of corruption with organized crime and money-laundering, by:

(*a*) Encouraging Member States to become parties to and to implement the terms of relevant international conventions and other instruments aimed at fighting corruption;

(*b*) Inviting Member States to participate in conferences and other forums for the advancement of international efforts against corruption;

(*c*) Also inviting Member States to explore the possibilities of developing a global system for peer review regarding the adequacy of practices aimed at combating corruption;

5. *Directs* the Ad Hoc Committee on the Elaboration of a Convention against Transnational Organized Crime to incorporate into the draft Convention measures against corruption linked to organized crime, including provisions regarding the sanctioning of acts of corruption involving public officials;

6. *Requests* the Ad Hoc Committee, using such time as its schedule permits and with extrabudgetary resources provided for that purpose, to explore the desirability of an international instrument against corruption, either ancillary to or independent of the Convention, to be developed after the finalization of the Convention and the three additional instruments referred to in General Assembly resolution 53/111, and to present its views to the Commission on Crime Prevention and Criminal Justice;

7. *Invites* Member States to keep the Office for Drug Control and Crime Prevention of the Secretariat informed of progress made in the implementation of the recommendations of the Expert Group Meeting on Corruption and its Financial Channels;

8. *Requests* the Office for Drug Control and Crime Prevention:

(*a*) To ensure that the ongoing revision of the manual prepared by the Secretariat on practical measures against corruption incorporates the recommendations of the Expert Group Meeting on Corruption and its Financial Channels and takes note of the conclusions of the first Global Forum on Fighting Corruption;

(*b*) To continue to develop, in consultation with Member States, an effective global programme for providing technical assistance to fight corruption;

(*c*) To explore ways to convince underregulated financial centres to adopt rules enabling them to trace and take action against the proceeds of organized crime and corruption, to participate actively in international cooperation aimed at preventing and controlling related forms of financial crime and, if necessary, to consider measures to protect the international financial system from the underregulated financial centres and mechanisms for the establishment of such minimum rules;

(*d*) To report to the Commission on Crime Prevention and Criminal Justice no later than at its tenth session on the progress made in the implementation of the present resolution and the steps taken by Member States to combat corruption and its proceeds;

9. *Requests* the Secretary-General to undertake, within existing or extrabudgetary resources, technical cooperation activities to combat corruption, in consultation with Member States that may be able to provide assistance.

On 22 December [meeting 87], the Assembly, on the recommendation of the Second (Economic and Financial) Committee [A/54/586], adopted **resolution 54/205** without vote [agenda item 98 (*b*)].

Prevention of corrupt practices and illegal transfer of funds

The General Assembly,

Recalling its resolution 53/176 of 15 December 1998 on action against corruption and bribery in international commercial transactions,

Concerned about the seriousness of problems posed by corruption, which may endanger the stability and security of societies, undermine the values of democracy and morality and jeopardize social, economic and political development,

Recognizing the importance of existing international and national laws for combating corruption in international commercial transactions,

Recognizing also the important role of the business community, in particular the private sector, in enhancing the dynamic process of the development of the agricultural, industrial and service sectors and the need to create an enabling environment for business in order to facilitate economic growth and development of developing countries, most especially African countries,

Mindful of the very important role that the private sector can play in fostering economic growth and development and of the active involvement of the United Nations system in facilitating the constructive participation and orderly interaction of the private sector in the development process by embracing universal principles and norms, such as honesty, transparency and accountability,

1. *Condemns* corruption, bribery, money-laundering and the illegal transfer of funds;

2. *Calls* for further international and national measures to combat corrupt practices and bribery in international transactions and for international cooperation in support of these measures;

3. *Also calls* for, while recognizing the importance of national measures, increased international cooperation, inter alia, through the United Nations system, in devising ways and means of preventing and addressing illegal transfers, as well as in repatriating illegally transferred funds to their countries of origin, and calls upon all countries and entities concerned to cooperate in this regard;

4. *Requests* the international community to support the efforts of all countries aimed at strengthening institutional capacity for preventing corruption, bribery, money-laundering and the illegal transfer of funds;

5. *Decides* to keep this matter under review, and in this regard requests the Secretary-General, in consultation with Member States and relevant bodies of the United Nations system, to include in the report called for in its resolution 53/176, to be submitted at its fifty-fifth session, information on progress in the implementation of the present resolution and recommendations, inter alia, with regard to repatriating illegally transferred funds to their countries of origin.

UN standards and norms

Pursuant to Economic and Social Council resolution 1992/22 [YUN 1992, p. 842], the Secretary-General submitted to the Commission on Crime Prevention and Criminal Justice a March report on the use and application of UN standards and norms in crime prevention and criminal justice [E/CN.15/1999/7].

In accordance with Council resolution 1998/21 [YUN 1998, p. 1047], the report incorporated the views of Member States, requested by the Secretary-General, on the plan of action for implementing the Declaration of Basic Principles of Justice for Victims of Crime and Abuse of Power, annexed to General Assembly resolution 40/34 [YUN 1985, p. 743]; on the establishment of an international fund for those victims; and on the creation of a coordination panel or other mechanism to promote implementation of the Declaration. The Secretary-General stated that all responding countries supported the plan of action and the establishment of a coordination panel or other mechanism to ensure concerted action among organizations of the UN system and other concerned entities to promote the Declaration's implementation. A number of States, however, had reservations on establishing the international fund.

The Secretary-General described the activities of the Coordination Panel on Technical Advice and Assistance in Juvenile Justice, established pursuant to Council resolution 1997/30 [YUN 1997, p. 1158] to ensure coordinated UN response. The Centre for International Crime Prevention, in cooperation with the United Nations Children's Fund, had initiated activities in Bangladesh, Guatemala and Lebanon, which were at various stages of implementation.

In response to Council resolution 1997/37 [YUN 1997, p. 1285], the Secretary-General summarized the replies of 21 Member States regarding prison conditions under their respective jurisdictions and any alternatives they had established to imprisonment.

In accordance with Council resolution 1998/21, the Centre, based on information received from questionnaires distributed to Member States, would provide to the Commission at its ninth (2000) session an update on the use and application of the United Nations Standard Minimum Rules for Non-custodial Measures (The Tokyo Rules), annexed to Assembly resolution 45/110 [YUN 1990, p. 752], and of Guidelines on the Role of Prosecutors and Basic Principles on the Role of Lawyers, both adopted by the Eighth (1990) Crime Congress [ibid., p. 701]. The Centre had prepared survey instruments on the United Nations Declaration against Corruption and Bribery in International Commercial Transactions, adopted by the Assembly in resolution 51/191 [YUN 1996, p. 1038]; the United Nations Declaration on Crime and Public Security, annexed to Assembly resolution 51/60 [ibid., p. 1028]; and the International Code of Conduct for Public Officials, adopted in Assembly resolution 51/59 [ibid., p. 1036].

ECONOMIC AND SOCIAL COUNCIL ACTION

On 28 July [meeting 43], the Economic and Social Council, on the recommendation of the Commission on Crime Prevention and Criminal Justice [E/1999/30], adopted three resolutions. **Resolution 1999/27** was adopted without vote [agenda item 14 *(c)*].

Penal reform

The Economic and Social Council,

Recalling its resolution 1997/36 of 21 July 1997 on international cooperation for the improvement of prison conditions and the Kampala Declaration on Prison Conditions in Africa, annexed to that resolution,

Recalling also its resolution 1998/23 of 28 July 1998 on international cooperation aimed at the reduction of prison overcrowding and the promotion of alternative sentencing and the Kadoma Declaration on Community Service, contained in annex I to that resolution,

Bearing in mind the recommendations of the African Regional Preparatory Meeting for the Tenth United Nations Congress on the Prevention of Crime and the Treatment of Offenders, held at Kampala from 7 to 9 December 1998, on topics III and IV,

Bearing in mind also the relevant United Nations standards and norms in crime prevention and criminal justice, in particular the Standard Minimum Rules for the Treatment of Prisoners, the Basic Principles for the Treatment of Prisoners, the United Nations Standard Minimum Rules for the Administration of Juvenile Justice (The Beijing Rules) and the United Nations Standard Minimum Rules for Non-custodial Measures (The Tokyo Rules),

Taking note of the Arusha Declaration on Good Prison Practice, annexed to the present resolution,

1. *Urges* Member States that have not yet done so, to the extent needed:

(a) To take specific action and to establish time-bound targets to address the serious problems confronting many Member States as a result of prison overcrowding, recognizing that the conditions in overcrowded prisons may affect the human rights of prisoners and that many States lack the necessary resources to alleviate prison overcrowding;

(b) In accordance with the Kampala Declaration on Prison Conditions in Africa and the Kadoma Declaration on Community Service, to devise, where necessary, and further to promote measures to reduce the number of prisoners on remand and awaiting trial;

(c) In this context, to make increased use of alternatives to imprisonment, such as pre-trial release, release on own recognizance, conditional release, restitution, community service or labour, the use of fines and payment by instalments and the introduction of conditional and suspended sentences;

2. *Recommends* to Member States that they consider the following, subject to the provisions of their national law:

(a) Conducting research on new approaches to penal and justice reform, including promoting alternatives to imprisonment, alternative forms of dispute resolution, new approaches to prison and traditional forms of justice, alternatives to custody, alternative ways of dealing with juveniles, restorative justice, mediation and the role of civil society in penal reform;

(b) The possible use of new modes of accessible justice for minor offences, with a view to the following:

(i) Reviewing existing trends in and issues concerning people's access to criminal justice systems;

(ii) Examining models of pre-trial dispute resolution;

(iii) Assessing the use of mechanisms for expediting justice;

3. *Invites* international and regional financial institutions such as the World Bank and the International Monetary Fund to incorporate in their technical assistance programmes measures to promote examination of those issues;

4. *Invites* the Tenth United Nations Congress on the Prevention of Crime and the Treatment of Offenders, to be held at Vienna from 10 to 17 April 2000, to consider those issues;

5. *Requests* the Secretary-General to report to the Commission on Crime Prevention and Criminal Justice at its tenth session on the implementation of the present resolution.

ANNEX

Arusha Declaration on Good Prison Practice

Aware of the fact that the management of prisons is a social service and that it is important to keep the public informed about the work of prison services,

Also aware of the need to promote transparency and accountability in the management of prisons and of prisoners in Africa,

Recalling the Kampala Declaration on Prison Conditions in Africa, which sets out an agenda for penal reform in Africa,

Taking note of the Kadoma Declaration on Community Service, which recommends greater use of non-custodial measures for offences committed at the lower end of the criminal scale,

Taking note also of the provisions of the African Charter on Human and Peoples' Rights, the International Covenant on Civil and Political Rights and the International Covenant on Economic, Social and Cultural Rights, and the Convention against Torture and Other Cruel, Inhuman or Degrading Treatment or Punishment that safeguard the right to life, to a prompt trial and to human dignity,

Bearing in mind the Standard Minimum Rules for the Treatment of Prisoners, the Basic Principles for the Treatment of Prisoners, the United Nations Standard Minimum Rules for the Administration of Juvenile Justice (The Beijing Rules), the Body of Principles for the Protection of All Persons under Any Form of Detention or Imprisonment and the Code of Conduct for Law Enforcement Officials,

Bearing in mind also that prison officers who comply with national and international standards for the protection of prisoners deserve the respect and the cooperation of the prison administration where they serve and the community as a whole,

Noting that conditions in most African prisons fall short of these minimum national and international standards,

The participants in the Fourth Conference of the Central, Eastern and Southern African Heads of Correctional Services, meeting in Arusha from 23 to 27 February 1999, agree with the following principles:

(a) To promote and implement good prison practice, in conformity with the international standards mentioned above, and to adjust domestic laws to those standards, if this has not yet been done;

(b) To improve management practices in individual prisons and in the penitentiary system as a whole in order to increase transparency and efficiency within the prison service;

(c) To enhance the professionalism of prison staff and to improve their working and living conditions;

(d) To respect and protect the rights and dignity of prisoners as well as to ensure compliance with national and international standards;

(e) To provide training programmes to prison staff that incorporate human rights standards in a way that is meaningful and relevant and to improve the skills base of prison officers and, for this purpose, to establish a training board of the Conference of the Central, Eastern and Southern African Heads of Correctional Services;

(f) To establish a criminal justice mechanism comprising all the components of the criminal justice system that would coordinate activities and cooperate in the solution of common problems;

(g) To invite civil society groups into the prisons to work in partnership with the prison services in order to improve the conditions of imprisonment and the working environment of prisons;

(h) To call upon Governments and national and international organizations to give full support to the present declaration.

The Council adopted **resolution 1999/26** without vote [agenda item 14 *(c)*].

Development and implementation of mediation and restorative justice measures in criminal justice

The Economic and Social Council,

Recalling its resolution 1997/33 of 21 July 1997, entitled "Elements of responsible crime prevention: standards and norms", as well as its resolution 1998/23 of 28 July 1998, in which it recommended to Member States that they consider using amicable means of settlement to deal with petty offences, for example, by using mediation, acceptance of civil reparation or agreement to compensation, and to consider using non-custodial measures, such as community service, as alternatives to imprisonment,

Bearing in mind General Assembly resolution 52/90 of 12 December 1997, in which the Assembly reaffirmed the high priority attached to technical cooperation and advisory services in the field of crime prevention and criminal justice,

Taking note of the reports of the Secretary-General on crime prevention and on the use and application of United Nations standards and norms in crime prevention and criminal justice and of the report of the Expert Group Meeting on Community Involvement in Crime Prevention, held at Buenos Aires from 8 to 10 February 1999,

Recalling the existing regional instruments, including Council of Europe recommendations No. R (85) 11 on the position of victims in criminal law and procedural criminal law and No. R (98) 1 on family mediation, adopted by the Committee of Ministers on 28 June 1985 and 21 January 1998, respectively,

Bearing in mind that crime prevention in all its aspects is a fundamental issue to be considered at the Tenth United Nations Congress on the Prevention of Crime and the Treatment of Offenders, to be held at Vienna from 10 to 17 April 2000, and that the issue of community involvement in crime prevention will be the subject of a workshop to be organized during the Tenth Congress,

1. *Recognizes* that, while a significant number of minor offences jeopardize citizens' security and comfort, traditional criminal justice mechanisms do not always provide an appropriate and timely response to those phenomena, whether from the perspective of the victim or in terms of adequate and appropriate penalties;

2. *Stresses* that an important means of settlement of minor disputes and offences can be represented, in appropriate cases, by mediation and restorative justice measures, especially measures that, under the supervision of a judicial or other competent authority, facilitate the meeting of the offender with the victim, compensation for damages suffered or the provision of community services;

3. *Emphasizes* that mediation and restorative justice measures, where appropriate, can lead to satisfaction for victims as well as to the prevention of future illicit behaviour and can represent a viable alternative to short terms of imprisonment and to fines;

4. *Welcomes* the development in many countries of experience in mediation and restorative justice in the field of criminal justice, where appropriate, in the areas of, inter alia, minor offences, family problems, school and community problems, and problems involving children and youth;

5. *Calls upon* States to consider, within their legal systems, the development of procedures to serve as alternatives to formal criminal justice proceedings and to formulate mediation and restorative justice policies, with a view to promoting a culture favourable to mediation and restorative justice among law enforcement, judicial and social authorities, as well as local communities, and to consider the provision of appropriate training for those involved in the implementation of such processes;

6. *Calls upon* interested States, international organizations and other entities to exchange information and experience on mediation and restorative justice, including in the framework of the United Nations Crime Prevention and Criminal Justice Programme, and to contribute actively to the discussion and consideration of mediation and restorative justice policies in the framework of the Tenth United Nations Congress on the Prevention of Crime and the Treatment of Offenders and in particular in its workshop on community involvement in crime prevention;

7. *Requests* the Commission on Crime Prevention and Criminal Justice to examine ways and means of facilitating an effective exchange of information concerning national experience in this area and possible ways to promote awareness among Member States of the issues of mediation and restorative justice;

8. *Recommends* to the Commission that it consider the desirability of formulating United Nations standards in the field of mediation and restorative justice, which are intended to ensure fairness in the resolution of minor offences;

9. *Requests* the Secretary-General to undertake, within existing or extrabudgetary resources, activities to assist Member States in developing mediation and restorative justice policies and to facilitate the exchange at the regional and international levels of experience on the issues of mediation and restorative justice, including dissemination of best practices;

10. *Also requests* the Secretary-General to prepare a report on work in progress in this area to be submitted to the Commission on Crime Prevention and Criminal Justice at its tenth session or as soon as possible, taking

into account, inter alia, relevant results of the Tenth United Nations Congress on the Prevention of Crime and the Treatment of Offenders.

The Council adopted **resolution 1999/28** without vote [agenda item 14 *(c)*].

Administration of juvenile justice

The Economic and Social Council,

Recalling its resolution 1997/30 of 21 July 1997 on the administration of juvenile justice and the Guidelines for Action on Children in the Criminal Justice System annexed to that resolution, and its resolution 1998/21 of 28 July 1998 on United Nations standards and norms in crime prevention and criminal justice,

Welcoming the fact that the Committee on the Rights of the Child places considerable emphasis on juvenile justice during its review of reports by States parties to the Convention on the Rights of the Child, and noting that its concluding observations often include recommendations to seek technical assistance in juvenile justice from, inter alia, the Office of the United Nations High Commissioner for Human Rights, the Centre for International Crime Prevention of the Office for Drug Control and Crime Prevention of the Secretariat, the United Nations Children's Fund and the network of non-governmental organizations concerned with juvenile justice issues, through the Coordination Panel on Technical Advice and Assistance in Juvenile Justice, established pursuant to Economic and Social Council resolution 1997/30,

Emphasizing the important preventive role of the effective use and application of existing United Nations standards and norms in juvenile justice,

Concerned about the situation of children and young people in conflict with the law and their treatment by the criminal justice system in a number of States,

Acknowledging that there are links between juvenile delinquency and drug abuse, and recognizing that there is an urgent need for adequate measures and enhanced cooperation between all relevant actors at the national and international levels,

Recognizing that young drug addicts in conflict with the law are often victims and offenders at the same time, vulnerable not only to drug-related criminal activities, but also to activities involving ordinary crime,

Taking note of the draft proposal by the Secretariat on the global programme against trafficking in human beings, taking into account the fact that children, especially the girl child, and young people are often victims of such trafficking,

Concerned about the fact that, in the view of the Committee on the Rights of the Child, there is a need to strengthen the juvenile justice system in the majority of States parties whose reports have been considered by the Committee,

1. *Takes note* of the report of the Secretary-General on the use and application of United Nations standards and norms in juvenile justice, in which the Secretary-General highlighted difficulties and deficiencies in the use and application of United Nations standards and norms in juvenile justice by Member States;

2. *Welcomes* the fact that the Centre for International Crime Prevention of the Office for Drug Control and Crime Prevention of the Secretariat has enhanced its cooperation with other United Nations entities and with other partners involved in assisting Member States in setting up separate juvenile justice systems or in improving existing juvenile justice systems by bringing them in line with United Nations standards and norms in juvenile justice;

3. *Also welcomes* the increased number of technical assistance projects in the field of juvenile justice, reflecting an increased awareness among Member States of the importance of juvenile justice reform in establishing and maintaining stable societies and the rule of law;

4. *Further welcomes* the establishment of the Coordination Panel on Technical Advice and Assistance in Juvenile Justice to coordinate activities in the field of juvenile justice, subject to the modalities set out in Economic and Social Council resolution 1997/30, and calls on the partners involved to increase their cooperation, share information and pool their capacities and interests in order to increase the effectiveness of programme implementation;

5. *Urges* States to include, where necessary, provisions for juvenile justice in their national development plans, calls upon States to include the administration of juvenile justice in their funding policies for development cooperation, and invites them to respond favourably to requests from other States seeking assistance from the Centre for International Crime Prevention, the Office of the United Nations High Commissioner for Human Rights or the United Nations Children's Fund in developing and improving juvenile justice systems;

6. *Stresses* the need to give timely assistance to children and young people in difficult circumstances, especially in drug-related situations, in order to prevent them from resorting to crime;

7. *Underlines* the importance of establishing, where possible and as appropriate, alternatives to imprisonment for young people in conflict with the law, including young drug addicts or users, such as the provision of treatment and vocational training, counselling, rehabilitation, reintegration and aftercare services;

8. *Requests* States to promote re-education and rehabilitation of children and young people who are in conflict with the law by encouraging, where appropriate, the use of methods of restorative justice, mediation, conflict resolution and victim/offender conciliation, as alternatives to judicial proceedings, as well as within the framework of community-based and custodial-based sanctions;

9. *Stresses* the need for close cooperation between all authorities and other actors working with children and young people, especially in the field of juvenile justice, such as the police, the judiciary, lawyers, prison staff, probation officers, social workers, health professionals, teachers and parents;

10. *Urges* Governments to consider including in policies, legislation and programmes on juvenile justice adequate prevention and rehabilitation measures targeting young offenders who are drug addicts or users or who commit drug-related criminal offences;

11. *Requests* the Secretary-General to ensure effective cooperation between the relevant United Nations entities active in the fields of juvenile justice and drug control, in particular between the United Nations International Drug Control Programme and the Centre for International Crime Prevention, and the other or-

ganizations mentioned in the Guidelines for Action on Children in the Criminal Justice System;

12. *Urges* States parties to the Convention on the Rights of the Child to ensure full implementation of their obligations under the Convention and to pursue the goals set forth in the Convention with regard to the treatment of children and young people in the administration of juvenile justice, and urges States to use and apply the United Nations standards and norms in juvenile justice and related instruments;

13. *Reaffirms* that juvenile justice remains a high priority in the work of the Centre for International Crime Prevention and the institutes comprising the United Nations Crime Prevention and Criminal Justice Programme network, in particular as children and young people, both those in conflict with the law and those in difficult circumstances who may be potential future criminals, are easy prey for criminal organizations;

14. *Calls upon* States parties to the Convention on the Rights of the Child to avail themselves fully of the existing programmes for technical assistance in juvenile justice;

15. *Calls upon* the Secretary-General to provide technical assistance in juvenile justice, in particular where States parties request assistance pursuant to recommendations of the Committee on the Rights of the Child, and to consider the provision of technical assistance in juvenile justice as a matter of high priority;

16. *Requests* the Secretary-General to submit to the Commission on Crime Prevention and Criminal Justice at its ninth session a programme proposal, involving all United Nations entities mentioned in the Guidelines for Action on Children in the Criminal Justice System, by which the timely and in-depth assessment of the needs of States parties to the Convention on the Rights of the Child regarding juvenile justice reform is ensured;

17. *Underlines* the need for mainstreaming a gender perspective into all policies and programmes relating to children and young people in the criminal justice system;

18. *Requests* the Secretary-General to report on the administration of juvenile justice, as well as on the activities of the Coordination Panel on Technical Advice and Assistance in Juvenile Justice, to the Commission on Crime Prevention and Criminal Justice at its tenth session.

Human resources

UN research and training institutes

UN Institute for Training and Research

A September note by the Secretary-General [A/54/390] transmitted a report approved by the Board of Trustees of the United Nations Institute for Training and Research (UNITAR) on the development and possible reformatting of the Institute. The Board noted that more than half of its members were scheduled to complete their tenure by year's end, changing the format and profile of the Board, which had participated in UNITAR's recent restructuring. The departure would mark the end of a phase at the Institute and the possible beginning of the next. The coincidence of the Board's reconstitution and the end of the century and millennium also encouraged reflection on the future of UNITAR.

The report presented a number of arguments in favour of change in the Institute, including the decline of official development assistance, UNITAR's narrow financial base and the growth of the private sector, and listed some possible avenues for initiating the change. The Board suggested that the next Board should continue deliberations on the matter.

In response to General Assembly resolution 53/195 [YUN 1998, p. 1056], the Secretary-General, in an October report [A/54/480], described progress made by UNITAR in cooperating with UN system partner organizations, and provided an assessment of a UNITAR survey on training of personnel from Member States by UN entities.

Cooperation was increasing in applying modern information and communication technologies, such as CD-ROMs and the Internet. Training and capacity-building programmes had been developed in the use of geographic information systems to facilitate the flow of institutional and scientific information among national and regional actors. Joint programmes had been introduced in developing countries, particularly in Africa, to better assess their environmental situation. UNITAR had designed and developed programmes with the United Nations Development Programme (UNDP) and the Global Environment Facility and others. The report concluded that despite progress made in strengthening cooperation between UNITAR and other programmes, more effort was required to avoid overlap and duplication.

An assessment of the UNITAR survey, which provided brief descriptions of training programmes offered to Member States by UN funds, programmes and entities concluded, among other factors, that training for governmental officials and civil society representatives constituted an important part of UN activity, with expenditures estimated at $65 million annually. It was noted that the prevalent pattern of financing training programmes was extrabudgetary; many programmes appeared to be directed at training trainers; and pragmatic cooperative links were used. It was not possible to discern from the survey the assessment and evaluation means employed. Moreover, it did not explain how the evaluation results were used to improve programmes. In addition, the survey did not offer any pedagogical quality assessment.

The report presented proposals for a broader study that could be conducted to obtain a complete and accurate picture of such training within the entire UN system. Meanwhile, the survey and the report of the Joint Inspection Unit on training institutions in the UN system [YUN 1997, p. 1178] shared the opinion that a clearing-house function within the UN system to provide governmental officials with a central reference point for information on training opportunities was desirable.

GENERAL ASSEMBLY ACTION

On 22 December [meeting 87], the General Assembly, on the recommendation of the Second Committee [A/54/590], adopted **resolution 54/229** without vote [agenda item 102].

United Nations Institute for Training and Research

The General Assembly,

Recalling its resolutions 48/207 of 21 December 1993, 49/125 of 19 December 1994, 50/121 of 20 December 1995, 51/188 of 16 December 1996, 52/206 of 18 December 1997 and 53/195 of 15 December 1998,

Having considered the report of the Secretary-General and the reflections of the Board of Trustees of the United Nations Institute for Training and Research on the development and possible reorganization of the Institute,

Welcoming the efforts towards consolidation of the restructuring process of the Institute and the recent progress made by the Institute in its various programmes and activities, including the improved cooperation that has been established with other organizations of the United Nations system and with regional and national institutions,

Expressing its appreciation to the Governments and private institutions that have made or pledged financial and other contributions to the Institute,

Noting that contributions to the General Fund of the Institute have not increased along with the increased participation of the developed countries in the training programmes, and stressing the urgent need to address this discrepancy,

Reiterating that training activities should be accorded a more visible and larger role in support of the management of international affairs and in the execution of the economic and social development programmes of the United Nations system,

1. *Reaffirms* the importance of a coordinated United Nations system-wide approach to research and training, and underlines the need for United Nations training and research institutions to avoid duplication in their work;

2. *Also reaffirms* the relevance of the United Nations Institute for Training and Research, in view of the growing importance of training within the United Nations and the training requirements of States, and the relevance of research activities related to training undertaken by the Institute within its mandate;

3. *Stresses* the need for the Institute to strengthen further its cooperation with other United Nations institutes and relevant national, regional and international institutes;

4. *Welcomes* the progress made in building partnerships between the Institute and other agencies and bodies of the United Nations system with respect to their training programmes, and, in this context, underlines the need to develop further and to expand the scope of these partnerships, particularly at the country level;

5. *Stresses* the need for continuity in the management of the Institute in order to ensure efficient and effective completion of the process of restructuring and revitalization;

6. *Requests* the Board of Trustees of the United Nations Institute for Training and Research to intensify its efforts to attract experts from developing countries and countries with economies in transition for the preparation of the relevant training materials for the programmes and activities of the Institute, and stresses that the Institute's courses should focus primarily on development issues;

7. *Renews its appeal* to all Governments, in particular those of developed countries, and to private institutions that have not yet contributed financially or otherwise to the Institute to give it their generous financial and other support, and urges the States that have interrupted their voluntary contributions to consider resuming them in view of the successful restructuring and revitalization of the Institute;

8. *Encourages* the Board of Trustees of the Institute to continue its efforts to address the discrepancy between the decline in contributions to the General Fund of the Institute and the increase in participation in its programmes;

9. *Also encourages* the Board of Trustees to consider organizing events of the Institute at additional sites, including the cities hosting regional commissions, in order to promote greater participation and to reduce costs;

10. *Requests* the Secretary-General, in consultation with the Institute and with United Nations funds and programmes, to continue to explore ways and means systematically to utilize the Institute in the execution of training and capacity-building programmes;

11. *Notes with appreciation* the services rendered by the Executive Director of the Institute in the light of the challenges emanating from the increased responsibilities encountered by his office;

12. *Renews its call* to the Secretary-General to continue to explore all possible ways and means to provide additional facilities to the Institute for maintaining its offices and for conducting programmes and training courses that are provided at no cost to States and to their representatives accredited to United Nations offices in New York, Nairobi, Geneva and Vienna;

13. *Requests* the Secretary-General to report to the General Assembly at its fifty-fifth session on the implementation of the present resolution.

United Nations University

The report of the United Nations University (UNU) Council [A/55/31], which described activities in 1999, stated that UNU had prepared its first strategic plan covering 1999-2002 and launched pilot initiatives within its new lines of development, bringing the University closer to the UN system and forming closer partnerships with international academia and stakeholders in UNU's host countries, particularly Japan. UNU also began new activities, including projects related to integrated capacity-building in water management and the pilot phase of the UNU International Courses. In the context of strategic planning, the issues that faced the United Nations in the twenty-first century were examined and efforts were made to determine areas on which the University's work would have the greatest impact.

During the year, the University concentrated on the thematic areas of peace and governance, and environment and sustainable development, as well as on knowledge networks, capacity-building, and dissemination and public lectures. In terms of peace and governance, the report outlined the challenges faced internationally by the conflicts in Kosovo, East Timor and Chechnya, noting that the University had made proposals for developing a new global message and institutional operations due to the international circumstances. Other initiatives included the launching of a Zero Emissions Forum, which brought together representatives from business, government and the scientific community to promote a development model in which all industrial inputs could be converted into final products. The College of Research Associates was launched by the UNU Institute for Natural Resources in Africa. With regard to capacity-building, UNU International Courses completed its pilot phase and global seminars were held in additional locations in Japan. UNU also provided fellowships to 119 young scientists, mostly from developing countries, and held over 40 brief training courses on various issues. In order to assist in developing a coordinated approach to environment policy, UNU convened a major international interlinkages conference on synergies and coordination between multilateral environmental agreements in July. The University's work also led to the publication of 24 books, of which 19 were published by the UNU Press.

UNU Council

The UNU Council, at its forty-sixth session (Tokyo, Japan, 29 November–3 December) focused on: reviewing the year's activities; discussing and adopting the 1999-2002 strategic plan; and approving the programme and budget for the 2000-2001 biennium. The Council also reviewed progress made in implementing recommendations of external evaluations and in developing a number of new UNU programmes.

University for Peace

A September report of the Secretary-General presented measures taken to revitalize the University for Peace by the Secretary-General, the UNESCO Director-General and the host Government, Costa Rica [A/54/312].

The Council of the University, which was reconstituted with new members, met in Paris on 29 and 30 March. It elected its President, who assumed the additional responsibilities of Rector until a new Rector was appointed, and established an Executive Committee. The Council had not met since 1994, largely because of financial constraints. The new administration had initiated a review of all existing programmes, capacities and facilities to develop a new long-term strategy with accompanying programme proposals, budget, work and management plans. The report described the programmes currently in operation and noted that although they had provided the University with valuable experience, they had not been on a scale or had the scope necessary to enable it to fulfil its global mission. Prospective programmes under consideration related to a culture of peace (see p. 593); environment, natural resources and peace; the establishment of peace parks; economic development and peace; the media and peace; and democracy and peace. Regarding the future of the University, political and financial support from members would reinvigorate its long-term prospects.

GENERAL ASSEMBLY ACTION

On 18 November [meeting 56], the General Assembly adopted **resolution 54/29** [draft: A/54/L.30 & Add.1, orally revised] without vote [agenda item 21].

University for Peace

The General Assembly,

Recalling that in its resolution 34/111 of 14 December 1979 it approved the idea of establishing the University for Peace as a specialized international centre for post-graduate studies, research and the dissemination of knowledge specifically aimed at training and education for peace and its universal promotion within the United Nations system,

Recalling also that in its resolution 35/55 of 5 December 1980 it approved the establishment of the University for Peace in conformity with the International Agreement for the Establishment of the University for Peace,

Recalling further its resolutions 45/8 of 24 October 1990, 46/11 of 24 October 1991 and 48/9 of 25 October 1993,

Recalling that in its resolution 46/11 it decided to include in the agenda of its forty-eighth session and biennially thereafter an item entitled "University for Peace",

Recalling also its resolution 50/41 of 8 December 1995, in which it decided to request the Secretary-General to consider ways of strengthening cooperation between the United Nations and the University for Peace and to submit a report thereon to the General Assembly at its fifty-second session,

Recalling further its adoption on 13 September 1999 of the Declaration and Programme of Action on a Culture of Peace,

Noting that in 1991 the Secretary-General, with the assistance of the United Nations Development Programme, established a Trust Fund for Peace consisting of voluntary contributions in order to provide the University with the means necessary to extend its sphere of activity to the whole world, taking full advantage of its potential capacity for education, research and support of the United Nations and to carry out its mandate of promoting peace in the world,

Noting with appreciation that the Government of Uruguay, by agreement with the University for Peace, established in 1997 a World Centre for Research and Information on Peace as regional sub-headquarters of the University for South America,

Noting also with appreciation the vigorous actions taken by the Secretary-General, in consultation with the Director-General of the United Nations Educational, Scientific and Cultural Organization and with the encouragement and support of the Government of Costa Rica, to revitalize the University,

Noting that the University has placed special emphasis on the area of conflict prevention, peacekeeping, peace-building and peaceful settlement of disputes, and that it has launched programmes in the areas of democratic consensus-building and training of academic experts in the techniques of peaceful settlement of conflicts,

Noting also that the University has launched a broad programme for building a culture of peace in Central America and the Caribbean in the context of the efforts being made by the United Nations and by the United Nations Educational, Scientific and Cultural Organization for the development and promotion of a culture of peace,

Noting with appreciation that the University is organizing a symposium in celebration of the International Year of Older Persons, 1999, at which it will emphasize the valuable contribution that older persons can make to the promotion of peace, solidarity, tolerance and the culture of peace,

Recognizing the important and varied activities carried out by the University during the period 1997-1999, within its financial limitations and with the valuable assistance and contributions of Governments, foundations and non-governmental organizations,

Considering the importance of promoting education for peace that fosters respect for the values inherent in peace and universal coexistence among persons, including respect for the life, dignity and integrity of human beings, as well as friendship and solidarity among peoples irrespective of their nationality, race, sex, religion or culture,

Considering that, by its resolution 52/15 of 20 November 1997, the General Assembly proclaimed the year 2000 as the International Year for the Culture of Peace and that it should be ushered in with One Day in Peace, 1 January 2000,

1. *Takes note with appreciation* of the report of the Secretary-General submitted pursuant to resolution 52/9 of 4 November 1997, on ways of strengthening cooperation between the United Nations and the University for Peace;

2. *Requests* the Secretary-General to consider using the services of the University in his conflict-resolution and peace-building efforts;

3. *Invites* Member States, intergovernmental bodies, non-governmental organizations and interested individuals to contribute directly to the Trust Fund for Peace or to the budget of the University;

4. *Invites* Member States to accede to the International Agreement for the Establishment of the University for Peace, thereby demonstrating their support for an educational institution devoted to the promotion of a universal culture of peace;

5. *Invites* Member States, intergovernmental and non-governmental organizations and all the peoples of the world to celebrate One Day in Peace, 1 January 2000;

6. *Decides* to include in the provisional agenda of its fifty-sixth session the item entitled "University for Peace".

Human resources for development

In response to General Assembly resolution 52/196 [YUN 1997, p. 1180], the Secretary-General, in a September report [A/54/408], examined the challenges and constraints that beset the development of human resources, including the Asian economic and financial crisis and its global impact, and identified possible new approaches to human resources development.

The Secretary-General emphasized that the comprehensive approach to human resources for development outlined in his 1997 note [YUN 1997, p. 1180] remained an overarching priority. Continued investments should be made in all factors of human development, such as education and training, health and nutrition, to achieve universal coverage, and everyone's well-being had to be the overall goal.

The report outlined the use of information technology as a new approach to human resources development. It could be applied to enhance learning through electronic community centres (also called tele-centres or cyber-centres), which facilitated networking, social communication and access to official data, among other advantages, and enhanced awareness of entitlements and opportunities in areas such as education, health, agricultural extension and social security. In addition, the centres created new opportunities for learning, income-earning, livelihoods and jobs, and would be key in bringing the information technology revolution to remote, unconnected and under-served communities. The report summarized strategies designed to build capacity to enter the information age in Brazil, Costa Rica, Egypt, Jamaica, Malaysia, South Africa and Thailand.

The UN system was supporting the efforts of developing countries to achieve universal access to information and communication technologies learning opportunities. A symposium on jobs in the information society of the twenty-first century (Damascus, Syrian Arab Republic), supported by UNDP Arab States, identified initiatives that Arab countries could take to enter the information age. The UN system could develop a global monitoring strategy to record and promote progress in information and communication technology. People development and empowering communities with universal access to learning opportunities could become a cross-cutting theme in UN country programmes.

GENERAL ASSEMBLY ACTION

On 22 December [meeting 87], the General Assembly, on the recommendation of the Second Committee [A/54/587/Add.4], adopted **resolution 54/211** without vote [agenda item 99 (*d*)].

Developing human resources for development

The General Assembly,

Reaffirming its resolutions 45/191 of 21 December 1990, 46/143 of 17 December 1991, 48/205 of 21 December 1993, 50/105 of 20 December 1995 and 52/196 of 18 December 1997, as well as the relevant sections of the Agenda for Development,

Recognizing that the well-being of people is the overall goal of sustainable development,

Stressing that Governments have the primary responsibility for defining and implementing appropriate policies for human resources development and that there is a need for continued support from the international community to complement the efforts of developing countries,

Stressing also that there is a need for a supportive and favourable national and international economic environment that will enhance human resources development in developing countries and promote sustained economic growth and sustainable development, in accordance with the relevant General Assembly resolutions and the outcomes of recent United Nations conferences,

Recognizing that there is a need to integrate human resources development into comprehensive strategies that mainstream a gender perspective, taking into account the needs of all people, in particular the needs of women and the girl child,

Recognizing also the vital role of South-South cooperation in supporting national efforts at human resources development,

Expressing concern at the increasing development gap between developed and developing countries, including the gap in knowledge, information and communication technologies, and at the increasing disparity of income in and among nations and its adverse impact on the development of human resources, in particular in the developing countries,

Stressing that developing countries should be assisted so that they can be well equipped with the knowledge of information technology that would enable them to benefit from the opportunities offered by globalization and to avoid the risk of marginalization in the process of globalization,

Emphasizing the continued need for coordination and integration among the organs and organizations of the United Nations system in assisting developing countries, in particular the least developed among them, to foster the development of their human resources, especially that of the most vulnerable groups, and for the United Nations to continue to give priority to human resources development in developing countries,

1. *Takes note* of the report of the Secretary-General;

2. *Recognizes* the importance of developing human resources as a means, inter alia, of participating more effectively in the world economic system and of benefiting from globalization;

3. *Urges* increased investments in all aspects of human development, such as education and training, health and nutrition, to achieve universal coverage and the well-being of all;

4. *Also urges* the adoption of comprehensive approaches to human resources development which combine, among other factors, economic growth, provision of basic social services, poverty eradication, sustainable livelihoods, empowerment of women, involvement of youth, the needs of vulnerable groups of society, political freedom, popular participation, respect for human rights, justice and equity, all of which are essential for enhancing human capacity to meet the challenge of development;

5. *Emphasizes* the need to ensure the full participation of women in the formulation and implementation of national policies to promote human resources development;

6. *Encourages* all countries to accord priority, in particular in national budgets, to human resources development in the context of the adoption of economic and social policies;

7. *Invites* international organizations, including international financial institutions, to continue to give priority to supporting the objectives of human resources development and to integrating them into their policies, programmes and operations;

8. *Recognizes* the need to direct concerted efforts at enhancing the technical skills and know-how of people living in rural and agricultural areas, with a view to improving their means of livelihood and material well-being, and in this regard encourages the allocation of more resources for this purpose so as to facilitate access to appropriate technology and know-how from within and from other countries, in particular the developed countries, as well as through South-South cooperation;

9. *Encourages* the adoption of policies, approaches and measures that serve to narrow the increasing gap between developed and developing countries in information and communication technologies in particular and in technology in general, including by:

(*a*) Encouraging the private sector, in collaboration with the United Nations system and non-governmental organizations, to donate voluntarily to designated centres in developing countries literary materials, information and communication technology equipment and training, in order to facilitate improved access, as well as to make funds available for these purposes;

(*b*) Taking advantage of the rapid turnaround in both the educational institutions and corporations in developed countries of literary material and information and communication technology equipment, through coordinated efforts involving the United Nations system, non-governmental organizations and recipients or interested developing countries;

(*c*) Promoting transparent, efficient regulatory regimes and other policies that encourage investment;

(*d*) Supporting targeted investments in infrastructure that would establish the physical foundation for the operation of Internet services and pave the way for commercial and development applications;

(*e*) Developing training in information technologies for users such as non-governmental organizations, universities and business service organizations, as well as key governmental agencies;

10. *Calls upon* developing countries, with the support of the international community, to establish information, communication and electronic community centres, where appropriate and in cooperation with the private sector, in order to provide connectivity and access to information and knowledge;

11. *Calls upon* the developed countries and the United Nations system to increase support to programmes and activities of developing countries for human resources development and capacity-building, in particular those geared towards harnessing information and communication technologies;

12. *Requests* the Secretary-General to include in his report to the General Assembly at its fifty-sixth session an assessment of the efficiency and effectiveness of the contribution made by the United Nations system to advancing human resources development in developing countries through its operational activities, and to make recommendations to enhance further its impact;

13. *Decides* to include in the provisional agenda of its fifty-sixth session, under the item entitled "Sustainable development and international economic cooperation", the sub-item entitled "Human resources development".

Education for all

The Secretary-General, in cooperation with the Director-General of the United Nations Educational, Scientific and Cultural Organization (UNESCO) and pursuant to General Assembly resolution 52/84 [YUN 1997, p. 1181], issued a June report on progress towards education for all [A/54/128-E/1999/70], which was being reviewed at the time by the ongoing Education for All (EFA) 2000 Assessment (see also PART THREE, Chapter XI). The assessment exercise was launched in 1997 under the auspices of the EFA Forum [YUN 1997, p. 1181], established to follow up the 1990 World Conference on Education for All [YUN 1990, p. 763]. The report discussed the feasibility of launching a United Nations decade to eradicate illiteracy. A final report was scheduled to be submitted following the World Education Forum in 2000 (Senegal).

GENERAL ASSEMBLY ACTION

On 17 December [meeting 83], the General Assembly, on the recommendation of the Third Committee [A/54/595], adopted **resolution 54/122** without vote [agenda item 106].

A United Nations literacy decade: education for all

The General Assembly,

Recalling that in the Universal Declaration of Human Rights, the International Covenant on Economic, Social and Cultural Rights and the Convention on the Rights of the Child the right of every individual to education is recognized as inalienable,

Recalling also its resolutions 42/104 of 7 December 1987, by which it proclaimed 1990 as International Literacy Year, 44/127 of 15 December 1989, 46/93 of 16 December 1991, 50/143 of 21 December 1995, in which it called for continuing international efforts to promote literacy, and 52/84 of 12 December 1997, in which it requested the Secretary-General, in cooperation with the Director-General of the United Nations Educational, Scientific and Cultural Organization and in consultation with Member States, to consider effective ways and means for achieving the goal of education for all, including the desirability and feasibility of launching a United Nations decade to eradicate illiteracy,

Deeply concerned about the persistence of the gender gap in education, which is reflected by the fact that nearly two thirds of the world's adult illiterates are women,

Convinced that literacy, especially functional literacy, and quality education represent a lifelong necessity for all and serve as an investment in human and social capital and a major tool for the empowerment of people,

Recalling its resolution 53/153 of 9 December 1998, entitled "United Nations Decade for Human Rights Education, 1995-2004, and public information activities in the field of human rights",

Confident that the International Literacy Year and the World Conference on Education for All, held at Jomtien, Thailand, in 1990, resulted in increased awareness and support for literacy efforts and became a turning point in the struggle for a literate world,

Underlining the importance of sustaining and further promoting the progress achieved since the International Literacy Year and the Jomtien Conference,

Welcoming the Amman Affirmation, adopted at the mid-decade meeting of the International Consultative Forum on Education for All, held at Amman from 16 to 19 June 1996, the report of the International Commission on Education for the Twenty-first Century to the United Nations Educational, Scientific and Cultural Organization and the Hamburg Declaration on Adult Learning, adopted at the Fifth International Conference on Adult Education, held at Hamburg, Germany, from 14 to 18 July 1997,

Recognizing that, despite the significant progress in basic education, especially the increase in primary school enrolment coupled with a growing emphasis on the quality of education, major problems, both emerging and continuing, still persist which require even more forceful and concerted action at the national and international levels so as to achieve the goal of education for all,

Urging Member States, in close partnership with international organizations, as well as non-governmental organizations, to promote the right to education for all and to create conditions for all for learning throughout life,

1. *Takes note* of the interim report of the Secretary-General and of the Director-General of the United Nations Educational, Scientific and Cultural Organization, entitled "Progress towards the goal of education for all: the year 2000 Assessment";

2. *Reaffirms* that basic education for all is essential for achieving the goals of eradicating poverty, reducing child mortality, curbing population growth, achieving gender equality and ensuring sustainable development, peace and democracy;

3. *Acknowledges* the efforts and the preparatory work at the national and regional levels for the year 2000 assessment of progress towards achieving the goals of education for all in identifying both continuing and emerging challenges, and stresses the need to meet those challenges and to accelerate the efforts to meet the basic needs of people of all age groups, in particular girls and women;

4. *Appeals* to all Governments to intensify their efforts to eradicate illiteracy and to direct education towards the full development of the human personality and to the strengthening of respect for all human rights and fundamental freedoms;

5. *Also appeals* to all Governments to redouble their efforts to achieve their own goals of education for all by setting firm targets and timetables, where possible, including gender-specific education targets and programmes to combat the illiteracy of women and girls, and, by working in active partnership with communities, associations, the media and development agencies, to reach those targets;

6. *Appeals anew* to Governments and to economic and financial organizations and institutions, both national and international, to lend greater financial and material support to the efforts to increase literacy and achieve the goals of education for all, through, inter alia, the 20/20 initiative, as appropriate;

7. *Invites* Member States, the specialized agencies and other organizations of the United Nations system as well as relevant intergovernmental and non-governmental organizations to intensify further their efforts to implement effectively the World Declaration on Education for All, the Amman Affirmation, the Hamburg Declaration on Adult Learning, adopted at the Fifth International Conference on Adult Education, and the Agenda for the Future, also adopted at the Fifth International Conference, and the relevant commitments and recommendations to promote literacy made in recent major United Nations conferences and at their five-year reviews with a view to better coordinating their activities and increasing their contribution to development;

8. *Welcomes* the convening of the World Education Forum, to be held in April 2000 in Senegal with a view to assessing the implementation of the goals of education for all and adopting an agenda for education in the twenty-first century;

9. *Requests* the Secretary-General, in cooperation with the Director-General of the United Nations Educational, Scientific and Cultural Organization and Member States and with other relevant organizations and bodies, to submit to the General Assembly at its fifty-sixth session, through the Economic and Social Council, a proposal for a United Nations literacy decade, with a draft plan of action and possible time frame for such a decade, on the basis of the outcomes of the World Education Forum and the special session of the General Assembly for the five-year review of the World Summit for Social Development;

10. *Also requests* the Secretary-General to bring the present resolution to the attention of all Member States as well as the relevant intergovernmental and non-governmental organizations;

11. *Decides* to include in the provisional agenda of its fifty-sixth session the question of a United Nations literacy decade.

Chapter X

Women

In 1999, the United Nations continued efforts to advance the status of women and ensure their rights, particularly through implementation of the Beijing Declaration and Platform for Action, adopted in 1995 at the Fourth World Conference on Women (Beijing). A triumvirate of UN bodies—the General Assembly, the Economic and Social Council and the Commission on the Status of Women—monitored Conference follow-up in the 12 critical areas of concern outlined in the Platform for Action.

During the year, preparations proceeded for the five-year review of the Platform's implementation, which was to be undertaken by a special session of the General Assembly in June 2000. The Assembly also addressed the issues of violence against women, women migrant workers, rural women, the girl child and traditional practices affecting the health of women and girls, and designated 25 November as the International Day for the Elimination of Violence against Women. In October, the Assembly adopted the Optional Protocol to the 1979 Convention on the Elimination of All Forms of Discrimination against Women. The Protocol, which was opened for signature on 10 December, introduced an individual and group complaints procedure to the Convention.

The Economic and Social Council, in July, held a high-level segment at which it adopted a ministerial communiqué on the role of employment and work in poverty eradication, especially with respect to the empowerment and advancement of women. The Council also took action with respect to the situation of women and girls in Afghanistan, Palestinian women, a new system-wide medium-term plan for the advancement of women for the period 2002-2005, and revitalization of the International Research and Training Institute for the Advancement of Women. The Council endorsed the agreed conclusions of the Commission on the Status of Women with respect to women and health and institutional mechanisms for the advancement of women.

The Commission reviewed gender mainstreaming within UN organizations, as well as emerging issues, trends and new approaches to issues affecting the situation of women or equality between women and men. It initiated a comprehensive review and appraisal of implementation of the Beijing Platform for Action and continued to serve as the preparatory committee for the Assembly's special session in 2000. Commission resolutions dealt with women and children taken hostage in armed conflicts, women and girls affected by HIV/AIDS, and the mental health of women, with emphasis on special groups.

The Committee on the Elimination of Discrimination against Women reviewed reports from 14 States parties to the 1979 Convention, which marked its twentieth anniversary.

In August, the Secretary-General issued the fourth edition of the *World Survey on the Role of Women in Development*. The survey examined the effect of current trends and policies on the economic and social situation of women, with particular emphasis on developing countries.

Follow-up to the Fourth World Conference on Women

The Commission on the Status of Women, at its forty-third session (New York, 1-12 March and 1 April) [E/1999/27], considered follow-up to the 1995 Fourth World Conference on Women, particularly the implementation of the Beijing Declaration and Platform for Action [YUN 1995, p. 1170]. Its work was organized around the 12 critical areas of concern set forth in the Platform for Action: women and poverty; education and training of women; women and health; violence against women; women and armed conflict; women and the economy; women in power and decision-making; institutional mechanisms for the advancement of women; human rights of women; women and the media; women and the environment; and the girl child. The Commission also reviewed the conclusions of the European Conference on Follow-up to the Beijing Platform for Action (Madrid, Spain, November 1998) [E/CN.6/1999/9] and the results of an information forum on national policies in the field of equality between women and men, convened by the Council of Europe (Tallinn, Estonia, November 1997) [E/CN.6/1999/7].

Preparations for special session of the General Assembly in 2000

In 1999, in accordance with Economic and Social Council **decisions 1999/213** and **1999/218**, the Commission on the Status of Women, acting as the preparatory committee for the special session of the General Assembly to be held in 2000, held its second session (15-29 March and 30 June) [E/1999/60 & Add.1]. In September, the Secretary-General transmitted the Commission's report on its session [A/54/354] to the Assembly. The Commission had before it a report of the Secretary-General [E/CN.6/1999/PC/3] outlining a framework for activities relevant to, and the scope of, the comprehensive five-year review. The report identified sources of information for the Secretariat's assessment of achievements and remaining gaps in the Platform's implementation. Among the planned activities were regional preparatory meetings, national-level reporting and other reports and reviews. A third edition of *The World's Women* would be prepared, updating data and analysis supplied in 1995 on the situation of women worldwide.

The Commission also had before it a January report of the Secretary-General [E/CN.6/1999/PC/2] proposing a framework for further actions and initiatives that were aimed at accelerating the Platform for Action and might be considered during the special session. The report suggested comprehensive and integrated strategies under five functional categories for action: demonstrating political will to create an enabling environment for implementation of the Platform for Action; capacity-building for women's advancement and gender mainstreaming; accountability for implementing the Platform's strategies and actions; cooperation and partnership for implementing the Platform; and assistance to women and girls subject to discrimination and disadvantage. It also outlined four broad, cross-cutting issues that had emerged since 1995: globalization and the economic empowerment of women, especially poor women; women, science and technology and the new information age; women's leadership; and human security and social protection. The Secretary-General recommended that the Commission endorse those themes as the basis for developing a vision for gender equality into the next millennium.

A February report of the Committee on the Elimination of Discrimination against Women [E/CN.6/1999/PC/4] on progress in the Platform's implementation, based on reports to the Commission received from States parties to the 1979 Convention on the Elimination of All Forms of Discrimination against Women, contained in Assembly resolution 34/180 [YUN 1979, p. 895], was also considered.

Inter-Agency Committee on Women. At its fourth session (New York, 23-26 February) [ACC/1999/3], the Inter-Agency Committee on Women and Gender Equality began work on a draft text to be adopted by the Administrative Committee on Coordination (ACC) as an input to the General Assembly's special session. The draft included a policy statement presenting the UN system's outlook on gender equality in the twenty-first century and measures for translating the policy statement into practice.

The Committee invited ACC to support a survey of management commitment to gender mainstreaming, to be conducted by the United Nations Population Fund (UNFPA) through a questionnaire to managers in all organizations. The Committee continued to prepare a compendium of good practices in implementing the Beijing Platform for Action and gender mainstreaming, based on the work of its task force. Other Committee activities included budget codes and financial monitoring systems, methodologies for gender impact analysis, compilation of a database on gender training materials, funding for its activities, a system-wide medium-term plan and collaboration with other ACC mechanisms.

ACC, at its second regular session of 1999 (New York, 29-30 October) [ACC/1999/20], agreed that the UN system should review progress made by and within organizations in the implementation of the Beijing Platform for Action prior to the Assembly's special session.

ECONOMIC AND SOCIAL COUNCIL ACTION

By **decision 1999/278** of 29 July, the Economic and Social Council took note of the report of the Commission acting as the preparatory committee at its second session and approved the provisional agenda and documentation for the third preparatory session. On 30 July, by **resolution 1999/55** on coordinated follow-up to major UN conferences, the Council urged the preparatory committees for the reviews of the Fourth World Conference on Women and of the World Summit for Social Development [YUN 1995, p. 1113] to consult with one another in order to avoid duplication and ensure cross-fertilization of ideas.

On 29 July [meeting 45], the Council, on the recommendation of the Commission on the Status of Women [E/1999/27], adopted **resolution 1999/50** without vote [agenda item 6].

Preparations for the special session of the General Assembly entitled "Women 2000: gender equality, development and peace for the twenty-first century"

The Economic and Social Council

Recommends to the General Assembly the adoption of the following resolution:

[For text, see General Assembly resolution 54/142 below.]

GENERAL ASSEMBLY ACTION

On 17 December [meeting 83], the General Assembly, on the recommendation of the Third (Social, Humanitarian and Cultural) Committee [A/54/599 & Corr.1], adopted **resolution 54/142** without vote [agenda item 110].

Preparations for the special session of the General Assembly entitled "Women 2000: gender equality, development and peace for the twenty-first century"

The General Assembly,

Recalling its resolutions 52/100 of 12 December 1997, 52/231 of 4 June 1998 and 53/120 of 9 December 1998 and Economic and Social Council resolution 1996/6 of 22 July 1996, and bearing in mind Council resolution 1999/50 of 29 July 1999,

Taking note of the reports of the Secretary-General on the initiation of the comprehensive review and appraisal of the implementation of the Platform for Action of the Fourth World Conference on Women, and on the framework for further actions and initiatives that might be considered during the special session of the General Assembly entitled "Women 2000: gender equality, development and peace for the twenty-first century",

Taking note with appreciation of the report of the Committee on the Elimination of Discrimination against Women on progress in the implementation of the Platform for Action by the States parties to the Convention on the Elimination of All Forms of Discrimination against Women,

1. *Reiterates its invitation* to Governments that have not yet done so to prepare national action plans and reports on the implementation of the Platform for Action of the Fourth World Conference on Women, and underlines the importance of involving relevant actors of civil society, especially non-governmental organizations;

2. *Invites* Member States, in preparing implementation plans and reports and responding to the questionnaire on the implementation of the Platform for Action, to report on good practices, positive actions, lessons learned, the use of qualitative and quantitative indicators for measuring progress and, wherever possible, on key challenges remaining in the critical areas of concern of the Platform for Action and obstacles encountered;

3. *Encourages* all the regional commissions and other intergovernmental regional organizations to carry out activities in support of the preparations for the special session of the General Assembly entitled "Women 2000: gender equality, development and peace for the twenty-first century", inter alia, by holding preparatory meetings to ensure a regional perspective on implementation and on further actions and initiatives, as well as on a vision for gender equality, development and peace in the twenty-first century, and to make their reports available in 2000 to the Commission on the Status of Women acting as the preparatory committee for the special session;

4. *Encourages* all entities of the United Nations system, including the programmes, funds and specialized agencies, and the Committee on the Elimination of Discrimination against Women, to be involved actively in preparatory activities and to participate at the highest level in the special session, including through presentations on best practices, obstacles encountered and a vision for the future to accelerate implementation of the Platform for Action and to address new and emerging trends;

5. *Decides* that the special session shall have a plenary and an ad hoc committee of the whole;

6. *Reaffirms* that the special session will be undertaken on the basis of and with full respect for the Platform for Action and that there will be no renegotiation of the existing agreements contained therein;

7. *Decides* that the provisional agenda shall include the following items:

(*a*) Review and appraisal of progress made in implementation in the twelve critical areas of concern of the Platform for Action;

(*b*) Further actions and initiatives for overcoming obstacles to the implementation of the Platform for Action;

8. *Requests* the Secretary-General to prepare, in time for the next session of the preparatory committee in 2000, comprehensive reports on progress made in the implementation of the Platform for Action nationally, regionally and internationally, taking into account all relevant information and inputs available to the United Nations system on the following:

(*a*) A review and appraisal of the implementation of the Platform for Action based on, inter alia, national action plans, reports submitted to the Committee on the Elimination of Discrimination against Women by the States parties under article 18 of the Convention on the Elimination of All Forms of Discrimination against Women, replies of Member States to the questionnaire on the implementation of the Platform for Action, statements made by delegations at relevant forums of the United Nations, reports of regional commissions and other entities of the United Nations system and follow-up to recent global United Nations conferences;

(*b*) Good practices, positive actions, lessons learned, examples of the use of any qualitative and quantitative indicators for measuring progress, successful strategies and promising initiatives for the implementation of the Platform for Action;

(*c*) Obstacles encountered and strategies for overcoming them;

(*d*) Further actions and initiatives, within the overall goals of gender equality, development and peace, to accelerate progress in implementation in the twelve critical areas of concern of the Platform for Action beyond 2000, recognizing the need for analytical tools and strategies for implementation, taking into account inputs, as well as comments of Member States on the report of the Secretary-General on the framework for further actions and initiatives, and, in this regard, invites Member States to provide inputs and comments thereon;

9. *Also requests* the Secretary-General to make available all necessary documentation in a timely manner for the special session, keeping in mind resolutions 52/231 and 53/120;

10. *Encourages* the United Nations system to continue to hold discussions with relevant actors of civil society, especially non-governmental organizations, in the exchange of views for the review and appraisal process on the implementation of the Platform for Action, including, wherever available, the use of electronic networking;

11. *Urges* Member States and observers to ensure their representation at the special session at a high political level;

12. *Confirms* that the special session will be open to the participation of all States Members of the United Nations, members of the specialized agencies and observers, in accordance with the established practice of the General Assembly;

13. *Calls* for the participation of associate members of the regional commissions in the special session, subject to the rules of procedure of the General Assembly, and in the preparatory process for the special session, in the same capacity of observer that applied to their participation in the Fourth World Conference on Women;

14. *Encourages* Member States to include relevant actors of civil society, especially non-governmental organizations and representatives of women's organizations, in their national preparatory processes as well as in their delegations to the preparatory committee and the special session;

15. *Emphasizes* the important role of non-governmental organizations in implementing the Platform for Action and the need for their active involvement in the preparations for the special session as well as the need to ensure appropriate arrangements for their contributions to the special session;

16. *Decides* that non-governmental organizations in consultative status with the Economic and Social Council, as well as the non-governmental organizations that were accredited to the Fourth World Conference on Women, may participate in the special session without creating a precedent for future sessions of the General Assembly;

17. *Also decides* to defer consideration of all the modalities for participation of non-governmental organizations in the special session until the next session of the preparatory committee;

18. *Invites* the Bureau of the Commission on the Status of Women, acting as the preparatory committee for the special session, to convene informal open-ended consultations, as appropriate, to consider preparations for the special session;

19. *Recommends* that the major portion of the three weeks scheduled for the forty-fourth session of the Commission on the Status of Women in March 2000 be allocated to the Commission acting as the preparatory committee for the special session of the General Assembly.

Implementation of Beijing Declaration and Platform for Action

Reports of Secretary-General. At its March session, the Commission on the Status of Women had before it the report of the Secretary-General on follow-up to the Fourth World Conference and implementation of the Beijing Declaration and Platform for Action [E/CN.6/1999/2]. The report emphasized efforts within the UN system in support of mainstreaming a gender perspective and follow-up activities, including activities by non-governmental organizations (NGOs) since his previous report [YUN 1998, p. 1061]. It also contained a joint work plan for the Office of the United Nations High Commissioner for Human Rights (OHCHR) and the UN Division for the Advancement of Women. In addition, the report covered the situation of Palestinian women and the release of women and children taken hostage in armed conflict and imprisoned (see below). An addendum [E/CN.6/1999/2/Add.1] presented an analysis of national action plans and implementation strategies submitted to the Secretariat since the Commission's 1998 session.

In a May report to the Economic and Social Council [E/1999/54], the Secretary-General focused on facilitating the Council's coordination function, in particular as to developments related to implementation of the Beijing Platform for Action in intergovernmental forums reporting to the Council, in the regional commissions and in the Inter-Agency Committee on Women and Gender Equality. By **decision 1999/288** of 30 July, the Council took note of the report.

An August report to the General Assembly [A/54/264] provided information on follow-up to the 1995 Conference by specialized agencies, international financial institutions and other entities in the UN system, as well as on implementation activities at the national level and by NGOs and other institutions of civil society.

GENERAL ASSEMBLY ACTION

On 17 December [meeting 83], the General Assembly, on the recommendation of the Third Committee [A/54/599 & Corr.1], adopted **resolution 54/141** without vote [agenda item 110].

Follow-up to the Fourth World Conference on Women and full implementation of the Beijing Declaration and the Platform for Action

The General Assembly,

Recalling its resolutions 52/100 of 12 December 1997, 52/231 of 4 June 1998 and 53/120 of 9 December 1998, in which it decided to convene a high-level plenary review as a special session of the General Assembly, which will take place from 5 to 9 June 2000, entitled "Women 2000: gender equality, development and peace for the twenty-first century",

Recalling also its resolutions 52/93 and 52/97 of 12 December 1997, 53/116, 53/117 and 53/118 of 9 December 1998, and bearing in mind its resolution 54/4 of 6 October 1999,

Stressing the importance of the special session and the need for strong, sustained political will and commitment at the national, regional and international levels towards achieving equality between women and men, and, in this regard, reaffirming that the full implementation of the Platform for Action of the Fourth World Conference on Women requires further action by all,

Reaffirming its decision that the special session will be undertaken on the basis of and with full respect for the Platform for Action and that there will be no renegotiation of the existing agreements contained therein,

Deeply convinced that the Beijing Declaration and the Platform for Action of the Fourth World Conference on Women are important contributions to the advancement of women worldwide in the achievement of gender equality and must be translated into effective action by all States, the United Nations system and other organizations concerned, as well as by non-governmental organizations,

Recognizing that the responsibility for the implementation of the Platform for Action rests primarily at the national level and that strengthened efforts are necessary in this respect, and reiterating that enhanced international cooperation is essential for the effective implementation of the Beijing Declaration and the Platform for Action,

1. *Takes note with appreciation* of the report of the Secretary-General on the follow-up to the Fourth World Conference on Women and full implementation of the Beijing Declaration and the Platform for Action;

2. *Commends* the work of the Commission on the Status of Women acting as the preparatory committee for the special session of the General Assembly entitled "Women 2000: gender equality, development and peace for the twenty-first century";

3. *Takes note* of the ministerial communiqué adopted by the Economic and Social Council at the high-level segment of its substantive session of 1999 on the theme "The role of employment and work in poverty eradication: the empowerment and advancement of women", as well as Council resolution 1999/55 of 30 July 1999 on integrated and coordinated implementation of and follow-up to major United Nations conferences and summits;

4. *Welcomes* the initiatives and actions taken by Governments, the United Nations system and other international organizations as well as by non-governmental organizations and other actors of civil society towards the accelerated implementation of the Beijing Declaration and the Platform for Action, and calls upon them to implement effectively all the critical areas of concern of the Platform for Action by promoting the empowerment of women at all levels and their full participation in all spheres of society through, inter alia, an active and visible policy of mainstreaming a gender perspective at all levels;

5. *Also welcomes* the replies from Governments to the questionnaire on the implementation of the Platform for Action, and once again invites Governments that have not yet done so to submit national evaluations of the implementation of the Platform for Action, in accordance with Economic and Social Council resolution 1999/50 of 29 July 1999;

6. *Recognizes* the importance attached to the regional and subregional monitoring of the global and regional platforms for action by regional commissions and other subregional or regional structures, within their mandates, in consultation with Governments, and calls for the promotion of cooperation in that respect among Governments and, where appropriate, national machineries of the same region;

7. *Reaffirms* that, in order to implement the Platform for Action, adequate mobilization of resources at the national and international levels, as well as new and additional resources for the developing countries, in particular those in Africa and the least developed countries, from all available funding mechanisms, including multilateral, bilateral and private sources, will also be required;

8. *Recognizes* that implementation of the Platform for Action in the countries with economies in transition requires continued national efforts and international cooperation and assistance, as indicated in the Platform for Action;

9. *Reaffirms* that, in order to implement the Platform for Action, a reformulation of policies and reallocation of resources may be needed, but that some policy changes may not necessarily have financial implications;

10. *Calls upon* Member States to allocate adequate resources for the provision of data disaggregated by sex and age for undertaking gender impact analysis and measuring progress in order to develop successful national implementation strategies for the Platform for Action;

11. *Encourages* all entities of the United Nations system, including the programmes, funds and specialized agencies, and the Committee on the Elimination of Discrimination against Women, to continue their active involvement in the preparations for the special session and to participate at the highest level in the special session, including through presentations on best practices, obstacles encountered and a vision for the future to accelerate implementation of the Platform for Action and address new and emerging trends;

12. *Welcomes* the initiatives and activities of all regional commissions and other intergovernmental organizations in support of the preparations for the special session;

13. *Reiterates* that participation in the special session should be at a high political level;

14. *Invites* Member States to include representatives of national machineries for the advancement of women in their delegations to the preparatory committee and the special session;

15. *Reiterates* the decision that non-governmental organizations in consultative status with the Economic and Social Council, as well as the non-governmental organizations that were accredited to the Fourth World Conference on Women, may participate in the special session without creating a precedent for future sessions of the General Assembly;

16. *Encourages* Member States to include relevant actors of civil society, especially non-governmental organizations and representatives of women's organizations, in their national preparatory processes as well as in their delegations to the preparatory committee and the special session;

17. *Requests* the Secretary-General to submit to the General Assembly at its fifty-fifth session a report on the special session;

18. *Decides* to include in the provisional agenda of its fifty-fifth session an item entitled "Implementation of the outcome of the Fourth World Conference on Women and of the special session of the General Assembly entitled 'Women 2000: gender equality, development and peace for the twenty-first century'".

By **decision 54/465** of 23 December, the Assembly decided that the agenda item on implementation of the outcome of the Fourth World Conference on Women would remain for consideration during its resumed fifty-fourth (2000) session.

Critical areas of concern

In 1999, the Commission considered as thematic issues 2 of the 12 critical areas of concern identified in the Beijing Platform for Action: women and health, and institutional mechanisms for the advancement of women [E/1999/27]. It had before it a report of the Secretary-General [E/CN.6/1999/4] presenting strategies for accelerating implementation of the Platform in relation to those issues, drawing on recommendations from expert group meetings convened by the Division for the Advancement of Women, as a basis for agreed conclusions. Following panel discussions, the Commission agreed to a set of conclusions with respect to those two areas, and recommended them to the Economic and Social Council for endorsement.

ECONOMIC AND SOCIAL COUNCIL ACTION

On 28 July [meeting 43], the Economic and Social Council, on the recommendation of the Commission on the Status of Women [E/1999/27], adopted **resolution 1999/17** without vote [agenda item 14 *(a)*].

Agreed conclusions of the Commission on the Status of Women on the critical areas of concern of the Beijing Platform for Action

The Economic and Social Council

Endorses the following agreed conclusions adopted by the Commission on the Status of Women with respect to the two critical areas of concern addressed by the Commission at its forty-third session:

I. Women and health

The Commission on the Status of Women

1. *Reaffirms* the Beijing Platform for Action, adopted by the Fourth World Conference on Women, notably chapter IV.C on women and health, the Programme of Action of the International Conference on Population and Development and the Convention on the Elimination of All Forms of Discrimination against Women;

2. *Recalls* the Constitution of the World Health Organization, which states that health is a state of complete physical, mental and social well-being and not merely the absence of disease or infirmity; that the enjoyment of the highest attainable standard of health is one of the fundamental rights of every human being without distinction of race, religion, political belief, economic or social condition; and that the health of all peoples is fundamental to the attainment of peace and security and is dependent upon the fullest cooperation of individuals and States;

3. *Requests* States parties to the Convention on the Elimination of All Forms of Discrimination against Women to consider, when preparing their initial and periodic reports under the Convention, including on article 12, general recommendations of the Committee on the Elimination of Discrimination against Women;

4. *Acknowledges* that the realization by women of their right to the enjoyment of the highest attainable standard of physical and mental health is an integral part of the full realization by them of all human rights, and that the human rights of women and of the girl child are an inalienable, integral and indivisible part of universal human rights;

5. *Also acknowledges* the link between the physical and mental health of women throughout the life cycle and the level of national development, including the availability of basic social services such as health services, the status and degree of empowerment of women in society, employment and work, poverty, illiteracy, ageing, race and ethnicity, and violence in all its forms, in particular harmful attitudes and traditional or customary practices affecting the health of women, as well as the importance of investing in the health of women for the well-being of women themselves and for the development of society as a whole;

6. *Recognizes* that lack of development is a major obstacle for women in many countries and that the international economic environment, through its impact on national economies, affects the capacity of many countries to provide and expand quality health services to women; further significant obstacles include competing governmental priorities and inadequate resources;

7. *Proposes,* in order to accelerate the implementation of the strategic objectives of chapter IV.C of the Beijing Platform for Action, that the following actions be taken:

Actions to be taken by Governments, the United Nations system and civil society, as appropriate

1. Universal access, on a basis of equality between women and men, to quality, comprehensive and affordable health care and health services and information by women throughout the life cycle

(a) Ensure universal access on a basis of equality between women and men to appropriate, affordable and quality health care and health services for women throughout the life cycle;

(b) Formulate policies favourable to investments in the health of women and intensify efforts to meet the targets identified in the Beijing Platform for Action, in order to bridge the gap between commitments and implementation;

(c) Ensure universal access for women throughout the life cycle, on a basis of equality between women and men, to social services related to health care, including education, clean water and safe sanitation, nutrition, food security and health education programmes;

(d) Integrate sexual, reproductive and mental health services, with emphasis on preventative measures, within the primary health-care system to respond to the broad health needs of women and men, in a life-cycle approach;

(e) Design and implement programmes, with the full involvement of young people, to educate and inform them on sexual and reproductive health issues, taking into account the rights of the child to access to information, privacy, confidentiality, respect and informed consent, and the responsibilities, rights and duties of parents and legal guardians;

(f) Allocate and reallocate, where appropriate, adequate resources to put in place the necessary measures which ensure that quality health services are accessible to those women throughout their life cycle who are living in poverty, are disadvantaged or socially excluded;

(g) Increase efforts directed towards poverty eradication by assessing the impact of broader macroeconomic policies on the feminization of poverty and

on the health of women and address the health needs of those vulnerable, throughout their life span;

(h) Adopt preventive and promotional health policies at an early stage where possible in order to prevent health problems and dependence of older women and enable them to lead independent and healthy lives;

(i) Ensure that special attention is given to supporting women with disabilities and empower them to lead independent and healthy lives;

(j) Address the need for appropriate screening services for women, within the context of national health priorities;

(k) Encourage women to practise regular sport and recreational activities that have a positive impact on the health, well-being and fitness of women throughout the life cycle, and ensure that women enjoy equal opportunities to practise sports, use sport facilities and take part in competitions.

2. Sexual and reproductive health

(a) Accelerate efforts for the implementation of the targets established in the Beijing Platform for Action with regard to universal access to quality and affordable health services, including reproductive and sexual health, reduction of persistently high maternal mortality and infant and child mortality and reduction of severe and moderate malnutrition and iron deficiency anaemia, as well as to provide maternal and essential obstetric care, including emergency care, and implement existing and develop new strategies to prevent maternal deaths, caused by, inter alia, infections, malnutrition, hypertension during pregnancy, unsafe abortion and post-partum haemorrhage, and child deaths, taking into account the Safe Motherhood Initiative;

(b) Promote and support breastfeeding unless it is medically contraindicated, as well as implement the International Code of Marketing of Breastmilk Substitutes and the Baby Friendly Hospital Initiative;

(c) Support scientific research into and the development of safe, affordable, effective and easily accessible female-controlled methods of family planning, including dual methods such as microbicides and female condoms that protect against both sexually transmitted diseases and human immunodeficiency virus/acquired immunodeficiency syndrome (HIV/AIDS) and prevent pregnancy, taking into account paragraph 96 of the report of the Fourth World Conference on Women;

(d) Support the development and widespread use of male contraceptive methods;

(e) Educate women and men, particularly young people, with a view to encouraging men to accept their responsibilities in matters related to sexuality, reproduction and child-rearing and to promoting equal relationships between women and men;

(f) Enhance the ability and knowledge of women, and empower them to make informed choices, to prevent unwanted pregnancies;

(g) Work with the media and other sectors to encourage the development of positive attitudes about major transitions in the reproductive lives of women and girls, such as the onset of menstruation and menopause, and provide appropriate support, where needed, for women undergoing these transitions;

(h) Eradicate the practice of female genital mutilation and other harmful traditional and customary practices affecting the health of women and girls, since such practices constitute a definite form of violence against women and girls and a serious form of violation of their human rights, including through the development of appropriate policies and enactment and/or reinforcement of legislation, ensure development of appropriate tools of education and advocacy and adopt legislation outlawing their practice by medical personnel;

(i) Take all necessary measures to prevent all harmful practices, such as early marriages, forced marriages and threats to the right to life of women.

3. HIV/AIDS, sexually transmitted diseases and other infectious diseases

(a) Support public education and advocacy and secure the highest level of political commitment to the prevention of and research into sexually transmitted diseases and HIV/AIDS, their care, treatment and the mitigation of their impact, including through the provision of social services and support, together with poverty alleviation;

(b) Increase prevention measures to reduce the spread of the HIV/AIDS pandemic worldwide and sexually transmitted diseases among the groups most heavily at risk, in particular young people, including through education and awareness-raising campaigns and improved access to high-quality condoms and improved accessibility to anti-retroviral therapy to prevent mother-to-child transmission of HIV, and treatment, care and support for HIV/AIDS-related illnesses;

(c) Enact laws and take measures to eliminate sexual violence against women and girls, which is one of the causes of HIV/AIDS infection and other sexually transmitted diseases, and review and enact laws and combat practices, as appropriate, that may contribute to the susceptibility of women to these infections, including enacting legislation against those sociocultural practices that contribute to AIDS, and implement legislation, policies and practices to protect women, adolescents and young girls from discrimination related to HIV/AIDS;

(d) Eliminate the stigmatization and social exclusion that surround HIV/AIDS, sexually transmitted diseases and other infectious diseases such as leprosy and filariasis, and lead to under-detection, lack of treatment and violence, especially for women, so that infected women who reveal their HIV/AIDS status are protected from violence, stigmatization and other negative consequences;

(e) Increase the preventative, as well as the therapeutic, measures against tuberculosis and malaria, and accelerate the research into the development of a vaccine against malaria, which has a harmful effect, especially on pregnant women, in most parts of the world, particularly in Africa;

(f) Educate, counsel and encourage men and women infected with HIV/AIDS and sexually transmitted diseases to inform their partners to help protect them from infection, and ensure that the spread of those diseases is curtailed.

4. Mental health and substance abuse

(a) Make available gender-sensitive and age-sensitive mental health services and counselling, as necessary, with particular attention to the treatment of psychiatric illness and trauma throughout the life cycle, inter alia, by integrating them into primary health-care systems and through appropriate referral support;

(b) Develop effective preventive and remedial health services to provide appropriate counselling and treatment for mental disorders related to stress, depression, powerlessness, marginalization and trauma since women and girls may suffer more from those ailments resulting from various forms of discrimination, violence and sexual exploitation, particularly in situations of armed conflict and displacement;

(c) Support research and dissemination of information on gender differences in the causes and effects of the use and abuse of substances, including narcotic drugs and alcohol, and develop effective gender-sensitive approaches to prevention, treatment and rehabilitation, including those specifically designed for pregnant women;

(d) Design, implement and strengthen prevention programmes aimed at reducing tobacco use by women and girls; investigate the exploitation and targeting of young women by the tobacco industry; support action to prohibit tobacco advertising and access by minors to tobacco products; and support smoke-free spaces, gender-sensitive cessation programmes and product labelling to warn of the dangers of tobacco use, noting the Tobacco Free Initiative proposed by the World Health Organization in July 1998;

(e) Promote equitable sharing of household and family responsibilities between women and men, and provide social support systems, where appropriate, to help women who, as a result of their multiple roles in the family, may often suffer from fatigue and stress;

(f) Support research on the relationship between the physical and mental health and self-esteem of women and girls and the extent to which women of all ages are valued in their societies, to address issues such as substance abuse and eating disorders.

5. Occupational and environmental health

(a) Support gender-specific research on the short- and long-term effects of the occupational and environmental health risks of work, including work in the formal and informal sector, performed by both women and men, and take effective legal and other measures to reduce these risks, including risks in the workplace, in the environment and from harmful chemicals, including pesticides, radiation, toxic waste and other such hazards that affect women's health;

(b) Protect the health of women workers in all sectors, including agricultural and domestic household workers, through effective environmental and occupational health policies for gender-sensitive work environments, free from sexual harassment and discrimination, which are safe and ergonomically designed to prevent occupational hazards;

(c) Take specific measures to protect the health of women workers who are pregnant or have recently given birth or are breastfeeding from harmful environmental and occupational hazards, and their children;

(d) Provide full and accurate information about environmental health risks to the public, in particular to women, and take steps to ensure access to clean water, adequate sanitation and clean air.

6. Policy development, research, training and evaluation

(a) Advance a comprehensive interdisciplinary and collaborative research agenda on the health of women which encompasses the entire lifespan of all women, including women from special and diverse groups within populations;

(b) Establish concrete accountability mechanisms at the national level for reporting on the implementation of the health and other related critical areas of the Beijing Platform for Action;

(c) Improve the collection, use and dissemination of data disaggregated by sex and age, and research findings, and develop collection methodologies that capture the differences between the life experiences of women and men, including through the use and, where necessary, further coordinated development of gender-specific qualitative and quantitative health indicators that go beyond morbidity, mortality and social indicators, capturing quality of life, and the social as well as mental well-being of women and girls;

(d) Promote research on the interrelationship between poverty, ageing and gender;

(e) Ensure participation of women at all levels in the planning, implementation and evaluation of health programmes; also ensure a gender perspective in the health sector at all levels, including through the elaboration of gender-sensitive and age-sensitive health policies and budgets, and the creation of an enabling environment supported by a legislative framework and monitoring, follow-up and evaluation mechanisms within individual countries;

(f) Mainstream a gender perspective into the curricula as well as the training of all health-care and service providers in order to ensure high-quality health services for women that can help eliminate discriminatory attitudes and practices by certain health professionals which impede the access of women to health services; and ensure that a gender perspective is developed and applied to treatment and prevention practice in the health sector;

(g) In order to ensure that the rights of women are addressed, the curricula of health-care providers should include relevant human rights topics to strengthen medical ethics and ensure that girls and women are treated with respect and dignity;

(h) Increase education and research among health service providers and users to address the unnecessary medicalization of health conditions affecting women;

(i) Ensure, where indicated, that clinical trials of pharmaceuticals, medical devices and other medical products include women with their full knowledge and consent and ensure that the resulting data is analysed for sex and gender differences;

(j) Collect data concerning scientific and legal developments on human genome and related genetic research and their implications for the health of women and their rights in general, and disseminate such information and the results of studies conducted in accordance with accepted ethical standards.

7. Health sector reform and development

(a) Take action, in the context of health sector reform and development and growing diversification of the provision of care, to secure equal and equitable access to care for women and to ensure that health sector reform and development efforts promote the health of women; and address under-provision of health care;

(b) Take the opportunity provided by health sector reform and development systematically to integrate the process of gender analysis in the health sector and undertake gender impact assessments and monitoring

of all health sector reforms and development to ensure that women benefit equally from them;

(c) Develop strategies designed to reduce occupational concentration by gender, to eliminate gender-based pay inequality, to ensure high-quality working conditions in the health workforce, and to provide appropriate skills training and development.

8. International cooperation

(a) Assure a strong political commitment by the international community to implementing strengthened international cooperation for development and to mobilizing domestic and international finance resources from all sources for development and the provision of health services for women;

(b) Promote progress in regard to external debt relief which, with improvement in the terms of trade, could help to generate resources, both public and private, to expand and upgrade health services, with special attention to the physical and mental health of women;

(c) Encourage the international community, including bilateral donors and multilateral development organizations, to assist developing countries in ensuring the provision of basic social services, including health-care services for women, in particular during periods of economic difficulty; socially and gender-sensitive approaches to structural adjustment policies are further encouraged;

(d) Encourage concerted efforts, through enhanced cooperation and coordination, to minimize the negative impacts and maximize the benefits of globalization and interdependence to enhance, inter alia, the provision of health-care services in developing countries, especially for women;

(e) Encourage sound macroeconomic policies and institutions, in the framework of international cooperation, to support, inter alia, the provision of health-care services for women.

II. Institutional mechanisms

The Commission on the Status of Women

1. *Reaffirms* the Beijing Platform for Action, adopted by the Fourth World Conference on Women, notably chapter IV.H on institutional mechanisms for the advancement of women, the Convention on the Elimination of All Forms of Discrimination against Women and Economic and Social Council agreed conclusions 1997/2 of 18 July 1997 on mainstreaming the gender perspective into all policies and programmes in the United Nations system;

2. *Recognizes* that the effectiveness and sustainability of national machineries are highly dependent on their embeddedness in the national context, the political and socio-economic system and the needs of and accountability to women, including those with the least access to resources; in addition, recognizes that sharing information at the regional and international levels is crucial for strengthening national machineries and other related institutional mechanisms, that gender equality is advanced through the promotion and protection of all human rights and fundamental freedoms, respect for democracy, peace and development, and that the full involvement of women and men is essential;

3. *Also recognizes* that gender mainstreaming is a tool for effective policy-making at all levels and not a substitute for targeted, women-specific policies and programmes, equality legislation, national machineries for the advancement of women and the establishment of gender focal points;

4. *Acknowledges* that national machineries are necessary for the implementation of the Beijing Platform for Action and that for national machineries to be effective, clear mandates, location at the highest possible level, accountability mechanisms, partnership with civil society, a transparent political process, adequate financial and human resources and continued strong political commitment are crucial;

5. *Stresses* the importance of international cooperation in order to assist the work of national mechanisms in all countries, especially developing countries;

6. *Welcomes* Economic and Social Council decision 1998/298 of 5 August 1998, by which the Council decided to devote the high-level segment of its 1999 substantive session to the advancement of women;

7. *Proposes,* in order to accelerate the implementation of the strategic objectives of chapter IV.H of the Beijing Platform for Action, that the following action be taken:

Actions by Governments, national machineries and other institutional mechanisms, and the international community, including the United Nations system, for the advancement of women and for gender equality

1. Actions to be taken by Governments

(a) Provide continued strong political commitment to supporting the strengthening of national machineries and the advancement of women;

(b) Ensure that national machineries are placed at the highest possible level of government and that all institutional mechanisms for the advancement of women are invested with the authority needed to fulfil their mandated roles and responsibilities;

(c) Provide adequate and sustainable financial and human resources to national machineries and other institutional mechanisms for the advancement of women through national budgets, while also granting national machineries the possibility of attracting funds from other bodies for the purpose of specific projects;

(d) Structure appropriately the functions of national machineries at all levels in order to ensure effectiveness in gender mainstreaming;

(e) Ensure that mainstreaming a gender perspective is fully understood, institutionalized and implemented. These efforts should include promoting awareness and understanding of the Beijing Platform for Action;

(f) Continue to take steps to ensure that the integration of a gender perspective in the mainstream of all government activities is part of a dual and complementary strategy to achieve gender equality. This should include a continuing need for targeted priorities, policies, programmes and positive action measures;

(g) Ensure that senior management in each ministry or agency takes responsibility for fulfilling gender equality commitments and integrating a gender perspective in all activities, and that appropriate assistance from gender experts or gender focal points is available;

(h) Promote and ensure, as appropriate, the establishment of effective gender focal points at all decision-making levels and in all ministries and other decision-

making bodies, develop close collaboration among them and create follow-up mechanisms;

(i) Create and/or encourage the creation and strengthening of institutional mechanisms at all levels, including taking all measures to ensure that national machineries as well as focal points within specific institutions are not marginalized in the administrative structure but supported at the highest possible level of government and entrusted with clearly defined mandates which define their function as a policy advisory body;

(j) Promote capacity-building, including gender training for both women and men in government ministries, so as to be more responsive to the needs and interests of women and gender equality, and develop their own capacity by making use of available national and international models and methodologies in the field of gender equality;

(k) Promote, where appropriate, and ensure accountability and transparency of government through effective monitoring mechanisms and tools such as gender-disaggregated statistics, gender budgeting, gender auditing and gender impact assessment, based on established benchmarks, and other performance indicators and regular public reporting, including under international agreements;

(l) Provide assistance, as appropriate, to agencies, including those outside government, in formulating gender-sensitive performance indicators, necessary to measure and review progress made in the field of gender equality, including the advancement of women and gender mainstreaming;

(m) Continuously improve the gathering and disaggregation of data and the development of statistics and indicators in all critical areas of the Platform for Action for use in analysis, policy development and planning;

(n) Give visibility to the relationship between remunerated and unremunerated work and its importance to gender analysis, and promote greater understanding among relevant ministries and organizations by developing methods for assessing its value in quantitative terms in order to develop appropriate policies in this respect;

(o) Recognize and acknowledge that unremunerated work by women in, for example, agriculture, food production, natural resources management, caring for dependants and household and voluntary work is a considerable contribution to society. Develop and improve mechanisms, for example time-use studies, to measure in quantitative terms unremunerated work in order to:

—Make visible the unequal distribution between women and men of remunerated and unremunerated work in order to promote changes;

—Assess the real value of unremunerated work and accurately reflect it in satellite or other official accounts that are separate from but consistent with core national accounts;

(p) Strengthen the relations among civil society, all governmental agencies and national machineries;

(q) Ensure that the needs, rights and interests of all women, including those who are not members of organizations and who live in poverty in rural and urban areas, are identified and mainstreamed into policy and programme development. This should be done in ways that value the diversity of women and recognize the barriers many women face that prohibit and prevent their participation in public policy development;

(r) Respect the involvement of non-governmental organizations in assisting Governments in the implementation of regional, national and international commitments through advocacy and raising awareness of gender equality issues. Women should be actively involved in the implementation and monitoring of the Platform for Action;

(s) Coordinate or consult with, as appropriate, non-governmental organizations and civil society in national and international activities, including the elaboration of national action plans, the preparation of reports to the Committee on the Elimination of Discrimination against Women and the implementation of the Beijing Platform for Action;

(t) Ensure transparency through open and participatory dialogue and the promotion of balanced participation of women and men in all areas of decision-making;

(u) Support autonomous organizations and institutions involved in research, analysis and evaluation of activities on gender issues and use the results to influence the transformation of policies and programmes;

(v) Create clear anti-discrimination regulations with adequate mechanisms, including a proper legal framework for addressing violations;

(w) Initiate, where necessary, gender equality legislation and create or strengthen, where appropriate, independent bodies, such as the ombudsperson and equal opportunity commission, with responsibility and authority for, inter alia, promoting and ensuring compliance with gender equality legislation;

(x) Involve parliaments and, wherever appropriate, the judiciary in monitoring progress in gender mainstreaming and strengthening gender-related aspects of all government reporting, and ensure transparency through open and participatory dialogue and the promotion of balanced participation of women and men in all areas and at all levels of decision-making.

2. Actions to be taken by national machineries and other institutional mechanisms

(a) Design, promote the implementation of, execute, monitor, evaluate and mobilize support for policies that promote the advancement of women and advocate gender equality and promote public debate;

(b) Act as catalysts for gender mainstreaming in all policies and programmes and not necessarily as agents for policy implementation. However, national machineries are partners in policy formulation and may also choose to implement and coordinate specific projects;

(c) Assist other parts of government in taking specific actions in the gathering and disaggregation of data and the development of statistics and indicators in all critical areas of the Beijing Platform for Action for use in analysis, policy development, planning and programming;

(d) Promote research and dissemination of research findings and information on women and gender equality, including disparities of income and workload between women and men and, where appropriate, among women;

(e) Take specific actions such as the establishment of documentation centres, to disseminate gender-relevant data and other information, including on the important contribution of women to society and re-

search results in easily accessible formats and places, in order to promote more informed public dialogue, including through the media, on gender equality and issues pertinent to the advancement of women;

(f) Ensure the ongoing training on gender issues, at all levels, of the personnel of the national machineries to promote programme and policy sustainability;

(g) Develop, as appropriate, policies to recruit technical staff with expertise in gender equality issues;

(h) Create or strengthen collaborative links with other agencies at local, regional, national and international levels;

(i) Recognize civil society as an important source of support and legitimacy, and therefore create and strengthen the relationship with civil society, through regular consultations with non-governmental organizations, the research community, social partners and other concerned groups. This will create a strong basis for gender-sensitive policy and the advancement of women;

(j) Establish partnerships, liaise and consult with women's organizations, non-governmental organizations, academic institutions, the media and other agencies on national and international policies relating to women and gender and inform them of the international commitments of their Governments;

(k) Engage the media in dialogue aimed at re-examining gender stereotypes and negative portrayal of both women and men;

(l) Create and strengthen collaborative relationships with the private sector, including through initiating advocacy dialogue and advising private companies to address the issues affecting women in the paid labour force, and set up ways and means to promote equality of women and men.

3. Actions to be taken by the international community, including the United Nations system

(a) Implement Economic and Social Council agreed conclusions 1997/2;

(b) Implement fully the revised system-wide medium-term plan for the advancement of women, 1996-2001;

(c) Ensure that individual managers are held accountable for implementing the strategic plan of action for the improvement of the status of women in the Secretariat (1995-2000) within their areas of responsibility, and that heads of departments and offices develop gender action plans which establish concrete strategies for the achievement of gender balance in individual departments and offices, with full respect for the principle of equitable geographical distribution and in conformity with Article 101 of the Charter of the United Nations, so as to ensure, as far as possible, that the appointment and promotion of women will not be less than 50 per cent, until the goal of 50/50 gender distribution is met;

(d) Request the Inter-Agency Committee on Women and Gender Equality of the Administrative Committee on Coordination to continue its work to implement the Beijing Platform for Action and to promote the integration of a gender perspective in the implementation of and follow-up to major United Nations conferences and summits;

(e) Support the implementation of the Beijing Platform for Action, including through support for the important activities of the United Nations Development Fund for Women and the International Research and Training Institute for the Advancement of Women in the fulfilment of their respective mandates;

(f) Support national Governments in their efforts to strengthen national mechanisms through official development assistance and other appropriate assistance;

(g) Encourage multilateral, bilateral, donor and development agencies to include in their programmes of assistance activities that strengthen national machineries;

(h) Encourage Governments and national machineries to undertake wide consultations with their civil societies when providing information on gender and women's issues to relevant international bodies;

(i) Document and publish "good practices", and provide logistical support and ensure equal access to information technology wherever appropriate. In this regard, the offices of United Nations resident coordinators, in particular the women in development programmes and gender units, should play a critical role;

(j) Develop and disseminate gender-disaggregated data and qualitative performance indicators to ensure effective gender-sensitive planning, monitoring, evaluation and implementation of programmes;

(k) Encourage multilateral development institutions, bilateral donors and international non-governmental organizations to make available methodology already developed on the collection and analysis of gender-disaggregated data measurement and valuation of unwaged work and to provide technical assistance and other resources, including financial resources as appropriate, to developing countries and countries with economies in transition;

(l) In order to elaborate a systematic and comprehensive approach to information on unremunerated work, the Division for the Advancement of Women of the Department of Economic and Social Affairs of the Secretariat should prepare and circulate among all States a detailed and well-structured questionnaire. The questionnaire should seek inputs on developments in measuring and valuing unremunerated work and on policies and programmes as well as laws that recognize and address such work;

(m) Request the Division for the Advancement of Women to expand the Directory of National Machinery for the Advancement of Women, by including, for example, mandates, number of staff, e-mail addresses, fax numbers and working-level contacts, so that this comprehensive information can facilitate better communication among national machineries around the world.

Violence against women

In January, the Secretary-General transmitted to the Commission on the Status of Women a report of the United Nations Development Fund for Women (UNIFEM) on its activities during the previous year to eliminate violence against women [E/CN.6/1999/6]. UNIFEM launched a series of inter-agency regional campaigns in Africa, Asia and the Pacific and Latin America and the Caribbean to raise public awareness about violence against women and highlight its economic and social costs. It increased the operational activities of the Trust Fund in Support of Actions to Eliminate Violence against Women, established in 1995 by General Assembly resolution 50/166 [YUN 1995, p. 1188]. The annual income of the Trust Fund in 1998 doubled that of the previous year, to approximately $1.8 million, and 29 new projects were approved for implementation, bringing the total number of projects funded worldwide to 71. In an effort to share the experience gained from implementation of Trust Fund projects, UNIFEM had created a new learning component, which would become a global resource centre to review, analyse and extract lessons from its grant-making activities and facilitate the identification of best methods on initiatives to combat violence against women across regions.

The Commission on Human Rights, at its fifty-fifth session, considered a follow-up report of the Special Rapporteur on violence against women, its causes and consequences (see p. 666).

Report of Secretary-General. The Secretary-General reported in March [A/54/69-E/1999/8 & Add.1] on crime prevention and criminal justice measures to eliminate violence against women, including implementation of the Model Strategies and Practical Measures on the Elimination of Violence against Women in the Field of Crime Prevention and Criminal Justice, adopted by the General Assembly in resolution 52/86 [YUN 1997, p. 1166]. The Model Strategies, which built on measures contained in the Beijing Platform for Action, were divided into 11 sections: criminal law, criminal procedure, police, sentencing and correction, victim support and assistance, health and social services, training, research and evaluation, crime prevention measures, international cooperation and follow-up activities. (See also PART THREE, Chapter IX.) The report summarized the responses of 26 Governments to the request of the Secretary-General for information on the implementation of the Model Strategies. It concluded that national strategies and measures introduced by Governments were not nearly as systematic and comprehensive as those recommended in the Model Strategies. Advisory services, gender-segregated data, research and other efforts were recommended to assist with national implementation efforts.

On 17 December, the General Assembly, by **decision 54/431**, took note of the report.

GENERAL ASSEMBLY ACTION

On 17 December [meeting 83], the General Assembly, on the recommendation of the Third Committee [A/54/598 & Corr.1,2], adopted **resolution 54/134** without vote [agenda item 109].

International Day for the Elimination of Violence against Women

The General Assembly,

Recalling the Declaration on the Elimination of Violence Against Women, adopted by the General Assembly in its resolution 48/104 of 20 December 1993, and its resolution 52/86 of 12 December 1997, entitled "Crime prevention and criminal justice measures to eliminate violence against women",

Recalling also the Universal Declaration of Human Rights, the International Covenant on Civil and Political Rights, the International Covenant on Economic, Social and Cultural Rights, the Convention on the Elimination of All Forms of Discrimination against Women and the Convention against Torture and Other Cruel, Inhuman or Degrading Treatment or Punishment,

Taking note of the Inter-American Convention on the Prevention, Punishment and Eradication of Violence Against Women adopted by the General Assembly of the Organization of American States at its twenty-fourth regular session, held in Belém, Brazil, from 6 to 10 June 1994, and general recommendation 19 on violence against women adopted by the Committee on the Elimination of Discrimination against Women at its eleventh session,

Concerned that violence against women is an obstacle to the achievement of equality, development and peace, as recognized in the Nairobi Forward-looking Strategies for the Advancement of Women and the Platform for Action of the Fourth World Conference on Women, which recommended a set of integral measures to prevent and eliminate violence against women, and to the full implementation of the Convention on the Elimination of All Forms of Discrimination against Women,

Concerned also that some groups of women, such as women belonging to minority groups, indigenous women, refugee women, migrant women, women living in rural or remote communities, destitute women, women in institutions or in detention, the girl child, women with disabilities, elderly women and women in situations of armed conflict, are especially vulnerable to violence,

Recognizing that violence against women is a manifestation of historically unequal power relations between men and women, which have led to domination over and discrimination against women by men and to the prevention of their full advancement, and that violence against women is one of the crucial social mechanisms by which women are forced into subordinate positions, compared with men,

Recognizing also that the human rights of women and of the girl child are an inalienable, integral and indivisible part of universal human rights, and recognizing further the need to promote and protect all human rights of women and girls,

Alarmed that women do not fully enjoy their human rights and fundamental freedoms, and concerned about the long-standing failure to protect and promote those rights and freedoms in relation to violence against women,

Recognizing with satisfaction the cooperation provided by the relevant agencies, bodies, funds and organs of the United Nations system to different countries in the fight to eradicate violence against women, in fulfilment of their respective mandates,

Recognizing the efforts made by civil society and non-governmental organizations that have contributed to creating a worldwide social conscience of the negative impact, both on social and on economic life, of violence against women,

Reiterating that, according to article 1 of the Declaration on the Elimination of Violence against Women, the term "violence against women" means any act of gender-based violence that results in, or is likely to result in, physical, sexual or psychological harm or suffering to women, including threats of such acts, coercion or arbitrary deprivation of liberty, whether occurring in public or in private life,

1. *Decides* to designate 25 November as the International Day for the Elimination of Violence against Women;

2. *Invites*, as appropriate, Governments, the relevant agencies, bodies, funds and programmes of the United Nations system, and other international organizations and non-governmental organizations, to organize on that day activities designed to raise public awareness of the problem of violence against women.

Women migrant workers

In September [A/54/342], the Secretary-General, in response to General Assembly resolution 52/97 [YUN 1997, p. 1194], reported on measures introduced by Governments and actions taken by the UN system to address violence against women migrant workers. Although several States had reported on measures to address violence against women in general and on measures to assist migrants, few reported on specific measures to address the particular issue of violence against women migrant workers. Those States that had introduced such measures had concentrated on information dissemination and raising the consciousness of potential migrants and their employers. More information and data were required on the situation of women migrant workers so that concrete strategies could be introduced. (See also p. 580.)

GENERAL ASSEMBLY ACTION

On 17 December [meeting 83], the General Assembly, on the recommendation of the Third Committee [A/54/598 & Corr.1,2], adopted **resolution 54/138** without vote [agenda item 109].

Violence against women migrant workers

The General Assembly,

Recalling all previous resolutions on violence against women migrant workers adopted by the General Assembly, the Commission on the Status of Women, the Commission on Human Rights and the Commission on Crime Prevention and Criminal Justice, as well as the Declaration on the Elimination of Violence against Women,

Reaffirming the outcome of the World Conference on Human Rights, held at Vienna from 14 to 25 June 1993, and its five-year review, the International Conference on Population and Development and its five-year review and the Fourth World Conference on Women, specifically as the results pertain to women migrant workers,

Emphasizing the need for objective, comprehensive, broad-based information and a wide exchange of experiences and lessons learned by individual Member States and civil society in the formulation of policies and concrete strategies to address the problem of violence against women migrant workers,

Encouraging the participation of civil society in developing and implementing appropriate measures to support innovative partnerships among public agencies, non-governmental organizations and other members of civil society for combating violence against women migrant workers,

Taking note with appreciation of the recommendations of the Working Group of Intergovernmental Experts on the Human Rights of Migrants of the Commission on Human Rights,

Noting the large numbers of women from developing countries and some countries with economies in transition who continue to venture forth to more affluent countries in search of a living for themselves and their families as a consequence of poverty, unemployment and other socio-economic conditions, and acknowledging the duty of the countries of origin to work for conditions that provide employment and security to their citizens,

Realizing that the movement of a significant number of women migrant workers may be facilitated and made possible through fraudulent or irregular documentation and arranged marriages and that, by the nature of their status and movement, women migrant workers are more vulnerable to abuse and exploitation,

Acknowledging the economic benefits that accrue to both the country of origin and the country of destination from the employment of women migrant workers,

Recognizing the importance of joint and collaborative approaches at the bilateral, regional, interregional and international levels in protecting and promoting the rights and welfare of women migrant workers,

Encouraged by some measures adopted by some countries of destination to alleviate the plight of women migrant workers residing within their areas of jurisdiction,

Underlining the important role of relevant United Nations treaty bodies in monitoring the implementation of human rights conventions and the relevant special procedures, within their respective mandates, in addressing the problem of violence against women migrant workers and in protecting and promoting their rights and welfare,

1. *Welcomes* the report of the Secretary-General;

2. *Also welcomes* the appointment of a Special Rapporteur on the human rights of migrants;

3. *Requests* all Governments to cooperate fully with the Special Rapporteur in the performance of the tasks and duties mandated and to furnish all information requested, including by reacting promptly to the urgent appeals of the Special Rapporteur;

4. *Encourages* Governments, in particular those of the countries of origin and destination, to share information on violence against women migrant workers with the Special Rapporteur with a view to requesting

the Special Rapporteur to recommend concrete measures and actions to address the problem;

5. *Also encourages* Governments to give serious consideration to inviting the Special Rapporteur to visit their countries so as to enable him or her to fulfil the mandate effectively;

6. *Urges* concerned Governments, in particular those of the countries of origin and destination, to strengthen further their national efforts to protect and promote the rights and welfare of women migrant workers, including through sustained bilateral, regional, interregional and international cooperation, by developing strategies and joint action and taking into account the innovative approaches and experiences of individual Member States, and to establish and maintain continuing dialogues to facilitate the exchange of information;

7. *Also urges* concerned Governments, in particular those of the countries of origin and destination, to support and allocate appropriate resources for programmes aimed at strengthening preventive action, in particular information for relevant target groups, education and campaigns to increase public awareness of this issue at the national and grass-roots levels, in cooperation with non-governmental organizations;

8. *Encourages* Member States to adopt appropriate measures to inform women migrant workers of their rights and the benefits to which they are entitled;

9. *Calls upon* concerned Governments, in particular those of the countries of origin and destination, if they have not done so, to put in place penal and criminal sanctions to punish perpetrators of violence against women migrant workers and, to the extent possible, to provide, and to encourage non-governmental organizations to provide, victims of violence with the full range of immediate assistance and protection, such as counselling, legal and consular assistance, temporary shelter and other measures, that will allow them to be present during the judicial process, as well as to establish reintegration and rehabilitation schemes for returning women migrant workers to their countries of origin;

10. *Encourages* concerned Governments, in particular those of the countries of origin and destination, to support and, if they have not done so, to formulate and implement training programmes for their law enforcers, prosecutors and service providers with a view to instilling among those public sector workers the necessary skills and attitude to ensure the delivery of proper and professional interventions for women migrant workers who are subjected to abuse and violence;

11. *Also encourages* concerned Governments, in particular those of the countries of origin and destination, to adopt measures or strengthen existing ones to regulate the recruitment and deployment of women migrant workers, including considering the adoption of appropriate legal measures against intermediaries who deliberately encourage the clandestine movement of workers and who exploit women migrant workers;

12. *Invites* Governments to identify the causes of undocumented migration and its economic, social and demographic impact, as well as its implications for the formulation and application of social, economic and migration policies, including those relating to women migrant workers;

13. *Encourages* concerned Governments, in particular those of the countries of origin, transit and destination, to avail themselves of the expertise of the United Nations, including the Statistics Division of the Secretariat and other relevant bodies, such as the International Research and Training Institute for the Advancement of Women, to develop appropriate national data-collection methodologies that will generate comparable data on violence against women migrant workers as bases for research and analyses on the subject;

14. *Encourages* Member States to consider ratifying and complying with International Labour Organization conventions and to consider signing and ratifying or acceding to the International Convention on the Protection of the Rights of All Migrant Workers and Members of Their Families, as well as the Slavery Convention of 1926;

15. *Encourages* the Committee on the Elimination of Discrimination against Women to consider developing a general recommendation on the situation of women migrant workers;

16. *Requests* the Secretary-General to submit to the General Assembly at its fifty-sixth session a report on the problem of violence against women migrant workers and on the implementation of the present resolution, taking into account updated information from the organizations of the United Nations system, in particular the International Labour Organization, the United Nations Development Programme, the United Nations Development Fund for Women and the International Research and Training Institute for the Advancement of Women, and the International Organization for Migration and other relevant sources, including non-governmental organizations.

Women in rural areas

As requested by the General Assembly in resolution 52/93 [YUN 1997, p. 1201], the Secretary-General reported in June [A/54/123-E/1999/66] on the current status of rural women and prospects for improving their situation. Issues related to rural women had been raised throughout the Beijing Platform for Action and were considered critical to the development discourse and strategy-making process because of rural women's central role in both agricultural production and caregiving. The report was prepared on the basis of a review of existing studies, in addition to the replies received from 14 Governments and 8 UN entities to a request for information from the Secretary-General. It outlined the impact of global trends and their policy implications for the situation of rural women and considered questions of access to productive resources, inputs and services. It showed that the process of globalization had direct and indirect effects on the situation of women. The changing patterns of financial flows, characterized by a decline in development assistance and increased but uneven equity capital flows to developing countries, were forcing countries to pursue policies, such as privatization of productive assets such as land, tending to exacerbate the socio-economic marginalization of rural women. There had been some benefits, particularly in providing opportunities for wage employment for rural women in new sectors, such as the non-traditional export sector in agriculture. In their replies, most Governments reported having passed laws to secure the access of rural women to productive resources, necessary inputs and services, and UN entities were engaged in supporting those national efforts. Future efforts to improve the situation of women in rural areas should be directed by research into the gender implications of globalization and rural change, the report concluded.

GENERAL ASSEMBLY ACTION

On 17 December [meeting 83], the General Assembly, on the recommendation of the Third Committee [A/54/598 & Corr.1,2], adopted **resolution 54/135** without vote [agenda item 109].

Improvement of the situation of women in rural areas

The General Assembly,

Recalling its resolution 52/93 of 12 December 1997,

Recalling also the importance attached to the problems of rural women by the Nairobi Forward-looking Strategies for the Advancement of Women, the Beijing Declaration and the Platform for Action adopted by the Fourth World Conference on Women and the Convention on the Elimination of All Forms of Discrimination against Women,

Noting that some effects of the evolving globalization process may deepen the socio-economic marginalization of rural women,

Noting also that the globalization process has had some benefits by providing opportunities for wage employment for rural women in new sectors,

Mindful of the fact that the available data and existing tools of measurement and analysis are insufficient for a full understanding of the gender implications of the processes of globalization and rural change, and their impact on rural women,

Recognizing the urgent need to take appropriate measures aimed at further improving the situation of women in rural areas,

1. *Takes note* of the report of the Secretary-General;

2. *Invites* Member States, in collaboration with United Nations organizations and civil society, to continue their efforts to implement the outcome of and to ensure an integrated and coordinated follow-up to United Nations conferences and summits, including their five-year reviews, and to attach greater importance to the improvement of the situation of rural women in their national, regional and global development strategies by, inter alia:

(*a*) Investing in and strengthening efforts to meet the basic needs of rural women through capacity-building and human resources development measures and the provision of a safe and reliable water supply, health services, including family planning services, and nutritional programmes as well as education and literacy programmes and social support measures;

(*b*) Designing and revising laws to ensure that, where private ownership of land and property exists, rural women are accorded full and equal rights to own land and other property, including through the right to inheritance, and undertaking administrative reforms and other necessary measures to give women the same right as men to credit, capital, appropriate technologies and access to markets and information;

(*c*) Integrating a gender perspective into the design, implementation, monitoring and evaluation of development policies and programmes;

(*d*) Providing microcredit and other financial and business services to a greater number of women in rural areas for generating self-employment among them and eradicating poverty;

(*e*) Pursuing the political and socio-economic empowerment of rural women by supporting their full and equal participation in decision-making at all levels, including in rural institutions;

(*f*) Placing a renewed focus on the issue of rural women within the context of the review and appraisal of the implementation of the Beijing Declaration and the Platform for Action adopted by the Fourth World Conference on Women;

(*g*) Taking steps towards ensuring that women's unpaid work and contributions to on-farm and off-farm production, including income generated in the informal sector, are visible and recorded in economic surveys and statistics at the local and national levels;

3. *Requests* the Secretary-General, in cooperation with the relevant international organizations, specialized agencies, funds and programmes, and in consultation with Member States, to prepare a comprehensive report on the situation of rural women and challenges faced by them, based, inter alia, on the outcome of an expert group meeting, which will draw from the contributions and case studies provided by experts from various regions, and to incorporate its findings and recommendations in his report to the General Assembly at its fifty-sixth session on the implementation of the present resolution.

Women and children in armed conflict

In March [E/1999/27 (res. 43/1)], the Commission on the Status of Women condemned violent acts in contravention of international humanitarian law against civilian women and children in areas of armed conflict, including those imprisoned, and called for an effective response. All parties to armed conflicts were urged to respect the norms of international humanitarian law and provide unimpeded access to humanitarian assistance for women and children. The Commission asked the Secretary-General and relevant international organizations to facilitate the release of women and children taken hostage in armed conflicts, including those subsequently imprisoned. The Secretary-General was also asked to submit a report to the Commission at its forty-fourth (2000) session.

The girl child

On 17 December [meeting 83], the General Assembly, on the recommendation of the Third Committee [A/54/601], adopted **resolution 54/148** without vote [agenda item 112].

The girl child

The General Assembly,

Recalling its resolution 53/127 of 9 December 1998 and all previous relevant resolutions, including the agreed conclusions of the Commission on the Status of Women, in particular those relevant to the girl child,

Recalling also all relevant United Nations conferences and the Declaration and Agenda for Action of the World Congress against Commercial Sexual Exploitation of Children, held at Stockholm from 27 to 31 August 1996, as well as the recent five-year review of the implementation of the Programme of Action of the International Conference on Population and Development,

Deeply concerned about discrimination against the girl child and the violation of the rights of the girl child, which often result in less access for girls to education, nutrition, physical and mental health care and in girls enjoying fewer of the rights, opportunities and benefits of childhood and adolescence than boys and often being subjected to various forms of cultural, social, sexual and economic exploitation and to violence and harmful practices such as female infanticide, incest, early marriage, prenatal sex selection and female genital mutilation,

Recognizing the need to achieve gender equality so as to ensure a just and equitable world for girls,

Deeply concerned that, in situations of poverty, war and armed conflict, girl children are among the victims most affected and that thus their potential for full development is limited,

Concerned that the girl child has furthermore become a victim of sexually transmitted diseases and the human immunodeficiency virus, which affects the quality of her life and leaves her open to further discrimination,

Noting that 1999 is the tenth anniversary of the Convention on the Rights of the Child and the twentieth anniversary of the Convention on the Elimination of All Forms of Discrimination against Women,

Reaffirming the equal rights of women and men as enshrined, inter alia, in the Preamble to the Charter of the United Nations, the Convention on the Elimination of All Forms of Discrimination against Women and the Convention on the Rights of the Child,

1. *Stresses* the need for full and urgent implementation of the rights of the girl child as guaranteed to her under all human rights instruments, including the Convention on the Rights of the Child and the Convention on the Elimination of All Forms of Discrimination against Women, as well as the need for universal ratification of those instruments;

2. *Urges* all States to take all necessary measures and to institute legal reforms to ensure the full and equal enjoyment by the girl child of all human rights and fundamental freedoms, to take effective action against violations of those rights and freedoms and to base programmes and policies for the girl child on the rights of the child;

3. *Urges* States to enact and to enforce strictly laws to ensure that marriage is entered into only with the free and full consent of the intending spouses, to enact and to enforce strictly laws concerning the minimum legal age of consent and the minimum age for marriage and to raise the minimum age for marriage where necessary;

4. *Urges* all States to fulfil their obligations under the Convention on the Rights of the Child and the Convention on the Elimination of All Forms of Discrimination against Women as well as the commitment to implement the Platform for Action of the Fourth World Conference on Women;

5. *Also urges* all States to enact and to enforce legislation to protect girls from all forms of violence, including female infanticide and prenatal sex selection, female genital mutilation, rape, domestic violence, incest, sexual abuse, sexual exploitation, child prostitution and child pornography, and to develop age-appropriate safe and confidential programmes and medical, social and psychological support services to assist girls who are subjected to violence;

6. *Calls upon* all States and international and non-governmental organizations, individually and collectively, to implement further the Platform for Action of the Fourth World Conference on Women, in particular the strategic objectives relating to the girl child;

7. *Urges* States to take special measures for the protection of children, in particular to protect girls from rape and other forms of sexual abuse and gender-based violence in situations of armed conflict, paying special attention to refugee and displaced girls and taking into account the special needs of the girl child in the delivery of humanitarian assistance;

8. *Also urges* States to formulate comprehensive, multidisciplinary and coordinated national plans, programmes or strategies to eliminate all forms of violence against women and girls, which should be widely disseminated and should provide targets and timetables for implementation, as well as effective domestic enforcement procedures through the establishment of monitoring mechanisms involving all parties concerned, including consultations with women's organizations, giving attention to the recommendations relating to the girl child of the Special Rapporteur of the Commission on Human Rights on violence against women, its causes and consequences;

9. *Calls upon* Governments, civil society, including the media, and non-governmental organizations to promote human rights education and the full respect for and enjoyment of the human rights of the girl child, inter alia, through the translation, production and dissemination of age-appropriate information materials on those rights to all sectors of society, in particular to children;

10. *Requests* the Secretary-General, as Chairman of the Administrative Committee on Coordination, to ensure that all organizations and bodies of the United Nations system, individually and collectively, in particular the United Nations Children's Fund, the United Nations Educational, Scientific and Cultural Organization, the World Food Programme, the United Nations Population Fund, the United Nations Development Fund for Women, the World Health Organization and the Office of the United Nations High Commissioner for Refugees, take into account the rights and the particular needs of the girl child in the country programme of cooperation in accordance with the

national priorities, including through the United Nations Development Assistance Framework;

11. *Requests* all human rights treaty bodies, special procedures and other human rights mechanisms of the Commission on Human Rights and its Subcommission on the Promotion and Protection of Human Rights to adopt regularly and systematically a gender perspective in the implementation of their mandates and to include in their reports information on the qualitative analysis of violations of the human rights of women and girls, and encourages the strengthening of cooperation and coordination in that regard;

12. *Calls upon* States and international and non-governmental organizations to mobilize all necessary resources, support and efforts to realize the goals, strategic objectives and actions set out in the Platform for Action of the Fourth World Conference on Women;

13. *Stresses* the importance of a substantive assessment of the implementation of the Platform for Action with a life-cycle perspective so as to identify gaps and obstacles in the implementation process and to develop further actions for the achievement of the goals of the Platform for Action;

14. *Calls upon* Governments, the United Nations system, in particular the Division for the Advancement of Women of the Secretariat, non-governmental organizations and women's organizations to ensure that, in the preparation for the special session of the General Assembly entitled "Women 2000: gender equality, development and peace for the twenty-first century", the needs and the rights of the girl child are duly taken into account and integrated into all activities;

15. *Requests* the Secretary-General to ensure that the needs and the rights of the girl child are specifically assessed in the five-year review of the implementation of the Programme of Action of the World Summit for Social Development, to be held in June 2000;

16. *Also requests* the Secretary-General, in consultation with the United Nations Development Programme, the United Nations Educational, Scientific and Cultural Organization, the United Nations Population Fund, the United Nations Children's Fund and the World Bank, to ensure that the needs and the rights of the girl child are given special attention in all preparatory processes at the national, regional and international levels, including the Education for All 2000 Assessment and the agenda of the World Education Forum, to be held in April 2000;

17. *Further requests* the Secretary-General to ensure that the needs and the rights of the girl child are integrated into the preparatory work for the special session of the General Assembly on the follow-up to the World Summit for Children in 2001, inter alia, by providing the General Assembly with a comprehensive report drawing on the experiences and outcomes of the five-year reviews of the International Conference on Population and Development, the Fourth World Conference on Women and the World Summit for Social Development, and the World Education Forum.

Women's health

In 1999, issues related to the health of women and girls were addressed by the General Assembly in **resolution 54/133** (see below), the Commission on Human Rights (see p. 669) and the Commission on the Status of Women in its agreed conclusions on critical areas of concern identified in the Beijing Platform for Action, which were endorsed by the Economic and Social Council in **resolution 1999/17** (see p. 1080).

Traditional practices affecting the health of women

In September [A/54/341], the Secretary-General, in response to General Assembly resolution 53/117 [YUN 1998, p. 701], reported on measures taken at the national and regional levels, and within the UN system, to eliminate traditional or customary practices affecting the health of women. Based on replies received from 20 Member States to a request of the Secretary-General for information on the issue, as well as information from UN entities and civil society organizations, the report noted that specific legal measures, information campaigns and research aimed at the eradication of such practices had been introduced in several States. The elimination of female genital mutilation had been addressed by the Commission on Human Rights (see p. 669), as well as by activities of the United Nations Children's Fund (UNICEF), UNFPA and the World Health Organization (WHO).

Important regional initiatives, particularly in Africa, had also been undertaken in 1999, indicating increased political will to address such practices. The important role of community and religious leaders, as well as NGOs, in advocating eradication of those practices was emphasized. The report called for the establishment and strengthening of national monitoring and implementation mechanisms and laws against all forms of harmful traditional practices. More research, education, training and public information campaigns on the issue were also crucial.

GENERAL ASSEMBLY ACTION

On 17 December [meeting 83], the General Assembly, on the recommendation of the Third Committee [A/54/598 & Corr.1,2], adopted **resolution 54/133** without vote [agenda item 109].

Traditional or customary practices affecting the health of women and girls

The General Assembly,

Reaffirming its resolution 53/117 of 9 December 1998 and its other relevant resolutions and decisions, as well as those of the Economic and Social Council, the Commission on Human Rights and the Subcommission on the Promotion and Protection of Human Rights,

Recalling the reports of the Special Rapporteur of the Subcommission on the Promotion and Protection of Human Rights on traditional practices affecting the health of women and children and of the Special Rapporteur of the Commission on Human Rights on violence against women, its causes and consequences,

Reaffirming the obligation of all States to promote and protect human rights and fundamental freedoms as stated in the Charter of the United Nations, and reaffirming also the obligations contained in later human rights instruments, in particular articles 5 and 12 of the Convention on the Elimination of All Forms of Discrimination against Women, article 24 of the Convention on the Rights of the Child and article 12 of the International Covenant on Economic, Social and Cultural Rights,

Bearing in mind article 2, paragraph *(a)*, of the Declaration on the Elimination of Violence against Women, and article 5, paragraph 5, of the Declaration on the Elimination of All Forms of Intolerance and of Discrimination Based on Religion or Belief,

Recalling the provisions of the outcome of the World Conference on Human Rights, held at Vienna from 14 to 25 June 1993, the International Conference on Population and Development, the Ninth United Nations Congress on the Prevention of Crime and the Treatment of Offenders, held at Cairo from 29 April to 8 May 1995, and the Fourth World Conference on Women pertaining to traditional or customary practices affecting the health of women and girls,

Recalling also general recommendation 14 concerning female circumcision adopted by the Committee on the Elimination of Discrimination against Women at its ninth session, as well as paragraphs 11, 20 and 24 *(l)* of general recommendation 19 concerning violence against women adopted by the Committee at its eleventh session and paragraphs 15 *(d)* and 18 of general recommendation 24 concerning article 12 of the Convention on the Elimination of All Forms of Discrimination against Women on women and health adopted by the Committee at its twentieth session,

Welcoming the fact that the First Ministerial Conference on Human Rights in Africa of the Organization of African Unity, in the Grand-Baie (Mauritius) Declaration and Plan of Action adopted on 16 April 1999, urged all African States to work assiduously towards the elimination of discrimination against women and the abolition of cultural practices which dehumanize or demean women and children,

Welcoming also the Ouagadougou Declaration adopted on 6 May 1999 at the Regional Workshop on the Fight against Female Genital Mutilation in the countries members of the West African Economic and Monetary Union,

Reaffirming that such traditional or customary practices constitute a definite form of violence against women and girls and a serious form of violation of their human rights,

Expressing concern at the continuing large-scale existence of these practices,

Stressing that the elimination of such practices requires greater efforts and commitment from Governments, the international community and civil society, including non-governmental and community organizations, and that fundamental changes in societal attitudes are required,

1. *Welcomes:*

(a) The report of the Secretary-General, which provides encouraging examples of national and international developments;

(b) The fact that the Commission on the Status of Women and the Commission on Human Rights addressed the issue of harmful traditional or customary practices at their sessions in 1999;

(c) The fact that the General Assembly, at its special session for the review and appraisal of the implementation of the Programme of Action of the International Conference on Population and Development, has addressed the issue of harmful practices;

(d) The efforts undertaken by United Nations bodies, programmes and organizations, including the United Nations Children's Fund, the United Nations Population Fund, the World Health Organization, the United Nations Educational, Scientific and Cultural Organization, the Office of the United Nations High Commissioner for Refugees and the United Nations Development Fund for Women, to address the issue of traditional or customary practices affecting the health of women and girls, and encourages them to continue to coordinate their efforts;

(e) The work carried out by the Special Ambassador for the Elimination of Female Genital Mutilation of the United Nations Population Fund, including her visits to a number of countries, and the fact that she has been invited to other countries;

(f) The work carried out by the Inter-African Committee on Traditional Practices Affecting the Health of Women and Children and other non-governmental and community organizations, including women's organizations, in raising awareness of the harmful effects of such practices, in particular of female genital mutilation;

(g) The fact that the progress made towards the elimination of traditional or customary practices affecting the health of women and girls will be considered during the special session of the General Assembly entitled "Women 2000: gender equality, development and peace for the twenty-first century";

2. *Emphasizes* the need for technical and financial assistance to developing countries working to achieve the elimination of traditional or customary practices affecting the health of women and girls from United Nations funds and programmes, international and regional financial institutions and bilateral and multilateral donors, as well as the need for assistance to non-governmental organizations and community-based groups active in this field from the international community;

3. *Calls upon* all States:

(a) To ratify or accede to, if they have not yet done so, the relevant human rights treaties, in particular the Convention on the Elimination of All Forms of Discrimination against Women and the Convention on the Rights of the Child, and to respect and implement fully their obligations under any such treaties to which they are parties;

(b) To implement their international commitments in this field, inter alia, under the Beijing Declaration and the Platform for Action of the Fourth World Conference on Women, the Programme of Action of the International Conference on Population and Development and the Vienna Declaration and Programme of Action adopted by the World Conference on Human Rights;

(c) To collect and disseminate basic data about the occurrence of traditional or customary practices affecting the health of women and girls, including female genital mutilation;

(*d*) To develop, adopt and implement national legislation and policies that prohibit traditional or customary practices affecting the health of women and girls, including female genital mutilation, and to prosecute the perpetrators of such practices;

(*e*) To establish or strengthen support services to respond to the needs of victims by, inter alia, developing comprehensive and accessible sexual and reproductive health services and providing training to health-care providers at all levels on the harmful health consequences of such practices;

(*f*) To establish, if they have not done so, a concrete national mechanism for the implementation and monitoring of relevant legislation, law enforcement and national policies;

(*g*) To intensify efforts to raise awareness of and to mobilize international and national public opinion concerning the harmful effects of traditional or customary practices affecting the health of women and girls, including female genital mutilation, in particular through education, the dissemination of information, training, the media, the arts and local community meetings, in order to achieve the total elimination of these practices;

(*h*) To promote the inclusion of the discussion of the empowerment of women and their human rights in primary and secondary education curricula and to address specifically traditional or customary practices affecting the health of women and girls in such curricula and in the training of health personnel;

(*i*) To promote men's understanding of their roles and responsibilities with regard to promoting the elimination of harmful practices, such as female genital mutilation;

(*j*) To involve, among others, public opinion leaders, educators, religious leaders, chiefs, traditional leaders, medical practitioners, women's health and family planning organizations, the arts and the media in publicity campaigns with a view to promoting a collective and individual awareness of the human rights of women and girls and of how harmful traditional or customary practices violate those rights;

(*k*) To continue to take specific measures to increase the capacity of communities, including immigrant and refugee communities, in which female genital mutilation is practised, to engage in activities aimed at preventing and eliminating such practices;

(*l*) To explore, through consultations with communities and religious and cultural groups and their leaders, alternatives to harmful traditional or customary practices, in particular where those practices form part of a ritual ceremony or rite of passage;

(*m*) To cooperate closely with the Special Rapporteur of the Subcommission on the Promotion and Protection of Human Rights on traditional practices affecting the health of women and the girl child and to respond to her inquiries;

(*n*) To cooperate closely with relevant specialized agencies and United Nations funds and programmes, as well as with relevant non-governmental and community organizations, in a joint effort to eradicate traditional or customary practices affecting the health of women and girls;

(*o*) To include in their reports to the Committee on the Elimination of Discrimination against Women, the Committee on the Rights of the Child and other relevant treaty bodies specific information on measures taken to eliminate traditional or customary practices affecting the health of women and girls, including female genital mutilation, and to prosecute the perpetrators of such practices;

4. *Invites:*

(*a*) Relevant specialized agencies, United Nations bodies and non-governmental organizations to exchange information on the subject of the present resolution, and encourages the exchange of such information between non-governmental organizations active in this field and the bodies monitoring the implementation of relevant human rights treaties;

(*b*) The Commission on Human Rights to address this subject at its fifty-sixth session, thus allowing a more comprehensive understanding of the impact of traditional or customary practices affecting the health of women and girls on the human rights of women;

(*c*) Governments, organizations and individuals in a position to do so to contribute to the trust fund that supports the work of the Special Ambassador for the Elimination of Female Genital Mutilation of the United Nations Population Fund;

5. *Requests* the Secretary-General:

(*a*) To make his report available to relevant meetings within the United Nations system;

(*b*) To report to the General Assembly at its fifty-sixth session on the implementation of the present resolution, with a special focus on recent national and international developments, including examples of national best practices and international cooperation.

HIV/AIDS

In March [res. 43/2], the Commission on the Status of Women, concerned that the proportion of women becoming infected with the human immunodeficiency virus (HIV) was growing in every region, called for the intensification of national efforts against the disease, particularly in favour of women and girls in the worst-hit regions of Africa and where the epidemic was severely setting back national development gains. Governments were urged to protect the rights of women and girls living with HIV/AIDS, provide counselling for those vulnerable to infection, support children orphaned by AIDS, and adopt a long-range prevention policy tailored to the needs of women and girls within their sociocultural contexts. The Joint United Nations Programme on HIV/AIDS was asked to assist Governments in determining the best policies and programmes to prevent the spread of HIV/AIDS, giving priority attention to African women and girls. The Commission recommended that gender policies and programmes integrating HIV/AIDS activities be mainstreamed by organizations in the UN system.

Mental health

In a resolution on women and mental health, with emphasis on special groups [res. 43/3], the

Commission called for urgent implementation of the health objectives of the Beijing Platform for Action with the integration of mental health as a priority issue. Concern was expressed for the tremendous health burdens borne by women due to, among other conditions, gender discrimination, violence, and lack of appropriate physical and mental health care. The Commission was also concerned that depression affected more women than men in many parts of the world due, in part, to their inferior social and economic status. Governments were asked to include in their national policies and action plans for women specific measures that would address mental health, especially the need for psychosocial care and counselling services. The Commission called on WHO, in partnership with other UN bodies, to develop a training manual on mental disorders resulting from trauma, all forms of discrimination, exploitation, abuse and oppression in relation to women and girls. Development of gender-sensitive psychosocial and mental health situation analyses and of women's mental health indicators was also recommended.

Situation of older women

The Commission on the Status of Women considered a January report of the Secretary-General [E/CN.6/1999/3], which outlined key global issues regarding the differential impact of population ageing on men and women as a contribution to the International Year of Older Persons, 1999 (see p. 1124). Noting that the Beijing Platform for Action referred explicitly to women at all stages of life, the report concluded that gender inequalities shaped older women's experiences, despite their majority status among the older population, and that age and gender inequalities were linked with poverty. Among its recommendations to Governments, the report called for the provision of minimal income for the elderly in need, social safety nets, housing and employment opportunities to improve the living conditions of elderly women. It recommended research on the interrelationship between poverty, gender and ageing and called for measures to empower older women, support their health and well-being and eliminate negative stereotypes. On 1 April [E/1999/27 (dec. 43/101)], the Commission took note of the report.

Palestinian women

In a report to the Commission on the Status of Women on follow-up to the Beijing Platform for Action [E/CN.6/1999/2], the Secretary-General described assistance provided by organizations of the UN system to Palestinian women, whose daily life continued to be adversely affected by the Israeli occupation, in particular by security-related measures imposed by the Israeli authorities. The Secretary-General stated that the measures had a detrimental impact on the socio-economic condition of Palestinian women, which was reinforced by existing inequalities in society between men and women.

In July, on the recommendation of the Commission, the Economic and Social Council adopted **resolution 1999/15**, by which it asked the Commission to continue to monitor and take action regarding the situation of Palestinian women and children (see p. 418).

Women in Afghanistan

On 28 July [meeting 43], the Economic and Social Council, on the recommendation of the Commission on the Status of Women [E/1998/27], adopted **resolution 1999/14** without vote [agenda item 14 *(a)*].

Situation of women and girls in Afghanistan

The Economic and Social Council,

Guided by the Charter of the United Nations, the Universal Declaration of Human Rights, the International Covenants on Human Rights, the Convention against Torture and Other Cruel, Inhuman or Degrading Treatment or Punishment, the Convention on the Elimination of All Forms of Discrimination against Women, the Convention on the Rights of the Child, the Beijing Declaration and the Platform for Action adopted at the Fourth World Conference on Women, and other instruments of human rights and international humanitarian law,

Recalling that Afghanistan is a party to the Convention on the Prevention and Punishment of the Crime of Genocide, the International Covenant on Civil and Political Rights, the International Covenant on Economic, Social and Cultural Rights, the Convention against Torture and Other Cruel, Inhuman or Degrading Treatment or Punishment, the Convention on the Rights of the Child, and the Geneva Convention relative to the Protection of Civilian Persons in Time of War, and that it has signed the Convention on the Elimination of All Forms of Discrimination against Women,

Deeply concerned by the continuing deterioration of the situation of women and girls in Afghanistan, in particular in all areas under the control of the Taliban, as documented by the continued and substantiated reports of grave violations of the human rights of women and girls, including all forms of discrimination against them, such as denial of access to health care, to all levels and types of education, to employment outside the home and, in repeated instances, to humanitarian aid, as well as restrictions upon their freedom of movement,

Welcoming the ongoing work of the Special Rapporteur of the Commission on Human Rights on the situation of human rights in Afghanistan, in particular his special focus on violations of the human rights of women and girls, especially in territories under the control of the Taliban faction,

Noting with concern the detrimental impact of these harmful conditions on the well-being of Afghan women and the children in their care,

Welcoming the United Nations Inter-Agency Gender Mission to Afghanistan in November 1997, led by the Special Adviser to the Secretary-General on Gender Issues and Advancement of Women, taking into account the report on the Mission, and hoping that the Mission will serve as a model for future efforts to address the gender dimension of crisis/conflict situations,

Expressing its appreciation for the international community's support of and solidarity with the women and girls of Afghanistan, being supportive of the women of Afghanistan who protest violations of their human rights, and encouraging women and men worldwide to continue efforts to draw attention to their situation and to promote the immediate restoration of their ability to enjoy their human rights,

1. *Condemns* the continuing grave violations of the human rights of women and girls, including all forms of discrimination and violence against them, in all areas of Afghanistan, particularly in areas under the control of the Taliban;

2. *Also condemns* the denial by the Taliban of the access of women to health care and the systematic violation of the human rights of women in Afghanistan, including the denial of access to education and to employment outside their home, freedom of movement, and freedom from intimidation, harassment and violence, which has a serious detrimental impact on the well-being of Afghan women and the children in their care;

3. *Urges* the Taliban and other Afghan parties to recognize, protect, promote and act in accordance with all human rights and fundamental freedoms, regardless of gender, ethnicity or religion, in accordance with international human rights instruments, and to respect international humanitarian law;

4. *Urges* all the Afghan parties, in particular the Taliban, to bring to an end without delay all violations of the human rights of women and girls and to take urgent measures to ensure:

(a) The repeal of all legislative and other measures that discriminate against women;

(b) The effective participation of women in civil, cultural, economic, political and social life;

(c) Respect for the equal right of women to work and their reintegration in employment;

(d) The equal right of women and girls to education without discrimination, the reopening of schools and the admission of women and girls to all levels of education;

(e) Respect for the right of women to security of person and that those responsible for physical attacks on women are brought to justice;

(f) Respect for freedom of movement for women;

(g) Respect for the equal access of women and girls to health care;

5. *Encourages* the continuing efforts of the United Nations, international and non-governmental organizations and donors to ensure that all United Nations-assisted programmes in Afghanistan are formulated and coordinated in such a way as to promote and ensure the participation of women in those programmes and that women benefit equally with men from such programmes;

6. *Appeals* to all States and to the international community to ensure that all humanitarian assistance to the people of Afghanistan, in conformity with the Strategic Framework for Afghanistan, is based on the principle of non-discrimination, integrates a gender perspective, and actively attempts to promote the participation of both women and men and to promote peace and respect for human rights and fundamental freedoms;

7. *Urges* States to continue to give special attention to the promotion and protection of human rights of women in Afghanistan and to mainstream a gender perspective into all aspects of their policies and actions related to Afghanistan;

8. *Welcomes* the establishment of the positions of Gender Adviser and Human Rights Adviser at the United Nations Office of the Resident Coordinator for Afghanistan, in order to ensure more effective consideration and implementation of human rights and gender concerns into all United Nations programmes within Afghanistan, taking into account the recommendations contained in the report of the United Nations Inter-Agency Gender Mission to Afghanistan led by the Special Adviser to the Secretary-General on Gender Issues and Advancement of Women in November 1997;

9. *Urges* the Secretary-General to ensure that all United Nations activities in Afghanistan are carried out according to the principle of non-discrimination against women and girls, and that a gender perspective and special attention to the human rights of women and girls are fully incorporated into the work of the Civil Affairs Unit established within the United Nations Special Mission to Afghanistan, including the training and selection of staff;

10. *Stresses* the importance of the Special Rapporteur of the Commission on Human Rights on the situation of human rights in Afghanistan giving special attention to the human rights of women and girls and fully incorporating a gender perspective in his work;

11. *Appeals* to States and the international community to implement the recommendations of the United Nations Inter-Agency Gender Mission to Afghanistan under the leadership of the Special Adviser to the Secretary-General on Gender Issues and Advancement of Women;

12. *Urges* all Afghan factions, in particular the Taliban, to ensure the safety and protection of all United Nations and humanitarian workers in Afghanistan and to allow them, regardless of gender, to carry out their work unhindered.

Women and development

The Economic and Social Council, at the high-level segment (New York, 5-7 July) of its 1999 substantive session [A/54/3/Rev.1], addressed the role of employment and work in poverty eradication, particularly in relation to the empowerment and advancement of women. The Council considered a report of the Secretary-General, prepared by the International Labour Organization (ILO) [E/1999/53], addressing the role of employment creation in poverty eradication, taking into account the processes of impoverishment, new types of vulnerability and the differential impact of those processes on women and men. Because the interrelated problems of poverty and employment differed between groups, particularly between women and men, successful poverty-reduction strategies needed to address both broad socio-economic and gender-specific policy issues, the report stated. A policy framework for employment growth and poverty reduction should include macroeconomic policies that would ensure fast, sustainable and stable growth that was employment-intensive, balanced and gender-sensitive. Public policies should provide an environment for the functioning of markets, and poverty-eradication strategies should aim at improving market outcomes for the poor. Public policies could also contribute to poverty reduction through the reallocation of public expenditure (education, health, skill formation), adoption of gender-sensitive policies for promoting employment, and extension of social protection through social safety nets. The report concluded with proposals for elements of an agenda for action, building upon previous work by the UN system, especially the 1998 ACC statement of commitment for action to eradicate poverty [YUN 1998, p. 782].

Other documents considered during the Council's high-level segment included a paper containing "A Comprehensive Employment Strategy" [A/54/171-E/1999/111], presented by the Group of Fifteen at the 1999 International Labour Conference (Geneva, 1-17 June); the report of the Committee for Development Policy on its first session (New York, 26-30 April) [E/1999/33], which considered the role of employment and work in poverty eradication in the context of globalization: the empowerment and advancement of women; and the *World Economic and Social Survey 1999* [Sales No. E.99.II.C.1].

ECONOMIC AND SOCIAL COUNCIL ACTION

On 7 July [A/54/3/Rev.1], the Economic and Social Council adopted a ministerial communiqué of the high-level segment submitted by the President, by which the ministers and heads of delegations affirmed their commitment to adopting effective poverty-eradication strategies that addressed employment creation and gender-specific policies. The Council recognized that women and men frequently suffered poverty for different reasons and faced different opportunities and constraints in coping with poverty and in accessing labour markets and sustainable livelihoods. The mainstreaming of a gender perspective into poverty-eradication policies was crucial as women constituted the majority of people living in poverty. Those policies had to be aimed at eliminating discrimination against women.

The Council stated that strategies to eradicate poverty, promote productive employment and achieve gender equality needed to be designed to address the conditions and needs of women and men on equal terms. Such strategies should be comprehensive in their approach while allowing for flexibility, pursued at both national and international levels, and supported by an enabling international environment. Women's empowerment was considered one of the prerequisites to effective poverty-eradication and employment-creation strategies.

In the communiqué, the Council suggested that an effective development strategy should target key economic sectors for employment-intensive growth, including agriculture and non-traditional sectors. It recognized the importance of small and medium-sized enterprises for creating employment, and the importance of micro-credit, non-standard forms of work, the informal employment sector, gender-sensitive labour policies, and laws protecting women who sought work in foreign countries. UN bodies were asked to translate the communiqué's recommendations into concrete actions and the Secretary-General was to submit a progress report to the Council at its 2000 substantive session.

On 30 July, by **resolution 1999/55**, the Council decided to transmit to the General Assembly the outcome of its consideration of the role of employment and work in poverty eradication as one of the inputs for the five-year reviews of the Fourth World Conference on Women and of the World Summit for Social Development.

World Survey

In August, the Secretary-General issued the 1999 *World Survey on the Role of Women in Development* [A/54/227], the fourth in a series begun in 1985. It examined the impact of current trends and policies on the overall economic and social situation of women, with particular emphasis on the difficult economic situation affecting women in the majority of developing countries. The *World Survey* examined three dimensions of economic development—reallocation of resources, adjustment costs and creation of new resources—in the context of five major new trends identified in the world of work: the casualization and informalization of employment; increased participation of women in paid work; downsizing of State and social expenditures; the growing importance of unpaid work; and increasing privatization and commercialization of agriculture. The report described the global forces and processes contributing to those trends, including globalization of trade and capital flows, the changing role of the State, new information technologies, and changing patterns of labour mobility and migration. It also presented a brief overview of women's status in relation to the 12 critical areas of concern in the Beijing Platform for Action, with the objective of assessing the progress women had made globally over recent decades.

On 30 July, the Economic and Social Council, by **decision 1999/286**, took note of the executive summary of the *World Survey* [E/1999/44].

GENERAL ASSEMBLY ACTION

On 22 December [meeting 87], the General Assembly, on the recommendation of the Second (Economic and Financial) Committee [A/54/587/Add.3], adopted **resolution 54/210** without vote [agenda item 99 (*c*)].

Women in development

The General Assembly,

Recalling its resolution 52/195 of 18 December 1997 and all its other resolutions on the integration of women in development, and also the relevant resolutions and the agreed conclusions, including those on women in the economy, adopted by the Commission on the Status of Women,

Reaffirming the Beijing Platform for Action and the outcomes of recent major United Nations conferences and summits,

Taking note of the ministerial communiqué of the high-level segment of the Economic and Social Council on the theme "The role of employment and work in poverty eradication: the empowerment and advancement of women",

Reaffirming that gender equality is of fundamental importance for achieving sustained economic growth and sustainable development, in accordance with the relevant General Assembly resolutions and recent United Nations conferences, and that investing in the development of women and girls has a multiplier effect, in particular on productivity, efficiency and sustained economic growth,

Recognizing the significant contribution that women make to the economy and the major force that they represent for change and development in all sectors of the economy, especially in key areas such as agriculture, industry and services,

Reaffirming that women are key contributors to the economy and to combating poverty through both remunerated and unremunerated work at home, in the community and in the workplace and that the empowerment of women is a critical factor in the eradication of poverty,

Recognizing that the rapid development of information technology and other new technologies presents both opportunities and challenges to women, in particular in developing countries,

Recognizing also that population and development issues, education and training, health, nutrition, the environment, water supply, sanitation, housing, communications, science and technology and employment opportunities are important elements for effective poverty eradication and the advancement and empowerment of women,

Recognizing further in this context the importance of respect for all human rights, including the right to development, and of a national and international environment that promotes, inter alia, justice, equity, popular participation and political freedom for the advancement and empowerment of women,

Concerned that the continued discrimination against women, the denial or lack of equal rights and access to education, training and credit facilities and the lack of control over land, capital, technology and other areas of production impede their full and equal contribution to, and equal opportunity to benefit from, development,

Recognizing that the difficult socio-economic conditions that exist in many developing countries, in particular the least developed countries, have resulted in the acceleration of the feminization of poverty and that the empowerment of women is a critical factor in the eradication of poverty,

Aware that, although globalization and liberalization processes have created employment opportunities for women in many countries, they have made women, especially in developing countries and in particular the least developed countries, more vulnerable to problems caused by increased economic volatility,

Recognizing that some effects of market liberalization may deepen the socio-economic marginalization of women in the agricultural sector, including through the loss of employment among small-scale farmers who are more likely to be women than men, and emphasizing that small-scale women farmers need special support and empowerment so as to be able to meet the challenges and opportunities of agricultural market liberalization,

Recognizing also that enhanced trade opportunities for developing countries, including through trade liberalization, will improve the economic condition of those societies, including women, which is of particular importance in rural communities,

Recognizing further the continued need to review the impact of structural adjustment programmes in order to reduce any adverse impact on women, especially in terms of cutbacks in social services, education and health and the removal of subsidies on food and fuel,

Emphasizing the promotion of programmes aimed at financial intermediation with a view to ensuring the access of rural women to credit and to agricultural inputs and implements and, in particular, to easing collateral requirements for access to finance by women,

Recognizing that the informal sector is a major source of entrepreneurship and employment for women in developing countries and that data collection on its important contribution should be improved,

Expressing its concern about the under-representation of women in economic decision-making, and stressing the importance of mainstreaming a gender perspective in all policy formulation, implementation and evaluation,

Recognizing that the increase in women's participation in paid employment contributes to the empowerment of women and gender equality by promoting the status, independence, self-esteem and decision-making power of women, but also that this alone may be insufficient, since, in general, the burden of household work and primary responsibility of women for childcare can give rise to an onerous double working day for most women,

Stressing the need for a family-friendly work environment, including appropriate working hours, affordable childcare and flexible working hours, and emphasizing the principle of shared responsibility between women and men for the achievement of gender equality,

Noting the importance of the organizations and bodies of the United Nations system, in particular its funds and programmes, including the United Nations Development Fund for Women and the International Research and Training Institute for the Advancement of Women, in facilitating the advancement of women in development,

1. *Takes note* of the report of the Secretary-General on the 1999 World Survey on the Role of Women in Development: Globalization, Gender and Work;

2. *Calls* for the accelerated and effective implementation of the Beijing Platform for Action and the relevant provisions contained in the outcomes of all other major United Nations conferences and summits, and in this regard expresses the hope that the special session of the General Assembly entitled "Women 2000: gender equality, development and peace for the twenty-first century", which will be held from 5 to 9 June 2000, can take tangible and significant steps to enhance the effective participation of women in development;

3. *Stresses* that a favourable and conducive national and international environment in all fields of life is necessary for the effective integration of women in development;

4. *Urges* Governments to develop and to promote methodologies for mainstreaming a gender perspective in all aspects of policy-making, including economic policy-making;

5. *Stresses* the importance of developing national strategies for promoting sustainable and productive entrepreneurial activities to generate income among disadvantaged women and women living in poverty;

6. *Urges* all Governments to ensure women's equal rights with men and their full and equal access to education, training, employment, technology and economic and financial resources, including credit, in particular for rural women and women in the informal sector, and to facilitate, where appropriate, the transition of women from the informal to the formal sector;

7. *Recognizes* the role of micro-finance including micro-credit in the eradication of poverty, the empowerment of women and the generation of employment and, in this regard, notes the importance of sound national financial systems and encourages the strengthening of existing and emerging micro-credit institutions and their capacities, including through the support of international financial institutions;

8. *Requests* Governments to ensure that the priorities of women are included in, and that women fully participate in, decisions on public investment programmes for economic infrastructure, technology, water supply and sanitation, electrification and energy conservation, transport and road construction and to promote the greater involvement of women beneficiaries at the project planning and implementation stages to ensure their access to jobs and contracts;

9. *Stresses* the need for assistance to enable women in developing countries, particularly grass-roots women's groups, to have full access to and use of new technologies, including information technologies, for their empowerment;

10. *Also stresses* the need to ensure that women and girls have full and equal access to all levels of education, vocational training and retraining programmes in order to improve their employment opportunities;

11. *Urges* States to design and revise laws that ensure that women are accorded full and equal rights as men to own land and other property, including through the right to inheritance, and to undertake administrative reforms and other necessary measures to give women the same right as men to credit, capital, appropriate technologies, access to markets and information;

12. *Requests* Governments to ensure the full participation of women in decision-making and policy formulation and implementation at all levels so that their priorities, skills and potentials can be adequately reflected in national policy;

13. *Calls upon* Governments to promote, inter alia, through legislation, family-friendly and gender-sensitive work environments and also to promote the facilitation of breastfeeding for working mothers;

14. *Stresses* the need for Governments and employers, as appropriate, to implement policies aimed at ensuring stability and security of work and to put in place social protection measures that cover temporary, part-time, informal sector and home workers, a majority of whom are women;

15. *Calls upon* the international community to make efforts to mitigate the effects of excess volatility and economic disruption, which have a disproportionately negative impact on women, and to enhance trade opportunities for developing countries in order to improve the economic conditions of women;

16. *Urges* the international community, the United Nations system and relevant organizations to give priority to assisting the efforts of developing countries to ensure the full and effective participation of women in deciding and implementing development strategies and integrating gender concerns into national programmes, including by providing adequate resources to operational activities for development in support of the efforts of Governments to ensure, inter alia, increased access of women to health care, capital, education, training and technology and full and equal participation in all decision-making;

17. *Calls upon* developed countries to strengthen their efforts to achieve, as soon as possible, the agreed target of 0.7 per cent of their gross national product for overall official development assistance and, where agreed, within that target to earmark 0.15 to 0.20 per cent of gross national product for the least developed countries, so as to assist the developing countries in implementing strategies to eradicate poverty and to promote development and gender equality;

18. *Urges* multilateral donors, international financial institutions and regional development banks to review and implement policies to support national efforts to ensure that a higher proportion of resources reach women, in particular in rural and remote areas;

19. *Calls upon* the United Nations system to integrate gender mainstreaming into all its programmes and policies, including in the integrated follow-up to

United Nations conferences, in accordance with agreed conclusions 1997/2 on gender mainstreaming adopted by the Economic and Social Council at its substantive session of 1997;

20. *Requests* the Secretary-General to update the World Survey on the Role of Women in Development for the consideration of the General Assembly at its fifty-ninth session; as in the past, this survey should focus on selective emerging development issues that have an impact on the role of women in the economy at the national, regional and international levels;

21. *Decides* to include in the provisional agenda of its fifty-sixth session the sub-item entitled "Women in development".

System-wide plan

In accordance with Economic and Social Council resolution 1996/34 [YUN 1996, p. 1057], a new draft system-wide medium-term plan for the advancement of women for the period 2002-2005 was to be prepared for review by the Commission on the Status of Women at its forty-fourth (2000) session.

ECONOMIC AND SOCIAL COUNCIL ACTION

On 28 July [meeting 43], the Economic and Social Council, on the recommendation of the Commission on the Status of Women [E/1999/27], adopted **resolution 1999/16** without vote [agenda item 14 *(a)*].

System-wide medium-term plan for the advancement of women, 2002-2005

The Economic and Social Council,

Recalling its resolution 1996/34 of 25 July 1996 on the system-wide medium-term plan for the advancement of women, 1996-2001, in which it called for a new draft plan to cover the period 2002-2005,

Considering that the new draft plan should take into consideration the outcome of the special session of the General Assembly on progress achieved in the implementation of the Beijing Platform for Action,

1. *Invites* the Secretary-General, in his capacity as Chairman of the Administrative Committee on Coordination, to formulate the plan for the period 2002-2005 in two phases, a first phase consisting of an assessment of activities undertaken by the United Nations system and of obstacles encountered and lessons learned from the present plan and the system-wide process of its implementation, and a second phase consisting of a new plan that reflects the growing emphasis on action and delivery;

2. *Decides* that the assessment should be submitted to the Economic and Social Council through the Commission on the Status of Women in 2000 and that the new plan for 2002-2005 should be submitted to the Council through the Commission in 2001.

Women in the Secretariat

The Commission on the Status of Women considered a January report of the Secretary-General [E/CN.6/1999/5], prepared in response to General Assembly resolution 53/119 [YUN 1998, p. 1316], which updated information on the status of women in the UN Secretariat. In 1998, the increase in the percentage of women on appointments subject to geographical distribution had been marginal, rising from 36.8 per cent to 37.1 per cent. The Secretary-General also provided information on measures taken for the achievement of gender equality. During 1999, priority was to be given to gender action plans in individual departments and offices. The Secretary-General reported to the General Assembly in September on the improvement of the status of women in the Secretariat [A/54/405], again noting that the increase of women on appointments subject to geographical distribution had been small, rising to 38.1 per cent since the end of 1998 (see p. 1333).

On 17 December, the General Assembly, in **resolution 54/139**, called on the Secretary-General to implement and monitor the strategic plan of action for the improvement of the status of women in the Secretariat (1995-2000) [YUN 1994, p. 1383] in order to achieve the goal of 50/50 gender distribution by 2000.

UN machinery

Convention on elimination of discrimination against women

As at 31 December 1999, 165 States were parties to the 1979 Convention on the Elimination of All Forms of Discrimination against Women, adopted by the General Assembly in resolution 34/180 [YUN 1979, p. 895]. During the year, the Niger and Tuvalu acceded to the Convention. Also at year's end, 23 States parties had accepted the amendment to article 20, paragraph 1, of the Convention in respect of the meeting time of the Committee on the Elimination of Discrimination against Women (CEDAW), which had been adopted by the States parties in 1995 [YUN 1995, p. 1178]. The amendment would enter into force when accepted by a two-thirds majority of States parties.

The Optional Protocol to the Convention, adopted by the General Assembly on 6 October (see next page) and opened for signature on 10 December, had 24 signatories by the end of 1999. The Protocol would enter into force following ratification by 10 States parties to the Convention.

The Secretary-General submitted his annual report to the General Assembly on the status of the Convention as at 1 August [A/54/224 & Corr.1].

Optional Protocol

In March, the Open-ended Working Group to elaborate a draft optional protocol to the Convention finalized its negotiations and submitted the draft and its enabling resolution to the Commission on the Status of Women for consideration [E/1999/27, annex II]. The draft text, which incorporated the complaints procedures contained in several international human rights treaties, would allow individuals or groups of individuals to submit claims of alleged violations of rights protected under the Convention. The Commission recommended the draft to the Economic and Social Council for adoption by the General Assembly.

ECONOMIC AND SOCIAL COUNCIL ACTION

On 28 July [meeting 43], the Economic and Social Council, on the recommendation of the Commission on the Status of Women [E/1999/27], adopted **resolution 1999/13** without vote [agenda item 14 *(a)*].

Optional Protocol to the Convention on the Elimination of All Forms of Discrimination against Women

The Economic and Social Council

Recommends to the General Assembly the adoption of the following draft resolution:

[For full text, see General Assembly resolution 54/4 below.]

GENERAL ASSEMBLY ACTION

On 6 October [meeting 28], the General Assembly adopted **resolution 54/4** [draft: A/54/L.4] without vote [agenda item 109].

Optional Protocol to the Convention on the Elimination of All Forms of Discrimination against Women

The General Assembly,

Reaffirming the Vienna Declaration and Programme of Action and the Beijing Declaration and Platform for Action,

Recalling that the Beijing Platform for Action, pursuant to the Vienna Declaration and Programme of Action, supported the process initiated by the Commission on the Status of Women with a view to elaborating a draft optional protocol to the Convention on the Elimination of All Forms of Discrimination against Women that could enter into force as soon as possible on a right-to-petition procedure,

Noting that the Beijing Platform for Action also called on all States that have not yet ratified or acceded to the Convention to do so as soon as possible so that universal ratification of the Convention can be achieved by the year 2000,

1. *Adopts and opens for signature, ratification and accession* the Optional Protocol to the Convention, the text of which is annexed to the present resolution;

2. *Calls upon* all States that have signed, ratified or acceded to the Convention to sign and ratify or to accede to the Protocol as soon as possible;

3. *Stresses* that States parties to the Protocol should undertake to respect the rights and procedures provided by the Protocol and cooperate with the Committee on the Elimination of Discrimination against Women at all stages of its proceedings under the Protocol;

4. *Stresses* also that in the fulfilment of its mandate as well as its functions under the Protocol, the Committee should continue to be guided by the principles of non-selectivity, impartiality and objectivity;

5. *Requests* the Committee to hold meetings to exercise its functions under the Protocol after its entry into force, in addition to its meetings held under article 20 of the Convention; the duration of such meetings shall be determined and, if necessary, reviewed by a meeting of the States parties to the Protocol, subject to the approval of the General Assembly;

6. *Requests* the Secretary-General to provide the staff and facilities necessary for the effective performance of the functions of the Committee under the Protocol after its entry into force;

7. *Also requests* the Secretary-General to include information on the status of the Protocol in her or his regular reports submitted to the General Assembly on the status of the Convention.

ANNEX

Optional Protocol to the Convention on the Elimination of All Forms of Discrimination against Women

The States Parties to the present Protocol,

Noting that the Charter of the United Nations reaffirms faith in fundamental human rights, in the dignity and worth of the human person and in the equal rights of men and women,

Also noting that the Universal Declaration of Human Rights proclaims that all human beings are born free and equal in dignity and rights and that everyone is entitled to all the rights and freedoms set forth therein, without distinction of any kind, including distinction based on sex,

Recalling that the International Covenants on Human Rights and other international human rights instruments prohibit discrimination on the basis of sex,

Also recalling the Convention on the Elimination of All Forms of Discrimination against Women ("the Convention"), in which the States Parties thereto condemn discrimination against women in all its forms and agree to pursue by all appropriate means and without delay a policy of eliminating discrimination against women,

Reaffirming their determination to ensure the full and equal enjoyment by women of all human rights and fundamental freedoms and to take effective action to prevent violations of these rights and freedoms,

Have agreed as follows:

Article 1

A State Party to the present Protocol ("State Party") recognizes the competence of the Committee on the Elimination of Discrimination against Women ("the Committee") to receive and consider communications submitted in accordance with article 2.

Article 2

Communications may be submitted by or on behalf of individuals or groups of individuals, under the jurisdiction of a State Party, claiming to be victims of a violation of any of the rights set forth in the Convention by that State Party. Where a communication is submitted on behalf of individuals or groups of individuals, this shall be with their consent unless the author can justify acting on their behalf without such consent.

Article 3

Communications shall be in writing and shall not be anonymous. No communication shall be received by the Committee if it concerns a State Party to the Convention that is not a party to the present Protocol.

Article 4

1. The Committee shall not consider a communication unless it has ascertained that all available domestic remedies have been exhausted unless the application of such remedies is unreasonably prolonged or unlikely to bring effective relief.

2. The Committee shall declare a communication inadmissible where:

(a) The same matter has already been examined by the Committee or has been or is being examined under another procedure of international investigation or settlement;

(b) It is incompatible with the provisions of the Convention;

(c) It is manifestly ill-founded or not sufficiently substantiated;

(d) It is an abuse of the right to submit a communication;

(e) The facts that are the subject of the communication occurred prior to the entry into force of the present Protocol for the State Party concerned unless those facts continued after that date.

Article 5

1. At any time after the receipt of a communication and before a determination on the merits has been reached, the Committee may transmit to the State Party concerned for its urgent consideration a request that the State Party take such interim measures as may be necessary to avoid possible irreparable damage to the victim or victims of the alleged violation.

2. Where the Committee exercises its discretion under paragraph 1 of the present article, this does not imply a determination on admissibility or on the merits of the communication.

Article 6

1. Unless the Committee considers a communication inadmissible without reference to the State Party concerned, and provided that the individual or individuals consent to the disclosure of their identity to that State Party, the Committee shall bring any communication submitted to it under the present Protocol confidentially to the attention of the State Party concerned.

2. Within six months, the receiving State Party shall submit to the Committee written explanations or statements clarifying the matter and the remedy, if any, that may have been provided by that State Party.

Article 7

1. The Committee shall consider communications received under the present Protocol in the light of all information made available to it by or on behalf of individuals or groups of individuals and by the State Party concerned, provided that this information is transmitted to the parties concerned.

2. The Committee shall hold closed meetings when examining communications under the present Protocol.

3. After examining a communication, the Committee shall transmit its views on the communication, together with its recommendations, if any, to the parties concerned.

4. The State Party shall give due consideration to the views of the Committee, together with its recommendations, if any, and shall submit to the Committee, within six months, a written response, including information on any action taken in the light of the views and recommendations of the Committee.

5. The Committee may invite the State Party to submit further information about any measures the State Party has taken in response to its views or recommendations, if any, including as deemed appropriate by the Committee, in the State Party's subsequent reports under article 18 of the Convention.

Article 8

1. If the Committee receives reliable information indicating grave or systematic violations by a State Party of rights set forth in the Convention, the Committee shall invite that State Party to cooperate in the examination of the information and to this end to submit observations with regard to the information concerned.

2. Taking into account any observations that may have been submitted by the State Party concerned as well as any other reliable information available to it, the Committee may designate one or more of its members to conduct an inquiry and to report urgently to the Committee. Where warranted and with the consent of the State Party, the inquiry may include a visit to its territory.

3. After examining the findings of such an inquiry, the Committee shall transmit these findings to the State Party concerned together with any comments and recommendations.

4. The State Party concerned shall, within six months of receiving the findings, comments and recommendations transmitted by the Committee, submit its observations to the Committee.

5. Such an inquiry shall be conducted confidentially and the cooperation of the State Party shall be sought at all stages of the proceedings.

Article 9

1. The Committee may invite the State Party concerned to include in its report under article 18 of the Convention details of any measures taken in response to an inquiry conducted under article 8 of the present Protocol.

2. The Committee may, if necessary, after the end of the period of six months referred to in article 8.4, invite the State Party concerned to inform it of the measures taken in response to such an inquiry.

Article 10

1. Each State Party may, at the time of signature or ratification of the present Protocol or accession thereto, declare that it does not recognize the competence of the Committee provided for in articles 8 and 9.

2. Any State Party having made a declaration in accordance with paragraph 1 of the present article may, at any time, withdraw this declaration by notification to the Secretary-General.

Article 11

A State Party shall take all appropriate steps to ensure that individuals under its jurisdiction are not subjected to ill treatment or intimidation as a consequence of communicating with the Committee pursuant to the present Protocol.

Article 12

The Committee shall include in its annual report under article 21 of the Convention a summary of its activities under the present Protocol.

Article 13

Each State Party undertakes to make widely known and to give publicity to the Convention and the present Protocol and to facilitate access to information about the views and recommendations of the Committee, in particular, on matters involving that State Party.

Article 14

The Committee shall develop its own rules of procedure to be followed when exercising the functions conferred on it by the present Protocol.

Article 15

1. The present Protocol shall be open for signature by any State that has signed, ratified or acceded to the Convention.

2. The present Protocol shall be subject to ratification by any State that has ratified or acceded to the Convention. Instruments of ratification shall be deposited with the Secretary-General of the United Nations.

3. The present Protocol shall be open to accession by any State that has ratified or acceded to the Convention.

4. Accession shall be effected by the deposit of an instrument of accession with the Secretary-General of the United Nations.

Article 16

1. The present Protocol shall enter into force three months after the date of the deposit with the Secretary-General of the United Nations of the tenth instrument of ratification or accession.

2. For each State ratifying the present Protocol or acceding to it after its entry into force, the present Protocol shall enter into force three months after the date of the deposit of its own instrument of ratification or accession.

Article 17

No reservations to the present Protocol shall be permitted.

Article 18

1. Any State Party may propose an amendment to the present Protocol and file it with the Secretary-General of the United Nations. The Secretary-General shall thereupon communicate any proposed amendments to the States Parties with a request that they notify her or him whether they favour a conference of States Parties for the purpose of considering and voting on the proposal. In the event that at least one third of the States Parties favour such a conference, the Secretary-General shall convene the conference under the auspices of the United Nations. Any amendment adopted by a majority of the States Parties present and voting at the conference shall be submitted to the General Assembly of the United Nations for approval.

2. Amendments shall come into force when they have been approved by the General Assembly of the United Nations and accepted by a two-thirds majority of the States Parties to the present Protocol in accordance with their respective constitutional processes.

3. When amendments come into force, they shall be binding on those States Parties that have accepted them, other States Parties still being bound by the provisions of the present Protocol and any earlier amendments that they have accepted.

Article 19

1. Any State Party may denounce the present Protocol at any time by written notification addressed to the Secretary-General of the United Nations. Denunciation shall take effect six months after the date of receipt of the notification by the Secretary-General.

2. Denunciation shall be without prejudice to the continued application of the provisions of the present Protocol to any communication submitted under article 2 or any inquiry initiated under article 8 before the effective date of denunciation.

Article 20

The Secretary-General of the United Nations shall inform all States of:

(a) Signatures, ratifications and accessions under the present Protocol;

(b) The date of entry into force of the present Protocol and of any amendment under article 18;

(c) Any denunciation under article 19.

Article 21

1. The present Protocol, of which the Arabic, Chinese, English, French, Russian and Spanish texts are equally authentic, shall be deposited in the archives of the United Nations.

2. The Secretary-General of the United Nations shall transmit certified copies of the present Protocol to all States referred to in article 25 of the Convention.

CEDAW

In 1999, the 23-member Committee on the Elimination of Discrimination against Women (CEDAW), established in 1982 [YUN 1982, p. 1149] to monitor compliance with the 1979 Convention, held two sessions in New York [A/54/38/Rev.1]. At its twentieth session (19 January–5 February), CEDAW reviewed the initial or periodic reports of Algeria, China, Colombia, Greece, Kyrgyzstan, Liechtenstein and Thailand on measures they had taken to implement the Convention. The Committee decided to elaborate a general recommendation on article 12, which addressed measures to eliminate discrimination against women in the field of health care. The recommendation called on States parties to implement comprehensive national strategies promoting women's health throughout their lifespan, including preventing and treating disease, responding to violence against women and ensuring universal access for all women to high-quality and affordable health care. The Committee also decided that representatives of NGOs should be invited to provide country-specific information on States parties whose reports were before the Committee.

At its twenty-first session (7-25 June), the Committee reviewed the initial or periodic reports of Belize, Chile, Georgia, Ireland, Nepal, Spain and the United Kingdom. It also adopted two decisions and a suggestion related to reporting procedural matters. On 7 June, a special ceremony was held at UN Headquarters to commemorate the twentieth anniversary of the adoption of the Convention.

GENERAL ASSEMBLY ACTION

On 17 December [meeting 83], the General Assembly, on the recommendation of the Third Committee [A/54/598 & Corr.1,2], adopted **resolution 54/137** without vote [agenda item 109].

Convention on the Elimination of All Forms of Discrimination against Women

The General Assembly,

Recalling its resolution 53/118 of 9 December 1998,

Bearing in mind that one of the purposes of the United Nations, as stated in Articles 1 and 55 of the Charter, is to promote universal respect for human rights and fundamental freedoms for all without distinction of any kind, including distinction as to sex,

Affirming that women and men should participate equally in social, economic and political development, should contribute equally to such development and should share equally in improved conditions of life,

Recalling the Vienna Declaration and Programme of Action adopted by the World Conference on Human Rights on 25 June 1993, in which the Conference reaffirmed that the human rights of women and the girl child were an inalienable, integral and indivisible part of universal human rights,

Acknowledging the need for a comprehensive and integrated approach to the promotion and protection of the human rights of women, which includes the integration of the human rights of women into the mainstream of United Nations activities system-wide, and, in this context, calling for the implementation of agreed conclusions 1998/2 of 28 July 1998 of the Economic and Social Council,

Noting that 1999 is the twentieth anniversary of the adoption of the Convention on the Elimination of All Forms of Discrimination against Women, welcoming the progress made in its implementation, but concerned about the remaining challenges,

Bearing in mind its resolution 54/4 of 6 October 1999, by which it adopted and opened for signature, ratification and accession the Optional Protocol to the Convention on the Elimination of All Forms of Discrimination against Women,

Bearing in mind also the recommendation of the Committee on the Elimination of Discrimination against Women that national reports include information on the implementation of the Platform for Action of the Fourth World Conference on Women,

Welcoming the growing number of States parties to the Convention on the Elimination of All Forms of Discrimination against Women, which now stands at one hundred sixty-five,

Noting the elaboration and adoption by the Committee, at its twentieth session, of general recommendation 24 on article 12 of the Convention, on women and health,

Having considered the report of the Committee on its twentieth and twenty-first sessions,

Expressing concern at the great number of reports that are overdue and that continue to be overdue, in particular initial reports, which constitutes an obstacle to the full implementation of the Convention,

1. *Welcomes* the report of the Secretary-General on the status of the Convention on the Elimination of All Forms of Discrimination against Women;

2. *Urges* all States that have not yet ratified or acceded to the Convention to do so as soon as possible, so that universal ratification of the Convention can be achieved by the year 2000;

3. *Emphasizes* the importance of full compliance by States parties with their obligations under the Convention;

4. *Notes with appreciation* the adoption by the General Assembly, by resolution 54/4, of the Optional Protocol to the Convention on the Elimination of All Forms of Discrimination against Women;

5. *Notes* that some States parties have modified their reservations, expresses satisfaction that some reservations have been withdrawn, and urges States to limit the extent of any reservations they lodge to the Convention, to formulate any such reservations as precisely and as narrowly as possible, to ensure that no reservations are incompatible with the object and purpose of the Convention or otherwise incompatible with international treaty law, to review their reservations regularly with a view to withdrawing them and to withdraw reservations that are contrary to the object and purpose of the Convention or that are otherwise incompatible with international treaty law;

6. *Urges* States parties to the Convention to make every possible effort to submit their reports on the implementation of the Convention in accordance with article 18 thereof and with the guidelines provided by the Committee on the Elimination of Discrimination against Women and to cooperate fully with the Committee in the presentation of their reports;

7. *Encourages* the Secretariat to extend further technical assistance to States parties, upon their request, in the preparation of reports, in particular initial reports, and invites Governments to contribute to these efforts;

8. *Commends* the Committee on its contributions to the effective implementation of the Convention;

9. *Urges* States parties to the Convention to take appropriate measures so that acceptance of the amendment to article 20, paragraph 1, of the Convention by a two-thirds majority of States parties can be reached as soon as possible in order for the amendment to enter into force;

10. *Expresses its appreciation* for the additional meeting time allowing the Committee to hold two sessions annually, each of three weeks' duration, preceded by a pre-session working group of the Committee;

11. *Emphasizes* the need to ensure adequate financing and staff support for the effective functioning of

the Committee, including for the dissemination of information;

12. *Invites* Governments, agencies and organizations of the United Nations system and intergovernmental as well as non-governmental organizations to disseminate the Convention and the Optional Protocol thereto;

13. *Encourages* all relevant entities of the United Nations system, within their mandates, to continue to assist States parties, upon their request, in implementing the Convention and, in this regard, to pay attention to the concluding comments as well as the general recommendations of the Committee;

14. *Encourages* all relevant parts of the United Nations system to continue to build women's knowledge and understanding of and capacity to utilize human rights instruments, in particular the Convention and the Optional Protocol thereto;

15. *Welcomes* the submission of reports by the specialized agencies at the invitation of the Committee on the implementation of the Convention in areas falling within the scope of their activities and the contribution of non-governmental organizations to the work of the Committee, and encourages those agencies to continue their submission of reports;

16. *Requests* the Secretary-General to submit to the General Assembly at its fifty-fifth session a report on the status of the Convention on the Elimination of All Forms of Discrimination against Women and the implementation of the present resolution.

Commission on the Status of Women

The Commission on the Status of Women, at its forty-third session (New York, 1-12 March and 1 April) [E/1999/27], adopted three resolutions related to improving the status of women and ensuring their rights and one decision by which it took note of four documents it had considered. Assessing and ensuring implementation of the Beijing Declaration and Platform for Action continued to be a primary focus of the Commission's work. Panel discussions were held during the session on 2 of the 12 critical areas of concern outlined in the Platform: women and health, and institutional mechanisms for the advancement of women (see p. 1080). The Commission recommended four draft resolutions for adoption by the Economic and Social Council. In addition, the Commission finalized work on the draft optional protocol to the 1979 Convention on the Elimination of All Forms of Discrimination against Women and recommended it to the Economic and Social Council for adoption by the General Assembly (see p. 1100). The Commission held its second session (15-19 March and 30 June) [E/1999/60 & Add.1] at which it acted as preparatory committee for the Assembly's special session in 2000 to review implementation of the Nairobi Forward-looking Strategies for the Advancement of Women [YUN 1985, p. 937] and the Beijing Platform for Action (see p. 1078).

ECONOMIC AND SOCIAL COUNCIL ACTION

On 25 March, the Economic and Social Council, by **decision 1999/213**, decided that the Commission should resume its forty-third session for one day on an exceptional basis, in order to complete its work.

By **decision 1999/257** of 28 July, the Council decided that the Commission should continue to meet annually for a period of 10 working days. On the same date, the Council, by **decision 1999/258**, took note of the report of the Commission on its forty-third session and approved the provisional agenda and documentation for its forty-fourth (2000) session.

Communications on the status of women

At a closed meeting on 10 March [E/1999/27], the Commission took note of the report of the Working Group on Communications on the Status of Women, established in 1993 [YUN 1993, p. 1050] to consider ways of making the communications procedure more transparent and efficient. The Working Group considered 13 confidential communications and two non-confidential communications received directly by the Division for the Advancement of Women and 83 confidential communications received by OHCHR. Regarding the confidential communications, the Working Group expressed deep concern for continuing grave violations of women's rights, as well as persistent and pervasive discrimination. In particular, the Working Group was concerned at the abusive treatment of women, including custodial deaths, torture, rape, abduction, disappearances, arbitrary arrests, forced abortions and sterilizations, and harassment and arson by security forces and other authorities. Concern was also expressed for the targeting of civilians, including women and children, for bombings; the mistreatment of those who were internally displaced in conflict situations; the failure of Governments to protect women and children in times of political instability and to punish those responsible for violation of their rights; the abusive treatment of wives, children and relatives of political opponents and prisoners; ongoing and large-scale trafficking in women and girls; continued discrimination against indigenous families; and the violation of the rights of women journalists, human rights defenders, migrant women workers and others. The Working Group was gravely concerned in one case by more than 35,000 communications regarding allegations of gross violations of all the basic human rights of women, particularly inhuman punishments that included women being beaten, tortured, shot, burnt alive and sprayed with acid. Regarding the non-confidential communications, the Working Group took note of the continued absence of women in decision-making processes in the context of conflict prevention and resolution. It expressed concern that women and children were the primary victims of war and poverty.

UN Development Fund for Women (UNIFEM)

During 1999 [A/55/271], the United Nations Development Fund for Women (UNIFEM) continued to focus on strengthening women's economic capacities, engendering governance and leadership, and promoting women's human rights and the elimination of violence against them.

UNIFEM's work on economic empowerment encompassed both global and regional issues. In Africa, the Fund emphasized links between women's products and markets, while the Asia/Pacific programme focused on engendering trade policies against the backdrop of the 1997 economic crisis. The Latin America and Caribbean programme stressed ensuring the rights of women in the informal sector. In Central and Eastern Europe and the Commonwealth of Independent States, projects highlighted market opportunities, including the use of new technologies. To promote women's leadership, UNIFEM activities focused on fostering women's participation in decision-making, peace-building and conflict resolution, as well as on engendering laws and supporting implementation of global commitments to achieve gender equality.

The Fund strengthened its efforts to ensure that learning in support of gender equality was made accessible to decision makers and programme planners. New information and communication technologies were utilized for knowledge sharing. During 1999, the <End-Violence> electronic discussion list enabled 2,300 participants to share strategies for promoting legal reform and strengthening protective services and overcoming other operational challenges for ending violence against women. With other partners, UNIFEM hosted 11 global discussions on the critical areas of concern in the Beijing Platform for Action. UNIFEM led an inter-agency task force to collect examples of good practice in gender mainstreaming, created a database, and made them available on the Internet (www.un.org/womenwatch). In March, UNIFEM convened an inter-agency global videoconference called "A World Free of Violence against Women".

By the end of 1999, the Trust Fund in Support of Actions to Eliminate Violence against Women, an inter-agency fund managed by UNIFEM, had financed 87 projects, ranging from promotion of gender-sensitive media reporting on violence against women to training of judiciary and law enforcement personnel, and provision of services for female victims of violence.

Total contributions for UNIFEM increased by $0.4 million in 1999, or 1.3 per cent, to $23.1 million from $22.7 million in 1998. The actual amount received for core contributions increased by $1 million, from $15.8 million in 1998 to $16.8 million in 1999. Cost-sharing and trust fund contributions decreased by $1.9 million, from $6.9 million in 1998 to $5 million in 1999. Project expenditure for regular resources increased by $0.1 million, or 1 per cent, to $10.2 million. Expenditures, including support costs for cost-sharing and sub-trust fund projects, increased by $0.5 million, or 12 per cent, to $4.8 million.

In September, the Secretary-General transmitted to the General Assembly a report on UNIFEM's activities during 1998 [A/54/225]. On 22 December, the Assembly, by **decision 54/448**, took note of the report.

GENERAL ASSEMBLY ACTION

On 17 December [meeting 83], the General Assembly, on the recommendation of the Third Committee [A/54/598 & Corr.1,2], adopted **resolution 54/136** without vote [agenda item 109].

United Nations Development Fund for Women

The General Assembly,

Recalling its resolution 39/125 of 14 December 1984, in which it decided to make the United Nations Development Fund for Women a separate and identifiable entity in autonomous association with the United Nations Development Programme, as well as its resolution 52/94 of 12 December 1997,

Recalling also the Platform for Action adopted by the Fourth World Conference on Women, which recognizes the special role of the Fund in the promotion of the empowerment of women,

Noting the importance of the work of the Consultative Committee on the United Nations Development Fund for Women in policy and programme directions, as stipulated in the annex to resolution 39/125,

Welcoming the contributions the Fund has made in supporting initiatives of Member States, United Nations organizations and non-governmental organizations to formulate and implement activities that promote gender equality and the empowerment of women, concentrating on three thematic areas: strengthening women's economic capacity, engendering governance and leadership and promoting women's human rights and the elimination of all forms of violence against women,

1. *Takes note with appreciation* of the note by the Secretary-General on the activities of the United Nations Development Fund for Women;

2. *Emphasizes* the important work that the Fund undertakes within the framework of the Platform for Action of the Fourth World Conference on Women and in supporting the implementation of recommendations related to the empowerment of women and gender mainstreaming from other United Nations world con-

ferences, such as the World Conference on Human Rights, held at Vienna from 14 to 25 June 1993, the International Conference on Population and Development, held at Cairo from 5 to 13 September 1994, and the World Summit for Social Development, held at Copenhagen from 6 to 12 March 1995;

3. *Notes* the progress achieved in the implementation of the Fund's strategy and business plan, 1997-1999, adopted in 1997;

4. *Encourages* the Fund to cooperate with other partners of the United Nations system, Governments and non-governmental organizations in assessment activities at all levels that will contribute to the five-year review of the Platform for Action, including efforts to improve capacity in the collection and dissemination of sex-disaggregated data and accountability mechanisms at the country level;

5. *Commends* the Fund for its leadership role in convening United Nations inter-agency campaigns to end violence against women in Latin America and the Caribbean, Africa and Asia and the Pacific throughout 1998 and continuing in 1999 and beyond, and the United Nations inter-agency global videoconference entitled "A World Free of Violence against Women", which was held on 8 March 1999;

6. *Recognizes* the progress achieved by the Fund in increasing the size and impact of its Trust Fund in Support of Action to Eliminate Violence against Women and the importance of incorporating a learning component to extract and share good practices in eliminating violence against women, and reiterates the call to Governments, non-governmental organizations and the public and private sectors to consider contributing or increasing contributions to the Trust Fund;

7. *Encourages* the Fund to continue to assist Governments in implementing the Convention on the Elimination of All Forms of Discrimination against Women in order to advance gender equality at all levels, including by reinforcing the cooperation between Governments and civil society, especially women's organizations;

8. *Requests* the Fund, in conjunction with other relevant United Nations agencies, to continue the activities that it is undertaking to raise awareness about and strengthen the capacities of women in situations of armed conflict and to contribute to promoting the integration of a gender perspective into all peace-building activities, including through support to the full and equal participation of women at all levels, in all forums;

9. *Also requests* the Fund to continue its efforts to mainstream a gender perspective in United Nations operational activities, in particular through its leadership of the Sub-Group on Gender of the United Nations Development Group and its convening of United Nations inter-agency thematic groups on gender to support the resident coordinator system;

10. *Commends* the Fund and the United Nations Development Programme, the United Nations Population Fund and the United Nations Volunteers as its collaborating partners for developing innovative mechanisms to expand the gender expertise available to the United Nations resident coordinator system at the country level, and encourages other United Nations organizations to develop similar initiatives that make use of the expertise and experience of the Fund in gender mainstreaming and the empowerment of women;

11. *Recognizes* that the Fund has been able to secure increased contributions for its work, and expresses its appreciation to Member States and private organizations, including the United Nations Foundation, and other foundations, whose increased contributions demonstrate their commitment to the issues on which the Fund is working;

12. *Urges* Member States, non-governmental organizations and members of the private sector that have contributed to the Fund to continue to contribute and to consider increasing their financial contributions, and invites others to consider contributing to the Fund.

International Research and Training Institute (INSTRAW)

The Board of Trustees of the International Research and Training Institute for the Advancement of Women (INSTRAW) held its nineteenth session in New York from 5 to 7 May [E/1999/57]. INSTRAW was an autonomous institution undertaking research and training programmes for the advancement and mobilization of women in development.

The Board recommended that Member States expedite payment of pledged contributions in order to increase the Institute's financial reserves and called for the establishment of a group entitled "Friends of INSTRAW" to bring visibility to the Institute and assist in securing financial and political support. With some modifications, the Board endorsed the INSTRAW strategic plan and work programme for 2000-2003, which provided for an early warning system and a clearing house, and for networking with other institutes on gender issues and the advancement of women. A working group was established to prepare a position paper on the future status of INSTRAW for consideration by the Economic and Social Council in 1999 (see next page).

In a September report on INSTRAW activities [A/54/352], the Secretary-General said that, within its current severe financial and staffing constraints, the Institute had been able to implement a modest but promising programme of work, demonstrating its institutional potential. INSTRAW research activities focused on engendering the political agenda, the temporary labour migration of women and women networking for conflict prevention and resolution. During the year, the Institute began a revision of its training approach based on recommendations regarding the need to link training activities to its research findings. Due to cost-reduction measures, the INSTRAW liaison office in New York was closed and the Institute's information and documentation work programme was substantially cut back. INSTRAW continued to collaborate with other UN agencies in many activities, including participation in the

Inter-Agency Committee on Women and Gender Equality, and to interact with its network of focal points in countries worldwide.

INSTRAW restructuring

The Economic and Social Council considered a July report of the President of the INSTRAW Board of Trustees containing an analysis of the Institute's financial and staffing crisis and its implications [E/1999/105]. The autonomous nature of INSTRAW had placed it in a vulnerable financial position, since voluntary donations—the Institute's only source of funding—had declined steadily since 1993, according to the report. As a result, INSTRAW's 1998-1999 budget had to be reduced from over $3.8 million to under $2.2 million (42 per cent), staffing resources for the same period were cut by 82 per cent, and the post of Director, which became vacant in March 1999, had not been filled. A strategic plan and work programme for 2000-2003 was approved by the Board, subject to available funds.

Appended to the report was a position paper of the Board of Trustees on revitalizing INSTRAW.

JIU report. In July [A/54/156-E/1999/102 & Add.1], the Secretary-General transmitted to the Economic and Social Council and the General Assembly an evaluation of INSTRAW by the Joint Inspection Unit (JIU), prepared in response to Council resolution 1998/48 [YUN 1998, p. 1089], along with his comments. The Unit made recommendations regarding the Institute's financial and staffing situations, as well as its administrative arrangements, autonomy and mandate in the context of UN programmes for the advancement of women. JIU concluded that the Institute had achieved remarkable success in spite of its scant resources. INSTRAW was experiencing a deep financial crisis that was threatening its continued operational existence, stated the Unit, noting that it would be regrettable if the only UN institution devoted entirely to research and training for the advancement of women ceased to exist as a result of financial attrition. On 22 December, the General Assembly, by **decision 54/443**, took note of the JIU report and the comments of the Secretary-General on the recommendations.

ECONOMIC AND SOCIAL COUNCIL ACTION

On 29 July [meeting 45], the Economic and Social Council adopted **resolution 1999/54** [draft: E/1999/L.41] without vote [agenda item 14 *(a)*].

Revitalization of the International Research and Training Institute for the Advancement of Women

The Economic and Social Council,

Recalling its resolution 1998/48 of 31 July 1998 on the International Research and Training Institute for the Advancement of Women,

Reiterating the importance of article I of the statute of the Institute, setting out its autonomous status,

Reiterating also the importance of paragraph 334 of the Beijing Platform for Action and the relevant provisions contained in its agreed conclusions 1997/2 of 18 July 1997,

Underlining the importance of research and training for the advancement of women,

Expressing grave concern at the financial situation of the Institute,

Taking note of the report of the Joint Inspection Unit containing an evaluation of the Institute,

Taking note also of the report of the Board of Trustees of the Institute on its nineteenth session,

Taking note further of the report of the President of the Board of Trustees of the Institute in compliance with paragraph 7 of resolution 1998/48 and the position paper prepared by the Board of Trustees,

Emphasizing the need to reorganize the structure of the Institute by maintaining administrative costs at a minimum and by funding its project activities through voluntary contributions,

Expressing appreciation to those Governments and organizations that have continuously contributed to or supported the activities of the Institute, in particular throughout the period of crisis that it has confronted,

1. *Decides* to engage in the revitalization of the International Research and Training Institute for the Advancement of Women;

2. *Requests* the Secretary-General, in consultation with the Board of Trustees of the Institute, to draw up a new structure and working method for the Institute and to report to the General Assembly at its fifty-fourth session, taking into consideration the views of interested States Members of the United Nations and building upon the following parameters:

(a) The core staff of the Institute should be constituted of a small number of persons, focusing on coordination and servicing;

(b) Each training and research activity should be structured in projects that are to be financed and managed separately;

(c) New technologies should be used for training, research and communications;

(d) The web site of the Institute should be developed to include categorizing and making accessible third-party gender research projects, thereby also providing a channel to include the results of these projects in United Nations policy-making for the advancement of women;

(e) An effective network of national and international research institutions should be created;

3. *Urges* the Secretary-General:

(a) To appoint, as expeditiously as possible, a Director of the Institute, in consultation with the Board of Trustees;

(b) To address the administrative anomalies noted in the report of the Joint Inspection Unit;

(c) To convene an ad hoc meeting of donors and other interested States Members of the United Nations to discuss the revitalization of the Institute and its immediate and long-term funding;

4. *Recommends* that the Institute:

(a) Strengthen its collaboration and the coordination of its activities with the Department of Economic and Social Affairs of the Secretariat, the Commission

on the Status of Women and the United Nations Development Fund for Women, as well as establish close collaboration with the United Nations University and other research and training institutes within and outside the United Nations system;

(b) Coordinate its research with other United Nations institutions, especially those involved with women and gender issues, and continue to participate in the Inter-Agency Committee on Women and Gender Equality of the Administrative Committee on Coordination in order to coordinate actions and establish collaboration;

5. *Requests* the Director of the International Research and Training Institute for the Advancement of Women, in close consultation with the Board of Trustees, to submit a report to the Council at its substantive session of 2000 on the implementation of the revitalization measures;

6. *Urges* States Members of the United Nations and intergovernmental and non-governmental organizations to consider contributing to the United Nations Trust Fund for the International Research and Training Institute for the Advancement of Women and to identify and consider contributing to specific research projects.

Report of Secretary-General. In October [A/54/500], the Secretary-General submitted a report to the General Assembly in which he outlined a new structure and working method for INSTRAW, based on parameters set out by the Economic and Social Council in resolution 1999/54. The revitalized INSTRAW would undertake a new strategic role and working method, whereby it would use primarily new information technologies as a means of producing, managing, disseminating and applying gender-aware knowledge and information on critical issues and trends, in order to promote the equal partnership of women and men in development. The centrepiece of the new working method would be the Gender Awareness Information and Networking System (GAINS), an integrated knowledge and information management system presented on an interactive web site. The GAINS project would aim to offer three core services: gathering, organization and dissemination of gender-aware research and information; creating networks of key users within and outside the UN system to facilitate information exchange; and using new information technologies for the development and dissemination of training materials and innovative methods of learning, targeted at a variety of audiences. To be completed in phases, the site would eventually include a database, online discussion forums, continuously updated gender-aware news on publications and research/training events, a good practices showcase and a gender-specific search service. In addition to the GAINS project, INSTRAW would continue to undertake research and training activities, which would be financed, staffed and managed as projects separate from the Institute's core operations.

GENERAL ASSEMBLY ACTION

On 17 December [meeting 83], the General Assembly, on the recommendation of the Third Committee [A/54/598 & Corr.1,2], adopted **resolution 54/140** without vote [agenda item 109].

Revitalization and strengthening of the International Research and Training Institute for the Advancement of Women

The General Assembly,

Bearing in mind Economic and Social Council resolution 1999/54 of 29 July 1999 on the revitalization of the International Research and Training Institute for the Advancement of Women,

Reaffirming article I of the statute of the Institute, which sets out its autonomous status,

Reaffirming also that the Institute continues to have a unique role to play, in that it is the only entity in the United Nations system devoted entirely to research, training and information in the context of the advancement of women in development,

Reaffirming further the objectives of the Institute to stimulate and assist, through research, training and the collection and dissemination of information, the advancement of women and their integration in the development process, both as participants and as beneficiaries,

Reiterating paragraph 334 of the Platform for Action of the Fourth World Conference on Women and the relevant provisions contained in agreed conclusions 1997/2 of 18 July 1997 of the Economic and Social Council,

Taking note of the recommendations contained in the report of the Joint Inspection Unit, which conducted an evaluation of the Institute,

Taking note also of the report of the Secretary-General on the activities of the Institute,

Taking note further of the report of the Secretary-General on the new structure and working method of the Institute,

1. *Takes note* of Economic and Social Council resolution 1999/54, and endorses the decision of Member States to engage in the revitalization of the International Research and Training Institute for the Advancement of Women;

2. *Takes note with appreciation* of the proposal for a new working method of the Institute through the establishment of an electronic Gender Awareness Information and Networking System, the principal activities of which are disseminating information from all countries, conducting research, capacity-building and networking, taking into account the special needs of developing countries;

3. *Urges* that the traditional methods of disseminating information also be improved and strengthened;

4. *Expresses its satisfaction* with the establishment of a new staffing structure for the Institute, consisting of a small number of persons, and urges that the approved posts be filled as soon as possible;

5. *Notes* the project-centred approach and the fact that the Gender Awareness Information and Network-

ing System and special research and training projects will be financed and managed separately;

6. *Acknowledges* the efforts of the Institute in producing outputs during the biennium 1998-1999, notwithstanding its current financial and institutional constraints;

7. *Welcomes* the recent appointment of the Director of the Institute, and urges the Secretary-General to ensure the stability and continuity of the post of Director;

8. *Requests* the Director of the Institute to ensure the preparation of a feasibility study of the Gender Awareness Information and Networking System, including the work plan and budget for the biennium 2000-2001, by an independent body funded by voluntary contributions, on the basis of the new structure and working method of the Institute, for approval by the Board of Trustees as established in article III, paragraph 2, of the statute of the Institute;

9. *Recommends* that the feasibility study provide, inter alia, information on how the new working method and work plan will benefit the advancement of women, in particular women from developing countries;

10. *Urges* that the use of all six official languages of the United Nations on the web site of the Institute be ensured as soon as possible, and in this context requests that the feasibility study, inter alia, examine the technical use of these languages on the web site of the Institute, and also requests the Secretary-General to report on the developments in this regard to the General Assembly at its fifty-fifth session;

11. *Requests* the Secretary-General to fulfil the commitment made to take the necessary measures to correct the administrative anomalies noted in the report of the Joint Inspection Unit, and urges that those measures be effected as soon as possible, given the critical financial situation of the Institute;

12. *Also requests* the Secretary-General to continue to provide support to the Institute, in particular in setting up the new structure and working method for the Institute, by encouraging voluntary contributions to the Institute and its special projects;

13. *Urges* Member States and intergovernmental and non-governmental organizations to contribute or to consider increasing their contributions to the United Nations Trust Fund for the International Research and Training Institute for the Advancement of Women in order to facilitate the immediate implementation of the programmes and activities of the Institute;

14. *Expresses its appreciation* to those Governments and organizations that continue to contribute to and support the activities of the Institute;

15. *Requests* the Secretary-General to report to the General Assembly at its fifty-fifth session on the implementation of the present resolution.

Chapter XI

Children, youth and ageing persons

In 1999, the United Nations Children's Fund (UNICEF) continued advocacy, alliance-building and other activities to improve the situation of children worldwide and ensure special protection for the most disadvantaged, including victims of war, disasters, extreme poverty and all forms of violence. Based on estimates that about 32,000 children under the age of five continued to die daily from preventable causes, UNICEF programmes gave priority to countries with the highest child mortality rates. The Fund's activities also continued to focus on achieving the goals established at the 1990 World Summit for Children. In December, the General Assembly established a preparatory committee to outline the agenda and outcome of its high-level special session in 2001 to review progress towards World Summit goals and to consider future action.

UNICEF efforts to protect children and women in situations of armed conflict were supported by the Security Council in an August resolution (see p. 672), by which it condemned the targeting of children in armed conflict and called on all parties concerned to comply strictly with their obligations under international law, including the 1989 Convention on the Rights of the Child (see p. 579). The Convention, which marked its tenth anniversary in 1999, served as the basis for UNICEF's ongoing efforts to integrate a human rights-based programming approach. During the year, both the Assembly and the Commission on Human Rights took action to protect children's rights, including meeting the needs of the girl child (see pp. 1090 and 670).

United Nations activities concerning young people focused on accelerating implementation of the 1995 World Programme of Action for Youth to the Year 2000 and Beyond, based on the results of two high-level global meetings convened in Portugal in 1998: the first World Conference of Ministers Responsible for Youth, which adopted the Lisbon Declaration on Youth Policies and Programmes, and the third session of the World Youth Forum of the United Nations System, which approved the Braga Youth Action Plan.

As part of United Nations efforts to support ageing persons, the International Year of Older Persons was observed in 1999. The Year, which promoted the 1991 United Nations Principles for Older Persons, culminated in the Assembly devoting four special plenary sessions to its commemoration. The Commission for Social Development considered follow-up to the Year, including options for improving implementation of the 1982 International Plan of Action on Ageing and elaboration of a long-term perspective strategy on ageing into the twenty-first century.

Children

United Nations Children's Fund

The United Nations Children's Fund continued to spearhead worldwide efforts to weave a global safety net to ensure that all children could grow up in good health in a world free from poverty and discrimination and safe from violence and exploitation. In 1999, UNICEF intensified its efforts to protect children from the impact of the HIV/AIDS pandemic and to provide all children, especially girls, with equal access to education. In accordance with the medium-term plan for 1998-2001 [YUN 1998, p. 1093], four main organizational priorities provided the focus for the Fund's activities: enhancing partnerships and promoting advocacy on children's rights; enhancing the survival, development, protection and participation of children; improving the availability and use of data in critical areas; and strengthening management and operations.

UNICEF programmes were committed to helping children obtain the best possible start in their early years, giving every child a quality basic education, and making sure that adolescents had adequate support and opportunities to develop their capabilities. Advocacy and programme development efforts continued to address the priority areas of health, nutrition, water, environment, sanitation, education, child protection, gender and programme partnerships. UNICEF partnerships, both within and beyond the UN system, aimed to mobilize broad support for programmes and policies for women and children; provide technical collaboration in support of field programmes; and develop and promote strategies for the advancement of women's and children's rights at the global, regional and national levels. The publication of two annual flagship reports provided analysis and data on key issues affecting children: *The State of the World's Children 1999* stressed the value of basic education as the key to reducing poverty and preventing gender discrimination and other child rights violations; *The Progress of Nations 1999* provided comparative data on advances made by countries towards achieving the goals of the 1990 World Summit for Children [YUN 1990, p. 797].

Ten years after its adoption by the General Assembly in resolution 44/25 [YUN 1989, p. 560] (see p. 579), the 1989 Convention on the Rights of the Child continued to provide the legal framework for establishing standards of behaviour towards children and addressing the conditions that inhibited fulfilment of their rights. During 1999, considerable progress was made in applying a human rights-based approach to UNICEF programme cooperation, within the broader context of the Convention. UNICEF's work was reoriented from a project-based response to different categories of children to a broader approach in which children were viewed as part of a wider society that had not been fully successful in protecting their rights. The General Assembly, in **resolution 54/149**, called for action to protect the rights of children, including implementation of the 1989 Convention (see p. 676). In addition, the Assembly, in **resolution 54/148**, addressed the needs and protection of the rights of the girl child (see p. 1090).

In 1999, UNICEF global advocacy efforts succeeded in increasing the prominence of children's issues on the UN agenda, including within the Security Council, which gave heightened attention to the situation of children in countries ravaged by war. In February, UNICEF presented to the Council a new "Peace and Security Agenda for Children", which included measures to end the use of child soldiers and protect children from the effects of sanctions. On 30 August, the Council adopted **resolution 1261(1999)**, in which it condemned the targeting of children in armed conflict and called on all parties to put an end to practices such as killing and maiming, sexual violence, abduction and forced displacement, recruitment and attacks on places that usually had a significant presence of children, such as schools and hospitals (see p. 672).

UNICEF cooperated with 161 countries, areas and territories during the year: 46 in sub-Saharan Africa; 35 in Latin America and the Caribbean; 33 in Asia and the Pacific; 20 in the Middle East and North Africa; and 27 in Central and Eastern Europe, the Commonwealth of Independent States (CIS) and the Baltic States.

Programme expenditure totalled $971 million in 1999, of which 33 per cent was spent on child and maternal health; 22 per cent on planning, advocacy and cross-sectoral support; 16 per cent on education and early childhood development; 14 per cent on community development, women's programmes and measures for children and women in need of special protection; 9 per cent on hygiene, water and environmental sanitation; and 6 per cent on child nutrition. In addition, $93 million, or 9 per cent of total expenditure, was spent on management, administration, write-offs and other charges. UNICEF operations in 1999 were described in the *2000 UNICEF Annual Report* and the report of its Executive Director [E/ICEF/2000/4 (Parts I & II)].

The UNICEF Executive Board held its first regular session of 1999 from 19 to 22 and on 25 January, the annual session from 7 to 11 June, and the second regular session from 7 to 10 September, all in New York [E/1999/34/Rev.1]. During those sessions, the Board adopted 21 decisions.

The Economic and Social Council, in **decision 1999/219** of 23 July, took note of the Board's report on its first regular session and of the annual report of the Executive Director covering 1998 [E/1999/9].

In September [dec. 1999/19], the Executive Board adopted the programme of work, including the dates, for its 2000 sessions. The first regular session would be held from 17 to 21 January, the annual session from 22 to 26 May, and the second regular session from 18 to 22 September.

Programme policies

In decisions related to UNICEF's programme policies, the Executive Board asked the Executive Director to continue to advocate for and support efforts by national Governments and civil society to achieve the end-decade goals of the World Summit for Children [dec. 1999/9] and authorized a three-year extension for the International Child Development Centre, based in Florence, Italy [dec. 1999/18]. It also adopted a new resource mobilization strategy, including a multi-year funding framework that conceptually integrated its organizational priorities and major areas of action, resources, budget and outcomes [dec. 1999/8] and approved the financial medium-term plan for 1999-2002 [dec. 1999/10] (see p. 1118). The medium-term plan was a rolling four-year plan that was updated every two years [YUN 1998, p. 1093], except for the financial plan, which was updated annually.

Follow-up to 1990 World Summit for Children

In April, UNICEF submitted to the Executive Board its annual progress report [E/ICEF/1999/9] on follow-up to the 1990 World Summit for Children [YUN 1990, p. 797], covering 1998. The report provided a global overview of progress by the international community towards World Summit goals, as well as information on actions taken to prepare for the General Assembly's end-decade review in 2001. In spite of general progress made during the decade, achieving the year 2000 goals would be difficult without a major acceleration in the pace of progress through efforts at both the national and international levels, the report stated.

Based on short-term priorities and consultations with country and regional offices, UNICEF had identified seven areas where progress towards the World Summit goals should be accelerated: reducing young child mortality and preventing child disability; reducing maternal deaths; improving access to and the quality of basic education; reducing exploitation, abuse and harm of children; improving early childhood care for child growth and development; improving young people's health and development; and improving the availability and use of data in critical areas.

In June [dec. 1999/9], the Executive Board urged Governments to adopt appropriate strategies and allocate the maximum resources possible for action and encouraged them to conduct periodic national and subnational reviews of progress in achieving the World Summit goals, and in the broader context of implementation of the Convention on the Rights of the Child. The Executive Director was asked to continue to support the efforts of Governments and civil society to achieve end-decade goals and to work with Governments to strengthen national capacities for the collection and use of data to monitor progress towards the goals. She was also asked to support the Secretary-General in preparing for the end-decade review in 2001, and to report in 2000. Donor Governments were asked to allocate the maximum resources possible to support the achievement of Summit goals and to ensure universal access to basic social services.

By **decision 1999/219** of 23 July, the Economic and Social Council took note of an extract from the Executive Board's report [E/1999/L.20] containing the June decision.

In an April report [E/ICEF/1999/10], UNICEF outlined preliminary recommendations for a future global agenda for children and the focus of its work beyond 2000. The proposals built on progress since the 1990 World Summit, drawing on lessons learned in the course of the decade and recommending actions to address remaining challenges requiring urgent collective action. The report argued that, although broad consensus existed on many of the issues that negatively influenced human development, those persistent problems were compounded by new concerns, such as the HIV/AIDS pandemic, sharply declining official development assistance (ODA), rising national debt among poor countries, a global economy that was creating both unprecedented wealth and growing disparities, and increasing instability and conflict in many countries. However, major new progress for children was possible within a single generation if the global community would commit to three key priorities: early childhood care and development; equal access to good quality basic education; and providing adolescents with the skills to develop fully their individual capacities. UNICEF proposed that the international community and Governments make a global pact to work in the next decade towards the universal realization of those outcomes. In its future work, UNICEF, while still emphasizing the importance of protecting children from various forms of preventable death, would go beyond survival to place the three priority areas at the centre of its global programme strategy.

General Assembly special session (2001)

In July [E/ICEF/1999/17], UNICEF submitted to the Executive Board a report outlining its support to the General Assembly special session to be held in 2001 on the follow-up to the World Summit. The report described UNICEF's follow-up activities since 1990, including the mid-decade reviews and the plan to ensure a successful review process for the mid-decade goals. The objectives of the special session were to review the implementation of the World Summit Declaration and the Plan of Action and agree on renewed commitments and future action for children and youth in the next decade. Additional events to mark the World Summit anniversary would unite the broadest possible alliance for children's rights, to be known as the Leadership Initiative for Children. The Initiative would mobilize a broad range of actors, including Governments, non-governmental organizations (NGOs), the private sector, and children and youth themselves, with the aim of intensifying world focus on children and enhancing responsibility for the realization of their rights. UNICEF was the secretariat for the 2001 special session and the coordinator of the Leadership Initiative.

In September [dec. 1999/12], the Executive Board, on the recommendation of the Executive Director, approved a supplementary-funded budget of $2 million for the UNICEF secretariat in the year 2000, subject to availability of specific-purpose contributions, for support to the special session and additional events.

GENERAL ASSEMBLY ACTION

On 7 December [meeting 72], the General Assembly adopted **resolution 54/93** [draft: A/54/L.51 & Add.1] without vote [agenda item 101 *(a)*].

Special session of the General Assembly in 2001 for follow-up to the World Summit for Children

The General Assembly,

Recalling its resolution 51/186 of 16 December 1996, in which it decided to convene in 2001 a special session to review the achievement of the goals of the World Summit for Children, and its resolution 53/193 of 15 December 1998,

Recalling also the report of the Secretary-General on progress on the implementation of the World Declaration and the Plan of Action of the World Summit for Children,

Recognizing the importance of achieving universal ratification of the Convention on the Rights of the Child,

1. *Decides* to convene the special session of the General Assembly to review the achievement of the goals of the World Summit for Children at the highest possible level;

2. *Invites* the participation of heads of State and Government in the special session;

3. *Decides* that the special session shall be convened in the month of September 2001;

4. *Also decides* that the special session, while reviewing the achievements in the implementation and results of the World Declaration on the Survival, Protection and Development of Children and Plan of Action for Implementing the World Declaration on the Survival, Protection and Development of Children in the 1990s, will undertake a renewed commitment and consider future action for children in the next decade;

5. *Recognizes* the importance of a participatory process at the national, regional and international levels with a view, inter alia, to establishing partnerships between a broad range of actors, including children and youth, in order to raise momentum for children's rights and needs;

6. *Decides* to establish an open-ended preparatory committee, also open to States members of the specialized agencies, to address organizational issues, including the form, the participation of a broad range of relevant actors and the agenda, and to prepare for the outcome of the special session;

7. *Strongly encourages* the full and effective participation of Member States, and invites the heads of State and Government to consider assigning personal representatives to the preparatory committee;

8. *Requests* the preparatory committee to convene one organizational session on 7 and 8 February 2000 and one substantive session from 30 May to 2 June 2000 and to propose to the General Assembly its requirements for further meetings in 2001;

9. *Requests* the Secretary-General, with the support of the United Nations Children's Fund, to assist the preparatory committee in providing substantive input to the preparatory process and at the special session, including a report on emerging issues to be considered at the substantive session of the preparatory committee in 2000;

10. *Invites* all other relevant organizations and bodies of the United Nations system, including the funds and programmes, specialized agencies and the international financial institutions, actively to participate in the preparations for the special session;

11. *Requests* the Secretary-General to ensure an effective and coordinated system-wide response to the preparations for the special session;

12. *Invites* the Committee on the Rights of the Child to provide its input to the preparatory process and at the special session;

13. *Invites* all relevant experts, including the Special Representative of the Secretary-General on the impact of armed conflict on children and the Special Rapporteur of the Commission on Human Rights on the sale of children, child prostitution and child pornography, to participate in the preparatory process and the special session in accordance with the established practice;

14. *Recognizes* the important role of all relevant actors, including non-governmental organizations, in implementing the Plan of Action, and stresses the need for their active involvement in the preparatory process, including in the preparatory committee, and at the special session, modalities for which will be addressed by the preparatory committee;

15. *Invites* Governments and relevant organizations, in particular the United Nations Children's Fund, as well as regional and subregional organizations, to undertake reviews of progress achieved since the World Summit for Children, and encourages appropriate national, regional and international preparatory activities with a view to contributing to the preparations for the special session and building partnerships for and with children;

16. *Reaffirms* its requests to the Secretary-General to submit to the special session, through the preparatory committee, a review of the implementation and results of the World Declaration and Plan of Action, including appropriate recommendations for further action, which also elaborates on the best practices noted and obstacles encountered in the implementation as well as on measures to overcome those obstacles;

17. *Decides* to invite States members of the specialized agencies that are not Members of the United Nations to participate in the work of the special session in the capacity of observers;

18. *Stresses* the importance of the full participation of the least developed countries in the special session and the preparations for the session, and invites Governments to make appropriate contributions to a trust fund to be established by the Secretary-General for that purpose;

19. *Requests* the Secretary-General to assist national Governments, at their request, in their assessment of and reporting on the implementation of the Plan of Action;

20. *Also requests* the Secretary-General, in close cooperation with the United Nations Children's Fund, to mount a public information programme to raise awareness of children's needs and rights and of the special session, its objectives and significance, and encourages Governments to do the same on a national basis;

21. *Further requests* the Secretary-General to submit a report during the main part of the fifty-fifth session on the state of the preparations for the special session;

22. *Decides* to include an item in the provisional agenda of its fifty-fifth session entitled "Special session of the General Assembly in 2001 for follow-up to the World Summit for Children".

Rights-based programming

An April report [E/ICEF/1999/11] described progress made by UNICEF in implementing a 1991 Executive Board decision [YUN 1991, p. 691] on the 1989 Convention on the Rights of the Child, adopted by the General Assembly in resolution 44/25 [YUN 1989, p. 560]. The report outlined ways in which the normative framework of international human rights standards systematically guided the practical work of UNICEF in fulfilling its mission and mandate and how the Fund was working to make its programmes of cooperation contribute more effectively to the realization of children's and women's rights.

The report concluded that consensus was emerging among UN country teams on the convergence between the human rights and development mandates of the various agencies. UNICEF had a leading role to play in ensuring that children's rights were a common concern for development partners and in providing advisory support. A human rights-based programming approach was crucial to the lasting impact of initiatives for children. By emphasizing partnerships and participation, a human rights perspective could provide the basis for making the goals and commitments of international conferences such as the World Summit for Children more binding.

Gender mainstreaming

As a follow-up to agreed conclusions adopted by the Economic and Social Council in 1997 [YUN 1997, p. 1186] on mainstreaming a gender perspective into all policies and programmes in the UN system, UNICEF reported in March [E/ICEF/1999/13] on progress achieved in integrating gender as a cross-cutting concern in UNICEF country programmes. Noting that UNICEF had recorded significant advances in mainstreaming a gender perspective into its work, the report analysed the organization's achievements and outlined areas for further action in relation to the development and application of tools, support for capacity-building, regional and country initiatives, and partnerships to support gender mainstreaming.

A framework for evaluating UNICEF efforts in mainstreaming gender was being developed and tested in 1999, based on regional trends and experiences in monitoring the situation of women and children, the gender audits conducted on the West Bank and Gaza and the Sudan and mid-term reviews and country evaluations in Burkina Faso and other countries. Resources for gender mainstreaming were included in country programme management plans, and supplementary funds had supported special initiatives on girls' education, ending female genital mutilation and violence against women and girls, and adolescent development in the promotion of women's and girls' rights. Gender focal points constituted UNICEF's core resource in its efforts to mainstream gender but capacity-building was needed, as was strengthening of institutional mechanisms, in order to sustain, expand and monitor the gains achieved in mainstreaming gender.

Strategies in basic education

In a March report [E/ICEF/1999/14], UNICEF described progress in achieving universal basic education and challenges faced in meeting goals and discussed future strategies. Some progress had been made in achieving the goals of the World Declaration on Education for All and its Framework for Action, adopted at the 1990 World Conference on Education for All [YUN 1990, p. 763], including remarkable success in some countries, but the general trends had been disappointing. Growth in school enrolment in some regions had barely kept pace with population growth and rates had actually declined in some countries. Significant progress was seen in defining learning outcomes and improving the measurement of learning achievement. Deepening poverty and reduced government resources for education in developing countries had increased the financial burden on many communities and households.

UNICEF's strategies for education in the twenty-first century related to: getting children ready for school through early childhood care; getting all children into school and keeping them there; ensuring children learned what they needed to learn; helping adolescents get educated and involved; empowering families and communities in education planning, financing and management; increasing the impact of education on HIV/AIDS prevention; improving the provision of education in unstable and emergency situations; and promoting child-friendly learning environments. New partnerships, including closer links with the World Health Organization (WHO), the Save the Children Alliance, the Joint United Nations Programme on HIV/AIDS, development agencies, NGOs and the private sector, as well as more intersectoral collaboration within UNICEF, would be crucial to implementing the new strategies. UNICEF was also working to ensure that its education programmes were developed from a rights perspective, based on nearly universal ratification of the Convention on the Rights of the Child and the resulting consensus that every child, regardless of resources and circumstances, had a right to a basic education of high quality (see also below, under "UNICEF programmes by sector").

Africa

In response to a 1997 Executive Board request [YUN 1997, p. 1212], UNICEF, in a March report [E/ICEF/1999/12], reviewed progress made in efforts to ensure children's rights to survival, development and protection in Africa. Children in Africa, particularly the sub-Saharan region, remained acutely vulnerable and exposed to the combined impact of economic crisis, unserviceable international debt, armed conflicts, spreading violence and the unrelenting HIV/AIDS pandemic. Those crises had, to varying degrees, diverted attention and resources away from longer-term development efforts, including investing in children and ensuring their rights. UNICEF priorities in Africa included: strengthening basic health care systems for child and maternal survival; ensuring access for all children, especially girls, to good quality basic education; strengthening community capacities for protecting women and children; promoting non-violence, gender equity and post-conflict recovery; and identifying viable approaches to improved family and community care for the survival and development of young children, including those affected by HIV/AIDS.

In March, members of the UNICEF Executive Board visited Mozambique and the United Republic of Tanzania, where they observed that the overall situation of children was poor in both countries, but the indicators in Mozambique were significantly worse. The team evaluated the incorporation of a rights-based approach in UNICEF programmes and reviewed the medical treatment of children, especially as it related to malaria and HIV/AIDS, in both countries. They also visited two refugee camps in the United Republic of Tanzania to learn more about UNICEF's emergency programmes.

Maurice Pate Award

The Executive Director recommended that the Maurice Pate Award for 1999 be presented to *kuleana*, an NGO based in the United Republic of Tanzania, and that an allocation of $25,000 be allocated from general resources for that purpose. Established in 1966 [YUN 1966, p. 385], the Award was presented to the Tanzanian NGO in recognition of its significant and innovative contribution to improving the situation of children in the country and inspiring other NGOs in the region to bring a child rights perspective to their work. On 21 January [dec. 1999/5], the Executive Board endorsed the recommendation and approved the allocation.

UNICEF programmes by region

During 1999, regional UNICEF expenditure in support of cooperation programmes totalled $934 million, $339 million of which (36 per cent) was spent for programmes in sub-Saharan Africa; $280 million (30 per cent) for programmes in Asia; $98 million (11 per cent) for programmes in the Americas and the Caribbean; $83 million (9 per cent) for programmes in the Middle East and North Africa; and $81 million (9 per cent) for programmes in Central and Eastern Europe, CIS and the Baltic States. In addition, $51 million (5 per cent) was spent for interregional programmes. Overall, the total programme expenditure represented an increase of $150 million, or about 19 per cent, over 1998.

As in previous years, the major portion of UNICEF resources was spent in the 63 low-income countries with a per capita gross national product of $785 or less. Those countries, which had a total child population of 1.3 billion or 69 per cent of all children worldwide, received 66 per cent of programme expenditure, the same as in 1998. Some 64 per cent of UNICEF programme expenditure went to countries where the child mortality rate (under five years of age) was classified as very high or high.

Field visits

In February, members of the UNICEF Executive Board visited Colombia and Peru to evaluate how the country offices had applied a rights-based approach to cooperation programmes, including the difference it made and the possible challenges to such an approach. They also reviewed emergency response, United Nations Development Assistance Framework processes (see p. 787) and resource mobilization in the two countries. The team found that the child rights approach had become an integral part of the programmes in both countries and that, in line with the approach, UNICEF had increased its focus on the most vulnerable groups—children at risk and those who were excluded. While the rights-based approach should be more effective and sustainable in the long term, the team saw the need for further discussion and analysis regarding whether the approach affected the time needed to realize certain goals for children.

(For information on a field visit to Mozambique and the United Republic of Tanzania, see above, under "Africa".)

UNICEF programmes by sector

The major share of UNICEF programme expenditure continued to be in the area of health ($256 million or 27 per cent) and child-focused advocacy, planning, capacity-building and other cross-sectoral programmes, including social mobilization and statistics ($167 million or 18 per cent). Significant shares of expenditure also went to basic education ($119 million or 13 per cent), water and environmental sanitation ($70 million or 7 per cent), nutrition ($43 million or 5 per cent), general emergencies ($28 million or 3 per cent) and other key developmental activities ($111 million or 12 per cent). Overall, the shares of expenditure among the various programme areas were very similar to 1998, with a slight increase in the share of health.

In accordance with a 1997 Executive Board decision [YUN 1997, p. 1220], the first 7 per cent of general resources was set aside to respond flexibly to the diversity of country situations and to evolving needs and special circumstances. The distribution of funds from the global set-aside aimed to achieve a catalytic effect or breakthrough in countries where clear opportunities or needs existed for accelerated efforts. In 1999, the first such set-aside was allocated by the Executive Director in support of the 1998-2000 programme priorities and for additional special needs. Of the $21.4 million available, some 53 per cent was allocated for accelerated actions in immunization; 11 per cent was provided for measures, mainly in eastern and southern Africa and South Asia, against HIV/AIDS; 9 per cent to combat malaria; 9 per cent for safe water and sanitation; 8 per cent for early childhood care; 5 per cent towards eradication of guinea worm disease; and 4 per cent for post-crisis rehabilitation efforts for children and women in Central America. Overall, 65 per cent of the set-aside was allocated to countries in sub-Saharan Africa and 19 per cent in Asia.

Child and adolescent health

UNICEF activities to reduce childhood death and disease, improve early childhood care, reduce maternal mortality, prevent childhood disability, and improve adolescent health and development focused in 1999 on accelerating action in relation to certain goals established at the 1990 World Summit for Children [YUN 1990, p. 797], including immunization, HIV/AIDS prevention and malaria control. UNICEF continued to concentrate on countries with the highest rates of infant and child mortality, particularly in sub-Saharan Africa. As in the past, immunization provided the foundation for other health and child development activities, with UNICEF providing support for national immunization days in over 100 countries. The challenge remained to reach all children, especially in the poorest countries, which depended substantially on UNICEF and other international partners to finance the purchase of vaccines. Substantial progress had been achieved in efforts to eradicate polio—a global cause of childhood disability—through a joint effort among UNICEF, WHO, Rotary International (United States) and others. The number of polio cases worldwide had fallen from about 350,000 in 1988 to a reported 6,000 in 1999. In conflict areas, where access to immunization was difficult, UNICEF worked with many parties to negotiate truces to allow health workers to vaccinate millions of children against polio and other child-killer diseases. UNICEF also continued to support efforts to prevent measles, reduce vitamin A deficiency and eradicate guinea worm disease, as well as prevent disabilities. Malaria control activities focused on developing community-based strategies for rapidly expanding the use and sustainable treatment of bed nets and improved access to antimalarial drugs within the global Roll-back Malaria Initiative, a partnership among UNICEF, WHO, the United Nations Development Programme (UNDP) and the World Bank.

Through the Integrated Management of Childhood Illnesses (IMCI) programme, developed in collaboration with WHO, UNICEF aimed to reduce childhood deaths by preventing and treating acute respiratory infections, diarrhoea, measles, malaria and malnutrition through coordinated strategies that included training health workers and improving the care provided by health facilities, communities and families. In 1999, IMCI was implemented in 63 countries and a dozen others were considering adopting the approach. UNICEF continued to play a major role in global advocacy and technical leadership in nutrition, particularly through efforts to strengthen the community and family dimensions of the IMCI initiative. National water and environmental sanitation programmes were supported in more than 80 countries, with the bulk of resources concentrated in South Asia and sub-Saharan Africa. In 1999, UNICEF helped some 9 million people gain access to improved water and 5 million to sanitation facilities.

Promoting the convergence of child health, nutrition and psychosocial and cognitive development within an overall approach to early childhood care was a major strategic concern. Activities in some 15 countries aimed at improving the knowledge and skills of parents and caregivers. Pilot programmes at the community level ranged from the use of volunteers to work with families in 20 provinces in the Philippines, to measures to address low birth weight in Nepal, to the use of television, radio or video to promote early childhood care in Jamaica and several other countries.

Implementation of the Baby-Friendly Hospital Initiative, a programme spearheaded by UNICEF and WHO, continued in 1999, but with slower progress, especially in sub-Saharan Africa. A total of 14,828 facilities worldwide were accredited as "baby-friendly", an increase of 2 per cent during the year, while improvements in breastfeeding rates were noted in 21 countries. UNICEF was active in efforts to reduce maternal mortality in 114 countries.

With regard to HIV/AIDS, UNICEF's goal was to address the underlying causes of the pandemic, reduce the vulnerability of children, adolescents and women and mitigate the impact of disease and death. In 1999, the Fund expanded staffing in the most-affected countries and continued to support communities in protecting the rights of children, young people and women affected by AIDS. It supported prevention programmes in more than 20 countries in eastern and southern Africa and helped to launch in 11 countries a pilot programme that offered voluntary and confidential counselling and testing for women and their partners; administered drugs that reduced HIV transmission from mother to child; and provided information about infant feeding options and improved prenatal care. During the year, UNICEF introduced 15 infant feeding pilot programmes which aimed to reduce mother-child transmission. UNICEF also worked to educate children and young people about AIDS and to provide support for children orphaned by the disease.

Basic education

In the context of meeting the goals of the 1990 World Summit on Education for All [YUN 1990, p. 763] in relation to children's rights to basic, quality education (see also above, under "Programme policies"), UNICEF worked with many partners to increase school enrolment, improve quality in the classroom and, as an increasing priority, open the doors of education to the more than 110 million school-age children who were not in school, especially girls, children in conditions of crisis, children living in remote areas, children of minorities, children in extreme poverty and those who worked. Studies were undertaken in some 35 countries to address why children were not in school or had dropped out. Other activities aimed at enabling children to enter school, including through multigrade teaching, bilingual education, school construction, social mobilization, parent education and making schools more welcoming to girls. In Nicaragua, children who were very poor, who worked or who were older than the primary school age benefited from a programme offering primary education with flexible schedules and mixed grade levels. Some 96,000 refugee children in the United Republic of Tanzania received primary schooling and nearly 30,000 Khmer and other minority children in Viet Nam enjoyed early grade instruction in their local languages in 1999. In Brazil, UNICEF joined a coalition of 42 national groups to launch a campaign to provide education to 50,000 children who survived by collecting and selling waste from garbage dumps. UNICEF supported school repairs, provided supplies and undertook training for psychosocial support and mine awareness in Kosovo province of the Federal Republic of Yugoslavia (FRY). In East Timor, education supplies and construction materials were distributed and some 6,000 teachers were registered in East Timor.

Among the results of UNICEF support, some 15,000 additional children were enrolled in school in Eritrea, 27,000 in Ethiopia, 36,000 in Peru and 37,000 in Nicaragua. Almost 1.5 million more children were enrolled in Bangladesh, India and Pakistan, and over a million more in several countries of the East Asia and Pacific region. Several UNICEF programmes for increased enrolment, particularly in the Middle East, North Africa and South Asia, focused on girls. In the Gambia, one of 30 countries taking part in the Africa Girls' Education Initiative, a UNICEF-led coalition of Governments, NGOs and other organizations, girls' enrolment jumped from 41 per cent in 1991/92 to 63 per cent in 1998/99. A wide range of broad-based school improvement projects undertaken in Bosnia and Herzegovina, Ecuador, Nepal, the Philippines, Tajikistan and Turkmenistan incorporated measures for health and child protection as a support for school-based learning. Globally, more teachers were being trained with UNICEF support, both in regular curriculum subjects and on issues such as health and gender.

Protection from armed conflict, exploitation and abuse

In areas affected by armed conflict and other emergency situations, UNICEF worked to ensure that children and their families received vital humanitarian assistance, as well as to restore school systems and to help families and children to deal with trauma from exposure to violence and other atrocities. In war-torn countries, including Angola, Burundi, the Democratic Republic of the Congo (DRC), East Timor, Sierra Leone, Sri Lanka and the Sudan, UNICEF, together with WHO, negotiated and organized "days of tranquillity" to immunize children. In Afghanistan, an agreement secured access by health workers to northern provinces for the first time in a year, allowing almost 4 million children to be vaccinated against polio. In Kosovo, 97 per cent of children whose schooling was disrupted were back in class by the end of the year as a result of UNICEF-led efforts.

Adolescents required special support during crises as they were particularly vulnerable to violence and abuse, including rape and exploitation as child soldiers. In Liberia, UNICEF supported the demobilization of more than 4,000 child soldiers and continued to build the capabilities of those and other war-affected adolescents, including girls abducted and raped during the war, so that they could lead productive lives. In six refugee camps for displaced Kosovars in Albania, UNICEF helped young people set up Youth Councils that planned and managed camp services, including schooling, cleaning crews, landmine awareness and inter-camp sporting events. UNICEF continued to support prevention, rehabilitation and reintegration programmes for children affected by landmines in a dozen countries, including Angola, Cambodia, FRY, including Kosovo, and Nicaragua and among refugees in the former Yugoslav Republic of Macedonia.

During 1999, UNICEF worked closely with the UN Department of Peacekeeping Operations and the Special Representative on Children and Armed Conflict (see PART TWO, Chapter II) on the deployment of child protection advisers for peacekeeping missions. The first advisers, whose role was to help ensure that the protection of children's rights was a priority concern throughout the peacekeeping process, were seconded by UNICEF to UN peacekeeping operations in the DRC and Sierra Leone. Assistance was also provided for the reunification of children separated during crises in a number of countries, including Angola, East Timor, Kosovo, Sierra Leone, the Sudan, Uganda and the United Republic of Tanzania.

UNICEF also strengthened its activities related to sexual exploitation and abuse in 1999, especially the trafficking of women and girls from countries in Central and Eastern Europe, CIS and the Baltic States region, and child prostitution and trafficking in Cambodia, the Lao People's Democratic Republic and Viet Nam.

Poverty reduction

In 1999, with an estimated 650 million children worldwide trapped in extreme poverty, UNICEF bolstered its poverty-alleviation efforts by increasing the percentage of resources allocated to the least developed countries and improving strategies to help the poorest children not only survive their early years but also achieve their potential for physical, emotional and intellectual development. As a result of UNICEF support for national efforts to improve social services for poor children, nearly three out of four children in developing countries had gained access to clean water and a larger percentage were in school than at any time previously. In Cambodia, a village-based programme that combined health, nutrition, sanitation, women's literacy and early childhood care had, in one year, from 1998 to 1999, reduced malnutrition among women and children under five by 10 per cent. As a result of a UNICEF-supported project to improve sanitation, launched in Zimbabwe in 1999, hundreds of families in poor neighbourhoods on the outskirts of Harare received low-cost, ecologically sound latrines in or near their homes.

Given that many of the world's poorest countries continued to service debt at the expense of basic social services, UNICEF, as the lead agency within the UN system for the 20/20 Initiative, endorsed by the 1995 World Summit for Social Development [YUN 1995, p. 1113], encouraged both developing and donor nations to allocate 20 per cent of their budgets and ODA, respectively, to basic social services. In Uganda, for example, resources freed from debt servicing were being used to ensure children's right to a quality basic education. By the end of 1999, UNICEF had participated in 40 national reviews to encourage the allocation of budgetary resources for basic social services. In addition, UNICEF collaborated in formulating the Principles of Good Social Policy, which were adopted by the World Bank's Development Committee in September.

Organizational and administrative matters

UNICEF finances

In 1999, UNICEF income amounted to $1,102 million, which was $93 million (9 per cent) higher than the $1,009 million estimated in the 1999 medium-term plan and $136 million (14 per cent) more than 1998 income. The main sources of income were contributions from Governments and intergovernmental organizations (63 per cent ($699 million) of total income); and non-governmental and private sector groups and individuals (34 per cent ($371 million)). Another 3 per cent ($32 million) came from other sources.

Budget appropriations

In January [dec. 1999/3], the Executive Board took note of a progress report on implementation of the biennial support budget for 1998-1999 [E/ICEF/1999/AB/L.1], prepared in response to the Board's 1998 request [YUN 1998, p. 1099]. In September [dec. 1999/20], the Board approved a biennial support budget totalling $545.5 million for UNICEF programme support and management and administration for 2000-2001, as recommended by the Executive Director [E/ICEF/1999/AB/L.7], and reviewed by the Advisory Committee on Administrative and Budgetary Questions (ACABQ) [E/ICEF/1999/AB/L.10]. Income estimates of $52 million would be used to offset the gross appropriations, resulting in estimated net appropriations of $493.5 million.

Also in September [dec. 1999/13], the Board approved the Executive Director's recommendations for funding 25 country programmes, one subregional programme for Central America and one multi-country programme for Central and Eastern Europe, CIS and the Baltic States [E/ICEF/1999/P/L.16 & Corr.1], amounting to the following respective amounts for general resources and supplementary funding for each region: Africa, $129.3 million and $127.6 million; Americas and the Caribbean, $7.6 million and $37.3 million; Asia, $26.5 million and $18 million; Central and Eastern Europe, CIS and the Baltic States, $45.8 million and $58.9 million; and the Middle East and North Africa, $9.7 million and $2.5 million.

As a result of the harmonization of the budgets of UNICEF, UNDP and the United Nations Population Fund (UNFPA), and in line with ACABQ recommendations, UNICEF proposals relating to intercountry programmes (previously categorized as advocacy and programme development for headquarters and regional offices) were presented separately from the support budget. Based on those proposals [E/ICEF/P/L.30], the Board, on 9 September [dec. 1999/14], approved a general resources 2000-2001 programme budget for programme activities at headquarters and regional offices of $21.1 million and an Emergency Programme Fund of $25 million. In addition, a supplementary-funded programme budget of $237 million was approved for the 2000-2001 biennium, subject to the availability of specific-purpose contributions.

On 7 September [dec. 1999/10], the Board approved the 1999-2002 financial medium-term plan [E/ICEF/1999/AB/L.11] as a flexible framework of projections, including the preparation of up to $656 million in programme expenditures from regular resources for submission in 2000. The amount was subject to the availability of resources and to the condition that estimates of income and expenditure made in the medium-term plan continued to be valid.

Audits

In January [dec. 1999/4], the Executive Board took note of the UNICEF financial report and audited statements for the biennium ended 31 December 1997 and report of the Board of Auditors [A/53/5/Add.2], and the 1998 UNICEF report to the Board of Auditors and ACABQ [E/ICEF/1998/AB/L.9].

In a May report [E/ICEF/1999/AB/L.8], UNICEF described to the Board of Auditors and ACABQ the steps taken or to be taken in response to the recommendations of the Board and ACABQ on the UNICEF accounts for the 1996-1997 biennium. It also presented the status of implementation of the recommendations on the UNICEF accounts for the 1994-1995 biennium. On 8 September [dec. 1999/11], the Executive Board took note of the report.

In June, the Office of Internal Audit issued its second annual report, which considered the results of its findings based on audits completed in 1998 [E/ICEF/1999/AB/L.14]. The report noted that the audit of field locations continued to receive high priority. There was particularly strong demand from offices in 1998 for assistance in introducing self-assessment techniques. The Executive Board, on 9 September [dec. 1999/15], took note of the report.

Also in September [dec. 1999/17], the Board took note of the interim financial report and statements for the year ended 31 December 1998 [E/ICEF/1999/AB/L.12].

Harmonization of budgets

The Executive Board, in January, considered proposals for revisions to the harmonized budget format submitted by UNDP, UNFPA and UNICEF [DP/1999/6-DP/FPA/1999/1-E/ICEF/1999/AB/L.2], in accordance with the Board's 1998 request [YUN 1998, p. 1099]. ACABQ presented its comments thereon [DP/1999/7-DP/FPA/1999/3-E/ICEF/1999/AB/L.4].

Amendments to financial regulations

In July [E/ICEF/1999/AB/L.9], UNICEF proposed several limited amendments to its financial regulations. The Executive Board, on 10 September [dec. 1999/21], approved the proposed changes, as reviewed by ACABQ in August [E/ICEF/1999/AB/L.10], and requested UNICEF to amend the relevant financial regulations and rules accordingly. It decided to examine the implications of the amendments when considering the report of the Board of Auditors for 1998-1999.

Resource mobilization strategy

In response to a 1998 Executive Board request [YUN 1998, p. 1100] and in accordance with General Assembly resolution 50/227 [YUN 1996, p. 1249] and Economic and Social Council resolution 1997/59 [YUN 1997, p. 846], UNICEF presented a resource mobilization strategy [E/ICEF/1999/5], which was the culmination of a series of reports and drafts reviewed by the Executive Board in 1998 [YUN

1998, p. 1100]. The resource mobilization strategy focused on increased contributions to core resources and burden-sharing, greater predictability of contributions to core resources, supplementary funds, supporting strategies and action and other means of mobilizing resources for UNICEF and for children.

In January [dec. 1999/8], the Executive Board adopted the resource mobilization strategy and endorsed the funding target of an annual growth in income of 7 per cent, to reach $1.5 billion by 2005, as a challenge for the mobilization of general resources and supplementary funds from Governments, the private sector and all other donors. The Board decided that UNICEF would adopt and develop a multi-year funding framework, which was annexed to the Board's decision, that conceptually integrated UNICEF organizational priorities and major areas of action, resources, budget and outcomes. It also outlined measures for UNICEF to adopt concerning contributions to supplementary funds. The Executive Director was asked to submit to the Board at its first regular session in 2000 a plan for the timing of the presentation of the various elements of the multi-year funding framework, including the medium-term plan, the biennial support budget, the analytical report of the Executive Director, and the announcement by Governments of their voluntary contributions, with a view to enhancing their linkages.

Private Sector Division

In a financial report on the Private Sector Division (PSD) for the year ended 31 December 1999 [E/ICEF/2000/AB/L.6], UNICEF stated that the total net income from PSD activities for the year was $202.9 million for regular resources, compared to $180.1 million in 1998. That amount included $65.2 million from the sale of UNICEF greeting cards and other products, $156.4 million from private sector fund-raising activities, and an offset of $18.7 million for other charges and adjustments. In addition, a total of $153.5 million ($92.5 million in 1998) was raised from private sector fund-raising activities, which was earmarked for other resources. The net consolidated income, including both regular and other resources, totalled $356.4 million ($272.6 million in 1998).

The Executive Board, in January [dec. 1999/2], approved for the fiscal year 1 January to 31 December 1999 budgeted expenditures of $88.8 million as presented in the proposed budget [E/ICEF/1999/AB/L.5]. It authorized the Executive Director to incur expenditures as summarized in the proposed budget and to increase expenditures up to the maximum proposed in the report, should there be an apparent net proceeds increase from product sales and/or private sector fund-raising, and, accordingly, to reduce expenditures should the net proceeds decrease. The Executive Director was also authorized to redeploy resources between the various budget lines up to 10 per cent of the amounts approved, and to spend additional funds between sessions of the Board, when necessary, due to currency fluctuations, to implement the 1999 work plan. The Board noted that PSD net proceeds for 1999 were budgeted at $284.3 million for general resources. It approved the proposed changes in posts contained in the budget (a net decrease of four posts) and renewed the Market Development Programme with $4 million for 1999 and the Fund-raising Development Programme with $8.5 million for 1999. It also renewed the Central and Eastern European National Committees Development Programme, which included nine countries, with a budget of $0.5 million for 1999. The Executive Director was authorized to incur expenditures in 1999 related to the cost of goods delivered for 2000 up to $37.1 million. In addition, the Board approved the PSD medium-term plan contained in the budget report.

In September [dec. 1999/17], the Board took note of the PSD financial report and statements for the year ended 31 December 1998 [YUN 1998, p. 1101].

Joint and coordinating committees

The seventh meeting of the United Nations Educational, Scientific and Cultural Organization (UNESCO)/UNICEF Joint Committee on Education (New York, 17-18 June) [E/ICEF/1999/18] approved recommendations on strengthening collaboration with State agencies and other bodies, particularly in the areas of: girls' education; early childhood care and education; the needs of children in Africa; the status, remuneration and training of teachers; education data and statistics; the assessment of the 1990 World Summit on Education for All [YUN 1990, p. 763]; further elaboration of the respective strengths and mandates of the two organizations; and reports of the Joint Committee. The Committee considered a presentation on the Framework Agreement between UNESCO and UNICEF on collaboration in the field of education, which was signed in February.

The Executive Board, on 9 September [dec. 1999/16], took note of the Committee's recommendations. In other action, the Board elected for 1999-2000 the members and alternates of the WHO/UNICEF/UNFPA Coordinating Committee on Health and of the UNESCO/UNICEF Joint Committee on Education [dec. 1999/1].

International Child Development Centre

In July [E/ICEF/1999/16], UNICEF submitted a progress report on the activities of the International Child Development Centre (ICDC), established in 1988 to strengthen the capacity of UNICEF and its cooperating institutions to respond to the evolving needs of children and to promote an emerging new global ethic for children [YUN 1988, p. 649]. The report observed that the Centre's most significant contributions had been in the areas of socio-economic policy analysis and children's rights. ICDC activities had helped to underpin UNICEF's ability to influence course corrections in global programmes of structural adjustment, debt and economic transition to market economies by demonstrating the crushing impact of fiscal measures on the poorest of children. The Centre had also undertaken efforts to increase global understanding of children's human rights and facilitated implementation of the 1989 Convention on the Rights of the Child, adopted by the General Assembly in resolution 44/25 [YUN 1989, p. 560]. Much of the Centre's early work had been incorporated into the future agenda of UNICEF and mainstreamed into its current work programme.

The UNICEF Executive Director recommended the extension of ICDC for the period 2000-2002 in order to strengthen UNICEF capacity to explore new dimensions of its future agenda and to document lessons learned from international experience. An allocation of $12.8 million in supplementary funding was proposed, of which the Government of Italy had pledged 10.5 billion lire (approximately $6 million) for the Centre's core activities, with the remainder to be sought from other donors for specific activities. In September, the Executive Board [dec. 1999/18] authorized a three-year extension for the Centre and approved the recommended allocation.

Communication and information

In an April report [E/ICEF/1999/AB/L.6], UNICEF outlined its information technology (IT) strategy and described progress in IT investments and projects. IT enabled UNICEF to fulfil its goals in advocacy, information-sharing and fund-raising and to achieve medium-term objectives in management and operations. It also facilitated the availability and use of data in critical areas. IT strategies addressed five critical areas: IT management, governance and organization; integrated systems for resource management; exploitation of the Internet and Intranet for knowledge management; global connectivity; and the IT infrastructure required to support those areas. IT areas requiring further development by UNICEF included communication channels; resource management systems; information management; information technology organization; and information technology infrastructure and support services.

Annual reports

In January [dec. 1999/6], the Executive Board asked the Executive Director to transmit her annual report covering 1998 [E/1999/9] to the Economic and Social Council and to ensure that future reports to the Council reflected greater analytical effort, selected focus on key issues, problem-oriented reporting and discussions of lessons learned.

Also in January [dec. 1999/7], the Board decided that, starting from 2000, information in part II of the Executive Director's annual report should be presented to the Board in a way that facilitated monitoring of progress in achieving the objectives in programmes and activities within the framework of organizational priorities in the medium-term plan. In addition, the report should be developed as an analytical report of annual global progress in the priority areas of the medium-term plan in a manner that linked planning, programming, budgeting and outcomes, including a review of objectives and results achieved, estimates of funds utilized for those purposes, main obstacles encountered and lessons learned, and other issues of special interest to the Board.

Youth

Implementation of the World Programme of Action for Youth

In 1999, United Nations policies and programmes involving youth continued to focus on implementation of the 1995 World Programme of Action for Youth to the Year 2000 and Beyond, adopted by the General Assembly in resolution 50/81 [YUN 1995, p. 1211]. The Programme of Action addressed the problems faced by youth worldwide and outlined meaningful ways to enhance youth participation in national and international policy- and decision-making. The 1998 Lisbon Declaration on Youth Policies and Programmes, adopted at the first World Conference of Ministers Responsible for Youth [YUN 1998, p. 1103], built on the 1995 Programme of Action by outlining further policy commitments by Governments in the areas of national youth policy, participation, development, peace, education, employment, health and drug abuse. Just prior to the World Conference, the third session of the World Youth Forum of the United Nations System adopted the Braga (Portugal) Youth Action Plan, a set of goals and actions aimed at fostering youth participation for human development [ibid.]. The Plan and the outcomes of the World Conference were submitted to the Assembly in 1999 through the Commission for Social Development.

Report of Secretary-General. In response to General Assembly resolution 52/83 [YUN 1997, p. 1225], the Secretary-General submitted a January report [A/54/59] in which he described progress in implementing the 1995 World Programme of Action, based on information submitted to the 1998 World Conference and Youth Forum by Member States, the UN system, youth NGOs and intergovernmental organizations, as well as on statements by Member States during the Assembly's 1998 session. The report reviewed implementation at the national, regional and global levels in relation to three indicators: youth policy, youth coordination and youth action. Those indicators illustrated significant progress by Member States in both formulation and implementation of national youth policies and programmes. States indicating that they had implemented a national youth programme grew from just 29 per cent in 1994 to 64 per cent in 1998. By the end of 1998, 153 (83 per cent) Member States had formulated cross-sectoral national youth policies; 167 (90 per cent) had designated a national youth coordinating mechanism (such as a ministry department, council or committee); 114 (62 per cent) had implemented a national youth programme of action; and 95 (51 per cent) had taken all three types of action to implement the Programme of Action. Despite such progress, the report indicated that many of the Member States that had adopted national youth policies had not done so on a cross-sectoral, inter-ministerial or interdepartmental basis. There had been an uneven reaction by the regional commissions regarding the follow-up to Assembly resolution 50/81 [YUN 1995, p. 1211] and Economic and Social Council resolution 1997/55 [YUN 1997, p. 1224] and there was a need for more serious cooperation between the regional commissions and regional intergovernmental youth organizations, which convened regional meetings of youth ministers, and the regional youth NGOs, which convened regional meetings of youth organizations, to better strengthen the capacities for formulating and implementing integrated national youth policies and programmes in the context of the Programme of Action.

Recommendations for future action by Governments, regional organizations and global mechanisms, including UN bodies, addressed the integration of youth concerns into overall economic and social policy; the impact of globalization on the lives of young people; the linkages between democracy and young people; regional integration and youth development; country experiences in formulating, implementing, monitoring and evaluating integrated national youth policies; and experiences of training and apprenticeship programmes for youth employment.

Communications. On 5 February [E/CN.5/1999/14], Turkey expressed its desire to organize the second World Conference of Ministers Responsible for Youth, together with the fifth session of the World Youth Forum and the World Youth Festival, in Turkey. On 12 February [A/54/66-E/1999/6], Senegal proposed hosting the fourth session of the World Youth Forum.

Commission for Social Development

The Commission for Social Development, at its thirty-seventh session (9-19 February) [E/1999/26], considered policies and programmes involving youth. It had before it the Secretary-General's report on the implementation of the World Programme of Action for Youth (see above) and a note [A/54/62] drawing attention to the report of the 1998 World Conference of Ministers Responsible for Youth [YUN 1998, p. 1103].

The Commission also held a panel discussion on youth, which addressed the results of the 1998 Conference and Forum, including follow-up action by Member States, NGOs, the UN system and other intergovernmental organizations. Priority concerns reflected in the discussion included: the achievements of the Conference and the Forum by bringing youth issues to the attention of the international community; the gravity of youth problems globally and the necessity for fund-raising to address youth problems; that youth should be seen as part of the solutions and not always as the source of problems; that policy makers should be encouraged to promote youth participation in all aspects of life; that the various youth-related agencies and organizations of the UN system should strengthen inter-agency cooperation to alleviate youth problems; that the effects of globalization on youth and the strategy to deal with that problem should be reviewed at the national level; the linkages of youth issues with other social policies and problems of society; and integrating the youth agenda in national development programmes of Member States. The panel made a series of recommendations regarding youth issues.

The Commission decided to include in its report the moderator's summary of the panel on youth [dec. 37/103] and recommended a draft resolution on youth policies and programmes to the Economic and Social Council for adoption.

ECONOMIC AND SOCIAL COUNCIL ACTION

On 28 July [meeting 43], the Economic and Social Council, on the recommendation of the Commission for Social Development [E/1999/26], adopted **resolution 1999/18** without vote [agenda item 14 *(b)*].

Policies and programmes involving youth

The Economic and Social Council

Recommends to the General Assembly the adoption of the following draft resolution:

[For text, see General Assembly resolution 54/120 below.]

GENERAL ASSEMBLY ACTION

On 17 December [meeting 83], the General Assembly, on the recommendation of the Third (Social, Humanitarian and Cultural) Committee [A/54/595], adopted **resolution 54/120** without vote [agenda item 106].

Policies and programmes involving youth

The General Assembly,

Recalling its resolution 50/81 of 14 December 1995, by which it adopted the World Programme of Action for Youth to the Year 2000 and Beyond, annexed thereto, as an integral part of that resolution,

Recalling also its resolutions 32/135 of 16 December 1977 and 36/17 of 9 November 1981, by which it adopted guidelines for the improvement of the channels of communication between the United Nations and youth and youth organizations, and 40/14 of 18 November 1985, entitled "International Youth Year: Participation, Development, Peace", by which it endorsed the guidelines for further planning and suitable follow-up in the field of youth as contained in the report of the Advisory Committee for the International Youth Year on its fourth session, held at Vienna from 25 March to 3 April 1985,

Noting especially that, according to paragraph 123 of the Programme of Action, current regional and interregional conferences of ministers responsible for youth affairs in Africa, Asia, Europe, Latin America and the Caribbean and Western Asia were invited to intensify cooperation among each other and to consider meeting regularly at the international level under the aegis of the United Nations to provide an effective forum for a focused global dialogue on youth-related issues,

Noting that, in paragraph 124 of the Programme of Action, youth-related bodies and organizations of the United Nations system were invited to cooperate with the above-mentioned conferences,

Recalling that, in paragraph 125 of the Programme of Action, the World Youth Forum of the United Nations system was invited to contribute to the implementation of the Programme of Action through the identification and promotion of joint initiatives to further its objectives so that they could better reflect the interests of youth,

Recalling also Economic and Social Council resolution 1997/55 of 23 July 1997 and General Assembly resolution 52/83 of 12 December 1997, in which the Council and the Assembly welcomed the offer of the Government of Portugal to host the World Conference of Ministers Responsible for Youth at Lisbon from 8 to 12 August 1998,

Welcoming the holding of the World Conference of Ministers Responsible for Youth, hosted by the Government of Portugal in cooperation with the United Nations, as well as the support of the Government of Portugal for the holding of the third session of the World Youth Forum at Braga, Portugal, from 2 to 7 August 1998,

1. *Takes note with appreciation* of the report of the Secretary-General on the implementation of the World Programme of Action for Youth to the Year 2000 and Beyond and the Lisbon Declaration on Youth Policies and Programmes, adopted at the World Conference of Ministers Responsible for Youth;

2. *Notes* the holding of the third session of the World Youth Forum of the United Nations system at Braga, Portugal, from 2 to 7 August 1998, and expresses its appreciation to the Government of Portugal for its support;

3. *Calls upon* all States, all United Nations bodies, the specialized agencies, the regional commissions and the intergovernmental and non-governmental organizations concerned, in particular youth organizations, to make every possible effort towards the implementation of the Programme of Action and to consider, within its framework, the appropriate ways and means to follow up the Lisbon Declaration, in accordance with their experience, situation and priorities;

4. *Invites* all relevant programmes, funds, specialized agencies and other bodies within the United Nations system, as well as other intergovernmental organizations and regional financial institutions, to give greater support to national youth policies and programmes within their country programmes as a way to follow up the World Conference;

5. *Reiterates* the call made by the World Conference to strengthen the Youth Unit of the Division for Social Policy and Development of the Secretariat through the provision of all regular staffing and resources necessary for the fulfilment of its mandate, including the provision of effective assistance in the implementation of the Programme of Action;

6. *Encourages* the regional commissions to follow up the World Conference in their respective regions, in coordination with regional meetings of ministers responsible for youth and regional non-governmental youth organizations, and to provide advisory services to support national youth policies and programmes in each region;

7. *Endorses* the recommendation made by the World Conference that 12 August be declared International Youth Day, and recommends that public information activities be organized at all levels to support the Day as a way to promote better awareness, especially among youth, of the Programme of Action;

8. *Invites* the Secretary-General to participate actively in the effective follow-up to the World Conference, bearing in mind General Assembly resolution 52/83 and Economic and Social Council resolution 1997/55 and within the framework of the Programme of Action;

9. *Recommends* that the second World Conference of Ministers Responsible for Youth be organized under the aegis of the United Nations, and notes with appreciation the offer made by the Government of Turkey to organize the second World Conference together with the fifth session of the World Youth Forum and the World Youth Festival;

10. *Welcomes* the offer of the Government of Senegal to host the fourth session of the World Youth Forum in 2001;

11. *Calls upon* Member States, all United Nations bodies and non-governmental organizations to continue to implement fully the guidelines for further planning and suitable follow-up in the field of youth,

which the General Assembly endorsed by its resolution 40/14, and the guidelines for the improvement of the channels of communication between the United Nations and youth and youth organizations, which the Assembly adopted by its resolutions 32/135 and 36/17, and in particular to facilitate, in accordance with these resolutions, the activities of youth mechanisms that have been set up by youth and youth organizations;

12. *Recognizes* the important role that could be played by the United Nations Youth Fund for the implementation of agreed programmes and mandates on youth, including the provision of support for youth activities promoting South-South cooperation;

13. *Invites* all Governments and intergovernmental and non-governmental organizations to contribute to the Fund, and requests the Secretary-General to take appropriate actions to encourage contributions;

14. *Recognizes* the important role of non-governmental youth organizations in the implementation of the Programme of Action at the national and international levels and in the development and evaluation of national policies, in particular concerning youth, and encourages Governments to ensure that the perspective of young people is reflected in national policies and programmes;

15. *Calls upon* all States, all United Nations bodies, the specialized agencies, the regional commissions and intergovernmental and non-governmental organizations to exchange knowledge and expertise on youth-related issues, upon setting up the ways and means to do so;

16. *Reiterates* the call made in the Programme of Action to Member States to consider including youth representatives in their delegations to the General Assembly and other relevant United Nations meetings, thus broadening the channels of communication and enhancing the discussion of youth-related issues, and requests the Secretary-General to convey this invitation again to Member States;

17. *Requests* the Secretary-General to report to the General Assembly at its fifty-sixth session on the implementation of the present resolution, in particular on progress made in the implementation of the Programme of Action.

By **decision 54/430** of 17 December, the Assembly took note of the Secretary-General's report on the implementation of the World Programme of Action on Youth to the Year 2000 and Beyond [A/54/59].

Ageing persons

International Year of Older Persons

The International Year of Older Persons, the theme of which was "A society for all ages", ended on 30 September. In accordance with resolution 52/80 [YUN 1997, p. 1227], the General Assembly devoted four plenary meetings to follow-up to the Year on 4, 5 and 6 October [A/54/PV.23-26].

The overall objective of the Year, designated by the Assembly in a 1992 Proclamation on Ageing contained in resolution 47/5 [YUN 1992, p. 889], was the promotion of the United Nations Principles for Older Persons, adopted by the Assembly in resolution 46/91 [YUN 1991, p. 698], which provided guidance in the areas of independence, participation, care, self-fulfilment and dignity.

Report of Secretary-General. In response to General Assembly resolution 53/109 [YUN 1998, p. 1104], the Secretary-General submitted an August report on the International Year of Older Persons, 1999: activities and legacies [A/54/268]. The report condensed the activities for the Year into the four facets of the policy framework for a society for all ages: the situation of older persons; lifelong individual development; multigenerational relationships; and population ageing and development. It also described initiatives with regard to women and ageing. The observance of the Year, which was launched with a multimedia information campaign on 1 October 1998, was highlighted by a special event at UN Headquarters on 30 September 1999. Activities undertaken during the Year by more than 80 national committees and numerous other entities included conferences, seminars, research studies and initiatives that explored and promoted various facets of the theme "A society for all ages". Promotional events included cultural, educational, art and social activities, as well as the launching of commemorative stamps, posters and calendars with the Year's logo.

The impact of the Year on the UN programme on ageing had already become evident said the Secretary-General. The programme had not only extended its exploration of the roles, opportunities, entitlements and contributions of older persons in fast-changing societies, but also was engaged in the ongoing formulation of a policy framework of a society for all ages, together with a research engine that could drive it. Future activities would include priority programmatic measures, meetings planned for 2000, reviews scheduled for 2001 and 2002 and mainstreaming in relation to ageing issues.

Highlights of an expert consultation on developing a policy framework for a society for all ages (Seoul, Republic of Korea, 11-16 June) were annexed to the report.

Follow-up arrangements

The Commission for Social Development (New York, 9-19 February) [E/1999/26] considered a note by the Secretary-General on follow-up arrangements to the International Year of Older

Persons [E/CN.5/1999/8], prepared in response to a 1998 Commission request [YUN 1998, p. 1106]. The note included suggestions for the development of a long-term perspective strategy on ageing into the twenty-first century; streamlining the review and appraisal of the International Plan of Action on Ageing, adopted at the 1982 World Assembly on Ageing [YUN 1982, p. 1184]; and the four General Assembly plenary meetings devoted to the follow-up to the Year.

On 19 February [E/1999/26 (res. 37/2)], the Commission asked the Secretary-General to solicit the views of States, NGOs and the private sector on updating the International Plan of Action on Ageing and on the desirability and feasibility of convening in 2002 a review of the outcome of the World Assembly on Ageing, including the interrelationship of ageing and development. Governments were urged to present to the Assembly, at the four plenary meetings devoted to follow-up to the Year at its fifty-fourth (1999) session, their national reports on observances of the Year, policy approaches to ageing and best practices for a society for all ages. The Secretariat was asked to incorporate those experiences, policies and best practices into a long-term strategy on ageing for the Assembly's consideration at its fifty-sixth (2001) session. The Commission also suggested exploring the feasibility of including an ageing-related development index in the *Human Development Report*.

GENERAL ASSEMBLY ACTION

On 10 November [meeting 51], the General Assembly adopted **resolution 54/24** [draft: A/54/L.6/Rev.1 & Add.1, orally revised] without vote [agenda item 106].

Follow-up to the International Year of Older Persons: a society for all ages

The General Assembly,

Recalling the World Assembly on Ageing, held in Vienna in 1982, which adopted the International Plan of Action on Ageing,

Recalling also the International Conference on Ageing, which it convened on 15 and 16 October 1992 on the occasion of the tenth anniversary of the adoption of the International Plan of Action on Ageing, and which, inter alia, recommended the observance of the International Year of Older Persons in 1999,

Recalling further its resolution 53/109 of 9 December 1998 and previous resolutions on ageing and the International Year of Older Persons,

Reaffirming the importance of the United Nations Principles for Older Persons, as adopted by its resolution 46/91 of 16 December 1991,

Taking note of the 1998 revision of the official United Nations population estimates and projections, which show that, with the continuation of the decline in fertility and the increase in life expectancy, the population of the world will age much faster in the next half-century than previously,

Also taking note that these population estimates and projections provide, for the first time, detailed information on the oldest of the old, which shows that the proportion of those who are eighty years of age or older will increase in all countries of the world, and illustrates two phenomena: the older the age group, the faster it grows, and the higher the proportion of older women,

Reaffirming the need to integrate a gender perspective in policies on ageing,

Conscious that the ageing of the world's population represents a far-reaching challenge to Governments as well as other relevant sectors of society, including non-governmental organizations and the private sector, to ensure that the needs of older persons, including their human resource potential to society, are adequately recognized and addressed,

Aware that a revolutionary change in the demographic structure of societies, as well as the rapidity of ageing of populations in developing countries, requires a fundamental change in the way in which societies cope with those challenges,

Conscious that discrimination and stereotyping of older persons constitute and lead to violations of their human rights,

Taking note of General Comment No. 6 (1995) of the Committee on Economic, Social and Cultural Rights on the economic, social and cultural rights of older persons,

Acknowledging the initiatives undertaken and the momentum generated, at all levels, towards addressing the challenge of ageing and the concerns and contributions of ageing and older persons by the celebration of the International Year of Older Persons,

Convinced of the necessity to ensure an action-oriented follow-up to the International Year of Older Persons with a view to sustaining that momentum,

Taking note of the report of the Secretary-General, and noting with satisfaction the focus in the annex to the report on the elaboration of a policy framework for a long-term perspective strategy on ageing, including a research agenda for the twenty-first century, in the context of a society for all ages,

Recalling resolution 37/2 adopted by the Commission for Social Development at its thirty-seventh session, in which the Commission requested the Secretary-General to solicit the views of States, non-governmental organizations and the private sector on updating the International Plan of Action on Ageing and on the desirability and feasibility of convening a review of the outcome of the World Assembly on Ageing in 2002, including the interrelationship of ageing and development,

1. *Notes with satisfaction* the successful celebration of the International Year of Older Persons, with the theme "A society for all ages", and resolves to maintain the momentum created by the Year;

2. *Emphasizes* the need to address the developmental aspects of ageing with particular attention to the situation of developing countries;

3. *Stresses* the importance of the collection of data and population statistics disaggregated by sex and by age on all aspects of population ageing for policy formulation by all countries, and encourages the relevant

entities of the United Nations to support national efforts, especially of developing countries, in capacity-building, and, in this context, takes note of the establishment by the United Nations of an Internet-accessible database on ageing, and invites States to submit, whenever possible, information for inclusion in the database;

4. *Encourages* the press and the media to play a central role in the creation of awareness of population ageing and related issues, in the elimination of stereotypes and discrimination of older persons in the media and in the promotion of solidarity among generations;

5. *Urges* the development of policies and programmes at the national, regional and international levels which respond to the rights, needs and abilities of older women;

6. *Also urges* Governments to take appropriate action to combat discrimination based on age;

7. *Requests* the Economic and Social Council and all its appropriate subsidiary bodies, in particular the Commission for Social Development, as well as the Executive Board of the United Nations Development Programme and the legislative and policy-making bodies of the concerned specialized agencies and intergovernmental organizations, to give careful consideration to the issue of ageing;

8. *Encourages* States Parties to include in their reports to the Committee on Human Rights, the Committee on the Elimination of Discrimination against Women and the Committee on Economic, Social and Cultural Rights information on older persons;

9. *Welcomes* activities in the field of ageing by United Nations funds and programmes, in particular the United Nations Development Programme and the United Nations Population Fund, as well as specialized agencies, including the World Health Organization, the United Nations Educational, Scientific and Cultural Organization, the International Labour Organization and the Bretton Woods institutions, and encourages them to continue to support activities in the field of ageing;

10. *Stresses* the importance of national follow-up activities to the International Year of Older Persons through involving older persons and consulting them on their needs;

11. *Encourages* regional initiatives to follow up on the International Year of Older Persons and to provide inputs into the process of revision of the International Plan of Action on Ageing, given the fact that different regions and countries are at different stages of population ageing and need to identify specific policy responses in order to achieve the goal of "A society for all ages";

12. *Takes note with appreciation* of the offer by the Government of Germany to host a regional ministerial conference on ageing under the aegis of the Economic Commission for Europe in 2002;

13. *Notes* that there is a need for guidelines and recommendations reflecting the current situation of societies and older persons in order to design and support adequate age-related policies;

14. *Decides* to entrust the Commission for Social Development with the revision of the International Plan of Action on Ageing and the elaboration of a long-term strategy on ageing, based on new developments since 1982 and on the experience of the International Year of Older Persons in 1999, with a view to the adoption of a revised plan of action and of a long-term strategy on ageing in 2002;

15. *Requests* the Secretary-General to consult Governments, intergovernmental organizations and non-governmental organizations in the preparation of a draft revised plan of action, including proposals on a review mechanism, to be submitted to the Commission for Social Development in 2001;

16. *Endorses* the request of the Commission for Social Development in its resolution 37/2, to the Secretariat, to incorporate, as feasible, the experiences, policies and best practices reported by States into a long-term strategy on ageing, encompassing periodic reviews, for the consideration of the General Assembly at its fifty-sixth session in 2001;

17. *Requests* the Commission for Social Development, at its thirty-eighth session, to adopt a recommendation on the desirability and feasibility of convening a second World Assembly on Ageing in 2002, devoted to reviewing the outcome of the First World Assembly as well as to considering a long-term strategy on ageing in the context of a society for all ages, and to report on this issue to the General Assembly at its fifty-fourth session through the Economic and Social Council;

18. *Takes note with appreciation* of the offer by the Government of Spain to host a second World Assembly on Ageing in 2002;

19. *Requests* the Secretary-General to submit a report to the General Assembly at its fifty-fifth session on the implementation of the present resolution under an item entitled "Follow-up to the International Year of Older Persons".

Chapter XII

Refugees and displaced persons

In 1999, the global population of concern to, and receiving assistance from, the Office of the United Nations High Commissioner for Refugees (UNHCR) totalled more than 22 million. They included almost 11.7 million refugees, 5.4 million internally displaced persons, 2.5 million repatriated refugees, 1.2 million asylum-seekers and 1.5 million affected by humanitarian and other crises.

The major challenges posed by the conflicts in Chechnya, East Timor and Kosovo, which generated new movements of refugees and displaced persons totalling almost 2 million, absorbed a large portion of UNHCR's resources.

While world attention was focused on those crises, African countries continued to host the world's largest refugee populations, internally displaced persons and other people of concern, totalling almost 6.3 million in 1999. The main refugee groups on the continent included half a million Sierra Leoneans in West Africa, 280,000 Burundians in the United Republic of Tanzania and 180,000 Congolese who had fled from the conflict in the Democratic Republic of the Congo (DRC) to various countries. More than 370,000 Sudanese were still refugees in Ethiopia and Uganda; 165,000 refugees from Western Sahara were in camps in Algeria and other countries; and 150,000 Angolan refugees were mostly based in the DRC. Guinea continued to host more than half a million refugees. The situation in the east and Horn of Africa continued to be dominated by the conflict between Ethiopia and Eritrea.

In Europe, the Kosovo crisis sparked one of the largest and most rapid refugee exoduses in modern times, with almost 850,000 Kosovar Albanians forced from their homes at the outbreak of hostilities in March. However, more than 400,000 voluntarily repatriated within two weeks following the restoration of peace. Elsewhere in Europe, the situation in Chechnya deteriorated in the second half of the year, forcing the displacement of more than 200,000 persons.

In Asia, East Timor experienced a fresh outbreak of violence, following the announcement of the results of the August referendum on independence, provoking the displacement of 75 per cent of the population, about 500,000 inside East Timor and an estimated 200,000 to West Timor and other areas of Indonesia. In October, UNHCR conducted a large-scale voluntary repatriation operation and signed a memorandum of understanding with the Government of Indonesia establishing a framework for protecting refugees and affirming the voluntary nature of the repatriation programme. In the Americas, a major displacement occurred in Colombia where 300,000 persons were forced to flee their homes because of the deteriorating conflict.

In October, the UNHCR Executive Committee considered as its annual theme "Strengthening partnership to ensure protection, also in relation to security". It recognized that all levels of partnership, including with States, other international organizations, regional organizations, local populations and other elements of civil society, including non-governmental organizations (NGOs), were important. The Committee reaffirmed that the 1951 Convention relating to the Status of Refugees and its 1967 Protocol remained the foundation of the international refugee regime. It recognized, however, that complementary forms of protection might need to be developed, and encouraged UNHCR, in consultation with others, to examine all aspects of the issue.

In December, the General Assembly urged that resources be mobilized to reduce the burden borne by States, in particular developing countries, that had received large numbers of asylum-seekers and refugees, and called on UNHCR to continue playing its catalytic role in mobilizing assistance from the international community to address the economic, environmental and social impact of large-scale refugee populations, especially in developing countries.

Office of the United Nations High Commissioner for Refugees

Programme policy

Executive Committee action. At its fiftieth session (Geneva, 4-8 October) [A/54/12/Add.1], the Executive Committee of the UNHCR Programme recognized that the presence of massive refugee populations in developing countries was putting considerable strain on their economies and environment and called on UNHCR to mobilize assistance from the international community to address the situation. Serious breaches of internationally recognized rights of refugees, asylum-seekers and other persons of concern over the past year were strongly deplored by the Committee, which remained preoccupied that systematic violations of human rights, blatant disregard of international humanitarian law, and policies of wholesale expulsions of populations and "ethnic cleansing" had caused significant displacement around the world. The Committee called on all interested parties to concentrate on revitalizing old partnerships and building new ones to support the international refugee protection system. Noting the fiftieth anniversary of the 1949 Geneva Conventions on the law of armed conflict, it also called on States and other parties to armed conflicts scrupulously to observe international humanitarian law. The Committee also addressed issues pertaining to access to protection, special protection needs, security of refugees, durable solutions, stateless persons and internally displaced persons and protection of the refugee's family.

For consideration of its annual theme, "Strengthening partnership to ensure protection, also in relation to security", the Committee had before it a note [A/AC.96/923] that raised issues and gave examples of how partnerships with a variety of actors had contributed to improving the protection of asylum-seekers, refugees and others of concern to UNHCR. The note contained suggestions as to both the potential limits of partnership and elements of success.

In her opening statement to the Committee, the High Commissioner said that 1999 had experienced one of the highest rates of deployment of emergency staff since UNHCR's response system was established in 1992. The year had also been marked by fresh conflicts and refugee crises in which civilians had been particularly targeted. The crises in Kosovo and East Timor had particularly challenged the international community. In Kosovo, the outflow of people was staggering and the return, only 10 weeks after the outflow started, was an even faster exodus in reverse. Despite the obstacles, the response to the crisis did meet immediate needs of safety and survival. The displacement situation in both East and West Timor was of extreme concern to UNHCR. It was imperative that the Office maintain its presence in West Timor with free and secure access to East Timorese refugees. Africa and the area stretching from the Black Sea to Central Asia were two other critical regions where the refugee problem had intensified.

With regard to management changes, the High Commissioner stated that the Office had completed a reorganization that had streamlined its overall management and was continuing to develop a comprehensive operations management system. The 2000 budget had abolished the separation between General and Special Programmes and a new human resources management package was scheduled to be launched in January 2000. The High Commissioner also addressed issues of humanitarian action and international responses to crises, stressing that while regional initiatives to bring peace to troubled areas were welcome, new complex aspects of the interventions needed to be addressed, particularly the role of the military in humanitarian operations and the overcrowding of humanitarian space in high-profile emergencies.

By **decision 1999/288** of 30 July, the Economic and Social Council took note of the High Commissioner's report for 1998/99 [E/1999/21 & Corr.1].

Coordination of humanitarian assistance

UNHCR concluded global or country-specific agreements with several partner organizations in 1999, as outlined in the Commissioner's 1999 report [A/55/12], including one with the International Organization for Migration (IOM) in Croatia and one with the International Association of Refugee Law Judges to jointly promote and encourage national systems for the identification, treatment and protection of asylum-seekers. The annual UNHCR/IOM meeting reviewed advances made and constraints faced in implementing the memorandum of understanding between them. The framework for cooperation with the World Bank was complemented by an agreement further defining the staff exchange programme. Secondments and staffing were the subject of three other cooperation agreements signed in 1999 with international organizations, NGOs and government agencies. UNHCR signed a memorandum of understanding with the International Organization of La Francophonie, whereby the latter would fund, recruit and deploy Junior Professional Officers from francophone countries and other members of the organization. Emergency staffing and other standby arrangements were the subject of cooperation agreements signed with the Danish and Norwegian Refugee Councils and the Russian State entity for civil defence, emergency response and disaster mitigation. Although UNHCR had no global cooperation agreement with the International Committee of the Red Cross (ICRC), annual meetings were held to review specific situations. The 1999 meeting addressed operating principles in large-scale humanitarian crises and the relationship between humanitarian, political and military actors.

UNHCR continued to strengthen cooperation and coordination with other UN agencies, funds and programmes, both bilaterally and within inter-agency forums. The annual meeting between UNHCR and the World Food Programme (WFP) addressed cooperation and implementation of programmes in the field. Guidelines to the field were issued concerning UNHCR participation in the resident coordinator system and the potential for inter-agency development management tools for strengthening humanitarian programmes and for addressing the matter of the gap from relief to development.

UNHCR continued to promote the UNHCR/NGO Partnership in Action process in 1999. Regional meetings on the process for national NGOs took place in Argentina and Sri Lanka.

In October [A/54/12/Add.1], the Executive Committee called on UNHCR to further strengthen its collaboration with ICRC, the International Federation of the Red Cross and Red Crescent Societies, and national Red Cross and Red Crescent societies.

Evaluation and inspection activities

By a 19 August report [A/AC.96/918], the Executive Committee was informed that in February responsibility for evaluation was transferred to a new Evaluation and Policy Analysis Unit and the Inspection and Evaluation Service was renamed the Inspector General's Office (IGO). During the 12 months ending 31 July, inspections were carried out in 14 countries. IGO inspected the Division of Human Resources Management in the second half of 1998 and undertook management reviews in response to specific requests. A report with recommendations for restructuring headquarters was issued in February and options for the new management structure for the regional bureau for Africa were proposed.

Evaluation activities were outlined in a 20 August report [A/AC.96/919], in which it was noted that the new Evaluation and Policy Analysis Unit had reviewed the UNHCR housing programme in Bosnia and Herzegovina; problems of access to land and its ownership in repatriation operations; UNHCR's strategy in the European Union (EU); the Mali/Niger repatriation operation; UNHCR's rehabilitation activities in the Great Lakes region of Africa; compliance with UNHCR's policies on refugee women, children and the environment; and UNHCR staff training.

The Executive Committee, in a general decision on administrative, financial and programme matters [A/54/12/Add.1], took note of the reports.

GENERAL ASSEMBLY ACTION

On 17 December [meeting 83], the General Assembly, on the recommendation of the Third (Social, Humanitarian and Cultural) Committee [A/54/600], adopted **resolution 54/146** without vote [agenda item 111].

Office of the United Nations High Commissioner for Refugees

The General Assembly,

Having considered the report of the United Nations High Commissioner for Refugees on the activities of her Office and the report of the Executive Committee of the Programme of the United Nations High Commissioner for Refugees on the work of its fiftieth session and the conclusions contained therein,

Recalling its resolution 53/125 of 9 December 1998,

Commending the High Commissioner and her staff for the competent, courageous and dedicated manner in which they discharge their responsibilities, paying tribute to those staff members whose lives have been endangered in the course of their duties, and deploring the injuries and deaths of staff members as a consequence of generalized as well as targeted violence,

Commending States that have successfully implemented durable solutions,

1. *Endorses* the report of the Executive Committee of the Programme of the United Nations High Commissioner for Refugees on the work of its fiftieth session and the conclusions contained therein;

2. *Strongly reaffirms* the fundamental importance and the purely humanitarian and non-political character of the function of the Office of the United Nations High Commissioner for Refugees of providing international protection to refugees and seeking permanent solutions to the problem of refugees, and reiterates the need for Governments to continue to facilitate the effective exercise of this function;

3. *Reaffirms* the fundamental importance of the 1951 Convention and the 1967 Protocol relating to the Status of Refugees, in particular their implementation in a manner fully compatible with the object and purpose of those instruments, notes with satisfaction that one hundred and thirty-nine States are now parties to one or to both instruments, and encourages the Office of the High Commissioner and States to strengthen their efforts to promote broader accession to these instruments and their full implementation;

4. *Notes* that the fiftieth anniversary of the Geneva Conventions on the law of armed conflict is being commemorated in 1999, and calls upon States and other parties to armed conflict to observe scrupulously international humanitarian law;

5. *Also notes* that the thirtieth anniversary of the Organization of African Unity Convention governing the specific aspects of refugee problems in Africa is also being commemorated in 1999, and acknowledges the contribution made by that Convention to the development of regional standards for the protection of refugees;

6. *Reaffirms* that, as set out in article 14 of the Universal Declaration of Human Rights, everyone has the right to seek and enjoy in other countries asylum from persecution, and calls upon all States to refrain from taking measures that jeopardize the institution of asylum, in particular by returning or expelling refugees or asylum-seekers contrary to international standards;

7. *Emphasizes* that the protection of refugees is primarily the responsibility of States, whose full and effective cooperation, action and political resolve are re-

quired to enable the Office of the High Commissioner to fulfil its mandated functions, and calls upon States, the Office of the High Commissioner and all interested parties to turn concentrated attention towards revitalizing old partnerships and building new ones in support of the international refugee protection system;

8. *Stresses* the importance of international solidarity and burden-sharing in reinforcing the international protection of refugees, urges all States and relevant non-governmental and other organizations, in conjunction with the Office of the High Commissioner, to cooperate and to mobilize resources with a view to reducing the burden borne by States, in particular developing countries, that have received large numbers of asylum-seekers and refugees, and calls upon the Office of the High Commissioner to continue to play its catalytic role in mobilizing assistance from the international community to address the economic, environmental and social impact of large-scale refugee populations, especially in developing countries;

9. *Condemns* all acts that pose a threat to the personal security and well-being of refugees and asylum-seekers, such as refoulement, unlawful expulsion and physical attacks, and calls upon all States of refuge, in cooperation with international organizations where appropriate, to take all necessary measures to ensure respect for the principles of refugee protection, including the humane treatment of asylum-seekers;

10. *Urges* States to uphold the civilian and humanitarian character of refugee camps and settlements, inter alia, through effective measures to prevent the infiltration of armed elements, to identify and separate any such armed elements from refugee populations, to settle refugees in secure locations and to afford the Office of the High Commissioner and other appropriate humanitarian organizations prompt, unhindered and safe access to asylum-seekers, refugees and other persons of concern;

11. *Welcomes* the coming into force of the Convention on the Safety of United Nations and Associated Personnel as well as the consideration of initiatives to widen its *ratione personae*, and calls upon States and all concerned parties to take all possible measures to safeguard the physical security and property of the staff of the Office of the High Commissioner and other humanitarian personnel, to investigate fully any crime committed against them and to bring to justice persons responsible for such crimes;

12. *Urges* all States and relevant organizations to support the High Commissioner's search for durable solutions to refugee problems, including voluntary repatriation, local integration and resettlement in a third country, as appropriate, reaffirms that voluntary repatriation is the preferred solution to refugee problems, and calls upon countries of origin, countries of asylum, the Office of the High Commissioner and the international community to act in a spirit of partnership to enable refugees to exercise their right to return home in safety and with dignity;

13. *Calls upon* all States to promote conditions conducive to the voluntary repatriation of refugees in safety and with dignity, including conditions furthering reconciliation and long-term development in countries of return, and to support the sustainable reintegration of returnees by providing countries of origin with necessary rehabilitation and development assistance in conjunction, as appropriate, with the Office of the High Commissioner and relevant development agencies, and urges the Office of the High Commissioner to strengthen its cooperation and coordination with relevant entities, including international financial institutions and non-governmental organizations;

14. *Reiterates* the right of all persons to return to their country of origin, emphasizes in this regard the obligation of all States to accept the return of their nationals, calls upon all States to facilitate the return of their nationals who have sought asylum and have been determined not to be in need of international protection, and affirms the need for the return of persons to be undertaken in a humane manner and with full respect for their human rights and dignity, irrespective of the status of the persons concerned;

15. *Acknowledges* the desirability of comprehensive approaches by the international community, including comprehensive regional approaches, to the problems of refugees and displaced persons, and notes in this regard that capacity-building in countries of origin and countries of asylum can play an important role in addressing the root causes of refugee flows, in strengthening emergency preparedness and response and in providing effective protection and achieving durable solutions;

16. *Urges* States, in cooperation with the Office of the High Commissioner and other relevant organizations, to explore and support fully capacity-building initiatives as part of a comprehensive approach to addressing refugee issues and to take necessary measures to promote sustainable development and to ensure the success of capacity-building activities, and reiterates that such initiatives may include those which strengthen legal and judicial institutions and civil society, those which promote the observance of human rights, the rule of law and accountability and those which enhance the capacity of States to fulfil their responsibilities with respect to persons of concern to the Office of the High Commissioner;

17. *Reiterates its support* for the role of the Office of the High Commissioner in providing humanitarian assistance and protection to internally displaced persons on the basis of criteria enumerated in paragraph 16 of its resolution 53/125, and underlines the continuing relevance of the Guiding Principles on Internal Displacement;

18. *Calls upon* States to adopt an approach that is sensitive to gender-related concerns and to ensure that women whose claims to refugee status are based upon a well-founded fear of persecution for reasons enumerated in the 1951 Convention and the 1967 Protocol, including persecution through sexual violence or other gender-related persecution, are recognized as refugees, and encourages the Office of the High Commissioner to continue and to strengthen its efforts for the protection of refugee women;

19. *Urges* States and relevant parties to respect and observe principles of international human rights, humanitarian and refugee law that are of particular relevance to safeguarding the rights of child and adolescent refugees, notes the particular vulnerability of refugee children to being forcibly exposed to the risks of injury, exploitation and death, in particular in the context of armed conflict, and to abduction with a view

to their forced participation in military activities, and urges all States and concerned parties to take all possible measures to protect child and adolescent refugees, including, in particular, from all forms of violence, exploitation and abuse and forced military service, and to prevent their separation from their families;

20. *Recognizes* the special role of elderly refugees within the refugee family, and, bearing in mind that 1999 has been declared the International Year of Older Persons, calls upon States and the Office of the High Commissioner to make renewed efforts to ensure that the rights, needs and dignity of elderly refugees are fully respected and addressed through appropriate programme activities;

21. *Recalls* that the family is the natural and fundamental group unit of society and that it is entitled to protection by society and the State, and calls upon States, working in close collaboration with the Office of the High Commissioner and other concerned organizations, to take measures to ensure that the refugee's family is protected, including through measures aimed at reuniting family members separated as a result of refugee flight;

22. *Notes* that forty-eight States are now parties to the 1954 Convention relating to the Status of Stateless Persons and that twenty States are parties to the 1961 Convention on the reduction of statelessness, recalls paragraphs 14 to 16 of its resolution 50/152 of 21 December 1995, and encourages the High Commissioner to continue her activities on behalf of stateless persons;

23. *Calls upon* Governments and other donors to demonstrate their international solidarity and burden-sharing with countries of asylum, in particular developing countries, countries with economies in transition and countries with limited resources that, owing to their location, host large numbers of refugees and asylum-seekers, stresses the need for the Office of the High Commissioner to be given adequate resources to fulfil its mandated functions, and in this regard calls upon Governments to contribute generously to the unified annual programme budget of the Office of the High Commissioner, to support efforts to widen the donor base so as to achieve greater burden-sharing among donors and to assist the High Commissioner in securing additional and timely income from traditional governmental sources, other Governments and the private sector to ensure that the needs of refugees, returnees and displaced persons of concern to the Office of the High Commissioner are fully met.

Enlargement of the Executive Committee

ECONOMIC AND SOCIAL COUNCIL ACTION

In accordance with decision 1998/302 [YUN 1998, p. 1111], the Economic and Social Council considered a note verbale from Côte d'Ivoire requesting admission to membership of the UNHCR Executive Committee [E/1998/97] and a draft decision on enlargement of the Committee [E/1998/L.53]. By **decision 1999/207** of 2 February, the Council took note of the request by Côte d'Ivoire and recommended that the General Assembly take a decision at its resumed fifty-third (1999) session on the question of enlarging the Committee's membership from 54 to 55.

At its substantive session in July, the Council had before it notes verbales from Chile [E/1999/112] and the Republic of Korea [E/1999/76] requesting membership of the Committee.

By **decision 1999/282** of 30 July, the Council took note of the requests from Chile and the Republic of Korea and recommended that the Assembly take a decision on the question of enlarging the Committee's membership from 55 to 57 States at its fifty-fourth (1999) session.

GENERAL ASSEMBLY ACTION

On 17 December [meeting 83], the General Assembly, on the recommendation of the Third Committee [A/54/600], adopted **resolution 54/143** without vote [agenda item 111].

Enlargement of the Executive Committee of the Programme of the United Nations High Commissioner for Refugees

The General Assembly,

Taking note of Economic and Social Council decisions 1999/207 of 2 February 1999 and 1999/282 of 30 July 1999 concerning the enlargement of the Executive Committee of the Programme of the United Nations High Commissioner for Refugees,

Taking note also of the requests regarding the enlargement of the Executive Committee contained in the note verbale dated 13 August 1998 from the Permanent Mission of Côte d'Ivoire to the United Nations addressed to the Secretary-General, the note verbale dated 26 May 1999 from the Permanent Mission of the Republic of Korea to the United Nations addressed to the Secretary-General and the note verbale dated 20 July 1999 from the Permanent Mission of Chile to the United Nations addressed to the Secretary-General,

1. *Decides* to increase the number of members of the Executive Committee of the Programme of the United Nations High Commissioner for Refugees from fifty-four to fifty-seven States;

2. *Requests* the Economic and Social Council to elect the additional members at its organizational session for 2000.

Financial and administrative questions

For 1999, UNHCR's initial budget (covering both General and Special Programmes) was $915 million [A/55/12], 10 per cent lower than that of 1998 ($1.1 billion). Of that amount, $413 million was allocated for General Programmes and $482 million for Special Programmes. The year was characterized by three successive emergencies (Kosovo, East Timor and the northern Caucasus) and by budget reductions due to funding shortfalls in several other General and Special Programmes, particularly in Africa. In the course of the year, overall requirements increased to $1,183.7 million, due mainly to the Kosovo emergency. Total contributions reached $911.6 million, an increase of $142.6 million over 1998. Despite the fact that the initial budget was $27 million lower than in 1998 and that some donors increased their contributions, General Programmes again faced a funding shortfall and UNHCR had to borrow $7.5 million from the Working Capital and Guarantee Fund to maintain the Emergency Fund at its statutory level. The Office was also forced to restrict or cancel a number of non-life-saving activities both in the field and at headquarters. Limited recourse to the Programme Reserve and the Voluntary Repatriation Fund also helped to match budgets with income.

During the year, the initial needs for Special Programmes were increased to $770.7 million, due mainly to the Kosovo debacle, and to small increased needs in Africa and in Asia. Some individual programmes began with little carry-over funds from 1998 and received only partial funding, resulting in the need to continually readjust operational budgets and programme implementation. Programmes particularly affected were the repatriation/rehabilitation programmes in West Africa, Rwanda, the Great Lakes region of Africa and Liberia. Programmes for the countries of the Commonwealth of Independent States (CIS), the Horn of Africa and south-eastern Europe also received insufficient funding to cover planned activities. Against the revised target, only $584.7 million was received during the year.

UNHCR continued informal consultations on a unified budget structure and on pledging mechanisms, scheduled to begin in January 2000. It also published its first *Global Report* (covering the 1998 programme year), providing comprehensive documentation for donors and others on programme implementation, achievement of objectives and financial reporting. Increased contributions from private and corporate sources reached $31.8 million, nearly three times more than in 1998.

UNHCR expenditures by region in 1999 were as follows: Africa, $292.2 million; Asia and the Pacific, $78.2 million; Europe (including the countries of the former Yugoslavia), $437.3 million; the Americas, $26.4 million; Central and South-West Asia, and North Africa and the Middle East, $76.1 million.

For 2000, the Executive Committee approved budgetary requirements of $933.5 million. By 31 December, total needs had increased to $965.2 million through the addition of supplementary programmes for Sierra Leonean refugees and for the situation in East Timor.

In October [A/54/12/Add.1], the Executive Committee approved the revised 1999 General Programmes budget amounting to $413 million and noted the new revised Special Programmes budget of $741.2 million. It also approved the (unified) programmes and budgets for regional operations, global operations and headquarters for 2000 (annual programme budget) amounting to $933.6 million, including an operational reserve of $82.1 million (representing 10 per cent of programmed activities). It requested the High Commissioner, within the resources available, to respond flexibly and efficiently to needs currently indicated under the annual programme budget for 2000 and as outlined in the Global Appeal.

Accounts (1998)

The audited financial statements on voluntary funds administered by UNHCR for the year ending 31 December 1998 [A/54/5/Add.5] showed total expenditures of $974.3 million and total income of $820.1 million, with a reserve balance of $190.6 million.

The Board of Auditors' main findings were: the financial statements and schedules of the voluntary funds generally conformed to UN accounting standards, except for recognition of income for trust funds and disclosure of liabilities for end-of-service benefits; of the $346.4 million advanced to implementing partners during 1998 and recorded as expenditure, financial reports had not been received for $92.8 million as at 31 March 1999, and audit certificates had not been received in respect of $97 million advanced to government partners and $234.5 million advanced to other implementing partners; projects reviewed at headquarters and in the field did not contain work plans or milestones for project implementation; of 2,565 projects implemented between 1994 and 1997, 2,123 (83 per cent) had not been closed as at November 1998; and although action in many of the key areas of Project Delphi was scheduled to have been completed by October 1997, the activity was either at the draft stage or was yet to commence as at April 1999.

The Board recommended that the Administration should: treat advances to implementing partners as accounts receivable at the time they were made and clear the advances to expenditure on receipt of satisfactory financial reports; assess the reasons for non-compliance by governmental and non-governmental implementing partners with the requirement to render audit certificates as prescribed in the sub-agreements and draw up a strategy for securing audit certificates; ensure that work plans were programme-specific and were prepared as an integral part of the project-planning and monitoring process; exercise stricter control of the progress of work of implementing partners in order to ensure achievement of stated objectives; review completed projects to ensure that they were promptly closed; and update plans still to be implemented under Project Delphi.

Reporting on measures taken or proposed to respond to the recommendations of the Board of Auditors [A/AC.96/917/Add.1], UNHCR noted that balances due from partners had been significantly reduced due to intensified efforts to obtain reports and the introduction of measures to withhold further instalments if those reports were not forthcoming. As to work plans, it was pointed out that while the requirement to prepare work plans was integral to the Office, many UNHCR projects covered recurrent activities to assist refugees and thus work plans would be repetitive. Also, in emergency situations, UNHCR needed to respond rapidly and work plans could easily become ineffectual when situations were volatile. Nevertheless, it was projected that a template would be provided for implementation, whenever applicable, in 2000. With regard to Project Delphi, it was recognized that actions foreseen in the 1996 Action Plan were overly ambitious in terms of the estimated time frame.

In an October report [A/54/441], the Advisory Committee on Administrative and Budgetary Questions (ACABQ) noted that, although considerable progress had been made in clearing outstanding balances of cash advances to implementing partners, the problem of timely receipt of audit certificates, especially from government implementing partners, persisted. It expressed concern that UNHCR referred to its influence over government partners as limited. The certification process was an important element of accountability and before a decision was made to pay government auditors, the cost effectiveness of such an option should be determined after all others had been explored. ACABQ recommended that UNHCR formulate the criteria for and conditions under which such assistance should be granted, including guidelines to ensure delivery of services to concerned implementing government partners.

In its general decision on administrative, financial and programme matters [A/54/12/Add.1], the Executive Committee asked to be kept informed of measures taken to address the recommendations and observations raised by ACABQ and the Board of Auditors.

GENERAL ASSEMBLY ACTION

On 23 December [meeting 88], the General Assembly, on the recommendation of the Fifth (Administrative and Budgetary) Committee [A/54/506/Add.1], adopted **resolution 54/13 B** without vote [agenda item 117].

Financial reports and audited financial statements, and reports of the Board of Auditors

The General Assembly,

Having considered, for the year ended 31 December 1998, the audited financial statements and the report of the Board of Auditors on voluntary funds administered by the United Nations High Commissioner for Refugees, the report of the Secretary-General on the implementation of the recommendations of the Board of Auditors, the report of the Board of Auditors on the implementation of its recommendations, the report of the Secretary-General on the year 2000 compliance issue, the report of the Secretary-General on the hiring and use of consultants in the Secretariat and the comments of the Board of Auditors thereon, and the report of the Advisory Committee on Administrative and Budgetary Questions,

1. *Notes* the measures taken by the United Nations High Commissioner for Refugees to implement the recommendations of the Board of Auditors;
2. *Accepts* the audited financial statements and the report of the Board of Auditors on voluntary funds administered by the United Nations High Commissioner for Refugees;
3. *Approves* all the recommendations and conclusions contained in the report of the Board of Auditors, and endorses the observations and recommendations contained in the report of the Advisory Committee on Administrative and Budgetary Questions, subject to the provisions of the present resolution;
4. *Commends* the Board of Auditors for the improvement in the format of its report;
5. *Takes note* of the report of the Secretary-General on the implementation of the recommendations of the Board of Auditors;
6. *Accepts* the report of the Board of Auditors on the implementation of its recommendations;
7. *Takes note* of the report of the Secretary-General on the hiring and use of consultants in the Secretariat and the comments of the Board of Auditors thereon;
8. *Requests* the Secretary-General to continue to implement the guidelines for the hiring and use of consultants and individual contractors in the Secretariat, in full conformity with the provisions of section VIII of its resolution 53/221 of 7 April 1999;
9. *Requests* the Board of Auditors to monitor the implementation of the guidelines for the hiring and use of consultants and individual contractors in the Secretariat as revised by the General Assembly in paragraph 11 of section VIII of its resolution 53/221;
10. *Also requests* the Board of Auditors to monitor the implementation of the provisions of section VIII of its resolution 53/221 on consultants and individual contractors.

Standing Committee

The Standing Committee held three meetings in 1999 (9-11 February [A/AC.96/913]; 28 June-1 July [A/AC.96/924]; and 28-29 September [A/AC.96/927]). It considered a number of recurrent items and conducted in-depth reviews of UNHCR programmes and activities in different regions. Africa and Central Asia, South-West Asia, and North Africa and the Middle East were reviewed in February; the Americas, Europe and the former Yugoslavia, in June; and Asia and the Pacific, in September. Updates on overall programme and funding issues, including a proposal for a new UNHCR budget structure, were also discussed. Programme/protection policy issues were reviewed, as were UNHCR's efforts on behalf of refugee women, the Office's emergency preparedness and response capacity, the economic and social impact of massive refugee populations on host developing countries, and issues relating to detention and family protection. In September, the Standing Committee received an update on the independent evaluation of UNHCR emergency preparedness for and response to the Kosovo refugee crisis.

In October [A/54/12/Add.1], the Executive Committee requested UNHCR to include in the documentation on each item of the Standing Committee's 2000 programme of work the relevant audit and recommendations of ACABQ, as well as steps taken to implement those recommendations and related Executive Committee decisions and conclusions. It authorized the Standing Committee to add and delete items, as appropriate, to its inter-sessional programme of work. The items adopted for the 2000 programme of work were: international protection; programme/protection policy; programme and funding; governance; coordination; and management, financial, oversight and human resources.

Safety of staff

At its fourteenth meeting (9-11 February) [A/AC.96/913], the Standing Committee discussed the issue of staff safety, including the release of Vincent Cochetel, head of the UNHCR office in the northern Caucasus, after 11 months of captivity. In that context, it noted that training remained an important element of UNHCR's efforts to protect its staff, but the responsibility of States and authorities on the ground was also crucial. The recent entry into force of the 1994 Convention on the Safety of United Nations and Associated Personnel, adopted by the General Assembly in resolution 49/59 [YUN 1994, p. 1289], was welcomed.

Refugee protection and assistance

Protection issues

In her annual report covering 1999 [A/55/12], the High Commissioner said that many States, particularly in Africa, continued to honour their humanitarian obligations towards refugees and generously offered protection to those in need. Other countries provided generous financial and material support or established special admission programmes. Despite those positive trends, however, systematic violations of human rights, blatant disregard of humanitarian law, wholesale expulsions of populations and large-scale ethnic cleansing caused significant displacement both internally and across borders in many regions. Denial of access to protection, including through closure of borders, non-admission to territory or to asylum procedures, or through direct or indirect refoulement and other acts that seriously endangered the life and physical security of refugees and asylum-seekers, continued to occur. Large numbers of individuals within UNHCR's mandate were also subject to detention or similar restrictive measures in different parts of the world.

In a July note [A/AC.96/914], the High Commissioner stated that the sheer magnitude of post-cold-war problems, the levels of national and regional insecurity they generated and State reluctance to continue to meet what were seen as the rising financial, political, environmental and social costs of maintaining large refugee populations or receiving a continuous flow, had a negative impact on countries' willingness to provide asylum.

UNHCR had detected a distinct trend in an increasing number of States to move away from a law- or rights-based approach to refugee protection towards more discretionary and ad hoc arrangements that gave greater primacy to domestic concerns rather than to international responsibilities. Some States blamed the present refugee problem on conflicts rather than on persecution as defined in the 1951 Convention relating to the Status of Refugees [YUN 1951, p. 520]. Consequently, calls had been made for an alternative refugee protection regime to that Convention. However, the General Assembly and the Executive Committee had continued to emphasize the primacy of both the Convention and its 1967 Protocol [YUN 1967, p. 477] and had confirmed that they formed the international legal basis for protecting refugees.

The High Commissioner pointed out that sovereign discretion as to the granting of protection to refugees was circumscribed by a plethora of human rights and refugee law responsibilities freely entered into. In balancing States' interests against those standards, it was fundamental to define clearly which responsibilities, irrespective of financial and political costs, could not be departed from. UNHCR had organized a series of regional seminars at which proposals were made for improving asylum activities and diminishing related costs. A consistent theme emanating from the discussions was the need to revitalize old and build new partnerships in support of the international refugee protection system. To that end, during 1999, UNHCR continued to promote collaboration on refugee protection through the "Reach Out" consultative process, initiated in

1998 to engage non-State actors in dialogues on the nature and dimensions of current protection challenges. UNHCR hoped that by the end of the century, a global partnership for refugee protection would re-emerge.

The High Commissioner also outlined the situation regarding refugee groups with special protection needs, such as women, children, the elderly, those with HIV/AIDS, those caught in situations of armed conflict and internally displaced persons. Other issues addressed included voluntary repatriation, resettlement and integration, statelessness and temporary protection.

In an October conclusion [A/54/12/Add.1], the Executive Committee reaffirmed that the 1951 Convention and its 1967 Protocol remained the foundation of the international refugee regime. However, it recognized that there might be a need to develop complementary forms of protection. In that context, it encouraged UNHCR to consult with States and relevant actors to examine all aspects of the issue. The Committee called on States to promote and protect the rights of all refugees and expressed concern that refugees with special protection needs, including women and children, were increasingly targets of exploitation, forced military service and various forms of violence. The Committee reiterated that voluntary repatriation, where and when feasible, remained the preferred solution in the majority of refugee situations.

International instruments

In 1999, Georgia and Kazakhstan became parties to the 1951 Convention relating to the Status of Refugees [YUN 1951, p. 520] and its 1967 Protocol [YUN 1967, p. 477], bringing the number of States party to one or both instruments to 134. Chad, Latvia, Saint Vincent and the Grenadines and Swaziland became parties to the 1954 Convention relating to the Status of Stateless Persons [YUN 1954, p. 416], bringing the number of States party to that instrument to 49. With the accession of Chad and Swaziland, the number of States party to the 1961 Convention on the Reduction of Statelessness [YUN 1961, p. 533] reached 21.

UNHCR continued its two-year global campaign, launched in 1998 [YUN 1998, p. 1114], to promote States' accession to the 1951 Convention and its Protocol, as well as to the 1954 and 1961 Conventions.

Promotional activities

UNHCR's promotional activities in 1999 were directed at raising public awareness and strengthening knowledge and understanding of refugee issues, in addition to fostering implementation of international legal standards on behalf of refugees, returnees and other persons of concern. Activities were also undertaken to strengthen linkages between refugee law, human rights law and international humanitarian law aimed at ensuring better measures to protect refugees. Those activities also aimed to promote incorporating relevant international legal standards into national legislation and administrative procedures. UNHCR increased its regional promotional activities and engaged in dialogue with non-governmental organizations (NGOs). The publication of a *Field Protection Guide for NGOs* was one result of those efforts.

UNHCR continued to strengthen its relationship with human rights bodies, monitoring the work of the Commission on Human Rights, the Commission's Subcommission on the Promotion and Protection of Human Rights and the six UN treaty bodies. It strengthened its monitoring of and collaboration with human rights components of regional bodies such as the Council of Europe, the European Court of Human Rights, the Organization for Security and Cooperation in Europe, the Organization of African Unity (OAU) and the Asian-African Legal Consultative Committee to reinforce understanding of international refugee protection within those groups.

Assistance measures

The global population of concern to UNHCR increased slightly during 1999, reaching 22.3 million, compared with 21.5 million in 1998. Those assisted included asylum-seekers, refugees, returning refugees in the early stages of their reintegration, internally displaced persons and other populations of concern, mainly victims of conflict. However, the global figure did not reflect the dramatic and massive humanitarian crises that arose during the year. Conflicts in Kosovo, East Timor and Chechnya dominated media reports and absorbed a large portion of UNHCR's resources, while many other humanitarian crises around the world, particularly in Africa, received less attention.

In Kosovo, some 350,000 people were displaced in the first three months of the year, and between March and June, more than 850,000 ethnic Albanians fled to other parts of the Federal Republic of Yugoslavia (FRY) or to neighbouring countries, mainly Albania and the former Yugoslav Republic of Macedonia (FYROM). The humanitarian challenges temporarily exceeded the capacities of UNHCR and its humanitarian partners. Following the establishment of the United Nations Interim Administration Mission in Kosovo (see PART ONE, Chapter V), the majority of the refugees returned to Kosovo almost as swiftly as they had fled.

UNHCR quickly transformed its programme from a refugee relief operation into an equally ambitious repatriation and reintegration effort. The eruption of violence in East Timor following the 30 August referendum on independence (see PART ONE, Chapter IV), provoked the displacement of some 500,000 persons within East Timor and an estimated 200,000 fled to West Timor and other areas of Indonesia. UNHCR responded to their immediate humanitarian needs by providing emergency relief, transportation and petrol. From October, UNHCR conducted a large-scale voluntary repatriation operation. With the outbreak of conflict in October in Chechnya, over 200,000 people fled into neighbouring republics, particularly Ingushetia. UNHCR provided assistance through a UN inter-agency emergency assistance programme (see PART THREE, Chapter III).

Meanwhile, in the absence of international support for other smaller but equally urgent humanitarian disasters, situations of fragile peace often deteriorated into renewed conflict and unresolved regional wars led to the outbreak of smaller sub-conflicts, precipitating further population displacements. The persistence of those situations underscored that stabilization and post-conflict recovery were essential if the consequences of conflicts were to be adequately addressed. UNHCR encouraged the international community to adopt broader, regionally based peace-building approaches to assist regions and countries aspiring to emerge from the spiral of conflict, poverty and human displacement. However, the gap between humanitarian and reconstruction activities continued to be very wide, which UNHCR sought to narrow both within the context of the Brookings process and the Inter-Agency Standing Committee. It also reviewed its responsibility to internally displaced persons, adopting a policy of preparedness to respond to calls by the international community to assist them, for example in Angola.

In 1999, UNHCR received over $900 million in voluntary contributions towards its General and Special Programmes. Assistance included emergency preparedness, response and assistance; care and maintenance; voluntary repatriation; local settlement; and resettlement. Following the emergency phase of an operation, the basic needs of refugees were covered by care and maintenance activities, which provided essential services such as the provision of food, household goods and cooking/heating materials; shelter; construction and maintenance of drinking water sources; and construction and operation of health and education facilities, among others.

Voluntary repatriation remained the preferred solution to refugee problems, but, unless convinced that refugees could return to their countries of origin in reasonable safety, UNHCR did not actively promote return. However, the Office did organize and facilitate a number of existing spontaneous return movements after ensuring that the legal framework existed to protect the rights and interests of returnees. It also facilitated reintegration of those who returned. Resettlement to third countries was promoted when no other durable solution was feasible.

Refugees and the environment

In 1999, responding to the need for improved monitoring of its environmental activities, UNHCR launched a three-year project to develop appropriate methods for conducting environmental assessments and monitoring in different phases of refugee operations and in varying environmental situations. The project, which used a combination of practical and sophisticated tools, ranging from simple participatory appraisals to remote sensing, focused primarily on Guinea and Uganda, while preliminary outputs were scheduled to be extensively tested in other countries. Expected outputs were a tool kit for UNHCR staff and implementing agencies, functional databases and a specially designed training component. With input from training events and feedback from the field, a training manual, *Environmental Management within Refugee Operations*, was revised.

Tailor-made demonstration projects, patterned after the 1996 *Environmental Guidelines* [YUN 1996, p. 1108], were designed and supported in Afghanistan (environmental protection and management), Djibouti (gender and environment), Liberia (strengthening environmental issues), the Sudan (community integration) and Zimbabwe (permaculture). Other projects provided essential support to natural resource management initiatives, forest-related activities, promotion of energy-saving devices and practices, environmental education, data collection and analysis, and environmental mapping.

Refugee women

During 1999, UNHCR continued to implement a targeted strategy for the advancement of refugee women and gender mainstreaming. A gender equality perspective was integrated in several key training packages, field guidelines and checklists, and the new project description format that specifically required field staff to indicate how each project would address the particular needs and rights of refugee women was introduced. Four senior regional advisers for refugee women were appointed to coordinate implementation of region-specific strategies. In Africa, those activities included a project targeting five sub-Saharan countries to prevent and respond to sexual and gender-based violence, reproductive rights-awareness training campaigns to eliminate harmful traditional practices, and gender-sensitive mine-awareness training.

In Eastern Europe and Central Asia, strategic frameworks for gender mainstreaming and gender-sensitive performance indicators were developed. In addition, income-generation projects for urban refugee women and rights-awareness seminars on issues such as domestic violence and human rights were held. In Mexico, migratory documents were provided to both female and male refugees and legislative reforms regarding land ownership by women refugees were adopted. In the Middle East, health programmes for women, education for girls, rights-awareness training and microcredit schemes for women remained priorities.

Promotion of gender-sensitive asylum procedures in countries of asylum included training and support to Governments and NGOs.

In October [A/54/12/Add.1], the Executive Committee encouraged States, UNHCR and other concerned actors to promote wider acceptance and inclusion in their protection criteria of the notion that persecution could be gender-related or effected through sexual violence. It encouraged UNHCR and other actors to develop, promote and implement guidelines, codes of conduct and training programmes on gender-related issues.

Refugee children and adolescents

UNHCR's activities relating to refugee children and adolescents included an increasingly concerted follow-up to the UN study on the impact of armed conflict on children (the Machel Study) [YUN 1996, p. 663], which improved its response in particular areas of concern. The Office made progress in the Action for the Rights of Children training and capacity-building project, a collaborative effort initiated in 1997 by UNHCR and the Save the Children Alliance. In 1999, it was extended to include the United Nations Children's Fund (UNICEF) and the Office of the United Nations High Commissioner for Human Rights. Child rights-based performance objectives for all phases of its operations in complex emergencies, with a fundamental requirement that girls and boys benefited equally from all programmes, were established, as were plans of action on protection and assistance measures at the country level, sexual exploitation and violence, underage military recruitment, education, and unaccompanied minors and adolescents.

Inter-agency coordination and cooperation with NGOs was actively pursued through initiatives, including the joint UNHCR and Save the Children Alliance Separated Children in Europe programme, UNHCR's participation in forums such as the Inter-Agency Group on Separated Children and through the Office's support for a study on the untapped potential of adolescents affected by armed conflict, undertaken by the Women's Commission for Refugee Women and Children. Four regional policy officers for refugee children oversaw UNHCR's protection and programming on behalf of refugee children and adolescents, and a senior regional policy officer was appointed in September to oversee the work of the Separated Children in Europe programme.

Report of Secretary-General. In response to General Assembly resolution 53/122 [YUN 1998, p. 1117], the Secretary-General submitted a September report on assistance to unaccompanied refugee minors [A/54/285], defined as those who were separated from both parents and were not being cared for by a legally responsible adult. The report reviewed new developments in family tracing and reunification, the Separated Children in Europe programme, the Action for the Rights of Children project, the 1989 Convention on the Rights of the Child, adopted by the Assembly in resolution 44/25 [YUN 1989, p. 560], action on behalf of internally displaced children and child soldiers, and efforts to strengthen UNHCR's field network. It also addressed issues of concern, such as the girl child (see p. 1090) and adoption of separated children.

The Secretary-General noted that a major outstanding challenge concerned the criteria for selecting foster families and systematic follow-up, for which resources were often limited. Although community-based strategies went some way in addressing the issues, separated children, particularly girls, remained at risk for some form of exploitation. Until civilians in general were protected from the impact of warfare or from serious human rights violations, increasing numbers of children would continue to be exposed to the additional trauma and danger of separation. Member States were urged to adhere to and promote the 1989 Convention.

Successful efforts by the United Nations and other agencies and organizations to assist unaccompanied refugee minors included the reunification of 62,000 children with their families in Rwanda by UNHCR, together with UNICEF and ICRC. However, 5,000 still remained in centres, many of whom were small children unable to give any information. The joint UNHCR/UNICEF Liberian Children's Initiative had been instrumental in reuniting 78 children with their families. In

1999, the Special Representative of the Secretary-General for children and armed conflict (see p. 674) proposed a "neighbourhood initiative", which aimed to obtain commitments from Governments and insurgency groups to protect children from cross-border threats and abuse. Three such neighbourhoods, in West Africa, East Africa and Kosovo, were proposed for implementation of the initiative. The Special Representative had also been active in seeking a solution to the problem of the abduction of children from northern Uganda to southern Sudan by members of an armed group, the Lord's Resistance Army. A small number of those children were released and their return to their families in Uganda was then facilitated by UNHCR, in coordination with UNICEF and local NGOs. Inter-agency cooperation involving UNHCR, ICRC and UNICEF also played an important role in tracing efforts during the Kosovo emergency. However, there were fewer child-family separations there than in other recent refugee crises. By early August, only 33 cases were pending solution.

GENERAL ASSEMBLY ACTION

On 17 December [meeting 83], the General Assembly, on the recommendation of the Third Committee [A/54/600], adopted **resolution 54/145** without vote [agenda item 111].

Assistance to unaccompanied refugee minors

The General Assembly,

Recalling its resolutions 49/172 of 23 December 1994, 50/150 of 21 December 1995, 51/73 of 12 December 1996, 52/105 of 12 December 1997 and 53/122 of 9 December 1998,

Aware of the fact that the majority of refugees are children and women,

Bearing in mind that unaccompanied refugee minors are among the most vulnerable refugees and the most at risk of neglect, violence, forced military recruitment, sexual assault and other abuses and therefore require special assistance and care,

Mindful of the fact that the ultimate solution to the plight of unaccompanied refugee minors is their return to and reunification with their families,

Noting the revised Guidelines on Refugee Children issued by the Office of the United Nations High Commissioner for Refugees in May 1994 and the development of an emergency kit to facilitate coordination and enhance the quality of responses to the needs of unaccompanied minors by the Office of the High Commissioner, the United Nations Children's Fund and non-governmental organizations,

Noting with appreciation the efforts of the Office of the United Nations High Commissioner for Refugees and the United Nations Children's Fund in the identification and tracing of unaccompanied refugee minors, and welcoming their efforts in reunifying families of refugees,

Welcoming the efforts exerted by the United Nations High Commissioner for Refugees to reunite refugees with their families,

Noting the efforts of the High Commissioner to ensure the protection of and assistance to refugees, including children and unaccompanied minors, and that further enhanced efforts need to be exerted to this effect,

Recalling the provisions of the Convention on the Rights of the Child and the 1951 Convention and the 1967 Protocol relating to the Status of Refugees,

1. *Takes note* of the report of the Secretary-General;

2. *Also takes note* of the report of the Special Representative of the Secretary-General for Children and Armed Conflict;

3. *Expresses its deep concern* at the continued plight of unaccompanied refugee minors, and emphasizes once again the urgent need for their early identification and for timely, detailed and accurate information on their number and whereabouts;

4. *Stresses* the importance of providing adequate resources for programmes of identification and tracing of unaccompanied refugee minors;

5. *Calls upon* the Office of the United Nations High Commissioner for Refugees, in cooperation with other relevant United Nations bodies, to incorporate into its programmes policies that aim at preventing the separation of refugee families, conscious of the importance of family unity;

6. *Calls upon* all Governments, the Secretary-General, the Office of the High Commissioner, all United Nations organizations, other international organizations and non-governmental organizations concerned to exert the maximum effort to assist and protect refugee minors and to expedite the return to and reunification with their families of unaccompanied refugee minors;

7. *Urges* the Office of the High Commissioner, all United Nations organizations, other international organizations and non-governmental organizations concerned to take appropriate steps to mobilize resources commensurate with the needs and interests of unaccompanied refugee minors and for their reunification with their families;

8. *Calls upon* all States and other parties to armed conflict to respect international humanitarian law, and, in this regard, calls upon States parties to respect fully the provisions of the Geneva Conventions of 12 August 1949 and related instruments, while bearing in mind resolution 2 adopted at the twenty-sixth International Conference of the Red Cross and Red Crescent, held at Geneva in December 1995, and to respect the provisions of the Convention on the Rights of the Child, which accord children affected by armed conflict special protection and treatment;

9. *Condemns* all acts of exploitation of unaccompanied refugee minors, including their use as soldiers or human shields in armed conflict and their forced recruitment into military forces, and any other acts that endanger their safety and personal security;

10. *Calls upon* the Secretary-General, the United Nations High Commissioner for Refugees, the Office for the Coordination of Humanitarian Affairs of the Secretariat, the United Nations Children's Fund, other United Nations organizations and other international organizations to mobilize adequate assistance to unaccompanied refugee minors in the areas of relief, education, health and psychological rehabilitation;

11. *Encourages* the Special Representative of the Secretary-General in his efforts to raise awareness

worldwide and to mobilize official and public opinion for the protection of children affected by armed conflict, including refugee minors;

12. *Requests* the Secretary-General to report to the General Assembly at its fifty-sixth session on the implementation of the present resolution and to give special attention to the girl-child refugee in his report.

Elderly refugees

With the observance of the International Year of Older Persons in 1999 (see PART THREE, Chapter XI), UNHCR was provided with an opportunity to re-examine its approaches to the mental and physical needs of elderly refugees and other older persons of concern to the Office. A range of materials featuring the situation of older refugees was published, and the Office, along with the Humanitarian Office of the European Community, jointly commissioned a study on the elderly in refugee emergencies, which covered all sectors, from health to shelter. UNHCR also formulated a policy on older refugees.

In a decision on special protection needs adopted in October [A/54/12/Add.1], the Executive Committee called on States, UNHCR and other concerned actors, taking into account that elderly refugees were particularly affected by social disintegration, chronic dependency and other adverse aspects of the refugee condition, to make renewed efforts to ensure that the rights, needs and dignity of elderly refugees were fully respected and addressed through appropriate programme activities.

Regional activities

Africa

Report of Secretary-General. In a September report on assistance to refugees, returnees and displaced persons in Africa [A/54/414], prepared in response to General Assembly resolution 53/126 [YUN 1998, p. 1119], the Secretary-General stated that some 15 African countries were currently embroiled in armed conflict (see PART ONE, Chapter II) and there were some 6 million persons of concern to UNHCR on the continent, namely refugees, internally displaced persons and returnees. The main refugee groups on the continent comprised over half a million Sierra Leoneans in West Africa, 280,000 Burundians in the United Republic of Tanzania and 180,000 Congolese who had fled from the conflict in the Democratic Republic of the Congo (DRC) to various countries. Movements also took place from the Republic of the Congo to the DRC and Gabon. Because of security problems in major returnee areas, the Liberian repatriation programme was interrupted and the planned repatriation of 250,000 people was put on hold.

Referring to older, unresolved conflict situations in Africa, the report noted that more than 370,000 Sudanese were still refugees in Ethiopia and Uganda; 165,000 Saharawi refugees were still in camps in Algeria and other countries; and there were 150,000 Angolan refugees, mostly in the DRC. In Angola and the Sudan, as well as in the war-torn areas on the border between Eritrea and Ethiopia, were tens of thousands of internally displaced people. In the DRC, UNHCR was providing assistance to 700,000 displaced persons in accessible areas within the country, while another 180,000 refugees were being assisted in Burundi, the Central African Republic, Rwanda, the United Republic of Tanzania and Zambia. In Liberia, 280,000 refugees had returned home and it was hoped that the remaining quarter of a million would be repatriated by mid-2000.

The situation in the Great Lakes region in 1999 continued to be volatile, engendering new waves of population movements. Consequently, with little prospect of rapid solutions for the resulting groups of refugees, UNHCR continued to provide care and maintenance assistance. Meanwhile, return movements had dwindled in Burundi because the optimism that accompanied the lifting of sanctions in January and improved relations with the United Republic of Tanzania gave way to disappointment as insecurity spread to provinces bordering Tanzania. Following a tripartite agreement signed in April by UNHCR with the Governments of the Republic of the Congo and the DRC, repatriation of refugees who had entered the DRC from the Republic during the conflict there was under way.

During 1999, countries in West Africa were hosting 2.1 million refugees and other persons of concern to UNHCR. Political situations in some parts of the area remained unstable, notably in Liberia where an armed confrontation had a destabilizing effect, leading to additional displacements and halting returns to Lofa county. However, repatriation to other counties continued. In Côte d'Ivoire and Guinea, UNHCR continued to protect and assist large numbers of refugees from Liberia, Sierra Leone and other countries; 350,000 Sierra Leoneans were residing in two provinces of Guinea alone. In Sierra Leone, the signing of the Lomé Peace Agreement (see PART ONE, Chapter II) opened prospects for the gradual return of hundreds of thousands of refugees and displaced persons. Another positive development was the improved situation in Guinea-Bissau as of May, when most of the over 350,000 internally displaced persons had returned to their homes. Elsewhere, notably in the Central

African Republic, Chad and Gabon, the year witnessed new refugee influxes resulting from conflict in the Republic of the Congo, the DRC and the Sudan.

In the East and Horn of Africa, the resumption of hostilities between Eritrea and Ethiopia caused population displacements in both countries and had repercussions on internal conflicts in Somalia, leading to new hostilities there. OAU mediation efforts revived hopes of greater stability and resumption of voluntary repatriation movements. The main groups concerned were Eritreans (mainly in the Sudan) and Somalis (with the largest groups in Ethiopia and Kenya).

Nearly 300,000 refugees, returnees and asylum-seekers were living in countries in the southern Africa region. In general, they were persons of rural background residing in villages and settlements, the largest single group being Angolans located mainly in Zambia (150,000). Also in Zambia, a new refugee emergency occurred with the arrival of some 25,000 Congolese refugees as of mid-June. In Botswana, there was an influx of Namibians from the Caprivi region.

There was little change in the refugee situation in North Africa, where UNHCR continued to provide basic care and assistance to refugees in countries of the region, pending voluntary repatriation and other long-term solutions. The slow process of implementing the UN settlement plan in Western Sahara (see PART ONE, Chapter II) caused further delays in UNHCR preparatory activities for repatriating Saharawi refugees from Algeria and Mauritania.

The Secretary-General stated that inter-agency cooperation had been of particular note in the specific areas of security, sustainable return, access to populations of concern, coordination of resources and unaccompanied minors. There had also been significant UNHCR cooperation with OAU and the Southern African Development Community.

The Secretary-General concluded that the human displacement problems in Africa were a source of concern for the United Nations, requiring coordinated action by UNHCR and other agencies. That was particularly true at a time when major emergencies elsewhere had drawn the world's attention and made heavy claims on available resources. Despite the serious situation in Africa, there had been some encouraging signs in 1999, such as the ceasefire agreements in the DRC and Sierra Leone, and the Framework Agreement in the dispute between Eritrea and Ethiopia (see PART ONE, Chapter II). However, the lasting success of such agreements, as well as solutions in other conflict situations that caused population movements, would require a renewed commitment by African Governments to take their future, and the future of their peoples, more resolutely into their own hands. The determination that lasting solutions to problems, including refugee problems, would only come through negotiations rather than force, was a fundamental precondition for international support. The international community, for its part, had to do all in its power to back such efforts.

Report of High Commissioner. In her annual report covering 1999 [A/55/12], the High Commissioner stated that a number of management changes had taken place in the structure of the UNHCR Africa Bureau that had resulted in the creation of three regional directorates based in Abidjan (Côte d'Ivoire), Addis Ababa (Ethiopia) and Pretoria (South Africa). By subregion, there were: 3.2 million persons of concern to UNHCR in Central and West Africa, who received $85 million in agency expenditures (Guinea continued to host by far the largest refugee population in the area; care and assistance was provided to more than half a million refugees there); 2.5 million of concern in the East and Horn of Africa and the Great Lakes region, who received $186 million; and 311,160 of concern in southern Africa, who received $21 million.

Communication. By a 13 December letter [A/54/682], Algeria transmitted the Khartoum Declaration and the Recommendations on Refugees, Returnees and Internally Displaced Persons in Africa, adopted by OAU at its December 1998 ministerial meeting.

Central African countries

In response to General Assembly resolution 53/1 N [YUN 1998, p. 1122], the Secretary-General submitted a September report on special assistance to Central and East African countries receiving refugees, returnees and displaced persons [A/54/421]. The report made particular reference to women and children, security access to populations in need and the environment. It also focused on the activities undertaken in areas where large numbers of refugees had repatriated. Activities consisted of providing emergency relief and assistance to thousands of refugees fleeing conflicts in the region and were undertaken in Burundi, the Central African Republic, the DRC, Gabon, Kenya, the Republic of the Congo, Rwanda, Uganda, the United Republic of Tanzania and Zambia. UNHCR, in collaboration with other UN agencies including WFP, the United Nations Development Programme (UNDP), UNICEF, the Food and Agriculture Organization of the United Nations (FAO), the United Nations Population Fund and the Office for the Coordination of Humanitarian Affairs (OCHA), together with international and local NGOs, also strove to lessen the political, economic and social impact of forced population movements.

Lack of funding remained a concern, said the Secretary-General, and the multiplication of smaller conflicts, with movements of refugees and displaced persons affecting a number of countries, posed particular challenges.

GENERAL ASSEMBLY ACTION

On 17 December [meeting 83], the General Assembly, on the recommendation of the Third Committee [A/54/600], adopted **resolution 54/147** without vote [agenda item 111].

Assistance to refugees, returnees and displaced persons in Africa

The General Assembly,

Recalling its resolution 53/126 of 9 December 1998,

Recalling also the provisions of its resolution 2312(XXII) of 14 December 1967, by which it adopted the Declaration on Territorial Asylum,

Recalling further the Organization of African Unity Convention governing the specific aspects of refugee problems in Africa of 1969 and the African Charter on Human and Peoples' Rights,

Recalling the Khartoum Declaration and the Recommendations on Refugees, Returnees and Internally Displaced Persons in Africa adopted by the Organization of African Unity at the ministerial meeting held at Khartoum on 13 and 14 December 1998,

Welcoming decision CM/Dec.459(LXX) on the situation of refugees, returnees and displaced persons in Africa adopted by the Council of Ministers of the Organization of African Unity at its seventieth ordinary session, held at Algiers from 8 to 10 July 1999,

Commending the First Ministerial Conference on Human Rights in Africa of the Organization of African Unity, held at Grand-Baie, Mauritius, from 12 to 16 April 1999, and welcoming the attention paid to issues relevant to refugees and displaced persons in the Declaration and Plan of Action adopted by the Conference,

Recognizing the contributions made by African States to the development of regional standards for the protection of refugees and returnees, and noting with appreciation that countries of asylum are hosting refugees in a humanitarian spirit and in a spirit of African solidarity and brotherhood,

Recognizing also the need for States to address resolutely the root causes of forced displacement and to create conditions that facilitate durable solutions for refugees and displaced persons, and stressing in this regard the need for States to foster peace, stability and prosperity throughout the African continent,

Convinced of the need to strengthen the capacity of States to provide assistance and protection for refugees, returnees and displaced persons and of the need for the international community, within the context of burden-sharing, to increase its material, financial and technical assistance to the countries affected by refugees, returnees and displaced persons,

Acknowledging with appreciation that some assistance is already rendered by the international community to refugees, returnees and displaced persons and host countries in Africa,

Noting with great concern that, despite all the efforts deployed so far by the United Nations, the Organization of African Unity and others, the situation of refugees and displaced persons in Africa, especially in the West African and Great Lakes regions and in the Horn of Africa, remains precarious,

Stressing that the provision of relief and assistance to African refugees by the international community should be on an equitable, non-discriminatory basis,

Considering that, among refugees, returnees and internally displaced persons, women and children are the majority of the population affected by conflict and bear the brunt of atrocities and other consequences of conflict,

1. *Takes note* of the reports of the Secretary-General and of the United Nations High Commissioner for Refugees;

2. *Notes with concern* that the declining socio-economic situation, compounded by political instability, internal strife, human rights violations and natural disasters, has led to increased numbers of refugees and displaced persons in some countries of Africa, and remains particularly concerned about the impact of large-scale refugee populations on the security, socio-economic situation and environment of countries of asylum;

3. *Notes* the commemoration in 1999 of the thirtieth anniversary of the adoption of the Organization of African Unity Convention governing the specific aspects of refugee problems in Africa of 1969, appeals to African States that have not yet done so to accede to the Convention, and calls upon States parties to the Convention to reaffirm their commitment to its ideals and to respect and observe its provisions;

4. *Also notes* the commemoration in 1999 of the fiftieth anniversary of the signature of the Geneva Conventions of 12 August 1949, and, bearing in mind that armed conflict is one of the principal causes of forced displacement in Africa, calls upon States and other parties to armed conflict to observe scrupulously the letter and spirit of international humanitarian law;

5. *Notes* the need for States to address the root causes of forced displacement in Africa, and calls upon African States, the international community and relevant United Nations organizations to take concrete action to meet the needs of refugees, returnees and displaced persons for protection and assistance and to contribute generously to national projects and programmes aimed at alleviating their plight;

6. *Also notes* the link, inter alia, between human rights violations, poverty, natural disasters and environmental degradation and population displacement, and calls for redoubled and concerted efforts by States, in collaboration with the Organization of African Unity, to promote and protect human rights for all and to address these problems;

7. *Encourages* the Office of the United Nations High Commissioner for Refugees to continue to cooperate with the Office of the United Nations High Commissioner for Human Rights and the African Commission on Human and Peoples' Rights, within their respective mandates, in the promotion and protection of the human rights and fundamental freedoms of refugees, returnees and displaced persons in Africa;

8. *Notes with appreciation* the positive outcome of all mediation and conflict resolution efforts carried out by African States, the Organization of African Unity and subregional organizations, as well as the establishment of regional mechanisms for conflict prevention and resolution, and urges all relevant parties to address the humanitarian consequences of conflicts;

9. *Expresses its appreciation and strong support* for those African Governments and local populations that, in spite of the general deterioration of socio-economic and environmental conditions and overstretched national resources, continue to accept the additional burden imposed upon them by increasing numbers of refugees and displaced persons, in compliance with the relevant principles of asylum;

10. *Expresses its gratitude* to the international community and to the Office of the United Nations High Commissioner for Refugees for the humanitarian assistance they have continued to render to refugees and displaced persons and to countries of asylum;

11. *Expresses its concern* about instances in which the fundamental principle of asylum is jeopardized by unlawful expulsion or refoulement or by threats to the life, physical security, integrity, dignity and well-being of refugees;

12. *Calls upon* States, in cooperation with international organizations, within their mandates, to take all necessary measures to ensure respect for the principles of refugee protection and, in particular, to ensure that the civilian and humanitarian nature of refugee camps is not compromised by the presence or the activities of armed elements;

13. *Urges* States and all other actors to take all necessary measures to protect activities related to humanitarian assistance, to prevent attacks on and kidnapping of national and international humanitarian workers and to ensure their safety and security, and requests organizations and aid workers to abide by the national laws and regulations of the countries in which they operate;

14. *Calls upon* the Office of the High Commissioner, the Organization of African Unity, subregional organizations and all African States, in conjunction with United Nations agencies, intergovernmental and non-governmental organizations and the international community, to strengthen and revitalize existing partnerships and forge new ones in support of the international refugee protection system;

15. *Calls upon* the Office of the High Commissioner, the international community and other concerned entities to intensify their support to African Governments through appropriate capacity-building activities, including training of relevant officers, disseminating information about refugee instruments and principles, providing financial, technical and advisory services to accelerate the enactment or amendment and implementation of legislation relating to refugees, strengthening emergency response and enhancing capacities for the coordination of humanitarian activities;

16. *Reaffirms* the right of return and also the principle of voluntary repatriation, appeals to countries of origin and countries of asylum to create conditions that are conducive to voluntary repatriation, and recognizes that, while voluntary repatriation remains the pre-eminent solution, local integration and third-country resettlement, as appropriate, are also viable options for dealing with the situation of African refugees who, owing to prevailing circumstances in their respective countries of origin, are unable to return home;

17. *Notes with satisfaction* the voluntary return of millions of refugees to their homelands following the successful repatriation and reintegration operations carried out by the Office of the High Commissioner, with the cooperation and collaboration of countries hosting refugees and countries of origin, and looks forward to other programmes to assist the voluntary repatriation and reintegration of all refugees in Africa;

18. *Reiterates* that the Plan of Action adopted by the Regional Conference on Assistance to Refugees, Returnees and Displaced Persons in the Great Lakes Region, held at Bujumbura from 15 to 17 February 1995, as endorsed by the General Assembly in its resolution 50/149 of 21 December 1995, continues to be a viable framework for the resolution of the refugee and humanitarian problems in that region;

19. *Appeals* to the international community to respond positively, in the spirit of solidarity and burden-sharing, to the third-country resettlement requests of African refugees, and notes with appreciation that some African countries have offered resettlement places for refugees;

20. *Welcomes* the programmes carried out by the Office of the High Commissioner with host Governments, the United Nations, non-governmental organizations and the international community to address the environmental impact of refugee populations;

21. *Calls upon* the international donor community to provide material and financial assistance for the implementation of programmes intended for the rehabilitation of the environment and infrastructure affected by refugees in countries of asylum;

22. *Expresses its concern* about the long stay of refugees in certain African countries, and calls upon the Office of the High Commissioner to keep its programmes under review, in conformity with its mandate in the host countries, taking into account the increasing needs of refugees;

23. *Emphasizes* the need for the Office of the High Commissioner to collate statistics, on a regular basis, on the number of refugees living outside refugee camps in certain African countries, with a view to evaluating and addressing the needs of those refugees;

24. *Urges* the international community, in a spirit of international solidarity and burden-sharing, to continue to fund generously the refugee programmes of the Office of the High Commissioner and, taking into account the substantially increased needs of programmes in Africa, to ensure that Africa receives a fair and equitable share of the resources designated for refugees;

25. *Requests* all Governments and intergovernmental and non-governmental organizations to pay particular attention to meeting the special needs of refugee women and children and displaced persons, including those with special protection needs;

26. *Calls upon* States and the Office of the High Commissioner to make renewed efforts to ensure that the rights, needs and dignity of elderly refugees are fully respected and addressed through appropriate programme activities;

27. *Expresses grave concern* about the plight of internally displaced persons in Africa, calls upon States to

take concrete action to pre-empt internal displacement and to meet the protection and assistance needs of internally displaced persons, takes note in this regard of the Guiding Principles on Internal Displacement, and urges the international community, led by relevant United Nations organizations, to contribute generously to national projects and programmes aimed at alleviating the plight of internally displaced persons;

28. *Requests* the Secretary-General to submit a comprehensive report on the situation of refugees, returnees and displaced persons in Africa to the General Assembly at its fifty-fifth session, taking fully into account the efforts expended by countries of asylum, under the item entitled "Report of the United Nations High Commissioner for Refugees, questions relating to refugees, returnees and displaced persons and humanitarian questions", and to present an oral report to the Economic and Social Council at its substantive session of 2000.

The Americas

In 1999, deterioration of the conflict in Colombia led to the massive forced displacement of almost 300,000 persons, as well as cross-border movements into Panama and Venezuela. Ecuador and Venezuela were both hosting large populations of undocumented Colombians who preferred to remain anonymous. Those influxes triggered a shift in the Office's humanitarian interventions from advocacy and promotional activities to technical advice and legal expertise for adopting or amending national legislation, capacity-building and emergency response at the national and local levels. Consequently, UNHCR established a liaison office in Ecuador and a field presence on Venezuela's common border with Colombia.

In southern South America, about 30 per cent of refugee needs were met by civil society institutions in Argentina and Brazil and, in Argentina, the foundation *Argentina con ACNUR* was established in December to support UNHCR activities worldwide.

The last collective return of Guatemalan refugees in July signalled the closure of UNHCR's repatriation programme there. Some 43,000 refugees had benefited from the programme since 1992. UNHCR intensified its efforts to involve returnees and their communities in government and civil society and advocated for their inclusion in national and regional plans. The migratory stabilization plan for 20,000 Guatemalan refugees in south-eastern Mexico continued to be implemented by the Government of Mexico, UNHCR and NGOs. In Chiapas, 96 per cent of the refugee population had received their migratory documents and remaining refugees in Mexico requesting naturalization were expected to benefit from UNHCR's assistance towards self-sufficiency. UNHCR facilitated acquisition of residency permits and naturalization for refugees in all countries of the sub-continent, and Belize and Costa Rica offered amnesty programmes for illegal aliens who had arrived in those countries during the Central American conflict in the 1980s.

In Canada and the United States, UNHCR continued to advocate for the application of international protection principles, promoting resettlement as a durable solution and reinforcing public awareness of and support for refugees and the Office's humanitarian programmes. In the Caribbean, UNHCR focused on building the foundation for refugee protection.

Asia and the Pacific and the Arab States

South Asia

As a result of procedural difficulties in the clearance by the Myanmar authorities of those willing to repatriate, only 1,500 Muslim refugees returned from camps in Bangladesh to Myanmar in 1999 under the voluntary repatriation programme, which had resumed in November 1998. UNHCR urged both Governments to expedite returns. Following discussions with UNHCR, Bangladesh agreed to introduce refugee self-help activities within camps for those unable or unwilling to return in the near future. UNHCR also facilitated the establishment of a five-year UN integrated development plan in Myanmar, which was expected to allow development agencies to take over UNHCR-funded activities in northern Rakhine State by the end of 2000. As a precursor, FAO, UNICEF and the United Nations Office for Project Services were engaged as implementing partners for UNHCR activities.

Bilateral talks between Bhutan and Nepal on the 97,000 refugees in camps in Nepal had made slow progress during the year. In Sri Lanka, the continuation of armed conflict between the Sri Lankan authorities and the separatist Liberation Tigers of Tamil Ealam sparked further population displacements in the northern Vanni region where an estimated 600,000 persons were displaced. UNHCR attempted to facilitate access to national protection for persons in the region affected by the conflict; an open relief centre, maintained with the Office's support, provided an area of relative safety. An estimated 70,000 Sri Lankan refugees also remained in camps in India during 1999. UNHCR's efforts to promote self-reliance among 16,000 urban refugees in India, mainly from Afghanistan, were impeded by difficulties in issuing and renewing residential permits by the Indian authorities due to security considerations.

East Asia and the Pacific

As planned, UNHCR phased out its local settlement assistance to Vietnamese refugees in China at the end of 1999, maintaining, however, a revolving credit scheme, initiated in 1994, through which refugees achieved self-reliance and which allowed them and host communities to continue to benefit from employment opportunities created under the scheme. In July and August, tripartite consultations between the Lao People's Democratic Republic, Thailand and UNHCR led to the organized return of the remaining 1,160 Lao in Thailand who did not meet internationally recognized refugee criteria, marking the end of the former Comprehensive Plan of Action for Indo-Chinese Refugees in Thailand. Returnee reintegration and monitoring assistance were scheduled to continue in Laos throughout 2000, and UNHCR was expected to seek resettlement solutions for the remaining 116 refugees in the Ban Napho camp.

In May, UNHCR completed registering almost 98,000 refugees, mainly of Karen and Karenni origin from Myanmar, located in 11 camps along the border between Thailand and Myanmar. The Office also continued to cooperate actively with the Thai Government on the admission of new arrivals to the camps. Despite several security incidents during the year, Thailand reiterated its policy of providing temporary asylum to Myanmar refugees. In addition, the repatriation of the remaining 47,000 Cambodian refugees in camps in Thailand was completed in March, and UNHCR continued to monitor protection of returnees in Cambodia and to promote their reintegration through community-based projects.

Timor

The eruption of violence in East Timor following the August referendum on independence (see PART ONE, Chapter IV) provoked the displacement of 75 per cent of the population, about 500,000 inside East Timor and an estimated 200,000 to West Timor and other areas of Indonesia. There was also large-scale destruction of private housing, public buildings and utilities. UNHCR responded to immediate humanitarian needs by providing emergency relief, transportation and petrol for the displaced persons and refugees. In October, the Office launched a large-scale voluntary repatriation operation and concluded a memorandum of understanding with Indonesia, which established a framework for protecting refugees and affirmed the voluntary nature of the repatriation programme to East Timor. Nevertheless, access to refugees in West Timor remained problematic and it was difficult to determine how many were located there. UNHCR was neither deterred by the difficulties, nor by threats and intimidation by militias, and continued its activities in West Timor, including mass information campaigns to promote repatriation.

Central Asia, South-West Asia, North Africa and the Middle East

Despite the lack of political settlement and general peace in Afghanistan, more than 160,000 Afghan refugees returned home in 1999, but a large majority of the 2.6 million Afghan refugees remaining in Pakistan and Iran were unlikely to return to Afghanistan in the near future. UNHCR's main operation in Central Asia was the repatriation of 4,670 Tajik refugees from Turkmenistan and Kyrgyzstan. In North Africa, pending implementation of a durable solution for the Saharan refugees, UNHCR continued its protection role and provided care and maintenance assistance.

UNHCR protected and assisted some 132,000 refugees in the Middle East in 1999. Most lived in urban settings, although there were also camp-based refugee populations in Iraq, Saudi Arabia and the Syrian Arab Republic. During the year, UNHCR attempted to strengthen its refugee status determination and resettlement processing capacities in the region, which resulted in enhanced protection, more opportunities for durable solutions for eligible refugees and reduced frequency of irregular movements of asylum-seekers in the region. As a result, almost 5,500 refugees were resettled in third countries from the Middle East and 17,000 returned home.

Europe

South-Eastern Europe

The conflict in the Kosovo province of FRY led to renewed displacement and suffering on a massive scale in 1999. Some 350,000 people had already been displaced when, on 24 March, the North Atlantic Treaty Organization (NATO) launched airstrikes against FRY (see PART ONE, Chapter V) and almost 1 million Kosovo Albanians fled their homes. Between March and June alone, more than 850,000 ethnic Albanians fled to other parts of FRY or to neighbouring countries, mainly to Albania and FYROM.

Despite the difficulties of one of the most complex and intensely political refugee emergencies in history, the humanitarian operation achieved its objective, namely to ensure the security and meet the immediate life-sustaining needs of the refugees. However, the humanitarian challenges posed by the size of the crisis initially overwhelmed the response capacity of the host Governments and temporarily exceeded the capacities of UNHCR and its humanitarian partners.

In addition to the relief efforts of civilian agencies, NATO's rapid logistical support proved vital to ensure refugee admission and to bring the humanitarian crisis under control. Other important factors included Albania's liberal asylum policy; the hospitality extended by host families in Albania, FYROM and Montenegro; and international burden-sharing through a humanitarian evacuation programme under which some 90,000 refugees were assisted in moving temporarily from FYROM to third countries.

Following the establishment of the United Nations Interim Administration Mission in Kosovo, the majority of the recently displaced refugees returned to Kosovo, almost as swiftly and dramatically as they had fled. UNHCR quickly transformed its programme from a refugee relief operation into an equally ambitious repatriation and reintegration effort, including a major emergency shelter programme for the hundreds of thousands who returned before the winter. Despite logistical difficulties, including bottlenecks at the border between FYROM and Kosovo, a humanitarian crisis during the winter was avoided.

Regrettably, the massive return of refugees to Kosovo resulted in an exodus of hundreds of thousands of non-Albanians, mainly to other parts of FRY, and there was a climate of violence and impunity, as well as widespread discrimination and intimidation directed against non-Albanians. That situation remained a major concern for all humanitarian agencies in Kosovo.

A critical protection issue for UNHCR in western Europe in 1999 was the outflow of thousands of refugees from Kosovo. In June alone, nearly 20,000 Kosovars arrived spontaneously to seek asylum. Although western European Governments generally responded positively and generously to the Kosovo crisis, UNHCR followed with concern the legislative, judicial and policy developments that had an impact on asylum possibilities. At the national level and at the level of the EU, policy directions continued to focus on restrictive practices designed to control migration.

Although 1999 was the fourth year of peace in Bosnia and Herzegovina and in Croatia, and despite sustained efforts to promote return and reconciliation, the number of refugees and internally displaced persons in and from the region remained high. In the second half of the year, some encouraging progress was achieved. In Bosnia and Herzegovina, there was a steady increase of minority returns to areas considered to be particularly difficult. Returns to and within Croatia numbered some 100,000. UNHCR played a catalytic role in establishing special return projects for both countries.

In **resolution 1239(1999)** of 14 May (see PART ONE, Chapter V), the Security Council invited UNHCR and other international humanitarian relief organizations to extend assistance to the internally displaced persons in Kosovo, the Republic of Montenegro and other parts of FRY.

Eastern Europe

The situation around Chechnya in the Russian Federation deteriorated in the second half of 1999, causing the displacement of more than 200,000 persons who fled into neighbouring republics, particularly Ingushetia. While several thousand Chechens returned home to parts of Chechnya under Russian control, many left again due to ongoing insecurity, the destruction of their homes and the poor state of the infrastructure. UNHCR provided assistance to approximately 180,000 persons in Ingushetia through a UN inter-agency emergency assistance programme.

The UNHCR assistance programme in Armenia increasingly focused on promoting naturalization of ethnic Armenian refugees, adopting relevant legislation and building local implementation capacity to reduce statelessness and facilitate integration of refugees into Armenian society. UNHCR also assisted in drafting a national refugee law, which was passed by the Armenian Parliament in March.

In Azerbaijan, UNHCR placed stronger emphasis on integration of refugees and internally displaced persons, which entailed closer interagency cooperation with the World Bank, UNDP and government agencies in efforts to rehabilitate territories of the country damaged by war. Azerbaijan passed a new law on refugees in May and UNHCR assisted the Government with developing implementation procedures.

The conflict in Georgia over the status of Abkhazia remained unresolved, but the situation in South Ossetia showed some signs of progress. UNHCR provided limited material assistance to 7,000 refugees who had fled to Georgia as a result of the Chechnya conflict.

Conference on refugees of CIS countries and neighbouring States

Report of Secretary-General. In an August report [A/54/286] submitted in response to General Assembly resolution 53/123 [YUN 1998, p. 1125], the Secretary-General described follow-up to the 1996 Regional Conference to Address the Problems of Refugees, Displaced Persons, Other Forms of Involuntary Displacement and Returnees in the Countries of the Commonwealth of Independent States and Relevant Neighbouring States (CIS Conference) [YUN 1996, p. 1117]. Regarding implementation of the Programme of Action adopted at the Conference, the Secretary-General, citing the mechanisms established within UNHCR and IOM, working in cooperation with concerned States, observed that perhaps the major achievement of the CIS Conference process might have been the establishment of an international forum to exchange information and pursue constructive dialogue on a broader humanitarian and migration agenda. It had served to galvanize international attention on issues relevant to refugees, forced migration and other migratory movements in the region.

In 1999, the third of the four years of the follow-up process, stakeholders had begun to concentrate on its sustainability and consolidation beyond 2000, and States in the region had recognized that refugee problems needed to be addressed by creating legislative and institutional frameworks consistent with international standards. Capacity-building and training activities intensified to assist States in implementing the Programme of Action and, with the support of IOM, national management systems were established in eight countries in the region. Headway was made in addressing the situation of formerly deported people, a group specifically identified in the CIS Conference process as requiring a durable settlement solution. States in the region also demonstrated greater readiness to tackle problems relevant to citizenship and statelessness. UNHCR and the Council of Europe actively promoted recognition of the role of NGOs in civil society, the establishment of a legal framework at the national level defining their status and the creation of an environment that would enable NGOs to play a more active role in CIS Conference follow-up. The World Bank, UNDP and OCHA were supporting follow-up efforts.

The Steering Group established to monitor follow-up to the CIS Conference met on 24 and 25 June.

UNHCR Executive Committee action. In an October conclusion [A/54/12/Add.1], the UNHCR Executive Committee, noting that a number of provisions of the Programme of Action could not be achieved by 2000, endorsed establishment of a working group to address the issue of the follow-up and hoped that the Steering Group would work out concrete proposals for the next meeting on modalities of the conference process after 2000. It called on all CIS Governments to strengthen their practical and political commitment to implementing the Programme of Action for more consistent and far-reaching progress.

GENERAL ASSEMBLY ACTION

On 17 December [meeting 83], the General Assembly, on the recommendation of the Third Committee [A/54/600], adopted **resolution 54/144** without vote [agenda item 111].

Follow-up to the Regional Conference to Address the Problems of Refugees, Displaced Persons, Other Forms of Involuntary Displacement and Returnees in the Countries of the Commonwealth of Independent States and Relevant Neighbouring States

The General Assembly,

Recalling its resolutions 48/113 of 20 December 1993, 49/173 of 23 December 1994, 50/151 of 21 December 1995, 51/70 of 12 December 1996, 52/102 of 12 December 1997 and, in particular, 53/123 of 9 December 1998,

Having considered the reports of the Secretary-General and of the United Nations High Commissioner for Refugees,

Recognizing the ongoing acuteness of the migration and displacement problems in the countries of the Commonwealth of Independent States and the necessity to follow up the Regional Conference to Address the Problems of Refugees, Displaced Persons, Other Forms of Involuntary Displacement and Returnees in the Countries of the Commonwealth of Independent States and Relevant Neighbouring States and the subsequent conclusions of the Executive Committee of the Programme of the United Nations High Commissioner for Refugees,

Reaffirming the view of the Conference that the primary responsibility for tackling population displacement problems lies with the affected countries themselves and that these issues are to be regarded as national priorities, while at the same time recognizing the need for enhancing international support for the national efforts of the countries of the Commonwealth of Independent States aimed at the effective implementation of such responsibilities within the framework of the Programme of Action adopted by the Conference,

Noting with satisfaction the efforts of the Office of the United Nations High Commissioner for Refugees, the International Organization for Migration and the Organization for Security and Cooperation in Europe in developing strategies and practical tools for more effective capacity-building in countries of origin and enhancing programmes to address the needs of various categories of concern to the countries of the Commonwealth of Independent States,

Welcoming the contributions of those countries that responded to the 1999 appeal launched by the Office of the United Nations High Commissioner for Refugees and the International Organization for Migration, and appreciating this tangible encouragement to the countries of the Commonwealth of Independent States and to further inter-agency cooperation,

Taking note of the positive results emanating from the implementation of the Programme of Action adopted by the Conference,

Bearing in mind that a number of the provisions of the Programme of Action are still at the stage of practical formulation and cannot be achieved by 2000,

Taking into account the decision made by the steering group of the Conference to establish a working group to address the issue of follow-up to the Conference,

Convinced of the necessity of continuing to maintain the regional approach for the achievement of effective implementation of the Programme of Action,

Recalling that the protection and promotion of human rights and the strengthening of democratic institutions are essential to prevent mass population displacement,

Mindful that the effective implementation of the recommendations contained in the Programme of Action should be facilitated and can be ensured only through cooperation and coordinated activities undertaken in this respect by all interested States, intergovernmental and non-governmental organizations and other actors,

Noting and reaffirming the importance of the 1951 Convention and the 1967 Protocol relating to the Status of Refugees,

1. *Takes note* of the reports of the Secretary-General and of the United Nations High Commissioner for Refugees;

2. *Calls upon* the Governments of the countries of the Commonwealth of Independent States, in cooperation with the Office of the United Nations High Commissioner for Refugees, the International Organization for Migration and the Organization for Security and Cooperation in Europe, to strengthen their efforts and mutual cooperation relating to the follow-up to the Regional Conference to Address the Problems of Refugees, Displaced Persons, Other Forms of Involuntary Displacement and Returnees in the Countries of the Commonwealth of Independent States and Relevant Neighbouring States, and welcomes the positive results achieved by them in the implementation of the Programme of Action adopted by the Conference;

3. *Endorses* the broad consensus reached by the participants in the steering group of the Conference that implementation of the issues outlined in the Programme of Action should be continued and that consideration should be given to a continuation of the follow-up to the Conference after 2000;

4. *Calls upon* the countries of the Commonwealth of Independent States and other interested States, in cooperation with the Office of the United Nations High Commissioner for Refugees, the International Organization for Migration and the Organization for Security and Cooperation in Europe, to elaborate concrete proposals for a mechanism for possible follow-up to the Conference after 2000;

5. *Invites* all States that have not yet done so to accede to and implement fully the 1951 Convention and the 1967 Protocol relating to the Status of Refugees, while welcoming the accession of Georgia and Kazakhstan to the Convention;

6. *Calls upon* States and interested international organizations, in a spirit of solidarity and burden-sharing, to provide appropriate forms and levels of support for the practical implementation of the Programme of Action;

7. *Invites* international financial and other institutions to contribute to the financing of projects and programmes within the framework of the implementation of the Programme of Action;

8. *Invites* the countries of the Commonwealth of Independent States to intensify bilateral, subregional and regional cooperation in maintaining the balance of commitments and interests in the process leading up to the implementation of the Programme of Action;

9. *Calls upon* the Governments of the countries of the Commonwealth of Independent States to continue to strengthen their commitment to the principles underpinning the Programme of Action, in particular principles of human rights and refugee protection, and to lend high-level political support to ensure progress in its implementation;

10. *Invites* the Office of the United Nations High Commissioner for Refugees and the International Organization for Migration to enhance their mutual relationship with other key international actors, such as the Council of Europe, the European Commission and human rights, development and financial institutions, in order better to address the wide-ranging and complex issues in the Programme of Action;

11. *Welcomes* the progress made in building civil society, in particular through the development of the non-governmental sector and the development of cooperation between non-governmental organizations and the Governments of a number of countries of the Commonwealth of Independent States, and notes in this regard the relationship between the progress made in implementing the Programme of Action and the success in promoting civil society, especially in the field of human rights;

12. *Encourages* the involvement of intergovernmental and non-governmental organizations in the follow-up to the Conference, and invites them to demonstrate stronger support for the process of multinational constructive dialogue among a wide range of countries concerned and further action with a view to the full implementation of the recommendations of the Conference;

13. *Emphasizes* the necessity of fulfilling the recommendations contained in the Programme of Action relating to ensuring respect for human rights as an important factor in the management of migration flows, the consolidation of democracy, the rule of law and stability;

14. *Recognizes* the importance of taking measures, on the basis of strict adherence to all of the principles of international law, including humanitarian law and international human rights standards, to prevent situations that lead to new flows of refugees, displaced persons and other forms of involuntary displacement;

15. *Requests* the Secretary-General to report to the General Assembly at its fifty-fifth session on the progress achieved in the follow-up to the Conference;

16. *Decides* to continue its consideration of the question at its fifty-fifth session.

Chapter XIII

Health, food and nutrition

In 1999, the United Nations continued to take action to promote human health, coordinate food aid and food security, and support research in nutrition.

The total number of people living with HIV/AIDS worldwide at the end of 1999 was 33.6 million, according to the Joint United Nations Programme on Human Immunodeficiency Virus/Acquired Immunodeficiency Syndrome (UNAIDS) and the World Health Organization (WHO). There were 5.6 million new infections and an estimated 2.6 million deaths due to the epidemic, the highest number ever in a single year. UNAIDS was working at various levels to fight the epidemic and had effectively promoted HIV/AIDS as a priority on international agendas. Progress was achieved in expanding both the prevention and the care agendas.

Another health concern for the United Nations continued to be tobacco and its ill effects. In May, the WHO World Health Assembly adopted a resolution that mapped out the political process for negotiation of a framework convention on tobacco control and related protocols. The Inter-Agency Task Force on Tobacco Control, established in 1999, held its first session in September. The Task Force, under the leadership of WHO, was designated to intensify a joint UN response and to galvanize support for tobacco control.

The World Food Programme (WFP)—a joint undertaking of the United Nations and the Food and Agriculture Organization of the United Nations (FAO)—provided food aid to 89 million people, an increase of some 17 per cent over 1998. Global food aid deliveries amounted to 14.5 million tons, up from 8.3 million in 1998. Follow-up to the 1996 World Food Summit continued under the Committee on World Food Security, which submitted its first report to the Economic and Social Council.

Health

AIDS prevention and control

The Joint United Nations Programme on Human Immunodeficiency Virus/Acquired Immunodeficiency Syndrome (UNAIDS) (formerly the Joint and Co-sponsored UN Programme), which became fully operational in 1996 [YUN 1996, p. 1121], continued to coordinate UN activities for AIDS prevention and control. The Programme, which served as the main advocate for global action on HIV/AIDS, had seven co-sponsors: the United Nations Development Programme (UNDP), the United Nations Children's Fund (UNICEF), the United Nations Educational, Scientific and Cultural Organization (UNESCO), the United Nations International Drug Control Programme (UNDCP), the United Nations Population Fund (UNFPA), the World Bank and WHO. UNDCP became a new co-sponsor in 1999. The role of UNAIDS was to lead, strengthen and support an expanded response to the epidemic, mainly through facilitation and coordination, best practice development and advocacy.

According to UNAIDS/WHO, provisional estimates indicated that 33.6 million people were living with HIV/AIDS worldwide at year's end. In 1999, some 5.6 million people were newly infected and about 2.6 million people died, the highest number ever in a single year, despite antiretroviral therapy which staved off AIDS and AIDS deaths in the richer countries. By the end of the year, the epidemic had left behind a cumulative total of 11.2 million AIDS orphans, defined as children who had lost their mother before reaching the age of 15. Many of them had also lost their father. The overwhelming majority of people with HIV—some 95 per cent of the global total—lived in developing countries. Sub-Saharan Africa continued to bear the brunt of HIV/AIDS, with close to 70 per cent of the global total of HIV-positive people. However, there was evidence that infections were on the rise in Central America and in the Caribbean basin, which had some of the worst HIV epidemics outside Africa. The world's steepest HIV curve in 1999 was in the Commonwealth of Independent States (CIS), where the proportion of the population living with HIV doubled between the end of 1997 and the end of 1999, mainly due to the unsafe injection of drugs. In 1999, an estimated 570,000 children worldwide aged 14 or younger became infected. Over 90 per cent were babies born to HIV-positive women, who acquired the virus at birth or through their mother's breast milk. Of those, almost nine tenths were in sub-Saharan Africa.

In response to Economic and Social Council resolution 1997/52 [YUN 1997, p. 1253], the Secretary-General, in a June note [E/1999/64], transmitted a report of the UNAIDS Executive Director describing progress made in response to HIV/AIDS and its impact on the countries affected. Among other things, the Executive Director recommended intensifying action in sub-Saharan Africa and stepping up action in Asia; developing strategies for women and young people, especially adolescent girls, and addressing the issue of male responsibility; and improving data collection and analysis on the economic causes and consequences of HIV. In the context of the reform of the United Nations, he recommended increased and better coordinated efforts by the UNAIDS co-sponsors and the secretariat on integrated planning at the country, regional and global levels, particularly in the context of the International Partnership against HIV/AIDS in Africa, and attention to HIV/AIDS issues by the broader UN system organizations, as relevant to their mandates, in cooperation with UNAIDS.

UNAIDS had been successful in persuading the global business community to engage in a more active response to AIDS. On 6 May, Bristol-Myers Squibb launched a $100 million initiative, "Secure the Future", to support community programmes, training and clinical research in five southern African countries. An evaluation of the development, dissemination and use of UNAIDS best practice materials began in May 1999. The best practice collection comprised advocacy documents, technical updates, case studies and key materials, covering some 50 topics. The UNAIDS secretariat remained actively involved in the follow-up processes of recent UN global conferences and summits. In his conclusions, the Executive Director drew to the Council's attention the unprecedented human disaster in southern Africa; the need for increased efforts and targeted programmes to address the vulnerability of young people to HIV infection; and the need to intensify and widen UN partnerships with governmental and non-governmental entities.

By **decision 1999/284** of 30 July, the Council took note of the Secretary-General's note.

The Programme Coordinating Board of UNAIDS, at its eighth meeting (Geneva, 28-29 June), encouraged its secretariat and co-sponsors to intensify their efforts towards developing a UN system strategic plan for HIV/AIDS for the years 2001-2005, in consultation with the UN system and other partners. It recommended that the secretariat include Central America and the Caribbean as priority regions for strategic support and approved the UNAIDS unified budget and work plan for 2000-2001. It asked the Executive Director to ask the Secretary-General to bring the HIV/AIDS crisis and the urgent need for an intensified response to the attention of the Council and the General Assembly.

The 1999 World AIDS Campaign, developed by UNAIDS and partner organizations, focused on the need to listen to children and young people in order for AIDS prevention and care efforts to be effective and on strengthening AIDS programmes with them in 10 action areas.

ECONOMIC AND SOCIAL COUNCIL ACTION

On 28 July [meeting 44], the Economic and Social Council adopted **resolution 1999/36** [draft: E/1999/L.36] without vote [agenda item 7 (*c*)].

Human immodeficiency virus/ acquired immunodeficiency syndrome

The Economic and Social Council,

Recalling its resolutions 1994/24 of 26 July 1994, 1995/2 of 3 July 1995, 1996/47 of 26 July 1996 and 1997/52 of 23 July 1997,

Noting with great concern the accelerating spread of human immunodeficiency virus (HIV), which has already infected millions of people worldwide, and the resulting increase in cases of acquired immunodeficiency syndrome (AIDS),

Noting with great concern also that young people, especially adolescent girls, children and women are particularly vulnerable to the infection,

Recognizing that no country in the world has been spared by the AIDS epidemic, and that 90 per cent of the people living with HIV/AIDS live in the developing world, in particular in sub-Saharan Africa, which has been very severely affected,

Mindful that the AIDS epidemic has become a development crisis in many countries, with devastating consequences for human, social and economic progress, which is already undermining the gains of many years of development efforts,

Recognizing that the needs in countries to address AIDS far outweigh both the human and the financial resources being made available and that high-level political commitment is critical to strengthen the response to the epidemic,

Recalling that a multisectoral approach is needed to reduce the transmission of HIV and to increase the quality and accessibility of treatment, care and support of people with HIV/AIDS,

Acknowledging in this regard that the Joint United Nations Programme on Human Immunodeficiency Virus/Acquired Immunodeficiency Syndrome (HIV/AIDS), co-sponsored by the United Nations Children's Fund, the United Nations Development Programme, the United Nations Population Fund, the United Nations International Drug Control Programme, the United Nations Educational, Scientific and Cultural Organization, the World Health Organization and the World Bank, has played a critical role in leading, strengthening and supporting an expanded multisectoral response to the epidemic and constitutes an important example of effective system-wide coordination in the context of the United Nations reform efforts,

Noting the end of the period of the first strategic plan, 1996-2000, and of the development of a United Nations system strategic plan for HIV/AIDS for 2001-2005,

Recognizing the critical role of the United Nations theme groups on HIV/AIDS in enhancing the United Nations response to the epidemic at the field level,

Noting the increased commitment efforts of the Secretary-General to generate strengthened support to the joint United Nations programme on HIV/AIDS,

1. *Notes* the change in name of the Programme from the Joint and Co-sponsored United Nations Programme on Human Immunodeficiency Virus/ Acquired Immunodeficiency Syndrome (HIV/AIDS) to the Joint United Nations Programme on Human Immunodeficiency Virus/Acquired Immunodeficiency Syndrome (HIV/AIDS) (UNAIDS) and welcomes the admission of the United Nations International Drug Control Programme as a co-sponsor of the Programme;

2. *Urges* Governments worldwide, with the assistance of the co-sponsoring organizations of the Programme, the Secretariat, other relevant United Nations programmes, funds and agencies, and intergovernmental and non-governmental organizations, to intensify their efforts in combating AIDS;

3. *Encourages* all countries and Governments, in particular those worst affected, to intensify their efforts to develop and implement multisectoral action aimed at reducing transmission and the vulnerability of individuals and communities, diminishing the stigma, denial and discrimination associated with AIDS, ensuring equitable access to care and mitigating the wider social impact of the epidemic;

4. *Recognizes* that such multisectoral action will require additional human and financial resources and therefore urges Governments to foster strong national partnerships with the private sector, non-governmental organizations and people living with HIV/AIDS;

5. *Urges* multilateral and bilateral donors, the Programme and its co-sponsors and the wider United Nations system to adequately support and strengthen these national efforts, especially in the worst-affected countries, particularly in sub-Saharan Africa;

6. *Recognizes* that AIDS is a major obstacle to development which has already reversed many hard-won development gains, strongly endorses the International Partnership against AIDS in Africa, and urges Governments, the United Nations system and intergovernmental and non-governmental organizations to participate actively in the activities of the Programme and its co-sponsors aimed at achieving the goals and objectives of the Partnership;

7. *Reiterates* the importance of focusing AIDS-related activities on especially vulnerable people, and commends the efforts of the Programme and its co-sponsors and the larger United Nations community to address the special vulnerability of young people, especially adolescent girls, children and women;

8. *Urges* Governments, with the assistance of the United Nations system, intergovernmental and non-governmental organizations and donors, to make efforts towards assuring access to HIV/AIDS information, education and services for all people, particularly males and females aged 15 to 24, and to ensure that by 2005 HIV prevalence in this particular age group is reduced globally;

9. *Re-emphasizes* the importance of coordination of activities, and therefore:

(*a*) Commends the Programme for the development of the unified budget and work plan, 2000-2001, distinguishing (i) activities to be implemented and funded jointly by two or more co-sponsors, (ii) activities to be funded by core budgets and implemented by the co-sponsoring organizations and (iii) coordination activities to be implemented by its secretariat;

(*b*) Urges the co-sponsors of the Programme and other organizations of the United Nations system to complete the development of their institutional strategies, as the tool to integrate AIDS-related activities into their operational activities for the implementation of the unified budget and work plan, 2000-2001, at the global, regional and country levels;

(*c*) Also urges the co-sponsors of the Programme and other organizations of the United Nations system to submit to their governing bodies their proposed contribution to the United Nations system strategic plan for HIV/AIDS for 2001-2005;

(*d*) Requests the United Nations programmes and funds, and invites the specialized agencies, to ensure that the United Nations theme groups on HIV/AIDS follow the principles under which administrative arrangements are provided within the United Nations Resident Coordinator system and that the role of chairman rotate between co-sponsors, and complete as soon as possible their respective joint strategies at the country level, with the participation of the Government of the host country to respond effectively to its national strategies and priorities and to participate actively in its implementation;

10. *Welcomes* the recommendations on HIV/AIDS in the follow-up to United Nations conferences and summits, and urges Governments and the United Nations system to further enhance their response in order to reach the goals articulated therein;

11. *Invites* the Secretary-General, in collaboration with the Programme, to set system-wide goals to mobilize further Member States and the international community in the fight against AIDS and in the mitigation of its effects;

12. *Urges* Governments, civil society and bilateral and multilateral donors to increase their funding efforts for AIDS-related activities in order to ensure a level of financial and other resources that is fully commensurate with the multisectoral challenges of the epidemic, and also to provide the required assistance for capacity-building;

13. *Requests* the Programme to transmit the conclusions and recommendations of the meetings of the Committee of Co-sponsoring Organizations and the Programme Coordinating Board to the Economic and Social Council and to the governing bodies of the co-sponsoring organizations;

14. *Requests* the Secretary-General to transmit to the Council at its substantive session of 2001 a comprehensive report prepared by the Executive Director of the Joint United Nations Programme on Human Immunodeficiency Virus/Acquired Immunodeficiency Syndrome (HIV/AIDS) (UNAIDS) in collaboration with other relevant organizations of the United Nations system, which should also include the progress made in the implementation of the present resolution in the response to the epidemic and its impact on reducing the

transmission of HIV and increasing the quality and accessibility of treatment, care and support for people living with HIV or AIDS.

Tobacco or health

In 1999, total world production of tobacco leaves was 7.09 million tons. World production had increased steadily during the 1970s and 1980s and stabilized in the 1990s. World production increased from 4.7 million tons in 1970 to 7.13 million in 1990. In the early 1990s, an estimated 1.1 billion individuals used tobacco worldwide, which had increased to almost 1.25 billion by 1998. Assuming no change in global prevalence, the global number of smokers was expected to reach 1.69 billion in 2020.

Framework convention

On 24 May, the WHO World Health Assembly adopted a resolution that mapped out the political process for negotiation of a framework convention on tobacco control and related protocols. The resolution established two intergovernmental bodies as WHO subsidiary bodies, a working group on the WHO framework convention on tobacco control, and an intergovernmental negotiating body (INB). In October, the working group laid the technical foundation for formal negotiations by INB, which were scheduled to begin in 2000.

Inter-agency task force

At the request of the WHO Director-General, and following an agreement between the Director-General and the Secretary-General of the United Nations Conference on Trade and Development (the body designated as focal point for multisectoral collaboration on economic and social aspects of tobacco production and consumption), the UN Secretary-General, in order to intensify a joint UN response and to galvanize global support for tobacco control, agreed to the designation of an ad hoc inter-agency task force on tobacco control, under the leadership of WHO. The establishment of the task force was endorsed by the Administrative Committee on Coordination (ACC) in April [ACC/1999/2].

The first session of the Task Force (New York, 19-30 September), attended by 13 UN organizations, the World Bank and the International Monetary Fund, sought to outline current and future actions of ACC members in respect of tobacco control and to develop an operational approach to ensure that one United Nations voice was heard throughout the framework convention on tobacco control process.

Note by Secretariat. A July note by the Secretariat [E/1999/114] stated that the report called for in an Economic and Social Council draft resolution [E/1999/L.53] would be prepared through the Inter-Agency Task Force and would be submitted by the Secretary-General in 2000.

By **decision 1999/284** of 30 July, the Council took note of the Secretariat's note.

ECONOMIC AND SOCIAL COUNCIL ACTION

On 30 July [meeting 46], the Economic and Social Council adopted **resolution 1999/56** [draft: E/1999/L.53] without vote [agenda item 7].

Tobacco or health

The Economic and Social Council,

Noting that, since the adoption of its first resolution on tobacco or health, resolution 1993/79 of 30 July 1993, the Council adopted two other resolutions, 1994/47 of 29 July 1994 and 1995/62 of 28 July 1995, in which the Secretary-General was requested to submit to the Council at subsequent substantive sessions reports on progress made by the United Nations focal point on tobacco or health in the implementation of the multisectoral collaboration on tobacco or health,

Noting with appreciation that so far the Secretary-General has submitted to the Council three reports on progress made in the implementation of multisectoral collaboration on tobacco or health, upon receipt of which the Council congratulated the Secretary-General for their high quality,

Recognizing the initiatives taken within the United Nations system, other international organizations and Member States to address the issue of tobacco or health,

Expressing concern that tobacco control has yet to reverse the negative trends in terms of the death toll from tobacco,

Acknowledging the recent initiatives within the United Nations system to intensify a system-wide response to tobacco control through the establishment of an Ad Hoc Inter-Agency Task Force on Tobacco Control and the support of the Secretary-General for this initiative,

Requests the Secretary-General to report to the Council at its substantive session of 2000 on progress made by the Ad Hoc Inter-Agency Task Force on Tobacco Control in the implementation of multisectoral collaboration on tobacco or health, with particular emphasis on the development of appropriate strategies to address the social and economic implications of the impact of tobacco or health initiatives.

Inter-agency coordination in health policy

The WHO/UNICEF/UNFPA Coordinating Committee on Health, at its second session (Geneva, 2-3 December) [E/ICEF/2000/7], considered follow-up to the 1994 International Conference on Population and Development [YUN 1994, p. 956], particularly maternal mortality and morbidity, adolescent health and development, HIV/AIDS and coordination of the follow-up to the Conference. The three organizations gave an overview of progress in the area of immunization and plans for the eradication of poliomyelitis, the elimination of maternal and neonatal tetanus, the expansion of immunization services and improvement in the quality of immunization services. In other action, the Committee reviewed the resolutions and decisions of the WHO, UNICEF and UNFPA governing bodies, as well as its terms of reference.

Food and agriculture

Food aid

World Food Programme

In July, the Economic and Social Council examined two reports pertaining to the work of the World Food Programme (WFP) in 1998: the annual report of the Executive Director [E/1999/58] and a report of the WFP Executive Board containing an overview of activities in 1998 and the decisions and recommendations of its four 1998 sessions [E/1999/36].

By **decision 1999/219** of 23 July, the Council took note of the report of the WFP Executive Board and the annual report of the Executive Director for 1998.

The WFP Executive Board [E/2000/36] decided on organizational and programme matters and approved a number of projects at its 1999 sessions, all held in Rome: first regular session (20-22 January), second regular session (13-14 May), annual session (17-20 May) and third regular session (18-22 October). In May, the Board approved the preparation of a consolidated 2000-2001 budget of some $2.6 billion for activities, including programme support and administrative costs totalling not more than $195 million. In October, it approved a net programme support and administrative appropriation of $194 million.

WFP activities

During 1999 [E/2000/54], the number of people assisted by WFP increased by some 17 per cent over 1998, to 89 million. Recipients of relief assistance accounted for nearly 80 per cent of all WFP beneficiaries in 1999, including a large number of people affected by natural disasters in late 1998, who continued to receive emergency assistance in early 1999. Of those assisted by WFP, 41 million people were victims of natural disasters, 18 million were affected by man-made disasters such as wars and civil unrest, 11 million were beneficiaries in protracted relief and recovery operations, and 19 million were in development programmes. Included among the beneficiaries were 19 million internally displaced persons in 35 countries and 3 million refugees in 31 countries.

In 1999, contributions to the Programme's operations amounted to $1,555 million from 45 donor countries, plus the European Commission (EC), various intergovernmental organizations, NGOs and private donors, including $45 million received in bilateral contributions. The five largest donors (United States, EC, Japan, Canada, Netherlands) contributed 77 per cent of all resources.

Global food aid deliveries amounted to 14.5 million tons, up from 8.3 million in 1998. Nearly half of the food aid delivered during 1999 was channelled as programme food aid provided bilaterally on a government-to-government basis as balance-of-payments support, largely from the United States. Programme food aid deliveries increased by 160 per cent compared to 1998. Emergency food aid, which accounted for 32 per cent of 1999 global deliveries, reflected an increase of 57 per cent over 1998. Project food aid deliveries remained at nearly the same level as in 1998. Targeted food aid, composed of emergency and project food aid, represented 49 per cent of total food aid deliveries.

The largest proportion of WFP assistance went to sub-Saharan Africa, with 44.1 per cent of its operational expenditures spent in 45 countries in the region; Asia and the Pacific received 34.8 per cent for 20 countries; Eastern Europe and CIS States, 7.7 per cent for 11 countries; Latin America and the Caribbean, 7.7 per cent for 25 countries; and the Middle East and North Africa, 3.2 per cent for 12 countries.

Administrative and financial matters

Resources and financing

WFP operational expenditure for 1999 amounted to $1,430 million for development and relief activities in the least developed countries and in low-income, food-deficit countries. Contributions totalled $1,555 million, of which $275 million was contributed to development, $863 million to emergency operations, $382 million to protracted relief and recovery operations, and $35 million was provided as "other contributions". Total quantities of food provided amounted to 3.4 million tons, with 0.8 million tons for development projects, 2 million tons for emergency operations and 0.6 million tons for protracted relief and recovery operations.

Revisions to General Regulations

Following the Executive Board's approval in January of WFP's resource and long-term financing policies, the Board endorsed the revision of article XIII.2 of the General Regulations relating to donor contributions. Subject to the approval of that recommendation, it approved the revision of general rule XIII.4. The revised Regulations and Rules would take effect from 1 January 2000, subject to the approval of article XIII.2 by the General Assembly and the Conference of FAO, on the advice of the Economic and Social Council and the FAO Council. In a June note, the Secretary-General transmitted to the Economic and Social Council the proposed amendment to the General Regulations [E/1999/87]. The recommendation was also made available to the FAO Council. By **decision 1999/219** of 23 July, the Council took note of the Secretary-General's note.

The amendment was endorsed by the FAO Council at its one hundred and sixteenth session in June 1999. By **decision 1999/220** of 23 July, the Economic and Social Council endorsed the proposed amendment to the General Regulations.

Regarding the General Regulations pertaining to the distribution of seats of the WFP Executive Board, the Council, by **decision 1999/209** of 5 February, decided to continue consideration of the subject at its resumed organizational session for 1999, with a view to arriving at a recommendation for submission to the General Assembly. It also decided to postpone action on a draft text on the item.

ECONOMIC AND SOCIAL COUNCIL ACTION

On 25 March [meeting 5], the Economic and Social Council adopted **resolution 1999/3** [draft: E/1999/L.12] without vote [agenda item 2].

Revision of the General Regulations of the World Food Programme

The Economic and Social Council

Recommends to the General Assembly the adoption of the following draft resolution:

[For text, see General Assembly resolution 53/223 below.]

GENERAL ASSEMBLY ACTION

On 7 April [meeting 97], the General Assembly, on the recommendation of the Economic and Social Council [A/53/899], adopted **resolution 53/223** without vote [agenda items 8 & 12].

Revision of the General Regulations of the World Food Programme

The General Assembly,

Recalling its resolutions 48/162 of 20 December 1993 and 50/8 of 1 November 1995,

1. *Decides,* subject to the concurrence of the Conference of the Food and Agriculture Organization of the United Nations, that the members of the Executive Board of the World Food Programme shall be elected on an interim basis for a term of three years from among the States included in the lists set out in the Basic Texts of the World Food Programme, in accordance with the following distribution of seats, it being understood that this allocation of seats creates no precedent for the composition of other United Nations bodies of limited membership:

(a) Eight members from the States included in list A, four members to be elected by the Economic and Social Council and four by the Council of the Food and Agriculture Organization of the United Nations;

(b) Seven members from the States included in list B, four members to be elected by the Economic and Social Council and three by the Council of the Food and Agriculture Organization of the United Nations;

(c) Five members from the States included in list C, two members to be elected by the Economic and Social Council and three by the Council of the Food and Agriculture Organization of the United Nations;

(d) Twelve members from the States included in list D, six members to be elected by the Economic and Social Council and six by the Council of the Food and Agriculture Organization of the United Nations;

(e) Three members from the States included in list E, two members to be elected by the Economic and Social Council and one by the Council of the Food and Agriculture Organization of the United Nations;

(f) One additional member rotating among the States included in lists A, B and C to be elected by the Council of the Food and Agriculture Organization of the United Nations in accordance with the following pattern of rotation:

(i) One State from list A is to be elected to occupy the additional seat every other term out of four, starting from 1 January 2000;

(ii) One State from list B is to be elected to occupy the additional seat the second term out of four, starting from 1 January 2003;

(iii) One State from list C is to be elected to occupy the additional seat the fourth term out of four, starting from 1 January 2009;

2. *Requests* the Economic and Social Council to elect one member from the States included in list E for a term of three years beginning on 1 January 2000;

3. *Decides* that the above-mentioned distribution of seats shall be reviewed two years before the end of one full rotation scheme of four terms, as referred to in paragraph 1 *(f)* of the present resolution. Such a review shall be in accordance with the relevant provisions of General Assembly resolutions 48/162 and 50/8, taking into account the relevant inputs of the Economic and Social Council and the Council of the Food and Agriculture Organization of the United Nations; the result of the review shall enter into force on 1 January 2012;

4. *Decides also,* subject to the concurrence of the Conference of the Food and Agriculture Organization of the United Nations, that the revised General Regulations shall enter into force on 1 January 2000.

On 13 November, the FAO Conference adopted a resolution regarding the General Regulations pertaining to the distribution of seats of the WFP Executive Board by which it concurred with Assembly resolution 53/223.

Food security

Follow-up to 1996 World Food Summit

The Economic and Social Council, by **decision 1999/212** of 25 March, decided to discontinue its quadrennial consideration of progress reports on the implementation of the decisions of the 1979 World Conference on Agrarian Reform and Rural Development [YUN 1979, p. 500]. It invited the FAO Director-General to transmit to the Council every four years, starting in 1999, a report prepared by the Committee on World Food Security on progress in the implementation of the Plan of Action adopted at the 1996 World Food Summit [YUN 1996, p. 1129], highlighting its linkages with the coordinated and integrated follow-up to major UN conferences and summits undertaken by the UN system. Accordingly, the Secretary-General, by a June note [E/1999/81], transmitted the Committee's report.

The report was based on information received from 68 countries and the EC, 14 UN agencies, 13 international organizations and six regional bodies, plus an additional 27 country reports that had reached the Secretariat at the time of the Committee's session. Many reporting countries provided highlights of major issues and objectives in implementing the Plan of Action. Food insecurity, affecting large shares or specific groups of the population, was underlined by many developing countries, with emphasis on the growing food deficit and/or instability of food production. Under- and malnutrition, affecting in particular children but also adults, was documented, even in cases where the general food security situation was satisfactory. Poverty was universally acknowledged as a major cause of food insecurity at the household level, and human development, mainly through education and health improvement, received much attention. Pursuing policies aimed at sound macroeconomic conditions and taking advantage of international trade were highlighted by several countries; sustainable development of agriculture and food production was widely considered an essential objective, often in connection with developing the agri-food sector. Intensification of production and diversification, particularly towards animal products and fish in certain cases, were sought. Productivity improvements benefiting the poor and environmental sustainability were emphasized. In the food chain, marketing, food quality and safety, and improved processing were frequently cited concerns. Decentralization and developing rural infrastructure were also repeatedly mentioned. The report concluded that the information received showed a universal commitment to implementing the Plan of Action. Mechanisms had been put in place, where they had not existed, to promote, coordinate and monitor follow-up to the Summit. However, several factors had prevented the Secretariat in its first review from drawing general substantive conclusions on progress in implementing the Plan of Action. Information provided in reports on policies for pursuing food security for all showed the predominance of continuing actions already in place at the time of the Summit. New actions undertaken as a consequence of the Summit were documented as well. However, results of those could not be observed or analysed given that the reports covered the year that immediately followed the Summit. It was also observed that a broad scope of reporting could be detrimental to a fruitful concentration of reporting and analysis on the most important issues; selecting a smaller number of commitments for each monitoring session would help in overcoming that issue.

By **decision 1999/283** of 30 July, the Council took note of the Secretary-General's note transmitting the Committee's report.

Nutrition

ACC activities

The ACC Subcommittee on Nutrition held its twenty-sixth session (Geneva, 12-15 April) [ACC/1999/9]. It kept under review working groups on such questions as life cycle consequences of fetal and infant malnutrition; vitamin A and iron deficiencies; breastfeeding and complementary feeding; nutrition, ethics and human rights; household food security; nutrition in emergencies; and iodine deficiency disorders.

The Subcommittee approved the core 2000-2001 budget in the amount of $861,000. Proposed programme activities for the biennium totalled $964,000. The Subcommittee approved the programme activities, subject to funds becoming available.

Given the changing needs of the Subcommittee on Nutrition and its secretariat, as well as the growth in professional expertise within the Subcommittee, the Subcommittee decided to hold the Advisory Group on Nutrition in abeyance and not make any appointments to it. The current two-year term of all Advisory Group members would expire at the close of the Subcommittee's twenty-sixth session. UN agencies proposed that an interim programme steering committee should be appointed with a one-year lifespan. Its terms of reference would include identifying the best way to execute tasks that had traditionally been carried out by the Advisory Group on Nutrition. The steering committee would be made up of FAO, UNDP, UNICEF, the World Bank, WHO, a representative of the non-governmental organizations, a representative of the bilaterals and the current Advisory Group Chairman.

The Commission on Nutrition Challenges of the Twenty-first Century, charged with examining nutritional problems emerging in the twenty-first century, presented its report.

The Advisory Group met (Geneva, 8-9 April) and, among other things, noted the overall approach of the *Fourth Report on the World Nutrition Situation.* The full draft was to be circulated in late July and published in December.

UNU activities

The United Nations University (UNU) continued its food and nutrition programme in 1999, as described in the report of the UNU Council to the General Assembly [A/55/31]. The programme, undertaken in collaboration with WHO, UNICEF and FAO, addressed major nutrition concerns in developing countries. During 1999, it maintained six major global projects and a number of minor ones, and provided 15 fellowships for various kinds of advanced training. The topics of some of the projects under the programme were: international network of food data systems; international iron nutrition; international dietary energy consultative group; multi-country growth reference study; global initiative for enhancing institutional capacity in food and nutrition: African leadership initiative (a joint project with the International Union of Nutritional Sciences); and harmonization of approaches for setting national dietary standards. The programme continued its quarterly publication of the *Food and Nutrition Bulletin* and the *Journal of Food Composition and Analysis.*

The programme's priority in 1999 was to work more effectively in strengthening capacity in Africa. A workshop in Capetown, South Africa, focused on the development of an African nutrition leadership initiative to strengthen and build up a cadre of nutrition leaders at the regional, national and local levels. Such leaders would be drawn from different fields, including health, agriculture, education and community development, and different sectors, including public, private and non-profit sectors.

Chapter XIV

International drug control

During 1999, the United Nations, through the Commission on Narcotic Drugs, the International Narcotics Control Board (INCB) and the United Nations International Drug Control Programme (UNDCP), renewed its commitment to strengthen international cooperation and increase efforts to counter the world drug problem, in accordance with the obligations of States under the United Nations drug control conventions, and on the basis of the general framework provided by the 1990 Global Programme of Action on narcotic drugs and psychotropic substances and the outcome of the General Assembly's twentieth special session, held in 1998. The Assembly urged competent authorities to implement the outcome of the special session within the agreed time frames, and adopted the Action Plan for the Implementation of the Declaration on the Guiding Principles of Drug Demand Reduction, which served as a guide to Member States in adopting strategies and programmes for reducing illicit drug demand in order to achieve significant results by the year 2008.

UNDCP stimulated action at the national, regional and international levels through technical cooperation programmes and supported the international community in pursuing the objectives agreed upon by the Assembly at its special session. It assisted States in complying with international treaties and supported them in establishing business plans to reduce the illicit cultivation of the opium poppy, coca bush and cannabis.

The Commission on Narcotic Drugs—the main UN policy-making body on drug control—addressed a number of issues, primarily the reduction of illicit demand for drugs, and illicit drug production and trafficking. It also considered the implementation of the Global Programme of Action and international treaties. The Subcommission on Illicit Drug Traffic and Related Matters in the Near and Middle East adopted the Lucknow Accord on the Adoption of Uniform Measures to Control International Trade in Precursors and Other Chemicals Used in the Illicit Manufacture of Narcotic Drugs and Psychotropic Substances. In July, the Economic and Social Council invited Member States to promote awareness within the chemical industry concerning the Accord's provisions.

INCB continued to oversee the implementation of the three major international drug control conventions, to analyse the drug situation worldwide and to draw Governments' attention to gaps and weaknesses in national control and treaty compliance, making suggestions and recommendations for improvements at the national and international levels.

Follow-up to the twentieth special session

The Secretary-General, in an August report [A/54/186], provided an overview of the implementation of the outcome of the twentieth special session of the General Assembly on the world drug problem, held in 1998 [YUN 1998, p. 1135]. The report, prepared in response to resolution 53/115 [ibid., p. 1170], covered the action plans and measures adopted and presented the activities already undertaken, as well as those envisaged, by UNDCP to meet the new mandates with regard to: the revised medium-term plan for international drug control, 1998-2001; designation of the twentieth special session as a major global conference, thereby requiring review of implementation of its outcome; an action plan for the implementation of the Declaration on the Guiding Principles of Drug Demand Reduction; elimination of illicit cultivation of the opium poppy, coca bush and cannabis through alternative development; measures to promote judicial cooperation; the Action Plan against Illicit Manufacture, Trafficking and Abuse of Amphetamine-type Stimulants and Their Precursors; control of precursors; efforts to counter money-laundering; and mobilization of the Commission on Narcotic Drugs to fulfil its mandates.

In a December report on follow-up to the twentieth special session [E/CN.7/2000/2], the UNDCP Executive Director listed the goals and targets set by the Assembly and described the role of the Commission in the implementation process, as well as action by the Assembly at its fifty-fourth (1999) session.

(For information on follow-up activities in specific areas, see below.)

Action Plan

A January note by the Secretariat [E/CN.7/1999/7] on reduction of illicit demand for drugs contained the report on the meeting of the intergovernmental working group on the elaboration of the action plan for the implementation of the Declaration on the Guiding Principles of Drug Demand Reduction, annexed to resolution S-20/3, adopted by the General Assembly at its twentieth special session [YUN 1998, p. 1137]. The working group (Vienna, 14-16 December 1998) discussed a preliminary draft of the action plan prepared by UNDCP following the special session, and agreed that it should be used as the basis for the elaboration of the action plan. The group emphasized that the Declaration and the action plan should provide Member States with an overall framework for cooperation and a structure within which demand reduction programmes could be adapted to meet the needs of local communities. The action plan should follow closely the structure of the Declaration and translate its content into practical action; it should also respect cultural and religious affiliation, human rights, national sovereignty and territorial integrity. Following consideration of 33 objectives suggested by Member States, specialized agencies and intergovernmental organizations, the working group agreed on 16 objectives to be covered by the plan.

The Commission on Narcotic Drugs, at its forty-second session [E/1999/28/Rev.1] (see p. 1187), expressed support for the action plan as a guide for Member States in developing programmes to reduce the demand for drugs.

ECONOMIC AND SOCIAL COUNCIL ACTION

On 28 July [meeting 43], the Economic and Social Council, on the recommendation of the Commission on Narcotic Drugs [E/1999/28/Rev.1], adopted **resolution 1999/29** without vote [agenda item 14 *(d)*].

Action Plan for the Implementation of the Declaration on the Guiding Principles of Drug Demand Reduction

The Economic and Social Council

Recommends to the General Assembly the adoption of the following draft resolution:

"*The General Assembly*

"*Adopts* the Action Plan for the Implementation of the Declaration on the Guiding Principles of Drug Demand Reduction annexed to the present resolution.

[For annex, see annex to General Assembly resolution 54/132 below.]

GENERAL ASSEMBLY ACTION

On 17 December [meeting 83], the General Assembly, on the recommendation of the Third (Social, Humanitarian and Cultural) Committee [A/54/597], adopted **resolution 54/132** without vote [agenda item 108].

International cooperation against the world drug problem

The General Assembly,

Recalling its resolutions 52/92 of 12 December 1997 and 53/115 of 9 December 1998,

Reaffirming its commitment to the outcome of the twentieth special session of the General Assembly devoted to countering the world drug problem together, held in New York from 8 to 10 June 1998, and welcoming the continued determination of Governments to overcome the world drug problem by a full and balanced application of national, regional and international strategies to reduce the demand for, production of and trafficking in illicit drugs, as reflected in the Political Declaration, the Declaration on the Guiding Principles of Drug Demand Reduction and the measures to enhance international cooperation to counter the world drug problem,

Gravely concerned that, despite continued increased efforts by States, relevant international organizations, civil society and non-governmental organizations, there is a global expansion of the drug problem, which constitutes a serious threat to the health, safety and well-being of all mankind, in particular young people, in all countries, undermines development, including efforts to reduce poverty, socio-economic and political stability and democratic institutions, entails an increasing economic cost for Governments, also threatens the national security and sovereignty of States, as well as the dignity and hope of millions of people and their families, and causes irreparable loss of human lives,

Concerned that the demand for, production of and trafficking in illicit drugs and psychotropic substances continue to threaten seriously the socio-economic and political systems, stability, national security and sovereignty of an increasing number of States, especially those involved in conflicts and wars, and that trafficking in drugs could make conflict resolution more difficult,

Deeply alarmed by the growing and spreading violence and economic power of criminal organizations and terrorist groups engaged in drug-trafficking activities and other criminal activities, such as money-laundering and illicit traffic in arms, precursors and essential chemicals, and by the increasing transnational links between them, and recognizing the need for international cooperation and implementation of effective strategies on the basis of the outcome of the twentieth special session of the General Assembly, which are essential to achieving results against all forms of transnational criminal activities,

Deeply convinced that the special session made a significant contribution to a new comprehensive framework for international cooperation, based on an integrated and balanced approach with strategies, measures, methods, practical activities, goals and specific targets to be met, that all States, the United Nations system and other international organizations must implement them with concrete actions and that the international financial institutions, such as the World Bank, and the regional development banks should be invited to include action against the world drug problem in their programmes, taking into account the priorities of States,

Convinced that civil society, including non-governmental organizations, can make an effective contribution to and should play an active role in addressing the world drug problem,

Emphasizing the importance of the adoption of the Action Plan for the Implementation of the Declaration on the Guiding Principles of Drug Demand Reduction annexed to the present resolution, which introduces a global approach, recognizing a new balance between illicit supply and demand reduction, under the principle of shared responsibility, aims at preventing the use of drugs and at reducing the adverse consequences of drug abuse, ensuring that special attention is paid to vulnerable groups, in particular youth, and constitutes one of the pillars of the new global strategy and an important initiative of the United Nations Decade against Drug Abuse, 1991-2000, and reaffirming the need for demand reduction programmes,

Emphasizing equally the importance of supply reduction as an integral part of a balanced drug control strategy under the principles enshrined in the Action Plan on International Cooperation on the Eradication of Illicit Drug Crops and on Alternative Development, reaffirming the need for alternative development programmes that are sustainable, welcoming the achievements of some States on their way to eradicating illicit drug crops, and inviting all other States to make similar efforts,

Underlining the role of the Commission on Narcotic Drugs as the principal United Nations policy-making body on drug control issues, the leadership role and commendable work of the United Nations International Drug Control Programme as the main focus for concerted multilateral action and the important role of the International Narcotics Control Board as an independent monitoring authority, as set out in the international drug control treaties,

Recognizing the efforts of all countries, in particular those that produce narcotic drugs for scientific and medical purposes, and of the International Narcotics Control Board in preventing the diversion of such substances to illicit markets and in maintaining production at a level consistent with licit demand, in line with the Single Convention on Narcotic Drugs of 1961 and the Convention on Psychotropic Substances of 1971,

Acknowledging that there are links, under certain circumstances, between poverty and the increase in the illicit production of and trafficking in narcotic drugs and psychotropic substances and that the promotion of the economic development of countries affected by the illicit drug trade requires appropriate measures, including strengthened international cooperation in support of alternative and sustainable development activities in the affected areas of those countries, which have as their objectives the reduction and elimination of illicit drug production,

Stressing that respect for all human rights is and must be an essential component of measures taken to address the drug problem,

Ensuring that women and men benefit equally, and without any discrimination, from strategies directed against the world drug problem, through their involvement in all stages of programmes and policy-making,

Recognizing that the use of the Internet poses new opportunities and challenges to international cooperation in combating drug abuse and illicit production and trafficking, and recognizing also the need for increased cooperation among States and the exchange of information, including with reference to national experiences, on how to counteract the promotion of drug abuse and illicit drug trafficking through this instrument and on ways to use the Internet for information concerning drug demand reduction,

I

Respect for the principles enshrined in the Charter of the United Nations and international law in the fight against the world drug problem

1. *Reaffirms* that the fight against the world drug problem is a common and shared responsibility which must be addressed in a multilateral setting, requiring an integrated and balanced approach, and must be carried out in full conformity with the purposes and principles of the Charter of the United Nations and international law, and in particular with full respect for the sovereignty and territorial integrity of States, the principle of non-intervention in the internal affairs of States and all human rights and fundamental freedoms;

2. *Calls upon* all States to take further action to promote effective cooperation at the international and regional levels in the efforts to combat the world drug problem so as to contribute to a climate conducive to achieving that end, on the basis of the principles of equal rights and mutual respect;

3. *Urges* all States to ratify or accede to and implement all the provisions of the Single Convention on Narcotic Drugs of 1961 as amended by the 1972 Protocol, the Convention on Psychotropic Substances of 1971 and the United Nations Convention against Illicit Traffic in Narcotic Drugs and Psychotropic Substances of 1988;

II

Action Plan for the Implementation of the Declaration on the Guiding Principles of Drug Demand Reduction

1. *Adopts* the Action Plan for the Implementation of the Declaration on the Guiding Principles of Drug Demand Reduction as contained in the annex to the present resolution;

2. *Requests* the Executive Director of the United Nations International Drug Control Programme to report to the Commission on Narcotic Drugs at its forty-third session on the follow-up to the Action Plan;

3. *Urges* all Member States to implement the Action Plan in their respective national, regional and international actions and to strengthen their national efforts to fight the use of illicit drugs among their population, in particular among children and youth;

III

International cooperation to counter the world drug problem

1. *Urges* competent authorities, at the international, regional and national levels, to implement the outcome of the twentieth special session, within the agreed timeframes, in particular the high-priority practical measures at the international, regional or national level, as indicated in the Political Declaration, the Declaration on the Guiding Principles of Drug Demand Reduction and the Action Plan for its implementation and the measures to enhance international cooperation to counter the world drug problem, including the Action

Plan against Illicit Manufacture, Trafficking and Abuse of Amphetamine-type Stimulants and Their Precursors, the measures to prevent the illicit manufacture, import, export, trafficking, distribution and diversion of precursors used in the illicit manufacture of narcotic drugs and psychotropic substances, the measures to promote judicial cooperation, the measures to counter money-laundering and the Action Plan on International Cooperation on the Eradication of Illicit Drug Crops and on Alternative Development;

2. *Stresses* its resolve to strengthen the United Nations machinery for international drug control, in particular the United Nations International Drug Control Programme, in order to enable it to fulfil its mandate, and takes note of the recommendations contained in Economic and Social Council resolution 1999/30 of 28 July 1999;

3. *Renews its commitment* to further strengthening international cooperation and substantially increasing efforts to counter the world drug problem, in accordance with the obligations of States under the United Nations drug control conventions, on the basis of the general framework given by the Global Programme of Action, and the outcome of the special session, and taking into account experience gained;

4. *Calls upon* all States to adopt effective measures, including national laws and regulations, to implement the mandates and recommendations of the Global Programme of Action, to strengthen national judicial systems and to carry out effective drug control activities in cooperation with other States in accordance with those international instruments, in order to implement the outcome and the goals of the special session, within the agreed time-frame of 2003 and 2008;

5. *Calls upon* the relevant United Nations bodies, the specialized agencies, the international financial institutions and other concerned intergovernmental and international organizations, within their mandates, and all actors of civil society, notably non-governmental organizations, community-based organizations, sports associations, the media and the private sector, to continue their close cooperation with Governments in their efforts to promote and implement the Global Programme of Action, the outcome of the special session and the Action Plan for the Implementation of the Declaration on the Guiding Principles of Drug Demand Reduction, including through public information campaigns;

6. *Urges* Governments, the relevant United Nations bodies, the specialized agencies and other international organizations to assist and support, upon request, transit States, in particular developing countries in need of such assistance and support, aiming at enhancing their capacity to fight illicit trafficking of narcotic drugs and psychotropic substances, taking into account national plans and initiatives, and emphasizes the importance of subregional, regional and international cooperation in combating illicit drug trafficking;

7. *Reaffirms* that preventing the diversion of chemicals from legitimate commerce to illicit drug manufacture is an essential component of a comprehensive strategy against drug abuse and trafficking, which requires the effective cooperation of exporting, importing and transit States, takes note of the progress made in developing practical guidelines to prevent such diversion of chemicals, including those of the International Narcotics Control Board and the recommendations on implementing article 12 of the 1988 Convention, and calls upon all States to adopt and implement measures to prevent the diversion of chemicals to illicit drug manufacture, in cooperation with competent international and regional bodies and, if necessary and to the extent possible, with the private sector in each State, in accordance with the objectives targeted for 2003 and 2008 in the Political Declaration of the special session and the resolution on the control of precursors adopted at the special session;

8. *Calls upon* States in which cultivation and production of illicit drug crops occur to establish or reinforce, where appropriate, national mechanisms to monitor and verify illicit crops, and requests the Executive Director of the United Nations International Drug Control Programme to report to the Commission on Narcotic Drugs at its forty-third session, in March 2000, on the follow-up to the Action Plan on International Cooperation on the Eradication of Illicit Drug Crops and on Alternative Development;

9. *Requests* the Commission on Narcotic Drugs, with the support of the United Nations International Drug Control Programme, to continue its work expeditiously, within the established time-frames, on the elaboration of guidelines to facilitate biennial reporting by Governments on the implementation of the Global Programme of Action and progress achieved in meeting the goals and targets for 2003 and 2008, as set out in the Political Declaration of the special session, and to encourage an efficient collection of reliable data, an increase in the number of Governments that report updated information on a regular basis and an improvement in the quality of their responses, as well as the avoidance of the duplication of activities;

10. *Calls upon* the Commission on Narcotic Drugs to mainstream a gender perspective into all its policies, programmes and activities, and requests the Secretariat to integrate a gender perspective into all documentation prepared for the Commission;

11. *Recalls* the World Programme of Action for Youth to the Year 2000 and Beyond adopted by the General Assembly on 14 December 1995, notes with satisfaction the commitment of young people to a drug-free society made at various forums, stresses the importance of youth continuing to contribute their experiences and to participate in the decision-making processes and, in particular, putting into effect the Action Plan for the Implementation of the Declaration on the Guiding Principles of Drug Demand Reduction, and, in this context, recalls the holding of the World Conference of Ministers Responsible for Youth in Lisbon from 8 to 12 August 1998, and also recalls the holding of the third World Youth Forum of the United Nations system in Braga, Portugal, from 2 to 7 August 1998;

12. *Calls upon* States to adopt effective measures, including possible national legislative measures, and to enhance cooperation to stem the illicit trade in small arms, which, as a result of its close link to the illicit drug trade, is generating extremely high levels of crime and violence within the societies of some States, threatening the national security and the economies of those States;

13. *Notes* the progress achieved in the elaboration of an international convention against transnational organized crime and the three related international instruments, within the framework of the Ad Hoc Com-

mittee on the Elaboration of a Convention against Transnational Organized Crime, and urges the Committee to intensify its work in order to complete it in 2000;

14. *Reaffirms* the importance of the achievement of the objectives of the United Nations Decade against Drug Abuse, 1991-2000, under the theme "A global response to a global challenge", by Member States, the United Nations International Drug Control Programme and the United Nations system;

IV

Action by the United Nations system

1. *Reaffirms* the role of the Executive Director of the United Nations International Drug Control Programme in coordinating and providing effective leadership for all United Nations drug control activities so as to increase cost-effectiveness and ensure coherence of action, as well as coordination, complementarity and non-duplication of such activities throughout the United Nations system;

2. *Emphasizes* that the multidimensional nature of the world drug problem calls for the promotion of integration and coordination of drug control activities throughout the United Nations system, including in the follow-up to major United Nations conferences;

3. *Invites* Governments and the United Nations International Drug Control Programme to attach high priority to the improvement of the coordination of United Nations activities related to the world drug problem so as to avoid duplication of such activities, strengthen efficiency and accomplish the goals approved by Governments;

4. *Urges* the specialized agencies, programmes and funds, including humanitarian organizations, and invites multilateral financial institutions, to include action against the world drug problem in their programming and planning processes in order to ensure that the integral and balanced strategy which emerged from the special session devoted to countering the world drug problem together is being addressed;

V

United Nations International Drug Control Programme

1. *Welcomes* the efforts of the United Nations International Drug Control Programme to implement its mandate within the framework of the international drug control treaties, the Comprehensive Multidisciplinary Outline of Future Activities in Drug Abuse Control, the Global Programme of Action, the outcome of the special session of the General Assembly devoted to countering the world drug problem together and relevant consensus documents;

2. *Expresses its appreciation* to the Programme for the support provided to different States in meeting the objectives of the Global Programme of Action and of the special session, especially in cases where significant and anticipated progress was achieved regarding the objectives targeted for 2003 and 2008;

3. *Requests* the United Nations International Drug Control Programme to continue:

(*a*) To strengthen cooperation with Member States and with United Nations programmes, funds and relevant agencies, as well as other relevant regional organizations and agencies and non-governmental organizations, and to provide, on request, assistance in implementing the outcome of the special session;

(*b*) To strengthen dialogue and cooperation with multilateral development banks and with international financial institutions so that they may undertake lending and programming activities related to drug control in interested and affected countries to implement the outcome of the special session, and to keep the Commission on Narcotic Drugs informed of further progress made in this area;

(*c*) To take into account the outcome of the special session, to include in its report on illicit traffic in drugs an updated assessment of worldwide trends in illicit traffic and transit in narcotic drugs and psychotropic substances, including methods and routes used, and to recommend ways and means of improving the capacity of States along those routes to deal with all aspects of the drug problem;

(*d*) To publish the *World Drug Report*, with comprehensive and balanced information about the world drug problem, and to seek additional extrabudgetary resources for its publication in all official languages;

4. *Urges* all Governments to provide the fullest possible financial and political support to the Programme by widening its donor base and increasing voluntary contributions, in particular general-purpose contributions, to enable it to continue, expand and strengthen its operational and technical cooperation activities;

5. *Urges* the International Narcotics Control Board to increase efforts to implement all its mandates under international drug control conventions and to continue to cooperate with Governments, including by offering advice to Member States that request it;

6. *Notes* that the Board needs sufficient resources to carry out all its mandates, and therefore urges Member States to commit themselves in a common effort to assigning adequate and sufficient budgetary resources to the Board, in accordance with Economic and Social Council resolution 1996/20 of 23 July 1996, and emphasizes the need to maintain its capacity, including through the provision of appropriate means by the Secretary-General and adequate technical support by the Programme;

7. *Stresses* the importance of the meetings of Heads of National Drug Law Enforcement Agencies, in all regions of the world, and the Subcommission on Illicit Drug Traffic and Related Matters in the Near and Middle East of the Commission on Narcotic Drugs, and encourages them to continue to contribute to the strengthening of regional and international cooperation, taking into account the outcome of the special session;

8. *Takes note* of the report of the Secretary-General, and, taking into account the promotion of integrated reporting, requests the Secretary-General to submit to the General Assembly at its fifty-fifth session a comprehensive report on the implementation of the outcome of the twentieth special session, including on the Action Plan for the Implementation of the Declaration on the Guiding Principles of Drug Demand Reduction, and the present resolution.

ANNEX

Action Plan for the Implementation of the Declaration on the Guiding Principles of Drug Demand Reduction

Preamble

1. In the Political Declaration adopted by the General Assembly at its twentieth special session, Member States:

(*a*) Recognized that demand reduction was an indispensable pillar in the global approach to countering the world drug problem and committed themselves:

(i) To introducing into their national programmes and strategies the provisions set out in the Declaration on the Guiding Principles of Drug Demand Reduction;

(ii) To working closely with the United Nations International Drug Control Programme to develop action-oriented strategies to assist in the implementation of the Declaration;

(iii) To establishing 2003 as a target date for new or enhanced drug demand reduction strategies and programmes set up in close collaboration with public health, social welfare and law enforcement authorities;

(iv) To achieving significant and measurable results in the field of demand reduction by 2008;

(*b*) Called upon all States to report biennially to the Commission on Narcotic Drugs on their efforts to meet the above-mentioned goals and targets for 2003 and 2008.

2. The present Action Plan for the Implementation of the Declaration on the Guiding Principles of Drug Demand Reduction is offered as guidance to Member States in implementing the above-mentioned commitments. Organizations of the United Nations system, other international organizations, regional organizations and non-governmental organizations are invited to provide support to Member States in implementing the Action Plan, according to their available resources, specific mandates and the different roles that they are to play in achieving the goals set out in the Declaration.

3. The Action Plan reflects the emphasis in the Declaration on the need for a comprehensive and balanced approach involving demand reduction and supply reduction, each reinforcing the other, together with the appropriate application of the principle of shared responsibility. It stresses the need for services responsible for prevention, including law enforcement agencies, to transmit the same message and use similar language.

4. The Action Plan is guided by the purposes and principles of the Charter of the United Nations and international law, in particular respect for the sovereignty and territorial integrity of States, non-interference in the internal affairs of States, human rights and fundamental freedoms and the principles of the Universal Declaration of Human Rights. It allows for flexible approaches to reflect social, cultural, religious and political differences and it acknowledges that efforts to reduce illicit drug demand are at different levels of implementation in different countries.

5. The Action Plan recognizes that progress to reduce the demand for illicit drugs should be seen in the context of the need for programmes to reduce the demand for substances of abuse. Such programmes should be integrated to promote cooperation among all concerned, should include a wide variety of appropriate interventions, should promote health and social well-being among individuals, families and communities and should reduce the adverse consequences of drug abuse for the individual and for society as a whole.

6. The Action Plan focuses on the need to design demand reduction campaigns and programmes to meet the needs of the population in general, as well as those of specific population groups, taking into account differences in gender, culture and education and paying special attention to youth. Demand reduction efforts should be developed with the participation of target groups, giving special attention to a gender perspective.

I. The commitment

7. *Objective 1.* To apply the Declaration on the Guiding Principles of Drug Demand Reduction in order to achieve significant and measurable results in reducing the demand for drugs by 2008 and to report on those results to the Commission on Narcotic Drugs. That would entail the following:

(*a*) *Impact.* Greater compliance with the spirit and principles of the Declaration and the achievement of significant and measurable results in reducing the demand for drugs;

(*b*) *Outputs.* Biennial reports by each country on the efforts to implement the Declaration and reduce the demand for drugs and on the results achieved;

(*c*) *National action.* Applying the Declaration and preparing a biennial report containing measurable results for submission to the Commission;

(*d*) *International and regional action.* The United Nations International Drug Control Programme to collate national reports and report on its findings to the Commission.

8. *Objective 2.* To secure, at the highest political level possible, a long-term commitment to the implementation of a national strategy for reducing illicit drug demand and to establish a mechanism for ensuring full coordination and participation of the relevant authorities and sectors of society. That would entail the following:

(*a*) *Impact.* Higher priority for and long-term commitment to demand reduction and effective coordination between relevant sectors of society;

(*b*) *Outputs.* A mechanism for ensuring ongoing commitment to the strategy by: (i) fostering linkages and integration with other relevant plans and programmes, for instance, those concerning health, including public health issues such as those relating to the human immunodeficiency virus, acquired immunodeficiency syndrome and hepatitis C, as well as education, housing, employment, social exclusion, law enforcement and crime prevention; (ii) encouraging the participation of all sectors of society; and (iii) providing for the assessment and reporting of results and refinement of the strategy as necessary;

(*c*) *National action.* Consultation and cooperation with potential partners in developing multisectoral plans and obtaining long-term commitments coordinated by the appropriate national authorities;

(*d*) *International and regional action.* The United Nations International Drug Control Programme and other relevant international and regional organizations to provide appropriate assistance in establishing coordination mechanisms for those requesting it.

9. *Objective 3.* To develop and implement, by 2003, national strategies fully incorporating the guiding principles set out in the Declaration. That would entail the following:

(*a*) *Impact.* An integrated, balanced, efficient and effective national strategy for addressing drug issues, with major emphasis on demand reduction;

(*b*) *Outputs.* A strategy document tailored to national needs, characteristics and cultures, specifying the role of agencies involved, the time-frame for activities and the goals;

(*c*) *National action.* This would include: (i) developing a national strategy by assessing the problem, defining the needs and resources, establishing priorities and goals, setting time-frames for specific activities and results and determining the roles of the agencies concerned; (ii) implementing the strategy through the development of a national action plan with a multisectoral approach, endorsed by an appropriate national body; and (iii) developing a framework for assessing and reporting results and reporting on the strategy and its implementation to the Commission on Narcotic Drugs;

(*d*) *International and regional action.* The United Nations International Drug Control Programme and other relevant international and regional organizations to provide guidance and assistance to those requesting it and to set up a database on national drug control strategies.

II. Assessing the problem

10. *Objective 4.* To assess the causes and consequences of the misuse of all substances in each country and to communicate those causes and consequences to policy makers, planners and the general public in order to develop practical measures, to establish a national system to monitor drug problems and trends and to record and evaluate intervention programmes and their impact on a regular basis using national indicators and, taking into account existing national and regional data systems for monitoring drug problems and trends, as well as the goals and targets established for 2003 and 2008 in the Political Declaration adopted by the General Assembly at its twentieth special session, to work towards establishing a core set of regionally and internationally recognized indicators. That would entail the following:

(*a*) *Impact.* Programmes and policies that are based on precise and timely evidence on the causes and consequences of drug abuse;

(*b*) *Outputs.* They would include: (i) a regular national report on the current drug situation and trends; and (ii) a periodic assessment of the health, social and economic costs of drug abuse and the benefits associated with different measures and actions, on both the demand and the supply sides;

(*c*) *National action.* This would include: (i) establishing a national system for data collection and analysis of drug abuse; (ii) undertaking periodic assessments of the costs to society of drug abuse and of the medium- and long-term benefits to society if the problem is reduced; and (iii) using the information for drug policy and programme development;

(*d*) *International and regional action.* The United Nations International Drug Control Programme and other relevant international and regional organizations: (i) to provide advice and technical assistance to countries requesting it on the establishment of national systems for monitoring the drug abuse problem, including regionally and internationally recognized core indicators; and (ii) to promote the development of methodologies for assessing the costs and consequences of drug abuse and for undertaking cost-benefit analyses of various measures and actions.

11. *Objective 5.* To develop research programmes at the national and regional levels in scientific fields concerning drug demand reduction and to disseminate widely the results so that strategies for reducing illicit drug demand may be elaborated on a solid scientific basis. That would entail the following:

(*a*) *Impact.* Improved drug demand reduction strategies based on scientific evidence;

(*b*) *Outputs.* Programmes for research on issues related to drug demand reduction;

(*c*) *National action.* Identifying research needs, developing research programmes, mobilizing the resources required and promoting the application of research findings;

(*d*) *International and regional action.* The United Nations International Drug Control Programme and other relevant international and regional organizations to encourage research into a wide range of drug demand reduction issues and the dissemination and application of research findings.

III. Tackling the problem

12. *Objective 6.* To identify and develop programmes for reducing illicit drug demand in a wide variety of health and social contexts and to encourage collaboration among those programmes, which should cover all areas of drug abuse prevention, ranging from discouraging the initial use of illicit drugs to reducing the negative health and social consequences of drug abuse, and should include continuing education, not only for all educational levels, beginning at an early age, but also in the workplace, the family and the community, and to develop programmes to make the public aware of the problem of drug abuse and of the full continuum of risks involved in such abuse and to provide information on and services for early intervention, counselling, treatment, rehabilitation, relapse prevention, aftercare and social reintegration to those in need. That would entail the following:

(*a*) *Impact.* Reduction of drug abuse and related health and social consequences;

(*b*) *Outputs.* Easily accessible drug demand reduction programmes, integrated into broader health and social programmes, covering where possible the full spectrum of services, including reducing the adverse health and social consequences of drug abuse;

(*c*) *National action.* Developing and implementing specific demand reduction activities at the primary, secondary and tertiary levels of prevention that meet the needs of various target groups and that are integrated into the health, education and other related sectors;

(*d*) *International and regional action.* The United Nations International Drug Control Programme and other relevant international and regional organizations to provide guidance and assistance to those requesting it and to facilitate the sharing of information on best strategies.

IV. Forging partnerships

13. *Objective 7.* To identify how different national and local institutions and organizations may contribute to efforts to reduce illicit drug demand and to promote the linking of those institutions and organizations. That would entail the following:

(*a*) *Impact.* More efficient utilization of resources and local ownership of programmes;

(*b*) *Outputs.* Identification of the roles of national and local institutions and organizations and of networking arrangements between them with a view to improving their contribution to and the effectiveness of national strategies;

(*c*) *National action.* This would include: (i) identifying drug demand reduction programmes run by various agencies, governmental and non-governmental, and defining their role in the national strategy; and (ii) promoting and reinforcing collaboration and networking among them;

(*d*) *International and regional action.* The United Nations International Drug Control Programme and other relevant international and regional organizations to compile a collection of examples of collaborative and cooperative arrangements that are in place in Member States to promote and reinforce networking and to facilitate the sharing of information on best strategies.

V. Focusing on special needs

14. *Objective 8.* To enhance the quality of programmes for reducing illicit drug demand, especially in terms of their relevance to population groups, taking into account their cultural diversity and specific needs, such as gender, age and socially, culturally and geographically marginalized groups. That would entail the following:

(*a*) *Impact.* Improvement in the quality and relevance of services offered;

(*b*) *Outputs.* Guidelines for programmes and services, taking into consideration cultural diversity and specific needs;

(*c*) *National action.* This would include: (i) establishing guidelines for the development and implementation of programmes; and (ii) monitoring and evaluating programmes according to established guidelines in order to improve programme quality and increase cost-effectiveness;

(*d*) *International and regional action.* The United Nations International Drug Control Programme and other relevant international and regional organizations to promote the development of guidelines and to facilitate the sharing of information among Member States.

15. *Objective 9.* To target the particular needs of groups most at risk of abusing drugs, through the development, in cooperation with those groups, of specially designed communication strategies and effective, relevant and accessible programmes. That would entail the following:

(*a*) *Impact.* Reduction of drug abuse among groups at risk and a reduction in the adverse health and social consequences of drug abuse;

(*b*) *Outputs.* Development of programmes and communication strategies for specific risk groups, in particular youth;

(*c*) *National action.* This would include: (i) identifying risk factors and groups at risk and developing programmes and communication strategies in cooperation with such groups to address their specific needs; and (ii) establishing and supporting mechanisms, including networks that facilitate the participation of young people in the design and implementation of programmes intended for them;

(*d*) *International and regional action.* The United Nations International Drug Control Programme and other relevant international and regional organizations: (i) to promote the participation of target groups in the design of projects and facilitate the sharing of information on best strategies; and (ii) to facilitate the creation of an international network promoting regular contact among youth involved in demand reduction activities and allowing them to stay informed and learn from one another.

16. *Objective 10.* To provide prevention, education, treatment or rehabilitation services to offenders who misuse drugs, whether in prison or in the community, as an addition to or, where appropriate and consistent with the national laws and policies of Member States, as an alternative to punishment or conviction, and to provide, in particular, drug-abusing offenders held in prison with services to enable them to overcome their dependence and to facilitate their reintegration in the community. That would entail the following:

(*a*) *Impact.* A reduction of drug abuse among offenders and, where appropriate, positive social integration or reintegration;

(*b*) *Outputs.* Comprehensive drug prevention, education, treatment, rehabilitation and social integration programmes for offenders;

(*c*) *National action.* Cooperation among institutions and organizations, both governmental and non-governmental, offering health, social, justice, correctional, vocational training and employment services in order to provide preventive care, education, treatment and rehabilitation for offenders and, where appropriate, programmes to enable their integration into the community;

(*d*) *International and regional action.* The United Nations International Drug Control Programme and other relevant international and regional organizations to facilitate the sharing of information on best strategies.

VI. Sending the right message

17. *Objective 11.* To undertake public information campaigns aimed at the population in general to promote health, raise awareness in society and improve people's understanding of the drug problem in the community and of the need to curb that problem, to evaluate those campaigns by establishing a follow-up system to determine their impact and to carry out research into the requirements of particular population groups, such as parents, teachers, community leaders and drug users, with regard to information on drugs and services. That would entail the following:

(*a*) *Impact.* Enhanced knowledge and awareness of the drug problem, of the need to take action and of the available support mechanisms;

(*b*) *Outputs.* Appropriately targeted public information campaigns based on knowledge acquired from research to promote greater awareness of the drug problem and to provide information on available resources and services;

(*c*) *National action.* Assessing needs and including and evaluating public information activities as part of national drug strategies;

(*d*) *International and regional action.* The United Nations International Drug Control Programme and other relevant international and regional organizations to facilitate the sharing of information on best strategies.

18. *Objective 12.* To develop information campaigns that are relevant and precise so that they take into account the social and cultural characteristics of the target population. That would entail the following:

(*a*) *Impact.* Increased knowledge and awareness among drug users and specific social and cultural groups about drugs and the adverse health and social consequences of drug use, as well as the availability of services;

(*b*) *Outputs.* Effective and culturally appropriate information campaigns that encourage and help drug users to reduce their involvement with drugs and prevent or reduce adverse health and social problems and inform them about available services;

(*c*) *National action.* Providing information on drugs and drug abuse and on how to obtain help for those most in need, in particular drug users. Information should be based on knowledge acquired from research and developed in collaboration with the target audience;

(*d*) *International and regional action.* The United Nations International Drug Control Programme and other relevant international and regional organizations to facilitate the sharing of information on best strategies.

19. *Objective 13.* To promote information, education and communication programmes for social mediators, for example, political, religious, education, cultural, business and union leaders, peer educators and representatives of non-governmental organizations and the media worldwide, so that they may convey appropriate and accurate messages about drug abuse. That would entail the following:

(*a*) *Impact.* Enhanced knowledge and skills among social mediators in conveying information about drug abuse;

(*b*) *Outputs.* Programmes and other activities to inform and educate social mediators and to develop their communication skills;

(*c*) *National action.* Developing training strategies for social mediators;

(*d*) *International and regional action.* The United Nations International Drug Control Programme and other relevant international and regional organizations to facilitate the sharing of information on best strategies in this field.

VII. Building on experience

20. *Objective 14.* To train planners and practitioners of governmental agencies, non-governmental organizations, the private sector, and others within the community on a permanent basis in all aspects of demand reduction activities and strategic programming by identifying local, national, subregional and regional human resources and using their experience in the design of programmes in order to guarantee their continuity and to create and strengthen regional, subregional, national and local training and technical resource networks and, with the possible assistance of regional and international organizations, to facilitate the exchange of experiences and expertise by encouraging States to include demand reduction personnel from other States in training programmes that they have developed. That would entail the following:

(*a*) *Impact.* Improved knowledge and skills of practitioners in demand reduction, facilitating the development of more efficient, effective and sustainable services;

(*b*) *Outputs.* Strategies for the development and expansion of the pool of technical expertise supporting planning, implementing, monitoring and evaluation of national demand reduction programmes;

(*c*) *National action.* This would include: (i) identifying those involved in planning and implementing programmes, from planners to practitioners and institutions and individuals involved with service delivery, in order to enhance their capacity to respond to the problem; (ii) supporting the design and implementation of training programmes, reviewed and updated on a regular basis, to form part of a continuing education programme for trainers; and (iii) designing and instituting training programmes for the various sectors involved in demand reduction programmes;

(*d*) *International and regional action.* The United Nations International Drug Control Programme and other relevant international and regional organizations to facilitate: (i) the sharing of information on best strategies; (ii) the development of guidelines on the development of curricula and training programmes, including distance learning, and assistance for those requesting it; and (iii) the intercountry exchange of experts for training purposes and the participation of foreign personnel in national training programmes developed by Member States.

21. *Objective 15.* To evaluate strategies and activities for reducing illicit drug demand and to develop mechanisms for intercountry, regional and interregional advocacy coordination, cooperation and collaboration in order to identify, share and expand best practices and effective activities in the development and implementation of drug demand reduction programmes. That would entail the following:

(*a*) *Impact.* Demand reduction programmes that are based soundly on validated experience and evidence;

(*b*) *Outputs.* They would include: (i) domestic evaluation results of strategies and activities and mechanisms for cooperation and data sharing; and (ii) mechanisms for facilitating the exchange of evaluation results and other data assessing the effectiveness of strategies and activities at the domestic, regional and interregional levels;

(*c*) *National action.* This would include: (i) monitoring and evaluating demand reduction strategies and activities and utilizing the results to inform and improve national plans; and (ii) participating in coordinating mechanisms for intercountry, regional and international exchange of information;

(*d*) *International and regional action.* The United Nations International Drug Control Programme and other relevant international and regional organizations to facilitate the exchange of information by establishing coordination mechanisms.

22. *Objective 16.* To create an international system of information on illicit drug demand reduction by linking existing databases managed by international, regional and national organizations in order to provide a network of information on knowledge and experiences that, to the extent possible, would use the above-mentioned core set of regionally and internationally recognized indicators and to enable comparisons of national experiences to be made. That would entail the following:

(a) *Impact.* Improved access to information, experiences and practices to facilitate the better design of programmes and policies;
(b) *Outputs.* National, regional and international mechanisms allowing easy access to databases and networks for the exchange of knowledge and experience of demand reduction;
(c) *National action.* Establishing and maintaining databases and facilitating linkages for international networking;
(d) *International and regional action.* The United Nations International Drug Control Programme and other relevant international and regional organizations to participate in the creation of an international mechanism by facilitating networking and linkages between databases.

In a December report on the follow-up to the Action Plan [E/CN.7/2000/3], prepared in response to the Assembly's request, the Executive Director reviewed the role of UNDCP in supporting Governments in the implementation process, and called on the Commission on Narcotic Drugs to provide guidance to the follow-up activities. Two principal roles for UNDCP were identified: to provide assistance to those requesting it for the establishment of national information systems and for the development of demand reduction strategies and programmes in line with the Guiding Principles; and to facilitate the sharing of information on best strategies in a number of areas. The report stated that UNDCP already provided assistance, mainly through technical projects, and that the volume of work depended on the availability of extrabudgetary contributions, crucial for the success of the global programme for assessing the magnitude of drug abuse. With regard to the sharing of information, UNDCP had taken some initiatives, funded mainly by extrabudgetary contributions, including the development of guidelines for treatment and rehabilitation programmes and for community-based prevention. The report stressed the importance of ensuring that demand reduction was funded from the regular budget and was not dependent on voluntary contributions. The Executive Director invited the Commission to indicate how to ensure the provision of assistance to enable UNDCP to fulfil the tasks entrusted to it, either by continuing to provide assistance using the limited resources from the regular budget while trying to raise extrabudgetary resources, or by requesting the inclusion, under the UN regular budget, of services for identifying, sharing and promoting best strategies for implementation of the Declaration.

Eradication of illicit crops and alternative development

The UNDCP Executive Director reported on the follow-up to the Action Plan on International Cooperation on the Eradication of Illicit Crops and on Alternative Development [E/CN.7/1999/3], adopted by the General Assembly in resolution S-20/4 E [YUN 1998, p. 1148]. The report, prepared in response to resolution 53/115 [ibid., p. 1170], stated that, following the Assembly's special session, UNDCP and Governments incorporated the provisions of the Action Plan into ongoing and new alternative development activities. Governments renewed their commitment to design time-bound strategies for the elimination or significant reduction of illicit crops, and international financial institutions showed interest in cooperating with Governments and UNDCP in the development of rural development programmes that also took into account the needs of communities affected by illicit crops.

In March [E/1999/28/Rev.1 (res. 42/3)], the Commission on Narcotic Drugs urged Governments in all areas producing coca bush, cannabis and opium poppy to design, formulate and implement national mechanisms for the monitoring and verification of illicit crops used in the production of drugs, with a view to implementing the Action Plan. It recommended that UNDCP collaborate with Governments and relevant organizations in establishing an international network for monitoring the cultivation of illicit crops. The Commission requested UNDCP to establish a central data bank on the basis of information furnished by Governments, and to report annually on the world situation regarding illicit crops. It also requested UNDCP to provide Governments with technical assistance and to mobilize international support, with a view to establishing national mechanisms for monitoring the cultivation of illicit crops used in the production of drugs and developing an international network for the control of illicit cultivation for the purpose of implementing the Action Plan.

In a December report on follow-up to the Action Plan [E/CN.7/2000/6], the Executive Director stated that UNDCP had developed a four-year global programme for alternative development, costed at $1.5 million, to develop and systematize lessons learned and best practices arising from alternative development projects carried out around the world, and to improve the analysis and dissemination of project results. In April, the programme started to monitor the progress made in areas such as gender mainstreaming in rural development; credit schemes in illicit crop areas; development of agro-industries; income diversification; the role of community organizations; and sound project monitoring and management at local and national levels. Another major development was the setting up of an illicit crops monitoring programme. That programme focused on the six countries in which the bulk of world illicit crop cultivation occurred: Afghanistan, Bolivia, Colombia, the Lao People's Democratic Republic, Myanmar and Peru. For each of those priority countries, UNDCP drew up a national project, described in the report. With relevant partners, UNDCP elaborated a common methodology for monitoring illicit crops, using a combination of technologies such as satellite imagery, ground surveys and aerial surveys.

ECONOMIC AND SOCIAL COUNCIL ACTION

On 28 July [meeting 43], the Economic and Social Council, on the recommendation of the Commission on Narcotic Drugs [E/1999/28/Rev.1], adopted **resolution 1999/32** without vote [agenda item 14 *(d)*].

International regulation and control of trade in poppy seeds

The Economic and Social Council,

Recalling article 22 of the Single Convention on Narcotic Drugs of 1961, on the prohibition of the illicit cultivation of the opium poppy, and the Action Plan on International Cooperation on the Eradication of Illicit Drug Crops and on Alternative Development, contained in resolution S-20/4 E of 10 June 1998, adopted by the General Assembly at its twentieth special session,

Recalling also that the International Narcotics Control Board, in its report for 1995, expressed its concern about trade in seeds obtained from the *Papaver somniferum* (opium poppy) plant in countries where cultivation of the opium poppy is prohibited, and that the Board urged Governments to be vigilant in order to ensure that poppy seeds traded for food purposes are not derived from illicitly cultivated poppy plants,

Emphasizing the need to fight the illicit cultivation of the opium poppy by all possible means,

Noting that poppy seeds are still being exported on a large scale from countries where cultivation of the opium poppy is prohibited,

Aware that, under the terms of the Single Convention on Narcotic Drugs of 1961, trade in poppy seeds is not subject to international control,

Recognizing that there is a need to prohibit international trade in poppy seeds from sources of illicit cultivation of the opium poppy,

Recognizing also that the poppy plant of low morphine content that is used for food purposes is unsuitable for the production of opium or illicit use by drug abusers,

Resolving to fight the international trade in illicit poppy seeds by practical measures, such as attempting to ensure that export is made only from countries authorized to cultivate the opium poppy,

1. *Calls upon* Member States to take the following measures to fight the international trade in poppy seeds from countries where no licit cultivation of opium poppy is permitted:

(a) Poppy seeds should only be imported if they originate from those countries where opium poppy is grown licitly in accordance with the provisions of the Single Convention on Narcotic Drugs of 1961;

(b) Governments should be encouraged, to the extent possible, and where national circumstances so require, to obtain an appropriate certificate from the exporting countries on the country of origin of *Papaver somniferum* seeds as the basis for importation, and also to give notification of export of *Papaver somniferum* seeds, as far as possible, to the competent authorities of the importing countries;

(c) Information on any suspicious transactions involving poppy seeds should be shared with other Governments concerned and with the International Narcotics Control Board;

2. *Urges* all Member States that have not already done so to prohibit the cultivation of the opium poppy in accordance with article 22 of the Single Convention on Narcotic Drugs of 1961 or to permit the cultivation of the opium poppy for purposes other than the production of opium, taking all the necessary measures as stipulated in article 25 of the 1961 Convention;

3. *Requests* the International Narcotics Control Board and the United Nations International Drug Control Programme to take appropriate measures to ensure the full implementation of article 22 of the 1961 Convention by concerned Member States;

4. *Requests* the Secretary-General to transmit the text of the present resolution to all Governments for consideration and implementation.

Conventions

In 1999, international efforts to control narcotic drugs were governed by three global conventions: the 1961 Single Convention on Narcotic Drugs [YUN 1961, p. 382], which, with some exceptions of detail, replaced earlier narcotics treaties and was amended in 1972 by a Protocol [YUN 1972, p. 397] intended to strengthen the role of INCB; the 1971 Convention on Psychotropic Substances [YUN 1971, p. 380]; and the 1988 United Nations Convention against Illicit Traffic in Narcotic Drugs and Psychotropic Substances [YUN 1988, p. 690].

As at 31 December 1999, 157 States were parties to the 1961 Convention, as amended by the 1972 Protocol. During the year, Azerbaijan, Liechtenstein, Pakistan and the United Republic of Tanzania became parties.

The number of parties to the 1971 Convention stood at 161 as at 31 December 1999. Azerbaijan, Liechtenstein and Mongolia became parties during the year.

At year's end, 153 States and the European Community were parties to the 1988 Convention. Andorra and Indonesia became parties in 1999.

Commission action. At its forty-second session in March, the Commission on Narcotic Drugs reviewed implementation of the international drug control treaties. It had before it a February report by the Secretary-General [E/CN.7/1999/10 & Corr.1 & Add.1] on changes in the scope of control of substances, which contained notifications from Governments recommending the inclusion of certain substances and clarification of the scope of their control under the 1961 and 1971 Conventions. The Commission also had before it the INCB report for 1998 [YUN 1998, p. 1151]. The Commission stressed the key role of the Board in monitoring the implementation of the treaties, and emphasized the need to strengthen the Board to enable it to implement fully the mandates entrusted to it by the treaties. It urged Governments that had not done so to adhere to the treaties as a matter of priority and to implement their provisions, and it requested that the Board provide technical assistance to countries where national control systems for drugs and chemicals used in illicit manufacture needed improvement. The Commission recognized the need for universal action to implement the provisions of article 12 of the 1988 Convention regarding precursor control, and for tightening drug control to prevent loopholes that could be exploited by traffickers.

On 16 March, the Commission adopted three decisions [E/1999/28/Rev.1 (dec. 42/1, 42/2, 42/3)] by which it included two new substances to be controlled under Schedule I of the 1961 Convention, clarified the scope of control of certain substances under the 1971 Convention, and requested further review by the World Health Organization (WHO) of two other substances.

By a 23 March resolution on voluntary international control of norephedrine [res. 42/1], the Commission requested Governments to recognize the danger of its diversion as a precursor and to establish or strengthen measures and codes of conduct governing its trade, in cooperation with INCB and relevant branches of trade and industry. It also urged Governments to monitor suspicious movements of norephedrine, to initiate pre-export notification of its shipments and to provide information to INCB on the extent of its licit production, trade and use. In December [E/CN.7/2000/7], the Secretariat forwarded to the Commission the INCB recommendation that norephedrine, which was frequently used in the illicit manufacture of amphetamines, be included in Table I of the 1988 Convention. The Board noted that amphetamines had created public health and social problems. It stated that the international control of norephedrine was required to limit its availability to traffickers and reduce the quantity of amphetamines manufactured illicitly, but those controls would have no adverse effect on its legitimate trade or licit medical requirements.

With regard to measures to control precursors, the Commission stated that traffickers must not be allowed to subvert legitimate chemical industries to obtain precursor chemicals required for the illicit production of narcotic drugs and psychotropic substances. The Action Plan against Illicit Manufacture, Trafficking and Abuse of Amphetamine-type Stimulants and Their Precursors [YUN 1998, p. 1139] provided a framework for cooperation in controlling precursors. It was essential for INCB to continue to monitor progress and analyse trends on the basis of information on seized shipments provided by national authorities.

Also on 23 March [res. 42/2], the Commission adopted temporary measures for the control of potassium permanganate, an essential oxidizing agent in the production of cocaine. It encouraged Governments to adopt measures to prevent the diversion to illicit activities of potassium permanganate, which was included in Table II of the 1988 Convention, and requested INCB to prepare, in accordance with its mandate under the 1988 Convention, a report on the effects of those measures, to be submitted to the Commission at its next session in 2000.

INCB action. In its report covering 1999 [E/INCB/1999/1], INCB stated that the implementation of the provisions of both the 1961 and 1971 Conventions was a prerequisite for achieving the objectives of the 1988 Convention. It welcomed the fact that most of the States that were major manufacturers, exporters and importers of precursors had acceded to the 1988 Convention, and reiterated its request to those States that had not done so to take, as a matter of priority, the necessary steps to put into effect the measures required under the 1988 Convention and to accede to it as soon as possible.

International Narcotics Control Board

The 13-member International Narcotics Control Board held its sixty-sixth (10-21 May) and sixty-seventh (1-18 November) sessions, both in Vienna [E/INCB/1999/1].

In carrying out the responsibilities assigned to it under the international conventions, the Board maintained a continuous dialogue with Governments. The statistical data and other information received from them were used in analyses of the licit manufacture of and trade in narcotic drugs and psychotropic substances worldwide, in order to identify whether Governments had strictly enforced treaty provisions requiring them to limit to medical and scientific purposes the licit manufacture of, trade in and distribution and use of those substances. The international drug control treaties required the Board to prepare an annual report examining the drug control situation worldwide, noting gaps and weaknesses in national control and in treaty compliance, and making recommendations for improvements.

In 1999, the Board reiterated its concern that many States, including important manufacturers, exporters and importers of narcotic drugs and psychotropic substances, had furnished statistical information after the deadlines. It stressed that the timely submission, comprehensiveness and reliability of the statistical reports were important indicators of the extent to which Governments had implemented the provisions of the 1961 and 1971 Conventions, and trusted that those States would ensure their timely compliance with the reporting obligations. The Board noted that several States parties to the 1988 Convention had not provided data on precursors for at least the last three years, and invited States that had not done so to submit information on the licit movement of precursors, indispensable in uncovering unusual trade trends, thereby preventing their diversion into illicit channels.

Many States had failed to submit the requisite data on estimates of the medical need for narcotic drugs, an indication of shortcomings in their national drug control systems; and some furnished a large number of supplementary estimates, indicating inadequate planning of medical needs. States were reminded that the 1961 Convention allowed for the submission of supplementary estimates only in the case of unforeseen circumstances. The Board undertook a review of the data available to identify inadequacies, in particular low consumption levels of opiate analgesics, and found a correlation between the degree of economic and human development in a country and the consumption of, for example, acute painkillers such as morphine and pethidine: the 20 countries with the highest per capita gross national product together accounted for about 75 per cent of global morphine consumption. In regard to assessments of requirements for psychotropic substances, the Board invited those Governments which had not done so to review the assessments established for their countries or territories and to submit comments to the Board.

Despite the large quantities of substances involved and the large number of transactions, no cases involving the diversion of narcotic drugs from licit international trade into illicit traffic were reported during 1999. As for the diversion of psychotropic substances from licit trade into illicit channels, an analysis by the Board of data on international trade in substances included in Schedules III and IV of the 1971 Convention indicated a significant decrease in the number of such cases, apparently as a result of Governments' implementation of treaty provisions, in combination with additional controls over international trade. The Board invited all Governments to remain vigilant with respect to orders for those psychotropic substances and to confirm with the Governments of importing countries the legitimacy of those orders prior to approving export; it also requested the Governments that did not control the import and export of psychotropic substances in those schedules to do so. The Board noted with concern that some States parties to the 1971 Convention had not reflected in their national legislation the 1995 decisions of the Commission on Narcotic Drugs to add to schedules of that Convention six additional substances and to transfer one substance from Schedule IV to Schedule III [YUN 1995, p. 1285].

Reports from various countries on the abuse and seizure of psychotropic substances indicated that the diversion of pharmaceutical products containing such substances from licit domestic distribution channels became an increasingly important source for illicit drug suppliers, and that the diversion of precursors from licit trade for the illicit manufacture of narcotic drugs or psychotropic substances continued on a large scale. The Board requested all Governments to report promptly important seizures of psychotropic substances, including seizures of pharmaceutical products diverted from licit distribution channels. In exercising its functions under the 1988 Convention, INCB participated fully in "Operation Purple", an international initiative undertaken by regulatory and law enforcement authorities in order to identify suspicious shipments and prevent the diversion of precursors.

In **resolution 1999/32** (see p. 1166), the Economic and Social Council called on Member States to take measures to fight the international trade in poppy seeds from countries where no licit cultivation of opium poppy was permitted. The Board called on countries importing poppy seeds to pay special attention to the country of origin. It also urged Governments of exporting and importing countries of opiate raw materials and/or products to prevent international trade in such seized materials.

On 28 July, the Council, by **decision 1999/265**, took note of the INCB report for 1998 [Sales No. E.99.XI.1].

World drug situation

In its 1999 report [E/INCB/1999/1], INCB provided a regional analysis of world drug abuse trends and control efforts, so that Governments would be kept aware of situations that might endanger the objectives of the international drug control treaties.

Africa

In Africa, trafficking in and abuse of narcotic drugs and psychotropic substances were increasingly linked to various civil conflicts (see PART ONE, Chapter II), augmenting drug problems, especially among children and youth. In the Democratic Republic of the Congo and Liberia, for example, child combatants were provided with drugs in order to induce them to carry out dangerous operations with impunity. Illicit drugs were also used to finance civil conflicts and the purchase of arms, as was the case in Angola and Rwanda.

The main drug trafficked and abused in Africa was cannabis, although methaqualone trafficking and abuse were serious problems in the eastern and southern parts of the region. Many countries continued to have problems in countering the illicit cultivation of, trafficking in and abuse of cannabis, the cultivation and distribution of which were used to generate supplementary income. Morocco remained a major source of cannabis resin destined for Western Europe, and cannabis cultivation continued in Egypt and in countries in Western Africa, such as Ghana and Senegal. Several Governments increased eradication efforts; Côte d'Ivoire, Egypt, Ghana, Kenya, Nigeria, Senegal and South Africa achieved good results.

Cocaine and heroin, as well as amphetamines, were becoming increasingly popular among drug abusers and traffickers. The consumption of cocaine, "crack" and heroin was principally an urban phenomenon confined to large cities. The increasing prevalence of the injection of heroin and other substances in some capital cities was believed to be a factor in the high rate of human immunodeficiency virus (HIV) infection and of cases involving acquired immunodeficiency syndrome (AIDS). In Southern and Western Africa, trafficking in and abuse of cocaine increased. In South Africa, there was an increase in trafficking in and abuse of "crack" and cocaine, and Cape Verde witnessed increasing drug abuse as a spillover effect of drug trafficking. The increasing sophistication and flexibility of drug trafficking groups were a serious concern: in reaction to measures in Nigeria, for example, traffickers began using other African countries as transit for shipments to Europe and North America. Illicit drugs continued to be smuggled through Africa's major seaports, such as Mombasa in Kenya, Maputo in Mozambique, Durban in South Africa and Dar es Salaam in the United Republic of Tanzania, as well as through several ports in Western Africa. There were no indications that opium poppy was cultivated in Africa, but several countries, including Ghana, Kenya, Mauritius and Tanzania, were routes used by traffickers to transport heroin from Asia to Europe, North America and South Africa.

In several countries in Africa, self-medication, the sale of licit drugs through unregulated channels, the availability of fake drugs and their use by those segments of the population unable to buy from legitimate pharmacies contributed to the spread of psychotropic substance abuse. In Nigeria, more psychotropic substances were seized than in any other African country, and more depressants (benzodiazepines) were seized than in any other country in the world. The trafficking in and abuse of methaqualone remained a problem, mainly in Eastern and Southern Africa, and trafficking in and abuse of methylenedioxymethamphetamine (MDMA) ("ecstasy") increased in Western and Southern Africa.

INCB carried out missions to Cameroon, Kenya, the Libyan Arab Jamahiriya and Mauritania in 1999. In Cameroon, national control over drugs and precursors was weak. The Board was concerned that pharmaceutical products containing controlled substances were sold without restrictions on street markets, and requested the Government to increase vigilance. Since cannabis cultivation had increased and important seizures of cannabis originating in Cameroon were made in Europe, the Government was encouraged to continue its measures against cannabis cultivation and to emphasize the dangers of its abuse. In Kenya, drug abuse and illicit trafficking had increased, and one development which caused concern was the abuse of heroin by injection. Both cannabis and khat were cultivated and abused. The Board urged the Government to enhance drug control efforts and to put in place stricter controls over precursors as required under the 1988 Convention. In the Libyan Arab Jamahiriya, the Board was pleased to note that neither illicit cultivation of drug crops nor illicit manufacture of drugs had been uncovered, that controls over the licit manufacture and distribution of narcotic drugs and psychotropic substances were adequate, and that the Government had taken steps to improve the implementation of the 1988 Convention. After its mission to Mauritania, the Board expressed concern that the provisions of the 1961 and 1971 Conventions had not been applied, which indicated problems related to the control of psychotropic substances, and that a legal framework had never been introduced for monitoring the licit market for substances controlled by the treaties. It urged the Government to pass a bill on the control of the licit market for narcotic drugs, psychotropic substances and precursors.

As to regional cooperation, the Board welcomed the entry into force of the Southern African Development Community (SADC) protocol on combating illicit trafficking. It also welcomed the growing activities of SADC member States and of the secretariat of the Economic Community of West African States. Organizational changes were being finalized in the secretariat of the Organization of African Unity, where a drug control focal point was established. In January, Nigeria and Uganda signed a cooperation agreement on sharing information on illicit drug trafficking. Cape Verde and Senegal signed an agreement on cooperation in drug control matters and efforts to combat money-laundering. National Drug Control Coordinating Councils were established in Botswana, Malawi and Mozambique, enhancing subregional cooperation, cross-border controls, liaison and intelligence to counter drug trafficking.

Americas

Central America and the Caribbean

In Central America and the Caribbean, cannabis remained the most widely abused drug, and some countries, such as the Bahamas, reported a substantial increase in its abuse. Although it was illicitly cultivated in many parts of the region, mainly for local consumption, cannabis cultivated in Jamaica was destined for illicit markets in North America. While most countries reported either increased or stable levels of its trafficking, the Dominican Republic reported a substantial decrease.

The region was increasingly used to trans-ship substantial quantities of cocaine and cannabis from South America to the United States and Europe. The transit traffic increased the availability of cocaine in Central America and the Caribbean, and its abuse, as well as "crack" abuse, spread in a number of countries; however, it decreased in the Bahamas. Trafficking in and storage of cocaine hydrochloride and "crack", mainly from Colombia, continued unabated throughout the region. Cocaine seizures remained at the same level for the region as a whole, but the level varied from country to country. Haiti, where drug traffickers took advantage of the economic and political crisis (see p. 208), emerged as the main transit point for smuggling cocaine from Colombia into the United States. Employees of airlines and associated companies were found to be involved in drug trafficking, and regional Governments were urged to control areas, such as airports, through which illicit drug consignments often passed. Because of its proximity to cocaine producers in South America, Central America was vulnerable to the diversion of precursors, and those Governments were requested to ensure that the imported quantities were within the limits of their legitimate requirements.

Illicit cultivation of opium poppy continued only in isolated places in Guatemala, and reports of heroin abuse remained limited. Heroin originating in Colombia was seized mainly in Costa Rica and Panama, although small quantities were also seized in several Caribbean countries.

INCB sent missions to the Bahamas, Cuba and Guatemala in 1999. In the Bahamas, it called on the Government to strengthen control mechanisms to prevent misuse of the offshore banking system to launder money derived from drug trafficking, and encouraged it to maintain cooperation with neighbouring countries to combat illicit trafficking by sea. The Board encouraged Cuba to adopt comprehensive drug control legislation that would integrate all existing regulations and to focus on preventive measures. It also recommended that donor countries and relevant international organizations provide technical assistance to the Government, since traffickers took advantage of the strategic location of Cuba in the Caribbean to smuggle drugs through its waters. Guatemala, faced with problems involving transit traffic in narcotic drugs and psychotropic substances, had inadequate controls over those substances and precursors; therefore, the Board called on the Government to comply with the 1961 and 1971 Conventions.

The Board was concerned about the increasingly liberal approach of some Governments to the offshore banking and gambling industries in view of their potential for money-laundering. Most countries in the region had laws aimed at preventing money-laundering; the Board encouraged them to implement those laws effectively, and urged Governments that had not done so to introduce such legislation. As to regional cooperation, the Board noted the efforts of the Caribbean Governments to work together to reduce money-laundering and tax evasion in offshore banking centres. Subregional cooperation in drug control was enhanced within the framework of the Plan of Action on Drug Control Coordination and Cooperation in the Caribbean (Barbados Plan of Action).

North America

Cannabis remained the most popular drug of abuse in Canada, Mexico and the United States. The increasing popularity of hydroponically grown cannabis with a high tetrahydrocannabinol (THC) content in western Canada and in some parts of the United States was a major concern to law enforcement authorities. Seizure data indicated its movement from western Canada and Quebec to the United States, as well as from west to east in the United States. In addition, large quantities of cannabis were smuggled into Canada and the United States. The Board noted that the United States had issued new guidelines to ease the availability of cannabis for medical research, and that Canada had put forward a research plan on its use for medical purposes. INCB reiterated its position that the issue must be approached in a scientific way and that objective scientific research into medical use of cannabis should be carried out by the Governments concerned.

In Mexico, drug abuse was at a much lower level than in Canada and the United States; however, cocaine and heroin abuse increased, and the abuse of inhalants among street children and other vulnerable groups was of concern in large cities. In 1998, there was a decline in the amount of opium poppy that was destroyed and in the number of clandestine laboratories for illicit drug manufacture that were dismantled. Seizures of ephedrine and opium gum declined, as did seizures of cannabis, cocaine and heroin. Mexico strengthened its drug control efforts but it remained an important transit country for cocaine shipments bound for the United States, as well as a significant source of cannabis.

Drug abuse was at a lower level in Canada than in the United States. Cocaine abuse increased in some cities in Canada and it remained a major problem in many communities in the United States. The number of persons who abused heroin in the United States reportedly fell in 1998, and the number of emergency-room "episodes" involving heroin or morphine abuse stabilized between 1995 and 1997, after more than doubling between 1990 and 1995.

In the United States, methamphetamine was the most prevalent controlled synthetic substance clandestinely manufactured; the number of laboratory seizures almost doubled between 1996 and 1998, and its abuse and trafficking continued to increase. The consumption of methylphenidate for the treatment of attention deficit disorder remained at a very high level and the number of prescriptions for amphetamines had increased by 500 per cent since 1993. The Board reiterated its concern that vigilance should be exercised to prevent the inappropriate prescribing of methylphenidate and other stimulants. MDMA abuse, which had increased significantly from 1993 to 1997, was not as widespread as that of many other drugs. There continued to be reports in the United States of increased abuse of so-called club drugs: substances such as ketamine and flunitrazepam, as well as sodium oxybate and its precursor gamma-butyrolactone; therefore, the Board welcomed the United States decision to place ketamine in Schedule III of the Controlled Substances Act. The Board noted the slow progress made in Canada in controlling psychotropic substances and in participating in the efforts of the international community to monitor precursors.

Cooperation at the regional and international levels remained an important element of drug control strategies in the region. Mexico and the United States adopted "performance measures of effectiveness" to guide the implementation of the 1998 Bi-National Drug Strategy, and signed a joint declaration on reducing drug abuse at the Bi-National Demand Reduction Conference (Tijuana, Mexico, June). Joint cross-border operations and investigations by Canada and the United States included a project to improve the campaign against smuggling in the area of Lake Ontario. Mexico signed a bilateral agreement with Colombia aimed at improving the exchange of information and technology to combat drug trafficking.

In April, INCB sent a technical mission to Mexico to discuss the monitoring of scheduled chemicals and the measures taken by the Government against their diversion into illicit channels. The Board noted that the control of substances in Table I of the 1988 Convention functioned well; however, it urged the Government to establish a comprehensive regulatory framework to ensure implementation of the 1998 precursor control legislation.

South America

In South America as a whole, the potential production, productivity and availability of coca leaf for illicit purposes remained stable in 1999. Bolivia was on its way to achieving its goal of eradicating the cultivation of coca bush, and in Peru the total area under illicit cultivation decreased by more than 50 per cent between 1995 and 1998. In spite of those eradication efforts, the availability of coca leaf for the illicit manufacture of cocaine hydrochloride in South America and the supply of cocaine hydrochloride to illicit markets in Europe and North America were not significantly reduced. The achievements in reducing illicit coca bush cultivation in Bolivia and Peru were offset by increased production of coca leaf in Colombia. In that country, the deterioration of public safety and the fact that substantial illicit coca leaf production and cocaine manufacture took place in areas beyond government control were hampering efforts to fight illicit coca bush cultivation, coca leaf production and cocaine manufacture and trafficking. Colombia remained the world's leading cocaine producer and the country with the largest area under coca bush cultivation. Coca leaf was increasingly processed into cocaine paste in Peru and sent directly overseas, and cocaine was more widely available at low prices on illicit markets in that country. Colombia stepped up its opium poppy eradication efforts, causing sites for illicit cultivation to be abandoned in some areas, only to be replaced by new ones. Throughout South America, heroin abuse continued to be marginal, but had increased slightly.

Illicit trafficking in cocaine destined for Europe and North America continued unabated. New routes and methods were used to smuggle it out of South America as detection techniques became more sophisticated, and most international airports in the region and seaports of all countries, on both the Atlantic and the Pacific, were used. The routes used for illicit trafficking had diversified. Cocaine headed for Western Europe followed well-established paths via the Caribbean or Africa; however, countries in Central Asia, West Asia and Eastern Europe were increasingly used for trans-shipment to Western Europe. Seizures of controlled chemicals remained substantial and were increasing in South America.

In South America, cannabis remained the most common drug of abuse among young people aged 15 to 19 and was the most often reported drug of initiation. Data on the extent of its illicit cultivation were scarce. It continued to be produced mostly for local consumption, although consignments of cannabis produced in Brazil, Colombia, Guyana, Paraguay and Suriname were seized while being transported in neighbouring countries and in the Caribbean, Europe and North America. With few exceptions, authorities in South America seized increasing amounts of cannabis. South American Governments needed to remain vigilant to prevent the spread of the illicit cultivation of opium poppy and the illicit traffic in heroin. Seizures of opium poppy seeds and opium in Peru increased significantly in 1999.

One of the main concerns in South America remained the abuse of amphetamine-type stimulants in the form of anorectics manufactured by the pharmaceutical industry. Brazil was one of the countries most affected by the misuse of the prescription system for stimulants, and in Bolivia and Peru tranquillizers were the most often abused psychotropic substances, with prevalence close to that of cannabis. Stimulants and hallucinogens were abused to a considerably lesser extent.

Regional cooperation on drug abuse and illicit trafficking was developed by the members of the Andean Pact (Bolivia, Colombia, Ecuador, Peru, Venezuela) and the Common Market of the Southern Cone (MERCOSUR) (Argentina, Brazil, Paraguay, Uruguay). Through Operation Millennium, which involved close cooperation and the exchange of information, particularly between Colombia, Ecuador and the United States, success against drug trafficking organizations was achieved, including the arrest of major organizers of drug traffic and money-laundering operations. With regard to national legislation, policy and action, Ecuador launched its National Strategy to Face Drugs, 1999-2003, and it was hoped that the economic difficulties and the social unrest in the country would not hinder its implementation, considering that drug traffickers increasingly used Ecuador as a base for their illicit operations. The Board, welcoming the results achieved by Bolivia in its programme to eradicate illicit coca bush cultivation, launched in 1998 as part of its Anti-Drug Strategy 1998-2002, called on donor countries to support Bolivia in its efforts. About 1,000 tons of coca leaf of Bolivian origin were estimated to be smuggled yearly into the northern Argentinian provinces of Jujuy and Salta, where the possession and consumption (chewing) of coca leaf in its natural form and the preparation of *mate de coca* (coca tea) were not considered by law as possession and consumption of a narcotic drug. The Board trusted that Argentina and Bolivia would deal with the problem of coca leaf smuggling.

Following an INCB technical mission to Bolivia in July, the Board called on the Government to avoid a situation in which coca leaf production, considered licit under its legislation, could result in coca leaf being diverted to supplement the diminishing illicit supply. The Board was of the view that the cultivation of coca leaf for chewing and drinking coca tea was contrary to the 1961 Convention. INCB also carried out a mission to Brazil in July. It encouraged the Government to continue its reform efforts by strengthening the capacity of the national sanitary surveillance agency to enforce registration requirements and prescription regulations and called on it to assume an active role in fostering cooperation among South American countries in drug-related matters, such as combating drug and chemical trafficking in the Amazon river basin. Regarding the control of precursors, Brazil seemed to have the required structure, but the financial and technical resources at its disposal remained insufficient to control the large chemical industry in the country.

Asia

East and South-East Asia

In 1999, there was a major reduction in the total area under illicit opium poppy cultivation in the Lao People's Democratic Republic, Myanmar, Thailand and Viet Nam. However, the abuse of opiates in East and South-East Asia remained prevalent in many countries, and their abuse by injection contributed to increases in the prevalence of HIV infection in Myanmar, Viet Nam and other countries. China, Malaysia and Thailand remained important illicit markets for heroin and served as transit points for heroin destined for illicit markets in other parts of the region, in North America and in Oceania. Data for 1998 showed a significant increase in the quantity of heroin seized in China, indicating a possible increase in the use of its trafficking route through that country and/or strengthened activities by the Chinese law enforcement authorities, as well as a possible increase in its abuse.

Significant illicit cultivation of cannabis continued to occur in Cambodia, Indonesia, the Philippines and Thailand. Cambodia became a major source of the cannabis found on the illicit market in countries inside the region and outside, primarily in Australia. Cannabis was also illicitly cultivated in remote, mountainous areas of the Philippines, despite efforts by law enforcement authorities to deal with the problem. Seizures of cocaine in the region increased in 1998, partly as a result of a large seizure that was made in the Hong Kong Special Administrative Region of China in December; however, the region did not appear to have a cocaine abuse problem.

The abuse of and trafficking in amphetamine-type stimulants spread quickly across the entire region. In the area of the Golden Triangle, facilities that once had been used exclusively for the refining of heroin were increasingly used for the manufacture of metamphetamine as well. China remained a major source of clandestinely manufactured amphetamine-type stimulants, which were available in urban areas and were widely abused by students. China and Myanmar remained the major sources of metamphetamine abused locally or exported to other countries in East Asia; it was also illicitly transported from the Philippines. Seizure data indicated that ephedrine, a chemical used in the manufacture of methamphetamine, continued to be smuggled out of China and India and into Myanmar. Since seizures of ephedrine of Indian origin increased on both sides of the border between India and Myanmar, the Board reiterated its call for increased cooperation between the countries in the region and those in South Asia, and welcomed the decision by China to introduce stricter controls over it. The abuse of MDMA ("ecstasy") was reported with increasing frequency; most of it was smuggled into East and South-East Asia after being illicitly manufactured in Europe, but some attempts had been made to manufacture it clandestinely in the region. China remained a source of amfepramone found on illicit markets in the Russian Federation and in various parts of Asia.

Regional cooperation and bilateral efforts continued. In February, representatives of the six countries in the Mekong area (Cambodia, China, the Lao People's Democratic Republic, Myanmar, Thailand, Viet Nam) agreed to combat trafficking by strengthening border controls and training drug control officers. In June, INCB sent a technical mission to the Democratic People's Republic of Korea and invited the Government to cooperate with other Governments in the region in matters involving international drug control. With regard to the abuse of and trafficking in amphetamine-type stimulants, the Board urged the Governments in the region to formulate and implement effective strategies to reduce demand for them, and to increase cooperation with each other in regulatory and law enforcement activities.

The Board carried out missions to Japan and Mongolia. Japan, where drugs were abused to a much lesser extent than in other developed countries, was not affected by heroin or cocaine abuse. However, the abuse of stimulants, especially among young people, was a matter of concern to the Government. In Mongolia, the abuse of and trafficking in narcotic drugs and psychotropic substances were minimal, but the country was increasingly targeted by traffickers, particularly for the diversion and manufacture of ephedrine. *Ephedra*, the plant from which ephedrine was made, grew wild on the northern rim of the Gobi desert, and the Board noted with concern attempts by foreign investors to cultivate *Ephedra* and manufacture ephedrine without a licence.

South Asia

While cannabis and opium were traditionally the main drugs of abuse in South Asia, the abuse of heroin and synthetic drugs increased in 1999; however, the abuse of stimulants (cocaine and "ecstasy") was very limited. Because of the proximity of South Asia to the world's two main opiate-producing countries, Afghanistan and Myanmar, drug trafficking and abuse in the region were mainly transit-related; certain areas had emerged as major drug-trafficking centres and/or had witnessed a rapid deterioration of the trafficking or abuse situation.

Despite cannabis eradication campaigns in India, Nepal and Sri Lanka, illicit cultivation continued, particularly in remote and inaccessible areas. The illicit demand for cannabis resin from Nepal, which had a high THC content, rose in other countries and led to an increase in the cultivation of cannabis and trafficking in its resin and herb. It was estimated that 70 per cent of the cannabis cultivated in Nepal entered international routes. While the cannabis herb smuggled out of Nepal was mainly destined for India, the resin was shipped to Asia, Europe and North America. Sri Lanka was increasingly used as a transit point for cannabis and heroin from South Asia and South-West Asia.

Large quantities of heroin were smuggled out of Afghanistan through Pakistan and out of Myanmar and into South Asian countries, mainly to be shipped to Europe and North America but also abused in the region. Seizure data indicated an increase in trafficking in heroin from India to Africa, some of which was destined for the more profitable markets in the United States and Europe. The number of heroin abusers increased and was particularly high along the main routes and in major trafficking areas such as Mumbai in India and the south-western border area of Bangladesh with India. Because of the increasing abuse of heroin by injection, the number of HIV/AIDS cases rose in most countries. The supply of illicit opiates from South-West Asia continued, and new smuggling routes leading from Myanmar through India, mainly to markets overseas, were developed following intensified law enforcement activities in China and Thailand. The illicit cultivation of opium poppy and the production of opiates also took place in India and Nepal. Regarding licit opium production in India, there were reports of fraud involving licensed opium poppy growers.

The preparation Proxyvon, containing a synthetic opioid used as an analgesic and cheaper than heroin, was increasingly abused as a substitute for heroin in north-east India. In Bangladesh, India and Nepal, the abuse of codeine-based cough medicines continued. In India, pharmaceutical preparations, used as an alternative to heroin, contained narcotic drugs and psychotropic substances and were manufactured locally, readily available and cheaper than heroin.

The large-scale abuse of psychotropic substances, in particular benzodiazepines, continued in Bangladesh, India and Nepal. The pharmaceutical industry in India manufactured large amounts of psychotropic substances for medical purposes, and a number of them continued to be diverted from domestic distribution channels and were either abused in the country or smuggled outside. Methamphetamine tablets, illicitly manufactured in the Wa hill area of Myanmar, began to appear on the illicit market in India. In Sri Lanka, controls over psychotropic substances at the retail level had been lacking for a long time, resulting in their abuse as substitutes for, or in addition to, heroin.

With regard to regional cooperation, the Board welcomed the continuing bilateral cooperation efforts to prevent drug trafficking between India and its neighbouring countries, Bangladesh, Myanmar, Nepal and Pakistan.

West Asia

The abuse of opiates continued to rise in Afghanistan and Iran; in Pakistan, heroin abuse remained at a very high level and, although drug addiction was limited in most other countries in West Asia, increases were reported in a number of countries in the region (Azerbaijan, Jordan, Kazakhstan, Kyrgyzstan, Lebanon, Tajikistan, Turkmenistan, United Arab Emirates, Uzbekistan).

Approximately 75 per cent of the world production of opium took place in Afghanistan, and the large-scale illicit cultivation of opium poppy in that country spread to areas previously unaffected. The area under opium poppy cultivation exceeded 90,000 hectares in the 1998/99 growing season, increasing by over 40 per cent compared with the previous season. It was estimated that, duc to cxpanded areas of cultivation and favourable weather conditions, the production of opium in 1999 reached a record level of about 4,600 tons. According to the latest survey, 97 per cent of the area under opium poppy cultivation was on territory controlled by the Taliban, whose commitment to ban opium poppy cultivation and heroin manufacture remained questionable, despite its decree calling for a ban on laboratories for processing heroin. Heroin manufacture had moved from Pakistan to Afghanistan. In Pakistan, the Government eradicated over 60 per cent of the opium poppy cultivation during the 1998/99 growing season; however, national law enforcement authorities encountered difficulties resulting from large-scale production of and trafficking in opiates in Afghanistan.

Trafficking in opiates in Afghanistan, Pakistan and member States of the Commonwealth of Independent States (CIS) was organized by multinational trafficking groups based in Pakistan, as was trafficking in chemicals. Most countries in West Asia were used as transit points for opiates originating in Afghanistan and destined for Europe and, to a lesser degree, South Asia. While an increasing proportion was smuggled through Central Asia, the largest share continued to be transported through Iran to Turkey or from Pakistan to Iran and other countries in the Persian Gulf area before being sent to its final destination. Turkey remained the major transit point for heroin destined for Europe. Iran continued to intercept illicit consignments of opiates en route from Afghanistan to Turkey, CIS member States and other countries in Europe; more than 80 per cent of seizures of opium worldwide were carried out by Iranian authorities. The Caspian Sea was increasingly used to trans-ship large amounts of both opiates and cannabis from Afghanistan through Turkmenistan to the Russian Federation and other European countries.

Illicit opium poppy cultivation in countries in Central Asia (Kazakhstan, Kyrgyzstan, Tajikistan, Turkmenistan, Uzbekistan) and the Caucasus (Armenia, Azerbaijan, Georgia) remained limited. However, the Board was concerned about the rapid spread of illicit crop cultivation and trafficking in and abuse of drugs, especially heroin, in both of those areas. Central Asia was used as a transit point to transport from east to west consignments of opiates and cannabis originating in Afghanistan, and chemicals used in the illicit manufacture of heroin were trafficked in the opposite direction.

Many countries in West Asia were used as transit points for the diversion of precursors, predominantly imported from or smuggled out of China, India and Europe. The quantity of seized acetic anhydride, the main precursor used in the illicit manufacture of heroin, rose substantially in Pakistan and the United Arab Emirates and remained large in Turkey. Heroin was increasingly smuggled through Turkey, where it was no longer manufactured, to Europe along the Balkan route. Seizures related to the transit traffic in heroin also increased in Israel, Jordan and the Syrian Arab Republic. Drug trafficking through Pakistan and the countries in the Persian Gulf area continued unabated, and heroin abuse, in particular, sharply increased as Afghan refugees returned from Pakistan.

Cannabis remained the most frequently abused drug in West Asia. It continued to be illicitly cultivated and to grow wild on extensive areas in Afghanistan and Pakistan, where no eradication efforts where reported. Cannabis originating in Afghanistan and Pakistan was smuggled through many countries in the region, and seizures of resin from those two countries increased in Europe. The world's largest single area covered by wild-growing cannabis plants, estimated to be about 300,000 hectares, was in Kazakhstan, but limited illicit cultivation also occurred in the Palestinian Autonomous Areas and Israel, Jordan and Turkey. In Lebanon, efforts to eradicate its small-scale illicit cultivation continued.

While the extent of cocaine abuse and trafficking in the region was insignificant, in many countries seizures of cocaine increased. In Kazakhstan and Kyrgyzstan, the clandestine manufacture of methcathinone continued in small home laboratories. The principal precursor, ephedrine, was illicitly extracted from the *Ephedra* plant, which grew wild. There was increasing evidence of the abuse in Central Asia of MDMA that had been smuggled out of Europe. The large-scale smuggling of stimulants from Europe into the Persian Gulf area continued, as evidenced by seizures in transit countries such as Jordan, the Syrian Arab Republic and Turkey.

In April, an INCB mission visited Iran, where the situation with regard to drug abuse, in particular opiates, appeared to be deteriorating, and a lack of resources had prevented the authorities from dealing with the problem more effectively. The Board recommended that the assessment of the drug abuse situation be finalized and that the international community consider supporting appropriate projects to reduce illicit drug demand.

Regional cooperation and harmonized action on drug control was promoted by the Economic Cooperation Organization, including judicial cooperation in drug and money-laundering cases. The Board welcomed many new activities and drug control efforts among the countries in the eastern Mediterranean, as well as the first joint drug law enforcement operation involving Pakistan and Saudi Arabia and the signing by Pakistan of an extradition and judicial cooperation treaty with Egypt. Several West Asian countries signed new or revised existing memoranda of understanding or protocols on cooperation in drug control matters, or agreed with each other and other Governments and institutions outside the region to combat drug trafficking. The Board urged States in Central Asia and the Caucasus to accelerate the adoption of national drug control programmes, to make any necessary amendments to national drug control legislation and to strengthen their drug law enforcement activities. It welcomed the adoption in Uzbekistan of a comprehensive law for the control of narcotic drugs, psychotropic substances and precursors, and noted that Armenia, Azerbaijan, Tajikistan and Turkmenistan could enhance their control efforts by enacting comprehensive legislation on drug and precursor control. The Board was concerned that many countries in West Asia had not enacted legislation to identify and counter money-laundering activities, and that Lebanon was not taking steps to withdraw its reservation on the provisions against money-laundering in the 1988 Convention. It expressed concern that in many countries controls over the licit distribution of pharmaceutical products containing narcotic drugs and psychotropic substances were weak.

Europe

The availability of cannabis in Europe increased considerably in 1999. That was partly the result of intensified cannabis cultivation in Southern Europe, mainly Albania, and of soaring indoor cannabis cultivation in Western Europe, facilitated by the unrestricted sale of cannabis seeds and cannabis-growing accessories in so-called hemp shops and on the Internet. There were many web sites based in Europe, particularly in the Netherlands and the United Kingdom, offering to sell and deliver potent varieties of cannabis to almost any destination in the world. Its increased availability, coupled with greater tolerance towards the substance, had led to increases in abuse and an expanded market for the substance. The Board noted that it was the consensus of the international community to put cannabis under international control; its abuse should not be treated as harmless or inevitable, and Governments should emphasize its dangers in activities aimed at reducing illicit drug demand. The Board called on the Governments of all countries where indoor cultivation proliferated and where countermeasures had not been taken to deal with the problem. Albania had emerged as an important producer of cannabis, which was smuggled into Greece, Italy, Slovenia and other European countries. In Italy, seizures increased from 11 tons in 1996 to over 54 tons in 1998; it was estimated that 90 per cent of the cannabis herb trafficked in Slovenia was of Albanian origin and entered the country by sea. Belarus, Croatia and Lithuania reported increased illicit cultivation, while Slovakia and Slovenia reported a strong increase in trafficking in cannabis herb. Morocco remained a major source of the resin seized in Europe, despite the intensified activities of national law enforcement authorities. Colombia emerged as an important source of the cannabis herb sold on the illicit markets in Europe.

Heroin abuse declined in most Western European countries, but it became a growing problem in Eastern Europe, particularly along the main heroin trafficking routes. Eighty per cent of all the heroin seized in Europe passed along the Balkan route. Heroin from South-West Asia was smuggled through countries in Central Asia on its way to the Russian Federation or through countries in Eastern Europe on its way to European Union (EU) member States. Heroin seizures increased more than fivefold in 1998 in the Russian Federation. Countries in Central and Eastern Europe were increasingly used as storage points for drugs, heroin in particular, destined for sale in Western Europe. Heroin abuse in Western Europe was estimated to affect 1 million people, a figure that had stabilized during 1995-1997. Alarming trends were reported, however, including lower prices, enhanced purity and the spread of HIV in some Eastern European countries, attributable to the infection spreading among intravenous drug users.

Cocaine seizures throughout the region increased, and significant seizures, amounting to more than 1 ton each, were made in several countries in Western Europe, indicating that the illicit demand remained high. Illicit consignments were hidden on cargo ships travelling from South America to Spain, the leading point of entry. Seizures of illicit coca paste indicated that traffickers also attempted to manufacture cocaine in Europe. There was almost no information on the nature and patterns of cocaine abuse, attributable to the fact that its abusers rarely sought help in public centres for drug abuse treatment.

The abuse of synthetic drugs, in particular amphetamine and amphetamine-type stimulants, rose in almost all countries. In EU member States, the rise in the abuse of amphetamine-type stimulants was more pronounced than the rise in other substances, including cannabis, and stimulants emerged as the second most widely used illicit drug after cannabis, ahead of cocaine and heroin. A study undertaken in the United Kingdom revealed that young people considered drug abuse at dances as commonplace, the drugs most often used being MDMA ("ecstasy"), followed by amphetamine, cocaine and lysergic acid diethylamide (LSD). Europe became a major location for illicit drug manufacture, mostly amphetamine and amphetamine-type stimulants. The Netherlands remained the main country in which amphetamine and amphetamine-type stimulants were manufactured, but amphetamines were also manufactured in Belgium, France, Germany, Poland, Slovakia and the United Kingdom. Western Europe was the main supplier of MDMA for illicit markets worldwide, and the Netherlands remained an important source for MDMA and other amphetamine analogues, particularly for use in the United States. The increased abuse of "psychedelic mushrooms", containing psilocin and psylocybine, was reported in Europe, particularly in the Netherlands and Switzerland. Significant drug abuse problems had emerged in the Czech Republic, Hungary, Poland, Slovakia and Ukraine, which in the past had mainly been used by drug traffickers as transit countries.

INCB carried out missions to France, Germany, Hungary, Italy and the United Kingdom in 1999. In France, it appreciated the Government's strong stand against decriminalizing the non-medical use of drugs, and noted that the number of deaths caused by overdose had decreased since the introduction of drug substitution programmes; however, it was concerned about the diversion into illicit channels of buprenorphine, a substance used in those programmes, and its abuse by patients under treatment. In Germany, the Board was concerned by the decision to establish a legal basis for the operation of drug injection rooms, or so-called shooting galleries, where addicts could inject themselves with illicit substances. It reminded the Government that it could be in contravention of the relevant international treaties by facilitating illegal drug possession and use, as well as drug trafficking. Concern was also expressed over the possible proliferation of heroin experiments and the adoption of social policies, including heroin prescription, before projects had undergone evaluation. INCB urged Hungary, following the privatization of the manufacture of narcotic drugs, to ensure complete control over poppy straw cultivation and production, which were previously in the hands of a State-owned enterprise. In Italy, the Board welcomed the Government's rejection of measures that could lead to further decriminalization of drug abuse, and commended it for fighting organized crime and the linkage between Albanian and Italian organized crime. It remained concerned about the low level of morphine consumption for medical purposes, indicative of its insufficient availability for pain management. In the United Kingdom, the Board welcomed efforts to link the criminal justice system and treatment programmes and noted that, although for more than 70 years medical practitioners had been authorized to prescribe heroin legally, the number of addicts receiving heroin on prescription declined, which reflected the judgement of physicians that prescribing the drug to treat opioid addiction was of limited value.

The Board welcomed efforts made at the regional level to coordinate and strengthen legislation and measures to fight drug abuse and illicit trafficking, as well as national legislation and other measures adopted by many European countries. The Treaty of Amsterdam entered into force in May, enhancing the ability of the EU institutions to act in areas of drug control and providing for strengthened cooperation within the EU and at the international level. The Board took note of the draft action plan to combat drugs (2000-2004), which would improve coordination and ensure that the fight against drug abuse and trafficking would remain an EU priority. Many Governments stepped up their bilateral and subregional cooperation. In Eastern Europe, there were many bilateral meetings to promote joint efforts against illicit trafficking, and the network of agreements with authorities from Western Europe expanded. INCB welcomed the fact that Eastern European countries paid increased attention to the link between organized crime and drug trafficking, and appreciated the efforts of Governments and international agencies to assist Bosnia and Herzegovina in drug law enforcement. Bosnia and Herzegovina, Bulgaria, Croatia, Estonia, Latvia, Poland and Romania took action against money-laundering, and the Russian Federation and Slovakia adopted new drug control strategies. The Board was concerned over a draft law approved in Portugal, stipulating that the abuse and possession of drugs for personal use would no longer be criminal offences but only administrative offences, and over the Swiss programme and policy of heroin prescription, allowing the drug to be prescribed to opiate addicts. The Board made a technical mission to Estonia; it trusted that the Government would continue to strengthen its efforts to prevent drug abuse in response to the increasing availability of heroin on the illicit market.

Oceania

Cannabis remained the most widely abused narcotic drug in Oceania. The illicit cultivation of cannabis plants in Australia was expanding, and there was a noticeable shift from outdoor to indoor hydroponic cultivation. Australia was also a key market for cannabis cultivated in Cambodia and Papua New Guinea, where efforts to eradicate crops were hampered by the mountainous and swampy terrain.

In New Zealand, there was no significant cultivation of opium poppy for the illicit manufacture of heroin on a commercial scale; however, opium poppy was illicitly cultivated and consumed locally. Seizure data indicated that New Zealand was sometimes used as a transit point for South-East Asian heroin en route to Australia, where the purity level of the heroin available remained high, the average age of first-time use fell below 18 years and the heroin death rate increased. Heroin abuse was not a major problem in New Zealand, Papua New Guinea and the Pacific island States, but the abuse of opiate substitutes, such as morphine sulphate tablets and "homebake" derived from codeine-based tablets, was common in New Zealand.

Trafficking in and abuse of cocaine were minimal in all countries except Australia, where those trends increased. Seizures indicated that New Zealand and the Pacific island States were used as transit points for South American cocaine destined for Australia. Methamphetamine remained the principal drug manufactured in clandestine laboratories in Australia, and the Board was concerned that not all jurisdictions in Australia had enacted legislation covering the illicit use of precursor chemicals.

The Board welcomed the completion of the rapid assessment survey of drug abuse in Papua New Guinea, which confirmed that the level of cannabis abuse in the country was high. LSD was smuggled out of the United States and Europe and into New Zealand, where it was more widely abused than in many other developed countries.

Some Pacific island States were vulnerable to being exploited as offshore financial centres in money-laundering operations. The Board noted the efforts to improve cooperation among the countries in Asia and the Pacific in the fight against money-laundering and trusted that appropriate legislation and systems would soon be in place. Regarding national legislation and policy, the Board urged Australia not to permit the establishment of drug injection rooms, which would provide an outlet for illicit drug abuse and facilitate drug trafficking. It also commended New Zealand for banning drug-smoking paraphernalia, targeting doctors who excessively prescribed controlled drugs and calling for more research and information about drug problems among the Maori.

ECONOMIC AND SOCIAL COUNCIL ACTION

On 28 July [meeting 43], the Economic and Social Council, on the recommendation of the Commission on Narcotic Drugs [E/1999/28/Rev.1], adopted **resolution 1999/33** without vote [agenda item 14 *(d)*].

Demand for and supply of opiates for medical and scientific needs

The Economic and Social Council,

Recalling its resolution 1998/25 of 28 July 1998 and previous relevant resolutions,

Emphasizing that the need to balance the global licit supply of opiates against the legitimate demand for opiates for medical and scientific purposes is central to the international strategy and policy of drug abuse control,

Noting the fundamental need for international cooperation and solidarity with the traditional supplier countries in drug abuse control in general, and in the universal application of the provisions of the Single Convention on Narcotic Drugs of 1961 in particular,

Having considered the *Report of the International Narcotics Control Board for 1998,* in which the Board points out that in 1997 a balance between consumption and production of opiate raw materials was achieved, and noting that efforts were made by the two traditional supplier countries, India and Turkey, to maintain, together with other producing countries, the balance between supply and demand,

Noting the importance of opiates in pain relief therapy as advocated by the World Health Organization,

1. *Urges* all Governments to continue to contribute to the maintenance of a balance between the licit supply of and demand for opiate raw materials for medical and scientific needs, the achievement of which would be facilitated by maintaining, insofar as their constitutional and legal systems permit, support to the traditional supplier countries, and to cooperate in preventing the proliferation of sources of production of opiate raw materials;

2. *Urges* Governments of all producing countries to adhere strictly to the provisions of the Single Convention on Narcotic Drugs of 1961 and to take effective measures to prevent illicit production or diversion of opiate raw materials to illicit channels, especially when increasing licit production;

3. *Urges* consumer countries to assess their licit needs for opiate raw materials realistically and to communicate those needs to the International Narcotics Control Board in order to ensure easy supply, and urges concerned producing countries and the Board to increase efforts to monitor the available supply and to ensure sufficient stocks of licit opiate raw materials;

4. *Recommends* that, at the request of traditional suppliers, consumer countries provide continued or new support to efforts to estimate yields and supplies of licit opiate raw materials in future years;

5. *Commends* the Board for its efforts in monitoring the implementation of the relevant Economic and Social Council resolutions and, in particular:

(a) In urging the Governments concerned to adjust global production of opiate raw materials to a level corresponding to actual licit needs and to avoid unforeseen imbalances between licit supply of and demand for opiates caused by the exportation of products manufactured from seized and confiscated drugs;

(b) In inviting the Governments concerned to ensure that opiates imported into their countries for medical and scientific use do not originate from countries that transform seized and confiscated drugs into licit opiates;

(c) In arranging informal meetings, during sessions of the Commission on Narcotic Drugs, with the main States importing and producing opiate raw materials;

6. *Requests* the Secretary-General to transmit the text of the present resolution to all Governments for consideration and implementation.

UN action to combat drug abuse

UN International Drug Control Programme

The United Nations International Drug Control Programme (UNDCP), established in 1991 [YUN 1991, p. 721] to promote the application of international drug control treaties and the development of drug control strategies, was a catalyst in stimulating action at the national, regional and international levels. The Executive Director described UNDCP activities in a report to the Commission on Narcotic Drugs [E/CN.7/2000/9]. Through a portfolio of technical cooperation programmes supported by a network of field offices located in key regions and countries, it promoted subregional cooperation and furthered bilateral cooperation and direct consultations between Governments. In mounting a global response to the drug problem, UNDCP mobilized specialized agencies and other UN entities, the international financial institutions, other intergovernmental organizations and civil society, particularly non-governmental organizations (NGOs). In addition to assisting States in complying with drug control treaties, it supported the international community in pursuing the objectives agreed upon by the General Assembly at its twentieth special session [YUN 1998, p. 1135], with particular attention given to assisting Governments in meeting the Assembly's objectives for improving judicial and law enforcement cooperation in countering the world drug problem. In that regard, training was provided to law enforcement personnel, national administrations, judges, magistrates, prosecutors and personnel working in the field of demand reduction.

UNDCP served as the substantive secretariat of INCB. It provided information to the Board in the preparation and release of its annual report and initiated technical assistance activities to better support INCB in monitoring the functioning of the international drug control system and the flow of precursors. In particular, greater emphasis was given to law enforcement and operational issues, such as the detection of smuggling or diversion of precursor chemicals, conducting investigations and sharing the information. UNDCP also served as the substantive secretariat to the Commission on Narcotic Drugs at its forty-second (1999) session and assisted it in preparing the Action Plan for the Implementation of the Declaration on the Guiding Principles of Drug Demand Reduction, adopted by the Assembly in resolution 54/132 (see p. 1157). In cooperation with the UN specialized agencies and with regional organizations such as the European Monitoring Centre for Drugs and Drug Addiction and the Inter-American Drug Abuse Control Commission of the Organization of American States, UNDCP initiated a programme to assist Member States in adopting strategies for demand reduction, with a view to achieving results by 2008, as called for in the Political Declaration adopted by the Assembly in resolution S-20/2 [YUN 1998, p. 1136].

During the year, the financial situation of UNDCP continued its upward trend. The income of the UNDCP Fund increased by 35.2 per cent during 1998-1999 to reach $139.7 million. The improved financial situation enabled it to support the expansion of programmes, particularly those related to the follow-up to the Assembly's twentieth special session.

UNDCP strengthened its presence in key countries and regions, such as Iran, the Russian Federation, South Africa and the States of Central Asia. The thrust of the operational activities was to support national efforts and initiatives, giving attention to activities to reduce or eliminate illicit cultivation of narcotic crops through alternative development, to strengthening national capacities in demand reduction and to institution-building, particularly through the adoption of national drug control master plans and the establishment of coordinating and planning entities. The Programme supported Member States in establishing a series of business plans aimed at meeting the commitment made at the Assembly's special session to eliminate or significantly reduce illicit cultivation of opium poppy, coca bush and cannabis by 2008. As a follow-up to the Action Plan on International Cooperation on the Eradication of Illicit Crops and on Alternative Development, adopted in Assembly resolution S-20/4 E [YUN 1998, p. 1148], UNDCP drew up a four-year programme for alternative development, designed to develop and systematize lessons learned and best practices arising from the alternative development projects carried out around the world. In response to the Action Plan and Commission resolution 42/3 (see p. 1165), it initiated the illicit crops monitoring programme with the support of the European Space Agency, focusing on the six countries accounting for the bulk of the illicit cultivation of opium poppy and coca bush: Afghanistan, Bolivia, Colombia, the Lao People's Democratic Republic, Myanmar and Peru. With regard to the Action Plan against Illicit Manufacture, Trafficking and Abuse of Amphetamine-type Stimulants and Their Precursors, adopted in resolution S-20/4 A [YUN 1998, p. 1139], the UNDCP laboratory continued its profiling and characterization of amphetamines and methamphetamines and their precursors.

UNDCP worked with the Joint United Nations Programme on Human Immunodeficiency Virus/Acquired Immunodeficiency Syndrome (UNAIDS) to prevent the risk of HIV infection by preventing drug abuse. Programmes targeting drug abusers and HIV/AIDS were implemented in Brazil and Viet Nam and initiated in Central Asian States. The joint data-sharing project between UNDCP, Interpol and the World Customs Organization became operational at the beginning of the year; the established data pool would be used for preparing analyses of trafficking trends to be made available to States in order to improve their capacity to formulate, refine and evaluate law enforcement countermeasures. UNDCP continued to promote inter-agency cooperation, especially at the field level, in an effort to mobilize the agencies of the UN system to include drug control issues in their work programmes. Several initiatives were undertaken and there was a marked trend towards multi-agency joint initiatives, such as a four-year project implemented by Brazil in cooperation with UNAIDS, the United Nations Children's Fund (UNICEF) and the United Nations Educational, Scientific and Cultural Organization (UNESCO) on the prevention of drug abuse and HIV/AIDS, and a project involving health promotion and drug abuse preventive education in schools in Bolivia, carried out with the cooperation of UNICEF, the United Nations Population Fund (UNFPA), UNESCO and the World Health Organization (WHO).

UNDCP continued its programme to improve the performance of national drug-testing laboratories in providing accurate results to support law enforcement, judicial and health authorities. In 1999, it assisted 21 drug-testing laboratories in 14 countries and organized training courses for drug analysts from 21 countries. Research activities included participation in a new initiative on a global study of illegal drug markets, which would analyse 20 illegal urban markets in different regions of the world.

The Executive Director outlined UNDCP activities in 1999 on a regional basis, as summarized below.

Africa south of the Sahara

In 1999, UNDCP developed its programme framework for Africa, which set out drug control objectives adapted to the needs of the different subregions. Two five-year programmes for West Africa and Nigeria were developed under the programme framework, to be initiated in 2000. UNDCP prepared the draft integrated drug control programme for Nigeria (for the period 1999-2003) on the basis of the national master plan drawn up by the Government with its assistance; it also participated in the high-level fact-finding expert mission undertaken by the European Commission and the United States to support Nigeria in its drug control efforts and in countering money-laundering and organized crime. During the year, UNDCP completed 10 technical assistance projects, and 15 new projects were integrated into priority programmes for East, Southern and West Africa. It also fostered close working relations between regional organizations and African Governments in implementing regional drug control action plans: in April, UNDCP and the Southern African Development Community (SADC) signed a memorandum of understanding to promote joint programming and coordination in priority sectors of drug control and support the implementation of the SADC regional drug control action plan. The UNDCP technical assistance programme for West African States, completed in 1999, contributed to the establishment of a drug control unit in the secretariat of the Economic Community of West African States (ECOWAS) and a coordinating body for drug control in each of the 16 ECOWAS member States. The new regional five-year programme for West Africa was finalized.

With regard to prevention and reduction of drug abuse, UNDCP provided advisory services and training to several regional and national NGOs and community-based organizations in 20 countries in East and Southern Africa, and new demand reduction activities with particular emphasis on prevention in schools and among youth were initiated in Kenya and Madagascar. In South Africa, it supported the establishment of 10 community centres for counselling, treatment and rehabilitation of drug abusers, the training of staff and the provision of equipment. Two other projects for creating community-based resource centres against drug and alcohol addiction in four countries in Southern Africa were finalized and submitted for funding. In West Africa, UNDCP supported the undertaking of rapid drug abuse assessment surveys in Côte d'Ivoire, Ghana, Nigeria and Senegal; rapid assessment surveys were also initiated in Angola, Chad and Gabon. To address the linkage between drug abuse, HIV and AIDS, UNDCP and UNAIDS initiated a process to enhance field-level cooperation between experts in drug control and HIV, particularly in East, Southern and West Africa.

Two regional programmes aimed at suppressing illicit trafficking were carried out by UNDCP in cooperation with the World Customs Organization in East and Southern Africa, which resulted in improved communication between law enforcement authorities within and outside the regions. UNDCP completed the implementation of a regional law enforcement training programme in East Africa that provided basic training in the identification and investigation of drugs, as well as specialized training for border, airport and seaport control, to more than 100 law enforcement officers, mainly from Kenya, Uganda and the United Republic of Tanzania and from Indian Ocean island States.

North Africa and the Middle East

In the Middle East, UNDCP initiated cooperation between countries and territories through technical meetings, leading to a commitment to subregional cooperation in drug control. The first phase of a subregional drug control programme was initiated following meetings with heads of State and key government ministers. UNDCP assisted the Palestinian Authority in drafting drug control legislation to comply with the international drug control treaties, and provided training to social workers in the field of demand reduction. In the areas under Palestinian jurisdiction, it supported the upgrading of the Anti-Narcotics Administration through the provision of a laboratory and equipment for use in drug searches, and through the training of law enforcement officers. In Israel, it assisted the authorities in the establishment of a comprehensive anti-money-laundering framework.

Assistance was provided to Egypt and Lebanon to conduct an assessment study of drug abuse patterns. In Lebanon, UNDCP, in cooperation with others, completed the second phase of its programme in the Bekaa valley, aimed at sustaining the eradication of illicit opium cultivation, and initiated a multisectoral drug control programme of assistance to law enforcement agencies for the suppression of illicit trafficking.

Central and Eastern Europe

In 1999, UNDCP cooperation with the Russian Federation was enhanced, with the opening of a regional office in Moscow in July to provide direct support in the implementation of a comprehensive cooperation programme. In response to requests of Governments of the region affected by illicit trafficking from Afghanistan, UNDCP prepared a programme to support the drug interdiction efforts of the Russian Border Guard on the Afghan-Tajik border and thereby stem the increasing flow of drugs. In Estonia, Latvia and Lithuania, a new subregional school-based programme to prevent drug abuse was launched. In Central Europe, over 500 health professionals in five countries were trained in modern techniques for treating drug addiction. The drug law enforcement programme for Bulgaria, Romania and the former Yugoslav Republic of Macedonia, undertaken jointly by UNDCP and the EU, provided training in drug law enforcement skills to over 250 police and customs officers; drug-scenting dogs were also supplied and trained. In Bosnia and Herzegovina, two drug law enforcement projects assisted in training and equipping anti-narcotics units.

South Asia

UNDCP co-organized a regional technical workshop in New Delhi, India, in June, on the prevention of HIV/AIDS among drug abusers. In collaboration with the International Labour Organization (ILO), it provided support to India in launching an intervention aimed at reducing and preventing drug abuse among the general population, high-risk groups and drug addicts on a nationwide scale. During the year, the capacity of 18 NGOs in 10 Indian cities was strengthened, and a total of 286 persons from NGOs were trained for improved services to 25,000 recovering drug abusers and their families. In Bangladesh and Nepal, the UNDCP technical assistance programme covering law enforcement, preventive education, treatment and rehabilitation was to be completed at the end of 1999. A new programme of assistance to Nepal covering demand and supply reduction and strengthening institutional capacity was finalized, and a programme for Bangladesh, with emphasis on law enforcement and demand reduction, was developed. In Sri Lanka, activities were initiated to strengthen the collection of data on drug abuse, prevention, treatment and rehabilitation programmes. UNDCP strengthened cross-border cooperation in drug control between the different law enforcement agencies in Bangladesh, India and Myanmar. The UNDCP regional programme for precursor control in South Asia provided assistance to Governments in preventing the diversion of precursors to illicit traffic.

East Asia and the Pacific

UNDCP supported the countries of East Asia in their drug control efforts through the subregional action plan covering Cambodia, China, the Lao People's Democratic Republic, Myanmar, Thailand and Viet Nam. Governments in the region benefited from UNDCP assistance in enacting and implementing drug control legislation in line with the international drug control treaties. UNDCP assisted the Lao People's Democratic Republic, Viet Nam and the South Pacific countries in adopting national drug control plans. It conducted a training workshop in Fiji on master plans for selected Pacific countries, in collaboration with the South Pacific Forum, to increase the understanding of the drug problem in the region and to assist in developing national drug control plans.

The subregional programme to develop community, national and subregional capabilities to reduce drug abuse and deal with related social problems among selected highland ethnic minority groups reached the final stage of implementation. UNDCP started another subregional programme aimed at improving the capacity of governmental and non-governmental institutions to deal with emerging drug abuse problems among high-risk groups. Programme activities in 1999 included a joint intercountry training seminar on the assessment of high-risk groups for participants from Cambodia, the Lao People's Democratic Republic, Myanmar and Viet Nam, and a seminar on the development of a drug abuse assessment methodology for use in schools for participants from drug control coordinating agencies. A regional training programme on addiction rehabilitation and prevention in the workplace was developed in cooperation with ILO. In the Lao People's Democratic Republic, a national project was launched to activate the Drug Demand Reduction Resource Centre as a focal point for coordinating and providing information and training on demand reduction. In Viet Nam, the demand reduction projects under the country programme were put into operation, and in Myanmar, activities to reduce drug abuse and the related risk of HIV infection were initiated in Kachin State. Training materials were provided to groups involved in teaching about drug abuse and HIV/AIDS. UNDCP supported Papua New Guinea in undertaking a drug abuse rapid assessment survey.

Alternative development programmes to follow the elimination of illicit crops were elaborated in the three opium-producing countries—the Lao People's Democratic Republic, Myanmar and Viet Nam. UNDCP provided assistance to States in implementing law enforcement projects covering precursor control, law enforcement training, gathering and exchange of information, and the development of operational procedures. During the year, UNDCP completed two subregional law enforcement projects to strengthen cross-border cooperation along the borders between China and Myanmar, and assisted the Lao People's Democratic Republic and Viet Nam in strengthening their law enforcement capacity, especially border controls.

West and Central Asia

In 1999, UNDCP assisted countries of the region in mounting a collective response to the threat posed by illicit drugs from Afghanistan, which accounted for more than 75 per cent of world illicit opium production. It elaborated a new drug control programme for Afghanistan, incorporating ongoing pilot projects in alternative development and demand reduction, and developed a programme of assistance for countries bordering Afghanistan, to contain the flow of opiates to other countries. UNDCP maintained a dialogue with the Taliban authorities in Afghanistan, urging them to pursue a more effective drug control policy. The second meeting under the memorandum of understanding on subregional drug control cooperation in Central Asia was held in Kyrgyzstan in October. The agreement, signed by the Russian Federation, the Central Asian States, UNDCP and the Aga Khan Development Network, provided a framework for regional cooperation. In the context of the regional cooperation programme, UNDCP assisted Kyrgyzstan, Turkmenistan and Uzbekistan in countering illicit trafficking from Afghanistan, and two new projects were formulated to strengthen border controls in Turkmenistan and Uzbekistan. UNDCP also initiated a regional programme for the control of precursors to prevent their flow to Afghanistan for heroin production.

Within the framework of a memorandum of understanding signed with the Economic Cooperation Organization (ECO), UNDCP launched a programme aimed at coordinating drug control activities between ECO member States, including Afghanistan, Azerbaijan, Iran, Kazakhstan, Kyrgyzstan, Pakistan, Tajikistan, Turkey, Turkmenistan and Uzbekistan. In conjunction with UNAIDS, it launched four new drug abuse prevention programmes in Kyrgyzstan, Tajikistan, Turkmenistan and Uzbekistan to complement an ongoing project in Kazakhstan. In the Caucasus region, a memorandum of understanding on cooperation in drug control and activities against money-laundering was signed in June by the Ministers for Foreign Affairs of Armenia, Georgia and Iran and by the UNDCP Executive Director.

A high-level UNDCP appraisal mission to Turkey, conducted from 31 October to 7 November, assessed the drug control situation in the country with a view to preparing a new drug control programme. UNDCP opened an office in Iran, where a comprehensive drug control programme was signed in June, involving UNDCP support in supply and demand reduction, in community mobilization for demand reduction and in the development of legislation. A new programme for Pakistan was launched to strengthen national law enforcement capacities, promote cooperation between Iran and Pakistan and extend cooperation with the Persian Gulf States.

Latin America and the Caribbean

In 1999, UNDCP assistance focused on the implementation, in Bolivia, Colombia and Peru, of three business plans aimed at the elimination of illicit drug crops through alternative development. Covering the period 1998-2003, they comprised 18 projects, 12 of which were initiated in 1999. UNDCP supported the implementation of the Barbados Plan of Action for Drug Control Coordination and Cooperation in the Caribbean by functioning as a source of information and technical assistance, and continued to mobilize civil society in the area of demand reduction. A memorandum of understanding was signed with the Caribbean Development Bank to support drug control initiatives in the region. Law enforcement agencies were upgraded, and Bolivia, Brazil and Colombia received specialized support in precursor control.

With few exceptions, drug control action in Latin America and the Caribbean was coordinated at the national level by commissions encompassing government entities responsible for health, education, law enforcement and development issues; UNDCP attempted to upgrade their effectiveness in elaborating drug control policies to enhance managerial, advocacy and fundraising capacities. In Bolivia, Colombia and Ecuador, UNDCP initiated projects to strengthen national drug councils' efforts to coordinate and implement national drug control policies. In Peru, it supported a balanced programme approach focusing on the elimination of illicit crops, on drug abuse prevention and reduction and on the strengthening of the national drug control council. With regard to drug abuse prevention and reduction, in Peru, UNDCP supported school-based prevention under the integrated programme in primary education. In Bolivia, it initiated a school-based preventive education programme aimed at training teachers and parents' associations; and in Colombia, it completed four programmes aimed at preventing drug abuse, particularly among youths. The first phase of a UNDCP prevention programme with emphasis on HIV/AIDS was completed in Brazil. Over 67 governmental and non-governmental institutions were involved in producing relevant baseline data, providing training and strengthening treatment and rehabilitation capacities. Given the dimensions of the HIV/AIDS problem in Brazil, a second phase of the programme was initiated, with UNDCP support and financing by the World Bank, to control and prevent the AIDS epidemic. At the subregional level, UNDCP promoted common methods and standards for epidemiological surveillance under a project based on the memorandum of understanding on drug control cooperation signed by Argentina, Bolivia, Chile, Peru, Uruguay and UNDCP. As a result, the five countries established drug abuse information systems allowing cross-country comparisons of prevalence, incidence and trends.

The business plans developed with UNDCP assistance for Bolivia, Colombia and Peru targeted the elimination of illicit drug crops through alternative development. As a result of the combined impact of UNDCP projects, 13,800 farm families benefited from technical assistance through rural infrastructure and social services designed to create sustainable economic opportunities to earn a legal income, thereby reducing their dependence on income from illicit crops. Under the business plan for Peru, projects were initiated to cover major coca-growing areas. Improvements were introduced in growing traditional crops, product quality was upgraded and business-oriented management practices were applied in agro-industrial enterprises. Under the business plan for Bolivia, an agroforestry programme was enlarged to promote alternative development activities, and environmentally sound and sustainable agroforestry management plans and practices were introduced. UNDCP assisted Colombia in establishing a national system for monitoring illicit drugs and providing information on the illicit cultivation of narcotic crops, on eradication efforts and on progress in alternative development. It provided support to law enforcement agencies, in particular the police, customs and judiciary and forensic laboratories, in Bolivia, Brazil, Colombia, Ecuador, Mexico, Central America and the Caribbean region.

Administrative and budgetary matters

Programme and support budgets

The Commission on Narcotic Drugs, at its March session (see p. 1187), had before it a report of the UNDCP Executive Director [E/CN.7/1999/13] on the proposed revised biennial programme budget for 1998-1999 for the UNDCP Fund, amounting to $115,004,900. The difference between the proposed revised programme budget and the initial programme budget, approved by the Commission in 1997 [YUN 1997, p. 1285], was $4,502,900, an increase of 4 per cent, which reflected the expanded UNDCP work programme as a result of the General Assembly's twentieth special session, as well as UNDCP experience in implementing drug control activities in the various regions since the preparation of the initial programme budget. In financial terms, the net result of the changes would be a shift of expenditure from supply reduction to demand reduction and a modest increase in intersectoral activities. The report focused on a description of those elements that had been changed, compared with the approved budget, and on the reasons for the revision.

The Commission also considered the UNDCP Executive Director's report on the proposed revised biennial support budget for 1998-1999 for the UNDCP Fund [E/CN.7/1999/12]. The Executive Director stated that the initial support budget for 1998-1999 had been revised from $34,292,200 to $34,065,700, reflecting a decrease of $226,500, which included volume increases (for controllable elements) of $3,644,800 (10.6 per cent) and cost decreases (arising from changes in costs, prices and exchange rates) of $3,871,300 (11.2 per cent). The revised biennial support budget for 1998-1999 proposed an increase for delivering new programme activities and increased implementation of technical cooperation. In parallel with the reorientation of UNDCP following the Assembly's twentieth special session, it was proposed that the organizational reforms launched in 1998 should be continued. They involved the consolidation of decentralization, including adjustments in the field offices and enhanced arrangements for accountability and executive management through strengthening the Office of the Executive Director. Both the revised biennial support budget and the revised biennial programme budget were supported by the UNDCP Fund, which experienced a positive turnaround in 1998 as the result of an increase in contributing countries and in cost-sharing contributions, providing for a diversification of the funding base. Issues of concern were the stagnation of general-purpose resources used to fund biennial support budget and programme activities, as increases were attributed primarily to special-purpose contributions, and the lack of income predictability, as donors preferred to make contributions on an annual basis.

Also before the Commission was the Executive Director's report on the proposed outline for 2000-2001 for the UNDCP Fund [E/CN.7/1999/11]. The proposed outline amounted to $213,416,400, an increase of $60,151,400 compared with the revised budget for 1998-1999. It was supported by estimates of the financial situation for 2000-2001. Income was estimated at $175,000,000 for 2000-2001, as compared with the estimate of $148,210,000 for 1998-1999. The Fund balance was expected to decline from $55,421,400, as at 31 December 1999, to $17,005,000, as at 31 December 2001, a level appropriate for the operation of UNDCP. The increase in income was anticipated on the basis of positive results achieved during 1998-1999, attributed to the momentum created by the Assembly's twentieth special session and initiatives launched by the Executive Director. The estimate of $230,421,400 in resources available in the outline for 2000-2001 reflected an increase of $21,735,000, compared with the revised estimate for 1998-1999. The increase was attributed to a higher opening balance and an estimated increase in income of $26,790,000, particularly special-purpose income.

The Advisory Committee on Administrative and Budgetary Questions (ACABQ) considered the Executive Director's reports and issued its comments thereon in March [E/CN.7/1999/14].

By a 24 March resolution [E/1999/28/Rev.1 (res. 42/8)], the Commission endorsed the revised resource allocation for programme activities amounting to $115,000,000 for 1998-1999 funded by the UNDCP Fund; it approved the amount of $34,065,700 for the revised 1998-1999 support budget for programme support to field offices and headquarters, as well as management and administration, and the amount of $4,199,300 for the revised 1998-1999 support budget for programme support to agencies. It also took note of the outline for the 2000-2001 biennium, totalling $213,416,400 for the Fund, which provided the basis for an initial budget for 2000-2001.

At its reconvened forty-second session on 30 November, the Commission considered further reports on administrative and budgetary matters.

In an October report [E/CN.7/1999/17], the UNDCP Executive Director stated that the final biennial support budget for 1998-1999 amounted to $34,843,500 as compared to the revised support budget of $34,065,700. The difference between the approved revised budget and the proposed final budget was due to a decrease in costing adjustments of $59,800 (0.1 per cent) and an increase in volume changes of $837,600 (2.4 per cent). The initial biennial support budget for 2000-2001 amounted to $36,181,200, an increase of $1,337,700 over the proposed final biennial support budget for 1998-1999. There was a volume decrease of $1,544,500 as compared to the previous biennium and a cost increase of $2,882,200. The report noted that UNDCP had adopted the harmonized budget model used by other UN funds and programmes, including the United Nations Development Programme (UNDP), UNICEF and UNFPA.

In his report containing the proposed final biennial programme budget for 1998-1999 and the proposed initial biennial programme budget for 2000-2001 for the Fund [E/CN.7/1999/18], the UNDCP Executive Director stated that total estimated programme expenditure for 1998-1999 was calculated to reach $91.7 million, or 80 per cent of the originally approved budget. On that basis, UNDCP projected that total expenditure for 2000-2001 would reach $125.6 million, or 80 per cent of the proposed budget of $157 million. Compared to the previous biennium, the proposed programme budget represented an increase of 37 per cent. Programme priorities for 2000-2001 were determined on the basis of Assembly resolutions S-20/2 [YUN 1998, p. 1136] and S-20/4 A-E [ibid., p. 1139]. The Commission was urged to agree to a higher budget to maintain the momentum in programme delivery reached during 1999.

In September [E/CN.7/1999/22], the Executive Director submitted to the Commission a report on the activities funded by the UNDCP Fund during 1998-1999.

In a November report [E/CN.7/1999/20], ACABQ commented on the UNDCP budget report, as well as the report on UNDCP activities funded by the Fund during 1998-1999 and the Secretariat report on the implications of instituting a results-based budget for the Fund (see p. 1186).

By a 1 December resolution [res. 42/10], the Commission endorsed the final resource allocation for programme activities in the amount of $91,722,900 for 1998-1999 and the programme and budget strategy for 2000-2001; it further endorsed the initial resource allocation for programme activities in the amount of $157,011,500 for 2000-2001 under the Fund. It also approved an appropriation of $34,843,500 for the final 1998-1999 support budget and of $36,181,200 for the initial 2000-2001 support budget, both funded under the UNDCP Fund.

Review of UNDCP

During the general debate at the forty-second session of the Commission on Narcotic Drugs, representatives remarked that the General Assembly's twentieth special session had adopted a balanced approach between supply and demand reduction, established specific objectives and target dates, and given new mandates to UNDCP to assist Governments in translating their commitments into action at the national, regional and international levels.

ECONOMIC AND SOCIAL COUNCIL ACTION

On 28 July [meeting 43], the Economic and Social Council, on the recommendation of the Commission on Narcotic Drugs [E/1999/28/Rev.1], adopted **resolution 1999/30** without vote [agenda item 14 *(d)*].

Review of the United Nations International Drug Control Programme: strengthening the United Nations machinery for international drug control within the scope of the existing international drug control treaties and in accordance with the basic principles of the Charter of the United Nations

The Economic and Social Council,

Noting that the General Assembly, at its twentieth special session, conferred additional mandates on the Commission on Narcotic Drugs and strengthened both its role as the global forum for international cooperation in combating the world drug problem and its functions as the governing body of the United Nations International Drug Control Programme and as a treaty organ,

Stressing the need to enhance the functioning of the Commission to enable it to discharge its new mandates emanating from the twentieth special session of the General Assembly, at which Member States were called upon to report biennially to the Commission on their efforts to meet the goals and targets for 2003 and 2008 set out in the Political Declaration adopted by the Assembly at the special session, on 10 June 1998,

Noting that the twentieth special session of the General Assembly has been designated as a major global conference within the framework of the United Nations system and that follow-up will be reviewed in that context,

Recognizing the crucial role of the International Narcotics Control Board in monitoring the implementation of the international drug control treaties,

Noting with concern that the low level of contributions to the Fund of the United Nations International Drug Control Programme has adverse consequences for the ability of the Programme to fulfil its mandates and to respond to emerging priority needs,

Reiterating the need to strengthen inter-agency cooperation and coordination within the United Nations system to counter the world drug problem,

Recalling its resolution 1997/37 of 21 July 1997, in which the Secretary-General was requested to convene a high-level expert group to review the United Nations International Drug Control Programme and to strengthen the United Nations machinery for international drug control,

Commending the work carried out by the High-level Expert Group to Review the United Nations International Drug Control Programme and to Strengthen the United Nations Machinery for International Drug Control, and expressing appreciation for its report and comprehensive recommendations,

I. Enhancing the functioning of the Commission on Narcotic Drugs

1. *Decides* that the normative functions of the Commission on Narcotic Drugs should be made distinct from its role as governing body of the United Nations International Drug Control Programme and that, to that end, the agenda of the Commission should be structured in two distinct segments, as follows:

(a) A normative segment, during which the Commission would discharge its treaty-based and normative functions, including mandates received from the General Assembly and the Economic and Social Council, and deal with emerging drug control issues;

(b) An operational segment, during which the Commission would exercise its role as the governing body of the United Nations International Drug Control Programme and consider issues related to the provision of policy guidance to the Programme;

2. *Recommends* that the Commission convene, whenever appropriate, ministerial-level segments of its sessions to focus on specific themes related to the follow-up to the twentieth special session of the General Assembly, and requests the Commission at its forty-third session to consider the timing of and the theme for any such ministerial-level segment;

3. *Decides* that, with effect from the year 2000, the Commission should, at the end of its session, elect its Bureau for the subsequent session and encourage it to play an active role in the preparations for the regular as well as the informal inter-sessional meetings of the Commission, so as to enable the Commission to provide continuous and effective policy guidance to the Programme. The Chairman should, whenever appropriate, invite the chairmen of the five regional groups to participate in the meetings of the Bureau;

II. Enhancing the functioning of the International Narcotics Control Board

1. *Invites* the Secretary-General to provide the International Narcotics Control Board with resources commensurate with its mandates emanating from the international drug control treaties and from the twentieth special session of the General Assembly;

2. *Encourages* the Executive Director of the United Nations International Drug Control Programme and the President of the International Narcotics Control Board to continue their mutual efforts to develop closer cooperation in order to take full advantage of the potential synergies between the Board and the Programme;

3. *Invites* Member States and the World Health Organization, when selecting candidates for the International Narcotics Control Board, to ensure the necessary multidisciplinary expertise and the required inde-

pendence and impartiality for the effective discharge of the responsibilities of the Board;

III. Strengthening the financing of the United Nations International Drug Control Programme

1. *Recommends* that a sufficient share of the regular budget of the United Nations be allocated to the United Nations International Drug Control Programme to enable it to fulfil its mandates;

2. *Urges* all Governments to provide the fullest possible financial support to the Programme by widening its donor base and increasing voluntary contributions, in particular general-purpose contributions;

3. *Requests* the Executive Director, in pursuance of Commission resolution 10(XXXIX) of 25 April 1996, to continue his efforts to widen the donor base and increase voluntary contributions to the Fund of the United Nations International Drug Control Programme;

4. *Invites* Member States, as beneficiaries of technical assistance provided by the Programme, to contribute through an agreed cost-sharing mechanism to the financing of that assistance;

5. *Encourages* the Executive Director to explore ways and means to obtain additional funds from the private sector and non-governmental organizations;

6. *Requests* the Executive Director to analyse the implications of instituting a results-based budget for the Fund of the Programme, including the identification of possible performance indicators, taking into account the practices of other funds and programmes of the United Nations system, and to report to the Commission at its reconvened forty-second session;

7. *Recommends* that the budget of the Fund of the Programme continue to be harmonized with the budgets of other funds and programmes of the United Nations system;

8. *Requests* the Secretary-General and the Executive Director, with the assistance of the Chairman of the High-level Expert Group to Review the United Nations International Drug Control Programme and to Strengthen the United Nations Machinery for Drug Control, to continue to explore innovative means of increasing the resources for drug control programmes, including the creation of a global drug facility, for example, along the lines of the Global Environment Facility, and to report thereon to the Commission at its forty-third session;

IV. Framework for inter-agency cooperation and coordination

1. *Recommends* that the Administrative Committee on Coordination ensure that the United Nations System-wide Action Plan on Drug Abuse Control develops into a strategic planning tool and that drug issues are considered in the formulation of the United Nations Development Assistance Framework;

2. *Also recommends* that Member States report on the implementation of measures arising from the twentieth special session of the General Assembly in line with the Political Declaration adopted at the special session and consider the world drug problem as a cross-cutting issue in the context of the integrated and coordinated follow-up to major United Nations conferences and summits;

3. *Further recommends* that Member States ensure that drug issues—especially demand reduction—are regularly included in the agenda of the governing bodies of the Joint United Nations Programme on Human Immunodeficiency Virus/Acquired Immunodeficiency Syndrome, the United Nations Children's Fund, the United Nations Development Programme, the United Nations Population Fund, the International Labour Organization, the United Nations Educational, Scientific and Cultural Organization, the World Health Organization and other interested agencies;

4. *Invites* the United Nations International Drug Control Programme to increase its cooperation with United Nations agencies working in the field of development in implementing alternative development programmes;

5. *Calls* for a significant increase in cooperation between the United Nations International Drug Control Programme and the United Nations Development Programme, in view of the special role of the latter body as a coordinator for development activities within the United Nations system, and to that effect recommends that:

(*a*) Drug-related indicators be jointly developed by the United Nations International Drug Control Programme and the United Nations Development Programme for inclusion in the *Human Development Report* of the United Nations Development Programme;

(*b*) United Nations resident coordinators, in close consultation with Governments, give higher priority to the reduction of the demand for and supply of illicit drugs;

6. *Requests* the Executive Director to continue his efforts, in cooperation with Member States, to forge closer cooperation with regional and international financial institutions engaged in the field of development, in order to secure increased funding for drug-related activities as proposed by the High-level Expert Group to Review the United Nations International Drug Control Programme and to Strengthen the United Nations Machinery for Drug Control, and to encourage those institutions, in particular the World Bank, to accord higher priority to funding such activities;

V. Operations of the United Nations International Drug Control Programme

1. *Encourages* the Executive Director to strengthen further the information strategy of the United Nations International Drug Control Programme along the lines suggested by the High-level Expert Group to Review the United Nations International Drug Control Programme and to Strengthen the United Nations Machinery for Drug Control;

2. *Requests* the Programme to strengthen its evaluation capacity, as proposed by the High-level Expert Group, so as to focus more on the medium- and long-term impact of projects rather than on the completion of the project process.

In response to the Council's resolution, the Secretariat submitted to the Commission at its reconvened forty-second session an October note [E/CN.7/1999/19] that analysed the implications of instituting a results-based budget for the UNDCP Fund, including the identification of possible performance indicators and taking into account the practices of other UN funds and programmes. The note outlined a proposed course of action by the Secretariat, in which it proposed to adapt the current budget and performance reporting system to make it more effective in identifying, measuring and reporting results. The Secretariat would follow closely the work undertaken by UNICEF, UNDP and UNFPA in implementing the results-based concept, with a view to applying those aspects that yielded practical benefits.

UN Vienna Civil Society Award

By a 25 March resolution [res. 42/9], the Commission on Narcotic Drugs welcomed the joint initiative of the United Nations Office at Vienna, the Office for Drug Control and Crime Prevention of the United Nations Secretariat, the host Government of Austria and the city of Vienna in establishing the United Nations Vienna Civil Society Award to honour individuals, institutions and organizations for their contributions in the fight against drug abuse, crime and terrorism. It noted that the annual award would consist of a medal, a certificate and prize money to be funded from voluntary contributions raised by the co-sponsors; it also noted that the selection committee would be composed of the Executive Director of the Office for Drug Control and Crime Prevention, a representative of Austria, the mayor and governor of the city and province of Vienna and other eminent persons representing the major geographic regions of the world, including the chairmen of the Commission on Narcotic Drugs and the Commission on Crime Prevention and Criminal Justice.

Commission on Narcotic Drugs

The Commission on Narcotic Drugs held its forty-second session in Vienna from 16 to 25 March, during which it adopted nine resolutions and three decisions and recommended to the Economic and Social Council for adoption four draft resolutions and two draft decisions. On 30 November and 1 December, the Commission held its reconvened forty-second session, during which it adopted two resolutions.

By **decision 1999/264** of 28 July, the Council took note of the Commission's report on its forty-second session [E/1999/28/Rev.1] and approved the provisional agenda and documentation for the forty-third (2000) session, on the understanding that informal inter-sessional meetings would be convened in Vienna, at no additional cost, to finalize the items to be included in the provisional agenda and the documentation requirements for the forty-third session.

Demand reduction

At its forty-second session, the Commission had before it a January report by the Secretariat on youth and drugs [E/CN.7/1999/8], which gave an overview of the world situation and emerging trends. It stated that drug abuse remained a strategy among youth to cope with unemployment, neglect, violence and sexual abuse. At the same time, however, there was considerable abuse among socially integrated young people, in particular in the industrialized world, which might be attributed in part to the fact that significant portions of the world's youth population were exposed to a culture more tolerant towards the use of drugs. The data available presented a situation of concern in almost every region. Lifetime prevalence rates of abuse of cannabis was high and on the increase. Abuse of amphetamine-type stimulants was diffuse and abuse of "ecstasy", while stabilizing at a high level in some Western European countries, was rising in others and spreading to other regions. There were high variations in the prevalence of cocaine, which was reported to be increasing in the United States. Heroin injection was expanding in Eastern Europe, while there were signs of a rise in its abuse by smoking (United States and Western Europe). Abuse of inhalants remained a serious problem. The changing perception of cannabis among young people, the increasing abuse of amphetamine-type stimulants and the widespread abuse of other drugs indicated a need for innovative approaches and the adaptation of prevention strategies aimed at reducing the demand for illicit drugs. The report suggested that multiple strategies were the best way to approach the drug abuse problem; ideally a combination should include a knowledge, attitude, behaviour and health approach.

By a 23 March resolution on measures to reduce drug demand [res. 42/6], the Commission recommended that the Declaration on the Guiding Principles of Drug Demand Reduction, adopted by the General Assembly in resolution S-20/3 [YUN 1998, p. 1137], should be fully implemented, as well as the Action Plan for its implementation (see p. 1157) with its new objectives, strategies and programmes for future activities. It invited Member States to pay attention to the need for thorough preventive campaigns at all levels; to include measures to raise the awareness of the public and targeted population groups of the risks of drug use, as well as measures to enhance the quality and accuracy of information circulated by the mass media; to limit and counterweigh by positive messages the damage caused by information that conflicted with those strategies; and to use the Internet to disseminate factual information in accordance with the strategies and conveying positive lifestyle messages, particularly for youth.

In a December report [E/CN.7/2000/4], the Secretariat analysed the world situation with regard to drug abuse. The report was based on data received from the 112 countries that had submitted the annual reports questionnaire for 1998. Thirty-one countries in Africa, Asia, the Americas and Europe reported increased abuse of heroin; in the United States, it rose slowly, and in both Europe and the United States, the use of non-injecting modes of administration (smoking in Europe, snorting in the United States) increased. Thirty countries reported the growing abuse of amphetamine-type stimulants. A source of concern was the rising trend in the abuse of methamphetamine in South-East Asia, particularly in Thailand; and increasing abuse of amphetamine was also reported in EU countries. The number of countries reporting the existence of injecting drug users and their infection with HIV continued to grow. Developing countries became highly vulnerable to drug abuse, and in many countries (the Russian Federation, Central and Eastern Europe and various Asian countries), there was an outbreak of HIV. Hepatitis C infections among abusers and drug-related mortality (mainly by overdose) also caused concern in some countries. While data collection systems improved in some parts of the world, there remained a need for improvements to understand the patterns and scale of, and the trends in, the global problem of drug abuse. To facilitate that task, the Secretariat suggested that standardized indicators be developed and capacity-building exercises be conducted in developing countries.

Illicit trafficking

The Commission on Narcotic Drugs had before it a Secretariat report on illicit drug traffic and supply and the impact of communication networks, such as the Internet, on the drug problem [E/CN.7/1999/9]. The report stated that worldwide supplies of heroin and cocaine had stabilized and that estimates of production of opium and coca leaf and statistics on the volume of global seizures of heroin, cocaine and cannabis reflected no further increases since the mid-1990s. However, the increased flow of heroin and cocaine into non-traditional markets (heroin in the United States, cocaine in Western Europe and both drug types in Africa, Asia and Eastern Europe) and the rising level of abuse of and trafficking in amphetamine-type stimulants worldwide had added a global dimension to drug control.

By a 23 March resolution on illicit traffic by sea [res. 42/7], the Commission urged Member States to supply to the Secretary-General details of the authority authorized to respond to requests to board vessels engaged in the illicit traffic in narcotic drugs and psychotropic substances, and requested them to notify changes of competent authorities, so that the information could be transmitted to all Member States by UNDCP. It also urged Member States to consider improving and implementing procedures to allow a timely response to requests in cases where the nationality of a vessel was in doubt or registration could not be confirmed. On 25 March [res. 42/5], the Commission requested UNDCP to pay attention to the issue of abuse of and trafficking in illicit drugs during conflicts, with a view to determining the need for assistance for soldiers and the population, especially children who were victims of drug abuse. It also requested UNDCP to assess the relationship between illicit drugs, conflicts, wars, transnational crime, terrorism, money-laundering and the illicit arms trade, and to propose measures to counter the adverse impact of illicit drugs on those involved in conflicts and wars.

A December report by the Secretariat [E/CN.7/2000/5] provided an overview of the world situation with regard to illicit drug trafficking and action taken by the Commission's subsidiary bodies. It summarized information received from Governments in the annual reports questionnaires. Reference was made to opiates, coca, cannabis and psychotropic substances, and an update was provided on cultivation and production of drugs, patterns and trends in drug trafficking, global interception rates, availability of drugs to the world market, and farm-gate and street prices. The global supply of cocaine remained stable in 1999, but that of heroin increased substantially because of the large increase in opium production in Afghanistan. Trafficking patterns and trends, as reflected in seizures provided up to 1998 in the questionnaires, indicated an increase in the interdiction of cocaine, heroin, cannabis resin and amphetamine-type stimulants. Most of the increase related to the established producer, transit and consumer areas, rather than to emerging markets for illicit substances. Following the Commission's forty-second session, two meetings of its subsidiary bodies were held in 1999—the Ninth Meeting of Heads of National Drug Law Enforcement Agencies (HONLEA), Latin America and the Caribbean (Santiago, Chile, 22-26 November), and the Twenty-third Meeting of HONLEA, Asia and the Pacific (Bangkok, Thailand, 7-10 December). The subsidiary bodies made recommendations on measures to combat money-laundering and to improve interdiction efforts of law enforcement agencies; on countering corrupt practices within drug law enforcement agencies and improving their effectiveness; and on illicit manufacture and distribution of stimulants, illicit traffic in heroin and illicit traffic via mail systems.

Subcommission on Illicit Drug Traffic and Related Matters in the Near and Middle East

The Subcommission on Illicit Drug Traffic and Related Matters in the Near and Middle East, which had held its thirty-third session in Beirut, Lebanon, in 1998, met in Lucknow, India, from 1 to 5 February 1999 for its thirty-fourth session [E/CN.7/1999/9/Add.1]. It recommended to the Commission on Narcotic Drugs the approval of a draft resolution for adoption by the Economic and Social Council on the Lucknow Accord on measures to control international trade in precursors used in the illicit manufacture of narcotic drugs and psychotropic substances. The Subcommission also adopted recommendations on: means by which local or competent authorities could contribute to a balanced approach, emphasizing the reduction of the supply of and the demand for narcotic drugs and psychotropic substances; links between transnational organized crime and other activities related to illicit drug trafficking; and practical measures and the exchange of information to increase the effectiveness of international cooperation, including cross-border operations and targeting trafficking in illicit drugs and precursors.

ECONOMIC AND SOCIAL COUNCIL ACTION

On 28 July [meeting 43], the Economic and Social Council, on the recommendation of the Commission on Narcotic Drugs [E/1999/28/Rev.1], adopted **resolution 1999/31** without vote [agenda item 14 *(d)*].

Lucknow Accord on the Adoption of Uniform Measures to Control International Trade in Precursors and Other Chemicals Used in the Illicit Manufacture of Narcotic Drugs and Psychotropic Substances

The Economic and Social Council,

Convinced that the Lucknow Accord on the Adoption of Uniform Measures to Control International Trade in Precursors and Other Chemicals Used in the Illicit Manufacture of Narcotic Drugs and Psychotropic Substances, adopted by the Subcommission on Illicit Drug Traffic and Related Matters in the Near and Middle East at its thirty-fourth session, held in Lucknow, India, from 1 to 5 February 1999, will contribute to the enhancement of the struggle against illicit drug trafficking in the region,

1. *Takes note* of the Lucknow Accord on the Adoption of Uniform Measures to Control International Trade in Precursors and Other Chemicals Used in the Illicit Manufacture of Narcotic Drugs and Psychotropic Substances, annexed to the present resolution;

2. *Invites* the Secretary-General to inform all Member States, relevant specialized agencies and other entities of the United Nations system and other intergovernmental organizations of the adoption of the Lucknow Accord by the Subcommission on Illicit Drug Traffic and Related Matters in the Near and Middle East;

3. *Invites* Member States to consider the Lucknow Accord when implementing article 12 of the United Nations Convention against Illicit Traffic in Narcotic Drugs and Psychotropic Substances of 1988, in accordance with their existing national legislation;

4. *Also invites* Member States to promote awareness within the chemical industry concerning the provisions of the Lucknow Accord;

5. *Requests* the International Narcotics Control Board to consider the necessary measures, in accordance with article 12 of the 1988 Convention, for the transfer of acetic anhydride and potassium permanganate from Table II to Table I of the Convention.

ANNEX

Lucknow Accord on the Adoption of Uniform Measures to Control International Trade in Precursors and Other Chemicals Used in the Illicit Manufacture of Narcotic Drugs and Psychotropic Substances

We, the representatives of the States members of the Subcommission on Illicit Drug Traffic and Related Matters in the Near and Middle East and observers attending the thirty-fourth session of the Subcommission, held in Lucknow, India, from 1 to 5 February 1999,

Having considered the adoption of uniform measures to control international trade in precursors and other chemicals used in the illicit manufacture of narcotic drugs and psychotropic substances,

Deeply concerned about the diversion of precursors and other chemicals from licit to illicit channels, especially in the course of international trade, for the manufacture of narcotic drugs and psychotropic substances,

Deeply concerned also about the lack of uniformity in monitoring the international trade among various States parties to the United Nations Convention against Illicit Traffic in Narcotic Drugs and Psychotropic Substances of 1988,

Reaffirming our commitment to combat the diversion of precursors and other chemicals used in the illicit manufacture of narcotic drugs and psychotropic substances,

Deciding to take practical measures to implement General Assembly resolution S-20/4 B of 10 June 1998, entitled "Control of precursors", adopted by the Assembly at its twentieth special session,

Have agreed on the following:

1. In accordance with resolution S-20/4 B, adopted by the General Assembly at its twentieth special session, and considering the problems being faced because of different control mechanisms being adopted by Member States, there should be uniformity in the control of international trade in precursors, and a minimum uniform procedure, in conformity with the domestic law of each country, should be adopted to effect such control. The following steps should be taken to achieve those objectives:

(a) International trade in all substances in Table I of the United Nations Convention against Illicit Traffic in Narcotic Drugs and Psychotropic Substances of 1988,

as well as international trade in acetic anhydride and potassium permanganate, substances in Table II, should be subject to control by the competent authorities in all States, irrespective of whether those substances are prone to being diverted;

(*b*) The competent authorities may require all importers and exporters to notify them about each transaction prior to shipment and to furnish the particulars of the trading party in the other country, such as the name of the trading party, the mode of payment and proof of authorization by the competent authority of that country;

(*c*) On receipt of such a notification, the competent authority of the exporting country should send a pre-export notification to the competent authority of the importing country;

(*d*) Each Government should clearly identify and make known its competent authority responsible for international trade;

(*e*) On receipt of the pre-export notification, the competent authority of the importing country should investigate and assure itself of the legitimacy of the transaction and should inform the competent authority of the exporting country;

(*f*) If, fifteen days after having sent the pre-export notification, the competent authority of the exporting country has received no reply from the competent authority of the importing country, it will be presumed that there is no objection to the proposed export. In the case of a specific request by the competent authority of the importing country related to a particular consignment, however, the time-limit of fifteen days will not apply;

(*g*) Each State should establish a system of penalizing companies in its territory that do not comply with the condition of notification. Timely notification will ultimately help such trade, as it will be easy for the competent authorities to verify the legitimacy of the transactions and provide timely responses to the competent authorities of other countries;

(*h*) For a select percentage of imports of precursors into a country, the competent authorities should verify the ultimate use of the precursors. This step is necessary to ensure that the chances of precursors being diverted to illicit channels are minimized and that the companies do not resort to recording inflated figures for precursors used for legitimate purposes. Competent authorities may consider carrying out such an investigation at levels up to and including the level of wholesale trade and, in some cases, even at levels up to and including the level of retail trade;

2. In respect of substitute chemicals, which were discussed and identified by the Subcommission on Illicit Drug Traffic and Related Matters in the Near and Middle East at its thirty-fourth session using as a basis the limited international special surveillance list of substances currently not in Tables I and II of the 1988 Convention and for which substantial information exists of their use in illicit drug trafficking, established by the International Narcotics Control Board pursuant to Economic and Social Council resolution 1996/29 of 24 July 1996, a procedure for monitoring the international trade of substitute chemicals and the format to be used for such monitoring should be approved by the parties to the 1988 Convention. States may also consider notifying the Secretary-General with a view to including such substances in Tables I and II of the 1988 Convention, where appropriate;

3. The International Narcotics Control Board is urged to take the immediate measures necessary to transfer acetic anhydride and potassium permanganate from Table II to Table I of the 1988 Convention.

System-wide Action Plan

The Subcommittee on Drug Control of the Administrative Committee on Coordination held its seventh session (Paris, 15-17 September) [ACC/1999/17] to develop, as recommended by the Economic and Social Council in resolution 1999/30 (see p. 1185), an umbrella framework for inter-agency coordination in drug control as a strategic planning tool to replace the United Nations System-wide Action Plan on Drug Abuse Control. It also reviewed the interim action plan for coordinated inter-agency support for national implementation of the outcome of the twentieth special session of the General Assembly. The Subcommittee extended the applicability of the interim action plan for another year and expanded it to include nine additional countries. The Subcommittee stressed the importance of linking inter-agency collaboration to the United Nations Development Assistance Framework (UNDAF) process, which was the country-level planning tool.

Global Programme of Action

Implementation

In a January report [E/CN.7/1999/4], prepared in response to General Assembly resolution 53/115 [YUN 1998, p. 1170], the Secretariat described implementation of the Global Programme of Action on narcotic drugs and psychotropic substances, adopted by the Assembly in resolution S-17/2 [YUN 1990, p. 859]. The report provided information to the Commission on those provisions of the Global Programme of Action that were not covered by the action plans adopted at the Assembly's twentieth special session and that would require separate reporting on their implementation. Those provisions included the diversion of arms and explosives, the illicit traffic by aircraft and vehicles and the illegal activities of mercenaries and subversive or terrorist groups. The Commission was invited to examine whether those provisions warranted separate reporting, on the understanding that the other provisions could be dealt with in progress reports on the goals for 2003 and 2008, as set out in the Political Declaration adopted by the Assembly in resolution S-20/2 [YUN 1998, p. 1136]. The Commission was also invited to consider whether the questionnaire used by Governments since 1990 [YUN 1990, p. 867] should be discontinued, amended or replaced by another reporting procedure.

Guidelines for reporting

The Commission on Narcotic Drugs had before it a January report by the Secretariat on guidelines for reporting on the implementation of the Global Programme of Action and on the follow-up to the special session of the General Assembly [E/CN.7/1999/2]. The report considered action plans for the implementation of the Declaration on the Guiding Principles of Drug Demand Reduction; on elimination of illicit cultivation of the opium poppy, coca bush and cannabis through alternative development; and on amphetamine-type stimulants and their precursors. It also discussed control of precursors, countering money-laundering, measures to promote judicial cooperation, an overall framework for follow-up, experience acquired within the western hemisphere and the EU, and possible approaches to be taken by the Commission.

Noting the overlap between the measures contained in the Global Programme of Action and the Assembly action plans and measures adopted at its special session, the Commission supported the rationalization of reporting requirements to reduce unnecessary efforts by Governments and the Secretariat, and agreed that reporting on the Global Programme of Action should be integrated with the follow-up to the action plans and measures. In a 24 March resolution [E/1999/28/Rev.1 (res. 42/4)], the Commission decided to establish an inter-sessional working group to elaborate guidelines to facilitate reporting by Governments. It requested the working group to submit unified draft guidelines to the Commission, and requested the UNDCP Executive Director to provide support to the working group, including suggestions on the guidelines. At two inter-sessional meetings (Vienna, 1-3 June and 28-30 September) [E/CN.7/1999/21], the working group elaborated guidelines for reporting and suggested a working methodology for the Commission.

On 1 December [res. 42/11], the Commission adopted the unified questionnaire, as proposed by the working group, that included the information required on all action plans. It requested Member States to transmit their replies to the first biennial questionnaire to the UNDCP Executive Director by 30 June 2000. On the basis of those replies, the Executive Director would prepare a biennial report containing information on global trends, organized by region and covering the action plans and sets of measures. The Executive Director was requested to inform the Commission on UN action to assist Member States in meeting the objectives and target dates set out in the Political Declaration and the UNDCP mandates. The Commission decided to report to the Assembly in 2003 and 2008 on the progress achieved, and to assess the reporting guidelines and questionnaires at regular intervals. It requested UNDCP to discontinue the 1990 questionnaire on the implementation of the Global Programme of Action and decided to evaluate the Executive Director's biennial report and to present recommendations on, among other things, national, regional and international action and cooperation.

Strengthening UN mechanisms

In a December report on strengthening UN machinery for drug control [E/CN.7/2000/8], the UNDCP Executive Director stated that the recommendations identified by the Economic and Social Council in resolution 1999/30 (see p. 1185) to strengthen UN mechanisms had been implemented. The measures to enhance the functioning of the Commission on Narcotic Drugs were realized, and those to enhance the functioning of INCB were brought to the attention of WHO and the Council. With regard to strengthening UNDCP financing, the 2000-2001 UN regular budget had provided a substantial increase for UNDCP. To review UNDCP, strengthen UN machinery for drug control and explore innovative means of increasing resources for drug control programmes, the Executive Director initiated consultations with the World Bank, which was in favour of closer cooperation with UNDCP. With regard to inter-agency coordination and cooperation, UNDCP participated in UNDAF to ensure that drug control was recognized by Member States as a priority, thereby leading to joint multi-agency initiatives involving drug control. The Commission was invited to provide guidance on UN action to strengthen the Organization's role in drug control, particularly in supporting government efforts to implement, within the agreed time frames, the action plans and measures adopted by the General Assembly at its special session.

Chapter XV

Statistics

In 1999, the United Nations continued its international statistics work programme. In March, the Statistical Commission, the 24-member body that guided UN statistical activities, adopted a classification of expenditure according to purpose and revised recommendations for a vital statistics system. It also adopted practical guidelines for good practices in technical cooperation in statistics and decided to discontinue the Task Force on Environment Statistics. Progress was made in developing an updating mechanism for the 1993 System of National Accounts and on a proposed manual on statistics in international trade in services. The Intersecretariat Working Group on Price Statistics, responsible for the preparation of price index manuals, held its first meeting in February 1999.

On the Commission's recommendation, the Economic and Social Council decided that the Commission should meet annually instead of biennially, starting in 2000, and that the Working Group on International Statistical Programmes and Coordination should cease to function.

Work of Statistical Commission

The Statistical Commission held its thirtieth session in New York from 1 to 5 March 1999 [E/1999/24]. It adopted the Classifications of Expenditure According to Purpose, and Revised Principles and Recommendations for a Vital Statistics System. It also adopted practical guidelines for good practices in technical cooperation in statistics. In addition, it recommended to the Economic and Social Council the adoption of a draft resolution by which the Council would establish annual sessions of the Commission, and the Commission's Working Group on International Statistical Programmes and Coordination would cease to function. In following up the statistical implications of recent major UN conferences and summits, the Commission commended the UN Statistics Division on the trial compilation of the Minimum National Social Data Set, which the Commission had adopted in 1997 [YUN 1997, p. 1299], and the initial work to take stock of indicators being produced and disseminated by the international community, while recognizing the inventory of development indicators being compiled by the Division as a tool for more in-depth analysis of duplications. It urged international agencies to work towards harmonizing and rationalizing the various sets of indicators being used at the international level, and to improve coordination in their collection in order not to overburden countries, and urged international agencies and bilateral donors to assist countries in building sufficient statistical capacity in order to produce development information.

The Commission reviewed the ongoing work that groups of countries and international organizations were undertaking in various fields of economic, social and environment statistics. In particular, it re-emphasized the need for those groups to formulate clear objectives and agendas and make them available to the Commission; in relation to the evaluation of the International Comparison Programme, requested the Chairman to appoint a group to advise on further steps to address the shortcomings that had been identified, and requested the international organizations active in the Programme to set out plans to take account of relevant recommendations; and decided that the Task Force on Environment Statistics should be discontinued, and that coordination in that field should be carried out by the Administrative Committee on Coordination (ACC) Subcommittee on Statistical Activities, to the extent possible. Members of the Commission emphasized the need for sufficient flexibility in the Special Data Dissemination System of the International Monetary Fund (IMF), in order to allow countries to focus on specific priority areas of statistical development. The Commission requested the Statistics Division and IMF to improve the communication and consultation process.

The Commission reviewed its functioning and adopted new approaches in order to improve its operation. It endorsed the planned production of a document that would improve the understanding of the fundamental principles of official statistics adopted previously by the Commission, promote awareness and assist in their implementation. It also welcomed the establishment of the United Nations Educational, Scientific and Cultural Organization Institute of Statistics and called on existing agencies to integrate their formal and informal collaborative arrangements. The Commission endorsed the proposed work programme of the Statistics Division, including the implementation plan and timetable for realizing the recommendations of the in-depth review of the statistical programme carried out in 1997 by the Office of Internal Oversight Services.

By **decision 1999/223** of 26 July, the Economic and Social Council took note of the Commission's 1999 report, decided that the thirty-first session of the Commission should be held in New York from 29 February to 3 March 2000, and approved the provisional agenda and documentation for that session.

Functioning of Statistical Commission

In response to a request made by the Working Group on International Statistical Programmes and Coordination [YUN 1998, p. 1174], the Secretary-General submitted a report to the Statistical Commission's March session on options for meetings of the Commission and the Working Group [E/CN.3/1999/24]. Regarding the feasibility of holding annual instead of biennial Commission sessions, the report noted that annual sessions would allow the Commission to deal with emerging topics and urgent issues on a more timely basis. However, an additional workload would be placed on the Statistics Division and other parts of the UN Secretariat. Should it be decided to hold annual meetings of the Commission, the Working Group on International Statistical Programmes and Coordination would no longer be needed. Should the Commission decide to maintain its biennial meeting cycle, the report suggested that it might wish to adopt new terms of reference for the Working Group so as to delegate authority to it. A draft of some revised terms of reference was presented.

ECONOMIC AND SOCIAL COUNCIL ACTION

On 26 July [meeting 39], the Economic and Social Council, on the recommendation of the Statistical Commission [E/1999/24], adopted **resolution 1999/8** without vote [agenda item 13 *(c)*].

Functioning of the Statistical Commission

The Economic and Social Council,

Bearing in mind its resolutions 8(I) of 16 February 1946 and 8(II) of 21 June 1946 concerning the establishment and terms of reference of the Statistical Commission and 1566(L) of 3 May 1971, in which the Council further refined the terms of reference, and resolution 1306(XLIV) of 31 May 1968, by which the Council established the Working Group on International Statistical Programmes and Coordination and gave it its initial task,

Welcoming the series of reviews that the Statistical Commission has carried out since 1993 on its role and functioning and that of its Working Group on International Statistical Programmes and Coordination,

Taking into account General Assembly resolution 50/227 of 24 May 1996 on the restructuring and revitalization of the United Nations in the economic, social and related fields,

Recognizing the need to provide for more continuity of the Commission's decision-making and oversight of the global statistical process,

Recognizing also the need for a more flexible and rapid response to emerging and topical developments in international statistics than is possible through the biennial meetings of the Statistical Commission,

Wishing to enable the Statistical Commission to carry out on a more continuous basis its role in following up the statistical implications of the major United Nations conferences and summits and the agreed conclusions of the high-level and coordination segments of the Economic and Social Council and of its resolutions, thus providing enhanced support to the Council in carrying out its own responsibilities in this area,

1. *Decides* that the Statistical Commission shall meet annually, beginning in 2000, for a period of four working days in New York, and decides that the small additional cost shall come from existing resources;
2. *Also decides* that, with immediate effect, the Working Group on International Statistical Programmes and Coordination shall cease to function.

Economic statistics

National accounts

In March, the Statistical Commission had before it a report of the Secretary-General on the milestone assessment of the implementation of the System of National Accounts (1993 SNA) [YUN 1993, p. 1112] by member States [E/CN.3/1999/3], submitted in response to a 1997 Commission request [YUN 1997, p. 1303]. The report contained background information on the definition and measurement of the milestones for implementation of the 1993 SNA and tables of the milestone assessment for member States, covering the period 1992-1997. For comparison, the assessment for the period 1990-1995 was also included. The regional commissions presented qualifying country notes and comments on the assessment. The report also analysed changes in the assessment over the preceding two years. The purpose of the milestone assessment was to create an instrument to detect progress and/or to identify difficulties encountered by countries or groups of countries in their implementation efforts, as well as to focus technical cooperation activities.

The Commission also had before it the report of the 1998 meeting of the Task Force on National Accounts [YUN 1998, p. 1175].

The Statistical Commission, at its March session, approved the Task Force's proposal for an updating mechanism for the 1993 SNA with one change: the period within which the 24 member countries of the Statistical Commission could approve an amendment of the type "interpretation" or "change" should be extended to 60 days. It also emphasized that all the steps of the amendment process, in particular those calling for review by all national statistical offices, should be strictly observed. The Statistical Commission agreed in principle with the proposed amendment referring to the treatment of financial derivatives and asked the Intersecretariat Working Group on National Accounts (ISWGNA) to consider specific comments made by member States, and to circulate the redrafted text to all national statistical offices and thereafter to the members of the Commission. It noted the proposals for further work in gross domestic product volume measures; national accounts and employment; measurement of insurance output; financial intermediation services indirectly measured; asset transfer costs; government accounting; exhaustiveness/measurement of the non-observed economy; and dissemination standards. The Commission asked the UN Secretariat to strengthen the analytical portion of future assessment papers, highlighting why progress had or had not been made within or between regions and requested ISWGNA to determine whether there was a match between its work programme and the needs of countries.

By a December 1999 note [E/CN.3/2000/2] to the Statistical Commission, the Secretary-General submitted the report of the Task Force on National Accounts, which provided an update on the status of the two concrete processes that had been initiated so far (treatment of financial derivatives, and functional classifications), and described other topics where electronic discussion had already begun, such as the cost of transferring ownership of assets. The report described the standard integrated presentation of ISWGNA's work programme in support of SNA implementation; reports on those areas where further and/or new conceptual and methodological work was proposed by the Commission; and ISWGNA's response to the particular needs of countries currently assessed at the pre-SNA phase and phase 1.

International trade statistics

During its March discussion on international trade statistics, the Statistical Commission considered the report of the Task Force on International Trade Statistics [E/CN.3/1999/4]. The Task Force endorsed a work plan that would result in the completion in the year 2000 of a compiler's manual for international trade statistics. It also amended and endorsed a questionnaire on customs areas of the world and noted work by the Statistical Division on technical information regarding index numbers of international trade; provision by countries to the Division of international trade statistics in terms of the Harmonized System; revised concepts and definitions for international merchandise trade statistics; possible rationalization of the commodity classifications in the Commodity Trade Statistics Database; and other matters. In an addendum to the Task Force's report [E/CN.3/1999/4/Add.1], the Secretary-General submitted a note in follow-up to the Task Force's discussions on the Commodity Trade Statistics Database and the Central Product Classification (CPC).

The Commission, among other things, agreed that the treatment of electronic commerce in international trade statistics should be clarified; endorsed the proposed work on the manual for international trade statistics and requested the Statistics Division to give special attention in the manual to the measurement of adjustments to customs statistics for balance-of-payments purposes; and considered that it was important to evaluate the usefulness and applicability of trade statistics according to CPC aggregates for economic analysis and welcomed the intention of the Statistics Division to produce a data set of merchandise trade statistics according to CPC (goods part) on diskette as an input into reviewing and evaluating CPC and its use. In addition, the Commission reconfirmed its support for the work of the Statistics Division on producing the planned publication on the statistical territories of the world for use in international merchandise trade statistics and agreed that, in the short term, the Division should maintain the Commodity Trade Statistics Database and develop a strategic plan for its rationalization. It also endorsed the efforts of the Division, the Organisation for Economic Cooperation and Development (OECD) and the Statistical Office of the European Commission (Eurostat) to rationalize their data collection, processing and storage systems to reduce duplicate processing and increase the compatibility of their databases.

Service statistics

In March, the Statistical Commission had before it the report of the Task Force on Statistics of International Trade in Services [E/CN.3/1999/5], which described action taken to produce a manual to help national statisticians compile statistics on international trade in services.

The Commission took note of the completed activities and proposed schedule put forward by the Task Force for the manual's completion.

Finance statistics

In March, the Statistical Commission considered the report of the Task Force on Finance Statistics [E/CN.3/1999/6], which held two meetings in 1998, the first meeting hosted by IMF (Washington, D.C., 13-14 July) and the second by OECD (Paris, 29-30 October). In the context of the financial crises in Asia, the Task Force launched several initiatives to improve collaboration with regard to disseminating statistics in two areas: international reserves and external debt.

The Statistical Commission recognized the concerns of countries about the complexities and high resource-intensiveness of measuring external debt, and the need to compile and publish components of external debt based on both creditor and debtor sources for improved data quality and accuracy. It took note of ongoing efforts to compare alternative methods of measuring external debt and to enable the advantages and disadvantages of the available methods to be determined. The Commission noted IMF's work in developing the *Manual on Monetary and Financial Statistics* and the *Manual on Government Finance Statistics.*

Other economic statistics

City groups

The Statistical Commission considered a report of seven city groups in the economic statistics area [E/CN.3/1999/7]; an addendum [E/CN.3/1999/7/Add.1] contained the terms of reference and functioning of the Intersecretariat Working Group on Price Statistics (ISWGPS), prepared by the International Labour Organization (ILO).

The city group report described the meetings and planned activities of the Canberra (Australia) Group on Household Income Statistics; the Delhi (India) Group on Informal Sector Statistics; the Expert Group on Capital Stock Statistics; the Expert Group on Intangibles; the Ottawa (Canada) Group on Price Indexes; the Paris Group on Labour and Compensation; and the Round Table on Business Survey Frames.

The Statistical Commission, among other things, noted the various efforts under way in Latin America, Asia, francophone West Africa and Europe to measure activities of the informal sector and encouraged the Delhi Group on Informal Sector Statistics to draw on relevant information and experiences. It also noted the establishment of ISWGPS with a mandate to prepare price index manuals, and welcomed IMF's offer to advance the work on a producer price index manual. ISWGPS was asked to communicate its needs to the Ottawa Group and to encourage the Group to make specific contributions to the manuals on leading edge thinking on theoretical and practical problems.

International Comparison Programme

The Commission had before it a consultant's report on the evaluation of the International Comparison Programme (ICP) [E/CN.3/1999/8] and an addendum [E/CN.3/1999/8/Add.1] containing the World Bank's observations on that report. The ICP evaluation recommended that, in order for the Programme to become more credible and useful, the Statistics Division should find a world coordinator to bring about required changes. The coordinator should be asked to put together a financing consortium consisting of national statistical offices and international agencies to ensure the success of a next phase of ICP; rewrite the *Handbook of the International Comparison Programme;* and find a way of getting the results to users in a timely fashion. The World Bank endorsed the consultant's findings.

The Commission accepted that ICP had significant timeliness and quality problems and agreed to request the Chairman to appoint a group to advise on further steps to address ICP's shortcomings; to request OECD/Eurostat to prepare a report describing future plans for their Purchasing Power Parity programme; and to rely on joint efforts by a group composed of the World Bank, IMF and the Statistics Division to prepare within three months an implementation plan setting out practical steps to be taken in order to address issues raised in the consultant's report.

ISWGPS

The Intersecretariat Working Group on Price Statistics held two meetings in 1999 (Geneva, February, November) [E/CN.3/2000/10]. A technical expert group on the consumer price index was established and also met in February and November in Geneva. The Ottawa Group on Price Indexes had a special session (Reykjavik, Iceland, 25-27 August) on the revision of the ILO *Manual on Consumer Price Indices.* A technical expert group on the producer price index was formed under the coordination of IMF.

Social and demographic statistics

Demographic, social and migration statistics

The Statistical Commission had before it in March a report on progress in demographic, social and migration statistics [E/CN.3/1999/9], which stated that the draft of the revised *Principles and Recommendations for a Vital Statistics System* had been prepared and submitted to an expert group (see below). The report noted that the Statistics Division, in partnership with the United Nations Population Fund, was undertaking interregional and regional training to assist countries in conducting a census of population and housing in the 2000 census decade. The Commission also considered the reports of the Expert Group on Draft Principles and Recommendations for a Vital Statistics System [YUN 1998, p. 1177] and of the Siena Group for Social Statistics [E/CN.3/1999/11], which highlighted the Group's planned activities.

The Statistical Commission endorsed the draft *Principles and Recommendations for a Vital Statistics System*, as revised by the Expert Group; requested the Secretariat to publish them as quickly as possible in all the United Nations official languages; and took note of the rescheduling of the next issue of the *Compendium of Human Settlements Statistics* to the 2000-2001 biennium.

Environment statistics

At its March session, the Statistical Commission considered a report on environment statistics [E/CN.3/1999/12], which listed recent recommendations on environment statistics made by the Statistical Commission, its Working Group on International Statistical Programmes and Coordination, and the ACC Subcommittee on Statistical Activities. Annexed to the report was a paper by the Statistics Division describing the nature, source and scope of environment statistics. The paper concluded that the large variety of user needs justified the diversity of approaches in the relatively new area of environment statistics, and efforts aimed at full harmonization and standardization were therefore deemed premature.

Also before the Commission was a report of the London Group on Environmental Accounting [E/CN.3/1999/13], which described the Group's mandate and work, including the planned revision of the UN draft handbook on the system of integrated environmental-economic accounting (SEEA). The Group had established working groups to begin drafting the material that would eventually be recommended to the Statistics Division for inclusion in a revised SEEA manual.

The Statistical Commission approved the suggestion made by the ACC Subcommittee on Statistical Activities in 1998 [YUN 1998, p. 1176] that the Task Force on Environment Statistics should be discontinued and that the Subcommittee should carry out coordination in environment statistics. It welcomed the work of the London Group leading to the revision of SEEA.

Technical cooperation

In March, the Statistical Commission had before it a Secretariat report on some guiding principles for good practices in technical cooperation for statistics [E/CN.3/1999/19]. The report was a result of the 1997 Workshop on Improving Technical Cooperation in Statistics [YUN 1997, p. 1305]. It also benefited from comments by the Commission's Working Group on International Statistical Programmes and Coordination and various national statistical offices and regional statistical commissions.

The Commission endorsed the guiding principles for good practices in technical cooperation for statistics, except that it agreed to rename them "practical guidelines for good practices in technical cooperation for statistics". It agreed to the wide dissemination of the practical guidelines to national statistics offices and regional and international organizations, and agreed that the guidelines would be reviewed after two or three years, taking into account relevant experiences in the field of technical cooperation.

Other statistical activities

Coordination and integration of international statistical programmes

In March, the Statistical Commission had before it a report of the Secretary-General on the global integration presentation of the work plans of the international organizations in statistical methodology [E/CN.3/1999/25]. The report responded to matters raised by the Commission's Working Group on International Statistical Programmes and Coordination in 1998 [YUN 1998, p. 1179] and comments made that year by the ACC Subcommittee on Statistical Activities [ibid., p. 1180]. The UN Secretariat believed there should be a companion document to the global presentation, comprising an annotated list of previously adopted standards, to be prepared and maintained by the Statistics Division; it would be placed on the Division web site with hyperlinks to available sites containing detailed information about each standard. The Secretariat also believed that the global presentation would be successful only if all organizations were included. To resolve the problem of both OECD and Eurostat having indicated that they would not provide information, the Division would enter their information for them. The report also presented observations on recommendations made in 1998 by the ad hoc group established by the Statistical Commission [ibid., p. 1179].

The Commission also considered the reports of the ACC Subcommittee's 1997 [YUN 1997, p. 1302] and 1998 [YUN 1998, p. 1175] sessions, and the report of the Expert (Prague) Group on Some Best Practices for Official Statistics [ibid.].

The Commission requested the Statistics Division to proceed with the database and integrated presentation of the work plans in statistical methodology of the international organizations, and requested all organizations to participate in that endeavour. The Division was also asked to prepare an annotated list of previously adopted statistical standards as a companion document to the integrated presentation. The Commission welcomed the work of the Prague Group and the follow-up working session on best practices in statistics (Singapore, 12-14 January). It endorsed the planned production of a document that would improve the understanding of the fundamental principles of official statistics, promote awareness of them and assist in their implementation; endorsed the establishment by the Statistics Division of the framework for a web site that would feature that document and serve as a referral system for relevant country practices; and requested the Division to prepare a revision of its handbook on statistical organizations.

Inter-agency cooperation

The ACC Subcommittee on Statistical Activities, at its thirty-third session (Madrid, Spain, 14-16 September) [E/CN.3/2000/19], noted, among other things, the work of the Statistics Division in the development of a web site for the global integrated presentation of the work of the international organizations in statistical methodology; the creation of the Intersecretariat Working Group on Price Statistics; and the discontinuation of the Task Force on Environment Statistics. It agreed that coordination in environment statistics should be carried out by the ACC Subcommittee.

Statistical implications of UN conferences

For its consideration of the statistical implications of the major UN conferences held during the 1990s, the Statistical Commission had before it a report on harmonization and rationalization of development indicators in the UN system, which was considered by the Economic and Social Council Executive Committee in 1998 [YUN 1998, p. 1178], and the report of the Rio Group on Poverty Statistics on its 1998 meeting [ibid.].

The Statistical Commission recognized the inventory of development indicators being compiled by the Statistics Division as a tool for more in-depth analysis of duplications, overlaps and inconsistencies; noted that the large number of indicators requested by different international agencies often overtaxed the capacity of countries, particularly developing countries; urged international agencies to work towards harmonizing and rationalizing the various sets of indicators being used at the international level, including the use of common definitions and methods; affirmed that the Minimum National Social Data Set was useful and could provide guidance to countries interested in developing a basic social statistics system; and encouraged UN funds and programmes to make statistical capacity-building a priority within the United Nations Development Assistance Framework. As to the Rio Group report, the Commission noted that development indicators, especially poverty indicators, were most useful when linked directly or indirectly to policy formulation and administrative operations; and requested the Rio Group to continue its activities, paying special attention to the nature of the data required for analysing the causes of poverty, the relation between poverty and social exclusion, and the effect of public services on poverty alleviation.

The Rio Group on Poverty Statistics (Lisbon, Portugal, 22-24 November 1999) [E/CN.3/2000/16] discussed, among other things, poverty indicators and poverty statistics oriented towards policy design and monitoring; absolute and relative poverty; statistical sources used for poverty measurements; and institutional agreements towards comparability of measurements in different regions.

International economic and social classifications

In March, the Statistical Commission considered the Secretary-General's report on evaluation of progress in the implementation of the International Standard Industrial Classification of All Economic Activities (ISIC), Revision 3, and the Central Product Classification (CPC), Version 1.0 [E/CN.3/1999/16]. The report examined whether the necessary coordination mechanisms for implementation, maintenance, updating and revision of ISIC, designed to be a standard classification of productive economic activities, were in place for the development of statistics of production, consumption, expenditure and trade. The Commission also considered the Secretary-General's 1998 report on international economic and social classifications [YUN 1998, p. 1177] and the 1998 Voorburg Group on Service Statistics report [ibid.].

The Statistical Commission recommended that the future work programme of the Voorburg Group be focused on problems of service product prices. As to classifications issues, the Commission agreed in principle with the strategies laid out in the reports; recommended that the Expert Group on International Economic and Social Classifications be the central coordinating body for implementing the proposed work programme, and that its tasks should include classification revisions and practical proposals to bring about the convergence of existing international and multinational classifications; called on the Expert Group to improve the supporting materials for ISIC and the implementation, assessment and future revisions of ISIC and CPC; and noted that the Statistics Division was prepared to host Expert Group meetings and provide funds for the participation of developing countries.

In 1999, two regional training workshops on classifications were conducted: the first, on SNA and classifications, was held for Caribbean countries (Curaçao, Netherlands Antilles, 31 May-4 June); the second, on classifications, was held for the Asia-Pacific region (Canberra, 27 September-1 October).

The Expert Group on International Economic and Social Classifications established a Technical Sub-group to take action on the implementation of the proposed programme on ISIC and CPC. It held its first meeting in November.

Economic and social information system

The Statistical Commission considered in March the Secretary-General's report on draft standards of the United Nations Economic and Social Information System (UNESIS) for data structure and metadata in international data exchange and dissemination [E/CN.3/1999/27]. UNESIS was a comprehensive project of the Statistics Division, in cooperation with the regional commissions and other parts of the global statistical system, designed to re-engineer its basic statistical data system so as to respond to new user demands, using new client-server and network technologies. The report described the state of development of metadata standards, the objectives for the system over the 2000-2001 biennium, and cooperation in development undertaken with the regional commissions and national experts.

The Statistical Commission took note of the report.

UNESCO Institute for Statistics

In March, the Statistical Commission considered a report of the United Nations Educational, Scientific and Cultural Organization (UNESCO) on its proposed institute for statistics [E/CN.3/1999/28]. The primary reason for establishing such an institute was to enable UNESCO to provide effective responses to the ever-increasing demands that emanated from member States and the international community for more diversified, policy-oriented and reliable statistical products and services in UNESCO's fields of competence: education, science and technology, and culture and communication. Its mission was to provide statistical information to help decision-making in member States and thereby enhance policy and programme development.

The Statistical Commission welcomed the establishment of the UNESCO Institute for Statistics and the broad nature of its mandate, and emphasized that the Institute should work in full collaboration with the existing agencies doing related work.

PART FOUR

Legal questions

Chapter I

International Court of Justice

In 1999, the International Court of Justice (ICJ) delivered two Judgments and one advisory opinion and made 33 Orders. It had pending before it 25 contentious cases and one advisory case during the year.

In a 26 October address to the General Assembly, the ICJ President noted that the Court had been seized of more new contentious cases in the period under review (1 August 1998–31 July 1999) than during any prior period, a trend that continued through the latter half of 1999. He remarked that many cases before the Court concerned major international crises, such as the hostilities in the Kosovo province of the Federal Republic of Yugoslavia and in the Democratic Republic of the Congo. The President noted that some 53 years after its creation, the Court had more than justified the perception that a world court could fundamentally foster peace and international cooperation through the adjudicated settlement of international disputes and the development of a body of international law.

With regard to the Court's advisory function and the proliferation of other international tribunals, the President suggested that such other tribunals be encouraged to turn to the Court to minimize and resolve conflicting interpretations of international law.

Judicial work of the Court

During 1999, the Court delivered a Judgment on the *Request for Interpretation of the Judgment of 11 June 1998 in the Case concerning the Land and Maritime Boundary between Cameroon and Nigeria (Cameroon v. Nigeria), Preliminary Objections (Nigeria v. Cameroon)* and a Judgment on the merits in the case concerning *Kasikili/Sedudu Island (Botswana/ Namibia)*. It rendered an advisory opinion in the case concerning the *Difference relating to Immunity from Legal Process of a Special Rapporteur of the Commission on Human Rights*.

The Court made Orders on requests for the indication of provisional measures made by Germany in the case concerning *LaGrand (Germany v. United States of America)*, and by the Federal Republic of Yugoslavia in the cases concerning the *Legality of Use of Force (Yugoslavia v. Belgium) (Yugoslavia v. Canada) (Yugoslavia v. France) (Yugoslavia v. Germany) (Yugoslavia v. Italy) (Yugoslavia v. Netherlands) (Yugoslavia v. Portugal) (Yugoslavia v. Spain) (Yugoslavia v. United Kingdom)* and *(Yugoslavia v. United States of America)*. The Court or its President further made Orders on the conduct of the proceedings in the cases concerning *Maritime Delimitation and Territorial Questions between Qatar and Bahrain (Qatar v. Bahrain), Questions of Interpretation and Application of the 1971 Montreal Convention arising from the Aerial Incident at Lockerbie (Libyan Arab Jamahiriya v. United Kingdom)* and *(Libyan Arab Jamahiriya v. United States of America), Land and Maritime Boundary between Cameroon and Nigeria (Cameroon v. Nigeria), Sovereignty over Pulau Litigan and Pulau Sipadan (Indonesia/Malaysia), LaGrand (Germany v. United States of America), Legality of Use of Force (Yugoslavia v. Belgium) (Yugoslavia v. Canada) (Yugoslavia v. France) (Yugoslavia v. Germany) (Yugoslavia v. Italy) (Yugoslavia v. Netherlands) (Yugoslavia v. Portugal) (Yugoslavia v. Spain) (Yugoslavia v. United Kingdom)* and *(Yugoslavia v. United States of America), Armed activities on the territory of the Congo (Democratic Republic of the Congo v. Burundi) (Democratic Republic of the Congo v. Uganda)* and *(Democratic Republic of the Congo v. Rwanda), Aerial Incident of 10 August 1999 (Pakistan v. India), Ahmadou Sadio Diallo (Republic of Guinea v. Democratic Republic of the Congo)* and *Application of the Convention on the Prevention and Punishment of the Crime of Genocide (Croatia v. Yugoslavia)*.

The 1999 activities of ICJ were covered in two reports to the General Assembly, for the periods 1 August 1998 to 31 July 1999 [A/54/4] and 1 August 1999 to 31 July 2000 [A/55/4]. By **decision 54/411** of 26 October 1999, the Assembly took note of the 1998/1999 report.

Maritime delimitation and territorial questions (Qatar v. Bahrain)

Qatar instituted proceedings in 1991 [YUN 1991, p. 820] against Bahrain in respect of disputes relating to sovereignty over the Hawar islands, sovereign rights over the shoals of Dibal and Qit'at Jaradah and the delimitation of the maritime areas of the two States.

In 1992, a Memorial by Qatar and a Counter-Memorial by Bahrain were filed [YUN 1992, p. 982], as were their respective Reply and Rejoinder.

Following hearings, the Court delivered on 1 July 1994 a Judgment [YUN 1994, p. 1279].

The Court received a letter from Qatar on 30 November 1994 transmitting an "Act to comply with paragraphs (3) and (4) of the operative paragraph 41 of the Judgment of the Court dated 1 July 1994". On the same day, Bahrain transmitted a "Report of the State of Bahrain to the International Court of Justice on the Attempt by the Parties to Implement the Court's Judgment of 1 July 1994".

At a public sitting held on 15 February 1995, the Court delivered a Judgment on jurisdiction and admissibility [YUN 1995, p. 1305], by which it found that it had jurisdiction and that the Application of Qatar as formulated on 30 November 1994 was admissible.

In 1996, each Party filed a Memorial on the merits [YUN 1996, p. 1176]. Counter-Memorials of the Parties were filed on 23 December 1997 [YUN 1997, p. 1312].

On 17 March 1998, the President held a meeting to ascertain the views of the Parties on a procedure concerning the authenticity of documents produced by Qatar [YUN 1997, p. 1312]. By an Order of 30 March 1998 [YUN 1998, p. 1184], the Court fixed 30 September 1998 as the time limit for the filing of an interim report by Qatar on the authenticity of the documents and directed the filing of a Reply by each of the Parties within the time limit of 30 March 1999. In its interim report filed in September 1998, Qatar stated that it would not rely on the disputed documents for the purposes of the present case so as to enable the Court to address the merits of the case without further procedural complications. In December 1998, Qatar requested "a two-month extension of the time limit for the filing of a Reply by each of the Parties, to 30 May 1999" [ibid.].

By an Order dated 17 February 1999, the Court placed on record Qatar's decision to disregard the 82 documents annexed to its written pleadings, which had been challenged by Bahrain, and decided that the Replies yet to be filed by Qatar and by Bahrain would not rely on those documents. After filing their Replies within the extended time limit, Qatar and Bahrain submitted, with the approval of the Court, certain additional expert reports and historical documents.

Questions of interpretation and application of the 1971 Montreal Convention arising from the aerial incident at Lockerbie (Libyan Arab Jamahiriya v. United Kingdom) (Libyan Arab Jamahiriya v. United States)

The Libyan Arab Jamahiriya instituted in 1992 [YUN 1992, p. 982] separate proceedings against the United Kingdom and the United States in respect of a dispute over the interpretation and application of the 1971 Montreal Convention for the Suppression of Unlawful Acts against the Safety of Civil Aviation [YUN 1971, p. 739], which arose from its alleged involvement in the crash of Pan Am flight 103 over Lockerbie, Scotland, on 21 December 1988. In the Applications, Libya referred to the charging and indictment of two of its nationals by the Lord Advocate of Scotland and by a United States Grand Jury for having caused a bomb to be placed aboard Pan Am flight 103, which exploded, caused the aircraft to crash and killed all 270 persons aboard.

The United Kingdom and the United States, on 16 and on 20 June 1995, respectively [YUN 1995, p. 1306], filed preliminary objections to the jurisdiction of the Court to entertain Libya's Applications. Libya presented a written statement of its observations and submissions on the preliminary objections raised by the United Kingdom and the United States within the prescribed time limits set by the Court. Public sittings to hear the oral arguments of the Parties on the preliminary objections raised by the United Kingdom and the United States were held in October 1997 [YUN 1997, p. 1313].

At public sittings held on 27 February 1998 [YUN 1998, p. 1184], the Court delivered the two Judgments on the preliminary objections, by which it rejected the objection to jurisdiction raised by the United Kingdom and the United States on the basis of the alleged absence of a dispute between the Parties concerning the interpretation or application of the Montreal Convention; found that it had jurisdiction, on the basis of article 14, paragraph 1 of the Convention, to hear the disputes between Libya and the United Kingdom and Libya and the United States concerning the interpretation or application of the provisions of the Convention; rejected the objection to admissibility derived by the United Kingdom and the United States from Security Council resolutions 748(1992) [YUN 1992, p. 55] and 883(1993) [YUN 1993, p. 101]; found that the Applications filed by Libya on 3 March 1992 were admissible; and declared that the objection raised by both countries, according to which the same Council resolutions had rendered the claims of Libya without object, did not, in the circumstances of the case, have an excessively preliminary character.

The time limit of 30 December 1998 fixed by the Court [YUN 1998, p. 1185] for the filing of the Counter-Memorials of the United Kingdom and the United States was extended to 31 March 1999 following a proposal of the United Kingdom and the United States, which referred to diplomatic initiatives [ibid., p. 163], and after the views of Libya had been ascertained. The Counter-Memorials were filed within the time limit.

Taking account of the agreement of the Parties and the special circumstances of the case, the Court, by Orders of 29 June 1999, authorized the submission of a Reply by Libya and a Rejoinder by the United Kingdom and the United States, which fixed 29 June 2000 as the time limit for the filing of the Reply. The Court fixed no date for the filing of the Rejoinders; the representatives of the Respondent States had expressed the desire that no such date be fixed at that stage of the proceedings, "in view of the new circumstances consequent upon the transfer of the two accused to the Netherlands for trial by a Scottish court" (see p. 148).

Oil platforms (Iran v. United States)

Iran instituted proceedings against the United States in 1992 [YUN 1992, p. 983] regarding a dispute in which Iran alleged that the destruction by United States warships, on 19 October 1987 and 18 April 1988, of three offshore oil production complexes owned and operated by the National Iranian Oil Company constituted a breach of international law and the 1955 Iran/United States Treaty of Amity, Economic Relations and Consular Rights. Iran requested the Court to rule on the matter.

Orders of the Court in 1992 [YUN 1992, p. 983] and 1993 [YUN 1993, p. 1183] fixed time limits for the filing of the Memorial by Iran and for a Counter-Memorial by the United States. Iran filed its Memorial, while the United States filed certain preliminary objections to the jurisdiction of the Court. In 1994 [YUN 1994, p. 1280], Iran presented a written statement of its observations and submissions on the United States objections, in accordance with an Order of the Court.

The Court delivered its Judgment in 1996 [YUN 1996, p. 1178], by which it rejected the preliminary objection of the United States and found that it had jurisdiction to entertain the claims made by Iran.

By an Order of 16 December 1996 [YUN 1996, p. 1178], the President of the Court fixed 23 June 1997 as the time limit for the filing of the Counter-Memorial of the United States. Within that time limit, the United States filed the Counter-Memorial and a Counter-Claim [YUN 1997, p. 1313].

In November and December 1997, Iran and the United States, respectively, submitted written observations on the question of the admissibility of the United States Counter-Claim.

In 1998 [YUN 1998, p. 1185], the Court found that the Counter-Claim presented by the United States in its Counter-Memorial was admissible. It further directed Iran to submit a Reply and the United States to submit a Rejoinder, fixing the time limits for those pleadings at 10 September 1998 and 23 November 1999, respectively.

By an Order of 26 May 1998 [YUN 1998, p. 1185], the Vice-President of the Court, Acting President, extended, at the request of Iran and taking into account the views expressed by the United States, the time limits for Iran's Reply and the United States Rejoinder to 10 December 1998 and 23 May 2000, respectively. By an Order of 8 December 1998, the Court further extended those time limits to 10 March 1999 for Iran's Reply and 23 November 2000 for the United States Rejoinder. Iran's Reply was filed within the time limit thus extended.

Application of the Convention on the Prevention and Punishment of the Crime of Genocide (Bosnia and Herzegovina v. Yugoslavia)

Bosnia and Herzegovina instituted proceedings in 1993 [YUN 1993, p. 1138] against the Federal Republic of Yugoslavia (Serbia and Montenegro) (FRY) for alleged violations of the 1948 Convention on the Prevention and Punishment of the Crime of Genocide, adopted by the General Assembly in resolution 260 A (III) [YUN 1948-49, p. 959]. The time limits were fixed for the filing of a Memorial by Bosnia and Herzegovina and a Counter-Memorial by FRY [YUN 1993, p. 1138]. The Memorial by Bosnia and Herzegovina was filed within the prescribed time limit [YUN 1994, p. 1281].

The time limit for the filing of the Counter-Memorial by FRY was extended in 1995 [YUN 1995, p. 1307]. Within the time limit, FRY filed certain preliminary objections. The objections related, first, to the admissibility of the Application and, second, to the jurisdiction of the Court to deal with the case. By virtue of the Rules of Court, proceedings on the merits were suspended. Pursuant to an Order of the Court [ibid.], Bosnia and Herzegovina presented a written statement of its observations and submissions on the preliminary objections raised by FRY, within the prescribed time limit.

The Court delivered its Judgment in 1996 on the preliminary objections [YUN 1996, p. 1179], by which it rejected the objections raised by FRY. In accordance with an Order of 23 July 1996 [ibid.], FRY filed a Counter-Memorial that included Counter-Claims against Bosnia and Herzegovina [YUN 1997, p. 1315].

Both Parties accepted in 1997 that their respective Governments would submit written observations on the question of the admissibility of the FRY Counter-Claims and did so. The Court found that the Counter-Claims submitted by FRY in its Counter-Memorial were admissible and directed Bosnia and Herzegovina to submit a Reply and FRY to submit a Rejoinder, fixing the time limits for those pleadings at 23 January and 23 July 1998, respectively. By an Order of 22 January 1998 [YUN 1998, p. 1186], those time limits were extended to 23 April 1998 and 22 January 1999, respectively. The Reply of Bosnia and Herzegovina was filed within the prescribed time limit. The Court, by an Order of 11 December 1998 [ibid.], extended the time limit for the filing of FRY's Rejoinder to 22 February 1999, which was filed within the time limit.

In 1999, several exchanges of letters took place concerning new procedural difficulties in the case.

Land and maritime boundary between Cameroon and Nigeria

Cameroon instituted proceedings against Nigeria in March 1994 [YUN 1994, p. 1281] in a dispute concerning the question of sovereignty over the peninsula of Bakassi and requested the Court to determine the course of the maritime frontier between the two States in so far as that frontier had not already been established in 1975. The Application was amended by an Additional Application in June 1994. Cameroon's Memorial was filed in 1995 [YUN 1995, p. 1308]. On 13 December 1995, within the time limit for the filing of its Counter-Memorial, Nigeria filed certain preliminary objections to the jurisdiction of the Court and to the admissibility of the claims of Cameroon.

In 1996 [YUN 1996, p. 1180], Cameroon presented a written statement of its observations and submissions on the preliminary objections raised by Nigeria. Following hearings in March 1996, the Court made an Order [ibid.] indicating that neither Party should take any action of any kind and that both should lend every assistance to a fact-finding mission to be sent by the United Nations Secretary-General [YUN 1996, p. 146].

On 11 June 1998 [YUN 1998, p. 1187], the Court delivered its Judgment on the preliminary objections, by which it rejected seven of Nigeria's eight preliminary objections; declared that the eighth preliminary objection did not have, in the circumstances of the case, an exclusively preliminary character; and found that, on the basis of Article 36, paragraph 2, of the ICJ Statute, it had jurisdiction to adjudicate on the dispute and that the Application filed by Cameroon on 29 March 1994, as amended by the Additional Application of 6 June 1994, was admissible. The Court, having been informed of the views of the Parties, fixed 31 March 1999 as the time limit for the filing of the Counter-Memorial of Nigeria.

On 28 October 1998, Nigeria filed a request for an interpretation of the Court's Judgment on the preliminary objections [YUN 1998, p. 1187]. The request for interpretation formed a separate case, in which the Court delivered its Judgment on 25 March 1999 (see below).

On 23 February 1999, Nigeria requested an extension of the time limit for the deposit of its Counter-Memorial, as it did not know the scope of the case it had to answer on State responsibility until the outcome of its request for interpretation was known. By a letter of 27 February 1999, the Agent of Cameroon informed the Court that Cameroon was resolutely opposed to Nigeria's request, as its dispute with Nigeria called for a rapid decision.

By an Order of 3 March 1999, the Court extended to 31 May 1999 the time limit for the filing of Nigeria's Counter-Memorial, which was filed within the time limit.

The Counter-Memorial included counter-claims. At the end of each section dealing with a particular sector of the frontier, Nigeria asked the Court to declare that the incidents referred to "engage the international responsibility of Cameroon, with compensation in the form of damages, if not agreed between the parties, then to be awarded by the Court in a subsequent phase of the case".

The seventh and final submission set out by Nigeria in its Counter-Memorial read as follows: "as to Nigeria's counter-claims as specified in . . . of this Counter-Memorial, [the Court is asked to] adjudge and declare that Cameroon bears responsibility to Nigeria in respect of those claims, the amount of reparation due therefor, if not agreed between the parties within six months of the date of judgment, to be determined by the Court in a further judgment". In an Order of 30 June 1999, the Court found that Nigeria's counter-claims were admissible and formed part of the proceedings; decided that Cameroon should submit a Reply and Nigeria a Rejoinder, relating to the claims of both Parties, and fixed the time limits for those pleadings at 4 April 2000 and 4 January 2001, respectively.

On 30 June 1999, Equatorial Guinea filed an Application for permission to intervene in the case, stating that the purpose was to protect its legal rights in the Gulf of Guinea and to inform the Court of Equatorial Guinea's legal rights and interests so that they might remain unaffected as the Court proceeded to address the question of the maritime boundary between Cameroon and Nigeria. Equatorial Guinea clarified that it did not seek to intervene in those aspects of the proceedings that related to the land boundary between Cameroon and Nigeria, nor to become a Party to the case. It further stated that, although it would be open to a request to the Court from the three countries not only to determine the Cameroon-Nigeria maritime boundary but also to determine Equatorial Guinea's maritime boundary with those two States, Equatorial Guinea had made no such request and wished to continue to determine its maritime boundary with its neighbours by negotiation.

The Court fixed 16 August 1999 as the time limit for the filing of written observations by Cameroon and Nigeria on Equatorial Guinea's Application, which were filed within the prescribed time limits.

By an Order of 21 October 1999, the Court handed down its decision on Equatorial Guinea's Application for permission to intervene, by which it unanimously decided that Equatorial Guinea could intervene in the case, pursuant to Article 62 of the Statute, to the extent, in the manner and for the purposes set out in its Application for permission to intervene; fixed the time limits for the filing of the written statement and the written observations at 4 April 2001 for the written statement of Equatorial Guinea and 4 July 2001 for the written observations of Cameroon and Nigeria; and reserved the subsequent procedure for further decision.

Interpretation of Judgment

In its request for an interpretation of the 11 June 1998 Judgment [YUN 1998, p. 1187], Nigeria stated that "One aspect of the case before the Court is the alleged international responsibility borne by Nigeria for certain incidents said to have occurred at various places in Bakassi and Lake Chad and along the length of the frontier between those two regions". Nigeria contended that Cameroon had made "allegations involving a number of such incidents in its Application of 29 March 1994, its Additional Application of 6 June 1994, its Observations of 30 April 1996 on Nigeria's Preliminary Objections, and during the oral hearings held from 2-11 March 1998", and that Cameroon had also said that it "would be able to provide information as to other incidents on some unspecified future occasion". In the view of Nigeria, the Court's Judgment "[did] not specify which of these alleged incidents [were] to be considered as part of the merits of the case" and, accordingly, "the meaning and scope of the Judgment require[d] interpretation".

The Senior Judge, Acting President, fixed 3 December 1998 as the time limit for Cameroon to submit its written observations on Nigeria's request for interpretation, which were filed within the time limit. In the light of the dossier thus submitted, the Court did not deem it necessary to invite the Parties to furnish further written or oral explanations.

At a public sitting held on 25 March 1999, the Court delivered its Judgment, in which it decided by 13 votes to 3, that the request for interpretation of the Judgment of 11 June 1998, presented by Nigeria, was inadmissible; and unanimously rejected Cameroon's request that Nigeria bear the additional costs caused to Cameroon by the request for interpretation.

Vice-President Weeramantry, Judge Koroma and Judge ad hoc Ajibola appended dissenting opinions to the Judgment.

Kasikili/Sedudu Island (Botswana/Namibia)

Botswana and Namibia by Special Agreement jointly submitted to the Court on 29 May 1996 a dispute concerning the boundary around Kasikili/Sedudu Island and the island's legal status [YUN 1996, p. 1181]. Each of the Parties had filed a Memorial and Counter-Memorial in 1997 [YUN 1997, p. 1319].

In a joint letter dated 16 February 1998 [YUN 1998, p. 1188], the Parties requested further written pleadings pursuant to article II, paragraph 2 *(c)* of the Special Agreement, which provided, in addition to the Memorials and Counter-Memorials, for "such other pleadings as may be approved by the Court at the request of either of the Parties, or as may be directed by the Court".

By an Order of 27 February 1998 [YUN 1998, p. 1188], the Court fixed 27 November 1998 as the time limit for the filing of a Reply by each of the Parties, which were filed within the prescribed time limit.

Public sittings to hear the oral arguments of the Parties were held from 15 February to 5 March 1999. At a public sitting held on 13 December 1999, the Court delivered its Judgment, in which it decided, by 11 votes to 4, that the boundary between Botswana and Namibia followed the line of deepest soundings in the northern channel of the Chobe River around Kasikili/Sedudu Island; by 11 votes to 4, found that Kasikili/Sedudu Island formed part of the territory of Botswana; and unanimously found that, in the two channels around Kasikili/Sedudu Island, the nationals of, and vessels flying the flags of, Botswana and Namibia should enjoy equal national treatment.

Judges Ranjeva, Koroma and Higgins appended declarations to the Judgment of the Court. Judges Oda and Kooijmans appended separate opinions. Vice-President Weeramantry, Judges Fleischhauer, Parra-Aranguren and Rezek appended dissenting opinions.

Sovereignty over Pulau Ligitan and Pulau Sipadan (Indonesia/Malaysia)

On 2 November 1998 [YUN 1998, p. 1189], Indonesia and Malaysia jointly notified the Court of a

Special Agreement between them, signed at Kuala Lumpur on 31 May 1997, which entered into force on 14 May 1998, in which they requested the Court "to determine on the basis of the treaties, agreements and any other evidence furnished by the Parties, whether sovereignty over Pulau Ligitan and Pulau Sipadan belongs to the Republic of Indonesia or to Malaysia". By an Order of 10 November 1998 [ibid.], the Court fixed 2 November 1999 and 2 March 2000 as the time limits for the filing by each of the Parties of a Memorial and a Counter-Memorial, respectively.

By an Order of 14 September 1999, the Court, at the joint request of the Parties, extended the time limit for the filing of the Counter-Memorials to 2 July 2000.

The Memorials were filed within the time limit of 2 November 1999, as fixed by the Court's Order of 10 November 1998.

Ahmadou Sadio Diallo (Guinea v. Democratic Republic of the Congo)

On 28 December 1998 [YUN 1998, p. 1190], Guinea instituted proceedings against the Democratic Republic of the Congo (DRC) by an "Application with a view to diplomatic protection", in which it requested the Court to condemn the DRC for the grave breaches of international law perpetrated upon the person of a Guinean national, Ahmadou Sadio Diallo.

According to Guinea, Mr. Diallo, a businessman who had been a resident of the DRC for 32 years, was "unlawfully imprisoned by the authorities of that State" during two and a half months, "divested from his important investments, companies, bank accounts, movable and immovable properties, then expelled". The expulsion took place on 2 February 1996, as a result of his attempts to recover sums owed to him by the DRC (especially by Gécamines, a State enterprise and mining monopoly) and by oil companies operating in that country (Zaïre Shell, Zaïre Mobil and Zaïre Fina) by virtue of contracts concluded with businesses owned by him, namely Africom-Zaïre and Africontainers-Zaïre.

As a basis of the Court's jurisdiction, Guinea invoked its own declaration of acceptance of the compulsory jurisdiction of the Court of 11 November 1998 and the declaration of the DRC of 8 February 1989.

By an Order of 25 November 1999, the Court, taking into account the agreement of the Parties, fixed 11 September 2000 as the time limit for the filing of a Memorial by Guinea and 11 September 2001 for the filing of a Counter-Memorial by the DRC.

Vienna Convention on Consular Relations (Germany v. United States)

On 2 March 1999, Germany instituted proceedings against the United States in a dispute concerning alleged violations of the 1963 Vienna Convention on Consular Relations [YUN 1963, p. 510]. In its Application, Germany based the jurisdiction of the Court on Article 36, paragraph 1, of the Statute and on article I of the Optional Protocol concerning the Compulsory Settlement of Disputes, which accompanied the Vienna Convention and which provided that the "disputes arising out of the interpretation or application of the Convention shall be within the compulsory jurisdiction of the International Court of Justice".

In the Application, Germany stated that in 1982 the authorities of Arizona (United States) detained two German nationals, Karl and Walter LaGrand; that the individuals were tried and sentenced to death without having been informed, as was required under article 36, subparagraph 1 (*b*), of the Vienna Convention, of their rights under that provision (which required the competent authorities of a State party to advise, without delay, a national of another State party whom such authorities arrested or detained of the national's right to consular assistance guaranteed by article 36). Germany also alleged that the failure to provide the required notification precluded it from protecting its nationals' interests in the United States, as provided for by the 1963 Convention, at both the trial and the appeal level in the United States courts.

Germany stated that it had been, until very recently, the contention of the authorities of the State of Arizona that they had been unaware of the fact that Karl and Walter LaGrand were German nationals, and that it had accepted that contention as true. However, during the proceedings before the Arizona Mercy Committee on 23 February 1999, the State Attorney admitted that the authorities of the State of Arizona had indeed been aware since 1982 that the two detainees were German nationals. Germany further stated that Karl and Walter LaGrand, finally with the assistance of German consular officers, did claim violations of the Vienna Convention before the Federal District Court (the federal court of first instance). In addition, it claimed that the Court, applying the municipal law doctrine of "procedural default", decided that, because the individuals in question had not asserted their rights under the Vienna Convention in the previous legal proceedings at the State level, they could not assert them in the Federal *habeas corpus* proceedings; and the intermediate federal appellate court, the last means of legal recourse in the

United States available to them, had affirmed that decision.

Germany asked ICJ to adjudge and declare that: the United States, in arresting, detaining, trying, convicting and sentencing the LaGrands, had violated its international legal obligations to Germany, in its own right and in the exercise of its right of diplomatic protection of its nationals, as provided by articles 5 and 36 of the Vienna Convention; Germany was therefore entitled to reparation; the United States was under an international legal obligation not to apply the doctrine of "procedural default", or any other doctrine of its internal law, so as to preclude the exercise of the rights accorded under the Vienna Convention; and the United States was under an international obligation to carry out in conformity with the foregoing international legal obligations any future detention of or criminal proceedings against the LaGrands or any other German national in its territory, whether by a constituent, legislative, executive, judicial or other power, whether that power held a superior or subordinate position in the organization of the United States, and whether that power's functions were of an international or internal character. The foregoing international legal obligations held that: any criminal liability imposed on the LaGrands in violation of international legal obligations was void, and should be recognized as void by the United States legal authorities; the United States should provide reparation, in the form of compensation and satisfaction, for the execution of Karl LaGrand on 24 February 1999; the United States should restore the status quo ante in the case of Walter LaGrand, which meant reestablishing the situation that existed before the detention of, proceedings against and conviction and sentencing of Walter LaGrand, whose execution had been set for 3 March; and the United States should provide Germany a guarantee of the non-repetition of the illegal acts.

On 2 March, Germany also submitted an urgent request for the indication of provisional measures, asking the Court to indicate that "the United States should take all measures at its disposal to ensure that Walter LaGrand is not executed pending the final decision in these proceedings, and should inform the Court of all the measures which it has taken in implementation of that Order"; it asked the Court moreover to consider its request as a matter of the greatest urgency "in view of the extreme gravity and immediacy of the threat of execution of a German citizen".

By a letter of the same date, the Vice-President of the Court addressed the United States Government in the following terms: "Exercising the functions of the presidency in terms of Articles 13 and 32 of the Rules of Court, and acting in conformity with Article 74, paragraph 4, of the said Rules, I hereby draw the attention of [the] Government [of the United States] to the need to act in such a way as to enable any Order the Court will make on the request for provisional measures to have its appropriate effects".

At a public sitting on 3 March, the Court rendered its Order on the request for the indication of provisional measures by which it indicated that: the United States should take all measures at its disposal to ensure that Walter LaGrand was not executed pending the final decision in the proceedings, and should inform the Court of all the measures which it had taken in implementation of the Order; and the United States should transmit the Order to the Governor of the State of Arizona. It decided that, until the Court had given its final decision, it would remain seized of the matters which formed the subject matter of the Order.

Judge Oda appended a declaration to the Order and President Schwebel a separate opinion.

By an Order of 5 March, the Court, taking into account the views of the Parties, fixed 16 September 1999 and 27 March 2000 as the time limits for the filing of the Memorial of Germany and the Counter-Memorial of the United States, respectively. The Memorial was filed within the prescribed time limit.

Use of force (Yugoslavia v. Belgium) (Yugoslavia v. Canada) (Yugoslavia v. France) (Yugoslavia v. Germany) (Yugoslavia v. Italy) (Yugoslavia v. Netherlands) (Yugoslavia v. Portugal) (Yugoslavia v. Spain) (Yugoslavia v. United Kingdom) and (Yugoslavia v. United States)

FRY instituted proceedings on 29 April 1999 against Belgium, Canada, France, Germany, Italy, the Netherlands, Portugal, Spain, the United Kingdom and the United States for alleged violation of the obligation not to use force. In the cases against Belgium, Canada, the Netherlands, Portugal, Spain and the United Kingdom, FRY invoked the jurisdiction of the Court based on Article 36, paragraph 2, of the Statute and on article IX of the 1948 Convention on the Prevention and Punishment of the Crime of Genocide, adopted by the General Assembly in resolution 260 A (III) [YUN 1948-49, p. 959], and, in the cases against France, Germany, Italy and the United States, on article IX of the Convention and Article 38, paragraph 5, of the Rules of Court.

In its Applications, FRY stated that the disputes involved acts of the [Respondent State concerned] "by which it has violated the international obligation banning the use of force against another

State, the obligation not to intervene in the internal affairs of another State, the obligation not to violate the sovereignty of another State, the obligation to protect the civilian population and civilian objects in wartime, the obligation to protect the environment, the obligation relating to free navigation on international rivers, the obligation regarding fundamental human rights and freedoms, the obligation not to use prohibited weapons, the obligation not to deliberately inflict conditions of life calculated to cause the physical destruction of a national group".

FRY requested the Court to adjudge and declare that [the Respondent State concerned] had acted against it by taking part in the bombing of the territory of FRY, breaching its obligation not to use force against another State; by taking part in the training, arming, financing, equipping and supplying of terrorist groups, i.e. the Kosovo Liberation Army, breaching its obligation not to intervene in the affairs of another State; by taking part in attacks on civilian targets, breaching its obligation to spare the civilian population and civilian objects; by taking part in destroying or damaging monasteries and cultural monuments, breaching its obligation not to commit any act of hostility directed against historical monuments, works of art or places of worship that constituted people's cultural or spiritual heritage; by taking part in the use of cluster bombs, breaching its obligation not to use prohibited weapons, i.e. weapons calculated to cause unnecessary suffering; by taking part in the bombing of oil refineries and chemical plants, breaching its obligation not to cause considerable environmental damage; by taking part in the use of weapons containing depleted uranium, breaching its obligation not to use prohibited weapons and not to cause far-reaching health and environmental damage; by taking part in killing civilians, destroying enterprises, communications, health and cultural institutions, breaching its obligation to respect the rights to life, to work, to information, to health care as well as other basic human rights; by taking part in destroying bridges on international rivers, breaching its obligation to respect freedom of navigation on international rivers; and by taking part in activities listed above, and in particular by causing enormous environmental damage and by using depleted uranium, breaching its obligation not to deliberately inflict on a national group conditions of life calculated to bring about its physical destruction, in whole or in part. In addition, the [Respondent State concerned] was responsible for the violation of the above international obligations; was obliged to stop immediately the violation of the above obligations vis-à-vis FRY; and was obliged to provide compensation for the damage to FRY and to its citizens and juridical persons.

Also on 29 April, FRY submitted, in each of the cases, a request for the indication of provisional measures, asking the Court to indicate that "the [Respondent State concerned] shall cease immediately its acts of use of force and shall refrain from any act of threat or use of force" against FRY. Hearings on the requests for the indication of provisional measures were held between 10 and 12 May.

At a public sitting on 2 June, the Vice-President of the Court, Acting President, read the Orders, by which, in the cases *(Yugoslavia v. Belgium)*, *(Yugoslavia v. Canada)*, *(Yugoslavia v. France)*, *(Yugoslavia v. Germany)*, *(Yugoslavia v. Italy)*, *(Yugoslavia v. Netherlands)*, *(Yugoslavia v. Portugal)* and *(Yugoslavia v. United Kingdom)*, the Court rejected the requests for the indication of provisional measures and reserved the subsequent procedure for further decision. In the cases of *(Yugoslavia v. Spain)* and *(Yugoslavia v. United States of America)*, the Court—having found that it manifestly lacked jurisdiction to entertain FRY's Application; that it could not therefore indicate any provisional measure whatsoever in order to protect the rights invoked therein; and that, within a system of consensual jurisdiction, to maintain on the General List a case upon which it appeared certain that the Court would not be able to adjudicate on the merits would most assuredly not contribute to the sound administration of justice—rejected FRY's requests for the indication of provisional measures and ordered that those cases be removed from the List.

In each of the cases *(Yugoslavia v. Belgium)*, *(Yugoslavia v. Canada)*, *(Yugoslavia v. Netherlands)* and *(Yugoslavia v. Portugal)*, Judge Koroma appended a declaration to the Order of the Court; Judges Oda, Higgins, Parra-Aranguren and Kooijmans appended separate opinions; and Vice-President Weeramantry, Acting President, Judges Shi and Vereshchetin and Judge ad hoc Kreca appended dissenting opinions.

In each of the cases *(Yugoslavia v. France)*, *(Yugoslavia v. Germany)* and *(Yugoslavia v. Italy)*, Vice-President Weeramantry, Acting President, and Judges Shi, Koroma and Vereshchetin appended declarations to the Order of the Court; Judges Oda and Parra-Aranguren appended separate opinions; and Judge ad hoc Kreca appended a dissenting opinion.

In the case *(Yugoslavia v. Spain)*, Judges Shi, Koroma and Vereshchetin appended declarations to the Order of the Court; and Judges Oda, Higgins, Parra-Aranguren and Kooijmans and Judge ad hoc Kreca appended separate opinions.

In the case *(Yugoslavia v. United Kingdom)*, Vice-President Weeramantry, Acting President, and Judges Shi, Koroma and Vereshchetin appended declarations to the Order of the Court; Judges Oda, Higgins, Parra-Aranguren and Kooijmans appended separate opinions; and Judge ad hoc Kreca appended a dissenting opinion.

In the case *(Yugoslavia v. United States of America)*, Judges Shi, Koroma and Vereshchetin appended declarations to the Order of the Court; Judges Oda and Parra-Aranguren appended separate opinions; and Judge ad hoc Kreca appended a dissenting opinion.

By Orders of 30 June, the Court, having ascertained the views of the Parties, fixed the time limits for the filing of the written pleadings in each of the eight cases maintained on the List as at 5 January 2000 for the Memorial of FRY and 5 July 2000 for the Counter-Memorial of the Respondent State concerned.

Communication. On 27 May [A/53/992], Bosnia and Herzegovina, Croatia, Slovenia and the former Yugoslav Republic of Macedonia, referring to a depositary notification made by FRY on 25 April concerning the declaration under Article 36, paragraph 2, of the Statute, stated that the notification could have no legal effect because FRY was not a UN State Member, nor was it a State party to the Statute. Thus, there was no legal basis to accept or circulate the invalid document.

Armed activities on the territory of the Congo (Democratic Republic of the Congo v. Burundi) (Democratic Republic of the Congo v. Uganda) and (Democratic Republic of the Congo v. Rwanda)

The DRC instituted proceedings against Burundi, Uganda and Rwanda on 23 June 1999 for acts of armed aggression perpetrated in flagrant violation of the Charter of the United Nations and the Charter of the Organization of African Unity.

In its Applications, the DRC contended that "such armed aggression . . . involved inter alia violation of the sovereignty and territorial integrity of the [DRC], violations of international humanitarian law and massive human rights violations". The DRC sought the cessation of the aggression against it, which constituted a serious threat to peace and security in central Africa in general and in the Great Lakes region in particular; reparation for acts of intentional destruction and looting; and restitution of national property and resources appropriated for the benefit of the respective Respondent States.

In the cases against Burundi and Rwanda, the DRC invoked the bases for the jurisdiction of the Court Article 36, paragraph 1, of the Statute, which provided that the jurisdiction of the Court comprised all cases which the parties referred to it and all matters specially provided for in the UN Charter or in treaties and conventions in force; the Convention against Torture and Other Cruel, Inhuman or Degrading Treatment or Punishment, adopted by the General Assembly by resolution 39/46 [YUN 1984, p. 813]; the Convention for the Suppression of Unlawful Acts against the Safety of Civil Aviation [YUN 1971, p. 739]; and Article 38, paragraph 5, of the Rules of Court, which contemplated the situation where a State filed an application against another State that had not accepted the jurisdiction of the Court. In the case against Uganda, the DRC based the jurisdiction on Article 36, paragraph 2, of the Statute.

The DRC requested the Court to adjudge and declare that: [the Respondent State concerned] was guilty of an act of aggression as defined by article 1 of Assembly resolution 3314(XXIX) [YUN 1974, p. 847] and of the jurisprudence of the Court, contrary to Article 2, paragraph 4, of the UN Charter; [the Respondent State concerned] committed repeated violations of the Geneva Conventions for the protection of war victims of 1949 and the two Additional Protocols of 1977 [YUN 1977, p. 706], in flagrant disregard of the elementary rules of international humanitarian law in conflict zones, and was also guilty of massive human rights violations in defiance of the most basic customary law; [the Respondent State concerned], by taking forcible possession of the Inga hydroelectric dam and deliberately and regularly causing massive electrical power cuts, in violation of the provisions of article 56 of the Additional Protocol of 1977, was responsible for very heavy loss of life in the city of Kinshasa (5 million inhabitants) and the surrounding area; and [the Respondent State concerned] had violated the Convention on International Civil Aviation signed in Chicago on 7 December 1944, the 1970 Convention for the Suppression of Unlawful Seizure of Aircraft and the 1971 Convention for the Suppression of Unlawful Acts against the Safety of Civil Aviation by shooting down, on 9 October 1998 at Kindu, a Boeing 727, the property of Congo Airlines, thereby killing 40 civilians.

The DRC requested the Court to adjudge and declare that: all armed forces [of the Respondent State concerned] participating in acts of aggression should forthwith vacate its territory; [the Respondent State concerned] should secure the immediate and unconditional withdrawal from Congolese territory of its nationals, both natural and legal persons; and the DRC was entitled to compensation from [the Respondent State concerned] in respect of all acts of looting, destruction, removal of property and persons and other unlawful acts attributable to [the Respondent State concerned], in respect of which the DRC reserved the right to determine at a later date the precise amount of the damage suffered, in addition to its claim for the restitution of all property removed.

In each of the cases against Burundi and Rwanda, the Court, by an Order of 21 October, taking into account the agreement of the Parties, as expressed at a meeting between the President and the Agents of the Parties on 19 October, decided that the written proceedings should first address the questions of the jurisdiction of the Court to entertain the Application and of its admissibility and fixed 21 April 2000 as the time limit for the filing of a Memorial on those questions by Burundi and Rwanda, and 23 October 2000 for the filing of a Counter-Memorial by the DRC.

In the case against Uganda, the Court, taking into account the agreement of the Parties, as expressed at a meeting held with them by the President of the Court on 19 October, fixed, by an Order of 21 October, 21 July 2000 as the time limit for the filing of a Memorial by the DRC and 21 April 2001 for the filing of a Counter-Memorial by Uganda.

Application of the genocide convention (Croatia v. Yugoslavia)

Croatia instituted proceedings against FRY on 2 July for alleged violations of the 1948 Convention on the Prevention and Punishment of the Crime of Genocide, adopted by the General Assembly in resolution 260 A (III) [YUN 1948-49, p. 959], said to have been committed between 1991 and 1995.

In its Application, Croatia contended that by "directly controlling the activity of its armed forces, intelligence agents, and various paramilitary detachments, on the territory of ... Croatia, in the Knin region, eastern and western Slovenia, and Dalmatia, [Yugoslavia] is liable [for] the 'ethnic cleansing' of Croatian citizens from these areas ... and is required to provide reparation for the resulting damage". It further alleged that, "by directing, encouraging, and urging Croatian citizens of Serb ethnicity in the Knin region to evacuate the area in 1995, as ... Croatia reasserted its legitimate governmental authority ... [Yugoslavia] engaged in conduct amounting to a second round of 'ethnic cleansing'". Croatia invoked the jurisdiction of the Court based on Article 36, paragraph 1, of the Statute and on article IX of the Convention.

Croatia requested the Court to adjudge and declare that FRY breached its legal obligations towards Croatia under articles I, II (a, b, c, d), III (a, b, c, d, e), IV and V of the 1948 Convention; and that FRY had an obligation to pay to Croatia, in its own right and as *parens patriae* for its citizens, reparations for damages to persons and property, as well as to the Croatian economy and environment caused by the foregoing violations of international law in a sum to be determined by the Court. Croatia reserved the right to introduce to the Court at a future date a precise evaluation of the damages.

By an Order of 14 September, the Court took account of an agreement of the Parties expressed on 13 September and fixed 14 March 2000 as the time limit for the filing of the Memorial of Croatia and 14 September 2000 for the filing of the Counter-Memorial of FRY.

Aerial incident (Pakistan v. India)

Pakistan instituted proceedings against India on 21 September regarding a dispute in which Pakistan alleged that, on 10 August, India destroyed a Pakistani aircraft. Pakistan founded the jurisdiction of the Court on Article 36, paragraphs 1 and 2, of the Statute and the declarations whereby the two Parties had recognized the Court's compulsory jurisdiction.

In a letter of 2 November, the Agent of India filed preliminary objections to the assumption of jurisdiction by the Court on the basis of Pakistan's Application.

At a meeting between the President of the Court and representatives of the Parties on 10 November, pursuant to Article 31 of the Rules of Court, the Parties provisionally agreed to request the Court to determine separately the question of its jurisdiction. The agreement was subsequently confirmed in writing by both Parties.

By an Order of 19 November, the Court, taking into account the agreement, decided that the written pleadings should first be addressed to the question of the jurisdiction of the Court to entertain the Application and fixed 10 January 2000 and 28 February 2000 as the time limits for the filing of a Memorial by Pakistan and a Counter-Memorial by India, respectively.

Maritime delimitation (Nicaragua v. Honduras)

On 8 December, Nicaragua instituted proceedings against Honduras in respect of a dispute concerning the delimitation of the maritime zones appertaining to each of those States in the Caribbean Sea.

In its Application, Nicaragua stated that it had maintained for decades the position that its maritime Caribbean border with Honduras had not been determined, while the position of Honduras, allegedly, was that a delimitation line was fixed by the King of Spain in an Arbitral Award of 23 December 1906, which was found valid and binding by ICJ on 18 November 1960 [YUN 1960, p. 536]. According to Nicaragua, the position adopted by Honduras had brought repeated confrontations and mutual capture of vessels of both nations in and around the general border area, and that diplomatic negotiations had failed. Nicaragua founded jurisdiction of the Court on declarations under Article 36, paragraph 2, of the Court's Statute, by which both States accepted the compulsory jurisdiction of the Court, and also article XXXI of the American Treaty on Pacific Settlement (officially known as the "Pact of Bogotá"), signed on 30 April 1948, to which both Nicaragua and Honduras were parties.

Nicaragua requested the Court to determine the course of the single maritime boundary between areas of territorial sea, continental shelf and exclusive economic zone appertaining to Nicaragua and Honduras.

Difference relating to immunity from legal process of a Special Rapporteur of the Commission on Human Rights

In April, the Court delivered an advisory opinion on the privileges and immunities of a Special Rapporteur of the Commission on Human Rights, Dato' Param Cumaraswamy (Malaysia).

In a 1995 interview with the publication *International Commercial Litigation*, Mr. Cumaraswamy, the Special Rapporteur on the independence of judges and lawyers, had commented on certain litigations that had taken place in Malaysian courts. Subsequently, commercial companies in Malaysia filed suit against him for damages. The UN Legal Counsel and the Secretary-General in 1997 informed Malaysia of the Special Rapporteur's immunity from legal process with respect to the complaint. However, the judge for the case was unable to maintain that the defendant was protected by the immunity he claimed to have.

The Economic and Social Council, in decision 1998/297 [YUN 1998, p. 1191], requested ICJ to give an advisory opinion on a difference that had arisen between the United Nations and Malaysia on the interpretation or application of the 1946 Convention on the Privileges and Immunities of the United Nations, adopted by the General Assembly by resolution 22 A (I) [YUN 1946-47, p. 100]. The Secretary-General officially communicated the Council's decision to the Court [YUN 1998, p. 1190].

At a public sitting held on 29 April 1999, the Court delivered its advisory opinion, the final paragraph of which read as follows:

"For these reasons,
The Court
Is of the opinion:

(1) *(a)* By fourteen votes to one,

That Article VI, Section 22, of the Convention on the Privileges and Immunities of the United Nations is applicable in the case of Dato' Param Cumaraswamy as Special Rapporteur of the Commission on Human Rights on the Independence of Judges and Lawyers;

In Favour: President Schwebel; *Vice-President* Weeramantry; *Judges* Oda, Bedjaoui, Guillaume, Ranjeva, Herczegh, Shi, Fleischhauer, Vereshchetin, Higgins, Parra-Aranguren, Kooijmans, Rezek;

Against: Judge Koroma;

(b) By fourteen votes to one,

That Dato' Param Cumaraswamy is entitled to immunity from legal process of every kind for the words spoken by him during an interview as published in an article in the November 1995 issue of *International Commercial Litigation;*

In Favour: President Schwebel; *Vice-President* Weeramantry; *Judges* Oda, Bedjaoui, Guillaume, Ranjeva, Herczegh, Shi, Fleischhauer, Vereshchetin, Higgins, Parra-Aranguren, Kooijmans, Rezek;

Against: Judge Koroma;

(2) *(a)* By thirteen votes to two,

That the Government of Malaysia had the obligation to inform the Malaysian courts of the finding of the Secretary-General that Dato' Param Cumaraswamy was entitled to immunity from legal process;

In Favour: President Schwebel; *Vice-President* Weeramantry; *Judges* Bedjaoui, Guillaume, Ranjeva, Herczegh, Shi, Fleischhauer, Vereshchetin, Higgins, Parra-Aranguren, Kooijmans, Rezek;

Against: Judges Oda, Koroma;

(b) By fourteen votes to one,

That the Malaysian courts had the obligation to deal with the question of immunity from legal process as a preliminary issue to be expeditiously decided *in limine litis;*

In Favour: President Schwebel; *Vice-President* Weeramantry; *Judges* Oda, Bedjaoui, Guillaume, Ranjeva, Herczegh, Shi, Fleischhauer, Vereshchetin, Higgins, Parra-Aranguren, Kooijmans, Rezek;

Against: Judge Koroma;

(3) Unanimously,

That Dato' Param Cumaraswamy shall be held financially harmless for any costs imposed upon him by the Malaysian courts, in particular taxed costs;

(4) By thirteen votes to two,

That the Government of Malaysia has the obligation to communicate this advisory opinion to the Malaysian courts, in order that Malaysia's international obligations be given effect and Dato' Param Cumaraswamy's immunity be respected;

In Favour: President Schwebel; *Vice-President* Weeramantry; *Judges* Bedjaoui, Guillaume, Ranjeva, Herczegh, Shi, Fleischhauer, Vereshchetin, Higgins, Parra-Aranguren, Kooijmans, Rezek;

Against: Judges Oda, Koroma."

Vice-President Weeramantry, Judges Oda and Rezek appended separate opinions to the advisory opinion; Judge Koroma appended a dissenting opinion.

Communications. Further to his letter of 5 May transmitting to the President of the Economic and Social Council the Court's advisory opinion [E/1999/49], the Secretary-General, on 21 July, informed the Council President that the Legal Counsel officially had transmitted a copy of the advisory opinion to Malaysia [E/1999/49/Add.1]. He stated that the Government of Malaysia had conveyed the advisory opinion to the competent judicial authorities. In the absence of a reply from Malaysia, the Legal Counsel, in July, requested further information as to the manner in which the Government would give effect to its obligations and to the Special Rapporteur's immunity from legal process. Notwithstanding the Legal Counsel's efforts and Mr. Cumaraswamy's motions to dismiss the four lawsuits pending against him, the competent judicial authorities fixed the first suit for case management on 6 August. It fixed the application to strike the second and third suits for hearing on 5 August, and postponed the application to strike the fourth suit.

ECONOMIC AND SOCIAL COUNCIL ACTION

On 30 July [meeting 46], the Economic and Social Council adopted **resolution 1999/64** [draft: E/1999/L.45] without vote [agenda item 14 *(h)*].

Applicability of the Convention on the Privileges and Immunities of the United Nations in the case of Dato' Param Cumaraswamy as Special Rapporteur of the Commission on Human Rights on the independence of judges and lawyers

The Economic and Social Council,

Considering that a difference has arisen between the United Nations and the Government of Malaysia, within the meaning of article VIII, section 30, of the Convention on the Privileges and Immunities of the United Nations, with respect to the immunity from legal process of Dato' Param Cumaraswamy, the Special Rapporteur of the Commission on Human Rights on the independence of judges and lawyers,

Considering also that Malaysia has acknowledged its obligations under article VIII, section 30, of the Convention, according to which the advisory opinion given by the International Court of Justice shall be accepted as decisive by the parties to the dispute,

Having requested, on a priority basis, in its decision 1998/297 of 5 August 1998, an advisory opinion of the International Court of Justice on the legal question of the applicability of article VI, section 22, of the Convention in the case of Dato' Param Cumaraswamy as Special Rapporteur of the Commission on Human Rights on the independence of judges and lawyers, taking into account the circumstances set out in paragraphs 1 to 15 of the note by the Secretary-General, and on the legal obligations of Malaysia in that case,

1. *Expresses its appreciation* to the International Court of Justice for having given the advisory opinion on 29 April 1999, which is contained in the annex to the letter dated 5 May 1999 from the Secretary-General to the President of the Economic and Social Council, and which states, inter alia:

"That article VI, section 22, of the Convention on the Privileges and Immunities of the United Nations is applicable in the case of Dato' Param Cumaraswamy as Special Rapporteur of the Commission on Human Rights on the independence of judges and lawyers;

"That Dato' Param Cumaraswamy is entitled to immunity from legal process of every kind for the words spoken by him during an interview as published in an article in the November 1995 issue of *International Commercial Litigation;*

"That the Government of Malaysia had the obligation to inform the Malaysian courts of the finding of the Secretary-General that Dato' Param Cumaraswamy was entitled to immunity from legal process;

"That the Malaysian courts had the obligation to deal with the question of immunity from legal process as a preliminary issue to be expeditiously decided *in limine litis;*

"That Dato' Param Cumaraswamy shall be held financially harmless for any costs imposed upon him by the Malaysian courts, in particular taxed costs,

"That the Government of Malaysia has the obligation to communicate this advisory opinion to the Malaysian courts, in order that Malaysia's international obligations be given effect and Dato' Param Cumaraswamy's immunity be respected;"

2. *Takes note* of the stated commitment by the Government of Malaysia to abide by the advisory opinion, and notes in this regard that the Government has conveyed the advisory opinion to the competent judicial authorities;

3. *Also takes note* of the letter dated 21 July 1999 from the Secretary-General to the President of the Council;

4. *Stresses* the obligation of Malaysia as a State party to the Convention on the Privileges and Immunities of the United Nations to make further efforts, in order that its international obligations thereunder be given effect and Dato' Param Cumaraswamy's immunity be respected, in accordance with the advisory opinion of the International Court of Justice.

Communications. On 19 October [E/1999/121], the Secretary-General informed the Council President that proceedings in the four civil suits had continued. Moreover, on the issue whether the courts of Malaysia should follow the advisory opinion, a competent judicial authority of the Malaysian courts ruled on 18 October that the 1946 Convention was not a final and binding authority and dismissed Mr. Cumaraswamy's application to set aside one of the suits and ordered him to file a defence for purposes of a full trial on the merits of the case. The Secretary-General stated that, as a party to the Convention, Malaysia had an obligation to give effect to its terms. Pursuant to section 30 of the Convention, the advisory opinion should be accepted as decisive by the parties.

In a 15 December letter to the Council President [E/1999/124], the Secretary-General, referring to the legal expenses incurred by Mr. Cumaraswamy, stated that since the Special Rapporteur was acting in the course of the performance of his mission when he spoke the words that gave rise to the subject proceedings, the United Nations was obliged to indemnify him for any costs, expenses or damages arising out of the proceedings. The United Nations had maintained that the Government of Malaysia was ultimately responsible for those costs, expenses or damages and the advisory opinion confirmed that fact. Therefore, the United Nations had submitted a claim to the Government of Malaysia for reimbursement for legal expenses it had paid on behalf of Mr. Cumaraswamy, which amounted to $110,886.91.

Composition of the Court

On 24 November [S/1999/1197], the Secretary-General informed the Security Council that Judge Stephen Schwebel, the President of the Court, whose term was to expire on 5 February 2006, intended to resign effective 29 February 2000. In accordance with the Statute, the Secretary-General asked the Council to fix the date of the election of a replacement.

Also in November, the Secretary-General informed the General Assembly of the vacancy [A/54/624].

SECURITY COUNCIL ACTION

On 30 November [meeting 4075], the Security Council adopted **resolution 1278(1999)** without vote. The draft [S/1999/1205] was prepared during Council consultations.

The Security Council,

Noting with regret the resignation of Judge Stephen Schwebel, taking effect on 29 February 2000,

Noting that a vacancy in the International Court of Justice for the remainder of the term of office of Judge Stephen Schwebel will thus occur and must be filled in accordance with the terms of the Statute of the Court,

Noting also that, in accordance with Article 14 of the Statute, the date of the election to fill the vacancy shall be fixed by the Security Council,

Decides that the election to fill the vacancy shall take place on 2 March 2000 at a meeting of the Security Council and at a meeting of the General Assembly at its fifty-fourth session.

Election of judges

In September, the Secretary-General informed the General Assembly and the Security Council that the terms of five judges would expire on 5 February 2000 [A/54/305-S/1999/939]. Thus, the Assembly and the Council would elect five judges for a term of office of nine years, beginning on 6 February 2000. The Secretary-General described the procedure in the Assembly and in the Council for the election. Nominations from the national groups of States parties to the Statute of the Court were circulated in September [A/54/307-S/1999/941] and in October [A/54/306-S/1999/940/Rev.1 & Add. 1].

Chapter II

International tribunals

In 1999, the judicial activities of the International Tribunal for the Prosecution of Persons Responsible for Serious Violations of International Humanitarian Law Committed in the Territory of the Former Yugoslavia since 1991 (ICTY) reached an unprecedented level, with events in the Kosovo province of the Federal Republic of Yugoslavia (FRY) dominating the work of the Office of the Prosecutor. On 22 May, Slobodan Milosevic, the President of FRY, and four others were indicted for crimes against humanity in Kosovo. A third Trial Chamber became operational during the year, and all three Trial Chambers and the Appeals Chamber were seized of cases.

At the International Criminal Tribunal for the Prosecution of Persons Responsible for Genocide and Other Serious Violations of International Humanitarian Law Committed in the Territory of Rwanda and Rwandan Citizens Responsible for Genocide and Other Such Violations Committed in the Territory of Neighbouring States between 1 January and 31 December 1994 (ICTR), a third Trial Chamber became operational in February. During the year, the Office of the Prosecutor continued to pursue its activities based on the theory of conspiracy to commit genocide by consolidating cases in joint indictments, grouping them by theme or by region.

International Tribunal for the Former Yugoslavia

In August, the Secretary-General transmitted to the General Assembly and the Security Council the sixth annual report of ICTY [A/54/187-S/1999/846], which was established by Council resolution 827(1993) [YUN 1993, p. 440]. By **decision 54/413** of 8 November, the Assembly took note of the report, which covered the period from 28 July 1998 to 31 July 1999.

In 1999, ICTY's judicial activities increased significantly, and the Tribunal provided fair trials for the accused while maintaining a high degree of protection for victims and witnesses. Nevertheless, events in the Kosovo province of the Federal Republic of Yugoslavia (FRY) (see PARTS ONE and THREE, Chapters V and III, respectively) and non-compliance by several States in the region continued to pose barriers to the Tribunal's operations.

The Chambers

The judicial activities of the Chambers of the Tribunal comprised trials, appellate proceedings and proceedings pertaining to the exercise of the primacy of the Tribunal, as well as contempt proceedings. Furthermore, the judicial activities of the Chambers involved reviewing indictments submitted by the Prosecutor, issuing arrest warrants and conducting hearings. The Chambers also engaged in regulatory activities to improve procedures for ensuring that trials were fair and expeditious.

In 1999, a third Trial Chamber, established by Security Council resolution 1166(1998) [YUN 1998, p. 1196], became operational. All three Trial Chambers and the Appeals Chamber were seized of cases.

New trials and cases

On 24 May, an indictment was confirmed against Slobodan Milosevic, President of FRY, Milan Milutinovic, President of Serbia, Nikola Sainovic, Deputy Prime Minister of FRY, Dragoljub Ojdanic, Chief of Staff of the Yugoslav Army, and Vlajko Stojiljkovic, Minister of Internal Affairs of Serbia, charging them with crimes against humanity with respect to criminal conduct in Kosovo. Consequently, arrest warrants were issued for each accused and ordered to be transmitted by the ICTY Registrar to FRY, Member States of the United Nations and Switzerland. Further orders were issued to those States requesting them to inquire whether any of the accused's assets were located in their territories and, if so, to freeze such assets provisionally until the accused were taken into custody. The last measure was taken in the light of the non-cooperation of FRY with the Tribunal and the possibility that such assets could be used to evade arrest.

The existence of an indictment against Zeljko Raznjatovic (also known as Arkan) was made public on 31 March, although the indictment itself was not made public.

The trial of Dario Kordic and Mario Cerkez began on 12 April. The two were charged with crimes against humanity, grave breaches of the Geneva Conventions for the protection of war victims of 12 August 1949 (Geneva Conventions) and violations of the laws and customs of war against the Bosnian Muslims in the Lasva Valley region of central Bosnia.

An indictment against Gojko Jankovic, Janko Janjic, Zoran Vukovic, Dragan Zelenovic and Radovan Stankovic was confirmed on 7 October. Mr. Vukovic appeared together with the accused Dragoljub Kunarac and Radomir Kovac (see below), all charged with crimes against humanity and violations of the laws or customs of war.

Dragan Kolundzija, Damir Dosen and Dusko Sikirica were charged with grave breaches of the Geneva Conventions, violations of the laws or customs of war and crimes against humanity in the Keraterm camp in the municipality of Prijedor. Mr. Kolundzija was arrested in June by the multinational Stabilization Force (SFOR) and on 29 September pleaded not guilty to all counts against him in an amended indictment that was confirmed on 30 August. Mr. Dosen, who was detained by SFOR in October, pleaded not guilty on 8 November at his initial appearance to all counts against him. Mr. Sikirica, who was still at large, was also charged with genocide.

An amended indictment of 17 December charged Radoslav Brdjanin and Momir Talic with their alleged participation in the ethnic cleansing of non-Serbs from the autonomous region of Krajina between April and December 1992. Mr. Brdjanin, who was arrested by SFOR in July, pleaded not guilty to all charges at his initial appearance on 12 July before the Trial Chamber. Mr. Talic, who was arrested on 25 August, pleaded not guilty to the charges at his initial appearance on 31 August. The amended indictment charged the accused with two counts of genocide, five counts of crimes against humanity, two counts of violations of the laws or customs of war and three counts of grave breaches of the Geneva Conventions.

The three accused in the case of Kunarac and Others were charged in connection with their alleged participation in the detention, degrading treatment and rape of women and girls in Foca and surrounding municipalities. Radomir Kovac was arrested on 2 August and pleaded not guilty to all counts of the indictment. On 3 September, a second amended indictment was confirmed, joining him with Dragoljub Kunarac and adding two new counts against him. Both pleaded not guilty to all counts. On 23 December, Zoran Vokovic was arrested and transferred to the Tribunal. At his initial appearance on 29 December, he pleaded not guilty to all charges.

General Stanislav Galic was accused of committing crimes against humanity and violations of the laws or customs of war between September 1992 and August 1994 during a campaign against civilians in Sarajevo. Arrested by SFOR, he was transferred to ICTY on 21 December. At his initial appearance on 29 December, he pleaded not guilty to the charges against him. The Trial Chamber designated its presiding judge to conduct pre-trial proceedings.

Communications. On 27 May [S/1999/625], FRY issued a statement asserting that the indictment of its President and four senior officials represented another manipulation by North Atlantic Treaty Organization (NATO) aggressors against FRY and an attempt to mislead the world public in order to cover up responsibility for the crime of genocide against the people of Yugoslavia. On the same date [S/1999/617], the Foreign Ministry of the Russian Federation stated that the indictment was motivated by strictly political considerations.

Ongoing trials

The Trial Chamber, on 7 May, found Zlatko Aleksovski, whose trial began in 1998 [YUN 1998, p. 1193], guilty of one count of a violation of the laws or customs of war and not guilty of two other charges. He was sentenced to two years' and six months' imprisonment. Considering that Mr. Aleksovski was entitled to credit for his time served in the UN Detention Unit (2 years, 10 months and 29 days), the Trial Chamber ordered his immediate release, notwithstanding any appeal. Both the accused and the prosecution appealed against the judgement.

On 7 July, the Trial Chamber began contempt proceedings against Milan Simic, one of the accused in the case of Simic and Others [YUN 1998, p. 1192], and his then lead counsel Branislav Avramovic, based on allegations of witness interference, intimidation and bribery. The Chamber suspended trial preparations pending the outcome of the contempt proceedings, including vacating the trial date, originally set for 22 June. Another of the accused, Stevan Todorovic, had filed a number of motions challenging the legality of his arrest, as well as ancillary motions seeking to obtain evidence from both the prosecution and SFOR as to the manner of his transfer to SFOR authority. In November, the Trial Chamber heard evidence from the accused as to the circumstances of his arrest. Yet another of the accused, Miroslav Tadic, on 28 July, was granted leave to appeal against a decision of the Trial Chamber denying his application for provisional release.

During the trial of General Tihomir Blaskic, who was charged with grave breaches of the Geneva Conventions, violations of the laws or customs of war and crimes against humanity, 158 witnesses testified, including the accused. The proceedings ended on 30 July with judgement reserved to a later date. On 11 June [A/53/1001], the Secretary-General sought the concurrence of the General Assembly with respect to a two-month extension of the services of a remaining individual brought in as gratis personnel, who had been the leading prosecution co-counsel in Mr. Blaskic's trial. On 23 June [A/53/PV.102], the Assembly approved the extension until the end of August.

In the case of Martinovic and Naletilic, Vinko Martinovic, who was being held in respect of a different case in Croatia, was transferred to ICTY custody on 9 August on the basis of an indictment dated 21 December 1998 [YUN 1998, p. 1194]. The accused pleaded not guilty to crimes against humanity, war crimes and grave breaches of the Geneva Conventions. His co-accused, Mladen Naletilic, however, remained in detention in Croatia for another case. On 25 August, the President of the Tribunal reported to the Security Council that the Croatian authorities had failed to transfer Mr. Naletilic (see below, under "State non-compliance").

In November, the Trial Chamber heard closing arguments in the 1993 case of Kupreskic and Others [YUN 1998, p. 1194] who were charged in connection with their alleged role in the 1993 attack on the Bosnian town of Ahmici.

In the case of Kvocka and Others [YUN 1998, p. 1192], four persons were charged with crimes alleged to have occurred in the Omarska camp in Bosnia and Herzegovina. The Trial Chamber dealt with many related questions, and in particular dismissed the Prosecutor's motion to join the case to the Kolundzija case (see p. 1215). In November, the Chamber decided that depositions taken by a legal officer could be accepted.

In the case of Dusko Tadic, who appealed his 1997 conviction and sentencing [YUN 1997, p. 1321], the Appeals Chamber rendered its judgement on the appeal against the Trial Chamber's judgement. Reversing the judgement in certain respects, the Appeals Chamber found him guilty on a number of additional counts. On 11 November, the designated Trial Chamber issued its sentencing judgement on the additional counts, imposing sentences ranging from 6 to 25 years. It stipulated that the new sentences were to run concurrently both inter se and in relation to each of the sentences imposed by the 1997 sentencing judgement. Mr. Tadic appealed against the second sentencing judgement and, on 3 December, the Appeals Chamber joined his two appeals; thus, the sentencing appeal judgement would relate to the appeals against both the 1997 and the 1999 sentencing judgements.

In December, the Trial Chamber completed the trial of Goran Jelisic [YUN 1998, p. 1192], who had pleaded guilty to war crimes and crimes against humanity, but not guilty to the count of genocide. The Trial Chamber, in October, had orally acquitted him of genocide because the mens rea required for constitution of the offence had not been proved, a decision appealed by the Prosecutor. On 14 December, the Trial Chamber rendered its reasoned written judgement on all the crimes ascribed to the accused, sentencing him to 40 years in prison for war crimes and crimes against humanity. Mr. Jelisic appealed against that judgement.

At an initial appearance on 14 September, Milorad Krnojelac, who was arrested in 1998 [YUN 1998, p. 1193], pleaded not guilty to charges of breaches of the Geneva Conventions, violations of the laws or customs of war and crimes against humanity contained in an amended indictment alleging that the accused, as camp commander at a detention centre in Foca, Bosnia and Herzegovina, in 1992 and 1993, had subjected both Muslim and non-Serb males to prolonged and routine imprisonment, confinement, torture and countless killings.

Upon a Prosecution request, the Trial Chamber on 12 March issued a binding order to the Republika Srpska for the production of documents in the case of General Radislav Krstic [YUN 1998, p. 1193]. Furthermore, on 6 May, the Trial Chamber granted, in part, a defence motion challenging the form of the indictment, thereby ordering the Prosecution to clarify the indictment in respect of the responsibility of the accused and his co-accused. Further to defence motions and discussions, an amended indictment was filed on 27 October, to which the accused pleaded not guilty.

State request for review

The Trial Chamber, on 4 February, granted, in substantial part, an application by the Prosecution by issuing an order to Croatia for the production of documents. Following Croatia's request for a review of the order, the Appeals Chamber, on 26 March, held that Croatia was directly affected by the order, which concerned issues relating to the Tribunal's powers. Consequently, the Appeals Chamber found Croatia's request for review admissible and suspended the order pending the outcome of the review. On 9 September, the Appeals Chamber confirmed the validity of the binding order on the basis that it conformed to the criteria established by the Appeals Chamber in the case of General Tihomir Blaskic (see p. 1216).

State non-compliance

The President of the Tribunal, in a letter of 2 November [S/1999/1117], requested the Security Council to take steps to address the issue of State non-compliance with the Tribunal's statute. Areas of non-compliance involved failure to arrest and transfer individuals indicted by the Tribunal; failure to recognize the Tribunal's jurisdiction over certain operations; and failure to permit ICTY investigators access to Kosovo sites where criminal activity allegedly occurred. Recently, the latter category had been largely resolved, and the Prosecutor herself had been in Kosovo. The first two categories, however, remained unresolved. The Prosecutor noted that the Tribunal lacked coercive mechanisms and had to rely on the international community to give effect to its arrest warrants and other orders. Annexed to the letter was a list of previous reports of non-compliance.

Bosnia and Herzegovina

In Bosnia and Herzegovina, the Republika Srpska had continued its policy of refusing to execute arrest warrants against the approximately 25 indictees believed to be residing in its territory.

Croatia

On 19 July, Croatia's Minister of Justice advised the Prosecutor that his Government would not consider the transfer to the Tribunal of Vinko Martinovic and Mladen Naletilic (see p. 1216), indicted in 1998 [YUN 1998, p. 1194], until they had completed sentences in Croatia relating to previous convictions. That position was contrary to the principle that the Tribunal enjoyed primacy over national courts. Subsequently, Croatia indicated that it was prepared to transfer the individuals following the completion of court proceedings in Croatia.

As a result of Croatia's persistent failure to comply with Prosecution requests, the Prosecutor requested the Tribunal President on 28 July to find that Croatia had failed to comply with its obligations towards the Tribunal and to report the matter to the Security Council. On 25 August [S/1999/912], the President of the Tribunal, in a letter to the Council, said that Croatia had refused to recognize the jurisdiction of the Tribunal over alleged criminal activity that occurred during the 1995 military offensive launched by the Croatian Army on Western Slavonia (Operation Flash) [YUN 1995, p. 571] and on Krajina (Operation Storm) [ibid., p. 580]. In addition, Croatia refused to surrender and to transfer Mr. Naletilic to the Tribunal. It transferred Mr. Martinovic to ICTY custody on 9 August.

In reply, Croatia transmitted to the Council a Government statement of 26 August [S/1999/923], which asserted that the Tribunal's claim of Croatia's alleged non-cooperation was unfounded. A further letter of 1 September [S/1999/936] from Croatia's Minister for Foreign Affairs stated that the problems encountered in Croatia's cooperation with ICTY were mostly of a legal and procedural nature, and easy to overcome.

On 22 September, the Minister of Justice of Croatia sent a letter of justification to the Council President. To clarify the record, the President of the Tribunal sent a letter on 27 September.

Federal Republic of Yugoslavia

On 2 February, the Prosecutor requested the President of the Tribunal to find non-compliance by FRY and to report such non-compliance to the Security Council. The request was based on a pattern of non-compliance, including the failure to defer to the competence of the Tribunal, failure to execute warrants, failure to provide evidence and information, and refusal to permit the Prosecutor and her investigators into Kosovo in 1998 [YUN 1998, p. 1195]. On 12 February, the President invited FRY to respond to the Prosecutor's request. No response was received. On 16 March, the President made a determination that FRY was in non-compliance with its obligations under the Tribunal's statute, and informed the Council accordingly [S/1999/383].

Composition of the Chambers

By a letter of 21 June [S/1999/727], the Secretary-General informed the President of the Security Council that Judge Gabrielle Kirk McDonald (United States) had resigned as a judge of the Chambers, effective 17 November 1999. The United States had presented as a replacement the candidacy of Patricia McGowan Wald, who, in the Secretary-General's view, had met the qualifications prescribed in the Tribunal's statute. The curriculum vitae of Ms. Wald was annexed to the Secretary-General's letter. Following consultations with Council members, the Council President, on 28 June [S/1999/728], stated that he supported the Secretary-General's intention to appoint Ms. Wald. In a letter of 29 June to the Council President [S/1999/739], the Secretary-General stated that he had received a corresponding letter from the General Assembly President [A/53/1042] and had appointed Ms. Wald, effective 17 November 1999, for the remainder of the term of office of Judge McDonald, to expire on 16 November 2001.

In a letter of 20 December [S/1999/1304], the Secretary-General informed the Council President that Italy had presented the candidacy of Fausto Pocar to replace Judge Antonio Cassese, who had resigned as a judge, effective 1 February 2000. In the Secretary-General's view, Mr. Pocar met the qualifications prescribed in the statute of the Tribunal. The Secretary-General wished to proceed to consultation with the Council President on Mr. Pocar's appointment. Annexed to the letter was the curriculum vitae of Mr. Pocar. On 29 December [S/1999/1305], the Council President stated that following consultations with Council members, he concurred with the Secretary-General's intention to appoint Mr. Pocar. On 30 December [S/1999/1306], the Secretary-General informed the Council President that he had received a corresponding letter from the General Assembly President [A/INF/54/7]. Accordingly, he had appointed Mr. Pocar, effective 1 February 2000, for the remainder of the term of office of Judge Cassese, to expire on 16 November 2001.

Regulatory activity

A series of amendments to the ICTY Rules of Procedure and Evidence and several new rules were adopted in 1999. Many of the amendments were intended to speed up trials and the pre-trial process and to minimize delays, while others were required to promote internal efficiency and linguistic consistency. Amendments were also made with regard to the powers and role of the pre-trial judge and to improve pre-trial management.

On 1 October, the Tribunal President issued a Practice Direction on the procedure for filing written submissions in appeal proceedings before the Tribunal. The President also adopted two Practice Directions relating to enforcement of sentences.

Office of the Prosecutor

The Office of the Prosecutor was engaged in intensive investigative work in Kosovo, once access to the territory became possible following the end of the NATO air campaign. On 12 June, Tribunal investigators entered Kosovo with NATO international security force (KFOR) troops. The focus of the work was to support the existing charges in the indictment of Slobodan Milosevic (see above, under "The Chambers") through additional witness interviews and examination of crime scenes, including mass graves, and to bring additional indictments against others. A few days later, forensic teams seconded to the Tribunal by Member States arrived in Kosovo to carry out exhumations from mass graves and crime scenes. Initial results were made public by the Prosecutor, who informed the Security Council in November that work had been completed at 195 of 529 identified grave sites and that 2,108 bodies had been exhumed.

In Bosnia and Herzegovina, investigative work continued, including forensic programmes. The Office of the Prosecutor continued to locate and exhume bodies in mass graves associated with the fall of Srebrenica [YUN 1995, p. 529] and deaths in the detention camps in Prijedor. In addition to the field team exhuming mass graves, a separate mortuary team carried out post-mortem examinations on the bodies recovered. In all, 838 bodies and partial remains were recovered from Kozluk, Nova Kasaba, Konjevic Polje and Glogova. An additional site in Bosnia and Herzegovina was exhumed in Kevljani where 172 bodies and partial remains were recovered.

Trial work and appellate work increased significantly, with the Office of the Prosecutor actively engaged in prosecuting and preparing trials.

On 15 September, Carla Del Ponte (Switzerland) assumed the position of Prosecutor of both ICTY and ICTR, after Justice Louise Arbour (Canada) resigned.

Communication. On 9 June [S/1999/665], the Secretary-General informed the Security Council President that the Prosecutor had requested some 300 experts to form forensic investigation teams for a period of six months to conduct on-site crime scene investigations in Kosovo. The Secretary-General stated that it was his intention to proceed with issuing invitations to all Member States to offer gratis personnel, and to accept experts for specialized functions identified by the Prosecutor, for a period of six months.

SECURITY COUNCIL ACTION

On 11 August [meeting 4033], the Security Council unanimously adopted **resolution 1259(1999)**. The draft [S/1999/863] was prepared during consultations among Council members.

The Security Council,

Recalling its resolutions 808(1993) of 22 February 1993, 827(1993) of 25 May 1993, 936(1994) of 8 July 1994, 955(1994) of 8 November 1994, and 1047(1996) of 29 February 1996,

Noting with regret the resignation of Mrs. Louise Arbour taking effect on 15 September 1999,

Having regard to article 16, paragraph 4, of the statute of the International Tribunal for the Prosecution of Persons Responsible for Serious Violations of International Humanitarian Law Committed in the Territory of the Former Yugoslavia since 1991 and article 15

of the statute of the International Tribunal for Rwanda,

Having considered the nomination by the Secretary-General of Ms. Carla Del Ponte for the position of Prosecutor of the above-mentioned Tribunals,

Appoints Ms. Carla Del Ponte as Prosecutor of the International Tribunal for the Prosecution of Persons Responsible for Serious Violations of International Humanitarian Law Committed in the Territory of the Former Yugoslavia and the International Tribunal for Rwanda with effect from the date on which the resignation of Mrs. Louise Arbour takes effect.

The Registry

The Registry of the Tribunal continued to exercise court management functions and provide administration and service to the Chambers and the Office of the Prosecutor. In addition, it provided information to the media and the public, administered the legal aid system under which it assigned defence counsel to indigent accused, supervised the UN Detention Unit and maintained diplomatic contacts with States and their representatives. The Registry was also responsible for budgetary matters.

Sweden and Austria, in February and July, respectively, signed the Agreement with the United Nations on the Enforcement of Sentences imposed by the Tribunal, allowing convicted persons to serve their sentences in those countries. Finland, Italy and Norway had previously signed the Agreement. On 16 September [S/1999/1014], Austria informed the Security Council that it was willing to carry out imprisonment sentences imposed by the Tribunal on a case-by-case basis in accordance with its laws and the Agreement with the United Nations.

In September, an outreach programme was established to improve understanding of the Tribunal's work and its relevance in the former Yugoslavia. The programme, with offices in The Hague, Netherlands, and the region, sought to ensure that the Tribunal's activities were transparent and accessible to the communities of the former Yugoslavia through such activities as conferences, seminars, workshops, transmission of court proceedings and Internet access.

Functioning of the Tribunal

Pursuant to General Assembly resolution 53/212 [YUN 1998, p. 1199], the Secretary-General transmitted, in November [A/54/634], the report of the Expert Group to Conduct a Review of the Effective Operation and Functioning of ICTY and ICTR. The Expert Group identified obstacles to the effective functioning of the Tribunals and made a series of recommendations to overcome them, focusing in particular on expediting pre-trial, trial and appeal proceedings.

The Judicial Practices Working Group, created in September, was the first multidisciplinary group established at ICTY. The Working Group was responsible for reviewing the Expert Group report. It also focused on possible changes to the practices of the different Chambers.

The Working Group on the Appeals Chamber was mandated to evaluate the structure and operation of the ICTY and ICTR Appeals Chambers. It was also responsible for resolving problems encountered by the Appeals Chambers regarding translation and transmission of documents between the two Tribunals.

Financing ICTY

1998 budget performance/ revised 1999 estimates/2000 requirements

Reports of Secretary-General. Pursuant to General Assembly resolution 52/217 [YUN 1997, p. 1326], the Secretary-General, in September [A/54/395], presented the fourth annual budget performance report of the Tribunal for the year ended 31 December 1998, including actual performance indicators. Of the total net appropriation of $61,941,400, actual expenditures recorded for 1998 totalled $59,363,300, reflecting an unencumbered balance of $2,578,100, or some 4 per cent of the appropriation. The balance was due to an unutilized amount in mission subsistence allowance and decreases in spending for other staff costs, travel, contractual services, general operating expenses, supplies and materials, and furniture and equipment.

On 1 November [A/54/518 & Corr.1], the Secretary-General submitted the proposed 2000 resource requirements of the Tribunal, amounting to $110,670,900 gross ($100,251,100 net) and reflecting an increase of $6,147,300 net and an additional 98 posts over the 1999 appropriation and authorized staffing level.

Also in November [A/C.5/54/30], the Secretary-General, in a report on judges' conditions of service, presented options for establishing a survivors' benefit for the survivors of ICTY and ICTR judges.

ACABQ action. In December [A/54/645], the Advisory Committee on Administrative and Budgetary Questions (ACABQ) recommended that the General Assembly approve an appropriation of $106,149,400 gross ($95,942,600 net) for the operation of the Tribunal in 2000.

Regarding the survivors' benefit for the survivors of judges of both Tribunals, ACABQ, also in December [A/54/646 & Add.1], recommended the option of a lump-sum payment equivalent to one month of base salary for each year of service, subject to a minimum of one month and a maximum of four months. It recommended that the financial implications be worked out and provided to the Fifth (Administrative and Budgetary) Committee.

GENERAL ASSEMBLY ACTION

On 23 December [meeting 88], the General Assembly, on the recommendation of the Fifth Committee [A/54/678], adopted **resolution 54/239 A** without vote [agenda item 142].

Financing of the International Tribunal for the Prosecution of Persons Responsible for Serious Violations of International Humanitarian Law Committed in the Territory of the Former Yugoslavia since 1991

The General Assembly,

Taking note of the report of the Secretary-General on the financing of the International Tribunal for the Prosecution of Persons Responsible for Serious Violations of International Humanitarian Law Committed in the Territory of the Former Yugoslavia since 1991 and the related report of the Advisory Committee on Administrative and Budgetary Questions,

Recalling its resolution 47/235 of 14 September 1993 on the financing of the International Tribunal for the Former Yugoslavia and its subsequent resolutions thereon, the latest of which was resolution 53/212 of 18 December 1998,

Taking note of the report of the Secretary-General on the budget performance of the International Tribunal for the Former Yugoslavia for 1998 and the comments of the Advisory Committee thereon,

1. *Deeply regrets* the delay in the submission of the report of the Secretary-General on the financing of the International Tribunal for the Prosecution of Persons Responsible for Serious Violations of International Humanitarian Law Committed in the Territory of the Former Yugoslavia since 1991, as well as the failure to submit to the General Assembly the report of the expert review group on the effective operation and functioning of that Tribunal and the International Criminal Tribunal for the Prosecution of Persons Responsible for Genocide and Other Serious Violations of International Humanitarian Law Committed in the Territory of Rwanda and Rwandan Citizens Responsible for Genocide and Other Such Violations Committed in the Territory of Neighbouring States between 1 January and 31 December 1994, as requested in its resolution 53/212;

2. *Notes with concern* that, owing to the late submission of the report on the financing of the International Tribunal for the Former Yugoslavia, the General Assembly did not have adequate time to consider it properly;

3. *Requests* that future reports on the financing of the International Tribunal for the Former Yugoslavia be submitted by 1 October of the year in which they are to be considered;

4. *Requests* the Secretary-General to issue, as a matter of priority, the report of the expert review group in the six official languages of the United Nations;

5. *Also requests* the Secretary-General to obtain comments and observations from the International Tribunal for the Former Yugoslavia on the report of the expert review group, and to submit them, through the Advisory Committee on Administrative and Budgetary Questions, to the General Assembly for consideration at its resumed fifty-fourth session;

6. *Further requests* the Secretary-General to improve further the workload indicators and to use them, as much as possible, as the basis for supporting the resources requested in the budget estimates;

7. *Approves* the recommendations of the Advisory Committee on the note of the Secretary-General on conditions of service for the judges of the International Tribunal for the Former Yugoslavia and the International Tribunal for Rwanda concerning the establishment of a lump-sum payment for survivors of the judges;

8. *Also approves* the budgetary recommendations of the Advisory Committee, as contained in paragraph 77 of its report, subject to the provisions of the present resolution;

9. *Decides* to appropriate, on a provisional basis, subject to further review at its resumed fifty-fourth session, to the Special Account for the International Tribunal for the Prosecution of Persons Responsible for Serious Violations of International Humanitarian Law Committed in the Territory of the Former Yugoslavia since 1991, a total amount of 106,149,400 United States dollars gross (95,942,600 dollars net) for the year 2000;

10. *Decides also* that the financing of the appropriation for the year 2000 under the Special Account shall take into account the amount of 2,740,700 dollars gross (2,578,100 dollars net), being the unencumbered balance for the year 1998, the estimated unencumbered balance of 8,200,000 dollars gross and net from the appropriation for the year 1999 and the estimated income of 5,200 dollars for the year 2000, which shall be set off against the aggregate amount of the appropriation, as detailed in the annex to the present resolution;

11. *Decides further* to apportion the amount of 47,601,750 dollars gross (42,582,250 dollars net) among Member States in accordance with the scale of assessments applicable to the regular budget of the United Nations for the year 2000;

12. *Decides* to apportion the amount of 47,601,750 dollars gross (42,582,250 dollars net) among Member States in accordance with the scale of assessments applicable to peacekeeping operations for the year 2000;

13. *Decides also* that, in accordance with the provisions of its resolution 973(X) of 15 December 1955, there shall be set off against the apportionment among Member States, as provided for in paragraphs 11 and 12 above, their respective share in the Tax Equalization Fund of the estimated staff assessment income of 10,039,000 dollars approved for the International Tribunal for the Former Yugoslavia for the year 2000;

14. *Welcomes* contributions already made to the Voluntary Fund to support the activities of the International Tribunal for the Former Yugoslavia, and invites Member States and other interested parties to make further voluntary contributions to the Tribunal;

15. *Decides* to continue its consideration of this question during its resumed fifty-fourth session.

ANNEX
Financing of the International Tribunal for the Prosecution of Persons Responsible for Serious Violations of International Humanitarian Law Committed in the Territory of the Former Yugoslavia since 1991

	Gross	*Net*
	(United States dollars)	
Appropriation for the year 2000	106,149,400	95,942,600
Less:		
Estimated unencumbered balance for the year 1999	(8,200,000)	(8,200,000)
Unencumbered balance for the year 1998	(2,740,700)	(2,578,100)
Estimated income for the year 2000	(5,200)	—
Balance to be assessed for the year 2000	95,203,500	85,164,500
Including:		
Contributions assessed on Member States in accordance with the scale of assessments applicable to the regular budget of the United Nations for the year 2000	47,601,750	42,582,250
Contributions assessed on Member States in accordance with the scale of assessments applicable to the peacekeeping budget of the United Nations for the year 2000	47,601,750	42,582,250

By **decision 54/462 A** of 23 December, the Assembly decided that the Fifth Committee should continue to consider the item on financing of ICTY. On the same date, by **decision 54/465**, the Assembly decided that the item would remain for consideration during its resumed fifty-fourth (2000) session.

Board of Auditors

The Secretary-General submitted his financial report on the ICTY accounts for the 1998-1999 biennium, including the report of the Board of Auditors for the same period [A/55/5/Add.12].

The budget for the biennium totalled $171.7 million, with actual expenditures amounting to $151.4 million, leaving an unencumbered balance of $20.3 million. The actual expenditures for 1998-1999 represented an increase of 107 per cent of the total expenditures for 1996-1997.

Following an audit of the financial statements and a management audit of courtroom resources and defence expenditure, the Board of Auditors found that the Tribunal did not disclose the liabilities for end-of-service benefits, post-retirement benefits and annual leave. It also found that as at 31 December, after six years of operation and expenditure of $225 million, the Tribunal had convicted six accused, acquitted one and released seven. In addition, the Tribunal did not use its three courtrooms for 58 per cent of the available 1,614 sessions between July 1998 and August 1999, and between 1997 and 1999, defence expenditure increased by 364 per cent (from $3.3 million to $12 million), while prosecution costs increased by 100 per cent (from $12.5 million to $25 million). The Board recommended that the Tribunal disclose the liabilities for those benefits, review procedures for using courtrooms, and review its legal aid system to establish tighter controls over defence costs.

International Tribunal for Rwanda

In September [A/54/315-S/1999/943], the Secretary-General transmitted to the General Assembly and the Security Council the fourth annual report of ICTR, covering the period from 1 July 1998 to 30 June 1999. By **decision 54/414** of 8 November, the Assembly took note of the report.

The Chambers

Trials and cases

On 5 February, the Trial Chamber sentenced Omar Serushago, who was found guilty in 1998 of the crime of genocide and of crimes against humanity (murder, extermination and torture) [YUN 1998, p. 1202], to a single term of 15 years' imprisonment. The accused lodged an appeal against the sentence.

A judgement and sentence were rendered on 21 May in the case against Clément Kayishema and Obed Ruzindana [YUN 1998, p. 1202]. Both were found guilty of genocide and not guilty of crimes against humanity (murder, extermination and other inhumane acts) and of violations of the Geneva Conventions and of Additional Protocol II thereto [YUN 1977, p. 706]. Mr. Kayishema was sentenced to life imprisonment and Mr. Ruzindana to a term of 25 years' imprisonment. Both accused and the Prosecutor lodged appeals against the judgement and the sentences.

The trial of Georges Anderson Rutaganda, the second Vice-President of the Interahamwe in Rwanda in 1994, was completed and deliberations on the judgement commenced on 17 June. He was charged with one count of genocide, four counts of crimes against humanity and four counts of violations of the Geneva Conventions and of Additional Protocol II. On 6 December, the accused was convicted of genocide and two counts of crimes against humanity (murder and extermination), and sentenced to life imprisonment. He appealed the judgement.

In the case of Bernard Ntuyahaga, charged in 1998 with a single count, crimes against humanity for the murder of Agathe Uwilingiyimana, former Prime Minister of Rwanda, and 10 Belgian peacekeepers of the United Nations Assistance Mission for Rwanda [YUN 1998, p. 1202], the Prosecutor, on 23 February, sought to withdraw the indictment against the accused. The Prosecutor made the request on the basis that prosecution of a single count would not serve her objective of exposing the totality of crimes committed in Rwanda in 1994, and she wished to withdraw the indictment to facilitate prosecution by national courts. She requested that the accused be transferred to the Government of the United Republic of Tanzania. The Government of Belgium, authorized by the Trial Chamber to appear before it as amicus curiae, requested that Mr. Ntuyahaga be handed over to Belgium to be tried before its courts, should the indictment be withdrawn. On 18 March, the Trial Chamber authorized the Prosecutor to withdraw the indictment and that Mr. Ntuyahaga be released, as it was not within its powers to hand over a released person to the authorities of any State. Thus, he was released on 29 March. Mr. Ntuyahaga appealed the withdrawal of his indictment, arguing that he should have been acquitted. The Appeals Chamber dismissed the appeal on the grounds that it was not an appeal against a conviction and that it had not been raised on the basis of a challenge to the Trial Chamber's jurisdiction. Mr. Ntuyahaga was later arrested by the authorities of the United Republic of Tanzania, who had received applications for his extradition from Belgium and Rwanda.

On 3 June, the Appeals Chamber delivered its decisions on two interlocutory appeals in the Nsengiyumva and Kanyabashi cases. The appeals stemmed from the composition of Trial Chambers that had been reconstituted by the Tribunal President for the purpose of hearing Prosecution motions for amendment of the indictments and Prosecution motions for joinder of the indictments. The President had acted because several of the judges who had confirmed the indictments against the accused were, in terms of the rules, disqualified from sitting in their trials. In a majority decision, the Appeals Chamber affirmed the President's powers to temporarily assign or rotate a member of one Trial Chamber to another, but ruled that motions for amendment of the indictment on a textual reading might be heard only by the Chamber before which the initial appearance of the accused had been held.

Following the Trial Chamber's denial of a motion to nullify the arrest in April 1996 and detention of Jean-Bosco Barayagwiza in Arusha, United Republic of Tanzania, in November 1997 [YUN 1997, p. 1328], the accused appealed the latter decision. On 3 November 1999, the Appeals Chamber dismissed the indictment against the accused on the grounds that his fundamental rights had been violated by his prolonged detention without a trial, and directed his release. The Prosecutor filed for a motion for review of the decision on the grounds of new facts. On 8 November [S/1999/1148], Rwanda transmitted a statement by its Minister of Foreign Affairs and Regional Cooperation on the release of the accused, registering the Government's strong protest against the action, which it said was not commensurate with the seriousness of the crime of genocide.

The Office of the Prosecutor continued to pursue the strategy of joint trials of multi-defendant cases by filing joint indictments, or by filing motions for joinder of accused to consolidate several indictments in a single proceeding for trial, in order to expedite the proceedings. Joint indictments were thematically based upon the accused's spheres of intervention, or regionally specific, on the basis of the accused's sphere of influence. In mid-August, the Trial Chambers organized a marathon session of pre-trial motions for all pending indictments, specifically calling for the disposition of pending and anticipated motions for amendments of indictments and motions for joinder of accused. The cases were consolidated as follows. In the Butare cases the following four indictments were amended and consolidated for trial: Sylvain Nsabimana [YUN 1997, p. 1328] and Alphonse Nteziryayo; Pauline Nyiramasuhuko [ibid.] and Arsène Shalom Ntahobali [ibid.]; Joseph Kanyabashi; and Elie Ndayambaje. The Cyangugu cases consolidated the indictment against André Ntagerura with the joint indictment of Immanuel Bagambiki and Samuel Imanishimwe [ibid.]. The military cases consolidated the indictments against Théoneste Bagosora [YUN 1998, p. 1202]; Gratien Kabiligi and Aloys Ntabakuze [YUN 1997, p. 1328]; and Anatole Nsengiyumva. Several indictments against Jean-Bosco Barayagwiza [YUN 1998, p. 1202], Ferdinand Nahimana and Hassan Ngeze were consolidated for trial of the media cases. The motion to consolidate four separate indictments of the Government cases was denied. However, the Government cases already consisted of three joint indictments: Augustin Bizimana, Edouard Karemera, Callixte Nzabonimana, André Rwamakuba, Mathieu Ngirumpatse, Joseph Nzirorera and Felicien Kabuga; Casimir Bizimungu, Justin Mugenzi, Jerôme Bicamumpaka and Prosper Mugiraneza; Jean de Dieu Kamuhanda and one other; and the single indictment against Eliezer Niyitegeka. Despite a plethora of defence motions for severance, the Trial Chamber only granted the motion to sever filed by Juvénal Kajelijeli. (For details of the charges related to some of the cases, see below, under "New arrests and cases".)

New arrests and cases

The trial of Alfred Musema, which began on 25 January, was completed on 28 June. The accused was charged with genocide, conspiracy to commit genocide, crimes against humanity and serious violations of the Geneva Conventions and of Additional Protocol II. Judgement and sentencing were scheduled for 2000.

In February 1999, Eliezer Niyitegeka, Minister of Information of the interim Government, Casimir Bizimungu, Minister of Health of the interim Government and Ignace Bagilishema, Bourgmestre (Mabanza Commune, Kibuye), were arrested and transferred to the Tribunal's Detention Facility in Arusha. Mr. Bagilishema, on 1 April, pleaded not guilty to 13 counts charging him with genocide, crimes against humanity and violations of the Geneva Conventions. On 15 April, Mr. Niyitegeka pleaded not guilty to six counts of genocide, crimes against humanity and violations of the Geneva Conventions. On 3 September, Mr. Bizimungo pleaded not guilty to eight counts of genocide and crimes against humanity.

On 6 April, the investigators of the Office of the Prosecutor, with the assistance of the Cameroon police, arrested three members of the interim Government: Jérôme Bicamumpaka, former Minister of Foreign Affairs; Mugenzi Justin, former Minister of Trade; and Prosper Mugiraneza, former Minister for Civic Activities. The three were transferred to the Detention Facility on 31 July, and on 17 August pleaded not guilty to charges of genocide and crimes against humanity.

Five senior officials of the 1994 interim government of Rwanda—former Minister of Interior, Edouard Karemera; former Minister of Primary and Secondary Education, André Rwamakuba; former Speaker of Parliament, Joseph Nzirorera; former Director General of Foreign Affairs in the President's Office, Mathieu Ngirumpatse; and former Bourgmestre of Mukingo, Juvénal Kajelijeli—pleaded not guilty to 11 counts jointly charging them with genocide, crimes against humanity and violations of the Geneva Conventions.

On 19 April, former Prefect of Cyangugu, Emmanuel Bagambiki, pleaded not guilty to seven counts charging him with genocide, crimes against humanity and violations of the Geneva Conventions.

Laurent Semanza, former Bourgmestre of Bicumbi, on 24 June, pleaded not guilty to seven new counts of alleged rapes of Tutsi women and other outrages upon their personal dignity.

On 11 August, Pauline Nyiramasuhuko, former Rwandan Minister for the Family and Women's Affairs, pleaded not guilty to fresh charges of encouraging sexual violence, including rape.

Following the arrest in November in the United Republic of Tanzania of Mikaeli Muhimana, Councillor in Gishyita commune (Kibuye Prefecture), the Trial Chamber entered a plea of not guilty on his behalf. The accused, charged with genocide, crimes against humanity and violations of the Geneva Conventions, had refused to enter a plea on his own.

On 25 November, Ferdinand Nahimana, former Director of Radio Télévision Libre des Mille Collines, a radio station in Rwanda, entered a plea of not guilty to three new counts charging him with genocide and crimes against humanity.

Jean de Dieu Kamuhanda, former Minister of Culture and Higher Education in the interim Government, was arrested in France on 26 November. The process to transfer him to the Detention Facility was in progress by year's end.

Trial Chamber I ruled on 16 pre-trial motions in the case of Ignace Bagilishema, of which six were filed by the Prosecutor and 10 by the defence. The accused, who was arrested in South Africa on 20 February and transferred to the Detention Facility on the same date, pleaded not guilty to seven counts in an amended indictment on 18 September. The trial began on 27 October.

Election of judges

The establishment of a third Trial Chamber by Security Council resolution 1165(1998) [YUN 1998, p. 1203] increased the number of judges from six to nine. Of the nine judges elected for a four-year term by the General Assembly on 3 November 1998 [ibid., p. 1204], four were re-elected. Three of the five new judges took their oath of office on 22 February 1999, while the remaining two did so on 31 May. One of the new judges, Dionysios Kondylis (Greece), resigned on 22 March and his replacement, Asoka de Zoysa Gunawardena (Sri Lanka), appointed by the Secretary-General [S/1999/448, S/1999/449, A/53/1003], took the oath of office on 31 May.

In other action, in identical letters of 17 May addressed to the President of the Council and the President of the Assembly [A/53/960-S/1999/566], the Secretary-General transmitted a request of the Tribunal President for an extension beyond 24 May of the term of office of a non-elected judge, Judge Lennert Aspegren, in order to allow him to dispose of two ongoing cases (Rutaganda and Musema). The Secretary-General stated that to restart both trials with a new panel of judges and order the rehearings of witnesses and testimonies would unnecessarily prolong the trials and violate the rights of the accused to due process of law. He estimated the cost of the proposed extension at $261,800. A 19 May note [A/53/963] by the Secretary-General stated that in order to enable the Assembly to consider the extension, it would be necessary to reopen consideration of agenda item 47.

SECURITY COUNCIL ACTION

On 19 May [meeting 4006], the Security Council unanimously adopted **resolution 1241(1999)**. The draft [S/1999/576] was prepared during consultations among Council members.

The Security Council,

Taking note of the letter dated 17 May 1999 from the Secretary-General to the President of the Security Council, to which he attached a letter to him dated 14 May 1999 from the President of the International Tribunal for Rwanda,

Endorses the recommendation of the Secretary-General that Judge Aspegren, once replaced as a member of the Tribunal, finish the Rutaganda and Musema cases which he has begun before expiry of his term of office, and takes note of the intention of the Tribunal to finish these cases if possible before 31 January 2000.

On 19 May [A/53/964], the Council President transmitted the text of resolution 1241(1999) to the Assembly President.

GENERAL ASSEMBLY ACTION

By **decision 53/309 B** of 24 May, the General Assembly endorsed the Secretary-General's recommendation to extend the term of Judge Aspegren.

Organizational activities

On 4 June, Judge Navanethem Pillay (South Africa) was elected President of the Tribunal, replacing Judge Laïty Kama (Senegal). Judge Erik Møse (Norway) was elected Vice-President, replacing Judge Yakov Ostrovsky (Russian Federation).

The Tribunal adopted several amendments to the Rules of Procedure and Evidence and the Directive on assignment of Defence Counsel.

In November, the newly established Working Group on the Appeals Chamber, tasked with reviewing the situation of the ICTY and ICTR Appeals Chambers, focused on amendment of the Rules and structural changes.

Office of the Prosecutor

The Office of the Prosecutor placed priority on investigations into the conspiracy to commit genocide. It conducted investigations into the preparation and execution of the conspiracy and formed new investigation teams, on the basis of the political, administrative, military and other institutions that operated in Rwanda at the time of those acts, since certain officials of those institutions were implicated in crimes.

Pending the conclusion of an agreement that would regulate the establishment and functioning of the Tribunal in Rwanda, the United Nations and the Government of Rwanda, on 3 June, signed a Memorandum of Understanding to regulate matters of concern relating to the ICTR office in Rwanda. The privileges and immunities provided for in the 1946 Convention on the Privileges and Immunities of the United Nations, adopted by the General Assembly in resolution 22 A (I) [YUN 1946-47, p. 100], would be extended to the Office of the Prosecutor and its staff. The Memorandum facilitated the work of the Office of the Prosecutor by allowing its key members to circulate freely throughout Rwanda, to have access to all prisoners and necessary documents, to have direct contact with national and local authorities and to question victims and witnesses.

On 11 August, the Security Council unanimously appointed Carla Del Ponte as Prosecutor of ICTR and ICTY (see p. 1218).

The Registry

The Registry administered and serviced the Chambers and the Prosecutor in the performance of their respective functions.

The Unit for Gender Issues and Assistance to Victims, which aimed to improve gender sensitivity in protecting and supporting witnesses in trials, carried out a mission assessment in January during a visit to women who had come to testify in the case of Jean-Paul Akayesu [YUN 1998, p. 1201].

Financing ICTR

1998 budget performance/ revised 1999 and 2000 estimates/ 2000 requirements

Reports of Secretary-General. In accordance with General Assembly resolution 49/251 [YUN 1995, p. 1324], the Secretary-General, in October [A/54/496 & Corr.1], presented the fourth annual budget performance report of the Tribunal covering 1998. Actual expenditures amounted to $50,430,000 net, resulting in an overexpenditure of $2,386,600. The overexpenditure consisted of increases of $2,781,000 under the Registry, partly offset by decreases under the Chambers and the Office of the Prosecutor. The report contained performance indicator statistics for 1998.

In a report of 3 November on ICTR financing [A/54/521], the Secretary-General stated that the resource requirements requested for 2000 amounted to $87,819,400 gross ($79,753,900 net), which reflected an increase of $12,558,800 gross ($11,222,000 net) over the 1999 appropriation and 60 additional posts.

ACABQ action. In December [A/54/646 & Add.1], ACABQ recommended that the General Assembly appropriate the amount of $86,154,900 gross ($78,170,200 net) for ICTR in 2000, representing a reduction of $1,664,500 gross ($1,583,700 net) of the requested amount. The report contained a summary of post reductions recommended by the Committee.

(For information on the report of the expert group to review the operation of ICTY and ICTR, and on the conditions of service for ICTY and ICTR judges, see above, under "Functioning of the Tribunal" and "Financing ICTY", respectively.)

Board of Auditors

The Secretary-General transmitted the financial report on ICTR accounts for the 1998-1999 biennium [A/55/5/Add.11], which contained the report of the Board of Auditors for that period.

The budget for the biennium totalled $127.6 million, with actual expenditures amounting to $124.6 million, leaving an unencumbered balance of $3 million. The 1998-1999 expenditures represented an increase of 91.7 per cent of the total expenditures for the 1996-1997 biennium.

Following an audit of the operations of the Tribunal and validation of its financial statements for 1998-1999, the Board made recommendations to improve the submission of financial reports and consolidated accounts, to tighten control over the reservation of credits in the accounts for travel and purchase of goods and services, to strengthen the imprest accounting of the Prosecutor's Office and to tighten internal control over procurement and contract management.

GENERAL ASSEMBLY ACTION

On 23 December [meeting 88], the General Assembly, on the recommendation of the Fifth Committee [A/54/679], adopted **resolution 54/240 A** without vote [agenda item 143].

Financing of the International Criminal Tribunal for the Prosecution of Persons Responsible for Genocide and Other Serious Violations of International Humanitarian Law Committed in the Territory of Rwanda and Rwandan Citizens Responsible for Genocide and Other Such Violations Committed in the Territory of Neighbouring States between 1 January and 31 December 1994

The General Assembly,

Taking note of the report of the Secretary-General on the financing of the International Criminal Tribunal for the Prosecution of Persons Responsible for Genocide and Other Serious Violations of International Humanitarian Law Committed in the Territory of Rwanda and Rwandan Citizens Responsible for Genocide and Other Such Violations Committed in the Territory of Neighbouring States between 1 January and 31 December 1994 and the related report of the Advisory Committee on Administrative and Budgetary Questions,

Recalling its resolution 49/251 of 20 July 1995 on the financing of the International Tribunal for Rwanda and its subsequent resolutions thereon, the latest of which was resolution 53/213 of 18 December 1998,

Taking note of the report of the Secretary-General on the budget performance of the International Tribunal for Rwanda for 1998 and the comments of the Advisory Committee thereon,

1. *Deeply regrets* the delay in the submission of the report of the Secretary-General on the financing of the International Criminal Tribunal for the Prosecution of Persons Responsible for Genocide and Other Serious Violations of International Humanitarian Law Committed in the Territory of Rwanda and Rwandan Citizens Responsible for Genocide and Other Such Violations Committed in the Territory of Neighbouring States between 1 January and 31 December 1994, as well as the failure to submit to the General Assembly the report of the expert review group on the effective operation and functioning of that Tribunal and the International Tribunal for the Prosecution of Persons Responsible for Serious Violations of International Humanitarian Law Committed in the Territory of the Former Yugoslavia since 1991, as requested in its resolution 53/213;

2. *Notes with concern* that, owing to the late submission of the report on the financing of the International Tribunal for Rwanda, the General Assembly did not have adequate time to consider it properly;

3. *Requests* that future reports on the financing of the International Tribunal for Rwanda be submitted by 1 October of the year in which they are to be considered;

4. *Requests* the Secretary-General to issue, as a matter of priority, the report of the expert review group in the six official languages of the United Nations;

5. *Also requests* the Secretary-General to obtain comments and observations from the International Tribunal for Rwanda on the report of the expert review group, and to submit them, through the Advisory Committee on Administrative and Budgetary Questions, to the General Assembly for consideration at its resumed fifty-fourth session;

6. *Further requests* the Secretary-General to improve further the workload indicators and to use them, as much as possible, as the basis for supporting the resources requested in the budget estimates;

7. *Approves* the recommendations of the Advisory Committee on the note of the Secretary-General on conditions of service for the judges of the International Tribunal for Rwanda and the International Tribunal for the Former Yugoslavia concerning the establishment of a lump-sum payment for survivors of the judges;

8. *Also approves* the budgetary recommendations of the Advisory Committee as contained in paragraph 71 of its report, subject to the provisions of the present resolution;

9. *Decides* to appropriate, on a provisional basis, subject to further review at its resumed fifty-fourth session, to the Special Account for the International Criminal Tribunal for the Prosecution of Persons Re-

sponsible for Genocide and Other Serious Violations of International Humanitarian Law Committed in the Territory of Rwanda and Rwandan Citizens Responsible for Genocide and Other Such Violations Committed in the Territory of Neighbouring States between 1 January and 31 December 1994, a total amount of 86,154,900 United States dollars gross (78,170,200 dollars net) for the year 2000;

10. *Decides also* that the financing of the appropriation for the year 2000 under the Special Account shall take into account the amount of 2 million dollars gross (1,816,000 dollars net), being the estimated unencumbered balance as at the end of 1999 after absorption of overexpenditure recorded as at the end of 1998 for the biennium 1998-1999, which shall be set off against the aggregate amount of the appropriation, as detailed in the annex to the present resolution;

11. *Decides further* to apportion the amount of 42,077,450 dollars gross (38,177,100 dollars net) among Member States in accordance with the scale of assessments applicable to the regular budget of the United Nations for the year 2000;

12. *Decides* to apportion the amount of 42,077,450 dollars gross (38,177,100 dollars net) among Member States in accordance with the scale of assessments applicable to peacekeeping operations for the year 2000;

13. *Decides also* that, in accordance with the provisions of its resolution 973(X) of 15 December 1955, there shall be set off against the apportionment among Member States, as provided for in paragraphs 11 and 12 above, their respective share in the Tax Equalization Fund of the estimated staff assessment income of 7,800,700 dollars approved for the International Tribunal for Rwanda for the year 2000;

14. *Welcomes* contributions already made to the Voluntary Fund to support the activities of the International Tribunal for Rwanda, and invites Member States and other interested parties to make further voluntary contributions to the Tribunal;

15. *Decides* to continue its consideration of this question during its resumed fifty-fourth session.

ANNEX

Financing of the International Criminal Tribunal for the Prosecution of Persons Responsible for Genocide and Other Serious Violations of International Humanitarian Law Committed in the Territory of Rwanda and Rwandan Citizens Responsible for Genocide and Other Such Violations Committed in the Territory of Neighbouring States between 1 January and 31 December 1994

	Gross	*Net*
	(United States dollars)	
Appropriation for the year 2000	86,154,900	78,170,200
Less:		
Estimated unencumbered balance as at the end of 1999 after absorption of overexpenditure recorded as at the end of 1998	(2,000,000)	(1,816,000)
Balance to be assessed for the year 2000	84,154,900	76,354,200
Including:		
Contributions assessed on Member States in accordance with the scale of assessments applicable to the regular budget of the United Nations for the year 2000	42,077,450	38,177,100
Contributions assessed on Member States in accordance with the scale of assessments applicable to the peacekeeping budget of the United Nations for the year 2000	42,077,450	38,177,100

By **decision 54/462 A** of 23 December, the Assembly decided that the Fifth Committee should continue to consider the item on financing the Tribunal. On the same date, by **decision 54/465**, the Assembly decided that the item would remain for consideration during its resumed fifty-fourth (2000) session.

Chapter III

Legal aspects of international political relations

The International Convention for the Suppression of the Financing of Terrorism was adopted by the General Assembly in December 1999; Assembly committees had been working on the text since 1996. Parties to the Convention, when ratified, would, among other things, take steps to identify, detect, freeze or seize any funds used or allocated for the purpose of carrying out terrorist acts. The Convention was to open for signature in January 2000.

In October, the Security Council adopted a resolution condemning all acts of terrorism as criminal and unjustifiable and called on States to cooperate with each other to prevent such acts and protect their nationals and other persons against them. The Assembly also condemned all terrorism as criminal in December and invited States to provide the Secretary-General with information on their national laws and regulations regarding its prevention and suppression.

Throughout 1999, the Rome Statute of the International Criminal Court, adopted in 1998, remained open for signature. By the end of the year, the Statute, which would enter into force when 60 States had become parties to it, had received six ratifications.

At its fifty-first session, the International Law Commission (ILC) adopted a draft preamble and 26 draft articles on nationality in relation to succession of States and recommended to the Assembly their adoption in the form of a declaration. In December, the Assembly, which decided to consider that recommendation at its 2000 session, invited Governments to submit comments on the question of a convention on the subject. Other topics considered by ILC included State responsibility, reservation to treaties, jurisdictional immunities of States and their property and unilateral acts of States.

Establishment of the International Criminal Court

Throughout 1999, the Rome Statute of the International Criminal Court, which in 1998 [YUN 1998, p. 1209] established the Court as a permanent institution with the power to exercise jurisdiction over persons for the most serious crimes of international concern—genocide, crimes against humanity, war crimes and the crime of aggression—remained open for signature at United Nations Headquarters in New York.

The Statute would enter into force after 60 States had become parties to it. As at 31 December, 92 States had signed and six had become parties.

Preparatory Commission. In accordance with General Assembly resolution 53/105 [YUN 1998, p. 1210], the Preparatory Commission for the International Criminal Court was established. During 1999, the Preparatory Commission held three sessions in New York (16-26 February, 26 July-13 August, 29 November-17 December) [PCNICC/2000/1]. In February [PCNICC/1999/L.3/Rev.1], the Commission agreed that its work plan would focus on two essential instruments necessary for the functioning of the Court: the Rules of Procedure and Evidence; and the Elements of Crimes. It established several working groups to consider those issues. In July/August [PCNICC/1999/L.4/Rev.1], the Commission continued its consideration of those two matters and agreed on arrangements concerning the question of the crime of aggression. In November/December [PCNICC/1999/L.5/Rev.1], the Commission noted that it had completed the first reading of the Elements of Crimes [PCNICC/1999/L.5/Rev.1/Add.2] and the Rules of Procedure and Evidence [PCNICC/1999/L.5/Rev.1/Add.1]. The Working Group on the Crime of Aggression met during the third session.

GENERAL ASSEMBLY ACTION

On 9 December [meeting 76], the General Assembly, on the recommendation of the Sixth (Legal) Committee [A/54/613], adopted **resolution 54/105** without vote [agenda item 158].

Establishment of the International Criminal Court

The General Assembly,

Recalling its resolutions 47/33 of 25 November 1992, 48/31 of 9 December 1993, 49/53 of 9 December 1994, 50/46 of 11 December 1995, 51/207 of 17 December 1996, 52/160 of 15 December 1997 and 53/105 of 8 December 1998,

Noting that the Rome Statute of the International Criminal Court was adopted on 17 July 1998 and is open for signature in New York at United Nations Headquarters until 31 December 2000, and taking note of the Final Act of the United Nations Diplomatic Conference of Plenipotentiaries on the Establishment of an International Criminal Court done at Rome on 17 July 1998,

Noting in particular that the Conference decided to establish a Preparatory Commission for the Court and that the Commission has held three sessions, from 16 to 26 February, 26 July to 13 August and 29 November to 17 December 1999,

Bearing in mind the mandate of the Preparatory Commission, as set out in resolution F adopted by the Conference, with regard to the preparation of proposals for practical arrangements for the establishment and coming into operation of the Court, including the finalization before 30 June 2000 of the draft texts of the rules of procedure and evidence and of the elements of crimes,

Recalling, with regard to the future work of the Preparatory Commission and related working groups, the specific arrangements agreed upon by the Commission and referred to in paragraph 8 of the summary of the proceedings of its second session,

Recognizing the continuing need for making available adequate resources and secretariat services to the Preparatory Commission in order to enable it to discharge its functions efficiently and expeditiously,

Emphasizing the need to make the necessary arrangements for the commencement of the functions of the International Criminal Court in order to ensure its effective operation,

Noting that a number of States have deposited their instruments of ratification and that a significant and growing number of States have signed the Rome Statute,

1. *Reiterates* the historic significance of the adoption of the Rome Statute of the International Criminal Court;

2. *Calls upon* all States to consider signing and ratifying the Rome Statute, and encourages efforts aimed at promoting awareness of the results of the Conference and of the provisions of the Statute;

3. *Requests* the Secretary-General to convene the Preparatory Commission, in accordance with resolution F adopted by the Conference, from 13 to 31 March, 12 to 30 June and 27 November to 8 December 2000, to carry out the mandate in that resolution and, in that connection, to discuss ways to enhance the effectiveness and acceptance of the Court;

4. *Also requests* the Secretary-General to make available to the Preparatory Commission secretariat services, including the preparation of working documents if so requested by the Commission, to enable it to perform its functions;

5. *Further requests* the Secretary-General to invite, as observers to the Preparatory Commission, representatives of organizations and other entities that have received a standing invitation from the General Assembly, pursuant to its relevant resolutions, to participate in the capacity of observers in its sessions and work, and also to invite as observers to the Commission representatives of interested regional intergovernmental organizations and other interested international bodies, including the international tribunals for the former Yugoslavia and Rwanda;

6. *Notes* that non-governmental organizations may participate in the work of the Preparatory Commission by attending its plenary and other open meetings, in accordance with the rules of procedure of the Commission, receiving copies of the official documents and making available their materials to delegates;

7. *Encourages* States to make voluntary contributions to the trust funds established pursuant to General Assembly resolutions 51/207 and 52/160, the mandates of which were expanded pursuant to Assembly resolution 53/105, towards meeting the costs of the participation in the work of the Preparatory Commission of the least developed countries and of those developing countries not covered by the trust fund established pursuant to resolution 51/207;

8. *Requests* the Secretary-General to report to the General Assembly at its fifty-fifth session on the implementation of the present resolution;

9. *Decides* to include in the provisional agenda of its fifty-fifth session the item entitled "Establishment of the International Criminal Court".

International Law Commission

The International Law Commission (ILC) held its fifty-first session in Geneva from 3 May to 23 July [A/54/10 & Corr.1,2]. The thirty-fifth session of the International Law Seminar (14 June–2 July) was held during the session. It was attended by 23 participants, mostly from developing countries, who observed Commission meetings, attended specially arranged lectures and participated in working groups on specific topics.

Under the topic nationality in relation to the succession of States, the Commission adopted the draft preamble and a set of 26 draft articles on second reading and recommended that the General Assembly adopt them in the form of a declaration.

The Commission also considered the topics of State responsibility, reservations to treaties, jurisdictional immunities of States and their property, unilateral acts of States, and international liability for injurious consequences arising out of acts not prohibited by international law (prevention of transboundary damage from hazardous activities). It also discussed its long-term programme of work, procedures to improve relations with the Sixth Committee and cooperation with scientific institutions, individual experts and international and national organizations concerned with international law. ILC continued traditional exchanges of information with the International Court of Justice, the Asian-African Legal Consultative Committee, the Inter-American Juridical Committee and the Committee of Legal Advisers on Public International Law of the Council of Europe.

In response to General Assembly resolution 53/102 [YUN 1998, p. 1212], ILC examined advantages and disadvantages of holding split sessions as of 2000. The Commission recommended split sessions as it believed they would be more efficient and effective and allow the uninterrupted attendance of more members. It agreed that its next session should be held in Geneva from 1 May to 9 June and from 10 July to 18 August 2000.

GENERAL ASSEMBLY ACTION

On 9 December [meeting 76], the General Assembly, on the recommendation of the Sixth Committee [A/54/610], adopted **resolution 54/111** without vote [agenda item 155].

Report of the International Law Commission on the work of its fifty-first session

The General Assembly,

Having considered the report of the International Law Commission on the work of its fifty-first session,

Emphasizing the importance of furthering the progressive development of international law and its codification as a means of implementing the purposes and principles set forth in the Charter of the United Nations and in the Declaration on Principles of International Law concerning Friendly Relations and Cooperation among States in accordance with the Charter of the United Nations,

Emphasizing also the role of the International Law Commission in the fulfilment of the objectives of the United Nations Decade of International Law,

Recognizing the desirability of referring legal and drafting questions to the Sixth Committee, including topics that might be submitted to the International Law Commission for closer examination, and of enabling the Sixth Committee and the Commission further to enhance their contribution to the progressive development of international law and its codification,

Recalling the need to keep under review those topics of international law which, given their new or renewed interest for the international community, may be suitable for the progressive development and codification of international law and therefore may be included in the future programme of work of the International Law Commission,

Welcoming the holding of the International Law Seminar, and noting with appreciation the voluntary contributions made to the United Nations Trust Fund for the International Law Seminar,

Stressing the usefulness of structuring the debate on the report of the International Law Commission in the Sixth Committee in such a manner that conditions are provided for concentrated attention to each of the main topics dealt with in the report,

Wishing to enhance further the interaction between the Sixth Committee as a body of governmental representatives and the International Law Commission as a body of independent legal experts, with a view to improving the dialogue between the two organs,

1. *Takes note* of the report of the International Law Commission on the work of its fifty-first session;

2. *Expresses its appreciation* to the International Law Commission for the work accomplished at its fifty-first session, in particular with respect to the topic "Jurisdictional immunities of States and their property" and the completion of the second reading of the draft articles on nationality of natural persons in relation to the succession of States, and notes that the Commission has completed its work on the topic "Nationality in relation to the succession of States";

3. *Draws the attention* of Governments to the importance for the International Law Commission of having their views on the various aspects involved in the topics on the agenda of the Commission, in particular on all the specific issues identified in chapter III of its report;

4. *Reiterates its invitation* to Governments to submit comments and observations in writing by 1 January 2000 on the draft articles on international liability for injurious consequences arising out of acts not prohibited by international law (prevention of transboundary damage from hazardous activities), and invites them, within the context of paragraph 3 above, to respond in writing by 1 March 2000 to the questionnaire on unilateral acts of States circulated by the Secretariat to all Governments on 30 September 1999;

5. *Also reiterates its invitation* to Governments to submit the most relevant national legislation, decisions of domestic courts and State practice relevant to diplomatic protection in order to assist the International Law Commission in its future work on the topic "Diplomatic protection";

6. *Recommends* that, taking into account the comments and observations of Governments, whether in writing or expressed orally in debates in the General Assembly, the International Law Commission should continue its work on the topics in its current programme;

7. *Takes note* of paragraph 608 of the report of the International Law Commission with regard to the procedure to be followed with respect to the topic "International liability for injurious consequences arising out of acts not prohibited by international law", and requests the Commission to resume consideration of the liability aspects of the topic as soon as the second reading of the draft articles on the prevention of transboundary damage from hazardous activities is finalized, taking into account developments in international law and comments by Governments;

8. *Also takes note* of the consideration by the International Law Commission of its long-term programme of work, and encourages the Commission to proceed with the selection of new topics for its next quinquennium corresponding to the wishes and preoccupations of States and to present possible outlines for new topics and information related thereto in order to facilitate decision thereon by the General Assembly;

9. *Welcomes with appreciation* the steps that have been taken by the International Law Commission in relation to its internal matters to enhance its efficiency and productivity, and invites the Commission to continue taking such measures, taking into consideration the discussion held by the General Assembly;

10. *Decides*, without prejudice to any future decision, that the next session of the International Law Commission shall be held at the United Nations Office at Geneva from 1 May to 9 June and from 10 July to 18 August 2000;

11. *Requests* the International Law Commission to implement arrangements in accordance with paragraph 639 of its report;

12. *Stresses* the desirability of enhancing dialogue between the International Law Commission and the Sixth Committee, and in this context takes note with appreciation of the comments made by the Commission in paragraphs 612 to 617 of its report;

13. *Requests* the International Law Commission to continue to pay special attention to indicating in its annual report, for each topic, any specific issues on which expressions of views by Governments, either in the Sixth Committee or in written form, would be of particular interest in providing effective guidance for the Commission in its further work;

14. *Also requests* the International Law Commission to continue the implementation of article 16, paragraph *(e)*, and article 26, paragraphs 1 and 2, of its statute in order to further strengthen cooperation between the Commission and other bodies concerned with international law, having in mind the usefulness of such cooperation, and in that regard takes note with appreciation of comments made by the Commission in paragraphs 618 to 632 of its report;

15. *Notes* that consulting with national organizations and individual experts concerned with international law may assist Governments in considering whether to make comments and observations on drafts submitted by the International Law Commission and in formulating their comments and observations;

16. *Reaffirms* its previous decisions concerning the role of the Codification Division of the Office of Legal Affairs of the Secretariat and those concerning the summary records and other documentation of the International Law Commission;

17. *Notes* the inclusion of information about the work of the International Law Commission in its web site;

18. *Expresses the hope* that the International Law Seminar will continue to be held in connection with the sessions of the International Law Commission and that an increasing number of participants, in particular from developing countries, will be given the opportunity to attend those seminars, and appeals to States to make urgently needed voluntary contributions to the United Nations Trust Fund for the International Law Seminar;

19. *Requests* the Secretary-General to provide the International Law Seminar with adequate services, including interpretation, as required, and encourages him to continue considering ways to improve the structure and content of the Seminar;

20. *Also requests* the Secretary-General to forward to the International Law Commission, for its attention, the records of the debate on the report of the Commission at the fifty-fourth session of the General Assembly, together with such written statements as delegations may circulate in conjunction with their oral statements, and to prepare and distribute a topical summary of the debate, following established practice;

21. *Requests* the Secretariat to circulate to States, as soon as possible after the conclusion of the session of the International Law Commission, chapter II of its report containing a summary of the work of that session and the draft articles adopted on either first or second reading by the Commission;

22. *Recommends* that the debate on the report of the International Law Commission at the fifty-fifth session of the General Assembly commence on 23 October 2000.

State succession

ILC had before it a memorandum by the Secretariat on nationality in relation to the succession of States [A/CN.4/497], which contained an overview of the comments and observations of Governments, made either orally in the Sixth Committee or in writing, on the draft preamble and set of draft articles, with commentaries, on nationality of natural persons in relation to the succession of States, which had been adopted on first reading at the Commission's forty-ninth session [YUN 1997, p. 1333].

The Commission re-established the Working Group on nationality in relation to the succession of States [A/54/10 & Corr.1,2], considered its report and referred the draft articles to the Drafting Committee. The draft preamble and draft articles, which addressed, among other things, the right to nationality, prevention of statelessness, legislation on nationality and other connected issues, non-discrimination, and attribution of the nationality of the successor State and withdrawal of nationality of the predecessor State, were adopted by the Commission along with the commentaries. The Commission recommended that the General Assembly adopt the draft articles in the form of a declaration.

Having concluded that States were not interested in the study of the second part of the topic—the nationality of legal persons in relation to the succession of States—given the absence of positive comments from them, the Commission recommended that with the adoption of the draft articles, its work on the topic be considered concluded.

GENERAL ASSEMBLY ACTION

On 9 December [meeting 76], the General Assembly, on the recommendation of the Sixth Committee [A/54/610], adopted **resolution 54/112** without vote [agenda item 155].

Nationality of natural persons in relation to the succession of States

The General Assembly,

Having considered chapter IV of the report of the International Law Commission on the work of its fifty-first session, which contains final draft articles on nationality of natural persons in relation to the succession of States,

Noting that the International Law Commission decided to recommend the draft articles to the General Assembly for their adoption in the form of a declaration,

1. *Expresses its appreciation* to the International Law Commission for its valuable work on nationality of natural persons in relation to the succession of States and to the Special Rapporteur and the Chairman of the Working Group of the Commission for their contribution to that work;

2. *Decides* to include in the provisional agenda of its fifty-fifth session an item entitled "Nationality of natural persons in relation to the succession of States", with a view to the consideration of the draft articles and their adoption as a declaration at that session;

3. *Invites* Governments to submit comments and observations on the question of a convention on nationality of natural persons in relation to the succession of States, with a view to the General Assembly considering the elaboration of such a convention at a future session.

State responsibility

During its 1999 session, ILC considered comments and observations received from two Governments [A/CN.4/492], additional to those received in 1998 [YUN 1998, p. 1213], on the draft articles on State responsibility, which had been provisionally adopted on first reading in 1996 [YUN 1996, p. 1207]. ILC also had before it the second report of the Special Rapporteur, James Crawford (Australia) [A/CN.4/498 & Add.1-4], which dealt with draft articles in the light of Governments' comments and developments in State practice, judicial decisions and in the literature. The five-part report dealt with the breach of an international obligation; the implication of a State in the internationally wrongful act of another State; a range of extremely important questions relating to circumstances precluding wrongfulness; an annex containing a brief comparative review of the unexplored question of interference with contractual rights; and certain questions of principle concerning countermeasures.

The Commission referred some draft articles in the report to the Drafting Committee and later took note of that Committee's report on chapters III, IV and V. It also noted the deletion of several articles.

International liability

At its fifty-first session, ILC had before it the second report by Special Rapporteur Pemmaraju Sreenivasa Rao (India) on prevention of transboundary damage from hazardous activities [A/CN.4/501]. Among other things, the report reviewed the status of ongoing negotiations on liability. The Special Rapporteur recommended that the Commission suspend its work on international liability, at least for the time being, until the regime of prevention was finalized in its second reading, and await developments in the negotiation of some of the protocols on liability. Having considered his recommendation and on the basis of discussion, ILC deferred consideration of the question of international liability, pending completion of the second reading of the draft articles on the prevention of transboundary damage from hazardous activities [A/54/10 & Corr.1,2].

Unilateral acts of States

At its 1999 session, ILC considered the second report on unilateral acts of States [A/CN.4/500 & Add.1] by Special Rapporteur Victor Rodríguez Cedeño (Venezuela). The report contained the texts of seven draft articles: the scope of the draft articles; definition of unilateral legal acts (declarations) of States; capacity to formulate unilateral legal acts; representatives of a State who could engage a State by formulating unilateral legal acts; subsequent confirmation of acts formulated without authorization; expression of consent; and formulation of reservations and conditional unilateral acts. The Commission reconvened the Working Group, which submitted a report to the Commission which was then amended and adopted. It was agreed that the Secretariat, in consultation with the Special Rapporteur, should elaborate and send to Governments, by October 1999, a questionnaire for possible reply within a reasonable deadline, requesting material and inquiring about their practice in the area of unilateral acts, as well as their position on certain aspects of the Commission's study of the topic. The questionnaire was circulated on 30 September.

International State relations and international law

Jurisdictional immunities of States and their property

In response to General Assembly resolution 52/151 [YUN 1997, p. 1344], the Secretary-General requested States to submit comments on a convention on jurisdictional immunities of States and their property, for which ILC had drafted articles in 1991 [YUN 1991, p. 829]. Replies received from two States were submitted to the Assembly in an August report [A/54/266].

ILC action. In May, the Commission established the Working Group on Jurisdictional Immunities of States and Their Property to prepare preliminary comments, as requested in Assembly resolution 53/98 [YUN 1998, p. 1215]. The Commission took note of the Working Group's report and adopted its suggestions, as amended in the course of discussions, and annexed it to the report on its fifty-first session [A/54/10 & Corr.1,2].

Sixth Committee consideration. In accordance with Assembly resolution 53/98, the Sixth Committee established an open-ended working group to consider outstanding substantive issues related to the draft articles on jurisdictional immunities of States and their property, which met in November 1999. In his report to the Committee [A/C.6/54/L.12], the Working Group's Chairman stated that progress seemed feasible towards achieving an instrument on the topic and it seemed advisable to continue attempts towards elaborating an instrument in order to maintain and intensify the momentum obtained in the Working Group's discussions.

GENERAL ASSEMBLY ACTION

On 9 December [meeting 76], the General Assembly, on the recommendation of the Sixth Committee [A/54/607], adopted **resolution 54/101** without vote [agenda item 152].

Convention on jurisdictional immunities of States and their property

The General Assembly,

Recalling its resolution 53/98 of 8 December 1998,

Having considered the report of the Working Group on Jurisdictional Immunities of States and Their Property of the International Law Commission, set forth in the annex to the report of the Commission on the work of its fifty-first session,

Having considered also the report presented to the Sixth Committee by the Chairman of the open-ended working group of the Committee established under resolution 53/98,

Having considered further the report of the Secretary-General,

1. *Takes note with appreciation* of the report of the Working Group on Jurisdictional Immunities of States and Their Property of the International Law Commission, set forth in the annex to the report of the Commission on the work of its fifty-first session;

2. *Urges* States, if they have not yet done so, to submit their comments to the Secretary-General in accordance with General Assembly resolution 49/61 of 9 December 1994, and also invites States to submit in writing to the Secretary-General, by 1 August 2000, their comments on the report of the Working Group;

3. *Decides* that the open-ended working group of the Sixth Committee established under resolution 53/98 will continue its work at the fifty-fifth session of the General Assembly to consider the future form of, and outstanding substantive issues related to, the draft articles on jurisdictional immunities of States and their property adopted by the International Law Commission at its forty-third session;

4. *Also decides* to include in the provisional agenda of its fifty-fifth session the item entitled "Convention on jurisdictional immunities of States and their property".

International terrorism

Convention on financing of terrorism

On 9 December, the General Assembly adopted the International Convention for the Suppression of the Financing of Terrorism (see below), the draft text of which was prepared by the Ad Hoc Committee established by Assembly resolution 51/210 [YUN 1996, p. 1208] and the Working Group of the Sixth Committee. The Convention was to be open for signature from 10 January 2000 to 31 December 2001.

The Ad Hoc Committee, which was established to elaborate an international convention for the suppression of terrorist bombings and, subsequently, an international convention for the suppression of acts of nuclear terrorism, as well as to address means of further developing a comprehensive legal framework of conventions dealing with international terrorism, held its third session in New York from 15 to 26 March [A/54/37]. The Assembly had adopted the International Convention for the Suppression of Terrorist Bombings by resolution 52/164 [YUN 1997, p. 1347].

In March, the Ad Hoc Committee completed the first and second readings of the main provisions of the draft convention for the suppression of the financing of terrorism and a number of articles were revised.

Work on the draft convention continued in the Working Group of the Sixth Committee, as decided by the Assembly in resolution 53/108 [YUN 1998, p. 1217], which met between 27 September and 8 October. It annexed the draft text of the convention to its report [A/C.6/54/L.2] and submitted it to the Sixth Committee for consideration.

GENERAL ASSEMBLY ACTION

On 9 December [meeting 76], the General Assembly, on the recommendation of the Sixth Committee [A/54/615], adopted **resolution 54/109** without vote [agenda item 160].

International Convention for the Suppression of the Financing of Terrorism

The General Assembly,

Recalling all its relevant resolutions, including resolution 46/51 of 9 December 1991, resolution 49/60 of 9 December 1994, by which it adopted the Declaration on Measures to Eliminate International Terrorism, and resolutions 51/210 of 17 December 1996 and 53/108 of 8 December 1998,

Having considered the text of the draft international convention for the suppression of the financing of terrorism prepared by the Ad Hoc Committee established by General Assembly resolution 51/210 of 17 December 1996 and the Working Group of the Sixth Committee,

1. *Adopts* the International Convention for the Suppression of the Financing of Terrorism annexed to the

present resolution, and requests the Secretary-General to open it for signature at United Nations Headquarters in New York from 10 January 2000 to 31 December 2001;

2. *Urges* all States to sign and ratify, accept, approve or accede to the Convention.

ANNEX

International Convention for the Suppression of the Financing of Terrorism

Preamble

The States Parties to this Convention,

Bearing in mind the purposes and principles of the Charter of the United Nations concerning the maintenance of international peace and security and the promotion of good-neighbourliness and friendly relations and cooperation among States,

Deeply concerned about the worldwide escalation of acts of terrorism in all its forms and manifestations,

Recalling the Declaration on the Occasion of the Fiftieth Anniversary of the United Nations, contained in General Assembly resolution 50/6 of 24 October 1995,

Recalling also all the relevant General Assembly resolutions on the matter, including resolution 49/60 of 9 December 1994 and the annex thereto on the Declaration on Measures to Eliminate International Terrorism, in which the States Members of the United Nations solemnly reaffirmed their unequivocal condemnation of all acts, methods and practices of terrorism as criminal and unjustifiable, wherever and by whomever committed, including those which jeopardize the friendly relations among States and peoples and threaten the territorial integrity and security of States,

Noting that the Declaration on Measures to Eliminate International Terrorism also encouraged States to review urgently the scope of the existing international legal provisions on the prevention, repression and elimination of terrorism in all its forms and manifestations, with the aim of ensuring that there is a comprehensive legal framework covering all aspects of the matter,

Recalling paragraph 3 *(f)* of General Assembly resolution 51/210 of 17 December 1996, in which the Assembly called upon all States to take steps to prevent and counteract, through appropriate domestic measures, the financing of terrorists and terrorist organizations, whether such financing is direct or indirect through organizations which also have or claim to have charitable, social or cultural goals or which are also engaged in unlawful activities such as illicit arms trafficking, drug dealing and racketeering, including the exploitation of persons for purposes of funding terrorist activities, and in particular to consider, where appropriate, adopting regulatory measures to prevent and counteract movements of funds suspected to be intended for terrorist purposes without impeding in any way the freedom of legitimate capital movements and to intensify the exchange of information concerning international movements of such funds,

Recalling also General Assembly resolution 52/165 of 15 December 1997, in which the Assembly called upon States to consider, in particular, the implementation of the measures set out in paragraphs 3 *(a)* to *(f)* of its resolution 51/210,

Recalling further General Assembly resolution 53/108 of 8 December 1998, in which the Assembly decided that the Ad Hoc Committee established by General Assembly resolution 51/210 of 17 December 1996 should elaborate a draft international convention for the suppression of terrorist financing to supplement related existing international instruments,

Considering that the financing of terrorism is a matter of grave concern to the international community as a whole,

Noting that the number and seriousness of acts of international terrorism depend on the financing that terrorists may obtain,

Noting also that existing multilateral legal instruments do not expressly address such financing,

Being convinced of the urgent need to enhance international cooperation among States in devising and adopting effective measures for the prevention of the financing of terrorism, as well as for its suppression through the prosecution and punishment of its perpetrators,

Have agreed as follows:

Article 1

For the purposes of this Convention:

1. "Funds" means assets of every kind, whether tangible or intangible, movable or immovable, however acquired, and legal documents or instruments in any form, including electronic or digital, evidencing title to, or interest in, such assets, including, but not limited to, bank credits, travellers cheques, bank cheques, money orders, shares, securities, bonds, drafts and letters of credit.

2. "State or government facility" means any permanent or temporary facility or conveyance that is used or occupied by representatives of a State, members of Government, the legislature or the judiciary or by officials or employees of a State or any other public authority or entity or by employees or officials of an intergovernmental organization in connection with their official duties.

3. "Proceeds" means any funds derived from or obtained, directly or indirectly, through the commission of an offence set forth in article 2.

Article 2

1. Any person commits an offence within the meaning of this Convention if that person by any means, directly or indirectly, unlawfully and wilfully, provides or collects funds with the intention that they should be used or in the knowledge that they are to be used, in full or in part, in order to carry out:

(a) An act which constitutes an offence within the scope of and as defined in one of the treaties listed in the annex; or

(b) Any other act intended to cause death or serious bodily injury to a civilian, or to any other person not taking an active part in the hostilities in a situation of armed conflict, when the purpose of such act, by its nature or context, is to intimidate a population, or to compel a Government or an international organization to do or to abstain from doing any act.

2. *(a)* On depositing its instrument of ratification, acceptance, approval or accession, a State Party which is not a party to a treaty listed in the annex may declare that, in the application of this Convention to the State Party, the treaty shall be deemed not to be included in the annex referred to in paragraph 1, subparagraph *(a)*. The declaration shall cease to have effect as soon as the

treaty enters into force for the State Party, which shall notify the depositary of this fact;

(b) When a State Party ceases to be a party to a treaty listed in the annex, it may make a declaration as provided for in this article, with respect to that treaty.

3. For an act to constitute an offence set forth in paragraph 1, it shall not be necessary that the funds were actually used to carry out an offence referred to in paragraph 1, subparagraph *(a)* or *(b)*.

4. Any person also commits an offence if that person attempts to commit an offence as set forth in paragraph 1 of this article.

5. Any person also commits an offence if that person:

(a) Participates as an accomplice in an offence as set forth in paragraph 1 or 4 of this article;

(b) Organizes or directs others to commit an offence as set forth in paragraph 1 or 4 of this article;

(c) Contributes to the commission of one or more offences as set forth in paragraph 1 or 4 of this article by a group of persons acting with a common purpose. Such contribution shall be intentional and shall either:

(i) Be made with the aim of furthering the criminal activity or criminal purpose of the group, where such activity or purpose involves the commission of an offence as set forth in paragraph 1 of this article; or

(ii) Be made in the knowledge of the intention of the group to commit an offence as set forth in paragraph 1 of this article.

Article 3

This Convention shall not apply where the offence is committed within a single State, the alleged offender is a national of that State and is present in the territory of that State and no other State has a basis under article 7, paragraph 1 or 2, to exercise jurisdiction, except that the provisions of articles 12 to 18 shall, as appropriate, apply in those cases.

Article 4

Each State Party shall adopt such measures as may be necessary:

(a) To establish as criminal offences under its domestic law the offences as set forth in article 2;

(b) To make those offences punishable by appropriate penalties which take into account the grave nature of the offences.

Article 5

1. Each State Party, in accordance with its domestic legal principles, shall take the necessary measures to enable a legal entity located in its territory or organized under its laws to be held liable when a person responsible for the management or control of that legal entity has, in that capacity, committed an offence as set forth in article 2. Such liability may be criminal, civil or administrative.

2. Such liability is incurred without prejudice to the criminal liability of individuals who have committed the offences.

3. Each State Party shall ensure, in particular, that legal entities liable in accordance with paragraph 1 above are subject to effective, proportionate and dissuasive criminal, civil or administrative sanctions. Such sanctions may include monetary sanctions.

Article 6

Each State Party shall adopt such measures as may be necessary, including, where appropriate, domestic legislation, to ensure that criminal acts within the scope of this Convention are under no circumstances justifiable by considerations of a political, philosophical, ideological, racial, ethnic, religious or other similar nature.

Article 7

1. Each State Party shall take such measures as may be necessary to establish its jurisdiction over the offences set forth in article 2 when:

(a) The offence is committed in the territory of that State;

(b) The offence is committed on board a vessel flying the flag of that State or an aircraft registered under the laws of that State at the time the offence is committed;

(c) The offence is committed by a national of that State.

2. A State Party may also establish its jurisdiction over any such offence when:

(a) The offence was directed towards or resulted in the carrying out of an offence referred to in article 2, paragraph 1, subparagraph *(a)* or *(b)*, in the territory of or against a national of that State;

(b) The offence was directed towards or resulted in the carrying out of an offence referred to in article 2, paragraph 1, subparagraph *(a)* or *(b)*, against a State or government facility of that State abroad, including diplomatic or consular premises of that State;

(c) The offence was directed towards or resulted in an offence referred to in article 2, paragraph 1, subparagraph *(a)* or *(b)*, committed in an attempt to compel that State to do or abstain from doing any act;

(d) The offence is committed by a stateless person who has his or her habitual residence in the territory of that State;

(e) The offence is committed on board an aircraft which is operated by the Government of that State.

3. Upon ratifying, accepting, approving or acceding to this Convention, each State Party shall notify the Secretary-General of the United Nations of the jurisdiction it has established in accordance with paragraph 2. Should any change take place, the State Party concerned shall immediately notify the Secretary-General.

4. Each State Party shall likewise take such measures as may be necessary to establish its jurisdiction over the offences set forth in article 2 in cases where the alleged offender is present in its territory and it does not extradite that person to any of the States Parties that have established their jurisdiction in accordance with paragraphs 1 or 2.

5. When more than one State Party claims jurisdiction over the offences set forth in article 2, the relevant States Parties shall strive to coordinate their actions appropriately, in particular concerning the conditions for prosecution and the modalities for mutual legal assistance.

6. Without prejudice to the norms of general international law, this Convention does not exclude the exercise of any criminal jurisdiction established by a State Party in accordance with its domestic law.

Article 8

1. Each State Party shall take appropriate measures, in accordance with its domestic legal principles, for the

identification, detection and freezing or seizure of any funds used or allocated for the purpose of committing the offences set forth in article 2 as well as the proceeds derived from such offences, for purposes of possible forfeiture.

2. Each State Party shall take appropriate measures, in accordance with its domestic legal principles, for the forfeiture of funds used or allocated for the purpose of committing the offences set forth in article 2 and the proceeds derived from such offences.

3. Each State Party concerned may give consideration to concluding agreements on the sharing with other States Parties, on a regular or case-by-case basis, of the funds derived from the forfeitures referred to in this article.

4. Each State Party shall consider establishing mechanisms whereby the funds derived from the forfeitures referred to in this article are utilized to compensate the victims of offences referred to in article 2, paragraph 1, subparagraph *(a)* or *(b)*, or their families.

5. The provisions of this article shall be implemented without prejudice to the rights of third parties acting in good faith.

Article 9

1. Upon receiving information that a person who has committed or who is alleged to have committed an offence set forth in article 2 may be present in its territory, the State Party concerned shall take such measures as may be necessary under its domestic law to investigate the facts contained in the information.

2. Upon being satisfied that the circumstances so warrant, the State Party in whose territory the offender or alleged offender is present shall take the appropriate measures under its domestic law so as to ensure that person's presence for the purpose of prosecution or extradition.

3. Any person regarding whom the measures referred to in paragraph 2 are being taken shall be entitled:

(a) To communicate without delay with the nearest appropriate representative of the State of which that person is a national or which is otherwise entitled to protect that person's rights or, if that person is a stateless person, the State in the territory of which that person habitually resides;

(b) To be visited by a representative of that State;

(c) To be informed of that person's rights under subparagraphs *(a)* and *(b)*.

4. The rights referred to in paragraph 3 shall be exercised in conformity with the laws and regulations of the State in the territory of which the offender or alleged offender is present, subject to the provision that the said laws and regulations must enable full effect to be given to the purposes for which the rights accorded under paragraph 3 are intended.

5. The provisions of paragraphs 3 and 4 shall be without prejudice to the right of any State Party having a claim to jurisdiction in accordance with article 7, paragraph 1, subparagraph *(b)*, or paragraph 2, subparagraph *(b)*, to invite the International Committee of the Red Cross to communicate with and visit the alleged offender.

6. When a State Party, pursuant to the present article, has taken a person into custody, it shall immediately notify, directly or through the Secretary-General of the United Nations, the States Parties which have established jurisdiction in accordance with article 7, paragraph 1 or 2, and, if it considers it advisable, any other interested States Parties, of the fact that such person is in custody and of the circumstances which warrant that person's detention. The State which makes the investigation contemplated in paragraph 1 shall promptly inform the said States Parties of its findings and shall indicate whether it intends to exercise jurisdiction.

Article 10

1. The State Party in the territory of which the alleged offender is present shall, in cases to which article 7 applies, if it does not extradite that person, be obliged, without exception whatsoever and whether or not the offence was committed in its territory, to submit the case without undue delay to its competent authorities for the purpose of prosecution, through proceedings in accordance with the laws of that State. Those authorities shall take their decision in the same manner as in the case of any other offence of a grave nature under the law of that State.

2. Whenever a State Party is permitted under its domestic law to extradite or otherwise surrender one of its nationals only upon the condition that the person will be returned to that State to serve the sentence imposed as a result of the trial or proceeding for which the extradition or surrender of the person was sought, and this State and the State seeking the extradition of the person agree with this option and other terms they may deem appropriate, such a conditional extradition or surrender shall be sufficient to discharge the obligation set forth in paragraph 1.

Article 11

1. The offences set forth in article 2 shall be deemed to be included as extraditable offences in any extradition treaty existing between any of the States Parties before the entry into force of this Convention. States Parties undertake to include such offences as extraditable offences in every extradition treaty to be subsequently concluded between them.

2. When a State Party which makes extradition conditional on the existence of a treaty receives a request for extradition from another State Party with which it has no extradition treaty, the requested State Party may, at its option, consider this Convention as a legal basis for extradition in respect of the offences set forth in article 2. Extradition shall be subject to the other conditions provided by the law of the requested State.

3. States Parties which do not make extradition conditional on the existence of a treaty shall recognize the offences set forth in article 2 as extraditable offences between themselves, subject to the conditions provided by the law of the requested State.

4. If necessary, the offences set forth in article 2 shall be treated, for the purposes of extradition between States Parties, as if they had been committed not only in the place in which they occurred but also in the territory of the States that have established jurisdiction in accordance with article 7, paragraphs 1 and 2.

5. The provisions of all extradition treaties and arrangements between States Parties with regard to offences set forth in article 2 shall be deemed to be modified as between States Parties to the extent that they are incompatible with this Convention.

Article 12

1. States Parties shall afford one another the greatest measure of assistance in connection with criminal investigations or criminal or extradition proceedings in respect of the offences set forth in article 2, including assistance in obtaining evidence in their possession necessary for the proceedings.

2. States Parties may not refuse a request for mutual legal assistance on the ground of bank secrecy.

3. The requesting Party shall not transmit or use information or evidence furnished by the requested Party for investigations, prosecutions or proceedings other than those stated in the request without the prior consent of the requested Party.

4. Each State Party may give consideration to establishing mechanisms to share with other States Parties information or evidence needed to establish criminal, civil or administrative liability pursuant to article 5.

5. States Parties shall carry out their obligations under paragraphs 1 and 2 in conformity with any treaties or other arrangements on mutual legal assistance or information exchange that may exist between them. In the absence of such treaties or arrangements, States Parties shall afford one another assistance in accordance with their domestic law.

Article 13

None of the offences set forth in article 2 shall be regarded, for the purposes of extradition or mutual legal assistance, as a fiscal offence. Accordingly, States Parties may not refuse a request for extradition or for mutual legal assistance on the sole ground that it concerns a fiscal offence.

Article 14

None of the offences set forth in article 2 shall be regarded for the purposes of extradition or mutual legal assistance as a political offence or as an offence connected with a political offence or as an offence inspired by political motives. Accordingly, a request for extradition or for mutual legal assistance based on such an offence may not be refused on the sole ground that it concerns a political offence or an offence connected with a political offence or an offence inspired by political motives.

Article 15

Nothing in this Convention shall be interpreted as imposing an obligation to extradite or to afford mutual legal assistance, if the requested State Party has substantial grounds for believing that the request for extradition for offences set forth in article 2 or for mutual legal assistance with respect to such offences has been made for the purpose of prosecuting or punishing a person on account of that person's race, religion, nationality, ethnic origin or political opinion or that compliance with the request would cause prejudice to that person's position for any of these reasons.

Article 16

1. A person who is being detained or is serving a sentence in the territory of one State Party whose presence in another State Party is requested for purposes of identification, testimony or otherwise providing assistance in obtaining evidence for the investigation or prosecution of offences set forth in article 2 may be transferred if the following conditions are met:

(a) The person freely gives his or her informed consent;

(b) The competent authorities of both States agree, subject to such conditions as those States may deem appropriate.

2. For the purposes of the present article:

(a) The State to which the person is transferred shall have the authority and obligation to keep the person transferred in custody, unless otherwise requested or authorized by the State from which the person was transferred;

(b) The State to which the person is transferred shall without delay implement its obligation to return the person to the custody of the State from which the person was transferred as agreed beforehand, or as otherwise agreed, by the competent authorities of both States;

(c) The State to which the person is transferred shall not require the State from which the person was transferred to initiate extradition proceedings for the return of the person;

(d) The person transferred shall receive credit for service of the sentence being served in the State from which he or she was transferred for time spent in the custody of the State to which he or she was transferred.

3. Unless the State Party from which a person is to be transferred in accordance with the present article so agrees, that person, whatever his or her nationality, shall not be prosecuted or detained or subjected to any other restriction of his or her personal liberty in the territory of the State to which that person is transferred in respect of acts or convictions anterior to his or her departure from the territory of the State from which such person was transferred.

Article 17

Any person who is taken into custody or regarding whom any other measures are taken or proceedings are carried out pursuant to this Convention shall be guaranteed fair treatment, including enjoyment of all rights and guarantees in conformity with the law of the State in the territory of which that person is present and applicable provisions of international law, including international human rights law.

Article 18

1. States Parties shall cooperate in the prevention of the offences set forth in article 2 by taking all practicable measures, *inter alia*, by adapting their domestic legislation, if necessary, to prevent and counter preparations in their respective territories for the commission of those offences within or outside their territories, including:

(a) Measures to prohibit in their territories illegal activities of persons and organizations that knowingly encourage, instigate, organize or engage in the commission of offences set forth in article 2;

(b) Measures requiring financial institutions and other professions involved in financial transactions to utilize the most efficient measures available for the identification of their usual or occasional customers, as well as customers in whose interest accounts are opened, and to pay special attention to unusual or suspicious transactions and report transactions suspected of stemming from a criminal activity. For this purpose, States Parties shall consider:

(i) Adopting regulations prohibiting the opening of accounts, the holders or beneficiaries of which are unidentified or unidentifiable, and measures to ensure that such institutions verify the identity of the real owners of such transactions;

(ii) With respect to the identification of legal entities, requiring financial institutions, when necessary, to take measures to verify the legal existence and the structure of the customer by obtaining, either from a public register or from the customer or both, proof of incorporation, including information concerning the customer's name, legal form, address, directors and provisions regulating the power to bind the entity;

(iii) Adopting regulations imposing on financial institutions the obligation to report promptly to the competent authorities all complex, unusual large transactions and unusual patterns of transactions, which have no apparent economic or obviously lawful purpose, without fear of assuming criminal or civil liability for breach of any restriction on disclosure of information if they report their suspicions in good faith;

(iv) Requiring financial institutions to maintain, for at least five years, all necessary records on transactions, both domestic and international.

2. States Parties shall further cooperate in the prevention of offences set forth in article 2 by considering:

(a) Measures for the supervision, including, for example, the licensing, of all money-transmission agencies;

(b) Feasible measures to detect or monitor the physical cross-border transportation of cash and bearer negotiable instruments, subject to strict safeguards to ensure proper use of information and without impeding in any way the freedom of capital movements.

3. States Parties shall further cooperate in the prevention of the offences set forth in article 2 by exchanging accurate and verified information in accordance with their domestic law and coordinating administrative and other measures taken, as appropriate, to prevent the commission of offences set forth in article 2, in particular by:

(a) Establishing and maintaining channels of communication between their competent agencies and services to facilitate the secure and rapid exchange of information concerning all aspects of offences set forth in article 2;

(b) Cooperating with one another in conducting inquiries, with respect to the offences set forth in article 2, concerning:

(i) The identity, whereabouts and activities of persons in respect of whom reasonable suspicion exists that they are involved in such offences;

(ii) The movement of funds relating to the commission of such offences.

4. States Parties may exchange information through the International Criminal Police Organization (Interpol).

Article 19

The State Party where the alleged offender is prosecuted shall, in accordance with its domestic law or applicable procedures, communicate the final outcome of the proceedings to the Secretary-General of the United Nations, who shall transmit the information to the other States Parties.

Article 20

The States Parties shall carry out their obligations under this Convention in a manner consistent with the principles of sovereign equality and territorial integrity of States and that of non-intervention in the domestic affairs of other States.

Article 21

Nothing in this Convention shall affect other rights, obligations and responsibilities of States and individuals under international law, in particular the purposes of the Charter of the United Nations, international humanitarian law and other relevant conventions.

Article 22

Nothing in this Convention entitles a State Party to undertake in the territory of another State Party the exercise of jurisdiction or performance of functions which are exclusively reserved for the authorities of that other State Party by its domestic law.

Article 23

1. The annex may be amended by the addition of relevant treaties:

(a) That are open to the participation of all States;

(b) That have entered into force;

(c) That have been ratified, accepted, approved or acceded to by at least twenty-two States Parties to the present Convention.

2. After the entry into force of this Convention, any State Party may propose such an amendment. Any proposal for an amendment shall be communicated to the depositary in written form. The depositary shall notify proposals that meet the requirements of paragraph 1 to all States Parties and seek their views on whether the proposed amendment should be adopted.

3. The proposed amendment shall be deemed adopted unless one third of the States Parties object to it by a written notification not later than 180 days after its circulation.

4. The adopted amendment to the annex shall enter into force 30 days after the deposit of the twenty-second instrument of ratification, acceptance or approval of such amendment for all those States Parties that have deposited such an instrument. For each State Party ratifying, accepting or approving the amendment after the deposit of the twenty-second instrument, the amendment shall enter into force on the thirtieth day after deposit by such State Party of its instrument of ratification, acceptance or approval.

Article 24

1. Any dispute between two or more States Parties concerning the interpretation or application of this Convention which cannot be settled through negotiation within a reasonable time shall, at the request of one of them, be submitted to arbitration. If, within six months from the date of the request for arbitration, the parties are unable to agree on the organization of the arbitration, any one of those parties may refer the dispute to the International Court of Justice, by application, in conformity with the Statute of the Court.

2. Each State may at the time of signature, ratification, acceptance or approval of this Convention or accession thereto declare that it does not consider itself

bound by paragraph 1. The other States Parties shall not be bound by paragraph 1 with respect to any State Party which has made such a reservation.

3. Any State which has made a reservation in accordance with paragraph 2 may at any time withdraw that reservation by notification to the Secretary-General of the United Nations.

Article 25

1. This Convention shall be open for signature by all States from 10 January 2000 to 31 December 2001 at United Nations Headquarters in New York.

2. This Convention is subject to ratification, acceptance or approval. The instruments of ratification, acceptance or approval shall be deposited with the Secretary-General of the United Nations.

3. This Convention shall be open to accession by any State. The instruments of accession shall be deposited with the Secretary-General of the United Nations.

Article 26

1. This Convention shall enter into force on the thirtieth day following the date of the deposit of the twenty-second instrument of ratification, acceptance, approval or accession with the Secretary-General of the United Nations.

2. For each State ratifying, accepting, approving or acceding to the Convention after the deposit of the twenty-second instrument of ratification, acceptance, approval or accession, the Convention shall enter into force on the thirtieth day after deposit by such State of its instrument of ratification, acceptance, approval or accession.

Article 27

1. Any State Party may denounce this Convention by written notification to the Secretary-General of the United Nations.

2. Denunciation shall take effect one year following the date on which notification is received by the Secretary-General of the United Nations.

Article 28

The original of this Convention, of which the Arabic, Chinese, English, French, Russian and Spanish texts are equally authentic, shall be deposited with the Secretary-General of the United Nations who shall send certified copies thereof to all States.

IN WITNESS WHEREOF, the undersigned, being duly authorized thereto by their respective Governments, have signed this Convention, opened for signature at United Nations Headquarters in New York on 10 January 2000.

ANNEX

1. Convention for the Suppression of Unlawful Seizure of Aircraft, done at The Hague on 16 December 1970.

2. Convention for the Suppression of Unlawful Acts against the Safety of Civil Aviation, done at Montreal on 23 September 1971.

3. Convention on the Prevention and Punishment of Crimes against Internationally Protected Persons, including Diplomatic Agents, adopted by the General Assembly of the United Nations on 14 December 1973.

4. International Convention against the Taking of Hostages, adopted by the General Assembly of the United Nations on 17 December 1979.

5. Convention on the Physical Protection of Nuclear Material, adopted at Vienna on 3 March 1980.

6. Protocol for the Suppression of Unlawful Acts of Violence at Airports Serving International Civil Aviation, supplementary to the Convention for the Suppression of Unlawful Acts against the Safety of Civil Aviation, done at Montreal on 24 February 1988.

7. Convention for the Suppression of Unlawful Acts against the Safety of Maritime Navigation, done at Rome on 10 March 1988.

8. Protocol for the Suppression of Unlawful Acts against the Safety of Fixed Platforms located on the Continental Shelf, done at Rome on 10 March 1988.

9. International Convention for the Suppression of Terrorist Bombings, adopted by the General Assembly of the United Nations on 15 December 1997.

Measures to eliminate terrorism

In response to General Assembly resolution 50/53 [YUN 1995, p. 1330], the Secretary-General submitted a report, with later addendum [A/54/301 & Corr.1 & Add.1], containing responses from States and international organizations to his request for information on their implementation of the Declaration on Measures to Eliminate Terrorism, contained in resolution 49/60 [YUN 1994, p. 1293]. As at 28 October, replies had been received from 22 States and seven international organizations, as well as from the United Nations Office for Drug Control and Crime Prevention.

GENERAL ASSEMBLY ACTION

On 9 December [meeting 76], the General Assembly, on the recommendation of the Sixth Committee [A/54/615], adopted **resolution 54/110** by recorded vote (149-0-2) [agenda item 160].

Measures to eliminate international terrorism

The General Assembly,

Guided by the purposes and principles of the Charter of the United Nations,

Recalling all its relevant resolutions, including resolution 49/60 of 9 December 1994, by which it adopted the Declaration on Measures to Eliminate International Terrorism, and resolutions 50/53 of 11 December 1995, 51/210 of 17 December 1996, 52/165 of 15 December 1997 and 53/108 of 8 December 1998, as well as Security Council resolution 1269(1999) of 19 October 1999,

Recalling also the Declaration on the Occasion of the Fiftieth Anniversary of the United Nations,

Deeply disturbed by the persistence of terrorist acts, which have been carried out worldwide,

Stressing the need to strengthen further international cooperation between States and between international organizations and agencies, regional organizations and arrangements and the United Nations in order to prevent, combat and eliminate terrorism in all its forms and manifestations, wherever and by whomsoever committed,

Mindful of the need to enhance the role of the United Nations and the relevant specialized agencies in combating international terrorism, and of the proposals of the Secretary-General to enhance the role of the Organization in this respect,

Convinced of the importance of the consideration of measures to eliminate international terrorism by the General Assembly as the universal organ having competence to do so,

Recalling the Declaration on Measures to Eliminate International Terrorism, contained in the annex to resolution 49/60, wherein the General Assembly encouraged States to review urgently the scope of the existing international legal provisions on the prevention, repression and elimination of terrorism in all its forms and manifestations, with the aim of ensuring that there was a comprehensive legal framework covering all aspects of the matter,

Taking note of the final communiqué of the meeting of Ministers for Foreign Affairs and Heads of Delegation of the Movement of Non-Aligned Countries, held in New York on 23 September 1999, which reiterated the collective position of the Movement of Non-Aligned Countries on terrorism and reaffirmed the previous initiative of the Twelfth Conference of Heads of State or Government of Non-Aligned Countries, held at Durban, South Africa, from 29 August to 3 September 1998, calling for an international summit conference under the auspices of the United Nations to formulate a joint organized response of the international community to terrorism in all its forms and manifestations,

Recalling its decision in resolution 53/108 to address at its fifty-fourth session the question of convening a high-level conference in 2000 under the auspices of the United Nations to formulate a joint organized response of the international community to terrorism in all its forms and manifestations,

Noting regional efforts to prevent, combat and eliminate terrorism in all its forms and manifestations, wherever and by whomsoever committed, including through the elaboration of and adherence to regional conventions,

Having examined the report of the Secretary-General,

1. *Strongly condemns* all acts, methods and practices of terrorism as criminal and unjustifiable, wherever and by whomsoever committed;

2. *Reiterates* that criminal acts intended or calculated to provoke a state of terror in the general public, a group of persons or particular persons for political purposes are in any circumstances unjustifiable, whatever the considerations of a political, philosophical, ideological, racial, ethnic, religious or other nature that may be invoked to justify them;

3. *Reiterates its call* upon all States to adopt further measures in accordance with the relevant provisions of international law, including international standards of human rights, to prevent terrorism and to strengthen international cooperation in combating terrorism and, to that end, to consider in particular the implementation of the measures set out in paragraphs 3 *(a)* to *(f)* of resolution 51/210;

4. *Also reiterates its call* upon all States, with the aim of enhancing the efficient implementation of relevant legal instruments, to intensify, as and where appropriate, the exchange of information on facts related to terrorism and, in so doing, to avoid the dissemination of inaccurate or unverified information;

5. *Reiterates its call* upon States to refrain from financing, encouraging, providing training for or otherwise supporting terrorist activities;

6. *Reaffirms* that international cooperation as well as actions by States to combat terrorism should be conducted in conformity with the principles of the Charter of the United Nations, international law and relevant international conventions;

7. *Urges* all States that have not yet done so to consider, as a matter of priority, becoming parties to relevant conventions and protocols as referred to in paragraph 6 of resolution 51/210, as well as the International Convention for the Suppression of Terrorist Bombings, and calls upon all States to enact, as appropriate, domestic legislation necessary to implement the provisions of those conventions and protocols, to ensure that the jurisdiction of their courts enables them to bring to trial the perpetrators of terrorist acts, and to cooperate with and provide support and assistance to other States and relevant international and regional organizations to that end;

8. *Reaffirms* the Declaration on Measures to Eliminate International Terrorism contained in the annex to resolution 49/60 and the Declaration to Supplement the 1994 Declaration on Measures to Eliminate International Terrorism contained in the annex to resolution 51/210, and calls upon all States to implement them;

9. *Notes* the establishment of the Terrorism Prevention Branch of the Centre for International Crime Prevention in Vienna, and welcomes its efforts, after reviewing existing possibilities within the United Nations system, to enhance through research and technical cooperation the capabilities of the United Nations in the prevention of terrorism;

10. *Invites* States that have not yet done so to submit to the Secretary-General information on their national laws and regulations regarding the prevention and suppression of acts of international terrorism;

11. *Invites* regional intergovernmental organizations to submit to the Secretary-General information on the measures they have adopted at the regional level to eliminate international terrorism;

12. *Decides* that the Ad Hoc Committee established by General Assembly resolution 51/210 of 17 December 1996 shall continue to elaborate a draft international convention for the suppression of acts of nuclear terrorism with a view to completing the instrument, shall address means of further developing a comprehensive legal framework of conventions dealing with international terrorism, including considering the elaboration of a comprehensive convention on international terrorism, and shall address the question of convening a high-level conference under the auspices of the United Nations to formulate a joint organized response of the international community to terrorism in all its forms and manifestations;

13. *Decides also* that the Ad Hoc Committee shall meet from 14 to 18 February 2000, devoting appropriate time to the consideration of the outstanding issues relating to the elaboration of a draft international convention for the suppression of acts of nuclear terrorism, and that it shall address the question of convening a high-level conference under the auspices of the United Nations to formulate a joint organized response of the international community to terrorism in

all its forms and manifestations, and that the work shall continue, including beginning consideration with a view to the elaboration of a comprehensive convention on international terrorism within a comprehensive legal framework of conventions dealing with international terrorism, during the fifty-fifth session of the General Assembly from 25 September to 6 October 2000, within the framework of a working group of the Sixth Committee, and that the Ad Hoc Committee shall be convened in 2001 to continue its work;

14. *Requests* the Secretary-General to continue to provide the Ad Hoc Committee with the necessary facilities for the performance of its work;

15. *Requests* the Ad Hoc Committee to report to the General Assembly at its fifty-fourth session in the event of the completion of the draft international convention for the suppression of acts of nuclear terrorism;

16. *Also requests* the Ad Hoc Committee to report to the General Assembly at its fifty-fifth session on progress made in the implementation of its mandate;

17. *Decides* to include in the provisional agenda of its fifty-fifth session the item entitled "Measures to eliminate international terrorism".

RECORDED VOTE ON RESOLUTION 54/110:

In favour: Algeria, Andorra, Angola, Antigua and Barbuda, Argentina, Armenia, Australia, Austria, Azerbaijan, Bahamas, Bahrain, Bangladesh, Barbados, Belarus, Belgium, Belize, Benin, Bhutan, Bolivia, Botswana, Brazil, Brunei Darussalam, Bulgaria, Burkina Faso, Cambodia, Cameroon, Canada, Cape Verde, Chile, China, Colombia, Congo, Costa Rica, Côte d'Ivoire, Croatia, Cuba, Cyprus, Czech Republic, Denmark, Dominican Republic, Ecuador, Egypt, El Salvador, Equatorial Guinea, Eritrea, Estonia, Ethiopia, Fiji, Finland, France, Georgia, Germany, Ghana, Greece, Grenada, Guatemala, Guinea, Guinea-Bissau, Guyana, Haiti, Honduras, Hungary, Iceland, India, Indonesia, Iran, Ireland, Israel, Italy, Jamaica, Japan, Jordan, Kazakhstan, Kenya, Kuwait, Lao People's Democratic Republic, Latvia, Lesotho, Libyan Arab Jamahiriya, Liechtenstein, Lithuania, Luxembourg, Madagascar, Malawi, Malaysia, Maldives, Mali, Malta, Mauritius, Mexico, Monaco, Morocco, Mozambique, Myanmar, Namibia, Nepal, Netherlands, New Zealand, Nigeria, Norway, Oman, Pakistan, Panama, Paraguay, Peru, Poland, Portugal, Qatar, Republic of Korea, Republic of Moldova, Romania, Russian Federation, Saint Lucia, Saint Vincent and the Grenadines, Samoa, San Marino, Saudi Arabia, Senegal, Sierra Leone, Singapore, Slovakia, Slovenia, Solomon Islands, South Africa, Spain, Sri Lanka, Sudan, Swaziland, Sweden, Tajikistan, Thailand, The former Yugoslav Republic of Macedonia, Togo, Trinidad and Tobago, Tunisia, Turkey, Turkmenistan, Uganda, Ukraine, United Arab Emirates, United Kingdom, United Republic of Tanzania, United States, Uruguay, Uzbekistan, Venezuela, Viet Nam, Yemen, Zambia.

Against: None.

Abstaining: Lebanon, Syrian Arab Republic.

On 23 December, the Assembly decided that the item on measures to eliminate terrorism would remain for consideration at its resumed fifty-fourth (2000) session (**decision 54/465**).

Security Council condemnation of terrorism

On 19 October, the Security Council met, at the initiative of the Russian Federation, to discuss the question of international terrorism and the threat it presented to international peace and security. Several Council members spoke before voting on a draft resolution on the subject. A number of members referred to terrorist attacks on their territory or nationals, including the recent attacks in Russia in which apartment buildings were destroyed and hundreds of their inhabitants killed. Argentina and Brazil referred to the increasing link between terrorism and drug trafficking and other forms of organized crime. Most members expressed the hope that the General Assembly would continue to draw up new instruments and conventions in the area of international terrorism.

SECURITY COUNCIL ACTION

On 19 October [meeting 4053], the Security Council unanimously adopted **resolution 1269(1999)**. The draft [S/1999/1071] was prepared in consultations among Council members.

The Security Council,

Deeply concerned by the increase in acts of international terrorism which endangers the lives and well-being of individuals worldwide as well as the peace and security of all States,

Condemning all acts of terrorism, irrespective of motive, wherever and by whomever committed,

Mindful of all relevant resolutions of the General Assembly, including resolution 49/60 of 9 December 1994, by which it adopted the Declaration on Measures to Eliminate International Terrorism,

Emphasizing the necessity to intensify the fight against terrorism at the national level and to strengthen, under the auspices of the United Nations, effective international cooperation in this field, on the basis of the principles of the Charter of the United Nations and norms of international law, including respect for international humanitarian law and human rights,

Supporting the efforts to promote universal participation in, and implementation of, the existing international anti-terrorist conventions, as well as to develop new international instruments to counter the terrorist threat,

Commending the work done by the General Assembly, relevant United Nations organs and specialized agencies and regional and other organizations to combat international terrorism,

Determined to contribute, in accordance with the Charter, to the efforts to combat terrorism in all its forms,

Reaffirming that the suppression of acts of international terrorism, including those in which States are involved, is an essential contribution to the maintenance of international peace and security,

1. *Unequivocally condemns* all acts, methods and practices of terrorism as criminal and unjustifiable, regardless of their motivation, in all their forms and manifestations, wherever and by whomever committed, in particular those which could threaten international peace and security;

2. *Calls upon* all States to implement fully the international anti-terrorist conventions to which they are parties, encourages all States to consider as a matter of priority adhering to those to which they are not parties, and encourages also the speedy adoption of the pending conventions;

3. *Stresses* the vital role of the United Nations in strengthening international cooperation in combating terrorism, and emphasizes the importance of enhanced coordination among States, international and regional organizations;

4. *Calls upon* all States to take, inter alia, in the context of such cooperation and coordination, appropriate steps:

—To cooperate with each other, particularly through bilateral and multilateral agreements and arrangements, to prevent and suppress terrorist acts, protect their nationals and other persons against terrorist attacks and bring to justice the perpetrators of such acts;

—To prevent and suppress in their territories through all lawful means the preparation and financing of any acts of terrorism;

—To deny those who plan, finance or commit terrorist acts safe havens by ensuring their apprehension and prosecution or extradition;

—To take appropriate measures in conformity with the relevant provisions of national and international law, including international standards of human rights, before granting refugee status, for the purpose of ensuring that the asylum-seeker has not participated in terrorist acts;

—To exchange information in accordance with international and domestic law, and cooperate on administrative and judicial matters in order to prevent the commission of terrorist acts;

5. *Requests* the Secretary-General, in his reports to the General Assembly, in particular those submitted in accordance with its resolution 50/53 of 11 December 1995 on measures to eliminate international terrorism, to pay special attention to the need to prevent and fight the threat to international peace and security as a result of terrorist activities;

6. *Expresses its readiness* to consider relevant provisions of the reports mentioned in paragraph 5 above and to take necessary steps in accordance with its responsibilities under the Charter of the United Nations in order to counter terrorist threats to international peace and security;

7. *Decides* to remain seized of this matter.

Communications. By a 27 October letter [A/54/547], Germany forwarded to the Secretary-General a statement against terrorism, adopted at the Ministerial Conference of the Group of Eight industrialized countries (Moscow, 19-20 October). It emphasized that all States should prevent and suppress in their territories the preparation for and financing of terrorist actions and included a communiqué on combating transnational organized crime.

On 29 October [A/54/519-S/1999/1114], Ukraine forwarded to the Secretary-General the text of a statement by Ministers for Foreign Affairs of the Commonwealth of Independent States on joint actions in connection with the increase of the threat of terrorism.

Burkina Faso, in its capacity as Chairman of the Islamic Group, transmitted a 19 November letter to the Secretary-General [A/54/637-S/1999/1204] enclosing the text of the Convention of the Organization of the Islamic Conference on Combating International Terrorism, adopted by the Islamic Conference of Foreign Ministers at its twenty-sixth session (Ouagadougou, Burkina Faso, 28 June-1 July).

Diplomatic relations

Protection of diplomatic and consular missions and representatives

As at 31 December 1999, the number of parties to the various international conventions relating to the protection of diplomats and diplomatic and consular relations was as follows: 179 States were parties to the Vienna Convention on Diplomatic Relations [YUN 1961, p. 512], 48 States were parties to the Optional Protocol concerning acquisition of nationality [ibid., p. 516] and 62 States were parties to the Optional Protocol concerning the compulsory settlement of disputes [ibid.].

The 1963 Vienna Convention on Consular Relations [YUN 1963, p. 510] had 163 parties, 38 States were parties to the Optional Protocol concerning acquisition of nationality [ibid., p. 512] and 45 States were parties to the Optional Protocol concerning the compulsory settlement of disputes [ibid.].

The 1973 Convention on the Prevention and Punishment of Crimes against Internationally Protected Persons, including Diplomatic Agents [YUN 1973, p. 775] had 102 States parties.

Report of Secretary-General. In accordance with General Assembly resolution 53/97 [YUN 1998, p. 1222], the Secretary-General invited Member States to communicate their views on measures to enhance the protection, security and safety of diplomatic and consular missions and representatives as provided for in Assembly resolution 42/154 [YUN 1987, p. 1068] and to report to him serious violations. In an October report [A/INF/54/5], the Secretary-General presented the texts and analytical summary of information received. Austria, Denmark, Estonia, Sweden and Switzerland provided information on incidents involving offences against other States committed by groups in their countries. Most incidents involved occupation of embassies or attacks on them. Israel reported on violations in connection with its embassies in Brussels and Oslo and an attack on the Israeli Consulate General in Berlin. The Secretary-General sent four reminders to States that had not responded to a case reported by another State.

Treaties and agreements

Reservations to treaties

In 1999, ILC considered the fourth report of Special Rapporteur Alain Pellet (France) on the law and practice relating to reservations to treaties [A/CN.4/499], as well as part of his third report which it could not consider at its fiftieth session [YUN 1998, p. 1223]. The Commission, having referred a number of draft guidelines to the Drafting Committee, considered its report and provisionally adopted on first reading 18 draft guidelines and new versions of two draft guidelines. The texts of the draft guidelines and related commentaries were included in ILC's report [A/54/10 & Corr.1,2]. The Special Rapporteur also submitted to ILC the revised bibliography on reservations to treaties [A/CN.4/478/Rev.1], which he first submitted in 1996 [YUN 1996, p. 1213].

Treaties involving international organizations

The 1986 Vienna Convention on the Law of Treaties between States and International Organizations or between International Organizations [YUN 1986, p. 1006], which had not yet entered into force, had 26 parties as at 31 December 1999.

Registration and publication of treaties by the United Nations

During 1999, 1,194 international agreements and 1,097 subsequent actions were received by the Secretariat for registration or filing and recording. In addition, there were 1,204 registrations of formalities concerning agreements for which the Secretary-General performed depositary functions.

The texts of international agreements registered or filed and recorded were published in the United Nations *Treaty Series* in the original languages, with translations into English and French where necessary. In 1999, 132 volumes of the *Treaty Series* covering treaties registered or filed and recorded from 1990 through 1997 were issued.

Volumes 24 and 25 of the Cumulative Index to the UN *Treaty Series* were published in English and French in 1999.

Multilateral treaties

The UN *Treaty Series* (approximately 1,850 printed volumes) and the regularly updated status of multilateral treaties deposited with the Secretary-General were available on the Internet at the UN Treaty Collection web site (http://untreaty.un.org).

New multilateral treaties concluded under UN auspices

The following treaties, concluded under UN auspices, were deposited with the Secretary-General during 1999:

Food Aid Convention, 1999, adopted at London on 13 April 1999

Protocol on Water and Health to the 1992 Convention on the Protection and Use of Transboundary Watercourses and International Lakes, adopted at London on 17 June 1999

International Convention on Arrest of Ships, 1999, adopted at Geneva on 12 March 1999

Optional Protocol to the Convention on the Elimination of All Forms of Discrimination against Women, adopted at New York on 6 October 1999

Protocol to the 1979 Convention on Long-range Transboundary Air Pollution to Abate Acidification, Eutrophication and Ground-level Ozone, adopted at Gothenburg, Sweden, on 30 November 1999

International Convention for the Suppression of the Financing of Terrorism, adopted at New York on 9 December 1999

Basel Protocol on Liability and Compensation for Damage resulting from Transboundary Movements of Hazardous Wastes and their Disposal, adopted at Basel on 10 December 1999

Multilateral treaties deposited with the Secretary-General

The number of multilateral treaties for which the Secretary-General performed depositary functions stood at 511 at the end of 1999. During the year, 226 signatures were affixed to treaties for which he performed depositary functions and 1,430 instruments of ratification, accession, acceptance, approval or notification were transmitted to him. In addition, he received 110 communications from States expressing observations or declarations and reservations made at the time of signature, ratification or accession.

The following multilateral treaties in respect of which the Secretary-General acted as depositary came into force in 1999:

Convention on the Safety of United Nations and Associated Personnel, concluded at New York on 9 December 1994

Convention on the Prohibition of the Use, Stockpiling, Production and Transfer of Anti-Personnel Mines and on their Destruction, concluded at Oslo on 18 September 1997

Amendment to the Montreal Protocol on Substances that Deplete the Ozone Layer, adopted by the Ninth Meeting of the Parties, concluded at Montreal on 17 September 1997

European Agreement on Main Inland Waterways of International Importance (AGN), concluded at Geneva on 19 January 1996

Food Aid Convention, 1995, concluded at London on 5 December 1994

International Coffee Agreement, 1994, as extended until 30 September 2001, with modifications, by Resolution No. 384 adopted by the International Coffee Council in London on 21 July 1999, concluded at London on 30 March 1994

Information for 1999 regarding all multilateral treaties deposited with the Secretary-General was contained in *Multilateral Treaties Deposited with the Secretary-General: Status as at 31 December 1999,* vols. I & II (ST/LEG/SER.E/18), Sales No. E.00.V.2.

Chapter IV

Law of the sea

During 1999, the United Nations continued to promote the universal acceptance of the 1982 United Nations Convention on the Law of the Sea and the two related Agreements. The three institutions created by the Convention—the International Seabed Authority, the International Tribunal for the Law of the Sea and the Commission on the Limits of the Continental Shelf—held sessions in 1999. The Council of the Authority completed the first reading of a draft seabed mining code; the Tribunal was concerned with two cases; and the Commission considered data and other material submitted by coastal States concerning the outer limits of the continental shelf where those limits extended beyond 200 nautical miles.

UN Convention on the Law of the Sea

Signatures and ratifications

In 1999, Ukraine and Vanuatu ratified the United Nations Convention on the Law of the Sea, bringing the number of parties to 132.

The Convention, which was adopted by the Third United Nations Conference on the Law of the Sea in 1982 [YUN 1982, p. 178], entered into force on 16 November 1994 [YUN 1994, p. 1301]. It was closed for signature in 1984, having received 159 signatures [YUN 1984, p. 108].

Meeting of States Parties. The ninth Meeting of States Parties to the Convention (New York, 19-28 May) [SPLOS/48] dealt primarily with budgetary matters of the International Tribunal, the rules of procedure of the Meeting and the Meeting's role in reviewing ocean and law of the sea issues. Elections to replace seven members of the Tribunal whose terms had expired on 30 September took place during the Meeting. Several items submitted by the Commission on the Limits of the Continental Shelf were considered.

Agreement relating to the implementation of Part XI of the Convention

During the year, the number of States parties to the Agreement relating to the Implementation of Part XI of the Convention, which was adopted in 1994 by the General Assembly in resolution 48/263 [YUN 1994, p. 1301], reached 96. The Agreement was to be interpreted and applied together with the Convention as a single instrument, and in the event of any inconsistency between the Agreement and Part XI of the Convention, the provisions of the Agreement would prevail. Any ratification or accession to the Convention made after 28 July 1994 represented consent to be bound by the Agreement as well. States that were parties to the Convention prior to the adoption of the Agreement had to establish their consent to be bound by the Agreement separately, by depositing an instrument of ratification or accession.

Agreement on conservation and management of straddling fish stocks and highly migratory stocks

As at 31 December 1999, the 1995 Agreement for the Implementation of the Provisions of the Convention on the Law of the Sea of 10 December 1982 relating to the Conservation and Management of Straddling Fish Stocks and Highly Migratory Fish Stocks [YUN 1995, p. 1334] had been ratified or acceded to by 26 States. It would enter into force 30 days after the date of deposit of the thirtieth instrument of ratification or accession.

Report of Secretary-General. In response to General Assembly resolution 52/28 [YUN 1997, p. 1356], the Secretary-General presented, in October, information provided by States, specialized agencies and other UN bodies, and non-governmental organizations relating to the conservation and management of straddling fish stocks and highly migratory fish stocks [A/54/461].

GENERAL ASSEMBLY ACTION

On 24 November [meeting 62], the General Assembly adopted **resolution 54/32** [draft: A/54/L.28 & Add.1] without vote [agenda item 40 *(b)*].

Agreement for the Implementation of the Provisions of the United Nations Convention on the Law of the Sea of 10 December 1982 relating to the Conservation and Management of Straddling Fish Stocks and Highly Migratory Fish Stocks

The General Assembly,

Recalling the relevant provisions of the United Nations Convention on the Law of the Sea, including Part VII, section 2,

Recognizing that the Agreement for the Implementation of the Provisions of the United Nations Convention on the Law of the Sea of 10 December 1982 relating to the Conservation and Management of Straddling Fish Stocks and Highly Migratory Fish Stocks ("the Agreement") sets forth the rights and obligations of States in authorizing the use of vessels flying their flags for fishing on the high seas,

Noting that while twenty-four States or entities have ratified or acceded to the Agreement, the Agreement has not yet entered into force,

Conscious of the need to promote and facilitate international cooperation, especially at the regional and subregional levels, in order to ensure the sustainable development and use of the living marine resources of the world's oceans and seas, consistent with the present resolution,

Noting that the stock situation for some species of straddling fish stocks and highly migratory fish stocks is of great concern owing to the fact that those stocks have not been subject to adequate regulatory measures,

Recognizing the importance of actions States and other entities should take in order to share responsibly in the use of high seas fishery resources, including straddling fish stocks and highly migratory fish stocks, as outlined in Parts III and IV of the Agreement,

Recognizing also the duty provided in the Agreement and reiterated as a principle in the Code of Conduct for Responsible Fisheries of the Food and Agriculture Organization of the United Nations for flag States to exercise effective control over fishing vessels flying their flag and vessels flying their flag which provide support to such vessels, and to ensure that the activities of such vessels do not undermine the effectiveness of conservation and management measures taken in accordance with international law and adopted at the national, subregional, regional or global levels,

Recognizing further that a number of regional fishing organizations and arrangements with competence to establish conservation and management measures regarding straddling fish stocks and/or highly migratory fish stocks are already taking significant conservation measures to promote the recovery and long-term sustainable use of fish stocks worldwide, and that in order for those efforts to succeed it is important that all States and entities, including those which are not members of these organizations or party to these arrangements, cooperate and observe these conservation and management measures,

Taking note of the obligation of States and other entities and regional and subregional fishery management organizations and arrangements to take measures to prevent or eliminate overfishing, and encouraging all States to participate in the work of the Food and Agriculture Organization of the United Nations on the subject,

Noting that some regional fisheries organizations and arrangements, including those mentioned in the report of the Secretary-General, have recently taken measures to ensure that fishing vessels flying the flags of non-members of those organizations or non-parties to those arrangements do not undermine the regionally adopted conservation and management measures,

Recognizing that the Agreement to Promote Compliance with International Conservation and Management Measures by Fishing Vessels on the High Seas builds upon the legal framework established by the United Nations Convention on the Law of the Sea, and also recognizing the importance of that Agreement and noting that it also has not yet entered into force,

Taking note with concern that straddling fish stocks and highly migratory fish stocks in some parts of the world have been subject to heavy and little-regulated fishing efforts, and that some stocks continue to be overfished, mainly as a result of unauthorized fishing,

Concerned that illegal, unregulated and unreported fishing, including that noted in the report of the Secretary-General, threatens serious depletion of populations of certain fish species, and in that regard urging States and entities to collaborate in efforts to address these types of fishing activities,

Noting the importance of the wide application of the precautionary approach to the conservation, management and exploitation of straddling fish stocks and highly migratory fish stocks, in accordance with the Agreement,

Reaffirming the importance it attaches to compliance with its resolution 46/215 of 20 December 1991, in particular those provisions calling for full implementation of a global moratorium on all large-scale pelagic driftnet fishing on the high seas of the world's oceans and seas, including enclosed seas and semi-enclosed seas,

Reaffirming also its resolution 49/116 of 19 December 1994 on unauthorized fishing in zones of national jurisdiction and its impact on the living marine resources of the world's oceans and seas, as well as its resolution 52/28 of 26 November 1997 and other relevant resolutions,

1. *Welcomes* the report of the Secretary-General on recent developments and current status of the Agreement for the Implementation of the Provisions of the United Nations Convention on the Law of the Sea of 10 December 1982 relating to the Conservation and Management of Straddling Fish Stocks and Highly Migratory Fish Stocks;

2. *Calls upon* all States and other entities referred to in article 1, paragraph 2 *(b)*, of the Agreement that have not done so to ratify or accede to it and to consider applying it provisionally;

3. *Emphasizes* the importance of the early entry into force and effective implementation of the Agreement;

4. *Reaffirms* the importance it attaches to compliance with its resolutions 46/215, 49/116, 49/118 of 19 December 1994 and 52/28, and urges States and other entities to enforce such measures fully;

5. *Calls upon* all States and other entities referred to in article X, paragraph 1, of the Agreement to Promote Compliance with International Conservation and Management Measures by Fishing Vessels on the High Seas that have not done so to accept that instrument;

6. *Calls upon* all States to ensure that their vessels comply with the conservation and management measures in accordance with the Agreement that have been adopted by subregional and regional fisheries management organizations and arrangements;

7. *Calls upon* States not to permit vessels flying their flag to engage in fishing on the high seas without having effective control over their activities and to take specific measures to control fishing operations by vessels flying their flag;

8. *Calls upon* the International Maritime Organization, in cooperation with the Food and Agriculture Organization of the United Nations, regional fisheries management organizations and arrangements and

other relevant international organizations, and in consultation with States and entities, to define the concept of the genuine link between the fishing vessel and the State in order to assist in the implementation of the Agreement;

9. *Urges* all States to participate in the efforts of the Food and Agriculture Organization of the United Nations to develop an international plan of action to address illegal, unregulated and unreported fishing, in particular the Meeting of Experts and Technical Consultation in the Food and Agriculture Organization of the United Nations scheduled for 2000, and in all efforts to coordinate all the work of the Food and Agriculture Organization of the United Nations with other international organizations, including the International Maritime Organization;

10. *Encourages* all States and entities concerned to work with flag States and the Food and Agriculture Organization of the United Nations in developing and implementing measures to combat or curb illegal, unregulated and unreported fishing;

11. *Calls upon* States to provide assistance to developing States as outlined in the Agreement, and notes the importance of participation by representatives of developing States in forums in which fisheries issues are discussed;

12. *Encourages* States and other entities to integrate in an appropriate manner the requirements for the protection of the environment, notably those resulting from multilateral environmental agreements, in the management of straddling fish stocks and highly migratory fish stocks;

13. *Requests* the Secretary-General to bring the present resolution to the attention of all members of the international community, relevant intergovernmental organizations, the organizations and bodies of the United Nations system, regional and subregional fisheries management organizations or arrangements and relevant non-governmental organizations, and invites them to provide the Secretary-General with information relevant to the implementation of the present resolution;

14. *Also requests* the Secretary-General to submit to the General Assembly at its fifty-sixth session a report on further developments relating to the implementation of the present resolution;

15. *Decides* to include in the provisional agenda of its fifty-sixth session, under the item entitled "Oceans and the law of the sea", the sub-item entitled "Agreement for the Implementation of the Provisions of the United Nations Convention on the Law of the Sea of 10 December 1982 relating to the Conservation and Management of Straddling Fish Stocks and Highly Migratory Fish Stocks".

Other developments related to the Convention

Report of Secretary-General. In October, the Secretary-General, in accordance with General Assembly resolution 53/32 [YUN 1998, p. 1230], submitted his annual report on developments pertaining to the status of the Convention and the related Agreements, the activities of institutions created under the Convention and issues relating to ocean affairs and the law of the sea [A/54/429 & Corr.1].

On a regional basis, the Secretary-General reviewed developments in legislation, delimitation treaties and State practice. He emphasized that, despite the positive trend of States adapting their legal practice to the provisions of the Convention, several examples existed where national legislation departed from the rules set out in it, and many States, both parties and non-parties, still had legislation in force that had not been harmonized with the Convention. He pointed out that delimitation of maritime boundaries was becoming increasingly important in the practice of States since it promoted peace and stability at the regional level and helped create the legal and political certainties required to attract investment in such fields as oil and gas exploitation and fisheries. In order to assist States, the Division for Ocean Affairs and the Law of the Sea was preparing a handbook providing basic legal, technical and practical information on maritime boundary delimitation. The Secretary-General presented information concerning the deposit and due publicity of charts and lists of geographical coordinates relating to baselines and various maritime areas. He highlighted developments in the dispute settlement mechanism, including choice of procedures, and additions to the lists of conciliators, arbitrators and experts for special arbitration.

The report dealt with issues concerning States with special geographical characteristics, such as small island States and landlocked States. Other parts of the report were devoted to issues related to combating crimes at sea, including illicit traffic in narcotic drugs, illegal trafficking in and transporting of migrants, and piracy and armed robbery; navigation, including safety and seaworthiness of ships, seafarers' condition, safety of navigation, maritime transport and carriage of dangerous goods. The Secretary-General described activities that had taken place in the development and management of marine resources and the protection and preservation of the marine environment, including pollution from land-based sources, vessels, the atmosphere and dumping. He provided a comprehensive review of marine fisheries in all regions, and information on ecosystems, habitats and species. He also reviewed regional sea programmes and action plans. The report focused on issues of marine science and technology and on cooperative mechanisms within the UN system, including capacity-building and information dissemination. The report highlighted the review of the sectoral theme of oceans and seas by the Commission on Sustainable Development (see p. 993).

Institutions created by the Convention

International Seabed Authority

Through the International Seabed Authority, established by the Convention on the Law of the Sea and the 1994 Implementing Agreement, States organized and conducted exploration and exploitation of the resources of the seabed and ocean floor and subsoil beyond the limits of national jurisdiction. As at 31 December, the Authority had 132 members.

In 1999, the Authority held its fifth session (Kingston, Jamaica, 9-27 August). The session emphasized early approval of the draft Regulations on Prospecting and Exploration for Polymetallic Nodules in the Area (seabed mining code). The Council of the Authority completed the first reading of the draft code. Following discussions, a revised draft was prepared. Early approval was stressed so that the Authority might enter into contracts for exploration with the seven pioneer investors whose work plans had been approved in 1997 [YUN 1997, p.1357]. The session also considered draft guidelines to assess the possible environmental impact arising from the exploration for polymetallic nodules in the Area. In other action, the Council adopted the draft financial regulations of the Authority, which applied provisionally until approved by the General Assembly. The Headquarters Agreement between the Government of Jamaica and the International Seabed Authority was formally signed by the parties.

The Protocol on the Privileges and Immunities of the International Seabed Authority, adopted in 1998 [YUN 1998, p. 1226], had 23 signatories as at 31 December. The Protocol would remain open for signature until 16 August 2000. It would enter into force 30 days after the date of deposit of the tenth instrument of ratification or accession.

International Tribunal for the Law of the Sea

The International Tribunal for the Law of the Sea held its seventh (25 February–16 April) and eighth (28 September–8 October) sessions in Hamburg, Germany [SPLOS/50].

In May, the ninth Meeting of States Parties to the Convention approved the budget of the Tribunal for 2000, which totalled $7,657,019. The Tribunal requested the Meeting to approve an adjustment in the remuneration of the members of the Tribunal in the light of General Assembly resolution 53/214 [YUN 1998, p. 1301], whereby the annual salary of the judges of the International Court of Justice (ICJ) was set at $160,000. The Meeting upheld the principle of equivalence of remuneration of the judges of ICJ and the Tribunal and set the level of approved remuneration of members of the Tribunal at a maximum of $160,000, effective 1 January 2000. The Meeting also considered the draft financial regulations of the Tribunal and agreed that the draft would be taken up at its tenth session with a view to its adoption.

On 1 July 1999, the 1997 Agreement on the Privileges and Immunities of the Tribunal [YUN 1997, p. 1361] closed for signature, having been signed by 21 States. The Agreement, which required ratification by 10 States to enter into force, had been ratified by the Netherlands and Norway at year's end.

Regarding the judicial work of the Tribunal, it was seized of a case between Saint Vincent and the Grenadines and Guinea concerning the arrest and detention off the coast of Sierra Leone by Guinean authorities of the oil tanker M/V *Saiga,* including its crew, which flew the flag of Saint Vincent and the Grenadines. A further case involved Australia and New Zealand on the one side and Japan on the other concerning the conservation of the southern bluefin tuna, a highly migratory fish species that traversed the territorial sea and the exclusive economic zone of several countries and the high seas.

At the request of Croatia and Bosnia and Herzegovina, the Tribunal, acting in its judicial capacity, nominated the seventh member of a Commission established by the two States to supervise, monitor, interpret and arbitrate the 1998 Agreement on Free Transit through the Territory of the Republic of Croatia to and from the Port of Ploce and through the Territory of Bosnia and Herzegovina at Neum [A/53/702-S/1998/1118].

Commission on the Limits of the Continental Shelf

During 1999, the Commission on the Limits of the Continental Shelf, established in 1997 [YUN 1997, p. 1362], held its fifth (3-14 May) and sixth (30 August–3 September) sessions in New York [A/54/429 & Corr.1]. The 21-member Commission, composed of experts in geology, geophysics or hydrography, made recommendations to coastal States on matters related to the establishment of the outer limits of their continental shelf beyond 200 nautical miles.

At those sessions, the Commission adopted the Scientific and Technical Guidelines [CLCS/11], which were intended to provide assistance to coastal States in their submission of technical data to the Commission, as well as annexes to the Guidelines [CLCS/11/Add.1], which included flow charts providing a simplified outline of the procedures described in the relevant parts of the Guidelines. The Commission considered the issue of training to develop knowledge and skills for preparation of submissions on the outer limits of the continental shelves, as required by the Convention. Among other matters, the Commission studied the issue of establishing a trust fund to assist in financing the participation of its members from developing countries. The Commission elected its officers for the remaining period of its current membership.

GENERAL ASSEMBLY ACTION

On 24 November [meeting 62], the General Assembly adopted **resolution 54/31** [draft: A/54/L.31 & Add.1] by recorded vote (129-1-4) [agenda item 40 *(a)*].

Oceans and the law of the sea

The General Assembly,

Recalling its resolutions 49/28 of 6 December 1994, 52/26 of 26 November 1997 and 53/32 of 24 November 1998 and other relevant resolutions adopted subsequent to the entry into force of the United Nations Convention on the Law of the Sea ("the Convention") on 16 November 1994,

Recalling also its resolution 2749(XXV) of 17 December 1970, and considering that the Convention, together with the Agreement relating to the implementation of Part XI of the United Nations Convention on the Law of the Sea of 10 December 1982 ("the Agreement"), provides the regime to be applied to the Area and its resources as defined in the Convention,

Emphasizing the universal character of the Convention and its fundamental importance for the maintenance and strengthening of international peace and security, as well as for the sustainable use and development of the seas and oceans and their resources,

Conscious that the problems of ocean space are closely interrelated and need to be considered as a whole,

Noting with satisfaction the increase in the number of States parties to the Convention and the Agreement,

Recognizing the impact on States of the entry into force of the Convention and the Agreement and the increasing need, particularly of developing States, for advice and assistance in their implementation in order to benefit thereunder,

Noting that developing countries, in particular small island developing States, may need assistance in the preparation and publication of charts under articles 16, 22, 47, 75 and 84 and annex II to the Convention,

Taking note with concern of the financial situation of the International Seabed Authority ("the Authority") and of the International Tribunal for the Law of the Sea ("the Tribunal"),

Conscious of the need to promote and facilitate international cooperation at the subregional, regional and global levels in order to ensure the orderly and sustainable development of the uses and resources of the seas and oceans,

Conscious also of the importance of education and training in the field of ocean affairs and the law of the sea,

Reaffirming the strategic importance of the Convention as a framework for national, regional and global action in the marine sector, as recognized also by the United Nations Conference on Environment and Development in chapter 17 of Agenda 21,

Welcoming the review by the Commission on Sustainable Development on oceans and seas and the adoption of the recommendations made by the Commission through the Economic and Social Council,

Taking note of the major challenges as well as the areas of particular concern facing the international community, as formulated in the recommendations on oceans and seas made by the Commission on Sustainable Development through the Economic and Social Council,

Expressing its concern in this context at the continuing threat posed to the sea by the dumping of nuclear waste and other toxic substances,

Recognizing the positive benefits for the marine environment that can be achieved through cooperative work within the regional seas programme of the United Nations Environment Programme,

Expressing its concern at the increasing threat to shipping from piracy and armed robbery at sea and its appreciation and support for the ongoing work of the International Maritime Organization in this area,

Reaffirming the importance of enhancing the safety of navigation as well as the necessity for cooperation in this regard,

Emphasizing the importance of the protection of the underwater cultural heritage, and recalling in this context the provisions of article 303 of the Convention,

Expressing its appreciation once again to the Secretary-General for his efforts in support of the Convention and in its effective implementation, including providing assistance in the functioning of the institutions created by the Convention,

Noting the responsibilities of the Secretary-General under the Convention and related resolutions of the General Assembly, in particular resolutions 49/28 and 52/26, and emphasizing the importance of the performance of such responsibilities for the effective and consistent implementation of the Convention,

Taking note of the report of the Secretary-General, and reaffirming the importance of the annual consideration and review by the General Assembly of the overall developments pertaining to the implementation of the Convention, as well as of other developments relating to the law of the sea and ocean affairs,

1. *Calls upon* all States that have not done so, in order to achieve the goal of universal participation, to become parties to the Convention and the Agreement;

2. *Reaffirms* the unified character of the Convention;

3. *Calls upon* States to harmonize as a matter of priority their national legislation with the provisions of the Convention, to ensure the consistent application of those provisions and to ensure also that any declarations or statements that they have made or make when signing, ratifying or acceding are in conformity with the Convention and to withdraw any of their declarations or statements that are not in conformity;

4. *Encourages* States parties to the Convention to deposit with the Secretary-General charts and lists of geographical coordinates, as provided for in the Convention;

5. *Urges* the international community to assist, as appropriate, developing countries, including small island developing States, in the preparation and publica-

tion of charts under articles 16, 22, 47, 75 and 84 and annex II to the Convention;

6. *Requests* the Secretary-General to convene the tenth Meeting of States Parties to the Convention in New York from 22 to 26 May 2000;

7. *Notes with satisfaction* the continued contribution of the Tribunal to the peaceful settlement of disputes in accordance with Part XV of the Convention, and underlines its important role and authority concerning the interpretation or application of the Convention and the Agreement;

8. *Encourages* States parties to the Convention to consider making a written declaration choosing from the means set out in article 287 for the settlement of disputes concerning the interpretation or application of the Convention and the Agreement, and invites States to note the provisions of annexes V, VI, VII and VIII to the Convention concerning, respectively, conciliation, the Tribunal, arbitration and special arbitration;

9. *Requests* the Secretary-General to circulate lists of conciliators and arbitrators drawn up and maintained in accordance with annexes V and VII to the Convention and to update these lists accordingly;

10. *Notes* the current work of the Authority, and emphasizes the importance of the commitment of its members to work expeditiously towards the adoption during 2000 of the regulations on prospecting and exploration for polymetallic nodules;

11. *Notes with appreciation* the adoption of the Headquarters Agreement between the Government of Jamaica and the Authority;

12. *Calls upon* States that have not done so to consider ratifying or acceding to the Agreement on the Privileges and Immunities of the Tribunal and to the Protocol on the Privileges and Immunities of the Authority;

13. *Appeals* to all States parties to the Convention to pay their assessed contributions to the Authority and to the Tribunal, respectively, in full and on time in order to ensure that they are able to carry out their functions as provided for in the Convention, and appeals also to the States which are former provisional members of the Authority to pay any outstanding contributions;

14. *Notes* the progress in the work of the Commission on the Limits of the Continental Shelf ("the Commission"), including the adoption of the scientific and technical guidelines and annexes thereto aimed at facilitating the preparation of submissions regarding the outer limits of the continental shelf in accordance with article 76 and annex II to the Convention, and the adoption of an action plan on training, taking into account, in particular, the needs of developing States;

15. *Welcomes* the decision of the Commission to convene an open meeting during its seventh session, aimed at familiarizing States with the necessity to implement the provisions of article 76 and annex II to the Convention relating to the establishment of the outer limits of the continental shelf beyond 200 nautical miles, and encourages States to attend the meeting;

16. *Approves* the convening by the Secretary-General of the seventh session of the Commission in New York from 1 to 5 May 2000 and, if necessary, an eighth session from 28 August to 1 September 2000;

17. *Urges* States to take all practicable steps to prevent the pollution of the sea by dumping of radioactive materials and industrial wastes, in accordance with the relevant provisions of the 1972 Convention on the Prevention of Marine Pollution by Dumping of Wastes and Other Matter and its amendments;

18. *Calls upon* States to become parties to and to implement the 1996 Protocol to the Convention on the Prevention of Marine Pollution by Dumping of Wastes and Other Matter;

19. *Encourages* States to continue to support the regional seas programme, which has achieved success in a number of geographic areas, and to work within the United Nations Environment Programme to enhance cooperation in the protection of the marine environment;

20. *Calls upon* States to cooperate fully with the International Maritime Organization to combat piracy and armed robbery against ships, including by submitting reports on incidents to that organization;

21. *Also calls upon* States to implement the International Maritime Organization guidelines on preventing attacks of piracy and armed robbery and to cooperate with the International Maritime Organization Correspondence Group, established to draw up standard guidelines for Governments in investigating attacks against ships and prosecuting offenders, and with other initiatives of the organization in this area;

22. *Urges* all States, in particular coastal States in affected regions, to take all necessary and appropriate measures to prevent and combat incidents of piracy and armed robbery at sea, including through regional cooperation, and to investigate or cooperate in the investigation of such incidents wherever they occur and bring the alleged perpetrators to justice, in accordance with international law;

23. *Urges* States to become parties to the Convention for the Suppression of Unlawful Acts against the Safety of Maritime Navigation and its Protocol, and to ensure its effective implementation;

24. *Expresses its appreciation* to the Secretary-General for the annual comprehensive report on oceans and the law of the sea prepared by the Division for Ocean Affairs and the Law of the Sea of the Office of Legal Affairs of the Secretariat, as well as for the other activities of the Division, in accordance with the provisions of the Convention and the mandate set forth in resolutions 49/28 and 52/26;

25. *Requests* the Secretary-General to ensure that the institutional capacity of the Organization adequately responds to the needs of States, the newly established institutions under the Convention and other competent international organizations by providing timely advice, information, including the information in his report, and assistance, taking into account the special needs of developing countries;

26. *Also requests* the Secretary-General to continue to carry out the responsibilities entrusted to him in the Convention and related resolutions of the General Assembly, including those mentioned in paragraph 11 of resolution 52/26, and to ensure that the performance of such activities is not adversely affected by savings as may be realized under the approved budget for the Organization;

27. *Reaffirms* the importance of ensuring the uniform and consistent application of the Convention and a coordinated approach to its overall implementation, and of strengthening technical cooperation and financial assistance for this purpose, stresses once again the

continuing importance of the efforts of the Secretary-General to these ends, and reiterates its invitation to the competent international organizations and other international bodies to support these objectives;

28. *Invites* Member States and others in a position to do so to contribute to the further development of the Hamilton Shirley Amerasinghe Memorial Fellowship Programme on the Law of the Sea established by the General Assembly in resolution 35/116 of 10 December 1980;

29. *Also invites* Member States to support the training activities under the TRAIN-SEA-COAST programme of the Division for Ocean Affairs and the Law of the Sea;

30. *Notes* the continued work of the United Nations Educational, Scientific and Cultural Organization towards a convention for the implementation of the provisions of the Convention, relating to the protection of the underwater cultural heritage, and re-emphasizes the importance of ensuring that the instrument to be elaborated is in full conformity with the relevant provisions of the Convention;

31. *Requests* the Secretary-General to bring the present resolution to the attention of the Director-General of the United Nations Educational, Scientific and Cultural Organization;

32. *Reaffirms* its decision to undertake an annual review and evaluation of the implementation of the Convention and other developments relating to ocean affairs and the law of the sea, taking into account resolution 54/33 of 24 November 1999;

33. *Requests* the Secretary-General to report to the General Assembly at its fifty-fifth session on the implementation of the present resolution, including other developments and issues relating to ocean affairs and the law of the sea, in connection with his annual comprehensive report on oceans and the law of the sea, and to provide the report in accordance with the modalities set out in resolution 54/33;

34. *Decides* to include in the provisional agenda of its fifty-fifth session the item entitled "Oceans and the law of the sea".

RECORDED VOTE ON RESOLUTION 54/31:

In favour: Algeria, Andorra, Angola, Argentina, Armenia, Australia, Austria, Bahamas, Bahrain, Belarus, Belgium, Benin, Bhutan, Bolivia, Brazil, Brunei Darussalam, Bulgaria, Burkina Faso, Cameroon, Canada, Chad, Chile, China, Congo, Costa Rica, Côte d'Ivoire, Croatia, Cuba, Cyprus, Czech Republic, Denmark, Djibouti, Egypt, Equatorial Guinea, Eritrea, Estonia, Ethiopia, Fiji, Finland, France, Gabon, Germany, Ghana, Greece, Grenada, Guatemala, Guinea-Bissau, Guyana, Haiti, Hungary, Iceland, India, Indonesia, Iran, Ireland, Italy, Jamaica, Japan, Jordan, Kazakhstan, Kenya, Kuwait, Lao People's Democratic Republic, Lebanon, Libyan Arab Jamahiriya, Liechtenstein, Lithuania, Luxembourg, Malawi, Malaysia, Maldives, Malta, Marshall Islands, Mauritius, Mexico, Micronesia, Monaco, Morocco, Mozambique, Myanmar, Namibia, Nepal, Netherlands, New Zealand, Nigeria, Norway, Oman, Pakistan, Panama, Papua New Guinea, Paraguay, Philippines, Poland, Portugal, Qatar, Republic of Korea, Republic of Moldova, Romania, Russian Federation, Samoa, San Marino, Saudi Arabia, Senegal, Seychelles, Sierra Leone, Singapore, Slovakia, Slovenia, Solomon Islands, South Africa, Spain, Sri Lanka, Sudan, Sweden, Syrian Arab Republic, Thailand, Togo, Trinidad and Tobago, Tunisia, Ukraine, United Arab Emirates, United Kingdom, United Republic of Tanzania, United States, Uruguay, Uzbekistan, Viet Nam, Yemen, and Zambia.

Against: Turkey.

Abstaining: Colombia, Ecuador, Peru, and Venezuela.

Division for Ocean Affairs and the Law of the Sea

During 1999, the Division for Ocean Affairs and the Law of the Sea of the Office of Legal Affairs continued to fulfil its role as the substantive unit of the Secretariat responsible for the review and monitoring of all developments related to the law of the sea and ocean affairs, as well as for the implementation of the Convention and related General Assembly resolutions. The Division developed and maintained facilities for the deposit by States of charts and geographical coordinates concerning maritime zones, including lines of delimitation, and gave publicity thereto through its "Maritime Zone Notifications" and the *Law of the Sea Information Circular.* It also maintained and expanded its web site: www.un.org/Depts/los.

Training activities were carried out under the TRAIN-SEA-COAST programme [YUN 1998, p. 1232], designed to build up in-country capacity to improve skills in integrated ocean and coastal management among policy makers and practitioners in developed and developing countries.

The fourteenth Hamilton Shirley Amerasinghe Memorial Fellowship on the Law of the Sea, established in 1981 [YUN 1981, p. 139], was presented to Fathima Razni Mulafer of Sri Lanka.

Chapter V

Other legal questions

In 1999, the United Nations continued to work on various aspects of international law, including international economic law.

The Special Committee on the Charter of the United Nations and on the Strengthening of the Role of the Organization met in April and discussed proposals for the maintenance of international peace and security and the peaceful settlement of disputes between States, including implementation of Charter provisions relating to assistance to third States affected by the application of sanctions under Chapter VII.

The United Nations Decade of International Law (1990-1999) concluded with a plenary meeting of the General Assembly on 17 November dedicated to the closure and with the centennial celebrations held in The Hague, Netherlands, and Saint Petersburg, Russian Federation, of the first International Peace Conference.

The United Nations Commission on International Trade Law made progress on receivables financing, electronic commerce, privately financed infrastructure projects and the legislative implementation of the 1958 Convention on the Recognition and Enforcement of Foreign Arbitral Awards.

The Committee on Relations with the Host Country, which increased its membership by four in 1999, discussed the security of missions, the safety of their personnel and travel regulations.

International organizations and international law

Strengthening the role of the United Nations

Special Committee on UN Charter

At its 1999 session (New York, 12-23 April) [A/54/33 & Corr.1], the Special Committee on the Charter of the United Nations and on the Strengthening of the Role of the Organization continued to consider proposals for the maintenance of international peace and security, the peaceful settlement of disputes between States and the strengthening of the role of the United Nations in those contexts. It also continued to discuss implementation of the provisions of the Charter related to third States affected by the application of sanctions. In addition, the Special Committee considered proposals concerning the role of the Trusteeship Council and whether to add new subjects to the Special Committee's agenda.

In connection with the maintenance of international peace and security, the Special Committee had before it the following documents submitted by the Russian Federation: two working papers on basic conditions and criteria for imposing and implementing sanctions and other enforcement measures [A/AC.182/L.94 & L.100]; two working papers on a draft declaration on basic principles and criteria for UN peacekeeping missions [A/AC.182/L.89 & Add.1]; and a working paper on the legal basis for UN peacekeeping operations in the context of Chapter VI of the UN Charter [A/AC.182/L.89/Add.2 & Corr.1]. Regarding the strengthening of the role of the United Nations, the Special Committee considered working papers submitted by Cuba [A/AC.182/L.93/Add.1], the Libyan Arab Jamahiriya [A/AC.182/L.99] and the Russian Federation [A/AC.182/L.104/Rev.1].

As to the peaceful settlement of disputes between States, the Special Committee considered a revised proposal from Sierra Leone on establishing a dispute prevention and early settlement service [A/AC.182/L.96] and two working papers by Guatemala regarding a proposed extension of the jurisdiction of the International Court of Justice (ICJ) in contentious cases to disputes between States and intergovernmental organizations [A/AC.182/L.101 & L.103 & Corr.1]. It also considered a working paper by Mexico on the need to provide ICJ with financial resources to adequately carry out its functions [A/AC.182/L.105].

Report of Secretary-General. In response to General Assembly resolution 53/106 [YUN 1998, p. 1234], the Secretary-General submitted a September progress report [A/54/363] describing his efforts to expedite the preparation and publication of supplements to the *Repertory of Practice of United Nations Organs* and the *Repertoire of the Practice of the Security Council.* He assessed the work required and proposed measures that might facilitate the process of preparation and publication.

GENERAL ASSEMBLY ACTION

On 9 December [meeting 76], the General Assembly, on the recommendation of the Sixth (Legal) Committee [A/54/614], adopted **resolution 54/106** without vote [agenda item 159].

Report of the Special Committee on the Charter of the United Nations and on the Strengthening of the Role of the Organization

The General Assembly,

Recalling its resolution 3499(XXX) of 15 December 1975, by which it established the Special Committee on the Charter of the United Nations and on the Strengthening of the Role of the Organization, and its relevant resolutions adopted at subsequent sessions,

Recalling also its resolution 47/233 of 17 August 1993 on the revitalization of the work of the General Assembly,

Recalling further its resolution 47/62 of 11 December 1992 on the question of equitable representation on and increase in the membership of the Security Council,

Taking note of the report of the Open-ended Working Group on the Question of Equitable Representation on and Increase in the Membership of the Security Council and Other Matters Related to the Security Council,

Recalling the elements relevant to the work of the Special Committee contained in its resolution 47/120 B of 20 September 1993,

Recalling also its resolution 51/241 of 31 July 1997 on the strengthening of the United Nations system and its resolution 51/242 of 15 September 1997, entitled "Supplement to an Agenda for Peace", by which it adopted the texts on coordination and the question of sanctions imposed by the United Nations, which are annexed to that resolution,

Recalling further that the International Court of Justice is the principal judicial organ of the United Nations, and reaffirming its authority and independence,

Considering the desirability of finding practical ways and means of strengthening the Court,

Taking note of the report of the Secretary-General on the *Repertory of Practice of United Nations Organs* and the *Repertoire of the Practice of the Security Council,*

Recalling its resolution 53/106 of 8 December 1998,

Having considered the report of the Special Committee on the work of its session held in 1999,

1. *Takes note* of the report of the Special Committee on the Charter of the United Nations and on the Strengthening of the Role of the Organization;

2. *Decides* that the Special Committee shall hold its next session from 10 to 20 April 2000;

3. *Requests* the Special Committee, at its session in 2000, in accordance with paragraph 5 of General Assembly resolution 50/52 of 11 December 1995:

(*a*) To continue its consideration of all proposals concerning the question of the maintenance of international peace and security in all its aspects in order to strengthen the role of the United Nations and, in this context, to consider other proposals relating to the maintenance of international peace and security already submitted or which may be submitted to the Special Committee at its session in 2000;

(*b*) To continue to consider on a priority basis the question of the implementation of the provisions of the Charter of the United Nations related to assistance to third States affected by the application of sanctions under Chapter VII of the Charter, taking into consideration the reports of the Secretary-General, the proposals submitted on this question, the debate on the question in the Sixth Committee at the fifty-fourth session of the General Assembly and the text on the question of sanctions imposed by the United Nations contained in annex II to Assembly resolution 51/242, and also the implementation of the provisions of Assembly resolutions 50/51 of 11 December 1995, 51/208 of 17 December 1996, 52/162 of 15 December 1997 and 53/107 of 8 December 1998;

(*c*) To continue its work on the question of the peaceful settlement of disputes between States and, in this context, to continue its consideration of proposals relating to the peaceful settlement of disputes between States, including the proposal on the establishment of a dispute settlement service offering or responding with its services early in disputes and those proposals relating to the enhancement of the role of the International Court of Justice;

(*d*) To continue to consider proposals concerning the Trusteeship Council in the light of the report of the Secretary-General submitted in accordance with General Assembly resolution 50/55 of 11 December 1995, the report of the Secretary-General entitled "Renewing the United Nations: a programme for reform" and the views expressed by States on this subject at the previous sessions of the General Assembly;

(*e*) To continue to consider, on a priority basis, ways and means of improving its working methods and enhancing its efficiency with a view to identifying widely acceptable measures for future implementation;

4. *Takes note* of paragraph 33 of the report of the Secretary-General, commends the Secretary-General for his continued efforts to reduce the backlog in the publication of the *Repertory of Practice of United Nations Organs*, and endorses the efforts of the Secretary-General to eliminate the backlog in the publication of the *Repertoire of the Practice of the Security Council;*

5. *Invites* the Special Committee at its session in 2000 to continue to identify new subjects for consideration in its future work with a view to contributing to the revitalization of the work of the United Nations, to discuss how to offer its assistance to the working groups of the General Assembly in this field and, in this regard, to consider ways and means of improving coordination between the Special Committee and other working groups dealing with the reform of the Organization, including the role of the Chairperson of the Special Committee for this purpose;

6. *Requests* the Special Committee to submit a report on its work to the General Assembly at the fifty-fifth session;

7. *Decides* to include in the provisional agenda of its fifty-fifth session the item entitled "Report of the Special Committee on the Charter of the United Nations and on the Strengthening of the Role of the Organization".

On the samc date [mccting 76], the Assembly, having considered a 1998 report on ICJ's observations on its increased workload [YUN 1998, p. 1234], also on the recommendation of the Sixth Committee [A/54/614], adopted **resolution 54/108** without vote [agenda item 159].

Strengthening of the International Court of Justice

The General Assembly,

Recalling that the International Court of Justice is the principal judicial organ of the United Nations,

Noting an increase in the recourse to the Court by States and the effects of such an increase on its operation,

Recalling its resolution 53/106 of 8 December 1998, in which it requested the Special Committee on the Charter of the United Nations and on the Strengthening of the Role of the Organization to consider practical ways and means of strengthening the International Court of Justice,

Bearing in mind the comments and observations submitted by the Court and by States on the consequences that the increase in the volume of cases before the Court has on its operation,

1. *Expresses its appreciation* to the International Court of Justice for the measures adopted to operate an increased workload with maximum efficiency;

2. *Invites* the Court to keep its working methods under periodic review and to adopt additional measures aimed at expediting its proceedings;

3. *Invites* States that appear before the Court to consider favourably the guidance offered by the Court in paragraph 3 of the annex to the report of the Secretary-General containing the comments and observations of the Court, and to adopt, whenever possible, any other measure that may help to expedite the proceedings.

Assistance to third States affected by Chapter VII sanctions

Report of Secretary-General. In response to General Assembly resolution 53/107 [YUN 1998, p. 1236], the Secretary-General submitted a September report with later addendum on implementation of the provisions of the UN Charter related to assistance to third States affected by the application of sanctions [A/54/383 & Add.1]. The report contained measures to further improve procedures and working methods of the Security Council and its sanctions committees, and presented information on Secretariat arrangements to provide better information and early assessments regarding the effects of sanctions on third States and international assistance available to them. Views communicated by Governments, the specialized agencies, UN bodies and other international and regional organizations regarding the report of the ad hoc expert group meeting on assistance to third States affected by sanctions [YUN 1998, p. 1235] were summarized in the report (see also PART THREE, Chapter III).

Security Council consideration. In a January note on the work of the sanctions committees [S/1999/92], the Security Council President made proposals to improve the work of those committees.

The President suggested that the sanctions committees should establish arrangements and channels of communication within the UN system, as well as with other intergovernmental and regional organizations, neighbouring countries and other countries and parties concerned, to improve the monitoring of the implementation of the sanctions regimes and the assessment of their humanitarian consequences on the target State population and their economic consequences on neighbouring and other States. The chairpersons of sanctions committees should visit the regions concerned to obtain first-hand accounts of the impact of sanctions regimes and the results of and difficulties in their implementation. The technical effectiveness of the mandatory measures should also be periodically assessed by the sanctions committees on the basis of inputs from Member States, reports prepared by the Secretariat and other available sources of information. The Secretariat should provide, whenever necessary, its assessment of the humanitarian and economic impact of sanctions.

Other proposals dealt with the committees' guidelines; the practice of hearing technical presentations of information by organizations assisting the Council; the impact of sanctions on diplomatic efforts towards implementing Council resolutions; humanitarian exemptions for humanitarian agencies; the exemption of foodstuffs, pharmaceuticals, medical supplies and equipment, educational items and agricultural equipment; and increased transparency of the committees' work, including the availability of summary records and public information on the Internet.

The Council President stated that all Council members had indicated their agreement that the proposals would be used to improve the work of the committees in accordance with the relevant resolutions.

By a 25 February note [S/1999/204], the Secretary-General drew the attention of Council members to General Assembly resolution 53/107 [YUN 1998, p. 1236] on assistance to third States affected by sanctions.

GENERAL ASSEMBLY ACTION

On 9 December [meeting 76], the General Assembly, on the recommendation of the Sixth Committee [A/54/614], adopted **resolution 54/107** without vote [agenda item 159].

Implementation of the provisions of the Charter of the United Nations related to assistance to third States affected by the application of sanctions

The General Assembly,

Concerned about the special economic problems confronting certain States arising from the carrying out of preventive or enforcement measures taken by the Security Council against other States, and taking into account the obligation of Members of the United Nations under Article 49 of the Charter of the United Nations to join in affording mutual assistance in carrying out the measures decided upon by the Security Council,

Recalling the right of third States confronted with special economic problems of that nature to consult the Security Council with regard to a solution of those problems, in accordance with Article 50 of the Charter,

Recognizing the desirability of the consideration of further appropriate procedures for consultations to deal in a more effective manner with the problems referred to in Article 50 of the Charter,

Recalling:

(a) The report of the Secretary-General entitled "An Agenda for Peace", in particular paragraph 41 thereof,

(b) Its resolution 47/120 A of 18 December 1992, entitled "An Agenda for Peace: preventive diplomacy and related matters", its resolution 47/120 B of 20 September 1993, entitled "An Agenda for Peace", in particular section IV thereof, entitled "Special economic problems arising from the implementation of preventive or enforcement measures", and its resolution 51/242 of 15 September 1997, entitled "Supplement to an Agenda for Peace", in particular annex II thereof, entitled "Question of sanctions imposed by the United Nations",

(c) The position paper of the Secretary-General entitled "Supplement to an Agenda for Peace",

(d) The statement by the President of the Security Council of 22 February 1995,

(e) The report of the Secretary-General prepared pursuant to the statement by the President of the Security Council regarding the question of special economic problems of States as a result of sanctions imposed under Chapter VII of the Charter,

(f) The reports of the Secretary-General on economic assistance to States affected by the implementation of the Security Council resolutions imposing sanctions against the Federal Republic of Yugoslavia and General Assembly resolutions 48/210 of 21 December 1993, 49/21 A of 2 December 1994, 50/58 E of 12 December 1995, 51/30 A of 5 December 1996 and 52/169 H of 16 December 1997,

(g) The reports of the Special Committee on the Charter of the United Nations and on the Strengthening of the Role of the Organization on the work of its sessions held in the years 1994 to 1999,

(h) The reports of the Secretary-General on the implementation of the provisions of the Charter related to assistance to third States affected by the application of sanctions under Chapter VII of the Charter,

Taking note of the most recent report of the Secretary-General, submitted in accordance with General Assembly resolution 53/107 of 8 December 1998,

Recalling that the question of assistance to third States affected by the application of sanctions has been addressed recently in several forums, including the General Assembly and its subsidiary organs and the Security Council,

Recalling also the measures taken by the Security Council in accordance with the statement by the President of the Security Council of 16 December 1994 that, as part of the effort of the Council to improve the flow of information and the exchange of ideas between members of the Council and other States Members of the United Nations, there should be increased recourse to open meetings, in particular at an early stage in its consideration of a subject,

Stressing that, in the formulation of sanctions regimes, due account should be taken of the potential effects of sanctions on third States,

Stressing also, in this context, the powers of the Security Council under Chapter VII of the Charter and the primary responsibility of the Council under Article 24 of the Charter for the maintenance of international peace and security in order to ensure prompt and effective action by the United Nations,

Recalling that, under Article 31 of the Charter, any Member of the United Nations that is not a member of the Security Council may participate, without vote, in the discussion of any question brought before the Council whenever the latter considers that the interests of that Member are specially affected,

Recognizing that the imposition of sanctions under Chapter VII of the Charter has been causing special economic problems in third States and that it is necessary to intensify efforts to address those problems effectively,

Taking into consideration the views of third States which could be affected by the imposition of sanctions,

Recognizing that assistance to third States affected by the application of sanctions would further contribute to an effective and comprehensive approach by the international community to sanctions imposed by the Security Council,

Recognizing also that the international community at large and, in particular, international institutions involved in providing economic and financial assistance should continue to take into account and address in a more effective manner the special economic problems of affected third States arising from the carrying out of preventive or enforcement measures taken by the Security Council under Chapter VII of the Charter, in view of their magnitude and of the adverse impact on the economy of those States,

Recalling the provisions of its resolutions 50/51 of 11 December 1995, 51/208 of 17 December 1996, 52/162 of 15 December 1997 and 53/107 of 8 December 1998,

1. *Renews its invitation* to the Security Council to consider the establishment of further mechanisms or procedures, as appropriate, for consultations as early as possible under Article 50 of the Charter of the United Nations with third States which are or may be confronted with special economic problems arising from the carrying out of preventive or enforcement measures imposed by the Council under Chapter VII of the Charter, with regard to a solution of those problems, including appropriate ways and means for increasing the effectiveness of its methods and procedures applied in the consideration of requests by the affected States for assistance;

2. *Welcomes once again* the further measures taken by the Security Council since the adoption of General Assembly resolution 50/51, most recently the note by the President of the Security Council of 29 January 1999 aimed at improving the work of the sanctions committees, including increasing the effectiveness and transparency of the sanctions committees, invites the

Council to implement those measures, and strongly recommends that the Council continue its efforts to further enhance the functioning of the sanctions committees, to streamline their working procedures and to facilitate access to them by representatives of States that find themselves confronted with special economic problems arising from the carrying out of sanctions;

3. *Requests* the Secretary-General to pursue the implementation of General Assembly resolutions 50/51, 51/208, 52/162 and 53/107 and to ensure that the competent units within the Secretariat develop the adequate capacity and appropriate modalities, technical procedures and guidelines to continue, on a regular basis, to collate and coordinate information about international assistance available to third States affected by the implementation of sanctions, to continue developing a possible methodology for assessing the adverse consequences actually incurred by third States and to explore innovative and practical measures of assistance to the affected third States;

4. *Welcomes* the report of the Secretary-General containing a summary of the deliberations and main findings of the ad hoc expert group meeting on developing a methodology for assessing the consequences incurred by third States as a result of preventive or enforcement measures and on exploring innovative and practical measures of international assistance to the affected third States, and invites States and relevant international organizations within and outside the United Nations system which have not yet done so to provide their views regarding the report of the ad hoc expert group meeting;

5. *Requests* the Secretary-General to present to the General Assembly his views on the deliberations and main findings, including the recommendations, of the ad hoc expert group on the implementation of the provisions of the Charter related to assistance to third States affected by the application of sanctions, taking into account the views of States, the organizations of the United Nations system, international financial institutions and other international organizations, and to provide the relevant information, where appropriate, on other developments in this context, particularly on the work of the sanctions committees as referred to in the note by the President of the Security Council;

6. *Reaffirms* the important role of the General Assembly, the Economic and Social Council and the Committee for Programme and Coordination in mobilizing and monitoring, as appropriate, the economic assistance efforts by the international community and the United Nations system to States confronted with special economic problems arising from the carrying out of preventive or enforcement measures imposed by the Security Council and, as appropriate, in identifying solutions to the special economic problems of those States;

7. *Takes note* of the decision of the Economic and Social Council, in its resolution 1999/59 of 30 July 1999, to continue consideration of the question of assistance to third States affected by the application of sanctions, and decides to transmit the most recent report of the Secretary-General on the implementation of the provisions of the Charter related to assistance to third States affected by the application of sanctions to the Council at its substantive session of 2000;

8. *Invites* the organizations of the United Nations system, international financial institutions, other international organizations, regional organizations and Member States to address more specifically and directly, where appropriate, special economic problems of third States affected by sanctions imposed under Chapter VII of the Charter and, for this purpose, to consider improving procedures for consultations to maintain a constructive dialogue with such States, including through regular and frequent meetings as well as, where appropriate, special meetings between the affected third States and the donor community, with the participation of United Nations agencies and other international organizations;

9. *Requests* the Special Committee on the Charter of the United Nations and on the Strengthening of the Role of the Organization, at its session in 2000, to continue to consider on a priority basis the question of the implementation of the provisions of the Charter related to assistance to third States affected by the application of sanctions under Chapter VII of the Charter, taking into consideration all the related reports of the Secretary-General, in particular the 1998 report containing a summary of the deliberations and main findings of the ad hoc expert group meeting convened pursuant to paragraph 4 of General Assembly resolution 52/162, together with the most recent report of the Secretary-General on this question, the proposals submitted on the question, the debate on the question in the Sixth Committee during the fifty-fourth session of the Assembly and the text on the question of sanctions imposed by the United Nations contained in annex II to Assembly resolution 51/242, as well as the implementation of the provisions of Assembly resolutions 50/51, 51/208, 52/162 and 53/107 and the present resolution;

10. *Decides* to consider, within the Sixth Committee, or if necessary within a working group of the Committee, at the fifty-fifth session of the General Assembly, further progress in the elaboration of effective measures aimed at the implementation of the provisions of the Charter related to assistance to third States affected by the application of sanctions under Chapter VII of the Charter;

11. *Requests* the Secretary-General to submit a report on the implementation of the present resolution to the General Assembly at its fifty-fifth session, under the agenda item entitled "Report of the Special Committee on the Charter of the United Nations and on the Strengthening of the Role of the Organization".

UN Decade of International Law

In response to General Assembly resolution 53/100 [YUN 1998, p. 1238], the Secretary-General submitted a September report with later addendum [A/54/362 & Add.1] summarizing actions taken by States and international organizations to implement the United Nations Decade of International Law (1990-1999), which the Assembly had declared in resolution 44/23 [YUN 1989, p. 848]. The Decade's objectives were to promote acceptance of and respect for the principles of international law and encourage its progressive development and codification; to promote means and methods of peaceful settlement of disputes between States, including resort to and full respect for ICJ; and to encourage the teaching, study, dissemination and wider application of international law. The Assembly had adopted the programme of activities for the final term of the Decade (1997-1999) in resolution 51/157 [YUN 1996, p. 1226].

Sixth Committee consideration. In response to General Assembly resolution 53/100, the Sixth Committee's Working Group on the United Nations Decade of International Law continued its work in 1999, holding 12 meetings between 18 October and 10 November. The Chairperson of the Working Group presented an oral report [A/C.6/54/SR.33] to the Sixth Committee on the work accomplished and introduced a draft resolution on the Decade.

GENERAL ASSEMBLY ACTION

On 17 November [meeting 55], the General Assembly, on the recommendation of the Sixth Committee [A/54/609], adopted **resolution 54/28** without vote [agenda item 154 *(a)*].

United Nations Decade of International Law

The General Assembly,

Recalling its resolution 44/23 of 17 November 1989, by which it declared the period 1990-1999 the United Nations Decade of International Law,

Recalling also that the main purposes of the Decade, according to resolution 44/23, should be, *inter alia:*

(a) To promote acceptance of and respect for the principles of international law,

(b) To promote means and methods for the peaceful settlement of disputes between States, including resort to and full respect for the International Court of Justice,

(c) To encourage the progressive development of international law and its codification,

(d) To encourage the teaching, study, dissemination and wider appreciation of international law,

Noting the conclusion of the Decade,

Reaffirming its resolution 53/101 of 8 December 1998, entitled "Principles and guidelines for international negotiations", adopted within the framework of the Decade,

Greatly encouraged by the significant achievements in the development and promotion of international law which occurred during the Decade, which has contributed to the strengthening of the rule of international law,

Recognizing that, *inter alia*, the establishment of the International Tribunal for the Former Yugoslavia in 1993, the International Tribunal for Rwanda in 1994 and the International Tribunal for the Law of the Sea in 1996 and the adoption of the Rome Statute of the International Criminal Court in 1998 constitute significant events within the Decade,

Recognizing also efforts made during the Decade by Legal Advisers of the Ministries of Foreign Affairs worldwide to create a common understanding of their role through annual informal consultations at United Nations Headquarters,

Convinced that the end of the Decade affords the international community an opportunity to reflect on those achievements and that States, international organizations and educational institutions should continue to encourage and promote activities in the legal field aimed at contributing to its main purposes,

Convinced also of the need to continue aiming towards the implementation of the main purposes of the Decade,

Welcoming the significant increase in the recourse to the International Court of Justice by States for the settlement of disputes,

Noting that international humanitarian law has been an important topic during the Decade, and mindful of the contributions made in this field by the International Committee of the Red Cross and the international conferences of the Red Cross and Red Crescent,

Noting also that the year 1999 marks the fiftieth anniversary of the adoption of the four Geneva Conventions of 12 August 1949,

Expressing its appreciation to the Governments of the Kingdom of the Netherlands and the Russian Federation for their efforts in realization of the programme of action dedicated to the centennial of the first International Peace Conference, which could be regarded as a significant contribution to the Decade,

Taking note with interest of the consideration of the outcome of the action dedicated to the 1999 centennial of the first International Peace Conference in the General Assembly during its fifty-fourth session,

Expressing its gratitude to the rapporteurs and all organizations, groups and individuals who contributed to the discussion of the centennial themes,

Having considered the report of the Secretary-General, and expressing its appreciation therefor,

Noting the deposit by the Secretary-General, on 21 December 1998, of an act of formal confirmation, on behalf of the United Nations, of the Vienna Convention on the Law of Treaties between States and International Organizations or between International Organizations of 21 March 1986,

Welcoming the progress that has been made towards eliminating the backlog in the publication of the United Nations *Treaty Series* by the implementation of a plan to be completed in 2001, and stressing the need for the elimination of such a backlog, as well as for a comprehensive electronification of the work of the Treaty Section of the Office of Legal Affairs of the Secretariat,

Recalling that, at the forty-fifth session of the General Assembly, the Sixth Committee established the Working Group on the United Nations Decade of International Law,

Noting that the Working Group continued its work during the fifty-fourth session in accordance with resolution 53/100 of 8 December 1998,

Having considered the oral report presented by the Chairperson of the Working Group to the Sixth Committee,

1. *Expresses its appreciation* for the work done by the Working Group on the United Nations Decade of International Law;

2. *Acknowledges* that the Decade has contributed significantly to the strengthening of the rule of international law;

3. *Reaffirms* the continued validity of the main objectives of the Decade, the fulfilment of which is essential to achieve the purposes of the United Nations;

4. *Expresses its appreciation* to States and international organizations and institutions that have undertaken activities in the implementation of the programme for the activities for the final term (1997-1999) of the Decade;

5. *Requests* the Secretary-General to continue developing the electronic database of the Treaty Section of the Office of Legal Affairs of the Secretariat, with a view to providing Member States expeditiously with a wider range of easily accessible treaty-related information in the electronic medium, and to keep the list, now available on the Internet, of the titles of multilateral treaties deposited with him updated in all official languages of the Organization;

6. *Urges* States and international organizations, in particular depositaries, to continue assisting the Secretariat in its efforts to expedite the registration of treaties and their publication by providing it with paper copies of treaties, or electronic copies, including maps, for registration and, wherever possible, translations of treaties in English or French;

7. *Requests* the Secretary-General to implement vigorously the plan to eliminate the backlog in the publication of the United Nations *Treaty Series*, and highlights, in this context, the relevance of timely translations;

8. *Expresses its appreciation* to the Office of Legal Affairs for the establishment during the Decade of various Internet web sites and the United Nations Audiovisual Library in International Law, and takes note of its efforts to maintain those sites and the Library;

9. *Notes* the publication by the Office of Legal Affairs of the *Collection of Essays by Legal Advisers of States, Legal Advisers of International Organizations and Practitioners in the Field of International Law*[a] and its intention to issue in 2000 two publications on international instruments related to the prevention and suppression of international terrorism and on the United Nations and the development of international law during the 1990s, in order to highlight the work accomplished in this area during the Decade;

10. *Invites* States, organs of the United Nations, international organizations and other relevant international forums to continue to give attention to the themes and outcome of the centennial of the first International Peace Conference;

11. *Congratulates* the Permanent Court of Arbitration on its one hundredth anniversary, commends it for its role in the international system of peaceful resolution of disputes, and invites States to consider making full use of the facilities of the Court and to support its work;

12. *Expresses its appreciation* to the International Committee of the Red Cross for the activities undertaken in the field of international humanitarian law, including with regard to the protection of the environment in times of armed conflict;

13. *Invites* States and international organizations to continue promoting the acceptance of and respect for the rules and principles of international law;

14. *Welcomes* the achievements during the Decade in the codification and progressive development of international law, and calls upon States, in order to contribute further to the rule of international law, to consider, if they have not yet done so, becoming parties to the multilateral treaties adopted during the Decade, including those listed in the annex to the report of the Secretary-General;

15. *Invites* States and international organizations to continue promoting the strengthening of the use of means and methods of peaceful settlement of disputes;

16. *Recalls* that States have the obligation to solve their disputes by peaceful means, including resort to the International Court of Justice, and that one of the main purposes of the Decade is to promote the full respect for the Court in accordance with the relevant provisions of the Charter of the United Nations;

17. *Invites* States to continue to pay attention to the identification of areas of international law that might be ripe for progressive development or codification, and to promote discussion thereon in the competent forums;

18. *Invites* States and international organizations to continue encouraging the publication of books or other materials on subjects of international law and the holding of symposia, conferences, seminars or other meetings aimed at promoting a wider appreciation of international law;

19. *Invites* States to continue encouraging educational institutions to introduce or increase the number of courses of international law;

20. *Requests* the Secretary-General to bring the present resolution to the attention of States, international organizations and institutions working in the field of international law;

21. *Decides* to continue considering developments in the progress made in the implementation of the purposes of the Decade beyond its conclusion, in the framework of the agenda item entitled "United Nations Programme of Assistance in the Teaching, Study, Dissemination and Wider Appreciation of International Law".

[a]UN Sales No. E/F/S.99.V.13.

First International Peace Conference centennial and end of Decade

In September, pursuant to General Assembly resolution 53/99 [YUN 1998, p. 1240], the Netherlands and the Russian Federation submitted to the Secretary-General a report [A/54/381] on the conclusions of the centennial of the first International Peace Conference, which emerged from an expert meeting (The Hague, 18-19 May), and of the international conference "Centennial of the Russian Initiative: from the First Peace Conference, 1899—to the Third, 1999" (Saint Petersburg, 22-25 June). The report reflected the outcome of and discussions on the themes of the 1899 first International Peace Conference and its 1999 centennial celebrations—disarmament questions (regional security organizations, nuclear disarmament/non-proliferation, missiles, biological and chemical weapons, anti-personnel landmines, conventional arms/small arms, Conference on Disarmament, control/verification mechanisms, the role of civil society); humanitarian law and laws of war (*ius in bello, ius ad bellum,* neutrality, naval warfare, belligerent occupation, UN military operations, internal armed conflicts, compliance); and peaceful settlement of disputes (prevention and resolution, negotiations and consultations, Permanent Court of Arbitration, ICJ, role of Security Council and Secretary-General, regional courts, international court of appeals, international constitutional court, specialized methods and procedures, permanent conciliation committee, codification of international law, world school of international law, mediation and role of technical bodies). Those activities were undertaken within the framework of the United Nations Decade of International Law, with a view to serving as a useful basis for carrying the results of the Decade of International Law into the next millennium.

Communication. On 17 May [A/54/98], Bangladesh transmitted the text of the Hague Agenda for Peace and Justice for the Twenty-first Century, which emerged from the Hague Appeal for Peace Conference (The Hague, 12-15 May). The Agenda reflected the four major strands of the Hague Appeal: root causes of war/culture of peace; international humanitarian and human rights law and institutions; prevention, resolution and transformation of violent conflict; and disarmament and human security.

GENERAL ASSEMBLY ACTION

On 17 November [meeting 55], the General Assembly, on the recommendation of the Sixth Committee [A/54/609], adopted **resolution 54/27** without vote [agenda item 154 *(b)*].

Outcome of the action dedicated to the 1999 centennial of the first International Peace Conference

The General Assembly,

Reaffirming the commitment of the United Nations and its Member States to the adherence to and the development of international law as a basis for conducting international relations,

Recognizing the historical importance of the first International Peace Conference, held at the Hague in 1899, for the rule of international law, the peaceful settlement of disputes, the development and codification of international law and the practice of multilateral diplomacy,

Recalling that, in accordance with its previous resolutions, the centennial of the first International Peace Conference coincides with the closing of the United Nations Decade of International Law and could be considered as a third international peace conference,

Recalling also that the Decade was closed by the General Assembly in plenary meeting on 17 November 1999,

Recalling with gratitude the initiatives for the celebration of the centennial of the first International Peace Conference by the Governments of the Kingdom of the Netherlands and the Russian Federation with regard to the themes of the Conference: development of international law relating to disarmament and arms control, humanitarian law and laws of war, and peaceful settlement of disputes,

Recalling that those initiatives called for, *inter alia,* discussions on the themes on the basis of in-depth reports at the global, regional and national levels by intergovernmental, governmental, diplomatic, academic and civil society experts at conferences, seminars and other meetings, as well as through the Internet, to be reported on to the General Assembly for consideration at its fifty-fourth session,

Noting that the general outcome of those discussions was that, while progressive development and codification of international law remains important, the furtherance of the rule of international law would best be served by the faithful compliance of States with existing international obligations, focusing more on the timely implementation of these obligations,

Noting also that the year 1999 marks the fiftieth anniversary of the adoption of the four Geneva Conventions of 12 August 1949,

Noting further that the Permanent Court of Arbitration was established in 1899 as a result of the first International Peace Conference,

Convinced that the legacies of the first International Peace Conference have been enhanced by the centennial initiatives and by the discussions in the General Assembly in plenary meeting at the closing of the Decade,

1. *Takes note with interest* of the outcome of the action dedicated to the centennial of the first International Peace Conference, reported by the co-hosts, the Governments of the Kingdom of the Netherlands and the Russian Federation;

2. *Commends* all who, through their efforts, wisdom and expertise, contributed to the success of the celebration of the centennial of the first International Peace Conference;

3. *Also commends* the International Committee of the Red Cross for its work in promoting adherence to and compliance with the four Geneva Conventions of 12 August 1949 and other instruments of international humanitarian law;

4. *Congratulates* the Permanent Court of Arbitration on its one hundredth anniversary;

5. *Expresses its appreciation* to the Secretary-General for bringing the outcome of the action dedicated to the centennial of the first International Peace Conference to the attention of the relevant international forums;

6. *Invites* States, organs of the United Nations, international organizations and other relevant international forums to take note of the outcome of the action dedicated to the centennial of the first International Peace Conference and to consider, where appropriate:

(a) Giving attention to the outcome of the thematic discussions within the sphere of their respective competencies or mandates;

(b) Making use in the future of the format of the discussions of the centennial of the first International Peace Conference in accordance with any relevant rules and procedures;

7. *Invites:*

(*a*) The Governments of the Kingdom of the Netherlands and the Russian Federation to file the records of the centennial of the first International Peace Conference in their archives and to provide access to those records to interested parties;

(*b*) All who contributed to the centennial of the first International Peace Conference to file their records in this respect with either of these Governments.

UN Programme for the teaching and study of international law

In response to General Assembly resolution 52/152 [YUN 1997, p. 1373], the Secretary-General submitted an October report [A/54/515] on the implementation of the United Nations Programme of Assistance in the Teaching, Study, Dissemination and Wider Appreciation of International Law during 1998-1999. The report gave an account of the activities undertaken by the United Nations and described contributions made by the United Nations Institute for Training and Research (UNITAR) and the United Nations Educational, Scientific and Cultural Organization (UNESCO). The Advisory Committee on the Programme held its thirty-third and thirty-fourth sessions on 10 December 1998 and 20 October 1999, respectively.

During the biennium, staff of the UN Office of Legal Affairs (OLA) continued to perform various functions connected with the Programme's goals. Pursuant to resolution 52/152, the Assembly approved the establishment of the United Nations Audio-visual Library in International Law. In the interim, OLA's Codification Division continued to catalogue the tapes received and to assist in disseminating information regarding UN work on codification and the progressive development of international law, as well as aspects regarding its application via the Internet. OLA issued publications covering issues such as treaties and the law of the sea.

UN fellowship programmes for the study of international law included the Fellowship Programme in International Law, provided by OLA in cooperation with UNITAR. The Office made various arrangements relating to the general orientation of the Programme, such as the selection of fellows and lecturers. Other programmes included the Hamilton Shirley Amerasinghe Memorial Fellowship on the Law of the Sea, awarded by OLA; and the UNITAR/International Peace Academy fellowship programme in peacemaking and preventive diplomacy.

The International Law Commission (ILC) organized the annual International Law Seminar for advanced students and young professors or government officers. The Seminar, held in Geneva, was funded by voluntary contributions from Member States and through national fellowships. The activities of the United Nations Commission on International Trade Law (UNCITRAL) were aimed at acquainting lawyers, government officials and scholars, particularly from developing countries, with the Commission's work and legal texts. UNCITRAL organized seminars and symposia in developing countries to assist them in adapting and implementing UNCITRAL texts. UNESCO continued to disseminate human-rights standard-setting instruments and UNESCO declarations. The number of Chairs in UNESCO's network of Chairs on human rights, democracy, peace and tolerance rose to 41.

The report also contained guidelines and recommendations for the execution of the Programme during the 2000-2001 biennium, as requested by Assembly resolution 52/152.

GENERAL ASSEMBLY ACTION

On 9 December [meeting 76], the General Assembly, on the recommendation of the Sixth Committee [A/54/608], adopted **resolution 54/102** without vote [agenda item 153].

United Nations Programme of Assistance in the Teaching, Study, Dissemination and Wider Appreciation of International Law

The General Assembly,

Taking note with appreciation of the report of the Secretary-General on the implementation of the United Nations Programme of Assistance in the Teaching, Study, Dissemination and Wider Appreciation of International Law and the guidelines and recommendations on future implementation of the Programme which were adopted by the Advisory Committee on the Programme and are contained in section III of that report,

Considering that international law should occupy an appropriate place in the teaching of legal disciplines at all universities,

Noting with appreciation the efforts made by States at the bilateral level to provide assistance in the teaching and study of international law,

Convinced, nevertheless, that States and international organizations and institutions should be encouraged to give further support to the Programme and increase their activities to promote the teaching, study, dissemination and wider appreciation of international law, in particular those activities which are of special benefit to persons from developing countries,

Reaffirming its resolutions 2464(XXIII) of 20 December 1968, 2550(XXIV) of 12 December 1969, 2838(XXVI) of 18 December 1971, 3106(XXVIII) of 12 December 1973, 3502(XXX) of 15 December 1975, 32/146 of 16 December 1977, 36/108 of 10 December 1981 and 38/129 of 19 December 1983, in which it stated or recalled that in the conduct of the Programme it was desirable to use as far as possible the resources and facilities made available by Member States, international organizations and others, as well as its resolutions 34/144 of 17 December 1979, 40/66 of 11 December 1985, 42/148 of 7 December 1987, 44/28 of 4

December 1989, 46/50 of 9 December 1991 and 48/29 of 9 December 1993, in which, in addition, it expressed or reaffirmed the hope that, in appointing lecturers for the seminars to be held within the framework of the fellowship programme in international law, account would be taken of the need to secure the representation of major legal systems and balance among various geographical regions,

Welcoming the establishment of the United Nations Audiovisual Library in International Law,

1. *Approves* the guidelines and recommendations contained in section III of the report of the Secretary-General and adopted by the Advisory Committee on the United Nations Programme of Assistance in the Teaching, Study, Dissemination and Wider Appreciation of International Law, in particular those designed to achieve the best possible results in the administration of the Programme within a policy of maximum financial restraint;

2. *Authorizes* the Secretary-General to carry out in 2000 and 2001 the activities specified in his report, including the provision of:

(a) A number of international law fellowships in both 2000 and 2001, to be determined in the light of the overall resources for the Programme and to be awarded at the request of Governments of developing countries;

(b) A minimum of one scholarship in both 2000 and 2001 under the Hamilton Shirley Amerasinghe Memorial Fellowship on the Law of the Sea, subject to the availability of new voluntary contributions made specifically to the fellowship fund;

(c) Subject to the overall resources for the Programme, assistance in the form of a travel grant for one participant from each developing country, who would be invited to possible regional courses to be organized in 2000 and 2001;

and to finance the above activities from provisions in the regular budget, when appropriate, as well as from voluntary financial contributions earmarked for each of the activities concerned, which would be received as a result of the requests set out in paragraphs 13 to 15 below;

3. *Expresses its appreciation* to the Secretary-General for his constructive efforts to promote training and assistance in international law within the framework of the Programme in 1998 and 1999, in particular for the organization of the thirty-fourth and thirty-fifth sessions of the International Law Seminar, held at Geneva in 1998 and 1999, respectively, and for the activities of the Office of Legal Affairs of the Secretariat related to the fellowship programme in international law and to the Hamilton Shirley Amerasinghe Memorial Fellowship on the Law of the Sea, carried out, respectively, through its Codification Division and its Division for Ocean Affairs and the Law of the Sea;

4. *Requests* the Secretary-General to consider the possibility of admitting, for participation in the various components of the Programme, candidates from countries willing to bear the entire cost of such participation;

5. *Also requests* the Secretary-General to consider the relative advantages of using available resources and voluntary contributions for regional, subregional or national courses, as against courses organized within the United Nations system;

6. *Further requests* the Secretary-General to continue to provide the necessary resources to the programme budget for the Programme for the next and the future bienniums with a view to maintaining the effectiveness of the Programme;

7. *Welcomes* the efforts undertaken by the Office of Legal Affairs to bring up to date the United Nations *Treaty Series* and the *United Nations Juridical Yearbook*, as well as efforts made to place on the Internet the *Treaty Series* and other legal information;

8. *Expresses its appreciation* to the United Nations Institute for Training and Research for its participation in the Programme through the activities described in the report of the Secretary-General;

9. *Also expresses its appreciation* to the United Nations Educational, Scientific and Cultural Organization for its participation in the Programme through the activities described in the report of the Secretary-General;

10. *Further expresses its appreciation* to the Hague Academy of International Law for the valuable contribution it continues to make to the Programme, which has enabled candidates under the fellowship programme in international law to attend and participate in the Programme in conjunction with the Academy courses;

11. *Notes with appreciation* the contributions of the Hague Academy of International Law to the teaching, study, dissemination and wider appreciation of international law, and calls upon Member States and interested organizations to give favourable consideration to the appeal of the Academy for a continuation of support and a possible increase in their financial contributions, to enable the Academy to carry out its activities, particularly those relating to the summer courses, regional courses and programmes of the Centre for Studies and Research in International Law and International Relations;

12. *Urges* all States and relevant international organizations, whether regional or universal, to make all possible efforts to implement the goals and carry out the activities contemplated in section IV of the programme of activities for the final term (1997-1999) of the United Nations Decade of International Law, dealing with the encouragement of the teaching, study, dissemination and wider appreciation of international law and contained in the annex to resolution 51/157 of 16 December 1996;

13. *Requests* the Secretary-General to continue to publicize the Programme and periodically to invite Member States, universities, philanthropic foundations and other interested national and international institutions and organizations, as well as individuals, to make voluntary contributions towards the financing of the Programme or otherwise to assist in its implementation and possible expansion;

14. *Reiterates its request* to Member States and to interested organizations and individuals to make voluntary contributions, inter alia, for the International Law Seminar, the fellowship programme in international law, the Hamilton Shirley Amerasinghe Memorial Fellowship on the Law of the Sea and the United Nations Audiovisual Library in International Law, and expresses its appreciation to those Member States, institutions and individuals which have made voluntary contributions for this purpose;

15. *Urges* in particular all Governments to make voluntary contributions for the organization of regional refresher courses in international law by the United Nations Institute for Training and Research, especially with a view to covering the amount needed for the financing of the daily subsistence allowance for up to twenty-five participants in each regional course, thus alleviating the burden on prospective host countries and making it possible for the Institute to continue to organize the regional courses;

16. *Requests* the Secretary-General to report to the General Assembly at its fifty-sixth session on the implementation of the Programme during 2000 and 2001 and, following consultations with the Advisory Committee on the Programme, to submit recommendations regarding the execution of the Programme in subsequent years;

17. *Decides* to appoint twenty-five Member States, six from Africa, five from Asia, three from Eastern Europe, five from Latin America and the Caribbean and six from Western Europe and other States, as members of the Advisory Committee on the United Nations Programme of Assistance in the Teaching, Study, Dissemination and Wider Appreciation of International Law, for a period of four years beginning on 1 January 2000;

18. *Also decides* to include in the provisional agenda of its fifty-sixth session the item entitled "United Nations Programme of Assistance in the Teaching, Study, Dissemination and Wider Appreciation of International Law".

Host country relations

In 1999, the Committee on Relations with the Host Country continued to consider aspects of relations between the UN diplomatic community and the United States—the host country. At six meetings held between 18 November 1998 and 5 November 1999 [A/54/26], the Committee considered its membership and composition; the security of UN permanent missions and safety of their personnel; acceleration of immigration and customs procedures; security arrangements for the fifty-fourth (1999) session of the General Assembly; and claims of financial indebtedness and procedures to be followed with a view to resolving related issues. Since there were no new developments with regard to the use of diplomatic motor vehicles, parking and related matters, the Working Group established in 1997 to consider those issues [YUN 1997, p. 1376] held no meetings during the reporting period. The Working Group on indebtedness also did not meet during the reporting period.

Committee membership and composition

In response to General Assembly resolution 53/104 [YUN 1998, p. 1243], the Committee's membership increased in 1999 by four members, one each from African, Asian, Latin American and Caribbean, and Eastern European States. The four new members were Cuba, Hungary, the Libyan Arab Jamahiriya and Malaysia. In 1999, the Committee's membership was as follows: Bulgaria, Canada, China, Costa Rica, Côte d'Ivoire, Cuba, Cyprus, France, Honduras, Hungary, Iraq, Libyan Arab Jamahiriya, Malaysia, Mali, Russian Federation, Senegal, Spain, United Kingdom and United States. The Bureau of the Committee held two meetings and, among other things, considered the composition and membership of the Committee and organizational issues related to its work.

Security of missions and safety of their personnel

Costa Rica remarked in November 1998 that security measures adopted during the general debate at the fifty-third (1998) session of the General Assembly had been excessive and at times insulting to certain dignitaries. The Russian Federation stated that lack of coordination between the UN Security and Safety Service and host country security authorities was manifested in the frequent and unwarranted checks of diplomats and other delegation members. It suggested that the Committee consider measures aimed at improving cooperation with the host country authorities and make appropriate recommendations. The United States maintained that the security arrangements were not excessive. Decisions relating to security at Headquarters were made by the Secretary-General and handed down through the Chief of the Security and Safety Service. With regard to the alleged indignities, the United States would not respond to generalities but required specific information. The Chief of the Security and Safety Service said that, in order to ensure all delegations proper protection and to make sure that the Headquarters district remained a safe venue, a security plan had been implemented by the host country law-enforcement authorities. There had been some delays in permitting access by pedestrians and vehicles and the Security and Safety Service had brought those concerns to the attention of the competent authorities.

Implementation of the Agreement between the United Nations and the United States of America regarding Headquarters of the United Nations

On 15 September, the Committee discussed security arrangements undertaken by the host country in connection with the fifty-fourth (1999) session of the General Assembly. The United States said that the Secretariat had specifically requested, pursuant to the United Nations Headquarters Agreement, the assistance of host country law enforcement agencies. The Chief of the UN Security and Safety Service said another briefing on security arrangements would be arranged prior to the session's opening and every effort would be made to ensure that all missions received information about it.

Travel regulations

In October, Cuba drew the Committee's attention to the imposition of restrictions by the host country on movement of the personnel of its Permanent Mission to the United Nations in New York [A/AC.154/326]. In November, the United States responded that it did not impose any such impediments on members of the Mission [A/AC.154/327]. It had, however, for reasons of national security, denied requests for travel to attend events that were non-UN related. The Libyan Arab Jamahiriya, in November, noted that, despite the many General Assembly resolutions that called for lifting travel restrictions imposed by the host country on officials of certain missions and on officials of the UN Secretariat who were of certain nationalities, the host country continued to accord discriminatory treatment to some diplomatic missions, including the Libyan Mission [A/AC.154/328]. The letter also mentioned that the Libyan Mission, as a member of the Committee on Relations with the Host Country, would like to receive formal notification from the Secretariat of any Committee meetings.

Belarus stated that the host country had refused to grant visas to its officials to attend UN-related meetings, which constituted a serious violation of the Headquarters Agreement. The United States replied that the invitation to the meeting in question had been extended by the Secretary-General of the Inter-Parliamentary Union, rather than by the United Nations; thus, the Headquarters Agreement did not apply.

Financial indebtedness

In March, the United States expressed appreciation of the fact that the United Nations would now voluntarily deduct funds from salaries and emoluments of staff members who were under a court order to provide support for spouses and children and had failed to do so.

Other matters

Malaysia raised the question of housing problems faced by diplomats in New York. There had been cases where diplomats had been requested to sign a letter revoking their immunity as a condition for renting an apartment. The United States said that the reason for those demands was the indebtedness of some members of the diplomatic community, and that the problem should be studied by the Bureau of the Committee and its working group on indebtedness.

GENERAL ASSEMBLY ACTION

On 9 December [meeting 76], the General Assembly, on the recommendation of the Sixth Committee [A/54/612], adopted **resolution 54/104** without vote [agenda item 157].

Report of the Committee on Relations with the Host Country

The General Assembly,

Having considered the report of the Committee on Relations with the Host Country,

Recalling Article 105 of the Charter of the United Nations, the Convention on the Privileges and Immunities of the United Nations, the Agreement between the United Nations and the United States of America regarding the Headquarters of the United Nations and the responsibilities of the host country,

Recognizing that effective measures should continue to be taken by the competent authorities of the host country, in particular to prevent any acts violating the security of missions and the safety of their personnel,

Noting the spirit of cooperation and mutual understanding that has guided the deliberations of the Committee on issues affecting the United Nations community and the host country,

Noting also that the membership of the Committee has been increased by four additional Member States, and welcoming their participation in the work of the Committee,

1. *Endorses* the recommendations and conclusions of the Committee on Relations with the Host Country contained in paragraph 43 of its report;

2. *Considers* that the maintenance of appropriate conditions for the normal work of the delegations and the missions accredited to the United Nations is in the interest of the United Nations and all Member States, and requests the host country to continue to take all measures necessary to prevent any interference with the functioning of missions;

3. *Expresses its appreciation* for the efforts made by the host country, and hopes that the issues raised at the meetings of the Committee will continue to be resolved in a spirit of cooperation and in accordance with international law;

4. *Notes* that during the reporting period the travel controls previously imposed by the host country on staff of certain missions and staff members of the Secretariat of certain nationalities remained in effect, and requests the host country to consider removing such travel controls, and in this regard notes the positions of affected States, of the Secretary-General and of the host country;

5. *Requests* the host country to continue to take steps to resolve the problem relating to the parking of diplomatic vehicles in a fair, balanced and non-discriminatory way, with a view to responding to the growing needs of the diplomatic community, and to continue to consult with the Committee on this important issue;

6. *Requests* the Secretary-General to remain actively engaged in all aspects of the relations of the United Nations with the host country;

7. *Requests* the Committee to continue its work in conformity with General Assembly resolution 2819(XXVI) of 15 December 1971;

8. *Decides* to include in the provisional agenda of its fifty-fifth session the item entitled "Report of the Committee on Relations with the Host Country".

International economic law

In 1999, legal aspects of international economic law continued to be considered by the United Nations Commission on International Trade Law (UNCITRAL) and by the Sixth Committee of the General Assembly.

International trade law

At its thirty-second session (Vienna, 17 May-4 June) [A/54/17], UNCITRAL considered privately financed infrastructure projects; electronic commerce; assignment in receivables financing; implementation of the 1958 Convention on the Recognition and Enforcement of Foreign Arbitral Awards (New York Convention) [YUN 1958, p. 390]; case law on UNCITRAL texts; training and technical assistance; status and promotion of UNCITRAL texts; and relevant General Assembly resolutions on the Commission's work.

GENERAL ASSEMBLY ACTION

On 9 December [meeting 76], the General Assembly, on the recommendation of the Sixth Committee [A/54/611], adopted **resolution 54/103** without vote [agenda item 156].

Report of the United Nations Commission on International Trade Law on the work of its thirty-second session

The General Assembly,

Recalling its resolution 2205(XXI) of 17 December 1966, by which it created the United Nations Commission on International Trade Law with a mandate to further the progressive harmonization and unification of the law of international trade and in that respect to bear in mind the interests of all peoples, in particular those of developing countries, in the extensive development of international trade,

Reaffirming its conviction that the progressive harmonization and unification of international trade law, in reducing or removing legal obstacles to the flow of international trade, especially those affecting the developing countries, would contribute significantly to universal economic cooperation among all States on a basis of equality, equity and common interest and to the elimination of discrimination in international trade and, thereby, to the well-being of all peoples,

Emphasizing the need for higher priority to be given to the work of the Commission in view of the increasing value of the modernization of international trade law for global economic development and thus for the maintenance of friendly relations among States,

Stressing the value of participation by States at all levels of economic development and from different legal systems in the process of harmonizing and unifying international trade law,

Having considered the report of the Commission on the work of its thirty-second session,

Mindful of the valuable contribution to be rendered by the Commission within the framework of the United Nations Decade of International Law, in particular as regards the dissemination of international trade law,

Concerned that activities undertaken by other bodies of the United Nations system in the field of international trade law without coordination with the Commission might lead to undesirable duplication of efforts and would not be in keeping with the aim of promoting efficiency, consistency and coherence in the unification and harmonization of international trade law, as stated in its resolution 37/106 of 16 December 1982,

Stressing the importance of the further development of the Case Law on United Nations Commission on International Trade Law Texts in promoting the uniform application of the legal texts of the Commission and its value for government officials, practitioners and academics,

1. *Takes note with appreciation* of the report of the United Nations Commission on International Trade Law on the work of its thirty-second session;

2. *Commends* the Commission for the progress made in its work on receivables financing, electronic commerce, privately financed infrastructure projects and the legislative implementation of the Convention on the Recognition and Enforcement of Foreign Arbitral Awards, done at New York on 10 June 1958;

3. *Appeals* to Governments that have not yet done so to reply to the questionnaire circulated by the Secretariat in relation to the legal regime governing the recognition and enforcement of foreign arbitral awards;

4. *Invites* States to nominate persons to work with the private foundation established to encourage assistance to the Commission from the private sector;

5. *Reaffirms* the mandate of the Commission, as the core legal body within the United Nations system in the field of international trade law, to coordinate legal activities in this field, and in this connection:

(*a*) Calls upon all bodies of the United Nations system and invites other international organizations to bear in mind the mandate of the Commission and the need to avoid duplication of effort and to promote efficiency, consistency and coherence in the unification and harmonization of international trade law;

(*b*) Recommends that the Commission, through its secretariat, continue to maintain close cooperation with the other international organs and organizations, including regional organizations, active in the field of international trade law;

6. *Also reaffirms* the importance, in particular for developing countries, of the work of the Commission concerned with training and technical assistance in the field of international trade law, such as assistance in the

preparation of national legislation based on legal texts of the Commission;

7. *Expresses the desirability* for increased efforts by the Commission, in sponsoring seminars and symposia, to provide such training and technical assistance, and in this connection:

(*a*) Expresses its appreciation to the Commission for organizing seminars and briefing missions in Argentina, Azerbaijan, Bahrain, Bolivia, Brazil, Bulgaria, Cameroon, China, Guatemala, Mexico, Mongolia, Peru, Romania, Venezuela and Zambia;

(*b*) Expresses its appreciation to the Governments whose contributions allowed the seminars and briefing missions to be organized, and appeals to Governments, the relevant United Nations organs, organizations, institutions and individuals to make voluntary contributions to the United Nations Commission on International Trade Law Trust Fund for Symposia and, where appropriate, to the financing of special projects, and otherwise to assist the secretariat of the Commission in financing and organizing seminars and symposia, in particular in developing countries, and in the award of fellowships to candidates from developing countries to enable them to participate in such seminars and symposia;

8. *Appeals* to the United Nations Development Programme and other bodies responsible for development assistance, such as the International Bank for Reconstruction and Development and the European Bank for Reconstruction and Development, as well as to Governments in their bilateral aid programmes, to support the training and technical assistance programme of the Commission and to cooperate and coordinate their activities with those of the Commission;

9. *Appeals* to Governments, the relevant United Nations organs, organizations, institutions and individuals, in order to ensure full participation by all Member States in the sessions of the Commission and its working groups, to make voluntary contributions to the trust fund for travel assistance to developing countries that are members of the Commission, at their request and in consultation with the Secretary-General;

10. *Decides,* in order to ensure full participation by all Member States in the sessions of the Commission and its working groups, to continue, in the competent Main Committee during the fifty-fourth session of the General Assembly, its consideration of granting travel assistance to the least developed countries that are members of the Commission, at their request and in consultation with the Secretary-General;

11. *Requests* the Secretary-General to ensure and enhance the effective implementation of the programme of the Commission;

12. *Stresses* the importance of bringing into effect the conventions emanating from the work of the Commission for the global unification and harmonization of international trade law, and to this end urges States that have not yet done so to consider signing, ratifying or acceding to those conventions.

Model law on corporate insolvency

In 1999, UNCITRAL had before it a proposal by Australia on possible future work in the area of insolvency law [A/CN.9/462/Add.1]), which referred to recent regional and global financial crises and the work undertaken in international forums in response to those crises. Reports from those forums stressed the need to strengthen the international financial system in three areas—transparency, accountability and the management of international financial crises by domestic legal systems. The proposal before the Commission recommended that, in view of its universal membership, its work on cross-border insolvency and its working relations with international organizations that had expertise and interest in the law of insolvency, the Commission was an appropriate forum to consider insolvency law. The proposal urged the Commission to entrust a working group with the development of a model law on corporate insolvency to foster the adoption of national corporate insolvency regimes.

The Commission was invited by the Secretariat [A/CN.9/WG.V/WP.50] to consider devoting one session of a working group to ascertain what would be an appropriate product. The prevailing view in the Commission was that an exploratory session of a working group should be convened to prepare a feasibility proposal for consideration by the Commission at its thirty-third session. Subsequently, it was decided that the Working Group on Insolvency Law would hold that exploratory session.

The Working Group on Insolvency Law, composed of all the States members of the Commission, held its twenty-second session (Vienna, 6-17 December) and submitted its report [A/CN.9/469] to the Commission. The Group recommended that the Commission give it the mandate to prepare: a comprehensive statement of key objectives and core features for a strong insolvency, debtor-creditor regime, including consideration of out-of-court restructuring; and a legislative guide containing flexible approaches to the implementation of such objectives and features, including alternative approaches and the benefits and detriments of such approaches. A legislative guide similar to the one being prepared by the Commission for privately financed infrastructure projects would be useful and could contain model legislative provisions, where appropriate.

International commercial arbitration

Privately financed infrastructure projects

The Commission considered a March report [A/CN.9/458 & Add.1-9] by the Secretary-General containing draft chapters of the UNCITRAL legislative guide on privately financed infrastructure projects. In response to the Commission's 1998 request [YUN 1998, p. 1245], the Secretariat changed the overall structure of the guide, combined some of its chapters, revised the documents considered by UNCITRAL in 1998 and prepared initial drafts of the remaining chapters, with the assistance of outside experts and in consultation with other international organizations.

The Commission generally approved the structure of the legislative guide. Following discussion of model legislative provisions on privately financed infrastructure projects, it was felt that the Commission should continue to consider the desirability of formulating the provisions when discussing the legislative recommendations contained in the draft chapters, and in that connection identify issues for which the formulation of the provisions would increase the guide's value. It was agreed that the legislative recommendations contained in each chapter needed to be reformulated for greater uniformity. The Commission was of the view that the Secretariat, with the assistance of experts, should review recommendations in their entirety, so as to make them more coherent and consistent with one another.

Electronic commerce

The Commission considered the report of the Working Group on Electronic Commerce on the work of its thirty-third (New York, 29 June-10 July 1998) [A/CN.9/454] and thirty-fourth (Vienna, 8-19 February 1999) [A/CN.9/457] sessions. It expressed appreciation for the efforts of the Working Group in preparing draft uniform rules on electronic signatures. While it was generally agreed that significant progress was made in understanding the legal issues of electronic signatures, it was also felt that the Working Group had been faced with difficulties in building a consensus as to the legislative policy on which the uniform rules should be based. Following discussions on the Working Group's approach, the need for the uniform rules and the Group's focus on public key infrastructure models, the Commission urged the Working Group to proceed expeditiously with the completion of the draft rules.

The Commission decided that, upon completing that task, the Working Group would be expected, in the context of its general advisory function regarding electronic commerce, to examine: electronic transactional and contract law; electronic transfer of rights in tangible goods; electronic transfer of intangible rights; rights in electronic data and software; standard terms for electronic contracting; applicable law and jurisdiction; and on-line dispute settlement, as well as additional items.

Assignment in receivables financing

The Commission discussed the report of the Working Group on International Contract Practices on the work of its twenty-ninth (Vienna, 5-16 October 1998) [A/CN.9/455] and thirtieth (New York, 1-12 March 1999) [A/CN.9/456] sessions. The Working Group continued its work on preparing a uniform law on assignment in receivables financing, tentatively entitled the draft Convention on Assignment in Receivables Financing. In October 1998, the Working Group adopted the substance of the preamble and draft articles on scope of application, definitions, debtor's discharge, priority and private international law rules and final provisions. In March 1999, it adopted the title, preamble and draft articles 1 to 24. As a result, the whole text of the draft convention was adopted, with the exception of the optional substantive law priority rules.

The Commission noted that a number of specific questions remained to be addressed by the Working Group, including: whether the draft convention would apply only to assignments in a financing context or to other assignments as well; and whether certain assignments, such as those involved in securities and clearing-house transactions, should be excluded or simply dealt with differently.

The Commission expressed appreciation for the work accomplished by the Working Group and requested it to make possible the draft's circulation, along with the Group's report on its next session, to Governments for comments in time for the draft to be considered for adoption in 2000.

Implementation of the 1958 New York Convention

The Commission noted that the secretariat had received 59 replies to the questionnaire it had sent relating to the legal regime governing the recognition and enforcement of foreign awards in States parties to the 1958 Convention on the Recognition and Enforcement of Foreign Arbitral Awards (New York Convention) [YUN 1958, p. 390]. The Commission called on the remaining States parties to submit their replies and requested the secretariat to prepare an analysis of the information gathered. The Commission considered a March note of the secretariat [A/CN.9/460], which presented possible topics for future work in the area of international commercial arbitration, with reference to the discussions at the fortieth commemoration of New York Convention Day, held in 1998. Other international conferences of arbitration practitioners were taken into account. The Commission, after exchanging views on its future work in the area of international commercial arbitration, decided to entrust the work to a working group and requested the secretariat to prepare the necessary studies. It was agreed that the priority items for the working group should be conciliation, requirement of written form for the arbitration agreement, enforceability of interim measures of protection and possible enforceability of an award that had been set aside in the State of origin.

Case law on UNCITRAL texts (CLOUT)

The Commission noted the work of national correspondents in collecting relevant decisions and arbitral awards and preparing case abstracts for compilation and distribution by the secretariat. However, whereas 58 jurisdictions had appointed national correspondents, another 30 had not yet done so. It was further noted that the number of States adhering to conventions or enacting legislation based on model laws enacted by the Commission had increased significantly. Strong concern was expressed as to the resultant increase of workload for the secretariat.

Training and technical assistance

UNCITRAL had before it a secretariat note [A/CN.9/461] on training and technical assistance activities that had taken place since its 1998 session. It reported that 21 seminars and briefing missions were held to explain the salient features of UNCITRAL texts and the benefits derived from their adoption by States. The Commission appealed to all States, international organizations and other interested entities to contribute to the UNCITRAL trust funds. It decided to recommend that the General Assembly request the Secretary-General to increase substantially the resources available to its secretariat.

PART FIVE

Institutional, administrative and budgetary questions

Chapter I

United Nations reform

In 1999, further progress was made in implementing the Secretary-General's programme of reform of the Organization. The streamlining of procedures in the context of his new vision of management advanced, including implementation of productivity measures, realization of efficiency savings to be deposited in the new Development Account and the adoption of a results-based approach to financial budgeting. Preparations continued for the holding of the Millennium Summit and Forum as part of the Millennium Assembly to begin on 6 September 2000. The Secretary-General proposed that the overall theme should be "The United Nations in the twenty-first century".

The General Assembly, in October, adopted further measures to make UN procurement procedures more transparent, effective and efficient and a set of procedures to assist the Secretary-General in fulfilling his oversight responsibilities in respect of the Organization's resources and staff.

Discussions continued on increasing the membership of the Security Council within the Open-ended High-level Working Group on the Question of the Equitable Representation on and Increase in the Membership of the Security Council and Other Matters Related to the Security Council. The Economic and Social Council continued its efforts to restructure and revitalize the United Nations in the economic and social fields by harmonizing and coordinating the agendas and work programmes of its functional commissions and providing them with clear policy direction in that regard. It also recommended ways to improve cooperation with the Bretton Woods institutions (the World Bank Group and the International Monetary Fund).

Programme of reform

General aspects

The Secretary-General's reform programme, first introduced in 1997 [YUN 1997, p. 1389], continued in 1999. In his annual report on the work of the Organization (see p. 3), he said that a new vision of management was central to his programme of reform and steady progress was being made towards the goals of streamlining procedures across a range of areas. The Management Policy Office had established an ongoing dialogue with programme managers regarding implementation of productivity measures, and efficiency savings would be deposited in a new Development Account and made available for additional projects. Advanced information technologies had improved communication with staff and encouraged discussion on reform throughout the Organization, and the establishment of a Human Resources Cyber Forum had allowed an on-line exchange of views on reform issues. Implementation of the human resources management strategy was progressing steadily, with managerial delegation, empowerment and accountability being pursued on an incremental basis. An electronically accessible performance assessment system had been put in place and the Secretariat's managerial resources were being built through an integrated series of staff development and career support programmes. The development of the results-based approach to financial budgeting continued. Upgrades to the Secretariat's information technology infrastructure had improved the Organization's ability to disseminate information internally, and the development and installation of an up-to-date integrated management information system at all duty stations was advancing. To meet the challenges of the twenty-first century, the Department of Public Information was implementing a new outreach strategy to find new ways to publicize the Organization's activities and highlight its successes.

Millennium Assembly

The Secretary-General, in response to General Assembly resolution 53/202 [YUN 1998, p. 598], by which the Assembly designated its fifty-fifth (2000) session as "The Millennium Assembly of the United Nations" and convened as part of that Assembly session a Millennium Summit, submitted a May report with later addendum [A/53/948 & Add.1] containing his proposals for the Summit's thematic framework. He reported that the Assembly President had held informal consultations to discuss the Millennium Assembly, including the Summit's thematic content. The Secretary-General benefited from those consultations to obtain the views of Member States, members of specialized agencies and observers on the overall theme and sub-topics. The views of non-governmental organizations (NGOs) and the Senior Management Group at Headquarters were also sought. During informal consultations, a number of overarching themes and sub-topics were suggested. It was felt that the selected theme or themes should emphasize the relationship between development on the one hand and peace and security on the other, and thus reflect a common aspiration for the promotion of development and peace and the establishment of a new international political and economic order.

Although the intergovernmental process with respect to the thematic content of the Millennium Summit was ongoing, the Secretary-General proposed as the overall theme "The United Nations in the twenty-first century" and as sub-topics: peace and security, including disarmament; development, including poverty eradication; human rights; and strengthening the United Nations.

He concluded that the third millennium presented a timely opportunity for the only global organization, in terms of its membership and work, to identify future challenges and engage in an imaginative exercise to enhance and strengthen a unique institution. The Millennium Summit would prove to be more than a celebratory event; it would provide an opportunity for a moral recommitment to the purposes and principles laid down in the UN Charter and spur new political momentum for the international cooperation and solidarity that the peoples of the world increasingly demanded.

GENERAL ASSEMBLY ACTION

On 8 June [meeting 101], the General Assembly adopted **resolution 53/239** [draft: A/53/L.77] without vote [agenda items 30 & 58].

United Nations reform: measures and proposals; and strengthening of the United Nations system

The General Assembly,

Recalling its resolution 53/202 of 17 December 1998, by which it decided, inter alia, to designate the fifty-fifth session of the General Assembly "The Millennium Assembly of the United Nations" and to convene, as an integral part of the Millennium Assembly of the United Nations, a Millennium Summit of the United Nations for a limited number of days on dates to be decided by the General Assembly at its resumed fifty-third session,

Recalling also its resolution 53/224 of 7 April 1999, by which it decided, inter alia, that the fifty-fourth session of the General Assembly would open on Tuesday, 14 September 1999,

Mindful that a decision on the duration of the Millennium Summit is predicated on its format and contents,

1. *Decides* that the fifty-fourth session of the General Assembly shall close on Tuesday, 5 September 2000, in the morning, and that the fifty-fifth session of the General Assembly shall open on Tuesday, 5 September 2000, in the afternoon;

2. *Also decides* that the Millennium Summit shall begin on Wednesday, 6 September 2000.

Follow-up to specific measures

Implementation of pilot projects on budgetary practices and procedures

The Secretary-General, in response to General Assembly decision 53/456 [YUN 1998, p. 1251], reported in a February note [A/C.5/53/53 & Corr.1] on the impact of the implementation of pilot projects on budgetary practices and procedures, one of the elements of the UN programme of reform that called for more managerial accountability through greater delegation of authority. He said that the first pilot project on delegataion of authority was initiated in 1998 [YUN 1998, p. 1250] at the Economic Commission for Latin America and the Caribbean (ECLAC). A Department of Management evaluation mission to ECLAC was scheduled for March/April and its report would be issued in May, allowing it to benefit from the Fifth (Administrative and Budgetary) Committee's discussion on human resources management.

The Assembly, by **decision 53/468** of 7 April, took note of the Secretary-General's note and expressed regret that the information it had requested had not been submitted. It deferred consideration of the issue until the second part of its resumed fifty-third (1999) session.

In May, the Secretary-General submitted the mission's report [A/53/947], annexed to which was a list of actions taken by ECLAC with regard to delegation of authority and their results. The team had examined implementation of the pilot project in relation to human and financial resources management and concluded that the extended delegation to ECLAC had been satisfactory and beneficial to ECLAC and the Office of Human Resources Management (OHRM). The scope of the delegation should be maintained at its current level and OHRM should continue to provide full support to maintain the efficiency of the recruitment process and strengthen the capacity of ECLAC's human resources management functions.

ECLAC management had decided not to pursue the delegation of authority regarding the application of revenues for the sale of goods/services to its accounts, as the necessary revolving fund had not yet been established and ECLAC member States continued to discuss reform issues. The requested increase of procurement authority from $200,000 to $1,000,000 was never given since it was felt that the $200,000 ceiling was adequate and the team found no instance of cases over that amount.

The Secretary-General concluded that the pilot project had been implemented without any impact on budgetary practices and procedures and within the existing regulations and rules. Close monitoring of the delegation of authority at the current level would continue.

By **decision 53/474** of 8 June, the Assembly deferred consideration of the Secretary-General's report, his February note and his March 1998 note [YUN 1998, p. 1250] until its fifty-fourth session.

Managerial reform and oversight

Administrative and financial functioning

In response to resolution 45/254 A [YUN 1990, p. 1010], by which the General Assembly invited the Secretary-General to report annually on the administrative, structural and other aspects of the improvement of the efficiency of the Organization, the Secretary-General, in a February report [A/54/67], recalled that his reform programme covered those issues, as well as follow-up action under specific agenda items, such as procurement and human resources management reform, the Development Account, results-based budgeting and the Revolving Credit Fund. He therefore suggested that the Assembly discontinue the submission of the report mandated in Assembly resolution 45/254 A and agree that the issues related to the efficiency of the administrative and financial functioning of the United Nations would be considered under specific agenda items.

On 23 December, the Assembly decided that the item on the review of the efficiency of the administrative and financial functioning of the United Nations would remain for consideration during its resumed fifty-fourth (2000) session (**decision 54/465**) and that the Fifth Committee should continue consideration of the item at that session (**decision 54/462 A**).

Procurement reform

GENERAL ASSEMBLY ACTION

The General Assembly, at its resumed fifty-third session, continued consideration of the item on procurement reform. It had before it the Secretary-General's 1998 reports on procurement [YUN 1998, pp. 1255 & 1256] and the related report of the Advisory Committee on Administrative and Budgetary Questions (ACABQ) [ibid., p. 1257].

On 7 April, the Assembly decided to resume consideration of the question of procurement reform at the second part of its resumed fifty-third (1999) session (**decision 53/467 A**) and, on 8 June, it deferred consideration of the item to the main part of its fifty-fourth (1999) session, with a view to concluding it (**decision 53/467 B**).

On 29 October [meeting 43], the Assembly, on the recommendation of the Fifth Committee [A/54/511], adopted **resolution 54/14** without vote [agenda item 118].

Procurement reform

The General Assembly,

Recalling its resolutions 52/214 B and 52/220 of 22 December 1997, 52/212 B of 31 March 1998, 52/252 of 8 September 1998 and 53/204 and 53/208 B of 18 December 1998,

Reaffirming its resolutions 49/216 C of 23 December 1994, 51/231 of 13 June 1997 and 52/226 A of 31 March 1998,

Having considered the reports of the Secretary-General on procurement reform and the related report of the Advisory Committee on Administrative and Budgetary Questions,

Recognizing that the procurement procedures should be more transparent, effective and efficient and should fully reflect the international character of the United Nations,

Noting the initial efforts to increase procurement opportunities for vendors from developing countries and countries with economies in transition, and stressing the need for further improvement in this respect,

I

General comment

1. *Recognizes* the recent improvements made by the Secretary-General in procurement reform;

2. *Notes with concern* that some of the provisions of its resolution 52/226 A have not been fully and adequately implemented, and requests the Secretary-General to complete the implementation of all outstanding provisions;

3. *Stresses* the need for the procurement system to be transparent, open, impartial and cost-effective, based on competitive bidding and fully reflecting the international character of the United Nations;

II

Procurement Manual

4. *Welcomes* the publication of the Procurement Manual, and requests the Secretary-General to update it, as appropriate, taking into account the recommendations of the Board of Auditors in paragraphs 99 to 104 of its report and including a step-by-step discussion of procedures required for field personnel to perform their duties;

III

General procurement process

5. *Requests* the Secretary-General to take the necessary measures to ensure that the bids received through electronic means are not compromised and to report on this in his next report on procurement reform;

6. *Endorses* the observations of the Advisory Committee on Administrative and Budgetary Questions re-

garding the need to take steps to ensure that specifications are not deliberately tailored to predetermine the choice of supplier and that the principle of separation of responsibilities of the requisitioning and approving officers is maintained;

7. *Requests* the Secretary-General to continue his efforts to ensure wider participation of suppliers from all Member States, taking into account the principles enshrined in the Charter of the United Nations;

8. *Also requests* the Secretary-General to improve further the competitive bidding process in order to ensure that vendors are granted reasonable time for the submission of bids;

9. *Welcomes* the increased use by the Secretary-General of modern electronic means of communication to disseminate information regarding requests for proposals, invitations to bid and requests for expression of interest, and requests him to continue to utilize traditional means of communication for such information upon request;

10. *Requests* the Secretary-General to consider ways to increase the transparency of procurement decisions, including the possibility of reviving the practice of the reading of prices and other decisive elements at public bid openings for requests for proposals, and to report thereon in his next report on procurement reform;

11. *Also requests* the Secretary-General to enhance and expedite the procurement process and to improve communication with suppliers;

IV

United Nations roster and common supplier database

12. *Notes* the efforts of the United Nations system to establish a common supplier database whereby participating organizations will be able to share information on suppliers, including evaluations of performance;

13. *Regrets* that the supplier roster is still not representative of the membership of the United Nations, and reiterates its request to the Secretary-General to intensify further and to focus his efforts to broaden the geographical base of the roster;

14. *Requests* the Secretary-General to improve further the registration process for the supplier roster;

15. *Also requests* the Secretary-General to send invitations to tender, to the fullest extent possible, to all vendors registered under specific categories and services on the supplier roster;

16. *Further requests* the Secretary-General to explore the possibility of using the harmonized system of classification of goods for United Nations procurement and to report thereon in his next report on procurement reform;

V

Procurement planning

17. *Encourages* the Secretary-General to continue to improve annual procurement planning for all offices and departments and to make such plans publicly available, including to all permanent missions to the United Nations;

VI

Exigency

18. *Notes with concern* the observations of the Advisory Committee that the definition of exigency as outlined in the report of the Secretary-General appears too broad to be of any real value in exercising the required control over the use of the exigency provision, and urges the Secretary-General to submit a sharper and clearer definition of exigency needs to the General Assembly, through the Advisory Committee, at its fifty-fourth session;

VII

Increasing procurement from developing countries

19. *Notes with appreciation* the acknowledgement by the Secretary-General of the need to increase procurement opportunities for vendors from developing countries and countries with economies in transition and the steps taken in this regard, and requests him to enhance those efforts;

20. *Requests* the Secretary-General to submit in his next report on procurement reform detailed information on the awarding of contracts for procurement, at Headquarters and in the field, to developing countries, in particular least developed and African countries and countries with economies in transition;

21. *Regrets* the initial delay in implementing the provisions of paragraph 13 of its resolution 52/226 A, and reiterates its request to the Secretary-General to take all possible measures to increase procurement from developing countries and countries with economies in transition, including the following:

(*a*) All invitations to tender should be posted on the Procurement Division website as soon as they are prepared;

(*b*) All invitations to tender should be sent to all permanent missions to the United Nations, as well as to all United Nations information centres and other United Nations offices away from Headquarters for wider dissemination among Member States;

(*c*) Procurement Division officials may undertake visits to developing countries and countries with economies in transition with a view to identifying potential vendors from those countries;

22. *Notes with concern* the observations of the Advisory Committee in paragraph 9 of its report that, out of the eleven countries visited by the procurement officials pursuant to paragraph 13 (*c*) of its resolution 52/226 A, only four were from the developing world and none were countries with economies in transition;

23. *Requests* the Secretary-General to make all possible efforts to facilitate the identification of vendors in developing countries and countries with economies in transition, including through the expeditious dissemination of information relating to procurement to those countries and the organization of seminars at the country and regional levels between the business community and United Nations offices in those countries;

24. *Also requests* the Secretary-General to direct field offices to encourage interested local vendors to apply for registration on the Procurement Division vendor roster with a view to broadening its geographical base;

25. *Encourages* the use of procurement within the region for the requirements of missions, taking into account efficiency and cost-effectiveness;

VIII

Question of preferential treatment

26. *Reaffirms its request* to the Secretary-General to examine ways to increase opportunities for developing countries in the awarding of procurement contracts, in particular for least developed countries, African countries and countries with economies in transition, taking

into account the experience of preferential treatment in this regard in the funds and programmes of United Nations organizations and other intergovernmental institutions, and to report thereon to the General Assembly in his next report on procurement reform;

27. *Requests* the Secretary-General to continue to explore ways to increase the procurement of goods and services from developing countries, in particular from least developed and African countries, and to report thereon to the General Assembly at its fifty-fifth session;

28. *Also requests* the Secretary-General to submit a report on due attention paid to offers for procurement submitted by vendors from developing countries and countries with economies in transition, without prejudice to the Financial Regulations and Rules of the United Nations and taking into account the provisions of the present resolution;

IX

Regulations and Rules

29. *Reiterates the request* contained in paragraph 4 of its resolution 52/226 A;

30. *Regrets* that the request contained in paragraph 28 of its resolution 52/226 A for the submission of proposals on possible amendments to the Financial Regulations and Rules of the United Nations, in order to address issues of potential conflict of interest, has not been fulfilled, and requests the Secretary-General to submit the proposals as a matter of priority, but not later than the end of its fifty-fourth session;

31. *Looks forward* to the submission of the text of the additional rules requested in paragraph 10 of its resolution 52/252, as a matter of priority, but not later than the end of its fifty-fourth session;

32. *Requests* the Secretary-General to make proposals for improving the system of payment to suppliers, including possible mechanisms similar to letters of credit;

X

Performance measurement

33. *Requests* the Secretary-General to develop a comprehensive system to measure the efficiency and cost-effectiveness of the procurement function, by taking into account the best practices of other organizations of the United Nations system in his next report on procurement reform;

XI

Reports of the Board of Auditors

34. *Requests* the Secretary-General to implement fully the provisions of paragraphs 3 and 4 of its resolution 52/212 B regarding the implementation of the recommendations of the Board of Auditors;

35. *Reiterates the request* contained in paragraph 6 of its resolution 53/204 addressed to the Secretary-General and the executive heads of the United Nations funds and programmes to ensure timely implementation of the recommendations of the Board of Auditors as approved in that resolution;

XII

Format for reports

36. *Requests* the Secretary-General to develop a standard format for future reports on procurement reform;

37. *Emphasizes* that the reports of the Secretary-General and the Advisory Committee on procurement reform should be submitted in accordance with paragraphs 24 and 25 of its resolution 52/214 B and paragraphs 10 to 12 of its resolution 53/208 B;

XIII

Method of determining the basis of statistical reports

38. *Endorses* the observations of the Advisory Committee in paragraph 8 of its report, and requests the Secretary-General to indicate on what basis the country of procurement is determined and how this methodology compares with recognized international practice.

In December, the Secretary-General submitted a report [A/54/650] in response to the request in resolution 54/14 for a sharper definition of the term "exigency needs" as it pertained to procurement reform. According to the revised definition, exigency was "an urgent and compelling need, not resulting from poor planning or from concerns over the availability of funds, that would lead to serious damage, loss or injury to property or persons or to considerable additional expenditure if not addressed immediately". The Secretary-General also set out the specific circumstances under which waiver from formal procurement procedures would be permitted and identified situations in which exigency would not be an accepted rationale.

Oversight

Internal oversight

Office of Internal Oversight Services (OIOS)

The Secretary-General, in transmitting the report on the 1998/99 activities of the Office of Internal Oversight Services to the General Assembly (see p. 1275), noted ongoing OIOS efforts to coordinate its programme with other oversight bodies, including the Board of External Auditors and the Joint Inspection Unit (JIU). He concurred with the observations of the Under-Secretary-General for Internal Oversight Services that the independence of the Office had never been compromised during his tenure and he enjoyed the Secretary-General's complete support.

On 8 June (**decision 53/474**), the Assembly deferred to its fifty-fourth session consideration of the Secretary-General's 1997 report on enhancing the internal oversight mechanism in operational funds and programmes [YUN 1997, p. 855] and his notes transmitting OIOS reports for the periods 1 July 1995 to 30 June 1996 [YUN 1996, p. 1268], 1 July 1996 to 30 June 1997 [YUN 1997, p. 1398] and 1 July 1997 to 30 June 1998 [YUN 1998, p. 1258].

On 13 September (**decision 53/496**), the Assembly included the item "Report of the Secretary-General on the activities of OIOS" in the draft agenda of its fifty-fourth (1999) session.

Appointment of Under-Secretary-General. By **decision 53/489** of 13 September, the Assembly included the item on the appointment of the Under-Secretary-General for Internal Oversight Services in the draft agenda of its fifty-fourth session.

In November [A/54/531], the Secretary-General informed the Assembly President that, as the term of office of the current Under-Secretary-General for OIOS was due to expire on 14 November and pending the completion of consultations regarding a possible successor, he had decided to request Hans Corell, Under-Secretary-General for Legal Affairs, the Legal Counsel, to oversee the Office. He would soon submit the name of a new appointee to the Assembly for its consideration and approval.

The Assembly, by **decision 54/415** of 10 November, took note of the Secretary-General's letter.

Implementation of resolution 48/218 B. On 7 April, the Assembly decided to defer consideration of the item entitled "Review of the implementation of General Assembly resolution 48/218 B" [YUN 1994, p. 1362], by which OIOS was established, to the second part of its resumed fifty-third session (**decision 53/471 A**). On 8 June, it deferred consideration of the item to its fifty-fourth (1999) session (**decision 53/471 B**).

On 23 December [meeting 88], the Assembly, on the recommendation of the Fifth Committee [A/54/673], adopted **resolution 54/244** without vote [agenda item 163].

Review of the implementation of General Assembly resolution 48/218 B

The General Assembly,

Reaffirming the relevant Articles of the Charter of the United Nations,

Recalling its resolution 48/218 B of 29 July 1994,

Having evaluated and reviewed the functions and reporting procedures of the Office of Internal Oversight Services, as called for in paragraph 13 of resolution 48/218 B,

Reaffirming its role as one of the principal organs of the Organization as laid down in the Charter,

Reaffirming also that the purpose of the Office of Internal Oversight Services is to assist the Secretary-General in fulfilling his internal oversight responsibilities in respect of the resources and staff of the Organization,

Reaffirming further its resolution 41/213 of 19 December 1986 and the regulations and rules of the United Nations,

Reaffirming the separate and distinct roles of internal and external oversight mechanisms,

1. *Reaffirms* its resolution 48/218 B, subject to the provisions of the present resolution;

2. *Also reaffirms* its role as the principal oversight organ of the Organization;

3. *Recognizes* the importance of the Office of Internal Oversight Services in continuing to assist the Secretary-General in fulfilling his internal oversight responsibilities;

Reporting

4. *Requests* the Secretary-General to transmit the reports of the Office of Internal Oversight Services to the General Assembly for its consideration and action, in conformity with the relevant provisions of the Charter of the United Nations and the rules of procedure of the General Assembly;

5. *Also requests* the Secretary-General to make substantive comments, as appropriate, on the findings and recommendations, and to ensure that the views of the departments concerned on the recommendations are included in the body of the report;

Functions

6. *Emphasizes* that the Office of Internal Oversight Services shall conduct its internal oversight activities strictly in full conformity with General Assembly resolution 48/218 B and subject to the provisions of the present resolution;

7. *Reaffirms* that the Office of Internal Oversight Services, with respect to its inspection and evaluation functions, shall evaluate the efficiency and the effectiveness of the implementation of the programmes and legislative mandates of the Organization, in accordance with paragraph 5 *(c)* (iii) of General Assembly resolution 48/218 B;

8. *Emphasizes* that the approval, change and discontinuation of legislative mandates are the exclusive prerogatives of intergovernmental legislative bodies;

9. *Stresses* that the Office of Internal Oversight Services shall not propose to the General Assembly any change in the legislative decisions and mandates approved by intergovernmental legislative bodies;

10. *Recognizes* that the Secretary-General can submit to the General Assembly any proposal for change in the legislative decisions and mandates through the appropriate channels;

Coordination

11. *Emphasizes* the importance of coordination among oversight bodies, and welcomes the periodic meetings between the Office of Internal Oversight Services and the external oversight bodies;

12. *Reaffirms* that the Board of Auditors and the Joint Inspection Unit shall be provided with copies of all reports produced by the Office of Internal Oversight Services, requests that these be made available within one month of their finalization, and emphasizes the need for comments by the Board and the Unit, as appropriate;

Funds and programmes

13. *Decides* to revert to the question referred to in paragraph 11 of its resolution 48/218 B in the context of its consideration of the report of the Secretary-General on enhancing the internal oversight mechanisms in operational funds and programmes, and in this connection requests the Secretary-General to update the information in that report;

14. *Decides also* to consider this question at an early stage at its fifty-fifth session;

15. *Decides further* that institutional arrangements governing reimbursements of costs between the Office of Internal Oversight Services and United Nations funds and programmes should be made in accordance with the relevant rules and regulations of the respective funds and programmes, including decisions, as appropriate, by their legislative bodies;

Investigations

16. *Stresses* that, in respect of the investigation function of the Office of Internal Oversight Services, the Secretary-General shall provide procedures to protect individual rights of staff, including those of staff members making reports to the Investigations Section, and to regulate due process and fairness for all parties concerned;

17. *Requests* the Secretary-General to submit to the General Assembly for its consideration and action, in conformity with the relevant provisions of the Charter and the rules of procedure of the General Assembly, rules and procedures to be applied for the investigation functions performed by the Office of Internal Oversight Services, in order to ensure fairness and avoid possible abuse in the investigation process;

Operational independence

18. *Emphasizes* that, in accordance with paragraph 5 *(a)* of its resolution 48/218 B, the operational independence of the Office of Internal Oversight Services is related to the performance of its internal oversight functions;

19. *Also emphasizes* that the recruitment and promotion of staff of the Office of Internal Oversight Services shall be in accordance with the provisions of the Charter, the relevant resolutions and decisions of the General Assembly and Staff Regulations and Rules of the Organization, taking into account Article 101, paragraph 3, of the Charter;

20. *Decides* to evaluate and review at its fifty-ninth session the functions and reporting procedures of the Office of Internal Oversight Services and any other matter which it deems appropriate, and to that end to include in the provisional agenda of that session an item entitled "Review of the implementation of General Assembly resolutions 48/218 B and 54/244".

Report of Secretary-General. In September, the Secretary-General transmitted to the General Assembly the fifth annual report of OIOS covering its activities from 1 July 1998 to 30 June 1999 [A/54/393].

The report stated that the number of reports issued by OIOS had steadily increased to 20 in 1998 and a similar number was envisaged for 1999. Emphasis on full implementation of its recommendations continued to be a strong focus of the Office and resulted in a continuous dialogue with its clients. More effort was being spent before recommendations were finalized to ensure their quality and usefulness to management. The implementation rate for the 6,675 recommendations issued between 1 October 1994 and 30 June 1999 was as follows: in the audit area, 6,201 recommendations were issued with a 72 per cent implementation rate; the Investigations Section had an 85 per cent implementation rate for its 324 recommendations; and of the Central Evaluation Unit's 159 recommendations, 82 per cent were implemented. During the current reporting period, the Audit and Management Consulting Division issued 744 recommendations, of which 37 per cent were implemented, while the Investigations Section issued 97 recommendations, of which 57 were implemented.

The report gave an overview of activities in the three oversight priority areas: peacekeeping; humanitarian and related activities; and procurement. It also reviewed the problem of establishing new bodies; human resources management; and information technology management, including UN efforts to prepare for the year 2000 computer problem.

In addition to expanding the audit coverage of the Department of Peacekeeping Operations, OIOS conducted audits at eight field missions. Audits of the Office of the United Nations High Commissioner for Refugees (UNHCR) focused on programme implementation by field offices and their implementing partners and on the UNHCR field office administration. OIOS also conducted three audits at UNHCR headquarters. In response to UNHCR's efforts to decentralize, OIOS established auditor positions in Abidjan, Côte d'Ivoire, and Nairobi, Kenya, and decided to assign a resident auditor for UNHCR operations in Kosovo, Federal Republic of Yugoslavia.

As to procurement, OIOS audits confirmed that continued progress had been made in addressing the major systemic issues identified by the High-level Expert Group on Procurement Reform [YUN 1995, p. 1457]. The Office had reviewed procurement-related arbitration cases (see p. 1315), management of service and ration contracts and the use of aviation services.

Regarding the problems in establishing new bodies, OIOS reviewed the International Tribunals for the Former Yugoslavia and Rwanda and the secretariat for the Basel Convention on the Control of Transboundary Movement of Hazardous Wastes and their Disposal and made recommendations regarding their administrative and financial functioning.

In the area of human resources management, OIOS found that inefficient administrative procedures continued to impede the accomplishment of the Organization's substantive and operational objectives. It noted that future success of key reform issues related to managerial empowerment and accountability would depend largely on specific elements of the OHRM implementation plan. OIOS conducted audits of the employment of retirees, resulting in the issuance of a new administrative instruction in that regard. It also conducted audits of the United Nations Field Service, the personnel administration of the United Nations Compensation Fund and management consulting activities.

With regard to managing information technology, OIOS found that not all clients were aware of the full scope of the year 2000 computer problem or fully compliant with best practices recommended by experts to deal with the problem. It had provided the International Computing Centre with suggestions to accelerate the preparation process and minimize the impact of the problem. OIOS also recommended ways to strengthen management and accountability of the Integrated Management Information System.

As part of its oversight function, the OIOS Audit and Management Consulting Division audited assets of $308 million, income of $75 million and total expenditures of $726 million, identifying some $33.8 million in potential savings and actual savings and recoveries of $23.2 million. The 100 audit assignments opened during the reporting period resulted in 83 audit reports addressed to senior management, with 744 key recommendations on cash management; payroll/personnel; travel and transportation; accounting/budgeting/financial reporting; procurement; property management; programme/project management; information technology systems; and general administration and management.

The Investigations Section devoted its resources to the principle of accountability through recommendations aimed at holding responsible those who violated UN regulations and rules or national laws. Its activities also included proactive investigations in areas of probable risk of fraud, such as education and personnel security grants. The Section received 247 reports and suggestions, compared to 173 in the previous reporting period, a 43 per cent increase. Of the caseload, 95 were in the Americas; 54 in Europe; 41 in Africa; 11 in Asia; and 46 in the Middle East.

OIOS conducted a new inspection review of the common services of the United Nations [A/54/157] (see p. 1376). Follow-up monitoring of implementation of OIOS recommendations was carried out in the International Trade Centre and the Crime Prevention and Criminal Justice Division [YUN 1998, p. 1035]. In-depth evaluations were undertaken of the disarmament programme [E/AC.51/1999/2] and of the electoral assistance programme [E/AC.51/1999/3 & Corr.1].

In two notes dated 30 September, the Secretary-General transmitted to the Assembly JIU's comments on the OIOS reports on the review of common services in the United Nations [A/54/157/Add.1] and on the review of the Office for the Coordination of Humanitarian Affairs [A/54/334/Add.1].

OIOS also conducted triennial reviews of the in-depth evaluations of the Departments of Peacekeeping Operations and of Public Information.

On 23 December, the Assembly decided that the item on the report of OIOS would remain for consideration at its resumed fifty-fourth (2000) session (**decision 54/465**). On the same date, it decided that the Fifth Committee should continue its consideration of the item at that session (**decision 54/462 A**).

External oversight mechanisms

JIU activities

The Joint Inspection Unit, in its thirty-first report to the General Assembly [A/55/34], gave an overview of its activities between 1 January and 31 December 1999, thus reverting to its previous reporting cycle. During that period, it issued reports on the following topics: review of the Administrative Committee on Coordination and its machinery [A/55/288]; an evaluation of the United Nations International Research and Training Institute for the Advancement of Women [A/54/156-E/1999/102]; results-based budgeting: the experience of UN system organizations [A/54/287]; review of management and administration in the International Labour Office [A/54/635]; use of contractual services to support established staff resources in the International Civil Aviation Organization [JIU/REP/99/5]; private sector involvement and cooperation with the UN system [A/54/700]; policies and practices in the use of the services of private management consulting firms in the organizations of the United Nations [A/53/702].

JIU continued to pursue measures to enhance further its functioning and impact. It stated that its impact could come only from the implementation of approved recommendations; improvement in the handling of its reports by participating organizations was also important. In that regard, the Unit issued 10 notes on the subject. In addition, serious consideration should be given to providing JIU with more adequate resources so as to allow it better to discharge its mandate.

In a February note [A/53/841], the Secretary-General transmitted to the Assembly the JIU work programme for 1999 and the preliminary listing of potential reports for 2000 and beyond.

The Assembly, by **decision 53/481** of 8 June, deferred consideration of the item "Joint Inspection Unit" until the main part of its fifty-fourth session.

In a 16 August report [A/54/223], the Secretary-General transmitted information on the status of implementation of recommendations contained in JIU reports on involvement of the UN system in providing and coordinating humanitarian assistance; advancement of the status of women in the UN Secretariat in an era of "human resources management" and "accountability"; advancement of women in and through the programmes of the UN system with a focus on the aftermath of the Fourth World Conference on Women; staffing of the UN peacekeeping and related missions (civilian component); investigation of the relationship between humanitarian assistance and peacekeeping operations; the military component of UN peacekeeping operations; requirements for successful implementation of the system of performance appraisal in the UN Secretariat; inspection of the application of UN recruitment, placement and promotion policies; comparison of methods of calculating equitable geographical distribution within the UN common system; communication for development programmes in the UN system; national execution of projects; UN system support for science and technology in Asia and the Pacific; and managing works of art in the United Nations.

GENERAL ASSEMBLY ACTION

On 29 October [meeting 43], the General Assembly, on the recommendation of the Fifth Committee [A/54/507], adopted **resolution 54/16** without vote [agenda item 123].

Joint Inspection Unit

The General Assembly,

Reaffirming its previous resolutions on the Joint Inspection Unit, hereafter referred to as the Unit, in particular resolution 50/233 of 7 June 1996,

Having considered the annual reports of the Unit for the periods 1 July 1995 to 30 June 1996 and 1 July 1996 to 30 June 1997, its programme of work for 1996-1997 and for 1997-1998, the note by the Secretary-General transmitting the note by the Unit regarding the cycle for its programme of work and the report of the Secretary-General on the implementation of the recommendations of the Unit,

Reaffirming the statute of the Unit, the only independent system-wide inspection, evaluation and investigation body,

Stressing again that the impact of the Unit on the cost-effectiveness of activities within the United Nations system is a shared responsibility of the Member States, the Unit and the secretariats of the participating organizations,

1. *Takes note with appreciation* of the annual reports of the Unit for the periods from 1 July 1995 to 30 June 1996 and 1 July 1996 to 30 June 1997, of its programme of work for 1996-1997, for 1997-1998, and for 1999, of the note by the Secretary-General transmitting the note by the Unit regarding the cycle for its programme of work and of the report of the Secretary-General on the implementation of the recommendations of the Unit;

2. *Invites* the Unit, while preparing its annual programme of work, to give priority to the reports requested by the participating organizations;

3. *Recognizes* the improvements made in the functioning of the Unit, encourages the Unit to continue its efforts in this respect, and decides to revert to the issue of the functioning of the Unit at its fifty-sixth session;

4. *Endorses* the system of follow-up to the reports of the Unit, as contained in annex I to the annual report of the Unit for the period from 1 July 1996 to 30 June 1997, and, in this connection, invites the Unit:

(*a*) To send reminders/notices for the implementation of recommendations to the executive heads of the participating organizations;

(*b*) To include in its annual reports approved recommendations that have not been implemented;

5. *Requests* that the system be implemented expeditiously;

6. *Requests* the Unit to report on experience with the system, including action taken and comments made by participating organizations, to the General Assembly at its fifty-sixth session.

In other action, the Assembly, by **decision 54/454** of 23 December, took note of the report of JIU for the period 1 July 1997 to 31 December 1998 [A/54/34], the Unit's programme of work for 1999 and the listing of potential reports for 2000 and beyond, as well as the report of the Secretary-General on the implementation of the Unit's recommendations, and requested the Secretary-General to further improve the quality, conciseness and clarity of the reports on implementation of the Unit's recommendations.

In **resolution 54/251, section II**, the Assembly, on the same date, approved the gross budget for JIU for the 2000-2001 biennium in the amount of $7,334,400. Also on the same date, in **resolution 54/249**, the Assembly stressed the need to ensure that JIU's independence, as the only system-wide external oversight body, was not compromised through the budgetary process and reaffirmed the Unit's statute, in particular article 20, paragraph 1. By **decision 54/465** of 23 December, the Assembly decided that the item on JIU would remain for consideration at its resumed fifty-fourth (2000) session.

Intergovernmental machinery

Strengthening of the UN system

Revitalization of the work of the General Assembly

In 1999, the General Assembly again took up the item on follow-up to resolution 51/241 [YUN

1997, p. 1402], by which it had adopted the recommendations of the Open-ended High-level Working Group on the Strengthening of the UN System, and considered the Secretary-General's 1998 report on the implementation of that resolution [YUN 1998, p. 1260].

GENERAL ASSEMBLY ACTION

On 7 April [meeting 97], the General Assembly adopted **resolution 53/224** [draft: A/53/L.74] without vote [agenda item 58].

Strengthening of the United Nations system

The General Assembly,

Recalling its resolution 51/241 of 31 July 1997, by which it adopted the recommendations of the Open-ended High-level Working Group on the Strengthening of the United Nations System as contained in the annex to the resolution,

Recalling also the report of the Secretary-General on the implementation of resolution 51/241,

Recalling further its resolution 52/232 of 4 June 1998, by which it decided that the fifty-second session of the General Assembly would close on Tuesday, 8 September 1998, and that the fifty-third session of the General Assembly would open on Wednesday, 9 September 1998, and by which it decided that the International Day of Peace would continue to be observed on the opening day of the regular sessions,

Mindful that, for practical reasons, the closing of the regular sessions of the General Assembly should be on a Monday, which should not be a holiday, and the opening of the regular sessions should be on the following day, that is, on a Tuesday,

1. *Decides* that the fifty-third session of the General Assembly shall close on Monday, 13 September 1999, and that the fifty-fourth session of the General Assembly shall open on Tuesday, 14 September 1999;

2. *Also decides* to consider further during its fifty-third session the question of the opening and closing dates of future regular sessions of the General Assembly.

On 13 September, the Assembly decided to include in the draft agenda of its fifty-fourth (1999) session the item entitled "Revitalization of the work of the General Assembly" (**decision 53/491**).

On 23 December, by **decision 54/465**, the Assembly decided that the item should remain for consideration during its resumed fifty-fourth (2000) session.

Review of Security Council membership and related matters

Open-ended Working Group. The Open-ended Working Group on the Question of the Equitable Representation on and Increase in the Membership of the Security Council and Other Matters Related to the Security Council submitted a report on its work during the General Assembly's fifty-third session [A/53/47]. Between 8 February and 30 July, the Group held 53 meetings at six substantive sessions.

At the first session (8-19 February), the Working Group adopted its programme of work and began in-depth discussions on the item "Working methods of the Security Council and transparency of its work", also referred to as cluster II, and on "Expansion of the Security Council", referred to as cluster I. It had before it a conference room paper prepared by the Bureau on the relationship between the Council and other principal organs of the United Nations.

At the second session (8-12 and 22-24 March), the Working Group focused on cluster II issues and took up two additional items "Decision-making in the Security Council, including the veto" and "Periodic review of the enlarged Security Council". At the third (12-23 April) and fourth (10-14 May) sessions, the Working Group considered revised working papers on the expansion of the Council and its decision-making, including the veto, and on the working methods of the Council and transparency of its work. At its fifth session (16-25 June), in addition to the papers submitted by the Bureau, the Working Group had before it a paper submitted by Colombia on behalf of 17 other Member States. Discussions on cluster I and II items continued. The question of institutionalization, namely the form in which provisions would be finally recorded, was also considered. At the sixth session (19-30 July), the Working Group continued its deliberations on both clusters and received working papers from: the Permanent Representative of Egypt, in his capacity as Chairman of the Working Group of the Movement of Non-Aligned Countries on the reform and restructuring of the Council; Algeria, transmitting the African position on equitable representation on and increase in the membership of the Council; and the Republic of Korea, transmitting a letter from the 10 elected members of the Council.

Concerning cluster II issues, provisional agreement was recorded on a number of subparagraphs in the conference room paper dealing with the working methods of the Council and transparency of its work. A revised version of that paper was issued indicating areas where provisional agreement was reached and those where no agreement was reached and listing all proposed amendments.

The Working Group also considered its report to the General Assembly and recommended that consideration of the agenda item should continue at the fifty-fourth session, building upon the work of all previous sessions.

The Assembly, by **decision 53/487** of 13 September, took note of the Working Group's report and decided that the Group should continue its work, taking into account the progress achieved during the Assembly's forty-eighth through fifty-third sessions, as well as views expressed during the fifty-fourth session, and submit a report, including any agreed recommendations, before the end of the fifty-fourth session.

On 23 December, by **decision 54/465**, the Assembly decided that the item should remain for consideration during its resumed fifty-fourth (2000) session.

Revitalization of the United Nations in the economic, social and related fields

In 1999, the Economic and Social Council continued consideration of the process of restructuring and revitalization in the economic, social and related fields of the United Nations, which began in 1991 [YUN 1991, p. 749], in particular the review of the functioning of its subsidiary bodies.

Implementation of General Assembly resolutions 50/227 and 52/12 B

The Secretariat, in a January note [E/1999/3], submitted to the Economic and Social Council, in response to Assembly resolution 50/227 [YUN 1996, p. 1249], a consolidated report on the outcomes of the functional commissions of the Economic and Social Council in 1998. The report identified and highlighted linkages between those outcomes to assist the Council in harmonizing and coordinating agendas and work programmes of functional commissions by promoting a clear division of labour among them and by providing clear policy guidance. The report also aimed to provide a means of communication among functional commissions themselves so that they could be more aware of each other's work and to overcome the isolation in which they operated. The report noted that there was no formal mechanism by which the functional commissions communicated among themselves; whatever communication existed took place largely in an ad hoc manner, often dependent on personal initiatives by chairpersons. The report contained several recommendations for the Council's consideration.

The Council also had before it in February the Secretary-General's 1998 reports on the restructuring and revitalization of the United Nations in the economic, social and related fields and on the joint exploratory review of cooperation between the United Nations and the Bretton Woods institutions (the World Bank Group and the International Monetary Fund) [YUN 1998, p. 1269].

ECONOMIC AND SOCIAL COUNCIL ACTION

On 2 February [meeting 2], the Economic and Social Council adopted **resolution 1999/1** [draft: E/1999/L.6 & Corr.1] without vote [agenda item 4].

Restructuring and revitalization of the United Nations in the economic, social and related fields

The Economic and Social Council,

Recalling its resolutions 1996/43 of 26 July 1996, 1998/46 and 1998/47 of 31 July 1998 and 1998/49 of 16 December 1998, and General Assembly resolutions 50/227 of 24 May 1996 and 52/12 B of 19 December 1997,

1. *Takes note with appreciation* of the reports of the Secretary-General on restructuring and revitalization of the United Nations in the economic, social and related fields and on the joint exploratory review of cooperation between the United Nations and the Bretton Woods institutions, and of the consolidated report by the Secretariat on the outcomes of the functional commissions of the Economic and Social Council in 1998;

I. Restructuring and revitalization of the United Nations in the economic, social and related fields

2. *Welcomes* the progress made in implementing the provisions of General Assembly resolutions 50/227 and 52/12 B;

3. *Decides* to inform the General Assembly of progress made by the Economic and Social Council in implementing Assembly resolutions 50/227 and 52/12 B, and, to that end, requests the President of the Council to write to the President of the Assembly, as a follow-up to the letter of the President of the Council dated 21 August 1998 pursuant to Council resolution 1998/46;

4. *Takes note* of the recommendations contained in the report of the Secretary-General on restructuring and revitalization of the United Nations in the economic, social and related fields related to the work of the Council which include elements for continued deliberations of the Council on the further implementation of General Assembly resolutions 50/227 and 52/12 B;

5. *Looks forward* to the annual progress report of the Secretary-General on the further implementation of General Assembly resolutions 50/227 and 52/12 B and resolution 1998/46, to be submitted to the Council at its substantive session of 1999;

II. Joint exploratory review of cooperation between the United Nations and the Bretton Woods institutions

6. *Welcomes* the joint exploratory review of cooperation between the United Nations and the Bretton Woods institutions as the first such joint review, and reaffirms that cooperation between the United Nations and the Bretton Woods institutions should cover cooperation at all levels, including intergovernmental, country and secretariat levels, as mandated by the Assembly in resolution 50/227;

7. *Also welcomes* the progress made in strengthening cooperation between the United Nations and the Bret-

ton Woods institutions at the intergovernmental, country and secretariat levels, and encourages further cooperation in that regard;

8. *Encourages* the organizations that participated in the joint exploratory review of cooperation between the United Nations and the Bretton Woods institutions collectively to undertake a renewed effort to concert policy approaches and give new impetus to collaborative actions by the organizations and agencies of the United Nations system, in particular in the area of poverty eradication;

9. *Welcomes* the increased dialogue and cooperation between the United Nations and the Bretton Woods institutions at the intergovernmental level, and decides to make further efforts to promote an open dialogue with a view to building a strategic partnership and integrated development approaches;

10. *Takes note* of the recommendations of the Secretary-General on cooperation between the United Nations and the Bretton Woods institutions contained in his report, and encourages the organizations to continue to pursue cooperation at the country and Secretariat levels, bearing in mind those recommendations;

11. *Requests* the Secretary-General to prepare a progress report on cooperation between the United Nations and the Bretton Woods institutions at all levels;

III. Outcomes of the functional commissions of the Economic and Social Council in 1998

12. *Recognizes* that a consolidated report on the outcomes of the functional commissions of the Economic and Social Council is a useful tool with respect to supporting its coordination function;

13. *Requests* the functional commissions that have not yet done so to implement Assembly resolution 50/227 with regard to the provision of summaries of their resolutions or decisions for action by, and for the attention of, the Economic and Social Council;

14. *Welcomes* recommendations 1, 3, 4, 5 and 6 of section 1, recommendation 1 of section 2 and the recommendations contained in sections 3 to 9 of the consolidated report on the outcomes of the functional commissions of the Economic and Social Council in 1998, decides to transmit the recommendations to the appropriate functional commissions for their implementation, and requests the functional commissions to report to the Council at its substantive session of 1999 on the follow-up actions taken;

15. *Requests* the Secretary-General to prepare a further consolidated report on the work of the functional commissions of the Economic and Social Council in 1999 for consideration at its substantive session.

As requested in resolution 1999/1, a May progress report [E/1999/56] reflected the ongoing cooperation between the United Nations and the Bretton Woods institutions (see p. 890).

Reports of Secretary-General. The Secretary-General submitted to the Economic and Social Council's substantive session a June report [A/54/115-E/1999/59] on progress in the implementation of General Assembly resolutions 50/227 [YUN 1996, p. 1249] and 52/12 B [YUN 1997, p. 1392] and Council resolution 1998/46 [YUN 1998, p. 1262]. The Secretary-General made a number of recommendations for the Council's consideration concerning the Assembly; documentation; the Council and its functional commissions; inter-agency coordination; and the relationship between the United Nations and international finance and trade institutions.

In response to Council resolution 1999/1, the Secretary-General issued in June another consolidated report on the work of the functional commissions [E/1999/101 & Corr.1]. The report focused on a limited number of activities, chosen with a view to facilitating the Council's coordinating and guiding role, primarily regarding the major cross-cutting themes.

The report provided an overview of the work of the commissions in 1999, identified the main focus of their work programmes and relationship to priority topics and major system-wide events, identified thematic linkages and complementarities among the activities of the functional commissions on the basis of sessional documents and outcomes of the commissions' sessions, and described the existing modalities of addressing those linkages, such as coordination and consultation mechanisms that were established between some functional commissions, and attempted to identify remaining weaknesses of the existing coordination arrangements. The Secretary-General made a number of recommendations for the harmonization and coordination of the work programmes of the functional commissions.

The Secretary-General also noted that, following the consolidation of the economic departments of the United Nations, five of the nine functional commissions were serviced by the Department of Economic and Social Affairs, which greatly facilitated and improved communication, coordination and collaboration within the Secretariat in terms of servicing the functional commissions.

In July, the Secretary-General submitted a report [E/1999/108] on the joint meetings between the Council's Bureau and the bureaux of its functional commissions. It provided recommendations for improving not only the working methods of the functional commissions but also the coordination and collaboration among them. He suggested that the Council might wish to: reiterate that the adoption of multi-year thematic programmes for the functional commissions responsible for follow-up to major conferences could be helpful to ensure greater collaboration; and invite the commissions to re-elect one member of the outgoing bureau to the incoming bureau to allow for continuity. As to better collaboration between functional commissions, he suggested that the Council might wish to: review the modalities of participation of NGOs; encourage the commissions to enhance cooperation on cross-cutting issues; invite the commissions to hold regular bilateral meetings on issues addressed by two or more commissions; invite them to ensure that resolutions and agreed conclusions contained clear guidance on how to operationalize the Council's guidance; and request the commissions to include an item on each agenda specifically devoted to follow-up to the guidance of the Council and coordination and collaboration with other functional commissions.

ECONOMIC AND SOCIAL COUNCIL ACTION

On 29 July [meeting 45], the Economic and Social Council adopted **resolution 1999/51** [draft: E/1999/L.46] without vote [agenda item 8].

Restructuring and revitalization of the United Nations in the economic, social and related fields and cooperation between the United Nations and the Bretton Woods institutions

The Economic and Social Council,

Recalling its resolutions 1996/43 of 26 July 1996, 1998/46 and 1998/47 of 31 July 1998, 1998/49 of 16 December 1998 and 1999/1 of 2 February 1999 and General Assembly resolutions 50/227 of 24 May 1996 and 52/12 B of 19 December 1997,

1. *Takes note* of the report of the Secretary-General on restructuring and revitalization of the United Nations in the economic, social and related fields, the progress report on cooperation between the United Nations and the Bretton Woods institutions, the consolidated report on the work of the functional commissions of the Economic and Social Council in 1999 and the report of the Vice-President of the Council on the joint meetings held between the Bureau of the Council and the bureaux of its functional commissions;

I. Restructuring and revitalization of the United Nations in the economic, social and related fields

2. *Requests* the full implementation of paragraph 1 *(l)* of its resolution 1982/50 of 28 July 1982, and paragraph 2 *(f)* (i) of its resolution 1988/77 of 29 July 1988 regarding the scheduling of meetings of subsidiary bodies of the Council at least eight weeks before the session of the Council, where feasible, and submission of the reports of these bodies well in advance for the consideration of the Council;

3. *Welcomes* the progress made in ensuring an increased interaction of the Council with its subsidiary bodies, including through joint bureau meetings, and in strengthening its coordinating functions, and supports the effort further to ensure the regular exchange of information on their programmes of work, including a more systematic transmission of documentation to other subsidiary bodies when it is of relevance to their work;

4. *Encourages* annual meetings of its Bureau with the chairpersons of the functional commissions to facilitate an exchange of views and information on the direction of the programmes of work of the commissions;

5. *Invites* the bureaux of the functional commissions to develop interaction among themselves to improve collaboration and coordination on issues that are addressed by two or more commissions, using information technology as required;

6. *Invites* the functional commissions to implement, where they have not yet done so, relevant provisions of its resolution 1998/46, in particular as it relates to the adoption of multi-year programmes of work and to the coordinated follow-up to major United Nations conferences and summits, and requests the Secretary-General to submit a progress report on this matter to the Council at its substantive session of 2000;

7. *Invites* the Commission on Crime Prevention and Criminal Justice, the Commission on Narcotic Drugs, the Statistical Commission and the Commission on Science and Technology for Development to consider adopting multi-year programmes of work;

8. *Encourages* the functional commissions, in formulating the titles of the items in their programmes of work, to provide, where appropriate, an explicit indication of linkages of their planned activities with those of other commissions and/or with major planned United Nations events, and also encourages the functional commissions, assisted by their secretariats, to enhance coordination and collaboration at the programme planning and formulation stage;

9. *Invites* the functional commissions, in designing their multi-year programmes of work, to take fully into account the multi-year programmes of work of other functional commissions to ensure complementarity between them;

10. *Stresses* the need for consistency and complementarity between the programmes of work of the subsidiary bodies of the Council, while keeping in mind the need to avoid overlapping and duplication of their mandates;

11. *Welcomes* the holding of open and informal dialogue sessions, including by the Council, on cross-cutting themes of various functional commissions, and encourages the further development of this practice, bearing in mind the importance of providing adequate time for intergovernmental debate, as well as the need to focus on issues within their mandates;

12. *Stresses* the importance of ensuring continuity on the bureaux of the functional commissions, and, therefore, invites the functional commissions to consider re-electing at least one member of the outgoing bureau to the incoming bureau, without prejudice to the rules of procedure of the functional commissions of the Economic and Social Council regarding the election of the bureau;

13. *Invites* the Committee for Development Policy to improve its methods of work in order better to contribute to the work of the Council, and decides that the future programme of work of the Committee should be determined at the substantive session of the Council;

14. *Welcomes* the high-level special meeting of the Council with the Bretton Woods institutions, and decides to maintain such meetings while focusing the agenda, in consultation with the Bretton Woods institutions, on one or two major substantive issues in order to provide sufficient time to share views and to explore the relationship with the high-level segment of the Council;

II. Progress report on cooperation between the United Nations and the Bretton Woods institutions

15. *Welcomes* the continued strengthening of a productive partnership, in all its aspects and at all levels, between the United Nations and the Bretton Woods institutions;

16. *Also welcomes* the series of events and initiatives in 1998 and 1999 which have strengthened and advanced the policy-oriented interaction and dialogue at the intergovernmental level, including dialogue between governing bodies of the United Nations and the Bretton Woods institutions;

17. *Further welcomes* the broad agreement reached in the context of the Ad Hoc Open-ended Working Group of the General Assembly on Financing for Development on the need to involve the Bretton Woods institutions in the process on financing for development, as reflected in the report of the Working Group;

18. *Recommends* in this context that the General Assembly consider exploring, during its fifty-fourth session, the possibility of inviting the Bretton Woods institutions to participate in a joint task force with the United Nations with the aim of facilitating the further involvement of the Bretton Woods institutions in this process;

19. *Encourages* further intensification and deepening of collaboration at the secretariat level and, especially important, at the country level, with a view to ensuring coherence, complementarity and synergy of development activities and to promoting national ownership;

20. *Reiterates its call* to the United Nations and the Bretton Woods institutions to undertake collectively a renewed effort further to coordinate policy approaches and give new impetus to collaborative and complementary actions by the organizations and agencies of the United Nations system, in particular in the area of poverty eradication;

III. Outcomes of the functional commissions of the Economic and Social Council in 1999

21. *Invites* the functional commissions to continue to give particular attention to the situation of African countries and the least developed countries in their consideration of relevant issues, especially in view of the Third United Nations Conference on the Least Developed Countries to be held in 2001 and the review of the United Nations New Agenda for the Development of Africa in the 1990s to be carried out in 2002;

22. *Encourages* the bureaux of the functional commissions to continue to support the cooperation among the functional commissions, in particular by implementing fully the guidance given by the Council in its resolution 1999/1, and encourages further strengthening and intensification of collaboration between and among the secretariats of the functional commissions; such collaboration can be in the form of, inter alia, preparation of joint reports on linked issues, systematic exchange of relevant information and documentation and participation in relevant activities, where feasible and appropriate;

23. *Requests* the functional commissions to report on the follow-up actions to the present resolution to the Council at its substantive session of 2000;

24. *Requests* the Secretary-General to submit a progress report on the implementation of the present resolution to the Council at its substantive session of 2000.

General Assembly action. By **decision 53/492** of 13 September, the General Assembly decided to include in the draft agenda of its fifty-fourth (1999) session the item entitled "Restructuring and revitalization of the United Nations in the economic, social and related fields".

On 23 December, the Assembly decided that the item would remain for consideration during its resumed fifty-fourth (2000) session (**decision 54/465**).

Chapter II

United Nations financing and programming

In 1999, the United Nations financial outlook improved appreciably, with higher end-of-year balances and lower unpaid assessments, as well as reduced debt to Member States for troops and contingent-owned equipment. Unpaid assessments at the end of 1999 stood at $1,758 million, compared to $2,031 million a year earlier. For the first time since 1995, no cross-borrowing of funds from peacekeeping accounts at the end of the year was required. The improved situation was due to consistent payment in full of regular budget assessment and substantially higher payments from the largest contributor. A record 126 Member States had paid their budget assessments for 1999 and all previous years in full. However, the Secretary-General warned that the overall improvement in the financial situation might be upset by new special missions launched during the year.

The General Assembly, in December, adopted revised budget appropriations of $2.5 billion, or a decrease of $42 million, compared to the initial appropriations approved for the 1998-1999 biennium, and approved appropriations of $2,535,689,200 for the 2000-2001 biennium, including $1,267,844,600 for 2000. The Assembly considered the experience gained by UN agencies and organizations with results-based budgeting and the Secretary-General's proposals to improve the current format. It established the Development Account—a special multi-year account for supplementary development activities—and decided that saving to be achieved as a result of efficiency measures should be transferred to that account, with the Assembly's approval. The United Nations International Partnership Trust Fund, established in 1998, had so far programmed $190 million for development projects, with the majority of grants going to children's health.

The Committee on Contributions continued to review the methodology for preparing the scale of assessments of Member States' contributions to the UN budget, in particular the procedural aspects for considering requests for exemption under Article 19 of the Charter, as well as new proposals for arriving at the rates of assessment for non-member States. On the Committee's recommendation, the Assembly granted a number of exemptions under Article 19 and agreed to consider the issues further in 2000.

The Assembly accepted the financial reports and audited financial statements and audit opinions of the Board of Auditors for peacekeeping operations for the 1998-1999 biennium and those on the voluntary funds administered by the Office of the United Nations High Commissioner for Refugees for the period 1 January to 31 December 1998. It reviewed the Secretary-General's reports on the implementation of the recommendations of the Board of Auditors, and the Board's report on the implementation of its recommendations by UN entities and organizations.

Financial situation

In March [A/53/514 & Add.1,2], the Secretary-General reported to the General Assembly that, as at 28 February, a total of 49 Member States had paid in full their regular budget estimates for 1999, 10 more than at the comparable date in 1998, and only 37 Member States remained under the provision of Article 19 of the Charter to lose their vote in the Assembly. As at that date, $405 million in regular budget assessments had been paid, $88 million more than in 1998. However, the Secretary-General noted that, despite the positive improvements in regular budget cash balance and unpaid assessments, numerous unstable conditions still held the Organization's financial future hostage.

By **decision 53/494** of 13 September, the Assembly deferred consideration of the item entitled "Improving the financial situation of the United Nations" and included it in the draft agenda of its fifty-fourth (1999) session.

As at 30 September [A/54/454], the Secretary-General reported that unpaid assessments aggregated $2,510 million, slightly more than a year earlier. Of that amount, $644 million was for the regular budget, $1,831 million for peacekeeping and $35 million for the international tribunals. The situation was due largely to the growth of peacekeeping arrears, the fact that payments by the major contributor would begin in October at the start of the Member State's new budget year and significant amounts owed by two of the next 14 principal contributors.

The regular budget contributions of $857 million received were actually lower than at the same time the previous year, or 79 per cent of the $1,084 million assessed for 1999. As at 30 September, 104 Member States had paid their regular budget contributions in full for 1999 and all prior years, showing continued improvement over previous years. In September, the Organization was in a positive cash balance position due to the payment by Japan of the $155 million balance of its regular budget contribution.

In an end-of-year review of the financial situation [A/54/454/Add.1], the Secretary-General noted that 1999 was a year of financial turnaround with higher end-of-year balances and lower unpaid assessments, as well as lower debt to Member States for troops and contingent-owned equipment. The aggregate cash balances for the regular budget, peacekeeping and the tribunals combined increased to a high of $1,093 million from $736 million in 1998. Unpaid assessments stood at $1,758 million, down from $2,031 million a year earlier. At the end of the year, 126 Member States had paid their regular budget assessment for 1999 and all earlier years in full, 9 more than in 1998. The consistent payment in full of regular budget assessment was the prime measure of the Organization's financial stability. The largest contributor also made substantially higher payments totalling $452 million. As a result, for the first time since 1995, no cross-borrowing of funds from peacekeeping accounts was needed at year's end.

Amounts due to Member States for troops and contingent-owned equipment totalled $800 million, significantly lower than during the previous three years. Unpaid peacekeeping assessments aggregated $1,482 million, a decrease of $112 million from 1998, while those of the international tribunals were over $32 million or 20 per cent of the 1999 assessment level.

The Secretary-General said that there was a danger that the overall improvement in the financial situation might be upset by the new special challenges, such as missions to the Kosovo province of the Federal Republic of Yugoslavia (FRY) (see p. 363) and East Timor (see p. 295). However, for 1999 as a whole, after a period of several years, a degree of financial stability had returned for activities funded from the regular budget, though that stability was less for activities funded by peacekeeping assessments.

On 23 December, the Assembly decided that the item on improving the financial situation of the United Nations would remain for consideration at its resumed fifty-fourth (2000) session (**decision 54/465**), and that the Fifth (Administrative and Budgetary) Committee should continue to consider it at that session (**decision 54/462 A**).

UN budget

Results-based budgeting

JIU report. As requested in General Assembly resolution 53/205 [YUN 1998, p. 1273], the Secretary-General transmitted in August [A/54/287] the Joint Inspection Unit (JIU) report entitled "Results-based budgeting: the experience of United Nations system organizations".

JIU found that the experience of other UN system organizations with results-based budgeting was mixed and indicated problems or difficulties that required special attention in considering the Secretary-General's proposal to apply it to the United Nations. However, overall, there was a growing common understanding among UN system organizations of, and support for, results-based budgeting techniques as a tool for achieving increased budget transparency and accountability.

JIU recommended that the *Glossary of financial and budgetary terms* should be reviewed and commented on by UN system organizations to resolve the problem of the lack of agreed definitions of key results-based budgeting terms; an open-ended working group of the Fifth Committee should be established; the United Nations Institute for Training and Research should conduct seminars and workshops to help familiarize staff and Member States' representatives with results-based budgeting; the Secretary-General's reports should include a comprehensive assessment of changes required to ensure UN readiness in areas such as regulations, procedures, a management information system and training; and the Secretary-General should submit recommendations on the matter along with the comments of the Advisory Committee on Administrative and Budgetary Questions (ACABQ) and the Committee for Programme and Coordination (CPC).

The Secretary-General's comments on the JIU report were transmitted to the Assembly in a November note [A/54/287/Add.1].

Reports of Secretary-General. The Secretary-General, also in response to Assembly resolution 53/205, submitted an October report on results-based budgeting [A/54/456], which further described the proposed format by highlighting the expected improvements over the current format and providing further justification for the proposals.

According to the report, results-based budgeting would build on existing processes and consolidate various elements of the programming, planning, budgeting, monitoring and evaluation cycle that had hitherto been applied in relative isolation from each other. A results-based budget format differed from the current format in its emphasis on expected accomplishments and would serve as a policy tool for Member States and as a basis for determining the effectiveness and continuing relevance of UN work. The accountability of programme managers would increase by focusing on objectives, expected accomplishments and performance indicators at the beginning of the programme cycle and during budget formulation. The programme budget could be used to its full potential to serve as a medium of communication between Member States and the Secretariat on the purpose and direction of the Organization.

The Secretary-General recommended further development of the performance indicators for use in all substantive and support programmes and that they be included in all sections of the 2002-2003 proposed programme budget, in addition to statements of objectives and expected accomplishments in a single coherent framework. He also recommended the preparation of a prototype report on accomplishments based on the prototype fascicles (see below) for consideration in 2001, and the further development of mechanisms and skills to successfully implement performance measurement as a basis for improved programme monitoring and evaluation within the existing programme budget cycle.

The Secretary-General also submitted in subsequent addenda, for illustrative purposes only, prototype fascicles in results-based budget format in five sections of the 2000-2001 budget: section 3, Political affairs [A/54/456/Add.1]; section 11A, Trade and development [A/54/456/Add.2]; section 15, International drug control [A/54/456/Add.3]; section 18, Economic development in Europe [A/54/456/Add.4]; and section 27B, Office of Programme Planning, Budget and Accounts [A/54/456/Add.5].

The report of the Secretary-General sought the endorsement of the Assembly to a gradual approach to the introduction of results-based budgeting in the programme planning, budgeting, monitoring and evaluation cycle. The Secretary-General proposed the inclusion of performance indicators in the programme budget for 2002-2003, in addition to statements of objectives and expected accomplishments, while maintaining the current level of detail on post and non-post requirements.

Further steps envisaged were: measurement of the performance of the five budget sections covered in the prototype fascicles against a limited number of expected accomplishments, using selected performance indicators at the end of the 2000-2001 biennium; and other internal measures designed to increase the knowledge of staff and the development of mechanisms and procedures that would support a gradual implementation of performance measurement as a basis for improved programme monitoring and evaluation.

Budget for 1998-1999

Final appropriations

In 1999, the General Assembly adopted final budget appropriations for the 1998-1999 biennium, decreasing the amount of $2,488.3 million approved in 1998 by resolution 53/215 [YUN 1998, p. 1275] by $41.6 million. It reduced approved income estimates by $6.3 million to $356.4 million.

Report of Secretary-General. In the second performance report [A/54/631 & Corr.1], the Secretary-General provided estimates of the anticipated final levels of expenditure and income for the 1998-1999 biennium, based on actual expenditures for the first 20 months and projected requirements for the last four months, as well as changes in inflation and exchange rates and cost-of-living adjustments. The estimates proposed represented a decrease of $35.3 million, or 1.6 per cent, compared with the revised appropriations and estimates of income approved in 1998. The net reduced requirement reflected an increase of $4.8 million for commitments entered into under the provisions of resolution 52/223 [YUN 1997, p. 1438] on unforeseen and extraordinary expenses, and commitments arising from Economic and Social Council resolution 1999/293 on the situation of human rights in East Timor (see p. 709). That was offset by a decrease of $40.1 million, attributable to changes in exchange rate assumptions ($17.2 million), changes in inflation ($2 million), variations in posts and common staff costs ($12.3 million) and adjustments to non-post expenditures, based on actual anticipated requirements ($14.9 million) and a decrease in income of $6.3 million. Proposed expenditure amounted to $2,488.3 million, or a decrease of $41.6 million or 1.6 per cent, compared with the revised appropriations and estimates of income approved in 1998 [YUN 1998, p. 1275]. Income was estimated at $2,131.9 million, or a decrease of $6.3 million.

In view of the Organization's chronic cash shortage, the Secretary-General sought the Assembly's concurrence to suspend financial regulations 4.3, 4.4 and 5.2 *(d)* in respect of surpluses arising at the end of the financial period.

ACABQ report. In its comments on the Secretary-General's report [A/54/7/Add.7], ACABQ observed that the net reduced requirement of $35.3 million for the biennium represented only a theoretical surplus and requested the Secretary-

General to deliver a clear statement of the current cash flow situation to the Fifth Committee, as well as a complete analysis of the impact of the suspension of provisions of the financial regulations in respect of surpluses on all Member States, particularly on those that had paid their assessments in full and on time.

Regarding additional requirements for commitments relating to the maintenance of peace and security, the Committee recommended that the Secretary-General's authority to commit without its prior concurrence be increased from $5 million to $8 million (see p. 1308). ACABQ also reiterated its recommendation that future performance reports indicate the amount of unliquidated obligations included in estimated expenditures for the biennium.

ACABQ requested that information on the reasons for the persistent high vacancy rate, including the impact of recruitment freezes, be provided to the Fifth Committee and sought assurances that vacancies were not being used to achieve budgetary savings. It pointed out that, with proper planning and streamlining of personnel practices and procedures, the vacancy situation could be improved. Concerning the lower than anticipated vacancy rate as a result of reductions in requirements for temporary assistance in some budget sections, ACABQ requested the Secretariat to provide a more detailed analysis to the Fifth Committee of the $7 million savings under section 1B, General Assembly affairs, to allow it to determine whether the savings had affected the delivery of conference services.

It noted that additional requirements of $4.3 million at the UN Office at Vienna were related to reduced reimbursement from translation and associated reproduction and distribution requirements of the United Nations Industrial Development Organization (UNIDO) and the International Atomic Energy Agency (IAEA). It was concerned about the underutilization of the conference-servicing capacity and requested that the issue be analysed with a view to increasing efficiency and the results reported to the Assembly as soon as possible (see p. 1364).

Noting that the report did not identify any savings from efficiency measures that could be transferred to the Development Account (see p. 1305), ACABQ requested the Secretary-General to provide clarification to the Fifth Committee.

GENERAL ASSEMBLY ACTION

On 23 December [meeting 88], the General Assembly, on the recommendation of the Fifth Committee [A/54/508/Add.1], adopted **resolutions 54/247 A** and **B** without vote [agenda item 119].

A

Final budget appropriations for the biennium 1998-1999

The General Assembly

1. *Takes note* of the second performance report of the Secretary-General on the programme budget for the biennium 1998-1999 and the related report of the Advisory Committee on Administrative and Budgetary Questions;

2. *Also takes note* of the observations of the Advisory Committee concerning the second performance report;

3. *Notes* that the vacancy rate for the Professional level during the biennium 1998-1999 was higher than the rate on the basis of which the programme budget had been approved;

4. *Resolves* that for the biennium 1998-1999:

(a) The amount of 2,529,903,500 United States dollars appropriated in its resolutions 53/215 A of 18 December 1998 and 53/219 of 7 April 1999 shall be decreased by 41,601,500 dollars as follows:

Section	Amount approved in resolutions 53/215 A and 53/219	Increase/ (decrease)	Final appropriation
	(United States dollars)		
Part I. Overall policy-making, direction and coordination			
1A. Overall policy-making, direction and coordination	41,341,200	364,500	41,705,700
1B. General Assembly affairs and conference services	427,653,800	9,830,900	437,484,700
Total, part I	**468,995,000**	**10,195,400**	**479,190,400**
Part II. Political affairs			
2A. Political affairs	41,233,900	(183,500)	41,050,400
2B. Disarmament	12,975,900	(1,172,100)	11,803,800
3. Peacekeeping operations and special missions	181,423,700	(14,357,500)	167,066,200
4. Peaceful uses of outer space	3,934,800	242,900	4,177,700
Total, part II	**239,568,300**	**(15,470,200)**	**224,098,100**
Part III. International justice and law			
5. International Court of Justice	20,659,600	521,800	21,181,400
6. Legal affairs	32,449,200	(1,008,300)	31,440,900
Total, part III	**53,108,800**	**(486,500)**	**52,622,300**
Part IV. International cooperation for development			
7A. Economic and social affairs	106,958,400	(1,978,000)	104,980,400
8. Africa: New Agenda for Development	5,230,000	(262,900)	4,967,100
11A. Trade and development	93,296,400	(4,351,300)	88,945,100

Section	Amount approved in resolutions 53/215 A and 53/219	Increase/ (decrease)	Final appropriation
	(United States dollars)		
11B. International Trade Centre UNCTAD/ WTO	19,812,700	(1,291,500)	18,521,200
12. Environment	8,756,600	50,000	8,806,600
13. Human settlements	12,588,700	367,700	12,956,400
14. Crime control	5,357,300	(598, 600)	4,758,700
15. International drug control	14,728,400	(842,500)	13,885,900
Total, part IV	**266,728,500**	**(8,907,100)**	**257,821,400**
Part V. Regional cooperation for development			
16. Economic and social development in Africa	80,607,800	(3,053,200)	77,554,600
17. Economic and social development in Asia and the Pacific	56,675,900	(2,727,500)	53,948,400
18. Economic development in Europe	43,549,600	(1,018,600)	42,531,000
19. Economic and social development in Latin America and the Caribbean	82,684,000	(3,558,800)	79,125,200
20. Economic and social development in Western Asia	49,752,300	(7,968,700)	41,783,600
21. Regular programme of technical cooperation	42,655,200	(398,000)	42,257,200
Total, part V	**355,924,800**	**(18,724,800)**	**337,200,000**
Part VI. Human rights and humanitarian affairs			
22. Human rights	40,832,600	1,065,200	41,897,800
23. Protection of and assistance to refugees	45,051,000	1,469,400	46,520,400
24. Palestine refugees	21,804,800	3,077,500	24,882,300
25. Humanitarian assistance	17,583,200	34,400	17,617,600
Total, part VI	**125,271,600**	**5,646,500**	**130,918,100**
Part VII. Public information			
26. Communications and public information	135,574,000	(1,711,100)	133,862,900
Total, part VII	**135,574,000**	**(1,711,100)**	**133,862,900**
Part VIII. Common support services			
27. Management and central support services			
A. Office of the Under-Secretary-General for Management	11,090,300	(46,200)	11,044,100
B. Office of Programme Planning, Budget and Accounts	20,888,200	(692,200)	20,196,000
C. Office of Human Resources Management	44,675,800	1,282,400	45,958,200
D. Office of Central Support Services	226,894,000	(4,431,600)	222,462,400
F. Administration, Geneva	99,853,200	(2,279,400)	97,573,800
G. Administration, Vienna	30,701,400	(860,400)	29,841,000
H. Administration, Nairobi	12,194,900	1,139,500	13,334,400
Total, part VIII	**446,297,800**	**(5,887,900)**	**440,409,900**
Part IX. Office of Internal Oversight Services			
28. Internal oversight	17,941,500	(173,500)	17,768,000
Total, part IX	**17,941,500**	**(173,500)**	**17,768,000**
Part X. Jointly financed administrative activities and special expenses			
29. Jointly financed administrative activities	5,824,200	2,139,900	7,964,100
30. Special expenses	52,684,300	(8,227,800)	44,456,500
Total, part X	**58,508,500**	**(6,087,900)**	**52,420,600**
Part XI. Capital expenditures			
31. Construction, alteration, improvement and major maintenance	34,173,100	2,838,500	37,011,600
Total, part XI	**34,173,100**	**2,838,500**	**37,011,600**
Part XII. Staff assessment			
32. Staff assessment	314,746,600	(2,832,900)	311,913,700
Total, part XII	**314,746,600**	**(2,832,900)**	**311,913,700**
Part XIII. Development Account			
34. Development Account	13,065,000	—	13,065,000
Total, part XIII	**13,065,000**	**—**	**13,065,000**
Grand total	**2,529,903,500**	**(41,601,500)**	**2,488,302,000**

(*b*) The Secretary-General shall be authorized to transfer credits between sections of the budget, with the concurrence of the Advisory Committee;

(*c*) In addition to the appropriations approved under paragraph (*a*) above, an amount of 51,000 dollars is appropriated for each year of the biennium 1998-1999 from the accumulated income of the Library Endowment Fund for the purchase of books, periodicals, maps and library equipment and for such other expenses of the Library at the Palais des Nations as are in accordance with the objects and provisions of the endowment.

B

Final income estimates for the biennium 1998-1999

The General Assembly

Resolves that for the biennium 1998-1999:

(a) The estimates of income of 362,705,400 United States dollars approved by its resolution 53/215 B of 18 December 1998 shall be decreased by 6,326,200 dollars as follows:

Income sections	*Amount approved in resolution 53/215 B*	*Increase/ (decrease)*	*Final appropriation*
	(United States dollars)		
1. Income from staff assessment	324,796,600	(10,101,200)	314,695,400
Total, income section 1	**324,796,600**	**(10,101,200)**	**314,695,400**
2. General income	33,585,400	3,986,200	37,571,600
3. Services to the public	4,307,600	(211,200)	4,096,400
Total, income sections 2 and 3	**37,893,000**	**3,775,000**	**41,668,000**
Grand total	**362,689,600**	**(6,326,200)**	**356,363,400**

(b) The income from staff assessment shall be credited to the Tax Equalization Fund in accordance with the provisions of General Assembly resolution 973(X) of 15 December 1955;

(c) Direct expenses of the United Nations Postal Administration, services to visitors, catering and related services, garage operations, television services and the sale of publications, not provided for under the budget appropriations, shall be charged against the income derived from those activities.

On 23 December, by **decision 54/465**, the Assembly decided that the item would remain for consideration at its resumed fifty-fourth (2000) session.

Budget for 2000-2001

The programme budget for the 2000-2001 biennium [A/54/6/Rev.1 & Add.1] was the second to fall within the medium-term plan for the period 1998-2001. Introducing the programme budget before the Fifth Committee, the Secretary-General said that the level of the budget he was proposing, at $2,535 million, was virtually the same, in real terms, as the one for the preceding biennium. It contained small but important increases in certain priority areas, including increases for internal oversight and capital expenditures, as well as for special political missions. To accommodate the increases, savings would be achieved in administration and common support services and through efficiency measures. In response to the priorities established by Member States, he was also proposing that 500 posts should be deployed among the various programmes and subprogrammes. The budget also reflected the ongoing reform effort, including the first set of projects from the 1998-1999 biennium financed under the Development Account. The proposed budget represented the first step in the shift towards results-based budgeting (see p. 1284) and included statements of expected accomplishments for all substantive areas and a separate proposal to build on that approach and complete the shift. In formulating his proposals, the Secretary-General said that he had taken into account that the United Nations had had absolutely no increase in its budget for five years, even in nominal terms, and had cut spending by $350 million since 1994. However, there came a point at which further cuts would severely compromise its ability to deliver the services Member States had mandated. The Organization's agenda was long and demands continued to rise; therefore, the proposed budget was a reasonable and rational one.

CPC considered the proposed programme budget at its 1999 session [A/54/16] and noted the Secretary-General's efforts to meet the new requirements of the revised Regulations and Rules Governing Programme Planning, the Programme Aspects of the Budget, the Monitoring of Implementation and the Methods of Evaluation. CPC recommended that all sections of future proposed programme budgets be presented in the same standard format, in accordance with the Regulations and Rules and relevant resolutions. It also recommended that the Assembly approve the narratives of the majority of the budget sections and review the programme narrative for section 4, Disarmament. CPC was not in a position to comment on the programme narratives of section 11B, International Trade Centre UNCTAD/ World Trade Organization, as a result of the new administrative arrangements approved by the General Assembly in decision 53/411 B [YUN 1998, p. 888].With regard to the programme narratives for section 12, Environment; section 13, Human settlements; and section 27C, Office of Human Resources Management, the Committee recommended that the Assembly request the Secretary-General to reformulate the narratives to conform with the standard presentation of the other sections of the proposed programme budget and resubmit them at its fifty-fourth (1999) session. Regarding section 33, Development Account, the Committee noted that the programme narrative for the utilization of the amount approved for the Account had not been submitted, and recommended that the Assembly request the Secretary-General to submit proposals for utilization of the Account to the fifty-fourth session.

GENERAL ASSEMBLY ACTION

On 23 December [meeting 88], the General Assembly, on the recommendation of the Fifth Com-

mittee [A/54/691], adopted **resolution 54/249** without vote [agenda item 121].

Questions relating to the proposed programme budget for the biennium 2000-2001

I

The General Assembly,

Reaffirming its resolutions 41/213 of 19 December 1986 and 42/211 of 21 December 1987,

Recalling its resolution 53/206 of 18 December 1998, in which it invited the Secretary-General to prepare the budget outline for the biennium 2000-2001 on the basis of 2,545 million United States dollars,

Recalling also its resolution 52/220 of 22 December 1997,

Recalling further its resolutions 51/219 of 18 December 1996 and 53/207 of 18 December 1998,

Recalling the relevant paragraphs of resolutions 52/12 A and 52/12 B of 12 November and 19 December 1997, respectively, as well as resolutions 52/235 of 26 June 1998, 53/220 A of 7 April 1999, 53/220 B of 8 June 1999 and 54/15 of 29 October 1999, relating to the Development Account,

Recalling also paragraph 2 *(a)* of its resolution 1798(XVII) of 11 December 1962,

Reaffirming the respective mandates of the Advisory Committee on Administrative and Budgetary Questions and the Committee for Programme and Coordination in the consideration of the proposed programme budget,

Reaffirming also the requirement of all Member States to fulfil their financial obligations as set out in the Charter of the United Nations in full, on time and without conditions,

Recognizing the detrimental effect of the withholding of assessed contributions on the administrative and financial functioning of the United Nations,

Recognizing also that late payments of assessed contributions adversely affect the financial situation of the Organization,

Stressing that the established procedures for the formulation, implementation and approval of the programme budget must be strictly followed,

Having considered the proposed programme budget for the biennium 2000–2001 and the related reports of the Advisory Committee on Administrative and Budgetary Questions and the report of the Committee for Programme and Coordination on the work of the thirty-ninth session,

1. *Reaffirms* that the Fifth Committee is the appropriate Main Committee of the General Assembly entrusted with responsibilities for administrative and budgetary matters;

2. *Reaffirms also* rule 153 of its rules of procedure;

3. *Reaffirms further* the Regulations and Rules Governing Programme Planning, the Programme Aspects of the Budget, the Monitoring of Implementation and the Methods of Evaluation, and the Financial Regulations and Rules of the United Nations;

4. *Decides* that no changes to the budget methodology, to established budgetary procedures and practices or to the financial regulations may be implemented without prior review and approval by the General Assembly, in accordance with established budgetary procedures;

5. *Reaffirms* the role of the General Assembly in carrying out a thorough analysis and approval of posts and financial resources, as well as of human resources policies, with a view to ensuring full implementation of all mandated programmes and activities and the implementation of policies in this regard;

6. *Welcomes* the timely submission of the proposed programme budget and the continued efforts made by the Secretary-General to improve the format of the proposed programme budget;

7. *Notes with concern* the late submissions on section 11B, International Trade Centre (UNCTAD/WTO), and section 33, Development Account;

8. *Commends* the efforts and initiatives of the Secretary-General aimed at reforming the United Nations;

9. *Requests* the Secretary-General to ensure that, in the implementation of approved reform proposals, there should be no adverse impact on the fulfilment of legislative mandates;

10. *Also requests* the Secretary-General to ensure that the proposals contained in the individual sections of future proposed programme budgets include more precise information on the outputs, activities, objectives and expected accomplishments of the various departments, on the basis of which the General Assembly may later evaluate budget performance;

11. *Recognizes* that the General Assembly has not yet approved the proposal of the Secretary-General on results-based budgeting;

12. *Takes note* of the fact that the concepts of "expected accomplishments", "outputs", "objectives" and "activities" are not exclusively related to and should not be confused with the concept of "results-based budgeting";

13. *Decides* that any development related to results-based budgeting should be undertaken only with the prior approval of the General Assembly;

14. *Requests* the Secretary-General to continue to present the budget outline and the proposed programme budget to the General Assembly strictly in accordance with existing budgetary procedure;

15. *Emphasizes* that resources proposed by the Secretary-General should be commensurate with all mandated programmes and activities in order to ensure their full and effective implementation;

16. *Renews its appeal* to Member States to demonstrate their commitment to the United Nations by, inter alia, meeting their financial obligations in full, on time and without conditions, in accordance with the Charter of the United Nations and the Financial Regulations and Rules of the United Nations;

17. *Reiterates* that core functions of the United Nations, as a principle, should be financed through the regular budget and apportioned among Member States, and notes with concern the excessive reliance on extrabudgetary resources in some sections;

18. *Notes with concern* the current and projected decreasing trend in extrabudgetary resources, particularly for the United Nations funds and programmes;

19. *Expresses concern* that the decrease in extrabudgetary resources in some sections of the proposed programme budget for the biennium 2000-2001 could have an adverse impact on the effective implementation of programmes and activities, especially those pro-

grammes that are still heavily funded primarily through such resources;

20. *Recalls* its decision set out in section II, paragraph 2 *(b),* of its resolution 41/213, and emphasizes that, in future, proposed programme budgets shall be considered by the General Assembly in fascicle form, together with recommendations on them by the Committee for Programme and Coordination and the Advisory Committee on Administrative and Budgetary Questions, and that the programme budgets shall be issued in their final form after approval by the General Assembly, with the changes to the resource level annexed to the approved programme budget;

21. *Requests* the Secretary-General and the Advisory Committee to submit their reports in accordance with paragraphs 11 and 12 of resolution 53/208 B of 18 December 1998;

22. *Recognizes* the need for Member States to participate in budgetary preparation from its earliest stages and throughout the process;

23. *Encourages* the Secretary-General to improve coordination between departments and the major duty stations so as to use resources effectively in all areas, including information technology;

24. *Calls upon* the Secretary-General to explore the possibility of presenting in future proposed programme budgets one consolidated section for staff assessment inflows and outflows, with a view to improving the transparency of the presentation of the budget;

25. *Also calls upon* the Secretary-General to ensure that all sections of future proposed programme budgets are presented in the same standard format, in accordance with the relevant regulations and rules and relevant resolutions;

26. *Requests* the Secretary-General, in his programme budget submission for the biennium 2002-2003, to make further improvements to the proposed programme budget, as described by the Advisory Committee in paragraphs 6 and 7 of its report;

27. *Also requests* the Secretary-General to improve the presentation of future proposed programme budgets by including all relevant legislative mandates for all proposed programme narratives;

28. *Further requests* the Secretary-General, in his proposed programme budget for the biennium 2002-2003, to provide a better explanation of the use of standard costs and unit rates in the calculation of cost estimates;

29. *Requests* the Secretary-General, in his proposed programme budget for the biennium 2002-2003, to submit estimates of the total amount of resources, from all sources of financing, that he should have at his disposal to be able to implement fully the mandated programmes and activities;

II

30. *Reaffirms* that the medium-term plan, as approved by the General Assembly, shall continue to constitute the principal policy directive of the United Nations;

31. *Reiterates* that the priorities for the biennium 2000-2001 are the following:

(a) Maintenance of international peace and security;

(b) Promotion of sustained economic growth and sustainable development, in accordance with relevant General Assembly resolutions and recent United Nations conferences;

(c) Development of Africa;

(d) Promotion of human rights;

(e) Effective coordination of humanitarian assistance efforts;

(f) Promotion of justice and international law;

(g) Disarmament;

(h) Drug control, crime prevention and combating international terrorism in all its forms and manifestations;

32. *Endorses* the conclusions and recommendations contained in the report of the Committee for Programme and Coordination on the programme narrative of the proposed programme budget for the biennium 2000-2001, subject to the provisions of the present resolution;

33. *Notes with concern* that the request for resources in the proposed programme budget did not accurately reflect the priorities approved by the General Assembly in its resolution 51/219;

34. *Reiterates* the need for the Secretary-General to ensure that resources are utilized strictly for the purposes approved by the General Assembly;

35. *Emphasizes* that the budget proposals of the Secretary-General should reflect resource levels commensurate with the mandates for their full implementation;

36. *Reiterates* that the reports of the Committee for Programme and Coordination on the proposed programme budget should be considered by the General Assembly, through the Fifth Committee, only for the final approval of the programme budget;

37. *Expresses its concern* that a number of sections in the proposed programme budget for the biennium 2000-2001 were not prepared in complete conformity with the medium-term plan for the period 1998-2001;

38. *Requests* the Secretary-General to ensure that, in the future, the programme narratives of the programme budget fully conform to the provisions of the medium-term plan;

39. *Reaffirms* the need to implement strictly and fully the Regulations and Rules Governing Programme Planning, the Programme Aspects of the Budget, the Monitoring of Implementation and the Methods of Evaluation;

40. *Emphasizes* that programmes and activities mandated by the General Assembly must be respected and implemented fully;

41. *Reiterates* that the allocation of resources should reflect fully the priorities established in the medium-term plan;

42. *Also reiterates* that due consideration should be given to issues related to the development of Africa, as a matter of priority;

43. *Emphasizes* the need for mandated programmes and activities to be delivered in the most effective and efficient manner;

44. *Decides* to make changes, as contained in annex I to the present resolution, to the programme narratives in the final published version of the proposed programme budget for the biennium 2000-2001, as reflected in the conclusions and recommendations contained in the report of the Committee for Programme and Coordination and the provisions of the present resolution;

III

45. *Endorses* the conclusions and recommendations of the Advisory Committee contained in its reports on the proposed programme budget for the biennium 2000-2001, subject to the provisions of the present resolution;

46. *Reaffirms* paragraph 10 of resolution 53/206, whereby the General Assembly decided, inter alia, that additional requirements to the level of 86.2 million United States dollars included in the proposed programme budget for the financing of special political missions should be financed in conformity with the provisions of resolution 41/213;

47. *Notes* that the technical proposal on the treatment of the provision for special political missions in the programme budget, as recommended by the Advisory Committee in paragraph 7 of its third report on the biennium 1996-1997, has not been submitted, and requests the Secretary-General to submit the proposal as a matter of priority to the General Assembly during its fifty-fifth session;

48. *Reaffirms* its support for maintaining the international character of the Organization and to the principles of efficiency, competence and integrity enshrined in Article 101 of the Charter;

49. *Also reaffirms* the role of the General Assembly with regard to the structure of the Secretariat, including the creation, suppression and redeployment of posts, and requests the Secretary-General to provide the Assembly with comprehensive information on all decisions involving established and temporary high-level posts, including equivalent positions financed from the regular budget and from extrabudgetary resources;

50. *Expresses its concern* at the high vacancy rate in certain areas of the Organization, particularly in some of the regional commissions, and reiterates in this regard that a high vacancy rate hampers the delivery of mandated programmes and activities;

51. *Reaffirms* that the vacancy rate is a tool for budgetary calculations and should not be used to achieve budgetary savings;

52. *Also reaffirms* that deliberate management decisions to keep a certain number of posts vacant should not be taken, as this action makes the budget process less transparent and the management of human resources more difficult;

53. *Decides* that a vacancy rate of 6.5 per cent for Professional staff and 2.5 per cent for General Service staff shall be used as a basis for the calculation of the budget for the biennium 2000-2001;

54. *Notes* that, should the vacancy rates realized be lower than those budgeted, the General Assembly would provide additional resources, if required, in the first and/or second performance report so as to preclude the need for any constraint on the recruitment of staff;

55. *Requests* the Secretary-General to recruit staff expeditiously by proper planning and by streamlining personnel practices and procedures, in order to avoid any adverse impact of a high vacancy rate on the effective implementation and delivery of mandated programmes and activities;

56. *Also requests* the Secretary-General to ensure that posts are not deliberately left vacant to provide a cushion for absorbing the costs of special missions and other activities authorized "within available resources";

57. *Emphasizes* that the reclassification of posts should not be used as a promotion tool;

58. *Reiterates* that reclassified posts, as approved by the General Assembly, should be filled only in full conformity with the established procedures for recruitment and placement;

59. *Requests* the Secretary-General to undertake a comprehensive review of the post structure of the Secretariat, taking into account, inter alia, the introduction of new technology, and to make proposals in the proposed programme budget for the biennium 2002-2003 to address the top-heavy post structure of the Organization;

60. *Welcomes* the use of information technology as one of the tools for improving the implementation of mandated programmes and activities;

61. *Notes with regret* the lack of a comprehensive information technology strategy for the United Nations, and requests the Secretary-General to develop a comprehensive strategy for the development and implementation of information technology, to be submitted through the Advisory Committee to the General Assembly during the main part of its fifty-fifth session;

62. *Emphasizes* that the introduction of new technology should lead neither to the involuntary separation of staff nor necessarily to a reduction in staff;

63. *Decides* to reduce the resources proposed for allocation to information technology for the biennium 2000-2001 by 3,443,000 dollars;

64. *Reaffirms* that the use of temporary assistance should be limited strictly to requirements for peak workload, maternity and sick leave, and that it should not be used to supplant established posts;

65. *Decides* to reduce the level of resources proposed by the Secretary-General for allocation to general temporary assistance, with the exception of general temporary assistance for conference services, by 3.2 million dollars;

66. *Regrets* the continued tendency towards excessive use of consultants where in-house expertise is available, and urges the Secretary-General to resort to the use of consultants strictly in accordance with the existing regulations and rules and relevant resolutions;

67. *Decides* to reduce the level of resources proposed by the Secretary-General for consultants by 2,028,000 dollars, with the exception of resources for the Department of Economic and Social Affairs and the regional commissions;

68. *Emphasizes* the importance of the knowledge and skills of the staff of the Organization, and therefore requests the Secretary-General to develop a more coordinated and systematic approach to staff training, in particular with a view to enhancing skills and increasing expertise through training programmes, as recommended by the Advisory Committee;

69. *Requests* the Secretary-General to continue to comply strictly with the approved travel policies, standards, and regulations and rules, particularly with respect to ensuring that travel is undertaken by the most direct and economical route;

70. *Decides* to reduce the resources proposed for travel of staff on official business by 2,480,000 dollars;

71. *Requests* the Secretary-General to provide some flexibility in allowing the use of the external printing account for internal printing purposes, as appropriate;

72. *Decides* that the staffing table for each year of the biennium 2000-2001 shall be as contained in annex II to the present resolution;

IV

Section 1. Overall policy-making, direction and coordination

73. *Decides* to establish a P-5 post in the Office of the Deputy Secretary-General;

74. *Concurs* with the observations of the Advisory Committee contained in paragraphs I.5, I.6 and I.7 of its report on the need to ensure that the Office of the President of the General Assembly is provided with adequate resources, and decides that, in the interest of clarity and transparency, the resources proposed for support to the President of the Assembly shall be presented separately from the estimates for the travel of representatives of least developed countries to sessions of the Assembly;

75. *Decides* that the resources for the Office of the President of the General Assembly shall be allocated between the presidents of the sessions of the General Assembly to which they relate so as to ensure equitable provision of these resources, taking into account the duration of the term of each president;

76. *Reaffirms* section IV, paragraphs 13 and 14, of its resolution 53/214 of 18 December 1998;

77. *Requests* the Secretary-General to take additional measures to ensure that the representatives of least developed countries are fully and duly informed in a timely manner of their entitlements to travel to sessions of the General Assembly;

78. *Also requests* the Secretary-General to keep under review the activities of the Office of External Relations in order to avoid any possible duplication with other areas of the Secretariat, and to report thereon in the context of the proposed programme budget for the biennium 2002-2003;

Section 2. General Assembly affairs and conference services

79. *Requests* the Secretary-General to ensure that the use of contractual services does not have an adverse impact on conference services or result in additional costs to the Organization;

80. *Reiterates its request* in section III, paragraph 19, of its resolution 52/220 of 22 December 1997;

81. *Decides* to establish four P-4 posts in the Interpretation Section, United Nations Office at Vienna;

82. *Also decides* to redeploy the P-4 post for the Chief of the Spanish Unit, Copy Preparation and Proofreading Section, Headquarters, New York;

83. *Notes with concern* the proposed reduction of resources for conference services for the biennium 2000-2001, and requests the Secretary-General to ensure that efficiency measures are carefully analysed to avoid any negative impact on conference services, in the light of the level and quality of services provided to Member States;

Section 3. Political affairs

84. *Endorses* the observations and recommendations of the Advisory Committee contained in paragraph II.12 of its report with respect to the new Policy Planning Unit;

85. *Reiterates* that any expenditure in excess of the provision approved for special political missions in the proposed programme budget shall continue to be treated in accordance with General Assembly resolution 41/213;

Section 4. Disarmament

86. *Decides* to reclassify to the D-2 level the D-1 post of Deputy Secretary-General of the Conference on Disarmament and Chief of the Conference on Disarmament secretariat and Conference Support Branch, Geneva;

87. *Reiterates* paragraph 6 of its resolution 54/55 C of 1 December 1999 on the United Nations Regional Centre for Peace and Disarmament in Asia and the Pacific;

Section 5. Peacekeeping operations

88. *Emphasizes* that all peacekeeping missions shall be provided with adequate resources to ensure their effective functioning;

Section 7. International Court of Justice

89. *Notes with concern* that the resources proposed for the International Court of Justice are not proportionate with the workload envisaged, and requests the Secretary-General to propose adequate resources for this section in the context of the proposed programme budget for the biennium 2002-2003, commensurate with its increased workload and the large backlog of volumes of Court documents;

90. *Commends* the response of the Court to earlier requests that it explore vigorously the introduction of modern technology, and recommends that it continue to pursue further the use of such technology, in accordance with the relevant resolutions of the General Assembly;

Section 9. Economic and social affairs

91. *Decides* to reclassify to the D-1 level the P-5 post of Chief of the Non-Governmental Organizations Section;

92. *Notes* the rapid development of the partnership between the United Nations and the non-governmental organization community, and recognizes, therefore, the additional responsibilities and the increased workload of the Non-Governmental Organizations Section;

93. *Requests* the Secretary-General to submit a report to the General Assembly at its fifty-fourth session on the administrative and financial issues concerning the Non-Governmental Organizations Section, in particular with regard to the number and level of posts in that Section;

Section 10. Africa: New Agenda for Development

94. *Reaffirms* the important role of the programme entitled "Africa: New Agenda for Development" in addressing Africa's critical socio-economic situation, and reiterates the urgent need to provide the programme with adequate resources to enable it to achieve its objectives;

95. *Also reaffirms* the priority assigned to the development of Africa by the General Assembly, and in this regard reiterates section III, paragraph 48, of its resolution 52/220, in which it called upon the Secretary-General to continue his efforts to mobilize additional resources for the implementation of the programme of

action contained in the United Nations New Agenda for the Development of Africa in the 1990s;

96. *Requests* the Secretary-General to ensure, in a coordinated manner, the effective and timely implementation of the New Agenda;

97. *Emphasizes* the continuing need to focus on the priority areas of the New Agenda and to organize close consultations at both the policy and the operational levels among the various development partners in order to achieve the best results;

Section 11A. Trade and development

98. *Endorses* the agreed conclusions of the Working Party on the Medium-term Plan and Programme Budget of the United Nations Conference on Trade and Development;

99. *Emphasizes* the need to provide adequate resources to strengthen the capacity of the United Nations Conference on Trade and Development in priority areas;

100. *Invites* the Secretary-General to consider the establishment of a new subprogramme on Africa under section 11A, Trade and development, through redeployment subject to the approval of the General Assembly at its fifty-fifth session on the basis of such proposals as the United Nations Conference on Trade and Development may wish to make at its tenth session through the Committee for Programme and Coordination;

101. *Requests* the Secretary-General to strengthen the Office of the Special Coordinator for Least Developed, Landlocked and Island Developing Countries in order to enable it to address effectively the concerns of landlocked and transit developing countries;

102. *Notes with concern* that the level of staff and financial resources in the Office of the Special Coordinator is not commensurate with the increased responsibilities and activities deriving from its mandates;

103. *Decides* to re-establish the unit for landlocked developing countries and small island developing States within the Office of the Special Coordinator, and to establish one P-5, two P-4, one P-3 and three General Service posts related thereto, and requests the Secretary-General to report on the effectiveness of the functioning of the unit before the end of the biennium 2000-2001;

104. *Requests* the Secretary-General to review, as a matter of priority, resource requirements for the high-level intergovernmental event on financing for development and the Third United Nations Conference on the Least Developed Countries, and to submit a report to the General Assembly for consideration at the first part of its resumed fifty-fourth session;

105. *Deeply regrets* that its decision in section III, paragraph 49, of its resolution 52/220 has not been implemented, and stresses the need expeditiously to recruit the P-5 post of the Special Coordinator referred to in that resolution;

106. *Notes with concern* that the reference to and resources allocated for the Third United Nations Conference on the Least Developed Countries and the Fourth United Nations Conference to Review All Aspects of the Set of Multilaterally Agreed Equitable Principles and Rules for the Control of Restrictive Business Practices (2000) are not clearly presented under the policy-making organs and the programme support costs, and requests the Secretary-General to report thereon in the context of the programme budget performance report for the biennium 2000-2001;

107. *Takes note with concern* of the high vacancy rates for this programme and the adverse effect of this situation on the effective implementation of this programme;

108. *Requests* the Secretary-General, in this regard, urgently to take measures to correct this situation;

Section 12. Environment

109. *Decides* to approve the reformulated fascicle for section 12;

110. *Requests* the Secretary-General to review the proposed provisions for this section with a view to ensuring a stable, predictable and viable source of funding in order to avoid heavy reliance upon extrabudgetary resources;

Section 13. Human settlements

111. *Requests* the Secretary-General, in accordance with paragraph 229 of the Habitat Agenda and in consultation with the Commission on Human Settlements, to continue to ensure more effective functioning of the United Nations Centre for Human Settlements (Habitat) by, inter alia, providing sufficient human and financial resources within the regular budget of the United Nations;

112. *Decides* to approve the reformulated programme narrative for section 13;

113. *Requests* the Secretary-General, as a matter of urgency, to appoint, on a full-time basis and at the level of Under-Secretary-General, the Executive Director of the United Nations Centre for Human Settlements (Habitat);

114. *Also requests* the Secretary-General to review the proposed provisions for this section with a view to ensuring a stable, predictable and viable source of funding in order to avoid heavy reliance upon extrabudgetary resources;

Section 15. International drug control

115. *Takes note with concern* of the high dependence of the programme on extrabudgetary resources;

116. *Decides* to appropriate resources for printing under subprogramme 1 at the same level as in the biennium 1998-1999;

Sections 16 to 21. Regional cooperation for development

117. *Emphasizes* the need for greater interaction between the regional commissions and the respective regional organizations;

118. *Requests* the Secretary-General to continue to ensure that the regional commissions provide technical assistance to Member States, including through their respective regional organizations;

119. *Commends* the efforts of the regional commissions at reform and streamlining, and encourages them to continue to take, as appropriate and under the auspices of their respective intergovernmental bodies, further measures in this regard;

120. *Expresses deep concern* about the underutilization of the conference centres at Bangkok and Addis Ababa, and requests the Secretary-General to develop and implement a strategy for increasing their use, and to report thereon to the General Assembly by the end of its fifty-fourth session;

Section 16. Economic and social development in Africa

121. *Notes with deep concern* the high vacancy rate in the Economic Commission for Africa, and in this regard reiterates section II, paragraph 23, of its resolution 52/220;

122. *Recalls* section IV, paragraphs 7 and 12, of its resolution 53/214, in which, inter alia, it requested the Secretary-General to take all the necessary steps to achieve a vacancy rate of no more than 5 per cent for posts in the Professional and higher categories by the end of the biennium 1998-1999;

123. *Requests* the Secretary-General to take the necessary measures, as a matter of priority, to achieve a vacancy rate of no more than 5 per cent within the biennium in the Economic Commission for Africa, and to report thereon to the General Assembly at its fifty-fifth session;

124. *Expresses its deep concern* that the Economic Commission for Africa is still suffering from a significantly high vacancy rate at the Professional level, and requests the Secretary-General to ensure that all posts budgeted for the biennium 2000-2001 are filled;

125. *Welcomes* the reform process carried out by the Economic Commission for Africa to strengthen its programme of work, in particular with regard to the subregional development centres;

126. *Reiterates its request* that the Secretary-General redeploy to the subregional development centres any savings realized during the biennium as the result of reform measures and efficiency gains from within the Economic Commission for Africa;

127. *Requests* the Secretary-General to provide the African Institute for the Prevention of Crime and the Treatment of Offenders with the core Professional staff required to enable it to function effectively towards the fulfilment of its mandates;

Section 16B. Regional Commissions New York Office

128. *Emphasizes* the need to provide an adequate level of resources for the Regional Commissions New York Office for the effective implementation of its activities;

129. *Requests* the Secretary-General to review the classification of General Service posts of the Regional Commissions New York Office;

Section 17. Economic and social development in Asia and the Pacific

130. *Notes with concern* the high vacancy rate in the Economic and Social Commission for Asia and the Pacific, which could adversely affect the implementation of mandated programmes and activities, and requests the Secretary-General to take all necessary measures to redress the situation;

Section 18. Economic development in Europe

131. *Commends* the Economic Commission for Europe for the rationalization of its programmes and for the improved presentation of its narratives;

Section 19. Economic and social development in Latin America and the Caribbean

132. *Commends* the Economic Commission for Latin America and the Caribbean for the implementation of the reform programme for the Commission;

133. *Expresses its concern* at the decreasing trend in extrabudgetary resources and at its impact on the level of technical cooperation activities, and requests the Secretary-General to submit proposals to address the adverse impact of declining extrabudgetary resources for the Economic Commission for Latin America and the Caribbean;

134. *Requests* the Secretary-General to ensure that all the necessary means are provided for the full implementation of all subprogrammes and their respective activities;

135. *Reaffirms* section III, paragraph 73, of its resolution 52/220, in which it requested the Secretary-General to ensure that all activities included in subprogramme 2 would benefit all members of the region;

Section 22. Human rights

136. *Commends* the Secretary-General for having successfully reduced the vacancy rate in the programme;

137. *Approves* the proposed establishment of a P-4 post for the New York office;

138. *Notes with concern* that paragraph 8 of its resolution 53/78 A of 4 December 1998 has not been fully implemented, requests the Secretary-General to provide the Subregional Centre for Human Rights and Democracy in Central Africa with adequate financial resources, and in this regard decides to appropriate an amount of one million dollars in the programme budget for the biennium 2000-2001;

139. *Notes with concern* that resources proposed for activities related to the right to development are not clearly identified within subprogramme 1;

140. *Decides* to appropriate an additional amount of 160,000 dollars for activities of the Preparatory Committee related to the World Conference against Racism, Racial Discrimination, Xenophobia and Related Intolerance;

141. *Reaffirms* section XI, paragraph 2, of its resolution 44/201 B of 21 December 1989, and recalls section III, paragraphs 74 to 77 and 79, of its resolution 52/220;

142. *Notes* that the General Assembly has not taken action on the report of the Secretary-General requested in section XI, paragraph 2, of its resolution 44/201 B;

143. *Decides,* consistent with section III, paragraph 79, of its resolution 52/220 and pending consideration of the report requested in resolution 44/201 B, to appropriate the resources requested by the Secretary-General in the proposed programme budget for the biennium 2000-2001, and in this regard requests the Secretary-General to ensure that no funds directly related to non-mandated activities are committed to them;

144. *Also decides* to revert to this issue during its resumed fifty-fourth session;

Section 23. Protection of and assistance to refugees

145. *Notes with concern* that no concrete action was taken by the Secretary-General pursuant to its request in section III, paragraph 82, of its resolution 52/220;

146. *Deeply regrets* the continuing decline of the flow of extrabudgetary resources to the Office of the United Nations High Commissioner for Refugees;

147. *Emphasizes* that refugees all over the world shall be given equal and non-discriminatory treatment, taking into account provisions of the relevant international conventions, and stresses the importance of providing adequate assistance to countries hosting refugees;

Section 24. Palestine refugees

148. *Notes with concern* the direct impact of the decrease of extrabudgetary resources on the quality of services provided by the United Nations Relief and Works Agency for Palestine Refugees in the Near East;

149. *Decides* to restore to the regular budget the six international posts (1 D-2, 1 D-1, 1 P-5, 1 P-4, 1 P-3 and 1 General Service) currently financed from the Agency's extrabudgetary resources, in line with General Assembly resolution 3331 B (XXIX) of 17 December 1974;

Section 25. Humanitarian assistance

150. *Requests* the Secretary-General to submit to the General Assembly by the end of its fifty-fourth session the report requested in section III, paragraph 84, of its resolution 52/220 on the legislative basis and methodology for charging programme support costs for voluntary contributions, in cash or in kind;

Section 26. Public information

151. *Notes with regret* that the pilot web sites in Arabic, Chinese and Russian are being maintained through the use of limited general temporary assistance funds, and in this regard decides to convert the related positions to established posts so as to ensure the equitable representation of all six official languages on the United Nations web sites;

152. *Requests* the Secretary-General to take into account the views of host countries before deciding to merge or close United Nations information centres in Member States;

153. *Also requests* the Secretary-General to consult Member States in which United Nations information centres were merged or closed, with a view to reviving those centres, as appropriate;

154. *Further requests* the Secretary-General to review earlier cases where United Nations information centres were merged with the offices of the United Nations Development Programme, with a view to determining whether such mergers resulted in diminished dissemination of public information;

155. *Recognizes* that radio broadcasting is one of the most effective and far-reaching media available to the Department of Public Information;

156. *Reiterates* paragraph 32 of its resolution 54/82 B of 6 December 1999, and requests the Secretary-General to ensure implementation of the pilot project for the development of an international radio broadcasting capacity for the United Nations as soon as possible, utilizing extrabudgetary resources to the fullest extent possible as well as the resources (496,300 dollars) sought in paragraph 26.69 *(c)* of his proposals and, if required, other redeployable resources including general operating expenses, within section 26, and to report on progress in the context of the first performance report for the biennium 2000-2001;

157. *Expresses its appreciation* at the fact that there are fifteen languages used to diffuse United Nations radio programmes, news magazines, programmes and multi-segment regional magazines, including Kiswahili;

158. *Notes with concern* that the post of Kiswahili producer was abolished and that for the last fifteen years only one Kiswahili producer has been deployed under a special service agreement, notwithstanding the fact that the Kiswahili language is increasingly gaining ground as it is widely spoken in many African countries and understood in many more countries internationally;

159. *Requests* the Secretary-General to ensure that the permanent P-3 post of Kiswahili producer is reinstated and that one additional G-6 assistant is recruited to the Kiswahili programme in order to render it more effective;

160. *Emphasizes* the need for the United Nations to have a coordinated public information strategy, which would bring the activities of different parts of the Secretariat together in an integrated way;

161. *Also emphasizes* that the public information resources of the Organization must be targeted properly so as to ensure that the United Nations delivers a consistent message through a variety of outlets;

162. *Requests* the Secretary-General to review the role of the Public Affairs Division, the News and Media Division, the Office of the Spokesman for the Secretary-General and the Office of External Relations and to consider their staffing level in the context of the proposed programme budget for the biennium 2002-2003;

163. *Also requests* the Secretary-General, pursuant to resolutions 53/22 of 4 November 1998 and 54/113 of 10 December 1999, to optimize the capacity of the Department of Public Information to disseminate information effectively on all activities undertaken in preparation for the year 2001, proclaimed as the United Nations Year of Dialogue among Civilizations;

164. *Further requests* the Secretary-General to make all arrangements to optimize the capacity of the Department of Public Information to undertake adequately activities pertaining to the International Year for the Culture of Peace in 2000 and the International Decade for a Culture of Peace and Non-Violence for the Children of the World (2001-2010), pursuant to General Assembly resolutions 52/15 of 20 November 1997 and 53/25 of 10 November 1998;

Section 27A. Office of the Under-Secretary-General for Management

165. *Emphasizes* that the responsibilities and workload of the secretariat of the Fifth Committee, which also serves as the secretariat of the Committee for Programme and Coordination, require that the secretariat be strengthened;

166. *Decides* to reclassify from D-1 to D-2 and from P-4 to P-5 the posts of Secretary and Deputy Secretary, respectively, of the Fifth Committee of the General Assembly and of the Committee for Programme and Coordination;

Section 27C. Office of Human Resources Management

167. *Decides* to approve the proposed reformulation of paragraph 27C.6 of the proposed programme budget for the biennium 2000;

168. *Requests* the Office of Human Resources Management to be more focused on the establishment of a proper system of accountability and responsibility, as

well as on the improvement of an effective system of administration of justice, as an integral part of the human resources management reform process;

169. *Requests* the Secretary-General to review carefully the agenda and meeting schedule of the Staff-Management Coordination Committee, with a view to avoiding the holding of inter-sessional meetings, also taking into account the possibilities offered by video-conferencing;

Section 27D. Office of Central Support Services

170. *Decides* to reduce the allocation of resources proposed for general operating expenses by 8.5 million dollars;

171. *Requests* the Secretary-General to report to the General Assembly at its fifty-fifth session on progress made by the United Nations Common Services Task Force on the existing common services, and to expand and develop new ones as appropriate;

172. *Notes* the advanced level of the arrangements for common services and related cost indicators at the United Nations Office at Vienna;

173. *Reiterates* the importance of the security system and security guards of the United Nations, and requests the Secretary-General to address the level of resources related to the Security and Safety Service, including the reclassification of posts, in the context of the proposed programme budget for the biennium 2002-2003;

Section 27E. Administration, Geneva

174. *Requests* the Secretary-General to review the current security arrangements and to report thereon to the General Assembly at the main part of its fifty-fifth session;

Section 27G. Administration, Nairobi

175. *Welcomes* the commitment of the Secretary-General to increase gradually the regular budget component of the United Nations Office at Nairobi, with a view to easing the administrative costs levied on the substantive programmes of the United Nations Environment Programme and the United Nations Centre for Human Settlements (Habitat);

176. *Calls upon* the Secretary-General to present, in the proposed programme budget for the biennium 2002-2003, in a uniform manner, the cost of the United Nations Office at Nairobi and the rates of reimbursement for services rendered to other organizations at Nairobi;

177. *Requests* the Secretary-General to replace the charge-back procedure for the cost-sharing of expenses for the United Nations Office at Nairobi with a simpler, more reliable and predictable procedure;

178. *Reaffirms* section III, paragraph 101, of its resolution 52/220, in which it requested the Secretary-General to bring the financial arrangements of the United Nations Office at Nairobi into line with those of similar United Nations administrative offices;

179. *Expresses concern* that the conference facilities at the United Nations Office at Nairobi are still under-utilized, as recorded during the last reporting period;

180. *Decides* to establish a permanent interpretation service at the United Nations Office at Nairobi;

181. *Requests* the Secretary-General to submit to the General Assembly at its fifty-fifth session a strategic plan for the full use of conference facilities at Nairobi, so as to ensure that interpretation capacity will be fully utilized;

Section 29. Jointly financed administrative activities

182. *Stresses* the need to ensure that the independence of the Joint Inspection Unit, as the only system-wide external oversight body, is not compromised through the budgetary process;

183. *Reiterates* its decision 54/454 of 23 December 1999;

184. *Reaffirms* the statute of the Joint Inspection Unit, in particular article 20, paragraph 1;

185. *Requests* the Secretary-General, pending the outcome of the review of the Information Systems Coordination Committee, to identify appropriate resources to finance the United Nations share of the cost of the Committee for the first year of the biennium 2000-2001, and to report thereon in the context of the first performance report;

186. *Requests* the Board of Auditors to submit a report on the status of the implementation of the recommendations contained in its report and to make further recommendations in this regard;

Section 31. Construction, alteration, improvement and major maintenance

187. *Requests* the Secretary-General to submit to the General Assembly during its fifty-fourth session a detailed and comprehensive report addressing the asbestos problem, including, inter alia, the following elements:

(*a*) An assessment of the current situation;

(*b*) An assessment of the impact of the asbestos situation on the health of staff members, delegates and other persons working in and visiting the building;

(*c*) A specific proposal aimed at improving the asbestos situation in the building and a related timetable for its implementation;

(*d*) Information on the level of resources required for the implementation of the plan;

188. *Expresses its concern* at the serious situation of the United Nations Headquarters buildings and the absence of specific proposals in the proposed programme budget for the biennium 2000-2001 aimed at addressing the situation;

189. *Requests* the Secretary-General to submit the master plan for capital improvements requested in paragraph XI.6 of the report of the Advisory Committee no later than February 2000;

Section 33. Development Account

190. *Notes with concern* the late submission of budget proposals on section 33 of the proposed programme budget for the biennium 2000-2001, and requests the Secretary-General to ensure that, in future, all budget proposals are submitted in time in accordance with established budgetary procedure;

191. *Emphasizes* that the efficiency measures and the transfer of savings therefrom should not lead to a process of budgetary reduction and should not result in the involuntary separation of staff;

192. *Also emphasizes* that the efficiency measures and the redeployment of savings to the Development Account should not adversely affect the full implementation of all mandated programmes and activities;

193. *Reiterates* that savings to be achieved as a result of the efficiency measures can be identified in the con-

text of budget performance reports and shall be transferred to the Development Account section with the prior approval of the General Assembly;

194. *Also reiterates* that the savings transferred to the Development Account section in accordance with paragraph 4 of General Assembly resolution 54/15 shall form the maintenance base for that section in future proposed programme budgets;

195. *Reaffirms* that the Development Account should be operated strictly in accordance with the Financial Regulations and Rules of the United Nations and the Regulations and Rules Governing Programme Planning, the Programme Aspects of the Budget, the Monitoring of Implementation and the Methods of Evaluation;

196. *Reiterates* that the anticipated duration of the approved projects contained in the report of the Secretary-General shall not be used as a precedent for setting time limits for the programmes of the regular budget;

197. *Stresses* that in the implementation of the proposals, particular attention should be given to the utilization of technical, human and other resources available in the developing countries;

198. *Reiterates* its decision to keep the implementation of the Development Account under review, and requests the Secretary-General to submit reports in accordance with the relevant regulations and rules;

199. *Stresses* that, in accordance with the established budgetary procedure, comprehensive proposals in the context of the proposed programme budget should be submitted to the Committee for Programme and Coordination and the Advisory Committee on Administrative and Budgetary Questions for their recommendations on the proposals of the Secretary-General, for consideration by the Fifth Committee;

200. *Requests* the Secretary-General to ensure that, in the future, project design and implementation should focus on economic and social activities in developing countries and countries with economies in transition;

Income section 2. General income

201. *Notes with appreciation* the measures taken to increase the return on United Nations balances and investments, and urges the Secretary-General to continue his efforts to enhance further such returns.

ANNEX I

Changes to the programme narratives of the proposed programme budget for the biennium 2000-2001, as reflected in the conclusions and recommendations of the Committee for Programme and Coordination at its thirty-ninth session, and additional modifications

Foreword and introduction

1. Delete paragraph 43 and renumber the subsequent paragraphs accordingly

2. In former paragraph 189, the first sentence should read: "During the biennium, the Office will perform functions in accordance with General Assembly resolution 48/218 B of 29 July 1994."

Section 1. Overall policy-making, direction and coordination

3. In paragraph 1.50:

(a) After the second sentence, insert a new sentence reading "The functions and responsibilities of the Deputy Secretary-General are in accordance with paragraph 1 of resolution 52/12 B."

(b) In the penultimate sentence, replace the phrase "This organizational unit" with "The Executive Office of the Secretary-General", and move the sentence so that it follows the first sentence of the paragraph

4. In paragraph 1.65, first sentence, after "Economic and Social Council;", insert "responsibilities entrusted to the Director-General of the Conference on Disarmament;"

5. In paragraph 1.75:

(a) In the last sentence, replace "the functions" with "the core functions"

(b) In subparagraph *(b)*, after "non-governmental organizations", insert "in consultative status with the Economic and Social Council"

Section 2. General Assembly affairs and conference services

6. After paragraph 2.35, add a new paragraph reading:

> "The Division of General Assembly and Economic and Social Council Affairs will also conduct consultations and coordinate the assignment of responsibilities for the implementation of General Assembly and Economic and Social Council resolutions and decisions and follow-up to ensure timely action by relevant bodies."

and renumber the subsequent paragraphs accordingly

7. At the end of former paragraph 2.36 *(c)* (i), add "and consultations and coordination for the assignment of responsibilities for the implementation of General Assembly and Economic and Social Council resolutions"

8. After former paragraph 2.45, add a new paragraph reading:

> "Another objective will be to coordinate with relevant bodies to ensure compliance with General Assembly resolutions 52/214 B of 22 December 1997 and 53/208 B of 18 December 1998 regarding the format of reports."

and renumber the subsequent paragraphs accordingly

9. In former paragraph 2.46 *(c)* (ii), after "limitation of documentation;", insert "compliance with resolution 53/208 B on format of reports;"

10. In former paragraph 2.46 *(c)*, add:

"(iii) Provision of interpretation services for meetings of regional and other major groupings of Member States, on an ad hoc basis, in accordance with established practice;

"(iv) Provision of facilities for bilateral meetings of heads of State and Government during the sessions of the General Assembly on an 'as available' basis."

Section 3. Political affairs

11. In paragraph 3.2, after the first sentence, insert "A case in point is the promotion of a comprehensive, just and lasting settlement of the question of Palestine in accordance with all relevant United Nations resolutions."

12. In paragraph 3.37 *(c)* (i), replace "Participation in the activities of" with "Maintenance of contacts for exchanges of information with"

Section 4. Disarmament

13. Replace paragraph 4.2 with the following:

"The Department for Disarmament Affairs, headed by an Under-Secretary-General, was re-established by the Secretary-General in January 1998 to replace the Centre for Disarmament Affairs as part of his programme for reform. The Secretary-General sought to put in place a new structure that would have the capacity to respond more effectively to the priorities of Member States in the disarmament area. The Department will continue its activities in 2000 and 2001 in the field of disarmament, related to weapons of mass destruction and conventional arms."

14. Replace paragraph 4.3 with the following:

"In the biennium 2000-2001, the Department will continue to assist Member States in promoting, strengthening and consolidating multilateral principles and norms in all the fields of disarmament. It will expand its outreach activities, including its databases, to ensure the exchange of impartial and factual information on disarmament and security-related matters among the United Nations, Member States, regional organizations and non-governmental organizations and to enhance interaction and cooperation on such matters. The Department will, through its revitalized regional centres for peace and disarmament, assist Member States in promoting the pursuit of regional solutions to regional problems in the field of disarmament."

15. Replace paragraph 4.4 with the following:

"The legislative authority for the programme under this section derives from the Charter of the United Nations, the medium-term plan for the period 1998-2001, as revised (A/53/6/Rev.1), and relevant resolutions and decisions of the General Assembly and other legislative organs of the United Nations system."

16. After paragraph 4.4, insert new paragraph 4.5 reading:

"The Conference on Disarmament (until 1984, the Committee on Disarmament) was set up in accordance with paragraph 120 of the Final Document of the Tenth Special Session of the General Assembly (resolution S-10/2) as the single multilateral disarmament negotiating forum of the international community. The Conference is open to the 5 nuclear-weapon States and 61 other States. In addition, some 40 non-member States are invited, upon their request, to participate in its work. The Conference, inter alia, conducts its work by consensus, adopts its own rules of procedure, rotates its presidency among all its members on a monthly basis, adopts its own agenda, taking into account the recommendations made to it by the Assembly and the proposals presented by the members of the Conference, and submits a report to the Assembly annually, or more frequently. The Conference divides its annual sessions into three parts and, if necessary, continues its negotiations on priority issues during the inter-sessional periods. Meetings thus are held for seven to nine months each year."

17. After new paragraph 4.5, insert new paragraph 4.6 reading:

"The Disarmament Commission, a subsidiary organ of the General Assembly, was set up in accordance with paragraph 118 of the Final Document of the Tenth Special Session of the General Assembly (resolution S-10/2) as the specialized, deliberative body within the United Nations multilateral disarmament machinery that allows for in-depth deliberation on specific disarmament issues, leading to the submission of concrete recommendations on those issues (General Assembly resolution 53/79 A, para. 3)."

18. Replace former paragraph 4.5 with new paragraph 4.7 reading:

"The proposals under this section address current and future trends in the field of disarmament and international security in order to assist Member States, and to enable the Secretary-General also to assist them, in their search for agreement. Apart from substantive issues involved in the deliberative and/or negotiating process, these proposals should also address the challenges arising from the implementation of the relevant General Assembly resolutions as well as relevant treaties."

19. Delete former paragraphs 4.9, 4.10 and 4.11

20. Renumber former paragraphs 4.6, 4.7, 4.8 and 4.12 as paragraphs 4.8, 4.9, 4.10 and 4.11, respectively

21. Replace former paragraph 4.13 with new paragraph 4.12 reading:

"During the biennium 2000-2001, the following objectives will be pursued: to provide organizational and substantive secretariat support to multilateral bodies entrusted with deliberation and/or negotiations on disarmament issues; to follow and assess current and future trends in the field of disarmament and international security in order to assist Member States, and to enable the Secretary-General also to assist them, in their search for agreement; to support and promote regional disarmament efforts and initiatives using approaches freely arrived at by the States of the region and taking into account the legitimate requirements of States for self-defence and the specific characteristics of each region; to strengthen the capacity of the Department as well as that of the Secretary-General's Advisory Board on Disarmament Matters; to provide impartial, factual information on the disarmament efforts of the United Nations to Member States, parliamentarians, research and academic institutions, and specialized non-governmental organizations through the disarmament information programme and by providing Member States with full access to all relevant databases, including on disarmament; and to continue to inform the public on an objective and updated basis of the United Nations disarmament activities."

22. Replace former paragraph 4.14 with new paragraph 4.13 reading:

"Following the establishment of the Department and its reorganization, its activities have been carried out by five branches and three regional centres as follows: the Conference on Disarmament Secretariat and Conference Support Branch at Geneva, the Weapons of Mass Destruction Branch, the Conventional Arms (including Practical Disarmament Measures) Branch, the Monitoring, Database and Information Branch, the Regional Disarmament Branch and the regional centres for peace and disarmament in Africa, in Asia and the Pacific and in Latin America and the Caribbean."

23. Replace former paragraph 4.15 with new paragraph 4.14 reading:

"Gender mainstreaming can make a contribution to strengthening the Department's ability to carry out key elements of its mandate. In this regard, efforts are being made to increase the number of women on the Secretary-General's Advisory Board on Disarmament Matters. In the biennium 2000-2001, 25 per cent of the members will be women, up from 8.6 per cent. Gender mainstreaming will also be built into activities pertaining to the establishment of other disarmament and arms control mechanisms, including advocacy."

24. Replace former paragraph 4.16 with new paragraph 4.15 reading:

"The expected accomplishments during the biennium include: assistance in negotiations, deliberations, consensus-building and review conferences of States parties to various multilateral arms limitation and disarmament agreements; increased expertise in the field of arms limitation and disarmament among Member States as a result of the implementation of the disarmament fellowship, training and advisory services programme; assistance in negotiations, deliberations and consensus-building in the field of weapons of mass destruction and conventional weapons, and increased awareness and understanding by Member States of new trends and developments in those fields; promotion of participation in the United Nations Register of Conventional Arms and the United Nations standardized instrument for reporting of military expenditures; assistance in initiatives taken to address illicit trafficking in small arms and light weapons in all its aspects; a reinvigorated publications and outreach programme, including a well-developed web site for the Department; effective confidence-building and arms limitation measures in the Central African subregion; and development of politically sound and economically viable projects on demobilization and weapons collection and destruction at the request of Member States."

25. Renumber former paragraphs 4.17 and 4.18 as paragraphs 4.16 and 4.17, respectively

26. In former paragraph 4.17 *(a)* (ii) b. (new para. 4.16 *(a)* (ii) b.), replace "Ottawa Convention" (line 14) with "Convention on the Prohibition of the Use, Stockpiling, Production and Transfer of Anti-personnel Mines and on Their Destruction"

27. In former paragraph 4.17 *(a)* (xviii) (new para. 4.16 *(a)* (xviii)), replace "Ottawa Convention on landmines" with "Convention on the Prohibition of the Use, Stockpiling, Production and Transfer of Anti-personnel Mines and on Their Destruction"

28. In former paragraph 4.18 (new para. 4.17), replace "Ottawa Convention on landmines" (line 6) with "Convention on the Prohibition of the Use, Stockpiling, Production and Transfer of Anti-personnel Mines and on Their Destruction"

Section 5. Peacekeeping operations

29. In paragraph 5.5, last sentence, replace "other missions" with "good offices, preventive diplomacy, peacemaking and humanitarian missions"

30. At the beginning of paragraph 5.6, insert:

"Every effort will be made to seek the early resolution of conflicts through pacific settlement of disputes by the parties concerned through negotiation, inquiry, mediation, conciliation, arbitration, judicial settlement, resort to regional agencies or arrangements, or other peaceful means in accordance with the Charter of the United Nations. However, peacekeeping will be one of the key instruments available to the United Nations to resolve conflicts and to maintain international peace and security."

Section 6. Peaceful uses of outer space

31. In paragraph 6.4:

(a) At the end of the penultimate sentence, after "sustainable development", add "and sustained economic growth"

(b) At the end of the paragraph, delete " and landmine detection" and add ", at the request of Governments"

32. In paragraph 6.5, first sentence, after "sustainable development", insert "and sustained economic growth"

Section 9. Economic and social affairs

33. In paragraph 9.4, penultimate sentence, insert "landlocked countries" after "least developed countries,". This change should be reflected throughout the narrative of section 9, wherever reference is made to "least developed countries and small island developing States"

34. In paragraph 9.58, line 4, after "in particular its Second Committee, and,", delete "as appropriate"

35. In paragraph 9.98, line 6, after "(resolution S-19/2),", insert "the resolution endorsing the World Solar Programme 1996-2005 as a contribution to the overall sustainable development agenda, adopted by the General Assembly at its fifty-third session (resolution 53/7),"

36. After paragraph 9.103, add a new paragraph reading:

"In compliance with General Assembly resolution 53/7 of 16 October 1998, concrete action will be undertaken by the Secretary-General in consultation with the United Nations Educational, Scientific and Cultural Organization and in cooperation with the United Nations Environment Programme and other relevant organizations to ensure that the World Solar Programme 1996-2005 is fully integrated and brought into the mainstream of the efforts of the United Nations system to attain the objective of sustained economic growth and sustainable development."

and renumber the subsequent paragraphs accordingly

37. In former paragraphs 9.105 *(a)* (v), 9.105 *(b)* (iii) and 9.107, after "integrated water resource management", insert "and development". This change is to be reflected throughout the entire narrative of section 9, wherever reference is made to "integrated water resource management"

Section 10. Africa: New Agenda for Development

38. In paragraph 10.2:

(a) At the end of the third sentence, add ", in accordance with General Assembly resolution 53/90 of 7 December 1998 and in the context of the Cairo Agenda for Action: Relaunching Africa's Economic and Social Development"

(b) At the end of the paragraph, add a new sentence reading:

"In its resolution 53/92 of 7 December 1998, the General Assembly welcomed the recommendations of the Secretary-General and requested him to submit a progress report on their implementation to the Assembly at its fifty-fourth session."

Section 11A. Trade and development

39. In table 11A.23, delete the text relating to the Committee for Programme and Coordination

Section 12. Environment

40. Replace the programme narrative and resource tables contained in the proposed programme budget under section 12 with the reformulated fascicle contained in document A/C.5/54/20

Section 13. Human settlements

41. Revise the programme narrative contained in the proposed programme budget under section 13 in accordance with the reformulated narrative contained in document A/C.5/54/16

Section 14. Crime prevention and criminal justice

42. Throughout section 14, insert "in all its forms and manifestations" after "terrorism"

43. In paragraph 14.3 *(b)*, replace "to improve the capacity of States" with "to support the strengthening of the capacity of Governments, at their request"

44. In paragraph 14.5, replace "to reform legislation" with "to improve legislation"

45. In paragraph 14.8, third sentence, replace "including law reform" with "the improvement of their legislation"

46. Replace paragraph 14.18 with the following:

"The focus will be, in particular, on issues such as transnational organized crime, terrorism, the laundering of the proceeds of crime, corruption, environmental offences, illicit traffic in children and economic crime, which are all of primary concern to the international community."

47. In paragraph 14.21 *(a)* (iii), delete ", including early warning mechanisms"

48. Delete references to a proposed additional protocol on computer-related crime to the convention against transnational organized crime and a proposed international convention against corruption and bribery in the following paragraphs: 14.17 *(a)*, 14.20 *(b)*, 14.21 *(a)* (i) g. and h., 14.21 *(a)* (ii) i. and 14.24 *(a)*

Section 15. International drug control

49. In paragraph 15.4, replace the second sentence with the following:

"These include the provision of secretariat services to the International Narcotics Control Board and to the Commission on Narcotic Drugs, its subsidiary bodies, and to intergovernmental conferences, as well as initiatives which aim to promote adherence to the related conventions and the inclusion of their provisions in national legislation and their effective implementation, and to meet the goals and objectives adopted at the twentieth special session of the General Assembly held in June 1998."

50. In paragraph 15.32 *(d)*, replace "including those countries that are not members of the Association of South-East Asian Nations (ASEAN)," with "and other Asian countries"

51. In paragraph 15.35, after subparagraph *(b)*, insert a new subparagraph *(c)* reading:

"Contribution to the achievement of the goals and objectives adopted at the twentieth special session of the General Assembly;"

and renumber the subsequent subparagraphs accordingly

52. At the end of paragraph 15.36 *(a)* (ii) a., insert "biennial reports on the achievement by Member States of the goals and objectives adopted at the twentieth special session of the General Assembly"

53. In paragraph 15.44, insert a new subparagraph *(h)*, reading:

"Strengthening the capacity of the Board to prepare its report, taking into account information provided by the interested Governments."

54. In paragraph 15.48, after subparagraph *(a)*, insert a new subparagraph *(b)* reading:

"Facilitation of the examination of the biennial reports on the achievement by Member States of the goals and objectives adopted at the twentieth special session of the General Assembly;"

and renumber the subsequent subparagraphs accordingly

55. In paragraph 15.56, last sentence, after "the European Centre for Drugs and Drug Addiction", insert "the Economic Cooperation Organization (ECO)"

56. Insert ", including production in enclosed premises" in the following paragraphs, as indicated:

(a) Paragraph 15.63, fourth sentence, after "cannabis"

(b) Paragraph 15.64, last sentence, after "illicit cultivation"

(c) Paragraph 15.65:

(i) First sentence, after "crops" (in both instances)

(ii) Fourth sentence, after "illicit cultivation"

(d) Paragraph 15.67 *(c)* and *(d)*, after "cannabis"

(e) Paragraph 15.68 *(b)* (iv) k., line 2, after "illicit crops"

(f) Paragraph 15.68 *(d)*:

(i) Subparagraph (ii) after "crop cultivation"

(ii) Subparagraph (xiii), after "cultivation"

(iii) Subparagraph (xiv), after "crops"

(iv) Subparagraphs (xv) and (xvi), after "cultivation"

(g) Paragraph 15.69, fourth sentence:

(i) *(a)* and *(b)*, after "crops"

(ii) *(d)*, after "cultivated"

(iii) *(f)*, after "crops"

(h) Paragraph 15.70, line 9, after "cultivation"

57. In paragraph 15.65, second sentence, after "States", insert "at their request"

58. In paragraph 15.66:

(a) In the last sentence, after "Central and West Asia", insert "South-West Asia,"

(b) At the end of the paragraph, insert:

"Cooperation in North America on the reduction and elimination of illicit cultivation of cannabis, including, inter alia, in enclosed premises, will also be of particular importance."

Section 17. Economic and social development in Asia and the Pacific

59. In paragraph 17.4, replace "will be further reviewed by the Commission at its fifty-fifth session, scheduled for 22 to 28 April 1999" with "was further reviewed and approved by the Commission at its fifty-fifth session, held from 22 to 28 April 1999"

60. In paragraph 17.57 *(a)*, line 9, after "violence against women", insert ", including women migrant workers,"

Section 19. Economic and social development in Latin America and the Caribbean

61. In paragraph 19.4:

(a) Replace "three fundamental" with "programme 17 of the medium-term plan for the period 1998-2001 and the following"

(b) After "prevailing circumstances", delete the remainder of the paragraph

62. In paragraph 19.51, delete the last sentence

63. Replace paragraph 19.71 *(a)* with the following:

"support of the design and implementation of policies to strengthen domestic capacities in the macroeconomic field;"

64. In paragraph 19.87, delete the second sentence

Section 20. Economic and social development in Western Asia

65. In paragraph 20.3 *(b)*, the first sentence should read:

"In line with the revised medium-term plan, gender and issues pertaining to the right to development are mainstreamed in the proposed programme of work for the biennium 2000-2001."

Section 22. Human rights

66. In paragraph 22.1:

(a) First sentence, after "realization of", insert "all"

(b) Second sentence, after "the programme is based on", insert "the revised medium-term plan for the period 1998-2001 (A/53/6/Rev.1),"

67. Delete paragraph 22.5, and renumber the subsequent paragraphs accordingly

68. Replace former paragraph 22.26 with the following:

"Resource requirements for the Committee on the Protection of the Rights of All Migrant Workers and Members of Their Families in 2000-2001 will be submitted when the International Convention on the Protection of the Rights of All Migrant Workers and Members of Their Families enters into force."

69. In former paragraph 22.45, first sentence, replace "The activities will focus on" with "The primary objectives of this subprogramme will include promotion and protection of the right to development. In this regard, the activities will be"

70. In former paragraph 22.48, first sentence, replace "implementation" with "promotion and protection of"

71. In former paragraph 22.49, subparagraph *(b)* (iii) should read:

"Preparation of a consolidated list of indicators showing success in respecting economic, social and cultural rights in conjunction with the United Nations partner agencies and programmes, taking into account ongoing consideration on this issue."

72. In former paragraph 22.49 *(c)* (i), last line, after "ICRC", insert ", OIC, OAU and OAS"

73. In former paragraph 22.50, line 5, replace "and normative components" with "in consultation with and upon the request of the Member States concerned,"

74. In former paragraph 22.79 *(c)* (i), third sentence, replace "integration of human rights components in the United Nations Development Assistance Frameworks" with "increased coordination in support of human rights and fundamental freedoms within the United Nations system"

Section 25. Humanitarian assistance

75. In paragraph 25.17, line 7, replace "ensuring that the humanitarian response of the United Nations system is properly integrated with political and peacekeeping initiatives" with "ensuring a high degree of coherence between assistance and the political and human rights aspects of the United Nations response"

76. In paragraph 25.22, line 4, replace "strategic coordination of humanitarian assistance with political strategy and human rights objectives" with "ensuring a high degree of coherence between assistance and the political and human rights aspects of the United Nations response"

77. Renumber paragraph 25.34 *(a)* (iii) as paragraph 25.34 *(c)* (viii)

Section 26. Public information

78. In paragraph 26.4, first sentence, replace "all Member States" with "the peoples of the world"

79. At the end of paragraph 26.69 *(c)*, insert "by launching the pilot project regarding United Nations international radio broadcasting"

Section 27. Management and central support services

80. In paragraph 27A.27 *(d)* (iii), include a reference to the reports of the Joint Inspection Unit

81. In paragraph 27C.5, after the two first sentences, insert the following:

"The General Assembly decided, in its resolution 53/221 of 7 April 1999, that, before delegating such authority, well designed mechanisms of accountability, including the necessary internal monitoring and control procedures, as well as training, should be put in place. In this regard, the General Assembly requested a comprehensive report on the system of accountability and responsibility. It was also decided that the role of the Office of Human Resources Management and its responsibilities and authority in establishing human resources policies, in the monitoring and approval of the recruitment and placement of staff, as well as in ensuring the full implementation of human resources mandates set by the General Assembly, among its other functions, should be retained and reinforced."

82. Replace paragraph 27C.6 with the reformulated paragraph 27C.6 contained in document A/C.5/54/17

83. At the end of paragraph 27C.31, insert "and to conduct a review of the internal system of justice in order to ensure the timely, fair and effective administration of justice"

Section 28. Internal oversight

84. Replace paragraph 28.3 with the following:

"In its programme of work for the biennium 2000-2001, the Office of Internal Oversight Services will manage the responsibilities of each oversight unit within the Office to ensure coherence and in order to assist the Secretary-General in fulfilling his internal oversight responsibilities in respect of resources and staff of the Organization through the exercise of the functions enumerated in resolution 48/218 B."

85. Replace paragraph 28.20 with the following:

"The objectives of the subprogramme are:

"*(a)* To facilitate the assessment by intergovernmental bodies, as systematically as possible, of the relevance, efficiency, effectiveness and impact of the activities of programmes in relation to their objectives;

"*(b)* To enable the Secretariat and Member States to engage in systematic reflection with a view to increasing the effectiveness of the main programmes of the Organization by altering their content and, if necessary, reviewing their objectives;

"*(c)* To assist the departments and offices in the Secretariat in implementing approved evaluation recommendations;

"*(d)* To support the evaluation activities of departments and offices."

86. Replace paragraph 28.24 with the following:

"The expected accomplishments by the end of the biennium consist of increases in the implementation of approved recommendations contained in evaluation reports and the strengthening of the role of self-evaluation within the Organization."

87. Replace the two first sentences of paragraph 28.41 with the following:

"In its programme of work for the biennium 2000-2001, the Division plans to consolidate its resources to provide comprehensive internal audit coverage. The Division will deliver the following outputs during the biennium:

ANNEX II
Staffing table for 2000 and 2001

	2000	*2001*
Professional category and above		
Deputy Secretary-General	1	1
Under-Secretary-General	25	25
Assistant Secretary-General	18	18
D-2	79	79
D-1	254	254
P-5	693	693
P-4/3	2,237	2,244
P-2/1	436	436
Total	**3,743**	**3,750**
General Service category		
Principal level	272	272
Other levels	2,731	2,732
Total	**3,003**	**3,004**
Other categories		
Security Services	176	176
Local level	1,630	1,634
Field Service	189	189
Trades and crafts	185	185
Total	**2,180**	**2,184**
Grand total	**8,926**	**8,938**

On 23 December, the Assembly decided that the item would remain for consideration at its resumed fifty-fourth (2000) session (**decision 54/465**) and that the Fifth Committee should continue to consider it at that session (**decision 54/462 A**).

Appropriations

In his proposed programme budget for the 2000-2001 biennium [A/54/6/Rev.1], the Secretary-General proposed expenditures amounting to $2,655 million and income totalling $43.5 million, as well as staff assessment income of $326.9 million, an increase of $7.7 million over estimates for 1998-1999, resulting in a net estimate of $2,284 million. The proposed budget represented a 0.2 per cent real growth before recosting from the revised 1998-1999 budget.

Extrabudgetary resources for the 2000-2001 biennium were estimated at $3,659,782,700, comprising $217,001,100 for support services, $175,887,900 for substantive services and $3,266,893,700 for operational activities.

ACABQ, in its first report on the 2000-2001 proposed programme budget [A/54/7], concluded that there was no basis to change the overall level of resources proposed by the Secretary-General. It pointed out that the last two bienniums had been ones of budget stringency and restraint, with the cost of additional activities having to be absorbed and with reductions in posts. Fortuitous gains in currency and low inflation had helped offset the effects of those developments, but that might not always be the case, and steps were being taken to significantly reduce vacancies. ACABQ cautioned that continued deviations from the full application of Assembly resolution 41/213 [YUN 1996, p. 1024] in all its aspects would call into serious question the validity of the budgetary process.

In November [A/54/623], the Secretary-General recommended revised estimates to reflect the latest data on actual inflation experience, the outcome of salary surveys and the movement of post adjustment, and the effect of the evolution of operational rates of exchange on the proposed programme budget for the 2000-2001 biennium. The recosted level of expenditures amounted to $2,584.6 million and income of $365.7 million. The figures were revised again in December [A/54/623/Add.1 & Corr.1], due to the significant change in the performance of a number of currencies against the United States dollar. Revised proposed expenditure amounted to $2,561.9 million and income to $363.8 million.

ACABQ, in its tenth report on the programme budget [A/54/7/Add.9], found no technical basis for objecting to the Secretary-General's revised estimates and transmitted them to the Fifth Committee.

The Fifth Committee recommended approval of a gross appropriation of $2,535,689,200 and income estimate (other than income derived from staff assessment) of $361,298,900. The net expenditure for the 2000-2001 biennium was estimated at $2,174,390,300 [A/54/691].

GENERAL ASSEMBLY ACTION

On 23 December [meeting 88], the General Assembly, on the recommendation of the Fifth Com-

mittee [A/54/691], adopted **resolutions 54/250 A-C** without vote [agenda item 121].

A

Budget appropriations for the biennium 2000-2001

The General Assembly

Resolves that for the biennium 2000-2001:

1. Appropriations totalling 2,535,689,200 United States dollars are hereby approved for the following purposes:

Section	Thousands of United States dollars
Part I. Overall policy-making, direction and coordination	
1. Overall policy-making, direction and coordination	47,675.1
2. General Assembly affairs and conference services	425,970.2
Total, part I	**473,645.3**
Part II. Political affairs	
3. Political affairs	137,756.0
4. Disarmament	14,067.9
5. Peacekeeping operations	76,094.7
6. Peaceful uses of outer space	3,667.7
Total, part II	**231,586.3**
Part III. International justice and law	
7. International Court of Justice	20,864.5
8. Legal affairs	34,522.3
Total, part III	**55,386.8**
Part IV. International cooperation for development	
9. Economic and social affairs	113,112.6
10. Africa: New Agenda for Development	5,883.4
11A. Trade and development	87,685.5
11B. International Trade Centre UNCTAD/WTO	19,248.7
12. Environment	8,743.4
13. Human settlements	13,757.4
14. Crime prevention and criminal justice	5,299.1
15. International drug control	15,037.8
Total, part IV	**268,767.9**
Part V. Regional cooperation for development	
16. Economic and social development in Africa	78,455.2
17. Economic and social development in Asia and the Pacific	57,031.6
18. Economic development in Europe	40,554.6
19. Economic and social development in Latin America and the Caribbean	78,857.5
20. Economic and social development in Western Asia	50,336.2
21. Regular programme of technical cooperation	41,995.3
Total, part V	**347,230.4**
Part VI. Human rights and humanitarian affairs	
22. Human rights	41,163.4
23. Protection of and assistance to refugees	41,940.0
24. Palestine refugees	21,667.9
25. Humanitarian assistance	18,841.8
Total, part VI	**123,613.1**
Part VII. Public information	
26. Public information	143,605.5
Total, part VII	**143,605.5**
Part VIII. Common support services	
27. Management and central support services	441,857.4
Total, part VIII	**441,857.4**
Part IX. Internal oversight	
28. Internal oversight	19,220.6
Total, part IX	**19,220.6**
Part X. Jointly financed administrative activities and special expenses	
29. Jointly financed administrative activities	7,844.3
30. Special expenses	53,001.2
Total, part X	**60,845.5**
Part XI. Capital expenditures	
31. Construction, alteration, improvement and major maintenance	42,617.4
Total, part XI	**42,617.4**
Part XII. Staff assessment	
32. Staff assessment	314,248.0
Total, part XII	**314,248.0**
Part XIII. Development Account	
33. Development Account	13,065.0
Total, part XIII	**13,065.0**
Total, expenditure sections	**2,535,689.2**

2. The Secretary-General shall be authorized to transfer credits between sections of the budget, with the concurrence of the Advisory Committee on Administrative and Budgetary Questions;

3. The total net provision made under the various sections of the budget for contractual printing shall be administered as a unit under the direction of the United Nations Publications Board;

4. In addition to the appropriations approved under paragraph 1 above, an amount of 250,000 dollars is appropriated for each year of the biennium 2000-2001 from the accumulated income of the Library Endowment Fund for the purchase of books, periodicals, maps and library equipment and for such other expenses of the Library at the Palais des Nations as are in accordance with the objects and provisions of the endowment.

B

Income estimates for the biennium 2000-2001

The General Assembly

Resolves that for the biennium 2000-2001:

1. Estimates of income other than assessments on Member States totalling 361,298,900 United States dollars are approved as follows:

Income section	Thousands of United States dollars
1. Income from staff assessment	318,911.5
2. General income	37,178.0
3. Services to the public	5,209.4
Total, income sections	**361,298.9**

2. The income from staff assessment shall be credited to the Tax Equalization Fund in accordance with the provisions of General Assembly resolution 973(X) of 15 December 1955;

3. Direct expenses of the United Nations Postal Administration, services to visitors, catering and related services, garage operations, television services and the sale of publications, not provided for under the budget appropriations, shall be charged against the income derived from those activities.

C

Financing of appropriations for the year 2000

The General Assembly

Resolves that for the year 2000:

1. Budget appropriations consisting of 1,267,844,600 United States dollars, being half of the appropriations of 2,535,689,200 dollars approved for the biennium 2000-2001 by the General Assembly under paragraph 1 of resolution A above, less 41,601,500 dollars, being the decrease in revised appropriations for the biennium 1998-1999 approved by the Assembly in its resolution 54/247 A of 23 December 1999, shall be financed in accordance with regulations 5.1 and 5.2 of the Financial Regulations of the United Nations as follows:

(*a*) 24,968,700 dollars, consisting of 21,193,700 dollars, being the net of half of the estimated income other than staff assessment approved for the biennium 2000-2001 under resolution B above, plus 3,775,000 dollars, being the increase in income other than staff assessment for the biennium 1998-1999;

(*b*) 1,201,274,400 dollars, being the assessment on Member States in accordance with its resolution 52/215 A of 22 December 1997 and 54/237 A of 23 December 1999 on the scale of assessments for the year 2000;

2. There shall be set off against the assessment on Member States, in accordance with the provisions of General Assembly resolution 973(X) of 15 December 1955, their respective share in the Tax Equalization Fund in the total amount of 149,354,550 dollars, consisting of:

(*a*) 159,455,750 dollars, being half of the estimated staff assessment income approved for the biennium 2000-2001 under resolution B above;

(*b*) Less 10,101,200 dollars, being the decrease in income from staff assessment for the biennium 1998-1999 approved by the Assembly in its resolution 54/247 B of 23 December 1999.

Other questions related to the 2000-2001 programme budget

Working Capital Fund

In December, the General Assembly established the Working Capital Fund for the 2000-2001 biennium at $100 million, the same level as during 1998-1999. As in the past, the Fund was to be used to finance appropriations pending the receipt of assessed contributions, to pay for unforeseen and extraordinary expenses, as well as for miscellaneous and self-liquidating purchases and advance insurance premiums, and to enable the Tax Equalization Fund to meet current commitments pending the accumulation of credits.

GENERAL ASSEMBLY ACTION

On 23 December [meeting 88], the General Assembly, on the recommendation of the Fifth Committee [A/54/691], adopted **resolution 54/253** without vote [agenda item 121].

Working Capital Fund for the biennium 2000-2001

The General Assembly

Resolves that:

1. The Working Capital Fund shall be established for the biennium 2000-2001 in the amount of 100 million United States dollars;

2. Member States shall make advances to the Working Capital Fund in accordance with the scale adopted by the General Assembly for contributions of Member States to the budget for the year 2000;

3. There shall be set off against this allocation of advances:

(*a*) Credits to Member States resulting from transfers made in 1959 and 1960 from the surplus account to the Working Capital Fund in an adjusted amount of 1,025,092 dollars;

(*b*) Cash advances paid by Member States to the Working Capital Fund for the biennium 1998-1999 in accordance with General Assembly resolution 52/224 of 22 December 1997;

4. Should the credits and advances paid by any Member State to the Working Capital Fund for the biennium 1998-1999 exceed the amount of that Member State's advance under the provisions of paragraph 2 above, the excess shall be set off against the amount of the contributions payable by the Member State in respect of the biennium 2000-2001;

5. The Secretary-General is authorized to advance from the Working Capital Fund:

(*a*) Such sums as may be necessary to finance budgetary appropriations pending the receipt of contributions; sums so advanced shall be reimbursed as soon as receipts from contributions are available for the purpose;

(*b*) Such sums as may be necessary to finance commitments that may be duly authorized under the provisions of the resolutions adopted by the General Assembly, in particular resolution 54/252 of 23 December 1999 relating to unforeseen and extraordinary expenses; the Secretary-General shall make provision in the budget estimates for reimbursing the Working Capital Fund;

(*c*) Such sums as may be necessary to continue the revolving fund to finance miscellaneous self-liquidating purchases and activities which, together with net sums outstanding for the same purpose, do not exceed 200,000 dollars; advances in excess of the total of 200,000 dollars may be made with the prior concurrence of the Advisory Committee on Administrative and Budgetary Questions;

(*d*) With the prior concurrence of the Advisory Committee, such sums as may be required to finance payments of advance insurance premiums where the period of insurance extends beyond the end of the biennium in which payment is made; the Secretary-General shall make provision in the budget estimates of each biennium, during the life of the related policies, to cover the charges applicable to each biennium;

(*e*) Such sums as may be necessary to enable the Tax Equalization Fund to meet current commitments pending the accumulation of credits; such advances shall be repaid as soon as credits are available in the Tax Equalization Fund;

6. Should the provision in paragraph 1 above prove inadequate to meet the purposes normally related to the Working Capital Fund, the Secretary-General is

authorized to utilize, in the biennium 2000-2001, cash from special funds and accounts in his custody, under the conditions approved by the General Assembly in its resolution 1341(XIII) of 13 December 1958, or the proceeds of loans authorized by the Assembly.

Contingency fund

The contingency fund, created to accommodate additional expenditures relating to each biennium that were derived from legislative mandates not provided for in the proposed programme budget, was established by General Assembly resolution 41/213 [YUN 1986, p. 1024].

The Fifth Committee considered the Secretary-General's December report [A/C.5/54/46] containing a consolidated statement of all programme budget implications and revised estimates subject to the criteria for the use of the contingency fund, as set out in Assembly resolution 42/211 [YUN 1987, p. 1098]. The amount of $2,737,300 was within the available balance of the fund, which, as at December 1998, stood at $15,307,800.

On 23 December, the Assembly, in **resolution 54/251, section VI**, noted that a balance of $16,362,700 remained in the contingency fund.

Follow-up to General Assembly resolutions 50/227 and 52/12 B

Development Account

The Fifth Committee and the General Assembly continued their review of the Secretary-General's proposals for the utilization of the development dividend [YUN 1998, p. 1278], by which savings from budget efficiencies in the regular programme budget would be transferred to an account for development activities.

GENERAL ASSEMBLY ACTION (April)

On 7 April [meetings 97], the General Assembly, on the recommendation of the Fifth Committee [A/53/485/Add.2], adopted **resolution 53/220 A** without vote [agenda item 113].

Development Account

The General Assembly,

Recalling its resolutions 52/12 B of 19 December 1997, 52/220 and 52/221 A of 22 December 1997 and 52/235 of 26 June 1998,

Reaffirming its resolution 41/213 of 19 December 1986,

Reaffirming also the Financial Regulations and Rules of the United Nations and the Regulations and Rules Governing Programme Planning, the Programme Aspects of the Budget, the Monitoring of Implementation and the Methods of Evaluation,

Noting the proposals made by the Secretary-General for the utilization of the development dividend,

Stressing the need to use the Development Account for projects related to the development priorities of the medium-term plan,

1. *Approves,* from the eight proposals made in the report of the Secretary-General, proposals A, B, D and E below:

A. Promotion of electronic commerce (United Nations Conference on Trade and Development);

B. Capacity-building in economic and social policy analysis in Africa through the networking of expertise (Economic Commission for Africa);

D. Computer and telecommunication system for international and national drug control (United Nations International Drug Control Programme);

E. Capacity-building and networking for the implementation of the Habitat Agenda in least developed countries (United Nations Centre for Human Settlements),

on an ad hoc and one-time basis only, without setting a precedent and without prejudicing the outcome of its consideration of the sustainability and establishment of the mechanism and modalities of the Development Account;

2. *Emphasizes* that, in the implementation of those proposals, emphasis should be placed on the promotion of development activities, and that the implementation should demonstrate the benefits accruing in building national capacities, particularly in developing countries and also in countries with economies in transition;

3. *Stresses* that, in the implementation of the proposals, particular attention should be given to the utilization of technical, human and other resources available in the developing countries;

4. *Decides* that the proposals should be reformulated and implemented in accordance with the relevant Financial Regulations and Rules of the United Nations and the Regulations and Rules Governing Programme Planning, the Programme Aspects of the Budget, the Monitoring of Implementation and the Methods of Evaluation, as revised by the General Assembly in its resolution 53/207 of 18 December 1998;

5. *Requests* the Secretary-General to reformulate the other proposals contained in his report following criteria according to which projects should:

(*a*) Have multiplier effects and promote capacity-building primarily in developing countries;

(*b*) Promote regional and interregional economic and technical cooperation among the developing countries;

(*c*) Use available human and technical resources from the developing regions;

and to submit those reformulated proposals to the General Assembly at the second part of its resumed fifty-third session;

6. *Decides* to keep the implementation of the proposals under review, and requests the Secretary-General to submit a report to the General Assembly on the utilization of the development dividend, in accordance with relevant regulations and rules;

7. *Also decides* to continue consideration of the sustainability and establishment of the mechanism and modalities of the Development Account during the resumed fifty-third session.

Report of Secretary-General (April). As requested in resolution 53/220 A, the Secretary-General, in an April report [A/53/374/Add.1], submitted his reformulated proposals for the utilization of the Development Account. With the exception of the project relating to access by developing countries and countries with economies in transition to the Mercure satellite telecommunications system for interconnectivity in environmental information and data, which was being reconsidered by the United Nations Environment Programme (see p. 979), the other reformulated projects focused on helping to transmit data, information and learned experiences back to programme countries through a network of developing country experts in various areas. The proposal would also bring together policy makers and provide the basis for long-term interaction through the use of information networks, training, enhancement of skills and pooling of national and regional expertise. Resources required for the seven reformulated projects totalled $12,945,000.

Report of Secretary-General (May). In a May report [A/53/945], the Secretary-General clarified the modalities for operating the Development Account. The modalities comprised three distinct elements: the identification and transfer of resources released due to productivity gains to the Development Account budget section; the operation of the Development Account budget section; and operation of the special account for supplementary development activities. Recommendations for transfers of verifiable and sustainable gains achieved in any biennium would be reviewed and approved by the Assembly, and the section transfers would be reflected in the final appropriations for the biennium concerned.

During the biennium, transfers would be made at two points: after the initial appropriation of the programme budget, which would contain approved funds for supplementary development activities, and after the Assembly's approval, following consideration of the second performance report. At that time, additional charges to the Development Account budget section would be made as transfers to the multi-year special account.

A key element of the arrangement would be the special account for supplementary development activities established by the Assembly. During the second year of the biennium, the Secretary-General would prepare proposals for the subsequent biennium. The proposals would be considered by CPC, ACABQ and the Fifth Committee, prior to submission to the Assembly.

Annexed to the report were the proposed timetables for approving expenditure from the special account for supplementary development, estimated at $13.065 million for the 2000-2001 budget and an initial estimate of $40 million for 2002-2003; and the presentation format for the consideration of projects to be funded from that account.

ACABQ consideration (May). ACABQ, in its comments on the Secretary-General's report [A/53/7/Add.12], recommended that the Assembly approve the Secretary-General's proposals. It indicated that the amount of $40 million projected for 2002-2003 should be $53 million, to include the $13 million already appropriated for the 2001-2002 biennium. ACABQ believed that an interim report should be provided at the end of the first biennium on the status of projected productivity gains.

GENERAL ASSEMBLY ACTION (June)

On 8 June [meeting 101], the General Assembly, on the recommendation of the Fifth Committee [A/53/485/Add.4], adopted **resolution 53/220 B** without vote [agenda item 113].

Development Account

The General Assembly,

Recalling its resolutions 52/12 B of 19 December 1997, 52/220 and 52/221 A of 22 December 1997, 52/235 of 26 June 1998 and 53/220 A of 7 April 1999,

Having considered the report of the Secretary-General on the utilization of the development dividend and the related report of the Advisory Committee on Administrative and Budgetary Questions,

Noting the reformulations made by the Secretary-General for proposals A, B, D, E, F, G and H,

Noting also that proposal C is being reconsidered for subsequent submission to the General Assembly,

Noting further the reformulations of proposals F, G and H in accordance with paragraph 5 of resolution 53/220 A,

Reaffirming its resolution 41/213 of 19 December 1986,

Reaffirming also the Financial Regulations and Rules of the United Nations and the Regulations and Rules Governing Programme Planning, the Programme Aspects of the Budget, the Monitoring of Implementation and the Methods of Evaluation,

1. *Decides* that the title of proposal H should be changed to "Activities for capacity-building in developing countries in pursuance of the objectives of Agenda 21, the Copenhagen Declaration on Social Development and the Programme of Action of the World Summit for Social Development, and the Beijing Declaration and the Platform for Action";

2. *Approves* the following reformulated proposals contained in the report of the Secretary-General, on an ad hoc and one-time basis only, without setting a precedent and without prejudicing the outcome of its consideration of the sustainability and establishment of the mechanism and modalities of the Development Account:

F. On-line network of regional institutions for capacity-building in public administration and finance (Department of Economic and Social Affairs of the Secretariat);

G. Research network for economic policy analysis (Department of Economic and Social Affairs);

H. Activities for capacity-building in developing countries in pursuance of the objectives of Agenda 21, the Copenhagen Declaration on Social Development and the Programme of Action of the World Summit for Social Development, and the Beijing Declaration and the Platform for Action (Department of Economic and Social Affairs);

3. *Reiterates* that all projects shall be fully implemented in accordance with the provisions of paragraphs 2 and 3 of General Assembly resolution 53/220 A and the relevant Financial Regulations and Rules of the United Nations and the Regulations and Rules Governing Programme Planning, the Programme Aspects of the Budget, the Monitoring of Implementation and the Methods of Evaluation, as revised by the Assembly in its resolution 53/207 of 18 December 1998;

4. *Decides* that the anticipated duration of the approved projects contained in the report of the Secretary-General shall not be used as a precedent for setting time limits for the programmes of the regular budget;

5. *Decides also* to keep the implementation of the projects under review, and requests the Secretary-General to submit reports to the General Assembly in accordance with relevant regulations and rules.

On the same date, the Assembly, by **decision 53/476**, deferred consideration of the question of modalities for operating the Development Account until the main part of its fifty-fourth (1999) session, with a view to finalizing it prior to its consideration of the proposed programme budget for the 2000-2001 biennium.

GENERAL ASSEMBLY ACTION (October)

On 29 October [meeting 43], the General Assembly, on the recommendation of the Fifth Committee [A/54/508], adopted **resolution 54/15** without vote [agenda item 119].

Development Account

The General Assembly,

Recalling its resolutions 52/12 B of 19 December 1997 and 52/220 and 52/221 A of 22 December 1997,

Reaffirming its resolutions 52/235 of 26 June 1998, 53/220 A of 7 April 1999 and 53/220 B of 8 June 1999,

Having considered the report of the Secretary-General on the Development Account and the related report of the Advisory Committee on Administrative and Budgetary Questions,

Reaffirming its resolution 41/213 of 19 December 1986,

Reaffirming also the Financial Regulations and Rules of the United Nations and the Regulations and Rules Governing Programme Planning, the Programme Aspects of the Budget, the Monitoring of Implementation and the Methods of Evaluation,

1. *Decides* to establish a special multi-year account for supplementary development activities based on the priority objectives of the programmes of the approved medium-term plan;

2. *Emphasizes* that the efficiency measures and the transfer of savings therefrom should not lead to a process of budgetary reduction and should not result in the involuntary separation of staff;

3. *Also emphasizes* that the efficiency measures and the redeployment of savings to the Development Account should not adversely affect the full implementation of all mandated programmes and activities;

4. *Decides* that savings to be achieved as a result of the efficiency measures can be identified in the context of budget performance reports and shall be transferred to the Development Account section with the prior approval of the General Assembly;

5. *Also decides* that the savings transferred to the Development Account section in accordance with paragraph 4 above shall form the maintenance base for that section in future proposed programme budgets;

6. *Reaffirms* that the Development Account should be operated strictly in accordance with the Financial Regulations and Rules of the United Nations and the Regulations and Rules Governing Programme Planning, the Programme Aspects of the Budget, the Monitoring of Implementation and the Methods of Evaluation;

7. *Requests* the Secretary-General to ensure that all budget proposals are fully commensurate with the related mandates in order to ensure their full and effective implementation;

8. *Decides* to keep the implementation of the Development Account under review, and requests the Secretary-General to submit reports in accordance with the relevant regulations and rules.

Report of Secretary-General (November). In November [A/C.5/54/37], the Secretary-General submitted 16 new projects at an estimated cost of $13,185,000. The Secretary-General proposed financing those projects from the balance of $120,000 remaining from the amount appropriated under section 34 (Development Account) of the 1998-1999 programme budget and included under section 33 of the proposed programme budget for 2000-2001.

ACABQ consideration (December). ACABQ, in December [A/54/7/Add.8], recommended that the Assembly approve the Secretary-General's proposals and that, in future, a summary of project proposals should be submitted to CPC for comment on their programmatic aspects, to ACABQ for its comments on the financial aspects and to the Second (Economic and Financial) Committee for its comments on the substance of the projects.

Revised estimates resulting from Economic and Social Council decisions

In November [A/54/443], the Secretary-General submitted a request for an additional appropriation totalling $440,300 above the resources proposed under section 11A (Trade and development) and section 22 (Human rights) of the proposed 2000-2001 programme budget, resulting from action taken by the Economic and Social Council during its 1999 sessions. That provision would represent a charge against the contingency fund (see p. 1305).

ACABQ, in October [A/54/7/Add.2], recommended that the Fifth Committee take note of the estimate of $440,300, on the understanding that such appropriations as might be necessary would be requested by the Secretary-General in the context of a consolidated statement of programme budget implications and revised estimates to be submitted to the General Assembly.

In a December addendum [A/54/443/Add.1], the Secretary-General proposed an additional provision of $149,800 under section 18 (Economic development in Europe) of the proposed 2000-2001 programme budget to be charged against the contingency fund.

The Assembly, in **resolution 54/251, section IV**, of 23 December, took note of the revised estimates resulting from Economic and Social Council resolutions and decisions.

Estimates relating to special political missions

On 7 December [A/C.5/54/39], the Secretary-General submitted estimated requirements of $9,964,500 for eight political missions, resulting from action taken by the Security Council. That amount would be charged against a provision of $86,200,000 for special political missions included in section 3 (Political affairs) of the 2000-2001 proposed programme budget by the General Assembly in resolution 53/206 [YUN 1998, p. 1284].

ACABQ, in a 13 December report [A/54/7/Add.10], recommended that the Assembly approve the Secretary-General's proposal. It requested that future reports should include a consolidated table of requirements by object of expenditure, including an indication of the decrease or increase with relation to the previous biennium, and information on those missions previously in place and those terminated since the last report. The Secretary-General should monitor the continuation of special missions and, if a mission was likely to go beyond the biennium, requirements should be included in the initial estimates for the next biennium.

The Secretary-General, on 16 December [A/C.5/54/45], reported that, after recosting, the provision of $86,200,000 proposed in the 2000-2001 programme budget for special political missions was equivalent to $90,387,200. Charges against that sum, approved by the Assembly and the Council in 1999, totalled $55,363,100, leaving an unallocated balance of $35,024,100. Annexed to the Secretary-General's note was a breakdown of the utilization of the provision, including the $9,964,500 resulting from estimates in respect of matters of which the Council was seized.

The Assembly, in **resolution 54/251, section VIII**, noted that the current utilization of the provision for special political missions amounted to $55,363,100, with an unallocated balance of $35,024,100 remaining against the provision of $90,387,200 for special political missions.

Subvention for UNIDIR

In October [A/C.5/54/26], the Secretary-General transmitted to the General Assembly for approval the recommendation of the Board of Trustees of the United Nations Institute for Disarmament Research (UNIDIR) for a subvention of $213,000 from the UN regular budget to the Institute's 2000 work programme.

The Assembly approved the subvention on 23 December in **resolution 54/251, section I**.

Unforeseen and extraordinary expenses

Under very specific circumstances, the Secretary-General was authorized by the General Assembly to enter into commitments for activities of an urgent nature, without reverting to the Assembly for approval.

ACABQ, in its first report on the programme budget for the 2000-2001 biennium [A/54/7], said that it was time to review the levels specified in Assembly resolutions on unforeseen and extraordinary expenses and requested the Secretary-General to submit to the Assembly's fifty-fourth (1999) session an analysis of those levels, together with proposals for their adjustment.

In response to that request, the Secretary-General, in November [A/C.5/54/29], recommended that the authority to commit without prior concurrence of ACABQ be increased from $5 million to $10 million for activities relating to peace and security. Furthermore, if a decision of the Security Council resulted in the need for the Secretary-General to enter into commitments relating to the maintenance of peace and security, the Secretary-General should be authorized to enter into commitments, with ACABQ's prior concurrence, up to $25 million, in excess of which the Assembly would be convened to consider the matter. He also recommended a revision of commitments certified by the President of the International Court of Justice relating to: the designation of ad hoc judges from $300,000 to $330,000; payment of pensions and travel and removal expenses of retiring judges, and travel and removal expenses and installation grant of members of the Court from $180,000 to $410,000; and holding of sessions away from The Hague from $50,000 to $25,000.

GENERAL ASSEMBLY ACTION

On 23 December [meeting 88], the General Assembly, on the recommendation of the Fifth Committee [A/54/691], adopted **resolution 54/252** without vote [agenda item 121].

Unforeseen and extraordinary expenses for the biennium 2000-2001

The General Assembly

1. *Authorizes* the Secretary-General, with the prior concurrence of the Advisory Committee on Administrative and Budgetary Questions and subject to the Financial Regulations of the United Nations and the provisions of paragraph 3 below, to enter into commitments in the biennium 2000-2001 to meet unforeseen and extraordinary expenses arising either during or subsequent to the biennium, provided that the concurrence of the Advisory Committee shall not be necessary for:

(a) Such commitments, not exceeding a total of 8 million United States dollars in any one year of the biennium 2000-2001, as the Secretary-General certifies relate to the maintenance of peace and security;

(b) Such commitments as the President of the International Court of Justice certifies relate to expenses occasioned by:

(i) The designation of ad hoc judges (Statute of the International Court of Justice, Article 31), not exceeding a total of 330,000 dollars;

(ii) The calling of witnesses and the appointment of experts (Statute, Article 50) and the appointment of assessors (Statute, Article 30), not exceeding a total of 50,000 dollars;

(iii) The maintenance in office for the completion of cases of judges who have not been re-elected (Statute, Article 13, paragraph 3), not exceeding a total of 40,000 dollars;

(iv) The payment of pensions and travel and removal expenses of retiring judges, and travel and removal expenses and installation grant of members of the Court (Statute, Article 32, paragraph 7), not exceeding a total of 410,000 dollars;

(v) The work of the Court or its Chambers away from The Hague (Statute, Article 22), not exceeding a total of 25,000 dollars;

(c) Such commitments, in an amount not exceeding 500,000 dollars, in the biennium 2000-2001, as the Secretary-General certifies are required for interorganizational security measures pursuant to section IV of General Assembly resolution 36/235 of 18 December 1981;

2. *Resolves* that the Secretary-General shall report to the Advisory Committee and to the General Assembly at its fifty-fifth and fifty-sixth sessions all commitments made under the provisions of the present resolution, together with the circumstances relating thereto, and shall submit supplementary estimates to the Assembly in respect of such commitments;

3. *Decides* that, for the biennium 2000-2001, if a decision of the Security Council results in the need for the Secretary-General to enter into commitments relating to the maintenance of peace and security in an amount exceeding 10 million dollars in respect of the decision, that matter shall be brought to the General Assembly, or, if the Assembly is suspended or not in session, a resumed or special session of the Assembly shall be convened by the Secretary-General to consider the matter.

Contributions

Unpaid assessed contributions from Member States to the UN budget totalled $1,758 million at the end of 1999, down from $2 billion at the end of 1998. Unpaid regular budget assessments totalled $244 million, a reduction of $173 million compared with the end of 1998.

The number of Member States paying their regular budget assessment in full continued to climb. As at the end of 1999, 126 Member States, 9 more than the previous year, had done so.

Aggregate peacekeeping assessments outstanding at the end of 1999 was $1.4 billion, a decrease of $112 million from 1998, and unpaid assessments for the international tribunals were over $32 million.

Assessments

Committee on Contributions. Pursuant to General Assembly resolution 53/36 A [YUN 1998, p. 1286], a special session of the Committee on Contributions was convened (New York, 8-12 February) [A/53/11/Add.1 & Corr.1] to consider representations from Member States with respect to the application of Article 19 of the Charter, whereby a Member would lose its vote in the Assembly if the amount of its arrears should equal or exceed the amount of contributions due from it for the preceding two full years.

The Committee considered a number of issues relating to the application of Article 19 and decided that more general policy considerations should be examined further during its fifty-ninth session (see next page), including the issue of those Member States that regularly paid only enough to retain or regain their votes and the possibility of submitting payment schedules for their arrears in UN contributions. The Committee discussed the date of expiration of a waiver in the context of traditional dates for its regular session, and decided to explore the advantages and disadvantages of setting the two dates roughly at the same time.

The Committee took up the cases of Bosnia and Herzegovina, Cambodia, the Republic of the Congo, Georgia, Guinea-Bissau, Honduras, Iraq and Nicaragua. Having heard oral representations from those Member States and received statistical and other information from the Secretariat, the Committee determined that the failure to pay the amount necessary to avoid the application of Article 19 was due to conditions beyond their control, and recommended that Bosnia and Herzegovina, Cambodia and Georgia be permitted to vote in the Assembly until 30 June 1999, and that the Congo, Guinea-Bissau, Honduras and Nicaragua be permitted to vote until 30 June 2000.

With respect to Iraq, the Committee concluded that the political aspects of the issues raised in that context went beyond its technical advisory role.

By **decision 53/406 C** of 7 April, the Assembly approved the Committee's recommendations.

At its fifty-ninth session (New York 7-25 June) [A/54/11], the Committee continued to discuss elements of the methodology for the preparation of future scales of assessment: income measures; base period; conversion rates; debt-burden adjustment; low per capita income adjustment; floor; ceiling; schemes of limits; and annual recalculations. Concerning income measures, the Committee emphasized that it was in the interest of the Member States to provide the most complete, reliable and comparable statistics possible to the UN Statistics Division for use by the Committee at its sixtieth session in 2000 when it would consider the scale of assessments for 2001-2003. It reaffirmed its earlier recommendation that future scales should be based on estimates of gross domestic product (GDP).

The Committee considered the further reduction from six to three years of the base period for calculating the scale of assessments. It reaffirmed that the base period should be a multiple of the scale period so that data from some years would not be used more frequently than data from others and should be kept constant in successive scale periods.

The Committee emphasized the importance of realistic conversion rates in considering the relative capacity of Member States to pay. It also noted an analytical study by the Statistics Division on possible approaches to improving the methodology for computing price-adjusted rates of exchange (PAREs), which was at a preliminary theoretical stage.

Doubts were expressed concerning the rationale for inclusion of the debt burden in the scale methodology. The Committee reaffirmed its earlier recommendation that, should the Assembly decide to retain the debt-burden adjustment in calculations for the scale, it should be based on debt flow data. It reaffirmed the continuing relevance and importance of the principle of an adjustment for low per capita income, a basic element of the scale from the beginning.

Also considered by the Committee were the effects of the discontinuity experienced by Member States moving up through the low per capita income threshold between scale periods and by those States just above the threshold. It concluded that the situation was inequitable and that remedial measures should be considered, and suggested that the Assembly consider whether the scale methodology should be changed to eliminate or mitigate the effects of discontinuity. The Committee recommended that the minimum assessment rate for 2001-2003 should be maintained at 0.001 per cent. It agreed to consider the annual recalculations of the scale of assessments in the light of any guidance received from the Assembly.

The Committee reviewed the procedural aspects for considering requests for exemption of Article 19 of the Charter, as requested by the Assembly in resolution 52/215 B [YUN 1997, p. 1444]. In that regard, it discussed the problem of timing of meetings of the Committee as they related to the application of Article 19, recalling that Member States in danger of falling under Article 19 in the coming year were so advised by the Secretariat before the end of the current year and that the Committee's regular session was normally held in June. Therefore, the Committee recommended that the Assembly encourage Member States that wished to avail themselves of the procedure to do so early enough before the Committee's regular session.

As to the question of tightening the application of Article 19, it decided to consider the matter at a forthcoming session in the light of any policy guidelines from the Assembly.

Other elements considered by the Committee included the use of budgetary surpluses, incentive payments and credits, interest on or indexation of arrears, ineligibility for election and recruitment and procurement issues. The Committee noted the proposal for the establishment of a new assessed fund in which the contributions of each Member State would depend on its recent payment record: the greater its passed due assessed contribution, the greater its contribution to the fund, and agreed to consider it further.

The Committee considered requests for exemptions under Article 19 from Bosnia and Herzegovina, the Comoros, Georgia, the Republic of Moldova and Tajikistan. Four of them requested an extension of an exemption; two of them had received exemptions in 1996. The Committee emphasized that exemptions should be regarded as exceptional measures and expressed concern at the evident tendency to extend them for long periods.

The Committee determined that Bosnia and Herzegovina's failure to pay the amount necessary to avoid application of Article 19 was beyond its control and recommended that it be permitted to vote until 30 June 2000, in the expectation that it would be the final extension.

The Committee noted that the Comoros had benefited from exemptions since 1996 and no payments had been received since October 1996. It expected that the Comoros would make serious efforts to make payments as soon as possible, but agreed that its failure to pay the necessary amounts was due to conditions beyond its control and recommended to the Assembly that the Comoros be permitted to vote until 30 June 2000.

The Committee was not in a position to consider Georgia's request for an exemption due to its late receipt. However, in December the Assembly took action on the matter (see p. 1313).

The Committee agreed that the failure of the Republic of Moldova to pay the amount necessary to avoid the application of Article 19 was due to conditions beyond its control and recommended that it be permitted to vote until 31 December.

The Committee, having recognized the continuing and severe economic and political problems facing Tajikistan, noted that it had granted waivers since 1996. The extension it sought would be the fourth such exemption. The Committee also noted Tajikistan's continuing efforts to make payments towards its outstanding assessed contributions and that it had reduced its arrears in both 1998 and 1999. The Committee concluded that failure to pay was due to conditions beyond the country's control and recommended to the Assembly that Tajikistan be permitted to vote until 30 June 2000, on the expectation that it would be the final extension of its exemption under Article 19.

At the conclusion of the Committee's session, 24 Member States were in arrears in the payment of their assessed contributions under Article 19 and had no vote in the Assembly: Burundi, Central African Republic, Democratic Republic of the Congo, Dominica, Equatorial Guinea, Gambia, Grenada, Guinea, Iraq, Kyrgyzstan, Liberia, Mauritania, Mongolia, Niger, Republic of Moldova, Rwanda, Sao Tome and Principe, Seychelles, Sierra Leone, Somalia, Togo, Turkmenistan, Vanuatu, Yugoslavia. The Committee also noted that Bosnia and Herzegovina, Cambodia and Georgia were permitted to vote until 30 June 1999, and the Republic of the Congo, Guinea-Bissau and Nicaragua until 30 June 2000, pursuant to Assembly decision 53/406 C (see previous page). The Committee noted that eight Member States had availed themselves, under resolution 52/215 B, of the opportunity of paying the equivalent of $2.2 million in contributions in currencies other than United States dollars.

The Committee, pursuant to resolution 53/36 E [YUN 1998, p. 1287], reviewed the rates of assessment for non-member States and the issue of whether those States should be assessed at a somewhat higher rate. It was suggested that a flat percentage should be applied to the notional assessment rates of non-member States, with rates varying from 50 and 75 per cent, without reference to participation in UN activities. However, it was felt that there was no technical rationale for a flat percentage rate and that the last revision of rates had been the subject of consultations with the States concerned. Although the next quinquennial review would not take place until 2003, the Committee decided that it would consider the matter further in 2001. Information had been received from the Holy See following the Committee's review of the issue at its fifty-eighth session, when it had recommended that the flat annual fee applied for the Holy See should be 10 per cent. However, the information indicated a significant increase in the participation by the Holy See in UN activities. The Committee recommended that the flat annual fee should be increased to 25 per cent beginning in 2000.

On 1 July [A/C.5/53/64], the Assembly President transmitted to the Fifth Committee Chairman a 28 June letter of the Committee on Contributions Chairman containing sections of the Committee's report on its fifty-ninth session dealing with requests for exemption under Article 19 of the Charter from Bosnia and Herzegovina, the Comoros, Georgia, the Republic of Moldova and Tajikistan.

On 12 July [A/C.5/53/65], the Acting Assembly President transmitted to the Fifth Committee Chairman an 8 July letter from Georgia containing its request for Article 19 consideration in view of its economic problems.

GENERAL ASSEMBLY ACTION

On 28 July [meeting 105], the General Assembly, on the recommendation of the Fifth Committee [A/53/464/Add.5], adopted **resolutions 53/36 F** and **G** without vote [agenda item 118].

Scale of assessments for the apportionment of the expenses of the United Nations

F

The General Assembly,

Having considered the recommendations of the Committee on Contributions on a number of requests for exemption under Article 19 of the Charter of the United Nations, transmitted by a letter dated 28 June 1999 from the Chairman of the Committee on Contributions to the President of the General Assembly through a letter dated 1 July 1999 from the President of the Assembly to the Chairman of the Fifth Committee,

1. *Decides* that:

(a) The failure of the Republic of Moldova to pay the amount necessary to avoid the application of Article 19 of the Charter of the United Nations is attributable to conditions beyond its control and that, accordingly, it is permitted to vote until 31 December 1999;

(b) The failure of Bosnia and Herzegovina, the Comoros and Tajikistan to pay the amount necessary to avoid the application of Article 19 of the Charter is attributable to conditions beyond their control and that, accordingly, they are permitted to vote until 30 June 2000;

2. *Reaffirms* its role in accordance with the provisions of Article 19 of the Charter and the advisory role of the Committee on Contributions in accordance with rule 160 of the rules of procedure of the General Assembly;

3. *Decides* to revert to the procedural aspects of the consideration of requests for exemption under Article 19 of the Charter at the fifty-fourth session of the General Assembly.

G

The General Assembly,

Having considered the letter dated 12 July 1999 from the Acting President of the General Assembly addressed to the Chairman of the Fifth Committee,

1. *Reaffirms* its role in accordance with the provisions of Article 19 of the Charter of the United Nations and the advisory role of the Committee on Contributions in accordance with rule 160 of the rules of procedure of the General Assembly;

2. *Requests* the Committee on Contributions to consider the request of Georgia, under Article 19 of the Charter, on the subject of the country's arrears, as a matter of priority, taking into account the views expressed by Member States, and to transmit its views, also as a matter of priority, to the General Assembly, to the extent possible before the end of its fifty-third session;

3. *Decides* to grant Georgia temporary exemption under Article 19 of the Charter so that it may be permitted to vote until a final decision on the matter is taken by the General Assembly;

4. *Decides also* that the procedural arrangements in the present resolution will not set a precedent for the future.

In August [A/53/1046], the Chairman of the Committee on Contributions informed the Assembly President that the Committee would consider, as a matter of priority, Georgia's request as mandated by the Assembly.

By **decision 53/406 D** of 2 September, the Assembly took note of the letter from the Chairman of the Committee on Contributions to the Assembly President.

GENERAL ASSEMBLY ACTION (December)

On 23 December [meeting 88], the General Assembly, on the recommendation of the Fifth Committee [A/54/685], adopted **resolutions 54/237 A-C** without vote [agenda item 125].

Scale of assessments for the apportionment of the expenses of the United Nations

A

The General Assembly,

Recalling its resolutions 54/1, 54/2 and 54/3 of 14 September 1999,

Recalling also the recommendations of the Committee on Contributions with respect to the assessment of the Republic of Kiribati, the Republic of Nauru and the Kingdom of Tonga as non-member States,

Recalling further its resolutions 52/215 A of 22 December 1997 and 53/36 E of 18 December 1998 and its decision 47/456 of 23 December 1992,

1. *Decides* that the rate of assessment for the Republic of Kiribati, the Republic of Nauru and the Kingdom of Tonga, admitted to membership of the United Nations on 14 September 1999, should be 0.001 per cent for the years 1999 and 2000;

2. *Also decides* that the contributions of the Republic of Kiribati, the Republic of Nauru and the Kingdom of Tonga for the year 1999 should be calculated on the basis of one twelfth of their rate of assessment for the year 1999 per full calendar month of membership and that a corresponding adjustment should be made in their assessments for the year 1999 as non-member States;

3. *Further decides* that the contributions of the Republic of Kiribati, the Republic of Nauru and the Kingdom of Tonga for the years 1999 and 2000 should otherwise be applied to the same basis of assessment as for other Member States, except that, in the case of appropriations or apportionments approved by the General Assembly for the financing of peacekeeping operations, the contributions of the Republic of Kiribati, the Republic of Nauru and the Kingdom of Tonga, as determined by the group of Member States to which they may be assigned by the Assembly, should be calculated in proportion to the calendar year;

4. *Decides* that the 1999 assessments of the Republic of Kiribati, the Republic of Nauru and the Kingdom of Tonga should be taken into account as miscellaneous income in accordance with regulation 5.2 *(c)* of the Financial Regulations and Rules of the United Nations;

5. *Also decides* that, for the year 2000, the rate of assessment for the Republic of Kiribati, the Republic of Nauru and the Kingdom of Tonga should be added to the scale of assessments established by the General Assembly in its resolution 52/215 A;

6. *Further decides* that, in accordance with financial regulation 5.8, the advances of the Republic of Kiribati, the Republic of Nauru and the Kingdom of Tonga to the Working Capital Fund should be calculated by the application of their rate of assessment of 0.001 per cent to the authorized level of the Fund and

should be added to the Fund pending the incorporation of their rate of assessment in a 100 per cent scale.

B

The General Assembly,

Having considered the relevant part of the report of the Committee on Contributions on its fifty-ninth session,

Recalling its resolution 53/36 C of 18 December 1998,

1. *Decides* that the Committee on Contributions should not consider further the questions covered in paragraphs 69 and 70 as well as 73 and 74 of its report;

2. *Requests* the Committee further to consider measures to encourage the timely, full and unconditional payment of assessed contributions and to make appropriate recommendations, pursuant to its general mandate under paragraph 3 of General Assembly resolution 14 A (I) of 13 February 1946.

C

The General Assembly,

Recalling its resolutions 50/207 B of 11 April 1996, 52/215 B of 22 December 1997 and 53/36 B to D of 18 December 1998,

Having considered the relevant parts of the report of the Committee on Contributions on its fifty-ninth session,

Reaffirming the obligation of all Member States to bear the expenses of the United Nations, as apportioned by the General Assembly, in conformity with Article 17, paragraph 2, of the Charter of the United Nations,

Reaffirming also the fundamental principle that the expenses of the Organization should be apportioned among Member States broadly according to their capacity to pay, as specified in rule 160 of the rules of procedure of the General Assembly,

1. *Urges* all Member States to pay their assessed contributions in full, on time and without imposing conditions, to prevent financial difficulties for the United Nations;

2. *Reaffirms* its role in accordance with the provisions of Article 19 of the Charter of the United Nations and the advisory role of the Committee on Contributions in accordance with rule 160 of the rules of procedure of the General Assembly;

3. *Urges* all Member States in arrears requesting exemption under Article 19 of the Charter to provide the fullest possible supporting information, including information on economic aggregates, government revenues and expenditure, foreign exchange resources, indebtedness, difficulties in meeting domestic or international financial obligations and any other information that might support the claim that failure to make necessary payments had been attributable to conditions beyond the control of the Member States;

4. *Decides* that requests for exemption under Article 19 of the Charter must be submitted by Member States to the President of the General Assembly at least two weeks before the session of the Committee, so as to ensure a complete review of the requests.

On the same date, the Assembly, by **decision 54/455 A**, decided that Georgia should be permitted to vote in the Assembly until 30 June 2000, and if it were to request further exemptions under Article 19, it should do so at least two weeks before the session of the Committee on Contributions.

The Assembly, by **decision 54/455 B** of 23 December, decided to continue consideration of the item on the scale of assessments for the apportionment of expenses as a matter of priority at its resumed fifty-fourth (2000) session, and to approve, no later than the last day of the first part of that session, the methodology that would instruct the Committee on Contributions to recommend to the Assembly at its fifty-fifth (2000) session a scale of assessments for the period 2001-2003. On the same date, the Assembly decided that the item would remain for consideration during the resumed fifty-fourth session (**decision 54/465**) and that the Fifth Committee should continue to consider the item at that session (**decision 54/462 A**).

Accounts and auditing

The General Assembly, at its resumed fifty third (1999) session, considered the report of the Board of Auditors on UN peacekeeping operations for the period 1 July 1997 to 30 June 1998 [A/53/5, vol. II], the Secretary-General's April report on implementation of the Board's recommendations thereon [A/53/932] and ACABQ's comments and recommendations [A/53/940].

By **decision 53/473** of 8 June, the Assembly deferred consideration of those reports until the main part of its fifty-fourth (1999) session.

On 29 October, the Assembly, in **resolution 54/13 A**, endorsed the Board of Auditors' report (see p. 64).

In September [A/54/140/Add.2], the Secretary-General updated his earlier report (see above) on the implementation of Board's recommendation concerning peacekeeping operations.

Report of Board of Auditors. The Assembly had before it the report of the Board of Auditors and audited financial statements of the voluntary funds administered by the United Nations High Commissioner for Refugees (UNHCR) for the period 1 January to 31 December 1998 [A/54/5/Add.5].

Also before the Assembly were the Secretary-General's annual reports, pursuant to resolution 52/212 B [YUN 1998, p. 1288], updating information on the implementation of the Board's recommendations [A/54/140]; replies of the executive heads of organizations and programmes relating to the Board's recommendations in its reports for the period ending 31 December 1997 and covering those organizational activities that had hitherto been reported on biennially [A/54/140/Add.1]; the Board's report on implementation of its recommendations [A/54/159 & Corr.1]; the Board's comments on the hiring and use of consultants in the Secretariat, pursuant to section VIII of Assembly resolution 53/221 [A/54/165] (see p. 1333); measures taken or proposed in response to the Board's recommendations on the accounts of the voluntary funds administered by UNHCR for the period ended 31 December 1998 [A/AC.96/917/Add.1]; and the Secretary-General's report on the year 2000 computer compliance issue [A/C.5/54/3] (see p. 1373).

ACABQ's comments and recommendations on those reports were contained in an October report to the Assembly [A/54/441]. With respect to UNHCR's voluntary funds, ACABQ noted that the problem of the timely receipt of audit certificates persisted and stressed the importance of implementing fully the Board's recommendation that the Administration assess reasons for noncompliance and draw up a strategy for dealing with the question. It recommended that UNHCR formulate the criteria for and the conditions under which UNHCR's assistance should be granted to implementing partners, including guidelines to ensure delivery of services. The Assembly took action on the Board of Auditors' report and ACABQ's comments in **resolution 54/13 B** (see p. 1133).

ACABQ noted that the bulk of the Board of Auditors' recommendations, 100 of 156, had been partially implemented. It requested that in its next report, the Board further analyse the recommendations being implemented and those partially implemented, but for which no further action was contemplated. Information on the time taken to implement recommendations would also be useful in demonstrating the efficiency and priority attention of the administrations concerned. It noted that the report on the year 2000 computer problem contained little information on measures taken to maintain the logistical and operational readiness of the UN Department of Peacekeeping Operations in the field, and that there was no system-wide picture of the state of preparedness of the UN system with regard to the year 2000 compliance issue. It requested the Secretary-General to draw the attention of the members of the Administrative Committee on Coordination to that need.

On 23 December, the Assembly decided that the item entitled "Financial reports and audited financial statements, and reports of the Board of Auditors" would remain for consideration during its resumed fifty-fourth (2000) session (**decision 54/465**) and that the Fifth Committee should continue consideration of the item at that session (**decision 54/462 A**).

Common accounting standards

In response to General Assembly decision 53/455 [YUN 1998, p. 1291], the Secretary-General submitted an October report on the Guidelines for Internal Control Standards [A/54/427], approved by the International Organization of Supreme Audit Institutions [YUN 1998, p. 1291]. The Secretary-General stated that, as recommended by ACABQ [ibid.], the UN administration would publicize the Guidelines as widely as possible, including on the UN Intranet.

Internal control and accountability

Management irregularities causing financial losses

The General Assembly, at its resumed fifty-third session, considered the Secretary-General's March report on management irregularities causing financial losses to the Organization [A/53/849], submitted in response to General Assembly decision 51/469 B [YUN 1997, p. 1415]. The report examined the meaning of "management irregularities"; outlined applicable statutory provisions under the staff rules and regulations for recovering such losses and disciplinary measures taken in cases of staff misconduct; distinguished between the different categories of such irregularities; and summarized applicable disciplinary, recovery and reporting procedures.

By **decision 53/466** of 7 April, the Assembly decided to resume consideration of the issue during the second part of its resumed fifty-third (1999) session, pending receipt of information from the Secretariat and ACABQ.

In May [A/53/954], ACABQ, in its comments on the report, noted that procedures had not yet been established for determining gross negligence in a specific instance and what financial responsibility, if any, should be incurred by those responsible. It recommended that the Secretariat prepare a more detailed report for submission to the Assembly through ACABQ, which should include procedures for determining gross negligence and the financial responsibility to be incurred by those committing the negligence. It noted that in cases where amounts recovered from accrued salary and other emoluments were insufficient to compensate the UN fully for staff wrongdoing, the Organization had no other means of obtaining a full recovery and that limitations existed to referring those matters to national authorities. It requested the Secretary-General to provide detailed information on steps taken in that connection. He should also take further preventive measures to identify risk factors that exposed the United Nations to management irregularities so that improvements in internal control and accountability could be instituted.

GENERAL ASSEMBLY ACTION

On 8 June [meeting 101], the General Assembly, on the recommendation of the Fifth Committee [A/53/533/Add.2], adopted **resolution 53/225** without vote [agenda item 113].

Management irregularities causing financial losses to the Organization

The General Assembly,

Having considered the report of the Secretary-General and the related report of the Advisory Committee on Administrative and Budgetary Questions,

1. *Endorses* the observations and recommendations contained in the report of the Advisory Committee on Administrative and Budgetary Questions;

2. *Requests* the Secretary-General to submit a detailed report to the General Assembly at its fifty-fourth session, through the Advisory Committee, on management irregularities causing financial losses to the Organization, taking into account the reports mentioned in paragraph 4 of the report of the Committee, including procedures for determining gross negligence and the financial and other responsibilities to be incurred by those who have committed such negligence, and preventive measures to identify the risk factors that expose the Organization to management irregularities and measures to improve internal control and accountability.

Arbitration of contract disputes

In March, the Secretary-General transmitted to the General Assembly an Office of Internal Oversight Services (OIOS) report on a comprehensive review of procurement-related arbitration cases [A/53/843], conducted in response to Assembly resolution 52/226 A [YUN 1998, p. 1254].

OIOS reviewed five cases involving claims totalling $52.6 million, of which $11.9 million was settled through negotiations. However, the Organization incurred interest costs of $4.8 million, as well as $2.3 million in legal and staff costs. The cases related to peacekeeping operations established in the early 1990s.

OIOS considered arbitration to be a costly method of dispute resolution and recommended that it be prevented to the extent possible through improved contract preparation and administration. It identified a number of shortcomings both at Headquarters and in the field that contributed to the situation. OIOS recommended that peacekeeping missions, especially in the early stages, be staffed with qualified, experienced procurement and contract administration personnel and legal advisers; administration in the field and at Headquarters ensure that material deviations from contracts were documented and brought to the attention of the relevant Headquarters officials; vendor performance be routinely evaluated; and all aspects of arbitration and settlement cases be reviewed to ensure that possible claims against third parties were considered and lessons learned identified and disseminated.

GENERAL ASSEMBLY ACTION

On 7 April [meeting 97], the General Assembly, on the recommendation of the Fifth Committee [A/53/521/Add.2], adopted **resolution 53/217** without vote [agenda item 112].

Procurement-related arbitration

The General Assembly,

Having considered the report of the Office of Internal Oversight Services on the review of procurement-related arbitration cases,

1. *Expresses deep concern* about the increase of pending procurement-related arbitration claims instituted against the United Nations, which total 56 million United States dollars as at 19 March 1999;

2. *Requests* the Secretary-General to submit to it, for consideration at an early stage during its fifty-fourth session, a comprehensive report, taking into account the recommendations of the Office of Internal Oversight Services and the views expressed by Member States on the issue of arbitration, which should cover, inter alia:

(*a*) The reasons for arbitration cases;

(*b*) The roles and mandates of various Secretariat structures and negotiating teams in arbitration and settlement processes;

(*c*) The sources of funding for arbitration awards and settlement payments;

(*d*) The selection of outside legal counsels and provisions to preclude conflict of interest;

(*e*) Disciplinary action taken against staff members responsible for wrongdoing that resulted in arbitration;

(*f*) Pending arbitration cases;

(*g*) Measures taken or proposed to prevent or reduce contract disputes which might lead to arbitration in the future;

3. *Also requests* the Secretary-General, without prejudice to the obligations of the United Nations under the Arbitration Rules of the United Nations Commission on International Trade Law, to keep Member States duly informed of all arbitration and settlement cases, inter alia, by clearly identifying such cases as separate items in corresponding financial performance reports and indicating corrective and disciplinary measures taken in this regard.

Report of the Secretary General. In response to the Assembly's request, the Secretary-General, in October [A/54/458], reported that the arbitration cases identified by OIOS were largely the consequence of the sudden exponential growth in peacekeeping activities in the late 1980s and early

1990s and the use of commercial vendors rather than reliance on Member States for support services. Most disputes did not arise from contractual or other legal issues, but rather were of an operational nature. To date, contractor claims were handled in an ad hoc manner and settlement discussions undertaken to reach amicable settlements. The amount of award or settlement, as well as arbitration costs, including legal fees, was charged to the budget of the peacekeeping mission concerned.

Outside legal counsel was selected through a transparent and competitive process and the Office of Legal Affairs closely supervised all law firms engaged to avoid conflict of interest and to protect the Organization's interests.

Procedures for the preparation of clear and sound contracts were implemented and training for field staff in contract administration and claim negotiation was being prepared. A system for contractor evaluation was also introduced. A means for contractors to raise complaints was included in the web page of the Procurement Division, reviews of arbitration cases for lessons learned regularly took place and alternate methods of dispute resolution, such as conciliation, were being explored.

Programme planning

Medium-term plan

The Secretary-General, in response to General Assembly resolution 53/207 [YUN 1998, p. 1294], submitted in June [A/54/125] further revisions to the Regulations and Rules Governing Programme Planning, the Programme Aspects of the Budget, the Monitoring of Implementation and Methods of Evaluation, originally adopted in resolution 37/234 [YUN 1982, p. 1430] and most recently revised in 1998 [YUN 1998, p. 1291]. The proposed revisions related mainly to the revised format of the medium-term plan and programme budget; the numbering of the Regulations; and a new rule that took into account Regulation 3.2 on the budget process, which referred to the deadline of 15 August in the off-budget year for submission by the Secretary-General of the budget outline. The Rules were also changed to incorporate gender-sensitive language.

CPC, in June [A/54/16], amended the proposed revisions and recommended their approval by the Assembly, and that the Secretary-General bring to the Assembly's attention, along with the revised Rules, a rule giving guidance to programme managers for better implementation of regulation 5.4. In response, the Secretary-General, in an October note [A/C.5/54/12], submitted the text of an additional paragraph in rule 105.4 that aimed to provide better guidance on the formulation of expected accomplishments by clarifying the relation of the element of expected accomplishments to objectives and outputs.

Proposed medium-term plan 2000-2005

In April [A/54/89], the Secretary-General, pursuant to General Assembly resolution 51/219 [YUN 1996, p. 1306], reported on measures for sectoral, functional and regional bodies to review the proposed medium-term plan for 2002-2005. The report described the measures taken by the Secretary-General to submit proposals to the relevant intergovernmental bodies and contained the schedule of reviews by sectoral, functional and regional intergovernmental bodies of the programmes and subprogrammes of the proposed plan prior to submission to the Assembly through CPC, the Economic and Social Council and ACABQ.

CPC, in June [A/54/16], recommended that the Fifth Committee should receive all comments prior to its consideration of the proposed medium-term plan and revisions, and that CPC should receive at its 2000 session the reviews by intergovernmental bodies of the Secretary-General's proposed plan.

Programme performance 1996-1997

The General Assembly, at its resumed fifty-third (1999) session, by **decision 53/469** of 7 April, transmitted to CPC for consideration a Secretariat note on UN programme performance for the 1996-1997 biennium [A/C.5/53/CRP.1/Rev.1].

In an April note to CPC [E/AC.52/1999/7], the Secretariat, pursuant to Assembly resolution 53/207 [YUN 1998, p. 1294], provided information on the reasons for the further postponement of the delivery of outputs from the 1996-1997 biennium to 1998-1999 and on the Secretary-General's proposal to delete 57 outputs carried over from the 1994-1995 biennium. The report noted that, of those 57 outputs, 14 had been implemented in 1997-1998, 12 would be implemented in 1999, and 2 had been further postponed to 2000. Twenty outputs were considered ongoing, of which six were pending decisions by intergovernmental mechanisms. Nine outputs had been recommended for termination.

CPC, in June [A/54/16], regretted that the opinion of relevant intergovernmental bodies on the Secretary-General's proposal to delete some outputs had not been submitted, as requested in resolution 53/207, and asked the Secretariat to ensure that future programme performance reports provided clear justification and criteria for termination.

Evaluation and programme planning

In June [A/54/117], the Secretary-General submitted a report, pursuant to General Assembly resolution 53/207, on ways in which the full implementation and the quality of mandated programmes and activities could be ensured and better assessed by and reported to Member States. The report proposed three options to improve the methodology through which full implementation and quality of mandated programmes and activities could be ensured and better assessed: mandate specialized intergovernmental bodies that oversaw each programme with the responsibility for making judgements about the quality of programme performance; address the utility of the programme performance report, and change its timing to present it as part of the review of the programme budget proposals by both the specialized intergovernmental body and CPC; and relate outputs to outcomes in the programme performance report. The Secretary-General concluded that the three options were not mutually exclusive and that any or all of them could be adopted.

CPC, in June [A/54/16], recommended that the Secretary-General be requested to further explore ways in which the full implementation of mandates could be ensured and better assessed, taking into account the Regulations and Rules Governing Programme Planning, the Programme Aspects of the Budget, the Monitoring of Implementation and the Methods of Evaluation, and budgetary procedures, and giving due consideration to the views of Member States, and report thereon to the Committee in 2000.

The Secretary-General transmitted to CPC, in a series of notes, OIOS reports on: the in-depth evaluation of the programme on disarmament [E/AC.51/1999/2]; the in-depth evaluation of the electoral assistance programme [E/AC.51/1999/3 & Corr.1]; the triennial review of the implementation of CPC recommendations at its thirty-sixth session in 1996 on the evaluation of the Department of Public Information [E/AC.51/1999/4]; and the triennial review of the implementation of CPC recommendations at its 1996 session on the evaluation of peacekeeping operations: termination phase [E/AC.51/1999/5].

CPC's comments and recommendations on those reports were contained in the report on its thirty-ninth (1999) session [A/54/16].

GENERAL ASSEMBLY ACTION

On 23 December [meeting 88], the General Assembly, on the recommendation of the Fifth Committee [A/54/676], adopted **resolution 54/236** without vote [agenda item 120].

Programme planning

The General Assembly,

Having considered the report of the Committee for Programme and Coordination on the work of its thirty-ninth session,

1. *Takes note with appreciation* of the report of the Committee for Programme and Coordination on the work of its thirty-ninth session;

2. *Endorses* the conclusions and recommendations contained in the report of the Committee regarding the review of the efficiency of the administrative and financial functioning of the United Nations, programme planning and the provisional agenda for the fortieth session of the Committee;

3. *Also endorses* the conclusions and recommendations on coordination questions contained in paragraphs 560 to 565, 567 and 568, and 587 to 596 of the report of the Committee;

4. *Notes* that, in the context of coordination questions, the proposals relating to performance indicators requested by the Committee and contained in the report of the Secretary-General on the implementation of the United Nations System-wide Special Initiative for the Implementation of the United Nations New Agenda for the Development of Africa in the 1990s have not been approved by the General Assembly;

5. *Also notes* that the matter addressed in paragraph 566 of the report of the Committee is being considered by the General Assembly under a separate agenda item;

6. *Urges* the Secretary-General to issue, as soon as possible, the revisions to the relevant rules of the revised Regulations Governing Programme Planning, the Programme Aspects of the Budget, the Monitoring of Implementation and the Methods of Evaluation adopted by the General Assembly at its fifty-third session, taking fully into account the recommendations of the Committee contained in paragraph 47 of its report;

7. *Decides* to continue its consideration of the item entitled "Programme planning" during its resumed fifty-fourth session.

On 23 December, the Assembly decided that the item on programme planning would remain for consideration at its resumed fifty-fourth (2000) session (**decision 54/465**) and that the Fifth Committee should continue to consider the item at that session (**decision 54/462 A**).

UN International Partnership Trust Fund

The Secretary-General reported in March on the United Nations Fund for International Partnership (UNFIP) [A/53/700/Add.1], established in 1998 [YUN 1998, p. 1297] to manage the process of grant allocations through the United Nations Foundation (UNF), a public charity founded by Robert Edward Turner to manage his gift to the United Nations of 18 million shares of Time Warner stock valued at some $1 billion. On 2 February, UNF announced approval of its third round of grants, the last funding cycle of the first year of UNFIP/UNF operations, totalling some

$31.7 million for 25 projects involving 14 UN organizations. Annexed to the report was a list of approved projects, showing the breakdown by theme, region and executing agency. As at February 1999, UNF had awarded a total of approximately $87 million for UN projects, with 35 per cent earmarked for population and women; 20 per cent for the environment; 25 per cent for children's health; and 19 per cent for other areas.

Based on the first year's experience, the United Nations and UNF reached agreement on a revised and more streamlined process of programme development for funding by UNF. The goal of the revised programming approach was to work more closely with UNF in defining priorities and focus within the broad areas of programmatic concentration already identified, and to promote greater inter-agency consultation in defining opportunities to be pursued by the UN system with UNF funding. The new approach entailed the establishment of Programme Framework Groups (PFGs) to provide guidance for the preparation of specific projects, identify programmatic opportunities and propose the most effective use of UNF support. PFGs on population and women and on children's health had been established and had commenced work by mid-February.

ACABQ, in May [A/53/7/Add.11], indicated its intention to review the UNFIP Assistant Secretary-General-level post of the Executive Director after 31 December in the context of its examination of UNFIP's administrative budget for 2000. It would also provide additional comments on the report in the context of its consideration of the 2000-2001 programme budget.

By **decision 53/475** of 8 June, the Assembly took note of the Secretary-General's report and of ACABQ's observations, and requested the Secretary-General to continue to keep the Assembly informed on a regular basis.

In response to that request, the Secretary-General provided additional information on UNFIP activities in December [A/54/664 & Add.1]. Data was provided on the outcome of the two funding cycles for 1999, as was information on progress in respect of PFGs on children's health, population and women, and the environment. A total of $108 million was programmed for the year, with the majority of grants ($59 million) awarded for projects concerning children's heath; over $15 million was granted for population and women's projects; $25 million, for projects on the environment; and $8 million, for humanitarian and other areas. Since UNFIP's inception, over $190 million had been programmed.

The UNFIP secretariat continued to play a facilitating role within the UN system. It supported the Secretary-General's reform initiatives, particularly in terms of development activities at the country level, and developed a solid collaboration with the Office of the United Nations Development Group and with resident coordinators and UN country teams.

Chapter III

United Nations staff

A number of issues concerning the conditions of service of United Nations staff members were considered by the General Assembly during 1999. Some arose from recommendations of the International Civil Service Commission (ICSC) and others resulted from the Secretary-General's programme for reform.

ICSC action included proposals regarding the base/floor salary scale, staff assessment, performance management and education grant, and the establishment of working groups on the framework of human resources management and on the draft standards of conduct for the international civil service. The Administrative Committee on Coordination proposed an amendment to the ICSC statute regarding its establishment of advisory panels.

The Assembly requested the Secretary-General to phase out the acceptance of certain types of gratis personnel.

The United Nations Joint Staff Pension Fund reported that its reserves had increased to more than $25.8 billion.

Conditions of service

International Civil Service Commission

In 1999, ICSC, a 15-member body established in 1974 by General Assembly resolution 3357(XXIX) [YUN 1974, p. 875], continued to regulate and coordinate the conditions of service of the UN common system of salaries and allowances. Thirteen organizations had accepted the ICSC statute: the United Nations; the International Labour Organization (ILO); the Food and Agriculture Organization of the United Nations; the United Nations Educational, Scientific and Cultural Organization (UNESCO); the World Health Organization; the International Civil Aviation Organization; the Universal Postal Union; the International Telecommunication Union; the World Meteorological Organization; the International Maritime Organization; the World Intellectual Property Organization; the United Nations Industrial Development Organization; and the International Atomic Energy Agency. One other organization, the International Fund for Agricultural Development, had not formally accepted the statute but participated fully in ICSC work.

The Commission held its forty-ninth (Geneva, 12-30 April) and fiftieth (New York, 19-30 July) sessions in 1999, examining issues that derived from decisions and resolutions of the General Assembly, as well as from its own statute. A summary of the Commission's deliberations, recommendations and decisions was provided in its twenty-fifth annual report [A/54/30], on which the Assembly acted in December (see resolution 54/238 on p. 1321).

In a 4 October statement on the administrative and financial implications of ICSC decisions and recommendations [A/54/434], the Secretary-General said that there would be an increase of $1,725,300, net of staff assessment, in the regular budget for the 22-month period from 1 March 2000 to 31 December 2001.

Functioning of ICSC

Review of ICSC

As follow-up to the 1998 endorsement by the Administrative Committee on Coordination (ACC) of his proposal to establish a group to examine the mandate, membership and functioning of ICSC [YUN 1998, p. 1300], the Secretary-General submitted to the General Assembly in October his recommendations concerning the composition of and terms of reference for the group [A/54/483].

The Assembly, in section V of resolution 54/238 (see p. 1322), decided to revert to the consideration of the modalities of the review of ICSC at its fifty-fifth (2000) session.

Proposed amendment to ICSC statute

At its first regular session of 1999 (Geneva, 9-10 April) [ACC/1999/4], ACC endorsed a draft amendment to the ICSC statute, proposed by the legal advisers of the UN system. The amendment would allow ICSC to request advisory opinions on the legality of ICSC decisions or recommendations, before they were implemented, from an ad hoc panel, composed of judges of the Administrative Tribunals of the United Nations and ILO, designated by the Presidents of the Tribunals, and a third person chosen by them. ACC requested ICSC to place the draft amendment before the General Assembly for consideration.

At its July session [A/54/30], ICSC noted that neither it nor its secretariat had been consulted by ACC or the legal advisers on the proposed amendment to the statute. Most Commission members opposed the creation of advisory panels, noting that there was no need for such a review mechanism since so few ICSC decisions and recommendations had been successfully challenged before the Administrative Tribunals. Also, the panels would result in adding a step in an already long and complex judicial process and their usefulness was doubtful since their opinions would not be binding on the Tribunals, the organizations and the staff representatives. The Presidents and members of the Tribunals favoured the option of having the organizations consult the legal advisers of the UN system, an approach that was also favoured by most ICSC members.

The Commission decided to submit its observations on the ACC proposal to the Assembly and to request its Chairman to forward them to the UN Legal Counsel.

In October [A/C.5/54/24], the Secretary-General, on behalf of ACC, transmitted to the Assembly the text of the draft amendment to the ICSC statute and ICSC's comments on it.

In section IV of resolution 54/238 (see p. 1322), the Assembly reaffirmed the ICSC statute.

Remuneration issues

Noblemaire principle

Under a standing mandate from the General Assembly [YUN 1992, p. 1055], ICSC continued to review the relationship between the net remuneration of UN staff in the Professional and higher categories in New York and that of the current comparator, United States federal civil service employees in comparable positions in Washington, D.C. ICSC reported to the Assembly that the margin forecast between United Nations and the United States employees' net remuneration would be 114.1 for 1999. It informed the Assembly that the comparator had not fully implemented recommended pay reforms, but there were indications that future adjustments to the salaries of the comparator employees could be higher than those in the past. ICSC requested its secretariat, the ACC Consultative Committee on Administrative Questions and representatives of the staff to discuss the imbalance in the margin levels with a view to formulating alternative proposals that would be available to the Commission before it made a recommendation on a real salary increase.

Effective 1 January 1999, the salary scale for the comparator civil service increased by 3.68 per cent gross (3.42 per cent net), calling for an upward adjustment of the common system salary scale by 3.42 per cent. The Commission recommended to the Assembly revised procedures for determining the base/floor salary scale and the single rate of staff assessment, and the consolidation of 3.42 per cent of post adjustment on a no-loss/no-gain basis with effect from 1 March 2000.

With regard to the remuneration of the General Service and other locally recruited categories of staff, ICSC reviewed the basis for the dependent children's allowance, recalling that in 1982 it had established a floor amount for the allowance at 3 per cent of the mid-point of net salary [YUN 1982, p. 1477]. The Commission decided that the social benefit approach for the payment of the allowance should continue to be maintained and that the floor formula should be reviewed, to the extent possible, in 2000 and not later than 2001.

On the basis of the revised methodology for surveys of best prevailing conditions of employment at headquarters and non-headquarters duty stations, adopted in 1997 [YUN 1997, p. 1453], ICSC conducted a survey of best prevailing conditions of service for the General Service and other locally recruited categories of staff of the common system in Paris, with a reference date of April 1999. ICSC attached to its report [A/54/30] the General Service salary scale that it had recommended to the Director-General of UNESCO. The Commission also recommended revised amounts of spouse and children's allowances, determined on the basis of tax abatement, social benefit provided by the French Government and additional amounts paid by outside employers. The Assembly took action on the remuneration of those categories of staff in section II of resolution 54/238 (see p. 1322).

Post adjustment

In the context of a renewed General Assembly request in resolution 53/209 [YUN 1998, p. 1304] for ICSC to conduct a comprehensive review of the post adjustment system as a whole, the Commission informed the Assembly that it had carried out several such reviews, most recently in 1996 [YUN 1996, p. 1316]. It was the Commission's view that if the post adjustment system was to continue to be responsive to developments in the world economy and the changing needs in the common system, it should, as a system dealing with remuneration, be transparent, stable and predictable. ICSC therefore believed that the post adjustment system should be allowed to function for a meaningful period of time so that any future review would take place on the basis of experience with its operation.

At the request of the Assembly, ICSC had examined the issue of the post adjustment in Geneva in 1995 [YUN 1995, p. 1409], 1996 [YUN 1996, p. 1317], 1997 [YUN 1997, p. 1453] and 1998 [YUN 1998, p. 1303]. On each occasion, it had concluded that any change to the methodology had attendant legal, technical and administrative difficulties that militated against the changes envisaged by the Assembly. As those difficulties were beyond the Commission's mandate, it requested the Assembly, in consultation with the governing bodies of the organizations of the common system, to take action in that regard.

The Assembly took action on the Geneva post adjustment and on the question of separation of housing from post adjustment in section I of resolution 54/238 (see below).

GENERAL ASSEMBLY ACTION

On 23 December [meeting 88], the General Assembly, on the recommendation of the Fifth (Administrative and Budgetary) Committee [A/54/677], adopted **resolution 54/238** without vote [agenda item 126].

United Nations common system: report of the International Civil Service Commission

The General Assembly,

Having considered the report of the International Civil Service Commission for the year 1999 and other related reports,

Reaffirming its commitment to a single, unified United Nations common system as the cornerstone for the regulation and coordination of the conditions of service of the United Nations common system,

Convinced that the common system constitutes the best instrument to secure staff of the highest standards of efficiency, competence and integrity for the international civil service, as stipulated under the Charter of the United Nations,

Reaffirming the central role of the Commission in the regulation and coordination of the conditions of service of the United Nations common system,

Reaffirming also the statute of the Commission,

I

Conditions of service of staff in the Professional and higher categories

A. *Noblemaire principle and its application*

Recalling its resolution 44/198 of 21 December 1989 and other relevant resolutions,

1. *Reaffirms* the continued application of the Noblemaire principle;

2. *Also reaffirms* the need to continue to ensure the competitiveness of the conditions of service of the common system;

B. *Evolution of the margin*

Recalling section I.B of its resolution 52/216 of 22 December 1997 and the standing mandate from the General Assembly, in which the Commission is requested to continue its review of the relationship between the net remuneration of the United Nations staff in the Professional and higher categories in New York and that of the comparator civil service (the United States federal civil service) employees in comparable positions in Washington, D.C. (referred to as "the margin"),

Recalling also section IX, paragraph 3, of its resolution 46/191 A of 20 December 1991, in which it requested the Commission to include in its work a review of the differences between the United Nations and the United States net remuneration at individual grade levels,

Recalling further section II.B, paragraph 3, of its resolution 48/224 of 23 December 1993, wherein it considered that the Commission should address the imbalance in the United Nations/United States remuneration ratios in the context of overall margin considerations,

1. *Notes* the view of the Commission that, bearing in mind the imbalance in the margin levels, a recommendation for a differentiated salary increase by grades would need to be submitted to the General Assembly at the time of any future recommendation for a real salary increase;

2. *Also notes* that the margin between the net remuneration of United Nations staff in grades P-1 to D-2 in New York and that of officials in comparable positions in the United States federal civil service for 1999 is 114.1;

C. *Base/floor salary scale*

Recalling section I.H of its resolution 44/198, by which it established a floor net salary level for staff in the Professional and higher categories by reference to the corresponding base net salary levels of officials in comparable positions serving at the base city of the comparator civil service (the United States federal civil service),

1. *Approves*, with effect from 1 March 2000, the revised base scale of gross and net salaries for staff in the Professional and higher categories, contained in annex I to the present resolution, and the consequential amendment to the Staff Regulations of the United Nations, as reflected in section A of annex II to the present resolution;

2. *Decides* that, with effect from 1 March 2000, the staff assessment amounts at various grades and steps for those receiving remuneration at the single rate will be determined in accordance with the procedure outlined in section B of annex II to the present resolution;

D. *Post adjustment at Geneva*

Recalling section I.B of its resolution 50/208 of 23 December 1995, section I.E of its resolution 51/216 of 18 December 1996, section I.D of its resolution 52/216 and section I.G of its resolution 53/209 of 18 December 1998, related to the establishment of a single post adjustment index in respect of staff members whose duty station is Geneva,

1. *Takes note* of the views and conclusions of the Commission contained in paragraphs 36 and 37 of its report;

2. *Reiterates its request* to the Commission to prepare a comprehensive review of the post adjustment system

along the lines requested in section I.G of resolution 53/209 and to include in that report indicative statistics and its views on legal and administrative aspects of the following options:

(a) Establishment of a single post adjustment index based on prices at Geneva and the bordering areas in France;

(b) Establishment of two separate post adjustment indices, one based on Geneva prices and the other based on prices in the bordering areas in France;

(c) Establishment of a single post adjustment index for Geneva and the surrounding cantons;

(d) Establishment of a single post adjustment index based on the comparison of prices of goods and services at Geneva with those applicable in New York (Manhattan only);

(e) Maintenance of the status quo;

E. *Separation of housing from post adjustment*

Recalling section III, paragraph 4, of its resolution 45/241 of 21 December 1990, in which it requested the Commission to establish a pilot project designed to simulate the operation of the proposals of the Commission in a limited number of duty stations in the field where valid housing comparisons were difficult or impossible,

Takes note of the decision of the Commission, set out in paragraph 99 of its report, not to pursue further the issue of the separation of housing from post adjustment at small field duty stations;

II

Remuneration of the General Service and other locally recruited categories of staff

A. *Review of the basis for the dependent children's allowance*

Recalling section II.C of its resolution 52/216,

1. *Endorses* the decision of the Commission, set out in paragraph 110 *(a)* of its report, that the social benefit approach for the payment of the children's allowance should continue to be maintained;

2. *Notes* the intention of the Commission to review the floor formula under the above-mentioned approach in 2001;

B. *Survey of best prevailing conditions of employment in Paris*

Recalling section II.A of its resolution 52/216, in which it reaffirmed that the Flemming principle should continue to serve as the basis for determining the conditions of service of the General Service and related categories and endorsed the revised methodology for surveys of best prevailing conditions of employment for these categories,

Takes note of the results of the salary survey conducted in Paris, as reported in paragraphs 111 to 118 of the report of the Commission;

III

Conditions of service applicable to both categories of staff

A. *Framework for human resources management*

Recalling its resolutions 51/216, 52/216 and 53/209,

1. *Welcomes* the progress made by the Commission regarding the development of an integrated framework for human resources management;

2. *Takes note* of the conclusions and decisions of the Commission contained in paragraphs 173 to 177 of its report;

3. *Requests* the Commission to continue its work in accordance with the programme outlined in paragraph 176 of its report;

B. *Standards of conduct for the international civil service*

Recalling paragraph 13 of its resolution 52/252 of 8 September 1998,

Takes note of the decisions of the Commission contained in paragraphs 200 and 201 of its report;

C. *Education grant*

Recalling section II.D, paragraph 2, of its resolution 48/224, in which it requested the Commission to study expatriate entitlements with a view to harmonizing the practices of organizations with those of the United Nations and to make recommendations thereon to the General Assembly at its fifty-first session,

1. *Requests* the Commission to complete the review of the methodology for the education grant, as well as a review of the purpose, scope, application of and controls for the education grant, and to report the results to the General Assembly at its fifty-fifth session;

2. *Also requests* the Commission, in conjunction with that review, to report specifically on harmonizing education grant practices with those of the United Nations, as called for in General Assembly resolution 48/224;

IV

Amendment proposed by the Administrative Committee on Coordination to the statute of the International Civil Service Commission regarding the establishment of an ad hoc advisory panel of the United Nations system

Having considered the note by the Secretary-General,

1. *Takes note* of the comments of the Commission as outlined in paragraphs 206 to 215 of its report;

2. *Reaffirms* the statute of the Commission;

V

Review of the International Civil Service Commission

Recalling paragraph 22 of its resolution 52/12 B of 19 December 1997,

Having considered the note by the Secretary-General on the review of the Commission,

1. *Emphasizes* that the review process should be impartial and transparent, and that the Commission shall participate fully in the process;

2. *Decides* to revert to the consideration of the modalities of the review of the Commission, including the proposal of the Secretary-General contained in his note, at the main part of its fifty-fifth session, subject to the submission by the Secretary-General of the information requested in paragraph 22 of General Assembly resolution 52/12 B;

3. *Requests* the Secretary-General to include the following elements in the information to be submitted to the General Assembly:

(a) Concrete and specific reasons, if any, for such a review;

(b) Identification of specific problems, if any, to be addressed;

(c) Objectives to be achieved by the review;

(d) Possible impact on the common system of such a review;

(e) Information on progress achieved as a result of previous reviews of the working methods and functioning of the Commission.

ANNEX I

Salary scale for staff in the Professional and higher categories showing annual gross salaries and net equivalents after application of staff assessment*

(United States dollars)

(Effective 1 March 2000)

Level		Steps I	II	III	IV	V	VI	VII	VIII	IX	X	XI	XII	XIII	XIV	XV
Under-Secretary-General																
USG	Gross	158,132														
	Net D	108,242														
	Net S	97,411														
Assistant Secretary-General																
ASG	Gross	143,674														
	Net D	99,278														
	Net S	89,899														
Director																
D-2	Gross	117,550	120,165	122,777	125,389	128,002	130,615									
	Net D	83,081	84,702	86,322	87,941	89,561	91,181									
	Net S	76,325	77,683	79,041	80,398	81,756	83,113									
Principal Officer																
D-1	Gross	103,763	106,000	108,239	110,471	112,710	114,947	117,185	119,423	121,658						
	Net D	74,533	75,920	77,308	78,692	80,080	81,467	82,855	84,242	85,628						
	Net S	68,893	70,112	71,329	72,545	73,763	74,972	76,135	77,297	78,459						
Senior Officer																
P-5	Gross	91,215	93,239	95,265	97,289	99,313	101,335	103,361	105,385	107,408	109,434	111,458	113,481	115,505		
	Net D	66,753	68,008	69,264	70,519	71,774	73,028	74,284	75,539	76,793	78,049	79,304	80,558	81,813		
	Net S	62,014	63,164	64,267	65,370	66,471	67,572	68,674	69,776	70,878	71,980	73,082	74,183	75,262		
First Officer																
P-4	Gross	75,424	77,282	79,135	80,986	82,844	84,697	86,552	88,406	90,279	92,252	94,224	96,202	98,174	100,148	102,124
	Net D	56,380	57,606	58,829	60,051	61,277	62,500	63,724	64,948	66,173	67,396	68,619	69,845	71,068	72,292	73,517
	Net S	52,503	53,629	54,751	55,872	56,996	58,116	59,238	60,360	61,481	62,603	63,701	64,778	65,852	66,926	68,002
Second Officer																
P-3	Gross	61,730	63,473	65,217	66,956	68,700	70,441	72,182	73,926	75,668	77,411	79,153	80,894	82,636	84,377	86,121
	Net D	47,342	48,492	49,643	50,791	51,942	53,091	54,240	55,391	56,541	57,691	58,841	59,990	61,140	62,289	63,440
	Net S	44,191	45,248	46,307	47,364	48,422	49,479	50,536	51,594	52,650	53,708	54,762	55,816	56,870	57,923	58,977
Associate Officer																
P-2	Gross	50,349	51,779	53,206	54,635	56,063	57,490	58,919	60,377	61,938	63,495	65,052	66,612			
	Net D	39,251	40,281	41,308	42,337	43,365	44,393	45,422	46,449	47,479	48,507	49,534	50,564			
	Net S	36,815	37,749	38,680	39,612	40,543	41,477	42,424	43,368	44,317	45,263	46,208	47,155			
Assistant Officer																
P-1	Gross	38,988	40,363	41,735	43,108	44,479	45,851	47,226	48,599	49,969	51,343					
	Net D	31,071	32,061	33,049	34,038	35,025	36,013	37,003	37,991	38,978	39,967					
	Net S	29,310	30,221	31,131	32,043	32,953	33,863	34,775	35,674	36,568	37,465					

D = Rate applicable to staff members with a dependent spouse or child.

S = Rate applicable to staff members with no dependent spouse or child.

*This scale will be implemented in conjunction with a consolidation of 3.42 per cent of post adjustment. There will be consequential adjustments in post adjustment indices and multipliers at all duty stations effective 1 March 2000. Thereafter, changes in post adjustment classifications will be implemented on the basis of the movements of the consolidated post adjustment indices.

ANNEX II
Amendments to the Staff Regulations of the United Nations

Regulation 3.3

Replace the second table in paragraph *(b)* (i) with the following:

Staff assessment rates to be used in conjunction with gross base salaries

(Effective 1 March 2000)

A. *Staff assessment rates for staff members with dependants*

Assessable payments (United States dollars)	*Staff assessment rates for staff members with a dependent spouse or a dependent child (Percentage)*
First 30,000 per year	18
Next 30,000 per year	28
Next 30,000 per year	34
Remaining assessable payments	38

B. *Staff assessment for staff members without dependants*

Staff assessment amounts for staff members with neither a dependent spouse nor a dependent child are equal to the differences between the gross salaries at different grades and steps and the corresponding net salaries at the single rate.

Also on 23 December, the Assembly decided that the agenda item on the UN common system would remain for consideration during its resumed fifty-fourth (2000) session (**decision 54/465**). On the same date, the Assembly, by **resolution 54/251, section III**, approved a gross budget of $12,254,800 for ICSC for the 2000-2001 biennium.

Other staff matters

Personnel policies

Human resources management

At its resumed fifty-third session in 1999, the General Assembly considered the agenda item on human resources management, which it had deferred from 1998 by decision 53/460 [YUN 1998, p. 1309]. The Assembly had before it reports of the Secretary-General, issued in 1998, dealing with: internal vacancies [ibid.]; a strategy for the management of human resources [ibid.]; human resources management reform [ibid.]; the employment of retirees [ibid., p. 1310]; the use of consultants [ibid., p. 1311]; the performance appraisal system [ibid., p. 1314]; staff composition [ibid., p. 1315]; and staff rules and regulations [ibid., p. 1317]. It also considered related reports by the Office of Internal Oversight Services (OIOS) and the Advisory Committee on Administrative and Budgetary Questions (ACABQ).

GENERAL ASSEMBLY ACTION

On 7 April [meeting 97], the General Assembly, on the recommendation of the Fifth Committee [A/53/748/Add.1], adopted **resolution 53/221** without vote [agenda item 119].

Human resources management

The General Assembly,

Recalling Articles 8, 97, 100 and 101 of the Charter of the United Nations,

Recalling also its resolutions 52/214 of 22 December 1997, 52/252 of 8 September 1998 and 53/208 of 18 December 1998,

Reaffirming its resolutions 49/222 A and B of 23 December 1994 and 20 July 1995, 51/226 of 3 April 1997 and 52/219 of 22 December 1997, as well as its other relevant resolutions and decisions, subject to the provisions of the present resolution,

Having considered the relevant reports on human resources management questions submitted by the Secretary-General to the General Assembly for consideration during its fifty-third session and the related report of the Advisory Committee on Administrative and Budgetary Questions,

Aware of the views expressed by the staff representatives in the Fifth Committee in accordance with General Assembly resolution 35/213 of 17 December 1980, as transmitted to the Assembly in a note by the Secretary-General,

Reaffirming that the staff of the United Nations is an invaluable asset of the Organization, and commending its contribution to furthering the purposes and principles of the United Nations,

Paying tribute to the memory of all staff members who have lost their lives in the service of the Organization,

Requests the Secretary-General to ensure that reports on human resources management are submitted in accordance with the relevant provisions of General Assembly resolutions 52/214 and 53/208;

I

Principles

1. *Reaffirms* the role of the General Assembly in carrying out a thorough analysis and approval of posts and financial resources as well as of human resources policies with a view to ensuring full implementation of all mandated programmes and activities and the implementation of all policies in this regard;

2. *Also reaffirms* that the Fifth Committee is the appropriate Main Committee of the General Assembly entrusted with responsibility for administrative, budgetary and human resources management matters;

3. *Emphasizes* that proposals on the reform of human resources management should be in conformity with the Charter of the United Nations, regulations and rules and the relevant resolutions of the General Assembly and that those proposals which require an amendment of the regulations and rules or a departure from provisions of prior Assembly resolutions shall be submitted to the Assembly for its consideration and approval before their implementation;

4. *Decides* that all issues relating to human resources management, including its reform, shall continue to be considered by the Fifth Committee in the context of the item entitled "Human resources management";

5. *Reiterates* its full support for the Secretary-General as the chief administrative officer of the Organization, and underlines its full respect for his prerogatives and responsibilities under the Charter;

6. *Reaffirms* its support for the integrity and independence of the international civil service;

7. *Reiterates* that no human resources management reform should be either a budget reduction or a staff reduction exercise;

8. *Requests* the Secretary-General to include in his budget proposals provisions for all resources necessary for the implementation of human resources management policies, and stresses that activities relating to human resources management, including its reform, should be financed according to the Financial Regulations and Rules of the United Nations and that, where there are requirements for additional resources, the decision should be taken by the General Assembly in accordance with established budgetary procedures and the Financial Regulations and Rules;

9. *Recognizes* that the staff of the United Nations is an invaluable asset of the Organization, commends its contribution to furthering the purposes and principles of the United Nations, and stresses that staff representatives should participate in the process of human resources management reform in accordance with article VIII of the Staff Regulations and Rules of the United Nations;

II

Role of the Office of Human Resources Management of the Secretariat

1. *Reiterates* the role, authority and responsibility of the Office of Human Resources Management of the Secretariat in establishing human resources policies and guidelines as well as in ensuring compliance with recruitment, placement and career development procedures throughout the Secretariat;

2. *Decides* that the Office of Human Resources Management shall remain the central authority for the monitoring and approval of the recruitment and placement of staff and for the interpretation of the regulations and rules of the Organization and their enforcement;

3. *Notes* the intentions of the Secretary-General outlined in his report on human resources management reform, and looks forward to the proposals the Secretary-General intends to submit to the General Assembly for its consideration;

4. *Recognizes* the central role of the Office of Human Resources Management in ensuring the full implementation of basic human resources mandates set by the General Assembly in the context of recruitment and placement processes;

III

Human resources planning

Cognizant of the relationship between human resources planning and programme and budgetary planning processes,

Emphasizing that effective human resources planning has an impact on all aspects of human resources management,

1. *Recognizes* the continuing need for central human resources planning within the Office of Human Resources Management of the Secretariat to ensure full implementation of the principles of the Charter of the United Nations and the relevant resolutions of the General Assembly;

2. *Notes* the intention of the Secretary-General to establish a Secretariat-wide integrated human resources planning system under the central authority of the Office of Human Resources Management, and requests him to report thereon to the General Assembly at its fifty-fifth session;

3. *Expresses concern* at the growing number of resignations of staff in the Secretariat, in particular of those in the Professional category, and requests the Secretary-General to carry out a study to ascertain the causes of such separations and to report thereon to the General Assembly at its fifty-fifth session;

4. *Emphasizes* the importance of a human resources planning system, including an integrated approach to recruitment policy, job classification and contractual policies, based on the fundamental principles of the Charter and the Staff Regulations and Rules of the United Nations;

5. *Regrets* that some regional commissions and duty stations of the Organization, particularly those in developing countries, have a high vacancy rate, which consequently hampers the execution of their respective mandates, and in this regard requests the Secretary-General to ensure the proper mobility of staff between all the regional commissions and duty stations to correct this situation;

6. *Reaffirms* that staff members are subject to the authority of the Secretary-General and to assignment by him to any of the activities and offices of the United Nations, in accordance with staff regulation 1.2;

7. *Emphasizes* the requirement of mobility of all internationally recruited staff of the Organization as an integral part of their obligation, and requests the Secretary-General to give full consideration to the need for greater mobility in the context of human resources planning, in accordance with staff regulation 1.2 *(c)*, and to include any problems in increasing staff mobility and possible measures for their solution, as appropriate, in his report on human resources management to be submitted to the General Assembly at its fifty-fifth session;

8. *Requests* the Secretary-General to establish mechanisms towards, and to implement a policy of, enhanced mobility across functions, departments and duty stations, and encourages him to explore, through the Administrative Committee on Coordination, the possibility of enhancing mobility among organizations of the United Nations system and to report to the General Assembly at its fifty-fifth session on progress made;

IV

Delegation of authority and accountability

Recalling its resolution 49/222 A, by which it endorsed the new strategy for human resources management,

1. *Recognizes* the need to promote responsibility and accountability of staff members at all levels;

2. *Notes* the intention of the Secretary-General to streamline administrative procedures further and to

eliminate duplication in relation to human resources management through the delegation of authority to programme managers, and requests him to ensure, before delegating such authority, that well-designed mechanisms of accountability, including the necessary internal monitoring and control procedures, as well as training, are put in place, and to report thereon to the General Assembly at its fifty-fifth session;

3. *Also notes* that no comprehensive system of accountability and responsibility has been established;

4. *Requests* the Secretary-General, while preparing his report on the system of accountability and responsibility, to include the following elements as well as the elements enumerated in section E, paragraph 5, of General Assembly resolution 48/218 A of 23 December 1993:

(*a*) A mechanism to review the decisions of the programme managers;

(*b*) Back evaluation;

(*c*) The role of the appointment and promotion bodies and the departmental panels;

(*d*) The role of the programme managers in the preparation and submission of budget proposals as well as programme delivery;

(*e*) The role of coordination, supervision and leadership;

(*f*) The accountability of staff to the Secretary-General in exercising his delegated authority;

(*g*) The degree to which programme evaluation influences personnel performance appraisal;

5. *Emphasizes* that the administrative and managerial discretionary powers of the Secretary-General should be in conformity with the relevant provisions of the Charter of the United Nations and the staff, financial and programme planning regulations and mandates given by the General Assembly;

6. *Notes with concern* that some administrative instructions on the delegation of authority do not conform to the provisions of decisions of the General Assembly on this matter, and requests the Secretary-General to comply fully with the decision of the Assembly in this respect;

7. *Reiterates* that every staff member of the United Nations shall be responsible and accountable to the Secretary-General, in accordance with financial rule 114.1 and staff rule 112.3;

8. *Emphasizes* that any delegation of authority should be in accordance with the Charter and regulations and rules of the Organization and should entail clear lines of authority and accountability as well as improvements in the administration of justice, taking into account the central role played by the Office of Human Resources Management in setting the policies and guidelines in respect of the human resources management of the Organization and monitoring their observance and implementation;

9. *Requests* the Secretary-General to submit, through the Advisory Committee on Administrative and Budgetary Questions, at the main part of the fifty-fourth session of the General Assembly, a consolidated and comprehensive compendium of all administrative circulars on the delegation of authority;

10. *Reiterates its request* to the Secretary-General in section II, paragraph 2, of its resolution 51/226 to enhance managerial accountability with respect to human resources management decisions, including imposing sanctions in cases of demonstrated mismanagement of staff and wilful neglect of or disregard for established rules and procedures, while safeguarding the right of due process of all staff members, including managers;

11. *Requests* the Secretary-General to review the internal system of justice in order to ensure the timely, fair and effective administration of justice;

V

Recruitment and placement

Recognizing the value of staff mobility to the Organization,

1. *Requests* the Secretary-General to ensure that the highest standards of efficiency, competence and integrity serve as the paramount consideration in the employment of staff, with due regard to the principle of equitable geographical distribution, in accordance with Article 101, paragraph 3, of the Charter of the United Nations;

2. *Reiterates* that the recruitment, appointment and promotion of staff shall be made without distinction as to race, sex or religion, in accordance with principles of the Charter and the provisions of the Staff Regulations and Rules of the United Nations;

3. *Requests* the Secretary-General, as a matter of priority, to ascertain whether racial discrimination exists in recruitment, promotion and placement, in order to ensure full compliance with the provisions of the Charter, the regulations and rules of the Organization and the relevant resolutions of the General Assembly, and to report thereon to the Assembly at the main part of its fifty-fifth session;

4. *Reiterates* that external vacancy announcements should continue to be submitted to the permanent missions of Member States and be displayed on the notice boards in United Nations premises, as well as posted on the United Nations home page, and decides that they should be effectively circulated on the date of issue and that the deadline for the submission of applications should be at least two months from the date of issue;

5. *Requests* the Secretary-General to circulate internal vacancy announcements to permanent missions when issued;

6. *Endorses* the recommendation of the Advisory Committee on Administrative and Budgetary Questions in paragraph 8 of its report on internal vacancies in the Secretariat;

7. *Reaffirms* the policy of the Secretary-General to circulate vacancies for posts at the P-5 level and above both internally and externally;

8. *Decides* that the Secretary-General may consider external candidates for posts at the P-4 level, while giving fullest regard, in filling these posts, to the requisite qualifications and experience of staff already in the service of the United Nations;

9. *Notes with concern* that the Secretary-General, in his report on human resources management, approved seventeen exceptions for the recruitment of gratis personnel in the International Tribunal for the Prosecution of Persons Responsible for Serious Violations of International Humanitarian Law Committed in the Territory of the Former Yugoslavia since 1991, in contravention of section III.B, paragraph 26, of General Assembly resolution 51/226;

10. *Reaffirms* the provisions of section III.B, paragraph 26, of its resolution 51/226, and requests the Secretary-General to ensure full compliance in the future;

11. *Requests* the Secretary-General not to extend the current contracts of the personnel mentioned in paragraph 9 above and, in this context, to ensure full compliance with the current recruitment procedures of the International Tribunal;

12. *Also requests* the Secretary-General, while filling vacant posts in language services in the Secretariat, to ensure the highest performance of translation and interpretation in all six official languages;

13. *Further requests* the Secretary-General to continue to improve existing recruitment and placement procedures with a view to making them simpler, more transparent and more timely;

14. *Requests* the Secretary-General to ensure, without exception, uniform application of the regulations and rules of the Organization in all departments of the Secretariat, in accordance with the relevant resolutions of the General Assembly;

15. *Urges* the Secretary-General, when making appointments to posts subject to geographical distribution, to continue and intensify his efforts to ensure that all Member States, in particular unrepresented and under-represented Member States, are adequately represented in the Secretariat, bearing in mind the need to increase the number of staff recruited from Member States below the mid-point of their desirable ranges;

16. *Reaffirms* that the national competitive examination programme is a useful tool for selecting the best-qualified candidates from inadequately represented Member States, and requests the Secretary-General to continue to hold the examinations for posts subject to geographical distribution at the P-2 and, if necessary, P-3 levels;

17. *Urges* the Secretary-General strictly to comply with the principle that appointment to P-2 posts and to posts requiring special language competence for conference services be made exclusively through competitive examinations, and requests, in this context, that he include in his future reports the information justifying non-compliance with that principle;

18. *Reaffirms* the policy that appointments at the P-3 level shall normally be made through competitive examinations;

19. *Requests* the Secretary-General to ensure that candidates selected through national competitive examinations are placed in a timely fashion and that special efforts are made to recruit candidates from the national competitive examinations roster against existing vacancies until these rosters are cleared;

20. *Also requests* the Secretary-General to adapt the number of occupational groups selected for national competitive examinations to the requirements of the Organization, with a view to facilitating the placement and future mobility of selected candidates in the Organization, and to report on the number of candidates placed by department or office as well as on possible failures to place successful candidates, including the reasons therefor, in his report on human resources management to be submitted to the General Assembly at its fifty-fifth session;

21. *Further requests* the Secretary-General to offer or to continue to offer probationary appointments to all staff members who have passed a competitive recruitment examination and to consider such staff members for conversion to permanent appointment after successful completion of the period of probationary service;

22. *Requests* the Secretary-General to complete the realignment with the national competitive examination of the competitive examination for promotion to the Professional category and above of staff members from other categories, in particular regarding academic qualifications and equitable geographical distribution, as well as equal treatment with regard to probationary appointments;

23. *Also requests* the Secretary-General to continue his efforts to implement section V, paragraph 2, of resolution 51/226, and encourages him to continue his efforts with a view to increasing the share of fixed-term appointments throughout the Secretariat;

24. *Reaffirms* that secondment from government service is consistent with Articles 100 and 101 of the Charter and is beneficial to both the Organization and Member States, and urges the Secretary-General to pursue this practice on a wider scale, as appropriate;

25. *Notes* the intention of the Secretary-General to present detailed proposals on the dual-track system of career and non-career appointments, and requests him to submit them to the General Assembly, taking into account the experience of other international and regional organizations in human resources management and benefiting from worldwide experience in human resources management outside the Organization as well as from the work being done in this field by the International Civil Service Commission;

26. *Requests* the Commission to prepare a study on the question of the fixed-term contracts in the United Nations, taking into account the needs and interests of the Organization and current trends in personnel management;

VI

Staff development: performance management and career development

Recognizing that career development is an indispensable part of effective personnel management,

Noting the objectives of the Secretary-General with regard to staff development, performance management and career support,

1. *Requests* the Secretary-General to ensure that the performance appraisal system is applicable to all staff within the meaning of Article 97 of the Charter of the United Nations;

2. *Also requests* the Secretary-General to continue his efforts for the consistent application of the performance appraisal system throughout the Secretariat;

3. *Approves* the step-by-step approach to performance recognition as set forth in paragraphs 24 to 34 of the report of the Secretary-General on performance management;

4. *Takes note* of the proposals on the need to address the issue of underperformance in paragraphs 35 to 43 of the report referred to in paragraph 3 above, and requests the Secretary-General to submit revised policy proposals to deal systematically and effectively with underperformance;

5. *Notes with concern* that no comprehensive and systematic career development policy has yet been developed by the Secretary-General, and reiterates its request that such a policy be developed on a priority basis in the interest of maintaining a strong and efficient international civil service, in accordance with the principles enshrined in Article 101 of the Charter;

6. *Requests* the Secretary-General, in the further enhancement of the career development system of the Organization, to implement a transparent promotion policy, augmented by the effective use of a simplified and appropriate performance appraisal system, adequate training and competitive examinations, in order to provide for the recognition of competence and outstanding performance and to facilitate the continuous professional growth of staff at all levels;

7. *Notes* the initiatives undertaken so far by the Secretary-General with regard to staff training;

8. *Requests* the Secretary-General to consider opening staff training courses, as appropriate, to members of permanent missions, within the framework of the approved budget, and without prejudice to meeting the staff training needs of the Organization;

9. *Also requests* the Secretary-General to streamline the personnel manual;

VII

Employment of retirees

1. *Endorses* the observations and recommendations on the employment of retirees, contained in the report of the Advisory Committee on Administrative and Budgetary Questions;

2. *Requests* the Secretary-General to have recourse to the employment of retirees only if the operational requirements of the Organization cannot be met by existing staff;

VIII

Consultants and individual contractors

1. *Endorses* the new definitions of consultants and individual contractors as contained in the report of the Secretary-General on comprehensive guidelines for the use of consultants in the Secretariat;

2. *Notes with concern* the observation of the Board of Auditors that the inadequacies earlier identified by the Board in the hiring of consultants persist;

3. *Reiterates its request* that the recommendations of the Board of Auditors as endorsed in General Assembly resolution 51/226 and its resolution 53/204 of 18 December 1998 be fully implemented, and requests the Secretary-General to submit a report through the Board to the Assembly at the main part of its fifty-fourth session;

4. *Requests* the Secretary-General to continue to submit an annual report to the General Assembly on consultants hired by the United Nations during the preceding year, with an indication of their functions;

5. *Takes note* of the comments on consultants made by the Advisory Committee on Administrative and Budgetary Questions in paragraph 15 of its report, and requests the Secretary-General to ensure full compliance with the provisions of section VI, paragraph 7, of its resolution 51/226;

6. *Reiterates* that the Secretary-General should refrain from using consultants to carry out functions assigned to established posts and that consultants should be hired only in accordance with the existing rules and relevant resolutions of the General Assembly and where in-house expertise is not available in the Organization;

7. *Emphasizes* that, in areas where consultants are frequently hired for a period of more than one year, the Secretary-General should submit proposals, where necessary, for the establishment of posts;

8. *Stresses* that consultants should generally not receive training at the expense of the United Nations;

9. *Notes with concern* that 31 per cent of contractors were hired from only four Member States and were paid 38 per cent of total fees during the biennium 1996-1997, and requests the Secretary-General to take remedial measures in this regard;

10. *Reaffirms* the principle contained in a recommendation of the Board of Auditors and endorsed in General Assembly resolution 51/226 that the objective of attracting consultants on a wider geographical basis should be achieved, inter alia, by fixing appropriate norms and by closer interaction with substantive offices and requesting units at all duty stations;

11. *Takes note* of the guidelines contained in the report of the Secretary-General subject to the following provisions:

(a) There should be a separation of functions between the requesting officers and the officer who processes the contract;

(b) The approved terms of reference should form part of the contract;

(c) The selection of consultants and individual contractors should be on a wider geographical basis and the question of travel expenses should not distort the geographical balance in the awarding of contracts;

(d) In the awarding of contracts, gender balance should be achieved without prejudice to wide geographical distribution;

(e) The Office of Human Resources Management of the Secretariat should have authority to take a final decision on whether further contracts should be awarded to contractors in the case of an unsatisfactory performance evaluation by a programme manager;

12. *Requests* the Secretary-General to circulate the revised guidelines as a matter of priority, throughout the Secretariat, with a view to ensuring full compliance;

IX

Composition of the Secretariat

1. *Notes with concern* that twenty-four Member States were unrepresented and ten under-represented in the Secretariat as at 30 June 1998;

2. *Also notes with concern* the significant reduction in the number of posts subject to geographical distribution at the P-2 and P-3 levels, as well as the increase in such posts at the D-2 and Assistant Secretary-General levels;

3. *Urges* the Secretary-General to take the necessary measures, as a matter of priority, to address the imbalance in the post structure of the Secretariat in the context of the proposed programme budget for the biennium 2000-2001, bearing in mind that more than one hundred posts subject to geographical distribution at the director level will be vacated by 2002 owing to the retirement of the present incumbents;

4. *Requests* the Secretary-General, when submitting future reports on the composition of the Secretariat, to discontinue the established practice of showing the representation of staff according to major geographical groupings as referred to in annex II to his report, and to list countries in alphabetical order;

5. *Recalls* that, in accordance with Article 97 of the Charter of the United Nations, the Secretariat shall comprise a Secretary-General and such staff as the Organization may require;

6. *Reaffirms* that no post should be considered the exclusive preserve of any Member State or group of States, including at the highest levels, and requests the Secretary-General to ensure that, as a general rule, no national of a Member State succeeds a national of that State in a senior post and that there is no monopoly on senior posts by nationals of any State or group of States;

7. *Requests* the Secretary-General to take all the necessary measures to ensure, at the senior and policy-making levels of the Secretariat, the equitable representation of Member States, especially those unrepresented and under-represented, in particular developing countries, in accordance with the relevant resolutions of the General Assembly, and to include relevant information thereon in all future reports on the composition of the Secretariat;

8. *Reiterates its request* to the Secretary-General to increase further his efforts to improve the composition of the Secretariat by ensuring a wide and equitable geographical distribution of staff in all departments;

9. *Takes note* of the observation in the report of the Secretary-General on the composition of the Secretariat with regard to the anticipated vacancies in posts subject to geographical distribution, and requests the Secretary-General, when filling those vacancies, to take into account the continuing inequitable representation among the Member States;

10. *Urges* all Member States, in particular those with inadequate representation in the Secretariat, to make every effort to identify qualified candidates for consideration for appointment in the Secretariat, and in this regard requests the Secretary-General to ensure that, among equally qualified candidates, preference is given to candidates from under-represented Member States;

X

Status of women in the Secretariat

Reaffirming section VI of its resolution 45/248 B of 21 December 1990,

Reaffirming also that the Fifth Committee is the appropriate Main Committee of the General Assembly entrusted with responsibility for the administrative and budgetary matters relating to the question of the status of women in the Secretariat,

1. *Decides* that all reports dealing with administrative and budgetary aspects of the status of women in the Secretariat shall be considered by the Fifth Committee;

2. *Notes* that, while there has been improvement in the status of women in the Secretariat, the rate of progress in the representation of women from developing countries, particularly at the senior level, has been very slow, and in this context urges the Secretary-General to make greater efforts to redress this situation in accordance with Article 101, paragraph 3, of the Charter of the United Nations, and to report thereon to the General Assembly at its fifty-fifth session;

3. *Recalls* its resolution 53/119 of 9 December 1998, including the reaffirmation of the goal of 50/50 gender distribution by the year 2000 in all categories of posts within the United Nations system, especially at the D-1 level and above, with full respect for the principle of equitable geographical distribution, in conformity with Article 101 of the Charter, and taking into account the continuing lack of representation or underrepresentation of women from certain countries, in particular from developing countries as well as countries with economies in transition;

4. *Notes with concern* the imbalance in the representation of women from different regions, and requests the Secretary-General to take appropriate remedial action when pursuing the goal of 50/50 gender distribution;

5. *Decides* that the objective of 50/50 gender distribution by the year 2000 should be pursued in compliance with the provisions of Articles 8 and 101 of the Charter and staff regulation 4.3 in order to ensure equal opportunities for qualified women and men in recruitment and promotion;

XI

Staff-management consultations

1. *Takes note* of the views of the staff representatives;

2. *Emphasizes* the need further to improve the staff-management consultative process in all issues relating to human resources management;

3. *Reaffirms* the need for the Secretary-General to use, to the fullest extent, the staff-management consultative mechanisms set out in staff rule 108.2;

4. *Requests* the Secretary-General to take into account the views of staff representatives, in accordance with article VIII of the Staff Regulations and Rules of the United Nations and its resolution 35/213;

XII

Amendments to the Staff Regulations and Rules

Recalling its resolution 52/252,

1. *Requests* the Secretary-General to expedite the issuance of the report requested in paragraph 10 of its resolution 52/252;

2. *Decides* that staff rule 101.3 *(c)* should read:

"*(c)* Performance reports shall be prepared regularly for all staff members, including at the Assistant Secretary-General level and above, in accordance with procedures promulgated by the Secretary-General.";

3. *Requests* the Secretariat to publish an index to the Staff Regulations and Rules of the United Nations;

4. *Requests* the Secretary-General to ensure that revised staff regulations and rules, or amendments thereto, are issued in a timely manner after their approval by the General Assembly.

On 23 December, the Assembly decided to continue consideration of the agenda item on human resources management, as a matter of priority, at its resumed fifty-fourth (2000) session (**decision 54/460 A**). On the same date, the Assembly decided that the Fifth Committee should continue consideration of that agenda item at the resumed fifty-fourth session (**deci-**

sion 54/462 A). Also on the same date, the Assembly decided that the agenda item would remain for consideration at the resumed session (**decision 54/465**).

Framework for human resources management

The working group on the framework for human resources management, established by ICSC in 1998 [YUN 1998, p. 1309], met four times in 1999 (24-26 February, 19 April, 22-28 June, 19-20 July).

The Commission requested the working group to meet a final time to complete work on the integrated framework for human resources management, including the drafting of guiding principles. The complete framework would be presented to the General Assembly in 2000. The Commission reviewed the topics discussed by the working group and grouped the priority items in a work programme, together with delivery dates as follows: ethics/standards of conduct and the pay and benefits system (2000); contractual arrangements/types of appointment and mobility (2001); staff well-being and information policy (date to be determined); and administration of justice (date to be determined).

Draft standards of conduct for the international civil service

In accordance with its 1998 decision to place on its work programme the updating of the 1954 Standards of Conduct in the International Civil Service of the International Civil Service Advisory Board, ICSC forwarded a questionnaire to all organizations and staff associations in the common system.

On the basis of the responses received, the ICSC secretariat prepared a note containing proposed standards, which, although they largely reproduced the 1954 Standards, reflected changes in several areas. New sections dealt with gender equality, harassment, conflict of interest and protection of confidential information, and provisions of the 1954 Standards that were dated or did not reflect current realities were omitted. The proposed standards were forwarded to the organizations of the common system and the comments received were considered by the Commission.

ICSC felt that a balance had to be maintained between the obligations of staff and their rights. It agreed that the purpose of updating and modernizing the Standards was to promote ethical behaviour, and the proposed standards should therefore take a less punitive approach and focus more on encouraging proper behaviour. Fair and open management, characterized by transparent procedures, was increasingly the basis of public service ethics. It was evident from the views expressed by the representatives of organizations and staff that consensus-building with the two parties was necessary; the Commission therefore formed a two-tier working group to that end.

The Commission decided that it would report to the General Assembly in 2000.

Post structure

In response to General Assembly resolution 52/220 [YUN 1997, p. 1421], the Secretary-General submitted a May report [A/53/955] on developments in the post structure of the Secretariat over the preceding 10 years, on the forward-looking human resources management policy that he intended to develop, for both the short and the medium term, with a view to rejuvenating the Organization, and on the impact that such a policy should have on developments in post structure in the future.

The Secretary-General pointed out that the post structure was an integral part of the review and approval process for the biennial programme budget and directly linked to the functions to be discharged by each organizational entity responsible for programme delivery. From 1988 to 1999, the total number of authorized posts declined by 1,155 or 11.7 per cent; Professional posts declined by 216 and those in the General Service and related categories by 939. Although posts at the Under-Secretary-General level remained relatively constant, those at the Assistant Secretary-General level declined by 18 per cent, those at the D-2 level by 12 per cent, D-1 posts by 5 per cent, P-4 posts by 4 per cent, P-3 posts by 1.5 per cent and P-2/1 posts by 23 per cent. The number of P-5 posts increased by 0.6 per cent. The ratio between posts in the Professional and higher categories and the General Service and related categories had not altered significantly over the decade.

With regard to a forward-looking human resources management policy, the Secretary-General cited the overall vision contained in his 1997 report "Renewing the United Nations: a programme for reform" [YUN 1997, p. 1390], in which he called for a simplified structure that avoided duplication and achieved greater impact; empowered and responsible staff and managers; a leaner and more efficient Secretariat; and an organization that fostered management excellence and was accountable for achieving results determined by the Member States. He also pointed to his 1998 report on human resources management reform [YUN 1998, p. 1309], in which he outlined the overall strategic direction, work in progress and future actions that he intended to take to develop further a modern human resources management capability within the Organization. Each of the components were interrelated and, taken together, represented his policy for revitalizing the Organization.

The Secretary-General noted that the Department of Management would monitor changes in the post structure of each department/office and would work with programme managers to ensure that proposals for posts took into account not only programmatic needs but the need for career development of staff.

By **decision 53/474** of 8 June, the Assembly deferred consideration of the Secretary-General's report on the post structure of the Secretariat until its fifty-fourth session later in the year.

On 23 December, the Assembly decided to continue its consideration of human resources management, as a matter of priority, at its resumed fifty-fourth (2000) session (**decision 54/460 A**).

Staff composition

In August, the Secretary-General submitted to the General Assembly his annual report on staff composition of the UN Secretariat, by nationality, gender, grade and contractual status [A/54/279 & Corr.1]. The report also updated information on changes in the desirable ranges of Member States and described measures taken to ensure the equitable representation of Member States at the senior and policy-making levels.

As at 30 June 1999, the staff totalled 14,319, of whom 7,394 were paid from the regular budget and 6,925 from extrabudgetary sources. There were 4,304 in the Professional category and above, 9,256 in the General Service and related categories and 759 project personnel.

Staff in posts subject to geographical distribution numbered 2,410. As at 30 June, there were 24 unrepresented Member States, the same as at 30 June 1998, and 13 underrepresented Member States, compared to 10 the year before. Changes in representation derived not only from staff appointments and separations from service, but also from such factors as adjustments in desirable ranges resulting from an increase or decrease in the number of posts subject to geographical distribution, changes in the number of Member States, variations in assessed contributions or population of individual Member States, and changes in the status of some staff members. The report also provided information on groupings of Member States, representation of developing and other countries among staff at the senior levels, representation of women and recruitment activities.

Between 1 July 1998 and 30 June 1999, 123 appointments were made to posts subject to geographical distribution. Of those, 1 (0.9 per cent) was a national of a non-member State, 20 (16.1 per cent) of underrepresented Member States, 97 (78.9 per cent) of within-range Member States and 5 (4.1 per cent) of overrepresented Member States.

Gratis personnel

In response to General Assembly resolution 51/243 [YUN 1997, p. 1469], the Secretary-General submitted in February the first quarterly report of 1999 on the use of gratis personnel covering the period from 1 October to 31 December 1998 [A/C.5/53/54], during which time type II gratis personnel decreased from 134 to 94. The report also contained information on the specific cases pertaining to the UN Office at Nairobi and the International Tribunal for the Former Yugoslavia (ICTY).

In accordance with resolution 51/243, which requested the phase-out of gratis personnel throughout the Secretariat, and resolution 53/11 [YUN 1998, p. 1313], which requested the Secretary-General to report on the implementation of the phase-out of type II gratis personnel at its resumed fifty-third session, the Secretary-General, in a March report [A/53/847], noting that all such personnel were to be replaced by staff members by 28 February 1999, stated that, with the exception of one individual who had been involved in a major trial at ICTY, all type II gratis personnel were phased out by that date.

ACABQ, in a March report [A/53/417/Add.1], again expressed the view that the hiring of gratis personnel had not been consistent with Assembly resolutions and reiterated that the functions being carried out by gratis personnel should have been performed by staff members as they did not require specialized expertise. As to the one remaining type II gratis personnel, the Committee believed that, whether or not the extension was justified, the Assembly's concurrence should have been sought. ACABQ also found that 17 gratis personnel were considered as an exception in the recruitment for ICTY, in contravention of the provisions of resolution 51/226 [YUN 1997, p. 1459].

GENERAL ASSEMBLY ACTION

On 7 April [meeting 97], the General Assembly, on the recommendation of the Fifth Committee [A/53/533/Add.1], adopted **resolution 53/218** without vote [agenda items 112 & 119].

Gratis personnel provided by Governments

The General Assembly,

Recalling Articles 97, 100 and 101 of the Charter of the United Nations,

Reaffirming its resolutions 51/243 of 15 September 1997, 52/234 of 26 June 1998 and 53/11 of 26 October 1998,

Recalling its resolutions 51/226 of 3 April 1997 and 52/219 of 22 December 1997,

Having considered the reports of the Secretary-General and the related report of the Advisory Committee on Administrative and Budgetary Questions,

1. *Notes* that, with the exception of one type II gratis personnel, all type II gratis personnel were phased out by 28 February 1999;

2. *Notes with concern* that its resolutions on gratis personnel have not been fully implemented, and reiterates the need for full compliance in future;

3. *Also notes with concern* the observations of the Advisory Committee on Administrative and Budgetary Questions in paragraphs 2, 4 and 5 of its report;

4. *Decides* to consider, under the item entitled "Human resources management", the question of the recruitment of seventeen gratis personnel in the International Tribunal for the Prosecution of Persons Responsible for Serious Violations of International Humanitarian Law Committed in the Territory of the Former Yugoslavia since 1991 as the recruitment was in contravention of General Assembly resolution 51/226;

5. *Endorses* the observation of the Advisory Committee in paragraph 6 of its report that, at the end of June 1999, confirmation should be given that, without exception, all type II gratis personnel have been phased out;

6. *Decides* to continue, at the main part of its fifty-fourth session, its consideration of the question of gratis personnel provided by Governments.

In May [A/C.5/53/59], the Secretary-General provided information on the use of gratis personnel for the period from 1 January to 31 March. He stated that 93 type II gratis personnel had left the Organization during the period and one remained at ICTY.

By a 9 June letter to the Assembly President [A/53/1000], the Secretary-General forwarded a copy of a letter received from the Prosecutor of ICTY, Justice Louise Arbour. It outlined the need to carry out forensic investigations as soon as international forces were permitted to enter Kosovo province of the Federal Republic of Yugoslavia. Following a determination of the scale of required operations and the need to act immediately, the Prosecutor concluded that the only way to allow immediate investigations was through the use of gratis personnel and sought approval to seek and accept a number of gratis personnel from Member States. The Prosecutor, after detailing the requirements, indicated the need for 12 teams, or up to 300 personnel. The level and quantity of expertise was not available within the United Nations in the time frame required. The Secretary-General informed the Assembly of his intention to approve the request.

On 11 June [A/53/1001], the Secretary-General sought the Assembly's concurrence for a two-month extension of the services of the remaining individual brought in as gratis personnel at ICTY. The extension was necessary because of various delays in the presentation of the case, in which the individual was the leading prosecution co-counsel. The Prosecutor stressed that it would be impossible to replace the individual at such a critical stage of the case.

By **decision 53/483** of 23 June, the Assembly, on the proposal of the Secretary-General, extended until 31 August the services of the one remaining gratis personnel in ICTY.

In July [A/53/1028], the Secretary-General provided information on the use of gratis personnel for the period from 1 April to 30 June. He noted that one type II gratis personnel remained at ICTY and drew attention to his 9 June letter regarding the request for 300 gratis personnel for ICTY.

In October [A/54/470], ACABQ pointed to deficiencies in the Secretary-General's July report, specifically with regard to provisions of Assembly resolution 52/234 [YUN 1998, p. 1312] that called for accurate, comprehensive, complete and integrated reports on the subject. With regard to the 300 gratis personnel requested by ICTY, ACABQ was of the view that information should have been provided on the procedure for selecting such personnel, the involvement of the Office of Human Resources Management, the list of Member States invited to offer the personnel, the dates of requests, functions performed, duration of service and specific expertise of the gratis personnel.

In November [A/54/533], the Secretary-General submitted both his quarterly and annual reports on the use of gratis personnel. The quarterly report covered the period from 1 July to 30 September, while the annual report described the situation between 1 October 1998 and 30 September 1999. The absence of figures for type I gratis personnel was due to the suspension of the activities of the United Nations Special Commission on the disarmament of Iraq [YUN 1998, p. 251]. The total of 98 type II gratis personnel represented a decrease of 27 per cent from a year earlier. In compliance with resolution 53/11 [YUN 1998, p. 1313], all such personnel but one serving with ICTY were phased out in February. In June, 105 forensic investigators were accepted by ICTY, followed by 83 in July, 112 in August and 63 in September. Six experts in civil affairs were accepted in August for Kosovo. Compared to a year earlier, the number of nationalities represented decreased from 27 to 10.

Consultants and individual contractors

In accordance with section VIII of resolution 53/221 (see p. 1328), the Secretary-General submitted two reports on the hiring of consultants.

In his July report [A/54/164], which dealt with the hiring and use of consultants in the Secretariat, the Secretary-General described action taken to implement recommendations made by the Board of Auditors. As recommended, the Administration had issued in 1998 [YUN 1998, p. 1311] detailed guidelines regarding terms of reference for consultants. The guidelines, which were circulated in April 1999, stipulated that heads of departments would be responsible for their implementation. The report also addressed questions of identification of candidates, maintenance of rosters, selection from a wider geographical base, lead time for selection, level of remuneration, management of consultants and evaluation of performance. In conclusion, it was stated that the development of the Integrated Management Information System (IMIS) to accommodate enhanced data and roster facilities would enable improved monitoring of the implementation of the guidelines.

In August [A/C.5/54/4], the Secretary-General provided information on consultants hired during 1998. While acknowledging the deficiencies noted by the Board of Auditors and OIOS in 1998 [YUN 1998, p. 1311], the Secretary-General stated that it would not be possible to rectify the presentation of information until IMIS was fully deployed at all duty stations in 2000. The report provided statistics on all consultancy engagements that began in 1998, covering the number of consultants engaged, the number of contracts by type and their duration, the number of women, educational level, fees, nationality, purpose of engagement by occupational groups and the aggregate data for each duty station.

Reports of Board of Auditors and ACABQ. In July, the Secretary-General transmitted to the Assembly the comments of the Board of Auditors [A/54/165] on his report on the hiring and use of consultants in the Secretariat [A/54/164]. The Board welcomed the issuance of the comprehensive guidelines, which substantially addressed its concerns. The Board expressed its intention to monitor the application of the guidelines and looked forward to the system-wide introduction of IMIS.

In an October report [A/54/450], ACABQ recognized that the issuance of the guidelines and the establishment of a roster and arrangements for reporting to the Assembly had addressed the issues raised by the Board of Auditors. With the development of IMIS, there would be improved monitoring of their implementation. However, ACABQ recommended that, to the extent possible, there should be a monitoring mechanism in place to ensure impartial evaluation of the performance of consultants. In addition, it welcomed the Secretary-General's August report [A/C.5/54/4] and noted the valuable assistance in collecting data rendered by IMIS.

Status of women in the Secretariat

In a January report [E/CN.6/1999/5] to the Commission on the Status of Women (see p. 1104), the Secretary-General provided a statistical update of the gender distribution of staff at the Professional and higher levels in the UN Secretariat, described special measures being taken for the achievement of gender equality and outlined the work programme for developing and implementing gender action plans during 1999.

In response to General Assembly resolution 53/119 [YUN 1998, p. 1316], the Secretary-General submitted a September report on improvement of the status of women in the Secretariat [A/54/405]. As at 30 June 1999, the percentage of women in Professional and higher-level posts subject to geographical distribution stood at 38.1 per cent, compared to 36.9 per cent in 1998. The percentage of women at the D-1 level and above had increased since the last report [YUN 1998, p. 1316] from 25.2 to 29.1 per cent. However, while visible progress was made in improving the representation of women at the senior and policy-making levels, progress in improving women's representation overall in the Professional and higher categories was slow. The goal of 50/50 gender distribution had nearly been met at the P-2 level (48.2 per cent) but the percentage increase in women's representation at the P-3 to P-5 levels was very small, ranging from 0.1 per cent at the P-3 level to 1.4 per cent at the P-4 level. The highest concentration of women was at the P-3 level, whereas that of men was at the P-4 level.

Work had begun on developing action plans on human resources management for individual departments and offices. One of the objectives set in those plans related to improving gender balance; the performance of departments under the plans with respect to gender would be monitored by the Special Adviser on Gender Issues and Advancement of Women. Other elements of the Secretary-General's strategy to achieve gender balance in the Secretariat included the review of the pool of women candidates within the Secretariat for projected vacancies by departments and occupations and the identification of external sources of women candidates, particularly in Member States that were unrepresented or underrepresented, in developing countries and in countries with economies in transition and in occupations in which women were underrepresented. Attention would also be paid to the further development of policies and practices to support the reconciliation of staff members' work and family responsibilities with the aim of attracting and retaining the best-qualified staff and enhancing their morale and productivity.

GENERAL ASSEMBLY ACTION

On 17 December [meeting 83], the General Assembly, on the recommendation of the Third (Social, Humanitarian and Cultural) Committee [A/54/598 & Corr.1,2], adopted **resolution 54/139** without vote [agenda item 109].

Improvement of the status of women in the Secretariat

The General Assembly,

Recalling Articles 1 and 101 of the Charter of the United Nations, as well as Article 8, which provides that the United Nations shall place no restrictions on the eligibility of men and women to participate in any capacity and under conditions of equality in its principal and subsidiary organs,

Recalling also the goal, contained in the Platform for Action adopted by the Fourth World Conference on Women, of the achievement of overall gender equality, particularly at the Professional level and above, by the year 2000,

Taking into account the continuing lack of representation or underrepresentation of women from certain countries, in particular developing countries, including least developed countries and small island developing States, and countries with economies in transition,

Recalling its resolutions 53/119 of 9 December 1998 on the improvement of the status of women in the Secretariat and 53/221 of 7 April 1999 on human resources management,

Welcoming the progress made in improving the representation of women at the D-1 level, but concerned that the representation of women at the senior and policy-making levels remains significantly below the goal of 50/50 gender distribution at these levels,

Welcoming also the fact that the percentage of women appointed at the D-2 level and promoted to the D-1 level exceeded the goal of 50 per cent,

Concerned that the appointment of women at all other levels, with the exception of the P-2 level, falls significantly below the goal of 50 per cent, and concerned at the incremental pace at which the overall representation of women in the Secretariat has increased,

Concerned also that some existing arrangements with Member States may impede the employment of spouses of United Nations staff members,

1. *Welcomes* the report of the Secretary-General and the framework for action contained therein;

2. *Reaffirms* the urgent goal of achieving 50/50 gender distribution in all categories of posts within the United Nations system, especially at the D-1 level and above, with full respect for the principle of equitable geographical distribution, in conformity with Article 101, paragraph 3, of the Charter of the United Nations, and also taking into account the continuing lack of representation or underrepresentation of women from certain countries, in particular developing countries and countries with economies in transition;

3. *Regrets* that the goal of 50/50 gender distribution will not be met by the year 2000, and urges the Secretary-General to intensify his efforts to realize significant progress towards this goal by the end of 2000;

4. *Requests* the General Assembly, at its special session entitled "Women 2000: gender equality, development and peace for the twenty-first century", to be held in June 2000, to consider further forward-looking strategies for achieving 50/50 gender distribution in all categories of posts within the United Nations system, especially at the D-1 level and above, with full respect for the principle of equitable geographical distribution, in conformity with Article 101, paragraph 3, of the Charter, and also taking into account the continuing lack of representation or underrepresentation of women from certain countries, in particular developing countries and countries with economies in transition;

5. *Welcomes* the ongoing personal commitment of the Secretary-General to meeting the goal of gender equality and his assurance that gender balance will be given the highest priority in his continuing efforts to bring about a new management culture in the Organization, including full implementation of the special measures for the achievement of gender equality;

6. *Also welcomes* the continued provision of specific training programmes on gender mainstreaming and gender issues in the workplace, tailored to meet the special needs of individual departments, and commends those heads of departments and offices who have launched gender training for their managers and staff;

7. *Strongly encourages* heads of departments and offices who have not yet organized such training to do so by the end of the next biennium;

8. *Calls upon* the Secretary-General to implement fully and to monitor the strategic plan of action for the improvement of the status of women in the Secretariat (1995-2000) in order to make notable progress towards the goal of 50/50 gender distribution by the end of the year 2000, especially at the D-1 level and above;

9. *Requests* the Secretary-General to ensure that individual managers are held accountable for implementing the strategic plan within their areas of responsibility;

10. *Encourages* the Secretary-General to appoint more women as special representatives and envoys and to pursue good offices on his behalf, especially in matters related to peacekeeping, peace-building, preventive diplomacy and economic and social development, and in operational activities, including as resident coordinators, as well as to appoint more women to other high-level positions;

11. *Welcomes* the inclusion of the objective of improving gender balance in action plans on human resources management for individual departments and offices, and encourages cooperation between the Special Adviser on Gender Issues and Advancement of Women and the Office of Human Resources Management of the Secretariat in the further elaboration and monitoring of these plans, which will include concrete strategies and specific targets for improving women's representation in each department and office;

12. *Requests* the Secretary-General to monitor closely the progress made by departments and offices in meeting the goal of gender balance and to ensure that the appointment and promotion of suitably qualified women will be no less than 50 per cent of all ap-

pointments and promotions until the goal of 50/50 gender distribution is met, including through full implementation of the special measures for women and the development of mechanisms to encourage, monitor and assess effectively the performance of programme managers in meeting targets for improving women's representation;

13. *Takes note* of the revised terms of reference of the Steering Committee for the Improvement of the Status of Women in the Secretariat issued by the Secretary-General in June 1999, in particular its role in monitoring the implementation of the special measures for the achievement of gender balance;

14. *Requests* the Secretary-General to develop innovative recruitment strategies to identify and attract suitably qualified women candidates, in particular in developing countries and countries with economies in transition, in other Member States that are unrepresented or underrepresented in the Secretariat and in occupations in which women are underrepresented;

15. *Also requests* the Secretary-General to continue his work to create within existing resources a gender-sensitive work environment supportive of the needs of his staff, both women and men, including through the development of policies for flexible working time, flexible workplace arrangements and child-care and elder-care needs, as well as through the provision of more comprehensive information to prospective candidates and new recruits on spouse-employment opportunities and the expansion of gender-sensitivity training in all departments and offices;

16. *Further requests* the Secretary-General to develop further the policy against harassment, including sexual harassment, and to issue clear, detailed guidelines for its application at Headquarters and in the field;

17. *Requests* the Secretary-General to enable the Office of the Special Adviser on Gender Issues and Advancement of Women to monitor effectively and facilitate progress in the implementation of the strategic plan and the special measures for women, including by ensuring access to the information required to carry out that work;

18. *Strongly encourages* Member States to support the efforts of the United Nations and the specialized agencies to achieve the goal of 50/50 gender distribution, especially at the D-1 level and above, by identifying and regularly submitting more women candidates for appointment to intergovernmental, judicial and expert bodies, identifying and proposing national recruitment sources that will assist the organizations of the United Nations system in identifying suitable women candidates, in particular from developing countries and countries with economies in transition, and encouraging more women to apply for positions within the Secretariat, the specialized agencies, funds and programmes and the regional commissions, including in areas in which women are underrepresented, such as peacekeeping, peace-building and other non-traditional areas;

19. *Also strongly encourages* Member States to identify women candidates for assignment to peacekeeping missions and to improve the representation of women in military and civilian police contingents;

20. *Requests* the Secretary-General to report to the Commission on the Status of Women at its forty-fourth session and to the General Assembly at its fifty-fifth session on the implementation of the present resolution, including by providing statistics on the number and percentage of women in all organizational units and at all levels throughout the United Nations system and on the implementation of departmental action plans for the achievement of gender balance.

Multilingualism

In response to General Assembly resolution 52/23 [YUN 1997, p. 1472], the Secretary-General submitted an October report on efforts to promote multilingualism in the Secretariat [A/54/478]. He described the types of language programmes provided at major duty stations, language incentives offered, the use of working languages, translation of documents, recruitment and promotion, and the simultaneous distribution of language versions of documents. The Department of Public Information produced and disseminated a broad range of information materials in all mediums in both the working languages (English and French) and to the extent possible the other official languages of the Organization (Arabic, Chinese, Russian and Spanish).

GENERAL ASSEMBLY ACTION

On 6 December [meeting 70], the General Assembly adopted **resolution 54/64** [draft: A/54/L.37 & Add.1] without vote [agenda item 23].

Multilingualism

The General Assembly,

Recalling its resolutions 50/11 of 2 November 1995 and 52/23 of 25 November 1997,

1. *Takes note* of the report of the Secretary-General;

2. *Requests* the Secretary-General to appoint a senior Secretariat official as coordinator of questions relating to multilingualism throughout the Secretariat;

3. *Also requests* the Secretary-General to submit to it at its fifty-sixth session a comprehensive report on the implementation of resolution 50/11 and of the present resolution;

4. *Decides* to include in the provisional agenda of its fifty-sixth session the item entitled "Multilingualism".

Staff rules and regulations

In response to General Assembly resolution 52/252 [YUN 1998, p. 1318], the Secretary-General submitted an August report containing the text of the Staff Regulations [A/54/276], which had been drafted in gender-neutral terms. The Regulations had also been amended to reflect the fact that the basis for calculation of termination indemnity and repatriation grant for all staff members was "gross salary less staff assessment"; "gross salary" would replace the term "pensionable remuneration".

In another August report [A/54/272], the Secretary-General submitted to the Assembly amendments to the Staff Rules under the 100 series, covering salary advances, special leave, maternity leave, travel expenses, excess baggage and unaccompanied shipments, insurance, termination indemnity, repatriation grant and last day for pay purposes; under the 200 series, covering hours of work and official holidays, travel expenses, excess baggage and unaccompanied shipments, insurance, repatriation grant and conditions governing payment of that grant and last day for pay purposes; and under the 300 series, covering hours of work and official holidays, subsistence allowance, excess baggage and unaccompanied shipments and insurance.

By **decision 54/460 A** of 23 December, the Assembly approved the Secretary-General's proposed amendments to the Staff Regulations and took note of the amendments to the Staff Rules as set out in his report.

Safety and security

The Economic and Social Council and the Security Council both took action with regard to the safety and security of UN personnel in 1999. On 15 January, the 1994 Convention on the Safety of United Nations and Associated Personnel, adopted by the General Assembly by resolution 49/59 [YUN 1994, p. 1289], entered into force, 30 days after the receipt of its twenty-second instrument of ratification.

The Economic and Social Council, in agreed conclusions of 23 July [A/54/3/Rev.1 (agreed conclusions 1999/1)], adopted at the humanitarian affairs segment of its substantive session (see p. 824), called on all parties to conflicts to respect international humanitarian and human rights law and to take measures to ensure the safety and security of international and local humanitarian personnel.

In **resolution 1265(1999)** of 17 September on the protection of civilians in armed conflict (see p. 649), the Security Council took note of the entry into force of the 1994 Convention and condemned attacks and the use of force against UN and associated personnel, as well as personnel of international humanitarian organizations, and affirmed the need to hold accountable those who committed such acts.

GENERAL ASSEMBLY ACTION

On 17 December [meeting 84], the General Assembly adopted **resolution 54/192** [draft: A/54/L.70] without vote [agenda item 20].

Safety and security of humanitarian personnel and protection of United Nations personnel

The General Assembly,

Reaffirming its resolution 46/182 of 19 December 1991 on strengthening of the coordination of humanitarian emergency assistance of the United Nations,

Recalling its resolutions 53/87 of 7 December 1998 on safety and security of humanitarian personnel and protection of United Nations personnel, 52/167 of 16 December 1997 on safety and security of humanitarian personnel and 52/126 of 12 December 1997 on protection of United Nations personnel,

Welcoming agreed conclusions 1999/1 adopted by the Economic and Social Council at the humanitarian affairs segment of its substantive session of 1999,

Taking note of the report of the Secretary-General on protection of civilians in armed conflicts, Security Council resolution 1265(1999) of 17 September 1999 and the recommendations made therein, the statement of the President of the Security Council of 12 February 1999 and the range of views expressed during the open debates of the Security Council on 12 February 1999 and 16 and 17 September 1999, on protection of civilians in armed conflicts, and bearing in mind the statements made by the President of the Council on 19 June 1997 and 29 September 1998, on protection for humanitarian assistance to refugees and others in conflict situations, as well as the statement made by the President of the Council on 8 July 1999 on maintenance of peace and security and post-conflict peace-building,

Recalling the fiftieth anniversary on 12 August 1999 of the Geneva Conventions of 12 August 1949, which reaffirmed the need to promote and ensure respect for the principles and rules of international humanitarian law,

Noting with satisfaction the entry into force on 15 January 1999 of the Convention on the Safety of United Nations and Associated Personnel of 9 December 1994,

Deeply concerned by the growing number of complex humanitarian emergencies in the last few years, in particular in armed conflicts and in post-conflict situations, which have dramatically increased the loss of human lives, in particular of civilians, the suffering of victims, flows of refugees and internally displaced persons, as well as material destruction, which disrupt the development efforts of countries affected, in particular those of developing countries,

Concerned by the increasingly difficult context in which humanitarian assistance takes place in some areas, in particular the continuous erosion, in many cases, of respect for the principles and rules of international humanitarian law,

Strongly deploring the rising toll of casualties among national and international humanitarian personnel and United Nations and its associated personnel in complex humanitarian emergencies, in particular in armed conflicts and in post-conflict situations, and strongly condemning the acts of murder and other forms of physical violence, abduction, hostage-taking, kidnapping, harassment and illegal arrest and detention to which those participating in humanitarian operations are increasingly exposed, as well as acts of destruction and looting of their property,

Recalling that primary responsibility under international law for the security and protection of humanitarian personnel and United Nations and its associated personnel lies with the Government hosting a United Nations operation conducted under the Charter of the United Nations or its agreements with relevant organizations,

Urging all other parties involved in armed conflicts, in compliance with their obligations under the 1949

Geneva Conventions and the Additional Protocols thereto, to ensure the security and protection of all humanitarian personnel and United Nations and its associated personnel,

Expressing concern that the occurrence of attacks and threats against humanitarian personnel and United Nations and its associated personnel is a factor that increasingly restricts the ability of the Organization to provide assistance and protection to civilians in fulfilment of its mandate and Charter,

Recognizing the fundamental requirement that consideration be given to incorporating into all new and ongoing United Nations field operations appropriate modalities for the safety and security of humanitarian personnel and United Nations and its associated personnel,

Emphasizing the need to give further consideration to the safety and security of locally recruited humanitarian personnel and United Nations and its associated personnel, who count for the majority of casualties,

Welcoming the inclusion of attacks intentionally directed against personnel involved in a humanitarian assistance or peacekeeping mission in accordance with the Charter of the United Nations as a war crime in the Rome Statute of the International Criminal Court, adopted on 17 July 1998, and noting the role that the Court could play in bringing to justice those responsible for serious violations of international humanitarian law,

Commending the courage and commitment of those who take part in humanitarian operations, often at great personal risk,

Guided by the relevant provisions on protection contained in the Convention on the Privileges and Immunities of the United Nations, the Convention on the Privileges and Immunities of the Specialized Agencies, the Convention on the Safety of United Nations and Associated Personnel, the Fourth Geneva Convention of 12 August 1949 and Additional Protocols of 8 June 1977 and Protocol II to the Convention on Prohibitions or Restrictions on the Use of Certain Conventional Weapons Which May Be Deemed to Be Excessively Injurious or to Have Indiscriminate Effects of 10 October 1980,

1. *Urges* all States to take the necessary measures to ensure the full and effective implementation of the relevant principles and rules of international humanitarian law, as well as relevant provisions of human rights law related to the safety and security of humanitarian personnel and United Nations personnel;

2. *Also urges* all States to take the necessary measures to ensure the safety and security of humanitarian personnel and United Nations and its associated personnel and to respect and ensure respect for the inviolability of United Nations premises, which are essential to the continuation and successful implementation of United Nations operations;

3. *Calls upon* all Governments and parties in complex humanitarian emergencies, in particular in armed conflicts and in post-conflict situations, in countries where humanitarian personnel are operating, in conformity with the relevant provisions of international law and national laws, to cooperate fully with the United Nations and other humanitarian agencies and organizations and to ensure the safe and unhindered access of humanitarian personnel in order to allow them to perform efficiently their task of assisting the affected civilian population, including refugees and internally displaced persons;

4. *Strongly condemns* any act or failure to act which obstructs or prevents humanitarian personnel and United Nations personnel from discharging their humanitarian functions, or which entails their being subjected to threats, the use of force or physical attack frequently resulting in injury or death, and affirms the need to hold accountable those who commit such acts;

5. *Requests* the Secretary-General to take the necessary measures to ensure full respect for the human rights, privileges and immunities of United Nations and other personnel carrying out activities in fulfilment of the mandate of a United Nations operation and to continue to consider ways and means to strengthen the protection of United Nations and other personnel carrying out activities in fulfilment of the mandate of a United Nations operation, notably by seeking the inclusion, in negotiations of headquarters and other mission agreements concerning United Nations and its associated personnel, of the applicable conditions contained in the Convention on the Privileges and Immunities of the United Nations, the Convention on the Privileges and Immunities of the Specialized Agencies and the Convention on the Safety of United Nations and Associated Personnel;

6. *Urges* all States to ensure that any threat or act of violence committed against humanitarian personnel on their territory is fully investigated and to take all appropriate measures, in accordance with international law and national legislation, to ensure that the perpetrators of such acts are prosecuted;

7. *Also urges* all States to provide adequate and prompt information in the event of arrest or detention of humanitarian personnel or United Nations personnel, to afford them the necessary medical assistance and to allow independent medical teams to visit and examine the health of those detained, and further urges all States to take the necessary measures to ensure the speedy release of United Nations and other personnel carrying out activities in fulfilment of the mandate of a United Nations operation who have been arrested or detained in violation of their immunity, in accordance with the relevant conventions referred to in the present resolution and applicable international humanitarian law;

8. *Calls upon* all States to consider signing and ratifying the Rome Statute of the International Criminal Court;

9. *Reaffirms* the obligation of all humanitarian personnel and United Nations and its associated personnel to observe and respect the national laws of the country in which they are operating, in accordance with international law and the Charter of the United Nations;

10. *Requests* the Secretary-General to take the necessary measures, falling within his responsibilities, to ensure that security matters are an integral part of the planning for existing and newly mandated United Nations operations and that such precautions extend to all United Nations and its associated personnel;

11. *Also requests* the Secretary-General, in consultation with United Nations agencies and other relevant international organizations, to compile examples of best practices, obstacles encountered and lessons

learned with regard to the safety and security of humanitarian personnel and United Nations personnel, to ensure that this information is widely disseminated in the field and to include in his comprehensive report to it at its fifty-fifth session on the subject of the present resolution detailed information in this regard;

12. *Further requests* the Secretary-General to take the necessary measures to ensure that United Nations and other personnel carrying out activities in fulfilment of the mandate of a United Nations operation are properly informed about the conditions under which they are called to operate, including relevant customs and traditions in the host country, and the standards that they are required to meet, including those contained in relevant domestic and international law, and that adequate training in security, human rights and humanitarian law, as well as stress counselling, are provided so as to enhance their security and effectiveness in accomplishing their functions, and reaffirms the necessity for all other humanitarian organizations to provide their personnel with similar support;

13. *Encourages* all States to contribute to the Trust Fund for Security of personnel of the United Nations system, and welcomes the inclusion of security components in the consolidated appeals to advance the cause of inter-agency security coordination;

14. *Recognizes* the need to strengthen the Office of United Nations Security Coordinator and the need for a full-time Security Coordinator to enable the Office to enhance its capacity in the discharge of its duties, in consultation with the Office for the Coordination of Humanitarian Affairs of the Secretariat and appropriate agencies within the Inter-Agency Standing Committee;

15. *Encourages* all States to become parties to and respect fully their obligations under the relevant international instruments, including the Convention on the Safety of United Nations and Associated Personnel;

16. *Welcomes* the addendum on the safety and security of United Nations and humanitarian personnel to the Secretary-General's report on strengthening of the coordination of emergency humanitarian assistance of the United Nations, and requests the Secretary-General to submit to it at its fifty-fifth session a comprehensive report on the safety and security situation of humanitarian personnel and protection of United Nations personnel, including an account of the measures taken by Governments and the United Nations in prevention of and in response to all individual security incidents involving the arrest, hostage-taking or death of United Nations and its associated personnel;

17. *Recognizes* the urgency to consult further to address the recommendations contained in the above-mentioned addendum, to that end requests the Secretary-General to submit by May 2000, for its consideration during its fifty-fourth session, a report containing a detailed analysis and recommendations addressing the scope of legal protection under the 1994 Convention on the Safety of United Nations and Associated Personnel, and in this regard takes note of the report of the Secretary-General on protection of civilians in armed conflicts and the range of views expressed during the open debates of the Security Council on 12 February 1999 and 16 and 17 September 1999, on protection of civilians in armed conflicts.

Personnel practices

Pursuant to a request made by ACABQ in its first report on the proposed programme budget for the 2000-2001 biennium [A/54/7], the Secretary-General submitted to the General Assembly a note on personnel practices and policies [A/C.5/54/21]. ACABQ noted that, although the Secretary-General was frequently assisted by decisions of the Assembly in carrying forward the human resources management reform effort, in certain cases problems were encountered in implementing the Assembly resolutions, which had affected his efforts to move forward.

The Secretary-General observed that the Secretariat would require more experience with implementation of the most recent resolution on human resources management (resolution 53/221, p. 1324), before presenting an analysis. With respect to the major problems identified by ACABQ, the Secretariat was working on simplification of the complex personnel regulations, development of a new recruitment and placement procedure and mechanisms to expedite the mobility of staff.

The Secretary-General's intention was to review the implementation of resolution 53/221 and, in the light of that experience, submit his views in detail to the Assembly at its fifty-fifth (2000) session within the context of his comprehensive report on human resources management reform.

Delegation of authority

In response to a request contained in General Assembly resolution 53/221 (see p. 1324), the Secretary-General submitted, through ACABQ, a note containing a compendium of all administrative circulars issued on the delegation of authority in the context of human resources management [A/54/257]. The note focused on the delegation of the authority exercised by the Secretary-General as chief administrative officer of the Organization under Article 97 of the Charter.

Commenting on the Secretary-General's note in its report on human resources management [A/54/450], ACABQ stated that procedures should be in place to monitor the implementation of the delegation of authority throughout the Organization and that there was an urgent need to carry out an exercise to simplify and streamline the rules on delegation of authority.

Competitive examination

In response to General Assembly resolution 53/221 (see p. 1324), the Secretary-General transmitted a note [A/C.5/54/2] on the realignment of the competitive examinations for promotion to the Professional category of staff members from other categories (G to P) with the national competitive examinations, in particular regarding academic qualifications, equitable geographical distribution and equal treatment with regard to probationary appointments. The Secretary-General drew attention to the fundamental difference between the two examinations: the former was a promotion exercise and the latter a recruitment exercise. In response to earlier resolutions, the two had been brought into broad alignment in that the same examination was offered to all candidates and all needed to possess a university degree in the subject matter of the examination. However, as the objective of the external examination was recruitment, there was an upper age limit for candidates (32), while there was none for the G to P. On the other hand, G-to-P candidates had to possess five years of experience within the Organization.

Following the inclusion of the new element of "equitable geographical distribution" for the G-to-P examination in resolution 53/221, staff members expressed grave concern about the negative impact on career development if the application of that principle took effect. The Assistant Secretary-General for Human Resources Management had informed the staff that, although the examination would take place, the marking of the papers of candidates from over-represented countries would be subject to the outcome of a review of the issue by the Assembly at its fifty-fourth session.

The Secretary-General was particularly concerned about the potential for inequitable treatment of staff, which might not be consistent with the Charter. Any treatment of serving staff members based solely on nationality would be of questionable legality and very damaging to staff morale. In addition, it would be contrary to the Assembly's repeated requests to promote the career development of staff at all levels and the implementation of the new provision would deny specific staff members any possibility of promotion because of their nationality. Lastly, it would have a negative effect on the Secretary-General's efforts to increase the number of women in the Professional category since nearly two thirds of those sitting for and succeeding in the examination were women.

The Secretary-General requested the Assembly to reconsider the issue with a view to removing the concept of equitable geographical distribution as a factor for the alignment of the examinations.

In its October report on human resources management [A/54/450], ACABQ stated that the issue that needed to be addressed was whether the G-to-P examination was a promotion exercise or a means of recruitment. It noted the discrepancies in the initial Joint Inspection Unit (JIU) recommendation and Assembly resolutions 33/143 [YUN 1978, p. 988] and 35/210 [YUN 1980, p. 1164] related to the introduction of the examination. ACABQ recommended that the Assembly should decide whether the examination was a promotion or recruitment exercise, which in turn would determine how the necessity for equitable geographical distribution would be recognized. If the examination was determined to be a recruitment exercise, that would be a decision determining that there were two entirely separate and distinct categories of staff and career tracks and that there could be no internal movement between them. Under those circumstances, the Assembly might wish to consider discontinuing the G-to-P examination and limiting recruitment to the national competitive examination. If, on the other hand, the Assembly confirmed that the G-to-P examination was a promotion exercise, then other considerations would apply, primarily the question of equitable geographical distribution. ACABQ was of the view that JIU took that element into consideration when it limited the movement of staff through the G-to-P examination to 30 per cent of posts available at the P-1 and P-2 levels. In not considering equitable geographical distribution solely, the Organization could make full use of the capabilities and acquired knowledge and skills of its staff by encouraging career development, as well as fostering gender equality.

Staff College

The Economic and Social Council, by **decision 1999/271** of 28 July, noting the importance of specific training and upgrading of the skills of UN personnel, with a view to increasing the effectiveness of UN programme activities in the area of development and improving the implementation of follow-up action to major UN conferences, invited the General Assembly to discuss the activities of the United Nations Staff College (Turin, Italy) during its fifty-fourth session, with a view to further considering the question at its fifty-fifth (2000) session, on the basis of recommendations of the Secretary-General on the future status and operations of the College at the conclusion of its pilot phase in December 2000.

In October [A/54/481], the Secretary-General submitted to the Assembly a progress report by the Director of the College. He recalled that the rationale for the College, which was established in 1996 for an initial period of five years [YUN 1996, p. 1050] to train international civil servants throughout the UN system, was to strengthen collaboration within the system in areas that cut across traditional lines of organizational responsibility. The College, entrusted for implementation to the ILO International Training Centre in Turin, was conceived as a global network of training centres and academic and professional institutions. It collaborated closely with the United Nations University and the United Nations Institute for Training and Research. The main training areas to be covered were: international peace and security, human rights and humanitarian emergency management; economic and social development; coordination training; and management development and organizational change in the UN system.

Voluntarily funded by UN Member States and UN organizations, the College's total income was $4 million in 1998 and an estimated $7 million in 1999. The goal for 2000 was $10 million. In the three and a half years of its existence, 3,500 middle and senior UN staff participated in its programmes, with special attention paid to key positions of inter-agency concern in development support and related areas, such as resident coordinators and UN country teams. In October 1998, the College undertook a major review and needs analysis and developed a new future strategy for the design and implementation of training and learning activities, focusing on the change and reform process of the United Nations, especially at the field level. It redefined its strategic direction into four product areas: executive/learning forums on issues of global concern; learning and training workshops; expert services; and networking/clearing house providing specific support services.

The Secretary-General stated in his transmittal note that, pursuant to Economic and Social Council decision 1999/271 and taking into account the outcome of discussions in the Assembly, he intended, in consultation with ACC, to elaborate arrangements that would enable the Staff College to be placed on a more secure and stable footing, beyond the initial project phase, and to report thereon to the Assembly at its fifty-fifth session.

GENERAL ASSEMBLY ACTION

On 22 December [meeting 87], the General Assembly, on the recommendation of the Second (Economic and Financial) Committee [A/54/590], adopted **resolution 54/228** without vote [agenda item 102].

United Nations Staff College in Turin, Italy

The General Assembly,

Recalling the decision taken by the Secretary-General in January 1996 to establish, in Turin, Italy, the United Nations Staff College project for an initial period of five years,

Reaffirming the importance of a coordinated United Nations system-wide approach to research and to training based on an effective division of labour among the relevant institutions and bodies,

Noting, in this respect, the pertinent recommendations of the Joint Inspection Unit,

Taking note of Economic and Social Council decision 1999/271 of 28 July 1999,

1. *Takes note with appreciation* of the progress report submitted by the Director of the United Nations Staff College on the activities undertaken so far by the College, in particular those aimed at strengthening the performance of the United Nations in the areas of economic and social development and international peace and security and promoting a common United Nations management culture;

2. *Notes with appreciation* the relevant technical, logistic and administrative contributions provided by the International Training Centre of the International Labour Organization;

3. *Requests* the Secretary-General to consult with the Administrative Committee on Coordination and the relevant United Nations organizations and to submit to the General Assembly at its fifty-fifth session a report on the College, based on a full and independent evaluation of the implementation and the completion of the activities undertaken by the College, incorporating the College's corporate plan and programme of action, and including recommendations on the future status, funding and operations of the College after the conclusion of its pilot phase in December 2000.

General temporary assistance

ACABQ, in its first report on the proposed programme budget for the 2000-2001 biennium [A/54/7], indicated that general temporary assistance (GTA) should not be used to compensate for reductions in established posts and noted a number of instances where staff requirements of a continuing nature had been met or were proposed to be met through GTA rather than by requesting temporary or established posts. It requested the Secretary-General to provide information to the General Assembly on the disposition of resources for the specific GTA positions reflected in the proposed programme budget for the 2000-2001 biennium [A/54/6/Rev.1], with proposals for either temporary or established posts or an explanation of why continued use of GTA would be necessary.

In response to that request, the Secretary-General submitted to the Assembly a November note on the use of GTA for specific positions [A/C.5/54/33]. He stated that the GTA positions proposed for 2000-2001 ranged from relatively long-term arrangements to new proposals. Generally, such positions had been associated with some degree of uncertainty as to the need for them to be retained in the definite future, either at their existing level or pattern of grades and categories. The Secretary-General gave reasons for the requests for specific positions related to the Integrated Management Information System (IMIS), the United Nations Office of the Special Coordinator in the Occupied Territories, human rights, subregional development centres of the Economic Commission for Africa and the United Nations Office at Nairobi (UNON). With regard to the posts for IMIS and UNON, he stated that the issue would be addressed in the context of the proposed programme budget for the 2002-2003 biennium, based on the experience gained in 2000-2001.

In its sixth report on the proposed programme budget for 2000-2001 [A/54/7/Add.5], ACABQ noted that, in many cases, the requested GTA positions were not converted to temporary posts because of the need for flexibility. ACABQ was of the opinion that ample flexibility was afforded through the use of short-term or fixed-term contracts. It stressed that the Secretary-General should be guided solely by Assembly resolutions in the area of administrative and budgetary practice and pointed out that the funding of positions of a continuing nature under GTA was a departure from approved budgetary practice.

The Assembly, in **resolution 54/251, section XIII**, of 23 December, took note of the Secretary-General's note and endorsed the recommendations in ACABQ's sixth report.

UN Joint Staff Pension Fund

During the biennium ended 31 December 1999, the number of participants in the United Nations Joint Staff Pension Fund (UNJSPF) increased from 67,740 to 68,935, or by 1.8 per cent; the number of periodic benefits in award increased from 43,149 to 46,199, or by 7.1 per cent. On 31 December, the breakdown of the periodic benefits in award was as follows: 14,599 retirement benefits, 9,499 early retirement benefits, 6,501 deferred retirement benefits, 6,957 widows' and widowers' benefits, 7,796 children's benefits, 803 disability benefits and 44 secondary dependants' benefits. In the course of the year, 4,762 lump sum withdrawal and other settlements were paid.

With the withdrawal of the World Trade Organization, effective 31 December 1998, the number of member organizations of the Fund stood at 19.

The Fund was administered by the 33-member United Nations Joint Staff Pension Board, which did not meet in 1999 due to the biennialization of the work of the Fifth Committee. Instead, its Standing Committee met on its behalf (New York, 13-16 July) [A/54/206]. It discussed matters related to the administration and operation of the Fund, revised budget estimates for the 1998-1999 biennium, budget estimates for the 2000-2001 biennium and the authorization for contributions to the Emergency Fund for 2000-2001.

In October [A/54/7/Add.1], ACABQ, commenting on the Standing Committee's report, concurred with the recommendation for revised appropriations for administrative expenses amounting to $57,514,000 for the 1998-1999 biennium and $62,301,100 for the 2000-2001 biennium. It also agreed with the proposal to supplement the voluntary contributions to the Emergency Fund by an amount not exceeding $200,000 for 2000-2001.

GENERAL ASSEMBLY ACTION

On 23 December [meeting 88], on the recommendation of the Fifth Committee [A/54/691], the General Assembly adopted **resolution 54/251, section V**, without vote [agenda item 121].

Administrative expenses of the United Nations Joint Staff Pension Fund

The General Assembly . . .

Having considered the report of the Standing Committee of the United Nations Joint Staff Pension Board to the General Assembly and to the member organizations of the United Nations Joint Staff Pension Fund, and the related report of the Advisory Committee on Administrative and Budgetary Questions,

1. *Concurs* with the recommendations contained in the report of the Advisory Committee on Administrative and Budgetary Questions on the administrative expenses of the United Nations Joint Staff Pension Fund;

2. *Approves* expenses, chargeable directly to the Fund, totalling 62,301,100 dollars net for the biennium 2000-2001 and an increase of 3,282,800 dollars net for the biennium 1998-1999, for the administration of the Fund;

3. *Also approves* an addition to the regular budget of the United Nations for the biennium 2000-2001 in the amount of 401,400 dollars for the United Nations share of the cost of the administrative expenses of the central secretariat of the Fund, and an increase of 18,400 dollars in the estimates of income from rental of premises;

4. *Authorizes* the United Nations Joint Staff Pension Board to supplement the voluntary contributions to the Emergency Fund for the biennium 2000-2001 by an amount not exceeding 200,000 dollars;

. . .

Pension Fund investments

The market value of UNJSPF assets as at 31 December 1999 was $25.9 billion, an increase of $4 billion over the previous year. The total investment return for the year was 19.9 per cent, which, after adjusting for inflation, represented a "real" rate of return of 16.9 per cent. Investment income from interest and dividends amounted to $682 million. New funds that became available for investment (contributions plus investment income, less benefit payment and administrative expenses) totalled $1.1 billion. The Fund's investment income during the 1998-1999 biennium amounted to $2.2 billion, comprising $1.4 billion in interest and dividends and $839 million in net profit on sales of investments. After deductions of investment management costs amounting to $37 million, net investment income was $2.2 billion.

The Fund remained one of the most diversified pension funds in the world, with 56.8 per cent of its assets exposed to currencies other than the United States dollar, which was the Fund's unit of account.

Administration of justice

In its annual note to the General Assembly [A/INF/54/6], the United Nations Administrative Tribunal reported in December that it had delivered 32 judgements during 1999, its fiftieth anniversary year. They related to cases brought by staff against the Secretary-General or the executive heads of other UN bodies to resolve disputes involving terms of appointment and related issues and regulations.

The Tribunal met in plenary session in New York on 23 November and held two panel sessions (Geneva, 28 June–30 July; New York, 25 October–24 November).

Review of statute

In accordance with decision 53/430 [YUN 1998, p. 1329], the General Assembly had on the agenda of its fifty-fourth session an item on the review of the statute of the Administrative Tribunal, which was discussed in the Sixth (Legal) Committee. France, Ireland and the United Kingdom sponsored a draft resolution [A/C.6/54/L.13/Rev.1], which, among other things, proposed various amendments to the Tribunal's statute. The Committee took no action on the draft.

On 9 December, the Assembly decided to include in the provisional agenda of its fifty-fifth (2000) session the item "Review of the statute of the United Nations Administrative Tribunal" (**decision 54/429**).

Chapter IV

Institutional and administrative matters

A number of institutional and administrative matters were reviewed by the United Nations in 1999. The General Assembly held its fifty-fourth session and resumed fifty-third session. It also convened its twenty-first and twenty-second special sessions and resumed its tenth emergency special session. The Assembly granted observer status to the Customs Cooperation Council, the Black Sea Economic Cooperation Organization, the Community of Portuguese-speaking Countries and the International Union for the Conservation of Nature and Natural Resources. Three States were admitted to United Nations membership, bringing the total number to 188.

During the year, the Security Council held 124 formal meetings to deal with regional conflicts, peacekeeping operations and a wide variety of other issues related to the maintenance of international peace and security.

The Economic and Social Council held its 1999 organizational session in January, February, March, May and June and its substantive session in July, September, October, November and December. The Council adopted resolutions on a wide range of economic, social and related issues. It also granted consultative status in various categories to a number of non-governmental organizations (NGOs).

UN bodies concerned with administrative and coordination matters, including the Administrative Committee on Coordination, the Committee for Programme and Coordination and the Joint Inspection Unit, also continued their work in 1999.

The Committee on Conferences examined requests for changes to the calendar of conferences and meetings for 1999. It recommended measures to improve utilization of conference-servicing resources, including the introduction of new technologies, and to improve career prospects for language staff. The Economic and Social Council continued its review of timely and effective responses to the year 2000 computer challenge. Progress was reported in the implementation of the Integrated Management Information System, implementation of the Secretary-General's common services strategy and on the harmonization of UN informatic systems. Efforts to enhance the safety and security of UN staff at all duty stations were also reviewed.

Institutional machinery

Admission to UN membership

During 1999, three States—Kiribati, Nauru and Tonga—were admitted to the United Nations, bringing the total membership of the Organization to 188.

The Security Council recommended the Republic of Kiribati and the Republic of Nauru for membership on 25 June and the Kingdom of Tonga on 28 July. On 14 September, the General Assembly admitted them to UN membership.

Admission of Kiribati

On 25 June [meeting 4016], the Security Council, acting on the application of the Republic of Kiribati [A/53/426-S/1999/477], adopted **resolution 1248(1999)** without vote. The draft [S/1999/715] was prepared by the Committee on the Admission of New Members.

The Security Council,

Having examined the application of the Republic of Kiribati for admission to the United Nations,

Recommends to the General Assembly that the Republic of Kiribati be admitted to membership in the United Nations.

Following the adoption of the resolution, the Council President made statement **S/PRST/1999/18** congratulating Kiribati on behalf of the Council members, who had taken note of Kiribati's commitment to uphold the UN Charter and fulfil all of its obligations.

The General Assembly, in **resolution 54/1** of 14 September, admitted the Republic of Kiribati to membership in the United Nations.

Admission of Nauru

On 25 June, the Security Council considered the application of the Republic of Nauru for UN membership [A/53/927-S/1999/478]. China, speaking before the vote, stated that it was most essential that the purposes and principles of the Charter be fully complied with, that General Assembly resolution 2758(XXVI) [YUN 1971, p. 136] be implemented and that all new Members comply with Assembly resolutions. On the basis of that principled position, China could not support the Council's recommendation to the Assembly, but would not block it. It hoped that after joining the United Nations, Nauru would strictly comply with UN resolutions, including resolution 2758(XXVI).

On 25 June [meeting 4017], the Council adopted **resolution 1249(1999)** by vote (14-0-1). The draft [S/1999/716] was prepared by the Committee on the Admission of New Members.

The Security Council,

Having examined the application of the Republic of Nauru for admission to the United Nations,

Recommends to the General Assembly that the Republic of Nauru be admitted to membership in the United Nations.

VOTE ON RESOLUTION 1249(1999):

In favour: Argentina, Bahrain, Brazil, Canada, France, Gabon, Gambia, Malaysia, Namibia, Netherlands, Russian Federation, Slovenia, United Kingdom, United States.

Against: None.

Abstaining: China.

Following the adoption of the resolution, the Council President made statement **S/PRST/1999/19** congratulating Nauru on behalf of the Council members, who had taken note of Nauru's commitment to uphold the UN Charter and fulfil all of its obligations.

The Assembly, in **resolution 54/2** of 14 September, admitted the Republic of Nauru to UN membership.

Admission of the Kingdom of Tonga

On 28 July [meeting 4026], acting on the application of the Kingdom of Tonga [A/53/1022-S/1999/793], the Security Council adopted **resolution 1253(1999)** without vote. The draft [S/1999/823] was prepared by the Committee on the Admission of New Members.

The Security Council,

Having examined the application of the Kingdom of Tonga for admission to the United Nations,

Recommends to the General Assembly that the Kingdom of Tonga be admitted to membership in the United Nations.

Following the adoption of the resolution, the Council President made statement **S/PRST/1999/23** congratulating Tonga on behalf of the Council members, who had taken note of Tonga's commitment to uphold the UN Charter and fulfil all of its obligations.

The General Assembly, in **resolution 54/3** of 14 September, admitted the Kingdom of Tonga to UN membership.

General Assembly

The General Assembly met throughout 1999; it resumed and concluded its fifty-third session and held the major part of its fifty-fourth session. The fifty-third session was resumed in plenary meetings on 18 February, 23 and 24 March, 7 and 23 April, 24 and 25 May, 8, 23 and 29 June, 12 and 28 July and 2 and 13 September. The fifty-fourth session opened on 14 September and continued until its suspension on 23 December.

The Assembly also held its twenty-first special session on the review and appraisal of the implementation of the Programme of Action of the International Conference on Population and Development from 30 June to 2 July (see p. 1005); its twenty-second special session to review and appraise the implementation of the Barbados Programme of Action for the Sustainable Development of Small Island Developing States on 27 and 28 September (see p. 771); and resumed the tenth emergency special session to discuss "Illegal Israeli actions in Occupied East Jerusalem and the rest of the Occupied Territory" from 5 to 9 February (see p. 402).

Organization of Assembly sessions

1999 sessions

On 17 September, by **decision 54/401**, the General Assembly, on the recommendation of the General Committee [A/54/250 & Corr.1], adopted a number of provisions concerning the organization of the fifty-fourth session.

The Committee's recommendations concerned rationalization of the Assembly's work; closing date of the session; schedule of meetings; general debate; explanations of vote, right of reply, points of order and length of statements; resolutions; documentation; questions related to the programme budget; observances and commemorative meetings; special conferences; and meetings of subsidiary organs. The Committee made observations and proposals on the organization of future Assembly sessions and recommendations concerning the agenda.

On 7 April, the Assembly, in **resolution 53/224**, decided that the fifty-third session should close on Monday, 13 September, and that the fifty-fourth session should open on Tuesday, 14 September.

By **decision 54/401** of 11 October, the Assembly decided to hold the commemoration of the tenth anniversary of the Convention on the Rights of the Child in the morning of Thursday, 11 November (see p. 579).

The Assembly authorized a number of bodies to meet during its fifty-fourth session: the Executive Board of the United Nations Development

Programme (UNDP)/United Nations Population Fund (UNFPA) and the Committee on Relations with the Host Country (**decision 54/403 A** of 14 September); the Committee on the Exercise of the Inalienable Rights of the Palestinian People and the Working Group on the Financing of the United Nations Relief and Works Agency for Palestine Refugees in the Near East (**decision 54/403 B** of 17 September); the Preparatory Committee for the Twenty-fourth Special Session of the General Assembly (**decision 54/403 C** of 20 September); and the Committee on Information (**decision 54/403 D** of the same date).

Credentials

The Credentials Committee, at its first meeting on 15 October [A/54/475], had before it a memorandum from the Secretary-General indicating that, as at 14 October, 133 Member States had submitted the formal credentials of their representatives. The Legal Counsel stated that information concerning representatives of other Member States whose formal credentials had not yet been received would be reported on later by the Secretary-General.

The Committee also examined the credentials of Afghanistan, from which it had received two separate sets of credentials: a communication signed by Burhanuddin Rabbani, "President of the Islamic State of Afghanistan", presenting a delegation whose head was identified as the "Vice-Minister for Foreign Affairs"; and the other signed by Mullah Mohammad Rabbani, "President of the Acting Council of the Islamic Emirate of Afghanistan", presenting a delegation whose head was identified as the "Deputy Foreign Minister". The Committee deferred a decision on those credentials on the understanding that the current representatives accredited to the United Nations would continue to participate in the work of the Assembly.

The Committee adopted a resolution accepting the credentials received and recommended to the Assembly a draft resolution for adoption. On 25 October, the Assembly, by **resolution 54/6 A**, approved the report of the Credentials Committee.

At its second meeting on 3 December [A/54/475/Add.1], the Committee considered a memorandum from the Secretary-General of 2 December, which was updated by the Assistant Secretary-General for Legal Affairs, indicating that formal credentials had been received from an additional 20 Member States. Information concerning representatives of 33 other Member States had been communicated also.

The Committee adopted a resolution accepting the credentials received and recommended to the Assembly a draft resolution for adoption. On 9 December, the Assembly, by **resolution 54/6 B**, approved the second report of the Credentials Committee.

Agenda

During its resumed fifty-third session, the General Assembly took a number of actions relating to its agenda, which were listed in **decision 53/402 B**: it included an additional item on observer status for the Customs Cooperation Council in the Assembly (18 February); reopened consideration of the items on human rights questions (23 March) and on the report of the Economic and Social Council (7 April); included an additional sub-item on the confirmation of the appointment of the UNDP Administrator (23 April); reopened consideration of the election of judges of the International Criminal Tribunal for Rwanda (24 May); decided to consider the agenda items on the review of the efficiency of the administrative and financial functioning of the United Nations and on human resources management in order to consider the request contained in the Secretary-General's letter to the Assembly President [A/53/1001] (23 June); included an additional item on the financing of the United Nations Interim Administration Mission in Kosovo and reopened consideration of the item on implementation of the outcome of the World Summit for Social Development to consider the request contained in the letter addressed to the Assembly President from the Chairman of the Preparatory Committee for the Special Session of the General Assembly on the Implementation of the Outcome of the World Summit for Social Development and Further Initiatives [A/53/1015] (12 July); and decided to consider the sub-item on appointment of members of the Advisory Committee on Administrative and Budgetary Questions (ACABQ) so as to consider the Secretary-General's note [A/53/101/Add.1] and the item on the scale of assessments for the apportionment of the expenses of the United Nations in plenary to consider the letter from the Chairman of the Committee on Contributions to the Assembly President [A/53/1046] (2 September).

On 13 September, the Assembly decided to include in the draft agenda of the fifty-fourth session the following items: armed aggression against the Democratic Republic of the Congo (**decision 53/488**); appointment of the Under-Secretary-General for Internal Oversight Services (**decision 53/489**); question of the Comorian island of Mayotte (**decision 53/490**); revitalization of the work of the General Assembly (**deci-**

sion 53/491); restructuring and revitalization of the United Nations in the economic, social and related fields (**decision 53/492**); question of Cyprus (**decision 53/493**); improving the financial situation of the United Nations (**decision 53/494**); financing of the United Nations Operation in Mozambique (**decision 53/495**); and report of the Secretary-General on the activities of the Office of Internal Oversight Services (**decision 53/496**).

On 17 September, by **decision 54/402 A**, the Assembly, on the recommendation of the General Committee [A/54/250 & Corr.1], adopted the agenda [A/54/251] and the allocation of agenda items for the fifty-fourth session to the plenary or appropriate Main Committee [A/54/252 & Corr.1]. It deferred consideration of the item on the question of the Malagasy islands of Glorieuses, Juan de Nova, Europa and Bassas da India and included it in the provisional agenda of its fifty-fifth (2000) session.

On 11 October, by the same decision, the Assembly, on the recommendation of the General Committee [A/54/250/Add.1], included an additional item on its agenda, observer status for the Community of Portuguese-speaking Countries in the Assembly, and an additional sub-item on relocation of South Africa to the group of Member States set out in paragraph 3 *(c)* of Assembly resolution 43/232 (see p. 62). At the same meeting, the Assembly, recalling its decision to allocate consideration of the sub-item on operational activities for development of the UN system to the Second (Economic and Financial) Committee, decided to consider only the topic of follow-up to the World Summit for Children directly in plenary.

On 1 November, the Assembly, by the same decision, included an additional item on financing of the United Nations Mission in Sierra Leone.

On 6 December, the Assembly, also by the same decision, on the recommendation of the General Committee [A/54/250/Add.2], included an additional item on international recognition of the Day of Vesak and, on the Secretary-General's proposal, included an additional item on financing of the United Nations Transitional Administration in East Timor and reopened consideration of the sub-item on election of five members of the International Court of Justice.

The Assembly, on 9 December, deferred consideration of the item entitled "Implementation of the resolutions of the United Nations" and included it in the provisional agenda of its fifty-fifth session (**decision 54/427**).

On 23 December, the Assembly decided to retain 71 items for consideration during its resumed fifty-fourth session in 2000 (**decision 54/465**).

Second, Third and Fifth Committees

The General Assembly, by **decision 54/452** of 22 December, approved the biennial programme of work of the Second Committee for 2000-2001.

On 17 December, by **decision 54/437**, the Assembly approved the organization of work of the Third (Social, Humanitarian and Cultural) Committee and its 2000-2001 programme of work.

On 23 December, the Assembly, by **decision 54/463**, approved the biennial programme of work of the Fifth (Administrative and Budgetary) Committee for 2000-2001.

Security Council

The Security Council held 124 formal meetings in 1999, adopted 65 resolutions and issued 34 presidential statements. It considered 42 agenda items (see APPENDIX IV). In September [A/54/398], the Secretary-General, in accordance with Article 12, paragraph 2, of the Charter of the United Nations and with the consent of the Council, notified the General Assembly of 35 matters relative to the maintenance of international peace and security that the Council had discussed since his previous annual notification [YUN 1998, p. 1333] and listed 36 matters that the Council had not discussed since then. On 25 October, the Assembly, by **decision 54/410**, took note of the Secretary-General's note.

By **decision 54/409** of 21 October, the Assembly took note of the report of the Security Council for the period 16 June 1998 to 15 June 1999 [A/54/2].

Documentation

Working methods and procedures

The Security Council President, in a January note on the work of the sanctions committees [S/1999/92], issued a set of practical proposals for improving their work, agreed to by all Council members. In a February note [S/1999/165], he stated that all Council members should be allowed to participate fully in the preparation of Council resolutions and statements of the President. Contributions by members of groups of friends and other similar arrangements were welcome and sufficient time should be allowed for consultation among all Council members and their consideration of the drafts prior to action by the Council.

In December [S/1999/1291], the President reported that the Council had agreed that every effort should be made to determine which matters, including situations involving specific countries, could usefully be considered in public meetings of the Council, in particular in the early stage in its consideration of a subject. The President should make draft resolutions and presidential statements available to non-Council members as soon as they were introduced within informal consultations of the whole. Briefings of non-Council members by the presidency should cover elements presented by the President to the press, and should take place shortly after informal consultations of the whole. The Council President should make available to non-Council members copies of statements provided to the media following informal consultations, as well as briefing notes on peacekeeping field operations distributed to Council members.

The Council also agreed, in an effort to advance the resolution of a matter under consideration, to use a range of meeting options. The President also set out the formats for meetings to be held in public and private.

Membership

The General Assembly continued to examine the issue of expanding the membership of the Security Council, and received the report [A/53/47] of its Open-ended Working Group on the Question of Equitable Representation on and Increase in the Membership of the Security Council and Other Matters related to the Security Council, established by Assembly resolution 48/26 [YUN 1993, p. 212] (see p. 1278).

On 13 September, the Assembly, by **decision 53/487**, took note of the Working Group's report and decided that it should continue its work and report before the end of the Assembly's fifty-fourth session.

Economic and Social Council

In 1999, the Economic and Social Council held its organizational session on 20 January and on 2, 3 and 5 February, a resumed organizational session on 25 March, 6 and 7 May and 23 June and a special high-level meeting with the Bretton Woods institutions (the World Bank Group and the International Monetary Fund) on 29 April, all in New York. The Council held its substantive session on 23 June in New York and from 5 to 30 July in Geneva. The resumed substantive session was held in New York on 16 September, 26 October, 15 November and 16 December.

On 20 January and 2 February, the Council elected five members to its Bureau—the President for 1999 and four Vice-Presidents (see APPENDIX III). On 20 January, it adopted the agenda of its organizational session [E/1999/2 & Add.1]. On 2 February, by **decision 1999/201**, it approved the provisional agenda for the 1999 substantive session. By **decision 1999/211** of 25 March, it approved the working arrangements for the substantive session.

On 23 June, the Council adopted the agenda of its 1999 substantive session [E/1999/100 & Add.1] and approved the programme of work of the session [E/1999/L.16]. On 7 July, it approved requests by NGOs to be heard [E/1999/95 & Add.1].

(For agenda lists, see APPENDIX IV.)

Sessions and segments

During 1999, the Economic and Social Council adopted 67 resolutions and 100 decisions. By **decision 1999/204** of 2 February, the Council decided that: the informal meeting of the Council to consider work carried out by the UN system on basic indicators measuring progress on implementation and follow-up to major UN conferences and summits should be held in New York on 10 and 11 May; and the 1999 session of the Committee on NGOs should be held in New York from 1 to 18 June. By **decision 1999/211** of 25 March, the Council decided that the high-level segment of its substantive session would be held from 5 to 7 July, the ceremony for the commemoration of the tenth anniversary of the Convention on the Rights of the Child should be held on 8 July, the operational activities segment should be held from 8 to 13 July, the humanitarian affairs segment from 13 to 15 July, the coordination segment from 16 to 20 July, the general segment from 21 to 28 July, and 30 July should be devoted to the adoption of proposals and the conclusion of the session.

The 1999 work of the Council was summarized in its report to the Assembly [A/54/3/Rev.1]. On 17 (**decision 54/438**), 22 (**decision 54/451**) and 23 (**decisions 54/461** and **54/464**) December, the Assembly took note of various chapters of that report.

2000 and 2001 sessions

On 29 July, by **decision 1999/280**, the Economic and Social Council approved the calendar of conferences and meetings for 2000 and 2001 in the economic, social and related fields [E/1999/L.18 & Add.1,2].

By **decision 1999/281** of 30 July, the Council decided on the following themes for its substantive session in 2000: the high-level segment would be devoted to "Development and international cooperation in the twenty-first century: the role of information technology in the context of a knowledge-based global economy"; the coordination segment would be devoted to "Assessment of the progress made within the United Nations system, through the conference reviews, in the promotion of an integrated and coordinated implementation of and follow-up to major United Nations conferences and summits in the economic, social and related fields"; and the sectoral theme would be "Coordinated implementation by the United Nations system of the Habitat Agenda".

By **decision 1999/291** of 26 October, the Council decided that the election of the President of the Council for the year 2000 would take place on 27 January.

Work programme

On 2 February, the Economic and Social Council considered its basic programme of work for 1999 and 2000 [E/1999/1]. By **decision 1999/202**, the Council took note of the list of questions for inclusion in the programme of work for 2000.

On 16 December, by **decision 1999/295**, the Council further postponed consideration of the Secretary-General's report on the ninth meeting of the Ad Hoc Group of Experts on International Cooperation in Tax Matters to its 2000 substantive session.

Restructuring issues

The Economic and Social Council continued consideration of General Assembly resolutions 50/227 [YUN 1996, p. 1249] and 52/12 B [YUN 1997, p. 1392] on further measures for the restructuring and revitalization of the United Nations in the economic, social and related fields. By **resolution 1999/1** of 2 February, the Council noted: the Secretary-General's report on restructuring and revitalization of the United Nations in the economic, social and related fields (see p. 1279); the joint exploratory review of cooperation between the United Nations and the Bretton Woods institutions (see p. 890); and the Secretariat's consolidated report on the outcomes of the functional commissions of the Council in 1998 (see p. 1279).

Coordination, monitoring and cooperation

Institutional mechanisms

ACC activities

During 1999, the Administrative Committee on Coordination (ACC) elaborated efforts to strengthen the dialogue between ACC and the central intergovernmental machinery, particularly the Economic and Social Council, as well as inter-agency coordination efforts to meet the challenges of the twenty-first century. In its annual overview report for 1999 [E/2000/53], ACC stated that, as the UN system entered a new century and addressed the challenges of globalization, the content and purpose of inter-agency coordination were taking on a new policy significance and a new, central place in the policy concerns and initiatives of the organizations of the system. ACC examined the interactions with the private sector and the UN system's institutional and programmatic capacity to respond to the challenges of the twenty-first century. ACC agreed that, in pursuing a "compact" or understanding with the private sector, the development dimension should be stressed and drawn particularly from the programmes of action agreed by the international community at the series of global conferences. It endorsed the common strands emerging from the retreat held in April 1999 and subsequent contributions from executive heads as guidance for further inter-agency work, including providing a common agenda for the future work of the system, addressing the mobilization of resources to overcome the major constraint to promoting the global agenda, and the need to build new and broader partnerships to achieve regional and global objectives.

Other issues receiving attention were follow-up to UN conferences and summits in the 1990s, peace and sustainable development in Africa and HIV/AIDS. ACC agreed to address a statement to the General Assembly's special session in 2000 entitled "Women 2000: gender equality, development and peace for the twenty-first century", which would present a compelling vision stressing the link between poverty reduction and gender issues (see p. 1075). ACC endorsed the conclusions of the first inter-agency meeting for the Africa region (Nairobi, Kenya, March) (see p. 849). It expressed strong support for the decisions of the Joint UN Programme on HIV/AIDS and its co-sponsors to intensify action in Africa, through the International Partnership against AIDS in Africa (see p. 1148).

ACC also discussed the functioning of the International Civil Service Commission (see p. 1319), UN staff security and safety (see p. 1336) and elements of its programme of work for 2000.

During the year, ACC held two regular sessions (Geneva, 9-10 April, and New York, 29-30 October). Its principal subsidiary bodies met as follows:

Organizational Committee (Geneva, 17-19 March, 12-13 April; New York, 1-2 and 4 October); Consultative Committee on Administrative Questions (Personnel and General Administrative Questions), ninetieth (Geneva, 6-9 April) and ninety-first (New York, 14-16 July) sessions; Consultative Committee on Administrative Questions (Financial and Budgetary Questions), eighty-ninth (Rome, 15-19 February) and ninetieth (New York, 30 August-3 September) sessions; Consultative Committee on Programme and Operational Questions, fourteenth (Geneva, 10-12 March) and fifteenth (New York, 21-24 September) sessions.

Bodies on specific subjects met as follows:

Subcommittee on Oceans and Coastal Areas, seventh session (Monaco, 8-12 February); Inter-Agency Committee on Women and Gender Equality, fourth session (New York, 23-26 February); Inter-Agency Committee on Sustainable Development, thirteenth (New York, 8-9 March) and fourteenth (Vienna, 9-10 September) meetings; Subcommittee on Nutrition, twenty-sixth session (Geneva, 12-15 April); Ad Hoc Inter-Agency Meeting on Security (Washington, D.C., 11-13 May); Joint United Nations Information Committee, twenty-fifth session (Vienna, 6-8 July); Subcommittee on Statistical Activities, thirty-third session (Madrid, 14-16 September); Subcommittee on Drug Control, seventh session (Paris, 15-17 September); Information Systems Coordination Committee, seventh session (New York, 15-17 September and 21 October); Subcommittee on Water Resources, twentieth session (Geneva, 4-8 October) .

Report for 1998

ACC's annual overview report for 1998 [E/1999/48] was considered on 11 June by the Committee for Programme and Coordination (CPC) [A/54/16]. CPC noted improvements in the report, stating that it was more comprehensive, analytical and focused on specific issues. It recommended that future reports should contain more information on levels of aid flows and provide details on follow-up action taken on past ACC decisions. It requested information on implementation by the UN system of Economic and Social Council legislative mandates, those mandates not implemented and the reasons why. The Committee supported the priority attention given to Africa by ACC and the latter's agreement that there should be no lessening of support for African development. Support for ACC's conclusions on poverty eradication was also expressed and CPC indicated that it was important for ACC to continue to deal with the issue of globalization and monitor the impact of the financial crisis and other negative consequences of globalization. CPC recommended that priority be given to follow-up on outcomes of UN conferences and summits, as well as assurance of adequate financial resources. The Committee took note of ACC's treatment of Article 50 of the Charter and strongly indicated that action was required to assist those countries affected by the impact of sanctions on third-party States. It supported ACC's attention to the safety and security of UN staff and encouraged universal ratification of the 1994 Convention on the Safety of United Nations and Associated Personnel, adopted by General Assembly resolution 49/59 [YUN 1994, p. 1289].

The Economic and Social Council, by **resolution 1999/57** of 30 July, took note of the ACC report.

Review of ACC

In an August note [A/54/288], the Secretary-General transmitted a Joint Inspection Unit (JIU) report on the review of ACC and its machinery. The review was conducted in the context of ongoing initiatives aimed at strengthening ACC's effectiveness and impact and improving its interaction with intergovernmental bodies.

JIU found that, as the only forum that brought together the executive heads of all UN organizations, recent initiatives in line with ACC's agreed guiding principles had brought a better sense of leadership and ownership among its members, and it should strive to remain relevant in a constantly evolving international environment.

JIU recommended that to enhance further the coherence of UN system-wide plans and activities, executive heads should reinforce the Secretary-General's leadership role as ACC Chairman, and the lead role of other executive heads and their respective organizations in their specific mandates and competencies. ACC should continue to demonstrate the relevance and impact of its work by addressing issues that lent themselves to system-wide scrutiny, developing policy-oriented and forward-looking agendas and ensuring that the outcomes of its meetings and those of its subsidiary bodies were more action-oriented. Executive heads should propose to the Economic and Social Council a new name for ACC that would better reflect the changes in its scope and functions.

JIU also made a number of recommendations regarding ACC machinery and interaction between ACC and intergovernmental bodies.

In a November note [A/54/288/Add.1], the Secretary-General transmitted his comments and those of ACC on the JIU report. In their general comments, ACC members welcomed the objectives of the report and its timeliness, in the context of UN reforms and ACC's own efforts for transformation and change to meet effectively the new challenges ahead. They said the report gave a balanced assessment of the evolution of the Committee and highlighted the new culture of consultation and cooperation within which ACC was currently operating.

The Secretary-General also transmitted the JIU report and the related comments on it to the Economic and Social Council [E/1999/123 & Add.1].

ECONOMIC AND SOCIAL COUNCIL ACTION

On 16 December [meeting 51], the Economic and Social Council adopted **resolution 1999/66** [draft: E/1999/L.61] without vote [agenda item 7 *(a)*].

Report of the Joint Inspection Unit on the review of the Administrative Committee on Coordination and its machinery

The Economic and Social Council,

Recalling General Assembly resolution 50/227 of 24 May 1996 on further measures for the restructuring and revitalization of the United Nations in the economic, social and related fields,

Recalling also Economic and Social Council resolution 1999/55 of 30 July 1999 on integrated and coordinated implementation of and follow-up to major United Nations conferences and summits,

1. *Takes note with appreciation* of the report of the Joint Inspection Unit on the review of the Administrative Committee on Coordination and its machinery and the comments thereon of the Secretary-General and the Administrative Committee on Coordination;

2. *Notes* the measures under way to enhance the functioning of the Committee and its contribution to greater unity of purpose and programme coherence and impact within the United Nations system, and to reinforce, to that end, secretarial support to the Committee, through the Office for Inter-Agency Affairs of the Department of Economic and Social Affairs of the Secretariat, and invites the Committee to continue to improve its capacity for promoting inter-agency cooperation and complementarities within the United Nations system;

3. *Welcomes in particular* the recent initiatives taken by the Committee, under the leadership of the Secretary-General, to strengthen its interactions with intergovernmental bodies, in particular the Economic and Social Council, and invites the Committee to consider ways in which its members, individually and collectively, can maximize their support to the Council in the exercise of its responsibilities for system-wide guidance and coordination;

4. *Reaffirms in particular its appreciation* for the efforts of the Committee and its standing machinery to assist the Council and the functional and regional commissions in their work, in particular in coordinating the follow-up to major United Nations conferences and summits, and encourages them and the United Nations system to pursue and deepen their efforts in this area;

5. *Invites* the Committee to consider ways in which its annual reports can contribute to this effort by bringing to the attention of the Council, in a timely manner, major developments in United Nations bodies and organizations of system-wide interest, as well as steps taken by the Committee and its subsidiary machinery to enhance system-wide effectiveness, in particular as a follow-up to recommendations and directives of the General Assembly and the Economic and Social Council;

6. *Takes note* of the decision adopted by the Committee at its second regular session of 1999 on United Nations staff security and safety, and requests all States and organizations of the United Nations system to extend their full support to its objectives;

7. *Invites* the Committee to give special attention, in its annual overview report for 1999, to progress being made towards system-wide coordinated management of information, including the role and contribution of its Information Systems Coordination Committee, pursuant to recommendation B1 contained in the report of the Joint Inspection Unit;

8. *Also invites* the Committee to continue to report on its deliberations concerning the recommendations of the Joint Inspection Unit in the context of its own reporting on its functioning and methods of work;

9. *Decides* to revert, in the context of its consideration of coordination questions, including annual overview reports of the Committee, to the follow-up to the report of the Joint Inspection Unit and the related comments of the Committee in the light of the outcome of further intergovernmental deliberations thereon, inter alia, by the governing bodies of the specialized agencies.

Programme coordination

The Committee for Programme and Coordination held an organizational meeting on 7 May and its thirty-ninth session from 7 June to 2 July, all in New York [A/54/16].

It considered the review of the efficiency of the administrative and financial functioning of the United Nations; programme performance for the 1996-1997 biennium; regulations and rules governing programme planning, the programme aspects of the budget, the monitoring of implementation and the methods of evaluation (see PART FIVE, Chapter II); the medium-term plan for 1998-2001; the proposed programme budget for 2000-2001; in-depth evaluation of the programme on disarmament and of the electoral assistance programme; a triennial review of the Department of Public Information; and the termination phase of the evaluation of peacekeeping operations. Coordination issues considered included ACC's annual report for 1998 (see p. 1349); the UN System-wide Special Initiative for the Implementation of the United Nations New Agenda for the Development of Africa in the 1990s (see p. 848); a JIU report on more coherence and enhanced oversight in the UN system [YUN 1998, p. 1257]; improvement of CPC's working methods and procedures; and the provisional agenda for its fortieth session.

ECONOMIC AND SOCIAL COUNCIL ACTION

On 30 July [meeting 46], the Economic and Social Council adopted **resolution 1999/57** [draft: E/1999/L.50] without vote [agenda item 7 *(a)*].

Report of the Committee for Programme and Coordination on the work of its thirty-ninth session

The Economic and Social Council,

Having considered the report of the Committee for Programme and Coordination on the work of its thirty-ninth session,

1. *Takes note* of the report of the Committee for Programme and Coordination on the work of its thirty-ninth session;

I. Improving the working methods and procedures of the Committee for Programme and Coordination

2. *Welcomes* the effort to improve the working methods and procedures of the Committee, and requests the Committee to take steps to ensure further improvement;

3. *Urges* the Committee, given the importance of its work in the areas of coordination, programming, planning and evaluation, to schedule its spring session so as to make its report available well in advance of the substantive session of the Economic and Social Council in order to allow the Council to devote adequate time to its consideration;

II. Programme planning

4. *Re-emphasizes* the importance of the planning, programming and coordination functions carried out by the Committee in accordance with its mandate and in the context of a continuing need for greater efficiency and effectiveness in the United Nations system;

5. *Reiterates* that the effectiveness of the instruments at the disposal of the Committee to fulfil its functions, inter alia, in-depth evaluations and triennial reviews of the implementation of its recommendations thereon, annual overview reports of the Administrative Committee on Coordination, programme budget mechanisms and medium-term plans, should continue to be improved;

6. *Invites* the specialized intergovernmental bodies, as well as the Economic and Social Council and the Main Committees of the General Assembly, to include in their programmes of work an agenda item on programme planning for the review of the proposed medium-term plan and its revisions;

III. Proposed programme budget for the biennium 2000-2001

7. *Notes* the improved format and the timely submission of the proposed programme budget for the biennium 2000-2001 to the Committee;

8. *Also notes* that the general level of resources was lower than indicated in the proposed budget outline;

9. *Further notes* a trend towards an increasing use of extrabudgetary funds for activities that should be funded under the regular budget;

IV. Annual overview report of the Administrative Committee on Coordination

10. *Takes note* of the annual overview report of the Administrative Committee on Coordination for 1998;

V. United Nations System-wide Special Initiative for the Implementation of the United Nations New Agenda for the Development of Africa in the 1990s

11. *Takes note* of the report of the Secretary-General and of the results achieved in the United Nations System-wide Special Initiative for the Implementation of the United Nations New Agenda for the Development of Africa in the 1990s;

12. *Invites* the Administrative Committee on Coordination to consider broadening the coverage of countries and clusters of priority areas to reflect the original commitment in the New Agenda;

13. *Notes* the contribution of the programmes, funds and organizations of the United Nations system and, in particular, the United Nations Conference on Trade and Development, to the follow-up to the New Agenda, and recommends that they continue their important role in assisting African countries in that regard;

14. *Welcomes* the closer collaboration between the Office of the Special Coordinator for Africa and the Least Developed Countries of the Department of Economic and Social Affairs of the Secretariat, the Economic Commission for Africa and the secretariat of the Special Initiative, and requests the Secretary-General to ensure that those entities work closely on the harmonization of the various initiatives on Africa, and to enhance the linkages and common elements among them;

VI. Report of the Joint Inspection Unit

15. *Concurs* with the recommendation of the Committee for Programme and Coordination that the Secretary-General should expedite the comments by the Administrative Committee on Coordination for due consideration of the reports of the Joint Inspection Unit by the Committee for Programme and Coordination and take concrete steps to ensure the full implementation of the recommendations contained in the reports of the Joint Inspection Unit as approved by the General Assembly.

Joint Inspection Unit

The Joint Inspection Unit, in its thirtieth annual report to the General Assembly [A/54/34], gave an overview of its activities from 1 July 1997 to 31 December 1998, pursuant to its decision [YUN 1998, p. 1336] to revert to a January-December reporting cycle. The report examined measures to further enhance JIU's functioning and impact, and relations and cooperation with Member States, participating organizations and other oversight bodies. In terms of its staff, JIU concluded that serious consideration should be given in the future to more appropriate resources requirements to allow the Unit to better discharge its mandate. It said that implementation by the Secretariat of article 20.1 of its statute, which described the procedure for consideration of its budget, compromised its operational independence, and suggested that the Assembly might wish to clarify the provision of that article. JIU reported that no action had so far been taken on its proposal entitled "Towards a more effective system of follow-up on reports of the Joint Inspection Unit" [YUN 1997, p. 1488]. Its endorsement by the Assembly would give the Unit an important tool to enhance its functioning and better assess its impact. In August [A/54/223], the Secretary-General submitted a report on the implementation of JIU recommendations.

The Assembly, in **resolution 54/16** of 29 October, endorsed the system of follow-up to the Unit's reports (see p. 1277).

Other coordination matters

Follow-up to international conferences

Economic and Social Council consideration. In accordance with its decision 1998/290 [YUN 1998, p. 1339], the Economic and Social Council held a two-day informal meeting on 10 and 11 May on basic indicators for the integrated and coordinated implementation of and follow-up to the major UN conferences and summits. It considered an April report of the Secretary-General [E/1999/11], containing a critical review of the development of indicators in the context of conference follow-up. According to the report, accurate, timely and unbiased information was crucial to sound policy decisions, particularly in the context of conference follow-up. Objective assessments of the achievement of goals were possible only if benchmark data and reliable indicators were available. At the international level, the coordination of data collection suffered from inconsistencies between data disseminated, as well as in definitions and methodologies. However, the major problems were the serious gaps in the international databases. There was an enormous mismatch between the demand for information, which had increased as a result of global conferences, and the ability of most countries to supply the required information.

To correct the situation, the Secretary-General proposed improving partnerships at the international level and strengthening statistical capacity at the national level. Coordination of data collection at the international level and the development of concepts and methods would address problems related to inconsistencies, as well as a common development indicator platform on the Internet. Coordination was also necessary to focus the information demands placed on countries. In terms of strengthening national capacity, the report recommended the formation of a high-level working group consisting of major donor agencies and the UN Department of Economic and Social Affairs to coordinate data-collection and statistical capacity-building programmes in countries, as well as a targeted international programme to build national capacity in the areas of censuses and sample surveys.

The Council President, in a June summary of the informal meeting [E/1999/77], stated that the main issues raised in the debate centred on the importance of indicators, strengthening national statistical capacity, coordination at the international level, developing a core set of common indicators, means of implementation, and the Council's role. The Council stressed that national capacity-building should be done at all stages of the information process and called for a collaborative effort by the UN system, including the World Bank and the International Monetary Fund (IMF), as well as the Organisation for Economic Cooperation and Development. There was a need to establish effective coordination mechanisms among all information-producing units at the national level, strengthen the status and independence of statistical offices, intensify the national dialogue between producers and users of information, establish clear priorities to address the problem of data gaps, improve data quality in terms of timeliness, reliability and relevance, and encourage regional or subregional collaborative networks to share experiences and develop common methodologies and practices, with the support of donors. International agencies should better coordinate their data requests to countries, avoid duplicative requests and share data collected. The Council could provide stronger guidance in that endeavour. However, the proposal for a high-level working group on coordination required further clarification. The common country assessment indicator was a good starting point for working towards a core set of indicators.

By **decision 1999/283** of 30 July, the Council took note of its President's summary of the informal meeting.

The Council also had before it a June report of the Secretary-General on integrated follow-up to major UN conferences and summits [E/1999/65], which examined developments related to cross-cutting conference themes, progress in the Council's coordination and management roles at the intergovernmental level, inter-agency coordination, integrating and coordinating conference implementation at the country level and evaluating integrated conference implementation. The report contained a number of recommendations for adoption by the Council.

In response to resolution 1998/44 [YUN 1998, p. 1337], the Council also considered a June report of the Secretary-General [E/1999/63] on possible modalities for a review by the Council in 2000 of progress within the UN system in promoting an integrated and coordinated implementation of major UN conferences and summits. The Secretary-General suggested that, since the Council had undertaken reviews of specific cross-cutting themes over the past five years, it should undertake, at its high-level segment in 2000, an overall review of progress on common and cross-cutting themes emerging from conferences. Moreover, there was a solid basis and effective avenues for better integrating efforts in guiding and coordinating system-wide efforts related to conference goals at national, regional, headquarters and intergovernmental levels. The Council should also review progress of major themes common to all conferences to enable it to further integrate the implementation of major conferences and summits within the UN system. It should also undertake in 2000 a review of conference implementation, as a special contribution to the Millennium Assembly, and decide on the scope and content of the review and the modalities for concluding it.

ECONOMIC AND SOCIAL COUNCIL ACTION

On 30 July [meeting 46], the Economic and Social Council adopted **resolution 1999/55** [draft: E/1999/L.57] without vote [agenda item 6].

Integrated and coordinated implementation of and follow-up to major United Nations conferences and summits

The Economic and Social Council,

Recalling its agreed conclusions 1995/1 of 28 July 1995, its resolutions 1996/36 of 26 July 1996, 1997/61 of 25 July 1997 and 1998/44 of 31 July 1998 and its decision 1998/290 of 31 July 1998,

Taking note of the reports of the Secretary-General on an integrated and coordinated implementation of and follow-up to major United Nations conferences and summits, on a critical review of the development of indicators in the context of conference follow-up and on the possible modalities of a review by the Economic and Social Council in 2000 of progress made within the United Nations system in promoting an integrated and coordinated implementation of and follow-up to major United Nations conferences and summits,

I. Ways to enhance an integrated and coordinated implementation of and follow-up to major United Nations conferences and summits

1. *Calls upon* Governments, at the national and international levels, to renew their efforts to implement the commitments they have undertaken and make more tangible progress towards the targets, goals and objectives set by major United Nations conferences and summits;

2. *Decides* to transmit to the General Assembly, as inputs for the five-year reviews of the Fourth World Conference on Women and of the World Summit for Social Development, the outcomes of the Council on *(a)* the role of employment and work in poverty eradication: the empowerment and advancement of women, *(b)* operational activities, in particular poverty eradication and capacity-building, and *(c)* coordination of implementation and coordinated follow-up by the United Nations system of initiatives on African development;

3. *Urges* its functional commissions and other relevant bodies of the United Nations system to enhance coordination and complementarity among the five-year reviews, and, to that effect, encourages the bureaux of the preparatory committees for the forthcoming five-year reviews of the Fourth World Conference on Women and of the World Summit for Social Development to consult with one another to avoid duplication and ensure cross-fertilization of ideas;

4. *Recommends* that the end-of-decade assessment of progress towards the goals of the World Conference on Education for All be taken into account in the five-year reviews of other conferences;

5. *Reaffirms* the importance of ensuring the policy guidance of the General Assembly and the coordination role of the Economic and Social Council in the follow-up to major United Nations conferences and summits, calls for further cooperation between the functional commissions of the Council and the rest of the United Nations system in order to complement major United Nations conferences and summits in a coherent way, and recalls in this context that the adoption of multi-year thematic programmes for the functional commissions responsible for follow-up to major conferences can be helpful;

6. *Encourages* the functional commissions, in their outcomes, to identify more clearly actions that require a coordinated United Nations system-wide response as well as to highlight recommendations specifically addressed to organizations of the United Nations system and to identify areas in which the Council could provide guidance to the programmes, funds and agencies regarding the decisions and recommendations of the functional commissions addressed to them;

7. *Invites* the regional commissions to strengthen further their active participation relating to the implementation at the regional level of the results of major United Nations conferences and summits and the five-year reviews;

8. *Welcomes* the efforts made by some of the governing bodies of the programmes, funds and agencies to address relevant aspects of themes from conferences to ensure greater coherence and complementarity in their work, including at the country level, and requests that further efforts be made in this regard and that the results of their deliberation be brought to the attention of the Council;

9. *Invites* concerned specialized agencies to advise the Council on how to improve the way in which the outcomes of the Council, together with proposed follow-up actions, can be brought to the attention of their governing bodies, in particular those concerning conference follow-up;

10. *Welcomes* the efforts of the Administrative Committee on Coordination and its standing machinery to assist the work of the Council and the functional and regional commissions, in particular in coordinating the follow-up to major United Nations conferences and summits, and encourages them and the United Nations system to pursue and deepen their efforts in this area;

11. *Decides* to review the follow-up by the functional commissions of the decisions and recommendations of the Council addressed to them and invites the commissions to discuss follow-up to the outcomes of the Council under a specific agenda item at their sessions;

12. *Invites* the functional commissions, in accordance with their rules and regulations, to consider innovative modalities for further engaging non-governmental

organizations and other actors, as appropriate, in conference follow-up;

II. Basic indicators for the integrated and coordinated implementation of and follow-up to major United Nations conferences and summits at all levels

13. *Requests* the Secretariat, in particular the Statistics Division, to serve as a focal point to promote networking among national and international institutions in the area of statistics and indicators relating to the follow-up to major United Nations conferences and summits so as to facilitate the exchange of relevant information and metadata;

14. *Recognizes* the importance of relevant, accurate and timely statistics and indicators for evaluating the implementation of the outcomes of major United Nations conferences and summits at all levels;

15. *Also recognizes* the progress made in the development of basic indicators in developing countries which require international support for national efforts to build national statistical capacity in data collection, analysis and dissemination;

16. *Stresses* the need further to develop indicators on means of implementation to evaluate progress towards conference goals in creating an enabling environment for development;

17. *Welcomes* the efforts already undertaken by the various bodies of the United Nations system, including the Administrative Committee on Coordination, to harmonize and rationalize the basic indicators used in the context of follow-up to major United Nations conferences, and encourages them to continue their efforts in order to lessen the burden on Member States;

18. *Invites* the Statistical Commission, with the assistance of the Statistics Division and in close cooperation with other relevant bodies of the United Nations system, including the Administrative Committee on Coordination, and, as appropriate, other relevant international organizations, to review, with a view to facilitating future consideration by the Council, the work undertaken in harmonizing and rationalizing basic indicators in the context of follow-up to major United Nations conferences and summits, taking fully into account the decisions taken in other functional and regional commissions and, in that process, to identify a limited number of common indicators from among those currently accepted and widely used by the States Members of the United Nations, in order to lessen the data provision burden on Member States, bearing in mind the work done so far in this area;

19. *Reaffirms* the important role that the functional commissions have to play in the integrated and coordinated follow-up and the evaluation of the implementation of the outcome of major United Nations conferences and summits;

20. *Urges* countries, United Nations programmes and funds, the Secretariat, bilateral funding agencies, the Bretton Woods institutions and regional funding agencies to work together closely in order to mobilize the required resources to support national statistical capacity-building in developing countries and coordinate their statistical capacity-building programmes;

21. *Requests* the Secretary-General to prepare a progress report on the implementation of this section of the present resolution for consideration by the Council at its substantive session of 2000;

III. Modalities for a review by the Council in 2000 of progress made in the promotion of an integrated and coordinated implementation of and follow-up to major United Nations conferences and summits

22. *Decides* to assess, at the coordination segment of its substantive session of 2000, the progress made within the United Nations system, through the conference reviews, in the promotion of an integrated and coordinated implementation of and follow-up to major United Nations conferences and summits in the economic, social and related fields as a possible contribution to the Millennium Assembly;

23. *Invites* the functional and regional commissions, programmes, funds, and specialized agencies, and encourages non-governmental organizations, to make substantive contributions to the review by the Council;

24. *Requests* the Secretary-General to prepare a report to support the review by the Council in collaboration with organizations of the United Nations system.

The UN and other organizations

Cooperation with organizations

Economic Cooperation Organization

In a September report [A/54/168], the Secretary-General described cooperation between the United Nations and the Economic Cooperation Organization (see p. 935). The General Assembly took action on the report by **resolution 54/100**.

Latin American Economic System

The Secretary-General submitted a report [A/53/420] on cooperation between the United Nations and the Latin American Economic System (see p. 947). The General Assembly took action thereon in **resolution 54/8**.

League of Arab States

In response to General Assembly resolution 53/8 [YUN 1998, p. 1340], the Secretary-General submitted a report on cooperation between the United Nations and the League of Arab States [A/54/180]. The report highlighted activities undertaken by the two organizations in areas of cooperation and stated that their secretariats continued to maintain close contact on matters of mutual concern. The report summarized the action taken by UN bodies and organizations in follow-up to previous joint meetings of the two organizations. The 1999 general meeting on cooperation between them was held in Vienna from 7 to 9 July. The meeting identified a number of areas to further consolidate and strengthen cooperation.

GENERAL ASSEMBLY ACTION

On 26 October [meeting 39], the General Assembly adopted **resolution 54/9** [draft: A/54/L.14 & Add.1] without vote [agenda item 26].

Cooperation between the United Nations and the League of Arab States

The General Assembly,

Recalling its previous resolutions on cooperation between the United Nations and the League of Arab States,

Having considered the report of the Secretary-General on cooperation between the United Nations and the League of Arab States,

Recalling article III of the Charter of the League of Arab States, which confers upon the Council of the League the task of deciding upon the means by which the League is to cooperate with the international bodies to be created in the future in order to guarantee security and peace and regulate economic and social relations,

Noting the desire of both organizations to consolidate, develop and enhance further the ties existing between them in the political, economic, social, humanitarian, cultural, technical and administrative fields,

Taking into account the report of the Secretary-General entitled "An Agenda for Peace", in particular section VII, concerning cooperation with regional arrangements and organizations, and the "Supplement to An Agenda for Peace",

Convinced of the need for more efficient and coordinated utilization of available economic and financial resources to promote common objectives of the two organizations,

Acknowledging the need for closer cooperation between the United Nations system and the League of Arab States and its specialized organizations in realizing the goals and objectives of the two organizations,

Welcoming the third meeting on cooperation between the United Nations and regional organizations, held on 28 and 29 July 1998, and the follow-up meeting held on 10 and 11 December 1998,

1. *Takes note with satisfaction* of the report of the Secretary-General;

2. *Commends* the continued efforts of the League of Arab States to promote multilateral cooperation among Arab States, and requests the United Nations system to continue to lend its support;

3. *Expresses its appreciation* to the Secretary-General for the follow-up action taken by him to implement the proposals adopted at the meetings between the representatives of the secretariats of the United Nations and other organizations of the United Nations system and the General Secretariat of the League of Arab States and its specialized organizations, including the latest general meeting, held in Vienna in 1999;

4. *Requests* the Secretariat of the United Nations and the General Secretariat of the League of Arab States, within their respective fields of competence, to intensify further their cooperation with a view to the realization of the purposes and principles embodied in the Charter of the United Nations, the strengthening of international peace and security, economic and social development, disarmament, decolonization, self-determination and the eradication of all forms of racism and racial discrimination;

5. *Requests* the Secretary-General to continue his efforts to strengthen cooperation and coordination between the United Nations and other organizations and agencies of the United Nations system and the League of Arab States and its specialized organizations in order to enhance their capacity to serve the mutual interests and objectives of the two organizations in the political, economic, social, humanitarian, cultural and administrative fields;

6. *Calls upon* the specialized agencies and other organizations and programmes of the United Nations system:

(*a*) To continue to cooperate with the Secretary-General and among themselves, as well as with the League of Arab States and its specialized organizations, in the follow-up of multilateral proposals aimed at strengthening and expanding cooperation in all fields between the United Nations system and the League of Arab States and its specialized organizations;

(*b*) To maintain and increase contacts and improve the mechanism of consultation with the counterpart programmes, organizations and agencies concerned regarding projects and programmes, in order to facilitate their implementation;

(*c*) To associate whenever possible with organizations and institutions of the League of Arab States in the execution and implementation of development projects in the Arab region;

(*d*) To inform the Secretary-General, not later than 14 July 2000, of the progress of their cooperation with the League of Arab States and its specialized organizations, in particular the follow-up action taken on the multilateral and bilateral proposals adopted at the previous meetings between the two organizations;

7. *Also calls upon* the specialized agencies and other organizations and programmes of the United Nations system to intensify cooperation with the League of Arab States and its specialized organizations in the priority sectors of energy, rural development, desertification and green belts, training and vocational training, technology, environment and information and documentation;

8. *Requests* the Secretary-General of the United Nations, in cooperation with the Secretary-General of the League of Arab States, to encourage periodic consultation between representatives of the Secretariat of the United Nations and of the General Secretariat of the League of Arab States to review and strengthen coordination mechanisms with a view to accelerating implementation of, and follow-up action on, multilateral projects, proposals and recommendations adopted at the meetings between the two organizations;

9. *Recommends* that the United Nations and other organizations of the United Nations system should utilize, insofar as possible, Arab institutions and technical expertise in projects undertaken in the Arab region;

10. *Reaffirms* that, in order to enhance cooperation and for the purpose of review and appraisal of progress, a general meeting between the United Nations system and the League of Arab States should take place once every two years, and inter-agency sectoral meetings should also be organized once every two years on areas of priority and wide importance in the development of the Arab States, on the basis of agreement between the counterpart programmes of the United

Nations system and the League of Arab States and its specialized organizations;

11. *Emphasizes* the importance of holding the next general meeting on cooperation between the representatives of the secretariats of organizations of the United Nations system and of the General Secretariat of the League of Arab States and its specialized organizations during 2001;

12. *Recommends* that a sectoral meeting entitled "Youth and Employment" should be held between the United Nations and the League of Arab States and their specialized organizations at the headquarters of the Economic and Social Commission for Western Asia in Beirut from 22 to 26 May 2000;

13. *Requests* the Secretary-General to submit to the General Assembly at its fifty-fifth session a report on the implementation of the present resolution;

14. *Decides* to include in the provisional agenda of its fifty-fifth session the item entitled "Cooperation between the United Nations and the League of Arab States".

International Organization of la Francophonie

In response to General Assembly resolution 52/2 [YUN 1997, p. 1491], the Secretary-General submitted a report [A/54/397] on cooperation between the United Nations and the International Organization of la Francophonie, formerly the Agency for Cultural and Technical Cooperation [YUN 1998, p. 1344]. The report highlighted activities relating to political cooperation, as well as cooperation in the economic, social and cultural fields with the programmes and funds of the United Nations and its specialized agencies.

At the biennial summit of la Francophonie (Moncton, New Brunswick, Canada, 3-5 September), the two organizations reviewed issues on their respective agendas.

The Secretary-General observed that cooperation between the two organizations embraced areas of common interest and was characterized by concern for complementarity and an awareness of their respective advantages.

GENERAL ASSEMBLY ACTION

On 15 November [meeting 53], the General Assembly adopted **resolution 54/25** [draft: A/54/L.25] without vote [agenda item 25].

Cooperation between the United Nations and the International Organization of la Francophonie

The General Assembly,

Recalling its resolutions 33/18 of 10 November 1978, 50/3 of 16 October 1995 and 52/2 of 17 October 1997, as well as its decision 53/453 of 18 December 1998,

Recalling also the Articles of the Charter of the United Nations which encourage the promotion of the purposes and principles of the United Nations through regional cooperation,

Having considered the report of the Secretary-General on cooperation between the United Nations and the International Organization of la Francophonie,

Noting the desire of the two organizations to consolidate, develop and tighten the ties that exist between them in the political, economic, social and cultural fields,

Noting with satisfaction the substantial progress achieved in cooperation between the United Nations, its specialized agencies and other United Nations bodies and programmes and the International Organization of la Francophonie,

Convinced that strengthening cooperation between the United Nations and the International Organization of la Francophonie serves the purposes and principles of the United Nations,

Considering that the International Organization of la Francophonie brings together a considerable number of States Members of the United Nations, among which it promotes multilateral cooperation in areas of interest to the United Nations,

Appreciating the will shown by the heads of State and Government of countries that use French as a common language at their eighth summit session, held in Moncton, Canada, from 3 to 5 September 1999, to play an active part in resolving the main political and economic problems of the contemporary world and to consolidate the partnership with the United Nations to that end,

1. *Takes note* of the report of the Secretary-General on cooperation between the United Nations and the International Organization of la Francophonie

2. *Notes with satisfaction* the positive evolution and development of cooperation between the two organizations;

3. *Expresses its appreciation* to the Secretary-General of the United Nations and the Secretary-General of the International Organization of la Francophonie for their sustained efforts to strengthen cooperation and coordination between the United Nations and the International Organization of la Francophonie, thereby serving the mutual interests of the two organizations in the political, economic, social and cultural fields;

4. *Notes with satisfaction* that the International Organization of la Francophonie is participating more frequently in the work of the United Nations, to which it makes a valuable contribution;

5. *Welcomes* the involvement of the countries that use French as a common language, particularly through the International Organization of la Francophonie, in United Nations activities, including the preparation for, conduct of and follow-up to world conferences organized under United Nations auspices;

6. *Commends* the International Organization of la Francophonie for its efforts in relation to conflict prevention, management and resolution, promotion of human rights and strengthening of democracy and the rule of law, as well as its action in favour of the development of multilateral cooperation among countries with French as a common language, particularly in the areas of economic, social and cultural development, and the promotion of new information technologies, and requests United Nations bodies to give it their support;

7. *Commends also* the high-level meetings held periodically between the secretariats of the United Nations and the International Organization of la Francophonie, and advocates the participation of those secretariats in major meetings of the two organizations;

8. *Notes with satisfaction* the outcome of the meeting held in New York on 29 and 30 April 1999 between senior officials of the two organizations to exchange information and coordinate their action in certain of the organizations' member countries affected by crises;

9. *Expresses its appreciation* to the Secretary-General for including the International Organization of la Francophonie in the periodic meetings he holds with the heads of regional organizations, and invites him to continue to do so, taking into account the role played by the International Organization of la Francophonie in conflict prevention and support for democracy and the rule of law;

10. *Recommends* to the United Nations and the International Organization of la Francophonie that they should continue and intensify their consultations with a view to ensuring greater coordination in the areas of conflict prevention, peace-building, support for the rule of law and democracy and promotion of human rights;

11. *Notes with satisfaction* the strengthening of collaboration between the United Nations and the International Organization of la Francophonie in the area of electoral monitoring and assistance, and advocates the strengthening of cooperation between the two organizations in that area;

12. *Requests* the Secretary-General, acting in cooperation with the Secretary-General of the International Organization of la Francophonie, to encourage the holding of periodic meetings between representatives of the United Nations Secretariat and representatives of the secretariat of the International Organization of la Francophonie in order to promote the exchange of information, coordination of activities and identification of new areas of cooperation;

13. *Invites* the Secretary-General to take the necessary steps, in consultation with the Secretary-General of the International Organization of la Francophonie, to continue to promote cooperation between the two organizations;

14. *Invites* the specialized agencies, funds and programmes of the United Nations, as well as the regional commissions, including the Economic Commission for Africa, to collaborate to this end with the International Organization of la Francophonie by identifying new synergies in favour of development, in particular in the areas of poverty elimination, energy, sustainable development, education, training and the development of new information technologies;

15. *Requests* the Secretary-General to submit to the General Assembly at its fifty-sixth session a report on the implementation of the present resolution;

16. *Decides* to include in the provisional agenda of its fifty-sixth session the item entitled "Cooperation between the United Nations and the International Organization of la Francophonie".

Preparatory Commission for the Comprehensive Nuclear-Test-Ban Treaty Organization

By **resolution 54/65**, the General Assembly invited the Secretary-General to take appropriate steps with the Executive Secretary of the Preparatory Commission for the Comprehensive Nuclear-Test-Ban Treaty Organization to conclude an agreement to regulate the relationship between the organizations and to present the negotiated draft to the Assembly for approval (see p. 472).

Inter-Parliamentary Union

In response to General Assembly resolution 53/13 [YUN 1998, p. 1341], the Secretary-General submitted a September report on cooperation between the United Nations and the Inter-Parliamentary Union (IPU) [A/54/379], highlighting activities undertaken by the two organizations. The Secretary-General especially welcomed the progress in preparation for a conference of presiding officers of national parliaments organized by IPU in conjunction with the Millennium Assembly in September 2000. IPU signed a cooperation agreeement with the International Labour Organization in May and a Memorandum of Understanding with the Office of the United Nations High Commissioner for Human Rights in July. Other areas of cooperation included the promotion of peace and security and of democracy, and follow-up to major UN conferences. The United Nations received increasing support from IPU in providing technical assistance and advisory services to parliamentarians, sometimes in the context of peacekeeping operations. In 1999, IPU implemented projects or supported national parliaments in Fiji, Gabon, the Gambia, Kyrgyzstan, the Lao People's Democratic Republic and Yemen. UNDP provided funding and support to IPU projects to assist parliamentarians as part of its promotion of good governance.

GENERAL ASSEMBLY ACTION

On 27 October [meeting 41], the General Assembly adopted **resolution 54/12** [draft: A/54/L.9 & Add.1] without vote [agenda item 27].

Cooperation between the United Nations and the Inter-Parliamentary Union

The General Assembly,

Recalling its resolution 53/13 of 28 October 1998, in which it looked forward to continued close cooperation between the United Nations and the Inter-Parliamentary Union,

Having considered the report of the Secretary-General that describes the recent enhanced cooperation between the United Nations and the Inter-Parliamentary Union in pursuance of the 1996 cooperation Agreement concluded between the two organizations,

Taking note with appreciation of the resolutions adopted and activities carried out by the Inter-Parliamentary Union during the past year in support of United Nations actions in the fields of peace and security, economic and social development, international law and human rights, democracy, good governance and gender issues,

1. *Welcomes* the support provided to the United Nations by national parliaments through their world organization, the Inter-Parliamentary Union, and ex-

presses the wish that the cooperation between the two organizations will be further strengthened and enhanced in the third millennium;

2. *Also welcomes* the information contained in the report of the Secretary-General regarding preparations made with his support by the Inter-Parliamentary Union to hold a conference of presiding officers of national parliaments in conjunction with the fifty-fifth session of the General Assembly, designated the Millennium Assembly of the United Nations, in the General Assembly hall from 30 August to 1 September 2000;

3. *Requests* the Secretary-General to examine the possibilities of inviting the Inter-Parliamentary Union to report to the General Assembly at its fifty-fifth session (Millennium Assembly) on the outcome of the conference of presiding officers of national parliaments, and to report thereon before the end of the fifty-fourth session of the General Assembly;

4. *Also requests* the Secretary-General to submit a report to the General Assembly at its fifty-fifth session on the various aspects of cooperation between the United Nations and the Inter-Parliamentary Union;

5. *Decides* to include in the provisional agenda of its fifty-fifth session the item entitled "Cooperation between the United Nations and the Inter-Parliamentary Union".

By **decision 54/465** of 23 December, the Assembly decided that the item would remain for consideration during its resumed fifty-fourth (2000) session.

Organization of African Unity

The Secretary-General submitted an October report [A/54/484] on cooperation between the United Nations and the Organization of African Unity (see p. 190). The General Assembly took action on that report in **resolution 54/94**.

Organization of the Islamic Conference

In response to General Assembly resolution 53/16 [YUN 1998, p. 1342], the Secretary-General submitted a September report on cooperation between the United Nations and the Organization of the Islamic Conference (OIC) [A/54/308]. During the period under review, regular consultations were held and information exchanged between the secretariats of the United Nations and OIC with regard to the ongoing peacemaking efforts of the two organizations, particularly in Afghanistan, Somalia and Tajikistan.

The report summarized action taken by UN organizations and agencies serving as focal points for cooperation with OIC to follow up the recommendations of earlier meetings, and described cooperation between the two organizations in economic and social development.

GENERAL ASSEMBLY ACTION

On 25 October [meeting 38], the General Assembly adopted **resolution 54/7** [draft: A/54/L.12] without vote [agenda item 29].

Cooperation between the United Nations and the Organization of the Islamic Conference

The General Assembly,

Recalling its resolutions 37/4 of 22 October 1982, 38/4 of 28 October 1983, 39/7 of 8 November 1984, 40/4 of 25 October 1985, 41/3 of 16 October 1986, 42/4 of 15 October 1987, 43/2 of 17 October 1988, 44/8 of 18 October 1989, 45/9 of 25 October 1990, 46/13 of 28 October 1991, 47/18 of 23 November 1992, 48/24 of 24 November 1993, 49/15 of 15 November 1994, 50/17 of 20 November 1995, 51/18 of 14 November 1996, 52/4 of 22 October 1997 and 53/16 of 29 October 1998,

Recalling also its resolution 3369(XXX) of 10 October 1975, by which it decided to invite the Organization of the Islamic Conference to participate in the sessions and the work of the General Assembly and of its subsidiary organs in the capacity of observer,

Having considered the report of the Secretary-General on cooperation between the United Nations and the Organization of the Islamic Conference,

Taking into account the desire of both organizations to continue to cooperate closely in the political, economic, social, humanitarian, cultural and technical fields and in their common search for solutions to global problems, such as questions relating to international peace and security, disarmament, self-determination, decolonization, fundamental human rights and economic and technical development,

Recalling the Articles of the Charter of the United Nations that encourage the activities through regional cooperation for the promotion of the purposes and principles of the United Nations,

Noting the strengthening of cooperation between the United Nations, its funds and programmes and specialized agencies and the Organization of the Islamic Conference, its subsidiary organs and its specialized and affiliated institutions,

Noting also the encouraging progress made in the ten priority areas of cooperation between the two organizations, as well as in the identification of other areas of cooperation between them,

Convinced that the strengthening of cooperation between the United Nations and other organizations of the United Nations system and the Organization of the Islamic Conference and its organs and institutions contributes to the promotion of the purposes and principles of the United Nations,

Noting with appreciation the determination of both organizations to strengthen further the existing cooperation by developing specific proposals in the designated priority areas of cooperation, as well as in the political field,

1. *Takes note with satisfaction* of the report of the Secretary-General;

2. *Notes with satisfaction* the active participation of the Organization of the Islamic Conference in the work of the United Nations towards the realization of the purposes and principles embodied in the Charter of the United Nations;

3. *Requests* the United Nations and the Organization of the Islamic Conference to continue to cooperate in their common search for solutions to global problems, such as questions relating to international peace and security, disarmament, self-determination, decolonization, fundamental human rights, social and economic development and technical cooperation;

4. *Welcomes* the efforts of the United Nations and the Organization of the Islamic Conference to continue to strengthen cooperation between the two organizations in areas of common concern and to review the ways and means for enhancing the actual mechanisms of such cooperation;

5. *Welcomes with appreciation* the continuing cooperation between the United Nations and the Organization of the Islamic Conference in the field of peacemaking and preventive diplomacy, and takes note of the close cooperation between the two organizations in continuing the search for a peaceful and lasting solution to the conflict in Afghanistan;

6. *Welcomes* the efforts of the secretariats of the two organizations to strengthen information exchange, coordination and cooperation between them in areas of mutual interest in the political field and their ongoing consultations with a view to developing the modalities of such cooperation;

7. *Welcomes also* the periodic high-level meetings between the Secretary-General of the United Nations and the Secretary-General of the Organization of the Islamic Conference, as well as between senior secretariat officials of the two organizations, and encourages their participation in important meetings of the two organizations;

8. *Recommends* that, in accordance with its resolution 50/17, in order to enhance cooperation and for the purpose of review and appraisal of progress, a general meeting of representatives of the secretariats of the United Nations system and the Organization of the Islamic Conference should be held in 2000;

9. *Also recommends* that, in accordance with resolution 50/17, coordination meetings of focal points of the organizations and agencies of the United Nations system and the Organization of the Islamic Conference and its subsidiary organs and specialized and affiliated institutions should be held concurrently with the general meeting in 2000;

10. *Encourages* the specialized agencies and other organizations of the United Nations system to continue to expand their cooperation with the subsidiary organs and specialized and affiliated institutions of the Organization of the Islamic Conference, particularly by negotiating cooperation agreements, and invites them to multiply the contacts and meetings of the focal points for cooperation in priority areas of interest to the United Nations and the Organization of the Islamic Conference;

11. *Urges* the United Nations and other organizations of the United Nations system, especially the lead agencies, to provide increased technical and other forms of assistance to the Organization of the Islamic Conference and its subsidiary organs and specialized and affiliated institutions in order to enhance cooperation;

12. *Expresses its appreciation* to the Secretary-General for his continued efforts to strengthen cooperation and coordination between the United Nations and other organizations of the United Nations system and the Organization of the Islamic Conference and its subsidiary organs and specialized and affiliated institutions to serve the mutual interests of the two organizations in the political, economic, social and cultural fields;

13. *Requests* the Secretary-General to report to the General Assembly at its fifty-fifth session on the state of cooperation between the United Nations and the Organization of the Islamic Conference;

14. *Decides* to include in the provisional agenda of its fifty-fifth session the item entitled "Cooperation between the United Nations and the Organization of the Islamic Conference".

Organization for Security and Cooperation in Europe

The Secretary-General, as requested in resolution 53/85 [YUN 1998, p. 419], submitted a November report [A/54/537 & Corr.1] on cooperation between the United Nations and the Organization for Security and Cooperation in Europe (see p. 393). The General Assembly, by **resolution 54/117**, took action on the report.

Observer status

Customs Cooperation Council

By a 25 January letter to the General Assembly President [A/53/236], Chile requested the inclusion in the agenda of the Assembly's fifty-third (resumed) session of an item entitled "Observer status for the Customs Cooperation Council in the General Assembly". In an explanatory memorandum, it noted that the Council, also known as the World Customs Organization, was an independent intergovernmental organization, comprising 147 States, with headquarters in Brussels, Belgium. Its mission was to enhance the effectiveness and efficiency of customs administrations in their compliance with trade regulations, protection of society and revenue collection. It had already concluded eight memoranda of understanding with UN bodies. Observer status in the Assembly would enable both organizations to promote and strengthen the integration of their social, economic and law enforcement efforts and to establish joint policies, thus avoiding contradiction in their definition and duplication.

GENERAL ASSEMBLY ACTION

On 23 March [meeting 95], the General Assembly adopted **resolution 53/216** [draft: A/53/L.75] without vote [agenda item 169].

Observer status for the Customs Cooperation Council in the General Assembly

The General Assembly,

Wishing to promote cooperation between the United Nations and the Customs Cooperation Council,

1. *Decides* to invite the Customs Cooperation Council to participate in the sessions and the work of the General Assembly in the capacity of observer;

2. *Requests* the Secretary-General to take the necessary action to implement the present resolution.

Black Sea Economic Cooperation Organization

Greece, in a 9 August letter to the Secretary-General [A/54/192], requested the inclusion of a supplementary item in the agenda of the General Assembly's fifty-fourth session entitled "Granting of observer status in the General Assembly for the Black Sea Economic Cooperation Organization". It was a regional organization comprising eleven members: Albania, Armenia, Azerbaijan, Bulgaria, Georgia, Greece, the Republic of Moldova, Romania, the Russian Federation, Turkey and Ukraine. The basic purpose of the organization was to facilitate economic cooperation. The heads of State or Government, at their summit in Yalta, Ukraine (4-5 June 1998), expressed the conviction that obtaining observer status in the Assembly would greatly assist future cooperation and achieve more effective results.

GENERAL ASSEMBLY ACTION

On 8 October [meeting 31], the General Assembly adopted **resolution 54/5** [draft: A/54/L.8 & Add.1] without vote [agenda item 168].

Observer status for the Black Sea Economic Cooperation Organization in the General Assembly

The General Assembly,

Considering the importance of the Black Sea Economic Cooperation Organization, an intergovernmental organization dedicated to enhancing mutual respect and confidence, dialogue and cooperation, and economic collaboration among its member States,

Considering also the need, frequently noted by the United Nations, to promote and support every effort towards the development of bilateral and multilateral cooperation on the basis of international law,

Taking into account that the Charter of the Black Sea Economic Cooperation Organization stresses regional cooperation as part of the process of integration in Europe, based on human rights and fundamental freedoms, promoting social justice and stability,

Wishing to promote cooperation between the United Nations and the Black Sea Economic Cooperation Organization,

1. *Decides* to invite the Black Sea Economic Cooperation Organization to participate in the sessions and work of the General Assembly in the capacity of observer;

2. *Requests* the Secretary-General to take the necessary action to implement the present resolution.

Community of Portuguese-speaking Countries

By a 10 September letter to the Secretary-General [A/54/232], Angola, Brazil, Cape Verde, Guinea-Bissau, Mozambique, Portugal and Sao Tome and Principe requested the inclusion in the agenda of the General Assembly's fifty-fourth session of an item entitled "Observer status for the Community of Portuguese-speaking Countries in the General Assembly". They stated that the general objectives of the Community, created in 1996, were aimed at concerted action to assert their presence in international forums; cooperation, particularly in the economic, social, cultural, legal and scientific spheres; and implementation of projects to promote and disseminate the Portuguese language. It already had relations with the Food and Agriculture Organization of the United Nations (FAO), UNDP and the World Intellectual Property Organization (WIPO). Observer status would enhance cooperation between the two organizations, as well as with the various UN agencies.

GENERAL ASSEMBLY ACTION

On 26 October [meeting 39], the General Assembly adopted **resolution 54/10** [draft: A/54/L.15 & Add.1] without vote [agenda item 171].

Observer status for the Community of Portuguese-speaking Countries in the General Assembly

The General Assembly,

Bearing in mind that the purposes of the Community of Portuguese-speaking Countries, as enunciated in its constitutive declaration, are consistent with those of the United Nations,

Considering that, accordingly, it is mutually advantageous to provide for cooperation between the United Nations and the Community of Portuguese-speaking Countries,

Taking note of the desire of the Community of Portuguese-speaking Countries for the establishment of that cooperation,

1. *Decides* to invite the Community of Portuguese-speaking Countries to participate in the sessions and the work of the General Assembly in the capacity of observer;

2. *Requests* the Secretary-General to take the necessary action to implement the present resolution.

International Union for the Conservation of Nature and Natural Resources

On 17 December, the General Assembly resumed consideration of the request for the International Union for the Conservation of Nature and Natural Resources to be granted observer status in the General Assembly, submitted in 1998 by the Dominican Republic [YUN 1998, p. 1344].

GENERAL ASSEMBLY ACTION

On 17 December [meeting 84], the General Assembly adopted **resolution 54/195** [draft: A/54/L.7/Rev.2] without vote [agenda item 162].

Observer status for the International Union for the Conservation of Nature and Natural Resources in the General Assembly

The General Assembly,

Recalling its decision 49/426 of 9 December 1994,

Considering the importance of the International Union for the Conservation of Nature and Natural Resources,

Considering also the need, frequently noted by the United Nations, to promote and support every effort towards the conservation of nature,

Taking into account that the main objective of the International Union for the Conservation of Nature and Natural Resources is to encourage and assist the international community in conserving the integrity and diversity of nature,

Wishing to promote cooperation between the United Nations and the International Union for the Conservation of Nature and Natural Resources,

1. *Decides* to invite the International Union for the Conservation of Nature and Natural Resources to participate in the sessions and work of the General Assembly in the capacity of observer;

2. *Decides also* that, in future, any request by an organization for the granting of observer status in the General Assembly will be considered in plenary session after the consideration of the issue by the Sixth Committee of the General Assembly;

3. *Requests* the Secretary-General to take appropriate measures to bring to the attention of all the States Members of the General Committee and General Assembly the criteria and procedures laid down by the General Assembly whenever a request is made by an organization seeking observer status in the General Assembly;

4. *Also requests* the Secretary-General to take the necessary action to implement the present resolution.

Participation of organizations in UN work

Non-governmental organizations

In accordance with General Assembly decision 53/452 [YUN 1998, p. 1345], the Secretary-General submitted a September report [A/54/329] containing the views of Member States, members of specialized agencies, observers, and intergovernmental and non-governmental organizations on the Secretary-General's report on arrangements and practices for the interaction of NGOs in all activities of the UN system [YUN 1998, p. 1344].

The Secretary-General stated that nearly all Member States recognized the important contribution of NGOs to UN activities, especially in the conceptualization and implementation of decisions taken at major UN conferences. Some States suggested that more consideration should be given to legal issues governing the interaction of NGOs in UN activities, the financial implications of the relationship between the United Nations and NGOs, the participation of NGOs from developing countries and performance review. The specialized agencies said that the report was useful in underlining the commonalities and differences in practices within the UN system, in line with particular mandates, needs and NGO constituencies. Almost all NGOs welcomed the Secretary-General's report, but some were concerned that it created the perception that the increasing number of NGOs represented a threat to the system or a problem that needed to be dealt with. They stressed that the growth of NGOs was very positive for the UN system, providing an opportunity for making the United Nations a more relevant, vibrant and forceful institution. Others felt that the report did not sufficiently address the NGO role in shaping UN decisions and did not offer suggestions with respect to building support for NGOs among Governments and within the Secretariat. In their view, the report should have attempted to build that support and provide examples of NGO best practices at all levels. Views and recommendations were presented on specific issues, such as institutional arrangements, participation of NGOs from all regions and establishment of a trust fund, appointment of NGO liaison officers and focal points, access to information, participation in the work of the Assembly and access to UN Headquarters.

Committee on NGOs

The Economic and Social Council, by **decision 1999/205** of 2 February, approved the 1999 provisional agenda and documentation for the Committee on Non-Governmental Organizations.

On 7 May (**decision 1999/215**), the Council granted general consultative status to two NGOs, special consultative status to 80 NGOs and Roster status to three. It reclassified two NGOs from special to general consultative status. It approved the participation of two organizations of indigenous peoples not in consultative status with the Council in the open-ended inter-sessional Working Group of the Commission on Human Rights (**decision 1999/216**).

The Committee on NGOs, at its 1999 session (New York, 1-18 June) [E/1999/109], considered a number of applications for consultative status with the Council that had been deferred from its 1998 session, as well as new applications. It also considered 1988 and 1999 quadrennial reports submitted by NGOs in general and special consultative status with the Council. The Committee reviewed its methods of work relating to implementation of resolution 1996/31 [YUN 1996, p. 1360], including the process of accreditation of NGO representatives, and decision 1995/304 [YUN 1995, p. 1445] on arrangements for consultation with NGOs. It considered in particular a complaint filed by the Sudan regarding the accreditation of Christian Solidarity International (CSI), an NGO with Roster status, according to which "the commander of the terrorist separatist group of southern Sudan" was allowed to speak at the fifty-fifth session of the Commission on Human Rights in Geneva under the umbrella of CSI. During consideration of the complaint, a number of procedural issues were raised. The Committee recommended withdrawal of CSI's consultative status.

The Committee recommended one draft resolution and three draft decisions for adoption by the Council.

On 28 July (**decision 1999/266**), the Council granted general consultative status to four NGOs, special consultative status to 95 NGOs and Roster status to seven NGOs. It also authorized the Committee to hold a resumed session for two weeks to complete its work for 1999 (**decision 1999/267**).

On 30 July (**decision 1999/268**), the Council considered that the complaint filed by the Sudan presented concerns warranting a review of CSI's status, in accordance with resolution 1996/31, and decided that the Committee on NGOs should complete consideration of the matter as expeditiously as possible. To that end, CSI should be given until 31 August to submit a response to the Committee, which should make a recommendation to the Council at its resumed substantive session on 16 September. In the interim, CSI's consultative status should be temporarily suspended.

Also on 30 July, the Council took note of the Committee's report on its 1999 session (**decision 1999/269**).

At the second part of its 1999 session (7 September) [E/1999/109/Add.1], the Committee on NGOs further considered the Sudan's complaint and recommended that the Council adopt its previous recommendation that CSI's consultative status with the Council be withdrawn.

By **decision 1999/292** of 26 October, the Council so decided.

Requests for hearings

The Committee on NGOs met in New York on 18 June to hear requests from NGOs in consultative status to address the Economic and Social Council in connection with items on its agenda [E/1999/95]. The Committee recommended that three NGOs be heard by the Council at its 1999 substantive session and that, on an exceptional basis, three coalitions of NGOs that had concrete action-oriented proposals on the theme of the high-level segment of the Council be heard during that segment. Five additional requests for hearings by NGOs were received by the Bureau of the Council [E/1999/95/Add.1] after the Committee's meeting. The Bureau requested the Council to decide on those requests.

Strengthening the Secretariat NGO Section

The Committee on NGOs, at its 1999 session [E/1999/109], discussed strengthening the NGO Section of the Secretariat. It recognized that its efficient functioning was dependent upon the work of the Section.

ECONOMIC AND SOCIAL COUNCIL ACTION

On 28 July [meeting 44], the Economic and Social Council, on the recommendation of the Committee on NGOs [E/1999/109], adopted **resolution 1999/34** without vote [agenda item 12].

Strengthening the Non-Governmental Organizations Section of the Secretariat

The Economic and Social Council,

Recalling the provisions of its resolution 1996/31 of 25 July 1996 which update the procedure on the consultative relationship between the United Nations and non-governmental organizations,

Aware of the evolving relationship between the United Nations and the non-governmental organizations community resulting from the broader and more substantive involvement of non-governmental organizations with the Economic and Social Council and the United Nations at large, and appreciative of the breadth of expertise of non-governmental organizations and their unique capacity to support the work of the Council and its subsidiary bodies,

Appreciative of the need to encourage greater participation of non-governmental organizations from developing countries and countries with economies in transition in the work of the Council and its subsidiary bodies,

Mindful of the significant increase in the number of non-governmental organizations in consultative status that has taken place in recent years, and conscious of the fact that the number will continue to increase in the foreseeable future,

Mindful also of the demand that the expansion of the participation of non-governmental organizations has on the workload and resources of the Non-Governmental Organizations Section of the Department of Economic and Social Affairs of the Secretariat,

Recalling paragraph 68 of its resolution 1996/31 regarding the requirement for adequate Secretariat support to fulfil the mandate defined for the Committee on Non-Governmental Organizations with respect to carrying out the wider range of activities in which the enhanced involvement of non-governmental organizations is envisaged,

Reaffirming the vital role of the Non-Governmental Organizations Section, as described in the report of the Secretary-General on the work of the Non-Governmental Organizations Section of the Secretariat, in accordance with resolution 1996/31, and emphasizing the need to ensure that the Section is able to operate efficiently in carrying out its mandate as well as in initiating new activities, as required, at the optimal level of performance,

1. *Requests* the Secretary-General to submit a report to the General Assembly at the main part of its fifty-fourth session containing a comprehensive analysis of the organizational structure and technical, personnel and financial resources of the Non-Governmental Organizations Section, commensurate with the increased workload and the level of responsibility necessary to implement the mandate of the Secretariat, as contained in Council resolution 1996/31, parts X and XI;

2. *Urges* the Secretary-General, in view of the increased workload and responsibilities of the Section, as an interim measure, to provide to the Section the resources necessary, from within existing resources, without diverting resources from development programmes, to enable it to carry out its responsibilities efficiently, effectively and expeditiously.

Pursuant to the Council's request, the Secretary-General submitted a November report [A/54/520] that provided an analysis of the organizational structure and technical, personnel and financial resources of the NGO Section of the Secretariat.

The Secretary-General noted that, since his last report [YUN 1998, p. 1346], the number of NGOs granted consultative status with the Council had risen by 582, bringing the total to 1,938. That had led to an increase in the volume of the work of the NGO Section. The Committee on NGOs also had to extend the length of its resumed sessions to accommodate its increased workload, and the number of meetings originally forecast in the 2000-2001 programme budget had already doubled. The Secretary-General observed that CPC, at its thirty-ninth session (7 June–2 July) [A/54/16], had noted that the increasing workload and responsibilities had prevented the Section from carrying out its activities effectively and expeditiously and welcomed the proposal to strengthen it by allocating adequate resources in the 2000-2001 programme budget.

The report analysed the Section's activities, including key tasks, with an estimate of work-months required to perform them in the 2000-2001 biennium. It also described special projects undertaken in 1999, those proposed for 2000-2001 to increase the Section's effectiveness and the Section's outreach and liaison activities, and provided details of its organizational structure.

ACABQ, in its first report on the 2000-2001 programme budget [A/54/7], said that the Secretariat had not addressed the question of the total level of resources proposed for the 1998-1999 biennium and reiterated its view that the time had come to appraise the impact on the programme budget of the large increase in NGOs involved in UN work. It recommended that that information be included in future budgets both as to programmatic and financial aspects.

In a December report [A/54/657], ACABQ stated that the Secretariat had procedurally mishandled the matter, making full consideration of it at the fifty-fourth session impracticable. No proposals had been put forward to address the issues raised in the report, in particular with regard to the number and level of posts in the Section. ACABQ recommended that the Secretary-General address its concerns without further delay, together with the administrative and financial issues raised in his November report for consideration at the resumed fifty-fourth (2000) session.

Conferences and meetings

The Committee on Conferences held organizational meetings on 21 April and on 23 and 24 June and its substantive session from 30 August to 2 September [A/54/32]. It examined requests for additions and changes to the approved calendar of conferences and meetings for 1999 [A/AC.172/1999/2] and adopted a draft biennial plan for 2000-2001. It considered improved use of conference-servicing resources, reviewed the proposed programme budget for 2000-2001 for the Department of General Assembly Affairs and Conference Services, as well as the draft medium-term plan for the period 2000-2005 related to conference services, and discussed the participation of observers in its sessions.

The Committee approved requests from the Advisory Board on Disarmament Matters to convene its thirty-third session (20-22 January), the International Civil Service Commission to convene its forty-ninth session (12-30 April) and the expert group on the establishment of a nuclear-weapon-free zone in Central Asia to convene (April), all in Geneva rather than in New York; from the United Nations Conference on Trade and Development meeting of governmental experts of landlocked and transit developing countries, representatives of donor countries and financial development institutions to convene in New York (23-26 August) rather than in Geneva; and from the United Nations Environment Programme/High-level Committee of Ministers and Officials to convene in Bonn (1 November) rather than Nairobi. It recommended that the General Assembly authorize a number of bodies to meet in New York during the fifty-fourth session (see above, under "Organization of Assembly sessions").

The Committee recommended that the Assembly adopt the biennial calendar of conferences and meetings for 2000-2001 and authorize the Committee to make adjustments to that calendar as a result of Assembly action. It noted that the Secretariat had taken into account the arrangements referred to in Assembly resolution 53/208 A [YUN 1998, p. 1348] regarding the inclusion of Id al-Fitr and Id al-Adha in the list of official holidays and that no UN meetings would be held on those days, and concerning Orthodox Good Friday. The Committee also noted that the Secretariat had merged into one section the draft list of meetings of treaty bodies established under UN auspices, including the meetings of the Preparatory Commission for the Comprehensive Nuclear-Test-Ban Treaty Organization, and the draft calendar of conferences and meetings of the principal organs of the specialized agencies and the International Atomic Energy Agency. The Committee recommended that, when planning the calendar of conferences and meetings, every effort should be made to avoid simultaneous peak periods at the various duty stations.

Intergovernmental meetings

At the request of the host Governments of several intergovernmental conferences held in 1999, the main documents of those meetings were transmitted to the Secretary-General for circulation to the General Assembly, the Security Council or both, as follows:

Seventieth ordinary session of the Organization of African Unity (OAU) Council of Ministers (Algiers, Algeria, 8-10 July) [S/1999/829]; thirty-fifth session of the Assembly of Heads of State and Government of OAU (Algiers, 12-14 July) [A/54/424], fourth extraordinary session (Sirte, Libyan Arab Jamahiriya, 8-9 September) [A/54/621]; one hundred and first Inter-Parliamentary Conference (Brussels, 10-16 April) [A/54/126], one hundred and second Inter-Parliamentary Conference (Berlin, 10-16 October) [A/54/617]; Annual Coordination Meeting of the Ministers for Foreign Affairs of the Organization of the Islamic Conference (OIC) (New York, 1 October) [A/54/632-S/1999/1194]; twenty-sixth session of the Conference of Foreign Ministers of OIC (Ouagadougou, Burkino Faso, 28 June–1 July) [A/53/1044-S/1999/924]; Ministerial Council of the Gulf Cooperation Council, twenty-third special session (Abu Dhabi, United Arab Emirates, 4 March) [S/1999/236], seventieth session (Riyadh, Saudi Arabia, 14-15 March) [A/53/869-S/1999/308], seventy-first session (Jeddah, Saudi Arabia, 3 July) [A/53/1014-S/1999/761], seventy-second session (Jeddah, 10-11 September) [S/1999/974]; twentieth session of the Supreme Council of the Gulf Cooperation Council (Riyadh, 27-29 November) [A/54/649-S/1999/1216]; eighth summit of la Francophonie (Moncton, Canada, 3-5 September) [A/54/453]; Ministerial Meeting of the Coordinating Bureau of the Movement of Non-Aligned Countries (New York, 23 September) [A/54/469-S/1999/1063]; twenty-third annual meeting of Ministers for Foreign Affairs of the Group of 77 (New York, 24 September) [A/54/432]; and first Summit of Heads of State and Government of Latin America and the Caribbean and the European Union (Rio de Janeiro, Brazil, 28-29 June) [A/54/448].

Use of conference services

The Secretary-General submitted to the Committee on Conferences a July report on improved utilization of conference-servicing resources, including meeting statistics of UN organs for 1998 [A/AC.172/1999/3].

The Committee noted that the overall utilization factor for 1998 exceeded the benchmark of 80 per cent and those for Geneva and Vienna were 87 and 88 per cent, respectively. It noted with concern that the utilization factor for New York had dropped to 77 per cent and that only 56 per cent of bodies in the sample utilized 80 per cent or more of their available conference-servicing resources. The Committee requested its Chairperson to continue to consult with the chairpersons of those bodies that had consistently utilized less than the applicable benchmark figure (80 per cent) of their allocated resources for the past three years, and to make recommendations to achieve optimum use of conference-servicing resources. It noted the oral report on improved coordination of conference services and requested the Secretariat, when preparing the agenda for its next substantive session, to take into account the proposals regarding the inclusion and timing of the videoconference. It encouraged the Secretariat to continue the dialogue between Conferences Services and the secretariats of intergovernmental bodies and looked forward to the issuance of a revision of the relative administrative instruction with regard to conference-servicing responsibility to include the UN Offices at Vienna and Nairobi. The Committee encouraged expanded efforts towards a coordinated approach within Conference Services to provide services efficiently and effectively from all duty stations.

Impact of economy measures on conference services

The Secretary-General, as requested in resolution 53/208 B [YUN 1998, p. 1353], submitted a February report on the impact of economy measures on the delivery of mandated conference services [A/53/833]. The report showed that between the 1994-1995 and 1998-1999 bienniums, the net appropriated resources for conference services had decreased by $14,053,400. At the same time, some 203 posts had been abolished (55 in the Professional category and above and 148 in the General Service and Trades and Crafts categories).

In the light of that reduction, improvements in productivity resulting from investments in technology, adjustments in work flow management and priority setting, and a decline in the demand for services, particularly in the volume of material submitted for translation, allowed Conference Services to cope with the overall workload in 1996-1997, albeit at a certain cost in quality and timeliness. Efficiency gains were achieved through savings in overtime, keeping document print runs under tight control and the introduction of off-site reporting in the production of verbatim records using advanced technology.

However, some inadequacies remained. There was insufficient excess interpretation capacity to attend to meetings of regional groups and other major groupings of Member States, and Conference Services could no longer compensate for late submission of documents by using overtime work and abundant staff resources for rapid turnover. Although the recent extensive delays in the issuance of summary records had been largely corrected, almost all of those had to be translated contractually, making it harder to ensure consistency and quality. Verbatim records still became backlogged during peak periods. Issuance was thus delayed and simultaneous circulation in all languages could not be strictly implemented. Conference Services hoped to address those situations through further use of technology and adjustments to resource allocations.

By **decision 53/470** of 7 April, the General Assembly decided to transmit the Secretary-General's report to ACABQ for consideration in the context of the proposed 2000-2001 programme budget, taking into account the views of Member States in the Fifth Committee.

ACABQ, in its first report on the 2000-2001 programme budget [A/54/7], said that it did not appear that the programme budget had taken into account its observations concerning resource reductions for conference services in Geneva and Vienna.

Temporary assistance for meetings

ACABQ noted reductions in the 2000-2001 programme budget, relating to temporary assistance for meetings [A/54/7]. Those reductions reflected the impact of measures applied in the control of resources and capacity utilization, the expanded use of remote translation for meetings held away from Headquarters and anticipated savings resulting from the implementation of cost-saving measures, better planning of resources and control over the issuance of documentation. ACABQ, bearing in mind the level and quality of services to be provided, requested the Secretary-General to provide further justification to the General Assembly at its fifty-fourth session.

In response to that request, the Secretary-General submitted an October note on requirements in 2000-2001 for temporary assistance for meetings [A/C.5/54/19]. He said that the overall proposed decrease in temporary assistance amounted to $5,126,200 (New York, $2,110,400; Geneva, $1,832,700; and Vienna, $1,483,100). The estimated conference-servicing workloads for 2000-2001 projected a level of demand broadly equivalent to the servicing requirements in 1998-1999. He therefore proposed that the staffing of conference services at Headquarters, Geneva and Vienna, both permanent and temporary, be maintained through the next biennium at its current levels. Consequently, actual expenditure for temporary assistance for meetings in 1998-1999 was considered a sound basis to estimate requirements for 2000-2001.

The Secretary-General further pointed out that perceived problems in the delivery of Conference Services were being addressed through managerial efforts to enhance quality control and utilization of capacity, and some shortcomings had causes outside the responsibility of Conference Services. While increased levels of temporary assistance could help overcome those problems, it would have to be considered in relation to relevant provisions of Assembly resolutions and to concerns about cost-efficiency.

ACABQ, in its December report on the 2000-2001 programme budget [A/54/7/Add.5], said that the Secretary-General's note did not address the concerns raised in its earlier report (see above), nor did it reflect the specific problems faced by the Department of General Assembly Affairs and Conference Services with regard to the impact of resources on the effective delivery of services. It believed that the estimates of requirements for conference services should be based, in addition to past experience, on meetings scheduled in the calendar of conferences, conferences and meetings arising from new legislative mandates and meetings of regional and other major groupings.

Regional and other major groupings

In February [A/53/826], the Secretary-General, pursuant to resolution 53/208 A [YUN 1998, p. 1348], reported on the provision of interpretation services to meetings of regional and other major groupings of Member States. For the period July 1998 to January 1999, almost 100 per cent of requests for conference facilities were met, including 151 out of 169 requests for interpretation services, or 89 per cent.

By **decision 53/470** of 7 April, the General Assembly noted the Secretary-General's report.

In an August update [A/54/208], the Secretary-General reported, for the period February to June 1999, that the figure had increased to 96 per cent in Geneva, with New York meeting all of its 510 requests. The report also showed that over the past three years, the percentage of meetings held by regional and other major groupings provided with interpretation services had risen from 68 per cent to 83 per cent. The Secretary-General concluded that further improvements could be realized if bodies planned their work programmes well in advance and more flexibility was exercised by regional groupings in rescheduling meetings, which would increase the likelihood of interpretation services being made available to them.

The Committee on Conferences regretted that 17 per cent of the requests for interpretation services by regional and other major groupings of Member States had not been met. It urged intergovernmental bodies to spare no effort at the planning stage to take into account meetings of regional and other major groupings of Member States, to make provision for such meetings in their programmes of work and to notify Conference Services well in advance of any cancellations so that unutilized conference-servicing resources might be reassigned to meetings of regional and other major groupings of States.

Improving conference facilities at Nairobi

Pursuant to General Assembly resolution 52/214 A [YUN 1997, p. 1501], the Secretary-General reported in February on improved utilization of conference facilities at the UN Office at Nairobi (UNON) [A/53/827]. He stated that UNON had an efficient and up-to-date conference centre, which was constantly being modernized and upgraded. Interpretation services were provided whenever needed, even in the absence of a permanent interpretation capacity. However, the utilization of conference facilities at Nairobi could increase only if intergovernmental and expert bodies took the decision to meet there. In that regard, efforts were being made to attract to UNON meetings of treaty bodies and other environment-related bodies, as well as bodies that currently did not meet regularly or occasionally away from their established headquarters. In addition, the Secretariat would explore the possibility of establishing a permanent interpretation service at UNON, including the provision of remote interpretation services from permanent interpretation structures (see next page for details).

By **decision 53/470** of 7 April, the Assembly noted the Secretary-General's report.

In August [A/54/221], in a further elaboration of his February report, the Secretary-General indicated that the number of meetings generated in 1999 by the sessions of the Nairobi-based bodies—the Commission on Human Settlements and the Governing Council of the United Nations Environment Programme—was relatively low compared to 1997, 20 as opposed to 84. He estimated that some 300 meetings would have been held in Nairobi in 1999, with 280 comprising meetings of intergovernmental or expert groups. Of those meetings, 200 would have been provided with interpretation services in two or more languages. The total figure represented an increase of 108 per cent in the level of meeting activity compared to 1998 when 144 meetings were held there.

The Secretary-General concluded that, despite the increased activity, the meeting capacity in Nairobi remained underutilized to a considerable degree, and, given the current circumstances, it was unlikely that the utilization rate of conference facilities would increase dramatically. That led inevitably to a policy question as to whether the satisfactory utilization rate of a UN conference centre should be made contingent upon its use by non-UN entities.

The Secretary-General, in another August report [A/54/262], explored the possibility of establishing a permanent interpretation service in Nairobi. He said that, to establish such a service, 20 Professional posts would have to be provided, at a cost of $3.2 million per biennium. He concluded that the current programme of meetings in Nairobi did not justify the cost of establishing a permanent team, and the current practice of providing interpretation services by staff deployed from New York, Geneva and Vienna or by freelance staff was the most cost-effective.

The Committee on Conferences noted the Secretary-General's reports and urged the Secretariat to continue to encourage increased utilization of UNON conference facilities. It expressed concern at the low number of meetings held at UNON and encouraged all bodies concerned to make better use of those facilities. The Committee requested the Secretariat to prepare detailed proposals on the utilization of UNON conference facilities, including by non-UN entities, and a comprehensive report on the possible establishment of a permanent interpretation service at UNON, taking into account the Committee's views. It considered that holding its sessions in Nairobi or other duty stations could provide an excellent opportunity for further evaluation of the provision of conference services.

Documents control

The Committee on Conferences took note of a conference room paper on the late issuance of documentation, as well as the Secretariat's observation that, when all the documents were issued by the opening of the session, an organ was three times more likely to have a high utilization factor of conference services than to have one below the benchmark rating. The Committee recommended that the General Assembly reaffirm that if a report was submitted late, the reasons should be included in a footnote to the document. The Committee reviewed the provision of written meeting records to the Assembly's subsidiary organs and reiterated its request to them to consider the use of unedited verbatim transcripts of their proceedings. It took note of the very limited number of subsidiary organs that had resorted to the use of unedited transcripts.

UN web sites

The Secretary-General submitted a March report [A/AC.198/1999/6] on the continuous development, maintenance and enrichment of UN web sites, which contained recommendations addressing the issue of the equitable treatment of all official languages, with a view to achieving full parity among them on those web sites (see p. 550).

Interpretation and translation-related matters

Remote interpretation

The Secretary-General submitted a July report on the provision of interpretation services to other locations from permanent interpretation structures in New York, Geneva and Nairobi [A/54/176]. He noted that recent interest in remote simultaneous interpretation of intergovernmental meetings had been prompted by several factors, including the need to ascertain whether more cost-effective alternatives to current methods of work existed, the attempt to improve the utilization of conference centres in certain locations, the use of remote servicing techniques in related conference-servicing activities, including videoconferencing, and the advent of new low-cost communications links. However, experience and knowledge in the field were still limited and did not allow for estimations of its relative cost advantages. The United Nations had conducted an experiment in early 1999 on remote simultaneous interpretation, the results of which were very promising in some aspects but revealed deficiencies in others. The Secretary-General recommended that another experiment be conducted in early 2000, involving a full-scale intergovernmental meeting, with six languages.

The Committee on Conferences noted the Secretary-General's report and requested the Secretariat to refine further the cost considerations of remote interpretation, taking into account technological possibilities, as well as the cost benefits, including the relative cost advantages of the different conference centres likely to provide remote interpretation services.

Career development in language services

The Secretary-General, as requested in resolution 53/208 B [YUN 1998, p. 1353], reported in April on career development in language services [A/53/919], which provided an analysis of the current staffing table situation and grade structure. The analysis revealed that the promotion possibilities for language staff at the P-3 and P-4 levels varied according to their function and the size of the organizational unit to which they were assigned. While opportunities for reaching the P-5 level in language services also varied, they were, overall, limited. The Secretary-General therefore proposed a comprehensive review of post gradings in the context of the preparation of the 2002-2003 programme budget; further efforts to facilitate increased mobility of staff between functions and duty stations, including common examinations for English and French editors, translators and verbatim reporters in 2000; continued consultations on the modalities for a limited system of managed reassignment to duty stations away from Headquarters; promoting greater flexibility and coordination in the administration of staffing tables for language services among conference services in New York, Geneva and Vienna; and paying increased attention to career development in line with the Assembly's concerns for the enhancement of the quality of conference services.

In a May addendum [A/53/919/Add.1], the Secretary-General reported on the the post of reviser. He said that staffing tables of translation services at all conference centres provided for a revision capacity that allowed for the revision of translations effected by junior staff and the revision of important or sensitive material. Out of a total of 521 language posts in New York, Geneva, Vienna and Nairobi, 83 were senior reviser (P-5) and 232 reviser/self-revising translator (P-4) posts, or 60.4 per cent. No curtailment of the revision capacity was reflected in the proposed programme budget for 2000-2001 and not for the foreseeable future.

The Committee on Conferences noted the Secretary-General's report and expressed concern that the rate of self-revision had exceeded the established benchmark and was increasing at all duty stations. The Committee requested the Department of General Assembly Affairs and Conference Services to continue to utilize new technologies, such as computer-assisted translation, terminology databases and speech recognition, to enhance further the productivity of language staff. It recommended that efforts continue to ensure that training opportunities were available to all UN language staff and to improve quality control at all duty stations.

In another May addendum [A/53/919/Add.2], the Secretary-General, in reporting on the possibility of introducing a system of managed assignments as a means of reducing the excessive vacancy rates in language services at some duty stations (Vienna and most regional commissions), stated that direct assignment of newly recruited staff and calls for experienced staff at Headquarters to volunteer for assignments of several years in the field had not proved very effective in resolving that problem. However, radical measures, such as establishing a system of managed assignments, might not be well suited to the nature and the magnitude of the issue. He suggested making assignments away from Headquarters more attractive, through enhanced career prospects as one alternative.

The Committee on Conferences took note of the Secretary-General's report and asked him to finalize proposals on a system of managed assignments based on career incentives. Information should also be provided on the cost elements in the employment of local and international freelance staff. UNON should be included in any arrangement to address the problem.

Responding to that request, the Secretary-General reported in November [A/C.5/54/28] that, as from 1 January 2000, a managed assignment system based on incentives would be put in place to alleviate the vacancy problem of language services at the duty stations concerned. The system would involve measures to fill vacancies at the entry level. Information on all successful candidates having passed a competitive examination would be systematically sent to those duty stations, which would be given priority for the selection of candidates on the roster. Contracts of all new recruits would provide that staff members could be assigned to any duty station at the discretion of the Organization. In addition, rather than relying almost exclusively on volunteers, management would select individuals to fill vacancies at duty stations away from Headquarters. The report outlined the incentives to be put in place in connection with those assignments.

GENERAL ASSEMBLY ACTION

On 23 December [meeting 88], the General Assembly, on the recommendation of the Fifth Committee [A/54/690], adopted **resolution 54/248** without vote [agenda item 124].

Pattern of conferences

The General Assembly,

Recalling its relevant resolutions and decisions, including resolutions 40/243 of 18 December 1985, 43/222 A to E of 21 December 1988, 47/202 A to D of 22 December 1992, 48/222 A and B of 23 December 1993, 49/221 A to D of 23 December 1994, 50/11 of 2 November 1995, 50/206 A to F of 23 December 1995, 51/211 A to E of 18 December 1996 and 51/211 F of 15 September 1997, 52/23 of 25 November 1997, 52/214 of 22 December 1997 and 53/208 A to E of 18 December 1998 and decisions 38/401 of 23 September 1983 and 52/468 of 31 March 1998,

A

Calendar of conferences and meetings

Having considered the report of the Committee on Conferences,

1. *Notes with appreciation* the work of the Committee on Conferences, and takes note of its report, subject to the provisions of the present resolution;

2. *Approves* the draft biennial calendar of conferences and meetings for 2000-2001, as submitted by the Committee on Conferences, subject to the provisions of the present resolution;

3. *Authorizes* the Committee on Conferences to make adjustments to the calendar of conferences and meetings for 2000-2001 that may become necessary as a result of actions and decisions taken by the General Assembly at its fifty-fourth session;

4. *Requests* the Secretary-General to provide all the conference services required as a result of decisions taken by the General Assembly at its fifty-fourth session, taking into account, as necessary, the procedures established by the Assembly in its resolutions 41/213 of 19 December 1986 and 42/211 of 21 December 1987;

5. *Reaffirms* its decision that the headquarters rule shall be adhered to by all bodies, and decides that waivers to the headquarters rule shall be granted solely on the basis of the calendar of conferences and meetings of the United Nations recommended by the Committee on Conferences for adoption by the General Assembly;

6. *Notes with satisfaction* that the Secretariat took into account the arrangements referred to in paragraph 10 of General Assembly resolution 53/208 A with regard to the two holidays of Id al-Fitr, which falls on 8 January (to be observed on 7 January) and 27 December 2000, and Id al-Adha, which falls on 16 March 2000, when drafting the biennial calendar of conferences and meetings for 2000-2001;

7. *Also notes with satisfaction* that the Secretariat took into account the arrangements referred to in paragraph 11 of General Assembly resolution 53/208 A concerning Orthodox Good Friday (which fell on 9 April 1999), which falls on 28 April 2000 and 13 April 2001 in the calendar for the next biennium, and requests all intergovernmental bodies to observe this decision when planning their meetings;

8. *Requests* the Secretary-General, when planning the calendar of conferences and meetings, to make every effort to avoid simultaneous peak periods at the various duty stations;

9. *Reaffirms* the provisions established by the General Assembly in its resolution 50/11 regarding multilingualism;

10. *Notes* that the procedure proposed in paragraph 172 of the report of the Committee on Conferences precludes observers from participating fully in the work of the Committee;

11. *Invites* the Committee on Conferences to keep under review its procedure regarding the participation of observers;

B

Utilization of conference-servicing resources and facilities

Having considered the report of the Secretary-General on the provision of interpretation services to meetings of regional and other major groupings of Member

States, the report of the Secretary-General on the improved utilization of conference facilities at the United Nations Office at Nairobi, the report of the Secretary-General on the possibility of establishing a permanent interpretation service at the United Nations Office at Nairobi, the report of the Secretary-General on the impact of economy measures on the delivery of mandated conference services, the report of the Advisory Committee on Administrative and Budgetary Questions on these issues and the report of the Secretary-General on career development in language services,

1. *Notes with concern* the proposed reduction of resources for conference services for the biennium 2000-2001, and requests the Secretary-General to ensure that efficiency measures are carefully analysed to avoid any negative impact on conference services, in the light of the level and quality of services provided to Member States;

2. *Emphasizes* the importance of providing adequate conference-servicing resources to all United Nations conference centres;

3. *Notes with appreciation* that the overall utilization factor for 1998 exceeded the benchmark of 80 per cent, in particular at Geneva and Vienna;

4. *Encourages* the optimum utilization of conference services in New York, taking into full consideration issues of efficiency and effectiveness, including the limitations of small delegations;

5. *Emphasizes*, therefore, the need to ensure equal opportunity for all Member States to participate fully in meeting their obligations under the Charter of the United Nations, and in this connection urges intergovernmental bodies when adopting their programmes of work to avoid as much as possible, inter alia, the scheduling of simultaneous, parallel and/or late night meetings;

6. *Reiterates its request* to the Committee on Conferences to continue to consult with those bodies that consistently utilized less than the applicable benchmark figure of their allocated resources for the past three sessions, with a view to making appropriate recommendations in order to achieve the optimum utilization of conference-servicing resources;

7. *Requests* the Chairperson of the Committee on Conferences to transmit a letter to the chairpersons of all bodies that utilized less than the applicable benchmark figure (80 per cent) of their allocated conference resources in the previous year, informing them of the problem and drawing their attention to the significant loss of meeting time, with a view to encouraging appropriate action on their part so as to improve the utilization of conference-servicing resources;

8. *Notes* the importance of meetings of regional and other major groupings of Member States for the smooth functioning of sessional bodies, in view of the increased requests for meetings of regional and other major groups, and welcomes the fact that 83 per cent of the requests for interpretation services for such meetings were met, while 100 per cent of the requests for facilities only were met;

9. *Notes with concern* the difficulties experienced by some Member States owing to the lack of conference services for some meetings of regional and other major groupings of Member States;

10. *Regrets* that 17 per cent of the requests for interpretation services made by regional and other major groupings of Member States were not met, while recognizing that meetings of Charter and mandated bodies must be serviced as a priority;

11. *Decides* to include all necessary resources in the budget for the biennium 2000-2001 to provide interpretation services for meetings of regional and other major groupings of Member States upon request by those groupings, on an ad hoc basis, in accordance with established practice, and requests the Secretary-General to submit to the General Assembly at its fifty-fifth session, through the Committee on Conferences, a report on the implementation of this decision;

12. *Urges* intergovernmental bodies to spare no effort at the planning stage to take into account meetings of regional and other major groupings of Member States, to make provision for such meetings in their programme of work and to notify conference services, well in advance, of any cancellations so that unutilized conference-servicing resources may, to the extent possible, be reassigned to meetings of regional and other major groupings of States;

13. *Decides* that full interpretation services, in the six official languages, must be ensured for the meetings of intergovernmental bodies for the full duration of those meetings;

14. *Expresses concern* that the conference facilities at the United Nations Office at Nairobi are still underutilized, as recorded during the last reporting period;

15. *Reiterates its call* for better utilization of the conference facilities at Nairobi;

16. *Urges* all subsidiary bodies of the Governing Council of the United Nations Environment Programme and the Commission on Human Settlements, and encourages Member States, intergovernmental bodies and regional and other major groupings to increase their use of the conference facilities at Nairobi;

17. *Reiterates its request* to the Secretary-General to assist the aforementioned bodies in improving this situation, and requests the Secretary-General to report to the General Assembly at its fifty-fifth session, through the Committee on Conferences, on the actions taken to that end;

18. *Takes note with appreciation* of the decision of the Department of Economic and Social Affairs to hold the Fifth Expert Group Meeting on Financial Issues of Agenda 21 in December 1999 at the United Nations Office at Nairobi;

19. *Encourages* other departments, intergovernmental bodies and regional and other major groupings to follow the example set by the Department of Economic and Social Affairs;

20. *Also encourages* all United Nations bodies and expert groups not subject to the headquarters rule to hold some of their meetings at the United Nations Office at Nairobi;

21. *Reaffirms* the general principle established in the headquarters rule, and in particular, that all meetings related to environment and human settlements that are organized by the United Nations Environment Programme and the United Nations Centre for Human Settlements (Habitat), respectively, should be held at Nairobi, being the headquarters of the Programme and Habitat;

22. *Discourages strongly* any invitation for hosting meetings which would violate the headquarters rule, in particular for United Nations centres with a low utilization level;

23. *Requests* the Committee on Conferences to consider the possibility of holding its 2000 substantive session at the United Nations Office at Nairobi;

24. *Decides* to establish a permanent interpretation service at the United Nations Office at Nairobi no later than January 2001;

25. *Also decides* to strengthen the interpretation service at the United Nations Office at Vienna;

26. *Encourages* the Secretariat to continue further the active dialogue between conference services and the secretariats of intergovernmental bodies, with a view to improving the provision of conference services;

27. *Requests* the Secretary-General to ensure an increase in the utilization of the regional centres in future work programmes and to report thereon to the General Assembly at its fifty-fifth session;

28. *Reiterates its request* to the Secretary-General to update the administrative instruction of 8 May 1987 on guidelines for the preparation of host Government agreements falling under General Assembly resolution 40/243 of 18 December 1985;

29. *Notes with appreciation* the renovation of the Economic and Social Council Chamber with the voluntary contribution of a Member State;

C

Documentation and publication-related matters

1. *Reiterates its decision* that, if a report is submitted late to the conference services, the reasons therefor should be included in a footnote to the document;

2. *Requests* the Secretary-General to ensure that the texts of the resolutions adopted by the General Assembly are communicated to Member States within fifteen days after the close of the session;

3. *Also requests* the Secretary-General to ensure that the *Official Records* of resolutions adopted by the General Assembly include information on the adoption of the resolutions, such as voting records and sponsors, before the text of each resolution, in the six official languages of the Organization;

4. *Notes with deep concern* the low rate of compliance with the six-week rule for the issuance of documentation;

5. *Reiterates its request* to the Secretary-General to ensure that documentation is available in accordance with the six-week rule for the distribution of documents simultaneously in the six official languages of the General Assembly;

6. *Notes with deep concern* that the provisions of paragraphs 24 and 25 of section B of its resolution 52/214 and paragraphs 11 and 12 of its resolution 53/208 B are not being fully implemented;

7. *Reiterates its request* that the Secretary-General direct all departments to include, where appropriate, the following elements in reports originating in the Secretariat:

(*a*) A summary of the report;

(*b*) Consolidated conclusions, recommendations and other proposed actions;

(*c*) Relevant background information;

8. *Reiterates* that all documents submitted to legislative organs by the Secretariat and expert bodies for consideration and action should have conclusions and recommendations in bold print;

9. *Reiterates its request* to the Advisory Committee on Administrative and Budgetary Questions to submit its reports in accordance with paragraph 12 of General Assembly resolution 53/208 B;

10. *Recalls* its decision in paragraph 2 (*b*) of section II of its resolution 41/213, and emphasizes that, in future, proposed programme budgets should be considered by the General Assembly in fascicle form, together with recommendations on them by the Committee for Programme and Coordination and the Advisory Committee on Administrative and Budgetary Questions, and that the programme budgets should be issued in their final form after approval by the Assembly with the changes to the resource level annexed to the approved programme budget;

11. *Notes with concern* the decline in the number of documents submitted to conference services in time for processing before the beginning of a session, and requests the Secretary-General to take urgent remedial measures to rectify this alarming situation, including the introduction of a system of responsibility and accountability;

12. *Requests* the Secretary-General to publish, prior to the fifty-fifth session of the General Assembly, updated versions of the Financial Regulations and Rules of the United Nations and the Regulations and Rules Governing Programme Planning, the Programme Aspects of the Budget, the Monitoring of Implementation and the Methods of Evaluation in the six official languages of the Organization;

13. *Also requests* the Secretary-General to publish the Staff Regulations and Rules of the United Nations in the six official languages of the Organization when their consolidation is completed;

14. *Urges* intergovernmental bodies, when feasible, to become more actively involved in rationalizing their meeting schedules in order to ensure the timely distribution of all related documentation, and requests the Secretary-General to submit proposals based on the reviews, through the Committee on Conferences, to the General Assembly at its fifty-fifth session;

D

Translation- and interpretation-related matters

Having considered the report of the Secretary-General on the provision of interpretation services to other locations from permanent interpretation structures in New York, Geneva, Vienna and Nairobi and the report of the Secretary-General entitled "Career development in language services: the post of reviser",

1. *Requests* the Secretary-General to continue the efforts to utilize new technologies, such as computer-assisted translation, remote translation, terminology databases and speech recognition, in the six official languages so as to enhance further the productivity of conference services, and to keep the General Assembly informed of the introduction and use of any other new technology;

2. *Also requests* the Secretary-General to continue the efforts to ensure that training opportunities in the six official languages are equally available to all language staff, including those at duty stations away from Headquarters;

3. *Decides* that, in the absence of a General Assembly decision to the contrary, the use of remote interpretation shall not constitute an alternative to the current institutionalized system of interpretation;

4. *Also decides* that the use of remote interpretation should not affect the quality of interpretation or in itself lead to any further reduction in language posts, nor will it affect the equal treatment of the six official languages;

5. *Requests* the Secretary-General to keep under review the introduction and use of any new technology, in particular remote interpretation, and to report thereon to the General Assembly on a regular basis;

6. *Requests* that efforts continue to be made to improve the quality control of language services at all duty stations;

7. *Takes note with appreciation* of the note by the Secretary-General entitled "Career development in language services—Measures aimed at reducing excessive vacancy rates at some duty stations: elements of a system of managed assignments", and requests the Secretary-General to keep the General Assembly informed of developments in this area;

8. *Notes with concern* that the rate of self-revision exceeded the established benchmark and even tended to increase at all duty stations;

9. *Recognizes* that an increase in the use of temporary assistance and contractual translation services could increase the need for revision at the senior levels;

10. *Notes with concern* that some documents issued in Arabic tend to follow a consistent pattern of excessively literal translation, by focusing more on the vocabulary and not on the content of the original language, and requests the Secretary-General to ensure that this situation is rectified;

11. *Requests* the Secretary-General to ensure that translation, in principle, reflects the specificity of each language;

12. *Also requests* the Secretary-General, in order to improve further the quality of translation of documents issued in the six official languages, to ensure continuous dialogue between translation staff and interpretation staff, among United Nations headquarters at New York, Geneva, Vienna and Nairobi, and between translation divisions and Member States with regard to the standardization of the terminology used;

13. *Further requests* the Secretary-General to ensure that Member States, which are the main users of United Nations documents, are briefed periodically on the terminology used;

14. *Decides* to keep the matter under review through consultations with Member States concerned;

E

Information technology

Having considered the report of the Secretary-General on the continuous development, maintenance and enrichment of United Nations web sites,

1. *Notes* the request of the Committee on Information that the Secretary-General continue to develop and enhance the United Nations web sites in all the official languages of the Organization and continue to develop proposals for consideration by the Committee on Information at its next session in May 2000;

2. *Requests* the Secretary-General to improve and update document access and retrieval from the United Nations web sites and from the optical disk system, equally in the six official languages, at all duty stations by March 2000;

3. *Also requests* the Secretary-General, in formalizing the structure of the Information Technology Section, to ensure that the six official languages are treated equally;

4. *Further requests* the Secretary-General to ensure that the goal of the equal treatment of the six official languages is taken into account in the course of the continuous development, maintenance and enrichment of United Nations web sites;

5. *Requests* the Secretary-General to take necessary measures to improve access to the web page of the Procurement Division;

6. *Also requests* the Secretary-General to report on the measures taken by the end of April 2000, pursuant to requests made under this section, and decides to revert to this matter during its resumed fifty-fourth session;

F

Recalling its decision 38/401, section E of its resolution 52/214 and its resolution 53/208 E concerning the prohibition of smoking in small conference rooms and the discouragement of smoking in large conference rooms,

1. *Calls upon* representatives of Member States to abide by its decision 38/401, section E of its resolution 52/214 and its resolution 53/208 E;

2. *Encourages* all users of United Nations conference facilities, in order to avoid involuntary exposure to passive smoking, to refrain from smoking, in particular in conference rooms.

The Assembly, in **resolution 54/249** of 23 December, requested the Secretary-General to submit at its fifty-fifth (2000) session a strategic plan for the full use of conference facilities at Nairobi, so as to ensure that interpretation capacity would be fully utilized. On the same date, the Assembly decided that the Fifth Committee should continue consideration of the pattern of conferences at the resumed fifty-fourth (2000) session (**decision 54/462 A**).

UN information systems

In response to Economic and Social Council resolution 1998/29 [YUN 1998, p. 1356], the Secretary-General submitted a June report on international cooperation in the field of informatics [E/1999/74], in which he summarized activities of the Ad Hoc Open-ended Working Group on Informatics on the need to harmonize UN information systems for optimal utilization and accessibility by all States. The Group focused at its 1999 meetings on the year 2000 computer problem and issues related to providing Member States with better electronic access. The report also addressed action taken by the Secretariat and UNDP in response to issues raised in the Working Group.

The Secretary-General stated that the Working Group, in cooperation with the Information

Technology Services Division, the Department of Public Information and UNDP, would continue to improve and expand electronic information services provided to Member States and permanent missions and assure that the technologies employed were abreast of technological development. At the country level, UNDP would intensify efforts to promote the use of information technology in the pursuit of sustainable development. The Working Group would reinforce efforts to promote year 2000 awareness and contingency planning at the regional, national and international levels. By **decision 1999/284** of 30 July, the Council took note of the Secretary-General's report.

The ACC Information Systems Coordination Committee (ISCC) held its seventh session in New York from 15 to 17 September and on 21 October [ACC/1999/19]. It recommended to ACC for endorsement the work planned for 2000-2001 to support ACC and its sub-organizations in information technology. It noted the increased interest in coordination of information technology and the management of information throughout the UN system. ISCC believed that it was important to recommend strategies, concepts, architectures, recognized standards and guidelines to help harmonize solutions across different organizations in the UN system. Annexed to the report were a number of high-priority projects approved by ISCC.

ECONOMIC AND SOCIAL COUNCIL ACTION

On 30 July [meeting 46], the Economic and Social Council adopted **resolution 1999/58** [draft: E/1999/L.54] without vote [agenda item 7 *(d)*].

The need to harmonize and improve United Nations informatics systems for optimal utilization and accessibility by all States

The Economic and Social Council,

Aware of the interest of Member States in taking full advantage of information and communications technologies for the acceleration of economic and social development,

Recalling its resolutions 1991/70 of 26 July 1991, 1992/60 of 31 July 1992, 1993/56 of 29 July 1993, 1994/46 of 29 July 1994, 1995/61 of 28 July 1995, 1996/35 of 25 July 1996, 1997/1 of 18 July 1997 and 1998/29 of 29 July 1998 on the need to harmonize and improve United Nations information systems for optimal utilization and accessibility by all States, with due regard to all official languages,

Welcoming the report presented by the Chairman of the Ad Hoc Open-ended Working Group on Informatics on the progress achieved so far in fulfilling the mandate of the Working Group,

1. *Reiterates once again* the high priority that it attaches to easy, economical, uncomplicated and unhindered access for States Members of the United Nations, observers and non-governmental organizations accredited to the United Nations to the computerized databases and information systems and services of the United Nations, provided that the unhindered access of non-governmental organizations shall not prejudice the access of Member States and that it shall not impose an additional financial burden for the use of databases and other systems;

2. *Requests* the President of the Economic and Social Council to convene the Ad Hoc Open-ended Working Group on Informatics for one more year to carry out its work from within existing resources, for the due fulfilment of the provisions of Council resolutions on this item, for facilitating the successful implementation of the initiatives being taken by the Secretary-General with regard to the use of information technology and for continuing the implementation of measures required to achieve its objectives, through, inter alia, the continuation of the following activities:

(a) Improving electronic connectivity via the Internet for all Member States in their capitals and at major United Nations locations, inter alia, through the enhanced connectivity of permanent missions to the Internet and the United Nations databases;

(b) Intensifying efforts to provide electronic connectivity to those Member States that do not currently have this service;

(c) Improving the access of Member States to a wider range of United Nations information on economic and social issues, development, political issues and other substantive programming areas, and having all official documents available via the Internet;

(d) Improving electronic mail links between Member States and the United Nations, the specialized agencies and each other;

(e) Providing specialized training for the staff of missions to enable them to take advantage of the facilities being developed for Member States, in particular electronic mail and Internet web pages;

(f) Enhancing the capacity of Member States to access United Nations data online, using low-cost telecommunications links or providing other modalities, for example, CD-ROM, whereby Member States can have access to specialized databases not available on the Internet;

(g) Making arrangements, as appropriate, to provide permanent missions of developing countries with the hardware platform to utilize Internet technology;

(h) Intensifying the use of videoconferencing to further communication and interaction between the United Nations, permanent missions and academic institutions;

(i) Addressing the year 2000 problem (the so-called "millennium bug") within the Secretariat and ensuring that remedial action is being taken, as appropriate, and that contingency plans are being developed;

(j) Building awareness of the year 2000 problem among Member States and, if necessary, providing a platform for Governments to address the issue at the global and regional levels;

(k) Promoting the active support of relevant international organizations for national efforts to deal with emergency situations which may arise from disruptions related to the year 2000, in particular in the aviation, telecommunications, maritime and health sectors;

(l) Encouraging greater information-sharing on year 2000 preparedness in order to help countries and organizations to take the necessary remedial actions and contingency planning and to share detailed year 2000 readiness information with the public;

(m) Broadening access to information about the United Nations at the country level, especially in developing countries;

(n) Developing an information management strategy;

3. *Commends* the Working Group for the success of the two global meetings of national year 2000 coordinators, held at United Nations Headquarters on 11 December 1998 and on 22 June 1999, which respectively raised the awareness of Member States, especially the developing countries, of the gravity of the year 2000 problem, reviewed the state of preparedness of Member States for meeting the challenge of the problem and enabled them to share experiences on remedial action and contingency planning;

4. *Expresses its appreciation* to the Governments of the United Kingdom of Great Britain and Northern Ireland and the United States of America for the financial assistance they provided for the organization of the meetings and the participation of national coordinators;

5. *Notes with appreciation* the efforts made to bring the Economic and Social Council in line with new information technologies, through a more user-friendly Council web page and the broadcasting on the Internet of the work of the high-level segment of the current substantive session;

6. *Reaffirms* the continuing need for representatives of States to be consulted closely and associated actively with the respective executive and governing bodies of United Nations institutions dealing with informatics within the United Nations system, so that specific needs of States as end-users can be given priority;

7. *Urges* the Working Group to intensify its contacts with the private sector so as to bring its wealth of expertise and experience to bear on the work of the Group;

8. *Welcomes* the efforts of the Information Systems Users' Group in Geneva to ensure connectivity to all Geneva-based permanent missions, and notes with appreciation that extensive work has been done, with the assistance of the various United Nations agencies, in particular the International Telecommunication Union, the World Intellectual Property Organization and the United Nations Office at Geneva, to provide training and equipment to permanent missions in Geneva;

9. *Expresses its gratitude* to the International Telecommunication Union and private sector sponsors for the contribution they have made to the Geneva Diplomatic Community Network, and hopes that this project will be extended to all permanent missions and to those of developing countries on concessional terms;

10. *Suggests* that one possibility for the theme of its high-level segment in 2001 could be "Information and communications technology for social and economic development" in order to underscore the importance of modern information technology for the development activities of the United Nations and the need for international cooperation in this field;

11. *Requests* the Secretary-General to extend full cooperation to the Working Group and to give priority to implementing its recommendations;

12. *Also requests* the Secretary-General to report to the Council at its substantive session of 2000 on the follow-up action taken on the present resolution, including the findings of the Working Group.

Year 2000 computer problem

In response to General Assembly resolution 53/86 [YUN 1998, p. 1359], the Secretary-General submitted a November report [A/54/525] on action taken by UN funds, programmes and specialized agencies, as well as by Member States, to resolve the year 2000 date conversion of computers. It updated the Secretary-General's August report [A/C.5/54/3], submitted in response to the ACABQ request that the Secretariat coordinate the preparation of a report by the UN system on the issue.

ACC, at its first regular session (Geneva, 9-10 April) [ACC/1999/4], adopted a note on the year 2000 issue, in which it recognized that UN system organizations were working diligently to ensure that they were prepared to meet potential problems arising out of possible worldwide computer system malfunctions.

GENERAL ASSEMBLY ACTION

On 15 December [meeting 79], the General Assembly adopted **resolution 54/114** [draft: A/54/L.61 & Add.1, orally revised] without vote [agenda item 45].

Global implications of the year 2000 date conversion problem of computers

The General Assembly,

Recalling its resolutions 52/233 of 26 June 1998 and 53/86 of 7 December 1998, entitled "Global implications of the year 2000 date conversion problem of computers",

Welcoming the report of the Secretary-General entitled "Steps taken within the United Nations system and with Member States to resolve the year 2000 date conversion of computers",

Recognizing that the effective operation of Governments, companies and other organizations is threatened by the year 2000 date conversion problem of computers, or "millennium bug",

Underlining the need for effective action to address the problem to be intensified as the inflexible date of 31 December 1999 draws nearer and nearer, beyond which important systems might cease to function,

Recognizing the potentially serious impact that the year 2000 problem could have in all countries whose economies are increasingly interdependent,

Emphasizing that the year 2000 problem could affect both computer systems and much electronic control equipment containing embedded chips and internal clocks, with wide-ranging effects on such important areas as power supplies, telecommunications, financial systems, transport, public health, building and factory systems, food supplies, emergency services and government services, including the organization of social welfare,

Emphasizing also that continued coordinated efforts by Governments and private, public and international organizations are required to address the year 2000 problem,

Noting that year 2000 effects are not limited to 1 January 2000, but may continue throughout the year as systems continue to use date-based information for monthly calculations and operations,

Appreciating the establishment of a trust fund by the World Bank to assist in the efforts to resolve the year 2000 problem and the voluntary contributions made to it by the Member States,

Appreciating also the efforts of the Ad Hoc Open-ended Working Group on Informatics of the Economic and Social Council in raising the level of awareness of the year 2000 problem,

1. *Requests* all Member States to continue their efforts to solve the year 2000 problem before the rollover date of 31 December 1999, including by working to ensure that the private sector is fully engaged in addressing the problem and by tackling it in those systems under their own control;

2. *Urges* Member States to take "best practices" measures, such as virus scanning, against the additional potential risk of malicious software which could be injected into systems with the intent of causing malfunctions or facilitating illegal access to information and which are meant to be mistaken for lack of year 2000 compliance;

3. *Urges* all Member States to emphasize the importance of contingency planning and to finalize such plans in order to address the potential for possible large-scale failures in the public and private sectors;

4. *Urges* Member States to set up and participate in national and regional mechanisms for service restoration in the event of service outages after 1 January 2000 attributable to the year 2000 problem;

5. *Appeals* to all Member States to forge global cooperation to ensure a timely and effective response to the year 2000 challenge and to work together to address the threats the problem poses globally and, in this regard, to cooperate with each other in the event of some Member States not having the capacity to correct service outages, through sharing information on significant events and on countermeasures taken, as well as causes, results and prospects of restoration of services, sharing resources in terms of knowledge, skills, products and solutions to offset the significant events and, where feasible, sending sector-specific experts and/or consultants to neighbouring countries;

6. *Calls upon* Governments, public and private sector organizations and civil society generally to share, locally, regionally and globally, information about their experiences in addressing the year 2000 problem;

7. *Requests* the Secretary-General to ensure that the United Nations system closely monitors actual and potential sources of funding to support the efforts of the developing countries and countries with economies in transition to address the year 2000 problem and to facilitate the dissemination of relevant information on those funding possibilities to the Member States;

8. *Urges* the Office for the Coordination of Humanitarian Affairs of the Secretariat to be ready to respond to any humanitarian emergencies that could be caused by serious year 2000 failures;

9. *Requests* the Secretary-General to submit to the General Assembly at its fifty-fifth session a final report on the evaluation of the outcome of the steps taken within the United Nations system and with Member States to resolve the year 2000 problem.

Integrated Management Information System

The Secretary-General, in February [A/53/829], transmitted the report of the Office of Internal Oversight Services (OIOS) on the increased costs of the Integrated Management Information System (IMIS) development contract, as requested in General Assembly resolutions 48/218 B [YUN 1994, p. 1362] and 52/227 [YUN 1998, p. 1360].

OIOS noted that the original price of the contract, awarded in 1991 for an amount of $17 million, had increased, following contract amendments for out-of-scope work, to $45.7 million, or 169 per cent of the original cost. The underlying reasons for the cost increase included underestimation of the level of effort required to develop, implement and maintain the project, lack of prior experience, contracting on the basis of inadequate and/or incomplete specifications, inadequate participation by main user departments in the development process and delays in addressing deficiencies.

OIOS recommended that to reduce the risk of delays and cost escalation in the implementation of the remaining IMIS releases and to ensure that IMIS was effectively institutionalized, the Administration should establish and communicate strategies and plans for the smooth implementation of revised Release 3 and Releases 4 and 5 and enforce management accountability for their implementation; and ensure that training in the use and operation of IMIS was strengthened and adequate funds were made available. Strategies, plans, organizational structures and resources for effective systems maintenance and support should be established, and heads of departments should identify further opportunities for streamlining administrative processes through the effective use of IMIS.

In a February addendum [A/53/573/Add.1] to his tenth progress report on the IMIS project [YUN 1998, p. 1361], the Secretary-General said that he concurred with the OIOS recommendations. They were in line with those made earlier by OIOS itself, the UN Board of Auditors and the independent experts [ibid., p. 1362]. He said that the Administration had reviewed, in the light of the comments and concerns expressed by OIOS, the estimated resource requirements contained in the tenth progress report and had concluded that they appeared adequate for completing the tasks related to the final stages of the development and implementation of the project. He therefore requested approval of the amount of $3.2 million for the 1998-1999 biennium and $9.5 million for the completion of the project at a total cost of $77.6 million.

GENERAL ASSEMBLY ACTION

On 7 April [meeting 97], the General Assembly, on the recommendation of the Fifth Committee [A/53/485/Add.2], adopted **resolution 53/219** without vote [agenda item 113].

Integrated Management Information System

The General Assembly,

Recalling its resolution 52/212 B of 31 March 1998,

Reaffirming its resolution 52/227 of 31 March 1998 and section VII of its resolution 53/214 of 18 December 1998,

Having considered the tenth progress report of the Secretary-General and the addendum thereto, the study of the Integrated Management Information System conducted by independent experts, the related report of the Advisory Committee on Administrative and Budgetary Questions, and the report of the Office of Internal Oversight Services on the increase in costs of the Integrated Management Information System development contract,

1. *Takes note with concern* of the findings contained in the report of the Office of Internal Oversight Services on the increase in costs of the Integrated Management Information System development contract, in particular that:

(a) With careful planning, proper identification of needs and more adequate preparations, the cost increase could have been reduced;

(b) Delays in promptly addressing deficiencies through concerted action in each phase of the development and implementation process have led the Organization to place undue reliance on the contractor;

(c) Insufficient progress has been made with respect to long-term operational support, software maintenance and staff training functions and, consequently, the reliance on the Integrated Management Information System project team and perhaps even the contractor is unlikely to diminish in the near future;

(d) There is no assurance that implementation problems similar to those experienced in previous years will not recur in the case of remaining releases, resulting in the possibility of further cost escalations;

2. *Notes* the observations of the Office of Internal Oversight Services that in large and complex software development contracts some out-of-scope work is a common occurrence;

3. *Regrets* the lack of adequate participation of the main user departments in the development and implementation phases of the system, which led to increased costs;

4. *Requests* the Secretary-General to ensure that the institutionalization of the Integrated Management Information System by the main user departments is completed as soon as possible;

5. *Reiterates its deep concern* about the time and cost overruns for the completion of the project;

6. *Requests* the Secretary-General to ensure that problems similar to those experienced previously do not recur;

7. *Notes* that the services required from the main contractor will be completed by the end of 1999, with the exception of warranty-related activities;

8. *Encourages* the Secretary-General to make use of any potential for improving efficiency by streamlining existing work flows and processes through more effective use of the Integrated Management Information System;

9. *Requests* the Secretary-General to take all corrective measures required to make the system fully operational and avoid further delays and unnecessary cost increases in the implementation of the project, taking into account the observations and recommendations contained in the report of the Office of Internal Oversight Services and the study conducted by independent experts;

10. *Decides* that the resources required to conclude the development of the Integrated Management Information System by August 2000 shall not exceed 77.6 million United States dollars;

11. *Reiterates* the need for a comprehensive programme for Integrated Management Information System training to be included as part of the ongoing training programme offered to staff at all duty stations concerned;

12. *Requests* the Secretary-General to include information on the implementation of paragraphs 3 and 4 of its resolution 52/212 B in future progress reports on the Integrated Management Information System;

13. *Also requests* the Secretary-General clearly to establish roles, responsibilities and accountability of all offices and staff concerned in the implementation of the remaining releases and to report thereon in his next progress report;

14. *Further requests* the Secretary-General to maintain an effective monitoring system to ensure that implementation problems are addressed properly as they arise;

15. *Decides* to approve an additional appropriation of 3.2 million dollars under section 27D, Support services, of the programme budget for the biennium 1998-1999, to be charged to the contingency fund and to be reflected in the assessment to be determined on the basis of the final appropriation for the biennium 1998-1999.

In October, the Secretary-General submitted the eleventh progress report on the IMIS project [A/54/474]. Since the last report, IMIS had been fully institutionalized and was implemented at all major duty stations. Its maintenance was fully assumed by UN staff and the costs for completion of the project remained within the projections given in the tenth report.

Over the past year, the new version of Release 2 (staff entitlements) was implemented in Nairobi, Kenya, two new versions of Release 3 (finance and support services) were implemented in New York, Release 3 was successfully implemented in Vienna and Beirut, Lebanon, and the "time and attendance" component was implemented at Headquarters. Progress had been achieved in the development of Releases 4 (payroll and related functionalities) and 5 (operational applications);

the reporting facility continued to be enhanced and new human resources functionalities were introduced. Globally, the usage of the system had increased.

The next steps for the completion of the system would be the implementation of Release 3 at all offices away from Headquarters by November 2000, and the implementation of Releases 4 and 5 in New York by the first quarter of 2000 and at all major duty stations by December 2000. Although major progress had been achieved, the implementation of Release 3 at five duty stations and the implementation of payroll at all duty stations would continue to require a very high level of effort on the part of staff at Headquarters and at the offices concerned.

In December, ACABQ, in its fifth report on the project [A/54/7/Add.4], requested the Secretary-General to provide information on the development of the system for field missions and for the tribunals for the former Yugoslavia and Rwanda in his next progress report, including resources to overcome technical and personnel constraints. He should implement IMIS expeditiously in the peacekeeping operations and the tribunals and a pilot project should be established in a peacekeeping mission, with the implementation costs included in that mission's budget. ACABQ recommended that the Secretary-General submit a comprehensive final report on the implementation of the system, including a full analysis of lessons learned and experience gained and addressing the issue of a long-term strategy for the further development of the system. ACABQ was concerned about the gap between the stated intention of the Secretary-General to create an "electronic United Nations" and the relatively low level of financial and human resources allocated to achieve that goal. It noted from the additional information provided on various information systems used in the UN system for financial and administrative applications that each agency continued to develop its own system, with little coordination, leading to unnecessary expenditures and duplication.

Other matters

Common services

JIU report. The Secretary-General, in January, transmitted a JIU report entitled "United Nations system common services at Geneva, part I, Overview of administrative cooperation and coordination" [A/53/787]. JIU found that, despite their close physical proximity and institutional commonalities, the Geneva-based secretariats operated very few services in common. No services were shared by the five specialized agencies located in the city and parallel support services existed among UN entities governed by the same Charter. That led to fragmentation and duplication of overhead structures and costs, aggravated by the absence of an intergovernmental consultative or review body and the lack of effective and cohesive institutional leadership of the UN Office at Geneva (UNOG).

The Inspectors recommended a basic framework for common services for Geneva-based organizations and that the Secretary-General refine and implement the revitalization measures proposed in the report, including the establishment of a UNOG common services committee and the possible appointment of a high-level official to foster common services objectives. JIU also recommended a more active role for the Geneva Diplomatic Committee, as well as meetings of ACABQ in Geneva focused specifically on issues of administrative and budgetary coordination among Geneva-based secretariats and entities. By **decision 53/474** of 8 June, the General Assembly deferred consideration of the JIU report until its fifty-fourth session.

OIOS reports. In June [A/54/157], the Secretary-General transmitted an OIOS report on the review of common services in the United Nations. The OIOS review, conducted at UN Headquarters in New York and at UN offices in Geneva and Vienna, examined progress achieved in strengthening common services in the areas identified in the Secretary-General's common services strategy, which was part of the new vision of management set out in his programme of reform [YUN 1997, p. 1389]. It also assessed efforts to improve the effectiveness and efficiency of UN support services in those areas. The review confirmed that the Secretary-General's reform measures gave new impetus to the need to seek cost-effectiveness through possible expansion of common services. Specific action was taken to implement those measures in New York, including the establishment of a Task Force on Common Services, which created working groups for specific areas, adopted plans of action and implemented them. OIOS said that it was important to ensure that the UN offices in Geneva and Vienna were included in the overall implementation strategy and that other duty stations were kept informed of lessons learned and best practices identified. It found that common services arrangements had led to the development of differing cost-sharing formulas and monitoring mechanisms. However, while common arrangements involving direct provision of services, such as payroll and pouch services, were more easily acceptable, there was reluctance to share processes requiring managerial decision-making, such as procurement or recruitment procedures. The perceived inefficiency of some central support services was cited as a deterrent to expanding common services. Some of the difficulties identified by departments/offices at all three duty stations included the need for each organization to control its own resources and staff, distrust of other entities' ability to prioritize services equitably, individual mandates from governing bodies and lack of interaction and communication among heads of organizations.

OIOS made a number of recommendations aimed at enhancing central support services and removing some of the barriers to their expansion. Among those recommendations were proposals for the Department of Management to expedite the delegation of authority and responsibility to line managers, and to UNOG and the UN Office at Vienna (UNOV) for human resources and financial and general support servicing. The Task Force on Common Services and UNOG should assess how common services might be expanded in Geneva, and the latter should streamline administrative processes to avoid duplication. UNOV should analyse the costs of maintaining administrative support structures and identify areas for reducing costs through shared procurement. The Department of Management should also promote common services within the UN system, working with ACC. Clear criteria and transparency of cost accounting to users should be developed for expanding common services.

In September [A/54/157/Add.1], the Secretary-General transmitted JIU's comments on the OIOS review of common services. JIU recommended that the General Assembly should encourage the Secretary-General and ACC to take steps to enhance common services and report to the Assembly's fifty-sixth (2001) session.

The Assembly, in **resolution 54/249** of 23 December, requested the Secretary-General to report at its fifty-fifth (2000) session on progress made by the UN Common Services Task Force on the existing common services and to expand and develop new ones as appropriate. It noted the advanced level of arrangements for common services and related cost indicators at UNOV.

Outsourcing practices

The Secretary-General, as requested in General Assembly resolution 52/226 B [YUN 1998, p. 1364], submitted a February report [A/53/818] setting out the basic policy and guidelines to be followed in considering the use of outsourcing, which took into account the JIU [YUN 1997, p. 1511] and OIOS [YUN 1998, p. 1253] reports on the subject. The report committed the United Nations to viewing outsourcing as one of the options to be considered by programme managers in providing or upgrading the quality and cost-effectiveness of the Organization's non-core activities and services. It did not mandate that specific non-core activities be outsourced, only that outsourcing be considered in a meaningful manner as part of the Organization's regular management decision-making process.

ACABQ, in a May report [A/53/942], concluded that the identification of functions that could be contracted out, as set out in the report, was not specific as to what could and could not be contracted out. The report did not analyse experience within the UN Secretariat and the statistical data provided was insufficient and inconclusive. The Committee recommended that the classification of activities as "core" and "non-core" should be dispensed with, since it had no utility value and had the potential for endless debate and disagreement as to those activities that should or should not be contracted out.

The Assembly, by **decision 53/474** of 8 June, deferred consideration of the 1997 JIU report and the 1998 ACC report [YUN 1998, p. 1364] on outsourcing and that of ACABQ until its fifty-fourth session.

Internal and external printing

In its first report on the proposed programme budget for the biennium 2000-2001 [A/54/7], ACABQ expressed concern about the need for a rational basis for determining the mix of external and "in-house" printing, and repeated its request that comparative data for all UN headquarters on in-house versus outsourcing of printing be provided at the General Assembly's fifty-fourth session. It also requested a comprehensive report for its review, including information on the total cost of operating all printing facilities in Geneva and New York and the capacity of all the plants and the printing workload of all organizations concerned. Additionally, information should be provided on the external printing programme and comparative costs for in-house and external printing. The report was to be submitted in time for the Committee to submit its recommendations to the Assembly at its fifty-fifth (2000) session.

In October, the Secretary-General submitted a provisional report on internal and external printing practices of the Organization [A/C.5/54/18]. He stated that the United Nations had traditionally used a mix of internal and external printing services. Improved technology had progressively reduced the range of services and materials that needed to be outsourced and the introduction of electronic pre-press equipment had shortened reproduction deadlines further. ACABQ had encouraged the trend towards increased use of internal capacity. System-wide expenditure on printing decreased from some $8 million in 1988-1989 to $6 million in 1996-1997, mainly at Headquarters where expenditure fell from $5.6 million to $3.4 million. However, the 2000-2001 proposed programme budget provided for an increase in external printing resources in some areas. While in-house facilities offered the advantages of an integrated production process not subject to outside controls, external services provided even greater product diversification than did the recently expanded internal plants. External printing was also an effective means of eliminating backlogs and meeting demand during specific periods.

As to costs, only limited ad hoc cost comparisons could be made between the two options. The Reproduction Section in New York had written a computer program to estimate the cost of individual jobs, but that did not include capital costs or items like power, maintenance and overheads. It was used selectively to provide indicative information as to whether a job should be done internally or outsourced and did not cover parliamentary documents. Geneva intended to develop a somewhat similar system. Using that costing system analysis, the Secretariat intended to submit a comprehensive report to the Assembly's fifth-fifth (2000) session.

In its sixth report on the proposed programme budget for 2000-2001 [A/54/7/Add.5], ACABQ noted the considerable improvement in efficiency in the printing programme in New York through the introduction of new technologies. It encouraged the further development of the computer program in the Reproduction Section, which should be coordinated with the development of a similar system in Geneva. The Committee was of the opinion that a method to figure in maintenance and overhead should also be developed and reported on in the context of the next proposed programme budget. However, the Committee felt that the Secretary-General's report only partially addressed its concerns; it requested a comprehensive report to the Assembly's fifty-fifth session to address the issues raised, in particular the situation in Geneva, and to assess the implementation of the conclusions and recommendations of the 1994 comprehensive study on conference services [YUN 1994, p. 1403]. That report should also include information on measures taken to ensure coordination between printing facilities at different duty stations, to achieve economies of scale, including through the development of common services among all UN entities at a duty station, and to ensure that the measurement of outputs was consistent. The Committee further requested information on the potential for further reducing the printing budget, given the 25 per cent reduction in hard-copy output since 1992-1993 and the productivity gains achieved.

By **resolution 54/251, section X**, of 23 December, the General Assembly took note of the Secretary-General's report on internal and external printing practices and ACABQ's recommendations and requested the Secretary-General to submit a comprehensive report on the printing practices of the Organization to its fifty-fifth (2000) session.

Measures to increase profitability of UN commercial activities

The Secretary-General, responding to a General Assembly request in resolution 52/220 [YUN 1997, p. 1421], submitted a January report on proposed measures to improve the profitability of UN commercial activities [A/53/794]. He indicated that a comprehensive review of the use of public spaces at Headquarters was currently in progress, including an examination of the commercial activities available to visitors to determine the extent to which they were in harmony with the goal of making the United Nations a safe and welcoming environment, and to what extent they would lend themselves to off-site application. In view of the comprehensive nature of the review, the Secretary-General planned to report on those issues and other related questions in the context of the proposed programme budget for the 2000-2001 biennium.

In the interim, the Secretary-General observed that, over the last two bienniums, the Geneva and New York Sales and Marketing Sections had increased income to the Organization through the sale of publications. In addition, electronic publications were expected to generate an increasingly larger share of revenue, saving the Organization mailing costs and expediting deliveries. With respect to the sale of publications in Geneva, he proposed a number of measures, including the diversification of sales, privatization of the UN Bookstore, active promotion of sales in Arabic and Russian, and the creation of new souvenir/gift items, extension of successful lines and the formation of joint ventures.

In the proposed 2000-2001 programme budget [A/54/6/Rev.1, vol. III], the Secretary-General projected, under income section 3, Services to the public, an increase in anticipated net revenue for the biennium of $1,282,900 compared with the revised estimates of $4,307,600 for the 1998-1999 biennium. The increase was largely attributable to the sale of UN publications and the gift shop and garage operations, partly offset by a projected reduction in income under the philatelic items.

ACABQ, in its first report on the 2000-2001 programme budget [A/54/7], noted the information concerning developments related to the sale of publications in Geneva.

UN premises and property

Facilities management

As requested in General Assembly resolution 52/220 [YUN 1997, p. 1421], the Secretary-General submitted a November update [A/54/628] on the principal properties of the United Nations worldwide, focusing on their replacement value. It discussed the implications for long-range major maintenance and the modernization of existing buildings.

Total gross floor area in use by the United Nations at locations surveyed was 1,252,621 square metres. The estimated total value of all land and buildings (owned or rented at nominal cost) was approximately $5,186,950,291. By the middle of the 2000-2001 biennium, 46 per cent of the total gross floor area of owned buildings would be over 40 years old. The Headquarters building had already passed the threshold for obsolescence and deterioration, having reached 50 years of age, and some 76 per cent of building space leased at nominal or no cost was 10 years old or more. Those buildings would require large increases in major maintenance expenditures and there was a need to clarify the relative responsibilities of the United Nations and the building owners for such costs.

The Secretary-General suggested that a more focused, integrated approach be adopted for facilities management. The activities of that subprogramme would be further elaborated in the capital master plan of the proposed programme budget for the 2000-2003 biennium. During the current medium-term plan period (1998-2001), technical support for and consultation with the administrations at principal locations would be increased in administration, programme identification and implementation. The implementation of projects for the modernization of existing facilities would include the continued introduction of building automation systems, energy conservation, modern electronic communications and planned improvements in the use of space.

The Secretary-General concluded that the physical condition of UN buildings had an important impact on the efficiency of the Secretariat and conference activities of the Organization. Owing to budgetary constraints, the amount of funding available was consistently below the industry benchmark standard. In collaboration with an Organization-wide team and a focal point from each duty station, the Headquarters' Office of Central Support Services would provide a coordinating role for monitoring, information exchange and policy dissemination with respect to locations outside of Headquarters. The United Nations had already taken additional Organization-wide initiatives to improve the efficiency and services of Headquarters and overseas facilities, including the creation of working groups on facilities management and a Joint Advisory Standing Committee on Environmental and Occupational Health and Safety Issues and the development of a capital master plan and a database of all office and conference spaces.

Rental premises

In response to an ACABQ request [A/54/7] that he survey the terms of agreements under which the press and other entities occupied space in buildings owned and rented by the United Nations free of change or at less than commercial rates, the Secretary-General submitted an October report on the subject [A/C.5/54/25].

A review of the current UN practice of charging rent to outside entities occupying space on its premises indicated that, while rents were generally based on local commercial rates, the rates varied by group of tenants and were affected by specific factors and conditions prevailing at each duty station. Rents were set according to the type of tenants housed and on the level of their contribution to the Organization's work. Thus, several different rates might apply at a particular location. Press and other media entities, as well as staff-affiliated bodies and entities, were exempt from paying rent, while other tenants were charged rent at commercial or concessional/reduced rates.

The Secretary-General was of the opinion that the agreements were based on established policies and took into account both tenant and local conditions, and he intended to continue to apply those practices.

In its sixth report on the programme budget for 2000-2001 [A/54/7/Add.5], ACABQ stated that the criteria for charging rent were too general and could be open to different interpretations, and the current practice, as set out in the Secretary-General's report, led to several inconsistencies. It requested a complete listing of UN tenants, including those occupying rent-free space, as well as information on the square footage of space occupied by each organization or tenant, rent paid per square foot, maintenance and overhead charges, the actual percentage formula applied in relation to market rates, and the type of contract or agreement.

By **resolution 54/251, section XI**, of 23 December, the General Assembly took note of the reports of the Secretary-General and ACABQ and requested the Secretary-General to provide the outstanding information requested by ACABQ. It decided to revert to the subject at its resumed fifty-fourth (2000) session.

Addis Ababa conference facilities

The Secretary-General submitted a February report [A/53/347/Add.1], in response to General Assembly resolution 53/214, section VI [YUN 1998, p. 1365], in which he was requested to take urgent measures to find a solution to the dispute concerning the telecommunications system installed at the new conference facilities in Addis Ababa. The Secretary-General reported that discussions were held with the host Government, leading to a satisfactory resolution of the problem and the release of the requested items from customs on 16 December 1998. As a result, the contractor commenced work to correct the identified deficiencies within the warranty period, which expired on 24 February 1999. The Secretary-General reported that the 10 per cent retention ($302,549) of the contract amount would not be released until the contractor had corrected the identified deficiencies. Claims for additional compensation would not be discussed until the completion of the contract. However, the Secretary-General did not request any additional resources beyond the amount ($115,228,494) already approved.

By **decision 53/474** of 8 June, the Assembly deferred consideration of the report until its fifty-fourth session.

In October [A/54/431], the Secretary-General reported that the deficiencies that had been identified had been resolved. Regarding claims for additional compensation, it was agreed that the United Nations would pay $34,756.53 for work performed out of the scope of the contract. The contractor agreed not to make any further claims either for extra work or for compensation for work-time loss. As at 30 June, total disbursements for the project amounted to $114,084,919, leaving a balance of $1,143,575. It was anticipated that all remaining accounts would be finalized within the 1998-1999 biennium to enable the construction-in-progress account to be closed and the project capitalized.

In its sixth report on the proposed programme budget for 2000-2001 [A/54/7/Add.5], ACABQ recommended that the Assembly take note of the Secretary-General's report, which it did in **resolution 54/251, section IX**, of 23 December.

Management audit of ECA and ESCAP conference centres

In September [A/54/410], the Secretary-General transmitted an OIOS report on the management audit of the conference centres at the Economic Commission for Africa (ECA) and the Economic and Social Commission for Asia and the Pacific (ESCAP), in response to General Assembly resolution 48/218 B [YUN 1994, p. 1362].

OIOS believed that the decision to construct two facilities of that magnitude was flawed. Their physical capacity requirements were vastly overestimated and the ongoing financial implications were not properly assessed. To date, the proper use and management of the two centres had not been a priority, despite their increasing financial burden to the Organization. Their current estimated annual operating costs were $1.16 million for ECA and $1.53 million for ESCAP, and revenue from external users covered no more than one eighth of either centre's annual operating costs.

The five major meeting rooms at both centres were empty between 60 and 85 per cent of the time. The ECA system of debt recovery from external users was inadequate and Secretariat offices and common system agencies rarely selected those two facilities for large conferences and meetings. Neither centre was established as a legitimate revenue-producing operation for the Organization, and no resources were earmarked for the marketing and promotion of the centres within or outside the UN system.

OIOS recommended that the ESCAP Executive Secretary should develop a comprehensive proposal for the management and promotion of the Bangkok centre, comprising a cost-benefit and market analysis, a detailed cost plan and a discussion of options, which might include outsourcing; the new ECA Conference Centre Chief should finalize a marketing cost plan and determine the feasibility of implementing additional service and facility enhancements; and the executive secretaries of the two commissions, in conjunction with the Department of General Assembly Affairs and Conference Services, should formulate a plan for using the two centres for major UN events and meetings.

Other recommendations dealt with management and customer service improvements. Both commissions had since addressed most of them. Specifically, the ECA secretariat had set up the Business Centre within the conference facility and was developing the Technology Centre for Africa, which would include both permanent and temporary exhibitions and a training centre. It was also working to streamline financial procedures and controls. The ESCAP secretariat had also initiated discussions to promote the centre.

Staff security

ACC, at its first regular session (Geneva, 9-10 April) [ACC/1999/4], agreed that all UN organizations should systematically report incidents involving the safety of UN staff to the Security Coordinator, who would examine them from a legal perspective to identify the need for enhanced legal protection.

The Ad Hoc Inter-Agency Meeting on Security (Washington, D.C., 11-13 May) made a number of recommendations to ACC on issues related to residential security measures, funding of security, security implications of the year 2000 computer problem for UN staff, inter-agency training, communications, revision of the field security handbook, field security officers and other related matters [ACC/1999/10].

In a decision on UN staff security, adopted at its second regular session (New York, 29-30 October) [ACC/1999/20], ACC decided that: a comprehensive approach needed to be fully and urgently implemented and concerted action taken by Member States and the secretariats at Headquarters and in the field to ensure the security of staff, including local staff, in all duty stations; every effort would be made to raise with Member States and parties to conflict their responsibility and accountability for the safety of staff and the full investigation of security incidents; steps would be taken to ensure that adequate funds and staff were available for security measures, including dedicated funding, preferably from programme budgets; and the adequacy and timeliness of the compensation to families of all staff members killed in the line of duty would be reviewed.

International recognition of Day of Vesak

On 15 December [meeting 79], the General Assembly adopted **resolution 54/115** [draft: A/54/L.59 & Add.1] without vote [agenda item 174].

International recognition of the Day of Vesak at United Nations Headquarters and other United Nations offices

The General Assembly,

Acknowledging the hope expressed by the International Buddhist Conference, held in Sri Lanka in November 1998, that the Day of Vesak, the Day of the Full Moon in the month of May each year, be recognized internationally and, in particular, at United Nations Headquarters and other United Nations offices,

Recognizing that the Day of the Full Moon in the month of May each year is the day most sacred to Buddhists, who commemorate on that day the birth of the Buddha, his attainment of enlightenment and his passing away,

Considering that international recognition at United Nations Headquarters and other United Nations offices would constitute acknowledgement of the contribution that Buddhism, one of the oldest religions in the world, has made for over two and a half millennia and continues to make to the spirituality of humanity,

Resolves that, without cost to the United Nations, appropriate arrangements shall be made for international observances of the Day of Vesak at United Nations Headquarters and other United Nations offices, in consultation with the relevant United Nations offices and with permanent missions that also wish to be consulted.

PART SIX

Intergovernmental organizations related to the United Nations

blank page -- (1384)

Chapter I

International Atomic Energy Agency (IAEA)

The International Atomic Energy Agency (IAEA), continued its activities in 1999 under what its medium term strategy (2001-2005) identified as the pillars of the IAEA programme: technology, safety and verification.

At its forty-third session (Vienna, 27 September–1 October), the IAEA General Conference adopted a series of resolutions on: strengthening of international cooperation in nuclear safety, radiological protection and waste management, and of IAEA's technical cooperation activities; improving the safeguards system and the application of the 1997 Model Protocol Additional to Safeguards Agreements [YUN 1997, p. 1519]; the early application of full-scope safeguards to all nuclear activities in the Middle East; and the full implementation of IAEA's safeguards agreement with the Democratic People's Republic of Korea and of UN Security Council resolutions on Iraq. Other resolutions concerned the safety of radiation sources and the security of radioactive materials, the safe transport of those materials, the radiological protection of patients, measures against illicit trafficking in nuclear and other radioactive materials, the development of nuclear technologies for producing potable water economically and the extensive use of isotope hydrology for water resources management.

During the year, IAEA's membership rose to 130 with the admission of Angola and Benin.

Activities

Nuclear safety

IAEA continued to foster a global nuclear safety culture, comprising legally binding conventions, internationally agreed safety standards and measures to apply those conventions and standards. Activities centred on developing standards on siting, design and operation of nuclear power plants and research reactors, providing a variety of expert services, promoting information exchange on safety issues and supporting coordinated research in member States. Operational safety review services emphasized safety management, safety culture and self-assessment.

Safety missions were undertaken during the year by the Operational Safety Review Team to Bulgaria, France, Pakistan and Switzerland, and by the Assessment of Safety Significant Events Team to Armenia, India, Slovakia and Ukraine. The International Nuclear Event Scale facilitated the communication and understanding of nuclear and other radiation incidents to the public. Fifty-nine countries provided information on 24 such incidents, among them the September accident at the nuclear fuel-processing facility in Tokaimura, Japan. To assist member States in preparing for possible Y2K computer problems at nuclear power plants, IAEA issued a guidance document, held three workshops and conducted 20 missions to nine member States.

In 1999, three States (Cyprus, Sri Lanka, United States) adhered to the 1994 Convention on Nuclear Safety [YUN 1994, pp. 925 & 1417], bringing the number of parties to 52.

Radiation safety

IAEA's radiation safety programme had two complementary objectives: development of a unified set of safety standards based on consensus and application of those standards in member States and through other international organizations. The programme emphasized research, development of requirements-level consensus documents and supporting guides, and preparation of manuals to assist in standards implementation. Technical cooperation projects included the Model Project on strengthening radiation and waste-safety infrastructures in over 50 member States. Considerable effort was devoted to emergency response activities, to support which a number of research programmes, training courses, conferences and other meetings were organized. A new service, the Transport Safety Appraisal Service, was introduced to provide reviews of national implementation of IAEA's Regulations for the Safe Transport of Radioactive Material.

Nuclear power

The nuclear power programme, as reformulated in 1999, emphasized the use of small and medium-sized reactors in developing countries. Work in nuclear power planning, implementation and performance sought to facilitate the exchange of experience and provide assistance to member States, including cost-benefit analysis of upgrades to nuclear plants. Assistance was provided to Bangladesh, Egypt, Morocco, Turkey and Viet Nam in nuclear power planning, feasibility studies and infrastructure development. The International Nuclear Desalination Advisory Group, in June, reviewed member States' national programmes and projects, stressing the importance of international cooperation in nuclear desalination demonstration activities.

Nuclear fuel cycle

Activities in the nuclear fuel cycle area focused on: uranium supply and demand and environmental issues related to uranium mining and milling; immediate challenges in reactor materials and fuel technology, such as those associated with increased burn-up; spent fuel management; and nuclear fuel cycle issues and databases. A symposium was held (Vienna, 17-21 May) on mixed-oxide fuel cycle technologies for medium- and long-term deployment. A report on the adverse environmental effects from uranium mining and milling operations and mitigation thereof was prepared jointly by IAEA and the Nuclear Energy Agency of the Organisation for Economic Co-operation and Development.

Radioactive waste management

The radioactive waste technology programme covered: sources of radioactive waste, with emphasis on inventories, minimization and decommissioning of facilities; implementation of waste management activities, focusing on disposal issues; and technology transfer and exchange. An international symposium (Taejon, Republic of Korea, 30 August–3 September) reviewed worldwide experience in implementing technologies to manage radioactive wastes in ways that were safe, economical and environmentally sound. Regional demonstrations of pre-disposal waste management methods and procedures were held in operating waste processing and storage facilities in Chile, the Philippines, the Russian Federation and Turkey. IAEA also assisted China, Costa Rica, Jamaica, Pakistan, Peru and the United Republic of Tanzania in the safe management of spent, sealed radiation sources, particularly unused radium sources.

Marine environment and water resources

Activities in the marine environment continued to focus on the protection of the oceans and coastal seas through radioactivity monitoring and assessment, and the use of nuclear and isotopic techniques to understand pollutant behaviour. Capacity-building, quality assurance, provision of reference materials and methods, training and participation in the collection of marine samples in the Southern Ocean and along the coast of Morocco were among IAEA's most important contributions in 1999. In addition, it developed an isotope methodology to assess groundwater renewal where water was scarce. The IAEA Marine Environment Laboratory in Monaco also developed an innovative system for monitoring marine radioactivity using stationary gamma monitors with satellite data transmission.

The tenth symposium on isotope techniques in water resources development and management (Vienna, 10-14 May) discussed isotope applications in surface-water hydrology, groundwater resource management, climate change phenomena and environmental management.

Food and agriculture

Progress was made in developing technologies and formulating environmentally sound practices for enhancing food security. Isotope and radiation techniques provided new scientific information on nitrogen fertilizer and water use in wheat cultivation, leading to practices that improved or maintained yields, while saving on nitrogen fertilizer applications and reducing nitrate pollution of groundwater. Mutation techniques combined with modern biotechnology led to the generation of economically useful traits in crop plants. The use of radioimmunoassay and related methods provided member States with recommendations for improving artificial insemination, increasing milk production and controlling important livestock diseases. The sterile insect technique continued to play a major role in the control and eradication of pests of both crops and livestock, while the role of irradiation as a sanitary phytosanitary treatment of food and agricultural commodities continued to gain recognition. The latter was highlighted by an international conference (Antalya, Turkey, 19-22 October) on ensuring the safety and quality of food through radiation processing.

Human health

The main thrust of IAEA's human health programme continued to be cancer control and combating infection and malnutrition through preventive measures. In nuclear medicine, cost efficacy studies of inexpensive radiopharmaceuticals and the application of isotopes in molecular biology and new radioimmunoassay-related procedures were emphasized. In radiation therapy and radiobiology, development of quality assurance was the main topic and included the development of patient immobilization devices and protocols for HIV-infected cancer patients. In health-related environmental studies, new strategies for nutrition intervention schemes were identified and the global network of analytical laboratories was strengthened.

Technical cooperation

During the year, IAEA began implementing its 1999-2000 technical cooperation programme and planning for the 2001-2002 programme.

To ensure the programme's relevance and impact, regional meetings were organized to discuss priorities, to train in project design and to plan specific projects; the programme's objectives were also aligned with those of other UN agencies, and links were forged with the private sector. In South Africa, where the main effort of the World Health Organization was combating communicable diseases, among them tuberculosis, IAEA began working with that country to develop isotope-based molecular techniques for the rapid and accurate detection of multi-drug-resistant strains of the disease. In West Asia, planning of water resources management was harmonized with the work of other UN bodies and intergovernmental organizations. The East Asia and Pacific region sponsored a seminar to assist project counterparts in marketing their capabilities to end-users.

Safeguards responsibilities

All information available to IAEA in 1999 supported the conclusion that nuclear material and related items placed under safeguards remained in peaceful nuclear activities or were otherwise adequately accounted for. As at 31 December, 224 safeguards agreements with 140 States (and with Taiwan, Province of China) were in force. Safeguards agreements that satisfied the requirements of the 1968 Treaty on the Non-Proliferation of Nuclear Weapons, adopted by the General Assembly in resolution 2373(XXII) [YUN 1968, p. 17], were in force in 128 States. Protocols Additional to Safeguards Agreements [YUN 1997, p. 1519] for 46 States were approved by the Board of Governors. Eight such Protocols were in force in Australia, the Holy See, Indonesia, Japan, Jordan, Monaco, New Zealand and Uzbekistan.

During 1999, 2,495 safeguards inspections were performed in 70 States, covering 196 nuclear power reactors, 156 research reactors and critical assemblies, 13 conversion plants, 43 fuel fabrication plants, 6 nuclear reprocessing plants, 14 uranium enrichment plants, 69 separate storage facilities and 86 other facilities.

IAEA was unable to fulfil its safeguards mandates in the Democratic People's Republic of Korea and Iraq (see PART ONE, Chapter IV).

Nuclear information

During the year, IAEA's *WorldAtom* Internet site was redesigned to improve its ability to handle an expanding number of external inquiries.

The Internet site of the journal *Nuclear Fusion* was enhanced, and work on an IAEA e-commerce site for sales publications began. Publishing activities included the production of a total of 142 books, reports, journal issues and booklets in English, plus two publications each in Chinese and French and one each in Russian and Spanish.

Participating members of the International Nuclear Information System (INIS) numbered 122, including 103 countries and 19 international organizations. A distance-learning project through the Internet was launched to provide training to INIS users, with the first phase completed in 1999.

Secretariat

At the end of 1999, IAEA secretariat staff totalled 2,212, including 944 in the Professional and higher categories and 1,286 in the General Service category. Ninety-two nationalities were represented in posts subject to geographical distribution.

Budget

The 1999 regular budget amounted to $221.8 million, of which $210.8 million was financed from assessed contributions by member States on the basis of the 1999 assessment scale and $4.9 million from income from reimbursable work for others. Actual expenditure from the budget amounted to $221.6 million. A total of $26.1 million in extrabudgetary funds was provided by member States, the United Nations, international organizations and other sources.

NOTE: For further information, see *The Annual Report for 1999*, published by IAEA.

HEADQUARTERS AND OTHER OFFICE

HEADQUARTERS

International Atomic Energy Agency
Wagramerstrasse 5
(P. O. Box 100, Vienna International Centre)
A-1400 Vienna, Austria
Cable address: INATOM VIENNA
Telephone: (43) (1) 26000
Fax: (43) (1) 26007
Internet: http://www.iaea.org/worldatom
E-mail: Official.Mail@iaea.org

LIAISON OFFICE

International Atomic Energy Agency Liaison Office at the United Nations
1 United Nations Plaza, Room 1155
New York, NY 10017, United States
Telephone: (1) (212) 963-6010, 6011, 6012
Fax: (1) (212) 751-4117

Chapter II

International Labour Organization (ILO)

In 1999, the International Labour Organization (ILO) continued to promote social justice and economic stability and improve labour conditions. Its four strategic objectives were: to promote and realize fundamental principles and rights at work; to create greater opportunities for women and men to secure decent employment and income; to enhance the coverage and effectiveness of social protection for all; and to strengthen tripartism and social dialogue.

In 1999, ILO membership remained at 174.

Meetings

The eighty-seventh session of the International Labour Conference (ILC) (Geneva, 1-17 June) unanimously adopted the Worst Forms of Child Labour Convention, 1999, which applied to all persons under the age of 18 and called for immediate and effective measures to secure the prohibition and elimination of the worst forms of child labour as a matter of urgency. ILC also adopted an unprecedented resolution against Myanmar for consistent violations of the Forced Labour Convention and failure to respond to repeated rulings by supervisory bodies to put an end to forced labour, a practice that an ILO Commission of Inquiry found to be widespread in the country. The Committee on Maternity Protection agreed to revise the Maternity Protection Convention (No. 103) and its accompanying Recommendation No. 95 to take account of developments since the latest provisions for maternity protection were adopted in 1952.

Sectoral and other meetings convened in Geneva during 1999 included: Meeting of Experts on Ambient Factors at the Workplace (27 January–2 February); Tripartite Meeting on Voluntary Initiatives Affecting Training and Education on Safety, Health and Environment in the Chemical Industries (22-26 February); Tripartite Meeting on Managing the Privatization and Restructuring of Public Utilities (12-16 April); International Symposium on the Future of Employers' Organizations (19-21 April); Tripartite Meeting on Social and Labour Issues in Small-scale Mines (17-21 May); Symposium on the Social and Labour Consequences of Technological Developments, Deregulation and Privatization of Transport (20-24 September); Meeting of Experts on Labour Inspection and Child Labour (27 September–1 October); International Symposium on Trade Unions and the Informal Sector (18-22 October); Tripartite Meeting on the Human Resource Implications of Globalization and Restructuring in Commerce (25-29 October); International Consultation concerning Follow-up on the World Summit for Social Development (2-4 November); Second ILO Enterprise Forum (5-6 November); and the Tripartite Meeting on Safety and Health in the Fishing Industry (13-17 December). The Fourteenth American Regional Meeting was held in Lima, Peru, from 24 to 27 August.

International standards

ILO activities with regard to conventions and recommendations during 1999 included standard-setting and the supervision and promotion of the application of standards. Supervisory bodies reviewed existing procedures and standard-setting policy.

Standard-setting

In June, ILC adopted an eighth fundamental convention, the Worst Forms of Child Labour Convention, 1999 (No. 182).

During the biennium 1998-1999, 83 ratifications of the eight fundamental conventions were registered: 6 for the Forced Labour Convention, 1930 (No. 29); 6 for the Freedom of Association and Protection of the Right to Organize Convention, 1948 (No. 87); 8 for the Right to Organize and Collective Bargaining Convention, 1949 (No. 98); 8 for the Equal Remuneration Convention, 1951 (No. 100); 15 for the Abolition of Forced Labour Convention, 1957 (No. 105); 12 for the Discrimination (Employment and Occupation) Convention, 1958 (No. 111); 26 for the Minimum Age Convention, 1973 (No. 138); and 5 for the Worst Forms of Child Labour Convention, 1999 (No. 182).

Supervision of standards

The Committee of Experts on the Application of Conventions and Recommendations, at its seventieth session (Geneva, 25 November–10 December), noted 27 instances in which Governments had changed their law and practice to conform with ratified conventions. The total number of cases in which the Committee had been led to express satisfaction with the progress achieved had risen to 2,230 since 1964.

The Governing Body Committee on Freedom of Association met three times during the year to examine complaints of violations of freedom of association received from employers' and workers' organizations.

Employment and development

ILO continued in 1999 to help constituents combat unemployment and poverty through the creation of employment opportunities and improvement of existing jobs. It also provided advice and guidance on employment, labour market policies and information and statistical systems, and supported the development of entrepreneurship through the creation of cooperatives and small and micro-enterprises, particularly by vulnerable groups, such as women, migrant workers, indigenous and tribal peoples and persons with disabilities.

Working environment

In April, ILO informed the Fifteenth World Congress on Occupational Safety and Health (São Paulo, Brazil) that 1 million work-related deaths occurred every year; 250 million work-related accidents caused absences from work every year; and 3,000 people were killed every work day. ILO activities in the field of occupational safety and health included creating alliances and partnerships by launching activities to be used by Governments, social partners, non-governmental organizations and human rights groups in advocacy campaigns and supporting, through technical assistance, national action regarding hazardous occupations.

Field activities

In 1999, expenditure on operational activities, under all sources of funding, totalled $97.1 million compared with $93.7 million in 1998. The three leading programmes in terms of annual expenditure (representing 52 per cent of total expenditure) were in employment and training ($17.1 million), enterprise and cooperative development ($16.2 million) and development policies ($15.8 million). Other programmes dealt with working conditions and environment ($13.7 million), including the International Programme for the Elimination of Child Labour ($10.5 million). Interregional and global activities accounted for some $18.8 million. In terms of regional distribution, Africa accounted for 35 per cent of total expenditure ($33.8 million), Asia and the Pacific for 20 per cent ($19.5 million) and Latin America and the Caribbean for 14 per cent ($13.8 million). Expenditure in Europe increased from $5.2 million in 1998 to $6.85 million in 1999, and the Arab States programme almost doubled from $2.3 million in 1998 to $4.3 million in 1999.

Educational activities

In 1999, the Turin Centre continued to carry out training and related activities in a wide range of technical areas as an integral part of ILO technical cooperation activities. The International Institute for Labour Studies conducted research and encouraged networking related to emerging labour policy issues, and acted as a catalyst for future ILO programme development.

The United Nations Staff College, by the end of October 1999, had trained a total of 145 UN staff members from 21 departments, agencies, programmes and offices.

The objectives of the Interactive Conference on Organized Labour in the Twenty-first Century, launched in September and scheduled to run for a year, were to establish an international forum in which a wide range of people could share ideas and strategies for strengthening and broadening the role of organized labour in 2000 and beyond, and to foster debate, build links and support research in relevant areas.

Secretariat

As at 31 December 1999, ILO employed a total of 2,219 full-time staff at its Geneva headquarters and in 40 field offices around the world. Of those, 925 were in the Professional and higher categories and 1,284 were in the General Service category.

Budget

In June 1999, ILC adopted a budget of $467 million for the 2000-2001 biennium.

NOTE: For further information on ILO, see *Report of the Director-General, Activities of the ILO, 1998-99.*

HEADQUARTERS, LIAISON AND OTHER OFFICES

HEADQUARTERS
International Labour Organization
4 Route des Morillons
CH-1211 Geneva 22, Switzerland
Telephone: (41) (22) 799-6111
Fax: (41) (22) 798-8685
Internet: http://www.ilo.org
E-mail: doscom@ilo.org

LIAISON OFFICE
International Labour Organization
Liaison Office with the United Nations
Suite 3101
220 East 42nd Street
New York, NY 10017, United States
Telephone: (1) (212) 909-7800
Fax: (1) (212) 909-7816
E-mail: newyork@ilo.org

ILO maintained regional offices in Abidjan, Côte d'Ivoire; Bangkok, Thailand; Geneva, Switzerland; and Lima, Peru.

Chapter III

Food and Agriculture Organization of the United Nations (FAO)

The Food and Agriculture Organization of the United Nations (FAO) continued to work towards the achievement of sustainable global food security by raising nutrition levels and living standards, improving agricultural productivity and advancing the condition of rural populations. It expanded the operational reach of its Special Programme for Food Security (SPFS) and established a secretariat for the inter-agency initiative Food Insecurity and Vulnerability Information and Mapping Systems. It brought early warning of potential food shortages to the world's attention through conferences, meetings and information campaigns and, in 1999, began publication of a new series of reports, *The State of Food Insecurity in the World.*

In 1999, FAO's membership rose to 180 countries, plus the European Community, with the admission of Kiribati, the Marshall Islands, Niue, Palau and San Marino.

The FAO Conference, the agency's governing body, held its thirtieth biennial session (Rome, Italy, 12-23 November). It approved the FAO Strategic Framework for 2000-2015, reviewed the follow-up activities to the 1996 World Food Summit [YUN 1996, p. 1129], examined the global state of food and agriculture and discussed issues on gender mainstreaming, the International Undertaking on Plant Genetic Resources for Food and Agriculture, the outcome of several international conferences related to agricultural issues, as well as several cooperation agreements with organizations dealing with food-related matters.

FAO's activities, carried out within the context of its mandate and the Strategic Framework, were in the areas of crops and livestock, forestry, fisheries, food standards and nutrition, commodities and trade, environment and natural resources management, plant and animal genetic resources, agricultural services, ethics in food and agriculture, rural development and gender in development.

In June, major donors approved the new Food Aid Convention (FAC) for an initial period of three years, from July 1999. FAC called for a more flexible approach to food aid by expanding the list of eligible commodities and methods of distribution. As expanded, the list included products that were part of the traditional diet of vulnerable groups or components of supplementary feed programmes, and micronutrients and fortified food products.

World food situation

World cereal production in 1999 reached 1,865 million tonnes (including rice in milled terms), slightly below the previous year's level but above the average of the preceding five years. The decline was mostly a result of lower wheat and coarse grain production. Severe drought in the Near East and parts of North Africa and excessive rainfall at planting time in northern Europe were the main causes of decline in wheat production, partially offset, however, by favourable weather and high yields in a number of other countries, including Argentina, Australia, Bangladesh, Canada, China, India and the Russian Federation. Global output of coarse grains in 1999, estimated at 876 million tonnes, was about 4 per cent below that of the previous year due to smaller harvests and declines among some major producers. In 1998/99, total cereal utilization rose slightly above the level of the previous season, to 1,875 tonnes, all of which occurred in the developing countries. Overall, the growth in world food consumption slightly exceeded the rise in population, resulting in a small increase in per capita food consumption of cereals in 1998/99.

FAO's Global Information and Early Warning System (GIEWS) continued to provide early warnings of imminent food crises in an environment of dramatic increases in natural and/or man-made emergencies worldwide, including, in 1999, drought, floods and civil strife. In cooperation with the World Food Programme, GIEWS fielded a number of crop and food-supply assessment missions to affected countries and issued Special Alerts to the international community. To manage vast amounts of information from many different sources, GIEWS developed an integrated information system, the GIEWS Workstation, and maintained a reference database for crop monitoring and early warning, with information pertaining to food security at global, regional, national and sub-national levels.

Activities

Emergency assistance

FAO's Special Relief Operations Service (TCOR) continued to respond to requests for emergency assistance in the agricultural, livestock, fisheries and forestry sectors, submitted by developing countries affected by exceptional natural or human-induced calamities. During the year, TCOR obtained funding of $45 million for a total of 120 projects from donor countries ($26 million), FAO's Technical Cooperation Programme ($16 million) and other UN system organizations ($3 million). In addition, $139 million was allocated to TCOR for the execution of the agricultural component of the "oil-for-food" programme in Iraq (see p. 269).

Field programmes

Through its field programmes, FAO continued to provide technical advice and support in all areas of food and agriculture, fisheries, forestry and rural development. Related expenditures during 1998-1999 totalled $588.4 million, provided by the Technical Cooperation Programme ($73 million) and SPFS ($7.4 million) under the FAO regular budget; by the United Nations Development Programme ($58 million); and by the Trust Fund Programme ($450 million). FAO's Investment Centre assisted 134 developing and transition countries in identifying and assessing investment opportunities, as well as member countries in formulating 79 agricultural and rural development projects for an approved total investment of some $4.7 billion. Participation in the South-South Cooperation initiative, launched by SPFS in 1997, increased as it gained momentum. Under that initiative, more advanced developing (cooperating) countries provided technicians and experts to work for two to three years with farmers in rural communities of other developing (host) countries. The associated costs were borne by the cooperating and host countries and donors, with FAO facilitating the process.

Crops and livestock

FAO continued in 1999 to participate in activities related to the conservation and use of plant biological diversity, crop management and diversification, seed production and improvement, crop protection, agricultural engineering, prevention of food losses, and food and agricultural industries. Specifically, it contributed to the development of programmes and strategies for livestock production and health; and to the support of smallholder, specialized and mixed livestock farming through better resource utilization, improved processing and commercialization, and better control of animal diseases. Through its Emergency Prevention System for Transboundary Animal and Plant Pests and Diseases, FAO continued to promote cooperation among countries on early warning, control and research on the desert locust, in the prevention and control of significant transboundary diseases, and in the global eradication of rinderpest by 2010.

Fisheries

FAO continued efforts to secure the long-term sustainable development and utilization of the world's fisheries and aquaculture. Its priorities included the implementation of the FAO Code of Conduct for Responsible Fisheries, with particular attention to the problem of excess fishing capacity and strengthening of regional fisheries bodies; and the promotion of increased contribution of responsible fisheries and aquaculture to world food supplies and food security, with a focus on the reduction of waste in fisheries, safety and quality of food fish, economic and social policy analysis, fish trade and responsible aquaculture development. Databases and information systems were developed for improved dissemination of fishery statistics and information.

Food standards and nutrition

In 1999, the Codex Alimentarius Commission, responsible for implementing the Joint FAO/World Health Organization Food Standards Programme, significantly expanded its work programme to include the development of guidelines governing animal feeding and foods derived from biotechnology. The Commission agreed to strengthen in general its work on food microbiology and on other aspects of food safety. With 165 member countries, it developed international food standards, guidelines and other recommendations for the protection of consumer health and for ensuring fair practices in food trade. To promote better nutrition, FAO continued to provide member countries with information and technical assistance in the formulation and implementation of national food policies and nutrition programmes, technical and legal advice on measures to ensure the quality and safety of food, and assessment and monitoring of the effects on nutrition of food and agricultural policies and development activities.

Commodities and trade

FAO continued to implement the Plan of Action of the 1996 World Food Summit [YUN 1996, p. 1129]. In addition, it engaged in a wide range of activities to enhance the capacity of developing countries to analyse the implications of the Uruguay Round of multilateral trade agreements [YUN 1994, p. 1474] in agriculture, forestry and fisheries, and to take advantage of new trading opportunities. Several regional workshops, global seminars, training courses, expert meetings and analytical studies were conducted on issues of concern to developing countries at the Uruguay Round.

Environment and natural resources

FAO continued its wide-ranging activities aimed at achieving more productive and efficient utilization of the earth's natural resources to meet current and future food and agricultural needs in a sustainable manner. To facilitate natural resources assessment and planning, it maintained over 30 land and water resource databases, available electronically on CD-ROM or over the World Wide Web. It also continued to develop AQUASTAT, its information system on water in agriculture, as well as an environmental database and decision-support tools.

Plant and animal genetic resources

FAO continued to provide technical assistance in plant breeding and safe movement of germ plasm and associated systems. Its Commission on Genetic Resources for Food and Agriculture continued negotiations on the revision of the International Undertaking on Plant Genetic Resources, in harmony with the 1992 Convention on Biological Diversity [YUN 1992, p. 683], to regulate access to and benefit-sharing of plant genetic resources in food and agriculture. FAO's Global Strategy for the Management of Farm Animal Genetic Resources supported projects in Asia, sub-Saharan Africa and Europe, with 91 national coordinators to facilitate preparation of the first report on the state of the world's genetic resources. FAO assisted member countries in complying with the World Trade Organization Agreement on Trade-Related Aspects of Intellectual Property Rights, specifically those relating to plant varieties, animal breeds, related technology and germ plasm.

Information

FAO continued to function as an information centre, collecting, analysing, interpreting and disseminating information through various media, including publishing, radio, television, video, film and photographic displays and exhibitions.

Major regular periodicals included the annual *The State of Food and Agriculture*, the *FAO Quarterly Bulletin of Statistics*, the annual *Food and Agricultural Legislation*, the forestry quarterly *Unasylva* and the quarterlies *World Animal Review* and *Plant Protection Bulletin*.

FAO increasingly disseminated information electronically through the World Agricultural Information Centre (WAICENT), its corporate strategic programme for the management and dissemination of information. WAICENT included statistical databases, among them FAOSTAT, containing international statistics on food, agriculture, fisheries, forestry and nutrition, dating back to 1961, as well as over 1 million time-series records for 210 countries and Territories.

Secretariat

As at 31 December 1999, staff at FAO headquarters numbered 2,242, of whom 938 were in the Professional or higher categories and 1,304 in the General Service category. Field project personnel and those in regional and country offices totalled 1,830, with 637 in the Professional or higher categories and 1,193 in the General Service category.

Budget

The regular programme budget for the 1998-1999 biennium was $650 million, the same as for the previous biennium.

NOTE: For further information, see *The State of Food and Agriculture 2000*.

HEADQUARTERS AND OTHER OFFICES

HEADQUARTERS
Food and Agriculture Organization of the United Nations
Viale delle Terme di Caracalla
00100 Rome, Italy
Telephone: (39) (06) 57051
Fax: (39) (06) 5705 3152
Internet: http://www.fao.org
E-mail: mailserv@mailserv.fao.org

NEW YORK LIAISON OFFICE
Food and Agriculture Organization Liaison Office with the United Nations
1 United Nations Plaza, Room 1125
New York, NY 10017, United States
Telephone: (1) (212) 963-6036
Fax: (1) (212) 888-6188
E-mail: FAO-LONY@field.fao.org

FAO also maintained liaison offices in Brussels, Geneva, Washington, D.C., and Yokohama, Japan; regional offices in Accra, Ghana; Bangkok, Thailand; Cairo, Egypt; and Santiago, Chile; and subregional offices in Apia, Samoa; Bridgetown, Barbados; Budapest, Hungary; Harare, Zimbabwe; and Tunis, Tunisia.

Chapter IV

United Nations Educational, Scientific and Cultural Organization (UNESCO)

The United Nations Educational, Scientific and Cultural Organization (UNESCO) continued in 1999 to promote cooperation in education, science, culture and communication among its member States.

The General Conference convened its thirtieth session (Paris, 26 October–17 November). In addition to electing Koichiro Matsuura as Director-General for a six-year term, it adopted a number of resolutions, among them one on the 2000-2001 programme budget, covering major programme appropriations for basic education for all, sciences in the service of development, the preservation and revitalization of the cultural and natural heritage, and the free flow of ideas and access to information and communication technologies. The 58-member Executive Board held its one hundred and fifty-sixth (25 May–11 June), one hundred and fifty-seventh (5-22 October) and one hundred and fifty-eighth (18-19 November) sessions, all in Paris.

The membership of UNESCO increased to 188 in 1999, with the admission of Micronesia and Palau.

Activities

Education

UNESCO continued to promote international cooperation in the enhancement of education and to bolster national capacities for expanding and extending education as a vital tool for development and for building a culture of peace. It sought to strengthen the commitment of its members and the international community at large to give absolute priority to basic education for all as a fundamental human right, and to the renewal of education systems, formal and non-formal, taking account of the current contradictions and future challenges identified by major UN and UNESCO international conferences.

Activities in preventive education against HIV/AIDS and drug abuse focused on mobilizing education ministries to formulate national action plans for the implementation of school-based programmes and teacher-training seminars. UNESCO launched the international campaign on "Youth Mobilizing Youth on Drug Abuse Prevention", which led more than 4 million young people to sign the Youth Charter for a Twenty-first Century Free of Drugs. It continued to collaborate with the European Commission in implementing the Prevention Education Drugs network, aimed at fostering exchange of knowledge and experience among professionals in the field.

As a follow-up to the Second International Congress on Technical and Vocational Education (Seoul, Republic of Korea, 26-30 April), UNESCO launched a new programme on technical and vocational education and created an international centre in Bonn, Germany, to serve as a global clearing house for technical information. Following a series of regional conferences in Africa, Asia and the Arab States, organized within the framework of the Plan of Action for the United Nations Decade for Human Rights Education, 1995-2004 [YUN 1994, p. 1038], UNESCO, as the focal point for the International Year for the Culture of Peace, 2000 [YUN 1998, p. 638], provided assistance for the elaboration of strategies aimed at further strengthening the teaching of human rights. It collaborated with the Committee on Economic, Social and Cultural Rights and played an active role in implementing article 13, on the right to education in international human rights law, of the 1966 International Covenant on Economic, Social and Cultural Rights, adopted by General Assembly resolution 2200 A (XXI) [YUN 1966, p. 419].

The network of Associated Schools continued to expand, promoting such activities as the distribution to 130 countries of the educational resource kit "World Heritage in Young Hands".

Sciences

Under its programme of sciences in the service of development, UNESCO continued to promote the advancement, sharing and transfer of knowledge. It emphasized the fostering of synergies between the exact and natural sciences and the social and human sciences.

Natural sciences

UNESCO, jointly with the International Council for Science (ICSU), convened the World Conference on Science for the Twenty-first Century: a New Commitment (Budapest, Hungary, 26 June-1 July), which provided a forum for scientists, political decision makers and representatives of society at large to discuss future services that science could provide to society. The Conference adopted two principal documents that ICSU and UNESCO endorsed: the Declaration on Science and the Use of Scientific Knowledge, underscoring the political commitment to the scientific endeavour and to finding solutions to problems between science and society; and the Science Agenda—Framework for Action, containing specific commitments and recommendations on capacity-building in science and the use of science for sustainable development.

Activities in the exact and natural sciences were dedicated towards the advancement, sharing and transfer of scientific and technological knowledge. UNESCO continued to enhance human resources development and capacity-building through fellowships, grants, workshops, seminars and production of training tools. Other activities aimed at modernizing university curricula and training teachers nationally and regionally in the basic and engineering sciences.

Through the International Geological Correlation Programme, UNESCO contributed to the understanding of Earth's history, pressing environmental problems and humankind's vulnerability to natural hazards. The Man and the Biosphere Programme, in partnership with the 1992 Convention on Biological Diversity [YUN 1992, p. 683], helped to develop a joint initiative on biodiversity education and to promote the ecosystem approach. UNESCO hosted the secretariat of a major global initiative: the development of a Vision for Water, the Environment and Life for the Twenty-first Century.

Within the framework of the environment and development in coastal regions and in small islands platform, 23 pilot projects were established involving some 60 countries, uniting decision makers, local communities, cultural heritage experts and scientists.

Social and human sciences

Activities in the social and human sciences included strengthening research and training capacities, mainly through the establishment of UNESCO chairs, networks and mechanisms for inter-university cooperation; building bridges between social scientists and decision makers under the programme called Management of Social Transformations; and publication of the first issue of *World Social Science Report*. As a follow-up to the Plan of Action for the UN Year of Tolerance (1995) [YUN 1995, p. 1126], UNESCO undertook a number of initiatives to promote tolerance and non-violence and awarded the UNESCO Prize for Peace Education to the Association of the Mothers of the Plaza de Mayo, Argentina.

UNESCO also continued to promote a culture of peace at the national, regional and international levels through mobilization campaigns, pilot projects and international meetings, and member States' initiatives aimed at the fuller development of that culture.

Culture

Cultural development activities concentrated on follow-up action to the 1998 Conference on Cultural Policies for Development [YUN 1998, p. 1382]. The 1999 General Conference approved a new programme designed to collect and disseminate policy-relevant knowledge and information, to build national and local capacities in the management and administration of cultural institutions, and to foster recognition among decision makers of the growing significance of culture as a dimension of public policy.

A worldwide evaluation of the application of the UNESCO 1989 Recommendation on the Safeguarding of Traditional Culture and Folklore was completed, for which three regional seminars, an international conference and two international training workshops had been held. With the World Intellectual Property Organization, UNESCO organized five regional consultation meetings in search of legal means for the international protection of the expression of folklore. Within the framework of the "Proclamation by UNESCO of Masterpieces of the Oral and Intangible Heritage of Humanity", a nine-member international jury was established and an implementation guide for the Proclamation was drafted.

Efforts to promote international and national standards for the better protection of movable and immovable cultural heritage continued. A second protocol to the 1954 Convention for the Protection of Cultural Property in the Event of Armed Conflict was adopted by the March 1999 Hague Diplomatic Conference. As at 31 December, the signatories to the second protocol numbered 39. Inscribed on the World Heritage List were 48 new sites. Currently protected under the Convention for the Protection of the World Cultural and Natural Heritage were 630 sites (in 118 States), comprising 480 cultural, 128 natural and 22 cultural/natural sites.

The General Conference proclaimed 21 March as World Poetry Day.

Communications

UNESCO promoted activities in favour of press freedom, notably the worldwide celebration of

World Press Freedom Day on 3 May, highlighted by a seminar on unpunished crimes against journalists (Bogotá, Colombia).

UNESCO organized a meeting on ways to combat paedophilia and child pornography on the Internet (Paris, 18-19 January), attended by more than 300 specialists in child care and child protection, Internet specialists and service providers, media practitioners, Interpol, law enforcement agencies and government representatives.

UNESCO's International Programme for the Development of Communication funded 56 new projects totalling $2,258,000. To confront the problem of the digital divide, UNESCO continued its efforts to encourage cultural diversity and endogenous production of digital content through pilot projects on public service telematics consortia and multi-purpose community telecentres in Africa.

UNESCO published 105 titles and produced five CD-ROMS, among them *Blue Gold Interactive Encyclopaedia of Water,* which won the Möbius Prize for the best science CD-ROM and was nominated for Prince's Award, a European prize for the best multimedia on the environment.

Secretariat

As at 31 December 1999, UNESCO had a full-time staff of 2,348, of whom 1,090 were in the Professional or higher categories, drawn from 153 nationalities, and 1,258 were in the General Service category.

Budget

The UNESCO General Conference, at its 1999 session, approved a budget of $544,367,250 for the 2000-2001 biennium.

HEADQUARTERS AND OTHER OFFICES

HEADQUARTERS
UNESCO House
7, Place de Fontenoy
75352 Paris 07-SP, France
Telephone: (33) (1) 45-68-10-00
Fax: (33) (1) 45-67-16-90
Internet: http://www.unesco.org

NEW YORK LIAISON OFFICE
United Nations Educational, Scientific and Cultural Organization
2 United Nations Plaza, Room 900
New York, NY 10017, United States
Telephone: (1) (212) 963-5995
Fax: (1) (212) 963-8014
E-mail: newyork@unesco.org

UNESCO also maintained liaison offices in Geneva, Vienna and Washington, D.C.

Chapter V

World Health Organization (WHO)

The World Health Organization (WHO) moved forward in 1999 with its new corporate strategy of health for all, comprising four interrelated priorities: reducing excess mortality, morbidity and disability, especially in poor countries; promoting healthy lifestyles and reducing factors of risk to human health arising from environmental, economic, social and behavioural causes; developing more equitable and financially fair health systems; and developing an enabling policy and institutional environment in the health sector.

The World Health Assembly, WHO's governing body, held its fifty-second session (Geneva, 17-25 May) and adopted resolutions on a range of subjects, including active ageing, smallpox eradication through the destruction of variola virus stocks, the roll-back-malaria approach, a WHO framework convention on tobacco control, a revised drug strategy, reforming the Health Assembly, poliomyelitis eradication, strengthening health systems in developing countries and prevention and control of iodine deficiency disorders.

The one hundred and third session of the WHO Executive Board (Geneva, 25 January-3 February) discussed shaping a clear strategy to put health at the core of the international development agenda, with concomitant headquarters structural changes and streamlining of working relations with regions and countries; the essential goals of health systems for a better understanding of world health trends and challenges; and engagement of high-level policy makers in the Health Assembly's work. The Board's one hundred and fourth session (Geneva, 26-27 May) took up the question of a research strategy and mechanisms for cooperation, in addition to institutional matters.

The World Health Report 1999—Making a Difference reviewed the accomplishments and challenges in world health and highlighted their implications for WHO's future approach, priorities and work. It explained how lessons learned from past successes and failures could guide a more targeted and pragmatic approach to current and emerging health challenges, offering strategic directions for tackling them in the next decade.

In 1999, WHO membership remained at 191, with two associate members and four observers.

Health policy

WHO laid emphasis on policy based on hard evidence, such as clear positive or negative trends in health. Priorities took into consideration four key drivers of health change: ageing, the HIV and the tobacco epidemics, and childhood mortality due to communicable diseases. To advance programmes towards their goals, WHO reached out to old partners and decided to conclude a larger number of influential partnerships with various entities, including Governments, other UN bodies, financial institutions and foundations, research institutes, professional associations, non-governmental organizations (NGOs) and private firms. For example, in 1999, a Global Alliance for the Elimination of Leprosy was established, whose core members consisted of a dozen endemic countries, a private Japanese foundation, the pharmaceutical company Novartis, and a federation of some 20 NGOs.

Health and development

WHO was being strengthened to ensure that its support for health systems development was effective. A new Global Programme on Evidence for Health Policy was established to improve and expand the knowledge base in key areas of epidemiology and disease burden measurement, assessment of service quality and cost-effectiveness and comparative analysis of financing, organizational, regulatory and legislative options. A regrouping of headquarters programmes in the cluster on Health Systems and Community Health ensured that priority interventions, such as the Integrated Management of Childhood Illness, and strengthening of health systems worked together in WHO's technical support to countries. A time-limited project, entitled Partnerships for Health Sector Development, was created to change the way that WHO worked on health sector-wide development with national and international development agencies, within and beyond the UN system.

In the light of its comparative analysis of health systems in a number of countries, WHO advocated a "new universalism" that recognized the limits of Governments but retained their responsibility for the leadership and finance of health systems. The new universalism welcomed diversity and, subject to appropriate guidelines, competition in the provision of services. It recognized private providers as important sources of care in many countries; welcomed private sector involvement in supplying service providers with drugs and equipment; and encouraged increased public and private investment in generating new drugs, equipment and vaccines to underpin long-term improvement in health.

A concerted effort was made to anchor health on the global political agenda for development, since poor health was intrinsically linked to poverty. Mounting evidence showed that health measures aimed at improving the health of the poor could reap real development gains. WHO was thus strengthening its focus on the poor, with Africa as a key priority. Its target was halving the number of people living in poverty by 2015.

Disease trends and control efforts

A priority for intensive work was the control of tobacco and malaria because of the high morbidity and mortality rates associated with them. Accordingly, the World Health Assembly, in May, unanimously supported a resolution calling for work to begin on a framework convention on tobacco control, which would constitute the first multilaterally negotiated set of rules focusing on global tobacco control. A working group subsequently met (Geneva, 25-29 October) to outline the basic parameters of the proposed framework convention and related protocols. WHO also developed a strategy to roll back the resurgence of malaria. The goal was to halve the burden from the disease by 2010, by raising awareness; providing anti-malaria treatments, from drugs to insecticide-treated bed nets; identifying malaria incubation areas; promoting proper management of the environment; and strengthening the health systems of affected countries.

Secretariat

At the end of 1999, WHO had a staff of 3,452, including 1,259 in the Professional and higher categories and 2,193 in the General Service category.

Budget

The fifty-second (1999) World Health Assembly adopted a budget of $1,800,854,000 for the 2000-2001 biennium.

NOTE: For further details of WHO activities, see *The World Health Report 1999* and *2000*, published by the organization.

HEADQUARTERS AND OTHER OFFICES

HEADQUARTERS
World Health Organization
20 Avenue Appia
CH-1211 Geneva 27, Switzerland
Telephone: (41) (22) 791-21-11
Fax: (41) (22) 791-31-11
Internet: http://www.who.int/
E-mail: info@who.ch

WHO OFFICE AT THE UNITED NATIONS
2 United Nations Plaza
New York, NY 10017, United States
Telephone: (1) (212) 963-4388
Fax: (1) (212) 963-8565

WHO also maintained regional offices in Alexandria, Egypt; Copenhagen, Denmark; Harare, Zimbabwe; Manila, Philippines; New Delhi, India; and Washington, D.C.

Chapter VI

World Bank (IBRD and IDA)

The World Bank consisted of the International Bank For Reconstruction and Development (IBRD) and the International Development Association (IDA). Collectively, the following five institutions were known as the World Bank Group: IBRD, IDA, the International Finance Corporation, the Multilateral Investment Guarantee Agency and the International Centre for Settlement of Investment Disputes.

In fiscal 1999 (1 July 1998–30 June 1999), IBRD, together with IDA (see below), continued to promote economic and social progress in developing countries and to assist them towards stable, sustainable and equitable growth. The challenges of fiscal 1999, brought about by the consequences of the East Asian financial crisis and compounded by failing investor confidence in Brazil and the Russian Federation, as well as by falling commodity prices in Africa and the crisis in Kosovo, forced the Bank to stretch itself into new boundaries in order to respond rapidly and in a manner commensurate with the wide-ranging emergency and long-term needs.

Through the Comprehensive Development Framework (CDF), launched in fiscal 1999, the Bank established mechanisms to bring people together and build consensus, forged stronger partnerships, reduced wasteful competition and emphasized the achievement of concrete results. In addition, CDF enhanced development effectiveness and contributed towards the central goal of poverty reduction.

The Bank strengthened its fight against poverty through the Country Assistance Strategies; new lending and non-lending services; IDA replenishment; debt relief; and aid coordination.

At the end of fiscal 1999, IBRD membership remained at 181.

Lending operations

Gross disbursements by IBRD totalled $18.2 billion, a decrease of nearly 5 per cent over fiscal 1998. The Bank's new loan commitments totalled $22.1 billion, a slight increase over the previous fiscal year. For the first time in the Bank's history, adjustment lending accounted for more than half of total commitments in fiscal 1999, reflecting the continued focus on responding to the financial crisis that started in East Asia and spread to other parts of the world. Adjustment lending had been in many instances accompanied by technical assistance.

Total IBRD lending commitments in the fiscal year amounted to $22.2 billion for 131 new operations in 39 countries. The five largest borrowers were Argentina ($3.2 billion), Indonesia ($2.7 billion), China ($2.1 billion), the Republic of Korea ($2 billion) and the Russian Federation ($1.9 billion). Lending for multisector projects ($8.8 billion) led all sectors by volume, followed by finance ($2.6 billion) and the social sector ($2.3 billion).

The Bank approved the introduction of new loans and hedging products, including the fixed-spread London Inter Bank Offered Rate-based (LIBOR-based) loan, in order to give borrowers greater flexibility with debt management. The Bank also considered guidelines and financial terms for two new instruments: the Programmatic Structural Adjustment Loan and the Special Structural Adjustment Loan, designed to enhance the effectiveness of Bank support for structural and social reforms for sustainable growth.

International Development Association

Established in 1960 as the Bank's concessional lending arm, the International Development Association provided concessionary assistance to low-income developing countries to reduce poverty and improve the quality of life. In 1999, IDA assistance continued to those with an annual per capita gross national product of $925 or less (in 1997 United States dollars), for which 81 countries were eligible. IDA credits to those countries totalled $6.8 billion.

At the end of fiscal 1999, IDA membership remained at 160.

Fiscal year 1999 was the third year of the eleventh replenishment of IDA (IDA-11), which was designed to provide IDA with resources to fund credits committed during the period 1 July 1996–30 June 1999. The total expected commitment authority for IDA-11 was $14.5 billion, including the Interim Trust Fund (ITF) administered by IDA. ITF was established by all IDA donors, except the United States, to fund operations while the United States became current on IDA-10. The commitment authority for IDA-11 comprised 4.6 billion special drawing rights (SDR) from IDA-11 donor contributions, SDR 2.1 billion from ITF donor contributions, SDR 1.3 billion from the unreleased portion of contributions carried over from the IDA-10 period, SDR 0.1 billion from special contributions from Brazil, Denmark and the Republic of Korea, and SDR 6.4 billion from advanced commitment authority from expected repayments of past IDA credits and IBRD net income transfers. As at 30 June, available IDA-11 resources totalled SDR 5.7 billion.

In fiscal 1999, total IDA lending commitments reached $6.8 billion for 145 new operations in 53 countries. The largest commitment was made to Bangladesh ($1,012 million), followed by India ($654.8 million) and Honduras ($283.7 million). The majority of lending went for multisector projects ($1,457.9 million), agriculture ($1,020 million) and transportation ($981.3 million).

Although IDA was legally and financially distinct from IBRD, it shared the same staff, and the projects it supported had to meet the same criteria as IBRD.

International Centre for Settlement of Investment Disputes

The International Centre for Settlement of Investment Disputes (ICSID), established in 1966 to help promote international investment, continued to provide facilities for the settlement, by conciliation or arbitration, of investment disputes between member countries and nationals of other member countries. Provisions referring to arbitration under the auspices of ICSID were a common feature of international investment contracts, investment laws and bilateral and multilateral investment treaties.

In 1999, ICSID's membership totalled 131.

Multilateral Investment Guarantee Agency

The Multilateral Investment Guarantee Agency (MIGA), established in 1988, continued to encourage the flow of foreign direct investment to its developing member countries by providing investment guarantees against non-commercial risks. MIGA had its own operating and legal staff, but drew on the Bank for administrative and other services. In 1999, MIGA had a total of 149 members.

In fiscal 1999, MIGA issued $1.3 billion in guarantee coverage in 72 guarantee contracts to ensure investment projects in 29 developing member countries. MIGA also broadened its portfolio in fiscal 1999 by issuing its first guarantee contracts covering investments in Côte d'Ivoire, Malaysia and Zambia.

World Bank Institute

In March, the Economic Development Institute became the World Bank Institute (WBI), as the Bank merged its client and staff learning activities to maximize synergies from external and internal learning. WBI stressed the Bank's priority areas: training and seminars focused on poverty, crisis response, governance and corruption. WBI's contributions in fiscal 1999 included support for building anticorruption strategies; training for financial sector supervision; and promoting learning on clean air issues. It was also leading the process of consultations with civil society and researchers worldwide on the 2000/01 poverty issue of the *World Development Report*. In East Asia, WBI aimed to encourage knowledge and experience-sharing across client countries, build understanding on corruption and facilitate civic participation in national debate. In learning efforts oriented to Africa, WBI worked with the African Development Bank (ADB) and the International Monetary Fund to establish the Joint Africa Institute; developed pilot on-line Internet courses with the African Economic Research Consortium and 13 partner universities; and advanced the African Virtual University.

In fiscal 1999, the Bank launched the World Bank Learning Network, a distance learning programme that offered interactive video- and web-based courses, linking participants across the globe.

Scholarships

The Joint Japan/World Bank Graduate Scholarship Programme awarded 198 new scholarships to individuals applying for advanced studies in fields related to public policy-making.

In 1999, the Robert S. McNamara Fellowships Programme awarded 16 postgraduate fellowships for the study of globalization and poverty, and social inclusion, social capital and poverty reduction.

Co-financing

In fiscal 1999, co-financing amounted to $11.3 billion in 103 operations, an increase of 17 per cent over the previous year. Official bilateral and multilateral partners continued to be the largest source of co-financing, accounting for 89 per cent of the total share. The largest co-financing partners included the Inter-American Development Bank ($4.6 billion); Japan ($2 billion); European Union institutions ($491 million); ADB ($473 million); and the United Kingdom ($323 million). By sector, co-financing was concentrated in macroeconomic and financial sector reform and social protection operations, generally involving official partners, and in electric power, which attracted private co-financing partners as well. The Bank collaborated with donors to deal with the Asian financial crisis, most notably with Japan in the context of the New Miyazawa Initiative, whereby the Government would provide support measures totalling $30 billion, of which $15 billion would be made available for medium- to long-term financial needs for economic recovery in Asia.

Financing activities

During fiscal year 1999, IBRD raised $22.4 billion in medium- and long-term debt, compared to $28 billion the previous year. The majority of new funding continued to be initially swapped into floating rate United States dollars, with conversion to other currencies or fixed-rate funding being carried out subsequently in accordance with funding requirements. The currency composition continued to be concentrated in United States dollars, with its share at 30 June 1999 rising to 79 per cent of the borrowing portfolio, compared to 66 per cent at 30 June 1998. Borrowing was carried out in 12 currencies, resulting in 185 transactions during the fiscal year.

As at 30 June 1999, outstanding borrowing stood at $118.6 billion, after swaps. The average cost of all borrowing, after swaps, was 5.92 per cent. The borrowers continued to prefer single-currency loans, as they selected LIBOR-based single-currency loan terms for $15.8 billion and fixed-rate single-currency loan terms for $5.9 billion.

Capitalization

As at 30 June 1999, the total subscribed capital of IBRD was $188.2 billion, or 98.7 per cent of authorized capital of $190.8 billion. The outstanding loans and callable guarantees totalled $114 billion, or 56 per cent of IBRD's statutory lending limit.

Income, expenditures and reserves

IBRD'S gross revenues totalled $9.6 billion in fiscal 1999, an increase of $1.1 billion over 1998. Net income was $1.5 billion, up from $1.24 billion in fiscal 1998. Expenses increased to $7.9 billion from $7.3 billion a year earlier. Administrative costs rose to $849 million from $763 million in 1998, a 10 per cent increase. At the end of fiscal 1999, the Bank's liquidity totalled $30 billion, and the reserves-to-loan ratio fell to 13.69 per cent from 14.06 per cent in 1998 due to IBRD's increased emphasis on the equity-to-loans measure and de-emphasis of the reserves-to-loans measures it had used in the past.

Secretariat

As at 31 December 1999, IBRD's regular, fixed-term, long-term consultants, and long-term temporary staff in Washington, D.C., and local offices numbered 9,245.

NOTE: For further details regarding the Bank's activities, see *The World Bank Annual Report 1999*.

HEADQUARTERS AND OTHER OFFICES

The World Bank
1818 H Street N.W.
Washington, DC 20433, United States
Telephone: (1) (202) 477-1234
Fax: (1) (202) 477-6391
Internet: http://www.worldbank.org

The World Bank Mission to the United Nations
809 UN Plaza, Suite 900
New York, NY 10017, United States
Telephone: (1) (212) 963-6008
Fax: (1) (212) 697-7020

The World Bank also maintained offices in Paris and Tokyo.

Chapter VII

International Finance Corporation (IFC)

The International Finance Corporation (IFC), part of the World Bank Group, continued in 1999 to promote growth in developing countries by financing private sector investments and providing technical assistance and advice to Governments and businesses. In fiscal 1999 (1 July 1998–30 June 1999), IFC faced formidable challenges as recovery began from the global financial crises in many of its developing member countries. Despite those challenges, IFC delivered increases in net income, investment commitments and new project approvals. It also sought out new investment, especially in reformed and high-development-impact sectors, such as financial and physical infrastructure; preserved the viability of companies in its existing portfolio through restructuring and recapitalization support; developed trade finance products that matched the needs of struggling companies; and strengthened its operational focus on those developing countries and sectors that had attracted comparatively less foreign investment flows.

During fiscal 1999, IFC membership remained at 174.

Financial and advisory services

In fiscal 1999, IFC's Board of Directors approved a total of $5.3 billion in financing for 255 projects in 77 countries, compared with $5.9 billion for 304 projects in 83 countries in fiscal 1998. The project cost of fiscal 1999 approvals was $15.6 billion; the ratio of IFC funding to costs was 1 to 3.7. IFC approved an investment in one new country, Saint Kitts and Nevis.

The "Extending IFC's Reach" initiative, begun in 1997 as a pilot programme to promote investment in selected countries where difficult conditions had constrained IFC activity, was expanded to cover 20 countries and regions where IFC previously had only limited activity. Under the initiative, the Corporation approved 160 projects totalling $1 billion. Of those, 67 investments totalling $68.3 million were through the Small Enterprise Fund. In addition, IFC mobilized $446.2 million from participants and provided $12.2 million through its Technical Assistance Trust Funds Programme for 108 projects.

During fiscal 1999, IFC approved eight risk management projects, including projects for clients from Bangladesh, Côte d'Ivoire, Ecuador, Mozambique, Panama, Peru and the Republic of Korea, and undertook more than 100 financial market advisory projects in some 50 countries and regions.

Demand for technical assistance and advisory services continued throughout the fiscal year. IFC provided a broad range of services, including capital markets technical assistance; advisory work in the infrastructure area; privatization and corporate restructuring; project development facilities; investment and project-specific advisory services; and the Foreign Investment Advisory Service.

Regional projects

IFC approved 255 projects in 77 countries and regions in fiscal 1999.

In sub-Saharan Africa, IFC's development priorities included strengthening the financial sector through direct investment in financial institutions; support for indigenous entrepreneurship; and the development of a sound physical infrastructure. It approved 80 projects in 26 countries in fiscal 1999, compared to 80 projects in 23 countries in fiscal 1998. As at 30 June 1999, IFC's committed portfolio, including loans and investments, totalled $1.33 billion, up from $1.18 billion in fiscal 1998.

In Asia and the Pacific, IFC's strategy was directed at rehabilitating and consolidating the financial and corporate sectors of those economies hardest hit by the East Asian financial crisis. IFC played a pivotal role in the establishment of the Asia Opportunity Fund. With $100 million in equity, IFC joined Chase Capital Partners and several Asian investors in one of the largest emerging-markets restructuring funds ever. Up to $750 million in investments was expected to be placed over a three- to five-year period. In addition, IFC established the Asian Debt Facility to provide loans and guarantees directly to companies about to be restructured. The Corporation approved 33 projects in 8 countries in fiscal 1999, compared to 50 projects in 14 countries in fiscal 1998. Its committed portfolio of loans and investments totalled $5.96 billion, down from $6.18 billion in fiscal 1998.

In the Middle East and North Africa, IFC focused on financial sector development, infrastructure and industries that created jobs and generated foreign exchange, while in Central Asia it supported natural resource development, small and medium-sized enterprises (SMEs), financial sector growth and the rehabilitation and modernization of selected post-privatization companies. IFC approved 34 projects in fiscal 1999 in 11 countries, compared to 32 projects in 11 countries in fiscal 1998. IFC's committed portfolio of loans and investments totalled $2.08 billion, compared to $1.96 billion in fiscal 1998.

In Europe, IFC worked closely with project owners and managers to develop joint responses and advised on possible protective measures as the financial turmoil unfolded in the Russian Federation, causing varying degrees of economic decline in Central, Southern and Eastern Europe. IFC supported institution-building throughout the region to strengthen the banking sectors, financial infrastructure and capital market efficiency. It placed increased emphasis on restructuring banks and improving the regulatory framework and its enforcement; provided technical assistance and financing for privatization; and supported SMEs. IFC approved 49 projects in 16 countries in fiscal 1999, compared to 74 projects in 18 countries in fiscal 1998. Its committed portfolio of loans and investments totalled $3.44 billion, compared with $2.78 billion in fiscal 1998.

In Latin America and the Caribbean, IFC deployed its resources to ensure the health of its portfolio companies; continued assisting high-development-impact sectors, such as financial and physical infrastructure; and concentrated on middle-market firms and SMEs. It approved 58 projects in 16 countries, compared to 67 projects in 17 countries in fiscal 1998. Its committed portfolio totalled $8.23 billion in fiscal 1999 compared to $8.32 billion in fiscal 1998.

Foreign Investment Advisory Service

The Foreign Investment Advisory Service (FIAS), jointly operated by IFC and the World Bank, continued to advise Governments on policies, law, regulations and procedures needed to increase inflows of productive foreign direct investment. Of particular importance in fiscal 1999 were projects in Central and Eastern Europe, where FIAS provided recommendations to 10 countries. FIAS teams also examined ways to improve the legal and institutional framework in Costa Rica, Nepal and Zambia to facilitate large-scale infrastructure investments on a project finance basis. In other assignments, FIAS identified bureaucratic impediments to private investments and recommended ways to address them in Bolivia, Indonesia, Jordan, Latvia, Madagascar, Mali, Mauritania and the Philippines.

Financial performance

In fiscal 1999, IFC's net income totalled $249 million, up from $246 million in fiscal 1998. The loan portfolio showed a small profit of $10 million in fiscal 1999, while net income from the equity/quasi-equity portfolio declined to $76 million from $94 million in fiscal 1998, mainly because of sizeable loss provisions taken early in the fiscal year. Net income from IFC's invested net worth and treasury activities totalled $155 million.

IFC's committed portfolio at the end of the fiscal year was $12.9 billion, up from $11.5 billion in fiscal 1998. The portfolio consisted of loans and equity investments in 1,280 companies in 112 countries.

Capital and retained earnings

As at 30 June 1999, IFC's net worth reached $5.3 billion, compared to $5.1 billion at the end of fiscal 1998.

Secretariat

As at 30 June 1999, IFC employed 1,818 staff, including consultants and temporary staff.

NOTE: For further details of IFC activities, see *International Finance Corporation 1999 Annual Report*, published by the Corporation.

HEADQUARTERS AND OTHER OFFICE

HEADQUARTERS
International Finance Corporation
2121 Pennsylvania Avenue, NW
Washington, DC 20433, United States
Telephone: (1) (202) 473-7711
Fax: (1) (202) 974-4384
Internet: http://www.ifc.org
E-mail: Webmaster@ifc.org

NEW YORK OFFICE
International Finance Corporation
809 U.N. Plaza, Suite 900
New York, NY 10017, United States
Telephone: (1) (212) 963-6008
Fax: (1) (212) 697-7020

Chapter VIII

International Monetary Fund (IMF)

During 1999, the International Monetary Fund (IMF) promoted international monetary cooperation, exchange stability and orderly exchange arrangements; fostered economic growth and high levels of employment; and provided temporary financial assistance to countries to help ease balance-of-payments adjustment. The continued repercussions of the 1997 Asian financial crisis and the spread of the financial stress to Brazil and the Russian Federation in 1998 posed challenges for IMF and the international community. Strong macroeconomic stabilization measures coupled with important structural reforms helped abate the crisis by the end of the fiscal year (1 May 1998–30 April 1999). The financial crises gave the Fund a powerful impetus to focus on proposals to strengthen the structure and transparency of the international financial system. IMF continued to help its members strengthen their financial sectors and worked towards identifying ways to involve the private sector in preventing and managing crises and in improving the functioning of international capital markets. IMF enhanced assistance to countries in post-conflict situations and, in collaboration with the World Bank, considered ways to reduce further the debt of low-income countries, undertaking strong adjustment programmes under the Heavily Indebted Poor Countries Debt Initiative (HIPC Initiative).

During fiscal 1999, IMF membership remained at 182.

IMF facilities and policies

IMF provided financial assistance to its members through several facilities and policies to help them achieve sustainable economic growth, balance-of-payments viability and establish normal relations with their creditors. Credit for short-term balance of payments for deficits of a temporary or cyclical nature was made available under standby arrangements. Credit for longer periods was made available under the extended funding facility (EFF).

The Fund provided concessional financial support to low-income countries under the enhanced structural adjustment facility (ESAF), which in 1999 was renamed the poverty reduction and growth facility. The HIPC Initiative, a joint IMF–World Bank project, provided debt-servicing relief to heavily indebted poor countries. During fiscal 1999, the IMF Executive Board reviewed the operation and financing of ESAF and the HIPC Initiative in order to improve their effectiveness in helping poor countries attain growth and reduce poverty.

Other IMF facilities consisted of the compensatory and contingency financing facility (CCFF) and the supplemental reserve facility, established in April.

Financial assistance

During fiscal 1999, the Fund approved 19 new standby, extended and ESAF arrangements, totalling 29.4 billion special drawing rights (SDR) in new commitments (SDR 14.32 billion in standby arrangements for five countries; SDR 14.09 billion for four EFF arrangements; and SDR 1 billion for 10 ESAF arrangements), compared with commitments of SDR 32.1 billion in fiscal 1998. The Fund also committed SDR 2.6 billion under CCFF. The largest credit commitments were for Brazil (SDR 13 billion), Indonesia (SDR 6.4 billion) and the Russian Federation (SDR 8.5 billion, including under CCFF).

As at 30 April, nine standby arrangements, 12 extended arrangements and 35 ESAF arrangements were in effect with members. Net of repayment of previous drawings, outstanding IMF credit reached a record SDR 67.2 billion, up from SDR 56 billion in fiscal 1998.

In April, the IMF Executive Board established contingent credit lines, a crisis-prevention mechanism intended for member countries with strong policies, as a precautionary line of defence against potential balance-of-payments problems arising from financial contagion.

Liquidity

In the aftermath of the financial crisis that began in Asia in 1997, heavy demand for the use of IMF resources continued in fiscal 1999, heightened by the emergence of crises in the Russian Federation in mid-1998 and in Brazil in December 1998. During December 1998, IMF's liquidity ratio fell to below 30 per cent, about the minimum needed for IMF to maintain operational manoeuverability. Prior to the quota increase under the Eleventh General Review—which took effect on 22 January 1999—IMF had to resort to borrowing: first in July 1998 in connection with the augmentation of the extended arrangement for Russia, and subsequently in December 1998 in connection with the standby arrangement for Brazil. Following the quota increase, IMF repaid the amount borrowed. IMF's usable resources increased sharply towards the end of the financial year as a result of quota payments amounting to SDR 46 billion in usable currencies and SDRs. Also, the inclusion of three additional members in the list of sufficiently strong countries during the fiscal year added SDR 1.7 billion to usable resources. Consequently, uncommitted and adjusted resources totalled SDR 56.7 billion at the end of fiscal 1999, compared with SDR 22.6 billion in fiscal 1998.

At the end of April 1999, the Fund's liquid liabilities totalled SDR 63.6 billion, consisting entirely of reserve tranche positions (as all borrowing undertaken during the year had been repaid), compared with SDR 50.3 billion a year earlier. The ratio of the Fund's net uncommitted usable resources to its liquid liabilities increased to 89.2 per cent at the end of April 1999 from 44.8 per cent a year earlier.

SDR activity

In fiscal 1999, total transactions of SDRs reached a record SDR 49.1 billion, from SDR 20.3 billion in fiscal 1998. The increase was due to flows associated with the quota increase under the Eleventh General Review, as well as to steep increases in purchases and repurchases under IMF arrangements, and the repayment of borrowings by the Fund. The dominant cause, however, was that of the quota increase, which led to a large rise in IMF holdings of SDRs in the general resources account (GRA), only partially offset during the year by transfers from the GRA to participants.

Transfers of SDRs from participants to the GRA increased dramatically to SDR 16.2 billion in 1998/99 from SDR 4.8 billion in 1997/98. Those transfers were boosted, in part, by exceptional flows associated with quota payments. IMF attempted during 1998/99 to reduce rapidly the SDR holdings of the GRA to more normal levels (SDR 1-1.5 billion). Accordingly, SDR transfers from the GRA to participants and prescribed holders more than doubled, to SDR 13.4 billion in 1998/99 from SDR 5.6 billion in 1997/98, reflecting the substantial use of SDRs by the GRA to finance purchases and to repay IMF borrowing under general arrangements and new arrangements to borrow. Purchases in SDRs in 1998/99 reached a record SDR 9.5 billion, including some SDR 2.3 billion in reserve tranche drawings by members availing themselves of the same-day loan facility to make quota payments.

Transfers of SDRs among participants and prescribed holders nearly doubled to SDR 19.4 billion in 1998/99, owing mainly to the substantial increase in transactions by agreement and to the use of the same-day SDR loan facility by members paying the reserve asset portion of their quota subscriptions. The SDR holdings of non-industrial countries declined to 52.5 per cent from 69.4 per cent during fiscal 1999, and those of industrial countries to 94.6 per cent from 107 per cent. The SDR holdings of prescribed holders increased to SDR 0.6 billion in fiscal 1999 from SDR 0.4 billion a year earlier.

Policy on arrears

Total overdue financial obligations to IMF increased slightly to SDR 2.3 billion during fiscal 1999, from SDR 2.26 billion a year earlier. All of the overdue obligations were protracted (overdue by six months or more). No new cases of protracted arrears emerged during the fiscal year, nor were any of the existing cases cleared, leaving the number of members in protracted arrears to IMF at seven. Overdue financial obligations continued to be concentrated among four members (Democratic Republic of the Congo, Liberia, Somalia, Sudan), whose arrears accounted for 94 per cent of total overdue obligations. As at 30 April, those four members were ineligible to use the Fund's general resources.

Technical assistance and training

In fiscal 1999, technical assistance activity represented about 15 per cent of IMF's total administrative expenditures. Demand for such assistance remained strong and continued to focus on the monetary and fiscal aspects of macroeconomic management, statistics, financial law, social security reform, IMF financial organization and operations and information technology.

The IMF Institute, faced with expanded demand and limited capacities, increased its collaborative arrangements with partners to provide overseas training to strengthen the institutional capacity of member countries in economic management. In 1999, the Joint Africa Institute was established in Côte d'Ivoire, in equal partnership with the African Development Bank and the World Bank. Also in 1999, the Institute, in partnership with the Arab Monetary Fund, established in the United Arab Emirates the Regional Training Programme to meet the training needs of the region by allowing both organizations to mobilize their human and financial training resources.

Secretariat

As at 31 December 1999, IMF employed 2,297 staff members, of whom 1,604 were Professional staff and 693 assistant staff.

Budget

The Fund's administrative budget for fiscal 1999 was $519.5 million. For the capital budget, $14.4 million was approved for projects beginning in fiscal 1999. Actual administrative expenses during the fiscal year totalled $520.6 million and capital project disbursements totalled $43.9 million, including $25.3 million for major building projects.

NOTE: For details of IMF activities during the 1999 fiscal year, see *Annual Report of the Executive Board for the Financial Year Ended April 30, 1999.*

HEADQUARTERS AND OTHER OFFICE

HEADQUARTERS
International Monetary Fund
700 19th Street, NW
Washington, DC 20431 United States
Telephone: (1) (202) 623-7000
Fax: (1) (202) 623-4661
Internet: http://www.imf.org
E-mail: publicaffairs@imf.org

IMF OFFICE, UNITED NATIONS, NEW YORK
International Monetary Fund
828 Second Avenue
New York, NY 10017, United States
Telephone: (1) 917-332-2140
Fax: (1) 917-332-2150

Chapter IX

International Civil Aviation Organization (ICAO)

The International Civil Aviation Organization (ICAO) continued to promote the safety and efficiency of civil air transport by prescribing standards and recommending procedures for facilitating civil aviation operations. Its objectives were set forth in annexes to the Convention on International Civil Aviation, adopted in Chicago, United States, in 1944, known as the Chicago Convention.

In 1999, domestic and international scheduled traffic carried by the airlines of ICAO's Contracting States increased to some 369 billion tonne-kilometres. The airlines carried a total of about 1.56 billion passengers and some 28 million tonnes of freight. The passenger load factor on total scheduled services remained at 69 per cent, and the overall weight load factor at 60 per cent. Air freight increased some 6 per cent to 108 billion tonne-kilometres, and airmail traffic totalled 5.7 billion tonne-kilometres. During the year, both the overall and international passenger/ freight/mail tonne-kilometres increased by some 6 per cent.

The Council of ICAO held three regular sessions (22 February-19 March, 31 May-25 June, 28 October-19 December), during which, among other things, it adopted a declaration urging all States to refrain from the use of weapons against civil aircraft in flight.

In January, ICAO launched its Universal Safety Oversight Audit Programme, which aimed at assessing the degree to which Contracting States had implemented the safety-related Standards and Recommended Practices (SARPs) contained in the 1944 Chicago Convention and its annexes. At year's end, 49 States had been audited.

Following the entry into force in 1998 of the Convention on the Marking of Plastic Explosives for the Purpose of Detection, the International Explosive Technical Commission was appointed to evaluate technical developments relating to the manufacture, marking and detection of explosives and to make recommendations to the ICAO Council for amendments. The Commission held its first meeting in Montreal, Canada, from 13 to 15 December.

In 1999, ICAO membership remained at 185 countries.

Activities

Air navigation

ICAO continued to update and implement international specifications and regional plans, emphasizing the introduction of communications, navigation, and surveillance/air traffic management (CNS/ATM) systems. The specifications consisted of SARPs contained in 18 technical annexes to the 1944 Chicago Convention and Procedures for Air Navigation Services (PANS). Regional plans covered air navigation facilities and services required for implementation of CNS/ATM systems and other international air navigation elements in ICAO regions.

Six navigation meetings, convened in Montreal in 1999, made recommendations to amend ICAO specifications. The Accident Investigation and Prevention Divisional Meeting (14-24 September) developed 14 recommendations for SARPs. Among other things, it formulated new provisions for medical examinations in investigations and for voluntary incident reporting systems. The remaining five air navigation panel meetings developed SARPs and guidance material for the aeronautical mobile satellite services; an initial package of SARPs for the global navigation satellite system; provisions relating to various subjects for the amendment of the *Procedures for Air Navigation Services—Aircraft Operations*; provisions to facilitate the implementation of available technology in relation to a number of data link applications; and provisions regarding the safe transport of dangerous goods by air.

The Council of ICAO adopted amendments to seven technical annexes to the 1944 Chicago Convention and approved amendments to two PANS documents.

Other projects that were given special attention in 1999 included accident investigation; accident and incident data reporting; accident prevention; aerodromes; aerodrome rescue and fire fighting; aeronautical electromagnetic spectrum; aeronautical information services; assistance to civil aviation accident victims and their families; audio-visual aids; aviation environmental matters; aviation medicine; bird strikes to aircraft; CNS/ATM systems; controlled flight into terrain; flight safety and human factors; licensing/certification of aerodromes; meteorology; personnel licensing and training; safety oversight audits; the TRAINAIR programme; and year 2000 (Y2K) planning.

Air transport

ICAO's air transport programmes were directed towards economic analysis, economic policy, forecasting and economic planning, collection and publication of air transport statistics, airport and route facility management, economic and organizational aspects of CNS/ATM systems, economic and coordination aspects of environmental protection and the promotion of greater facilitation in international air transport.

The Council of ICAO adopted a resolution on the organization's policy on the taxation of international air transport.

The Technical Advisory Group on Machine Readable Travel Documents (Montreal, 1-3 September) finalized work on machine readable official travel documents. Six workshops in air transport regulatory policy, forecasting and economic planning, statistics, and airport and route facility management, a seminar on airport and route facility management and a Facilitation Area Meeting were held during the year.

ICAO continued to provide secretariat services to three independent regional civil aviation bodies—the African Civil Aviation Commission, the European Civil Aviation Conference and the Latin American Civil Aviation Commission.

The organization maintained its responsibilities for the administration of the Danish and Icelandic Joint Financing Agreements, to which 23 Governments were contracting parties in 1999. The two agreements, which were signed in 1956 and amended in 1982, concerned the provision in Greenland and Iceland of air traffic control, communications and meteorology facilities and services to North Atlantic flights.

Legal matters

The International Conference on Air Law (Montreal, 10-18 May) adopted the Convention for the Unification of Certain Rules for International Carriage by Air, which provided new compensation levels for victims of air accidents.

The Protocol relating to an amendment to the Convention on International Civil Aviation (Final Clause/Russian text) entered into force on 17 August. Accordingly, the Protocol on the Authentic Quadrilingual Text of the Convention on International Civil Aviation entered into force on 16 September.

Additional conventions and protocols on international air law concluded under ICAO auspices registered new ratifications, adherences or successions in 1999.

Technical cooperation

In 1999, ICAO undertook 126 technical cooperation projects in 72 countries. The technical cooperation programmes, financed by the United Nations Development Programme (UNDP), trust funds, management service agreements and the Civil Aviation Purchasing Service, had total expenditures of $54.3 million. Some 95 per cent of that amount was provided by Governments to fund their own projects on the basis of trust funds and cost sharing with UNDP.

ICAO had resident missions in 39 countries, and 92 others received assistance through fellowships and visits from experts assigned to intercountry and sub-contractual arrangements. A total of 581 fellowships were awarded in 1999, of which 540 were implemented. ICAO employed 371 experts from 41 countries, of whom 135 were on assignment under UNDP and 236 worked on trust fund projects. Registered with ICAO under its Civil Aviation Purchasing Service were 85 Governments and organizations. Equipment purchases during the year totalled $21.23 million.

Secretariat

In 1999, ICAO employed a total of 778 staff members, including 336 in the Professional and higher categories and 442 in the General Service and related categories. Of the total, 84 were technical cooperation funded posts.

Budget

Appropriations for the ICAO budget in 1999 were $52,578,000.

NOTE: For further details on the activities of ICAO in 1999, see *Annual Report of the Council 1999.*

HEADQUARTERS AND OTHER OFFICES

International Civil Aviation Organization
999 University Street
Montreal, Quebec, Canada H3C 5H7
Telephone: (1) (514) 954-8219
Fax: (1) (514) 954-6077
Internet: http://www.icao.int
E-mail: icaohq@icao.int

ICAO maintained regional offices in Bangkok, Thailand; Cairo, Egypt; Dakar, Senegal; Lima, Peru; Mexico, D. F.; Nairobi, Kenya; and Neuilly-sur-Seine, France.

Chapter X

Universal Postal Union (UPU)

The Universal Postal Union (UPU) continued to promote a fast and reliable universal postal service at affordable prices through international collaboration among its member countries. In 1999, the Universal Postal Congress, UPU's supreme legislative body, adopted the Beijing Postal Strategy, the Union's strategic document for 2000-2004. The year marked the one hundred and twenty-fifth anniversary of UPU.

UPU's 189 member countries remained the largest physical distribution network in the world, with some 6 million postal employees working in more than 700,000 post offices worldwide.

Activities of UPU organs

Universal Postal Congress

The Universal Postal Congress, which met every five years and was composed of all member States, held its twenty-second session in 1999 (Beijing, China, 23 August–15 September). It adopted the Beijing Postal Strategy, a blueprint for action by Governments, postal administrations and UPU bodies. The Congress laid out action plans to help member countries improve postal service in areas such as mail security, quality of service and the development of markets, including letter-mail, parcels, postal financial services and philately. The Congress reiterated its support of postal reform and cooperation as a means of reducing the operational and financial performance gap between developed and developing countries. To that end, it authorized the establishment of a Quality Service Fund, whereby special assessments on developed countries would be paid out to developing countries in the form of specific quality of service improvement projects. Recommendations concerning the future role and structure of UPU were debated, and a 25-member high-level group was formed to propose changes in UPU within two years. In order to increase stakeholder participation in the Union's work, an Advisory Group, open to regional postal unions and non-governmental organizations, as well as a selected number of postal administrations, was set up.

Council of Administration

The Council of Administration, which ensured the continuity of the Union's work between Congresses and studied regulatory, administrative, legislative and legal issues of concern to the Union, held two sessions in 1999. The first session (Berne, Switzerland, 15-18 February) focused on the recommendations to be presented to the twenty-second UPU Congress, while the second (Beijing, 10-15 September) assigned tasks to be undertaken during the five-year period leading to the next Congress.

Postal Operations Council

The Postal Operations Council, which dealt with the operations, economic and commercial aspects of international postal services, assisted those services to modernize and upgrade their postal products, including letter post, express mail service, postal parcels and postal financial services. The Council met twice in Berne in 1999. The first session (8-12 February) approved proposals for submission to the UPU Congress, and the second (22 November–1 December), in addition to setting up new committees and work plans, approved the Union's Letter Post Regulations, the Parcel Post Regulations and the Regulations of the Postal Payment Services Agreement, as well as the respective Final Protocols.

The Council, after four years of study of costs, tariffs, the regulatory environment and market behaviour, formulated its proposal for a new terminal dues system in February 1999. Terminal dues were the payment postal services made to each other for the delivery of inland foreign letter post. Country-specific rates for terminal dues would come into effect in developed countries at the beginning of 2001 as part of a new terminal dues system adopted during the UPU Congress.

International Bureau

The International Bureau, under the supervision of the Council of Administration, was the area of the UPU secretariat that provided support, liaison, information and consultation to the postal administrations of member countries. It continued to act as a clearing house for the settlement of various inter-administration charges related to the exchange of postal items and international reply coupons. The Bureau undertook studies on developments in the postal environment, monitored the quality of postal service on a global scale and published information and statistics on international postal services. Its Postal Technology Centre managed the postal application of the electronic data interchange.

As at 31 December 1999, the number of permanent staff members employed by the Bureau was 151, of whom 63 were in the Professional or higher categories and 88 were in the General Service category.

Budget

Under the Union's self-financing system, contributions were payable in advance by member States based on the following year's budget. Since the early 1990s, UPU had adopted the principle of zero real growth, and for the last two years it had followed zero nominal growth. Therefore, the budget approved for 2000 was 35.7 million Swiss francs, the same amount as in 1999. The twenty-second Congress authorized the introduction of a biennial budget cycle starting from the year 2001.

NOTE: For further details of UPU activities, see the following: *Comprehensive report on the work of the Council of Administration 1994-1999; Comprehensive report on the work of the Postal Operations Council 1994-1999; Director General's Report 1994-1999;* and *Director General's report on the finances of the Union 1994-1999.*

HEADQUARTERS

Universal Postal Union
Weltpoststrasse 4
3015 Berne, Switzerland
Postal address: Union postale universelle
Case postale
3000 Berne 15, Switzerland
Telephone: (41) (31) 350 31 11
Fax: (41) (31) 350 31 10
Internet: http://www.upu.int
E-mail: ib.info@upu.int

Chapter XI

International Telecommunication Union (ITU)

The International Telecommunication Union (ITU) continued to promote development and efficient operation of telecommunication systems and to provide technical assistance.

At its annual session, the ITU Council (Geneva, 14-25 June) focused on strengthening ITU's policy-making role, the ongoing ITU reform process and new cost-recovery strategies to help fund the Union's growing areas of responsibility, while minimizing the financial impact on its members. The Council approved the establishment of an annual strategic planning workshop to focus on topics of interest to regulators and policy makers, and moved to set up a working group on ITU reform. Also approved was the establishment of a group of experts to study the impact of changes in the regulation and operation of international telecommunication services. The Council endorsed a schedule of charges for processing satellite filings; agreed to ITU's participation in the Protocol Supporting Organization of the Internet Corporation for Assigned Names and Numbers; and, in regard to Internet names, endorsed the Union's management of the .int top-level domain, intended primarily for use by intergovernmental organizations. A new strategy for providing assistance to least developed countries was approved.

During the year, ITU membership increased to 189 with the admission of Seychelles.

A major event in 1999 was World TELECOM 99 + INTERACTIVE 99 (Geneva, 10-17 October), a forum and exhibition organized by ITU every four years on new technological developments in the telecommunication sector. The event attracted more than 4,000 delegates, who participated in five summits covering topics from industry convergence, technology and interactivity to policy and regulatory issues and telecommunication development.

Radiocommunication Sector

ITU's Radiocommunication Sector (ITU-R) coordinated the development of timely standards for new and evolving wireless communication systems and established the global framework for management of the radio frequency spectrum and the procedures for coordinating the use of frequencies and the orbits used by communication satellites. Preparations for the World Radiocommunication Conference in 2000 continued, while the ITU-R study groups prepared new and updated recommendations on spectrum issues, including standards for next-generation cellular mobile systems. The Radiocommunication Bureau continued to provide services to administrations and users in the application of regulatory, administrative and operational procedures. It also processed notifications for frequency assignments to new or modified terrestrial radiocommunication systems.

Telecommunication Standardization Sector

In 1999, the Telecommunication Standardization Sector (ITU-T) adopted 362 new or revised global standards, on which the world's telecommunication networks were based, including standards for advanced technologies such as optical switching and wave division multiplexing. It developed key standards for systems from digital television and audio broadcasting to cable television and digital image formats. The Telecommunication Standardization Bureau assigned an additional 3,100 universal international freephone numbers (UIFNs). At the end of 1999, 18,485 UIFNs had been assigned.

ITU-T became a founding member of the Internet Corporation for Assigned Names and Numbers (ICANN) Protocol Supporting Organization. Through a Memorandum of Understanding signed in July between ICANN and a number of standard development organizations (SDOs), ITU would work in partnership with international and regional SDOs to facilitate the growth of the Internet.

Telecommunication Development Sector

Through the Electronic Commerce for Developing Countries Initiative, the Telecommunication Development Bureau, the executive arm of the Telecommunication Development Sector, helped extend the power of emerging electronic commerce networks to local merchants in developing countries. Workshops and seminars held in 1999 covered a diverse range of technologies, from digital sound and television broadcasting and global mobile personal communication satellite services to new telemedicine systems.

The Bureau assisted developing countries with their training needs through a wide range of initiatives. One of the most important was the establishment of four new Centres of Excellence in East and West Africa, the Americas, and Asia and the Pacific. The Centres would train public officials in policy and regulatory issues, while serving as a resource for telecommunication companies and service providers throughout the three regions. All four Centres delivered their first pilot courses during 1999, in partnership with leading vendors and operators. The Bureau continued to develop a special tele-education programme under the auspices of its Global Telecom University/Global Telecom Training Institute project, and undertook a range of ad hoc activities, which included convening the Second World Telemedicine Symposium (Buenos Aires, Argentina, 22-25 March) and the implementation of regional workshops.

Secretariat

As at 31 December 1999, ITU had 770 staff members.

Budget

The budget for ITU in 1998-1999 amounted to 327,644,000 Swiss francs (SwF). The ITU Council set the 2000-2001 budget at SwF 332,621,000.

NOTE: For further details regarding ITU activities, see *ITU 1999 Annual Report*, published by the Union.

HEADQUARTERS

International Telecommunication Union
Place des Nations
CH-1211, Geneva 20, Switzerland
Telephone: (41) (22) 730-5111
Fax: (41) (22) 733-7256
Internet: http://www.itu.int
E-mail: itumail@itu.int

Chapter XII

World Meteorological Organization (WMO)

The World Meteorological Organization (WMO) continued in 1999 to facilitate cooperation related to meteorological and hydrological information and the application of meteorology to aviation, shipping, water problems, agriculture and other activities. WMO also promoted operational hydrology and encouraged research and training in meteorology.

The Thirteenth World Meteorological Congress (Geneva, 4-26 May), WMO's governing body, which met every four years, approved the Fifth Long-term Plan (2000-2009), and the programme and budget for 2000-2003. The Congress adopted the Geneva Declaration, which reaffirmed the importance of the National Meteorological and Hydrological Services (NMHSs) for sustainable development, and urged Governments to uphold the free and unrestricted international exchange of meteorological data and products. It established a Joint WMO/Intergovernmental Oceanographic Commission (IOC) Technical Commission for Oceanography and Marine Meteorology (JCOMM) to serve WMO and IOC of the United Nations Educational, Scientific and Cultural Organization (UNESCO).

WMO membership remained at 179 States and six Territories in 1999. Members were grouped in six regional associations (RAs)—Africa (RA I), Asia (RA II), South America (RA III), North and Central America (RA IV), South-West Pacific (RA V) and Europe (RA VI).

World Weather Watch Programme

The World Weather Watch Programme (WWW), the backbone of WMO scientific and technical programmes, through its Commission for Basic Systems (CBS), collected, analysed and disseminated meteorological data and products needed by member States to run their meteorological services efficiently. WWW offered up-to-the-minute worldwide weather information though its Global Observing System (GOS), Global Telecommunications System (GTS), Global Data-processing System (GDPS), and data management and system support activities, collectively known as the basic systems. It also included the Tropical Cyclone Programme, the Instruments and Methods of Observation Programme and WMO satellite and environmental emergency response activities.

World Weather Watch implementation

During the year, WWW's main activities focused on the implementation of the new working structure of CBS; a review of the impact of observing systems, particularly radiosondes, on numerical weather predictions (NWPs); a survey on the use of the Internet on national meteorological services; the international exchange of meteorological data and products; and the further implementation of advanced telecommunication technology for the collection and distribution of data. Procedures for the provision of forecast model guidance on the occurrence of severe weather, pollution transport model products and extended/ monthly and long range/seasonal forecasts were established. Expert meetings were held to redesign and establish a new composite GOS.

The implementation of the Regional Meteorological Telecommunications Networks of all regions made steady progress through the upgrading of circuits and centres. Special efforts were made to support and assist member countries in ensuring year-2000 compliance of the GTS services and systems. Activities also focused on enhancing and developing members' facilities at advanced GDPS centres and National Meteorological Centres.

Instruments and methods of observation

In 1999, activities were carried out to better meet users' needs regarding observations. A joint CBS/Commission for Instruments and Methods of Observation Expert Meeting on Requirements and Representation of Data from Automatic Weather Stations (AWS) (De Bitt, Netherlands, 19-23 April) developed users' requirements related to AWS and conventional surface observations with a view to broadening instrument standardization. An Expert Meeting on Capacity-Building (Beijing, China, 23-25 September) developed proposals on capacity-building related to the activities of Regional Instrument Centres, and guidance material on the choice of instruments for developing countries and for the preparation of an instrument catalogue.

A third Expert Meeting on Operational Issues for Radiosonde Applications in the Tropics and Sub-tropics (Geneva, 18-22 October) dealt with the performance of operationally used upper-air sounding systems.

Tropical Cyclone Programme

During the year, all five regional tropical cyclone centres in Miami, Florida (United States), Nadi (Fiji), New Delhi (India), Réunion and Tokyo (Japan) accelerated the implementation of their regional cooperation programmes, including the regionally coordinated plan for future development of services by NMHSs and agencies involved in disaster prevention and preparedness. Tropical cyclone forecasters were trained to promote capacity-building.

World Climate Programme

In 1999, overall coordination of the World Climate Programme was carried out by the Inter-Agency Coordinating Committee for the Climate Agenda (IACCA). At its third session (Paris, 11-12 March), IACCA discussed, among other things, the possibility of convening a Third World Climate Conference; actions required to improve inter-agency cooperation; priorities and strategies of international funding organizations; and the future of the Climate Agenda and role of IACCA.

During 1999, emphasis was placed on identifying overall priorities for WMO under the framework of the Climate Agenda. Particular attention was given to the Climate Information and Prediction Services project and to the Global Climate Observing System activities that were critical to obligations emerging under the environmental conventions related to climate change, desertification and biodiversity. Another major activity was the completion of the scientific and technical review of the 1997/98 El Niño event, which would serve as the basis for further studies on the social and economic impacts of El Niño.

Under the World Climate Applications and Services Programme, the International Conference on Urban Climatology was held jointly with the International Congress on Biometeorology (Sydney, Australia, 8-12 November). The joint conferences provided platforms for examining a broad spectrum of climate-related issues and their impacts on human activities.

Regional climate outlook forums were held in many parts of the world and plans were in place to examine their long-term sustainability as an effective mechanism for ensuring dialogue between seasonal forecast providers and users.

World Climate Research Programme

The World Climate Research Programme, undertaken jointly by WMO, the International Council of Scientific Unions and IOC, continued studies to provide the scientific basis for predictions of global and regional climate variations on all timescales and made projections of the magnitude and rate of human-induced climate change. One of its principal projects was the climate variability and predictability study, which included specific regionally focused investigations of the variability of the American monsoon system, the Asian-American monsoon systems and the African climate variability. The Global Energy and Water Cycle Experiment continued the collection of global climatological datasets of key climate parameters, including cloudiness, surface radiation budget, water vapour and aerosols.

Atmospheric Research and Environment Programme

The Atmospheric Research and Environment Programme continued to coordinate and encourage research in atmospheric and related sciences. The Seventh WMO Scientific Conference on Weather Modification (Chiang Mai, Thailand, 17-22 February) reviewed the latest developments in weather modification techniques, including inadvertent weather modification. The Sixth Regional Workshop on Asian/African Monsoon Emphasizing Training Aspects (Nairobi, Kenya, January) updated meteorologists from monsoon-affected countries on the latest developments in Asian/African monsoon research.

The Global Atmosphere Watch held numerous scientific advisory group meetings that considered programme components, such as greenhouse gases, ultraviolet monitoring and instrumentation, ozone, aerosols, precipitation chemistry and observations. The WMO/United Nations Environment Programme Fourth Meeting of Ozone Research Managers of the Parties to the Vienna Convention and Meeting of the Bureau of the Vienna Convention for the Protection of the Ozone Layer (Geneva, 28-30 April) reviewed the current state of ozone monitoring and research activities.

Applications of meteorology

Agricultural meteorology

The International Workshop on Agrometeorology in the Twenty-first Century (Accra, Ghana, 15-17 February) discussed important issues facing agrometeorology in the next millennium, including initiatives to strengthen services for agricultural production. Roving seminars on crop-yield weather modelling were held in Pune, India (19-30 July), and Ljubljana, Slovenia (6-17 September). Roving seminars on instrumentation and operation of AWS for applications in agrometeorology were held in Casablanca, Morocco (28 June–9 July), and Tehran, Iran (27 November–8 December). Roving seminars were held on data management for applications to agriculture (Tashkent, Uzbekistan, 8-19 November) and on the application of climatic data for drought preparedness and management of sustainable agriculture (Accra, 1-12 November).

Aeronautical meteorology

In 1999, the Aeronautical Meteorology Programme held five training events related to the application of NWP products to aviation and to the recovery of costs for the provision of meteorological service to aviation. The second Aircraft Meteorological Data Relay Panel Meeting (Geneva, 19-22 October) reviewed coordination of national and regional programmes and improvements of data exchange and quality control.

Marine meteorology

In 1999, the first transition planning meeting for JCOMM, established to provide the institutional umbrella and coordinating/integrating mechanism for all existing and future operational marine-related activities of WMO and IOC/UNESCO, was held in Saint Petersburg, Russian Federation, in July.

Public weather services

During 1999, the Public Weather Services (PWS) Programme continued to assist WMO members in the observation, monitoring and prediction of weather patterns. The Programme's work was carried out through three expert teams and an implementation and coordination team. Several training seminars and workshops were organized in different regions with the objective of improving participants' national public weather services. PWS also ensured the provision of meteorological information in support of UN humanitarian missions related to natural disasters and other crises.

Hydrology and water resources

A major achievement in 1999 was the launch of the regional Hydrological Cycle Observing System project for Western and Central Africa, with the aim of securing a regional information system.

The Thirteenth World Meteorological Congress adopted a resolution on the free exchange of hydrological data and products, in consonance with the requirements of WMO's scientific and technical programmes. The Fifth UNESCO/WMO International Conference on Hydrology (Geneva, 8-12 February) reviewed the results achieved within the framework of both organizations' programmes in freshwater and considered their respective plans for future work.

Technical cooperation

In 1999, WMO technical assistance, valued at $16.53 million, was financed by trust funds (28.6 per cent), the WMO Voluntary Cooperation Programme (51.7 per cent), the United Nations Development Programme (13.7 per cent) and the WMO regular budget (6 per cent). Regional offices continued to implement WMO programmes.

Secretariat

As at 31 December 1999, the number of full-time staff employed by WMO totalled 264. Of those, 121 were in the Professional and higher categories and 143 were in the General Service and related categories.

Budget

The WMO Executive Council, in 1997, approved a regular budget of 125,100,000 Swiss francs (SwF) for the 1998-1999 biennium. Unspent balances remaining from the budget of the prior biennium (1996-1997), amounting to SwF 9,110,758, were reappropriated to the 1998-1999 biennium. Thus, the approved budget for the biennium amounted to SwF 134,210,758.

In 1999, the Council approved a regular budget of SwF 126,100,000 for the 2000-2001 biennium. The Thirteenth World Meteorological Congress approved a maximum expenditure of SwF 252,300,000 for the thirteenth financial period (2000-2003).

NOTE: For further details regarding WMO activities, see *World Meteorological Organization Annual Report 1999*, published by WMO.

HEADQUARTERS

World Meteorological Organization
7 bis, avenue de la Paix
(Case postale No. 2300)
CH 1211 Geneva 2, Switzerland
Telephone: (41) (22) 730-8111
Fax: (41) (22) 730-8181
Internet: http://www.wmo.ch
E-mail: ipa@gateway.wmo.ch

Chapter XIII

International Maritime Organization (IMO)

In 1999, the International Maritime Organization (IMO) continued to improve the safety of international shipping and prevent marine pollution from ships.

The IMO Assembly, the organization's governing body, at its twenty-first session (London, 15-26 November), elected a new Council for the 2000-2001 biennium, approved budget appropriations and a work programme for the biennium and adopted technical resolutions relating to IMO's work. The Assembly adopted 28 resolutions, including several submitted by the Maritime Safety Committee (MSC), IMO's senior technical body, the Marine Environment Protection Committee (MEPC) and other subsidiary bodies.

In 1999, IMO membership remained at 157.

Activities in 1999

The IMO Council awarded the International Maritime Prize for 1998 to the International Lifeboat Federation, which included both voluntary and government-supported sea rescue organizations, with 57 members in 44 countries. The Prize was awarded annually to the person, organization or other entity judged to have done the most to advance IMO objectives.

The Council was informed that some $1.5 million had been contributed or pledged to the Seafarers Memorial Trust Fund, established in 1998 [YUN 1998, p. 1405].

Prevention of pollution

At its forty-third session (28 June–2 July), MEPC decided to propose to the IMO Council the holding of a conference in the next biennium to adopt a legal instrument to effect the phasing out of organotins acting as biocides in anti-fouling systems on ships. An MEPC Working Group proposed new regulations intended to address the environmental damage caused by the introduction of harmful aquatic organisms in ballast water, used to stabilize vessels at sea. The Committee adopted regulations to ensure that certain sized tankers carrying persistent oils (such as heavy fuel oil) as cargo were subject to the same stringent requirements as crude-oil tankers. Amendments to the International Convention for the Prevention of Pollution from Ships, 1973 [YUN 1973, p. 964], as modified by the 1978 Protocol relating thereto (MARPOL 73/78), would make existing oil tankers between 20,000 and 30,000 tons deadweight carrying persistent product oil, including heavy diesel and fuel oil, subject to the same construction requirements as crude-oil tankers. The amendments, expected to enter into force on 1 January 2001, related to Regulations for the Prevention of Pollution by Oil and the control of noxious liquid substances. MEPC approved new procedures for the designation of a "particularly sensitive sea area" (PSSA). In an area approved as a PSSA, measures could be used to control maritime activities, such as routeing measures, strict application of MARPOL discharge and equipment requirements for ships, such as oil tankers, and installation of Vessel Traffic Services. There were currently two designated PSSAs: the Great Barrier Reef (Australia) and the Sabana-Camagüey Archipelago (Cuba). The Committee adopted a resolution on Guidelines for Monitoring the Worldwide Average Sulphur Content of Residual Fuel Oils Supplied for Use on Board Ships, intended to establish an agreed method of monitoring.

Ship security and safety at sea

At its seventy-first meeting (19-28 May), MSC adopted amendments to the International Convention for the Safety of Life at Sea (SOLAS), 1974 [YUN 1974, p. 1030], aimed at making mandatory the International Code for the Safe Carriage of Packaged Irradiated Nuclear Fuel, Plutonium and High-Level Radioactive Wastes on Board Ships (INF Code). The amendments were expected to enter into force on 1 January 2001. The Code applied to all ships, regardless of the date of construction and size, engaged in the carriage of INF cargo, but was not applicable to warships, naval auxiliary or other ships used only on government non-commercial service, although administrations were expected to ensure that such ships were in compliance with the Code. Specific regulations in the Code covered damage stability, fire protection, temperature control of cargo spaces, structural consideration, cargo securing arrangements, electrical supplies, radiological protection equipment and management, training and shipboard emergency plans. The Committee reviewed progress in implementing the 1995 amendments to the 1978 International Convention on Standards of Training, Certification and Watchkeeping for Seafarers [YUN 1978, p. 1161], which required parties to communicate to IMO information on compliance with the 1995 amendments. As at 21 May, 95 of the 133 parties had communicated information and 15 panels had completed their work and reported to the Secretary-General, 40 panels had completed initial evaluations and clarifications, and, of those, 20 panels were considering clarifications provided by the parties. The Committee agreed to a draft IMO Assembly resolution on the issue of fraudulent certificates of competency to highlight the problem and encourage member States to eliminate the circulation of fraudulent certificates. MSC established a Working Group on Bulk Carrier Safety to review relevant submissions. It also reviewed progress in carrying out a formal safety assessment study of bulk carriers to aid future IMO decision-making on bulk carrier safety and agreed to a framework setting out project objectives, scope and application. MSC established a Correspondence Group to prepare a preliminary draft text of an instrument for the investigation and prosecution of the crime of piracy and armed robbery against ships. It also agreed to a definition of fatigue, which had been recognized as a contributor to many accidents involving means of transport, and developed guidance on dealing with the problem.

Secretariat

As at 31 December, IMO had 271 staff members, of whom 114 were in the Professional and higher categories and 157 in the General Service category.

Budget

The IMO Assembly, at its twentieth biennial session in 1997, approved budgetary appropriations of 36,612,200 pounds sterling for the 1998-1999 biennium, of which 18,666,100 pounds sterling was for 1999. At its twenty-first session in 1999, the Assembly approved budgetary appropriations of 36,612,200 pounds sterling for the 2000-2001 biennium, of which 18,155,000 pounds sterling was for 2000 and 18,457,200 pounds sterling was for 2001.

NOTE: For further information, see the organization's quarterly magazine, *IMO News*.

HEADQUARTERS

International Maritime Organization
4 Albert Embankment
London SE1 7SR, United Kingdom
Telephone: (44) (207) 735-7611
Fax: (44) (207) 587-3210
Internet: http://www.imo.org
E-mail: info@imo.org

Chapter XIV

World Intellectual Property Organization (WIPO)

In 1999, the World Intellectual Property Organization (WIPO) continued development cooperation, norm-setting and registration activities to promote respect for the protection and use of intellectual property. The organization's main areas of work continued to focus on strengthening the intellectual property systems of developing countries; promoting new or revised norms for the protection of intellectual property at the national, regional and multilateral levels; and facilitating the acquisition of intellectual property protection through international registration systems.

The governing bodies of WIPO and the Unions administered by the organization held their thirty-fourth series of meetings (Geneva, 20-29 September).

During 1999, WIPO membership increased to 173 States, with the accession of Antigua and Barbuda and Seychelles to the 1967 Convention establishing WIPO, amended in 1979. The number of States adhering to treaties administered by WIPO also increased: as at 31 December 1999, there were 157 States parties to the Paris Convention for the Protection of Industrial Property; 142 to the Berne Convention for the Protection of Literary and Artistic Works; and 106 to the Patent Cooperation Treaty (PCT).

Activities in 1999

Development cooperation

Much of the work of WIPO's regional cooperation programme continued to be shaped by the 1 January 2000 deadline for developing countries that were members of the World Trade Organization (WTO) to make their national legislation and administrative structures compatible with the provisions of the WTO Agreement on Trade-Related Aspects of Intellectual Property Rights. Towards that end, WIPO prepared 61 draft laws for 33 developing countries and regional organizations and provided written comments on another 66 draft laws received from 31 countries or secretariats of regional organizations.

The Nationally Focused Action Plans (NFAPs), which were established jointly between individual Governments and WIPO and were aimed at helping developing countries to reach a significantly higher level of efficient management and use of the national intellectual property system, continued to be implemented. In 1999, 13 new NFAPs were launched and a total of 69 were being implemented.

Several national and regional projects aimed at capacity-building in the area of collective management were introduced, ranging from software development, legal advice and guidelines on model statutes to human resources development. In parallel, the evolution of the digital environment and its impact on collective management systems was monitored closely, in order to meet the challenges posed and to ensure that copyright protection would not be adversely affected by those changes. Besides formal training, many regional and national symposia and meetings were held to create a greater awareness of the role of intellectual property.

The WIPO Worldwide Academy, an Internet-based nine-module course on intellectual property in English, French and Spanish, was launched in 1999 with a total of some 480 registered students in the three languages. To consolidate the foundations of the Academy, cooperation agreements were concluded with a number of universities for the participation of their students in the Academy's on-line courses.

Intellectual property law

By year's end, 12 countries had ratified the WIPO Copyright Treaty and 11 countries had ratified the WIPO Performances and Phonogram Treaty (WPPT). For each treaty to enter into force, at least 30 States were required to adhere to it. The treaties, both adopted in 1996, updated the legal principles underpinning international protection of copyright and the rights of performers and phonogram producers in the digital age, particularly regarding the Internet.

Regarding the harmonization of patent laws, the Standing Committee on the Law of Patents adopted the draft Patent Law Treaty (PLT), which covered formal administrative requirements for the filing of patent applications in patent offices. The Committee agreed that a diplomatic conference would be held in 2000, to which the draft text of PLT would be submitted for negotiation.

In June, the Standing Committee on the Law of Trademarks, Industrial Designs and Geographical Indications (SCT) reached agreement on a set of new guidelines to improve protection for well-known marks. SCT continued discussions on the protection of well-known marks, trademark licences, use of marks on the Internet, geographical indications and international nonproprietary names.

The Standing Committee on Copyright and Related Rights, at meetings in May and November, discussed the protection of audio-visual performances, databases and the rights of broadcasting organizations. It recommended that a preparatory committee and an extraordinary session of the WIPO Assembly be convened in April 2000 to consider holding a diplomatic conference on a new treaty on audio-visual performances, as WPPT only covered audio performers.

WIPO Arbitration and Mediation Centre

The Arbitration and Mediation Centre continued to provide less expensive and speedier alternatives to costly court proceedings in commercial disputes involving intellectual property rights. In 1999, the Centre finalized development of its online dispute resolution service, which would allow involved parties to communicate via the Internet, thus greatly reducing the time and cost of reaching a solution. The service was especially helpful for parties exploiting their intellectual property rights across borders, which needed an international facility for resolving disputes. Following the adoption by the Internet Corporation for Assigned Names and Numbers (ICANN) of the Uniform Dispute Resolution Policy applicable to top-level domain names, the Centre was accredited by ICANN to administer cases filed under the Uniform Policy.

International registration activities

PCT. In 1999, over 74,000 international applications were filed, representing an increase of 10.5 per cent over the total for 1998 and the equivalent of 5.82 million national patent applications.

Madrid Agreement. In the trademark system under the Madrid Agreement concerning the International Registration of Marks and its 1989 Protocol, the number of international registrations was just over 20,000, maintaining the figure reached in 1998.

Hague Agreement. A Geneva Act of the Hague Agreement concerning the International Deposit of Industrial Designs was adopted at a diplomatic conference (Geneva, July). The new treaty was expected to result in a much-expanded coverage of countries of the Hague system, which offered users from business and industry a more practical and cost-effective way to obtain international protection for their designs. In 1999, the number of international deposits of industrial designs under the Hague Agreement rose to 4,093, a 3 per cent increase over 1998. Renewals of deposited designs also rose by 7 per cent compared to 1998.

Secretariat

As at 31 December 1999, WIPO employed 752 staff members representing 82 countries; 276 were in the Professional or higher categories and 476 were in the General Service category.

Budget

WIPO's principal sources of income in 1998-1999 were fees paid by private sector users of the international registration services (85 per cent), contributions paid by the member States (9 per cent) and the sale of WIPO publications and interest earnings (6 per cent). In September, member States approved the results-based programme and budget for the 2000-2001 biennium. The approved expenditure of 410 million Swiss francs (SwF) was an increase of 8 per cent over that of the 1998-1999 biennium. Projected income for the same period was estimated at SwF 410 million. Thus, the surplus for the period was expected to be negligible. In 1999, the organization's budgeted income was SwF 218,686,000 and budgeted expenditure was SwF 221,807,000.

NOTE: For further information on the organization, see *WIPO Annual Report 1999*, published by WIPO.

HEADQUARTERS AND OTHER OFFICE

HEADQUARTERS

World Intellectual Property Organization
34, chemin des Colombettes (P.O. Box 18)
CH-1211 Geneva 20, Switzerland
Telephone: (41) (22) 338-9111
Fax: (41) (22) 733-5428
Internet: http://www.wipo.int
E-mail: wipo.mail@wipo.int

WIPO OFFICE AT THE UNITED NATIONS

2 United Nations Plaza, Suite 2525
New York, NY 10017, United States
Telephone: (1) (212) 963-6813
Fax: (1) (212) 963-4801
E-mail: wipo@un.org

Chapter XV

International Fund for Agricultural Development (IFAD)

In 1999, the International Fund for Agricultural Development (IFAD) continued to promote the economic advancement of the rural poor, mainly by improving the productivity of on- and off-farm activities, and by designing and implementing innovative, cost-effective and replicable programmes that had a sustainable impact.

IFAD's Governing Council, at its twenty-second session (Rome, 17-18 February), established the Consultation to Review the Adequacy of the Resources Available to the Fund to consider IFAD's mandate and proposed work programme. The Executive Board held three regular sessions (April, September, December), during which it approved loans for 30 projects and programmes; one project and two programmes were for direct supervision by IFAD. The Board approved a contribution to Mali to help reduce its debt to IFAD within the framework of IFAD's participation in the World Bank's Heavily-Indebted Poor Countries Debt Initiative. It approved a programme of work for the year 2000 of $482.2 million for loans and grants under the Regular Programme and endorsed a budget of $55.4 million, including a contingency of $400,000 and $141,000 to fund meetings of the Consultation in 2000.

IFAD membership remained at 161 in 1999. As at 31 December 1999, of its member countries, 22 were in List A (developed countries), 12 in List B (oil-exporting developing countries), and 127 in List C (other developing countries), 49 in Sub-List C1 (Africa), 47 in Sub-List C2 (Europe, Asia and the Pacific) and 31 in Sub-List C3 (Latin America and the Caribbean).

Resources

The fourth replenishment of IFAD's resources, totalling $460 million, allowed IFAD to make commitments worth over $1,350 million for new projects and grant financing during 1997-1999. The Consultation to Review the Adequacy of the Resources Available to IFAD focused on the need for a fifth replenishment of the Fund to cover the next three years of operation.

Activities in 1999

Loans approved in 1999 under IFAD's Regular Programme totalled $432.7 million for 30 projects and $30.2 million, which financed 124 technical assistance grants.

Regular Programme lending was distributed by region as follows: eastern and southern Africa, $112.7 million for 7 projects in 20 countries (26.1 per cent); Asia and the Pacific, $104.2 million for 6 projects in 21 countries (24.1 per cent); western and central Africa, $85.7 million for 7 projects in 24 countries (19.8 per cent); Latin America and the Caribbean, $76 million for 5 projects in 28 countries (17.6 per cent); the Near East and North Africa region (included Djibouti, Somalia and the Sudan), $54.1 million for 5 projects in 21 countries (12.5 per cent).

Secretariat

As at 31 December 1999, the IFAD secretariat comprised 290 staff, including 132 staff in the Professional and higher categories and 158 in the General Service category.

Income and expenditure

Total revenue under the Regular Programme in 1999 was $240 million, consisting of $196.5 million of investment income and $43.5 million from interest and service charges on loans. The excess of revenue over expenses for the year was $62.8 million, compared to $363 million in 1998.

NOTE: For further details on IFAD activities in 1999, see *Annual Report 1999*, published by the Fund.

HEADQUARTERS AND OTHER OFFICES

HEADQUARTERS
International Fund for Agricultural Development
Via del Serafico, 107
00142 Rome, Italy
Telephone: (39) (06) 54591
Fax: (39) (06) 5043463
Internet: http://www.ifad.org
E-mail: ifad@ifad.org

IFAD LIAISON OFFICES
1 United Nations Plaza, Room 1460
New York, NY 10017, United States
Telephone: (1) (212) 963-0546
Fax: (1) (212) 963-2787

1775 K Street, N.W., Suite 410
Washington, DC 20006, United States
Telephone: (1) (202) 331-9099
Fax: (1) (202) 331-9366

Chapter XVI

United Nations Industrial Development Organization (UNIDO)

In 1999, the United Nations Industrial Development Organization (UNIDO) completed its reform programme and embarked on a new and more direct path towards the industrialization of developing countries and economies in transition. Throughout the year, UNIDO focused on adjusting and refining its programming and implementation methods, and on introducing quality control for its programmes and activities.

The Industrial Development Board, at its twenty-first session (Vienna, 23-25 June), adopted decisions relating to the implementation of the Business Plan in Latin America and the Caribbean; the Industrial Development Fund; and administrative matters.

The eighth session of the General Conference (Vienna, 29 November–3 December) adopted the programme and budget for 2000-2001 and set the agenda for industrial development in the new millennium. The adoption of resolutions on sustainable industrial development and on the Global Environment Facility (GEF) strengthened UNIDO's mandate as a knowledge-based specialized agency in environment and energy.

UNIDO membership remained at 168.

New integrated programmes

At the end of 1999, UNIDO's new system of integrated programmes, which represented a holistic approach to industrial development, had completed a full year of operation. The programmes provided a series of interlinked activities within a given country based on the accumulated expertise and experience of the organization as a whole rather than individual organizational units. As at 31 December, a total of 29 programmes were in place, of which 5 had been under implementation for almost a year. Although coverage was for all regions, the focus remained on Africa, where 15 programmes were in place. The 29 ongoing programmes had a total budget of $212,415,000.

Service modules

An important component of UNIDO's transformation was the grouping of services into 16 modules, thus aligning the programmatic focus of activities with the organization's long-term goals of sustainable industrial development—the so-called "3 Es": competitive economy, productive employment and sound environment. The integrated programmes developed and launched in 1999 combined those service modules to meet the initial industrial development requirements of countries assisted by UNIDO.

The service modules under competitive economy included: industrial policy formulation and implementation; statistics and information networks; metrology, standardization, certification and accreditation; continuous improvement and quality management; and investment and technology promotion. Industrial policy and research efforts were spearheading the convergence of technical cooperation with the organization's global forum function. The new orientation was reflected by integrating global forum activities, such as information assessment, analysis and diffusion, with technical cooperation provided through the service module. The overall objective was to encourage good industrial governance by providing policy advice, facilitating public-private consultations, policy implementation, monitoring and auditing, and institutional capacity-building. Innovation in investment and technology promotion was further strengthened by the new Investment and Technology Promotion Network, which embraced a broad cross-section of industrial stakeholders. The service module on statistics and information networks defined much of UNIDO's activities in delivering industrial information to client countries and assisted countries to improve their own capacity to collect, process and provide information. Progress was achieved in programmes featuring standardization, metrology, certification and accreditation as keys to competitiveness and efficiency in the global market. Within the continuous improvement and quality management service module, UNIDO assistance to Albania, Algeria, Romania and Sri Lanka helped local services to restructure and upgrade industries for enhanced competitiveness.

Under productive employment, the service modules were: small and medium enterprise (SME) policy framework; women entrepreneurship development; industrial business development services; and upgrading agro-industries and related technical skills. The need to establish an effective policy and institutional environment for promoting SMEs was reflected in integrated programmes such as those for Bolivia, Cuba, Eritrea, Ghana, Guinea, Rwanda, the Sudan, the United Republic of Tanzania, Viet Nam and Yemen. To promote productive employment and gender equality within small and micro industries, UNIDO provided capacity-building services and policy support to address the needs of women entrepreneurs. Programmes in Central America and in Tanzania were producing substantial results in improving women's entrepreneurial skills in agro-based food processing to enable them to manage their own businesses. UNIDO addressed the needs of entrepreneurs in developing countries and in economies in transition by providing them with specialized support. In addition, UNIDO assisted rural economies through the upgrading of agro-industries and related technical skills module, which included services in food, leather, textiles and wood-processing technologies and skill upgrading.

Service modules under the environment comprised: environmental policy framework; the 1992 United Nations Framework Convention on Climate Change [YUN 1992, p. 681] and the 1997 Kyoto Protocol thereto [YUN 1997, p. 1048]; energy efficiency; rural energy development; cleaner production; pollution control and waste management; and the 1987 Montreal Protocol on Substances that Deplete the Ozone Layer [YUN 1987, p. 686]. The first UNIDO-executed GEF-financed programme on water pollution control and biodiversity conservation of the Gulf of Guinea marine ecosystem was completed in 1999. Policies for sustainable environmental growth were launched in Benin, Cameroon, China, Côte d'Ivoire, Ghana, India, Nigeria, Togo and Viet Nam. Under the service module of the 1992 Climate Convention and 1997 Kyoto Protocol thereto, UNIDO assisted countries with capacity-building and technical assessment for the Kyoto mechanisms. Regarding energy in general and industrial energy efficiency in particular, UNIDO cooperated with the United Nations Development Programme in formulating and implementing a number of GEF-financed large-scale projects. The national cleaner production centres programme, a centrepiece of the cleaner production service module, was expanded in 1999 with the inauguration of new centres in Guatemala, Morocco and the Russian Federation. The pollution control and waste management service module provided advice on waste management technology to enterprises and helped increase awareness of the value of pollution control services. During the year, the Multilateral Fund for the Implementation of the Montreal Protocol approved for implementation by UNIDO 132 projects valued at $36.6 million in 37 countries to eliminate 4,230 ozone depletion potential tonnes.

Secretariat

As at 31 December 1999, UNIDO employed a total of 669 staff members; 247 were in the Professional or higher categories and 422 were in the General Service category.

Budget

The seventh (1997) session of the UNIDO General Conference approved the organization's 1999 regular budget of $68.5 million. In addition, UNIDO received $83.5 million in voluntary contributions for technical cooperation activities. In 1999, new project approvals, including net changes to ongoing projects, amounted to $81.6 million, compared with $57.1 million in 1998.

In December 1999, the General Conference approved UNIDO's 2000-2001 regular budget in the amount of $167.7 million, which represented a 22.7 per cent increase over the budget of the previous biennium.

NOTE: For further information on UNIDO, see *Annual Report of UNIDO 1999*.

HEADQUARTERS AND OTHER OFFICES

HEADQUARTERS

United Nations Industrial Development Organization
Vienna International Centre
P.O. Box 300
A-1400 Vienna, Austria
Telephone: (43) (1) 26026-0
Fax: (43) (1) 269-26-69
Internet: http://www.unido.org

LIAISON OFFICES

UNIDO Office at Geneva
Le Bocage
Pavillion I/Palais des Nations
CH-1211 Geneva 10, Switzerland
Telephone: (41) (22) 917-3367
Fax: (41) (22) 917-0059

UNIDO Office in New York
1 United Nations Plaza, Room DC1-1110
New York, NY 10017, United States
Telephone: (1) (212) 963-6890
Fax: (1) (212) 964-4116

Chapter XVII

World Trade Organization (WTO)

The World Trade Organization (WTO), which was the legal and institutional foundation of the multilateral trading system, continued in 1999 to oversee the rules of international trade, settle trade disputes between Governments and organize trade negotiations.

The third WTO Ministerial Conference, which was WTO's highest authority and comprised all of its members, was held in Seattle, United States, from 30 November to 3 December. The Conference failed to reach agreement either on the launch of a new round of trade negotiations or on the other important points that had emerged in the course of the preparatory process. Furthermore, WTO found itself at the centre of a wave of resentment against many aspects of the global economy, for which the Ministerial Conference became a focus.

WTO's General Council, the body entrusted with carrying out the functions of the organization in the interval between Conferences, continued to monitor the implementation and operation of the multilateral trading system embodied in the WTO Agreement. In addition to making preparations for the Ministerial Conference, it continued to oversee the implementation of the Work Programme on Electronic Commerce, followed the review of the Dispute Settlement Understanding and granted waivers from obligations under the WTO Agreement.

During the year, WTO membership increased to 135 with the admission of Estonia and Latvia.

General activities

The three working groups set up by the 1996 Ministerial Conference [YUN 1996, p. 1441] met during 1999. The Working Group on the Relationship between Trade and Investment, at meetings in March, June and September, continued to examine implications of the relationship between trade and investment for development and economic growth; the economic relationship between trade and investment; and stocktaking and analysis of existing international instruments and activities regarding trade and investment. The Working Group on Transparency in Government Procurement, which met in February, June and October, discussed the definition and scope of government procurement; procurement methods; publication of information on national legislation and procedures; information on procurement opportunities, tendering and qualification procedures; time periods; transparency of decisions on qualification; contract awards; domestic review procedures; maintenance of records; information technology, language, and the fight against bribery and corruption; notification to other Governments; dispute settlement procedures; technical cooperation; and special and differential treatment for developing countries. The Working Group on the Interaction between Trade and Competition Policy, which met in April, June and September, continued to discuss the relevance of fundamental WTO principles of national treatment, transparency and most-favoured-nation treatment to competition policy and vice versa; approaches to promoting cooperation and communication in technical cooperation; and the contribution of competition policy in achieving WTO objectives, including the promotion of international trade.

During the year, the Trade Policy Review Body carried out reviews of Argentina, Bolivia, Egypt, Guinea, Israel, Nicaragua, Papua New Guinea, the Philippines, Romania, Thailand, Togo and the United States.

WTO continued to provide technical cooperation and training to developing countries and economies in transition through courses, seminars and symposia to widen participants' understanding of trade policy matters, the multilateral trading system, international trade law and other relevant trade and development issues.

Trade in goods

The Council for Trade in Goods continued to monitor the implementation of agreements and examined and approved requests for waivers and waiver extensions from members in connection with the transposition of their Schedules into the Harmonized Systems. It also reviewed the operation of the Trade-related Investment Measures Agreement; took note of the situation with respect to the compliance of notification obligations; and adopted the draft status report on exploratory work undertaken on trade facilitation. Discussions continued on the best way to implement the provisions of the Agreement on Textiles and Clothing for the integration of textile and clothing products into the General Agreement on Tariffs and Trade rules by 2005.

The Committee on Agriculture reviewed the implementation of commitments to the WTO Agreement on Agriculture in market access, domestic support and export subsidies and export restrictions. Since 1995, the Committee had received 834 notifications submitted by member States. In the area of market access, the Committee reviewed the administration of tariff quotas, imports and the application of the special agricultural safeguard.

The Committee on Sanitary and Phytosanitary Measures reviewed the implementation of the Agreement on the Application of Sanitary and Phytosanitary Measures (the "SPS Agreement"), which set out the rights and obligations of members to ensure food safety, protect human health from plant- or animal-spread diseases, or protect plant and animal health from pests and diseases. In November, the Committee discussed specific trade concerns and the need for a more focused approach on the discussion of developing countries' implementation of the Agreement and the transparency of the Agreement.

The Committee on the Agreement on Safeguards completed its review of national safeguard legislation; monitored the notifications of WTO members on the timetables for the phase-out of their "grey area" measures (voluntary export restraints); and reviewed notifications of findings of serious injury due to increased exports.

The following groups continued to review relevant legislation and regulations of members: the Committee on Subsidies and Countervailing Measures; the Committee on Anti-Dumping Practices; the Committee on Technical Barriers to Trade; the Committee on Import Licensing; the Committee on Rules of Origin; the Committee on Customs Valuation; the Working Party on Preshipment Inspection; the Working Party on State Trading Enterprises; and the Committee on Trade-related Investment Measures.

Trade in services

The Council for Trade in Services held substantive discussions on the negotiating guidelines and procedures of the General Agreement on Trade in Services (GATS), which called on member States to enter into successive rounds of negotiations, beginning not later than 2000, with a view to achieving a progressively higher level of liberalization. The Working Party on GATS rules continued to negotiate new rules on safeguards, government procurement and subsidies.

Intellectual property

The WTO Agreement on Trade-related Aspects of Intellectual Property Rights (TRIPS) provided for minimum international standards of protection in copyright, trademarks, geographic indications, industrial designs, patents, layout designs of integrated circuits and undisclosed information. During the year, the Council for TRIPS considered notifications concerning the implementation of the so-called "mail-box" and exclusive marketing rights for countries that did not yet provide product patent protection for pharmaceuticals and/or agricultural chemicals. It also discussed implementation of the Agreement, which required developed-country members to provide incentives to enterprises in their territories to promote and encourage technology transfer to least developed country members. In addition, discussions continued regarding geographic indications and intellectual property issues connected with electronic commerce.

Regional trade agreements

The Committee on Regional Trade Agreements continued to examine regional trade agreements (RTAs). By the end of 1999, it had concluded the factual examination of 52 of the 77 RTAs under its purview.

Trade and development

The Committee on Trade and Development discussed the funding of technical assistance activities; examined the secretariat's plan for technical cooperation for the period 2000-2002; and held preliminary discussions on its 2000 work programme.

Trade and environment

In 1999, the Committee on Trade and Environment discussed, among other things, trade in services and the environment; the linkages between the multilateral environment and trade agendas; market access; the environmental effects of removing trade restrictions and distortions in the agriculture, fisheries, forestry and environmental services sectors; the export of domestically prohibited goods; and the relationship between the 1992 Convention on Biological Diversity [YUN 1992, p. 683] and the TRIPS Agreement.

Plurilateral agreements

The Agreement on Government Procurement called on parties, not later than three years from its entry into force on 1 January 1996, to undertake further negotiations to improve the Agreement in order to achieve the greatest possible extension of its coverage among the parties and eliminate any remaining discriminatory measures and practices. In October, the parties considered the timetable for the completion of the negotiations and the overall work programme.

The Agreement on Trade in Civil Aircraft eliminated all customs duties and other charges on imports of civil aircraft products and repairs, bound them at zero level, and required the adoption or adaptation of end-use customs administration. Although the Agreement was part of the WTO Agreement, it remained outside the WTO framework. In 1999, signatories discussed a draft protocol rectifying the Agreement.

International Trade Centre

The International Trade Centre (ITC), operated jointly by WTO and the United Nations Conference on Trade and Development (see p. 880), continued to undertake technical cooperation activities as a follow-up to the Uruguay Round Agreements. In 1999, ITC agreed to assume day-to-day management of the Integrated Technical Assistance Programme in Selected Least Developed Countries and Other African Countries.

Budget

The WTO budget for 1999 amounted to 120.2 million Swiss francs. Beginning in 1996, WTO members' contributions were determined according to their share in total trade in goods, services and intellectual property rights.

Secretariat

At the end of 1999, WTO staff numbered 533, of whom 291 were in the Professional and higher categories and 242 in the General Service category.

NOTE: For further information on WTO activities, see the organization's *Annual Report 1999.*

HEADQUARTERS

World Trade Organization
Centre William Rappard
154 rue de Lausanne
CH-1211 Geneva 21, Switzerland
Telephone: (41) (22) 739-5111
Fax: (41) (22) 731-4206
Internet: www.wto.org
E-mail: enquiries@wto.org

Appendices

blank page -- (1426)

Appendix I

Roster of the United Nations

There were 188 Member States as at 31 December 1999.

MEMBER	DATE OF ADMISSION	MEMBER	DATE OF ADMISSION	MEMBER	DATE OF ADMISSION
Afghanistan	19 Nov. 1946	El Salvador	24 Oct. 1945	Mauritania	27 Oct. 1961
Albania	14 Dec. 1955	Equatorial Guinea	12 Nov. 1968	Mauritius	24 Apr. 1968
Algeria	8 Oct. 1962	Eritrea	28 May 1993	Mexico	7 Nov. 1945
Andorra	28 July 1993	Estonia	17 Sep. 1991	Micronesia (Federated States of)	17 Sep. 1991
Angola	1 Dec. 1976	Ethiopia	13 Nov. 1945	Monaco	28 May 1993
Antigua and Barbuda	11 Nov. 1981	Fiji	13 Oct. 1970	Mongolia	27 Oct. 1961
Argentina	24 Oct. 1945	Finland	14 Dec. 1955	Morocco	12 Nov. 1956
Armenia	2 Mar. 1992	France	24 Oct. 1945	Mozambique	16 Sep. 1975
Australia	1 Nov. 1945	Gabon	20 Sep. 1960	Myanmar	19 Apr. 1948
Austria	14 Dec. 1955	Gambia	21 Sep. 1965	Namibia	23 Apr. 1990
Azerbaijan	2 Mar. 1992	Georgia	31 July 1992	Nauru	14 Sep. 1999
Bahamas	18 Sep. 1973	Germany[3]	18 Sep. 1973	Nepal	14 Dec. 1955
Bahrain	21 Sep. 1971	Ghana	8 Mar. 1957	Netherlands	10 Dec. 1945
Bangladesh	17 Sep. 1974	Greece	25 Oct. 1945	New Zealand	24 Oct. 1945
Barbados	9 Dec. 1966	Grenada	17 Sep. 1974	Nicaragua	24 Oct. 1945
Belarus	24 Oct. 1945	Guatemala	21 Nov. 1945	Niger	20 Sep. 1960
Belgium	27 Dec. 1945	Guinea	12 Dec. 1958	Nigeria	7 Oct. 1960
Belize	25 Sep. 1981	Guinea-Bissau	17 Sep. 1974	Norway	27 Nov. 1945
Benin	20 Sep. 1960	Guyana	20 Sep. 1966	Oman	7 Oct. 1971
Bhutan	21 Sep. 1971	Haiti	24 Oct. 1945	Pakistan	30 Sep. 1947
Bolivia	14 Nov. 1945	Honduras	17 Dec. 1945	Palau	15 Dec. 1994
Bosnia and Herzegovina	22 May 1992	Hungary	14 Dec. 1955	Panama	13 Nov. 1945
Botswana	17 Oct. 1966	Iceland	19 Nov. 1946	Papua New Guinea	10 Oct. 1975
Brazil	24 Oct. 1945	India	30 Oct. 1945	Paraguay	24 Oct. 1945
Brunei Darussalam	21 Sep. 1984	Indonesia[4]	28 Sep. 1950	Peru	31 Oct. 1945
Bulgaria	14 Dec. 1955	Iran (Islamic Republic of)	24 Oct. 1945	Philippines	24 Oct. 1945
Burkina Faso	20 Sep. 1960	Iraq	21 Dec. 1945	Poland	24 Oct. 1945
Burundi	18 Sep. 1962	Ireland	14 Dec. 1955	Portugal	14 Dec. 1955
Cambodia	14 Dec. 1955	Israel	11 May 1949	Qatar	21 Sep. 1971
Cameroon	20 Sep. 1960	Italy	14 Dec. 1955	Republic of Korea	17 Sep. 1991
Canada	9 Nov. 1945	Jamaica	18 Sep. 1962	Republic of Moldova	2 Mar. 1992
Cape Verde	16 Sep. 1975	Japan	18 Dec. 1956	Romania	14 Dec. 1955
Central African Republic	20 Sep. 1960	Jordan	14 Dec. 1955	Russian Federation[6]	24 Oct. 1945
Chad	20 Sep. 1960	Kazakhstan	2 Mar. 1992	Rwanda	18 Sep. 1962
Chile	24 Oct. 1945	Kenya	16 Dec. 1963	Saint Kitts and Nevis	23 Sep. 1983
China	24 Oct. 1945	Kiribati	14 Sep. 1999	Saint Lucia	18 Sep. 1979
Colombia	5 Nov. 1945	Kuwait	14 May 1963	Saint Vincent and the Grenadines	16 Sep. 1980
Comoros	12 Nov. 1975	Kyrgyzstan	2 Mar. 1992	Samoa	15 Dec. 1976
Congo	20 Sep. 1960	Lao People's Democratic Republic	14 Dec. 1955	San Marino	2 Mar. 1992
Costa Rica	2 Nov. 1945	Latvia	17 Sep. 1991	Sao Tome and Principe	16 Sep. 1975
Côte d'Ivoire	20 Sep. 1960	Lebanon	24 Oct. 1945	Saudi Arabia	24 Oct. 1945
Croatia	22 May 1992	Lesotho	17 Oct. 1966	Senegal	28 Sep. 1960
Cuba	24 Oct. 1945	Liberia	2 Nov. 1945	Seychelles	21 Sep. 1976
Cyprus	20 Sep. 1960	Libyan Arab Jamahiriya	14 Dec. 1955	Sierra Leone	27 Sep. 1961
Czech Republic[1]	19 Jan. 1993	Liechtenstein	18 Sep. 1990	Singapore[5]	21 Sep. 1965
Democratic People's Republic of Korea	17 Sep. 1991	Lithuania	17 Sep. 1991	Slovakia[1]	19 Jan. 1993
Democratic Republic of the Congo	20 Sep. 1960	Luxembourg	24 Oct. 1945	Slovenia	22 May 1992
Denmark	24 Oct. 1945	Madagascar	20 Sep. 1960	Solomon Islands	19 Sep. 1978
Djibouti	20 Sep. 1977	Malawi	1 Dec. 1964	Somalia	20 Sep. 1960
Dominica	18 Dec. 1978	Malaysia[5]	17 Sep. 1957	South Africa	7 Nov. 1945
Dominican Republic	24 Oct. 1945	Maldives	21 Sep. 1965	Spain	14 Dec. 1955
Ecuador	21 Dec. 1945	Mali	28 Sep. 1960	Sri Lanka	14 Dec. 1955
Egypt[2]	24 Oct. 1945	Malta	1 Dec. 1964	Sudan	12 Nov. 1956
		Marshall Islands	17 Sep. 1991		

MEMBER	DATE OF ADMISSION	MEMBER	DATE OF ADMISSION	MEMBER	DATE OF ADMISSION
Suriname	4 Dec. 1975	Tunisia	12 Nov. 1956	United States of America	24 Oct. 1945
Swaziland	24 Sep. 1968	Turkey	24 Oct. 1945	Uruguay	18 Dec. 1945
Sweden	19 Nov. 1946	Turkmenistan	2 Mar. 1992	Uzbekistan	2 Mar. 1992
Syrian Arab Republic[2]	24 Oct. 1945	Uganda	25 Oct. 1962	Vanuatu	15 Sep. 1981
Tajikistan	2 Mar. 1992	Ukraine	24 Oct. 1945	Venezuela	15 Nov. 1945
Thailand	16 Dec. 1946	United Arab Emirates	9 Dec. 1971	Viet Nam	20 Sep. 1977
The former Yugoslav Republic of Macedonia	8 Apr. 1993	United Kingdom of Great Britain and Northern Ireland	24 Oct. 1945	Yemen[8]	30 Sep. 1947
Togo	20 Sep. 1960	United Republic of Tanzania[7]	14 Dec. 1961	Yugoslavia[9]	24 Oct. 1945
Tonga	14 Sep. 1999			Zambia	1 Dec. 1964
Trinidad and Tobago	18 Sep. 1962			Zimbabwe	25 Aug. 1980

[1]Czechoslovakia, which was an original Member of the United Nations from 24 October 1945, split up on 1 January 1993 and was succeeded by the Czech Republic and Slovakia.

[2]Egypt and Syria, both of which became Members of the United Nations on 24 October 1945, joined together—following a plebiscite held in those countries on 21 February 1958—to form the United Arab Republic. On 13 October 1961, Syria, having resumed its status as an independent State, also resumed its separate membership in the United Nations; it changed its name to the Syrian Arab Republic on 14 September 1971. The United Arab Republic continued as a Member of the United Nations and reverted to the name of Egypt on 2 September 1971.

[3]Through accession of the German Democratic Republic to the Federal Republic of Germany on 3 October 1990, the two German States (both of which became United Nations Members on 18 September 1973) united to form one sovereign State. As from that date, the Federal Republic of Germany has acted in the United Nations under the designation Germany.

[4]On 20 January 1965, Indonesia informed the Secretary-General that it had decided to withdraw from the United Nations. By a telegram of 19 September 1966, it notified the Secretary-General of its decision to resume participation in the activities of the United Nations. On 28 September 1966, the General Assembly took note of that decision and the President invited the representatives of Indonesia to take their seats in the Assembly.

[5]On 16 September 1963, Sabah (North Borneo), Sarawak and Singapore joined with the Federation of Malaya (which became a United Nations Member on 17 September 1957) to form Malaysia. On 9 August 1965, Singapore became an independent State and on 21 September 1965 it became a Member of the United Nations.

[6]The Union of Soviet Socialist Republics was an original Member of the United Nations from 24 October 1945. On 24 December 1991, the President of the Russian Federation informed the Secretary-General that the membership of the USSR in all United Nations organs was being continued by the Russian Federation.

[7]Tanganyika was admitted to the United Nations on 14 December 1961, and Zanzibar, on 16 December 1963. Following ratification, on 26 April 1964, of the Articles of Union between Tanganyika and Zanzibar, the two States became represented as a single Member: the United Republic of Tanganyika and Zanzibar; it changed its name to the United Republic of Tanzania on 1 November 1964.

[8]Yemen was admitted to the United Nations on 30 September 1947 and Democratic Yemen on 14 December 1967. On 22 May 1990, the two countries merged and have since been represented as one Member.

[9]Refers to the former Socialist Federal Republic of Yugoslavia.

Appendix II

Charter of the United Nations and Statute of the International Court of Justice

Charter of the United Nations

NOTE: The Charter of the United Nations was signed on 26 June 1945, in San Francisco, at the conclusion of the United Nations Conference on International Organization, and came into force on 24 October 1945. The Statute of the International Court of Justice is an integral part of the Charter.

Amendments to Articles 23, 27 and 61 of the Charter were adopted by the General Assembly on 17 December 1963 and came into force on 31 August 1965. A further amendment to Article 61 was adopted by the General Assembly on 20 December 1971 and came into force on 24 September 1973. An amendment to Article 109, adopted by the General Assembly on 20 December 1965, came into force on 12 June 1968.

The amendment to Article 23 enlarges the membership of the Security Council from 11 to 15. The amended Article 27 provides that decisions of the Security Council on procedural matters shall be made by an affirmative vote of nine members (formerly seven) and on all other matters by an affirmative vote of nine members (formerly seven), including the concurring votes of the five permanent members of the Security Council.

The amendment to Article 61, which entered into force on 31 August 1965, enlarged the membership of the Economic and Social Council from 18 to 27. The subsequent amendment to that Article, which entered into force on 24 September 1973, further increased the membership of the Council from 27 to 54.

The amendment to Article 109, which relates to the first paragraph of that Article, provides that a General Conference of Member States for the purpose of reviewing the Charter may be held at a date and place to be fixed by a two-thirds vote of the members of the General Assembly and by a vote of any nine members (formerly seven) of the Security Council. Paragraph 3 of Article 109, which deals with the consideration of a possible review conference during the tenth regular session of the General Assembly, has been retained in its original form in its reference to a "vote of any seven members of the Security Council", the paragraph having been acted upon in 1955 by the General Assembly, at its tenth regular session, and by the Security Council.

WE THE PEOPLES
OF THE UNITED NATIONS
DETERMINED

to save succeeding generations from the scourge of war, which twice in our lifetime has brought untold sorrow to mankind, and

to reaffirm faith in fundamental human rights, in the dignity and worth of the human person, in the equal rights of men and women and of nations large and small, and

to establish conditions under which justice and respect for the obligations arising from treaties and other sources of international law can be maintained, and

to promote social progress and better standards of life in larger freedom,

AND FOR THESE ENDS

to practice tolerance and live together in peace with one another as good neighbours, and

to unite our strength to maintain international peace and security, and

to ensure, by the acceptance of principles and the institution of methods, that armed force shall not be used, save in the common interest, and

to employ international machinery for the promotion of the economic and social advancement of all peoples,

HAVE RESOLVED TO
COMBINE OUR EFFORTS TO
ACCOMPLISH THESE AIMS

Accordingly, our respective Governments, through representatives assembled in the city of San Francisco, who have exhibited their full powers found to be in good and due form, have agreed to the present Charter of the United Nations and do hereby establish an international organization to be known as the United Nations.

Chapter I
PURPOSES AND PRINCIPLES

Article 1

The Purposes of the United Nations are:

1. To maintain international peace and security, and to that end: to take effective collective measures for the prevention and removal of threats to the peace, and for the suppression of acts of aggression or other breaches of the peace, and to bring about by peaceful means, and in conformity with the principles of justice and international law, adjustment or settlement of international disputes or situations which might lead to a breach of the peace;

2. To develop friendly relations among nations based on respect for the principle of equal rights and self-determination of peoples, and to take other appropriate measures to strengthen universal peace;

3. To achieve international co-operation in solving international problems of an economic, social, cultural or humanitarian character, and in promoting and encouraging respect for human rights and for fundamental freedoms for all without distinction as to race, sex, language or religion; and

4. To be a centre for harmonizing the actions of nations in the attainment of these common ends.

Article 2

The Organization and its Members, in pursuit of the Purposes stated in Article 1, shall act in accordance with the following Principles:

1. The Organization is based on the principle of the sovereign equality of all its Members.

2. All Members, in order to ensure to all of them the rights and benefits resulting from membership, shall fulfil in good faith the obligations assumed by them in accordance with the present Charter.

3. All Members shall settle their international disputes by peaceful means in such a manner that international peace and security, and justice, are not endangered.

4. All Members shall refrain in their international relations from the threat or use of force against the territorial integrity or political independence of any state, or in any other manner inconsistent with the Purposes of the United Nations.

5. All Members shall give the United Nations every assistance in any action it takes in accordance with the present Charter, and shall refrain from giving assistance to any state against which the United Nations is taking preventive or enforcement action.

6. The Organization shall ensure that states which are not Members of the United Nations act in accordance with these Principles so far as may be necessary for the maintenance of international peace and security.

7. Nothing contained in the present Charter shall authorize the United Nations to intervene in matters which are essentially within the domestic jurisdiction of any state or shall require the Members to submit such matters to settlement under the present Charter; but this principle shall not prejudice the application of enforcement measures under Chapter VII.

Chapter II
MEMBERSHIP

Article 3

The original Members of the United Nations shall be the states which, having participated in the United Nations Conference on International Organization at San Francisco or having previously signed the Declaration by United Nations of 1 January 1942, sign the present Charter and ratify it in accordance with Article 110.

Article 4

1. Membership in the United Nations is open to all other peace-loving states which accept the obligations contained in the present Charter and, in the judgment of the Organization, are able and willing to carry out these obligations.

2. The admission of any such state to membership in the United Nations will be effected by a decision of the General Assembly upon the recommendation of the Security Council.

Article 5

A Member of the United Nations against which preventive or enforcement action has been taken by the Security Council may be suspended from the exercise of the rights and privileges of membership by the General Assembly upon the recommendation of the Security Council. The exercise of these rights and privileges may be restored by the Security Council.

Article 6

A Member of the United Nations which has persistently violated the Principles contained in the present Charter may be expelled from the Organization by the General Assembly upon the recommendation of the Security Council.

Chapter III
ORGANS

Article 7

1. There are established as the principal organs of the United Nations: a General Assembly, a Security Council, an Economic and Social Council, a Trusteeship Council, an International Court of Justice, and a Secretariat.

2. Such subsidiary organs as may be found necessary may be established in accordance with the present Charter.

Article 8

The United Nations shall place no restrictions on the eligibility of men and women to participate in any capacity and under conditions of equality in its principal and subsidiary organs.

Chapter IV
THE GENERAL ASSEMBLY

Composition

Article 9

1. The General Assembly shall consist of all the Members of the United Nations.

2. Each Member shall have not more than five representatives in the General Assembly.

Functions and Powers

Article 10

The General Assembly may discuss any questions or any matters within the scope of the present Charter or relating to the powers and functions of any organs provided for in the present Charter, and, except as provided in Article 12, may make recommendations to the Members of the United Nations or to the Security Council or both on any such questions or matters.

Article 11

1. The General Assembly may consider the general principles of co-operation in the maintenance of international peace and security, including the principles governing disarmament and the regulation of armaments, and may make recommendations with regard to such principles to the Members or to the Security Council or to both.

2. The General Assembly may discuss any questions relating to the maintenance of international peace and security brought before it by any Member of the United Nations, or by the Security Council, or by a state which is not a Member of the United Nations in accordance with Article 35, paragraph 2, and, except as provided in Article 12, may make recommendations with regard to any such questions to the state or states concerned or to the Security Council or to both. Any such question on which action is necessary shall be referred to the Security Council by the General Assembly either before or after discussion.

3. The General Assembly may call the attention of the Security Council to situations which are likely to endanger international peace and security.

4. The powers of the General Assembly set forth in this Article shall not limit the general scope of Article 10.

Article 12

1. While the Security Council is exercising in respect of any dispute or situation the functions assigned to it in the present Charter, the General Assembly shall not make any recommendation with regard to that dispute or situation unless the Security Council so requests.

2. The Secretary-General, with the consent of the Security Council, shall notify the General Assembly at each session of any matters relative to the maintenance of international peace and security which are being dealt with by the Security Council and shall similarly notify the General Assembly, or the Members of the United Nations if the General Assembly is not in session, immediately the Security Council ceases to deal with such matters.

Article 13

1. The General Assembly shall initiate studies and make recommendations for the purpose of:

a. promoting international co-operation in the political field and encouraging the progressive development of international law and its codification;

b. promoting international co-operation in the economic, social, cultural, educational and health fields, and assisting in the realization of human rights and fundamental freedoms for all without distinction as to race, sex, language or religion.

2. The further responsibilities, functions and powers of the General Assembly with respect to matters mentioned in paragraph 1 (b) above are set forth in Chapters IX and X.

Article 14

Subject to the provisions of Article 12, the General Assembly may recommend measures for the peaceful adjustment of any situation, regardless of origin, which it deems likely to impair the general welfare or friendly relations among nations, including situations resulting from a violation of the provisions of the present Charter setting forth the Purposes and Principles of the United Nations.

Article 15

1. The General Assembly shall receive and consider annual and special reports from the Security Council; these reports shall include an account of the measures that the Security Council has decided upon or taken to maintain international peace and security.
2. The General Assembly shall receive and consider reports from the other organs of the United Nations.

Article 16

The General Assembly shall perform such functions with respect to the international trusteeship system as are assigned to it under Chapters XII and XIII, including the approval of the trusteeship agreements for areas not designated as strategic.

Article 17

1. The General Assembly shall consider and approve the budget of the Organization.
2. The expenses of the Organization shall be borne by the Members as apportioned by the General Assembly.
3. The General Assembly shall consider and approve any financial and budgetary arrangements with specialized agencies referred to in Article 57 and shall examine the administrative budgets of such specialized agencies with a view to making recommendations to the agencies concerned.

Voting

Article 18

1. Each member of the General Assembly shall have one vote.
2. Decisions of the General Assembly on important questions shall be made by a two-thirds majority of the members present and voting. These questions shall include: recommendations with respect to the maintenance of international peace and security, the election of the non-permanent members of the Security Council, the election of the members of the Economic and Social Council, the election of members of the Trusteeship Council in accordance with paragraph 1 (c) of Article 86, the admission of new Members to the United Nations, the suspension of the rights and privileges of membership, the expulsion of Members, questions relating to the operation of the trusteeship system, and budgetary questions.
3. Decisions on other questions, including the determination of additional categories of questions to be decided by a two-thirds majority, shall be made by a majority of the members present and voting.

Article 19

A Member of the United Nations which is in arrears in the payment of its financial contributions to the Organization shall have no vote in the General Assembly if the amount of its arrears equals or exceeds the amount of the contributions due from it for the preceding two full years. The General Assembly may, nevertheless, permit such a Member to vote if it is satisfied that the failure to pay is due to conditions beyond the control of the Member.

Procedure

Article 20

The General Assembly shall meet in regular annual sessions and in such special sessions as occasion may require. Special sessions shall be convoked by the Secretary-General at the request of the Security Council or of a majority of the Members of the United Nations.

Article 21

The General Assembly shall adopt its own rules of procedure. It shall elect its President for each session.

Article 22

The General Assembly may establish such subsidiary organs as it deems necessary for the performance of its functions.

Chapter V

THE SECURITY COUNCIL

Composition

Article 23[1]

1. The Security Council shall consist of fifteen Members of the United Nations. The Republic of China, France, the Union of Soviet Socialist Republics, the United Kingdom of Great Britain and Northern Ireland and the United States of America shall be permanent members of the Security Council. The General Assembly shall elect ten other Members of the United Nations to be non-permanent members of the Security Council, due regard being specially paid, in the first instance to the contribution of Members of the United Nations to the maintenance of international peace and security and to the other purposes of the Organization, and also to equitable geographical distribution.
2. The non-permanent members of the Security Council shall be elected for a term of two years. In the first election of the non-permanent members after the increase of the membership of the Security Council from eleven to fifteen, two of the four additional members shall be chosen for a term of one year. A retiring member shall not be eligible for immediate reelection.
3. Each member of the Security Council shall have one representative.

Functions and Powers

Article 24

1. In order to ensure prompt and effective action by the United Nations, its Members confer on the Security Council primary responsibility for the maintenance of international peace and security, and agree that in carrying out its duties under this responsibility the Security Council acts on their behalf.
2. In discharging these duties the Security Council shall act in accordance with the Purposes and Principles of the United Nations. The specific powers granted to the Security Council for the discharge of these duties are laid down in Chapters VI, VII, VIII and XII.
3. The Security Council shall submit annual and, when necessary, special reports to the General Assembly for its consideration.

Article 25

The Members of the United Nations agree to accept and carry out the decisions of the Security Council in accordance with the present Charter.

Article 26

In order to promote the establishment and maintenance of international peace and security with the least diversion for armaments of the world's human and economic resources, the Security Council shall be responsible for formulating, with the assistance of the Military Staff Committee referred to in Article

47, plans to be submitted to the Members of the United Nations for the establishment of a system for the regulation of armaments.

Voting

Article 27[2]

1. Each member of the Security Council shall have one vote.

2. Decisions of the Security Council on procedural matters shall be made by an affirmative vote of nine members.

3. Decisions of the Security Council on all other matters shall be made by an affirmative vote of nine members including the concurring votes of the permanent members; provided that, in decisions under Chapter VI, and under paragraph 3 of Article 52, a party to a dispute shall abstain from voting.

Procedure

Article 28

1. The Security Council shall be so organized as to be able to function continuously. Each member of the Security Council shall for this purpose be represented at all times at the seat of the Organization.

2. The Security Council shall hold periodic meetings at which each of its members may, if it so desires, be represented by a member of the government or by some other specially designated representative.

3. The Security Council may hold meetings at such places other than the seat of the Organization as in its judgment will best facilitate its work.

Article 29

The Security Council may establish such subsidiary organs as it deems necessary for the performance of its functions.

Article 30

The Security Council shall adopt its own rules of procedure, including the method of selecting its President.

Article 31

Any Member of the United Nations which is not a member of the Security Council may participate, without vote, in the discussion of any question brought before the Security Council whenever the latter considers that the interests of that Member are specially affected.

Article 32

Any Member of the United Nations which is not a member of the Security Council or any state which is not a Member of the United Nations, if it is a party to a dispute under consideration by the Security Council, shall be invited to participate, without vote, in the discussion relating to the dispute. The Security Council shall lay down such conditions as it deems just for the participation of a state which is not a Member of the United Nations.

Chapter VI

PACIFIC SETTLEMENT OF DISPUTES

Article 33

1. The parties to any dispute, the continuance of which is likely to endanger the maintenance of international peace and security, shall, first of all, seek a solution by negotiation, enquiry, mediation, conciliation, arbitration, judicial settlement, resort to regional agencies or arrangements, or other peaceful means of their own choice.

2. The Security Council shall, when it deems necessary, call upon the parties to settle their dispute by such means.

Article 34

The Security Council may investigate any dispute, or any situation which might lead to international friction or give rise to a dispute, in order to determine whether the continuance of the dispute or situation is likely to endanger the maintenance of international peace and security.

Article 35

1. Any Member of the United Nations may bring any dispute, or any situation of the nature referred to in Article 34, to the attention of the Security Council or of the General Assembly.

2. A state which is not a Member of the United Nations may bring to the attention of the Security Council or of the General Assembly any dispute to which it is a party if it accepts in advance, for the purposes of the dispute, the obligations of pacific settlement provided in the present Charter.

3. The proceedings of the General Assembly in respect of matters brought to its attention under this Article will be subject to the provisions of Articles 11 and 12.

Article 36

1. The Security Council may, at any stage of a dispute of the nature referred to in Article 33 or of a situation of like nature, recommend appropriate procedures or methods of adjustment.

2. The Security Council should take into consideration any procedures for the settlement of the dispute which have already been adopted by the parties.

3. In making recommendations under this Article the Security Council should also take into consideration that legal disputes should as a general rule be referred by the parties to the International Court of Justice in accordance with the provisions of the Statute of the Court.

Article 37

1. Should the parties to a dispute of the nature referred to in Article 33 fail to settle it by the means indicated in that Article, they shall refer it to the Security Council.

2. If the Security Council deems that the continuance of the dispute is in fact likely to endanger the maintenance of international peace and security, it shall decide whether to take action under Article 36 or to recommend such terms of settlement as it may consider appropriate.

Article 38

Without prejudice to the provisions of Articles 33 to 37, the Security Council may, if all the parties to any dispute so request, make recommendations to the parties with a view to a pacific settlement of the dispute.

Chapter VII

ACTION WITH RESPECT TO THREATS TO THE PEACE, BREACHES OF THE PEACE, AND ACTS OF AGGRESSION

Article 39

The Security Council shall determine the existence of any threat to the peace, breach of the peace, or act of aggression and shall make recommendations, or decide what measures shall be taken in accordance with Articles 41 and 42, to maintain or restore international peace and security.

Article 40

In order to prevent an aggravation of the situation, the Security Council may, before making the recommendations or deciding upon the measures provided for in Article 39, call upon the parties concerned to comply with such provisional measures as it deems necessary or desirable. Such provisional measures shall be without prejudice to the rights, claims or position of the parties concerned. The Security Council shall duly take account of failure to comply with such provisional measures.

Article 41

The Security Council may decide what measures not involving the use of armed force are to be employed to give effect to its decisions, and it may call upon the Members of the United Nations to apply such measures. These may include complete or partial interruption of economic relations and of rail, sea, air, postal, telegraphic, radio and other means of communication, and the severance of diplomatic relations.

Article 42

Should the Security Council consider that measures provided for in Article 41 would be inadequate or have proved to be inadequate, it may take such action by air, sea or land forces as may be necessary to maintain or restore international peace and security. Such action may include demonstrations, blockade, and other operations by air, sea, or land forces of Members of the United Nations.

Article 43

1. All Members of the United Nations, in order to contribute to the maintenance of international peace and security, undertake to make available to the Security Council, on its call and in accordance with a special agreement or agreements, armed forces, assistance and facilities, including rights of passage, necessary for the purpose of maintaining international peace and security.
2. Such agreement or agreements shall govern the numbers and types of forces, their degree of readiness and general location, and the nature of the facilities and assistance to be provided.
3. The agreement or agreements shall be negotiated as soon as possible on the initiative of the Security Council. They shall be concluded between the Security Council and Members or between the Security Council and groups of Members and shall be subject to ratification by the signatory states in accordance with their respective constitutional processes.

Article 44

When the Security Council has decided to use force it shall, before calling upon a Member not represented on it to provide armed forces in fulfilment of the obligations assumed under Article 43, invite that Member, if the Member so desires, to participate in the decisions of the Security Council concerning the employment of contingents of that Member's armed forces.

Article 45

In order to enable the United Nations to take urgent military measures, Members shall hold immediately available national air-force contingents for combined international enforcement action. The strength and degree of readiness of these contingents and plans for their combined action shall be determined, within the limits laid down in the special agreement or agreements referred to in Article 43, by the Security Council with the assistance of the Military Staff Committee.

Article 46

Plans for the application of armed force shall be made by the Security Council with the assistance of the Military Staff Committee.

Article 47

1. There shall be established a Military Staff Committee to advise and assist the Security Council on all questions relating to the Security Council's military requirements for the maintenance of international peace and security, the employment and command of forces placed at its disposal, the regulation of armaments, and possible disarmament.
2. The Military Staff Committee shall consist of the Chiefs of Staff of the permanent members of the Security Council or their representatives. Any Member of the United Nations not permanently represented on the Committee shall be invited by the Committee to be associated with it when the efficient discharge of the Committee's responsibilities requires the participation of that Member in its work.
3. The Military Staff Committee shall be responsible under the Security Council for the strategic direction of any armed forces placed at the disposal of the Security Council. Questions relating to the command of such forces shall be worked out subsequently.
4. The Military Staff Committee, with the authorization of the Security Council and after consultation with appropriate regional agencies, may establish regional sub-committees.

Article 48

1. The action required to carry out the decisions of the Security Council for the maintenance of international peace and security shall be taken by all the Members of the United Nations or by some of them, as the Security Council may determine.
2. Such decisions shall be carried out by the Members of the United Nations directly and through their action in the appropriate international agencies of which they are members.

Article 49

The Members of the United Nations shall join in affording mutual assistance in carrying out the measures decided upon by the Security Council.

Article 50

If preventive or enforcement measures against any state are taken by the Security Council, any other state, whether a Member of the United Nations or not, which finds itself confronted with special economic problems arising from the carrying out of those measures shall have the right to consult the Security Council with regard to a solution of those problems.

Article 51

Nothing in the present Charter shall impair the inherent right of individual or collective self-defence if an armed attack occurs against a Member of the United Nations, until the Security Council has taken measures necessary to maintain international peace and security. Measures taken by Members in the exercise of this right of self-defence shall be immediately reported to the Security Council and shall not in any way affect the authority and responsibility of the Security Council under the present Charter to take at any time such action as it deems necessary in order to maintain or restore international peace and security.

Chapter VIII
REGIONAL ARRANGEMENTS

Article 52

1. Nothing in the present Charter precludes the existence of regional arrangements or agencies for dealing with such matters relating to the maintenance of international peace and security as are appropriate for regional action, provided that such arrangements or agencies and their activities are consistent with the Purposes and Principles of the United Nations.
2. The Members of the United Nations entering into such arrangements or constituting such agencies shall make every effort to achieve pacific settlement of local disputes through such regional arrangements or by such regional agencies before referring them to the Security Council.
3. The Security Council shall encourage the development of pacific settlement of local disputes through such regional arrangements or by such regional agencies either on the initiative of the states concerned or by reference from the Security Council.
4. This Article in no way impairs the application of Articles 34 and 35.

Article 53

1. The Security Council shall, where appropriate, utilize such regional arrangements or agencies for enforcement action under its authority. But no enforcement action shall be taken under regional arrangements or by regional agencies

without the authorization of the Security Council, with the exception of measures against any enemy state, as defined in paragraph 2 of this Article, provided for pursuant to Article 107 or in regional arrangements directed against renewal of aggressive policy on the part of any such state, until such time as the Organization may, on request of the Governments concerned, be charged with the responsibility for preventing further aggression by such a state.

2. The term enemy state as used in paragraph 1 of this Article applies to any state which during the Second World War has been an enemy of any signatory of the present Charter.

Article 54

The Security Council shall at all times be kept fully informed of activities undertaken or in contemplation under regional arrangements or by regional agencies for the maintenance of international peace and security.

Chapter IX

INTERNATIONAL ECONOMIC AND SOCIAL CO-OPERATION

Article 55

With a view to the creation of conditions of stability and well-being which are necessary for peaceful and friendly relations among nations based on respect for the principle of equal rights and self-determination of peoples, the United Nations shall promote:

a. higher standards of living, full employment, and conditions of economic and social progress and development;
b. solutions of international economic, social, health, and related problems; and international cultural and educational co-operation; and
c. universal respect for, and observance of, human rights and fundamental freedoms for all without distinction as to race, sex, language, or religion.

Article 56

All Members pledge themselves to take joint and separate action in co-operation with the Organization for the achievement of the purposes set forth in Article 55.

Article 57

1. The various specialized agencies, established by intergovernmental agreement and having wide international responsibilities, as defined in their basic instruments, in economic, social, cultural, educational, health, and related fields, shall be brought into relationship with the United Nations in accordance with the provisions of Article 63.

2. Such agencies thus brought into relationship with the United Nations are hereinafter referred to as specialized agencies.

Article 58

The Organization shall make recommendations for the coordination of the policies and activities of the specialized agencies.

Article 59

The Organization shall, where appropriate, initiate negotiations among the states concerned for the creation of any new specialized agencies required for the accomplishment of the purposes set forth in Article 55.

Article 60

Responsibility for the discharge of the functions of the Organization set forth in this Chapter shall be vested in the General Assembly and, under the authority of the General Assembly, in the Economic and Social Council, which shall have for this purpose the powers set forth in Chapter X.

Chapter X

THE ECONOMIC AND SOCIAL COUNCIL

Composition

Article 61[3]

1. The Economic and Social Council shall consist of fifty-four Members of the United Nations elected by the General Assembly.

2. Subject to the provisions of paragraph 3, eighteen members of the Economic and Social Council shall be elected each year for a term of three years. A retiring member shall be eligible for immediate re-election.

3. At the first election after the increase in the membership of the Economic and Social Council from twenty-seven to fifty-four members, in addition to the members elected in place of the nine members whose term of office expires at the end of that year, twenty-seven additional members shall be elected. Of these twenty-seven additional members, the term of office of nine members so elected shall expire at the end of one year, and of nine other members at the end of two years, in accordance with arrangements made by the General Assembly.

4. Each member of the Economic and Social Council shall have one representative.

Functions and Powers

Article 62

1. The Economic and Social Council may make or initiate studies and reports with respect to international economic, social, cultural, educational, health, and related matters and may make recommendations with respect to any such matters to the General Assembly, to the Members of the United Nations, and to the specialized agencies concerned.

2. It may make recommendations for the purpose of promoting respect for, and observance of, human rights and fundamental freedoms for all.

3. It may prepare draft conventions for submission to the General Assembly, with respect to matters falling within its competence.

4. It may call, in accordance with the rules prescribed by the United Nations, international conferences on matters falling within its competence.

Article 63

1. The Economic and Social Council may enter into agreements with any of the agencies referred to in Article 57, defining the terms on which the agency concerned shall be brought into relationship with the United Nations. Such agreements shall be subject to approval by the General Assembly.

2. It may co-ordinate the activities of the specialized agencies through consultation with and recommendations to such agencies and through recommendations to the General Assembly and to the Members of the United Nations.

Article 64

1. The Economic and Social Council may take appropriate steps to obtain regular reports from the specialized agencies. It may make arrangements with the Members of the United Nations and with the specialized agencies to obtain reports on the steps taken to give effect to its own recommendations and to recommendations on matters falling within its competence made by the General Assembly.

2. It may communicate its observations on these reports to the General Assembly.

Article 65

The Economic and Social Council may furnish information to the Security Council and shall assist the Security Council upon its request.

Article 66

1. The Economic and Social Council shall perform such functions as fall within its competence in connexion with the carrying out of the recommendations of the General Assembly.

2. It may, with the approval of the General Assembly, perform services at the request of Members of the United Nations and at the request of specialized agencies.

3. It shall perform such other functions as are specified elsewhere in the present Charter or as may be assigned to it by the General Assembly.

Voting

Article 67

1. Each member of the Economic and Social Council shall have one vote.

2. Decisions of the Economic and Social Council shall be made by a majority of the members present and voting.

Procedure

Article 68

The Economic and Social Council shall set up commissions in economic and social fields and for the promotion of human rights, and such other commissions as may be required for the performance of its functions.

Article 69

The Economic and Social Council shall invite any Member of the United Nations to participate, without vote, in its deliberations on any matter of particular concern to that Member.

Article 70

The Economic and Social Council may make arrangements for representatives of the specialized agencies to participate, without vote, in its deliberations and in those of the commissions established by it, and for its representatives to participate in the deliberations of the specialized agencies.

Article 71

The Economic and Social Council may make suitable arrangements for consultation with non-governmental organizations which are concerned with matters within its competence. Such arrangements may be made with international organizations and, where appropriate, with national organizations after consultation with the Member of the United Nations concerned.

Article 72

1. The Economic and Social Council shall adopt its own rules of procedure, including the method of selecting its President.

2. The Economic and Social Council shall meet as required in accordance with its rules, which shall include provision for the convening of meetings on the request of a majority of its members.

Chapter XI

DECLARATION REGARDING NON-SELF-GOVERNING TERRITORIES

Article 73

Members of the United Nations which have or assume responsibilities for the administration of territories whose peoples have not yet attained a full measure of self-government recognize the principle that the interests of the inhabitants of these territories are paramount, and accept as a sacred trust the obligation to promote to the utmost, within the system of international peace and security established by the present Charter, the well-being of the inhabitants of these territories and, to this end:

a. to ensure, with due respect for the culture of the peoples concerned, their political, economic, social, and educational advancement, their just treatment, and their protection against abuses;
b. to develop self-government, to take due account of the political aspirations of the peoples, and to assist them in the progressive development of their free political institutions, according to the particular circumstances of each territory and its peoples and their varying stages of advancement;
c. to further international peace and security;
d. to promote constructive measures of development, to encourage research, and to co-operate with one another and, when and where appropriate, with specialized international bodies with a view to the practical achievement of the social, economic, and scientific purposes set forth in this Article; and
e. to transmit regularly to the Secretary-General for information purposes, subject to such limitation as security and constitutional considerations may require, statistical and other information of a technical nature relating to economic, social, and educational conditions in the territories for which they are respectively responsible other than those territories to which Chapters XII and XIII apply.

Article 74

Members of the United Nations also agree that their policy in respect of the territories to which this Chapter applies, no less than in respect of their metropolitan areas, must be based on the general principle of good-neighbourliness, due account being taken of the interests and well-being of the rest of the world, in social, economic, and commercial matters.

Chapter XII

INTERNATIONAL TRUSTEESHIP SYSTEM

Article 75

The United Nations shall establish under its authority an international trusteeship system for the administration and supervision of such territories as may be placed thereunder by subsequent individual agreements. These territories are hereinafter referred to as trust territories.

Article 76

The basic objectives of the trusteeship system, in accordance with the Purposes of the United Nations laid down in Article 1 of the present Charter, shall be:

a. to further international peace and security;
b. to promote the political, economic, social, and educational advancement of the inhabitants of the trust territories, and their progressive development towards self-government or independence as may be appropriate to the particular circumstances of each territory and its peoples and the freely expressed wishes of the peoples concerned, and as may be provided by the terms of each trusteeship agreement;
c. to encourage respect for human rights and for fundamental freedoms for all without distinction as to race, sex, language, or religion, and to encourage recognition of the interdependence of the peoples of the world; and
d. to ensure equal treatment in social, economic, and commercial matters for all Members of the United Nations and their nationals, and also equal treatment for the latter in the administration of justice, without prejudice to the attainment of the foregoing objectives and subject to the provisions of Article 80.

Article 77

1. The trusteeship system shall apply to such territories in the following categories as may be placed thereunder by means of trusteeship agreements:

a. territories now held under mandate;
b. territories which may be detached from enemy states as a result of the Second World War; and
c. territories voluntarily placed under the system by states responsible for their administration.

2. It will be a matter for subsequent agreement as to which territories in the foregoing categories will be brought under the trusteeship system and upon what terms.

Article 78

The trusteeship system shall not apply to territories which have become Members of the United Nations, relationship among which shall be based on respect for the principle of sovereign equality.

Article 79

The terms of trusteeship for each territory to be placed under the trusteeship system, including any alteration or amendment, shall be agreed upon by the states directly concerned, including the mandatory power in the case of territories held under mandate by a Member of the United Nations, and shall be approved as provided for in Articles 83 and 85.

Article 80

1. Except as may be agreed upon in individual trusteeship agreements, made under Articles 77, 79 and 81, placing each territory under the trusteeship system, and until such agreements have been concluded, nothing in this Chapter shall be construed in or of itself to alter in any manner the rights whatsoever of any states or any peoples or the terms of existing international instruments to which Members of the United Nations may respectively be parties.

2. Paragraph 1 of this Article shall not be interpreted as giving grounds for delay or postponement of the negotiation and conclusion of agreements for placing mandated and other territories under the trusteeship system as provided for in Article 77.

Article 81

The trusteeship agreement shall in each case include the terms under which the trust territory will be administered and designate the authority which will exercise the administration of the trust territory. Such authority, hereinafter called the administering authority, may be one or more states or the Organization itself.

Article 82

There may be designated, in any trusteeship agreement, a strategic area or areas which may include part or all of the trust territory to which the agreement applies, without prejudice to any special agreement or agreements made under Article 43.

Article 83

1. All functions of the United Nations relating to strategic areas, including the approval of the terms of the trusteeship agreements and of their alteration or amendment, shall be exercised by the Security Council.

2. The basic objectives set forth in Article 76 shall be applicable to the people of each strategic area.

3. The Security Council shall, subject to the provisions of the trusteeship agreements and without prejudice to security considerations, avail itself of the assistance of the Trusteeship Council to perform those functions of the United Nations under the trusteeship system relating to political, economic, social, and educational matters in the strategic areas.

Article 84

It shall be the duty of the administering authority to ensure that the trust territory shall play its part in the maintenance of international peace and security. To this end the administering authority may make use of volunteer forces, facilities, and assistance from the trust territory in carrying out the obligations towards the Security Council undertaken in this regard by the administering authority, as well as for local defence and the maintenance of law and order within the trust territory.

Article 85

1. The functions of the United Nations with regard to trusteeship agreements for all areas not designated as strategic, including the approval of the terms of the trusteeship agreements and of their alteration or amendment, shall be exercised by the General Assembly.

2. The Trusteeship Council, operating under the authority of the General Assembly, shall assist the General Assembly in carrying out these functions.

Chapter XIII

THE TRUSTEESHIP COUNCIL

Composition

Article 86

1. The Trusteeship Council shall consist of the following Members of the United Nations:

a. those Members administering trust territories;
b. such of those Members mentioned by name in Article 23 as are not administering trust territories; and
c. as many other Members elected for three-year terms by the General Assembly as may be necessary to ensure that the total number of members of the Trusteeship Council is equally divided between those Members of the United Nations which administer trust territories and those which do not.

2. Each member of the Trusteeship Council shall designate one specially qualified person to represent it therein.

Functions and Powers

Article 87

The General Assembly and, under its authority, the Trusteeship Council, in carrying out their functions, may:

a. consider reports submitted by the administering authority;
b. accept petitions and examine them in consultation with the administering authority;
c. provide for periodic visits to the respective trust territories at times agreed upon with the administering authority; and
d. take these and other actions in conformity with the terms of the trusteeship agreements.

Article 88

The Trusteeship Council shall formulate a questionnaire on the political, economic, social, and educational advancement of the inhabitants of each trust territory, and the administering authority for each trust territory within the competence of the General Assembly shall make an annual report to the General Assembly upon the basis of such questionnaire.

Voting

Article 89

1. Each member of the Trusteeship Council shall have one vote.

2. Decisions of the Trusteeship Council shall be made by a majority of the members present and voting.

Procedure

Article 90

1. The Trusteeship Council shall adopt its own rules of procedure, including the method of selecting its President.

2. The Trusteeship Council shall meet as required in accordance with its rules, which shall include provision for the convening of meetings on the request of a majority of its members.

Article 91

The Trusteeship Council shall, when appropriate, avail itself of the assistance of the Economic and Social Council and of the specialized agencies in regard to matters with which they are respectively concerned.

Chapter XIV

THE INTERNATIONAL COURT OF JUSTICE

Article 92

The International Court of Justice shall be the principal judicial organ of the United Nations. It shall function in accordance with the annexed Statute, which is based upon the Statute of the Permanent Court of International Justice and forms an integral part of the present Charter.

Article 93

1. All Members of the United Nations are *ipso facto* parties to the Statute of the International Court of Justice.
2. A state which is not a Member of the United Nations may become a party to the Statute of the International Court of Justice on conditions to be determined in each case by the General Assembly upon the recommendation of the Security Council.

Article 94

1. Each Member of the United Nations undertakes to comply with the decision of the International Court of Justice in any case to which it is a party.
2. If any party to a case fails to perform the obligations incumbent upon it under a judgment rendered by the Court, the other party may have recourse to the Security Council, which may, if it deems necessary, make recommendations or decide upon measures to be taken to give effect to the judgment.

Article 95

Nothing in the present Charter shall prevent Members of the United Nations from entrusting the solution of their differences to other tribunals by virtue of agreements already in existence or which may be concluded in the future.

Article 96

1. The General Assembly or the Security Council may request the International Court of Justice to give an advisory opinion on any legal question.
2. Other organs of the United Nations and specialized agencies, which may at any time be so authorized by the General Assembly, may also request advisory opinions of the Court on legal questions arising within the scope of their activities.

Chapter XV

THE SECRETARIAT

Article 97

The Secretariat shall comprise a Secretary-General and such staff as the Organization may require. The Secretary-General shall be appointed by the General Assembly upon the recommendation of the Security Council. He shall be the chief administrative officer of the Organization.

Article 98

The Secretary-General shall act in that capacity in all meetings of the General Assembly, of the Security Council, of the Economic and Social Council, and of the Trusteeship Council, and shall perform such other functions as are entrusted to him by these organs. The Secretary-General shall make an annual report to the General Assembly on the work of the Organization.

Article 99

The Secretary-General may bring to the attention of the Security Council any matter which in his opinion may threaten the maintenance of international peace and security.

Article 100

1. In the performance of their duties the Secretary-General and the staff shall not seek or receive instructions from any government or from any other authority external to the Organization. They shall refrain from any action which might reflect on their position as international officials responsible only to the Organization.
2. Each Member of the United Nations undertakes to respect the exclusively international character of the responsibilities of the Secretary-General and the staff and not to seek to influence them in the discharge of their responsibilities.

Article 101

1. The staff shall be appointed by the Secretary-General under regulations established by the General Assembly.
2. Appropriate staffs shall be permanently assigned to the Economic and Social Council, the Trusteeship Council, and, as required, to other organs of the United Nations. These staffs shall form a part of the Secretariat.
3. The paramount consideration in the employment of the staff and in the determination of the conditions of service shall be the necessity of securing the highest standards of efficiency, competence, and integrity. Due regard shall be paid to the importance of recruiting the staff on as wide a geographical basis as possible.

Chapter XVI

MISCELLANEOUS PROVISIONS

Article 102

1. Every treaty and every international agreement entered into by any Member of the United Nations after the present Charter comes into force shall as soon as possible be registered with the Secretariat and published by it.
2. No party to any such treaty or international agreement which has not been registered in accordance with the provisions of paragraph 1 of this Article may invoke that treaty or agreement before any organ of the United Nations.

Article 103

In the event of a conflict between the obligations of the Members of the United Nations under the present Charter and their obligations under any other international agreement, their obligations under the present Charter shall prevail.

Article 104

The Organization shall enjoy in the territory of each of its Members such legal capacity as may be necessary for the exercise of its functions and the fulfilment of its purposes.

Article 105

1. The Organization shall enjoy in the territory of each of its Members such privileges and immunities as are necessary for the fulfilment of its purposes.
2. Representatives of the Members of the United Nations and officials of the Organization shall similarly enjoy such privileges and immunities as are necessary for the independent exercise of their functions in connexion with the Organization.
3. The General Assembly may make recommendations with a view to determining the details of the application of paragraphs 1 and 2 of this Article or may propose conventions to the Members of the United Nations for this purpose.

Chapter XVII
TRANSITIONAL SECURITY ARRANGEMENTS

Article 106

Pending the coming into force of such special agreements referred to in Article 43 as in the opinion of the Security Council enable it to begin the exercise of its responsibilities under Article 42, the parties to the Four-Nation Declaration, signed at Moscow, 30 October 1943, and France, shall, in accordance with the provisions of paragraph 5 of that Declaration, consult with one another and as occasion requires with other Members of the United Nations with a view to such joint action on behalf of the Organization as may be necessary for the purpose of maintaining international peace and security.

Article 107

Nothing in the present Charter shall invalidate or preclude action, in relation to any state which during the Second World War has been an enemy of any signatory to the present Charter, taken or authorized as a result of that war by the Governments having responsibility for such action.

Chapter XVIII
AMENDMENTS

Article 108

Amendments to the present Charter shall come into force for all Members of the United Nations when they have been adopted by a vote of two thirds of the members of the General Assembly and ratified in accordance with their respective constitutional processes by two thirds of the Members of the United Nations, including all the permanent members of the Security Council.

Article 109[4]

1. A General Conference of the Members of the United Nations for the purpose of reviewing the present Charter may be held at a date and place to be fixed by a two-thirds vote of the members of the General Assembly and by a vote of any nine members of the Security Council. Each Member of the United Nations shall have one vote in the conference.

2. Any alteration of the present Charter recommended by a two-thirds vote of the conference shall take effect when ratified in accordance with their respective constitutional processes by two thirds of the Members of the United Nations including all the permanent members of the Security Council.

3. If such a conference has not been held before the tenth annual session of the General Assembly following the coming into force of the present Charter, the proposal to call such a conference shall be placed on the agenda of that session of the General Assembly, and the conference shall be held if so decided by a majority vote of the members of the General Assembly and by a vote of any seven members of the Security Council.

Chapter XIX
RATIFICATION AND SIGNATURE

Article 110

1. The present Charter shall be ratified by the signatory states in accordance with their respective constitutional processes.

2. The ratifications shall be deposited with the Government of the United States of America, which shall notify all the signatory states of each deposit as well as the Secretary-General of the Organization when he has been appointed.

3. The present Charter shall come into force upon the deposit of ratifications by the Republic of China, France, the Union of Soviet Socialist Republics, the United Kingdom of Great Britain and Northern Ireland and the United States of America, and by a majority of the other signatory states. A protocol of the ratifications deposited shall thereupon be drawn up by the Government of the United States of America which shall communicate copies thereof to all the signatory states.

4. The states signatory to the present Charter which ratify it after it has come into force will become original Members of the United Nations on the date of the deposit of their respective ratifications.

Article 111

The present Charter, of which the Chinese, French, Russian, English, and Spanish texts are equally authentic, shall remain deposited in the archives of the Government of the United States of America. Duly certified copies thereof shall be transmitted by that Government to the Governments of the other signatory states.

IN FAITH WHEREOF the representatives of the Governments of the United Nations have signed the present Charter.

DONE at the city of San Francisco the twenty-sixth day of June, one thousand nine hundred and forty-five.

---

[1] Amended text of Article 23, which came into force on 31 August 1965.
(The text of Article 23 before it was amended read as follows:
1. The Security Council shall consist of eleven Members of the United Nations. The Republic of China, France, the Union of Soviet Socialist Republics, the United Kingdom of Great Britain and Northern Ireland and the United States of America shall be permanent members of the Security Council. The General Assembly shall elect six other Members of the United Nations to be non-permanent members of the Security Council, due regard being specially paid in the first instance to the contributions of Members of the United Nations to the maintenance of international peace and security and to the other purposes of the Organization, and also to equitable geographical distribution.
2. The non-permanent members of the Security Council shall be elected for a term of two years. In the first election of the non-permanent members, however, three shall be chosen for a term of one year. A retiring member shall not be eligible for immediate re-election.
3. Each member of the Security Council shall have one representative.)

[2] Amended text of Article 27, which came into force on 31 August 1965.
(The text of Article 27 before it was amended read as follows:
1. Each member of the Security Council shall have one vote.
2. Decisions of the Security Council on procedural matters shall be made by an affirmative vote of seven members.
3. Decisions of the Security Council on all other matters shall be made by an affirmative vote of seven members including the concurring votes of the permanent members; provided that, in decisions under Chapter VI, and under paragraph 3 of Article 52, a party to a dispute shall abstain from voting.)

[3] Amended text of Article 61, which came into force on 24 September 1973.
(The text of Article 61 as previously amended on 31 August 1965 read as follows:
1. The Economic and Social Council shall consist of twenty-seven Members of the United Nations elected by the General Assembly.
2. Subject to the provisions of paragraph 3, nine members of the Economic and Social Council shall be elected each year for a term of three years. A retiring member shall be eligible for immediate re-election.
3. At the first election after the increase in the membership of the Economic and Social Council from eighteen to twenty-seven members, in addition to the members elected in place of the six members whose term of office expires at the end of that year, nine

additional members shall be elected. Of these nine additional members, the term of office of three members so elected shall expire at the end of one year, and of three other members at the end of two years, in accordance with arrangements made by the General Assembly.

4. Each member of the Economic and Social Council shall have one representative.)

[4] Amended text of Article 109, which came into force on 12 June 1968.
(The text of Article 109 before it was amended read as follows:

1. A General Conference of the Members of the United Nations for the purpose of reviewing the present Charter may be held at a date and place to be fixed by a two-thirds vote of the members of the General Assembly and by a vote of any seven members of the Security Council. Each Member of the United Nations shall have one vote in the conference.

2. Any alteration of the present Charter recommended by a two-thirds vote of the conference shall take effect when ratified in accordance with their respective constitutional processes by two thirds of the Members of the United Nations including all the permanent members of the Security Council.

3. If such a conference has not been held before the tenth annual session of the General Assembly following the coming into force of the present Charter, the proposal to call such a conference shall be placed on the agenda of that session of the General Assembly, and the conference shall be held if so decided by a majority vote of the members of the General Assembly and by a vote of any seven members of the Security Council.)

Statute of the International Court of Justice

Article 1

The International Court of Justice established by the Charter of the United Nations as the principal judicial organ of the United Nations shall be constituted and shall function in accordance with the provisions of the present Statute.

Chapter I
ORGANIZATION OF THE COURT

Article 2

The Court shall be composed of a body of independent judges, elected regardless of their nationality from among persons of high moral character, who possess the qualifications required in their respective countries for appointment to the highest judicial offices, or are jurisconsults of recognized competence in international law.

Article 3

1. The Court shall consist of fifteen members, no two of whom may be nationals of the same state.

2. A person who for the purposes of membership in the Court could be regarded as a national of more than one state shall be deemed to be a national of the one in which he ordinarily exercises civil and political rights.

Article 4

1. The members of the Court shall be elected by the General Assembly and by the Security Council from a list of persons nominated by the national groups in the Permanent Court of Arbitration, in accordance with the following provisions.

2. In the case of Members of the United Nations not represented in the Permanent Court of Arbitration, candidates shall be nominated by national groups appointed for this purpose by their governments under the same conditions as those prescribed for members of the Permanent Court of Arbitration by Article 44 of the Convention of The Hague of 1907 for the pacific settlement of international disputes.

3. The conditions under which a state which is a party to the present Statute but is not a Member of the United Nations may participate in electing the members of the Court shall, in the absence of a special agreement, be laid down by the General Assembly upon recommendation of the Security Council.

Article 5

1. At least three months before the date of the election, the Secretary-General of the United Nations shall address a written request to the members of the Permanent Court of Arbitration belonging to the states which are parties to the present Statute, and to the members of the national groups appointed under Article 4, paragraph 2, inviting them to undertake, within a given time, by national groups, the nomination of persons in a position to accept the duties of a member of the Court.

2. No group may nominate more than four persons, not more than two of whom shall be of their own nationality. In no case may the number of candidates nominated by a group be more than double the number of seats to be filled.

Article 6

Before making these nominations, each national group is recommended to consult its highest court of justice, its legal faculties and schools of law, and its national academies and national sections of international academies devoted to the study of law.

Article 7

1. The Secretary-General shall prepare a list in alphabetical order of all the persons thus nominated. Save as provided in Article 12, paragraph 2, these shall be the only persons eligible.

2. The Secretary-General shall submit this list to the General Assembly and to the Security Council.

Article 8

The General Assembly and the Security Council shall proceed independently of one another to elect the members of the Court.

Article 9

At every election, the electors shall bear in mind not only that the persons to be elected should individually possess the qualifications required, but also that in the body as a whole the representation of the main forms of civilization and of the principal legal systems of the world should be assured.

Article 10

1. Those candidates who obtain an absolute majority of votes in the General Assembly and in the Security Council shall be considered as elected.

2. Any vote of the Security Council, whether for the election of judges or for the appointment of members of the conference envisaged in Article 12, shall be taken without any distinction between permanent and non-permanent members of the Security Council.

3. In the event of more than one national of the same state obtaining an absolute majority of the votes both of the General Assembly and of the Security Council, the eldest of these only shall be considered as elected.

Article 11

If, after the first meeting held for the purpose of the election, one or more seats remain to be filled, a second and, if necessary, a third meeting shall take place.

Article 12

1. If, after the third meeting, one or more seats still remain unfilled, a joint conference consisting of six members, three appointed by the General Assembly and three by the Security Council, may be formed at any time at the request of either the General Assembly or the Security Council, for the purpose of choosing by the vote of an absolute majority one name for each seat still vacant, to submit to the General Assembly and the Security Council for their respective acceptance.

2. If the joint conference is unanimously agreed upon any person who fulfils the required conditions, he may be included in its list, even though he was not included in the list of nominations referred to in Article 7.

3. If the joint conference is satisfied that it will not be successful in procuring an election, those members of the Court who have already been elected shall, within a period to be fixed by the Security Council, proceed to fill the vacant seats by selection from among those candidates who have obtained votes either in the General Assembly or in the Security Council.

4. In the event of an equality of votes among the judges, the eldest judge shall have a casting vote.

Article 13

1. The members of the Court shall be elected for nine years and may be re-elected; provided, however, that of the judges elected at the first election, the terms of five judges shall expire at the end of three years and the terms of five more judges shall expire at the end of six years.

2. The judges whose terms are to expire at the end of the above-mentioned initial periods of three and six years shall be chosen by lot to be drawn by the Secretary-General immediately after the first election has been completed.

3. The members of the Court shall continue to discharge their duties until their places have been filled. Though replaced, they shall finish any cases which they may have begun.

4. In the case of the resignation of a member of the Court, the resignation shall be addressed to the President of the Court for transmission to the Secretary-General. This last notification makes the place vacant.

Article 14

Vacancies shall be filled by the same method as that laid down for the first election, subject to the following provision: the Secretary-General shall, within one month of the occurrence of the vacancy, proceed to issue the invitations provided for in Article 5, and the date of the election shall be fixed by the Security Council.

Article 15

A member of the Court elected to replace a member whose term of office has not expired shall hold office for the remainder of his predecessor's term.

Article 16

1. No member of the Court may exercise any political or administrative function, or engage in any other occupation of a professional nature.

2. Any doubt on this point shall be settled by the decision of the Court.

Article 17

1. No member of the Court may act as agent, counsel, or advocate in any case.

2. No member may participate in the decision of any case in which he has previously taken part as agent, counsel, or advocate for one of the parties, or as a member of a national or international court, or of a commission of enquiry, or in any other capacity.

3. Any doubt on this point shall be settled by the decision of the Court.

Article 18

1. No member of the Court can be dismissed unless, in the unanimous opinion of the other members, he has ceased to fulfil the required conditions.

2. Formal notification thereof shall be made to the Secretary-General by the Registrar.

3. This notification makes the place vacant.

Article 19

The members of the Court, when engaged on the business of the Court, shall enjoy diplomatic privileges and immunities.

Article 20

Every member of the Court shall, before taking up his duties, make a solemn declaration in open court that he will exercise his powers impartially and conscientiously.

Article 21

1. The Court shall elect its President and Vice-President for three years; they may be re-elected.

2. The Court shall appoint its Registrar and may provide for the appointment of such other officers as may be necessary.

Article 22

1. The seat of the Court shall be established at The Hague. This, however, shall not prevent the Court from sitting and exercising its functions elsewhere whenever the Court considers it desirable.

2. The President and the Registrar shall reside at the seat of the Court.

Article 23

1. The Court shall remain permanently in session, except during the judicial vacations, the dates and duration of which shall be fixed by the Court.

2. Members of the Court are entitled to periodic leave, the dates and duration of which shall be fixed by the Court, having in mind the distance between The Hague and the home of each judge.

3. Members of the Court shall be bound, unless they are on leave or prevented from attending by illness or other serious reasons duly explained to the President, to hold themselves permanently at the disposal of the Court.

Article 24

1. If, for some special reason, a member of the Court considers that he should not take part in the decision of a particular case, he shall so inform the President.

2. If the President considers that for some special reason one of the members of the Court should not sit in a particular case, he shall give him notice accordingly.

3. If in any such case the member of the Court and the President disagree, the matter shall be settled by the decision of the Court.

Article 25

1. The full Court shall sit except when it is expressly provided otherwise in the present Statute.

2. Subject to the condition that the number of judges available to constitute the Court is not thereby reduced below eleven, the Rules of the Court may provide for allowing one or more judges, according to circumstances and in rotation, to be dispensed from sitting.

3. A quorum of nine judges shall suffice to constitute the Court.

Article 26

1. The Court may from time to time form one or more chambers, composed of three or more judges as the Court may determine, for dealing with particular categories of cases; for example, labour cases and cases relating to transit and communications.

2. The Court may at any time form a chamber for dealing with a particular case. The number of judges to constitute such a chamber shall be determined by the Court with the approval of the parties.

3. Cases shall be heard and determined by the chambers provided for in this Article if the parties so request.

Article 27

A judgment given by any of the chambers provided for in Articles 26 and 29 shall be considered as rendered by the Court.

Article 28

The chambers provided for in Articles 26 and 29 may, with the consent of the parties, sit and exercise their functions elsewhere than at The Hague.

Article 29

With a view to the speedy dispatch of business, the Court shall form annually a chamber composed of five judges which, at the request of the parties, may hear and determine cases by summary procedure. In addition, two judges shall be selected for the purpose of replacing judges who find it impossible to sit.

Article 30

1. The Court shall frame rules for carrying out its functions. In particular, it shall lay down rules of procedure.

2. The Rules of the Court may provide for assessors to sit with the Court or with any of its chambers, without the right to vote.

Article 31

1. Judges of the nationality of each of the parties shall retain their right to sit in the case before the Court.

2. If the Court includes upon the Bench a judge of the nationality of one of the parties, any other party may choose a person to sit as judge. Such person shall be chosen preferably from among those persons who have been nominated as candidates as provided in Articles 4 and 5.

3. If the Court includes upon the Bench no judge of the nationality of the parties, each of these parties may proceed to choose a judge as provided in paragraph 2 of this Article.

4. The provisions of this Article shall apply to the case of Articles 26 and 29. In such cases, the President shall request one or, if necessary, two of the members of the Court forming the chamber to give place to the members of the Court of the nationality of the parties concerned, and, failing such, or if they are unable to be present, to the judges specially chosen by the parties.

5. Should there be several parties in the same interest, they shall, for the purpose of the preceding provisions, be reckoned as one party only. Any doubt upon this point shall be settled by the decision of the Court.

6. Judges chosen as laid down in paragraphs 2, 3 and 4 of this Article shall fulfil the conditions required by Articles 2, 17 (paragraph 2), 20, and 24 of the present Statute. They shall take part in the decision on terms of complete equality with their colleagues.

Article 32

1. Each member of the Court shall receive an annual salary.

2. The President shall receive a special annual allowance.

3. The Vice-President shall receive a special allowance for every day on which he acts as President.

4. The judges chosen under Article 31, other than members of the Court, shall receive compensation for each day on which they exercise their functions.

5. These salaries, allowances, and compensation shall be fixed by the General Assembly. They may not be decreased during the term of office.

6. The salary of the Registrar shall be fixed by the General Assembly on the proposal of the Court.

7. Regulations made by the General Assembly shall fix the conditions under which retirement pensions may be given to members of the Court and to the Registrar, and the conditions under which members of the Court and the Registrar shall have their travelling expenses refunded.

8. The above salaries, allowances, and compensation shall be free of all taxation.

Article 33

The expenses of the Court shall be borne by the United Nations in such a manner as shall be decided by the General Assembly.

Chapter II

COMPETENCE OF THE COURT

Article 34

1. Only states may be parties in cases before the Court.

2. The Court, subject to and in conformity with its Rules, may request of public international organizations information relevant to cases before it, and shall receive such information presented by such organizations on their own initiative.

3. Whenever the construction of the constituent instrument of a public international organization or of an international convention adopted thereunder is in question in a case before the Court, the Registrar shall so notify the public international organization concerned and shall communicate to it copies of all the written proceedings.

Article 35

1. The Court shall be open to the states parties to the present Statute.

2. The conditions under which the Court shall be open to other states shall, subject to the special provisions contained in treaties in force, be laid down by the Security Council, but in no case shall such conditions place the parties in a position of inequality before the Court.

3. When a state which is not a Member of the United Nations is a party to a case, the Court shall fix the amount which that party is to contribute towards the expenses of the Court. This provision shall not apply if such state is bearing a share of the expenses of the Court.

Article 36

1. The jurisdiction of the Court comprises all cases which the parties refer to it and all matters specially provided for in the Charter of the United Nations or in treaties and conventions in force.

2. The states parties to the present Statute may at any time declare that they recognize as compulsory *ipso facto* and without special agreement, in relation to any other state accepting the same obligation, the jurisdiction of the Court in all legal disputes concerning:

a. the interpretation of a treaty;

b. any question of international law;

c. the existence of any fact which, if established, would constitute a breach of an international obligation;

d. the nature or extent of the reparation to be made for the breach of an international obligation.

3. The declarations referred to above may be made unconditionally or on condition of reciprocity on the part of several or certain states, or for a certain time.

4. Such declarations shall be deposited with the Secretary-General of the United Nations, who shall transmit copies thereof to the parties to the Statute and to the Registrar of the Court.

5. Declarations made under Article 36 of the Statute of the Permanent Court of International Justice and which are still in force shall be deemed, as between the parties to the present Statute, to be acceptances of the compulsory jurisdiction of the International Court of Justice for the period which they still have to run and in accordance with their terms.

6. In the event of a dispute as to whether the Court has jurisdiction, the matter shall be settled by the decision of the Court.

Article 37

Whenever a treaty or convention in force provides for reference of a matter to a tribunal to have been instituted by the League of Nations, or to the Permanent Court of International Justice, the matter shall, as between the parties to the present Statute, be referred to the International Court of Justice.

Article 38

1. The Court, whose function is to decide in accordance with international law such disputes as are submitted to it, shall apply:

a. international conventions, whether general or particular, establishing rules expressly recognized by the contesting states;
b. international custom, as evidence of a general practice accepted as law;
c. the general principles of law recognized by civilized nations;
d. subject to the provisions of Article 59, judicial decisions and the teachings of the most highly qualified publicists of the various nations, as subsidiary means for the determination of rules of law.

2. This provision shall not prejudice the power of the Court to decide a case *ex aequo et bono*, if the parties agree thereto.

Chapter III
PROCEDURE

Article 39

1. The official languages of the Court shall be French and English. If the parties agree that the case shall be conducted in French, the judgment shall be delivered in French. If the parties agree that the case shall be conducted in English, the judgment shall be delivered in English.

2. In the absence of an agreement as to which language shall be employed, each party may, in the pleadings, use the language which it prefers; the decision of the Court shall be given in French and English. In this case the Court shall at the same time determine which of the two texts shall be considered as authoritative.

3. The Court shall, at the request of any party, authorize a language other than French or English to be used by that party.

Article 40

1. Cases are brought before the Court, as the case may be, either by the notification of the special agreement or by a written application addressed to the Registrar. In either case the subject of the dispute and the parties shall be indicated.

2. The Registrar shall forthwith communicate the application to all concerned.

3. He shall also notify the Members of the United Nations through the Secretary-General, and also any other states entitled to appear before the Court.

Article 41

1. The Court shall have the power to indicate, if it considers that circumstances so require, any provisional measures which ought to be taken to preserve the respective rights of either party.

2. Pending the final decision, notice of the measures suggested shall forthwith be given to the parties and to the Security Council.

Article 42

1. The parties shall be represented by agents.

2. They may have the assistance of counsel or advocates before the Court.

3. The agents, counsel, and advocates of parties before the Court shall enjoy the privileges and immunities necessary to the independent exercise of their duties.

Article 43

1. The procedure shall consist of two parts: written and oral.

2. The written proceedings shall consist of the communication to the Court and to the parties of memorials, counter-memorials and, if necessary, replies; also all papers and documents in support.

3. These communications shall be made through the Registrar, in the order and within the time fixed by the Court.

4. A certified copy of every document produced by one party shall be communicated to the other party.

5. The oral proceedings shall consist of the hearing by the Court of witnesses, experts, agents, counsel, and advocates.

Article 44

1. For the service of all notices upon persons other than the agents, counsel, and advocates, the Court shall apply direct to the government of the state upon whose territory the notice has to be served.

2. The same provision shall apply whenever steps are to be taken to procure evidence on the spot.

Article 45

The hearing shall be under the control of the President or, if he is unable to preside, of the Vice-President; if neither is able to preside, the senior judge present shall preside.

Article 46

The hearing in Court shall be public, unless the Court shall decide otherwise, or unless the parties demand that the public be not admitted.

Article 47

1. Minutes shall be made at each hearing and signed by the Registrar and the President.

2. These minutes alone shall be authentic.

Article 48

The Court shall make orders for the conduct of the case, shall decide the form and time in which each party must conclude its arguments, and make all arrangements connected with the taking of evidence.

Article 49

The Court may, even before the hearing begins, call upon the agents to produce any document or to supply any explanations. Formal note shall be taken of any refusal.

Article 50

The Court may, at any time, entrust any individual, body, bureau, commission, or other organization that it may select, with the task of carrying out an enquiry or giving an expert opinion.

Article 51

During the hearing any relevant questions are to be put to the witnesses and experts under the conditions laid down by the Court in the rules of procedure referred to in Article 30.

Article 52

After the Court has received the proofs and evidence within the time specified for the purpose, it may refuse to accept any further oral or written evidence that one party may desire to present unless the other side consents.

Article 53

1. Whenever one of the parties does not appear before the Court, or fails to defend its case, the other party may call upon the Court to decide in favour of its claim.

2. The Court must, before doing so, satisfy itself, not only that it has jurisdiction in accordance with Articles 36 and 37, but also that the claim is well founded in fact and law.

Article 54

1. When, subject to the control of the Court, the agents, counsel, and advocates have completed their presentation of the case, the President shall declare the hearing closed.

2. The Court shall withdraw to consider the judgment.
3. The deliberations of the Court shall take place in private and remain secret.

Article 55

1. All questions shall be decided by a majority of the judges present.
2. In the event of an equality of votes, the President or the judge who acts in his place shall have a casting vote.

Article 56

1. The judgment shall state the reasons on which it is based.
2. It shall contain the names of the judges who have taken part in the decision.

Article 57

If the judgment does not represent in whole or in part the unanimous opinion of the judges, any judge shall be entitled to deliver a separate opinion.

Article 58

The judgment shall be signed by the President and by the Registrar. It shall be read in open court, due notice having been given to the agents.

Article 59

The decision of the Court has no binding force except between the parties and in respect of that particular case.

Article 60

The judgment is final and without appeal. In the event of dispute as to the meaning or scope of the judgment, the Court shall construe it upon the request of any party.

Article 61

1. An application for revision of a judgment may be made only when it is based upon the discovery of some fact of such a nature as to be a decisive factor, which fact was, when the judgment was given, unknown to the Court and also the party claiming revision, always provided that such ignorance was not due to negligence.
2. The proceedings for revision shall be opened by a judgment of the Court expressly recording the existence of the new fact, recognizing that it has such a character as to lay the case open to revision, and declaring the application admissible on this ground.
3. The Court may require previous compliance with the terms of the judgment before it admits proceedings in revision.
4. The application for revision must be made at latest within six months of the discovery of the new fact.
5. No application for revision may be made after the lapse of ten years from the date of the judgment.

Article 62

1. Should a state consider that it has an interest of a legal nature which may be affected by the decision in the case, it may submit a request to the Court to be permitted to intervene.
2. It shall be for the Court to decide upon this request.

Article 63

1. Whenever the construction of a convention to which states other than those concerned in the case are parties is in question, the Registrar shall notify all such states forthwith.
2. Every state so notified has the right to intervene in the proceedings; but if it uses this right, the construction given by the judgment will be equally binding upon it.

Article 64

Unless otherwise decided by the Court, each party shall bear its own costs.

Chapter IV

ADVISORY OPINIONS

Article 65

1. The Court may give an advisory opinion on any legal question at the request of whatever body may be authorized by or in accordance with the Charter of the United Nations to make such a request.
2. Questions upon which the advisory opinion of the Court is asked shall be laid before the Court by means of a written request containing an exact statement of the question upon which an opinion is required, and accompanied by all documents likely to throw light upon the question.

Article 66

1. The Registrar shall forthwith give notice of the request for an advisory opinion to all states entitled to appear before the Court.
2. The Registrar shall also, by means of a special and direct communication, notify any state entitled to appear before the Court or international organization considered by the Court, or, should it not be sitting, by the President, as likely to be able to furnish information on the question, that the Court will be prepared to receive, within a time limit to be fixed by the President, written statements, or to hear, at a public sitting to be held for the purpose, oral statements relating to the question.
3. Should any such state entitled to appear before the Court have failed to receive the special communication referred to in paragraph 2 of this Article, such state may express a desire to submit a written statement or to be heard; and the Court will decide.
4. States and organizations having presented written or oral statements or both shall be permitted to comment on the statements made by other states or organizations in the form, to the extent, and within the time limits which the Court, or, should it not be sitting, the President, shall decide in each particular case. Accordingly, the Registrar shall in due time communicate any such written statements to states and organizations having submitted similar statements.

Article 67

The Court shall deliver its advisory opinions in open court, notice having been given to the Secretary-General and to the representatives of Members of the United Nations, of other states and of international organizations immediately concerned.

Article 68

In the exercise of its advisory functions the Court shall further be guided by the provisions of the present Statute which apply in contentious cases to the extent to which it recognizes them to be applicable.

Chapter V

AMENDMENT

Article 69

Amendments to the present Statute shall be effected by the same procedure as is provided by the Charter of the United Nations for amendments to that Charter, subject however to any provisions which the General Assembly upon recommendation of the Security Council may adopt concerning the participation of states which are parties to the present Statute but are not Members of the United Nations.

Article 70

The Court shall have power to propose such amendments to the present Statute as it may deem necessary, through written communications to the Secretary-General, for consideration in conformity with the provisions of Article 69.

Appendix III

Structure of the United Nations

General Assembly

The General Assembly is composed of all the Members of the United Nations.

SESSIONS

Resumed tenth emergency special session: 5, 8 and 9 February 1999 (suspended).
Resumed fifty-third session: 18 February–13 September 1999.
Twenty-first special session: 30 June–2 July 1999.
Fifty-fourth session: 14 September–23 December 1999 (suspended).
Twenty-second special session: 27-28 September 1999.

OFFICERS

Resumed tenth emergency special, resumed fifty-third and twenty-first special sessions
President: Didier Opertti (Uruguay).[1]
Vice-Presidents:[2] Brunei Darussalam, Cameroon, China, France, Georgia, Germany, Lesotho, Liberia, Morocco, Myanmar, Nicaragua, Russian Federation, San Marino, Senegal, Suriname, Syrian Arab Republic, Turkmenistan, Uganda, United Kingdom, United States, Yemen.

Fifty-fourth and twenty-second special sessions
President: Theo-Ben Gurirab (Namibia).[3]
Vice-Presidents:[4] Algeria, Bolivia, China, Congo, Côte d'Ivoire, Cuba, Democratic People's Republic of Korea, France, Grenada, Iceland, Iran, Iraq, Lithuania, Monaco, Nigeria, Russian Federation, Seychelles, Tajikistan, Thailand, United Kingdom, United States.

The Assembly has four types of committees: (1) Main Committees; (2) procedural committees; (3) standing committees; (4) subsidiary and ad hoc bodies. In addition, it convenes conferences to deal with specific subjects.

Main Committees

Six Main Committees have been established as follows:

Disarmament and International Security Committee (First Committee)
Special Political and Decolonization Committee (Fourth Committee)
Economic and Financial Committee (Second Committee)
Social, Humanitarian and Cultural Committee (Third Committee)
Administrative and Budgetary Committee (Fifth Committee)
Legal Committee (Sixth Committee)

The General Assembly may constitute other committees, on which all Members of the United Nations have the right to be represented.

OFFICERS OF THE MAIN COMMITTEES

Resumed fifty-third session

Fifth Committee[5]

Chairman: Movses Abelian (Armenia).
Vice-Chairmen: Manlan Ahounou (Côte d'Ivoire), Miles Armitage (Australia), Sharon Brennen-Haylock (Bahamas).
Rapporteur: Tamman Sulaiman (Syrian Arab Republic).

Twenty-first special session[6]

First Committee

Acting Chairperson: Akmaral Arystanbekova (Kazakhstan).

Fourth Committee

Chairman: Pablo Macedo (Mexico).

Second Committee

Chairman: Bagher Asadi (Iran).

Third Committee

Chairman: Ali Hachani (Tunisia).

Fifth Committee

Chairman: Movses Abelian (Armenia).

Sixth Committee

Chairman: Jargalsaikhany Enkhsaikhan (Mongolia).

Ad Hoc Committee of the Whole of the Twenty-first Special Session

Chairman: Anwarul Karim Chowdhury (Bangladesh).[7]
Vice-Chairmen: Elza Berquo (Brazil), M. Patricia Durrant (Jamaica), Armi Heinonen (Finland), Ross Hynes (Canada), Matia Mulumba Semakula Kiwanuka (Uganda), Alexandru Niculescu (Romania), Jacob Botwe Wilmot (Ghana), Ryuichiro Yamazaki (Japan).
Vice-Chairperson/Rapporteur: Gabriella Vukovich (Hungary).

Fifty-fourth session[8]

First Committee

Chairman: Raimundo González (Chile).
Vice-Chairmen: Tarig Ali Bakhit (Sudan), Kestutis Sadauskas (Lithuania), Günther Siebert (Germany).
Rapporteur: Carlos D. Sorreta (Philippines).

Fourth Committee

Chairman: Sotirios Zacheos (Cyprus).
Vice-Chairmen: Yuri Kazhura (Belarus), Matia Mulumba Semakula Kiwanuka (Uganda), Carlos Morales (Spain).
Rapporteur: Gualberto Rodriguez San Martin (Bolivia).

Second Committee

Chairman: Roble Olhaye (Djibouti).
Vice-Chairmen: Giovanni Brauzzi (Italy), Daul Matute (Peru), Alexandru Niculescu (Romania).
Rapporteur: Hassam Edin A'Ala (Syrian Arab Republic).

Third Committee

Chairman: Vladimir Galuska (Czech Republic).
Vice-Chairmen: Kirsten Geelan (Denmark), Mónica Martínez (Ecuador), Amina Mesdoua (Algeria).
Rapporteur: Naif Bin Bandar Al-Sudairy (Saudi Arabia).

Fifth Committee

Chairman: Penny A. Wensley (Australia).

Vice-Chairmen: Judith Maria Cardoze (Panama), Ahmed H. Darwish (Egypt), Amjad B. Sial (Pakistan).
Rapporteur: Jan Jaremczuk (Poland).

Sixth Committee

Chairman: Phasiko Mochochoko (Lesotho).
Vice-Chairmen: Victoria Hallum (New Zealand), Hiroshi Kawamura (Japan), Andres Franco Vasco (Colombia).
Rapporteur: Josko Klisavic (Croatia).

Twenty-second special session[9]

First Committee

Chairman: Raimundo González (Chile).

Fourth Committee

Chairman: Sotirios Zackheos (Cyprus).

Second Committee

Chairman: Roble Olhaye (Djibouti).

Third Committee

Chairman: Vladimir Galuska (Czech Republic).

Fifth Committee

Chairman: Penny A. Wensley (Australia).

Sixth Committee

Chairman: Phasiko Mochochoko (Lesotho).

Ad Hoc Committee of the Whole of the Twenty-second Special Session[10]

Chairman: John William Ashe (Antigua and Barbuda).
Rapporteur: Navid Hanif (Pakistan).

Procedural committees

General Committee

The General Committee consists of the President of the General Assembly, as Chairman, the 21 Vice-Presidents and the Chairmen of the six Main Committees [at the twenty-first and twenty-second special sessions, the Chairman of the Ad Hoc Committee of the Whole was also a member of the General Committee (dec. S-21/15 & S-22/15)].

Credentials Committee

The Credentials Committee consists of nine members appointed by the General Assembly on the proposal of the President.

Resumed tenth emergency special, resumed fifty-third and twenty-first special sessions[11]

China, Fiji, Jamaica, Mali, New Zealand, Russian Federation, United States, Venezuela, Zimbabwe.

Fifty-fourth and twenty-second special sessions [12]

Austria, Bolivia, China, Philippines, Russian Federation, South Africa, Togo, Trinidad and Tobago, United States.

Standing committees

The two standing committees consist of experts appointed in their individual capacity for three-year terms.

Advisory Committee on Administrative and Budgetary Questions

To serve until 31 December 1999: Denise Almao (New Zealand); Ammar Amari (Tunisia); Gérard Biraud (France); Norma Goicochea Estenoz (Cuba); Vladimir V. Kuznetsov (Russian Federation).[13]

To serve until 31 December 2000: Ioan Barac (Romania); Hasan Jawarneh (Jordan); Mahamane Amadou Maiga (Mali); Ernest Besley Maycock, *Vice-Chairman* (Barbados); C. S. M. Mselle, *Chairman* (United Republic of Tanzania).

To serve until 31 December 2001: Nazareth A. Incera (Costa Rica); Ahmad Kamal (Pakistan); Rajat Saha (India); Nicholas A. Thorne (United Kingdom); Fumiaki Toya (Japan); Gian Luigi Valenza (Italy).

On 15 November 1999 (dec. 54/312 A), the General Assembly appointed the following for a three-year term beginning on 1 January 2000 to fill the vacancies occurring on 31 December 1999: Gérard Biraud (France), Norma Goicochea Estenoz (Cuba), Vladimir V. Kuznetsov (Russian Federation), Susan M. Shearouse (United States), Roger Tchongui (Cameroon).

Committee on Contributions

To serve until 31 December 1999: Iqbal Akhund (Pakistan); Alvaro Gurgel de Alencar Netto (Brazil); Eduardo Iglesias (Argentina); Ju Kuilin (China); Isabelle Klais (Germany); Sergei I. Mareyev (Russian Ferderation); Ugo Sessi, *Vice-Chairman* (Italy).

To serve until 31 December 2000: Uldis Blukis (Latvia); Sergio Chaparro Ruiz (Chile); David Etuket, *Chairman* (Uganda); Ihor V. Humenny (Ukraine); David A. Leis (United States); Prakash Shah (India); Kazuo Watanabe (Japan).

To serve until 31 December 2001: Pieter Johannes Bierma (Netherlands); Paul Ekorong A Ndong (Cameroon); Neil Hewitt Francis (Australia); Henry Hanson-Hall (Ghana).

On 15 November 1999 (dec. 54/313 A), the General Assembly appointed the following for a three-year term beginning on 1January 2000 to fill the vacancies occurring on 31 December 1999: Alvaro Gurgel de Alencar Netto (Brazil), Ju Kuilin (China), Sergei I. Mareyev (Russian Federation), Angel Marrón (Spain), Hae-Yun Park (Republic of Korea), Ugo Sessi (Italy). (Bernardo Greiver (Uruguay) was to serve a two-year term beginning on 1 January 2000 [YUN 1998, p. 1437].)

Subsidiary and ad hoc bodies

The following is a list of subsidiary and ad hoc bodies functioning in 1999, including the number of members, dates of meetings/sessions in 1999, document numbers of 1999 reports (which generally provide specific information on membership), and relevant decision numbers pertaining to elections. (For other related bodies, see p. 1453.)

Ad Hoc Committee established by General Assembly resolution 51/210 of 17 December 1996

Session: Third, New York, 15-26 March
Chairman: Philippe Kirsch (Canada)
Membership: Open to all States Members of the United Nations or members of the specialized agencies or of IAEA
Report: A/54/37

Ad Hoc Committee on the Elaboration of a Convention against Transnational Organized Crime

Sessions: First, second, third, fourth, fifth and sixth, Vienna, 19-29 January, 8-12 March, 28 April–3 May, 28 June–9 July, 4-15 October, 6-17 December
Chairman: Luigi Lauriola (Italy) (acting in his personal capacity)
Membership: Open to the participation of all States
Reports: A/AC.254/9, A/AC.254/11, A/AC.254/14, A/AC.254/17, A/AC.254/19 & Add.1, A/AC.254/23

Ad Hoc Committee on the Indian Ocean

Meeting: New York, 14 July
Chairman: John de Saram (Sri Lanka)
Membership: 44
Report: A/54/29

Advisory Committee on the United Nations Programme of Assistance in the Teaching, Study, Dissemination and Wider Appreciation of International Law

Session: Thirty-fourth, New York, 20 October
Chairman: Henry Hanson-Hall (Ghana)

Membership: 25
Report: A/54/515
Decision: GA 54/319

Board of Auditors

Sessions: Fifty-third, New York, 28-30 June; twenty-ninth special, Accra, Ghana, 9 December
Chairman: Osei Tutu Prempeh (Ghana)
Membership: 3
Decision: GA 54/314

Committee for the United Nations Population Award

Meetings: New York, 25 February, 1 April
Chairman: José Luis Barbosa Leao Monteiro (Cape Verde)
Membership: 10 (plus 5 honorary members, the Secretary-General and the UNFPA Executive Director)
Report: A/54/407
Decision: ESC 1999/210 A

Committee on Conferences

Sessions: New York, 21 April (organizational), 30 August–2 September (substantive)
Chairman: Peter Van De Velde (Belgium)
Membership: 21
Report: A/54/32
Decision: GA 54/308

Committee on Information

Sessions: Twenty-first, New York, 3 May (organizational), 3-14 May (substantive), 1-5 November (resumed)
Chairman: El Hassane Zahid (Morocco)
Membership: 93 (95 from 6 December)
Reports: A/54/21 & Add.1
Decision: GA 54/318

Committee on Relations with the Host Country

Meetings: New York, 10 March,13 May, 15 September, 27 October, 5 November
Chairman: Sotirios Zackheos (Cyprus)
Membership: 18 from 18 February, 19 from 4 November (including the United States as host country)
Report: A/54/26
Decisions: GA 53/322, 54/311

Committee on the Exercise of the Inalienable Rights of the Palestinian People

Meetings: Throughout the year
Chairman: Ibra Deguène Ka (Senegal)
Membership: 25
Report: A/54/35

Committee on the Peaceful Uses of Outer Space

Session: Forty-second, Vienna, 14-16 July
Chairman: U. R. Rao (India)
Membership: 61
Report: A/54/20 & Corr.1

Disarmament Commission

Sessions: New York, 19 March (organizational), 12-30 April (substantive), 2 December (organizational)
Chairman: Maged A. Abdelaziz (Egypt)
Membership: All UN Members
Reports: A/54/42, A/55/42

High-level Committee on the Review of Technical Cooperation among Developing Countries

Sessions: New York, 4 May (organizational), 1-4 June (eleventh)
President: M. Patricia Durrant (Jamaica)
Membership: All States participating in UNDP
Report: A/54/39

International Civil Service Commission

Sessions: Forty-ninth, Geneva, 12-30 April; fiftieth, New York, 19-30 July
Chairman: Mohsen Bel Hadj Amor (Tunisia)
Membership: 15
Report: A/54/30
Decision: GA 53/317 B

ADVISORY COMMITTEE ON POST ADJUSTMENT QUESTIONS

Session: Did not meet in 1999
Membership: 6

International Law Commission

Session: Fifty-first, Geneva, 3 May–23 July
Chairman: Zdzislaw Galicki (Poland)
Membership: 34
Report: A/54/10 & Corr.1,2

Investments Committee

Meetings: New York, 22-23 February, 10-11 May, 13-14 September, 22-23 November
Chairman: Emmanuel Noi Omaboe (Ghana)
Membership: 9
Decision: GA 54/315

Joint Advisory Group on the International Trade Centre UNCTAD/WTO

Session: Thirty-second, Geneva, 19-23 April
Chairman: J.-M. Noirfalisse (Belgium)
Membership: Open to all States members of UNCTAD and all members of WTO
Report: ITC/AG(XXXII)/173

Joint Inspection Unit

Chairman: Louis-Dominique Ouedraogo (Burkina Faso)
Membership: 11
Report: A/55/34
Decision: GA 53/320

Office of the United Nations High Commissioner for Refugees (UNHCR)

EXECUTIVE COMMITTEE OF THE HIGH COMMISSIONER'S PROGRAMME

Session: Fiftieth, Geneva, 4-8 October
Chairman: Raimundo Pérez-Hernández y Torra (Spain)
Membership: 54
Report: A/54/12/Add.1
Decision: ESC 1999/210 C

High Commissioner: Sadako Ogata

Panel of External Auditors

Membership: Members of the UN Board of Auditors and the appointed external auditors of the specialized agencies and IAEA

Preparatory Committee for the Special Session of the General Assembly on the Implementation of the Outcome of the World Summit for Social Development and Further Initiatives

Session: First, New York, 17-29 May and 15 July; resumed first, New York, 21 September
Chairman: Cristian Maquieira (Chile)
Membership: Open to the participation of all States Members of the United Nations and members of the specialized agencies
Reports: A/54/45 & Corr.1 & Add.1

Scientific and Technical Committee of the International Decade for Natural Disaster Reduction

Session: Eleventh (final), Canberra, Australia, 15-19 February
Chairman: Robert Hamilton (United States)
Membership: 20-25 (24 in 1999)
Report: A/54/132/Add.1-E/1999/80/Add.1

Special Committee on Peacekeeping Operations

Meetings: New York, 24-26 March (general debate), 30 March–23 April (open-ended working group)
Chairman: Ibrahim A. Gambari (Nigeria)
Membership: 100
Report: A/54/87

Special Committee on the Charter of the United Nations and on the Strengthening of the Role of the Organization

Meetings: New York, 12-23 April
Chairperson: Marja Lehto (Finland)
Membership: Open to all States Members of the United Nations
Report: A/54/33 & Corr.1

Special Committee on the Situation with regard to the Implementation of the Declaration on the Granting of Independence to Colonial Countries and Peoples

Session: New York, 22 February, 31 March (first part); 21 June–21 July, 28 July (second part)
Chairman: Peter D. Donigi (Papua New Guinea)
Membership: 24
Report: A/54/23

Special Committee to Investigate Israeli Practices Affecting the Human Rights of the Palestinian People and Other Arabs of the Occupied Territories

Meetings: Geneva, 3-5 March, 17-18 May; Damascus, Syrian Arab Republic, 19-21 May; Amman, Jordan, 22-25 May; Cairo, Egypt, 26-30 May
Chairman: John de Saram (Sri Lanka)
Membership: 3
Report: A/54/325

Special Committee to Select the Winners of the United Nations Human Rights Prize

Meeting: Did not meet in 1999
Membership: 5

United Nations Administrative Tribunal

Sessions: Geneva, 28 June–30 July; New York, 25 October–24 November
President: Hubert Thierry (France)
Membership: 7
Report: A/INF/54/6
Decisions: GA 53/316 B, 54/316

United Nations Capital Development Fund

EXECUTIVE BOARD

The UNDP/UNFPA Executive Board acts as the Executive Board of the Fund.

Managing Director: James Gustave Speth (until 30 June), Mark Malloch Brown (from 1 July) (UNDP Administrator)

United Nations Commission on International Trade Law (UNCITRAL)

Session: Thirty-second, Vienna, 17 May–4 June
Chairman: Reinhard G. Renger (Germany)
Membership: 36
Report: A/54/17

United Nations Conciliation Commission for Palestine

Membership: 3
Reports: A/54/338, A/55/329

United Nations Conference on Trade and Development (UNCTAD)

Membership: Open to all States Members of the United Nations or members of the specialized agencies or of IAEA
Secretary-General of UNCTAD: Rubens Ricupero
Decision: GA 53/321

TRADE AND DEVELOPMENT BOARD

Sessions: Twentieth, twenty-first and twenty-second executive, forty-sixth, twenty-third executive (first part), Geneva, 5 February, 1 July, 15 October, 18-29 October, 17 December
President: Chak Mun See (Singapore) (twentieth to twenty-second executive sessions), Philippe Petit (France) (forty-sixth and twenty-third executive sessions)
Membership: Open to all States members of UNCTAD
Reports: A/54/15 (Parts II-V), A/55/15 (Part I)

SUBSIDIARY ORGANS OF THE TRADE AND DEVELOPMENT BOARD

COMMISSION ON ENTERPRISE, BUSINESS FACILITATION AND DEVELOPMENT

Session: Fourth, Geneva, 19-23 July
Chairperson: Hasnudin Hamzah (Malaysia)
Membership: Open to all States members of UNCTAD
Report: TD/B/46/11

COMMISSION ON INVESTMENT, TECHNOLOGY AND RELATED FINANCIAL ISSUES

Session: Fourth, Geneva, 4-8 October
Chairperson: Magda Shahin (Egypt)
Membership: Open to all States members of UNCTAD
Report: TD/B/46/12

Intergovernmental Group of Experts on Competition Law and Policy

Session: Second, Geneva, 7-9 June
Chairperson: D. J. Pathirana (Sri Lanka)
Membership: Open to all States members of UNCTAD
Report: TD/B/COM.2/19

Intergovernmental Working Group of Experts on International Standards of Accounting and Reporting

Session: Sixteenth, Geneva, 17-19 February
Chairperson: Alicja Jaruga (Poland)
Membership: 340
Report: TD/B/COM.2/16
Decisions: ESC 1999/210 B-F

COMMISSION ON TRADE IN GOODS AND SERVICES, AND COMMODITIES

Session: Fourth, Geneva, 11-14 October
Chairperson: Federico Alberto Cuello (Dominican Republic)
Membership: Open to all States members of UNCTAD
Report: TD/B/46/14

WORKING PARTY ON THE MEDIUM-TERM PLAN AND THE PROGRAMME BUDGET

Sessions: Thirty-third, Geneva, 25-29 January; thirty-fourth, Geneva, 27 September–1 October
Chairperson: Philippe Merlin (France) (thirty-third session), Angelina Catalina (Philippines) (thirty-fourth session)
Membership: Open to all States members of UNCTAD
Reports: TD/B/46/2, TD/B/46/9

United Nations Development Fund for Women (UNIFEM)

CONSULTATIVE COMMITTEE

Session: Thirty-ninth, New York, 25-26 February
Chairperson: Victoria Sandru (Romania)
Membership: 5

Director of UNIFEM: Noeleen Heyzer
Deputy Director: Flavia Pansieri

United Nations Environment Programme (UNEP)

GOVERNING COUNCIL

Session: Twentieth, Nairobi, Kenya, 1-5 February

President: László Míklos (Slovakia)
Membership: 58
Report: A/54/25
Decision: GA 54/307

Executive Director of UNEP: Klaus Töpfer

United Nations Institute for Disarmament Research (UNIDIR)

BOARD OF TRUSTEES

Sessions: Thirty-second, Geneva, 20-22 January; thirty-third, New York, 28-30 June
Chairperson: Thérèse Delpech (France)
Membership: 20 in 1999
Reports: A/54/201, A/54/218 & Corr.1

Director of UNIDIR: Patricia Lewis
Deputy Director: Christophe Carle

United Nations Institute for Training and Research (UNITAR)

BOARD OF TRUSTEES

Sessions: Thirty-seventh, Geneva, 30 March–2 April; extraordinary, Geneva, 1-3 September
Chairman: Ahmad Kamal (Pakistan)
Membership: Not less than 11 and not more than 30, plus 4 ex-officio members

Executive Director of UNITAR: Marcel A. Boisard

United Nations Joint Staff Pension Board

Session: Did not meet in 1999
Membership: 33

United Nations Relief and Works Agency for Palestine Refugees in the Near East (UNRWA)

ADVISORY COMMISSION OF UNRWA

Meeting: Amman, Jordan, 28 September
Chairperson: Marguerite Rivera Houze (United States)
Membership: 10
Report: A/54/13

WORKING GROUP ON THE FINANCING OF UNRWA

Meetings: New York, 10 September, 13 October
Chairman: Volkan Vural (Turkey)
Membership: 9
Report: A/54/477

Commissioner-General of UNRWA: Peter Hansen
Deputy Commissioner-General: Dr. Mohamed Abdelmoumène

United Nations Scientific Committee on the Effects of Atomic Radiation

Session: Forty-eighth, Vienna, 12-16 April
Chairman: L. E. Holm (Sweden)
Membership: 21
Report: A/54/46

United Nations Staff Pension Committee

Meetings: New York, 21 January, 13 April, 12 July, 29 October
Chairperson: Susan Shearouse (United States)
Membership: 12 members and 8 alternates
Decisions: GA 54/317 A, 54/462 A

United Nations University

COUNCIL OF THE UNITED NATIONS UNIVERSITY

Session: Forty-sixth, Tokyo, 29 November–3 December
Chairperson: Ingrid Moses (Australia)
Membership: 24 (plus 3 ex-officio members and the UNU Rector)
Report: A/55/31

Rector of the University: Johannes A. van Ginkel

United Nations Voluntary Fund for Indigenous Populations

BOARD OF TRUSTEES

Session: Twelfth, Geneva, 12-14 April
Chairperson: Victoria Tauli-Corpuz (Philippines)
Membership: 5
Report: E/CN.4/Sub.2/AC.4/1999/6

United Nations Voluntary Fund for Victims of Torture

BOARD OF TRUSTEES

Session: Eighteenth, Geneva, 17-28 May
Chairman: Jaap Walkate (Netherlands)
Membership: 5
Report: A/54/177

United Nations Voluntary Trust Fund on Contemporary Forms of Slavery

BOARD OF TRUSTEES

Session: Fourth, Geneva, 24-26 March
Chairperson: Swami Agnivesh (India)
Membership: 5
Report: A/54/348

Conference

Third United Nations Conference on the Exploration and Peaceful Uses of Outer Space (UNISPACE III)

Session: Vienna, 19-30 July
President: U. R. Rao (India)
Attendance: 100 States, plus UN bodies and programmes, specialized agencies and intergovernmental and non-governmental organizations
Report: A/CONF.184/6

Security Council

The Security Council consists of 15 Member States of the United Nations, in accordance with the provisions of Article 23 of the United Nations Charter as amended in 1965.

MEMBERS

Permanent members: China, France, Russian Federation, United Kingdom, United States.

Non-permanent members: Argentina, Bahrain, Brazil, Canada, Gabon, Gambia, Malaysia, Namibia, Netherlands, Slovenia.

On 14 October 1999 (dec. 54/306), the General Assembly elected Bangladesh, Jamaica, Mali, Tunisia and Ukraine for a two-year term beginning on 1 January 2000, to replace Bahrain, Brazil, Gabon, the Gambia and Slovenia whose terms of office were to expire on 31 December 1999.

PRESIDENT

The presidency of the Council rotates monthly, according to the English alphabetical listing of its member States. The following served as President during 1999:

Month	*Member*	*Representative*
January	Brazil	Celso L. N. Amorim
February	Canada	Robert R. Fowler
		Lloyd Axworthy

Month	Member	Representative
March	China	Qin Huasun
April	France	Alain Dejammet
May	Gabon	Denis Dangue Réwaka
June	Gambia	Baboucarr-Blaise Ismaila Jagne
July	Malaysia	Hasmy Agam Syed Hamid Albar
August	Namibia	Martin Andjaba Theo-Ben Gurirab
September	Netherlands	A. Peter van Walsum Wim Kok
October	Russian Federation	Sergey V. Lavrov
November	Slovenia	Danilo Türk Boris Frlec
December	United Kingdom	Sir Jeremy Greenstock, KCMG Peter Hain

Military Staff Committee

The Military Staff Committee consists of the chiefs of staff of the permanent members of the Security Council or their representatives. It meets fortnightly.

Standing committees

Each of the three standing committees of the Security Council is composed of representatives of all Council members:

Committee of Experts (to examine the provisional rules of procedure of the Council and any other matters entrusted to it by the Council)

Committee on the Admission of New Members

Committee on Council Meetings Away from Headquarters

Peacekeeping operations and special missions

United Nations Truce Supervision Organization (UNTSO)

Chief of Staff: Major-General Timothy Ford.

United Nations Military Observer Group in India and Pakistan (UNMOGIP)

Chief Military Observer: Major-General Jozsef Bali.

United Nations Peacekeeping Force in Cyprus (UNFICYP)

Special Adviser to the Secretary-General on Cyprus: Diego Cordovez (until April).

Special Representative of the Secretary-General and Chief of Mission: Ann Hercus (until September), James Holger (Acting, from October).

Force Commander: Major-General Evergisto Arturo de Vergara (until 15 December), Major-General Victory Rana (from 16 December).

United Nations Disengagement Observer Force (UNDOF)

Force Commander: Major-General Cameron Ross.

United Nations Interim Force in Lebanon (UNIFIL)

Force Commander: Major-General Jioji Konousi Konrote (until 30 September), Brigadier-General James Sreenan (Acting, 1 October–30 November), Major-General Seth Kofi Obeng (from 1 December).

United Nations Iraq-Kuwait Observation Mission (UNIKOM)

Force Commander: Major-General Esa Kalervo Tarvainen (until 30 November), General John Augustine Vize (from 1 December).

United Nations Mission for the Referendum in Western Sahara (MINURSO)

Personal Envoy of the Secretary-General: James A. Baker III.

Special Representative of the Secretary-General: Charles F. Dunbar (until 31 March), Robert Kinloch (Acting, 1 April–20 May), William Eagleton (from 21 May).

Force Commander: Major-General Bernd S. Lubenik (until 31 October), Brigadier-General Claude Buze (from 1 November).

United Nations Observer Mission in Georgia (UNOMIG)

Special Representative of the Secretary-General and Head of Mission: Liviu Bota (until 23 November), Dieter Boden (from 24 November).

Chief Military Observer: Major-General Tariq Waseem Ghazi.

United Nations Mission of Observers in Tajikistan (UNMOT)

Special Representative of the Secretary-General and Head of Mission: Ján Kubiš (until 16 June), Ivo Petrov (from 20 September).

Chief Military Observer: Brigadier-General Tengku Ariffin Bin Tengku Mohammed (until 4 April), Brigadier-General John Hvidegaard (from 5 April).

United Nations Preventive Deployment Force (UNPREDEP)[14]

Special Representative of the Secretary-General and Chief of Mission: Fernando Valenzuela Marzo.

Force Commander: Brigadier-General Ove Johnny Stromberg.

United Nations Mission in Bosnia and Herzegovina (UNMIBH)

Special Representative of the Secretary-General and Coordinator of United Nations Operations in Bosnia and Herzegovina: Elisabeth Rehn (until 1 August), Jacques Paul Klein (from 2 August).

Deputy Special Representative of the Secretary-General: Julian Harston (from September).

Commissioner of the United Nations International Police Task Force: Richard Monk (until 1 March), Brigadier-General Detlef Buwitt (from March).

United Nations Mission of Observers in Prevlaka (UNMOP)

Chief Military Observer: Lieutenant-Colonel Graeme Williams.

United Nations Observer Mission in Angola (MONUA)[15]

Special Representative of the Secretary-General: Issa B. Y. Diallo.

Force Commander/Chief Military Observer: Major-General Seth Kofi Obeng.

United Nations Civilian Police Mission in Haiti (MIPONUH)

Special Representative of the Secretary-General and Head of Mission: Julian Harston (until 18 September), Alfredo Lopes Cabral (from 20 October).

Police Commissioner: Colonel Claude Grudé (until May), Colonel George Gabbardo (from May).

United Nations Mission in the Central African Republic (MINURCA)

Special Representative of the Secretary-General and Head of Mission: Oluyemi Adeniji (until 11 December).

Force Commander: Major-General Barthélémy Ratanga.

United Nations Observer Mission in Sierra Leone (UNOMSIL)[16]

Special Representative of the Secretary General and Chief of Mission: Francis G. Okelo.

Chief Military Observer: Brigadier-General Subhash C. Joshi.

United Nations Interim Administration Mission in Kosovo (UNMIK)[17]

Special Representative of the Secretary-General: Bernard Kouchner (from 7 July).

Prinicpal Deputy Special Representative: James Peter Covey (from 13 July).

United Nations Mission in East Timor (UNAMET)[18]

Special Representative of the Secretary-General and Head of Mission: Ian Martin.

United Nations Mission in Sierra Leone (UNAMSIL)[19]

Special Representative of the Secretary-General and Head of Mission: Francis G. Okelo (until November), Oluyemi Adeniji (from 12 December).

Chief Military Observer: Brigadier-General Subhash C. Joshi (until 30 November).

Force Commander: Major-General Vijay Kumar Jetley (from 7 December).

United Nations Tranitional Administration in East Timor (UNTAET)[20]

Special Representative of the Secretary-Gernal for East Timor: Jamsheed K. A. Marker.

Special Representative of the Secretary-General and Head of Mission: Sergio Vieira de Mello (from 8 November).

Force Commander: Lieutenant-General Jaime de los Santos.

United Nations Organization Mission in the Democratic Republic of the Congo (MONUC)[21]

Special Representative of the Secretary-General and Head of Mission: Kamel Morjane.

Economic and Social Council

The Economic and Social Council consists of 54 Member States of the United Nations, elected by the General Assembly, each for a three-year term, in accordance with the provisions of Article 61 of the United Nations Charter as amended in 1965 and 1973.

MEMBERS

To serve until 31 December 1999: Cape Verde, Chile, Cuba, Djibouti, El Salvador, France, Gambia, Germany, Iceland, Japan, Latvia, Mexico, Mozambique, Republic of Korea, Spain, Sri Lanka, Turkey, Zambia.

To serve until 31 December 2000: Algeria, Belarus, Belgium, Brazil, Colombia, Comoros, India, Italy, Lesotho, Mauritius, New Zealand, Oman, Pakistan, Poland, Saint Lucia, Sierra Leone, United States, Viet Nam.

To serve until 31 December 2001: Bolivia, Bulgaria, Canada, China, Czech Republic, Democratic Republic of the Congo, Denmark, Guinea-Bissau, Honduras, Indonesia, Morocco, Norway, Russian Federation, Rwanda, Saudi Arabia, Syrian Arab Republic, United Kingdom, Venezuela.

On 29 October 1999 (dec. 54/309), the General Assembly elected the following for a three-year term beginning on 1 January 2000 to fill the vacancies occurring on 31 December 1999: Angola, Austria, Bahrain, Benin, Burkina Faso, Cameroon, Costa Rica, Croatia, Cuba, Fiji, France, Germany, Greece, Japan, Mexico, Portugal, Sudan, Suriname.

SESSIONS

Organizational session for 1999: New York, 20 January and 2, 3 and 5 February.

Resumed organizational session for 1999: New York, 25 March, 6 and 7 May and 23 June.

Special high-level meeting with the Bretton Woods institutions: New York, 29 April.

Substantive session of 1999: New York, 23 June; Geneva, 5-30 July.

Resumed substantive session of 1999: New York, 16 September, 26 October, 15 November and 16 December.

OFFICERS

President: Paolo Fulci (Italy).

Vice-Presidents: Percy Metsing Mangoaela (Lesotho), Alyaksandr Sychov (Belarus), Alfonso Valdivieso (Colombia), Makarim Wibisono (Indonesia).

Subsidiary and other related organs

SUBSIDIARY ORGANS

The Economic and Social Council may, at each session, set up committees or working groups, of the whole or of limited membership, and refer to them any items on the agenda for study and report.

Other subsidiary organs reporting to the Council consist of functional commissions, regional commissions, standing committees, expert bodies and ad hoc bodies.

The inter-agency Administrative Committee on Coordination also reports to the Council.

Functional commissions

Commission for Social Development

Session: Thirty-seventh, New York, 9-19 February
Chairman: Aurelio Fernández (Spain)
Membership: 46
Report: E/1999/26
Decisions: ESC 1999/210 A & C

Commission on Crime Prevention and Criminal Justice

Session: Eighth, Vienna, 27 April–6 May
Chairperson: Ana María Cortez de Soriano (Bolivia)
Membership: 40
Report: E/1999/30
Decision: ESC 1999/210 C

Commission on Human Rights

Sessions: Fifty-fifth, Geneva, 22 March–30 April; fourth special, Geneva, 23, 24 and 27 September
Chairperson: Anne Anderson (Ireland)
Membership: 53
Reports: E/1999/23 & Add.1
Decision: ESC 1999/210 C

SUBCOMMISSION ON THE PROMOTION AND PROTECTION OF HUMAN RIGHTS

Session: Fifty-first, Geneva, 2-27 August
Chairperson: Ribot Hatano (Japan)
Membership: 26
Report: E/CN.4/2000/2

Commission on Narcotic Drugs

Session: Forty-second, Vienna, 16-25 March, 30 November and 1 December
Chairman: Mohammad S. Amirkhizi (Iran)
Membership: 53
Report: E/1999/28/Rev.1
Decision: ESC 1999/210 C

Commission on Population and Development

Session: Thirty-second, New York, 22, 23 and 26 March
Chairman: Robert Louis Cliquet (Belgium)
Membership: 47
Report: E/1999/25
Decisions: ESC 1999/210 A-C

Commission on Science and Technology for Development

Session: Fourth, Geneva, 17-21 May

Chairperson: Henri Hogbe Nlend (Cameroon)
Membership: 33
Report: E/1999/31
Decisions: ESC 1999/210 A & B

Commission on Sustainable Development

Sessions: Seventh (second part), New York, 19-30 April; eighth (first part), New York, 30 April
Chairman: Simon Upton (New Zealand) (seventh session), Juan Mayr Maldonado (Colombia) (eighth session)
Membership: 53
Reports: E/1999/29, E/2000/29
Decisions: ESC 1999/210 A, C & E

Commission on the Status of Women

Session: Forty-third, New York, 1-12 March and 1 April
Chairperson: Patricia Flor (Germany)
Membership: 45
Report: E/1999/27
Decision: ESC 1999/210 C

Statistical Commission

Session: Thirtieth, New York, 1-5 March
Chairman: Guest Charumbira (Botswana)
Membership: 24
Report: E/1999/24
Decision: ESC 1999/210 C

Regional commissions

Economic and Social Commission for Asia and the Pacific (ESCAP)

Session: Fifty-fifth, Bangkok, Thailand, 22-28 April
Chairperson: Nyam-Osoryn Tuya (Mongolia)
Membership: 51 members, 9 associate members
Report: E/1999/39

Economic and Social Commission for Western Asia (ESCWA)

Session: Twentieth, Beirut, Lebanon, 27-28 May
Chairman: Nasser Saidi (Lebanon)
Membership: 13
Report: E/1999/41/Rev.1 & Corr.1

Economic Commission for Africa (ECA)

Session: Thirty-third (twenty-fourth meeting of Conference of Ministers), Addis Ababa, Ethiopia, 6-8 May
Chairman: Nigeria
Membership: 53
Report: E/1999/38

Economic Commission for Europe (ECE)

Session: Fifty-fourth, Geneva, 4-6 May
Chairman: Miroslav Somol (Czech Republic)
Membership: 55
Report: E/1999/37

Economic Commission for Latin America and the Caribbean (ECLAC)

Session: Did not meet in 1999
Membership: 41 members, 6 associate members

Standing committees

Commission on Human Settlements

Session: Seventeenth, Nairobi, Kenya, 5-14 May
Chairman: Germán Garcia Durán (Colombia)
Membership: 58
Report: A/54/8
Decisions: ESC 1999/210 A-C

Committee for Programme and Coordination

Sessions: Thirty-ninth, New York, 7 May (organizational), 7 June–2 July (substantive)
Chairman: Michel Tommo Monthe (Cameroon)
Membership: 34
Report: A/54/16
Decisions: ESC 1999/210 A-C, GA 53/308 B & C, GA 54/305

Committee on Non-Governmental Organizations

Session: New York, 1-18 June and 7 September
Chairman: Wahid Ben Amor (Tunisia)
Membership: 19
Reports: E/1999/109 & Add.1
Decision: ESC 1999/210 A

Expert bodies

Ad Hoc Group of Experts on International Cooperation in Tax Matters

Meeting: Ninth, New York, 3-7 May
Membership: 25
Report: E/1999/84 & Corr.1

Committee for Development Policy[22]

Session: First, New York, 26-30 April
Chairman: Just Faaland (Norway)
Membership: 24
Report: E/1999/33

Committee of Experts on the Transport of Dangerous Goods

Session: Did not meet in 1999
Membership: 22 (23 from 6 May)
Decision: ESC 1999/217

Committee on Economic, Social and Cultural Rights

Sessions: Twentieth, Geneva, 26 April–14 May; twenty-first, Geneva, 15 November–3 December
Chairperson: Virginia Bonoan-Dandan (Philippines)
Membership: 18
Report: E/2000/22 & Corr.1

Committee on Energy and Natural Resources for Development

Session: First, New York, 5-16 April
Chairman: Christian M. Katsande (Zimbabwe)
Membership: 24
Report: E/1999/32
Decisions: ESC 1999/210 A & B

United Nations Group of Experts on Geographical Names

Session: Did not meet in 1999
Membership: Representatives of the 21 geographical/linguistic divisions of the Group of Experts

Ad hoc bodies

Commission on Human Settlements acting as the Preparatory Committee for the special session of the General Assembly for an overall review and appraisal of the implementation of the Habitat Agenda

Session: Organizational, Nairobi, Kenya, 13 May
Chairman: Germán Garcia Durán (Colombia)
Membership: Open to the participation of all States
Report: A/54/322

Commission on Population and Development acting as the preparatory committee for the twenty-first special session of the General Assembly

Session: New York, 24 March–1 April, 24-29 June
Chairman: Anwarul Karim Chowdhury (Bangladesh)
Membership: Open to the participation of all States
Reports: A/S-21/2 & Add.1,2

Commission on the Status of Women acting as the preparatory committee for the special session of the General Assembly entitled "Women 2000: gender equality, development and peace for the twenty-first century"

Session: Second, New York, 15-19 March (first part), 30 June (resumed)

Chairperson: Irma Engelbrecht (South Africa) (first part), Roselyn Ruth Asumwa Odera (Kenya) (resumed)
Membership: Open to the participation of all States Members of the United Nations and members of the specialized agencies
Reports: E/1999/60 & Add.1

Administrative Committee on Coordination

Sessions: Geneva, 9-10 April; New York, 29-30 October
Chairman: The Secretary-General
Membership: Organizations of the UN system
Reports: ACC/1999/4, ACC/1999/20

Other related bodies

International Research and Training Institute for the Advancement of Women (INSTRAW)

BOARD OF TRUSTEES

Session: Nineteenth, New York, 5-7 May
President: Amaryllis Torres (Philippines)
Membership: 11
Report: E/1999/57
Decision: ESC 1999/210 C

Director of INSTRAW: Yakin Ertürk (until 28 February), Eleni Stamiris (from 5 September)

Joint United Nations Programme on Human Immunodeficiency Virus/Acquired Immunodeficiency Syndrome (UNAIDS)

PROGRAMME COORDINATING BOARD

Meeting: Eighth, Geneva, 28-29 June
Chairperson: Dr. Juan Ramón de la Fuente (Mexico)
Membership: 22
Report: UNAIDS/PCB(8)/99.7
Decisions: ESC 1999/210 A, C & E

Executive Director of the Programme: Peter Piot

United Nations Children's Fund (UNICEF)

EXECUTIVE BOARD

Sessions: First and second regular, New York, 19-22 and 25 January, 7-10 September; annual, New York, 7-11 June
Chairman: Ibrahim A. Gambari (Nigeria)
Membership: 36
Report: E/1999/34/Rev.1
Decision: ESC 1999/210 C

Executive Director of UNICEF: Carol Bellamy

United Nations Development Programme (UNDP)/ United Nations Population Fund (UNFPA)

EXECUTIVE BOARD

Sessions: First, second and third regular, New York, 25-29 January, 12-16 April, 13-17 September; annual, New York, 14-22 June
President: Asda Jayanama (Thailand)
Membership: 36
Report: E/1999/35
Decisions: ESC 1999/210 C, GA 53/323

Administrator of UNDP: James Gustave Speth (until 30 June), Mark Malloch Brown (from 1 July)
Associate Administrator: Rafeeuddin Ahmed (until January), Zéphirin Diabré (from 15 January)
Executive Director of UNFPA: Dr. Nafis I. Sadik

United Nations Interregional Crime and Justice Research Institute (UNICRI)

BOARD OF TRUSTEES

Session: Tenth, Rome, Italy, 2-3 December
President: Adedokun A. Adeyemi (Nigeria)
Membership: 7 (plus 4 ex-officio members)
Decision: ESC 1999/263

Director of UNICRI: Alberto Bradanini (Officer-in-Charge until 31 July)

United Nations Research Institute for Social Development (UNRISD)

BOARD OF DIRECTORS

Session: Thirty-seventh, Geneva, 1-2 July
Chairperson: Emma Rothschild (United Kingdom)
Membership: 11 (plus 7 ex-officio members)
Report: E/CN.5/2001/3

Director of the Institute: Thandika Mkandawire

World Food Programme (WFP)

EXECUTIVE BOARD

Sessions: First, second and third regular, Rome, Italy, 20-22 January, 13-14 May, 18-22 October; annual, Rome, 17-20 May
President: Laurie Tracy (United States)
Membership: 36
Report: E/2000/36
Decision: ESC 1999/210 F

Executive Director of WFP: Catherine A. Bertini

Trusteeship Council

Article 86 of the United Nations Charter lays down that the Trusteeship Council shall consist of the following:

Members of the United Nations administering Trust Territories;
Permanent members of the Security Council that do not administer Trust Territories;
As many other members elected for a three-year term by the General Assembly as will ensure that the membership of the Council is equally divided between United Nations Members which administer Trust Territories and those which do not.[23]
Members: China, France, Russian Federation, United Kingdom, United States.

International Court of Justice

Judges of the Court

The International Court of Justice consists of 15 Judges elected for nine-year terms by the General Assembly and the Security Council.

The following were the Judges of the Court serving in 1999, listed in the order of precedence:

Judge	*Country of nationality*	*End of term*[24]
Stephen M. Schwebel, *President*	United States	2006
Christopher G. Weeramantry, *Vice-President*	Sri Lanka	2000
Shigeru Oda	Japan	2003
Mohammed Bedjaoui	Algeria	2006
Gilbert Guillaume	France	2000
Raymond Ranjeva	Madagascar	2000
Géza Herczegh	Hungary	2003
Shi Jiuyong	China	2003
Carl-August Fleischhauer	Germany	2003
Abdul G. Koroma	Sierra Leone	2003
Vladlen S. Vereshchetin	Russian Federation	2006
Rosalyn Higgins	United Kingdom	2000
Gonzalo Parra-Aranguren	Venezuela	2000
Pieter H. Kooijmans	Netherlands	2006
Francisco Rezek	Brazil	2006

On 3 November 1999, the General Assembly (dec. 54/310 A) and the Security Council elected the following for a nine-year term beginning on 6 February 2000 to fill the vacancies occurring on 5 February: Awn Shawkat Al-Khasawneh (Jordan), Gilbert Guillaume (France), Rosalyn Higgins (United Kingdom), Gonzalo Parra-Aranguren (Venezuela), Raymond Ranjeva (Madagascar).

Registrar: Eduardo Valencia-Ospina.
Deputy Registrar: Jean-Jacques Arnaldez.

Chamber of Summary Procedure

Members: Stephen M. Schwebel (ex officio), Christopher G. Weeramantry (ex officio), Géza Herczegh, Shi Jiuyong, Abdul G. Koroma.
Substitute members: Rosalyn Higgins, Gonzalo Parra-Aranguren.

Chamber for Environmental Matters

Members: Stephen M. Schwebel (ex officio), Christopher G. Weeramantry (ex officio), Mohammed Bedjaoui, Raymond Ranjeva, Géza Herczegh, Carl-August Fleischhauer, Francisco Rezek.

Parties to the Court's Statute

All Members of the United Nations are ipso facto parties to the Statute of the International Court of Justice. Also party to it is the following non-member: Switzerland.

States accepting the compulsory jurisdiction of the Court

Declarations made by the following States, a number with reservations, accepting the Court's compulsory jurisdiction (or made under the Statute of the Permanent Court of International Justice and deemed to be an acceptance of the jurisdiction of the International Court) were in force at the end of 1999:

Australia, Austria, Barbados, Belgium, Botswana, Bulgaria, Cambodia, Cameroon, Canada, Colombia, Costa Rica, Cyprus, Democratic Republic of the Congo, Denmark, Dominican Republic, Egypt, Estonia, Finland, Gambia, Georgia, Greece, Guinea, Guinea-Bissau, Haiti, Honduras, Hungary, India, Japan, Kenya, Liberia, Liechtenstein, Luxembourg, Madagascar, Malawi, Malta, Mauritius, Mexico, Nauru, Netherlands, New Zealand, Nicaragua, Nigeria, Norway, Pakistan, Panama, Paraguay, Philippines, Poland, Portugal, Senegal, Somalia, Spain, Sudan, Suriname, Swaziland, Sweden, Switzerland, Togo, Uganda, United Kingdom, Uruguay, Yugoslavia.

United Nations organs and specialized and related agencies authorized to request advisory opinions from the Court

Authorized by the United Nations Charter to request opinions on any legal question: General Assembly, Security Council.

Authorized by the General Assembly in accordance with the Charter to request opinions on legal questions arising within the scope of their activities: Economic and Social Council, Trusteeship Council, Interim Committee of the General Assembly, ILO, FAO, UNESCO, ICAO, WHO, World Bank, IFC, IDA, IMF, ITU, WMO, IMO, WIPO, IFAD, UNIDO, IAEA.

Committees of the Court

BUDGETARY AND ADMINISTRATIVE COMMITTEE
Members: Stephen M. Schwebel (ex officio), Christopher G. Weeramantry (ex officio), Mohammed Bedjaoui, Gilbert Guillaume, Shi Jiuyong, Carl-August Fleischhauer, Vladlen S. Vereshchetin, Pieter H. Kooijmans.

COMMITTEE ON RELATIONS
Members: Christopher G. Weeramantry (ex officio), Géza Herczegh, Gonzalo Parra-Aranguren.

COMPUTERIZATION COMMITTEE
Members: Open to all interested members of the Court.

LIBRARY COMMITTEE
Members: Shi Jiuyong, Abdul G. Koroma, Rosalyn Higgins, Pieter H. Kooijmans, Francisco Rezek.

RULES COMMITTEE
Members: Shigeru Oda, Gilbert Guillaume, Carl-August Fleischhauer, Abdul G. Koroma, Rosalyn Higgins, Francisco Rezek.

Other United Nations–related bodies

The following bodies are not subsidiary to any principal organ of the United Nations but were established by an international treaty instrument or arrangement sponsored by the United Nations and are thus related to the Organization and its work. These bodies, often referred to as "treaty organs", are serviced by the United Nations Secretariat and may be financed in part or wholly from the Organization's regular budget, as authorized by the General Assembly, to which most of them report annually.

Commission against Apartheid in Sports

Session: Has not met since 1992
Membership: 15

Committee against Torture

Sessions: Twenty-second, Geneva, 26 April–14 May; twenty-third, Geneva, 8-19 November
Chairman: Peter Burns (Canada)
Membership: 10
Reports: A/54/44, A/55/44

Committee on the Elimination of Discrimination against Women

Sessions: Twentieth, New York, 19 January–5 February; twenty-first, New York, 7-25 June
Chairperson: Aída González Martínez (Mexico)
Membership: 23
Report: A/54/38/Rev.1

Committee on the Elimination of Racial Discrimination

Sessions: Fifty-fourth, Geneva, 1-19 March; fifty-fifth, Geneva, 2-27 August
Chairman: Mahmoud Aboul-Nasr (Egypt)
Membership: 18
Report: A/54/18

Committee on the Rights of the Child

Sessions: Twentieth, twenty-first and twenty-second, Geneva, 11-29 January, 17 May–4 June, 20 September–8 October
Chairperson: Sandra Prunella Mason (Barbados) (twentieth session), Nafsiah Mboi (Indonesia) (twenty-first and twenty-second sessions)
Membership: 10
Reports: A/55/41, CRC/C/84, CRC/C/87, CRC/C/90

Conference on Disarmament

Meetings: Geneva, 18 January–26 March, 10 May–25 June, 26 July–8 September
President: United States, Venezuela, Viet Nam, Algeria, Argentina, Australia (successively)
Membership: 61 (66 from 5 August)
Report: A/54/27

Human Rights Committee

Sessions: Sixty-fifth, New York, 22 March–9 April; sixty-sixth, Geneva, 12-30 July; sixty-seventh, Geneva, 18 October–5 November
Chairperson: Cecilia Medina Quiroga (Chile)
Membership: 18
Reports: A/54/40, vol. I, A/55/40, vol. I

International Narcotics Control Board (INCB)

Sessions: Sixty-sixth and sixty-seventh, Vienna, 10-21 May and 1-18 November
President: António Lourenço Martins (Portugal)
Membership: 13
Report: E/INCB/1999/1
Decisions: ESC 1999/210 A & C

Principal members of the United Nations Secretariat

(as at 31 December 1999)

Secretariat

The Secretary-General: Kofi A. Annan
Deputy Secretary-General: Louise Fréchette

Executive Office of the Secretary-General

Under-Secretary-General, Chef de Cabinet: Iqbal Syed Riza
Under-Secretary-General, Adviser: Diego Cordovez
Under-Secretary-General, Special Adviser: Ismat Kittani
Under-Secretary-General, Special Adviser: Jamsheed K. A. Marker
Under-Secretary-General, Special Adviser: Mohamed Sahnoun
Under-Secretary-General, Special Adviser: Maurice F. Strong
Assistant Secretary-General, Special Adviser: John Ruggie
Assistant Secretary-General for External Relations: Gillian M. Sorensen
Assistant Secretary-General, Coordinator for Preparations for the Millennium Assembly: Miles Stoby

Office of Internal Oversight Services

Under-Secretary-General: Vacant

Office of Legal Affairs

Under-Secretary-General, Legal Counsel: Hans Corell
Assistant Secretary-General: Ralph Zacklin

Department of Political Affairs

Under-Secretary-General: Kieran Prendergast
Under-Secretary-General, Adviser for Special Assignments in Africa: Ibrahim A. Gambari
Assistant Secretaries-General: Ibrahima Fall, Alvaro de Soto

Department for Disarmament Affairs

Under-Secretary-General: Jayantha Dhanapala

Department of Peacekeeping Operations

Under-Secretary-General: Bernard Miyet
Assistant Secretaries-General: Hédi Annabi, Young-Jin Choi

Office for the Coordination of Humanitarian Affairs

Under-Secretary-General, Emergency Relief Coordinator: Sergio Vieira de Mello

Department of Economic and Social Affairs

Under-Secretary-General: Nitin Desai
Assistant Secretaries-General: Angela E. V. King, Patrizio M. Civili

Department of General Assembly Affairs and Conference Services

Under-Secretary-General: Yongjian Jin
Assistant Secretary-General: Federico Riesco-Quintana

Department of Public Information

Under-Secretary-General: Kensaku Hogen

Department of Management

Under-Secretary-General: Joseph E. Connor

OFFICE OF PROGRAMME PLANNING, BUDGET AND ACCOUNTS
Assistant Secretary-General, Controller: Jean-Pierre Halbwachs

OFFICE OF HUMAN RESOURCES MANAGEMENT
Assistant Secretary-General: Rafiah Salim

OFFICE OF CENTRAL SUPPORT SERVICES
Assistant Secretary-General: Toshiyuki Niwa

Office of the Iraq Programme

Under-Secretary-General, Executive Director: Benon V. Sevan
Assistant Secretary-General, Humanitarian Coordinator: Hans von Sponeck

Economic and Social Commission for Asia and the Pacific

Under-Secretary-General, Executive Secretary: Adrianus Mooy

Economic and Social Commission for Western Asia

Under-Secretary-General, Executive Secretary: Hazem El-Beblawi

Economic Commission for Africa

Under-Secretary-General, Executive Secretary: K. Y. Amoako

Economic Commission for Europe

Under-Secretary-General, Executive Secretary: Yves Berthelot

Economic Commission for Latin America and the Caribbean

Under-Secretary-General, Executive Secretary: Jose Antonio Ocampo

United Nations Centre for Human Settlements (Habitat)

Under-Secretary-General, Acting Executive Director: Klaus Töpfer

United Nations Office at Geneva

Under-Secretary-General, Director-General of the United Nations Office at Geneva: Vladimir Petrovsky

Office of the High Commissioner for Human Rights

Under-Secretary-General, High Commissioner: Mary Robinson
Assistant Secretary-General, Deputy High Commissioner: Gangapersaud Ramcharan

United Nations Office at Vienna

Under-Secretary-General, Director-General of the United Nations Office at Vienna and Executive Director of the United Nations International Drug Control Programme: Giuseppe Arlacchi

International Court of Justice Registry

Assistant Secretary-General, Registrar: Eduardo Valencia-Ospina

Secretariats of subsidiary organs, special representatives and other related bodies

International Trade Centre UNCTAD/WTO

Executive Director: J. Denis Bélisle

Office of the Secretary-General in Afghanistan and Pakistan

Under-Secretary-General, Special Envoy of the Secretary-General for Afghanistan: Lakhdar Brahimi

Assistant Secretary-General, Head of the Special Mission to Afghanistan: Norbert Heinrich Holl

Office of the Special Representative of the Secretary-General for the Great Lakes Region

Assistant Secretary-General, Special Representative: Berhanu Dinka

Office of the Special Representative of the Secretary-General for Children and Armed Conflict

Under-Secretary-General, Special Representative: Olara A. Otunnu

Office of the United Nations High Commissioner for Refugees

Under-Secretary-General, High Commissioner: Sadako Ogata

Assistant Secretary-General, Deputy High Commissioner: Frederick Barton

Office of the United Nations Security Coordinator

Under-Secretary-General, United Nations Security Coordinator: Benon V. Sevan

Personal Representative of the Secretary-General on the Guyana-Venezuela border dispute

Under-Secretary-General, Personal Representative: Oliver Jackman

Regional Coordinator for the Balkans

Under-Secretary-General, Special Envoy of the Secretary-General: Carl Bildt

Under-Secretary-General, Special Envoy of the Secretary-General: Eduard Kukan

Special Adviser to the Secretary-General on European Issues

Under-Secretary-General, Special Adviser: Bernard Merimee

Special Assignments in support of the Secretary-General's preventive and peacemaking efforts

Under-Secretary-General: Lakhdar Brahimi

Special Envoy of the Secretary-General

Under-Secretary-General, Special Envoy: Yuli Vorontsov

Special Envoy of the Secretary-General for Humanitarian Affairs in the Sudan

Under-Secretary-General, Special Envoy: Tom Eric Vraalsen

United Nations Children's Fund

Under-Secretary-General, Executive Director: Carol Bellamy

Assistant Secretaries-General, Deputy Executive Directors: Karin Sham Poo, Stephen Lewis

United Nations Civilian Police Mission in Haiti

Special Representative of the Secretary-General and Head of Mission: Alfredo Lopes Cabral

Police Commissioner: Colonel George Gabbardo

United Nations Compensation Commission

Assistant Secretary-General, Executive Secretary: Jean-Claude Aime

United Nations Conference on Trade and Development

Under-Secretary-General, Secretary-General of the Conference: Rubens Ricupero

Assistant Secretary-General, Deputy Secretary-General of the Conference: Carlos Fortin Cabezas

United Nations Coordinator for Humanitarian Assistance in Iraq

Assistant Secretary-General, Coordinator: Denis John Halliday

United Nations Development Programme

Administrator: Mark Malloch Brown

Under-Secretary-General, Associate Administrator: Zéphirin Diabré

Assistant Secretary-General, Special Adviser to the Administrator: Richard Jolly

Assistant Administrator and Director, Bureau of Management: Jan Mattson

Assistant Administrator and Director, Bureau for Development Policy: Eimi Watanabe

Assistant Administrator and Director, Bureau for Resources and External Affairs: Normand R. Lauzon

Assistant Administrator and Chief Procurement Officer: Veronique Lavorel

Assistant Administrator and Regional Director, UNDP Africa: Thelma Awori

Assistant Administrator and Regional Director, UNDP Arab States: Fawaz Fokeladeh

Assistant Administrator and Regional Director, UNDP Asia and the Pacific: Nay Htun

Assistant Administrator and Regional Director, UNDP Europe and the Commonwealth of Independent States: Anton Kruiderink

Assistant Administrator and Regional Director, UNDP Latin America and the Caribbean: Elena Martinez

United Nations Disengagement Observer Force

Assistant Secretary-General, Force Commander: Major-General Cameron Ross

United Nations Environment Programme

Under-Secretary-General, Executive Director: Klaus Töpfer

Assistant Secretary-General, Deputy Executive Director: Shafqat S. Kakakhel

United Nations Institute for Training and Research

Executive Director: Marcel A. Boisard

United Nations Interim Administration Mission in Kosovo

Under-Secretary-General, Special Representative of the Secretary-General: Bernard Kouchner

Assistant Secretary-General, Principal Deputy Special Representative of the Secretary-General: James Peter Covey

Assistant Secretary-General, Deputy Special Representative of the Secretary-General: Tom Koenigs

Assistant Secretary-General, Deputy Special Representative of the Secretary-General: Dennis R. McNamara

United Nations Interim Force in Lebanon

Assistant Secretary-General, Force Commander: Major-General Seth Kofi Obeng

United Nations Iraq-Kuwait Observation Mission

Assistant Secretary-General, Force Commander: General John Augustine Vize

United Nations Joint Staff Pension Fund

Assistant Secretary-General, Chief Executive Officer: Raymond Gieri

United Nations Military Observer Group in India and Pakistan

Chief Military Observer: Major-General Jozsef Bali

United Nations Mission for the Referendum in Western Sahara

Under-Secretary-General, Personal Envoy of the Secretary-General: James A. Baker III

Under-Secretary-General, Special Representative of the Secretary-General: William Eagleton

Force Commander: Brigadier-General Claude Buze

United Nations Mission in Bosnia and Herzegovina

Assistant Secretary-General, Special Representative of the Secretary-General and Coordinator of United Nations Operations in Bosnia and Herzegovina: Jacques Paul Klein

Commissioner of the United Nations International Police Task Force: Brigadier-General Detlef Buwitt

United Nations Mission in Sierra Leone

Under-Secretary-General, Special Representative of the Secretary-General and Head of Mission: Oluyemi Adeniji

Force Commander: Major-General Vijay Kumar Jetley

United Nations Mission in the Central African Republic

Special Representative of the Secretary-General and Head of Mission: Vacant

Force Commander: Major-General Barthélémy Ratanga

United Nations Mission of Observers in Prevlaka

Chief Military Observer: Lieutenant-Colonel Graeme Williams

United Nations Mission of Observers in Tajikistan

Assistant Secretary-General, Special Representative of the Secretary-General and Head of Mission: Ivo Petrov

Chief Military Observer: Brigadier-General John Hvidegaard

United Nations Observer Mission in Georgia

Assistant Secretary-General, Special Representative of the Secretary-General and Head of Mission: Dieter Boden

Chief Military Observer: Major-General Tariq Waseem Ghazi

United Nations Office for Project Services

Assistant Secretary-General, Executive Director: Reinhart Helmke

United Nations Organization Mission in the Democratic Republic of the Congo

Under-Secretary-General, Special Representative of the Secretary-General and Head of Mission: Kamel Morjane

United Nations Peacekeeping Force in Cyprus

Special Adviser to the Secretary-General on Cyprus: Vacant

Assistant Secretary-General, Special Representative of the Secretary-General and Chief of Mission: James Holger (Acting)

Force Commander: Major-General Victory Rana

United Nations Population Fund

Executive Director: Dr. Nafis I. Sadik

Deputy Executive Director, Policy and Administration: Hirofumi Ando

Deputy Executive Director, Programme: Kerstin Trone

United Nations Relief and Works Agency for Palestine Refugees in the Near East

Under-Secretary-General, Commissioner-General: Peter Hansen

Assistant Secretary-General, Deputy Commissioner-General: Dr. Mohamed Abdelmoumène

United Nations Special Coordinator for the Middle East Peace Process and Personal Representative of the Secretary-General to the Palestine Liberation Organization and the Palestine Authority

Under-Secretary-General, Personal Representative of the Secretary-General: Terje Roed-Larsen

United Nations Transitional Administration in East Timor

Under-Secretary-General, Special Representative of the Secretary-General for East Timor: Jamsheed K. A. Marker

Under-Secretary-General, Special Representative of the Secretary-General and Head of Mission: Sergio Vieira de Mello

Force Commander: Lieutenant-General Jaime de los Santos

United Nations Truce Supervision Organization

Assistant Secretary-General, Chief of Staff: Major-General Timothy Ford

United Nations University

Under-Secretary-General, Rector: Johannes A. van Ginkel

Director, World Institute for Development Economics Research: Andrea Cornia

---

On 31 December 1999, the total number of staff of the United Nations Secretariat with continuous service or expected service of a year or more was 13,264. Of these, 4,335 were in the Professional and higher categories, 757 were experts (200-series Project Personnel staff) and 8,172 were in the General Service and related categories.

[1]On 30 June 1999 (dec. S-21/12), the Assembly decided that the President at its fifty-third session would serve in the same capacity at the twenty-first special session.

[2]On 30 June 1999 (dec. S-21/13), the Assembly decided that the Vice-Presidents of the fifty-third session would serve in the same capacity at the twenty-first special session.

[3]Elected on 14 September 1999 (dec. 54/302); on 27 September (dec. S-22/12), the Assembly decided that the President at its fifty-fourth session would serve in the same capacity at the twenty-second special session.

[4]Elected on 14 September 1999 (dec. 54/304); on 27 September (dec. S-22/13), the Assembly decided that the Vice-Presidents at its fifty-fourth session would serve in the same capacity at the twenty-second special session.

[5]The only Main Committee to meet at the resumed session.

[6]On 30 June 1999 (dec. S-21/14), the Assembly decided that the Chairmen of the Main Committees of the fifty-third session would serve in the same capacity at the twenty-first special session; in the absence of the First Committee Chairman, a Vice-Chairperson served as Acting Chairperson.

[7]Elected by the Assembly on 30 June 1999 (dec. S-21/15); other officers elected by the Ad Hoc Committee.

[8]Chairmen elected by the Committees; announced by the Assembly President on 14 September 1999 (dec. 54/303).

[9]On 27 September 1999 (dec. S-22/14), the Assembly decided that the Chairmen of the Main Committees of the fifty-fourth session would serve in the same capacity at the twenty-second special session.

[10]Chairman elected on 27 September 1999 (dec. S-22/15); Rapporteur elected by the Ad Hoc Committee on 28 September.

[11]On 30 June 1999 (dec. S-21/11), the Assembly decided that the Credentials Committee for the twenty-first special session would have the same composition as that of the fifty-third session.

[12]Appointed on 14 September 1999 (dec. 54/301); on 27 September (dec. S-22/11), the Assembly decided that the Credentials Committee for the twenty-second special session would have the same membership as that of the fifty-fourth session.

[13]Appointed on 2 September 1999 (dec. 53/312 B) to fill the vacancy created by the resignation of Leonid E. Bidnyi (Russian Federation).

[14]Mandate ended on 28 February 1999.

[15]Mandate expired on 26 February 1999.

[16]Terminated on 22 October 1999 on the establishment of UNAMSIL.

[17]Established on 10 June 1999.

[18]Established on 11 June 1999; mandate expired on 30 November.

[19]Established on 22 October 1999.

[20]Established on 25 October 1999.

[21]Established on 30 November 1999.

[22]Formerly Committee for Development Planning.

[23]During 1999, no Member of the United Nations was an administering member of the Trusteeship Council, while five permanent members of the Security Council continued as non-administering members.

[24]Term expires on 5 February of the year indicated.

Appendix IV

Agendas of United Nations principal organs in 1999

This appendix lists the items on the agendas of the General Assembly, the Security Council and the Economic and Social Council during 1999. For the Assembly, the column headed "Allocation" indicates the assignment of each item to plenary meetings or committees.

Agenda item titles have been shortened by omitting mention of reports, if any, following the subject of the item. Where the subject matter of an item is not apparent from its title, the subject is identified in square brackets; this is not part of the title.

General Assembly

Agenda item considered at the resumed tenth emergency special session (5, 8 and 9 February 1999)

Item No.	*Title*	*Allocation*
5.	Illegal Israeli actions in occupied East Jerusalem and the rest of the occupied Palestinian territory.	Plenary

Agenda items considered at the resumed fifty-third session (18 February–13 September 1999)

Item No.	*Title*	*Allocation*
2.	Minute of silent prayer or meditation.	Plenary
8.	Adoption of the agenda and organization of work.	Plenary
12.	Report of the Economic and Social Council.	Plenary[1]
16.	Elections to fill vacancies in subsidiary organs and other elections:	
	(a) Election of seven members of the Committee for Programme and Coordination.	Plenary
17.	Appointments to fill vacancies in subsidiary organs and other appointments:	
	(a) Appointment of members of the Advisory Committee on Administrative and Budgetary Questions;	[2]
	(e) Appointment of members of the United Nations Administrative Tribunal;	5th
	(f) International Civil Service Commission:	
	(i) Appointment of members of the Commission;	5th
	(ii) Designation of the Chairman and Vice-Chairman of the Commission;	5th
	(h) Appointment of a member of the Joint Inspection Unit;	Plenary
	(i) Confirmation of the appointment of the Secretary-General of the United Nations Conference on Trade and Development;	Plenary
	(j) Appointment of the Under-Secretary-General for Internal Oversight Services;	Plenary
	(l) Confirmation of the appointment of the Administrator of the United Nations Development Programme.[3]	Plenary
30.	United Nations reform: measures and proposals.	Plenary
31.	Culture of peace.	Plenary
37.	Implementation of the outcome of the World Summit for Social Development.	Plenary
47.	Election of judges of the International Criminal Tribunal for the Prosecution of Persons Responsible for Genocide and Other Serious Violations of International Humanitarian Law Committed in the Territory of Rwanda and Rwandan Citizens Responsible for Genocide and Other Such Violations Committed in the Territory of Neighbouring States between 1 January and 31 December 1994.	Plenary
57.	Question of the Comorian island of Mayotte.	Plenary
58.	Strengthening of the United Nations system.	Plenary

Item No.	*Title*	*Allocation*
59.	Question of equitable representation on and increase in the membership of the Security Council and related matters.	Plenary
60.	Revitalization of the work of the General Assembly.	Plenary
61.	Restructuring and revitalization of the United Nations in the economic, social and related fields.	Plenary
62.	Question of Cyprus.	[4]
93.	Sustainable development and international economic cooperation:	
	(f) Implementation of the Programme of Action of the International Conference on Population and Development.	[5]
94.	Environment and sustainable development:	
	(c) Implementation of the outcome of the Global Conference on the Sustainable Development of Small Island Developing States.	[5]
111.	Financial reports and audited financial statements, and reports of the Board of Auditors.	5th
112.	Review of the efficiency of the administrative and financial functioning of the United Nations.	5th
113.	Programme budget for the biennium 1998-1999.	5th
114.	Programme planning.	5th
115.	Improving the financial situation of the United Nations.	[2]
117.	Pattern of conferences.	5th
118.	Scale of assessments for the apportionment of the expenses of the United Nations.	5th
119.	Human resources management.	5th
122.	Financing of the United Nations peacekeeping forces in the Middle East:	
	(a) United Nations Disengagement Observer Force;	5th
	(b) United Nations Interim Force in Lebanon.	5th
123.	Financing of the United Nations Angola Verification Mission and the United Nations Observer Mission in Angola.	5th
124.	Financing of the activities arising from Security Council resolution 687(1991):	
	(a) United Nations Iraq-Kuwait Observation Mission.	5th
125.	Financing of the United Nations Mission for the Referendum in Western Sahara.	5th
126.	Financing and liquidation of the United Nations Transitional Authority in Cambodia.	5th
127.	Financing of the United Nations Protection Force, the United Nations Confidence Restoration Operation in Croatia, the United Nations Preventive Deployment Force and the United Nations Peace Forces headquarters.	5th
128.	Financing of the United Nations Operation in Somalia II.	5th
129.	Financing of the United Nations Operation in Mozambique.	[2]
130.	Financing of the United Nations Peacekeeping Force in Cyprus.	5th
131.	Financing of the United Nations Observer Mission in Georgia.	5th
132.	Financing of the United Nations Mission in Haiti.	5th
133.	Financing of the United Nations Observer Mission in Liberia.	5th
134.	Financing of the United Nations Assistance Mission for Rwanda.	5th
136.	Financing of the United Nations Mission of Observers in Tajikistan.	5th
138.	Financing of the United Nations Mission in Bosnia and Herzegovina.	5th
139.	Financing of the United Nations Transitional Administration for Eastern Slavonia, Baranja and Western Sirmium and the Civilian Police Support Group.	5th
140.	Financing of the United Nations Preventive Deployment Force.	5th
141.	Financing of the United Nations Support Mission in Haiti, the United Nations Transition Mission in Haiti and the United Nations Civilian Police Mission in Haiti.	5th
142.	Financing of the Military Observer Group of the United Nations Verification Mission in Guatemala.	5th
143.	Administrative and budgetary aspects of the financing of the United Nations peacekeeping operations:	
	(a) Financing of the United Nations peacekeeping operations.	5th
144.	Report of the Secretary-General on the activities of the Office of Internal Oversight Services.	[2]
145.	Review of the implementation of General Assembly resolution 48/218 B.	5th
152.	Report of the Committee on Relations with the Host Country.	[6]
161.	Financing of the United Nations Mission in the Central African Republic.	5th
165.	Joint Inspection Unit.	5th
167.	Armed aggression against the Democratic Republic of the Congo.	Plenary
169.	Observer status for the Customs Cooperation Council in the General Assembly.[7]	Plenary
170.	Financing of the United Nations Interim Administration Mission in Kosovo.[7]	5th

Agenda of the twenty-first special session (30 June–2 July 1999)

Item No.	*Title*	*Allocation*
1.	Opening of the session by the Chairman of the delegation of Uruguay.	Plenary
2.	Minute of silent prayer or meditation.	Plenary
3.	Credentials of representatives to the twenty-first special session of the General Assembly:	
	(a) Appointment of the members of the Credentials Committee;	Plenary
	(b) Report of the Credentials Committee.	Plenary
4.	Election of the President.	Plenary
5.	Report of the Commission on Population and Development acting as the preparatory committee for the twenty-first special session of the General Assembly.	Plenary
6.	Organization of the session.	Plenary
7.	Adoption of the agenda.	Plenary
8.	Overall review and appraisal of the implementation of the Programme of Action of the International Conference on Population and Development.	Plenary[8]
9.	Adoption of the final document.	Plenary

Agenda of the fifty-fourth session (first part, 14 September–23 December 1999)

Item No.	*Title*	*Allocation*
1.	Opening of the session by the Chairman of the delegation of Uruguay.	Plenary
2.	Minute of silent prayer or meditation.	Plenary
3.	Credentials of representatives to the fifty-fourth session of the General Assembly:	
	(a) Appointment of the members of the Credentials Committee;	Plenary
	(b) Report of the Credentials Committee.	Plenary
4.	Election of the President of the General Assembly.	Plenary
5.	Election of the officers of the Main Committees.	Plenary
6.	Election of the Vice-Presidents of the General Assembly.	Plenary
7.	Notification by the Secretary-General under Article 12, paragraph 2, of the Charter of the United Nations.	Plenary
8.	Adoption of the agenda and organization of work.	Plenary
9.	General debate.	Plenary
10.	Report of the Secretary-General on the work of the Organization.	Plenary
11.	Report of the Security Council.	Plenary
12.	Report of the Economic and Social Council.	Plenary, 4th, 2nd, 3rd, 5th
13.	Report of the International Court of Justice.	Plenary
14.	Report of the International Atomic Energy Agency.	Plenary
15.	Elections to fill vacancies in principal organs:	
	(a) Election of five non-permanent members of the Security Council;	Plenary
	(b) Election of eighteen members of the Economic and Social Council;	Plenary
	(c) Election of five members of the International Court of Justice.	Plenary
16.	Elections to fill vacancies in subsidiary organs and other elections:	
	(a) Election of twenty members of the Committee for Programme and Coordination;	Plenary
	(b) Election of twenty-nine members of the Governing Council of the United Nations Environment Programme.	Plenary
17.	Appointments to fill vacancies in subsidiary organs and other appointments:	
	(a) Appointment of members of the Advisory Committee on Administrative and Budgetary Questions;	5th
	(b) Appointment of members of the Committee on Contributions;	5th
	(c) Appointment of a member of the Board of Auditors;	5th
	(d) Confirmation of the appointment of members of the Investments Committee;	5th
	(e) Appointment of members of the United Nations Administrative Tribunal;	5th
	(f) Appointment of a member of the United Nations Staff Pension Committee;	5th

Item No.	*Title*	*Allocation*
	(g) Appointment of members of the Committee on Conferences;	Plenary
	(h) Appointment of members of the Joint Inspection Unit;	Plenary
	(i) Appointment of the Under-Secretary-General for Internal Oversight Services.	Plenary
18.	Implementation of the Declaration on the Granting of Independence to Colonial Countries and Peoples.	Plenary, 4th
19.	Admission of new Members to the United Nations.	Plenary
20.	Strengthening of the coordination of humanitarian and disaster relief assistance of the United Nations, including special economic assistance:	
	(a) Strengthening of the coordination of emergency humanitarian assistance of the United Nations;	Plenary
	(b) Special economic assistance to individual countries or regions;	Plenary
	(c) Strengthening of international cooperation and coordination of efforts to study, mitigate and minimize the consequences of the Chernobyl disaster;	Plenary
	(d) Participation of volunteers, "White Helmets", in activities of the United Nations in the field of humanitarian relief, rehabilitation and technical cooperation for development;	Plenary
	(e) Assistance to the Palestinian people;	Plenary
	(f) Emergency international assistance for peace, normalcy and reconstruction of war-stricken Afghanistan.	Plenary
21.	University for Peace.	Plenary
22.	Building a peaceful and better world through sport and the Olympic ideal.	Plenary
23.	Multilingualism.	Plenary
24.	Return or restitution of cultural property to the countries of origin.	Plenary
25.	Cooperation between the United Nations and the International Organization of la Francophonie.	Plenary
26.	Cooperation between the United Nations and the League of Arab States.	Plenary
27.	Cooperation between the United Nations and the Inter-Parliamentary Union.	Plenary
28.	Cooperation between the United Nations and the Economic Cooperation Organization.	Plenary
29.	Cooperation between the United Nations and the Organization of the Islamic Conference.	Plenary
30.	Cooperation between the United Nations and the Organization for Security and Cooperation in Europe.	Plenary
31.	Cooperation between the United Nations and the Organization of African Unity.	Plenary
32.	Cooperation between the United Nations and the Latin American Economic System.	Plenary
33.	Necessity of ending the economic, commercial and financial embargo imposed by the United States of America against Cuba.	Plenary
34.	Dialogue among civilizations.	Plenary
35.	Assistance in mine action.	Plenary
36.	Bethlehem 2000.	Plenary
37.	Implementation of the outcome of the World Summit for Social Development.	Plenary
38.	Question of equitable representation on and increase in the membership of the Security Council and related matters.	Plenary
39.	Support by the United Nations system of the efforts of Governments to promote and consolidate new or restored democracies.	Plenary
40.	Oceans and the law of the sea:	
	(a) Law of the sea;	Plenary
	(b) Agreement for the Implementation of the Provisions of the United Nations Convention on the Law of the Sea of 10 December 1982 relating to the Conservation and Management of Straddling Fish Stocks and Highly Migratory Fish Stocks;	Plenary
	(c) Results of the review by the Commission on Sustainable Development of the sectoral theme of "oceans and seas".	Plenary
41.	Zone of peace and cooperation of the South Atlantic.	Plenary
42.	The situation in Bosnia and Herzegovina.	Plenary
43.	The situation in the Middle East.	Plenary
44.	Question of Palestine.	Plenary
45.	Global implications of the year 2000 date conversion problem of computers.	Plenary
46.	Causes of conflict and the promotion of durable peace and sustainable development in Africa.	Plenary
47.	The situation in Central America: procedures for the establishment of a firm and lasting peace and progress in fashioning a region of peace, freedom, democracy and development.	Plenary
48.	The situation of democracy and human rights in Haiti.	Plenary
49.	United Nations reform: measures and proposals:	

Item No.	*Title*	*Allocation*
	(a) United Nations reform: measures and proposals;	Plenary
	(b) The Millennium Assembly of the United Nations.	Plenary
50.	The situation in Afghanistan and its implications for international peace and security.	Plenary
51.	Report of the International Criminal Tribunal for the Prosecution of Persons Responsible for Genocide and Other Serious Violations of International Humanitarian Law Committed in the Territory of Rwanda and Rwandan Citizens Responsible for Genocide and Other Such Violations Committed in the Territory of Neighbouring States between 1 January and 31 December 1994.	Plenary
52.	Question of the Falkland Islands (Malvinas).	Plenary, 4th
53.	Report of the International Tribunal for the Prosecution of Persons Responsible for Serious Violations of International Humanitarian Law Committed in the Territory of the Former Yugoslavia since 1991.	Plenary
54.	Declaration of the Assembly of Heads of State and Government of the Organization of African Unity on the aerial and naval military attack against the Socialist People's Libyan Arab Jamahiriya by the present United States Administration in April 1986.	Plenary
55.	Armed Israeli aggression against the Iraqi nuclear installations and its grave consequences for the established international system concerning the peaceful uses of nuclear energy, the non-proliferation of nuclear weapons and international peace and security.	Plenary
56.	Consequences of the Iraqi occupation of and aggression against Kuwait.	Plenary
57.	Implementation of the resolutions of the United Nations.	Plenary
58.	Launching of global negotiations on international economic cooperation for development.	Plenary
59.	Strengthening of the United Nations system.	Plenary
60.	Revitalization of the work of the General Assembly.	Plenary
61.	Restructuring and revitalization of the United Nations in the economic, social and related fields.	Plenary
62.	Question of the Comorian island of Mayotte.	Plenary [9]
63.	Question of Cyprus.	
64.	Reduction of military budgets:	
	(a) Reduction of military budgets;	1st
	(b) Objective information on military matters, including transparency of military expenditures.	1st
65.	Prohibition of the development and manufacture of new types of weapons of mass destruction and new systems of such weapons.	1st
66.	Question of Antarctica.	1st
67.	Compliance with arms limitation and disarmament and non-proliferation agreements.	1st
68.	Verification in all its aspects, including the role of the United Nations in the field of verification.	1st
69.	Implementation of the Declaration of the Indian Ocean as a Zone of Peace.	1st
70.	African Nuclear-Weapon-Free-Zone Treaty.	1st
71.	Developments in the field of information and telecommunications in the context of international security.	1st
72.	Role of science and technology in the context of international security and disarmament.	1st
73.	Establishment of a nuclear-weapon-free zone in the region of the Middle East.	1st
74.	Conclusion of effective international arrangements to assure non-nuclear-weapon States against the use or threat of use of nuclear weapons.	1st
75.	Prevention of an arms race in outer space.	1st
76.	General and complete disarmament:	
	(a) Notification of nuclear tests;	1st
	(b) Transparency in armaments;	1st
	(c) Establishment of a nuclear-weapon-free zone in Central Asia;	1st
	(d) Assistance to States for curbing the illicit traffic in small arms and collecting them;	1st
	(e) Prohibition of the dumping of radioactive wastes;	1st
	(f) Small arms;	1st
	(g) Reducing nuclear danger;	1st
	(h) Observance of environmental norms in the drafting and implementation of agreements on disarmament and arms control;	1st
	(i) Relationship between disarmament and development;	1st
	(j) Consolidation of peace through practical disarmament measures;	1st
	(k) Regional disarmament;	1st
	(l) Conventional arms control at the regional and subregional levels;	1st
	(m) Nuclear-weapon-free southern hemisphere and adjacent areas;	1st

Item No.	*Title*	*Allocation*
	(n) Implementation of the Convention on the Prohibition of the Development, Production, Stockpiling and Use of Chemical Weapons and on Their Destruction;	1st
	(o) Illicit traffic in small arms;	1st
	(p) Follow-up to the advisory opinion of the International Court of Justice on the *Legality of the Threat or Use of Nuclear Weapons;*	1st
	(q) Nuclear disarmament;	1st
	(r) Towards a nuclear-weapon-free world: the need for a new agenda;	1st
	(s) Convening of the fourth special session of the General Assembly devoted to disarmament.	1st
77.	Review and implementation of the Concluding Document of the Twelfth Special Session of the General Assembly:	
	(a) Regional confidence-building measures: activities of the United Nations Standing Advisory Committee on Security Questions in Central Africa;	1st
	(b) United Nations Regional Centre for Peace and Disarmament in Asia and the Pacific;	1st
	(c) United Nations Regional Centre for Peace and Disarmament in Africa;	1st
	(d) Convention on the Prohibition of the Use of Nuclear Weapons;	1st
	(e) United Nations regional centres for peace and disarmament.	1st
78.	Review of the implementation of the recommendations and decisions adopted by the General Assembly at its tenth special session:	
	(a) Report of the Disarmament Commission;	1st
	(b) Report of the Conference on Disarmament;	1st
	(c) Advisory Board on Disarmament Matters;	1st
	(d) United Nations Institute for Disarmament Research.	1st
79.	The risk of nuclear proliferation in the Middle East.	1st
80.	Convention on Prohibitions or Restrictions on the Use of Certain Conventional Weapons Which May Be Deemed to Be Excessively Injurious or to Have Indiscriminate Effects.	1st
81.	Strengthening of security and cooperation in the Mediterranean region.	1st
82.	Consolidation of the regime established by the Treaty for the Prohibition of Nuclear Weapons in Latin America and the Caribbean (Treaty of Tlatelolco).	1st
83.	Convention on the Prohibition of the Development, Production and Stockpiling of Bacteriological (Biological) and Toxin Weapons and on Their Destruction.	1st
84.	Review of the implementation of the Declaration on the Strengthening of International Security.	1st
85.	Comprehensive Nuclear-Test-Ban Treaty.	1st
86.	Effects of atomic radiation.	4th
87.	International cooperation in the peaceful uses of outer space.	4th
88.	United Nations Relief and Works Agency for Palestine Refugees in the Near East.	4th
89.	Report of the Special Committee to Investigate Israeli Practices Affecting the Human Rights of the Palestinian People and Other Arabs of the Occupied Territories.	4th
90.	Comprehensive review of the whole question of peacekeeping operations in all their aspects.	4th
91.	Questions relating to information.	4th
92.	Information from Non-Self-Governing Territories transmitted under Article 73 *e* of the Charter of the United Nations.	4th
93.	Economic and other activities which affect the interests of the peoples of the Non-Self-Governing Territories.	4th
94.	Implementation of the Declaration on the Granting of Independence to Colonial Countries and Peoples by the specialized agencies and the international institutions associated with the United Nations.	4th
95.	Offers by Member States of study and training facilities for inhabitants of Non-Self-Governing Territories.	4th
96.	Question of East Timor.	Plenary, 4th
97.	Macroeconomic policy questions:	
	(a) High-level international intergovernmental consideration of financing for development;	2nd
	(b) Financing of development, including net transfer of resources between developing and developed countries;	2nd
	(c) Trade and development;	2nd
	(d) Science and technology for development;	2nd
	(e) External debt crisis and development.	2nd
98.	Sectoral policy questions:	
	(a) Industrial development cooperation;	2nd

Item No.	*Title*	*Allocation*
	(b) Business and development.	2nd
99.	Sustainable development and international economic cooperation:	
	(a) Implementation of the commitments and policies agreed upon in the Declaration on International Economic Cooperation, in particular the Revitalization of Economic Growth and Development of the Developing Countries, and implementation of the International Development Strategy for the Fourth United Nations Development Decade;	2nd
	(b) Implementation of the outcome of the United Nations Conference on Human Settlements (Habitat II);	2nd
	(c) Women in development;	2nd
	(d) Human resources development;	2nd
	(e) International migration and development, including the question of the convening of a United Nations conference on international migration and development to address migration issues;	2nd
	(f) Implementation of the Programme of Action for the Least Developed Countries for the 1990s;	2nd
	(g) Renewal of the dialogue on strengthening international economic cooperation for development through partnership;	2nd
	(h) Implementation of the Programme of Action of the International Conference on Population and Development.	Plenary, 2nd
100.	Environment and sustainable development:	
	(a) Implementation of Agenda 21 and the Programme for the Further Implementation of Agenda 21;	2nd
	(b) International Decade for Natural Disaster Reduction;	2nd
	(c) Convention on Biological Diversity;	2nd
	(d) Protection of global climate for present and future generations of mankind;	2nd
	(e) Implementation of the United Nations Convention to Combat Desertification in those Countries Experiencing Serious Drought and/or Desertification, particularly in Africa;	2nd
	(f) Implementation of the outcome of the Global Conference on the Sustainable Development of Small Island Developing States.	2nd
101.	Operational activities for development:	
	(a) Operational activities for development of the United Nations system;	Plenary, 2nd
	(b) Economic and technical cooperation among developing countries.	2nd
102.	Training and research.	2nd
103.	Permanent sovereignty of the Palestinian people in the occupied Palestinian territory, including Jerusalem, and of the Arab population in the occupied Syrian Golan over their natural resources.	2nd
104.	Globalization and interdependence.	2nd
105.	Implementation of the first United Nations Decade for the Eradication of Poverty (1997-2006).	2nd
106.	Social development, including questions relating to the world social situation and to youth, ageing, disabled persons and the family.	Plenary, 3rd
107.	Crime prevention and criminal justice.	3rd
108.	International drug control.	3rd
109.	Advancement of women.	Plenary, 3rd
110.	Implementation of the outcome of the Fourth World Conference on Women.	3rd
111.	Report of the United Nations High Commissioner for Refugees, questions relating to refugees, returnees and displaced persons and humanitarian questions.	3rd
112.	Promotion and protection of the rights of children.	3rd
113.	Programme of activities of the International Decade of the World's Indigenous People.	3rd
114.	Elimination of racism and racial discrimination.	3rd
115.	Right of peoples to self-determination.	3rd
116.	Human rights questions:	
	(a) Implementation of human rights instruments;	3rd
	(b) Human rights questions, including alternative approaches for improving the effective enjoyment of human rights and fundamental freedoms;	3rd
	(c) Human rights situations and reports of special rapporteurs and representatives;	3rd
	(d) Comprehensive implementation of and follow-up to the Vienna Declaration and Programme of Action;	3rd
	(e) Report of the United Nations High Commissioner for Human Rights.	3rd
117.	Financial reports and audited financial statements, and reports of the Board of Auditors:	
	(a) United Nations peacekeeping operations;	5th
	(b) United Nations Institute for Training and Research;	5th
	(c) Voluntary funds administered by the United Nations High Commissioner for Refugees.	5th

Item No.	*Title*	*Allocation*
118.	Review of the efficiency of the administrative and financial functioning of the United Nations.	5th
119.	Programme budget for the biennium 1998-1999.	5th
120.	Programme planning.	5th
121.	Proposed programme budget for the biennium 2000-2001.	5th
122.	Improving the financial situation of the United Nations.	5th
123.	Joint Inspection Unit.	5th
124.	Pattern of conferences.	5th
125.	Scale of assessments for the apportionment of the expenses of the United Nations.	5th
126.	United Nations common system.	5th
127.	Report of the Secretary-General on the activities of the Office of Internal Oversight Services.	5th
128.	Financing of the United Nations peacekeeping forces in the Middle East:	
	(a) United Nations Disengagement Observer Force;	5th
	(b) United Nations Interim Force in Lebanon.	5th
129.	Financing of the United Nations Angola Verification Mission and the United Nations Observer Mission in Angola.	5th
130.	Financing of the activities arising from Security Council resolution 687(1991):	
	(a) United Nations Iraq-Kuwait Observation Mission;	5th
	(b) Other activities.	5th
131.	Financing of the United Nations Mission for the Referendum in Western Sahara.	5th
132.	Financing and liquidation of the United Nations Transitional Authority in Cambodia.	5th
133.	Financing of the United Nations Protection Force, the United Nations Confidence Restoration Operation in Croatia, the United Nations Preventive Deployment Force and the United Nations Peace Forces headquarters.	5th
134.	Financing of the United Nations Operation in Somalia II.	5th
135.	Financing of the United Nations Operation in Mozambique.	5th
136.	Financing of the United Nations Peacekeeping Force in Cyprus.	5th
137.	Financing of the United Nations Observer Mission in Georgia.	5th
138.	Financing of the United Nations Mission in Haiti.	5th
139.	Financing of the United Nations Observer Mission in Liberia.	5th
140.	Financing of the United Nations Assistance Mission for Rwanda.	5th
141.	Financing of the United Nations Mission of Observers in Tajikistan.	5th
142.	Financing of the International Tribunal for the Prosecution of Persons Responsible for Serious Violations of International Humanitarian Law Committed in the Territory of the Former Yugoslavia since 1991.	5th
143.	Financing of the International Criminal Tribunal for the Prosecution of Persons Responsible for Genocide and Other Serious Violations of International Humanitarian Law Committed in the Territory of Rwanda and Rwandan Citizens Responsible for Genocide and Other Such Violations Committed in the Territory of Neighbouring States between 1 January and 31 December 1994.	5th
144.	Financing of the United Nations Mission in Bosnia and Herzegovina.	5th
145.	Financing of the United Nations Transitional Administration for Eastern Slavonia, Baranja and Western Sirmium and the Civilian Police Support Group.	5th
146.	Financing of the United Nations Preventive Deployment Force.	5th
147.	Financing of the United Nations Support Mission in Haiti, the United Nations Transition Mission in Haiti and the United Nations Civilian Police Mission in Haiti.	5th
148.	Financing of the Military Observer Group of the United Nations Verification Mission in Guatemala.	5th
149.	Financing of the United Nations Mission in the Central African Republic.	5th
150.	Financing of the United Nations Observer Mission in Sierra Leone.	5th
151.	Administrative and budgetary aspects of the financing of the United Nations peacekeeping operations:	
	(a) Financing of the United Nations peacekeeping operations;	5th
	(b) Relocation of Ukraine to the group of Member States set out in paragraph 3 *(c)* of General Assembly resolution 43/232;	5th
	(c) Relocation of South Africa to the group of Member States set out in paragraph 3 *(c)* of General Assembly resolution 43/232.	5th
152.	Convention on jurisdictional immunities of States and their property.	6th
153.	United Nations Programme of Assistance in the Teaching, Study, Dissemination and Wider Appreciation of International Law.	6th
154.	United Nations Decade of International Law:	
	(a) United Nations Decade of International Law;	Plenary, 6th

Item No.	Title	Allocation
	(b) Outcome of the action dedicated to the 1999 centennial of the first International Peace Conference.	6th
155.	Report of the International Law Commission on the work of its fifty-first session.	6th
156.	Report of the United Nations Commission on International Trade Law on the work of its thirty-second session.	6th
157.	Report of the Committee on Relations with the Host Country.	Plenary, 6th
158.	Establishment of an international criminal court.	6th
159.	Report of the Special Committee on the Charter of the United Nations and on the Strengthening of the Role of the Organization.	6th
160.	Measures to eliminate international terrorism.	6th
161.	Review of the Statute of the United Nations Administrative Tribunal.	6th
162.	Observer status for the International Union for the Conservation of Nature and Natural Resources in the General Assembly.	Plenary
163.	Review of the implementation of General Assembly resolution 48/218 B.	5th
164.	Human resources management.	5th
165.	Commemoration of the tenth anniversary of the Convention on the Rights of the Child.	Plenary
166.	Financing of the United Nations Interim Administration Mission in Kosovo.	5th
167.	Cooperation between the United Nations and the Preparatory Commission for the Comprehensive Nuclear-Test-Ban Treaty Organization.	Plenary
168.	Granting of observer status in the General Assembly for the Black Sea Economic Cooperation Organization.	Plenary
169.	Financing of the United Nations Mission in East Timor.	5th
170.	Armed aggression against the Democratic Republic of the Congo.	Plenary
171.	Observer status for the Community of Portuguese-speaking Countries in the General Assembly.	Plenary
172.	Financing of the United Nations Mission in Sierra Leone.	5th
173.	Financing of the United Nations Transitional Administration in East Timor.	5th
174.	International recognition of the Day of Vesak.	Plenary

Agenda of the twenty-second special session (27 and 28 September 1999)

Item No.	Title	Allocation
1.	Opening of the special session by the Chairman of the delegation of Namibia.	Plenary
2.	Minute of silent prayer or meditation.	Plenary
3.	Credentials of representatives to the twenty-second special session of the General Assembly:	
	(a) Appointment of the members of the Credentials Committee;	Plenary
	(b) Report of the Credentials Committee.	Plenary
4.	Election of the President.	Plenary
5.	Report of the Commission on Sustainable Development acting as the preparatory body for the twenty-second special session of the General Assembly.	Plenary
6.	Organization of the session.	Plenary
7.	Adoption of the agenda.	Plenary
8.	Review and appraisal of the implementation of the Programme of Action for the Sustainable Development of Small Island Developing States.	Plenary[10]
9.	Adoption of the final documents.	Plenary

Security Council

Agenda items considered during 1999

Item No.[11]	Title
1.	The situation in Sierra Leone.
2.	The situation in Angola.

Item No.[11]	*Title*
3.	The situation in Croatia.
4.	Letter dated 11 March 1998 from the Deputy Permanent Representative of the United Kingdom of Great Britain and Northern Ireland to the United Nations addressed to the President of the Security Council; letter dated 27 March 1998 from the Permanent Representative of the United States of America to the United Nations addressed to the President of the Security Council [situation in Kosovo].
5.	Promoting peace and security: humanitarian activities relevant to the Security Council.
6.	The situation in the Middle East.
7.	The situation concerning Western Sahara.
8.	The situation in Georgia.
9.	The situation between Eritrea and Ethiopia.
10.	Protection of civilians in armed conflict.
11.	The situation in the Central African Republic.
12.	The situation in Tajikistan and along the Tajik-Afghan border.
13.	The situation in the former Yugoslav Republic of Macedonia.
14.	The situation concerning the Democratic Republic of the Congo.
15.	Letter dated 24 March 1999 from the Permanent Representative of the Russian Federation to the United Nations addressed to the President of the Security Council [situation in Kosovo].
16.	The situation in Guinea-Bissau.
17.	Letters dated 20 and 23 December 1991 from France, the United Kingdom of Great Britain and Northern Ireland and the United States of America [mandatory sanctions against the Libyan Arab Jamahiriya in connection with the bombing of Pan Am flight 103].
18.	Admission of new Members.
19.	The situation in East Timor.
20.	Letter dated 7 May 1999 from the Permanent Representative of China to the United Nations addressed to the President of the Security Council [situation in Kosovo].
21.	Security Council resolutions 1160(1998), 1199(1998) and 1203(1998) [situation in Kosovo].
22.	International Criminal Tribunal for the Prosecution of Persons Responsible for Genocide and Other Serious Violations of International Humanitarian Law Committed in the Territory of Rwanda and Rwandan Citizens Responsible for Genocide and Other Such Violations Committed in the Territory of Neighbouring States between 1 January and 31 December 1994.
23.	The situation between Iraq and Kuwait.
24.	The situation in Somalia.
25.	Security Council resolutions 1160(1998), 1199(1998), 1203(1998) and 1239(1999) [situation in Kosovo].
26.	The situation in Bosnia and Herzegovina.
27.	The situation in Cyprus.
28.	Maintenance of peace and security in post-conflict peace-building.
29.	Promoting peace and security: humanitarian assistance to refugees in Africa.
30.	International Tribunal for the Prosecution of Persons Responsible for Serious Violations of International Humanitarian Law in the Territory of the Former Yugoslavia since 1991; International Criminal Tribunal for the Prosecution of Persons Responsible for Genocide and Other Serious Violations of International Humanitarian Law Committed in the Territory of Rwanda and Rwandan Citizens Responsible for Genocide and Other Such Violations Committed in the Territory of Neighbouring States between 1 January and 31 December 1994.
31.	Children and armed conflict.
32.	The situation in Afghanistan.
33.	Consideration of the draft report of the Security Council to the General Assembly.
34.	The situation in Africa.
35.	Small arms.
36.	The responsibility of the Security Council in the maintenance of international peace and security.
37.	Election of five members of the International Court of Justice.
38.	Security Council resolutions 1160(1998), 1199(1998), 1203(1998), 1239(1999) and 1244(1999) [situation in Kosovo].
39.	The situation in Burundi.
40.	Role of the Security Council in the prevention of armed conflicts.
41.	The question concerning Haiti.
42.	Date of an election to fill a vacancy in the International Court of Justice.

Economic and Social Council

Agenda of the organizational and resumed organizational sessions for 1999 (20 January and 2, 3 and 5 February; 25 March, 6 and 7 May and 23 June 1999)

Item No. *Title*

1. Election of the Bureau.
2. Adoption of the agenda and other organizational matters.
3. Basic programme of work of the Council.
4. Implementation of General Assembly resolutions 50/227 and 52/12 B.
5. Review of the distribution of seats in the Executive Board of the World Food Programme.
6. Enlargement of the Executive Committee of the Programme of the United Nations High Commissioner for Refugees.
7. Work programme for the Committee for Development Policy.
8. Elections, nominations and confirmations.

Agenda of the substantive and resumed substantive sessions of 1999 (23 June and 5-30 July; 16 September, 26 October, 15 November and 16 December 1999)

Item No. *Title*

1. Adoption of the agenda and other organizational matters.

High-level segment (5-7 July)

2. The role of employment and work in poverty eradication: the empowerment and advancement of women.

Operational activities of the United Nations for international development cooperation segment

3. Operational activities of the United Nations for international development cooperation:
   (*a*) Poverty eradication and capacity-building;
   (*b*) Follow-up to policy recommendations of the General Assembly;
   (*c*) Reports of the Executive Boards of the United Nations Development Programme/United Nations Population Fund, the United Nations Children's Fund and the World Food Programme;
   (*d*) Economic and technical cooperation among developing countries.

Coordination segment

4. Coordination of the policies and activities of the specialized agencies and other bodies of the United Nations system related to the following theme: Development of Africa: implementation and coordinated follow-up by the United Nations system of initiatives on African development.

Humanitarian affairs segment

5. Special economic, humanitarian and disaster relief assistance.

General segment

6. Integrated and coordinated implementation of and follow-up to major United Nations conferences and summits.
7. Coordination, programme and other questions:
   (*a*) Reports of coordination bodies;
   (*b*) Proposed programme budget for the biennium 2000-2001;
   (*c*) Joint and Co-sponsored United Nations Programme on Human Immunodeficiency Virus/Acquired Immunodeficiency Syndrome (HIV/AIDS);
   (*d*) International cooperation in the field of informatics;
   (*e*) Calendar of conferences and meetings in the economic, social and related fields.
8. Implementation of General Assembly resolutions 50/227 and 52/12 B.
9. Implementation of the Declaration on the Granting of Independence to Colonial Countries and Peoples by the specialized agencies and the international institutions associated with the United Nations.
10. Regional cooperation.
11. Economic and social repercussions of the Israeli occupation on the living conditions of the Palestinian people in the occupied Palestinian territory, including Jerusalem, and the Arab population in the occupied Syrian Golan.

Item No.	Title
12.	Non-governmental organizations.
13.	Economic and environmental questions:
	(a) Sustainable development;
	(b) Science and technology for development;
	(c) Statistics;
	(d) Human settlements;
	(e) Environment;
	(f) Women in development;
	(g) Transport of dangerous goods;
	(h) International Decade for Natural Disaster Reduction;
	(i) Population and development;
	(j) International cooperation in tax matters;
	(k) Energy and natural resources for development.
14.	Social and human rights questions:
	(a) Advancement of women;
	(b) Social development;
	(c) Crime prevention and criminal justice;
	(d) Narcotic drugs;
	(e) United Nations High Commissioner for Refugees;
	(f) Implementation of the Programme of Action for the Third Decade to Combat Racism and Racial Discrimination;
	(g) Programme of activities for the International Decade of the World's Indigenous People;
	(h) Human rights.

[1] Allocated also to the Fourth, Second, Third and Fifth Committees at the first part of the session in 1998.

[2] Allocated to the Fifth Committee at the first part of the session in 1998 but considered only in plenary meeting at the resumed session.

[3] Sub-item added at the resumed session.

[4] Not allocated; consideration deferred to the fifty-fourth session.

[5] Allocated to the Second Committee at the first part of the session in 1998 but considered only in plenary meeting at the resumed session.

[6] Allocated to the Sixth Committee at the first part of the session in 1998 but considered only in plenary meeting at the resumed session.

[7] Item added at the resumed session.

[8] Also allocated to the Ad Hoc Committee of the Whole of the Twenty-first Special Session.

[9] On 17 September 1999, the General Assembly adopted the General Committee's recommendation that the item be allocated at an appropriate time during the session.

[10] Also allocated to the Ad Hoc Committee of the Whole of the Twenty-second Special Session.

[11] Numbers indicate the order in which items were taken up in 1999.

Appendix V

United Nations information centres and services

(as at 15 November 2001)

ACCRA. United Nations Information Centre
Gamel Abdul Nassar/Liberia Roads
(P.O. Box 2339)
Accra, Ghana

Serving: Ghana, Sierra Leone

ADDIS ABABA. United Nations Information Service, Economic Commission for Africa
P.O. Box 3001
Addis Ababa, Ethiopia

Serving: Ethiopia, ECA

ALGIERS. United Nations Information Centre
9A Rue Emile Payen, Hydra
(Boîte Postale 823, Alger-Gare)
Algiers, Algeria

Serving: Algeria

ANKARA. United Nations Information Centre
197 Atatürk Bulvari
(P.K. 407)
Ankara, Turkey

Serving: Turkey

ANTANANARIVO. United Nations Information Centre
22 Rue Rainitovo, Antasahavola
(Boîte Postale 1348)
Antananarivo, Madagascar

Serving: Madagascar

ASUNCION. United Nations Information Centre
Avda. Mariscal López esq. Saraví
Edificio Naciones Unidas
(Casilla de Correo 1107)
Asunción, Paraguay

Serving: Paraguay

ATHENS. United Nations Information Centre
36 Amalias Avenue
GR-10558 Athens, Greece

Serving: Cyprus, Greece, Israel

BANGKOK. United Nations Information Service, Economic and Social Commission for Asia and the Pacific
United Nations Building
Rajdamnern Avenue
Bangkok 10200, Thailand

Serving: Cambodia; Hong Kong, China; Lao People's Democratic Republic; Malaysia; Singapore; Thailand; Viet Nam; ESCAP

BEIRUT. United Nations Information Centre/United Nations Information Service, Economic and Social Commission for Western Asia
UN House
Riad El-Solh Square
(P.O. Box 11-8575-4656)
Beirut, Lebanon

Serving: Jordan, Kuwait, Lebanon, Syrian Arab Republic, ESCWA

BOGOTA. United Nations Information Centre
Calle 100 No. 8A-55, Piso 10
(Apartado Aéreo 058964)
Bogotá 2, Colombia

Serving: Colombia, Ecuador, Venezuela

BONN. United Nations Information Centre
United Nations Premises in Bonn
Martin-Luther-King Strasse 8
D-53175 Bonn, Germany

Serving: Germany

BRAZZAVILLE. United Nations Information Centre
Avenue Foch, Case Ortf 15
(P.O. Box 13210 or 1018)
Brazzaville, Congo

Serving: Congo

BRUSSELS. United Nations Information Centre
UN House
14 Rue Montoyer
B-1000 Brussels, Belgium

Serving: Belgium, Luxembourg, Netherlands; liaison with the EC

BUCHAREST. United Nations Information Centre
16 Aurel Vlaicu
(P.O. Box 1-701, Bucharest)
Bucharest 79362, Romania

Serving: Romania

BUENOS AIRES. United Nations Information Centre
Junín 1940 (1er piso)
1113 Buenos Aires, Argentina

Serving: Argentina, Uruguay

BUJUMBURA. United Nations Information Centre
117 Avenue de la Révolution
(Boîte Postale 2160)
Bujumbura, Burundi

Serving: Burundi

CAIRO. United Nations Information Centre
1 Osiris Street, Garden City
(Boîte Postale 262)
Cairo, Egypt

Serving: Egypt, Saudi Arabia

COLOMBO. United Nations Information Centre
202/204 Bauddhaloka Mawatha
(P.O. Box 1505, Colombo)
Colombo 7, Sri Lanka

Serving: Sri Lanka

COPENHAGEN. United Nations Information Centre
Midtermolen 3
DK-2100 Copenhagen East, Denmark

Serving: Denmark, Finland, Iceland, Norway, Sweden

DAKAR. United Nations Information Centre
12 Avenue Leopold S. Senghor, Immeuble UNESCO
(Boîte Postale 154)
Dakar, Senegal

Serving: Cape Verde, Côte d'Ivoire, Gambia, Guinea, Guinea-Bissau, Mauritania, Senegal

DAR ES SALAAM. United Nations Information Centre
Marogoro Road/Sokoine Drive
Old Boma Building (ground floor)
(P.O. Box 9224)
Dar es Salaam, United Republic of Tanzania

Serving: United Republic of Tanzania

DHAKA. United Nations Information Centre
IDB Bhaban (14th floor)
Begum Rokeya Sharani
Sher-e-Bangla Nagar
(G.P.O. Box 3658, Dhaka-1000)
Dhaka-1207, Bangladesh

Serving: Bangladesh

GENEVA. United Nations Information Service, United Nations Office at Geneva
Palais des Nations
1211 Geneva 10, Switzerland

Serving: Bulgaria, Switzerland

HARARE. United Nations Information Centre
Sanders House (2nd floor)
First Street/Jason Moyo Avenue
(P.O. Box 4408)
Harare, Zimbabwe

Serving: Zimbabwe

ISLAMABAD. United Nations Information Centre
House No. 26, Street: 88, G-6/3
(P.O. Box 1107)
Islamabad, Pakistan

Serving: Pakistan

JAKARTA. United Nations Information Centre
Gedung Dewan Pers (5th floor)
32-34 Jalan Kebon Sirih
Jakarta 10100, Indonesia

Serving: Indonesia

KABUL. United Nations Information Centre
(not operational)

KATHMANDU. United Nations Information Centre
Pulchowk, Patan
(P.O. Box 107, UN House)
Kathmandu, Nepal

Serving: Nepal

KHARTOUM. United Nations Information Centre
United Nations Compound
Gamma'a Avenue
(P.O. Box 1992)
Khartoum, Sudan

Serving: Somalia, Sudan

KINSHASA. United Nations Information Centre
Bâtiment Deuxième République
Boulevard du 30 Juin
B.P. 7248
Kinshasa 1, Democratic Republic of the Congo

Serving: Democratic Republic of the Congo

LAGOS. United Nations Information Centre
17 Kingsway Road, Ikoyi
(P.O. Box 1068)
Lagos, Nigeria

Serving: Nigeria

LA PAZ. United Nations Information Centre
Calle 14 esq. S. Bustamante
Edificio Metrobol II. Calacoto
(Apartado Postal 9072)
La Paz, Bolivia

Serving: Bolivia

LIMA. United Nations Information Centre
Lord Cochrane 130
San Isidro (L-27)
(P.O. Box 14-0199)
Lima, Peru

Serving: Peru

LISBON. United Nations Information Centre
Rua Latino Coelho, 1
Edificio Aviz, Bloco A-1, 10°
1050-132 Lisbon, Portugal

Serving: Portugal

LOME. United Nations Information Centre
107 Boulevard du 13 Janvier
(Boîte Postale 911)
Lomé, Togo

Serving: Benin, Togo

LONDON. United Nations Information Centre
Millbank Tower (21st floor)
21-24 Millbank
London SW1P 4QH, England

Serving: Ireland, United Kingdom

LUSAKA. United Nations Information Centre
Revenue House (ground floor)
Cairo Road (Northend)
(P.O. Box 32905, Lusaka 10101)
Lusaka, Zambia

Serving: Botswana, Malawi, Swaziland, Zambia

MADRID. United Nations Information Centre
Avenida General Perón, 32-1
(P.O. Box 3400, 28080 Madrid)
28020 Madrid, Spain

Serving: Spain

MANAGUA. United Nations Information Centre
Palacio de la Cultura
(Apartado Postal 3260)
Managua, Nicaragua

Serving: Nicaragua

MANAMA. United Nations Information Centre
United Nations House
Building 69 Road 1901
(P.O. Box 26004)
Manama 319, Bahrain

Serving: Bahrain, Qatar, United Arab Emirates

MANILA. United Nations Information Centre
NEDA sa Makati Building
106 Amorsolo Street
Legaspi Village, Makati City, 1229
(P.O. Box 7285 ADC (DAPO), Pasay City)
Metro Manila, Philippines

Serving: Papua New Guinea, Philippines, Solomon Islands

MASERU. United Nations Information Centre
United Nations Road
UN House
(P.O. Box 301, Maseru 100)
Maseru West, Lesotho

Serving: Lesotho

MEXICO CITY. United Nations Information Centre
Presidente Masaryk, 29-6° piso
Col. Chapultepec Morales
11570 México, D.F., Mexico

Serving: Cuba, Dominican Republic, Mexico

MONROVIA. United Nations Information Centre
UNDP
Dubar Building
Monrovia, Liberia

Serving: Liberia

MOSCOW. United Nations Information Centre
4/16 Glazovsky pereulok
Moscow 121002, Russian Federation

Serving: Russian Federation

NAIROBI. United Nations Information Centre
United Nations Office
Gigiri
(P.O. Box 30552)
Nairobi, Kenya

Serving: Kenya, Seychelles, Uganda

NEW DELHI. United Nations Information Centre
55 Lodi Estate
New Delhi 110 003, India

Serving: Bhutan, India

OUAGADOUGOU. United Nations Information Centre
14 Avenue Georges Konseiga
Secteur No. 4
(Boîte Postale 135)
Ouagadougou 01, Burkina Faso

Serving: Burkina Faso, Chad, Mali, Niger

PANAMA CITY. United Nations Information Centre
Calle Gerardo Ortega y Ave. Samuel Lewis
Banco Central Hispano Building (1st floor)
(P.O. Box 6-9083 El Dorado)
Panama City, Panama

Serving: Panama

PARIS. United Nations Information Centre
1 Rue Miollis
75732, Paris Cedex 15, France

Serving: France

PORT OF SPAIN. United Nations Information Centre
2nd floor, Bretton Hall
16 Victoria Avenue
(P.O. Box 130)
Port of Spain, Trinidad, W.I.

Serving: Antigua and Barbuda, Bahamas, Barbados, Belize, Dominica, Grenada, Guyana, Jamaica, Netherlands Antilles, Saint Kitts and Nevis, Saint Lucia, Saint Vincent and the Grenadines, Suriname, Trinidad and Tobago

PRAGUE. United Nations Information Centre
nam. Kinskych 6
150 00 Prague 5, Czech Republic

Serving: Czech Republic

PRETORIA. United Nations Information Centre
Metro Park Building
351 Schoeman Street
(P.O. Box 12677)
Pretoria, South Africa

Serving: South Africa

RABAT. United Nations Information Centre
6 Angle Charii Ibnou Ziyad et Zankat Roudana
(Boîte Postale 601, Casier ONU, Rabat-Chellah)
Rabat, Morocco

Serving: Morocco

RIO DE JANEIRO. United Nations Information Centre
Palácio Itamaraty
Av. Marechal Floriano 196
20080-002 Rio de Janeiro, RJ Brazil

Serving: Brazil

ROME. United Nations Information Centre
Palazzetto Venezia
Piazza San Marco 50
00186 Rome, Italy

Serving: Holy See, Italy, Malta, San Marino

SANA'A. United Nations Information Centre
St. 5, Off Al-Bonyia Street
Handlal Zone, Beside Handhal Mosque
(P.O. Box 237)
Sana'a, Yemen

Serving: Yemen

SAN SALVADOR. United Nations Information Centre
(not operational)

SANTIAGO. United Nations Information Service, Economic Commission for Latin America and the Caribbean
Edificio Naciones Unidas
Avenida Dag Hammarskjöld
Vitaoura
(Avenida Dag Hammarskjöld s/n, Casilla 179-D)
Santiago, Chile

Serving: Chile, ECLAC

SYDNEY. United Nations Information Centre
46-48 York Street (5th floor)
(G.P.O. Box 4045, Sydney, N.S.W. 2001)
Sydney, N.S.W. 2000, Australia

Serving: Australia, Fiji, Kiribati, Nauru, New Zealand, Samoa, Tonga, Tuvalu, Vanuatu

TEHRAN. United Nations Information Centre
185 Ghaemmagham-Farahani St.
(P.O. Box 15875-4557, Tehran)
Tehran-15868, Iran

Serving: Iran

TOKYO. United Nations Information Centre
UNU Building (8th floor)
53-70 Jingumae 5-chome, Shibuya-ku
Tokyo 150-0001, Japan

Serving: Japan

TRIPOLI. United Nations Information Centre
Muzzafar Al-Aftas St.
Hay El-Andalous (2)
(P.O. Box 286)
Tripoli, Libyan Arab Jamahiriya

Serving: Libyan Arab Jamahiriya

TUNIS. United Nations Information Centre
61 Boulevard Bab-Benat
(Boîte Postale 863)
Tunis, Tunisia

Serving: Tunisia

VIENNA. United Nations Information Service, United Nations Office at Vienna
Vienna International Centre
Wagramer Strasse 5
(P.O. Box 500, A-1400 Vienna)
A-1220 Vienna, Austria

Serving: Austria, Hungary, Slovakia, Slovenia

WARSAW. United Nations Information Centre
Al. Niepodleglosci 186
(P.O. Box 1, 02-514 Warsaw 12)
00-608 Warszawa, Poland

Serving: Poland

WASHINGTON, D.C. United Nations Information Centre
1775 K Street, N.W., Suite 400
Washington, D.C. 20006, United States

Serving: United States

WINDHOEK. United Nations Information Centre
372 Paratus Building
Independence Avenue
(Private Bag 13351)
Windhoek, Namibia

Serving: Namibia

YANGON. United Nations Information Centre
6 Natmauk Road
(P.O. Box 230)
Yangon, Myanmar

Serving: Myanmar

YAOUNDE. United Nations Information Centre
Immeuble Tchinda, Rue 2044
Derrière camp SIC TSINGA
(Boîte Postale 836)
Yaoundé, Cameroon

Serving: Cameroon, Central African Republic, Gabon

For more information on UNICs, access the Internet: http://www.un.org/aroundworld/unics

Indexes

USING THE SUBJECT INDEX

To assist the researcher in reading and searching the *Yearbook* index, three typefaces have been employed.

ALL BOLD CAPITAL LETTERS are used for major subject entries, including chapter topics, (e.g., **DEVELOPMENT**, **DISARMAMENT**), as well as country names (e.g., **TAJIKISTAN**), region names (e.g., **AFRICA**) and principal UN organs (e.g., **GENERAL ASSEMBLY**).

CAPITAL LETTERS are used to highlight major sub-topics (e.g., POVERTY), territories (e.g., MONTSERRAT), subregions (e.g., CENTRAL AMERICA) and official names of specialized agencies (e.g., UNIVERSAL POSTAL UNION) and regional commissions (e.g., ECONOMIC COMMISSION FOR EUROPE).

Regular body text is used for single entries and cross-reference entries, e.g., armed conflict, juvenile detention, social development.

1—An asterisk (*) next to a page number indicates the presence of a text (reproduced in full) of General Assembly, Security Council or Economic and Social Council resolutions and decisions, or Security Council presidential statements.

2—Entries, which are heavily cross-referenced, appear under key substantive words, as well as under the first word of official titles.

3—United Nations bodies are listed under major subject entries and alphabetically.

Subject Index

Index of resolutions and decisions

Resolution/decision numbers in italics indicate that the text is summarized rather than reprinted in full. (For dates of sessions, refer to Appendix III.)

GENERAL ASSEMBLY,
54th SESSION *(cont.)*

Index of 1999 Security Council presidential statements

Statement numbers in italics indicate that the text is summarized rather than reprinted in full.

How to obtain volumes of the *Yearbook*

Recent volumes of the *Yearbook* may be obtained in many bookstores throughout the world, as well as from United Nations Publications, Room DC2-853, United Nations, New York, N.Y. 10017, or from United Nations Publications, Palais des Nations, CH-1211 Geneva 10, Switzerland.

Older editions are available in microfiche.

Yearbook of the United Nations, 1998
Vol. 52. Sales No. E.01.I.1 $150.

Yearbook of the United Nations, 1997
Vol. 51. Sales No. E.00.I.1 $150.

Yearbook of the United Nations, 1996
Vol. 50. Sales No. E.97.I.1 $150.

Yearbook of the United Nations, 1995
Vol. 49. Sales No. E.96.I.1 $150.

Yearbook of the United Nations, 1994
Vol. 48. Sales No. E.95.I.1 $150.

Yearbook of the United Nations, 1993
Vol. 47. Sales No. E.94.I.1 $150.

Yearbook of the United Nations, 1992
Vol. 46. Sales No. E.93.I.1 $150.

Yearbook of the United Nations, 1991
Vol. 45. Sales No. E.92.I.1 $115.

Yearbook of the United Nations, 1990
Vol. 44. Sales No. E.98.I.16 $150.

Yearbook of the United Nations, 1989
Vol. 43. Sales No. E.97.I.11 $150.

Yearbook of the United Nations, 1988
Vol. 42. Sales No. E.93.I.100 $150.

Yearbook of the United Nations, 1987
Vol. 41. Sales No. E.91.I.1 $105.

Yearbook of the United Nations, 1986
Vol. 40. Sales No. E.90.I.1 $95.

Yearbook of the United Nations, 1985
Vol. 39. Sales No. E.88.I.1 $95.

Yearbook of the United Nations, 1984
Vol. 38. Sales No. E.87.I.1 $90.

Yearbook of the United Nations, 1983
Vol. 37. Sales No. E.86.I.1 $85.

Yearbook of the United Nations, 1982
Vol. 36. Sales No. E.85.I.1 $75.

Yearbook of the United Nations
Special Edition
UN Fiftieth Anniversary
1945-1995
Sales No. E.95.I.50 $95

The Yearbook *in microfiche*

Yearbook volumes 1-46 (1946-1992) and 49 (1995) are available in microfiche. Individual volumes are also available, and prices can be obtained by contacting the following: United Nations Publications, Room DC2-853, United Nations, New York, N.Y. 10017, or United Nations Publications, Palais des Nations, CH-1211 Geneva 10, Switzerland.

NOTES

NOTES

NOTES

NOTES

NOTES

NOTES

NOTES

NOTES

NOTES